Federal Regulatory Directory

Seventeenth Edition

Federal Regulatory Directory

Seventeenth Edition

Los Angeles | London | New Delhi
Singapore | Washington DC

Los Angeles | London | New Delhi
Singapore | Washington DC

FOR INFORMATION:

CQ Press

An Imprint of SAGE Publications, Inc.

2455 Teller Road

Thousand Oaks, California 91320

E-mail: order@sagepub.com

SAGE Publications Ltd.

1 Oliver's Yard

55 City Road

London EC1Y 1SP

United Kingdom

SAGE Publications India Pvt. Ltd.

B 1/I 1 Mohan Cooperative Industrial Area

Mathura Road, New Delhi 110 044

India

SAGE Publications Asia-Pacific Pte. Ltd.

3 Church Street

#10-04 Samsung Hub

Singapore 049483

Printed in the United States of America

ISBN 978-1-4833-8477-1

Editor: Laura Notton

Editorial Assistant: Jordan Enobakhare

Production Editor: David C. Felts

Contributors: Rebecca Adams, Mary Marshall, David Masci

Research: Mollie Maxon, Meisha Mossayebi

Typesetter: C&M Digitals (P) Ltd.

Proofreaders: Ellen Brink, Bonnie Moore

Cover Designer: Michael Dubowe

Marketing Managers: Carmel Schrire, Teri Williams

This book is printed on acid-free paper.

15 16 17 18 19 10 9 8 7 6 5 4 3 2 1

Contents

REGULATORY OVERSIGHT AND COORDINATION AGENCIES 861

NAME INDEX 947

SUBJECT INDEX 985

Thematic Table of Contents

EDUCATION

ELECTIONS

ENERGY

ENVIRONMENT AND NATURAL RESOURCES

FEDERAL BUDGET AND TAX POLICY

FEDERAL GOVERNMENT OPERATIONS AND CIVIL SERVICE

HEALTH, SAFTEY, AND NUTRITION

Preface

Over the last few years, the U.S. Supreme Court has played a prominent role in defining the path forward for recent federal regulation amidst continuing highly-partisan congressional gridlock. The passage of health care reform legislation—specifically the Patient Protection and Affordable Care Act of 2010 (ACA)—has become President Barack Obama's defining and most significant policy achievement to date, and the law has been met with contention at every turn, repeatedly requiring the Supreme Court to weigh in. In March 2014 *Burwell v. Hobby Lobby* came before the Court arguing that some closely held for-profit companies should not be required to provide contraceptive coverage as mandated under the ACA if the company leadership had religious objections. The Court ruled 5–4 in favor of Hobby Lobby, and the Department of Health and Human Services (HSS) promptly engaged in compliance efforts by issuing regulations that allowed women to instead obtain coverage directly from the insurer when their employers notified them in writing of their religious objections.

The following year, the Supreme Court heard another challenge to the ACA in *King v. Burwell*, involving four plaintiffs in Virginia who did not want to buy health insurance, arguing that the law only provides for subsidies through exchanges "established by the state." In this case, the subsidized health coverage of an estimated eight million consumers hung in the balance in 34 states that use the federal health care marketplaces. The plaintiffs' argument focused on the wording of the legislation and whether the intent of Congress was to provide subsidies to low-income consumers who purchased only through the state marketplaces, or whether the intent was to also extend subsidies to coverage purchased through exchanges established by the federal government. In a 5–4 decision handed down on June 25, 2015, the U.S. Supreme Court upheld the ACA subsidies in states that opted to use the federal exchange, thereby allowing the IRS to continue to issue the tax-credit subsidies.

Recent debates around same-sex marriage also reached the Court's docket with implications for the regulatory status quo. On June 26, 2013, the U.S. Supreme Court ruled Section 3 of the Defense of Marriage Act (DOMA) unconstitutional in *Windsor v. the United States*. Section 3 of DOMA, signed into law in 1996, had defined marriage as a legal union of one man and one woman

for the purposes of "any act of Congress . . . any ruling, regulation, or interpretation of the various administrative bureaus and agencies of the United States." In some cases, such as the determination of Social Security benefits, the *Windsor* ruling specifically impacted federal government laws and regulations only in states where same-sex marriage was recognized. In the weeks after the *Windsor* ruling, the Justice Department provided guidance to various federal agencies to remove barriers to federal programs for same-sex spouses. By the end of 2013 the Social Security Administration (SSA) began processing claims for retirement benefits and survivor's benefits for same-sex spouses. Also following this outcome, Medicare is no longer prevented by DOMA from recognizing same-sex marriages for determining entitlement to, or eligibility for, Medicare. Beneficiaries in private Medicare plans additionally have access to equal coverage when it comes to care in a nursing home where their same-sex spouses live.

In a historic decision two years later, same-sex marriage was legalized across the nation on June 26, 2015, in a 5–4 ruling in *Obergefell v. Hodges*, which asked the Court to decide whether the Fourteenth Amendment requires states to issue marriage licenses to same-sex couples and whether states are required to recognize same-sex marriages lawfully performed out of state. Any state bans on same-sex marriage were effectively struck down and declared unconstitutional, and this decision will undoubtedly lead to the further removal of barriers regarding health care coverage, veterans' benefits, and Social Security, amongst other benefits, for married same-sex couples in the months to follow.

In recent years, the Supreme Court has also entered the election finance fracas by weighing in on a two high-profile campaign finance cases that have vastly altered the election landscape. The 2010 *Citizens United v. FEC* decision paved the way for Super PACs, which have become major players in the campaign finance game, to gain a firm toehold in the election process. The widely controversial ruling in *Citizens United* supported the idea that corporate media political spending is a form of free speech protected by the First Amendment and should not be subject to, or stifled by, government regulation. While corporations and unions cannot give money directly to campaigns to support or denounce candidates, they may seek to persuade the voting public through other means such as ads. In the three federal elections since *Citizens United*, Super PACs have spent more than $1 billion on electioneering communications. This dramatic growth of soft and dark money, which is unlimited, largely unregulated money contributed primarily to political parties, has opened new avenues of undisclosed giving and is already influencing election outcomes.

And in the 2014 *McCutcheon v. FEC* case, the Court struck down McCain-Feingold's combined limits on political donations by individuals, with the interpretation that campaign giving is considered free speech under the First Amendment and that the imposed contribution limits do not further the federal government's pursuit to prevent quid pro quo corruption. Previously, the total amount an individual could give in a two-year election cycle was $123,200, and while there are still limits on the amount that individuals can give to national and state parties per year, the *McCutcheon* decision allows wealthy donors to contribute unlimited sums to as many candidates as they wish, as long as they stay within the per-candidate contribution limits.

Despite the stalemate in Congress, after three long years of discussions the Farm Bill—known as the Agricultural Act of 2014—finally passed in 2014 with the intention of recasting a range of food, nutrition, and agriculture programs that is projected to save $16 billion in federal spending over the next ten years. For one, direct subsidies provided to farmers would end, and instead farmers would be allowed to take advantage of crop insurance: individual or county level Agriculture Risk Coverage or Price Loss Coverage. When crop losses due to market shifts are extensive and beyond the control of farmers, the Actual Production History provision will allow for yield adjustments, and the USDA provides online tools to assist farmers in choosing an insurance option. Open enrollment in the program began June 17, 2015, and by the end of the month more than 1.76 million farmers had signed up for either ARC or PLC.

The Farm Bill also cut roughly $8 billion in funding for the Supplemental Nutrition Assistance Program (SNAP),

formerly known as food stamps, by altering the eligibility requirements and implementing mechanisms to prevent fraud and abuse of the SNAP program and also sought to improve nutrition availability and store participation in the program. Under the new bill, affluent college students, lottery winners, and convicted felons are not eligible for SNAP assistance; stores must stock more perishable food in order to provide more healthy options; and states must implement systems to verify immigration status. The law also requires states to phase out the participation of women, infants, and children in the Commodity Supplemental Food Program, which will serve only low-income senior citizens going forward. To further alleviate the need for food assistance, the bill also allows for up to ten states to pilot employment and training programs providing job training. "The work pilot projects are a response to a need to help struggling Americans find employment and earn higher wages so they are no longer dependent on federal food assistance," said then House Agricultural Committee chair Frank Lucas.

The Seventeenth edition of the *Federal Regulatory Directory* continues its legacy of guiding readers through the intricacies of the federal agencies and regulation. Offering both a directory of contacts for economic, environmental, safety, health, and other regulatory agencies as well as a discussion of how each agency regulates policies and programs, the *Federal Regulatory Directory* provides a broad but comprehensive exploration of the history and current issues facing regulatory agencies and information on major regulatory legislation.

CQ Press seeks to continue the *Federal Regulatory Directory*'s reputation as an invaluable and authoritative reference of its kind. We welcome feedback related to the book's quality and functionality, as well as suggestions for future editions.

Laura Notton
Editor

List of Abbreviations

AARC	Alternative Agricultural Research and Commercialization Center
ABA	American Bar Association
ABA	Architectural Barriers Act of 1968
ACA	Patient Protection and Affordable Care Act
ACAs	Agricultural Credit Associations
ACEP	Agricultural Conservation Easement Program
ACF	Administration for Children and Families
ACL	Administration for Community Living
ACYF	Administration for Children, Youth, and Families
ADA	Americans with Disabilities Act
ADAAG	ADA Accessibility Guidelines
ADEA	Age Discrimination in Employment Act
ADR	Alternative Dispute Resolution
ADS-B	Automatic Dependent Surveillance–Broadcast
AEC	Atomic Energy Commission
AEFLA	Adult Education and Family Literacy Act
AFA	American Fisheries Act of 1998
AFDC	Aid to Families with Dependent Children
AHP	Affordable Housing Program
AIA	American Institute of Architects
AIDD	Administration on Intellectual and Developmental Disabilities
ALFD	Advertising, Labeling and Formulation Division
ALJ	administrative law judge
AMA	American Medical Association
AMID	Air and Marine Interdiction Division
AMS	Agricultural Marketing Service
ANDA	Abbreviated New Drug Application
ANPR	Advance Notice of Proposed Rulemaking
ANWR	Alaskan National Wildlife Refuge
AoA	Administration on Aging
APA	Administrative Procedure Act of 1946
APHIS	Animal and Plant Health Inspection Service
APO	army post office
AQI	Agricultural Quarantine Inspection
ARC	Agriculture Risk Coverage
ARCP	Agricultural Resource Conservation Program
ARM	adjustable-rate mortgage
ARRA	American Recovery and Reinvestment Act of 2009
AS	American Samoa
ASCS	Agricultural Stabilization and Conservation Service
ASH	Office of the Assistant Secretary for Health
ASOS	Automated Surface Observing Stations
ATBCB	Architectural and Transportation Barriers Compliance Board
ATF	Bureau of Alcohol, Tobacco, Firearms and Explosives
ATFI	Automated Tariff Filing and Information System
ATL	Alcohol and Tobacco Laboratory
ATP	Advanced Technology Program
ATSA	Aviation and Transportation Security Act
ATV	all-terrain vehicle
AWA	Animal Welfare Act
AYP	adequate yearly progress
BBS	electronic bulletin board system
BCAP	Biomass Crop Assistance Program
BCIS	Bureau of Citizenship and Immigration Services
BCRA	Bipartisan Campaign Reform Act of 2002
BEHT	Bill Emerson Humanitarian Trust
BIA	Bureau of Indian Affairs
BIE	Bureau of Indian Education
BIS	Bureau of Industry and Security
BJA	Bureau of Justice Assistance
BJS	Bureau of Justice Statistics
BLM	Bureau of Land Management
BLS	Bureau of Labor Statistics
BOEM	Bureau of Ocean Energy Management
BOEMRE	Bureau of Ocean Energy Management, Regulation, and Enforcement (now BOEM and BSEE)
BOP	Federal Bureau of Prisons
BRS	Bibliographic Retrieval System
BSEE	Bureau of Safety and Environmental Enforcement

BTS	Bureau of Transportation Statistics
BXA	Bureau of Export Administration (now BIS)
CAA	Civil Aeronautics Authority
CAB	Civil Aeronautics Board
CAFÉ	Corporate Average Fuel Efficiency
CAP	Citizen Advocacy Panel
CAT	catastrophic level
CBO	Congressional Budget Office
CBP	Customs and Border Protection
CCC	Commodity Credit Corporation
CCF	Capital Construction Fund
CCL	Commerce Control List
CCP	Cooperative Compliance Program
CCS	carbon capture and storage
CDAP	Center for Disability and Aging Policy
CDC	Centers for Disease Control and Prevention
CEA	Council of Economic Advisers
CEBA	Competitive Equality Banking Act of 1987
CEQ	Council on Environmental Quality
CERCLA	Comprehensive Environmental Response, Compensation, and Liability Act (Superfund)
CETA	Comprehensive Employment and Training Act
CFCs	chlorofluorocarbons
CFPB	Consumer Financial Protection Bureau
CFR	Code of Federal Regulations
CFTC	Commodity Futures Trading Commission
CHAP	chronic hazard advisory panel
CHIP	Children's Health Insurance Program
CIC	Consumer Information Center
CITES	Convention of International Trade in Endangered Species of Wild Fauna and Flora
CLIA	Clinical Laboratory Improvement Amendments
CMS	Centers for Medicare and Medicaid Services
CNS	Corporation for National Service
COA	Certificate of Waiver or Authorization
COBRA	Consolidated Omnibus Budget Reconciliation Act of 1985
COMPETES Act	America Creating Opportunities to Meaningfully Promote Excellence in Technology, Education, and Science Reauthorization Act of 2010
COOL	Country of Origin Labeling
COPS	Community Oriented Policing Services
COSHI	Clearinghouse for Occupational Safety and Health Information
CPD	Community Planning and Development
CPSC	Consumer Product Safety Commission
CRA	Community Reinvestment Act

CREP	Conservation Reserve Enhancement Program
CRP	Conservation Reserve Program
CSAB	Center for the Study of American Business
CSRA	Civil Service Reform Act
CSSPAB	Computer System Security and Privacy Advisory Board
D&D	deactivation and decommissioning
DACA	Deferred Action for Childhood Arrivals
DAPA	Deferred Action for Parental Accountability
DART	Deep-ocean Assessment and Reporting of Tsunami
DASP	Disaster Assistance Support Program
DEA	Drug Enforcement Administration
DEAC	Deemed Export Advisory Committee
DHS	Department of Homeland Security
DIF	Deposit Insurance Fund
DMSP	Defense Meteorological Satellite Program
DNFSB	Defense Nuclear Facilities Safety Board
DOE	Department of Energy
DOJ	Department of Justice
DOL	Department of Labor
DOMA	Defense of Marriage Act
DOT	Department of Transportation
DPC	Domestic Policy Council
DRA	Deficit Reduction Act
DTV	digital television
EA	Office of Enterprise Assessment
EAA	Export Administration Act
EAC	Election Assistance Commission
EAR	Export Administration Regulations
EBSA	Employee Benefits Security Administration
EBT	Electronic Benefit Transfer
ECD	Early Childhood Development
ECP	Emergency Conservation Program
ECR	Export Control Reform
EDA	Economic Development Administration
EDGAR	Electronic Data Gathering Analysis and Retrieval system
EEOC	Equal Employment Opportunity Commission
EEOICPA	Energy Employees Occupational Illness Compensation Program Act
EERE	Energy Efficiency and Renewable Energy
EFIN	Environmental Financing Information Network
EHP	environmental and historic preservation
EHSS	Office of Environment, Health, Safety and Security
EIA	Energy Information Administration
EIS	Environmental Impact Statement
ELAIN	Export License Application and Information Network
ELAP	Emergency Assistance for Livestock, Honey Bees, and Farm-Raised Fish

ELVIS	Electronic License Voice Information System	FEMA	Federal Emergency Management Agency
EM	Office of Environmental Management (Energy Dept.)	FEPC	Fair Employment Practices Committee
E-mail PMO	Electronic Messaging Program Management Office	FERC	Federal Energy Regulatory Commission
		FERN	Food Emergency Response Network
		FERPA	Family Educational Rights and Privacy Act
EPA	Environmental Protection Agency	FFEL	Federal Family Education Loans
EPA	Equal Pay Act	FFIs	foreign financial institutions
EPUB	Electronic Publishing System	FFIEC	Federal Financial Institutions Examination Council
EQC	Environmental Quality Council		
ERA	Economic Regulatory Administration	FFP	Feedstock Flexibility Program for Bioenergy Producers
ERDA	Energy Research and Development Administration		
		FGIS	Federal Grain Inspection Service
ERIC	Educational Resources Information Center	FHA	Federal Housing Administration
		FHEO	Office of Fair Housing and Equal Opportunity
ERISA	Employee Retirement Income Security Act of 1974		
		FHFA	Federal Housing Finance Agency
EROD	Education Resources Organization Directory	FHFB	Federal Housing Finance Board
		FHLB	Federal Home Loan Bank
ERS	Economic Research Service	FHLMC	Federal Home Loan Mortgage Corporation (Freddie Mac)
ESA	Employment Standards Administration		
ESEA	Elementary and Secondary Education Act of 1965	FHWA	Federal Highway Administration
		FIFRA	Federal Insecticide, Fungicide, and Rodenticide Act
ESH	Office of Environment, Safety and Health		
ESRL	Earth Systems Research Laboratory (NOAA-Commerce)	FIN	Federal Information Network
		FIPSE	Fund for the Improvement of Postsecondary Education
ESTA	Electronic System for Travel Authorization		
		FIRREA	Financial Institutions Reform, Recovery, and Enforcement Act of 1989
ETA	Employment and Training Administration		
		FISA	Foreign Intelligence Surveillance Act
ETF	exchange traded funds	FLBA	Federal Land Bank Association
ETRAC	Emerging Technology and Research Advisory Committee	FLSA	Fair Labor Standards Act
		FMCSA	Federal Motor Carrier Safety Administration
EUC	Emergency Unemployment Compensation		
		FMAP	Federal Medical Assistance Percentage
		FMC	Federal Maritime Commission
FAA	Federal Aviation Administration	FmHA	Farmers Home Administration
FAFSA	Free Application for Federal Student Aid	FNS	Food and Nutrition Service
FAIR	Federal Agricultural Improvement and Reform	FOI	freedom of information
		FOIA	Freedom of Information Act
Fannie Mae	Federal National Mortgage Association	FOMC	Federal Open Market Committee
Farmer Mac	Federal Agricultural Mortgage Corporation	FPC	Federal Power Commission
		FPCO	Family Policy Compliance Office
FAS	Foreign Agricultural Service	FPDC	Federal Procurement Data Center
FASB	Financial Accounting Standards Board	FPDS	Federal Procurement Data Center—Next Generation
FATCA	Foreign Account Tax Compliance Act of 2010		
		FPO	fleet post office
FBI	Federal Bureau of Investigation	FRA	Federal Railroad Administration
FCA	Farm Credit Administration	FRCS	Federal Reserve Communications System
FCC	Federal Communications Commission	Freddie Mac	Federal Home Loan Mortgage Corporation
FCIC	Federal Crop Insurance Corporation		
FCS	Food and Consumer Service	FRP	Federal Radionavigation Plan
FCSBA	FCS Building Association	FRSO	Federal Relay Service Online
FDA	Food and Drug Administration	FSA	Family Support Administration
FDC	Food, Drug, and Cosmetic Act	FSA	Farm Service Agency
FDIC	Federal Deposit Insurance Corporation	FSIS	Food Safety and Inspection Service
FEA	Federal Energy Administration	FSLIC	Federal Savings and Loan Insurance Corporation
FEC	Federal Election Commission		
FECA	Federal Election Campaign Act	FTA	Federal Transit Administration
Fed	Federal Reserve Board	FTC	Federal Trade Commission

FTS	Federal Technology Service	ISP	Internet service provider
FWP	Farmable Wetlands Program	ISPR	Incident Specific Preparedness Review
FWS	United States Fish and Wildlife Service	ISTEA	Intermodal Surface Transportation Efficiency Act of 1991
GAO	Government Accountability Office	ITA	International Trade Administration
GATT	General Agreement on Tariffs and Trade	ITD	International Trade Division
GEAR UP	Gaining Early Awareness and Readiness for Undergraduate Programs	ITS	Information Technology Service
		ITU	International Telecommunication Union
GFN	Good Faith Negotiations		
GIPSA	Grain Inspection, Packers, and Stockyards Administration	JOBS	Job Opportunities and Basic Skills program
		JTPA	Job Training Partnership Act of 1982
GNMA	Government National Mortgage Association (Ginnie Mae)		
		LDC	local distribution companies
GPO	U.S. Government Printing Office	LEA	local educational agency
GPS	Global Positioning System	LEP	limited English proficiency
GSA	General Services Administration	LFP	Livestock Forage Disaster Program
		LIBOR	London Interbank Offered Rate
HAVA	Help America Vote Act of 2002	LIHEAP	Low Income Home Energy Assistance Program
HEA	Higher Education Amendments of 1998		
HEARTH	Helping Expedite and Advance Responsible Tribal Homeownership Act of 2012	LIP	Livestock Indemnity Program
		LMRDA	Labor-Management Reporting and Disclosure Act
HEARTH	Homeless Emergency Assistance and Rapid Transition to Housing Act	LNG	liquefied natural gas
		LPTV	low-power television
HEP	Higher Education Programs	LSA	local service area
HERA	Housing and Economic Recovery Act of 2008	LWA	limited work authorization
HEW	Department of Health, Education, and Welfare	MAP-21	Moving Ahead for Progress in the 21st Century Act of 2012
HHI	Healthy Homes Initiative	MARAD	Maritime Administration
HHS	Department of Health and Human Services	MBS	Mortgage-Backed Securities
		MCSAC	Motor Carrier Safety Advisory Committee
HIPAA	Health Insurance Portability and Accountability Act of 1996	MEDLARS	Medical Literature Analysis and Retrieval System
HIRE	Hiring Incentives to Restore Employment Act of 2010	MEP	Manufacturing Extension Partnership
HITECH	Health Information Technology for Economic and Clinical Health Act	MFN	most-favored-nation
		MHPA	Mental Health Parity Act
HMEP	Hazardous Materials Emergency Preparedness	MINER	Mine Improvement and New Emergency Response Act of 2006
HPCs	high performance computers	MMDS	Multipoint Microwave Distribution Services
HUBZone	historically underutilized business zone		
HUD	Department of Housing and Urban Development	MMS	Minerals Management Service
		MOA	memorandum of agreement
		MODU	mobile offshore drilling units
ICC	Interstate Commerce Commission	MP	Northern Mariana Islands
ICE	Immigration and Customs Enforcement	M.S.	mail stop
ICVI	Interstate Certificate of Veterinary Inspection	MSHA	Mine Safety and Health Administration
		MSPB	Merit Systems Protection Board
IDEA	Individuals with Disabilities Education Act		
		NAAQS	National Ambient Air Quality Standard
IFLE	International and Foreign Language Education	NACOSH	National Advisory Committee on Occupational Safety and Health
IHAs	Indian Housing Authorities	NAFTA	North American Free Trade Agreement
IHS	Indian Health Service	NAIS	National Animal Identification System
INA	Immigration and Nationality Act	NAP	Noninsured Crop Disaster Assistance Program
INS	Immigration and Naturalization Service		
IOM	Institute of Medicine	NAS	National Airspace System
IRS	Internal Revenue Service	NASD	National Association of Securities Dealers
ISDN	Integrated Services Digital Network		

NCCC	National Civilian Community Corps	NOSB	National Organic Standards Board
NCE	new chemical entity	NPDES	National Pollution Discharge Elimination System
NCEI	National Centers for Environmental Information	NPR	National Performance Review
NCES	National Center for Education Statistics	NPS	National Park Service
NCJRS	National Criminal Justice Reference Service	NRA	National Rifle Association
		NRA	Negotiated Rates Act of 1993
NCLB	No Child Left Behind Act of 2002	NRC	Nuclear Regulatory Commission
NCUA	National Credit Union Administration	NRCS	Natural Resources Conservation Service
NCUSIF	National Credit Union Share Insurance Fund	NRTs	National Response Teams
		NSC	National Security Council
NDA	new drug application	NTIA	National Telecommunications and Information Administration
NEA	National Endowment for the Arts		
NEC	National Economic Council	NTIS	National Technical Information Service (Commerce)
NEDRES	National Environmental Data Referral Service		
		NTSB	National Transportation Safety Board
NEPA	National Environmental Policy Act	NVOCC	non-vessel operating common carrier
NESDIS	National Environmental Satellite, Data, and Information Service	NVRA	National Voter Registration Act of 1993
		NWS	National Weather Service
NEXRAD	next generation radar		
NextGen	Next Generation Air Transportation System	OAR	Office of Air and Radiation (EPA)
		OASHI	Office of AIDS and Special Health Issues
NEW	Native Employment Works program	OAW	Office of the American Workplace
NFA	National Futures Association	OCA	Office of Consumer Affairs
NGPA	Natural Gas Policy Act of 1978	OCC	Office of the Comptroller of the Currency
NHS	National Highway System		
NHTSA	National Highway Traffic Safety Administration	OCR	Office for Civil Rights (HHS)
		OCRM	Ocean and Coastal Resource Management
NIBIN	National Integrated Ballistic Information Network		
		OCS	Outer Continental Shelf
NIC	National Institute of Corrections	OCST	Office of Commercial Space Transportation
NICS	National Instant Criminal Background Check System		
		OCTAE	Office of Career, Technical, and Adult Education
NIDILRR	National Institute on Disability, Independent Living, and Rehabilitation Research		
		OEA	Office of Environmental Analysis
		OECD	Organization for Economic Cooperation and Development
NIDRR	National Institute on Disability and Rehabilitation Research		
		OESE	Office of Elementary and Secondary Education
NIDSIs	National Integrated Drought Information System		
		OFBCI	Office of Faith-based and Community Initiatives
NIES	National Import Export Services		
NIJ	National Institute of Justice	OFBNP	Office of Faith-based and Neighborhood Partnerships
NIOSH	National Institute of Occupational Safety and Health		
		OFCCP	Office of Federal Contract Compliance Programs
NIRA	National Industrial Recovery Act		
NIST	National Institute of Standards and Technology	OFLH	Office of Federal Lands Highway
		OFSA	Office for Federal Student Aid
NLB	National Labor Board	OGC	Office of General Counsel
NLCS	National Landscape Conservation System	OGHA	Office of Global Health Affairs
NLECTC	National Law Enforcement Corrections Technology Center	OGP	Office of Governmentwide Policy
		OGSM	Office of the General Sales Manager
NLM	National Library of Medicine	OHA	Office of Health Affairs
NLRA	National Labor Relations Act	OHMS	Office of Hazardous Materials Safety
NLRB	National Labor Relations Board	OHRP	Office for Human Research Protections
NMB	National Mediation Board	OID	Office of Integration and Disposition
NOAA	National Oceanic and Atmospheric Administration	OIE	World Organization for Animal Health (*Office International des Epizooties*)
NOP	National Organic Program	OIG	Office of the Inspector General (HHS)
NOPR	Notice of Proposed Rulemaking	OIRA	Office of Information and Regulatory Affairs
NOS	National Ocean Service		

OJJDP	Office of Juvenile Justice and Delinquency Prevention	PRC	Postal Regulatory Commission
OJP	Office of Justice Programs	PRISM	Performance and Registration Information Systems Management
OLE	Office of Law Enforcement	PSA	Packers and Stockyards Administration
OLMS	Office of Labor Management Standards	PSP	Packers and Stockyards Programs
OLS	online library system	PSQIA	Patient Safety and Quality Improvement Act of 2005
OMB	Office of Management and Budget	PSS	Program Support Services
ONAP	Office of National AIDS Policy	PTC	positive train control
ONAP	Office of Native American Programs	PTO	Patent and Trademark Office
ONDCP	Office of National Drug Control Policy	PUHCA	Public Utility Holding Company Act
ONRR	Office of Natural Resources Revenue	PURPA	Public Utilities Regulation Policy Act
OPA	Office of Public Affairs	PWBA	Pension and Welfare Benefits Administration
OPAGAC	Office of Public Assistance, Governmental Affairs, and Compliance		
OPE	Office of Postsecondary Education	QHWRA	Quality Housing and Work Responsibility Act of 1998
OPHS	Office of Public Health and Science		
OPPT	Office of Pollution Prevention and Toxics	RARG	Regulatory Analysis Review Group
OPS	Office of Pipeline Safety	RBC	Regulatory Barriers Clearinghouse
ORA	Office of Regulatory Activities	RBS	Rural Business-Cooperative Service
ORIC	online research and information center	RCPP	Regional Conservation Partnership Program
OSC	Office of Site Closure	RCRA	Resource Conservation and Recovery Act of 1976
OSERS	Office of Special Education and Rehabilitative Services	RDA	Rural Development Administration
OSG	Office of the Surgeon General	REA	Rural Electrification Administration
OSHA	Occupational Safety and Health Administration	REAP	Rural Economic Area Partnership
OSHS	Office of Safety, Health and Security	RECA	Radiation Exposure Compensation Act
OSMRE	Office of Surface Mining Reclamation and Enforcement	REFCORP	Resolution Funding Corporation
OSRA	Ocean Shipping Reform Act	REMIC	Real Estate Mortgage Investment Conduit
OSRP	Oil Spill Response Plans	RESPA	Real Estate Settlement Procedures Act of 1974
OSTP	Office of Science and Technology Policy		
OTA	Office of Technology Assessment	RESTORE Act	Resources and Ecosystems Sustainability, Tourist Opportunities, and Revived Economies of the Gulf Coast States Act of 2012
OTC	over-the-counter		
OTS	Office of Thrift Supervision		
OVC	Office for Victims of Crime		
OVW	Office on Violence Against Women	RFA	Regulatory Flexibility Act
OWCP	Office of Workers' Compensation Programs	RHS	Rural Housing Service
		RIK	Royalty-in-Kind
PAC	political action committee	RIMS	Records and Information Management System
PAYE	Pay As You Earn		
PBGC	Pension Benefit Guaranty Corporation	RITA	Research and Innovative Technology Administration
PCAOB	Public Company Accounting Oversight Board	RMA	Risk Management Agency
PEIS	Programmatic Environmental Impact Statement	RPD	Office of Railroad Policy and Development
PHAs	Public Housing Authorities	RRF	Ready Reserve Fleet
PHMSA	Pipeline and Hazardous Materials Safety Administration	RSPA	Research and Special Programs Administration (Transportation)
PHS	Public Health Service	RTC	Resolution Trust Corporation
PHS	Public Health Service Act of 1944	RTECS	Registry of Toxic Effects of Chemical Substances
PIH	Public and Indian Housing		
PL	Public Law	RUS	Rural Utilities Service
PLC	Price Loss Coverage		
POV	pattern of violations	S&S	significant and substantial
PPI	Policy, Planning, and Innovation	SAC	special-agent-in-charge
PPQ	Plant Protection and Quarantine	SADA	Supplemental Agriculture Disaster Assistance
PPRA	Protection of Pupil Rights Amendment		
PRA	Paperwork Reduction Act		

SAFE Act	Secure and Fair Enforcement for Mortgage Licensing Act of 2008		TAP	Taxpayer Advocacy Panel
SAFETEA	Safe, Accountable, Flexible, and Efficient Transportation Equity Act of 2005		TAP	Tree Assistance Program
			TARP	Troubled Asset Relief Program
SAIC	Special Agent in Charge		TASC	Technical Assistance for Specialty Crops Program
SAIF	Savings Association Insurance Fund		TCE	Tax Counseling for the Elderly program
SAMHSA	Substance Abuse and Mental Health Services Administration		TDD	Telecommunications Device for the Deaf
SAVE	Systematic Alien Verification for Entitlements program		TEA-21	Transportation Equity Act for the 21st Century
SBA	Small Business Administration		TEFAP	The Emergency Food Assistance Program
SBIC	Small Business Investment Company			
SBREFA	Small Business Regulatory Enforcement Fairness Act		TERAs	Tribal Energy Resource Agreements
			TIRC	Toxicology Information Response Center
SBTE	Small Business Tax Education program		TOLA	Tribal Law and Order Act of 2010
SCO	Supplemental Coverage Option		TRR	Trade Regulation Rules
SCS	Soil Conservation Service		TSA	Transportation Security Administration
SCSRs	self-contained self-rescue devices			
SEC	Securities and Exchange Commission		TSC	Transportation Systems Center
SESD	Special Examination and Supervision Division		TSI	Transportation Safety Institute
			TSR	Transportation Security Regulation
SILS	Science Information and Library Services		TTB	Alcohol and Tobacco Tax and Trade Bureau
SIPC	Securities Investor Protection Corporation		TTRC	Training Technology Resource Center
SLSA	Saint Lawrence Seaway Authority		TTY	text telephone
SLSDC	Saint Lawrence Seaway Development Corporation		TWIC	Transportation Worker Identification Credentials program
SMART	Sex Offender Sentencing, Monitoring, Apprehending, Registering, and Tracking		UIT	unit investment trusts
SMCRA	Surface Mining Control and Reclamation Act of 1977		UMTA	Urban Mass Transportation Administration
SMI	supplementary medical insurance		URI	University Research Institute
SMSA	standard metropolitan statistical area		USACE	U.S. Army Corps of Engineers
SNAP	Supplemental Nutrition Assistance Program		USAID	U.S. Agency for International Development
SORNA	Sex Offender Registration and Notification Act		U.S.C.	United States Code
			USCBP	U.S. Customs and Border Protection
SPR	Strategic Petroleum Reserve		USCIS	U.S. Citizenship and Immigration Service
SPRS	Surveillance, Preparedness and Response			
SRO	self-regulatory organization		USCS	U.S. Customs Service
SRS	Secure Rural Schools and Community Self-Determination Act		USDA	U.S. Department of Agriculture
			USEC	U.S. Enrichment Corporation
SSA	Social Security Administration		USES	U.S. Employment Service
SSI	Supplemental Security Income program		USFA	U.S. Fire Administration
STAA	Surface Transportation Assistance Act		USFCS	U.S. and Foreign Commercial Service
STAS	Science, Technology and Analysis		USGS	U.S. Geological Survey
STAX	Stacked Income Protection Plan		USITC	U.S. International Trade Commission
STB	Surface Transportation Board		USML	U.S. Munitions List
STELA	System for Tracking Export License Applications		USN	U.S. Navy
			USPHSCC	U.S. Public Health Service Commissioned Corps
Superfund	Comprehensive Environmental Response, Compensation, and Liability Act		USPS	U.S. Postal Service
			USPTO	U.S. Patent and Trademark Office
TA	teaching assistant		USTR	Office of the U.S. Trade Representative
TAACCCT	Trade Adjustment Assistance Community College and Career Training grant program		UTC	University Transportation Center
			V2V	vehicle-to-vehicle
TACs	Technical Advisory Committees		VA	Department of Veterans Affairs
TANF	Temporary Assistance for Needy Families program		VACAA	Veterans Access, Choice, and Accountability Act of 2014

VAWA	Violence Against Women Act	WHD	Wage and Hour Division
VETS	Veterans' Employment and Training Service	WHTI	Western Hemisphere Travel Initiative
		WIA	Workforce Investment Act
VITA	Volunteer Income Tax Assistance program	WIC	Women, Infants, and Children food program
VPA-HIP	Voluntary Public Access and Habitat Incentive Program	WIOA	Workforce Innovation and Opportunity Act
VRAP	Veterans Retraining Assistance Program	WRRDA	Water Resources Reform and Development Act of 2014
VSS	voting system standards	WTO	World Trade Organization

Key to Congressional Addresses

U.S. Capitol. Abbreviated as CAP; the letters H and S before the room number indicate the House or Senate side of the building. Zip codes are 20510 for the Senate, and 20515 for the House.

Senate Office Buildings. Mail for delivery to Senate office buildings does not require a street address. The zip code is 20510. Abbreviations, building names, and street locations are as follows:

SD	Dirksen Senate Office Bldg., Constitution Ave. between 1st and 2nd Sts. N.E.
SH	Hart Senate Office Bldg., 2nd St. and Constitution Ave. N.E.
SR	Russell Senate Office Bldg., Constitution Ave. between Delaware Ave. and 1st St. N.E.

House Office Buildings. Mail for delivery to House office buildings does not require a street address. The zip code is 20515. Abbreviations, building names, and street locations are as follows:

CHOB	Cannon House Office Bldg., Independence Ave. between New Jersey Ave. and 1st St. S.E.
FHOB	Ford House Office Bldg., 2nd and D Sts. S.W.
LHOB	Longworth House Office Bldg., Independence Ave. between S. Capitol St. and New Jersey Ave. S.E.
OHOB	O'Neill House Office Bldg., 300 New Jersey Ave. S.E.
RHOB	Rayburn House Office Bldg., Independence Ave. between S. Capitol and 1st Sts. S.W.

Federal Regulatory Directory

Federal Regulation: An Introduction

For much of U.S. history, regulation was a modest and relatively obscure government function. Conflict over regulation, when it occurred, generally was muted and played out in court. Over time, as the role of regulation in American society grew, so too did the controversy that attended each manifestation of its considerable power. Because regulation continues to be a pervasive presence in American economic and social affairs, controversy over it provides much of the fuel for the U.S. political system.

Conflict is inevitably a part of virtually every significant element of regulation. Statutes creating or amending regulatory programs are hotly contested when under consideration by Congress. Affected parties frequently challenge regulations mandated or authorized by legislation during the agency rulemaking process or in court after the rules are completed. The implementation and enforcement of regulations generate thousands of hearings and lawsuits. Students and practitioners of regulation debate virtually all aspects of regulatory programs, from their origins in American political culture to their actual impact on society. They even disagree on an issue as basic as the definition of *regulation*.

Anyone asked to provide a defensible definition of regulation is well advised to err on the side of generality. Many experts, including members of the Senate Committee on Governmental Affairs and the staff of the Office of Management and Budget (OMB), have attempted to be specific. But they have found regulation is difficult to capture because of its many variations and nuances. Even efforts to develop comprehensive lists of regulatory programs or regulated activities usually are frustrated by the remarkable diversity of forms and functions. One scholar on regulation, Kenneth Meier, offers a definition that may be sufficiently general: regulation is "any attempt by the government to control the behavior of citizens, corporations, or subgovernments." This definition encompasses programs and activities in which regulation is either the primary goal or secondary effect. After all, many programs in which the primary mission is to deliver benefits or services in fact develop eligibility criteria, reimbursement policies, and other requirements that in effect serve to regulate program participants.

Regulation is also a complex and continuous process that occurs in identifiable stages—legislation, rulemaking, implementation, enforcement, judicial review, and dispute resolution. But the sequence of these stages is neither neat nor predictable. For example, any stage can lead directly to dispute resolution. Rulemaking by an agency can stimulate interest groups to demand new legislation. While the institutional focus shifts from stage to stage, regulation engages the time and resources of all the major institutions and actors in the U.S. political system: Congress, the president, agencies, departments, and commissions of all sorts, the courts, the ubiquitous interest groups, the press, business, and individuals.

In a real sense, regulation is always being redefined. Once it was confined largely to economic concerns, such as entry to markets by individual companies, the rates they charged, and the products or services provided in defined industries. This form of regulation has declined in importance, overshadowed today by programs that seek broader social objectives—equity, health, safety, protection, aesthetics—and cut across all economic sectors

and activities. Regulation is today the dominant form of domestic policy, and the regulatory process is the chosen method of policy making.

■ REASONS FOR REGULATION

Proponents of regulation justify the implicit limitations on freedom by arguing that the free market and private decisions either create inequitable and inefficient conditions or fail to achieve optimal social benefits. Opponents frequently scoff at such justifications, arguing that regulation usually substitutes one type of inequity or inefficiency for another and that purported benefits rarely are achieved because regulatory programs are either fundamentally misguided or mismanaged. The debate reached a crescendo in the late 1970s and early 1980s, when some of the most thoughtful critiques and defenses of regulation were offered by scholars and professionals.

After an ebb, the 1994 elections that brought the first Republican Congress to power since the Eisenhower administration reinvigorated the regulatory debate. As long as the Republicans controlled Congress and Democrat Bill Clinton occupied the White House, the legislative branch's efforts to bring about major regulatory change was doomed to yield more debate than legislation. But with the election of George W. Bush in 2000, the landscape changed. One of Bush's first actions on Inauguration Day in 2001 was to slap a sixty-day freeze on new rules and regulations, during which time the new White House vowed to review hundreds of measures proposed in the final months of Clinton's administration. Emboldened, the Republican Congress immediately moved to begin its review of the Clinton regulatory legacy.

While a number of the late Clinton administration regulations, such as the rules on arsenic levels in drinking water, ultimately took effect, many were rolled back permanently. The Bush administration also changed the paradigm for justifying new regulations—focusing more on cost-benefit analysis, especially on those regulations that affected businesses. But the changes under Bush were just the latest salvo in a long war between those who favor a more thorough regulatory scheme as a means to soften the sharper edges of the market economy and those who view such a scheme as an obstacle to wealth creation and prosperity. The November 2006 elections leading to Democratic majorities in both houses of Congress brought about yet another shift in emphasis. After twelve years of Republican rule on Capitol Hill, Democrats announced their intention to increase oversight of the executive branch, including federal regulatory agencies. In November 2008 the nation elected a Democratic president, Barack Obama, resulting in less tension between the legislative and executive branches over regulatory policy. Indeed, many of the people chosen for important administrative posts, especially in the smaller, more regulation-heavy agencies, have come from the staff of Democratic members of Congress.

This section reviews some of the classic arguments for and against regulation.

Economic Regulation

Competition is the cornerstone of the American economy, and a major purpose of economic regulation is to ensure the proper continuation of a competitive atmosphere. The justification for regulation is that it corrects market failures that occur when competition either does not exist in an industry or does not allocate resources efficiently.

NATURAL MONOPOLY

One such failure is the existence of a "natural monopoly," or exclusive control of a commodity or service in a specified area. Unregulated monopolies can restrict output and elevate prices compared with those in a competitive market structure. The regulation of public utilities is the classic example of government controls on natural monopolies. A public utility commission determines what the single supplier (the monopolist) may charge for output, the minimum quality of the service, and what profit the monopolist is entitled to earn. During the late 1990s, the debate in Congress over proposed deregulation of the electricity industry highlighted the limits and lengths lawmakers and regulators have gone to end such "natural monopolies." The electricity industry stood as the last major regulated monopoly in the country. But the deregulatory fiasco in California that led to rolling blackouts and nearly bankrupt utilities in the winter of 2000–2001 may have doomed efforts for complete deregulation of the industry.

In fact, what once seemed a natural monopoly often ceases to be one with changes in the market or the advent of new technology. The railroads, for example, were considered natural monopolies in the nineteenth century; as such, the rates they could charge, as well as other aspects of their business, were regulated. But with the development of other viable methods of transportation in the twentieth century, this natural-monopoly rationale for government regulation ceased to exist. The same held true for providers of local telephone service, which were regulated as monopolies until the Telecommunications Act of 1996 allowed the phase-in of competition for local service.

Monopolies may also occur when a company or a group of companies takes deliberate action to set prices or control supply and thus drive other competitors out of business. Since it was enacted in 1890, the Sherman Antitrust Act has made such combinations in restraint of trade illegal. Critics of this justification for regulation scrutinize any activity for which natural-monopoly status is proposed. The Department of Justice in 1998 moved against two powerful corporations consolidating power in the computer age, Intel and Microsoft. Both were accused of unfair trade practices that had left them with near-total control over their markets—microprocessors (Intel) and software (Microsoft). Intel quietly settled its antitrust case with the government, but in 1999 U.S. District Court Judge Thomas Penfield Jackson ordered a defiant Microsoft to be broken up into two companies; he set into motion the most momentous antitrust action since AT&T was broken up in the 1980s.

Although Jackson's order to break up Microsoft was overturned by a federal appeals court in 2001, his contention that the company was an illegal monopoly was affirmed. Still, the reversal gave impetus to the Bush Justice Department—which was much less enthusiastic about breaking up the software maker than was the department under President Clinton—to cut a deal with the company later that year. Under the agreement, Microsoft remained whole in exchange for altering certain business practices that had allowed it to use the monopoly it enjoyed with its Windows operating system to shut competitors out of certain parts of the software market.

Overall, antitrust activity subsided substantially by the end of President Bush's term. Huge mergers in telecommunications, media, banking, and other industries went ahead or were expected to go ahead with the blessing of the federal government. Even the Democratic takeover of Congress did little to slow this trend: in 2007 huge mergers in telecommunications, energy, and other industries were announced and expected to win regulatory approval. Ironically, European regulators have been more aggressive in their pursuit of possible U.S. monopolists. For instance, General Electric's bid to buy Honeywell was approved by U.S. regulators only to be nixed in July 2001 by their European counterparts, who worried that the two firms would unfairly dominate the world market for jetliner components. But the change in administrations has shifted the emphasis back to the consumer and away from business. Indeed, in May 2009 the head of the Justice Department's Antitrust Division, Christine Varney, announced that she would aggressively enforce the nation's antitrust laws, particularly against large corporations.

DESTRUCTIVE COMPETITION

Overly vigorous competition within an industry can lead to a deterioration in product quality, bankruptcy, and monopoly. The railroad price wars that raged in the 1870s and 1880s demonstrated the harm imposed by destructive competition—prices and services fluctuated wildly, consumer demands went unsatisfied, and industry planning became increasingly difficult. Both the railroads and the public suffered from this instability. The Interstate Commerce Commission (ICC) was created in 1887 in part to end the destructive competition.

Advocates of free markets note that such industry-threatening conditions are sometimes caused by those seeking monopoly or oligopoly through predatory pricing. For example, they argue that the savings and loan problems in the 1980s arose as much because of conflict of interest, fraud, and mismanagement as because of destructive competition. Cases of unadulterated destructive competition are rare; anticompetitive and illegal practices are usually lurking in the background.

EXTERNALITIES

Another form of market imperfection involves what economists call "externalities," or spillovers, which develop when the production or use of a product has an effect on third parties. Positive externalities are benefits enjoyed by third parties; negative externalities are costs borne by third parties.

Air pollution, which harms the health of the public in general, is a negative externality. Resources such as clean air and water are scarce and exhaustible, but manufacturers treat them as a "free" input in the production process; consequently production costs do not include the expenses of the pollution. From a social point of view, therefore, the company's goods will not reflect the true costs of production. The public shares those costs, and the price can include illness and expensive health care.

No one seriously questions the existence of externalities or the inefficiencies and inequities they create. However, many take issue with the regulatory mechanisms that deal with them. The use of "command and control" regulation, with its uniform rules and enforcement through monitoring and sanctioning, frequently is criticized as inappropriate, ineffective, and inefficient. Critics much prefer regulations that set standards (but leave to regulated parties decisions as to how to comply). This type of system, critics argue, avoids a cumbersome bureaucracy and draws on the ingenuity of U.S. business and proven market forces to achieve important social goals such as pollution reduction. Programs launched by the Environmental Protection Agency (EPA), the Department of Agriculture, and the Occupational Safety and Health Administration (OSHA) during the Clinton administration sought to do just that, setting goals in areas as diverse as workplace safety, pollution control, and food safety—then letting industry find the way to reach those goals. Proponents of the existing mode of regulation question the ability and willingness of the private sector to find these solutions.

But if anything, such cooperative programs are expanding. Under the George W. Bush administration, agencies such as the EPA and OSHA worked to increase their outreach efforts to the businesses they regulate and, in some cases, have pushed for forms of voluntary or self-regulation. An example of this is Bush's Clear Skies Initiative, a 2002 proposal that aimed to lower smog and acid rain–causing emissions by allowing utilities to buy and sell pollution credits. Introduced in Congress as the Clear Skies Act of 2003, the proposal never won passage in either house through the end of Bush's last term. Since the election of President Obama, however, the emphasis has shifted to greater and more direct regulation on environmental issues. An example is the administration's cap-and-trade environmental measure, which passed the House in spring 2009 and aimed to reduce carbon emissions through a complex regulatory scheme.

SPECIAL GOODS AND SERVICES

Some goods and services have characteristics that prevent the free market from handling them in an efficient manner. Many socially beneficial goods or services would not be produced without government intervention, such as highways, air traffic control, national defense, and clean air. Other goods and services might be exploited, depleted, or foreclosed for other beneficial purposes if use was unregulated. The government typically regulates the use of resources such as ground water, common grazing areas, and free-flowing rivers.

Again, critics find fault with the typical regulatory response. Some support more user charges for the goods and services government provides to ensure that those who enjoy the benefits pay the costs. Some would provide access to resources that could be threatened by unlimited use through an auction, with use going to the highest bidder. Others prefer to entrust such decisions to regulatory agencies, which are charged with the responsibility to define and defend an always elusive "public interest."

Social Aspects of Economic Regulation

Many, if not most, types of economic regulation are social in nature. The nation seeks to control damage from pollution, illness, or injuries to workers and consumers; preserve multiple uses of rivers; and protect endangered species for more than economic reasons. Issues of social equity have driven a number of other regulatory programs, notably in employment. Arguments over equal employment opportunity regulations have raged since 1964 and show no signs of abating. Charges of quotas and reverse discrimination arising from these programs are all too familiar and still unresolved.

The rationing of energy supplies or controls on their prices also can be seen as social regulation, and these practices often are attacked on efficiency grounds. "Supplement incomes," say the critics, "and let the market determine prices." Ultimately, they claim, the market eliminates shortages by encouraging production or generating substitutes.

There is another form of social regulation the mere mention of which triggers fierce reactions. The content of art and entertainment can offend the moral code or aesthetic sensibilities of some viewers or listeners. What might otherwise be protected by basic constitutional rights of free expression becomes a potential object of regulation when public monies or licenses are involved. The Federal Communications Commission (FCC) took similar action to prevent its radio and television licensees from exposing children to "indecent" programming. The Telecommunications Act of 1996 ordered that new televisions contain circuitry capable of blocking programs rated for violence or adult content. These new indecency rules were put to the test by a series of subsequent incidents on television and radio, particularly the exposure of part of singer Janet Jackson's breast during the February 2004 broadcast of the Super Bowl halftime show. These incidents ultimately led Congress, in summer 2006, to pass a new, tougher indecency law. The legislation, which did not regulate cable or satellite television providers, increased by tenfold the amount the FCC could fine each television or radio broadcaster for each incident of indecency, raising the total from $32,500 to $325,000.

The 1996 and 2006 telecommunications laws and the recent decision that followed them are an example of the kinds of tensions that social regulations can produce. Balancing the desire to set community standards with the need to protect liberty often leads to prolonged and difficult political and legal conflicts.

The 1996 telecommunications law also broke new and controversial ground in other, newer media by barring the transmission or display of indecent material to a minor on an interactive computer service such as the Internet. Indecency in this case extended not just to sexually explicit material but also to information about drugs and devices for producing abortions. The reaction to such initiatives has been predictable, with civil libertarians decrying limits to speech and social and religious conservatives calling for even greater restrictions. What is most significant about these cases is that they illustrate how deeply regulation affects fundamental constitutional freedoms and personal values.

However sophisticated and esoteric they become, the arguments for and against the regulatory system always return to fundamental questions of effectiveness, efficiency, and equity. That regulatory programs fall short of achieving the goals set for them is indisputable, but this fact ignores the extraordinary tasks set before them. The Occupational Safety and Health Act, for example, called upon OSHA to "set . . . standard(s) which most adequately assures to the extent feasible, on the basis of the best available evidence, that no employee will suffer material impairment of health or functional capacity even if such employee has regular exposure to the hazard dealt with by such standard for the period of his working life."

The 1972 Clean Water Act required the EPA to issue regulations governing all point sources of water pollution within one year and to bring all regulated parties into compliance with strict standards within ten years. Realistic criteria for an "effective" program are elusive when regulatory statutes promise so much to so many. If taken literally, these laws doom their regulatory progeny to failure and the public to disappointment.

■ EARLY HISTORY AND GROWTH OF REGULATION

Article I, Section 8, of the U.S. Constitution empowers Congress to "regulate Commerce with foreign Nations, and among the several States." One of the earliest cases in American administrative law involved delegation of a regulatory power—the imposition and suspension of tariffs—to the president of the United States. The federal government in its first 100 years established numerous offices that performed regulatory functions. Designed largely to promote and develop the young nation and its industries, these agencies included the Army Corps of Engineers (1824), the Patent and Trademark Office (1836), the Comptroller of the Currency (1863), the Copyright Office of the Library of Congress (1870), and the Bureau of Fisheries (1871). Two other agencies, the Internal Revenue Service (1862) and the Civil Service Commission (1883), were established to facilitate administration of the government.

In 1887, in response to widespread dissatisfaction with the state of the railroads, Congress created the Interstate Commerce Commission (ICC) to regulate that industry. The ICC can be seen as the start of the modern era of regulation for a number of reasons. It represented a shift of regulatory power from the states to the federal government, a trend that continues today, though a strong current of "federalism" is seeking to reshift the balance toward the states. The "independent commission," multimember and politically balanced, became a model used in regulation of other industries and economic activities. The original statute, the Interstate Commerce Act, was amended several times to correct perceived defects in its design or alleged abuses and limitations in the responsible agency. Early on, the judiciary emerged as a major force in railroad regulation, as the ICC's decisions were routinely and successfully challenged by regulated parties. These aspects in the development of the ICC have been repeated to some degree in all the other regulatory agencies. The ICC's later history is less typical, though it may also provide a prototype for the critics of government regulation: deregulation in the 1980s led to the ICC's elimination in 1995, with its remaining regulatory functions being transferred to the new Surface Transportation Board in the Transportation Department.

Between 1915 and the beginning of the New Deal, Congress created seven more agencies and commissions to regulate parts of the nation's commercial and financial systems. These were the Coast Guard (1915), the Tariff Commission (1916), the Commodity Exchange Authority (1922), the Customs Service (1927), the Federal Radio Commission (1927), the Federal Power Commission (1930—to replace the Water Power Commission, which was established in 1920), and the Food and Drug Administration (1931). Some of these agencies were later absorbed into larger departments.

The New Deal marks the next major landmark in the history of regulation. A network of entities designed to regulate the economy out of the Great Depression, President Franklin D. Roosevelt's program was an unprecedented incursion by government into the private sector. The regulatory legacy of the New Deal was threefold. The first legacy was economic regulation. Some of the agencies and legislation dealing with economic regulation and created during the New Deal are

- The Federal Home Loan Bank Board (FHLBB), established in 1932 to regulate federally chartered savings and loan associations.
- The Federal Deposit Insurance Corporation (FDIC), created in 1933 to be the primary regulator and insurer of state-chartered banks that were not members of the Federal Reserve System.
- The Securities and Exchange Commission (SEC), started in 1934 to protect the public against fraud and deception in the securities and financial markets.
- The National Labor Relations Board (NLRB), established by the Wagner Act of 1935 to prevent "unfair labor practices" and to protect the right of employees to bargain collectively.
- The Motor Carrier Act of 1935, which gave the ICC authority over the burgeoning trucking industry.
- The U.S. Maritime Administration, created in 1936 to oversee shipbuilding and ship operations during World War II. Eventually these functions, among others, were transferred to the Transportation Department and the independent Federal Maritime Commission (FMC).

At Roosevelt's urging, Congress in 1934 established the independent Federal Communications Commission to consolidate federal regulation of all common carriers in interstate communications, which then were radio, telephone, and telegraph. During this period, the growing competition among airlines necessitated coordination of airline routes and regulation of flight operations. Because the ICC was already heavily burdened with increased responsibility for surface transportation, Congress in 1938 created the Civil Aeronautics Authority (CAA) to promote and regulate the industry, and then replaced it in 1940 with the Civil Aeronautics Board (CAB), an independent commission.

The second legacy of the New Deal was the establishment of a federal responsibility for social welfare through Social Security and related programs. In this way the New Deal set the stage for the massive expansion of benefit programs in the 1960s and regulatory programs concerned with social problems in the 1970s. The third legacy was the revolution in administrative procedure that still influences the operation of regulatory programs. Perceived abuses by New Deal agencies in the way they made and implemented regulatory decisions led directly, if slowly, to the Administrative Procedure Act of 1946 (APA). Both social regulation and regulatory procedures will be discussed subsequently.

From the end of World War II until the mid-1960s, relatively few new programs of federal regulation appeared. The Atomic Energy Commission and the expansion of aviation regulation were the major additions.

■ THE DEVELOPMENT OF SOCIAL REGULATION

The origins of much contemporary social regulation can be traced back to the 1960s. This new form of regulation was characterized by broad social objectives, greatly diversified government activities, and a vastly expanded reach into the private sector. Some mark the beginning with passage of the Civil Rights Act of 1964; others point to the National Environmental Policy Act of 1969. Whichever date is chosen as the start, the 1970s were unquestionably the most significant years in the history of regulation. More than 100 regulatory statutes were enacted during this decade alone, and many new regulatory institutions were created.

Consumer Protection

The consumer movement reached its zenith in the early 1970s and made a deep imprint on American life and the marketplace. Before his foray into electoral politics—and his role as Green Party spoiler in the 2000 election—Ralph Nader was, above all, a regulatory crusader. In the 1970s consumers, led by Nader, organized to demand safer, higher-quality products; goods that lived up to advertised claims; and lower prices for food, medical care, fuel, and other products. Nader's activities influenced passage of auto safety legislation in 1966. The new law established federal motor vehicle and tire safety standards and brought the automobile industry under permanent regulation for the first time. In 1970 the National

Highway Traffic Safety Administration (NHTSA) was created within the Transportation Department with authority to set auto safety and fuel efficiency standards as well as standards for state highway safety programs. Other agencies created to protect consumers of transportation included the Federal Highway Administration (FHWA) in 1966, which establishes highway safety standards, and the Federal Railroad Administration (FRA) also in 1966, which sets rail safety standards.

Financial and banking matters also came under new regulations. Between 1968 and 1977 Congress enacted the Truth in Lending Act, the Fair Credit Billing Act, the Equal Credit Opportunity Act, the Home Mortgage Disclosure Act, the Consumer Leasing Act, and the Fair Debt Collection Practices Act. Congress in 1975 also passed legislation strengthening regulation of consumer warranties. The National Credit Union Administration (NCUA) was created in 1970 to regulate member credit unions.

Consumers also won passage of the Consumer Product Safety Act in 1972. That law established the Consumer Product Safety Commission (CPSC) as an independent regulatory commission to protect the public against unreasonable risk of injury from hazardous products.

From the 1990s through much of the 2000s, the importance of consumer issues ebbed as conservatives in Congress, the White House, and elsewhere successfully pushed to reduce intense oversight and regulation of industry, arguing that it could leave U.S. business at a severe disadvantage over increasingly competitive rivals. But evidence of particularly unsafe or defective products occasionally brought the issue back into the headlines. For instance, problems in 2007 with Chinese products, including unsafe toys, tires, and pet food, called attention to the thin safety and inspection regime for overseas imports. As a result, politicians from both parties called for greater oversight of imported goods, particularly from China. As perhaps an indication of the swing back toward greater scrutiny of consumer goods, the Democratic Congress in 2008 passed a new consumer law, the Consumer Product Safety Improvement Act, and Republican Bush signed it. The act authorized substantial yearly budget increases for the CPSC until 2014. Besides agreeing with the increased budget for consumer safety, President Obama in 2009 showed additional support for the CPSC by increasing the number of commissioners from three to five.

Environmental Quality

Paralleling consumer activism was an equally enthusiastic public voice calling for a cleaner environment. Disasters, such as the 1969 oil spill off the coast of Santa Barbara, CA, strengthened the environmentalists' case.

One result of the environmental movement was the consolidation of the federal government's widespread environmental protection efforts into a single agency. The EPA, created in 1970 by President Richard Nixon's executive order, soon became one of the most controversial agencies in government. It remains so today. In the course of a single decade, Congress delegated vast authority to the EPA, through the Clean Air Act (1970, amendments in 1977), the Clean Water Act (1972, amendments in

1977), the Safe Drinking Water Act (1974, amendments in 1996), the Toxic Substances Control Act (1976), and the Resource Conservation and Recovery Act (1976).

Other regulatory agencies were established to protect certain elements of the environment, such as the Office of Surface Mining Reclamation and Enforcement (now the Office of Surface Mining) created in 1977 to regulate the strip-mining industry.

Workplace Safety

Safety in the workplace was the focus of another new regulatory agency that had an immense impact on U.S. business. OSHA was created in 1970 as an agency within the Labor Department to promulgate and enforce worker safety and health standards. The agency was authorized to conduct workplace inspections, require employers to keep detailed records on worker injuries and illness, and conduct research. Within one month of its creation, the agency adopted 4,400 standards from existing federal regulations, industry codes, and the American National Standards Institute. The agency also was authorized to issue standards for health hazards such as exposure to toxic chemicals.

Congress in 1973 established the Mining Enforcement and Safety Administration within the Interior Department to promulgate and enforce mine safety and health standards. In 1977 the agency was reorganized as the Mine Safety and Health Administration (MSHA) and placed in the Labor Department.

Energy Regulation

Another major area of expanded federal regulation in the 1970s was the energy sector, in which the United States was repeatedly confronted with the twin problems of dwindling energy supply and soaring costs. In 1973 Congress set up the Federal Energy Administration (FEA) to manage short-term fuel shortages. In 1974 Congress abolished the Atomic Energy Commission (AEC), creating in its place the Energy Research and Development Administration (ERDA), which was authorized to develop nuclear power and new energy sources while maintaining the nation's nuclear arsenal. That year, Congress also created an independent Nuclear Regulatory Commission (NRC), which assumed the AEC's nuclear safety and regulatory responsibilities.

In 1977 President Jimmy Carter created the cabinet-level Department of Energy (DOE) to consolidate the array of evolving energy powers, programs, and agencies throughout the government. The DOE assumed the powers and functions of the Federal Power Commission (FPC), the FEA, and ERDA, all of which were abolished. Authority to set prices for natural gas, oil, and electricity was given to the Federal Energy Regulatory Commission (FERC), an independent commission set up within, but separate from, the DOE.

The Ronald Reagan and George H. W. Bush Administrations

If the 1970s demonstrated extraordinary faith in regulation as an instrument for achieving social objectives, the 1980s were a decade of doubt, criticism, and reconsideration. Elected in 1980 on a platform highly critical of government roles in society in general and the economy in particular, President Ronald Reagan acted quickly, broadly, and decisively to alter the federal regulatory process.

In 1981 President Reagan issued Executive Order 12291 (*see appendix*), which gave the OMB extensive powers over the regulatory apparatus—perhaps the single most important reform of the rulemaking process since the Administrative Procedure Act (APA) in 1946. The order empowered the OMB to identify duplication, overlap, and conflict in rules, which federal agencies then were required to rectify; and to review existing and new rules for consistency with administration policies. The order required the use of cost-benefit analysis and established a "net benefit" criterion for rulemaking. The order also called for the serious consideration of alternatives, including nonregulatory options, when attempting to solve problems, and selecting the approach that creates the least burden for affected parties.

In the 1980s both the process and substance of regulation changed. The deregulation movement, which actually had begun in the late 1970s, accelerated and engulfed airlines, telecommunications, securities, trucking, railroads, buses, cable television, oil, natural gas, financial institutions, and even public utilities. In some areas the changes were profound. For example, the ICC, the institution that started it all in 1887, was left a shadow of its former self by deregulation legislation of the early 1980s. (The ICC was finally abolished in 1995.) Almost all the areas affected by deregulation were economic: rates, entry to markets, or business practices that critics believed were better left to the free market.

The Reagan administration attacked social regulation with different, subtler means. Administration officials imposed a temporary moratorium on new rules, altered procedures, cut budgets, and questioned policy decisions. New regulations faced a more arduous path from initiation to publication in the *Federal Register*.

It must also be said that an examination of the 1980s also finds new regulatory statutes, but these statutes usually were amendments to earlier legislation. Examples include the Government Securities Act (1986); the Hazardous and Solid Waste Amendments of 1984, which amended the Resource Conservation and Recovery Act; the Safe Drinking Water Act Amendments (1986); and the Electric Consumers Protection Act (1986), which amended the Federal Power Act. There were some new initiatives as well, such as the Commercial Space Launch Act of 1984 and Superfund hazardous waste regulations of 1980.

During the administration of George H. W. Bush, the president was often described, perhaps unfairly, as lacking interest in domestic policy. He attempted to respond to these criticisms with numerous assertions of intent, including his widely quoted aspiration to be known as the "environmental president." Whatever his interests and hopes, it was certainly true that regulatory activity during the first years of his presidency continued a revival that had begun in Reagan's second term.

Alarmed by apparent backsliding on the regulation issue, Bush's conservative supporters mounted an organized and concerted effort to drag their president back to the path of reduction and reform. He imposed and then extended a moratorium on new rules and tightened cost-benefit analysis requirements for those that were issued. He began instituting programs to set standards, then allowing businesses to develop the means to meet them. The EPA's 33/50 program, developed under the Bush administration, was one example. The program allowed more than 1,300 companies to cut back voluntarily toxic emissions 33 percent by 1993 and 50 percent by 1995. In exchange, EPA regulators would ease up on oversight and compliance rules. But Bush's most dramatic response was the creation of the Council on Competitiveness, chaired by Vice President Dan Quayle. The council was given authority to roam the full range of regulation in search of relief for U.S. business, and it soon became an aggressive advocate for relaxed requirements. A major source of controversy concerned the way the council conducted its business. It attempted to maintain strict secrecy in its deliberations and repeatedly refused to disclose those people in the private sector with whom it communicated or consulted. Those critics who were upset earlier with the possibilities of "backdoor rulemaking" were livid when they learned about the council's operations.

The Bill Clinton Administration

President Clinton's arrival in Washington was greeted with relief by liberal groups who felt the Reagan and Bush administrations had eased up too much on protection for the environment, workplace safety, and public health. Clinton's actions, however, elicited both applause and concern from those groups. Ironically, business groups also gave Clinton mixed reviews, approving of many industry-friendly initiatives but decrying a few tough new regulations. Clinton geared his reforms toward easing the regulatory burden on industry, the interest group that offered him the least political support. But his advocacy of "keeping the regulatory cop on the beat" quieted the criticism of liberal interest groups, as did the more public process his agencies instituted for rulemaking. A remarkable slew of "midnight" regulations—issued in the waning days of the Clinton White House—solidified his reputation as a regulatory activist. Forty-six finalized regulations—from sweeping rules governing repetitive motion injuries in the workplace to antidiscrimination protections for homosexuals—were published between Election Day, Nov. 2, 2000, and the day Clinton left office.

From 1994 to the end of his term, Clinton's attitudes toward regulation could not be seen in isolation from those of Congress. The 1994 elections brought to power a group of Republicans whose contempt for regulation was unprecedented. Although they failed to enact their most ambitious legislative items, the self-described Republican revolutionaries forced the Democratic administration to institute regulatory changes that preempted and defused some antiregulatory zeal. The Republican Congress succeeded in invigorating Clinton's reform efforts. At times, they even pushed agencies further to the right than they

would have gone otherwise. On the other hand, a hostile Congress emboldened Clinton to use his regulatory powers where his legislative powers failed him. From homosexual rights to patient protections against managed care insurers, Clinton was able to use the power of the presidency to circumvent Congress.

The Clinton approach to regulation and the regulatory process was outlined in two different documents. His Executive Order 12866, "Regulatory Planning and Review" (*for text of order, see the appendix*), established the principles guiding the development of regulations in federal agencies and the review of those regulations in the White House. The National Performance Review (NPR), written under the direction of Vice President Al Gore, contained a number of proposals to "reinvent" regulation. While Clinton was generally viewed as more sympathetic to regulatory programs than his Republican predecessor, Clinton's program for improving regulation contained much that is familiar from previous administrations.

The executive order, under the section titled "The Principles of Regulation," established twelve policies that the president expected agencies to observe in their regulatory work. These included

- Identification of problems to be addressed by regulation and their magnitude.
- Review of existing regulations for possible elimination or modification.
- Assessment of nonregulatory alternatives to solving problems.
- Use of risk assessment to establish regulatory priorities.
- Establishing steps to ensure that the benefits of regulation justify the costs and that regulations adopted are cost effective.
- Use of the best available information when developing regulations.
- Use of performance objectives whenever possible. Wide consultation with state, local, and tribal governments. Avoidance of inconsistent, incompatible, or duplicative regulations.
- Tailoring of regulations to produce the least burden possible on society.
- Writing regulations that are simple and understandable.

The NPR, in a brief chapter titled "Eliminating Regulatory Overkill," provided a number of more specific objectives that the Clinton administration sought to achieve. These were mostly related in some way to the principles set forth in Executive Order 12866. Among these objectives were ambitious plans to reduce existing rules—50 percent—within three years and set up better interagency coordination to reduce "red tape."

Interagency coordination would be heightened through the creation of a high-level Regulatory Working Group. An NPR report noted the need for such coordination with the example of chocolate manufacturers who faced conflicting regulations from separate agencies. OSHA demanded porous insulation to reduce noise from machinery, while the Food and Drug Administration (FDA) insisted such insulation could not be kept clean enough to meet food safety standards. The group also assumed the task of identifying priority rules for OMB review. By easing the review burden on OMB, the coordinating group allowed rule reviewers to consider new rules in new ways, such as using more detailed cost-benefit analyses and examining the various segments of society and the economy the rule was impacting. The group also quieted criticism of "backdoor" rulemaking by taking away from OMB some of the responsibility Reagan and Bush had given it.

The administration also let it be known, both in the NPR and at the press conference announcing Executive Order 12866, that it strongly supported the expanded use of regulatory negotiation. The administration subsequently named the EPA, OSHA, and FDA as the vanguard agencies for its reform efforts, stressing cooperation and consultation over punishment and oversight.

To complement the Bush administration's 33/50 program, the EPA under Clinton created Project XL and the Common Sense Initiative. Project XL allowed large companies with good environmental track records to demonstrate their paths toward emissions reduction outside those prescribed by EPA rule-writers. The Common Sense Initiative identified six industry sectors—automobiles, electronics, iron and steel, metal finishing, petroleum refining, and printing—and then formed teams of business, environmental, and community representatives to come up with industry-specific ways to cut red tape, reduce emissions, and end the one-size-fits-all approach to environmental regulations. Through the program, the EPA reached an agreement with the metal finishing industry, granting it regulatory relief in exchange for efforts that went beyond mere compliance with environmental law. About 11,000 metal finishing shops would be brought under the agreement, which envisioned slashing emissions by up to 75 percent of 1992 levels.

Starting in 1993 OSHA's Maine 200 Program identified companies with high injury rates, then gave those firms the choice between partnering with OSHA to develop new worker safety programs or facing stepped-up enforcement. In December 1997 OSHA transformed the Maine pilot program into a national effort involving 12,250 employers, dubbed the Cooperative Compliance Program (CCP). But cooperation could only go so far. About 10,000 out of 12,000 employers invited to join the CCP had signed up by February 1998, but that month, the program was thrown out by a federal appeals court, responding to a major lawsuit by the U.S. Chamber of Commerce, the National Association of Manufacturers, the American Trucking Associations, and the Food Marketing Institute. The court found that the program amounted to an unfair club in the hands of the regulators. OSHA could promise fewer inspections, but to participate, businesses would have to institute some workplace safety programs that had not gone through a formal rulemaking procedure. That, the court ruled, was an end run around the regulatory process.

In 1996 the FDA announced a series of new cooperative programs. One pilot effort allowed medical device manufacturers to select an FDA-recognized third-party reviewer to assess the safety of low-risk and moderate-risk products, thus speeding the regulatory process. A series of meetings between the FDA and medical device manufacturers produced changes to FDA inspection procedures to permit advance notification of inspections and an opportunity for firms to note on inspection records that a violation had been immediately corrected.

In July 1996 the Department of Agriculture's (USDA) Food Safety and Inspection Service announced the first overhaul of its meat and poultry inspection system in ninety years, and again, cooperation was a key component. Slaughterhouses and processing plants, with the help of USDA inspectors, were required to develop hazard analysis plans and sanitation standards. Regulators had to approve those plans and standards, and their implementation was to be monitored. But administration officials stressed that the new system allowed plants to develop strategies best suited to their situations rather than follow a system devised in Washington, D.C.

But just as it emphasized cooperation with industry, the Clinton administration also moved to protect its regulatory powers, in some cases flouting the notion of regulatory relief. By executive order, the EPA was given new authority to force polluters to clean up toxic waste sites. The USDA's new meat inspection rules may have involved cooperation, but they also tightened safety controls. The rules mandated, for instance, that slaughter plants regularly test carcasses for the generic *E. coli* bacteria to verify the effectiveness of plant procedures designed to prevent fecal contamination. The rules also created the first regulatory performance standard for salmonella contamination rates.

Bridling under such regulations, a coalition of industry groups in 1997 mounted perhaps the most significant challenge to the government's regulatory authority since the modern regulatory era began in 1970. The group's lawsuit was triggered by tough new smog- and soot-reduction standards adopted in 1997 by the EPA under the authority of the Clean Air Act. Industry lawyers contended that Congress had ceded too much of its lawmaking power to regulators when it approved the Clean Air Act, and that the EPA should be obligated to balance compliance costs against health benefits when setting standards. But in February 2001 the Supreme Court ruled unanimously in *Whitman v. American Trucking Associations* that the EPA—and by extension, all regulatory agencies—had the right to issue rules under the authority vested by Congress. Specifically, the justices ruled, the Clean Air Act bars the EPA from weighing compliance costs against health benefits. The Court would later rule in 2007 that the EPA was in fact obligated, under the Clean Air Act, to regulate greenhouse gas emissions.

The ruling was a victory for Clinton, whose second term was marked by an increasing interest in new regulatory efforts. The Department of Agriculture approved new rules to regulate food labeled "organic." In 1997 the White House signed the international agreement reached in Kyoto, Japan, to stem global warming through strict new limits on emissions of greenhouse gases such as carbon dioxide. Although there was not enough support in Congress to ratify the Kyoto accords immediately, the Clinton administration continued to work on emissions piecemeal. In 1999 the White House completed new emissions standards for the rapidly growing numbers of minivans and sport utility vehicles, so-called light trucks. These vehicles escaped automotive regulatory standards through a loophole originally intended for trucks used for business purposes, such as hauling and construction.

A Congress once marked by antiregulatory zeal was also joining the act. Its Congressional Review Act, passed in March 1996 to give lawmakers the authority to overturn any regulation by a simple majority vote, lay dormant for the remainder of the Clinton years. That same year, the Telecommunications Act created a new discount "e-rate" that firms must provide schools, libraries, and nonprofit groups for access to the Internet. In 1998 Congress again waded into the telecommunications market and drafted legislation banning the practice of "slamming," where companies unilaterally change an unsuspecting customer's long-distance service provider.

Any credit the Clinton administration may have gotten for regulatory innovation was swamped by the ill will of business over the increased cost of regulation. In an August 1996 report, Thomas D. Hopkins of the Center for the Study of American Business (CSAB) at Washington University in St. Louis calculated that the total costs of regulation during the Clinton administration increased from $642 billion in 1992 and 1993 to $677 billion in 1996, using constant 1995 dollars. Those costs were to climb steadily to $721 billion by 2000.

The growth in funding and staffing for both economic and social regulation was considerable from 1970 to 1980. The rate of growth slowed in the 1980s, but by the end of the decade it was increasing once again. Staffing levels during the early years of the Clinton administration declined because of cuts mandated by the NPR and others necessitated by congressional and administration budget cuts. OSHA employment declined from 2,409 in 1992 to 2,208 in 1997, bouncing back to 2,370 in 2001. EPA employment declined to 16,790 in 2000 from 18,398 in 1992. Still, by 2001, total staffing at fifty-four regulatory agencies was expected to rebound to a record 131,983, according to CSAB. The administrative costs of running those agencies were forecast to reach $19.8 billion, a 4.8 percent increase over 2000.

Another barometer of regulatory activity, the number of pages printed annually in the *Federal Register,* showed a similar trend. In 1970 the *Federal Register* had 20,032 pages; in 1980, it had 87,012. The number had declined to 47,418 by 1986 but stood at 68,530 pages in 1997. Then the numbers soared. In 2000, the final full year of the Clinton administration, 83,178 pages were published. Clinton's final three months alone saw 25,605 pages printed in the *Federal Register.* On January 22, 2001, three days after Clinton officially left office, last-minute rules, regulations, and other measures still in the pipeline filled 944 *Federal Register* pages.

The George W. Bush Administration

From the day of his inauguration, George W. Bush signaled his regulatory approach would be more similar to Reagan's than Clinton's—or even his father's. As Reagan had done, Bush immediately froze all new rules and regulations, pending a sixty-day review by the new administration. He also quickly put a conservative ideological stamp on his executive decision making. In his first month in office, Bush ordered that all companies contracting with the federal government notify unionized employees that they had the right to withhold the portion of their union dues slated to be used for political purposes. Republicans had been trying for years to enact this so-called paycheck protection measure as a way to curb funding for union political activities that were heavily biased toward the Democratic Party. Bush also rescinded Clinton-era orders favoring unionized contractors that bid on federally funded construction projects.

President Bush tapped John Graham, a vocal critic of business regulation, to head his Office of Information and Regulatory Affairs (OIRA), the regulatory gatekeeper within the OMB. OIRA was created during the last days of the Carter administration but was first staffed and shaped during Reagan's tenure in the White House. The office aims to watch over and guide regulators. In this role, it reviews regulations—roughly 700 per year—and guards against bureaucratic overreach. A strong advocate of cost-benefit analyses, Graham lost no time in applying his tough standards to regulations under review. During his first six months in office, the new OIRA head sent twenty rules back to their agencies of origin for redrafting. During the previous seven years under Clinton, the office had sent back just seven regulations.

But Graham was not entirely predictable. For instance, early in his tenure he argued against an administration decision not to regulate carbon dioxide as a pollutant. The decision was a reversal of a pledge Bush had made during the 2000 campaign. Such regulation would have been a powerful tool to combat global climate change, but the administration argued that the cost to industry—especially to energy producers—would have been too high. Like Graham, though, Bush also defied predictions, making decisions that surprised opponents and supporters alike. For example, during his first few months in office he earned the praise of environmentalists by declining to reverse Clinton's decision to set aside millions of acres of land as national monuments.

Meanwhile, with the White House canceling or at least reviewing many Clinton-era regulations, the Republican-controlled Congress dusted off the 1996 Congressional Review Act in March 2001 and put it to use for the first time to overturn the Clinton administration's tough new rule guarding against repetitive motion disorders, such as carpal tunnel syndrome and tendonitis. The review act had passed with little fanfare as a means to diffuse stronger regulatory "reform" measures. But it granted Congress extraordinary new powers to combat regulatory efforts. The act sets aside traditional legislative procedures, such as hearings, bars filibusters, disallows amendments to so-called resolutions of disapproval, and forbids an agency from reissuing a regulation that is "substantially the same" without explicit congressional approval. The highly controversial ergonomics rule—developed by the Department of

Labor during the course of a decade—would have covered 6 million workplaces and 100 million workers. Annual compliance cost estimates ranged wildly, from $4.5 billion to more than $100 billion.

But seven months before the rule was to go into force, Congress scuttled it with remarkable speed. Bush's signature sent a clear signal that the regulatory activism of the Clinton era was over. "There needs to be a balance between and an understanding of the costs and benefits associated with federal regulations," Bush said in a statement the day the rule was officially revoked.

In 2001 the administration sought regulatory change by formalizing the process of OIRA review by actively soliciting groups—business associations, nonprofit organizations, think tanks, and universities, as well as government agencies—to suggest regulations for review and possible change. The nominated regulations, seventy-one in all, were handed over to Graham and his staff at OIRA, where they were subjected to strict cost-benefit analysis. Of these, twenty-three were categorized as "high priority" and many were eliminated or changed. For example, a Clinton-era regulation mandating greater energy efficiency on new air conditioners was scaled back. Another rule banning the use of snowmobiles in national parks was largely rescinded.

But despite the work of OIRA, regulatory activity did not grind to a halt under Bush. During the president's first year in office, the federal government issued 4,132 regulations, while 4,313 were issued in 2000, the last year of the Clinton presidency. The number of *Federal Register* pages, another measure of regulatory activity, declined slightly under President Bush. In 2002, 80,332 pages were published, a little less than Clinton's last year in office. That number dropped further to 75,798 pages in 2003. The numbers are a testament to the fact that though regulatory philosophy may change one way or another with the comings and goings of presidents, the work of regulating goes on. After all, most regulation is the fruit of legislation, often enacted long before a president arrives at the White House.

The shock of the terrorist attacks on September 11, 2001, quickly changed the political and social dynamic of the nation. Bush and his administration asked Congress for $40 billion in new funds to help a devastated New York City and to begin waging the new war on terrorism, both at home and abroad. Legislation appropriating the funds cleared Congress a mere three days after the attack. The administration also asked for new law enforcement powers, such as new wiretapping and search authority as well as broader power to detain and deport immigrants. The USA PATRIOT Act that cleared Congress on Oct. 25, 2001, granted expanded regulatory authority to a large number of agencies, including the Immigration and Naturalization Service (INS), the Customs Service, and the Federal Bureau of Investigation (FBI).

In November 2001 Congress created the Transportation Security Administration (TSA) within the Department of Transportation, charged with administering security at airports. Under the legislation creating the new agency, the federal government replaced all 28,000 privately employed airport baggage screeners with federal workers. It was the first major agency created since 1977, the year the Department of Energy came into existence. It would not be the last.

One criticism that came out of the 2001 attacks was that federal agencies did not adequately coordinate their counterterrorism activities. The charge stuck especially to intelligence and law enforcement agencies—notably the FBI and the Central Intelligence Agency (CIA). Bush sought to overcome this handicap by creating an Office of Homeland Security, to coordinate the government's domestic response to terrorism. The president appointed popular Pennsylvania governor Thomas Ridge to fill the post. Many in Congress, however, called for legislation that would define the powers of the new office and subject the president's choice to confirmation. While Congress was beginning to float other proposals, the White House released a new plan for homeland security, one that was much broader and more far-reaching than most of the congressional proposals.

The Bush plan called for reorganizing large parts of the federal government to create a whole new department, the Department of Homeland Security. After initial congressional enthusiasm for the new department, the issue became bogged down over labor issues. The administration wanted to be able to design a new personnel system, setting pay and performance rules free of the strictures of the civil service rules. The president also wanted to be able to rearrange parts of the agencies and their budgets without congressional approval. Finally, on November 22, 2002, Congress cleared a bill that virtually mirrored Bush's initial proposal and that largely gave the president his way on personnel issues.

The new Department of Homeland Security was created out of twenty-two different agencies with just under 170,000 employees and a budget approaching $40 billion. After the Department of Defense, it was the largest cabinet department (in terms of personnel) in the federal government. The new department merged agencies in four basic areas: border and transportation security; emergency preparedness; countermeasures against weapons of mass destruction; and information analysis and infrastructure protection. It included the Coast Guard, the Customs Service, the INS, the Federal Emergency Management Agency, the Secret Service, and the new TSA. The new department also absorbed smaller functions of other agencies, such as the Department of Health and Human Service's National Pharmaceutical Stockpile, the Department of Agriculture's Animal and Plant Health Inspection Service, and the Department of Energy's Nuclear Energy Search Team.

The organizational fallout from the 2001 terrorist attacks did not end with the creation of the Department of Homeland Security. Terrorism analysts had bemoaned the lack of adequate intelligence since the day of the attacks, focusing particularly on a lack of coordination between the government's fifteen intelligence-gathering agencies. These included the CIA, the FBI, the National Security Agency (NSA), the National Reconnaissance Office, the Defense Intelligence Agency, and intelligence bureaus in the State Department, Treasury Department, and the newly created Department of Homeland Security.

Calls for greater intelligence coordination were not new. Some forty studies in the five decades before 2001 recommended the creation of some sort of intelligence czar. But pressure for an intelligence overhaul gained momentum after the attacks, especially when it was learned that the hijackers had lived in the country for months before the attacks and had openly engaged in suspicious activities.

Pressure for change increased even more after the release of the report of the 9/11 Commission on July 22, 2004. The commission had been charged with determining why the government failed to predict and stop the terrorist attacks. The cornerstone of the commission's proposed changes was the creation of a national intelligence director (NID), who would oversee and coordinate the activities of the fifteen agencies and would be the chief intelligence liaison to the president. Most significantly, the NID would have operational control over all of the intelligence agencies' budgets. The panel also called for the creation of a National Counterterrorism Center to act as an intelligence clearinghouse, conducting joint operational planning and analysis for use by the fifteen agencies.

Intense negotiations during fall 2004 produced a compromise on a major obstacle—control of the defense intelligence budget. Under the language eventually signed into law, the new director could shift only relatively small amounts of money—5 percent of an agency's budget and no more than $150 million—at any given time. In addition, the NID could not "abrogate" the military chain of command. The intelligence overhaul became law on December 8, 2004, and within four months, the first NID, longtime diplomat John Negroponte, had been nominated by President Bush and confirmed by the Senate. In addition, the Counterterrorism Center was up and running.

While Congress and the White House spent a significant amount of time and energy focusing on terrorism-related issues, domestic concerns were not entirely set aside in this new era. Probably the most important and far-reaching action on the domestic front occurred in late 2003, when Congress passed legislation making significant changes to Medicare, the government's health insurance program for seniors. The new prescription drug benefit—estimated to cost more than $500 billion—was the largest expansion of an entitlement program since the 1960s "Great Society" legislation that created Medicare and Medicaid.

Meanwhile, the administration continued to push for what it called a more commonsense policy toward regulation, focusing on easing the regulatory burden on business. In August 2004 the NHTSA issued what consumer advocates claimed was an important new regulation that would prohibit the public release of some automobile safety data. Public Citizen, a consumer advocacy group, filed suit to block the new rule, claiming that motorists needed this data to make informed choices when buying a car. The administration responded that the data was rarely, if ever, seen by consumers and that regulators needed to weigh the overall utility of the information with the burden of requiring businesses to release it. But the issue received little media attention.

The NHTSA rule came on the heels of other significant rule changes that also were little noticed. For example, in May 2003 the administration killed a rule, proposed during the first Clinton administration, which would have required hospitals to establish facilities to protect their workers against tuberculosis. A month later OSHA eliminated proposed rules that would have significantly toughened ergonomic standards for employers. In both cases, the administration argued that the gains realized by the proposed rules did not outweigh the burden they would have imposed on businesses.

In August 2003 the White House relaxed Clean Air Act rules by allowing power plants to upgrade and expand without installing expensive new pollution control equipment. This move came on the heels of a rewrite of proposed new rules by the Energy Department that aimed at toughening the energy efficiency of newly manufactured air conditioners. The standards—originally proposed during the Clinton administration—were weakened, although the new Bush-era rules still required new air conditioners to be more energy efficient.

OIRA's Graham defended these and other similar decisions. While he admitted that the administration generally favored the business community, Graham claimed that the White House was willing and able to impose tough new requirements on industry when they were provided with "adequate scientific and economic justification." He cited recent reductions in diesel-engine exhaust emissions, new more transparent nutritional labeling requirements, and tougher criteria for side-impact air bags as examples of cases in which new regulations were warranted, even though they imposed substantial costs on business.

OMB claimed that this approach was balanced and that the administration had cut back the growth of costly new regulations by 75 percent, as compared with the Clinton and first Bush administrations. But consumer advocates, Democrats in Congress, and liberal activists argued that the administration's efforts at "regulatory reform" were threatening the welfare of the American people. "Regulatory reform has generally been a way for this administration to avoid having the government act to protect the health and safety of the American public," said Henry Waxman, ranking Democrat on the House Government Reform Committee.

Opponents of the administration's regulatory efforts won some important victories in court. At the end of 2003, for instance, a federal court of appeals blocked the administration's relaxation of Clean Air Act rules for power plants. A month later, another court of appeals ruled that the administration did not have the authority to weaken the new air conditioner efficiency rule.

One of the major initiatives of Bush's first term was bipartisan passage of the No Child Left Behind Act in 2002. The act gave major regulatory powers to the Education Department in its attempt to hold schools accountable for student achievement levels. The law required annual testing of students from third through eighth grade and withheld federal funds from failing schools.

Some states and local school districts viewed the law as an unfunded mandate, claiming that Congress did not provide adequate funding to implement the act's provisions.

Under pressure, the Education Department began allowing flexibility in the No Child Left Behind program by 2004. These efforts continued throughout Bush's second term as groups from various states filed suits claiming, among other things, that the law was unconstitutional. While many of these legal actions were dismissed or appealed, the administration's attempt at reauthorization in 2007 failed in the face of strong Democratic attempts to make major changes to the law. While provisions of the act remained in place in 2009, the Obama administration indicated that it wanted Congress to overhaul the law to lessen its reliance on standardized testing but toughen the requirements for teacher quality and academic standards.

In August 2005 Hurricane Katrina struck the Gulf Coast, bringing devastation to the states of Louisiana, Mississippi, Alabama, and Florida. Thousands of homes and businesses were destroyed, and New Orleans suffered a catastrophic flood. The death toll eventually exceeded 1,700, and in addition to billions in property damage, the aftermath of the hurricane was characterized by chaos and looting. Problems were particularly acute in New Orleans, where many of the city's poor, largely African American residents were stranded in the flooded city with little local, state, or federal government support.

Many criticized the lumbering response of the Federal Emergency Management Agency (FEMA), the agency within the Department of Homeland Security responsible for managing federal aid to disaster-stricken areas. Bush accepted blame for the slowness in the federal response. "And to the extent that the federal government didn't fully do its job right, I take responsibility," he stated. Still, problems associated with the government's inability to quickly alleviate the suffering caused by the hurricane damaged public confidence in Bush and in the federal government.

Indeed, the long, costly road to recovery for the Gulf Coast brought the Bush administration its greatest challenge since the terrorist attacks of 2001. One of the first acts of the administration was to loosen regulation, especially of the energy industry to keep gasoline and electricity flowing to the nation. However, it was evident that to rebuild the region, including most of the city of New Orleans, the full regulatory apparatus of the federal government would have to be employed—from agencies such as the EPA, to clean up the toxic mess left behind in New Orleans, to the Housing and Urban Development Department, to provide temporary and permanent housing to thousands of displaced residents.

Under intense scrutiny from Congress, the media, and others, Homeland Security Secretary Michael Chertoff promised to thoroughly reengineer FEMA. During this time, the government also announced that the Army Corps of Engineers would completely rebuild the floodwalls and strengthen the levees that protect New Orleans. The project was slated to be fully completed by 2010, although some initial protection was put in place by summer 2006 to ensure the city was not flooded during hurricane season, which traditionally begins in June.

In September 2006 Congress passed legislation significantly boosting FEMA's funding and expanding its role and responsibilities. Under the new law, the FEMA director became the president's chief adviser on disaster relief, superseding the authority of even the secretary of homeland security in this capacity. The statute also reversed an earlier decision by Chertoff to remove FEMA's responsibility for the nation's emergency preparedness. The agency now was charged with both emergency preparedness and emergency response—its previous role.

At the same time President Bush was struggling with the fallout from Hurricane Katrina, he also was fighting for another domestic priority: the reauthorization of the USA PATRIOT Act. Although there was little doubt that the act would be reauthorized, many in Congress, particularly Democrats, saw the debate over the bill as an opportunity to publicize and even curb what they saw as the administration's excessive disregard for civil liberties in the years following the 2001 attacks. Of particular concern, they said, was the NSA's illegal practice of monitoring the communications of terrorism suspects without a warrant from a federal court. Administration officials and others countered that the practice was not illegal and was necessary to effectively keep tabs on people who might be trying to plan and perpetrate terrorist attacks on the United States.

But while the debate over warrantless eavesdropping delayed the Patriot Act reauthorization, it did not ultimately prevent it. The bill cleared Congress in March 2006 and was signed by the president that same month. Furthermore, GOP control of Congress ensured that the president was able to push through a measure that accomplished most of what he wanted. In particular, the administration was able to convince Congress to permanently reauthorize most provisions of the act. The original USA PATRIOT Act had contained a four-year authorization.

In the November 2006 elections, the Republicans lost control of both houses of Congress, giving the Democrats complete control of the legislative branch for the first time in twelve years. Congressional Democrats—through their control of committees—began much more vigorous oversight of certain industries. Congress passed the Housing and Economic Recovery Act of 2008, which tightened regulatory oversight and accounting requirements for Freddie Mac and Fannie Mae, the two government-chartered mortgage lenders. There was also a renewed effort to pass legislation allowing the FDA to regulate tobacco. The measure had bipartisan support, in both houses, but stalled due to opposition from the White House.

In addition to congressional action, significant regulatory initiatives in 2007 also originated from the White House, the courts, and the agencies themselves. For instance, in January 2007 the president issued an executive order aimed at giving the White House more control over the making of regulations (*for the text of order, see appendix*). The order required each federal agency to have a regulatory policy office headed up by a political appointee. The idea was to have someone who shared the president's policy priorities in each agency to review and to conduct a cost-benefit analysis of regulations. The order also required that agencies issue new business regulations only if there was a specific need for the government to intervene.

Industry groups hailed the new directive, arguing that it would be a check on a government bureaucracy that often regulated without fully considering the cost to citizens and business. But Democrats criticized it, arguing that the president was replacing the judgment of the impartial experts who staff the agencies with those who put political considerations first. They also argued that the White House was trying to compensate for the GOP loss of Congress by exerting tighter control over agency rulemaking.

Meanwhile, in April 2007 the Supreme Court ruled that the EPA was obliged, under the Clean Air Act, to regulate greenhouse gas emissions that likely cause global warming. The ruling delegated a significant new regulatory responsibility to the EPA, even though the agency, under President Bush, had not sought it. The administration reacted quickly to the ruling, announcing in May that it was ordering the EPA and three other federal agencies to write new regulations by the end of 2008 aimed at reducing greenhouse gas emissions from cars and trucks. But Democrats and many environmentalists argued that the president could immediately order a tightening of fuel efficiency and auto emissions standards. By asking agencies to take almost two years to come up with new regulations, Bush was merely delaying any meaningful action until the end of his term, they charged. The White House countered that the issue was complicated and difficult and could only be resolved with adequate time for study and deliberation.

At the same time the Supreme Court gave the EPA powers for which it had not asked, the FCC moved in the opposite direction, issuing a report, also in April 2007, urging Congress to give it more authority, in this case to regulate violence on television. The agency, which already regulated obscene language and images on broadcast television, argued that there was growing evidence that television violence could hurt children and thus should be subject to oversight and regulation. Although the proposal received a lot of attention in the media and on Capitol Hill, Congress never moved to act on the recommendation.

President Bush was not idle during his last year or so in office. Near the end of 2007, Bush successfully fought largely Democratic efforts in Congress to expand the State Children's Health Insurance Program (SCHIP), which provided federal matching funds to states to ensure children from families too poor to afford health insurance but not poor enough to qualify for Medicaid. Democrats in Congress had hoped to expand SCHIP eligibility to children from higher income families who still lacked insurance, raising the number of participants in the program from 6 million to an estimated 10 million. They proposed paying for the expansion by raising the federal tax on cigarettes.

The president opposed the move on the grounds that it was a step toward socialized medicine. In October and then November of 2007, Bush vetoed measures containing the SCHIP expansion. Efforts to override the president's veto fell short and Congress ended 2007 by passing legislation reauthorizing the existing program, a measure that Bush signed. The expansion ultimately did become law in early February 2009 when newly elected Democratic President Obama signed it into law.

In April 2008 Bush lifted an executive branch ban on offshore drilling of oil and natural gas. With gasoline prices hovering around $4 a gallon at the time, the move was popular but largely symbolic since Congress had earlier passed its ban on new offshore exploration in certain areas. Bush called on Congress to follow his example and open up restricted areas to exploration and drilling, but Democratic leaders in both the House and Senate refused. Expanding offshore drilling became a 2008 campaign issue, with Republicans—including GOP presidential candidate, Arizona senator John McCain—calling for restricted areas to be opened up to drilling.

Indeed, while energy usage and its impact on the environment appeared, at one point, to be shaping up to be one of the most important issues in the campaign, it and everything else took a back seat in the minds of voters to concerns that the economy was sliding into a recession and possibly even a full-scale depression. While economists had been predicting that the United States and other parts of the world would fall into a recession sometime in late 2008 or early 2009, almost all experts believed that the downturn would be relatively short and mild. As it turned out, many banks and other financial firms had tied their fortunes to the U.S. housing market, where mortgage companies had begun to offer increasingly opaque and disadvantageous loans, especially to those in the subprime mortgage market (loans to those with a greater risk of default). In turn, U.S. financial institutions bundled these disadvantageous, subprime mortgages together and packaged them as securities.

When housing prices began to fall dramatically in 2007 and 2008, many of these subprime borrrowers could no longer pay their loans, leading to growing losses in the financial sector in both the United States and Europe. These losses were much greater than almost anyone had anticipated, and soon many of the most storied names in the finanical world, including Citibank, Lehman Brothers, and American Insurance Group (AIG), faced bankruptcy. By October 2008, most banks and financial firms were hoarding what cash they had in an effort to survive, while not lending to businesses and individuals. Economists predicted that unless this situation improved, the world economy could be heading for an economic collapse that could rival the Great Depression of the 1930s.

It soon became clear to Bush's Treasury Secretary, Henry Paulson, Federal Reserve Chairman Ben Bernanke, and other high-ranking officials that many financial firms would not survive without an infusion of funds from the government. In September 2008 Paulson (himself the former president of Goldman Sachs) asked Congress for up to $700 billion to allow the federal government to bail out banks and other firms. Without the money, Paulson said, the financial sector would be unable to begin lending again and the broader economy would fall deeper into recession or even depression. After the collapse of Lehman Brothers in September, Congress heeded Paulson's warning and passed legislation in early October creating the Troubled Assets Relief Program (TARP). Congress appropriated half of the requested funds ($350 billion) immediately and promised to give the Treasury Department the remainder, if needed, in early 2009. At the same time, the Federal Reserve under Bernanke began pumping what would eventually become a total of $2 trillion into the banking system to shore up its liquidity and encourage more lending.

Originally, the TARP money was to be used to purchase subprime loans and other troubled assets from banks, hence directly relieving them of the major cause of their problems. But soon after TARP was enacted, Paulson changed his mind and began directly lending the money to banks by purchasing preferred shares of stock in these institutions. Many in Congress, on both sides of the aisle, criticized this new direction, accusing the secretary of lying to them when he originally requested the money in September. Paulson countered that the situation in the financial sector was highly fluid and volatile and that he had changed his mind as to how to best deploy the TARP funds because his understanding of the problem and how to best solve it had changed.

As already noted, the troubled financial sector and the worsening economy became the focus of the 2008 presidential campaign during its last months. Both candidates voted in the Senate for the passage of TARP and both criticized banking executives and others in high finance for being so reckless. Senator McCain also criticized government regulators for not seeing the problem until it was too late. He even called for SEC chair, Christopher Cox, to resign. In the end many Americans blamed President Bush and, more broadly, the Republican Party, for at least some of the problems, making it hard for McCain to cast himself as the agent of change and reform. In the November 2008 election, Obama won a convincing victory over his rival, garnering 53 percent of the popular vote.

The Barack Obama Administration

President Obama came into office vowing to tackle the economic crisis with immediate and longer-term fixes. The incoming president argued that the nation needed to do more than simply prop up the banks and stimulate the economy; it needed to fix what he deemed fundamental, structural problems to make the country stronger and to avoid another economic meltdown. With this in mind, Obama linked his broader reform agenda in education, health care, energy, and other areas to the financial crisis and the recession and announced his intention to push all of his major policy initiatives in his first year in office.

Still, the president determined that his priority as president would be passage of a major economic stimulus bill. Although it was becoming apparent that the TARP and other actions had saved the financial sector from total collapse, Obama and his economic team argued that without a major dollop of federal spending to boost the economy, the nation could still slide into a severe recession. The administration's stimulus measure (which in its original form would have totaled nearly $900 billion),

however, hit some snags, as congressional Republicans and moderate Democrats balked at the high levels of spending. In the end, Obama settled for a $787 billion package that ultimately won the support of only three Republicans in the Senate and none in the House. The 1,100-page bill moved from first draft to law in less than a month, and three-quarters of the money was expected to reach state capitals, businesses, and individual taxpayers by the end of September 2010.

Signed into law in February 2009, a chief beneficiary of the measure (called the American Recovery and Reinvestment Act) were the unemployed, who received extended benefits and subsidies to continue health insurance coverage. The act also included tax breaks for individuals and businesses, investments in health care and alternative energy, and substantial investments in Medicaid and education. To ensure that the legislation passed, Democratic lawmakers and the White House added billions in new spending and tax breaks that benefited a handful of specific companies and industries, including $8 billion in spending for regional high-speed rail projects.

Republican opponents criticized the measure for devoting too much money to Democratic pet projects—such as health and education spending as well as money to pad state and local government budgets. At the same time, they said, there was too little money for programs that would quickly create private-sector jobs, such as road and bridge building. Sen. Tom Coburn of Oklahoma spoke for many in the GOP when he said that Congress had "reverted to its bad habit of larding up bills with special interest pork projects that stimulate reelection campaigns rather than the economy."

After his victory on the stimulus bill, Obama turned his attention to the rest of his agenda. First to be addressed was regulatory legislation aimed at lowering carbon emissions believed to cause global warming. After months of horse-trading, a climate change bill narrowly passed in the House in June 2009, but only after furious lobbying by the White House to win over Democrats from agricultural states, who complained that it would too heavily penalize farmers. The president also had to coax support from some liberals, who were complaining that the measure was too watered down to be effective. In the end, the bill passed the House swiftly but narrowly, 219 to 212.

The bill—which would regulate U.S. emissions, requiring them to decline 17 percent by 2020 and set national limits on greenhouse gases—would create a complex "cap and trade" system to allow polluters to buy and sell emission permits, and would provide tax and other incentives aimed at changing the way individuals and businesses used energy. House conservatives argued that the bill would sharply increase energy bills for American households and impose new costs on businesses, resulting in the shipment of millions of jobs overseas to countries, such as China, that did not have strict climate regulations.

The president urged the Senate to follow the House's lead and take up the legislation. Obama hoped a law regulating greenhouse gas emissions would be enacted before a major climate summit in Copenhagen, Denmark, set to occur in December 2009. But the legislation faced a stiffer challenge in the Senate, where Republicans and Democrats from energy and industrial states had traditionally opposed efforts to dramatically reduce fossil fuel use.

After efforts to push through a measure that was similar to the House-passed bill failed, Senate supporters attempted to broaden its appeal by linking it with other energy initiatives, such as provisions offering new support for nuclear power and offshore oil production. But this effort also failed, and by the summer of 2010 the legislation was essentially dead. Republican gains in the Senate in November of that same year killed any hopes that the bill might be revived in 2011.

The president had better luck with the second and most important major plank of his domestic agenda: health reform. Still, the White House faced enormous difficulties in pushing its plans to reform the nation's health care system through Congress, doing so only after significantly scaling back the measure to attract enough moderate Democratic support.

A number of presidents before Obama, including Truman, Nixon, and Clinton, had tried to overhaul the nation's health care system only to find themselves stymied. Part of the difficulty in making substantial change rests in the fact that the health care industry, which is nearly one-sixth of the American economy, has huge vested interests that are naturally resistant to change. In addition, many Americans with health insurance are satisfied with their quality of care, making wholesale changes a difficult sell. Obama and others pointed out that health care costs had been rising at far above the rate of inflation for decades, making the current situation unsustainable both for the government (which insures more than 40 percent of the population via Medicare, Medicaid, and other programs) and businesses that provide insurance to their employees. In addition, by the time Obama took office at the beginning of 2009, roughly 45 million Americans had no health insurance, forcing many people to delay important medical treatments or rely on expensive visits to hospital emergency rooms for routine care.

As with the climate bill, Obama turned to his allies in Congress to actually come up with the details of the plan. In the House, Democrats produced a measure that would have allowed those without insurance to purchase it from the government—a so-called public option. Those in lower-income brackets would receive this public insurance at subsidized rates and no one would be denied coverage due to a preexisting condition. The measure also tried to save money by cutting $500 billion from Medicare over ten years. But by the end of 2009, the health bill had yet to pass the House, held up mostly by opposition from Republicans, who worried about cost estimates for the legislation of more than $1 trillion for the next decade. Others also worried that the public option would drive private insurers out of business and create a situation in which the government not only regulated but ran the entire national health care system. Opposition also came from moderate and conservative Democrats, over cost issues as well, but also over concerns about the possibility that a greater government role in the health system would lead to more taxpayer funded abortions.

In the Senate, three Democratic and three Republican members of the Finance Committee negotiated through the summer to come up with a plan that could garner bipartisan support. The "gang of six," led by Sen. Max Baucus of Montana, unveiled a plan in September that would expand eligibility for Medicaid, create a system of "insurance exchanges" where people could buy government-subsidized insurance, and levy fees on those who did not purchase health insurance. The bill, which would expand health insurance coverage without adding to the federal deficit, attracted little Republican support, however. Even Democrats criticized it for requiring that middle-income Americans buy expensive insurance policies. In a major address to Congress that month, President Obama reiterated his intention to get health reform passed in 2009. The White House, however, began talking about scaling back its ambitions to get a bill that many in Congress could support. In particular, the president indicated a willingness to possibly forgo the public option, a move that produced vigorous protests from the more liberal wing of his party.

In spite of the impasse on climate change and delays on health care, the president could point to some important victories during the first year of his tenure. In late January 2009, for instance, Obama signed the Lilly Ledbetter Fair Pay Act, a priority for civil rights advocates and women's groups that extended the amount of time someone could sue in pay discrimination cases. The act was named for Ms. Ledbetter, a Goodyear Rubber and Tire employee who alleged pay discrimination but was prevented from bringing legal action against her employer because she initiated the lawsuit after the statute of limitations had run out.

In May 2009 Obama signed legislation aimed at protecting consumers from excessive charges and other unpopular practices common among some credit card companies. The law, called the Credit Card Responsibility, Accountability and Disclosure Act, made it more difficult for card issuers to charge consumers penalties or excessive fees and required companies to clearly warn cardholders of any changes to the terms of their contracts.

On June 11, 2009, Congress passed landmark legislation giving the FDA sweeping new powers to regulate tobacco, from the amount of nicotine in cigarettes to their packaging and marketing. President Obama, himself an occasional smoker, applauded the bill and quickly signed it. Previous attempts to regulate tobacco had been hampered by opposition from the powerful tobacco lobby, but changing social attitudes in the past decade had led to greater intolerance for a product that the medical community had long considered addictive and deadly. The legislation imposed restrictions aimed most particularly at preventing children from acquiring the smoking habit, including requiring warning labels to cover 50 percent of a cigarette pack and banning the use of Joe Camel and other cartoon characters that tobacco industry opponents said were clearly directed at children.

In spite of these legislative achievements, the administration's biggest goals remained unrealized. As already noted, legislation aimed at reducing carbon emissions would die in Congress by the middle of 2010. The president's biggest legislative priority—health care reform—looked to be heading for a similar fate. Indeed, in August 2009, the greatest champion of health reform in Congress, Sen. Edward Kennedy, D-MA, died of brain cancer, dealing supporters a huge blow. But in the wake of Kennedy's death, Democratic congressional leaders made a new push to pass health care reform and succeeded, passing legislation in December of that year in both the House and Senate.

It was a victory for supporters of reform, but a victory tempered by a number of factors. First, no Republican in either the House or Senate voted for the bill, leaving the most significant legislative initiative in a generation without even token bipartisan support. Perhaps more importantly, the House-passed and Senate-passed versions differed in key areas. In particular, the House-passed bill contained the so-called public option and the Senate bill did not—a major point of contention between House and Senate Democratic leaders. Still, as Congress went home for the Christmas holiday, the president and Democratic congressional leaders confidently predicted that these differences would be ironed out and that the legislation would be finalized and passed soon after the New Year.

At the beginning of 2010, however, this optimism collapsed, caused by the election of Republican Scott Brown to the Senate seat held by the recently deceased Kennedy. Brown, who was behind in the polls until the last few days before the election, had campaigned vigorously against health care reform. Brown's election to the seat of the most revered liberal in the Senate and in one of the most liberal states in the nation seemed to be a rebuke of the president, his party, and his plans for the nation's health care system. But his victory was more than symbolic. Replacing Kennedy with a Republican gave the Democrats only 59 seats in the Senate, one short of the 60 needed to stop a filibuster.

Many saw Brown's election and the loss of the Democrat's filibuster-proof majority as the final straw for health care reform, at least health care reform on a grand scale. As already noted, none of the Senate's Republicans supported the administration's health care reform effort, despite intense lobbying by the president of more moderate GOP senators, Obama's willingness to forgo the public option, and the efforts of the "gang of six" to hammer out a compromise that at least some Republicans could support. In addition, some national polls showed that a slim majority of the American people opposed health care reform, with many worrying that an overhaul would degrade their current health care options.

By early 2010, some supporters of the president were arguing that the best course was to attempt to pass much smaller, more incremental reforms instead of a big, sweeping bill. But Obama decided to press ahead with a comprehensive overhaul. The key obstacle remained the Senate, where the entire GOP caucus threatened to filibuster the measure, leaving the Democrats one vote short of being able to move a bill forward. To get around this obstacle, Democratic leaders used a technicality—bringing up the legislation as part of budget reconciliation—which allowed it to pass with only a simple majority. On March 21, 2010, the Senate passed the measure, over strenuous Republican protests, by a vote of 56–43. Later that day, the House passed the Senate bill, 220–207.

On the evening the measure cleared Congress, President Obama (who would sign the bill into law two days later) remarked that passage of health reform "proved that we are still capable of doing big things. We proved that this government—a government of the people and by the people—still works for the people." Republicans countered that the law was rammed through Congress using procedural tricks and was passed in defiance of the wishes of the American people. GOP leaders promised to retake Congress in November 2010 and to make the repeal of the law their top priority.

The new law—called the Patient Protection and Affordable Care Act—more closely mirrors the original Senate-passed bill and does not contain everything that the administration had hoped for—particularly the public option. Still, the act makes dramatic changes to the health care landscape. For instance, it forbids insurers from refusing to cover someone with a preexisting condition and allows children to continue to be covered by their parents' insurance plans until the age of twenty-six. The law also authorizes $875 billion over the next decade (mostly after 2014) to expand insurance coverage. This provision makes an estimated 24 million working people who lack access to affordable coverage through their employers eligible for tax credits to buy insurance. In addition, it expands Medicaid eligibility. Everyone who earns less than 133 percent of the federal poverty level—an estimated 16 million people—would become eligible for Medicaid.

The new law also calls for the creation of a health insurance "exchange" in each state aimed at offering consumers different insurance options at competitive prices. Perhaps most controversially, the act (starting in 2014) requires all uninsured adults to buy insurance or face fines of at least $750 a year. This last provision has already been the basis for a number of lawsuits challenging its constitutionality. At the end of September 2011, the Department of Justice asked the Supreme Court to hear one of these challenges, a development that almost guaranteed that the high court would decide whether the requirement to purchase insurance and, indeed, potentially the entire statute, were constitutional. In June 2012, in *National Federation of Independent Business v. Sebelius,* the court upheld the bulk of the law, including the "individual mandate," ruling that Congress had power under the Taxing Clause to impose a penalty on individuals for failing to obtain health insurance but exceeded its power under the Spending Clause by threatening to withhold all Medicaid funds from states that did not agree to expand coverage under the program.

Just months after the health care bill was signed into law, the president scored another big victory with the enactment of financial reform legislation. Introduced in the wake of the financial crisis, debated for more than a year, and signed into law on July 21, 2010, the Wall Street Reform and Consumer Protection Act of 2010 (also called "Dodd-Frank" after its chief sponsors, Sen. Christopher Dodd, D-Conn., and Rep. Barney Frank, D-Mass.) was the most sweeping overhaul of the financial system since the Great Depression.

Although the law was considered a major legislative victory for President Obama and for its supporters in Congress, Dodd-Frank's journey from bill to law was not without major hurdles, especially in the Senate. Criticism for the proposal came from both sides of the aisle, with Republicans arguing that it would entail excessive and burdensome regulation that would only make it more difficult and costly for businesses and consumers to raise or borrow money. And while most Democrats saw the law as a victory that demonstrated to their constituents that they could be tough on Wall Street, some in the party felt the package did not go far enough and left too many critical decisions to the same federal regulators who had missed the warning signs in the run-up to the financial crisis of 2008.

Among the key provisions of the new law was the establishment of a council of federal regulators to watch for and assess any potential threats to the financial system. The overhaul also gave shareholders a non-binding advisory vote on executive compensation and gave federal agencies new powers to regulate and even liquidate financial institutions that posed a threat to the nation's financial health.

Perhaps the most important and controversial provision of the new law involved the establishment of the Consumer Financial Protection Bureau (CFPB). The CFPB's mandate was to track consumer-related issues with an eye toward protecting ordinary people from unscrupulous banks and financial services firms. Although the bureau was to be technically part of the Federal Reserve, it was to operate independently, with a director appointed by the president who was not answerable to the Federal Reserve Board.

Democrats, consumer advocates, and others praised the creation of the new agency as a new bulwark against greedy banks and other financial services companies that prey on consumers. But many Republicans as well as business groups worried that the bureau would expand the "nanny state" to new levels and take away citizens' rights to make their own decisions.

This debate continued after the bill became law. Democrats wanted President Obama to appoint Harvard law professor Elizabeth Warren (who is credited with coming up with the idea for the bureau) as director. Many Republicans in Congress, however, said they could not support Ms. Warren, whom they saw as too stridently anti-business. Warren also did not have the full backing of the administration, where she was seen as a little too outspoken by some people on the president's economic team.

In the end, the president passed over Warren and, on July 16, 2011, nominated former Ohio Attorney General Richard Cordray to head the new agency. Cordray, who had built a reputation in his state and nationally for successfully prosecuting financial crime (particularly against mortgage lenders), also was not favored by many Republicans, some of whom declared him "dead on arrival" soon after his nomination was announced. Indeed, some senators said they would not support any nominee until the president agreed to discuss changes to the agency to make it more "accountable." In particular, some GOP senators wanted the bureau's budget to be provided by Congress. As things stand, the CFPB receives its funding through the Federal Reserve and, thus, is not required to ask congressional appropriators for money, leaving Congress with

little oversight authority over the agency. At the beginning of 2012, after nearly six months of wrangling with Senate Republicans over Cordray's nomination, President Obama used a recess appointment to put the former Ohio attorney general atop the new agency.

While the Federal Reserve was on the sidelines of the CFPB fight, it was at the center of another battle—this one over whether to continue to "prime the economic pump" with the tools at its disposal. Throughout 2010 and into 2011, Fed Chairman Ben Bernanke resisted calls to raise long-term interest rates, which had been lowered to near zero during the financial crisis in an effort to help jump-start the economy. By 2010, however, some prominent economists and bankers, including a number of people sitting on the Fed's Board of Governors, were warning that keeping interest rates low could lead to inflation, which in turn could stall the economic recovery. Bernanke argued that low rates were still needed because the economic recovery continued to be very tenuous.

In early November 2010, Bernanke upped the ante when he had the Federal Reserve begin a second round of quantitative easing—known as QE2. QE2 involved pumping additional money into the economy by having the Fed purchase about $600 billion in Treasury bills (T-bills) over the next six to eight months. This came on the heels of the first round of easing in 2008 and 2009, in which the Fed pumped almost $2 trillion into the American economy, also by purchasing T-bills, as well as bonds and stocks.

QE1 had been initiated during the worst days of the financial crisis, a time when many economists worried that the nation and the world would be thrust into a severe economic depression. As a result, QE1 was relatively uncontroversial. QE2, on the other hand, was initiated during a time when the economy was growing and the nation was supposedly recovering from the recession. Supporters of QE2 argued that the economy was still scarred by the financial crisis and the recession of 2008 and 2009 and that the recovery was weak. QE2, they said, would provide a necessary monetary lubricant to help keep the economy growing. In particular, Bernanke and others argued, QE2 would help keep stock prices high, which in turn would put more money in consumers' hands and help drive economic growth. Others, however, warned that the Fed was playing a dangerous game with QE2. After all, they pointed out, the program was financed by simply printing more money and injecting it into the economy, a tactic that could easily devalue the currency and lead to much higher inflation. And if that happened, they said, the Fed would have to dramatically raise interest rates to tamp down inflation, which in turn would almost certainly restrain economic growth or even produce another recession.

By the summer of 2011 a consensus had formed among economy watchers that QE2 had not fulfilled the expectations of either the optimists or pessimists. The economy was growing, but slowly, and unemployment remained stubbornly above 9 percent. On the other hand, the much-feared rise in inflation had largely failed to materialize. By mid-July some economists were expressing concern that the country could be headed into another recession, and

Bernanke held open the possibility of another round of quantitative easing—QE3.

These debates over interest rates and quantitative easing did not involve President Obama, who has no authority over the Federal Reserve beyond appointing its leadership. But during this time the president was also working to boost economic growth. By the time QE2 was being debated in late 2010, Obama's first big attempt to help the nation's economy—the nearly $800 billion stimulus package—had largely run its course. And like QE2, the stimulus had many detractors, who could point to high unemployment and uneven growth as evidence that the enormous spending package had not actually provided much help to the economy.

Many Democratic lawmakers and liberal pundits called on Obama to put together another stimulus, arguing that the economy needed an additional injection of government funds to prevent the recovery from losing steam. But the election, in November 2010, of a Republican majority in the House as well as Republican gains in the Senate, ended any chance that Congress would enact another stimulus, even a much smaller one. Instead, in December 2010, the president sat down with incoming House Speaker John Boehner and other Republican leaders and worked out an $858 billion deal that kept in place all of the tax cuts that had been enacted under President George W. Bush, in exchange for expanded unemployment benefits and other tax incentives aimed at stimulating the economy.

The Bush tax cuts had been scheduled to expire at the end of 2010 and Republicans had campaigned to keep them in place, arguing that the nation could ill afford what amounted to a major tax increase during difficult economic times. The deal struck between Obama and GOP leaders kept all of the Bush cuts, including lower rates for the wealthiest Americans (something the president had campaigned against vigorously in 2008) and lower capital gains rates. In exchange, Republicans agreed to a $57 billion extension of emergency federal unemployment benefits, allowing the long-term unemployed to draw up to 99 weeks of benefits until the end of 2011. There was also a provision allowing businesses to deduct the cost of all equipment purchases until the end of 2011. Allowing an upfront deduction gives businesses an incentive to accelerate their capital investment plans, which in turn should benefit equipment manufacturers.

While many Democrats in Congress criticized the measure, particularly the continuation of tax cuts for the wealthy, many in the president's party ultimately voted for it because it contained the unemployment extension and a continuation of tax cuts for middle-income Americans. The president acknowledged this ambivalence when he admitted that "there are some elements of this legislation that I don't like." But, he said, "that's the nature of compromise, yielding on something each of us cares about to move forward on what all of us care about. And right now, what all of us care about is growing the American economy and creating jobs for the American people."

Around the same time, Obama made another attempt at boosting growth, this time by looking for ways to help the nation's business community. During the first half of the president's first term, many business leaders had accused Obama of treating them with neglect and, at times, even hostility. The business community was particularly troubled by what Obama considered to be some of his signature achievements—namely, the overhaul of health care and the new financial reform law.

In the wake of 2010 midterm elections, the president made it clear that he was eager for a détente with the business community. As evidence of this attitude, Obama called for federal agencies to look for rules that were "outdated, duplicative, or 'just plain dumb.' " And by June 2011, the administration had identified hundreds of regulations that were unnecessary and burdensome to businesses. These rules would be eliminated or rewritten, the president promised, saving companies and consumers hundreds of millions of dollars annually.

Around this time, the Obama administration and the still relatively new Republican leadership in the House locked horns in a new budget battle. It occurred less than six months after the same parties had come to an agreement on extending the Bush tax cuts and unemployment benefits. This time, the fight would be over the debt ceiling. But the issue was essentially the same: how to best reduce the deficit.

The debt ceiling represents the maximum amount of money that the U.S. can borrow. Until recently, Congress routinely raised this ceiling with little debate, giving the government the authority to borrow more money. In recent years, however, deficit hawks in the Republican Party have come to view the debt ceiling as an opportunity to call attention to the government's rising debt and as a bargaining chip in their efforts to bring down spending.

In the months leading to 2011, the debt ceiling of nearly $14.3 trillion was about to be exceeded. By March 2011, the ceiling had technically been breached, but the Department of the Treasury was able to use accounting tricks to keep an actual default on American debt at bay until the middle of the summer. As the summer began and GOP leaders in Congress started negotiating in earnest with their Democratic counterparts and the White House, it became clear that both sides were far apart, even though both claimed they wanted to cut the deficit and raise the debt ceiling. One huge sticking point was taxes: Republicans didn't want to raise them, even for the wealthy. Democrats wanted a mix of tax increases and spending cuts but were unwilling to tackle significant cuts in entitlements, such as Social Security and Medicare, which are big drivers of deficit growth.

By July, both sides were looking to Republican House Speaker John Boehner and President Obama to come together and negotiate a "Grand Bargain" that would provide long-term deficit reduction and raise the debt ceiling by a substantial amount. The two men almost struck a deal that would have reduced future debt by $4 trillion over 10 years, the amount budget experts estimated was needed to stabilize government deficits. But the negotiations fell apart after each man accused the other of making new, unacceptable demands just as they were about to close the deal.

At the last minute, just before an unprecedented U.S. default on its debt, a new, much smaller deal was forged that effectively increased the debt ceiling by $900 billion. The bill, which was passed by bipartisan majorities in both houses of Congress and signed into law on August 2, 2011, also contained $917 billion in spending cuts over the next 10 years. Finally, and perhaps most important, the new law, named the Budget Control Act of 2011, created a mechanism, called sequestration, aimed at prodding Congress to cut an additional $1.2 billion or more in spending before the end of 2012. If Congress failed to cut at least $1.2 trillion by the end of 2012, automatic, across-the-board spending cuts would kick in over the next 10 years to make up for the missing cuts. If Congress managed to pass some spending cuts but didn't reach the $1.2 trillion mark, the automatic cuts would cover the difference.

Sequestration, as this mechanism is called, largely left politically sensitive entitlement spending alone, meaning that virtually all cuts would come from discretionary and defense spending. Still, many in both parties viewed sequestration as an outcome so unpalatable that it likely would prompt both sides to make the necessary cuts before the deadline at the beginning of 2013.

Just two days after President Obama signed the Budget Control Act, Standard and Poor's (S&P) downgraded the debt of the United States, from its top AAA rating to its second-best AA+ rating. S&P (one of the world's three largest credit rating agencies) pointed to the inability of U.S. political leaders to hammer out a more substantial budget deal. While the new AA+ is still a good rating, this was the first time in modern history that U.S. debt had anything but the highest rating. In addition, there was worry that the downgrade would have a global impact, as the United States is the world's largest economy and the dollar is, in effect, the world's currency.

While some economists and market watchers predicted that the S&P downgrade would make it more expensive for the U.S. to borrow money, interest rates on U.S. debt actually fell slightly in the days following the announcement. Investors, both foreign and domestic, clearly still thought the United States was the safest harbor for their money. In addition, the other two large credit rating agencies, Moody's and Fitch, kept their top ratings for American debt, leading many observers to charge that S&P had jumped the gun. Indeed, as 2011 wound down, economists were predicting that the American economy was finally moving from slow, post-recession growth to something more robust, if not quite full-speed.

By the time the 2012 presidential campaign was in full swing, questions about how fast the economy was growing and how to make it grow faster had taken center stage. While Obama advocated federal spending on education and new energy sources, his opponent, Republican Mitt Romney derided this approach as "trickle down government," which would entail raising taxes on the middle class and already-struggling small businesses. This criticism carried some weight, as Obama faced reelection at a time of tepid economic growth and an unemployment rate that seemed forever locked above 8 percent. Mr. Romney also attacked a number of policies implemented during Obama's first term, including Dodd-Frank, the legislation that brought about significant changes to financial regulation in the United States, as well as Obamacare, the president's health insurance reform legislation. Romney argued that both laws would ultimately be a drag on the economy. But Obama fought back, criticizing Romney's refusal to cut taxes even for the wealthy and arguing that Romney had not clearly explained what he would replace Dodd-Frank with. The president added that his federal health care plan was very similar to the one Romney himself had instituted while governor of Massachusetts.

At the end of June, just before the presidential nominating conventions, the Supreme Court handed the administration what may be the most important regulatory decision of the decade. The ruling saved the president's most important first-term legislative achievement: the law overhauling the heath care system.

Almost immediately after the Affordable Care Act (ACA) was enacted in 2010, the law was challenged in court on a host of different fronts. Eventually, two of those challenges were combined into one case by the high court. The first, and by far the most important part, of the two issues before the Court involved the law's mandate that everyone must buy health insurance or pay a penalty. Opponents of this provision, known as the "individual mandate," argued that Congress did not have the power to force people to choose between purchasing something or paying a penalty. Proponents argued that the government did have the authority to require certain purchases—such as auto insurance—and did so all the time. Both sides agreed that if the high court struck down the individual mandate, it would effectively gut the health care law.

The second major issue involved the ACA's requirement that all 50 states participate in an expansion of Medicaid coverage—aimed at significantly increasing the number of poor people who are eligible for health insurance. As with the individual mandate, those states opposed to this requirement argued that Congress did not have the authority to order them to expand their Medicaid programs, while the administration and others claimed that Congress' authority to regulate interstate commerce (known as the "Commerce Clause"), as well as other powers, gave it the right to require states to participate in the Medicaid expansion.

When the Supreme Court finally ruled in June 2012, it struck down the Medicaid mandate, handing states a huge victory. The Court ruled that in mandating state participation, the federal government had been unreasonably coercive and had exceeded its authority under federalism, which is the constitutional principle that the states and the federal government each have their own powers and authority. And indeed, over 20 states have opted out of the expansion.

Nevertheless, the law survived the more important challenge involving the individual mandate. The lawyers who defended the mandate argued that it was constitutional under the Commerce Clause, but in the end, the Court ruled that Congress had the right to impose the requirement or fine based on its power to tax, rather than its authority to regulate interstate commerce. In other words, the fine for not purchasing insurance was judged to be a tax and, thus, constitutional. By squarely rejecting the Constitution's Commerce Clause as a justification for keeping the individual mandate, the Court may have clipped Congress' wings for the future, as many laws that impose requirements on the states do so claiming the Commerce Clause as the source of this authority.

Just months after this decision, the administration lost a key player in the regulatory realm. In August 2012 regulatory "Czar" Cass Sunstein announced that he would be leaving his government post overseeing the administration's regulatory policy to return to his previous job as a professor at Harvard Law School. As chief of the Office of Information and Regulatory Affairs (OIRA), a unit in the White House's Office of Management and Budget (OMB), Sunstein reviewed and ruled on hundreds of regulations, from major environmental initiatives to revamping of the decades-old food pyramid. He had also played a significant role in the regulatory work resulting from the enactment of Dodd-Frank, the Affordable Care Act, and other major laws.

While Sunstein was at times criticized by business interests, the sharpest criticism of his polices came from unions, environmentalists, and others who accused Sunstein of worrying too much about the cost of regulations and not enough about the problems that prompted agencies to draft them in the first place.

Meanwhile, just a month after Sunstein's resignation and two months before the presidential election, the Federal Reserve announced its long-anticipated third round of quantitative easing (QE3). Under the plan, released in September, the Federal Reserve would buy about $85 billion in mortgage-backed securities and government bonds each month. In addition, Bernanke promised that the Fed would hold down short-term interest rates to zero until the middle of 2015, extending an earlier deadline by an additional six months. Perhaps most important, the chair and his colleagues promised to keep buying securities and bonds until the recovery was firmly in place.

The announcement of QE3 came in the wake of a big policy shift at the central bank. Since the 1960s, the Fed has had two core macroeconomic missions: fight inflation and keep unemployment low. And in the 1970s and 1980s, under then Fed Chairman Paul Volcker, the central bank had in effect made inflation-fighting its first priority. However, in June 2012 Chairman Bernanke announced that the Fed would rebalance the bank's mission. Bernanke said that from now on, the Fed would be willing to tolerate inflation as high as 2.5 percent. At the same time, he said, the bank would not consider raising interest rates until either unemployment was down to 6.5 percent or lower or inflation rose above 2.5 percent.

In many ways the shift in Fed policy was to be expected. After four years of keeping interest rates at near zero, as well as two rounds of quantitative easing, the new policy statement was more a reflection of existing reality than a set of guidelines for the future. For some time, Bernanke had been viewed as too lax about inflation and too concerned with economic stimulus. The new policy announcement merely fed these fears.

Still, with many economists and others talking about a "jobless recovery," Bernanke's focus on unemployment was welcomed in many quarters. In July 2012, a month after the announcement of the new policy, unemployment ticked up from 8.2 percent to 8.3 percent. Many saw this higher unemployment number as proof that the Fed's policy shift had been the correct course. A few months later, the Fed launched QE3.

It is unclear what role, if any, QE3 played in Obama's reelection. But while polls showed that the American people were still unhappy about the state of the economy, they were happy enough with the president's efforts to restart economic growth to give him another four years in office. Indeed, while many thought the race would be close or that Romney would tap enough economic discontent to win, Obama was reelected with just over 51 percent of the vote.

A president's second term is often characterized by frustration and scandal, and just months after being handily reelected, President Obama was experiencing both. But first, the president chalked up a big legislative victory, getting some of the tax increases he had fought for unsuccessfully during his first term.

The 2010 budget agreement that extended all of the Bush tax cuts was set to expire at the end of 2012. If nothing was done, all of the cuts would end and substantial tax increases would automatically go into effect. This massive tax increase, called the "fiscal cliff" for obvious reasons, gave the president a lot of leverage over Republicans, who were loath to see the Bush cuts expire. At the same time, if the Republicans called Obama's bluff and let the tax cuts expire, all taxpayers, including those in the middle class, would pay more. Obama, who had declared himself a champion of the middle class during the 2012 campaign, did not want to see middle-income taxes rise, which gave the GOP at least some counter leverage. Still, fresh off his reelection win, the president clearly had the advantage in these negotiations.

Since the president's relationship with Speaker Boehner had soured after their failed debt ceiling negotiations in 2011, Obama turned to his vice president, former senator Joe Biden, to be the lead White House negotiator. Biden in turn appealed to his old colleague, Senate Minority Leader and Republican Mitch McConnell, to help him hammer out a deal. The two worked through the Christmas holiday and came up with an agreement that Republicans didn't like, but could live with. Taxes would be raised for individuals making $400,000 or more and couples making $450,000 or more. The estate tax, which had been phased out, was phased back in—at 40 percent for anything more than $5 million. Finally, the 2 percent cut in the payroll tax that had been instituted in 2010 to help stimulate the sluggish economy was allowed to expire. The deal was quickly passed by both houses on New Year's Day 2013 and signed into law the next day.

Many Democrats criticized the deal, saying that the president should have used his leverage to extract tax increases for people at the $250,000 threshold, rather than at $400,000. Republicans also were critical, asserting that small-business owners would suffer disproportionately under the new law and, as a result, would hire fewer people.

Still, it was clear that the president had won this round, an assessment that led many political observers to say that he was gaining momentum as he entered his second term.

The president's momentum seemed to extend to his establishment of an almost entirely new cabinet. As is customary in second-term presidencies, there was a significant cabinet shuffle following Obama's reelection. By June 2013, the president had nearly completed overhauling his cabinet, although he came under fire for a lack of diversity at the top. In addition, some of his nominations caused fierce partisan resistance. Obama's first choice for secretary of state, U.N. Ambassador Susan Rice, ran into heavy turbulence over her role in what some alleged was a cover-up on the part of the administration concerning the September 2012 attack on the U.S. Consulate in Benghazi, Libya. Rice was ultimately named Obama's national security adviser, while his second choice for State, Massachusetts Senator John Kerry, easily won confirmation to replace the popular Hilary Clinton, who had announced her retirement after the president was reelected. Chuck Hagel, a former Nebraska senator and a Republican, also ran into turbulence in his quest to succeed the retiring Leon Panetta as secretary of Defense. Hagel, known as a maverick within his own party, was deemed by some in the GOP to be not supportive enough of Israel, a charge Hagel successfully refuted on his way to confirmation.

Of special note were the successful confirmations of Sally Jewell as Interior secretary (replacing former senator Ken Salazar) and former White House Chief of Staff Jack Lew as Treasury secretary (replacing Timothy Geithner, who resigned at the end of Obama's first term). Other appointments included that of Penny Pritzker to replace John Bryson as Commerce secretary and Thomas Perez to replace Hilda Solis as Labor secretary, as well as Ernest Moniz as Energy secretary, and Anthony Foxx as Transportation secretary. Early criticism concerning lack of diversity (Kerry, Hagel, Lew, Jewell, Moniz, and Pritzker are all white) may have helped prompt Obama's nomination of Perez, a first-generation Dominican American and Foxx, an African American.

But success for the president was short-lived and the second-term "curse" seemed to arise less than two months after his inauguration. The trouble began at the start of March 2013, when the president and Congress gave up on their effort to reach an agreement to forestall more than $85 billion in automatic spending cuts that would be triggered under the Budget Control Act of 2011. The sequester had been scheduled to begin on January 2, 2013, but Congress gave itself and the White House two additional months to make the $1.2 trillion in cuts needed to avoid sequestration.

The extra time proved inadequate. While the White House and some Republicans hoped to avoid the sequester, some in the GOP were content to let it take effect, reasoning that virtually any spending cut was good when the government is running annual deficits of more than $1 trillion. Some Democrats, meanwhile, felt that the defense cuts included in the sequester were overdue, and last-ditch Republican efforts to excise the defense portion of the sequester only strengthened this perspective.

In the lead-up to the sequester trigger in March, Obama warned that many Americans would suffer under the cuts because they would be across the board and indiscriminate. But while there were some high-profile closures (the White House stopped giving tours to the public), the anticipated breakdown in government services never materialized, leaving the president with some egg on his face. The sense of doom diminished further when, in April, Congress passed, and the president signed, legislation giving the Pentagon and air traffic controllers more leeway in determining how to make the cuts, meaning they would be less likely to jeopardize national security or air safety.

In addition to these policy setbacks, the administration, by May, found itself on the defensive as a cascade of embarrassing scandals came to light. The first issue was the continuing fallout from the killing by Islamist radicals of the U.S. ambassador to Libya and three other American officials at the consulate in Benghazi, Libya, in September 2012. Problems for the administration stemmed not only from questions about whether the personnel had been given adequate security but whether the administration had tried to issue and stand by a false story about who attacked the consulate because, as Republicans and others maintained, the White House didn't want to contradict its campaign narrative that the war on terror was essentially over by admitting that the attack had been executed by an al Qaeda affiliate. The White House countered that it had initially given out wrong information because it did not immediately know what had happened. Interest in the Benghazi attack faded for a time but was revived in May 2013, after a number of State Department and intelligence officials came forward to contradict some of the administration's claims about what it knew and when.

A second and potentially more damaging revelation came in May 2013, when IRS officials admitted that in 2011 and 2012 inspectors in the agency's Cincinnati office had specifically targeted hundreds of conservative groups for investigations and audits when they had applied for tax-exempt status. While these revelations resulted in the dismissal of the acting director of the IRS and substantial concern about the whether the government could be trusted to be impartial, no substantive evidence was produced implicating the White House or the 2012 Obama campaign.

The same week the IRS scandal broke, the Justice Department admitted to having wiretapped the phones of 20 reporters at the Associated Press as part of an investigation aimed at determining who in the government was leaking classified information to journalists. The revelations caused concern about the government's commitment to press freedom—particularly a reporter's right to protect the identity of his or her source—in cases involving national security.

Less than two weeks after the news of the Justice Department probe surfaced, a 29-year-old information technology contractor named Edward Snowden revealed that the National Security Agency maintained a database of all the recent phone records of every American. Snowden also revealed that the NSA ran a program, called PRISM, which allowed it to access phone, e-mail, and Internet search records of practically everyone in the world. He also later revealed that the United States had bugged dozens of foreign embassies, including those of allies, such as France and Germany.

While accessing the phone records of Americans requires a lawful search warrant, critics charged that the special intelligence court tasked with issuing such warrants was essentially a rubber stamp. International records obtained through PRISM or via embassy eavesdropping did not require a warrant since the subjects of the search were not American citizens and, thus, were not protected by the Constitution.

For some, Snowden was a hero who had pulled back the curtain on a secret government program that was almost certainly abusing its power. For others, including the president and most members of Congress, Snowden was a traitor who had compromised the nation's national security by letting America's enemies see how it keeps tabs on them. These critics also pointed out that both programs had been authorized and were overseen by Congress and that the national security court charged with issuing domestic warrants was not a rubber stamp but a real court manned by respected federal judges.

Even before these four scandals broke, public trust in government was near an all-time low—at 26 percent in April 2013, according to a survey conducted by the Pew Research Center. In 1958 nearly three times as many Americans (73%) said they trusted their government. This was bad news for President Obama and Democrats, who saw an expanding role for the federal government, not only in providing health care via the Affordable Care Act, and protecting the environment, but in creating more social mobility and economic growth with more spending on infrastructure, research, and education.

On top of this general mistrust of the government, the administration continued battling in court to protect many of its signature priorities, particularly the Affordable Care Act (ACA). Indeed, although the ACA was upheld in 2012, parts of the law continued to be challenged in federal court. In particular, challenges to the law's subsidy scheme and to provisions mandating that most employers provide free contraceptive coverage to female employees were working their way through the federal court system, with virtually all Supreme Court–watchers predicting final resolution at the high court. In addition to these troubles, one of the most important parts of the law—the creation of state-run "exchanges" offering a range of low-cost health insurance to individuals—was imperiled in the short term because some states were saying they would not be ready to start the program on October 1, 2013, the date mandated by the law. And on top of these problems, almost half of all states (twenty-two, including Texas, Pennsylvania, and both Carolinas) had refused to participate in the ACA's expansion of Medicaid, citing fears that future costs for states will spiral out of control. And in early July, the administration announced that a key section of the bill that requires employers with fifty employees or more to offer benefits (the "employer mandate") would not be implemented on January 1, 2014, but instead was postponed to January 1, 2015.

While various factions continued to fight over the constitutionality of the president's health and environmental plans, a new debate with profound regulatory implications was unfolding. Indeed, in June 2013 the Supreme Court handed down a number of landmark decisions that will likely have a significant regulatory impact in years to come. While none of these decisions had quite the heft of 2012's health care ruling, two cases in particular were milestones in their own right.

In one of these landmark decisions, the high court ruled that a core provision of the Voting Rights Act of 1965 was unconstitutional. The part of the civil rights law at issue was the section that targets certain states and counties for heightened federal scrutiny due to their history of discriminating against minority voters. The Court ruled that this section was no longer valid because it relied on decades-old data and did not reflect today's reality—one in which African Americans generally do not face the same challenges in voting or registering to vote as during the days of segregation. The Court concluded that if Congress redrafted this section of that act, this time using up-to-date information, the section would no longer be unconstitutional.

Until the ruling, nine states (all but one in the South) and a host of counties in other states around the country were required to submit any new election laws, regulations, or other electoral changes to the Justice Department for review. The department could and often did reject these changes if it believed that they would imperil or hinder minority voting. By striking down this section, the Court effectively took away the Justice Department's authority to hold these states and counties especially accountable. The department did retain the right to investigate and prosecute efforts to impede voting by minorities.

The final, and from a regulatory standpoint, the most important, ruling handed down by the high court in the early summer of 2013 involved the decision to strike down part of the federal Defense of Marriage Act of 1996 (DOMA). At issue in the case was the part of the law that banned same-sex marriage for purposes of federal law. This meant that even if a gay or lesbian couple married in a state where gay marriage was legal, they would not be eligible for federal spousal benefits, from Social Security to veterans' benefits. The court ruled that in enacting DOMA, the federal government had overreached into an area that had traditionally been the states' power to regulate and define. In addition, said the Court majority, by denying basic benefits and rights to legally married same-sex couples, DOMA violated the equal rights guarantees contained in the Fifth Amendment of the Constitution.

As marital status directly or indirectly affects eligibility for more than 1,000 federal benefits, the invalidation of DOMA required a substantial number of regulatory and other changes to accommodate legally married gays and lesbians. In addition, same-sex couples who are legally married but who lived in a state that did not give marital rights to gays and lesbians were at first still not eligible for most federal benefits. President Obama, who supported the ruling striking down DOMA, quickly convened a task force to see how many federal benefits could be given to couples living in states that don't recognize same-sex marriage via new regulations and executive orders. While many benefits were soon conferred, there were statutory roadblocks for other agencies (such as the Social Security Administration).

Beyond its important regulatory implications, the gay rights decision had another, even greater impact: gay marriage advocates used the rationale given by the Court's majority to strike down DOMA to launch federal court challenges to same-sex marriage bans in more than thirty states, arguing that these prohibitions violated the U.S. Constitution's promise of equal protection under the law. By early 2015 federal courts in roughly half of these states had overturned prohibitions on gay marriage, bringing the total number of states that allowed gay marriage to thirty-six and creating an opportunity for the Supreme Court to finally rule on the constitutionality of same-sex unions.

Around the same time constitutional scholars were dissecting the Supreme Court's landmark rulings on voting rights and gay rights, economists were paying special attention to a raft of economic data in an effort to determine whether the American economy was finally entering a period of high and sustained growth. Generally, they liked what they saw. By the middle of 2013 the Fed's third round of quantitative easing (QE3) seemed to be working. First quarter economic growth had come in at a respectable annual rate of 2.4 percent and the unemployment rate (by May) had dropped to 7.6 percent and seemed to be heading lower. In addition, the stock market was booming, with the Dow Jones Industrial Average up more than 15 percent in the first six months of 2013, adding cash in some peoples' pockets and boosting consumer confidence. Perhaps most important, the housing market was showing real growth, with prices up more than 12 percent in May from the same period the year before and new home construction picking up to meet increased demand.

By June 2013 Bernanke felt enough confidence in the health of the economy to begin publicly speculating about gradually throttling back on QE3. But global stock markets plummeted in reaction to his comments, and the chair and others were soon forced to clarify that they would maintain the $85 billion bond-buying program as long as fundamental weaknesses remained in economy.

In spite of the good economic news and reassuring words from Bernanke and others, some economists predicted that stock market volatility would remain, due to continuing fears that the Fed was waiting for an opportunity to wind down QE3 as well as rumors that Bernanke would not be reappointed for another term as chair once his current tenure ended in January 2014. When asked about his future at the Fed, Bernanke repeatedly hinted that he might not stay for a third time, arguing that he was not the only person capable of managing "the exit" from QE3 and the other important policies implemented during the 2008 financial crisis, such as keeping short-term interest rates near zero. And indeed, during the summer of 2013 the White House made it clear that it would chose someone other than Bernanke to be the nation's top banker.

Obama had reportedly intended to nominated former Treasury Secretary Lawrence Summers as Fed chair but was forced to consider another candidate after more liberal Democratic senators objected to Summers on the grounds that he was too close to Wall Street and not attuned enough to the needs of average working Americans. So, in October 2013 President Obama nominated the person many considered to be his second choice, Vice Chair Janet Yellen, to be the next Fed chair. "She's a proven leader and she's tough—not just because she's from Brooklyn," the president said in announcing Yellen's nomination. At the same ceremony, Yellen seemed to acknowledge the Summers critics when she said that "too many Americans still can't find a job, and worry how they'll pay their bills and provide for their families. The Federal Reserve can help if it does its job effectively."

In the wake of the Yellen nomination, Fed watchers began speculating on how she might impact the fate of QE3. Some worried that ending QE3 would endanger a still weak economic recovery and possibly pull the nation back into recession. But in December 2013, a month before Yellen was confirmed, the Fed's open market committee (still chaired by Bernanke) voted to scale back QE3, cutting monthly bond buying from $85 billion to $75 billion. And while both Bernanke and Yellen signaled that the Fed would continue scaling back QE3 in the coming months (the program would ultimately end in October 2014), they also made clear that interest rates would remain near zero for the time being. The combination of scaling back QE3 and keeping low interest seemed to work: the economy suffered no appreciable damage during this time.

The big story of the second half of 2013 was supposed to be immigration reform. Throughout much of the year, the White House and the Senate negotiated the contours of a massive new immigration reform plan, one that would give the estimated 11 million illegal immigrants in the United States a path to legalization and possibly even citizenship. Efforts in the Senate were led by a freshman Republican senator from Florida, Marco Rubio, who had won an upset election in 2010 with support from the Tea Party. Pro-reform strategists in both parties hoped that Rubio's imprimatur on an immigration measure would give it a fair hearing among conservative Republicans in the Senate and then the House.

The strategy seemed to be working when, in late June 2013, the Senate passed a measure that would have granted permanent residency to those already here illegally, if they paid a fine and any back taxes owed. Under the bill, unauthorized immigrants would be able to stay and work in the U.S. but would not be eligible for citizenship until it could be shown that the U.S. border was secure. Toward that end, the measure would have authorized $40 billion in new spending for border security, including the completion of a 700-mile fence from one end of the border with Mexico to the other.

But the bill never gained traction in the House, where Speaker Boehner was unable to generate enough support among Republicans to move the bill forward. While some GOP lawmakers were open to allowing some illegal immigrants to stay permanently, many opposed the path to citizenship offered under Rubio's measure. By the end of 2013 the immigration reform proposal was dead.

In addition to its failure to pass immigration reform, Congress also gridlocked on spending for fiscal year 2014, a battle that ended up shutting down the government for more than two weeks. The disagreement centered on providing money for the government to implement the Affordable Care Act. In mid-September 2013, House Republicans passed a spending bill for the entire government for the new fiscal year (which begins every year on October 1) that also contained provisions to defund the new health care law. A week later, the Senate and its Democratic majority passed the same spending bill with one key difference: it restored funding for implementing the ACA. A few days later, the House took up the same bill and added the ACA defunding provision back in.

This standoff was in place when, on October 1, fiscal year 2014 began. Since Congress had not appropriated any money to fund government operations, 1.3 million federal employees were furloughed and only essential personnel were told to report to their offices. During the next ten days, Congressional Republicans and officials from the Obama administration met a number of times in an unsuccessful effort to forge an agreement.

As the shutdown entered its second week, many Republicans began looking for a way to end the stalemate. Polls showed the voters were unhappy about the shutdown and that many blamed GOP lawmakers for the situation. At this point, Senate leaders from both parties worked out a deal that gave the White House and congressional Democrats virtually everything they wanted. The new measure did not defund the ACA. Indeed, the only concession the Democrats made was to agree to stricter income verification requirements for those receiving government subsidies when they buy health insurance from government exchanges set up under the new law. The measure quickly passed the Senate with significant Republican support. In the House, Speaker Boehner relied on Democrats (all 198 of whom voted for the bill) to give him the majority he needed to clear the measure for the president's desk. A full seventeen days after the shutdown had begun, the government reopened for business.

Still, while the administration and congressional Democrats saved the ACA, the law remained deeply unpopular, with polls routinely showing a large majority of Americans opposed to it. This problem for the president and his allies in Congress was compounded when, in March 2014, it became clear that the president's claims about one important aspect of the law proved untrue. During the 2012 presidential campaign, Obama repeatedly claimed that under the ACA no one would be forced to give up their insurance or even their doctors. But as those parts of the law that impact individuals began to be implemented in 2013, millions of self-insured individuals with policies purchased prior to the ACA received notices from their insurance companies canceling their policies. The cancellations came because many of these individual policies did not offer the array of services required for all health insurance policies under the new law. Those who lost their pre-ACA insurance were required to purchase a new policy—and many were livid. Obama's words came back to haunt him, with many Republicans accusing the president of outright lying

to the American people. The president was forced to admit that he had been wrong about his claim but denied he had lied.

Things went from bad to worse for the administration when, in April, it was revealed that 40 military veterans in Phoenix, Arizona, had died while waiting for care from the Veterans Administration (VA). By June an internal audit revealed that more than 120,000 veterans had either been made to wait too long before receiving care or had simply been ignored by the VA and had never received any treatment.

Obama's chief of staff, Denis McDonough, said that the president was "madder then hell" about the problem and had vowed to fix it. Veterans Affairs secretary Eric Shinseki, resigned amidst the scandal and was replaced by Robert McDonald, former CEO of Procter and Gamble. Meanwhile, Congress passed the Veterans Access, Choice, and Accountability Act of 2014, which appropriated $10 billion to allow veterans to receive private medical care at the government's expense. Another $6 billion was appropriated to bring on additional staff at the VA with the aim of eliminating the agency's backlog.

Meanwhile, in the spring and summer of 2014 the high court handed the administration a number of defeats, including a ruling that invalidated President Obama's "recess appointments" to the National Labor Relations Board (NLRB). The Constitution gives the president the power to make temporary, high-level appointments without Senate approval when the Senate is "in recess," a point no one disputes and one that was not at issue in the case. But Obama had made the NLRB picks during a "pro forma" session of the Senate, when no official business was being conducted but when the chamber was not technically in recess.

The justices rebuked the president for overstepping his authority, saying that only the Senate, not the White House or anyone else, can determine when it is in recess. The decision called into question roughly 300 NLRB decisions that had been made during the time the now-invalid appointees had sat on the board.

The Supreme Court also ruled against the administration in the case regarding birth control, *Burwell v. Hobby Lobby*, deciding that a regulation stemming from the Affordable Care Act mandating that employers provide free contraception to female workers could not be applied to employers who object to doing so on religious grounds. The ruling applied only to closely held companies (those that are directly run by a person or a family) and not big public corporations. Still, religious liberty advocates hailed the decision as a major victory that would protect small-business owners, such as Catholics, who might object to all artificial birth control; or evangelical Protestants, Orthodox Jews, Mormons, and Muslims, some of whom object to emergency contraception because they see it as de facto abortion.

By the fall of 2014 it was clear that Obama was not having his best year. But in the midterm elections in November, things got even worse for the president. Republicans took control of the Senate, bringing their total up from 45 to 54. Republican Sen. Mitch McConnell of Kentucky became the Senate Majority leader, replacing Nevada Democrat Harry Reid. Republicans also solidified their hold on the House of Representatives, growing their majority to 247, up from 233 before the election. At the state level, the GOP now controls 31 of the nation's governor's mansions and controls 68 of the nation's 98 state legislative bodies, the most since the 1920s.

In the days following the election, McConnell signaled that he wanted to "start passing legislation." And while he wanted to pass some measures that Obama opposed, such as authorization of the long-stalled Keystone XL Pipeline, he also indicated that he would work with the president to move bills in areas where there was agreement, such as trade and, to a lesser extent, taxes. McConnell also announced that he wanted to "get the Senate to normal," passing a budget, allowing members from both parties to offer amendments to bills, and working more through the committee system.

But in December, before McConnell and Speaker Boehner could begin moving the GOP's agenda forward, President Obama issued an executive order that threatened to derail any possible goodwill between the White House and Congress. In November 2014 the president issued an order prohibiting the deportation of an estimated 4 million undocumented aliens, or about a third of all illegal immigrants in the country. The order covers those who were illegally brought into the country as children and their parents and siblings. It also allows adults within this group to apply for legal work permits.

Obama argued that his action was necessary, given the inability of the Congress to pass any immigration reform. He also said it was perfectly legal, invoking a concept known as "prosecutorial discretion," which essentially gives the executive branch the authority to decide who it will and will not prosecute. But the immigration order produced howls of protest from Republicans, who argued that the president was pandering to Latino voters and that he did not have the authority to grant de facto amnesty to millions of illegal immigrants. Indeed, they said, prosecutorial discretion is intended to be employed on a case-by-case basis not as a tool to stop enforcing the law against millions of people.

Within weeks of the action, 26 states sued to have the order blocked. In May 2015 the 5th Circuit Court of Appeals upheld a lower court decision, putting the order on hold until a final ruling can be issued. The fact that the appeals court stayed implementation of the order means that the court could well strike it down when it issues a final ruling later in 2015. But regardless of how the appeals court rules, the case is likely to end up in the Supreme Court in 2016.

Meanwhile, in February 2015 the Federal Communications Commission (FCC) issued one of the most important decisions in its eighty-year history when it voted—3-2 along party lines—to classify the Internet as a "utility," bringing it under the commission's full regulatory authority. Along with the new classification came new "net neutrality" rules, which prohibit Internet providers from offering some business customers faster service in exchange for higher fees.

At the commission meeting, FCC Chair Tom Wheeler said that the commission was using "all the tools in our toolbox to protect innovators and consumers" and that the Internet "was too important to let broadband providers be the ones making the rules." But the two Republicans on the commission were highly critical of the move, arguing that the Internet has been a platform for innovation in large part because it has remained largely unregulated. "The Internet is not broken," said Republican Commissioner Ajit Pai. "There is no problem to solve."

Around this time, the new Congress sworn in in January 2015 began in earnest to fulfill McConnell's promise to get things done. The first order of business was passing legislation mandating the construction of the Keystone XL Pipeline. The project, which had been held up by the Obama administration for six years, would run a pipeline from Nebraska to the Gulf Coast, allowing Canadian and American companies to ship 830,000 barrels of oil per day both for shipment by sea to other parts of the country, as well as destinations outside the United States. Proponents of the measure contend that the pipeline would create more than 20,000 high-paying construction, engineering, and maintenance jobs and help defray the need for the U.S. to buy oil from the Middle East, Africa, and Latin America. But environmentalists argue that the pipeline would inevitably break and despoil natural areas and that it would be used to ship oil extracted from Canadian tar sands, which burns much dirtier than normal crude, causing unusually high amounts of pollution.

In February 2015, with Republicans firmly in control of both houses of Congress, the Keystone XL bill passed easily and was sent to the president's desk. Obama, while not officially opposed to XL, vetoed the bill saying still more time was needed to review the project. Efforts to override the president's veto failed and the fate of the project remained in Obama's hands.

Other legislative initiatives proved more successful, even if their paths to passage were difficult. Throughout much of April and May, Congress debated the reauthorization of the USA Freedom Act (also known as the Patriot Act), which was due to expire on May 31, 2015. The debate was unusually fraught due to continued unease in the wake of Edward Snowden's 2011 revelations about activities at the National Security Agency, particularly the NSA's collection of domestic phone records.

Initially, McConnell had hoped to simply reauthorize the existing law, allowing the NSA to continue bulk data collection of phone records. But efforts to scale back the NSA's reach found a champion in Sen. Rand Paul, a Kentucky Republican who had just announced that he was running for president. Paul managed to bring together the more libertarian elements within his own party, with many liberal Democrats also concerned that the government could be unnecessarily violating the privacy of its own citizens. In the end, McConnell and other Senate Republican leaders realized that they did not have the 60 votes needed to get a simple reauthorization of the law through their chamber.

Just as the law was set to expire, a compromise was fashioned that would grant the NSA the authority to collect phone records for six months, and then pass that responsibility over to phone companies. These private firms will be required to keep records of people's calls and to make them available to the government in cases where a search warrant had been obtained. In early June, just two days after parts of the law had expired, the reauthorization cleared Congress and was quickly signed by Obama.

Another major piece of legislation, which cleared Congress just weeks after the Patriot Act bill, concerned efforts to give the president what is known as fast track authority to negotiate trade deals. For years, the administration has been negotiating free trade deals with all of the major countries, with the exception of China, that border the Pacific Ocean. The Trans Pacific Partnership (TPP) is intended to help maintain American economic leadership in East Asia by creating a free trade zone with Japan, Korea, and nine other countries on both sides of the Pacific. The administration has also been working with the European Union to create a similar free trade zone, known as the Transatlantic Trade and Investment Partnership (TTIP). But the TPP negotiations are farther along and, as of July 2015, are nearing completion.

As the trade talks have moved forward, the administration has stepped up its efforts to spur Congress to pass fast track authority. Fast track, which last expired in July 2007, allows the president to submit trade deals to Congress for simple up or down votes. Trade deals can be rejected, but they cannot be amended or filibustered. The idea behind fast track is that the prospect of congressional amendments makes it very hard for the president to negotiate deals with foreign countries, given that they can later be changed when Congress considers the agreement.

Ironically, the president's chances of getting fast track authority improved dramatically after his party lost control of the Senate in 2014. Liberal Democrats are particularly wary of free trade, arguing that giving countries with lower labor costs unfettered access to the American market leads to job losses, particularly in the manufacturing sector. Proponents contend that while free trade can disrupt certain industries, it produces many more jobs than it destroys.

The debate over trade pitted the president and congressional Republicans against many of his traditional allies on the left. House Democrats thought they had ended fast track when, in mid-June, they killed part of the Senate-passed bill that included funds to retrain workers let go due to trade-related layoffs. But near the end of June, Senate Republicans and moderate Democrats reconvened and passed the House fast track bill without the retraining provisions and sent it to Obama, who signed it days later. Set to expire in 2021, the trade bill handed Obama and his successor a huge victory.

The good news for Obama continued in the weeks that followed. At the end of June, the Supreme Court handed the administration a huge victory in the last major legal challenge to the Affordable Care Act. The ACA contains language granting subsidies to those who buy health insurance through "an exchange established through the state." This case asked whether the federal government can provide subsidies to low-income individuals who buy insurance through the federal health care exchange in states that did not set up their own exchanges.

Opponents of the law argued that this language was meant to encourage each state to create its own health care exchange. However, for various reasons, only twenty-three states have set up such exchanges, leaving many Americans in states that did not set up their own exchanges able to purchase insurance only through the federal exchange. The IRS ruled that, in spite of the statute's language, people buying insurance on the federal exchange could receive subsidies and the high court agreed, ruling that while a narrow reading of the plain language of the statute might limit subsidies only to those who are able to use a state exchange, the whole thrust of the Affordable Care Act is to expand insurance coverage for those who otherwise could not afford it. "Congress passed the Affordable Care Act to improve health insurance markets, not destroy them," wrote Chief Justice John Roberts in the majority opinion. President Obama, who was clearly happy and relieved that his signature legislative achievement had not been significantly damaged, strode into the White House rose garden minutes after the ruling had been announced and declared that "the Affordable Care Act is here to stay."

A day after the ACA decision, the Court gave the president another victory when it handed down a landmark ruling granting same-sex couples a constitutional right to marry. The movement toward nationwide legalization of gay marriage had been gaining momentum since the Court's 2013 ruling striking down DOMA. Indeed, in the wake of that decision, federal courts had struck down same-sex marriage bans in fourteen states, and national public opinion had shifted solidly in favor of allowing gays and lesbians to wed. By the time the court decided that same-sex marriage was a constitutionally protected right, 36 states (including many of the most populous) already allowed gays and lesbians to legally wed.

Still, gay marriage supporters and their allies saw the ruling as a major victory. Not only did the decision legalize same-sex unions nationwide, but it enshrined in the U.S. Constitution gay and lesbian couples' right to marry. Supporters' views were summed up by the author of the decision's majority opinion, Justice Anthony Kennedy, who wrote: "No union is more profound than marriage, for it embodies the highest ideals of love, fidelity, devotion, sacrifice, and family." Kennedy went on to say that gay and lesbian couples "ask for equal dignity in the eyes of the law. The Constitution grants them that right."

The decision was a major defeat for social conservatives and other Americans in the still-sizable minority who oppose same-sex marriage. Just ten years earlier, all but a few states banned the practice, and a solid majority of the nation's adults opposed gay marriage. Opponents had long argued that same-sex marriage would redefine marriage into a meaningless institution, further degrade the nuclear family, and leave most American children without the ideal nurturing environment provided by a mother and father.

The ruling also created new questions about both the rights and obligations of religious institutions, such as the Roman Catholic Church, many evangelical Protestant denominations, and Orthodox Judaism, amongst others, who oppose gay marriage for theological reasons. While it does not follow from the ruling that a minister, priest, or rabbi who opposes gay marriage will be required to officiate at a same-sex wedding ceremony, questions have already arisen about religiously affiliated institutions, such as hospitals, schools, and charities. For example, will a religious college that offers housing to opposite-sex married couples be required to do the same for legally married same-sex couples? Indeed, in the wake of the decision, both supporters and opponents of gay marriage called on state and the federal governments to enact laws spelling out what religious institutions are and are not required to do to accommodate married same-sex couples.

In addition to the continued debate about same-sex marriage and, more broadly, sexual orientation, questions about race and racism also have been coming to the fore. One part of this debate was prompted by a number of highly publicized killings of young black men in the last year by law enforcement officers in cities such as Ferguson, Missouri; New York City; and Baltimore, Maryland. In these and other cases, the police have been accused of using unnecessary deadly force—something many believe the police would not do with white suspects.

Mostly Democratic politicians, including President Obama and New York City Mayor Bill DeBlasio, have argued that some police officers are unnecessarily targeting, harassing, and, at times, harming young black men, often with tragic consequences. The police and their political allies counter that most young black men are killed by other young black men and that while tragedies occasionally occur, their proactive crime-fighting methods have helped bring down the nation's crime rate.

The debate has taken a number of different turns. People on different sides of the issue have shown interest in placing small body cameras on police officers as a way of better documenting incidents in which deadly force has been used. Others, including the president, have called for criminal justice reform, including less severe sentencing guidelines for nonviolent drug offenders.

President Obama has said that he plans to make his last eighteen months in office extremely productive. In addition to criminal justice reform and the Pacific and European trade deals, some Washington observers hold out hope that White House and congressional Republicans can move forward on reform of the corporate tax code. Both liberals and conservatives argue that the corporate taxation system is broken. With its high rate of 35 percent on all profits and its myriad loopholes, many say that it discourages investment in the U.S. and encourages large companies to keep as much of their profits as possible overseas.

Both the administration and the GOP say they are open to a deal that would lower overall rates, close loopholes, and make it harder for companies to avoid taxation by keeping money in foreign countries.

Also on the agenda is a deal with Iran to contain its alleged ambitions to build nuclear weapons in exchange for a lifting of international economic sanctions against the country. In March Congress cleared legislation that gives it the authority to approve any deal the administration negotiates with the Iranians. While both sides say they are close to finalizing an agreement, many worry that the administration will give Iran too much leeway or that Iran will agree to tough limits on its nuclear program only to cheat and ultimately acquire the weapons clandestinely.

Other issues on the administration's to-do list include new spending on infrastructure. A reauthorization of highway spending will be debated in the second half of 2015. Also on the agenda is the continued implementation of the Affordable Care Act, with signs that congress-men on both sides of the aisle may be looking for ways to make the law more effective.

Entering into calculations for both Republicans and Democrats are the upcoming presidential and congressional elections, which will occur in November of 2016. For example, if, as some predict, the continued expansion of the ACA leads to huge increases in health insurance premiums next year, it could damage the candidacy of whoever receives the Democratic nomination for president. Conversely, new infrastructure spending and other measures to boost the economy could help Democratic candidates as they run, at least in part, on the record of the current administration.

◾ REGULATORY TOOLS

The wide variety of issues and conditions dealt with by regulation requires similarly diversified mechanisms and procedures. Nevertheless, there are common elements that, taken together, form the outlines of contemporary regulation.

Legislation

Contrary to views held by some, regulation does not grow mushroom-like in the dark recesses of Washington bureaucracy. All regulation starts with an act of Congress. Statutes define the goals of regulatory programs, identify the agency responsible for achieving them, and contain substantive and procedural guidance as to how the agency is to conduct its work. The first and most important tool of regulation is the law that establishes the authority and basic architecture of the program.

In the matter of guidance, regulatory statutes vary tremendously. A perennial criticism of regulatory statutes is that they are vague, giving far too much substantive and procedural discretion to bureaucrats in the programs they administer. There is no question that the provisions of some statutes are quite general. The Federal Power Act, for example, directs FERC to license those hydroelectric power projects that "are best adapted to a comprehensive plan for development of the waterway." The comprehensive plan and what constitutes a project that is "best adapted" is left to FERC's discretion. Similarly, the statutory language that created OSHA gave that agency a broad mandate. More recently, critics of President Obama's health care reform law, the Affordable Care Act, have argued that in spite of its size (the law is more than 2,000 pages long), too many decisions have been left to the Department of Health and Human Services, the Internal

Revenue Service, and the other agencies involved in issuing implementing regulations.

On the other hand, statutes can be quite specific when establishing the substantive jurisdiction of agencies. The Safe Drinking Water Act amendments of 1996 upheld regulations the EPA had been drafting on the by-products of disinfectants, such as chlorine. The Delaney Amendment to the Food, Drug, and Cosmetic Act gave the FDA strict guidelines for dealing with suspected carcinogens. The "zero-tolerance" standard of Delaney was replaced in 1996 by a new pesticide law establishing a uniform safety standard to ensure that the chemicals on both raw and processed foods pose a "reasonable certainty" of no harm. Such a standard is commonly interpreted to mean a lifetime cancer risk of no more than one in a million. In some instances, the subject matter of the regulatory statute is so narrow, such as the Surface Transportation Assistance Act's provisions relating to tandem truck trailers, that substantive discretion is negligible.

The trend since 1965 is toward more narrowly defined statutes and limiting amendments, which are the result of accumulated experience with programs. For example, the first Clean Air Act in 1970 was much less specific about hazardous air pollutants.

Procedural guidance in statutes varies as well. But as with substantive provisions, the trend is for Congress to provide more direction to agencies on how to make decisions and what factors to take into account when doing so. The 1996 safe drinking water law rescinded a requirement that the EPA set standards for twenty-five new drinking water contaminants every three years. Instead, the agency must publish every five years a list of unregulated contaminants found in drinking water. The EPA would then use that list to propose the regulation of new contaminants, taking the costs and benefits of any new regulation into account. Some statutes require agencies to balance conflicting interests or to conduct specified analyses during the process of making regulatory decisions. Amendments to the Federal Power Act tell FERC to balance power and nonpower interests in hydropower licensing, and they make it plain that environmental and recreational concerns are the nonpower interests most important to Congress. In addition to balancing multiple interests, Congress expects regulatory agencies to study different facets of proposed regulations.

Rules and Rulemaking

Rulemaking is usually the most important function performed by regulatory agencies. It transforms the provisions of statutes into specific mandates that, in turn, structure the behaviors of implementing officials and affected parties in the private sector. Since the earliest Congresses, which required the president to write rules related to trade with Native Americans and uses of public lands, rulemaking has been the source of law people use to learn exactly what they can expect from government and what government can expect from them.

The process by which rules are made can be quite complex. Congress first established uniform methods for rulemaking in the APA in 1946. The rulemaking provisions of that statute stressed three principles that remain central today: information, participation, and accountability. The act required a notice in the *Federal Register* that described the rule the issuing agency was proposing, opportunity for the public to comment in writing on the proposal, and a notice of the final rule and its effective date. The act promoted accountability by authorizing the courts to review any rule that was challenged as illegal. Still, the provisions were quite flexible, balancing a modest degree of public scrutiny and involvement with considerable discretion for rulemaking agencies.

Since 1946 the number of legal requirements for creating new rules has grown enormously, although most requirements apply selectively to individual rulemakings. Virtually all of these additional requirements enhance in some way one or more of the principles established in the APA. There are general statutes such as the Regulatory Flexibility Act, Paperwork Reduction Act, National Environmental Policy Act, and Unfunded Mandates Act of 1995, which require additional studies and forms of public participation when rules affect the interests that these laws seek to protect. Agency-specific and program-specific authorizing and appropriations bills establish similar procedures. Presidential executive orders impose additional requirements, ranging from cost-benefit analysis to special consideration of private property, the family, and state and local governments. Individual judicial decisions can require agencies to conduct special studies or consult extensively with interest groups. Overall, the weight of these requirements is to transform the APA model of rulemaking into a process that may be so encumbered that Thomas McGarrity of the University of Texas has used the term "ossification" to describe it. The pendulum has clearly swung away from agency flexibility in favor of public participation, especially by interest groups, broadly defined.

Any governmental function that is so important, frequent, and complex is bound to attract controversy and criticism, and rulemaking is certainly no exception. The complaints are numerous and, at times, contradictory. Some charge there is simply too much rulemaking and that it is choking the private sector. Others argue for more rulemaking, either because they favor more extensive regulation or they believe government too often makes law or policy without observing the proper procedures. Critics also fault the time it takes to issue rules; in some agencies the average is measured in years. Finally, there are persistent concerns in both the private and public sectors about the quality of the rules that the process ultimately produces.

The private sector has questioned the quality of information and analysis on which rules are based and has found them difficult to understand and comply with, and, most disturbing, biased in favor of large, established firms and organizations. Some in the public sector undoubtedly share some or all of these views, but they focus more on the difficulties created by unrealistic deadlines set by Congress and the courts, rules that are written in Washington without regard for resources available to implement them in the field, and ambiguous or otherwise faulty language in rules that impede their enforcement. The battle between the Department of Energy and Congress over the establishment of a permanent nuclear waste repository at Yucca Mountain, Nevada, is a case in point. Members of Congress, echoing the anger of the nuclear power industry, complained bitterly when the federal government failed to meet its statutory obligation in accepting commercial nuclear waste by January 1998. But Energy Department officials snapped back that Congress created that deadline in 1982 without a realistic assessment of the difficulty in creating a repository that must remain safe and stable for 10,000 years. As of September 2013, funding for the development of the Yucca Mountain nuclear waste repository was canceled.

It should not be surprising that rulemaking is a function that requires a substantial amount of proactive management. It is now common to find priority-setting, budgeting, and scheduling systems in agencies that issue a substantial number of rules. Most use some form of cross-agency working group to write rules to ensure that all relevant legal, technical, and political issues are considered. Rulemaking also attracts the attention of Congress, which conducts oversight by a variety of means; of the White House, which reviews both proposed and final rules; and of the courts when litigation over rules occurs.

However troubled and difficult, rulemaking is and will continue to be an elemental regulatory function that structures much of what follows.

Licenses and Permits

Granting licenses and issuing permits are common regulatory activities. States license doctors, lawyers, and a variety of other professionals and service providers to protect the public from the unqualified or unscrupulous. At the federal level the focus is different. There, it is more common to find programs that license activities, usually those with implications for health, safety, or the environment. For example, licenses are required to build and operate nuclear power plants and hydroelectric facilities. The National Pollution Discharge Elimination System (NPDES) issues permits to discharge all sources of pollution into America's waterways. The handling of pesticides and hazardous wastes must be cleared through the EPA.

Control of licenses and permits serves several interrelated purposes. In some instances those seeking the government's permission to engage in certain activities, such as operating a nuclear power plant, are expected to demonstrate that they are competent to perform them or that the activity poses no risk to health, safety, or the environment. Permits and licenses also are used to impose conditions on the activity for which the permission is being granted. A pesticide registration may be accompanied by the limitations on its use or the precautions those administering it are required to take.

Because a considerable amount of environmental, health, safety, and natural resource regulation involves licenses and permits, the procedures used to issue them are painstaking. Most require an applicant to submit extensive background information. The government then evaluates the applicant's qualifications; the threats that the proposed activity might pose to health, safety, or environmental quality; and the steps the applicant will take to eliminate or lessen the potential for harm.

For environmental, safety, and natural resource licenses, the agency's rules usually require that applicants consult in advance with other agencies or groups and report the comments they receive from these third parties in the application. In its procedures for licensing hydroelectric power plants, FERC requires preapplication consultation with federal and state agencies responsible for fisheries, wildlife, recreation, aesthetics, water quality, geology and soils, historic preservation, and Native American lands.

It is also common for the licensing agency to circulate the completed applications it receives to other agencies for formal comment. Notices to the public about the proposed action are published in the *Federal Register* and other outlets. Negotiations between the applicant and agencies or groups often result in agreements written into the license or permit.

At some point, the agency decides whether to issue a license or permit and what, if any, conditions to impose. Looking again at the hydropower licensing process, it is not uncommon for FERC to issue such a license containing dozens of conditions, or "articles," designed to protect natural resources and historic sites and to preserve other values and uses of the waterway on which the project will be built. Most agencies also have procedures to reconsider the content of licenses or permits at the request of the applicant or a third party, and, as with rules, licenses and permits can be challenged in court.

Because licenses and permits have policy implications that affect multiple interests and are in effect for long periods of time, the procedures employed to issue them have come to resemble those associated with rulemaking.

▉ IMPLEMENTATION TECHNIQUES

Once the rules or licenses are written, their provisions must be implemented. At this stage the behavior of regulated parties becomes important, and regulatory agencies engage in a variety of activities to ensure compliance.

Informing the Public

The *Federal Register* is the official means of communicating regulatory policies and decisions to the public, yet few in the regulated community learn about their obligations through it. Many have on-staff specialists to track new and changing requirements and to fashion approaches to compliance. Others rely on trade associations and professional newsletters to supply information; some hire expert consultants. The Internet has become a new resource for public participation. The *Federal Register* is available at www.federalregister.gov; the *Code of Federal Regulations* is available at www.gpo.gov/fdsys/browse/collectionCfr.action?collectionCode=CFR; and the *Electronic Code of Federal Regulations* is available at www.ecfr.gov. The federal government's website www.regulations.gov (*see appendix*) is a further resource.

To keep the public better informed, regulatory agencies provide information beyond what is found in the *Federal*

Register. At times, agencies may communicate directly with regulated parties, especially in emergency situations, such as when defects are discovered in aircraft. Agencies also provide technical supplements to rules to assist regulated parties. The NRC provides this type of guidance with each new rule that requires significant changes in equipment or operations. The supplement tells what the NRC considers acceptable, effective means of complying with new requirements and standards. OSHA has taken this approach a step further by performing "regulatory audits" for businesses. Under this program, OSHA officials conduct a no-fault survey of the company's compliance record and make recommendations for change. In this way, the company obtains authoritative information about how to avoid noncompliance without the threat of an enforcement action. The audit program has been explored by other agencies as well; it is perhaps the most ambitious method of keeping regulated parties aware of their obligations.

Monitoring

However they communicate requirements to the regulated parties, agencies do not rely solely on the provision of information to ensure that obligations are met. Agencies use a variety of means to monitor restricted activities and behaviors. Some programs require regulated parties to monitor their activities and to submit periodic reports. The reports might consist of raw data or summaries that follow a standard format. In some instances, data and reports may not be required routinely but must be made available to the agency on request when an inspector visits.

Inspection is the customary way to monitor for workplace safety, protection of natural resources, and compliance in some environmental programs. For some programs, such as OSHA's, the number of regulated premises far outnumber the available staff. OSHA's 2,000 inspectors cannot possibly visit all 7 million workplaces that fall under their jurisdictions. Such programs rely on complaints from the public when establishing their inspection priorities. An inspection program can become so intensive that it resembles supervision of the regulated activity. The USDA's 8,400 food safety inspectors in 2013 are a constant presence at the nation's 6,500 slaughterhouses and processing plants, although furloughs due to the 2013 budget sequestration stretched the inspectors even more. There tends to be a direct relationship between the potential danger to the public posed by the regulated activity and the amount of agency monitoring.

Intervention and Enforcement

When an agency discovers that a violation has occurred, it must intervene to bring the offending party into compliance. Some inspectors, notably those associated with occupational safety, have been criticized for issuing citations for minor offenses and, in the process, trivializing the program and infuriating the affected businesses. But many cases have been reported of inspectors overlooking minor, often inadvertent violations to get quick agreements from regulated parties to correct more serious problems. Citations may or may not be issued in

such instances. In a few cases, corruption—inspectors overlooking violations in return for personal rewards—is uncovered and programs are revamped.

Sanctions

The approach an agency takes to intervention depends to some extent on the nature and severity of sanctions it can impose on parties who fail to comply. Generally, regulatory statutes establish a range of sanctions that agencies can impose. Agencies match the type of sanction to the type of noncompliance through rules and management directives to their inspection staff.

Sanctions come in the form of warnings, fines, more frequent inspections, product recalls, temporary or permanent cessation of activities, suspension or termination of licenses or permits, and criminal penalties. Sanctions also have serious indirect consequences. An airline, such as ValuJet in 1996, which has its airworthiness certification suspended by the Federal Aviation Administration (FAA) can suffer a loss of consumer confidence. ValuJet shut down and reopened under the name AirTran. A manufacturing plant cited for polluting a waterway can suffer serious public relations problems. Both may expect to lose business.

The mechanisms by which sanctions are imposed also vary across programs. Some regulatory statutes grant significant authority to agencies to impose sanctions; others require the responsible agency to seek court orders. The EEOC had to file a federal lawsuit against Mitsubishi in April 1996 to take action on one of the biggest sexual harassment cases in history. When criminal penalties may be involved, the agency usually refers the matter to the Department of Justice for prosecution. The FDA in June 1996 asked Justice Department prosecutors to investigate whether the Upjohn Co. hid safety concerns about its controversial sleeping pill Halcion. In 1999 the Justice Department, using a racketeering statute created to pursue organized crime, sued the tobacco industry for health care costs incurred by taxpayers. In 2000 the Department of Housing and Urban Development, with the Justice Department's help, threatened to sue gun manufacturers if they did not cooperate with state and local governments pursuing their lawsuits to restrict the sale and marketing of firearms.

In recent years, financial services and accounting firms have come under increased state and federal scrutiny as a result of a series of scandals ranging from shady accounting practices to the defrauding of investors. As a result, an increasing number of fines have been levied against these companies. For instance, in March 2003 Merrill Lynch, one of the nation's top brokerage houses, paid an $80 million fine to the SEC in exchange for the agency's dropping charges against the firm. Merrill Lynch had been accused of aiding bankrupt energy giant Enron in its efforts to hide losses and inflate earnings. In May 2003 the SEC fined telecommunications giant WorldCom $500 million for its uncovered accounting fraud. At the end of 2004 corporate giant American International Group (AIG) was fined $126 million for accounting and other financial irregularities. In fall 2006 Boeing agreed to pay a $615 million fine to avoid prosecution related to a host of alleged improprieties in its bid to replace the nation's military air refueling fleet. Three years later, in 2009, pharmaceutical giant Eli Lilly was fined $1.5 billion for marketing one of its drugs for uses not approved by the FDA. And three years after that, Hong Kong-based bank HSBC agreed to pay a $1.9 billion fine for money laundering in violation of U.S. sanctions against Iran.

■ DISPUTE RESOLUTION

Conflict is common between an agency enforcing regulations and the regulated parties. Disputes arise regarding alleged violations and the sanctions imposed for noncompliance. Congress has established a two-tiered system for resolving these disputes. The first tier is based in the agencies; the second is in the federal court system.

Adjudication of disputes in agencies is governed by provisions in the APA and the procedural regulations of individual agencies that apply to the conduct of hearings. Adjudication usually involves fewer parties and is more judicial in nature than other forms of regulatory procedure. Formal adjudication involves a court trial in which the agency charges a named individual or company with violating a law or regulation. The APA outlines a strict format of notice, hearings, procedures, evidence, oral argument, and formal judicial decision that adjudication proceedings must follow. Consequently, adjudication is often a time-consuming and cumbersome process.

Participation

Companies and industries affected by federal regulations always have been well represented at agency proceedings. But intervention by citizens and consumer groups involves the question of standing—whether petitioners have a legitimate right to be heard before an agency because their interests and well-being are affected. While the right to appeal an agency decision before the courts is subject to limits imposed by the Constitution and court decisions, agencies enjoy broad discretion in setting and enforcing rules for participation in their proceedings.

The ability of groups other than the regulated industries to participate has been influenced by the regulatory system itself. Delay in the procedure is costly, and many small businesses and interest groups have found that they cannot afford to participate in a lengthy series of hearings and appeals. Although notice is required to be given in the *Federal Register,* unless a group has been following a particular issue closely, it may not be aware of a proposed ruling. Moreover, there might not always be adequate notice of a pending case, necessitating a hasty response by interested parties. In general, the regulated industries are better equipped to keep themselves abreast of forthcoming rules that fall within their interests.

The expense of participation has raised the question of whether there is a need to facilitate representation by consumer and citizen groups. It has been argued that their greater representation would provide the agencies with new or different information and lead to better informed judgments. Others have contended that because regulation exists to protect consumers and workers as well as industry interests, such views should be heard. Congress, however, has been unwilling to create an agency to represent consumer interests before other regulatory agencies. Programs to reimburse citizens who take part in agency proceedings also have met with mixed success and spotty government support. The Clinton administration broadened federal outreach to "stakeholder" groups, including activists and citizens, but with mixed results. Business groups complained that the citizens participating in hearings and roundtable discussions were really the representatives of special interests, such as environmental groups. The citizens complained that their opinions carried no weight in the final decisions.

Adjudicatory Process

Many disputes are resolved by consent order, which is a regulatory "plea bargain." Using this device a regulated party agrees to cease violation of regulations. A proposed order is drafted, published in the *Federal Register* for comment, and then recommended by the agency. Comments are considered part of the record of the case and, based on them, the agency may issue a consent order in final form. This substantial role for the public is another manifestation of the importance of participation in regulatory procedure. If a case is not dropped or settled through a consent order, the agency may initiate adjudicatory proceedings by issuing a formal complaint against the alleged violators.

Formal adjudication is conducted in a manner similar to a court proceeding. After the agency's complaint has been served, the charged party (the respondent) must provide a written response within a stipulated period of time. The case is assigned to an administrative law judge (ALJ) who presides over the trial. The litigating parties usually meet in an informal pretrial conference, at which oral arguments are presented and documents exchanged.

After the case has been narrowed to the substantive issues involved, the formal trial begins. The APA requires the agency to notify the affected parties of the hearing's time and place, the statute involved, and the factual dispute to be decided. The parties may submit oral or written evidence, present a defense and rebuttal, and cross-examine witnesses. The ALJ is prohibited from consulting any party on an issue of fact unless all parties have a chance to participate. Generally, regulatory agencies are more lenient than law courts on the evidence that may be admitted; this leniency is based on the assumption that regulatory officials are experts and thus highly qualified to evaluate evidence. But agencies must be careful that the evidence they admit will stand in a court of law should the decision in the case be appealed.

The record is closed when the hearing ends. Each party then submits a memorandum to the ALJ and responds to the other side's presentation. After reviewing the record, the ALJ issues a decision with respect to the facts of the case and the applicable law. A proposed order to remedy any found violations of law is then served on the involved parties.

Appeals

After an agency order has been served, the parties may appeal the ALJ's decision to the full commission or the agency administrator. After completion of its review, which may range from cursory to thorough, the agency can adopt the ALJ's decision, reject it, or return it for further consideration. At this point the agency's determination of the facts of the case is considered final.

This review of regulatory tools, while brief, underscores the complexities of the regulatory process, which is properly seen as a process by which a fundamental decision to regulate passes through successively finer procedural filters until the obligations of individual parties are established in specific terms. The procedures vary at each stage and become more formal when they shift from essentially legislative decisions and executive actions to judicial determinations. Perhaps the most compelling characteristic of regulatory procedure is the interdependence of the procedural steps and its appearance of perpetual motion. Decisions made at each point are being continually reexamined, altered, or supplemented at the next. At each stage of the regulatory process, analysis of some kind is being conducted.

■ ANALYSIS IN THE REGULATORY PROCESS

Analysis plays a role at each stage of every significant decision made during the regulatory process. Congressional staffers perform analyses when regulatory legislation is considered; the clerks of federal judges prepare analyses of conflicting testimony when a policy or decision is challenged in a lawsuit. But in terms of cumulative effect, the analyses performed in agencies by bureaucrats and their surrogates during the rulemaking process are the most important and wide-ranging in regulatory program operations.

Legal Analysis

Every rulemaking begins with an assessment of the provisions in legislation or judicial decisions that will govern the development of the regulation. What the statute mandates or allows the agency to do must be determined. Legislation may impose deadlines, require certain types of studies, or call for specific forms of public participation beyond the written comment mandated by the APA. Usually, this legal analysis is straightforward because legislative provisions are easy to understand. At times, the staff responsible for writing the rule may have to consult the agency's office of general counsel to determine what is expected under the statute. Legal analysis of this sort is an essential prerequisite to other rulemaking activities.

Policy Analysis

As noted earlier, President Reagan at the outset of his first term announced a set of "regulatory principles" that he expected agencies of the executive branch to follow when they developed rules or made other regulatory decisions. Other presidents have done the same. In addition to the president's general policies, rule-writers must be aware of the priorities and preferences of the political leadership of their agencies. During the Clinton administration, EPA rule-writers showed a keen awareness of EPA Administrator Carol M. Browner's background as an environmental agency chief for the state of Florida when they crafted their state "performance partnership grants," which give state governments more flexibility with federal environmental funds. While many of Clinton's agency heads were relatively low-key, FDA Commissioner David A. Kessler was notably aggressive in his regulatory role. FDA rule-writers took their cue, especially with their tough tobacco regulations. In contrast, a succession of free market FERC chairs kept that regulatory agency's hands off the increasingly deregulated wholesale electricity market. When California began facing severe electricity shortages and soaring power costs during the 2000–2001 winter, state officials implored FERC to step in to cap wholesale electricity prices, at least temporarily. First, FERC's Clinton-appointed chair, James Hoecker, then FERC's Bush-appointed chair, Curt Hebert Jr., declined. Indeed, throughout the crisis that lasted into 2002, the White House argued that such controls would only discourage the building of new power-generating facilities and prolong the shortage.

Failure to incorporate policy preferences into rules can lead to problems when the rules are reviewed at higher levels. Therefore, at the outset of rulemaking, agencies analyze the policy issues associated with the regulation to determine whether a particular substantive approach or set of procedures should be adopted.

Scientific and Technical Analysis

Every rule has a purpose that its substantive content is expected to achieve. In many cases the content deals with comparatively minor matters, and staff draws on readily available information. Analysis is minimal. For example, when it first came into being, OSHA simply adopted as rules more than 4,000 standards that a panoply of testing and professional societies had developed to protect worker safety. Other rules respond to individual problems as they arise. An airline disaster caused by a technical malfunction usually brings a wave of new rules, as aviation experts in the FAA analyze the problem and take steps to prevent its recurrence.

In still other cases, rules change to incorporate state-of-the-art practices and innovations. In fact, the NRC has been criticized for engaging in the serial "ratcheting up" of engineering requirements that draw on newly developed equipment or practices that promise increases in safety. Similarly, the EPA is required to locate and mandate the "best available technology" to limit pollution or its discharge into the water and air. This requirement also involves analysis of available means and how they perform. As science develops techniques capable of detecting the presence of even minute traces of a pollutant, industries and even the scientists themselves fear regulators will become more and more strict with allowable exposures.

On the other hand, technical analyses to support new rules are most difficult to perform when Congress mandates regulatory solutions for problems about which little is known. Environmental and worker health programs frequently are pushed beyond available knowledge. For example, the disputes over regulation of benzene in the workplace, asbestos in schools, and radon in houses hinge, at least in part, on studies of long-term health effects that cannot be conducted quickly or cheaply. Congress has thus far prevented OSHA from developing regulations on repetitive stress injuries in the workplace, fearing that effective solutions could be difficult to find and expensive to implement.

Agencies are organized to perform these analyses in a variety of ways. Many have offices of research and development to conduct studies. In a distinctive arrangement, all worker health regulations written by OSHA originate with research conducted by the National Institute for Occupational Safety and Health (NIOSH), a separate agency. More common is the use of contractors to supplement agency staff in conducting the basic data collection and analysis. Bottlenecks develop in studies when the necessary data is in the hands of the very industries to be regulated. Claiming proprietary rights, these sources often are loath to release information to help the agency write a rule that will end up costing them money.

Delays in completing rules, and successful legal challenges to completed ones, often result from the unavailability of information or its poor quality. But technical analysis is about more than time or potential litigation. The accuracy of technical analysis determines the success of a regulatory program. If problems are inadequately assessed or their solutions improperly devised, regulations will fail to achieve their goals.

Risk Analysis

Environmental, health, and safety regulatory programs are premised on conceptions of risk to human life or to valuable animal and plant life. Determining the nature and degree of risk posed by a given substance or activity is essential to any regulatory effort aimed at its elimination, reduction, or mitigation. This is the goal of a scientific technique known as risk analysis or risk assessment. A number of statutes require agencies to conduct studies of risk and use the results as the basis for regulation.

A number of high-profile regulatory disputes, such as occupational exposure to benzene and dioxin contamination in the food chain, have hinged on the quality of risk assessments. In those cases determining acceptable levels of exposure or ingestion has been stalled by protracted disagreements among scientists regarding the conduct of the risk analyses. Overall research designs, the ability to measure minute amounts of substances thought to be highly toxic, methods of data collection, statistical techniques used to analyze available data, conclusions drawn from statistical analyses, and proposed levels of pollution control based on the results of analyses have all been disputed in these and other cases. Further, Congress has not adopted uniform standards to guide risk assessment. Even in a single agency the criteria can vary across programs. EPA administers at least three statutes—the Safe Drinking Water Act; the Federal Insecticide, Fungicide and Rodenticide Act; and the Toxic Substances Control Act—that

seek different levels of risk reduction. Clinton's Executive Order 12881 established the National Science and Technology Council within the White House. The council's risk assessment subcommittee has been reviewing federal risk assessment research to help improve its quality and implementation.

Beginning in 1995 Congress dramatically raised the issue's profile when it made risk assessment and cost-benefit analysis cornerstones of its regulatory efforts. The 1996 safe drinking water law mandated that EPA publish a nonbinding analysis of the costs, benefits, and risks of new drinking water regulation. In response, some regulators have complained that Congress should not call for increased risk assessment while simultaneously cutting agency budgets.

While the overuse of risk analysis can stop or slow the regulatory process, high-quality risk analysis and assessment remains a powerful tool in efforts to build regulatory programs that work. As a scientific technique it is developing rapidly. But these methodological advances do not transfer automatically to the regulatory process, and the day that risk analyses are no longer disputed is well in the future.

Cost-Benefit Analysis

If there was a dominant theme in the Reagan administration's assault on the regulatory process, it was the simple, appealing notion that a regulatory action should generate more benefit than cost. That theme reemerged in 1995 with the swearing in of the Republican-led 104th Congress. The vehicle offered by the Republicans to ensure "net benefit" was cost-benefit analysis. This technique had been in use long before the Reagan administration. President Gerald R. Ford in 1974 directed agencies to prepare "inflation impact statements" to accompany their rules. At the end of 1976 the program was extended and its title changed to the economic impact statement program. Although the cost estimates were reasonably accurate, the assessment of benefits usually was weak, as was the study of alternatives. Agencies found that the program was useful in formulating their regulations and that the paperwork and time involved were not excessive.

President Carter also supported this approach. Shortly after taking office in 1977 he asked that full consideration be given to the "economic cost of major government regulations, through a more effective analysis of their economic impact." In March 1978 Carter issued Executive Order 12044, which set criteria for agencies to follow in performing regulatory impact analyses (*for text of order, see appendix*). The analysis had to include a description of the major alternative ways of dealing with the problem that were considered by the agency; an analysis of the economic circumstances of each of these alternatives; and a detailed explanation of the reasons for choosing one alternative over the others. The order did not extend to independent commissions, nor did it require a strict cost-benefit analysis.

Carter also created the Regulatory Analysis Review Group (RARG), chaired by a member of the Council of Economic Advisers, to improve such analysis. The Carter administration "always took pains to stress that its requirements for regulatory analysis should not be interpreted as subjecting rules to a [strict] cost-benefit test," said former RARG chair George C. Eads.

In contrast, in February 1981 Reagan issued Executive Order 12291, which replaced Carter's Executive Order 12044, and required a cost-benefit analysis from agencies. It required executive agencies to prepare a regulatory impact analysis for all new and existing major regulations. Major rules were defined as those likely to have an annual effect on the economy of $100 million or more, lead to a major increase in costs or prices, or have "significant adverse effects" on business.

Regulatory analyses had to be submitted to OMB for review sixty days before publication in the *Federal Register*. However, OMB was empowered to waive the regulatory impact analysis for any rule. Agencies had to apply cost-benefit analyses to all rulemaking and adopt the least costly alternative.

The rise of cost-benefit analysis as a decision-making tool in the development of specific regulations remains controversial. As an analytical technique, cost-benefit analysis is limited, sometimes severely, by the lack of data or skepticism about the data's sources and accuracy. Even more fundamental are problems in measuring benefits and costs that may occur over a long period of time or involve intangibles that are difficult to value. It has been widely reported, for example, that different agencies use different estimates for the value of a human life that might be saved by a given regulatory intervention. Many people are appalled by the very notion of placing dollar values on life, health, or safety. The fact that studies are conducted before regulations are actually implemented means agencies should be estimating compliance rates, another complicating factor.

The administration of George H. W. Bush retained Executive Order 12291's approach to cost-benefit analysis. The Clinton administration embraced the technique as well, often using it as a means to justify many of its regulatory initiatives. For instance, in 1997 the Clinton administration estimated the cost of a new nutritional labeling campaign for food at $4 million per year, with a benefit ranging from $275 million to $360 million a year. The FDA's proposed regulations of tobacco were estimated to cost $180 million a year at a benefit of up to $10.4 billion.

But it was the Republican 104th Congress that pushed hardest for its broad implementation, and with some success. The unfunded mandates law of 1995 requires the Congressional Budget Office (CBO) to estimate the impacts of all new mandates that would cost state or local governments $50 million or more a year. The CBO also must estimate the impacts of any mandate that would cost private companies $100 million or more a year. Before issuing rules that would cost businesses more than $100 million yearly, regulatory agencies now must prepare a cost-benefit analysis. A rider attached to a 1996 law raising the federal debt ceiling instructs the EPA and OSHA to collect advice and recommendations from small businesses to improve their analyses of a proposed regulation's impact.

Such mandates are not necessarily cheap. A 1998 study by CBO found that eighty-five randomly selected "regulatory impact analyses" finished in 1997 cost federal agencies anywhere from $14,000 to $6 million to implement. OSHA spent as much as $5 million performing risk assessments and regulatory analyses on the single rule it issued in 1997. The EPA spends about $120 million a year on regulatory analyses.

Not surprisingly, compliance with these mandates has been spotty at best. In a 2000 report, the CSAB concluded that OMB had largely failed to supply independent cost-benefit analyses, relying instead on the regulatory agencies' efforts—efforts that have been suspect. For instance, in 1997 EPA reported—and OMB dutifully repeated—that the annual benefits of environmental regulation were worth $3.2 trillion. At EPA's request, the number was revised radically downward, to $1.45 trillion in 2000 to respond to charges of gross exaggeration.

Meanwhile the cost to businesses of all regulation has remained high. According to a study issued by the Weidenbaum Center at Washington University in St. Louis, regulations cost the private sector $1.13 trillion in 2002. Possibly in response to these continuing concerns, President Obama appointed Harvard Law professor Cass Sunstein to head up the OIRA. Sunstein, although politically liberal, is known for his advocacy of cost-benefit analysis in the regulation of business, and his appointment surprised and even angered some on the left.

Other Analyses Required by Statutes

As noted above, several types of analysis may be required by legislation. For example, the Regulatory Flexibility Act (RFA) requires agencies to determine the effects of rules on small business. The National Environmental Policy Act (NEPA) may require an environmental impact statement (EIS) if the rule is likely to have major ecological effects.

An EIS is a significant analytical task and is governed by guidelines issued by the Council on Environmental Quality (CEQ). In addition to covering a wide range of potential impacts, the EIS must be made available in draft form for review and comment by the public. Hence, the process side of NEPA is substantial, as well.

Since its passage in 1980, one piece of analytical legislation has created tremendous controversy and difficulty for the regulatory process. The Paperwork Reduction Act (PRA) was intended to force discipline in the government's information collection efforts (*for text of act, see appendix*). The act established the OIRA as a principal unit of OMB. Its main task is to oversee the actions of regulatory agencies to determine if the paperwork required in any regulatory effort is the least burdensome, not duplicative, and "of practical utility." The goal of obtaining good quality, useful information was as important as the more widely known objective of reducing the burden of paperwork on the public. Clearly the PRA requires agencies to think carefully about their information requests. But OMB's role in this process has been the object of intense controversy in Congress. (*See Accountability and Oversight, below.*)

REGULATORY PERSONNEL

Much of the debate on reforming the federal regulatory process centers on two important areas—the people chosen to direct the agencies and the procedures they use to regulate. The president appoints and the Senate confirms the heads of most regulatory agencies, but there are few guidelines for the selection process. Many critics believe that federal regulators are not as well qualified for their jobs as they should be.

Numerous experts, task forces, and study commissions have examined the twin problems of the quality of administrators and regulatory procedures, and they have made hundreds of recommendations for improvements. But few of these recommendations have been implemented in any formal way, and the debate on how to solve these problems is likely to continue.

Selection of Officials

Most regulatory agency heads and commissioners are selected in accordance with Article II, Section 2, of the Constitution, which states that the president "shall nominate, and by and with the Advice and Consent of the Senate, shall appoint Ambassadors, other public Ministers and Consuls, Judges of the Supreme Court, and all other Officers of the United States." Dividing the power of appointment between the president and the Senate was one of the checks the framers of the Constitution felt was necessary to ensure that one branch of government did not dominate the others.

The president may remove for any or no reason heads of regulatory agencies who are within the executive branch. Once the Senate has confirmed a nominee and he or she has been sworn in, the Senate may not reconsider the nomination. Independent regulatory commission members generally may be removed only for cause, such as inefficiency, neglect of duty, or misconduct.

The Constitution does not specify any qualifications to be a regulator. Congress, however, has required that appointees to particular agencies sit for fixed terms and meet certain criteria. For example, the act establishing the Federal Reserve Board stipulates that members be chosen with "due regard to a fair representation of the financial, agricultural, industrial, and commercial interests and geographical divisions of the country." The requirements can be even more precise. For example, the FAA administrator is to "be a civilian and shall have experience in a field directly related to aviation."

To ensure a degree of bipartisanship in regulatory decisions, Congress has required that most independent regulatory commissions have no more than a simple majority of commissioners from the same political party. The president is authorized to designate the chairs of most independent regulatory commissions, and most presidents choose someone of their political party.

NOMINATIONS

There is no established formal process for the selection of presidential appointees, although recent administrations have followed roughly the same procedures. Generally the president has an appointments adviser who oversees the process of searching out, screening, and recommending potential nominees. Members of Congress and special interest groups are often consulted in an effort to obtain informal clearance for the candidate. But few people will be nominated who are not politically acceptable to the White House, and in some cases politics and patronage may be the chief determinant in a person's selection.

The president, along with advisers, will consider several other points in deciding whom to nominate to a regulatory agency. These factors can include the potential nominee's educational background and employment record, familiarity with the matter to be regulated, age, health, minority status, and the region of the country from which he or she comes.

Another connection that has been useful to dozens of regulatory agency appointees is congressional sponsorship. In its study of thirty-eight regulatory appointments to four agencies over a fifteen-year period, the Senate Governmental Affairs Committee found that congressional sponsorship was often an important, if not the predominant, factor in the selection process.

President Clinton explicitly introduced diversity as a criterion in presidential appointments. In order to form a government that "looks like America," his White House personnel office sought qualified women, African Americans, Hispanics, and other minorities to fill vacancies in regulatory and other agencies. Presidents George W. Bush and Barack Obama carried on the practice, appointing women and minorities to top positions, including cabinet posts and heads of White House offices, such as secretary of state and attorney general.

CONFIRMATIONS

The purpose of congressional confirmation proceedings is to determine the character and competence of the nominee. The committee with oversight for the agency holds hearings at which the nominee and others may testify. Once the committee has approved a nominee, the name is submitted to the full Senate. The Senate may approve, reject, or recommit a nomination to the committee that considered it. Controversial nominations sometimes are debated at length, but few are brought to the floor if there is any chance the nominee will be rejected. A nominee having that much opposition usually withdraws before the full Senate considers the appointment.

The Senate's advice and consent role gives Congress an important mechanism for monitoring the quality of regulatory agency appointments. Critics have charged, however, that the Senate does not take full advantage of this power. In general, the Senate does not closely examine presidential choices for regulatory positions in the executive branch on the theory that presidents should be allowed to choose their staffs. A check of the candidate's basic qualifications, rather than a full-scale examination of his or her views, generally suffices.

Appointments to the independent regulatory commissions are a somewhat different matter. Until the early 1970s presidential nominations to the independent agencies also were routinely confirmed. But after the Watergate scandal heightened sensitivity to potential abuses of government office, the Senate began to scrutinize nominations more carefully, looking at a nominee's economic views and political philosophy, as well as potential conflicts of interest.

QUESTION OF QUALITY

The quality of regulatory commissioners has been an issue for many decades. James M. Landis, President John F. Kennedy's regulatory adviser, wrote in 1960 that poor administrators can "wreak havoc with good law." Landis attributed many of the agencies' shortcomings to "a deterioration in the quality of our administrative personnel" since World War II, "both at the top level and throughout the staff."

Studying the problem seventeen years later, the Senate Governmental Affairs Committee did not find the situation much improved. "[T]here is something lacking in overall quality," the committee wrote. "It is not a matter of venality or corruption or even stupidity; rather, it is a problem of mediocrity."

There is little agreement on the reasons for the lack of quality and even less agreement on what should be done about it. Some have argued that the multimember structure of the independent commissions, not the personnel, is responsible for mediocrity. "Even if the best qualified person filled each position, the collegial structure would impede effective performance," the Ash Council, a task force set up by President Nixon, wrote in 1971.

The selection process is also blamed for the lack of qualified regulators in government service. Critics say it is haphazard and too often governed by factors other than a candidate's professional qualifications. Finding a candidate who is politically acceptable is oftentimes more important than finding one who is technically qualified.

The Regulatory Civil Service

The quality of political leadership in regulatory institutions is unquestionably important. These individuals have the power to influence the policies implemented by their agencies and are constantly involved in important decisions. But concern for top officials should not obscure the crucial importance of career staff in the performance of regulatory agencies. It is the civil servant whose work determines if and how well higher-level policies are carried out and priorities met. They draft the rules, carry out the inspections, and resolve most disputes. The problems associated with these regulatory personnel are different from, but every bit as serious as, those that affect the political leadership of any agency.

The education, skills, and experiences that are represented in the professional staff of regulatory agencies constitute a microcosm of American society. For every regulated activity there must be appropriate expertise. A large number of professions are represented in the regulatory civil service. The FCC requires the services of a substantial number of attorneys as well as engineers, economists, accountants, and electrical technicians. A review of the professional backgrounds of employees of the EPA would find attorneys, economists, engineers, chemists, biologists, statisticians, and persons with advanced degrees in public administration and policy analysis.

Additionally, those working in each of these agencies, whatever their academic training, must have, or acquire on the job, intimate working knowledge of the private industry or activity they are engaged in regulating. It goes without saying that persons with these combinations of education, skills, and experience are often sought after by the private or nonprofit sectors. Attracting highly qualified persons to government service is only part of the challenge; keeping them there when government salaries, benefits, working conditions, and promotional opportunities may lag behind the private sector has become difficult. Qualified persons must be recruited for public service, and once in place they must be retained.

The report of the National Commission on the Public Service, "Leadership for America: Rebuilding the Public Service," points to a gradual erosion in the caliber of government personnel due mainly to the difficulty of attracting and keeping qualified workers. Those familiar with regulatory requirements, procedures, and compliance techniques are much in demand in affected industries, businesses, and organizations where salaries, benefits, and opportunities are greater. This dilemma has no easy solution. The investment the nation needs to make to attract experienced and talented professionals to leave the private sector for careers in regulatory agencies is substantial indeed.

▨ ACCOUNTABILITY AND OVERSIGHT

There is intense conflict over the accountability of those who make regulatory decisions. A few observers find nothing less than a total perversion of the constitutional system, with unelected bureaucrats wielding vast regulatory powers essentially unchecked by direct popular will. Others find the governmental agencies greatly hindered by external checks. There is no question that bureaucrats in regulatory agencies make important decisions, but in doing so they are constrained. They are accountable to the popular will, but indirectly, through the actions of elected representatives—Congress and the president—and those of the unelected branch of government—the judiciary.

Presidential Influence

Presidents sought to exert control over regulation almost as soon as the first agency came into being. In 1908 President Theodore Roosevelt urged that all independent commissions be placed in the executive branch under the immediate supervision of a cabinet secretary. A task force appointed in 1937 by Franklin Roosevelt amplified that view. It found that "important powers of policy and administration" were routinely parceled out "to a dozen or more irresponsible agencies."

In 1949 the Hoover Commission recommended that the "purely executive functions of quasi-legislative and quasi-judicial agencies" be brought within the regular executive departments. In 1971 the Ash Council proposed that rulemaking functions of the independent commissions be placed directly under the president. Although Congress ignored these proposals, the powers of the president remained formidable.

The appointment process (discussed in a previous section) obviously is an important mechanism to ensure accountability of regulatory officials to the president. The use of the budget and executive orders are other controls available.

BUDGET CONTROL

The budget is one of the most important controls presidents have over the regulatory agencies. Presidents, not the agencies, decide how much money to request from Congress and for what purposes. In this way presidents can cut back regulatory efforts they disapprove of and give a boost to those they favor. Although the budget is one of its main oversight tools, Congress in the past generally made only insignificant changes to the presidential budget request for the regulatory agencies. That changed dramatically in 1995. The Republican-led Congress used the appropriations process to try to curb regulations through attrition. House appropriators tried to slash the EPA's budget by a third. OSHA's budget was slated for a 16 percent cut. Budgetary attacks on regulatory agencies, coupled with riders on appropriations bills to curb the agencies' enforcement powers specifically, helped lead to the government shutdowns of 1995 and 1996. Most of the funds were eventually restored. The EPA, for instance, wound up with a 9.8 percent cut. But fiscal uncertainties during the budget battles had the temporary effect of curbing much regulatory action.

In the latter years of the Clinton administration, many regulatory agencies made remarkable budgetary recoveries. With his March 2001 budget blueprint, President George W. Bush signaled a return to austerity for some agencies, while other, more politically favored offices would thrive. The EPA and the Labor Department faced budget cuts, while the EEOC would remain flush, a sign of the new president's outreach to minorities. These trends continued in the president's succeeding budget requests, although the EEOC in Bush's second term faced cuts as well. The new Democratic Congress from 2007 to 2009, however, indicated its willingness to confront Bush over cuts to regulatory agencies. President Obama has moved to increase some regulatory budgets, at agencies such as OSHA and the CPSC, even though the federal government's debt has risen dramatically in recent years.

Since 1921, when the Budget and Accounting Act was passed, presidents have had the authority to review and revise budget estimates for all executive branch agencies before they were submitted to Congress. In 1939 that authority was extended to the independent regulatory commissions.

Congress did not object to this executive control over the independent commissions' budgets until President Nixon created the OMB in 1970. Built around the nucleus of the old Budget Bureau, OMB was given new authority to coordinate the executive branch budget requests and legislative proposals. Unlike its predecessor, which had retained an image of neutrality, OMB was quickly identified as the president's agency, a tool for pushing the presidential budget and legislative proposals through Congress.

President Reagan, for example, used the budget to promote his antiregulation policies. The biggest cuts in regulatory spending, 37 percent from 1981 to 1985, occurred in agencies that regulate specific industries such as airlines, trucking, railroads, and intercity bus lines. On the other hand, the budgets of agencies concerned with banking and finance and general business matters, such as the FDIC, the SEC, and the Patent and Trademark Office, increased substantially during Reagan's first term. Staffing reductions occurred across the board, but safety, health, and energy and environmental programs took the biggest cuts. The CPSC lost 225 employees between 1981 and 1985. OSHA had lost 654 full-time staffers by the end of Reagan's first term, and the EEOC, 285. Most of the cuts occurred during the first year Reagan had full control over agency budgets and personnel.

After 1985 the cuts slowed down and in some cases were reversed. The change in direction was attributed to several factors. Observers of the regulatory scene noted that the analytical requirements called for by Executive Order 12291 would be expensive for the agencies to implement. In addition, the Democratic-controlled Congress appeared to be less willing to acquiesce in regulatory budget cutting after the EPA was convulsed by scandal in 1983. Stung by charges of being anti-environment, the Republican 104th Congress began showing similar reluctance to cut in 1996.

EXECUTIVE ORDERS

In addition to the appointments and budget powers, presidents also are free to issue directives and statements to the agencies in the form of executive orders. In February 1981 President Reagan issued Executive Order 12291, which imposed strict new rules on cabinet and agency regulators, gave OMB extensive powers, and required the use of cost-benefit analysis. In January 1985 Reagan issued Executive Order 12498, which required agencies to clear their regulations with OMB while they were in the early stages of development (*for text of order, see appendix*). The order called for each agency to submit to OMB in January of each year lists of significant regulatory actions it expected to propose in the coming year. According to OMB, this procedure would give the agency the opportunity to clear regulations while they were under development instead of when they were about to be proposed to the public. The executive order also called for the annual publication of the rules each agency planned to propose.

The changes wrought by these executive orders were among the most significant alterations in the regulatory process since passage of the APA. Their significance was underscored by the firestorm of criticism, litigation, and political conflict they generated. OMB critics charged that the agency improperly altered proposed regulations and was a secret conduit for industry lobbyists who wished to weaken regulatory proposals. Lawsuits challenged the constitutionality of OMB's intervention. Although the use of OMB by the president to manage the regulatory process emerged largely intact from this litigation, the controversy did not go away.

Soon after taking office, President Clinton issued Executive Order 12866, which repealed the Reagan executive orders and outlined the Clinton approach to presidential oversight of rulemaking. In addition to articulating a number of principles to guide rulemakers, he limited the use of OMB review and cost-benefit analysis to "significant" rules, as determined by a number of criteria set out in the order. The president required that the OIRA disclose all manner of communication with agencies and outside parties during the course of its review and imposed strict time periods for completion of the review process. The order also established a "Regulatory Working Group"— consisting of the vice president, the director of OIRA, and the heads of all government agencies involved in domestic regulation—which was charged with developing "innovative regulatory techniques."

Like Reagan and Clinton before him, President George W. Bush also put his stamp on the rulemaking process. At the beginning of 2007 Bush issued an executive order requiring each federal agency to have a regulatory policy office headed up by a political appointee. The aim was to have someone who shared the president's policy priorities in each agency to review and to conduct a cost-benefit analysis of regulations. While business leaders and many economists praised the new directive, Democrats, consumer advocates, and others argued that the president was politicizing the rulemaking process. In similar fashion, when President Obama arrived at the White House, he quickly reached for an executive order to help set his regulatory agenda. Ten days after he became president, Obama issued Executive Order 13497, which revoked several of his predecessor's executive orders on regulatory planning, including Bush's 2007 order.

In all, Clinton issued 364 executive orders during his eight years in office, fewer than Reagan's 381 but still a respectable total. In his eight years in office President George W. Bush issued 291 executive orders, and President Obama issued 213 executive orders by July 2015 of his second term—an annual pace similar to that of George W. Bush.

Congressional Oversight

Although any president can exert a strong influence on the regulatory process through the powers of appointment, budget, and executive order, congressional powers are also substantial. In its 1977 study of regulation, the Senate Governmental Affairs Committee listed six primary goals of congressional oversight. They were (1) ensuring compliance with legislative intent; (2) determining the effectiveness of regulatory policies; (3) preventing waste and dishonesty; (4) preventing abuse in the administrative process; (5) representing the public interest; and (6) preventing agency usurpation of legislative authority.

"[O]versight is not simply hindsight," the report noted. "Oversight involves a wide range of congressional efforts to review and control policy implementation by regulatory agencies. Congressional oversight thus includes both participation before agency action and review after the fact."

The fundamental congressional control over independent and executive branch regulatory agencies is statutory—the passage of legislation establishing new agencies and commissions, and spelling out their powers and limitations. Once the agencies are created, Congress exercises its control by assigning new responsibilities to them. Members of Congress also may influence the selection of nominees to head the commissions and agencies, and even more important is the Senate's authority to confirm them.

After the agencies are established and their members confirmed, Congress uses several tools to ensure that the agencies remain politically accountable to the legislative branch. One tool is investigation: Congress can examine agency practices in light of possible abuses, costs and benefits of regulation, potential reforms, and agency responsiveness to the elusive "public interest." But the two principal tools are appropriations and authorization statutes.

The appropriations process enables the House and Senate appropriations committees to scrutinize proposed agency budgets. Oversight through appropriations has been strengthened through the annual review of most agency budgets. In approving them, Congress may specify the purposes for which funds are to be used—a direct and unambiguous method of control.

At times, Congress has been unable to ensure that appropriated funds actually are spent. Nevertheless, Congress has used the appropriations process to order the agencies to take specific regulatory actions or to refrain from them. For example, Congress repeatedly used a rider to an appropriations bill to prevent the Agriculture Department from abolishing certain marketing orders targeted for elimination by Reagan's OMB staff in the early 1980s. In 1995 House members tried to use a rider to bar OSHA from developing standards or issuing regulations on repetitive motion injuries, such as carpal tunnel syndrome. After Republicans battled for months with the Clinton administration, a compromise was reached to allow the standards to be developed but to block new regulations. After the GOP came to power in 1995, a little-noticed provision in the energy and water development appropriations bill prevented federal regulators from tightening corporate average fuel efficiency (CAFE) standards for automakers. The congressional prohibition has recently taken on more urgency with the booming popularity of "light trucks"—sport utility vehicles and minivans—because such vehicles are exempt from the tougher CAFE standards for cars. In 1998 House Republicans inserted a provision into the spending plan for the departments of Veterans Affairs and Housing and Urban Development, blocking the Consumer Products Safety Commission from developing a new standard for upholstery flammability.

Traditionally, the appropriations review has not focused on the agencies' policies and goals. If it has occurred at all, such scrutiny has come during the authorization process when Congress determines whether to continue the agency. Again, the 104th Congress broke from this tradition, although it ultimately failed to get its plans enacted. Riders on its fiscal 1996 appropriations bill would have severely curtailed OSHA's enforcement power while increasing funds for counseling and technical assistance, essentially changing it from an enforcement agency to one focused on safety awareness and technical support.

The House's original 1996 budget for the EPA contained seventeen legislative provisions aimed at limiting EPA's ability to enforce regulations on sewer systems, wetlands, refineries, oil and gas manufacturing, radon in water, pesticides in processed foods, lead paint, and water pollution. The budget wars of 1995 and 1996 chased Congress back to the position that substantive changes to agency policies should be the purview of authorizing committees. A number of agencies have been given permanent authorization status, among them the FCC and the EPA. Aware that permanent authorizations decrease its ability to oversee regulatory actions, Congress in recent years has required periodic authorization for some of the more controversial agencies, including the CPSC and the Federal Trade Commission (FTC).

More often than not, Congress gives up some of its control by couching agency authorizing statutes in vague generalities, giving the regulators considerable leeway in the performance of their functions. Occasionally, agencies have taken actions that run counter to congressional intent. In a few such cases, Congress then has felt obliged to narrow the agency's mandate.

Besides these formal oversight powers, Congress has other ways to regulate the regulators, among them hearings; informal contacts; and directives contained in committee reports, sunset provisions, and individual casework. These nonstatutory controls may be the most common form of congressional oversight. A number of statutes require regulatory agencies to submit detailed reports to committees. Committee investigations not only provide information but also publicize the performance of agencies.

Casework is intervention by a member of Congress on behalf of a constituent who is involved in a proceeding before an agency. There are no reliable figures on the number of times members attempt to assist constituents with regulatory problems. Anecdotes suggest that a significant percentage of "congressional mail" received by some regulatory agencies involves this type of inquiry. It may be too strong to characterize this political ombudsman role as oversight, but it clearly puts affected agencies on notice that Congress is watching their decisions as they affect individuals, as well as overall programs and general policies.

The legislative veto, once a popular device, allowed Congress to manage the regulatory process through rejection of individual rules. In 1983 the Supreme Court ruled its use unconstitutional in *Immigration and Naturalization Service v. Chadha.*

Limits on Oversight

The Senate Governmental Affairs Committee in 1977 detailed a number of major roadblocks to effective oversight, which remain in place today. These include

Committee Structure. Because several committees usually share jurisdiction over an agency, oversight is fragmented, and coordination and cooperation among legislative panels is difficult to achieve, particularly among House and Senate committees.

Information Lag. Committees sometimes have experienced difficulties and delays in obtaining requested information. Agencies may refuse to supply information, or they simply may not have it available. Moreover, filtering most regulatory agency budget and legislative requests through OMB reduces the ability of Congress to obtain independent information.

Inadequate Staff. According to the committee report, the professional staff members on legislative committees having oversight responsibility for the regulatory agencies numbered only several hundred, reflecting the great disparity in size between congressional staffs and the agencies they oversee. Perhaps more important is the problem of developing the necessary staff expertise for effective oversight, the committee said.

Other intangible factors can hinder congressional oversight, among them the demand on members' time and the belief that members gain more politically from sponsoring new legislation than from policing what has already been enacted. Bonds that develop between congressional committees and agencies also may impede a full and critical review of regulatory performance.

Judicial Review

As with the other branches, the courts have always been significantly involved in regulatory decision making. The Supreme Court's decisions invalidating New Deal regulatory programs set the stage for the APA. More recently, the courts have played a profoundly important role in setting the limits of congressional, presidential, and even judicial influence over regulatory policy making in the agencies. Their rulings have altered whole regulatory programs and countless individual decisions. Although critics of judicial activism deplore such decisions, judicial review is not without substantial constraints.

The judiciary is the most passive branch, awaiting the filing of lawsuits before it can take action. The courts are empowered to hear a variety of challenges to regulatory decisions, ranging from the delegation of authority to agencies by Congress to the legality and fairness of agency dealings with individual regulated parties. There are, however, criteria that must be satisfied before the courts can hear a case brought by a complaining party.

Litigants must establish standing to sue; the court must agree that the timing of the lawsuit is correct; and all other possible remedies must be exhausted. To establish standing, potential litigants must demonstrate that they have a personal stake in the outcome of the lawsuit and that the damage suffered is related to the regulatory action in dispute. Courts will not entertain a lawsuit until an agency has completed its work on the matter in question. The principles of "finality" and "ripeness for review" are well-settled tenets of administrative law; they prevent premature review of issues that may be resolved by agency deliberations. "Exhaustion of remedies" is a similar concept that forecloses court review if there are opportunities remaining in the administrative process to redress the grievances. Lawsuits also must be brought to the proper level of court. Most regulatory statutes contain provisions that determine which federal courts have the authority to hear cases arising from different types of regulatory actions.

If a litigant satisfies these criteria and presents the lawsuit in the proper court, a decision of some sort will be rendered on the merits of the case. A critical question is the extent to which courts will question the judgment of regulators when they are sued. This is the "scope of review" issue, and on this matter the judiciary has sent decidedly mixed signals. In 1983 the Supreme Court announced in the case of *Motor Vehicle Manufacturers v. State Farm* that the courts would take a "hard look" when regulators made decisions to ensure that they were doing what Congress had intended in a careful and well-reasoned manner. One year later, however, the Court appeared to back off from this aggressive approach in its decision in *Chevron USA v. NRDC,* which stated that the judicial inquiry should end as soon as the judges satisfied themselves that the agency had interpreted the statute in question in a manner that is "permissible."

Courts continue to shape regulatory issues. A 1996 Supreme Court ruling in *Seminole Tribe v. Florida* could affect the enforcement of federal statutes and regulations against states deemed in violation. The ruling did not directly involve regulation. Instead, it was prompted by a dispute over Native American gaming. But if the decision is broadly interpreted, regulators may be unable to sue states in federal court. States could find themselves protected against federal regulations by the 11th Amendment, which states in part, "The judicial power of the United States shall not be construed to extend to any suit in law or equity, commenced or prosecuted against one of the United States." Protections for state governments against federal regulation were bolstered again in 2001, when a divided Supreme Court ruled 5–4 that a woman employed by the state of Alabama could not sue the state under the Americans with Disabilities Act.

A wide variety of decisions are possible when a court reviews actions of regulatory agencies. Courts can uphold the agency decision, invalidate the agency decision, or specify corrective procedures for the agency or litigant. Courts may even decide whether an agency has jurisdiction at all, as in 1997, when a federal court in Greensboro, NC, ruled that the FDA could regulate tobacco and its contents as a drug but did not have the power to regulate tobacco advertising. Both the Clinton administration and the tobacco industry appealed the ruling, and understandably so. Different courts facing different circumstances at different times will reach different results. In 1998 a three-judge panel from the 4th Circuit U.S. Court of Appeals in Richmond overturned the ruling. Finally, in 1999 the Supreme Court ruled that the FDA had no jurisdiction over tobacco.

But just as the judiciary can restrict regulatory activity, it can affirm the power of regulators to do their jobs. The Supreme Court's February 2001 *Whitman v. American Trucking Associations* decision may prove to be a landmark. The ruling unambiguously found that the EPA was not taking too much lawmaking power away from Congress by filling in the blanks left by vague congressional requests in the Clean Air Act. Such fill-in-the-blank exercises have become part of the daily routine for all federal regulatory agencies.

Whatever the prevailing general philosophy of judicial review, there is no question that judges and their decisions influence the regulatory process. In some instances, courts have been quite aggressive in substituting their judgment for those of agency experts. In July 1998 U.S. District Court Judge William Osteen of North Carolina undercut all regulation of indoor smoking by striking down a landmark 1993 EPA finding that secondhand tobacco smoke increases the risk of cancer. Almost fifteen years later, the Supreme Court ruled in 2007 that the EPA had erred when it claimed that it did not have the authority to regulate carbon dioxide emissions from cars. The Court went on to rule that the agency must either use this authority or give good reasons why it will not. In other cases, courts have ordered a redistribution of agency resources, a reduction in agency discretion, and redistributions of power among the various types of professionals in regulatory agencies.

Overall, then, the view that holds that regulatory agencies are subject to an elaborate network of controls is most certainly true. The issue is not whether agencies are accountable; rather, the issue is how agencies sort out the multiple and often conflicting messages they get from the president, Congress, the courts, and interest groups.

■ REFORM AND THE FUTURE

Frequently, reform triggers reaction. Consider the calls in 1990 for reregulation in many areas deregulated since 1975. To varying degrees, reform restored unfettered market forces in civil aviation, trucking, telecommunications, energy, and banking. These returns to the free market have indeed paid dividends. The CSAB estimated the consumer benefits of airline deregulation amount to $10 billion annually while accident rates have fallen. Deregulation of railroads has led to savings of between $3.5 and $5 billion a year for shippers. Trucking deregulation more than doubled the number of carriers, increased jobs by 30 percent, and saved the economy $7.8 billion per year. But experience with some of the side effects of deregulation—concerns for safety in air travel, poor quality service in cable television, the monumental mismanagement and fraud in the savings and loan industry, and the distributional consequences of market-based prices generally—have convinced many that only a return to regulation will restore satisfaction with and confidence in these industries.

Consider also the reaction to presidents' attempts to better manage the regulatory process, particularly rule-making. President Reagan's uses of OMB review of new rules, cost-benefit analysis, the Paperwork Reduction Act, and regulatory planning were attacked by powerful, vocal critics who saw them as thinly veiled efforts to usurp congressional powers, delay essential regulations, and provide a convenient back channel by which special interests could influence the content of regulatory policy. Bitter exchanges between Congress and the White House over continued authorization and funding for some of these OMB functions became a hallmark of the late 1980s and early 1990s. Legislation proposed in the 104th Congress would have shifted responsibility for rulemaking from the regulatory agencies back to the Capitol, a reaction to growing presidential power but a recipe for legislative gridlock, critics contend.

Regulatory negotiation, an innovation in rulemaking, may offer a way to alleviate conflict. But even ideas that have wide appeal may take a long time to put into practice. This idea, developed in the early 1980s, calls for the development of rules through a form of collective bargaining. Regulatory negotiation brings together parties interested in the content of a new rule with the responsible agency in an effort to draft the rule in a collective and consensual process. The advantages to this approach are many. It eliminates the distant and often adversarial relations between the regulators and the regulated that characterize much important rulemaking. Information flows freely, and the resulting rule is based on an informed consensus, which eases the task of implementation, compliance, and enforcement.

Regulatory negotiation is not appropriate for all rules. There are limits on the types of issues and numbers of affected parties that this form of rulemaking can accommodate. Nevertheless, in 1990 Congress enacted legislation that required agencies to consider this method of rulemaking for new regulations. Several agencies, including the EPA, OSHA, and the FAA, have used the device. The OSHA Compliance Act of 1998, signed by President Clinton that summer, directed OSHA by statute to establish and fund consultation programs that allow employers to identify violations and correct them without penalty. But this innovation has not caught on in the regulatory agencies to the extent justified by its many apparent advantages.

Although the regulatory negotiations attempted to date have not been uniformly successful, at the worst they should be characterized as encouraging. Why, then, with the thousands of regulations written and planned since the concept first emerged have only a few dozen such negotiations taken place? There is no definitive answer, but in all likelihood a complex mix of economic, political, and bureaucratic factors have retarded its growth. Up-front costs of participating in regulatory negotiation for an interest group may be higher than those of participating in conventional rulemaking. For groups working with limited budgets and concerned with a large number of issues, cost may be an obstacle. Moreover, some groups may prefer the distance and tension of conventional rulemaking to the collaboration and tacit acceptance of regulation that involvement in negotiation implies. Corporate attorneys fear that a regulatory compliance plan negotiated with an agency may not protect their clients from third-party lawsuits. If the EPA allows a company to operate outside its rigid regulatory framework to reduce emissions, who is to say an environmental group will not file suit to force the firm back into that framework? Clinton administration officials found just such wariness.

Agencies may resist change because of bureaucratic inertia or because regulatory negotiation involves the sacrifice of the obscurity and relative autonomy of normal rulemaking. Analysts working on Vice President Al Gore's NPR team in the 1990s conceded they had been asking regulatory agencies to change an entrenched, confrontational culture, a process that has been far slower than they had anticipated. Whatever the reasons, the acceptance of regulatory negotiation is widespread in theory but so far limited in practice.

While eschewing the harsh rhetoric of Reagan and George H. W. Bush and seemingly dedicated to a better, more open process, Clinton set in motion a number of initiatives that created great stress in the regulatory process. Compounded by congressional attacks, his proposals in the NPR to cut 252,000 federal jobs, reduce the number of existing regulations by 50 percent, and eliminate the deficit meant leaner, more difficult times for regulators. Agencies complained that the ongoing reviews of existing rules took huge amounts of their time, leaving precious little for traditional enforcement or nontraditional negotiations. Because rule-writers tend to be the more powerful, senior members of staff, budget cuts may be taking a disproportionate toll on enforcement staff.

Clinton's success in implementing his ambitious agenda was also spotty. On the NPR's fifth anniversary in April 1998, Vice President Gore appeared to have plenty to boast about: the elimination of more than 200 federal programs; the cutting of more than 16,000 pages of regulations; and the saving, by Gore's estimate, of more than $137 billion. The surge in new regulations during the administration's final days, however, showed the limits of Clinton's efforts.

As it turns out, many of these last-minute regulations were overturned by the incoming administration of George W. Bush. New workplace ergonomic standards and 175 new environmental regulations were nullified. Bush justified the action by arguing that he should not be bound by decisions made by his predecessor at the last minute.

The process of rolling back previous regulations gathered steam in the Bush administration. The OIRA reviewed 267 rules in 2002 and 189 in 2004. The numbers greatly exceeded the 71 regulations chosen in 2001 for its first referendum on regulations to review. Most of the regulations nominated for review came from just a few agencies: the Departments of Health and Human Services, Labor, and Transportation as well as EPA and the FCC.

In other areas, regulatory activity has increased dramatically, largely as a result of the 2001 terrorist attacks, and mostly from agencies now under the Homeland Security Department's umbrella. Indeed, new rules have touched all areas of domestic security. For instance, the new TSA promulgated a large number of new regulations—from tougher baggage screening requirements to the rules on the storage of guns in airliner cockpits—all aimed at improving air travel security.

A host of other new regulatory schemes have arisen since the enactment of the 2001 Patriot Act. The Customs Service, for example, implemented new safety guidelines for freight shippers and movers in an effort to improve security without slowing down the speed of shipping. The INS also promulgated new regulations requiring men visiting the United States, from twenty-five mostly Muslim countries, to register with the agency. The men also are fingerprinted and questioned by INS agents. The Department of Homeland Security took this a step further when it began in 2004 to fingerprint and photograph all foreign visitors arriving with visas in the United States. The department hoped this would allow it to screen for possible terrorists and to keep track of visitors during their U.S. stays.

Even in realms other than domestic security, the administration moved the regulatory ball forward. The EPA, for instance, added tough new standards to reduce pollution from diesel fuel as well as regulations requiring higher fuel efficiency for light trucks. Meanwhile the FDA announced that it would regulate ephedra, a popular diet drug that was deemed harmful by some. Under the 1994 Dietary Supplement and Health Education Act, the agency must prove a health supplement, such as a diet aid or vitamin pill, is harmful before taking it off the market. The reverse is true with prescription drugs; pharmaceutical companies must prove their safety before winning FDA approval to market it to the public.

Indeed, one of the biggest outcomes of the terrorist attacks and subsequent war on terrorism, many analysts said, was a change in the administration's philosophy that was previously focused on limiting the role of government in people's lives. Still, the impetus to rein in regulation did not disappear after September 2001. In addition to the work of OIRA, many agencies have sought alternatives to regulation on their own. For instance, when the Department of Homeland Security announced that it was going to create a huge database to catalog and track all of the nation's vital infrastructure in sectors such as transportation and energy, it indicated it wanted to avoid drafting new regulations to do so. Deputy Secretary Gordon England told business leaders at a U.S. Chamber of Commerce meeting that the department would instead create incentives for businesses to cooperate. Clinton-era officials would have been more likely to set down disclosure and reporting requirements for businesses.

The coming years will likely see new challenges for the regulatory community. Recently enacted laws include the Telecommunications Act, the pesticide and safe drinking water amendments, the Patriot Act, and the Consumer Product Safety Improvement Act, the Affordable Care Act, and the Wall Street Reform and Consumer Protection Act. Some of these laws, such as the safe drinking water amendments, call for increased flexibility, more cost-benefit analysis, and the novel "right to know" concept. Others, such as the Affordable Care Act, are more rigid, imposing sweeping mandates on many individuals and businesses. Indeed, the ACA's requirements that uninsured individuals purchase health insurance or pay a fine and that employers with 50 or more employees do the same have been seen by some as an innovation that will lead to better health outcomes and greater cost-savings and by others as a one-size fits all "solution" that will not make health care delivery better or cheaper. But regardless of who is right, these major ACA initiatives may in the coming years succeed or fail on the backs of regulatory agencies, such as the IRS and the Department of Health and Human Services, which have been tasked with adding the regulatory muscle needed to put the new law into motion.

The coming years may also see a host of completely new regulatory challenges. If President Obama succeeds in enacting his second term legislative agenda—which, in part, calls for overhauls of the immigration, environment, and trade sectors—many agencies will have new regulatory and oversight duties. Immigration reform alone could involve tremendous new regulatory activity on the part of agencies such as the Department of Homeland Security, which is charged with policing the border and enforcing immigration laws, and the IRS, which would be tasked with collecting taxes from the undocumented immigrants who would be legalized under the proposed law. Even if some of the president's legislative agenda is not enacted, the volume of regulation is likely to increase.

Regardless of which party or president is in power, regulation will remain a primary vehicle for domestic public policy in America. The varied processes of rulemaking will continue to attract the interest and efforts of powerful political forces. Americans will rely on it to formulate and implement solutions to some of the most serious, intractable, and contentious problems that face society. Regulation will command ever-increasing shares of the attention and resources of public and private institutions. The results it achieves will have a profound effect on the quality of American life.

Major Regulatory Agencies

Consumer Product Safety Commission

4330 East-West Hwy., Bethesda, MD 20814
Internet: www.cpsc.gov

▨ INTRODUCTION

The Consumer Product Safety Commission (CPSC) is an independent regulatory agency that was established by the 1972 Consumer Product Safety Act and began operations on May 14, 1973. It was created to be composed of five commissioners, appointed to seven-year terms by the president and confirmed by the Senate. In 1986 Congress restricted funds for two commissioners and their staffs, effectively reducing the CPSC to a three-member commission. In 2009, with additional funding, the CPSC returned to being a five-member commission, not more than three of whom may be members of the same political party. The president designates one of the commissioners to serve as chair.

Responsibilities

The commission's statutory purposes are to (1) protect the public against unreasonable risks of injury associated with consumer products; (2) assist consumers in evaluating the comparative safety of consumer products; (3) develop uniform safety standards for consumer products and minimize conflicting state and local regulations; and (4) promote research and investigation into the causes and prevention of product-related deaths, illnesses, and injuries.

The CPSC

- Works with industry to develop voluntary product standards.
- Establishes mandatory safety standards governing the performance and labeling of more than 15,000 consumer products when voluntary efforts prove inadequate.
- Develops rules and regulations to enforce standards.
- Bans the sale of products that present unreasonable risk of injury.
- Researches and develops test methods for consumer product standards.
- Establishes flammability standards for fabrics.
- Develops broad consumer and industry education programs.
- Requires manufacturers, distributors, and retailers to notify consumers and/or recall, repair, or replace consumer products that present a substantial hazard.
- Prohibits introduction into interstate commerce of misbranded or banned substances and products.
- Establishes packaging requirements for poisonous substances.
- Enforces standards through litigation and administrative actions.
- Collects data on hazardous consumer products and accidents involving consumer products through the National Injury Information Clearinghouse.
- Requires manufacturers of products subject to consumer product safety standards to certify that the products conform to all applicable safety standards.
- Works with U.S. Customs and Border Protection to identify and prevent the entry of hazardous consumer products into the United States.

Powers and Authority

In addition to the authority assigned to the commission when it was created by the Consumer Product Safety Act, major consumer programs were transferred to the new agency from the Food and Drug Administration; the Health, Education, and Welfare Department; and the Commerce Department. Included were the Federal Hazardous Substances Act of 1960, as amended by the Toy Safety Acts of 1969 and 1984 and the Child Protection Amendments of 1966, the Poison Prevention Packaging Act of 1970, the Flammable Fabrics Act of 1953, and the Refrigerator Safety Act of 1956.

The 1984 Toy Safety amendments to the Federal Hazardous Substances Act give the CPSC authority to recall dangerous toys from the market immediately when warranted. When the CPSC was created, it was given authority under the Consumer Product Safety Act to order a recall when a substantial hazard is discovered. But the recall of toys was left under different procedures in the Federal Hazardous Substances Act.

The CPSC's power to regulate products containing substances such as asbestos and formaldehyde, which present risks of cancer, birth defects, or gene mutations, is tempered by a requirement that the agency form a chronic hazard advisory panel (CHAP) to review the available scientific data. The commission must consider the CHAP report before issuing an advance notice of proposed rulemaking involving the substance.

In 1988 the Labeling of Hazardous Art Materials Act was passed giving the CPSC power to regulate art products that pose a chronic health hazard. In 1992 the agency issued guidelines for evaluating these products.

Certain consumer products, including foods, drugs, and automobiles, continue to be regulated by other agencies and do not fall under the commission's broad domain. However, responsibility for administration of several existing consumer programs was transferred from other agencies when the CPSC was created.

Any differing state or local law cannot preempt standards set by the CPSC. However, states and localities may obtain permission to set different product safety standards if the resulting standard produces a greater degree of protection than that offered by the CPSC and if there would be no undue burden on interstate commerce. The Consumer Product Safety Act also gives the commission flexibility in choosing which of the five laws it administers to use in regulating a particular product. It can choose the Consumer Product Safety Act over the others if it publishes a formal explanation of the decision in the *Federal Register*. The CPSC may not regulate firearms, tobacco products, aviation and boating equipment, motor vehicles, food and drugs, cosmetics, insecticides, fungicides, and rodenticides.

SECTION 15

The heart of the Consumer Product Safety Act is the requirement under Section 15(b) that any importer, distributor, or manufacturer who knows of a product defect that poses a substantial product hazard must report that product to the CPSC in a timely manner or face severe civil penalties. The Office of Compliance and Field Operations *(see p. 61)* is responsible for identifying product defects that present substantial product hazards but are not subject to safety standards or banning regulations. The office also identifies products that violate existing standards and guidelines. In addition, it is responsible for developing and enforcing adequate corrective action plans designed to remove such products from the marketplace. A substantial product hazard is defined in the act as a product defect that because of the pattern of defect, the number of products distributed in commerce, or the severity of the risk, creates a substantial risk of injury to the public. In most cases companies work cooperatively with the CPSC to develop and implement voluntary corrective action plans to recall or otherwise correct products that may present possible substantial hazards.

The Consumer Product Safety Improvement Act, signed by President George H. W. Bush in 1990, gave a major boost to the commission's power. This legislation increased industry's obligation to report substantial product hazards to the CPSC. The act made reporting requirements tougher by requiring companies to report not only products that create "an unreasonable risk of serious injury or death" but also products that fail to comply with applicable voluntary standards upon which the commission has relied under Section 9 of the Consumer Product Safety Act.

The Improvement Act also created a new Section 37, an automatic lawsuit-reporting requirement. Under this provision, manufacturers and importers must report to the CPSC if a "particular model" of a product is the subject of three or more civil actions—alleging death or grievous bodily injury and resulting in a final settlement or in a judgment in favor of the plaintiff—filed in federal or state courts in a prescribed two-year period.

This latest fine-tuning of the Section 15 reporting requirements followed a 1984 policy statement clarifying industry's obligation and the 1989 *Recall Handbook,* which spelled out in detail the substantial hazard reporting requirements. The handbook listed the various types of product hazards the commission considered serious enough to report. Since publication of the handbook and the issuance of stricter reporting requirements, the number of Section 15 reports and product recalls has steadily increased.

STANDARDS DEVELOPMENT

Since its establishment, the CPSC has assisted industry in developing hundreds of voluntary standards. Voluntary standards often are arrived at by revising existing industry standards, by repealing existing mandatory standards, or after notifying an industry of an emerging hazard.

Since 1973 the CPSC opted for voluntary negotiated guidelines over mandatory standards and bans. When industry has adopted a voluntary rule dealing with a risk of injury, the commission must find that compliance with the voluntary standard is not likely to result in adequate reduction of the risk or that it is unlikely that there will be substantial compliance before it can issue mandatory safety rules. The benefits of such a mandatory rule also must bear a reasonable relationship to the costs of compliance and impose the least burdensome requirement in preventing or adequately reducing the risk of injury.

The commission also is responsible for monitoring enforcement of existing mandatory standards, bans, or labeling requirements (among them toys and children's articles), restrictions on the sale of clothing treated with the chemical Tris (a flame retardant identified as a carcinogen), and compliance with provisions of the Poison Prevention Packaging Act that require child-resistant tops on oral prescription drugs. The Consumer Product Safety Act also allows the commission to issue a rule that prohibits manufacturers from stockpiling products that may be banned or that will fail to comply with a standard that has been issued but has not yet gone into effect.

Information from surveillance activities that uncovers violations of standards or regulations under the Consumer Product Safety Act, the Federal Hazardous Substances Act, and the Poison Prevention Packaging Act is transmitted to commission headquarters where, if voluntary action is not forthcoming, federal court action may result. Violations of standards issued under the Flammable Fabrics Act may be turned over to an administrative law judge who will preside over an administrative hearing and make an initial decision on the case. A judge's decision may be appealed to the full commission.

The CPSC also has the authority to impose civil fines for violations of its standards and for failure to observe cease-and-desist orders. In some cases the commission negotiates consent agreements whereby a company agrees to stop engaging in activities that violate commission rules but does not admit any wrongdoing.

Background

The CPSC was created early in the consumer movement. In 1968 President Lyndon B. Johnson, heeding the demand for safer products, established the National Commission on Product Safety. In June 1970 this fact-finding commission recommended establishment of a permanent agency. Just two years later, Congress created the CPSC, the first independent agency since the New Deal.

The national commission based its recommendation on the finding that an estimated 20 million Americans were injured annually by consumer products. Of those injured, the commission stated, approximately 110,000 were permanently disabled and 30,000 killed. The commission's chair, Arnold Elkind, told Congress that an effective agency could prevent as many as 4 million injuries and 6,000 deaths each year.

President Richard Nixon, who took office while Congress was debating the need for a product safety agency, supported the establishment of such a function in the executive branch but opposed establishment of an independent commission. Nevertheless, Congress passed the Consumer Product Safety Act, which granted the new agency unusual independence from the executive branch. Its chair was to serve a fixed term. (This practice was changed in 1976.) Other innovative provisions required the agency to open its proceedings to the public and to ensure public participation.

These provisions, some of which inhibited the commission's progress, were intended to answer the often-heard criticism of regulatory agencies—that they become captives of the industries they regulate. The congressional intent was to keep business and industry at arm's length and to substitute consumers as the primary participants in the agency's decision-making processes.

In another attempt to give the CPSC independence, the legislation required the agency to deliver its budget requests to Congress at the same time they were forwarded to the Office of Management and Budget (OMB). Nixon had created OMB just two years earlier to screen agency requests for funds or changes in the law before they were sent to Congress.

The law establishing the CPSC incorporated elaborate mechanisms for ensuring maximum public participation in agency proceedings. Money was authorized to underwrite some of the costs of public participation. Through a procedure called the "offeror" process, any interested and competent outside group was invited to offer, or propose, mandatory consumer product safety standards for eventual adoption by the agency. Until 1978 the CPSC was permitted to develop its mandatory safety standards only when no acceptable outside group had offered to do so.

The innovative procedures prescribed by Congress absorbed a good deal of the commission's attention during its formative years. Some procedures, such as the offeror process, were repealed; but the agency's original rules regarding open proceedings stand, having been amended just once to open the originally closed commission meetings.

Another forerunner of change in all regulatory agencies was the requirement that CPSC regulations take economic considerations into account. The requirement to perform cost-benefit analysis eventually became part of most substantive federal regulatory activities.

The greatest change in the agency during its first decade was in its relationship to the industries it regulates. Amendments to the law gradually shifted the commission's functions from handing down mandatory design standards and bans to promoting and nurturing the voluntary industry standard-setting process. Fostered by the shift from mandated consumer protection to deregulation and helped by a consumer activist constituency that has, in some part, developed its ability to work with business and industry, successive commissions have abandoned their hostility toward manufacturers of consumer products.

EARLY HISTORY

Lacking the wholehearted support of Nixon (who delayed appointing a commission for five months after Congress authorized its creation), the CPSC's first chair, Richard Simpson, spent much of his three-year term asserting the independence of the agency. The White House and OMB followed traditional patterns, recommending party-loyal candidates for top staff positions and expecting to agree informally on a budget without congressional advice. Simpson found neither procedure consistent with the CPSC's congressional mandate.

Congress supported Simpson, passing an amendment exempting agency employees from political clearance at the White House. Simpson was not reappointed to the commission when his term expired.

President Gerald R. Ford chose S. John Byington to succeed Simpson in 1976. Byington was a known opponent of consumer legislation pending before Congress. In addition to the enmity of consumerists—both those in Congress and those who sought to influence the developing CPSC—Byington soon faced a barrage of critical government evaluations of the agency, including studies by the General Accounting Office, the Civil Service Commission, and the House Commerce Oversight and Investigations Subcommittee.

Matters came to a head in early 1978 when a Civil Service Commission report alleged thirty cases of CPSC abuse of government personnel rules. The violations occurred, the report stated, "against a backdrop of management unconcern for and, in some instances, outright contempt for principles of merit." Amid calls for a change at the agency, Byington resigned to "depoliticize" congressional hearings on extending the agency's authorization.

REAUTHORIZATION AND REFORM

By 1978 President Jimmy Carter had appointed a number of consumer advocates to top administration positions. Congress, while it was beginning to talk about deregulation, was still giving regulatory agencies substantial funds and support. Susan King, Carter's appointee to head the CPSC, was the first commission chair to enjoy good relations simultaneously with the White House, Congress, and consumer activists.

Midway through Carter's term, some of the president's advisers recommended that the agency be abolished and that its functions be transferred to other agencies to streamline federal health and safety regulatory activities. However, after vigorous lobbying by the commissioners and consumer advocates, the president announced in April 1978 that he would support a three-year reauthorization. Congress reauthorized the agency through 1981, but it also agreed to the following changes requested by Carter:

- Authorized the commission to participate directly in the development of mandatory safety standards in certain circumstances.
- Authorized the commission to make existing voluntary standards mandatory and to delay imposition of a mandatory standard to permit an industry to develop a voluntary standard.
- Required manufacturers to notify the commission if they planned to export products that the commission had banned or that were not in conformity with applicable mandatory standards. The commission, in turn, would notify the government of the country that would be receiving the goods.
- Required that the commission make a study of its goals, accomplishments, effectiveness, and impact of its regulatory activities on industry and the economy. As a result, the agency initiated a program to review existing standards to determine if any of them were conflicting, overlapping, obsolete, or ineffective. Regulations were reviewed for clarity and the burden they imposed on industry. The commission's

approach to its regulatory mission was to target the most significant product hazards in a manner that least impinged on product utility, consumer demand, manufacturers' costs, and marketplace competition.

CPSC IN THE 1980s

After the 1980 election of Ronald Reagan, the fortunes of the CPSC took a decidedly downward turn. In 1981 OMB director David Stockman announced that the Reagan administration wanted to dismantle the CPSC because it had "adventured too far in some areas of regulation." Others in the administration wanted to reorganize it into an executive branch agency or put it into the Commerce Department where it would be accountable to the president.

Consumer groups won the battle to keep the CPSC independent, but the Product Safety Amendments of 1981 cut the agency's budget authorization and circumscribed its powers in several respects, most notably by directing the commission not to set a mandatory safety standard without exhausting every possible means of arriving at a voluntary one.

These amendments reinforced the commission's duty to make economic analyses before regulatory decisions. They abolished the process through which outside organizations drafted standards for the commission to approve; they restricted the release of information business considered confidential; and they allowed one chamber of Congress to veto CPSC regulations if the other chamber did not object. This type of congressional veto provision, however, was found unconstitutional in 1983 by the Supreme Court in *Immigration and Naturalization Service v. Chadha.*

It fell to Nancy Harvey Steorts, Reagan's first appointment to the CPSC chair, to change direction under the 1981 amendments and accompanying budget slashing. The amendments also

- Eliminated CPSC authority to issue safety standards containing product design requirements and required the agency to express standards in terms of performance requirements, warnings, and instructions.
- Directed the CPSC to amend its controversial mandatory safety standard for lawn mowers, which required mowers to stop when the user was not touching the handle and to restart automatically. The commission was required to provide an alternative that would allow the engine to be started manually.
- Abolished three of the four statutory advisory committees: the Product Safety Advisory Council, the National Advisory Committee for the Flammable Fabrics Act, and the Technical Advisory Committee on Poison Prevention Packaging. The Toxicological Advisory Board continued in existence.

Steorts is credited with creating an atmosphere of cooperation with industry. She began by reevaluating mandatory standards established by earlier commissions. Among these was the unvented gas heater standard, which was revoked in favor of a voluntary industry standard. This regulatory philosophy also was applied to enforcement, substituting voluntary corrective action plans, whenever possible, for outright bans of products found defective by the agency. Still, Steorts was not reappointed to a second term—perhaps because she never completely embraced the Reagan deregulatory philosophy, and she appealed to OMB to restore agency funds that had been cut.

The reductions in the CPSC's 1982 budget were dramatic. In fiscal 1980 the CPSC had a budget of $41 million and 871 full-time positions. In fiscal 1982 Congress agreed to Reagan's request of $32 million and a ceiling of 631 full-time employees—30 percent lower than Carter's budget recommendation for fiscal 1982, and a 27 percent cut in its staff.

In an attempt to set priorities and to increase efficiency, the commission established in 1981 a priority list of twelve hazard projects. Criteria for selecting priorities focused on the severity of the risk involved, size and characteristics of the population exposed, and the circumstances of the exposure. A number of the agency's former critics applauded this more focused approach. They noted that in the early years of the CPSC the agency had listed more than 180 priorities.

By fiscal 1986 the list of priorities was down to five: electrocution hazards, fire toxicity, gas heating systems, portable electric heaters, and riding mowers. In its request for funds for fiscal 1986, the CPSC explained that by selecting priority projects the commission was able "to focus its very limited resources" on the most serious consumer safety problems. In practice, however, priority projects sometimes were postponed, having been superseded by a more immediate serious hazard.

Terrence Scanlon, appointed to a four-year term as chair in 1984, favored increasing cooperation with state and local government through contracts under which local inspectors would spend a portion of their time working for the CPSC. In fiscal 1986 nearly one-fourth of the agency's budget was allocated to field activity with the continuing aim of reducing the ratio of administrators to investigators.

Scanlon also attempted to foster the development of voluntary standards. By 1990 the commission staff had participated in the development of nearly 300 voluntary standards. Some notable accomplishments included revision of the National Electrical Code to require ground fault circuit interrupters in household wiring to help prevent electrocutions; modification of swimming pool standards to help prevent child drownings; changes in the kerosene heater voluntary standard to require nitrogen dioxide sensors; changes in the voluntary standard for hair dryers to include protection from water immersion electrocution; and limiting the amount of methylene chloride in consumer products such as paint strippers, paint thinners, spray paints, and adhesive removers.

CPSC IN TROUBLE

For the last half of the 1980s the CPSC faced three major problems—dwindling resources, a bitter internal power struggle among the commissioners, and a protracted battle with the all-terrain vehicle (ATV) industry. From 1985 to 1990 the CPSC's budget was between $33 million and $36 million. Each year the commission's operating plan was trimmed to accommodate the figures set by OMB and Congress, and contract money for major research projects was eliminated. Priority setting became narrower and more focused.

By 1990 the CPSC had resources sufficient to select only two priority projects for fiscal year 1992—smoke detectors and carbon monoxide/fuel gas detection. Although some observers and agency officials said that budget and staff reductions had resulted in increased efficiency, streamlined procedures, and improved management techniques, critics argued that the cuts were designed more to hamper the CPSC's ability to function than to effect real savings.

The internal power struggle began in 1986 with the resignation of two commissioners—leaving the agency with only three sitting commissioners. The House and Senate Appropriations committees restricted funds for the salaries for the two vacancies. In effect the CPSC had, by the funding cuts, been changed from a five-member to a three-member commission. When Scanlon attempted a staff reorganization without consulting the other two commissioners, months of public squabbling resulted. The ill will remained until Scanlon resigned in January 1989.

The commission's involvement with ATVs began in 1985 with the publication of an *Advance Notice of Proposed Rulemaking*, which was based on reports of 161 deaths and 89,000 injuries, primarily to young children. Public hearings were held around the nation, and by October 1986 the CPSC recommended a ban of ATVs for children under twelve and an extensive consumer notification program. In December the CPSC asked the Justice Department to represent it in a lawsuit against the ATV manufacturers; the suit sought a refund program for all three-wheel ATVs, development of a voluntary standard, consumer notification, and driver training for new purchasers. After a year of negotiations, the commission entered into a consent agreement with the industry that included everything except the refund program for current owners of ATVs.

Critics called the agreement a sellout and a victory for the industry. By June 1990 the industry stopped work on developing a voluntary standard, saying it could not produce one that would be satisfactory to the commission. In 1992 the CPSC officially terminated rulemaking proceedings for ATVs. A coalition of consumer groups brought a suit against the commission saying that its decision was "arbitrary and capricious." The U.S. District Court for the District of Columbia upheld the commission's decision, however.

CPSC IN THE 1990s

The commission was without its third member—and thus without a quorum—for ten months until President George H. W. Bush appointed Jacqueline Jones-Smith as the new chair in November 1989. One of the major accomplishments of Jones-Smith was the relocation of the CPSC headquarters staff from several Washington, DC, offices to one building in Bethesda, MD. The major regulatory achievement of her four years as chair proved to be the development of a mandatory standard for child-resistant cigarette lighters. The standard was the result of a cooperative effort between the commission and lighter manufacturers, who favored the idea of a safety standard as a defense against product liability lawsuits. The standard was built on research started in 1988 and was issued in 1992.

Two significant developments that occurred during Jones-Smith's term came about not through commission initiative, but rather because of the intervention of Congress. First was the passage of the Consumer Product Safety Improvement Act, which created tighter reporting requirements under Section 15. Second was the passage of the Child Safety Protection Act, which mandated placing labels that warned of choking hazards on certain toys and the reporting of choking incidents to the commission.

In March 1994 President Bill Clinton replaced Jones-Smith as chair with consumer advocate Ann Brown. Brown came to the commission with a reputation as an activist with a flair for gaining media attention. She was widely known for her annual Christmas toy hazard list, which she announced at a preholiday press conference highlighted by dangerous toys being dumped into a trash can. During the first four months of her term more rule-making proceedings were initiated by the commission than in the entire four years of the previous term. Proposed rules were published to address such hazards as fireworks that could kill and strings on children's garments that could strangle.

During her first year Brown held news conferences that received nationwide news coverage. A news conference announcing the recall of crayons that contained lead garnered one of the largest consumer responses in the commission's history in terms of calls to the agency's hotline. Lead, if ingested, can stunt a child's brain development and, in rare cases, can lead to death.

Brown also made frequent radio and television appearances promoting CPSC activities, and she often called in industry and consumer representatives to discuss safety problems and regulatory approaches. For example in 1995 the CPSC launched an educational program called "baby safety showers," aimed at informing new parents of infants of safe products and potential hazards. Brown also instituted an annual public relations push to review the previous year's recalls and actions.

Confronting the budget-cutting proposals of the Republican Congress in 1995, Brown declared that "regulation is a last resort" and offered the CPSC, with its perennially small appropriations and staff, as a model for government regulatory agencies in the new era of federal downsizing. Brown's proactive stance helped the CPSC survive essentially intact against a hostile Congress from 1995 through 2000. Budget requests at the agency reflected the need to keep up with inflation but not the addition of new programs.

Under Brown, voluntary recalls that gained attention included those for plastic lawn chairs that were prone to collapse, net minihammocks without spreader bars, and tubular metal bunk beds. In the area of indoor air pollution, CPSC laboratory tests confirmed in 1996 that some imported vinyl miniblinds contained lead. Manufacturers of the blinds agreed to change the formula for the plastic in the blinds, and some retailers voluntarily pulled the products from their shelves. Later, the agency worked with industry to prevent the accidental strangulation deaths of children caught in window blind and drapery pull cords.

In another area of child safety, the CPSC in June 1996 issued recommendations on safer new protective equipment for children's baseball, citing the statistic that the sport caused 162,000 injuries to children in 1995. In the highly controversial report, the commission urged baseball leagues to use softer baseballs. The CPSC study found eighty-eight deaths between 1973 and 1995—sixty-eight of them caused by balls hitting children in the head or chest and thirteen caused by bat impact. A few leagues adopted the recommendations while most clung to the traditional ball.

Another study released by the CPSC in June 1996 found that child-resistant packaging has reduced the death rate for children who accidentally swallow medicine by 45 percent since 1974. The commission in 1995 had ordered a further redesign of child-resistant packaging of medicine, to take effect by January 1998; the new design was tested both by children and by adults aged fifty to seventy and received strong industry support.

In 1997 the commission targeted for voluntary recall the popular halogen torchiere lamps that had been linked to 100 fires and ten deaths since 1992. After negotiations, Underwriters Laboratories (UL), the nation's leading independent product testing service, agreed to distribute for free in-home repair kits for the 40 million lamps sold as well as update the store packages with wire guards.

In 1998 the commission settled a lawsuit with Central Sprinkler Co. by recalling 8.4 million Omega fire sprinklers. The commission found that the popular fire sprinklers—a dozen of which were installed in the East and West Wings of the White House—contained a basic defect that could cause them to fail during a fire. The incident increased scrutiny of the safety of fire sprinklers and of UL, which had vouched for the sprinkler's efficacy. In June 2000, in part because of the controversy that was generated by concern about the testing performed on the sprinklers, UL announced that it would improve its safety standards and allow more public oversight over the testing process.

In 1998 the CPSC continued its focus on children's products and toys by issuing a voluntary recall of old-style rolling baby walkers and urged parents instead to buy newer, wider walkers that do not fit through doorways and cannot fall down stairs. In conjunction with the National Highway Traffic Safety Administration, the commission also issued a massive recall of 800,000 Evenflo On My Way infant car seat/carriers. The agency said that while the seats/carriers met rigorous crash standards when used inside the car, they caused numerous injuries, including skull fractures, concussions, and bruises, when used as a carrier, due to defective latches on the carrying handle.

In 1999 there were more than 300 federal recalls of faulty products. However, most of these recalls were voluntary rather than mandatory.

CPSC IN THE 2000s

The commission continued to take a particular interest in regulating products for children. In early 2001 voluntary recalls included the removal of about 171,000 baby bungee jumpers that allow babies to bounce while supported by a seat that is suspended from a doorway. Additionally, about 125,000 fleece pants were recalled voluntarily because a cord had a tendency to break off. The commission also blocked Burger King Corp. from giving out 400,000 toys with children's meals and another 234,000 toys from McDonald's Happy Meals program that posed a choking hazard.

By 2000 the commission had finished consolidating its information systems into one comprehensive system to make them more available to business officials and consumers than they had been in past years. The new computer system integrated information received from various sources, including industry, consumer groups, and the National Electronic Injury Surveillance System. In addition to an expanded hotline service, the commission's website was improved so that consumers could get quick information about recalls and safety alerts.

The commission received unwanted attention in 2001 when President George W. Bush's nominee to head the agency, Mary Sheila Gall, was widely rejected on Capitol Hill. Gall, who had been a CPSC commissioner since 1991, had upset consumer groups by voting against recalls and safety standards. Democrats cited her vote in 1994 against beginning a safety review for a type of baby walker. She said the review was unnecessary because the injuries related to that style of walker could have been prevented by better supervision of the child. After the Democratic-led Senate Commerce Committee rejected her nomination in August 2001 on a party-line vote, Gall asked Bush to withdraw her name from consideration.

In July 2002 the Senate confirmed Bush's second nominee, Harold D. Stratton Jr. At his confirmation hearing, Stratton told lawmakers what while he was philosophically opposed to regulation, the government must play a role in consumer safety issues. Noting that he was the father of two young daughters, Stratton said, "We all believe in the safety of our consumer products when it comes to kids." Stratton's tenure, however, was marred by charges from consumer advocates that he was too close to the industries he was supposed to regulate. Stratton drew fire for taking what the *Washington Post* described as "dozens" of industry-funded trips both domestically and abroad while holding few public meetings and issuing even fewer safety rules.

The uproar only grew louder when in February 2005 the CPSC, in revisiting ATV regulation, recommended that the government not ban the sale of new, adult-sized ATVs for use by children under the age of sixteen. The vehicles continued to be linked to hundreds of deaths of adults and children. Agency staff said that a ban would be impractical because it would deal only with sales of new ATVs, which accounted for more than one-third of sales.

Industry representatives and other agency watchers, however, said that Stratton had struck a far more conciliatory note than Brown, his predecessor. "He's gone out there and tried to stress that the agency is not one to be feared but one to work with," said Frederick Locker, general counsel for the Toy Industry Association. The *Washington Post* reported that Stratton blamed the agency's slowness to issue rules on the commission's authorizing law, which forces the CPSC to defer to voluntary industry standards unless those regulations do not eliminate a safety hazard or bring about substantial compliance.

Indeed, under Stratton, many of the agency's initiatives were aimed at voluntary compliance and education rather than enforcement. For instance, during his tenure the CPSC created the Resale Roundup Campaign, which worked in conjunction with consignment and thrift shops to prevent the resale of recalled or banned products. Also the new Neighborhood Safety Network communicated important safety messages to hard-to-reach and non–English-speaking populations.

In addition, the CPSC continued working to encourage manufacturers in all consumer-oriented industries to recall products they know to be defective voluntarily, rather than wait for the agency to force their hand. As a result, the number of products recalled voluntarily increased to 397 by 2005, the highest number in a decade and significantly greater than the annual average of roughly 300 voluntary recalls.

While consumer advocates remained unimpressed with Stratton's leadership, some agency critics were heartened by the arrival in 2005 of Nancy A. Nord as vice chair. Nord, who a year earlier had criticized an administration proposal to open more federal land to off-road vehicles, had held a variety of posts in both the public and private sectors that were focused on consumer products and environmental issues.

Some critics also welcomed evidence of a slight uptick in the commission's enforcement of consumer laws and collection of fines from companies that violate those laws. From late 2004 through April 2005, the CPSC levied a record $8.76 million in penalties against businesses. In March 2005 the agency announced its largest-ever civil penalty against child product manufacturer Graco, which agreed to pay $4 million to settle charges that it belatedly reported problems with child car seats, high chairs, strollers, and other products that resulted in hundreds of injuries and at least six deaths.

During this time the commission also investigated the prevalence of lead in certain kinds of metal jewelry sold to children. Lead in this type of jewelry, which was often small and easy for children to put in their mouths, could be particularly dangerous. From 2004 through 2006, more than 160 million jewelry items were recalled and by the end of 2006 the commission approved a rule that banned all lead from children's jewelry.

In 2006 the commission also approved a new flammability standard for mattresses. The new requirements, which went into effect on July 1, 2007, aimed to make mattresses less likely to ignite from threats such as smoldering cigarettes and slower to burn if a fire did start.

Meanwhile, in July 2006 Stratton announced that he was stepping down as chair. With only two remaining commissioners, the CPSC lacked a quorum. Republican Nord, who became acting chair, and Democrat Thomas

Moore continued to vote on new rules (such as the vote in December 2006 to ban lead in children's jewelry) for six months. After that, no new rules could be approved without a quorum of three.

In August 2006 the CPSC announced the voluntary recall of 4 million lithium ion batteries used in thirty-three different laptop and notebook computers sold between 2004 and 2006. Because lithium ion batteries are able to hold a lot of energy in a small space, they are prone to overheating and can even burst into flames, as was happening with the recalled batteries, all of which were made by Sony. In the months following the initial recall notice, additional Sony batteries were added to the list, bringing the total number recalled to a staggering 9.4 million.

The CPSC began 2007 facing strong criticism from outside and unrest among its employees. To make matters worse, on Jan. 16, 2007, the commission effectively lost its authority. Because the Bush administration had not named a replacement for Stratton, Nord and Moore were left without the power to approve new rules. Consumer advocates, frustrated with the delay in naming a new commissioner, were not satisfied when the administration in March finally tapped Michael Baroody as the new chair. Baroody, who was the executive vice president and top lobbyist for the National Association of Manufacturers, was seen by advocates as an unapologetic booster for big business at the expense of consumer interests. "This really is a slap in the face of consumer protection," said Ed Mierzwinski, consumer program director for U.S. Public Interest Research Group.

The administration and industry supporters countered that Baroody would be able to balance the need to protect consumers without bankrupting companies with needless and inefficient regulations. However, the strong opposition mounted by Democrats, who had taken control of the Senate confirmation process, eventually led Baroody to withdraw from consideration. For the remainder of Bush's second term, the CPSC would have only two commissioners.

The agency was back in the news in summer 2007, when a string of recalls of Chinese-made toys and other products became front-page stories. In early August, Fisher-Price announced that it was recalling almost 1 million toys because they contained excessive amounts of lead. That action led to a flood of additional recalls of Chinese-made goods, including a series of announcements by toymaker Mattel asking consumers to return a total of 21 million toys.

As the number of recalls increased, critics questioned whether the agency had sufficient resources. In mid-September 2007, a government panel appointed by Bush issued a report arguing that the CPSC had not been satisfactorily policing the safety of imported products. Congressional criticisms by Sen. Richard Durbin (D-IL) and others on Capitol Hill ultimately led to the enactment of the Consumer Product Safety Improvement Act (CPSIA), which Bush signed into law on Aug. 14, 2008. With strong bipartisan support, the CPSIA provided the most substantive overhaul of the nation's product safety system since the 1970s. The new law aimed to increase the size and

effectiveness of the CPSC, raising its budget authorization from $80 million in fiscal 2008 to $136 million by fiscal 2014 and restoring the number of commissioners to five.

The statute also contained provisions raising safety standards for specific products, most of which, not surprisingly, were for children. Indeed, beginning Feb. 10, 2009, the law prohibited the sale of children's products of any kind if they contained a total lead content of more than 600 parts per million (ppm). In addition to the lead restrictions, the statute banned the sale of children's products that contained more than 0.1 percent of certain specific phthalates, which are chemicals found in soft plastic products such as teethers and pacifiers. Phthalates can interfere with the endocrine system and may cause reproductive problems.

Backers of the new law claimed that it signified a major change in the government's approach to consumer safety, shifting regulation and enforcement from a reactive stance to a proactive one. The statute gives the CPSC much greater authority to dictate the terms of product recalls, significantly increases its ability to impose civil penalties (up to $15 million), and provides for five-year prison sentences as well as asset forfeiture for those who knowingly violate the statute.

However, the new law also created consternation and confusion among manufacturers and even among consumer advocates. Toymakers and other manufacturers argued, among other things, that the act did not give them sufficient time to meet the new lead and other standards. Their concern was exacerbated by a legal opinion issued soon after the statute's enactment and aimed at clarifying specific provisions of the law—in this case, the lead provisions. The opinion, drafted by the agency's general counsel, Cheryl Falvey, stated that under the new law, any children's product that exceeded the lead limit, regardless of whether it was manufactured before or after the law was enacted, would be in violation of the statute when it took effect on Feb. 10, 2009.

Manufacturers responded to Falvey's ruling by arguing that it put too much pressure on businesses already struggling through the deepening recession in 2008. They urged the CPSC to pass more far-reaching exemptions or loopholes to the lead requirements that could be put in place before the ban on lead in toys took effect. Indeed, some owners of medium and small businesses asserted that they did not have the time—or the money—to comply with the tough new provisions, and a number of international companies, such as German toy manufacturer Selecta, opted to withdraw from the U.S. market due to what they deemed the excessive cost of doing business.

On the other hand, consumer advocates were troubled and disappointed when, around the same time, Falvey issued another opinion, this time stating that the phthalates ban applied only to merchandise manufactured after the law took effect on Feb. 10, 2009. Retailers could continue to sell products containing phthalates even after that date, as long as they were manufactured before the ban took effect. Consumer advocates argued that this decision violated the intent of the law and would cause confusion in the marketplace. Makers of children's products, however, found it a welcome reprieve, as independent testing for phthalates could be quite costly.

Amid this swirl of complaints from both sides, the commission in January 2009 voted to delay enforcement of certain provisions of the law, including postponing by one year a requirement that companies test their children's products to verify that they are in compliance. The agency also backed a proposal to exempt electronic goods and products with lead embedded inside from the new legislation. However, U.S. District Judge Paul Gardephe ruled on Feb. 6, 2009, that the CPSC could not allow toys containing toxic manufacturing chemicals (phthalates) to stay on shelves after the ban took effect, effectively reversing Falvey's opinion.

Meanwhile, in November 2008 the agency was able to report good news when it announced that toy recalls were down 46 percent from the year before. Acting chair Nord attributed the decline in recalls to tougher surveillance methods at the agency and stronger voluntary safety standards imposed by toy manufacturers themselves. In spite of these successes, the CPSC faced new challenges around this time. Most notably, the agency grappled with the issue of unsafe cribs that killed a number of small children for reasons that included detached side rails and falling mattress supports, which in both cases could potentially trap and even suffocate infants. One company in particular, Simplicity, faced repeated recalls, including a September 2007 recall involving one million cribs after two infants died earlier that year.

The problems with Simplicity helped to prompt the CPSC in October 2008 to announce that it would issue new regulations aimed at addressing some of the hardware durability problems that were at the center of crib recalls. Over time, metal and other parts could wear out, and parents might be unaware of the dangers in cribs that were often reused, resold, or passed on to them by someone else. Although certain crib parts, such as mattress supports and side rails, were tested to meet durability standards, no comprehensive standards existed.

In December 2010, more than two years after the agency announced it would issue new crib safety regulations, the new rules were published. Among other things, the regulations strengthened durability standards for mattresses and crib hardware and prohibited the sale of dropside cribs. The new rules took effect in June 2011.

CPSC IN THE 2010s

The CPSIA authorized yearly budget increases for the CPSC, reaching $118 million in fiscal year 2010 and $122 million for fiscal 2011. President Barack Obama addressed another chronic problem at the agency: commission vacancies. In summer 2009 the president announced three nominations to bring the number of commissioners up to five. Obama chose Inez Moore Tenenbaum, a former South Carolina education superintendent, to be CPSC chair. Upon being sworn in to her office, Tenenbaum identified her aims. "First, I want CPSC to be more accessible and transparent to parents and consumers," she said, adding that the cornerstone of this goal was the creation of a user-friendly product database to help consumers stay away from products that might be dangerous. "By creating an electronic database of product incident reports that consumers can search and by collaborating with state and local agencies and consumer groups, we can give the public confidence that CPSC is working openly and in their best interest," she added.

In addition to Tenenbaum, Obama filled the two remaining vacancies on the commission by picking Democrat Robert Adler and Republican Anne Northrup. Adler, a legal scholar and ethicist at University of North Carolina, had previously spent eleven years at the commission as a staff attorney. Northrup, a Kentucky native, served five terms in the House of Representatives, where she gained a reputation as an advocate for education. With Nord and Moore remaining on the commission, the CPSC had five commissioners for the first time since 1986.

On March 11, 2011, the $3 million CPSC database—www.SaferProducts.gov—successfully launched. The searchable database allows consumers to report events of harm, or potential harm, caused by products that range from toys to household cleaners. Although consumer advocates lauded the new database as an "early warning system" for consumers that would revolutionize the way they make buying decisions, others in Congress pointed to the potential abuses of a system that allows virtually anyone to file a complaint. The commission, however, insisted that there were built-in safeguards to prevent abuses and that every posted report was screened to ensure it contained accurate information that pertains to the safety of the product and not its performance.

The agency also continued to deal with a steady stream of allegedly unsafe products, particularly from China. In a preliminary study released in October 2009, federal investigators found that imported Chinese drywall had higher levels of some chemicals than domestic drywall and that these higher chemical levels could cause health and other problems for those living in homes built with the product. Cheaper and more plentiful, Chinese drywall had been used in thousands of homes, primarily in the Gulf Coast region of the South, where home construction increased significantly due to damage suffered as a result of Hurricane Katrina in 2005.

In April 2010 the CPSC recommended that homeowners remove the Chinese drywall and replace the electrical wiring, gas pipes, and sprinkler systems in their homes. Homeowners would have to absorb the cost of replacement and repairs, a process that can amount to as much as $100,000. The commission recommended that the IRS allow drywall-related costs to be deducted from tax returns, but many homeowners have been brought to the brink of bankruptcy by the costly repairs or have been forced to find alternative housing.

Perhaps in recognition of the high costs associated with drywall-related repairs, the commission, in March 2011, revised its drywall remediation guidelines to recommend that some, but not all, electrical wiring and components be removed. This change was based on findings that some components corroded faster than others depending on the amount of usage, how well the components were installed, and other factors. The new guidelines have concerned consumer groups as well as many homeowners affected by contaminated drywall (now numbering more than 10,000), who have expressed concern that not removing all the electrical wiring can cause a fire hazard.

The safety of children's products, from toys to strollers, also continued to take up a significant amount of the agency's time and energy. Two of the agency's primary concerns involved toxicity levels of lead and cadmium in a variety of children's products. In June 2009 toymaker Mattel and its Fisher-Price subsidiary agreed to pay a $2.3 million civil penalty for selling toys with hazardous levels of lead. Fisher-Price came under scrutiny again when, in October 2010, it was forced to recall more than 11 million tricycles, toys, and highchairs over safety concerns. The tricycles, for instance, had a protruding plastic ignition key near the seat that children could sit or fall on, leading to injuries including genital bleeding.

Another child safety concern involved traces of cadmium found in promotional glasses sold to children by McDonald's. Concern about the substance caused the fast food chain to proactively recall 12 million pairs of glasses, potentially costing the company $15 million in refunds. Although the commission said the level of cadmium in the glasses posed a low risk to consumers, the McDonald's recall came on the heels of three recalls earlier in the year related to cadmium levels in children's jewelry.

Cribs and strollers also remained an ongoing concern for the agency. Two companies, Maclaren Strollers and Graco Children's Products, recalled millions of strollers after reports that children were getting their fingertips severed in the strollers' hinge mechanisms. Graco also had to address the growing problem of secondhand stroller purchases, a more prevalent practice now because of the economic recession. Graco urged owners of 2 million older-model strollers to stop using them due to concerns about possible strangulation, when children who crawl through the opening between the seat bottom and stroller tray become trapped.

Another issue the agency has tackled that touches the lives of children involves standards used in the manufacture of football helmets for students. Specifically, the agency took to task the National Operating Committee on Standards for Athletic Equipment (NOCSAE) for refusing to toughen safety standards for football helmets in spite of the growing problem of head injuries, specifically concussions, in student football. According to one study, approximately 500,000 concussions are sustained annually by the 4.4 million students who play organized football. Yet NOCSAE, which is largely financed by the sporting goods industry, has modified the standard for football helmets only once since 1973.

In 2010 CPSC stated that student helmets are held to "below-science" standards and are thus responsible for many injuries. But NOCSAE's executive director, Mike Oliver, disagreed, countering that the science is "all over the place," and that the reasons football concussions occur are too numerous and complex to assume that different helmets might protect against them any better than do those currently in use.

Still, pressure from the CPSC as well as some on Capitol Hill ultimately prompted the industry to act. In March 2011 the National Athletic Equipment Reconditioners Association (NAERA), another industry group, announced that it would no longer recondition and sell helmets more than ten years old. In addition, both NAERA and NOCAE said they would pursue a new test standard for youth and high school helmets that takes into consideration that not all concussions result from a single hard blow but can be caused by several less severe impacts.

Meanwhile, three years after it was enacted in 2008, the Consumer Product Safety Improvement Act (CPSIA) was still causing consternation among small toymakers and others who argued that the provisions of the law on toy safety were threatening their livelihood, due to what they claimed were vague child product definitions and extensive and costly testing requirements. The toymakers also argued that the new regulations unfairly heaped additional costs on small, American-based businesses when most of the toys deemed most problematic had been manufactured in China for large companies. In addition, they said, the new product testing required smaller manufacturers to employ expensive third-party testing services, while larger companies could use their labs to do the work.

The CPSC responded to these concerns by trying to draft regulations that had enough flexibility to address the legitimate concerns of the small toymakers while still upholding the purpose of the law. For example, in 2012, the agency approved new rules requiring testing of toy components rather than the final product. This idea won support from many small toymakers, who were now able to forgo final product testing as long as they made toys with components that had already passed the safety tests.

In June 2011 the CPSC opened a high-profile investigation into a more dramatic danger: a liquid gel fuel for ceramic firepots used to provide light at evening outdoor social events. The manufacturer, Napa Home and Garden, Inc., of Duluth, Georgia, had sold hundreds of thousands of containers of the fuel, a form of ethanol, since December 2009. Sold under the names "FireGel" and "Napafire," and marketed as "the Safe Pourable Gel," the product had since caused dozens of horrific injuries, including two near-fatal ones in the New York City area.

Witnesses and victims likened the fuel gel explosions to a Molotov cocktail or napalm. The flash explosions covered victims in a flaming, jellied fuel that stuck to skin and clothing and would not stop burning even when victims dropped to the ground and rolled over or when bystanders tried to smother the flames with blankets or clothing. Although the fuel gel and firepots carried warnings not to refill the pots if they were still lit or even hot, many victims reported that these warnings were understated and gave no sense of how dangerous the product could be to operate. Also, because the product did not have a wick, it was often difficult to determine that it was lit.

After opening its investigation, the commission issued a public warning to consumers to take precautions when using what it called "illuminating fuels" in firepots and Tiki torches and to only add fuel when the vessel is "cool to the touch." Numerous accidents, including the two in New York, prompted Napa Home & Garden to recall a half-million bottles and to ask Bed Bath & Beyond to stop selling the product. The company would later file for bankruptcy following a flood of civil lawsuits.

By the beginning of 2013, the CPSC indicated that it would continue its technical review of the safety of fire pots and fuel gels with an eye toward possible future rule-making. But consumer advocates and others argued that these products should have never hit the shelves to begin with. Clearly, critics said, they had fallen outside even the most basic safety regulations.

Meanwhile, disagreement over the CPSC consumer safety database continued. In April 2011, Representative Mike Pompeo (R-Kan.), a pro-business conservative, unsuccessfully attempted to insert language cutting all funds for the project into a stopgap spending agreement between the White House and leaders of Congress. While the budget negotiators did not adopt Pompeo's proposal, they did include language directing the General Accountability Office to study the database's effectiveness and report back to Congress.

Six months later, the new database faced its first legal challenge when a company tried to block the CPSC from posting what the firm termed "baseless allegations" against its product, in relation to an incident that allegedly harmed a child. In October 2012, a federal court judge sided with the manufacturer (which was allowed to proceed in the case without revealing its identity), arguing that the complaint made against it was confusing and contradictory and the agency should never have allowed it to be published.

The CPSC "SaferProducts" database continues to be a divisive issue for the commission. Critics, including the commission's two Republican appointees, contend that the site unfairly threatens companies' reputations and that the reporting system is highly prone to inaccuracy. Indeed, as of September 2011, 383 companies had formally complained to the commission about inaccuracies. At the same time, the site was clearly popular with the public. In its first three years in operation, consumers filed more than 11,000 reports of allegedly unsafe products.

The consumer complaints database was just one of a number of issues during this time that helped divide the five-member commission. Some of the blame was because of the Consumer Product Safety Improvement Act, which calls on the board to expand its regulatory role and tasks it with issuing a series of new rules under rigorous deadlines. The law's new mandate meant much more activity and, thus, much more opportunity for disagreement among board members.

The problem became more acute when, in late 2011, Democrat Thomas Moore departed the board after serving 16 years. The agency now found itself evenly divided, with two Democrats and two Republicans. Just days before Moore stepped down, the commission had endured a contentious vote on setting timetables on the testing of children's products. Republicans on the board had slammed the Democratic majority for holding the vote before addressing the cost implications of the timetables, with Republican Nancy Nord accusing Democrats of "regulatory malpractice." Chairwoman Inez Tenenbaum countered by

accusing her Republican colleagues of launching "a coordinated campaign to delay and distort our actions in an attempt to circumvent the will of American families and Congress."

Sensing that the two-two split would lead to a logjam, consumer groups urged President Obama to quickly select someone to fill the board's open seat to avoid perpetual gridlock. In January 2012, the president nominated Marietta S. Robinson (D) to fill Moore's vacated seat. Robinson, a Michigan trial lawyer, specialized in medical malpractice cases and had served eight years as a federally appointed trustee of the Dalkon Shield Trust, which paid out $2.5 billion to women who had used the contraceptive. But by the end of 2012, nearly a year after her nomination, the Senate had still not voted on Robinson. In addition, in October 2012, Republican Anne Northup left the board, creating a second vacancy.

In May 2013, with two seats empty on the board, Obama moved to fill the vacancies by re-nominating Marietta Robinson and nominating Anne Marie Buerkle, a former Republican congresswoman from New York who is also a lawyer and a registered nurse. Senate Republicans, who had vowed not to allow Robinson's nomination to move forward until the president picked a Republican replacement for Northup, now allowed both women to quickly win approval. They were sworn in in June 2013.

The agency also continued its efforts to address the fallout from homebuilders' use of contaminated Chinese drywall. In January 2013 the commission received a new mandate in this area when President Barack Obama signed into law the Drywall Safety Act of 2012. The bipartisan act was an attempt to ensure that homes are never again built with defective drywall, regardless of its origin.

The new law tasked the CPSC to draft regulations for the manufacture and distribution of drywall, aimed at ensuring high quality and safety. It also mandated the creation of a labeling system so any new contaminated drywall can be traced directly to a manufacturer. Finally, the commission was required to establish chemical standards for domestic and imported drywall.

In August 2013 the agency's regulations governing play yards went into effect. Play yards are large portable cribs for infants that can be folded up and put in the car. But play yards also can be very dangerous. According to commission records, between 2007 and 2011, there were more than 2,100 reported incidents involving children and play yards, resulting in 170 serious injuries and 60 fatalities.

The new regulations, which were mandated by the Consumer Product Safety Act of 2008, included requiring newly sold play yards to be more stable to prevent them from tipping over. Better latches and locks were also mandated to prevent the play yard from folding up while in use. Finally, a number of design changes were required to make it less likely that any part or parts of the crib would entrap a child's hand, foot, or head.

In October 2013 Chairwoman Tenenbaum announced that she would leave the agency at the end of November to return to her home state of South Carolina and practice law. Tenenbaum's move was expected, but the White House did not immediately announce a nominee to replace her.

Indeed, the new nominee, Elliot F. Kaye, was not named until March 2014. Prior to his nomination, Kaye served as the commission's executive director and had taken the lead in the agency's high profile efforts to reduce head injuries in youth football. Kaye was confirmed by the Senate and sworn in as chairman in July 2014.

Meanwhile the CPSC continued reviewing and, at times, recalling products deemed unsafe. In December 2013 the commission recalled the recharging cords for some of Hewlett-Packard's popular Chromebook laptops. The recall was initiated after the agency began receiving reports from consumers (one of whom was burned) that the chargers could overheat and even melt. A similar problem prompted the agency to recall the My Sweet Love Baby Doll three months later, in March 2014. The doll has a circuit board in its chest that overheats, causing its surface to heat up and potentially burn children who play with it.

Larger items also posed dangers. In April 2014, for instance, the commission issued a recall of 30,000 golf carts after it became clear that they might have loose steering wheels. The carts are all made by EZ-Go, a division of multinational conglomerate Textron. The investigation into the steering systems was prompted after a golf cart spun out of control and lightly injured the driver.

Four months later, in August, the commission recalled a whopping 2.2 million bean bag chairs after 2 children died choking on the beads used to fill the bag chairs. The agency found that children can easily unzip the bag chairs, climb inside, and access the beads.

In addition to recalling specific products, the commission during this time also continued warnings about broader dangers. For instance, just before the 2014 Fourth of July holiday, it released a report detailing the rising number of fireworks-related injuries from the year before. According to the report, on and around Independence Day 2013 there were 11,400 injuries and 8 deaths as a result of amateurs setting off fireworks, an increase of 31 percent from the year before. Part of the increase can be blamed on recent laws in some states, such as those in Arizona and Michigan, which make it easier for nonprofessionals to buy more sophisticated fireworks.

During this time, the commission also moved to effectively ban the sale of certain types of small magnets used in toys and games. At issue were high-powered magnet sets, basically hundreds of small magnetic balls or pieces that can be put together to create different shapes. If more than one of these small magnets is ingested, they can stick together in the intestines, pinching or cutting off the normal digestive flow. The result can be serious injury or, if left untreated, even death.

Each year, according to the commission, roughly 2,900 children are brought to hospital emergency rooms as the result of ingesting one or more high-powered magnets. Most victims are toddlers, but others include teens who have accidently swallowed the magnets after using them to simulate tongue piercings.

The commission became interested in the dangers posed by magnets as early as 2006. In 2010 it began legal action against Maxfield & Oberton, the maker of "Buckyballs," a set of magnetic spheres that can be stacked into different shapes. By early 2014 Buckyballs had been taken off the market and the sets that were sold had been recalled. Another suit, against magnet set maker Zen Magnets, is ongoing.

In September 2014 the commission announced new rules that required toy magnets to either be large enough so that a child cannot swallow them or magnetically weak enough so that they cannot stick together inside a person's intestines. The rules, which took effect April 1, 2015, were applauded by consumer groups and others.

Just after the New Year, in the middle of one of the snowiest winters in recent memory, the agency made news by releasing data showing that in the last decade, roughly 9,000 Americans had lost one or more fingers to snow blower-related accidents. According to the January 2015 release, the accidents most often occurred when a person reached into his or her snow blower after the snow blower became stuck, and the person was unable to get his or her hand out quickly enough once the blades started moving again.

Current Issues

A little more than a month into 2015, the CPSC issued an important report warning about the hazards to children posed by televisions. The report spoke of the large number of precariously perched televisions (often old and heavy) that fall on and crush children. Also detailed were the hazards posed by the furniture holding the televisions, which could collapse or tip along with televisions.

Dubbed the "tip-over report" by the media, the commission revealed that between 2011 and 2013 a staggering 15,400 children were brought to emergency rooms for injuries caused by falling televisions or televisions and furniture. During this two-year period 279 children had died, the agency said in its report, recommending that televisions either be mounted on walls or placed on low pieces of stable furniture. It also urged parents not to place toys atop TVs so that children would not be enticed to climb up the television set.

After the release of the tip-over report, the commission announced that it would roll out a $400,000 advertising campaign, dubbed "Anchor It," in the spring and summer of 2015. The agency hopes the ads, which will run on television as well as radio and in print, will raise awareness among parents of the dangers to their children of wobbly and badly placed TVs.

In early March 2015 the Senate Committee on Commerce, Science, and Transportation publicly urged the CPSC, as well as the Federal Trade Commission and the Centers for Disease Control, to begin investigating the safety of laminate flooring that has been imported from China and is being sold by the retail chain, Lumber Liquidators. Laminate flooring is popular among homeowners and building contractors because it is easy to install and tends to be inexpensive. But the committee, following media reports, alleged that some Chinese-made flooring contained unacceptably high levels of formaldehyde, which can cause certain kinds of cancer as well as, more commonly, skin, eye, and throat irritations. The accusations echoed similar charges made a number of years before against Chinese-produced drywall, which led Congress to pass the Drywall Safety Act of 2012.

No one was yet ready propose a similar bill governing laminate flooring. Instead, the committee called on the CPSC and the other agencies to thoroughly test the Chinese flooring sold at Lumber Liquidators so that any toxic brands could be taken off the shelves and tainted flooring already installed in homes could be removed. "Because this could affect millions of homeowners, it's imperative we get some answers quickly," said Senator Bill Nelson (D-Fla.), the committee's ranking member. The next day, the commission announced it would begin looking into the charges.

Also in March, Democrats in both houses of Congress introduced legislation that would authorize the commission to set safety standards for liquid detergent pods, the small soap balls that can be dropped in the washing machine in lieu of pouring in liquid or powder. The bills were prompted by research that showed that 700 children were hospitalized each year after ingesting the detergent pods, which are often quite colorful and can look like candy to younger children.

The measure would require the CPSC to set mandatory standards for the sale of detergent pods, including child safe packaging and warning labels. Sponsors of the bills, including Senators Dick Durbin (D-Ill.) and Charles Schumer (D-N.Y.), have promised to withdraw them if the detergent industry agrees to work with the commission to develop adequate voluntary standards to better protect children.

▪ AGENCY ORGANIZATION

Biographies

ELLIOT F. KAYE, CHAIR
Appointment: Nominated by President Barack Obama on March 31, 2014, and confirmed by the U.S. Senate on July 28, 2014; sworn in on July 30, 2014, to a term that expires in October 2020.
Education: Medill School of Journalism at Northwestern University, B.S.J.; New York University School of Law, J.D.
Profession: Lawyer.

Political Affiliation: Democrat.
Previous Career: From 2007 to 2010, Kaye was an attorney at Hogan Lovells. Prior, he was an attorney at cooley godward kronish LLP and a judicial clerk for the honorable Sterling Johnson Jr. of the U.S. district court for the Eastern District of New York. He has served as chief of staff and legislative director for U.S. representative John Tierney as well as chief of staff and communications director for U.S. Representative Pat Danner. At the U.S. Consumer Product Safety Commission (CPSC), he served as the senior counsel to the chairman from 2010 to 2011, and as deputy chief of staff and senior counsel to the chairman from 2012 to 2013. Kaye served as the CPSC's executive director from 2013 until his confirmation as chairman.

ROBERT S. ADLER, COMMISSIONER
Appointment: Nominated by President Barack Obama on May 5, 2009, and confirmed by the U.S. Senate on August 7, 2009, to a term that expired in October 2014. Renominated and confirmed on December 2, 2014, to a term expiring in October 2021.
Education: University of Pennsylvania, B.A., 1966; University of Michigan, J.D., 1969.
Profession: Lawyer, educator.
Political Affiliation: Democrat.
Previous Career: Adler served on the Obama Transition Team and co-authored a report on the CPSC for the Obama administration. He served as a professor of legal studies at the University of North Carolina, as the Luther Hodges Jr. Scholar in Ethics and Law at Chapel Hill's Kenan-Flagler Business School. At the University of North Carolina, he served as the associate dean of the MBA Program and as associate dean for the school's bachelor of science in business administration program. Prior to his service at UNC, he spent nine years as an attorney-adviser to two commissioners at the U.S. Consumer Product Safety Commission. Subsequently, he served as counsel to the Subcommittee on Health and the Environment of the Committee on Energy and Commerce in the U.S. House of Representatives. While on the subcommittee, he worked on legislation relating to product liability, childhood vaccines, the Food and Drug Administration, medical malpractice, and the Consumer Product Safety

Consumer Product Safety Commission

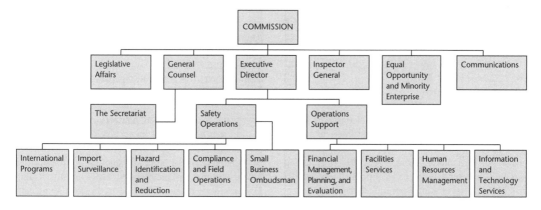

Commission. Adler has been involved in numerous consumer protection and education activities for many years. He was elected six times to the board of directors of Consumers Union, publisher of *Consumer Reports* magazine.

MARIETTA ROBINSON, COMMISSIONER

Appointment: Nominated by President Barack Obama on January 29, 2013, and confirmed by the U.S. Senate on June 27, 2013. She was sworn in on July 2, 2013, to a term expiring October 2017.

Born: Platteville, Wisc.

Education: University of Michigan at Flint, B.A.; UCLA School of Law, J.D.

Profession: Lawyer.

Political Affiliation: Democrat.

Previous Career: With 33 years of experience as a trial lawyer, Robinson serves as a fellow at the International Society of Barristers, an organization she led as president from 2010 to 2011. Her background includes significant experience in medical malpractice; she also served eight years in a federal appointment to the board of the Dalkon Shield Claimants Trust. In 2011, Robinson was the independent legal counsel to the chair of the United Nations Peacebuilding Commission in Liberia.

ANN MARIE BUERKLE, COMMISSIONER

Appointment: Nominated by President Barack Obama on May 24, 2013, and confirmed by the U.S. Senate on June 27, 2013. She was sworn in on July 5, 2013, to a term expiring October 2018.

Born: May 5, 1951; Auburn, N.Y.

Education: St. Joseph's Hospital School of Nursing, R.N., 1972; LeMoyne College, B.S., 1977; Syracuse University School of Law, J.D., 1994.

Profession: Assistant attorney general, elected official.

Political Affiliation: Republican.

Previous Career: From 2011 until her appointment, Buerkle was a member of the U.S. House for New York's 25th congressional district. She began her nursing career at Columbia-Presbyterian Hospital in New York City and at St. Joseph's and served as a substitute school nurse for many years before obtaining her law degree. She was assistant New York State attorney general from 1997 to 2009. She also served one term on the Syracuse, New York Common Council.

JOSEPH MOHOROVIC, COMMISSIONER

Appointment: Nominated by President Barack Obama on October 13, 2013, confirmed by the U.S. Senate on July 28, 2014; term expires in October 2019.

Education: University of Texas at Austin, B.A.; University of New Mexico, M.B.A.

Profession: Executive.

Political Affiliation: Republican.

Previous Career: Mohorovic was previously the senior vice president of intertek. Before joining Intertek, Mohorovic's public service included two terms as state representative for New Mexico's 28th District before resigning elected office to serve in the CPSC administration of former Chairman Hal Stratton from 2002 through 2007.

Headquarters and Divisions

OFFICE OF THE COMMISSIONERS

The chair is the principal executive officer of the commission and has authority over all executive and administrative functions. The commission annually elects a vice chair to act in the absence of the chair. The commissioners have general authority over all functions of the CPSC. These responsibilities are generally delegated to various offices within the CPSC; the commissioners retain the final approval over their recommendations.

The commissioners set the commission's agenda and priorities; vote on staff proposals for new regulations; oversee the staff's work with various voluntary standards organizations (e.g., ANSI and ASTM); approve/disapprove civil penalty recommendations; vote on the commission's budgets and operating plans; approve the strategic plan, which sets out the death/injury reduction goals and strategies of the commission; and are responsible for ensuring that its media tools are used to alert and educate the public.

Chair

Elliot F. Kaye . . . . (301) 504–7881

Commissioners

Robert S. Adler . . . . (301) 504–7731

Marietta Robinson . . . . (301) 504–7253

Ann Marie Buerkle . . . . (301) 504–7978

Joseph Mohorovic . . . . (301) 504–7901

Chief of Staff

Jason Levine . . . . (301) 504–7853

OFFICE OF THE EXECUTIVE DIRECTOR

The executive director acts as the agency's chief operating manager under the broad direction of the chair; assists with development of the agency's budget and operating plan; and, after commission approval, manages execution of those plans. The executive director oversees the offices of Hazard Identification and Reduction; Import Surveillance; Compliance and Field Operations; Education, Global Outreach, and Small Business Ombudsman; Financial Management, Planning, and Evaluation; Facilities Services; Human Resources Management; and Information and Technology Services. The commission's directorates report to the executive director.

Main Office . . . .**(301) 504–7907**

Executive Director

Patricia Adkins . . . . (301) 504–7854

Fax. . . . . (301) 504–0461

Deputy Executive Director, Safety Operations

Jay Howell . . . . (301) 504–7949

Fax. . . . . (301) 504–0407

Deputy Executive Director, Operations Support

DeWane Ray. . . . . (301) 504–7547

OFFICE OF COMMUNICATIONS

Responsible for the development, implementation, and evaluation of a comprehensive national information and public affairs program designed to promote product safety. This includes maintaining relations with consumer organizations; business groups; trade associations; state and local government entities; labor organizations; medical, legal, scientific, and other professional associations; and other federal health, safety, and consumer agencies. Prepares literature for the national print and broadcast media, develops and disseminates news releases, and organizes news conferences.

Director

Scott Wolfson..................... (301) 504–7051

Fax........................... (301) 504–0124

OFFICE OF COMPLIANCE AND FIELD OPERATIONS

Identifies and takes action to have manufacturers correct or recall any defective consumer product already in distribution; establishes industry compliance with existing safety standards through development of surveillance and enforcement programs as well as the conduct of enforcement litigation; and provides case guidance to field offices. Responsible for all commission field operations.

Main Office ....(301) 504–7912

Assistant Executive Director

Jay Howell (acting) .... (301) 504–7700

Fax........................... (301) 504–0008

Deputy Director

Marc J. Schoem .... (301) 504–7520

Director of Field Investigations

Ray Aragon .... (301) 504–7578

Director of Defect Investigations

Scott Simmons.................... (301) 504–7574

Director of Regulatory Enforcement

Mary Toro....................... (301) 504–7586

OFFICE OF EQUAL OPPORTUNITY AND MINORITY ENTERPRISE

Oversees CPSC compliance with laws, regulations, and internal policies relating to equal employment opportunity and ensures compliance with relevant provisions of the Small Business Act.

Director

Kathy Buttrey.................... (301) 504–7904

Fax........................... (301) 504–0107

OFFICE OF FACILITIES SERVICES

Manages the facilities-related services for all CPSC leased space in three locations (headquarters building, laboratory facility, and sample storage facility). Handles preparation, procurement, and distribution of printed and duplicated material originating within the agency. Manages internal print shop and U.S. Government Printing Office printing services. Responsible for management, use, and control of government-owned/leased vehicles and privately-owned vehicles by employees in performing official business, as well as the Transit Subsidy Benefit Program. Handles all safety and employee emergency programs and is responsible for reporting the agency's environmental sustainability to the Executive Office of the President.

Director

Douglas Brown .... (301) 504–7846

OFFICE OF FINANCIAL MANAGEMENT, PLANNING, AND EVALUATION

Responsible for developing the commission's funds control system, long-range strategic plans, annual performance budgets, and operating plans. Analyzes major policy and operational issues, performing evaluations and management studies. Ensures that commission resources are procured and expended according to purchasing regulations. Recommends actions to enhance the effectiveness of commission programs and procurement activities. Serves as the staff support to the commission chief financial officer.

Director

Jay Hoffman .... (301) 504–7207

OFFICE OF THE GENERAL COUNSEL

Prepares the commission's legislative program and reviews legislative proposals originating elsewhere, conducts or supervises the conduct of litigation to which the commission is a party, and reviews and approves the litigation aspects of enforcement matters. Staff also provides final legal review of and makes recommendations to the commission on proposed product safety standards, rules, laws, regulations, petition actions, and substantial consumer hazard actions; provides legal review of certain procurement, personnel, and administrative actions; and drafts documents for publication in the *Federal Register*.

Main Office ....(301) 504–7922

General Counsel

Stephanie Tsacoumis............... (301) 504–7612

Fax........................... (301) 504–0403

Deputy General Counsel

Mary Boyle....................... (301) 504–7859

Assistant General Counsel for Enforcement and Information

Melissa Hampshire .... (301) 504–7631

Assistant General Counsel for General Law

Melissa Buford.................... (301) 504–7636

Assistant General Counsel for Regulatory Affairs

Vacant........................... (301) 504–7922

Office of the Secretary

The major point of contact for consumer information, prepares the agenda; prepares, distributes, and stores official records; and schedules and coordinates commission business at official meetings. Exercises joint responsibility with the Office of the General Counsel for interpretation and implementation of the Privacy Act, the Freedom of Information Act, and the Government in the Sunshine Act. Staff prepares and coordinates reports required by law under these acts, issues *Federal Register* documents, supervises and administers the dockets of adjudicative proceedings before the commissioners, administers the public reading room, maintains a master calendar of commission meetings, publishes the Public Calendar, and operates the National Injury Information Clearinghouse (see Information Sources: Data and Statistics below).

Director

Todd Stevenson................ (301) 504–7923

OFFICE OF HAZARD IDENTIFICATION AND REDUCTION

Manages hazard-related programs delineated in the commission's operating plan or assigned by the executive director; analyzes petitions requesting development of standards submitted to the commission; provides direction and support to all projects including mandatory and voluntary standards and petitions, data collection and analysis, and emerging hazards, especially where responsibility involves more than one directorate. Staff ensures that technical, environmental, economic, and social impacts of projects are coordinated when presented to the commission for decision; exercises program review and is active in setting commission priorities; oversees CPSC involvement with voluntary standard-setting groups.

Main Office ....**(301) 504–7949**
Assistant Executive Director
    George Borlase.................... (301) 504–7547
    Fax........................... (301) 504–0407

Directorate for Economic Analysis

Conducts studies to determine the impact of CPSC regulations on consumers, the economy, industry, and production. Also studies potential environmental effects of commission actions. Most of the directorate's resources are located in the hazard programs, where they provide the economic information necessary to make decisions concerning the best options to reduce unreasonable risks of injury associated with consumer products.

Associate Executive Director
    Gregory Rodgers.................. (301) 504–7705

Directorate for Engineering Sciences

Provides scientific and technical expertise to the commission to support voluntary standards development and agency regulatory activities. Develops and evaluates product performance criteria, design specifications, and quality control standards; conducts engineering tests; evaluates test methods; provides advice on proposed safety standards; performs and monitors research in the engineering sciences.

Associate Executive Director
    Joel Recht ....(301) 987-2036

Directorate for Epidemiology

Collects data on consumer product–related hazards and potential hazards; determines the frequency, severity, and distribution of the various types of injuries and investigates their causes; and assesses the effects of product safety standards and programs on consumer injuries. Staff also conducts epidemiological studies and research in the fields of consumer-related injuries.

Assistant Executive Director
    Kathleen Stralka .... (301) 504–7416

Directorate for Health Sciences

Responsible for reviewing and evaluating the human health effects and hazards related to consumer products and assessing exposure, uptake, and metabolism, including information on population segments at risk. Directorate staff conducts health studies and research in the field of consumer product–related injuries. The directorate performs risk assessments for chemical, physiological, and physical hazards based on methods such as medical injury modeling; and on injury and incident data for mechanical, thermal, chemical, and electrical hazards in consumer products. The directorate is the commission's primary source of expertise for implementation of the Poison Prevention Packaging Act, and the directorate provides technical liaison with the National Toxicological Program, the National Cancer Institute, the Environmental Protection Agency, and other federal programs related to chemical hazards. It also manages activities of the chronic hazard advisory panels.

Associate Executive Director
    Alice Thaler .... (301) 987–2240

Directorate for Laboratory Sciences

Conducts engineering analyses and testing of consumer products, supports the development of voluntary and mandatory standards, and supports the agency's compliance activities through product safety assessments.

Associate Executive Director
    Andrew Stadnik................... (301) 504–7705

OFFICE OF HUMAN RESOURCES MANAGEMENT

Provides management support to the commission in the areas of recruitment and placement, training and executive development, employee and labor relations, benefits and retirement assistance, disciplinary actions, and grievances and appeals.

Director
    Donna Simpson................... (301) 504–7925
    Fax........................... (301) 504–0432

OFFICE OF IMPORT SURVEILLANCE

Works closely with U.S. Customs and Border Protection (CBP) to identify and examine imported shipments of consumer products; maintains staff investigators at many of the largest ports of entry. Works to educate importers, manufacturers, and customs brokers on CPSC standards and procedures.

Director
    Carol Cave .... (301) 504–7677

OFFICE OF INFORMATION AND TECHNOLOGY SERVICES

Oversees all areas related to information technology systems and general policy and planning issues, including but not limited to OMB A-130, the Federal Information Security Management Act, the Government Paperwork Elimination Act, Section 508 of the Disabilities Act, and the E-Government Act under the President's Management Agenda. Responsible for the design, implementation, and support of the CPSC information technology systems, as well as the public and internal websites.

Assistant Executive Director
    Patrick D. Weddle.............. (301) 504–7654
Director of IT Policy and Planning
    Mary James .... (301) 504–7213

Director of Technology Services
Deane Ray . . . . (301) 504–7547

OFFICE OF THE INSPECTOR GENERAL
Reviews, analyzes, and reports on commission programs and organization to assess compliance with appropriate laws, regulations, and procedures. Recommends ways to promote economy, efficiency, and effectiveness within the commission's programs and operations. Receives complaints and investigates possible violations of law, rules, and regulations; mismanagement; abuse of authority; and waste of funds. The inspector general is selected by and reports directly to the CPSC chair.
Inspector General
Christopher W. Dentel . . . . (301) 504–7644
Fax. . . . . (301) 504–7004
Toll-free hotline. . . . . (800) 638–2772

OFFICE OF INTERNATIONAL PROGRAMS
Coordinates international and intergovernmental efforts with respect to consumer product safety standards development, harmonization efforts, inspection and enforcement coordination, manufacturer education, bilateral and multilateral government safety initiatives, and information dissemination.
Director
Richard O'Brien. . . . . (301) 504–7651
Small Business Ombudsman
Neal S. Cohen . . . . (888) 531–9070
International Programs
Richard W. O'Brien. . . . . (301) 504–7054
Intergovernmental Affairs
N. J. Scheers . . . . (301) 504–7670

OFFICE OF LEGISLATIVE AFFAIRS
Provides information and assistance to Congress on matters of commission policy; coordinates written and oral testimony by commissioners and agency personnel before Congress.
Director
Jason Levine. . . . . (301) 504–7660
Fax. . . . . (978) 967–2797
Congressional Liaison
Jenilee Keefe Singer. . . . . (301) 504–7488

◼ CONGRESSIONAL ACTION

Congressional Liaison
Jenilee Keefe Singer. . . . . (301) 504–7488

Committees and Subcommittees

HOUSE APPROPRIATIONS COMMITTEE
Subcommittee on Financial Services and General Government
B300 RHOB, Washington, DC 20515–6015
(202) 225–7245

HOUSE ENERGY AND COMMERCE COMMITTEE
Subcommittee on Commerce, Manufacturing and Trade
2125-RHOB, Washington, DC 20515–6115
(202) 225–2927
Fax (202) 225–1915

SENATE APPROPRIATIONS COMMITTEE
Subcommittee on Financial Services and General Government
SDOB-133, Washington, DC 20510–6025
(202) 224–2104

SENATE COMMERCE, SCIENCE, AND TRANSPORTATION COMMITTEE
Subcommittee on Consumer Protection, Product Safety, Insurance, and Data Security
SDOB-512, Washington, DC 20510–6125
(202) 224–1251

Legislation
The CPSC was established under authority of the **Consumer Product Safety Act,** signed by the president Oct. 27, 1972. The act was later amended by the **Consumer Product Safety Commission Improvements Act of 1976** (90 Stat. 503, 15 U.S.C. 2051 note), the **Emergency Interim Consumer Product Safety Standard Act of 1978** (92 Stat. 386), the **Consumer Product Safety Amendments of 1981** (Title 12, subtitle A, 95 Stat. 703), and the **Consumer Product Safety Improvement Act of 1990** (104 Stat. 3110, 15 U.S.C. 2051 note).

Major legislation administered by the CPSC includes **Flammable Fabrics Act** (67 Stat. 111, 15 U.S.C. 1191). Signed by the president June 30, 1953. Prohibited the introduction or movement in interstate commerce of highly flammable clothing or material.

Refrigerator Safety Act (70 Stat. 953, 15 U.S.C. 1211). Signed by the president Aug. 2, 1956. Required that all refrigerators sold in interstate commerce be equipped with a safety device enabling them to be easily opened from the inside.

Federal Hazardous Substances Act (74 Stat. 372, 15 U.S.C. 1261). Signed by the president July 12, 1960. Required precautionary labels and regulated distribution and sale of hazardous substances suitable for household use.

Poison Prevention Packaging Act of 1970 (84 Stat. 1670, 15 U.S.C. 1471). Signed by the president Dec. 30, 1970. Required special packaging to protect children from serious injury or illness from handling or swallowing household substances.

Consumer Product Safety Act (86 Stat. 1207, 15 U.S.C. 2051). Signed by the president Oct. 27, 1972. Established the CPSC to protect consumers against unreasonable risk of injury from hazardous products.

Lead Contamination Control Act of 1988 (102 Stat. 2884, 42 U.S.C. 201 note). Signed by the president Oct. 31, 1988. Amended the Safe Drinking Water Act to allow the CPSC to recall drinking-water coolers with lead-lined tanks.

Regulations Regarding Lawn Darts (102 Stat. 3183, 16 C.F.R. 1500.86(a)(3)). Signed by the president Nov. 5, 1988. Banned the sale of lawn darts and similar sharp-pointed toys.

Labeling of Hazardous Art Materials (102 Stat. 4568, 15 U.S.C. 1277). Signed by the president Nov. 18, 1988. Amended the Federal Hazardous Substances Act by adding Sec. 23, which sets forth requirements for labeling art materials that the commission deems potentially hazardous to the health of children and adults.

Consumer Product Safety Improvement Act of 1990 (104 Stat. 3110, 15 U.S.C. 2051 note). Signed by the president Nov. 16, 1990. Title I amended the Consumer Product Safety Act, the Federal Hazardous Substances Act, and the Flammable Fabrics Act to require the commission to devise procedures to monitor compliance with certain voluntary standards and to terminate a proposed consumer product safety rule only if a voluntary standard has been approved. Title II required the commission to issue a standard for automatic garage door openers to protect against entrapment.

Child Safety Protection Act (108 Stat. 722, 15 U.S.C. 1261 note). Signed by the president June 16, 1994. Title I required legible and conspicuous choking hazard warning labels on packages of balloons, marbles, small balls, and toys with small parts intended for children over age three. Title II, the Children's Bicycle Helmet Safety Act of 1994, authorized funding for helmets and helmet safety programs through the National Highway Traffic Safety Administration and specified that helmets must meet CPSC standards.

Product Packaging Protection Act of 2002 (116 Stat. 2445, 18 U.S.C. 1365). Signed by the president Dec. 2, 2002. Amended the federal criminal code to prohibit intentionally tampering with consumer products and to increase penalties for tampering with products.

Amendment to Consumer Product Safety Act (116 Stat. 2776, 15 U.S.C. 2085). Signed by the president Dec. 4, 2002. Amended the Consumer Product Safety Act to provide that low-speed electric bicycles are consumer products and subject to CPSC regulations.

Consumer Product Safety Improvement Act (CPSIA) (122 Stat. 3016, 15 U.S.C. 2051 note). Signed by the president Aug. 14, 2008. Amended the Consumer Product Safety Act and other statutes. Prohibited the sale of any product for children that contained more than 600 parts per million of total lead content or more than 0.1 percent of certain specific phthalates. Banned three-wheeled ATVs and developed a mandatory standard for four-wheeled ATVs.

Drywall Safety Act of 2012 (126 Stat. 2437, 15 U.S.C. 2056c) Signed by the president on January 15, 2013. Amended the Consumer Product Safety Act. Sets chemical standards for domestic and imported drywall and establishes remediation procedures for the disposal of existing, installed drywall that fails to meet the law's standards.

■ INFORMATION SOURCES

Internet

Agency website: www.cpsc.gov; E-mail: info@cpsc.gov. News releases about recalls and product hazards along with the CPSC's news releases are available online.

Information on hazardous products and how consumers can report hazardous products to the agency also is available at www.SaferProducts.gov.

Telephone Contacts

Consumer Hotline . . . . (800) 638–2772
General Information. . . . . (301) 504–7923
Compliance Information . . . . (301) 504–7912
Inspector General Hotline . . . . (800) 638–2772
Federal Relay Service TTY. . . . . (301) 595–7054
Compliance Information. . . . .(301) 504–7912
Commission Meeting Agendas. . . . . . (301) 504–7923
Employment Information . . . . (301) 504–7925
Freedom of Information Act . . . . (301) 504–7923
Media . . . . (301) 504–7908
National Injury Information
    Clearinghouse . . . . (301) 504–7921
Safety Guides . . . . (301) 504–7921
Small Business Ombudsman . . . . (888) 531–9070

Information and Publications

KEY OFFICES

CPSC Office of Communications

4330 East-West Hwy.
Bethesda, MD 20814–4408
(301) 504–7051
Fax (301) 504–0399
E-mail: publicaffairs@cpsc.gov
Scott Wolfson, director

Distributes health and safety information to the news media and issues press releases. Coordinates media coverage of commission events and information activities within the commission. Distributes commission publications. Manages the commission's consumer hotline, which provides information on recalls and handles consumer complaints about unsafe products or product-related injuries; it operates at all times, with staff available weekdays from 8:30 a.m. to 5:00 p.m.

CPSC Office of Information and Technology Services

4330 East-West Hwy.
Bethesda, MD 20814–4408
(301) 504–7654
E-mail: pweddle@cpsc.gov
Patrick Weddle, chief information officer

Manages the commission's data-processing resources and networks and Internet and fax-on-demand services. Works to improve agency operations through information technology.

Freedom of Information

4330 East-West Hwy.
Bethesda, MD 20814–4408
(301) 504–7923
Fax (301) 504–0127

E-mail: cpsc-os@cpsc.gov
Deborah Acosta, FOIA liaison
(301) 504–6821

Requests should specify person's address; product or manufacturer's name; and exact titles, dates, file designation, or other information to identify the records requested. Fees for search and reproduction costs vary.

Office of Education, Global Outreach, and Small Business Ombudsman

4330 East-West Hwy.
Bethesda, MD 20814–4408
Toll-free (888) 531–9070
Fax (978) 967–2857
E-mail: sbo@cpsc.gov
Internet: www.cpsc.gov/smallbiz
Neal S. Cohen, ombudsman

Provides guidance and advice about compliance with CPSC laws and regulations as well as technical assistance in resolving problems.

PUBLICATIONS

Call the consumer hotline or send e-mail to info@cpsc.gov to order publications or to request the *Publications Listing*. Publications lists are also available, searchable by title or by subject, on the website: www.cpsc.gov/en/Safety-Education/Safety-Guides/General-Information/Publications-Listing. Some publications are available only online. CPSC publications cover all aspects of consumer product safety, including children's products, helmet safety, playground equipment, toys, electrical wiring, and avoiding fire and carbon monoxide hazards. Titles available include

Annual Report. Summarizes commission activities; lists policies, advisory opinions, regulations, and proposals.

Hotline Brochure. Fact sheet outlining the functions and purpose of the hotline, as well as how the hotline operates.

The Invisible Killer: Carbon Monoxide

Outdoor Home Playground Safety Handbook

Regulated Products Handbook. A guide for manufacturers, importers, distributors, and retailers to help in understanding obligations and responsibilities under the Consumer Product Safety Act.

Sleep Safer: A Fire Resistant Mattress Can Save Your Life.

Which Helmet for Which Activity?

Which Toy for Which Child? Lists toys by appropriate age (birth to 5 years; 6 to 12 years)

Home Electrical Safety Checklist

Who We Are, What We Do For You. General brochure on CPSC organization and activities.

DATA AND STATISTICS

The CPSC *Annual Report* lists data on deaths, injuries, and costs of injuries from consumer products; it also provides an index of products regulated by the commission. More information is available from

CPSC National Injury Information Clearinghouse

4330 East-West Hwy.
Bethesda, MD 20814–4408
(301) 504–7921
Toll free (800) 638–8095, ext.7431
Fax (301) 504–0127
E-mail: clearinghouse@cpsc.gov
Thomas Schroeder, Division Director, Hazard and Injury Data Systems

Maintains databases on product-related deaths and injuries. Obtains data and statistics from state agencies such as police departments and coroners' offices, from consumers, and through the National Electronic Surveillance System. Most data requests are answered free of charge; however, when costs exceed $50, the requester will be notified of the amount due. Information on the following databases is available from the clearinghouse or through the agency's Internet services:

Accident Investigations. Information on accident sequence, product brand name, involvement of product, environmental circumstances, behavior of people involved, photographs, or diagrams. Police, fire, or coroners' reports may be included as supplemental data. Investigation reports are filed by calendar year, area office or contractor, type of injury, type of consumer product, age, sex, and so on.

DTHS—Death Certificate System. Information on age, sex, race and ethnicity, date and place of accident, accident mechanism, manner of death, whether or not the accident was work related, nature of injuries, external causes, consumer products involved, general location of the accident, and up to two lines of narrative detail.

NEISS—National Electronic Injury Surveillance System. Data on product-related injuries collected from statistically representative hospital emergency rooms nationwide. Data include victim's age, sex, diagnosis, body part affected, disposition of the case, product involved, any indication of a second product involved, and the general location of the accident.

Reported Incidents. Narrative reports of actual or potential product hazards taken from reports submitted on www.SaferProducts.gov, consumers' letters to the CPSC, hotline calls, newspaper articles, and notices from coroners and medical examiners.

MEETINGS

The commissioners' meetings are usually open to the public, but participation is limited to observation. Notices of meetings, with a tentative agenda, are published in the *Public Calendar* seven days in advance of the meeting and in the "Sunshine Act Meetings" section of the *Federal Register*.

The CPSC Office of the Secretary maintains the master calendar of the agency, which it distributes through a mailing list. The secretary's office can provide notices, agendas, and minutes of executive session meetings. Call (301) 504–6836.

Reference Resources

LIBRARY

The CPSC no longer maintains a physical library. Reference materials have been digitized and are accessible through the agency's website: www.cpsc.gov/en/Research--Statistics.

DOCKETS

CPSC Office of the Secretary

4330 East-West Hwy.
Bethesda, MD 20814–4408
(301) 504–6833
Rocky Hammond, docket control specialist
Hours: 8:30 A.M. to 5:00 P.M.

Maintains a reading room containing CPSC documents and other records that are available for public inspection. An electronic reading room is also available on the website: www.cpsc.gov. Federal dockets are also available at www.regulations.gov. *(See appendix for Searching and Commenting on Regulations: Regulations.gov.)*

RULES AND REGULATIONS

CPSC rules and regulations are published in the *Code of Federal Regulations,* Title 5, Chapter LXXI, Part 8101; Title 16, Chapter II, Part 1000 to the end. Proposed rules, new final rules, and updates to the *Code of Federal Regulations* are published in the *Federal Register.* (*See appendix for information on how to obtain and use these publications.*) The *Federal Register* may be accessed at www.federalregister.gov and the *Code of Federal Regulations* at www.archives.gov/federal-register/cfr; also see the federal government's website www.regulations.gov (*see appendix*).

Other Information Sources

RELATED AGENCY

Consumer Information Center

General Services Administration
    (*See appendix, Ordering Government Publications.*)

NONGOVERNMENTAL RESOURCES

The following are some key resources for information on the CPSC and consumer product safety issues.

Consumer Federation of America

1620 Eye St. N.W., #200
Washington, DC 20006
(202) 387–6121
E-mail: cfa@consumerfed.org
Internet: www.consumerfed.org

Consumers Union of United States

101 Truman Ave.
Yonkers, NY 10703–1057
(914) 378–2000
Publishes *Consumer Reports* magazine.
Internet: www.consumersunion.org
    Washington office
    1101 17th St. N.W., #500
    Washington, DC 20036
    (202) 462–6262
    Fax (202) 265–9548

Council of Better Business Bureaus

3033 Wilson Blvd., #600
Arlington, VA 22201
(703) 276–0100
Internet: www.bbb.org

National Consumers League

1701 K St. N.W., #1200
Washington, DC 20006
(202) 835–3323
Fax (202) 835–0747
Internet: www.nclnet.org

Public Citizen

1600 20th St. N.W.
Washington, DC 20009
(202) 588–1000
Internet: www.citizen.org

United States Public Interest Research Group (U.S. PIRG)

294 Washington St., 500
Boston, MA 02108
(617) 747–4370
Internet: www.uspirg.org
    Washington office
    218 D St. S.E., 1st Floor
    Washington, DC 20003–1900
    (202) 546–9707

Environmental Protection Agency

1200 Pennsylvania Ave. N.W., #3000, MC 1101A
Washington, DC 20460
Internet: www.epa.gov

▨ INTRODUCTION

Established in 1970, the Environmental Protection Agency (EPA) is an independent agency in the executive branch. It is headed by an administrator who is assisted by a deputy and nine assistant administrators, all nominated by the president and confirmed by the Senate.

Responsibilities

In the area of air quality, the EPA

- Establishes U.S. air quality standards.
- Sets limits on the level of air pollutants emitted from stationary sources such as power plants, municipal incinerators, factories, and chemical plants.
- Establishes emission standards for new motor vehicles.
- Sets allowable levels for toxic substances such as lead, benzene, and toluene in gasoline.
- Establishes emission standards for hazardous air pollutants such as beryllium, mercury, and asbestos.
- Supervises states in their development of state implementation plans (SIPs).

In the area of water quality and protection, the EPA

- Issues permits for the discharge of any pollutant into navigable waters.
- Coordinates with the Coast Guard to clean up oil and chemical spills in U.S. waterways.
- Develops "effluent guidelines" to control discharge of specific water pollutants, including radiation.
- Develops criteria that enable states to set water quality standards.
- Administers grants program to states to subsidize the cost of building sewage treatment plants.
- Regulates disposal of waste material, including sludge and low-level radioactive discards, into the oceans.
- Cooperates with the Army Corps of Engineers to issue permits for the dredging and filling of wetlands.
- Sets national drinking water standards to ensure that drinking water is safe.
- Regulates underground injection of wastes to protect purity of ground water.

To control the disposal of hazardous waste, the EPA

- Maintains inventory of existing hazardous waste dump sites.
- Tracks more than 500 hazardous compounds from point of origin to final disposal site.
- Sets standards for generators and transporters of hazardous wastes.
- Issues permits for treatment, storage, and disposal facilities for hazardous wastes.
- Assists states in developing hazardous waste control programs.
- Maintains a multibillion-dollar fund, the "Superfund," from industry fees and general tax revenues to provide for emergency cleanup of hazardous dumps when no responsible party can immediately be found.

GLOSSARY

Chlorofluorocarbons (CFCs)—Chemical compounds, such as refrigerants, suspected of causing the depletion of the ozone layer in the atmosphere.

Greenhouse effect—The trapping of carbon dioxide and other gases within the atmosphere, leading to climate change and health hazards.

Radon—An odorless and colorless gas produced from the decay of radium 226 in soil and rocks. High levels of radon trapped indoors can pose health hazards.

State implementation plans (SIPs)—Plans created by the states in place of national EPA directives. The EPA oversees the development of such plans, which must be at least as stringent as EPA plans.

Superfund—A multibillion-dollar fund set up in 1980 to provide for emergency cleanup of hazardous sites when no responsible party can be found.

Wetlands—Marshes, swamps, or bogs that provide wildlife habitat and, according to environmentalists, perform other valuable ecological functions.

- Pursues identification of parties responsible for waste sites and eventual reimbursement of the federal government for Superfund money spent cleaning up these sites.

To regulate chemicals, including pesticides, and radioactive waste, the EPA

- Maintains inventory of chemical substances now in commercial use.
- Regulates existing chemicals considered serious hazards to people and the environment, including fluorocarbons, asbestos, and polychlorinated biphenyls (PCBs).
- Issues procedures for the proper safety testing of chemicals and orders them tested when necessary.
- Requires the registration of insecticides, herbicides, and fungicides intended for sale in the United States.
- Requires pesticide manufacturers to provide scientific evidence that their products will not injure humans, livestock, crops, or wildlife when used as directed.
- Classifies pesticides for either general public use or restricted use by certified applicators.
- Sets standards for certification of applicators of restricted-use pesticides. (Individual states may certify applicators through their programs, based on the federal standards.)
- Cancels or suspends the registration of a product on the basis of actual or potential unreasonable risk to humans, animals, or the environment.
- Issues a "stop sale, use, and removal" order when a pesticide already in circulation is found to be in violation of the law.
- Requires registration of pesticide-producing establishments.
- Issues regulations concerning the labeling, storage, and disposal of pesticide containers.

- Issues permits for pesticide research.
- Monitors pesticide levels in the environment.
- Monitors and regulates the levels of radiation in drinking water, oceans, and air.
- Conducts research on toxic substances, pesticides, air and water quality, hazardous wastes, radiation, and the causes and effects of acid rain.
- Provides overall guidance to other federal agencies on radiation protection matters that affect public health.

Powers and Authority

The EPA encourages voluntary compliance by government agencies, private industries, and communities and, as mandated by federal environmental laws, encourages state and local governments to perform direct enforcement activities needed to meet local environmental standards. If state and local agencies fail to produce effective plans for pollution abatement, or if they do not enforce the programs they develop, the EPA is authorized to do so under provisions of major environmental laws.

The EPA carries out national enforcement functions where delegation to the states is not practical. For example, the EPA inspects and tests automobiles to ensure compliance with air pollution control standards. The agency also can recall vehicles that fail to meet those standards. The agency maintains a staff of inspectors who spot-check compliance with unleaded gasoline regulations, monitor air and water quality, check radiation levels in the environment, and collect other data to use in enforcing environmental laws.

The Office of Enforcement and Compliance Assurance is responsible for overseeing all of the EPA's enforcement activities. The office gathers and prepares evidence and conducts enforcement proceedings for water quality, stationary and mobile sources of air pollution, radiation, pesticides, solid wastes, toxic substances, hazardous wastes, and noise pollution (see p. 85).

EPA's ten regional counsels review administrative enforcement actions and develop judicial enforcement cases for headquarters' review. In addition they provide regional administrators and regional program managers with legal advice and assistance for all program areas in an attorney-client relationship.

Under the terms of most statutes administered by the agency, the alleged polluter is notified of a violation of EPA standards and ordered to stop. If the violation is not corrected, informal negotiations begin. If the informal meeting fails, the agency has authority to start civil court proceedings to force compliance. Penalties for violations of environmental laws can be severe. For example, a court can order civil penalties for violations of the Clean Air Act Amendments of up to $25,000 per day for as long as each violation continues and impose a one-year jail sentence or, if the violator knowingly endangers human health, a longer term.

Without going into federal court the EPA may revoke or suspend licenses and permits for activities regulated by the agency. Under the Toxic Substances Control Act, for example, the EPA may order the seizure of any substances found to be toxic. The agency also may order the manufacturer of the toxic substances to publicize the violation and issue a notice of possible risk of injury.

The Resource Conservation and Recovery Act mandated a record-keeping system to keep track of the handling and disposal of hazardous wastes. The system was designed specifically to thwart "midnight dumpers," who dump toxic wastes in sewers, woods, fields, or streams under cover of darkness.

The Enforcement Office also has a criminal investigation unit to prosecute persons who willfully discharge wastes into waterways, engage in midnight dumping of toxic substances, or deliberately destroy or falsify vital environmental reports. Willful violators may be subject to imprisonment and be personally liable for fines.

Among the major laws administered by the EPA are those dealing with clean air and water, safe drinking water, pesticides, waste treatment and disposal, control of toxic substances, and the Superfund program to deal with release of hazardous substances in spills and abandoned disposal sites.

The statutes take two basic approaches in their civil enforcement provisions: administrative and judicial. Administrative enforcement encompasses a wide range of responses, including informational orders, notices of noncompliance, notices of violation, administrative orders, and administrative penalty complaints. An administrative penalty complaint is a notice sent to a violator informing the recipient that he or she is in violation and that he or she is entitled to an administrative hearing. An administrative law judge presides over the hearing and renders a final decision that may in turn be appealed to the EPA administrator. The administrator's decision may be further appealed to the federal court system and ultimately to the Supreme Court. However, the vast majority of these administrative cases never reach the courts.

The second basic approach to enforcement is judicial action. Here the violator again receives notice that he or she is in violation. If the problem cannot be resolved at this level, the EPA refers the case to the Justice Department for prosecution. The Justice Department reviews the case and then sends it to a U.S. attorney who initiates the case at the federal district court level. The authority to take enforcement action varies under each statute.

Background

Since its establishment, the EPA has evolved into one of the most closely watched, as well as most criticized, federal regulatory agencies. Controversy over the agency stems partly from its wide-ranging responsibilities, involving the administration of a multitude of complex and costly laws. In most cases of EPA action or inaction to implement those statutes, environmentalists and industry representatives square off to fight for or against a deadline, a delay, or a new standard. At times the agency has been the target of complaints from both supporters and opponents of the environmental movement. Nonetheless, over time it has succeeded in forcing significant reductions in the levels of pollutants in the environment.

EARLY HISTORY

When the EPA came into being in 1970, it took control of air pollution, water pollution, solid waste, pesticide, and radiation programs scattered around the federal government. Between the EPA's establishment and the early 1980s those programs were broadened and improved, and Congress heaped major new responsibilities on the agency. "Many of EPA's difficulties over the years can be traced to the fact that Congress loaded the agency with far more statutory responsibilities within a brief period of time than perhaps any agency could effectively perform," commented Russell Train in 1982. Train served as EPA administrator from 1973 to 1977.

The EPA was established at a time when the nation was becoming increasingly concerned about declining air and water quality and a general deterioration of the environment. The dramatic blowout of an oil well in the channel off the coast of Santa Barbara, CA, in January 1969 focused public attention on the seriousness of environmental problems. Miles of beaches were covered with oil, and thousands of fish and wildfowl were killed.

Some months after the Santa Barbara incident, on June 3, President Richard Nixon established by executive order the cabinet-level Environmental Quality Council (EQC). Congress was not satisfied and in December 1969 it passed the National Environmental Policy Act (NEPA), which made environmental protection a matter of national importance. The act required federal agencies to submit environmental impact statements for all proposed actions and created the three-member Council on Environmental Quality (CEQ) within the Executive Office of the President to replace the EQC. Many industry groups denounced NEPA, but conservation organizations such as the Sierra Club hailed it as "an environmental Magna Carta."

During the early days of his administration, Nixon was widely criticized for lacking a strong commitment to environmental protection. As the pressure for corrective action mounted, the president in 1970 submitted to Congress a plan to consolidate the federal government's widespread environmental protection efforts into a single agency. Against little congressional opposition, the EPA was created by executive order. Most existing environmental programs were transferred to the EPA from other government departments. The EPA's first administrator was William D. Ruckelshaus, a vigorous enforcer of water and air quality standards; he infused the EPA with an enthusiasm and sense of mission not unlike that associated with the Peace Corps.

The CEQ continued to exist as an advisory and policy-making body. While the EPA was charged with setting and enforcing pollution control standards, the CEQ focused on broad environmental policies and coordination of the federal government's environmental activities.

Enthusiasm for environmental legislation continued throughout the early 1970s. Congress passed several laws designed to limit or halt the entry of pollutants into the environment, including the Water Quality Improvement Act and the Clean Air Act Amendments, both of 1970, and the Federal Environmental Pesticide Control Act; the Noise Control Act; the Marine Protection, Research, and Sanctuaries Act; and the Water Pollution Control Act Amendments, all of 1972. Responsibility for enforcing these laws was given to the EPA.

The energy shortage created by the 1973 Arab oil embargo slowed the rush of environmental programs as legislators sought to balance the benefits of a sometimes costly antipollution program against the need for a stable and productive economy. Opponents of stricter environmental standards argued that the costs of complying with EPA regulations slowed industrial expansion. In some cases companies reportedly closed their doors rather than attempting to meet EPA-imposed standards. Moreover, the environmental movement, which was the impetus behind some of the environmental laws passed by Congress, had lost some of its momentum by the mid-1970s.

Nonetheless, the EPA's responsibilities expanded in certain areas. The Safe Drinking Water Act of 1974 set standards for chemical and bacteriological pollutants in water systems. The Toxic Substances Control Act of 1976 gave the EPA responsibility for studying the risks attached to toxic substances and protecting the public from them. The Resource Conservation and Recovery Act (RCRA) of 1976 was intended to ensure that hazardous and nonhazardous wastes were disposed of in environmentally sound ways. During 1977 clean water standards were redefined and deadlines extended.

President Jimmy Carter's EPA head, Douglas M. Costle, who had served on an advisory council that recommended establishing the agency, focused on dealing with the concerns of industry while continuing to protect the environment. The EPA undertook a review of existing regulations and attempted to streamline its regulatory process and to be more cost conscious in its enforcement procedures.

During Costle's tenure in office, the innovative "bubble" and "offset" methods of getting private industry to comply with air emission standards were introduced. Instead of determining emission standards for every process within a factory, in the first approach, the EPA puts an imaginary bubble over the plant and sets allowable standards for the entire operation. This procedure gives factory managers greater incentive to make changes in basic plant operations rather than just adding pollution control devices.

The second approach is to grant "offsets" in areas where pollution standards are not being met. If a new factory wants to move into an overpolluted area, it must induce existing factories to reduce their pollution levels by more than the amount the new factory will produce. Another variation allows a company having more than one factory in the same area to offset higher-than-standard emissions at one factory by lower-than-standard emissions at another.

SUPERFUND

More responsibilities in the hazardous waste area were given to the EPA with the passage of the controversial Superfund legislation in the waning days of the 96th Congress. In December 1980 President Carter signed the Comprehensive Environmental Response, Compensation and Liability Act of 1980, which established a $1.6 billion emergency fund to clean up toxic contaminants spilled or dumped into the environment. The major part of the Hazardous Substance Response Trust Fund (Superfund)—86 percent—was scheduled to come from the chemical and oil industries; appropriations of general revenue in fiscal years 1981–1985 would provide the remaining 14 percent. The EPA was given responsibility for administering the fund.

Under the Superfund authority, the EPA first notifies responsible parties of their potential liability. If the responsible parties are unwilling to perform appropriate abatement measures, the EPA will either issue an order requiring cleanup (the violation of which subjects the respondent to punitive damages); bring suit to obtain a judicial order requiring cleanup; or tap Superfund monies to finance the necessary removal or remediation activities. If the EPA performs the cleanup, the agency will later bring an action against the responsible parties to recover the costs.

Complaints about the way the EPA carried out the Superfund law prompted congressional investigations through the years. Congressional probers found that the EPA was slow in spending money in the fund, preferred to negotiate rather than litigate against dumpers to collect costs, and settled for inadequate cleanups at some sites. The agency also has been criticized for spending more on lawyers than on site cleanup.

EPA IN THE 1980s

President Ronald Reagan's first term produced little in the way of new legislation. The RCRA, which had governed "cradle-to-grave" handling of hazardous wastes since its enactment in 1976, was reauthorized at the end of 1984 with stronger controls. But the legislative mandates for other major environmental laws, such as the Clean Water Act, the Clean Air Act, the Safe Drinking Water Act, the Ocean Dumping Act, and laws governing the use of pesticides, expired and were funded only on a year-to-year basis.

Personalities, scandal, and internal problems dominated the agency in the early 1980s. Critics of Reagan's first administrator, Anne M. Gorsuch Burford, complained that she circumvented the legislative process by using regulatory decisions and budget cuts to undermine the agency's effectiveness. In response Burford claimed that she was carrying out her mandate from the president to make the agency more efficient and cost conscious. She tried to reduce the agency's budget and to cut funding for many of its programs, but Congress consistently appropriated more money for the EPA than the administration requested.

Of particular concern to environmentalists and their supporters in Congress was the reduction Burford made in the Office of Enforcement and the number of enforcement cases earmarked for court action. She defended the moves, saying violations should be dealt with at the lowest appropriate level wherever possible. Burford also claimed her enforcement methods, which stressed voluntary compliance, were yielding better results than those of the Carter administration.

The House Energy and Commerce Subcommittee on Oversight and Investigations disagreed. In an October 1982 report, the panel criticized the EPA's enforcement program and noted a 69 percent decline between calendar years 1980 and 1981 in the number of civil case referrals from the agency to the Justice Department under the major acts the EPA administered.

In December 1982 the House cited Burford for contempt for refusing—on Reagan's orders—to turn over documents sought by a subcommittee regarding the agency's management of the Superfund program. She was the highest executive branch official ever cited for contempt by Congress, but the constitutional issue of executive privilege—Reagan's justification for withholding the documents—was never resolved. In the end, administration and congressional representatives struck a compromise that allowed the committees to examine nearly all the documents they sought. In August 1983 the House dropped the contempt citation.

The political damage to the agency was enormous. The controversy drew widespread publicity to charges that some EPA officials had been lax in enforcing toxic waste laws, made "sweetheart deals" with polluters, stood to profit from conflicts of interest, manipulated toxic cleanup grants to influence elections, shredded papers subpoenaed by Congress, and used political "hit lists" to terminate the appointments of science advisers and career employees who disagreed with the administration's environmental policies. Although none of the charges was prosecuted by the Justice Department, the White House began distancing itself from Burford. She resigned in March 1983.

More than a dozen top EPA aides resigned or were fired during the turmoil of this period. Among them was Rita M. Lavelle, head of the Superfund program and the only EPA official to face criminal charges in the scandal. Lavelle was convicted of perjury and obstructing a congressional investigation. In January 1984 she was sentenced to six months in prison and fined $10,000.

With the EPA in disarray, Reagan tapped the EPA's first administrator, Ruckelshaus, to restore public and congressional confidence in the beleaguered agency. Ruckelshaus convinced the administration to reverse several years of decline in its operating budget. He also made several significant regulatory decisions.

Under the new administrator's direction, a 91 percent reduction in the lead content of gasoline was initiated. Despite requirements in effect since 1975 that all new cars sold in the United States use unleaded gasoline, leaded fuel accounted for nearly 40 percent of total gasoline sales in 1984. The EPA found that to be disproportionately high given the number of late-model vehicles in operation. It estimated that 16 percent of all cars that should be using lead-free gasoline were using leaded gasoline. The agency's revised rules on lead were issued March 4, 1985. They required gasoline lead content to be cut from 1.1 grams per gallon to 0.5 grams by July and to 0.1 gram by Jan. 1, 1986.

Another major Ruckelshaus action was the EPA's move against the pesticide ethylene dibromide (EDB), widely used as a fumigant of grains and food products. The agency declared an emergency ban on EDB as a grain fumigant Feb. 4, 1984, and placed interim limits on its content in food still in the pipeline. Later it limited its use on citrus fruits before banning it altogether on Sept. 1, 1984.

But Ruckelshaus was frustrated in his effort to get the administration to take action on acid rain. With studies linking sulfur dioxide emissions from coal-burning power plants in the Midwest to acid rain problems in the northeastern United States and Canada, the issue divided lawmakers along regional lines and became an irritant in U.S.-Canadian relations. Debate over acid rain stalled renewal of the Clean Air Act.

Central to the dispute was the cost of cutting emissions and who would pay. The administration took the coal and utility industry position that not enough scientific evidence had been gathered to justify costly controls and proposed doubling acid rain research funding. The move was announced by President Reagan in his 1984 State of the Union address.

Ruckelshaus left the EPA soon after and was replaced by Lee Thomas, former head of the EPA's toxic waste programs. Under Thomas, the EPA established a major enforcement precedent in May 1985 when it reached an agreement with Westinghouse Corp. that required the company to spend up to $100 million, the largest such settlement to date, to clean up toxic waste sites it used at six locations in Indiana.

But in February 1988 the EPA imposed an even larger fine for environmental damage. Shell Oil Co. and the U.S. Army pledged to spend up to $1 billion to clean up toxic contamination from production of chemical weapons at the Rocky Mountain Arsenal in Denver. The settlement required the parties to clean up the dump site for the debris from two decades of chemical weapons development. The EPA was to supervise the project, with the costs shared by Shell and the army.

In 1986 Congress enacted a major expansion of the Superfund program. The bill set strict standards for cleaning up sites and required the EPA to begin work at 375 sites within five years. It stressed the use of permanent cleanup methods, calling for detoxifying wastes whenever possible, instead of burying them in landfills. The measure also required industries to provide local communities with information on what chemicals they handled or dumped, and it gave victims of toxic dumping a longer opportunity to sue those responsible.

After the low environmental focus of the Reagan administration, environmental issues again moved to the front burner of national concerns when George H. W. Bush moved into the White House. Bush promised during his campaign that he would be "the environmental president," and he pleased many environmentalists by appointing William Reilly as administrator of the EPA. Reilly was the first professional environmentalist to hold the post; he had been head of an important mainstream environmental group, the U.S. branch of the Swiss-based World Wildlife Fund. Reilly had gained attention by promoting the use of economic incentives as a way to break the logjam between industry and environmental activists over the cost of pollution controls. Instead of mandating what each utility should do to curb pollution, Reilly advocated the trading of "pollution credits" between polluters who cleaned up and those who could not or who needed to expand plants that might add pollution.

This formula might allow Utility A, which spent $5 million to install new smoke-cleaning equipment, to gain a credit that could be swapped with Utility B, which needed a credit to avoid penalties imposed by the EPA. This market-based approach, he argued, would help finance cleanup efforts and provide incentives lacking in the usual environmental government-by-directive regulations.

In 1989 the EPA released a report claiming that indoor pollution, especially exposure to radon gas, posed one of the greatest environmental risks to Americans. Indoor pollutants were thought to cause more than 14,000 deaths annually.

Also in 1989, Reilly's activist approach gained impetus from an environmental disaster that alarmed the nation. The *Exxon Valdez*, running aground at Valdez, Alaska, spilled more than 11 million gallons of crude oil, spreading a slick over hundreds of miles of pristine coastline. This oil spill, the worst in the nation's history, set the tone for debate in Congress over major environmental legislation, much like the earlier Santa Barbara spill.

Although the captain of the *Valdez* was convicted for the negligent discharge of oil, it was Exxon, target of lawsuits totaling billions of dollars in damages, which was put on trial by the public. Despite spending about $2 billion and enlisting thousands of Alaskans in an effort to clean up the mess, Exxon was portrayed as an environmental villain. A poll taken in the wake of the *Valdez* spill found renewed interest in environmental issues. More than 70 percent of Americans considered themselves environmentalists.

In October 1991 Exxon agreed, as part of an out-of-court settlement, to pay the government more than $1 billion in fines and damages. The bulk of the money—$900 million—was set aside over a ten-year period to pay civil claims brought as a result of the damage. Additionally, on Sept. 16, 1994, a federal court ordered Exxon to pay a record $5 billion in punitive damages to 34,000 Alaskan residents affected by the spill. (After years of litigation, however, in 2008 the Supreme Court reduced the punitive damages to $507.5 million.)

EPA IN THE 1990s

The Alaska disaster set the stage for the G. H. W. Bush administration to rewrite the nation's major pollution law, the Clean Air Act, which had last been revised in 1977. Signed into law on Nov. 15, 1990, the overhaul of the act was designed to markedly improve air quality by the end of the century and became the most significant environmental achievement of the Bush administration.

The act imposed new standards for smog-producing emissions: reducing nitrogen oxides by 60 percent and hydrocarbons by 40 percent by 1994. Further reductions in these emissions would be required in 2003 unless the EPA determined that they were not technologically possible. In addition, cars had to be built to meet the new emissions standards for ten years or 100,000 miles, by 1996.

In provisions to reduce sulfur dioxide and nitrogen oxide emissions from utilities that cause acid rain, the act established five classes of nonattainment for smog problems in each metropolitan area, ranging from marginal to extreme. The timetable for cleanup—which would involve refitting many industries with pollution control devices—depended on the severity of the problem. Areas with marginal smog problems had only three years to achieve attainment, while extreme areas would be granted twenty years to reduce smog to acceptable levels. All but marginal areas would be required to reduce nonautomotive smog by 15 percent annually for the first six years and 3 percent for each year after that.

The act also sought by 2000 to phase out U.S. production of chlorofluorocarbons and methyl chloroform, two chemicals widely used as refrigerants and in electronics. These chemicals were blamed for the depletion of the ozone shield in the upper atmosphere, which allowed more dangerous ultraviolet rays from the sun to penetrate, raising the risk of cancers.

The global focus on the environment reached its apex in May 1992, when representatives of more than 150 countries met in Rio de Janeiro, Brazil, to discuss environmental issues. The conference hit a snag when the Bush administration balked at international caps on the emission of carbon dioxide and other gases causing the greenhouse effect, which in turn is believed by most scientists to lead to global warming and health hazards. The European Community and Japan had already agreed to limit greenhouse gases to their 1990 levels by the year 2000.

American negotiators argued that the United States was already doing its part to combat global warming. They pointed out that the country had banned some greenhouse gases, namely chlorofluorocarbons, and had initiated a program to plant one billion trees. In the end, a treaty limiting greenhouse gas emissions to 1990 levels was passed, but at U.S. insistence, no timetables were set.

The conference passed a second treaty requiring a full inventory of all of the world's plants and animals and the development of a strategy for preserving biodiversity. But the United States initially refused to sign the so-called Biodiversity Treaty, arguing that it would ultimately impose limitations on the pharmaceutical and biotechnology industries. The U.S. position on the treaty changed with administrations, and President Bill Clinton signed the pact in 1993.

Clinton chose Carol M. Browner to be EPA administrator in 1993. Browner served as secretary of the Florida Department of Environmental Regulation, where she built a reputation as a tough environmentalist with a commensurate understanding of business concerns. Browner's first major challenge as administrator was to help negotiate and sell an environmental side agreement for the North American Free Trade Agreement (NAFTA) among the United States, Canada, and Mexico. The treaty, completed in the last year of the Bush administration, was designed to eliminate tariffs and other trade barriers among the three countries. During the 1992 campaign, Clinton had been in favor of NAFTA but had conditioned his support on the negotiation of additional side agreements aimed at strengthening treaty provisions on the environment, labor laws, and other areas.

Environmental groups had worried that NAFTA would allow Mexico to successfully challenge tough U.S. state and local environmental laws as trade barriers. They also feared that provisions of the treaty requiring the three countries to work toward common environmental standards would lead to weakening of laws, because Mexico's standards were much lower than those of its northern neighbors. The final agreement did not require harmonization of laws. Instead, the countries were encouraged to adopt the highest standard. The agreement also established a Commission for Environmental Cooperation, responsible for monitoring environmental laws.

Browner put her philosophy to work in programs that favored broad goals, not prescriptive solutions. Browner's marquee program was Project XL, which required companies to meet standards but gave them flexibility in how to do so. In June 1996 Browner announced administrative changes to the Superfund program to free some small businesses and municipalities from the program's costly web of litigation by no longer making them responsible for cleanup costs. The Clinton administration ostensibly reflected an approach to environmental protection that favored consensus over confrontation.

Despite Browner's background and new regulatory approaches, the Clinton administration still found itself early on the target of a backlash toward what many perceived as overly restrictive rules and regulations. During the Democratic-controlled 103rd Congress, Republicans and some conservative Democrats lambasted the EPA for offering programs they considered only a token response to the call for more leeway in environmental laws.

A bill to elevate the EPA to cabinet-level status died after being caught up in a larger movement to curb regulations, by requiring the EPA and other agencies to weigh the costs and benefits of new rules. Clinton continued to have Browner sit in on cabinet meetings, underlining the importance of the agency and its administrator.

Ironically, it was the Republican-controlled 104th Congress that resurrected the environment as a vibrant issue and trained the president's attention on it. The ground began to shift in spring and summer 1995 when the Republicans in Congress attempted to push through a rewrite of the Clean Water Act and endorsed environment-related legislative provisions in appropriation bills. Both moves were roundly criticized as regulatory rollbacks, and Republicans faced harsh criticism. Clinton seized the opening, exploiting the Republican's credibility gap to paint the GOP Congress as "extremists" and positioning himself as the chief protector of the environment.

By August 1996 the political ground had shifted sharply as Congress, hoping to shore up its environmental image, sent Clinton a sweeping bipartisan rewrite of the federal drinking water law. The drinking water act gave more flexibility to regulators in revising health standards, created a grant and loan fund to pay for water system improvements, and required that drinking water suppliers inform customers of contaminants. The contamination of drinking water in the United States was more widespread than was commonly believed. According to the EPA, there were more than 700 harmful contaminants in drinking water. Long-term exposure to some of these chemicals can lead to problems such as birth defects. The 1996 act was seen as an important step in improving the nation's drinking water quality.

President Clinton also signed in 1996 an overhaul of pesticide regulations. The Food Quality Protection Act sought to protect people from dangerous levels of cancer-causing pesticides in food. At the same time, the act allowed some chemical residues in food, enabling farmers to continue to use certain pesticides. In addition, provisions sought to safeguard the health of infants and children, restrict the ability of states to pass laws stricter than federal regulations, and educate the public about the risks and benefits of agricultural chemicals.

At the end of 1996, the EPA proposed stringent new clear air standards. The regulations, the most significant rewrite of the Clean Air Act since the 1970s, tightened an existing rule for ozone, the main component of smog. In addition, the act created a new standard for airborne particles of soot produced by sources such as diesel engines and power plants fueled by coal.

The proposed regulations produced a firestorm of criticism, especially from the business community. Industries, including utilities and automobile manufacturers, argued that the new rules would cost millions of dollars to implement and produce no appreciable environmental benefit. These and other critics lobbied the Clinton administration to eliminate or at least significantly soften the EPA's clean air plan. But in July 1997 environmentalists scored a huge victory when the president announced that he would support the agency's new rules. The announcement outraged many Republicans and some Democrats in Congress. But an effort to reverse the regulations legislatively stalled after supporters of the bill realized that they could not muster the two-thirds majority needed in both houses to override a promised presidential veto.

After being accused by environmentalists and others of inflexibility and foot-dragging, the administration signed an agreement on global warming at a 1997 world conference in Kyoto, Japan. Under what became known as the Kyoto protocol, the United States agreed to deep cuts in national greenhouse gases, produced largely through the burning of oil and coal, lowering emissions to 7 percent below 1990 levels during the following fifteen years.

Many Republicans and a few Democrats in Congress, joined by business groups, criticized the need for the Kyoto agreement, especially one so far-reaching. They argued that global warming was a theory that had yet to be proven. In addition, they said, the treaty would cost businesses billions and leave millions of U.S. workers jobless. While President Clinton signed the treaty in November 1998, intense opposition to it in Congress forced him to delay sending it to the Senate for ratification. Soon after, the administration realized that any attempt at ratification would have to wait until after the 2000 elections, producing more charges of foot-dragging from the Europeans and others.

In 1998 EPA began its review of potentially dangerous pesticides, as required by the 1996 Food Quality Protection Act. The action pitted chemical producers and farmers against environmentalists and public health advocates. In 1999 the agency banned most applications of methyl parathion and increased restrictions on azinphos methyl. Both substances were popular pesticides, which had been shown to cause illness in farm workers and others. The EPA was particularly concerned that the two pesticides might cause neurological disorders in small children. In 2000 the agency banned chlorpyrifos (used in insecticides and flea collars) and reached a voluntary agreement with the chemical company Syngenta to phase out home and garden use of diazinon, a commonly used pesticide for controlling roaches and other pests.

EPA IN THE 2000s

By 2000 the EPA had come under fire for its role in encouraging the use of methyl tertiary butyl ether (MTBE), a gasoline additive that makes fuel burn cleaner by reducing the amount of carcinogens cars emit. The EPA touted MTBE as a way for states with high levels of air pollution to meet tougher air quality standards under the Clean Air Act Amendments of 1990. But while the substance did help improve air quality, it also leaked from underground storage tanks, contaminating water supplies everywhere.

In March 2000 the EPA called for a prohibition on the use of MTBE and urged oil companies to use the more expensive ethanol instead. Ethanol, derived from corn, is another petroleum additive that some believe makes gasoline burn cleaner. The agency was criticized, however, for its decision regarding ethanol. Some environmentalists charged that the substance was not an appropriate substitute because it actually boosted emissions of some smog-forming chemicals.

As it grappled with the fuel additive issue, the agency also proposed new regulations aimed at reducing emissions from trucks and buses that burn diesel fuel, which causes a disproportionate amount of air pollution. The new regulations, which were proposed in May 2000, called for removing 97 percent of the sulfur found in diesel fuel. Along with other steps, EPA aimed to reduce pollution caused by diesel emissions by 90 percent during the following decade.

The agency's efforts to clean up the nation's air received a boost from the Supreme Court in winter 2001. In late February the Court ruled that when setting new clean air standards, the EPA did not have to consider their potential economic impact on industry. Although U.S. businesses had claimed that new regulations on ozone and soot would cost untold billions of dollars in unnecessary expense, the Court ruled that the agency only had to weigh public health considerations when deciding on acceptable levels of pollution.

The results of the 2000 presidential election created a dramatically new situation for the EPA. The agency lost its biggest champion with the defeat of presidential candidate Gore, a longtime environmentalist. In his place were a new president and vice president who had spent part of their professional lives in the oil industry. Moreover, during the campaign, the Republican presidential nominee, Gov. George W. Bush of Texas, had alarmed environmentalists by advocating oil drilling in Alaska's Arctic National Wildlife Refuge.

On the other hand, most EPA boosters were satisfied with Bush's pick to run the agency—Gov. Christine Todd Whitman of New Jersey. While Whitman, a moderate Republican, did not have her predecessor's direct experience in environmental policy, she had a reputation as a good manager and a familiarity with some environmental concerns—such as Superfund cleanup and coastal management issues—from her six-year tenure as the governor of a highly industrial state.

At her confirmation hearing in January 2001, Whitman signaled a new direction for the agency by promising to emphasize market-based solutions to problems. Moreover she indicated that in the future, the EPA would more thoroughly consider the economic impact of a policy before proposing new regulations. She tried to assuage the concerns of environmentalists by promising that the EPA would be more "flexible" in reaching solutions by cooperating with all sides in the environmental debate, including business, environmental advocacy groups, and state governments.

The administration's early moves on the environment, however, guaranteed that Whitman would have no honeymoon period with environmentalists. The battle began on the day Bush took office, when he put a hold on 175 new environmental regulations promulgated by Clinton in the waning days of his administration. Among these were new rules lowering the allowable levels of arsenic in drinking water. Putting the new arsenic regulations on hold set off a furor among Democrats and earned the new president some of his first bad press.

In the months immediately following, Bush also announced that he would not submit the Kyoto protocol to the Senate for consideration. While the protocol was unlikely to win Senate approval anyway, Bush's action nonetheless incensed environmentalists around the globe, who said that such a stark repudiation by the world's top economy and largest producer of greenhouse gases would seriously dilute the efforts of other countries that had signed the treaty. Bush countered that Kyoto would cost the American economy a total of $400 billion and 4.9 million jobs. Instead, the president promised to come up with a new plan to limit greenhouse gases that would not damage the economy.

After these first rocky months, the administration made more of an effort to shore up its green credentials, beginning by reinstating the arsenic rules. It also unveiled a number of large and small policy proposals in key environmental areas. The most significant of these new proposals, the Clear Skies Initiative, was the Bush plan to amend the Clean Air Act to cut power plant emissions of sulfur dioxide, nitrogen oxide, and mercury—pollutants that contribute to smog and acid rain—by 70 percent. This would be accomplished through a market-based system that would allow utilities to buy and sell pollution credits. In other words, those firms with emissions below prescribed levels would be able to sell the difference to utilities with power plants that were exceeding the limits.

But the environmental lobby argued that Clear Skies itself was a misnomer, allowing polluters to avoid cleaning up dirty plants by using bookkeeping tricks. Only mandated pollution reductions, such as those already in the Clean Air Act, would improve air quality, they said. Even industry groups expressed concern over the proposal, especially planned reductions in mercury, much of which is produced by coal-burning power plants. Clear Skies quickly became bogged down in Congress, receiving only lukewarm support from Republican congressional leaders, and the legislation languished through 2003 and 2004. The administration later achieved some of the goals of the legislation through regulation when it issued the Clean Air Interstate Rule and the Clean Air mercury rule in March 2005 (*see below*). Additionally, a voluntary carbon emissions trading program in Chicago involving many of America's largest companies was established in 2003.

Meanwhile, the EPA was taking action in another major environmental sphere: water. In July 2001 the agency announced it was delaying the implementation of major new clean water rules that would have required states to come up with plans to protect and clean up some 21,000 streams, rivers, and lakes that had already been declared "impaired" by the EPA. A year later, the agency gave the first indications of how it was going to change the rules, saying that states would be given more flexibility in how they clean up waterways. Efforts would be made to encourage voluntary compliance. The agency also said it was considering a market-based system that would allow polluters to buy and sell credits, similar to the one proposed in the president's Clear Skies Initiative.

The rules, originally drafted during the Clinton administration, had come under heavy fire from states, farm groups, and many members of Congress, who worried that they would impose high costs on local governments and the agricultural industry. Environmental groups countered that the administration was using the strong objections from these groups as an opportunity to weaken the rules so as to make them ineffective.

Environmentalists also were angered by a delay of other Clinton-era clean water rules requiring small construction sites to develop plans for storm water runoff. In March 2002 the EPA announced that the rules, which were just coming into force, would not apply to oil and gas companies for at least another two years. Energy companies had argued that the new regulations should not apply to them because unlike other kinds of construction, oil and gas drilling was usually set up quickly. The EPA said that it would study the issue during the two-year exemption and then decide what to do. But environmentalists and their allies argued that the exemption was a payoff to the Bush administration's many allies in the oil and gas industry.

On the other hand, the EPA surprised environmentalists in August 2001 when it ordered General Electric to pay $500 million to clean up toxic materials it had dumped into the Hudson River. The agency order came even as the company and business groups lobbied the administration, saying that the dredging required to clean the river floor would do more harm than good.

Environmentalists also lauded Whitman's statement that the nation's water infrastructure—including pipes and water treatment facilities—was aging and that $535 billion above the current spending levels would be needed over twenty years to ensure that drinking water was safe and rivers and lakes were not further polluted. The agency also pleased the environmental community with its announcement that it would thoroughly review cleanup efforts, past, present, and future, at many of the nation's 1,500 Superfund sites because of recent research showing that one contaminant, trichloroethylene, was more toxic than previously thought. The substance, used as a solvent to clean electronic parts, could be between five and sixty-five times more toxic for pregnant women than originally estimated.

Meanwhile a group of northeastern governors, led by New York Governor George Pataki, began collaborating in 2003 on efforts to reduce power plant emissions of the greenhouse gas carbon dioxide that scientists believe traps heat within the atmosphere. This effort, known as the Regional Greenhouse Gas Initiative (RGGI, or "Reggie") aimed to create a regional cap-and-trade program, limiting carbon dioxide emissions. By summer 2007 the compact stretched from Maryland to Maine, with state officials actively debating the details of putting a trading program in place. The initiative began in September 2008 auctioning permits to emit carbon for power plants in Connecticut, Delaware, Maryland, Maine, Massachusetts, New Hampshire, New York, New Jersey, Rhode Island, and Vermont.

In 2003 Whitman announced she would leave her post in June. President Bush replaced her with Michael O. Leavitt, a three-term Republican governor of Utah. Business groups hailed Leavitt as a pragmatic consensus builder, but the reaction from the environmental community was decidedly mixed—with some groups saying that he favored development in general and the oil and gas industry in particular, over the environment. Leavitt pointed out his environmental record as governor, which included steps to improve the air quality at the Grand Canyon. "To me there is an inherent human responsibility to care for the earth," he said. Leavitt was confirmed on Oct. 27, 2003.

One of Leavitt's first major decisions as EPA head left him at odds with environmentalists. In early December 2003 the EPA proposed altering planned regulations that would have imposed strict limits on mercury under the Clean Air Act. The decision, which had been in the works long before Leavitt arrived, reversed rules drafted during the Clinton administration that would have regulated mercury emissions from coal-burning power plants with the same stringency as the most toxic air pollutants, such as asbestos and lead. These earlier regulations would have required all power plants to begin installing new pollution control equipment by 2007.

The new proposed rules, which would not have taken effect until 2010 if they had been implemented, would place mercury under that part of the Clean Air Act that governs the emission of less harmful pollutants, such as sulfur dioxide, which causes acid rain. The centerpiece of the new proposal was the establishment of a market-based "cap and trade" system, which would allow utilities to buy and sell the right to discharge mercury. The utility industry applauded the approach—which was similar to the one proposed in the president's Clear Skies Initiative—saying that it would bring overall mercury levels down without forcing every power plant to install expensive new equipment.

Environmentalists argued that while overall mercury levels might drop, a system that allowed particularly dirty power plants to buy emissions credits from others could lead to high levels of contamination in certain areas. They also pointed out that unlike sulfur dioxide—which is harmful to the environment but does not directly threaten human health—mercury is a neurotoxin, which can accumulate in tissue and cause neurological damage, especially in children, as well as birth defects. Pressure from these groups, as well as congressional Democrats, caused Leavitt to publicly "rethink" the market-based system, leaving the issue to his successor.

Leavitt earned plaudits from the environmental community, however, for another major decision early in his tenure. At the time of his becoming administrator, the agency had been drafting new regulations that would have removed millions of acres of wetlands from protection under the Clean Water Act. Many of the wetlands targeted were small and isolated. The move was opposed by environmentalists as well as most state governments. It was supported by the home-building trade, which argued that the current rules were not only overly restrictive but confusing as well. But a little more than a month after taking office, Leavitt announced that the proposed changes were being shelved, in large part, he said, because of the Bush administration's commitment to "no net loss of wetlands."

Leavitt also won praise from environmentalists when he announced in May 2004 new regulations that further strengthened the agency's already tough diesel emissions standards. New diesel rules had been proposed during the final days of the Clinton administration and had already been strengthened once, early in President Bush's first term. The new rules expanded the stricter standards from buses and trucks to all nonroad diesel vehicles, requiring most of them to reduce the fuel's sulfur content from 500 parts per million to 15 parts per million by 2010. Locomotives and boats were given an additional two years to meet the standard.

In addition, Leavitt and the agency were applauded for increasing grants to states to clean up so-called brownfields, urban industrial and commercial sites that had been abandoned. The June 2004 announcement detailed $75.4 million for sites in forty-two states and Puerto Rico.

Soon after President Bush's reelection, Leavitt left the EPA and Bush nominated Stephen L. Johnson to head the agency. Having worked for the EPA for twenty-four years before becoming acting administrator on Leavitt's departure, Johnson was the first scientist nominated to the top job at the agency. During his time at the agency, he held a number of senior posts, including heading up the office on pesticides and other toxic substances.

Even before Johnson was officially confirmed, the agency moved to implement one of the Bush administration's top priorities—new clean air regulations that were largely embraced by industry. The Clean Air Interstate Rule affected twenty-eight eastern states and the District of Columbia. It aimed to reduce sulfur dioxide by 5.4 million tons, or 57 percent, from 2003 levels, by 2010. Officials also expected it to reduce power plant nitrogen oxide (NOx) emissions by 2 million tons, a 61 percent reduction from

2003. The agency noted that sulfur dioxide and nitrogen oxides contribute to the formation of fine particles and NOx contributes to the formation of ground-level ozone, or smog. Fine particles and ozone are associated with thousands of premature deaths and illnesses each year, the agency said in announcing the rule.

The rule, which mirrored the goals of the administration's Clear Skies legislation that had been stuck in Congress, allowed plants to buy and sell pollution credits under a cap and trade approach. Plants that did not meet their pollution-reduction goals would have to buy credits from others who had exceeded their requirements. Although some environmentalists said the rule was better than the status quo, a number of environmental activists and state officials criticized the rule as too limited. They said that the agency should have been far more aggressive in limiting pollution, with deeper cuts and faster implementation schedules.

Five days after announcing the new interstate air rules, the agency also finalized its cap-and-trade policy limiting mercury emissions from coal-fired power plants. The mercury rule aimed to reduce emissions from forty-eight tons a year to thirty-eight tons annually by 2010, a cut of more than 20 percent. Environmentalists once again assailed the policy as too weak and argued that the cap-and-trade approach should not be used for mercury, because so-called hot spots, or concentrated areas of pollution, could be quite toxic to human health. Many state officials agreed and ultimately decided to impose stricter state standards rather than follow the federal rule.

In late summer 2005 the EPA, along with other federal agencies, suddenly faced the tremendous challenge of cleaning up after Hurricane Katrina, which had devastated the Gulf Coast, including flooding the city of New Orleans. The EPA dispatched a team of 650 personnel to help assess the damage and prepare for cleanup of the stricken areas. One immediate concern was the water quality in the flooded city. EPA tests determined extremely unhealthful levels of sewage-related bacteria and lead, among other toxic chemicals. These findings were a major factor in a mandatory evacuation order of the remaining New Orleans residents. The EPA also planned on advising the city when parts of the city would be safe again for habitation.

The hurricane also had flooded thirty-one other Superfund sites in coastal areas of Louisiana, Mississippi, and Alabama. Johnson called Hurricane Katrina "the largest national disaster that we at EPA or we believe the nation has faced." Johnson gathered a panel of experts to assist the EPA in cleaning up the toxic mess left behind in New Orleans, Lake Pontchartrain, and other areas of the Gulf.

In 2006, a year after Katrina first hit, the EPA reported it had taken approximately 1,800 sediment and soil samples in the New Orleans area to test for contaminants. Some samples found elevated levels of arsenic, lead, benzo(a)pyrene, and diesel and oil range organic petroleum chemicals. Further study suggested that the highest concentrations of arsenic were likely associated with herbicides used at golf courses. Despite the elevated level of contamination in some areas, however, the EPA said that "in general, the sediments left behind by the flooding from the hurricanes are not expected to cause adverse health impacts to individuals returning to New Orleans."

On a controversial front, the EPA announced in 2005 that it would change reporting requirements for polluting companies. These pollution reports were available to the public through a database known as the Toxics Release Inventory. The EPA proposed relaxing the reporting rules for companies by changing annual reporting requirements to be biennial. The agency also wanted to increase the minimum threshold for when companies should report releases of certain toxics—up from 500 pounds to 5,000 pounds. After Democrats won control of Congress in the November 2006 elections, EPA officials initially said that they would drop the plans to lessen the reporting frequency. But in December 2006 the agency finalized the rule to increase the reporting threshold, slightly modifying the language to 2,000 pounds for certain toxins. Democrats were unable to stop the change.

In 2007, with Democrats in control of Congress, environmentalists and their advocates in Congress had hopes that they could combat the Bush regulatory agenda. Those hopes began to be realized to some degree in the waning days of the Bush administration and were helped in part by the courts, which intervened to overturn a number of the administration's regulatory policies. One of the biggest questions involved how the United States would regulate greenhouse gas emissions that scientists say contribute to climate change.

Public attention to climate change had grown in recent years as the International Intergovernmental Panel on Climate Change continued its work documenting the evidence that climate change has been occurring. The panel of acclaimed scientists released its fourth report in 2007, finding that it was virtually certain that human activity had been contributing to climate change. The report predicted that as many as 30 percent of species could become extinct if temperatures rose 3.6 degrees above historical averages.

During this period, with the EPA unwilling to act on climate change, states stepped up to regulate greenhouse gases on their own. In 2002 California had passed a law requiring significant new reductions in the greenhouse gases that come from tailpipe emissions. That law required a federal waiver from the EPA. California's decision prompted an eventual thirteen other states to pass similar measures. In 2005 California requested that EPA give it a waiver to allow the state the right to control greenhouse gas emissions from motor vehicles. U.S. automakers opposed the state rules, which they said would cost billions and would make little progress in slowing global warming because other nations would probably continue to emit greenhouse gases. EPA administrator Johnson ultimately denied the request in early 2008. Bush administration officials said there was too much scientific uncertainty surrounding the issue to approve the waiver. The denial was unusual because federal law generally allows California the flexibility to experiment with clean air policies that are stricter than those of the federal government.

The resulting friction over greenhouse gas emission rules between state and federal government was among the factors that prompted a dozen states, including California and Massachusetts, to challenge in court the EPA's reluctance to regulate carbon dioxide as a pollutant under the Clean Air Act. In 2007 the Supreme Court ruled in *Massachusetts v. EPA* that the EPA did have the authority to regulate the gases in automobile emissions and that the agency could not ignore its responsibility to regulate greenhouse gases without providing a scientific rationale. The Court's decision did not require new regulations but found that the "EPA can avoid taking further action only if it determines that greenhouse gases do not contribute to climate change or if it provides some reasonable explanation as to why it cannot or will not exercise its discretion to determine whether they do."

Agency observers said that the decision would have long-lasting implications for the regulation of greenhouse gases stretching far beyond the auto industry alone. U.S. autos account for about 20 percent of U.S. greenhouse gas emissions. Many legal experts predicted that the decision would lead to full-scale greenhouse gas regulation for all industries, including factories, power plants, and other polluting entities. Some of the legal arguments that the Court rejected have also been used in other lawsuits.

Massachusetts v. EPA was not the only court case that reversed Bush administration policies. A number of Bush administration policies—including the 2005 rule affecting mercury and the 2005 rule known as the Clean Air Interstate Rule, affecting sulfur dioxide, nitrogen oxides, and other pollutants—had been sent back to the agency to be rewritten.

The U.S. Court of Appeals for the D.C. Circuit ruled against the Clean Air Interstate Rule in July 2008, saying that the judges found "more than several fatal flaws in the rule." However, the parties to the litigation asked the court to leave the rules in place temporarily until the EPA rewrote them, arguing that striking them entirely would create too much uncertainty. The court complied in December 2008. The agency proposed new rules in 2010 but left the existing rules in place, while officials underwent a long process of finalizing them. In July 2011 the EPA finalized the regulations, which came to be known under a new name, the Cross-State Air Pollution Rule. The rule required twenty-seven states to improve air quality by reducing power plant emissions that contribute to ozone or fine particle pollution in other parts of the country. The agency also issued a final rule in December 2011 to require five of the states and one other state to make summertime nitrogen oxide reductions.

The implementation of the Cross-State Air Pollution Rule was delayed because of court actions. But in 2014 the agency scheduled implementation of the first phase in 2015 and the second phase in 2017.

The D.C. Court of Appeals struck down the mercury rules as well and did not leave those rules intact temporarily. The panel said that the Bush administration's EPA had ignored the clear intent of Congress in the Clean Air Act because the agency sought to set aside the act's framework for regulating pollutants, such as mercury, and substitute the administration's own alternative means of regulating the toxin. The court said that the preordained decisions by the administration in the regulation "deploy[ed] the logic of the Queen of Hearts, substituting EPA's desires for the plain text of" the law, adding that "EPA can point to no persuasive evidence suggesting that [the law's] plain text is ambiguous."

When Barack Obama was inaugurated in January 2009, it was clear that his EPA would take a different approach to the environment, particularly on global warming and Clean Air Act issues, than the Bush administration. Obama brought back former Clinton administration EPA administrator Browner as a White House coordinator on energy and environmental policies. Obama's EPA administrator, Lisa P. Jackson, had worked for sixteen years at the EPA before serving as the top environmental official in New Jersey. She was confirmed three days after Obama's inauguration as the nation's first African American EPA administrator.

Obama administration officials made it clear that they wanted Congress to spend more money on protecting the environment. One of the first laws that Obama signed was the economic stimulus package in February 2009, which contained $62.2 billion in direct spending on green initiatives and $20 billion in green tax incentives, including money for renewable energy, fuel efficiency, improved energy transmission, smart-grid technology, low-income housing retrofits, rail transit, and green jobs training.

Obama's EPA also reversed the Bush 2006 policy on reporting requirements for polluting companies. Democratic lawmakers included a provision in a catch-all omnibus budget law that required the EPA to rewrite the reporting rules. EPA administrator Jackson reinstated the previous, more extensive reporting requirements in late April 2009, with the restored requirements taking effect in July. "People have a right to information that might affect their health and the health of their children—and EPA has a responsibility to provide it," Jackson said.

In November 2010 the EPA finalized a rule adding sixteen toxic chemicals to the list of substances that polluters have to report to the agency under the Toxics Release Inventory program. That marked the first time in more than a decade that new chemicals had been added to the requirements. The sixteen chemicals are classified by the National Toxicology Program as "reasonably anticipated to be a human carcinogen." The new requirements took effect in January 2011.

One early decision in the Obama administration came when the president signed a memo requiring the EPA to review a Bush decision affecting the right of California and other states to regulate greenhouse gases on their own. On Jan. 26, 2009, Obama requested that the EPA revisit the denial. The EPA then announced at the end of June that it was granting California's waiver, allowing the state to enforce its greenhouse gas standards for new motor vehicles starting with the current model year. That decision cleared the way for thirteen other states and Washington, DC, to enforce similar standards.

Obama took a similar stance on other policies affecting greenhouse gases. Upon taking office, Obama and the EPA quickly released a response to the Supreme Court's 2007 ruling in *Massachusetts v. EPA*. In April 2009 Jackson issued a proposed finding that greenhouse gases contribute to air pollution that may endanger public health or welfare. The EPA targeted six gases—carbon dioxide, methane, nitrous oxide, hydrofluorocarbons, perfluorocarbons, and sulfur hexafluoride—that had been linked by scientists to climate change. The EPA said that greenhouse gases not only can result in higher concentrations of smog but also can contribute to problems associated with climate change, such as drought, more intense storms and flooding, heat waves and wildfires, and a rise in sea levels.

The finding was expected, given that Obama promised on the 2008 presidential campaign trail to address the problems associated with climate change, but it was significant nonetheless for the huge policy and political shift it represented. The Bush administration had focused for eight years on reducing the burden of environmental regulation on business and studying the effects of climate change, which environmental activists believed was an effort to stand in the way of more ambitious action to reduce greenhouse gases. The EPA's finding that greenhouse gases potentially harm humans was a sign that Obama was taking more aggressive steps to reduce the gases, even though the world was in the midst of a significant economic downturn that conservatives said would be exacerbated by tougher environmental regulations. The agency collected comments on the finding until late June, when it prepared to finalize the finding and moved toward writing rules that would govern emission of greenhouse gases.

However, Jackson and Obama said they would prefer that Congress act on legislation to regulate greenhouse gases through a cap-and-trade system rather than leave the issue to the agency. Congress could make broader, more comprehensive changes than the agency. The House of Representatives passed legislation in June 2009 to control carbon dioxide emissions. The House bill, which narrowly passed in the Democratic-controlled House, by 219–212, would have established a federal cap-and-trade program to reduce the emissions of other greenhouse gases, such as carbon dioxide, from current levels, by 17 percent in 2020 and 83 percent in 2050. The EPA would have restricted emissions and issued emission credits that polluters could buy and sell under a trading system in order to meet the limits.

However, the measure stalled in the Senate.

EPA IN THE 2010s

When Republicans took control of the House in November 2010, they made it clear they would not pass a cap-and-trade climate change bill. As congressional efforts stalled, the EPA took steps to use its regulatory muscle to impose new controls on carbon dioxide. The agency also separately proposed that some industry sources begin reporting the amount of carbon dioxide that they emit on an annual basis. The EPA proposed that the first annual report be submitted to EPA in 2011 for the previous calendar year, except for car manufacturers, who would begin reporting for the model year 2011.

EPA officials responded in May 2010 to concerns that the greenhouse gas regulations the agency was charged with writing would overreach and affect small businesses. To address those fears, the EPA released the so-called tailoring rule, which detailed what types of companies and facilities would be affected by rules on carbon dioxide. Small farms, restaurants, and some commercial facilities were among those that were exempt. EPA officials said that the national greenhouse gas standards would eventually require about 70 percent of stationary sources to comply with permitting requirements.

Later, in June 2014, the Supreme Court partially struck down the tailoring rule. The high court said in its *Utility Air Regulatory Group v. Environmental Protection Agency* ruling that facilities could not be required to get permits based solely on their greenhouse gas emissions. However, the Court also said that EPA has the authority to regulate greenhouse gases under permit programs if the facilities are already otherwise required to get permits for conventional criteria pollutants, such as sulfur dioxide and nitrogen oxides.

The Obama administration also signaled that it would be active and more aggressive than the Bush administration in regulating hazardous waste sites. In April 2009 the EPA added nine new hazardous waste sites that it said pose risks to human health and the environment to the National Priorities List of Superfund sites, which are often the most complex hazardous waste sites in the nation. The agency also took the preliminary step of proposing to add thirteen other sites to the list. The actions brought the total of final and proposed sites to 1,331 areas. The agency continued periodically updating the list. When the administration announced in March 2011 that it was adding another ten sites to the final list, the total of final and proposed sites tallied 1,350 areas.

Current Issues

The EPA has continued to implement new air policies to replace those of the Bush administration. The mercury rule that was vacated by the courts was replaced on March 16, 2011, with a tougher proposed rule that will limit emissions from power plants. The rules restrict emissions of heavy metals, including mercury, arsenic, chromium, and nickel, and acid gases such as hydrogen chloride and hydrogen fluoride. The final rules for these toxic air pollutants, also known as air toxics, were released on Feb. 16, 2012, in compliance with a court consent decree.

EPA officials said the new rules will keep about 91 percent of the mercury in coal from being released to the air. They estimated that the standards could prevent as many as 17,000 premature deaths each year, at a cost of about $3 to $4 a month in household utility bills when the regulation was fully in force after 2015. By then, approximately one-third of states would have set their own restrictions on mercury, but the EPA proposal served as the first national standard. The agency said that more than half of the nation's coal- and oil-fired generating units would be able to meet the EPA standards already because they had already installed pollution control equipment.

The Supreme Court heard a challenge to the mercury rule in 2015. A key question was when the agency should consider the costs of the program. The court ruled that the EPA acted unreasonably and that the agency must

consider costs, including the cost of compliance, before deciding whether regulation is needed.

The agency further tightened another air quality program, the New Source Review policy, in May 2011 by eliminating some grandfathering provisions for particulate matter that had allowed polluters to continue operating under outdated rules.

Environmentalists largely cheered most of the administration's actions, but there were some policies that they felt did not go far enough.

One major disappointment for environmentalists came in late summer 2011, when the White House ordered the EPA to back down from plans to tighten rules affecting ground-level ozone, or smog. The EPA typically reassesses national smog standards, which are part of a larger Clean Air program known as National Ambient Air Quality Standard (NAAQS), every five years. But in 2010, Jackson announced that she planned to revise the standards set in 2008 by the Bush administration earlier than normal. The 2008 rules had been somewhat controversial because the Bush administration had decided not to follow the advice of the agency's scientific advisory committee, which recommended a tougher standard of between 60 and 70 parts per billion. Instead, the Bush administration tightened the standards only slightly by setting them to 75 parts per billion. Jackson indicated that she wanted to follow the committee's more stringent advice.

However, business leaders and local government officials warned the White House that it would be difficult to comply with the tougher standard pursued by Jackson. Counties that are out of compliance risk losing federal funds. They also argued that the new rules could weaken the fragile economy. One week before President Obama gave a major speech on employment and the economy to Congress, the administration announced that further revisions to the smog standards would be delayed until they were scheduled for routine review in 2013. Environmentalists were dismayed, wondering whether the announcement signaled a change in the administration's environmental philosophy. But defenders of Obama's decision said that other rules Jackson was putting in place would achieve at least some of the same outcomes of the national smog standard update. For instance, rules to regulate air toxins such as mercury were still expected to move forward. The new Cross-State Air Pollution Rule would also reduce smog emissions, although the cross-state rule affects pollution only from power plants, rather than the multiple sources, including motor vehicles, which would have had to comply with the national smog standards.

The environmental community's worries eased as the administration continued pursuing additional regulatory proposals aimed at reducing climate change and pollution.

The administration was particularly aggressive in reducing emissions from vehicles. In August 2011, EPA and the National Highway Traffic Safety Administration finalized greenhouse gas emission standards and fuel economy standards for medium- and heavy-duty trucks and other vehicles. The standards were to be phased in between 2014 and 2018, affecting models made in those years. When implemented fully, the regulations were expected to reduce greenhouse gas emissions by 17 percent for diesel trucks and 12 percent for gasoline-powered trucks.

The administration followed up in October 2012, when it issued greenhouse gas emission standards for model year 2017–2025 light-duty vehicles. Under the standards, greenhouse gas emissions from new cars and light trucks are projected to decline about 50 percent by 2025 compared with 2010. The average fuel economy standards will increase to about 50 miles per gallon. The new standards follow the previous emission standards for model years 2012–2016 vehicles and for 2014–2018 model year medium- and heavy-duty trucks. The agency said the new standards represented a significant reduction in the emissions that contribute to climate change. Supporters, such as the environmental group the Sierra Club, said that by 2030 the actions would be equivalent to shutting down 65 coal-fired power plants for a year.

In the spring of 2013 the EPA released a proposed rule that tackled the issue of tailpipe emissions in another way. The regulation, also known as the "Tier 3" rule, required that oil refineries reduce the sulfur content of gasoline and that automakers use advanced technology to slash tailpipe emissions. The tailpipe emission standards include different phase-in schedules that vary by vehicle class but phase in between the vehicle model years of 2017 and 2025.

EPA also required in the rule that federal gasoline contain no more than 10 parts per million of sulfur on an annual average basis by January 1, 2017. The lower-sulfur fuel requirements will mirror those in California.

The EPA finalized the Tier 3 proposal in March 2014. When the regulation is fully implemented in model year 2025, EPA officials said that tailpipe emissions that contribute to smog such as non-methane organic gases and nitrogen oxides will be reduced by about 80 percent and emissions of particulate matter will be required to decline by about 70 percent. The agency estimated that the reductions would reduce respiratory illnesses in the United States and prevent about 770 to 2,000 premature deaths per year.

EPA officials said that the proposal would quickly improve U.S. air quality and help counties meet their Clean Air goals under the NAAQS program. NAAQS standards include specific rules affecting a variety of pollutants, including ozone and particulate matter, which are adjusted every five years.

In December 2012 the agency released a final rule revising the NAAQS standards for fine particle pollution (known as PM 2.5), including soot. The agency strengthened the annual health standard, setting it at 12 micrograms per cubic meter. The EPA kept the daily standard for coarse particles and the daily standard for fine particles the same. The agency predicted that fewer than 10 counties, out of the more than 3,000 U.S. counties, will need to take actions to reduce fine particle pollution to meet the new standard by 2020.

Another Clean Air rule that the EPA issued in 2012 included the first regulation of emissions from natural gas wells that use hydraulic fracturing (also known as "fracking"). The new standards were to be implemented by 2015 and affect about 11,000 new wells annually.

On water quality, environmentalists forced the EPA to propose tougher antipollution rules for power plants. A coalition of environmental groups filed a lawsuit in 2010 that required action by the agency. The agency put forward a series of options in 2013 that would reduce toxic metals such as mercury, arsenic, and lead. The EPA planned to release a final rule in the fall of 2015.

President Obama took on the issue of climate change with greater force in the summer of 2013 by releasing a climate action plan that set the framework for further actions to regulate greenhouse gas emissions.

Leading that charge was Gina McCarthy, who took over the agency after Jackson resigned early in Obama's second term. Environmentalists were strongly supportive of the nomination of McCarthy, who had led the EPA's air pollution division. Environmental groups created a lobbying campaign to pressure the Senate to approve McCarthy. They pointed to her involvement in Clean Air Act rules as evidence that she would push the administration to address climate change. They noted that she had the support of some industry executives as well, and pointed out that she had worked for Republican governors on the state level in the Northeast. She had been confirmed by the Senate for her post overseeing air and radiation policies on a voice vote in 2009. On July 18, 2013, the Senate confirmed McCarthy's nomination to head the agency by 59–40.

McCarthy used her experience in regulating air emissions to drive forward the administration's approach to regulating greenhouse gas emissions. In the summer of 2014 the EPA announced changes to its Significant New Alternatives Policy that would promote the use of refrigerants that are less harmful to the atmosphere and reduce the use of hyrdofluorocarbons that EPA officials said contribute to climate change. The agency identified hydrofluorocarbons used in aerosols, motor vehicle air conditioning, retail food refrigeration and vending machines, and foam blowing as unacceptable for use.

The next moves by the agency got more attention. In September 2013 the EPA released a proposed rule that would limit the amount of carbon pollution that coal-fired and natural gas-powered plants that are constructed in the future can release. The agency received about two million comments from the public by the time the comment period closed in 2014.

In June 2014 the EPA added to that approach by releasing national regulations on carbon dioxide from existing power plants. The final version of the proposal, which the administration called the Clean Power Plan, is intended to reduce carbon pollution from power plants by more than 30 percent by 2030 from 2005 levels. Power plants were the largest source of carbon pollution in the U.S. The plan also would reduce pollution that contributes to smog and soot.

Under the final plan, which was released in August 2015, every state would have its own emissions rate reduction goal to comply with. State regulatory agencies will create implementation plans to submit to the EPA. States could use a variety of options to cut carbon dioxide emissions, such as using more renewable energy, boosting energy efficiency programs, or creating regional cap-and-trade programs.

Republicans and some Democrats, especially from coal-producing states, said that the EPA overreached with the regulatory plan. EPA officials argued that the proposal was justified because it would prevent as many as 3,600 premature deaths and a number of health problems, including up to 90,000 asthma attacks in kids. The administration also predicted that electricity bills would not increase but would decline by about $85 per year by 2030 due to increased energy efficiency and other factors. The rule for existing power plants also received enormous public discussion and generated more than two million comments from the public.

■ AGENCY ORGANIZATION

Biographies

GINA MCCARTHY, ADMINISTRATOR

Appointment: Nominated by President Barack Obama on March 4, 2013. Confirmed by the Senate on July 18, 2013.

Born: Boston, Mass.

Education: University of Massachusetts at Boston, B.A.; Tufts University, M.S.

Profession: Public administrator.

Political Affiliation: Democrat.

Previous Career: McCarthy held the position of assistant administrator at the U.S. Environmental Protection Agency (EPA) from 2009 to 2013. Prior to 2009, she was commissioner for the Connecticut Department of Environmental Protection for five years. She was deputy secretary of the Massachusetts Office of Commonwealth Development from 2003 to 2004, and under secretary for policy at the Massachusetts Executive Office of Environmental Affairs from 1999 to 2000.

STAN MEIBURG, DEPUTY ADMINISTRATOR

Appointment: Appointed by President Barack Obama to serve as deputy administrator on January 29, 2015, after serving as acting deputy administrator.

Born: Atlanta, Ga.

Education: Wake Forest University, B.A.; Johns Hopkins University, M.A.

Profession: Public administrator.

Political Affiliation: Democrat.

Previous Career: Meiburg spent eighteen years as deputy regional administrator of EPA's Region 4 office in Atlanta, Georgia, following service as deputy regional administrator in EPA's Region 6 office in Dallas, Texas. From 1990 to 1995, Meiburg was director of Region 6's Air, Pesticides and Toxics Division. From 1985 to 1990, he was director of the planning and management staff of EPA's Office of Air Quality Planning and Standards in Durham, North Carolina. Meiburg joined EPA in 1977.

Environmental Protection Agency

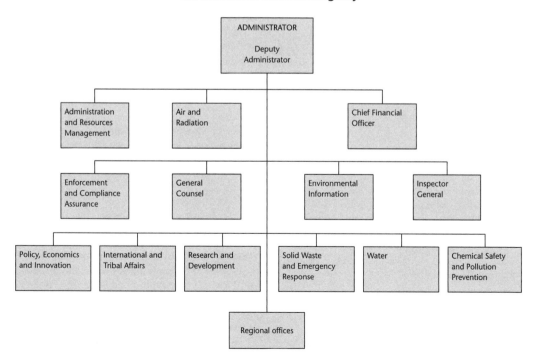

GWEN KEYES FLEMING, CHIEF OF STAFF
Appointment: Appointed on June 3, 2013.
Born: Succasunna, N.J.
Education: Douglass College, B.A.; Emory University School of Law, J.D.
Profession: Lawyer.
Political Affiliation: Democrat.
Previous Career: Appointed Region 4 (Atlanta) regional administrator in 2010 by President Barack Obama. Previously, she served as the first African American and first female attorney and solicitor general for the DeKalb County district.

Headquarters and Divisions

OFFICE OF THE ADMINISTRATOR
The administrator is responsible to the president for overall supervision of the agency.
Administrator
   Gina McCarthy . . . . (202) 564–4700
Deputy Administrator
   A. Stanley Meiburg (acting) . . . . (202) 564–4711
Chief of Staff
   Gwendolyn Keyes Fleming . . . . (202) 564–6999

Office of Administrative Law Judges
The administrative law judges conduct formal administrative hearings.
Chief Administrative Law Judge
   Susan L. Biro . . . . (202) 564–6255

Environmental Appeals Board
The final EPA body responsible for appeals under all major EPA administrative statutes. Duties include adjudicating appeals in the implementation and enforcement of environmental regulations. The board's caseload consists primarily of permit and civil penalty decisions and Superfund cases.
Environmental Appeals Judges
   Kathie A. Stein. . . . . (202) 233–0122
      E-mail: stein.kathie@epa.gov
   Leslye Fraser. . . . . (202) 564–2476
   E-mail: fraser.leslye@epa.gov
   Catherine R. McCabe . . . . (212) 637–5025
      E-mail: mccabe.catherine@epa.gov
   Randolph L. Hill . . . . (202) 564–5474
      E-mail: hill.randolph@epa.gov
   Fax. . . . . (202) 233–0121

Office of Children's Health Protection
Supports and facilitates EPA efforts to protect children's health from environmental risks through regulatory guidance, benefit-cost and other economic analyses, and sponsorship of reports and studies. Provides educational resources to increase public awareness and knowledge of environmental issues and challenges.
Director
   Ruth A. Etzel . . . . (202) 564–2188

Office of Civil Rights
Implements and monitors the agency's equal employment opportunity program and processes discrimination complaints. Monitors recipients of EPA grants for compliance with various sections of the civil rights acts.
Main Office . . . .**(202) 564–7272**
Director
   Velveta Golightly-Howell . . . . (202) 564–7272
      E-mail: golightly-howell.velveta@epa.gov

Office of Congressional and Intergovernmental Relations
The principal adviser to the administrator for communications and public affairs with respect to congressional activities and the main point of congressional contact with the agency. Develops and drafts legislative initiatives for the EPA. Prepares EPA testimony before congressional committees; prepares reports and recommendations on pending and enacted legislation; and represents the agency in legislative dealings with Congress, other departments, and agencies.
Associate Administrator
   Laura Vaught . . . . (202) 564–5200
      E-mail: vaught.laura@epa.gov
Principal Deputy Associate Administrator
   Joyce Frank. . . . . (202) 564–5200
      E-mail: frank.joyce@epa.gov
Congressional Affairs
   Nichole Distefano . . . . (202) 564–7178

Information and Management
Coordinates responses to congressional mail, notifies members of Congress of EPA grants and awards, and edits congressional transcripts.
Director
   Aretha Brockett . . . . (202) 564–0911
Intergovernmental Relations
   Mark Rupp . . . . (202) 564–7178

Office of the Executive Secretariat
Manages executive correspondence for the Office of the Administrator. Handles Freedom of Information Act inquiries and records.
Director
   Eric E. Wachter . . . . (202) 564–7311
      E-mail: wachter.eric@epa.gov

Office of Executive Services
Provides administrative, financial management, automatic data processing, and budget support services to all of the component offices of the Office of the Administrator.
Director
   Diane N. Bazzle . . . . (202) 564–0396
      E-mail: bazzle.diane@epa.gov

Office of Federal Advisory Committee Management and Outreach (OFACMO)
Provides the administrator with technical assistance and focused information dissemination on issues concerning technology transfer.
Main Office . . . .**(202) 564–2294**
Director
   Cynthia Jones-Jackson (acting) . . . . . . (202) 564–2321
      E-mail: Jones-Jackson.Cynthia@epa.gov

Office of Homeland Security

Coordinates homeland security activities and policy development across all EPA program areas. Serves as the agency's central liaison for homeland security matters to the White House Homeland Security Council, Department of Homeland Security, and other federal agencies.

Associate Administrator
Sam Wiggins (acting) . . . . (202) 564–6978

Office of Policy

The principal adviser to the administrator for environmental policy and innovation, environmental economics, and business and community innovation.

Associate Administrator
Joel Beauvais . . . . (202) 564–4332
General e-mail: PolicyOffice@epa.gov
Principal Deputy Associate Administrator
Shannon Kenny . . . . (202) 564–4332
General e-mail: PolicyOffice@epa.gov
Climate Change Adaptation Activities
Joel Scheraga . . . . (202) 564–3385
National Center for Environmental Economics
Albert M. (Al) McGartland . . . . (202) 566–2244
Regulatory Policy and Management
Alexander Cristofaro . . . . (202) 564–4332
Strategic Environmental Management
Sandra Connors. . . . . (202) 564–0495
Sustainable Communities
Matthew Dalbey . . . . (202) 566–2860

Office of Public Affairs

Oversees the agency's distribution of information to inform the public of its environmental initiatives, policies, and compliance assistance programs.

Associate Administrator
Thomas Reynolds . . . . (202) 564–8368
Principal Deputy Associate Administrator
Roxanne Smith . . . . (202) 564–4455
Deputy Associate Administrator
Liz Purchia. . . . . (202) 564–8368
Media Relations
George Hull . . . . (202) 564–4355
National Press Secretary
Melissa Harrison . . . . (202) 564–8368

Office of Public Engagement and Environmental Education

Establishes and maintains close working relationships with a broad range of public-sector and private-sector organizations.

Associate Administrator
Brian Bond. . . . . (202) 564–1785
Environmental Education
Sarah Sowell (acting) . . . . (202) 564–0145
Email: sowell.sarah@epa.gov
Public Engagement
Micah Ragland. . . . . (202) 564–1785
Email: ragland.micah@epa.gov

Office of Regional Operations

Serves as the primary communications link between the EPA administrator and the regional administrators.

Director
Khanna Johnston (acting) . . . . (202) 564–3100
E-mail: Johnston.khanna@epa.gov

Office of Small Business Programs

Advocates for and advances the business, regulatory, and environmental compliance concerns of small and socio economically disadvantaged businesses and minority academic institutions. Assists small, small disadvantaged, minority-owned, and women-owned businesses in applying for EPA grants and contracts.

Director
Jeanette L. Brown . . . . (202) 566–2075
E-mail: brown.jeanettel@epa.gov
Asbestos and Small Business Ombudsman
Joan B. Rogers . . . . (202) 564–6568
E-mail: rogers.joanb@epa.gov
Disadvantaged Business Enterprise
Vacant. . . . . (202) 566–2222
Minority Academic Institutions Program
Lester Facey . . . . (202) 566–1321
E-mail: facey.lester@epa.gov

Science Advisory Board

Advises the administrator on scientific and technical information pertaining to the environment and human health.

Main Office . . . .**(202) 564–2221**
Director
Thomas Carpenter . . . .(202) 564-4885
E-mail: carpenter.thomas@epa.gov

OFFICE OF ADMINISTRATION AND RESOURCES MANAGEMENT

Has primary responsibility for policy and procedures governing internal resources management, sustainability initiatives and environmental health and safety at EPA facilities, administration, organization and management analyses and systems development, facilities management, information management, automated data processing systems, procurement through contracts and grants, and human resource management. Also serves as liaison to the Office of Management and Budget and other federal agencies involved in the conduct of budget and administrative activities.

Assistant Administrator
Karl Brooks (acting) . . . . (202) 564–4600
E-mail: aaoarm@epa.gov
Policy and Resource Management
John Showman. . . . . (202) 564–5341
Director (Cincinnati, OH)
Rick Carter. . . . . (513) 569–7910
Director (Research Triangle Park, NC)
Peter Johnson. (919) 541–2258

Office of Administration

Responsible for security and health and safety procedures. Oversees property and space management, personal and property security, and occupational health and safety programs.

Director
Vaughn Noga. (202) 564–8400

Office of Acquisition Management

Responsible for the policies, procedures, operations, and support of the EPA's procurement and contracts management program, from contract planning through closeout.

Director
John Bashista . . . . (202) 564–4310

Office of the Federal Sustainability

Coordinates and assists environmental and sustainability efforts of the federal government, including waste prevention, recycling, and the acquisition of recycled and environmentally preferable products and services, including vehicles and bio-based products. Housed in the White House Council on Environmental Quality; administered by the EPA; website http://ofee.gov.

Federal Environmental Executive
Kate Brandt . . . . (202) 395–5750

Office of Grants and Debarment

Responsible for the administrative management of the EPA's grants, cooperative agreements, and interagency agreements; and for the management of EPA's suspension and debarment program.

Director
Howard Corcoran . . . . (202) 564–1903

Office of Human Resources

Oversees human resources, information management and systems, labor and employee relations, organization and management consulting services, planning and budgeting, and strategic planning and policy systems.

Director
Susan Kantrowitz . . . . (202) 564–4606

OFFICE OF AIR AND RADIATION

Advises the administrator and oversees the air activities of the agency. Air activities include development of national programs, technical policies, and regulations for air pollution control.

Assistant Administrator
Janet McCabe . . . . (202) 564–7404

Office of Air Quality Planning and Standards

Develops national air quality standards, including emission standards for new stationary sources of pollution and for hazardous pollutants. Assesses national air pollution control programs and provides assistance to states, industry, and other groups through personnel training and technical information. Maintains the national air programs data system, which includes information on air quality, emissions, and other technological data. Also devises ways to apply technological advances to pollution control procedures. Located in Research Triangle Park, NC.

Director
Steve Page . . . . (919) 541–5616
Fax . . . . (919) 541–0501
Air Quality Assessment
Richard Wayland . . . . (919) 541–5455
Air Quality Policy
Anna Marie Wood . . . . (919) 541–5676

Health and Environmental Impacts
Erika Sasser . . . . (919) 541–3889
Outreach and Information
Gregory Green . . . . (919) 541–2808
Sector Policies and Programs
Peter Tsirigotis . . . . (919) 541–5536

Office of Atmospheric Programs

Develops technical policy, procedures, and regulations for programs to control acid deposition. Also develops policy and regulations regarding the impact of ozone-depleting chemicals on the stratospheric ozone layer and implements voluntary pollution prevention programs to control global warning.

Director
Sarah Dunham . . . . (202) 343–9140
Clean Air Markets
Reid Harvey . . . . (202) 343–9429
Climate Protection Partnership
Jean Lupinacci (acting) . . . . (202) 343–9137
Climate Change
Paul Gunning . . . . (202) 343–9836
Stratospheric Protection
Drusilla Hufford . . . . (202) 343–9410
Toll-free . . . . (800) 296–1996

Office of Transportation and Air Quality

Identifies characteristics of mobile source emissions (vehicles and engines) and fuels. Assesses technology to control such emissions. Develops emission standards for mobile sources and works to ensure compliance.

Director
Christopher Grundler . . . . (202) 564–1682
The following division is in Ann Arbor, Mich.
Assessment and Standards
Bill Charmley (acting) . . . . (734) 214–4466
Testing and Advanced Technology
David Haugen . . . . (734) 214–4366
The following divisions are in Ann Arbor, Mich., and Washington, DC.
Compliance
Byron Bunker . . . . (734) 214–4155
Transportation and Climate
Karl Simon . . . . (202) 564–7918

Office of Radiation and Indoor Air

Develops radiation and indoor air pollution protection criteria, standards, and policies. Works with other EPA programs and other agencies to control radiation and indoor air pollution exposure and provides technical assistance to states through EPA's regional offices. Also directs an environmental radiation monitoring program, responds to radiological emergencies, and evaluates the overall risk and impact of radiation and indoor air pollution. Serves as EPA's lead office for intra- and interagency activities coordinated through the Committee for Indoor Air Quality. Responsibilities also include establishing standards for disposal of radioactive wastes and guidelines relating to control of radiation exposure under the Atomic Energy Act, the Clean Air Act, and other applicable legislation.

Director
Mike Flynn . . . . (202) 343–9320
Fax . . . . (202) 343–2395
Indoor Environments
David Rowson . . . . (202) 343–9370
Program Management
Kia Logan . . . . (202) 343–9285
Radiation Protection
Jonathan Edwards . . . . (202) 343–9290
National Analytical Radiation Environmental Laboratory (Montgomery, AL)
John Griggs . . . . (334) 270–3401
E-mail: griggs.john@epa.gov
National Center for Radiation Field Operations (Las Vegas, NV)
Ronald G. Frass . . . . (702) 784–8200

OFFICE OF CHEMICAL SAFETY AND POLLUTION PREVENTION

Develops strategies for toxic substance control; establishes criteria for assessing chemical substances, including new chemicals. Develops and enforces procedures for industry reporting and regulations for controlling hazardous substances. Promotes reduced use of pesticides, establishes tolerance levels for pesticides in food, and investigates pesticide accidents.
Assistant Administrator
Jim Jones . . . . (202) 564–2902

Office of Pesticide Programs

Responsible for control of pesticide pollution and the review of research and monitoring programs. Establishes tolerance levels for pesticide residues in or on food; requires registration of pesticides; and monitors pesticide residues in food, people, and certain fish and wildlife and their environments. Also imposes restrictions on the sale and use of pesticides and investigates accidents and incidents involving pesticides. Establishes guidelines for inspection of products, prepares model legislation to be used by the states to improve pesticide control, provides assistance to technical and personnel training programs related to pesticides, and reviews environmental impact statements that relate to pesticide use.
Director
Jack Housenger . . . . (703) 305–7090
Antimicrobials
Jennifer McLain (acting) . . . . (703) 308–6411
Biological and Economic Analysis
Yu-Ting Guilaran . . . . (703) 308–8200
Biopesticides and Pollution Prevention
Robert McNally . . . . (703) 308–8712
Environmental Fate and Effects
Donald Brady . . . . (703) 305–7695
Field and External Affairs
Jacqueline Mosby . . . . (703) 305–7102
Health Effects
Dana Vogel (acting) . . . . (703) 305–0874
Information Technology and Resources Management
Mark Hartman (acting) . . . . (703) 305–5440
Pesticide Re-Evaluation
Rick P. Keigwin Jr. . . . . (703) 308–8000

Registration
Susan Lewis . . . . (703) 305–5447

Office of Pollution Prevention and Toxics

Responsible for administration of the Toxic Substances Control Act (TSCA). Develops policies for programs designed to control toxic substances; determines research priorities; and develops scientific, technical, economic, and social databases for the health evaluation of toxic substances. Also responsible for communicating with the industrial community on implementation of the regulations.
Director
Wendy Cleland-Hamnett . . . . (202) 564–3810
Chemical Control
Maria Doa . . . . (202) 564–0104
Chemistry, Economics and Sustainable Strategies
David Widasky . . . . (202) 566–2215
Environmental Assistance
Felecia Fort (acting) . . . . (202) 564–6239
Information Management
Pamela Myrick (acting) . . . . (202) 564–9838
National Program Chemicals Division
Tanya Mottley . . . . (202) 564–3152
Risk Assessment
Tala Henry . . . . (202) 564–2959
TSCA Interagency Testing Committee
John D. Walker . . . . (202) 564–7526

Office of Science Coordination and Policy

Oversees exposure assessment coordination and policy and hazard assessment coordination and policy.
Director
David J. Dix . . . . (202) 564–8430
Fax . . . . (202) 564–8452
Exposure Assessment Coordination and Policy
Steven Knott . . . . (202) 564–2827
Science Advisory Panel, Executive Secretary
Laura Bailey . . . . (202) 564–3181

OFFICE OF THE CHIEF FINANCIAL OFFICER

Responsible for the agency's budget, resources management, financial management, program analysis and planning, funding allotments and allocations, and accounting and payroll systems.
Chief Financial Officer
David Bloom (acting) . . . . (202) 564–1151
General e-mail: ocfoinfo@epa.gov

OFFICE OF ENFORCEMENT AND COMPLIANCE ASSURANCE

Serves as the EPA's national program manager and principal adviser to the administrator for matters concerning national crime enforcement, including of air, water, drinking water, and toxic substances acts; forensics; and training programs. Also manages the agency's regulatory, site remediation, and federal facilities enforcement and compliance assurance programs, as well as the agency's environmental justice program responsibilities.

Assistant Administrator
Cynthia Giles . . . . (202) 564–2440
E-mail: giles-aa.cynthia@epa.gov

Administration and Policy
Mark Badalamente . . . . (202) 564–2350
E-mail: badalamente.mark@epa.gov

Civil Enforcement
Susan Shinkman . . . . (202) 564–2220
E-mail: shinkman.susan@epa.gov

Compliance
Cynthia Giles . . . . (202) 564–2440
E-mail: giles-aa.cynthia@epa.gov

Criminal Enforcement, Forensics, and Training
Henry Barnet . . . . (202) 564–2480
E-mail: barnet.henry@epa.gov

Environmental Justice
Matthew Tejada . . . . (202) 564–2515
Toll-free (800) 962–6215
E-mail: tejada.matthew@epa.gov

Federal Activities
Susan Bromm . . . . (202) 564–5400
E-mail: bromm.susan@epa.gov

Federal Facilities Enforcement
David Kling . . . . (202) 564–2510
E-mail: kling.dave@epa.gov

Site Remediation Enforcement
Cyndy Mackey . . . . (202) 564–5110
E-mail: mackey.cyndy@epa.gov

OFFICE OF ENVIRONMENTAL INFORMATION

Advances the creation, management, and use of data as a strategic resource to enhance public health and environmental protection, inform decision making, and improve public access to information about environmental conditions.

Chief Information Officer
Ann Dunkin . . . . (202) 564–6665

Assistant Administrator and Principal Deputy Assistant Administrator
Renee Wynn . . . . (202) 564–6665

Office of Information Analysis and Access

Oversees environmental analysis, information access, and the Toxic Release Inventory Program.

Director
Arnold E. Layne . . . . (202) 566–0600

Environmental Analysis
Megan Carroll (acting) . . . . (202) 564–2814

Information Access
Gilberto Irizarry (acting) . . . . (202) 564–7982

Toxic Release Inventory Program
Steven Knizner . . . . (202) 566–0292

Office of Information Collection

Plans and coordinates collection services and strategies.

Director
Matthew Leopard (acting) . . . . (202) 566–1630

Information Exchange and Services
Connie Dwyer . . . . (202) 566–1650

Collection Strategies
Constance Downs (acting) . . . . (202) 566–1640

Office of Technology Operations and Planning

Oversees technology operations and planning.

Director
Harrell Watkins (acting) . . . . (202) 566–0300

Enterprise Desktop Solutions
Kenneth Tindal (acting) . . . . (202) 566–0190

Mission Investment Solutions
Fawn Freeman . . . . (202) 564–2762

National Computer Center (Research Triangle Park, NC)
Tim Thorpe (acting) . . . . (919) 541–4470

OFFICE OF THE GENERAL COUNSEL

Provides legal support for all programs and activities of the agency, including legal opinions, counsel, and litigation support; and assists as legal adviser in the formulation and administration of the agency's policies and programs.

General Counsel
Avi Garbow . . . . (202) 564–8040
Fax . . . . (202) 564–1777

Air and Radiation Law
Lorie Schmidt . . . . (202) 564–7606

Alternative Dispute Resolution
Richard (Rich) Kuhlman . . . . (202) 564–2922

Civil Rights and Finance Law
Elise Packard . . . . (202) 564–2738

Cross-Cutting Issues
Carol Ann Siciliano . . . . (202) 564–7622

Ethics
Justina Fugh . . . . (202) 564–1786

General Law
Wendy Blake (acting) . . . . (202) 564–5323

Pesticides and Toxic Substances Law
Kevin McLean . . . . (202) 564–5375

Resource Management
Kraig Lattimore . . . . (202) 564–1757

Solid Waste and Emergency Response Law
Mary Kay Lynch . . . . (202) 564–7706

Water Law
Steve Neugeboren . . . . (202) 564–7700

OFFICE OF THE INSPECTOR GENERAL

Conducts and supervises audits and investigations of EPA programs and operations. Reviews existing and proposed legislation and regulations to promote effectiveness and prevent fraud or abuse in agency programs. Reports semiannually to the EPA administrator and Congress.

Inspector General
Arthur A. Elkins Jr. . . . . (202) 566–0847
Fax . . . . (202) 566–0857
Inspector General Hotline . . . . (888) 546–8740

Audit
Kevin Christensen . . . . (202) 566–0824

Congressional and Public Affairs
Alan Larsen . . . . (202) 566–2391

Counsel
Alan Larsen . . . . (202) 566–0863

Electronic Crimes

Melody Upah . . . . (703) 347–8310

Investigations

Patrick Sullivan . . . . (202) 566–0819

Mission Systems

Ed Shields (acting) . . . . (202) 566–2683

Program Evaluation

Carolyn Copper. . . . . (202) 566–0828

OFFICE OF INTERNATIONAL AND TRIBAL AFFAIRS

Coordinates the EPA's international activities and assists the administrator in determining policies and programs conducted by the EPA overseas. Coordinates agency's effort to strengthen public health and environmental protection in Indian country, emphasizing working with tribes to administer their own environmental programs.

Assistant Administrator

Vacant . . . . (202) 564–6600

General e-mail: oiainternet-comments@epa.gov

Principal Deputy Assistant Administrator

Jane Nishida. . . . . (202) 564–6600

American Indian Environmental Office

JoAnn K. Chase. . . . . (202) 564–0303

E-mail: chase.joann@epa.gov

Global Affairs and Policy

Walker B. Smith. . . . . (202) 564–6455

E-mail: smith.walker@epa.gov

Management and International Services

Katrina D. Cherry . . . . (202) 564–6605

E-mail: cherry.katrina@epa.gov

Regional and Bilateral Affairs

Neilima Senjalia (acting) . . . . (202) 564–6400

E-mail: senjalia.neilima@epa.gov

OFFICE OF RESEARCH AND DEVELOPMENT

Performs research and development to identify, understand, and solve current and future environmental problems. Provides responsive technical support to EPA's mission. Provides leadership in addressing emerging environmental issues and in advancing the science and technology of risk assessment and risk management.

Assistant Administrator

Lek Kadeli (acting) . . . . (202) 564–6620

Aging Initiative

Conducts science-based educational and outreach activities. These include educating health care providers and persons living with heart disease about the health effects of air particle pollution; educating older adults and their caregivers about environmental hazards and chronic health conditions through a series of fact sheets; and distributing a monthly electronic newsletter with environmental health research findings. Website www.epa.gov/ORD/aging.

Senior Adviser

Kathy Sykes . . . . (202) 564–3651

E-mail: aging.info@epa.gov

National Center for Computational Toxicology

Assesses chemical hazards and risks to human health and the environment through the development of computer screening methods; offers grants to research institutions and partners with other government and private entities to develop methods for screening thousands of chemicals for toxicity. Headquartered in Research Triangle Park, NC.

Director

Rusty Thomas . . . . (919) 541–4219

E-mail: thomas.russell@epa.gov

National Center for Environmental Assessment

Serves as a resource center for the overall process of risk assessment. Operates branches in Cincinnati, OH; Research Triangle Park, NC; and Washington, DC.

Director

Kenneth Olden . . . . (703) 347–8600

E-mail: olden.kenneth@epa.gov

National Center for Environmental Research

Promotes scientific research by the EPA. Operates the Science to Achieve Results (STAR) program, which seeks to focus the work of leading research scientists from universities and nonprofit centers to meet specific science needs of the agency. Offers grants and graduate fellowships.

Director

James H. Johnson . . . . (703) 347–8200

General e-mail: ord.grants@epamail.epa.gov

National Exposure Research Laboratory

Conducts human and ecosystem exposure assessments. Headquartered in Research Triangle Park, NC.

Director

Jennifer Orme-Zavaleta . . . . (919) 541–2106

National Health and Environmental Effects Research Laboratory

Performs laboratory and field research on health and ecological effects of exposures to man-made stressors, particularly under conditions of environmental exposure. Located in Research Triangle Park, NC.

Director

William H. Benson (acting). . . . . (919) 541–2508

E-mail: benson.william@epa.gov

National Homeland Security Research Center

Provides scientific research to protect the nation from terrorist threats to human health and the environment posed by biological, chemical, and radiological agents. Headquartered in Cincinnati, OH.

Director

Gregory Sayles (acting) . . . . (513) 569–7607

E-mail: sayles.gregory@epa.gov

National Risk Management Research Laboratory

Provides the scientific basis for risk management involving pollutants. Conducts research to reduce the uncertainty associated with making and implementing risk management decisions. Headquartered in Cincinnati, OH.

Director

Cynthia Sonich-Mullin. . . . . (513) 569–7923

E-mail: sonich.mullin.cynthia@epa.gov

Office of the Science Adviser

Facilitates the integration of high-quality science and technology into the agency's policies and decisions. Draws on the expertise of scientists, engineers, and policy advisers through intra- and interagency networks.

Deputy Assistant Administrator

Thomas Burke . . . . (202) 564–6620

Office of Science Policy

Administers the Science and Technology Policy Council, the Risk Assessment Forum, the Program in Human Research Ethics and the Human Studies Review Board, the Global Earth Observation System, the Council for Regulatory Environmental Modeling, and the Forum on Environmental Measurement and Environmental Laboratory Advisory Board. Oversees issues related to hydraulic fracturing ("fracking").

Director

Fred Hauchman . . . . (202) 564–6705

OFFICE OF SOLID WASTE AND EMERGENCY RESPONSE

Provides agency-wide policy, guidance, and direction for solid waste and emergency response programs. Responsibilities include program policy development and evaluation, development of appropriate hazardous waste standards and regulations, program policy guidance and overview, technical support and evaluation of regional solid waste and emergency response activities, and development of programs for technical and programmatic assistance to state and local governments. Administers Superfund and Brownfields programs.

Assistant Administrator

Mathy Stanislaus . . . . (202) 566–0200
    E-mail: aastanislaus@epa.gov

Environmental Emergencies Hotline

Toll-free . . . . (800) 424–8802

Federal Facilities Restoration and Reuse

Charlotte Bertrand (acting) . . . . (703) 603–0049

Innovation, Partnership, and Communication

Marsha Minter . . . . (202) 566–1885

Organizational Management and Integrity

Lora Culver . . . . (202) 566–1897

Program Management

Nigel Simon . . . . (202) 566–1910

Center for Program Analysis

Brigid Lowery . . . . (202) 566–0198

Office of Brownfields and Land Revitalization

Supports land revitalization efforts and the strengthening of state and tribal voluntary cleanup programs through brownfield grants, including environmental assessment, cleanup, job training grants, and categorical grants to support state and tribal response programs.

Director

David R. Lloyd . . . . (202) 566–2731

Office of Emergency Management

Responsible for emergency program implementation and coordination.

Director

Reggie Cheatham (acting) . . . . (202) 564–8003

Office of Superfund Remediation and Technology Innovation

Coordinates with regional offices on Superfund remedial responses to cleanup sites. This includes screening, evaluating, ranking, and planning. The planning process includes determination of the states' role, remedial investigation, solution selection, remedial design/construction, oversight of potentially responsible parties (PRP) cleanups, and post-construction activities.

Director

Jim Woolford . . . . (703) 603–8960

Office of Resource, Conservation, and Recovery

Establishes program policy for the regulation of solid and hazardous waste management throughout the country.

Director

Barnes Johnson . . . . (703) 308–8895

Office of Underground Storage Tanks

Controls releases of petroleum products and other regulated substances from underground storage tanks.

Director

Carolyn Hoskinson . . . . (703) 603–7166

OFFICE OF WATER

Responsible for the agency's drinking water and surface water quality activities, which represent a coordinated effort to restore the nation's drinking waters and surface waters. In addition, furnishes technical direction, support, and evaluation of regional water activities. The office oversees the provision of training in the fields of drinking water, water quality, economic and long-term environmental analysis, and marine and estuarine protection.

Deputy Assistant Administrator

Ken Kopocis . . . . (202) 564–5700
    E-mail: kopocis.ken@epa.gov

Office of Ground Water and Drinking Water

Develops standards for drinking water quality and promulgates regulations to preserve underground sources of drinking water. Monitors and evaluates compliance. Develops and coordinates the agency's ground water policy; distributes grants to states for the development of ground water strategies. Also maintains an information program and develops plans to handle water emergencies.

Director

Peter C. Grevatt . . . . (202) 564–8954
    E-mail: grevatt.peter@epa.gov

Drinking Water Protection

Ann Codrington . . . . (202) 564–3751
    E-mail: codrington.ann@epa.gov

Standards and Risk Management

Eric Burneson . . . . (202) 564–5250
    E-mail: burneson.eric@epa.gov

Water Security

David Travers . . . . (202) 564–4638
E-mail: travers.david@epa.gov

Office of Science and Technology

Coordinates national water-related activities and sets effluent and water quality guidelines. Maintains data systems on water quality, discharge, and programs.

Director

Betsy Southerland . . . . (202) 566–0430
E-mail: southerland.elizabeth@epa.gov

Engineering and Analysis

Robert Wood . . . . (202) 566–1822
E-mail: wood.robert@epa.gov

Health and Ecological Criteria

Betsy Behl . . . . (202) 566–0788
E-mail: behl.betsy@epa.gov

Standards and Health Protection

Sara Hisel-McCoy . . . . (202) 566–1649

Office of Wastewater Management

Develops and oversees programs to protect the nation's watersheds and conserve water resources in cooperation with EPA regional offices, states, municipalities, and the public. Administers permit programs for sewage treatment plants and industrial waste, regulates sewage sludge disposal and storm water collection systems, and manages revolving funds for municipalities to finance publicly owned treatment works.

Director

Andrew Sawyers . . . . (202) 564–0748
E-mail: sawyers.andrew@epa.gov

Municipal Support

Raffael Stein . . . . (202) 564–5385
E-mail: anderson.bill@epa.gov

Water Permits

Deborah Nagle . . . . (202) 564–1185
E-mail: nagle.deborah@epa.gov

Office of Wetlands, Oceans, and Watersheds

Oversees EPA programs that manage, protect, and restore the aquatic sewage systems of inland and coastal watersheds. Promotes wetlands protection through both regulatory and cooperative programs, develops criteria to evaluate ocean-dumping proposals and issuing permits for the dumping of all wastes, oversees the marine sanitation device program, manages grants programs for abating nonpoint source pollution, and oversees surface water quality monitoring and water quality assessment activities.

Director

Benita Best-Wong . . . . (202) 566–1155
E-mail: best-wong.benita@epa.gov

Assessment and Watershed Protection

Tom Wall . . . . (202) 564–4179
E-mail: wall.tom@epa.gov

Oceans and Coastal Protection

Paul Cough . . . . (202) 566–1200
E-mail: cough.paul@epa.gov

Wetlands

Jim Pendergast (acting) . . . . (202) 566–0398
E-mail: pendergast.jim@epa.gov

Regional Offices

REGION 1

(CT, MA, ME, NH, RI, VT, 10 tribal nations)
5 Post Office Square, #100
Boston, MA 02109–3912
(617) 918–1111
Fax (617) 918–1809
(888) 372–7341
TTY (800) 439–2370
H. Curtis (Curt) Spalding, regional administrator
E-mail: EPA-region01-RA@epa.gov

REGION 2

(NJ, NY, PR, VI, 8 tribal nations)
290 Broadway
New York, NY 10007–1866
(212) 637–3000
(877) 251–4575
Judith A. Enck, regional administrator
E-mail: Enck.Judith@epa.gov
(212) 637–5000

REGION 3

(DC, DE, MD, PA, VA, WV)
1650 Arch St. (3PM52)
Philadelphia, PA 19103–2029
(215) 814–5000
(800) 438–2474
E-mail: r3public@epa.gov
Shawn Garvin, regional administrator

REGION 4

(AL, FL, GA, KY, MS, NC, SC, TN, 6 native tribes)
61 Forsyth St., SW
Atlanta, GA 30303–3104
(404) 562–9900
Fax: (404) 562–8174
(800) 241–1754
Heather McTeer Toney, regional administrator
(404) 562– 9900

REGION 5

(IL, IN, MI, MN, OH, WI, 35 native tribes)
77 W. Jackson Blvd.
Chicago, IL 60604–3507
(312) 353–2000
(800) 621–8431
Fax: (312) 353–1120
Susan Hedman, regional administrator
(312) 886–3000
E-mail: hedman.susan@epa.gov

REGION 6

(AR, LA, NM, OK, TX, 66 native tribes)
1445 Ross Ave., #1200
Dallas, TX 75202–2733
(214) 665–2200
(800) 887–6063
Ron Curry, regional administrator

(214) 665–2200

E-mail: curry.ron@Epa.gov

REGION 7

(IA, KS, MO, NE, 9 tribal nations)

11201 Renner Blvd.

Lenexa, KS 66219

(913) 551–7003

(800) 223–0425

E-mail: r7actionline@epa.gov

Karl Brooks, regional administrator

(913) 551–7006

REGION 8

(CO, MT, ND, SD, UT, WY, 27 tribal nations)

1595 Wynkoop St.

Denver, CO 80202–1129

(303) 312–6312

(800) 227–8917

E-mail: r8eisc@epa.gov

Shaun McGrath, regional administrator

(303) 312–6308

REGION 9

(AZ, CA, HI, NV, the Pacific Islands, 148 tribal nations)

75 Hawthorne St.

San Francisco, CA 94105

(415) 947–8000

(866) 372–9378

Fax: (415) 947–3553

E-mail: r9info@epa.gov

Jared Blumenfeld, regional administrator

(415) 947–8702

E-mail: blumenfeld.jared@epa.gov

REGION 10

(AK, ID, OR, WA, 271 native tribes)

1200 Sixth Ave., #900

Seattle, WA 98101–3123

(206) 553–1200

(800) 424–4372

Fax: (206) 553–2955

Criminal Investigation Division hotline (206) 553–8306

Dennis McLerran, regional administrator

(206) 553–1234

E-mail: mcLerran.dennis@epa.gov

▓ CONGRESSIONAL ACTION

Congressional Affairs

Deputy Associate Administrator

Joyce Frank. . . . . (202) 564–5200

Committees and Subcommittees

HOUSE APPROPRIATIONS COMMITTEE

Subcommittee on Interior, Environment, and Related Agencies

B308 RHOB, Washington, DC 20515–6015

(202) 225–3081

HOUSE ENERGY AND COMMERCE COMMITTEE

Subcommittee on Energy and Power

2125 RHOB, Washington, DC 20515–6115

(202) 225–2927

Subcommittee on Environment and the Economy

2125 RHOB, Washington, DC 20515–6115

(202) 225–2927

HOUSE OVERSIGHT AND GOVERNMENT REFORM COMMITTEE

2157 RHOB, Washington, DC 20515–6143

(202) 225–5074

HOUSE SCIENCE, SPACE, AND TECHNOLOGY COMMITTEE

Subcommittee on Energy

2321 RHOB, Washington, DC 20515–6301

(202) 225–6371

Subcommittee on Environment

2321 RHOB, Washington, DC 20515–6301

(202) 225–6371

HOUSE TRANSPORTATION AND INFRASTRUCTURE COMMITTEE

Subcommittee on Water Resources and Environment

B370A RHOB, Washington, DC 20515

(202) 225–4360

SENATE APPROPRIATIONS COMMITTEE

Subcommittee on Interior, Environment, and Related Agencies

SDOB-131, Washington, DC 20510–6025

(202) 224–7233

SENATE ENERGY AND NATURAL RESOURCES

SDOB-304, Washington, DC 20510–6150

(202) 224–4971

SENATE ENVIRONMENT AND PUBLIC WORKS COMMITTEE

SDOB-410, Washington, DC 20510–6175

(202) 224–6176

Legislation

The EPA was established by Reorganization Plan No. 3, an executive order submitted to Congress July 9, 1970, by President Nixon. The House of Representatives defeated a resolution to block approval of the plan creating the new agency; there was no formal opposition to the reorganization in the Senate.

The EPA administers most of the environmental statutes in force. (The Agriculture Department has responsibility for parts of some laws governing pesticide use and the Interior Department has responsibility for some conservation measures related to environmental law.) The following laws are administered by the EPA:

National Environmental Policy Act of 1969 (83 Stat. 852, 42 U.S.C. 4321). Signed by the president Jan. 1, 1970. Established the Council on Environmental Quality (CEQ) and required the development of a national policy on the environment.

Water Quality Improvement Act of 1970 (84 Stat. 94, 33 U.S.C. 1251). Signed by the president April 3, 1970. Made oil companies partially liable (up to $14 million) for oil spills and outlawed flushing of raw sewage from boats. Increased restrictions on thermal pollution from nuclear power plants. Created the Office of Environmental Quality to serve as staff for the CEQ.

Clean Air Act Amendments of 1970 (84 Stat. 1676, 42 U.S.C. 1857b). Signed by the president Dec. 31, 1970. Set initial deadlines for auto emission standards and gave the EPA administrator power to establish the standards. Gave citizens and public interest groups the right to bring suit against alleged polluters, including federal agencies.

Federal Environmental Pesticide Control Act of 1972 (86 Stat. 975, 7 U.S.C. 135). Signed by the president Oct. 1, 1972. Required the registration of pesticides and gave the EPA authority to ban the use of hazardous pesticides.

Federal Water Pollution Control Act Amendments of 1972 (Clean Water Act) (86 Stat. 816, 33 U.S.C. 1254). Vetoed by the president Oct. 17, 1972; veto overridden Oct. 18, 1972. Set up a program of grants to the states for construction of sewage treatment plants. Established industrial and municipal pollutant discharge permit programs.

Marine Protection, Research, and Sanctuaries Act of 1972 (86 Stat. 1052, 33 U.S.C. 1401). Signed by the president Oct. 23, 1972. Outlawed dumping of waste in oceans without an EPA permit and required the EPA to designate sites to be used by permit holders.

Noise Control Act of 1972 (86 Stat. 1234, 42 U.S.C. 4901). Signed by the president Oct. 27, 1972. Gave the EPA the authority to set national noise standards for commercial products. Required the EPA to assist the Federal Aviation Administration in developing noise regulations for airports and aircraft.

Safe Drinking Water Act (88 Stat. 1661, 42 U.S.C. 300f). Signed by the president Dec. 16, 1974. Set standards for allowable levels of certain chemicals and bacteriological pollutants in public drinking water systems.

Toxic Substances Control Act (90 Stat. 2005, 15 U.S.C. 2601). Signed by the president Oct. 11, 1976. Banned use of polychlorinated biphenyls (PCBs) and gave the EPA power to require testing of chemical substances that present a risk of injury to health and the environment.

Resource Conservation and Recovery Act of 1976 (RCRA) (90 Stat. 95, 42 U.S.C. 6901). Signed by the president Oct. 21, 1976. Set safety standard regulations for handling and storage of hazardous wastes and required permits for the operation of hazardous waste treatment, storage, and disposal facilities.

Clean Air Act Amendments of 1977 (91 Stat. 685, 42 U.S.C. 7401). Signed by the president Aug. 7, 1977. Delayed auto emission deadlines for an additional two years and tightened emission standards for 1980 and 1981 model year automobiles. Set new standards to protect areas with clean air from deterioration of air quality. Extended air quality standards for most cities and industries.

Clean Water Act of 1977 (91 Stat. 1566, 33 U.S.C. 1251). Signed by the president Dec. 27, 1977. Created "best conventional technology" standard for water quality by 1984, continued grants to states, and raised liability limit on oil spill cleanup costs.

Comprehensive Environmental Response, Compensation and Liability Act of 1980 (CERCLA) (94 Stat. 2767, 42 U.S.C. 9601 note). Signed by the president Dec. 11, 1980. Created a $1.6 billion Hazardous Substance Response Trust Fund (Superfund) to clean up toxic contaminants spilled or dumped into the environment. Imposed liability for government cleanup costs and natural resource damages of up to $50 million on anyone releasing hazardous substances into the environment.

Hazardous and Solid Waste Amendments of 1984 (98 Stat. 3221, 42 U.S.C. 6901 note). Signed by the president Nov. 8, 1984. Revised and strengthened EPA procedures for regulating hazardous waste facilities. Prohibited land disposal of certain hazardous liquid wastes. Authorized EPA to regulate underground storage tanks containing petroleum products and hazardous materials.

Safe Drinking Water Act Amendments of 1986 (100 Stat. 642, 42 U.S.C. 201 note). Signed by the president June 19, 1986. Revised EPA safe drinking water programs, including grants to states for drinking water standards enforcement and ground water protection programs.

Comprehensive Environmental Response, Compensation and Liability Act Amendments of 1986 (CERCLA) (100 Stat. 1613, 42 U.S.C. 9601 note). Signed by the president Oct. 17, 1986. Provided $8.5 billion for the Hazardous Substance Response Trust Fund (Superfund) for fiscal years 1987 through 1991. Required the EPA to start work on 375 sites within the five-year funding period.

Water Quality Act of 1987 (101 Stat. 7, 33 U.S.C. 1251 note). Signed by the president Feb. 4, 1987. Amended the Clean Water Act of 1972 and expanded EPA enforcement authority. Revised EPA water pollution control programs, including grants to states for construction of wastewater treatment facilities and implementation of mandated nonpoint source pollution management plans. Established a national estuary program.

Federal Insecticide, Fungicide, and Rodenticide Act Amendments of 1988 (FIFRA) (102 Stat. 2654, 7 U.S.C. 9601 note). Signed by the president Oct. 25, 1988. Required chemical companies to determine, over a nine-year period, whether their pesticide products had adverse health effects.

Toxic Substances Control Act Amendments of 1988 (102 Stat. 2755, 15 U.S.C. 2601). Signed by the president Oct. 28, 1988. Authorized federal aid to help states develop programs to mitigate the effects of radon gas in homes, schools, and other buildings.

Ocean Pollution Dumping Act of 1988 (102 Stat. 3213, 16 U.S.C. 1438). Signed by the president Nov. 7, 1988. Amended the Marine Protection, Research, and Sanctuaries Act of 1972 to end all ocean disposal of sewage sludge and industrial waste by Dec. 31, 1991. Established dumping fees, permit requirements, and civil penalties for violations of ocean dumping laws.

Pollution Prevention Act of 1990 (104 Stat. 1388, 42 U.S.C. 13101 note). Signed by the president Nov. 5, 1990. Established the Office of Pollution Prevention in the EPA to coordinate agency efforts at source reduction. Mandated that businesses submit a source reduction and recycling report to accompany annual toxic release inventory.

Clean Air Act Amendments of 1990 (104 Stat. 2399, 42 U.S.C. 7407 note). Signed by the president Nov. 15, 1990. Set new requirements and deadlines for major urban areas to meet federal clean air standards. Imposed new emissions standards for motor vehicles and mandated cleaner fuels. Required reduction in emissions of sulfur dioxide and nitrogen oxides by power plants to limit acid deposition. Prohibited the use of chlorofluorocarbons (CFCs) by the year 2000 and established phase-out schedules for other ozone-depleting chemicals.

Reclamation Projects Authorization and Adjustment Act of 1992 (106 Stat. 4600, 43 U.S.C. 371 note). Signed by the president Oct. 30, 1992. Authorized completion of major water projects. Mandated extensive wildlife and environmental protection, mitigation, and restoration programs.

Waste Isolation Pilot Plant Act (106 Stat. 4777). Signed by the president Oct. 30, 1992. Authorized the storage of certain defense-related nuclear waste at the Energy Department's underground storage facility near Carlsbad, NM.

Small Business Regulatory Enforcement Fairness Act of 1996 (110 Stat. 847, 5 U.S.C. 601 note). Signed by the president March 29, 1996. Required SBA to assist small businesses with regulatory compliance through community information clearinghouses and resource centers; to establish a Small Business and Agriculture Regulatory Enforcement Ombudsman; and to establish a Small Business Regulatory Fairness Board in each SBA regional office.

Food Quality Protection Act of 1996 (110 Stat. 1489, 7 U.S.C. 136 note). Signed by the president Aug. 3, 1996. Amended the Federal Insecticide, Fungicide, and Rodenticide Act of 1947 and the Federal Food, Drug, and Cosmetic Act of 1958 (FFDCA) to allow the EPA to issue an emergency order to suspend pesticides that pose a risk to public health before a pesticide goes through the cancellation process.

Safe Drinking Water Amendments of 1996 (42 U.S.C. 201 note). Signed by the president Aug. 6, 1996. Changed the process by which new contaminants become regulated. Required the EPA to publish a cost-benefit analysis of all proposed regulation.

Chemical Safety Information, Site Security and Fuels Regulatory Relief Act (113 Stat. 207, 42 U.S.C. 7401 note). Signed by the president Aug. 5, 1999. Amended the Clean Air Act to exempt propane and similar flammable fuels from EPA emergency management requirements.

Beaches Environmental Assessment and Coastal Health Act of 2000 (114 Stat. 870, 33 U.S.C. 1251 note). Signed by the president Oct. 10, 2000. Amended the Federal Water Pollution Control Act to require states to establish water quality standards and monitoring programs for coastal recreational areas.

Small Business Liability Relief and Brownfields Revitalization Act (115 Stat. 2356, 42 U.S.C. 9601 note). Signed by the president Jan. 11, 2002. Title I, the Small Business Liability Protection Act, amended the Comprehensive Environmental Response, Compensation and Liability Act of 1980 (CERCLA) to provide small businesses certain relief from liability under CERCLA. Title II, the Brownfields Revitalization and Environmental Restoration Act of 2001, amended CERCLA to provide grants to states for the cleanup and reuse of contaminated industrial sites, or brownfields.

Public Health Security and Bioterrorism Preparedness and Response Act of 2002 (116 Stat. 594, 42 U.S.C. 201 note). Signed by the president June 12, 2002. Amended the Safe Drinking Water Act to require communities with more than 3,330 residents to evaluate the vulnerability of their water systems to a terrorist attack or other act intended to affect the safety and reliability of the water supply. Required the establishment of an emergency response plan based upon the evaluation.

Great Lakes Legacy Act of 2002 (116 Stat. 2355, 33 U.S.C. 1268). Signed by the president Nov. 27, 2002. Amended the Federal Water Pollution Control Act to authorize the EPA to carry out projects and conduct research for remediation of sediment contamination in areas of concern in the Great Lakes.

Water Supply, Reliability, and Environmental Improvement Act (118 Stat. 1681). Signed by the president Oct. 25, 2004. Authorized the EPA and other agencies to protect drinking water quality, restore ecological health, improve water supply, and protect levees. Authorized the EPA to carry out planning activities and feasibility studies for specific projects (dams and reservoirs in California) and to develop and implement ground water management and storage projects and comprehensive water management planning.

Energy Policy Act of 2005 (119 Stat. 594, 42 U.S.C. 15801 note). Signed by the president Aug. 8, 2005. Amended the Energy Policy and Conservation Act to establish a voluntary program at the EPA to identify and promote energy-efficient products and buildings (Energy Star Program). Directed the EPA to establish a program for awarding grants on a competitive basis to entities for the installation of hybrid retrofit and electric conversion technologies for combustion engine vehicles.

■ INFORMATION SOURCES

Internet

Agency website: www.epa.gov. Provides links to many EPA offices, programs, and publications. (*See also Reference Resources and Other Information Sources, below.*)

Telephone Contacts

The EPA maintains many hotline, information, and clearinghouse numbers, which are directed to state and local agencies, the private sector, environmental and health groups, and the public.

Aerometric Information Retrieval
    System (AIRS)......................(800) 367–1044
Antimicrobial Information Hotline......(703) 308–6411
Asbestos Ombudsman Hotline......... (800) 368–5888;
    .... (202) 566–1970 (DC area)
Clean Air Markets Hotline ....(202) 343–9620
Clean Air Technology Center ....(919) 541–0800
Compliance Assistance Centers ....(202) 564–7076
Endangered Species Protection
    Bulletin (Pesticides) Hotline ....(800) 447–3813
Energy Efficiency and Renewable
    Energy Information Center ....(877) 337–3463

Energy Star . . . .(888) 782–7937
Environmental Emergencies Hotline . . . .(800) 424–8802
Environmental Finance
    Information Network. . . . .(202) 564–4994
Environmental Justice Hotline . . . .(800) 962–6215
EPA Test Methods . . . .(617) 918–1881
Inspector General Hotline; Fraud,
    Waste, and Abuse . . . . (888) 546–8740;
    . . . . (202) 566–2476 (DC area)
Ground Water and Ecosystem Information
    Center (GWERIC) . . . .(580) 436–8502
Imported Vehicles and Engines Public
    Help Line. . . . .(734) 214–4100
Local Government Reimbursement
    Program Helpline. . . . .(800) 431–9209
Mexico Border Hotline . . . .(800) 334–0741
National Lead Information Center . . . . . .(800) 424–5323
National Pesticide Information Center . . .(800) 858–7378
National Poison Control Hotline . . . .(800) 222–1222
    (emergencies); . . . . (202) 362–3867 (DC area)
National Radon Hotline . . . .(800) 557–2366
National Response Center, to report oil and chemical spills
    and radiation emergencies . . . . (800) 424–8802;
    . . . . (202) 267–2675 (DC area)
National Service Center for Environmental Publications
    (NSCEP) . . . . (800) 490–9198
National Small Flows Clearinghouse
    Hotline . . . . (800) 624–8301;
    . . . .(304) 293–4191 (West Virginia)
Office of Water Resource Center . . . .(202) 566–1729
Ozone Protection Hotline . . . . (800) 296–1996;
    . . . . (202) 343–9210 (DC area)
Pay-As-You-Throw Helpline . . . .(888) 372–7298
Pollution Prevention Information
    Clearinghouse . . . .(202) 566–0799
Safe Drinking Water Hotline . . . .(800) 426–4791
Small Business Ombudsman . . . . (800) 368–5888;
    . . . .(202) 566-1970 (DC area)
SmartWay Program Hotline . . . .(734) 214–4767
Superfund and EPCRA Call Center, oil information
    center hotline . . . . (800) 424–9346;
    . . . . (703) 412–9810; (DC area)
    TTY . . . .(800) 553–7672
    TTY, DC area . . . .(703) 412–3323
Toxic Release Inventory Information
    Center Hotline . . . . (800) 424–9346;
    . . . . (703) 412–9810 (DC area)
    TTY . . . . (800) 553–7672
Toxic Substances Control Act Hotline . . . . .(202) 554–1404
WasteWise Helpline . . . .(800) 372–9473
Wetlands Information Helpline . . . . (800) 832–7828;
    . . . . (202) 566–1730 (DC area)

Information and Publications

KEY OFFICES

National Service Center for Environmental Publications (NSCEP)
    P.O. Box 42419
    Cincinnati, OH 45242–0419

(800) 490–9198
E-mail: nscep@lmsolas.com
Fax (301) 604–3408
Internet: www.epa.gov/nscep

Distributes information to the public, including numerous EPA publications.

EPA Office of External Affairs
    1200 Pennsylvania Ave. N.W.
    Washington, DC 20460
    (202) 564–8368
    Tom Reynolds, associate administrator
    Melissa Harrison, press secretary

Oversees the agency's distribution of information to inform the public of its environmental initiatives, policies, and compliance assistance programs.

Freedom of Information
    National Freedom of Information Officer
    U.S. EPA, Records, FOIA and Privacy Branch
    1200 Pennsylvania Ave. N.W. #2822T
    Washington, DC 20460
    (202) 566–1667
    Fax (202) 566–2147
    E-mail: hq.foia@epa.gov
    Internet: www.epa.gov/foia

GRANTS
Information on competitive EPA grants can be found on the Internet at www.grants.gov. Information on EPA grants and fellowships, including application instructions and forms, can be obtained at www.epa.gov/ogd. This site also contains links to EPA regional grant offices and links to websites listing grant opportunities from all federal grant-making agencies. For information by phone, call the nearest EPA regional office or the headquarters grants office at (202) 564–5315.

PUBLICATIONS
General information. The National Service Center for Environmental Publications (NSCEP) maintains and distributes EPA publications in hard copy, CD ROM, and other multimedia formats. The publication inventory includes more than 7,000 titles in stock and 31,000 digital titles.

NSCEP also develops and distributes (on the website and by CD ROM) the annual EPA National Publications Catalog. To order publications, see NSCEP contact information under Key Offices, above. For additional sources of Internet publications, see Online, below.

DATA AND STATISTICS
EPA data and statistics are available on a wide range of topics. There is no central office that provides all EPA information; good places to start include the EPA Headquarters Library, the National Service Center for Environmental Publications (*see Publications, above*), and the agency's Internet sites.

Reference Resources

LIBRARIES
The EPA National Library Network is composed of libraries and repositories located in the agency's headquarters,

regional and field offices, research centers, and specialized libraries, as well as Web-based access to electronic collections. The libraries in the network provide access to information about the environment and related scientific, technical, management, and policy information. Detailed information about the EPA National Library Network, including a listing of libraries, may be accessed at www.epa.gov/libraries.

The EPA Online Library System (OLS) is the network's online catalog of library holdings, and the National Service Center for Environmental Publications (NSCEP) is the agency's gateway for EPA publications (*see Online, below*). The National Technical Information Service (NTIS) also holds EPA documents (1–800–553–6847, www.ntis.gov).

EPA National Library Network

EPA Headquarters, MC 3404T
1200 Pennsylvania Ave. N.W.
Washington, DC 20460–0001
E-mail: epalibrarynetwork@epa.gov
Internet: www2.epa.gov/libraries
(202) 566–0556

EPA Headquarters and Chemical Libraries

EPA West Bldg., Room 3340
1301 Constitution Ave. N.W.
Washington, DC 20004
Mailing address:
MC 3404T
1200 Pennsylvania Ave. N.W.
Washington, DC 20460
(202) 566–0556
Hours: Mon.–Fri., 8:30 a.m. to 4:30 p.m.
E-mail: hqchemlibraries@epa.gov

Borrowing privileges are limited to EPA staff and on-site contractors; available to the public via interlibrary loan. All public visitors must have photo identification to enter.

EPA Research Triangle Park Library

109 T. W. Alexander Dr., Room C261
Research Triangle Park, NC 27711
Mailing address:
EPA-RTP Library
U.S. Environmental Protection Agency
MD C267–01
109 T. W. Alexander Dr.
Research Triangle Park, NC 27711
(919) 541–2777
E-mail: library.rtp@epa.gov
Hours: EPA staff—Mon.–Fri. 8:00 a.m. to 4:30 p.m.;
    Public—Mon.–Fri. 9:00 a.m. to 3:00 p.m.

Borrowing privileges are limited to EPA staff and on-site contractors; available to the public via interlibrary loan. Microfiche reader/printers and copy machines are available for public use. All visitors must have photo identification to enter the facility.

Andrew W. Breidenbach Environmental Research Center Library

26 W. Martin Luther King Dr., Room 406
Cincinnati, OH 45268

Mailing address:
AWBERC Library
U.S. Environmental Protection Agency
26 W. Martin Luther King Dr.
Cincinnati, OH 45268
(513) 569–7703
Fax (513) 569–7709
E-mail: CI_Awberc_Library@epamail.epa.gov
Hours: EPA staff—Mon.–Fri. 7:30 a.m. to 5:00 p.m.

Major subject areas of the collection include bacteriology, biotechnology, hazardous waste, risk assessment, toxicology, wastewater treatment, water pollution, and water quality. Not open to the public for walk-ins, but visitors to the reading room are permitted by appointment. Information on the reading room is available at www2.epa.gov/libraries/andrew-w-breidenbach-environmental-research-center-library-services. Borrowing privileges are limited to EPA staff; available to the public via interlibrary loan.

DOCKETS

Dockets relating to EPA actions can be found at the centralized EPA Docket Center–Public Reading Room. Federal dockets from 2001 on are also available at www.regulations.gov. (*See appendix for Searching and Commenting on Regulations: Regulations.gov.*)

EPA Docket Center—Public Reading Room

EPA West Bldg., Room 3334
1301 Constitution Ave. N.W.
Washington, DC 20004
Hours: Mon.–Fri., 8:30 a.m. to 4:30 p.m.
(202) 566–1744
Internet: www.epa.gov/dockets
E-mail: Docket-customerservice@epa.gov

All visitors must have photo identification to enter the facility.

ONLINE

National Service Center for Environmental Publications (NSCEP). EPA's largest electronic documents site, including some documents that are no longer available in print form. See description under Publications, above. Internet address: www.epa.gov/nscep.

Publications on the EPA Site. Publication pages that provide access to full-text publications or information about the publications produced by various offices and programs. Internet address: www.epa.gov/nscep.

EPA Online Library System (OLS). Several related databases that can be used to locate books, reports, journals, and audiovisual materials on a variety of topics. The National Catalog database contains the holdings for most of the 28 EPA regional libraries and laboratories, as well as EPA documents available from the National Technical Information Service (NTIS). Also indexed are documents available from the National Service Center for Environmental Publications; see Publications, above. The OLS website is located at www2.epa.gov/libraries/epa-national-library-catalog.

Ground Water and Ecosystems Restoration Information Center (GWERIC). Maintains a database providing highly specialized scientific and technical information relating to ground water protection and remediation. Accessible via OLS (see above) or by contacting GWERIC, 919 Kerr Research Dr., P.O. Box 1198, Ada, OK 74821–1198; (580) 436–8502.

See Other Information Sources, below, for related online services that are not maintained by the EPA.

RULES AND REGULATIONS

EPA rules and regulations are published in the *Code of Federal Regulations,* Title 5, Chapter LIV, Part 6401; Title 40, Chapter I, Parts 1–1068; Title 40, Chapter IV, Part 1400; Title 40, Chapter VII, Part 1700. Proposed rules, new final rules, and updates to the *Code of Federal Regulations* are published in the daily *Federal Register. (See appendix for information on how to obtain and use these publications.)* The *Federal Register* may be accessed at www.federal-register.gov and the *Code of Federal Regulations* at www .archives.gov/federal-register/cfr; also see the federal government's website www.regulations.gov (*see appendix*).

Other Information Sources

Contaminated Site Clean-Up Information (CLU-IN). Offers numerous databases and publications on hazardous waste remediation projects and technologies at www.clu-in.org.

Education Resources Information Center (ERIC). Provides a database of more than 1.4 million bibliographic records of journal articles and other education-related materials, including some EPA publications, through its website at www.eric.ed.gov. Sponsored by the U.S. Department of Education, Institute of Education Sciences.

Environmental Finance Center Network (EFCN). A network of regional university-based programs in the ten regions collaborating and sharing innovative ways to manage the costs of environmental protection and improvement. For further assistance, contact the EFIN librarian at (202) 564–4994 or www.epa.gov/envirofinance.

Environmental Financing Information Network (EFIN). Provides abstracts of publications and other relevant materials on environmental financing on its website at www.epa.gov/efinpage. For further assistance, call the EFIN librarian at (202) 564–4994 or e-mail efin@epa.gov.

National Environmental Services Center (NESC). Home of the National Small Flows Clearinghouse, the National Drinking Water Clearinghouse, the National Onsite Demonstration Program, and the National Environmental Training Center for Small Communities. Assists small and rural communities with their drinking water, wastewater, environmental training, solid waste, infrastructure security, and utility management needs. Maintains searchable online databases and hosts discussion groups on the website, www.nesc.wvu.edu. Many free and low-cost educational products are available. Staff of certified operators, engineers, and scientists provide technical assistance: call (800) 624–8301 or (304) 293–4191; e-mail info@mail.nesc.wvu.edu; or write to P.O. Box 6893, Morgantown, WV 26506–6893. Supported by the USDA.

National Technical Information Service (NTIS) Database. Supported by the Commerce Department. It lists U.S. government-sponsored research, development, and engineering reports from the EPA and other agencies. Call NTIS at (703) 605–6000, toll-free (800) 553–6847; or visit the website at www.ntis.gov. NTIS Visitor Center is open 8:30 A.M. to 5:00 P.M., Mon.–Fri., 5301 Shawnee Rd., Alexandria, VA 22312.

All the publications below are available from ProQuest, 789 E. Eisenhower Pkwy., Ann Arbor, MI 48103, (800) 521–0600; or visit the website at www.csa.com.

ASFA 3: Aquatic Pollution and Environmental Quality. An abstracts journal devoted exclusively to research and policy on the contamination of oceans, seas, lakes, rivers, and estuaries.

Digests of Environmental Impact Statements. Government-released environmental impact statements are indexed and offered in full text or abstracted.

Environmental Sciences and Pollution Management. More than 6,000 serials covering a wide variety of the environmental science disciplines are abstracted and indexed, including scientific journals, conference proceedings, books, and government publications.

Pollution Abstracts. International technical literature is abstracted and indexed.

NONGOVERNMENTAL RESOURCES

The following are some key resources for information on the EPA and environmental protection issues.

American Rivers

1101 14th St. N.W., #1400
Washington, DC 20005
(202) 347–7550
Internet: www.americanrivers.org

Environmental Defense Fund

257 Park Ave. South
New York, NY 10010
(212) 505–2100
Internet: www.edf.org
Washington office
1875 Connecticut Ave. N.W. #600
Washington, DC 20009
(800) 684–3322

Environmental Working Group

1436 U St. N.W., #100
Washington, DC 20009–3987
(202) 667–6982
Internet: www.ewg.org

Greenpeace USA

702 H St. N.W., #300
Washington, DC 20001
(202) 462–1177
(800) 722–6995
E-mail: info@wdc.greenpeace.org
Internet: www.greenpeace.org

The Keystone Center
1628 Saints John Rd.
Keystone, CO 80435
(970) 513–5800
Internet: www.keystone.org
> **Washington office**
> 1730 Rhode Island Ave. N.W., #509
> Washington, DC 20036
> (202) 452–1138

League of Conservation Voters
1920 L St. N.W., #800
Washington, DC 20036
(202) 785–8683
Internet: www.lcv.org

National Wildlife Federation
11100 Wildlife Center Dr.
Reston, VA 20190–5362
(703) 438–6000
(800) 822–9919
Internet: www.nwf.org
> **Washington office**
> 901 E St. N.W., #400
> Washington, DC 20004
> (202) 797–6800

Natural Resources Defense Council
40 W. 20th St.
New York, NY 10011–4231
(212) 727–2700
Internet: www.nrdc.org
> **Washington office**
> 1152 15th St. N.W., #300
> Washington, DC 20005
> (202) 289–6868

Ocean Conservancy
1300 19th St. N.W., 8th Floor
Washington, DC 20036
(202) 429–5609
(800) 519–1541
Internet: www.oceanconservancy.org

Property and Environment Research Center (PERC)
2048 Analysis Dr., Suite A
Bozeman, MT 59718
(406) 587–9591
Fax (406) 586–7555
E-mail: perc@perc.org
Internet: www.perc.org

Resources for the Future
1616 P St. N.W.
Washington, DC 20036
(202) 328–5000
Fax (202) 939–3460
E-mail: info@rff.org
Internet: www.rff.org

Sierra Club
85 2nd St., 2nd Floor
San Francisco, CA 94105–3459
(415) 977–5500
Internet: www.sierraclub.org
> **Washington office**
> 50 F St. N.W., 8th Floor
> Washington, DC 20001
> (202) 547–1141

The Wilderness Society
1615 M St. N.W.
Washington, DC 20036
(202) 833–2300
(800) 843–9453
Internet: www.wilderness.org

World Wildlife Fund
1250 24th St. N.W.
P.O. Box 97180
Washington, DC 20090–7180
(202) 293–4800
(800) 960–0993
Internet: www.worldwildlife.org

Equal Employment Opportunity Commission

131 M St. N.E., Washington, DC 20507
Internet: www.eeoc.gov

▓ INTRODUCTION

The Equal Employment Opportunity Commission (EEOC) is an independent agency that was established in 1965. It is composed of five commissioners, not more than three of whom may be members of the same political party. The commissioners are appointed by the president and confirmed by the Senate for five-year terms. The president designates one member to serve as chair and another to serve as vice chair. In addition, the general counsel is nominated by the president and confirmed by the Senate for a four-year term.

Responsibilities

The EEOC is charged with enforcing laws that

- Prohibit employment discrimination on the basis of race, color, national origin, religion, or sex.
- Prohibit employment discrimination based on pregnancy, childbirth, or related medical conditions.
- Protect workers against pay discrimination based on sex.
- Protect workers of ages forty or older from arbitrary age discrimination in hiring, discharge, pay, promotions, and other aspects of employment.
- Prohibit discrimination against individuals with disabilities within the federal government.

Also, the commission

- Coordinates all federal equal employment efforts.
- Oversees affirmative action plans to eliminate discriminatory practices.
- Has jurisdiction over federal employees' complaints concerning equal employment discrimination.

Powers and Authority

The EEOC has the authority to investigate, conciliate, and litigate charges of discrimination in employment. It also has the authority to issue guidelines, rules, and regulations and to require employers, unions, and others covered by Title VII of the Civil Rights Act of 1964 to report regularly on the race, ethnic origin, and sex of their employees and members. In cases where a charge of discrimination cannot be conciliated, the EEOC has the authority to file a lawsuit in federal district court to force compliance with Title VII.

Under Title VII, as amended, the EEOC has broad authority. The commission is charged with prohibiting employers from discriminating in hiring on the basis of race, color, religion, sex, or national origin. The law applies to all private concerns that ship or receive goods across state lines and employ fifteen workers. EEOC enforces the Equal Pay Act of 1963, which requires equal pay for equal work, and the Age Discrimination in Employment Act of 1967, as amended. This legislation formerly came under the jurisdiction of the Labor Department.

GLOSSARY

Alternative dispute resolution (ADR)—A less formal and less adversarial method of resolving employment practice disputes, such as mediation.

Charging party—A person or group making a charge of employment discrimination.

Deferral—The process whereby the EEOC turns over a discrimination charge it has received to a state or local fair employment practices agency (706 agency) for action.

FEP agencies—State and local government agencies, known as FEPAs, that enforce fair employment practice (FEP) laws.

No cause—A finding by the commission that a charge of discrimination does not have merit under the law.

Respondent—The firm, union, employment agency, or individual against whom a charge of employment discrimination is filed.

706 agencies—State and local agencies described in Section 706(c) of Title VII of the Civil Rights Act. They are FEP agencies that meet certain criteria. The 706 agencies enforce state and local laws prohibiting job discrimination as well as Title VII on a contract basis with the EEOC.

Systemic discrimination—Employment "systems" that show a pattern or practice of employment discrimination throughout an industry or large company, as opposed to individual acts of discrimination.

The EEOC is responsible for the administration of Executive Order 11478, which protects people with disabilities and aged workers from discrimination in federal government employment. It also administers the employment sections of the 1990 Americans with Disabilities Act, which outlawed discrimination against Americans with disabilities (more than 54 million in 2009) in employment, public services, and public accommodations. It took effect July 26, 1992, for employers with twenty-five or more employees. Beginning on July 26, 1994, the law applied to employers with fifteen or more employees.

The EEOC administers Executive Order 12067, which requires oversight and coordination of all federal equal employment opportunity regulations, practices, and policies. The commission enforces the Pregnancy Discrimination Act, which was written into Title VII and forbids discrimination on the basis of pregnancy, childbirth, or related medical conditions; and Section 501 of the Rehabilitation Act of 1973, which pertains to employment discrimination against individuals with disabilities in the federal government.

The EEOC currently uses a system of "negotiated rulemaking," meaning it tries to bring all potentially affected parties into a working group during the drafting of a proposed rule, rather than relying on traditional procedures of receiving public comment after a rule has been devised and proposed. Under this system, the agency creates a committee made up of labor, industry, and other representatives to work out the details of a proposed rule. While admitting this does not solve all differences, the agency says it reduces legal challenges to new rules.

Employees of the U.S. Congress are protected by the EEOC under the Congressional Accountability Act.

SYSTEMIC DISCRIMINATION

The commission has the authority to investigate and prosecute cases of systemic discrimination—a pattern or practice of employment discrimination throughout an entire company or industry. Systemic Investigations and Review Programs, under the Office of the General Counsel, monitors equal employment opportunity reports from private employers to identify possible cases of systemic discrimination. Regional offices take the worst-first approach by targeting companies whose profiles show the greatest underrepresentation of minorities and women. An investigation is carried out if a pattern or practice of discrimination is discovered.

Based on the evidence developed, one of the commissioners then decides whether to lodge a charge. After a charge has been filed, the office requests additional information from the company about its employment practices. During the investigation, the EEOC tries to make a predetermination settlement. If the matter is not settled and discrimination is found to exist, the regional office issues an administrative decision and tries to settle the matter through conciliation. If this fails, the regional office seeks the commission's authority to litigate the matter in federal district court.

Class action suits, as with systemic cases, deal with patterns or practices of discrimination within an industry or group. Class action cases are initiated by individuals rather than by a commissioner.

Any member of the public or any organization or agency may request that the commission investigate a case of systemic discrimination, but the EEOC is not required to undertake investigations based on outside requests.

AFFIRMATIVE ACTION

Congress enacted Title VII to overcome the effects of past and present employment practices that perpetuated discrimination. In addition to prohibiting specific acts of employment discrimination, Title VII encouraged voluntary affirmative action by employers to eliminate barriers to equal employment opportunity. Since the enactment of Title VII, therefore, many employers, labor organizations, and others have developed programs to improve employment opportunities for groups that previously suffered from discrimination. These programs include efforts to recruit women and minorities and to offer them special training to improve their chances of promotion. Some of these actions and programs have been challenged under Title VII. These so-called reverse discrimination cases charge that affirmative action programs are in conflict with requirements that employment decisions not be based on race, color, religion, sex, or national origin.

The EEOC has published guidelines to help employers develop programs that would encourage increased employment opportunities for minorities and women while at the same time meeting the requirements of Title VII.

PROCEDURES

In 1983 the EEOC decided that it would no longer rely on its rapid charge processing system, which had been instituted in the 1970s, and instead should consider in each and every case whether the charge deserved investigation and perhaps litigation. The processing takes place at the nearest field office or at a 706 agency, with assistance from headquarters. The person making the charge (the charging party) first meets with an EEOC investigator (the intake officer) to determine whether the charge falls under the commission's jurisdiction (that is, discrimination in employment). If it does, a formal complaint is drawn up. Then the field office makes a decision as to whether the charge deserves rapid processing aimed at settlement or extended processing aimed at litigation and assigns it to the appropriate unit. The business, group, or individual against whom the charge is filed (the respondent) is then notified of the charge and asked to provide information. If the respondent fails to provide the information, the commission may issue a subpoena. After the EEOC field office gets the information, it may hold a fact-finding conference attended by both parties. The charging party and the respondent may reach a settlement during this process. If no settlement is reached, or if the charge is in extended processing, a formal investigation then commences.

The formal investigation uses the administrative powers of the commission. Witnesses are interviewed, field visits are made, and relevant documents are examined. The investigator then confers with an EEOC attorney to make a determination of "reasonable cause"—a decision as to whether the charge has merit under the law.

An effort of conciliation (a Title VII term signaling a settlement only after issuance of a decision) among the parties is made. However, according to a 1985 policy statement, the EEOC is committed to seeking "full remedial, corrective, and preventive relief" in every case where reasonable cause was found to believe that there had been illegal discrimination. Yet the statement also said that "reasonable compromise" could be considered during conciliation efforts.

If conciliation does not occur, the investigator and attorney then make a recommendation to the district director. If the director agrees, the case is recommended to the general counsel who, in turn, recommends it to the commission. The commission, at its weekly meeting, makes the final decision on filing a suit. If the commission decides to sue, the case is sent back to the office where it originated and charges are filed against the respondent in federal district court. If the commission decides against litigation, the claimant is informed and issued a right-to-sue notice. Claimants who have been issued right-to-sue notices may file suit on their own, if they wish, but the EEOC will not provide any further assistance.

Age, Pay, and Disability Discrimination

Procedures for filing age, pay, and disability discrimination complaints and charges are similar to those used for Title VII charges. Anyone alleging age, pay, or disability discrimination can file either a complaint or a charge at the nearest EEOC district or area office.

For charges filed under the Equal Pay Act and the Age Discrimination Act, the complaint protects the identity of the individual making the filing, and the respondent is not notified of an investigation until the commission makes a determination of reasonable cause. When a charge is filed, the respondent is notified within ten days and the identity of the person making the charge is not protected.

Charges filed under the Americans with Disabilities Act and Title VII do not carry the same confidentiality provision for employees but, as in all cases, charges are kept confidential from the public. Concurrent charges that allege discrimination under Title VII in addition to pay or age bias also may be filed.

Federal Employment Discrimination

Federal employment discrimination complaints are first made informally to the accused agency's equal employment opportunity counselor, who makes an inquiry and seeks a solution. If the matter cannot be resolved, a formal complaint may be filed with the agency's director of equal employment opportunity or other appropriate official, who investigates the complaint and proposes a disposition. The complainant may request a hearing, in which case the agency asks the EEOC to assign an administrative judge to conduct a hearing. After the hearing, the administrative judge makes a recommendation to the agency head (or designee), who then makes a final decision. The complainant has the right to appeal the decision to the EEOC's Office of Federal Operations or to file a civil suit in federal district court. If dissatisfied with the appellate decision, the complainant still may file a civil suit.

If the complaint is of age discrimination, the complainant may avoid this administrative process by filing a Notice of Intent to Sue and giving the EEOC thirty days' notice of intent to file suit. Complaints of violations of the Equal Pay Act (EPA) must be filed directly with the EEOC at any of its district or area offices. In addition, an EPA suit may be brought in federal court before filing an administrative complaint.

In October 1992 new regulations about the federal agency complaint process went into effect. Under the so-called Part 1614 regulations, EEOC's administrative judges must close new requests for hearings within 180 days. An employee or applicant also generally must contact a counselor within forty-five days of the discriminatory event, but the time is also allowed to be extended when warranted. Part 1614 limited the time spent in counseling to thirty days, with the possibility of extending an additional sixty days if agreed to by both parties. It also required the agency to complete its investigation and issue a notice of final action on a complaint within 180 days of its filing. The EEOC reported that this procedure increased average hearings productivity for each administrative judge by 11 percent during fiscal 1993, its first year of implementation.

In May 1998 President Bill Clinton expanded the list of categories that are protected from federal hiring and contracting discrimination. Along with such classifications as age and gender, Clinton by executive order said sexual orientation could not be the basis of discrimination.

REPORTING REQUIREMENTS

The commission enforces several reporting requirements that apply to employers, unions, and employment agencies. Generally only aggregate and nonconfidential information from these reports is available to the public (*see Other Information Sources, p. 120*).

Private employers of 100 or more individuals must annually file reports (EEO-1 reports) on the composition of their workforces by occupational category, broken down by race, sex, and national origin. All government contractors and subcontractors with fifty or more employees and contracts in excess of $50,000 also must file this report.

Others required to file EEOC reports include

- Local unions with 100 or more members (EEO-3 reports, biennial).
- State and local governments with 15 or more employees (EEO-4 reports, biennial).
- Elementary and secondary school districts that employ 100 or more individuals (EEO-5 reports, biennial).
- Private and public colleges and universities that employ 15 or more individuals (EEO-6 reports, biennial).

Employers are required to post in a conspicuous place a notice that gives a summary of fair employment laws and information on the procedures for filing a charge of employment discrimination.

Background

The EEOC was established by Title VII of the Civil Rights Act of 1964 and began operations July 2, 1965. The creation of the EEOC was the culmination of more than two decades of effort by civil rights activists to establish a federal fair employment agency. In 1941 President Franklin D. Roosevelt set up a Fair Employment Practices Committee (FEPC). Largely advisory, the committee sought to end discrimination in hiring by the federal government and its defense contractors. Four years later, after a bitter debate over appropriations, Congress directed that the agency end its activities in 1946.

President Harry S. Truman in 1948 submitted a civil rights program to Congress calling for a new fair employment agency, but bills to establish such an agency were kept from the floor of both chambers until 1950. During that year the House of Representatives passed a fair employment bill, but a Republican-sponsored amendment, supported by southern Democrats, deleted the agency's enforcement powers. Efforts to pass a stronger measure in the Senate also failed that year.

In 1961 President John F. Kennedy, by executive order, established the Equal Employment Opportunity Committee, headed by Vice President Lyndon B. Johnson. Kennedy told the committee to use its powers "to remove permanently from government employment and work performed for the government every trace of discrimination."

A governmentwide racial employment census was undertaken for the first time, and all government departments and agencies were directed to report to the committee their plans and recommendations for eliminating employment discrimination. The committee sought to persuade corporations doing business with the government to adopt "Plans for Progress," designed to provide for the training and employment of African Americans. Such agreements were voluntary, however, and the reach of the committee's authority was uncertain.

EARLY HISTORY

In 1963, when the drive for civil rights began to dominate national headlines, legislation again was introduced in Congress to create a fair employment agency. It came in the form of an amendment to a civil rights package submitted by Kennedy. With the strong backing of President Johnson, the Civil Rights Act, including a section creating the EEOC, was enacted by Congress in 1964.

As originally structured, the EEOC had authority to encourage compliance with the equal employment provisions of Title VII by using conciliation proceedings. If conciliation failed, the commission could recommend that the U.S. attorney general file suit in federal district court to force compliance. If the attorney general declined to prosecute, the aggrieved individual (the charging party) could file a suit. The commission lacked the power to compel an employer to obey the law.

The enactment of the Equal Employment Opportunity Act of 1972 amended Title VII and gave the commission authority to file lawsuits against private employers, employment agencies, and unions when conciliation efforts failed. It also allowed the commission to file suit in cases of alleged systemic discrimination. Authority to file suit against alleged discriminatory practices in state and local governments, however, was not given to the EEOC; that power remained in the Justice Department.

During the commission's first decade of operation, it gained the reputation of being among the worst-managed government agencies. By 1976 it had gone through six chairs and several acting chairs, as well as a similar number of executive directors. It also was burdened with a backlog that by some estimates exceeded 120,000 cases.

Criticism of the commission came from all sides. Minorities and women asserted that it took so long to process charges that the victims often lost patience and dropped their complaints. Employers and unions, on the other hand, argued that the commission provoked confrontation and was biased in favor of employees. The EEOC also was accused of encouraging preferential hiring and using discriminatory quota systems.

Eleanor Holmes Norton, who was appointed chair by President Jimmy Carter in 1977, instituted several revisions. She reorganized the commission's internal structure and field offices and established a new system for handling complaints. Norton's system, called rapid charge processing, reduced the commission's case backlog, which had been significantly increased by the transfer of age and equal pay regulation from the Labor Department in 1979. By 1981 the commission's backlog had been reduced to fewer than 33,000 cases. The average case required less than three months to process and resolve, as compared with two years under the former procedures.

EEOC IN THE 1980s

During the course of the presidency of Ronald Reagan, the EEOC underwent a complete change in leadership and direction. With the appointment of Clarence Thomas, the assistant secretary for civil rights in the Education Department, as chair in 1982, the EEOC scrapped the use of goals and timetables to promote the hiring of minorities and women. In fact, Thomas was so vehemently opposed to goals and timetables that during his term of office, EEOC attorneys inserted new clauses in some of the consent decrees obtained during the Carter administration. The clauses announced that the EEOC would not enforce any sections of the decrees calling for the use of goals and timetables to increase the hiring of minorities and women.

In 1985 the commission adopted a statement of policy to seek "full remedial, corrective, and preventive relief" in every case where reasonable cause was found to suspect illegal discrimination. That policy statement was widely seen as heralding a shift in EEOC emphasis—away from systemic discrimination cases against large companies or entire industries and toward cases involving discrimination against specific individuals.

Criticism of the agency continued, in large part because of the backlog of cases—due, as some critics charged, to Thomas's belief in litigating as many valid cases as possible. The backlog affected both the private-sector enforcement activities of the commission and its role in enforcing laws against discrimination in federal employment. Congress continued to be frustrated with the federal equal employment opportunity complaint process and pressed Thomas and the commission to come up with a better system.

Federal workers and civil rights organizations condemned the system as containing built-in conflicts of interest. In 1989 Congress introduced a bill to give the EEOC full responsibility for handling discrimination complaints in the federal government, just as it had in the private sector. But Thomas resisted the measure, saying that the agency did not have the money or the staff to handle federal workers' complaints on top of its existing workload.

In September 1987 the Senate Special Committee on Aging made inquiries into the way the EEOC handled claims of discrimination filed under the Age Discrimination in Employment Act (ADEA), focusing on the EEOC's failure to file class action suits that would have a broad impact on discrimination against older workers. At the same time, Senate investigators discovered that the statute of limitations had expired on approximately 7,500 cases and the EEOC had failed to notify the complainants of that fact in many of the cases. To preserve the rights of older workers to sue under the ADEA, in 1988 the House and Senate passed, and President Reagan signed, the Age

Discrimination Claims Assistance Act, giving older workers an additional eighteen months to file a lawsuit once the statute of limitations expired.

In response to criticism about the agency's lack of work on discrimination on the basis of national origin, the EEOC set up "expanded presence" offices—temporary facilities located in churches or other community gathering places in areas removed from the EEOC district offices. Thomas also attempted to mend EEOC relations with the small-business community by starting the Voluntary Assistance Program, in which district offices held seminars for business owners to educate them about antidiscrimination laws.

One final set of events significant to the future course of the EEOC was the six 1989 Supreme Court rulings that narrowed the scope of antibias laws and put the responsibility for proving discrimination on employees rather than the employer. The best known of these decisions was *Wards Cove Packing Co. v. Antonio,* which required the worker to identify a particular employment practice that resulted in an underrepresentation of minorities in the workplace and gave the worker the job of proving the practice was not required in the course of running a business.

CIVIL RIGHTS LEGISLATION

Two major pieces of legislation redefined the work of the EEOC in the 1990s: the Civil Rights Act of 1991 and the Americans with Disabilities Act of 1990. These laws greatly increased the workload and the complexity of cases under the jurisdiction of the EEOC.

Congress first addressed civil rights discrimination issues when it sought to counter the effects of the six 1989 Supreme Court decisions that made it harder for workers to sue their employers for discrimination. While Democrats in Congress proposed legislation to give women and religious and ethnic minorities the right to seek monetary damages in job discrimination cases, the administration of President George H. W. Bush opposed the bill, maintaining that the introduction of monetary damages and a jury trial would turn the EEOC mediation process into an adversarial one. However, on Nov. 7, 1991, Congress passed a compromise civil rights bill that Bush signed. The Civil Rights Act of 1991 allowed limited monetary damages for harassment victims and those discriminated against on the basis of sex, religion, or disability, permitting women for the first time the right to seek limited monetary damages for sex discrimination.

It required the EEOC to establish a Technical Assistance Training Institute to provide training and technical assistance on the laws and regulations enforced by the commission. It also required the EEOC to carry out educational and outreach activities, including targeting those who historically had been targets of discrimination and distributing information in other languages besides English.

The second major piece of legislation, the Americans with Disabilities Act (ADA), was signed into law July 26, 1990. It outlawed discrimination at that time against the estimated 43 million Americans with disabilities in employment, public services, and public accommodations.

The EEOC was responsible for enforcing the sections of the ADA dealing with employment. Although changes that would involve "undue hardship" were excluded, employers were required to make "reasonable accommodations" for workers who have disabilities. The law did not spell out what these accommodations might be.

The ADA created a special challenge for the EEOC because the commission had to develop manuals and pamphlets for use by people with disabilities. This requirement meant publishing materials in Braille or on tape for the blind and expanding the use of telecommunication devices for the deaf. Moreover, the ADA required the EEOC to determine whether certain specific conditions should be regarded as disabilities. For example, persons with acquired immune deficiency syndrome (AIDS) were covered under the law "implicitly," under an interpretation of the Rehabilitation Act of 1973, issued by the Justice Department, which described AIDS patients as disabled. In July 1998 the Supreme Court ruled that those people with the human immunodeficiency virus (HIV), which causes AIDS, were covered by the act. By a 5–4 vote, the Court said it did not matter whether a person had developed symptoms of the disease.

The agency itself made clear the scope of the law in 1997, issuing guidelines stating that mental illness is a disability and that employers must accommodate those suffering from it. The guideline raised the ire of many who worried about unstable workers being protected. For the EEOC, the law meant a broad expansion of its jurisdiction and workload. In subsequent years the EEOC requested increasing appropriations from Congress to keep up with its increased workload under the ADA.

In October 1990 Congress also passed the Older Workers Benefit Protection Act, legislation to reverse a 1989 Supreme Court ruling that allowed age-based discrimination in employee benefits. Regulations dating from 1969 prohibited age-based differentials in benefits unless they were justified by "significant cost considerations." Those so-called equal cost or equal benefit regulations were invalidated by a 1989 Court decision. The 1990 act codified the equal cost or equal benefit regulations. As the act was originally opposed by many business groups, members incorporated a compromise that gave employers exemptions for two widely used early retirement incentive plans.

EEOC IN THE 1990s

In addition to having major legislative additions to its responsibility, the EEOC also remained under public scrutiny with ongoing criticism and investigations. In 1990, when EEOC chair Thomas won confirmation to the U.S. Court of Appeals for the District of Columbia Circuit, some Senate Judiciary Committee members expressed concern about the commission's handling of age discrimination cases and halting of efforts to meet minority hiring goals and timetables under Thomas's stewardship.

Thomas brought the EEOC back into the spotlight a year later, during his Supreme Court nomination hearings. During the initial hearings, Thomas again was criticized on age discrimination; some groups also complained that he failed to challenge gender-based wage discrimination. University of Oklahoma law school professor Anita Hill then came forward to testify in a second set of hearings that Thomas had sexually harassed her while both worked at the EEOC. Thomas denied the charges and later won confirmation to the Court, although not without sparking national dialogue about sexual harassment in the workplace.

The EEOC's guidelines on sexual harassment, ironically, had come to be the accepted workplace standard: "Unwelcome sexual advances, requests for sexual favors, and other verbal or physical conduct of a sexual nature constitute sexual harassment when (1) submission to such conduct is made either explicitly or implicitly a term or condition of an individual's employment, (2) submission to or rejection of such conduct by an individual is used as the basis for employment decisions affecting such individual, or (3) such conduct has the purpose or effect of unreasonably interfering with an individual's work performance or creating an intimidating, hostile, or offensive working environment."

A series of hearings and reports in the early 1990s marked a trail of ongoing criticism of the agency. A General Accounting Office (GAO) report in July 1993 detailed concerns about the EEOC's operations, including the increasing time it took the commission to investigate and process charges, the inventory of charges awaiting investigation, and the adequacy of investigations. The GAO also expressed concerns about the high proportion of findings that the discrimination charges were not warranted and the limited number of litigation actions and systemic investigations initiated by the EEOC.

Another concern had been the hiring and promotion of women and minorities in the federal workforce. In October 1991 the GAO testified before the Senate Governmental Affairs Committee that representation of women and minorities in the federal workforce had improved overall between 1982 and 1990, but the GAO noted that white women and minorities still had fewer numbers in upper-level positions. The GAO recommended that the EEOC require agencies to analyze hiring, promotion, and other personnel action data to identify equal employment barriers better. In March 1993 the GAO still found white women and minorities underrepresented in key higher-level government jobs.

Revisions to the EEOC's structure and procedures continued to be a topic of discussion. In a report to the Senate Special Committee on Aging in February 1994, the GAO warned that the EEOC's workload would continue to increase unless the agency changed its policies and practices. Among the options mentioned in the report were using alternative dispute resolution (ADR) approaches such as mediation to achieve agreement through less formal and less adversarial procedures. The report also suggested that the EEOC could increase its systemic actions by working with constituency groups and making greater use of testers—people who apply for jobs with the sole purpose of uncovering discriminatory hiring practices.

In 1994 President Bill Clinton nominated Gilbert Casellas as EEOC chair. That year the agency's backlog of complaints continued to swell, nearing the 100,000 mark by late 1994. Under Casellas, however, the EEOC made some attempt to answer its critics, through both greater efficiency and increased activism. Coming from a career in corporate law rather than in civil rights organizations, Casellas set up a task force to increase the use of alternative methods of dispute resolution in cases handled by the EEOC.

A second task force, headed by EEOC commissioner Paul Igasaki, recommended that the agency divide complaints into three categories and stop fully examining complaints that were deemed to have little merit. Field offices were given authority to dismiss some complaints and were relieved of the burden of writing letters to explain each dismissal. By April 1995 the EEOC had enacted these recommendations.

The EEOC under Casellas increased both its activism and its pragmatism, resulting in a somewhat mixed and ambiguous record. A case in point was the agency's handling of the ADA, which many critics faulted for a dramatic increase in the number of discrimination cases filed with the EEOC. In April 1995 the EEOC expanded its interpretation of the ADA to include employment discrimination based on a worker's genetic predisposition toward particular diseases or disorders, thereby staking out new authority over a type of case that was anticipated but not yet common. In October 1995, on the other hand, the EEOC refined its guidelines on the ADA to relax the rules on questions about "reasonable accommodations" that employers can ask job applicants: this came in response to businesses' confusion under the initial guidelines.

The EEOC's handling of its most high-profile cases also brought mixed results. In 1996 the EEOC took up a class-type lawsuit against Mitsubishi Motors, alleging sexual harassment of some 500 women at an Illinois factory. In April the company staged a worker rally against the EEOC, but on July 11, 1998, the agency announced it had secured the largest sexual harassment litigation payment in history. The $34 million settlement, along with the company's apology to more than 300 female workers, gave the agency a well-publicized victory.

Ida L. Castro, a former labor lawyer, became the first Hispanic woman to head the agency in October 1998 and quickly showed herself to be an aggressive advocate of workers. In controversial moves, the agency issued new rules in 1999 making clear that a company did not have to know about a particular case of worker harassment to be held liable. The EEOC also ruled in late 2000 that an employer who did not offer contraception as part of an insurance drug benefit was guilty of sexual discrimination.

In other policy guidelines, the agency tackled the salary differentials of male and female coaches at the high school and college level and the rights of temporary employees. In a highly publicized announcement, the agency said pay variances among male and female coaches were acceptable, as long as they could be justified. The guideline addressed the common practice of paying male coaches more than their female counterparts and took into account the fact that men's sports often bring in more revenue than female athletics.

In March 1999 the agency worked out a $2.1 million settlement against a Missouri nursing home that discriminated against Filipino registered nurses. The agency, however, was not involved in a 1999 settlement between African American workers and Coca-Cola Co. The $492.5 million settlement was the largest racial discrimination settlement in history.

In a turnabout in the late 1990s, a series of Supreme Court rulings limited the scope of the commission's enforcement of the ADA. In two cases, one involving a mechanic who suffered from hypertension and another concerning nearsighted pilots, the agency had argued that under the ADA such conditions negatively affect the ability of individuals to gain employment. The Court disagreed, ruling that such workers whose conditions could be corrected by medication or other treatments, such as glasses, were exempted from the law. The Court also ruled that state government workers cannot sue their employers in federal court under the ADA.

In a major victory for the agency, however, the Court in 1999 overturned an appellate court ruling that said the agency did not have the power to impose compensatory damages. The lower court ruling, if left intact, would have stripped the agency of much of its power, backers said. The agency in the latter part of the decade focused its attention on those workers who reported allegations of discrimination. With a nearly double increase in retaliation complaints since 1991, the EEOC issued guidelines in 1997 clarifying that it was illegal to retaliate against workers, or former workers, who file discrimination complaints.

EEOC IN THE 2000s

Until her tenure ended in August 2001, Castro stressed the need to educate employers, especially small businesses, about the ways to avoid ending up on the receiving end of a complaint. Under her leadership the agency urged workers and employers to mediate, rather than litigate, cases. The rate of voluntary mediations rose dramatically.

In fiscal 2000 the EEOC won $245.7 million in settlements. In one case the EEOC successfully filed suit on behalf of a man who was fired by a Ryder Systems subsidiary because he suffered from epilepsy. The man, a former trucker, received $5.5 million. The agency ruled that temporary employment agencies and contracting companies are responsible for ensuring workers with disabilities are treated fairly. In June 2000 the agency secured a $1 million settlement of a class action lawsuit on behalf of twenty-two Hispanic women against Grace Culinary Systems and Townsend Culinary. The agency had alleged wide-ranging sexual harassment against the women at the Maryland food processing plant.

Castro took additional steps to protect immigrant and migrant workers, pointing to statistics that show harassment allegations against workers based on their nationality have been increasing. The agency issued guidelines in 2000 stating that undocumented workers "are entitled to the same remedies as any other workers: back pay, reinstatement if the employee was unlawfully terminated, hiring ... except in the very narrow situations where an award would directly conflict with the immigration laws."

In early 2001 the agency convinced Burlington Northern Santa Fe Railroad to stop testing its workers for genetic defects. The case, supporters said, was an important step toward protecting the medical privacy of workers and complemented a Clinton administration executive order blocking the federal government from basing hiring decisions on such information.

The agency's authority was strengthened in some respects through a 2002 Supreme Court decision. *EEOC v. Waffle House Inc.* affirmed that the EEOC could sue employers who discriminate against workers, even if the workers had signed an arbitration agreement that sought to bar employees from suing their employers for discrimination.

The appointment of Cari M. Dominguez by President George W. Bush in 2001 as the new chair of the commission marked a shift in direction for the agency. In early 2002 Dominguez introduced a five-point plan encouraging the agency to use more cost-efficient techniques. The five elements of Dominguez's plan were (1) proactive prevention of discrimination through educational outreach; (2) cost-effective and timely resolution of charges; (3) strategic enforcement that targets the most egregious cases; (4) expansion of mediation and arbitration techniques; and (5) strict antidiscrimination safeguards at the EEOC for its workers.

Dominguez used the media and the agency's website as low-cost ways to educate the public about discrimination and how to prevent it. Her second stated goal—to streamline and expedite the resolution of cases—was intended to save both time and money. The purpose of Dominguez's third point was to litigate cases that would "provide the greatest benefit to the greatest number of people," such as situations involving widespread, systemic discrimination. An expanded emphasis on mediation and arbitration, which had been used extensively in the Clinton administration as well, was another way that Dominguez believed the agency could reduce the funding and time involved in resolving cases. The fifth point of her plan simply involved making the EEOC a "model workplace" and improving coordination among its offices.

The EEOC addressed 84,442 cases during the 2002 budget year—the highest level since 1995, when it addressed 87,529 cases. In 2003 the number of complaints dropped to 81,293 and then to 79,432 in 2004. With the number of complaints falling, the agency saw a corresponding drop in resolutions during this same period. The total number of cases resolved dropped to 85,259 in 2004, down from 95,222 cases in 2002. Moreover, resolving a complaint in 2004 took an average of 165 days, a sharp drop from the 216 days it took to process a claim in 2000. Dominguez credited part of the reason for this improved timeliness to the agency's increased use of alternative dispute resolution approaches, notably mediation and arbitration, to keep the annual number of case resolutions high.

In 2004 the threat of EEOC court action led Morgan Stanley, one of the biggest U.S. brokerage houses, to settle in a sex discrimination claim for $54 million—the second largest out-of-court settlement in the agency's history. The case involved allegations of denial of equal pay and promotions by 340 women employees of Morgan Stanley's investment banking division.

The agency also was involved in another, high-profile sex discrimination case—against retailing giant Walmart. In June 2004 a federal district court judge in San Francisco ruled that 1.6 million women could proceed to trial in a class action sex discrimination case against the retailer. Walmart appealed the decision, but in February 2007 a federal appeals court affirmed the lower court ruling. However, in June 2011 the Supreme Court reversed the 2007 decision, ruling that the women could not proceed with their class action suit because they could not show that there had been a company-wide policy of gender discrimination. The decision was a huge victory—not just for Walmart but for American business—since it made it harder to bring large class action lawsuits against companies.

In addition to lawsuits against specific companies, the EEOC also was involved in legal actions challenging agency policies. In March 2005 the commission won a legal victory of sorts when the Supreme Court ruled that workers who sued their employers for age discrimination did not need to prove that the bias was intentional. Instead, the Court said plaintiffs needed only to show an employer's policies had a "disparate impact" on older workers. In accepting this less stringent standard, the Court also affirmed the EEOC's long-standing policy in discrimination claims.

A federal district court also backed an agency rule allowing companies to drop promised health coverage for retiring workers who become eligible for Medicare at age sixty-five. The American Association of Retired Persons (AARP), which brought the lawsuit against the EEOC, had argued that the new rule was unfair and inherently discriminatory because it would deny millions of retired workers benefits that their former employers had promised them. Business groups and others defended the rule, arguing that rising health care costs meant that without a Medicare opt-out, many employers would be disinclined to offer health benefits to retirees under age sixty-five. The district court, in February 2005, had blocked the rule. But later that year, in September, the same judge reversed her earlier decision and allowed the new rule change to go forward.

Meanwhile, the agency labored to do its job with a budget that had become flat. During three fiscal years beginning in 2005, the EEOC received $327 million, a significant decrease (after inflation) from its budgets of its first two decades. These reductions took a toll on the agency's workforce, which shrunk from 3,800 employees in 1979 to 2,400 by 2005.

Mindful of these budget constraints, Dominguez continued to look for ways to increase efficiency. On May 10, 2005, she announced that she was streamlining the agency's operations outside of Washington, DC, changing eight of twenty-three district offices into smaller field offices. The move, which took effect on Jan. 1, 2006, did not result in any layoffs, although some positions were eventually eliminated through attrition.

At the same time, Dominguez continued to strengthen the alternative dispute process. She pushed the expansion of the EEOC's voluntary National Mediation Program, under which the agency steers disputes to mediators rather than to courts. In April 2003 the EEOC signed mediation agreements with its counterparts in nine states, including the large states of New York and Florida. Under these agreements, each state equal employment office agreed to provide mediation services for parties in EEOC complaints within their jurisdiction. On May 10, 2005, the agency issued new guidelines aimed at making it easier for people with disabilities who have workplace discrimination complaints to take advantage of the mediation process.

The following year, in October 2006, the EEOC announced an initiative aimed at encouraging other federal agencies to hire more workers with disabilities. The action was prompted by a steep decline in the number of people with disabilities in the federal workforce. From a peak of 31,337 federal employees with disabilities in 1994, the number had dropped to 24,086 by 2004.

The agency addressed this issue again in January 2008 when it released a report indicating that 43 percent of federal agencies with more than 1,000 employees had not established recruitment and hiring goals as specified in a 2003 EEOC management directive. Although the government workforce grew by 135,732 between fiscal years 1997 and 2006, the number of employees with severe disabilities decreased by 4,229, a loss of about 15 percent. The report cited a number of factors for this decline, including lack of training for managers, an increase in contractors who fill jobs at lower pay grades, and managerial "misperceptions" and "bias."

Also in 2006, the agency won a significant victory when the Supreme Court accepted its broad definition of what constitutes retaliation by an employer against an employee who has complained about workplace discrimination. In the June decision, the Court determined that any "materially adverse" action by an employer that might dissuade a reasonable employee from complaining is "retaliation" under Title VII of the Civil Rights Act of 1964. The ruling would make it easier for the agency to act against businesses and other employers who allegedly punish workers who have complained about discrimination.

Also during this time, the board underwent a near complete changeover, most notably with the existing vice chair, Naomi Churchill Earp, becoming chair when Dominguez left the commission. Earp, who had served on the board since 2003, had worked for the commission in the 1980s as an adviser and had later led internal equal opportunity programs at the National Institutes of Health and the Department of Agriculture.

A major setback for the agency occurred in May 2007, when the Supreme Court issued a ruling revoking an important EEOC policy concerning when employees could sue over discrimination in pay. The main federal statute on workplace discrimination, Title VII of the Civil Rights Act of 1964, required employees who accuse employers of unfair pay disparity to sue within 180 days of the discriminatory act. The EEOC had interpreted the law to allow the 180-day clock to start running each time the employee received a paycheck. But the Court ruled that the suit must be filed 180 days after the initial discriminatory act. This meant that employees with grievances going back more than six months could no longer sue under the act.

In August 2008 the EEOC released its Annual Report on the Federal Workforce for the 2007 fiscal year, which showed that discrimination complaints in the federal workplace had dropped slightly, from 16,723 in fiscal year 2006 to 16,363 in 2007. In spite of this decline, the agency expressed concern that the representation of Asians, Latinos, and African Americans in the federal workforce had only slightly increased, while the number of people with disabilities had actually declined. Indeed, these trends had already prompted the commission to establish a number of working study groups to explore these issues.

In October 2007 the first of these working groups was formed to examine how Asian Americans are treated and promoted across the government. This action was prompted, in part, by an audit issued by the Office of Personnel Management (OPM). The OPM audit found that while the overall representation of Asian Americans in the federal government (5.9 percent) was satisfactory when measured against the entire national workforce, relatively few Asian Americans attained high-ranking positions. Indeed, Asian Americans constituted less than 1 percent of the Senior Executive Service.

The EEOC and Social Security Administration established a similar working group in May 2008 to look at hiring and promotion issues facing Hispanics in the federal government. The EEOC estimates that of the 2.6 million people in the government, 7.74 percent are Hispanic, an underrepresentation compared with the presence in the nation's overall labor force. More significantly, Hispanics make up less than 4 percent of federal executives.

In January 2009 the commission released two reports highlighting the recommendations of the Asian American and Hispanic working groups. Both reports recommended holding senior hiring officials as well as senior managers at federal agencies accountable for improving diversity. The documents also recommended providing Hispanic and Asian American federal workers with better training to improve their skills and tasked federal agencies to improve their outreach to minority communities to better inform them about opportunities for federal employment and advancement.

In addition to its work on minority issues, the EEOC also widened the scope of antidiscrimination protection for workers who are caring for children, parents, or other family members in need. In May 2007 the commission released new enforcement guidance related to caregiver discrimination, considered one of the most open and widespread forms of discrimination in the workplace. While such guidance does not have the force of law, courts often use it when interpreting existing antidiscrimination statutes. Among other things, the guidance on caregivers made it clear that employers cannot make "assumptions" about how mothers or other care-giving employees will behave and that any such stereotyping, whether conscious or unconscious, is evidence of employment discrimination.

Some months later, at the beginning of 2008, the agency found itself in the media spotlight as a result of its role in two high-profile job discrimination cases. In the first case, the EEOC announced in January its largest-ever settlement for an individual racial discrimination claim. As a result of agency action, defense contractor Lockheed Martin was required to pay $2.5 million to Charles Daniels, a black aviation electrician who was subjected to verbal harassment and physical threats by white employees while repairing military aircraft for the company in 1999.

While the Lockheed settlement represented a major victory for the EEOC, this triumph was tempered by a public scolding the agency received at roughly the same time from the Supreme Court. The case before the courts involved an age discrimination claim by a former courier for Federal Express, Patricia Kennedy. Kennedy had filed what she thought were appropriate documents with the EEOC initiating her discrimination claim, but neither she nor Federal Express ever heard from the agency, leading Kennedy to miss the deadline to correctly file a complaint. During oral argument before the Supreme Court in November 2007, some of the justices, including Antonin Scalia and John G. Roberts, were publicly critical of the EEOC's perceived lapses in the case, with Scalia telling the agency "to get its act in order." In February 2008 the Court ruled that as a result of EEOC mistakes, Kennedy's case could move forward, even though she had missed the filing deadline.

The first piece of legislation President Barack Obama signed into law concerned pay discrimination, a major responsibility of the EEOC. The Lilly Ledbetter Fair Pay Act of 2009, which became law on Jan. 29, 2009, was named for a retired supervisor at a tire plant who learned too late to bring suit that she was being paid less than her male counterparts. The statute effectively nullified the May 2007 Court ruling pertaining to the length of time that can pass between the alleged discriminatory action and the filing of a lawsuit under the Civil Rights Act of 1964. Under the old law, as interpreted by the Court, such cases had to be brought within six months of the discrimination's onset. Under the new legislation, a worker can bring a lawsuit for up to six months after receiving his or her last paycheck. The new law was expected to produce an increase in the number of gender-related pay discrimination complaints that the agency handled each year.

In early 2009 Obama elevated Democrat commissioner Stuart Ishimaru to be acting chair of the agency. In September, Obama nominated Jacqueline Berrien to be permanent chair, but Berrien, who had worked as a civil rights lawyer for the NAACP and the American Civil Liberties Union, was opposed by some Republican senators who were concerned that she was too liberal. As a result her nomination languished for more than six months. In March 2010 Obama bypassed the Senate and moved Berrien into the top position using a recess appointment, allowing her to serve as chair until the end of 2010.

Just before Berrien's recess term ended, in December 2010, the Senate finally confirmed her, along with two other Obama nominees: Democrat Chai Feldblum and Republican Victoria Lipnic. Feldblum, a law professor at Georgetown University and noted gay rights advocate, was the first openly lesbian member of the commission. Lipnic, a labor lawyer, had served as U.S. sssistant secretary of Labor for Employment Standards during the second George W. Bush administration.

In addition to personnel changes, the agency continued to confront significant staffing, budgetary, and morale problems. All of this occurred at a time when the EEOC was carrying its largest caseload in twenty-five years; more than 95,400 charges of job bias in the private sector were filed in fiscal year 2008 alone, up 15.2 percent from the previous year, and up 26 percent from 2006. In early 2009 the backlog of unresolved cases stood at 73,951, a 35 percent increase from the backlog in 2007. Meanwhile, staff continued to decrease in size, meaning continued delays that could leave complainants vulnerable to retaliation at their jobs. These staffing pressures probably contributed to another problem. In March 2009 the EEOC came under fire for violating the Fair Labor Standards Act. According to a union representing the employees, the commission had a practice of pressuring employees to work overtime without offering them compensatory pay, amounting to a kind of "forced volunteering." Ishimaru, who was still acting chair at the time, said the EEOC would examine its overtime practices and "make any changes necessary."

Still, in spite of these problems, the commission continued to press ahead in its efforts to combat workplace discrimination. Indeed, it made history in February 2009 with its path-breaking proposed rules for the enforcement of the Genetic Information Nondiscrimination Act, a law that prohibits discrimination by insurers and employers based on genetic test results. The first significant expansion of employment discrimination law since the 1990 Americans with Disabilities Act, the genetics bias law arose in response to breakthroughs in genetic testing that allow individuals to check whether they are at risk of certain diseases or other medical conditions. These genetic testing advances have raised alarms that employers and insurers might deny coverage or employment to those whose results showed them to be at greater risk.

EEOC IN THE 2010s

One area of growing concern for the agency was the rise in religious discrimination claims made by Muslim workers. Although they represent a small share of the workforce, Muslim workers made nearly four times as many religious discrimination complaints as Protestants or Catholics, a spike that coincided with rising tensions between Muslim Americans and those of other faiths. Muslim workers filed a record 803 claims in the year ending Sept. 30, 2009, up nearly 60 percent from 2005 and exceeding the number filed in the year following the 2001 terrorist attacks.

The EEOC filed several prominent lawsuits in 2010 on behalf of Muslim workers. Two of the most prominent suits concerned JBS Swift meatpacking plants in

Colorado and Nebraska, where Muslim workers alleged company supervisors disrupted their efforts to worship during Ramadan (the holy month in which Muslims are expected to fast until sunset). Workers claimed that they were harassed when they tried to pray during scheduled breaks, that their requests to pray during bathroom breaks were denied, and that they were terminated in retaliation. In 2013 the courts ruled in favor of JBS Swift, finding that the employees' requests for religious accommodations would have caused an undue burden to the employer, and that the employees were not disciplined or terminated for praying but rather for walking out of the plant and withholding work. Other high-profile EEOC cases involving discrimination against Muslims were filed against entertainment giant Disney and clothing retailer Abercrombie and Fitch. In June 2015, the Court ruled in favor of the EEOC, finding Abercrombie and Fitch should not have failed to hire a Muslim woman because she wore a headscarf for religious reasons. Justice Antonin Scalia wrote, "An employer may not make an applicant's religious practice, confirmed or otherwise, a factor in employment decisions." *(See Current Issues, below.)*

The agency also continued its work fighting what it saw as racial discrimination. In late December 2010, for instance, the commission sued Kaplan Higher Education, alleging that the company discriminated against black job applicants by refusing to hire people based on their credit histories. Although the consideration of credit histories when making hiring decisions is not illegal and is used by many employers, the commission argued that the practice violates civil rights laws when it has the effect of discriminating on the basis of race and is not justified by the needs of the business. In fact, several states, including Hawaii, Washington, Oregon, and Illinois, have banned or severely limited the use of credit reports in hiring, partly out of a rising concern that the practice may be preventing financially pressed and unemployed Americans from returning to the workforce.

Kaplan, bought by the Washington Post Company in 1984, operates a chain of for-profit colleges and training schools around the country. The EEOC said it would seek to stop the credit history practice and win wages, benefits, and offers of employment for people who were not hired by Kaplan because of the alleged wrongdoing. For its part, the company argued that it conducts background checks on all potential employees, including credit histories for job applicants whose responsibilities touch on financial matters, such as giving students financial aid advice. As Kaplan pointed out, the Consumer Data Industry Association strongly defends using credit histories in hiring decisions as employers endeavor to create work environments that are free from fraud and theft. Indeed, in a letter to the agency, Eric J. Ellman, the association's vice president for public policy and legal affairs wrote: "In a climate of economic uncertainty, where employers are likely choosing from a large employment pool, they need to be critically careful about protecting their businesses and their customers."

Ultimately, in January 2013 a federal district court in Ohio dismissed the case after granting Kaplan's motion to exclude an EEOC expert witness. The judge concluded that the way the witness determined which applicants were black was unscientific and unreliable. Kaplan welcomed the ruling, maintaining that the company's practices were consonant with the standard practices of many private companies and even some government agencies.

Meanwhile, many labor experts during this time worried that the rise in unemployment following the 2007–2008 recession had left workers in many industries vulnerable to layoffs and hiring discrimination. In particular, these experts said, employment pressures had led to an increase in age discrimination, a charge that seemed substantiated by the fact that the number of discrimination claims with the EEOC by older workers rose by 30 percent, from 2007 to 2008 alone.

Pro-labor and civil rights advocates argued that many employers had fallen prey to the stereotype that older workers are more costly and less adaptable to change. Subsequently, when downsizing decisions were made, older workers were often the first to be let go, regardless of their long-term contributions to the companies or organizations. While the Age Discrimination in Employment Act of 1967 prohibits age discrimination against workers aged forty and older, many labor advocates and others claimed that the effectiveness of the law has been severely curtailed by a 2009 Supreme Court decision that made it harder to prove age discrimination. In that case, *Gross v. FBL Financial Services,* the Court ruled that workers claiming they were let go due to age discrimination had the burden of showing that the discrimination was the major factor in the dismissal. Previously, some lower federal courts had ruled that the 1967 act allows workers to successfully sue for age discrimination even if they show that the employer's discriminatory behavior was only one of a number of factors leading to the employee's dismissal.

In the wake of the *Gross* decision as well as the rise in age discrimination claims, then chair Ishimaru felt compelled to speak out against what he saw as a crisis in the American workplace. "Age discrimination is an equal opportunity plague," he said. "It is not limited to members of a particular class or a particular race. It is not limited to particular industries or particular regions. And it is not limited to a particular gender."

But business groups applauded the *Gross* decision, saying that it would cut down on the number of frivolous claims by disgruntled employees who had been legitimately let go. Small businesses were particularly susceptible to frivolous age discrimination claims, they said, because they often lack the resources to mount an effective legal defense and so end up settling out of court even when former workers had tenuous claims.

Meanwhile, the agency reported that more workers had been complaining of employer discrimination than ever before, a trend that was linked to widespread layoffs and a tough job market. Accusations of workplace discrimination soared to 99,922 in the year ending September 30, 2010, up from 93,277 the previous year, an increase of 7.2 percent. The largest increase was from individuals who said they had been discriminated against because of a disability, a spike that may have been due to recent changes in the legal definition of disability that makes it more expansive.

A similar uptick in claims occurred following the 2001 recession, and many employers this time around argued that many of these extra cases were baseless and were made by disgruntled workers or applicants with few or no job opportunities. This seemed to be supported by the fact that there was an actual decline in the number of enforcement suits (as opposed to claims) that were filed by the commission and resolved in federal courts in 2010. In addition, some workers may have been preemptively filing claims if they thought they were about to be laid off. Workers knew that once they filed a discrimination charge with the EEOC they were legally protected from retaliation by their employers, making it much more difficult for employers to fire them until the claim was resolved.

Workers countered that the poor job climate brought out the often hidden prejudices of employers, particularly in hiring. Women felt they were being passed over in favor of men; blacks believed they were being passed over for whites and Hispanics; and older workers pointed to the preference for younger, and often lower-paid, employees.

Noting the tough job environment, the Obama administration pushed the commission to be more aggressive in pursuing claims of discrimination, particularly gender discrimination. "More enforcement will happen," promised Andrea Baran, supervisory attorney in the agency's Arizona district office, adding that the agency did not need a formal complaint by a woman to begin an investigation.

Pressure on gender issues also came from outside the government, as civil and woman's rights activists pressured the commission to focus more on battling what they claimed was a growing wage gap between men and women. Indeed, in spite of the passage of the EPA a few years before, companies were still offering lower starting salaries to women. In 2011, it was reported that women made 20 cents less on the dollar than their male counterparts. According to a 2011 GAO report, the situation was less pronounced in the federal government, where women earned 11 cents less on the dollar than their male counterparts. The General Schedule (GS), the government's highly structured job and pay classification system, was credited with lessening the gender pay disparity. Still, while the disparity might be smaller in the federal government, it was not insubstantial. In addition, the GAO reported, women continued to be underrepresented in government leadership posts.

There were other problems in the federal workforce too. Perhaps due to the expectation that the federal government would be a "model workplace," federal job discrimination complaints increased nearly 4 percent in fiscal year 2010, with management retaliation as the most common allegation. Dexter Brooks, director of EEOC's federal-sector programs, noted to the commission that this was a serious concern and cautioned federal agencies to ensure that reprisals were not the typical response to employees who lodged discrimination complaints. Outstripping all agencies and cabinet-level departments in complaints was the U.S. Postal Service. Postal employees make up 18.6 percent of the federal workforce, but they accounted for a whopping 31.2 percent of all discrimination complaints filed in 2010. Overall, filings of job bias both in and outside of the public sector hit an all-time high in 2011—99,947 allegations were filed, ranging from claims of religious and disability discrimination to discrimination on the basis of a person's genetic history. This was the largest number of claims since the Civil Rights Act of 1964 was passed.

Meanwhile, in July 2011 the EEOC, as part of its efforts to fight age discrimination, made headlines when it announced that manufacturing giant 3M had agreed to pay $3 million to older workers it had laid off. The company, which publicly admitted no wrongdoing, also pledged to completely overhaul its employment policies to ensure that older employees were treated fairly.

The agency was also involved in a high-profile disability discrimination and religious rights case, *EEOC v. Hosanna-Tabor Lutheran Church and School,* which came before the Supreme Court in 2011. In the landmark lawsuit, the EEOC and a disabled teacher sued a Lutheran day school claiming the teacher had been dismissed in violation of the Americans with Disabilities Act (ADA). The Lutheran school did not dispute that the teacher's disability (in this case, narcolepsy) was partly responsible for her dismissal. However, the school argued that lower courts have long recognized that laws like the ADA do not apply when churches and other religious institutions are exercising their First Amendment right to hire and fire employees who have important religious functions (like clergy) without government interference—a practice known as the "ministerial exception." The Supreme Court agreed with the school, handing religious-rights activists a major victory—and civil and disability rights supporters, as well as the agency—a major judicial defeat.

But while the commission may have been disappointed with the Supreme Court's decision in *Hosanna-Tabor,* it was very pleased after President Obama issued a long-awaited executive order regarding federal workforce diversity. The order, which was issued in August 2012, called for a coordinated, governmentwide strategic plan to promote inclusion and diversity. The EEOC, along with the Office of Personnel Management and the Office of Management and Budget, was required to issue the strategy within 90 days, with specific plans from each federal agency or department due 120 days after that.

The president's order may have been prompted by the findings of a new book—*Documenting Desegregation*—written by sociologists Kevin Stainback and Donald Tomaskovic-Devey—which underscored the need for more practical mechanisms for achieving the aims of the Civil Rights Act. The authors analyzed the trajectory of antidiscrimination efforts in workplaces from 1964 to 2005, noting that the pace of change was very uneven and was often negatively impacted by a host of outside factors, from prevailing political trends to changing human resources practices to specific legislation aimed at increasing workplace efficiency. The authors also noted what they termed "predictable patterns" in positions of authority within organizations, stating, "White men are often in positions in management over everyone; white women tend to supervise other women; black men to supervise black men, and black women tend to supervise black women." A separate report from the Federal Equal Opportunity Recruitment Program backed up many of these claims with numbers. According to the report, whites still hold more than 81 percent of senior-level pay positions, while African Americans hold only 7 percent, and Latinos a mere 4 percent. In addition, women constitute only 31 percent of senior-level positions.

In 2012 the agency also updated its policy for employers who are considering hiring someone with a criminal background, making it more difficult for them to use background checks to systematically rule out anyone with a prior criminal record. Arguing that blanket exclusion practices can be discriminatory, the agency called for employers to conduct individualized assessments that looked at a number of other factors, such as the nature and gravity of the criminal offense, the amount of time that had passed since the offense was committed, and the nature of the job applied for. The commission was prompted to change its ruling in part because of current incarceration rates, where one in six Hispanic men and one in three African American men are expected to serve time in prison compared with one in seventeen white men. The higher conviction rates among blacks and Hispanics could unfairly impact their employment chances, the EEOC asserted. The new guidance, which applies to companies with more than fifteen employees, requires employers to establish procedures to show that they are not using criminal records to discriminate by race or national origin. The agency also recommends that employers distinguish between "arrests" and "convictions," arguing that arrests are not proof of criminal conduct. An employer can, however, investigate the conduct that led to the arrest and make an employment decision if that conduct makes the individual unfit for the position.

The new rules concerning felons are not without controversy, especially at a time when more than 90 percent of employers conduct criminal background checks of applicants, up 51 percent since 1996. Andrea Herran, a human resources consultant in the Chicago area, argued that the new rules would subject small businesses to a legal quagmire, especially those businesses with employees that work in the field, which makes companies liable for the actions of their employees in a client's home or office. Others find the criteria too subjective and painstaking—first an employer has to decide which criminal convictions might rule out a potential job applicant for a specific job and then judge each prospect against the job in question.

Also in December 2012, the Supreme Court handed federal employees who allege workplace discrimination a big victory. In *Kloeckner v. Solis,* a unanimous Supreme Court ruled that a federal employee who claims to have been a victim of job-related discrimination can, after EEOC review, take the case directly to federal district court instead of having to appeal to a special federal tribunal first. The decision makes it easier and faster for federal workers with discrimination claims to get a ruling on the merits.

Also in 2012, the EEOC broke new ground in the area of sex discrimination when it ruled that the Civil Rights Act protects transgender people from sexual discrimination in the workplace. The ruling stemmed from a case involving Mia Macy, a military veteran and former police detective, who had been promised a job at the Bureau of Alcohol, Tobacco, Firearms, and Explosives in early 2011. Later that year, after making the decision to transition from male to female, Macy informed officials at the bureau that she intended to legally live as a woman. Shortly after that, she was told that the position was no longer available but later learned that the position had been filled by a different candidate.

Macy filed a complaint with the EEOC in 2011. Initially, the agency responded by denying the complaint, saying that transgender people were not covered under EEOC complaint procedure. But a year later, the commission reversed itself and ruled that transgender people are protected under the act.

In the wake of the EEOC ruling, the Department of Health and Human Services issued a letter clarifying that the provisions in the Affordable Care Act prohibiting sex discrimination in health insurance also apply to transgender people. In the past, insurers had often denied transgender individuals coverage, claiming they have a preexisting condition. Under the new health law, which took effect in 2014, insurers could no longer deny coverage on that basis. However, the law does not require insurers to cover surgery costs related to the actual gender transition, only to health issues that may follow.

In December 2012 the EEOC approved a new strategic enforcement plan for 2013–2016. The plan noted that over the next few years, the agency's priorities would be to fight discrimination in hiring and pay, as well as to combat sexual and other kinds of harassment in the workplace. The inclusion of pay in addition to hiring as a priority in the strategic enforcement plan surprised some, as it had not been included in previous plans or even in the original draft of this latest one. However, President Obama drew attention to the issue as a priority when, at the very beginning of his first term, he signed the Lilly Ledbetter Fair Pay Act early in 2008.

The question of workplace discrimination came up a few months later, in March 2013, when the agency issued a report detailing long-standing obstacles for African Americans in the federal workforce. Among the obstacles cited by the EEOC report was a lack of adequate mentors for African American employees and insufficient training for black federal workers. The report also called on Congress to give the EEOC greater authority to enforce antidiscrimination laws within the federal government.

At the same time the agency was calling for more authority, however, it was chaffing under the requirements of the budget sequester and considering furloughing some employees. At $367 million, the agency's presequester budget for fiscal 2013 was already unchanged from its 2011 level. The sequester, which imposed 5 percent across-the-board cuts in spending at all federal agencies, created new pressures at the EEOC. Furloughs could increase the already sizable backlog of discrimination cases by 40 percent, the agency warned.

In the late spring and early summer of 2013, all EEOC employees were required to take five days off without pay. Due to some last minute cuts elsewhere in the commission budget, the furlough was only half as long as originally planned. In part because of the shorter furloughs, the impact on the discrimination caseload turned out to be minimal, the commission later said.

In May 2013 the commission won a landmark intellectual disability case in an Iowa state court. The case involved 32 mentally disabled men who had worked for years at a turkey processing plant in Atalissa, Iowa. The men, were paid $65 a month and given room and board by their employer, Henry's Turkey Service. The EEOC charged that the company was violating the Americans with Disabilities Act by not only grossly underpaying the men, but regularly physically and emotionally abusing them in order to cow them into continuing to work for low wages and accepting poor living conditions.

A jury awarded $7.5 million to each of the 32 workers, for a total of $240 million. The staggering award was the largest in a lawsuit in EEOC history. However, the judge reduced the total award to $1.6 million due to a state law capping discrimination damage awards. Even that much lower amount will probably not be paid in its entirety, as Henry's Turkey Service had gone out of business several years before. Still, the verdict was seen as a victory for mentally disabled people, many of whom work in difficult menial jobs for low pay.

A month after the Henry's Turkey Service verdict, the Supreme Court handed the commission a major defeat when it issued two rulings that effectively made it harder for workers to prove employment discrimination. One ruling, *Vance v. Ball State University*, narrowed the definition of what constitutes a "supervisor," rejecting the definition that the EEOC had crafted as someone who is authorized to take "tangible employment actions." Writing for the majority, Justice Samuel Alito determined that the EEOC's definition was too vague and that a supervisor ultimately was someone with the ability to hire and fire workers. This narrower definition is important because if someone who discriminates against an employee is not a supervisor, the company cannot be held liable for that person's actions unless the aggrieved worker shows that the employer knew of the discriminatory actions and did not act to stop them.

In the second case, *University of Texas Southwestern Medical Center v. Nassar*, the Court toughened the standard of proof used when employees try to prove their employers retaliated against them after they claimed they were discriminated against. Prior to the ruling, an employee suing for discrimination could claim retaliation as well if they could show that the retaliation was "motivated" by the employee's discrimination claim. But the Court in *Nassar* said that employees claiming retaliation had to show that their discrimination claim was the "determining factor"—a harder standard to meet—in their employer's subsequent actions.

In the fall of 2013 the commission filed a number of lawsuits against big employers, including Honeywell, arguing that their "employee wellness plans" were coercive rather than voluntary and that they violated the Americans with Disabilities Act (ADA). Many employers reward their employees with reduced health insurance premiums if they participate in wellness programs and, in certain circumstances, can even penalize those who do not take part in the programs with higher premiums. The commission contends that these policies are in direct violation of the ADA, because they coerce and penalize those who do not take part in a wellness program.

The commission's wellness lawsuits have run into some opposition from Congress and the Obama administration, in part because the Affordable Care Act encourages the use of wellness plans—even providing financial incentives for employers to create such plans—as a way to cut health care costs. So far, courts have not been sympathetic to the EEOC's position. While none of the lawsuits has yet gone to trial, requests by the commission to grant emergency relief and shut down certain wellness programs have all been denied.

In July 2014 the commission issued two new sets of guidelines aimed at helping both men and women with childbearing as well as childrearing. One set of guidelines called on employers to give fathers the same parental leave rights as mothers. The guidelines, which merely clarified existing federal laws, recognized that women might still need more time, due to medical issues related to pregnancy and birth. But, the commission stated, in seeking to take time off for child care, a workplace's policy should be the same for both men and women.

The set of second guidelines were aimed at ensuring that employers provide reasonable accommodations to pregnant women. Again, the new guidelines did not make new law, only clarified and explained the real world application of a patchwork of existing federal antidiscrimination statutes. For instance, the guidelines made it clear that workers cannot be demoted or fired after they tell their employers they are pregnant. They also reminded employers that they must allow pregnant workers to take sufficient bathroom breaks. Perhaps most importantly, the guidelines stated that pregnancy-related conditions, such as lactation, could be considered a disability under the Americans with Disabilities Act and should be treated as such.

The new guidelines are, in part, a response to an increase in pregnancy-related complaints filed with the agency. From 1997 to 2011 the annual number of pregnancy discrimination complaints has increased by 46 percent, said EEOC general counsel P. David Lopez in the summer of 2014. The issue also has caught the attention of the White House, where President Obama called on Congress to pass more rigorous antidiscrimination protections for pregnant workers.

The commission's new pregnancy guidelines came as the Supreme Court was preparing to hear arguments in an important case involving the rights of pregnant workers. The case, which was heard by the Court in December 2014, concerns a pregnant United Parcel Service (UPS) package handler who, on the advice of her doctor, had requested to be transferred to a less physically strenuous job. UPS refused to do so and, instead, forced the package handler, Peggy Young, to take unpaid leave.

At the end of March 2015 the high court ruled with Young and against UPS. The justices stated that the Pregnancy Discrimination Act of 1978, which prohibits discrimination on the basis of pregnancy, means that a pregnant worker must be given the same leeway on the job as someone who is temporarily disabled.

Current Issues

In late February 2015 the Supreme Court heard oral arguments in another employment discrimination case, this one involving alleged religious discrimination. The case—*EEOC v. Abercrombie and Fitch*—centers on how far an employer needs to go to accommodate an employee's religion. It was prompted after clothing retailer, Abercrombie, decided not to hire Samantha Elauf because she did not meet the company's dress code. Elauf, who is a Muslim, wore a headscarf to her interview for a job as a sales clerk at a store owned by the company.

Abercrombie's dress code requires that store employees not wear hats or headgear of any kind. The company says that Ms. Elauf never specifically requested to be exempted from the requirement for religious or other reasons. Elauf and the EEOC, which is suing the retailer on her behalf, say that someone's religious liberty rights do not disappear just because they are not asserted. In addition, they argued, Abercrombie had an obligation to inquire about the headscarf and ask Ms. Elauf whether she would be wearing it at work.

The case, which was decided in June 2015, will dramatically impact the law of religion in the workplace. Are employers required to accommodate an employee's religion, even if he or she doesn't assert rights to it? Abercrombie and other companies say that if the answer is "yes," it would burden businesses by forcing them to constantly guess as to an employee's religious needs even when that person is silent.

Around the same time the Abercrombie case was being argued, pressure was mounting to build on and expand the EEOC's 2012 ruling requiring employers with 15 or more employees to lessen the importance of criminal background checks in hiring. A new report from the National Employment Law Project, an employee advocacy group, urged President Obama to make the federal government a model in hiring more ex-convicts. Along with other advocacy and civil rights groups, NELP asked the president to issue an executive order requiring all federal agencies to make a conditional job offer to all potential employees before conducting a criminal background check.

Meanwhile, the agency continued to make news, launching a high profile lawsuit in a state court in Oregon against nationwide restaurant chain, Ruby Tuesday. The suit, which was filed in February 2015, alleges that the restaurant discriminated against men in seeking to hire wait staff for lucrative positions at its Park City, Utah, restaurant as well as eateries in Arizona, Colorado, Iowa, Missouri, Minnesota, Nebraska, Nevada, and Oregon. The firm explicitly stated its preference for women in its advertisements for the jobs. The lawsuit is not expected to go to trial until at least 2016.

■ AGENCY ORGANIZATION

Biographies

JENNY R. YANG, CHAIR

Appointment: Nominated by President Barack Obama on Sept. 1, 2014; confirmed by the Senate on April 25, 2013, for a term expiring July 1, 2017.

Education: Cornell University, B.A. in government; New York University School of Law, J.D.

Profession: Lawyer.

Political Affiliation: Democrat.

Previous Career: Ms. Yang was a partner of Cohen, Milstein, Sellers & Toll PLLC. She joined the firm in 2003 and served as chair of its hiring and diversity committee. From 1998 to 2003 she served as a senior trial attorney with the U.S. Department of Justice, Civil Rights Division, Employment Litigation Section. Before that she worked at the National Employment Law Project to enforce the workplace rights of garment workers. Ms. Yang clerked for the Hon. Edmund Ludwig on the U.S. District Court for the Eastern District of Pennsylvania. At the New York University School

Equal Employment Opportunity Commission

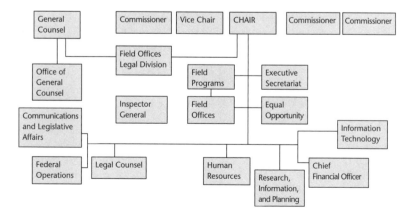

of Law, she was a note and comment editor of the Law Review and a Root-Tilden Public Interest Scholar.

CONSTANCE S. BARKER, COMMISSIONER

Appointment: Originally nominated by President George W. Bush on March 31, 2008; unanimously confirmed by the Senate June 27, 2008, to a term expiring July 1, 2011. Renominated for a second term by President Barack Obama; confirmed by the Senate to a term expiring July 1, 2016.

Born: Florence, Ala.

Education: University of Notre Dame, B.A., 1973; University of Alabama, J.D., 1977.

Profession: Lawyer.

Political Affiliation: Republican.

Previous Career: Barker provided advice regarding the prevention of discrimination complaints and defended clients in employment discrimination lawsuits. Her public sector experience includes four years as an assistant district attorney for the 11th and 13th Judicial Circuits of Alabama and eleven years as the general counsel for the Mobile County Public School System.

CHAI R. FELDBLUM, COMMISSIONER

Appointment: Nominated by President Barack Obama and confirmed by the Senate for a term expiring July 1, 2013. Nominated by Barack Obama for a second term ending July 1, 2018.

Born: New York, N.Y.

Education: Barnard College, B.A.; Harvard Law School, J.D., 1985.

Profession: Lawyer, educator.

Political Affiliation: Democrat.

Previous Career: Feldblum was a professor of law at the Georgetown University Law Center where she had taught since 1991. At Georgetown, she founded the Law Center's Federal Legislation and Administrative Clinic. She also founded and co-directed Workplace Flexibility 2010, a policy enterprise focused on finding common ground between employers and employees on workplace flexibility issues. As legislative counsel for the American Civil Liberties Union from 1988 to 1991, Feldblum was involved in drafting and negotiating the Americans with Disabilities Act of 1990. Later, as a law professor representing the Epilepsy Foundation, she was instrumental in the drafting and negotiating of the ADA Amendments Act of 2008. Feldblum has also worked to advance lesbian, gay, bisexual, and transgender rights, has been one of the drafters of the Employment Nondiscrimination Act, and is the first openly lesbian commissioner of the EEOC.

VICTORIA A. LIPNIC, COMMISSIONER

Appointment: Nominated on Nov. 3, 2009, by President Barack Obama; confirmed by the Senate for a term expiring July 1, 2015.

Born: Carrolltown, Pa.

Education: Allegheny College, B.A.; George Mason University School of Law, J.D.

Profession: Lawyer.

Political Affiliation: Republican.

Previous Career: Before coming to the EEOC, Lipnic was counsel to the law firm of Seyfarth Shaw LLP in its Washington, DC, office. She had worked with federal labor and employment laws, most recently as the U.S. Assistant Secretary of Labor for Employment Standards, a position she held from 2002 until 2009. In that position, she oversaw the Wage and Hour Division, the Office of Federal Contract Compliance Programs, the Office of Workers' Compensation Programs, and the Office of Labor Management Standards. Under her tenure, the Wage and Hour Division revised regulations regarding overtime under the Fair Labor Standards Act and reissued regulations under the Family and Medical Leave Act, and the Office of Federal Contract Compliance Programs issued new guidance and regulations for evaluating compensation discrimination. Her government experience also included service as workforce policy counsel to the then majority (Republican) members of the Committee on Education and the Workforce in the U.S. House of Representatives. She had previously served as in-house counsel for labor and employment matters to the U.S. Postal Service for six years. She also served as a special assistant for business liaison to the U.S. Secretary of Commerce, Malcolm Baldrige.

CHARLOTTE A. BURROWS, COMMISSIONER

Appointment: Nominated by President Barack Obama on Sept. 12, 2014; confirmed by the Senate on Dec. 3, 2014, to serve a term expiring July 1, 2019.

Education: Princeton University, A.B.; Yale Law School, J.D.

Profession: Lawyer.

Political Affiliation: Democrat.

Previous Career: Prior to her appointment at the EEOC, Ms. Burrows served as associate deputy attorney general at the Department of Justice (DOJ), where she worked on a broad range of legal and policy issues. She previously served as general counsel for Civil and Constitutional Rights to Senator Edward M. Kennedy on the Senate Committee on Health, Education, Labor, and Pensions in 2009, and on the Senate Judiciary Committee from 2007 to 2008, after having served as legal counsel on the Senate Judiciary Committee from 2003 to 2007. Prior to that, Burrows served in the Civil Rights Division's Employment Litigation Section at DOJ, first as a trial attorney, and later as special litigation counsel and then as deputy chief. She served as a judicial clerk for the Honorable Timothy K. Lewis of the U.S. Court of Appeals for the Third Circuit and an associate at Debevoise & Plimpton.

Headquarters and Divisions

COMMISSION

The commission is responsible for receiving and investigating charges of employment discrimination. Individual commissioners may initiate charges if they receive information that indicates the law has been violated. The commission approves the filing of lawsuits under Title VII of the Civil Rights Act of 1964, as amended; the Equal Pay Act of 1963; the Age Discrimination in Employment Act of 1967; and the Americans with Disabilities Act of 1990. It conducts public and closed hearings on employment discrimination in various industries and on proposed employment guidelines. It also rules on the designation of state and local 706 agencies and makes final judgments on appeals of denials of Freedom of Information Act requests. The commission reviews selected decisions of the Merit Systems Protection Board in which federal employment discrimination is an issue.

The chair, as executive officer, is responsible for the implementation of commission policy and the supervision of the commission staff. The chair recommends policies, procedures, and programs for consideration by the commission.

Chair

Jenny R. Yang. (202) 663–4002
E-mail: jennyyang@eeoc.gov
TTY. . . . . (202) 663–4141

Vice Chair

Vacant

Commissioners

Chai Feldblum . . . . (202) 663–4090
E-mail:chai.feldblum@eeoc.gov
Victoria A. Lipnic (202) 663–4099 or (202) 663–4271
E-mail: victoria.lipnic@eeoc.gov
Constance S. Barker . . . . (202) 663–4027
E-mail: constance.barker@eeoc.gov
Charlotte A. Burrows . . . . (202) 663–4052
E-mail: charlotte.burrows@eeoc.gov
TTY. . . . . (202) 663–7129

OFFICE OF CHIEF FINANCIAL OFFICER

Establishes, monitors, and maintains control over federal funds appropriated for commission operations. Responsible for accounting for such funds. Administers the commission's contracts and procurement programs.

Director

Germaine Roseboro . . . . (202) 663–4238
E-mail: germaine.roseboro@eeoc.gov

Planning and Systems Services Division

Vacant. . . . . (202) 663–4238

Acquisitions Services Division

Patrick Mealy . . . . (202) 663–4824

Financial Operations

Raj Mohan . . . . (202) 663–4203

OFFICE OF THE CHIEF HUMAN CAPITAL OFFICER

Provides leadership in the design, planning, development, and administration of human resources management. Institutes procedures and standards to achieve customer satisfaction, hiring reform, and employee satisfaction and wellness.

Chief Human Capital Officer

Lisa M. Williams . . . . (202) 663–4306
TTY. . . . . (202) 663–4399
E-mail: lisa.williams@eeoc.gov

OFFICE OF COMMUNICATIONS AND LEGISLATIVE AFFAIRS

The Legislative Affairs Division responds to congressional communications and tracks, researches, and analyzes legislation and issues. Communications division staff inform employees, employers, the general public, and all other stakeholders about EEOC policies and programs, participate in seminars and exhibits, produce publications and annual reports, and serve as liaisons to the media. The Public Information Unit answers general public inquiries. Agency public information publications are available free of charge through a toll-free number and on the website. Reports and fact sheets are available in many languages and in various formats (including Braille and large print).

Director

Beverly L. Barnes. . . . . (202) 663–4191

Deputy Director

Brett Brenner . . . . (202) 663–4191

Communications Director

Christine Nazer (acting). . . . . (202) 663–4191

Legislative Affairs

Patricia Crawford (acting) . . . . (202) 663–4191
Fax. . . . . (202) 663–4912

Public Information Unit

All areas . . . . (202) 663–4191

Public Affairs Specialist

Joseph J. Olivares. . . . . (202) 663–4110
E-mail: joseph.olivares@eeoc.gov

Publications Distribution Center

All areas . . . . (800) 669–3362
TTY. . . . . (800) 669–3302
E-mail: Legis.Affairs@eeoc.gov

OFFICE OF EQUAL OPPORTUNITY

Counsels, investigates, and recommends disposition of complaints of commission employees and applicants for employment who believe they have experienced discrimination in the workplace or in the application process. Provides alternative dispute resolution opportunities (principally mediation) at all steps of the foregoing processes. Coordinates with other EEOC components to promote affirmative employment and diversity, and establishes and monitors special employment programs for disabled and veteran employees.

Director

Matthew Murphy . . . . (202) 663–7081
TTY. . . . . (202) 663–7002
E-mail: matthew.murphy@eeoc.gov

OFFICE OF THE EXECUTIVE SECRETARIAT

Serves as the focal point for the receipt, documentation, review, coordination, and monitoring of all policy-related activities and all the decisions flowing to and from the chair, commissioners, and program offices. Responsible for the coordination of the commission meetings and the administration of responsibilities under the Government in the Sunshine Act.

Director

Bernadette B. Wilson . . . . (202) 663–4070
TTY. . . . . (202) 663–4074

OFFICE OF FEDERAL OPERATIONS

Provides leadership and guidance to federal agencies regarding the federal government's equal employment opportunity program; develops proposed policies; and implements programs to ensure hiring, placement, and advancement of women, minorities, and individuals with disabilities.

Also receives appeals of discrimination decisions handed down by the Merit Systems Protection Board (MSPB) and from final action taken on discrimination complaints made by the heads of federal agencies. Drafts proposed decisions for the commissioners, who then adopt a recommendation for a ruling.

Director
    Carlton M. Hadden................ (202) 663–4599
        TTY......................... (202) 663–4593
        Fax.......................... (202) 663–7022
Appellate Review Programs
    Robbie Dix....................... (202) 663–4599
Federal Sector Programs
    Dexter R. Brooks.................. (202) 663–4511
FSMS Program Manager
    Gerard Thomson.................. (202) 663–4560
        TTY.........................(202) 663–4593
        E-mail: gerard.thomson@eeoc.gov
Special Services
    Robert Barnhart (acting) .... (202) 663–4599
        (Phone calls returned on Wednesdays.)
        E-mail: fed.adr@eeoc.gov or oso.eeoc@eeoc.gov

OFFICE OF THE GENERAL COUNSEL

Responsible for litigation authorized by the commission, represents the commission in litigation, and provides legal advice to the commission and its officers. Also concurs in the appointment of regional attorneys and advises them on litigation. Oversees, along with the Office of Field Programs, enforcement litigation programs in the headquarters and field offices. The division of Systemic Investigations and Review Programs advises the Office of Field Programs during the investigation of systemic and individual charges to ensure EEOC standards are met before cases are litigated. Develops programs designed to encourage compliance with EEO laws and reports to the commission on legal issues raised in enforcement litigation that may affect commission policy.

General Counsel
    P. David Lopez................... (202) 663–4702
        TTY......................... (202) 663–7181
Deputy General Counsel
    James L. Lee .... (202) 663–4702
Associate General Counsel, Appellate Services
    Lorraine Davis .... (202) 663–4735
Associate General Counsel, Litigation Management Services
    Gwendolyn Young Reams .... (202) 663–7028
Research and Analytic Services
    Joseph Donovan .... (202) 663–4745

OFFICE OF INFORMATION TECHNOLOGY

Provides information technology operations; data management; network infrastructure; customer support; systems development; technical consulting; innovation; and voice, data, and audio/video services to all EEOC offices.

Director/Chief Information Officer
    Kimberly Hancher................ (202) 663–4447
        E-mail: cio@eeoc.g

OFFICE OF THE INSPECTOR GENERAL (OIG)

Principal responsibilities under the Inspector General Act of 1978, as amended, include providing policy direction and conducting, supervising, and coordinating independent internal and external audits, investigations, and evaluation of all EEOC programs and operations. Works to promote economy and efficiency in the administration of—and to prevent and detect fraud, waste, and abuse in—EEOC programs and operations. OIG keeps the chair and Congress fully and currently informed about commission problems and deficiencies and the need for corrective action. OIG focuses its resources on issues that represent the greatest risk and maximum opportunity to add value to the agency.

    Hotline .... (800) 849–4230
Inspector General
    Milton A. Mayo Jr.................. (202) 663–4327
        E-mail: inspector.general@eeoc.gov
Deputy Inspector General
    Joyce T. Willoughby .... (202) 663–4327
        Mailing address: Office of the Inspector General
        P.O. Box 77067, Washington DC 20013-7067

OFFICE OF LEGAL COUNSEL

Serves as principal adviser to and representative of the commission on legal matters. Provides legal advice to federal agencies, state and local governments, fair employment practice agencies, and members of Congress. Drafts regulations, enforcement guidance, and compliance manual sections for commission approval; responds to requests under the Freedom of Information Act (FOIA); manages the administration of Executive Order 12067, which calls for governmentwide coordination of equal employment opportunity statutes, regulations, and policies; and provides advice on the EEOC's ethics program. Subject matter experts respond to media inquiries.

Legal Counsel
    Peggy R. Mastroianni .... (202) 663–4640
        Fax.......................... (202) 663–4697
        TTY......................... (202) 663–7026
        E-mail: peggy.mastroianni@eeoc.gov
ADA/GINA
    Christopher J. Kuczynski .... (202) 663–4640
Advice and External Litigation Division
    Thomas J. Schlageter.............. (202) 663–4640
FOIA Programs and Assistant Legal Counsel
    Stephanie D. Garner .... (202) 663–4634
        E-mail: stephanie.garner@eeoc.gov
Title VII, ADEA, and EPA Division
    Carol Miaskoff.................... (202) 663–4640
Coordination
    Corbett L. Anderson............... (202) 663–4640
        Mailing address:
        Office of Legal Counsel, 131 M St.
        N.E., #5NW02E
        Washington, DC 20507
        E-mail: FOIA@eeoc.gov
        FOIA requests website: www.eeoc.gov/foia

OFFICE OF RESEARCH, INFORMATION, AND PLANNING

Researches, collects, and analyzes enforcement data; reviews and analyzes organizational activities; makes recommendations to improve operations; manages agency website and library services; and provides resource, technical, and research support to the commission and the public.

Director

Deidre Flippen. . . . . (202) 663–4844
    E-mail: deidre.flippen@eeoc.gov

Program Research and Surveys Division

Patrick Ronald Edwards. . . . . (202) 663–4949
    E-mail: Ronald.Edwards@eeoc.gov

Program Planning and Analysis

Deidre Flippen. . . . . (202) 663–4844
    E-mail: Deidre.Flippen@eeoc.gov

Library and Information Services

Holly Wilson . . . . (202) 663–4630
    E-mail: Holly.Wilson@eeoc.gov

Website Contact Manager

Adam Guasch-Melendez . . . . (202) 663–4632
    E-mail: Adam.Guasch@eeoc.gov

OFFICE OF FIELD PROGRAMS

Manages EEOC's 53 field offices. Advises and assists field offices in meeting the challenges of managing large and complex workloads. Coordinates field office enforcement and litigation, as well as hearings and federal affirmative action functions. Gathers and assembles data from field offices to present to Congress and oversight agencies. Designs and develops national training programs for field office staff, coordinates outreach programs aimed at EEOC's stakeholders, including fee-based training under the EEOC revolving fund, and oversees the national mediation program. Manages and supports the resolution of charges by state and local agencies under work-sharing agreements and contracts, and contracts with Tribal Employment Rights Offices to protect Title VII and special preference rights of Native Americans. Also works with the commission's management offices to administer budgetary, financial, and training services to the field offices.

Director

Nicholas Inzeo. . . . . (202) 663–4801
    TTY. . . . . (202) 663–7063

State/Local Programs

Michael Dougherty. . . . . (202) 663–4801

Field Coordination Programs

John Schmelzer (acting). . . . . (202) 663–4801

Regional Offices

The EEOC has 15 district offices, 9 field offices, 15 area offices, and 14 local offices. Offices are responsible for the receipt, mediation, investigation, conciliation, and litigation of charges of employment discrimination. Offices also provide education outreach and technical assistance to employers and others on the laws EEOC enforces. Certain offices also have hearings and federal affirmative action functions.

Section 706 of Title VII provides that the EEOC may contract with designated state and local fair employment practice agencies; the 706 agencies play a major role in processing discrimination charges within their jurisdictions.

Below is a list of EEOC district and field offices. For information about area, local, and 706 agency offices, contact the closest district office or call toll-free (800) 669–4000 (voice) or (800) 669–6820 (TTY).

ALBUQERQUE (New Mexico except southwestern New Mexico, see "San Antonio")

505 Marquette Ave. N.W., #900
Albuquerque, NM 87102
(800) 669–4000
TTY (800) 669–6820
Internet: www.eeoc.gov/field/albuquerque/index.cfm
Derick Newton, director

ATLANTA (Georgia; southeastern South Carolina)

Sam Nunn Atlanta Federal Center
100 Alabama St., #R430
Atlanta, GA 30303
(800) 669–4000
TTY (800) 669–6820
Internet: www.eeoc.gov/field/atlanta/index.cfm
Bernice Williams-Kimbrough, director

BALTIMORE (Maryland)

City Crescent Bldg.
10 S. Howard St., 3rd Floor
Baltimore, MD 21201
(410) 962–3932
TTY (410) 962–6065
Fax (410) 962–4270
Internet: www.eeoc.gov/field/baltimore/index.cfm
Rosemary Rhodes, director

BIRMINGHAM (Alabama; central and southern Mississippi)

Ridge Park Place
1130 22nd St. South, #2000
Birmingham, AL 35205
(800) 669–4000
TTY (800) 669–6820
Internet: www.eeoc.gov/field/birmingham/index.cfm
Delner Franklin-Thomas, director

CHARLOTTE (North Carolina; South Carolina except southeastern South Carolina, see "Atlanta")

129 W. Trade St., #400
Charlotte, NC 28202
(800) 669–4000
TTY (800) 669–6820
Internet: www.eeoc.gov/field/charlotte/index.cfm
Reuben Daniels Jr., director

CHICAGO (Illinois)

500 W. Madison St., #2000
Chicago, IL 60661

(800) 669–4000
TTY (800) 669–6820
Internet: www.eeoc.gov/field/chicago/index.cfm
John P. Rowe, director

CLEVELAND (eastern Ohio)
Anthony J. Celebrezze Federal Bldg.
1240 E. 9th St., #3001
Cleveland, OH 44199
(800) 669–4000
TTY (800) 669–6820
Internet: www.eeoc.gov/field/cleveland/index.cfm
Cheryl Mabry-Thomas, director

DALLAS (northern Texas)
207 S. Houston St., 3rd Floor
Dallas, TX 75202–4726
(800) 669–4000
TTY (800) 669–6820
Internet: www.eeoc.gov/field/dallas/index.cfm
Janet V. Elizondo, director

DENVER (Colorado; Wyoming)
303 E. 17th Ave., #410
Denver, CO 80203
(800) 669–4000
TTY (800) 669–6820
Internet: www.eeoc.gov/field/denver/index.cfm
John C. Lowrie, director

DETROIT (Michigan; northwestern Ohio)
Patrick V. McNamara Bldg.
477 Michigan Ave., #865
Detroit, MI 48226–9704
(800) 669–4000
TTY (800) 669–6820
Internet: www.eeoc.gov/field/detroit/index.cfm
Gail Cober, director

HOUSTON (southeastern Texas)
Total Plaza
1201 Louisiana St., 6th Floor
Houston, TX 77002
(800) 669–4000
TTY (800) 669–6820
Internet: www.eeoc.gov/field/houston/index.cfm
R.J. Ruff Jr., director

INDIANAPOLIS (Indiana; western Ohio)
101 W. Ohio St., #1900
Indianapolis, IN 46204–4203
(800) 669–4000
TTY (800) 669–6820
Internet: www.eeoc.gov/field/indianapolois/index.cfm
Webster Smith, director

LOS ANGELES (southern California; southern Nevada; Hawaii; American Samoa; Guam; Northern Mariana Islands; Wake Island)
Roybal Federal Bldg.
255 E. Temple St., 4th Floor

Los Angeles, CA 90012
(213) 894–1000
TTY (800) 669–6820
Internet: www.eeoc.gov/field/losangeles/index.cfm
Rosa Viramontes (acting), director

LOUISVILLE (Kentucky)
600 Dr. Martin Luther King Jr. Place, #268
Louisville, KY 40202
(800) 669–4000
TTY (800) 669–6820
Internet: www.eeoc.gov/field/louisville/index.cfm
Randy G. Poynter, director

MEMPHIS (Arkansas; Tennessee; northern Mississippi)
1407 Union Ave., #901
Memphis, TN 38104
(901) 544–0115
TTY (800) 669–6820
Internet: www.eeoc.gov/field/memphis/index.cfm
Katharine Kores, director

MIAMI (Florida except the Panhandle, see Birmingham; Puerto Rico; U.S. Virgin Islands)
Miami Tower
100 S.E. 2nd St., #1500
Miami, FL 33131
(800) 669–4000
TTY (800) 669–6820
Internet: www.eeoc.gov/field/miami/index.cfm
Malcolm S. Medley, director

MILWAUKEE (Iowa; Minnesota; Wisconsin; North Dakota; South Dakota)
Reuss Federal Plaza
310 W. Wisconsin Ave., #800
Milwaukee, WI 53203–2292
(800) 669–4000
TTY (800) 669–6820
Internet: www.eeoc.gov/field/milwaukee/index.cfm
Rosemary Fox (acting), director

NEW ORLEANS (Louisiana)
1555 Poydras St., #1900
New Orleans, LA 70112
(504) 595–2825
TTY (504) 595–2958
Internet: www.eeoc.gov/field/neworleans/index.cfm
Keith T. Hill, director

NEW YORK (New York; Connecticut; Massachusetts; Maine; New Hampshire; Rhode Island; Vermont; northern New Jersey)
33 Whitehall St., 5th Floor
New York, NY 10004
(212) 336–3620
TTY (800) 669–6820

Internet: www.eeoc.gov/field/newyork/index.cfm
Kevin J. Berry, director

NORFOLK (Virginia except northern Virginia)

Federal Bldg.
200 Granby St. # 739
Norfolk, VA. 23510
(800) 669–4000
TTY (800) 669–6820
Internet: www.eeoc.gov/field/norfolk/index.cfm
Michael Johnson (acting), director

PHILADELPHIA (Delaware; southern New Jersey; Pennsylvania; West Virginia)

801 Market St., #1300
Philadelphia, PA 19107–3127
(800) 669–4000
TTY (800) 669–6820
Internet: www.eeoc.gov/field/philadelphia/index.cfm
Spencer H. Lewis Jr., director

PHOENIX (Arizona; Utah)

3300 N. Central Ave., #690
Phoenix, AZ 85012–2504
(800) 669–4000
TTY (800) 669–6820
Internet: www.eeoc.gov/field/phoenix/index.cfm
Rayford O. Irving, director

SAN ANTONIO (southern, central, and western Texas; southwestern New Mexico)

Legacy Oaks Bldg. A
5410 Fredericksburg Rd., #200
San Antonio, TX 78229–3555
(210) 281–2550
TTY (800) 669–6820
Internet: www.eeoc.gov/field/sanantonio/index.cfm
Travis Hicks, director

SAN FRANCISCO (northern California, northern Nevada)

350 The Embarcadero, #500
San Francisco, CA 94105–1260
(800) 669–4000
TTY (800) 669–6820
Internet: www.eeoc.gov/field/sanfrancisco/index.cfm
Michael Baldonado, director

SEATTLE (Alaska; Idaho; Montana; Oregon; Washington)

Federal Office Bldg.
909 First Ave., #400
Seattle, WA 98104–1061
TTY (800) 669–6820
Internet: www.eeoc.gov/field/seattle/index.cfm
Nancy Sienko, director

ST. LOUIS (Kansas; Missouri; eastern St. Louis, Missouri; Oklahoma; Nebraska)

Robert A. Young Bldg.
1222 Spruce St., #8100

St. Louis, MO 63103
(314) 539–7800
TTY (800) 669–6820
Internet: www.eeoc.gov/field/stlouis/index.cfm
James R. Neely Jr., director

TAMPA (western and central Florida except the Panhandle, see "Birmingham")

501 E. Polk St., #1000
Tampa, FL 33602
(813) 228–2310
TTY (800) 669–6820
Internet: www.eeoc.gov/field/tampa /index.cfm
Georgia Marchbanks, director

WASHINGTON, DC (Washington, DC; northern and western Virginia)

131 M St. N.E., #4NW02F
Washington, DC 20507–0100
(202) 419–0713
TTY (800) 669–6820
Internet: www.eeoc.gov/field/washington/index.cfm
Mindy Weinstein (acting), director

◼ CONGRESSIONAL ACTION

Congressional Liaison

Director of Legislative Affairs
Patricia Crawford (acting) . . . . (202) 663–4191

Committees and Subcommittees

HOUSE APPROPRIATIONS COMMITTEE

Subcommittee on Commerce, Justice, Science, and Related Agencies
H-310 CAP, Washington, DC 20515
(202) 225–3351

HOUSE EDUCATION AND THE WORKFORCE COMMITTEE

2181 RHOB, Washington, DC 20515–6100
(202) 225–4527
Subcommittee on Health, Employment, Labor, and Pensions
2181 RHOB, Washington, DC 20515
(202) 225–4527
Subcommittee on Higher Education and Workforce Training
2181 RHOB, Washington, DC 20515
(202) 225–4527
Subcommittee on Workforce Protection
2181 RHOB, Washington, DC 20515
(202) 225–4527

HOUSE OVERSIGHT AND GOVERNMENT REFORM COMMITTEE

2157 RHOB, Washington, DC 20515–6143
(202) 225–5074
Subcommittee on Economic Growth, Job Creation, and Regulatory Affairs
2157 RHOB, Washington, DC 20515–6143
(202) 225–5074

Subcommittee on the Federal Workforce, U.S. Postal Service, and the Census
2157 RHOB, Washington, DC 20515
(202) 225–5074

Subcommittee on Government Operations
2157 RHOB, Washington, DC 20515
(202) 225–5074

Subcommittee on Energy Policy, Health Care, and Entitlements
2157 RHOB, Washington, DC 20515
(202) 225–5074

SENATE APPROPRIATIONS COMMITTEE
Subcommittee on Commerce, Justice, Science, and Related Agencies
SDOB-142, Washington, DC 20510
(202) 224–7277

SENATE COMMITTEE ON LABOR, HEALTH AND HUMAN SERVICES, EDUCATION, AND RELATED AGENCIES
SDOB-135, Washington, DC 20510–6300
(202) 224–7230

SENATE COMMITTEE ON HOMELAND SECURITY
SDOB-131, Washington, DC 20510–6250
(202) 224–4319

Legislation

The EEOC was created by **Title VII of the Civil Rights Act of 1964** (78 Stat. 241, 42 U.S.C. 2000e), signed by the president July 2, 1964. Title VII contained the provisions of the law to be enforced by the EEOC. It outlawed discrimination in employment on the basis of race, color, religion, national origin, and sex (pregnancy-related discrimination was specifically prohibited by the **Pregnancy Discrimination Act of 1978**, 92 Stat. 2076, 42 U.S.C. 2000e). It also applies to employers of 15 or more employees, state and local government, employment agencies, and labor unions.

The provisions of Title VII did not apply to elected officials, their personal assistants, and appointed policy-making officials. Title VII also provided that employers could make distinctions on the basis of sex, religion, or national origin if sex, religion, or national origin was a bona fide occupational qualification for the job.

Enforcement powers contained in the 1964 law gave the EEOC authority only to investigate, find cause, and attempt conciliation. However, passage of the **Equal Employment Opportunity Act** (86 Stat. 103, 42 U.S.C. 2000e), signed by the president March 24, 1972, gave EEOC authority to prosecute cases of employment discrimination against private employers. It also brought all federal employees under the protection of Title VII, with enforcement initially assigned to the Civil Service Commission.

A 1978 presidential reorganization plan gave EEOC authority to enforce the EEO laws prohibiting discrimination by the federal government.

The same reorganization also transferred responsibility for equal pay and age discrimination statutes from the Labor Department to the EEOC. In 1990 EEOC was given responsibility for the enforcement of the Americans with Disabilities Act.

In addition to Title VII, EEOC currently enforces the following laws:

Equal Pay Act of 1963 (77 Stat. 56, 29 U.S.C. 206). Signed by the president June 10, 1963. Forbade discrimination in wages and fringe benefits based on sex.

Age Discrimination in Employment Act of 1967 (81 Stat. 602, 29 U.S.C. 621). Signed by the president Dec. 15, 1967. Outlaws discrimination against workers or applicants over the age of forty. It applies to private employers of twenty or more workers; federal, state, and local governments and employment agencies; and labor unions with twenty-five or more members or that operate a hiring hall or office that recruits or attempts to recruit employees for a covered employer.

Rehabilitation Act of 1973, Section 501 (86 Stat. 355, 29 U.S.C. 791). Signed by the president Sept. 26, 1973. Prohibits disability-based discrimination against federal employees and requires federal agencies to undertake affirmative action in connection with the employment of persons with disabilities.

Title I of the **Americans with Disabilities Act** (104 Stat. 327, 42 U.S.C. 1201 note). Signed by the president July 26, 1990. Prohibits employment discrimination against qualified individuals with disabilities. Applies to employers with fifteen or more employees, unions, employment agencies, and state and local government.

Civil Rights Act of 1991 (105 Stat. 1071, 42 U.S.C. 1981 note). Signed by the president Nov. 21, 1991. Amended the Civil Rights Act of 1964 by strengthening the scope and effectiveness of civil rights protections. Provided compensatory and punitive damages for intentional discrimination under Title VII of the Civil Rights Act and under the Americans with Disabilities Act.

Lilly Ledbetter Fair Pay Act of 2009 (123 Stat. 5, 42 U.S.C. 2000a note). Signed by the president Jan. 29, 2009. Amended Title VII of the Civil Rights Act of 1964 and the Age Discrimination in Employment Act of 1967, and modified the Americans with Disabilities Act of 1990 to clarify that an individual may file a discriminatory compensation charge up to six months after receiving his or her last paycheck.

▇ INFORMATION SOURCES

Internet

The EEOC can be reached via the Internet using the host address: www.eeoc.gov. The site is comprehensive, including contact information, an introduction to the commission, publications, enforcement guidelines, and links to other relevant sites. News is also distributed via Twitter: @EEOCNews and @EEOCespanol

Telephone Contacts

Publications Orders . . . .(800) 669–3362
Information Line . . . .(800) 669–4000
TTY. . . . .(800) 669–6820

Information and Publications

KEY OFFICES

EEOC Communications and Legislative Affairs

131 M St. N.E.
Washington, DC 20507
(202) 663–4191
TTY (202) 663–4494
E-mail: newsroom@eeoc.gov
Internet: www.eeoc.gov/eeoc/newsroom/index.cfm
Patricia Crawford (acting), director

Answers general questions from the press and the public. Also issues news releases and publications in many languages and alternate formats (Braille and large print).

Freedom of Information

Office of Legal Counsel
131 M St. N.E., #5NW02E
Washington, DC 20507
(202) 663–4634
TTY (202) 663–7026
E-mail: foia@eeoc.gov
Stephanie Garner, contact

EEOC Office of Field Programs

131 M St. N.E.
Washington, DC 20507
(202) 663–4801
TTY (202) 663–7063
Call Center: (800) 669–4000
Nicholas Inzeo, director

Provides information on complaints and charges. Complaints alleging employment discrimination must be made at the EEOC field office nearest the dispute or at a 706 agency. If conciliation fails to settle the matter, the commissioners vote on whether to litigate on behalf of the party alleging discrimination.

An individual may file a charge up to six months after receiving his or her last paycheck (up to 300 days if a state or local fair employment practices agency was first contacted).

To file a charge, a claimant must use Form EEOC-5, which is available from any EEOC office. The initial charge may be made without this form, but it must be in writing. This initial charge need contain only the claimant's name, address, place of employment, and a statement indicating that an employer has discriminated against him or her.

This information constitutes a charge, although the claimant should be willing to give further information at later stages of the investigation.

Charges are kept confidential. A charge may be filed by one party on behalf of another party.

PUBLICATIONS

The EEOC publishes an extensive series of reports and fact sheets, available on the website at www1.eeoc.gov/eeoc/publications/index.cfm?; or contact the EEOC Publications Distribution Center (800) 669–3362, TTY (800) 800–3302.

Publications are available in alternative formats (Braille and large print) and in many languages, including Arabic, Bosnian, Chinese, Farsi, French, Haitian Creole, Hindi, Korean, Punjabi, Russian, Spanish, Vietnamese, and Urdu. The following titles, which are available at no cost, are a sampling of what is available:

The ADA: Your Rights as an Individual with a Disability. Explains rights under the Americans with Disabilities Act.

Equal Employment is the Law Poster. Every employer covered by the nondiscrimination and EEO laws is required to display this poster on its premises. The notice must be posted prominently, where it can be readily seen by employees and applicants for employment. Provides information concerning the laws and procedures for filing complaints of violations of the laws with the Office of Federal Contract Compliance Programs (OFCCP). Also available in Spanish, Arabic, and Chinese.

Federal Sector Complaint Processing Manual. Provides federal agencies with EEOC policies, procedures, and guidance relating to the processing of employment discrimination complaints governed by the EEOC's regulations in 29 C.F.R. Part 1614.

National Origin Discrimination. Includes overview and background of revised guidelines on discrimination because of national origin.

Pregnancy Discrimination. Includes overview of guidelines for compliance with the Pregnancy Discrimination Act of 1978.

Religious Discrimination. Provides brief overview and background of revised guidelines on discrimination because of religion.

Sexual Harassment. Gives brief overview of sexual harassment as a form of discrimination.

Age Discrimination. Provides overview of age as a form of discrimination and guidelines pertaining thereto.

Questions and Answers about the Workplace Rights of Muslims, Arabs, South Asians, and Sikhs under the Equal Opportunity Laws.

Employment Rights of Immigrants under Federal Anti-Discrimination Laws. Gives information for all immigrants, regardless of nationality.

Questions and Answers: The Application of Title VII and the ADA to Applicants or Employees Who Experience Domestic or Dating Violence, Sexual Assault, or Stalking.

Mediation! Fair, Efficient and Everyone Wins: How to Use Mediation in the Early Stages of Issues.

Filing a Charge of Job Discrimination.

DATA AND STATISTICS

Program Research and Survey Division

Office of Research, Information, and Planning
(202) 663–4949
E-mail: Deirdre.flippen@eeoc.gov
Deidre Flippen, director

Provides information on reports required by the EEOC, which supply data on the composition of the nation's working population. (Most information has been "sanitized" to protect the confidentiality of employers and employees alike.) The following reports are available on the EEOC website and by request from this office:

Elementary and Secondary Staff Information (EEO-5). Data provided biennially by public school districts with 100 or more full-time employees. Full-time employees are categorized by race, ethnicity, and gender groups and by 18 job assignment classes. Part-time and new hire data also are collected. Aggregate data available to the public.

Employer Information Report (EEO-1). Annual data provided by all private employers with 100 or more employees and all government contractors with 50 or more employees and a contract of $50,000 or more. Collected by race, ethnicity, and gender groups, by ten occupational categories and by the North American Industrial Classification system; currently reported for any payroll period in July through September. Data available to the public.

Local Union Report (EEO-3). Data provided biennially by all local referral unions with 100 or more members; data include total and race and ethnicity group membership, job referrals, applicants for membership and referrals, sex of members, trades, and geographic location. Aggregate data available to the public.

State and Local Government Information (EEO-4). Employment data on state and local governments with 100 or more full-time employees are collected biennially by race, ethnicity, and gender categories, in eight job categories, and in eight salary intervals for full-time employment. Data also collected for part-time employment and new hires. Aggregate listings available to the public.

MEETINGS

The commission members meet formally as needed. Notices of upcoming meetings are posted in the lobby of the EEOC headquarters outside the offices of the executive secretariat, the chair, and the legal counsel, and on the website, www.eeoc.gov. Notices are published in the *Federal Register* and are available from a 24-hour telephone recording: (202) 663-7100.

At open sessions, the commission considers EEOC policy, proposed guidelines, proposals to fund various agencies and programs, and the general operations of the EEOC. Closed EEOC sessions typically involve litigation, complaints filed and/or internal personnel matters, and federal sector (employee or applicant) adjudication.

Reference Resources

LIBRARY

EEOC Library
131 M St. N.E., #4SW16N
Washington, DC 20507
(202) 663-4630
TTY (202) 663-4641
Holly Wilson, director
E-mail: Holly.Wilson@eeoc.gov

Hours: 9:00 A.M. to 5:00 P.M.
Open to the public by appointment.

INTERPRETATIONS AND OPINIONS

Office of Legal Counsel
131 M St. N.E., #5NW02E
Washington, DC 20507
(202) 663-4634
TTY (202) 663-7026
E-mail: foia@eeoc.gov
Peggy R. Mastroianni, legal counsel

DECISIONS

Commission decisions, regulations, sub-regulatory guidance, informal staff discussion letters, and technical assistance are available on the EEOC website and at EEOC field offices, or contact the Office of Legal Counsel.

DOCKETS

A number of important EEOC publications are available on the agency's website at www.eeoc.gov. Federal dockets are also available at www.regulations.gov. (*See appendix for Searching and Commenting on Regulations: Regulations.gov.*)

RULES AND REGULATIONS

EEOC rules and regulations are published in the *Code of Federal Regulations,* Title 5, Chapter LXII, Part 7201; Title 29, Chapter XIV, Parts 1600–1699. Proposed rules, new final rules, and updates to the *Code of Federal Regulations* are published in the *Federal Register.* (*See appendix for information on how to obtain and use these publications.*) The *Federal Register* may be accessed at www.federalregister.gov and the *Code of Federal Regulations* at www.archives.gov/federal-register/cfr; also see the federal government's website www.regulations.gov (*see appendix*).

All EEOC rules, regulations, and policies are also available on its website.

Other Information Sources

RELATED AGENCY

Office of Personnel Management
Workforce Information
1900 E St. N.W.
Washington, DC 20415
(202) 606-1800
E-mail: general@opm.gov
Internet: www.opm.gov; www.opm.gov/about-us/contact-us

Compiles and distributes statistical data on federal affirmative employment, covering race and national origin, sex, disability, veteran status, years of service, and age. Publications include *Demographic Profile of the Federal Workforce.*

COMPLIANCE MANUAL

The EEOC also prepares a compliance manual detailing requirements of Title VII. The manual is not distributed or sold by the government, but it is available from private publishers who have been given the right to reprint it. The compliance manual also is available for use at all EEOC district offices and at the EEOC Library. Selected guidance documents and newly revised sections are also available on the EEOC website: www.eeoc.gov/laws/guidance/compliance.cfm.

NONGOVERNMENTAL RESOURCES

The following are some key resources for information on the EEOC and equal employment opportunity issues.

Bureau of National Affairs, Inc.
1801 S. Bell Street
Arlington, VA 22202
Mailing address:
Bloomberg BNA's Customer Contact Center
3 Bethesda Metro Center, #250
Bethesda, MD 20814
(800) 372–1033
Internet: www.bna.com

CCH, A Wolters Kluwer business
(Formerly Commerce Clearing House)
2700 Lake Cook Rd.
Riverwoods, IL 60015
(847) 267–7000
(800) 248–3248 or (800) 234–1660
Internet: www.cchgroup.com

Center for Equal Opportunity
7700 Leesburg Pike, #231
Falls Church, VA 22043
(703) 442–0066
Internet: www.ceousa.org

Equal Employment Advisory Council
1501 M St. N.W., #400
Washington, DC 20005
(202) 629–5650
Internet: www.eeac.org

Equal Rights Advocates
1170 Market St, #700
San Francisco, CA 94102
(415) 621–0672
(800) 839–4372
E-mail: info@equalrights.org
Internet: www.equalrights.org

Gale [part of Cengage Learning]
27500 Drake Rd.
Farmington Hills, MI 48331–3535
(248) 699–4253
(800) 877–4253
Internet: www.cengage.com

Human Rights Campaign
1640 Rhode Island Ave. N.W.
Washington, DC 20036–3278
(202) 628–4160
(800) 777–4723
TTY (202) 216–1572
Internet: www.hrc.org

ILR Press
Cornell University Press
512 East State Street
Ithaca, NY 14850
(607) 277–2338
Internet: www.ilr.cornell.edu/ilrpress;
    www.cornellpress.cornell.edu/contacts

Leadership Conference on Civil Rights
1629 K St. N.W., 10th Floor, #1000
Washington, DC 20006
(202) 466–3311
Internet: www.civilrights.org

NAACP Legal Defense and Educational Fund
40 Rector St, 5th floor
New York, NY 10006
(212) 965–2200
Internet: www.naacpldf.org
    Washington office
    1444 Eye St. N.W., 10th Floor
    Washington, DC 20005
    (202) 682–1300

National Organization for Women (NOW)
1100 H St. N.W., #300
Washington, DC 20005
Mailing address:
P.O. Box 1848
Merrifield, VA 22116–9899
(202) 628–8669
TTY (202) 331–9002
Internet: www.now.org

National Organization on Disability
77 Water St., #204
New York, NY 10005
(646) 505–1191, ext. 122
Media contact: Zach Chizar
E-mail: zchizar@a-g.com
Internet: www.nod.org
    Washington office
    1625 K St. N.W., #850
    Washington, DC 20006
    (202) 293–5960

9 to 5, National Association of Working Women
207 E. Buffalo St., #211
Milwaukee, WI 53202
(414) 274–0925
Job problems helpline: (800) 522–0925
E-mail: info@9to5.org
Press (303) 628–0925
Press e-mail: pr@9to5.org
Internet: www.9to5.org

Federal Communications Commission

445 12th St. S.W., Washington, DC 20554
Internet: www.fcc.gov

■ INTRODUCTION

The Communications Act of 1934 established the Federal Communications Commission (FCC) as an independent regulatory agency. The FCC is composed of five commissioners, not more than three of whom may be members of the same political party. The president nominates commissioners who are then confirmed by the Senate. The president designates one of the members to serve as chair. The commissioners' five-year terms have staggered expiration dates so that no two terms expire in the same year. Originally there were seven commissioners with longer terms, but legislation enacted by Congress in 1982 reduced both. The change to five commissioners became effective June 30, 1983. The FCC's offices are located primarily in Washington, DC.

Responsibilities

The FCC oversees all interstate and foreign communication by means of radio, television, wire, cable, and satellite. The agency controls licenses for about three million companies and individuals that rely on the airwaves for communications, ranging from amateur radio operators to regional Bell telephone companies and cable television systems.

Specifically, the FCC

- Allocates portions of the radio spectrum to nongovernmental communications services and assigns specific frequencies within those spectrum bands to individual users. The FCC also governs the use of the spectrum for other purposes, such as remote-control devices.
- Licenses and regulates all commercial audio, video, and communications services that use the radio spectrum.
- Regulates common carriers in interstate and foreign communications by telegraph, telephone, and satellite. The FCC also sets national standards for competition in local telephone service.
- Regulates cable television and video services provided over telephone lines.
- Promotes safety through the use of radio on land, water, and in the air.

The commission also participates in an advisory capacity in U.S. delegations to international communications forums of the International Telecommunication Union (ITU). The ITU coordinates international spectrum allocations by treaty.

The FCC does not control every aspect of communications or broadcasting, largely because of the limits imposed by the First Amendment to the U.S.

GLOSSARY

Broadcasting—The multidirectional transmission of sound, images, data, or other electronically encoded information over the air by means of electromagnetic radiation in the radio spectrum, such as in radio or television.

Cable—Transmission of sound, images, data, and other electronically encoded information by means of wires, usually a combination of fiber-optic and coaxial cables capable of carrying hundreds of video channels simultaneously.

Cellular telephone—Transmission of telephone calls via radio to mobile receivers. Metropolitan areas are divided into "cells," each with an antenna to relay signals to and from the mobile phones. The call is handed off from one cell to the next as the receiving phone moves, allowing the first cell to use the same frequency for a new call.

Common carrier—A regulatory category that includes any company offering telecommunications services to the general public, such as telephone and telegraph companies. Common carriers must offer their transmission services at nondiscriminatory rates to any interested customer and for regulatory purposes are treated much like electric or gas utilities.

Direct broadcast satellite (DBS)—The transmission of video images and sound directly from a programming source to viewers' homes via satellite. The service typically is offered via subscriptions, such as cable, and the satellite dishes are roughly eighteen inches in diameter.

Low power television—Television stations with ranges of only a few miles. The FCC licenses low-power stations to increase the number of channels serving a community without electronically interfering with transmissions in nearby communities.

Multipoint microwave distribution services (MMDS), or wireless cable—Television broadcasting systems that transmit over the microwave portion of the radio spectrum. Microwave broadcasts can carry multiple channels but have a limited range because their signals do not pass through objects.

Open Internet—Ability of Internet consumers to go where they want, when they want. FCC rules stipulate that broadband service providers may not block access to legal content, applications, services, or non-harmful devices; impair or degrade lawful Internet traffic; or favor some lawful Internet traffic; over other lawful traffic in exchange for payment of any kind. Also known as net neutrality.

Personal communications service (PCS)—A digital version of cellular telephone service that the FCC started licensing in 1994. Typically, PCS phones are capable of more functions than other mobile units. For example, they can simultaneously act as phones, pagers, and answering machines.

Radio spectrum—The range of radio frequencies available for use by the broadcasting and mobile communications services. These frequencies are divided into discrete channels and allocated to the various users by the FCC.

Telecommunications—Transmission of information chosen by a customer to points selected by the customer, without changing the form or content of the information.

Constitution. It has little oversight over the broadcast networks or programming practices of individual stations or cable franchises. It does not control the content of broadcasts, although it has rules governing obscenity, slander, and political programs. It also does not regulate the advertising practices of broadcasters or claims made by advertisers on radio or television, other than limiting the amount of advertising during children's television programs. Instead, the Federal Trade Commission (FTC) handles those matters.

The FCC has no authority over any form of government communication, nor does it have jurisdiction over communications media other than broadcasters, cable, and telecommunications companies. For example, it does not regulate the motion picture industry, newspapers, or book publishers.

Finally, the FCC has only a limited role in local telephone or telecommunications services, which are regulated primarily by state utility commissions. In 1996 Congress gave the FCC authority to promote competition in local phone service and encourage the availability of low-cost telecommunications services in all areas, a policy known as "universal service." The FCC was given the power to preempt any state or local rule that was inconsistent with its regulations in those areas.

Powers and Authority

The five FCC commissioners adopt regulations to implement the telecommunications laws enacted by Congress. The regulations are developed and carried out by several FCC bureaus, including Wireline Competition, Wireless Telecommunications, Media, International, and Enforcement. All of the bureaus are assisted when necessary by the Office of the General Counsel and the Office of Engineering and Technology.

The commission's power to regulate is strictly limited by Congress, but its power to deregulate is broad and discretionary. In the Telecommunications Act of 1996, Congress instructed the FCC to stop enforcing any regulation that was no longer needed to protect consumers or the public interest. That provision effectively gave the FCC the power to deregulate any segment of the industry that had become competitive, such as long-distance phone service.

Some of the specific areas the FCC controls are broadcast licenses, radio and television technical matters, interstate telephone and telegraph rates and charges, international communications by satellite and undersea cable, amateur (ham) radio equipment and practices, maritime communications, police and fire department communications, cable and pay television rates and program distribution, data transmission services, educational broadcasting, antitrust cases involving broadcast and telephone companies, consumer electronics standards (that is, specifications for radio and television receivers), industrial radio use such as radio dispatch of motor vehicle fleets, and aviation radio communication. The commission also is responsible for the equal employment opportunity practices of the industries it regulates.

WIRELINE COMPETITION

Communications common carriers provide telephone, telegraph, facsimile, data, telephoto, audio and video broadcast program transmission, satellite transmission, and other electronic communications services for hire. The Communications Act requires common carriers to charge reasonable and nondiscriminatory prices, and the FCC's Wireline Competition Bureau assumes most of the responsibility for enforcing this provision of the act. Technically, the commission has jurisdiction only over interstate and related telephone and telegraph services. Its reach extends to local phone companies, however, because those companies' networks are financed in part by interstate calls carried by long-distance companies.

Through the Wireline Competition Bureau, the commission sets caps on the prices that phone companies charge for interstate and related services, writes accounting and depreciation rules, and determines whether companies may build new telephone facilities or discontinue or reduce services. It also requires regular financial and operating reports, reviews proposed phone company mergers and acquisitions, and promotes competition in the telephone markets.

Other duties include evaluating new technologies and use of facilities; conducting economic studies and investigations in industry structure and practice; overseeing telephone numbering, network reliability, and equipment registration; and regulating the rates and conditions for cable companies' use of utility poles.

The commission attempts to clear the way for new services through proceedings such as the Computers 2 and 3 inquiries, which determined the computer services that were properly subject to FCC regulation, and the Open Network Architecture proposal, designed to provide the building blocks for enhanced services. The FCC completed all three proceedings in the 1980s.

In the late 1990s the commission ended the requirement that phone companies file tariffs for domestic long-distance service because of the extensive competition in that market. The move all but deregulated prices in the interstate telephone business, although the FCC still retained the power to investigate complaints about excessive rates.

WIRELESS TELECOMMUNICATIONS

Cellular telephone, paging, public-safety dispatching, private radio, aviation radio, and other mobile communications services must obtain licenses from the FCC to use frequencies in the radio spectrum. The job of assigning those frequencies and issuing licenses falls to the Wireless Telecommunications Bureau, which the FCC established in 1994 to replace the Private Radio Services Bureau.

In the case of commercial services, the FCC has been given temporary power to conduct auctions and assign licenses to the highest-qualified bidders. The bureau also promotes competition in wireless services and regulates the frequencies used, transmitting power, call signals, permissible communications, and related matters.

Unlike the landline local phone companies, wireless operators face at least one competitor in every market. For that reason, they are subject to less regulation by the FCC and state authorities than their wireline counterparts. For example, the FCC does not require mobile communications companies to file tariffs, and Congress in 1993 barred state and local governments from regulating those companies' rates.

MEDIA

Radio and television stations also must obtain licenses from the FCC before going on the air. The commission assigns the task of issuing licenses and developing broadcast regulations to the Media Bureau. The bureau also sets technical standards and power limits for transmissions, assigns call letters, sets operating hours, and licenses the technicians who operate broadcast equipment.

In the interest of promoting competition and diversity of media ownership, the commission exerts a limited degree of control over television and radio networks. For example, the FCC reviews the restrictions that networks place on their affiliates' programs and advertising, and it limits the number of stations under common ownership locally and (in the case of television stations) nationally.

The FCC's principal leverage over broadcasters is its control over license renewals. When a station seeks to renew its license, the Media Bureau reviews its performance to determine whether it has met the requirement to serve the public interest. For new licenses, the bureau conducts lotteries to determine which of the competing applicants will be authorized.

The commission has limited power over the content of programs because, in addition to their First Amendment rights, broadcasters are not common carriers—they are not compelled to provide airtime to all would-be programmers or advertisers. The commission can and does restrict obscene and indecent programming, require television broadcasters to carry a certain amount of educational programming, and limit advertising during children's programs.

The commission's political broadcasting rules require stations that sell air time to one candidate to provide equal time to other major candidates for that office and to keep strict records of candidate requests for air time. The FCC also acts as arbiter in disputes concerning political broadcasts. The commission no longer requires stations to present contrasting views on nonpolitical programs, having concluded in 1987 that its Fairness Doctrine was unconstitutional. The decision continues to be a sore point with Congress, where proponents of restoring the policy remain vocal.

In addition to the typical television and radio stations, the Media Bureau licenses and regulates noncommercial educational stations, low-power television stations, and instructional television fixed service (ITFS) for in-school reception. ITFS uses higher frequencies than broadcast television and is not considered a broadcast service. It also licenses microwave-based "wireless cable" systems, a competitor to conventional cable television systems that the commission has tried to promote.

The FCC's Media Bureau also regulates cable television. As in phone service, the regulation of cable television operators is split between the FCC and state and local agencies. Generally, local agencies are allowed to regulate franchising, basic subscriber rates, and leased access services. The FCC reviews rates for certain cable services, sets standards for customer service and picture quality, and enforces the federal requirements on cable programming. The latter includes the mandates that cable systems carry local broadcast stations, pay for the broadcast programs they retransmit, and make channels available to public, educational, and governmental programmers.

The commission also regulates other forms of video service and program distribution, ensures compatibility of programming with home electronic equipment, restricts indecent cable programs, monitors competition in video services, and oversees certain technical aspects of cable operation.

Previously, the FCC had a separate Cable Services Bureau, which had been split off from the Mass Media Bureau in 1993 to heighten the oversight of the rapidly expanding cable industry. Congress ordered the increased regulation in 1992, giving the FCC and local authorities the power to set "reasonable" rates for basic and expanded basic services, equipment rentals, and installation in areas where there was no effective competition.

In 1996 Congress reduced the FCC's control over cable rates and system ownership, particularly in relation to small cable systems. The same law also set out new regulatory requirements for telephone companies' video systems, and the Cable Services Bureau developed rules for such "open video systems" later that year. In 2001 the Cable Services Bureau was folded back into the Media Bureau.

INTERNATIONAL

In addition to communications within the United States, the FCC also has domestic authority over satellite communications systems, telephone services that link the United States with foreign countries, and international broadcasting stations. The commission established the International Bureau in 1994 to consolidate the commission's international policies and activities. It licenses satellite communications systems, regulates international telecommunications and broadcasting services, and represents the FCC at international telecommunications organizations.

The FCC's international mission includes enhancing U.S. competitiveness overseas and promoting an interconnected, global telecommunications network. Through the International Bureau, it researches the development of international telecommunications regulations and facilities, promotes the international coordination of spectrum use and orbital assignments, advises the U.S. Trade Representative on international telecommunications negotiations and standard-setting, monitors compliance with licenses, and conducts training programs for foreign telecommunications officials.

ENFORCEMENT

The job of enforcing federal radio law and FCC rules generally falls to the Enforcement Bureau, formerly known as the Compliance and Information Bureau. It operates sixteen field offices and thirteen automated monitoring facilities across the United States, serving as the commission's window onto the communications world it regulates. In addition to acting as the commission's police, it also educates the public and the communications industries about FCC rules and policies.

Through the bureau, the FCC monitors the use of the spectrum to identify violations of the law or license terms. Its staff inspects radio stations and investigates complaints of interference, unauthorized transmission, or unlawful interception of calls. The bureau also is a leading authority on direction finding and other methods to identify the source of transmissions.

In 1996 the bureau began operating a national call center to field complaints about communications companies and other matters within its jurisdiction. In addition to providing information to the public, the bureau also advises the commission on the impact of regulations, the level of compliance, problems in the communications industries, and the merits of discontinuing old rules.

ENGINEERING AND TECHNOLOGY

To guard against conflicts in the radio spectrum, the FCC regulates most equipment that makes or interferes with radio transmissions—including computers, garage-door openers, cordless telephones, radio and television transmitters, and microwave ovens. New equipment in that category must meet FCC specifications and be authorized by the commission before it can be marketed.

The commission's Office of Engineering and Technology tests and authorizes equipment to ensure compliance. The office also works on technical standards, monitors and experiments with new technology, coordinates use of the frequencies shared by U.S. companies and international users or federal agencies, and provides the bureaus with scientific and technical advice.

Background

Federal regulation of interstate electrical communication began with the Post Roads Act in 1866, which authorized the postmaster general to fix rates annually for government telegrams. In 1887 Congress gave the Interstate Commerce Commission (ICC) authority to require telegraph companies to interconnect their lines for more extended service to the public.

Government regulation of the accounting practices of wire communication carriers began with the Mann-Elkins Act of 1910. That act authorized the ICC to establish uniform systems of accounts for telegraph and telephone carriers and to require certain reports of them. The Mann-Elkins Act also gave the ICC certain powers over radiotelegraph (wireless) carriers. This statute, in effect, extended provisions of the Interstate Commerce Act of 1887 to cover wireless telegraph.

As the number of radio users increased, it became necessary to organize the way the radio spectrum was used. A series of international radio conferences, starting in 1903, led to the development of regulations specifying uniform practices for radiotelegraph services. The enforcement of the regulations in the United States was delegated to the secretary of commerce and labor.

In 1912 Congress passed the Radio Act, the first law for the domestic regulation of radio communications in general. The Radio Act governed the character of emissions and transmissions of distress calls. The act also set aside certain frequencies for government use and placed licensing of wireless stations and operators under the secretary of commerce and labor. The first stations were licensed that year.

After World War I commercial radio broadcasting began to grow. Because the Radio Act of 1912 had not anticipated commercial broadcasting, no federal safeguards had been adopted to prevent stations from interfering with or overpowering one another's signals. These problems were dealt with on an ad hoc basis by four National Radio Conferences held during the early 1920s.

In 1926 President Calvin Coolidge urged Congress to rewrite the 1912 law. The result was the Dill-White Radio Act of 1927. It created a five-member Federal Radio Commission with regulatory powers over radio, including the issuance of station licenses, the allocation of frequency bands to various services, the assignment of specified frequencies to individual stations, and the control of station power. The secretary of commerce was delegated the authority to inspect radio stations, examine and license radio operators, and assign radio call signals.

Although the creation of the Federal Radio Commission solved many problems, the responsibility for electronic communications remained divided. The ICC still retained major responsibilities, and some aspects of telegraph service were under the jurisdiction of the Post Office Department and the State Department.

EARLY HISTORY

In 1933 President Franklin D. Roosevelt urged the creation of a new agency to regulate all interstate and foreign communication by wire and radio, including telephone, telegraph, and broadcasting. In response, Congress enacted the Communications Act of 1934, which consolidated in the new Federal Communications Commission the regulatory authority previously exercised by the Federal Radio Commission (which was abolished), the secretary of commerce, and the ICC.

The 1934 act would stand for sixty-two years as the foundation for federal telecommunications policy. It provided the basis for strict federal regulation of the communications media, a level of control intended to protect consumers and the public interest in the face of powerful monopolies. The most significant changes during the next six decades were the Communications Satellite Act of 1962, which created the Communications Satellite Corporation (Comsat) and gave the FCC authority to regulate the corporation and its activities; the 1984 and 1992 cable acts, which deregulated and reregulated the cable industry; and the Omnibus Budget Reconciliation Act of 1993, which required the FCC to auction off portions of the radio spectrum instead of awarding those frequencies by lottery.

Congress tried repeatedly and unsuccessfully in the 1970s, 1980s, and early 1990s to overhaul the 1934 act. With competing interest groups facing off over the complex legislation, lawmakers demurred rather than appearing to take sides.

FROM TELEPHONE MONOPOLY TO COMPETITION

For many years, the FCC and state officials agreed with the American Telephone and Telegraph (AT&T) Company that the phone system was a natural monopoly; indeed, one effect of state and federal regulation was to sustain that monopoly against would-be competitors. In the local phone arena, the country was divided into regional monopolies dominated by AT&T's twenty-two Bell affiliates. In long-distance service, AT&T was effectively the sole provider. In addition, AT&T purchased all of its equipment from its Western Electric subsidiary, and all Bell customers were required to use that equipment.

To give consumers some degree of protection, the FCC and state utility commissions regulated telephone rates and limited the profits earned by AT&T and the local phone companies. The FCC also imposed surcharges to shift costs from local to long-distance services; this shift was designed to hold down the cost of local phone lines. The main principles observed by the FCC were promoting the availability of low-cost phone service and ensuring nondiscriminatory pricing.

The commission's approach to telephone service began to change in the 1960s, when it made two major moves toward competition: it allowed MCI and other upstart long-distance companies to offer specialized services in markets already served by AT&T, and it ended the requirement that consumers use the telephone sets and office switchboards provided by AT&T. In the early 1970s the commission's Common Carrier Bureau (now Wireline Competition) allowed the competing long-distance companies to expand their offerings to the public, extending the battle with AT&T into more types of service.

AT&T responded by underpricing the competition, a move that the FCC tried repeatedly to block. Meanwhile, the Justice Department filed another antitrust lawsuit against AT&T—its third—seeking to split the Bells from the long-distance operations of AT&T and Western Electric. The Justice Department argued that AT&T was using the Bells' regulated monopoly power in local phone service to gain an illegal advantage in the newly competitive field of long-distance service.

That lawsuit led in 1982 to the consent decree that split the Bells from AT&T. The decree also released AT&T from the restrictions imposed under a previous settlement with the Justice Department, which had confined AT&T to markets regulated by the government. Those restrictions had kept AT&T out of the data-processing business and other computer- and information-related markets. At the same time, the Bells were barred from carrying long-distance calls, providing information services, and manufacturing telecommunications equipment until the federal courts ruled that there would be no threat of anticompetitive behavior.

The consent decree took effect Jan. 1, 1984, requiring a major new undertaking by the FCC: ensuring that all long-distance companies had equal access to the local phone companies' customers. The agency also came up with a new mechanism for shifting costs from local to long-distance services, establishing "access charges" that the local companies applied to each long-distance call.

DEREGULATION AT THE FCC

During the period of the breakup of AT&T, the FCC was transforming its interpretation of the law, moving toward a less strict regulatory regime. The move was prompted partly by political philosophy and partly by the rapid advance of technology, which strained the restrictions imposed by the FCC.

Deregulation first began in the common carrier area under Richard Wiley, a Republican chair appointed by President Richard Nixon. A series of court cases started to chip away AT&T's monopoly over long-distance telephone service. Using the court decisions as precedent, the FCC made several decisions that had the effect of promoting competition in long-distance services.

When Charles Ferris, a Democrat appointed by President Jimmy Carter, became chair, deregulation spread to the other communications services regulated by the FCC. By the time Mark Fowler, President Ronald Reagan's chair, was sworn in, the nature of the FCC's role in regulating telecommunications had undergone a fundamental change. Rather than restrict the development of new technologies and tightly regulate each component of the nation's communications network, the commission began to allow a free and open marketplace in telecommunications products and services.

Lotteries were introduced in the 1980s to grant low-power television, multichannel and multipoint distribution, cellular mobile telephone, electronic paging, and private radio services. Minority ownership rules were suspended. The Fairness Doctrine and other content-oriented broadcast regulations were dropped. Marketplace regulations based on pricing replaced traditional rate-of-return rules for common carriers. Tariff proceedings were expedited to speed delivery of new long-distance services to businesses and consumers. Station antitrafficking rules were eliminated. The multiple station ownership rules were eased. Regulation after regulation was dismantled for AT&T.

In the process, the commission reduced the paperwork burden imposed on many of its licensees and the backlog of some license applications, but the FCC also alienated the more regulatory-minded majority in Congress. The result was several confrontations in the late 1980s and early 1990s as lawmakers tried to reassert their leadership on communications issues.

FCC IN THE 1990s

Congress reacted to the efforts of Fowler and Dennis Patrick, the succeeding FCC chair, by seeking to influence, obstruct, or overturn FCC decisions. With tensions growing, President George H. W. Bush appointed a Republican moderate, Alfred Sikes, who was well liked in Congress, to be his commission chair. The appointment of Sikes, however, did not stop Congress from approving sweeping legislation in 1992 to reregulate the cable industry, even overriding Bush's veto.

President Bill Clinton's choice for FCC chair, Reed Hundt, drew mixed reviews from the industry and Congress. The broadcasters, for example, accused him of heavy-handedness in pushing to mandate three hours of educational television programming per week, and the cable companies decried his implementation of the 1992 cable act. Their complaints found a sympathetic ear among Republicans on Capitol Hill. Some leading congressional Democrats, on the other hand, praised Hundt for trying to protect consumers while also looking for ways to lighten the industry's regulatory load.

When Republicans took control of Congress in 1995, GOP conservatives targeted the FCC for cuts and even elimination. Most deregulatory proposals were opposed by many segments of the industry, however, for fear that the Bells would run roughshod over their competition. Instead, a consensus gradually emerged in favor of a regulated transition to competition overseen by the FCC. Lawmakers worked to fashion a rewrite of the 1934 act that satisfied most segments of the industry, their allies in Congress, and the Clinton administration. The Telecommunications Act of 1996 expanded competition in the telephone and cable industries while paring the amount of regulation on all telecommunications companies and broadcasters. The new law represented a 180-degree shift in policy from the 1934 act as Congress sought to have competition and market forces take the place of strict federal and state controls.

As competition flourished in the long-distance market, the FCC gradually eased its regulation of AT&T's long-distance services. In 1995 the FCC declared that AT&T was no longer a "dominant" carrier in the domestic long-distance market, lifting the added regulatory burden that AT&T had been forced to meet.

State regulators also were warming to the idea of competition in the local phone markets, but many technical and regulatory barriers stood in the way. The 1996 act eliminated the legal obstacles to competition in those markets, and it instructed the FCC to help remove the technical barriers on two main fronts: interconnection and universal service.

"Interconnection"—hooking into the incumbent local phone company's network—enables customers on competing phone networks to make calls to one another. Otherwise, a competitor would have to install new lines and phones in every home and business. The 1996 act required the incumbent phone companies to allow their competitors to interconnect with their networks at reasonable and nondiscriminatory rates. It also required them to give competitors a wholesale discount if the competitors chose to resell the incumbent's services rather than installing their own networks.

The FCC was left to translate the act's general instructions into specific rules within six months. In August 1996 the commission adopted a set of minimum interconnection standards that left many of the details to be negotiated by competitors or ironed out by state regulators. For example, the FCC established a method for determining what prices incumbents could charge their competitors, as well as default ceilings for those prices, but left the states to set the actual prices. Similarly, the FCC established rules to help the states calculate an appropriate wholesale discount, as well as set a default discount of 17 to 25 percent below the retail price.

New FCC rules dealing with universal service were also not well received. State and federal universal service policies had posed a threat to competition because they distorted prices, with businesses and toll callers paying higher rates to keep the prices for residential lines low and affordable. The 1996 act required the FCC to create a new, competitively neutral system of explicit subsidies that would ensure the wide availability of low-cost phone service. Under the FCC's rules released in May 1997, companies had to use forward-looking formulas to determine how much a typical telephone line in an area would cost to replace five years in the future. The FCC then stipulated that the federal Universal Service Fund would cover 25 percent of those costs incurred over a national benchmark price. The other 75 percent would be left to the states to pay.

These May 1997 rules drew sharp criticism and litigation from the states and the Bells. As the 1990s drew to a close, the federal court system, including the Supreme Court, began sorting out these rules and lawsuits. Although the act and FCC rules left the states in primary control of the move to local-phone competition, the FCC was given the power to intervene if a state strayed from the mandates of the new law or failed to resolve disputes among competitors.

The act also gave the FCC, not the courts, control over the Bells' expansion into long-distance service and telecommunications equipment manufacturing. Before applying to the FCC, a Bell was required to face competition in at least a portion of its local phone market, meet a fourteen-point test that its network and operational support systems could handle interconnection, and be in the public interest.

Cable Reversals

For cable companies, the 1996 act represented the third major shift in regulatory policy in twelve years. The 1984 Cable Communications Policy Act had deregulated the cable industry and relieved the commission and local municipalities of their rate and other regulatory authority. To give the fledgling cable companies a buffer against competition, the act barred the local phone companies from offering video programming services over the phone lines—a major restriction that the Bells would eventually challenge in court.

The deregulation was followed by the explosion of the cable industry into a $20 billion giant and complaints of poor service and discriminatory business practices. After a three-year fight, Congress reversed itself in 1992, giving the commission the power to set certain rates and requiring that cable program producers, such as MTV and ESPN, offer their programs to cable competitors at fair prices and terms.

The FCC was left to implement the 1992 act, and its interpretation won plaudits from consumer advocates but complaints from the industry. Using its authority, the commission ordered rates reduced up to 10 percent in 1993 and an additional 7 percent in 1994, cuts that saved consumers an estimated $4 billion. Hundt called the cuts "one of the greatest cost savings in the face of monopoly pricing in the history of American business regulation."

The 1996 act lifted the federal price controls on "cable programming services"—channels in the expanded basic tier, such as CNN and ESPN—after March 31, 1999. The act also made it much harder for the FCC to review a proposed rate increase before the price controls were lifted and allowed cable operators to escape price controls earlier in the face of threatened competition. Finally, the act eliminated price controls on "cable programming services" for many small cable systems.

Some GOP congressional leaders wanted additional limits on the FCC's authority over cable. Consumers did not need regulators to protect them, these Republicans argued, because cable was hardly the only source of video entertainment. But opposition from the White House forced Republicans to agree to leave some price controls in place for three years.

The 1996 act also gave the FCC jurisdiction over the telephone companies' video efforts, although the companies were allowed to choose how extensively they would be regulated. One new option, called "open video systems," required the operator to make two-thirds of its channels available to unaffiliated programmers. It also exempted the operator, however, from many of the regulations on cable systems.

The FCC adopted its rules for open video systems in June 1996, prohibiting operators from discriminating among programmers, favoring their programs, or charging unaffiliated programmers excessively to use the system. The rules, such as the regulations adopted in 1993 for cable systems, also required operators to carry the signals of local television stations and obtain permission before retransmitting a station's broadcasts.

Mass Media

The FCC loosened the reins significantly on broadcasters in the 1980s and 1990s, opening the door to more players and new services. One of the early deregulatory moves came in April 1981, when the commission eliminated many of its radio record-keeping requirements, all of its requirements governing minimum amounts of news and public affairs programming, and its rules requiring station executives to poll their communities regularly to ascertain their listeners' concerns and programming preferences.

In June 1984 the FCC extended those changes to television broadcasters when it eliminated guidelines concerning minimum amounts of news and public affairs programs and maximum amounts of commercial time. The commission also abolished program logs and requirements that stations meet certain program needs of the communities in which they operate.

More recently, the commission granted a major new freedom to television networks in 1995 when it repealed its twenty-five-year-old financial interest and syndication rules. Those rules had deterred CBS, NBC, and ABC from owning television programming. It also repealed the old prime-time access rule that had prohibited those networks and their affiliates in large cities from filling their prime-time schedules with network-originated programs.

In addition to giving broadcasters more control over their schedules and programs, the rule changes eased the path to license renewal. In the 1996 act, Congress extended the terms of licenses to eight years—up from seven for radio and five for television stations—and ordered the FCC to renew a license automatically if a station had served the public interest, made no serious violations of FCC rules or federal communications law, and committed no pattern of abuse of FCC rules or federal law. In deciding whether to renew a license, the FCC could not consider whether the public interest would be served better by another applicant for that license.

The FCC and Congress also steadily increased the number of stations that a network or ownership group could control. For radio, the limit rose from twelve AM and twelve FM stations in late 1984 to twenty AM and twenty FM stations in 1994, and to an unlimited number in the 1996 act. For television, the limit rose from twelve stations reaching no more than 25 percent of the national viewing audience in late 1984 to an unlimited number of stations reaching no more than 35 percent of the national audience in the 1996 act.

Congress also eased the limits on local ownership of radio stations, allowing a single company or group to control as many as eight stations in large markets. It left intact the ban on networks owning more than one television station in a single market, although the FCC was ordered to reconsider that restriction and other ownership limits every two years. The law also ordered the FCC to let broadcast networks own cable systems. The FCC would have to ensure, however, that cable systems controlled by a network did not discriminate against broadcasters not affiliated with that network.

The 1996 changes in ownership limits sparked a flurry of mergers and buyouts. Two of the biggest deals, announced while the legislation was still moving through Congress, came in the area of television and cable: Walt Disney's purchase of Capital Cities/ABC and Westinghouse's purchase of CBS. In 1997 Time Warner acquired Turner Broadcasting Company to form another notable media titan. The merger wave quickly swept up radio stations and the "Baby Bells," and by 1998 deals were pending that would combine the original seven Bells into four telephone giants.

The FCC and Congress generally justified the diminished control over broadcasters by citing the numerous and expanding sources of audio and video programming. Indeed, the FCC authorized almost 700 new FM stations in the mid-1980s and authorized a new, satellite-based digital audio broadcasting service in the 1990s. It also oversaw the emergence of direct broadcast satellites and attempted to speed the deployment of multipoint microwave distribution services (also known as wireless cable).

One significant potential source of video programming that emerged in the mid-1990s was digital television. In 1993 a group of manufacturers formed the Grand Alliance to develop a standard format for digital broadcasts. They eventually proposed a flexible format that would allow stations to transmit multiple channels on a single frequency or to broadcast one "high definition" signal with enhanced sound and picture quality. In May 1996 the FCC proposed to make the Grand Alliance format mandatory for all digital broadcasts. In April 1997 the FCC set a timetable for build-out of the digital television system that would have all broadcasters converted to digital television and relinquishing their analog frequencies by 2006. Those frequencies were to be reauctioned at that time (a 2004 law pushed the digital conversion date to 2009).

One area where the FCC and Congress resisted the deregulatory tide was in television programming for children. In 1974 the commission issued the Children's Television Report and Policy Statement, which established guidelines for broadcasters. Sixteen years later, Congress enacted the Children's Television Act in a bid to improve the quality of commercial programming for children. The law ordered the FCC to determine whether a television station had served the educational needs of children before renewing its license.

After adopting an initial set of rules for children's programming in 1991, the FCC struggled for almost five years to clarify the requirements for broadcasters. Democrats sought to mandate a specific amount of educational programming that stations had to broadcast and Republicans resisted any quantitative standard. The logjam broke in August 1996, when the commission ordered stations to carry at least three hours of educational programming per week for viewers under the age of seventeen. The order represented a compromise among the commissioners, the White House, and broadcasters.

In 1997 the FCC approved a set of TV ratings developed by the broadcasting industry. The system, which displays a series of letters at the start of the program warning parents of sexual situations, violence, language, or dialogue, works with the "V-chip"—a device that can block the display of programs with certain ratings.

License Fees and Auctions

For many years the FCC has offset its expenses by charging fees to the telecommunications industry, but by the early 1990s the revenue had fallen far behind the commission's costs. In 1993 Congress approved an FCC plan for doubling new user fees ranging from $200 to $900 for radio stations and from $4,000 to $18,000 for television stations.

Congress also authorized the FCC to auction portions of the radio spectrum for commercial use. Long advocated by the FCC, the auctions represented a radical change in the way the spectrum was parceled out to users. They also reflected the growing role played by wireless technologies in telecommunications. The bulk of the usable spectrum has been reserved for the Defense Department and other federal agencies. The next largest users are radio and television broadcasters; the FCC awards those licenses for free after holding hearings to decide which applicants would best serve the public interest.

The FCC used similar "comparative hearings" to award licenses for the early mobile communications systems, which were akin to two-way radios. As technology advanced and competition for licenses increased, the commission switched to a lottery system that awarded licenses on the basis of luck, not public interest.

The FCC started using lotteries to award cellular-phone licenses in 1983, and it followed the same route for paging systems. An unintended byproduct, however, was a new industry of license speculators who would apply for licenses only for the sake of selling whatever they won to the highest bidder. By auctioning licenses, the FCC effectively transferred the speculators' bounty to the U.S. Treasury. The first licenses offered at auction were for a new, digital form of mobile phone and paging called "personal communications services." Those auctions raised an estimated $10 billion.

The enormous amount of money raised by the auctions led numerous lawmakers to call for more of the government-reserved spectrum to be converted to private use through auctions. By summer 1998 the commission had raised $23 billion through these auctions, with the broadband C-block auction pulling in nearly $10 billion. However, several of the C-block license winners defaulted on their loans. Congress, as part of its Balanced Budget Act of 1997, also required the commission to set minimum prices for each license after the April 1997 Wireless Communications Services auction ended with several winning bids of less than $5 for major metropolitan licenses.

Mergers and Consolidations

The 1996 Telecommunications Act spurred more than $500 billion in mergers, as telephone companies, broadcast and cable system owners, and content providers retrenched in the deregulated environment. Major deals included America Online's purchase of Time-Warner—which combined the nation's largest Internet service provider with the second-largest cable-system owner; Bell Atlantic's purchase of GTE; AT&T's acquisition of cable giants MediaOne and Tele-Communications; and WorldCom's purchase of MCI. The FCC under William Kennard, who succeeded Hundt as chair in 1997 and had served as the commission's general counsel, was responsible for assessing whether these combinations ultimately benefited consumers. Because some merged entities began "bundling" services—simultaneously selling voice, cable, and high-speed Internet, all transmitted over high-capacity fiber-optic lines—the agency also was thrust into the role of regulating some new digital services that had previously fallen outside of its purview.

The FCC came under particular scrutiny for its role in promoting competition in local telephone service. One area the Bells coveted was the transmission of computer data over long distances. Several Bells submitted to lengthy FCC reviews of whether they had opened their local phone markets to competition—for instance, by allowing smaller vendors to install equipment in the Bells' central switching offices—hoping in exchange to win approval to begin to offer long-distance service. Verizon Communications, formed by the merger of Bell Atlantic and GTE Corp., won approval for long-distance service in New York early in 2000, and SBC Communications later

that year similarly received approval in Texas, Oklahoma, and Kansas. However, congressional Republicans and some Democrats traditionally sympathetic to the Bells complained the FCC was not opening local markets quickly enough. Conversely, consumer groups bitterly criticized the agency for not doing enough to prevent a "re-monopolization" of the telecommunications market.

The act also gave the FCC control over the Bells' expansion into long-distance service. Before FCC approval, however, a Bell was required to face competition in at least a portion of its local phone market. But by summer 1998, no Bell companies had been admitted into the long-distance market, although several had applied. Southwestern Bell Communications prevailed in a Texas district court with its claims that Section 271 of the Telecommunications Act, which bars the Bell companies from long-distance service until the FCC gives its consent, constituted a bill of attainder—an obscure section of the U.S. Constitution that prohibits Congress from singling out an individual for punishment without due process. The lower court ruling was stayed pending the FCC's appeal. In 1998 the Supreme Court upheld all but one of the FCC rules that were challenged. The Court struck down only the rule that ensured new telephone companies access to most of the "elements" of the local phone system. The Court ruled that the FCC had exceeded its authority in drafting so broad a rule.

FCC IN THE 2000s

Kennard's efforts to offset media consolidation also were evident in a January 2000 initiative to license approximately 1,000 new low-power FM radio stations. The permits for 100-watt, noncommercial stations were intended to give schools, churches, and community groups an opportunity to create niche programming at low cost. Central to the plan was allowing the tiny stations to be located closer to existing stations on the FM dial than had been previously permitted. But the proposal triggered an intense lobbying effort by opponents including the National Association of Broadcasters and National Public Radio, who charged spacing the signals closer would result in signal interference. Upset at what some viewed as an independent, activist agenda, Congress late in 2000 included a provision in a year-end spending bill disallowing the closer spacing, which eliminated 70 to 80 percent of qualified applicants. Only applicants in outlying areas where signal interference was not likely were allowed to proceed.

In January 2001 President George W. Bush elevated commissioner Michael K. Powell to FCC chair. Powell, the son of former Secretary of State Colin Powell, had served on the commission since 1997, and before that in the antitrust division of the Justice Department. Early in his tenure, the new FCC chair vowed to adopt a less activist agenda and argued for a scaled back role for telecommunications regulators in the marketplace. Indeed, he proposed deregulating many parts of the industry, especially local telephone companies and large media firms.

Powell arrived at the FCC at just the moment when the telecommunications industry was tipping into crisis. Companies had overbuilt capacity (especially fiber-optic cable) and had taken on enormous debt to do so. As a result, a number of large firms, including giants such as WorldCom and rising stars such as Global Crossing and PSINet, slipped into bankruptcy. In the first eighteen months of the new commissioner's tenure, the industry as a whole lost $2 trillion in market valuation and shed 500,000 jobs. At the same time, broadcasters and cable operators were reeling from a slowdown in the advertising market, cutting deeply into their revenues and profits.

Industry contraction led to less competition in some areas. For instance, during the first six months of 2001, the cost of broadband Internet service provided by the Baby Bells rose 25 percent, reflecting a dearth of other providers. Instead of calling for new regulations, Powell proposed doubling fines the agency levied against those Baby Bells that did not adequately open their local networks to competitors, as mandated by the 1996 Telecommunications Act.

At the same time, Powell faced intense pressure from these same Bell companies to undo a number of restrictions imposed on them as a result of the 1996 act. In particular, the phone companies no longer wanted to lease out their local phone lines to outside competitors at discount rates. The act required the discounts—ultimately determined by state regulators with guidelines provided by the FCC—in an effort to create an environment by which other phone companies could crack the Bells' traditional local phone monopoly. But Verizon, SBC, and other former Bells argued that the discounts allowed their competitors an unfair advantage in the fight for local phone customers.

Competitors, such as AT&T and MCI, complained that the Bells were stalling by mounting legal challenges to the efforts of many state regulators to establish a discount fee for new local providers. In addition, these companies said that the Baby Bells often took days or even weeks to hand over the records of those customers who were switching to a new provider. The discounts also were supposed to ensure the viability of a class of small vendors known as competitive local exchange carriers (CLECs). However, regional Bells complained that some CLECs had struck exclusive agreements with Internet service providers and were only routing one-way calls to the provider, ensuring that they only receive payments for connecting the calls.

In an effort to split the difference, Powell proposed a two-year phase-out of the FCC guidelines, which raised the ire of the new big competitors and CLECs, who argued that eliminating the discounts too soon would slow their progress, just as they were beginning to take market share away from the Bells and create a competitive environment. The debate continued with the federal courts weighing in on both sides. First, on May 14, 2002, the Supreme Court affirmed the part of the 1996 law that required the discounts. But on May 25, the D.C. Circuit Court of Appeals struck down a part of those rules, when it decided that the discounts from the Bells did not apply to phone lines the CLECs were using to provide customers with Internet access.

The resulting confusion was a powerful argument for Powell's proposed phase-out of the discounts. On Feb. 20, 2003, the FCC voted on Powell's proposal. Given the fact

that the commission had three Republicans (all appointed by Bush) and only two Democrats, industry watchers expected the chair to win the day. But the vote to phase out local discounted rates was defeated 3–2.

The vote was a huge blow to Powell. The local discount rate had clearly been the most important issue before the commission since he had assumed the chair, and it had not gone his way. Even worse, the dissenting Republican, Kevin J. Martin, was now deemed to be a swing vote, which gave him enormous leverage. Martin emerged as a powerful force on the commission and a rival to Powell. The ruling was also a blow to the Bells. Not only were the discounts not phased out, but the state role in determining rates remained, leaving in place a chaotic fifty-state patchwork of rules.

Powell was more successful in his efforts to repeal a prohibition on large mergers in the cell phone industry. There were six national carriers, including Verizon Wireless, Cingular, AT&T Wireless, and Sprint PCS, and the commission previously had effectively banned consolidation among these providers by restricting the amount of wireless spectrum one company could own in each market. The restriction was intended to prevent one or two firms from dominating a market, but studies showed the ban was hurting the industry. The big six had national networks and all could compete in every market, which would make competition especially fierce and prices low, benefiting consumers. So, on Nov. 1, 2001, the agency voted to phase out the cap on spectrum ownership by 2003.

At first, none of the wireless giants took advantage of the easing of restrictions on mergers. One reason was that the companies each used one of three incompatible cell phone technologies. For instance, while Verizon used a technology called CDMA, Cingular and AT&T Wireless used another called GSM. Because these technologies were incompatible, only those companies that used the same standard could realistically combine their operations. Eventually, the rule change led to a number of huge mergers among those companies that did share the same technologies. In 2004 Cingular purchased AT&T Wireless for $41 billion. Sprint and Nextel—who also used compatible wireless technologies—combined in a $36 billion deal that created Sprint Nextel. The big six had become the big four.

The FCC struck another blow for industry consolidation on June 2, 2003, when it voted 3–2 to significantly scale back the cross-ownership rules that prohibited one company from owning a large number of media outlets—such as television and radio stations and newspapers—in one market. The old rules also prevented a business from owning television stations that reach more than 35 percent of all households nationwide. Under the new FCC-approved guidelines, one company could own up to three television stations, eight radio outlets, one daily newspaper, and one cable operator in one large market. Companies could also own television stations reaching up to 45 percent of all households in the country.

Powell defended the decision, arguing that the old rules were anachronistic in the fast-paced information

age, where the Internet and cable have caused a proliferation of new sources of information. Moreover, he said,
the FTC and the Justice Department's Antitrust Division
would still have the authority to review media mergers and stop those deals that would hurt consumers. But
consumer advocates, entertainers, and others decried the
change, arguing that eliminating the rules further threatened the independence of the press as well as that of independently owned radio and television stations, which tend
to provide communities with more local programming
than network-owned stations.

Later, these opponents hailed a June 2004 decision by
the Third Circuit Federal Court of Appeals blocking the
implementation of the new rules. The decision did not
criticize the ownership guidelines per se but instead took
issue with the methodology the agency had used in formulating them. The FCC appealed the case. Meanwhile,
Congress stepped into the debate. A bill restoring most
of the old guidelines won the approval of the Senate
Commerce Committee on June 19, 2003. The measure
was seen as a direct rebuke to Powell. The Senate committee issued Powell another reprimand the following week
when it adopted language as part of an FCC reauthorization package creating a complex new ownership formula
that would have restricted the number of television stations one firm could own beyond even the original 35
percent cap.

Meanwhile, both the Senate and House Appropriations
Committees adopted legislation that reversed the agency's
media ownership decision. The same language passed the
full Senate but ran into serious opposition from the House
Republican leadership and the White House. Still, the surprisingly strong congressional support for the proposal
led both sides to sit down and negotiate a compromise.
Under an agreement reached in mid-November, the 35
percent cap was increased to 39 percent, rather than the
45 percent proposed by the agency.

But no sooner had the agency put the ownership issue
behind it than it found itself embroiled in the middle of
another controversy—this time over broadcast indecency.
The issue first surfaced at the beginning of February 2004,
when Janet Jackson inadvertently bared part of one breast
during a musical number at the Super Bowl halftime
show. The incident sparked a popular campaign among
religious conservatives and others to rein in what many
claimed was a dramatic increase in sexually explicit material on the airwaves.

In Congress, existing legislative proposals that would
significantly raise indecency fines gained new support and
momentum after they had languished for months before
the Jackson incident. On March 11, 2004, one indecency
bill overwhelmingly passed the House. But a similar
Senate bill also contained a provision blocking the new
FCC's media ownership rules, throwing in doubt the just-
negotiated compromise and reigniting that contentious
debate. Subsequent efforts by House and Senate conferees
to find some sort of compromise failed.

Early in 2005 the House took up and, once again,
overwhelmingly passed an indecency bill that mirrored
the one it had approved the year before. But a companion

measure did not see action in the Senate by summer 2005.
Meanwhile, the FCC responded to the Jackson flap by
stepping up its enforcement efforts in this area. The agency
toughened its definition of indecency, making it easier to
bring future actions against broadcasters. Furthermore,
Powell personally supervised the investigation into the
Jackson incident to signal his commitment to the issue.
Eventually, the agency judged CBS to be culpable and, in
early July 2004, proposed fining twenty affiliate CBS stations a total of $550,000—the largest penalty ever imposed
for broadcast indecency.

A few months later, in October, the Jackson penalty
was topped by a proposed $1.2 million fine levied against
169 Fox affiliates for the broadcast of the reality TV show
Married in America, which depicted digitally obscured
nudity. The following month, Viacom paid a record $3.5
million to the agency to settle indecency charges stemming from two radio shows.

A major FCC leadership shake-up occurred in early
2005 with Powell resigning as the agency's chair. President
Bush named sitting commissioner Martin as his replacement. Like Powell, Martin was young (thirty-eight years
old) and well connected in Republican circles. Many in
the telecom industry were pleased with his record of support for deregulation. But Martin's willingness to split
with Powell on preserving local discount rates gave consumer advocates and other industry watchdogs hope that
his agenda would be customer friendly as well. Social
conservatives also hailed his appointment because he had
criticized Powell and other commissioners for being too
soft on indecency.

Among the first issues facing Martin after he assumed
the chair involved the provision of services by companies
that provide phone service over the Internet. In May 2005
the commission passed a rule requiring that Internet
phone providers such as Vonage ensure its subscribers
have access to local 911 emergency services. Vonage and
other companies challenged the rule in court, arguing
that the agency had no jurisdiction over Internet telephony. In June 2006 Congress settled the matter, passing
legislation requiring the Internet telephone providers to
offer 911 service.

Also facing Martin early in his tenure was a revival of
the indecency issue, which had been largely quiescent for
more than a year. On March 15, 2006, the FCC announced
that it was proposing a record $4 million in fines for a
number of shows that had allegedly violated the agency's
indecency standards. The March 15 ruling prompted a
number of television networks and more than 800 affiliate
stations to sue the agency, arguing that it had overstepped
its authority in issuing these indecency fines. More specifically, the broadcasters accused the FCC of violating their
First Amendment rights to free speech. In November 2006
the agency voted to withdraw two of its smaller indecency
fines that had led to the lawsuit. However, the bulk of the
fines levied on March 15 remained in place and the lawsuit continued to advance in the courts.

In 2006 Congress worked again on indecency legislation. Supporters in May managed to quickly push through
the Senate a measure that was slightly less far-reaching

than the bills Congress had previously considered. This new version increased by tenfold the amount the FCC could fine each television or radio broadcaster for each incident of indecency, raising the total from $32,500 to $325,000. As with earlier bills, only broadcasters, not cable or satellite providers, were liable. Soon after Senate passage, the measure was rapidly taken up and passed by the House; President Bush signed it into law on June 15, 2006.

Meanwhile, the agency was grappling with a number of huge telecommunications mergers that promised to dramatically alter the industry landscape and to affect consumer interests. In November 2005 the agency approved two large mergers. The first involved the purchase of MCI by Verizon Wireless. The second merger involved "Baby Bell" SBC Communications absorbing its former parent, AT&T, making the new combined firm (which adopted the much better known AT&T name) the largest telecommunications provider in the world. Consumer groups criticized both mergers, arguing that they would lead to monopoly-like conditions in many markets and, ultimately, price increases. In an effort to answer this criticism, the FCC required the companies in both deals to sell customers broadband DSL Internet access without requiring that they buy traditional phone service as well.

In March 2006, just a few months after the first mergers were approved, AT&T upped the ante, proposing to buy Bell South, yet another Baby Bell. The $86 billion deal, which gave AT&T a third of the nation's wireless market and increased its reach in other major telecommunications businesses, produced a seven-month deadlock on the commission. While two Republican commissioners supported the merger, the commission's two Democrats opposed it, expressing concern about the impact the new, huge firm would have on consumers. The tie-breaking vote was held by the third Republican commissioner, the newly seated Robert M. McDowell, who refrained from voting because of a possible conflict of interest, due to his previous telecommunications lobbying activity. The deadlock was finally broken in December 2006, when AT&T presented a package of concessions to allay the Democratic concerns, and the deal was approved by the FCC at the end of the year.

In the same month, the commission handed AT&T and other large telephone companies, such as Verizon and Sprint, another victory, when it approved, by a 3–2 party-line vote, a rule severely limiting the authority state and local regulators have over telephone carriers trying to offer cable service in their area. Among other things, the measure required local regulators to rule on cable franchise applications within ninety days and prohibited officials from forcing applicants to offer cable service to everyone in their jurisdictions.

Supporters of the cable rule, including Martin, argued that it would ultimately lower rates for consumers by bringing more competition to areas where there was currently only one cable provider. But Democratic commissioner Jonathan Adelstein countered that the FCC had exceeded its legal authority and that the new rule would lead to a flood of legal challenges from local regulators and cable companies.

Just three months later, in early March 2007, AT&T, Verizon, and other big firms scored yet another victory when the commission approved a rule requiring small, rural telephone companies to grant access to their phone lines to companies, such as AT&T, Verizon, and Time–Warner Cable, that want to offer phone service through the Internet. The Democratic takeover of Congress in January 2007 had an almost immediate impact on the FCC. In March 2007 the five commissioners were summoned before the House Energy and Commerce Committee Subcommittee on Telecommunications, where they were rebuked by the powerful chair, John Dingell (D-MI), and others for not being responsive enough to consumer needs, from not setting new rules for cable service in apartment buildings to not resolving disputes over the distribution of telecommunications development funds in rural areas.

The agency also has found itself facing pressure from the private sector, especially over the future allocation of valuable radio spectrum. A law that Congress passed in 2004 mandated that television broadcasters complete the conversion to digital signals by Feb. 17, 2009, a move that would free up a substantial part of the radio spectrum then being used by television stations. While the agency was required to set aside at least some of the new space for public safety and emergency communication uses, it could allocate a portion of the freed-up space for commercial use as well. The television frequencies, particularly UHF, would be particularly useful to cell phone companies and satellite television providers because they travel long distances, are barely affected by weather, and penetrate buildings more effectively than many other parts of the spectrum. Called the C-block, these 700-megahertz frequencies are considered the "last beachfront property in the ether."

In August 2007 the FCC announced that those who bought a part of the spectrum would have to allow consumers to purchase any service, using any device. The ruling was a major victory for consumer advocates as well as Internet providers such as Google and Microsoft, who wanted to use the new spectrum to offer a host of new wireless Internet and other services. Both wanted to prevent wireless service providers from forcing their subscribers to use certain search engines when they surfed the Internet using their cell phones.

The eight-week spectrum auction, which closed on March 18, 2008, netted $19.6 billion for the federal government and set the stage for the first nationwide network open to all devices and software. The nation's two largest carriers, Verizon and AT&T, garnered 80 percent of the airwaves auctioned. Google, which also bid on a slice of the new spectrum, did not win any of the 1,090 licenses sold. But the Internet search giant had already won a huge victory by helping to convince the agency to attach the open access requirement to the spectrum, regardless of who won the auction.

FCC chair Martin hailed the C-block auction, pointing out that it raised more than all past auctions of radio spectrum combined. But a simultaneous auction of the D-block spectrum, the designation of airwaves set aside for first responders, failed to find a buyer. The public safety portion of the airwaves was to be developed as a partnership between a corporate buyer and police, firefighters, and other public safety groups. The plan stipulated that the private buyer who bought the spectrum would develop it and then lease it to first responders and others. But there was only one bidder for the D-block, and the bid was far below the $1.3 billion minimum price set by the FCC.

An investigative report on the D-block auction, issued by the commission's inspector general's office in April 2008, found that the FCC terms of the auction—including an unwillingness to establish how much public renters of the spectrum would have to pay the company that controlled it—may have dissuaded some firms from getting involved. By June 2009 the issue of what to do with the D-block had still not been resolved, although a growing number of state and local governments were calling on the FCC to give over control of the spectrum to public entities.

Meanwhile, in late April 2007 the FCC released a report recommending that Congress enact legislation giving the commission new authority to limit violent content on television. The FCC report, which had been commissioned by Congress in 2004, suggested the agency be granted the power to fine TV stations and networks for excessively violent programming, similar to the system then in place for regulating indecency. The proposal, however, would expand the agency's reach, allowing it to regulate not only broadcasters but basic cable channels as well.

The report has been hailed by child advocacy and parents' rights groups, who have argued that depictions of excessive violence on television have become commonplace, are harmful to children, and can lead to aggressive and even violent behavior. But civil liberties groups and media companies have countered that regulations could violate free speech protections contained in the First Amendment. Indeed, they say, parents, not television stations, have an obligation to police what children do and do not watch. But the proposal to give the agency the extra authority was never taken up by Congress, and the issue ultimately faded from the public eye.

Later in 2007, the agency turned its attention to another sensitive area: media ownership. Tough market conditions—particularly in the newspaper industry, but also in radio and television broadcasting—had led media firms in recent years to pressure the commission to relax ownership rules and allow for greater consolidation. These firms also argued that the thirty-five-year-old ban on "cross-ownership" was outdated in the current era of multiple news and information sources. The Newspaper Association of America agreed, arguing that lifting of the ban was a way to help struggling newspapers by allowing them to buy television stations whose advertising revenues could help pay for the cost of newsgathering.

Martin proposed to lift the ban as a way of "forestalling the erosion in local news coverage." Critics of Martin's proposal argued that it would threaten media diversity and lead to corporate monopolies in various markets. On Dec. 18, 2007, in a 3–2 party-line vote, the commission partially lifted the ban, allowing a newspaper in one of the country's top twenty media markets to merge with a radio or television station in the same market, as long as the television station is not among the four highest-rated in that city. In a separate 3–2 vote, the agency reestablished a national cable television ownership ceiling at 30 percent, meaning one company could not have more than 30 percent of all cable subscribers.

Meanwhile, the commission attempted to resolve another dispute, this time involving empty airwaves—called "white spaces"—that exist between broadcast channels 2 to 51. These airwaves were slated to become available after the transition from analog to digital television programming. Public interest groups believe the white space transmission could be used to bring broadband and other services to poorly served parts of the country and might also provide improved communications for various emergency response groups. But entertainers and others who currently use wireless microphones that operate on these frequencies lobbied against opening these white spaces to other uses, arguing that doing so could disrupt various events, from concerts to church services.

However, the commission was heavily lobbied by technology companies, such as Microsoft and Google, who argued that opening up white spaces would greatly expand wireless options and make it easier to create new and cheaper wireless products and services. The FCC ultimately agreed with the corporate viewpoint and on Nov. 4, 2008, voted unanimously to open white spaces for general use.

In June 2008 FCC chair Martin reported that the agency had received 3,700 complaints on high early cancellation fees for cell phone contracts. Wireless providers argued that the penalty fees recoup the costs they incur from subsidies that enable new customers to get cheap phones. At the same time, the nation's largest wireless firms—Verizon, AT&T, Sprint Nextel, and T-Mobile—were lobbying the FCC to adopt a federal rule on cancellation fees that would supersede the patchwork of state laws and protect them from a raft of class action lawsuits in various state courts.

For their part, consumer groups opposed federal regulations in this area if they superseded state laws, arguing that state regulators are the best watchdogs of consumer abuse. In addition, states worried that an overarching federal policy would effectively eliminate the right of a citizen charged high cancellation fees to sue for damages in state courts. Martin supported the large wireless providers and pushed to establish a federal policy on early cancellation fees. But the issue languished at the agency and the issue lost some of its potency after wireless companies began lowering their cancellation fees.

In August 2008 the FCC ruled that Comcast had violated federal policy when it unlawfully blocked Internet traffic for some subscribers by disrupting the transfer of certain digital files. Although Comcast was not fined, the agency ordered the firm to change the way it managed its network. This precedent-setting ruling sent a message to other Internet carriers that they must fully disclose how they manage the flow of traffic over their networks.

A few years earlier, in 2005, the FCC had outlined a set of principles aimed at ensuring that broadband networks are "widely deployed, open, and affordable and accessible to all consumers." Comcast had argued that the agency's "network neutrality principles" were part of a policy statement and were not enforceable rules. With the August ruling, the agency established categorically that the neutrality principles are more than a statement of intent and are enforceable.

A few months later, the commission became involved in a number of controversial mergers. In November 2008 the FCC approved the merger of Verizon and Alltel, forming the country's largest cell phone operator, with 83.8 million subscribers. The merger had been opposed by public interest groups who felt it would deprive consumers of choice while shackling them with higher prices. The commission also approved Sprint Nextel's merger with wireless broadband provider Clearwire, adding another large competitor to the broadband wireless industry.

In addition to the wireless mergers, the government, upon the agency's recommendation, approved the merger of XM and Sirius, the nation's only satellite radio companies. Both firms had been struggling financially under increased competition from music-enabled cell phones, iPods, music websites, and traditional radio stations. The merger allowed the companies to eliminate overlapping transmission towers and programming. Although the merger was opposed by consumer groups, broadcasters, and lawmakers who argued it would create a radio monopoly, the agency asserted that the marketplace had changed dramatically and that the joining of the companies could occur without a threat to competition with traditional radio.

Meanwhile, the much ballyhooed switch from analog to digital television was hitting some last-minute snags. Seven months prior to the long-awaited switch, the Government Accountability Office (GAO) released a report indicating that many consumers were still confused about how to prepare for the transition. Nationwide, between 30 and 80 million TVs relied on antennas to receive over-the-air-signals. To continue watching TV after the transition, these owners would need to buy converter boxes. For those who applied for them, $40 coupons were made available to offset the cost. But according to the report, two-thirds of the people who wanted a coupon did not know how to get one.

Two agencies had been tasked with managing the process—the FCC was to handle the technical aspects of the switch, while the National Telecommunications and Information Administration was responsible for educating consumers and running the $1.5 billion coupon program. But critics of the transition argued that neither agency took a lead in keeping consumers informed and prepared. As the time to switch to digital approached, millions of consumers began requesting coupons in ever greater numbers. By early January 2009, the coupon program had run out of money and millions had to be put on a waiting list. In response, Congress postponed by nearly four months the deadline for stations to drop the old signals—from Feb. 17 to June 12.

However, the delay created a slew of new problems. In particular, broadcasters were unhappy shouldering the expense of having to maintain both analog and digital signals on the air at the same time. In spite of these issues, the digital switch moved ahead in nearly 500 full-power stations around the country in winter and spring 2009. The switch-off of all analog television signals occurred fairly seamlessly in June, although in some areas, consumers complained of reception issues.

On another contentious issue before the commission, the Supreme Court ruled in April 2009 that the FCC had the right to penalize broadcasters for the occasional use of certain expletives on the airwaves, even if they were unscripted and isolated. The ruling upheld a 2004 change in FCC policy that allowed broadcasters to be fined up to $325,000 every time certain words were spoken on the air. The decision was a big win for the FCC and it was hailed by children's rights groups, such as the Parents Television Council, as "an incredible victory for families."

Meanwhile, the changeover of administrations led to turnover on the commission. President Barack Obama nominated Democrat Julius Genachowski as FCC chair on March 3, 2009. Genachowski was widely praised for his experience both in business and as a Washington telecom policy adviser. During his confirmation hearing, Genachowski said that he planned to tackle issues such as "net neutrality" and bringing broadband Internet to rural and low-income areas, a key component of Obama's larger economic stimulus plan.

The president also filled other vacancies on the commission. With Democrat Michael J. Copps, who was reappointed to a second term in 2006, remaining on the commission, Obama reappointed Republican Robert M. McDowell, a telecommunications lawyer who had joined the FCC in 2006. For the final two commissioners, Obama chose Democrat Mignon Clyburn, former head of the South Carolina Public Service Commission and daughter of House Majority Whip Jim Clyburn (D-SC), and Republican Meredith Attwell Baker, the former administrator of the National Telecommunications and Information Administration.

FCC IN THE 2010s

In November 2009 Comcast, the largest cable system operator in the United States, and NBC-Universal, owner of broadcast networks and a portfolio of popular cable channels, announced that they would, in effect, merge. The proposed deal would give Comcast a 51 percent stake in NBC, allowing the cable company effective control over the network. The remainder of NBC would be held by the network's existing owner, General Electric (GE), with an option for Comcast to eventually acquire GE's remaining stake.

The deal was regarded by many as a major test of President Obama's call during the campaign for closer inspection of media mergers and greater diversity in the information made available to TV viewers. The two companies hoped for approval by the close of 2010, in part because Comcast's stock had lost value due to the uncertainty surrounding the deal.

Public interest groups expressed strong reservations about the merger, concerned about the implications of allowing one company to control both the creation and the distribution of so much content. They argued that Comcast could block competitors' access to NBC's prime-time shows and local newscasts. Coming at a time when there was intense focus on online video, the merger also displeased some critics in Congress who were concerned that a media merger of this size had the potential to leave consumers with less programming and higher rates.

Comcast argued that the merger would fulfill its vision of "anytime, anywhere access to content," and it was prepared for a fight. In addition to advertising, donations, and investments, the company had about thirty lobbying firms on its payroll and spent $6.9 million on lobbyists in the first half of 2010, which opponents of the deal held up as evidence that Comcast was trying to "buy" government approval. Comcast also began to cash in on its years of charitable giving by urging the beneficiaries of its funding to write letters of support to the FCC.

Typically, merger reviews take 180 days, but by late December 2010 officials indicated the deal would not be completed by the end of the year, as Comcast executives had hoped. It was not until Jan. 19, 2011, that the merger finally received FCC approval in a 4–1 vote. Democratic commissioner Copps cast the sole dissenting vote: "The Comcast-NBCU joint venture opens the door to the cableization of the open Internet. The potential for walled gardens, toll booths, content prioritization, access fees to reach end users, and a stake in the heart of independent content production is now very real." Hoping to temper such concerns, FCC Chair Genachowski asserted that the conditions imposed by the FCC included "carefully considered steps to ensure that competition drives innovation in the emerging online video marketplace."

Indeed, the deal did not come without a long list of conditions intended to ensure that Comcast played fair when dealing with rival programmers, cable providers, and broadband Internet providers. Notable among those conditions was the requirement that Comcast give up NBC-Universal's management stake in Hulu, the premier online TV website.

Meanwhile, in the first half of 2010, the agency was the subject of two important court decisions. The first came in March, when the U.S. Court of Appeals, District of Columbia Circuit upheld an FCC rule requiring cable operators that also own programming channels to offer those channels to competitors. In other words, if a cable operator also owned a sports channel, it could not prohibit other cable operators from purchasing the right to offer the channel as well.

The rule, which also applies to Satellite TV providers, was the subject of a bitter challenge by cable giants Comcast and Cablevision, who argued that given the huge array of choices in television, such rules were unnecessary and counterproductive. But the rule and the court ruling were hailed by consumer advocates and others, who argued that it would ensure greater competition and choice for consumers.

The ruling was deemed timely and important, coming just months after cable giant Comcast had announced its intention to purchase a controlling stake in NBC-Universal, potentially giving it ownership of dozens of channels, from the NBC broadcast network to cable offerings such as A&E, USA, and Bravo. While Comcast criticized the ruling, its executives indicated that the firm would abide by the requirement, a move that industry analysts said would help the company win FCC approval for the merger with NBC.

While the cable programming decision was a major victory for the agency, less than one month after that ruling, the same court handed the FCC a huge defeat. This decision, issued by the DC Circuit Court of Appeals in April 2010, largely struck down an FCC requirement that Internet providers treat all websites equally. The rule, which was the cornerstone of the agency's "net neutrality" policy, aimed to ensure that providers would not offer faster service to its own sites or to those websites that agreed to pay a fee. In other words, the agency wanted to ensure that there would not be a "fast lane" and "slow lane" for traffic and that all websites, regardless of their origin or pedigree, would be treated equally.

The case involved not only the same court but the same plaintiff: Comcast. The cable giant pointed out that it did not now nor did it have plans to offer different levels of Internet service to different websites. However, Comcast and others said, the FCC had no legal authority to regulate this aspect of Internet traffic. The court agreed. The decision put the agency's net neutrality strategy in serious jeopardy. After the ruling was announced, FCC Chair Genachowski said his agency was "firmly committed to promoting an open Internet" and that he would look for other ways to regulate Internet providers to make sure they offered every website the same service.

True to his word, Genachowski joined the other two Democrats on the five-person commission in voting to propose a new rule giving the agency authority to regulate broadband Internet as part of the FCC's powers to regulate telephony. The proposed rule, approved by the commission in June 2010, classified broadband Internet as a "telecommunications service" and thus subject to FCC statutory authority. The idea behind the action was to restore the agency's authority to mandate net neutrality in the wake of the April appeals court ruling.

With its authority to regulate the Internet restored, at least temporarily, the commission moved on to drafting and considering net neutrality rules. In December 2010, by a party line vote of 3–2, the commission approved regulations that prevent Internet providers from blocking lawful Internet traffic except when they are performing "reasonable network management." In addition, the new rules prevent "unreasonable discrimination" by prohibiting providers from allowing some websites to download faster than others. Finally, the regulations do not apply to providers of wireless broadband—which means that mobile devices such as smartphones and tablets are exempt.

The approval of the new net neutrality rules seemed to please no one. Democrats and consumer advocates argued that the wireless exemption made the regulations largely meaningless, since more and more people were accessing the Internet wirelessly through phones and tablets. Other net neutrality advocates argued that by prohibiting "unreasonable discrimination" the commission created confusion and potentially a great loophole, since the rule seemed to allow "reasonable" discrimination. "The commission could have established clear rules that would give more protections to Internet users than the one approved today," said Gigi Sohn, president of Public Knowledge, a consumer advocacy group.

Opponents questioned whether the agency even had the authority to regulate the Internet, in light of the April ruling denying the FCC such authority. By the beginning of January 2011, a group of Internet providers, led by Verizon, had filed lawsuits accusing the commission of overreaching. While the agency has moved to dismiss all of these cases, the lawsuits were expected to move forward in the coming year.

One of the biggest issues the FCC faced in the second decade of the 21st century involved its review of the proposed merger of AT&T and T-Mobile. Like the Comcast-NBC/Universal merger that the FCC approved in 2010 (and for which it was roundly criticized), the AT&T and T-Mobile merger would have been an industry game-changer. In this case, the $39 billion deal would have created the largest wireless phone provider in the country, bigger even than Verizon, which is currently the largest company in the market. Perhaps more important, the number of big companies with national reach in the wireless market would have fallen from four to three—Verizon, AT&T (with T-Mobile), and Sprint. According to some analysts, the market would really have just two national players—Verizon and AT&T—since Sprint would be a distant third in subscribers and revenue.

Consumer advocates and others quickly criticized the proposed deal, saying that in many markets consumers would be at the mercy of a few big players and, as a result, would likely be subjected to increased rates. "AT&T is already a giant in the wireless marketplace," said Paul P. Desai, policy counsel for the Consumers Union, an advocacy group. "From a consumer's perspective, it's difficult to come up with any justification or benefits from letting AT&T swallow up one of its few major competitors."

AT&T countered this criticism by pointing out that the cost of wireless had actually fallen by 50 percent in the past decade, a time when the industry was consolidating and consumer advocates were warning of higher costs for phone users. In addition, they said, combining AT&T's network with T-Mobile's would give the merged firm the ability to offer unparalleled service to consumers. Smartphone users, who complained that AT&T's wireless system did not always have the capacity to handle their voice and data needs, would particularly benefit from this new capacity. Furthermore, the company said, in most large markets (where the majority of users are) there are a host of smaller providers, driving the level of competition up and rates down.

But AT&T's efforts to win approval for the deal ran into two difficulties. First, in May 2011, FCC commissioner Baker announced that she would be leaving the agency to become a lobbyist for Comcast. Baker, a Republican appointee, had supported the Comcast-NBC merger and was expected to favor AT&T's tie-up with T-Mobile. Also in August 2011, the Department of Justice sued AT&T and T-Mobile on antitrust grounds to prevent the deal. The lawsuit did not mean that the merger was dead. Indeed, the federal judge handling the case quickly urged both sides to settle. However, the lawsuit also meant that AT&T might have to agree to a raft of conditions to move the merger forward. In fact, the company already sought to offer concessions that might win it regulatory approval, including potentially selling more than a quarter of T-Mobile's customers and spectrum to a competitor, such as Leap Wireless.

However, as 2011 came to a close, AT&T decided to withdraw its application for approval from the agency. Chairman Genachowski had aggressively sought to derail the deal, informing the other three commissioners that he intended to refer the proposed merger to an administrative law judge for a trial-like hearing in which AT&T would have to demonstrate that the deal was "in the public interest." Although AT&T had substantial lobbying clout and seemed prepared to do battle, the FCC's opposition, coupled with the Justice Department suit, proved too much, prompting the wireless phone company to drop its bid on Thanksgiving—ending its hopes for growth in the domestic wireless market and leaving T-Mobile with an uncertain future. The phone giant may have withdrawn its application in part to prevent the FCC from making public AT&T and T-Mobile records about the potential effects of the merger, records that could then be used by the Justice Department in the upcoming antitrust trial. But even if AT&T were to win its case with the Justice Department, it would still require FCC approval to be able to take over T-Mobile's licenses to operate its network on the public airwaves. AT&T CEO Randall Stephenson would later say that the company had not "executed well" in the deal and that the failed merger was one of his worst moments as CEO. By 2013, AT&T was running attack ads against T-Mobile, the company it had once courted.

In addition to its impact on the AT&T/T-Mobile merger, Baker's decision to leave the FCC made news for another reason. Although she denied that her new job as head of Comcast's governmental affairs office was in any way connected to her decision to support the company's takeover of NBC, the move prompted a storm of criticism and accusations of a "revolving door" between regulatory agencies and the companies they oversee. Some consumer advocates called for new rules to make it harder for a government official to move from regulating a certain industry to working in it.

Baker's departure also left the commission with one vacancy and a temporary three-to-one split in favor of Democrats. A second vacancy occurred with Democratic commissioner Copps's resignation at the end of 2011, when his second term was due to expire. The two vacancies left by Baker and Copps were filled in May 2012—Jessica Rosenworcel, a Democrat, who served as senior communications counsel for the United States Senate Committee on Commerce, Science, and Transportation, and also as a legal adviser to former commissioner Copps, was sworn in on May 11th. Republican Ajit Pai, who held several positions in the FCC's Office of General Counsel, as well as several private sector positions, including as associate general counsel at Verizon Communications, Inc., was sworn in on May 14.

The soon-to-be refurbished commission would tackle a wide range of issues, with varying degrees of success over the next several years.

In December 2011 the FCC's position on multiple media ownership took a new direction when it announced plans to relax a long-standing rule that limited the ability of a company to own both a newspaper and a television or radio station in the same local market. Only five months before, a federal appeals court had overturned a 2008 decision by the FCC to loosen restrictions on cross-ownership because, the court ruled, the agency failed to allow sufficient time for official notice and public comment on the new rules. This effectively bounced the ball back to the FCC, which was undergoing a mandatory reevaluation of ownership rules anyway (one that is required every four years).

The agency's modified stance on ownership has been due, in part, to the dramatic evolution of the media landscape in recent years. More and more people are now obtaining their news online, which has caused many newspapers to close. Those who support the relaxed rules believe that broadcasters might offer financial support to newspapers in some markets if the two share resources. The changes to the rules would affect only the top twenty media markets, where the FCC perceives there to be more competition among media outlets. Ownership combinations in smaller markets would still be limited.

As of March 2013, the FCC's efforts to finalize this new rule had not made much progress. First, it was delayed to allow for public comment on ownership information—specifically, whether relaxation of the rules would adversely affect minority ownership. When some public comments suggested that minorities would be hurt by the new rules, the FCC responded by commissioning a new study on the issue from the Minority Media and Telecommunications Council, a Washington DC-based nonprofit. In March, the *New York Times* quoted sources within the agency who predicted that a final decision on the rules could come in the summer of 2013, but as the summer wore on, a decision did not seem imminent.

The FCC suffered several setbacks in its indecency policy, with one resuscitated case dating back to 2004. First, in June 2012 the Supreme Court ruled that the Fox and ABC television networks had not been given fair notice of a new FCC policy, which asserted that fleeting or briefly heard expletives and momentary nudity could be found actionably indecent. The two networks faced potential fines for their violations. In the case of Fox, it was for the broadcast of fleeting expletives by celebrities on awards shows. For ABC, it was the partial nudity of one of its characters on the series *NYPD Blue*. The justices sidestepped the First Amendment questions, however, disappointing free speech advocates who were looking for a clearer ruling as to whether the government

still has the authority to regulate indecency on broadcast television, especially as the broadcast landscape has changed so significantly. The Court has long relied on what it called "the uniquely pervasive nature of broadcast media and its unique accessibility to children." Now, with the rise of cable television and the Internet, that principle may be less relevant.

Later that same month, the Supreme Court dealt the agency another blow when it refused to consider an appeal by the FCC of a federal appeals court ruling that had overturned the agency's fine against CBS for broadcasting a fleeting image of Janet Jackson's breast during the 2004 Super Bowl halftime show. The appeals court ruled that while the FCC had authority to police fleeting images, it had acted arbitrarily by not announcing that it had stiffened its "fleeting material" policy until after it decided to fine the network. However, in a two-page opinion explaining the high court's decision not to hear the case, Chief Justice John G. Roberts warned that because of changes in the agency's rules since then, any similar offense could be punished. Roberts wrote: "It is now clear that the brevity of an indecent broadcast—be it word or image—cannot immunize it from FCC censure."

The Supreme Court has been critical, at times even baffled, by federal regulation in the area of indecency violations. For example, the commission said that swearing in Stephen Spielberg's film, *Saving Private Ryan,* was not indecent, while swearing by blues musicians in a documentary was. While nudity was deemed acceptable in *Schindler's List,* another Spielberg movie, the partial nudity in *NYPD Blue* was not. As Justice Elena Kagan quipped, "The way that this policy seems to work . . . it's like nobody can use dirty words or nudity except for Steven Spielberg." Justice Ruth Bader Ginsburg also questioned whether restricting swearing made sense in a society in which "expletives are in common parlance."

But while the agency was losing its appeals at the Supreme Court, there were some notable successes during this period as well. In October 2011, for instance, the commission unfurled a well-received plan to transform the Universal Service Fund, an $8 billion fund that is paid for by the country's telephone customers and used to subsidize basic telephone service in rural areas. The new fund, now called the "Connect America Fund," will help expand broadband Internet service to 18 million Americans who lack high-speed connection. According to then Chair Genachowski, the new fund will provide for broadband in hundreds of thousands of homes and businesses in 2012 and cut in half the number of Americans without broadband access by 2017. "Broadband has gone from being a luxury to being a necessity for full participation in our economy and our society," the chairman said.

In general, consumer groups and telecommunications companies commended the commission for the plan. However, some industry groups were concerned by the lack of details about how it would affect phone companies and broadband providers. On the other side, the Consumers Union also expressed concern that the plan could lead to higher fees for customers with telephone landlines.

The FCC has explored other ways to encourage more Americans to use high-speed Internet, including assembling a group of private companies, such as Best Buy and Microsoft, which would offer free computer training to people in disadvantaged communities. The agency is also pursuing a pilot project that will lead to expanding the number of libraries, which teach people how to use computers and apply for jobs online. In places such as South Korea, 90 percent of citizens with access to high-speed Internet are using it, while in the United States usage among those with access is only at 68 percent. Studies have shown that the biggest impediments to Internet usage are the cost of Internet services, the cost of computers, and a lack of understanding of how to use a computer and how to install a computer with an Internet connection. In the ongoing effort toward moving the nation to full computer literacy, the agency is looking for a variety of ways to topple those barriers.

The FCC's continuing battle to bring broadband Internet service under its jurisdiction also gained some ground. While in recent years the commission lost some of its authority over Internet communications, in December 2012, a federal appeals court ruled that the agency's free roaming policy, which allows mobile wireless customers to automatically receive voice service even when they are "roaming" outside of the area covered by their home provider's network, also applies to mobile data services. In other words, services such as e-mail and Internet access for customers using smartphones, tablets, and other wireless devices also come within the commission's jurisdiction.

The appeals court ruling was greeted enthusiastically by the agency, which saw it as confirmation of its authority to promote broadband competition. It was also hailed by smaller cell phone companies who wanted to offer national service to compete with Verizon and AT&T and looked to the FCC's free roaming rules to help pry open the wireless market. Not surprisingly, large wireless providers were not pleased with this development, countering that the data roaming order would give them less incentive to invest in their networks because it would benefit competitors that didn't need to bear any of the cost of building infrastructure. In addition, Verizon raised the more philosophical question of what type of business the Internet really is—a utility or an information service. It argued that the Internet is an information service that should be subject to few, if any, regulations and that the agency did not have the authority to impose "common carrier" regulations on Internet services in the same way they might do with a public utility, such as telephone service.

Meanwhile, in March 2013 the FCC began lobbying Congress to overturn a 2012 ruling by the copyright office of the Library of Congress that made it illegal for consumers to unlock their cell phones. The FCC argued that consumers should be able to switch carriers and keep their actual phones, making it easier for them to take advantage of lower rates once the terms of their initial contract are fulfilled. Under the Digital Millennium Copyright Act, the potential penalties for unauthorized unlocking, which involves opening the software that restricts use of a phone to a certain carrier's network, are nothing to sniff at—a $500,000 fine and five years in prison.

But major wireless carriers viewed the agency's concerns as a "nonissue," saying they already had policies that allowed users to unlock a phone on request once they had fulfilled the terms of the initial contract. The reason these carriers locked the phones for the duration of the contract was so that they could recover some of the cost of their initial subsidies that reduced the purchase price of the phone. (Unlocked phones are usually several times the subsidized price at which carriers offer phones with a two-year contract.) They also pointed out that there were places where you could buy an unlocked phone to use on a pay-as-you-go basis.

By 2014, however, the momentum in Congress was clearly with the commission and the consumer groups that supported its position on phone unlocking. In July 2014 Congress passed legislation requiring wireless carriers to allow their customers to unlock their phones. The measure, which was signed by President Obama at the beginning of August, mandated unlocking for only a year. The sunset provision was included after the all the major carriers pledged to adopt voluntary unlocking standards, which they did in the spring of 2015.

In March 2013, after serving on the commission for four years, Chairman Julius Genachowski resigned. Genachowski, who announced he would be taking a position at the Aspen Institute, said he was proud of the work that he and the commission had done to promote net neutrality. He also pointed to his successful expansion of broadband Internet service, his work to free up the airwaves for sale to mobile phone companies, and his opposition to the merger of AT&T and T-Mobile as other high points of his tenure. But his time at the FCC was not without controversy or obstacles. Indeed, his critics pointed to what they said were a number of large missteps, such as his approval of the purchase of NBC Universal by Comcast and his effort to reform the Universal Service Fund, which actually raised rates for consumers instead of cutting down on corporate fraud and waste.

Two months later, in May, President Obama named telecommunications lobbyist and investor Tom Wheeler to replace Genachowski. Wheeler, who headed up the National Cable Television Association as well as the Cellular Telecommunications and Internet Association before becoming a venture capitalist, was seen as a steady and experienced hand by members of both parties. At his Senate confirmation hearings in June, he repeatedly said that his two priorities as chairman would be to increase both consumer choice and industry competition. Statements like these won plaudits from both Democrats and Republican and led to his unanimous Senate approval in late October. A few days later, in early November, Wheeler was sworn in as the commission's thirty-first chairman.

On his first day on what President Obama has called "one of the toughest jobs in Washington," Wheeler addressed the commission staff, urging them to take inspiration from the industries they regulate. "The connective technology that will define the 21st century flows through the FCC," Mr. Wheeler said at FCC headquarters on Nov. 4, 2013. "Our challenge is to be as nimble as the innovators and network builders who are creating these great opportunities."

While Wheeler's nomination was still working its way through the Senate, the agency, under the leadership of acting chairman Mignon Clyburn, continued to make important decisions. In July, for example, it voted to approve the $21.6 billion sale of Sprint, at the time the country's fourth-largest wireless provider, to Japan's Softbank. The sale had run into some headwinds after satellite broadcaster, Dish Corporation, made a rival offer for the company, arguing that for national security purposes, Sprint should not be sold to a foreign firm. But the commission viewed the deal as fostering more competition, since Softbank did not already have a big presence in the American market and had the resources to make Sprint a more powerful wireless provider.

And in late October 2013, just a day before the Senate confirmed Wheeler, the commission adopted new rules aimed at strengthening wireless service in rural areas. The action was prompted by reports that as many as one in five long-distance calls made in rural areas do not go through. The new rules, which sunset in three years, require phone companies to track and collect data on the percentage of rural calls that are successfully made and completed. It also offered these companies fee reductions and other financial incentives to improve their rural infrastructure.

In November, with Wheeler now sworn in as chairman, the commission announced that it would likely draft new rules giving airlines the option of allowing passengers to use cell phones and other wireless devices in flight. The move followed the Federal Aviation Administration's decision in October to allow passengers to use some electronic devices, such as e-readers and MP3 players, during takeoff and landing. But the new FAA rules did not involve phones, which are the purview of the FCC.

The FCC's announcement set off a flood of comment, much of it from people and organizations who argued that allowing passengers to speak on flights would only make already tough flying experiences more unpleasant. "Do we really need this?" tweeted motivational speaker Tony Robbins. Particularly upset were the unions representing flight crews and attendants, who argued that it would lead to distracted passengers and only make their jobs harder. The commission responded that airlines would still be free to ban calls on flights.

Weeks after the airlines proposal, the commission made news again, this time announcing that it would drop a proposal it had been considering to relax existing rules that generally ban one company from owning a newspaper and television station in the same media market. In 2012 Chairman Genachowski proposed scraping the limits in the nation's top twenty markets, arguing that rules no longer made any sense in today's much more diverse media environment. But Wheeler argued that the rules should not be eliminated until the issue is studied further. While he did not say he favored keeping the current rules in place indefinitely, he expressed concern that lifting the limits could make it harder for minorities and women to own and run media outlets.

Just a few weeks into the new year, the commission was handed a partial defeat when a federal appeals court ruled that Internet service providers could offer businesses faster service at a higher price. In theory, the decision allowed providers such as Verizon and Comcast the option of charging customers such as Netflix or Amazon more money to stream their content at a faster speed. Since tiered pricing had first been proposed a number of years before, the commission had been trying to stop it, arguing that it would be the end of the open Internet, as large corporate customers paid for better service and crowded out smaller, poorer businesses, nonprofits and individuals. Verizon, which brought the suit against the FCC, argued that it had spent tens of billions of dollars building its Internet infrastructure and that it should be allowed to sell access to it as it saw fit.

The decision, which set off a debate about "net neutrality" that has yet to subside, did contain a silver lining for the agency. The case gave the court an opportunity to determine whether the Internet is a public utility and thus open to regulation by the FCC under the Telecommunications Act of 1934. But while the appeals court judges struck down the regulations preventing tiered pricing, they did not specifically prohibit the commission from future regulation of the Internet; indeed, the decision alluded to the possibility of future regulation. More importantly, the court did not address the question of whether the Internet is or is not a "utility" for purposes of the 1934 act, leaving it for another time and possibly another court to decide.

Still, many pro-business groups and others hailed the ruling as a victory for free markets and innovation.

Wheeler said he was considering his next move, holding open the possibility of an appeal to the Supreme Court or possibly new rules.

In the months following the decision, while the net neutrality issue simmered, the commission took a number of small but significant steps. In February it announced that over the next two years it would double, from $1 billion each year to $2 billion annually, spending on its program to bring high-speed Internet to schools and libraries. The money, which comes from fees paid by the telecommunications industry, will be spent to realize President Obama's goal of equipping 15,000 of the nation's schools and libraries with broadband.

In March 2014 the commission unanimously voted to increase by 100 MHz, or 15 percent, the amount of available spectrum for Wi-Fi routers, which are now used in many Americans' homes and businesses. The move, which had been an unrealized goal of former Chairman Genachowski, was recognition by Wheeler and the other commissioners that Wi-Fi use was growing, not only in homes but also in airports, coffee shops, and hotels, where more and more people are accessing data-hungry devices such as tablets and smartphones. Indeed, a growing number of mobile phone users are now tapping Wi-Fi networks not just for data, but for voice phone calling services as well, supplanting their traditional wireless carriers. As a result of this increasing reliance on Wi-Fi, many analysts said that the commission would likely act again in the coming years to open another block of spectrum to meet this growing need.

During this time, the agency also found itself presented with a number of large proposed mergers. The nation's now third-largest wireless provider, Sprint (now a subsidiary of

Softbank) wanted to buy the nation's fourth-largest wireless phone provider, T-Mobile. The nation's largest cable provider, Comcast, wanted to buy its next-largest rival, Time Warner Cable. And finally, AT&T was interested in acquiring satellite television provider, DirecTV.

By the summer of 2014 Sprint had dropped its bid for T-Mobile after it became clear that regulators at the FCC, as well as the Justice Department's antitrust division, were wary of the country dropping from four to three major wireless carriers—the other two being Verizon and AT&T. However, Comcast and AT&T continued their efforts to successfully complete their deals, working through the rest of the year and into the next to try to convince the commission that the public would benefit if their bids went through.

Meanwhile the net neutrality debate continued. In April 2014 the commission proposed creating a limited number of Internet "fast lanes" that would give service providers some space to sell at a higher price. The decision, meant as a compromise, pleased virtually no one. A few months later, President Obama felt obliged to weigh in. After pointing out that the FCC is an independent agency and thus not under his purview, he argued against allowing even limited fast lanes, stating that doing so could stifle "the next Google or the next Facebook" before they have a chance to succeed. Whether or not the agency felt compelled to listen to the president—who would repeat his views a number of times in the coming month— they soon indicated that they would revisit their proposed fast lane rules and take their time in formulating their next proposal.

But while the commission vacillated on net neutrality, it moved forward forcefully in other areas. In October 2014 it voted unanimously to eliminate the so-called Blackout Rule that allows the National Football League to cancel the television broadcast of a game if a certain percentage of stadium tickets remain unsold seventy two hours before kickoff. The rule was crafted in the 1970s, during an era when teams still derived a substantial portion of their revenue from ticket sales. In justifying the decision, the commission pointed out that today the rule is used by owners to threaten broadcasters during contract negotiations rather than to encourage ticket sales.

And as 2014 approached its end, the agency held the biggest and most successful spectrum auction in its history, fetching $45 billion for a 65-megahertz block of new spectrum. The record sale, fetching more than twice as much as the last big spectrum auction in 2008, was seen as a sign that wireless providers, such as AT&T and Verizon, expected demand for their services to continue to grow.

As 2015 began, it became clearer that new net neutrality regulations would soon be proposed and that the new rules would likely please the White House and consumer advocates much more than the telecommunications industry. Indeed, at a public appearance just week after new year began, Wheeler made a clear argument for regulating the Internet as a utility and for preventing service providers from offering faster speeds for a higher charge.

In February the predictions panned out when the commission took the historic step of voting—3–2 along party lines—to classify the Internet as a utility, bringing it under the commission's full regulatory authority. Along with the new classification came new rules prohibiting Internet providers from offering some business customers faster service in exchange for higher fees.

At the commission meeting, Wheeler said that his agency was using "all the tools in our toolbox to protect innovators and consumers" and that the Internet "was too important to led broadband providers be the ones making the rules." But the two Republicans on the commission were highly critical of the move, arguing that the Internet has been a platform for innovation in large part because it has remained largely unregulated. "The Internet is not broken," said Republican commissioner Ajit Pai. "There is no problem to solve."

Current Issues

The commission's vote in late February to approve the new proposed net neutrality rules is probably the most important decision it has made in a decade or more. It set off a media firestorm and drew heaps of both praise and criticism from politicians, analysts, businessmen, and others. Both sides promised to fight either for or against the rules—in Congress, in court and in the court of public opinion.

But while the commission approved a general policy in its February meeting, the actual rules were not made available to the public until weeks later, in the middle of March. The release of this document, 313 pages of detail and explanation, now sets the stage for the fight that will come. Already, committees in both houses of the Republican-controlled Congress have started to hold hearings to examine the regulations and determine whether Congress should intervene. These hearings are expected to continue into the summer and possibly fall months of 2015.

Most Congressional Republicans as well as many in the business community say that the decision to regulate the Internet as a utility is a gross overreach that should not and probably will not survive judicial challenge. They also dismiss statements made by Chairman Wheeler, who says that even though applying the 1934 act to the Internet gives the commission far-reaching regulatory powers, he has no intention of using most of them. Finally, GOP members say President Obama inappropriately "strong armed" the commission, when he publicly and repeatedly told them to adopt net neutrality rules.

But while Congress may debate and even pass legislation repealing all or part of the net neutrality regulations, any bill they send to President Obama will likely be vetoed. Therefore opponents say that their best chance of reversing the regulations lies in the courts. And here, the action is just beginning.

By the end of March the first of what will likely be many lawsuits challenging the rules had been filed. The two suits, filed by a trade group (the United States Telecomm Association) and a small Internet provider (Alamo Broadband) charge that the FCC has exceeded its authority and that the Internet is not a utility and thus not open to the kind of regulation that the agency has proposed.

But Wheeler has confidently predicted that the rules will survive court challenge, arguing that the earlier court of appeals decision in the Verizon case left the agency a window to use the 1934 act to regulate the Internet. In addition, Wheeler and others believe the public will support these new regulations because they keep the control of the Internet out of the hands of large corporate interests and guarantee that fairness and openness will be maintained online.

Meanwhile, roughly one year after it was first proposed, Comcast ended its proposal to acquire Time Warner Cable amidst FCC scrutiny and public outcry. The deal was once thought to be highly likely to win government approval, especially after Comcast came out in favor of the commission's proposed net neutrality rules. The Comcast-Time Warner merger would have combined the nation's first-and second-largest cable operators, creating a cable behemoth with enormous power over television entertainment as well as the Internet, since many people access the web through their cable providers. "The proposed merger would have posed an unacceptable risk to competition and innovation," Wheeler said in a statement.

The commission has yet to act on AT&T's intention to buy DirecTV, eliciting criticism that it is taking far too long to decide the fate of the deal. The AT&T-DirecTV deal is seen as likely to win approval, in part because in buying DirecTV, AT&T would not be altering the competitive landscape too much. DirecTV is an entertainment programming provider while AT&T is a telephone and Internet service company. Hence combining the two firms does not create a player in any of these industries that would be significantly larger and thus potentially anticompetitive.

Looking forward, the commission is moving ahead with its plans to open up another large block of unused spectrum, either for free or at low cost, for Wi-Fi and other forms of inexpensive wireless services. The frequency the agency would make available, 3.5 gigahertz, is good for low-cost services because it does not penetrate walls as well as other frequencies and therefore is not as prized as some of the other parts of the spectrum currently used by wireless phone companies and broadcasters. The idea is to make the new spectrum available to retailers and other businesses in order to spur creation of more Wi-Fi hotspots.

■ AGENCY ORGANIZATION

Biographies

TOM WHEELER, CHAIR

Appointment: Nominated by President Barack Obama, confirmed by the Senate, and sworn in on November 4, 2013.

Born: April 5, 1946.

Education: The Ohio State University, B.A.

Profession: Businessman.

Political Affiliation: Democrat.

Previous Career: Prior to joining the FCC, Wheeler was managing director at Core Capital Partners. He served as president and CEO of Shiloh Group, LLC and co-founded SmartBrief. From 1979 to 1984, Wheeler was the president and CEO of National Cable Television Association (NCTA). Following NCTA, he was CEO of several high-tech companies, including the first company to offer high-speed delivery of data to home computers and the first digital video satellite service. From 1992 to 2004, he served as president and CEO of the Cellular Telecommunications & Internet Association (CTIA).

MIGNON L. CLYBURN, COMMISSIONER

Appointment: Nominated by President Barack Obama on June 25, 2009; confirmed by the Senate on July 24, 2009; and sworn in on Aug. 3, 2009, to a term expiring June 30, 2012. Currently serving a second term, sworn in February 19, 2013.

Born: March 22, 1962.

Education: University of South Carolina, B.S. (banking, finance, and economics), 1984.

Federal Communications Commission

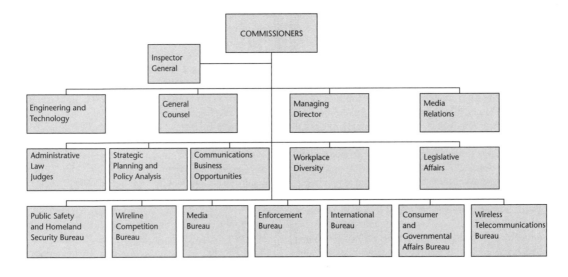

Profession: Public official, publisher.

Political Affiliation: Democrat.

Previous Career: Prior to becoming commissioner, Clyburn served for eleven years as the representative of South Carolina's Sixth District on the Public Service Commission of South Carolina (PSC). She was sworn in for her first term in July 1998 and was subsequently reelected in 2002 and 2006. She served as chair of the PSC from July 2002 through June 2004. During her tenure at the PSC, she participated in many national and regional state-based utility organizations. Most recently, she served as the chair of the National Association of Regulatory Utility Commissioners' (NARUC) Washington Action Committee and as a member of both the association's Audit Committee and Utilities Market Access Partnership Board. She is also a former chair of the Southeastern Association of Regulatory Utility Commissioners (SEARUC). Before being elected to the South Carolina PSC, she served for fourteen years as the publisher and general manager of *The Coastal Times,* a family-founded, Charleston-based weekly newspaper that focused primarily on issues affecting the African American community.

JESSICA ROSENWORCEL, COMMISSIONER

Appointment: Nominated by President Barack Obama on November 1, 2011, and unanimously confirmed on May 7, 2012. Sworn in on May 11, 2012.

Born: July 12, 1971.

Education: Wesleyan University, B.A., 1993; New York University School of Law, J.D., 1997.

Profession: Attorney.

Political Affiliation: Democrat.

Previous Career: Rosenworcel served as senior communications counsel for the United States Senate Committee on Commerce, Science, and Transportation. Before joining the staff of the committee, she served as legal adviser to former FCC Commissioner Copps. She also served at the agency as legal counsel to the chief of the Wireline Competition Bureau, as well as an attorney adviser. Prior to entering public service, she practiced communications law at Drinker Biddle and Reath.

AJIT PAI, COMMISSIONER

Appointment: Nominated by President Barack Obama November 1, 2011, and confirmed unanimously by the Senate on May 7, 2012. Sworn in on May 14, 2012, for a term that concludes on June 30, 2016.

Born: January 10, 1973.

Education: Harvard University, B.A., 1994; University of Chicago, J.D., 1997.

Profession: Attorney.

Political Affiliation: Republican.

Previous Career: Partner in Communications Practice at Jenner & Block LLP prior to his swearing in. Held several positions in the FCC's Office of General Counsel from 2007 to 2011, most prominently as deputy general counsel. Prior to that he was deputy chief counsel for the Senate Judiciary Committee's Subcommittee on Administrative Oversight and the Courts, as well as chief counsel to the Senate Judiciary Committee's Subcommittee

on Constitution, Civil Rights, and Property Rights. He also served as senior counsel in the Office of Legal Policy at the Department of Justice. His first post upon moving to Washington, DC, was with the Department of Justice's Antitrust Division as Honors Program trial attorney on the Telecommunications Task Force.

MICHAEL O'RIELLY, COMMISSIONER

Appointment: Nominated by President Barack Obama on August 1, 2013, and unanimously confirmed on October 29, 2013. Sworn in on November 4, 2013. Sworn in for a second term on January 29, 2015.

Education: University of Rochester, B.A.

Profession: Political adviser.

Political Affiliation: Republican.

Previous Career: Prior to joining the agency Commissioner O'Rielly served as a Policy Advisor in the Office of the Senate Republican Whip since January 2013. He worked in the Republican whip's office since 2010 as an Adviser from 2010 to 2012 and deputy chief of staff and policy director from 2012 to 2013 for U.S. Senator Jon Kyl. He previously worked for the Republican Policy Committee in the U.S. Senate as a Policy Analyst for Banking, Technology, Transportation, Trade, and Commerce issues from 2009 to 2010. Prior to this, O'Rielly worked in the Office of U.S. Senator John Sununu, as Legislative Director from 2007 to 2009, and Senior Legislative Assistant from 2003 to 2007. Before his tenure as a Senate staffer, he served as a Professional Staff Member on the Committee on Energy and Commerce in the United States House of Representatives from 1998 to 2003, and Telecommunications Policy Analyst from 1995 to 1998. He began his career as a Legislative Assistant to U.S. Congressman Tom Bliley from 1994 to 1995.

Headquarters and Divisions

COMMISSION

The commissioners hold final authority (subject to review by federal courts) in all matters under the jurisdiction of the FCC. The commissioners also coordinate FCC activities with other federal agencies and with state regulatory bodies.

The chair presides at all commission meetings, coordinates and organizes commission work, and represents the FCC in legislative matters and in relations with other departments and agencies.

Chair

Tom Wheeler .... (202) 418–1000

Commissioners

Mignon L. Clyburn................ (202) 418–2100

Michael O'Rielly .... (202) 418–2200

Ajit Pai .... (202) 418–2000

Jessica Rosenworcel. .... (202) 418–2400

OFFICE OF THE ADMINISTRATIVE LAW JUDGES

The administrative law judges are responsible for presiding at and conducting proceedings assigned by the commission in cases requiring adjudicatory hearings. The assigned judge prepares initial decisions and forwards them to the commissioners for final decision.

Administrative Law Judge

Richard L. Sippel . . . . (202) 418–2280

OFFICE OF COMMUNICATIONS BUSINESS OPPORTUNITIES

The main contact for small business owners and investors in communications services. Provides research materials on small businesses and on minority and female ownership and employment in the communications industry. Advises the commission on policy and rules that affect small businesses.

Director

Thomas Reed . . . . (202) 418–0990

OFFICE OF ENGINEERING AND TECHNOLOGY

Advises the commission on characteristics of the radio frequency spectrum, its uses, and the types of equipment using the spectrum. Responsible for the examination and approval of equipment, domestic and international frequency allocation, and research into spectrum propagation and innovation in the field. Identifies and reviews new developments in telecommunications and related technologies. The chief engineer also advises the commission on the development of U.S. telecommunications policy.

Chief Engineer

Julius Knapp. . . . . (202) 418–2470

Deputy Office Chief

Ira Keltz . . . . (202) 418–0616

Electromagnetic Compatibility

Walter Johnston. . . . . (202) 418–0807

Laboratory

Rashmi Doshi . . . . (301) 362–3011

Policy and Rules

Mark Settle . . . . (202) 418–1569

OFFICE OF THE GENERAL COUNSEL

Handles legal matters for the commission including litigation, recommendations on legislation, interpretation of statutes and treaties, and review of rules for consistency and legality. Works with the chief engineer on frequency allocation proceedings and advises on rulemaking proceedings involving more than one bureau. Also advises the commission on the preparation and revision of rules and the implementation and administration of the Freedom of Information, Privacy, and Sunshine acts.

General Counsel

Jonathan Sallet . . . . (202) 418–1700

Fax. . . . . (202) 418–2822

Administrative Law

Linda Oliver (acting) . . . . (202) 418–1758

Ethics

Patrick J. Carney . . . . (202) 418–1712

Litigation

Jacob M. Lewis . . . . (202) 418–1740

OFFICE OF THE INSPECTOR GENERAL

Conducts independent internal audits and investigations of the commission's operations and reports directly to Congress and the chair of the FCC.

Inspector General

David L. Hunt . . . . (202) 418–0473

Fax. . . . . (202) 418–2811

Hotline . . . . (202) 418–0473

(Outside of Washington, DC) . . . . (888) 863–2244

OFFICE OF LEGISLATIVE AFFAIRS

Advises the commission on legislative proposals and responds to congressional inquiries.

Director

Andrew Woelfling (acting) . . . . (202) 418–1953

Fax. . . . . (202) 418–2806

E-mail: andrew.woelfling@fcc.gov

OFFICE OF THE MANAGING DIRECTOR

Responsible for internal administrative matters, including personnel, budget planning, labor relations, information processing, records, security, data automation, health and safety, and implementation of the Public Information Act of 1966.

Also serves as principal adviser to and spokesperson for the commission on matters of administration and management and has management and administrative responsibilities over the agency's bureau and staff offices.

Managing Director

Jon Wilkins . . . . (202) 418–1919

OFFICE OF MEDIA RELATIONS

Responsible for the commission's media information and Internet programs. Also issues daily news releases and other FCC publications.

Director

Shannon Gilson . . . . (202) 418–0500

News Media . . . . (202) 418–0503

Information Service . . . . (888) 225–5322

OFFICE OF THE SECRETARY

Oversees the receipt and distribution of documents filed by the public through electronic and paper filing systems and gives effective legal notice of commission decisions by publishing them in the Federal Register and the FCC Record.

Secretary

Marlene H. Dortch . . . . (202) 418–0300

OFFICE OF STRATEGIC PLANNING AND POLICY ANALYSIS

Responsible for working with the chair, commissioners, bureaus, and offices to develop a strategic plan identifying short- and long-term policy objectives for the agency; helping to prepare the agency's annual budget ensuring that budget proposals mesh with agency policy objectives and plans; and working with the office of the chair and the managing director in developing a workforce strategy consistent with agency policy-related requirements.

OSP is responsible for monitoring the state of the communications industry to identify trends, issues, and overall industry health; producing staff working papers; and acting as expert consultants to the commission in areas of economic, business, and market analysis and in other areas that cut across traditional lines, such as the Internet. OSP also reviews legal trends and developments not necessarily related to current FCC proceedings, such as intellectual property law, Internet, and e-commerce issues.

Chief
Jonathan Chambers .... (202) 418–2030

OFFICE OF WORKPLACE DIVERSITY
Responsible for promoting diversity in the FCC workplace and ensuring equal employment opportunities within the agency.

Director
Thomas Wyatt .... (202) 418–1799

CONSUMER AND GOVERNMENTAL AFFAIRS BUREAU
Handles public inquiries and informal consumer complaints. Works with the disability community, especially the hearing impaired. Also responsible for promoting partnerships with other FCC bureaus and offices, consumer groups, industry groups, and state and local municipalities to enhance consumer awareness, solicit feedback, and encourage more public participation in the work of the commission.

Bureau Chief
Alison Kutler (acting)............. (202) 418–1400
Deputy Bureau Chief
Michael Carowitz .... (202) 418–0026
Deputy Bureau Chief
Mark Stone...................... (202) 418–0816
Deputy Bureau Chief
Karen Peltz Strauss .... (202) 418–2388
Associate Bureau Chief and Chief of Staff
D'wana Terry .... (202) 418–0643
Associate Bureau Chief
Roger Goldblatt.................. (202) 418–1035
Consumer Affairs and Outreach
Lyle Ishida .... (202) 418–7868
Consumer Inquiries and Complaints Division (Gettysburg, PA)
Sharon Bowers, Chief............. (717) 338–2533
Consumer Policy Division
Kurt Schroeder .... (202) 418–0966
Disability Rights Office
Greg Hlibok..................... (202) 418–8124
Intergovernmental Affairs
Greg Vadas...................... (202) 418–1798
Native Affairs and Policy
Geoffrey Blackwell .... (202) 418–3629
Reference Information Center
Melissa Askew .... (202) 418–1400
Web and Print Publishing Division
Howard Parnell, Chief .... (202) 418–7280
Consumer Centers
Toll-free .... (888) 225–5322

ENFORCEMENT BUREAU
Primary FCC organization responsible for enforcement of the Communications Act, as well as commission rules, orders, and authorizations.

Chief
Travis LeBlanc .... (202) 418–7450
Investigations and Hearings
Jeffrey Gee .... (202) 418–1420
Market Disputes Resolution
Christopher Killion .... (202) 418–7330
Management and Resources
Noelle Green .... (202) 418–7450
Regional and Field Offices
William Davenport............... (202) 418–1034
Spectrum Enforcement Division
Bruce Jacobs .... (202) 418–1160
Telecommunications Consumers
Richard Hindman .... (202) 418–7320

INTERNATIONAL BUREAU
Administers the FCC's international telecommunications policies and obligations; promotes a high-quality, reliable, globally interconnected, and interoperable international infrastructure; and promotes U.S. interests in international communications and the competitiveness of U.S. industry domestically and abroad.

Chief
Mindel De La Torre............... (202) 418–0437
Management and Administrative Staff
Sarah Van Valzan................. (202) 418–0409
Policy Division
James Ball....................... (202) 418–1460
Satellite Division
José J. Albuquerque .... (202) 418–0751
Strategic Analysis and Negotiations Division
Olga Madruga-Forti .... (202) 418–2489

MEDIA BUREAU
Develops, recommends, and administers the policy and licensing programs relating to electronic media, including cable television, broadcast television, and radio in the United States and its territories. Also handles post-licensing matters regarding direct broadcast satellite service.

Chief
William T. Lake .... (202) 418–7200
Senior Deputy Bureau Chief
Kris A. Monteith .... (202) 418–2606
Audio Services Division
Peter Doyle...................... (202) 418–2700
Communications and Industry Information
Michael S. Perko .... (202) 418–7021
Engineering Division
John Wong .... (202) 418–7012
Industry Analysis Division
Hillary De Nigro .... (202) 418–2330
Management and Resources
India Malcolm .... (202) 418–1723
Policy Division
Mary Beth Murphy............... (202) 418–2120
Video Services Division
Barbara Kreisman .... (202) 418–1600

PUBLIC SAFETY AND
HOMELAND SECURITY BUREAU

Responsible for developing, recommending, and administering the agency's policies pertaining to public safety communications issues, including 911 and E911; operability and interoperability of public safety communications; communications infrastructure protection and disaster response; and network security and reliability. Also serves as a clearinghouse for public safety communications information and takes the lead on emergency response issues.

Chief
David G. Simpson .... (202) 418–1300
Cybersecurity and Communications Reliability
Jeffery Goldthorp (acting) .... (202) 418–2478
Policy and Licensing
Thomas Beers .... (202) 418–0952
Public Communications Outreach and Operations
William Lane .... (202) 418–1199
Chief Engineer
William Lane .... (202) 418–1199

WIRELINE COMPETITION BUREAU

Develops and recommends policy goals, programs, and plans for the commission on matters concerning wireline telecommunications. Overall objectives include (1) ensuring choice, opportunity, and fairness in the development of wireline telecommunications services and markets; (2) developing deregulatory initiatives; (3) promoting economically efficient investment in wireline telecommunications infrastructure; (4) promoting the development and widespread availability of wireline telecommunications services; and (5) fostering economic growth. The Wireline Competition Bureau is organized into four divisions and an administrative and management office.

Bureau Chief
Matthew DelNero .... (202) 418–1500
Competition Policy Division
Randy Clarke .... (202) 418–1580
Industry Analysis Technology Division
Roger Woock .... (202) 418–0940
Pricing Policy Division
Pamela Arluk .... (202) 418–1520
Telecommunications Access Policy Division
Ryan Palmer .... (202) 418–7400

WIRELESS TELECOMMUNICATIONS BUREAU

Handles all FCC domestic wireless telecommunications programs and policies, except those involving satellite and public safety communications or broadcasting, including licensing, enforcement, and regulatory functions. Wireless communications services include cellular telephone, paging, personal communications services, and other commercial and private radio services. Also responsible for implementing competitive bidding authority for spectrum auctions, as authorized by the 1993 Omnibus Budget Reconciliation Act. Some divisions are based in Gettysburg, PA.

Chief
Roger C. Sherman .... (202) 418–0600
Auctions and Spectrum Access
Margaret Wiener .... (202) 418–2176

Broadband Division
Blaise Scinto .... (202) 418–1380
Competition and Infrastructure Policy
Joel Taubenblatt .... (202) 418–0634
Management and Resources
Stephen Ebner .... (202) 418–2147
Mobility Division
Roger Noel .... (202) 418–0620
Technologies, Systems and Innovation (Gettysburg, PA)
Stephen Ebner (acting) .... (717) 338–2656

Regional Offices

People interested in contacting the regional or district offices may dial (888) 225–5322 to reach the FCC's Consumer Centers for referral to the appropriate office.

NORTHEAST REGION

(CT, DC, DE, IL, IN, KY, MA, MD, ME, MI, MN, ND, NH, NJ, NY, OH, PA, RI, SD, VA, VT, WI, WV)
Park Ridge Office Center
1550 Northwest Hwy., #306
Park Ridge, IL 60068–1460
G. Michael Moffit, regional director
(847) 813–4660

Boston District
1 Batterymarch Park
Quincy, MA 02169–7495
Dennis Loria, district director
(617) 786–7746

Chicago District
Park Ridge Center
1550 Northwest Hwy., #306
Park Ridge, IL 60068–1460
James Roop, district director
(847) 813–4660

Columbia District
9200 Farm House Lane
Columbia, MD 21046
Soloman Satche, district director
(301) 725–1996

Detroit District
24897 Hathaway St.
Farmington Hills, MI 48335–1552
James A. Bridgewater, district director
(248) 471–5661

New York District
201 Varick St., #1151
New York, NY 10014–4870
Steve Maguire, district director
(212) 337–1865

Philadelphia District
One Oxford Valley Bldg., #404
2300 East Lincoln Hwy.
Langhorne, PA 19047–1859

David Dombroski, district director
(215) 741–3016

SOUTH CENTRAL REGION
(AL, AR, FL, GA, IA, KS, LA, MO, MS, NC, NE, OK,
PR, SC, TN, TX, VA, VI)
520 NE Colbern Rd., 2nd Floor
Lee's Summit, MO 64086
Dennis P. Carlton, regional director
(816) 316–1248

Atlanta District
3575 Koger Blvd., #320
Duluth, GA 30096–4958
Douglas Miller, district director
(770) 935–3370

Dallas District
9330 LBJ Freeway, #1170
Dallas, TX 75243–3429
James D. Wells, district director
(214) 575–6361

Kansas City District
520 NE Colbern Rd., 2nd Floor
Lee's Summit, MO 64086
Ronald Ramage, district director
(816) 316–1248

New Orleans District
2424 Edenborn Ave., #460
Metairie, LA 70001
Loyd Perry, district director
(504) 219–8999

Tampa District
4010 West Boy Scout Blvd., #425
Tampa, FL 33607
Ralph M. Barlow, district director
(813) 348–1741

WESTERN REGION
(AK, AZ, CA, CO, HI, ID, MT, NM, NV, OR, SD, UT,
WA, WY)
5653 Stoneridge Dr., #105
Pleasanton, CA 94588–8543
Rebecca L. Dorch, regional director
(925) 416–9717

Denver District
215 S. Wadsworth Blvd., #303
Lakewood, CO 80226–1544
Nikki Shears, district director
(303) 231–5212

Los Angeles District
Cerritos Corporate Tower
18000 Studebaker Rd., #660
Cerritos, CA 90701–3684

Charles A. Cooper, district director
(562) 860–7474

San Diego District
Interstate Office Park
4542 Ruffner St., #370
San Diego, CA 92111–2216
James T. Lyon, district director
(858) 496–5111

San Francisco District
5653 Stoneridge Dr., #105
Pleasanton, CA 94588–8543
David Hartshorn, district director
(925) 416–9717

Seattle District
11410 NE 122nd Way, #312
Kirkland, WA 98034–6927
Vacant, district director
(425) 820–6271

■ CONGRESSIONAL ACTION

Congressional Correspondence
Connie Chapman . . . . (202) 418–1900

Committees and Subcommittees

HOUSE APPROPRIATIONS COMMITTEE
Subcommittee on Financial Services and General
Government
B300 RHOB, Washington, DC 20515–6015
(202) 225–7245

HOUSE ENERGY AND COMMERCE COMMITTEE
Subcommittee on Oversight and Investigations
2125 RHOB, Washington, DC 20515–6115
(202) 225–2927
Subcommittee on Communications and Technology
2125 RHOB, Washington, DC 20515–6115
(202) 225–2927

HOUSE HOMELAND SECURITY COMMITTEE
Subcommittee on Emergency Preparedness, Response,
and Communications
Majority side
H2–176 FHOB, Washington, DC 20515–6480
(202) 226–8417
Minority side
H2-117 FHOB, Washington, DC 20515–6480
(202) 226–2616

HOUSE JUDICIARY COMMITTEE
Subcommittee on Courts, Intellectual Property, and
the Internet
6310 OHOB, Washington, DC 20515–6216
(202) 226–7680

SENATE APPROPRIATIONS COMMITTEE

Subcommittee on Financial Services and General Government

SDOB-133, Washington, DC 20510–6025

(202) 224–2104

SENATE COMMERCE, SCIENCE, AND TRANSPORTATION COMMITTEE

Subcommittee on Communications, Technology, Innovation, and the Internet

SDOB-512, Washington, DC 20510–6125

(202) 224–1251

SENATE HOMELAND SECURITY AND GOVERNMENTAL AFFAIRS

Majority side

SDOB-340, Washington, DC 20510–6250

(202) 224–4751

Minority side

SHOB-442, Washington, DC 20510–6250

(202) 224–2627

SENATE JUDICIARY COMMITTEE

Majority side

SDOB-224, Washington, DC 20510–6275

(202) 224–5225

Minority side

SDOB-152, Washington, DC 20510–6275

(202) 224–7703

Legislation

The FCC exercises authority under the following major pieces of legislation:

Communications Act of 1934 (48 Stat. 1064, 15 U.S.C. 21, 47 U.S.C. 35, 151–609). Signed by the president June 19, 1934. Created the FCC and gave it basic authority to regulate interstate and international communications by wire and radio. Numerous amendments over the years have expanded the commission's power.

A copy of the Communications Act of 1934 and its amendments, the Administrative Procedures Act, the Judicial Review Act, and selected sections of the criminal code pertaining to broadcasting is available from the GPO (*see appendix, Ordering Government Publications*).

Communications Satellite Act of 1962 (76 Stat. 419, 47 U.S.C. 701–744). Signed by the president Aug. 31, 1962. Created the Communications Satellite Corp. and gave the FCC authority to regulate the corporation.

Cable Communications Policy Act of 1984 (98 Stat. 2779, 47 U.S.C. 521). Signed by the president Oct. 30, 1984. Maintained the dual roles of the FCC and local government in regulating cable and eliminated the regulation of cable rates by local governments in markets where there was effective competition after 1987. Designated the FCC to define effective competition and oversee equal employment opportunity in cable operations.

Children's Television Act of 1990 (104 Stat. 996–1000, 47 U.S.C. 303a, 303b, and 394). Signed by the president Oct. 17, 1990. Required each TV station in the United States to serve the educational and information needs of children through its overall programming.

National High-Performance Computer Technology Act (105 Stat. 1594, 15 U.S.C. 5501). Signed by the president Dec. 9, 1991. Provided for a coordinated federal research program to ensure continued U.S. leadership in high-performance computing. Created a high-capacity national research and education network to link up supercomputers and databases in the United States.

Automated Telephone Consumer Protection Act of 1991 (105 Stat. 2394, 47 U.S.C. 227 note). Signed by the president Dec. 20, 1991. Prohibited sending an unsolicited ad by fax; using automated telephone equipment to call emergency telephone lines, pagers, or cellular telephones; or initiating unsolicited, auto-dialed telephone calls to residences, except as regulated by the FCC.

Cable Television Consumer Protection and Competition Act of 1992 (106 Stat. 1460, 47 U.S.C. 521 note). Signed by the president Oct. 5, 1992. Amended the Communications Act of 1934 to provide increased consumer protection and to promote increased competition in the cable television and related markets.

Telephone Disclosure and Dispute Resolution Act (106 Stat. 4181, 15 U.S.C. 5701). Signed by the president Oct. 28, 1992. Provided regulation and oversight of the applications and growth of the pay-per-call industry to protect public interest.

Telecommunications Act of 1996 (47 U.S.C. 609 note). Signed by the president Feb. 8, 1996. Revised provisions of the Communications Act of 1934 to reduce regulation and increase competition in communications markets and to speed deployment of new telecommunications technologies. Also included provisions regarding obscenity in broadcast and Internet transmissions. Charged the FCC with more than eighty rulemakings required to implement the new provisions.

Satellite Home Viewer Improvement Act of 1999 (SHVIA) (113 Stat. 1501, 47 U.S.C. 325e, et seq.). Signed by the president Nov. 29, 1999. Incorporated into the fiscal 2000 omnibus spending bill, the SHVIA amended the Communications Act of 1934 to permit satellite carriers to air local television broadcasts. Required the FCC to establish rules for satellite companies with regard to mandatory carriage of broadcast signals, retransmission consent, and program exclusivity.

Open-Market Reorganization for the Betterment of International Telecommunications Act (ORBIT) (114 Stat. 48, 47 U.S.C. 701/761 note). Signed by the president March 17, 2000. Amended the Communications Satellite Act of 1962 to add a new chapter concerning competition and privatization in satellite communications. Required the privatization of Intelsat, the International Telecommunications Satellite Organization, and Inmarsat, the International Maritime Satellite Organization.

FCC Regulations Regarding Use of Citizens Band Radio Equipment (114 Stat. 2438). Signed by the president Nov. 22, 2000. Amended the Communications Act of 1934 to authorize state and local governments to enforce FCC regulations that limit the signal strength of citizens band (CB) radio amplifiers. Under previous law, state and local governments were unable to stop such broadcasts because the FCC had total regulatory authority over the use of CB radios.

Auction Reform Act of 2002 (116 Stat. 715, 47 U.S.C. 609 note). Signed by the president June 19, 2002. Amended the Communications Act of 1934 to require the FCC to determine the deadlines for competitive bidding and auctioning of electromagnetic spectrum used by analog television broadcasters. Required the FCC to postpone indefinitely auctions of portions of the 700-megahertz band of spectrum. Directed the FCC to submit a report to Congress within a year describing the agency's progress in promoting the transition to digital television (DTV) and developing a comprehensive spectrum allocation plan for advanced wireless communications services.

Do-Not-Call Implementation Act (117 Stat. 557, 15 U.S.C. 6101 note). Signed by the president March 11, 2003. Authorized the Federal Trade Commission (FTC) to implement and enforce provisions relating to the "do-not-call" registry of the Telemarketing Sales Rule promulgated under the Telephone Consumer Fraud and Abuse Prevention Act. Individuals must be relisted every five years. Directed the FTC and the FCC to align their telemarketing regulations for the purposes of consistency.

Controlling the Assault of Non-Solicited Pornography and Marketing (CAN-SPAM) Act of 2003 (117 Stat. 2699, 15 U.S.C. 7701–7713). Signed by the president Dec. 16, 2003. Required the FCC to protect consumers from unwanted mobile service commercial messages, or commercial electronic mail messages, including rules to provide subscribers with the ability to avoid receiving such messages unless they have provided express prior authorization; and allow recipients to indicate electronically their desire not to receive such messages in the future.

To Amend the National Telecommunications and Information Administration Organization Act (118 Stat. 3986, 3991, 47 U.S.C. 928). Signed by the president Dec. 23, 2004. Amended the National Telecommunications and Information Administration Organization Act to facilitate the reallocation of spectrum from governmental to commercial users; and to improve homeland security, public safety, and citizen-activated emergency response capabilities through the use of enhanced 911 services.

Junk Fax Prevention Act of 2005 (119 Stat. 359, 47 U.S.C. 227). Signed by the president July 9, 2005. Amended the Communications Act of 1934 to prohibit a person from using any telephone facsimile (fax) machine, computer, or other device to send, to another fax machine, an unsolicited advertisement to a person who has requested that such sender not send such advertisements.

Broadcast Decency Enforcement Act of 2005 (120 Stat. 491, 47 U.S.C. 609 note.). Signed by the president June 15, 2006. Amended the Communications Act of 1934 to increase the maximum penalties for obscene, indecent, and profane broadcasts. Gave the FCC authority to levy fines up to $325,000 per violation, with a limit of $3 million per violator.

■ INFORMATION SOURCES

Internet

Agency website: www.fcc.gov. Provides links to many FCC offices, programs, and publications. Includes consumer information and details on the Telecommunications Act of 1996. The FCC Electronic Document Management System (EDOCS) Advanced Search Engine, found under "search" of the fcc.gov website, gives online access to the *Daily Digest*, a searchable database for FCC documents posted on the FCC website since March 1996. EDOCS displays information in three formats: full record, condensed record, and Citator. The Citator format displays citations to the FCC Record Index, FCC Reports 2nd series, and the *Federal Register*. The database contains citations for documents back to 1982.

Telephone Contacts

Inspector General Hotline . . . .(202) 418–0473
Inspector General Hotline (toll-free) .(888) 863–2244
National Call Center (toll-free) . . . . . .(888) 225–5322
TTY (toll-free) . . . .(888) 835–5322
Fax (toll-free) . . . .(866) 418–0232
Elections and political candidate matters (202) 418–1440

Information and Publications

KEY OFFICES

FCC Media Relations

445 12th St. S.W., #CY-C314
Washington, DC 20554
(202) 418–0500
Fax (202) 418–7286
Shannon Gilson, director and press contact

Provides general information; issues news releases daily. Also issues the *Daily Digest,* an index and summary of each day's releases. Does not maintain a mailing list. Provides a list of commercial messenger and press services that will pick up and forward releases upon request.

Freedom of Information

445 12th St. S.W., #1-A836
Washington, DC 20554
(202) 418–0440 or (202) 418–0212
Fax (202) 418–0521
E-mail: foia@fcc.gov
Stephanie Kost, FOIA public liaison
(202) 418–1379

FCC Consumer Centers

445 12th St. S.W.
Washington, DC 20554
(888) 225–5322
Fax (202) 418–0232
TTY (888) 835–5322

If a direct complaint to a broadcast station, a telephone or telegraph company, or a cable television system does not resolve the problem, contact the FCC's Consumer Centers, the nearest regional office, or the agency headquarters. Staff can assist in filing a complaint. Written complaints should be specific, including when and where the problem occurred and other pertinent details. Include copies of all correspondence with the station or company when you contact the FCC. Regional offices handle complaints involving private radio.

PUBLICATIONS

Contact the FCC Office of the Secretary (202) 418–0300.

FCC Record. Biweekly; a comprehensive listing of FCC actions, including texts released to the public daily. Contains proposed rulemaking and some other public notices. Publications are available to print in PDF format at www.fcc.gov/encyclopedia/fcc-search-tools.

MEETINGS

The commission usually meets once a month at the FCC, 445 12th St. S.W., Washington, DC 20554. Meetings are generally open to the public at the Washington, DC, headquarters and online at FCC.gov/Live. Agendas for meetings are published one week in advance in the "Sunshine Act Meetings" section of the *Federal Register,* www.federalregister.gov. They also are available on the FCC website: www.fcc.gov. For more details and information on last-minute changes in schedule and agenda, contact the Office of Media Relations (202) 418–0500.

Reference Resources

LIBRARIES

FCC Library

445 12th St. S.W., #TWB-505A
Washington, DC 20554
(202) 418–0450
Lisa Leyser, library staff
(202) 418–0456
Hours: 8:00 A.M. to 5:30 P.M.

Maintains a collection of books and periodicals on broadcasting and telecommunications and a complete collection of FCC opinions. Not open to the public, but telephone inquiries are accepted.

FCC Reference Information Center

445 12th St. S.W., #CY-A257, Portals 2
Washington, DC 20554
(202) 418–0270
Melissa Askew (acting), chief
Hours: Mon.–Thurs. 8:00 A.M. to 4:30 P.M.,
Fri. 8:00 A.M. to 11:30 A.M.

The Reference Information Center (RIC) contains all publicly available files, including International and Broadcast Station files, Cable and Wireless files and microfilm, and active Docket and Rulemaking files. The RIC research area has a seating capacity for 100 visitors and is equipped with ten public computer workstations. The RIC provides electronic access to the commission's public information databases, allowing the capability to query data for immediate status, research, verification, and printing by the FCC copy contractor.

DOCKETS

For important FCC documents, news, and actions, consult the *Daily Digest* that is released daily via e-mail, in hard copy, and on the FCC website: www.fcc.gov. The FCC's Electronic Document Management System allows users to search issues of the *Daily Digest* back to 1994. Federal dockets are also available at www.regulations .gov. (*See appendix for Searching and Commenting on Regulations: Regulations.gov.*)

RULES AND REGULATIONS

FCC rules and regulations are published in the *Code of Federal Regulations,* Title 5, Chapter XXIX, Parts 3900–3999; Title 47, Chapter I, Parts 0–199. Chapter I is divided into four volumes: (1) General, parts 1–19; (2) Common Carrier Services, parts 20–69; (3) Broadcast Radio Services, parts 70–79; and (4) Safety and Special Radio Services, parts 80–end. Proposed rules, new final rules, and updates to the *Code of Federal Regulations* are published in the daily *Federal Register.* (*See appendix for information on how to obtain and use these publications.*) The *Federal Register* may be accessed at www.federal register.gov and the *Code of Federal Regulations* at www .archives.gov/federal-register/cfr; also see the federal government's website www.regulations.gov (*see appendix*).

Other Information Sources

NONGOVERNMENTAL ORGANIZATIONS

The following are some key organizations that monitor the FCC, telecommunications issues, and emerging technologies.

Association of Public Television Stations

2100 Crystal Dr., #700
Arlington, VA 22202
(202) 654–4200
Fax (202) 654–4236
Internet: www.apts.org

Association of TeleServices International

222 S. Westmonte Dr., #101
Altamonte, FL 32714
(866) 896–2874
Fax (407) 774–6440
Internet: www.atsi.org

ATIS (Alliance for Telecommunications Industry Solutions)

1200 G St. N.W., #500
Washington, DC 20005
(202) 628–6380

Fax (202) 393–5453
Internet: www.atis.org

Broadcast Education Association
1771 N St. N.W.
Washington, DC 20036–2891
(202) 429–5355
Internet: www.beaweb.org

Cellular Telecommunications Industry Association
1400 16th St. N.W., #600
Washington, DC 20036
(202) 785–0081
Fax (202) 785–0721
Internet: www.ctia.org

Center for Democracy and Technology
1634 Eye St. N.W., #1100
Washington, DC 20006
(202) 637–9800
Fax (202) 637–0968
Internet: www.cdt.org

Communications Workers of America
501 3rd St. N.W.
Washington, DC 20001–1279
(202) 434–1100
Fax: (202) 434–1375
Internet: www.cwa-union.org

COMPTEL–Competitive Communications Association
1200 G St. N.W, #350,
Washington, DC 20005
(202) 296–6650
Fax (202) 296–7585
Internet: www.comptel.org

Electronic Frontier Foundation
815 Eddy St.
San Francisco, CA 94109
(415) 436–9333
Fax (415) 436–9993
Internet: www.eff.org

Enterprise Wireless Alliance
2121 Cooperative Way, #225
Herndon, VA 20171
(703) 528–5115
(800) 482–8282
Fax (703) 524–1074
Internet: www.enterprisewireless.org

Federal Communications Bar Association
1020 19th St. N.W., #325
Washington, DC 20036
(202) 293–4000
Fax (202) 293–4317
Internet: www.fcba.org

Independent Telephone and Telecommunications Alliance
1101 Vermont Ave. N.W., #501
Washington, DC 20005
(202) 898–1514
Fax (202) 898–1589
Internet: www.itta.us

InfoComm International
11242 Waples Mill Rd., #200
Fairfax, VA 22030
(703) 273–7200
(800) 659–7469
Internet: www.infocomm.org

The Internet Society
1775 Wiehle Ave., #201
Reston, VA 20190–5108
(703) 439–2120
Fax (703) 326–9881
Internet: www.isoc.org

National Association of Broadcasters
1771 N St. N.W.
Washington, DC 20036
(202) 429–5300
Fax (202) 429–5315
Internet: www.nab.org

National Cable Telecommunications Association
25 Massachusetts Ave. N.W., #100
Washington, DC 20001–1413
(202) 222–2300
Fax (202) 222–2514
Internet: www.ncta.com

NTCA—The Rural Broadband Association
4121 Wilson Blvd., #1000
Arlington, VA 22203
(703) 351–2000
Fax (703) 351–2001
Internet: www.ntca.org

PCIA—Wireless Infrastructure Association
500 Montgomery St., #500
Alexandria, VA 22314
(703) 739–0300
(800) 759–0300
Fax (703) 836–1608
Internet: www.pcia.com

Telecommunications Industry Association
1320 N. Courthouse Rd., #200
Arlington, VA 22201
(703) 907–7700
Fax (703) 907–7727
Internet: www.tiaonline.org

U.S. Telecom Association
607 14th St. N.W., #400
Washington, DC 20005

(202) 326–7300
Fax (202) 315–3603
Internet: www.ustelecom.org

PUBLISHERS

The following companies and organizations publish books, periodicals, or electronic media on the FCC and related issues.

Artech House Publishers

685 Canton St.
Norwood, MA 02062
(781) 769–9750
(800) 225–9977
Fax (781) 769–6334
Internet: www.artechhouse.com

Bloomberg BNA

3 Bethesda Metro Center, #250
Bethesda, MD 20814–5377
(800) 960–1220
Fax (732) 346–1624
Internet: www.bna.com

Broadcasting and Cable Magazine

28 East 28th Street, 12th floor,
New York, NY 10016
(212) 378–0463
Fax (212) 378–0470
Internet: www.broadcastingcable.com

Crain Communications Inc.

National Press Bldg.
529 14th St. N.W., #814
Washington, DC 20045
(202) 662–7200
Internet: www.crain.com

NewBay Media

28 East 28th St., 12th Floor
New York, NY 10016
(212) 378–0400

Fax (212) 378–0470
Internet: www.newbaymedia.com

R.R. Bowker

630 Central Ave.
New Providence, NJ 07974
(888) 269–5372
Internet: www.bowker.com

Radio Television Digital News Association (RTDNA)

RTDNA Headquarters: The National Press Building
529 14th St. N.W., #1240
Washington, D.C. 20045
(202) 659–6510
Fax (202) 223–4007
Internet: www.rtdna.org

SNL Financial

212 7th St. N.E.
Charlottesville, VA 22902
(434) 977–1600
Fax (434) 977–4466
Internet: www.snl.com

TechAmerica

1525 Wilson Blvd., #540
Arlington, VA 22209
(202) 682–9110
Fax (202) 682–9111
www.techamerica.org

Warren Communications News

2115 Ward Ct. N.W.
Washington, DC 20037
(202) 872–9200
(800) 771–9202
Internet: www.warren-news.com

Wolters Kluwer's Legal Education

76 Ninth Ave., 7th Floor
New York, NY 10011
(212) 771–0600
Internet: www.wklegaledu.com

Federal Deposit Insurance Corporation

550 17th St. N.W., Washington, DC 20429
Internet: www.fdic.gov

▓ INTRODUCTION

The Federal Deposit Insurance Corporation (FDIC) is an independent agency of the federal government; it is also a corporation receiving no taxpayer money. It is managed by a five-member board of directors. One of the directors is the comptroller of the currency; another is the director of the Consumer Finance Protection Board. The three others are appointed by the president and confirmed by the Senate. One of the appointed members is designated chair, and all three serve six-year terms. No more than three of the board members may be of the same political party.

Responsibilities

The FDIC insures funds at about 8,300 U.S. banks and savings associations up to a $250,000 limit on deposit and individual retirement accounts. In March 2011 insured deposits at all institutions totaled about $6.4 trillion. The agency also acts as the primary federal regulator of about 5,200 insured commercial banks, including small savings banks and banks that hold state charters and are not members of the Federal Reserve System (state nonmember insured banks). The FDIC

- Operates an insurance fund—the Deposit Insurance Fund (DIF)—for commercial banks and thrifts.
- Assesses premiums on all insured deposit accounts of commercial banks and thrifts.
- Requires periodic reports of condition and income and other financial data about regulated banks.
- Examines banks annually to determine their condition.
- Approves proposals to relocate main offices and relocate or establish branch offices.
- Approves reduction or retirement of capital.
- Approves bank mergers when the resulting institution will be a bank subject to FDIC regulation.
- Issues cease-and-desist orders to, or obtains agreements from, banks and bank officers to stop engaging in unsound, unsafe, dishonest, or illegal practices.
- Acts as receiver for failed insured national banks and, when appointed by state authorities, for failed state-chartered banks.
- Enforces fair credit, consumer, community reinvestment, and truth-in-lending legislation affecting banks.
- Administers the regulations and reporting provisions of the Securities Exchange Act with respect to banks whose securities are publicly traded.
- Requires reports of changes in ownership of outstanding voting stock of a bank that results in a change in control of the bank.
- Approves the acquisition of controlling interest of a bank by an individual or group.
- Requires banks to maintain an adequate security system to discourage burglaries and robberies.
- Has authority to terminate insurance coverage of a bank that continues, after notice and hearing, to

GLOSSARY

National bank—A bank that is chartered and regulated by the comptroller of the currency. National banks are required to have FDIC insurance.

State member bank—A bank that is chartered by a state and is a member of the Federal Reserve System. State member banks are required to have FDIC insurance.

State nonmember bank—A bank that is chartered by a state, has FDIC insurance, but is not a member of the Federal Reserve System. The FDIC monitors the performance of all banks it insures, but it is the principal federal regulator of state nonmember banks and mutual savings banks (which are a form of a thrift owned and operated by its depositors).

engage in unsafe and unsound practices in violation of laws and regulations.

- Publishes quarterly reports on the condition of the commercial banking industry.

Powers and Authority

Unlike most other government agencies, the FDIC receives no annual appropriation from Congress. The corporation received its initial funding from assessments levied against the members of the Federal Reserve System and a $150 million loan from the U.S. Treasury, which was paid back in full by 1948. Since then it has been funded by assessments on deposits held by insured banks and from interest on the required investment of its surplus funds in government securities.

Most states require state-chartered banks that are not members of the Federal Reserve System to apply to the FDIC for federal insurance coverage. After receiving the application, the agency undertakes a thorough investigation of the bank. The factors reviewed include the bank's financial history and current condition, the adequacy of its capital structure, its prospects for future earnings, the general character of the bank's management, and the needs of the community in which the bank is located.

National banks and state banks that are members of the Federal Reserve System receive FDIC insurance with their charters and do not require investigation by the corporation before becoming members. The FDIC granted 165 new charters in 1990. The number dropped to 50 by 1994 but then increased over the following years as the nation experienced a stronger economy and troubles in the industry faded. The number of new charters peaked at 231 in 1999 but then, as the economy stumbled, began declining again. Charters hit a recent low in 2002 with 94, but a rebound lifted the number to 128 in 2004 and a high of 196 in 2006, before falling with the banking crisis to 98 in 2008. In 2010, there were 9 new charters, and 2011, there were only 3 (and these were specially created to acquire failed banks). In 2012, there was none at all.

REPORTING REQUIREMENTS

All federally insured banks are required to file reports on condition and income with the FDIC. Reports on condition must be filed quarterly; reports on income are required twice a year for most banks and quarterly for banks with assets in excess of $300 million. The data is used to keep track of economic conditions and trends in the banking industry. The data also is fed into the Integrated Monitoring System (IMS), a computerized analysis system for monitoring bank performance between examinations. Summaries of the reports are available from the Office of Public Information Center (*p. 178*).

BANK EXAMINATIONS

The FDIC Improvement Act of 1991 requires an annual examination of all banks to determine their financial health. Before that, regulators had set the priorities, focusing mainly on troubled banks. The corporation makes four types of examinations—safety and soundness, compliance with consumer protection and civil rights laws and regulations, performance of fiduciary responsibilities in trust departments, and adequacy of internal controls in electronic data processing operations.

A full-scale examination includes evaluation of assets, capital structure, income and changes in capital, loan policies, concentrations of credit, loans to bank officers and stockholders, investment policies, borrowing practices, management, internal controls, compliance with laws and regulations, and review of the bank's premises and other real estate. A less rigorous checkup, called a modified examination, emphasizes management policies and the bank's financial performance.

The number of banks examined for safety and soundness peaked in 1990 at 6,234. More than 11,000 examinations were carried out that year when other types of exams were included. In each of the next three years, the FDIC completed more than 5,300 safety and soundness exams. By 1998 that number was down to 2,399, though the number increased slightly to 2,540 in 1999. Since that time the number of exams has generally hovered in the 2,400 to 2,600 range: there were 2,566 in 2001; 2,421 in 2003; and 2,416 in 2008. This has continued apace through the financial crisis but has not increased. In August 2011, for instance, FDIC officials told the House Financial Services Subcommittee on Financial Institutions and Consumer Credit that they had conducted a little more than 2,500 bank examinations in 2010.

The FDIC also relies on the states to share the burden of periodic bank examinations. Because state-chartered banks are examined regularly by both federal and state regulators, the FDIC follows a program of divided responsibility, under which the states and the corporation alternate their examinations.

ENFORCEMENT ACTIVITIES

If the FDIC examiners determine that a bank is faltering, in poor condition, or engaged in illegal activities, the corporation can respond in several ways. Usually the FDIC attempts to work with the bank management informally by obtaining its approval of a corrective agreement or privately issuing a proposed notice of charges and a proposed cease-and-desist order. If, after a meeting with the bank and the appropriate state supervisory authority, the bank does not consent to comply with the proposed order, the FDIC will initiate formal proceedings by publicly issuing the notice of charges and holding a hearing before an administrative law judge.

Banking practices that might result in an informal cease-and-desist action or hearing include inadequate capital in relation to the kind and quality of assets, inadequate provisions for liquidity, failure of the bank to diversify its portfolio resulting in a risk to capital, extension of credit to officers and affiliates of the bank who are not creditworthy, poor management practices, hazardous lending practices involving extension of credit with inadequate documentation or for the purpose of speculation in real estate, an excessive portfolio of poor-quality loans in relation to capital, and failure to comply with consumer protection laws and regulations.

The FDIC also has the authority to terminate a bank's insurance if it finds that the bank has been conducting its affairs in an unsound and unsafe manner. The bank is notified when termination-of-insurance proceedings are started and has 120 days to correct the problems cited by the FDIC. If the deficiencies are not corrected, an administrative hearing is held. If the hearing results in a decision to terminate, depositors are given notice that the insured status of the bank has been revoked and that two years from the date of termination their funds no longer will be insured.

The FDIC also has the authority to remove an officer, director, or other manager if it determines that the person has engaged in illegal or unsafe activities that have caused substantial financial damage to the insured bank. To protect the bank, the corporation also has the power to suspend such persons until the removal proceedings can be completed.

If all of the preventive activities of the FDIC fail and a bank becomes insolvent, the corporation acts as the receiver for the bank; it assumes the bank's liabilities and assets and pays out funds to the depositors up to the $250,000 limit. In most cases, the FDIC arranges for a takeover of a failed bank by a healthy one and does not make direct deposits to the failed bank. From 1934 through 1994, a total of 2,069 banks failed, of which 2,050 required disbursements by the FDIC to pay off insured depositors. More than two-thirds of the failures took place in the ten years from 1983 to 1992. The deposits in all failed banks for the period 1934–1994 totaled nearly $212 billion.

In 1996 five banks and one thrift failed. For a fifteen-month period from mid-1996 until the end of 1997 there was not a single bank failure. Though failures did pick up slightly over the next seven years—there were three failures in 1998, seven in 2000, eleven in 2002, and four in 2004—the FDIC went ten consecutive quarters from June 2004 through December 2006 without a bank failure. This was the longest period in U.S. history without the failure of an FDIC-insured bank. That streak ended with three bank failures in 2007. A sharp change occurred with the banking crisis that began in the closing months of 2008; that year a total of only twenty-five banks failed. In the two years that followed the number of insolvent banks ballooned, to 140 in 2009 and 157 in 2010.

Background

The FDIC was created by the Banking Act of 1933 to help stem the rash of bank failures that swept the country after the stock market crash of October 1929. A root cause of the failures was the involvement of many banks in investment companies that had speculated extensively in securities and real estate, often with their depositors' funds. At the time of the crash and during the Great Depression that followed, both the investment companies and their parent banks suffered tremendous losses: 9,106 banks were forced to close their doors between 1930 and 1933. Depositors in failed banks could not always recover their money, and those banks that did survive were badly damaged when their customers, fearful of the spreading failures, withdrew their funds.

To restore public confidence in the banking system, the FDIC offered federally guaranteed insurance for an individual's deposit up to $2,500. This insurance limit was soon raised to $5,000, and Congress periodically has increased the maximum coverage. In March 1980 the maximum limit was raised to $100,000. In 2006 the president signed into law changes allowing the FDIC to increase the $100,000 limit to account for inflation once every five years beginning in 2010. Additionally, in 2006 deposit insurance coverage for individual retirement accounts was increased to $250,000. In 2008 deposit insurance coverage for all other types of bank accounts was increased to $250,000.

EARLY HISTORY

The FDIC was the third agency created to regulate the U.S. banking industry. Federal regulation began with the National Currency Act of 1863, which established the Office of the Comptroller of the Currency (p. 839). The comptroller's office was given the power to charter and supervise national banks as a way to provide and promote a stable national currency. The comptroller of the currency remains the primary regulator of all nationally chartered banks. State regulation of banking had begun earlier in the nineteenth century when state legislatures passed chartering laws for local banks.

The Federal Reserve Act that created the Federal Reserve System was passed by Congress in 1913. Under that law, national banks were required to become members of the Federal Reserve; state-chartered banks were given the option of joining, but membership was not mandatory. The Federal Reserve System assumed responsibility as primary regulator of those state banks that chose to join the system (state member banks).

When first established, the FDIC's insurance coverage was made mandatory for all members of the Federal Reserve that could meet the corporation's requirements for admission, including adequate capitalization, reserve strength, and financial stability. Originally, only members of the Federal Reserve System could obtain FDIC insurance. In 1939 that requirement was dropped, and the availability of FDIC coverage was extended to state-chartered banks that were not members of the Federal Reserve System.

Under the 1933 Banking Act, a group of amendments to the 1913 Federal Reserve Act, the FDIC was to institute a program of bank examinations to detect potential problem areas in bank management and funding. It was authorized to promulgate regulations to promote safe and sound banking practices and thereby protect both banks and their depositors. The original legislation also forced banks to divest themselves of ownership or control of investment companies. FDIC examiners were authorized to review the operations of banks under FDIC jurisdiction, including loans, status of investments, assets, and liabilities. The legislation further established the FDIC as receiver for all failed national banks and declared that the FDIC could be appointed receiver of failed state banks if requested by a state banking authority.

Two years later, the Banking Act of 1935 gave the FDIC power to cancel insurance for banks engaging in unsafe banking practices and banks in violation of laws or regulations. It also authorized the FDIC to approve the reduction or retirement of capital and the establishment of branch offices for banks under its jurisdiction, to require reports of a bank's condition, to regulate payment of interest on deposits, and to issue regulations necessary to carry out its functions. The 1935 law also authorized the FDIC to make loans or purchase assets to facilitate the absorption of a faltering bank by an insured bank in sound financial condition.

GROWING AUTHORITY

In 1951 authority for the FDIC was withdrawn from the Federal Reserve Act and made part of a separate law called the Federal Deposit Insurance Act. This new legislation gave the FDIC two additional powers: (1) It permitted the corporation to provide funds through loans or deposits to a bank experiencing difficulty, if the FDIC determined that continued operation of the bank was crucial for the local community; (2) it extended FDIC examination authority to national and state-chartered banks that are members of the Federal Reserve System, a power seldom exercised.

The Bank Mergers and Consolidation Act of 1960 gave the FDIC power to approve mergers between insured and noninsured banks when the resulting institution would be a state-insured bank that would not be a member of the Federal Reserve System. In 1966 the supervisory powers of the corporation again were increased when Congress authorized the FDIC to issue cease-and-desist orders to institutions persisting in unsafe banking practices and to remove bank officers engaging in dishonest or illegal dealings.

During the 1960s and 1970s the corporation also was given enforcement responsibility for various consumer laws that apply to banks regulated by the FDIC. These include the Truth in Lending Act, the Fair Credit Reporting Act, the Real Estate Settlement Procedures Act, the Equal Credit Opportunity Act, the Open Housing Act, the Home Mortgage Disclosure Act, and the Community Reinvestment Act.

REFORMS IN THE 1970s

Except for the disasters of the Depression era, until the mid-1970s only a handful of banks had failed. Since the mid-1970s, however, the number of bank closings increased steadily. A number of well-publicized failures called into question the adequacy of the existing regulatory system. A 1977 study by the FDIC showed that 60 percent of bank failures between 1960 and 1975 were because of "insider loans," which are preferential or excessive loans provided to bank officers and stockholders.

In 1978 Congress passed the Financial Institutions Regulatory and Interest Rate Control Act, which limited loans that could be made to a bank's officers and major stockholders to no more than 10 percent of the capital accounts of the bank. Banks were required to report loans to their officers, and preferential loans to insiders and overdrafts by bank officers were prohibited. The act also restricted most forms of interlocking directorates (overlapping memberships on the board of directors) among financial institutions. Enforcement powers were increased, allowing the FDIC to impose civil penalties, issue cease-and-desist orders to individual officers, order the removal of executives and directors who threatened the safety and soundness of financial institutions, and require depository holding companies to divest themselves of holdings that endangered the soundness of banking subsidiaries. The measure required individuals wishing to acquire a bank or savings institution to give sixty days' notice to the appropriate regulatory agency. The agencies were given the authority to reject such acquisitions.

The 1978 legislation also created the Federal Financial Institutions Examination Council to coordinate the regulatory activities of the agencies responsible for supervising financial institutions. The purpose of the council is to promote uniform supervision of financial institutions. In addition, consumer safeguards were increased by the 1978 law. Most important was a provision limiting to $50 the liability of a customer for unauthorized fund transfers involving automated bank tellers and other forms of electronic banking.

The FDIC's involvement in international banking also increased significantly under the 1978 regulatory act as well as under the International Banking Act of 1978. The regulatory act required state nonmember insured banks to obtain the prior written consent of the FDIC before establishing or operating a foreign branch and before obtaining any interest in a foreign bank or financial institution. The act also gave the FDIC primary examining authority over U.S. branches of foreign banks that are chartered by a state and carry FDIC insurance but are not members of the Federal Reserve System. FDIC insurance of commercial deposits in branches of foreign banks is available but is not mandatory. However, FDIC insurance is mandatory if the branch accepts retail domestic deposits.

Also in 1978 Congress approved legislation authorizing the General Accounting Office to audit the performance of the FDIC, the Federal Reserve System, and the Office of the Comptroller of the Currency.

DEREGULATION IN THE 1980s

In March 1980 Congress passed the Depository Institutions Deregulation and Monetary Control Act, which made far-reaching changes in the federal regulation of the nation's banking industry and opened the door to the eventual deregulation of depository institutions. Among its provisions, the landmark banking reform legislation more than doubled FDIC insurance protection from $40,000 to $100,000 per depositor. Although the 1980 law did not provide for any significant increase in FDIC funding, it stipulated a revised formula by which the corporation computed deposit insurance assessment credits. Banks were required to pay the cost of FDIC insurance through assessments based on their volume of deposits.

The Monetary Control Act was intended to allow for increased competition between commercial banks and traditional thrift institutions. The bill also phased out interest rate ceilings on time and savings accounts.

In October 1982 President Ronald Reagan signed into law the Depository Institutions Act, a bill intended to help banks cope with the highly competitive financial environment that had developed in the early 1980s during the rapid growth of money market mutual funds. The money markets' higher yields had drained banks of a large proportion of the funds that consumers previously had deposited in checking accounts and low-interest savings accounts. The 1982 law allowed banks to develop new products to compete with these money market funds, including checking accounts that paid interest—NOW accounts—and their money market accounts, which paid higher interest. But banks had to pay more for the funds they needed to operate, straining profit margins and weakening the industry's financial health.

The 1982 legislation gave the FDIC greater flexibility and additional powers to deal with troubled and failed banks through financial aid and merger assistance. It permitted financial institutions with plunging net worths to obtain emergency infusions of capital from the FDIC to help prevent them from going under. The FDIC was authorized to provide new forms of assistance, including assumptions of liabilities, deposits and contributions, and the purchase of securities.

For the first time, the agency was authorized to arrange for interstate and interindustry acquisitions of failing or failed institutions under certain limited circumstances. To help equalize competition between banks and savings and loan associations, the legislation provided for the elimination of all federal interest rate ceilings by Jan. 1, 1984. The ceilings originally were established to ensure savings and loan associations a slight competitive edge over commercial banks in attracting savings deposits, thus indirectly encouraging the home mortgage marketplace.

The Competitive Equality Banking Act of 1987 gave the FDIC power to establish a bridge bank when an insured bank is closed, no immediate buyer is available, it would be less expensive to continue operating the bank than to liquidate it and pay off depositors, and the continued operation of the bank is in the best interest of depositors and the public. A bridge bank is a full-service national bank that can be operated for up to three years by a board of directors appointed by the FDIC. The FDIC used its bridge bank authority for the first time Oct. 30, 1987, when it closed the Capital Bank & Trust Co. in Baton Rouge, LA.

At the time of the 1987 legislation, farmers were being hurt by declining land values, depressed crop prices, and soft export markets. The legislation permitted agricultural banks to amortize losses on agricultural loans and losses resulting from reappraisal of other related assets over a seven-year period.

Both the industry and its federal regulators were unprepared for the upheaval in the financial services industry unleashed by congressional actions of the early 1980s. These moves resulted in the rapid expansion by securities brokers, insurance companies, and even retailers such as Sears, Roebuck and Company and the Kroger Company into the markets formerly reserved for banks. In the newly competitive financial marketplace, consumers began to turn more and more toward these alternative providers of financial services, causing the banks to founder.

To meet the challenge of these new less-regulated rivals, many states enacted laws that allowed banks to engage in nontraditional banking activities such as securities brokerage, real estate investment, and insurance operations. The FDIC accommodated these changes by allowing these operations through separate subsidiaries.

To help commercial banks avoid losing corporate customers, the banking regulators pressed Congress to allow commercial banks to engage in more investment banking activities, including underwriting and dealing in corporate securities, commercial paper, and municipal bonds. Many banks also faced new competition from other commercial banks as interstate banking restrictions began to crumble with the development of regional banking pacts. These agreements allowed banks to set up operations in states within the pact. By the late 1980s only a few states were not part of regional banking pacts. Ironically, the regulatory changes designed to prop up the banking industry ended up laying the foundation for the demise of many institutions. By the late 1980s the banking industry had suffered the largest number of failures since the Depression. Banks concentrating in energy and agriculture loans were particularly vulnerable because of falling oil and farm prices. Problems also spread to commercial real estate loans.

The number of banks on the FDIC's problem bank list jumped from 848 in 1984 to a peak of 1,575 at the end of 1987 and hovered around the 1,100 mark until 1992. In 1988 the insurance fund suffered the first operating loss in its fifty-five-year history. It did not see a profit until four years later. In 1989 the number of bank failures peaked at 206. The trend reversed after that but each of the next four years saw more than 100 banks close because of financial difficulties. The growing number of banks in trouble, especially in the oil and farm belts, prompted federal regulators to tighten capital standards. The FDIC and other regulators adopted capital standards stipulating that banks with the riskiest investment portfolios would have to build larger capital cushions against potential losses.

Although the number of bank failures was making post-Depression records, it was the more widespread and much larger failures of savings and loan institutions insured by the FDIC's sister agency, the Federal Savings and Loan Insurance Corporation (FSLIC), which forced attention on the future of the federal deposit insurance system. In 1989 President George H. W. Bush signed into law the historic Financial Institutions Reform, Recovery, and Enforcement Act (FIRREA), which established a financing corporation to raise the money needed to close failed savings and loan associations and pay off insured depositors. The process was projected to cost U.S. taxpayers more than $500 billion over forty years.

The FSLIC fund, although broke, was placed under the FDIC, and the name was changed to the Savings Association Insurance Fund (SAIF). The FDIC board was assigned to manage the Resolution Trust Corporation (RTC), a temporary agency created to take control of failed savings and loan associations and sell their assets. (The bill also expanded the FDIC board to five members.)

To strengthen the FDIC fund, the bill raised the insurance premium on bank deposits. The bill added enforcement powers of both thrift and banking regulators and significantly increased civil penalties for unsafe and abusive activities by bank directors and officers. It also made it easier for regulators to take control of banks operating with insufficient capital.

FDIC IN THE 1990s

The early 1990s were a time of rebuilding for the FDIC and the banking industry, as regulators and banks alike faced a dire need for new capital, while the late 1990s saw financial institutions basking in a wave of unprecedented prosperity. The new century came, however, with concerns about the health of the industry. Before the prosperity could be enjoyed, the Bank Insurance Fund (BIF) had to be restored to health to avert the need for Treasury support and the threat of a taxpayer bailout. The insurance fund dropped to 7 cents for every $100 of insured bank deposits by the end of 1989—well below the historic level of $1.25 for every $100 in deposits.

To increase the fund, the Omnibus Budget Reconciliation Act of 1990 waived caps on the FDIC's insurance premiums and allowed the agency to make midyear premium adjustments, rather than only annual changes. The premium later shifted from a flat rate to a risk-related system on Jan. 1, 1993; the premium banks pay is determined by a formula based on an institution's capital level and its management strength.

During the administration of President Bill Clinton, the FDIC saw restored prosperity both in the BIF and in the banking industry. In 1995 the FDIC lowered deposit-insurance premiums twice for most banks: first from 23 cents to 4 cents per $100 of deposits, then to the statutory minimum requirement of $2,000 a year per insured institution. The latter move, which took effect in January 1996, came after the insurance fund passed the $25 billion mark, at the time a record in FDIC history. By late 1995 the insurance fund had exceeded the requirement of 1.25 percent of insured deposits, where it remained by the end of the decade.

In 1991, when the insurance fund was still severely undercapitalized, the FDIC Improvement Act put a time frame on getting the fund back to the 1.25 percent level, requiring the FDIC to meet this goal within fifteen years. To ensure that the agency could continue to protect deposits in failed banks without having to tap taxpayer funds, the act also increased a direct line of credit from the Treasury from $5 billion to $30 billion.

Meanwhile, to avoid having the FDIC dip into bank insurance funds for savings and loan cleanups, the SAIF was given separate appropriations authority. The SAIF, too, was experiencing unprecedented financial success by the latter part of the 1990s, reaching a record balance of $9.5 billion in the first quarter of 1998.

In September 1996 Congress passed legislation to merge the BIF and SAIF in 1999, provided an additional law was passed to eliminate the SAIF charter. However, by summer 2005, Congress had yet to act. Because the insurance fund for thrifts continued to lag behind the fund for banks, the 1996 law more immediately levied a one-time assessment on thrifts, of 68 cents per $100, to bring the SAIF to its required 1.25 percent level.

The 1991 FDIC Improvement Act also changed the way the agency approached its regulatory role. First, the act required the FDIC to examine every bank every year, a departure from the past method of giving troubled banks priority over healthy banks. Second, the 1991 law changed the way the FDIC handled failed banks. Previously, regulators used a "least-costly resolution," which gave them latitude to consider how a community might be affected by a failed bank, allowing them more time to find a prospective buyer or otherwise dispose of assets. Now they must use a "least cost resolution," making their decisions dollar-driven only, with no regard for the economic condition of the area.

The FDIC Improvement Act also phased out the "too big to fail" doctrine, which led regulators to prop up such behemoths as the Bank of New England because of the potentially damaging ripple effect its failure would have had on the people of Boston. The 1991 law also prohibited state charter banks from engaging in activities not allowed for national banks, which took many more bankers out of the real estate business once and for all.

After the banking crisis of the late 1980s and the resulting tightening of lending restrictions, it did not take long for bank owners to claim those restrictions hurt business. Such pressure led Congress in 1992 to pass a number of tax laws to ease the regulatory burden. For example, the value of property requiring a certified appraisal for a loan was raised from $100,000 to $250,000, which translated into less red tape for the majority of home loans.

Barriers to interstate banking also fell in the 1990s. Since 1933, branching across state lines had been prohibited. Large banking empires had to charter new banks in each state, hiring separate bank presidents and boards of directors. Bank industry lobbyists claimed this restriction cost the industry billions of dollars each year. The Interstate Banking Efficiency Act, passed in 1994, removed these restrictions, allowing banks to operate in more than one state under the same corporate structure.

In 1994 Clinton appointed Ricki Helfer as the FDIC's first female chair. Helfer instituted an extensive reorganization of the agency, whereby most divisions reported to three deputies rather than directly to the chair. The 1993 RTC Completion Act also required the RTC to consolidate its staff and functions with the FDIC by the end of 1995. Helfer also created a task force to study how derivatives and other new financial instruments affect deposit insurance funds; a so-called early warning system, to help prevent bank failures; and increased consumer education. The FDIC sought to help member banks clarify to customers the differences between federally insured investments, such as certificates of deposit (CDs), and uninsured investments, including mutual funds—especially when these two types of investments are marketed by the same financial institution.

In 1998 under Helfer's successor, Donna Tanoue, the FDIC continued efforts to streamline regulations; expedite application procedures for well-capitalized, well-managed banks; and simplify deposit insurance rules. Additionally, FDIC worked with other financial regulators to coordinate the handling of merger requests. The FDIC began downsizing in the late 1990s, as the number of bank failures diminished and the workload decreased. It closed regional offices, offered employee buyouts, and relied on traditional attrition. By 2001 the agency employed 6,700 workers, a decrease of about 5,000 employees over four years.

In the midst of the economic boom of the 1990s, regulators became increasingly concerned that lending standards were slipping dangerously. Although the thriving economy had brought tremendous benefits for banks, it also had led to increased competition for loans. That meant lower profit margins and increased lending to those with tarnished credit histories. Fears that a downturn in the economy would have seriously negative consequences for many banks led the FDIC in May 1997 to issue a letter warning banks about risky subprime lending.

As the twentieth century came to a close the agency's image was tarnished by missteps. Under pressure in 1999, it dropped a highly criticized plan calling for banks to track the actions of their customers. The agency also agreed to a $14 million race discrimination settlement of a lawsuit filed by former African American workers. In 1999 the agency announced a "diversity strategic plan," which called for increased recruiting of minority job applicants.

In November 1999 President Clinton signed into law a major banking overhaul bill, known as Gramm-Leach-Bliley, for its sponsors, which broke down many of the Depression-era barriers that had separated banks, brokerages, and insurance firms. The FDIC then spent several months crafting rules dealing with various provisions in the new law and preparing for a potential increase in its oversight responsibilities.

FDIC IN THE 2000s

The FDIC in 2000 adopted new "sunshine" guidelines called for by Gramm-Leach-Bliley, setting disclosure requirements for agreements that banks and private groups reach to abide by the 1977 Community Reinvestment Act.

The agency adopted guidelines requiring new safeguards to protect consumer information and records. Also related to the legislation, the agency in May 2000 approved a consumer privacy regulation that required financial institutions to describe their privacy policies clearly and allow customers to "opt out of disclosures to nonaffiliated third parties."

President George W. Bush nominated Texas banker Donald E. Powell as FDIC chair. Powell promised to continue efforts to overhaul deposit insurance, including merging the two insurance funds—the BIF and the SAIF, indexing insurance coverage limits to inflation, and increasing the insurance limit for retirement accounts. The FDIC in early 2001 issued guidelines making clear it would more closely scrutinize "subprime lending programs," those aimed at borrowers with sketchy credit histories and a willingness to pay higher interest rates.

In 2002 and 2003, lawmakers in the House made an aggressive push to complete the deposit insurance overhaul advocated by Tanoue and Powell. Twice the House passed legislation that would have boosted the federal deposit insurance limit from $100,000 to $130,000 and merged the BIF and SAIF. The legislation, however, stalled in the Senate. The Bush administration and Federal Reserve also opposed the increase, saying it would increase the risk to taxpayers without benefiting consumers.

On the regulatory front, the massive corporate accounting scandals at companies, such as Enron, spurred the FDIC to boost oversight of troubled financial institutions, despite Powell's attempt to take an industry-friendly approach in daily relations with banks. Similar to other federal regulators, agency officials reviewed auditor independence requirements, ethics policies, and the practices of FDIC-supervised institutions.

Beginning in 2004, the FDIC joined other federal regulators in pushing industry-supported proposals to ease requirements under the 1977 Community Reinvestment Act (CRA), which directed federal regulators to encourage banks to offer credit to low- and moderate-income neighborhoods. The agency's proposed measure would have raised to $1 billion from $250 million the level of assets a bank could have to qualify for a streamlined CRA examination.

Backers of the change said small- and moderate-sized banks, including local community banks, were being burdened by the paperwork and preparation costs associated with CRA examinations by the FDIC, OTS, and the Office of the Comptroller of the Currency (OCC). Critics countered that the change severely diluted the original intent of the legislation, and opposition groups submitted more than 12,000 comment letters to the FDIC complaining about the proposal.

Banking regulators from the Group of Ten (G-10) countries also came together in 2004 following six years of negotiations to reach an accord on international capital standards for the world's largest banks. Known as Basel II, the agreement created a framework to determine appropriate risk-based capital requirements for internationally active banking institutions. The agreement went into effect in 2008.

Entering into 2005, the FDIC turned its focus to the high-profile issue of identity theft. The agency, along with other federal banking regulations, issued new guidance in March 2005 after a series of well-publicized breaches at firms such as ChoicePoint allowed identity thieves access to personal information databases. The guidance directed firms to immediately notify federal regulators of any security breach involving sensitive customer information. Additionally, the regulators said companies should implement programs to improve customer authentication programs, as well as address any vulnerabilities in systems storing personal information and procedures for notifying customers in case sensitive information was compromised.

At the same time, the FDIC also continued with its controversial push to ease CRA requirements for moderate-to small-sized banks. In 2005 the FDIC, Federal Reserve, and OCC approved a rule submitting intermediate-sized banks—those between $250 million and $1 billion in assets—to a new "community development test," less onerous than the traditional CRA examinations for banks with greater than $250 million in assets.

Throughout 2005, Congress wrestled with whether to increase the $100,000 federal deposit insurance limit. Legislation raising the deposit insurance limit, which was nearly identical to the bills passed by the House in 2002 and 2003, overwhelmingly passed the House in May 2005. Critics in the Senate remained wary of making the federal government, and thus the taxpayers, responsible for insuring larger amounts than under current law. Still, in late 2005 the two sides found room to compromise and announced an agreement to include deposit insurance reform language in a larger budget reconciliation package. As signed into law by President Bush, the legislation allowed the FDIC to determine whether to increase deposit insurance levels to account for inflation beginning in April 2010, and once every five years after that time. The law increased the deposit insurance coverage for individual retirement accounts to $250,000 from $100,000, permitted inflationary increases after 2010, and merged the FDIC's two funds—the BIF and the SAIF—into a single Deposit Insurance Fund (DIF) covering all insured banks and thrifts.

As 2005 came to a close, the FDIC and other regulators started to express concerns about the increase in so-called exotic or nontraditional mortgage products being offered by lending institutions. These loans, which typically allow borrowers to exchange lower initial payments for higher payments down the road, included "interest-only" mortgages and "payment option" adjustable-rate mortgages. The loans became popular during the housing boom of those years, as low interest rates and rising housing prices led to record numbers of mortgage loans and refinances being offered by lenders. For banking regulators, however, these nontraditional loans raised concerns that lenders were not properly assessing the risk levels associated with loans that were subject to large increases in the monthly payments owed by borrowers. In September 2006 the FDIC, Federal Reserve, and other regulators declined to issue any new rules governing the loans, instead offering guidance to regulated financial institutions to be prudent when offering nontraditional mortgages to borrowers.

Likewise, the FDIC and other banking regulators raised similar concerns about the concentration of commercial real estate loans being offered by some banks. Regulators feared that banks whose lending was concentrated in a particular area could face increased risk from any changes in commercial real estate markets. Similar to the guidance offered to lenders offering nontraditional mortgage products, federal regulators finalized guidance in December 2006 that encouraged banks to be aware of the risks associated with concentrations of commercial real estate loans and to implement the appropriate risk management procedures and capital levels to deal with any adverse market conditions that should arise.

The most publicized regulatory issue for the FDIC in recent years was the application by retail behemoth Walmart Stores Inc. for federal deposit insurance for a proposed Utah-based industrial loan company. Walmart said it wanted to own the state-chartered and FDIC-insured bank to process the millions of transactions made in its stores monthly. Though a number of other firms—notably Walmart rival Target Corp.—already owned industrial loan companies (ILCs), the application by the world's largest retailer set off a firestorm in Congress and throughout the banking industry. Opponents of the application flooded the FDIC with comment letters. Spurred by some lawmakers and an intense lobbying effort by the banking industry—which feared Walmart wanted to start a nationwide bank—the FDIC in July 2006 issued a six-month moratorium on all applications for deposit insurance by ILCs.

On June 26, 2006, Sheila C. Bair was sworn in to a five-year term heading up the FDIC. Bair had previously served as assistant secretary for financial institutions at the U.S. Department of the Treasury, as well as on the FDIC's Advisory Committee on Banking Policy. Bair took charge of an agency that had overhauled its employment practices and streamlined its operations. The agency went from a high of 23,000 employees in 1992 to about 4,600 employees in 2006.

The FDIC continued to grapple with a number of the same regulatory issues that garnered the greatest attention in recent years, particularly the ongoing debate over federal deposit insurance for ILCs. In January 2007 the FDIC extended for one year its moratorium on ILC applications from commercial firms, including Walmart, although the agency said it would make decisions on applications from financial firms. That delay, and what Walmart called a "manufactured controversy," led the retailer to withdraw its application for federal deposit insurance in March 2007.

The other major issue of regulatory concern for the FDIC at this time—as well as the other federal banking agencies—was the rapid rise in foreclosures caused by nontraditional mortgage products. Though the agencies issued guidance warning lenders about the products in 2006, it was too late to prevent a rapid increase in the number of borrowers unable to keep up with their monthly mortgage payments. Nationwide, foreclosures climbed 42 percent in 2006, with particular problems in the subprime market, where typically more expensive loans were offered to borrowers with spotty credit histories.

In March 2007 the FDIC, Federal Reserve, OCC, and OTS issued joint guidance on subprime lending requiring lenders to consider borrowers' ability to repay their loans when offering a mortgage loan or refinance. Additionally, the agencies said lenders should provide "clear and balanced" information about the risks and benefits of a particular type of loan, especially more exotic adjustable-rate mortgages. The regulators followed that guidance with an April 2007 statement that encouraged lenders to make every effort to work with homeowners to restructure loans where a borrower is no longer able to make the monthly payment. Despite those efforts, however, Bair and others admitted that not all homeowners could be kept from foreclosure. This admission raised the ire of some members of Congress, who faulted the regulators for not doing more to regulate nontraditional mortgage products and ensuring regulated firms were properly underwriting loans.

By mid-2007 lawmakers in both the House and Senate were considering legislation to help homeowners already in trouble with their loans, as well as to prevent similar problems from occurring in the future. The proposed legislation included regulatory changes affecting the FDIC and other banking regulators. But Bair argued against new legislative action. Even though there was concern about the growing number of troubled home loans, Bair said, new regulations from her agency and other government financial watchdogs would better address concerns than legislation. Ultimately, Congress followed this advice; in both the House and Senate the proposed "fixes" to the home lending market did not advance.

By late summer and early fall 2008, however, the situation had changed dramatically. The prospect of a crisis in the mortgage lending market was no longer a fear; it was a reality. Indeed, a collapse in housing prices throughout much of 2008 coupled with a large number of subprime mortgages created a perfect storm that threatened not only the U.S. banking sector but the entire global financial system. At the center of this storm were a growing number of troubled banks and financial services providers. During this time and into the first months of 2009, the FDIC found itself dealing with an increasing number of bank failures, a situation that stretched the agency's financial and staff resources.

The largest bank failure occurred on Sept. 25, 2008, when federal regulators seized Washington Mutual, or WaMu, the country's largest savings and loan. The FDIC then turned around and sold much of the company to JPMorgan Chase for $1.9 billion, creating the largest bank in the nation. Initially, there was great concern about WaMu's demise, as it would have put significant stress on the FDIC to cover depositors, costing the agency an estimated $24 billion, which was approximately half of the assets in the agency's insurance fund. But the company's greater troubles were linked to its role in selling option ARMS, mortgage loans that resemble a credit card in that they allow the borrower to pay less than the total

due each month. The default rate on such loans is much higher than with conventional mortgage loans, resembling the high failure rate of credit cards. Thousands of defaulted loans left the company saddled with billions of dollars in bad debts.

Close in scale to the WaMu collapse was the demise of IndyMac in summer 2008, which was purchased in March 2009 for $13.9 billion by OneWest. A California company that had thrived during the housing boom, IndyMac collapsed largely due to Alt-A mortgages, which cater to borrowers who provide less documentation about income or employment than traditional loans require. Although regulators prefer to sell failed banks to healthy banks, which are best equipped to operate them, there were at the time fewer and fewer banks in a position to close such large deals. As a result, more private investors outside of the banking industry such as OneWest were viewed as a prime source of much-needed money.

IndyMac's failure, the fourth largest in U.S. history, would ultimately cost the FDIC between $8.5 billion and $9.4 billion. But out of IndyMac's wreckage, the FDIC began to forge a new model for reworking mortgages and rescuing homeowners that they hoped more banks throughout the country would adopt. These "modified" loans aimed to assist 25,000 delinquent IndyMac borrowers by granting them new interest rates as low as 3 percent. Regulators also applied a more formulaic approach to determining whether someone should be saved from foreclosure or not. But this initiative faced some challenges. Even after receiving a loan modification, there was considerable risk that these homeowners would still default. According to a Credit Suisse report released in fall 2008, about 40 percent of homeowners were delinquent again within a year of a traditional loan modification.

In early October 2008 the FDIC came under criticism for its handling of a merger involving struggling Wachovia, the nation's third-largest retail and commercial banking franchise, headquartered in North Carolina. Initially, the FDIC had tried to broker a deal between Citigroup and Wachovia. It would have also made the federal government a $12 billion stakeholder in the nation's largest bank. The proposed deal made San Francisco-based Wells Fargo, also interested in the distressed bank, walk away from the bidding table. However, Wachovia shareholders objected to Citigroup's offer as being too low.

The situation dramatically changed after Congress passed a tax law that would allow whichever bank bought Wachovia to use Wachovia's losses to shelter its profits from taxation. Wells Fargo renewed its pursuit, offering to buy all of Wachovia for about $15 billion, an offer Wachovia shareholders happily accepted because it was substantially larger than Citigroup's earlier tender. Although initially it did not give up the legal fight for Wachovia, Citigroup eventually yielded to pressure from the Federal Reserve, which was concerned that a delay would compromise Wachovia's ability to stay in business.

Citigroup had its own problems that year. In November 2008 the bank's stock fell about 60 percent. In a move that was partly symbolic to assure markets that the government still had faith in the bank, the Treasury

Department, Federal Reserve, and FDIC announced they would protect Citigroup against potential losses on $306 billion in troubled assets. Although at the time Citigroup had $2 trillion on its books and was considered "too big to fail," government officials still feared that a low stock price would prompt those who did business with the company to pull their money, raising the risk of a downward spiral for the company. Stocks surged in November 2008, as investors greeted the government announcement that it would bail out Citigroup. As a condition of the bailout, the company had to adhere to new restrictions on what it pays its executives and carry out an FDIC program to help homeowners avoid foreclosure, using the same approach established at IndyMac. Government intervention seemed to have a reassuring impact on investors.

Apart from the fall of three of the country's largest financial institutions, dozens of other smaller banks throughout the country failed in 2008 and the first half of 2009, among them Silver Falls Bank of Oregon, First Bank Financial Services of Georgia, Silver State Bank of Nevada, National Bank of Commerce of Illinois, and several banks in California, including 1st Centennial Bank. According to the agency, the list of troubled banks shot up by 46 percent in the third quarter of 2008. Approximately 13 percent of the institutions on the list ended up failing.

The bank bailouts were just one of several government efforts to stabilize the financial sector, culminating in the Bush administration and Congress enacting the $700 billion bailout of the banking sector, known as the Troubled Asset Relief Program (TARP) in November 2008. Many members of the Congress as well as consumer groups, however, complained that the administration was overlooking homeowners. In an effort to answer these concerns, Bair presented a loan guarantee plan to the board of directors wherein a lender would get a government guarantee that troubled loans would be repaid. In exchange, the lender would be required to significantly drop the interest rate, reduce the principal, or extend the life of the affected loan.

But the loan modification program, long opposed by some in the Bush administration and many in the financial industry, was highly controversial. Critics of foreclosure aid questioned why a homeowner who took on an unaffordable loan should be entitled to government help, while those who had honored their mortgage payments would receive nothing. Others questioned how to target the right homeowners and how much risk the government should bear to boost the housing market.

The loan modification controversy intensified in November 2008, after the FDIC seized Downey Savings and Loan Association, the third-largest bank to fail that year, and announced that all those who held Downey mortgage loans and were delinquent would now be eligible for reduced monthly payments to help them avoid foreclosure. Never before had such a decision been made in conjunction with a bank failure.

In an attempt to break the logjam in bank-to-bank lending, the FDIC in October 2008 established the Temporary Liquidity Guarantee Program that covered new senior unsecured debt, which banks issue to one another.

A key beneficiary of this program was GE Capital, which received federal backing of up to $139 billion of its debt. GE Capital qualified because it owned GE Money Bank, a federally chartered thrift. In March 2009 the FDIC board voted unanimously to extend the program through 2009.

In October 2008 Congress passed the Economic Emergency Stabilization Act, which, among other things, raised the amount the FDIC covered for each depositor in each bank from $100,000 to $250,000, until Dec. 31, 2009. While the change was seen by many as long overdue and necessary to restore depositor confidence, the temporary nature of the boost was criticized. In May 2009 President Barack Obama signed the Helping Families Save Their Homes and the Fraud Enforcement and Recovery Act, which extended the insurance coverage to Dec. 31, 2013.

Meanwhile, the sharp rise in bank failures depleted the agency's federal insurance fund. In 2008 twenty-five banks failed, dropping the $52.4 billion fund to $18.9 billion. By September 2009, another 140 banks failed. Moreover, at the beginning of 2010, the agency announced that more than 700 additional banks with assets in excess of $400 billion were in danger of failing, with the fund dropping below $15 billion. The FDIC was required to maintain the fund at a fixed 1.15 percentage of the total deposits it insured, but by mid-2008 the fund fell below this mandated percentage and reached 0.22 percent in summer 2009.

In late February the board voted to collect $12 billion in quarterly fees and gave preliminary approval to a special assessment of about $15 billion. Objections to this assessment were presented during a March 2009 hearing of the Senate Banking, Housing, and Urban Affairs Subcommittee on Financial Institutions, in which William Grant, chairman and chief executive officer of First United Bank and Trust of Oakland, MD, testified on behalf of the American Bankers Association, arguing that the assessment would impose "a significant burden that will impact earnings, capital, and cost of funds—all of which makes it far more difficult [for banks] to lend." Grant and others also pointed out that healthy banks, which had acted prudently in recent years and not dabbled in risky mortgages, were being asked to pay for those financial institutions that had created the crisis through their careless lending practices.

In response to this criticism, the FDIC approved a number of changes that would require banks with riskier business practices to pay a larger share of the assessment. Former FDIC general counsel John L. Douglas described this policy prodding as similar to an insurance company saying, "If you drink and drive, you are going to pay more premiums."

In March 2009 FDIC Chair Sheila Bair also proposed an alternative to the emergency assessment, agreeing to halve the fee charged to banks in exchange for Congress more than tripling the agency's borrowing authority to tap federal aid, if needed to replenish the insurance fund. With the passage of the Helping Families Save Their Homes Act of 2009, Congress gave Bair exactly what she asked for. The FDIC's line of credit with the Treasury Department increased from $30 billion to $100 million.

Meanwhile, in August 2009 the FDIC issued new rules governing the regulation of newly created or "newly chartered" banks—those that were less than seven years old. In announcing these new rules, the agency noted that banks that have only recently been established are statistically much more likely to fail than firms that have been in business for longer than seven years. The announced regulations would raise capital requirements for newer banks and require a full FDIC examination each year, rather than every eighteen months as is the case for older institutions.

FDIC IN THE 2010s

In addition to raising the capital requirements for newer banks, the FDIC issued new broad-based accounting rules that required banks to have larger capital reserves, specifically to protect against losses on asset-backed securities. Banks resisted these stiffer rules, complaining that they would limit the availability of credit, which was already tight, and make it more challenging and expensive for consumers and companies to borrow. Obama Treasury Secretary Timothy F. Geithner and Federal Reserve Chair Ben S. Bernanke in March 2009 argued that strengthening the rules was essential for guarding against another financial meltdown, but they also recognized that the securitization of mortgage loans and other credit instruments was critical to the health of the economy: "No financial recovery plan will be successful unless it helps restart securitization markets for sound loans made to consumers and businesses, large and small," said Geithner, before unveiling the new administration's plan for overhauling financial regulation. In an attempt to strike a balance, the agency kept the new requirements but gave banks an additional six months to raise the additional capital required by the new regulation, moving the effective date of the requirement from Jan. 1, 2010, to July 1 of the same year.

While these new rules were important, they paled in comparison to the Wall Street Reform and Consumer Protection Act of 2010—also called the Dodd-Frank Act after its chief sponsors, Sen. Chris Dodd, D-CT, and Rep. Barney Frank, D-MA. Introduced in the wake of the financial crisis and signed into law on July 21, 2010, Dodd-Frank was the most sweeping overhaul of the financial system since the Great Depression.

Although the law was considered a major legislative victory for President Obama and for its supporters in Congress, Dodd-Frank's journey from bill to law was not without major hurdles, especially in the Senate. Criticism for the proposal came from both sides of the aisle, with Republicans arguing that it would entail excessive and burdensome regulation that would only make it more difficult and costly for businesses and consumers to get credit. While most Democrats saw the law as a victory that demonstrated to their constituents that they could be tough on Wall Street, some in the party felt the package did not go far enough and left too many critical decisions to the same federal regulators who had missed the warning signs before the financial crisis of 2008.

Among the key provisions of the new law was the establishment of an independent consumer bureau, aimed at protecting borrowers against abuses in mortgage, credit card, and other types of lending. In addition, the law established a council of federal regulators to be on the lookout for any incipient threats to the financial system. The overhaul also gave shareholders a nonbinding advisory vote on executive compensation.

For the FDIC specifically, Dodd-Frank gave the agency the authority to wind down and close large troubled financial firms in an orderly manner. This new power, known as "resolution authority," was designed to avoid a repeat of an event like the September 2008 bankruptcy of Lehman Brothers, which destabilized markets around the world and forced the U.S. government to bail out many of its largest banks and financial services companies to avoid an economic disaster.

Dodd-Frank also gave the agency new authority to change the fee structure it used to assess how much banks owe the agency's deposit insurance fund. Soon after the bill was enacted, the commission unanimously approved new regulations requiring large financial institutions to pick up a greater portion of the cost of the deposit insurance fund. The law directed the agency to reevaluate fees according to the value of total assets held by each bank rather than simply the level of deposits, as had been the case up to that point. This change was aimed at decreasing the burden on small banks, who had been complaining that they were bearing a disproportionate amount of the cost of replenishing the fund even though the failure of the larger banks had been the primary cause of its depletion. As a result, 110 of the nation's largest banks, in April 2011, began to cover approximately 80 percent of the premiums paid into the government's deposit insurance fund each year, an increase of about 12 percent from the year before. In addition, this new fee structure will allow the agency to collect more overall each year from the banking industry. These new funds were needed if the FDIC was to ever adequately replenish its deposit insurance fund, which had been severely depleted as a result of the large number of bank failures in recent years.

Meanwhile, the agency was still dealing with the fallout from the failure, in September 2008, of WaMu. In April 2010 a federal commission issued a report blaming the FDIC and the OTS for not properly supervising WaMu, even as the bank took on risky subprime mortgages. While the Office of Thrift Supervision (OTS) was tasked with ensuring the company's safeness and soundness, the FDIC was responsible for assessing the risks the bank's failure would pose to its deposit insurance fund.

As it turns out, the risks were great. With more than $300 billion in assets, WaMu was the largest institution regulated by the OTS. Although the FDIC had questioned OTS assessments of WaMu's soundness, both agencies were sharply criticized for not intervening even as the bank became increasingly unstable. Even in summer 2008, with the bank on the brink of failure, the two agencies could not agree on the proper tactic to take, and it was only in September of that year, merely a few weeks before WaMu declared bankruptcy, that both agencies were ready to concede that the bank was "unsafe and unsound." The report ultimately concluded that the FDIC should make its own assessment of institutions large enough to pose significant risk to its insurance fund and, if necessary, act alone to mitigate that risk.

Although the demise of WaMu came at no cost to the FDIC's deposit insurance fund (because the bank was taken over by JPMorgan Chase), the agency had taken the bank into receivership before its sale to JPMorgan and retained the right to sue former directors and officers of the failed bank if it believed WaMu was harmed by their actions. In fact, the FDIC has, so far, brought claims against 158 individuals at about twenty banks that failed during the crisis. The case against WaMu, however, was the biggest and most prominent.

As many predicted, 2010 set the high-water mark for bank failures—157—the highest number since 1992. Most of these failures were due to mortgage loan losses, and some states, notably Florida, Georgia, and Alabama, were especially hard hit. Florida led the way for bank failures in 2010, with twenty-nine. In spite of these losses, it looked as if the banking industry was beginning to regain its footing in 2010. Industry-wide profits were up ($87.5 billion), and loan losses were down. Only twenty-four lenders were added to the government's list of troubled banks. For the first time in six years, the number of institutions reporting a loss decreased.

Meanwhile, the agency began looking beyond just banks to pick up the tab for the cost of bank failures, including directing its attention to those high-ranking executives whose careless risk-taking helped lead to the financial crisis. In April 2011, the agency proposed rules for recovering compensation from executives and directors—as much as two years' pay—if they were found responsible for the systematic failure of an important financial company. Known as "clawbacks," this recovered compensation was aimed in particular at those executives of "too big to fail" financial institutions that had failed anyway.

Under the new rules, which were approved by the agency in July 2011, executives could be held financially responsible for an institution's failure if they failed to conduct their responsibilities with "the requisite degree of skill and care required by that position." The vagueness of this language had many questioning whether the new rules were largely symbolic, with no real punitive clout. Still, the financial services industry strenuously opposed clawbacks, which indicated that at least the executives themselves took them seriously.

Clawbacks became a very real issue after the FDIC filed a civil lawsuit against Kerry Klinger, WaMu's former chief executive, and two of his top lieutenants, former bank president Stephen Rotella, and former loans president David Schneider. While the lawsuit asked for an astronomical $900 million in damages from the three men, the agency in December 2011 settled for substantially less: $64.7 million. In addition, the executives only paid $400,000, with the rest of the settlement coming from directors' and officers' liability insurance policies paid for by the bank and other sources.

Many criticized the agency's handling of the WaMu settlement, characterizing it as a mere "wrist slapping." These critics pointed out that in addition to having to pay

what amounted to a pittance for top banking executives, the settlement did not require the three WaMu officers to admit any wrongdoing or mistakes. Senator Carl Levin, the Michigan Democrat who led the Senate's 2010 investigation into the origins of the financial crisis, summed up what many agency critics felt when he called the settlement "pretty soft."

The collapse of WaMu was the source of another headache for the FDIC. In 2009, Deutsche Bank filed a $10 billion lawsuit against the agency, claiming that it was responsible for losses suffered by the German bank as a result of its purchase of bad mortgages that had been securitized by WaMu. The FDIC requested the lawsuit against it be dismissed, arguing that Deutsche Bank should bring its claims against JPMorgan, which, the agency argued, had assumed WaMu's liabilities as well as its assets when it purchased the failed bank in 2008. JPMorgan countered that it had not assumed WaMu liabilities when it took over WaMu and, thus, was not responsible. In August 2011, a federal judge agreed with JPMorgan and let the lawsuit against the FDIC proceed.

The ruling on the Deutsche Bank lawsuit came just before the agency recovered $787 million in damages from the huge German bank in a different case. In early 2012, Deutsche Bank agreed to settle with the FDIC and pay the sizeable sum to resolve charges that it allegedly sold fraudulent mortgages to IndyMac, a California bank that ultimately collapsed, leaving the FDIC to pay off depositors.

Although Deutsche Bank won the right to bring the suit, it has not fared so well on the merits of its claim. So far, the FDIC has won the first two rounds, with a federal district court and an appeals court both ruling it is not responsible for the damages suffered by Deutsche Bank. Nevertheless, the lawsuit remained unresolved, as cited by a May 2013 appeals court decision barring a group of direct WaMu shareholders from getting involved in the suit. An October 2013 settlement between JPMorgan and the Federal Housing Finance Agency (FHFA) regarding the WaMu liabilities revived the possibility that the American bank and not the FDIC could be on the hook for the liabilities, pending further court decisions.

In March 2011, the FDIC and several other agencies proposed a set of new rules that would prohibit banks from selling packages of risky mortgages without retaining at least 5 percent of the ownership of those securities. This proposed requirement was aimed at ensuring that banks have a stake in maintaining those mortgages and not simply unloading them onto unsuspecting clients. The new rules would not apply to government-backed mortgages (which make up more than 80 percent of all mortgages) or to qualified residential mortgages (QRMs)—the safest form of mortgages.

Even though the new proposed QRM rules would apply to roughly 10 percent of mortgages, the FDIC's proposal prompted banks to begin a massive lobbying campaign, aimed at broadening the definition of a QRM and hence the exemption. Specifically, the banking industry expressed concern that the rules might curtail access to future mortgages sought by low- and moderate-income borrowers. In addition, some argued that the new rules would not make the system safer from future upheaval because a 5 percent retention requirement on 10 percent of mortgages issued was not substantial enough to dramatically change the industry's behavior. A more logical course, they said, would be to enforce existing rules that make mortgage lending safer by simply restricting the amount of debt borrowers can take on when they seek a mortgage. The intense pushback over the proposed QRM rules from bankers and others prompted the agency to put the regulations on hold, where they remained two years later, in spring 2013.

The argument over the QRM rules mirrored a broader debate in the monetary policy community. In the years following the 2008 financial meltdown, federal policymakers had been trying to strike a balance between encouraging banks to lend more, while making sure these institutions keep enough capital on hand to avoid another round of debilitating loan losses. On one level, at least, the policies put in place seemed to be working: In the first five months of 2011, only 44 banks failed, nearly half the rate of 2010.

Fewer bank failures helped to restore the agency's severely depleted deposit insurance fund. At the beginning of the financial crisis, the fund had a surplus of more than $50 billion. At one point in 2010, that surplus had been transformed into a $21 billion deficit. By mid-2011, thanks to fewer failures and higher bank fees, this deficit had shrunk to $1 billion.

Meanwhile, in May 2011, Bair announced that she would be leaving the FDIC after five years. She was one of the first federal regulators to publicly warn about the aggressive and risky lending practices that flooded the mortgage industry during the housing market boom years. Indeed, soon after her appointment by President Bush, she advised that the government demand that banks modify their mortgage lending practices, as by then borrowers were beginning to default at a disturbing rate. Her counsel went unheeded and her aggressive stance during the financial crisis would go on to alienate both her fellow Republicans, as well as Obama administration officials, such as Treasury Secretary Timothy F. Geithner.

On June 13, 2011, President Obama nominated the FDIC's vice chair, Martin Gruenberg, to replace Bair as chair. Before becoming vice chair of the agency in 2005, Gruenberg built a career on Capitol Hill, working for the Senate Banking Committee and then for Sen. Paul S. Sarbanes, D-MD, where he played a key role in drafting the 2002 "Sarbanes-Oxley" financial overhaul law.

Given his experience, Gruenberg was hailed by both Republicans and Democrats as a solid choice to replace Bair. However, his nomination was held up until November 2012. Republicans wanted to wait until after the election to vote on the nominee, arguing that if GOP presidential candidate Mitt Romney won the election, he should have a free hand to choose the FDIC chair. Right after Obama's reelection in November, the Senate approved Gruenberg's nomination. Meanwhile, during the more than 16 months Gruenberg had to wait to win Senate confirmation, he ran the agency as acting chair.

Sheila Bair's exit from the agency was far from quiet. In 2012, the former chair released a book—*Bull by the*

Horns: Fighting to Save Main Street From Wall Street and Wall Street From Itself—that took a fresh swipe at her foes and the bankers she blamed for the crisis. Bair's targets included fellow regulators, especially then-Treasury Secretary Geithner, whom she depicted as being in the pocket of Wall Street, referring to him as the "bailouter in chief."

Bair, who characterized herself as a lifelong Republican with a populist streak, described how difficult it was being "the only woman in the room" and wrote that she was often purposely kept in the dark by top Obama economic advisers. She also questioned whether Geithner's effort to inject billions of dollars into nine big banks masked a rescue intended solely for Citigroup, which received more government support than any other bank.

Meanwhile, in October 2012, the agency announced publication of its final rule regarding "stress testing" required under Dodd-Frank. The final rule required all financial companies with total consolidated assets of more than $10 billion that are regulated by a primary federal financial regulatory agency to conduct an annual company-run stress test, beginning in October 2013. The rule also required institutions with assets greater than $50 billion to begin conducting annual stress tests in 2012, although the FDIC reserved the authority to allow covered institutions above $50 billion to delay implementation on a case-by-case basis where warranted.

But the need for the stress testing of banks seemed, if not unnecessary, at least less urgent than it had during the height of the financial crisis in 2008 and 2009. Indeed, by mid-2012, a number of indicators revealed steady but slow recovery in the banking sector. In August, the FDIC reported that bank earnings rose 20.7 percent in the second quarter, continuing a trend that began in the first quarter with the highest level of earnings in five years. The agency also reported a $102 billion increase in lending, as well as a drop in the percentage of troubled loans for the ninth quarter in a row—an encouraging shift. Perhaps most encouraging, loans in the troubled real estate sector showed the sharpest decline in delinquency, to nearly 18 percent.

At the same time, however, bank revenue growth remained sluggish and earnings continued to be impacted by low interest rates. Moreover, banks' net interest margins—the difference between what they earn on loans and pay out on deposits—remained very tight. And while many large and medium banks, by 2012, had the emergency funds they needed to guard against losses, smaller banks, especially community banks, were still struggling to build their reserves. Consumer lending also continued to be low, reflecting the ongoing weakness in the all-important housing market. James Chessen, chief economist at the American Bankers Association explained, "One of the consequences of really low interest rates is borrowers know that there is no urgency to borrow. They can wait for the next two years and see what happens with the debt levels in the U.S., what happens to their foot traffic."

Meanwhile, the nation's largest bank, JPMorgan, appeared to be losing some of its luster in Washington, DC, particularly with regulators. By 2013 eight federal agencies, including the FDIC, were investigating the bank over a number of different allegations, among them failing to fully alert authorities to suspicions about jailed swindler Bernard Madoff and misstating how the bank harmed more than 5,000 homeowners due to botched reviews of troubled mortgages.

The investigations represented a stunning turnaround for the bank. Up to this time, JPMorgan's chief executive Jamie Dimon had been widely praised for successfully shepherding his bank, largely unscathed, through the 2008 financial crisis. But now perceptions about Chase and Dimon were changing. The FDIC focused its particular attention on the notorious $6.2 billion trading loss, known as the "London Whale," which took place in 2012. The London Whale, named after a JPMorgan trader based in the British capital, caught the attention of regulators and members of Congress who were concerned about another big bank collapsing and requiring a huge federal bailout—the so-called too big to fail scenario that occurred with many banks in 2008 and 2009.

Dimon initially characterized all the attention paid to the colossal loss as "a complete tempest in a teapot." But later he changed his tune, apologizing for the incident several times and calling it "the stupidest and most embarrassing situation I have ever been a part of." But Dimon's apology did little to stem the "tempest" over the Whale, especially after a Senate report in early 2013 accused the bank of understating the risks taken by its traders, including Bruno Iksil, the derivatives trader known as "The Whale," who worked out of Chase's London trading division.

A Senate hearing that followed on the heels of the report raised even more questions. The bank originally asserted all along that Iksil's trades were "hedges"—investments designed to offset risks being taken elsewhere in the bank. But Senate investigators, who examined more than 90,000 documents and conducted more than 50 interviews, could not identify the assets that Iksil's trades were supposed to be hedging or how his trades were meant to reduce risk.

In September 2013 it was announced that the bank would pay American and British regulators $920 million to settle charges related to the London Whale. The announced fine came just a month after two of Iksil's colleagues (although not Iksil) were criminally charged with conspiring to illegally conceal more than $500 million in losses related to the London Whale trades. The cases have yet to come to trial.

JPMorgan's multibillion-dollar trading loss had another, broader outcome: It brought renewed attention to the Volcker Rule, a controversial provision of the Dodd-Frank reform bill that restricts banks from making risky investments with their own money, a practice known as proprietary trading. Proprietary trading has produced impressive profits for financial firms, but it has also been blamed for the huge losses that took place during the height of the financial crisis. Named after former Federal Reserve chairman Paul Volcker, who was a vocal critic of bank practices that led to the financial crisis, the Volcker Rule was designed to prevent Wall Street banks that benefit from government safety nets, such as the FDIC's deposit insurance, from making certain kinds of risky trades that benefit only themselves.

Supporters of the rule say that it will do just that, discouraging the "casino culture" at proprietary trading operations of large banks that caused JP Morgan's London Whale debacle as well as other less-publicized losses. But critics argue that the rule unnecessarily limits some safe forms of trading and will severely curtail the profit at some of the nation's largest banks, particularly investment banks such as JPMorgan and Goldman Sachs, which derive a large percentage of their revenue from trading in derivatives and other financial instruments. Indeed, they say, it will not only completely change the way Wall Street does business but will threaten New York's status as the world's financial capital.

The FDIC unanimously approved the Volcker Rule in October 2011. But it languished in an intrgovernmental agency debate over various issues, including a highly publicized lawsuit by some banks claiming that they should be allowed to continue trading certain kinds of mortgage backed securities. The rule was not finalized until January 2014, after the FDIC and other agencies carved out an exception, allowing banks to continue trading the securities that had been the subject of the lawsuit. In addition, at the end of 2014 the Federal Reserve announced that the implementation of the rule would be delayed until July 2016 and possibly for an additional year after that.

Meanwhile, in the wake of one of the worst recessions in U.S. history, many Americans were opting out of traditional banking. According to a 2013 FDIC report, roughly 17 million adults were without a checking or savings account, and the percentage of the "unbanked" population had grown from 7.6 percent to 8.2 percent of U.S. households between 2009 and 2011. In addition, the agency report claimed, one in five American adults was "underbanked" in the sense that they had a checking or savings account but often relied on payday loans, check-cashing services, and similar nonbank institutions to manage their money. Moreover, the report noted, many of the unbanked or underbanked were among the poor or working poor.

Perhaps with an eye on helping those less likely to use a traditional bank, the agency, in March 2013 voted to provide full deposit insurance to American Express prepaid debit cards. These cards, called Bluebird cards, are currently sold at Walmart stores and operate much like a debit card or credit card. The agency's move reflected the rise in the use of these cards—with nearly 18 percent of American households using them in 2012.

Around the same time the agency ended a four-year program that had provided an unlimited insurance guarantee for the $1.5 trillion in accounts at the nation's small banks. This guarantee, known as the Transaction Account Guarantee, was instituted by the agency during the worst period of the financial crisis as a means of preventing the migration of risk-averse customers from smaller banks to larger ones that were viewed (incorrectly, as it turned out) as being less likely to fail. The accounts that lost the special insurance are used primarily by businesses, municipalities, and entities like nonprofits for regular cash-flow needs. Of course, these accounts still receive the FDIC's $250,000 coverage available to everyone else.

Community banks, in particular, had benefited from the guarantee, and there was widespread concern that customers would respond to the end of the program by withdrawing large sums out of these banks. But this did not happen, in part because many of the smaller banks turned to specialized cash-management firms that helped customers split up larger deposits into multiple, insurable $250,000 chunks and distributed them among a network of banks.

Meanwhile, in July 2013, the agency moved to further shore up the credibility of the nation's largest banks, instituting new capital requirements. Under the new rules, the country's largest banks are required to have cash on hand equal to at least 5 percent of their total assets—or 2 percent higher than the existing international requirements.

The new rules were meant to ensure that banks have enough liquid assets to weather a financial crisis like the one that befell them in the recession of 2008. The agency initially had proposed a 6 percent requirement, but the Federal Reserve argued that requiring banks to keep too much cash on hand would leave them too little to lend out and, thus, hurt the economy. Under Fed pressure, the FDIC lowered the requirement to 5 percent.

Banks were given until 2019 to fully comply with the higher capital requirements. In addition, the rules did not apply to smaller banks, which successfully argued that since they had not caused the financial crisis, they should not be penalized for the reckless actions of the larger banks that had actually been responsible for the problems the rule was meant to address.

At the same time the FDIC was trying to help to create a new regulatory regime for banks, it also was moving aggressively in court to punish directors and officers from banks that had failed in the wake of the 2008 crisis. During the first eight months of 2013, the agency filed 32 lawsuits against directors and officers, almost as many as it had filed in the previous four years. The suits revolved around claims that officers and directors had negligently contributed to their banks' failures and were thus civilly liable to the agency for the money it had paid to those banks' depositors whose accounts had been wiped out.

In the five years between the beginning of the crisis and 2013, 483 banks (many of them small) had failed, requiring the agency to reimburse insured depositors to the tune of $89 billion. But by the start of 2013, the agency had recouped only $727 million from litigation against high-level employees and directors at these failed banks, prompting critics to say that the agency was not moving fast enough against those who had contributed to the losses.

FDIC officials countered that it often takes years after a bank fails to build a case that the institution collapsed due, at least in part, to negligence rather than a tough business environment or bad luck. The surge in lawsuits in 2013 reflected this lag, they said.

In October 2013 the FDIC, along with the Federal Reserve, the Department of Housing and Urban Development, and three other federal agencies proposed a rule that would require prospective homebuyers to pay 30 percent of a home's value up front if they wanted the lowest interest mortgages available. In addition to the 30 percent down payment, these borrowers also would have to show that they had a sterling credit rating.

In proposing the new rule, the agency argued that it would strengthen the mortgage market and ultimately help prevent another housing sales collapse like the one that helped spark the Great Recession of 2008. But the new proposed requirement provoked a strong response from the banking and real estate industries, which predicted that it would unnecessarily depress new home sales just when the housing market was beginning to show real signs of improvement. In addition, these industries argued, the new requirement would unnecessarily favor the rich and make it harder for middle-income people to buy a house.

Following intense lobbying, the arguments by the housing and banking industry won the day. And soon after the proposed rule had been made public, the FDIC and its sister agencies withdrew it.

As 2013 drew to a close, the agency once again found itself in tense negotiations with Jamie Dimon and his bank, JP Morgan. Instead of the London Whale, however, the object of the dispute concerned the bank's role in the sale of faulty mortgage securities, a much bigger and more costly problem. While JP Morgan agreed to pay a whopping $13 billion to the government to settle claims against it for selling bad mortgage securities, it balked at covering more than $1 billion in liabilities of Washington Mutual, a huge, bankrupt mortgage lender Morgan had purchased in 2008 at the urging of the government.

Dimon argued that the FDIC had promised to assume some of WaMu's liabilities (in this case, unpaid state taxes owed on the sale of mortgage securities) in an effort to entice JP Morgan to purchase the bank. The government wanted a healthy bank such as Morgan to buy WaMu to help stabilize the banking system, he claimed. But the agency denied making such a promise, contending that JP Morgan had assumed both WaMu's assets and its liabilities when it bought the failed lender.

In December 2013, JP Morgan sued the FDIC for $2.75 billion to cover some of the costs associated with the WaMu purchase. But in December of that year, the bank dropped the lawsuit after tax authorities in the some of the states owed money by WaMu agreed to abandon their claims against the Morgan.

In March 2014 the agency launched its most ambitious action against the international banking industry when it sued 16 of the world's largest banking institutions, accusing them of conspiring to manipulate interest rates in an effort to defraud smaller banks. The suit involved global heavyweights, including JP Morgan and Bank of America from the U.S. as well as Britain's Barclays, Germany's Deutsche Bank, and Switzerland's UBS.

At the heart of the suit is the London Interbank Offered Rate, or Libor, which is the name for the interest rate banks set when lending money to one another as well as to other financial institutions. Rates for at least $550 trillion in loans and other financial products are tied to the Libor, making it extremely important.

FDIC lawyers claim that from 2007 to 2011 the sixteen banks involved in the lawsuit colluded to change the Libor rate to their advantage, which in turn drove ten banks in the United States into receivership. Since the agency was required to pay off depositors in these bankrupt institutions, it sued to recover the cost of doing so. "Financial institutions around the world, including the closed banks, reasonably relied on Libor as an honest and accurate benchmark of a competitively determined interbank lending rate," the agency stated in its lawsuit. "Defendants' wrongful conduct . . . caused substantial losses to the closed banks."

The suit, which has yet to go to trial, came on the heels of an agreement by four banks, including Barclays and UBS, to pay a $3.6 billion fine to settle Libor-related charges made by European regulators.

Meanwhile, during the summer of 2014 two large American banks accused of fraudulently selling mortgage-backed securities agreed to settle with the government. First, in July, Citigroup agreed to pay $7 billion to settle allegations against it. Then, one month later, Bank of America agreed to a record $16.65 billion settlement. In both cases, no one from the banks was prosecuted and the institutions were not required to admit any wrongdoing.

The summer also saw the agency sounding an alarm on the crisis contingency plans of the nation's eleven largest banks. Under the Dodd-Frank law, large banks (those with $50 billion or more in assets outside of traditional banking, such as derivatives) are required to create a "living will" with clear plans detailing how they will unwind their assets in the event that a financial crisis bankrupts them. The living wills are intended to prevent banks from chaotically collapsing, as happened during the 2008 crisis. The idea is that banks would dispose of assets in an orderly manner, preventing the need for the government to step in and prop them up, as happened during the financial crisis.

But in August 2014 officials from the FDIC and the Federal Reserve issued a joint statement warning the large banks that their first attempt at crafting livings wills had failed. "Each plan . . . is deficient and fails to convincingly demonstrate how, in failure, any one of these firms could overcome obstacles to entering bankruptcy without precipitating a financial crisis," FDIC chairman Hoenig said.

Specifically, the Fed and the FDIC said that the plans to spin off subsidiaries were still too complex and would take too much time. The eleven banks, which include Bank of American, JP Morgan, Goldman Sacs, and Morgan Stanley, were sent back to the drawing board and told to submit revised plans by July 1, 2015.

In November 2014 the agency along with the Fed and the Treasury Department warned banks about making loans to companies with low credit ratings. The agencies noted that banks have been making more and more of these risky, high interest moves in the last few years. While these so-called leveraged loans are usually subsequently sold by banks to hedge funds and other investors, regulators fear that an increase in high-risk lending could ultimately hurt the country's financial system. Still, the warning was not a demand and banks were under no legal obligation to take the regulators' advice.

Current Issues

The agency was once again in the news at the very end of the 2014, as the now lame-duck Congress and the White House negotiated a $1.1 trillion, fiscal 2015 omnibus spending bill. At the behest of parts of the finance industry, House Republican leaders added language to the huge measure reversing derivative trading limits for banks that had been included in the 2010 Dodd-Frank financial reform law.

Derivatives are financial contracts that specify that a certain payment will be made under certain circumstances. Like insurance, they are often used to hedge bets in those industries—such as agriculture or airline travel—where unforeseen circumstances such as bad weather or a terrorist attack can severely damage a businesses' short-term prospects.

Among its many provisions, Dodd-Frank required that banks spin off some of their riskier derivative trading operations into separate entities not insured by the FDIC. The idea was to reduce risk of huge losses, both to banks and to the government. But while trading in derivatives can be risky, it also can be profitable.

Not surprisingly, the spin-off idea had never been popular with the banking industry, which had been lobbying for Congress to revoke the provision from the time it had been enacted. Their chance came after the midterm election of November 2014, which resulted in the GOP taking control of the Senate and adding to its already solid majority in the House.

Republicans in Congress had never liked Dodd-Frank, arguing that it was an overreaction to the financial crash that was unnecessarily hobbling the nation's banking industry through overregulation. Although Democrats retained control of the Senate in the two months following the election, incoming GOP Senate leaders were able to press their Democratic counterparts to include language striking the derivative trading prohibitions as part of a huge deal to pass a governmentwide spending bill that was working its way through the lame-duck Congress.

Republicans see the repeal as the first step in dismantling Dodd-Frank. But House Democratic Minority Leader, Nancy Pelosi, said the provision allows banks to gamble wildly with depositors' money, putting taxpayers on the hook if the bet does not pay off. It is "the same old Republican formula" she said during the debate over the measure, adding, "Privatize the gain, nationalize the risk. You succeed, it's in your pocket. You fail, the taxpayer pays the bill. It's just not right."

The new year saw the agency working in a number of different areas. In February 2015 it helped shutter Doral Financial, a once high-flying Puerto Rico bank that had suffered chronic losses and mismanagement in recent years. The bank, which at one time was the island territory's top mortgage lender, suffered a severe blow in 2011 when one of its leaders, Maurice Spagnoletti, was killed by a gunman while driving in San Juan. Doral also had been the subject of a number of criminal probes involving misuse of bank funds. The bank's closure and subsequent payout to depositors was ultimately expected to cost the FDIC about $750 million, its largest loss since 2010.

Also in February, the agency issued new regulatory guidance that seemed to backtrack from an earlier position it had taken on banks providing services to certain industries. In 2013 the FDIC and the Department of Justice had urged financial institutions to cut-off or curtail banking services to payday lenders, gun dealers, producers of pornography, and other industries that it judged could routinely skirt the law.

Congressional Republicans and other critics had complained that under "Operation Chokehold," as the FDIC–Justice initiative was called, certain entirely legitimate businesses were treated as quasicriminal enterprises without benefit of due process. Some even charged that the Obama administration was using the Justice Department and the FDIC to punish industries it does not like, particularly gun dealers.

The new FDIC guidance effectively closed down Operation Chokehold. It urged banks not to cut off entire industries when deciding whether or not to offer them banking services. Instead, the agency recommended that banks judge each business on a case-by-case basis.

Around the same time the agency was ending Operation Chokehold, it issued an important report detailing a crisis in the African American banking sector. The report found that in 2013 there were only twenty-five banks that were majority owned by African Americans, down from fourty-eight in 2001. Even among those black-owned banks that were still in business, fully 60 percent lost money in 2013, the agency said.

Reasons for the decline range from difficulties faced by the banking sector in general during the Great Recession to a failure on the part of many black-owned banks to modernize services, such as installing automated teller machines (ATMs) at branches. Ironically, the report noted, the declines in black-owned banks came as the total number of minority-owned banks (those owned by Latinos, Asian Americans, as well as African Americans) actually increased during the same twelve-year period, from 164 to 174. The reduction in the number of African American banks also coincided with an increased need for banking services in the black community, particularly among poorer African Americans.

Meanwhile, the agency is preparing to once again review the living wills of the nation's largest banks. The revised plans were due July 1, 2015, and failure to satisfy officials at the FDIC and the Fed could lead to requirements to set aside more assets to cover potential losses. Banks that repeatedly fail to come up with satisfactory plans could be forced to divest from entire lines of business.

■ AGENCY ORGANIZATION

Biographies

MARTIN J. GRUENBERG, CHAIR

Appointment: Nominated by President George W. Bush on July 27, 2005, as member and vice chair of the FDIC Board of Directors; confirmed by the Senate on July 29, 2005 for a five-year term, which expired on December 27, 2012. He served as acting chair from November 2005 to June 2006 and again from July 2011 to November 2012. Nominated chair by President Barack Obama on June 10, 2011, for a five-year term; confirmed by the Senate on November 15, 2012.

Born: April 4, 1953; New York, N.Y.

Education: Princeton University, Woodrow Wilson School of Public and International Affairs, A.B.; Case Western Reserve Law School, J.D.

Profession: Lawyer.

Political Affiliation: Democrat.

Previous Career: Prior to his appointment, Gruenberg served as senior counsel to Sen. Paul S. Sarbanes while the senator was on the Committee on Banking, Housing, and Urban Affairs, advising on all issues of domestic and international financial regulation, monetary policy, and trade. Gruenberg also served as counsel to Senator Sarbanes from 1993 to 2005, advising on all issues under the jurisdiction of the Banking Committee, and as staff director of the Banking Committee's Subcommittee on International Finance and Monetary Policy from 1987 to 1992. Gruenberg's congressional experience with finance and banking issues dates to 1979. He served as chair of the executive council and president of the International Association of Deposit Insurers from November 2007 to November 2012.

THOMAS M. HOENIG, VICE CHAIR

Appointment: Nominated by President Barack Obama and confirmed by the Senate to a six-year term beginning on April 16, 2012. Appointed vice chair on November 15, 2012.

Born: Fort Madison, Iowa.

Education: St. Benedict's College, B.A.; Iowa State University, M.A.

Profession: Economist.

Political Affiliation: Republican.

Previous Career: Hoenig served on the Federal Reserve for thirty-eight years, as an economist and as a senior officer in banking supervision during the 1980s banking crisis in the U.S. He was president of the Kansas City Federal Reserve Bank from 1991 to 2011, directing the oversight of more than 1,000 banks and bank holding companies. He was also a member of the Federal Reserve System's Federal Open Market Committee. He serves as a member of the executive board of the International Association of Deposit Insurers.

VACANT, DIRECTOR

THOMAS J. CURRY, DIRECTOR, COMPTROLLER OF THE CURRENCY

Appointment: Nominated for the FDIC board by President George W. Bush on June 12, 2003; confirmed by the Senate Dec. 9, 2003; sworn in Jan. 12, 2004, for a six-year term expiring Jan. 12, 2010. Since becoming comptroller of the currency in 2012, serves on the FDIC board in that capacity.

Born: 1955.

Education: Manhattan College, B.A.; New England School of Law, J.D.

Federal Deposit Insurance Corporation

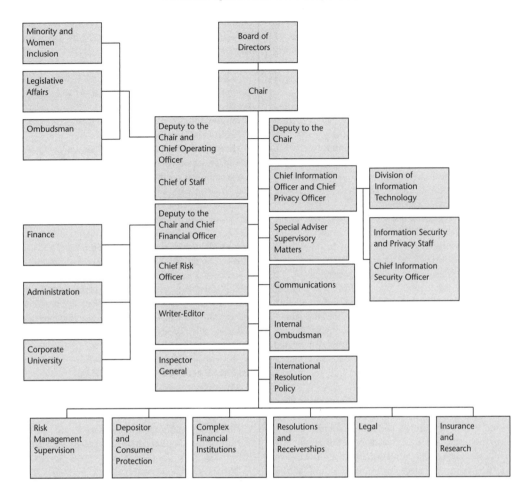

Profession: Lawyer.

Political Affiliation: Independent.

Previous Career: Curry was sworn in as comptroller of the currency for the U.S. Treasury Dept. on April 9, 2012; named chair of the Federal Financial Institutions Examination Council on April 1, 2013; and as chair of the NeighborWorks America Board of Directors. He served five Massachusetts governors as the commonwealth's commissioner of banks from 1990 to 1991 and from 1995 to 2003. Prior to that, he served as an acting bank commissioner and as first deputy commissioner after first joining Massachusetts's Division of Banks in 1986. Curry also served as chair of the Conference of State Bank Supervisors from 2000 to 2001.

RICHARD CORDRAY, DIRECTOR, CONSUMER FINANCIAL PROTECTION BUREAU

Appointment: Since January 2012, serves on the FDIC board in his capacity as director of the Consumer Financial Protection Bureau.

Born: Columbus, Ohio.

Education: Michigan State University, B.A.; Oxford University, M.A.; University of Chicago Law School, J.D.

Profession: Lawyer.

Political Affiliation: Democrat.

Previous Career: Cordray served as attorney general of Ohio from 2009 to 2011; treasurer of Ohio from 2007 to 2009; treasurer of Franklin County, Ohio, from 2002 to 2007; solicitor general of Ohio; and member of the Ohio House of Representatives for the 33rd District. He clerked for U.S. Supreme Court Justices Byron White and Anthony Kennedy, and was an adjunct professor at the Ohio State University College of Law. He has argued seven cases before the U.S. Supreme Court, including those by special appointment of the Clinton and Bush Justice Departments.

Headquarters and Divisions

BOARD OF DIRECTORS

The board is responsible for formulating and executing policy and administering the affairs of the corporation. It bears final responsibility for FDIC activities involving protection of bank depositors and is accountable to the president and Congress. The board adopts rules and regulations, supervises state nonmember insured banks, determines the course of action to take when an insured bank has difficulties, and decides how to deal with potential and actual bank failures. The board makes final decisions on conversions, mergers, and consolidations of banks; proposals to reduce or retire capital; requests to establish or move branch offices; issuance of cease-and-desist orders; and applications for insurance by noninsured banks.

Chair
    Martin J. Gruenberg . . . . (202) 898–3888
Vice Chair
    Thomas M. Hoenig. . . . . (202) 898–6616
Directors
    Vacant, Director . . . . (202) 898–3957
    Thomas J. Curry, Comptroller
      of the Currency . . . . (202) 649–6800
    Richard Cordray, Director of the Consumer
      Financial Protection Bureau . . . . . (202) 906–6590
    (The Comptroller of the Currency and the Director of the Consumer Financial Protection Bureau are required by law to be members of the FDIC Board of Directors.)
Deputy to the Chair and Chief Financial Officer
    Steven O. App . . . . (202) 898–8732
    Special Adviser to the CFO
      Chris Aiello . . . . (202) 898–3966
Deputy to the Chair and Chief Operating Officer, Chief of Staff
    Barbara A. Ryan. . . . . (202) 898–3811
Deputy to the Chair
    Kymberly K. Copa. . . . . (202) 898–3858
Senior Adviser to the Chair
    David S. Hoelscher . . . . (202) 898–6714
Chief Information Officer and Chief Privacy Officer
    Barry C. West . . . . (703) 516–5781
Internal Ombudsman
    Robert D. Harris . . . . (202) 898–6622
Deputy to the Director, Comptroller of the Currency
    William A. Rowe III . . . . (202) 898–6960
Deputy to the Director, CFPB
    Elizabeth Ellis . . . . (202) 435–7000
Deputy to Director
    Patricia A. Colohan (acting) . . . . (202) 898–6548
Chief of International Affairs
    Galo Cevallos (acting) . . . .(202) 898–7439

OFFICE OF COMMUNICATIONS
See Information Sources.

OFFICE OF COMPLEX FINANCIAL INSTITUTIONS
Oversees and reviews bank holding companies with more than $100 billion in assets and some non-bank financial companies, and liquidates those companies that fail.
Director
    Arthur J. Murton. . . . . (202) 898–6714
Assistant Director, Organizational Planning and Resource Management
    Krista Hughes . . . .(202) 898–3773
Deputy Director, Resolution Planning, Policy Review, and Enforcement
    Ricardo Delfin . . . . (202) 898–6591

Deputy Director, Systemic Resolution and Planning Implementation Group
    Herbert Held . . . . (202) 898–6681

OFFICE OF CORPORATE RISK MANAGEMENT
Provides analysis of external and internal risks to the FDIC that require consideration by the board of directors and senior executives.
Chief Risk Officer
    Stephen A. Quick . . . . (202) 898–6959

OFFICE OF THE INSPECTOR GENERAL
Conducts audits, evaluations, and investigations related to the programs and operations of the FDIC.
Inspector General
    Fred W. Gibson (acting) . . . . (703) 562–2166
      Hotline . . . . (800) 964–3342
Principal Deputy Inspector General
    Vacant . . . . (703) 562–6339
Deputy Assistant Inspector General
    Trina Petty . . . . (703) 562–6305
Assistant Inspector General for Audits
    Mark Mulholland . . . . (703) 562–6316
Assistant Inspector General for Evaluations
    E. Marshall Gentry . . . . (703) 562–6378
Assistant Inspector General for Investigations
    Matthew T. Alessandrino. . . . . (703) 562–6373
Assistant Inspector General for Management
    Deborah L. Schweikert. . . . . (703) 562–2774

OFFICE OF LEGISLATIVE AFFAIRS
Advises the FDIC on legislative policy, which includes developing congressional testimony, as well as responding to congressional inquiries regarding pending legislation and to congressional constituent complaints and inquiries.
Director
    Eric Spitler . . . . (202) 898–7140
Deputy Director
    Vacant. . . . . (202) 898–7140

OFFICE OF MINORITY AND WOMEN INCLUSION
Directs equal opportunity programs and affirmative employment programs for FDIC employees and employment applicants; handles outreach to small disadvantaged women and minority-owned businesses.
Director
    Segundo Pereira . . . . (703) 562–6090
      Fax. . . . . (703) 562–6059
Deputy Director
    Melodee Brooks . . . . (703) 562–6041

OFFICE OF THE OMBUDSMAN
An independent, neutral, and confidential source of assistance for bankers and the public. Provides answers to bankers and the public in the areas of depositor concerns, loan questions, asset information, bank-closing issues, and any FDIC regulation or policy.
Ombudsman
    Cottrell L. Webster . . . . (703) 562–6040
      Fax. . . . . (703) 562–6057

CORPORATE UNIVERSITY

Manages five schools for the training and development of FDIC's workforce: *Supervision and Consumer Protection* for core examiner training; *Resolutions and Receiverships* for training in receivership management and resolutions, franchise marketing, and loan management; *Insurance* for education in risk analysis and assessment; *Corporate Operations* for development of employees in functional support operations; and *Leadership Development* for development of current and future executives.

Chief Learning Officer
Suzannah Susser .... (703) 516–1061

DIVISION OF ADMINISTRATION

Branches and sections handle a variety of support services within the FDIC, such as acquisitions and human resources.

Director
Arleas Upton Kea .... (703) 562–2100
Fax.......................... (703) 562–2513

DIVISION OF DEPOSITOR AND CONSUMER PROTECTION

Promotes stability and public confidence in the nation's financial system by examining and supervising insured financial institutions to ensure that they operate in a safe and sound manner, that consumers' rights are protected, and that FDIC-supervised institutions invest in their communities. This division also provides timely and accurate deposit insurance information to financial institutions and the public.

Director
Mark Pearce...................... (202) 898–7088
Deputy Director, Consumer Protection and Community Affairs
Elizabeth Ortiz.................... (202) 898–3911
Deputy Director, Policy and Research
Jonathan Miller .... (202) 898–3587

DIVISION OF FINANCE

Manages the FDIC's corporate and receivership funds; provides necessary financial statements and reports; operates according to the Chief Financial Officers Act, and conducts audits of and collects premiums from insured financial institutions; and provides other services, including accounting, budgeting, travel, and relocation.

Director
Craig Jarvill .... (703) 562–6206
Deputy Director, Assessments
Donna Saulnier .... (703) 562–6167
Deputy Director, Controller
Karen J. Hughes................... (703) 562–6181
Deputy Director, Corporate Management Control
James H. Angel Jr................. (703) 562–6456
Deputy Director, Corporate Planning and Performance Management
Thomas E. Peddicord III .... (703) 562–6252
Deputy Director, Financial Operations
Thompson Sawyer................. (703) 562–6398

DIVISION OF INFORMATION TECHNOLOGY

Coordinates the FDIC's computer operations and data analysis used by agency officials involved in regulation and insurance activities; fosters the sharing and integration of information.

Director and Chief Information Officer
Russell Pittman .... (703) 516–5781

DIVISION OF INSURANCE AND RESEARCH

Researches, analyzes, and develops policy on banking and deposit insurance; identifies existing and emerging risks to the deposit insurance funds; manages and evaluates the risk-related premium system; and provides comprehensive and statistical information on banking.

Director
Diane Ellis .... (202) 898–3940
Deputy Director, Research and International Affairs
Fred Carns .... (202) 898–3940
Deputy Director, Risk Analysis and Pricing
Pat Mitchell (acting) .... (202) 898–3927

DIVISION OF RESOLUTIONS AND RECEIVERSHIPS

Coordinates the FDIC's response to failed and failing banks and savings associations, including the development, negotiation, and monitoring of all aspects of the resolution process; manages and disposes of equity positions acquired in resolutions; and develops related policies and financing strategies. Supervises the liquidation of failed insured banks and savings associations, verifies claims of depositors, and pays out insurance up to the $250,000 limit per depositor for all account types. Administers a portfolio of assets of failed insured banks and savings associations and keeps a complete record of the details of each liquidation case.

Director
Bret D. Edwards.................. (703) 562–6101
Deputy Director, Receivership Operations
Randy Taylor* .... (972) 761–8555
  * in Dallas, Texas
Deputy Director, Franchise and Asset Marketing
Pamela Farwig.................... (202) 898–6714
Field Operations Manager
David Davis .... (202) 898–7083

DIVISION OF RISK MANAGEMENT SUPERVISION

Director
Doreen R. Eberley................. (202) 898–3858
Fax........................... (202) 898–3638
Deputy Director, Policy
George E. French................. (202) 898–3929
Deputy Director, Strategic Planning and Resource Management
Melinda West..................... (202) 898–7221
Deputy Director, Supervisory Examinations
James C. Watkins................. (202) 898–6556

LEGAL DIVISION

Handles all legal matters affecting the FDIC, including litigation; legal correspondence; interpretation of federal and state laws; and preparation of rules, regulations, opinions, and legal documents.

General Counsel
Charles Yi . . . . (202) 898–3706
Deputy General Counsel, Consumer, Enforcement/ Employment, Insurance and Legislation
Roberta K. McInerney . . . . (202) 898–3830
Deputy General Counsel, Litigation and Resolutions
Richard Osterman Jr. . . . . (703) 562–2451
Deputy General Counsel of Supervision and Corporate Operations
John V. Thomas . . . . (202) 898–7417

Legal Division, Executive Secretary Section
Responsible for the maintenance and custody of official records of the board of directors and any standing or special committees. Certifies and seals documents, issues certificates of insurance to insured banks, and issues public notices of all meetings of the board and any standing or special committees. Publishes proposed and final rules in the *Federal Register*.

Associate General Counsel/Executive Secretary
Michelle Adams . . . . (202) 898–7043
Fax. . . . . (202) 898–8788
Operations Unit, Supervisory Counsel
Valerie Best. . . . . (202) 898–3812

Regional Offices

DIVISION OF SUPERVISION AND CONSUMER PROTECTION

ATLANTA
(AL, FL, GA, NC, SC, VA, WV)
10 Tenth St. N.E., #800
Atlanta, GA 30309–3906
(678) 916–2200
(800) 765–3342
Michael J. Dean (acting), regional director
(678) 916–2244

BOSTON
(CT, MA, ME, NH, RI, VT)
15 Braintree Hill Office Park, #100
Braintree, MA 02184–8701
(781) 794–5500
(866) 728–9953
John Vogel, regional director*
*in the New York Regional Office
350 Fifth Avenue, #1200
New York, NY 10118–0110
(917) 320–2500

CHICAGO
(IL, IN, KY, MI, OH, WI)
300 S. Riverside Plaza, #1700
Chicago, IL 60606
(312) 382–6000
(800) 944–5343
M. Anthony Lowe, regional director
(312) 382–6000

DALLAS
(CO, NM, OK, TX)
1601 Bryan St.
Dallas, TX 75201
(214) 754–0098
(800) 568–9161
Kristie K. Elmquist, regional director
(972) 761–8215

KANSAS CITY
(IA, KS, MN, MO, ND, NE, SD)
1100 Walnut St., #2100
Kansas City, MO 64106
(816) 234–8000
(800) 209–7459
James D. LaPierre, regional director
(816) 234–8170

MEMPHIS
(AR, LA, MS, TN)
5100 Poplar Ave., #1900
Memphis, TN 38137
(901) 685–1603
(800) 210–6354
Kristi K. Elmquist*, regional director,
(972) 761–8215
*in the Dallas Regional Office

NEW YORK
(DC, DE, MD, NJ, NY, PA, PR, VI)
350 Fifth Ave., #1200
New York, NY 10118–0110
(917) 320–2500
(800) 334–9593
John Vogel, regional director,
(917) 320–2500

SAN FRANCISCO
(AK, AZ, CA, GU, HI, ID, MT, NV, OR, UT, WA, WY)
25 Jessie St. at Ecker Square, #2300
San Francisco, CA 94105–2780
(415) 546–0160
(800) 756–3558
Stan Ivie, regional director
(415) 546–0160

■ CONGRESSIONAL ACTION

Congressional Liaison
Director, Office of Legislative Affairs
Eric Spitler . . . . (202) 898–7140

Committees and Subcommittees

HOUSE APPROPRIATIONS COMMITTEE
Subcommittee on Financial Services and General Government

B300 RHOB, Washington, DC 20515–6015
(202) 225–7245

HOUSE FINANCIAL SERVICES COMMITTEE
Subcommittee on Capital Markets and Government Sponsored Enterprises
2129 RHOB, Washington, DC 20515–6050
(202) 225–7502
Subcommittee on Monetary Policy and Trade
2129 RHOB, Washington, DC 20515–6050
(202) 225–7502
Subcommittee on Financial Institutions and Consumer Credit
2129 RHOB, Washington, DC 20515–6050
(202) 225–7502
Subcommittee on Housing and Insurance
2129 RHOB, Washington, DC 20515–6050
(202) 225–7502
Subcommittee on Oversight and Investigations
2129 RHOB, Washington, DC 20515–6050
(202) 225–7502

HOUSE OVERSIGHT AND GOVERNMENT REFORM COMMITTEE
Subcommittee on Government Operations
2157 RHOB, Washington, DC 20505
(202) 225–5074
Subcommittee on Health Care, Benefits, and Administrative Rules
2157 RHOB, Washington, DC 20505
(202) 225–5074
Subcommittee on National Security
2157 RHOB, Washington, DC 20505
(202) 225–5074

SENATE APPROPRIATIONS COMMITTEE
Subcommittee on Financial Services and General Government
133 SDOB, Washington, DC 20510–6075
(202) 224–2104

SENATE BANKING, HOUSING, AND URBAN AFFAIRS COMMITTEE
Subcommittee on Housing, Transportation, and Community Development
SROB 167, Washington, DC 20510–6075
(202) 224–6121
Subcommittee on Securities, Insurance, and Investment
SDOB-239, Washington, DC 20510–6075
(202) 224–6142
Subcommittee on Financial Institutions and Consumer Protection
SROB-248, Washington, DC 20510–6075
(202) 224–4254

Legislation
The FDIC was organized under the **Banking Act of 1933** (48 Stat. 162, 12 U.S.C. 227), signed by the president June 16, 1933, which added a new section (12B) to the **Federal Reserve Act** (38 Stat. 251, 12 U.S.C. 226), signed by the president Dec. 23, 1913. The **Banking Act of 1935** (49 Stat. 684, 12 U.S.C. 228), signed by the president Aug. 23, 1935, extended and expanded the power of the FDIC. In 1951 Section 12B of the Federal Reserve Act was withdrawn from that act and enacted as a separate law known as the **Federal Deposit Insurance Act** (64 Stat. 873, 12 U.S.C. 1811–1831), signed by the president Sept. 21, 1951. This law embodies the basic authority for the operations of the FDIC.

The FDIC also is responsible for the administration of several other laws, many of them having to do with fair consumer practices. In almost all cases where the FDIC holds authority under a law, that authority extends only to insured state nonmember banks regulated by the agency.

Major legislation administered by the FDIC includes
Securities Exchange Act of 1934 (48 Stat. 881, 15 U.S.C. 78b). Signed by the president June 6, 1934. Required the registration of securities by U.S. banking institutions.

Bank Holding Company Act of 1956 (70 Stat. 133, 12 U.S.C. 1841). Signed by the president May 9, 1956. Regulated the creation and expansion of bank holding companies.

Bank Mergers Act of 1960 (74 Stat. 129, 12 U.S.C. 1828). Signed by the president May 13, 1960. Required bank mergers to receive prior approval from the federal regulatory agency having jurisdiction over the surviving bank.

Bank Service Corporation Act (76 Stat. 1132, 12 U.S.C. 1861). Signed by the president Oct. 23, 1962. Permitted certain federally supervised banks to form service corporations to perform clerical, bookkeeping, and data processing services.

Truth in Lending Act (82 Stat. 146, 15 U.S.C. 1601). Signed by the president May 29, 1968. Required lenders and merchants to inform consumers of the total cost of loans and installment purchase plans and to clearly state annual percentage rate. Also prohibited unsolicited distribution of credit cards and limited owners' liability for unauthorized use of lost or stolen cards.

Bank Protection Act of 1968 (82 Stat. 294, 12 U.S.C. 1881). Signed by the president July 7, 1968. Required establishment of minimum security system standards for banking institutions.

Fair Credit Reporting Act (84 Stat. 1128, 15 U.S.C. 1681). Signed by the president Oct. 26, 1970. Regulated credit information collection and use.

NOW Accounts Act (87 Stat. 342, 12 U.S.C. 1832). Signed by the president Aug. 16, 1973. Regulated interest-bearing checking accounts.

Equal Credit Opportunity Act (88 Stat. 1521, 15 U.S.C. 1691). Signed by the president Oct. 28, 1974. Prohibited credit discrimination against women. Amended by the **Equal Credit Opportunity Act Amendments of 1976** (90 Stat. 251, 15 U.S.C. 1691 note). Signed by the president March 23, 1976. Barred credit discrimination based on age, race, religion, or national origin.

Real Estate Settlement Procedures Act of 1974 (88 Stat. 1724, 12 U.S.C. 2601–2616). Signed by the president Dec. 22, 1974. Minimized settlement charges for home buyers; confirmed the authority of the Department of Housing and Urban Development to set standards for settlement charges on homes financed through federally backed mortgages.

Home Mortgage Disclosure Act (89 Stat. 1125, 12 U.S.C. 2801). Signed by the president Dec. 31, 1975. Required lending institutions within standard metropolitan statistical areas (SMSAs) to disclose the number and amount of mortgage loans made yearly to determine if banks are discriminating against certain city neighborhoods by refusing to make mortgage loans regardless of the creditworthiness of the potential borrower (practice known as "redlining").

Fair Debt Collection Practices Act (91 Stat. 874, 15 U.S.C. 1692). Signed by the president Sept. 20, 1977. Regulated methods used by debt-collecting agencies.

Community Reinvestment Act of 1977 (91 Stat. 1147, 12 U.S.C. 2901–2905). Signed by the president Oct. 12, 1977. Required federal bank regulators to encourage institutions they regulate to help meet the credit needs of their communities, including low- and moderate-income neighborhoods, consistent with safe and sound operations.

International Banking Act of 1978 (92 Stat. 607, 12 U.S.C. 3101–3108). Signed by the president Sept. 17, 1978. Provided for. the federal regulation of foreign banks in domestic financial markets.

Electronic Fund Transfer Act of 1978 (92 Stat. 3728, 15 U.S.C. 1601 note). Signed by the president Nov. 10, 1978. Established rules relating to consumer liability for unauthorized use of an electronic fund transfer card and unsolicited issuance of cards by financial institutions. Prohibited creditors from making automatic repayment of loans a condition of extending credit; overdraft credit plans were exempted.

Financial Institutions Regulatory and Interest Rate Control Act of 1978 (92 Stat. 3641, 12 U.S.C. 226 note). Signed by the president Nov. 10, 1978. Regulated the activities of individual bank officers; provided for tighter controls on insider lending and interlocking directorates among financial institutions and expanded the authority of bank regulators.

Depository Institutions Deregulation and Monetary Control Act of 1980 (94 Stat. 132, 12 U.S.C. 226 note). Signed by the president March 31, 1980. Extended reserve requirements to all financial institutions, phased out interest rate ceilings over a six-year period, and allowed thrift institutions to offer a wider range of financial services. Established the Depository Institutions Deregulation Committee. Increased FDIC insurance coverage to $100,000 per depositor.

Garn-St. Germain Depository Institutions Act of 1982 (96 Stat. 1469, 12 U.S.C. 226 note). Signed by the president Oct. 15, 1982. Expanded the FDIC's powers to assist troubled banks by allowing either direct or merger-related assistance (1) to prevent the closing of or to reopen any insured bank, or (2) when severe financial conditions threaten the stability of a significant number of banks or banks with substantial financial resources. Increased the powers of federally chartered savings and loan associations and savings banks (thrift institutions) to conduct a wider range of commercial operations and thus be able to compete with recently established investment institutions.

Federal Deposit Insurance Act, Amendment (97 Stat. 189, 96 U.S.C. 1492). Signed by the president May 16, 1983. Provided that the issuance of net worth certificates did not constitute default under existing debt obligations. This amendment took effect retroactively on Oct. 15, 1982, the date of enactment of the Garn-St. Germain Depository Institutions Act of 1982.

Supplemental Appropriations Act, 1984; Domestic Housing and International Recovery and Financial Stability Act, Titles VII and IX (97 Stat. 1153, 12 U.S.C. 1701a note). Signed by the president Nov. 30, 1983. Title VII amended the Federal Deposit Insurance Act by permitting any sitting member of the FDIC board of directors to remain in office until a successor is confirmed by the Senate. Title IX, the International Lending Supervision Act of 1983, increased FDIC supervisory and regulatory powers over banking institutions engaged in international borrowing and lending.

Bankruptcy Amendments and Federal Judgeship Act of 1984 (98 Stat. 333, 28 U.S.C. 151 note). Signed by the president July 10, 1984. Permitted the FDIC to act as a member of an unsecured creditor's committee when acting as a receiver or liquidator of banks failing after Oct. 9, 1984.

Continuing Appropriations, 1985–Comprehensive Crime Control Act of 1984 (98 Stat. 1837, 43 U.S.C. 1715). Signed by the president Oct. 12, 1984. Prohibited the receipt of stolen property from a bank and the bribing of bank personnel.

The Competitive Equality Banking Act of 1987 (101 Stat. 552, 12 U.S.C. 226 note). Signed by the president Aug. 10, 1987. Granted the FSLIC new borrowing authority to reimburse depositors as it shut down bankrupt thrifts. Suspended the expansion of banks into insurance, securities underwriting, and real estate and prohibited the expansion of limited service banks. Eased regulatory requirements for savings and loans in economically depressed areas and required faster clearing of depositors' checks.

Technical and Miscellaneous Revenue Act of 1988 (102 Stat. 3342, 26 U.S.C. 1 note). Signed by the president Nov. 10, 1988. Extended until Dec. 31, 1989, special tax treatment to troubled banks assisted by the FDIC.

Financial Institutions Reform, Recovery, and Enforcement Act of 1989 (FIRREA) (103 Stat. 183, 12 U.S.C. 1811 note). Signed by the president Aug. 9, 1989. Approved the use of $50 billion to finance the closing of insolvent savings and loans. Created the RTC to manage the disposal of the assets of bankrupt thrifts. Dissolved the Federal Home Loan Bank Board, assigning its regulatory responsibilities to the Treasury Department and assigning its role in insuring depositors through the FSLIC to the FDIC. Savings and loans were required to maintain a minimum amount of tangible capital equal to 1.5 percent of total assets.

Federal Deposit Insurance Corporation Improvement Act of 1991 (105 Stat. 2236, 12 U.S.C. 1811 note). Signed by the president Dec. 19, 1991. Required banks to increase capital and pay higher deposit insurance premiums. Provided Treasury funding to the BIF.

Depository Institutions Disaster Relief Act of 1992 (106 Stat. 2771, 12 U.S.C. 1811 note). Signed by the president Oct. 23, 1992. Facilitated recovery from disasters by providing greater flexibility for depository institutions and their regulators.

Housing and Community Development Act of 1992 (106 Stat. 3672, 42 U.S.C. 5301 note). Signed by the president Oct. 28, 1992. Established regulatory structure for government-sponsored enterprises, combated money laundering, and provided regulatory relief to financial institutions.

Resolution Trust Corporation Completion Act (107 Stat. 2369, 12 U.S.C. 1421 note). Signed by the president Dec. 17, 1993. Amended the Inspector General Act of 1978. Changed the inspector general position into a presidential appointment. Set forth structural changes for the FDIC as well as the RTC. Prescribed the termination of the RTC on Oct. 1, 1995, and delegated all remaining authorities, duties, responsibilities, and activities to the FDIC thereafter. Directed the FDIC to prescribe regulations regarding conflicts of interest, ethical responsibilities, and the use of confidential information; and established minimum standards of competence, experience, and integrity for FDIC contractors.

Interstate Banking Efficiency Act of 1994 (108 Stat. 2338, 12 U.S.C. 1811 note). Signed by the president Sept. 29, 1994. Permitted banks to operate networks of branch offices across state lines without having to set up separately capitalized subsidiary banks.

Gramm-Leach-Bliley Act (113 Stat. 1338, 12 U.S.C. 1811 note). Signed by the president Nov. 12, 1999. Title I repealed provisions of the Banking Act of 1933 and the Bank Holding Company Act of 1956 to allow affiliations between banks and any financial company, including brokerage and insurance firms. Required the FDIC to enforce privacy and fair credit reporting standards.

American Homeownership and Economic Opportunity Act of 2000 (114 Stat. 2944, 12 U.S.C. 1701). Signed by the president Dec. 27, 2000. Title I, the Housing Affordability Barrier Removal Act of 2000, amended the Housing and Community Development Act of 1992 to authorize $15 million for the next five years for states, local government, and consortiums to create regulatory relief strategies. Title XII, the Financial Regulatory Relief and Economic Efficiency Act of 2000, provided regulatory relief to banks, including permitting banks to own some of their stock.

Uniting and Strengthening America by Providing Appropriate Tools Required to Intercept and Obstruct Terrorism Act of 2001 (USA Patriot Act) (115 Stat. 272, 18 U.S.C. 1 note). Signed by the president Oct. 26, 2001. Title III, the International Money Laundering Abatement and Anti-Terrorist Financing Act of 2001, amended various federal banking laws, including the Bank Holding Company Act of 1956, the Fair Credit Reporting Act, the Federal Reserve Act, and the Federal Deposit Insurance Act. Directed certain government agencies, principally the Treasury Department in consultation with the Federal Reserve (Fed), to investigate and curtail money laundering and other activities that might be undertaken to finance terrorist actions or disrupt legitimate banking operations.

Investor and Capital Markets Fee Relief Act (115 Stat. 2390, 15 U.S.C. 78a note). Signed by the president Jan. 16, 2002. Amended the Securities Exchange Act of 1934 to reduce fees on the purchase and sale of securities, on trades of single stock futures, on merger and tender offers, and on fees companies pay to register securities. Eliminated fees on Trust Indenture applications. Required the SEC to adjust its fees annually after fiscal 2002 to account for changing market conditions. Increased SEC staff salaries by authorizing the SEC to establish an employee compensation system outside of the existing federal civil service system.

Check Clearing for the 21st Century Act or Check 21 Act (117 Stat. 1177, 12 U.S.C. 5001–5018). Signed by the president Oct. 28, 2003. Made substitute checks the legal equivalent of the original during processing by banks so that the bank where the original check was deposited could transmit it electronically to the originating bank. Significantly shortened the time period between when a check is deposited and when the money is deducted from the check writer's account.

Fair and Accurate Credit Transactions Act (117 Stat. 1952, 15 U.S.C. 1601 note). Signed by the president Dec. 4, 2003. Made permanent the federal consumer protection standards originally created by the Fair Credit Reporting Act. Prevented states from imposing new restrictions on how banks and other financial services firms share consumer information. Mandated that credit card and debit card issuers disclose credit scores when approving certain loans and requires fraud alerts and blocks in consumer credit files.

Bankruptcy Abuse Prevention and Consumer Protection Act of 2005 (119 Stat. 23, 11 U.S.C. 101 et seq.). Signed by the president April 20, 2005. Amended the Federal Deposit Insurance Act (FDIA) to redefine specified contracts, agreements, and transfers entered into with an insolvent insured depository institution before a conservator or receiver was appointed. Amended the Federal Deposit Insurance Corporation Improvement Act of 1991 to make conforming amendments with respect to (1) bilateral netting contracts; (2) security agreements; (3) clearing organization netting contracts; (4) contracts with uninsured national banks; and (5) contracts with uninsured federal branches or agencies.

Deficit Reduction Act of 2005 (120 Stat. 4, 42 U.S.C 1305 note). Signed by the president Feb. 8, 2006. Amended the Federal Deposit Insurance Act to allow the FDIC to review federal deposit insurance levels once every five years, beginning in April 2010, and increase the current $100,000 limit to account for inflation. Raised the deposit insurance coverage for individual retirement accounts to $250,000 from $100,000 and merged the BIF and SAIF into the DIF. Permitted the FDIC to assess and adjust risk-based premiums charged to firms that receive deposit insurance coverage.

Financial Services Regulatory Relief Act of 2006 (120 Stat. 1966, U.S.C. 1811 note). Signed by the president Oct. 13, 2006. Amended the Federal Deposit Insurance Act to direct the federal banking agencies to reduce or eliminate mandatory condition reports filed by certain insured depository institutions and increase to $500 million the maximum total assets of a bank or thrift eligible for examinations every eighteen months. Prescribed certain conditions, including prior FDIC approval, under which a federal savings association may convert to a national or state bank.

Authorized federal banking agencies to share certain types of confidential interagency supervisory information.

Housing and Economic Recovery Act of 2008 (122 Stat. 2654, 5 U.S.C. 301 and 552). Signed by the president July 30, 2008. Strengthened the existing state-run nationwide mortgage originator licensing and registration system and required a parallel registration system for FDIC-insured banks to prevent fraud. Authorized $10 billion in mortgage revenue bonds for refinancing sub-prime mortgages. Increased the maximum loan amount for reverse mortgages guaranteed by the Federal Housing Administration, imposed a cap on fees, and permitted reverse mortgages to be used to buy a home.

Emergency Economic Stabilization Act of 2008 (12 U.S.C. 5201–5261). Signed by the president Oct. 3, 2008. Title I, Troubled Asset Relief Program (TARP), increased the amount of deposit and share insurance coverage offered under the Federal Deposit Insurance Act and the Federal Credit Union Act from $100,000 to $250,000.

Helping Families Save Their Homes and the Fraud Enforcement and Recovery Act (123 Stat. 1632, 12 U.S.C. 5201 note). Signed by the president May 20, 2009. Extended deposit and share insurance coverage offered under the Federal Deposit Insurance Act and the Federal Credit Union Act to Dec. 21, 2013. Increased the FDIC's borrowing authority from the U.S. Treasury to $100 billion.

Dodd-Frank Wall Street Reform and Consumer Protection Act of 2010 (124 Stat. 1376, 12 U.S.C. 5201 note). Signed by the president July 21, 2010. Established an independent consumer bureau to protect borrowers against abuses in mortgage, credit card, and other types of lending. Created a council of federal regulators to help spot threats to the financial system. Gave the FDIC the authority to close large troubled financial firms.

▨ INFORMATION SOURCES

Internet

Agency website: www.fdic.gov. Provides general information and links to specific FDIC offices, programs, and publications.

Telephone Contacts

Call Center/Public Information Center

Mon.–Fri., 8:00 a.m. to 8:00 p.m.; Sat.–Sun.,
    9:00 a.m. to 5:00 p.m. . . . . (877) 275–3342
TTY . . . . (800) 925–4618
Email: publicinfo@fdic.gov

Consumer Response Center

Investigates consumer complaints about FDIC-supervised institutions and responds to consumer questions about consumer laws, regulations, and banking practices.

1100 Walnut St., Box 11
Kansas City, MO 61406
Mon.–Fri., 8:00 a.m. to 8:00 p.m. ET . (877) 275–3342
TTY . . . . (800) 925–4618

Secure fax . . . . (703) 812–1020
E-mail: For an electronic customer assistance form, visit the website www.fdic.gov and click on "Contact Us."
Internet: www.fdic.gov/consumers/consumer/ccc

Closed Banks and Asset Sales

The FDIC liquidates a variety of assets including real estate and loans in its capacity as court-appointed receiver. The FDIC may also be able to provide assistance to consumers who have loans with failed banks.

FDIC, Division of Resolutions and Receiverships
1601 Bryan St.
Dallas, TX 75201
(888) 206-4662
E-mail: Closed banks: cservicefdicdal@fdic.gov; Asset sales: assetmarketing@fdic.gov
Internet: Closed banks: www.fdic.gov/bank/individual/failed/index.html; Asset sales: www.fdic.gov/buying/index.html

Inspector General Hotline

Individuals may use the hotline to report fraud, misuse of government property or funds, misconduct, conflicts of interest, or other unethical or illegal activities. Callers may remain anonymous.

(800) 964–3342
E-mail: ighotline@fdic.gov
Internet: www.fdicig.gov/hotline.shtml

Information and Publications

KEY OFFICES

FDIC Office of Communications

550 17th St. N.W.
Washington, DC 20429
(202) 898-6993
E-mail: communications@fdic.gov
Barbara Hagenbaugh, deputy to the chair

Issues news releases; topics include notices of failed banks, policy statements, addresses by FDIC officials, and personnel changes. Distributes most FDIC publications.

Freedom of Information

FDIC FOIA/Privacy Act Group
550 17th St. N.W.
Washington, DC 20429
(202) 898-7021
Fax (202) 898-6910
Charles Yi, Chief FOIA officer

FOIA Service Center
Hours: Mon.–Fri., 8:30 a.m. to 5:00 p.m.
(202) 898-7021
Internet: www.fdic.gov/about/freedom
FOIA electronic reading room: www.fdic.gov/about/freedom/readingroom.html

PUBLICATIONS

For a list or to order a specific title, contact FDIC Office of Public Affairs or

FDIC Public Information Center

3501 N. Fairfax Dr., Room E-1005

Arlington, VA 22226

(877) 275–3342, ext. 52

Fax (703) 562–2296

Internet: www.fdic.gov/news/publications/
PIChardcopies.html

E-mail: publicinfo@fdic.gov

Hours: Mon.–Fri., 9 a.m. to 5 p.m. ET, by
appointment only

Most publications are free and available on the FDIC website. FDIC policy manuals have various prices, which must be prepaid. Contact the Public Information Center for more information on available policy manuals and payment options. Fees are charged for all materials that must be printed from the electronic version ($.20 per page) or faxed ($.50 per page). Most requests can be filled in less than twenty-four hours. Orders exceeding five documents or twenty-five pages may require additional processing time.

Annual Report. Describes FDIC operations and performance, enforcement actions, and statistics on closed banks and deposit insurance.

FDIC Consumer News. (Quarterly) Information on the latest regulatory developments and a wide range of topics of interest to consumers presented in a non-technical manner. This and other consumer pamphlets, including *Money Smart Training Program, Your Investments: Consumer Facts About Investments, Putting Your Home on the Loan Line Is a Risky Business,* are available from www.fdic.gov/news/publications; many also available in Spanish. Bulk quantities may be ordered free of charge.

A History of the FDIC 1933–1983. Includes information on the antecedents to federal deposit insurance, the creation of the FDIC in 1933–35, and a general history of the FDIC with a focus on the corporation's insurance coverage and financial operations, its role in handling bank failures, and its function as a bank supervisor and examiner. The agency website provides a detailed table of contents.

Your Insured Deposit. Provides examples of insurance coverage under the FDIC's rules on certain types of accounts commonly held by depositors in insured banks; provides answers to common consumer questions.

FDIC Quarterly. Summarizes current financial results for the banking industry. Analyzes economic and banking trends that may affect FDIC-insured institutions.

Failed Bank List. Provides information for customers and vendors of failed banks for which the FDIC is receiver. Includes information on how customer accounts and loans are affected and how vendors can file claims. Visit the website: http://fdic.gov/bank/individual/failed/banklist.html.

Information on relevant laws and regulations is available at the website: www.fdic.gov/regulations. Information useful to minority depository institutions can be found at the website: www.fdic.gov/regulations/resources/minority.

In addition, the Executive Secretary section of the Legal Division issues a Loose-Leaf Service on the laws, regulations, and related acts that affect the operation of insured banks. This four-volume reporting service is updated every two months and is available free at the FDIC website at www.fdic.gov/regulations/laws/rules/index.html or by subscription. For details, contact regs@fdic.gov.

Finally, subscriptions to a number of FDIC publications are available, including *FDIC Consumer News (Quarterly)* and *FDIC Quarterly.* If interested, visit https://service.govdelivery.com/accounts/USFDIC/subscriber/new.

DATA AND STATISTICS

FDIC Division of Insurance and Research

550 17th St. N.W.

Washington, DC 20429–9990

(202) 898–3938

Diane Ellis, director

E-mail: insurance-research@fdic.gov

Internet: www2.fdic.gov/Call_TFR_Rpts (this site
provides call report information and thrift
financial reports for the banking community);
www.fdic.gov/regulations/resources/call/call2.html
(this site provides electronic documents including
quarterly reports of condition and income on
FDIC-supervised banks).

Compiles statistics on bank deposit insurance and banking in general. Prepares special reports, surveys, and studies; and analyzes policy issues, proposed legislation, economic trends, and other developments affecting financial institutions and markets. The following titles are available in printed form via the FDIC Public Information Center or the website listed above:

Historical Statistics on Banking. Contains annual data on FDIC-insured institutions from 1934. Includes state-level tables and annual lists of failed commercial banks and savings institutions.

Quarterly Banking Profile. Published within seventy-five days after the end of each quarter; provides the earliest comprehensive summary of financial results from all insured institutions.

QBP Statistics at a Glance. Provides the latest quarterly and historical data for FDIC-insured institutions and for the deposit insurance fund.

Statistics on Banking. Quarterly; provides aggregate financial information on FDIC-insured institutions, such as assets, income, and liabilities.

State Banking Performance Summary. Provides key financial data quarterly, by state and charter type.

Institution Directory. Provides a searchable directory of individual bank data including financial statements, locations of bank branches, and bank history. See the website: www2.fdic.gov/IDASP/.

MEETINGS

The directors of the FDIC hold meetings approximately monthly. Notices are posted in the lobby of the FDIC headquarters, published in the *Federal Register,* and are available on FDIC's website at www.fdic.gov/news/board/index.html. Some meetings are Web cast live, and videos are made available at this website approximately one week after the meeting. The Executive Secretary section can provide further details at (202) 898–7043.

Reference Resources

LIBRARY

FDIC Library
550 17th St. N.W., #4060
Washington, DC 20429
(202) 898–3631
Fax (202) 898–3984
E-mail: library@fdic.gov
R. Teresa Neville, head librarian

Specializes in banking law and maintains separate banking, legal, and economic sections. Open to federal employees by appointment only.

RESEARCH

FDIC Center for Financial Research
3501 N. Fairfax Drive, MB-4012
Arlington, VA 22226
E-mail: cfr@fdic.gov
Internet: www.fdic.gov/bank/analytical/cfr/index.html

Encourages and supports research on topics that are important to the FDIC's role as deposit insurer and bank supervisor; sponsors conferences and workshops that encourage dialogue among industry, academia, and the public sector. Interests include developments affecting the banking industry, risk measurement and management methods, regulatory policy, and related topics of interest to the FDIC and the larger financial community. Solicits and selects research proposals annually; completed papers are distributed as CFR working papers. Organizes weekly research seminars, hosts short-term visiting scholars, and manages a visiting fellows program that sponsors long-term academic visitation.

DOCKETS
Federal dockets are available at www.regulations.gov. (*See appendix for Searching and Commenting on Regulations: Regulations.gov.*)

RULES AND REGULATIONS
FDIC rules and regulations are published in the *Code of Federal Regulations,* Title 5, Chapter XXII, Part 3201; Title 12, Chapter III, Parts 300–399. Proposed rules, new final rules, and updates to the *Code of Federal Regulations* are published in the daily *Federal Register.* (*See appendix for information on how to obtain and use these publications.*) The *Federal Register* may be accessed at www.federalregister.gov and the *Code of Federal Regulations* at www.archives.gov/federal-register/cfr; also see the federal government's website www.regulations.gov (*see appendix*).

Other Information Sources

NONGOVERNMENTAL RESOURCES
The following are some key resources for information on the FDIC and banking issues.

American Bankers Association
1120 Connecticut Ave. N.W.
Washington, DC 20036
(202) 663–5000
(800) 226–5377
Internet: www.aba.com

American Financial Services Association
919 18th St. N.W., #300
Washington, DC 20006
(202) 296–5544, ext. 606
Internet: www.afsaonline.org

Bank Administration Institute
115 S. LaSalle St., #3300
Chicago, IL 60603–3801
(312) 683–2464
(888) 224–9889
Publications and customer service: (800) 224–9889
Internet: www.bai.org

Conference of State Bank Supervisors
1129 20th St. N.W., 9th Floor
Washington, DC 20036
(202) 296–2840
Internet: www.csbs.org

Consumer Bankers Association
1225 Eye St. N.W., #550
Washington, DC 20005
(202) 552–6380
Internet: www.cbanet.org

Elsevier
Journal of Banking and Finance
525 B St., #1800
San Diego, CA 92101
(619) 231–6616
E-mail: JournalCustomerService-usa@elsevier.com
Internet: www.elsevier.com

Financial Services Roundtable
600 13th St N.W., #400
Washington, DC 20005
(202) 289–4322
Internet: http://fsroundtable.org

Independent Community Bankers of America
1615 L St. N.W., #900
Washington, DC 20036

(202) 659–8111
(800) 422–8439
Internet: www.icba.org

Moody's Investors Service
7 World Trade Center at 250
   Greenwich St.
New York, NY 10007
(212) 553–1653
Internet: www.moodys.com

John Wiley & Sons
Journal of Money, Credit and Banking
350 Main St.
Malden, MA 02148
(781) 388–8598
(800) 835–6770
E-mail: cs-journals@wiley.com
Internet: http://onlinelibrary.wiley.com/

Federal Energy Regulatory Commission

888 1st St. N.E., Washington, DC 20426
Internet: www.ferc.gov

■ INTRODUCTION

Established as an independent regulatory agency, the Federal Energy Regulatory Commission (FERC) is within, but separate from, the Department of Energy (DOE). It was created by the Department of Energy Organization Act of 1977 to replace the Federal Power Commission (FPC).

The commission has five members appointed by the president and confirmed by the Senate. Before 1990, members served four-year terms. In April 1990 President George H. W. Bush signed a law providing for five-year terms of office for members. The president appoints one commissioner to serve as chair.

Responsibilities

The commission

- Regulates the transmission of natural gas in interstate commerce.
- Regulates the construction, operation, and abandonment of interstate pipeline facilities.
- Reviews curtailment plans proposed by gas companies to reduce service to certain areas.
- Oversees construction and operation of facilities needed by pipelines at the point of entry to import or export natural gas.
- Reviews rates set by the federal power marketing administrations and certifies small power production and cogeneration facilities.
- Regulates the rates and practices of oil pipeline companies engaged in interstate transportation.
- Regulates the transmission and sale (wholesale) of electricity in interstate commerce.
- Authorizes the conditions, rates, and charges for interconnections among electric utilities.
- Issues licenses, conducts safety inspections, and reviews environmental compliance for nonfederal hydroelectric projects.
- Regulates security (stock) issues and mergers of electric utilities; approves interlocking directorships among electric utilities.
- Reviews appeals from DOE remedial orders and denials of adjustments.
- Authorizes onshore liquefied natural gas import facilities.
- Oversees mandatory reliability rules for interstate grid.
- Provides backstop transmission siting authority.

Powers and Authority

NATURAL GAS REGULATION

The natural gas industry consists of three major segments: natural gas producers; pipeline companies, which transport gas from producing areas to consuming markets; and local distribution companies (LDCs), which sell gas to ultimate consumers. The commission sets the rates that interstate pipeline companies may charge for the transmission of natural gas. LDCs, which buy gas from

GLOSSARY

Abandonment—The cessation of service certificated under the Natural Gas Act from a gas well or facilities dedicated to the interstate market.

Blanket certificate—Allows pipelines to conduct certain transactions and services on a self-implementing basis.

Curtailment—A cutback in acceptance of delivery by pipelines from gas producers during periods of oversupply; a cutback in the availability of "interruptible" transportation service during periods of high demand.

Electronic bulletin board—The use of computerized information systems to exchange information about pipeline capacity, rates, and deliveries. FERC, in Order 889, required electric utilities to obtain information about their transmission using the Open Access Same-time Information System (OASIS), sharing information about available transmission capacity with competitors.

Interconnection—A joining of the transmission networks of two or more electric utilities. Interconnection allows utilities to share facilities and power reserves and provides service to larger areas.

ISO—Independent system operator.

LDC—Local distribution company.

NOPR—Notice of proposed rulemaking.

Open-access transportation program—A program that allows pipelines to apply for "blanket" transportation certificates that require transportation to be carried out on a nondiscriminatory basis. Transportation requests are fulfilled on a first-come, first-served basis.

Pooling—The voluntary agreement among utilities to sell power to each another. Pooling offers a sales outlet for power produced in excess of immediate system requirements, and a supply source when demand exceeds immediate system generating capacity. Pools may or may not be operated by independent system operators.

Stranded costs—Costs that a utility has incurred to serve wholesale requirements or retail franchise customers that are stranded when a customer stops buying power from the utility and simply pays for transmission services to reach a different supplier.

Take-or-pay—Requires pipelines either to buy and take the agreed-on volumes from the producer or to pay a fee to the producer if it fails to take the gas.

Unbundling—The separation of services into discrete components with separate charges for each service.

Wheeling—An arrangement in which one electric company allows another company to use its lines to transmit power to customers in its service area. Retail wheeling allows any customer to buy from any supplier.

pipelines and sell it to homes and industries, generally are regulated by state public utility commissions. The commission no longer regulates the rates for wellhead sales of natural gas and is phasing out regulation of rates charged by the gathering systems owned by interstate pipelines.

FERC approves construction of interstate pipeline facilities. In acting on a proposal to build a major pipeline facility, the commission must take into account a number of factors, including the market for the gas, environmental impact, and financial viability. FERC also reviews proposals by interstate pipeline companies to provide service to new customers or to modify existing service, to abandon pipeline facilities, and to transport gas directly to industrial and other end users.

The commission can exercise authority in several areas where little regulation has been required since the return of normal market conditions in the 1980s: authority over the siting, construction, and operation of liquefied natural gas (LNG) terminals to receive and regasify imported LNG; and the approval of curtailment plans, which are used by pipelines to allocate available supplies among customers during periods when gas supplies are inadequate to satisfy demand.

WHOLESALE ELECTRIC RATE REGULATION

The commission regulates the rate and service standards for wholesale electricity. These sales of electricity for resale—between utilities or by a utility to a municipality—make up more than a quarter of total U.S. electricity sales. Retail sales of electricity to consumers, such as homeowners and businesses, are regulated by state public utility commissions. The traditional split between state and federal jurisdiction has been complicated by the commission's assertion in Order 888 of jurisdiction over the rates for unbundled retail transmission in interstate commerce.

The commission ensures that rates for wholesale transactions in interstate commerce are just and reasonable and not unduly discriminatory. The commission reviews agreements for the interconnection of utility systems and the transfer of power among utilities, with the aim of achieving reliable service at just and reasonable rates.

In addition to the review of rates and service standards, the commission has authority over the mergers of regulated utilities, certain issuances of utility stock, and the existence of certain interlocking relationships between top officials in utilities and major firms doing business with utilities. It also approves the rates of the five power marketing agencies, which are federally owned utilities operated by the DOE. Finally, FERC determines whether the operations of independent power producers and cogeneration facilities qualify for purposes of selling electricity to utilities at preferential rates under the Public Utility Regulatory Policies Act of 1978.

HYDROELECTRIC POWER PROJECT LICENSING

FERC issues licenses to construct and operate hydroelectric power projects, except those owned by other federal agencies. Hydroelectric power generation represents 49 percent of the country's current renewable energy resources; hydropower projects under FERC's jurisdiction are approximately 50 percent of the national total. The commission seeks to preserve environmental quality at hydroelectric sites by including protective measures in its licensing orders. FERC is responsible for licensing and regulating all nonfederal hydroelectric projects. Licenses issued by the commission contain conditions for protection of fish and wildlife, water quality, historical and archeological sites, scenic and cultural values, as well as providing for recreational opportunities, flood control, and the efficient, safe operation of project dams.

OIL PIPELINE REGULATION

The commission regulates the rates and practices of the approximately 150 pipeline companies transporting oil in interstate commerce. The overall objective of FERC is to establish just and reasonable rates that will encourage the optimal use, maintenance, and construction of oil pipeline systems—a relatively inexpensive mode of oil transportation—while protecting consumers against unjustified costs. The commission also has the authority to prohibit certain anticompetitive oil pipeline company practices.

RELATIONSHIP TO DOE

The commission functions as an independent regulatory body within the DOE. The energy secretary exercises no control over the decisions of the commission, although the secretary may recommend issues for its consideration. Commission decisions are final for the DOE; they may be appealed to the U.S. Court of Appeals.

FERC also reviews certain rules proposed by the DOE. If a proposed rule could significantly affect its functions, FERC may consider the rule, receive comments from the public, and make recommendations to the secretary of energy on whether and how it should be implemented. The energy secretary must incorporate all changes proposed by the commission before a rule becomes final.

FORMAL PROCEEDINGS

The commission may initiate formal rulemakings, major rate cases, applications for curtailments, and other issues it considers of sufficient merit. Proposals for rulemaking may originate from within the commission or from the general public. FERC staff proposals are placed on the agenda of an open commission meeting and published in the *Federal Register*; important public proposals likewise are placed on the agenda and published. At the commission meeting the commissioners may accept the proposed rule, reject it, or send it back to the staff for further study. If approved, it is published in the *Federal Register* as a Notice of Proposed Rulemaking (NOPR) and public comment is solicited.

An administrative law judge (ALJ) presides over hearings on cases in which the commission wants an evidentiary record. A hearing is conducted similarly to a courtroom hearing; participants may examine and cross-examine witnesses, file briefs, and submit evidence and exhibits. After the hearing, the ALJ issues an "initial decision" or recommendation for the consideration of the commission. The commission may adopt the ALJ's recommendation or modify, reject, or remand it for further proceedings in an opinion that is published in the *Federal Register*. These opinions, along with other orders of the commission, are posted on the FERC's website. Parties to the decision may request a rehearing, which is held at the commission's discretion. FERC decisions may be appealed to the U.S. Court of Appeals.

Company requests for rate increases, adjustments, and curtailments follow a similar procedure. After the commission receives a request for action and the FERC staff reviews it, a Notice of Application is issued and published in the *Federal Register* to solicit public comment. Following further staff analysis, the case is placed on the commission meeting agenda. After considering the staff's recommendation, the commission may approve, modify, reject, or set certain issues for an evidentiary hearing before an ALJ.

ENFORCEMENT

FERC has the authority to enforce compliance with its statutes, rules, orders, and regulations. Most enforcement is by administrative or judicial action. Compliance orders may be appealed to the commission. Failure to comply may result in proceedings in a U.S. district court. Preliminary enforcement proceedings also can take the form of special investigations and examinations.

CERTIFICATES AND LICENSES

The commission requires several different types of licenses and certificates of regulated industries. Actions that require FERC approval include

- Construction of nonfederal hydroelectric projects (license). Similar to the certificates required for gas.
- Maintenance of facilities at international borders for the transmission of electric energy or natural gas between the United States and another country (permit).
- Construction of gas pipelines and facilities (certificate). This certificate is the most common authorized by FERC. It ensures that the builder's financial resources are in order and that the pipeline or facility will be able to meet anticipated demand. Relaxations under the blanket certificate program have enabled pipelines to start construction on certain projects without prior FERC authorization.

REPORTING REQUIREMENTS

FERC maintains a uniform system of accounts that almost all large electric utilities and pipelines use. FERC collects detailed financial information on the revenues, costs, and balance sheets of the larger industry participants. In recent years, authority to collect some types of data, such as gas storage operations, has been reassigned to the DOE's Energy Information Administration. Most of the detailed financial reports are available for public inspection.

Background

Although FERC technically is one of the newer federal agencies, its history stretches back more than three-quarters of a century. FERC was created by the Department of Energy Organization Act and began operations Oct. 1, 1977. Its primary responsibilities, however, are those previously administered by the FPC, which was established in 1920. In addition to taking over the FPC's functions, FERC assumed the oil pipeline valuation and rate regulation functions of the Interstate Commerce Commission.

EARLY HISTORY

The FPC, FERC's predecessor, was created by the Federal Water Power Act of 1920 in response to demands for the government to encourage and coordinate the construction of hydroelectric projects on federal lands and waterways. Before the FPC's creation, a special act of Congress was required before a private hydroelectric project could be built on federal lands or waterways. The FPC originally consisted of the secretaries of the departments of war, interior, and agriculture. However, as the demand for electric power expanded, this arrangement proved too unwieldy, and in 1930 the commission was reorganized into a five-member bipartisan group.

In the FPC's early days, the commission's sole responsibility was the approval or disapproval of hydroelectric projects, but during the 1930s the body's regulatory powers were increased. In 1935 the Federal Water Power Act of 1920 was made part of a new Federal Power Act. In addition to its existing functions, the FPC assumed responsibility for regulating electric utilities' wholesale rates and transactions. The bill also authorized the commission to prescribe a uniform system of accounts and to inspect the records of licensees and public utilities.

The Natural Gas Act of 1938 extended FPC jurisdiction to the wholesale sales and transportation of natural gas in interstate commerce by pipeline companies. In 1942 the Natural Gas Act was amended to make the FPC responsible for certifying, as well as regulating, facilities for the transportation and wholesale sale of natural gas in interstate commerce.

The FPC's interest in natural gas grew as demand for the fuel increased after World War II. In 1954 the Supreme Court ruled that independent local producers selling natural gas for resale in interstate commerce were subject to FPC regulation. Consequently, the rates for gas produced and sold within the same state were left to the discretion of state governments, but the FPC maintained responsibility for setting rates for natural gas sold by producers in interstate commerce.

During the 1950s and 1960s, when natural gas was relatively plentiful, these two different approaches to rate setting did not cause serious problems. However, as the difference in the average prices of interstate and intrastate gas began to widen, producers increasingly made the decision to sell their gas in the higher-priced intrastate market, which was free of federal regulation. By the mid-1970s only 19 percent of newly discovered natural gas was being sold on the interstate market.

Severe shortages, culminating in a natural gas crisis in the winter of 1976–1977, developed in the consuming states that were dependent on federally regulated gas, while gas surpluses grew in the producing states where prices usually were unregulated. The need for reform of natural gas pricing was evident. The Natural Gas Policy Act (NGPA) of 1978 extended federal price controls to the intrastate market to end the distortions caused by the dual system. The act also established a schedule for phased deregulation of new gas beginning in 1985. Gas drilled before April 20, 1977, was to remain under control.

NATURAL GAS REGULATION IN THE 1980s

The NGPA also established categories of natural gas that could be priced at different levels. The tiered pricing system was intended to encourage the discovery of new gas supplies. But proponents of ending federal price controls said the system only encouraged producers to drill for the most expensive gas.

By the winter of 1981–1982 natural gas prices began to surge. The highly regulated market did not conform to traditional supply-demand price and cost models. Long-term contracts signed during the 1970s when supplies were tight were blamed for some of the price increases. Because federal regulators allowed pipelines to earn a fixed rate of return on their costs, they had little incentive to keep gas costs down. Meanwhile, incremental demand was increasingly being met from the several tiers of deregulated gas permitted by the NGPA. Each new increment of supply was commanding historic high prices. Rising costs were simply averaged into the total supply mix, most of it purchased by pipelines at controlled prices, and passed on to consumers.

In many cases pipelines—which not only transported gas but also sold, stored, and processed some of it—had agreed to pay the highest price allowed by the NGPA. Many producer-pipeline contracts contained "take-or-pay" provisions requiring pipelines to pay for almost all of the gas they contracted for, even if they did not take delivery of it. Some pipelines were farsighted enough to protect themselves with "market out" clauses that dropped the take-or-pay obligation if demand for gas fell, but most were not. These pipelines were stuck with huge and growing liabilities once gas demand started to fall.

During the last months of 1984, FERC began a broad inquiry on gas transportation issues. In October 1985 FERC issued Order 436, which embodied comprehensive changes in its regulations governing the transportation of natural gas by pipelines. Among other things, Order 436 broadened access for shippers and consumers to transportation services offered by pipelines. The rules required pipelines that accepted federal authorization to carry gas for others to do so on a nondiscriminatory basis.

In April 1986 the DOE unveiled a bill designed to correct the flaws in Order 436 while also providing for decontrol of old-gas prices. Under the open-access transportation program, pipelines holding open-access blanket certificates had to transport gas on a nondiscriminatory, first-come, first-served basis.

Despite opposition from some producer-states, the DOE convinced FERC to develop a rule that would eliminate old-gas price "vintaging." (Gas was classified by vintage for pricing ceiling purposes, according to the date the gas well was drilled, the method used for drilling, and the degree of difficulty in drilling.) Order 451, which took effect in July 1986, obligated pipelines in certain situations to transport gas and required renegotiation of high gas prices if they were contained in multivintage contracts.

Congress repealed the incremental pricing provisions of the NGPA as well as the gas-use restrictions contained in the Power Plant and Industrial Fuel Use Act in January 1987. President Ronald Reagan signed the bill in

FERC MAJOR ORDERS

Order 436: Issued October 1985. Established the principle of open-access transportation by encouraging pipelines to apply for "blanket certificates" under which they provide carriage in a nondiscriminatory fashion. Transportation requests are fulfilled on a first-come, first-served basis. (D.C. Circuit Court of Appeals remanded to FERC in June 1987 so the commission could "more convincingly" address the take-or-pay issue.)

Order 451: Issued June 1986. Permitted first sellers of "old" natural gas—which may be contractually priced below current market levels—to initiate "good faith negotiations" (GFNs) to settle on a new price. If the seller and purchaser engaging in GFN are unable to agree on a price, each is entitled to abandon the sale or purchase. (Vacated in September 1989 by the 5th U.S. Circuit Court of Appeals, which ruled that FERC exceeded its statutory authority in establishing a new pricing structure for old gas that collapsed the previous vintage, or classification, system into a single, higher ceiling price. The court also criticized the abandonment provision. The Supreme Court upheld the order in 1991.)

Order 497: Issued June 1988. Set a number of requirements for natural gas pipelines and their marketing affiliates, including the separation of operating personnel "to the maximum extent practicable" and reports of affiliate transactions.

Order 500: Issued August 1987. Attempted to meet the D.C. Circuit Court of Appeals' remand with Order 436. Established mechanisms to prevent the accumulation of take-or-pay when a pipeline transports; spreads take-or-pay liabilities among all parties—producers, pipelines, and customers. (The D.C. Circuit Court of Appeals ruled October 1989 that Order 500 failed to provide the reasoned take-or-pay explanation it had sought in the Order 436 case. The court remanded the case again to FERC.)

Order 500-H: Issued December 1989. Met D.C. Circuit Court of Appeals' remand with Order 500. Revised the take-or-pay explanation for Order 436.

Order 636: Issued April 1992. Mandated the complete separation of pipeline services, or unbundling. Required pipelines to provide open-access firm and interruptible transportation services for all gas suppliers. Allowed pipelines to sell gas at unregulated prices.

Order 888: Issued April 1996. Required electric utilities and transmission companies to file tariffs that offered competitors open-access to transmission grids. Provided for the recovery of stranded costs. Asserted FERC jurisdiction over retail wheeling as a last resort where state regulatory commissions lacked jurisdiction to order recovery of stranded costs.

Order 2000: Issued December 1999. Called for the creation of regional transmission organizations (RTOs) to increase the operating efficiency of electric transmission systems while eliminating opportunities for discriminatory transmission practices.

Order 2005: Issued February 2005. Promoted the exploration, development, production, and transportation of natural gas in Alaska.

May 1987, spurring talk in the industry of new markets for natural gas.

Meanwhile, the take-or-pay problem was growing. Estimating that take-or-pay costs could go as high as $14 billion by the end of 1986, pipelines urged FERC to develop a mechanism allowing them to bill customers directly for expenses related to buying out expensive take-or-pay contracts. The commission responded in March 1987 with a plan allowing pipelines and their customers to split the costs on a 50–50 basis.

But FERC's solution was not satisfactory to the D.C. Circuit Court of Appeals. In June 1987 the court remanded Order 436 to FERC so the commission could "more convincingly address" the take-or-pay issue. Although the appeals court decision (*Associated Gas Distributors v. FERC*) generally upheld Order 436, the appeals court told FERC to give "reasoned consideration" to claims that the open-access transportation program would aggravate pipelines' take-or-pay obligations.

In August 1987 the commission issued an interim rule, Order 500, designed to meet the court's concerns. The commission established a crediting mechanism to prevent the accumulation of take-or-pay when an open-access pipeline transported gas. The rule also set out an equitable sharing mechanism to spread take-or-pay liability among all parties—producers, pipelines, and customers.

The commission at this time began to explore more fully a fee that would allow pipelines to recover future take-or-pay costs. FERC's open-access policies had prodded pipelines to "unbundle" or charge separately for services, rather than charge one fee for all services. The innovative "gas inventory charge" provided a mechanism for pipelines to recover costs of maintaining gas supplies to satisfy the demand of their remaining sales customers, whether or not the customers actually purchased the gas.

In fall 1989 the commission issued its "final" version of Order 500, which made few changes to the previous interim rule and concluded that pipelines had resolved the bulk of their take-or-pay problems. But the D.C. Circuit Court remanded the record to FERC, holding that the order failed to provide the reasoned explanation it had sought about whether the open-access transportation program would aggravate pipeline take-or-pay obligations. The Supreme Court resolved the issue. On Jan. 8, 1991, the Court unanimously upheld the validity of FERC's Order 451. The decision was lauded by consumer groups, who said that the ruling would ensure consumers got the most competitive price possible for gas.

NATURAL GAS RESTRUCTURING IN THE 1990s

During 1990 and 1991 the movement in federal government toward creating a more competitive natural gas industry intensified. In May 1991 a public conference was held to air views of new, overall pipeline regulations aimed at revising pipeline service obligations, rate structure, and comparability of service. The conference concluded with industry-wide agreement that any new regulations should reflect the natural gas industry's need for flexible guidelines for making a pipeline's merchant function comparable to its transportation function.

In August 1991 FERC proposed a new rule, officially known as Docket No. RM91–11. Industry observers dubbed it the "Mega-NOPR" because of its far-reaching implications for the natural gas industry. The rule had several key provisions:

- Pipelines could continue to market gas to customers. However, pipelines had to set up discrete marketing affiliates.
- Pipelines would have to unbundle their services. In the past, pipelines had worked package deals—but under Mega-NOPR, pipelines would not be allowed to force a customer to buy more than one of these services at a time.
- Pipelines would have to set separate prices for each of the services that they offered. This would allow customers to choose from a menu of services.
- Pipelines would retain the right to abandon service without first getting FERC approval in cases where they provided interruptible and short-term firm transportation service.
- Pipelines would have to use the straight-fixed variable method of rate design (placing all fixed costs in the demand component and all variable costs in the commodity component) and to provide customers access to that information.

The commission billed the new rule as a major step toward enhancing consumer benefits. Initially, there was some negative reaction to Mega-NOPR from pipelines as well as LDCs. Because the rule would force contract renegotiation, many were concerned that there would be increased litigation in the courts.

Pipeline companies also said the rule would affect their ability to secure short-term, no-notice supplies of gas—reliability had always been a key reason behind the industry's extensive regulation. Before Mega-NOPR, pipelines could offer access to stored gas on a no-notice basis under bundled rates. But LDCs and pipeline operators expressed concern that once access was stripped away under an unbundled system, they would lose control of the gas availability. Pipeline operators and gas utilities also argued that the new rule would impair their ability to secure supplies and could raise prices.

In March 1992 the commission outlined the rule officially. It retained many features of the initial guidelines and included a provision aimed at providing pipelines with greater operational control of their facilities. It also responded to LDC concerns about supply with a provision that required pipelines to provide no-notice, unbundled firm transportation service. On April 8, 1992, the commission issued Order 636, the long-awaited 250-page final version of Mega-NOPR.

In August FERC issued orders on rehearing, called 636-A, which kept largely intact the previous thrust of the regulations. Additional adjustments were made in December 1992, officially known as 636-B. On Jan. 8, 1993, the commission denied all requests for rehearings and set to work revising its regulations for all seventy-nine interstate pipelines.

Congress passed and signed into law the Energy Policy Act in fall 1992. Among other things, the law loosened existing restrictions on Canadian natural gas, blocked the need for special import approvals, and specified that neither federal nor state regulators could treat Canadian gas differently than domestic natural gas once it was in the country.

The law also directed FERC to simplify its method for setting "just and reasonable" rates for interstate oil pipelines. However, the statute allowed rates that were approved at least one year before enactment and that were not subject to challenge to remain in effect. It also directed the commission to streamline consideration of rate changes.

After the issuance of Order 636, restructuring in the natural gas industry continued. FERC decisions focused on some of the so-called leftover 636 issues. One of these centered on requirements in the order that interstate pipelines post information about their capacity release guidelines on electronic bulletin boards.

One of the primary reasons for the inclusion of electronic notification in Order 636 was to ensure that pipelines were able to use their storage and transportation space most efficiently. The electronic notification system was designed so that customers who contracted for firm capacity could resell that capacity if demand dropped—as during the summer months—by posting an electronic notice of freed-up capacity. FERC's aim was to standardize the computer systems and information so that businesses could download information and manipulate it according to their needs. The result was the Gas Pipeline Data bulletin board, available to anyone with a computer modem to download pipeline tariffs and similar information.

The commission moved to further standardize access and information, requiring by June 1, 1999, that pipelines provide all information and conduct all business using the public Internet and common protocols. This made it easier for shippers to move gas across multiple pipelines.

A second leftover 636 issue was reform of gas gathering systems—the methods by which interstate pipelines collect and retrieve the natural gas from suppliers. Interstate pipelines are not necessarily located near gas wells or gas fields. Gathering systems collect the gas from the wells or fields, take it to a processing plant, separate out the natural gas from the other petroleum liquids, and transport the gas to an appropriate pipeline.

During the time when natural gas was regulated, the gathering business had largely been done by independent companies. Only about a third of natural gas was gathered by pipelines. The gathering systems run by pipelines were regulated by FERC, but those run by independent companies were unregulated. As a result, pipeline operators were anxious to set up unregulated affiliates to take over their gathering requirements.

Following the introduction and enactment of Order 636, gathering regulation became increasingly divisive. Pipelines argued that their affiliated gathering systems could not compete against unregulated independents. The operators supported deregulation of gathering systems.

But producers maintained that sufficient competition did not exist in all cases and that protecting nonaffiliated gatherers could prove difficult in a deregulated environment. The challenge was to put protections in place for gathering systems that were already operating.

In a series of eight decisions on gathering, FERC announced policy changes that had the effect of phasing out federal regulation. Gathering systems run by pipelines were still regulated, but pipelines were permitted to sell gathering systems to unregulated affiliates or third parties so long as (1) the new arrangement did not operate to frustrate the commission's regulation over the interstate gas pipeline grid, and (2) the gathering system's customers agreed to new contracts or were offered a default contract at favorable rates.

The final deregulation issue concerned capacity release. Order 636 allows those who control a portion of a pipeline's capacity to release it either temporarily or permanently if they no longer need to use it. Usually, this means renting it out for short periods to a broker or large shipper who happens to need additional capacity. Many of these transactions are arranged over electronic bulletin boards.

The commission in March 1995 issued Order 577 to change the former rule that prearranged capacity releases had to be for less than thirty days. The revision permitted transactions for a full calendar month without meeting the commission's advanced notice and bidding requirements.

The benefits of natural gas restructuring became evident in the late 1990s. By 1998, six years after Order 636, markets had become dynamic and were being driven by short-term and even intraday transactions. However, providing adequate protection to captive customers—those who have no options in choosing their natural gas supplier—remained a concern for FERC. For this reason, the commission issued an NOPR in July 1998 that proposed expanding options for captive customers and examining ways to keep long-term contracts attractive. FERC's intention was to create a more open and efficient short-term market, while eliminating any regulation-based bias against long-term transactions. Pipelines also would be given greater flexibility in negotiating terms and conditions of service with individual customers.

NATURAL GAS RESTRUCTURING IN THE 2000s

Addressing some of the leftover issues that had arisen or remained after six years of operating under Order 636, FERC in 2000 issued Order 637, which changed the regulation of short-term pipeline services and interstate pipelines. It revised the regulatory structure in response to increased competition in the natural gas industry and in the transportation of natural gas. Particularly, it suspended price ceilings for the sale of short-term (less than one year) released capacity until Sept. 30, 2002, in an effort to respond to the formation of a significant "grey market" in the sale of bundled capacity during peak periods by marketers and LDCs that essentially circumvented the ceilings set by Order 636. Pipelines were required to file tariff revisions in summer 2000. The commission began issuing compliance orders in 2001 and completed initial compliance by the end of 2002.

Even with continued attempts to get a handle on pricing through revised regulations, natural gas prices swung wildly during the first years of the decade, as charges of deception and malfeasance were lodged against energy trading companies. FERC eventually found evidence that companies, including the giant El Paso Corp., withheld gas pipeline capacity, creating an artificial shortage in California that led to higher prices. Prices did not come down significantly until FERC imposed general price restraints in the western states in June 2001.

In summer 2002 FERC began a formal investigation into natural gas pricing. In addition to examining allegations of withholding pipeline capacity, the commission began looking into charges that natural gas traders fed inaccurate price data to trade journals in an effort to boost prices for the commodity. The price indexes, published by the trade journals, were used to calculate the value of contracts between natural gas providers and their customers. During this time, some large traders, including Enron, Dynegy, and Williams Transcontinental Gas Pipe Corp., admitted that some employees had reported false data in an effort to drive up prices. These revelations had an especially great impact in California. In November 2002 the state government filed a lawsuit against dozens of natural gas companies and two trade journals, alleging that the false data had driven up prices and contributed to the state's energy crisis during 2000–2001.

Other kinds of market-altering violations also came to light during this period. For instance, in March 2003 FERC imposed the largest fine to date on Williams Transcontinental, forcing the energy giant to pay $20 million over the following four years. Williams Transcontinental was found to have given price discounts to its gas marketing unit, which violated federal laws requiring pipeline owners to give equal treatment to all competitors.

In spring and summer 2002, natural gas prices began rising again, and home heating costs rose by nearly 70 percent within a year. This time though, legitimate market forces rather than manipulation were blamed. Demand for gas had been increasing, in large part because—unlike coal or oil—gas is a clean-burning fuel and therefore not environmentally controversial. As a result, nearly all U.S. power plants built since 1998 were fired by natural gas. By spring 2003 new gas drilling had increased by 25 percent. But supply was still running short, in part because much of the new drilling work had been done in gas fields that had already been heavily exploited, producing much lower returns.

In a significant policy shift, on Dec. 18, 2002, the commission voted to remove regulatory barriers to the construction of new LNG import regasification terminals. In the new policy, FERC terminated open access requirements (that is, tariff requirements and nondiscriminatory rates) for LNG import terminals in an attempt to encourage more LNG site development. The policy allowed for the new facilities to operate under market-based rates and terms rather than under regulated cost-of-service rates. Under the decision, LNG import facilities would be treated as supply sources rather than as part of the transportation chain. FERC stated that it hoped the new policy would encourage the construction of new LNG facilities by removing some of the economic and regulatory barriers to investment.

The 2002 decision marked a significant departure from previous FERC practice. The new rules were expected to reinvigorate the natural gas industry and begin to solve supply woes. The decision also made onshore terminal proposals competitive with proposed offshore LNG facilities. While FERC's decision reduced rules for marketing operations at onshore LNG terminals, other regulations, such as those involving siting, were unchanged by this new policy.

Included in the fiscal 2005 omnibus appropriations legislation, which President George W. Bush signed into law Dec. 8, 2004, were provisions that reinforced FERC's authority to site local LNG terminals over state objections. The law stated that federal authority—not state interests—should determine where LNG terminals were located. FERC officials justified the agency's position by pointing out that natural gas demand was expected to rise dramatically during the following twenty years—according to the Energy Information Administration—and that the country needed more LNG terminals to satisfy energy demands.

But by December 2004, local debates raged across the country over proposals to construct new LNG terminals. More than thirty proposals had been submitted, sparking debate over safety and environmental concerns. In another attempt to clarify the situation, the Energy Policy Act of 2005 clarified that FERC had primary jurisdiction over the construction, expansion, or operation of LNG terminals. However, battles, including court challenges, between FERC and the states over siting of new LNG terminals seemed destined to drag out for years ahead.

In February 2005 FERC issued Order 2005, which approved rules on proposals for a natural gas pipeline to carry oil from Alaska. The rules, mandated by the 2004 Alaska Natural Gas Pipeline Act, established standards for creating "open seasons" for voluntary capacity expansion—commercial opportunities for potential customers to compete for and acquire capacity on a proposed or existing pipeline. Order 2005 also promoted competition in the exploration, development, and production of Alaskan natural gas, and provided opportunities for the transportation of natural gas from sources other than Prudhoe Bay or Point Thomson if the open seasons exceed the initial capacity of a pipeline project.

After years of debate, Congress in summer 2005 passed sweeping new energy legislation. One part of the broad Energy Policy Act of 2005 clarified FERC's exclusive jurisdiction under the Natural Gas Act for site selection, construction, expansion, and operation of import/export facilities onshore or in state-controlled waters. The jurisdiction included oversight and review of new LNG facilities, which were also overseen by the states. While the bill granted FERC principal authority in selecting LNG sites, the agency was still required to work with states before a site is chosen. The measure addressed market manipulation, requiring price publishers to provide FERC with natural gas pricing and availability for evaluation. In 2007 the commission issued a final rule to encourage greater investment in natural gas storage expansion markets with the aim of mitigating gas price volatility. In mid-2007 FERC proposed another rule—this one requiring gas companies to report daily on how much is moved through pipelines. The rule, which went into effect in early 2008, aimed at improving gas market transparency and, again, preventing price spikes by energy firms.

ELECTRICITY RESTRUCTURING IN THE 1990s

While natural gas regulation dominated the commission's work during the 1980s and early 1990s, the restructuring of the interstate electricity market became the commission's main focus by the mid-1990s. This change was caused by the need to address serious financial problems faced by many large electricity generators and a desire to provide a competitive market for power generation. The problems the industry faced were similar to those that the commission had successfully addressed when restructuring interstate natural gas shipments.

Traditional electric utilities got into trouble because of changes in the underlying economics of electricity generation. During the 1970s the industry built too many large and sometimes ruinously expensive central generating facilities, which usually lacked the heat recovery facilities to be optimally efficient. This prompted larger industrial customers to either cogenerate their electricity from the process heat left over from manufacturing, or to buy electricity at cheaper rates from new, small independent power generators. The independent producers used highly efficient new technology, such as natural gas turbines, and could sell electricity at rates well below those charged by the traditional utilities. This reversed the long-term trend where unit production costs could only be lowered by taking advantage of the economies of scale inherent in ever larger generating plants. The new generating facilities could produce electricity at lower unit cost, even though they were many times smaller in scale. The only problem was whether they could get access to the transmission lines owned by the traditional utilities in order to deliver their power to their new customers.

The process of restructuring wholesale electricity sales got under way in early 1988 when the commission considered four NOPRs addressing revisions to regulation of the electricity industry. These proposals were never formalized but they were an important first step in restructuring.

The next step was taken by Congress in the Energy Policy Act of 1992. In the section of the law that amended the 1935 Public Utility Holding Company Act (PUHCA), FERC was authorized to order a utility to transmit the power from wholesale electricity generators whenever the transaction was in the public interest. Under the new law, wholesale producers who requested such a transmission would have to pay for it, and those charges had to cover the utility's transmission costs plus a reasonable return on investment. Mandatory transmission orders would not be allowed when they jeopardized the reliability of established electric systems.

Before 1992, it was not possible for an electric utility wholesale customer to purchase electricity from any other provider than the one that served the grid in their area. After the 1992 energy bill, wholesale customers—primarily rural electric cooperatives and municipalities—were able to shop around for electricity sources and could apply to FERC to ask the utilities to transmit the power.

The bill also created a category of wholesale power producers exempted from PUHCA. The change was added to allow utilities to operate independent wholesale plants outside their service territories and encourage independent producers to operate generating plants. Power producers had to apply to FERC for the designation on a case-by-case basis. The exemption applied only to producers who generated and sold electricity wholesale.

While implementing the new law's section 211 provisions, FERC saw the need for a broader rule (as opposed to a case-by-case approach). Meanwhile, nearly a dozen states announced plans to proceed with some version of restructuring on their own, and the financial problems of the traditional generating industry continued to grow. Often the financial problem was not actual losses, so much as concern over what would happen to the industry's balance sheet if the large, expensive, but inefficient generating facilities had to be written off as more and more traditional customers were lost to competition. For some utilities, the threat was not just to less efficient assets. All assets could be at risk if enough large industrial customers pursued other alternatives. These stranded costs could be substantial.

Finally, FERC took action. The commission issued a proposed rule on April 7, 1995, that called for open access to utility electricity transmission facilities and recovery of stranded costs by public utilities. Among the many controversial questions was the environmental impact of the proposed rule. This issue touched off a cross-agency dispute with the Environmental Protection Agency (EPA) that was resolved by the issuance of an environmental impact statement adopting FERC's view that the impact of a restructured electric utility industry would be minimal.

The many issues raised by the proposed rules were debated for nearly a year, until the commission took final action in the form of Orders 888 and 889, issued in April 1996. Order 888 specified how the electricity generation industry would be restructured, while Order 889 detailed the electronic information systems that would be used by utilities to make known how much transmission capacity was available at any given time.

Under Order 888, all public utilities that owned, controlled, or operated interstate transmission facilities were required to file new tariffs that specified the rates for nondiscriminatory access to their transmission facilities. Public utilities were required to file a single open access tariff that offered both network, load-based service, and point-to-point contract-based service. Related ancillary services incident to normal electricity generation had to be provided. These services were scheduling, system control, and dispatch; reactive supply and voltage control from generation sources service; regulation and frequency response service; energy imbalance service; operating reserve (spinning reserve service); and operating reserve (supplemental reserve service). The power company pools that handled bulk power transactions between utilities were required to revise their pooling agreements and joint poolwide transmission tariffs to remove provisions that discriminated against outsiders.

FERC asserted authority for the first time over the rates and terms for unbundled retail transmission of electricity in interstate commerce. The commission announced seven indicators for deciding where its jurisdiction ended and state regulatory authority began.

With regard to the recovery of stranded costs related to wholesale requirements contracts executed on or before July 11, 1994, FERC permitted a public utility to seek recovery from departing customers. Recovery of stranded costs related to wholesale requirements contracts executed after July 11, 1994, was permitted only if the contract provided for such recovery. FERC ordered that utilities seeking to recover stranded costs from retail wheeling should first look to the state regulatory commissions but that FERC would review cases when state commissions lacked authority at the time retail wheeling was required to order stranded cost recovery. Parties to requirements contracts entered into before July 11, 1994, could seek to have them modified on a case-by-case basis. Utilities seeking market rates for sales from new capacity did not need to show lack of generation dominance in new capacity.

The initial implementation phase went smoothly. FERC announced in July 1996 that it had received either the newly ordered tariffs or waiver requests from all of the 166 interstate utilities that had been expected to respond. Nearly 200 parties challenged the orders, however, and it took another four years to settle the dispute.

In June 2000 the U.S. Court of Appeals for the District of Columbia Circuit upheld FERC's Orders 888 and 889. The court ruled that FERC could use its powers under the Federal Power Act and the Energy Policy Act of 1992 to create regional wholesale power markets and to check anticompetitive behavior. The court turned away arguments from utilities that the orders represented an unconstitutional "taking" under the Fifth Amendment as well as claims from environmental groups and the EPA that the orders could lead to increased pollution from coal-fired power plants. The court sent two issues to the commission for review—one involving the treatment of energy costs under FERC's market option for stranded cost recovery, the other dealing with FERC's failure to provide a "reasonable" cap on contract extensions for transmission customers who wanted to renew contracts for transmission capacity.

ELECTRICITY RESTRUCTURING IN THE 2000s

In December 1999 FERC issued Order 2000, calling for the creation of regional transmission organizations (RTOs) throughout the country. The order required utilities that owned, operated, or controlled interstate electric transmission facilities—but had not already chosen to participate as an independent system operator (ISO) or other regional transmission entity—to file a proposal for joining an RTO by October 2000. Utilities that chose not to file this proposal could file an alternative plan.

Order 2000 also outlined any characteristics that proposed RTOs were required to meet and allowed utilities some flexibility in their proposals to meet FERC requirements. FERC hoped that the order would significantly increase the operating efficiency of electric transmission systems while eliminating opportunities for discriminatory transmission practices and improving the estimates of available transmission capacity, system reliability, and pricing.

California became the first state to introduce a statewide competitive electric industry, opening its market to competition in March 1998. By late 2000, however, not only had the lower prices not materialized, but the state found itself in a power crisis brought on by the combination of a lack of new electric generation and the increased demand for electricity. State residents were subjected to rolling blackouts during the winter months in 2000 and early in 2001.

With two of the state's largest electric utilities on the brink of bankruptcy and the system near collapse, President Bill Clinton in December 2000 directed FERC to authorize California officials to reimpose rate controls on most of the electricity generated in the state. After his January 2001 inauguration, President George W. Bush extended the rate caps for two additional weeks before allowing them to expire. Bush, and the newly appointed head of FERC, Curt Hebert Jr., were both opposed to price caps, saying they would not bring in new supplies of electricity. Although the state crisis began to ease by late February, one large electricity supplier filed for bankruptcy in April 2001. Customers of another large utility, San Diego Gas & Electric Co., were hit with higher costs because the utility had recovered its stranded costs through the sale of its generation facilities, a move that allowed it to fully deregulate prices.

With its utilities unable to act, the state government was forced to step in and buy power on their behalf. In spite of these steps, in April 2001 FERC issued an order requiring price restraints in California during times of emergency and defined such times as whenever the state's power reserves drop to below 7.5 percent. But by late spring the agency was under intense pressure from Congress to do more to alleviate California's energy crisis. In June the commission unanimously voted to make semi-permanent the existing price restraints on electricity sales. In addition, FERC expanded the restraints to eleven western states to ensure that utilities in California would not be tempted to send power to neighboring states to sell it at a higher price. Hebert called the order "a market-based decision" that was preferable to strict price caps, which critics say destroy incentives for power companies to add capacity.

But California governor Gray Davis called on the federal government to force electricity generators to refund $9 billion the governor said they overcharged California. FERC asked one of its administrative law judges to investigate the charges and propose a solution. The judge, Curtis Wagner Jr., tried to broker a deal between the state and its energy suppliers, which included Reliant Energy, Duke Energy, Enron, and Dynegy. After weeks of unsuccessful negotiations, Wagner issued his proposal, arguing that California was owed no more than $1 billion in refunds. However, the new price restraints, coupled with a milder summer and energy conservation measures, led to lower energy prices during July and August 2001, giving the state and consumers some much-needed relief.

With FERC chair Hebert stepping down in August 2001, Bush named Pat Wood III, former chief energy regulator of Texas, as the next FERC chair. Wood had been much more sympathetic to California's arguments that it had been grossly overcharged by energy providers.

The trouble in California alerted federal policymakers to the potential for energy shortages around the country and prompted FERC to take a number of actions aimed at preventing another power supply meltdown. The first of these occurred in July 2001, when the agency announced that it would ask most utilities to hand over control of their power lines to four new RTOs that would be established in 2002. These four regional authorities would have the power to build new lines to connect up power grids and ensure the free flow of electricity around the country.

The idea was to create the equivalent of an interstate highway system for electricity that would prevent price gouging by creating a free flow of power around the country and prevent large energy suppliers from enacting monopolistic pricing policies. With a larger, more integrated grid, a local utility that needed power would have a much greater number of suppliers to choose from, hence ensuring a more competitive pricing environment.

In September 2002 Wood put teeth in the new proposal by announcing that any electric utility that did not join one of the four RTOs would lose the right to set market-based prices for power. FERC took the proposal even further two months later, announcing in November that it would impose price controls on utilities that were in a position to raise prices because of their dominance in a local market. The new regional authorities and the price controls were opposed by many utilities and supporters of a free market, who argued that the actions amounted to unnecessary regulation that would stifle competition and lead to disincentives for power suppliers to build new plants. Wood countered that the advantage held by the big utilities had to be addressed to allow new energy producers to enter the market competitively.

Early in 2002 California was back in the news, once again accusing power suppliers—most notably fallen energy giant Enron—of overcharging in some of the long-term state contracts. Davis asked FERC to rescind $40 billion in long-term contracts he had signed during the crisis a year before, in an effort to guarantee the state sufficient power in the coming decade. By the late spring 2002 evidence had emerged showing that Enron and other companies had indeed used power shortages in California to manipulate the market. In August FERC launched its investigation into the matter.

The commission also faced severe criticism over the uncovered price gouging in California. In November the Senate Energy Committee released a report accusing

FERC of ignoring signs that power companies had been taking advantage of California during the energy crisis. Wood, who was not FERC chair during that period, agreed that the commission could have done more. A number of companies were ordered to pay $3.3 billion in refunds to California. Moreover, some energy companies were forced to renegotiate some of the long-term contracts they had signed with California.

With the investigation complete in February 2005, FERC recommended that Enron, then entangled in bankruptcy proceedings, pay $1.67 billion for improper trading in the electricity markets in the western states. It was the highest recommended sanction in FERC's history, signaling a new tough line by federal regulators who had been criticized for lax oversight. As part of the Energy Policy Act of 2005, Enron and other companies that manipulated wholesale power contracts in the late 1990s would also no longer be permitted to collect money from western state utilities.

The electricity market that had been focused on California received a jolt in August 2003 when a blackout left nearly 50 million consumers across eight states in the Northeast and Midwest and Canada without power. The blackout of 2003 highlighted the need for infrastructure improvements and standard operating rules. It also revealed the fragility of the U.S. electricity system. Congress unleashed a flurry of proposals to upgrade it, ranging from $56 billion to more than $400 billion. The White House and congressional leaders responded with demands for higher rates of profit for transmission owners, federal eminent domain powers to site new transmission lines, and inclusion of electricity reliability measures in a massive energy bill loaded with billions of dollars of additional incentives to the fossil fuel and nuclear industries.

By fall 2004 FERC's plan for establishing RTOs was falling into place. PJM Interconnection integrated American Electric Power Co. and Dayton Power and Light into its RTO; the Midwest Independent Transmission System Operator integrated Illinois Power into its RTO; and the California Independent System Operator implemented a new market design. FERC also directed the New England RTO to develop a more comprehensive transmission agreement with its neighboring New York Independent System Operator.

Congress addressed long-term national energy issues by passing the Energy Policy Act of 2005. The law provided tax credits for new energy development and gave FERC a host of new oversight responsibilities. The act required power companies to get permission from FERC before mergers or consolidations involving more than $10 million. After holding public hearings, FERC could approve such mergers or consolidations as long as the change would not have a negative effect on consumers or the public interest.

The law repealed the 1935 PUHCA, which restricted the ownership and operations of power companies and their ability to control electricity prices. It replaced PUHCA with language designed to provide disclosure of power company finances. Specifically, it gave FERC—and, to a lesser extent, state authorities—the power to examine all relevant books, records, accounts, and memorandums belonging to a company that owns or partly owns a power facility to ensure that costs are allocated fairly to public utilities.

The act also amended the Federal Power Act to direct FERC to replace voluntary reliability standards overseen by the industry with federal government rules aimed at ensuring reliability and reducing the cost of delivered power by reducing transmission congestion. The law required all operators of bulk-electric power-generating systems to comply with the reliability standards, which were intended to limit instability and cascading failures.

After Joseph T. Kelliher took over as FERC chair in July 2005, many of the commission's actions reflected the mandates dictated by the 2005 energy act. To implement the law the commission in 2006 issued nine final rules, three notices of proposed rules, and seven reports to Congress. The expanded duties resulted in the hiring of more staff at the commission. The new tasks for the commission included implementing penalty authority to prevent market manipulation; supplementing state transmission siting authority; adopting new rate incentives to encourage electric transmission investment; and reviewing certain company mergers and acquisitions of electric utility facilities.

In the wake of the Enron scandal, one of the biggest issues emerging from the law was FERC's responsibility to prevent market manipulation. The commission gained for the first time the ability to levy civil penalties when it uncovered market manipulation, with fines up to $1 million per day per transaction. Kelliher in 2006 called the new authority "one of the most important changes to the laws we administer made by the Energy Policy Act of 2005."

The final market manipulation rule, issued in January 2006, made it illegal for any entity, including a government or company, to commit fraud, make any untrue statement of fact, or engage in any deceit that affects the purchase of electricity or natural gas or transmission or transportation services. It clarified that the rules do not apply to oil pipeline transportation regulated by the commission.

The energy law required more changes in the electricity sector than any other. In addition to the market manipulation rule, FERC had to set up reliability standards, for instance. The rules, issued in February 2006, were aimed at preventing blackouts. Kelliher noted that the previous three blackouts, including the August 2003 blackout, were caused when utilities violated the unenforceable reliability standards overseen by industry and that the commission's new civil penalties should deter any future violations. To enforce the law, the commission certified an Electric Reliability Organization to oversee regional transmission.

In July 2006 the commission issued rules aimed at spurring new investment in interstate electricity transmission. The rules (1) allowed an incentive rate of higher return on equity for new investments by traditional utilities and transmission-only companies; (2) allowed a higher return on equity for transmission owners that join, and remain in, regional organizations; (3) gave companies full recovery of construction work and preoperation costs, within limits; (4) accelerated depreciation; (5) deferred cost recovery for utilities with frozen retail rates; and (6) permitted recovery of prudently incurred costs to comply with mandatory reliability standards as well as those related to infrastructure development in corridors sited by the federal government because they were deemed to be of national interest.

However, all of these incentives struck some critics as merely benefits for companies that did not guarantee actual improvements in the power grid. Consumer advocates worried that users would face higher prices driven by the incentives without getting much improvement in exchange. The California Public Utilities Commission said the rule offered "far more access to such undue riches than either transmission owners need or . . . is justified."

As a result, FERC modified its policy in December 2006. The new policy kept provisions in the rule that said there would be a rebuttable presumption that a transmission project is eligible for incentives "if it results from a fair and open regional planning process or has received state siting approval." The commission, however, also adjusted the policy to clarify that if approval processes did not require that a project ensure reliability or lower the cost of power by reducing congestion, the applicant bore additional burdens of demonstrating that its project was eligible.

The commission also issued a rule in November 2006 giving the federal government electric transmission siting authority for projects that the DOE considered to be of such vital national interest that they designated them as "national interest electric transmission corridors." FERC was allowed to issue a construction permit only if states did not have authority to site these facilities, if an applicant did not quality for siting under state law, or if the state siting body had withheld approval for more than a year. The rule was controversial because some state officials felt that it infringed on their authority.

FERC's siting authority, especially for LNG terminals for fuel transported from other nations, remained the most volatile issue for the agency. Although FERC was still expected to involve states and localities in the decision making, state and local officials objected to what they viewed as the commission's encroachment on their powers. Congress attempted to strike a balance between FERC authority, the demands of the energy industry, the expectations of the states and consumers, and the condition of the country's power supply.

In September 2007 federal energy regulators met to resolve accusations made against PJM, an energy management company that coordinated the operations of more than 1,000 generating plants owned by a host of power companies in Washington, DC, Maryland, Virginia, and eleven other East Coast states. Consumer electric bills were largely determined by PJM transmission charges and wholesale spot prices, which were prices set at certain points across the transmission grid every half hour. Spot prices depended on the prices and quantities of generation, level of demand, availability, and system operation requirements—and they could be quite volatile.

Earlier that year, PJM's internal market monitor, Joseph Bowring, alleged that customers in Maryland and other states had been overcharged. Although the market monitor was a PJM employee, he also served as an independent watchdog tasked with alerting regulators to problems and ensuring the market remain competitive. PJM responded to Bowring's charges by hinting that they would replace him and his staff with an outside firm. Bowring countered by filing a complaint with FERC in April 2007 claiming that PJM officials had censored his annual reports and had barred him from briefing PJM members about his concerns.

In the end, Bowring got the independence he wanted. In March 2008 FERC settled the complaint by ordering that internal market monitors be moved outside of the control of PJM. The new independent operation would allow monitors to take concerns directly to member companies and regulators. In addition, the commission ruled that Maryland consumers had been overcharged in 2006 by $87.5 million.

The PJM incident raised larger questions concerning the commission's legal duty to prevent "unjust and unreasonable" electricity rates that arise when wholesale markets favor large generating companies at the expense of smaller competitors. A broad coalition of industrial, governmental, and consumer groups petitioned the FERC in December 2007 to expand its investigation into the marketing of power, asserting that some companies that own both utilities and generating stations that sell into wholesale markets are earning far higher returns than those of other similarly regulated industries.

Many industry watchers agreed that one way to discourage price gouging was to expand generating and grid capacity. But efforts to expand capacity often ran into opposition from environmental groups as well as state environmental agencies. In an effort to ease this opposition, the government in October 2007 announced that it was giving power companies the opportunity to submit expansion plan proposals to FERC if they could show that they were being obstructed in state and local negotiations. A successful application to FERC would allow these companies to make use of "eminent domain condemnation," which gives a governmental agency the right to force landowners to sell whether they want to or not, but requires the government to pay market value for the property.

Utilities and others hailed the move, arguing that it would ease energy shortfalls that have led to such events as the East Coast's massive 2003 blackout. But environmentalists decried the decision, pointing out that environmentally damaging plans, such as Dominion Virginia Power's proposed 240-mile line that would extend through parks and Civil War battlefields, would now likely go forward.

Although President Barack Obama made alternative energy projects a central part of his campaign platform, several challenges confronted FERC as it worked out plans to help implement the president's mandate in a difficult fiscal environment. For instance, the country's enormous and complex electric power grid—a jumble of individual and regional systems—is antiquated and largely unable to connect with places where renewable power supplies are plentiful. Yet only $2 billion in the economic stimulus package, which was enacted in February 2009, was designated for Smart Grid transmission lines, falling far short of the $100 billion to $200 billion needed to overhaul the entire grid.

In addition to this financial shortfall, the administration and the agency faced opposition from environmental groups on some of the administration's new energy plans. These groups argued that the delivery of "green" energy carries with it heavy environmental costs. In addition to vast tracts of land required for solar panels, wind turbines, and transmission towers, opponents contend, the power lines needed to get the energy to consumers would have to be routed through many thousands of miles of unspoiled landscape.

Environmentalists also objected to aspects of wave farming, an alternative energy that uses high-tech buoys to strain clean, renewable power from the ocean. The buoys, which are anchored several miles offshore, gently move up and down with ocean swells and have the potential to produce 5 to 10 percent of the nation's energy supply, according to some estimates. But environmentalists and the fishing industry argued that too little is known about the effect wave farms might have on migrating fish and whales. FERC, which has issued several permits to conduct testing for wave energy farms off the U.S. coast, asserts that wave farming is a green technology whose promise warrants further investigation.

In March 2009 FERC reached an agreement with the Interior Department to divide responsibility for regulating offshore alternative energy sources, putting an end to a long-running interagency turf battle between the department and FERC that threatened to obstruct the administration's efforts to expand renewable energy capacity. In a joint statement the two agencies agreed to draw up a "Memorandum of Understanding" that would give Interior the right to decide on wind power proposals in federal waters, while FERC would have the right to oversee wave, tidal, and ocean-current projects.

Also in March, President Obama named Jon Wellinghoff chair of the commission. Wellinghoff, who had been a FERC commissioner since 2006 and acting chair since January 2009, had once served as Nevada's consumer advocate and also had helped to write that state's renewable electricity standard requiring utilities to increase their use of wind, solar, and geothermal technologies. In his first meeting as chair, Wellinghoff made clear that the agency's new priorities would be climate change, energy conservation, and Smart Grid technologies aimed at better coordinating fluctuations in wind and solar power with household, building, and factory demand. At the same meeting, the new chair stated that new nuclear power plants were not needed, a position that put him at odds with his boss, Obama, as well as with some environmentalists, who see nuclear energy as a way to increase the nation's power generation capacity without raising greenhouse gas emissions. Wellinghoff also announced the creation of a new office within FERC that would focus on the intersection of energy and climate policies.

Soon after Wellinghoff officially took the reins at FERC, the agency found itself in the middle of the debate over the climate change bill brought before Congress. The legislation, which began moving through the House early in 2009, aimed to curb the carbondioxide gases scientists have linked to climate change. Central to the bill was a cap-and-trade system that set a limit on overall emissions of heat-trapping gases, while allowing utilities, manufacturers and other emitters to trade pollution permits, or allowances, among themselves. Over time, this cap would become more stringent, increasing the cost of emissions and, it was hoped, goading the industry to find cleaner energy sources. FERC, along with the Commodity Futures Trading Commission (CFTC), would be tasked with regulating this new system and ensuring that the parties involved met their obligations.

While Obama declared that cap-and-trade was one of his top priorities, many potential obstacles remained before passage. Congressional Republicans viewed it as little more than an energy tax that would raise electricity and heating bills for consumers and manufacturers during an economic recession. While some environmentalists got behind the legislation, others opposed it as not being stringent enough. The business sector was also divided, with some large corporations in favor and many manufacturers opposed. Meanwhile more liberal West and East Coast Democrats found themselves pitted against more moderate members of their party from areas, especially in the Midwest and South, dependent on coal for electricity as well as heavy manufacturing for jobs.

In June 2009 the measure managed to pass the House by the slim margin of 219–212. Meanwhile, in the Senate, Democratic backers of a companion bill had difficulty gaining the sixty votes needed to avoid a filibuster. Senate Republicans called for major concessions, demanding new provisions promoting nuclear power and offshore drilling in exchange for cap-and-trade. As in the House, some Democrats from the industrial Midwest and the South were also wary of the legislation and its impact on future energy costs. Senator Majority Leader Harry M. Reid (D-NV) announced that he would not bring the climate bill to the Senate floor that summer. A few months later, the Senate Democrats lost six seats in the November election, effectively ending any chance for passage.

FERC IN THE 2010s

While action on cap-and-trade ultimately stalled, FERC did move forward on other fronts. For instance, during late 2009 and early 2010, the commission reviewed a number of utility company mergers, most notably the $8.5 billion deal by First Energy of Ohio to buy Allegheny Energy of Pennsylvania. The new company would become the largest utility in the country, made up of ten smaller utilities serving 6.1 million customers in seven states. It would generate electricity from a mix of coal, nuclear, natural gas, oil, and renewable energy sources.

While consumer watchdogs expressed concern that a bigger FirstEnergy could dominate the wholesale and retail markets and drive up prices for consumers, FERC approved the merger in December 2010, ultimately concluding that the combined companies would have no adverse effect on competition. The agency also determined that Allegheny's newer coal-fired plants would bode well for FirstEnergy's ability to generate more power with greater efficiency and less cost to the environment.

During this time, the commission also signed off on an important plan to finance the cost of new power lines in the western half of the country, part of the agency's larger vision of making the nation's power grid more suitable for carrying energy from renewable sources. The FERC-drafted regulation aimed to spread the costs for these new power lines among thirteen states, from Montana to Ohio, and to make the agency responsible for determining whether transmission pricing plans submitted by regional grid operators and utilities are "just and reasonable." The aim was for the Midwest cost-sharing plan to serve as a template for how transmission costs will be shared throughout the country. But utility companies, which would be tasked with paying much if not most of the bill, worried that the costs to states would not be borne proportionately and that some power companies would end up subsidizing consumers served in other states, by other utilities.

This concern was echoed on Capitol Hill, where Bob Corker (R-TN), with the backing of other Senate Republicans, introduced legislation that would require FERC to evaluate who would benefit from the transmission lines and then to assign costs proportionally. Some voices of opposition used even stronger language, calling the FERC rules unconstitutional, a tariff that would essentially "socialize the costs of renewable energy." But many Senate Democrats and other advocates of the transmission project argued that Corker's demands would take years to implement, prompt litigation, and delay the benefits of the grid update. This Democratic opposition stalled Corker's bill in the Senate, where it died.

While the issue of upgrading the country's power grid remained mired in legal and public relations battles, offshore wind power got a boost when, in October 2010, Google announced that it would become a major player in the Atlantic Wind Connection (AWC), a $5 billion, 350-mile-long power transmission corridor, or underwater spine, running along the coast from Virginia to New Jersey. The project would be built along the eastern seaboard in conjunction with a series of planned wind farms. When complete, AWC could supply wind power to 1.6 million households.

FERC Chair Wellinghoff praised the Google initiative as "one of the most interesting transmission projects that I've ever seen walk through the door." But in spite of Wellinghoff's support and the overall excitement generated over Google's efforts, by the spring of 2013, the project's first phase—the construction of the transmission line from waters off the coast of Jersey City, NJ, to south along the coast to Atlantic City, NJ—remained stalled, still awaiting regulatory approval from the New Jersey state regulators.

Meanwhile, the agency moved forward with more mundane duties, including its review of the proposed merger of Duke Energy and Progress Energy, both large power utilities based in the South and Midwest. In spite of protests from consumer groups and others that the merger would further limit competition and lead to higher energy prices, the deal for Duke to acquire its former rival won FERC and Nuclear Regulatory Commission approval in 2011. With $22.7 billion in annual revenue and more than 7 million customers in North Carolina, South Carolina, Florida, Indiana, Kentucky,

and Ohio, the combined company (still called Duke Energy) became the largest utility in the country.

In addition to the Duke-Progress merger, FERC also signed a $410 million settlement between California utility Sempra Energy and its southern California customers. Sempra was one of a number of companies charged with creating false energy shortages during the state's 2000–2001 energy crisis to justify overcharging consumers. Under the deal, which was negotiated with California's Attorney General, Jerry Brown, and approved by FERC, Sempra agreed to pay the cash settlement to millions of its customers but did not have to admit to any wrongdoing. Meanwhile, FERC was mentioned in a January 2011 report issued by the DOE that detailed the vulnerability of the nation's power grid to cyber-attack and other threats. The report, which criticized utilities as well as regulatory agencies like FERC for everything from weak computer security standards to insufficient oversight, came only seven months after the House had passed grid security legislation in June 2010. That measure, which stalled in the Senate, would have given FERC more authority to mandate greater security measures to protect the nation's electric grid from cyber-attacks and other threats such as solar flares. The House-passed bill also would have authorized the agency to issue emergency measures to protect critical electrical infrastructure if it was notified by the president of an imminent security threat to the grid. In 2012, in the wake of Superstorm Sandy, some members in both houses of Congress once again called for passage of a bill to protect the grid from cyber-attacks. Still, even though Sandy pounded most of the East Coast of the United States and caused tremendous damage in the mid-Atlantic region, Congress did not act. In November 2012 the bill was voted down in the Senate, and Majority Leader Harry Reid declared the issue dead for the time being.

Another threat to the power grid is oversupply—often caused by renewable sources of energy, notably wind power and hydropower. In June 2010, for example, a particularly intense storm in the Pacific Northwest caused high winds and rapid currents that, in turn, produced a severe overage of power from wind and water sources. As a result of this storm, the Bonneville Power Administration—a quasi-governmental entity that provides power for customers in eight Western states, including California, Oregon, and Washington—created a program to divert this excess energy and protect the grid from overload. One key component of this program involved simply disconnecting the power lines from wind turbines to the grid when the turbines are creating too much power, a policy that angered private wind energy producers, who were losing money whenever the connection between their wind farms and the grid was cut.

In 2011, several private wind power companies appealed to FERC, arguing that the Bonneville's policy of disconnecting the grid from their wind farms was discriminatory, in that other energy providers did not have their connections severed so as not to overload the grid. In December 2011, FERC agreed with the wind operators and ordered Bonneville to stop the practice. Instead, the commission ruled, Bonneville should pay customers with the capacity to do so to take and store the extra power. For example, homeowners with recently manufactured water heaters can have them adapted to store excess electricity that can later be used as needed.

While the commission was working on issues associated with the electric grid, it was also devoting time and resources to another important part of the nation's energy infrastructure: pipelines. Oil and natural gas producers have been using pipelines for more than a century, but in recent years, there has been a growing need for new lines because of substantial increases in domestic gas and oil production.

Until 2005 or so, most energy analysts predicted that the United States would soon import up to half of the natural gas it needed and that American businesses and consumers would pay top dollar for it, as natural gas is the cleanest burning of all fossil fuels. Coal, the dirtiest of the major fuel sources, seemed poised to retain its place as the cheapest and most common source of fuel for power generation. But even as these predictions were being made, new technologies were already beginning to turn them on their head. Starting in 2008, hydraulic fracturing or "fracking," which involves pumping huge amounts of water and chemicals in rock formations, began opening significant reserves of natural gas and, to a lesser extent, oil, long trapped in massive shale deposits. As a result, the United States quickly went from being a gas importer to a major exporter of natural gas. And by 2011 natural gas prices were roughly a quarter of what they had been as late as 2009, prompting many American utilities to begin to replace coal-fired plants with facilities that burn natural gas.

With the expanded production and use of natural gas has come a need in many parts of the country for more gas pipelines. In February 2013 a natural gas industry group estimated that the nation would need to build 450,000 miles of new pipeline in the next twenty-five years. But even before this estimate, FERC was receiving a larger number of requests for permits to build pipelines, from a single application in 2008 to nine in 2012. These requests, many of which were ultimately granted, often put the commission in a difficult position, as it tried to balance the growing need for energy with environmental and other concerns. For instance, a proposed forty-four–mile pipeline from Northern Pennsylvania to a terminal in Mahwah, NJ, was seen by many as necessary to bring needed natural gas from the Pennsylvania shale fields to energy-hungry New York City. But the commission took more than a year to approve the pipeline because of its route through forests and wetlands. Even after the commission approved the pipeline in 2012, lawsuits by environmental activists delayed the beginning of construction until March 2013.

On a different front, FERC moved against a number of large banks, including Barclays and JPMorgan after they were accused of manipulating the power market in California to boost profits. These banks have energy trading arms—divisions that buy and sell power to utilities on the open market. Energy trading firms play a particularly important role in areas that routinely suffer from power shortages, such as California.

A FERC investigation found that in 2010 and 2011, as California was experiencing rolling blackouts, JPMorgan, Barclays, and other banks withheld power in a successful effort to exacerbate power shortages and drive up the price of electricity. As a result, the commission determined, California consumers ended up paying hundreds of millions of dollars more for electricity than they would have otherwise. In 2012, after an investigation into the issue by the commission, Barclays was fined $470 million and JPMorgan was barred from power trading in California for six months, beginning in April of that year.

FERC was able to make decisions on fining banks, approving pipelines, and other issues, in part, because membership in the five-person commission remained remarkably stable during the two or three years leading up to 2013. Indeed, during this period, only one member, Marc Spitzer, left after his term expired in 2011. Spitzer was replaced by fellow Republican Tony Clark, who had served two terms in the North Dakota legislature and chaired the state's public service commission. In June of 2012, Clark was sworn in for a term that expires in 2015.

Meanwhile, in March 2013, the commission approved new rules governing the removal of vegetation near power lines. In a storm, tree branches and other vegetation often break and damage lines, causing power outages. A branch that takes down a single power line can cause loss of electricity to tens of thousands of homes and businesses. The new rules strengthen existing requirements that power companies and even private landowners keep tree branches and other plants trimmed and away from lines. The rules also expand the types of lines covered under the regulation to include those that carry less power. While the regulations are not intended to prevent large outages caused by hurricanes and other major storms, where whole trees often fall, they aim to prevent smaller, more routine outages.

In May 2013 Chairman Wellinghoff announced that after serving seven years on the commission, four as chair, he would be resigning when his term ended on June 30. A little more than a month after Wellinghoff's announcement, President Obama named Ronald Binz as his nominee to head up the commission. Binz, who served as chair of the Colorado Public Utilities commission and is a supporter of renewable energy, ran into fierce opposition from Senate Republicans, who claimed he was a radical environmentalist whose efforts at FERC would drive up energy prices for American consumers.

Roughly five months after he was tapped, Binz withdrew his nomination. A month later, in November, the president named sitting commissioner, Cheryl LaFleur, as acting chairman. LaFleur, who had served on the commission since 2010, had previously been an executive at National Grid, a New England electric utility that serves 3.4 million customers. Soon after she assumed her new duties, she was formally nominated for the chairmanship and was confirmed by the Senate in July 2014.

Also approved to sit on the commission in July 2014 was Norman Bay, who had previously headed up the enforcement division at FERC. After Binz's withdrawal, President Obama had intended to nominate Bay as chairman. But Bay also was opposed by Senate Republicans, who argued that he did not have the breadth of experience needed to chair the commission and urged the White House to formally tap LaFleur for the top slot. Eventually the GOP and the White

House cut a deal: Bay would serve on the commission to gain needed experience until April 2015, after which time he would replace LaFleur as commissioner.

Even in the midst of the fight over Binz, the agency was not idle. In July 2013, for instance, FERC imposed a record $410 million fine on JPMorgan. The banking giant agreed to the fine in order to resolve allegations that it had rigged energy markets in the Western and Midwestern states in order to profit from price swings. Although it was not required by the settlement, JPMorgan also subsequently agreed to sell its commodities trading division to Swiss company Mercuria Energy Group for $3.5 billion.

Around the same time it was settling with JPMorgan, the agency announced an even larger fine of $456 million would be levied against Barclays bank, also for energy market manipulation. But unlike JPMorgan, the British bank vowed to fight the fine in court. In 2014 Barclays succeeded in getting a federal district court in California to put payment of the fine on hold, pending resolution of the case, which still has not gone to trial.

The Barclays case was not the only legal battle at issue in 2014. In May of that year, the U.S. Court of Appeals for the District of Columbia Circuit ruled that FERC had overstepped its authority in regulating certain arrangements aimed at conserving energy during peak usage periods. In 2011 the agency had approved rules aimed at encouraging "demand-response," a system whereby consumers voluntarily agree to use less power during peak usage times, such as the early evening hours. Those who agree to use less during high volume periods are rewarded with overall lower electricity rates. The DC Circuit, which is second most powerful court in the nation after the Supreme Court, ruled that regulating usage at the customer level is a matter for state governments, not a federal agency.

Meanwhile, the agency continued to find itself caught in the middle of efforts by the administration to decide whether American energy firms should be allowed to export more liquid natural gas (LNG). As noted above, recent technological advances have dramatically expanded the country's production of natural gas and led to a huge drop in gas prices. This price drop was a boon to consumers, who paid less in heating and other energy costs, as well as to manufacturers, who started building more factories in the United States in energy intensive industries such as steel, chemicals, and plastics to take advantage of low-cost power.

But since the production boom began in 2010, producers of natural gas have wanted to liquefy some of it and sell it to foreign customers in Japan, Europe, and elsewhere. Many companies planned to convert existing natural gas importation facilities, which had been built before the current boom when it was believed that the United States would need to import much of its gas, into facilities that could be used to export gas. Manufacturers and other consumers of natural gas lobbied the Obama administration to prevent this, arguing that allowing large-scale exportation would dramatically raise gas prices at home and erode the competitive edge that the current environment gives manufacturers and other businesses. But energy exploration firms countered that exports would probably result in only modest price increases at home because there is a wealth of

recoverable gas and greater demand will inevitably lead to more production, more supply, and stable prices.

The debate took on geopolitical tones when in 2014 Russia effectively annexed the Ukrainian territory of Crimea and began to encroach into eastern Ukrainian provinces along its border, and Western European countries including Germany and France were criticized for not imposing tough economic sanctions on Russia because they were heavily reliant on natural gas imports from Russia. U.S. geopolitical thinkers argued that increased American LNG exports would break Europe's dependency on Russian gas and make them freer to ratchet up the pressure on Russia.

But, so far, the LNG export boom has failed to take off. In the roughly five years since the agency began considering applications, FERC has received thirty-eight proposals from energy firms either wanting to convert LNG importing facilities into exporting terminals or to build new ones. To date, the agency has granted only five permits, although two other projects may soon receive the final go ahead.

Current Issues

On April 15, 2015, Commissioner Bay was sworn in as chairman, replacing LaFleur, who remains on the commission serving a term that does not expire until 2019. Unlike LaFleur, who has been on good terms with Capitol Hill Republicans, Bay will need to shore up GOP support. In particular, he will need to forge a good working relationship with Sen. Lisa Murkowski (R-AK), the powerful chairman of the Senate Energy and Natural Resources Committee, who led the opposition to his 2014 nomination to the commission.

One issue that could strain the relationship is the controversial Keystone XL Pipeline, which is intended to carry oil from Western Canada through the United States to the Gulf of Mexico. FERC usually approves new pipelines, but because this pipeline crosses an international border, the decision must go through the State Department first. While pro-business and pro-environment advocates argue the merits of the project, President Obama has refused to make a final decision, saying that the project needs to be studied further.

House Republicans and some Democrats who favor moving forward with the pipeline immediately have repeatedly passed legislation that would direct FERC to approve the project. But until recently, the Senate has refused to take up a similar bill. That changed after November 2014 election, which led to GOP control of the Senate. Just weeks before power officially changed hands, Democratic leaders engineered a vote on a similar bill in an effort to help a Democratic senator from Louisiana, Mary Landrieu, who was in a tough runoff election in early December 2014. The bill failed to get the sixty votes needed to prevent a filibuster and went down to defeat—as did Landrieu. But after the GOP took control of the Senate, the measure was revived and passed in February 2015. However, just days after final passage, President Obama vetoed the bill. Supporters of Keystone in the Senate were just five votes shy of the sixty-seven needed to override the veto and have vowed to round up more support and try again.

While the fight over Keystone rages on, the commission has been busy drafting new regulations that would work in concert with the Environmental Protection Agency's proposal to dramatically reduce carbon dioxide emissions at power plants. FERC has been charged with making sure that in lowering carbon emissions, plants do not reduce the reliability and consistency of their power output. If power fluctuations are significant enough, they could damage the power grid. Some utilities have called on FERC to offer them a regulatory "safety valve," allowing them to waive the EPA requirements if implementing them is causing power swings. New proposed rules are expected to be released in the second half of 2015.

AGENCY ORGANIZATION

Biographies

NORMAN C. BAY, CHAIR

Appointment: Nominated by President Barack Obama and confirmed as a commissioner by the Senate to be groomed for the position of chair; sworn in as commissioner on August 4, 2014, and later sworn in as chair on April 15, 2015, to a term expiring on June 30, 2018.

Education: Dartmouth College, B.A.; Harvard Law School, J.D.

Profession: Lawyer.

Political Affiliation: Democrat.

Previous Career: From July 2009 to July 2014, Bay was the director of the Office of Enforcement (OE). Before coming to FERC, Bay was a professor of law at the university of ew Mexico School of Law, where he taught criminal law, evidence, and constitutional law. Bay served in the Department of Justice from 1989 to 2001. From 1989 to 2000, he was an assistant U.S. attorney in the District of Columbia and New Mexico. From 2000 to 2001, he was the U.S. Attorney in the District of New Mexico, having been nominated by President Clinton and confirmed by unanimous consent of the Senate. Prior to his Justice Department service, Bay was an attorney-adviser in the Office of Legal

Adviser at the State Department. He also clerked for the Hon. Otto R. Skopil of the U.S. Court of Appeals for the Ninth Circuit in Portland, Oregon. From 2013 to 2014, Bay was a member of the NCAA Division I Committee on Infractions.

PHILIP D. MOELLER, COMMISSIONER

Appointment: Nominated by President George W. Bush and confirmed by the Senate in July 2006; nominated by President Barack Obama and sworn in on July 16, 2010, for a term expiring in June 2015.

Born: Jan. 5, 1962; Chicago, Ill.

Education: Stanford University, B.A., 1983.

Profession: Energy executive.

Political Affiliation: Republican.

Previous Career: Before becoming a commissioner, Moeller headed the Washington, DC, office of Alliant Energy Corporation. Prior to Alliant Energy, Moeller worked in the Washington office of Calpine Corporation. From 1997 through 2000, Moeller served as an energy policy adviser to Sen. Slade Gorton (R-WA). Before joining Senator Gorton's staff, he served as the staff coordinator for the Washington State Senate Committee on Energy, Utilities, and Telecommunications, where he was responsible for a wide range of policy areas that included energy, telecommunications, conservation, water, and nuclear waste.

TONY CLARK, COMMISSIONER

Appointment: Nominated by President Barack Obama on January 23, 2012; confirmed by the Senate May 24, 2012; sworn in June 15, 2012; term expires June 30, 2016.

Born: Dec. 31, 1971; Platteville, WI.

Education: North Dakota State University, B.A.; University of North Dakota, M.P.A..

Profession: Politician.

Political Affiliation: Republican.

Previous Career: Before joining the commission, Clark served as a member of the North Dakota Public Service Commission (PSC) from 2001 until 2012, most recently as

Federal Energy Regulatory Commission

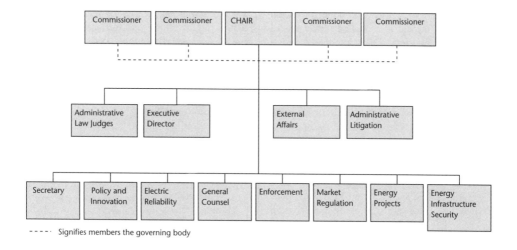

----- Signifies members the governing body

chair. In November 2010, he was elected to serve a one-year term as president of the National Association of Regulatory Utility Commissioners (NARUC), and he is a past chair of the NARUC Telecommunications Committee. Prior to his election to the PSC, he was North Dakota's labor commissioner as well as a state legislator in North Dakota's state House of Representatives from 1994 to 1997.

CHERYL A. LAFLEUR, COMMISSIONER

Appointment: Nominated by President Barack Obama and confirmed by the Senate; sworn in July 2010 for a term expiring June 30, 2014. Confirmed for a second term and sworn in July 29, 2014, to a term expiring on June 30, 2019. Served as commission chair from July 2014 to April 2015.

Education: Princeton University, B.A.; Harvard Law School, J.D.

Profession: Lawyer.

Political Affiliation: Democrat.

Previous Career: LaFleur retired in 2007 as executive vice president and acting chief executive officer of National Grid USA, which delivers electricity to 3.4 million customers in the Northeast. Her previous positions at National Grid USA and its predecessor, New England Electric System, included chief operating officer, president of the New England distribution companies, and general counsel. LaFleur is a frequent speaker on energy issues, particularly reliability and grid security, transmission planning, and enabling clean energy resources. She is a member of the National Association of Regulatory Commissioners Committees on Electricity and Critical Infrastructure.

COLETTE D. HONORABLE, COMMISSIONER

Appointment: Nominated by President Barack Obama in August 2014 and confirmed by the Senate in December 2014; sworn in January 5, 2015, for a term expiring June 30, 2017.

Education: University of Memphis, B.A.; University of Arkansas at Little Rock, School of Law, J.D.

Profession: Lawyer.

Political Affiliation: Democrat.

Previous Career: Before coming to FERC, Ms. Honorable served on the Arkansas Public Service Commission since October 2007 and led the commission as chair since January 2011. Commissioner Honorable began her career at Legal Services, and worked as a consumer protection attorney, civil litigation, and as a Medicaid fraud special prosecutor before serving as chief of staff to then Arkansas Attorney General Mike Beebe. As chair of the Arkansas PSC, Commissioner Honorable oversaw an agency charged with ensuring safe, reliable, and affordable retail electric service. Honorable is a past president of the National Association of Regulatory Utility Commissioners (NARUC), where she represented NARUC on an array of issues ranging from pipeline safety to reliability, resilience, and diversity of both energy supply and the workforce. She testified before Congress on multiple occasions and advocated for infrastructure development to ensure safe, clean, reliable, and affordable utility services. She also chaired the association's Pipeline Safety Task Force and its Anybody Can Serve, So Let's Conserve energy efficiency campaign.

Headquarters and Divisions

COMMISSION

The commissioners make all final decisions on matters regulated by FERC. These include setting limits on rates and charges for the interstate transportation and sale of natural gas; issuing certificates for the construction and operation of facilities for the transportation of gas by pipeline and approving abandonment of such facilities and service; setting rates, terms, and conditions for interstate transmission and wholesale sales of electric energy; issuing licenses and permits for hydroelectric plants; acting on proposed mergers involving electric utilities and dispositions of facilities; acting on certain issuances of securities and assumptions of liabilities by electric utilities; acting on certain interlocking directorates involving electric utilities; setting limits on oil pipeline rates, charges, and valuations; and requiring regulated electric and natural gas companies to follow a uniform system of accounts.

The chair is responsible for the executive and administrative operation of the commission, including appointment of administrative law judges, the selection of personnel (including the executive director), and the supervision of FERC personnel.

Chair
    Norman C. Bay . . . . (202) 502–8000
Commissioners
    Philip D. Moeller. . . . . (202) 502–8852
    Tony Clark . . . . (202) 502–6501
    Cheryl A. LaFleur . . . . (202) 502–8961
    Colette D. Honorable . . . . (202) 502–8798

OFFICE OF ADMINISTRATIVE LAW JUDGES AND DISPUTE RESOLUTION

Administrative law judges preside over hearings for the resolution of issues concerning the Federal Power Act and the Natural Gas Act, conduct hearings, and issue initial decisions on actions taken under the authority of the secretary of energy on which a departmental level hearing and on-the-record determination have been made. The office conducts hearings delegated to FERC under the Interstate Commerce Act, the Natural Gas Policy Act, and the Public Utility Regulatory Policies Act. The administrative law judges play a judicial role and are, in effect, the trial judiciary of the agency. On all cases set for hearing by the commission, the judges preside over the hearing and issue an initial decision at its conclusion.

Chief Administrative Law Judge
    Curtis L. Wagner Jr.. . . . . (202) 502–8500
Chief of Staff
    Martha E. Altamar . . . . (202) 502–8654
Administration Officer
    Susie J. Waller. . . . . (202) 502–8824
Administrative Law Judges
    Philip C. Baten. . . . . (202) 502–6697
    Michael J. Cianci Jr.. . . . . (202) 502–8309
    Carmen A. Cintron. . . . . (202) 502–8545
    David Coffman . . . . (202) 502–6504
    Judith A. Dowd . . . . (202) 502–8557
    John P. Dring . . . . (202) 502–6860

Steven A. Glazer . . . . (202) 502–6487
Michael J. Haubner . . . . (202) 502–8161
Karen V. Johnson. . . . . (202) 502–6412
Dawn Scholz . . . . (202) 502–8110
Steven L. Sterner . . . . (202) 502–6553
Jennifer Whang . . . . (202) 502–6744
H. Peter Young. . . . . (202) 502–8550

Dispute Resolution Service

The Dispute Resolution Service fosters the use of alternative dispute resolution (ADR) processes in oil, gas, electric, and hydroelectric proceedings, and for disputes within the commission. It is neutral and independent, and provides ADR services, such as convening sessions, facilitation, and mediation. It is available to assist parties in screening disputes for ADR application, and also helps develop programs for ADR education and training.

Director
Deborah M. Osborne . . . . (202) 502–8831
Toll-free . . . . (877) 337–2237

OFFICE OF ADMINISTRATIVE LITIGATION

The Office of Administrative Litigation litigates or otherwise resolves cases set for hearing. The lawyers and technical staff represent the public interest and seek to litigate or settle cases in a timely, efficient, and equitable manner while ensuring the outcomes are consistent with commission policy.

Director
Ted Gerarden. (202) 502–6100

OFFICE OF THE EXECUTIVE DIRECTOR

The Office of the Executive Director (OED) oversees and directs the executive and administrative operations of the commission including administrative support, information technology, human resources, organizational management, logistics, procurement, financial services, financial policy, budgets, internal control and evaluations, and management, administrative, and payroll system strategic plan. The OED advises the chair of potential issues and concerns in the areas of management studies and related financial reviews, productivity, and performance audits.

Executive Director
Anton C. Porter. . . . . (202) 502–8300

OFFICE OF THE SECRETARY

The Office of the Secretary serves as the official focal point through which all filings are made for all proceedings before the commission, notices of proceedings are given, and from which all official actions are issued by the commission. The secretary promulgates and publishes all orders, rules, and regulations of the commission and prescribes the issuance date for these unless such date is prescribed by the commission.

Secretary of the Commission
Kimberly D. Bose . . . . (202) 502–8400

OFFICE OF ELECTRIC RELIABILITY

The Office of Electric Reliability helps protect and improve the reliability of the nation's bulk power system through regulatory oversight. The office oversees the development and review of mandatory reliability and security standards and compliance with approved mandatory standards for the bulk power system.

Director
Michael Bardee . . . . (202) 502–8600

Deputy Director
Edward "Ted" Franks . . . . (202) 502–6311

Compliance
Mark Hegerle. (202) 502–8287

Engineering, Planning, and Operations
Nano Sierra . . . . (202) 502–8479

Reliability Standards and Security
Cynthia Pointer . . . . (202) 502–6069

OFFICE OF ENERGY INFRASTRUCTURE SECURITY

The Office of Energy Infrastructure Security (OEIS) provides leadership, expertise, and assistance to the commission to identify, communicate, and seek comprehensive solutions to potential risks to FERC-jurisdictional facilities from cyber-attacks and such physical threats as electromagnetic pulses.

Director
Joseph H. McClelland. . . . . (202) 502–8867

Deputy Director
David Andrejcak. . . . . (202) 502–6721

OFFICE OF ENERGY MARKETS REGULATION

The Office of Energy Markets Regulation (OEMR) was created to integrate the commission's economic regulation of the electric, natural gas, and oil industries. OEMR deals with matters involving markets, tariffs, and rates relating to electric, natural gas, and oil pipeline facilities and service; and the reliability of the electric grid. The office plays a lead role in monitoring, promoting, and maintaining competitive markets and refining compliance auditing. The OEMR looks at how it can ensure lighter-handed regulation for energy transactions in competitive markets, while standardizing terms and conditions for those transactions that will continue to be regulated on a cost basis. This office reflects the convergence of electric and natural gas concerns already taking place in the energy industry.

Director
Jamie Simler . . . . (202) 502–6700

Deputy Director
Anna V. Cochrane. . . . . (202) 502–6357

Administration and Operations Staff
Peggy Ford . . . . (202) 502–8505

Electric Power Regulation
Eastern Region: Kurt Longo . . . . (202) 502–8048
Central Region: Penny Murrell . . . . . . (202) 502–8531
Western Region: Steve Rodgers. . . . . . (202) 502–8227
Pipeline Regulation: Nils Nichols . . . . (202) 502–8638

OFFICE OF ENERGY POLICY AND INNOVATION

The Office of Energy Policy and Innovation (OEPI) provides leadership in the emerging issues affecting wholesale and interstate energy markets. OEPI focuses, among other things, on demand response, energy efficiency, smart grid standards, and electric vehicles, taking into account energy and environmental concerns.

Director
J. Arnold Quinn .... (202) 502–8693
Deputy Director
Jignasa Gadani .... (202) 502–8608
Policy Development
Jeffrey Dennis .... (202) 502–6532
Economic and Technical Analysis
Michael McLaughlin .... (202) 502–6135

OFFICE OF ENERGY PROJECTS

The mission of the office is to foster economic and environmental benefits for the nation through the approval and oversight of hydroelectric and natural gas pipeline energy projects that are in the public interest.

Director
Ann F. Miles .... (202) 502–8700
Deputy Director
Michael McGehee .... (202) 502–8700
Dam Safety and Inspections
William H. Allerton .... (202) 502–6025
Gas Environment and Engineering
Terry Turpin .... (202) 502–8558
Hydropower Administration and Compliance
Jennifer Hill .... (202) 502–6797
Hydropower Licensing
Vince Yearick..................... (202) 502–6174
Pipeline Certificates
John Wood (acting) .... (202) 502–8113

OFFICE OF ENFORCEMENT

The Office of Enforcement (OE) helps the commission improve its understanding of energy market operations and ensure vigilant and fair oversight of those areas under commission jurisdiction.

OE oversees and assesses the operations of the nation's gas, oil pipeline, and electricity markets. Its functions include understanding energy markets and risk management, measuring market performance, investigating compliance violations, and analyzing market data. The office has a multidisciplinary team of economists, engineers, attorneys, auditors, data management specialists, financial analysts, regulatory policy analysts, energy analysts, and support staff.

Director
Larry R. Parkinson .... (202) 502–8051
Deputy Director
Lee Ann Watson .... (202) 502–6317
Analytics and Surveillance
Sean Collins..................... (202) 502–8269
Audits and Accounting
Bryan Craig .... (202) 502–8741
Energy Market Oversight
Jerome Pederson .... (202) 502–8903
Investigations
David Applebaum (acting) .... (202) 502–8186
Enforcement Hotline
Toll-free .... (888) 889–8030

OFFICE OF EXTERNAL AFFAIRS

See Information Sources.

OFFICE OF THE GENERAL COUNSEL

The Office of the General Counsel (OGC) provides legal services to the commission. OGC represents the commission before the courts and Congress and is responsible for the legal phases of the commission's activities.

General Counsel
David Morenoff................... (202) 502–6000
Deputy General Counsel
Christy Walsh .... (202) 502–6523
Administration and Operations
Parthenia Campbell .... (202) 502–6160
Energy Markets—1
Lawrence R. Greenfield .... (202) 502–6415
Energy Markets—2
Deborah B. Leahy .... (202) 502–8378
Energy Projects
Jacqueline Holmes................. (202) 502–8198
Solicitor
Robert Solomon .... (202) 502–8257
General and Administrative Law
Charles Beamon .... (202) 502–8780

Regional Offices FERC/ Hydropower Licensing

ATLANTA

3700 Crestwood Pkwy. N.W., 9th Floor
Duluth, GA 30096
(678) 245–3075
Fax (678) 245–3010
Wayne King, regional engineer

CHICAGO

230 S. Dearborn St., #3130
Chicago, IL 60604
(312) 596–4437
Fax (312) 596–4460
John Zygaj, regional engineer

NEW YORK

19 West 34th St., #400
New York, NY 10001–3006
(212) 273–5911
Fax (212) 631–8124
Gerald Cross, regional engineer

PORTLAND

805 Southwest Broadway, #550
Portland, OR 97205
(503) 552–2715
Fax (503) 552–2799
Douglas Johnson, regional engineer

SAN FRANCISCO

100 1st St., #2300
San Francisco, CA 94105
(415) 369–3318

YBP Library Services

FEDERAL REGULATORY DIRECTORY.

             17TH ED.   Cloth   1044 P.
WASHINGTON: CQ PRESS, 2016
SER: FEDERAL REGULATORY DIRECTORY.

ANNUAL DIRECTORY.

ISBN 1483384772   **Library PO#** STANDING ORDERS

	List	215.00 USD
3421 METROPOLITAN STATE UNIVERS	**Disc**	6.0%
App. Date 1/13/16 2182-80	**Net**	202.10 USD

SUBJ: INDEPENDENT REGULATORY COMMISSIONS--U.S.--
DIRECT.

CLASS KF5406   DEWEY# 351.02573   LEVEL GEN-AC

YBP Library Services

FEDERAL REGULATORY DIRECTORY.

             17TH ED.   Cloth   1044 P.
WASHINGTON: CQ PRESS, 2016
SER: FEDERAL REGULATORY DIRECTORY.

ANNUAL DIRECTORY.

ISBN 1483384772   **Library PO#** STANDING ORDERS

	List	215.00 USD
3421 METROPOLITAN STATE UNIVERS	**Disc**	6.0%
App. Date 1/13/16 2182-80	**Net**	202.10 USD

SUBJ: INDEPENDENT REGULATORY COMMISSIONS--U.S.--
DIRECT.

CLASS KF5406   DEWEY# 351.02573   LEVEL GEN-AC

Fax (415) 369–3322
Frank Blackett, regional engineer

CONGRESSIONAL ACTION

Director, Government Affairs Division
Chris Murray . . . . (202) 502–8694

Committees and Subcommittees

HOUSE APPROPRIATIONS COMMITTEE
Subcommittee on Energy and Water Development, and Related Agencies
2362-B RHOB, Washington, DC 20515
(202) 225–3421

HOUSE ENERGY AND COMMERCE COMMITTEE
Subcommittee on Energy and Power
2125 RHOB Washington, DC 20515
(202) 225–2927

SENATE APPROPRIATIONS COMMITTEE
Subcommittee on Energy and Water Development
SDOB-142, Washington, DC 20510–6025
(202) 224–2104

SENATE ENERGY AND NATURAL RESOURCES COMMITTEE
Subcommittee on Energy
SDOB-301, Washington, DC 201510–6150
(202) 224–4971
Subcommittee on Water and Power
SDOB-304, Washington, DC 20510–6150
(202) 224–4971

Legislation
FERC was created by the **Department of Energy Organization Act** (91 Stat. 565, 42 U.S.C. 7101 note). Section 401(a) of that act assigned to FERC all of the responsibilities that had been carried out by the Federal Power Commission under the Federal Power Act, the Natural Gas Act, the Emergency Petroleum Allocation Act, and the Energy Policy and Conservation Act. The oil pipeline valuation and rate regulation functions of the Interstate Commerce Commission also were transferred to FERC. Signed by the president Aug. 4, 1977, the Energy Organization Act brought together in one central cabinet-level agency all the federal government's energy responsibilities. FERC began operations on Oct. 1, 1977.

The Energy Organization Act also gave FERC powers over oil pricing and some administrative procedures in the Energy Department. Although oil pricing has been deregulated, FERC still has jurisdiction over appeals of Economic Regulatory Administration decisions concerning oil pricing violations that occurred from 1973 to 1980.

FERC administers the following acts in full or in part:

Federal Water Power Act of 1920 (41 Stat. 1063, 16 U.S.C. 791). Signed by the president June 10, 1920. Established the Federal Power Commission (FPC), which then consisted of the secretaries of war, interior, and agri-culture. The FPC was empowered to grant preliminary licenses, to study potential sites, and to issue licenses for the development of hydroelectric power plants on the nation's waterways. The act became part I of the Federal Power Act in 1935.

Federal Power Act of 1935 (41 Stat. 1063, 16 U.S.C. 791–828c). Signed by the president Aug. 26, 1935. Incorporated the Federal Water Power Act and added two new parts. Part II gave the commission responsibility for regulating the interstate transmission and wholesale sale of electric energy and empowered the Federal Power Commission to encourage voluntary interconnection and coordination of facilities for the generation, transmission, and sale of electric energy. Part III gave the commission authority to prescribe a uniform system of accounts and to inspect the books and records of licensees and public utilities.

Natural Gas Act of 1938 (52 Stat. 821, 15 U.S.C. 717). Signed by the president June 21, 1938. Gave the Federal Power Commission jurisdiction over the interstate transportation of natural gas, the wholesale price of natural gas in interstate commerce, and the accounting systems used by natural gas companies.

Natural Gas Policy Act of 1978 (92 Stat. 3350, 15 U.S.C. 3301 note, 42 U.S.C. 7255). Signed by the president Nov. 9, 1978. One of five parts of the National Energy Act, the act deregulated the price of natural gas over a five-year period, established a program of incentive prices for newly discovered gas, and required the development of an incremental pricing plan to transfer the burden of higher gas prices to the largest users of natural gas.

Public Utility Regulatory Policies Act of 1978 (92 Stat. 3117, 16 U.S.C. 2601). Signed by the president Nov. 9, 1978. One of five parts of the National Energy Act, the act required state utility commissions and other regulatory agencies to consider energy-saving methods, such as pricing electricity at lower levels in off-peak hours. It also gave FERC greater control over electric ratemaking.

Electric Consumers Protection Act of 1986 (100 Stat. 1243, 16 U.S.C. 791a note). Signed by the president Oct. 16, 1986. Amended the Federal Power Act to enhance competition among applicants in hydroelectric power relicensing cases and to provide that equal consideration be given to developmental and environmental concerns in the licensing of hydroelectric power projects.

Natural Gas Wellhead Decontrol Act of 1989 (103 Stat. 157, 15 U.S.C. 3301 note). Signed by the president July 26, 1989. Provided for the phased elimination of all remaining wellhead price and nonprice controls on the first sale of natural gas by Jan. 1, 1993.

Federal Energy Regulatory Commission Member Term Act of 1990 (104 Stat. 135, 42 U.S.C. 7101 note). Signed by the president April 11, 1990. Amended the Department of Energy Organization Act to provide for five-year, staggered terms for members of the commission. The new terms apply only to those appointed or reappointed as members of the commission after the date of enactment.

Energy Policy Act of 1992 (106 Stat. 2775, 42 U.S.C. 13201 note). Signed by the president Oct. 24, 1992. Promoted energy conservation and efficiency and increased domestic energy production to ensure economic growth and to protect national security.

Energy Act of 2000 (114 Stat. 2029, 42 U.S.C. 6201 note). Signed by the president Nov. 9, 2000. Reauthorized a program under the Energy Policy and Conservation Act that provided for continued operation of U.S. strategic petroleum reserves. Amended the Federal Power Act to direct FERC to discontinue its licensing and regulatory authority over certain small hydroelectric power projects in Alaska. Directed FERC to review federal hydroelectric licensing procedures.

Pipeline Safety Improvement Act of 2002 (116 Stat. 2985, 49 U.S.C. 6201 note). Signed by the president Dec. 17, 2002. Directed FERC to study and report to specified congressional committees on a natural gas pipeline transmission network and storage facilities.

Energy Policy Act of 2005 (119 Stat. 594, 42 U.S.C. 15801 note). Signed by the president Aug. 8, 2005. Repealed the Public Utility Holding Company Act (PUHCA) of 1935. Established a long-range, comprehensive national energy policy. Provided incentives for increased domestic oil and natural gas production and for the development of energy-efficient technologies and conservation methods. Encouraged nuclear power plant construction. Required modernization of the national electric grid. Granted FERC authority over the construction, expansion, and operation of LNG terminals. Gave FERC additional powers to review mergers within the energy industry. Directed FERC to establish market-based rates for the interstate transmission of electric energy by public utilities to benefit consumers by ensuring reliability.

Federal Energy Independence and Security Act of 2007 (121 Stat. 1492, 42 U.S.C. 17001 note). Signed by the president Dec. 20, 2007. Prohibited manipulative or deceptive devices or contrivances in connection with the purchase or sale of natural gas, electric energy, or transportation or transmission services. Directed the National Institute of Standards and Technology (NIST) to coordinate the development of Smart Grid standards, which the FERC would promulgate through official rulemakings.

American Recovery and Reinvestment Act of 2009 (123 Stat. 115, 26 U.S.C. 1 note). Signed by the president Feb. 17, 2009. Required FERC to adopt standards and protocols necessary to facilitate the functionality and interoperability of Smart Grid technology in the interstate transmission of electric energy and in regional and wholesale electricity markets.

■ INFORMATION SOURCES

Internet

Agency website: www.ferc.gov. Comprehensive website provides access to documents filed with, and issued by, the commission; decisions and notices; dockets and submission guidelines; the dispute resolution service, publications; and extensive e-Library services.

Information on commission meetings is also posted on the website, along with FERC regulations and enabling legislation. FERC Online provides a range of e-Services,

www.ferc.gov/docs-filing/ferconline.asp. Available services include e-Filing, e-Register, e-Subscription, e-Service, and e-Library.

For assistance . . . . (202) 502–6652
Toll-free . . . . (866) 208–3676

Telephone Contacts

General information . . . . (202) 502–8200
Toll-free . . . . (866) 208–3372
Recorded information . . . . (202) 502–8627
TTY . . . . (202) 502–8659
E-Library and Online Support Hotline . . . .
. . . . (202) 502–6652; (866) 208–3676
Enforcement Hotline . . . . (888) 889–8030

Information and Publications

KEY OFFICES

FERC External Affairs

888 1st St. N.E.
Washington, DC 20426
(202) 502–8004
(866) 208–3372
Fax (202) 208–2106
Leonard Tao, director, (202) 502–8214
Andrea Spring, deputy director
E-mail: customer@ferc.gov

The Office of External Affairs is the commission's primary contact point with the Congress; the general public; international, federal, state, and local government offices; interest groups; and the news media. It is responsible for developing public relations and other outreach strategies for the commission.

Governmental Affairs Division

888 1st St. N.E.
Washington, DC 20426
(202) 502–8004
Fax (202) 208–2106
Chris Murray, director
John Peschke, Senate liaison
Jehmal Hudson, House liaison

Responsible for communication with the Congress and all federal agencies.

Division of State, International, and Public Affairs

888 1st St. N.E.
Washington, DC 20426
(202) 502–8092
Toll-free (866) 208–3372
Sandra Waldstein, director, (202) 502–8092
Mary O'Driscoll, press services, (202) 502–8680

Responsible for public outreach, including to state and local governments, as well as internationally, and Web services, along with all press services.

Public Inquiries

888 1st St. N.E.
Washington, DC 20426
(202) 502–6088
Toll-free (866) 208–3372
TTY (202) 502–8659
E-mail: customer@ferc.gov

Responds to questions from the public and other government agencies.

Public Reference Room

888 1st St. N.E., #2A
Washington, DC 20426
(202) 502–8371
E-mail: public.referenceroom@ferc.gov
Hours: 8:30 a.m. to 5:00 p.m.

The Public Reference Room, along with the website's e-Library, are the commission's primary channels for disseminating information, providing a wide range of holdings on the topic of energy. Interested parties may use the public workstations to access FERC's website and to view FERC documents at no charge. The website's e-Library system is a records information system that contains more than twenty years of documents submitted to and issued by FERC.

Freedom of Information/Critical Energy Infrastructure Information

Contact: Toyia Johnson
(202) 502–8389
E-mail: foia-ceii@ferc.gov

Members of the public may obtain nonpublic or privileged information by submitting a FOIA request. FERC is protecting energy facilities by restricting public access to Critical Energy Infrastructure Information.

PUBLICATIONS

Citizen's Guides are available on the website at www .ferc.gov/for-citizens/citizen-guides.asp or through the Public Reference Room. Publications are available through the Government Printing Office, (202) 512–1800 or book store.gpo.gov. Publications include information about FERC programs, electric power, gas, liquefied natural gas, hydropower, and oil pipelines. Titles include *An Interstate Natural Gas Facility on My Land: What Do I Need To Know?, Federal Guidelines for Dam Safety,* and *Annual Energy Outlook 2013 with Projections to 2040.* Some publications, such as *Guide to Electronic Information at FERC,* are available to view on www.ferc. gov as well. The Public Reference Room, along with the website's e-Library, are the commission's primary channels for disseminating information. E-Library is an online records information system that contains more than twenty years of documents submitted to and issued by FERC. Interested parties may use the public work-stations to access FERC's website and to view FERC documents at no charge.

DATA AND STATISTICS

FERC requires regulated industries to file various reports on production, income, expenditures, and other items. These reports generally adhere to a format designed by FERC and are assigned a form number and title. Reports are available through the Public Reference Room, and the FERC website.

MEETINGS

Commission meetings usually are scheduled the third Thursday of each month, except in August, and are held in Room 2C of FERC headquarters, 888 lst St. N.E., Washington, DC 20426.

Meetings are open to the general public, as are most hearings, conferences, and other regulatory proceedings. Transcripts of special meetings usually are available the morning following the hearing either in the Public Reference Room or online. Free Web casts are available as well.

The Office of the Secretary can supply details on meeting schedules and agendas; (202) 502–8400 or online at www.ferc.gov/EventCalendar.

Reference Resources

LIBRARY

See Public Reference Room (above).

DOCKETS

FERC Public Reference Room

888 1st St. N.E., #2A
Washington, DC 20426
(202) 502–8371
Hours: 8:30 a.m. to 5:00 p.m.

The files for rulemaking proceedings and other formal activities of the commission are under the jurisdiction of the Office of the Secretary; however, dockets may be examined and copied at the Public Reference Room. Docket numbers are included in all press releases and in *Federal Register* notices; they also can be obtained from FERC reference staff. Copying services may be arranged for those unable to visit. Transcripts from public hearings also are available for inspection and copying.

Dockets relating to FERC actions can be found at the FERC Online e-Library: http://elibrary.ferc.gov. Federal dockets are also available at www.regulations.gov. (*See appendix for Searching and Commenting on Regulations: Regulations.gov.*)

RULES AND REGULATIONS

FERC rules and regulations are published in the *Code of Federal Regulations,* Title 5, Chapter XXIV, Part 3401; Title 18, Chapter I, Parts 1–399. Proposed rules, new final rules, and updates to the *Code of Federal Regulations* are published in the *Federal Register.* (*See appendix for information on how to obtain and use these publications.*) The *Federal Register* may be accessed at www.federalregister.gov and the *Code of Federal*

Regulations at www.archives.gov/federal-register/cfr; also see the federal government's website www.regulations.gov (*see appendix*).

Other Information Sources

RELATED AGENCIES

National Energy Information Center

Energy Information Administration E1-30
1000 Independence Ave. S.W.
Washington, DC 20585
(202) 586–8800
Fax (202) 586–0114
E-mail: InfoCtr@eia.doe.gov
Internet: www.eia.gov

Provides statistical data on energy; publishes analytical reports and numerous periodicals approximately annually. Topics covered include supply-and-demand data, pricing, imports and exports, and projections.

DOE Office of Scientific and Technical Information

P.O. Box 62
Oak Ridge, TN 37831
(865) 576–1188
STI Documents Request (865) 576–8401
Fax (865) 576–2865
Internet: www.osti.gov

Handles inquiries about *National Library of Energy*, a resource for energy literacy, innovation, and security, which is national in scope; and *Energy Technology Data Exchange (ETDE),* which pertains to international energy-related information, also found at www.etde.org.

NONGOVERNMENTAL RESOURCES

The following are some key resources for information on FERC and related energy issues.

Access Intelligence

4 Choke Cherry Rd., 2nd Floor
Rockville, MD 20850
(301) 354–2000
Toll-free (888) 707–5814
Internet: www.accessintel.com

Advanstar Communications, Inc.

2450 E. Colorado Ave., # 300
Santa Monica, CA 90404
(310) 857–7500
Fax (310) 857–7510
Internet: www.advanstar.com

American Petroleum Institute

1220 L St. N.W., 12th Floor
Washington, DC 20005–4070
(202) 682–8000
Fax (202) 682–8110
Internet: www.api.org

American Public Power Association

2451 Crystal Drive, #1000
Arlington, VA 22202
(202) 467–2900
(800) 515–2772
Fax (202) 467–2910
Internet: www.publicpower.org

Association of Oil Pipelines

1808 Eye St. N.W., #300
Washington, DC 20006
(202) 408–7970
Fax (202) 280–1949
Internet: www.aopl.org

Barrows Company

116 E. 66th St., #1-B
New York, NY 10065
(212) 772–1199
(800) 227–7697
Fax (212) 288–7242
Internet: www.barrowscompany.com

Proquest (formally The Dialog)

2250 Perimeter Park, #300
Morrisville, NC 27560
(919) 804–6400
(800) 334–2564
Fax (919) 804–6410
Internet: www.proquest.com
Provides access to energy-related databases.

Edison Electric Institute

701 Pennsylvania Ave. N.W.
Washington, DC 20004–2696
(202) 508–5000
Fax (202) 508–5038
Internet: www.eei.org

Energy Bar Association

1990 M St. N.W., #715
Washington, DC 20036
(202) 223–5625
Fax (202) 833–5596
Internet: www.eba-net.org

Global Insight

24 Hartwell Ave.
Lexington, MA 02421–3158
(781) 301–9100
(800) 447–2273
Fax (781) 301–9407
Internet: www.globalinsight.net

Hart Energy

1616 S. Voss, #1000
Houston, TX 77057
(713) 260–6400
Internet: www.hartenergy.com

Virginia office
1749 Old Meadow Rd., #301
McLean, VA 22102
(703) 891–4800
Fax (703) 891–4880

McGraw-Hill Companies, E-Commerce
1221 Avenue of the Americas
New York, NY 10020
(212) 512–2000
(212) 904–2000
(877) 833–5524
Fax (614) 759–3749
Internet: www.mhfi.com

National Association of Regulatory Utility Commissioners
1101 Vermont Ave. N.W., #200
Washington, DC 20005–3521
(202) 898–2200
Fax (202) 898–2213
Internet: www.naruc.org

National Rural Electric Cooperative Association
4301 Wilson Blvd.
Arlington, VA 22203–1860
(703) 907–5500
Fax (703) 907–5511
Internet: www.nreca.coop

PennWell Publishing Co.
1421 S. Sheridan Rd.
Tulsa, OK 74112
(918) 835–3161
(800) 331–4463
Fax (918) 831–9497
Internet: www.pennwell.com

Platts (Division of McGraw-Hill)
2 Penn Plaza, 25th Floor
New York, NY 10121
(212) 904–3070
(800) 752–8878
Internet: www.platts.com

Utility Data Institute
1200 G St. N.W., #1000
Washington, DC 20005–3802
(202) 942–2000
Internet: www.platts.com/udi-data-directories

U.S. Chamber of Commerce
Environment, Technology, and
    Regulatory Affairs
1615 H St. N.W.
Washington, DC 20062–2000
(202) 659–6000
(800) 638–6582
Fax (202) 887–3445
Internet: www.uschamber.com

U.S. Energy Association
1300 Pennsylvania Ave. N.W., #550
Washington, DC 20004
(202) 312–1230
Fax (202) 682–1682
Internet: www.usea.org

Wolters Kluwer
(formerly Commerce Clearing House)
2700 Lake Cook Rd.
Riverwoods, IL 60015
(212) 771–0600
(800) 835–5224
Internet: www.wklawbusiness.com

Federal Reserve System

20th St. and Constitution Ave. N.W.,
Washington, DC 20551
Internet: www.federalreserve.gov

◼ INTRODUCTION

The Federal Reserve System (the Fed) is an independent regulatory and monetary policy-making agency, established by the Federal Reserve Act in 1913. The Fed is administered by a board composed of seven governors, nominated by the president and confirmed by the Senate. The president also designates two of the members to serve as chair and vice chair for four years. Both the chair and vice chair may be redesignated. A governor's term is fourteen years, but few serve that long, and often an individual is appointed to fill the remaining portion of a term. Members who have served a full term may not be reappointed.

Responsibilities

The Fed's major responsibility is to conduct the federal government's monetary policy. Through the buying and selling of government securities, the Fed directly influences the supply of credit and the level of key short-term interest rates, which in turn strongly affect the pace of economic activity, unemployment, and prices.

In addition, the Fed regulates certain credit activities, collects economic data, oversees the activities of bank holding companies, and acts as the primary federal government supervisor of state-chartered banks that have joined the Federal Reserve System. These banks are referred to as state member banks. State-chartered banks that are not members of the Fed are supervised by the Federal Deposit Insurance Corporation (FDIC) (p. 156); federally chartered banks are regulated by the Office of the Comptroller of the Currency (OCC) (p. 839).

In executing its monetary policy-making functions, the Fed

- Determines the level of reserves that must be kept on deposit with the twelve Federal Reserve district banks by all financial institutions.
- Lends money through its "discount window" to banks that encounter unexpected deposit fluctuations and need to enlarge their reserves or pay depositors. Serves as the "lender of last resort" when financial markets are in disarray. Reviews and confirms the "discount rate" charged on such loans by the Federal Reserve district banks.
- Buys and sells government securities in the open market, thereby directly increasing or reducing the amount of bank cash reserves and short-term market interest rates ("open market operations").
- Collects and analyzes extensive data on the money supply, credit, industrial production, and other economic activity.
- Supervises and examines the activities of the twelve Federal Reserve district banks.
- Supervises the issuance and distribution of Federal Reserve notes and monitors the amount of currency in circulation.
- Regulates various types of credit, such as for purchasing stocks and other equity securities.
- Serves as fiscal agent for the U.S. government, selling, servicing, and redeeming U.S. Treasury securities.
- Buys and sells foreign currencies, in cooperation with the Treasury Department or on behalf of foreign central banks, to counteract disorderly conditions in foreign exchange markets.
- Supervises the government securities broker and dealer activities of state member banks, foreign banks and

GLOSSARY

Bank holding company (BHC)—A company that owns or controls one or more banks. The Fed regulates and supervises BHCs, approves bank mergers and acquisitions, and maintains authority over a BHC even if the banks it owns are under the supervision of the FDIC or OCC.

Discount rate—The interest rate district Federal Reserve banks charge on loans to depository institutions (banks, savings banks, thrifts, and credit unions).

Discount window—An expression used to describe the mechanism by which the Fed makes loans to depository institutions.

Fed—A widely used nickname for the Federal Reserve System.

Federal funds rate—The rate commercial banks pay to borrow money from each other on a short-term basis, generally overnight, and typically to meet reserve requirements.

Interlocking directorates—Boards of directors having some members in common, so that the corporations concerned are to some extent under the same control.

National bank—Bank that is chartered and regulated by the OCC. National banks are required to be members of the Federal Reserve System.

NOW accounts (negotiable-order-of-withdrawal accounts)—These are interest-bearing accounts on which checks may be drawn.

Reserves—Money that financial institutions must keep as cash in their vaults.

State member bank—A bank that is chartered by a state and is a member of the Federal Reserve System, which supervises these banks.

State nonmember bank—A bank that is chartered by a state but is not a member of the Federal Reserve System. These banks are supervised by the FDIC.

their uninsured U.S. branches, and foreign branches and affiliates of U.S. banks.

As one of the five major federal regulatory agencies for financial institutions, the Fed

- Registers, regulates, and supervises bank holding companies; reviews acquisition and expansion plans of bank holding companies to ensure they do not foster anticompetitive and monopolistic behavior.
- Approves establishment of foreign branches of member banks and regulates their activities; regulates and supervises the foreign activities of U.S. banks.
- Charters and regulates international banking subsidiaries (known as Edge corporations) of member banks.
- Approves acquisitions of banks, thrifts, and commercial-lending offices in the United States by foreign-owned banks; approves opening of branch offices by

foreign banks; has authority to close state-chartered branches and affiliate offices of foreign banks that are not subject to comprehensive regulation in their home countries (and recommend such action to the OCC for federally chartered branches of foreign banks); supervises certain nonbank offices of state-chartered, foreign-owned banks; enforces consumer protection laws as they apply to foreign-owned U.S. banks; monitors capital standards for foreign banks in the United States.

- Provides check clearing, settlement, wire transfer, automated clearinghouse, and other services to the banking system.
- Issues regulations requiring meaningful disclosure of credit terms offered by state member banks.
- Issues rules prohibiting discrimination by banks in granting credit.
- Participates in the deliberations of the Federal Financial Institutions Examination Council, which was established in 1978 to develop uniform examination and supervision practices for all depository institutions' regulatory agencies. Other members of the council include the FDIC, OCC, the Consumer Financial Protection Bureau (*p. 387*), and the National Credit Union Administration (*p. 424*).

As the primary regulator of state-chartered banks that have joined the Federal Reserve System (state member banks), the Fed

- Regulates and supervises the activities of state member banks, including their lending practices and financial conditions.
- Approves establishment of new facilities and branches by state member banks.
- Authorizes the issuance of orders requiring state member banks and bank holding companies to cease and desist from violations of law and unsafe business practices.
- Authorizes the removal from office of bank officers and directors who violate the law, engage in unsafe and unsound practices, or engage in insider loans and arrangements.
- Regulates issuance of credit cards by state member banks.
- Establishes minimum standards for installing and maintaining security systems.
- Enforces statutory restrictions that greatly limit interlocking directorates and overlap of officers among banking companies.
- Regulates mergers, consolidations, and acquisitions when the resulting institution would be a state member bank.

Powers and Authority

The Federal Reserve System is the nation's central bank and is charged with making and administering policy for the nation's credit and monetary affairs. It also has supervisory and regulatory power over bank holding companies, state-chartered banks that are members of the system, overseas activities of U.S. banks, and U.S.-based operations of foreign-owned banks.

STRUCTURE

The Federal Reserve System consists of five major parts: (1) the board of governors, (2) the Federal Open Market Committee (FOMC), (3) the twelve Federal Reserve banks, (4) the three advisory councils, and (5) the member banks of the system.

The Board of Governors

The board is responsible for administering and supervising the Federal Reserve System. It consists of seven members who are appointed by the president and confirmed by the Senate. Board members are appointed for fourteen-year terms, and no two members may come from the same Federal Reserve district. The chair and vice chair of the board are named by the president to four-year terms and may be renamed as long as their terms have not expired.

Although the Fed is designed to be independent of political influences, the chair often meets with administration officials to discuss economic policy and since 1978 is required by law to appear biannually before the House and Senate Banking committees to give lawmakers an economic update. In practice, members of the board testify much more often than that on a wide variety of economic issues.

The board supervises the twelve Federal Reserve District banks and appoints some members of each bank's board of directors. Each bank's board appoints its president and vice presidents, but the Federal Reserve Board confirms those appointments. In addition, the Fed coordinates the Federal Reserve System's economic research and data collection and reviews all publications. It must vote to approve acquisitions by bank holding companies, some bank mergers, and certain other commercial bank actions.

The board's primary function, however, is the formulation of monetary policy. In addition to approving proposed changes in the discount rate, it has authority to change reserve requirements within specified limits and to set margin requirements for the financing of securities traded on national securities exchanges.

Federal Open Market Committee

The FOMC, with twelve voting members, is the system's most important monetary policy-making body. The committee meets eight times a year in Washington, DC, and consults by telephone when a change of policy is called for between meeting dates. It is composed of the board of governors plus the president of the New York Reserve Bank. Four other voting positions rotate among the eleven remaining Reserve bank presidents, though all twelve Reserve bank presidents typically attend each session of the FOMC and participate in discussions.

The committee's main responsibility is to establish open market operations and thereby the general course of monetary policy. The FOMC decides the extent to which the system buys and sells government and other securities. Purchases and sales of securities in the open market are undertaken to supply the credit and money needed for long-term economic growth, to offset cyclical economic swings, and to accommodate seasonal demands of businesses and consumers for money and credit. The

committee also issues regulations regarding administration of the discount window.

In addition, the committee oversees the system's operations in foreign exchange markets. Foreign currency transactions are undertaken in conjunction with the Treasury to safeguard the value of the dollar in international exchange markets and to facilitate growth in international liquidity in accordance with the needs of an expanding world economy.

The New York Reserve Bank serves as the committee's agent in making actual purchases and sales. Government securities bought outright are then prorated among the twelve Reserve banks according to a formula based upon their reserve ratios. The foreign department of the New York bank acts as the agent for foreign exchange transactions.

The Federal Reserve Banks

The operations of the Federal Reserve System are conducted through a nationwide network of twelve Federal Reserve banks located in Atlanta, Boston, Chicago, Cleveland, Dallas, Kansas City, Minneapolis, New York, Philadelphia, Richmond, San Francisco, and St. Louis. Branches of Reserve banks have been established in twenty-five additional cities (p. 230).

Each Reserve bank is an incorporated institution with its separate board of directors, consisting of nine members. The Federal Reserve Act requires that directors be divided into three classes. Class A directors, who represent member banks, and Class B directors, who are engaged in pursuits other than banking, are elected by the member banks in each Federal Reserve district. The board of governors appoints the three Class C directors and designates one of them as chair and another as deputy chair of the bank's board. No Class B or Class C director may be an officer, director, or employee of a bank; in addition, Class C directors are prohibited from being stockholders of any bank.

The directors of each Reserve bank oversee the operations of their banks under the overall supervision of the board of governors. They establish, subject to approval by the board, the interest rates the bank may charge on short-term collateral loans to member banks and on any loans that may be extended to nonmember institutions. The directors appoint the bank's president and first vice president subject to approval of the Fed board of governors.

Advisory Councils

To aid the Fed in its work, three advisory councils monitor various issues and offer suggestions to the board and the FOMC. The Federal Advisory Council consists of one member from each of the Federal Reserve districts. The board of directors of each bank annually selects one council member, usually a banker from the district. The council is required to meet in Washington, DC, at least four times a year. It confers with the board of governors on economic and banking matters and makes recommendations regarding the affairs of the system. The Consumer Advisory Council meets three times a year to discuss consumer issues relating to Fed responsibilities. The thirty-member body is made up of bankers, consumer group representatives, academics, and legal experts. The twelve-member Thrift Institutions Advisory Council provides the Fed with information and views on the needs and problems of thrifts. The council is composed of representatives from savings banks, savings and loan associations, and credit unions.

Agency Budget

The Fed receives no appropriation from Congress, and its budget is largely free from congressional scrutiny. Interest paid on government securities purchased by the Fed accounts for about 90 percent of the Fed's earnings. In addition, the Fed earns money from the fees it charges for its services, from interest on discount window loans, and from its foreign currency operations.

Technically, the Federal Reserve System is owned by its member banks. To be admitted to membership, a bank must subscribe a certain percentage of its capital stock and surplus to the Reserve bank in its district. Member banks receive a dividend of 6 percent annually on the value of their paid-in stock. The dividend is exempt from federal, state, and local tax.

The Fed's earnings go first to pay expenses and to pay the 6 percent dividend to member banks on their paid-in stock. Earnings also are used to make any additions to each Reserve bank's surplus to keep it equal to the bank's paid-in stock. Remaining earnings then are paid to the U.S. Treasury. About 90 percent of the Fed's annual income has been paid to the Treasury since the system was established.

Although Congress has no authority over the budgets of the Federal Reserve board of governors or the twelve district banks, since 1978 the General Accounting Office—now the Government Accountability Office (GAO)—has been authorized to audit certain records of the Fed. The GAO is barred from examining international monetary and financial transactions; monetary policy matters, including discount window operations, member bank reserves, securities credit, interest on deposits, and open market operations; FOMC activities; and all communications among Fed personnel relating to exempted activities. The comptroller general is required to report audit results to Congress.

MONETARY POLICY

The Fed closely monitors and takes regular steps to affect the supply of credit and its price, or interest rates, which in turn influence the level of spending and production in the economy. Long-term monetary policy is set by the Fed's board of governors through the discount rate and bank reserve requirements. But short-term policy, which is more central to the economy and market observers, is set in meetings of the FOMC.

The Fed requires all depository institutions to maintain reserves—in the form of cash in their vaults or held in non-interest-bearing accounts at Federal Reserve banks—equal to a certain percentage of their deposits. When the central bank buys Treasury securities from banks, it pays for them by crediting the banks' reserve accounts, giving banks additional money to lend to individuals and corporations. Conversely,

when the Fed sells Treasury securities, it prompts banks to draw down their reserves. To maintain the required level of reserves, banks are forced to pull money out of the system by slowing down their rate of lending or perhaps even calling in some loans.

Most banks meet their reserve requirements by borrowing, usually on an overnight basis, from other institutions that have a temporary surplus. The market-based interest rate for such short-term borrowing, dubbed the federal funds rate, is closely controlled by Fed open market operations, and it is closely watched by financial markets as a sign of changes in available credit. When the Fed seeks to move interest rates up or down, it buys or sells Treasury securities and thereby expands or contracts bank reserves, altering the supply of money to meet reserve requirements. A tighter supply of lendable reserves results in a higher price to borrow, or a higher federal funds rate; a looser supply results in a lower rate. Fed open market operations are carefully geared to keep the federal funds rate fairly steady and to move it generally in increments of a quarter of a percentage point.

The Fed often engages in open market transactions simply to iron out temporary fluctuations in the demand for money and credit in the economy. These shifts in demand can result from a variety of factors, such as seasonal variations in economic activity and the weather, among others. But open market transactions also influence longer-term trends in credit conditions.

Since the mid-1950s the Fed has used monetary policy to moderate the degree of inflation or recession in the economy. To counteract inflation, the central bank has followed a restrictive policy, making it more difficult for consumers, businesses, and governments to borrow money. Tighter credit tends to reduce the demand for goods, in turn decreasing inflationary pressures on prices, but it also risks increasing unemployment. At other times, to fight recession, the central bank has eased credit conditions, bringing down interest rates and encouraging borrowing. That tends to increase the demand for goods, raising production and employment, but it also creates the danger of inflationary wage and price scales.

The challenge to monetary policymakers has always been to find an appropriate guide for their activities. The effects of a change in policy on growth or inflation may not show up in the economy until many months after the change has occurred. As a result, the FOMC must predict the effects of its actions using imperfect indicators.

During World War II and immediately after, the FOMC was guided by the need to prevent interest rates on the government debt from rising. The government had borrowed heavily to finance the war, and increasing rates would add greatly to the federal budget. If the rates the Treasury had to pay to borrow money started to rise, the Fed would follow an easier policy, creating more reserves and encouraging interest rates to fall. Such a policy, however, was powerless to prevent inflation. As the rate of inflation began to rise during the Korean War, the Fed formally ended its support of Treasury financing.

The Fed continued to pay attention to interest rates, however, as well as to various measures of the money supply and other indicators of economic activity. It was not until October 1979 that the Fed decided to ignore interest rates and set a policy designed to slow the growth of the money supply in a vigorous attempt to curtail double-digit inflation.

The close focus on money supply measures came to an end in 1982. The FOMC claimed that the principal measure of the money supply—known as M1—had become distorted. M1 was supposed to include currency in circulation plus checking accounts, but not savings accounts. But the rise of NOW accounts and money market accounts made the line between checking and savings accounts increasingly vague. As a result, Fed officials claimed, M1 had become an unreliable guide to policy. Perhaps more important than those technical arguments, however, was the fact that the money supply was rising rapidly in late 1982, and the Fed knew that any attempt to rein it in would exacerbate an already deep recession and a looming international debt crisis. An increasingly global economy and a resulting increase in "Eurodollars"—U.S. dollars held and traded in Europe—added to the Fed's difficulty in controlling the money supply.

Since 1982 the FOMC has followed a varied set of policy guides. Because meetings are held in private, it is difficult to say precisely what determines committee decisions. A statement of policy directives adopted by the FOMC and minutes of the meetings are released five to eight weeks after they occur—typically a few days after the following meeting.

Not only is it difficult to know what guides Fed policy decisions, sometimes the decisions themselves are obscure. In fact, it has long been the Fed's practice to allow the financial markets, businesses, governments, and other observers to guess at its intentions. Its silence has led to severe criticism. In response to such objections, the Fed on several occasions in 1994 released public statements that the FOMC had decided to boost the federal funds rate.

Despite the apparent policy reversal, the FOMC's policy actions remain somewhat ambiguous, particularly the rationale for policy decisions. It is, however, apparent from a careful reading of FOMC policy statements and minutes that in making monetary policy the committee keeps a close eye not only on the behavior of money supply measures but also on other indicators, such as economic growth rates, including gross measures of the economy and narrow statistics of regional and sectoral activity; inflation; the value of the dollar on foreign exchange markets; lending activit; and the health of the financial system.

Moreover, it is plain that the Fed chair, being the most visible member of the Fed board and also serving as chair of the FOMC, wields enormous influence. To the extent that the chair's thinking reflects a general view of the board of governors and the FOMC, it is sometimes possible to discern what influences the committee. The Fed chair testifies twice yearly to the House and Senate Banking committees, explaining Fed monetary policy, and makes frequent other appearances before congressional committees to discuss economic concerns. Financial markets follow closely every statement the Fed chair makes, looking for clues to the direction of Fed monetary policy.

BANK SUPERVISION AND REGULATION

The Bank Holding Company Act of 1956 granted to the Federal Reserve regulatory authority over bank holding companies (BHCs). A BHC was defined as any company controlling at least 25 percent of a bank's voting stock or the election of a majority of its governing body.

The purpose of the act was to control BHC expansion, prevent the formation of monopolies, and discourage restraint-of-trade in banking. The act required a company to obtain prior approval from the Fed before becoming a BHC. It also required prior approval for a BHC to do any of the following: acquire more than 5 percent of a bank's voting stock, acquire a bank's assets or merge with another BHC, or acquire a bank's assets in another state unless state law specifically authorizes out-of-state acquisition. (The prohibition on out-of-state acquisitions was repealed in 1994.) It prohibited expansion into nonbanking areas, except those deemed by the Fed to be permissible bank-related activities or "so closely related to the business of banking or of managing or controlling banks as to be a proper incident thereto."

A 1970 amendment to the Bank Holding Company Act closed a major loophole by giving the Fed regulatory authority over bank holding companies that own only a single bank—companies that previously had been exempted.

The Bank Mergers Act of 1966 granted the board of governors partial authority to administer bank mergers. The Fed approves mergers between state member banks and national or state nonmember banks if the resulting institution is to be a state member bank.

Throughout the 1980s and 1990s, the Fed several times expanded its interpretation of closely related activities to allow some banking companies to engage in securities activities. Those decisions required a relaxed interpretation of the Glass-Steagall Act of 1933, the Depression-era barriers that barred banks from engaging in most securities sales and underwriting activities and from affiliating with companies "principally engaged" in those securities activities.

In November 1999 President Bill Clinton signed a historic overhaul of the Glass-Steagall Act, known as Gramm-Leach-Bliley. The long-awaited modernization of the financial services industry allowed banks, securities firms, and insurance companies to enter into each other's markets to a certain degree. Under the new system, banks could form BHCs that engage in traditional banking activities as well as insurance and securities underwriting, merchant banking, and real estate development. Each endeavor operated as a separate business under the umbrella of the new financial services conglomerates—still closely regulated by the Fed. Other federal agencies, such as the Securities and Exchange Commission (p. 339) and the OCC, continued to regulate activities within their jurisdictions, regardless of whether they were carried out by a bank.

International Banking

The Fed issues licenses for foreign branches of Federal Reserve member banks and regulates the scope of their activity. It also charters and regulates international banking subsidiaries, called Edge corporations after Sen. Walter Edge (R-NJ), who introduced the legislation in 1919; it authorizes overseas investments of commercial banks, Edge corporations, and BHCs.

The International Banking Act of 1978 gave the Fed the primary authority for regulating U.S. branches of foreign banks and overseas branches of U.S. banks. Two years later, the Monetary Control Act required U.S. branches of foreign banks and Edge corporations to meet the Fed's reserve requirements. The Foreign Bank Supervision Enhancement Act of 1991 greatly expanded the Fed's jurisdiction over U.S. activities of foreign banks by requiring advance approval of the Fed for the acquisition or establishment of a branch, agency, representative office, or commercial-lending company.

In addition to these regulatory responsibilities, the Fed advises and consults with agencies of the federal government in discussions with international organizations and maintains contacts with the central banks of other countries.

Consumer Credit Protection

The board shares with other banking regulators enforcement responsibility for several consumer-protection laws. These include the Truth in Lending Act, the Truth in Savings Act, the Fair Credit Billing Act, the Fair Debt Collection Practices Act, the Home Mortgage Disclosure Act, the Equal Credit Opportunity Act, the Community Reinvestment Act, and certain provisions of the Real Estate Settlement Procedures Act, the Federal Trade Commission Act, and the Wall Street Reform and Consumer Protection Act of 2010.

Bank Examinations

The Fed has the authority to conduct examinations of all member banks, including national as well as state-chartered banks. However, the OCC has primary responsibility for the supervision and regulation of nationally chartered member banks and furnishes the Fed with reports on their operations. The FDIC examines and regulates state nonmember insured banks.

Because its primary role is formulating monetary policy, the board of governors has delegated the responsibility for field examination of member banks to the twelve Federal Reserve banks around the country. The mechanics and standards of examinations, as well as enforcement activities, are similar to those carried out by the FDIC (*p. 153*).

Field examiners have the authority to examine a bank's financial condition, enforce regulations and statutory provisions, such as restrictions on asset holdings, and require that unsatisfactory operating conditions of member banks be corrected. Under a major banking law enacted in 1991, bank regulators, including the Fed, were required to take direct action to prevent financial institutions from becoming undercapitalized and to take control of or close institutions whose capital fell below a designated "critical" level.

Most state member banks must be examined by Federal Reserve bank officials every year. Only smaller banks that received the highest of five regulatory ratings are examined every eighteen months.

SUPPORT SERVICES

The Monetary Control Act of 1980 required the board to charge for Federal Reserve bank services, which include currency and coin services of a nongovernmental nature; check clearing and collection; wire transfers; automated clearinghouse; settlement; securities safekeeping; Federal Reserve float (the Fed gives one institution credit for a check before it has collected funds from the institution where the check was written); and payment services for electronic funds transfer.

Issuing Currency

Reserve banks provide a convenient and accessible source of currency and coin for banks. If a bank needs cash, it replenishes its supply by obtaining shipments from a Reserve bank. If a bank accumulates more currency and coin than it needs, it is allowed to return this money to a Reserve bank and receive credits to its reserve accounts.

Federal Reserve banks also replace worn or damaged currency or coin with new money obtained from the U.S. Mint or the Bureau of Engraving and Printing. The Federal Reserve collects substantial quantities of bank checks and noncash items such as drafts, promissory notes, and bond coupons for the public.

When a check remains in the community near the bank on which it is drawn, presentation for payment usually is made by an exchange of checks through a local clearing arrangement. For checks leaving the local community, however, the Federal Reserve assists the timely presentation of that check by accepting millions of checks daily and then sorting and directing them to the banks on which they are drawn. Banks receive credit for checks deposited with a Federal Reserve bank based on a published availability schedule, with credit being passed to the depositor the same day payment is scheduled to be received from the bank on which the check is written.

Securities Credit

Through Regulations T, U, and X, the board of governors sets the amount of credit that may be used to buy equity securities. These regulations are known as "margin" requirements.

Wire Transfer of Funds

A member bank may transfer funds from its reserve account to another member bank anywhere in the country within a matter of minutes. Such transactions formerly were processed on a private communications system known as the Federal Reserve Communications System. In 1994 the twelve Federal Reserve district banks and member banks began using a new completely interconnected Fednet system.

Automated Clearinghouses

Reserve banks and their branches operate automated clearinghouses (ACHs) that provide for the exchange of payments on magnetic tape. The ACH receives a tape of transaction information from a commercial bank and electronically directs each item to the appropriate receiving bank where customer accounts are posted. Examples of ACH transactions are the direct deposit of a payroll by an employer and payment of a customer's recurring bills such as mortgages. In 2010 the Fed processed more than 19.4 billion of these transactions, totaling $31.7 trillion.

Background

The Federal Reserve System was created by Congress in December 1913. It was the nation's third attempt to establish a central bank. The first Bank of the United States was chartered by Congress in 1791. When its twenty-year charter expired, Congress, fearing the central bank vested too much control over the economy in the hands of the federal government, refused to extend it.

In 1816 Congress established the second Bank of the United States. But again, members of Congress grew distrustful of their creation and allowed its charter to expire in 1836. Both national banks also were criticized for benefiting the moneyed aristocracy over the general population.

For the next twenty-five years, the banking system consisted of a network of unregulated state-chartered banks and was plagued by insufficient capital, a high level of risky loans, fluctuating currency values, and insufficient reserves to back bank notes and deposits. The situation continued to deteriorate until 1863, when Congress passed the National Bank Act, which established federally chartered banks and created the Office of the Comptroller of the Currency to regulate them. A primary purpose was to establish a uniform national currency that would be issued through national banks, with the intent of stabilizing money in the Union and devaluing that in the Confederacy during the Civil War. The economy continued to suffer from periodic banking and currency crises, however, leading Congress to pass the Federal Reserve Act in 1913.

EARLY HISTORY

The architects of the Federal Reserve System were concerned principally with the need for an efficient payments system that would allow money to be transferred among financial institutions across the nation. They also believed the new Federal Reserve banks could smooth out fluctuations in the nation's money supply and help avoid financial panics by making loans to banks through the discount window. Authors of the Federal Reserve Act said that the bill's purpose was "to provide for the establishment of Federal Reserve banks, to furnish an elastic currency, to afford a means of rediscounting commercial paper [and] to establish a more effective supervision of banking in the United States."

During the 1920s, however, the Fed learned that the sale and purchase of U.S. Treasury securities provided an even more powerful tool for influencing money creation than the discount window. When the Fed bought securities from a bank, it increased the bank's reserves and enabled it to make more loans; as a result, interest rates on loans tended to fall. When the Fed sold securities, on the other hand, bank reserves fell and credit shrank; as a result, interest rates tended to rise.

At first, sales and purchases of Treasury securities by the Federal Reserve district banks were uncoordinated, sometimes contributing to disarray in financial markets. But in 1922 the Fed established the Open Market Investment Committee to coordinate dealings in securities.

In spring 1933, in the midst of the Great Depression, the Fed failed to avert panic by providing sufficient cash to banks experiencing depositor runs. President Franklin D. Roosevelt was forced to declare a "bank holiday," closing all the banks in the nation on March 6, two days after he was sworn into office. Several thousand banks never reopened their doors. This severe crisis prompted passage of landmark banking laws in 1933 and 1935, which established the FDIC to insure bank deposits and stabilize banks.

The FDIC also was charged with supervising state-chartered banks that were not members of the Fed and, therefore, previously had not been subject to federal regulation. The Fed continued to supervise state-chartered banks that were members, and the comptroller regulated national banks.

The banking acts of the 1930s also increased the power and the autonomy of the Fed by removing the secretary of the Treasury and the comptroller from its board of governors. The acts also stripped the regional Fed banks of their power to buy and sell securities and concentrated that power in the hands of the Federal Open Market Committee—successor to the Open Market Investment Committee—which operated through the Federal Reserve Bank of New York.

From the outset, all national banks were required to be members of the Fed, and state-chartered banks could choose to be members if they wished. Member banks were required to keep interest-free reserves at the Fed, and in return they received certain Fed services. The rise of interest rates in the 1970s, however, caused dramatic growth in the cost to banks of keeping interest-free reserves at the Fed. As a result, many state banks withdrew from Fed membership, and some national banks converted to state charters so they also could withdraw.

Fearing that a loss of Fed members would hamper the central bank's ability to manage the money supply, Congress passed the Monetary Control Act in 1980. That law required all depository institutions to keep reserves at the Fed, regardless of whether they were members. The Fed also was required to charge fees for its check clearing and other services, and to offer them to nonmember banks.

THE FED IN THE 1980s

In the 1980s, confronted with major upheavals in the economy and the performance of financial markets, the Fed attracted severe criticism for its monetary policy. With inflation topping 10 percent in 1979, Fed chair Paul A. Volcker began a "war on inflation," convincing the FOMC to stop trying to control interest rates and focus on restraining the growth of the money supply. Prices had been brought under control by 1982, when inflation settled in at about 4 percent, as measured by the Consumer Price Index. But price stability came at the cost of soaring interest rates—prime rates charged by commercial banks exceeded 20 percent in 1981—and a pair of back-to-back recessions that stretched from January 1980 to November 1982.

The war on inflation was ultimately considered a success. Though Volcker was branded as a pariah in the early 1980s, by the time he left the Fed in 1987, the economy was in its fifth consecutive year of economic growth, and the chair was hailed for the prosperity.

But notwithstanding its success in reining in prices, the Fed was left struggling with interest rates that remained high, particularly as the economy grew with gusto in the mid-1980s. The prime rate fell in 1987 to just above 8 percent before it began climbing, and the central bank came under renewed pressure from policymakers—in Congress and the White House—who thought that rates were too high.

Alan Greenspan, who took the helm of the Fed in summer 1987, continued the vigorous approach of his predecessor, but whereas Volcker had battled inflation to get the economy back on track, Greenspan tried to prevent inflationary pressures from gaining a foothold to keep economic growth at a stable and sustained pace.

The Fed did not hesitate to intervene when the stock and futures markets were in disarray. After Oct. 19, 1987, when stock markets around the world crashed and the Dow Jones Industrial Average dropped 508 points, the central bank took steps to assure brokers that credit would be extended if needed. The move calmed investors' biggest fears—that credit would not be available to cover margin requirements and their stocks would have to be sold in a deeply depressed market.

Likewise, in October 1989, after the Dow dropped 190 points on a Friday, Fed officials spent the weekend assuring investors that money would be available to meet credit needs. When trading began the following Monday, the markets rebounded.

THE FED IN THE 1990s

Greenspan's emphasis on price stability often came at the expense of economic growth. The economy stalled again in July 1990 and recovered slowly from a recession that lasted until March 1991, in technical terms, and continued for a year or more after that in practical effect. The result, however, was a further decline in inflation and interest rates. In July 1991, expressing confidence in his inflation-fighting skills, President George H. W. Bush renominated Greenspan for a second four-year term as chair and a full fourteen-year term on the board of governors.

The Fed had taken a deliberate route of pulling rates down during the 1990 recession and after: in just twelve months, from late 1990 to late 1991, the Fed cut the discount rate in half, from 7 percent to 3.5 percent. Six months later, in mid-1992, the discount rate fell to 3 percent, a level where it had not been since 1962. "Real" short-term rates—or rates after the effects of inflation were discounted—were near zero, providing what the Fed later said was needed accommodation to the economy's recovery.

The Fed board took one other monetary policy step in the aftermath of the 1990 recession to ease what it viewed as a credit crunch threatening the economy. In April 1992 the board reduced from 12 percent to 10 percent the number of bank deposits above a threshold amount ($51.9 million in 1994) that must be set aside as reserves in vault cash or on deposit with the Fed. Deposits less than the threshold were subject to a statutory 3 percent reserve requirement.

The Fed also actively—and successfully—sought changes in international banking laws in 1991, following the scandal involving the Bank of Credit and Commerce International (BCCI) and its secret ownership of several large U.S. banks. The Fed eventually fined a top BCCI official $37 million. Nonetheless, the Fed's regulation of foreign banks suffered a blow in 1995: when it closed the U.S. operations of Japan's Daiwa Bank for fraud in bond trading, critics faulted both the Fed and the Federal Reserve Bank of New York for overlooking a problem that dated back more than a decade.

In February 1994, somewhat to the consternation of financial markets and policymakers, the FOMC began edging rates higher, as a stronger economy posed the threat of resurgent inflation. Six more hikes followed over twelve months. By late 1995 the rates began to lower, and from January through November 1996 the short-term interest rates held steady at 5.25 percent. Through all these fluctuations the Fed's objectives continued to be low inflation and an unemployment rate no lower than 6 percent. In return, the Fed received some credit for a recovery that, though never robust, had been fairly steady.

Even though the administration of President Bill Clinton in 1994 considered consolidating the federal government's banking regulators into a single agency—stripping the Fed of much of its bank regulatory authority—the president renominated Greenspan to his third term as chair in 1996; he was confirmed with strong bipartisan congressional support. Greenspan's consistent emphasis on "slow growth" had helped lower the unemployment rate to 5.1 percent and kept the annual inflation rate to 2.6 percent, a thirty-year low.

The Fed under Greenspan did not just focus on inflation but also worked aggressively to transform the U.S. financial services industry. In particular, the Fed pushed hard for repeal of the Glass-Steagall Act of 1933, which had prohibited banks from dealing in and underwriting securities other than those issued by the government and backed by tax receipts. The Glass-Steagall Act also had prevented banks from affiliating with companies "principally engaged" in prohibited securities activities.

Despite Greenspan's strong backing for financial services overhaul and the efforts of federal regulators, including the Fed, to allow banks to dabble in securities and insurance products, Congress several times during the 1980s and 1990s chose not to overturn Glass-Steagall, largely because compromise among the three main industry groups affected—banks, securities firms, and insurance companies—remained elusive.

In 1998 Congress again tried to overhaul the law. Greenspan argued publicly with opponents of repealing Glass-Steagall, namely Treasury Secretary Robert E. Rubin. The disagreement between Greenspan and Rubin centered on how new financial conglomerates in a post–Glass-Steagall world would organize their banking, brokerage, and insurance arms, and on who would regulate the new conglomerates. Greenspan favored a system in which banks could form holding companies that engaged in traditional banking activities as well as insurance and securities underwriting, merchant banking, and real estate development. The new financial services conglomerates would be regulated by the Fed. Rubin argued that such a structure would disadvantage smaller institutions that could not afford to set up an elaborate system. Rubin favored allowing the organization of operating subsidiaries without a holding company, which would essentially leave the brokerage and insurance operations as a part of the parent bank.

Greenspan's plan received a boost early in 1999, when Rubin's retirement as Treasury secretary removed a major opponent to the chair's proposal. At the same time, various finance-related industries put aside their differences and began aggressively pushing legislation that resembled Greenspan's proposal. Such a bill cleared Congress and was signed into law by Clinton in November of that year.

Meanwhile, the economy had continued to improve, culminating in record-breaking stock market highs during the late 1990s and into 2000. Despite the financial peaks, the Fed remained on guard for inflationary trends that could sidetrack the economy's growth. A brief dip in the stock market during summer 1998 prompted the Fed to make three quarter-point rate cuts, bringing the federal funds rate down to 4.75 percent, while the market rose to new highs.

But by the middle of 1999 the Fed had once again become concerned about the threat of inflation. These fears were reinforced when the unemployment rate reached a twenty-nine-year low of just above 4 percent, driving up demand for skilled workers. The Fed chair and others worried that the high demand for workers would drive up wages, which would in turn increase the cost of products, fueling inflation. Even the serious fiscal crisis in Asia in 1997 did not slow down the American economy. In June 1999—just a year after the slight decrease in rates—the bank had made the first of six interest rate increases, in an effort to slow down the economy and prevent inflation. Over the next year, the federal funds rate was increased from 4.75 percent to 6.5 percent. The goal of the increases was to engineer what financial analysts called a "soft landing," an economy with slower but steady growth, coupled with low inflation.

THE FED IN THE 2000s

At first the Fed's strategy to slow the economy seemed to be working. In the second half of 2000, economic growth began to slow down. However, by early 2001 the "soft landing," according to some indicators, appeared to be turning into a "hard landing." By spring 2001 economists agreed that it looked as though the country was in a recession. Growth in the first months of the year almost sputtered to a halt, slowing to 1 percent. The formerly high-flying stock market dropped precipitously. In particular, the tech-heavy Nasdaq lost more than half its value in the last quarter of 2000 and first quarter of 2001.

Greenspan, renominated to a fourth term in 2000, took a drubbing. Some members of the financial community questioned why the Fed chair, who in 1996 coined the term "irrational exuberance" to describe investors' feverish purchase of overvalued stock, had not done more to burst the bubble in its early stages. The new president, George W. Bush, met with the Fed chief before his inauguration to express total confidence in his abilities. Greenspan returned the favor in January 2001 by giving a general endorsement to tax cuts—the cornerstone of the new president's economic agenda—as a way of giving the economy a much-needed boost.

Bush's proposed tax cut was estimated to cost $1.6 trillion over ten years. In spite of his general support for tax cuts, Greenspan recommended several times during congressional testimony in 2001 that tax cuts be accompanied by a "trigger" that would limit cuts if certain surplus or debt targets were not met. In May 2001 Congress passed a reduced form of Bush's tax cut, worth $1.35 trillion over ten years, without any such trigger.

The Fed responded to the slowdown with a number of deep cuts in the federal funds interest rate. A half-point reduction in early January 2001 gave the markets a short-term boost. When the Fed cut rates for a third time that March—once again by a half point—short term rates went down to 5 percent, and the markets actually dropped precipitously. By August the Fed had slashed rates to 3.75 percent.

The terrorist attacks on Sept. 11, 2001, dealt a major blow to the already floundering economy. When the stock market reopened six days later, understandably skittish investors reacted by selling: equity markets tumbled by 7 percent on the first day and another 5 percent later that week. The Fed sought to reassure the markets with two cuts of 0.5 percent each within three weeks of the attacks. By December the Fed had cut rates a record eleven times in 2001, leaving rates at a forty-year low of 1.75 percent.

Greenspan gave a guardedly encouraging assessment of the economy in testimony to Congress early in 2002. It was at that time, however, when the country learned that the energy giant Enron had been using stock options bestowed on its executives to inflate its stock prices artificially. Corporate accountability leapt onto the congressional agenda. It was then that Greenspan and Bush had their first significant public disagreement over how to reform the expensing of stock options. As news broke of major companies—WorldCom, Tyco, and Xerox—also using stock options to inflate earnings, Greenspan advocated for corporations being required to state stock options as expenses. Meanwhile, Bush supported maintaining the status quo of requiring companies to include unexercised options in their calculations of the number of outstanding shares.

When Republicans took control of both chambers of Congress following the 2002 midterm elections, President Bush seemed poised to enact further tax cuts in 2003, touting them as a necessary stimulant to the still-skittish economy. But this time, Greenspan sent mixed signals regarding Bush's proposed tax cut. While stating that the elimination of dividend taxation was sound economic policy, the Fed chair noted that the effects would be negligible in the short term. Furthermore, he said that any cuts should be offset by cuts in spending to prevent further ballooning of the federal deficit.

Uncertainties tied to the U.S.-led war in Iraq, spikes in energy prices, and increases in unemployment continued to loom over the U.S. economy in 2003. By spring the Fed had cut interest rates to 1 percent, another historic low. As the United States made steady progress in toppling the Iraqi regime, energy prices dropped and the stock market rallied. Greenspan continued to be cautiously optimistic about the future of the economy, citing its ability in dealing with shocks of the past few years, including the terrorist attacks, the accounting scandals, and the decline in stock prices.

The Fed chair retained the confidence of the administration, and Bush reappointed Greenspan in 2004 to a record fifth term as chair of the Fed's board of governors. Although optimistic about the near future of the U.S. economy, Greenspan in November 2004 issued a warning to federal leaders against deficit complacency, saying that they could not expect foreign investors to continue to finance never-ending growth in America's already huge trade gap. He recommended that U.S. policymakers try to cut the record federal budget deficit.

By spring 2004 the federal funds rate had remained at the 1 percent rate for more than a year. Top Fed officials publicly agreed that the federal funds rate was too low and ran the risk of fueling inflation. Beginning in June, the Fed began to raise the rate at every meeting for the next fifteen months, even in summer 2004 when the economy hit what they later called a "soft patch" because of higher energy prices. By early 2005 Greenspan and Fed officials were incorporating new rhetoric into statements and congressional testimony, frequently dropping references to a "measured" pace for rate increases, but without really detailing what that would mean.

On Sept. 20, 2005, Fed commissioners raised rates a quarter-percentage point to 3.75 percent. It was also the eleventh straight increase since June 2004. Even the destructive havoc of Hurricane Katrina did not give the Fed reason to pause. Meanwhile, government-backed mortgage broker Freddie Mac's $5 billion manipulation of earnings, revealed in 2003, and news that sister broker Fannie Mae had overstated 2000 to 2003 earnings by about $12 billion in late 2004 shook up the financial world, already reeling from Enron, Tyco, and other such corporate financial scandals. In February 2005 testimony before the House Financial Services Committee, Greenspan argued that Fannie and Freddie had grown too large and could pose a real risk for the broader economy.

In October 2005 the House followed Greenspan's advice and overwhelmingly passed legislation that would create a new oversight body to regulate Fannie Mae and Freddie Mac. The Federal Housing Finance Agency (FHFA), as the new agency was to be called, would have had the authority to limit the size of the lenders' holdings of mortgages and securities as well as a mandate to review and approve or reject any new lending services of either company. The new regulator would have been independent of current agencies, exist outside of the appropriations process, and would have much broader authority than Freddie Mac and Fannie Mae's current regulator, the Office of Federal Housing Enterprise Oversight.

Early in 2006 Sen. Richard Shelby, chair of the Senate Banking Committee, began pushing a companion bill in the Senate, but a number of factors stalled the measure. First, Republicans and Democrats disagreed about a number of provisions, in particular a proposal (not included in the House bill) that would require the lenders to divest most of their huge investment portfolios. Also, after initially fighting federal efforts to uncover wrongdoing, Freddie Mac and Fannie Mae began working closely with investigators to clean up their books, soothing some congressional tempers. No bill passed the Senate that year.

While the fate of Freddie Mac and Fannie Mae was big news in 2005 and 2006, the biggest question facing the Fed concerned the Fed itself. After a record eighteen years as chair, Greenspan was poised to leave his post in January 2006. Next to the president, many consider the Fed chair the most powerful official in the federal government. On Oct. 24, 2005, Bush chose Ben Bernanke, his chair of the White House Council of Economic Advisers, to succeed Greenspan.

From the beginning, the reaction to the nomination, from the banking and financial industry and from Congress, was positive. Bernanke's past experience, which included a stint as a governor of the Federal Reserve and as an economics professor at Princeton University, made him well qualified for the job. Like Greenspan and Volcker, he also had a reputation as an inflation fighter. At his confirmation hearing before the Senate Banking Committee on Nov. 15, 2005, Bernanke was widely praised by all committee members. On Jan. 31, 2006, he was confirmed in the Senate by voice vote. In Bernanke's first months as chair, the board raised interest rates three times, with the benchmark rate hitting 5.25 percent in June 2006. The continued rate hikes were justified, the board said, by inflation fears, stoked by rising oil and other commodity prices and low unemployment.

But the increases also earned Bernanke criticism from some respected economists and financial analysts, who worried that the move came just as the all important housing market was turning sour. Indeed, after five years of impressive prices, sales, and new construction increases, the housing market began to show a real slowdown, both in the new and existing housing markets. For instance, in October, new home construction dropped almost 15 percent from the same time the year before. Housing has become particularly important for the nation's economic health. One in every ten jobs is dependent on the housing industry and the dramatic increase in the price of homes allowed many Americans to borrow against their home's rising value, helping to drive consumer spending.

Bernanke defended the rate increases as necessary to fight rising prices. He was helped by the fact that although short-term interest rates rose (along with the Fed rate increases), mortgage or long-term rates stayed relatively stable, helping potential home buyers.

By the beginning of 2007 Bernanke was winning more praise than criticism. The stock market was moving forward and housing prices were slumping but not collapsing. In addition, the gross domestic product had increased by a slower but still healthy 2.5 percent during the first quarter of 2007, a sign that after four years of strong growth the nation's economy seemed to be coming in for a "soft landing" as opposed to a recession. Federal deficits, another concern, were also falling, to an estimated $240 billion in fiscal 2008, due to increased government revenue from steady economic growth.

Finally, all important inflation numbers were coming down, to an annual rate of 2.5 percent in March 2007, from 3.4 percent in all of 2006. At the same time, unemployment in winter and spring 2007 had fallen to a low 4.4 percent. It seemed that Bernanke had calibrated the rate increases just enough to control inflation but not damage the economy.

Still, dangers loomed, particularly in the housing market. While sales and prices did not drop as fast as some had predicted, the market began to decline in earnest in 2007. A particular concern were high-risk subprime mortgages, usually given to people who did not have enough money or a good enough credit rating to afford a more desirable fixed-rate mortgage. Subprime loans are often adjustable rate (which can change over time) or "interest only," which means the borrower pays only the bank interest and does not pay down the loan's principle. These loans were popular during the height of the housing boom and were predicated on the expectation that housing prices would continue to rise and that borrowers who could not make their payments could always sell their homes for a profit and pay off the loan.

But when prices began to fall in late 2006, the number of people defaulting on mortgages, especially subprime mortgages, began to grow, doubling from January 2006 to June 2007. A number of large subprime loan companies declared bankruptcy and some analysts began to show concern that the subprime phenomenon might lead to a collapse in the housing market.

Bernanke remained cautiously optimistic about housing. While the number of foreclosures due to subprime loans "will continue to rise," he said in a speech in Chicago in May 2007, "we do not expect significant spillovers from the subprime market to the rest of the economy or to the financial markets." At the same time, Bernanke said, the Fed and government banking regulators might have to do more to protect consumers from abusive lending practices, which were common in the subprime industry.

Uncertainty and fear was stoked by wild up-and-down gyrations in the stock markets, which reacted to both the decline in housing and a reduction in credit caused by trouble in the home mortgage market. On Sept. 18, 2007, Bernanke and the board cut the federal funds rate by a half a percentage point, from 5.25 percent to 4.75 percent. On the day of the cut the Dow Jones Industrial Average gained more than 335 points, and in the following weeks the markets performed well, with the Dow hitting a new high. Still, in spite of the boost the rate cut gave to stocks, no one was sure whether it was enough to help fix the underlying problems in the housing and credit markets. In addition, worries about inflation and a weakening dollar—two conditions that often prompt the Fed to raise interest rates—made many financial analysts wonder whether the rate cut would be short-lived. Meanwhile, the new Democratic Congress revived efforts to tighten regulation on Fannie

Mae and Freddie. A measure that was in some ways similar to the 2005 House-passed bill won overwhelming approval in that chamber again in late May 2007. The Senate worked out its objections to the House bill, and President Bush signed the Housing and Economic Recovery Act in July 2008 to create the new FHFA, with greater authority over Fannie Mae and Freddie Mac.

Supporters of tighter regulation on Freddie and Fannie and greater regulation of the financial services industry in general, however, quickly saw their fears of an economic bust turned into reality. By early 2008 it was clear that the housing sector was in much more trouble than almost anyone had realized. Indeed, a growing number of economists were now saying that sector was in freefall rather than just decline. In addition, the damage done by rapidly falling housing prices and rising foreclosure rates quickly spread beyond traditional home lenders because millions of mortgages, including millions of riskier "subprime mortgages" had been bundled into different financial instruments and then sold to other financial institutions around the world.

The first evidence that the mortgage-lending crisis had spread through the financial system came in March 2008, when the Fed, along with the Treasury Department, moved to save Bear Stearns, one of the largest and most respected investment firms on Wall Street. In an effort to save the ailing firm, the Fed and Treasury backed its acquisition by JPMorgan Chase, a major Wall Street bank. Initially offering a "bargain basement price" of $2 a share for Bear, JPMorgan increased its offer to $10 after shareholders demanded more. The bank also was forced to take on the Bear's less attractive assets after the Fed agreed to put taxpayer dollars on the line, largely to avert a much greater financial crisis, to guarantee $30 billion of the Bear's most risky mortgages.

While the rescue plan did save Bear Stearns, it did not have the intended effect of keeping investors from panicking; on the day of the initial announcement of a deal, markets around the world plunged. Although many analysts agreed that the fall of Bear Stearns might have possibly led to other investment bank collapses, imploding the country's financial system, some voiced concern about the long-term risk to taxpayers. Vincent Reinhart, a former senior policy adviser to Greenspan, called the rescue "the worst policy decision in a generation," and one that would forever eliminate the possibility that the Fed could serve as an "honest broker" in the banking sector.

In spite of the Fed's offering an unprecedented line of credit to investment banks in March 2008, bank shares continued to plummet, with Lehman Brothers especially hard hit. Six months later it was filing for bankruptcy, the largest firm to fall in the global credit crisis. In spite of rescuing Bear Stearns and a number of other major financial institutions earlier in the year, the Fed and Treasury drew a line in the sand with Lehman Brothers, ignoring would-be buyers such as Bank of America and the British bank Barclays, suitors whose interest depended on federal protection against any losses arising from the bank's toxic assets.

Unlike Bear Stearns, whose collapse was relatively sudden and potentially shocking to the financial system,

Lehman's demise had been foretold for months, giving investors time to adapt and get ready. In the end, Bernanke and Treasury Secretary Henry M. Paulson gambled that financial markets would be able to withstand Lehman's collapse. Bernanke and Paulson argued that the government could not be expected to bail out every failing firm. But investor anxieties over the fall of such a large internationally active firm set off a global panic, causing the U.S. stock market to fall more than 500 points on Sept. 15, 2008. Within weeks, Paulson and Bernanke had switched tack and were bailing out other firms deemed too big to fail, most notably insurance giant AIG, which ended up requiring nearly $180 billion from the federal government to survive.

In the wake of Lehman's collapse, even markets generally thought to be "safe," such as money market funds, were not immune to financial woes. In October 2008 the Fed, worried about the overall health of the money market industry, created a program that would make up to $540 billion available to buy troubled assets from such funds. Nervous investors had started pulling money from a particular class of money market funds—about $480 billion in early September. Had that run on the funds continued, they might have been forced to sell assets into an already troubled market, potentially causing a snowballing series of losses to investors.

Meanwhile, the Fed began cutting interest rates, tentatively at first and then aggressively, in an effort to stave off a deep recession. Initially, rates were cut from 6.25 percent to 5.75 in August 2007. The Fed continued to show a disinclination to make dramatic moves, instead indicating that inflation remained its greatest concern. But as 2007 wore on, stock values continued to fall and the markets for mortgages and corporate debt came to a standstill. In November 2007, in spite of signs of a still strong economy, the rate dropped to 4.5 and then again to 4.25 in December.

In January 2008 the distress in financial markets had become a significant enough threat to ordinary Americans to warrant another cut—down to 3 percent. In May the rate was aggressively cut again to 2 percent. Between May and September the rate stayed constant but dipped twice in October to 1 percent. By January 2009 the rate was effectively at zero, where the Fed indicated it would be for some time while the country remained in a deep recession and fears about low interest rates and inflation had not been realized.

In addition to cutting rates, the Fed also sought to ease the crisis by working with the Treasury Department to accurately assess the health of the nation's top banks. The plan was to subject each of them to a "stress test" intended to determine whether each bank would have enough money in its capital reserves to cover projected losses on loans and other assets over the next two years. If a bank was determined to require new capital, it was hoped that most of that capital would come from private investors. If federal aid was required, that aid would come with conditions giving the bank incentives to pay back the money as soon as possible. These conditions, far tougher than those imposed by the Bush administration, would also require the bank

to submit reports proving that it was using the federal aid to do more lending. The announcement of the stress tests in February 2009 initially had a destabilizing effect on the financial markets. But the twelve-week wait before the results were released seemed to calm investor anxieties, especially as other government aid programs began to show a positive impact.

The results of the first round of stress tests, announced by Treasury and the Fed in early May 2009, indicated that of the nineteen banks tested, only two—GMAC and Citigroup—were likely to require additional taxpayer assistance. The report also concluded that ten of the banks would need to raise a combined $75 billion in common equity to withstand an even more serious financial crisis. But this figure was much lower than analysts expected. Officials also reported that banks continued to hold vast quantities of ill-considered loans and could suffer losses totaling $600 billion over the next twenty months as more borrowers defaulted, but the tests ultimately determined that the banks could absorb those losses.

When the U.S. Senate voted in 1991 to expand the Fed's emergency powers to lend financial institutions large amounts of money, it received little notice at the time. In the sixteen years that followed the creation of this new authority, it was rarely used. But from March 2008 to September 2009, the Fed invoked its emergency powers—which essentially allowed the institution to print more money to prop up failing banks—at least nineteen times, from containing the fallout from the collapse of Bear Stearns to limiting losses at Bank of America. In total, the Fed doled out more than $2 trillion to buy bonds and Treasury bills—all aimed at providing the financial system with greater liquidity.

By mid-2009 the Fed faced the strategic challenge of figuring out when was the best time to withdraw that money from the U.S. economy. Critics worried that as the economy showed signs of stabilizing, the money the Fed gave out, along with the government's stimulus spending, could cause inflation to surge and the dollar to lose a substantial amount of its value. These criticisms were not confined to domestic policymakers. Countries such as China, which held more than $1 trillion in U.S. dollars in 2009, voiced fears that the dollar might collapse as the currency loses value. The Fed countered that much of the new money was not actually in circulation but sitting in bank reserves, that a slow economic recovery would keep inflation and devaluation in check, and that the Fed had enough time to reverse course if needed.

But many in Congress pressured the Fed for greater accountability to voters, especially as the agency put more and more public money at risk. Those demanding transparency, especially concerning what companies the Fed had been lending money to, had become more insistent, but the Fed resisted such disclosure out of fear that it might spark runs on those firms by investors. In early June 2009 the agency began to release a wider range of information concerning its lending programs in a new monthly report. Although the report described the kinds of collateral the Fed has been taking in exchange for loans, it did not identify the specific banks involved.

Questions of transparency were brought into sharp relief by the controversy surrounding Bank of America's acquisition of Merrill Lynch, which occurred in January 2009. By June the bank's top executive, Kenneth Lewis, was claiming that federal officials, specifically Paulson and Bernanke, had threatened to oust him and the rest of his bank's senior management if they backed away from the purchase, a deal that the bank became increasingly wary of consummating due to accelerating losses at Merrill. The sale, which initially involved no federal assistance, went through only after the government agreed to provide $20 billion in federal aid and guaranteed up to $118 billion in losses by Bank of America. Although Bernanke quickly defended the central bank's actions and repeatedly denied applying undue pressure on Lewis to close the deal, the controversy came at a sensitive time when Congress had begun considering the prospect of overhauling the nation's financial regulations as well as its regulatory agencies—including the powers and authority of the Fed.

In June 2009 the new administration of President Barack Obama announced that it would allow the largest banks to repay billions in federal aid given to them in the form of direct investments. A number of banks had sought permission to return the money to avoid restrictions such as limits on executive pay and as a sign of economic recuperation. Almost no bank raised opposition to repaying the money.

On Aug. 25, 2009, President Obama reappointed Bernanke to a second term, giving the Fed chair the credit for helping to guide the financial sector through one of its most difficult periods. "Ben approached a financial system on the verge of collapse with calm and wisdom, with bold action and out-of-the-box thinking that has helped put the brakes on our economic free fall," Obama said. Bernanke was seen as a safe choice, given his steady performance during the financial crisis and the perceived need for continuity in leadership while the economy was still emerging from the recession.

Still, the Fed chair was not given an easy time in the Senate. Many senators, still smarting over the unpopularity of the 2008 bailout of the banking sector, known as the Troubled Asset Relief Program (TARP), were at least publicly wary of Bernanke. Many argued that the Fed had lost much of its credibility during the financial crisis and was in need of a new leader. Others worried that replacing Bernanke would send exactly the wrong signal to the markets and would risk unnecessary panic at a time when the global economy was just beginning to recover. This argument was driven home by Treasury Secretary Timothy Geithner and other administration officials, who vigorously lobbied senators on Bernanke's behalf. On Jan. 28, 2010, the Senate voted 70–30 to confirm Bernanke for another four-year term.

THE FED IN THE 2010s

But Bernanke's confirmation did not put an end to personnel questions at the Fed. In early March 2010 Donald L. Kohn, vice chair of the Fed, announced that he would retire in June, leaving President Obama with an important seat to fill on the agency's twelve-member board of governors. Kohn's announcement immediately generated pressure from liberals on Obama to nominate a replacement who would not just put an emphasis on the board's mission to check inflation but also rein in unemployment, which was nearing 10 percent at the time. The following month, Obama nominated Janet L. Yellen, who was serving as president of the Federal Reserve Bank of San Francisco. Yellen—no stranger to the central bank—had already served on the board from 1994 to 1997, and had been the chair of the Council of Economic Advisers from 1997 to 1999 under President Clinton.

Obama also announced two nominations to fill the two remaining vacancies on the Fed Board: Peter A. Diamond, an economics professor at the Massachusetts Institute of Technology, and Sarah Bloom Raskin, a law professor and the Maryland Commissioner of Financial Regulation. Diamond's confirmation stalled after several Republican senators, particularly ranking Banking Committee member Shelby, expressed concerns about his suitability for a slot on the board. Shelby argued that the MIT professor lacked the necessary real-world expertise to deal with the challenges confronted by the board. Democrats countered that Diamond had won a Nobel Prize for economics and that he was much more qualified than some of President Bush's nominees for the board, nominees that Shelby and others had voted to confirm. But Shelby refused to budge and his continued opposition to Diamond left the nomination in limbo. On June 6, 2011, the nominee bowed to the reality of the situation and announced that he would withdraw from consideration. The position was not filled until May 2012, when two new members (Jerome H. Powell and Jeremy C. Stein) were confirmed to bring the number of active board members back to a full seven. However, the 2013 resignations of Elizabeth A. Duke and Ben S. Bernanke left two vacancies again; although the need to fill those positions was overshadowed by Obama's failed nomination of Larry Summers to take over from Bernanke as Fed chair and the subsequent nomination of Vice Chair Janet Yellin.

At the same time Republicans and Democrats on Capitol Hill were fighting over Diamond's nomination, they were involved in a much bigger and more consequential battle over how to best overhaul the country's financial system, a battle that involved the Fed and Chair Bernanke. Introduced in the wake of the financial crisis, debated for more than a year, and signed into law on July 21, 2010, the Wall Street Reform and Consumer Protection Act of 2010 (also called "Dodd-Frank" after its chief sponsors, Sen. Chris Dodd, D-CT, and Rep. Barney Frank, D-MA) was the most sweeping overhaul of the financial system since the Great Depression.

Although the law was considered a major legislative victory for Obama and for its supporters in Congress, Dodd-Frank's journey from bill to law was not without major hurdles, especially in the Senate. Criticism for the proposal came from both sides of the aisle, with Republicans arguing that it would entail excessive and burdensome regulation that would only make it more difficult and costly for businesses and consumers to raise or borrow money. While most Democrats saw the law as a victory that demonstrated to their constituents that they could be tough on Wall Street, some in the party felt the package did not go far enough and left too many critical decisions to the same federal regulators who had missed the warning signs in the run-up to the financial crisis of 2008.

Among the key provisions of the new law was the establishment of a council of federal regulators to watch for and assess any potential threats to the financial system. The overhaul also gave shareholders a nonbinding advisory vote on executive compensation and gave federal agencies new powers to regulate and even liquidate financial institutions that posed a threat to the nation's financial health.

For the Fed, the new law meant new authority and responsibilities. For instance, the law established the Consumer Financial Protection Bureau, to track consumer-related issues to protect ordinary people from unscrupulous banks and financial services firms. Although the bureau is housed in the Fed, it operates independently, with a director appointed by the president who is not answerable to the Federal Reserve Board. Obama appointed Harvard Law professor, Elizabeth Warren (who is credited with coming up with the idea for the bureau) as acting director after some Republicans in the Senate let it be known that they would oppose Warren's nomination to the post. Subsequently, on July 18, 2011, Obama nominated Richard Cordray, the head of the bureau's Enforcement Division; he was not confirmed until July 16, 2013.

The new law also gave the president the power to appoint the president of the Federal Reserve Bank of New York, by far the most powerful of the Fed's twelve regional banks. Previously, this position had been appointed by a board made up of representatives of those banks that it regulated. The change is intended to scale back the influence that Wall Street banks have over this regional Fed bank that is first among equals.

Throughout the debate over Dodd-Frank, Bernanke pushed Congress to move forward with the law. In the year that followed the law's enactment, Bernanke defended it from critics of various stripes. "The Dodd-Frank Act addresses critical gaps and weaknesses of the U.S. regulatory framework," he said, just months after the bill was signed into law, adding, "The Federal Reserve is committed to working with the other financial regulatory agencies to effectively implement and execute the act."

In early November 2010 the Fed took a big and controversial step aimed at keeping the economy growing when it began a second round of quantitative easing—known as QE2. Quantitative easing involved pumping additional money into the economy by having the Fed purchase about $600 billion in Treasury bills (T-bills) over the next six to eight months. This came on the heels of the first round of easing in 2008 and 2009, in which the Fed pumped almost $2 trillion into the American economy, also by purchasing t-bills, as well as bonds and stocks. Supporters of quantitative easing say that it provides a necessary monetary lubricant to help an economy still scarred by the financial crisis and the recession. In particular, Bernanke and others argued, QE2 would help keep stock prices high, which in turn would put more money in consumers hands and help drive economic growth.

But others warned that the Fed was playing a dangerous game with QE2. After all, they pointed out, the program was financed by simply printing more money and injecting it into the economy, a tactic that could easily lead to much higher inflation. If inflation returned, critics said, the Fed would have to dramatically raise interest rates to tamp it down, which in turn would almost certainly restrain economic growth or even produce another recession.

In April 2011 Bernanke made history by becoming the first Fed chair in the agency's ninety-eight-year history to hold a press conference. In an effort to boost the central bank's image, Bernanke pledged to meet with the news media four times a year. Although the Fed has a long history of avoiding the media spotlight, the intense criticism of the agency following the financial crisis forced it to adopt a more forthcoming relationship with the American public. Bernanke addressed this new reality in 2009 when he said that "central banks should be as transparent as possible, both for reasons of democratic accountability and because many of our policies are likely to be more effective if they are well understood by the markets and the public."

In his first press briefing, Bernanke focused on predictions of moderate improvements in the economy with slow growth in jobs. When questioned about the seemingly slow growth of the economy, Bernanke pointed to a number of factors, including weather effects, weaker exports, and slower defense spending, which he anticipated being gone in the later part of the year. In spite of this good news, the Fed chair remained committed to keeping interest rates as low as possible until the economy was on a stronger footing. Vice Chair Yellen also argued for this policy, saying just two weeks before Bernanke's first press conference that keeping the benchmark rate so low "continues to be appropriate."

But opposition to near-zero rates was building. In April 2011, consumer prices edged up 0.4 percent, a much higher increase than had been expected. Inflation hawks responded by urging the Fed to reconsider its low interest rate policy to ensure that a flood of easy money did not ultimately cause inflation to spiral out of control. Indeed, opposition to holding down rates even came from within the Fed itself. On June 8, 2011, Federal Reserve Bank of Kansas City President Thomas Hoenig urged the Fed to increase interest rates by 1 percent in 2012 to tame inflation. "Zero is not the right rate," said Hoenig, the longest-serving member of the Fed board. Hoenig went on to warn that keeping the rate at zero would stoke not only inflation but property and other price bubbles.

Within days of this statement, however, the Fed board reaffirmed that it would not raise rates in the near future. This position was strengthened after a number of economic reports in June showed that unemployment was again rising (to 9.1 percent) and that the American economy was slowing (to 1.8 percent in the first quarter of 2011). These reports immediately sparked fears of a "double dip recession," and many called on the Fed to address these challenges.

At a June press conference, the second of his tenure, Bernanke acknowledged concerns about the economy.

But while he believed that the U.S. economy would slow, he did not foresee another recession. In addition, the Fed chair predicted (correctly as turns out) that the nation's economy would pick up steam in 2012 and 2013, with growth increasing and unemployment coming down below 9 percent. Still, Bernanke pledged to leave interest rates alone, at least in the short term.

Two months later, Bernanke gave global markets a temporary boost when he announced that the Fed would leave interest rates alone for an additional two years. This unprecedented action was intended to help stock markets reverse their downward slide, by giving businesses and consumers the certainty that credit would remain cheap for the foreseeable future. Some Fed watchers saw Bernanke's pledge as an act of desperation and proof that he had essentially run out of options for helping to right the economy.

Meanwhile, the second round of quantitative easing (QE2) came to an end. The $600 billion program ended in July. Given continued worries about the U.S. economy, many wondered whether Bernanke and the Fed would initiate a third round. But at the June press conference, Bernanke made clear that there would be no QE3. However, during an August meeting of the Fed board, Bernanke and others discussed whether the bank could do more to stimulate the lagging American economy. While the board of governors could not agree on a precise course of action, some Fed watchers predicted that QE3 might be a possibility, especially if the economy continued to slow.

Another issue clearly on the Fed chair's mind was the federal deficit, which was on track to surpass $1.3 trillion in 2011 alone. At a June 7, 2011, meeting of bankers in Atlanta, Bernanke argued that the country's long-term economic future looked bleak unless the administration and leaders in Congress came up with a real plan to bring the huge deficit down to more manageable levels. Even though the Fed had helped the country recover from the recession by keeping interest rates extremely low and by injecting trillions of new dollars into the economy, "monetary policy is not a panacea," he said.

After the White House and congressional Republicans reached a $2.4 trillion debt reduction deal in August 2011, the Fed chair urged both sides to reduce the deficit even more substantially. Bernanke's message was amplified by Standard and Poor's decision to downgrade U.S. government debt from its traditional AAA rating to AA+, the first such downgrade in the nation's history.

Around the same time the president and Congress were ironing out their deficit reduction plan, economists were expressing fear that the United States economy was running out of steam. Increasing oil prices, disruptions in Asian supply lines caused by the earthquake and tsunami in Japan and flooding in Thailand, and a reduction in U.S. government spending all combined to slow things down. In the first half of 2011, the U.S. economy grew at an anemic annualized rate of only 0.8 percent. By the summer of 2011, talk of a "double dip" recession was in the air.

With interest rates effectively at 0 percent and two rounds of quantitative easing behind it, the Federal Reserve had fewer tools left in its toolbox to help the economy. Still, in August 2011, Bernanke and his colleagues attempted to give the economy a jolt when they announced that short-term rates would stay at near zero until at least mid-2013, a little longer than they had promised earlier in the year. At the beginning of 2012, the central bank upped the ante, announcing that zero rates would probably remain in place through the end of 2014—a full year-and-a-half longer than its last pledge.

Still, economy-watchers hoped for more—specifically, a third round of quantitative easing. But at its open market committee meeting in March 2012, the Fed passed on a chance to announce QE3, as it would be called, and instead upgraded its outlook for the economy, from "modest" to "moderate." This more positive outlook was due to an uptick in retail sales, which usually bodes well for consumer spending. And since consumer spending drives 70 percent of U.S. economic activity, the new positive retail numbers were important.

Another cause for optimism at the March meeting was due to a report released by the Fed on the same day on the health of the nation's 19 largest banks. The report, the result of stress tests administered by the Fed to the Bank of America, Citi, Goldman Sachs, JPMorgan, and the country's other giant banking institutions, showed that almost all of the largest banks recovered from the 2008 crash and were now "healthy." Given the importance of a vibrant banking sector to the nation's economy, Bernanke and others hailed the report as good news and part of the reason for their upgrade.

But some analysts dismissed the importance of the stress test report, arguing that banks had passed the test by taking actions that shored up their balance sheets but did little or nothing to boost the economy. These economists and others charged that the banks that passed had underwritten very few mortgages or consumer loans and simply played it safe by buying Treasury bonds.

In addition, as spring turned into summer, the pressure on the Fed to "do something" remained, in large part due to continued high unemployment. Even though the "recovery" was three years old, the unemployment rate remained around 8 percent. Indeed, some economists said the real jobless rate was close to double the official number if those who were underemployed or who had given up looking for work were included.

Then, in June 2012, the Labor Department delivered some disheartening economic news, announcing that 64,000 jobs had been created that month, roughly a quarter of the number one would expect in a growing economy. Although the number rebounded to 163,000 in July, experts were still worried that high unemployment was becoming a chronic problem and urged the Fed, as well as the White House and Congress, to do more to stimulate hiring.

With the specter of chronic or near-chronic joblessness hanging in the air, the Fed finally acted. In the early fall of 2012, the central bank announced its long-anticipated third round of quantitative easing (QE3). Under the plan, released in September, the Federal Reserve would buy about $85 billion in mortgage-backed securities and government bonds each month. In addition, Bernanke promised that the Fed would hold down short-term interest rates to zero until the middle of 2015, extending the deadline by an additional six months. Perhaps most important, the chair and his colleagues promised to keep buying securities and bonds until the recovery was firmly in place.

The announcement of QE3 came in the wake of a big policy shift at the central bank. Since the 1960s, the Fed had had two core macroeconomic missions: fight inflation and keep unemployment low. In the late 1970s and 1980s, that mission shifted somewhat to favor inflation fighting. Then-Fed Chairman Paul Volcker had been willing to push the country into a deep recession with high interest rates to break the back of inflation that had reached 13.5 percent in 1981. In recent years, keeping inflation at or below 2 percent had been the central bank's biggest goal.

However, in June 2012, Chairman Bernanke announced that the Fed would rebalance the bank's mission. Bernanke said that from now on, the Fed would be willing to tolerate inflation as high as 2.5 percent. At the same time, he said, the bank would not consider raising interest rates until either unemployment was down to 6.5 percent or lower or inflation rose above 2.5 percent.

In many ways the shift in Fed policy was to be expected. After four years of keeping interest rates at near zero, as well as two (soon to be three) rounds of quantitative easing, the new policy statement was more a reflection of existing reality than a set of guidelines for the future. For some time, Bernanke had been seen as being too lax about inflation and too concerned with economic stimulus. The new policy announcement merely fed these fears.

Still, with many economists and others talking about a "jobless recovery," Bernanke's focus on unemployment was welcomed in many quarters. In July 2012, a month after the announcement of the new policy, unemployment ticked up from 8.2 percent to 8.3 percent. Many saw this higher unemployment number as proof that the Fed's policy shift had been the correct course. A few months later, the Fed launched QE3.

As summer moved into fall and the presidential election campaign, the Fed was blamed by both campaigns for working too hard to protect Wall Street at the expense of Main Street. Republicans also criticized the Fed for quantitative easing, which they said was falsely propping up the economy and would soon lead to severe inflation. GOP presidential candidate Mitt Romney went so far as to say that, if elected, he would not reappoint Bernanke as chair.

In the months following President Obama's reelection, Bernanke urged the president and congressional leaders to work together to responsibly bring the growth of deficit spending under control. At the same time, the chair urged the parties not to make draconian spending cuts or tax increases occur too quickly for fear that they would lead to recession. Bernanke was particularly troubled by the threatened "fiscal cliff," a set of large and automatic spending cuts and tax increases, which were scheduled to take effect on January 1, 2013. Republicans and Democrats created the fiscal cliff in 2011 as a kind of poison pill that would be so unpleasant that they would be compelled to come together and hammer out a long-term budget deal.

The fiscal cliff was averted at the last minute when President Obama and GOP congressional leaders agreed to a $1.3 billion deficit reduction package. But another automatic budget trigger, known as sequestration (which refers to budget caps) loomed in March. Bernanke was not as concerned about sequestration, in large part because it would cut only $110 billion in discretionary spending in 2013. Still, he once again urged leaders to find a way to avoid automatic cuts and come up with a more long-term plan to reduce the federal debt. This time, however, the president and congressional leaders were unable to come to agreement, and sequestration became reality.

In March 2013, the same month sequestration began, the Fed released its latest annual report detailing its stress test of the nation's 19 largest banks. Once again, most of the banks passed the test and the Fed hailed the results as evidence that the banking sector had fully recovered from the financial crisis. Only one bank, Ally Financial, failed and another, BB&T, passed with reservations.

But while the Fed reported the stress tests as good news, some critics (as they had in 2012) questioned the real-world value of the test, although for different reasons. Specifically, some members of Congress wondered how JPMorgan could have unconditionally passed the test after sustaining a nearly $6 billion trading loss at the bank's London office. In addition, challenges to the test results by Ally and BB&T were met with silence by the Fed, which refused to release any information about how it had come up with the results. This left some Fed watchers wondering whether to trust the test when the Fed was unwilling to be transparent about the way in which it was conducted.

By the summer of 2013, speculation was already mounting about who would replace Chair Bernanke, whose term was slated to end at the beginning of 2014. Some expressed a strong desire to have the chairman stay and serve a third term. After all, more than anyone, Bernanke was credited with keeping the country out of depression during the 2008 financial crisis.

But at a news conference in March 2013, Bernanke hinted that he would probably not seek a third term. When asked whether he should stay on to wind down the Fed's policies aimed at stimulating the economy, the chair said, "I don't think I'm the only person in the world who can manage the exit." Rumors of a third term were put to rest a few months later, in June, when President Obama publicly ruled out nominating Bernanke again.

While Obama did not speak of it at the time, the unofficial word from the White House indicated that the president was leaning toward appointing former Treasury Secretary Lawrence Summers to the job. No one questioned whether Summers was qualified for the post; the brilliant Harvard economist had been secretary of the Treasury under President Clinton and had been a key economic adviser to Obama during the president's first term.

But the prospect of Summers' nomination unleashed a firestorm of criticism, largely from the political left. Some of the Senate's most liberal members, such as Ohio Democrat Sherrod Brown, criticized the former Treasury secretary for being both difficult to work with and insufficiently concerned about the plight of the average, working Americans. Women's groups also came out against Summers over some remarks he had made almost a decade before while he was president of Harvard University, indicating that cognitive differences between the sexes might help explain why women are not well represented in many scientific disciplines.

At first, the administration stuck by Summers and pushed to get enough senators lined up behind him to win confirmation. But by the late summer, it was clear that Summers's nomination might not win Senate approval. In September 2013 Summers withdrew from consideration, stating that acrimony caused by his nomination would "not serve the interests of the Federal Reserve."

In the wake of Summers's withdrawal, Vice Chair, Janet Yellen, became the odds-on favorite to replace Bernanke. A Democrat with decades of experience at the Fed and other important economic posts, Yellen had supported Bernanke's efforts to stimulate the economy and was thought likely to continue these policies if promoted. She also was well liked, both within the Fed and on Capitol Hill.

Another possible candidate was Stanley Fischer, who had been governor of the Bank of Israel (the Israeli equivalent of the Fed) from 2005 until the beginning of 2013 and had been credited with successfully steering that country's economy through the 2008 financial meltdown. Fischer, who holds Israeli and American citizenship, was among the most highly respected economists in the world and was Bernanke's faculty adviser when the men were professor and student at MIT.

In October 2013 the wait was over. President Obama nominated Yellen for the Fed's top job and picked Fischer to take her place as vice chair. "She's a proven leader and she's tough—not just because she's from Brooklyn," the president said in announcing Yellen's nomination. At the same ceremony, Yellen seemed to acknowledge the Summers critics when she said that "too many Americans still can't find a job, and worry how they'll pay their bills and provide for their families. The Federal Reserve can help if it does its job effectively."

Even before Yellen was confirmed in January 2014, Fed watchers began speculating on how her nomination might impact the fate of QE3. Some worried that ending the third round of quantitative easing could hurt a still weak economic recovery and possibly pull the nation back into recession. They hoped that Yellen's interest in stoking economic growth and job creation would outweigh her fears of inflation and prompt her to keep the program in place for the time being.

But the pressure, both inside and outside of the Federal Reserve, to end or at least reduce the program had been building for months. In April 2013, for instance, Jeffrey Lacker, president of the Richmond Fed, made headlines when he openly criticized QE3 and, by association, Bernanke, saying that the program should not have been established and that it needed to be stopped immediately. Lacker and others argued that by pumping $85 billion of newly printed money into the economy and keeping interest rates at zero, the Fed was going to drive up inflation and create new asset bubbles, like the run-up in housing prices that contributed to the 2008 financial crash.

Lacker and others pointed to signs that asset bubbles were possibly already forming. For instance, the first three months of 2013 saw a substantial run-up in the stock market, with the Dow Jones Industrial Average increasing 13 percent and the broader S&P 500 stock index moving up 11 percent. And for the first time since the 2008 recession, housing prices also had begun to rise. In 2012, prices rose 6.5 percent nationwide and were on track to rise even more in 2013.

For his part, Bernanke gave conflicting signals about his intentions. For instance, comments he made in June 2013 almost seemed to echo Lacker's remarks and sparked a major stock market sell-off in both American and international markets. Although Bernanke later calmed the situation by offering reassurances that QE3 would continue as long as the American economy was growing sluggishly, the reaction of stock markets reinforced concerns that the world economy had become too dependent on the Fed's easy money policies and that scaling back both quantitative easing and low interest rates could lead to another global recession or at least significantly dampen already slow economic growth.

Ultimately these dangers proved unpersuasive. In December the open market committee voted to cut the bond and equities buying program from $85 billion per month to $75 billion. And at the last meeting chaired by Bernanke, at the end of January 2013, the Fed shaved another $10 billion per month from the program, to $65 billion, with $30 billion being directed to mortgage-backed securities and $35 billion to Treasury bills.

At the same time, however, Bernanke and his colleagues announced that the Fed could continue to keep interest rates at close to zero, even if unemployment dropped to below 6.5 percent unemployment, its earlier target for beginning to raise rates. This was important, because in January unemployment had dropped to 6.6 percent. But, as Bernanke, Yellen, and others pointed out, the falling unemployment rate was being driven in part by the fact that so many people had dropped out of the job market and thus were no longer being counted as unemployed. As a result, they said, the employment picture was still uncertain and low rates were required to encourage borrowing and, ultimately, job creation.

Upon assuming the chairmanship at the beginning of February, Yellen signaled that Bernanke's policies would largely remain in place. At her first press conference in March, she announced that in April the Fed would reduce its QE3 bond-buying program by another $10 billion, to $55 billion per month. Barring a dramatic change in the economy, she said, this gradual tapering would continue, with reductions of $10 billion each month until October 2014, when QE3 would end completely. Chair Yellen expressed confidence that the American economy, and even the stock market, would be strong enough to withstand the end of QE3.

At the same press conference, Yellen also reiterated her intention to keep interest rates in place for now, even if the unemployment rate fell below the earlier 6.5 percent target set in 2012 for raising rates. Henceforth, rate hikes would be triggered by more than just the unemployment rate. Instead, she said, a range of factors, including wage growth and inflation as well as the unemployment rate, would be used to determine when to raise rates and by how much.

Fed watchers interpreted Yellen's remarks to mean that rates would stay at near zero until at least the middle of 2015. This was reaffirmed a few months later in June when the Fed lowered its projections for growth in the U.S. in 2014 from 2.9 percent to 2.2 percent. Indeed, some economists began to think that rates might not start moving up until the end of 2015 or the beginning of 2016.

At the end of March, a few weeks after Yellen's first press conference, the Fed released the results from its latest round of "stress tests" for the world's largest private banks. While previous tests had largely been positive, the results this time around were mixed. Four major banks—Citi and the American operations of RBS, HSBC, and Santander—outright failed and were judged not to have the resources or operational structure needed to withstand the effects of a severe economic downturn. Goldman Sachs and Bank of America both passed the test, but just barely. To make matters worse, a month after the results were announced, Bank of America revealed that the data it submitted to the Fed had been wrong due to an accounting error and that it too likely had failed.

Meanwhile, the debate continued over when the Fed would raise interest rates. During the first quarter of 2014, the economy actually shrank by 2.1 percent, prompting some to predict a delay of rate hikes. But the bad news was tempered by the fact that a severely harsh winter had dampened economic activity in many parts of the country. Indeed, during the second quarter, the economy expanded by 4 percent. Furthermore, the private sector was adding an average of roughly 200,000 jobs a month, a sign that job growth was finally taking off. Meanwhile inflation remained at about 1 percent, well below the 2 percent target set by the Fed. Predictions of an early increase in interest rates came back into vogue.

All of this good economic news came as the Fed continued to taper its third round of QE3. In October, as planned, the central bank stopped buying bonds and other assets and QE3 officially came to an end. Yellen's prediction that tapering would not hurt the economy seemed correct. And again, the fact that QE3's end did not shake the economy led many to wonder whether a rate increase would come soon. The confidence of those predicting a rate hike sooner rather than later was further bolstered when the economy grew a whopping 5 percent in the third quarter of 2014.

But signals from the Fed were still mixed. Minutes released from its July 2014 meeting showed that most Fed governors wanted to see more evidence that the economy was on a sound footing before voting to raise interest rates. By the September meeting, the message was largely the same: they would continue to wait and watch the economy before making any decision on raising rates. For her part, Yellen said that a "considerable time" would likely pass before rates were raised, although she did not define exactly what "considerable" might mean in terms of months.

In December 2014 the Fed proposed a new rule that would increase capital requirements at the nation's eight largest banks, including Goldman Sachs, JPMorgan, and Bank of America. The rule will force these banks to hold larger cash reserves (between about 7 percent and 10 percent of assets, depending on a number of factors) in the hope that the extra money will help them survive another financial collapse. Traditionally, banks rely on short-term loans to meet their everyday liquidity needs. During the financial crisis, however, the market for short-term loans dried up, leaving banks without sufficient day-to-day funds and in need of the federal bailout they ultimately received.

With this new rule, the Fed was largely codifying the status quo, since all the eight banks covered by the requirement have significantly increased their cash reserves since bouncing back from the 2008–2009 recession. Most would already meet the new requirements without the need for more capital, Fed officials predicted. However, it was reported that the nation's largest bank, JPMorgan, might need to raise at least some new money to meet the new requirement.

Current Issues

The date by which the Fed would raise interest rates has continued to be a moving target. If raised too soon or too much, higher interest rates could slow or even stall the economic recovery. Higher rates also would make government borrowing more expensive, putting pressure on federal and state budgets.

As 2015 began, the consensus was that a faster growing economy and continued brisk hiring in the private sector would prompt the Fed to begin raising rates as early as June 2015. Indeed, while Europe, Japan, and most of emerging countries including China, were slated to perform relatively poorly, the U.S. was seen as a bright spot in the global economic sphere.

But some disappointing economic data early in the spring of 2015 threw into question both this rosy economic outlook and predictions for a summer rate increase. At the beginning of April, the Labor Department published data showing that the American economy had added a paltry 126,000 new jobs in March, about half of what was expected and the worst numbers since December 2013. The jobs numbers, in turn, generated concern that first quarter GDP would not be as robust as expected. By May the majority of economists were predicting the Fed would not begin raising rates until the fall of 2015 or even later.

The "will they, won't they" interest rate dance continued into the spring. For instance, at the end of April, William Dudley, who heads the influential Federal Reserve Bank of New York, said that he was still hopeful that the Fed could begin raising interest rates later in 2015. Dudley predicted that even if the economy slowed in the first quarter of the year, the rest of 2015 would likely see strong GDP and job growth.

Once it was clear that the economy was growing at a good pace, Dudley said, the Fed would begin phasing in an increase, from near zero to about 3.5 percent. If the Fed met this 3.5 percent target, he added, it would not suddenly mean that the central bank had shifted to a tight money policy of the sort used to fight inflation. "We simply will be moving from an extremely accommodative monetary policy to one that is only slightly less so," he said.

Dudley's remarks received a lot of attention, and not only because he is the chairman of the most important of the Fed's regional banks. He is also considered close to Chair Yellen, and his words on Fed policy are thought to reflect hers as well.

But the day after Dudley spoke, one of the nation's most influential bank analysts, Dick Bove, argued that the Fed would not raise rates in 2015, in large part because raising interest rates tends to strengthen a country's currency. When Bove made his comments, the dollar was near record highs against the Euro and the Yen, making it harder for U.S. companies to export their products overseas. Boosting an already too high dollar to even greater heights would further hurt American firms and thus the economy, he added.

Meanwhile, Republicans in the House and Senate revived plans to curtail some of the Fed's independence. Members of the GOP, including House Financial Services Committee chairman Jed Hensarling (R-TX), have argued that three rounds of quantitative easing as well as years of near-zero interest rates have created a "house of cards" economy built on cheap money. Critics also say that the vague and opaque nature of Fed policy making has created unnecessary uncertainty for businesses and others about what the central bank will or will not do, which in turn hurts the economy. "We are into an improvisation phase where an incredible amount of discretionary power has been imparted upon the unelected and relatively unaccountable," Hensarling said at a March hearing on Capitol Hill. "I don't think that is good for promoting long-term economic growth."

The concerns of Hensarling and others have prompted many congressional Republicans to support legislation that would require the Fed to follow a formula known as the "Taylor Rule," which pegs interest rates to the rate of inflation as well as economic output. The rule, named for economist John Taylor, would make the Fed's future actions much more predictable, creating more stability and thus growth in the greater economy, supporters say.

But many Democrats and other opponents of the change contend that no one formula can fit every economic circumstance. They point out that the institution's broad discretionary powers gave it the ability to act decisively during the 2008 financial crisis and stop a recession from becoming a depression. Since President Obama generally shares this view, it seems likely that he would veto any measure mandating the Taylor Rule that managed to pass both houses of Congress.

■ AGENCY ORGANIZATION

Biographies

JANET L. YELLEN CHAIR
Appointment: Appointed as chair of the Board of Governors of the Federal Reserve System on Feb. 3, 2014, for a four-year term ending Feb. 3, 2018.

Born: August 13, 1946; Brooklyn, New York.
Education: Brown University, B.S. in economics, 1967; Yale University, Ph.D. in economics, 1971.
Profession: Economist.
Previous Career: An assistant professor at Harvard University from 1971 to 1976, Yellen served as an economist with the Federal Reserve's Board of Governors in 1977 and 1978 and on the faculty of the London School of Economics and Political Science from 1978 to 1980. Yellen is professor emeritus at the University of California at Berkeley and has been a faculty member since 1980. Yellen took leave from Berkeley in 1994 and served as a member of the Board of Governors of the Federal Reserve System through February 1997; she then left the Federal Reserve to become chair of the Council of Economic Advisers through August 1999. She also chaired the Economic Policy Committee of the Organization for Economic Cooperation and Development from 1997 to 1999. Prior to her appointment as chair, Dr. Yellen served as vice chair of the Board of Governors, taking office in October 2010, when she simultaneously began a 14-year term as a member of the board that will expire January 31, 2024. She also served as president and chief executive officer of the Federal Reserve Bank of San Francisco from 2004 to 2010.

STANLEY FISCHER, VICE CHAIR
Appointment: Sworn in as vice chairman of the Board of Governors on June 16, 2014. His term as vice chairman expires on June 12, 2018.

Born: October 1943; Lusaka, Zambia
Education: London School of Economics, B.Sc. and M.Sc. in economics; Massachusetts Institute of Technology; Ph.D. in economics, 1969
Profession: Economist, professor.
Previous Career: Prior to his appointment to the board, Dr. Fischer was governor of the Bank of Israel from 2005 through 2013. From February 2002 to April 2005, Dr. Fischer was vice chairman of Citigroup. Dr. Fischer served as the first deputy managing director of the International Monetary Fund from September 1994 through August 2001. From January 1988 to August 1990, he was the chief economist of the World Bank. From 1973 to 1999, Dr. Fischer was a professor of economics at the Massachusetts Institute of Technology (MIT). Prior to joining the MIT faculty, Dr. Fischer was an assistant professor of economics and a postdoctoral fellow at the University of Chicago. He has been a fellow at the Guggenheim Foundation, the American Academy of Arts and Sciences, and the Econometric Society, as well as a research associate at the National Bureau of Economic Research and an honorary fellow at the London School of Economics.

DANIEL K. TARULLO, GOVERNOR
Appointment: Nominated by President Barack Obama and took office on Jan. 28, 2009, to fill an unexpired term ending Jan. 31, 2022.

Born: November 1952; Boston, Mass.
Education: Georgetown University, A.B., 1973; Duke University, M.A., 1974; University of Michigan, J.D., 1977.
Profession: Professor, lawyer.

Federal Reserve System

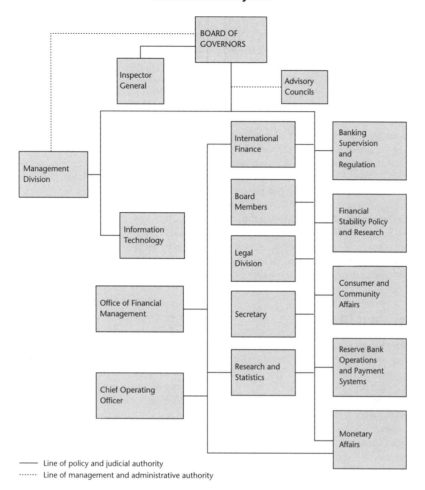

Board of Governors
Inspector General
Advisory Councils
Management Division
Information Technology
Office of Financial Management
Chief Operating Officer
International Finance
Board Members
Legal Division
Secretary
Research and Statistics
Banking Supervision and Regulation
Financial Stability Policy and Research
Consumer and Community Affairs
Reserve Bank Operations and Payment Systems
Monetary Affairs

——— Line of policy and judicial authority
········· Line of management and administrative authority

Previous Career: Prior to his appointment to the board, Tarullo was professor of law at Georgetown University Law Center, where he taught courses in international financial regulation, international law, and banking law. Prior to joining the Georgetown law faculty, he held several senior positions in the Clinton administration. From 1993 to 1998, he served, successively, as assistant secretary of state for economic and business affairs, deputy assistant to the president for economic policy, and assistant to the president for international economic policy. He also served as a principal on both the National Economic Council and the National Security Council. From 1995 to 1998, he also served as President Clinton's personal representative to the G7/G8 group of industrialized nations. He served as chief counsel for employment policy on the staff of Sen. Edward M. Kennedy (D-MA), and practiced law in Washington, DC. He also worked in the antitrust division of the Justice Department and as special assistant to the under secretary of the Commerce Department. From 1981 to 1987, he taught at Harvard Law School.

JEROME H. POWELL, GOVERNOR

Appointment: Powell took office as a member of the Board of Governors of the Federal Reserve System on May 25, 2012, to fill an unexpired term. He was reappointed and sworn in on June 16, 2014, for a term ending January 31, 2028.

Born: February 1953; Washington, D.C

Education: Princeton University, A.B., 1975 Georgetown University, J.D. 1979.

Profession: Lawyer and investment banker.

Previous Career: Prior to his appointment to the board, Powell was a visiting scholar at the Bipartisan Policy Center in Washington, D.C., where he focused on federal and state fiscal issues. From 1997 through 2005, Mr. Powell was a partner at The Carlyle Group. Powell served as an assistant secretary and as under secretary of the Treasury under President George H.W. Bush, with responsibility for policy on financial institutions, the Treasury debt market, and related areas. Prior to joining the administration, he worked as a lawyer and investment banker in New York City. In addition to service on corporate boards, Powell has served on the boards of charitable and educational institutions, including the Bendheim Center for Finance at Princeton University and The Nature Conservancy of Washington, D.C., and Maryland. He was editor-in-chief of the *Georgetown Law Journal*.

LAEL BRAINARD, GOVERNOR

Appointment: Took office on June 16, 2014, to fill an unexpired term ending January 31, 2026.

Born: 1962; Newton, Penn.

Education: Wesleyan University, B.A., 1983; Harvard University, M.S. and Ph.D. in economics, 1989.

Profession: Financial services.

Previous Career: Prior to her appointment to the board, from 1990 to 1996, Brainard was Assistant and associate professor of applied economics at the Massachusetts Institute of Technology's Sloan School of Management. Brainard served as the deputy national economic adviser and deputy assistant to President Clinton. She also served as President Clinton's personal representative to the G-7/G-8. From 2001 to 2008, Brainard was vice president and the founding director of the Global Economy and Development Program and held the Bernard L. Schwartz Chair at the Brookings Institution. Brainard served as counselor to the secretary of the Treasury in 2009 and under secretary of the U.S. Department of Treasury from 2010 to 2013 and counselor to the secretary of the Treasury in 2009.

Headquarters and Divisions

BOARD OF GOVERNORS

Establishes and implements the government's monetary policy. Has broad supervisory and regulatory responsibilities over state-chartered banks that are members of the Federal Reserve System, bank holding companies, and operations of foreign banks in the United States.

Establishes reserve requirements for all depository institutions that offer transaction accounts or non-personal time accounts, reviews and acts on discount rate recommendations of the boards of directors of Federal Reserve banks, and issues regulations governing the administration of the discount window at those banks.

Exercises supervisory and regulatory responsibilities over the laws that regulate foreign operations of member banks and administers the laws that regulate the actions of foreign bank operations in the United States. Directed by Congress to write rules for and to implement a number of major consumer credit protection laws, including the Truth in Lending Act and the Equal Credit Opportunity Act.

Submits an annual report to Congress and makes available detailed statistics and other information relating to the system's activities and the nation's money supply through a variety of publications, including the monthly *Federal Reserve Bulletin.*

Submits a biannual written report to Congress on the state of the economy and monetary policy.

Chair

Janet L. Yellen. (202) 452–3201

Vice Chair

Stanley Fischer. . . . . (202) 452–3761

Governors

Daniel K. Tarullo. . . . . (202) 452–3735

Jerome H. Powell. . . . . (202) 452–3000

Lael Brainard . . . . (202) 452–3217

FEDERAL OPEN MARKET COMMITTEE

The principal instrument used by the Federal Reserve to implement national monetary policy. Responsible for determining what transactions the Federal Reserve will conduct in the open financial marketplace. Through frequent buying and selling of U.S. government securities or the securities of federal agencies, the manager of the System Open Market Account increases or decreases bank reserves in keeping with the instructions and directives issued by the committee. When purchases are made on behalf of the Open Market Account, reserves are increased and more money is injected into the financial system. When the account manager makes sales, the buyers must take money out of circulation to pay for the securities acquired, thus reducing the money supply. In addition to operations in the domestic securities market, the FOMC authorizes and directs operations in foreign exchange markets. The Federal Reserve Bank of New York executes all such transactions and makes allocations among the Reserve banks according to a formula approved by the board of governors.

The FOMC is composed of twelve members—the seven members of the board of governors and five Reserve bank presidents, one of whom is the president of the Federal Reserve Bank of New York, who serves on a continuous basis. The other bank presidents serve one-year terms, January 1 to December 31, on a rotating basis. One member is elected from each of the following groups of Reserve banks: (1) Boston, Philadelphia, Richmond; (2) Cleveland, Chicago; (3) Atlanta, St. Louis, Dallas; and (4) Minneapolis, Kansas City, San Francisco. By statute the committee determines its own organization, and by tradition it elects the chair of the board of governors to serve as its chair and the president of the Federal Reserve Bank of New York as its vice chair. The committee meets in the board's offices in Washington, DC, eight times yearly.

Chair

Janet L. Yellen (Board of Governors)

Vice Chair

William C. Dudley (New York)

Other Members:

Lael Brainard (Board of Governors)

Charles L. Evans (Chicago)

Stanley Fischer (Board of Governors)

Jeffrey M. Lacker (Richmond)

Dennis P. Lockhard (Atlanta)

Jerome H. Powell (Board of Governors)

Daniel K. Tarullo (Board of Governors)

John C. Williams (San Francisco)

Alternate Members:

James Bullard (St. Louis)

Esther L. George (Kansas City)

Loretta J. Mester (Cleveland)

Eric S. Rosengren (Boston)

Michael Strine (first vice president, New York)

Economists

Andrea Ajello. (202) 912–7884

E-mail: andrea.ajello @frb.gov

Javed I. Ahmed . . . . (202) 912–4649

E-mail: javed.i.ahmed @frb.gov

General Counsel

    Scott Alvarez . . . . (202) 452–3583

Manager for Foreign Operations, System Open Market Account

    Simon M. Potter . . . . (212) 720–6309

        E-mail: simon.potter@ny.frb.org

Secretary

    William B. English . . . . (202) 736–5645

ADVISORY COUNCILS

Federal Advisory Council

Composed of twelve banking industry representatives from each Federal Reserve district. Members are selected annually by the board of directors of each Federal Reserve Bank and may be reappointed. Meets four times a year. Confers with the board of governors on banking, business conditions, credit, and monetary policies, and makes recommendations regarding the affairs of the Federal Reserve System.

    Members

    Richard E. Holbrook, First District

    James P. Gorman, Second District

    Scott V. Fainor, Third District

    Paul G. Greig, Fourth District

    Kelly S. King, Fifth District

    O.B. Grayson Hall Jr., Sixth District

    Frederick H. Waddell, Seventh District

    Ronald J. Kruszewski, Eight District

    Patrick J. Donovan, Ninth District

    Jonathan M. Kemper, Tenth District

    Ralph W. Babb Jr., Eleventh District

    John G. Stumpf, Twelfth District

Contact, Office of Visitor Services

    Main . . . . (202) 452–3324

    Wanda Quick . . . . (202) 452–3586

        E-mail: wanda.s.quick@frb.gov

        Internet: www.federalreserve.gov/aboutthefed/fac.htm

Community Depository Institutions Advisory Council

Provides input to the board on the economy, lending conditions, and other issues. Twelve members are representatives from banks, thrift institutions, and credit unions serving on local advisory councils at the 12 Federal Reserve Banks.

President for 2015

    John B. Dicus (Topeka, KS)

Vice President

    Michael J. Castellana (Albany, NY)

Contact, Office of Visitor Services

    Main . . . . (202) 452–3324

    Wanda Quick . . . . (202) 452–3586

        E-mail: wanda.s.quick@frb.gov

        Internet: www.federalreserve.gov/aboutthefed/cdiac.htm

OFFICE OF BOARD MEMBERS

Provides direct staff support to the seven members of the board, provides secretarial help, implements actions taken by the board, assists divisions in implementing policy actions, assists board members in speech preparation, conducts special surveys and research assignments for board members, and answers selected correspondence.

Special Adviser to the Chair

    Trevor A. Reeve . . . . (202) 452–3716

Advisers to the Board

    William English . . . . (202) 736–5645

    Stacey Tevlin . . . . (202) 452–2322

OFFICE OF THE INSPECTOR GENERAL

Investigates suspected cases of impropriety, wrongdoing, fraud, or waste and abuse in programs and operations administered or financed by the board.

Inspector General

    Mark Bialek . . . . (202) 973–5005

        Fax. . . . . (202) 973–5044

    IG Hotline (DC local). . . . . (202) 452–6400

    Toll-free . . . . (800) 827–3340

OFFICE OF THE SECRETARY

Coordinates and handles items requiring board action including the following: preparing agendas for board meetings; implementing actions taken at board meetings; preparing, indexing, and circulating minutes of board meetings; and participating in the drafting of Federal Reserve regulations, rules, and procedures. Also performs the same functions for the Federal Advisory Council and coordinates communication between the board and the conference of presidents and the conference of first vice presidents of Federal Reserve banks. Makes arrangements for individuals and groups visiting the board and maintains custody of and provides reference service for official records of the board. Produces the *Federal Reserve Regulatory Service* and handles correspondence and Freedom of Information requests.

Secretary

    Robert de V. Frierson . . . . (202) 452–3711

        Fax. . . . . (202) 452–3819

Deputy Secretary

    Margaret M. Shanks . . . . (202) 452–2200

Associate Secretary

    Michael J. Lewanodowski. . . . . (202) 736–1927

DIVISION OF BANKING SUPERVISION AND REGULATION

Informs the board about current developments in bank supervision and banking structure. Coordinates the system's bank supervision and develops and implements safety and soundness and other regulations for these entities under board direction and in collaboration with Reserve Banks and other domestic and international regulatory authorities. In addition, the division supports the conduct of monetary policy by monitoring current conditions and prospective developments affecting the banking industry and financial markets more generally.

Director

    Michael S. Gibson . . . . (202) 452–2495

        E-mail: michael.s.gibson@frb.gov

        Fax. . . . . (202) 452–2770

Deputy Director
Maryann F. Hunter . . . . (202) 452–6468
Application and Enforcement
Barbara Bouchard . . . . (202) 452–3072
Accounting Policy and Regulatory Reporting
Robert T. Maahs . . . . (202) 452–3000
Accounting Policy and Disclosure
Laurie F. Priest . . . . (202) 452–2750
Community Banking Organizations
Vitus Ukwuoma . . . . (202) 452–3163
Credit Risk
Brian Valenti . . . . (202) 452–3575
Domestic Applications
Michael J. Sexton . . . . (202) 452–3009
Financial Analysis, Surveillance, and Risk Assessment
Matt Mattson . . . . (202) 452–2943
Large Complex Banking Organizations
Tim Clark . . . . (202) 452–5264
Large Financial Institutions
William Charwat . . . . (202) 452–3006
Regulatory Reports
Douglas W. Carpenter . . . . (202) 452–2205

DIVISION OF CONSUMER AND COMMUNITY AFFAIRS

Drafts, interprets, and administers regulations governing consumer protection laws, community reinvestment, and fair lending. Coordinates the system's supervision and examining activities to make sure state member banks comply with consumer protection regulations, and investigates consumer complaints against banks. Oversees a community affairs program that encourages banks to engage in community development projects. The Consumer Advisory Council, established in 1976 and composed of thirty members from across the country, meets quarterly to represent consumer and creditor interests before the board.

Director
Eric Belsky . . . . (202) 452–2631
Fax . . . . (202) 872–4995
Senior Associate Director
Suzanne G. Killian . . . . (202) 452–2090
Associate Director
Allen J. Fishbein . . . . (202) 452–3000
James A. Michaels . . . . (202) 452–3667
Assistant Director
Marisa A. Reid . . . . (202) 452–3000

DIVISION OF INFORMATION TECHNOLOGY

Provides telecommunication and computer services for the board of governors, including maintenance and storage of data files and an extensive distribution processing network facility.

Director
Sharon Mowry . . . . (202) 452–3618
Fax . . . . (202) 872–7566

DIVISION OF INTERNATIONAL FINANCE

Provides the board, the Federal Open Market Committee, and other Federal Reserve officials with assessments of current international economic and financial developments, principally those relating to the effects on the U.S. economy and world activity, and the effects of the world economy on U.S. economic and financial conditions. Provides economic data and analyses for public release.

Director
Steven B. Kamin . . . . (202) 452–3339
E-mail: steven.kamin@frb.gov
Fax . . . . (202) 452–6424
Deputy Director
Thomas A. Connors . . . . (202) 452–3639
E-mail: tom.connors@frb.gov
Deputy Director
Michael Leahy . . . . (202) 452–3000
E-mail: michael.leahy@frb.gov
Senior Advisers
Stijin Claessens . . . . (202) 452–2089
Brian M. Doyle . . . . (202) 785–6011
Jane Haltmaier . . . . (202) 452–2374
Associate Director
Mark Carey . . . . (202) 452–2784
Associate Director
Charles P. Thomas . . . . (202) 452–3698

LEGAL DIVISION

Provides legal advice in support of board statutory and regulatory responsibilities. Prepares legal analyses and drafts proposals for use by the board in implementing statutory provisions. Represents the board in civil litigation and in administrative proceedings. Aids other divisions in the following areas: contracting; fiscal agency activities; Federal Reserve bank matters; environment and labor law; personnel and supervisory enforcement matters; preparing draft legislation or comments on proposed legislation; and assisting in the preparation of board member testimony. Also prepares, interprets, and distributes information about board decisions, regulations, rules, and instructions. Advises the board of governors and acts as general counsel to the FOMC.

General Counsel
Scott G. Alvarez . . . . (202) 452–3583
Fax . . . . (202) 452–3101
Deputy General Counsel
Richard M. Ashton . . . . (202) 452–3750
International Banking
Kathleen O'Day . . . . (202) 452–3786
Monetary and Reserve Bank Affairs
Stephanie Martin . . . . (202) 452–3198

MANAGEMENT DIVISION

Maintains the board's account books and directs its internal financial management program, draws up the annual budget, and supervises the receipt and disbursement of funds. Reviews and analyzes the board's use of resources and makes recommendations on developing new programs and improving existing ones.

Director
Michell C. Clark . . . . (202) 452–3000

DIVISION OF MONETARY AFFAIRS

Responsible for support of the board and the Federal Open Market Committee (FOMC) in the conduct of domestic monetary policy through open market operations, discount rates and the administration of the discount window, and reserve requirements. Serves as liaison with the domestic trading desk at the Federal Reserve Bank of New York in the daily conduct of open market operations, and monitors and analyzes the implications of open market operations and lending for the Federal Reserve's balance sheet. Monitors and interprets developments in financial markets, and analyzes and produces data on developments in money, reserves, and bank credit. Also conducts research on topics related to the conduct of monetary policy, both short-run implementation and more general issues related to formulating policy and analyzing the markets in which policy is carried out.

Director
Thomas Laubach . . . . (202) 452–3652
E-mail: thomas.laubach@frb.gov
Deputy Director
James Clouse . . . . (202) 452–3922
E-mail: james.a.clouse@frb.gov
Deputy Associate Director
Margaret DeBoeh . . . . (202) 452–3139
E-mail: Margaret.deboer@frb.gov
Deputy Director
William R. Nelson . . . . (202) 452–3579
E-mail: William.r.nelson@frb.gov
Deputy Director
Stephen A. Myer . . . . (202) 452–3985
E-mail: steve.meyer@frb.gov

DIVISION OF RESEARCH AND STATISTICS

Prepares and develops economic and financial information needed by Fed officials to formulate credit and monetary policies and to maintain current operations of the board and the Federal Reserve System. Also supplies economic data and analyses for public release. Most of the data is available in various publications (*see Publications, below*).

Director
David W. Wilcox . . . . (202) 452–2991
E-mail: david.w.wilcox@frb.gov
Deputy Directors
William L. Wascher . . . . (202) 452–2812
E-mail: william.l.wascher@frb.gov
Matthew J. Eichner . . . . (202) 452–2019
E-mail: matthew.j.eichner@frb.gov
Associate Director
David E. Lebow . . . . (202) 452–3057
E-mail: david.e.lebow@frb.gov
Deputy Associate Directors
Diana Hancock . . . . (202) 452–3019
E-mail: diana.hancock@frb.gov
Joshua H. Gallin . . . . (202) 452–2788
E-mail: Joshua.h.gallin@frb.gov
Sean D. Campbell . . . . (202) 452–3760
E-mail: sean.d.Campbell@frb.gov

DIVISION OF RESERVE BANK OPERATIONS AND PAYMENT SYSTEMS

Oversees the Federal Reserve banks' provision of financial services to depository institutions, fiscal agency services to the Treasury and other government agencies, and significant support functions such as information technology and financial and cost accounting. The division also develops policies and regulations to foster the efficiency and integrity of the U.S. payment system, works with other central banks and international organizations to improve payment systems more broadly, and conducts research on payment issues.

Director
Louise L. Roseman . . . . (202) 452–2789
Fax . . . . (202) 452–2746
Deputy Director
Jeffrey Marquardt . . . . (202) 452–2360
Associate Director
Paul W. Bettge . . . . (202) 452–3174
Associate Director
Paul Bajinder . . . . (202) 452–3646
Gregory L. Evans . . . . (202) 452–3945
Deputy Associate Director
Lisa K. Hoskins . . . . (202) 452–3437
Associate Director
Michael J. Lambert . . . . (202) 452–3376
Assistant Director
David C. Mills . . . . (202) 452–6265
E-mail: david.c.mills@frb.gov

OFFICE OF THE STAFF DIRECTOR FOR MANAGEMENT

Responsible for planning and coordinating the board's operations and activities, including building administration, budget preparation, accounting, and personnel management. Coordinates contingency planning operations and equal employment opportunity programs. The staff director is a designated official of the board's occupational safety and health program.

Staff Director
Donald Hammond . . . . (202) 452–3000
Fax . . . . (202) 728–5832

FEDERAL RESERVE BANKS

The twelve Federal Reserve districts were created on the basis of trade areas and related economic considerations and do not always follow state lines. There is a Federal Reserve bank in each district, and ten of the banks have branch offices. The Reserve banks are the principal medium through which the policies and supervisory powers of the Federal Reserve System are implemented. Responsibilities of the banks include providing local and nationwide facilities for the processing of checks and other monetary instruments, meeting the currency needs of the country, holding the reserve accounts required of financial institutions, extending credit to depository institutions, supervising and collecting data on the banking system, acting as a fiscal agent for the government, maintaining government accounts, selling and redeeming government securities, and administering regionally the policies of the board of governors and the FOMC. The chief executive officer of each bank is its president. The president and first vice president are appointed by the board of directors, with approval of the Fed's board of governors, for a term of five years.

Directors of Federal Reserve District Banks

Each of the twelve Federal Reserve district banks has nine directors, elected or appointed for staggered three-year terms. They are divided into three classes of three directors each; the term of one director in each class expires every year.

The classes represent member banks (Class A) and the public (Classes B and C). Class A and B directors are elected by the member banks in the district. Class C directors are appointed by the board of governors.

Member banks are divided into categories according to capitalization: Group 1 (large banks), Group 2 (medium banks), and Group 3 (small banks). Each group elects one Class A and one Class B director.

Class A directors are almost always member bank officers or directors. Class B directors are selected with consideration to agricultural, commercial, industrial service, labor, and consumer interests. Class B and C directors may not be officers, directors, or employees of any bank. Class A and B directors may be reelected.

One of the Class C directors is appointed by the board to act as chair, and another is appointed as deputy chair. In the absence of the chair and deputy chair, the third Class C director acts as chair. Class C directors are not reappointed if they have served two full terms of three years each.

The directors help formulate monetary policy through biweekly recommendations to the board of governors on the discount rate their banks charge on collateralized loans to depository institutions. They prescribe the bylaws under which the bank's general business is conducted and oversee management of the bank. The directors appoint all officers and recommend their salaries, decide on promotion or change in office personnel, supervise internal auditing, and approve the annual budget for their banks.

Directors of Federal Reserve Branch Banks

Branches have either five or seven directors. The board of directors of the parent Reserve bank appoints a majority of these; the others are appointed by the Fed's board of governors. The chair of a branch bank board is chosen from among the directors appointed by the board of governors. Branch bank directors must be individuals whose business and financial interests are primarily within and representative of the branch territory. Directors serve for three years when the branch board consists of seven people, or for two years when the branch board consists of five people.

Branches perform for their territories most of the functions performed at the district level.

Federal Reserve District Banks

DISTRICT 1

(northern CT, MA, ME, NH, RI, VT)

Federal Reserve Bank of Boston

600 Atlantic Ave.
Boston, MA 02210
(617) 973–3000
Eric S. Rosengren, president
Internet: www.bostonfed.org

DISTRICT 2

(southern CT, northern NJ, NY, PR, VI)

Federal Reserve Bank of New York

33 Liberty St.
New York, NY 10045
(212) 720–5000
William C. Dudley, president
Internet: www.newyorkfed.org

DISTRICT 3

(DE, southern NJ, eastern and central PA)

Federal Reserve Bank of Philadelphia

10 Independence Mall
Philadelphia, PA 19106
(215) 574–6000
Patrick T. Harker, president
Internet: www.phil.frb.org

DISTRICT 4

(eastern KY, OH, western PA, northern WV)

Federal Reserve Bank of Cleveland

1455 E. 6th St.
Cleveland, OH 44114
(216) 579–2000
Loretta Mester, president
(216) 579–2114
Internet: www.clevelandfed.org

Cincinnati Branch

150 E. 4th St.
Cincinnati, OH 45202
(800) 432–1343
(513) 721–4787
LaVaughn M. Henry, vice president
(513) 762–7100

Pittsburgh Branch

1 Oxford Center, #3000
301 Grant St.
Pittsburgh, PA 15219
(412) 261–7800
Guhan Venkatu, vice president
(412) 261–7806

DISTRICT 5

(DC, MD, NC, SC, VA, eastern and southern WV)

Federal Reserve Bank of Richmond

701 E. Byrd St.
Richmond, VA 23219
(804) 697–8000

Jeffrey M. Lacker president
Internet: www.richmondfed.org

Baltimore Branch

502 S. Sharp St.
Baltimore, MD 21201
(410) 576–3300
David E. Beck, senior vice president
(410) 576–3310
E-mail: dave.beck@rich.frb.org

Charlotte Branch

530 E. Trade St.
Charlotte, NC 28202
(704) 358–2100
Matthew Martin, vice president
(704) 358–2101

DISTRICT 6

(AL, FL, GA, southern LA, southern MS, central and
eastern TN)

Federal Reserve Bank of Atlanta

1000 Peachtree St. N.E.
Atlanta, GA 30309–4470
(404) 498–8500
Dennis P. Lockhart, president
Internet: www.frbatlanta.org

Birmingham Branch

524 Liberty Pkwy.
Birmingham, AL 35242–7531
(205) 968–6700
Julius Weyman, vice president

Jacksonville Branch

800 Water St.
Jacksonville, FL 32204
(904) 632–1000
Christopher Oakley, vice president

Miami Branch

9100 N.W. 36th St.
Miami, FL 33178–2425
(305) 591–2065
Juan Del Busto, vice president

Nashville Branch

301 Rosa L. Parks Ave.
Nashville, TN 37203–4407
(615) 251–7100
Lee Jones, vice president

New Orleans Branch

525 St. Charles Ave.
New Orleans, LA 70130–1630
(504) 593–3200
Robert J. Musso, vice president

DISTRICT 7

(IA, northern IL, central and northern IN, southern
MI, southern WI)

Federal Reserve Bank of Chicago

230 S. LaSalle St.
Chicago, IL 60604–1413
(312) 322–5322
Charles L. Evans, president
Internet: www.chicagofed.org

Detroit Branch

1600 E. Warren St.
Detroit, MI 48207–1063
(313) 961–6880
Robert Wiley, vice president

DISTRICT 8

(AR, southern IL, southern IN, western KY, northern
MS, eastern MO, western TN)

Federal Reserve Bank of St. Louis

One Federal Reserve Bank Plaza
Broadway and Locust Sts.
St. Louis, MO 63102
(314) 444–8444
(800) 333–0810
James Bullard, president
Internet: www.stlouisfed.org

Little Rock Branch

Stephens Building
111 Center St., #1000
Little Rock, AR 72201
(501) 324–8300
Robert A. Hopkins, vice president

Louisville Branch

National City Tower
101 S. Fifth St., #1920
Louisville, KY 40202
(502) 568–9200
Nikki Jackson, vice president

Memphis Branch

200 N. Main St.
Memphis, TN 38103
(901) 523–7171
Douglas Scarboro, vice president

DISTRICT 9

(northern MI, MN, MT, ND, SD, northwestern WI)

Federal Reserve Bank of Minneapolis

90 Hennepin Ave.
Minneapolis, MN 55401
(612) 204–5000
Narayana Kocherlakota, president
Internet: www.minneapolisfed.org

Helena Branch

100 Neill Ave.
Helena, MT 59601

(406) 447–3800
Susan Woodrow, assistant vice president

DISTRICT 10
(CO, KS, western MO, NE, northern NM, OK, WY)

Federal Reserve Bank of Kansas City
1 Memorial Drive
Kansas City, MO 64198
(816) 881–2000
(800) 333–1010
Esther L. George, president
Internet: www.kansascityfed.org

Denver Branch
1020 16th St.
Denver, CO 80202
(303) 572–2300
(800) 333–1020
Alison Felix, vice president

Oklahoma City Branch
211 North Robinson
Two Leadership Square, #300
Oklahoma City, OK 73102
(405) 270–8400
(800) 333–1030
Chad Wilkerson, vice president

Omaha Branch
2201 Farnam St.
Omaha, NE 68102
(402) 221–5500
(800) 333–1040
Nathan Kauffman, vice president

DISTRICT 11
(northern LA, southern NM, TX)

Federal Reserve Bank of Dallas
2200 N. Pearl St.
Dallas, TX 75201
(214) 922–6000
Helen Holcomb, interim president
Internet: www.dallasfed.org

El Paso Branch
301 E. Main St.
El Paso, TX 79901
(915) 521–5200
Roberto A. Coronado, vice president

Houston Branch
1801 Allen Pkwy.
Houston, TX 77019
(713) 483–3000
Daron D. Peschel, vice president

San Antonio Branch
402 Dwyer Ave
San Antonio, TX 78204
(210) 978–1200
Blake Hastings, vice president

DISTRICT 12
(AK, AZ, CA, HI, ID, NV, OR, UT, WA)

Federal Reserve Bank of San Francisco
101 Market St.
San Francisco, CA 94105
(415) 974–2000
TTY (415) 393–1900
John C. Williams, president
Media Inquiries (800) 227–4133, ext. 2
Internet: www.frbsf.org

Los Angeles Branch
950 S. Grand Ave.
Los Angeles, CA 90015
(213) 683–2300
Roger W. Replogle, vice president

Portland Branch
1500 S.W. 1st Ave., #100
Portland, OR 97201
(503) 276–3000
Mary Daly, vice president

Salt Lake City Branch
120 S. State St.
Salt Lake City, UT 84111
(801) 322–7900
Jim Narron, vice president

Seattle Branch
2700 Naches Ave. S.W.
Renton, WA 98057
(425) 203–0800
Mark A. Gould, vice president

■ CONGRESSIONAL ACTION

Congressional Liaison
Brian Gross. . . . . (202) 452–2013

Committees and Subcommittees

HOUSE FINANCIAL SERVICES COMMITTEE
Subcommittee on Monetary Policy and Trade
2129 RHOB, Washington, DC 20515–6050
(202) 225–7502

**U.S. SENATE COMMITTEE ON BANKING,
HOUSING, AND URBAN AFFAIRS**
SDOB-534, Washington, DC 20510–6075
(202) 224–7391

JOINT ECONOMIC COMMITTEE
G-01 SDOB, Washington, DC 20515–6432
(202) 224–5171

Legislation

The Federal Reserve System was established under authority of the **Federal Reserve Act,** approved Dec. 23, 1913 (38 Stat. 251, 12 U.S.C. 221). The act was substantially amended by the **Banking Act of 1933,** also known as the **Glass-Steagall Act** (48 Stat. 162, 12 U.S.C. 227) and the **Banking Act of 1935** (49 Stat. 684, 12 U.S.C. 228). This legislation, as amended, embodies the basic authorization for the activities of the Federal Reserve System.

The Fed also has responsibility for the administration of other legislation. Although it has supervisory powers over all member banks, its regulatory powers for the legislation listed below extend only to state-chartered banks that have voluntarily become members of the system. The following is a list of the major legislation administered in part by the Federal Reserve. The regulation letter in brackets after a statute refers to the Federal Reserve regulation that covers that law.

Federal Trade Commission Act of 1914 (38 Stat. 719, 15 U.S.C. 41). Signed by the president Sept. 26, 1914. Prohibited unfair or deceptive banking practices. [Regulation AA]

Securities Act of 1933 (48 Stat. 74, 15 U.S.C. 77a). Signed by the president May 27, 1933. Originally administered by the Federal Trade Commission, the act exempted banks from registering securities.

Securities Exchange Act of 1934 (48 Stat. 881, 15 U.S.C. 78b). Signed by the president June 6, 1934. Required registration of securities (applicable to state member banks with more than $1 million in assets and more than 500 stockholders). [Regulations T, U, G, and X]

Defense Production Act of 1950 and **Executive Order 10480** (64 Stat. 798, 50 U.S.C. app. 2091). Signed by the president Sept. 8, 1950. Guaranteed the financing of contractors, subcontractors, and others involved in national defense work. [Regulation V]

Bank Holding Company Act of 1956 (70 Stat. 133, 12 U.S.C. 1841). Signed by the president May 9, 1956. Regulated the creation and expansion of bank holding companies. [Regulation Y]

Bank Mergers and Consolidation Act of 1960 (74 Stat. 129, 12 U.S.C. 1828). Signed by the president May 13, 1960. Required that all proposed bank mergers receive prior approval from the federal regulatory agency that will have jurisdiction over the surviving bank.

Bank Service Corporation Act (76 Stat. 1132, 12 U.S.C. 1861). Signed by the president Oct. 23, 1962. Permitted certain federally supervised banks to form service corporations to perform clerical, bookkeeping, and data-processing functions.

Bank Mergers Act of 1966 (80 Stat. 7, 12 U.S.C. 1828). Signed by the president Feb. 21, 1966. Established a procedure for review of proposed bank mergers so as to eliminate the necessity for dissolution of merged banks.

Truth in Lending Act (82 Stat. 146, 15 U.S.C. 1601). Signed by the president May 29, 1968. Required lenders and merchants to inform customers of the total cost of loans and installment purchase plans in terms of annual rates to be charged; permitted customers to make valid cost comparisons between lending rates or installment plans of different stores or lending institutions. Also prohibited unsolicited distribution of credit cards and limited the owner's liability for unauthorized use of lost or stolen cards. [Regulation Z]

Bank Protection Act of 1968 (82 Stat. 294, 12 U.S.C. 1881). Signed by the president July 7, 1968. Required establishment of security system standards for banking institutions. [Regulation P]

Credit Control Act of 1969 (83 Stat. 376, 12 U.S.C. 1901). Signed by the president Dec. 23, 1969. Authorized the board of governors, at the direction of the president, to impose controls on all forms of consumer credit.

Currency and Foreign Transactions Reporting Act (84 Stat. 1118, 31 U.S.C. 1051). Signed by the president Oct. 26, 1970. Required banks, citizens, and businesses to maintain adequate records of foreign currency transactions. [Regulations M, N]

Fair Credit Reporting Act (84 Stat. 1128, 15 U.S.C. 1681). Signed by the president Oct. 26, 1970. Regulated credit information and use. [Regulation Z]

NOW Accounts Act (87 Stat. 342, 12 U.S.C. 1832). Signed by the president Aug. 16, 1973. Regulated interest-bearing checking accounts. [Regulation J]

Equal Credit Opportunity Act (88 Stat. 1521, 15 U.S.C. 1691). Signed by the president Oct. 28, 1974. Prohibited credit discrimination against women; amended in 1975 to include discrimination based on age, race, color, religion, or national origin. [Regulation B]

Home Mortgage Disclosure Act of 1975 (89 Stat. 1125, 12 U.S.C. 2801). Signed by the president Dec. 31, 1975. Required lending institutions within standard metropolitan statistical areas (SMSAs) to disclose the number and amount of mortgage loans made annually to determine if banks are discriminating against certain city neighborhoods by refusing to make mortgage loans regardless of the creditworthiness of the potential borrower (practice known as "redlining"). [Regulation C]

Consumer Leasing Act of 1976 (90 Stat. 257, 15 U.S.C. 1601). Signed by the president March 23, 1976. Required full disclosure of terms of leases of personal property, including vehicles, appliances, and furniture. [Regulation Z]

Community Reinvestment Act of 1977 (91 Stat. 1147, 12 U.S.C. 2901–2905). Signed by the president Oct. 12, 1977. Required federal regulators of banks and savings and loan associations to encourage institutions they regulate to help meet the credit needs of their communities, particularly low- and moderate-income neighborhoods. [Regulation BB]

International Banking Act of 1978 (92 Stat. 607, 12 U.S.C. 3101–3108). Signed by the president Sept. 17, 1978. Provided for the federal regulation of foreign banks in domestic financial markets.

Electronic Fund Transfer Act of 1978 (92 Stat. 3728, 15 U.S.C. 1601 note). Signed by the president Nov. 10, 1978. Established rules relating to consumer liability for unauthorized use of an electronic fund transfer card and unsolicited issuance of cards by financial institutions. Prohibited creditors from making automatic repayment of loans a condition of extending credit; overdraft credit plans were exempted. [Regulation E]

Financial Institutions Regulatory and Interest Rate Control Act of 1978 (92 Stat. 3641, 12 U.S.C. 226 note). Signed by the president Nov. 10, 1978. Regulated the activities of individual bank officers. Provided for tighter controls on insider lending and interlocking directorates among financial institutions and expanded the authority of bank regulators.

Depository Institutions Deregulation and Monetary Control Act of 1980 (94 Stat. 132, 12 U.S.C. 226 note). Signed by the president March 31, 1980. Extended reserve requirements to all financial institutions. Phased out interest rate ceilings over a six-year period. Allowed thrift institutions to offer a wider range of financial services.

Garn-St. Germain Depository Institutions Act of 1982 (96 Stat. 1469, 12 U.S.C. 226 note). Signed by the president Oct. 15, 1982. Expanded the FDIC's powers to assist troubled banks by allowing either direct or merger-related assistance. Allowed commercial banks and mutual savings banks, which were in danger of closing, to be acquired on an interstate and/or cross-industry basis. Provided increased powers for federally chartered savings and loan associations and savings, including more liberal chartering options; the ability to offer stock; the authority to accept certain types of demand deposits; expanded real estate investment authority; and the ability to invest in a broad range of government securities.

International Lending Supervision Act of 1983 (97 Stat. 1278, 12 U.S.C. 3901). Signed by the president Nov. 30, 1983. Increased the oversight responsibilities of the Federal Reserve in terms of the international lending procedures of U.S. banks. Required federal banking agencies to establish minimum capital levels for banking institutions, accounting fee regulations on international loans, and regulations for collection and disclosure of international lending data regarding the status of banks' outstanding loans to particular countries. Also required banks to maintain special reserves against loans that were unlikely to be paid off by a foreign borrower.

Competitive Equality Banking Act of 1987 (101 Stat. 581, 12 U.S.C. 1841 note). Signed by the president Aug. 10, 1987. Redefined "banks" as institutions that take deposits or write commercial loans. Prohibited limited service banks from engaging in banking activities without regulation.

Expedited Funds Availability Act (101 Stat. 635, 12 U.S.C. 4001). Signed by the president Aug. 10, 1987. Mandated timetables for check clearing and availability of funds. Required the Federal Reserve to reduce the amount of time for checks to clear.

Federal Deposit Insurance Corporation Improvement Act of 1991 (105 Stat. 2236, 12 U.S.C. 1811). Signed by the president Dec. 19, 1991. Required the most cost-effective method of resolving banks in danger of failing and improved supervisory and examination procedures. It also made additional resources available to the Bank Insurance Fund. Gave the Federal Reserve Board jurisdiction over all foreign banks in the United States.

Depository Institutions Disaster Relief Act of 1992 (106 Stat. 2771, 12 U.S.C. 1811 note). Signed by the president Oct. 23, 1992. Facilitated recovery from recent disasters by providing greater flexibility for depository institutions and their regulators.

Futures Trading Practices Act of 1992 (106 Stat. 3628, 7 U.S.C. 1 note). Signed by the president Oct. 28, 1992. Title 5 directed any contract market in stock index futures or options on stock index futures to submit to the board of governors any rule establishing or changing levels of either initial or maintenance margin on such contracts. Also permitted the board to delegate to the Commodity Futures Trading Commission its authority over margin levels for stock index contracts.

Housing and Community Development Act of 1992 (106 Stat. 3672, 42 U.S.C. 5301 note). Signed by the president Oct. 28, 1992. Established regulatory structure for government-sponsored enterprises, combated money laundering, and provided regulatory relief to financial institutions.

Depository Institutions Disaster Relief Act of 1993 (107 Stat. 752, 12 U.S.C. 4008 note). Signed by the president Aug. 12, 1993. Authorized the board to make exceptions to the Truth in Lending Act and Expedited Funds Availability Act within major disaster areas.

Government Securities Act Amendments of 1993 (107 Stat. 2344, 15 U.S.C. 78a note). Signed by the president Dec. 17, 1993. Extended and revised rulemaking authority with respect to government securities under the federal securities laws.

Home Ownership and Equity Protection Act of 1994 (108 Stat. 2160, 12 U.S.C. 4701 note). Signed by the president Sept. 23, 1994. Part of a larger bill. Under Title I, Subtitle B, Section 157, Fed's board of governors was directed to (1) study and report to Congress on the adequacy of federal consumer protections in connection with an open-ended credit transaction secured by the consumer's principal dwelling; (2) report to Congress on whether, for purposes of such transactions, a more appropriate interest rate index exists than the yield on Treasury securities; and (3) conduct periodic public hearings on the home equity loan market and the adequacy of existing consumer protection laws to protect low-income consumers.

Interstate Banking Efficiency Act of 1994 (108 Stat. 2338, 12 U.S.C. 1811 note). Signed by the president Sept. 29, 1994. Permitted banks to operate networks of branch offices across state lines without having to set up separately capitalized subsidiary banks.

Farm Credit System Reform Act of 1996 (110 Stat. 162, 12 U.S.C. 20001 note). Signed by the president Feb. 10, 1996. Required Federal Reserve banks to act as depositaries, fiscal agents, or custodians of the Federal Agricultural Mortgage Corporation (FAMC). Required the book-entry system of the Fed to be made available to FAMC.

Economic Growth and Regulatory Paperwork Reduction Act of 1996 (110 Stat. 3009–32, 5 U.S.C. 3109). Signed by the president Sept. 30, 1996. Authorized the board of governors to exempt transactions from the Truth in Lending Act (TILA) disclosure requirements when the board determined (1) they are not necessary to effectuate its purposes; or (2) they do not provide a measurable benefit in the form of useful information or consumer protection.

Required the board to publish its rationale for exemption at the time a proposed exemption is published for comment.

Gramm-Leach-Bliley Act (113 Stat. 1338, 12 U.S.C. 1811 note). Signed by the president Nov. 12, 1999. Title I repealed provisions of the Banking Act of 1933 and the Bank Holding Company Act of 1956 to allow affiliations between banks and any financial company, including brokerage and insurance firms. Gave the Federal Reserve supervisory oversight authority and responsibility for bank holding companies.

To Amend the Federal Reserve Act to Broaden the Range of Discount Window Loans (113 Stat. 1638). Signed by the president Dec. 6, 1999. Amended the Federal Reserve Act to allow the Federal Reserve to print more money for its "discount window," which extended credit to banks and served as a buffer against unexpected fluctuations in bank reserves. Permitted banks to offer additional types of collateral to receive credit at the discount window, including receipts of deposits and collections and agricultural securities.

Uniting and Strengthening America by Providing Appropriate Tools Required to Intercept and Obstruct Terrorism Act of 2001 (USA Patriot Act) (115 Stat. 272, 18 U.S.C. 1 note). Signed by the president Oct. 26, 2001. Title III, the International Money Laundering Abatement and Anti-Terrorist Financing Act of 2001, amended various federal banking laws, including the Bank Holding Company Act of 1956, Fair Credit Reporting Act, Federal Deposit Insurance Act, and Federal Reserve Act. Directed certain government agencies, principally the Treasury Department in consultation with the Fed, to investigate and curtail money laundering and other activities that might be undertaken to finance terrorist actions or disrupt legitimate banking operations. Required the Fed to consider an institution's ability to combat money laundering when evaluating proposed bank shares or mergers.

Terrorism Risk Insurance Act of 2002 (116 Stat. 2322, 15 U.S.C. 6701, note). Signed by the president Nov. 26, 2002. Amended the Federal Reserve Act to state that certain actions that previously required the affirmative vote of five members of the board may nevertheless be taken on the unanimous vote of all members then in office if fewer than five.

Check Clearing for the 21st Century Act or Check 21 Act (117 Stat. 1177, 12 U.S.C. 5001–5018). Signed by the president Oct. 28, 2003. Made substitute checks the legal equivalent of the original during processing by banks so that the bank where the original check was deposited can transmit it electronically to the originating bank. Significantly shortened the time period between when a check is deposited and when the money is deducted from the check writer's account.

Fair and Accurate Credit Transactions Act of 2003 (FACT Act) (117 Stat. 1952, 15 U.S.C. 1681a). Signed by the president Dec. 4, 2003. Directed the federal banking agencies, including the Fed, to coordinate regulations governing the accuracy and integrity of information provided by furnishers of consumer information to consumer reporting agencies.

Housing and Economic Recovery Act of 2008 (122 Stat. 2654, 5 U.S.C. 301 and 552). Signed by the president July 30, 2008. Merged the Office of Federal Housing Enterprise Oversight and the Federal Housing Finance Board into the newly created Federal Housing Finance Agency (FHFA). Prescribed regulatory actions for undercapitalized regulated entities. Prescribed the minimum capital level for each Federal Home Loan Bank.

Dodd-Frank Wall Street Reform and Consumer Protection Act of 2010, (124 Stat. 1376, 12 U.S.C. 5201 note). Signed by the president July 21, 2010. Established an independent consumer bureau to protect borrowers against abuses in mortgage, credit card, and other types of lending. Created a council of federal regulators to help spot threats to the financial system. Gave the FDIC the authority to close large troubled financial firms.

■ INFORMATION SOURCES

Internet
Board of Governors comprehensive website: www.federalreserve.gov. Includes information on Federal Reserve Banks nationwide and provides links to their Internet sites. Includes an extensive list of publications available.

Telephone Contacts
Main Line . . . . (202) 452–3000
TTY . . . . (202) 263–4869
Consumer Help . . . . (888) 851–1920
Federal Reserve Recording . . . . (202) 452–3206
Inspector General Hotline . . . . (202) 452–6400
Toll-free . . . . (888) 851–1920
Publications . . . . (202) 452–3245
TTY . . . . (877) 766–8533
Media Inquiries . . . . (202) 452–2955

Information and Publications

KEY OFFICES

Board of Governors Public Affairs
20th St. and Constitution Ave. N.W., MS N127
Washington, DC 20551
(202) 452–3204, ext. 3
Fax (202) 452–6481
Lucretia M. Boyer, special assistant to the board for public information

Acts as the spokesperson for the board of governors and prepares all press releases. Pamphlets and audiovisual materials are available from Publications Services, which also maintains all mailing lists for publications.

Board of Governors Consumer and Community Affairs
20th St. and Constitution Ave. N.W.
Washington, DC 20551
(202) 452–2631
Eric S. Belsky, director

Administers the board's consumer protection responsibilities. Writes rules to implement consumer-related laws for which the board has administrative responsibility; supervises enforcement with regard to state member banks; and operates a program to monitor and respond to consumer complaints. Oversees a program that encourages banks to engage in community economic development. Administers a program to educate financial institutions and assists the board's Public Affairs office in developing consumer education materials. Also produces consumer education pamphlets, available on the website and from Publications Services.

Federal Reserve Publications Services

20th St. and Constitution Ave. N.W.,
MS N127
Washington, DC 20551
(202) 452–3245
Fax (202) 728–5886
E-mail: publications-bog@frb.gov
Internet: federalreserve.gov/pubs/order.htm
Linda Kyles, manager

Provides publications and price lists.

Freedom of Information

Board of Governors Office of the Secretary
20th St. and Constitution Ave. N.W., #MP-500
Washington, DC 20551
Jeanne McLaughlin, FOIA Service Center Manager
(202) 452–2407
FOIA Service Center
(202) 452–3684
Fax (202) 872–7565
Internet: www.federalreserve.gov/foia/about_foia.htm

DATA AND STATISTICS

See the website and extensive list of publications, below, for titles that include statistical information.

MEETINGS

The board of governors meets about two or three times a month, usually every other Monday, to consider matters relating to its supervisory, regulatory, and monetary responsibilities. Notices of open meetings are listed on the website and published in the *Federal Register*, as well as usually being available in advance from the Freedom of Information and Public Affairs offices and the Treasury Department press rooms. The board also maintains a "Sunshine" mailing list to announce meetings to interested members of the public. Information about agenda items may be obtained from the website, www.federalreserve.gov, or from Public Affairs, (202) 452–3204.

Notices of meetings closed to the public are listed on the website and published in the *Federal Register*, identifying the official designated to provide information about the meeting. After the meeting has been held, a cassette recording and agenda are available. Special facilities are provided in the Freedom of Information Office, Room MP-500, for listening to recordings; cassettes may also be purchased.

PUBLICATIONS

An extensive series of publications is available from the website, including publications from the twelve Federal Reserve district banks. Also contact Federal Reserve Publications Services for specific titles. Titles include

The Federal Reserve System. Purposes and functions, an overview of the Federal Reserve System

Annual Report. Reviews monetary policy and the state of the economy for the previous year and reports on system operations. Also contains statistical charts and tables. Free.

Statistical Digest. Provides economic and financial data for a broad range of users. Provides historical perspective and detailed series of statistics for years covered. No text accompanying tables; all explanations contained in notes to the tables.

Federal Reserve Bulletin. Quarterly; includes articles on selected topics in economics, domestic and international business activity, and recent developments in banking. Separate tables include substantial statistics related to activity of various sectors of the economy.

Federal Reserve Regulatory Service. Monthly; CD-ROM or loose-leaf service that includes all board statutes, rulings, regulations, staff opinions, and related interpretations and documents. Consists of three publications, with subject and citation indexes. The service includes the *Securities Credit Transaction Handbook* (Regulations T, U, and X and a list of over-the-counter margin stocks); *Monetary Policy and Reserve Requirements Handbook* (Regulations A, D, and Q); *Payment Systems Handbook* (Regulations CC, J, and EE), and the *Consumer and Community Affairs Handbook* (Regulations B, C, E, G, H, P, V, M, Z, AA, BB, DD, and FF). Handbooks also available individually.

International Journal of Central Banking. Quarterly; features articles on central bank theory and practice, with emphasis on research relating to monetary and financial stability.

The Federal Reserve System: Purposes and Functions. A detailed explanation of the work of the system, especially in developing monetary policy. Free.

Index of Federal Reserve Economic Research.

In Plain English: Making Sense of the Federal Reserve. Booklet, bonus activities, DVD to download, and up to 35 free-of-charge.

Regulations of the Board of Governors of the Federal Reserve System. Full texts of regulations A through EE; each regulation is issued as an individual booklet, updated. Free.

Consumer Education Pamphlets. Issued by the board of governors and suited for classroom use. Single and multiple copies available at no charge. Most titles are available in English and Spanish. Titles include

A Consumer's Guide to Mortgage Lock-Ins
A Consumer's Guide to Mortgage Refinancing
A Consumer's Guide to Mortgage Settlement Costs
Consumer Handbook on Adjustable Rate Mortgages
Consumer Handbook to Credit Protection Laws
Five Tips for Avoiding Foreclosure
Five Tips for Dealing with a Home Equity Line Freeze or Reduction
Five Tips for Getting the Most from Your Credit Card
Five Tips for Improving Your Credit Score

A Guide to Business Credit for Women, Minorities, and Small Businesses

How to File a Consumer Complaint about a Bank

Making Deposits: When Will Your Money Be Available?

Privacy Choices for your Personal Financial Information

Tips for Shopping for a Mortgage

Tips for Protecting Your Checking Account

Tips for Protecting Your Home from Foreclosure

What You Should Know about Home Equity Lines of Credit

Series on the Structure of the Federal Reserve System:

- The Board of Governors of the Federal Reserve System
- The Federal Open Market Committee
- Federal Reserve Bank Board of Directors
- Federal Reserve Banks

Reference Resources

LIBRARIES

Federal Reserve Law Library

20th St. and Constitution Ave. N.W., #B-1066

MS 7

Washington, DC 20551

Scott Finet, law librarian

(202) 452–3040

Fax (202) 452–3101

E-mail: legal-law-library@frb.gov

Hours: 9:00 a.m. to 5:00 p.m.

Open to the public by appointment. Holds more than 26,000 volumes on banking legislation and regulation as well as an electronic collection. Interlibrary loan service available within the Washington, DC, area.

Federal Reserve Research Library

20th St. and Constitution Ave. N.W., #B-C-241

Washington, DC 20551

(202) 452–3398

Kris Vajs, chief librarian

Open to the public by appointment for research in fields of banking, finance, monetary and fiscal policy, economics, and the history and operation of the Federal Reserve System. Makes limited interlibrary loans within the Washington, DC, area.

DOCKETS

Individual copies of each regulation are available on the Federal Reserve's website. They include the text of each regulation, text of relevant statutes, and, in some cases, a section on interpretations. Federal dockets are also available at www.regulations.gov. (*See appendix for Searching and Commenting on Regulations: Regulations.gov.*)

RULES AND REGULATIONS

Federal Reserve System rules and regulations are published in the *Code of Federal Regulations*, Title 5,

Chapter LVIII, Part 6801; Title 12, Chapter II, Parts 200–299. Proposed regulations, new final regulations, and updates to the *Code of Federal Regulations* are published in the daily *Federal Register*. (*See appendix for information on how to obtain and use these publications.*) The *Federal Register* may be accessed at www.federalregister.gov and the *Code of Federal Regulations* at www.archives.gov/federal-register/cfr; also see the federal government's website www.regulations.gov (*see appendix*).

The pamphlet *A Guide to Federal Reserve Regulations* gives a brief summary of the regulations. The *Guide* may be obtained from Federal Reserve Publications Services. Individual copies of each regulation also are available. They include the full text of each regulation, text of relevant statutes, and, in some cases, a section on interpretations.

Other Information Sources

NONGOVERNMENTAL RESOURCES

The following are some key resources for information on the Federal Reserve and related economic issues.

American Banker

1 State St. Plaza, 27th Floor

New York, NY 10004

(212) 803–8200

(800) 221–1809

Fax (212) 843–9600

Internet: www.americanbanker.com

American Bankers Association

1120 Connecticut Ave. N.W.

Washington, DC 20036

(202) 663–5000

(800) 226–5377

Internet: www.aba.com

American Business Conference

1828 L St. N.W., #280

Washington, DC 20036

(202) 822–9300

Fax (202) 467–4070

Internet: www.americanbusinessconference.org

American Enterprise Institute for Public Policy Research

Economic Policy Studies

1150 17th St. N.W.

Washington, DC 20036

(202) 862–5800

Fax (202) 862–7177

Media (202) 862–5829

E-mail: mediaservices@aei.org

Internet: www.aei.org

Bank Administration Institute

115 S. La Salle St., # 3300

Chicago, IL 60603–3801

(312) 683–2464

(800) 224–9889
Fax (800) 375–5543
E-mail: info@bai.org
Internet: www.bai.org

The Brookings Institution
Economic Studies Program
1775 Massachusetts Ave. N.W.
Washington, DC 20036–2188
(202) 797–6000
Fax (202) 797–6181
Media: (202) 797–6105
Internet: www.brookings.edu

Bureau of National Affairs, Inc.
1801 S. Bell St.
Arlington, VA 22202
(800) 372–1033
Fax (703) 341–4634
Internet: www.bna.com

The Business Council
1901 Pennsylvania Ave. N.W., #701
Washington, DC 20006
(202) 298–7650
Fax (202) 785–0296
Internet: www.businesscouncil.com

The Business Roundtable
300 New Jersey Ave. N.W., #800
Washington, DC 20001
(202) 872–1260
Fax (202) 466–3509
Internet: www.businessroundtable.org

Economic Policy Institute
1333 H St. N.W., #300
East Tower
Washington, DC 20005
(202) 775–8810
Fax (202) 775–0819
E-mail: epi@epi.org
Internet: www.epi.org

The Heritage Foundation
214 Massachusetts Ave. N.E.
Washington, DC 20002–4999
(202) 546–4400
Fax (202) 546–8328
Media: (202) 675–1761
Internet: www.heritage.org

Journal of Money, Credit and Banking
(Published on behalf of Ohio State University)
Wiley-Blackwell, Inc.
350 Main St.
Malden, MA 02148
(781) 388– 8598
(800) 835–6770
Internet: http://onlinelibrary.wiley.com/
    journal/10.1111/(ISSN)1538–4616

U.S. Chamber of Commerce
Economic Policy
1615 H St. N.W.
Washington, DC 20062–2000
(202) 463–5620
Fax (202) 463–3174
E-mail: khirt@uschamber.com
Internet: www.uschamber.com

Federal Trade Commission

600 Pennsylvania Ave. N.W., Washington, DC 20580
Internet: www.ftc.gov

▨ INTRODUCTION

Created in 1914, the Federal Trade Commission (FTC) is an independent agency headed by five commissioners who are nominated by the president and confirmed by the Senate for seven-year terms. The president designates one commissioner as chair. No more than three of the commissioners may be members of the same political party. As a quasi-judicial and quasi-legislative administrative authority, the FTC deals with trade practices by identifying and seeking to end unfair competition and deceptive practices. Although it has no authority to punish, the commission uses its powers to prevent unfair practices or issue cease-and-desist orders. The agency also is charged with consumer protection. It works to ensure truth in advertising, marketing, and product labeling. Additionally, it seeks to prevent creditors from unlawful practices when issuing credit, operating collection services, and collecting debts.

Responsibilities

The FTC

- Promotes free and fair competition in interstate commerce through the prevention of trade restraints such as price-fixing, boycotts, illegal combinations of competitors, and similar unfair practices.
- Protects the public from false and deceptive advertising.
- Prevents practices that tend to lessen competition.
- Receives prior notice of large mergers and acquisitions. Such transactions cannot occur before the expiration of a waiting period during which the FTC may challenge them on antitrust grounds.
- Prohibits interlocking directorates that restrain competition.
- Prevents unlawful price discrimination.
- Prevents fraudulent telemarketing schemes and deceptive sales tactics.
- Regulates the packaging and labeling of consumer products to prevent deception.
- Requires accurate labels on fur, wool, and textile products.
- Informs consumers and industry of major FTC decisions, programs, statutes, and rules defining the legality of certain business practices.
- Prohibits credit discrimination on the basis of sex, race, marital status, national origin, age, or receipt of public assistance.
- Requires nondepository creditors including retailers and finance companies to give borrowers accurate and complete information about the true cost of credit.
- Prohibits debt-collection agencies from harassing consumers.
- Requires sellers to give consumers notice of their three-day cancellation rights for sales, such as door-to-door and telephone sales, made away from the seller's place of business.
- Prohibits the sending of unordered merchandise to consumers and then charging for it.
- Requires that consumers ordering merchandise through the mail, by telephone, or fax be informed if shipment cannot be made by the promised date (or within thirty days). Customers must then be given the opportunity to agree to a new shipping date or to cancel the order and receive a full refund.

GLOSSARY

Advisory opinion—Advice given by the commission in response to a request from an individual or company as to the legality of a specific course of action.

Consent orders—Orders issued by the commission in which a company, neither admitting nor denying it violated the law, agrees to discontinue certain practices.

Trade regulation rules (TRRs)—Rules that set standards and define which industry practices the commission holds to be unfair and deceptive. TRRs have the force of law.

- Requires funeral directors to disclose prices and other information about funeral goods and services.
- Requires operators of (900) number telephone services to disclose fees and to avoid sales to minors without parental consent.
- Requires packaging and labeling of energy-consuming appliances, other devices, and vehicles to assist consumers in selecting those that are most energy efficient.

Powers and Authority

The FTC derives its authority under the Federal Trade Commission Act and the Clayton Act, both passed in 1914. The FTC act prohibits the use of "unfair methods of competition" and "unfair or deceptive acts or practices." The Clayton Act makes illegal certain practices that may lead to monopolies. Since 1914, Congress also passed numerous other statutes expanding the duties of the commission (*see Background, p. 242*).

The FTC is authorized to investigate cases involving alleged unfair competition or deceptive practices. Once the FTC determines that a company may have engaged in illegal activities, the agency may either negotiate an agreement in which the company voluntarily agrees to stop the practice and, in appropriate cases, pays civil penalties and consumer redress, or it may initiate adjudicative proceedings. Investigations, consent agreements, and adjudication related to anticompetitive behavior are handled by the Bureau of Competition. Matters related to consumers and consumer problems are handled by the Bureau of Consumer Protection. Both bureaus have personnel assigned to monitor and enforce specific provisions of FTC statutes. The regional offices have staff assigned to both consumer protection and business competition.

ADMINISTRATIVE PROCEEDINGS

The FTC initially attempts to ensure compliance by voluntary means, usually through nonbinding staff advice. The commission also can issue advisory opinions, guides, and policy statements clarifying legal practices. However, enforcement largely depends on several administrative procedures used to inform the business community and consumers of the legality of certain acts or practices.

Advisory Opinions

The advisory opinion procedure was established to enable business executives to learn, before implementing a practice, whether the practice might violate the laws the FTC administers. Because they clarify and interpret the law regarding a specific proposed action, advisory opinions do not usually involve consumers.

Advisory opinions are promulgated by the commission at the request of a business or an individual and apply specifically to a practice that the business or the individual is considering. The opinions define the limits of the law as they relate to that particular business practice. The commission at any time may overturn an advisory opinion. If an opinion is overturned, however, the commission must give the individual or business originally affected by the opinion a reasonable amount of time to alter practices to conform to the new ruling. Any individual or any business may apply to the commission for an advisory opinion; the commission will issue an advisory opinion if it involves a substantial or novel question. The FTC staff may issue advice when a case does not warrant an advisory opinion.

Adjudicative Proceedings

Adjudicative proceedings are instituted to resolve a complaint that alleges a company is engaging in anticompetitive, unfair, or deceptive acts or practices. Complaints can arise from several sources: the public, Congress, the White House, other government agencies, consumer or business groups, or the commission itself. The adjudicative proceeding begins after the commission has conducted an investigation and issued a formal complaint alleging some form of illegal behavior. The party charged (respondent) is notified and given thirty days to respond to the complaint. If the respondent decides not to dispute the charge, the illegal practice must be stopped and, in some cases, restitution must be made to the consumers adversely affected by the behavior of the respondent. If the respondent wishes to dispute the charge, an administrative law judge is named and a hearing is scheduled.

At the hearing, both sides present their arguments to the administrative law judge. Witnesses are examined and cross-examined and exhibits can be placed in the record. After considering the case, the administrative law judge issues an initial decision. This decision automatically becomes the order of the commission within thirty days, if neither party files a notice of intention to appeal to the commission within ten days of being served the decision and if the commission unilaterally declines to review the decision. If a matter is appealed to the commission, an opinion is rendered. Respondents retain the right to appeal that decision to any U.S. Court of Appeals. If, after adjudication, it is determined that the violative conduct also is dishonest or fraudulent, the commission may begin a district court proceeding to seek redress for injured consumers.

Consent Orders

The commission often is able to stop lengthy adjudicative proceedings by negotiating a consent order with the respondent. Typically, the respondent neither admits nor denies any wrongdoing but agrees to discontinue the practice and, as appropriate, to take some type of affirmative action to rectify past actions. In such cases the commission issues a proposed consent order, spelling out any corrective action that must be taken.

This proposed order is placed on the public record, including publication in the *Federal Register,* and is open for public comment for sixty days. The comments become a part of the record and are considered by the commission in deciding whether to issue the order in final form. The comments may result in a commission decision, or if the respondent does not agree to the change, the matter may be adjudicated.

Trade Regulation Rules

The FTC's farthest-reaching power is the authority to issue trade regulation rules (TRRs). The commission was authorized to issue TRRs by the Magnuson-Moss Warranty–Federal Trade Commission Improvement Act of 1975. TRRs have the force of law and can apply to an entire industry or only to industries in a specific geographical region.

Generally, when the FTC staff finds an unfair or deceptive practice to be prevalent in an entire industry, it recommends that the commissioners begin rulemaking proceedings. Alternatively, the public may petition the commission to make a rule. However, before beginning the rulemaking process, the commission first publishes an advance notice of the proposed rule and solicits public comment.

If the FTC then decides to begin rulemaking, a presiding officer is appointed and a notice again is published in the *Federal Register* outlining the proposed rule and what the commissioners believe are the central issues to be discussed. At that time, individuals can comment, testify on the rule, or suggest additional issues to be discussed.

The presiding officer conducts public hearings that include cross-examination of witnesses on certain issues. When the hearings are completed, the FTC staff submits a report and the presiding officer recommends a decision on the issues. At that time the public can comment on the entire rulemaking record.

The matter then goes before the commission for deliberation on the record, which includes the presiding officer's decisions, the FTC staff report, and comments from the general public. The commission makes the final decision whether to issue the trade regulation rule. The commission can decide instead to make changes in the provisions of the rule and issue a Revised Version. The commission's rule may be challenged in an U.S. Court of Appeals. When a rule becomes final, it has the force of law.

ENFORCEMENT

If a respondent fails to comply with an FTC final cease-and-desist order or a TRR, the commission can request that the attorney general seek a district court order imposing a civil penalty of up to $10,000 for each violation of the rule or order. In the case of continuing violations, civil penalties of up to $11,000 per day may be requested. In the event of a court judgment for civil penalties and equitable relief, further failure to comply will result in contempt of court charges. The order becomes final sixty days after service, unless the respondent petitions a U.S. Court of

Appeals to review the order and petitions the commission to stay the order pending review. The appeals court can affirm, modify, or overturn the order. Depending on the action, the respondent can then petition the Supreme Court for redress.

The FTC act empowers the commission to seek a preliminary injunction to aid in obtaining effective relief, pending the outcome of subsequent administrative proceedings with respect to any law enforced by the commission. This provision often is used to obtain preliminary injunctions blocking mergers and acquisitions if there are commission administrative complaints challenging such transactions as anticompetitive. In one such 1989 case involving an acquisition (*FTC v. Elders Grain*), the 7th Circuit held that the parties' consummated acquisition could be rescinded.

In appropriate cases, often involving fraud, the commission may seek permanent injunctions in court. No administrative proceeding is required.

OTHER POWERS

The agency also devotes its efforts to consumer protection to fulfill its obligations under a variety of statutes: the Wheeler-Lea Act, the Clayton Act, the Consumer Protection Act, the Robinson-Patman Protection Act, the Magnuson-Moss Warranty–Federal Trade Commission Improvement Act, the Smokeless Tobacco Health Education Act of 1986, the Telephone Disclosure and Dispute Resolution Act, the FTC Improvement Act of 1994, the International Antitrust Enforcement Assistance Act of 1994, and the Telemarketing and Consumer Fraud and Abuse Prevention Act and FTC Act Amendments of 1994.

It focuses much of its consumer protection efforts on advertising and marketing, including health and nutrition claims, environmental advertising and labeling, telemarketing, and franchise investments. It works to ensure truthful, not misleading, advertising and to curtail fraudulent or deceptive marketing practices. Under the Consumer Protection Act, it seeks to prohibit creditors from illegal practices when issuing credit, maintaining credit information, collecting debts, and operating credit systems.

Under the Wool Products Labeling Act, the Fur Products Labeling Act, and the Textile Fiber Products Identification Act, the commission requires the registration of certain types of products, including labeling for content, country of origin, and identity of manufacturer. These statutes also give the FTC power to issue rules and regulations related to these products, to test and inspect products, to institute condemnation proceedings, and to issue cease-and-desist orders.

The commission's outreach program apprises the business community of laws and regulations. The FTC believes that most businesses will comply voluntarily, and it can then concentrate its enforcement on those who do not. The FTC also publishes guidelines, pamphlets, and other materials for consumers to warn them of fraudulent practices they may encounter and to inform them of their rights under the law. Publications often are prepared in cooperation with businesses or business associations.

REPORTING REQUIREMENTS

Section 6(a) of the FTC act gives the commission extensive power to request information from any business in the country. This power is backed up by the commission's authority to compel a business to submit the materials it wants to inspect. If the business does not comply, the FTC may seek a court order to enforce the process. The court then decides whether enforcement is appropriate.

The FTC is prohibited from publishing trade secrets or privileged financial information and is required to ensure the confidentiality of data collected in its statistical reporting program. Despite its power to seek information, the FTC does not maintain a single, across-the-board reporting program for the business community. It does, however, operate several separate reporting programs *(see Data and Statistics, p. 262).*

Background

The formation in the late nineteenth century of several large and extremely powerful industrial trusts led Congress in 1898 to create the Industrial Commission to study the monopolistic behavior of corporations. The commission recommended that Congress establish a federal bureau to collect information on corporations. This recommendation led to the creation in 1903 of the Bureau of Corporations, in what was then the Department of Commerce and Labor. The bureau had no enforcement powers, and its main activity was gathering data from businesses, often at the instigation of Congress, which at the time had few investigative staff.

The Federal Trade Commission Act of 1914 created the FTC, which was designed to act as the federal government's chief trust-buster. The Bureau of Corporations was merged into the FTC in 1915 and made up most of the original staff of the commission. The reliance on voluntary compliance was continued at the new commission, but the FTC was given additional power to investigate business practices and to order them stopped. The wording of the legislation was intentionally flexible; Section 5 of the act gave the FTC broad powers to define business practices that constituted "unfair methods of competition." Congress also passed the Clayton Act (frequently referred to as the Clayton Antitrust Act) in 1914. This statute prohibited specific business activities that tended to lessen competition or to create monopolies.

EARLY HISTORY

During its infancy the FTC issued broad orders designed to promote competition. However, Congress, after initial enthusiasm, ignored the commission. Court decisions limited the agency's power to take action against practices that injured consumers but not competition. The commission fell into a period of inactivity.

The FTC's authority was increased in 1938 with the passage of the Wheeler-Lea Amendment to the original FTC act. Designed to provide some degree of consumer protection to those who previously had been at the mercy of business interests, the amendment authorized the commission to prohibit "unfair or deceptive" business acts and practices. In this way the FTC could move against a

business on behalf of consumers without first proving the existence of anticompetitive behavior.

In the 1940s the commission again began the active pursuit of cases. The courts were especially willing to uphold commission orders related to false advertising, which, as a result, became one of the agency's main areas of investigation and enforcement. The commission also moved into specialized regulation with the passage of the Wool Products Labeling Act. Success in that area led to the passage of the Fur Products Labeling Act, the Textile Fiber Products Identification Act, and the Flammable Fabrics Act (implementation of which was shifted subsequently to the Consumer Product Safety Commission).

In the 1950s and 1960s the FTC made few waves, except for a 1964 rule that would have required cigarette packages and all cigarette advertising to carry a health-hazard warning. However, the tobacco industry lobbied successfully to weaken the rule. The result was passage of the 1965 Federal Cigarette Labeling and Advertising Act, which required warnings on packages only. Subsequent legislation strengthened this law. The Public Health Cigarette Smoking Act of 1969 prohibited radio and television cigarette advertising, required printed ads to include a health warning, and strengthened the wording of the messages. In 1973 the law was amended to include small cigars, and in 1984 the Comprehensive Smoking Education Act strengthened the warning again and required four different messages to appear on a quarterly, rotating basis. A 1986 amendment, the Smokeless Tobacco Health Education Act, added chewing tobacco and snuff to the list of tobacco products banned from television and radio advertisements and required that their packages also carry health warnings.

Revitalization of the Agency

In 1969 a group of students working for consumer activist Ralph Nader issued a study of the FTC, charging that the commission was mired in trivial matters, that its reliance on case-by-case enforcement slowed progress, and that voluntary compliance was not stopping illegal or unfair business practices. In reaction to the Nader report, President Richard Nixon requested that the American Bar Association (ABA) appoint a committee to study the FTC. The ABA committee report also was critical of the commission.

The Nader and ABA reports made it politically advantageous for Nixon to begin upgrading the agency. He appointed Caspar Weinberger, who had developed a reputation as a first-rate manager, to the chair's post in 1969, replacing him seven months later with Miles Kirkpatrick, who had coordinated the ABA report on the FTC.

Under Weinberger and Kirkpatrick the FTC hired a number of young, activist lawyers. Greater emphasis was placed on consumer affairs and public participation. As a result, the commission gained a favorable reputation among consumer groups, while some business people charged that the commission was ignoring its responsibilities toward industry.

The push for improvements at the FTC resulted in the passage, in 1975, of the Magnuson-Moss Warranty–Federal Trade Commission Improvement Act, which gave the FTC authority to use industry-wide rulemaking—having the force and effect of law—as an alternative to challenging unfair or deceptive advertising and trade practices of an entire industry. The legislation also granted funds to public participants in rulemaking procedures. This provision, designed to encourage greater public participation in the rulemaking process, was repealed in 1994. An additional warranties provision of the act authorized the FTC for the first time to spell out standards to be met by written warranties given by manufacturers or sellers of products priced at $10 or more.

Passage of the Magnuson-Moss bill, one of the major legislative successes of the consumer movement, was just one of several indications in the early 1970s that the public and its representatives on Capitol Hill still favored a vigorous FTC. The agency's activism was strongly supported by President Jimmy Carter, who appointed consumer proponent Michael Pertschuk to chair the FTC. Under Pertschuk, the FTC continued to push for consumer protection rules and regulations and took on some of the giants in the business and professional communities. The FTC reached its peak size of about 1,800 employees during the Carter administration.

Congress Curbs the FTC

A decade after it helped rouse the FTC from its somnolence, Congress began showing irritation with the agency. The FTC, using its broad mandate to ferret out "unfair or deceptive acts or practices," had antagonized a number of powerful industries and professional associations, as well as various individual retailers.

In 1977 the House of Representatives attempted to stall industry-wide rulemaking by attaching to the FTC's authorization bill a requirement that trade regulation rules be submitted to Congress for approval before taking effect. Both the Senate and President Carter objected to this legislative veto, calling it unconstitutional because it encroached on the authority of the executive branch. Because of this disagreement the agency was funded for the next three years by continuing resolutions, bypassing the normal authorization process. The stalemate continued until 1980, when certain House members announced they would not continue to fund the commission until an agreement was reached on the veto issue.

Compromise legislation that authorized FTC funds through fiscal 1982 provided for a two-house veto of the commission's rules and cut back other agency powers. Carter indicated that he would accept the legislative veto only if no major FTC proceedings would be terminated. Therefore, proposed rules to regulate children's advertising, funeral homes, and agricultural cooperatives survived when the compromise authorization bill was signed May 28, 1980.

The 1980 authorization bill also restricted FTC rulemaking authority governing commercial advertising to deceptive—not to unfair—practices. It prohibited the agency from providing citizens or consumer groups the funds necessary to enable them to participate in agency proceedings, and it prohibited the FTC from further study of the insurance industry. Congress also demanded that the FTC consider whether the children's advertising it sought to regulate was deceptive, not merely unfair. This forced the FTC to drop the children's advertising proceeding in 1981.

FTC IN THE 1980s

Groups that had chafed for years under FTC restrictions saw an opportunity when the Republican Party took over the White House and Senate in 1981. While President Ronald Reagan chose board members who were philosophically aligned with the administration's goal of reducing the regulatory burden on U.S. businesses, opposition groups also pressed Congress to rein in the FTC still further. Associations of doctors, lawyers, and other professionals; the U.S. Chamber of Commerce; dairy groups; advertising groups; and the National Association of Manufacturers were among leaders of the movement to curb the FTC. The pressure group campaign fit in neatly with the new administration's plans to cut the budget of the regulatory agency and thus limit its activity.

When the FTC authorization expired at the end of 1982, Congress took another two years to reauthorize the agency. Each time Congress tried and failed to reauthorize the FTC, new restrictions appeared in the bills that did not pass. Other restrictions in other unpassed bills, such as one requiring the FTC to notify Congress before it gave testimony or made comments before any other federal or state body, were similarly honored by the agency. Some of the numerous restrictions were included in the FTC authorization bill finally passed in 1984.

During this time the FTC issued rules in two controversial areas—used cars and funeral homes. These rules prompted Congress to use, for the first time, the veto power it had given itself in 1980. Consumer groups challenged the veto, and in July 1983 the Supreme Court ruled the veto unconstitutional. The used-car rule, after a further challenge on its merits, was repromulgated by the FTC in 1985 without a controversial provision that would have required used-car dealers to inform consumers of any major known defect in a used car.

Reagan's two terms brought eight consecutive years of budget and personnel cuts for the commission. The FTC workforce was cut in half, from 1,800 people when Pertschuk was chair, to fewer than 900. The budget shrank along with the size of the agency.

Although Reagan's first FTC chair, James Miller III, urged Congress to limit the FTC's authority to correct unfair and deceptive business practices to abuses that caused consumers "substantial injury," he fought off congressional and American Medical Association proposals to curb the FTC's antitrust authority over state-licensed professional groups. Begun under Miller, the agency's campaign against professionally imposed boycotts, restrictions on locations of clinics and doctors' offices, collusion to fix prices, and bans on advertising continued into the 1990s and was an acknowledged success. The FTC was aided by the Supreme Court which, in a unanimous 1986 decision, upheld a lower court in *FTC v. Indiana Federation of Dentists*. Subsequently, the agency challenged the practices of a range of associations including pharmacists, veterinarians, real estate professionals, and college football teams.

FTC IN THE 1990s

President George H. W. Bush appointed the first woman to chair the commission in 1989. Janet Steiger undertook to improve the FTC's image. Consumer groups, supported by former chair Pertschuk, had been critical of the commission's failure to act on what they saw as flagrantly deceptive advertising and evermore prevalent mergers. Steiger set up working groups with the agency's critics, most notably the National Association of Attorneys General (NAAG). She set three goals: (1) to eliminate the perception that the FTC had ceased to be a vigorous law enforcement agency; (2) to eliminate the appearance of a confrontational attitude toward Congress, the states, the legal community, and other public interest constituencies; and (3) to attempt to halt the decline in resources at the FTC.

Congress gave the agency its first budget boost in a decade soon after Steiger's appointment, and it continued to heed her requests for additional funds in subsequent years. To counter criticism of the commission's poor record of regulating mergers during the 1980s, Steiger embarked on an internal study of the agency's merger activities and, together with the state attorneys general and the Justice Department's Antitrust Division, formed an executive working group on antitrust. Not only did the agency challenge more mergers in the ensuing years, it also produced the first *Joint Horizontal Merger Guidelines* with Justice's Antitrust Division in 1992. In 1993 the same two entities cooperated to produce Statements of Antitrust Enforcement Policy in the health care area to help reduce business uncertainty about mergers and other conduct that might give rise to antitrust actions during a time of rapid change in the health care industry. These guidelines were supported by Congress and the legal profession.

Under Steiger, the agency's efforts on advertising brought mixed results. In 1994 the FTC announced that it would match its food advertising enforcement policies with the food labeling regulations of the Food and Drug Administration (FDA) that strictly limit health and other dietary claims. Also in 1994, however, the commission voted not to act on allegations that the "Joe Camel" cigarette ads were aimed at young people. The vote was a setback to Steiger, who had identified action on tobacco advertising as a priority early in her tenure.

However, the telemarketing law passed in late 1994 gave the FTC a clear mandate to make rules for the telemarketing industry. Rules implemented in 1995 barred telemarketers from repeatedly disturbing individual consumers with unsolicited telephone calls, limited the hours during which telephone sales could be solicited, and required telemarketers to "promptly and clearly disclose" the sales nature of any telephone call. The rules allowed nationwide injunctions against telemarketing companies, not merely refunds for individual consumers. Working with the NAAG, the FTC also set up the Telemarketing Fraud Data Base, which allowed law enforcement agencies to review consumer complaints and information about investigations and enforcement.

When Congress enacted a bill authorizing continued operation for the FTC in August 1994, it was seen as an indication of the FTC's improved relationship with lawmakers. The legislation reinstated the agency's power to make rules governing unfair conduct, although it first required the FTC to prove that any practice it deemed unfair was a prevalent practice. FTC attorneys suspected that the definition of unfair in the new law might limit them to bringing cases in which consumers have suffered economic injury and exclude those that charge that an act or practice is harmful to health. Another sign of a rejuvenated, well-run agency was the FTC's ability to attract top-notch law school graduates.

In April 1995 President Bill Clinton appointed Robert Pitofsky chair of the FTC—but the election of a Republican Congress in the meantime decreased the likelihood that Pitofsky's approach to the agency would diverge markedly from Steiger's. Under Pitofsky the FTC sought to update itself through regulatory reform and a fuller understanding of regulatory implications of new technology. Vowing to repeal 25 percent of its trade regulatory rules, the FTC in 1996 eliminated some 10,000 directives that were more than twenty years old and not frequently implemented. By September 1998 the agency had vacated 35 percent of its guides and rules. However, the agency had remained active on battling cases in court, winning more cases than previous administrations and losing only one case in three years.

Pitofsky approached the regulation of corporate mergers with a new emphasis. He gave more weight to increased efficiencies, such as lower unit and production costs, that pass on savings to consumers—whereas antitrust enforcement traditionally assumes that decreasing competition will raise prices. Pitofsky also directed FTC staff to examine how proposed mergers might affect market share and product development and innovation, especially in light of increased international competition.

At first glance, Pitofsky's appointment increased the antitrust activism of the FTC. In fiscal 1995 the agency challenged thirty-five corporate mergers—the highest since 1980—and observers remarked that the FTC was becoming more effective at enforcement than the Antitrust Division of the Justice Department. However, with the largest mergers in the media and defense industries, Pitofsky's FTC proved to be quite accommodating. In April 1996 the agency also approved Lockheed Martin's $9.1 billion acquisition of Loral Corp. (Lockheed Martin itself was the offspring of an FTC-approved merger in January 1995.) A year later, the commission approved a $15 billion merger between Boeing and McDonnell Douglas Corp. In mid-1998, running counter to the FTC, the Justice Department objected to a proposed merger of the last of the major defense contractors: Lockheed Martin Corp.'s proposed $12 billion purchase of Northrop Grumman Corp. In 1996 the FTC also approved the merger of Time Warner and Turner Broadcasting without any divestiture of assets.

The FTC was not reluctant to take on giants, particularly in the area of retail superstores. In July 1997 the commission blocked the proposed $4 billion merger of office suppliers Staples and Office Depot. The FTC contended that the proposed merger would essentially reduce competition to two major players, the new Staples and Office

Depot entity and OfficeMax. Countering the company's argument that additional competition would still exist with small stationery shops and large discount stores, such as Walmart, the commission said their unusual variety of office supply products constituted a unique market.

In 1998 the FTC charged that the largest manufacturer of computer microprocessors, Intel Corporation, used its monopoly power to dominate the entire market. The FTC alleged that Intel illegally used its market power against its three competitors who had sought to enforce patents in microprocessor technology. Similarly, the FTC alleged that Toys "R" Us forced all the leading toy manufacturers, including Hasbro and Mattel, into withholding best-selling merchandise from warehouse stores such as Sam's and Price Club, leading to higher prices for consumers. The company, which controlled nearly 20 percent of the U.S. toy market, also compelled manufacturers to sell those products only in combinations that made it difficult for consumers to compare prices, the agency argued.

In health care, the FTC in early 1996 rejected a merger of the Rite Aid and Revco drugstore chains, as well as launched an investigation into whether pharmaceutical companies conspired to overcharge independent pharmacies for drugs. Then again in 1998, the courts upheld the FTC's request to stop two mergers of wholesale drug manufacturers: McKesson Corp. from buying AmeriSource Health Corp., and Cardinal Health Inc. from acquiring Bergen Brunswig Corp. The FTC contended that the mergers would have left only two companies in control of nearly 80 percent of the drug wholesale market.

The FTC also overhauled its tar and nicotine ratings for cigarettes, a system that had been widely regarded as inaccurate for much of its history. The agency also continued its litigation against "Joe Camel," or "unfair" advertising aimed at children, in spite of a 1998 federal appeals court ruling that the FDA lacked jurisdiction in its fight against tobacco.

The FTC voiced concern that the Telecommunications Act of 1996 might infringe on privacy, as it allowed companies to share customer data in the name of increased competition. In an action hailed by privacy advocates, the agency in August 1998 targeted for the first time a popular website on the Internet to enforce laws against deception and the misuse of personal information. The agency forced GeoCities to stop releasing personal information about its users to advertisers without notification.

In 1997 the agency established the Consumer Response Center to receive consumer complaints and inquiries by mail, telephone, and the Internet. Toll-free numbers established in 1999 and 2000 also made the agency more accessible. In fiscal 2000 the FTC received more than 833,000 complaints and inquiries from the public—more than one-third above its target number of 600,000 for that year and producing an estimated $265 million in savings to consumers.

In handling complaints, the FTC strengthened its ties with partners such as the National Fraud Information Center of the National Consumers League; local chapters of the Better Business Bureau; and PhoneBusters, the Canadian fraud database. Fraud complaints are collected and analyzed to identify trends and patterns, new scams, and companies that engage in fraudulent, deceptive, or unfair business practices; the complaints are also shared with law enforcement agencies in the United States, Canada, and Australia via Consumer Sentinel, a secure website. The analysis allows the agency to stop unlawful or deceptive practices that included online auction fraud; pyramid schemes; scams for travel and health care; and unauthorized billing for unwanted services, known as "cramming."

The 1990s came to an end with corporate mergers continuing at an accelerated pace, rising to 4,642 in 1999. The dollar value of the mergers increased even more dramatically, from $169 billion to approximately $3 trillion. The FTC saw the rise in mergers, and a corresponding increase in their complexity, as requiring greater antitrust review to prevent mergers that could diminish healthy competition.

FTC IN THE 2000s

The merger wave continued into the 2000s. The FTC required divestitures before a $27 billion merger between BP Amoco and Atlantic Richfield Company (ARCO) was allowed to proceed in April 2000. That year the FTC also sanctioned the merger of America Online and Time Warner, after requiring the new AOL Time Warner to open its cable system to competitor Internet service providers (ISPs) and prohibiting the company from interfering with content passed along the bandwidth contracted for by nonaffiliated ISPs.

In 2004 the FTC issued three opinions addressing difficult competition policy issues. These opinions contained detailed antitrust analyses and provided guidance to businesses and the public on how the commission reviews mergers, potentially anticompetitive conduct, and antitrust defenses. Also that same year the FTC completed ten rules under the Fair and Accurate Credit Transactions (FACT) Act of 2003, proposed two additional rules, and published five studies to combat identity theft and improve the accuracy of consumers' credit records.

The FTC sought to bring the pre-merger notification filings required for companies seeking mergers up to date with the electronic era, announcing with the Department of Justice in June 2006 that the agencies were in the process of implementing a system to allow companies to file electronically. Before that system, companies had to submit hard copies of all documents to both agencies. In March 2006 the FTC and Justice jointly issued a new commentary on Horizontal Merger Guidelines, which the agencies use to scrutinize the likely competitive effects of such mergers.

The commission stepped up its merger enforcement program. In 2008 the commission addressed problems with competition involving companies such as hospitals, offshore waste disposal services for oil production, drug treatment companies, database systems for auto repair cost estimates, battery separators, and producers of outdoor paving stones. The agency's merger caseload had been constantly increasing as had the complexity of proposed transactions. Stopping mergers that substantially lessen competition ensured that consumers paid lower prices and had greater choice in their selections of goods and services.

In 2009 the FTC announced that it and Justice would consider updating its guidelines affecting mergers and acquisitions. The guidelines last underwent a major revision in 1992. The FTC and Justice held a series of workshop meetings and solicited public comments and, in April 2010, issued new guidelines that aimed to make the review process more flexible and fact-specific.

Health care remained a significant concern of the commission because of its profound effect on patients and on the nation's high medical costs. On the issue of competition from generic medicines, the FTC directed several companies to divest generic medicines before proceeding with mergers, in order to preserve competition.

Particularly notable in the nonmerger area were the FTC's actions to stop branded pharmaceutical company practices that delay generic drug entry. In July 2002 the FTC also released a comprehensive study of generic drug entry prior to patent expiration. In this report, the FTC recommended legislative changes to the Hatch-Waxman Amendments to ensure that provisions of this law do not delay generic drug entry into the market. The FTC also focused on competition in the pharmaceutical industry; for example, in 2000 its monopolization case against Mylan Laboratories resulted in a record $100 million settlement. Mylan was charged with conspiring to eliminate its competition for generic versions of two drugs used to treat anxiety, making unavailable the key active ingredients for those drugs.

The FTC sharpened its focus on deceptive health claims. In 2003 the commission, working with the FDA, brought twenty-six enforcement actions involving dietary supplements and other products—representing about $1 billion in sales—that were alleged to be deceptively marketed for their purported ability to treat or cure a wide variety of health conditions. In November 2004 the FTC filed complaints against six companies it says used deceptive marketing practices to sell weight-loss products. The FTC published a guide showing the media how to identify and screen for advertisers making bogus weight-loss claims.

In June 2004 Kentucky Fried Chicken settled a complaint filed by the agency over ads claiming its chicken is healthy. The settlement prohibited the company from making unproven claims about health or weight-loss benefits associated with its food. In June 2005 Tropicana Products Inc. also reached a settlement with the FTC over ads claiming the company's orange juice could lower blood pressure and cholesterol levels and reduce the risk of stroke. The company agreed to stop airing the ads.

The FTC suggested changes to food-labeling requirements to address concerns about obesity and to permit qualified health claims on food. The agency issued a report with the Department of Health and Human Services on childhood obesity in April 2006, following a two-day workshop on the issue. The report recommended ways to encourage industry and the media to promote healthier food and drinks to children.

One significant example of the agency's interest in health care issues came in 2008 when the FTC blocked a proposed merger of two hospitals in northern Virginia that would have given one of the hospital centers, Inova Health Systems, control over nearly 75 percent of hospital beds in the area. Inova and the other hospital, Prince William Health System, dropped their plans soon after the FTC brought a federal court complaint supported by the Virginia attorney general.

In a well-received move the FTC launched in June 2003 the National Do-Not-Call Registry, a centralized database of telephone numbers from consumers who have indicated they do not want to receive telemarketing calls. The registry was legally binding and allowed consumers to stop most telemarketing calls simply by clicking on a website or making a toll-free call. Within the first seventy-two hours of the registry's operation, consumers enrolled more than 10 million telephone numbers. In the years since the registry's creation, FTC has filed dozens of enforcement actions against individual and corporate defendants for civil penalties totaling about $20 million as well as consumer compensation totaling more than $11 million.

In 2007 members of Congress began to push to make FTC's National Do-Not-Call Registry permanent. Under the original version of the law, consumers had to reregister every five years. In 2008 President Bush signed two pieces of legislation aimed at extending and improving the do-not-call system. One bill permanently extended the authority of the FTC to collect fees from direct marketers to fund the registry. The other prevented the commission from purging phone numbers of consumers from the database so that individuals would not have to register again. By 2009 the database contained 175 million telephone numbers of people who had requested that marketers refrain from contacting them. The FTC reported that consumer surveys reflected high consumer satisfaction and telemarketer compliance with the do-not-call option.

In recent years a growing concern for the agency has been the misuse of new technology, especially in Internet commerce. In spring 2003 the FTC announced "Operation Bidder Beware"—a program to combat Internet auction fraud. Most auction fraud—the top complaint of consumers about the Internet—dealt with consumers paying for an auction item and then never receiving it. Under the program, the FTC worked with state and local law enforcement agencies to police Internet auction sites, while the agency launched a campaign to educate consumers about Internet auction fraud.

In 2004 the FTC issued two rules aimed at attacking Internet spam. The first required spammers to identify sexually explicit content in the subject line of e-mail, and the second established criteria to determine whether the e-mail's primary purpose was commercial and therefore covered by the Controlling the Assault of Non-Solicited Pornography and Marketing Act of 2003 (CAN-SPAM Act). The FTC also focused on other harmful computer practices, such as use of software programs that take control of or damage personal computers, commonly known as spyware. In April 2004 the FTC held a public workshop to learn more about spyware and on March 7, 2005, the agency released a staff workshop report.

Another privacy issue—so-called pretexting—rose to national attention in 2006. The term refers to the use of fraud or deception to obtain call logs and other confidential customer records from telephone companies. Pretexting became a top issue after revelations that investigators hired by Hewlett-Packard to track down the source of boardroom media leaks had used the practice to obtain the phone records of board members and reporters. Congress cleared legislation in December 2006 to criminalize the practice, and the president signed the bill into law in January 2007.

In May 2006 President George W. Bush created the Identity Theft Task Force, composed of eighteen federal regulatory agencies; the FTC chair was named co-chair. The new group was charged with charting a strategy for the federal government to better combat the problem of identity theft, coordinate prosecution, educate consumers and businesses, and ensure recovery for victims. The task force released its comprehensive plan in April 2007, which included several legislative proposals and other recommendations. Among the proposed policy changes, the group recommended broadening the law that criminalizes electronic data theft by removing the current requisite that information be stolen through interstate communications; modifying statutes to make it easier for federal prosecutors to bring charges against purveyors of malicious spyware and keyloggers; creating a National Identity Theft Law Enforcement Center to coordinate various agencies' efforts and information; and creating national standards for the use of personal information by private-sector businesses and notification procedures for when breaches occur.

The FTC also helped to pass the US SAFE WEB Act of 2006, which allowed the agency to engage in broader cooperation with foreign law enforcement authorities in cross-border fraud cases and other international issues. These new tools allowed the FTC to combat international online identity theft and the spyware programs that can track online behavior and steal sensitive personal data.

The commission also weighed in on the controversial practice by companies of tracking an individual's online activities to tailor advertising to the computer user's interests. The practice, known as "behavioral advertising," is widely used by companies such as Yahoo, Microsoft, and Google. The FTC released a report, *Self-Regulatory Principles for Online Behavioral Advertising*, which highlighted the benefits to consumers of these ads, such as the increased likelihood that consumers would see advertising of a service that suited their needs. On the other hand, the report also noted concerns from privacy advocates who are uncomfortable with the idea of large companies tracking their online searches and activities.

The report introduced four main principles for companies to follow: (1) companies collecting data should have clear information stating that they are tracking consumers' movements and give consumers the opportunity to opt out; (2) companies should provide reasonable security for the information and retain it only as long as necessary for a business or law enforcement need; (3) companies should keep prior commitments to use previously collected data only in accordance with consumers' wishes; and (4) companies should collect sensitive, personal data, such as health or financial information, only with the express consent of consumers.

The rise of social media has raised new questions about authenticity in advertising and what constitutes an endorsement. For instance, is there any difference between traditional product endorsements and those done by bloggers or via social media such as Twitter and Facebook? In October 2009 the agency essentially said "no," issuing new rules that treat new media like more traditional forms of broadcasting and print advertising.

The new rules clarified that when a blogger receives cash or an in-kind payment to review a product, that review is considered an endorsement. Bloggers must disclose the compensation they receive from companies they write about, including when they receive free products; this includes celebrities who often do not disclose their financial ties to companies whose products they promote. In addition, the new guidelines specified that advertisers who cite studies by a particular research institute they also help to fund must now disclose that financial connection. Punishments for violations could be as mild as a warning letter or as severe as an $11,000 fine per violation.

Traditional real estate agencies suffered a blow in 2006 as the FTC went after their efforts to block access by other brokers, such as those on the Internet, to the Multiple Listing Services (MLS). In October 2006 the FTC filed its first enforcement sweep, challenging rules in seven regions that either blocked other brokers' listings from MLS or prohibited the dissemination of such agents' listings to popular websites. As a result, five regional real estate MLS operators agreed to end the discriminating practices, and a sixth settled later after further action by the FTC.

As the housing crisis began to unfold in 2006 and 2007, some consumer groups argued that the panel had not done enough to curb abusive or fraudulent practices related to subprime lending or credit. In February 2007 FTC chair Deborah Platt Majoras said the agency would emphasize what she called the "ABCs" of financial practices: alternative mortgages, bad debt collection, and credit-related deception. As mortgage foreclosures surged across the country, the agency targeted deceptive and unfair mortgage lending practices, particularly deceptive advertising of nontraditional mortgages offering low "teaser" rates to start but sometimes carrying significant, long-term financial burden.

The commission increased enforcement efforts against mortgage scams that promised to rescue homeowners from foreclosure, fake debt relief and credit repair schemes, unlawful debt collection operations, and deceptive credit offers to consumers in the subprime lending market. One of the cases included enforcement against Bear Stearns and EMC Mortgage, who were accused of unlawful practices in servicing and collecting mortgage loans, many in the subprime market. The FTC alleged that the two companies misrepresented the amounts borrowers owed, charged unauthorized fees, and engaged in unlawful and abusive collection practices. The settlement returned $28 million to 86,000 consumers. The settlement, announced in September 2008, involved allegations of behavior before JPMorgan Chase acquired Bear Stearns in the spring of that year.

The commission also filed six actions against businesses promising foreclosure rescue, and it joined with twenty-four state agencies to challenge claims by thirty-six credit repair operations that they could remove accurate information from a consumer's credit report. "There can be no greater priority than addressing the credit crisis and protecting consumers in financial distress," said Majoras's successor, Jon Leibowitz, whom President Barack Obama moved from commissioner to FTC chair in March 2009.

As the decade neared its end, the agency showed an interest in issues related to energy and the environment, particularly as they affect the marketing of "green" products, which are supposed to be protective of the environment. In 2009 the commission embarked on a plan to gather information and begin making policies to ensure that consumers are not fooled by dubious claims that products protect the environment. The commission held workshops on how to certify carbon offsets and renewable energy certificates, undertook enforcement actions alleging deceptive claims for devices that were supposed to increase gas mileage or reduce energy use in homes, and began deliberating about how to regulate energy use labels for consumer products such as light bulbs and personal computers.

Green marketing came under scrutiny again later in the year when the agency proposed tighter rules on the advertising of how environmentally friendly products are advertised to consumers. This move came partly in response to the rapid rise in eco-labeling and the increased demand by consumers for more green products. New guidelines mandated that seals and certifications with environmental claims be more specific. They also provided marketers with parameters on other types of claims, such as what constitutes a "renewable" material. In addition, companies that use third-party certifications would need to make sure the certification companies actually performed the testing and could substantiate the claims they made.

The FTC also addressed credibility in advertising in another important area—credit reports. Credit scores have plummeted in recent years as recession-weary Americans have fallen behind on credit card payments, mortgages, and other debts. Lower scores prevent many consumers from obtaining a new mortgage or refinancing an old one. The desire to improve credit scores has made many more vulnerable to credit report scams, which have been on the rise.

Every person is entitled to a free credit report every twelve months from each of the three nationwide credit reporting bureaus—Equifax, Experian, and Transunion. Those reports are made available through a government-authorized site called AnnualCreditReport.com. But ever since FACT was signed into law in 2003 (which mandated free credit reports), there has been confusion among consumers about what information they can obtain free of charge and what they need to pay for. For example, many people have confused credit reports with credit scores. A credit report contains a person's credit history, which includes a list of past and current creditors and a record of the borrower's payment history, while a credit score assigns a numerical valuation to how creditworthy someone is. The bureaus are not required to provide free credit scores, only reports. As a result of this and other kinds of confusion, many consumers have found themselves paying for services that are free.

Further complicating the situation for consumers are companies that claim they can "clean up" or improve credit scores, in exchange for a fee. In September 2010 the agency filed a complaint against Clean Credit Report Services Inc. of North Miami, alleging that the firm promised clients it could boost their credit scores and make negative credit information, even if it was accurate, simply disappear. Disgruntled customers whose scores were not improved after paying the fees filed complaints with state and local authorities. Under the Credit Repair Organizations Act companies are prohibited from making "untrue statements" in their claims to fix consumers' credit files, and they may not charge or collect money in advance of rendering their services. The case against Clean Credit is pending.

FTC IN THE 2010s

With the collapse of the U.S. housing market at the end of the decade, the FTC increased its focus on the financial services industry, especially mortgage lending. In June 2010 the FTC announced a $108 million settlement against Bank of America's Countrywide Financial subsidiary. The money, in its entirety was to be paid in refunds to many thousands of homeowners who were charged excessive fees by Countrywide before it was purchased by Bank of America in 2008.

Prior to the settlement, the FTC alleged that Countrywide's servicing arm had deceived borrowers who had defaulted on their loans into paying inflated fees for property inspections, lawn mowing, and other services aimed at protecting the lender's interest in the home. Some home owners were charged as much as $2,500 for trustee fees, when the average rate for such a service is in the range of $600. The FTC also charged that Countrywide had inflated the amount owed to it by borrowers who had filed for Chapter 13 bankruptcy protection.

The investigation into these charges and the eventual settlement was another blow to what was once one of the most powerful lending institutions in the United States. During the first half of 2007, Countrywide held about one in five loans in the United States, and it serviced or collected payments from borrowers on 14 percent of all outstanding mortgages. The company thrived on its ability to grant subprime mortgages, quickly selling them to investors, and then using that money to fund more mortgages. After the mortgage market began to collapse in 2008, Countrywide assessed fees on customers who had sought to reorganize their debts and save their homes, or on homeowners who were in default on their loans. As FTC Chair Leibowitz described it, "Countrywide profited from making risky loans to homeowners during the boom years, and then profited again when the loans failed."

For its part, Bank of America neither admitted nor denied any wrongdoing, saying that the probe into Countrywide's lending practices began before it had acquired the California-based lender. While not admitting to any wrongdoing, the bank stated that it had settled the case "to avoid the expense and distraction of litigation."

Leibowitz declared that more than 200,000 people would be reimbursed for overcharges on loans that were serviced by Countrywide prior to acquisition, but this $108 million represented only the agency's estimate on consumer losses; the agency was not permitted to impose a penalty. In addition to the money for the refunds, the settlement required that Countrywide and its Bank of America parent establish internal procedures and an independent third party to verify that bills and claims filed in bankruptcy court were valid. The FTC has not yet established how much will be paid to each customer, in part because, according to Leibowitz, Countrywide's record keeping was "abysmal."

Another example was the agency's crackdown on "pay for delay" agreements between brand-name drug companies and generic drug companies that prevent or delay the introduction of cheaper generic drugs on the market. The commission challenged a settlement between Solvay Pharmaceuticals, the maker of a testosterone replacement drug worth $400 million a year in sales, and two generic drug companies. The companies agreed to Solvay's request to drop their patent challenges so that Solvay could continue dominating the marketing of the drug for another nine years. The commission challenged the deal in court, supported by the California attorney general. In 2012, the 11th Circuit U.S. Court of Appeals ruled against the agency and for the drugmakers, arguing that the deal didn't violate antitrust laws. But in June 2013, the U.S. Supreme Court reversed this decision and ordered a lower federal court to rehear the case under federal antitrust laws.

Rapid changes in the communications and technology industry have invited sustained FTC scrutiny. In 2010 the commission began an investigation into privacy breaches in connection with a Google project known as Street View. Street View began in 2007 and involved taking and uploading street level pictures of neighborhoods around the country and adding these images to Google's Maps feature. The idea was that when someone looked up a street on Google Maps, the service would also offer a photo of the area along with the map. These pictures were collected in 30 countries by cars that use cameras to capture 360-degree images, which were then linked with GPS data. The cars also recorded information about Wi-Fi networks in nearby homes and businesses, data that helps mobile devices determine their locations. However, Google went beyond merely noting the existence of such networks to collecting Internet users' information as well, potentially in violation of laws protecting privacy. When this information came out early in 2010, the company faced an FTC investigation as well as a parallel probe by 38 states' attorneys general.

In its defense, Google argued that it never used the payload data in any of its products or services and that it was taking appropriate steps to stop retrieving the information. In October 2010 the FTC ended its investigation. The agency announced that it was satisfied with the steps Google had taken to prevent a recurrence of the problem, including naming a director of privacy and improving its privacy training for employees. However, the states' attorneys general continued their probe, and in March 2013, they announced an agreement with Google that led the company to promise new privacy safeguards and pay the 38 states a $7 million settlement.

But just months after ending the Street View investigation, the agency found itself investigating Google again, this time over its Buzz social networking application. The company had not informed its estimated 200 million G-mail users that it would launch the application using information in their e-mail accounts, a step that was in direct contradiction of its privacy promises to consumers. Users complained that their contact lists and other data were publicly exposed and that they had difficulty opting out of Buzz. In March 2011, the agency and Google settled the Buzz investigation. This time, Google promised to create a comprehensive, company-wide privacy program and submit itself to an outside privacy audit every two years for the next 20 years.

In addition to consumer privacy breaches, the FTC and Google clashed over a number of antitrust issues. In particular, the commission became concerned that the presence of Google CEO Eric Schmidt on the board of directors of Apple Computer made the relationship between two of the most powerful technology firms in the world a little too close. In August 2009, before the agency launched a formal probe, the problem was resolved when Schmidt resigned from Apple's board. While the move preempted any potential antitrust problems, the growing competitiveness between two Silicon Valley giants, particularly in the mobile phone market, likely made the split inevitable.

Google also was under investigation over whether the company had been using its dominant position in the Internet search market to steer users to products and services that it promotes and away from those offered by competitors. In a situation reminiscent of the case against Microsoft's Windows operating system in the 1990s, critics alleged that Google had been illegally leveraging its popular search engine to unfairly knock out its competitors in areas where it offers services. For example, the travel site TripAdvisor.com complained that when users searched for hotels, Google put its results from its own travel service, Google Places, above other sites' results, meaning that fewer rival sites with their own hotel or restaurant listings had the chance of appearing on the all-important first page of a user search. In short, critics charged, with Google acting as the Internet's de facto gatekeeper, users did not always know what they might be missing when they hit "search."

But after two years of intense federal scrutiny and much fanfare, the FTC decided to close its antitrust investigation against Google in January 2013. The agency couldn't find enough evidence that Google was manipulating search results to benefit its own products while at the same time hurting competitors and curtailing choice. As Chair Leibowitz summed it up, "American antitrust laws protect competition, not competitors." After actively lobbying the Obama administration in 2011 to give it rather than the Justice Department the Google investigation, the FTC required only two concessions from the company in the end: that Google agree to make it easier for marketers to move their ads to rival search services, and that it stop appropriating content from other websites, such as the popular Yelp, which offer user reviews of movies, restaurants, and the like. Google was using this information without giving credit, making it appear as though it had generated the content. Noting the earlier hype around the case, retiring Commissioner J. Thomas Rosch (R) quipped, "After promising an elephant more than a year ago, the commission has instead brought forth a couple of mice."

In November 2011, the FTC made peace with another technology giant when it settled eight counts of privacy violations against Facebook, just prior to the company's public offering in 2012. The FTC alleged that the company allowed advertisers and others to access Facebook users' personal information. This happened in December 2009 when Facebook announced some changes that made some user-profile information public, much to the indignation of its members. Similar to the case with Google over its Buzz social networking application, Facebook did not face any monetary penalties. However, it did have to agree to obtain consent forms from consumers before changing privacy policies and also to agree that 30 days after someone deletes a Facebook account, none of his or her information will be available to advertisers or others. As part of the deal, Facebook also agreed to be subject to regular independent reviews of its practices for the next 20 years.

In addition to the investigations against Google and Facebook, the FTC (along with the Justice Department) helped review the proposed merger of two huge telecommunications firms, AT&T and T-Mobile, a deal that would have allowed AT&T to upgrade its network capacity and deliver wireless broadband to 95 percent of American households. The deal, announced in March 2011, would also have added 33.7 million T-Mobile wireless customers to the 95.5 million AT&T had already, allowing the new, merged company to eclipse Verizon as the nation's largest wireless carrier.

AT&T touted the deal as a great opportunity for consumers because, it said, the new, larger company would offer more and better services more efficiently and, thus, at a lower price. This would prompt other mobile phone companies to offer their customers similar quality at a similar price to compete, the company added. But consumer advocates worried that the merger would actually stifle competition and lead to higher prices because if the deal went through, it would reduce the number of national wireless carriers to just three—AT&T, Verizon, and Sprint—and possibly even two. That's because the AT&T/T-Mobile merger would have made it difficult for Sprint, the third-largest nationwide carrier, to compete with its two larger competitors, these advocates said. This, in turn, would have made Sprint an attractive acquisition target for Verizon. A Verizon-Sprint merger would then drop the number of major wireless carriers from three to two. These antitrust concerns prompted the Justice Department, the Federal Trade Commission, and the

Federal Communications Commission to try to block the deal in the summer of 2011. By the end of the year, AT&T withdrew from the deal, citing the government's strong opposition and the likelihood the merger would be successfully blocked.

Soon after the deal was blocked, the agency stepped back into the online privacy debate when, in March 2012, it submitted a report urging Congress to enact tougher Internet privacy laws. Specifically, the commission wanted to require data brokers—companies such as Lexis-Nexis and ChoicePoint, who take data collected online and merge it with offline data to create detailed consumer "profiles"—to reveal what information they buy and sell about consumers. However, the agency stopped short of suggesting antitracking buttons on websites, even though privacy advocates have argued they are an easy way to prevent browsers from depositing cookies that can store records of a user's purchasing, entertainment, and communications history.

Although the FTC devoted significant time and resources to technology and communications issues and would continue to do so, it also focused on other important areas of commerce. For instance, as part of President Obama's initiative to address the childhood obesity epidemic, an interagency group, with the FTC at its helm, proposed creating voluntary nutritional guidelines that would limit the sodium, fats, and added sugars in foods and drinks directed to children ages 2 to 17. A study released in early December 2011 identified nearly three-dozen brands of cereal in which sugar makes up more than a third of the product by weight, as well as three popular children's cereals that have more sugar in one serving than a Hostess Twinkie. The FTC proposal received major pushback from the industries that produce, sell, and market breakfast cereals. Calling themselves the "Sensible Food Policy Coalition," these companies, which included Viacom and Time Warner, characterized the proposal as backdoor "stealth" regulation that would effectively wipe out advertising to children, eliminate millions of jobs, and infringe on commercial free speech. They argued that the administration failed to show a direct link between the marketing of cereals and childhood obesity. The proposal received another setback when Congress in 2012 put a rider on the spending bill that barred the FTC from spending money on finalizing the proposal until they had performed a cost-benefit analysis.

Also in the agency's crosshairs during this time was the oil and gas industry, which was accused of anticompetitive conduct and price manipulation. Although collusion and price fixing are under the purview of the Justice Department, the FTC can impose civil penalties on companies that manipulate the prices of petroleum products. Sharp fluctuations in oil prices in early 2011 had many questioning whether day-to-day prices accurately reflected market conditions or were more the result of manipulation aimed at producing quick gains for energy traders and others. In June 2011 the FTC launched a well-publicized investigation into whether the energy industry was engaging in anticompetitive behavior. Since then, a Justice Department "Oil and Gas Price Fraud Working

Group" has been assisting the FTC in a probe into the practices of U.S. oil refiners, but nearly a year later, it had still not issued a report to the public. In March 2013, in response to questions about these delays from Senator Maria Cantwell, D-Wash., Chair Leibowitz described the investigation as "active and ongoing" and promised that the agency would move forward on it "expeditiously."

Meanwhile, the agency found itself deeply involved in the debate over how apps are marketed to children. In 1998, Congress enacted the Children's Online Privacy Protection Act (COPPA.) But many child advocates and others argued that the legislation had not kept up with the times, especially in light of the more recent explosion in smartphones and tablets. Children were increasingly accessing the Web through mobile devices and downloading harmful content or engaging in activities that could prove unsafe. This made some characterize the current environment as a "digital wild west," where children were especially vulnerable. The FTC—which agreed that the COPPA needs updating—expressed particular concern that parents are not being told if kids' apps contain advertisements (some of these ads are geared to mature audiences or promote junk food, etc.), but they were also concerned about games and other apps that encourage children to spend real money while online. After testing 400 leading apps sold in Apple's iTunes and Google's Google Play, the nation's two largest mobile apps stores, an FTC study found that developers of these software programs offered misleading privacy policies or buried their practices in fine print. Furthermore, the majority of them failed to inform parents about the data the app could gather about their children and who could access these data.

Web titans, including Google and Facebook, opposed updating the COPPA, arguing that though children should have special protections, some of the proposals would stifle creativity and innovation in a young and growing industry, as well as saddle small businesses with burdensome legal and technical costs. Others saw a lack of public awareness as the true culprit. More rules were not needed, they argued, but rather a better understanding of existing privacy policies.

After two years of debate and congressional inaction concerning how far the government should go to protect the privacy of children twelve and younger, the FTC attempted to tighten the rules on its own. In December 2012, the agency issued new regulations (which took effect in July 2013) that require companies to get permission from parents to collect a child's photographs, videos, and geolocational information—content that social media, online games, and mobile devices have made it all too easy to share. Companies must also have a parent's consent before using tracking tools, such as cookies, that use IP addresses and mobile device IDs to follow a child's Web activity across multiple sites and applications.

In February 2013 FTC Chair Jon Leibowitz announced plans to leave the agency. A collegial leader who took strong stands on health care matters and protections for children online, Leibowitz also was criticized by consumer groups and others who claimed he acted too tentatively when dealing with fast-moving technology industries. According to these critics, this cautiousness was exemplified by his handling of the antitrust complaint against Google, especially as the agency had aggressively lobbied for the case two years before, only to end with modest concessions from the tech giant that preserved the status quo.

Leibowitz's resignation created a two-two partisan split in the agency, which continued until his selected replacement, Edith Ramirez (D), was chosen from within the commission a month later. Ramirez, who took over as chair in March 2013, had served on the agency's board the previous three years and was a Harvard Law School classmate of President Obama. Her nomination was praised by consumer groups and Democrats on Capitol Hill, who predicted that she would be more sympathetic to consumer concerns than Leibowitz had been. The nomination also won plaudits because Ramirez, who is Mexican-American, would be the first Latina to hold the FTC's chair.

Meanwhile, in June the Supreme Court handed the agency a major victory when it ruled against a drug company that had paid makers of generics to keep less expensive versions of its drug off the market once the patent on that medication had expired. These agreements allow drugmakers to continue to charge high prices for drugs that no longer enjoy patent protection and can be produced and sold cheaply by other companies.

In this case, *Federal Trade Commission v. Actavis*, the high court gave the agency the green light to sue drugmakers who engage in these "pay to delay" agreements if it believes they run afoul of anticompetitive provisions of federal antitrust law. "The Supreme Court's decision is a significant victory for American consumers, American taxpayers and free markets," Ramirez said, adding, "With this finding, the court has taken a big step toward addressing a problem that has cost Americans $3.5 billion a year in higher drug prices."

Just weeks after the Supreme Court decision, the agency delved into a different area of patent law when it announced that it would begin a major investigation into the practices of firms called "patent trolls," companies that buy the patents from legitimate technology firms in order to use them to sue their competitors for patent infringement. Critics of patent trolls claim that they make money by trying to force makers of smartphones, computers, tablets, and other high-tech devices to settle out of court rather than endure the cost of a prolonged legal battle. The practice has been severely criticized by many technology companies as well as politicians from both parties, who claim that fighting frivolous lawsuits drains a firm's time and resources that otherwise could be used to develop new products and services.

Overhauling the patent system to make such suits harder has long had bipartisan support in Congress as well as from Republican and Democratic presidents. In December 2013 the House overwhelmingly passed legislation that aims to discourage frivolous patent suits by, among other things, making the loser pay the winner's legal costs. But the measure stalled in the Senate, where

Majority Leader Harry Reid (D-NV) refused to bring it up for a vote, a move opponents said was linked to his longtime closeness to lobbying groups associated with trial lawyers.

Almost a year and a half later, in December 2014 the FTC's investigation into patent trolls had not been completed. But that month, Commissioner Julie Brill warned that the agency would not wait until the investigation's completion or for Congress to act before enforcing existing laws against frivolous lawsuits and unfair business practices in this area.

Roughly a month after Brill's comments, the GOP took control of the Senate, following its victories in the November 2014 elections. Reid was no longer majority leader, and supporters of reining in patent trolls were more optimistic that a bill similar to that passed in the House would work its way through the Senate sometime in the next year or so.

In addition to its efforts to end allegedly abusive business practices, the FTC continued to bolster consumer privacy protection. For example, in September 2013 (the same time the FTC was beginning its investigation of patent trolls) the agency opened an inquiry into whether Facebook's new privacy policy violated its 2011 agreement with the agency. Under that agreement, Facebook had promised to obtain users' explicit consent before exposing their private information to advertisers or other new parties. The new investigation centered on a new consent form that Facebook required each of its users to sign, giving the social media site broad authority to share information with advertisers. Privacy advocates and others argued that the form, which all users were required to sign if they wanted to maintain their Facebook accounts, gave the company too much power and left consumers unprotected. But the company maintained that its actions were well within the terms of the 2011 FTC agreement.

The debate dragged on until May 2014, when Facebook announced some changes to its privacy policy. From now on, Facebook users would be able to limit what can be shared with third parties such as advertisers, including their e-mail addresses and the information on their public profiles, which anyone can already access. The move was an attempt by the company to mollify the FTC and many of its 1.3 billion users who had complained about Facebook's interest in sharing peoples' personal data with advertisers.

Meanwhile, enforcement actions continued apace. Early in January 2014 a commission investigation prompted four weight-loss products manufacturers to pay $34 million in refunds to consumers who claimed that their dietary supplements and other products had not produced advertised results. Later that same month, Apple agreed to pay $32.5 million in refunds to customers whose children had purchased apps from the company's App Store without first getting their parent's permission. The settlement also required Apple to tighten purchasing procedures to better ensure parental control. In addition, in September 2014 a similar settlement was announced with Google, which agreed to change its procedures and refund at least $19 million to consumers whose children had purchased apps without their permission.

Around the same time, the commission won an important ruling that extended its authority in the financial services area. In March 2014 a federal district court in Nevada ruled that the FTC has the authority to pursue complaints against payday lenders owned by Indian tribes. Payday lenders offer short-term loans, mostly to poorer people and often at exorbitantly high interest rates and with hidden fees. These lenders and practices have frequently been the target of regulators as well as law enforcement.

The tribes involved had argued that their status as quasi-independent nations immunizes them from the commission's jurisdiction. But the judge in the case ruled that federal law aimed at preventing unfair or deceptive practices applies to Indian tribes and thus the FTC has the authority to investigate and act against payday lenders accused of illegal activity.

Meanwhile, the agency's duels with technology firms continued. In August 2014, just months after Facebook had backed away from its efforts to share large amounts of its users' personal data with advertisers, the company was in hot water again, this time over revelations that it conducted a 2012 study that attempted to manipulate users' emotions without first obtaining their permission. The "emotion study" involved sending one group of Facebook users a high number of positive and affirming posts and another group more negative posts. The company then read what the members of each group subsequently wrote on their Facebook pages to see whether the group exposed to more positive material sounded more positive than the group exposed to negative material.

Under pressure from privacy advocates and the FTC, Facebook promised to subject future studies to greater internal scrutiny and review, a solution that pleased few of the company's critics. Still, the commission opted not to take legal action against the social media company, a move that elicited criticism from consumer groups as well as privacy advocates who contend that the agency is not policing large firms like Facebook aggressively enough.

Current Issues

Year 2015 has already seen its ups and downs for the agency. In January, Chair Ramirez received praise and plaudits from many privacy and consumer advocates with what many say was a farsighted speech focusing on technology and privacy. Speaking at a Las Vegas technology conference in March, Ramirez urged the next generation of tech companies to deal with issues of privacy up front, by acknowledging that such issues exist and then building privacy protections into their products from the very start.

Of particular concern to the chair is the growing field of wearable technology, such as watches and fitness trackers, as well as the so-called internet of things—appliances, cars, and other items that increasingly operate in concert with the Internet. "In the not-too-distant future, many, if not most, aspects of our everyday lives will be digitally observed and stored," Ramirez said. "That data trove will contain a wealth of revealing information that, when patched together, will present a deeply personal and startlingly complete picture of each of us."

But in the months following Ramirez' speech, many of the same people who had praised the chairwoman in January now found themselves criticizing her. The cause was the release of a controversial internal agency document detailing the 2012 investigation of Google. The document, which was inadvertently leaked, describes the debate within the FTC over whether or not to sue Google for anti-competitive practices. As already noted, in January 2013 all five commissioners voted not to initiate legal action. But while the investigation and vote may be old news, the release of the nearly three-year-old document has reopened the debate over whether the huge search engine company and similarly dominant technology firms, such as Facebook, are not being adequately regulated.

For many consumer advocates, the evidence presented in the document is confirmation that Google was and still is abusing its monopoly position in the Internet search market and that the FTC is not willing to do anything to stop it. The fact that, as the internal document reveals, some FTC staff at the time recommended that the commission take legal action against Google, makes advocates even more suspicious of the commission's leadership. These suspicions only grew worse when, in April 2014, European Union (EU) officials opened an antitrust investigation into Google (and a number of other American technology firms) to determine whether their market dominance is impeding technology competition with the EU.

Meanwhile, worries about the agency's will to act have been rivaled by concerns about its power to act. Specifically, many believe that a series of alleged bureaucratic turf wars could be severely curtailing the FTC's authority in key areas. The most important of these conflicts arises out of the Federal Communications Commission's efforts to regulate the Internet as a "utility" under the Telecommunications Act of 1934. If courts agree that under the 1934 act the Internet is indeed a utility, the FCC's power to regulate this area will grow dramatically and will almost certainly crowd out some of the power currently granted to the FTC in this area.

Another concern involves the newly created Consumer Financial Protection Bureau (CFPB), which has been bringing the types of actions that used to be largely within the purview of the FTC. For example, in December 2014 the bureau, which has a mandate to protect consumers from financial scams, brought a suit against wireless phone provider Sprint, contending that it is illegally adding unauthorized charges to its customers' bills, a practice known as "cramming." But in the year prior to this CFPB lawsuit, the FTC had brought similar legal actions against AT&T and T-Mobile, also for cramming. While the FTC, the CFPB, and the FCC have all publicly maintained that they are working well together, newspapers such as *The New York Times* have reported tensions among the three agencies over who has responsibility for regulating what.

AGENCY ORGANIZATION

Biographies

EDITH RAMIREZ, CHAIR

Appointment: Nominated as commissioner by President Barack Obama; sworn in on April 5, 2010, to a term expiring Sept. 25, 2015. Designated as chair March 4, 2013.

Born: California.

Education: Harvard University, A.B., 1989; Harvard Law School, J.D., 1992.

Profession: Lawyer.

Political Affiliation: Democrat.

Previous Career: Prior to joining the commission, Ramirez was a partner in the Los Angeles office of Quinn Emanuel Urquhart & Sullivan, LLP, where she handled a broad range of business litigation, including representing clients in intellectual property, antitrust, unfair competition, and Lanham Act matters. From 1993 to 1996, she was an associate at Gibson, Dunn & Crutcher, LLP, in Los Angeles. She clerked for the Hon. Alfred T. Goodwin in the U.S. Court of Appeals for the Ninth Circuit from 1992 to 1993. Throughout her career, she has been active in a variety of professional and community activities, most recently serving as the vice president on the board of commissioners for the Los Angeles Department of Water and Power.

JULIE BRILL, COMMISSIONER

Appointment: Nominated by President Barack Obama; sworn in on April 6, 2010, to a term expiring on Sept. 25, 2016.

Born: Houston, Texas.

Education: Princeton University, B.A.; New York University School of Law, J.D., 1985.

Profession: Lawyer.

Political Affiliation: Democrat.

Previous Career: Prior to her appointment as commissioner, Brill was the senior deputy attorney general and chief of Consumer Protection and Antitrust for the North Carolina Department of Justice from February 2009 to April 2010. She was also a lecturer in law at Columbia University's School of Law. From 1988 to 2009, she was an assistant attorney general for Consumer Protection and Antitrust for the State of Vermont. She has testified before Congress; published numerous articles; served on many national expert panels focused on consumer protection issues such as pharmaceuticals, privacy, credit reporting, data security breaches, and tobacco; and received several national awards for her consumer-protection work. She has served as vice-chair of the Consumer Protection Committee of the Antitrust Section of the American Bar Association. Earlier in her career, she was an associate at Paul, Weiss, Rifkind, Wharton & Garrison in New York from 1987 to 1988 and clerked for Vermont Federal District Court Judge Franklin S. Billings Jr. from 1985 to 1986.

MAUREEN K. OHLHAUSEN, COMMISSIONER

Appointment: Nominated by President Barack Obama on July 19, 2011; confirmed by the Senate

Federal Trade Commission

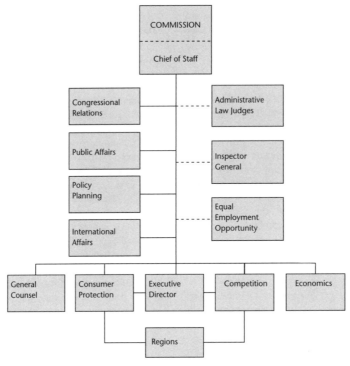

---- Denotes independent operation within the agency

March 29, 2012; sworn in April 4, 2012; term expires Sept. 2018.

Born: New York, N.Y.

Education: University of Virginia, B.A., 1984, Echols Scholar; George Mason University School of Law, J.D., 1991.

Profession: Lawyer, author, and professor of law.

Political Affiliation: Republican.

Previous Career: Ohlhausen joined the FTC from the law firm of Wilkinson Barker Knauer, LLP, where she was a leading partner in the firm's practice addressing privacy, data protection, and cybersecurity. Her previous FTC work spans eleven years, most recently as director of the Office of Policy Planning from 2004 to 2008, where she led the FTC's Internet Access Task Force. She also served as deputy director of that office. From 1998 to 2001, Ohlhausen was an attorney adviser for former FTC Commissioner Orson Swindle, focusing on competition and consumer protection matters. She started at the FTC General Counsel's Office in 1997. Before coming to the FTC, she served for five years at the U.S. Court of Appeals for the D.C. Circuit attorney, and from 1991 to 1992, clerked for Judge Robert Yock of the U.S. Court of Federal Claims. She has been a member of the adjunct faculty for George Mason University School of Law in privacy law and unfair trade practices and has written articles on competition law, privacy, and technology topics.

JOSHUA D. WRIGHT, COMMISSIONER

Appointment: Nominated by President Barack Obama on Sept. 10, 2012; confirmed by the Senate Jan. 1, 2013; sworn in Jan. 11, 2013; term expires in Sept. 2019.

Born: San Diego, California.

Education: University of California, San Diego, B.A. 1998, honors; UCLA, J.D., 2002; UCLA Ph.D., 2003, economics.

Profession: Lawyer, professor of law.

Political Affiliation: Republican.

Previous Career: Prior to joining the commission, Wright was a professor at George Mason University School of Law and held a courtesy appointment in the department of economics. He has done extensive research in antitrust law, economics, and consumer protection and has published more than sixty articles and book chapters; he was a co-author for a leading casebook on these issues. Wright also served as co-editor of the *Supreme Court Economic Review* and a senior editor of the *Antitrust Law Journal*. Wright previously served the commission in the Bureau of Competition as its inaugural Scholar-in-Residence from 2007 to 2008, where he focused on enforcement matters and competition policy. Wright also served as an intern in both the Bureau of Economics (1997) and Bureau of Competition (1998). Before his tenure at George Mason University School of Law, Wright clerked for Judge James V. Selna of the U.S. District Court for the Central District of California and taught at the Pepperdine University Graduate School of Public Policy.

TERRELL MCSWEENY, COMMISSIONER

Appointment: Nominated by President Barack Obama; sworn in on April 28, 2014, to a term expiring on Sept. 25, 2017.

Born: Washington, DC.

Education: Harvard University, B.A.; Georgetown University Law School, J.D.

Profession: Lawyer.

Political Affiliation: Democrat.

Previous Career: Prior to joining the Commission, McSweeny served as Chief Counsel for Competition Policy and Intergovernmental Relations for the U.S. Department of Justice Antitrust Division. She joined the Antitrust Division after serving as deputy assistant to the President and domestic policy adviser to the vice president from January 2009 until February 2012. Previously, McSweeny worked as an attorney at O'Melveny & Myers LLP.

Headquarters and Divisions

COMMISSION

The commissioners make final decisions on trade regulation rules (TRRs), advisory opinions, investigatory subpoenas, consent orders, and appeals of administrative law judges' decisions. They vote on ordering companies and individuals to file reports and answer questions in FTC investigations, and on issuing complaints alleging unfair competition and deceptive business practices. The commissioners grant extensions of deadlines, supervise the rule-making process, and approve the appointment of top FTC employees. The chair, as chief officer of the FTC, has final responsibility for the operations of the agency. The whole commission, however, votes on matters related to the FTC's policy-making, regulatory, and law enforcement activities.

Chair
 Edith Ramirez . . . . (202) 326–3400
Commissioners
 Julie Brill . . . . (202) 326–2626
 Maureen Ohlhausen . . . . (202) 326–2150
 Joshua D. Wright . . . . (202) 326–2488
 Terrell McSweeny . . . . (202) 326–2606
Chief of Staff
 Heather Hippsley . . . . (202) 326–3285
Executive Assistant to the Chair
 Monica Etheridge-Pyos . . . . (202) 326–2666
Attorney Advisers to the Chair
 Janis Kestenbaum . . . . (202) 326–2798
 Lisa Kimmel . . . . (202) 326–2672
 Mary Lehner . . . . (202) 326–3744
 Jon Nathan . . . . (202) 326–2457
 Evan Zullow . . . . (202) 326–2914
Staff Assistant to Commissioner Brill
 Judith Dickie . . . . (202) 326–2870
  Fax . . . . (202) 326–2441
Attorney Advisers to Commissioner Brill
 Kathleen Benway . . . . (202) 326–2024
 Abigail Slater . . . . (202) 326–3473

 Holly Vedova . . . . (202) 326–2896
 Shaundra Watson . . . . (202) 326–2777
Staff Assistant to Commissioner Ohlhausen
 Barbara A. Cook . . . . (202) 326–2150
  Fax . . . . (202) 326–3436
Attorney Advisers to Commissioner Ohlhausen
 Anna H. Davis . . . . (202) 326–3207
 Gregory P. Luib . . . . (202) 326–3249
 Alexander Okuliar . . . . (202) 326–2332
 Pablo Zylberglait . . . . (202) 326–3260
Staff Assistant to Commissioner Wright
 Kimberly M. Thompson . . . . (202) 326–2229
  Fax . . . . (202) 326–3446
Attorney Advisers to Commissioner Wright
 Elizabeth A. Delaney . . . . (202) 326–2903
 Derek Moore . . . . (202) 326–3367
 Jan Rybnicek . . . . (202) 326–2834
 Joanna Tsai . . . . (202) 326–2707
Staff Assistant to Commissioner McSweeny
 Joneta Saceda . . . . (202) 326–3131
  Fax . . . . (202) 326–2958
Attorney Advisers to Commissioner McSweeny
 Christine Lee DeLorme . . . . (202) 326–2095
 Brian A. O'Dea . . . . (202) 326–2227
 Jennifer Schwab . . . . (202) 326–2335
 Joshua Tzuker . . . . (202) 326–3279

OFFICE OF ADMINISTRATIVE LAW JUDGES

Performs the initial fact-finding in adjudicative cases, conducts hearings, examines evidence, and issues decisions. Initial decisions become final unless reviewed by the full commission or appealed. The judges also act as presiding officers assigned to conduct rulemaking proceedings, with the chief judge serving as chief presiding officer. All filings in adjudicative proceedings should be delivered or mailed to room H-135 at FTC headquarters.

Chief Administrative Law Judge
 D. Michael Chappell . . . . (202) 326–3637
  Fax . . . . (202) 326–2427
Attorney Adviser
 Victoria C. Arthaud . . . . (202) 326–2321
 Hillary Gebler . . . . (202) 326–2268
Legal Assistant
 Dana L. Gross . . . . (202) 326–3723
 Lynette Pelzer . . . . (202) 326–3150

OFFICE OF CONGRESSIONAL RELATIONS

Provides information for congressional members and staff who have questions concerning proposed legislation, commission activities, and constituent requests. Also advises the commission on congressional policies, procedures, interests, and pending legislative initiatives. For general inquiries, call (202) 326–2195.

Director
 Jeanne Bumpus . . . . (202) 326–2946
  Fax . . . . (202) 326–3585
Legislative Counsel
 Claudia Simmons . . . . (202) 326–2172
Congressional Liason
 Philip Runco . . . . (202) 326–2489

OFFICE OF THE EXECUTIVE DIRECTOR

The executive director has executive and administrative supervisory authority over all FTC offices, bureaus, and employees. Staff is responsible for publication of all commission documents and notices in the *Federal Register* and for other publications.

Executive Director
David B. Robbins................. (202) 326–2842
    Fax........................... (202) 326–3599
Deputy Executive Directors
Patricia Bak .... (202) 326–2842
Monique Fortenberry.............. (202) 326–2017
Chief Financial Officer
David Rebich .... (202) 326–2201
Chief Information Officer
Patricia Bak (acting).............. (202) 326–2842

OFFICE OF EQUAL EMPLOYMENT OPPORTUNITY

Director
Kevin D. Williams................. (202) 326–2064
Attorney Adviser
Namon C. Friends................. (202) 326–2582

OFFICE OF THE GENERAL COUNSEL

The general counsel acts as the commission's chief law officer and adviser and provides legal services to the commission, the operating bureaus, and other offices. The office participates in rulemaking proceedings, legislative matters, and policy deliberations; prepares legal opinions; represents the commission in most federal court proceedings; and ensures FTC compliance with the Freedom of Information and Privacy acts. The general counsel's office also issues a quarterly Litigation Status Report that summarizes the current status of pending court actions involving the commission. For general inquiries, call (202) 326–2424.

General Counsel
Jonathan E. Nuechterlein........... (202) 326–2828
    Fax........................... (202) 326–2477
Principal Deputy General Counsel
David C. Shonka .... (202) 326–2436
Deputy General Counsel for Legal Counsel
Christian S. White................. (202) 326–2476
Deputy General Counsel for Litigation
Joel Marcus....................... (202) 326–2244
Deputy General Counsel for Opinions and Analysis
William E. Cohen .... (202) 326–2110
Associate General Counsel for Energy
John H. Seesel .... (202) 326–2702
Associate General Counsel for Project Management
Sarah D. Mackey .... (202) 326–3254

OFFICE OF THE INSPECTOR GENERAL

Conducts and supervises audits and investigations of FTC programs and operations. Reviews existing and proposed legislation and regulations to promote effectiveness and to prevent fraud and abuse. For general inquiries and the Inspector General's hotline, call (202) 326–2800 or e-mail OIG@ftc.gov.

Inspector General
Roslyn A. Mazer .... (202) 326–2800
    Fax........................... (202) 326–2034
Investigator
Dena Davis....................... (202) 326–3602
Auditor
Mary Harmison................... (202) 326–2622

OFFICE OF INTERNATIONAL AFFAIRS

Coordinates all of the FTC's international activities. Works with foreign competition and consumer protection agencies abroad to promote cooperation and best practices. Collaborates with foreign competition agencies on cases affecting both countries, and promotes policy convergence through various channels. Works with foreign law enforcement agencies on cases and investigations that the FTC finds would affect U.S. consumers, sharing information and other investigative resources for law enforcement actions. Aids developing countries with advice and technical assistance to develop their own competition and consumer protection agencies. For general inquiries, call (202) 326–2600.

Director
Randolph W. Tritell............... (202) 326–3051
    Fax........................... (202) 326–3045
Deputy Director, Special Projects
Alden F. Abbott .... (202) 326–2881
Deputy Director, International Antitrust
Elizabeth Kraus .... (202) 326–2649
Deputy Director, International Consumer Protection
Hugh G. Stevenson .... (202) 326–3511
Deputy Director, International Technical Assistance
James C. Hamill................... (202) 326–2107

OFFICE OF POLICY PLANNING

Researches, develops, and drafts policy recommendations to the commission on a wide variety of issues, as guidance during commission deliberations or as proposals for future enforcement policy. Through its advocacy program, advises other governmental and self-regulatory organizations about the potential effects on consumers of proposed legislation, rules, or industry guides or codes.

Director
Marina Lao....................... (202) 326–3620
    Fax........................... (202) 326–3548
Deputy Directors
Tara Isa Koslov................... (202) 326–2386
Suzanne Munck................... (202) 326–2429

OFFICE OF PUBLIC AFFAIRS (PRESS OFFICE)

See Information Sources.

OFFICE OF THE SECRETARY

Responsible for the minutes of commission meetings and acts as the custodian of the FTC's seal, papers, and records, including all legal and public records gathered by the commission. Receives all incoming congressional correspondence and coordinates the agency's response. The secretary signs all commission orders and official correspondence and coordinates all liaison activities with the executive and administrative departments and agencies. The secretary also issues and serves all official agency documents and maintains the commission's rules of procedure.

Secretary
Donald S. Clark . . . . (202) 326–2514
Fax. . . . . (202) 326–2496
Minutes Section Supervisor
LaJuan Jeter . . . . (202) 326–2519
Congressional Correspondence
Susan Taylor. (202) 326–2671

BUREAU OF COMPETITION

Enforces antitrust laws that are under the administration of the FTC (Clayton Antitrust Act and Federal Trade Commission Act).

Investigates and litigates cases of alleged anticompetitive or monopolistic behavior, including antimerger enforcement, which are in violation of those acts, and advises the commission on rules and procedures. Also enforces the Export Trade Act, which allows the formation, monitoring, and regulation of certain export trade associations. Requires prior notice of certain mergers (typically in which a company worth $100 million or more plans to acquire or merge with a company worth $10 million or more) and reviews these cases to determine whether the action will reduce competition. For general inquiries, call (202) 326–3300 or e-mail antitrust@ftc.gov.

Director
Deborah L. Feinstein . . . . (202) 326–3630
Fax. . . . . (202) 326–2884
Deputy Directors
Marian R. Bruno . . . . (202) 326–2846
Stephen Weissman . . . . (202) 326–2030
Assistant Director, Anticompetitive Practices
Geoffrey Green . . . . (202) 326–2641
Fax. . . . . (202) 326–3496
Assistant Director, Compliance
Daniel P. Ducore . . . . (202) 326–2526
Fax. . . . . (202) 326–3396
Assistant Director, Healthcare Services and Products
Markus H. Meier. . . . . (202) 326–3759
Fax. . . . . (202) 326–3384
Assistant Director, Mergers 1
Michael R. Moiseyev. . . . . (202) 326–3106
Fax. . . . . (202) 326–2655
Assistant Director, Mergers 2
Catharine M. Moscatelli. . . . . (202) 326–2749
Fax. . . . . (202) 326–2071
Assistant Director, Mergers 3
Phillip L. Broyles . . . . (202) 326–2805
Fax. . . . . (202) 326–3383
Assistant Director, Mergers 4
Alexis Gilman . . . . (202) 326–2579
Fax. . . . . (202) 326–2286
Assistant Director, Policy and Coordination
Michael J. Bloom . . . . (202) 326–2475
Fax. . . . . (202) 326–2884
Assistant Director, Premerger Notification
Robert L. Jones . . . . (202) 326–2740
Fax. . . . . (202) 326–2624

BUREAU OF CONSUMER PROTECTION

Investigates, attempts to foster compliance, and litigates instances of alleged unfair, deceptive, or fraudulent business practices that harm the consuming public. Advises the commission on rules and proceedings and recommends cases for litigation. Seeks to educate both consumers and the business community about the laws it enforces, and informs Congress of the impact proposed actions could have on consumers. Administers product registration numbers for wool, fur, and textile fiber products through its enforcement division. The division operates the Identity Theft Data Clearinghouse, the federal government's centralized repository for consumer identity theft complaints. To register a complaint, go to www.identitytheft.gov or contact the call center at (877) 438–4338.

Director
Jessica L. Rich . . . . (202) 326–2148
Fax. . . . . (202) 326–3799
Deputy Directors
Christopher Olsen (acting) . . . . (202) 326–3621
Daniel Kaufman . . . . (202) 326–2675
Associate Director, Advertising Practices
Mary K. Engle . . . . (202) 326–3161
Fax. . . . . (202) 326–3259
Associate Director, Consumer and Business Education
Nat Wood (acting) . . . . (202) 326–3268
Fax. . . . . (202) 326–3574
Assistant Director, Consumer Response and Operations
David M. Torok. . . . . (202) 326–3075
Fax. . . . . (202) 326–3392
Assistant Director, Enforcement
James A. Kohm . . . . (202) 326–2640
Fax. . . . . (202) 326–2558
Assistant Director, Financial Practices
Reilly Dolan . . . . (202) 326–2148
Fax. . . . . (202) 326–3629
Assistant Director, Litigation Technology and Analysis
Laura DeMartino . . . . (202) 326–3030
Fax. . . . . (202) 326–3383
Assistant Director, Marketing Practices
Lois C. Greisman. . . . . (202) 326–3404
Fax. . . . . (202) 326–3395
Assistant Director, Privacy and Identity Protection
Maneesha Mithal. . . . . (202) 326–2771

BUREAU OF ECONOMICS

Advises the commission on the economic aspects and effects of FTC actions. Prepares economic surveys and reports for use by the commission and by other FTC bureaus. Areas of analysis include industry and trade practices and behavior, consumer protection, antitrust, and government and self-regulatory entities. For general inquiries, call (202) 326–3419.

Director
Francine Lafontaine . . . . (202) 326–2784
Fax. . . . . (202) 326–2380
Deputy Director, Antitrust
Kenneth Heyer. . . . . (202) 326–2032

Assistant Director, Antitrust I
Louis Silvia Jr. . . . . (202) 326–3471
    Fax. . . . . (202) 326–2625
Assistant Director, Antitrust II
Aileen J. Thompson . . . . (202) 326–3493
    Fax. . . . . (202) 326–3443
Associate Director, Competition Analysis
Timothy A. Deyak. . . . . (202) 326–3742
Deputy Director, Consumer Protection
Andrew E. Stivers . . . . (202) 326–3357
Assistant Director, Consumer Protection
Janice K. Pappalardo . . . . (202) 326–3380
Assistant Director, Accounting and Financial Analysis
H. Gabriel Dagen. . . . . (202) 326–2573
Deputy Director, R&D and Operations
Pauline M. Ippolito . . . . (202) 326–3477
Assistant Director, Applied Research and Outreach
David R. Schmidt . . . . (202) 326–2781
    Fax. . . . . (202) 326–3443

Regional Offices

EAST CENTRAL REGION
(DC, DE, MD, MI, OH, PA, VA, WV)
1111 Superior Ave., #200
Cleveland, OH 44114–2507
(216) 263–3455
Fax (216) 263–3426
Jon M. Steiger, regional director

MIDWEST REGION
(IA, IL, IN, KS, KY, ND, NE, MN, MO, SD, WI)
55 W. Monroe St., #1825
Chicago, IL 60603
(312) 960–5634
Fax (312) 960–5600
C. Steven Baker, regional director

NORTHEAST REGION
(CT, MA, ME, NH, NJ, NY, PR, RI, VI, VT)
1 Bowling Green, #318
New York, NY 10004
(212) 607–2829
Fax (212) 607–2822
William H. Efron, regional director

NORTHWEST REGION
(AK, ID, MT, OR, WA, WY)
915 2nd Ave., #2896
Seattle, WA 98174
(206) 220–6350
Fax (206) 220–6366
Charles A. Harwood, regional director

SOUTHEAST REGION
(AL, FL, GA, MS, NC, SC, TN)
225 Peachtree St. N.E., #1500
Atlanta, GA 30303
(404) 656–1390
Fax (404) 656–1379
Cindy Liebes, regional director

SOUTHWEST REGION
(AR, LA, NM, OK, TX)
1999 Bryan St., #2150
Dallas, TX 75201–6808
(214) 979–9350
Fax (214) 953–9374
Dama J. Brown, regional director

WESTERN REGION
(AZ, CA, CO, HI, NV, UT)
901 Market St., #570
San Francisco, CA 94103
(415) 848–5100
Fax (415) 848–5184
10877 Wilshire Blvd., #700
Los Angeles, CA 90024
(310) 824–4343
Fax (310) 824–4380
Thomas Dahdouh, regional director

■ CONGRESSIONAL ACTION

Congressional Liaison
Philip Runco . . . . (202) 326–2946

Committees and Subcommittees

HOUSE APPROPRIATIONS COMMITTEE
Subcommittee on Financial Services and General Government
B-300 RHOB, Washington, DC 20515
(202) 225–7245

HOUSE ENERGY AND COMMERCE COMMITTEE
Subcommittee on Commerce, Manufacturing and Trade
2125 RHOB, Washington, DC 20515–6115
(202) 225–2927
Fax (202) 225–1919
Subcommittee on Communications and Technology
2125 RHOB, Washington, DC 20515–6115
(202) 225–2927
Fax (202) 225–1919
Subcommittee on Oversight and Investigations
2125 RHOB, Washington, DC 20515–6115
(202) 225–2927
Fax (202) 225–1919

HOUSE FINANCIAL SERVICES COMMITTEE
Subcommittee on Financial Institutions and Consumer Credit
2129 RHOB, Washington, DC 20515
(202) 225–7502

HOUSE COMMITTEE ON OVERSIGHT AND GOVERNMENT REFORM
2157 RHOB, Washington, DC 20515
(202) 225–5074
Fax (202) 225–3974

HOUSE JUDICIARY COMMITTEE
Subcommittee on Courts, Intellectual Property, and the Internet
6310 OHOB, Washington, DC 20024
(202) 226–7680

SENATE APPROPRIATIONS COMMITTEE
Subcommittee on Financial Services and General Government
SDOB-133, Washington, DC 20510
(202) 224–2104

SENATE COMMERCE, SCIENCE, AND TRANSPORTATION COMMITTEE
Subcommittee on Consumer Protection, Product Safety, Insurance, and Data Security
SDOB-512, Washington, DC 20510–6125
(202) 224–1251
Subcommittee on Communications, Technology, Innovation, and the Internet
SDOB-512, Washington, DC 20510–6125
(202) 224–1251

SENATE JUDICIARY COMMITTEE
Subcommittee on Antitrust, Competition Policy, and Consumer Rights
SDOB-224, Washington, DC 20510
(202) 224–5225

SENATE BANKING, HOUSING, AND URBAN AFFAIRS COMMITTEE
SDOB-534, Washington, DC 20510
(202) 224–7391
Fax (202) 224–5137

SENATE FINANCE COMMITTEE
SDOB-219, Washington, DC 20510
(202) 224–4515
Fax (202) 228–0554

SENATE HOMELAND SECURITY AND GOVERNMENTAL AFFAIRS COMMITTEE
Subcommittee on Federal Spending Oversight and Emergency Management
SHOB-439, Washington, DC, 20510
(202) 224–2254
Permanent Subcommittee on Investigations
SROB-1099, Washington, DC, 20510
(202) 224–3721

SENATE SMALL BUSINESS AND ENTREPRENEURSHIP COMMITTEE
SROB-428A, Washington, DC 20510
(202) 224–5175
Fax (202) 224–5619

SENATE SPECIAL COMMITTEE ON AGING
Republican/Majority Office
SDOB-G31, Washington, DC 20510
Democrat/Minority Office

SHOB-628, Washington, DC 20510
(202) 224–5364
Fax (202) 224–9926

Legislation

The FTC was created by the **Federal Trade Commission Act of 1914** (38 Stat. 717, 15 U.S.C. 41). Signed by the president Sept. 26, 1914. The commission's primary function is to define and outlaw unfair methods of competition. The FTC Act was amended in 1938 by the passage of the **Wheeler-Lea Act** (52 Stat. 114, 15 U.S.C. 52). The 1938 amendment extended protection to consumers by forbidding unfair or deceptive acts or practices in commerce. The FTC Act was amended again with passage of the **Federal Trade Commission Improvements Act of 1980** (94 Stat. 374, 15 U.S.C. 58 note). Signed by the president May 28, 1980. Permitted Congress to veto FTC regulations or actions without presidential approval.

The commission also administers several other laws, all of which either prohibit anticompetitive practices or promote consumer protection. They include, as amended:

Sherman Antitrust Act (26 Stat. 209, 15 U.S.C. 1). Signed by the president July 2, 1890. Prohibited restraint of trade and the monopolization of any part of trade or commerce.

Clayton Act (38 Stat. 730, 15 U.S.C. 12). Signed by the president Oct. 15, 1914. Outlawed mergers or acquisitions that could substantially lessen competition or help to create monopolies.

Export Trade Act (40 Stat. 516, 15 U.S.C. 61). Signed by the president April 10, 1918. Promoted export trade by permitting certain types of cooperative business activities.

Robinson-Patman Protection Act (49 Stat. 1526, 15 U.S.C. 13). Signed by the president June 19, 1936. Prohibited specified practices, such as unlawful price discrimination and related acts.

Wool Products Labeling Act of 1939 (54 Stat. 1128, 15 U.S.C. 68). Signed by the president Oct. 14, 1940. Required manufacturers to disclose composition of spun, woven, knitted, felted, and other types of manufactured wool products.

Lanham Trademark Act of 1946 (60 Stat. 427, 15 U.S.C. 1051). Signed by the president July 5, 1946. Required registration and protection of trademarks used in commerce.

Fur Products Labeling Act (65 Stat. 175, 15 U.S.C. 69). Signed by the president Aug. 8, 1951. Prohibited false advertising, false invoicing, and false branding of furs and fur products.

Textile Fiber Products Identification Act (72 Stat. 1717, 15 U.S.C. 70). Signed by the president Sept. 2, 1958. Prohibited use of false brands or false advertising of the fiber content of textile fiber products.

Federal Cigarette Labeling and Advertising Act (79 Stat. 282, 15 U.S.C. 1331 note). Signed by the president July 27, 1965. Required health warnings on cigarette packages. This act was amended by the **Public Health Cigarette Smoking Act of 1969** (84 Stat. 87, 15 U.S.C. 1331 et seq.). Signed by the president April 1, 1970. Prohibited radio and television cigarette advertising, required printed ads to include a health warning, and strengthened the wording of the messages. The Federal Cigarette Labeling and Advertising Act was again amended by the **Little Cigar Act of 1973** (87 Stat. 352, 15 U.S.C. 1331), which was signed by the president Sept. 21, 1973, and brought little cigars under its jurisdiction. The final amendment to the 1965 act was the **Comprehensive Smoking Education Act of 1984** (98 Stat. 2200, 15 U.S.C. 1331 note). Signed by the president Oct. 12, 1984. This act strengthened the warning again and required four different messages to appear on a quarterly, rotating basis.

Fair Packaging and Labeling Act (80 Stat. 1296, 15 U.S.C. 1451). Signed by the president Nov. 3, 1966. Prohibited unfair or deceptive packaging and labeling of certain consumer products.

Truth in Lending Act (82 Stat. 146, 15 U.S.C. 1601). Signed by the president May 29, 1968. Required full disclosure of credit terms before a consumer credit account is opened or a credit transaction completed. Also established limits on a consumer's liability for unauthorized use of a credit card.

Fair Credit Reporting Act (84 Stat. 1128, 15 U.S.C. 1681). Signed by the president Oct. 26, 1970. Required that credit reports be accurate and allowed consumers to correct faulty information in their reports. Also required that credit reports be kept confidential and that only properly authorized parties be allowed access to the reports.

Equal Credit Opportunity Act (88 Stat. 1521, 15 U.S.C. 1691). Signed by the president Oct. 28, 1974. Prohibited the denial of credit on the basis of sex, marital status, age, race, religion, or national origin.

Fair Credit Billing Act (88 Stat. 1511, 15 U.S.C. 1666). Signed by the president Oct. 28, 1974. Amended the Truth in Lending Act by setting up a mechanism that consumers can use to dispute billing errors and requiring creditors to take steps to correct billing errors.

Magnuson-Moss Warranty–Federal Trade Commission Improvement Act (88 Stat. 2183, 15 U.S.C. 2301–12, 15 U.S.C. 45–58). Signed by the president Jan. 4, 1975. Authorized the FTC to establish standards for written warranties on products that cost more than $10; gave the FTC authority to promulgate trade regulation rules that carry the force of law to deal with unfair or deceptive practices throughout an industry rather than on a case-by-case basis; allowed the commission to represent itself in court and to request redress and civil penalties for violations of the Federal Trade Commission Act; and expanded the FTC's jurisdiction to cover activities "affecting commerce" as well as "in commerce."

Hart-Scott-Rodino Antitrust Improvement Act of 1976 (90 Stat. 1383, 15 U.S.C. 1311 note). Signed by the president Sept. 30, 1976. Required companies to notify the FTC and the Justice Department of an intention to merge if one of the companies involved is worth in excess of $100 million and the other company is worth in excess of $10 million and if the transaction would affect in excess of $50 million in stocks or assets, or 15 percent of the voting securities of the acquired company.

Fair Debt Collection Practices Act of 1977 (91 Stat. 874, 15 U.S.C. 1601 note). Signed by the president Sept. 20, 1977. Established a national system of controls on the activities of debt collection agencies.

Electronic Fund Transfer Act (92 Stat. 3728, 15 U.S.C. 1693). Signed by the president Nov. 11, 1978. Enacted as Title IX of the Consumer Credit Protection Act to provide a framework for consumer rights regarding electronic fund transfer systems. The FTC was given authority for the administrative enforcement of this statute, excepting oversight of financial institutions, air carriers, and securities brokers and dealers.

Smokeless Tobacco Health Education Act (100 Stat. 30, 15 U.S.C. 4401 note). Signed by the president Feb. 27, 1986. Required manufacturers of "smokeless tobacco" products such as chewing tobacco and snuff to print warning labels on their packages. Prohibited radio and television advertising of such products.

Telephone Disclosure and Dispute Resolution Act of 1992 (106 Stat. 4181, 15 U.S.C. 5701). Signed by the president Oct. 28, 1992. Title II amended the Communications Act of 1934 by adding 228 (42 U.S.C. 228). Authorized the FTC to regulate pay-per-call telephone services to protect consumers. Also authorized regulation of unfair and deceptive advertising regarding pay-per-call.

Telemarketing and Consumer Fraud and Abuse Prevention Act (108 Stat. 1545, 15 U.S.C. 6101). Signed by the president Aug. 16, 1994. Prohibited unfair or deceptive telemarketing practices. Required a limit on the hours during which telephone sales can be solicited; required telemarketers to "promptly and clearly disclose" the purpose of the call; barred telemarketers from repeatedly disturbing consumers with unsolicited calls.

Federal Trade Commission Act Amendments of 1994 (108 Stat. 1691, 15 U.S.C. 58 note). Signed by the president Aug. 26, 1994. Amended the Federal Trade Commission Act to deny authority to the FTC to study, investigate, or prosecute agricultural cooperatives for any action not in violation of antitrust acts; or to study or investigate agricultural marketing orders. Prohibited the FTC from instituting a civil action in cases involving consent orders, to obtain civil penalties for unfair or deceptive acts or practices. Prohibited the FTC from using authorized funds for submitting statements to, appearing before, or intervening in the proceeds of, any federal or state agency or legislative body concerning proposed rules or legislation that the agency or legislative body is considering, without notifying relevant congressional committees in a timely manner.

Consumer Credit Reporting Reform Act of 1996 (110 Stat. 3009–426, 15 U.S.C. 1601 note). Required the FTC to take action to achieve consumer standardization and comprehensibility. Authorized the FTC to commence a civil action to recover a civil penalty in a federal district court in the event of a knowing violation constituting a pattern or practice of the Fair Credit Reporting Act (FCRA) violations. Limited such penalty to $2,500. Precluded the FTC from promulgating trade regulation rules with respect to the FCRA.

Credit Repair Organizations Act (110 Stat. 3009–455, 15 U.S.C. 1601 note). Signed by the president Sept. 30,

1996. Authorized the FTC to enforce the following provisions: (1) prohibited any credit repair organizations (CRO) from advising consumers to make an untrue or misleading statement or to alter a consumer's credit record; (2) prohibited any fraud or deceptive actions by a CRO; and (3) prohibited a CRO from charging or receiving valuable consideration for any service before such service is fully rendered.

Do-Not-Call Implementation Act (117 Stat. 557, 15 U.S.C. 6101 note). Signed by the president March 11, 2003. Authorized the FTC to collect fees for use in establishing a National Do-Not-Call Registry for telemarketers. Directed the FTC and the Federal Communications Commission (FCC) to align their telemarketing regulations for the purposes of consistency.

Fair and Accurate Credit Transactions Act of 2003 (FACT Act) (117 Stat. 1952, 15 U.S.C. 1681a). Signed by the president Dec. 4, 2003. Directed the federal banking agencies, including the FTC, to coordinate regulations governing the accuracy and integrity of information provided by furnishers of consumer information to consumer reporting agencies. Directed the FTC to prepare a model summary of consumer rights regarding the procedures for remedying the effects of fraud or identity theft.

Fairness to Contact Lens Consumers Act (1117 Stat. 2024, 15 U.S.C. 7601a, 7603f, 7609a). Signed by the president Dec. 5, 2003. Authorized the FTC to implement a law requiring contact lens prescribers to provide patients with a copy of their contact lens prescription, whether or not requested by the patient, and to verify the prescription's accuracy.

Controlling the Assault of Non-Solicited Pornography and Marketing (CAN-SPAM) Act of 2003 (117 Stat. 2699, 15 U.S.C. 7701–7713). Signed by the president Dec. 16, 2003. Imposed limitations and penalties on the transmission of unsolicited commercial electronic mail via the Internet. Required the FTC to issue regulations covering the law and to submit to Congress a timetable for establishing a nationwide marketing Do–Not–E-mail registry.

Bankruptcy Abuse Prevention and Consumer Protection Act of 2005 (119 Stat. 23, 11 U.S.C. 101). Signed by the president April 20, 2005. Amended federal bankruptcy law to revamp guidelines governing dismissal or conversion of a Chapter 7 liquidation (complete relief in bankruptcy) to one under either Chapter 11 (reorganization) or Chapter 13 (adjustment of debts of an individual with regular income).

Energy Policy Act of 2005 (119 Stat. 607, 16 U.S.C. 824). Signed by the president Aug. 8, 2005. Established a long-range, comprehensive national energy policy. Directed the FTC to consider the effectiveness of the current consumer products labeling program. Authorized the FTC to issue rules (1) protecting the privacy of electric consumers; (2) prohibiting the change of selection of an electric utility without the electric consumer's informed consent (slamming); and (3) prohibiting the sale of goods and services to an electric consumer without express authorization by law or the electric consumer (cramming).

Undertaking Spam, Spyware, and Fraud Enforcement with Enforcers Beyond Borders (US SAFE WEB) Act of 2006 (120 Stat. 3372, 15 U.S.C. 58 note). Signed by the president Dec. 22, 2006. Empowered the FTC to work with foreign law enforcement officials to combat international online fraud. Authorized the FTC to seek court orders requiring third parties, such as Internet service providers, to provide confidential information without notifying targets of the investigations. Allowed FTC to share information with federal regulators to track proceeds of fraud and other illegal practices channeled through U.S. banks. Affirmed FTC's power to prosecute cross-border fraud cases and to work with the Justice Department in cases involving foreign litigation to freeze overseas assets and enforce U.S. court judgments abroad.

Energy Independence and Security Act of 2007 (121 Stat. 1492, 49 U.S.C. 32902). Signed by the president Dec. 19, 2007. Banned any manipulative or deceptive device in connection with the wholesale purchase or sale of crude oil, gasoline, or other petroleum distillate that would contradict any regulations the FTC might write. Required the FTC to issue rules for the labeling of biodiesel or biodiesel blend fuel sold at retail. Amended the Energy Policy and Conservation Act so that the FTC could oversee rulemaking in specified circumstances regarding energy efficiency labeling for certain heating and cooling equipment, lamps and lighting, consumer electronic products, and other consumer products as appropriate.

Do-Not-Call Improvement Act of 2007 (122 Stat. 633, 15 U.S.C. 6151 note). Signed by the president Feb. 15, 2008. Eliminated the automatic removal of telephone numbers registered on the National Do-Not-Call Registry.

Do-Not-Call Registry Fee Extension Act of 2007 (122 Stat. 635, 15 U.S.C. 6151 note). Signed by the president Feb. 15, 2008. Extended the fees that marketers are assessed for the National Do-Not-Call Registry of consumers who do not wish to be contacted by marketing agents.

▪ INFORMATION SOURCES

Internet

Agency website: www.ftc.gov. Provides information on FTC offices, programs, cases, meetings, and hearings, as well as news releases, consumer information, and an extensive collection of publications.

The FTC monitors and investigates Internet spam and phishing schemes. Unsolicited commercial e-mail (spam), including phishing messages, may be forwarded directly to the FTC at spam@uce.gov.

Telephone Contacts

Calendar (recording) . . . .(202) 326–2711
Main information number, including publication
    requests. . . . .(202) 326–2222
En Español . . . .(877) 382–4357
Federal Relay Service TTY . . . .(800) 877–8339

Complaints . . . . (877) 382–4357
Complaints TTY . . . . (866) 653–4261
Identity theft hotline . . . . (877) 438–4338
Identity theft TTY. . . . . (866) 653–4261
Inspector General's hotline. . . . . . . (202) 326–2800
National Do Not Call Registry. . . . . (888) 382–1222
National Do Not Call Registry TTY. . (866) 290–4236

Information and Publications

KEY OFFICES

FTC Public Affairs (Press Office)
600 Pennsylvania Ave. N.W.
Washington, DC 20580
(202) 326–2180
Fax (202) 326–3366
General e-mail: opa@ftc.gov
Justin Cole, director
(202) 326–2334
Frank Dorman, Betsy Lordan, and Jack Mayfield,
    press officers

Issues news releases on actions of the commission, including investigations, consent orders, settlements, court cases, trade regulation rules, staff reports, and hearings. The weekly calendar and notice of Sunshine Meetings are available online and via recorded messages (see Telephone Contacts, above). For general inquiries, call (202) 326–2180.

FTC Consumer Response Center
600 Pennsylvania Ave. N.W., Room 130
Washington, DC 20580
(202) 326–2222
Toll-free (877) 382–4357
Fax (202) 326–2012, Attn: CRC

Responds to inquiries from the public, the business community, and government. Distributes copies of FTC reports, speeches, regulations, publications, and press releases. Receives complaints involving antitrust matters and unfair or deceptive trade practices. Maintains complaint databases that are shared with other federal agencies, state attorney's general, and international partners. Operates a walk-in public reference room and a general information telephone line. Consumers may also contact the FTC regional office in their area.

FTC Consumer and Business Education
Bureau of Consumer Protection
600 Pennsylvania Ave. N.W.
Washington, DC 20580
(202) 326–3268
Fax (202) 326–3574
Carolyn S. Shanoff, associate director

Provides information about FTC programs to consumers, attorneys, law enforcement officials, and business executives.

Freedom of Information
Freedom of Information Act Request
Office of General Counsel
Federal Trade Commission
600 Pennsylvania Ave. N.W., Room 130
Washington, DC 20580
(202) 326–2430
Fax (202) 326–2477
E-mail: foia@ftc.gov
Richard Gold, FOIA public liaison
(202) 326–3355

FTC records are available on the website, and extensive information on FOIA requests, including a sample FOIA request letter, may be obtained at www.ftc.gov/about-ftc/foia/freedom-information-act-contacts

DATA AND STATISTICS
All FTC documents, studies, reports, summaries, dockets, files, and investigations that are open to the public are available for inspection and copying in the Consumer Response Center, as well as on the website. The *Annual Report* provides an overview of agency data and is available from the Consumer Response Center and in regional offices. Annual Reports from 1916 to 2014 are available on the website at www.ftc.gov/policy/reports/policy-reports/ftc-annual-reports.

MEETINGS
The commissioners usually meet in Room 432 of the FTC headquarters. Schedules and agendas for meetings are available on the website. This information is also available from the FTC Consumer Response Center and on a recorded message maintained by FTC Public Affairs: (202) 326–2711. Meetings are closed to the public.

PUBLICATIONS
Contact the FTC Consumer Response Center or visit the website at www.ftc.gov/bcp/consumer.shtm. More than 400 FTC publications are available, whether as single copies or ordered in bulk. Publications include information on automobiles and warranties; computers and the Internet; credit and loans; education, scholarships, and job placement; health; ID theft, privacy, and security; investments and business opportunities; shopping for products and services; and telemarketing and telephone services. Many publications are available in Spanish. FTC Annual Reports from 1916 to 2011 are available on the website at acpolicy/reports/policy-reports/ftc-annual-reports

Reference Resources

LIBRARIES

FTC Library
600 Pennsylvania Ave. N.W., Room 630
Washington, DC 20580
(202) 326–2395
Fax (202) 326–2732
Chris Westergard, production assistant director

Open to the public. Holds materials on law, related antitrust matters, and consumer and economic affairs. Subscribes to the following search services: EBSCO, Lexis-Nexis, HeinOnline, Westlaw, and JSTOR. Interlibrary loan service is available.

FTC Consumer Response Center
600 Pennsylvania Ave. N.W., #130
Washington, DC 20580
(202) 326–2222
Toll-free (877) 382–4357
Fax (202) 326–2012, Attn: CRC
Hours: 9:00 a.m. to 5:00 p.m.

Provides public dockets for all FTC proceedings for inspection and copying. Other information available to the public includes an index of opinions, orders, statements of policy, and interpretations; administrative staff manuals; a record of the final votes of commissioners in agency proceedings; records of adjudicative proceedings and hearings; petitions filed with the secretary regarding rules and regulations; transcripts of hearings and written statements filed in connection with rulemaking proceedings; published FTC reports on economic surveys and investigations; registration statements and annual reports filed by export trade associations; requests for advice on proposed mergers, divestitures, and acquisitions; reports of compliance; administrative interpretations; notices of rulemaking, including proposals; news releases; reprints of the FTC's principal laws; FTC annual reports; and *Federal Trade Commission Decisions*. This information is also available on the FTC website at www.ftc.gov.

DOCKETS
Contact the FTC Consumer Response Center. Federal dockets are available on the FTC website and at www.regulations.gov. (*See appendix for Searching and Commenting on Regulations: Regulations.gov.*)

RULES AND REGULATIONS
FTC rules and regulations are published in the *Code of Federal Regulations,* Title 5, Chapter LVII, Part 5701; Title 16, Chapter I, Parts 0–999. Proposed rules, new final rules, and updates to the *Code of Federal Regulations* are published in the daily *Federal Register*. (*See appendix for information on how to obtain and use these publications.*) The *Federal Register* may be accessed at www.federalregister.gov and the *Code of Federal Regulations* at www.archives.gov/federal-register/cfr; also see the federal government's website www.regulations.gov (*see appendix*).

Other Information Sources

RELATED AGENCIES

Antitrust Division
Justice Department, Antitrust *(see p. 726).*

Federal Citizen Information Center
General Services Administration (*see appendix, Ordering Government Publications*). The FCIC may be reached at (888) 878–3256 or online at www.gsa.gov/portal/category/101011.

NONGOVERNMENTAL RESOURCES
The following are some key resources for information on the FTC and related trade and consumer protection issues.

Action on Smoking and Health
701 4th St. N.W.
Washington, DC 20001
(202) 659–4310
Internet: www.ash.org

American Advertising Federation
1101 Vermont Ave. N.W., #500
Washington, DC 20005–6306
(202) 898–0089
Internet: www.aaf.org

Bureau of National Affairs, Inc.
3 Bethesda Metro Center, #250
Bethesda, MD 20814–5377
(703) 341–3500
(800) 372–1033
Fax (800) 253–0332
Internet: www.bna.com

The Business Roundtable
300 New Jersey Ave. N.W., #800
Washington, DC 20001
(202) 872–1260
Internet: www.businessroundtable.org

Consumer Federation of America
1620 Eye St. N.W., #200
Washington, DC 20006
(202) 387–6121
Internet: www.consumerfed.org

Consumers Union of the United States
101 Truman Ave.
Yonkers, NY 10703–1057
(914) 378–2000
Publishes *Consumer Reports* magazine.
Internet: www.consumersunion.org
Washington office
1101 17th St. N.W., #500
Washington, DC 20036
(202) 462–6262
Fax (202) 265–9548

Journal of Consumer Research
Oxford University Press
2001 Evans Road
Cary, NC 27513
(919) 677–0977

(800) 852–7323
Fax (919) 677–1714
Internet: www.ejcr.org

National Association of Attorneys General

2030 M St. N.W., 8th Floor
Washington, DC 20036
(202) 326–6000
Fax (202) 331–1427
Internet: www.naag.org

National Consumers League

1701 K St. N.W., #1200
Washington, DC 20006
(202) 835–3323

Fax (202) 835–0747
Internet: www.nclnet.org

Public Citizen

1600 20th St. N.W.
Washington, DC 20009
(202) 588–1000
Internet: www.citizen.org

U.S. Chamber of Commerce

1615 H St. N.W.
Washington, DC 20062–2000
(202) 659–6000
(800) 638–6582
Internet: www.uschamber.com

Food and Drug Administration

10903 New Hampshire Ave., Silver Spring, MD 20993
Internet: www.fda.gov

▓ INTRODUCTION

The Food and Drug Administration (FDA) is an agency within the Health and Human Services Department (HHS). The president appoints and the Senate confirms the FDA commissioner.

The FDA traces its authority back to the Food and Drug Act of 1906, which called for the protection of the public from the potential health hazards presented by adulterated and mislabeled foods, drugs, cosmetics, and medical devices. FDA powers were expanded by the Food, Drug and Cosmetic (FDC) Act of 1938 and various amendments to it (including the FDA Modernization Act of 1997), the Public Health Service Act (PHS) of 1944, the 1968 Radiation

Control for Health and Safety Act amending the PHS Act, the Fair Packaging and Labeling Act of 1966, the Drug Price Competition and Patent Term Restoration Act of 1984, and the Family Smoking Prevention and Tobacco Control Act of 2009. By force of these major laws, as well as others, the FDA regulates those foods, drugs, cosmetics, medical devices, and tobacco products found in interstate commerce. Meat and poultry are regulated by the Agriculture Department, and products such as child-proof medicine bottle caps are regulated elsewhere in the federal government.

Responsibilities

The FDA

- Regulates the composition, quality, safety, and labeling of food, food additives, food colors, and cosmetics and carries out some research in these areas.
- Monitors and enforces regulations through the inspection of food and cosmetics producers' facilities and some imported products, surveillance of advertising and media reports, and follow-up of consumer complaints.
- Regulates the composition, quality, safety, efficacy, and labeling of all drugs for human use and establishes, in part through research, scientific standards for this purpose.
- Requires premarket testing of new drugs and evaluates new drug applications and requests to approve drugs for experimental use.
- Develops standards for the safety and effectiveness of over-the-counter drugs.
- Develops guidelines on good drug manufacturing practices and makes periodic inspections of drug manufacturing facilities in the United States and overseas.
- Monitors the quality of marketed drugs through product testing, surveillance, and compliance and adverse reaction reporting programs.
- Conducts recalls or seizure actions of products found to violate federal laws and pose hazards to human health.
- Conducts research and establishes scientific standards for the development, manufacture, testing, and use of biological products.
- Inspects and licenses manufacturers of biological products.
- Requires premarket testing of new biological products and evaluates the claims for new drugs that are biologics, often on a lot-by-lot basis.

GLOSSARY

Adulterated—Products or materials that are defective and unsafe because they are contaminated or were produced under unsanitary conditions.

ANDA (abbreviated new drug application)—An application that must be filed and approved before a manufacturer can market a copy of an already approved drug. ANDAs require information showing that the copy is bioequivalent to the original product but do not require original test results proving safety and efficacy.

Bioequivalent—A drug product is considered a bioequivalent if it demonstrates the same therapeutic effect as the drug it copies.

Biologics—Medical products, such as vaccines and serums, derived from living organisms.

Carcinogen—A substance that is shown to cause cancer.

Delaney Amendment—A 1958 amendment to the Federal Food, Drug, and Cosmetic Act that requires the FDA to ban any food or color additive that has been shown to cause cancer in laboratory test animals. Named after the chief sponsor, Rep. James J. Delaney (D-NY).

Generic drug—A copy of an already-approved drug product whose patent protection has expired. To gain approval of a generic drug product, the manufacturer must submit an ANDA including laboratory tests demonstrating that the copy is bioequivalent to the original product.

Listed drug—A product with an approved NDA.

Misbranded—Products or materials with labels that mislead or lack necessary information.

NCE (new chemical entity)—A new chemical that has not been adequately characterized in the literature with regard to its physical and chemical properties.

NDA (new drug application)—An application that a pharmaceutical company must submit before the FDA will allow it to market a new drug. NDAs require supporting evidence that the new drug is both safe and effective.

OTC (over-the-counter)—A drug product that can be sold directly to the consumer without a doctor's prescription.

PMA (Premarket Approval)—An application that a medical device company must submit before the FDA will allow it to market a new device. PMAs require supporting evidence that the new drug is safe and effective. PMAs are required for high-risk devices, including those that support or sustain human life or that present a potentially significant risk of illness or injury. Device manufacturers also can receive clearance through the shorter 510(k) process to market a device that is substantially equivalent to another device that is already sold.

- Collects data on medical device experience and sets standards for medical devices.
- Regulates the safety, efficacy, and labeling of medical devices and requires premarket testing of medical devices categorized as potentially hazardous.

- Establishes standards and makes regulations for good manufacturing practices for medical devices and inspects manufacturers' facilities.
- Conducts research on the biological effects of radiation exposure and develops programs to reduce human exposure to radiation.
- Determines standards for the quality of radiation-emitting products, such as television sets and X-ray machines, inspects radiological product manufacturing facilities, and provides certification for products meeting FDA standards.
- Develops programs and standards dealing with veterinary drugs, particularly in the areas of good manufacturing practices and the handling of livestock destined for human consumption.
- Occasionally conducts or solicits research on potentially toxic substances and distributes information on toxic substances under agency jurisdiction.
- Regulates tobacco products.

Powers and Authority

The FDA commissioner is assisted by a principal deputy commissioner, five deputy commissioners, including officials who are responsible for policy and budget planning; operations; global affairs; foods; and medical products and tobacco. Four associate commissioners are responsible for external affairs; special medical affairs; regulatory affairs; and legislation. Three other associate commissioners supplement the work of international affairs; policy and planning; and foods and veterinary medicine. The FDA's investigations, analysis, research, and compliance monitoring take place through the Center for Devices and Radiological Health, the Center for Biologics Evaluation and Research, the Center for Drug Evaluation and Research, the National Center for Toxicological Research, the Centers for Food Safety and Applied Nutrition, the Center for Veterinary Medicine, and the Center for Tobacco Products.

ENFORCEMENT ACTIVITIES

In fulfilling its statutory duties, the FDA engages in three broad categories of activity: analysis, surveillance, and correction. Most, although not all, analytical work is preventive, occurring in the process of clearing new products for the market. Rather than conducting research on new drugs, food additives, veterinary drugs, biological drugs, and some medical devices from scratch, each section of the agency reviews scientific literature and test results and consults with advisory boards on the products under its jurisdiction. To the degree that the agency oversees and makes standards for bioresearch carried out by product sponsors (for example, drug manufacturers and processed food manufacturers), it has a hand in the analytical process itself. Insulin and a few other products must be tested batch by batch before going on the market; in September 1982 antibiotics were exempted from this process. In the FDA's field offices, chemists analyze samples from products already on the market to ensure that they meet FDA standards.

The FDA's surveillance duties are performed by field office inspectors authorized to inspect factories and other establishments that produce food, drugs, cosmetics, medical devices, and radiation-emitting products. Inspectors have access to every link in the commercial chain, overseeing research and development, production, distribution, and storage for the products regulated by the FDA. In addition, the FDA keeps track of developments in relevant markets by means of programs such as its "adverse reaction reporting system" and by attention to consumer complaints. The FDA licenses blood banks and manufacturers of biologic drugs.

Finally, when the FDA encounters violations of its rules—such as adulterated or misbranded products—it has several enforcement options:

Regulatory Letter. The FDA can send an enforcement document to the top management of a firm, stating that legal action will be taken unless the apparent violative product conditions are corrected.

Recall. After the FDA, or a manufacturer, finds that a product is defective, a recall may be initiated to remove the product from the marketplace. Recalls may be made voluntarily by the manufacturer or conducted at the request of the FDA. In some cases recalls may involve correction rather than removal of the product. The administration monitors the progress of recalls to ensure that all affected inventory is corrected or removed from sale.

Injunction. The FDA also may initiate civil court proceedings against the individual or company involved. Such actions usually seek to stop the continued manufacture or distribution of products that are in violation of the law.

Citation. In the event of a possible law violation, the FDA may send to a firm or to an individual notification that criminal action is contemplated and an invitation to provide information indicating that no violation has occurred.

Seizure. The FDA can initiate a seizure by filing a complaint with the U.S. District Court where the goods to be seized are located. A U.S. marshal is directed by the court to take possession of the goods until the matter is resolved.

Prosecution. On recommendation of the FDA, the U.S. attorney general may file a criminal action against an individual or a company that is charged with violating the laws administered by the agency.

Civil Money Penalty. On recommendation by the FDA that violations related to radiation-emitting electronic devices have occurred, monetary fines may be imposed by a court.

REGULATIONS AND STANDARDS

The FDA commissioner has initial authority to issue regulations and standards for the industries under the agency's jurisdiction. All regulations are subject to review by the HHS secretary. Major regulations administered by the FDA include

- FDA Food Standards, which establish specifications for foods and food products.
- Current Good-Manufacturing Practice Guidelines, which establish quality controls, including requirements for sanitation, inspection of materials, and finished products.

- New Drug Regulations, which establish requirements for new drug approvals and for a drug's continued safety and efficacy.
- Regulations may be formulated or amended by a process of hearings and other administrative proceedings.

Once a proposed regulation is published in the *Federal Register,* any party may submit comments to the commissioner on the proposal. After taking these public comments into account, the commissioner issues a final rule. The decisions of the commissioner may be appealed to a U.S. Circuit Court of Appeals.

The FDA also issues guidelines and advisory opinions. The guidelines state procedures or standards that are not legally binding, but they are recommended by the FDA. Guidelines are announced in the *Federal Register* and placed on file with the dockets management office. Advisory opinions are formulated, when feasible, upon receiving a request from any member of the public.

To assist the commissioner with decisions, the FDA has established advisory committees whose members review and recommend policy and technical decisions to the commissioner. There are currently more than fifty standing advisory committees. An advisory committee may be established to examine any area regulated by the FDA. The committees are composed of experts in particular areas, and they also may include representatives of consumer groups.

The advisory committees play a particularly crucial role in the drug approval process, holding lengthy detailed hearings on experimental therapies to determine whether there is sufficient scientific evidence to find the drugs safe and effective in their intended use. Although such hearings are not required under federal drug law, the FDA typically calls on the committees to screen any pending drug, especially one for which approval might engender controversy, to bolster the decision-making process. The committees' views are not binding on the FDA, but they typically carry great weight with agency decision makers.

ADMINISTRATIVE PROCEEDINGS

The FDA has several types of administrative proceedings for rulemaking: some are mandated by statute; others may be requested by interested persons or initiated by the commissioner. The rulemaking process is complex, with various opportunities for hearings depending on factors such as whether the rulemaking is considered formal or informal by the agency. Detailed information is contained in Title 21 of the *Code of Federal Regulations.*

The commissioner has several administrative proceedings by which to consider a petition from a member of the public; to issue, amend, or revoke a rule; or to otherwise review and discuss regulations. In several cases, the FDA commissioner has the authority to issue regulations without going through the process of administrative hearings. A hearing, required in certain rulemaking procedures, may be initiated in a number of ways, most frequently by objections to proposed FDA regulations or upon the initiative of the commissioner.

REPORTING AND REGISTRATION

The FDA has several reporting programs for its regulated industries. The major programs are

Drug Listing and Establishment Registration. Owners and operators of establishments that manufacture or process pharmaceuticals in the United States are required to register and list all of their products with the FDA. Products that must be listed include all drugs for human use, biologics, blood and blood derivatives, veterinary drugs, medicated premixes for animal feed, and in vitro diagnostic products (those that are drugs). Establishments that are required to register include all facilities that manufacture or process drugs and those that repackage or otherwise change the container, wrapper, or labels. Foreign drug manufacturers must list drugs as well, although they do not have to register.

Low-Acid Canned Foods Registration. All commercial processors of low-acid canned food must register their facilities and products with the FDA. Processors also are required to file processing information for each food product they handle.

Medical Device Registration. As with drug manufacturers, owners and operators of establishments that manufacture medical devices must register and list all of their products with the FDA.

Radiation Registration. Manufacturers of certain electronic products that emit radiation (such as microwave ovens, X-ray machines, and color television sets) must furnish the FDA with initial product reports prior to marketing as well as reports of model changes.

Cosmetics Registration. The FDA has a voluntary reporting program for the registration of cosmetics manufacturers and their products.

Background

The origins of the FDA can be traced to one individual, Harvey W. Wiley, chief chemist of the Agriculture Department's Bureau of Chemistry. Soon after joining the bureau in 1883, Wiley began experimenting with food and drug adulteration. Wiley's most famous experiments took the form of feeding small doses of poisons to a group of human volunteers. The substances fed to the volunteers were similar or identical to those found in food preservatives common at the time. Dubbed the "Poison Squad," the volunteers generated publicity for Wiley's experiments and created a public awareness of the dangers of eating adulterated foods. This publicity led Congress to enact the Food and Drug Act of 1906.

Wiley's Bureau of Chemistry began administering the act in 1907. Twenty years later, responsibility for administering the legislation was transferred to the Agriculture Department's newly created Food, Drug, and Insecticide Administration. In 1931 the name was changed to the Food and Drug Administration.

The FDA's powers were expanded in 1938 with the passage of the Federal Food, Drug, and Cosmetic Act. The most significant part of the legislation required that a manufacturer prove the safety of a new drug before the FDA would allow it to be placed on the market. Congress was spurred into action by the death in 1937 of more than one hundred people who had taken a dose of a seemingly harmless cure-all, elixir of sulfanilamide.

In 1940 the administration was transferred from the Agriculture Department to the Federal Security Agency, a new agency established to protect the public health. The Federal Security Agency was incorporated into the Department of Health, Education, and Welfare (HEW) when that department was created in 1953.

Today the FDA maintains a wide influence over U.S. products—it monitors the manufacture, import, transport, storage, and sale of more than $1 trillion worth of goods annually in the U.S. market, which is about one-fourth of the nation's economy.

EXPANDED POWERS

The regulatory authority of the administration was broadened in 1958 with the passage of an amendment to the Federal Food, Drug, and Cosmetic Act. Known as the Delaney Amendment, after its sponsor, New York representative James Delaney, it required manufacturers to prove the safety of food additives and required the FDA to prohibit the use of any food additive that induced cancer in humans or animals.

In 1962 it was discovered that pregnant women who had taken the drug thalidomide ran a high risk of giving birth to deformed children. Thalidomide had been widely marketed in Europe, but the drug had been kept off the U.S. market largely through the efforts of an FDA chemist who was not convinced of its safety. Again, public awareness of the problem roused Congress to enact stronger FDA legislation.

The Food and Drug Act Amendments of 1962 required drug manufacturers to prove the effectiveness as well as the safety of their products before they could be marketed. The FDA also was authorized to order the immediate withdrawal of dangerous drugs from the market. It was given additional powers in 1976 when Congress passed legislation requiring regulation of complex medical devices and diagnostic products.

In 1979 Congress passed legislation removing education functions from HEW to a new Education Department. What remained, including the Food and Drug Administration, was renamed the Health and Human Services Department.

FDA IN THE 1980s

In 1983 President Ronald Reagan signed into law a bill providing financial incentives to the developers of new therapies for diseases that were rare or otherwise had such small markets as to make them unprofitable. The FDA, two years earlier, had instituted a program to encourage the development of so-called orphan drugs, which the government defined as drugs intended for the treatment of diseases with 200,000 or fewer U.S. victims. But the 1983 law and its 1985 amendments formalized the FDA program and offered eligible orphan drug developers seven years' marketing exclusivity, tax credits, research grants, and other federal incentives and subsidies.

The Drug Price Competition and Patent Term Restoration Act, which became law in 1984, was intended by its drafters to make the drug industry more competitive by speeding the entry into the marketplace of generic drugs, which are copies of brand-name products whose patent protection has expired. The law allowed manufacturers of generic drugs simply to demonstrate that their product was "bioequivalent," or therapeutically identical, to the brand-name product they were copying. They accomplished this by filing an abbreviated new drug application (ANDA), a much shorter procedure than the new drug application (NDA) required for a new drug. At the same time the measure offered enhanced patent protection for brand-name drug products, to offset the growing period of time required for FDA review of new drug marketing applications.

The 1984 law had made immediately eligible for generic competition more than one-quarter of the 200 largest-selling prescription drugs, as well as many less popular products. Once the new law was in place, drug companies swamped the FDA with applications to market new generic drugs. In the first six months of the law's life, the FDA approved 206 ANDAs but was slow to finalize the formal regulations of the approval process for new generic drugs.

The law also enabled the holder of a patent for a drug, medical device, or food additive to extend it for a maximum of five years, depending on the time required by the FDA to complete its review of the product and provided the postapproval patent life did not exceed fourteen years. The longer patent life responded to the brand-name industry's complaints that lengthy FDA review times had decreased the effective life of a patent from sixteen years in 1961 to ten years by 1984.

A scandal uncovered in the FDA's Generic Drugs Division during 1989 devastated congressional and administration confidence in the FDA. The lack of regulations and controls had made it easier for unscrupulous FDA drug reviewers to act unfairly or arbitrarily by, for example, moving one company's applications through the bureaucracy at a faster pace than a competitor's or repeatedly "losing" another company's paperwork. By April 1992 Congress had passed legislation that provided stricter HHS oversight of the FDA and tightened the generic drug approval process.

FDA IN THE 1990s

In 1990 President George H. W. Bush appointed David A. Kessler, medical director of the Albert Einstein College of Medicine in New York, commissioner of the agency. Kessler, who had both medical and law degrees, waged an aggressive effort to improve the FDA's image, enforce regulations, and streamline its product-testing efforts. Kessler played a high-profile role, becoming one of the most recognized figures in the federal bureaucracy.

The FDA in 1990 completed a review of the safety and effectiveness of the active ingredients of all over-the-counter drugs, a project it had begun in 1972 under orders from Congress. In 1990 the FDA banned 111 unproven ingredients used in nonprescription diet aids and appetite suppressants and another 223 ingredients in nineteen other classes of over-the-counter drugs used to treat a wide variety of medical conditions. In August 1992 the FDA released a list of 415 ingredients that the agency said were not shown to be effective.

In the early 1990s the FDA approved important new drugs to treat cystic fibrosis and to combat Alzheimer's disease. It also approved Taxol, a drug used to treat advanced ovarian cancer, and Depo-Provera, a birth control drug for women that prevents pregnancy with four injections per year. The FDA also approved over-the-counter use of the painkiller naproxen sodium and the hair-growth drug Rogaine.

A furor over the safety of silicone breast implants prompted the FDA in April 1992 to ban almost all of their cosmetic uses, limiting them to breast cancer patients and others with valid medical needs. The agency said they would be banned until scientific proof of their safety was established. (In 2006, after years of study, the FDA approved the use of silicone gel for implants for cosmetic purposes.) With roughly 80 percent of implant surgery done for cosmetic purposes, saline breast implants became more popular. In 1994 the FDA opened an inquiry into the safety of saline breast implants. In succeeding years the agency continued to monitor the safety of all breast implants.

President Bill Clinton reappointed Kessler in 1993 as the FDA continued to cut bureaucratic delays and red tape, speed agency actions, and eliminate unnecessary regulation. With health concerns rising, the FDA continually found itself in the middle of several national debates, ranging from the health risks of dietary supplements and cigarettes to tighter regulation of medical devices.

The FDA in February 1994 ended a ten-year-long debate over a genetically engineered drug that boosts milk production in cows when it approved recombinant bovine somatotropin (rBST), a bovine growth hormone. Consumer groups had fought the approval, voicing concerns about genetic engineering. Numerous studies, however, found that milk from hormone-treated cows posed no risk to human health. The FDA also approved in 1994 the genetically engineered Flavr-Savr tomato, opening the door to more genetically modified foods in the future.

In May 1994 the agency promulgated new requirements for uniform and understandable food labels, culminating in a four-year process to give consumers more information about the food they buy. Manufacturers were barred from making certain nutritional claims about their products on the labels—such as promoting a product as "high fiber"—when other important information such as cholesterol level was not mentioned.

In a similar effort, the FDA in August 1995 unveiled an education program aimed at giving patients better written information on prescription drugs, such as a product's approved uses and listing serious adverse reactions. The program established quality standards for health professionals in distributing written leaflets with prescriptions. These standards focused on seven areas—scientific accuracy, consistency in a standard format, nonpromotional tone and content, specificity, comprehensiveness, understandable language, and legibility.

In 1995 the FDA turned its attention to claims by makers of dietary supplements. For two decades the agency had sought tighter regulations on the growing billion-dollar industry. New FDA rules forced makers of vitamins, minerals, and herbal remedies to back up the health claims made on their labels with evidence supported by "significant scientific agreement." Supporters of the labeling requirements contended that dietary supplement producers had misled consumers with exaggerated or unsubstantiated health claims.

The FDA in January 1996 approved the fat substitute olestra, developed over twenty-five years by Procter & Gamble at a cost of $300 million. The food additive, which adds no fat or calories, was marketed under the trademark Olean in certain snacks. Because the substance may inhibit the body's absorption of some vitamins and nutrients, the company was required to add the vitamins A, D, E, and K to products containing olestra. All products containing olestra also had to carry an explicit warning about the fat substitute's possible side effects. In June 1998 an FDA advisory panel recommended that the agency consider changes to the warning labels following industry-sponsored studies that reportedly showed no increased side effects among olestra users.

The FDA approved in July 1996 the first nicotine patch to be sold over-the-counter to adults who wish to stop smoking. The skin patches, which have been available by prescription since 1992, were designed to help adults overcome their craving for a cigarette by releasing nicotine through the skin. In a related move, the FDA approved in February 1996 an over-the-counter chewing gum called Nicorette that contains nicotine.

Although there was evidence that a few drug companies were making lavish profits from drugs brought to market under the 1983 orphan drug program, Congress and President Clinton extended the tax credit for manufacturers of orphan drugs in August 1996. The FDA counseled against altering the terms of the program, for fear changes might discourage the development of life-saving remedies for obscure maladies.

Clinton also signed into law in August 1996 bipartisan legislation that broke a decades-old logjam on pesticide regulations. The new law created a unified health standard for both raw and processed foods with guidelines to protect children from pesticides. The compromise wording imposed a safety standard to ensure that pesticide residues on foods pose no reasonable risk of harm, meaning that there likely would be no more than one in a million cases of cancer related to the residue in question.

The AIDS Epidemic

From the initial discovery of the first cases of acquired immune deficiency syndrome (AIDS), AIDS has remained a huge challenge for the FDA as well as the entire health-related federal bureaucracy. As the numbers of people infected with HIV, the virus that causes AIDS, dramatically increased from the early 1980s through the 1990s, AIDS activists pressured the FDA to reform its conservative approach to more aggressive testing of new drugs.

In May 1990, after months of study, HHS formally proposed what it labeled a "parallel track" mechanism for the evaluation of drugs for AIDS and related conditions. Under the parallel track plan, unproven drugs would be widely distributed to patients under minimal medical supervision at the same time FDA testing was taking place. FDA implemented the policy in April 1992, allowing certain drugs that showed promise of combating the AIDS virus to be made available to people unable to take standard therapy.

In June 1994 the FDA approved four drugs to treat AIDS and the HIV infection. None of these drugs was a cure for AIDS, but they delayed the onset of symptoms for some patients. In December 1995 the FDA approved Invirase (saquinavir), the first protease inhibitor, a new class of drugs that inhibit the production of an enzyme key to HIV reproduction. The drug was approved in just three months, prompting the agency to tout its ability to get promising new drugs to dying patients quickly. With the medical community struggling for a cure, the FDA and other federal agencies also focused on prevention. The FDA also approved the first home blood test kit for detecting the HIV virus in 1996 and an at-home urine HIV test in 1998.

The first broad-based international trial of a vaccine to protect against HIV was approved by the FDA in 1998, a year after Clinton issued a call for such a vaccine by 2007. A San Francisco-based company, VaxGen, began testing a vaccine composed of a genetically engineered molecule that resembles part of HIV. The vaccine trial, which lasted three years, had mixed results. As of mid-2015, efforts to prove the safety and efficacy of an AIDS vaccine were still ongoing after more than two decades of research.

Movement toward Tobacco Regulation

The decision by Congress in 2009 to allow the FDA to regulate tobacco had its roots in actions taken a generation earlier. In February 1994 FDA commissioner Kessler announced a major FDA policy change, asserting that the agency had the authority to regulate the sale of cigarettes. Kessler said evidence indicated that nicotine levels in cigarettes were being manipulated, which made cigarettes a drug and thus placed it under FDA jurisdiction.

Kessler's decision was followed by a number of allegations that Philip Morris, the nation's largest tobacco company, had suppressed a 1983 study concluding that nicotine was addictive. When Republicans gained control of Congress in 1995, congressional action on the issue was effectively halted. In summer 1996, however, the Clinton administration took the initiative by essentially recasting smoking as a "pediatric disease."

In August 1996 President Clinton announced that he would allow the FDA to regulate nicotine as an addictive drug and impose strict limits on tobacco advertising in an effort to prevent children and teenagers from smoking cigarettes or using smokeless tobacco. The president's decision was significant because for the first time the FDA was given oversight authority over tobacco advertising—a jurisdiction that had previously fallen to the Federal Trade Commission (FTC).

Coinciding with the White House announcement, the FDA issued its rule to reduce the access and appeal of tobacco products by making it harder for young people under eighteen to buy cigarettes and smokeless tobacco.

The rule required anyone who looked younger than twenty-six to show proof of age to buy cigarettes and that tobacco products be placed behind sales counters to deter youngsters from shoplifting. Cigarette vending machines were prohibited in many public places, and cigarette billboards were banned within 1,000 feet of schools and playgrounds. Tobacco ads in magazines with a high ratio of underage readers were restricted to black-and-white text.

Hours after the FDA's announced rule, tobacco and advertising industries filed a complaint in federal district court alleging that only Congress could give the FDA regulatory authority over tobacco. Moreover, they said the new regulatory action would affect adults because it restricted tobacco companies' ability to use billboards, sponsor major sporting events, and use in-store tobacco displays. In addition, critics of the government's action said the move to declare nicotine in tobacco an addictive drug could eventually lead to a ban on cigarette sales to adults.

In an about-face, the five major tobacco companies on June 20, 1997, agreed to many of the same or more stringent restrictions in a legal settlement with forty state attorneys general. Beginning in Mississippi in May 1994, state officials had filed lawsuits in state and federal courts seeking recoupment of Medicaid funds used to treat state smokers. In the June 1997 settlement, the five companies agreed to pay $368.5 billion over the first twenty-five years of the lawsuit and comply with a number of restrictions on marketing if they were granted legal protections, such as the settling of punitive damage claims based on past actions and the resolution of lawsuits brought by the state attorneys general. The settlement also would have capped the amount of money that the tobacco companies would have paid out for other lawsuits such as individual actions in any given year.

The enactment of the settlement proved to be more difficult than state officials or the industry had envisioned. Congress demanded a strong role in crafting a national tobacco policy By the time the bill reached the Senate floor in mid-1998, requirements on the industry had increased, with payments over twenty-five years rising to $516 billion, while legal protections had been stripped down essentially to an annual cap on payouts. The industry protested by launching a $40 million national ad campaign against the legislation. The full Senate conducted a freewheeling debate on the bill before the measure died on a pair of procedural votes in June 1998. With Congress no longer involved, the states were able to salvage a more modest $206 billion settlement with the tobacco companies in November 1998.

The tobacco industry, however, scored a courtroom victory in August 1998 when a circuit court panel ruled 2–1 that the FDA had no authority to impose any restrictions on tobacco products without congressional approval. The ruling reversed the April 1997 decision that allowed FDA regulation of tobacco sales to teenagers. The Justice Department quickly appealed the ruling, which reached the Supreme Court. In March 2000 the Court ruled 5–4 against FDA's authority to regulate tobacco, saying that only Congress could confer such authority on the agency.

In late 2004 lawmakers debated giving the FDA the power to regulate tobacco as part of a ten-year, $10 billion buyout for tobacco farmers. Senate supporters of FDA regulation of tobacco products said that pairing it with the tobacco farmer buyout was its best chance of passage. However, many House Republicans opposed giving that authority to the FDA, and the final legislation included the buyout but dropped the FDA regulatory power. Congress ultimately passed legislation giving FDA this authority in 2009 (*see below*).

FDA Drug and Device Overhaul

In 1997 the FDA underwent a major overhaul under the Food and Drug Administration Modernization Act. The impetus behind the legislation was to combat complaints that the FDA was dragging its feet in approving new drugs and medical devices. Congressional Republicans and some Democrats criticized the agency's extensive testing practices by saying they prevented needed, life-improving drugs from reaching the public.

Consumer advocates and other Democrats, concerned that a speedy approval process might unnecessarily endanger the lives and safety of Americans, opposed the bill. Opponents argued that the agency had already made great strides in reducing the review time of new drugs and medical devices. After months of negotiations, vocal opponents supported the final version of the bill. The overhaul affected almost every major responsibility of the FDA. The legislation laid out specific timelines for the FDA to act on various applications.

Among the requirements was a mandated faster review of clinical trials for new drugs. Before the law's enactment, the preapproval process took an average of about seven years as the drug companies evaluated the safety of the proposed drug on a pool of generally fewer than one hundred volunteers. After that stage, the companies were required to conduct another trial on a larger pool of patients to double-check the drug's effects because previous law mandated "substantial evidence of effectiveness." The 1997 law clarified that only one clinical trial could offer enough study for a new drug approval. The FDA was not required to accept more than one trial before approving a drug, but it was given the option if the trial was "well-controlled." In exchange for shortening the time frame for drug approval, drug companies were required to pay an increase of about 21 percent in user fees.

The law also expanded the parallel track process for approving new drugs, including vaccines and biological products that are intended to fight life-threatening or serious diseases. Producers may request that their applications be given the faster parallel track review. If the HHS secretary approves the product for parallel track consideration under certain criteria, the FDA would be able to review further studies and any proposed promotional materials at least thirty days before the product was released to the public. The FDA would still have the authority to withdraw its backing of a product if further tests raised concerns.

Further evidence of a desire to change the culture of the FDA was apparent in a new rule to require advisory panels of expert consultants to review drugs within sixty days of submission and to require the FDA to report the panel's recommendation within ninety days of receiving it. Medical devices, from pacemakers to hearing aids to bandages, also were affected by the legislation. Simple devices such as bandages, toothbrushes, and tongue depressors were exempted from approval procedures unless they posed a danger to society or were of "substantial importance." Priority for review was given to rare devices that are considered breakthrough technologies and are significantly different from products already on the market.

Most devices had been reviewed through a procedure, known as the 510(k) process, reserved for devices similar to others already on the market. The new legislation offered a more collaborative manner for the review of such applications by encouraging FDA officials to suggest minor improvements to manufacturers in the clinical review phase. Manufacturers would not have to submit an additional application for approval to implement suggested changes to the device or to clinical testing procedures.

HHS officials also were required to meet with manufacturers to determine what type of scientific evidence would be needed for the FDA to evaluate the efficacy of a device that the manufacturer planned to later submit for approval. Within thirty days of a meeting, officials would have to describe the necessary scientific evidence in writing to the manufacturer.

Evaluation of devices by outside third-party consultants was encouraged in the legislation. The measure expanded a demonstration project that allowed the HHS secretary to accredit reviewers. Manufacturers were to pay the reviewers to consult with them under the oversight of the secretary. Certain complicated devices were exempted.

Health and nutrient claims that food producers want to use in labeling were expected to be reviewed more quickly as a result of the law. Under the legislation, a proposed claim would be considered denied if officials did not approve it within one hundred days unless an extension was granted.

Another provision allows drug and device manufacturers to distribute information from a medical journal or textbook about a product's other, unapproved uses if the FDA approves it through a secondary "off-label" use application. The FDA could force the manufacturer to disclose conflicting reports of the secondary use or ban the manufacturer from distributing the information if the use was not legal. In October 1996 the FDA began allowing some limited uses of such information.

One of the first applications of the FDA's speedy parallel track process was the quick approval of the first approved oral pill to treat impotence dysfunction. The drug Viagra, or sildenafil citrate, was approved less than six months after submission. Viagra caused a stir among the public, with 2.7 million prescriptions dispensed between March and June 1998. Some concerns arose about its safety for elderly patients. During that time, at least seventy-seven patients reportedly died after being prescribed the drug, with twenty-four reported to have suffered from cardiac problems.

Some lawmakers remain concerned that the new procedures initiated by the 1997 overhaul could jeopardize consumer safety. The July 1998 approval by the FDA of the drug thalidomide for leprosy raised eyebrows. The agency had banned the drug in 1962 because of safety concerns. Later, it was established that the drug caused severe birth defects. The FDA said that its approval in 1998 was based on a limited use of the drug. Officials argued that the large amount of publicity that the drug had received lowered the likelihood that it would be misused.

However, some lawmakers pointed to this approval as evidence that public safety was taking second priority to the need to push through approval of drugs. The September 2000 report to Congress found that many of the required changes mandated in the FDA overhaul bill were occurring at the agency. The report found that new drugs and biologics were being approved in just six months and that in 1999 the agency had approved new drugs to treat several diseases, including osteoarthritis, influenza, obesity, HIV, and diabetes.

The report also found that nearly two-thirds of 4,000 manufacturers of drugs, biological agents, and medical devices said that the FDA's guidance on submission requirements made the approval process faster and easier than it was in 1997. The agency also had improved the safety of seafood by installing a quality control system in all domestic seafood plants, worked with other federal agencies to establish a nationwide food safety surveillance network, and launched a nationwide public information campaign to help reduce injuries and other adverse events caused by improper use of medicines, vaccines, medical devices, and foods.

The 1997 overhaul also required the FDA to compile a new publicly available database of clinical trials used to treat serious conditions, a goal the agency met during 1999. In November 2000 the agency launched an improved website to allow the public access to information about FDA activities, such as safety alerts and product approvals.

FDA IN THE 2000s

The year 2000 brought a variety of new challenges for the FDA that reflected the changing nature—and complexity—of the many issues under the agency's regulations. That year, for example, the FDA came under scrutiny for its monitoring of gene therapy trials after an eighteen-year-old volunteer died. Gene therapy is a process in which faulty genes linked to certain diseases are replaced by healthy ones. During congressional hearings lawmakers questioned whether both FDA and the National Institutes of Health (NIH), which share oversight of biomedical trials, had adequately monitored potentially serious side effects that may arise from gene therapy.

FDA clashed with Congress again in September 2000 when it approved the marketing of RU-486, the so-called abortion pill. Conservatives were outraged and HHS secretary Tommy G. Thompson expressed concerns about the safety of RU-486, but he took no action to ban use of the pill. In late 2004, however, when FDA officials linked a third death to the pill since its 2000 approval, FDA strengthened the warning label on the drug, urging physicians to redouble efforts at watching their patients carefully for signs of infection, excessive vaginal bleeding, or tubal pregnancies.

In late 2001 Mark B. McClellan, a Texas-born physician and economist named by President George W. Bush to head the agency, pledged to take tougher and quicker action against misleading drug ads and dietary supplement labels.

In December 2002 Congress reauthorized the drug user fee program and expanded it to include medical devices. The medical device industry had shied away from paying user fees to underwrite additional FDA staff, although the user fee program for the drug industry has been hailed for speeding up approvals for new drugs. The 2002 act allowed private contractors to assume some of the FDA's duties to inspect manufacturing facilities of medical devices. Democrats won inclusion of funding to expand FDA studies of the safety of new products after they reach the market. The bill also established new regulations for the sterilization and reuse of catheters and other products currently approved only for single use.

In 2002 the FDA approved a test that could detect within as little as twenty minutes if someone was infected with HIV. Experts said that advance might encourage thousands of Americans to get tested, which in turn might slow the spread of the disease. In March 2003 the agency approved the use of the drug Fuzeon to treat advanced HIV infection in adults and children ages six and older. According to the FDA, the drug was the first product in a new class of medications called fusion inhibitors to receive marketing approval. Drugs in that class interfere with the entry of HIV into cells by inhibiting the fusion of viral and cellular membranes. That inhibition blocks the virus's ability to infect certain components of the immune system. While AIDS advocates were pleased with the drug's approval, its price—$20,000 a year or more for patients—made the drug out of reach for many of patients.

While the FDA claimed it has jurisdiction over human cloning, some lawmakers, backed by President Bush, tried in both 2002 and 2003 to pass legislation that would ban the use of the procedure to create human embryos. Proponents of a ban said that there was no way that FDA could stop the practice, even if it did have the regulatory power to do so. Agency officials claimed that the act of taking an adult cell and implanting it into a woman's egg stripped of its DNA is subject to provisions in the Public Health Service Act of 1944 and the Federal Food, Drug and, Cosmetic Act of 1938.

The FDA was thrust into the spotlight in the 107th Congress when Democrats and some Republicans pushed proposals that would make it easier to import prescription drugs approved by the agency from nations that cap prices. Proponents of such measures say the practice, known as drug reimportation, would allow consumers to pay less—perhaps as much as 50 percent less in some cases—for the same drugs they now purchase at higher prices in the United States. Drug manufacturers said that drug importation should not be allowed because it would jeopardize patient safety by increasing the flow of counterfeit drugs into the country, and that it would be virtually impossible for the FDA to police how drugs are produced, shipped, or stored overseas. When the issue was debated in Congress in 2002, FDA officials, as well as HHS Secretary Thompson said that the agency could not guarantee the safety of "reimported" drugs, and the legislation was never enacted.

With prescription drug prices increasing—and much of the rise being attributed to ads that target some of the newest and most expensive drugs on the market—many lawmakers continue to push for the FDA to have rigorous oversight of so-called direct to consumer advertising, the proliferation of television and magazine advertising that drug companies have done since 1997 when the FDA loosened its rules on such ads. Pharmaceutical companies have said the advertising gives patients important information about drugs and may convince them to seek treatment for many medical conditions that often go undiagnosed, such as depression or hypertension. But critics say ads create undo pressure to prescribe a particular medication whether or not it is needed. Should the FDA move to regulate such ads, lawmakers sympathetic to the drug industry may try to block the agency's efforts.

In 2003 millions of American women learned that hormone replacement therapy (HRT), which had been touted as a protection against breast cancer and heart disease, could actually raise the risk of contracting those conditions. Based on that new data, the FDA approved revised labels for estrogen and estrogen with progestin therapies to help women and their physicians evaluate the risks and benefits of such treatment. The FDA's labeling changes included a new boxed warning, the highest level of warning information in labeling that highlights the increased risk for heart disease, heart attacks, strokes, and breast cancer.

In the 2000s the FDA had come under fire on a variety of fronts, including its attention to drug safety. Some lawmakers and consumer groups said the agency was not aggressive enough in its surveillance of prescription drugs once they were approved for use. Agency critics charged that the FDA had become too cozy with the drug industry it was supposed to regulate. Some lawmakers and consumer groups urged greater federal scrutiny of the agency after allegations surfaced that the FDA ignored evidence that a popular set of anti-inflammatory drugs, including painkillers Vioxx and Bextra, were linked to higher rates of heart attack and stroke. David Graham, a reviewer in the FDA's Office of Drug Safety, told Congress in late 2004 that FDA officials tried to suppress his research about the dangers of Vioxx, a claim that agency officials denied. Graham told the Senate Finance Committee that Vioxx was "the single greatest drug-safety catastrophe in the history of this country."

Graham's statements about the FDA followed allegations in 2004 that agency officials either missed or deliberately covered up evidence that antidepressants brought on suicidal tendencies in children and teenagers. News reports in spring 2004 revealed that the FDA and drug manufacturers had known about the link since the 1980s, but agency officials had ignored key findings by one of its epidemiologists. In October 2004 the FDA required antidepressant labels to indicate a potential for elevated suicide risk in children and teens. In September 2005 the FDA issued a specific warning for the antidepressant Paxil for possible increased risk for suicide in children and adolescents.

In late 2004 acting FDA commissioner Lester M. Crawford tried to help stem the landslide of bad press about the agency with an announcement that he would ask the Institute of Medicine to review FDA safety procedures for all drugs. Crawford also pledged to conduct a series of drug-safety workshops for doctors and health professionals and to publish risk-management guidelines for drug manufacturers.

As the pressure from Congress and outside lawmakers continued to intensify on the agency, HHS Secretary Michael Leavitt in February 2005 announced the creation of a new board to advise the agency on safety issues surrounding approved drugs. Lawmakers and many consumer groups also criticized the board's structure as weak, saying that it would need more authority and independent experts to make the nation's drug supply safer. While the panel would work with existing FDA agencies on drug safety, it would have no authority over those offices, FDA officials said. Leavitt also said the FDA would launch a new Drug Watch Web page to share quickly with health professionals and patients new information about newly approved drugs and those that have been on the market for long periods.

Some lawmakers pushed for legislation that would give FDA more power to monitor drugs once they hit the market. "During the last eighteen months, this country's confidence in the FDA has been shaken," said Senate Finance Committee Chair Charles E. Grassley (R-IA). Most in Congress, however, appeared uninterested in any sweeping legislation to dramatically restructure the agency. For Republicans in control of Congress, much of that reluctance stemmed from the GOP philosophy that less government regulation of industry is best. Democrats and Republicans alike also did not want to unravel the 1992 user fee act, which poured hundreds of millions of dollars each year into FDA's coffers. It was also difficult to ask the agency to take on additional responsibilities when there was little money to do so in an era of budget deficits.

In 2005 FDA officials clashed with lawmakers over the agency's delay in making a decision on over-the-counter sales of so-called morning-after birth control pills. The drug's manufacturer, Barr Laboratories, submitted a revised application in July 2004 asking the FDA to make the drug available behind the counter at pharmacies— meaning a woman would have to ask a pharmacist for it and prove she was at least seventeen years old. The FDA approved "Plan B," as the drug is known, as a prescription medication in 1999, but conservative and religious groups, such as the Family Research Council, opposed making Plan B more accessible, claiming it would encourage sexual promiscuity and accelerate the spread of sexually transmitted diseases.

Angry that the FDA was delaying approval of over-the-counter sales of Plan B, Democratic senators Patty Murray of Washington and Hillary Rodham Clinton of New York said in June 2005 they would place a "hold" on the nomination of acting FDA commissioner Crawford to head the agency. After HHS Secretary Michael O. Leavitt promised the two senators that the FDA would make its decision by September, Clinton and Murray withdrew their objections. The Senate confirmed Crawford as FDA commissioner on July 18, 2005.

In late August 2005, however, the FDA announced that because of difficulty in regulating how the morning-after pill was to be kept from being sold to adolescents under age seventeen, it was once again postponing its approval. Senators Murray and Clinton angrily accused the FDA of reneging on its agreement with them. Leavitt disagreed, saying that the agreement was that the FDA would act by September. "Sometimes action isn't always yes and no. Sometimes it requires additional thought."

In September 2005 Crawford, in a surprise announcement, resigned as FDA commissioner two months after being confirmed by the Senate as full agency chief. It appeared that he was asked to resign after the Justice Department began investigating complaints that Crawford filed numerous false disclosure reports stating incorrectly that he did not own stocks of companies that he regulated as head of the FDA. In 2006 Crawford pleaded guilty to misdemeanor charges alleging conflict of interest and false statements.

The Bush administration quickly named Andrew von Eschenbach, the director of the National Cancer Institute (NCI), to be acting FDA commissioner. A cancer fighter for decades, von Eschenbach had previously served as executive vice president and chief academic officer at the University of Texas Cancer Center. President Bush officially nominated von Eschenbach to be commissioner in March 2006, but once again Senators Clinton and Murray said that they would block his confirmation until the FDA announced a decision on whether the morning-after pill could be sold without a prescription. After the senators had lifted their hold, however, the agency reneged on its promise and again delayed an announcement. The senators hoped for a decision favoring over-the-counter sales, but they said that their only demand was that the agency resolve the matter.

On Aug. 24, 2006, the FDA approved over-the-counter sales of the emergency birth control for women age eighteen and older, an unusual structure that nonetheless removed some of the controversy surrounding the issue. Von Eschenbach said that it was appropriate to limit the use of the emergency birth control to older teens because the model "builds on well-established state and private sector infrastructures to restrict certain products to consumers eighteen and older," such as nicotine. The decision on Plan B helped to clear Democratic barriers to a confirmation vote for von Eschenbach, who was confirmed in December 2006.

In early 2007 von Eschenbach and other FDA officials announced a set of modest steps to improve oversight of drugs. The FDA's drug safety improvement plan included the creation of a pilot program to analyze the safety of some drugs eighteen months after they enter the market, efforts to collaborate with the Veterans Health Administration to monitor the reactions of patients to drugs that have been approved, the creation of an office of chief medical officer to oversee problems, and improvements to its database of adverse event reports.

The agency ventured again into the issue of birth control in 2007 when it approved a contraceptive drug that would stop the routine menstrual flow of women taking the pill. The Wyeth drug, Lybrel, worked in a similar way to other contraceptives in that it interrupted the body's monthly preparation for pregnancy by decreasing the production of hormones that make pregnancy possible. However, Lybrel was the first birth control pill regimen that did not include placebos or allow for short intervals in which the women would take no pills. Those intervals allow menstruation to take place. Early public reaction was mixed.

In 2007 Congress acted to overhaul the FDA's drug safety programs and reauthorize the Prescription Drug User Fee Act, which was to expire in September 2007. The renewal of the user fee law provided an opportunity to the new Democratic congressional leadership to make broader regulatory changes to the oversight of prescription drugs and medical devices. The Senate passed by a 93–1 vote its bipartisan bill. The House followed in July with the passage, 403–16, of a version that was tougher on industry.

One of the most divisive issues in the Senate involved language to allow consumers and pharmacies to import drugs from Canada, much of Europe, New Zealand, Japan, and a handful of other countries whose drug safety oversight mirrors the FDA's. Prescription drugs are often cheaper abroad than in the United States, often because other countries employ price controls.

However, the White House threatened to veto the bill if the drug reimportation provision was included. That provision was not included in the final version of the bill.

The underlying Senate bill added several provisions aimed at improving the monitoring of drugs, particularly after they had been approved. It would create a surveillance system to track problems with drugs sold in the United States. Higher-risk drugs would be reviewed periodically, and the FDA would have more authority to order additional postmarket studies. The measure would require disclosure of potential conflicts of interest, such as financial ties to drug companies, by drug review board members and FDA advisory board members. The measure required registration of clinical trials in a public database and narrowed the sales exclusivity agreements for drugs used in pediatric care from the current six months of exclusive sales rights to three months.

In July 2007 the House passed its version, which had similar provisions. However, the House version had more far-reaching drug safety provisions, more oversight, and stiffer fines for violators than the Senate measure. The final version of the measure passed both chambers and was signed by President Bush on Sept. 27, 2007. The Food and Drug Administration Amendments Act of 2007 gave the FDA the authority to require postapproval clinical studies of new drugs. The legislation also allowed the FDA to require that drug companies follow risk-reduction plans for pharmaceuticals that are suspected to have potentially dangerous side effects. If the companies did not comply,

the agency could levy higher fines against drug companies of $250,000 per violation, or $1 million for multiple violations. Repeated violations carried higher penalties.

The law also included new limits on conflicts of interest for members of FDA advisory panels that evaluate drugs. The law also contained incentives for drug manufacturers to develop other pediatric drugs and drug uses, including a period of market exclusivity for new products. Drug companies were required by the law to provide information to a database of drug trials by registering all new clinical trials and disclosing their results and any safety concerns. The law also addressed the issue of food and product safety by calling for an alert system to notify consumers of contaminated food and pet products.

As Congress debated the drug safety legislation in 2007, the FDA had to contend with additional bad publicity surrounding drug safety. Patients using a diabetes drug produced by GlaxoSmithKline, Avandia, were found to carry a significantly higher risk of heart attack and a 64 percent increase in the risk of cardiovascular death than those who did not use the drug, according to an analysis published in the *New England Journal of Medicine*.

Three years later, the FDA would take the unusual step of requiring a restricted access program for Avandia. Under the strategy, announced in 2010, Avandia became available to new patients only if they were unable to achieve glucose control on other medications and were unable to take Actos (pioglitazone), the only other drug in this class. Previous users of Avandia could continue using the medication if they chose to do so.

During the 2007 debate, congressional critics, particularly on the Senate Finance Committee, said that the news demonstrated that FDA was still too "cozy" with the companies it regulates. "Both the drug company and the FDA have some major explaining to do about what they knew about Avandia, when they knew it, and why they didn't take immediate action to protect patients," said Sen. Max Baucus (D-MT), echoing concerns voiced by Senator Grassley, the ranking Republican on the committee.

Grassley also criticized the agency not only for its safety lapses in 2004 and 2005, but also for its slow reaction in 2007 to reports that an antibiotic known as Ketek, by Sanofi Aventis, apparently could cause liver failure. Under pressure from Congress, the FDA limited Ketek's use to pneumonia and revoked its use for treating other diseases such as bronchitis and bacterial sinusitis.

In 2007 the agency found itself facing questions about its ability to ensure food safety after several food safety crises, including outbreaks of *E. coli* in spinach and salmonella in peanut butter, as well as the contamination of pet food imported from China that killed cats and dogs. The agency was only one of several charged with overseeing different aspects of food safety, although consumer safety critics argue that no single agency has enough authority because none has the ability to mandate immediate recalls of contaminated products, with the exception of infant formula. The FDA often works to persuade companies to voluntarily withdraw their products from the marketplace.

Congress addressed some of these issues in the Food and Drug Administration Amendments Act of 2007. The act requires the FDA, which largely oversees produce, dairy, seafood, and processed foods, to post a listing of all recalled products on the agency's website and to create a registry of tainted food incidents. The law also requires HHS to establish processing and ingredient standards for pet food and to update standards for pet food labeling that include ingredient information. HHS also was ordered to establish an early warning and surveillance system to identify adulteration of the pet food supply.

Food safety became more of a priority after a 2008 outbreak of salmonella in peanut products that sparked national outrage. Investigators believed that the Peanut Corporation of America knowingly shipped contaminated peanuts to producers of other food products who then used the peanuts as ingredients. The enormous recall of peanuts did not prevent hundreds of sicknesses and at least nine deaths, as well as thousands more suspected illnesses. The peanut recall was followed by reports in 2009 of *E. coli* in prepackaged cookie dough and of potential salmonella in instant nonfat dried milk and whey, which added to the momentum for an overhaul of the nation's food safety protections.

In 2009 President Barack Obama appointed Margaret A. Hamburg as FDA commissioner. Hamburg was a former health commissioner of New York City and assistant director of the National Institute of Allergy and Infectious Diseases. She joined principal deputy commissioner Joshua Sharfstein, a former Baltimore health commissioner, who pushed the Bush administration's FDA to warn against the use of over-the-counter cold and cough remedies for young children. Hamburg and Sharfstein said they wanted the agency to take a more aggressive stance than during the Bush administration in ensuring food safety, overseeing the drug and device industry, and communicating warnings quickly to the public.

On food safety, Hamburg said in 2009, "The number of recent outbreaks have underscored for the public and policymakers that things need to change." As the agency sought to be assertive in protecting the nation's food supply, one of the difficulties has been the increase in imported food from overseas facilities, which are often not inspected by the agency. Hamburg said she wanted to target the riskiest imported foods and the most likely sites for contamination to make the most of the FDA's limited inspection resources.

Another priority in the early days of the Obama administration for the FDA, also affected by events overseas, was the agency's response to a potential flu pandemic. In 2009 a global swine flu pandemic swept throughout the world. The virus, known as the H1N1 flu virus, spread to people within the United States in the spring, with many cases originating in Mexico. The agency, in cooperation with other government agencies, such as within HHS and the Department of Homeland Security, began working on a vaccine against the virus and, in the meantime, on efforts to make flu treatments and diagnostic tests available in ways that the FDA had not previously approved. The FDA also worked with the Centers for Disease Control, the National Institutes of Health, and the World Health Organization on lab studies of the virus. Another group

within the FDA was charged with monitoring the supply of antiviral drugs so that no shortages would occur.

The Obama administration also created a team of FDA officials to focus on consumer protection. The group's aim was to stop the marketing of fraudulent products that falsely claimed to diagnose, prevent, mitigate, treat, or cure the 2009 H1N1 flu virus. This was a more aggressive approach than under the Bush administration.

In 2009 the Democratic Congress and Obama administration also took a decidedly different approach on the issue of tobacco regulation. The FDA assumed greatly expanded regulatory powers when Congress passed a long-anticipated bill allowing the agency to regulate tobacco. The House had pushed its version of the legislation through in April on a tally of 298–112. The Senate passed the bill with some changes by 79–17, on June 11, 2009. The House cleared the Senate bill by a vote of 307–97 the next day. Obama, himself an occasional smoker, signed the legislation on June 22, 2009.

The Family Smoking Prevention and Tobacco Control Act, however, set boundaries on the power of the agency. For instance, the FDA could not ban an entire class of tobacco products under the law, or insist on the complete elimination of nicotine from tobacco products such as cigarettes. The law also protected farmers from oversight by the FDA. In the end, the largest cigarette maker, Philip Morris, supported the passage of the law because company officials favored regulatory certainty and believed that its competitors would suffer far more from the additional regulation than it would.

Some of the provisions of the new landmark legislation mirrored tools that then FDA Commissioner Kessler had included in the 1996 rule, which was later thrown out in 2000 by the Supreme Court. The 2009 law allowed the agency to bar flavor additives in tobacco products, to regulate—but not ban—nicotine, and to require tough new warning labels on cigarette packages and advertising. The agency carried out the ban on flavored cigarettes in September 2009. The law gave the FDA the authority to set nicotine levels as long as it did not require companies to eliminate nicotine entirely from their products. The agency also could set product content standards to eliminate harmful ingredients. Companies must submit the details of the ingredients, components, and additives in tobacco products and the effects of those products.

FDA IN THE 2010s

Hamburg's agency received more authority to oversee food products when Congress passed in December 2010 the most far-reaching food safety legislation in decades. The Food Safety Modernization Act, which President Obama signed in January 2011, expanded FDA authority for the inspection of imports. To bring food into the country, importers or producers were required to show documents, certified by foreign governments or third-party accreditors, that the products met safety standards which are equivalent to U.S. standards. The comprehensive law also increased the frequency of inspections at food facilities, toughened record-keeping requirements, and allowed the FDA to force companies to recall products if the producer did not do so voluntarily.

The new law required food processing, manufacturing, shipping, and other regulated facilities to analyze the most likely safety hazards and design controls to prevent problems, based on risk. The law also called for an improvement in the nation's surveillance systems to track foodborne diseases. Certain food processors and farms that produce less than $500,000 in food sold during the previous three years were exempt from some of the requirements. The food safety law calls for the FDA to produce more than 50 rules, studies, and guidelines. The FDA came under fire for taking a while to release some of the regulations related to the law.

The food safety law has seven fundamental rules that the FDA was supposed to release first in proposed form and then, after collecting public comments, in final form. Because the agency missed key deadlines for releasing the regulations, advocacy organizations sued the FDA in 2012. The agency agreed in 2014 to a consent order with new deadlines from 2015 to 2017.

One of the seven rules is known as the produce rule. It sets science-based standards for the harvesting of many unprocessed vegetables and fruits. Farmers would have to meet requirements affecting soil; hygiene; domesticated, and wild animals; and equipment, tools, and buildings.

Another, the preventive controls rule, requires domestic and foreign food operators to put in place safeguards against common hazards. The businesses will have to develop a written plan for preventing their food products from causing foodborne illness and written plans for correcting any problems that arise. A separate rule creates manufacturing requirements for animal feed.

A fourth rule requires importers to show that their suppliers overseas use the same type of preventive controls used in the United States.

A fifth policy puts in place standards for accreditation organizations of third-party food safety auditors.

Food facilities have to review their systems to see whether they are vulnerable to terrorist attacks under another rule.

The seventh rule requires food shippers to ensure that vehicles don't have contamination and have transported food under conditions using the correct temperature.

Other food-related agenda items during Hamburg's tenure included an initiative in the 2010 health care law to require calorie-count labels on restaurant menus and an effort to reduce trans-fats in food.

The FDA's Center for Tobacco Products, a division in the Office of Medical Products and Tobacco that was created by the 2009 tobacco law, is devoted entirely to regulating tobacco products. Companies that produce and import tobacco pay user fees to support the center, which oversees the marketing of products under new restrictions and new, much larger, and more explicit warning labels. The agency has moved toward approving graphic warning labels to accompany nine messages in the law. Tobacco products can no longer be labeled with claims such as "light," "mild," and "low" tar, which critics say could fool consumers into believing that the cigarettes with those labels are not

dangerous. The regulation of tobacco is expected to be a significant new focus for the FDA in the coming years.

Because lawmakers have been concerned about the percentage of new smokers who were youth, the 2009 law restricted sales and marketing to young people. The federal minimum age to purchase tobacco products is eighteen. The law added limits to sales from vending machines and banned the sale of packages with less than twenty cigarettes. A wide range of marketing restrictions were also overseen by the FDA under the tobacco law. Tobacco companies cannot sponsor entertainment or sports events or give out free cigarettes. Advertising is strictly limited.

Throughout Hamburg's tenure, the agency continued to maintain surveillance of drugs that may pose safety risks to consumers, an issue that regained prominence in the early part of the decade when cardiovascular risks were associated with drugs such as the painkiller Vioxx. The FDA has sought to conduct more postmarket surveillance in recent years. This has led to developments such as the voluntary withdrawal of the diet drug Meridia in 2010 because it may pose unnecessary cardiovascular risks.

Another industry that has come under increased scrutiny during the Obama administration has been the medical device sector. As Congress prepared to reauthorize legislation that faced expiration in 2012 and provide the FDA with authority to impose user fees on the drug and device industries, the agency launched an initiative to update the regulatory procedures affecting medical devices.

Jeffrey E. Shuren, the director of the Center for Devices and Radiological Health, embarked on an ambitious effort to update the most common path for medical devices to be approved, the so-called 510(k) process. The procedures had been established for devices that are similar to those already on the market, and the vast majority of devices were approved using this process. Shuren sought to revamp the process, saying that more certainty was needed.

Medical device manufacturers agreed with some of the changes, such as efforts to create a new approval pathway for moderate-risk devices and the creation of a Center Science Council to oversee clinical studies. However, these manufacturers said that other changes would be disruptive and would stifle innovation. For instance, officials for a major trade association representing the industry, the Advanced Medical Technology Association (AdvaMed), said that they opposed such recommendations as proposals to allow the FDA to consider an off-label use for a device in some circumstances when determining the intended use for a device that is being reviewed for approval. AdvaMed officials also opposed changes that would result in additional regulatory review, including a proposal to require each manufacturer to provide periodic updates to the FDA about any modifications made to a device, along with explanations of why the company did not submit a new application for approval because of the modifications.

Shuren asked the Institute of Medicine (IOM) to weigh in on some of the most controversial changes. The IOM's report, issued in late July 2011, was largely dismissed by many because it recommended moving away from the current system and creating an entirely new, undefined program—a recommendation that seemed to be radical and vague to many lawmakers, who would have had to create the new system.

As the FDA moved ahead on its priorities, the leadership shifted in 2011 as Sharfstein, the second-in-command who often appeared before Congress, left to become the secretary for health and mental hygiene for the state of Maryland. Hamburg announced a restructuring of the top layers of the agency in July 2011. She created four new offices to oversee foods, operations, medical products and tobacco, and global regulatory operations and policy. She hired Steven Spielberg, a former dean of Dartmouth Medical School, as a new deputy commissioner for medical products and tobacco. Deborah Autor, who was director of the Office of Compliance in the Center for Drug Evaluation and Research, was promoted to the new post of deputy commissioner for global regulatory operations and policy. Murray Lumpkin, who was deputy commissioner for international programs, took on a new role as senior adviser and representative for global issues. The agency planned to hire a chief operating officer to oversee the third directorate, a new Office of Operations to handle administrative functions. The existing Office of Foods was elevated into the fourth directorate, led by its previous leader, Mike Taylor.

The FDA also continued to play an important part in the treatment of Americans in its role as the decision maker of whether new drugs can come to market. In the case of HIV-AIDS treatment, the agency approved a new drug in 2011 to be used in combination with other antiretroviral drugs. The drug, Edurant (rilpivirine), is in the class of anti-HIV drugs known as nonnucleoside reverse transcriptase inhibitors and is for the treatment of HIV infection in adults who have never before taken HIV therapy.

The agency's functions were updated and expanded significantly when Congress passed the Food and Drug Administration Safety and Innovation Act, which was the reauthorization of the Prescription Drug User Fee Act. The new version was signed by President Obama in July 2012. The law reauthorizes the drug and medical device user fee programs for five years until Sept. 30, 2017. It also creates two new user fees programs: one for generic drugs and another for biosimilar biological products.

The provisions related to drugs were in some ways a continuation of the previous authorization. The user fee law reauthorized three types of user fees for drugs, setting the total fee revenue for fiscal 2013 at more than $693 million.

However, the law's new provisions affecting generic drug and biosimilar products involved significant changes. Generic drugs constituted about 80 percent of the prescriptions filled by patients at the time that the law passed. However, because there had not been any user fee money providing resources for FDA reviews of applications, a backlog of more than 2,500 applications for new generic drugs seeking approval built up. The median wait time to get a generic approved was 31 months. The new revenues from industry, which would total nearly $300 million over five years, were intended to speed up the process. By the fifth year of the generic user fee program, FDA officials committed to make review decisions on 90 percent of

electronic generic applications within 10 months after submission.

The FDA was authorized to approve biosimilar drugs under the 2010 health care reform law (PL 111–148). The 2012 user fee law strengthened the agency's ability to carry out reviews of applications and implement the new approval process.

Biosimilars, which are copycat biological products such as a drug or a vaccine made from living organisms, are more complex and difficult to replicate than chemical drugs, so they are not identical to the original brand-name product. Under the FDA approval process, manufacturers must show that a product is highly similar to another already-approved biologic.

Under the new biosimilar user fee program, the FDA promised to review 70 percent of applications for biosimilars within 10 months of submission in fiscal years 2013 and 2014, 80 percent in fiscal year 2015, 85 percent in fiscal year 2016, and 90 percent in fiscal year 2017.

The FDA later approved the first biosimilar in 2015. The agency allowed Sandoz, Inc., to make a biosimilar known as Zarxio, which is similar to Amgen Inc.'s Neupogen, or filgrastim. Amgen's drug was originally licensed in 1991 to help cancer patients. The agency noted that a biosimilar can only be approved if it has the same mechanism of action, route of administration, dosage form and strength as the original, and only for the uses that were approved for the first product. The user fee law also addressed concerns by lawmakers about the agency's handling of drug shortages in the United States, particularly of generic cancer drugs including injectables. Before the law passed, FDA largely received notifications from manufacturers about potential shortages of other products on a voluntary basis. Only the sole manufacturers of certain drug products for serious conditions were required by law to tell the FDA of shortages.

The law contained new authority for the agency to monitor shortages, with the goal of preventing them. It significantly broadened the types of drug manufacturers that have to report potential shortages.

Congress also made changes to provisions related to devices, building on the earlier discussions between Shuren of the FDA and the industry. Besides increasing the fees to about $600 million over five years and expanding the number of manufacturers that must pay the fees, the law also included provisions that updated the process for getting devices cleared for use in the United States. Currently, most devices are allowed on the market through the 510(k) process. In this process, a manufacturer must prove only that the new device is substantially equivalent to one already being sold. This way of getting permission to sell the device is faster and easier than the other route, known as the premarket approval (PMA) process. The PMA process typically requires clinical studies and evidence that the device is safe and effective.

The device provisions were the result of intense negotiations between manufacturers and the agency. The law included a commitment to reduce the review times of products after manufacturers submit an application through either the 510(k) or PMA process. FDA officials who oversee devices are required to provide quarterly and annual reporting of their progress toward meeting specific performance goals. The law created more opportunities for industry to consult with FDA staff before submitting an application for permission to sell the device.

The law also includes an FDA commitment to issue guidance documents with revised submission acceptance criteria. The guidance is supposed to include objective criteria and updated checklists for industry to use to make sure they are sending in complete submissions.

The FDA also said it would fully implement final guidance on factors to consider when making benefit-risk determinations in medical device premarket review. The guidance focuses on factors to consider in the review process before devices can be sold, including patients' tolerance for risk, the device's benefit, and the availability of other alternative treatments or tests.

FDA officials said that the additional funding available for the center that oversees devices could allow the agency to hire as many as 200 full-time employees, although those expectations were tempered somewhat after the FDA was hit by budget decreases in 2013 through an across-the-board funding cut for many domestic agencies.

As the user fee law was being implemented, the FDA was hit with another controversy—its oversight of compounding pharmacies that mix their own drugs. A 2012 outbreak of fungal meningitis caused by one of these pharmacies, New England Compounding Center of Framingham, raised questions about whether the agency had the authority it needs to monitor them. The outbreak sickened more than 750 people and killed at least 64 individuals.

Compounding pharmacies produce drugs and other products that are usually not required to be approved by the FDA because they are supposed to be tailor-made treatments for specific individuals. However, some of the facilities—including the New England Compounding Center, which closed after the outbreak—operated on a much wider scale that some experts say is tantamount to drug manufacturing. The FDA does have authority to inspect the facilities, but Hamburg asked Congress to give her more power.

"Our authorities are limited and not the right fit for FDA to provide appropriate and efficient oversight of this growing industry," Hamburg wrote in March 2013. "There should be legislation that establishes appropriate, minimum federal standards for firms that compound sterile drug products in advance of or without a prescription and ship them interstate. FDA must have clear authority to proactively inspect pharmacies to determine the scope and nature of their operations. Even during this time of heightened awareness, our inspectors are being delayed in their work or denied full access to records at some of the facilities we are inspecting."

Congress cleared a bill (PL 113-54) in late 2013 that broadened the FDA's authority and clarified when the federal government has oversight over compounding pharmacies. It also created a 10-year schedule for establishing a track-and-trace system for prescription drugs. The law also strengthened licensure requirements for wholesale distributors and logistics providers.

The FDA followed up with more than 90 inspections of compounding pharmacies in 2014, Hamburg said. Beyond the statutory changes to its authority, the agency continued its work in reviewing products for approval and regulating industry.

One issue that stirred controversy for more than a decade reemerged in the spring of 2013 when a federal judge for the U.S. District Court in the Eastern District of New York ordered the agency to make emergency contraception pills available for all women without a prescription. The pills, originally marketed as Plan B, were approved for over-the-counter use in 2006 for women 18 and older, or with a prescription to adolescents under the age of 18. Later, the FDA was ordered through a judicial ruling to make it available without a prescription to 17-year-olds in 2009. In 2011, the agency recommended that anyone, without age restrictions, be able to buy it without a prescription, but Health and Human Services Secretary Kathleen Sebelius used her authority to block that policy change from taking effect.

In April 2013 U.S. District Court Judge Edward R. Korman ruled that the agency acted in an arbitrary and capricious manner in restricting over-the-counter use to people of a certain age. Korman ordered the FDA to lift age and sale restrictions on the pill and generic versions within 30 days. He noted that young people who were old enough to buy it without a prescription still had to show proof of age to get it, which could be a deterrent.

The FDA announced on June 20 that it would comply with the court order by approving the use of one type of the levonorgestrel pill, Plan B One-Step, as a nonprescription product for all women without age restrictions. The agency on July 22 granted the manufacturer of the product, Teva Pharmaceuticals, exclusive marketing rights until April 2016. The FDA said generic manufacturers of the one-pill form of emergency contraception are expected to continue to face age restrictions so that only women ages 17 and over can buy it over-the-counter until the exclusivity rights expire.

Other routine duties of the FDA, such as drug and device approvals, continued to impact patient care in the United States.

One noteworthy approval was the permission granted in spring 2013 to Allergan to sell a new silicone breast implant. Because of concerns about safety issues, the agency imposed a set of conditions aimed at tracking long-term patient experience and durability of the devices after approval.

Another series of noteworthy approvals represented innovations in seasonal flu vaccines. One of the most significant came in early 2013, when the agency for the first time approved a flu vaccine that uses an insect virus rather than influenza and is not produced using chicken eggs. The technology, which had been used in other vaccines but not the flu vaccine, will allow the production of a greater amount of vaccine in a shorter amount of time than the traditional method of using eggs.

The agency also tried to help companies that are interested in developing drugs for early stage Alzheimer's, which is a major public health challenge for the future.

The FDA issued a guidance that walked the public through the FDA's thinking about the way researchers can identify and select patients with early Alzheimer's disease, or those who are at risk of developing the disease, for participation in clinical trials. The effort is part of a larger interagency effort to address Alzheimer's. It also provides an example of how the FDA is seeking to provide companies with more information about the agency's standards before the manufacturers begin clinical trials.

Current Issues

The pace of drug approvals quickened during the last years of the Obama administration. The FDA approved 51 drugs in 2014, which Hamburg said was the most in almost two decades. She said that the number of drugs approved for rare diseases, known as orphan drugs, was the most in more than three decades.

Some drugs were controversial because of their price tags. The FDA approved three hepatitis C drugs that generated as many headlines about their cost as about their medical advances. The drug that received the most attention was Gilead Science's Solvaldi, which cost about $1,000 per pill, in December 2013. The agency gave the green light to Olysio in November 2013 and the first hepatitis C genotype 1 infection combination drug, Harvoni, in October 2014. While supporters applauded the cures as breakthroughs, budget-conscious critics complained about the impact on Medicare and other health program spending.

Tobacco regulation moved forward in 2014 when the agency issued a proposed rule that would broaden the agency's tobacco product authority over more products including electronic cigarettes, cigars, pipe tobacco, nicotine gels, waterpipe or hookah tobacco, and dissolvables that are not already regulated. Public health advocates had complained that the rule took too long to be released. Advocates were disappointed that it would not ban online sales or flavoring and marketing that attract children but were pleased with many of its other provisions. Industry lobbyists want the agency to lighten the regulatory oversight of the rule.

The proposal, known as the " deeming rule," requires the companies that manufacture the previously unregulated tobacco products to register with the FDA, report their ingredients, get agency approval for new products, and include health warning labels. The manufacturers will not be able to sell to people under the age of 18 or sell e-cigarettes in vending machines unless they are located in certain places, such as a bar, where underage people are not allowed to be present. The companies also could not give out free samples.

The FDA also stopped allowing the sale of 11 tobacco products that manufacturers had claimed were equivalent to another product, but the agency ruled they were not similar enough.

A new era at the agency began in 2015 when Hamburg stepped down as commissioner in March after almost six years, a long tenure in the past few presidential administrations. Stephen Ostroff, the FDA's chief scientist and a former official at the Centers for Disease Control and Prevention, was named the acting commissioner.

■ AGENCY ORGANIZATION

Biography

STEPHEN OSTROFF, ACTING COMMISSIONER

Appointment: Nominated by President Barack Obama in March, 2015. Confirmed by the Senate on April 1, 2015.

Education: University of Pennsylvania School of Medicine, 1981; University of Colorado Health Sciences Center

Profession: Public administrator, physician.

Previous Career: Ostroff joined the FDA in 2013 as chief medical officer in the Center for Food Safety and Applied Nutrition and senior public health adviser to the Office of Foods and Veterinary Medicine. He has served as the FDA's chief scientist since January 2014. Prior to his career at the FDA, Ostroff served as deputy director of the National Center of Infectious Diseases at the Centers for Disease Control and Prevention (CDC), where he also served as acting director of CDC's Select Agent Program. He retired from the Commissioned Corps of the U.S. Public Health Service with the rank of rear admiral, and was also the director of the Bureau of Epidemiology for the Commonwealth of Pennsylvania.

Headquarters and Divisions

Listings for the FDA's research centers begin on p. 284.

OFFICE OF THE COMMISSIONER

The commissioner is the chief administrative officer of the FDA, an agency within the Department of Health and Human Services. The commissioner is responsible for making final decisions on actions against food and drug manufacturers and distributors. Any decision of the FDA commissioner is subject to review and revision by the secretary of health and human services. The Office of Management and Budget reviews proposed regulations with significant economic impact. The commissioner oversees all FDA operations and develops policy. The deputy commissioner/senior adviser assists the commissioner with the administration of the FDA centers and offices.

Commissioner
Stephen Ostroff (acting). . . . . (301) 796–5000
Senior Adviser to the Commissioner
Sally Howard . . . . (301) 796–7460
Principal Deputy Commissioner
John M. Taylor III (acting). . . . . (301) 796–7460
Chief of Staff
Denise Esposito. . . . . (301) 796–5000
Deputy Commissioner for Foods and Veterinary Medicine
Michael R. Taylor . . . . (301) 796–4500
Deputy Commissioner for Global Regulatory Operations and Policy
Howard Sklamberg . . . . (301) 796–8400
Deputy Commissioner for Operations
Walter S. Harris. . . . . (301) 796–4700
Deputy Commissioner for Policy, Planning, and Legislation
Jeremy B. Sharp . . . . (301) 796–4800

Food and Drug Administration

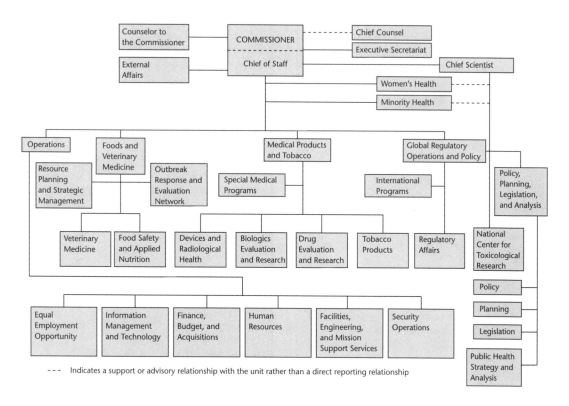

--- Indicates a support or advisory relationship with the unit rather than a direct reporting relationship

Deputy Commissioner for Medical Products and Tobacco
Robert Califf .... (301) 796–5000
Deputy Commissioner for Science and Public Health, Chief Scientist
Luciana Borio (acting).............. (301) 796–4880

Office of the Counselor to the Commissioner
Advises the commissioner on policy development, interpretation, and integration; provides leadership in emergency and crisis management for all FDA regulated products and agency programs.
Counselor to the Commissioner
Vacant........................... (301) 796–7460
Director, Office of Crisis Management
Mark Russo (acting) .... (301) 796–8257
Director, Office of Emergency Operations
Andrei Perlloni .... (301) 796–9655

Office of the Chief Counsel
Provides legal services involving FDA's regulatory activities. Supports public health and consumer protection missions by handling litigation matters and providing legal counsel. Represents FDA in judicial and administrative hearings by actively participating in case development and prosecution. Prepares legal opinions and participates in rulemaking proceedings, legislative matters, policy deliberations, and international negotiations.

Chief Counsel
Elizabeth H. Dickinson .... (301) 796–8540

OFFICE OF EXTERNAL AFFAIRS
Directs, coordinates, and oversees the agency's consumer activities and serves as the agency's central point of communication and education about the FDA's public health and regulatory activity. This includes the development and coordination of all FDA communications and outreach efforts to the news media, health professionals, patient advocates, industry, states, consumer groups, academia, trade associations, ethnic and minority groups, tribes, and the general public. Also serves as the focal point for internal employee communications, speechwriting, creative and editorial services, and digital and Web technology.
Assistant Commissioner
Virginia Cox...................... (301) 796–4631

Office of Communications
Oversees all print and online communications, directs all aspects of internal communications for employees, and acts as a liaison for the all of the agency's publications and audiovisual needs.
Assistant Commissioner
Lawrence Bachorik .... (301) 796–8234

Office of Health and Constituent Affairs
Works with patients and their advocates to encourage and support their active participation in the formulation

of FDA regulatory policy. Serves the public by answering questions about FDA activities related to HIV/AIDS, cancer, and other special health issues and providing information about the drug approval process and clinical trials.

Assistant Commissioner
Heidi C. Marchand . . . . (301) 796–8460

Office of Media Affairs

Serves as the agency's primary liaison with the news media and develops much of the material FDA uses to communicate its public health and consumer protection mission.

Assistant Commissioner
Heidi Rebello . . . . (301) 796–4540

Deputy Director of Strategy
Karen Riley . . . . (301) 796–4674

Deputy Director of Operations
Vacant . . . . (301) 796–4566

Web Communications
Chris Mulieri . . . . (301) 796–9315

OFFICE OF FOODS AND VETERINARY MEDICINE

Leads FDA Foods Program that addresses food and feed safety, nutrition, and other critical related areas. Includes three major operating units: the Center for Food Safety and Applied Nutrition (CFSAN), the Center for Veterinary Medicine (CVM), and the foods-related activities of the Office of Regulatory Affairs (ORA).

Deputy Commissioner
Michael R. Taylor . . . . (301) 796–4500
Fax . . . . (301) 847–3535

Associate Commissioner for Food Protection
Jeffrey A. Farrar . . . . (301) 796–4500

Office of Coordinated Outbreak Response and Evaluation Network

Manages outbreak response, surveillance, and post-response activities related to incidents involving multiple illnesses linked to FDA-regulated human and animal food and cosmetic products.

Director
Kathleen Gensheimer . . . . (240) 402–1608

Office of Resource Planning and Strategic Management

Provides overall guidance and leadership on cross-cutting resource and strategic management activities for the Office of Foods and Veterinary Medicine (OFVM). These include functional areas such as strategic planning, information systems, resource planning and evaluation, risk-based priority setting and resource allocation, human capital executive services, oversight of decentralized budget execution, internal controls/continuous improvements, long-range facility planning, and administrative support.

Director
Vacant . . . . (301) 796–9254

OFFICE OF GLOBAL REGULATORY OPERATIONS AND POLICY

Responsible for overall leadership, policy, and coordination of FDA international activities. Serves as focal point and liaison with foreign countries and international organizations. Coordinates FDA participation in a variety of international standard-setting and harmonization organizations and activities. Focal point for international agreements, including Memoranda of Understanding and mutual recognition activities. Also processes approvals for export of international drugs, manages requests for international technical assistance, develops strategies for international partnering activities, and develops international strategic plans.

Deputy Commissioner
Howard Sklamberg . . . . (301) 796–8400
Fax . . . . (301) 595–5063

Associate Commissioner, Global Regulatory Policy
Dara Corrigan . . . . (301) 796–8400

Associate Commissioner, International Programs
Mary Lou Valdez . . . . (301) 796–8400

OFFICE OF MEDICAL PRODUCTS AND TOBACCO

Provides high-level coordination and leadership across the centers for drug, biologics, medical devices, and tobacco products. The office also oversees the agency's special medical programs.

Deputy Commissioner
Robert Califf . . . . (301) 796–4566

Office of Special Medical Programs

Coordinates internal and external review of pediatric science, safety, ethical, and international issues and special programs and initiatives that are cross-cutting and clinical, scientific, and/or regulatory in nature.

Associate Commissioner
Jill H. Warner . . . . (301) 796–4810

Director, Combination Products
Thinh Nguyen . . . . (301) 796–4810

Director, Good Clinical Practice
Joanne Less . . . . (301) 796–4810

Director, Orphan Product Development
Gayatri Rao . . . . (301) 796–4810

Director, Pediatric Therapeutics
Dianne Murphy . . . . (301) 796–4810

OFFICE OF OPERATIONS

Oversees agency management activities, including budget and finance, human resources, ethics, grants and contracts, procurement information systems and management, and record keeping. Also processes public responses to proposed FDA rulemaking.

Deputy Commissioner
Walter Harris . . . . (301) 796–4700

Office of Equal Employment Opportunity and Diversity Management

Develops, implements, and monitors the FDA's affirmative action plans.

Director
Carol Moulton . . . . (301) 796–9400

Office of Ethics

Provides advice and assistance to current and former employees in order to help ensure that decisions they

make, and actions they take, are not, nor appear to be, tainted by any question of conflict of interest.
Director
Vince Tolino. . . . . (301) 796–8438

Office of Information Management and Technology
Develops and implements agency policy and procedure related to information technology. Plans and coordinates information technology development to support agency programs. Manages paperwork reduction activities.
Chief Information Officer
Walter Harris (acting). . . . . (301) 796–6700

Office of Finance, Budget and Acquisitions
Responsible for all duties associated with planning and implementing the annual FDA budget.
Chief Financial Officer
James Tyler. . . . . (301) 796–8836

Office of Financial Management Organization
Responsible for the execution of agency budget; development and maintenance of agency financial systems; oversight of the agency's financial audit activities; and management of all financial activities for FDA.
Director
William Collinson. . . . . (301) 796–7183

Office of Acquisitions and Grants Services
Executes all grants and contracts in the FDA.
Glenda Barfell . . . . (301) 827–7042

OFFICE OF POLICY, PLANNING, LEGISLATION, AND ANALYSIS
Deputy commissioner of the Office of Policy, Planning, and Legislation oversees all the offices below.
Deputy Commissioner
Sally Howard . . . . (301) 796–4800

Office of Policy and Planning
Provides strategic policy direction, planning, and data-driven analysis with the goal of increasing the effectiveness and efficiency of FDA activities.
Associate Commissioner
Peter Lurie (acting). . . . . (301) 796–4800
Fax. . . . . (301) 796–3533

Office of Planning
Leads all FDA planning and performance activities. Planning functions include program and policy evaluation studies; economic analyses; performance budget support activities; business process planning; and coordination of risk communication policy, research, and best practices.
Assistant Commissioner
Malcolm J. Bertoni . . . . (301) 796–4850
Fax. . . . . (301) 796–8616
Planning Staff Director
Timothy Kiang. . . . . (301) 796–4860

Program Evaluation and Process Improvement Staff Director
Don Lipkey. . . . . (301) 796–9170
Economics Staff Director
Clark Nardinelli. . . . . (301) 796–9100
Risk Communication Staff Director
Jodi Duckhorn. . . . . (301) 796–9150
Public Health Measurement and Risk Analysis Staff Director
Kara Morgan . . . . (301) 796–8808

Office of Policy
Advises the commissioner, the deputy commissioner for Policy, Planning, and Legislation, and other agency officials on matters relating to agency policy and regulations development. Acts as the agency's liaison for intergovernmental policy development. Oversees, directs, and coordinates the agency's rulemaking activities and regulations development system, including editing, processing, and preparing documents for publication in the *Federal Register,* and initiates new systems and procedures to make the agency's rulemaking process more efficient.
Assistant Commissioner
Leslie Kux. . . . . (301) 796–4830
Policy Development and Coordination
Catherine Lorraine (acting). . . . . (301) 796–9206
Regulations Policy and Management
Kenneth Cohen. . . . . (301) 796–7001
Regulations Editorial Section
Joyce Strong . . . . (301) 796–9148

Office of Legislation
Acts as liaison between the FDA and Congress; monitors hearings and legislation relevant to the agency; and prepares FDA reports, testimony, and position papers on proposed legislation. Drafts legislative proposals, provides explanations of the laws and regulations administered by the FDA, and provides technical assistance to members of Congress and their staffs on matters related to the FDA. (*See also Congressional Action.*)
Associate Commissioner
Thomas Kraus . . . . (301) 796–8900

Office of Public Health Strategy and Analysis
Acts as Office of the Commissioner and Agency resource for quantitative research and analysis on emerging issues. Helps to develop policy options and aids in understanding the expected impact of those options on public health outcomes.
Associate Commissioner
Peter Lurie . . . . (301) 796–7527

OFFICE OF THE CHIEF SCIENTIST
Fosters development and use of innovative technologies to meet public health needs; supports professional development of FDA scientists in all areas through continuing education, the Commissioner's Fellowship Program, and scientific interaction with universities and others; provides support and guidance for the National Center for Toxicological Resources; provides cross-agency

scientific coordination; supports science and public health activities to anticipate and respond to counterterrorism and emerging deliberate and natural threats (chemical, biological, radiological, and nuclear) through the Office of Counterterrorism and Emerging Threats; provides technical expertise to support FDA programs; leads agency's efforts to protect scientific integrity.

Deputy Commissioner for Science and Public Health, Chief Scientist
Luciana Borio (acting) . . . . (301) 796–4880
Fax. . . . . (301) 847–8617

Assistant Commissioner, Counterterrorism and Emerging Threats
Carmen Maher (acting) . . . . (301) 796–8510

Assistant Commissioner, Women's Health
Marsha B. Henderson. . . . . (301) 796–9440

Director
Luciana Borio. . . . . (301) 796–8510

Director, Critical Path Initiatives
Frank E. Weichold (acting) . . . . (301) 796–5370

Director, Minority Health
Jonca Bull . . . . (301) 796–8000

Director, Regulatory Science Innovation
Carol Linden . . . . (301) 796–5370

Director, Scientific Integrity
Nathan Doty. (301) 796–8556

Director, Scientific Professional Development
Leslie Wheelock. . . . . (301) 796–8450

Executive Assistant
Diane Rose. . . . . (301) 796–8733

Ombudsman (*see Information Sources: Information and Publications*)
Laurie Lenkel. . . . . (301) 796–8530

OFFICE OF REGULATORY AFFAIRS

Responsible for agency-wide programs to ensure compliance with FDA rules.

Associate Commissioner
Melinda K. Plaisier . . . . (301) 796–8800

Deputy Associate Commissioner
Steve M. Solomon . . . . (301) 796–8310

Operations
Ellen Morrison . . . . (301) 796–5170

Enforcement and Import Operations
Douglas Steam. . . . . (240) 796–3668

Criminal Investigations
George Karavetsos. . . . . (240) 276–9500

Resource Management
Karen Pane. . . . . (301) 796–4308

Communications and Quality Program Management
L'Tonya Davis. . . . . (301) 796–8804

Partnerships
Barbara J. Cassens . . . . (510) 590–3002

Policy and Risk Management
Kate Bent . . . . (301) 796–8211

OFFICE OF WOMEN'S HEALTH

Principal adviser to commissioner and other key agency officials on scientific, ethical, and policy issues relating to women's health. Advocates for participation of women in clinical trials and supports scientific research and collaboration with other government agencies and national organizations to sponsor scientific and consumer outreach programs.

Assistant Commissioner
Marsha B. Henderson . . . . (301) 796–9440
Fax. . . . . (301) 874–8604

Research and Development Program Director
Ameeta Parekh . . . . (301) 796–9440

OFFICE OF MINORITY HEALTH

Serves as the principal adviser to the commissioner on minority health and health disparities. Provides leadership, direction, and coordination in identifying agency actions that can help reduce health disparities.

Director
Jonca Bull . . . . (301) 796–8000
E-mail: omh@fda.hhs.gov

CENTER FOR BIOLOGICS EVALUATION AND RESEARCH

CBER ensures the safety and efficacy of biological products, from premarket review and clinical investigations, to manufacturing and inspections, to postmarketing requirements and enforcement actions. Conducts mission-related regulatory research that focuses on safety, provides supporting information to the review process, and establishes national standards.

Postmarketing activities include adverse event monitoring, both active and passive; inspections; lot release; surveillance; and enforcement. Responsible for the safety of the nation's blood supply and the products derived from blood, vaccines, allergenic extracts, anti-toxins, therapeutics, related drugs and devices, and a wide variety of the products of new technologies such as DNA-derived biotechnology products, somatic cell therapy, gene transfer products, conventional banked human tissues, and xenotransplantation.

Director
Karen Midthun . . . . (202) 402–8000

Deputy Director
Peter W. Marks. . . . . (240) 402–8000

Biostatistics and Epidemiology
Steven A. Anderson . . . . (240) 402–8577

Blood Research and Review
Jay S. Epstein . . . . (240) 402–8280

Cellular, Tissue, and Gene Therapies
Celia M. Whitten. . . . . (240) 402–8190

Communication, Outreach, and Development
Lorrie H. McNeill . . . . (240) 402–7800

Compliance and Biologics Quality
Mary Anne Malarkey . . . . (240) 402–9008

Information Technology
Theodore R. Stevens . . . . (240) 402–8357

Management
James Sigg. . . . . (204) 402–7990

Vaccines Research and Review
Marion F. Gruber . . . . (301) 796–1856

CENTER FOR DEVICES AND RADIOLOGICAL HEALTH

Helps ensure that medical devices are safe and effective, and helps reduce unnecessary exposure to radiation from medical, occupational, and consumer products. Medical devices under the center's jurisdiction range widely in complexity and potential risk, and include such products as contact lenses, heart valves, artificial joints, and condoms.

Radiation-emitting products include microwave ovens, television sets, sunlamps, and lasers. In regulating medical devices, the center has several functions: evaluating the safety and effectiveness of new devices before they can be marketed; conducting a postmarket surveillance program to identify and correct problems that occur with devices already on the market; working with the FDA field force in the inspection of medical device firms; educating health professionals and consumers about how to use devices safely; and conducting laboratory research to help make regulatory decisions and to identify safety problems that cross product lines. In regulating radiation-emitting products, the center promulgates and enforces performance standards with which manufacturers must comply.

Director
Jeffrey Shuren . . . . (301) 796–5900
Deputy Director, Policy
Paul Gadiock (acting). . . . . (301) 796–5736
Deputy Director, Science
William Maisel. (301) 796–5900
Management Operations
Denise Huttenlocker. . . . . (301) 796–5449
Compliance
Jan Welch (acting). . . . . (301) 796–5500
Device Evaluation
William Maisel (acting) . . . . (301) 796–5550
Communication, Education, and Radiation Programs
Lynne L. Rice . . . . (301) 796–5660
In Vitro Diagnostic Device Evaluation and Safety
Alberto Gutierrez . . . . (301) 796–5453
Science and Engineering Laboratories
Steven Pollack . . . . (301) 796–2530
Surveillance and Biometrics
Tom Gross . . . . (301) 796–5997

CENTER FOR DRUG EVALUATION AND RESEARCH

Regulates the testing, manufacture, and labeling of drugs; reviews and evaluates new drug and investigational drug applications; monitors the quality and safety of drug products; regulates the advertising and promotion of prescription drugs; provides ongoing surveillance for adverse events and use problems; and promotes informational and educational programs that address both medical and consumer interests. Additional information can be found at www.fda.gov/cder.

For general drug information, contact the Division of Drug Information at CDER Division of Drug Information (WO51–2201), 10903 New Hampshire Ave., Silver Spring, MD 20993, (301) 796–3400. To report an adverse event associated with the use of an FDA-regulated drug, biologic, device, or dietary supplement, call (800) 332–1088 or submit a report at www.fda.gov/medwatch.

Director
Janet Woodcock. . . . . (301) 796–5400

Deputy Center Director
Douglas Throckmorton . . . . (301) 796–5400
Business Process Support
Tanya Clayton (acting). . . . . (301) 796–0871
Compliance
Cynthia Schnedar . . . . (301) 796–3100
Controlled Substance Staff
Michael Klein. . . . . (301) 796–5402
Counter-Terrorism and Emergency Coordination
Rosemary Roberts. . . . . (301) 796–1740
Drug Safety Operations
Theresa Toigo. (301) 796–8473
Executive Programs
Marybeth Clarke . . . . (301) 796–1446
International Programs
Howard Sklamberg . . . . (301) 769-4600
Management
Melanie Keller . . . . (301) 796–3300
Strategic Programs
Theresa Mullin . . . . (301) 796–3800
Medical Policy
Jonathan Jarow (acting) . . . . (301) 796–0149
MedWatch
Norman S. Marks . . . . (301) 827–2287
Toll-free . . . . (800) 332–1088
New Drugs
John Jenkins. . . . . (301) 796–0700
Pharmaceutical Science
Keith Webber. . . . . (301) 796–2400
Regulatory Policy
Grail Sipes . . . . (301) 796–5122
Surveillance and Epidemiology
Gerald Dal Pan . . . . (301) 796–2380
Communications
Christine Shreeve . . . . (301) 796–3700
Translational Sciences
ShaAvhree Buckman-Garner. . . . . (301) 796–1721

CENTER FOR FOOD SAFETY AND APPLIED NUTRITION

5100 Paint Branch Pkwy., College Park, MD 20740–3835

Responsible for developing FDA policy, standards, and regulations on foods (with the exception of red meats and poultry, which are under the jurisdiction of the Agriculture Department), food additives, artificial colorings, and cosmetics. Develops programs to monitor the implementation of quality assurance programs, provides information on the levels of compliance achieved by the food and cosmetic industries, and plans and manages seminars and workshops on topics related to food and cosmetics, including the protection of consumers from economic fraud.

Also conducts research on composition and safety of foods; methods to detect and identify microorganisms in foods that may cause human illness; health hazards associated with cosmetics and color additives; food hygiene and sanitation; processing, packaging, and handling procedures for food and cosmetics; chemical composition of cosmetics and color additives; the nutritional composition of food; and methods to detect pesticides and chemical contaminants. Develops rules and guidelines for safety and sanitation of foods and inspecting facilities where food products and additives are manufactured. Also determines the accuracy of nutritional labeling statements and collects and studies data on food consumption patterns and food composition.

Director
Susan Mayne .... (240) 402–1600
Deputy Director for Compliance
William A. Correll................. (240) 402–3143
Deputy Director for Scientific Operations
Steven Musser .... (240) 402–1600
Analytics and Outreach
Ted Elkin .... (240) 402–2413
Applied Research and Safety Assessment
Vacant........................... (240) 402–3450
Cosmetics and Colors
Linda M. Katz .... (240) 402–1130
Dean, CFSAN Staff College
Wesley Long...................... (301) 436–1673
Compliance
William A. Correll .... (240) 402–2546
Food Additive Safety
Dennis Keefe .... (240) 402–1200
Food Safety
Nega Beru........................ (240) 402–1700
Management
Vacant........................... (240) 402–2114
Nutrition, Labeling, and Dietary Supplements
Vacant........................... (240) 402–2373
Regulations Policy and Social Sciences
Susan Bernard .... (240) 402–2379
Regulatory Science
Vincent K. Bunning .... (240) 402–2404

CENTER FOR TOBACCO PRODUCTS

Oversees the implementation of the Family Smoking Prevention and Tobacco Control Act. Responsibilities include setting performance standards, reviewing premarket applications for new and modified-risk tobacco products, and establishing and enforcing advertising and promotion restrictions. For general inquiries call the CTP Call Center (877) 287–1373 or e-mail: askCTP@fda.hhs.gov.

Director
Mitchell Zeller .... (301) 796–9200
Director, Health Communication and Education
Kathy Crosby .... (301) 796–9200
Director, Management
Janelle R. Barth (acting)............ (301) 796–9200
Director, Regulation
Beverly Chernaik.................. (301) 796–9200
Director, Policy
Eric Lindblom .... (301) 796–9185
Director, Compliance and Enforcement
Ann Simoneau..................... (301) 796–9200
Director, Science
David Ashley .... (301) 796–9200

CTP Ombudsman

Facilitates the resolution of disputes between the Center for Tobacco Products and the tobacco industry.

Ella Yeargin .... (301) 796–9239
Fax............................. (301) 276–3904
E-mail: CPTOmbudsman @fda.hhs.gov

CENTER FOR VETERINARY MEDICINE

7519 Standish Pl., Rockville, MD 20855

Develops FDA policy, standards, and regulations on the safety and efficacy of animal drugs, feed additives, and veterinary devices (instruments and implements intended for use in the diagnosis, cure, treatment, and prevention of disease). Works with federal and state agencies to ensure animal health and the safety of food derived from animals. Evaluates applications to market new animal drugs, food additives, feed ingredients, and devices; coordinates the veterinary medicine aspects of inspection and investigation programs; assesses the environmental impact of product approvals; and plans, directs, and evaluates the agency's surveillance and compliance programs for all animal drugs, feed additives, and devices.

Director
Bernadette M. Dunham .... (240) 402–7075
Deputy Director
Tracey Forfa .... (240) 402–5710
Management
Roxanne Schweitzer................ (240) 402–8537
Minor Use and Minor Species
Meg R. Oeller..................... (240) 402–0566
New Animal Drug Evaluation
Steven D. Vaughn .... (240) 276–8300
Research
John Graham .... (240) 402–0883
Science Policy
William T. Flynn .... (240) 402–5704
Surveillance and Compliance
Daniel G. McChesney.............. (240) 402–7140

NATIONAL CENTER FOR TOXICOLOGICAL RESEARCH

3900 NCTR Rd., Jefferson, AR 72079, Washington office: 10903 New Hampshire Ave., White Oak Bldg. 32, #2208, HF-10 Silver Spring, MD 20993

Conducts peer-reviewed fundamental research that is targeted to (1) develop new strategies, standards, and systems to predict toxicity and anticipate new product technology to support FDA's commitment to bringing this technology to market more rapidly; and (2) understand the mechanisms of toxicity and design better risk assessment/detection techniques for use in review and surveillance of FDA-regulated products. Key performance goals include the integration of new genetic systems and computer-assisted toxicology into the review process and the integration of gene chip, gene array, and proteomic technologies as standards for FDA review/risk management. NCTR actively involves its stakeholders in planning and evaluating its research agenda, and partners with other agencies, academia, and industry to address critical research issues such as individual susceptibility to drugs, toxicity due to drug interactions, standard markers for foodborne pathogens, and phototoxicity of cosmetics and foods.

Director

    William Slikker Jr.................. (870) 543–7517

Deputy Director, Research

    Daniel Acosta.................... (870) 543–7576

Executive Officer

    Jeanne F. Anson.................. (870) 543–7237

Associate Director for Management

    Winona Cason................... (870) 543–7351

Supervisory Program Analyst, Executive Programs and Services

    Moses Robinson .... (870) 543–7569

Associate Director for Regulatory Activities

    Margaret A. Miller .... (301) 796–8890

Associate Director for Regulatory Compliance and Risk Management

    Donna Mendrick................. (870) 543–8892

Associate Director for Scientific Coordination/FDA Liaison to National Toxicological Program

    Paul Howard .... (870) 543–7672

Director, Bioinformatics, and Biostatistics

    Weida Tong .... (870) 543–7142

Biochemical Toxicology

    Frederick A. Beland .... (870) 543–7205

Genetic and Molecular Toxicology

    Martha Moore .... (870) 543–7050

Microbiology

    Sung Duk Kim................... (301) 543–7341

Neurotoxicology

    Merle Paule..................... (870) 543–7203

Systems Toxicology

    Deborah Hansen (acting).......... (870) 543–7480

Senior Adviser for Science and Policy

    Thomas Flammang............... (870) 543–7291

Systems Biology

    Donna Mendrick................. (870) 543–7718

Veterinary Service

    Jefferson H. Carraway............. (870) 543–7347

Regional Offices

NORTHEAST REGION

(CT, MA, ME, NH, NY, RI, VT)
158–15 Liberty Ave., 5th Floor
Jamaica, NY 11433–1034
(781) 587–7500
Mutahar Shamsi (acting), regional director

CENTRAL REGION

(DC, DE, IL, IN, KY, MD, MI, MN, ND, NJ, OH, PA,
   SD, VA, WI, WV)
Chicago Office
20 N. Michigan Ave., #510
Chicago, IL 60602
(312) 596–6501
Joann Givens (acting), regional director

SOUTHEAST REGION

(AL, FL, GA, LA, MS, NC, PR, SC, TN)
60 Eighth St. N.E.
Atlanta, GA 30309

(404) 253–1171
Anne Reid (acting), regional director

SOUTHWEST REGION

(AR, CO, IA, KS, MO, NE, NM, OK, TX, UT, WY)
4040 N. Central Expwy., #900
Dallas, TX 75204
(214) 253–4904
Dennis Baker, regional director

PACIFIC REGION

(AK, AZ, CA, HI, ID, MT, NV, OR, WA)
1301 Clay St., #1180-N
Oakland, CA 94612–5217
(510) 287–2700
Mark S. Roh, regional director

CONGRESSIONAL ACTION

Congressional Liaison

Associate Commissioner for Legislation

    Tom Kraus .... (301) 796–8920

Committees and Subcommittees

HOUSE AGRICULTURE COMMITTEE

1301 LHOB, Washington, DC 20515–6001
(202) 225–2171

HOUSE APPROPRIATIONS COMMITTEE

Subcommittee on Agriculture, Rural Development, FDA, and Related Agencies
2362A RHOB, Washington, DC 20515
(202) 225–2638

HOUSE ENERGY AND COMMERCE COMMITTEE

2125 RHOB, Washington, DC 20515
(202) 225–2927
Subcommittee on Health
2125 RHOB, Washington, DC 20515
(202) 225–2927
Subcommittee on Oversight and Investigations
2125 RHOB, Washington, DC 20515
(202) 225–2927

HOUSE OVERSIGHT AND GOVERNMENT REFORM COMMITTEE

2157 RHOB, Washington, DC 20515–6143
(202) 225–5074

SENATE AGRICULTURE, NUTRITION, AND FORESTRY COMMITTEE

SROB-328A, Washington, DC 20510–6000
(202) 224–2035

SENATE APPROPRIATIONS COMMITTEE

Subcommittee on Agriculture, Rural Development, FDA, and Related Agencies
SDOB-127, Washington, DC 20510–6025
(202) 224–5270

SENATE HEALTH, EDUCATION, LABOR, AND PENSIONS COMMITTEE
SDOB-428, Washington, DC 20510–6300
(202) 224–5375

SENATE HOMELAND SECURITY AND GOVERNMENTAL AFFAIRS
Subcommittee on Permanent Investigations
SROB-1099, Washington, DC 20510–6250
(202) 224–3721

Legislation

The original legislation giving the federal government regulatory control over foods and drugs was the **Food and Drug Act of 1906** (34 Stat. 768, 21 U.S.C.). Signed by the president June 30, 1906. Prohibited interstate commerce in misbranded and adulterated foods, drinks, and drugs. The power to administer the law was placed in the Agriculture Department's Bureau of Chemistry.

A major overhaul of the basic food and drug legislation occurred in 1938 with the passage of the **Federal Food, Drug and Cosmetic (FFDCA) Act of 1938** (52 Stat. 1040, 21 U.S.C. 301–395). Signed by the president June 25, 1938. Broadened the original legislation by extending FDA regulatory power to cover cosmetics and medical devices; requiring predistribution approval of new drugs; requiring that tolerance levels be set for unavoidable poisonous substances; authorizing standards of identity, quality, and fill levels for containers for foods; authorizing inspections of factories where regulated products are manufactured; and adding court injunctions to FDA enforcement powers.

Other legislation administered by the FDA includes

Public Health Service Act (58 Stat. 682, 42 U.S.C. 201, et seq.). Signed by the president July 1, 1944. Gave the FDA authority to ensure safety, purity, and potency of vaccines, blood, serum, and other biological products. Also empowered the FDA to ensure safety of pasteurized milk and shellfish, as well as the sanitation of food services and sanitary facilities for travelers on buses, trains, and planes.

Humphrey Amendment (65 Stat. 648, 21 U.S.C. 333 note). Signed by the president Oct. 26, 1951. Required that drugs that cannot be safely used without medical supervision must be labeled for sale and dispensed only by prescription of a licensed practitioner.

Food Additives Amendment or **Delaney Amendment** (72 Stat. 1784, 21 U.S.C. 321, 331, 342, 346, 348). Signed by the president Sept. 6, 1958. Prohibited the use of new food additives until the manufacturer had proven they were safe for public consumption. The act further provided that any food containing a substance found to be carcinogenic had to be removed from the market.

Color Additive Amendments of 1960 (74 Stat. 397, 21 U.S.C. 321, 331, 333, 342, 343, 346, 351, 361, 362, 371, 376). Signed by the president July 12, 1960. Gave the FDA authority to establish standards for safe use of color additives.

Federal Hazardous Substances Act (74 Stat. 372, 15 U.S.C. 1261–1277). Signed by the president July 12, 1960. Gave the FDA power to declare as a hazardous substance any material containing a residue of an insecticide, pesticide, fungicide, or similar chemical.

Drug Amendments of 1962 (76 Stat. 780, 21 U.S.C. 321, 331, 332, 348, 351–353, 355, 357–360, 372, 374, 376, 381). Signed by the president Oct. 10, 1962. Authorized the administration to require that all drugs be proven effective as well as safe before they could be marketed. The Drug Amendments also gave the FDA responsibility to regulate prescription drug advertising.

Drug Abuse Control Amendments (79 Stat. 226, 18 U.S.C. 1114, 21 U.S.C. 321, 331, 333, 334, 360, 360a, 372). Signed by the president July 15, 1965. Established controls to prevent illicit traffic of groups of abused drugs—depressants, stimulants, and hallucinogens.

Fair Packaging and Labeling Act (80 Stat. 1296, 15 U.S.C. 1451–1461). Signed by the president Nov. 3, 1966. Gave the FDA authority to require that labels on packages of food, drugs, cosmetics, and medical devices be uniform and accurate.

Radiation Control for Health and Safety Act (82 Stat. 1173, 21 U.S.C. 360hh–360ss). Signed by the president Oct. 18, 1968. Authorized the FDA to set performance standards for television sets, microwave ovens, X-ray machines, and other products that emit radiation.

Drug Listing Act of 1972 (86 Stat. 559, 21 U.S.C. 331, 355, 360). Signed by the president Aug. 16, 1972. Required registration with the FDA of producers of drugs or medical devices and the filing of lists of drugs and devices produced by registrants.

Vitamins and Minerals Amendments (90 Stat. 410, 21 U.S.C. 321, 333, 334, 343, 350, 378). Signed by the president April 22, 1976. Amended the FFDCA to prevent the FDA from establishing standards limiting the potency of vitamins and minerals in food supplements or regulating such products as drugs.

Medical Device Amendments of 1976 (90 Stat. 539, 21 U.S.C. 321, 331, 334, 351, 352, 358, 360, 360c–360k, 374, 376, 379, 379a, 381). Signed by the president May 28, 1976. Empowered the FDA to regulate medical devices. The amendments allowed the FDA to ban risky medical devices, to establish categories for medical devices, to set performance standards for less hazardous devices, and to require that the safety of the most complex medical devices be demonstrated prior to their being marketed.

Infant Formula Act of 1980 (94 Stat. 1190, 21 U.S.C. 301 note, 321, 331, 350a, 374, 830, 841–843, 873). Signed by the president Sept. 26, 1980. Set standards for content and processing of infant formulas.

Orphan Drug Act of 1983 (96 Stat. 2049, 21 U.S.C. 301 note, 360aa–360dd, 904). Signed by the president Jan. 4, 1983. Authorized financial incentives for companies to develop drugs for the treatment of rare illnesses.

Federal Anti-Tampering Act (97 Stat. 831, 18 U.S.C. 1365). Signed by the president Oct. 13, 1983. Made it a felony to tamper with packaged consumer products such as foods, drugs, and cosmetics. Gave investigatory authority to the FDA where products within its jurisdiction are involved.

Drug Price Competition and Patent Term Restoration Act (98 Stat. 1585, 21 U.S.C. 301 note, 355, 360cc). Signed by the president Sept. 24, 1984. Designed to expedite the approval of generic versions of "pioneer" drugs and to extend patent protection to compensate sponsors for time required by the FDA to consider new drug approvals.

Orphan Drug Amendments of 1985 (99 Stat. 387, 21 U.S.C. 301 note, 360aa, 360aa note, 360bb, 360cc, 360ee). Signed by the president Aug. 15, 1985. Extended the authorizations for research grants, expanded the marketing protection to sponsors of approved orphan drugs, and established a National Commission on Orphan Diseases to evaluate government research activities on rare diseases.

Orphan Drug Amendments of 1988 (102 Stat. 90, 21 U.S.C. 301 note, 360aa note, 360bb, 360ee). Signed by the president April 18, 1988. Extended authorizations for grant money and required manufacturers of designated orphan drugs who intended to halt production to notify the FDA one year in advance so the agency could locate a new production source. Required a study to be completed by 1990 to determine the necessity of incentives to encourage companies to develop medical devices and foods for rare diseases and conditions.

Prescription Drug Marketing Act of 1987 (102 Stat. 95, 21 U.S.C. 301 note, 331, 333, 353, 353 notes, 381). Signed by the president April 22, 1988. Banned the reimportation of drugs produced in the United States, placed restrictions on the distribution of drug samples, banned certain resales of drugs by hospitals and charitable institutions, and required federal standards for the licensure of drug wholesalers.

Health Omnibus Programs Extension of 1988 (102 Stat. 3048, 21 U.S.C. 301 note, 393, 393 notes). Signed by the president Nov. 5, 1988. The Food and Drug Administration Act, Title V of this act, established in statute the FDA within the Health and Human Services Department and required that the FDA commissioner be appointed by the president and confirmed by the Senate. Title II of this act, the **AIDS Amendments of 1988** (102 Stat. 3062, 42 U.S.C. 201 note, 242c, 247d, 286, 289f, 300cc–300aaa), required development of research and education programs, counseling, testing, and health care for AIDS patients. It also required the FDA to develop a registry of experimental AIDS drugs.

Nutrition Labeling and Education Act (104 Stat. 2353, 21 U.S.C. 301 note, 321, 331–334, 335b, 341–343, 346a, 352, 355, 358, 360b–360i, 360cc, 360hh–360ss). Signed by the president Nov. 8, 1990. Mandated uniform nutrition labeling on packaged food items, including most processed food products and some raw agricultural products, fish, and shellfish. Required manufacturers' labels to provide detailed information on caloric levels and amounts of fat and cholesterol in food items. Directed the FDA to test products for such claims as "natural" and "low-fat" before those terms could be used on food labels.

Safe Medical Devices Act of 1990 (104 Stat. 4511, 21 U.S.C. 301 note, 321, 333, 333 note, 351, 353, 360, 360c, 360d–360j, 3601, 360gg–360ss, 383). Signed by the president Nov. 28, 1990. Strengthened FDA procedures for approving new medical devices and recalling defective products already on the market. Required medical facilities to report faulty or dangerous devices to manufacturers

and, in the case of a death, to the FDA. Imposed monetary fines for violations.

FDA Revitalization Act (104 Stat. 4583, 21 U.S.C. 301 note, 379b, 379c, 379d, 394). Signed by the president Nov. 28, 1990. Consolidated FDA headquarters offices and provided for the automation of the FDA approval application process. Authorized the commissioner to appoint technical and scientific review panels and to pay appointees not employed by the federal government.

Generic Drug Enforcement Act of 1992 (106 Stat. 149, 21 U.S.C. 301 note, 321, 335a, 335a notes, 335b, 335c, 336, 337, 355). Signed by the president May 13, 1992. Expanded FDA authority to oversee the generic drug industry. Prescribed civil penalties for fraud and abuse of the approval process for generic copies of brand-name prescription drugs, including monetary fines, debarment from future dealings with the FDA, withdrawal of FDA approval, and suspension of distribution.

Mammography Quality Standards Act of 1992 (106 Stat. 3547, 42 U.S.C. 201, 263b, 263b note). Signed by the president Oct. 27, 1992. Required all U.S. mammography facilities to be accredited and fully certified.

Prescription Drug User Fee Act of 1992 (106 Stat. 4491, 21 U.S.C. 321, 331, 342, 343, 346a, 351, 352, 360j, 361, 362, 372a, 376, 379c–379h, 453, 601, 1033); **Dietary Supplement Act of 1992** (106 Stat. 4500, 21 U.S.C. 301 note, 343 notes, 343–1 note, 393 note). Signed by the president Oct. 29, 1992. Required prescription drug manufacturers to pay "user fees" to help underwrite the cost of federal safety and efficiency reviews. Established rates for annual "facilities" fees and an "application fee," to be paid when a drug is submitted for approval.

Dietary Supplement Health and Education Act of 1994 (108 Stat. 4332, 21 U.S.C. 321, 331, 342, 343, 343–2, 350, 350b; 42 U.S.C. 281, 287c-11). Signed by the president Oct. 25, 1994. Established a regulatory framework and specific labeling requirements for dietary supplement manufacturers.

FDA Export Reform and Enhancement Act of 1996 (110 Stat. 1321–313, 21 U.S.C. 301 note, 331, 381, 382; 42 U.S.C. 262). Signed by the president April 26, 1996. Part of a larger bill. The act amended the Federal Food, Drug, and Cosmetic Act to revise requirements regarding the importing and exporting of any component of a drug, biological product (including a partially processed biological product), device, food or color additive, or dietary supplement.

Food Quality Protection Act of 1996 (110 Stat. 1489, 7 U.S.C. 136 note). Signed by the president Aug. 3, 1996. Amended the Federal Insecticide, Fungicide, and Rodenticide Act of 1947 and the Federal Food, Drug, and Cosmetic Act to allow the EPA to issue an emergency order to suspend pesticides that pose a risk to public health before the pesticides go through the cancellation process. Replaced the FFDCA's Delaney Amendment with a single health standard requiring the EPA to ensure that pesticide residue in both raw and processed food posed a "reasonable certainty of no harm." Required the EPA to establish programs to screen for estrogen-like substances and provide increased information to the public on the amounts of pesticides found in foods.

FDA Modernization Act of 1997 (111 Stat. 2296, 21 U.S.C. 301 note et seq.). Signed by the president Nov. 21, 1997. The act amended certain provisions in the FFDCA and the Prescription Drug User Fee Act of 1992. Streamlined the regulation and approval of a product by codifying FDA's regulations and practice to increase patient access to experimental drugs and medical devices and to accelerate review of important new medications. Made available for patients an expanded database on clinical trials. Enabled the FDA to contract outside experts to conduct the initial reviews of medical devices.

Best Pharmaceuticals for Children Act (115 Stat. 1408, 21 U.S.C. 301 note). Signed by the president Jan. 4, 2002. Amended the Federal Food, Drug and Cosmetic Act and the Public Health Service Act to improve the safety and efficacy of pharmaceuticals for children. Established an Office of Pediatric Therapeutics within the FDA to oversee activities that deal with pediatric health and pharmacy issues.

Public Health Security and Bioterrorism Preparedness and Response Act of 2002 (116 Stat. 594, 42 U.S.C. 201 note). Signed by the president June 12, 2002. Authorized the FDA and the Agriculture Department to hire new border inspectors and develop new methods for detecting crop and food contaminations. Mandated the annual registration of foreign manufacturers of drug and device products. Authorized the FDA to detain suspicious foods and required prior notice of all food imports.

Medical Device User Fee and Modernization Act (MDUFMA) of 2002 (116 Stat. 1588, 21 U.S.C. 301 note). Signed by the president Oct. 26, 2002. Amended the Federal Food, Drug, and Cosmetic Act to establish a new program that imposed fees on medical device manufacturers to help pay for faster FDA approval of their products. Allowed manufacturers to hire independent contractors to conduct safety inspections of their factories. Established new regulations governing the sterilization and reuse of catheters and other products originally approved for one-time use only.

Health Care Safety Net Amendments of 2002 (116 Stat. 1621, 42 U.S.C. 201 note). Signed by the president Oct. 26, 2002. Amended the Public Health Service Act to reauthorize and improve its Consolidated Health Center Program and the National Health Service Corps (NHSC). Established a grant program to improve the quality of health care by rural and other small health care providers.

Rare Diseases Act of 2002 (116 Stat. 1988, 42 U.S.C. 201). Signed by the president Nov. 6, 2002. Amended the Public Health Service Act to establish an Office of Rare Diseases at the National Institutes of Health and provide for rare disease regional centers of excellence.

Medicare Prescription Drug, Improvement, and Modernization Act of 2003 (117 Stat. 2322, 42 U.S.C. 1395x(s)(2)). Signed by the president Dec. 8, 2003. Amended title XVIII (Medicare) of the Social Security Act to add a new optional Medicare prescription drug benefit program. Amended the Federal Food, Drug, and Cosmetic Act to revise provisions with respect to abbreviated new drug applications (ANDAs). Prohibited the ANDA applicant from amending the application to include a drug different from that approved by FDA but allowed the applicant to amend the application for a different strength of the same drug.

Food and Drug Administration Amendments Act of 2007 (121 Stat. 823, 21 U.S.C. 301 note). Signed by the president Sept. 27, 2007. Amended the Federal Food, Drug, and Cosmetic Act to revise and extend the user-fee programs for prescription drugs and for medical devices. Enhanced the postmarket authorities of the FDA with respect to the safety of drugs. Reauthorized and amended the Prescription Drug User Fee Act and the Medical Device User Fee and Modernization Act.

Family Smoking Prevention and Tobacco Control Act of 2009 (123 Stat. 1776, 21 U.S.C. 301 note, 387 note). Signed by the president June 22, 2009. Provided the FDA with the authority to restrict and regulate the marketing and manufacturing of tobacco products. Amended the Federal Food, Drug, and Cosmetic Act, the Comprehensive Smokeless Tobacco Health Education Act of 1986, Federal Cigarette Labeling and Advertising Act, and the Copeland Pure Food and Drugs Act to authorize the FDA to regulate the levels of tar, nicotine, and other harmful components of tobacco products.

Food Safety Modernization Act (P.L. 111-353, 124 Stat. 3885). Signed by the president Jan. 4, 2011. Amended the Federal Food, Drug, and Cosmetic Act to expand food safety protections, increase inspections, and give the FDA the authority to order a mandatory recall. Required certain facilities to produce a written plan regarding their prevention measures and food safety law compliance. Allowed the FDA to collect fees connected with food recalls, facility inspections, and importer reinspections.

The Food and Drug Administration Safety and Innovation Act of 2012 (P.L. 112–144, 126 Stat. 993). Signed by the president July 9, 2012. Amended the Prescription Drug User Fee Act to reauthorize drug, device, and other industry user fees through September 30, 2017. Created new user fees for generic drugs and biological products. Permanently authorized the Best Pharmaceuticals for Children program, which was created in 1997 to support the assessment of safety and efficacy of drugs in children. Imposed reporting requirements on some drug manufacturers to try to prevent shortages. Created incentives to spur the development to antibiotics intended for use against serious diseases.

Drug Quality and Security Act (P.L. 113-54, 127 Stat. 587). Signed by the president Nov. 27, 2013. Required facilities to meet requirements of the Food, Drug, and Cosmetic Act for drug manufacturers unless they qualify for one of several exemptions or they register with the FDA as a so-called outsourcing facility. An outsourcing facility can qualify for exemptions from FDA approval requirements and the requirement to label products with adequate directions for use but must meet other requirements, such as those for good manufacturing practices. Removed certain provisions from section 503A of the Federal Food, Drug, and Cosmetic Act that the U.S. Supreme Court found unconstitutional in 2002.

Sunscreen Innovation Act (P.L. 113-195, 128 Stat. 2035). Signed by the president Nov. 26, 2014. Created an expedited process for the review and approval of sunscreens that are sold over-the-counter.

INFORMATION SOURCES

Internet

Agency website: www.fda.gov. Comprehensive website provides a range of information about the agency's activities, meetings, and regulatory operations, including the activities of all FDA centers. Press releases, reports, and newsletters also are available.

Telephone Contacts

FDA General Inquiries . . . . (888) 463–6332
FDA's 24-hour Emergency Line . . . . . .(301) 796–8240
Consumer Affairs and Inquiries . . . . .(888) 463–6332
Drug Information Line . . . .(301) 827–4573
Locator. . . . .(888) 447–3742

The FDA maintains the following hotline and clearinghouse numbers:

Advisory Committee Information
    Hotline. . . . .(800) 741–8138
AIDS Clinical Trials
    Information Service. . . . .(800) 874–2572
Center for Biologics Evaluation and Research
    Voice Information Service . . . .(800) 835–4709
Center for Devices and Radiological
    Health . . . .(800) 638–2041
Center for Drug Evaluation
    and Research. . . . .(301) 827–4573
Center for Food Safety and Applied
    Nutrition Outreach and Information
    SAFE-FOOD or . . . .(888) 723–3366
Adverse Event Reporting System/
    MedWatch. . . . .(800) 332–1088
Center for Veterinary Medicine Adverse Drug
    Reporting System. . . . .(888) 332–8387
Vaccine Adverse Event
    Reporting System. . . . .(800) 822–7967

Information and Publications

KEY OFFICES

Office of the Ombudsman

10903 New Hamphsire Ave., WO 32, #4231
Silver Spring, MD 20993
(301) 796–8530
Fax (301) 847–8628
E-mail: ombuds@oc.fda.gov
Laurie Lenkel, director
Andrew Moss, Deputy ombudsman

Addresses complaints and assists in resolving disputes between companies or individuals and FDA offices concerning application of FDA policy and procedures; serves as a neutral and independent resource for members of FDA-regulated industries when they experience problems with the regulatory process that have not been resolved at the center or district level; works to resolve externally and internally generated problems for which there are no legal or established means of redress. Cases include disputes from regulated industry regarding agency product center or district office actions; disputes about import detentions; complaints from small businesses, including those referred by the U.S. Small Business Administration; inquiries about the agency's handling of consumer complaints; and requests for information and assistance from regulated industry.

FDA Media Affairs

10903 New Hampshire Ave., Bldg. 32
Silver Spring, MD 20993
(301) 796–4540
Fax (301) 847–8620
Katie Conover, assistant commissioner
Jennifer Rodriguez, deputy director of strategy,
    (301) 796–8232
Heidi Rebello, deputy director of operations, (301)
    796–4566

Handles FDA press relations and news releases, distributes publications, and answers questions about programs and policies. Office handles press inquiries on food, cosmetics, human and animal drugs, vaccines, medical devices, or health fraud.

Office of Communications

10903 New Hampshire Ave., Bldg. 32, #5378
Silver Spring, MD 20993
(301) 796–8234
Fax (301) 847–8622
Jason D. Brodsky, director

Produces FDA publications, including the *Consumer Updates,* online articles on FDA actions and a wide variety subjects of interest to consumers, including nutrition, drugs, medical devices, and cosmetics. These updates and related resources are available through the website www .fda.gov/ForConsumers.

DATA AND STATISTICS

FDA Center for Drug Evaluation and Research

10903 New Hampshire Ave.
Silver Spring, MD 20993
(301) 796–5400
Janet Woodcock, director
E-mail: druginfo@fda.hhs.gov

Provides several FDA databases containing drug information. (Databases for other products under FDA jurisdiction are maintained by the various centers; see listings beginning on *p. 284.*)

Freedom of Information

Public Reading Room
5630 Fishers Ln., Room 1061
Rockville MD 20857
(301) 796–3900

Fax (301) 827–9267
Sarah Kotler, FOIA Director, (301) 796–8976

Public reading room open 9:00 a.m. to 4:00 p.m., Monday through Friday. FDA's website has a link for information on FOIA requests.

GRANTS

Office of Acquisitions and Grant Services
Office of Commissioner
5600 Fishers Lane
Rockville, MD 20857
(301) 827–7042
Fax (301) 827–7101
Glenda Barfell, director
E-mail: Glenda.barfell@fda.hhs.gov

Executes all grants and contracts on behalf of the FDA.

MEETINGS
Meetings are announced on the FDA's website www .fda.gov. All FDA Centers' Advisory Committee current and past meetings and agendas can be found on the FDA home page.

PUBLICATIONS
Many publications and documents are available from the FDA's website, www.fda.gov, including the *Everyday Health Newsletter* and the *Drug Safety Newsletter*. (*FDA Consumer* ceased publication in 2007. All back issues continue to be available on the website and some articles are updated.) The site also provides links and references to administrative reports; press announcements; historical, research, and scientific papers; and other publications currently available in the public domain as follows:

- Administrative (i.e., budget, policies, strategic priorities): www.fda.gov/aboutfda/reportsmanualsforms/defau lt.htm
- Consumers: www.fda.gov/ForConsumers/Consumer Updates/default.htm
- Press announcements: www.fda.gov/NewsEvents/ Newsroom/PressAnnouncements/default.htm
- Scientific publications (as categorized by medical product area, food, and tobacco): www.accessdata.fda .gov/scripts/publications
- Regulatory history: http://www.fda.gov/AboutFDA/ WhatWeDo/History/ResearchTools/default.htm

Other research to support FDA's public health mission can be found at: www.fda.gov/AboutFDA/CentersOffices/ OC/OfficeofScientificandMedicalPrograms/NCTR/ WhatWeDo/NCTRPublications/default.htm.

Reference Resources

LIBRARIES

FDA Biosciences Library
Main Library
White Oak, Bldg. 2
10903 New Hampshire Ave., 3rd Floor

Silver Spring, MD 20993
(301) 796–2039
Hours: 8:30 a.m. to 4:30 p.m.
Kathie McConnell, director

Collection scope covers all areas regulated by the FDA, including biologics, food safety, legal and regulatory issues, neurologic health, toxicology, pharmacology, veterinary medicine, and tobacco. Also includes technical literature related to the chemistry of food and cosmetic research. Open to the public by appointment.

National Center for Toxicological Research Library (NCTR)
3900 NCTR Rd.
Bldg. 10, Library and Conference Center
Jefferson, AR 72079
(870) 543–7603
Susan Laney-Sheehan, branch manager

A branch of the FDA Main Library, the NCTR maintains a collection of toxicology literature. Accessible to the public by appointment only.

DOCKETS

FDA Office of Management and Systems
Division of Dockets Management
5630 Fishers Lane, Room 1061, HFA-305
Rockville, MD 20852
(301) 827–6860
Fax (301) 827–6870
Karen Kennard, supervisory administrator

Serves as the official FDA repository for documents submitted to administrative proceedings and rulemaking and *Federal Register* documents. Types of documents include comments, transcripts, motions, briefs, and petitions to establish, amend, or revoke an FDA action. Advisory committee materials are accessible via the FDA website and can be found under individual offices. A search engine is available. Comments may be submitted electronically through the dockets website at www.regulations.gov. The Dockets Public Reading Room is open 9:00 a.m. to 4:00 p.m., Monday through Friday. Federal dockets are also available at www.regulations.gov. (*See appendix for Searching and Commenting on Regulations: Regulations.gov.*)

RULES AND REGULATIONS
FDA rules and regulations are published in the *Code of Federal Regulations,* Title 21, Chapter I, Parts 1–99. Proposed rules, new final rules, rulings by the commissioner, and updates to the *Code of Federal Regulations* are published in the daily *Federal Register*. (*See appendix for information on how to obtain and use these publications.*) The *Federal Register* may be accessed at www.federal register.gov and the *Code of Federal Regulations* at www .archives.gov/federal-register/cfr; also see the federal government's website www.regulations.gov (*see appendix*).

Two sources of information detailing the laws and regulations administered by the FDA, *Requirements of Laws and Regulations Enforced by the U.S. FDA* and *Food and Drug Administration Acts,* are available on the FDA website at www.fda.gov.

Other Information Sources

RELATED AGENCY

National Library of Medicine (NLM)
8600 Rockville Pike, Bldg. 38
Bethesda, MD 20894
(301) 594–5983
(888) 346–3656
Internet: www.nlm.nih.gov

Part of the National Institutes of Health. Maintains MEDLINE, a Web-based database of eleven million references and abstracts to medical journal articles. PubMed is the access system for MEDLINE. Other databases cover toxicology, chemical substances, and environmental health. MEDLINE Plus is an information service available on the Web containing health information for the public. Links are available at the NLM website to access these and other services. Many NLM fact sheets and reports are available via the agency website; other publications may be purchased from the GPO and NTIS (*see appendix, Ordering Government Publications*). Main reading room hours are 8:30 a.m. to 5:00 p.m., Monday through Friday.

NONGOVERNMENTAL RESOURCES
The following are some key resources for information on the FDA and related food and drug issues.

American Council on Science and Health
1995 Broadway, #202
New York, NY 10023–5882
(212) 362–7044
Internet: www.acsh.org

American Public Health Association
800 Eye St. N.W.
Washington, DC 20001–3710
(202) 777–2742
TTY (202) 777–2500
Internet: www.apha.org

CCH, a Wolters Kluwer business
(previously Commerce Clearing House, Inc.)
2700 Lake Cook Rd.
Riverwoods, IL 60015
(847) 267–7000
Internet: www.wolterskluwer.com

Center for Science in the Public Interest
1220 L St., N.W., #300
Washington, DC 20005
(202) 332–9110
Internet: www.cspinet.org

Consumer Federation of America
1620 Eye St. N.W., #200
Washington, DC 20006
(202) 387–6121
Internet: www.consumerfed.org

ECRI Institute
5200 Butler Pike
Plymouth Meeting, PA 19462–1298
(610) 825–6000
Internet: www.ecri.org

Food and Drug Law Institute
1155 15th St. N.W., #910
Washington, DC 20005
(202) 371–1420
(800) 956–6293
Internet: www.fdli.org

Food Chemical News
Informa Agra Customer Operations
Christchurch Court
10–15 Newgate St.
London, EC1A 7AZ
(888) 732–7070
Internet: www.agra-net.net/agra/food-chemical-news
E-mail: agrahelp@informa.com

Food Research and Action Center
1200 18th St. N.W., #400
Washington, DC 20036
(202) 986–2200
Internet: www.frac.org

National Academies Press
500 Fifth St. N.W.
Washington, DC 20001
(202) 334–3313
(800) 624–6242
Internet: www.nap.edu

National Consumers League
1701 K St. N.W., #1200
Washington, DC 20006
(202) 835–3323
Internet: www.nclnet.org

National Pharmaceutical Council
1717 Pennsylvania Ave. N.W., #800
Washington, DC 20006
(202) 827–2100
Internet: www.npcnow.org
E-mail: info@npcnow.org

U.S. Pharmacopoeia
12601 Twinbrook Pkwy.
Rockville, MD 20852–1790
(301) 881–0666
(800) 227–8772
Internet: www.usp.org

National Labor Relations Board

1015 Half St. S.E., Washington, DC 20570
Internet: www.nlrb.gov

▧ INTRODUCTION

The National Labor Relations Board (NLRB) is an independent agency established by the National Labor Relations Act (Wagner Act) of 1935. The board is composed of a general counsel and five members who are nominated by the president and confirmed by the Senate. The president designates one of the members to serve as chair. Board members serve five-year terms, and the general counsel serves a four-year term; incumbents may be reappointed.

Responsibilities

The NLRB

- Conducts elections to determine if workers in a plant, factory, or business want to be represented by a union.
- Conducts elections to determine which of two or more unions attempting to organize a workplace the workers prefer.
- Conducts elections to determine if workers want to remove their union.
- Certifies results of elections.
- Acts to prevent employers and unions from engaging in unfair labor practices.

Powers and Authority

The NLRB does not initiate cases; it has the power to act only when cases are brought before it and only in cases in which an employer's operation or a labor dispute affects commerce. In practice, this restriction means that the agency has authority to act in all but purely local cases. However, the board may decline to exercise jurisdiction over a category of employers when the labor dispute does not have a substantial impact on commerce.

The agency will not consider cases involving race tracks; owners, breeders, or trainers of horses; and real estate brokers. The following employees also are exempt from coverage under the act: agricultural laborers; domestic servants; individuals employed by a parent or spouse; independent contractors; managers or supervisors; individuals subject to the Railway Labor Act; federal, state, or local government employees; employees of Federal Reserve banks; and employees of church-affiliated schools.

Most NLRB activity takes place in the field offices, with less than 5 percent of unfair labor practice cases making it all the way to the board for review. In addition to the broad discretion that regional directors have because of this arrangement, they have the authority to define bargaining units.

PETITIONS

The NLRB may perform its duties only after the filing of a petition or charge. A petition, which requests the NLRB to hold a representation election, may be filed by an employee, a group of employees, any individual or labor organization acting on their behalf, or an employer.

GLOSSARY

Charge—Form used for filing an allegation of unfair labor practices.

Closed shop—An establishment in which the employer by agreement hires only union members in good standing.

Complaint—Formal allegation issued by an NLRB regional office after investigation indicates merit to a charge.

Jurisdictional standards—NLRB's criteria for acting on a case, based on an enterprise's annual amount of business or annual sales or purchases.

Petition—Form used to request a representation election.

Right-to-work laws—State laws that prohibit labor-management agreements requiring union membership to obtain or keep a job.

Union shop—An agreement that requires an employee to join a union to obtain or keep a job.

A petition filed by or on behalf of employees must show that at least 30 percent of the employees desire an election and that their employer refuses to acknowledge their representative.

ELECTIONS

Once a petition has been filed, the NLRB regional director must investigate it. The purpose of the investigation is to determine whether the agency has jurisdiction to conduct the election; if there is a sufficient showing of employee interest to justify an election; if a question of representation actually exists; whether the representative named in the petition is qualified; if there are any barriers to an election such as an existing contract or previous election; and the scope and composition of the appropriate bargaining unit.

An election may be held by agreement between the employer and individual or labor group claiming to represent the employees. In such a case, the parties determine who is eligible to vote and authorize the NLRB regional director to conduct the election. Employees are given a choice of one or more bargaining representatives, or they may choose not to have any representative at all. To be certified as the bargaining representative, an individual or labor organization must receive a majority of the votes cast.

If the parties are unable to reach an agreement, the NLRB must hold a hearing to resolve disputed issues and decide whether to direct a secret ballot election. Election details are left to the discretion of the regional director and are decided in accordance with established board rules and precedents. Elections generally are held thirty days after they are ordered.

Any party that believes a board election standard was not met may file an objection with the regional director who supervised the election. The director will then issue a ruling on the objection, which usually may be appealed to the NLRB for a decision. An election will be set aside if the board determines that one of the parties acted in such a way as to interfere with the employees' free expression of choice.

UNFAIR LABOR PRACTICES

To file an unfair labor practice complaint with the NLRB, a charge must be registered with the regional director for the district in which the practice occurred. Charges may be filed by employee representatives against an employer or vice versa. The regional director then investigates the charge to determine its validity. If the regional director agrees that an unfair labor practice was or is occurring, a complaint will be issued notifying the offending party that a hearing is to be held concerning the charges.

Every effort is made to resolve the dispute before the hearing date. If the decision reached between the participating parties is fair and acceptable to both parties and to the NLRB, the board may defer to that decision. If the arbitration procedure does not result in an acceptable agreement, the board resumes jurisdiction. Only one-third of the cases filed are found to have merit; another one-third are settled before the hearing stage.

Unsettled unfair labor practice cases are conducted before an NLRB administrative law judge in accordance with procedures that apply in U.S. District Court. The administrative law judge makes findings and recommendations to the board based on testimony taken at the hearing. Any party involved may appeal the administrative law judge's decision to the board. If the NLRB agrees that an unfair labor practice was or is occurring, it is authorized to issue a cease-and-desist order requiring the offending party to take appropriate affirmative action.

Any party to proceedings in an unfair labor practices case may appeal a board decision to the appropriate U.S. Court of Appeals. At this point, the general counsel represents the board and may not appeal its ruling. The court of appeals may enforce the order, remand it to the board for reconsideration, change it, or set it aside entirely.

Board cases provide more litigation in these courts than any other federal agency. The circuit courts are obligated to accept NLRB cases. Either party in an NLRB case may appeal proceedings to the Supreme Court.

If an employer or a union fails to comply with a board order, the board is empowered to petition the U.S. Court of Appeals for a court decree enforcing the order. Further failure to comply with the order can result in a fine or imprisonment for contempt of court.

Background

Until the 1930s federal and state laws favored management; union activity was discouraged by employers, who sometimes used force to prevent unions from coming into their plants or businesses. In spite of antiunion activity, the movement to organize employees into labor unions for self-protection gradually began to make progress.

During World War I, a National War Labor Board was created to establish policies covering labor relations. The board—operating from April 1918 until August 1919—served to protect the right of employees to bargain collectively and barred management from interfering in the process. Employers also were barred from discriminating against employees engaging in legitimate union activity.

The Railway Labor Act of 1926 required the railroads and their employees to exert every reasonable effort to make employment agreements through representatives chosen by each side, free from interference by the other. A board for mediation of disputes was established, and the act later was extended to cover airline employees. Employees covered by this act were exempted from the National Labor Relations Act.

The Norris-LaGuardia Act of 1932 restricted the federal courts' power to issue injunctions against unions engaged in peaceful strikes. It declared that workers had a right to organize and engage in collective bargaining. In addition, the act prohibited federal courts from enforcing "yellow dog" contracts in which employees promised not to join a union or to quit one if already a member.

LABOR AND THE NEW DEAL

The National Industrial Recovery Act (NIRA), symbolized by a blue eagle, took effect on June 16, 1933. The act sought to preserve employees' right to collective bargaining and to ensure that no employee would be required to join a union or refrain from joining a union as a condition of employment. Critics complained that employers were not complying with the codes and were refusing to recognize or meet with committees of employees to discuss grievances. The need for an agency to administer NIRA became apparent.

That administrative body, the National Labor Board (NLB), was created by President Franklin D. Roosevelt on Aug. 5, 1933, with Sen. Robert Wagner (D-NY, 1927–1949) as its first chair. In addition to the chair, the board consisted of three industry members and three labor members. To handle the volume of disputes brought before the NLB, twenty regional boards composed of industry and labor representatives were created to hold hearings wherever controversies arose. This procedure expedited cases as the parties involved were no longer required to travel to Washington to plead their cases.

However, flagrant defiance of the board, especially by large employers, soon became a serious obstacle to its effectiveness. Theoretically, the NLB could report violations to the U.S. attorney general for possible prosecution, but in reality the only sanction the board could apply was to take away from the offender the symbol of compliance, the agency's blue eagle. This lack of enforcement authority, coupled with a lack of explicit legislative authority, ultimately led to the board's demise.

NATIONAL LABOR RELATIONS ACT

The NLRB as it currently exists dates from the passage in 1935 of the National Labor Relations Act, commonly known as the Wagner Act, after its sponsor. The newly created board supplanted the earlier NLB that Wagner had chaired; the NLB had been declared unconstitutional by the Supreme Court. The Wagner Act went further in protecting the rights of workers than the Railway Labor

Act and the Norris-LaGuardia Act. It gave the board more enforcement tools, such as the power to issue subpoenas, cease-and-desist orders, and remedies. In addition to establishing the NLRB, the Wagner Act barred employers from engaging in five kinds of illegal labor practices. Prohibited were

- Interference with employees who exercise their right to organize (by threatening or even questioning employees about their union activities).
- Establishing or contributing to the support of a union (a so-called company, or sweetheart, union).
- Discrimination against actual or potential employees on the basis of union membership (by firing or refusing to hire union or nonunion members). This provision did not prohibit the closed shop agreement, under which an employer agrees to hire only union members, or the union shop agreement, in which employers agree to require all employees, once hired, to join a union.
- Discrimination against employees who testify or file charges under the act.
- Refusal to bargain collectively with employees' chosen union.

Thus protected from the sometimes violent antiunion practices of employers that characterized organizing activity before the Wagner Act became law, unions rapidly increased their membership, growing from 3.6 million in 1935 to more than 10 million by 1941. But the hard-won protection that unions had gained under the Wagner Act was not destined to remain unchallenged for long.

TAFT-HARTLEY ACT

The constitutionality of the Wagner Act was upheld by the Supreme Court in five challenges brought by employer groups. But the act was altered substantially by the Taft-Hartley amendments of 1947 and the Landrum-Griffin amendments of 1959. The 1947 Taft-Hartley Act was passed by Congress over President Harry S. Truman's veto and was bitterly opposed by organized labor groups. For the first time, a means to protect employers as well as employees was established. A detailed list of unfair labor activities that unions were forbidden to practice was added to the original legislation, along with a "free speech" amendment allowing employers to propagandize against unions before an NLRB election, if no threats or promises were made. After passage of Taft-Hartley, union election rates started dropping.

The Taft-Hartley Act still protected the employees' right to bargain collectively, join a union, strike, and petition the NLRB to hold a certification election to determine union representation, but it added their right to refrain from such activities and allowed a union to be sued for contract violations and held liable for damages resulting from illegal actions. Closed shops were forbidden but union shops remained legal. Union officials had to file financial reports and swear they were not communists. Strikes against the government were outlawed. Federal courts were empowered to issue injunctions against national emergency strikes, providing for an eighty-day cooling-off period.

Under other provisions of the act, the NLRB was reorganized to its present five-member form and the Federal Mediation and Conciliation Service and Joint Committee on Labor-Management Relations were established. The act also created an independent general counsel to remove the appearance of conflict between the board's dual roles as prosecutor and judge.

LANDRUM-GRIFFIN ACT

After a series of hearings on union corruption, Congress in 1959 passed a tough labor anticorruption bill entitled the Labor-Management Reporting and Disclosure (Landrum-Griffin) Act. The act required all unions to adopt constitutions and bylaws and to register them with the secretary of labor. In addition, unions were required to submit annual reports detailing assets, liabilities, revenue and sources, payments to union members exceeding $10,000, loans to union members and businesses, and other financial disbursements.

NLRB IN THE 1970s

In 1970 Congress passed the Postal Reorganization Act, which moved the U.S. Postal Service under NLRB jurisdiction. The National Labor Relations Act was further amended in 1974 to extend protection under the act to employees of all private health care institutions, whether or not they were profit-making enterprises.

Efforts on the part of organized labor to halt the gradual erosion by Congress and the courts of the protections granted to organized labor by the Wagner Act generally have failed. Many union leaders were optimistic that the tide would change under the administration of President Jimmy Carter. Carter was much more in tune with union interests than his Republican predecessors had been, but labor's agenda in Congress still fared poorly.

A big disappointment to labor was the 1977 defeat of a bill to legalize common-site picketing in the construction industry. A twenty-five-year battle had been waged by the construction trade unions to permit a form of secondary boycott by allowing unions with a grievance against one contractor to picket an entire construction site.

The following year, labor geared up to push a labor law reform bill that would have, among other things, simplified and expedited union certification elections. But a filibuster led by conservative senators defeated the measure. The bill was viewed suspiciously as an attempt to revive unions' lagging organizing successes. Nonetheless, critics in industry charged that Carter was attempting to bring about the reforms that Congress had refused to enact by appointing members to the board who were sympathetic toward labor's position.

Over the years several important Supreme Court cases have modified coverage for workers and employers under the National Labor Relations Act, as well as the scope of the NLRB's authority. In March 1979 the Court ruled that the NLRB did not have jurisdiction over teachers in church-affiliated schools; and in February 1980 the Court overturned a board decision that maintained faculty members at a private university had the right to bargain collectively under federal labor law. The Court held that if faculty members had authority over academic matters and institutional policies, they were, in effect, managers, and not entitled to the protections of the act if they organized a union.

NLRB IN THE 1980s

President Ronald Reagan came into office promising to rein in the government and reduce regulation. Nowhere did he have a better opportunity than at the NLRB. Attrition allowed him to appoint new board members who shared his conservative philosophy. Virtually all of his nominations to the NLRB were opposed by labor and supported by management.

During the Reagan administration, the NLRB handed down a number of decisions that reversed previous rulings. The board affirmed the right of employers to demand loyalty from supervisors, relaxed rules on management neutrality when rival unions compete to represent workers, and indicated it would refrain from involvement in minor workplace disputes.

In a ruling that was decried by labor groups, the board in January 1984, and again on remand in 1987, upheld the firing of a truck driver who refused to drive an unsafe truck. The NLRB said that while it was "outraged" by the action of Meyer Industries of Tennessee, the driver was not protected by the National Labor Relations Act because he did not act in concert with other employees. The ruling reversed the finding of an administrative law judge and also reversed a policy set in a 1975 case involving the Alleluia Cushion Co. In the earlier case, the board had said that an employee who acted to protect his own safety for good cause was engaged in "concerted activity" because safety involved all employees.

Also in 1984 the NLRB ruled that an employer could relocate work to another, nonunion plant to avoid the higher union labor costs, as long as relocation was not barred in the union contract. But three years later, the Supreme Court ruled in *Fall River Dyeing and Finishing Corp. v. NLRB* that in the case of a new owner, bargaining obligations carry over if they represent substantially the same operation and jobs.

According to an AFL-CIO study released in 1985, the NLRB had ruled in favor of employers in 60 percent of the cases it decided in 1984, more than double the promanagement decisions made by two previous boards examined by the study. The Reagan board's goal of keeping government out of the collective bargaining process had some success, as disgruntled labor officials sought other avenues, such as arbitration, to resolve disputes.

Some of the controversy surrounding the NLRB in the mid-1980s focused on a huge case backlog, a problem that has historically plagued the agency. A report issued by the Employment and Housing Subcommittee of the House Government Operations Committee following a series of hearings throughout the 1980s found the NLRB to be "in a crisis" because of slowness in decision making.

Unlike most federal regulatory agencies, the board has rarely initiated substantive rulemaking, which it considers a measure of last resort. Pressed by an ever-increasing number of cases in the health care field, the board in 1987 proposed to recognize eight appropriate bargaining units in acute care hospitals, replacing the old system of defining units on a case-by-case basis. In effect, the rule made it easier for hospital staff to organize unions. The hospital industry immediately challenged NLRB's authority to issue the rules, which were to have gone into effect in May 1989. A federal appeals court upheld the NLRB's authority in 1990, and, in a major victory for labor forces, a unanimous Supreme Court upheld the new NLRB rules in 1991.

In 1988 the Court in *Edward J. De Bartolo Corp. v. Florida Gulf Coast Building & Construction Trades Council* overturned a board decision that a union's peaceful distribution of handbills urging consumers to boycott secondary employers—not the employer with whom the union had a dispute—violated the act's secondary boycotting provision. The Court reasoned that unlike picketing, passing out handbills was not coercive and, therefore, not illegal. In 1992 however, the Court ruled in *Lechmere, Inc. v. National Labor Relations Board* that a store owner preventing union representatives who were not employees from giving out handbills in the parking lot in order to organize the labor force at his shop was acting within the scope of the National Labor Relations Act. The Court rejected the board's rule allowing the distribution of the handbills because the union had not proven that there was no other reasonable means of communicating with the employees.

In 1989 the board was rebuffed when it tried to force an employer to hire a union organizer. A federal appeals court ruled in *H. B. Zachry Co. v. NLRB* that the board "chose form over substance" in its attempt to prevent worker discrimination based on union sympathy. But workers won a major battle when the Court ruled in a 1994 case *ABF Freight Systems, Inc. v. National Labor Relations Board* that the NLRB was acting within its authority when it reinstated a fired worker, even though the worker had lied during the administrative proceedings in the case.

One controversial decision of the NLRB occurred in 1989 when the NLRB general counsel ruled that drug testing was a subject for collective bargaining and could not be unilaterally imposed. The board later overruled part of that order, saying that it applied only to current employees, leaving employers free to test job applicants.

NLRB IN THE 1990s

In 1990 President George H. W. Bush appointed James M. Stephens, former counsel of the Senate Labor and Human Resources Committee, to head the NLRB. Under Stephens's leadership, the board was credited by both labor and management with bringing a more balanced, impartial approach to board decisions.

By the 1990s there was a slight upturn in union victories in representational elections. In 1980 they won 3,498 elections, fewer than half of the 7,296 conducted by the NLRB, but by 1995 unions had won 1,468 of the 2,911 representation elections held, or a full 50 percent. Unions also did slightly better in the decertification elections. Whereas unions won only 24 percent of these elections in the early 1980s, between 1990 and 1995 they won 1,000 of the 3,278 decertification elections or roughly 31 percent.

Democrat Bill Clinton's election as president did not immediately produce positive results for labor. Unions and labor leaders suffered several major defeats in Congress and the courts. Notwithstanding vocal and intense labor opposition to the North American Free Trade Agreement (NAFTA), Congress approved the measure in 1993. The same battle was fought and lost against the General Agreement on Tariffs and Trade (GATT), which passed in 1994.

In 1992 the NLRB announced it would initiate rules to comply with the 1988 Supreme Court decision in *Beck v. Communications Workers of America*. The Court ruled that nonunion workers who had to pay fees to a union were entitled to withhold the portion of the fee that went to activities other than negotiating with the employer or administering the labor union. The nonunion workers did not have to pay the portion of the dues that went to lobbying, organizing new workers, supporting strikes elsewhere, or running community service activities. Though the NLRB had promulgated these rules since 1992, it was not until two 1995 cases, *California Saw and Knife Works* and *Weyerhaeuser*, that the board cited the *Beck* case in rendering decisions against organized labor.

In 1994 the Supreme Court struck down the NLRB's test to determine whether nurses should be considered supervisors. (Supervisors are not protected under the National Labor Relations Act.) In *National Labor Relations Board v. Health Care & Retirement Corporation of America*, the Court held that the NLRB's test—which relied on whether the nurse was acting for the benefit of the employer or the patient—was inconsistent with the act.

The outlook for organized labor took a decided turn for the better with the appointment of Stanford University law professor William B. Gould IV as NLRB chair, the first African American named to that position. Gould, who took office in March 1994 after an acrimonious nine-month Senate confirmation fight, made no secret of his belief that the board tilted too far toward management during the Reagan and George H. W. Bush administrations and that he was determined to correct that perceived bias.

When the Supreme Court sided with the NLRB in 1995 (*NLRB v. Town & Country Electric, Inc.*), ruling that union activists who take jobs in nonunion companies in order to organize from within cannot be fired for their prounion activities, Gould called the decision "a big victory," saying that this ruling was likely to increase such organizing efforts, which are called "salting" campaigns.

Gould also was openly opposed to the Teamwork for Employees and Management (TEAM) Act, which would have modified the 1935 National Labor Relations Act to make clear that U.S. businesses are permitted to form worker-management groups to address issues such as quality control, productivity, and safety. Organized labor strongly opposed the measure, fearing that it would lead to sham or "company" unions, while business argued such groups would provide for more flexibility and cooperation in the workplace. President Clinton vetoed the legislation in July 1996.

Gould was not invariably prounion, however. In January 1995 he cast the deciding vote in two rulings that union members had improperly picketed employers of other, nonunion workers. Gould cited a 1992 Court decision that employers are within their rights to bar nonemployee union members who attempt to organize workers on private property.

In 1995 the board issued a record number of injunctions ordering companies to reverse antiunion actions. This increase in injunctions signaled a major change in operations for the NLRB, which had previously depended far more on standard litigation to resolve cases.

Injunctions were part of a trend in labor relations that de-emphasized the strike in favor of legal action, thus increasing the importance of the NLRB in everyday collective bargaining. At the root of the trend was workers' fear of being permanently replaced if they were to go on strike. In 1994 labor failed to secure passage in Congress of a bill to prohibit the hiring of permanent replacements for some striking workers. The practice had been sanctioned by the Supreme Court in its 1938 decision *NLRB v. Mackay Radio and Telegraph Co.*, but it had not been widely practiced until the 1980s, when management seized on it as a method of breaking unions who were striking for better pay.

Because this practice is illegal if the strike is called because of unfair labor practices, it has become part of unions' defense against the threat of permanent replacement of workers to file complaints of unfair labor practices with the NLRB. For example, the United Auto Workers lodged more than 180 complaints of unfair labor practices during their seventeen-month-long strike against Caterpillar Inc. Caterpillar ultimately won the strike, however, by using managers, office workers, and skilled temporaries rather than permanent replacements to maintain production.

The NLRB's increasingly active role in labor disputes did not go unnoticed in Congress, where the pro-labor Democratic majority was replaced in 1995 by the more probusiness Republican one. Republican members accused Gould of being shamelessly prounion and claimed that he was unable to intervene fairly in labor disputes. Gould, for his part, argued that the Republicans and probusiness groups were angered by his willingness to apply laws designed to protect workers' rights. He also accused Republicans of directly interfering in specific NLRB cases, something members of Congress had never done before, he said.

The rhetoric heated up almost immediately after Republicans took charge of both houses of Congress in early 1995. That year Congress rescinded a recently proposed NLRB rule that would have allowed a company's employees at one workplace site to unionize, even if workers at its other nearby sites did not. In other words, even if workers did not vote to unionize company-wide, employees at one site could still form a union. Implementation of the rule was blocked in the fiscal 1996 spending bill funding the agency. This recision was renewed by Congress in the next two annual spending bills covering the NLRB. These bills also cut the agency's budget by 2 percent in fiscal 1996 and froze it the following two years.

Gould accused Congress of micromanaging and second-guessing the board. But on Feb. 18, 1998, over his objections, the entire board voted to withdraw the proposed regulation. Shortly afterward he announced that he would not seek another four-year term when his term as chair ended in August. In his place, Clinton nominated John C. Truesdale, a labor lawyer who joined the NLRB in 1948 and served in a variety of capacities. Uncontroversial, Truesdale promised to focus on reducing the agency's backlog of unresolved cases.

In spite of Gould's absence, the board continued to issue what many in the business community regarded as controversial, prounion decisions. One of the most highly publicized of these rulings came in August 1998 and involved a 1995 strike by workers at Detroit's two daily newspapers, the *News* and the *Free Press*. Claiming that the newspapers had not bargained in good faith, the NLRB ruled that both had to reinstate strikers, even if it meant laying off permanent replacements who had long ago been brought on to work at the papers. It also ordered the newspapers to pay strikers back wages, estimated at $80 million.

The agency also weighed in on the contentious issue of whether doctors should be able to unionize. Health maintenance organizations and private hospitals have long opposed collective bargaining for doctors, arguing that they are private contractors. While only about 5 percent of the nation's physicians belong to a union, their numbers grew dramatically during the 1990s. The NLRB gave a boost to these efforts in November 1999 by ruling that interns and residents at privately owned hospitals had the right to unionize.

NLRB IN THE 2000s

The agency raised its profile at the start of the new millennium with a potentially far-reaching decision, granting some temporary workers the right to organize and form unions. Under the ruling, handed down in September 2000, temporary employees were allowed to form a union if they were supervised by the company they were assigned to work for and if they did the same work as the firm's full-time employees. The decision had long-term implications, as more and more businesses relied on temporary workers to do jobs formerly held by permanent employees.

Two months later, the board weighed in on a similar issue, in this case involving graduate teaching assistants at private universities. Two decades earlier the NLRB had ruled that teaching assistants did not have the right to form a union. But a new case, brought by graduate students from New York University, prompted the board to reverse itself and allow unionization. The decision had a broad impact, fueling new labor organizing drives at scores of public and private universities around the country, including Columbia University, the University of Michigan, and the University of California.

It took Clinton's successor, Republican George W. Bush, a few years to fill vacancies on the board, giving it the traditional three-to-two split in favor of the administration's party. Bush also tapped Republican Robert J. Battista, at the end of 2002 to be the new chair. At his

Senate confirmation hearing, Battista, a well-respected labor lawyer from Detroit, said he wanted to reduce rancor and partisanship on the board.

President Bush began his term at odds with organized labor. A little more than a month after taking office, the president upset unions when he signed an executive order requiring federal contractors to post notices at the workplace informing their unionized employees of a 1988 Court decision giving them the right to withhold that portion of their dues that goes to political activities. At the same time, Bush signed another executive order reversing a policy that requires some federal contractors to be union shops. In February 2001, after labor talks between machinists and Northwest Airlines collapsed, the president moved to prohibit the workers temporarily from carrying out their threat to strike, arguing that it would unfairly hurt U.S. travelers.

During his first years in office, Bush continued to rankle labor groups. In October 2002 he invoked the Taft-Hartley Act to order longshore workers on the West Coast back to work, after a slowdown had prompted dockowners to shut down ports all along the coast. In January 2003 labor leaders were angered by the administration's refusal to allow 60,000 new federal airport safety screeners to unionize. The administration countered that collective bargaining agreements would make the new workforce much less flexible and could hamper the government's ability to change work assignments and implement other moves to respond quickly to terrorist threats.

With a new conservative board in place by the end of 2003, the NLRB moved to review and eventually reverse a number of controversial rulings that had been made under the more liberal, Clinton-appointed board. Conservatives and probusiness groups applauded this move, arguing that it was a much needed corrective after almost a decade of liberal activism at the agency.

Earlier NLRB decisions reversed included the 1999 Epilepsy Foundation decision, where the board held that nonunion workers could demand that a coworker be present during any questioning that could lead to disciplinary action or firing. In the past only union employees enjoyed these rights (referred to as "Weingarten rights"). In June 2004 the Epilepsy Foundation decision was reversed, taking away such rights for nonunion workers. Likewise, a 2000 decision that had allowed temporary workers to join a union representing permanent employees to create a single collective bargaining unit was reversed. Business groups and others felt that the decision had created great difficulties for firms, because temporary and permanent workers often had different needs and hence had difficulty bargaining together. The board also changed the NLRB ruling that gave graduate student teaching assistants the right to organize. Even though at many universities teaching assistants take on a substantial part of the teaching load, the board ruled that they were not "employees" under the National Labor Relations Act and hence not entitled to organize.

All of these decisions were handed down along a 3–2 party-line vote, with the two Democratic members strongly dissenting in each case. The board's turnaround

on these and other issues produced a storm of criticism from organized labor and their supporters, who said that the new decisions would hobble fundamental rights of workers. NLRB chair Battista defended the board's action. "All the cases that we've decided have been well reasoned," he told the *New York Times,* in a Jan. 2, 2005, article.

In June 2006 the board voted 4–1 to allow airport screeners who work for private contractors to unionize. The ruling affected a small percentage of screeners, most of whom were government employees, prohibited by Congress from unionizing. Indeed, only six airports use private contractors to screen luggage. Still the Transportation Security Administration, which was created in 2003 to oversee airport security, had argued that allowing private screeners to unionize could jeopardize its ability to perform vital national security functions. In issuing the ruling, however, the board majority argued that since Congress had not specifically prohibited private screeners from joining a union, they should be allowed to do so. By mid-2007 private screeners in only one of the six airports—Kansas City—had voted to unionize.

In October 2006 the board struck a blow to unions when it voted 3–2 along party lines, to broaden the definition of "supervisor" for purposes of determining whether someone can be in a union or not. Under the new rule, workers are considered supervisors if they have real supervisory authority—such as the power to assign coworkers to certain locations or duties. For instance, a nurse or teacher who helps determine where and how colleagues will perform their duties is, under this ruling, a supervisor. The change in definition is significant because supervisors are a part of management and cannot join a union. Labor supporters contend that as many as 8 million workers could lose the right to be in a union.

The following year began with a major victory for the board when in February 2007 a federal appeals court ruled that the nation's labor laws apply to more than 250,000 workers employed at Native American casinos. As a result, the court said, the NLRB has the authority to regulate labor conditions in the more than 400 casinos owned and operated by Native American tribes. Moreover, in the years that followed, workers at a number of Native American casinos have unionized. Most recently, in May 2011, bartenders and servers at a casino owned by the Mashantucket Pequot Tribal Nation voted to join the United Food and Commercial Workers Union.

In 2007 the board was involved in a number of high-profile actions against several well-established companies. In April the NLRB charged that coffee chain Starbucks was violating labor laws in its campaign against efforts to unionize stores in Manhattan. An official at Starbucks, which has built a reputation over the years as a model corporate citizen, denied the allegations, calling them "baseless." But the following year Starbucks faced additional complaints from the NLRB, involving employees who were fired, allegedly for promoting union activity. The two employees were eventually rehired and Starbucks agreed to settling with them and posting workers' rights notices in the stores.

Also in 2007, retail giant Walmart was subjected to a raft of bad publicity when Human Rights Watch issued a report providing the first comprehensive examination of recent NLRB rulings against the company. The report detailed NLRB findings of antiunion activity (from 2000 to 2005), including retaliation against workers who supported unionization and the illegal confiscation of prounion literature.

Probably the most important and illustrative case against Walmart involved its dealings with its meat-cutting employees. After meat-cutters in a Texas store voted to unionize in 2000, Walmart responded by closing the store's meat-cutting department and switching to a prepackaged meat supplied by other companies. In June 2003 the NLRB ruled that Walmart had illegally retaliated against its meat-cutters. It was not until March 2008, however, that a ruling by the 5th U.S. Circuit Court of Appeals upheld the NLRB's subsequent order that the company bargain with the union. Exactly one year after the court ruling, union representatives and Walmart management sat down at the negotiating table for the first time.

With Democrats winning back control of Congress in 2006, the labor movement expected to see its policy priorities put near the top of the legislative agenda. In March 2007 House Democrats took a big step toward obliging their labor allies by passing the Employee Free Choice Act. The bill would allow unionization if a majority of workers sign cards authorizing the formation of a union. While some companies, such as Cingular Wireless, had already voluntarily allowed the process, known as majority sign-up, employers still had the right to demand an election by secret ballot. The House-passed measure contained other labor-friendly provisions, including increased penalties for employers who discipline or fire workers because they are prounion. But the measure was opposed by President Bush and lacked sufficient support in the Senate, where it never came to a vote.

Later that year, labor suffered another defeat when the NLRB voted to give employees an opportunity to object to unionization and demand secret-ballot elections even if the company had agreed to a "card check" campaign. Card check allows workers to form a union by simply convincing a majority of employees in a workplace to sign prounion cards, instead of having to hold a secret-ballot election, as most employers insist on. Previous NLRB policy had banned decertification petitions for a "reasonable" amount of time if a company voluntarily agreed to a card check process. The new rule stipulated holding an NLRB secret-ballot election if employees opposed to unionization could get 30 percent of the eligible employees to sign a petition within forty-five days of union certification. While business groups hailed the ruling, unions argued that this would make it less likely that a company would voluntarily agree to a card check campaign.

In late 2007 the NLRB came under attack both by the public as well as Congress. In November hundreds of labor protestors decried a slew of NLRB decisions handed down two months earlier that would make it more difficult for unions to organize and easier for employees who do not support unions to protest and disband them. One decision that particularly troubled big labor involved the rejection of a petition put forth by six labor unions,

including the United Steelworkers, to require employers to bargain with small groups of union members even if they did not represent a majority of those in the workplace. The "mini-union" petition, described by NLRB and business leaders as "far-fetched," would force employers to recognize unions that would bargain only for their dues-paying members—so-called members-only unions.

Unions alleged that this decision and others were part of a "beat the clock" strategy by Bush appointees to render as many probusiness decisions as possible before the 2008 elections. The issue came to a head in December 2007, when House Democrats criticized NLRB board members during a hearing, accusing the Republican majority on the board of turning the nation's labor laws "inside out." Asked to defend this allegation, NLRB Chair Battista responded by saying that the board was focusing on what employees want, not on the demands of unions or companies.

That same month, the agency dealt another blow to labor unions when it ruled that employers have the right to ban employees from using e-mail for purposes of union organizing. The board ruled that so long as the employer (in this case the *Register Guard* newspaper in Eugene, OR) had a policy prohibiting the use of e-mail for nonwork-related functions, it could ban the sending of union-related messages. Six months after this December 2007 ruling, the issue surfaced again when two employees of online retailer ULoop.com were fired for posting a message on an online company forum urging workers to organize. Citing the *Register Guard* case, the NLRB dismissed the fired workers' complaints, ruling that employers could prohibit union-related material from online message boards.

At the beginning of 2008, Battista, who had served as the NLRB chair since 2002, was renominated by President Bush. The Senate was slow to act, however, and by May Battista asked the president to withdraw his nomination. In addition to Battista, the Democratic-controlled Senate also refused to confirm Gerald Morales and Dennis Walsh, the other two Bush NLRB nominees, leaving the board to operate with only two of its five members. A spokeswoman for the NLRB argued that in spite of the vacancies, the board was moving forward with its work.

NLRB IN THE 2010s

Soon after taking office in January 2009 President Barack Obama took a number of steps aimed at resolving vacancies on the agency's board, which had operated with only two members since 2008. First, Obama designated Wilma B. Liebman, who had been serving on the board since 1997, to be the NLRB chair. For the board's remaining three vacancies Obama nominated Craig Becker, Mark Gaston Pearce, and Brian Hayes. But all three nominations were held up, largely because of concern over Becker by Senate Republicans, who claimed that the former counsel for the Service Employees International Union was too prolabor. In particular, GOP lawmakers were troubled by an article the Chicago-based attorney had written in the 1990s, arguing that businesses should be barred from campaigning when unions are trying to organize their workers. They put a hold on Becker's nomination and urged the president to find a replacement. But on March 27, 2010, the president put Becker on the board as a recess appointment, thus circumventing the need for Senate confirmation.

On June 22, 2010, just months after the Becker appointment, the less controversial Pearce and Hayes were confirmed by the Senate. Pearce had previously worked for the agency as an attorney and had held several labor-relations jobs with the New York State government. Hayes, the sole Republican in the trio of new members, had worked as a labor lawyer in private practice and, more recently, as the labor policy director on the GOP staff of the Senate Committee on Health, Education, Labor, and Pensions. A mere two months after Becker, Pearce, and Hayes were sworn in, the term ended of the board's other Republican, Peter C. Schaumber, dropping the total number of board members from five to four.

At about the same time the Supreme Court, on June 17, 2010, dealt the agency a serious blow when it ruled that many decisions the NLRB had made over more than two years were invalid because the agency's board had consisted of only two members during this period. Both parties shared blame for the vacancies that left the board understaffed. When Democrats took control of Congress in 2006, they objected to then President Bush's labor policies and refused to confirm his nominees. This situation continued under Obama, when Republicans turned around and blocked one of the new president's nominees, complaining that he was biased in favor of union interests. Recognizing that they were soon going to be shorthanded, the then four member board, at the end of 2007, voted to delegate authority to the reduced board to keep making progress on cases.

By the time President Obama brought the board back to full strength, the two-member board, composed of Liebman, a Democrat, and Schaumber, a Republican, issued rulings on nearly 600, mostly routine, cases on which they could agree. Left undecided were approximately 60 cases in which they had deadlocked and another 60 that they had set aside because they might set a legal precedent. "We thought we were doing the right thing to keep the agency running," Liebman said. But the Court did not see it that way, ruling that a two-person board simply did not meet the standards for due process necessary to render decisions.

Just days after the Court decision, President Obama appointed three new members to the board—Democrats Craig Becker and Mark Pearce and Republican Brian Lewis. Obama used his power to make recess appointments to fill the board slots. While Republicans in Congress expressed satisfaction with Pearce and Lewis, they protested the appointment of Becker, a top lawyer with the Service Employees International Union, charging that he was much too hostile to business. But the White House defended Becker's appointment and refused to reconsider it.

Now at full strength, the agency began to take more concrete action. An important early step occurred in June 2011, when the board proposed new rules that would speed up union elections. Unions had long complained that it took too long after a petition was filed for a secret-ballot election

to take place. They claimed that the process gave management too much time to mount antiunion campaigns.

A few months later, in December, the NLRB ruled that companies must post notices to let their workers know of their right to organize under federal law. This was the first time since Congress had passed the National Labor Relations Act in 1935 that the labor board had required employers to post notices about employees' rights under the act. The rules also require employers to postpone any legal challenges to elections until after workers vote.

Business groups reacted negatively to the ruling, questioning whether the agency was more concerned with stemming the decline in union membership (now at just 7.2 percent of the workforce) than communicating to workers about their rights. Randel K. Johnson, senior vice president for labor policy at the United States Chamber of Commerce, went so far as to question whether the labor board had the statutory authority to impose such posting requirements and whether the new requirements would provide a "balanced view"—that is, inform employees of *all* of their rights, including the right not to join a union.

But by May 2012, the issue was moot. A federal judge struck down the rules on a technicality, saying that the board had not followed proper voting procedures when it approved them. Judge James E. Boasberg ruled that the board lacked a quorum when it voted on the rules. Although the board had the three members required for a quorum when it approved the rules in December, one of the members, Brian Hayes, did not formally vote on the rules. Thus, under the strict requirements of the law, a quorum was not present when the voting occurred.

During President Obama's first two years in office, the labor-supported Employee Free Choice bill, also called card check, did not fare well in Congress. Employers and other probusiness advocates contended that eliminating the secret ballot was undemocratic and would expose workers to union scare tactics. Unions countered that check cards would allow workers to express their preferences free of employer intimidation and would prevent employer stalling during bargaining. During his 2008 campaign, Obama favored card check, but the issue was never a priority for the new president—who decided to use his political capital to push for an overhaul of the nation's health care system in 2010. As a result, Democratic leaders in both houses of Congress, particularly the Senate, held off on trying to bring the legislation to a vote. The 2010 elections—with the Republican takeover of the House and gains in the Senate—spelled the effective end of any chance for passage of card check in either house of Congress. On August 27, 2011, President Obama named Mark G. Pearce as new chairman of the NLRB.

Meanwhile, the agency found itself in the middle of a number of tough, high-profile labor disputes, most notably a battle between the National Football League (NFL) team owners and the players' union. After roughly two years of unsuccessful negotiations over how to divide the league's projected $9.3 billion in annual revenue, team owners locked out the players in early March 2011, ending all athletic training and imperiling the 2011 football season. In response, the players' union decertified itself.

By disbanding their union, the players were no longer bound by an agreement that prohibited them from suing the owners, which they did just days after decertification. The owners then filed a complaint with the NLRB, alleging that by decertifying the union, the players were no longer bargaining in good faith.

The owners argued in court that the suit should be dismissed and that the NLRB was the proper venue for determining who was in the wrong. But in April 2011, Federal District Court Judge Susan Nelson ignored the owners' request and issued an injunction ordering them to end the lockout. In her ruling, Nelson pointed out that the NLRB could take years to come to a final decision, depriving the players of their livelihoods and football fans of one or more seasons of play. But on July 8, 2011, a federal appeals court reversed this decision, ruling that the owners' lockout of players could continue. The timing of the ruling seemed to catalyze and polarize both sides in the negotiating process. Now, with the lockout upheld, owners demanded more concessions from players, while some on the players' side wanted to press their case even harder.

But clearer heads prevailed, and two weeks later the league's owners approved a 10-year collective bargaining agreement and conditionally lifted the four-month lockout. The deal, which had been negotiated with union representatives and was later approved by the newly recertified players' union, split the league's annual revenues almost evenly, with players collectively receiving just less than a 50 percent share. In the end, the sport lost only one preseason game.

While the NFL negotiations were still going on, another dispute between professional sports team owners and players exploded into conflict. On May 24, 2011, the union representing basketball players filed a complaint with the board against the National Basketball Association (NBA), charging team owners with "grossly regressive contract demands," failing to provide the union with critical financial data and with repeatedly threatening players with a lockout in the absence of a new collective bargaining agreement. It would be the first of numerous legal salvos. The labor agreement, in place since 2005, was set to expire in June. In spite of nearly two years of negotiations on a new labor deal, the deadline for adopting a new collective bargaining agreement was fast approaching.

As with the NFL labor dispute, the only alternative to lockout was for the union to decertify. This would open the door for players to sue the league on antitrust grounds. Also similar to the NFL dispute was the cause of the impasse: how to fairly divide the financial pie. Despite annual revenues of about $3.8 billion, NBA league officials claimed that the league was losing more than $300 million a year, to 22 of 30 teams losing money. They wanted a complete overhaul of the system used to calculate players' salaries, including a 38 percent rollback in player pay—amounting to an $800 million cut. They also demanded that each team's payroll be reduced from $58 million to $45 million. The players union, which disputed the NBA's loss figures, offered a counterproposal that for the most part retained the existing system but included an offer to reduce the players' 57 percent guarantee of league revenues.

In August 2011, the league filed its own complaint with the board, saying that the union's threat to decertify and its complaint challenging the legality of the lockout were evidence "that the Players Association has failed to bargain in good faith." Four months later, in November, the players' union petitioned the NLRB for permission to formally disband, declaring that once the players were no longer unionized they would take their labor standoff into federal court. Just prior to this, the league's commissioner, David Stern, gave the players an ultimatum: either accept the current offer or see it withdrawn and replaced with something far less palatable.

Even as both sides were escalating the conflict, there also was outside pressure for the two sides to quickly settle their differences in time to begin a 66-game season on Christmas Day, traditionally a showcase for the league. On November 26, both sides came together and, after a 15-hour negotiating session, reached a handshake deal for a new collective bargaining agreement, narrowly eluding the embarrassment of becoming the second North American sports league in history to cancel an entire season due to a labor dispute. The deal allowed players to receive a 49 percent to 51 percent "band" of basketball related income, which would be linked to league profitability.

Not every high-profile case involving the NLRB was sports related. On April 20, 2011, the board sued airplane maker Boeing, alleging that a recent decision to put a factory in Charleston, SC, amounted to unlawful retaliation against the company's unions. In 2009, Boeing decided that it needed to have two assembly lines to build its popular 787 Dreamliner aircraft. One line was already being readied in Everett, WA, where the company builds most of its planes with union labor. But instead of adding a second line in Everett, Boeing decided to set up an assembly plant in Charleston, using nonunion labor.

After Boeing announced the move to Charleston, the company's chapter of the International Association of Machinists and Aerospace Workers (IAM) filed a complaint, alleging that the decision to move was aimed at punishing Boeing's unions. After a lengthy investigation, the NLRB agreed, finding that the move was motivated by "a desire to retaliate for past strikes and to chill further strike activity."

Boeing vowed to fight the suit, arguing that the NLRB had become radically prolabor, to the point of telling manufacturers where to build its factories. South Carolina—which is a "right to work" state—was also fighting the suit, arguing that the agency was trying to deprive it of its right to attract new businesses to the state. In September 2011, Congress became involved, with the House passing a Republican-backed bill that would prohibit the board from pursuing its case. Calling it the "Protecting Jobs from Government Interference Act," Republicans asserted that the board was overreaching its authority by dictating where companies can locate their operations. In addition, they said, the move against Boeing was causing some foreign companies to reconsider opening operations in the United States.

But before the case could go to trial, it was resolved. In December 2011, Boeing and the union representing its machinists agreed to a comprehensive labor agreement that raised wages, provided unusual job security provisions, and expanded jet production in the Puget Sound area of Washington state. As part of the deal, the union urged the board to drop the case and allow the nonunion factory in South Carolina to remain.

The Boeing case involved workers and management in a traditional industry grappling with a traditional labor union. But the agency vaulted into some new areas during this period as well, tackling its first case involving Facebook and the workplace implications of social media. The groundbreaking case involved the firing of an employee at American Medical Response (AMR) of Connecticut, an ambulance company. An employee of AMR—Dawnmarie Souza—posted Facebook comments from her home computer criticizing her supervisor. Earlier in the day, the supervisor reprimanded Souza when a customer complained about her work. The company argued that Souza was in violation of a policy that bars employees from negatively depicting the company. The company also asserted she was fired over multiple serious complaints about her behavior.

Near the end of 2010, the NLRB sued the company, asserting that employers were breaking the law when they disciplined workers who posted criticisms on social networking websites and that such comments are protected speech under federal labor laws, which allow workers to discuss wages, hours, and working conditions with coworkers. In February 2011, the company agreed to change its blogging and Internet policies and arrived at a private settlement with Souza.

The early months of 2011 also saw the reemergence of the card check controversy. In April the agency announced that it would sue the state of Arizona to nullify a recently approved constitutional amendment prohibiting workers from choosing to unionize through the card check process. Supporters of the amendment had pushed for its adoption after becoming concerned early in the Obama administration that the president and congressional Democrats would enact federal legislation mandating the right to card check.

In its suit, the NLRB contended that the amendment, and others like it adopted by South Carolina and a number of other states, conflicts with existing federal labor law, which allows employees to express a desire to form a union using card check, although management can choose to ignore this and require a secret-ballot election. Arizona and the other states defend the amendments in question, insisting that the opportunity to vote by secret ballot—uninfluenced by union bosses—is a fundamental employee right. Barring some agreement between the states and the agency, a trial in the Arizona case is expected to occur by early 2012.

Meanwhile, two board members left the agency. First to go was long-standing board member and chair Wilma B. Liebman, whose term expired in August 2011. The then 61-year-old Liebman, who was first appointed to the board by President Bill Clinton in 1997, asked not to be reappointed. Her departure left the board with three members. But just five months later (in December), the board dropped to two members when Craig Becker resigned to take a position as co-general counsel of the A.F.L.C.I.O.

Recognizing that Becker's departure left the board without a quorum, Obama once again made three recess appointments. In January 2012, the president appointed Democrats Sharon Block and Richard Griffin and Republican Terence Flynn. While the appointments were praised by Obama's union allies, they were harshly criticized by Republicans. Indeed, GOP members of the Senate said they would hold up nominees for other agencies to protest this and other recess appointments.

But troubles with President Obama's appointments to the board were only just beginning. In September 2012, Senate Republicans filed a friend-of-the-court brief challenging the president's "recess" appointments to the board, arguing that he had made these appointments while the Senate was still in session. The brief was filed as part of an existing case, *Noel Canning v. NLRB,* in which a Pepsi-Cola bottler disputed a board ruling that it had violated federal labor laws, arguing that the three Obama appointments were invalid and that the board had, therefore, lacked a quorum to take any action against it.

Meanwhile, in August 2013 the Senate approved four new members to the board: Democrats Nancy Schiffer and Kent Y. Hirozawa, and Republicans Philip A. Miscimarra and Harry I. Johnson III. In addition, Democrat Mark G. Pearce, who had been a board member since 2010 and chairman since 2011, was approved for a full term as chairman.

The approvals were part of broader deal whereby Senate Republicans agreed to stop stalling some Obama administration nominations in exchange for Senate Democrats agreeing not to change the chamber's rules allowing filibusters on nominations—the so-called nuclear option. The Senate action finally brought the board up to its full complement of five.

Even though these new board members replaced the recess appointees at the center of the *Noel Canning* case, the litigation continued, in large part because the Senate's action did not resolve fundamental dispute over when the president could and could not make recess appointments. There also remained a question about whether NLRB decisions made with the help of the recess appointees were valid.

In June 2014 the Supreme Court finally weighed in, siding with Senate Republicans and Pepsi, unanimously ruling that by appointing the board members when he did, the president had exceeded his constitutional authority. "The Senate is in session when it says it is," said Justice Stephen G. Breyer, writing for the majority.

The ruling invalidated more than 300 decisions the board had made between January 2012 and August 2013, the time between when the recess appointees took office and when they were replaced by the new members. While many of these decisions were appealed and remain unresolved, many others were simply dropped since the parties did not expect the new board to rule differently than the older one.

While the recess appointments question was still working its way through the courts, the agency found itself embroiled in another legal dispute. The question this time centered on whether the NLRB could require employers to put up posters in the workplace informing workers of their right to form a union. Pro-business groups argued that these posters were blatantly prounion and thus the government was violating employers' free speech rights by requiring them to be displayed.

In May and June of 2013 two federal appeals courts (the DC and 4th Circuits) in two separate but related cases agreed with the business groups and struck down the rule. The NLRB could have appealed these decisions to the Supreme Court. But in January 2014 the agency issued a statement saying it would not seek the high court's review and would let the appeals courts' decisions stand.

In December 2013 yet another federal appeals court, the Fifth Circuit, handed the agency yet another defeat. In this case, the court overturned an earlier board decision invalidating agreements between employers and employees in which workers waive their right to file a class action lawsuit in case of future workplace grievances. The NLRB had earlier ruled that such agreements, even if voluntary, violate the National Labor Relations Act because they limit workers' right to pursue collective action against an employer.

But while the string of legal defeats was a setback for the NLRB, they did not dampen the board's enthusiasm to act. Indeed, just weeks after 2014 began, the board filed a complaint against the nation's largest private employer, the retailer Walmart. The complaint centered on what the agency alleged were numerous incidents in which Walmart fired, disciplined, or threatened 60 employees (19 of whom were fired) in 13 states for engaging in legal activities to protest working conditions or wage levels. Walmart countered that the employees were disciplined because they had walked away from their jobs to engage in these activities when they were supposed to be working, and not because they were protesting company policies.

While most aspects of the complaint are still awaiting legal resolution, an NLRB judge in December 2014 handed an early victory to the agency when it ruled that employees in two California Walmart stores had been illegally disciplined by the company. Walmart has vowed to appeal the decision.

Another big corporation that became embroiled in a labor dispute in 2014 was German automaker Volkswagen (VW). But unlike Walmart VW was not accused of violating workers' rights. In fact, the car company sided with the United Auto Workers (UAW) and supported its efforts to unionize the company's huge car assembly plant in Chattanooga, Tennessee.

Opposing the union and VW were state political leaders, including Gov. Bill Haslam and Republican Senator Bob Corker. Haslam, Corker, and others argued that if the Chattanooga plant unionized it would jeopardize the state's reputation as a lower cost haven for manufacturers and lead to less job creation in the future. In February 2014, on the morning of the scheduled vote, Corker created substantial controversy when he stated that VW officials had told him that if the workers at the planted voted *not* to unionize, the company would build its new SUV at the plant, rather than at a VW facility in Mexico, and create up to 1,500 new jobs. Although VW denied making such a promise to Corker, the election went forward and the workers voted against unionizing.

The UAW initially moved to have the NLRB declare the election void and order a new vote, arguing that comments by Corker and others had improperly scared the workers into voting against unionizing. But in late April, the union withdrew its complaint, stating that a long drawn out fight for a new election would not be in the best interests of the workers or the company. The next day, the NLRB certified the election, preventing the union from trying to organize workers in the plant for one year.

Current Issues

One of the biggest and most controversial issues facing the board concerns how to define who is and who is not an employer for purposes of collective bargaining. At the center of this debate is fast food giant McDonald's, which has recently been the target of the Service Employees International Union and labor activist groups hoping to force the company to pay workers in its restaurants a minimum wage of $15 per hour.

McDonald's has resisted these efforts, arguing that the company does not formally employ these workers because each restaurant is an independently owned franchise. As a result, the company says, it is not responsible for employment issues at the thousands of McDonald's restaurants nationwide.

But in December 2014 the board found that McDonald's controls virtually every important aspect of its franchisees' businesses. The board is now trying to decide whether this finding makes the company a "joint employer," along with each franchise owner, and thus a potential target for unions hoping to organize all workers employed at McDonald's restaurants.

If the NLRB ultimately rules that McDonald's is an "employer," it would almost certainly impact other companies such as restaurants and retailers that use the franchise business model. It also could affect firms that rely on temporary staffing companies to provide much of their workforce. These businesses, as well as organizations representing franchisees, have been lobbying Congress, arguing that if the NLRB broadly defines "employer" it would reduce the independence of thousands of small businesses and force them to abide by agreements negotiated between labor unions and large corporations.

Also on the agency's agenda is an upcoming ruling on whether graduate students at universities are de facto employees who have the right to unionize and collectively bargain. The issue has come before the board before, most recently in 2004 when the then Republican majority ruled that universities could ban graduate student unions.

The students contend that they handle much of the teaching load at universities, often for meager compensation. Universities counter that grad students often receive free tuition and stipends in exchange for their work as teaching assistants. A decision on the issue is expected in the second half of 2015.

Meanwhile, in March both houses of the Republican-controlled Congress passed legislation that overturned a board rule allowing faster, more streamlined union elections. The rule could reduce the average time it takes to conduct an election campaign from 38 days to 11 days.

Critics say the rule would allow unions to spring elections on unsuspecting employers, giving them little time to make the case against unionizing to their workers. But, at the end of March, President Obama vetoed the measure, arguing that the NLRB rule would allow employers less to time to coerce and pressure workers and would enhance employees' ability to freely choose whether to form a union or not. Given that the measure passed in both houses without the two-thirds support needed to override Obama's veto, the issue is likely dead until at least after the 2016 election.

■ AGENCY ORGANIZATION

Biographies

MARK G. PEARCE, CHAIR

Appointment: Sworn in April 7, 2010, following a recess appointment by President Barack Obama; confirmed by the Senate on June 22, 2010, to a term expiring August 27, 2013. Sworn in for a second term expiring August 27, 2018.

Born: Brooklyn, N.Y.

Education: Cornell University, B.A. 1975; State University of New York at Buffalo, J.D. 1978.

Political Affiliation: Democrat.

Previous Career: Before joining the board, Pearce served as a member of the New York State Industrial Board of Appeals; owner of Creighton, Pearce, Johnson & Giroux; and district trial specialist at NLRB.

KENT Y. HIROZAWA, BOARD MEMBER

Appointment: Sworn in on August 5, 2013, to a term expiring August 27, 2016.

Education: Yale University B.A.; New York University School of Law, J.D.

Political Affiliation: Democrat.

Previous Career: Hirozawa served as chief counsel to National Labor Relations Board Chairman Mark Gaston Pearce from April 2010 until he was sworn in as a board member. Prior, Hirozawa was a field attorney in Region 2 of the board after clerking in the U.S. Court of Appeals for the Second Circuit. Prior to returning to the board, he represented unions, workers, and employee benefit funds for more than twenty years as a member of the New York City law firm of Gladstein, Reif & Meginniss LLP.

PHILIP A. MISCIMARRA, BOARD MEMBER

Appointment: Sworn in on August 7, 2013, to a term expiring Sept. 16, 2017.

Education: Duquesne University, B.A.; University of Pennsylvania's Wharton Business School, M.A.; University of Pennsylvania Law School, J.D.

Political Affiliation: Republican.

Previous Career: Miscimarra previously was a labor and employment law partner with Morgan Lewis & Bockius LLP in Chicago, and he was a senior fellow in the Center for Human Resources at the University of Pennsylvania's Wharton Business School. He is the author or co-author of several books involving labor law issues. Before joining Morgan Lewis in 2005, Miscimarra was a labor and employment attorney with Seyfarth Shaw LLP in Chicago from 1987–2005; Murphy Smith & Polk PC from 1986–87; and Reed Smith Shaw & McClay from 1982–1986.

National Labor Relations Board

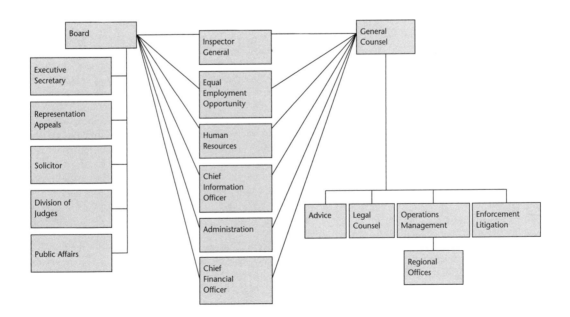

HARRY I. JOHNSON III, BOARD MEMBER

Appointment: Sworn in on August 12, 2013, to a term expiring August 27, 2015.

Education: Johns Hopkins University, B.A.; Tufts University's Fletcher School of Law, MALD; Harvard Law School, J.D.

Political Affiliation: Republican.

Previous Career: Johnson was a partner with law firm Arent Fox LLP, a position he held since 2010. Previously, Johnson worked at the Jones Day law firm as a partner from 2006 to 2010 and as an associate from 1994 to 2005.

LAUREN MCFERRAN, BOARD MEMBER

Appointment: Sworn in on December 17, 2014. Confirmed by the Senate on December 8, 2014, to a term expiring Dec. 17, 2019.

Education: Rice University, B.A.; Yale Law School, J.D.

Political Affiliation: Democrat.

Previous Ceer: McFerran served as chief labor counsel for the Senate Committee on Health, Education, Labor, and Pensions and had also served the committee as deputy staff director. She began on the HELP Committee as senior labor counsel for Senator Ted Kennedy and Senator Tom Harkin in 2005 and served in that capacity until 2010. Prior, McFerran was an associate at Bredhoff & Kaiser, P.L.L.C. from 2002 to 2005. She served as a law clerk for Chief Judge Carolyn Dineen King on the United States Court of Appeals for the Fifth Circuit from 2001 to 2002.

Headquarters and Divisions

BOARD

The NLRB has two principal functions under the National Labor Relations Act, as amended: (1) preventing statutorily defined unfair labor practices on the part of employers and labor organizations or their agents; and (2) conducting secret-ballot elections among employees in appropriate collective bargaining units to determine whether they desire to be represented by a labor organization.

The NLRB is further responsible for conducting secret-ballot elections among employees who have been covered by a union shop agreement, when requested by 30 percent of the employees, to determine whether they wish to revoke their union's authority to make such agreements; determining, in cases involving jurisdictional disputes, which of the competing groups of workers is entitled to perform the work involved; and conducting secret-ballot elections among employees concerning the final settlement offers of employers in national emergency labor disputes.

The board exercises full and final authority over the Office of the Solicitor, Office of the Inspector General, Office of Representation Appeals, and Office of Public Affairs. The board appoints administrative law judges and exercises authority over the Division of Administrative Law Judges subject to the Administrative Procedures Provisions of Title 5, U.S. Code, and the National Labor Relations Act, as amended. Each board member supervises staff counsel, each staff being under the immediate supervision of the chief counsel of the respective board member.

Along with the general counsel, the board approves the budget, opens new offices, and appoints the director of administration, regional directors, and officers-in-charge.

Chair
Mark G. Pearce . . . . (202) 273–1070
    Fax. . . . . (202) 273–4270
Board Members
Kent Y. Hirozawa. . . . . (202) 273–1740
Harry I. Johnson III . . . . (202) 273–1770
Lauren McFerran. . . . . (202) 273–1700
Philip A. Miscimarra . . . . (202) 273–1790
Board Staff
Chief Counsel to the Chair
Ellen Dichner. . . . . (202) 273–1070
Chief Counsel to Member Hirozawa
Peter Winkler. . . . . (202) 273–1740
Chief Counsel to Member Johnson
James Murphy . . . . (202) 273–1770
Chief Counsel to Member McFerran
Vacant
Chief Counsel to Member Miscimarra
Peter Carlton . . . . (202) 273–1790

OFFICE OF THE EXECUTIVE SECRETARY

Serves as administrative manager of the board's judicial affairs. Assigns cases to individual board members to initiate the judicial process; represents the board in dealing with parties to cases; receives, dockets, and acknowledges formal documents filed with the board; issues and serves board decisions and orders on the parties to all cases; and certifies copies of all documents that are part of the board's files or records.

Advises the board on interlocutory appeals and requests for special permission to appeal and advises regional offices about procedural matters in representation cases. Communicates on behalf of the board with employees, employers, labor organizations, Congress, other agencies, and the public. Handles FOIA requests that deal with the NLRB board.

Executive Secretary
Gary Shinners . . . . (202) 273–3737
Docket Order and Issuance Section
Bertha Dinkins . . . . (202) 273–1956
General Office Information and
    Services. . . . . (202) 273–1940

OFFICE OF CHIEF INFORMATION OFFICER

See Information Sources, below.

OFFICE OF EQUAL EMPLOYMENT OPPORTUNITY

Processes all complaints of alleged discrimination within the NLRB. Carries out its responsibilities under Title VII of the Civil Rights Act of 1964, the Rehabilitation Act of 1973, the Equal Pay Act of 1963, the Age Discrimination in Employment Act of 1967, and the Civil Rights Act of 1991.

Also monitors the agency's affirmative action employment plan and the agency's federal equal opportunity recruitment program plan. Offers advice and assistance to all managers, supervisors, and employees on EEO matters and issues.

Director

  Brenda V. Harris . . . . (202) 273–3891

OFFICE OF THE GENERAL COUNSEL

Supervises the agency's attorneys, regional offices, and headquarters divisions and offices (except those under the direct supervision of the board: the administrative law judges, staff counsel to board members, executive secretary, and solicitor). Investigates charges, issues complaints, and prosecutes those complaints before the board. On behalf of the board, prosecutes injunction proceedings; handles U.S. Court of Appeals proceedings, miscellaneous litigation, and efforts to obtain compliance with board orders. Together with the members of the board, the general counsel determines budget requests, appoints agency personnel, and administers the equal employment opportunity program. The general counsel is independent from the board.

General Counsel

  Richard F. Griffin Jr. . . . . (202) 273–3700

Deputy General Counsel

  Jennifer Abruzzo . . . . (202) 273–3700

OFFICE OF HUMAN RESOURCES

Provides employees, through a training program, with the skills that will benefit them in performing the mission of the NLRB.

Director

  Angela Wilson . . . . (202) 273–3801

OFFICE OF THE INSPECTOR GENERAL

Investigates allegations of waste, fraud, abuse, and mismanagement in federal programs and conducts audits of internal agency matters. Also recommends steps to increase the NLRB's effectiveness, efficiency, and integrity. Because focus is on matters internal to NLRB, not engaged in investigations relating to unfair labor practice or matters concerning union representation.

Inspector General

  David P. Berry . . . . (202) 273–1960

    1015 Half St. S.E. Washington, DC 20570

  IG hotline . . . . (800) 736–2983

    E-mail: OIGHOTLINE@nlrb.gov

Assistant Inspector General for Investigations

  Vacant 202–273–1965

Assistant Inspector General for Audits

  Robert Brennan . . . . (202) 273–1965

OFFICE OF PUBLIC AFFAIRS

See Information Sources, below.

OFFICE OF REPRESENTATION APPEALS

Handles appeals by parties of decisions issued by NLRB regional directors in representation cases.

Director

  Vacant . . . . (202) 273–1975

  Fax . . . . (202) 273–1962

OFFICE OF THE SOLICITOR

Advises the board on questions of law and procedure, on intervention in court proceedings to protect the board's jurisdiction, on the board's exercise of its discretion regarding injunctive relief, and on enforcement of board orders. Makes recommendations to the board on summary judgments, advisory opinions concerning the board's jurisdiction, and formal settlement proposals. Also advises the board on internal labor relations matters. Serves as the board's liaison to Congress, the White House, state officials, other agencies, and members of the bar.

Solicitor

  William B. Cowen . . . . (202) 273–2910

DIVISION OF ADMINISTRATION

Directs the administrative management functions of the agency. Responsible for financial management functions; personnel management; mail, graphic, printing, editorial, and transportation services; library and records management; procurement; facilities and communications management; and an occupational health and safety program.

Director

  Caroline Krewson . . . . (202) 273–3890

DIVISION OF ADVICE

Handles circuit court appeals cases from district courts; advises the general counsel in appeal and contempt matters; assists in injunction litigation under special circumstances; and makes recommendations for the general counsel to the board on handling requests for injunction.

The Regional Advice Branch advises the general counsel and regional directors on special issues of law and policy and performs legal research. This branch prepares the general counsel's quarterly reports and guideline memoranda on important legal issues for regional directors and the public.

The Research and Policy Planning Branch analyzes, digests, and indexes all board and related court decisions for publication and internal agency use. This branch is responsible for legal information retrieval systems. It also coordinates compliance with the Freedom of Information Act.

Associate General Counsel

  Barry J. Kearney. . . . . (202) 273–3800

    Fax . . . . (202) 273–4275

Injunction Litigation

  Elinor Merberg . . . . (202) 273–3833

Regional Advice Branch

  Jayme Sophir . . . . (202) 273–3837

Research and Policy Planning Branch

  Jacqueline A. Young . . . . (202) 273–3825

DIVISION OF ENFORCEMENT LITIGATION

Represents the agency in litigation before the U.S. Supreme Court, U.S. Court of Appeals, and federal district courts, including contempt litigation and enforcement and review of board decisions.

The division's Office of Appeals reviews appeals of refusals by regional directors to issue complaints in unfair labor practice cases and on occasion hears informal supportive or opposing oral presentations by counsel or other representatives of parties involved in such litigation, before recommending the action to be taken by the general counsel. The office also advises the general counsel on further legal action in appeals cases stemming from regional directors' refusals to provide documents under the Freedom of Information Act.

Associate General Counsel

John H. Ferguson . . . . (202) 273–2950

Fax. . . . . (202) 273–4244

Appeals

Deborah Yaffe . . . . (202) 273–3760

Appellate and Supreme Court Litigation

Linda F. Dreeben . . . . (202) 273–2960

Contempt Litigation and Compliance

Barbara O'Neill . . . . (202) 273–3739

Special Litigation

Abby Simms. . . . . (202) 273–2930

DIVISION OF JUDGES

Conducts all hearings in unfair labor practice cases and other hearings as assigned. Also rules on pretrial motions, requests for extension of time to file briefs, proposed findings, and conclusions. The chief, deputy chief, and associate chief administrative law judges designate administrative law judges to conduct hearings, make rulings, assign dates for hearings, and maintain a calendar of cases to be heard.

Chief Administrative Law Judge

Robert A. Giannasi . . . . (202) 501–8800

Fax. . . . . (202) 501–8686

Atlanta Branch Office

401 W. Peachtree St. N.W., #1708

Atlanta, GA 30308–3510

(404) 331–6652

Fax (404) 331–2061

William N. Cates, associate chief administrative law judge

New York Branch Office

120 W. 45th St., 11th Floor

New York, NY 10036–5503

(212) 944–2940

Fax (212) 944–4904

Joel P. Biblowitz, associate chief administrative law judge

San Francisco Branch Office

901 Market St., #300

San Francisco, CA 94103–1779

(415) 356–5255

Fax (415) 356–5254

Gerald Etchingham, associate chief administrative law judge

DIVISION OF OPERATIONS MANAGEMENT

Responsible for the operation and administration of all regional, resident, and subregional offices, including case processing; coordinates these operations with the case handling and administrative operations of the general counsel. Also provides advice to the general counsel on major policy questions.

Associate General Counsel

Anne Purcell . . . . (202) 273–2900

Regional Offices

REGION 1

(Boston)

Boston Federal Office Bldg.

10 Causeway St., 6th Floor

Boston, MA 02222–1072

(617) 565–6700

Fax (617) 565–6725

Jonathan Kreisberg, regional director

(Hartford subregional office)

450 Main St., 4th Floor

Hartford, CT 06103–3503

(860) 240–3552

Fax (860) 240–3564

Michael C. Cass, officer-in-charge

REGION 2

(New York)

Jacob K. Javits Federal Bldg.

26 Federal Plaza, #3614

New York, NY 10278–0104

(212) 264–0300

Fax (212) 264–2450

Karen Fernbach, regional director

REGION 3

(Buffalo)

Niagara Center Bldg.

130 S. Elmwood Ave., #630

Buffalo, NY 14202–2387

(716) 551–4931

Fax (716) 551–4972

Rhonda P. Ley, regional director

(Albany resident office)

Leo W. O'Brien Federal Bldg.

11A Clinton Ave., Room 342

Albany, NY 12207–2350

(518) 431–4155

Fax (518) 431–4157

Barnett Horowitz, resident officer

REGION 4

(Philadelphia)

One Independence Mall

615 Chestnut St., 7th Floor

Philadelphia, PA 19106–4404

(215) 597–7601

Fax (215) 597–7658

Dennis P. Walsh, regional director

REGION 5

(Baltimore)

Bank of America Center, Tower II

100 S. Charles St., 6th Floor

Baltimore, MD 21201

(410) 962–2822

Fax (410) 962–2198

Charles L. Posner, regional director

(Washington resident office)

310 • NATIONAL LABOR RELATIONS BOARD

1015 Half St. S.E.
Washington, DC 20570–0001
(202) 208–3000
Fax (202) 208–3013
Mark Baptiste-Kalaris, resident officer

REGION 6
(Pittsburgh)
William S. Moorehead Federal Bldg.
1000 Liberty Ave., #904
Pittsburgh, PA 15222–4111
(412) 395–4400
Fax (412) 395–5986
Nancy Wilson, regional director

REGION 7
(Detroit)
Patrick V. McNamara Federal Bldg.
477 Michigan Ave., #300
Detroit, MI 48226–2569
(313) 226–3200
Fax (313) 226–2090
Terry Morgan, regional director

(Grand Rapids resident office)
Gerald Ford Federal Bldg. and U.S. Court House
110 Michigan St. N.W., #299
Grand Rapids, MI 49503–2363
(616) 456–2679
Fax (616) 456–2596
Thomas M. Good, resident officer

REGION 8
(Cleveland)
Anthony J. Celebrezze Federal Bldg.
1240 E. 9th St., #1695
Cleveland, OH 44199–2086
(216) 522–3715
Fax (216) 522–2418
Allen Binstock, regional director

REGION 9
(Cincinnati)
John Weld Peck Federal Bldg.
550 Main St., #3003
Cincinnati, OH 45202–3271
(513) 684–3686
Fax (513) 684–3946
Garey Lindsay, regional director

REGION 10
(Atlanta)
233 Peachtree St. N.E.
Harris Tower, #1000
Atlanta, GA 30303–1531
(404) 331–2896
Fax (404) 331–2858
Claude T. Harrell Jr., regional director

(Birmingham resident office)
Ridge Park Pl., #3400
1130 South 22nd St.

Birmingham, AL 35205–2870
(205) 933–3018
Fax (205) 933–3017
Belinda Bennet, resident officer

(Nashville resident office)
810 Broadway, #302
Nashville, TN
(615) 736–5921
Fax (615) 736–7761
Stacee R. Smith, resident officer

(Winston-Salem subregional office)
Republic Square
4035 University Pkwy., #200
Winston-Salem, NC 27106–3325
(336) 631–5201
Fax (336) 631–5210
Scott C. Thompson, officer-in-charge

REGION 12
(Tampa)
South Trust Plaza
201 E. Kennedy Blvd., #530
Tampa, FL 33602–5824
(813) 228–2641
Fax (813) 228–2874
Margaret Diaz, regional director

(Puerto Rico resident office)
La Torre de Plaza
252 F.D. Roosevelt Ave., #1002
Hato Rey, PR 00918–1002
(787) 766–5347
Fax (787) 766–5478
Luis Padilla, officer-in-charge

(Miami resident office)
Federal Bldg., #1320
51 S.W. 1st Ave.
Miami, FL 33130–1608
(305) 536–5391
Fax (305) 536–5320
Shelley B. Plass, resident officer

REGION 13
(Chicago)
The Rookery Bldg.
209 S. LaSalle St., #900
Chicago, IL 60604–5208
(312) 353–7570
Fax (312) 886–1341
Peter Sung Ohr, regional director

REGION 14
(St. Louis)
1222 Spruce St., #8.302
St. Louis, MO 63103–2829
(314) 539–7770
Fax (314) 539–7794
Daniel Hubbel, regional director

(Tulsa resident office)
224 South Boulder Ave., #318
Tulsa, OK 24103
(918) 581–7951
Fax (918) 581–7970
Charles Hoskin, resident officer

(Overland Park subregional office)
8600 Farley St., #100
Overland Park, KS 66212
(913) 967–3000
Fax (913) 967–3010
Naomi Stuart, officer-in-charge

REGION 15
(New Orleans)
600 S. Maestri Pl., 7th Floor
New Orleans, LA 70130–3413
(504) 589–6362
Fax (504) 589–4069
M. Kathleen McKinney, regional director

(Little Rock subregional office)
425 West Capital Ave., #1615
Little Rock, AR 72201
(501) 324–6311
Fax (501)324–5009
Stacia Campbell, office-in-charge

(Memphis subregional office)
Brinkley Plaza Bldg.
80 Monroe Ave., #350
Memphis, TN 38103–2481
(901) 544–0018
Fax (901) 544–0008
Christopher Roy, resident officer

REGION 16
(Fort Worth)
Federal Office Bldg.
819 Taylor St., #8A24
Fort Worth, TX 76102–6178
(817) 978–2921
Fax (817) 978–2928
Martha Kinard, regional director

(Houston resident office)
Mickey Leland Federal Bldg.
1919 Smith St., #1545
Houston, TX 77002
(281) 228–5600
Fax (281) 228–5619
Nadine Littles, resident officer

(San Antonio resident office)
615 East Houston St., #559
San Antonio, TX 78205–1711
(210) 472–6140
Fax (210) 472–6143
Steve Martinez, resident officer

REGION 18
(Minneapolis)
Minneapolis Federal Office Bldg.
212 Third Ave. South, #200
Minneapolis, MN 55401
(612) 348–1757
Fax (612) 348–1785
Marlin O. Osthus, regional director

(Des Moines resident office)
210 Walnut St., #439
Des Moines, IA 50309–2103
(515) 284–4391
Fax (515) 284–4713
Jennifer Hadsall, resident officer

(Milwaukee subregional office)
310 W. Wisconsin Ave., #450W
Milwaukee, WI 53203–2211
(414) 297–3861
(414) 297–3800
Benjamin Mandelman, officer-in-charge

REGION 19
(Seattle)
Henry M. Jackson Federal Bldg.
915 2nd Ave., #2948
Seattle, WA 98174–1078
(206) 220–6300
Fax (206) 220–6305
Ronald K. Hooks, regional director

(Anchorage resident office)
Anchorage Federal Bldg.
605 West 4th Ave., #210
Anchorage, AK 99501–1936
(907) 271–5015
Fax (907) 271–3055
Vacant, resident officer

(Portland subregional office)
1220 S.W. Third St., #605
Portland, OR 97204–2170
(503) 326–3085
Fax (503) 326–5387
Jessica Dietz, officer-in-charge

REGION 20
(San Francisco)
901 Market St., #400
San Francisco, CA 94103–1735
(415) 356–5130
Fax (415) 356–5156
Joe Frankl, regional director

(Honolulu subregional office)
300 Ala Moana Blvd., #7–245
Honolulu, HI 96850–4980
(808) 541–2814
Fax (808) 541–2818
Thomas W. Cestare, officer-in-charge

REGION 21

(Los Angeles)
888 S. Figueroa St., 9th Floor
Los Angeles, CA 90017–5449
(213) 894–5200
Fax (213) 894–2778
Olivia Garcia, regional director

(San Diego resident office)
555 W. Beech St., #418
San Diego, CA 92101–2939
(619) 557–6184
Fax (619) 557–6358
Steven J. Sorenson, resident officer

REGION 22

(Newark)
20 Washington Pl., 5th Floor
Newark, NJ 07102–3110
(973) 645–2100
Fax (973) 645–3852
David Leach, regional director

REGION 25

(Indianapolis)
Minton-Capehart Federal Bldg.
575 N. Pennsylvania St., #238
Indianapolis, IN 46204–1577
(317) 226–7381
Fax (317) 226–5103
Rik Lineback, regional director

(Peoria subregional office)
101 S.W. Adams St., #400
Peoria, IL 61602
(309) 671–7810
Fax (309) 671–7095
Nathaniel E. Strickler, officer-in-charge

REGION 27

(Denver)
Byron Rogers Federal Office Bldg.
1961 Stout St., #13–103
Denver, CO 80294
(303) 844–3551
Fax (303) 844–6249
Wanda Pate Jones, regional director

REGION 28

(Phoenix)
2600 N. Central Ave., #1400
Phoenix, AZ 85004–3099
(602) 640–2160
Fax (602) 640–2178
Cornele A. Overstreet, regional director

(Albuquerque resident office)
421 Gold Ave. S.W., #310
P.O. Box 567
Albuquerque, NM 87103–2181
(505) 248–5125
Fax (505) 248–5134
David Garza, resident officer

(Las Vegas resident office)
300 Las Vegas Blvd. South, #2-901
Las Vegas, NV 89101
(702) 388–6416
Fax (702) 388–6248
Steve Wamser, resident officer

REGION 29

(Brooklyn)
Two Metro Tech Center
100 Myrtle Ave., 5th Floor
Brooklyn, NY 11201–4201
(718) 330–7713
Fax (718) 330–7579
James G. Paulsen, regional director

REGION 31

(Los Angeles)
11150 W. Olympic Blvd., #600
Los Angeles, CA 90064–1824
(310) 235–7352
Fax (310) 235–7420
Mori Rubin, regional director

REGION 32

(Oakland)
Oakland Federal Bldg.
1301 Clay St., #300N
Oakland, CA 94612–5211
(510) 637–3300
Fax (510) 637–3315
George P. Velastegui, regional director

■ CONGRESSIONAL ACTION

Congressional Liaison
Celine McNicholas . . . . (202) 273–0808

Committees and Subcommittees

HOUSE APPROPRIATIONS COMMITTEE
Subcommittee on Labor, Health and Human Services, Education, and Related Agencies
2358 BRHOB, Washington, DC 20515–6015
(202) 225–3508

HOUSE COMMITTEE ON EDUCATION AND THE WORKFORCE
2181 RHOB, Washington, DC 20515–6100
(202) 225–4527

SENATE APPROPRIATIONS COMMITTEE
Subcommittee on Labor, Health and Human Services, Education, and Related Agencies
SDOB-428, Washington, DC 20510–6025
(202) 224–7230

SENATE HEALTH, EDUCATION, LABOR, AND PENSIONS COMMITTEE
SDOB-428, Washington, DC 20510–6300
(202) 224–5375
TTY (202) 224–1975

Legislation

The NLRB administers the following acts in full or in part:

National Labor Relations Act of 1935 (Wagner Act) (49 Stat. 449, 29 U.S.C. 151). Signed by the president July 5, 1935. Defined rights of employees to bargain collectively and strike; determined unfair labor activities that employers are forbidden from practicing.

Labor-Management Relations Act of 1947 (Taft-Hartley Act) (61 Stat. 136, 29 U.S.C. 141). Signed by the president June 23, 1947. Added provisions to the 1935 act protecting employers as well as employees.

Labor-Management Reporting and Disclosure Act of 1959 (Landrum-Griffin Act) (73 Stat. 519, 29 U.S.C. 401). Signed by the president Sept. 14, 1959. Established an employee bill of rights and reporting requirements for union activities.

Postal Reorganization Act of 1970 (84 Stat. 719, 39 U.S.C. 1201–1209). Signed by the president Aug. 12, 1970. Provided NLRB jurisdiction over labor disputes and representation elections in the U.S. Postal Service.

National Labor Relations Act Amendments of 1974 (88 Stat. 395, 29 U.S.C. 152). Signed by the president July 26, 1974. Repealed the exemption for nonprofit hospital employees under the National Labor Relations Act as amended by the Taft-Hartley Act.

Information and Publications

KEY OFFICES

NLRB Office of Public Affairs
1015 Half St. S.E.
Washington, DC 20570–0001
(202) 273–1991
Fax (202) 273–1789
E-mail: publicinfo@nlrb.gov
Celine McNicholas, director
(202) 273–0222
Mary M. Davis, public inquiry assistant
(202) 273–1948
Tony Wagner, new media specialist
(202) 273–0187

Provides general information to the media and the general public; arranges for agency personnel to speak before groups; issues news releases and a weekly summary of board and administrative law judges' decisions; distributes publications; and publishes *Daily Labor News*. General information also is available from the regional offices.

Freedom of Information
1015 Half St. S.E., 4th Floor
Washington, DC 20570
(202) 273–3825
Fax (202) 273–3642
Dierdre MacNeil, FOIA officer

Information about FOIA requests and forms are available on the NLRB website. FOIA requests pertaining to the NLRB board should be made to the Office of the Executive Secretary (above).

DATA AND STATISTICS

Office of Chief Information Officer
1015 Half St. S.E.
Washington, DC 20570
(202) 273–2555
Bryan Burnett, chief information officer

Maintains the NLRB's computerized databases; prepares regular and special reports on case activity for the use of agency staff and the public. Much of this information appears in summary form in the *Annual Report*. More specific data is contained in the internal information system, which provides an accounting of all cases processed in the agency including median elapsed days and volume of cases at different stages of case handling. Statistical reports are generated monthly and summaries are published annually.

Research and Policy Planning Branch
NLRB Division of Advice
1015 Half St. S.E.
Washington, DC 20570
(202) 273–3825
Jacqueline A. Young, assistant general counsel

Maintains a Legal Research System that provides indexes of board decisions, court decisions, and related legal information. Case digests are available on the website, as are other publications of this office.

MEETINGS

In accordance with the Government in the Sunshine Act, NLRB oral arguments and advisory committee meetings are open to the public and are announced on the NLRB website. Meetings scheduled to consider specific litigation or the drafting of an opinion on a pending case are closed to the public.

For more information on scheduled board meetings, contact the NLRB Office of the Executive Secretary at (202) 273–3737.

PUBLICATIONS

An extensive listing of publications is available on the website, including many in Spanish. The E-Reading Room on the website contains links to frequently requested manuals and publications, as well as forms, rules and regulations, public notices, press releases, and many other NLRB materials. For a complete listing of publications regarding the NLRB and their prices (if any), consult the website or call the Government Printing Office at (202) 512–1800. The NLRB Division of Information distributes limited quantities of free pamphlets. These pamphlets include (*available online):

*Basic Guide to the National Labor Relations Act**

*The National Labor Relations Board: Protecting Employee Rights**

*An Outline of Law and Procedure in Representation Cases**

*Your Government Conducts an Election**

Other publications, including subscription services, are available on the website or may be purchased from the Superintendent of Documents, U.S. Government Printing Office (GPO) (*see appendix, Ordering Government Publications*). Titles include

Annual Report of the National Labor Relations Board

Classified Index of National Labor Relations Board Decisions and Related Court Decisions. Quarterly; covers all board-, administrative law judge-, and NLRB-related court decisions issued during the period. Available as a subscription service.

Decisions and Orders of the National Labor Relations Board. Contact the NLRB Office of Public Affairs for information on latest volumes available.

A Guide to Basic Law and Procedures Under the National Labor Relations Act*

The Guide for Hearing Officers in NLRB Representation and Section 10(k) Proceedings. Designed to assist agency employees in preparing for and conducting hearings in representation cases pursuant to Section 9(c) and in jurisdictional disputes, pursuant to Section 10(k) of the National Labor Relations Act.

National Labor Relations Board Casehandling Manual. Provides complete, updated general counsel procedural and operational guidelines to NLRB regional offices in processing cases received under the National Labor Relations Act. The three-part manual is available as a subscription service.

NLRB Election Report.* Lists the outcome of secret ballot voting by employees in NLRB-conducted representation elections in cases closed for each month. Compiled from results following resolution of post-election objections and/or challenges. Published monthly.

Weekly Summary of NLRB Cases.* Weekly subscription service containing a summary of each published NLRB decision in unfair labor practice and representation election cases; lists decisions of NLRB administrative law judges and directions of elections by NLRB regional directors.

■ INFORMATION SOURCES

Internet

The NLRB's Internet site is www.nlrb.gov; sections are available in Spanish. The comprehensive website includes publications, regional contact information, weekly summaries of decisions by the board, and forms used to file charges.

Telephone Contacts

Spanish language options are available in some cases. Also consult the NLRB Office of Public Affairs (above).

General information line. . . . .(202) 273–1000
Toll-free . . . .(866) 667–6572
TTY . . . .(866) 315–6572
Inspector General's Hotline . . . .(800) 736–2983

Reference Resources

LIBRARIES

NLRB Library

1015 Half St. S.E.
Washington, DC 20570
(202) 273–3720
Andrew Martin, librarian
Hours: 9:00 a.m. to 4:00 p.m.

Open to the public. Participates in the interlibrary loan program.

Public Information Room

1015 Half St. S.E., Room 3055
Washington, DC 20570
Stacy Byas, chief of records
(202) 273–3920
Appointment recommended

Maintains for public inspection the decision papers of the agency, including regional director's decisions, judge's decisions, appeals and advice papers, and regional director dismissal letters. Photocopying facilities are not available, but arrangements may be made to purchase copies. Federal dockets available (*see Dockets below*).

DOCKETS

Federal dockets are available in the Public Information Room; call chief of case records for appointment: (202) 273–2840. Federal dockets also available at www.regulations.gov. (*See appendix for Searching and Commenting on Regulations: Regulations.gov.*)

RULES AND REGULATIONS

NLRB rules and regulations are published in the *Code of Federal Regulations,* Title 5, Chapter LXI, Part 7101; Title 29, Chapter I, Parts 100–199. Proposed rules, new final rules, and amendments to the *Code of Federal Regulations* are published in the daily *Federal Register.* (*See appendix for information on how to obtain and use these publications.*) The *Federal Register* may be accessed at www.federalregister.gov and the *Code of Federal Regulations* at www.archives.gov/federal-register/cfr; also see the federal government's website www.regulations.gov (*see appendix*).

Other Information Sources

RELATED AGENCIES

DOL Bureau of Labor Statistics

2 Massachusetts Ave. N.E.
Washington, DC 20212–0001
(202) 691–5200
Internet: www.bls.gov
Erica Groshen, commissioner

Gathers and analyzes data relating to labor and industry, including employment, unemployment, industrial relations, industrial safety, and wages and prices.

DOL Office of Labor-Management Standards
See p. 774.

Equal Employment Opportunity Commission
See p. 97.

NONGOVERNMENTAL RESOURCES

The following are some key resources for information on the NLRB and labor relations issues.

AFL-CIO
Government Affairs
815 16th St. N.W.
Washington, DC 20006
(202) 637–5000
Fax (202) 637–5058
Internet: www.aflcio.org

American Arbitration Association
120 Broadway, 21st Floor
New York, NY 10271
(212) 716–5800
Fax (212) 307-4387
Internet: www.adr.org

American Law Institute–American Bar Association
Committee on Continuing Professional Education
4025 Chestnut St.
Philadelphia, PA 19104–3099
(215) 243–1614
(800) CLENEWS
Fax (215) 243–1664
Internet: www.ali-cle.org

Bureau of National Affairs, Inc.
1801 South Bell St.
Arlington, VA 22202
(703) 341–3000
(800) 372–1033
Fax (800) 253–0332
Internet: www.bna.com

Industrial and Labor Relations Review
381 Ives Hall East
Cornell University
Ithaca, NY 14853–3901
(607) 255–3295
Fax (607) 255–8016
E-mail: ilrr@cornell.edu
Internet: www.ilr.cornell.edu/ilrreview

Industrial Relations:
A Journal of Economy and Society
Institute for Research on Labor and
  Employment
University of California at Berkeley
2521 Channing Way, #5555
Berkeley, CA 94720–5555
(510) 643–8140
E-mail: ir_journal@berkeley.edu
Internet: http://onlinelibrary.wiley.com/
  journal/10.1111/(ISSN)1468-232X

National Association of Manufacturers
Human Resources Policy
733 10th St. N.W., #700
Washington, DC 20001
(202) 637–3000
(800) 814–8468
Fax (202) 637–3182
E-mail: manufacturing@nam.org
Internet: www.nam.org

Thomson Reuters
610 Opperman Dr.
Eagan, MN 55123
(651) 687–7000
(800) 344–5008
Internet: http://legalsolutions.thomsonreuters.com/
  law-products

U.S. Chamber of Commerce
Domestic Policy
1615 H St. N.W.
Washington, DC 20062–2000
(202) 659–6000
(800) 638–6582
Internet: www.uschamber.com

Occupational Safety and Health Administration

200 Constitution Ave. N.W., Washington, DC 20210
Internet: www.osha.gov

▨ INTRODUCTION

The Occupational Safety and Health Administration (OSHA) was established as an agency within the Labor Department by the Occupational Safety and Health Act of 1970. The assistant secretary of labor for occupational safety and health, who is nominated by the president and confirmed by the Senate, directs the agency.

Responsibilities

OSHA performs the following:

▪ Encourages employers and employees to reduce hazards in the workplace by improving existing safety and health programs or by implementing new ones.

▪ Establishes "separate but dependent responsibilities and rights" for employers and employees to improve safety and health conditions.

▪ Maintains reporting and record-keeping procedures to monitor job-related injuries and illnesses.

▪ Develops and enforces mandatory job safety and health standards.

▪ Encourages the states to assume responsibility for establishing and administering their own occupational safety and health programs.

▪ Monitors federal agency safety programs and receives an annual report from each agency about its job safety and health efforts.

▪ Establishes advisory committees when necessary to assist in developing standards.

▪ Imposes emergency temporary standards when workers are in danger because of exposure to new toxic substances or hazards.

▪ Grants variances for special circumstances.

▪ Provides free on-site consultation services to small businesses to assist them in meeting OSHA standards.

Powers and Authority

OSHA regulations and standards extend to all employers and their employees in the fifty states, the District of Columbia, Puerto Rico, and all other territories under federal jurisdiction. As defined by the Occupational Safety and Health Act, an employer is any "person engaged in a business affecting commerce who has employees, but does not include the United States or any state or political subdivision of a state." Therefore, the act covers employers and employees in varied fields such as construction, shipyards, agriculture, law, medicine, charity and disaster relief, organized labor, and private education. Coverage includes religious groups to the extent that they employ workers for secular purposes. Self-employed persons, family-owned and operated farms, and workplaces already protected by other federal agencies are not subject to OSHA regulations.

Federal agencies also are exempted from OSHA regulations and enforcement provisions, but each agency is required to establish and maintain an effective and comprehensive job safety and health program of its own. Such a program must be based, in part, on consultations with representatives of its employees and be consistent with

OSHA standards for private employers. OSHA monitors federal agency programs, and each agency must submit an annual report to OSHA on the status of job safety and health efforts.

STANDARDS

One of OSHA's major tasks is developing standards to protect workers. The agency's standards fall into four major categories—general industry, maritime, construction, and agriculture. When it first started operating, OSHA adopted many of the consensus standards developed over the years by the American National Standards Institute and the National Fire Protection Association. These standards, however, frequently either were outdated or represented minimum rather than optimal degrees of protection. OSHA has worked to update, revise, and add to these standards to cover as many potential workplace hazards as possible.

OSHA can begin standards-setting procedures on its initiative or on petitions from other parties, including the secretary of the Health and Human Services Department, the National Institute for Occupational Safety and Health, state and local governments, any nationally recognized standards-producing organization, employer or labor representatives, or any other interested person.

If OSHA determines that a standard is needed, it may call on its two standing advisory committees or appoint ad hoc committees to develop specific recommendations. The ad hoc committees, limited to a life span of 270 days, include representatives of labor, management, and state and federal agencies, as well as occupational safety and health professionals and the general public. Meetings and records of the committees are open to the public. Notices of committee meetings are published in the *Federal Register* at least seven days in advance and include the location of the meeting and a staff member to contact for additional information.

Anyone wishing to participate in a committee meeting should notify the Directorate of Standards and Guidance in advance. The directorate requests that participating persons provide it with at least twenty copies of statements to be presented or an estimate of the time required to speak and an outline of the view to be presented. Participation is limited to a designated time period and is subject to the discretion of the administrative law judge who presides over the meeting. The judge may call for additional opinions to be offered by anyone attending the meeting.

Usually the standards development process follows the rules set out in the Administrative Procedure Act. There must be publication of proposals in the *Federal Register,* followed by an adequate period of time for comments. After all evidence from committee meetings, hearings, and written submissions has been analyzed from a legal, technical, environmental, and economic viewpoint, OSHA must publish in the *Federal Register* either a final rule or a standard based on updated information or technological advances in the field. The legislation creating OSHA stressed that its standards should be feasible and based on research, experiments, demonstrations, past experience, and the latest available scientific data.

In some critically dangerous situations OSHA is authorized to set emergency temporary standards that take effect immediately. In those cases, OSHA must determine that workers are in grave danger because of exposure to toxic substances or new hazards and that an emergency standard is needed to protect them. After publication of such an emergency standard, regular standard-setting procedures must be initiated and completed within six months.

Any person adversely affected by a final or emergency standard may file a petition within sixty days of the rule's issuance for judicial review of the standard with the U.S. Court of Appeals for the circuit in which the person lives or has his or her principal place of business. Filing an appeals petition, however, does not delay enforcement of a standard unless the court specifically orders an injunction.

Employers may apply to OSHA for a variance from a standard or regulation if they lack the means to comply with it readily, or if they can prove that their facilities or methods of operation provide employee protection that is "at least as effective as" that required by OSHA. Standard or regulation variances may be temporary or permanent, depending on the situation.

To ensure that all workers are protected, the Occupational Safety and Health Act includes a provision making it the duty of all employers to provide a safe and healthful workplace. Thus, even if a specific standard has not been developed, all workers have at least minimum protection.

INSPECTIONS AND INVESTIGATIONS

To enforce its standards and regulations, OSHA is authorized under the Occupational Safety and Health Act to conduct workplace inspections. Every establishment covered by the act is subject to inspection by OSHA safety and health compliance officers. States with their own occupational safety and health programs conduct inspections using qualified compliance officers.

With few exceptions, inspections are conducted without advance notice. Before 1978, OSHA compliance officers were allowed to enter a workplace without a search warrant. However, in May 1978 the Supreme Court ruled that an employer has the right to refuse admission to an OSHA inspector who does not have a warrant. The ruling has not had a dramatic effect on the agency; most employers are willing to admit the compliance officers without a warrant. Should an employer refuse, a warrant can be obtained from a federal court relatively quickly. OSHA need not indicate a specific unsafe condition it is looking for to obtain a warrant. The agency need only indicate that the premises to be inspected have been chosen on the basis of a neutral plan to enforce OSHA standards.

Because OSHA has limited personnel to conduct workplace inspections, the agency has established a system of inspection priorities. Imminent danger situations are given top priority, followed in descending order by investigations of fatalities and catastrophes resulting in hospitalization of five or more employees; investigations of employee complaints of alleged violation of standards or unsafe or unhealthful working conditions; inspections aimed at specific high-hazard industries, occupations, or health substances; and follow-up inspections to determine whether previously cited violations have been corrected.

An employer has the right to accompany an OSHA inspector during a tour of the workplace. An employee representative also may accompany the inspector during the tour. In addition, the inspector must be given the opportunity to interview employees privately.

Employees or their representative may give written notification to the inspector of any violation they believe exists, and they must be provided with a written explanation if no citation is issued respecting the alleged violation. Employees or their representative also have the right to request a special inspection if they feel there are unsafe conditions in their workplace.

For an inspection, a compliance officer explains the purpose of the visit to the employer and provides copies of the safety and health standards that apply to that particular workplace. A copy of any employee complaint may also be provided. If so requested, the name of the employee making the complaint will not be revealed. After reviewing records of deaths, injuries, and illnesses that the employer is required to keep, the inspector determines the route and duration of the inspection. The inspector must keep confidential any trade secrets observed during an inspection.

Following the inspection tour, the compliance officer and the employer hold a closing conference. The compliance officer discusses with the employer what has been found on the inspection and advises the employer of all apparent violations for which a citation may be issued or recommended. During the closing conference the employer may provide the compliance officer with information to help OSHA determine how much time may be needed to correct an alleged violation.

CITATIONS

A citation in writing is issued to the employer if violations are discovered during an inspection. The citation describes the violation and allows a reasonable amount of time for its correction. A copy of the citation must be posted at or near the place of each violation. The compliance officer does not propose penalties.

Many relatively minor, or de minimis, violations are not sufficiently serious to warrant a citation. In such cases the compliance officer discusses the violation with the employer and recommends ways to correct the problem.

Employers who have received citations during an inspection by a compliance officer may request an informal settlement or file a "Notice of Contest" with the OSHA area director if they wish to contest the citation. Once a Notice of Contest is filed, the Occupational Safety and Health Review Commission (an independent government agency that adjudicates disputes) takes over the case from OSHA.

Employees may request an inspection if they believe unsafe conditions exist in their workplace. Employers are not allowed to take any action or discriminate against employees who complain to OSHA. If an inspection is conducted and no citations are issued, the employee or

employee representative may request an informal review of the decision not to issue a citation. Also, if the time limit allowed for correction of an unsafe condition seems unreasonably long, the employee or employee representative may submit a written objection to OSHA that will be forwarded to the Occupational Safety and Health Review Commission.

When an OSHA compliance officer finds that there exists an imminent danger—defined as "a condition or practice that could reasonably be expected to cause death or serious physical harm before such condition or practice can be abated"—the officer asks the employer to take immediate steps voluntarily to protect workers, including removal of employees from the dangerous area if necessary. If the employer refuses to take immediate action, a temporary restraining order or injunction requiring that steps be taken to correct, remove, and avoid the danger may be obtained from a U.S. district court.

ENFORCEMENT REVIEW

The Occupational Safety and Health Review Commission has responsibility for reviewing contested inspections. After an inspection or investigation has been completed and any citations issued, OSHA notifies the employer in writing of the period of time allowed to correct the violation (abatement period) and the proposed penalty, if any, for each violation. All of this information is turned over to the review commission. An employer has fifteen days to contest a citation or a proposed penalty, as do employees or their representative. Usually a notice of contest filed by employees challenges the reasonableness of the abatement period.

If no notice of contest is filed, the citation and proposed penalties become the final order of the commission. If a citation is contested, the review commission usually holds a hearing before an administrative law judge. After listening to the evidence and considering all arguments, the judge prepares a decision and mails copies of it to the parties involved. The judge also files all material related to the case with the commission.

The judge's decision becomes final thirty days after the commission receives it, unless a petition for discretionary review is filed. If such a petition is filed, the three-member commission reviews the administrative law judge's decision. In a few cases the commission will initiate a review of a decision even if a petition for discretionary review has not been filed.

Employers also may file a petition requesting modification of the abatement period specified in a citation. Such petitions are handled in much the same manner as a notice of contest.

PENALTIES

OSHA only proposes penalties; the final orders imposing them are issued by the Occupational Safety and Health Review Commission. The law requires the review commission to consider four factors when determining civil penalties: (1) the size of the business involved; (2) the gravity of the violation; (3) the good faith of the employer; and (4) the employer's history of previous violations.

No penalties are imposed for minor violations. For an "other than serious violation," one that has a direct relationship to job safety and health but probably would not cause death or serious injury, a fine of up to $1,000 may be imposed. If reinspection shows failure to correct the violation, penalties of up to $1,000 per day may be added.

For "serious violations," when there is substantial probability of death or serious physical harm and the employer knows about the hazard, or should know about it, a penalty of up to $5,000 is mandatory for each violation. Falsifying records, reports, and applications can bring a fine of $10,000 and six months in jail. Violations of posting requirements can bring a civil penalty of $3,000. Assaulting compliance officers or interfering with compliance officers in the performance of their duties is a criminal offense, subject to a fine of not more than $5,000 and imprisonment for not more than three years.

For employers who willfully or repeatedly violate the law, penalties of up to $70,000 for each violation may be assessed. If an employer is convicted of a willful violation that has resulted in the death of an employee, the employer may be fined not more than $70,000 and imprisoned for up to six months. A second conviction doubles the maximum penalties.

RECORD KEEPING AND REPORTING

OSHA requires employers of eleven or more employees to maintain records of occupational injuries and illnesses. In 2009 about 1.5 million U.S. employers had eleven or more employees. Employers with ten or fewer employees must keep such records only if selected by the Bureau of Labor Statistics to participate in periodic statistical surveys.

An occupational injury is any injury, such as a cut, fracture, sprain, or amputation, that results from a work-related accident or from exposure involving a single incident in the work environment. An occupational illness is any abnormal condition or disorder, other than one resulting from an occupational injury, caused by exposure to environmental factors associated with employment. Included are acute and chronic illnesses that may be caused by inhalation, absorption, ingestion, or direct contact with toxic substances.

Employers must record all occupational illnesses. Injuries must be recorded if they result in death (regardless of the length of time between the injury and death and regardless of the length of the illness); one or more lost workdays; restriction of work or motion; loss of consciousness; transfer to another job; or medical treatment (other than first aid).

Two record-keeping forms are used for data that must be maintained on a calendar-year basis. They are not sent to OSHA but are retained at the establishment and kept available for OSHA inspections for at least five years following the end of the year recorded.

The records required are a log of occupational illnesses and injury (OSHA No. 200) and a supplementary record of injury and illness (OSHA No. 101). Certain employers are chosen by OSHA to participate in the annual statistical survey (OSHA No. 200S).

In addition, if an on-the-job accident occurs that results in the death of an employee or in the hospitalization of five or more employees, the employer by law must report the accident in detail to the nearest OSHA office within forty-eight hours.

STATE PROGRAMS

OSHA's legislation requires the agency to encourage states to develop and operate their own occupational safety and health programs. These plans must be at least as effective as the federal program. By 2009 twenty-five states and the U.S. Virgin Islands had OSHA-certified programs.

OSHA retains the authority to enforce federal regulations in the state until the proposed state program is fully operational. Once the state has demonstrated that within three years its program will be as effective as the federal program, the plan may be approved by OSHA. The state in this interim period must exhibit legislative, administrative, regulatory, and procedural commitment to occupational safety as well as a sufficient number of enforcement personnel to meet OSHA's requirements. When a state plan is approved, OSHA agrees to pay up to 50 percent of the cost of operations.

The agency continues to receive summaries of enforcement and compliance activities from the state and submits an annual evaluation of progress to the state. When the state program has operated at a fully effective level for at least one year, final OSHA approval may be granted. At that time, agency enforcement authority will cease but monitoring activities continue to ensure compliance with federal standards.

If the state program does not continue to provide adequate safety and health protection, OSHA either can reintroduce federal enforcement personnel in the appropriate areas or begin proceedings to withdraw federal approval of the program.

Critics maintain that some state plans provide grossly inadequate enforcement of workplace safety and health standards. State officials reject such criticism, saying that their programs conduct more safety inspections than the federal agency. Some state officials also argue that they get insufficient federal funds. The federal contribution to state programs in fiscal year 2008 constituted 21 percent of OSHA's total budget.

CONSULTATION AND TRAINING

OSHA has developed a consultation program to help businesses comply with safety standards. Of the states administering OSHA-approved job safety and health programs, only one does not provide on-site consultation. For states without OSHA-approved plans, OSHA has issued rules under which they too may offer such consultation, using state personnel.

On-site consultation is intended primarily to provide aid to small businesses that do not have their own safety and health staffs. A consultative visit consists of an opening conference, an inspection tour of the workplace, a closing conference, and a written summary of findings. During the inspection tour the consultant explains to the employer which OSHA standards apply to the company and the technical language and application of the appropriate standards. The consultant also points out where the employer is not in compliance and may suggest ways to eliminate identified hazards.

No citations are issued and no penalties are proposed for alleged violations discovered during the consultation. An employer, however, must agree to eliminate hazardous conditions identified by the consultant. Failure to abide by this agreement can result in referral of the employer's establishment to the enforcement staff for inspection.

OSHA also offers training to safety and health specialists through its Training Institute in Des Plaines, IL, and through its field offices. In addition, OSHA has endorsed vocational safety and health training programs at schools of business administration throughout the country.

Background

OSHA was created by Congress in 1970 after years of debate over workplace safety and worker health. During the early 1960s the Labor Department came under increasing criticism for weak enforcement of a 1936 law directing the department to ensure safe work standards for federal contractors. Congress held hearings on the matter in 1964, and the following year the Public Health Service published a study drawing attention to health threats arising from new technologies.

President Lyndon B. Johnson endorsed a legislative package of safety and health measures in 1968, but business opposition defeated it, charging usurpation of states' rights by the federal government. In 1969 President Richard Nixon offered a bill, the Occupational Safety and Health Act, which gave the states the option to administer standards set by the federal government. Passage the following year created the agency, which was given a broad mandate "to assure so far as possible every working man and woman in the nation safe and healthful working conditions and to preserve our human resources." Twenty-three states immediately chose to conduct their own OSHA programs. By law these programs had to be "at least as effective" as the federal health and safety regulations.

EARLY HISTORY

As required by Congress, OSHA's start-up health and safety standards were adopted from existing federal regulations and national consensus standards set by groups such as the National Institute of Standards and Technology (NIST) and the National Fire Protection Association. The wholesale adoption of about 4,400 job safety and health rules during OSHA's first month of operation later proved to be a major source of irritation, especially for business. Even at the time, it was generally recognized that many of these standards were "outdated, unnecessarily specific and unrelated to occupational health and safety," according to a 1985 Office of Technology Assessment (OTA) report. The OTA was a nonpartisan research arm of Congress.

Business complained that penalties for first violations were unfair and that the cost of compliance was at times so burdensome as to drive small companies into bankruptcy. The paperwork requirements imposed on employers also came under attack as excessive and time-consuming. At the same time, labor groups complained that the agency's enforcement activities were sporadic and weak and that it failed to reduce workplace hazards significantly.

From 1974 to 1976 OSHA stepped up its efforts to develop health standards for substances linked to illnesses such as cancer and lung disease. Although evidence sometimes was inconclusive, OSHA often set stringent standards without waiting for more concrete scientific data. These standards required employers to reduce worker exposure to certain substances to the lowest feasible levels, even if the agency was not sure that those levels were necessary to prevent significant risk. Critics charged that OSHA paid little attention to how much the regulations cost industries.

STREAMLINING OSHA

The first wave of limitations on OSHA came in 1976, when Congress decided to exempt most small businesses—those with ten or fewer employees—from record-keeping requirements. In early 1977 President Jimmy Carter, who had made deregulation a theme of his presidential campaign, appointed Eula Bingham to head OSHA. In an effort to reduce complaints about the agency, Bingham pledged to adopt a set of "common sense" priorities and to make fundamental changes in administration and regulation policy. She promised to focus attention on the most dangerous industries and devote less time to inspecting small businesses (except those with a higher-than-average rate of serious injury).

Under Bingham, who served until 1981, streamlining and consolidation became the operative words in OSHA's efforts to develop safety standards. Nearly 1,000 safety standards were revoked during the first month of fiscal 1977. OSHA staff members also worked to simplify the rules and regulations in the areas of construction, fire protection, and electricity. Inspections became concentrated on the most dangerous industries, with less than 5 percent of inspections being done in small businesses.

During this period the agency further increased its emphasis on the development of health standards designed to protect workers from toxic substances, such as carcinogens and cotton dust. In a setback for the agency, however, the Supreme Court in two July 1980 cases (*Marshall v. American Petroleum Institute, Industrial Union Department* and *AFL-CIO v. American Petroleum Institute*) ruled that OSHA's standard for worker exposure to benzene was invalid because the rule was unsupported by sufficient evidence that it was necessary to protect the health of workers. Broadly applied, these decisions meant that OSHA could no longer require employers to reduce worker exposure to hazards to the lowest feasible levels unless it proved that a significant risk to workers existed above those levels. OSHA had to prove not only that the substance being regulated was hazardous but also that a significant risk existed above the exposure levels it set as permissible in its standards.

OSHA IN THE 1980s

Despite the reforms initiated by Bingham, OSHA remained a favorite target of labor and business. As a candidate for president in 1980, Ronald Reagan promised to abolish the agency. Once in office, however, he failed to muster the political support to fulfill his pledge.

Reagan's choice to head the agency, Thorne G. Auchter, shared his commitment to reduce the federal presence in workplace health and safety matters. As did many other Reagan appointees, he emphasized cost effectiveness and voluntary, rather than mandatory, compliance. Supporting this philosophy, the Reagan administration in January 1981 froze a number of pending OSHA regulations, including a safety standard limiting exposure to lead in the workplace and a requirement that employers pay workers who accompany federal safety officials on inspection tours.

The agency also announced that it would forgo inspections of businesses that reported below-average numbers of injuries. This move would allow the agency to concentrate on high-hazard companies. Critics maintained that this policy provided business with a powerful incentive to underreport. In 1983 an AFL-CIO report called the program of targeting plants with poor records a "paper tiger" and complained that inspectors spent too much time inspecting records rather than touring plants.

OSHA had been directed since its inception to balance worker health and safety against costs incurred by employers. President Reagan elevated cost-benefit analysis to even greater importance in 1981 when he issued Executive Order 12291, which required federal rulemaking agencies to show that "the potential benefits to society for [a proposed] regulation outweigh the potential costs." Unlike the previous orders, which only directed regulatory agencies to evaluate the economic impact of their decisions, Reagan's order made the application of cost-benefit analysis an explicit requirement.

The order's application to OSHA regulations, however, was soon declared invalid by the Supreme Court in *American Textile Manufacturing Institute v. Donovan,* a case involving permissible limits of cotton dust in textile mills. During the Carter administration, OSHA had issued a new standard to protect textile workers from byssinosis, or brown lung, which is caused by breathing cotton particles. Textile industry representatives argued that OSHA had exceeded its authority because it had not conducted an analysis to show that the benefits of the regulation exceeded the costs. Labor union representatives argued that the 1970 act required no such analysis. The Reagan administration asked the Court to refer the case back to OSHA for modification in accordance with cost-benefit analysis. But the Court denied the request and in June 1981 upheld OSHA's cotton-dust standard, saying that cost-benefit analysis was not required by the Occupational Safety and Health Act.

Although the ruling was hailed at the time as one of the most significant in the history of regulatory law, it did not deter Auchter's commitment to curb federal health and safety regulations. Following the Court decision, he announced that the agency would consider four points in issuing future regulations: whether a significant health risk existed; whether the proposed standard would protect workers from that risk; whether the standard was economically feasible for the industry affected; and whether the standard was cost effective—that is, was the least costly way to achieve the desired goal.

Applying Auchter's four-point guideline, OSHA made a number of controversial recommendations to postpone or revise existing regulations. It reopened the cotton-dust debate in June 1983 by proposing revisions to the regulations upheld by the Court. OSHA also proposed to revoke 194 safety and health standards that the agency said were unenforceable because they used the word "should" rather than "shall."

Auchter's zeal for curbing OSHA rulemaking appeared to wane by 1983. In the summer of that year, OSHA suddenly decided to set a stricter emergency standard for asbestos, bypassing normal rulemaking procedures. Auchter also promised additional safety standards and health standards by the end of 1984. Critics pointed out that OSHA's increased regulatory activities coincided with a scandal at the Environmental Protection Agency (EPA) in which its top administrator and her entire management team were forced to resign in 1983 over charges that the EPA had been lax in enforcement.

John A. Pendergrass began his tenure as head of OSHA in May 1986 at a time when President Reagan was signaling his interest in improving ties with organized labor. Under Pendergrass, the most visible signs of OSHA's change in direction came in the form of high-profile health and safety regulation enforcement that produced record proposed fines against some of the country's biggest employers. Among them were Chrysler, General Motors, Ford, General Dynamics, Caterpillar, Union Carbide, and IBP, the nation's leading meatpacker. In all, OSHA proposed fines totaling $24.7 million for health and safety violations in fiscal 1987, almost five times the amount proposed in 1982.

Most of the large fines, however, as critics noted, were settled for half of the proposed amount or less. In addition, most of the fines were imposed for record-keeping violations, not hazardous workplaces. Pendergrass maintained that he was more interested in encouraging companies to improve their record keeping and fostering a spirit of cooperation between government and business than collecting big fines. Sensitive to criticism of the agency's enforcement efforts, Pendergrass in March 1988 announced that OSHA's manufacturing safety inspectors would start checking factory floors in high-hazard businesses, rather than simply checking office records of injuries and illnesses, the procedure at the time.

A month later, a number of the agency's scientists and compliance officers, under subpoena to testify, criticized OSHA's performance during hearings before a Senate committee: OSHA had been slow to issue workplace safety standards; top administration officials, had weakened OSHA safety proposals; OSHA compliance officers had been pressured to rush their work to meet inspection quotas; and the agency lacked the budget and personnel to enforce all of its regulations.

Under the glare of congressional scrutiny, OSHA became more activist in the last year of the Reagan administration. In January 1989, in the first overhaul of exposure limits since the passage of the Occupational Safety and Health Act in 1970, OSHA issued new exposure standards for nearly 400 hazardous materials used in workplaces. Lumping so many substances together in a single package marked a major shift in the agency's approach to rulemaking. In the past, OSHA had developed exposure limits for toxic substances on a case-by-case basis, thus inviting endless debate over technical issues. By bundling 400 substances into one package, the agency hoped to disarm critics who would think twice about challenging the entire package just to object to a handful of the new standards. However, this approach was overturned by the Eleventh Circuit Court of Appeals in 1992, because OSHA had not made a separate scientific case for gauging the health risks of each individual chemical.

OSHA IN THE 1990s

The administration of President George H. W. Bush had what seemed to be a split personality in its policy toward OSHA. The administration worked hard to defeat a congressional effort to beef up OSHA's enforcement powers and called for more cost-benefit analysis in issuing health and safety regulations. At the same time, OSHA, headed by Gerard F. Scannell, issued one of the most controversial rules to date—one dealing with blood-borne pathogens. The public comment period on the rule went on for more than a year, and the agency received more comments on the proposed rule than any other in its history. The rule, which went into effect in March 1992, was largely aimed at preventing people, primarily health care workers, from contracting the HIV or hepatitis B viruses while on the job.

In other signs of activism under Bush, OSHA proposed the largest fine in its history, $7.3 million, against USX Corp., for more than 2,000 alleged safety, health, and record-keeping violations; worked out an agreement with the Sara Lee Corp.'s thirty-one meat processing plants to seek ways to reduce repetitive motion injuries; and issued final, controversial rules requiring companies to ensure that machinery shut down for maintenance cannot be turned on while employees work on it. Also OSHA, in an important policy shift, began referring flagrant cases of willful exposure of employees to hazards of all kinds to the Justice Department for criminal prosecution. OSHA had always had this authority but had seldom used it.

However, OSHA under George H. W. Bush, as it had been under Reagan, was greatly restricted by the enormous oversight power held by OMB. Between 1981 and 1990 OMB changed, disapproved, or forced the withdrawal of more than 40 percent of the Labor Department's proposed regulations—most of which were generated by OSHA. Defenders of OMB's regulatory oversight powers maintained that the review process served as a necessary check and balance over rulemaking by agencies under the president's authority. Critics countered that OMB had become a super-regulatory agency, operating outside the normal rulemaking procedures.

Many supporters of OSHA hoped that the arrival of a Democratic president in 1993 would mean a more proactive federal bureaucracy. In September 1993 Bill Clinton issued Executive Order 12866, which limited OMB's role in regulatory overview. Joseph Dear, Clinton's assistant secretary of labor for OSHA, pledged to reinvigorate and rededicate OSHA. As part of the administration's "Reinventing Government" initiative, OSHA's inspection programs were restructured to focus on the most dangerous workplaces. The agency also streamlined procedures for complaints, eliminated obsolete regulations, and began to rewrite guidelines and requirements in nonbureaucratic language. To improve cooperation between OSHA and state agencies and with inspected businesses and industry, OSHA undertook a redesign of its field offices.

Under Dear, the agency initiated standards for certain workplace hazards that earlier had been overshadowed by OSHA's emphasis on accidents and company noncompliance. When the Centers for Disease Control issued a report in 1993 stating that tuberculosis (TB) transmission was a recognized risk in health care facilities, OSHA began work on a rule designed to protect health care workers from exposure to TB. The final rule was promulgated in September 1996. In 1995 OSHA began to develop specific guidelines to prevent workplace violence, which was on the rise.

OSHA had long been a target of antiregulatory groups, and it faced a particularly forceful challenge from the 104th Congress and its new Republican majority. For many in the Republican ranks and the business community, OSHA remained a symbol of the invasiveness of the federal government. In 1995 and 1996 various legislative proposals advanced in Congress to ease safety regulations on small businesses; apply cost-benefit analysis requirements to worker safety regulations; limit inspections to those workplaces where worker complaints had been filed; and eliminate the National Institute for Occupational Safety and Health (NIOSH), the research arm of OSHA. None of these major initiatives became law, although in 1996 Congress was able to pass the Small Business Regulatory Enforcement Fairness Act, which simply required OSHA to be more responsive to the needs of small businesses.

In addition to its congressional efforts at restructuring the agency, the Republican majority also cut OSHA's budget, decreasing it by $6 million to $304.9 million in fiscal 1996. Despite President Clinton's request for $340 million, Congress cut OSHA's budget further to $298 million in fiscal 1997. Efforts to expand voluntary safety partnerships stalled because of reduced funds for employer and worker training, as did plans for redesign of field offices.

In November 1997, Charles N. Jeffress, the former OSHA director for North Carolina, was sworn in as the new head of the agency. Jeffress soon announced a controversial policy for encouraging voluntary compliance among businesses that have bad health and safety records. Under the plan, the owners of the 12,000 work sites that had injury rates twice the national average or higher would be asked by the agency to voluntarily institute new, rigorous plans aimed at improving worker safety and health. In exchange for agreeing to comply, companies would significantly reduce the likelihood of a surprise OSHA inspection. Those businesses that did not opt for voluntary compliance would inevitably be inspected.

OSHA officials and others argued that the plan would let the agency focus on the worst employers while allowing others to fix their problems.

Although 87 percent of the targeted work sites volunteered to establish the new safety plans, many in the business community opposed the policy. The U.S. Chamber of Commerce, the National Association of Manufacturers, and other business groups argued that there was nothing "voluntary" about complying with the plan because noncompliance guaranteed inspection. The business groups succeeded in 1998 in getting a federal court to stop the new program temporarily and force OSHA to revert to its old, random inspection regime. In April 1999 the U.S. Court of Appeals in Washington, DC, ruled that the new safety program was essentially a new federal regulation and should have, under the Administrative Procedures Act, been open to public comment before it was finalized.

OSHA IN THE 2000s

Soon after Republican George W. Bush took office in 2001, it became clear that the new administration's approach to workplace safety issues would differ considerably from that of the Clinton administration. Almost immediately, Republican leaders in Congress, with support from the White House, moved to overturn high-profile workplace ergonomics regulations, which had been finalized in November 2000 after a decade of study and controversy.

The draft ergonomics regulations—aimed at preventing musculoskeletal disorders caused by repetitive motions such as typing or lifting—had been issued under Dear. But opposition from Congress, with the support of big business, had forced delays in the publication of final rules. At the end of Clinton's term, Jeffress issued the final regulations. The move left the new rules in a precarious place, because lawmakers had been unable to find a compromise.

The final regulations would have applied to about 102 million workers and would have required employers to inform their employees about musculoskeletal disorders such as carpal tunnel syndrome and tendonitis. Businesses would have had to adjust job conditions when an injury occurred and allow workers who were unable to work to continue receiving up to 90 percent of their pay for ninety days.

Congressional Republicans overturned the final Clinton ergonomics rule through an unusual legislative procedure known as the Congressional Review Act. That procedure, which allows Congress to overturn any regulation by simple majorities in each chamber within a limited time frame, had never before been used successfully to rescind a rule. A Congressional Review Act resolution bans an agency from issuing a similar regulation that is in "substantially the same form." Bush Labor Secretary Elaine L. Chao said that she would work to create a more flexible program to "address injuries before they occur, through prevention and compliance assistance."

Regardless of Chao's promise, organized labor and its Democratic allies protested the loss of the ergonomics rule, saying the new administration was paying back big business for its support in the 2000 election at the expense of worker safety. Business groups and others countered that the causes of ergonomic injuries were still too vague to impose a broad and expensive mandate on businesses.

Another Clinton-era workplace-safety proposal that was dropped by the Bush administration would have banned smoking in virtually all workplaces. The rule, which never went into effect, was vigorously opposed by the tobacco industry but supported by the nation's public health community. OSHA announced it was setting aside the proposed rule so that it could "devote its resources to other projects." It also noted that nearly 70 percent of all workplaces were already smoke-free.

The first year of the new administration also saw the appointment of John Henshaw as OSHA's new head. While Henshaw came from the business sector—working on health and safety issues for a number of chemical companies—organized labor praised the nominee's relevant experience. He was confirmed by the Senate in August 2001.

The start of 2002 found labor unions and OSHA once again at odds. This time, the fight concerned the new ergonomic policy the administration had promised. The new policy called for companies to take voluntary steps to reduce repetitive motion injuries. OSHA hoped to assist employers by developing ergonomic guidelines for major industries, especially those with high rates of repetitive stress injuries such as meatpacking and nursing home care. Enforcement would be beefed up to encourage companies to take the steps needed to reduce ergonomic injuries and punish those who ignored the issue and allowed workers to be hurt. Finally, OSHA would create a National Advisory Committee on Ergonomics to help it set guidelines and conduct research on how best to reduce repetitive stress injuries.

Henshaw said the voluntary industry guidelines would give businesses flexibility to tailor their ergonomic efforts to their specific needs. But unions and their allies in Congress criticized the plan as a gift to big business. In spite of this criticism, OSHA moved ahead with its ergonomics plan. In January 2003 the agency also began working with industry groups and companies to produce voluntary guidelines for each major sector of the workplace. During the first few years of this plan, OSHA helped formulate ergonomic guidelines for the nursing home, poultry processing, retail grocery, and shipyard industries. Moreover, the agency set up alliances with other industrial sectors—including airline baggage handlers and construction workers—and began working on drafting their voluntary guidelines.

OSHA also greatly beefed up enforcement in this area. After conducting only eighty-seven inspections between 1993 and 2000, it made 1,300 ergonomics-related visits to businesses from July 2002 to January 2004. However, critics of the agency noted that in spite of an increase in ergonomic inspections, OSHA had issued only twelve citations in the two and a half years. Critics also pointed to a June 2003 repeal of a requirement that employers report repetitive stress injuries as further evidence that the agency was not serious about reducing ergonomic problems in the workplace. Labor unions had supported the reporting requirement, arguing that the data would help OSHA determine which industries were the most ergonomically hazardous and hence in need of the most attention.

Indeed, in place of promulgating rules, OSHA used voluntary ergonomic plans as part of a broader, agency-wide shift away from a regulatory regime and toward an approach that emphasized collaboration with business. For example, between 2002 and 2004, the agency formed 231 alliances with trade associations and companies, providing them with detailed information and guidance on making their workplaces safer.

At the same time, OSHA issued few regulations. Of the thirty-three agency rules that were in some stage of development when Clinton left office, twenty-four were subsequently withdrawn, according to OMB Watch, a government watchdog group. Among those withdrawn were new rules governing toxic chemicals, flammable and combustible liquids, and metalworking fluids. Of the nine regulations that were completed, none were of any great significance, the group claimed.

Henshaw defended the agency's new focus and methods, arguing that the change in direction had already produced results, in the form of decreases in injuries and illnesses on the job. Even though there was a slight increase in the number of people killed at work, Henshaw predicted that that number also would soon fall as the effect of OSHA's new policies spread to more and more businesses, which is exactly what happened. In 2006 the number of worker fatalities dropped to a near twenty-year low of 5,703.

Henshaw also pointed to stepped-up enforcement efforts as proof that the agency was not doing the bidding of big business. For instance, in March 2003 OSHA announced that it would dramatically increase the number of follow-up inspections of those work sites where there had been severe safety violations. One year later the agency announced that it would inspect 4,000 high-hazard work sites in 2004, a significant increase over previous years.

But Democrats and organized labor argued that these steps were not enough to offset the deficiencies of OSHA's "collaborative" approach, which, they claimed, left big business with little incentive to improve worker safety. Congressional Democrats introduced legislation that would have significantly stiffened criminal penalties for willful health and safety violations on the part of employers. But the legislation did not have the support of the administration or the Republican majority in either house of Congress and soon stalled.

In December 2004 Henshaw announced that he was stepping down. Labor Secretary Chao appointed as the agency's acting head Jonathon L. Snare, who had worked at the Labor Department as a senior adviser to the solicitor's office. Early in Snare's brief tenure, the agency announced that it was working more closely with the Environmental Protection Agency and the Justice Department's Environmental Crimes Section to better coordinate enforcement efforts. The initiative was prompted by the notion that employers who violated environmental regulations also were more likely to ignore

worker safety requirements, and vice versa. While the partnership received little attention, it has resulted in a number of successful criminal prosecutions, including guilty verdicts in 2006 against executives of McWane Inc. and ACS Environmental Services.

While Snare was at OSHA, the agency also set new limits on acceptable workplace exposure to airborne particles of hexavalent cromium, a toxic metal substance produced by makers of steel, paint, and other industrial products that has been shown to cause lung cancer, asthma, and other respiratory illnesses. The limits set by OSHA, five micrograms of dust per cubic meter of air, was one-tenth the amount allowed under the existing standards, which dated from the 1940s. Still, labor and environmental activists decried the new standards, pointing out that five micrograms was still five times higher than the levels OSHA had originally proposed. At the same time, industry groups argued that the new standard was too onerous and would lead many manufacturers to relocate factories in other countries.

Snare served as OSHA head for only about one year. In September 2005 President George W. Bush named Edwin G. Foulke Jr. to be assistant secretary of labor for OSHA. Foulke was a labor relations lawyer who had served four years as chair of the Occupational Safety and Health Review Commission, the adjudicatory body that settles disputes between OSHA and employers who have been cited for workplace safety violations. Foulke was easily confirmed by the Senate in March 2006.

Almost immediately after assuming his post, Foulke and OSHA found themselves at the center of a controversy. First, in April the Government Accountability Office (GAO) released a report criticizing the agency for neglecting to properly monitor workplace safety at federal government offices and facilities. According to the report, OSHA only rarely performed workplace safety inspections at federal facilities. In addition, although the agency was required by law to conduct annual worker safety evaluations at each federal department and agency, it had not done so since 2000. The report also noted that from 1995 to 2004, more than 800 federal employees had died in workplace-related accidents.

OSHA officials did not deny the report's conclusions and instead pointed out that the agency had relatively few staff members specifically dedicated to federal workplace safety. They also pointed out that OSHA was working to implement a 2004 White House initiative aimed at reducing worker compensation claims among federal employees by improving the collection of safety data at federal offices and using the information to better target inspections.

OSHA also faced complaints over delays in issuing a rule requiring employers to purchase adequate safety equipment, such as faceplates and rubber boots, for workers in hazardous jobs, particularly in the meatpacking, poultry, and construction industries. OSHA had initially proposed such a rule in 1999, while President Clinton was still in office. But the proposal was put on hold for the next eight years, prompting the AFL-CIO and the United Food and Commercial Workers to sue the agency in 2006 for failing to implement the requirement. The lawsuit was eventually dropped after the Labor Department, in March 2007, agreed to issue the rule.

In the wake of the November 2006 elections, George Miller (D-CA), the incoming head of the House Committee on Education and Labor, promised to be much more vigorous with OSHA oversight, starting with a review of the agency's voluntary compliance programs. Miller's first congressional hearing on OSHA in March 2007, however, turned into a lengthy denunciation of the agency's current practices. Congressional Democrats brought up a number of other worker safety issues, including the alleged slow pace at which OHSA had been implementing the voluntary ergonomics guidelines it first promised in 2002 and the high number of injuries among immigrant workers in industries such as meatpacking and construction.

Amidst this criticism, administration supporters argued that the White House was committed to worker safety. As evidence they pointed to President Bush's fiscal year 2008 budget for the agency, which included $490 million for OSHA, an increase of $17.9 million from the agency's 2007 budget. Much of the extra funding was slated to be used to increase enforcement efforts, especially in high-hazard industries, such as meatpacking. In addition, administration supporters pointed out that the agency planned 37,700 workplace inspections for 2008, 1,200 more than in 2007. While Foulke and others touted the additional funding for OSHA, union representatives argued that the administration was nonetheless shortchanging the agency, pointing out that the slightly larger budget was still $5 million less than 2006 funding levels, once inflation was factored in.

Meanwhile OSHA faced new challenges, including preparing for a possible deadly influenza pandemic. For more than a year, a rising number of bird flu cases in Asia, Europe, and Africa had stoked fears that the avian virus could mutate into a strain of influenza particularly deadly to humans, killing millions around the world. In February 2007 OSHA issued guidelines to help employers prepare their workplaces in the event of a major flu pandemic. Recommendations included preparing a "disaster plan" and training some employees to carry out critical business functions if a company were to lose a large part of its workforce to illness or death. "A severe pandemic in our country could have a devastating effect on our nation's workplaces," Foulke said at the time. "Proper planning and preparation now saves lives in the future."

Later in 2007 and in 2008, OSHA issued a number of large fines for safety violations across a number of industries. In August 2007, for instance, the agency found forty-six safety violations at a Cintas Corporation plant in Tulsa, OK, where one worker was killed, and levied a $2.76 million fine against the company. An $8.7 million penalty grew out of an incident that occurred in February 2008, when an explosion at an Imperial Sugar refinery in Port Wentworth, GA, killed thirteen workers and seriously burned ten others. The incident was the latest in approximately 300 such cases and 130 deaths since 1980 blamed on combustible sugar dust. Combustible dust buildup is a problem in a number of industries, including chemical, pharmaceutical, and recycling operations. OSHA asserted

that Imperial had known of the safety hazards associated with combustible dust as early as 2002 and did nothing to alleviate conditions at its plants.

In response to these high-profile incidents, the House in May 2008 passed a bill requiring OSHA to issue new standards for regulating industries that produce hazardous combustible dusts, based on recommendations from the National Fire Protection Association. The measure was never taken up by the Senate. However, in May 2009, under a Democratic White House, OSHA announced that it would adopt stricter rules for controlling combustible dust.

Later in 2008, the agency held Rapetti Rigging Services responsible for the collapse of a tower crane in midtown New York City that killed seven people and injured a dozen others. The incident generated a lot of media attention about workplace safety at construction sites, particularly heavily populated city sites as in this case. In September 2008 OSHA issued nearly three dozen citations against Rapetti as well as two other firms and levied fines of $220,000. In January 2009 owner William Rapetti was indicted by the Manhattan District Attorney's Office on charges of manslaughter and reckless homicide, among other charges.

Workplace safety violations hit closer to home when a twenty-seven-year Smithsonian Institution employee filed federal workplace safety complaints against his employer in 2008. Richard Pullman, a lighting specialist at the National Air and Space Museum, became alarmed when he learned during an asbestos safety class that there was asbestos in the museum walls. In his work, Pullman had frequently cut into interior walls to install and update artifacts. Because he had been experiencing shortness of breath, Pullman went to see a lung doctor who diagnosed asbestosis, a lung disease linked to breathing asbestos fibers.

Investigations by the agency revealed that although workers had been drilling, sanding, and cutting exhibit walls for more than thirty years, they had never been warned about asbestos in the walls until the 2008 asbestos safety class. Asbestos became an issue again when members of a steamfitters union claimed that asbestos dust had filled the air during renovation of the National Museum of American History in 2007 and that proper precautionary actions had not been taken to protect employees. Specifically, air circulation equipment continued to operate after the dust became airborne, exposing the museum's full-time staff—who continued to work in the building during the construction—to the contaminant.

In a statement before a congressional panel hearing on April 1, 2009, secretary of the Smithsonian Institution, G. Wayne Clough, said that he had ordered free health screenings for all employees and a complete review of the institution's safety policies and procedures, asserting that there had never been any indication of unacceptable levels of asbestos. A cleanup of the asbestos in the Air and Space Museum was initiated in March 2009.

While the agency received praise for its involvement in these high-profile cases, the criticism of its overall performance under President Bush continued. Indeed, even after the November 2008 elections, OSHA and the Bush administration were the subjects of a number of highly critical articles in major newspapers, charging gross neglect of worker safety. According to a December 2008 investigative article in the *Washington Post,* between 2001 and 2007 the agency issued 86 percent fewer significant workplace safety rules or regulations than their counterparts did during eight years under Clinton. The article also pointed out that the agency issued just two health standards during this period, in contrast to the thirty-two released between 1992 and 2000.

In the waning days of the Bush presidency, the administration worked to quickly push through a number of OSHA-related proposals that critics charged were last-minute gifts for big business. For instance, in August 2008 the Labor Department fast-tracked a new rule that would make it harder for OSHA to regulate potentially dangerous workplace chemicals by intensifying the standards for scientific data used to assess the risk of these chemicals and by requiring the agency to add another "advance" round of outside challenges to any proposed regulation. This last step was seen by critics as possibly adding up to two more years to the already long, eight-year process it took to put out a new rule for a complex chemical hazard.

In 2009, even with the new administration of Barack Obama in charge, criticisms of the Bush-era OSHA intensified after an April 2009 Labor Department audit reported that a 2003 initiative designed to improve worker safety in hazardous industries had rarely fulfilled its mission. The aim of what was called the "Enhanced Enforcement Program" had been to better use OSHA resources by focusing on improving safety conditions at companies with a troubled history of job-related fatalities. The Labor Department report found that OSHA did not follow correct procedures in 97 percent of the cases examined in the program. In addition, a 2008 procedural change at OSHA resulted in a significant drop in the number of companies targeted by the program, from 719 in 2007 to 475 in 2008. The agency had appeared to be leaning heavily on a strategy of "voluntary compliance," in which agreements are reached with industry associations and companies to police themselves.

Amidst these criticisms, President Obama lost little time in declaring his commitment to improving workplace safety. In his fiscal 2010 budget request, Obama proposed a 10 percent increase in funding for the agency, to $563.5 million. Ultimately, Congress gave the president most of what he wanted, appropriating $558.6 million for the agency, a 9 percent increase.

Meanwhile, the agency saw a change in leadership. In April 2009 Jordan Barab became the acting assistant secretary of labor for OSHA. Barab had had a long career in workplace safety, working at different times on health and safety issues for the House Education and Labor Committee; U.S. Chemical Safety and Hazard Investigation Board; and the American Federation of State, County, and Municipal Employees. Just a few months later, however, the president named David Michaels to be the assistant secretary of labor for OSHA. Michaels was a professor of environmental and occupational health at George Washington University. Barab, who was picked to be the

agency's number two, was confirmed as deputy assistant secretary for OSHA on the same day that Michaels won Senate approval.

OSHA IN THE 2010s

Early in Michael's tenure the agency became involved in a high-profile case involving Kleen Energy Systems, a power plant under construction in Middletown, CT. In early February 2010 an explosion at the still-unfinished plant killed six people, wounded fifty others, and shook homes in a wide area across the state. The explosion occurred as workers for O&G Industries, an industrial construction firm, were purging a pipeline of natural gas, a procedure that involves shooting flammable natural gas through a supply pipe to rid it of debris. The dangers of this procedure, known as "blow-down," have been well-documented. Indeed, a blow-down was the cause of a similar incident, which killed four workers, nearly a year before at a ConAgra Foods plant in Garner, NC.

After a six-month investigation, OSHA issued $16.6 million in fines to O&G and a number of other construction and maintenance firms, stemming from 371 alleged violations, including 255 considered "willful" in their blatant disregard of worker safety. Among the breaches the agency said it found were a failure to vent gas after it was no longer needed, neglecting to remove nonessential workers during the procedure, and allowing welders to continue working during the blow-down (welding torches are thought to be a possible cause of the explosion). Michaels also noted that O&G and other companies had been given "significant financial incentives" to meet deadlines and get the plant up and running by May 31, deadline pressure that may have contributed to the lapses in safety procedures.

In the wake of its investigation, OSHA issued a warning letter to other operators of gas-fired power plants, urging them to consider using alternatives to flammable gas when cleaning pipes. Still, the agency has yet to issue an emergency ban on the practice and has been instead reviewing whether a ban could sustain a legal challenge.

The agency levied an even heftier penalty against oil giant BP after a 2005 explosion that killed fifteen workers at its Texas City, Texas, refinery, the third-largest oil refinery in the country. The $50.6 million fine is the largest in the agency's history, and more than three times the size of any previous OSHA sanction. The explosion occurred when a 170-foot tower was being filled with liquid hydrocarbons—propane and other liquid fuels derived from natural gas. Workers, who had been logging in twelve-hour shifts for more than a month, failed to notice that the tower was filled too high. A geyser of unstable chemicals shot into the air, which then caught fire when a contractor, who had been trying to get away, repeatedly tried to start the engine on his stalled pickup truck.

BP initially disputed all of the 709 violations found during subsequent inspections of the refinery by OSHA. The company said that following the explosion it spent more than $1 billion to upgrade production and improve safety at the refinery. But OSHA countered that BP has long been lax when it comes to safety issues. In the agency's estimation, BP's zealous pursuit of growth and profits contributed to the company's shortcuts on safety procedures and put unreasonable production pressures on fatigued employees, who often worked with out-of-date equipment. In August 2010 BP agreed to pay the record $87 million and accepted the 270 citations for failing to fix problems following the deadly explosion.

The Texas City incident was unrelated to the April 20, 2010, explosion of the offshore drilling rig, Deepwater Horizon, in the Gulf of Mexico, an accident that killed eleven workers and injured seventeen. Work safety issues surrounding the incident, which led to the largest oil spill in U.S. history, were still under investigation in 2011. As the Texas City refinery case illustrates, fatigue can play a big role in workplace injuries. Moreover, fatigue-related injuries may be more common in times of economic recession, where many companies do more with fewer employees.

A panel of labor and corporate representatives in the transportation and petrochemical industries met in early May 2011 to discuss on-the-job fatigue issues. At the meeting, Jim Lefton, an official with the United Steelworkers Union, pointed out that OSHA does not set fatigue standards and that standards were being set by unions and management during contract negotiations.

Unions and worker safety advocates contend that fatigue is an area where regulations have not kept up with the changing times. This is especially evident in the airline industry, they say, where rules on the number of hours that pilots and other airline employees can work have not changed much since 1985. But business groups and others argue that there are no compelling reasons to set new standards, pointing out that the airlines and other industries where fatigue might be an issue generally have excellent safety records.

In addition to fatigue, repetitive motion injuries also received a lot of attention around this time. This type of injury is among the most common, causing 28 percent of American workers to miss at least one day of work in 2009. In March 2010 Michaels vowed that the agency would soon address the issue with new rules and standards. But less than a year later, in January 2011, OSHA withdrew a modest rule it had proposed just months before requiring employers to record repetitive motion injuries separately on injury logs. According to Michaels, the proposed rule was "temporarily" pulled because the agency needed to consult with small businesses to determine how the change would affect them. Unions cried foul, but agency observers pointed out the agency was probably responding to President Obama's Jan. 18, 2011, order that regulatory agencies review rules with an eye to eliminating those that are unnecessary or put "unreasonable burdens on businesses."

But while labor and business lobbies debated the necessity of a separate repetitive motion reporting requirement, a new report released by the GAO called into question the accuracy of existing workplace safety data. OSHA came in for particularly harsh criticism, with the report pointing to several academic studies that found the agency may have missed nearly two-thirds of workplace injuries and illnesses. Auditors cited numerous reasons for these inaccuracies, including underreporting by employees for fear of being fired, disciplined, or penalized; pressure felt by health practitioners to play down injuries or illnesses; and fears by employers that reporting injuries would increase their workmans' compensation costs or hurt their chances of winning contracts. In light of this evidence, the agency agreed to adopt the GAO's recommendations, which includes requiring inspectors to interview employees during all audits to verify the accuracy of employer-provided injury data.

At the same time that its data accuracy was under question, OSHA became involved in a number of high-profile worker safety cases. In August 2010, for instance, the agency fined SeaWorld $75,000 for safety violations related to the headline-grabbing death earlier in the year of a SeaWorld Orlando trainer who drowned after being dragged underwater by a killer whale named Tilikum. At a subsequent trial in 2012, an OSHA administrative law judge ruled that animal trainers must be better protected from mammals such as Tilikum, who ignored slaps in the water and other signals designed to keep him under control. The judge also questioned the theme park's tendency to blame trainers when things went wrong and to place too much faith in the predictability of the orca's behavior. But the judge also scaled back the agency's earlier sanction, downgrading one major violation from "willful" to "serious" and reduced the fines SeaWorld was required to pay from the original $75,000 to $12,000. The judge also stated that SeaWorld is "a safety-conscious employer with a highly detailed and thorough" safety training program.

In March 2011, in another high-profile case, the agency cited the Broadway musical production *Spider-Man: Turn off the Dark* for three serious workplace safety violations, stemming from several instances in which cast members were hurt. In one case, actor Christopher Tierney sustained broken ribs and a hairline fracture of his skull when he fell, untethered, from a platform stage into the orchestra pit. In March 2011, OSHA fined the musical's production company, 8 Legged Productions, $12,600.

In March 2012, the agency fined Verizon more than $140,000—the maximum allowed by law—for safety violations following the 2011 electrocution death of a technician in Brooklyn, New York. OSHA issued more than 10 citations against the telecommunications company, finding, among other things, that Verizon failed to provide technicians with lifesaving equipment and had not ensured that protective helmets and gloves were used during dangerous work operations. The agency also found that Verizon did not provide adequate training to those technicians who worked near high-voltage lines. Many of these violations were repeat offenses for Verizon. In fact, the company's lax safety record had been one of the issues that had prompted 45,000 Verizon employees to strike in August 2011.

Another high-profile case involved Walmart and its practice of allowing thousands of people to wait outside its stores before big storewide sales and then rush in when the building opens. This case was prompted by the trampling death of one of the company's employees at its Valley Stream, New York, store. The employee died of asphyxiation when 2,000 shoppers charged through the doors on Black Friday 2008, the day following Thanksgiving, when many stores traditionally run a major sales event.

In April 2011, with the Walmart case very much in mind, OSHA issued guidelines on retail crowd control, which included training employees in crowd control techniques and giving people tickets for popular items, such as electronics, to avoid a rush at opening. Although Walmart said that it was and would continue to abide by these guidelines, by spring of 2013, it was still appealing the $7,000 fine from the Valley Stream incident. The company's appeals had little to do with the money. Instead, Walmart and other retailers worry that if the ruling is upheld, OSHA could have much greater influence over retailers and their marketing campaigns.

Finally, in an incident reminiscent of the Rapetti Rigging Services crane collapse in 2008, a crane on the far west side of Manhattan spectacularly collapsed in April 2012, killing one worker and injuring four others. Just before it collapsed, a steel-wire cable on the crane snapped. Later, a commissioner of the city's building department confirmed that finding, reporting that engineers discovered defects in the hoisting system of the 24-year-old, 170-foot crane. OSHA charged that Yonkers Contracting did not meet national standards for the maintenance and operation of mobile cranes. More specifically, the agency cited the company for serious violations of workplace safety, including allowing a worker inside the crane's fall zone and failing to adequately inspect the wire ropes used to hoist materials. Yonkers Contracting is currently contesting the $68,000 in fines proposed by OSHA.

These various workplace injury cases are typical of the types of incidents OSHA spends most of its time pursuing. The agency has a history of rating safety threats a higher priority than health hazards, a pattern for which it would come under criticism in 2013 (see below). One exception during this period involved complaints OSHA received from stylists and hair salon owners with regard to formaldehyde exposure. OSHA first became aware of this issue in October 2010, when it began conducting air sampling at multiple salons and found formaldehyde in the air when stylists were using products such as Brazilian Blowout Acai Professional Smoothing Solution, a keratin-based hair-smoothing product.

In April 2011, the agency warned that Brazilian Blowout and other products like it had unacceptably high levels of formaldehyde. Salon workers who used the product had reported headaches, nosebleeds, vomiting, and asthma attacks. Some of these products were labeled "formaldehyde free" or did not list formaldehyde on the product label. This finding came just a couple of months before the Department of Health and Human Services issued a report identifying formaldehyde—which also is found in troublingly high quantities in plywood, particle board, and mortuaries—as a carcinogen. In January 2012, the distributer of Brazilian Blowout agreed to include "Caution" stickers on bottles of the hair smoother with warnings about formaldehyde exposure and a description of precautions that should be taken when using the product.

Another relatively unusual OSHA action during this period stemmed from complaints made by foreign exchange students who were working at Exel, which owns a Palmyra, Pennsylvania, factory that makes chocolate for Hershey. The students, who hailed from countries including China, Romania, and Nigeria, were employed through a foreign exchange program for work and travel offered by the State Department, which allows students to work for several months and then travel for a month as tourists. Two hundred of these students walked off their jobs in August 2011, complaining of low pay and overly strenuous work, including production lines that were moving too fast for them to keep up their work.

Hershey tried to improve the situation by asking the plant contractor to give the foreign students a fully paid week off. But OSHA initiated what would become a six-month long investigation of charges of safety violations at the Palmyra plant. In February 2012, the agency issued fines of $283,000—fairly steep for workplace safety offenses—against Exel, finding that it had failed to report 42 serious injuries over four years. Six of the nine cited violations were for "willful failure by Exel to protect its employees." These injuries were echoed in the exchange students' stories, in which they complained of neck, back, and arm injuries from repeatedly lifting and carrying boxes that weighed up to 60 pounds.

Meanwhile, OSHA became involved in alleged widespread safety violations connected to cleanup operations after Hurricane Sandy, which hit the Mid-Atlantic coast of the United States in October 2012. At the height of the cleanup, workers without protection fell from roofs, were shocked by exposed wires, or were injured by chemicals. Federal inspectors found 3,100 instances of unsafe job conditions when they patrolled hurricane-ravaged neighborhoods in New York City, New Jersey, and Long Island. Records obtained under the Freedom of Information Act revealed that there were a variety of safety violations, including instances in which some contractors blatantly disregarded rules, even after being caught and warned. In some cases, there appeared to be an intentional cover-up. While the agency removed approximately 7,900 workers from hazardous situations, few employers were ultimately punished. OSHA issued violations in only 32 cases, imposing fines that totaled just $141,934.

In the spring of 2013 OSHA made headlines after it completed investigations in a number of large-scale explosions at facilities in the southwest. The first, a September 2012 boiler explosion at an Oklahoma refinery, killed two workers. The refinery, which had been cited for a similar boiler explosion in 2008, was fined $281,000 for the 2012 accident. David Bates, director of the agency's Oklahoma City–area office, remarked: "If OSHA's standards had been followed, it is possible this tragedy could have been avoided." Some local residents expressed concern that the September explosion was due to a generally lax environment at the refinery and questioned whether some of the company's 265 workers might have been reluctant to complain for fear of losing their jobs.

Lack of regulatory oversight was even more glaring in the case of the April 2013 explosion at a fertilizer plant in the town of West, Texas. The facility had been inspected only once in its 51-year history, and that had been roughly three decades ago. In that 1985 inspection, the agency had detected multiple serious violations of federal safety requirements, for which the company had paid a mere $30 in fines. Because Texas does not have an occupational safety and health program that meets federal requirements, OSHA is responsible for ensuring the safety of potentially dangerous workplaces such as the one at West Texas Fertilizer. The chemical that caused the explosion is ammonium nitrate, a highly combustible substance and the same one that Timothy McVeigh used in the Oklahoma City bombing in 1995. The explosion in West Texas, which occurred 20 minutes after a fire had been reported at the plant, was so powerful that it resulted in 15 deaths and nearly 200 injuries.

In the weeks following the blast, regulators from OSHA and other agencies remained baffled as to how a plant with such obvious dangers had largely fallen through the regulatory cracks. For instance, facilities that house more than 400 pounds of ammonium nitrate are required to file regular security reports with the Department of Homeland Security. But no such reports were ever filed, even though the plant in West had 540,000 pounds of the substance. Also, federal officials were unclear as to how local officials had approved the placement of homes and even schools near the site. One early culprit, agency investigators determined, was an overreliance by state and federal agencies on self-reporting. Still, in October 2013 the agency levied $118,300 in fines to West Fertilizer Company, citing two-dozen serious safety violations.

Indeed, the number of deaths as well as the results of the initial investigation led to a wave of criticism from outside the agency as well as soul-searching within OSHA itself. To begin with, virtually everyone agreed that the agency simply did not have the resources to undertake the kinds of comprehensive inspections needed to ensure compliance with safety standards, especially at smaller, more remote facilities like the West Fertilizer Company. In 2013 the ratio of OSHA inspectors to workers under its jurisdiction was 1 to 60,000, compared with 1 to 30,000 in the 1970s. And with budget cuts brought about by the sequester, the number of inspectors was unlikely to rise and, if anything, could continue to fall.

In addition to a lack of resources, critics also faulted the agency for its overemphasis on safety at the expense of long-term health. While a crane collapse or trampling death that made news headlines understandably captured the agency's attention, long-term health dangers often took decades to be noticed, let alone addressed, they said. OHSA head David Michaels admitted that his agency's record regarding long-term dangers was inadequate: "I'm the first to admit this is broken . . . meanwhile, tens of thousands of people end up on the gurney," he told the New York Times in April 2013.

Around the same time Michaels was speaking about long-term health risks, the agency issued a report on the long-term and short-term health dangers posed to workers and even USDA inspectors in poultry processing plants. The issue involves exposure for long periods of time to potentially dangerous chemicals used processing the chickens and turkeys. Substances such as ammonia, which help kill bacteria and prevent diseases like salmonella, have been known to cause respiratory, eye, skin, and other ailments in workers and inspectors in the poultry industry.

According to the OSHA report, which was intended to raise awareness of the issue, recent snap inspections had shown serious problems at five processing facilities. These included failure on the part of management to adequately train workers in how to handle potentially toxic substances and failure to monitor levels of exposure to ensure that those working with these chemicals were not in any danger. But while the report received significant media attention, poultry industry representatives denied that the use of chemicals in plants was harmful to workers. In addition, they argued, chemicals with antibacterial properties are the most effective way to protect the public from poultry-related diseases such as salmonella.

A few months later, in August 2013 Michaels's new boss, Thomas Perez, was sworn in as the nation's secretary of Labor. Perez, who replaced Hilda Solis, had held a number of important jobs prior to his nomination, including assistant attorney general for civil rights. Known for his energy and ambition, Perez promised to hit the ground running at the department. Specifically, he was expected to push forward on new regulations that had been held up for one reason or another.

And indeed, a little more than a month after Perez was sworn in, OSHA proposed important and controversial new rules dramatically limiting workplace exposure to silica dust. Exposure to silica, which is used in the manufacture of glass, stone, and other building materials, causes severe respiratory trouble for thousands of workers each year. Effects include lung cancer and silicosis, which causes the lungs to swell and makes breathing increasingly difficult. Those at risk include people in factories as well as people working in the mining and construction industries.

The rule would cut the amount of silica workers could be exposed to by up to 80 percent from levels that are currently permitted. "We know that disease occurs at exposures below the current level," OSHA's Michaels said on the day the proposed rule was announced. "To truly protect the American worker, you need to lower the exposure level," he added.

Industry groups, however, argued that the proposed rule would be expensive to implement and that it would be very difficult for companies to continually and accurately measure the amount of silica particulates in the air. They vowed to fight the new standard and, two years later, the rule still had not taken effect.

But while the agency was stymied in some of its proposed rulemaking, it continued to move forward in its enforcement and other actions. In April 2014, for instance, Republic Steel agreed to pay an unusually high $2.4 million fine to OSHA to settle multiple allegations of worker health and safety violations at four of its factories in Ohio and New York. The agreement between the agency and company mandated not only that Republic fix the problems that led to the fine but that it create a comprehensive safety compliance program at all of its facilities to ensure that, going forward, worker safety is a priority.

And in July 2014 OSHA sounded an alarm about heat-related conditions in the workplace. The message was accompanied by an agency report that showed that in 2012, 31 outdoor workers died and 4,120 had become ill as a result of working in conditions that were too hot. Particularly at risk were people who often spend all day outside, including construction workers, farm laborers, and trash collectors. The report was a follow-up from a 2011 OSHA campaign and voluntary guidelines to encourage employers during the summer months to allocate a longer than usual time for rest and to make sure that outdoor workers had access to plenty of water and shade.

As 2014 neared its end, the agency issued a number of other voluntary guidelines aimed at helping employers deal with specific health and safety issues. For instance, in October OSHA released an advisory to help employers with workers who may have been exposed to the Ebola virus, which was killing thousands per month in sub-Saharan Africa at the time. OSHA urged employers with workers at risk of contracting the disease to be on the lookout for symptoms and to educate employees about self-monitoring.

A month later, in November, OSHA sent out a letter to major retailers warning about the dangers to employees working on Black Friday and recommending safety guidelines. Most retailers see Black Friday, the day after Thanksgiving, as the official beginning of the holiday shopping season. Stores often open at midnight and can be overwhelmed and overrun by crowds. In the past, workers have been badly injured (and in at least one case killed) by swarming and chaotic crowds of shoppers. The agency urged all retailers to plan ahead so that large numbers of shoppers can be controlled and employees are not put in difficult or even dangerous situations.

Current Issues

Because the workplace is constantly changing, OSHA has had to contend with a steady stream of new and often difficult challenges. For example, as factories and warehouses become more automated, a growing number of workers are being killed or injured by self-operating machines or robots. While many of these machines have, until recently, been stationary, new robots are becoming much more mobile and self-directed, which means they are more capable of inflicting injuries if they malfunction. In April 2015 OSHA cited Formed Fiber Technologies for not having proper safeguards on some of its autonomous machines. The company could end up paying $108,800 in fines.

Much larger fines also continue in more traditional settings. In February 2015, for instance, the agency fined Ashley Furniture $1.7 million for dozens of alleged violations of safety rules at its furniture factory in Arcadia, Wisconsin. According to the OSHA officials, workers at the plant had suffered more than 1,000 injuries over a three-and-a-half-year period.

In March the agency was thrust into the headlines when "Fight for $15," a group advocating a national $15 per hour minimum wage, alleged that workers at McDonald's

in 19 American cities had recently been injured due to lack of proper training and protective equipment. Injuries at the fast food restaurants included burns and sprains, the group claimed. While McDonald's has reiterated its commitment to worker safety, it has promised to look into the charges. For its part, OSHA also is planning to investigate the complaints.

That same month, the agency tightened its reporting requirements for employers with injured employees. Under the old rules, employers were required to report worker injuries to OSHA only if three or more workers were injured. Under the new rules, all serious injuries (those involving overnight stays in the hospital) must be reported to OSHA. The new requirement is aimed at giving the agency a more comprehensive picture of serious workplace injuries. That in turn will allow the agency to more efficiently deploy its inspectors and investigators.

Meanwhile, in April the agency issued updated guidance aimed at better protecting health care workers and other social service providers from violence. OSHA notes that these workers are four times more likely to suffer a violent attack on the job than the average American worker, largely because they often help troubled and even psychotic people. "It is unacceptable that people who dedicate their lives to care for our loved ones often work in fear of injury or death," Michaels said in a statement accompanying the release of the guidelines.

The agency recommends that employers create a "workplace violence prevention program" that monitors and tracks threats and regularly considers preventive measures. The new guidelines also identify risk factors that employers should work to mitigate, including crowded waiting areas and a lack of adequately trained security personnel.

▪ AGENCY ORGANIZATION

Headquarters and Divisions

ASSISTANT SECRETARY OF LABOR FOR OCCUPATIONAL SAFETY AND HEALTH

Advises and assists the secretary of labor on all matters related to worker safety and health and provides executive direction for developing and enforcing safety and health standards. Holds final authority over all departments within OSHA and provides leadership and direction for public affairs, policy analysis, legislative and interagency affairs, equal employment opportunities, and regional programs.

Assistant Secretary
    David Michaels . . . . (202) 693–2000
          Fax. . . . . (202) 693–1659
Deputy Assistant Secretaries
    Dorothy Dougherty . . . . (202) 693–2000
    Jordan Barab . . . . (202) 693–2000
Chief of Staff
    Kirk Sander . . . . (202) 693–2000
Senior Policy Adviser
    Deborah Berkowitz . . . . (202) 693–2000

Occupational Safety and Health Administration

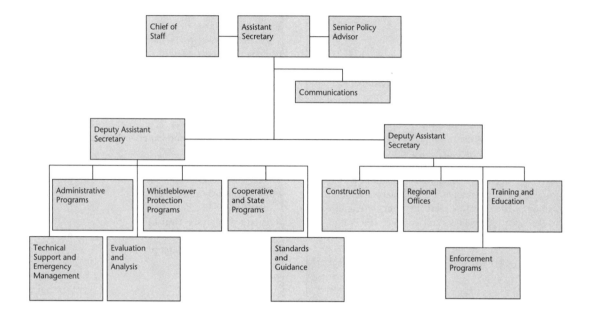

OFFICE OF COMMUNICATIONS
See Information Sources.

EQUAL EMPLOYMENT OPPORTUNITY
OSHA does not have an equal employment opportunity (EEO) office. The agency's EEO business is handled by the Department of Labor's Office of Civil Rights, which can be reached at (202) 693–6500.

DIRECTORATE OF ADMINISTRATIVE PROGRAMS
Responsible for general administrative services: personnel, labor-management relations, budgeting, contract management, data processing, and housekeeping. Compiles data and conducts studies on program policies and coordination with other management groups.

Director
Kimberly Locey . . . . (202) 693–1600
    Fax . . . . (202) 693–1660

Administrative Services
Heather LeMay . . . . (202) 693–2121
    Fax . . . . (202) 693–1660

Human Resources
Patricia Williams . . . . (202) 693–1800

Internet/Intranet Support Services
(see Salt Lake Technical Center)
Diane Childress . . . . (801) 233–4900
    Fax . . . . (801) 233–5004

Management Systems and Organization
Nancy Adams . . . . (202) 693–2002

Safety and Health Officer
Julia Navarro . . . . (202) 693–2151
    Fax . . . . (202) 693–1658

DIRECTORATE OF CONSTRUCTION
Advises OSHA on construction safety and engineering. Acts as technical construction adviser to the assistant secretary and supports all headquarters and regional organizations with regard to construction activities. Also serves as the focal point for requests for information from industry, labor, and other interest groups regarding OSHA's construction program.

Director
Jim Maddux . . . . (202) 693–2020
    Fax . . . . (202) 693–1689

Deputy Director
Dean McKenzie . . . . (202) 693–2020

Construction Services
Dean McKenzie . . . . (202) 693–2020

Construction Standards and Guidance
Paul Bolon . . . . (202) 693–2020

Engineering Services
Mohammad Ayub . . . . (202) 693–2020

DIRECTORATE OF COOPERATIVE AND STATE PROGRAMS
Develops, evaluates, and analyzes the performance of the state occupational safety and health programs. Trains and advises employers, employees, and their representative organizations on how to recognize, avoid, and prevent unsafe and unhealthful working conditions. Administers OSHA partnership programs including the Voluntary Protection Programs.

Director
Doug Kalinowski . . . . (202) 693–2200
    Fax . . . . (202) 693–1671

Deputy Director
Tina Jones . . . . (202) 693–2200

Outreach Services and Alliances
Manuel Gomez .... (202) 693–2340
Partnerships and Recognition
David Hamel .... (202) 693–2213
Small Business Assistance
Patrick Showalter .... (202) 693–2200
State Programs
Eric Lahaie .... (202) 693–2244

DIRECTORATE OF ENFORCEMENT PROGRAMS

Maintains occupational safety and health compliance directives and assistance programs for general industry, maritime, construction, health, and other areas; oversees an occupational safety and health program administered by federal agencies and submits evaluations and a summary report to the president; administers an antidiscrimination program that protects the rights of employees to make safety complaints; and conducts the cargo gear accreditation program.
Director
Thomas Galassi .... (202) 693–2100
Fax........................... (202) 693–1681
Chemical Process Safety and Enforcement Initiatives
Mary Lynn .... (202) 693–2341
Federal Agency Programs
Francis Yebesi.................... (202) 693–2122
General Industry and Agriculture Enforcement
Arthur Buchanan .... (202) 693–1850
Health Enforcement
Dionne Williams.................. (202) 693–2190
Maritime Enforcement
Stephen Butler .... (202) 693–2399

DIRECTORATE OF EVALUATION AND ANALYSIS

Evaluates and advises the assistant secretary on OSHA programs and policies, monitors congressional activities, and analyzes OSHA-related legislation. Also maintains liaison with other regulatory agencies such as the National Institute for Occupational Safety and Health, the Environmental Protection Agency, the Food and Drug Administration, and the Consumer Product Safety Commission.
Director
Francis Yebesi (acting) .... (202) 693–2400
Fax........................... (202) 693–1641
Evaluation and Audit Analysis
Jens Svenson..................... (202) 693–2400
Program Review
Audie Woolsey.................... (202) 693–2400
Statistical Analyses
David Schmidt .... (202) 693–1702

DIRECTORATE OF STANDARDS AND GUIDANCE

Studies and evaluates occupational safety standards. Is aided by the National Institute of Occupational Safety and Health (NIOSH).
Director
Bill Perry .... (202) 693–1950
Fax........................... (202) 693–1678

Deputy Directors
Andy Levinson .... (202) 693–1950
Lisa Long (acting) .... (202) 693–1950
Biological Hazards
Valentine Schaeffer (acting) .... (202) 693–2091
Chemical Hazards–Metal
David O'Connor .... (202) 693–2093
Chemical Hazards-Nonmetal
David O'Connor .... (202) 693–2090
Engineering Safety
Lisa Long .... (202) 693–2277
Information Quality and Paperwork Reduction
Todd Owen....................... (202) 693–2222
Maritime and Agriculture
Amy Wangdahl .... (202) 693–2086
Physical Hazards and Others
Lyn Penniman .... (202) 693–2092
Regulatory Analysis (Health)
Robert Stone .... (202) 693–1950
Regulatory Analysis (Safety)
Robert Burt .... (202) 693–2222
Safety Systems
Mark Hagemann .... (202) 693–2255
Technological Feasibility
Joseph Coble .... (202) 693–2222

DIRECTORATE OF TECHNICAL SUPPORT AND EMERGENCY MANAGEMENT

Provides technical guidance and support to OSHA compliance staff and oversees development of technical manuals and interactive software advisers for employers and employees. Maintains laboratories to analyze toxic substances and health hazards in the workplace and to test newly developed hazard detection equipment. Makes decisions on granting standards variances based on recommendations of the Directorate of Standards and Guidance.
Director
Amanda Edens.................... (202) 693–2300
Deputy Director
Lee Anne Jilings.................. (202) 693–2300
Fax........................... (202) 693–1644
Emergency Management and Preparedness
Denise Mathews .... (202) 693–2095
Science and Technology Assessment
Kelly Schnapp .... (202) 693–2095
Technical Data Center
Michelle Walker.................. (202) 693–2350
Technical Programs and Coordination Activities
David Johnson.................... (202) 693–2110

OSHA Cincinnati Technical Center

Maintenance and Calibration Laboratory
435 Elm St., #500
Cincinnati, OH 45202
(513) 684–3721
Robert T. Williams, director

Provides for development, evaluation, calibration, and repair of hazard measurement instrumentation and equipment.

Salt Lake Technical Center

660 S. Sandy Pkwy.
Sandy, UT 84070–6424
(801) 233–4900
Fax (801) 233–5000
Dean Lillquist, director
Todd Jordan, Health Response Team director

Conducts analyses, tests, and studies of all samples submitted by safety and health compliance officers and others to evaluate toxicity and the existence of health hazards. Health Response Team investigates accidents involving major health issues, fatalities, and catastrophes that receive nationwide attention; coordinates and leads OSHA's chemical, biological, radiological, and collapsed structures Specialized Response Teams.

DIRECTORATE OF TRAINING AND EDUCATION

Develops and manages OSHA's national training and education policies and procedures. Through its OSHA Training Institute, provides training and education in occupational safety and health for federal and state compliance officers, state consultants, other federal agency personnel, and the private sector. Offers training videos for loan and awards grants to nonprofit organizations to develop training and education programs.

Director
Henry E. Payne . . . . (847) 759–7771
    Fax . . . . (847) 759–7748
Deputy Director
Ernest B. Thompson . . . . (847) 759–7731
Training Institute
Front desk . . . . (847) 759–7700
Charlie Shields . . . . (847) 759–7729
Resource Center Loan Program
Joe Spevacek . . . . (847) 759–7736
    Fax . . . . (847) 759–7748

DIRECTORATE OF WHISTLEBLOWER PROTECTION PROGRAMS

Directs and manages OSHA's programs to improve the fairness, efficiency, effectiveness, and transparency of whistleblower programs.

Director
John Lewis . . . . (202) 693–2230

ADVISORY COMMITTEES

Four standing advisory committees and a varying number of special ad hoc committees make specific recommendations on the development of standards. All advisory committees must have members representing employers, employees, and state and federal agencies. The occupational safety and health professions as well as the general public also may be represented. Ad hoc committees are specially appointed to develop standards in specific areas and are limited in duration to 270 days.

Advisory Committee on Construction Safety and Health (ACCSH)

Advises the secretary of labor on the formulation of construction safety and health standards and related regulations.

Chair
Sarah M. Coyne . . . . (410) 564–5852
Contact (Designated Federal Officer)
Dean McKenzie . . . . (202) 693–2020

Federal Advisory Council on Occupational Safety and Health (FACOSH)

Advises the secretary of labor and the secretary of health and human services on matters pertaining to the occupational safety and health of federal employees.

Chair
David Michaels . . . . (202) 693–2000
Contact (Designated Federal Officer)
Francis Yebesi . . . . (202) 693–2122

Maritime Advisory Committee for Occupational Safety and Health (MACOSH)

Advises the secretary of labor and addresses the concerns of the maritime community in matters pertaining to the safety and health of workers in the maritime industry, with a focus on the shipbuilding, shipbreaking, ship repair, and longshoring and marine terminal industries.

Chair
Jim Thornton . . . . (757) 380–4651
Contact (Designated Federal Officer)
Amy Wangdahl . . . . (202) 693–2086

National Advisory Committee on Occupational Safety and Health (NACOSH)

Advises the secretary of labor and the secretary of health and human services on matters regarding the administration of the Occupational Safety and Health Act.

Chair
Lamont Byrd . . . . (202) 624–6960
Contact (Designated Federal Officer)
Amanda Edens . . . . (202) 693–2270

Whistleblower Protection Advisory Committee

Advises the secretary of the Labor Dept. and the administrator of OSHA on ways to improve the fairness, efficiency, effectiveness, and transparency of OSHA's administration of whistleblower protections.

Chair
Emily Spieler . . . . (202) 693–2230
Contact (Designated Federal Officer)
Anthony Rosa . . . . (202) 693–2199

Regional Offices

These offices monitor state safety and health programs and oversee area office compliance personnel. They coordinate regional activities with the Labor Department's Office of the Solicitor, the Field Operations Coordinator, National Institute of Occupational Safety and Health, and the Small Business Administration. There are area offices located within the regions that conduct inspections and provide compliance assistance and training to employers and employees.

REGION 1

(CT, MA, ME, NH, RI, VT)
JFK Federal Bldg.

25 New Sudbury St., Room E340
Boston, MA 02203
(617) 565–9860
Fax (617) 565–9827
Kim Stille, regional administrator

REGION 2
(NJ, NY, PR, VI)
201 Varick St., #670
New York, NY 10014
(212) 337–2378
Fax (212) 337–2371
Rich Mendelson (acting), regional administrator

REGION 3
(DC, DE, MD, PA, VA, WV)
Curtis Center, #740 West
170 S. Independence Mall West
Philadelphia, PA 19106–3309
(215) 861–4904
Fax (215) 861–4904
Robert Kulick (acting), regional administrator

REGION 4
(AL, FL, GA, KY, MS, NC, SC, TN)
61 Forsyth St. S.W., #6T50
Atlanta, GA 30303
(678) 237–0400
Fax (678) 237–0447
Kurt Petermeyer, regional administrator

REGION 5
(IL, IN, MI, MN, OH, WI)
230 S. Dearborn St., #3244
Chicago, IL 60604
(312) 353–2220
Fax (312) 353–7774
Nick Walters, regional administrator

REGION 6
(AR, LA, NM, OK, TX)
525 Griffin St., #602
Dallas, TX 75202
(972) 850–4145
Fax (972) 850–4149
John Hermanson, regional administrator

REGION 7
(IA, KS, MO, NE)
2 Pershing Square Bldg.
2300 Main St., #1010
Kansas City, MO 64108–2416
(816) 283–8745
Fax (816) 283–0547
Marcia Drumm, regional administrator

REGION 8
(CO, MT, ND, SD, UT, WY)
Cesar Chavez Memorial Bldg.
1244 Speer Blvd. #551

Denver, CO 80204
(720) 264–6550
Fax (720) 264–6585
Greg Baxter, regional administrator

REGION 9
(AS, AZ, CA, GU, HI, NV, MP)
San Francisco Federal Building
90 7th St., #18100
San Francisco, CA 94103
(415) 625–2547
Fax (415) 625–2534
Barbara Goto (acting), regional administrator

REGION 10
(AK, ID, OR, WA)
300 Fifth Ave., #1280
Seattle, WA 98104
(206) 757–6700
Fax (206) 757–6705
Ken Atha, regional administrator

■ CONGRESSIONAL ACTION

Congressional Liaison
Lora DeLatorre . . . . (202) 693–4600

Committees and Subcommittees

HOUSE APPROPRIATIONS COMMITTEE
Subcommittee on Labor, Health and Human Services, Education, and Related Agencies
2358B RHOB, Washington, DC 20515–6015
(202) 225–3508
Fax (202) 225–3509

HOUSE EDUCATION AND THE WORKFORCE
2181 RHOB, Washington, DC 20515–6100
(202) 225–4527
Fax (202) 225–9571
Subcommittee on Workforce Protections
2181 RHOB, Washington, DC 20515–6100
(202) 225–4527
Subcommittee on Health, Employment, Labor, and Pensions
2181 RHOB, Washington, DC 20515
(202) 225–4527

SENATE APPROPRIATIONS COMMITTEE
Subcommittee on Labor, Health and Human Services, Education, and Related Agencies
SDOB-135, Washington, DC 20510–6025
(202) 224–7230
Fax (202) 224–2100

SENATE HEALTH, EDUCATION, LABOR, AND PENSIONS COMMITTEE
SDOB-428, Washington, DC 20510–6300
(202) 224–5375
Fax (202) 228–5044

Subcommittee on Employment and Workplace Safety
SDOB-428, Washington, DC 20510–6300
(202) 224–5375
Fax (202) 228–5044

Legislation

OSHA was established by the **Occupational Safety and Health Act of 1970** (84 Stat. 1590, 29 U.S.C. 553, 651–678). In addition to creating OSHA, the act set up the Occupational Safety and Health Review Commission and the National Institute for Occupational Safety and Health.

The legislation gives OSHA the power to promulgate and enforce worker safety and health standards, conduct inspections and investigations, require employers to keep detailed records on worker injuries and illnesses, and provide education and training.

When OSHA became operational in 1971 it adopted the standards issued under several earlier acts. (The legal administration of these acts remains with the Labor Department.) As OSHA develops its own standards, they supersede the standards issued under the following acts:

Longshore and Harbor Workers' Compensation Act (44 Stat. 1444, 33 U.S.C. 941). Signed by the president March 4, 1927. Provided benefits for injured and disabled workers and dependents of deceased workers.

Walsh-Healey Act (49 Stat. 2036, 41 U.S.C. 35). Signed by the president May 13, 1936. Provided benefit and labor standards for persons employed by federal contractors.

National Foundation on the Arts and the Humanities Act (79 Stat. 845, 20 U.S.C. 951). Signed by the president Sept. 29, 1965. Provided health and safety standards for performers and personnel engaged in any project or production authorized under this act.

Service Contract Act of 1965 (79 Stat. 1034, 41 U.S.C. 351). Signed by the president Oct. 22, 1965. Provided labor standards for persons employed by federal contractors.

Construction Safety Act (83 Stat. 96, 40 U.S.C. 333). Signed by the president Aug. 9, 1969. Promoted health and safety in the building trades and construction industry for all federal and federally financed or assisted construction projects.

Small Business Regulatory Enforcement Fairness Act of 1996 (110 Stat. 857, 5 U.S.C. 601 note). Signed by the president March 29, 1996. Required the Small Business Administration to assist small businesses with regulatory compliance, to establish a Small Business and Agriculture Regulatory Enforcement Ombudsman, and to establish a Small Business Regulatory Fairness Board in each SBA regional office. Authorized Congress, through passage of a joint resolution of disapproval, to deny the enactment of the proposed regulation. However, the president could override the decision of Congress if the regulation affected national security, national health, or if necessary to implement an international trade agreement.

■ INFORMATION SOURCES

Internet

Agency website: www.osha.gov. Provides information on OSHA offices, programs, publications, and statistics. The public can also search through multiple databases at the agency's website.

Telephone Contacts

DOL Information . . . . (866) 487–2365
Report accidents and health
    & safety violations . . . . (800) 321–6742
TTY . . . . (877) 889–5627

Information and Publications

KEY OFFICES

OSHA Office of Communications
200 Constitution Ave. N.W., #N3647
Washington, DC 20210
(202) 693–1999
Fax (202) 693–1635
Frank Meilinger, director

Provides general information about OSHA to the news media and the public; publishes and distributes consumer information leaflets. Handles Freedom of Information requests for documents of a general nature.

To request documents related to a specific incident, contact the FOI officer in the area or regional office serving the location where the incident occurred. If an initial request for information is denied by either an area office or the national office, an appeal may be made to the solicitor of the Labor Department (see Other Information Sources).

Responsible for developing the OSHA consumer affairs program to give employers and employees a greater role in the rulemaking process. Provides information on upcoming meetings and works to increase public comment on new proposals.

OSHA Publications Office
200 Constitution Ave. N.W., #N3101
Washington, DC 20210
(202) 693–1888
Fax (202) 693–2498
Internet: www.osha.gov/pls/publications/publication
    .html
Heather LeMay, director

Distributes publications and training materials; extensive series of publications available on the website.

Freedom of Information
DOL Office of the Solicitor
200 Constitution Ave. N.W., Room N2428
Washington, DC 20210
(202) 693–1999
Email: foiarequests@dol.gov
Thomas G. Hicks, public liaison
(202) 693–5427

More information on FOI is available from the Office of Communications, above, and on the agency's website.

GRANTS

OSHA makes grants to state agencies to administer and enforce federally approved state programs for occupational safety and health. Arrangements for statistical operating grants are handled for OSHA by the Bureau of Labor Statistics; funds are also available from the National Institute for Occupational Safety and Health (*see Related Agencies, p. 337*).

PUBLICATIONS

Consumer Information

OSHA's Publications Office offers hundreds of free publications describing hazards, standards, and OSHA programs and policies, available by calling the office or from the website. Topics include job safety and health, eye protection, indoor air quality, OSHA consultation services, general record-keeping requirements, protection against asbestos, carbon monoxide poisoning, cotton dust, field sanitation standards, grain handling facilities standards, and hazardous waste/emergency response. OSHA also produces a free biweekly e-newsletter, *Quick–Takes*, about workplace safety and health; posters providing safety guidelines for employers and employees in specific industries; QuickCards providing brief, plain-language safety and health information for employees about OSHA standards that employers must meet; fact sheets, brochures, booklets, and pocket guides about the agency's focus industries; and guidance documents providing detailed examinations of safety and health issues. Many materials are also available in Spanish.

The public can view and download many of these publications via the agency's website at www.osha.gov/pls/publications/publication.html, or call (202) 693–1888.

Other General Publications

For information and specific titles, contact the OSHA Publications Office in Room N3101, Washington, DC 20210, (202) 693–1888, or a regional office. Publications are also available through the OSHA website, which contains the most recent listings.

Titles available include

All about OSHA. An outline of OSHA's activities and policies.

How to Plan for Workplace Emergencies and Evacuations. Details basic steps needed to prepare for handling emergencies such as accidental releases of toxic gases, chemical spills, fires, explosions, and personal injuries.

Job Safety and Health. It's the Law! Official poster required by law to be posted prominently in the workplace.

Maritime Standards: Parts 1911–1925. Contains all job safety and health rules and regulations pertaining to maritime terminals and longshoring operations. This publication also available from the Government Printing Office.

Worker Rights under the Occupational Safety and Health Act of 1970 Fact Sheet. Lists fourteen rights covered in the Occupation Safety and Health Act of 1970. Also includes employee responsibilities.

OSHA titles regarding standards and regulations are also available from the U.S. Government Printing Office (GPO) (*see appendix, Ordering Government Publications*). Topics include general health and safety guidelines for various industries; electrical hazards; emergency response and preparedness requirements; ergonomics; workplace violence; and materials on handling and storage.

Training Program Materials

OSHA has various training materials to help both employers and employees understand OSHA requirements. These include programmed courses of instruction and may be purchased from the National Technical Information Service (NTIS) (*see appendix, Ordering Government Publications*). Contact the Directorate of Training and Education *(see above)* for information about OSHA outreach training. See OSHA's website at www.osha.gov for up-to-date information and listings.

DATA AND STATISTICS

Office of Statistical Analysis

Department of Labor, OSHA
200 Constitution Ave. N.W., #N3641
Washington, DC 20210
(202) 693–1886
David Schmidt, director

Maintains inspection reports, citation and penalty data, notices of contest, complaints, and penalty payment amounts. Also maintains other data, many of which are produced by the Bureau of Labor Statistics (BLS) or the National Institute for Occupational Safety and Health (NIOSH). Information is also available on the website, and data collections include

Annual Survey of Occupational Injuries and Illnesses. Data collected by industry category on deaths, lost workdays, nonfatal cases not resulting in lost workdays, and seven categories of specific illnesses. For details contact the BLS.

Criteria Documents. Prepared by NIOSH and used by OSHA to develop new standards. Available at the OSHA Technical Data Center (see below) and at all area and regional offices; or contact NIOSH.

Supplementary Data System. Data from reports of injuries and illnesses that are submitted to state workers' compensation programs. Major categories of data collected are characteristics of the injury or illness, the firm, the worker, and the work situation. For details contact the BLS.

Work Injury Reports. Profiles of characteristics associated with selected types of workplace injuries. Compiled from questionnaires completed by injured workers. For more information contact the BLS.

MEETINGS

Schedules of upcoming advisory committee meetings are on the website and published in the *Federal Register* at least seven days in advance of the meeting. (*See appendix for details on how to use the Federal Register.*) Records of previous meetings are available for review by the public on the website and in the OSHA Technical Data Center.

Reference Resources

LIBRARY

OSHA Technical Data Center

200 Constitution Ave. N.W., #N2625
Washington, DC 20210
(202) 693–2350
Fax (202) 693–1648
Vacant, director
Hours: 8:15 a.m. to 4:45 p.m.

Open to the public; no appointment needed. Houses transcripts of advisory committee meetings, reports, opinions, periodicals, and books on safety and health issues. Interlibrary loan service is available. Federal dockets are also available at www.regulations.gov.

DOCKETS

All records of hearings dealing with proposed standards or standards development since December 18, 2006, have been moved to the Federal Docket Management System (FDMS) and may be viewed at www.regulations.gov. (*See appendix for Searching and Commenting on Regulations: Regulations.gov*). Older dockets will remain available on the OSHA system but will be moved periodically to the FDMS. Call the OSHA Docket Office for help in locating dockets and for information on the docket migration system at (202) 693–2350.

RULES AND REGULATIONS

OSHA rules, regulations, and standards are published in the *Code of Federal Regulations,* Title 29, Chapter XVII, Parts 1900–2006; Title 29, Chapter XX, Parts 2200–2400. Proposed regulations and standards, new final rules, and standards and updates to the *Code of Federal Regulations* are published in the daily *Federal Register. (See appendix for information on how to obtain and use these publications.)* The *Federal Register* may be accessed at www.federalregister.gov and the *Code of Federal Regulations* at www.archives.gov/federal-register/cfr; also see the federal government's website www.regulations.gov (*see appendix*).

OSHA standards are divided into three major categories—General Industry, Maritime, and Construction. Copies of each category of rules may be obtained from the Government Printing Office or from the OSHA website at www.osha.gov.

Other Information Sources

RELATED AGENCIES

DOL Bureau of Labor Statistics

Office of Safety, Health, and Working Conditions
Statistics
2 Massachusetts Ave. N.E., #3180
Washington, DC 20212
(202) 691–6170
Fax (202) 691–6196
Internet: www.bls.gov
Erica L. Groshen, commissioner

Provides many of the statistics used by OSHA.

DOL Office of the Solicitor

200 Constitution Ave. N.W., #S2002
Washington, DC 20210
(202) 693–5261
Fax (202) 693–5278
M. Patricia Smith, solicitor

Divisions include the Office of the Solicitor for OSHA. The co-counsel for administrative law provides information on the Freedom of Information appeals process for OSHA.

National Institute for Occupational Safety and Health (NIOSH)

Centers for Disease Control and Prevention
1600 Clifton Rd.
Atlanta, GA 30333
(800) 232–4636
TTY (888) 232–6348
Internet: www.cdc.gov/niosh
Washington office
395 E St. S.W., #9200
Washington, DC 20201
(202) 245–0625
John Howard, director

Conducts research and evaluation studies of occupational injuries and hazardous substances in the workplace. These criteria are used by OSHA for the basis of its standards development process. Also operates the Clearinghouse for Occupational Safety and Health Information (COSHI) and the Registry of Toxic Effects of Chemical Substances (RTECS). (The Centers for Disease Control and Prevention, which includes NIOSH, is a component of the Health and Human Services Department.)

NIOSH publications and documents can be ordered through the above toll-free number, and most NIOSH documents are available at the website, www.cdc.gov/pubs/niosh.aspx. NIOSH criteria documents are available, upon request, for inspection and copying at all OSHA regional and area offices, at the OSHA Technical Data Center, at NIOSH field offices, and on the website at www.cdc.gov/niosh/pubs/criteria_date_desc_nopubnumbers.html. They also may be obtained from the U.S. Government Printing Office (GPO) (*see appendix, Ordering Government Publications*).

Funds are available from NIOSH to any public or private institution wishing to conduct research in the field of occupational safety and health or to develop specialized professional personnel with training in occupational medicine, nursing, industrial hygiene, and safety.

Further information on application and award procedures may be obtained from

National Institute for Occupational Safety and Health

Office of Extramural Programs
1600 Clifton Rd.
Atlanta, GA 30333
(404) 498–2530
Internet: www.cdc.gov/niosh/oep
W. Allen Robison, director

Leads and supports occupational safety and health research and training programs in collaboration with global partners.

Occupational Safety and Health Review Commission

Office of Information
1120 20th St. N.W., 9th Floor
Washington, DC 20006
(202) 606-5370
Fax (202) 606-5050
Internet: www.oshrc.gov
Cynthia Attwood (acting), chair
Melik Ahmir-Abdul, press officer

An independent adjudicatory agency (not connected with the Labor Department). All citations issued by OSHA compliance and enforcement officers are subject to appeal to the review commission. For further information on agency administration and proceedings, contact this office.

NONGOVERNMENTAL RESOURCES

The following are some key resources for information on OSHA and issues of occupational health and safety.

American Industrial Health Council

(Contact through American Industrial Hygiene Association)
3141 Fairview Park Ave., #777
Falls Church, VA 22042
(703) 849-8888
Fax (703) 207-3561
Internet: www.aiha.org

Board of Certified Safety Professionals

2301 W. Bradley Ave.
Champaign, IL 61821
(217) 359-9263
Fax (217) 359-0055
Internet: www.bcsp.org

National Association of Manufacturers

703 10th St., #700
Washington, DC 20001
(800) 314-8468
(202) 637-3000
Fax (202) 637-3182
Internet: www.nam.org

National Safety Council

1121 Spring Lake Dr.
Itasca, IL 60143-3201
(800) 621-7615
(630) 285-1121
Fax (630) 285-1315
Internet: www.nsc.org
   Washington office
   1025 Connecticut Ave. N.W., #1210
   Washington, DC 20036-5405
   (202) 293-2270
   Fax (202) 567-5704

ProQuest

(formerly Cambridge Scientific Abstracts)
789 E. Eisenhower Pkwy.
Ann Arbor, MI 48103
(800) 521-0600
(734) 761-4700
Fax (734) 997-4222
Internet: www.proquest.com

Public Citizen Health Research Group

1600 20th St. N.W.
Washington, DC 20009
(202) 588-1000
Fax (202) 588-7796
Internet: www.citizen.org

Securities and Exchange Commission

100 F St. N.E., Washington, DC 20549
Internet: www.sec.gov

▨ INTRODUCTION

The Securities and Exchange Commission (SEC) is an independent regulatory agency established by the Securities Exchange Act of 1934. The commission is composed of five members, and not more than three may be members of the same political party. The commissioners are nominated by the president and confirmed by the Senate for five-year terms. The president also designates one of the members to serve as chair.

Responsibilities

The SEC functions as both a regulatory and investigatory agency. Its role is to police the securities markets and protect investors, both through public disclosure of information about corporate activities and securities transactions and through enforcement actions.

Because the nation's financial markets are closely interlinked and because the SEC does not have jurisdiction over all aspects of them, the agency works closely with other regulators. Among those are the Treasury Department, which regulates trading in federal government securities; the Commodity Futures Trading Commission (CFTC), which regulates commodity traders and exchanges (*p. 381*); the Federal Reserve System, which regulates bank holding companies and foreign banks and oversees monetary policy (*p. 206*); and the Office of the Comptroller of the Currency, which regulates federally chartered banks (*p. 839*).

As the world securities markets become increasingly linked, the SEC also works with foreign securities regulators to investigate and prevent fraud, to enhance public disclosure of foreign corporate financial activity, and to harmonize international financial reporting.

In its effort to regulate the securities markets, the SEC

- Requires broad disclosure of facts concerning public offerings of securities listed on national securities exchanges and certain securities traded over-the-counter (a market for buying and selling stock among broker-dealers without going through a stock exchange).

- Requires detailed periodic reports on the financial condition of companies that have made public securities offerings. Monitors and works with the Financial Accounting Standards Board, a private, self-regulatory association of public accountants who develop rules for corporate financial reporting. Also works with the Public Company Accounting Oversight Board, likewise a private, nonprofit corporation that oversees the auditing industry and sets standards for the preparation of public company financial reports.

- Regulates the trading of securities on the eight national securities exchanges and on over-the-counter markets; oversees the operations and rules of securities exchanges and the National Association of Securities Dealers (NASD), each of which functions as a self-regulatory organization; oversees the operations and rules of various clearing corporations that handle settlement of securities transactions.

GLOSSARY

Broker—A person who acts as an agent for customers in selling or buying securities for their accounts.

Dealer—A person who acts as a principal rather than as an agent in buying or selling securities. Typically, dealers buy for their accounts and sell to a customer from their inventories.

Holding company—A corporation organized to hold the stock of other corporations; usually a holding company owns or controls a dominant interest in one or more other corporations and is able to influence or dictate the management policies of the other corporations.

Insider trading—Violation of the antifraud provisions of federal securities laws; occurs when an individual profits in the stock market on the basis of confidential corporate secrets. For example, an insider could profit from knowledge of an impending corporate takeover, which would drive up the takeover target's stock price, or of a soon-to-be released disappointing earnings report, which typically would drive a stock price down.

Institutional investor—Commonly used phrase for bank mutual funds, insurance companies, pension funds, and large corporate investment accounts that, because of the size and frequency of their transactions, are eligible for preferential commissions and other services from broker-dealers.

Junk bonds—Colloquial expression for high-yield, high-risk bonds. Because they have received a low, or speculative, rating from the companies that rate bonds, these bonds pay a higher interest rate to attract buyers.

Margin trading—Purchasing securities that are paid for in part with a loan taken out using the same securities as collateral, in the hope that the price of the securities will increase, allowing the purchaser to pay off the loan and make a profit. Also called "buying on margin."

Mutual fund—An investment organization that issues stock to raise capital, which it then invests in other securities to generate funds for its operating costs and profits for its investors.

Program trading—Defined by the New York Stock Exchange as buy or sell orders for a group of fifteen or more stocks. Program trading usually employs computers to determine the optimum time for such trades and to execute them. Strategies include index arbitrage, the simultaneous trading of Big Board stocks and stock-index futures contracts to profit from brief price disparities and tactical asset allocation, which uses futures contracts to shift money among equities, bonds, and other types of investments.

Selling short—Borrowing securities and selling them in anticipation of a market decline; if the market goes down, the securities may be bought back at a lower price and returned to the party from which they were borrowed, with the short seller keeping the profit.

Tender offer—A public offer to purchase stock (usually the controlling interest) in a corporation within a specified time period and at a stipulated price, usually above the market price.

- Requires securities brokers, dealers, and investment advisers to register with the SEC and regulates their activities.
- Enforces disclosure requirements in the soliciting of proxies for meetings of security holders by companies whose securities are listed on exchanges, public utility holding companies and their subsidiaries, and investment companies.
- Investigates securities fraud, stock manipulation, and other violations of securities laws; imposes administrative sanctions for such violations and seeks judicial injunctive remedies and criminal prosecution.
- Supervises the activities of mutual funds (including money market funds) and other investment companies.
- Regulates the provisions of trust indentures under which debt securities are sold to the public.
- Regulates the purchase and sale of securities, utility properties, and other assets by registered public utility holding companies and their electric and gas utility subsidiaries; also regulates reorganizations, mergers, and consolidations of public utility holding companies.
- Advises federal courts regarding corporate reorganization proceedings under Chapter 11 of the Federal Bankruptcy Code.
- Regulates cash and exchange tender offers.
- Requires government securities dealers to register with the agency to improve protection for investors in the market for government securities; monitors records of government securities transactions to guard against fraud and other illegal trading activities.
- Enforces record-keeping provisions of the Foreign Corrupt Practices Act, which prohibits public companies from bribing officials of foreign governments.
- Oversees the Securities Investor Protection Corporation.
- Works toward the establishment of a national market system for securities and for the prompt and accurate clearance and settlement of transactions in securities.

Powers and Authority

Legislation enacted since the establishment of the SEC has required various companies, individuals, and institutions to register with the commission. Supervising these registrants is one of the commission's major tasks.

The Securities Act of 1933 requires that before a public offering of securities is made by a company, or any person controlling such a company, a registration statement must be filed with the SEC by the issuer. The statement must contain an adequate and accurate disclosure of the material facts concerning the company and the securities it proposes to sell. Generally, statements include a description of the registrant's properties and business, a description of the significant provisions of the security to be offered for sale and its relationship to the registrant's other capital securities, information about the management of the registrant, and financial statements certified by independent public accountants. The information contained in registration filings becomes public immediately, but sales of securities may not start until the effective date of the filing, which on average occurs about thirty-five days after the filing is made.

Security registration statements are reviewed for compliance with disclosure requirements by the Division of Corporation Finance. If the statement appears to be incomplete or inaccurate, and the issuing company takes no action to correct it, the commission has the authority to advance or suspend the statement's effective date. A hearing may be held if intentionally misleading information is included in the filing. If evidence of a deliberate attempt to conceal and mislead is developed during the hearing, a stop order barring the security from the market may be issued.

However, a stop order is not a permanent bar to the sale of securities. The order must be lifted and the statement declared effective if amendments are filed correcting the statement in accordance with the stop order decision.

The registration requirement applies to securities of both domestic and foreign private stock issues offered for sale in the United States, as well as to securities of foreign governments or their instrumentalities. Exempted from the registration requirement are (1) private offerings to a limited number of persons or institutions who have access to the kind of information registration would disclose; (2) offerings restricted to the residents of the state in which the issuing company is organized and doing business; (3) securities of municipal, state, federal, and other government instrumentalities, of charitable institutions, of banks, and of carriers subject to the Interstate Commerce Act; (4) offerings by smaller businesses of up to $7.5 million made in compliance with regulations of the commission; and (5) offerings of "small business investment companies."

In October 1980 Congress passed the Small Business Investment Incentive Act, which amended securities laws to make it easier for small companies to issue stock. The legislation exempted from registration certain employee benefit and retirement plans.

The Securities Exchange Act of 1934 requires the registration of "national securities exchanges" (those having a substantial trading volume) and of brokers and dealers who conduct an over-the-counter securities business in interstate commerce. To register, exchanges must show that they are able to comply with the provisions of the statute and the rules and regulations of the commission and that they operate under rules that adequately protect the investing public. While exchanges establish self-regulatory rules, the commission may "alter or supplement" them if it finds that those rules fail to protect investors.

Registered brokers and dealers must conform to business practices and standards prescribed by various laws and by the commission. The Office of Filings and Information Services, with assistance from the Division of Market Regulation, examines applications from brokers and dealers.

In 1986 Congress amended the Securities Exchange Act of 1934 to require all government securities dealers to register with the SEC. The Public Utility Holding Company Act of 1935 requires registration of interstate holding companies that are engaged through their subsidiaries in the electric utility business or in the retail distribution of natural or manufactured gas. Registered holding companies are subject to regulation by the commission.

The Investment Company Act of 1940 requires registration of mutual funds: companies that engage in the business of investing, reinvesting, and trading in securities and whose own securities are offered, sold to, and held by the investing public. Mutual funds and other investment companies are required to disclose their financial condition and investment policies. They are prohibited from changing the nature of their business or investment policies without the approval of the stockholders.

REPORTING REQUIREMENTS

Any company whose securities are registered with the SEC must file an annual report and other periodic reports with the commission to keep the information in the original filing up to date. The data in these reports are available to the public at the offices of the SEC, at the exchanges, and online. These reports also are used extensively by publishers of securities manuals, securities advisory services, investment advisers, trust departments, and securities brokers and dealers. There are penalties for filing false reports, as well as a provision for recovery by investors who suffer losses in the purchase or sale of registered securities due to incorrect information in the reports.

Proxies

When management or a group of stockholders is soliciting proxies for any reason, reports must be filed disclosing all the facts concerning the matters on which they are asked to vote. When a contest for control of the management of a corporation is involved, the rules require disclosure of the names and interests of all participants in the proxy contest. Proxy material must be filed in advance with the commission to permit staff review and to ensure that any interested securities holder may have access to it before the vote.

Acquisition

Amendments to the Securities Exchange Act of 1934 require that any effort to acquire control of a company through a tender offer or other planned stock acquisition be reported to the SEC. This applies to anyone attempting to obtain more than 5 percent of a company's equity securities.

Insider Trading

Officers, directors, and holders of more than 10 percent of a company's registered securities must file a report with the commission showing the amount of holdings. A report also must be filed for any month during which there is any change in the holdings.

INVESTIGATION AND ENFORCEMENT

Disclosure requirements of the federal securities laws, including registration and reporting requirements, are intended to safeguard the integrity of U.S. securities markets. It is the duty of the commission under the laws it administers to investigate complaints or other indications of possible law violations in securities transactions, most of which arise under the Securities Act of 1933 and the Securities Exchange Act of 1934 as amended. Investigation and enforcement work is the primary responsibility of the commission's Division of Enforcement.

Most of the commission's investigations are conducted privately; the facts are developed to the fullest extent possible through informal inquiry, interviewing of witnesses, examination of brokerage records, trading data, and other documents, and by similar means. The commission, however, has the authority to issue subpoenas requiring sworn testimony and the production of books, records, and other documents pertinent to the subject under investigation. In the event of refusal to respond to a subpoena, the commission may apply to a federal court for an order compelling compliance.

Inquiries and complaints from investors as well as news stories provide leads for detection of law violations in securities transactions. Violations also may be uncovered by unannounced inspections of the books and records of brokers and dealers by the SEC regional offices to determine whether the business practices of the companies being examined conform to prescribed rules. Inquiries into market fluctuations in particular stocks, when those fluctuations appear to be influenced by factors other than known developments affecting the issuing company or broad market trends, also may reveal securities laws violations.

The more general types of investigations concern the unregistered sales of securities subject to the registration requirement of the Securities Act of 1933 and misrepresentation or omission of material facts concerning securities offered for sale (whether or not registration is required). The antifraud provisions of the law apply equally to the purchase of securities, whether involving outright misrepresentations or the withholding or omission of pertinent facts to which the seller was entitled. For example, it is unlawful in certain situations to purchase securities from another person while withholding material information that would indicate that the securities have a value substantially greater than the purchase price. Such provisions of the law apply not only to transactions between brokers and dealers and their customers but also to the reacquisition of securities by an issuing company or its "insiders."

Other types of inquiries relate to the manipulation of the market prices of securities; the misappropriation or unlawful pledging of customers' funds or securities; the conduct of a securities business while insolvent; the purchase or sale of securities by a broker-dealer, from or to customers, at prices not reasonably related to the current market prices; and violation by the broker-dealer of a responsibility to treat customers fairly.

The most common of the latter type of violation involves broker-dealers who, on gaining the trust and confidence of customers and thereby establishing a relationship demanding the highest degree of integrity, take secret profits in their securities transactions with or for the customers over and above the agreed brokerage (agency) commission. For example, the broker-dealers may have purchased securities from customers at prices far below, or sold securities to customers at prices far above, their current market value. Or the firm may engage in large-scale buy and sell transactions for the customer's account (churning) to generate increased commissions.

STATUTORY SANCTIONS

SEC investigations are essentially fact-finding inquiries. The facts developed by the staff are considered by the commission only in determining whether there is prima facie evidence of a law violation and whether an action should be commenced to determine if a violation actually occurred and if some sanction should be imposed. If the facts show possible fraud or other law violation, the laws provide the following courses of action or remedies.

Civil Injunction

The commission may apply to an appropriate U.S. district court for an order enjoining those acts or practices alleged to violate the law or commission rules. The SEC also may issue cease-and-desist orders against persons who it believes are violating securities laws or commission rules when it fears continued activity would be significantly harmful to investors or the public interest, or would result in substantial dissipation or conversion of assets.

The SEC often secures consent agreements, in which an accused party voluntarily agrees not to engage in prohibited practices, while not admitting to prior violations. Such consent agreements have the effect of court-ordered injunctions. The parties who agree to them also can be subject to more severe sanctions if they do not adhere to the terms.

Civil Fines

For cases where the SEC believes a fraud or other securities law violation has occurred, it may seek civil fines as punishment. The authority to seek fines is relatively new (except in cases of insider trading, for which civil penalties have existed since 1984). It was granted by Congress in 1990 because the standard of proof for civil actions is less than that for criminal prosecution and thus often easier and quicker to meet.

Criminal Prosecution

If fraud or other willful law violation is indicated, the SEC may refer the facts to the Department of Justice with a recommendation for criminal prosecution of the offending persons. Through local U.S. attorneys, frequently assisted by SEC attorneys, the Justice Department may present the evidence to a federal grand jury and seek an indictment.

Administrative Remedy

The commission may, after a hearing, issue orders that suspend or expel members from exchanges or from the over-the-counter dealers association; deny, suspend, or revoke the registrations of broker-dealers; censure firms or individuals for misconduct; or bar individuals (temporarily or permanently) from employment with a registered firm.

All of the sanctions mentioned above may be applied to any person who engages in securities transactions that violate the law, whether or not the person is engaged in the securities business. The administrative remedy is invoked in the case of exchange or association members, as well as registered brokers, dealers, or individuals who may associate with any such firm. In an administrative proceeding, the commission issues an order specifying the acts or practices alleged to have been committed in violation of law and directing that a hearing be held. At the hearing, counsel for the Division of Enforcement (normally a regional office attorney) undertakes to establish for the record those facts that support the charge. The respondents have full opportunity to cross-examine the witnesses and to present evidence in their defense.

The initial decision in such a proceeding is delivered to the respondents by an agency administrative law judge and can be appealed to the full five-member SEC. The commission's final opinion in a proceeding of this type can be appealed directly to a federal court of appeals.

Background

The origins of the SEC may be traced to the stock market crash of Oct. 29, 1929. The crash and the ensuing economic depression focused public attention on the way securities were bought and sold during the feverish trading years of the 1920s. There were widespread reports of stock manipulations designed to make large profits quickly for small groups or "pools" of wealthy investors. Unscrupulous dealers and brokers promoted offers of securities that they knew to be almost worthless.

Public outrage at the practices on Wall Street caused the Senate in 1931 to pass a resolution calling for an extensive investigation of securities trading. The investigation led to passage of the Securities Act of 1933, also known as the "truth-in-securities" bill. The act required anyone offering securities for sale in interstate commerce or through the mail to file information with the Federal Trade Commission (FTC) on the financial condition of the issuing company. A prospectus containing a summary of the filed information had to be given to potential investors.

The Securities Exchange Act of 1934 created the SEC and transferred to it the functions that had been assigned to the FTC under the 1933 law. The 1934 act required companies whose securities were traded on national exchanges to file periodic financial reports. The measure also required that exchanges and over-the-counter dealers and brokers conduct business in line with principles of fair and equitable trade. Those who failed to comply could be forced to do so by the SEC.

Agitation for increased regulation of securities markets, primarily emanating from the administration of President Franklin D. Roosevelt, continued through the 1930s. The first three SEC chairs, Joseph P. Kennedy, James M. Landis, and William O. Douglas, provided strong leadership for the new agency. Douglas, who served as chair from 1937 until his appointment to the Supreme Court in 1939, was especially effective in forcing the reorganization of the New York Stock Exchange (NYSE), altering the character of the nation's largest exchange from a private men's club to a public institution.

Beginning in 1935 a number of laws greatly expanded the powers of the SEC. The first was the Public Utility Holding Company Act, which required utility companies to register with the SEC and submit to its regulation. That act was followed in 1938 by the addition of a new section to federal bankruptcy law, authorizing the commission to assist federal courts in the administration of corporations undergoing reorganization as a result of bankruptcy. In 1939 Congress passed the Trust Indenture Act, which was followed in 1940 by two related bills: the Investment Company Act and the Investment Advisers Act, requiring investment companies and advisers to register with the SEC.

From 1940 until the early 1960s, Congress showed little interest in securities regulation, primarily because the securities markets functioned smoothly. However, as the U.S. economy began to boom and international trade increased, the need for new industrial plants also grew. This development required commensurate growth in capital markets, from traditional banking to stocks, bonds, and other forms of investment. In response, the SEC in 1963 recommended numerous administrative and legislative changes to give added protection to investors. Chief among the recommendations were tightening regulations for over-the-counter trading, raising the quality of securities sales personnel, increasing supervision of brokers, and granting the SEC more flexibility in disciplining violators.

Most of the recommendations were incorporated in the Securities Acts Amendments of 1964. The amendments generally extended the same information disclosure requirements to companies whose stock was traded over-the-counter as already applied to those whose securities were traded on the national exchange. The law also required dealers in over-the-counter markets either to join the NASD or to accept SEC supervision. In addition, the NASD was required to adopt written standards of training, experience, and competence for its members and to establish minimum capital requirements for member firms.

The SEC then turned its attention to mutual funds. Neither the Investment Company Act nor the Investment Advisers Act had ever been substantially amended, and the acts were no longer adequate to deal with the multibillion-dollar industry. Passage of new legislation, however, was delayed until 1970.

While the SEC was concentrating on over-the-counter markets and mutual funds, other problems were emerging in the securities markets. The troubles stemmed, in part, from general economic conditions: prevailing high interest rates on debt instruments made equity stocks less attractive investments, and recession undercut corporate profits. But the primary difficulty lay in the failure of the industry and federal regulations to keep pace with the vast expansion of trading volume and the changing character of the securities market.

One such change was the growing importance of stock investments by institutions such as pension funds, insurance companies, banks, and other organizations that managed large portfolios. Institutional investors accounted for most of the rising stock market activity during the 1960s, and the existing exchange structure had difficulty adjusting to their rising prominence.

One problem involved the fixed brokerage commission rates that U.S. stock exchanges had been setting since the NYSE was founded in 1792. That system had prevented investors from negotiating the best possible price for stock transaction services offered by exchange members, thus curtailing competition among brokers who held stock exchange seats. During the 1960s institutional investors began to seek alternative ways to cut brokerage costs, including attempts to obtain stock exchange seats for themselves or affiliated firms that could offer preferential treatment. The NYSE, the most significant securities auction market in the nation, refused to admit institutional members and insisted that fixed brokerage rates were necessary as an incentive for holding expensive exchange seats and as protection for smaller firms and investors.

At the same time, the securities markets were becoming increasingly fragmented as more and more shares listed on the NYSE were traded in other regional exchanges or on the so-called third market (over-the-counter trading through securities dealers outside the exchanges). The situation complicated investors' efforts to find the best available price for stocks.

Stock markets encountered other problems as well, among them rapidly rising trading volume that occasionally overwhelmed an outmoded system for clearing and settling stock transactions. In fact, a 1968–1970 "paperwork crisis" almost closed down the markets. That development, along with inadequate capitalization for many firms and other difficulties, forced more than 100 brokerage firms into liquidation.

These problems worked to undermine public confidence in stock markets. Relatively low investment returns after 1968 discouraged stock purchases, and the growing dominance of institutional investors suggested to many potential investors that individuals making small investments were at a disadvantage. As a result, the number of persons investing directly in stocks began falling for the first time in many years.

SEC IN THE 1970s

To restore confidence in the securities markets, Congress passed the Securities Investor Protection Act of 1970. The law created the Securities Investor Protection Corporation (SIPC), a nonprofit membership organization that provided coverage for loss of cash and securities left on deposit with brokers who became insolvent. Although the SIPC was an independent, nongovernmental corporation, it was subject to close supervision by the SEC.

The SEC also promulgated a series of rules under its existing powers of supervision over the self-regulatory exchanges and the NASD. In 1973 the SEC adopted rules that ordered (1) the creation of a consolidated tape communications system for reporting the prices and volume of all transactions in listed stocks, whether sold on the NYSE, other exchanges, or the third market; (2) a limit on institutional membership on stock exchanges for firms that conducted at least 80 percent of their business with nonaffiliated persons; and (3) the replacement of fixed exchange commission rates with fully competitive fees on most transactions after May 1, 1975.

Congress in 1975 gave final approval to amendments to the Securities Act intended to encourage development of a national system for buying and selling stocks. The amendments banned practices that restricted investors' access to the nation's stock exchanges and the over-the-counter markets. While preserving the self-regulatory framework established under the Securities Exchange Act of 1934, the legislation significantly enlarged SEC oversight of the stock exchanges and the NASD.

Provisions prohibiting exchange members from buying or selling stocks for themselves or for an affiliated company and provisions upholding the SEC's earlier abolition of fixed brokerage commissions significantly changed the operation of the stock exchanges. Other major provisions extended SEC regulation to firms that process securities transaction paperwork and to banks that underwrite and trade state and local government bonds. The bill also required that banks, insurance companies, and other large-scale institutional investors be subject to certain SEC disclosure requirements.

SEC IN THE 1980s

In the 1980s a series of high-profile insider trading cases the SEC brought against well-known traders rocked Wall Street and captured banner headlines in newspapers throughout the country. As part of its crackdown on insider trading, the SEC sought to stiffen penalties for the offense. Existing law in the early 1980s empowered the SEC to order an inside trader to pay back illegal profits. In 1982 the commission sought legislation increasing the fine up to three times the value of an inside trader's illegal profits. The Insider Trading Sanctions Act was signed into law in 1984.

The serious nature of the SEC cases in the late 1980s led Congress to further stiffen the penalties for insider trading violations. In November 1988 Congress passed the Insider Trading and Securities Fraud Enforcement Act, raising the penalty for each violation of insider trading from five years to ten years in prison and increasing potential fines from $100,000 to $1 million. The legislation also authorized the SEC to pay bounties for information leading to an SEC insider trading case. The bill also included severe fines for Wall Street firms that do not supervise their employees.

Earlier, on Oct. 19, 1987, one of the worst stock market drops in history occurred. (The Dow Jones Industrial Average fell 508 points, losing 22.6 percent of its value.) An SEC staff study echoed the views of many market observers that sophisticated program trading strategies employed by institutional investors and brokerage firms accelerated and worsened the market's fall.

These trading strategies often used stock-index futures, a product developed and traded on the Chicago futures markets and regulated by the CFTC. Index futures were tied to the value of an index of stock prices, such as the S&P 500, and essentially allowed investors to bet on the direction of the stock market. Unlike most commodity futures contracts, stock-index futures were settled for cash, not the underlying commodity, when they came due. They were created and often used by institutional investors who wanted to hedge against the possibility that the stock market would move adversely to their stock investments.

The SEC asked Congress for jurisdiction over stock-index futures, but all that resulted were modified circuit breakers that stopped the use of computer-assisted trades after a 50-point rise or fall in the Dow Jones average. Pressure to reform the financial markets returned, following a major drop in the stock market in October 1989. The next year, President George H. W. Bush signed into law the Market Reform Act, which gave the SEC authority to order trading halts and take other steps to protect the integrity of the stock markets in times of emergency. It required brokers and dealers to keep records of large securities transactions and gave the SEC authority to require reports of such transactions.

The SEC also stepped up its pursuit of accounting fraud during the 1980s. Despite its enforcement efforts, however, the SEC came under heavy criticism from some members of Congress for its policy of encouraging the accounting industry to regulate its affairs through industry groups such as the Financial Accounting Standards Board and the American Institute of Certified Public Accountants. Following disclosures during the savings and loan debacle in the late 1980s that accounting firms had been complicit in allowing weak thrifts to disguise their financial difficulties to regulators, some members of Congress attempted to make outside auditors responsible for reporting evidence of financial fraud to the SEC.

The SEC moved slowly in developing the national market system, as mandated by the 1975 legislation. In January 1983 the commission formally approved the modest beginnings of such a system, which it called the Intermarket Trading System. The system consists of a permanent electronic linkage of the NASD's automated quotation system for trading over-the-counter stocks, the Nasdaq, and the eight U.S. exchanges. During its first year of operation, more than one billion shares of stock were traded through the system. The linkage also meant investors could obtain faster and more complete information about a stock's trading activity.

In late 1984 the commission approved new rules relaxing the standards used by the NASD to determine stocks eligible for use as collateral for margin loans by broker-dealers. Following the October 1987 market crash, additional concerns arose over the clearing and settling of stock transactions and the time it took (typically five business days) to close trades. The 1990 Market Reform Act gave the SEC authority to develop a national system for clearance and settlement. In a move toward that end, in 1993 the SEC issued a rule requiring settlement of stock trades handled by registered brokers and dealers within three business days. The change went into effect in 1995.

SEC IN THE 1990s

The Securities Enforcement Remedies and Penny Stock Reform Act of 1990 granted the SEC authority to seek civil monetary penalties in cases of securities law violations and also gave federal courts the power to bar anyone convicted of a securities law violation from serving as an officer or a director of a public company. The 1990 law also increased the SEC's authority in the area of so-called penny stocks—small, low-cost issues not traded on exchanges. Generally, the law required the SEC to monitor this market and to require brokers and dealers in penny stocks to provide buyers with a risk-disclosure document explaining that these stocks were often difficult to trade because the market for them was small and less liquid.

Congress in 1993 followed the lead of the SEC and imposed new disclosure requirements on brokers who put together deals to convert limited partnerships into public corporations. Often these restructurings involved real estate and oil-and gas-drilling ventures that had greatly declined in value. More than 2,000 partnerships worth billions of dollars were "rolled up" in the 1980s and 1990s. In many cases there were allegations that the results often enriched the general partners who managed the ventures and left limited partners holding stock whose prices fell precipitously.

The SEC and NASD had issued rules requiring broad disclosure of rollup proposals and to allow limited partners greater opportunity to communicate with each other about rollup deals. The bill enacted in 1993 essentially codified those rules and extended them to brokers not otherwise subject to SEC or NASD jurisdiction. It also allowed dissenters to a rollup to demand cash or other compensation rather than stock.

President Bill Clinton appointed Arthur Levitt Jr. chair of the SEC in 1993. Levitt, a former American Stock Exchange (Amex) chair, thrived in the deregulatory environment of the 1990s and was confirmed for a second five-year term in April 1998. He oversaw the slashing of dozens of securities rules and regulations considered redundant. At the same time, Levitt furthered the agency's efforts to build confidence in the securities market by allocating more staff to enforcement offices. In 1995 the agency moved most of its employees who formerly studied small business filings to a new centralized Washington, DC, Office of Compliance Inspections and Examinations.

To protect investors' principal against rapid interest rate changes similar to those seen in 1994, the SEC in 1996 approved a rule to tighten safeguards over money market funds that invest in tax-exempt municipal securities. The new rule placed stricter requirements on these funds to diversify, to improve credit quality, and to limit investments in more volatile securities. For example, a money market fund investing in tax-exempt securities in a single state could invest no more than 5 percent of its portfolio with a single issuer in that state.

Under pressure from House Republicans to further reduce securities regulations, the SEC spent much of 1996 making changes to simplify corporate offering procedures. Dozens of rules considered duplicative and obsolete were eliminated, while new rules were passed to make it easier for small companies to raise capital. The changes revamped insider trading rules designed to prevent the illegal manipulation of a company's securities when new financial products were being issued. Historically, corporate officers and directors were not allowed to turn profits within six months on transactions involving the companies' securities.

Under the rule changes approved in May 1996, corporate insiders would be exempt from the trading restrictions on many routine transactions involving employee-benefit plans, dividend reinvestment plans, and other investment plans, as long as the transactions were approved by the company's board, a panel of outside directors, or by shareholders. The new rules also narrowed the time frame in which trading restrictions apply during a new offering and exempted more than 2,000 large, actively traded companies from the restrictions altogether.

In June 1997 the Supreme Court issued a 6–3 ruling that made it easier for the SEC and the Department of Justice to prosecute investors who improperly benefited from confidential information by establishing a broader definition of insider trading. The Court defined insider trading as the illegal buying or selling of securities for personal gain using misappropriated information, regardless of the source of the information. This definition extended to those who profited from confidential information even if they did not work for the company or obtained the information from representatives of the company.

In what many financial experts considered a monumental achievement of Levitt's tenure, the SEC unanimously approved new rules for the Nasdaq. Phased in during 1997, the new rules narrowed the trading spreads (the differences between the prices at which dealers offer to buy and sell stock) by forcing Nasdaq dealers to publicly display all investor limit orders; notify the public of the absolute best prices for stocks, which had been available only to institutions and dealers, through such systems as Instinet and Nasdaq's SelectNet; and expand the size of any offered block of stock at the best market price to include a customer's limit order at the same price. The SEC postponed a decision on a more controversial proposal: a "price-improvement" rule that would have obligated dealers to improve prices in investors' favor if the market shifted after the customer orders were placed.

In a related move, the SEC in 1997 took action to revamp the U.S. trading system's long-standing practice of expressing stock prices in fractional terms. For more than two centuries, U.S. exchanges had quoted stock prices in increments of eighths of a dollar, such as 1/8 (12.5 cents). Critics said the fractional pricing system hurt small investors by keeping stock spreads artificially high. Fractional pricing also complicated trading between U.S. and foreign exchanges, because most of the world's industrialized countries expressed stock prices in decimal units.

Congress in March 1997 introduced a bill requiring a switchover to decimal units, but the legislative approach proved to be unnecessary. In June 1997 the governing board of the NYSE voted to phase out fractional pricing and to start expressing stock prices in dollars and cents as soon as it could revamp its computer system. In the interim, the NYSE, Nasdaq, Amex, and some regional exchanges started quoting prices in increments of 1/16 of a dollar, or 6.25 cents.

The SEC endorsed the concept of decimal pricing, but in October 1997 it recommended that the nation's exchanges delay the conversion until after Jan. 1, 2000, because of the potential for computer problems associated with the rollover from 1999 to 2000. However, fears about the so-called Y2K bug proved to be unfounded. The NYSE and Amex began trading in decimals in January 2001, and a number of regional exchanges soon followed suit. The Nasdaq became the last major U.S. exchange to switch over to decimals on April 9, 2001.

In early 1996 the SEC further refined its controversial stance on campaign contributions by bond dealers. In trying to combat the practice known as "pay to play," in which bond dealers contribute to state and local officials' campaigns in hopes of winning bond business, the SEC had set a $250 limit on contributions to candidates in jurisdictions where the bond dealers are entitled to vote. If their contributions exceeded that limit, their firms were barred from doing business in that jurisdiction for two years.

International Agreements

The SEC took its first enforcement action against a Russian investment fund in 1996, charging a Moscow-based fund with making an illegal public offering of securities without registering as an investment company under federal securities laws. Russ-Invest settled with the SEC without admitting wrongdoing and agreed not to raise money from U.S. investors. The case was unusual because the SEC had made a point of trying to accommodate foreign firms that have different standards for accounting and disclosure to encourage participation in the U.S. market and to sustain a sense of cooperation with other countries, especially in enforcement issues.

The SEC had been nurturing its foreign relationships for nearly two decades. In 1982 the agency negotiated an agreement with Switzerland aimed at helping U.S. law enforcement authorities get around Swiss bank secrecy laws in investigating suspected illegalities. This agreement was followed by similar arrangements with Japan and the United Kingdom. In 1988 the commission signed a memorandum of understanding with three Canadian provinces, permitting U.S. and Canadian officials to conduct full-scale investigations upon the request of their foreign counterparts. The SEC also worked with the International Organization of Securities Commissions to develop an international disclosure system. This system is based on the mutual recognition of each participating country's disclosure, accounting, and auditing requirements.

In 1990, to facilitate such international cooperation, Congress passed a law that permitted the SEC to exchange information with foreign enforcement agencies and insulated the SEC from Freedom of Information Act requests for information obtained from foreign sources. The law also gave the SEC and stock exchanges authority to bar persons convicted abroad of securities violations from U.S. exchanges. Acknowledging the reluctance of many foreign countries to submit to stiff U.S. financial reporting requirements, early in 1990 the SEC moved to allow privately placed securities to be traded freely among large investors and to permit foreign companies to issue private placements in the United States.

Investor Awareness

The SEC took several more steps in the latter part of the 1990s to protect the millions of Americans pouring money into the market through mutual funds, their 401(ks) and other retirements plans, and other methods that rely on investment advisers. Levitt called "appalling" the financial literacy levels of many of these new entrants to the market and the American public as a whole, and the SEC moved to require both greater disclosure of the risks and that sellers communicate investment information in "plain English."

In January 1997 the SEC adopted new rules to require any company trading or raising money in domestic markets to publicly disclose its potential losses that could be caused by sudden shifts in financial markets, such as volatility in stock prices, exchange rates, or interest rates.

Levitt also pressed for the use of straightforward and easy-to-understand language in introductory and other sections of investment documents. In January 1998 the SEC approved a rule requiring companies and mutual funds to write the cover page, summary, and risk-factor sections of their prospectuses in simple, concise language that even novice investors would be able to understand. Two months later, the SEC moved to allow mutual fund companies, for the first time, to sell shares to investors using only a short profile of the fund rather than distributing the full prospectus to potential buyers before making a sale. The latter move, combined with the plain English requirement, was intended to make it easier for the average investor to choose among competing mutual funds, the number of which had grown to 8,000 in 1998.

In April 2000 the commission extended its plain English initiative to investment advisers, requiring them to give clients an easily understandable brochure outlining their services. The rule, billed as the most significant commission initiative in regulating advisers since the Investment Advisers Act of 1940, also created an Internet database that allowed consumers to look up information on the services and fees of all registered financial advisers, and on any disciplinary actions taken against them.

The SEC also continued its efforts to give investors more information about the operation of mutual funds. In January 2001 the commission announced it would require mutual funds to disclose standardized after-tax returns so investors could compare tax consequences when choosing an investment. That same month the commission also signaled it expected mutual fund names to reflect the makeup of their portfolios accurately. It released specifications about the percentage of stocks or bonds that funds would have to own to include the term in their name. The most controversial of the recent agency rules designed to maximize investor information was known as "fair disclosure" or "Regulation FD," which barred public companies from releasing important corporate information to a select audience and not also to the general public.

EDGAR System

To help investors obtain accurate, up-to-date information, the commission in 1983 took the first steps toward making the periodic corporate reports filed with it available to the public in electronic form through the Electronic Data Gathering, Analysis, and Retrieval system (EDGAR). After more than a decade and about $111 million in investment, EDGAR finally went online in 1996 with corporate filings of 16,000 public companies. The SEC estimated that EDGAR eliminated more than 12 million pages of corporate material annually, and savvy investors with a personal computer and a phone line could daily monitor the financial details of any public company.

In July 1998 the SEC launched a three-year modernization of the EDGAR system that aimed to reduce costs and effort associated with the preparation and submission of SEC-required documents and improve the presentation of the information. The project was designed to convert the EDGAR system to an Internet-based system using HTML as the official filing format. By November 2000 filers were required to submit information directly to the Internet site.

Managing Competition

In December 1999 the commission adopted a rule that gave all regulated stock exchanges, such as the Nasdaq, full access to shares listed at the venerable NYSE. The rule expanded the Intermarket Trading System to give the NASD and other traders access to companies that had been listed on the NYSE before 1979, including mammoth corporations such as General Electric and IBM. The move was seen as a first step to allowing electronic communications networks, such as Island and Archipelago, unimpeded access to traditional exchanges. These networks allow traders to keep buying and selling after the stock markets close, by matching sell and buy orders.

SEC IN THE 2000s

The most significant challenge for the SEC in the early part of the new century was how to best regulate the burgeoning practice of Internet-based trading. The average number of online trades soared from about 455,000 per day in the first quarter of 1999 to more than 1.24 million per day in the first quarter of 2000, an increase of 173 percent. Likewise, the number of investors opening online trading accounts nearly doubled from 8.6 million in the first quarter of 1999 to more than 17.4 million in the second quarter of 2000.

The popularity of online trading spawned a host of Internet-based stock manipulation schemes. Some hustlers used the Internet to run "pump and dump" operations, driving up their stock prices by posing as interested investors, or "shills," on anonymous Internet message boards. Others conned unwary online traders out of their money using "spam" e-mails, electronic newsletters, and bogus websites.

The SEC launched five nationwide "Internet sweeps" beginning in 2000 in an effort to shut down companies and individuals engaged in such activities. By 2001 the agency had brought 200 enforcement actions against websites that gave out faulty information. The SEC also launched a campaign to educate investors about the potential risks of online trading.

The SEC also took action to strengthen its conflict-of-interest regulations for independent auditors. The ambitious, but controversial, move was prompted by an internal SEC review, made public in January 2000, that alleged widespread violations of auditor independence rules by employees of accounting giant PricewaterhouseCoopers (PwC). The review found that many PwC employees owned stock in companies they were hired to audit. Likewise, it found that PwC employees hired as auditors routinely negotiated lucrative consulting contracts with their clients for other professional services, such as tax advice and information technology services.

Alarmed by the findings, the SEC in March began talking with PwC and the other "Big Five" accounting firms about revamping the conflict of interest rules governing the accounting profession. Initially, Levitt sought to prohibit accounting firms from providing information technology and other nonaudit services to their audit clients altogether. Levitt maintained that audit firms might ignore or conceal their clients' financial problems so as not to jeopardize their lucrative nonaudit business ventures. The accounting firms, conversely, argued that performing nonaudit consulting services made them better auditors because they learned more about their clients' businesses.

The SEC formally adopted in February 2001 an updated conflict of interest rule that allowed accounting firms to continue to design information technology systems and to provide other nonaudit consulting services to their audit clients. However, it imposed a host of disclosure requirements on companies that maintain nonaudit business relationships with their auditors. Specifically, the rule required companies to disclose publicly how much they paid their auditors for both audit and nonaudit services. In addition, the rule required companies to disclose publicly any concerns they might have regarding their auditors' independence.

The SEC quickly showed that it intended to rigorously enforce the new regulation. The same month the rule was approved, the commission sanctioned KPMG, one of the "Big Five" accounting firms, for compromising its independence in a 1996 audit of Porta Systems, a telecommunications equipment manufacturer that was being run by KPMG BayMark, an affiliate of the accounting firm.

President George W. Bush nominated Harvey L. Pitt, a private-practice securities lawyer who served as the SEC's general counsel, to be SEC chair. Supporters said Pitt was eminently qualified for the job, but critics argued that he was too beholden to corporate interests to be an effective advocate for small investors. As a securities lawyer, critics noted, Pitt routinely advised Wall Street brokerage houses, accounting firms, corporate executives, and the NYSE on how to avoid getting into trouble with the SEC.

Pitt had been on the job only a few weeks when terrorists attacked the World Trade Center towers in New York City in September 2001. The attacks posed a host of daunting challenges for the SEC. The commission's northeast regional office in Lower Manhattan was destroyed in the attack, but incredibly no SEC employees were killed in the assault. The nation's securities markets also temporarily shut down, but the SEC played a key role in reestablishing their operations. Immediately following the attacks, Pitt and other SEC officials met in New York City with the leaders of the nation's major markets, securities firms, and banks to devise a strategy and a timetable for reopening

the markets. The nation's fixed-income and futures markets resumed trading just two days after the tragedy. The NYSE, Nasdaq, and the other major equities and options markets reopened six days after the attacks.

The SEC also for the first time in its history invoked certain "emergency powers" that it holds under the Securities Exchange Act of 1934. For example, the commission temporarily relaxed a regulation so that public companies could repurchase more of their own stock. The move, which was rescinded in mid-October 2001, was designed to provide companies with greater stability and liquidity in a time of market uncertainty.

Corporate Scandals

The SEC soon faced another crisis: a rash of business meltdowns and accounting scandals that wiped out many investors' life savings and raised serious questions about the integrity and soundness of corporate America. The crisis began in October 2001, when Enron Corp., one of the nation's largest public companies, unexpectedly reported a $618 million third-quarter loss and a $1.2 billion write-down in shareholder equity. The SEC launched investigations of the Texas-based energy trading company and its "Big Five" accounting firm, Arthur Andersen. The SEC soon found that Enron's once-mighty financial empire had been built on dubious accounting schemes and shady business arrangements, such as off-the-books partnerships designed to hide losses from investors and federal securities regulators. Enron filed for bankruptcy protection in December 2001, wiping out many employees' pension funds and socking investors with huge losses.

In the congressional hearings that followed, officials from Enron and Andersen blamed each other for the debacle. In the end, both companies collapsed. In March 2002 the Department of Justice indicted the Andersen firm for obstruction of justice. Andersen, admitting that its employees had destroyed thousands of Enron records after learning that the SEC had begun investigating its client, contended that it should not be criminally prosecuted as a firm. A jury disagreed, finding Andersen guilty in June 2002. The Supreme Court overturned that verdict in spring 2005, and in October 2011, government prosecutors determined they would not retry the case. Andersen, meanwhile, has been reduced to a shell of its former self and banned from performing public audits.

Enron has not fared much better. The company's creditors continue to seek more than $200 billion from the bankrupt firm, and many Enron executives have been brought up on federal criminal charges. By 2011 twenty-five Enron executives had pleaded guilty or had been convicted at trial, including former chief financial officer Andrew S. Fastow and former president and chief operating officer Jeffrey Skilling. Former Enron chief executive Kenneth Lay was convicted of fraud and conspiracy but died before sentencing.

Enron was only the tip of the corporate-scandal iceberg. In July 2002 WorldCom, the nation's second-largest long-distance telephone carrier, filed for bankruptcy protection after admitting that it had overstated its earnings for five quarters, by $3.8 billion. The company later reported additional accounting errors and increased the total overstatement to approximately $9 billion. The bankruptcy filing and alleged corporate fraud by WorldCom was, by far, the largest in U.S. history. The SEC charged WorldCom and four of its former employees with numerous violations of U.S. securities laws.

Other corporate scandals soon followed. In 2002 the SEC filed fraud charges against Adelphia Communications, Dynegy, Global Crossing, Halliburton, Rite Aid, Tyco International, and Xerox, to name a few. In most cases, the SEC also brought charges against individual executives of these companies. While the details of these cases varied, each revolved around allegations that the defendants purposely and knowingly overstated their earnings to bolster their stock prices and enrich themselves.

Dawn of Sarbanes-Oxley

Congressional leaders and federal regulators in Washington responded to the corporate scandals with a host of divergent proposals for reform. Of the various proposals, bills introduced by Democratic lawmakers called for the strongest crackdown on malfeasance by public companies and the accounting industry. Most Republicans, at least initially, backed weaker measures. SEC chair Pitt sided openly with the Republicans. But after WorldCom's implosion made it clear that the Enron debacle had not been an isolated incident, Republicans rushed to embrace many of the tougher reform provisions advocated by the Democrats. In July 2002 lawmakers passed an anticorporate fraud measure named after the sponsors of two competing bills, Sen. Paul Sarbanes (D-MD) and Rep. Michael Oxley (R-OH). President Bush signed the Sarbanes-Oxley Act into law on July 30, 2002, calling the bill "the most far-reaching reforms of American business practices since the time of Franklin Delano Roosevelt."

Among its other provisions, Sarbanes-Oxley made it a criminal offense—punishable by up to twenty years in prison—to knowingly destroy or falsify records pertaining to SEC or other federal investigations. The law created new criminal penalties for knowingly filing false financial reports. It also prohibited companies from hiring outside accountants to perform certain nonaudit consulting services contemporaneously with their official bookkeeping duties.

The most sweeping provision of the Sarbanes-Oxley Act created a new nongovernmental entity, the Public Company Accounting Oversight Board (PCAOB), to oversee the audits of public companies. The act empowers the PCAOB to inspect the auditing firms performing those audits, to set rules and standards for such audits, and to impose meaningful sanctions if warranted. To safeguard the board's independence, the act mandated that it be funded by fees from public companies. Moreover, no more than two of its five members were to be accountants. The act granted the SEC "general oversight and enforcement authority" over the board, including the approval of its rules and the appointment of its members.

Ironically, Pitt was forced to resign as SEC chair as a result of his efforts to appoint the first chair of the PCAOB. Pitt's controversial choice for the job, former FBI and CIA director William H. Webster, was initially approved by the SEC on Oct. 25, 2002, in a bitterly divided 3–2 vote. A political firestorm, however, soon developed when it became known that Webster had once headed the audit committee of a company accused of fraud by the SEC. Pitt, who had known about but had not shared that information about Webster with his fellow SEC commissioners, tendered his resignation, having served just fifteen months of his six-year term. Webster stepped down as chair of the PCAOB a week after Pitt resigned.

President Bush tapped William H. Donaldson to succeed as SEC chair. Donaldson, who co-founded a Wall Street investment bank and ran the NYSE from 1990 to 1995, said at his Senate confirmation hearing in February 2003 that he would "call on corporate America and Wall Street" to make honesty, integrity, and regard for shareholders' interests the motivating factors for all business decisions.

In May 2003 Donaldson and his fellow SEC commissioners unanimously appointed William J. McDonough, a former president of the Federal Reserve Bank of New York, to be chair of the fledgling PCAOB. In June 2003 the PCAOB approved a set of strict ethics rules in an apparent effort to stave off any conflicts of interest that could tarnish its work. The rules generally prohibit all board and staff members from either owing, or being owed, any money from any "former employer, business partner, publisher or client." Members of the PCAOB and their spouses and dependents were also prohibited from having any financial interests in or receiving any profit or payments from a public accounting firm. Likewise, they instructed PCAOB employees to "avoid investments that affect or reasonably create the appearance of affecting their independence or objectivity."

The SEC, meanwhile, completed the lengthy rulemaking process required by the landmark Sarbanes-Oxley Act. Early in 2003 the commission adopted rules for one of the most controversial sections of the act: consulting services prohibited to independent auditors. The rules defined nine nonaudit services that could potentially impair an auditor's independence, such as investment banking services, legal services, and the design and implementation of financial information systems. The SEC also adopted Sarbanes-Oxley–mandated rules relating to financial experts on audit committees; trading during pension fund blackout periods; retention of audit records; and standards of conduct for corporate attorneys, among other matters. In July 2003 the president signed into law the Accountant, Compliance, and Enforcement Staffing Act, a law that would help implement Sarbanes-Oxley by streamlining the hiring of key SEC positions.

Corporate Punishment

The commission continued to make headlines in its crackdown on corporate crime. In June 2003 the SEC filed securities fraud charges against lifestyle entrepreneur Martha Stewart and her former stockbroker, Peter Bacanovic. Both Stewart and Bacanovic were found guilty and served five months in jail and five months of home detention in 2005. In March 2004 a midlevel executive at Dynegy was sentenced to twenty-four years in prison after being convicted of hiding a $300 million loan to the company to improve its financial outlook. In June 2005 Adelphia founder and former chief executive John Rigas, convicted of conspiracy, securities fraud, and bank fraud, was sentenced to fifteen years in prison. In July 2005 former WorldCom chief executive Bernard J. Ebbers, guilty of securities fraud, conspiracy, and filing false reports with regulators, was sentenced to twenty-five years in prison.

The commission has also focused on discouraging companies from offering benefits to its executives that are hidden from shareholders. While the SEC has not endorsed reducing compensation for CEOs, it has sent a clear message that companies should award salaries responsibly and that performance should be strongly linked to pay. Donaldson said that pay and benefits packages for top executives could serve as a litmus test for improved board oversight of companies.

The SEC showed its seriousness in addressing inappropriate executive compensation when it fined Tyson Foods and its chairman, Donald J. Tyson, $2.2 million for not disclosing to shareholders the full extent of the $3 million in personal benefits the company paid Tyson. Tyson Foods settled with the SEC, paying a $1.5 million fine. Tyson agreed to pay a $700,000 fine.

During the same period, the commission approved a major new rule aimed at modernizing the regulatory structure of the U.S. equity markets. One of a number of commission ventures aimed at harnessing various technological advances to enhance the efficiency of stock markets, the rule required companies to seek the best price for electronic stock trades, even if the best price existed outside the company's system. Additionally, the rule established a uniform market access rule intended to promote nondiscriminatory access to quotations displayed by trading centers through a private linkage approach provided by commercial vendors. The rule also prohibited market participants from showing or accepting quotations in stocks that are priced in an increment of less than a penny, unless the price of the quotation is less than $1.00. If the price of the quotation is less than $1.00, the minimum increment would be $0.0001. Called the subpenny rule by SEC staff, this rule was seen as a way to facilitate greater price transparency and consistency, as well as to protect displayed limit orders.

One of Donaldson's key reform initiatives was to establish a more detailed definition of independence for directors of public companies, requiring the majority of members on companies' boards to satisfy that standard. One of the key complaints during scandals such as Enron and WorldCom was that corporate directors would too often defer to executives or ignore concerns raised by investor advocates. To combat this, the commission pushed new rules requiring independent director oversight of the corporate governance process, auditing, director nominations, and compensation for top executives. Other reform measures during this period include requiring companies to electronically report insider transactions within two days, and, for the first time, public reporting by management auditors on internal controls and their effectiveness.

Of all the new rules created by the Sarbanes-Oxley legislation, Donaldson said he believed the one with the most potential to improve financial reporting was the latter measure. Requiring these disclosures by both management and an independent auditor, Donaldson said, will likely result in companies reporting they cannot complete their assessments or audits of controls or that their internal controls are lacking. Donaldson said the goal should be for companies to improve controls over financial reporting, which will increase investor information and confidence.

On a theoretical level, Donaldson's approach was sound in the sense it was aimed at improving financial statement reporting. However, it also created uncertainty for companies and resulted in backlash from the corporate community because of what industry representatives considered overly strict rules that inhibited their economic vitality. Donaldson, and the commission as a whole, were not deaf to these arguments, particularly those from smaller publicly traded companies for whom compliance with various aspects of Sarbanes-Oxley was cost prohibitive. The SEC addressed these criticisms in a variety of ways under Donaldson, holding a series of roundtable discussions and eliciting written feedback from affected companies. Additionally, the SEC established the SEC Advisory Committee on Smaller Public Companies to examine the impact of Sarbanes-Oxley on small businesses.

In June 2005, after Donaldson stepped down, President Bush tapped Rep. Christopher Cox (R-CA) to be SEC chair. The choice was seen as an olive branch to the business community as Cox, a former securities lawyer, was known as a staunch business advocate during his nine terms in the House. The choice raised the ire of some consumer groups, who complained that Cox would seek to roll back major sections of Sarbanes-Oxley and other corporate governance reforms and unfairly favor business interests. During his Senate nomination, however, Cox said he understood a major responsibility of the position was to protect individual investors.

Electronic Innovation

In fall 2005 the commission sought to improve the availability of corporate and mutual fund information over the Internet. The focus of the effort was updating the EDGAR system to make it more useful for investors. To accomplish that, the commission tested a data format for company reports known as Extensible Business Reporting Language (XBRL), which would allow the information in company filings to be used more effectively by investors.

The commission's efforts to adjust to an Internet-based economy did not stop with EDGAR improvements. Also in November 2005 the commission voted to propose for public comment a rule allowing for proxy materials to be delivered over the Internet. Instead of providing shareholders with proxy materials and other information through the mail or by e-mail, the new rule imagined companies meeting their legal obligations by posting their materials on a website and then notifying shareholders of the availability of the information. The goal, the commission said, was to save companies money in distributing proxy materials and to make it easier for individuals offering competing proxy proposals to share alternate materials.

In addition the SEC hosted a series of roundtable discussions with a variety of stakeholders—investors, issuers, auditors, and corporations—throughout 2006 to discuss the modernization of SEC filing data. The focus, Cox explained, was on "implementing interactive data initiatives that can benefit investors as quickly as possible." To that end, in September 2006 the SEC awarded three contracts totaling $54 million to update EDGAR and make the commission's systems more interactive. Ultimately, the agency plans to require all corporations, mutual funds, and other related entities to file all of their data with the SEC electronically.

Dealing with Sarbanes-Oxley

In his first few months as chair, Cox focused on the same issues that occupied Donaldson during his tenure. At the top of that list was the ongoing effort to implement all of the Sarbanes-Oxley reforms Congress had passed three years before. But as with Donaldson, the commission delayed final implementation and painstakingly reviewed the new filing requirements, in part because of ongoing complaints from the business community. For example, many small businesses complained about the internal controls requirements of section 404 of Sarbanes-Oxley. In September 2005 the commission voted to postpone compliance of section 404 for companies with less than $75 million in assets until mid-July 2006.

In May 2006 the SEC announced a series of initiatives to continue the implementation of Sarbanes-Oxley. The announcement came after a series of roundtable discussions in winter and spring 2006, as well as a report from the Advisory Committee on Smaller Public Companies and feedback from larger filers that had already filed under the 404 requirements. The refrain from most quarters was that the cost of implementing Sarbanes-Oxley was higher than most had expected, in part because companies were required to implement internal controls for business functions that posed no real risks and because independent auditors were conducting overly excessive reviews of companies' financial statements.

The SEC plan introduced in May had two parts. In the first part, the SEC was to provide written guidance for companies on how to apply section 404 requirements. The goal, the commission said, was for companies to introduce internal controls based on the various levels of risk presented by their business models. New controls should focus on those areas posing the largest risk, while areas where there was little or no risk to the company's financial health could receive less rigorous scrutiny. The second part of the announced initiative was for the PCAOB to revise auditing standards dealing with section 404 so that external accounts focused on "areas that pose higher risk of fraud or material error." With this announcement came a further delay of section 404 compliance for smaller filers, until Dec. 16, 2006.

Commission work on fine-tuning section 404 for all publicly traded companies continued throughout 2006. The effort focused on streamlining the legislation's requirements for reporting on internal financial controls and giving companies time to make the necessary changes without facing penalties. In August 2006 the SEC, granting yet another delay to smaller public companies for full compliance with section 404, moved the deadline to December 2007. In December 2006 the SEC closed the year by voting to propose interpretative guidance directing companies to focus their internal control deliberations on the areas where there is the biggest risk for material problems or malfeasance.

Focus on Executives

Although Sarbanes-Oxley implementation was the top focus during Cox's first year on the job, the commission's work on another issue—executive compensation—was arguably more significant. In a move that received praise from both the business community and proponents of corporate governance reforms, the SEC in January 2006 proposed an overhaul of disclosure requirements for the compensation of top executives. The outsized pay packages received by disgraced executives at WorldCom, Enron, and other firms served as the impetus for the commission's decision to revamp its disclosure rules.

Cox and the SEC were careful to tailor the executive compensation proposal narrowly to focus solely on disclosure, as opposed to suggesting any sort of appropriate level of compensation. The goal was to simplify and extend existing disclosures included in company filings by requiring companies to disclose payment plans in a standardized chart form, as well as to include an extensive narrative, "provided in plain English," describing the various factors underlying the company's compensation policies. The commission approved the rule in late July 2006 with few changes, requiring companies to comply with the new rules beginning in December 2006.

Final approval of the new executive compensation disclosure requirements coincided, ironically enough, with another market-roiling scandal concerning the granting of stock options to top executives. At issue were a group of practices that collectively guaranteed that executives fortunate enough to receive options would profit handsomely from the stock options. Some companies timed option grants to take effect just ahead of announcements of good news; others waited to offer grants until after bad news was public and the share price had fallen. Known as spring-loading and bullet-dodging, these manipulations were designed to take advantage of expected stock price movements to enrich option holders. The most prevalent practice that came to the SEC's attention was the backdating of options to a time when a stock price was low, guaranteeing that the executive receiving the option would reap a greater profit.

One of the first backdating investigations revealed to the general public involved California-based Brocade Communications Systems. On July 20, 2006, the FBI and SEC jointly announced the filing of criminal and civil securities fraud charges against the company's former chief executive officer and vice president of human resources for routinely backdating options without recording the necessary compensation expenses. The commission said at the time that the charges were the result of an eighteen-month investigation. When a few weeks later charges were brought against executives at Comverse Technology for similar practices, across the country executives and boards of directors scrambled to examine their books for similar practices. Brocade later reached a settlement with the SEC in May 2007 and agreed to pay a penalty of $7 million.

Spurred on by research that suggested 29 percent of the companies that gave options to top executives between 1996 and 2005 manipulated the grants in some fashion, Congress quickly joined in the call for a major review of options practices. Household names such as Apple Computer and Home Depot faced inquiries about their options grants, and hundreds of companies initiated internal probes. Following so soon after the corporate scandals of a few years earlier, the business community quickly moved to assure investors and regulators that they were being proactive in dealing with the problem.

But the issue of executive compensation did not go away. When the 2008–2009 financial crisis broke, many called on the federal government to cap executive pay. Moreover, an uproar ensued in the opening months of 2009, when it was discovered that some of the firms that had received government bailout money were paying hefty bonuses to executives. By summer 2009 there were a number of proposals in Congress to give the SEC authority to regulate how executives at publicly traded firms were paid.

Procorporation Developments

In January 2006 consumer groups and investor advocates loudly criticized the SEC when it said it would scale back efforts to secure monetary civil penalties from corporations found guilty of wrongdoing or as part of settlement negotiations with corporations. The commission said its new policy generally would be to seek civil penalties against a company if the violation the firm was accused of had improperly benefited shareholders. Conversely, if shareholders had been hurt by a company's malfeasance, the SEC said it might pursue civil penalties against specific individuals rather than the firm as a whole so as not to pass on the cost to shareholders. In its announcement, the SEC argued that the action would benefit shareholders, but consumer groups saw this as a relaxing of rules against corporate America.

The business world also scored a pair of legal victories over the SEC in 2006, as rules championed by former chair Donaldson were overturned following lawsuits from industry groups. The first dealt with a rule that required 75 percent of a mutual fund's directors, including the chair, to be independent of company management. Pushed by Donaldson after a number of abuses were discovered in the mutual fund industry, the rule was controversial at best. A federal appeals court struck down the rule in June 2005, but the commission—in one of Donaldson's last actions as chair—voted in favor of a revised rule again just days after the court decision. Thus, the issue was left for Cox to deal with, even after the rule was once again struck down by a federal court in April 2006. Cox, for his part,

was not a vocal advocate for the rule, although the SEC did reopen the comment period for the rule through 2006. Ultimately, however, no further action was taken.

The second legal victory surrounded another rule adopted during Donaldson's tenure, this time regarding hedge funds. That rule required members of the secretive hedge fund industry to submit to basic oversight by the SEC, including registering as advisers and adopting a code of ethics. The theory was that as powerful funds continued to grow in popularity, it was important for the chief regulator of the securities market to have at least base-level information about them. But the hedge fund industry balked and once again an SEC rule was challenged by the business community. The mutual fund rule, like the SEC's hedge fund rule, was struck down by a federal court, this time because the new rule was "counterintuitive" and "arbitrary." The decision was a victory for the hedge fund industry and a setback for the SEC.

The biggest issue facing the commission in 2007 was the ongoing effort to implement section 404 of Sarbanes-Oxley, particularly for smaller publicly traded companies. SEC critics in Congress and in the business sector were emboldened by both anecdotal evidence and raw numbers that suggested companies had been avoiding selling their stock in the United States in favor of countries where less stringent reporting requirements were the norm. Initial public offerings by companies in the United States had been on the decline, and European investment banks had begun to keep pace with their American counterparts on deals and fees. Although observers said the phenomenon was not necessarily a Sarbanes-Oxley issue—the decline in the U.S. dollar and evolution of foreign stock markets likely played a large role in companies listing abroad—critics of the SEC's corporate governance law pointed to the growth of overseas listings as evidence of an overreach by lawmakers and the commission. Section 404 received the greatest scrutiny, targeted by an aggressive lobbying campaign of smaller public companies that saw auditing costs cutting into their profits to a greater extent than their larger rivals.

The SEC continued to adjust and streamline its new guidance proposal for section 404 that directed company management to focus on those internal controls where there was the greatest risk for fraud or for a material financial misstatement. The SEC's five commissioners unanimously approved the new section 404 guidance at a May 2007 meeting. Said Cox of the new guidance, "companies of all sizes will be able to scale and tailor their evaluation procedures according to the facts and circumstances."

Outside of Sarbanes-Oxley, one of the major issues for the SEC during this period continued to be the regulation of markets in an era of increased globalization and particularly the continued growth of multinational companies whose stock traded on multiple international exchanges. In spring 2006 Cox and his European counterparts at the Committee of European Securities Regulators reiterated past commitments to work together on a number of fronts, including modernizing technology governing financial reporting, dealing with differences in accounting principles, and setting up procedures for sharing information among regulators for affected companies.

In April 2007 the SEC signed an agreement with the German securities regulator to exchange information and consult on issues facing companies that do business in both countries. That same month, the SEC and financial regulators from the United Kingdom agreed to a framework for dealing with the accounting standards used by firms listed in the United Kingdom but registered with the SEC.

The SEC also finalized rules governing firms that offer ratings on the debt issued by private companies and municipalities. Officially known as "nationally recognized statistical rating organizations," these firms evaluate the investment quality of bond offerings and issue ratings based on a variety of standards. Under the Credit Rating Agency Reform Act of 2006, the agency was required to adopt final rules dealing with the registration and oversight of rating agencies. The new rules, which the commission issued in late May 2007, dictated how a credit rating agency could become nationally recognized, including the information and certifications it needed to provide to the SEC. Additionally, the new rules required credit rating agencies to retain certain records, as well as to provide certain financial reports and statements to the SEC on an annual basis. In spite of these rules, the power and influence of credit rating agencies would become a contentious issue in the financial crisis of the following year.

In 2008 the agency was involved in major enforcement action involving large banks and auction-rate securities. Auction-rate securities are instruments that resemble corporate debt, except that interest rates are reset at auctions, sometimes as frequently as once a week. Many companies and retail clients invest in these securities because they earn higher rates of return and yet can continue to treat their holdings almost like cash or money market investments. However, the $330 billion auction rate securities market collapsed in February 2008 during the downturn in the broader credit market. Their failure would soon catch the attention of state and federal regulators, which accused banks of fraudulently marketing auction-rate bonds to clients as safe, liquid investments when they were no such thing.

In summer 2008, the agency, along with New York State Attorney General Andrew M. Cuomo, formally announced a major investigation into alleged fraud concerning the sale of auction-backed securities. The probe resulted in a number of settlements with major banks, forcing them to buy back many of the auction-rate securities from clients. The first firm to be targeted was Citigroup, which had been a primary dealer in these specialized securities. Although Citigroup neither admitted nor denied wrongdoing, it agreed to buy back $7.3 billion in these securities and to pay $100 million in civil penalties. Other firms soon followed, including Swiss investment bank UBS, which under a settlement with the SEC and state regulators agreed to refund clients up to $18.6 billion. In August 2008 Cuomo announced that he was expanding his probe to include JPMorgan Chase, Morgan Stanley, Wachovia, Merrill Lynch, and Goldman Sachs.

But the agency's victory in the auction-backed securities probe was short-lived. By early fall 2008 the beginnings of an expected recession quickly turned into a full-blown global financial crisis. As banks, financial brokerages, and stock prices all fell, those in charge of regulating financial markets, including the SEC, were subjected to increasing criticism for not doing enough to prevent the meltdown. Bush continued to support Cox, while others noted that the parts of the financial sector hardest hit by the crisis—mortgage lenders, insurance companies and others—were not within the regulatory purview of the agency. Indeed, as the financial sector continue to collapse in fall 2008, the SEC was notably absent from much of the major decision-making process. It was the Treasury Department—first under Henry Paulson and then Timothy Geithner—and the Federal Reserve—under Ben Bernanke—that led the government response to the crisis.

The Madoff and Stanford Scandals

In December 2008 the financial sector was shocked to learn that one its own, well-known financier Bernard L. Madoff, was arrested and charged with running a Ponzi scheme that defrauded investors of an estimated $65 billion. Although the SEC had the authority to investigate Madoff's investment business, which for decades had managed tens of billions of dollars for wealthy investors, universities, charities, and hedge funds, it failed to find evidence of fraud in its investigation of Madoff in 2006.

One of the reasons Madoff may have escaped notice was because he also simultaneously operated a legitimate, regulated stock brokerage business. It was in this role that he helped to create and, for a time, run Nasdaq, the first electronic stock exchange, and even became an SEC adviser on electronic trading issues. A second, separate investment business was allowed to operate on the perimeter of regulation at a time when the government was intentionally permitting private, unregulated transactions to take place. In the days following Madoff's arrest, SEC Chair Cox reported that the defendant kept multiple sets of books and falsified documents that misled both investors and regulators.

But Cox, who criticized his staff for "apparent multiple failures" in the Madoff case offered some additional explanations—that his agency had inappropriately discounted outside allegations against Madoff, that staff did not relay their concerns to agency leaders, and that examiners relied on documents voluntarily supplied by Madoff rather than seeking subpoenas to obtain critical information. Critics pointed to darker reasons for the failure: Madoff, long considered a Wall Street legend, had what might be considered a "too cozy" relationship with regulators.

The agency received the full brunt of congressional disdain in February 2009 when SEC Enforcement Chief Linda Chatman Thomsen and acting General Counsel Andrew N. Vollmer appeared before members of a House Financial Services subcommittee to explain what had happened in the Madoff scandal. Rep. Gary L. Ackerman (D-NY) was particularly scathing in his rebuke: "The economy is in crisis. We thought the enemy was Mr. Madoff. I think it's you," Ackerman said. In March 2009 Madoff pleaded guilty to eleven felony charges, including securities fraud, mail fraud, and money laundering. Three months later, he was sentenced to 150 years in prison.

Under intense scrutiny for its oversight, the SEC made sure the alleged perpetrator of another Ponzi scheme did not slip through its fingers the way Madoff had. On Feb. 18, 2009, the SEC charged R. Allen Stanford and three companies under his control with orchestrating a $9.2 billion fraud involving the sale of certificates of deposit. Stanford allegedly lied to customers about how their money was being invested and how the firms' investment portfolios had performed. Posting double-digit returns consistently during the past fifteen years, Stanford International told investors that their deposits were safe, invested in easily sellable securities, and overseen by a team of more than twenty research analysts. In fact, the agency charged, the funds were largely invested in illiquid real estate and private equity holdings, managed solely by Stanford and James M. Davis, one of Stanford's top executives. In June 2009 the SEC charged the financier with multiple counts of money laundering and mail,wire and securities fraud.

A New SEC Team

By the end of 2008, the Madoff case and other issues had kept Cox in a near continuous defensive posture. Critics pointed to the collapse of the Bear Stearns investment firm in March 2008 as yet another example of Cox's and the agency's shortcomings. They argued that the SEC had been aware that the firm's exposure to mortgage securities had exceeded its internal limits yet made no effort to reduce that exposure. After the embarrassment of the Madoff case, there was a sense on Wall Street as well as on Capitol Hill that the SEC desperately needed to repair its tarnished reputation. The first step in this rebuilding effort was the 2009 appointment—by President Barack Obama—of Mary L. Schapiro as SEC chair.

The first woman to chair the SEC on more than an interim basis, Schapiro had a history of attracting support from both Republicans and Democrats. She was nominated to the SEC's board twice, first by President Reagan and then by President George H. W. Bush, and was named acting chair by President Clinton. Schapiro's beginning stance on oversight was proactive, vigorously pursuing wrongdoing in the investigation into the breakdown at Reserve Primary Fund, a $60 billion money market mutual fund that collapsed in September 2008. Furthermore, Schapiro quickly moved to reassert the SEC's institutional relevance, arguing for more authority rather than less and pushing to ensure that the SEC be an integral part of a proposed council of regulators, which would be responsible for spotting risks to the overall financial system.

In February 2009 Schapiro appointed Republican Robert Khuzami, a former federal prosecutor and lawyer at Deutsche Bank, as the agency's enforcement director. Khuzami made his reputation by prosecuting insider trading, Ponzi schemes, and accounting fraud. In confident language befitting his new position, Khuzami said that he wanted his agency to become more of a deterrent to financial crime and that he and his staff would "relentlessly pursue and bring to justice those whose misconduct infects our markets, corrodes investor confidence, and has caused so much financial suffering." Khuzami's words proved to be more than mere rhetoric: in his first six months in office, he brought a number of high-profile actions against Bank of America, General Electric, and Hank Greenberg, the former chief executive of failed insurance giant AIG. Under Khuzami the SEC also filed its first enforcement case against the controversial practice of "naked" short selling, which many believe helped drive stock prices unnecessarily low.

The financial crisis that began in 2008 prompted the SEC and other federal regulators to ramp up efforts to punish firms and executives who may have contributed to the problem. This included charges of fraud against General Electric, which agreed to pay $50 million in August 2009 for boosting its earnings by hundreds of millions of dollars through the use of improper accounting methods. The SEC complaint identified four separate instances of accounting violations, including one that involved improper accounting for sales of commercial aircraft engine spare parts.

In August 2009 charges were also brought against Bank of America for misleading shareholders by hiding their plans to pay billions of dollars in bonuses to employees of Merrill Lynch, which was purchased by Bank of America in fall 2008. While Merrill Lynch was on the brink of collapse, Bank of America had secretly authorized $5.8 billion in bonuses to be paid to Merrill executives. The penalty—$33 million—was, according to SEC officials, the largest ever imposed by the agency for a violation of the requirement that companies disclose relevant information to shareholders.

The financial crisis also focused regulators on reforming the rules by which markets operate. One area that the SEC focused on involves the powerful role played by credit-rating agencies. Many believe that the three largest credit-rating firms—Standard & Poor's, Fitch Rating, and Moody's Investors Service—played a significant role in helping to precipitate the financial crisis. In particular, these critics said, the rating agencies' overly optimistic assessments of subprime mortgages helped convince many firms to invest in this area. When these same agencies downgraded subprime securities, they effectively forced money market funds and investment banks to sell them, often at huge losses. Regulators and investors also argued that credit-rating agencies have a conflict of interest because they are paid by the investment banks issuing the securities, and thus are encouraged to give high ratings to win business.

By the end of 2008, the SEC approved rules aimed at increasing accountability among credit-rating agencies. The requirements forbid firms from rating securities if the agency has previously advised the company issuing the stock as to how to acquire the best credit rating. The rules also ban credit-rating agency employees from accepting more than $25 worth of gifts from companies issuing securities and require the agencies to provide detailed information about how they determine specific ratings and how those ratings hold up over time. Although the rules were deemed a step in the right direction toward greater transparency, some felt they were not stringent enough.

Dodd-Frank

As the SEC worked in 2009 to reform parts of the financial machinery, the Obama administration began work on a regulatory overhaul of the entire financial system. In July the White House sent to Congress a proposal to vastly expand federal oversight of previously unregulated markets, such as trading in derivatives, and to impose more rigorous regulations on financial firms and products, such as hedge funds and municipal bonds.

While the proposed overhaul has received positive reviews from some in the industry, it quickly became the subject of intense turf battles between various federal agencies, including the SEC. Introduced in the wake of the financial crisis, the bill's provisions were vigorously debated on Capitol Hill for more than a year. Finally signed into law on July 21, 2010, the Wall Street Reform and Consumer Protection Act of 2010 (also called "Dodd-Frank" after its chief sponsors, Senator Dodd, and Rep. Barney Frank, D-Mass.) was the most sweeping overhaul of the financial system since the Great Depression.

Although the law was considered a major legislative victory for President Obama and for its supporters in Congress, Dodd-Frank's journey from bill to law was not without major hurdles, especially in the Senate. Criticism for the proposal came from both sides of the aisle, with Republicans arguing that it would entail excessive and burdensome regulation that would only make it more difficult and costly for businesses and consumers to raise or borrow money. While most Democrats saw the law as a victory that demonstrated to their constituents that they could be tough on Wall Street, some in the party felt the package did not go far enough and left too many critical decisions to the same federal regulators who had fatally missed the warning signs in the run-up to the financial crisis of 2008.

Among the key provisions of the new law was the establishment of the Financial Stability Oversight Council, a group of federal regulators tasked with watching for and assessing any potential threats to the financial system. It also created the Consumer Financial Protection Bureau to track consumer-related issues with an eye toward protecting ordinary people from unscrupulous banks and financial services firms. The financial overhaul also gave shareholders a nonbinding advisory vote on executive compensation and gave federal agencies new powers to regulate and even liquidate financial institutions that posed a threat to the nation's financial health.

No agency was affected more by the enactment of Dodd-Frank than the SEC. The legislation left the agency with more than 100 new rules to draft as well as a host of new responsibilities and reporting requirements. Specifically, the new law required the SEC chair to serve on the Financial Stability Oversight Council and tasked the agency with drafting new rules governing a host of financial projects, from derivatives to secondary securities. In addition, the law enhanced the SEC's enforcement authority, giving the agency new powers to conduct investigations and bring lawsuits against accused wrongdoers. It also gave the SEC new authority to reward whistleblowers who provide essential information in criminal investigations.

As Congress and the administration worked to hash out differences over the financial overhaul, the SEC also continued to deal with the fallout from the crisis that precipitated the legislation. In September 2009, for instance, the SEC's inspector general issued a blistering report completely blaming the agency for failing to catch Madoff. A few days later, a federal court rejected a $33 million settlement between the Bank of America and the agency. The settlement had come after the SEC found out that the bank had secretly promised to pay billions in bonuses to executives at Merrill Lynch, a firm it had just acquired. The court, however, said that the SEC's $33 million fine was a "contrivance designed to provide the SEC with the façade of enforcement" and blamed the agency for not adequately protecting Bank of America shareholders.

SEC IN THE 2010s

Early in 2010 the SEC and Bank of America tried again, crafting a settlement that required the bank to pay the agency $150 million, or nearly five times the amount agreed to in the earlier settlement that had been rejected by the court. Although the judge ultimately accepted this second attempt by the parties to settle, he did so reluctantly, once again claiming that the agency was letting the bank off too easy.

Meanwhile, under Schapiro the SEC began devoting more time and resources to enforcement. During the first half of 2009, the agency opened 10 percent more cases than in the same period in 2008, more than doubled the number of formal orders of investigation that come with subpoena power, and filed 147 percent more temporary restraining orders.

This increase in activity prompted some to ask whether the agency had enough resources to do so much more, especially litigation resources needed to sustain the increase in legal action that naturally accompanies a greater emphasis on enforcement. Early in 2010, Schapiro brushed these concerns aside, saying that the SEC would continue to accelerate its investigatory work. With this in mind, the agency changed its rule regarding subpoenas: no longer would SEC lawyers need to get the approval of the agency's five-person commission before issuing subpoenas in ongoing investigations. This change was aimed at streamlining the process and allowing investigators to move more quickly during an investigation.

The new mandate to investigate and the enhanced authority to do so were steps aimed, in part, at giving the agency new momentum in the wake of the scandals of the financial crisis. The Madoff case, in particular, left a perception that the SEC was not tough enough on the people it was charged with regulating and overseeing. But this perception began to change as the agency pursued a long list of financial services firms and other companies accused of running afoul of the nation's securities laws.

The biggest and most watched of these cases was against financial powerhouse Goldman Sachs, which was charged with fraud in April 2010. The case arose after the SEC and others came to believe that Goldman had given advice to clients to buy mortgage-backed securities that at least some in the firm knew to be bad bets. Goldman, which invests its own money as well as advising others how to invest theirs, was accused of having an inherent conflict of interest. In this case, Goldman advisers were accused of urging clients to buy securities that the firm was not purchasing and that it urged other clients to bet against.

Although Goldman denied any wrongdoing, the SEC charges were a public relations nightmare for the firm, coming as the nation was still struggling to pull itself out of a recession that many blamed on Wall Street. The firm's president, Lloyd Blankfein, and other top executives endured hours of grilling by angry senators at a Senate Banking Subcommittee hearing in April. Within months of the hearing and the charges being filed, Goldman settled with the SEC, agreeing to pay a $550 million penalty to the agency, the highest ever paid by a Wall Street firm. Goldman also agreed to overhaul the system it uses to recommend mortgage securities to its clients. In exchange, the SEC promised to drop the charges and allow the firm to avoid having to admit to any wrongdoing.

Around the same time as the Goldman settlement, the agency scored another victory against a firm accused of financial wrongdoing, in this case allegedly fraudulent accounting practices. Computer giant Dell had been accused of using accounting tricks to meet earnings targets throughout much of the decade ending in 2010. By doing so, the SEC and others charged, the computer maker had been able to artificially inflate its stock price. As with the Goldman settlement, Dell agreed to pay a fine—$100 million in this case—and reform its accounting methods. While the fine could have been larger and Dell formally admitted to no wrongdoing, the penalty was intended to send a message to other firms that accounting tricks would not be tolerated.

Amid these investigations and settlements, the commission pushed forward new regulations aimed at reining in what many saw as bad corporate practices. Many of these regulatory efforts were mandated by the Dodd-Frank act and nearly all of them were, in one way or another, a response to practices that many claimed had led to the financial crisis. For instance, in September 2010 the commission approved rules that would require companies to publicly disclose more information about their short-term debt. The aim, in this case, was to give investors a better picture of a company's liabilities and make it harder for firms to use accounting gimmicks to deceive shareholders and the public at large.

In January 2011 the commission took aim at high corporate salaries when it adopted rules that would allow shareholders to vote on the pay of top executives. The rules would apply only to publicly traded companies and were not scheduled to take effect until 2013. Still, the new regulations were seen as a victory for shareholders who had long complained that top corporate executives awarded themselves lavish pay packages, even at times when their companies were struggling.

In May 2011 the SEC once again turned its attention to the credit-ratings agencies. Although the commission overhauled the rules governing these agencies in 2008, it proposed a second set of regulations aimed at better ensuring that these entities accurately assess the risk of each bond issue. The newly proposed rules, which were likely to take effect in fall 2011, aimed to mitigate the agencies' conflict of interest by not allowing employees of the agencies who market and sell their services to engage in any of the actual ratings work. In addition, if someone who helped rate certain bonds later were to work for the financial services firm that issued them, the rating of those bonds must immediately be reviewed and, if necessary, be revised.

Also in May, the agency won a major victory when a New York court convicted the head of a large hedge fund, Raj Rajaratnam, of 14 counts of securities fraud and conspiracy in connection with a series of incidents involving insider trading. Rajaratnam, the head of the Galleon Group, used a wide network of corporate executives to obtain and profit from proprietary information about a host of important firms, including Google, Goldman Sachs, and Intel.

The commission saw the Rajaratnum case as important beyond the obvious aim of fighting wrongdoing on Wall Street. According to Robert Khuzami, director of enforcement at the agency, the Galleon case was part of a broader effort to monitor suspicious behavior in the high-flying hedge-fund industry. In other words, the case was a warning to Wall Street to expect more investigations and arrests. Indeed, around the time Rajaratnam was being tried and convicted, a number of managers from another major hedge fund, SAC Capital, were arrested and charged with insider trading.

On June 24, 2011, the agency issued new rules aimed at preventing a "flash crash" of the sort that occurred in May 2011, when some automated trading systems drove the price of some stocks down to as low as one cent per share. Automated systems often sell stocks when their value drops to a certain level, which in turn can trigger other automated sales, producing a cascade of selling that pushes prices to extremely low levels. The new SEC rules, which went into effect in August, expanded an already existing pilot program that stopped the trading of certain stocks or mutual funds that lost or gained 10 percent of their value in five minutes or less. This "circuit breaker" was extended to all stocks and funds traded on all major exchanges in the nation.

New SEC rules set additional restrictions on mutual fund fees. Investors had long complained that mutual fund managers saddle investors with excessive and often hidden fees. "It's very difficult for investors to understand what they're paying and when," said Commissioner Elisse Walter in late April 2011. Under the new rules, long-term fees would be phased out and the upfront costs of buying into a mutual fund would be capped. But the commission slowed action on the proposed rules in response to stronger than expected pushback by the mutual fund industry. And by the summer of 2013 the rules still had not been adopted.

In spite of setbacks like this, by the summer of 2011, Schapiro was able to report that the agency had drafted more than two-thirds of the regulations mandated by Dodd-Frank. And yet some important regulatory requirements remained unfulfilled and the agency admitted that it was behind the schedule mandated under the law for writing new regulations. For instance, complex new rules regarding the closing of failing financial institutions had not been finished. These new rules were particularly important since most experts believe that confusion over whether and how to close failing banks and other financial institutions helped accelerate the 2007–2009 financial crisis.

On June 29, 2011, the agency took a big step toward finishing its remaining regulatory work under Dodd-Frank when it announced new rules governing—what had been largely unregulated in the past—derivatives. Derivatives are financial instruments used by investors and others to hedge risk, such as the future cost of a particular commodity—for instance, oil or wheat. The new rules particularly focused on derivative transactions known as "swaps," which involve promises from one party to another to pay cash if certain events occur, such as a rise in interest rates or bond prices or, again, movement in one direction or another in the price of a certain commodity. During the financial crisis, many investors were ruined because they failed to adequately assess the risk of buying swaps. The best known of these "victims" was AIG, which required a bailout by the federal government to the tune of $182.5 billion to prevent a collapse of the firm and further damage to the global financial system.

Under the new rules, those who sell swaps were required to fully disclose to the buyer the risks associated with the transaction. The rules also required sellers to disclose any conflicts of interest associated with the deal. Finally, sellers were required to ensure that a certain class of potential clients—municipalities, pension funds, charitable foundations—had hired independent and well-qualified financial advisers before going through with any sale.

Schapiro hailed the new rules, saying that they would "level the playing field . . . by bringing needed transparency to this market and by seeking to ensure that customers in these transactions are treated fairly." But another commissioner who also supported the rules, Republican Troy Paredes, worried publicly that the new requirements could make derivatives much more expensive and give people fewer options when trying to hedge risk.

One month after the release of the derivative rules, the agency suffered a big blow when the Court of Appeals for the District of Columbia (the second-highest federal court in the country) struck down another new rule, one that would have made it easier for shareholders to throw out directors on corporate boards and install their own candidates. The rule had been intended to make corporate boards more accountable to shareholders, but it ran into strong opposition from business groups, including the U.S. Chamber of Commerce, which filed the lawsuit, alleging the agency had not adequately considered the cost of implementing these requirements.

Managers of private and public pension funds (which often own large blocks of a corporation's stock), as well as shareholder rights groups, applauded the new regulations when they were issued in 2010, saying that corporate managers and directors had long ignored shareholders, seeing them as more of a nuisance than anything else. By making it easier for shareholders to

replace directors, rule supporters said, the SEC restored the true owners of corporations to their proper place as the ultimate decision makers.

But in striking down the regulations, the appeals court stated that the agency had "neglected its statutory responsibility" to consider both the costs and the benefits of the rule. Specifically, the court agreed with business groups, which argued that increasing shareholder rights would lead to near-constant battles over board directors and leave corporations in a state of chaos.

In spite of this defeat, the agency pressed ahead with its agenda. In October 2011, for instance, it issued new guidelines requiring publicly traded companies to report major instances of cyber-attack or cyber-theft. The guidelines were aimed at helping investors be better informed about a company's ability to protect its data network. Some investors might not want to consider funding companies that have difficulty protecting their networks, SEC officials said.

Also in October 2011 the commission adopted new rules requiring hedge funds, private equity firms, and other high-end financial investment services to disclose details of their operations to the SEC. Specifically, the new regulations require these firms to disclose basic business strategy, exposure to debt, and connections to other firms. The rules were intended to help the SEC and other regulators assess the risk that these firms would fail. The idea was to help companies that are deemed to be at risk to avoid the kind of complete collapse that occurred in 2008, when firms such as AIG and Lehman Brothers imploded and nearly took the entire financial system down with them.

But the SEC's respite from public attack was short-lived. In December 2011, just two months after one court struck down the agency's attempt to increase investor clout, another court rejected a settlement the commission had made with Citibank, ruling that it had not adequately considered investors. This latter ruling, coming from a federal district court judge, Jed Rakoff, invalidated an agreement by the bank to pay $285 million to investors after Citibank allegedly misled them when they sold them mortgage-backed securities that ultimately proved to be nearly worthless.

Rakoff stuck down the deal as being too lenient to Citibank, given that the size of investor losses was roughly $1 billion. Moreover, just weeks after the ruling, Rakoff criticized the SEC again, this time accusing the agency of making misleading statements when it appealed the case to a federal appeals court. In response to Rakoff's stinging rebukes, the agency reviewed its settlement procedures and set new, tougher guidelines aimed at ensuring that future settlements would not be criticized for being too small.

In February 2013, lawyers for the agency and Citibank appeared before a federal appeals court in Washington, DC, to defend the settlement, while a lawyer for Judge Rakoff argued against the deal. And while the court has yet to hand down a decision, there is some speculation that the parties will craft a new settlement more to Judge Rakoff's liking and ask that the case be dismissed.

During the time it was defending the Citibank settlement, the agency also found itself involved in another important lawsuit, this one involving the Securities Investors Protection Corporation (SIPC), a private firm established by the financial services industry that guarantees investments when brokerage houses and other financial services providers fail. The agency sued SIPC after it refused to compensate victims of R. Allen Stanford's $7.2 billion Ponzi scheme. As already noted, Stanford promised high returns to investors while at the same time absconding with their money. But in July 2012, a federal district ruled that losses due to Stanford's criminal behavior were not covered by the SIPC, which was created to protect investors who lost money with firms that collapsed due to legitimate business failure and bankruptcy rather than criminal fraud.

Meanwhile, in November 2012 the agency settled another high-profile case involving allegations of fraud against big banks, also in connection with the sale of mortgage-backed securities. This time, the case involved not Citibank, but two other giants: JPMorgan and Credit Suisse. The SEC accused the banks of fraudulently misleading investors about the health of the mortgages packaged into the securities they sold to investors. Specifically, the agency said, many of these mortgages were delinquent or not being paid at all while they were being marketed to clients. While neither bank admitted to any wrongdoing, they agreed to pay investors $417 million—with $297 million coming from JPMorgan and $120 million paid by Credit Suisse. In exchange, the SEC agreed to drop the case.

While some people applauded the deal, it had critics on both sides. Consumer advocates argued that the banks were being let off with a slap on the wrist, since they were clearly culpable and $417 million is not a lot of money to institutions such as JPMorgan and Credit Suisse. But others argued that JPMorgan was being unfairly treated because the securities were sold by Bear Stearns, which was taken over by JPMorgan in 2008. Normally, when one company buys another, it assumes its liabilities. But JPMorgan absorbed Bear Stearns after the federal government asked it to do so, leading some to argue that the bank should not be held responsible for what happened at Bear before it was purchased. This falls into the "no good deed goes unpunished" category, said Congressman Frank, after the settlement was announced.

In late November 2012, just weeks after President Obama had been reelected, Mary L. Schapiro announced that she would be leaving as chair of the agency, effective December 14. Both Republicans and Democrats generally viewed Schapiro's five-year tenure at the SEC as positive, crediting her with reviving what many saw as an agency in crisis. Under Schapiro, the agency's tarnished enforcement unit was overhauled, and she was seen as a much-needed calm presence during the darkest days of the financial crisis. However, she was not without her critics. Consumer advocates argued that she was not aggressive enough in fighting Wall Street fraud and protecting small investors. In addition, she was repeatedly criticized over the SEC's failure to spot Bernard Madoff's massive Ponzi scheme, even though she was not chair during virtually the entire time Madoff was active.

Obama appointed Commissioner Elisse B. Walter (D) to replace Schapiro as interim chair, while he searched for a permanent replacement. In an unusual move, Walter was actually sworn in as chair—rather than remaining acting chair. Her promotion did not require Senate approval since she had already won confirmation when originally appointed to the commission.

But Walter had little time to enjoy her new job. In January 2013 President Obama nominated Mary Jo White (D) to permanently replace Schapiro as chair of the SEC. Unlike so many of the president's other nominees, White was considered a noncontroversial pick and ran into virtually no Republican opposition. Prior to being tapped to run the SEC, she had won bipartisan plaudits as the U.S. attorney for the Southern District of New York, where she became famous for overseeing the successful prosecutions of mobster John Gotti as well as the terrorists responsible for the first attempt to bring down New York's Twin Towers in 1993. On April 8, 2013, the Senate approved White by voice vote. Two days later, she was sworn in as the agency's 30th chair.

In January 2013, just days before the president nominated White to fill the vacancy created by Schapiro, another high-level and well-respected member of the commission announced he was leaving. Robert Khuzami, who had headed up the important enforcement bureau for four years, said he wanted to move to the more lucrative private sector to "provide more" for his family.

Khuzami's departure was a blow to the agency. A former federal prosecutor, he had widely been credited with restoring the enforcement division's credibility in the wake of the Madoff scandal. Even Judge Rakoff, who criticized Khuzami for the Citibank settlement, praised him for restoring "a sense of pride and purpose to the enforcement division."

At the end of January, the agency named Khuzami's top deputy, George Canellos, acting head of enforcement. Prior to coming to the SEC with Khuzami in 2009, Canellos had spent two decades working as a securities lawyer in New York. In April, White formally appointed Canellos to head the office. In addition, she appointed a former federal prosecutor, Andrew Ceresney, to be his co-director. White's appointment of two people to lead the enforcement office was seen as a sign that she expected the division to be more active in the coming years.

Three months after appointing Canellos and Ceresney, White announced that in future criminal investigations, the SEC would more frequently seek public admissions of wrongdoing. In the past, the agency had been criticized for allowing banks and brokerages involved in alleged criminal activity to pay fines (sometimes for enormous sums) without having to admit any guilt or culpability. White said that in the future, the agency would decide whether to seek admissions of wrongdoing based on "how much harm has been done to investors [and] how egregious is the fraud."

Also in April 2013 the commission unanimously voted to approve new rules aimed at protecting investors from identity theft. The rules, which were mandated under the Dodd-Frank law, require stockbrokers, financial advisers, mutual fund companies, and other financial services providers to have in place by early 2014 a program to detect and protect clients against identity theft. In particular, the rules require financial services providers to train employees to identify "red flags" for identity theft. The companies must also have in place plans to deal with instances of identity theft.

Meanwhile, in early May the commission made history when, for the first time, it sued a city, Harrisburg, Pennsylvania, for allegedly misrepresenting its financial situation to investors who were purchasing its municipal bonds. Like many cities and towns in the years following the 2008 financial crash, Harrisburg had taken on more and more debt to meet its financial obligations. The SEC charged that from 2008 to 2011, city officials intentionally misled investors by not informing them of the true extent of the city's financial difficulties. For instance, in 2008 Harrisburg officials never informed potential bond investors that Moody's (a ratings agency) had downgraded the city's debt, information that would have made it harder to attract bond buyers and would have required the city to borrow money at higher interest rates.

This is first time the SEC had charged a city with violating federal antifraud rules, but it would not be the last. Indeed, just a few months later, in July, the commission sued Miami Florida, also for allegedly defrauding investors who had purchased the city's bonds. The SEC charged that in 2009 city officials, particularly its then-budget director, Michael Boudreaux, made patently false statements so that the city would pay lower interest rates on its municipal bonds.

In September 2013 the commission formally proposed a rule requiring publicly traded companies to calculate and disclose the ratio of what it pays its top executives as compared to its median pay for all workers. The announcement was greeted by relief in some quarters, particularly among those in the consumer and shareholder rights communities. They noted that the regulation was mandated under the Dodd-Frank law and had accused the agency of dragging its feet on what they claimed should be a simple and straightforward rule.

But what happened next was neither simple nor straightforward. The announcement prompted a chorus of protest from many large firms and others in the business community. These businesses and their allies argued that it would be difficult and time-consuming to calculate these ratios. In addition, they argued, the rule would serve no real purpose other than to provide fodder for enemies of free markets and large corporations. Supporters of the proposal countered that it was important to disclose to shareholders and the public how much more top executives earn than anyone else. They accused the business community of being opposed to disclosure for the simple reason that they were paying their top managers obscene amounts of money at the expense of workers and shareholders.

In the midst of this acrimonious debate, the SEC tried to ease the burden of implementation by creating a more flexible definition of "average median pay." Earlier versions of the draft regulation had required companies to consider all workers—including part-timers and even those working for the firm in other countries. The agency proposed allowing companies to create their own methodologies, as long as all full-time permanent American workers were included in the calculations.

But by the summer of 2015, nearly two years later, the rule still had not been finalized, prompting some consumer groups and their allies in Congress to once again criticize the agency for crumbling in the face of opposition. However, others (including some outside the business community) worried that implementing the rule would briefly shame some executives without appreciably closing the pay gap. Some even predicted that it would end up just demoralizing workers.

Meanwhile, just a week after proposing the new rule on executive pay, the commission made headlines again when it announced a $1 billion settlement with JPMorgan Chase over a trading scandal that had occurred in London in 2012. The scandal involved derivatives traders at the bank's London office making huge trades and concealing losses as they were building up. Known as the "London Whale affair," the trades resulted in a total of $6 billion in losses for JPMorgan. While a bank that size can absorb such a loss, all agreed that, given the amounts being wagered, the London Whale (named for the huge amounts of money involved) could have resulted in much larger losses and easily bankrupted the bank, possibly damaging the still-fragile global financial system.

While no one accused JPMorgan Chairman, Jamie Dimon, of authorizing the trades, he and his management team were taken to task for not properly supervising the London traders. The agency also accused Dimon and his team, once they knew what was going on, of initially concealing the extent of the losses from the bank's board of directors and from investors. Indeed, while applauding the $1 billion fine (which was announced in the middle of September 2013) many Wall Street watchers criticized the SEC for not bringing legal action against Dimon and others in JPMorgan's leadership.

A month after the JPMorgan fine, the agency suffered a blow when a federal district court in Dallas found well-known billionaire investor Mark Cuban not guilty of insider trading. After the Rajaratnam case, the Cuban prosecution was the SEC's most high-profile insider trading case. But unlike the successful Rajaratnam prosecution, the agency's lawyers failed to convince a jury that Cuban had known he was using inside information when he suddenly sold his stake in a Canadian Internet firm in 2009.

At the beginning of 2014 co-director of enforcement George Canellos announced that he would be leaving the agency to return to private legal practice. The January announcement left his partner, Andrew Ceresney, in charge of the important enforcement division. It also fed the impression among some Wall Street watchers that top enforcement official at the SEC and other financial regulators "go easy" on banks and brokerages because they hope one day to work for them. In Canellos's case, leaving the SEC meant returning to his old law firm, Milbank Tweed, where could find himself defending in court the very firms he had been charged with policing.

In June 2014 the agency adopted a new rule to limit derivative trading by foreign affiliates of American banks. With the huge losses by AIG's London unit in 2008 and the more recent "London Whale" losses by JPMorgan still fresh in their minds, the commissioners imposed new requirements on overseas trading. The rule requires banks to register their foreign trading operations with the SEC and to abide by the same tough reporting standards that currently apply to their American operations.

But the new rule contains a loophole that might allow many foreign operations to avoid the new scrutiny: It applies only to foreign affiliates that have been "legally guaranteed" by their American parents. This means that the home bank or firm has legally agreed to cover all its affiliates' losses. But if an American firm does not offer such a guarantee, it is not required to register its foreign operations. Critics of the loophole, including two commissioners who voted in favor of the new rule, argued that many financial institutions could simply remove guarantees from their foreign operations, making the new oversight meaningless.

In July 2014 an audit of the agency's progress in finalizing rules mandated under the Dodd-Frank law revealed that the SEC was moving more slowly than other financial regulators. While governmentwide, 52 percent of all Dodd-Frank rules had been finalized, only 44 percent of the SEC's portion had been completed. One reason given for the commission's slowness was that it was tasked with drafting some of the most technically complicated and difficult regulations involving complex financial instruments, such as the new foreign office derivative-trading rule.

In October 2014 the commission (along with the Federal Reserve and the Comptroller of the Currency) loosened restrictions on the kinds of mortgages that banks could sell to investors. Under 2011 regulations mandated by the Dodd-Frank law, a bank could sell a mortgage to an outside investor only if the borrower had put at least a 20 percent down payment on his or her house. The idea was that anyone who could put a large 20 percent down would likely be able to pay the mortgage. The rule was meant to avoid a repeat of the chief causes of the financial crisis, when banks sold millions of risky or underperforming mortgages to investors, causing a crash in the banking system and housing market.

Under the new rule approved by the three agencies, banks could sell mortgages with down payments lower than 20 percent if the borrower had a relatively low debt to income ratio. In other words, banks could sell mortgages issued to borrowers who clearly had sufficient income to make monthly payments on the loans.

The opening days of 2015 began with the commission announcing that it had set a record in its whistleblower program in 2014 by paying $30 million to one tipster in exchange for information in a securities fraud investigation. This was more than twice the previous record of $14 million, awarded to a whistleblower in 2014.

The program, which pays whistleblowers between 10 percent and 30 percent of what the agency recovers in fines, is meant to encourage people to come forward and reveal potential wrongdoing at financial institutions and within the government itself. Although the agency did not reveal the name of the person awarded the money or the business that had been the subject of the investigation, it publicized the award in an effort to encourage other employees to report wrongdoing when they see it.

Current Issues

A few months later, the commission's interest in whistleblowers was again in the news. In April 2015 the SEC ruled that defense contractor Kellogg Brown & Root (KBR) had improperly used an employee confidentiality agreement to "muzzle" workers who sought to report fraud and abuse in government contracts. "By requiring its employees and former employees to sign confidentiality agreements imposing pre-notification requirements before contacting the SEC, KBR potentially discouraged employees from reporting securities violations to us," said SEC Enforcement Chief Ceresney. "SEC rules prohibit employers from taking measures through confidentiality, employment, severance, or other type of agreements that may silence potential whistleblowers before they can reach out to the SEC," he added.

While KBR denied any wrongdoing, it did agree to pay a $130,000 fine. Even though some criticized the fine's relatively small amount, many involved in securities law said the ruling is unique and unprecedented and could have significant ramifications going forward. "The use of employment agreements to silence potential whistleblowers has been widespread and growing," said Jordan Thomas, an attorney who represents whistleblowers. "This landmark enforcement action is the first step in attacking this significant law enforcement investor-protection problem. This is just the beginning. I predict that the SEC will bring more cases like this in the coming years."

In early June the commission was back in the media spotlight after Sen. Elizabeth Warren, D-Mass., sent a well-publicized letter to Chair White, accusing her of "highly disappointing" leadership. Warren, who is one of the leaders of the populous wing of the Democratic Party and a constant critic of Wall Street, accused White of failing in a number of crucial areas and not living up to the promises she made when she took the reins at the commission.

To begin with, Warren wrote, the chairwoman continued to drag her heels on finalizing the proposed rule requiring disclosure of top executive pay at publicly traded firms. The Massachusetts senator also took the chairwoman to task for not getting companies to publicly admit to wrongdoing when they settle out of court with the SEC for fraud and other allegations.

The letter, which made headlines around the country, prompted a furious reaction on Wall Street and within the Obama administration. Warren had criticized the agency on other occasions but had never personally attacked White. The White House vigorously defended the chairwoman, saying that the president continued to have full confidence in her. Others directly criticized Warren, arguing that she had gone too far in personally attacking White. For her part, White brushed off the criticism, calling the letter a "mischaracterization" of her record and saying it would not detract from her work.

A few weeks later, the commission found itself at the center of a debate on Capitol Hill over whether publicly traded companies should be required to disclose their political spending. For years, some prominent people in the securities industry, including former SEC chairs Arthur Levitt and William Donaldson, have urged the commission to develop and implement a rule requiring firms to disclose spending on lobbying, campaign contributions and other political activities. They have argued that shareholders have a right to know the details of political spending.

But in the middle of June, the House Appropriations Committee included language in its spending bill for the agency that would prevent the SEC from implementing a political spending discloser rule. Even if the language is stripped out before the appropriations bill becomes law, there is little chance that such a disclosure rule will be drafted, let alone implemented. Recently, Chair White made it known that her priority for the foreseeable future is to complete drafting and implementing the backlog of regulations mandated under the Dodd-Frank law, including pending rules on executive pay and the regulation of crowdfunding, a list that does not include the proposed political disclosure rule.

On the same day as the House Appropriations Committee vote, the agency announced that it had fined most of the nation's largest banks, including Morgan Stanley, Bank of America, and Citibank, for making false statements when selling municipal bonds. In particular, the banks did not adequately disclose the risk of default to purchasers of these bonds, which provide funds to towns and cities around the country.

But once again, the agency was criticized for not extracting a large enough penalty. Indeed, each bank paid only $500,000 to the SEC. At the same time, the agency pointed out that going forward the settlement requires that all of the banks use outside consultants to ensure that all risks are disclosed in future bond sales.

◼ AGENCY ORGANIZATION

Biographies

MARY JO WHITE, CHAIR

Appointment: Nominated chair by President Barack Obama on Feb. 7, 2013; confirmed by the U.S. Senate on April 8, 2013; sworn in on April 10, 2013, to a term expiring June 5, 2019.

Born: Dec. 27, 1947; Kansas City, Mo.

Education: William and Mary, B.A., 1970; New School for Social Research, M.A. in psychology, 1971; Columbia Law School, J.D., 1974.

Profession: Lawyer.

Political Affiliation: Democrat.

Previous Career: Prior to her appointment, White was U.S. attorney for the Southern District of New York (1993–2002); first assistant U.S. attorney and acting U.S. attorney for the Eastern District of New York (1990–1993);

and assistant U.S. attorney for the Southern District of New York (1978–1981), becoming chief appellate attorney for the Criminal Division. After leaving her U.S. Attorney post, White was chair of the litigation department at Debevoise and Plimpton, New York, as partner (1983–1990) and as an associate (1976–1978). She has also served as a director of the Nasdaq Exchange and on its executive, audit, and policy committees. She is a member of the Council on Foreign Relations and has won numerous awards.

LUIS A. AGUILAR, COMMISSIONER

Appointment: Appointed by President George W. Bush on March 31, 2008; confirmed by the Senate on June 27, 2008; sworn in July 31, 2008, to a term expiring June 5, 2010. Appointed by President Barack Obama in May 2011 to another five-year term; confirmed by Senate on Oct. 21, 2011; second term expires June 5, 2015.

Born: Nov. 1953.

Education: Georgia Southern University, B.S., 1976; University of Georgia, J.D., 1979; Emory University, M.A. (Laws in Taxation), 1985.

Profession: Lawyer.

Political Affiliation: Democrat.

Previous Career: Prior to his appointment, Aguilar was a partner with the international law firm of McKenna Long & Aldridge, LLP, Atlanta (2005–2008), where he specialized in securities law. From 2003 to 2005 he was a partner at Alston & Bird, LLP, Atlanta; and from 1993 to 2002, he was with Kilpatrick & Cody LLP, also in Atlanta. He served as the managing director of Latin America, general counsel, executive vice president, and corporate secretary at INVESCO. He also served as an attorney at the Securities and Exchange Commission and is a sponsor of the SEC's Hispanic Employment Committee and the African American Council.

DANIEL M. GALLAGHER, COMMISSIONER

Appointment: Appointed by President Barack Obama; confirmed by U.S. Senate on Oct. 21, 2011; took office Nov. 7, 2011, for a term expiring June 5, 2016.

Born: May 31, 1972.

Education: Georgetown University, B.A., 1994; Catholic University of America, J.D., 1998.

Political Affiliation: Republican.

Profession: Lawyer.

Previous Career: Prior to his appointment, Gallagher was a partner at WilmerHale, Washington, DC. Previously he served at the SEC as co–acting director of the Trading and Markets Division (April 2009–Jan. 2010), deputy director of the Trading and Markets Division (2009–2009), counsel to SEC Chair Christopher Cox, and counsel to Commissioner Paul S. Atkins (Jan. 2006). Prior to his initial service at the SEC as a staff member, Gallagher was general counsel and senior vice president of FistServ Securities, Inc., where he was responsible for legal and regulatory matters.

KARA M. STEIN, COMMISSIONER

Appointment: Appointed by President Barack Obama; sworn in Aug. 9, 2013, to a term expiring June 5, 2017.

Securities and Exchange Commission

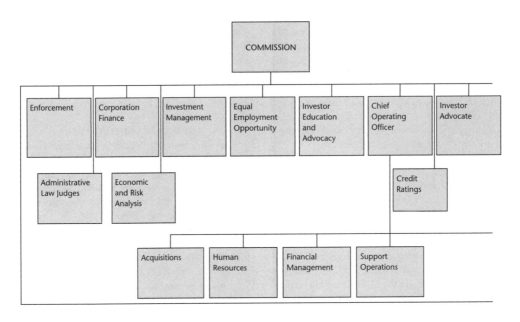

Education: Yale College, B.A.; Yale Law School, J.D.

Profession: Lawyer.

Political Affiliation: Democrat.

Previous Career: Prior to her appointment to the commission, Ms. Stein served as the legal counsel and senior policy adviser for securities and banking matters to Sen. Jack Reed. From 2009 to 2013, she was staff director of the Securities, Insurance, and Investment Subcommittee of the Senate Committee on Banking, Housing, and Urban Affairs. Prior to that, she was the legal counsel and senior policy Adviser to Sen. Reed from 2007 to 2009 and served as both the Majority and Minority staff director on the Banking Committee's Subcommittee on Housing and Transportation from 2001 to 2006. She served as legal counsel to Sen. Reed from 1999 to 2000, following two years as a legislative assistant to Sen. Chris Dodd. Before working on Capitol Hill, Ms. Stein was an associate at the law firm of Wilmer, Cutler & Pickering, a Skadden Public Interest Fellow, an advocacy fellow with the Georgetown University Law Center, and an assistant professor with the University of Dayton, School of Law.

MICHAEL S. PIWOWAR, COMMISSIONER

Appointment: Appointed by President Barack Obama on May 23, 2013; confirmed by the Senate on August 1, 2014; and sworn in August 9, 2013, to a term expiring June 5, 2018.

Education: Pennsylvania State University, B.A. (foreign service and international politics); Georgetown University, M.B.A.; Pennsylvania State University, Ph.D. (finance).

Profession: Professor, economist.

Political Affiliation: Republican.

Previous Career: Prior to his appointment to the commission, Dr. Piwowar was the Republican chief economist for the U.S. Senate Committee on Banking, Housing, and Urban Affairs under senators Mike Crapo (R-ID) and Richard Shelby (R-AL). Dr. Piwowar also worked on a number of important SEC-related oversight issues under the jurisdiction of the committee, such as securities, over-the-counter derivatives, investor protection, market structure, and capital formation. During the financial crisis and its immediate aftermath, Dr. Piwowar served in a one-year fixed-term position at the White House as a senior economist at the President's Council of Economic Advisers (CEA) in both the George W. Bush and Barack Obama administrations. While at the CEA, Dr. Piwowar also served as a staff economist for the Financial Regulatory Reform Working Group of the President's Economic Recovery Advisory Board. Before joining the White House, Dr. Piwowar worked as a principal at the Securities Litigation and Consulting Group (SLCG). Dr. Piwowar's first tenure at the SEC was in the Office of Economic Analysis as a visiting academic scholar on leave from Iowa State University and as a senior financial economist. Prior to that, he was an assistant professor of finance at Iowa State University where he focused his research on

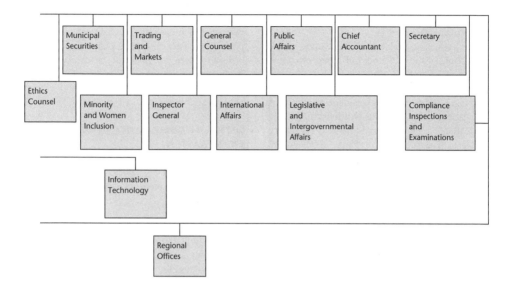

market microstructure and taught undergraduate and graduate courses in corporate finance and investments. He published a number of articles in leading academic publications and received several teaching and research awards.

Headquarters and Divisions

COMMISSION
Promulgates rules and regulations related to the statutes it administers and holds hearings on proposed changes in regulations. Considers results of staff investigations to determine if there is sufficient evidence of violation of the law to warrant prosecution or administrative sanctions. Can apply for civil injunctions ordering a halt to alleged violations; can recommend criminal prosecution; or can issue orders suspending or expelling members from exchanges and over-the-counter associations. Empowered to deny, suspend, or revoke the registration of broker-dealers and censure individuals for misconduct. Can bar individuals (temporarily or permanently) from employment with firms registered with the SEC. Can order stock exchanges and dealers' associations to comply with its rules and guidelines under penalty of the judicial and administrative sanctions mentioned. Handles SEC congressional liaison work.
Chair
 Mary Jo White . . . . (202) 551–2100
Commissioners
 Luis A. Aguilar. . . . . (202) 551–2500

 Daniel M. Gallagher . . . . (202) 551–2600
 Michael S. Piwowar. . . . . (202) 551–2700
 Kara M. Stein . . . . (202) 551–2800

OFFICE OF ADMINISTRATIVE LAW JUDGES
Conducts hearings on administrative proceedings instituted by the SEC.
Chief Judge
 Brenda P. Murray. . . . . (202) 551–6030

CHIEF OPERATING OFFICER
Oversees the operations of the SEC's Office of Information Technology; the Office of Financial Management, including financial reporting internal controls; the Office of Acquisitions; the Office of Human Resources; and the Office of Support Operations, including FOIA and Records Management Services.
Chief Operating Officer
 Jeff Heslop . . . . (202) 551–2200

Office of Acquisitions
Responsible for administrative services and acquisitions.
Director
 Vance Cathell . . . . 202) 551–8385

Office of Financial Management
Responsible for the financial management and programming functions of the commission. The comptrol-

ler serves as SEC liaison with the Office of Management and Budget, congressional appropriations committees, the Treasury Department, and the General Accounting Office and is jointly administered by the Executive Director and the Chief Operating Officer.

Chief Financial Officer
Kenneth Johnson.................. (202) 551–7840

Office of Human Resources

Provides leadership for the strategic management of the SEC's human capital by administering programs, establishing policies, and ensuring compliance with federal regulation. Develops, implements, and evaluates the commission's programs and policies for recruitment, staffing, retention, and separations; position management and classification; compensation and benefits counseling and processing; leadership and employee development; performance management and awards; employee relations; disability program, work/life programs, telework, employee records processing and maintenance, and employee financial disclosure.

Represents the commission as the liaison to the Office of Personnel Management, professional human resources organizations, other federal government agencies, educational institutions, and the private sector in matters relating to human capital management activities.

Director
Lacey Dingman.................. (202) 551–7500

Office of Information Technology

Responsible for the analysis, design programming, operation, and maintenance of all automated data processing (ADP) systems; developing and implementing long-range ADP plans and programs; coordinating all ADP and systems analysis activities being considered or carried out by other divisions and offices, and furnishing such organizations with appropriate assistance and support; providing technical advice to the staff in connection with development of commission rules and regulations having ADP implications; facilitating the commission's surveillance of ADP in the security industry; evaluating and recommending new information processing concepts and capabilities for application within the commission; and developing of microcomputer and office automation capabilities and support within the commission.

Supports all aspects of information technology, including systems that receive all electronically filed documents; operates and maintains the SEC's electronic data processing facilities; and operates systems that keep SEC official records and the Electronic Data Gathering, Analysis, and Retrieval (EDGAR) system. See EDGAR under Reference Resources.

Director and Chief Information Officer
Pamela C. Dyson .... (202) 551–8800

Office of Support Operations

Oversees Freedom of Information Act (FOIA) requests, Records Management Services, the Records Management Certification unit, Security Services, Building Operations, facilities, Publishing and Printing of SEC materials, and Mail.

Director
Barry Walters..................... (202) 551–8400
See Information Sources for Freedom of Information Act (FOIA) and Records Management Services.

OFFICE OF THE CHIEF ACCOUNTANT

Responsible for establishing and enforcing accounting and auditing policy to enhance the transparency and relevancy of financial reporting, and for improving the professional performance of public company auditors in order to ensure that financial statements used for investment decisions are presented fairly and have credibility.

Chief Accountant
James Schnurr .... (202) 551–5300

OFFICE OF COMPLIANCE INSPECTIONS AND EXAMINATIONS

Conducts all compliance inspection programs of brokers, dealers, self-regulatory organizations, investment companies, investment advisers, clearing agencies, and transfer agents.

Director
Maurice Wyatt (acting) .... (202) 551–6200
Associate Director (Office of Broker-Dealers)
Kevin Goodman .... (202) 551–6207
Associate Director (Market/SRO Oversight)
John Polise .... (202) 551–6200
Chief Counsel
Paula Drake .... (202) 551–6460
Investment Adviser/Investment Company
Jane Jarcho .... (202) 551–6300

OFFICE OF CREDIT RATINGS

Assists the commission in executing its responsibility for protecting investors, promoting capital formation, and maintaining fair, orderly, and efficient markets through the oversight of credit rating agencies registered with the commission as "nationally recognized statistical rating organizations" or "NRSROs." Monitors the activities and conducts examinations of registered NRSROs to assess and promote compliance with statutory and commission requirements.

Director
Thomas Butler* .... (212) 336–9080
*In New York, N.Y.

OFFICE OF EQUAL EMPLOYMENT OPPORTUNITY

Develops, implements, and monitors internal affirmative action plans. Initiates and conducts surveys to determine the effectiveness of existing programs and counsels employees as well as management officials on career development, and the complaint and appeals procedure.

Director
Alta G. Rodriguez................. (202) 551–6040

OFFICE OF THE ETHICS COUNSEL

Responsible for advising and counseling all commission employees and members on such issues as personal and financial conflicts of interest, securities holdings and transactions of commission employees and their immediate families, gifts, seeking and negotiating other employment, outside activities, financial disclosure, and post-employment restrictions. Drafts, comments on, and implements regulations concerning ethical conduct issues. Assists presidential appointees with various aspects of financial disclosure to the Senate and the U.S. Office of Government Ethics in connection with the confirmation process.

Director

Shira Pavis Minton . . . . (202) 551–5170

OFFICE OF THE GENERAL COUNSEL

Represents the commission in legal proceedings and reviews cases with the Division of Enforcement to determine which ones should be referred to the Justice Department for criminal prosecution. Interprets questions of law for the commission, assists in the preparation of SEC comments to Congress on pending legislation, and helps draft proposed legislation. Also reviews all SEC releases and speeches dealing with SEC statutes.

General Counsel

Anne K. Small . . . . (202) 551–5100

Associate General Counsel (Adjudication)

Vacant . . . . (202) 551–5169

Associate General Counsel (Appellate Litigation and Bankruptcy)

Jacob Stillman . . . . (202) 551–5130

Associate General Counsel (Regulatory Policy)

Lori Price . . . . (202) 551–5100

Associate General Counsel (Ethics)

Shira Minton . . . . (202) 551–5170

Associate General Counsel (Legal Policy)

Richard Levin . . . . (202) 551–5100

Associate General Counsel (Litigation and Administrative Practice)

Richard Humes . . . . (202) 551–5140

OFFICE OF THE INSPECTOR GENERAL

Conducts independent internal audits and investigations of the commission's operations.

Inspector General

Carl W. Hoecker . . . . (202) 551–6061

Hotline . . . . (877) 442–0854

Deputy Inspector General for Audits

Rebecca Sharek . . . . (202) 551–6035

Counsel to the Inspector General

Roderick Fillinger . . . . (202) 551–6039

OFFICE OF INTERNATIONAL AFFAIRS

Negotiates protocols between the SEC and foreign securities regulators and coordinates enforcement programs according to those agreements. Also handles inquiries from SEC offices and the general public regarding international securities regulation.

Director

Paul A. Leder . . . . (202) 551–6690

OFFICE OF INVESTOR ADVOCATE

Analyzes the potential impact on investors of regulations and rules that are proposed by the commission and any self-regulatory organization (SRO); identifies areas in which investors would benefit from changes in regulations or SRO rules; assists retail investors in resolving significant problems they have with the commission or SROs; identifies problems that investors have with financial service providers and investment products; proposes to the commission changes in regulations or orders of the commission that may be appropriate to mitigate problems identified and to promote the interests of investors; and proposes to Congress any legislative, administrative, or personnel changes that may be appropriate to mitigate problems identified and to promote the interests of investors.

Investor Advocate

Rick Fleming . . . . (202) 551–3302

Ombudsman

Tracey L. McNeil . . . . (202) 551–3330
Email: Ombudsman@sec.gov

OFFICE OF INVESTOR EDUCATION AND ADVOCACY

Serves and assists individual investors. Investor assistance specialists are available to answer questions and analyze complaints. However, the office cannot coerce a brokerage firm to resolve complaints. Actions taken by the office are not a substitute for private individuals taking action on their own. Individuals who have unresolved complaints are urged to seek counsel under federal and state laws.

The Office of Investor Education and Advocacy has three separate electronic mailboxes:

- oiea@sec.gov to file an investor complaint with SEC;
- help@sec.gov to submit general questions regarding federal securities laws or investments;
- publicinfo@sec.gov to obtain copies of SEC records and documents, historic commission filings, special reports and studies, speeches, and testimony.

Director

Lori Schock . . . . (202) 551–6500

General information . . . . (202) 551–6551

Toll-free . . . . (800) 732–0330

OFFICE OF LEGISLATIVE AND INTERGOVERNMENTAL AFFAIRS

Responsible for legislative and intergovernmental liaison. Responds to requests for information and assistance from Congress, produces the annual report to Congress, and supervises the production and distribution of SEC publications.

Director

Timothy Henseler . . . . (202) 551–2010

Deputy Director

Julie Z. Davis . . . . (202) 551–2010

OFFICE OF MINORITY AND WOMEN INCLUSION

Responsible for all matters related to diversity in management, employment, and business activities at the SEC. Committed to ensuring that diversity and inclusion are leveraged throughout the agency to advance the SEC's mission to protect investors; maintain fair, orderly, and efficient markets; and facilitate capital formation.

Director

Pamela A. Gibbs .... (202) 551–6046

OFFICE OF MUNICIPAL SECURITIES

Coordinates the SEC's municipal securities activities, advises the commission and SEC offices and divisions on policy matters relating to the municipal securities and the municipal bond market and provides technical assistance in the development and implementation of major SEC initiatives in the municipal securities area. Works closely with the municipal securities industry to educate state and local officials and conduit borrowers about risk management issues and foster a thorough understanding of the commission's policies. Reviews and processes rule filings of the Municipal Securities Rulemaking Board and acts as the commission's liaison with a variety of industry groups on municipal securities issues.

Director

Jessica Kane .... (202) 551–5680

OFFICE OF PUBLIC AFFAIRS

The public information office of the commission. Responds to requests for information and assistance from the news media and the public. Publishes the daily *SEC News Digest* and provides speakers for various forums.

Director

John Nester...................... (202) 551–4120

Fax........................... (202) 777–1026

Deputy Director

Florence Harmon .... (202) 551–5604

Public Affairs Specialist

Kevin Callahan .... (202) 551–4127

OFFICE OF THE SECRETARY

Prepares and maintains the record of all official commission actions. The commissioners have delegated to the secretary responsibility for the commission's rules of practice. Responsible for SEC Public Reference Room (*see Reference Resources*).

Secretary

Brent J. Fields .... (202) 551–5400

OFFICE OF THE WHISTLEBLOWER

Administers the SEC's whistleblower program.

Chief

Sean McKessy .... (202) 551–4790

DIVISION OF CORPORATION FINANCE

Assists the commission in executing its responsibility to oversee corporate disclosure of important information to the investigating public. Corporations are required to comply with regulations pertaining to disclosure that must be made when stock is initially sold and then on a continuing and periodic basis. The division's staff routinely reviews the disclosure documents filed by companies. The staff also provides companies with assistance interpreting the commission's rules and recommends to the commission new rules for adoption.

Director

Keith F. Higgins.................. (202) 551–3110

Office of the Director

Chief of Staff

Lona Nallengara .... (202) 551–3120

Deputy Director (Disclosure Operations)

Shelley Parratt .... (202) 551–3130

Associate Directors (Disclosure Operations)

James Daly .... (202) 551–3140

Karen Garnett .... (202) 551–3785

Cicely LaMothe .... (202) 551–3411

Kyle Moffatt .... (202) 551–3030

Barry Summer .... (202) 551–3160

Associate Director (Regulatory Policy)

Vacant .... (202) 551–3190

Chief Accountant

Mark Kronforst .... (202) 551–3400

Chief Counsel

David Fredrickson................ (202) 551–3500

Legal, Regulatory, and Capital Markets Offices

Answers questions about the provisions of the federal securities laws that the division administers. Each office handles a specific range of issues and has expertise in the substantive areas covered by their offices.

Capital Markets Trends

Amy Starr....................... (202) 551–3860

Disclosure Support

Patti Dennis .... (202) 551–3565

Enforcement Liaison

Mary Kosterlitz .... (202) 551–3425

Global Security Risk

Cecilia Blye...................... (202) 551–3470

International Corporate Finance

Paul Dudek...................... (202) 551–3450

Mergers and Acquisitions

Michele Anderson................ (202) 551–3440

Rulemaking

Felicia Kung .... (202) 551–3430

Small Business Policy

Sebastian Gomez................. (202) 551–3460

Structured Finance

Katherine Hsu .... (202) 551–3850

Disclosure Operations Offices

Reviews company security filings to monitor and enhance compliance with disclosure and accounting requirements.

Assistant Director (Beverages, Apparel, and Mining)

John Reynolds .... (202) 551–3790

Assistant Director (Consumer Products)

Mara Ransom.................... (202) 551–3720

Assistant Director (Electronics and Machinery)

Amanda Ravitz .... (202) 551–3528

Assistant Director (Financial Services I)

Dieter King...................... (202) 551–3770

Assistant Director (Financial Services II)

Suzanne Hayes................... (202) 551–3830

Assistant Director (Health Care and Insurance)

Jeffrey Riedler .... (202) 551–3710

Assistant Director (Information Technologies and Services)

Barbara Jacobs................... (202) 551–3730

Assistant Director (Manufacturing and Construction)
Pamela Long. (202) 551–3760
Assistant Director (Natural Resources)
H. Roger Schwall. . . . . (202) 551–3740
Assistant Director (Real Estate and Commodities)
Sonia Barros. (202) 551–3780
Assistant Director (Telecommunications)
Larry Spirgel. (202) 551–3810
Assistant Director (Transportation and Leisure)
Ann Nguyen Parker . . . . (202) 551–3750

DIVISION OF ECONOMIC AND RISK ANALYSIS

Provides analysis of all commission activities, including policy making, rulemaking, enforcement, and examinations, in order to identify risks or potential securities law violations in the capital markets. Analyzes new financial products and strategies.
Director
Mark Flannery. . . . . (202) 551–6642
Deputy Co-Directors
Scott W. Bauguess . . . . (202) 551–4350
Jennifer Marietta-Weisberg . . . . (202) 551–4350
Managing Executive
Kristin Kaepplein . . . . (202) 551–3539
Business Manager
Kim Coronel . . . . (202) 551–6641
Chief Counsel
Vanessa Countryman . . . . (202) 551–3522
Assistant Director (Office of Asset Management)
Christof W. Stahel . . . . (202) 551–6623
Assistant Director (Office of Corporate Finance)
Simona Mola Yost . . . . (202) 551–3110
Assistant Director (Office of Financial Intermediaries)
Adam Yonce. (202) 551–6659
Assistant Director (Office of Litigation Economics)
Chyhe Becker. . . . . (202) 551–6654
Assistant Director (Office of Markets)
Amy Edwards. . . . . (202) 551–6663
Assistant Director (Office Research and Data Services)
Harvey Westbrook . . . . (202) 551–6609
Associate Director (Office of Risk Assessment)
Christopher Arnold . . . . (202) 551–5359
Assistant Director (Office of Structured Disclosure)
Vacant. . . . . (202) 551–6660

DIVISION OF ENFORCEMENT

Supervises and conducts the enforcement activities required by each of the acts administered by the SEC. Reviews cases with the general counsel to determine which ones should be referred to the Justice Department for criminal prosecution. Supervises operations of the regional offices.
Director
Andrew Ceresney . . . . (202) 551–4500
Deputy Director
Vacant. . . . . (202) 551–4740
Chief Counsel
Joseph Brenner . . . . (202) 551–4930
Chief Litigation Counsel
Matthew Solomon. . . . . (202) 551–4481

Chief Accountant (Corporate Practice)
Howard Scheck . . . . (202) 551–4610
Asset Management
Julie M. Riewe (co-chief) . . . . (202) 551–4500
Marshall S. Sprung (co-chief) . . . . . . (202) 551–4500
Associate Directors of the Division of Enforcement
Antonia Chion. . . . . (202) 551–4842
Stephen Cohen . . . . (202) 551–4834
Gerald Hodgkins. . . . . (202) 551–4711
Scott Friestad . . . . (202) 551–4962
Associate Director (Foreign Corrupt Practices)
Kara Brockmeyer. . . . . (202) 551–4767
Associate Director (Market Intelligence)
Vincente L. Martinez . . . . (202) 551–4691
Associate Director (Structured and New Products)
Kenneth B. Lench . . . . (202) 551–4810
Regional Operations
Vacant. . . . . (202) 551–4500

DIVISION OF INVESTMENT MANAGEMENT

Regulates investment companies (such as mutual funds, closed-end funds, unit investment trusts, exchange-traded funds, and interval funds), including variable insurance products and federally registered investment advisers.
Director
David Grim . . . . (202) 551–6720
Deputy Director
Vacant. . . . . (202) 551–6720
Financial Analysis
Paul Goldman . . . . (202) 551–6715

Chief Counsel's Office
Associate Director and Chief Counsel
Douglas J. Scheidt . . . . (202) 551–6701
Associate Director and Deputy Chief Counsel
Elizabeth G. Osterman. . . . . (202) 551–6746
Legal Guidance Office #1
Nadya B. Roytblat
(assistant chief counsel) . . . . (202) 551–6825
Legal Guidance Office #2
Sara Crovitz (assistant chief counsel). (202) 551–6825
Legal Guidance Office #3
Dalia Blass (assistant chief counsel). . (202) 551–6825
Enforcement Liaison
Janet Grossnickle (assistant director) (202) 551–6785

Disclosure Review and Accounting Office
Associate Director
Barry D. Miller. . . . . (202) 551–6725
Associate Director and Deputy for Disclosure Policy
Susan Nash. . . . . (202) 551–6742
Public Inquiry Line (EDGAR) . . . . . . (202) 551–6989
Chief Accountant
Matthew Giordano . . . . (202) 551–6918
Disclosure Review #1
Michael Spratt . . . . (202) 551–6921
Disclosure Review #2
Christian Sandoe. . . . . (202) 551–6921
Insurance Investments
William J. Kotapish . . . . (202) 551–6921

Rulemaking Office

Associate Director

Diane Blizzard . . . . (202) 551–6702

Investment Adviser Regulation

Daniel S. Kahl (assistant director) . . . (202) 551–6999

Investment Company Regulation

Sarah ten Siethoff (assistant director) (202) 551–6792

Managing Executive's Office

Managing Executive

Eun Ah Choi . . . . (202) 551–6720

Business Manager

Denise Green . . . . (202) 551–6720

Communications

Vacant . . . . (202) 551–6720

Risk and Examinations

Jon Hetzke . . . . (202) 551–6706

Technology

Amy Lawson . . . . (202) 551–6720

DIVISION OF TRADING AND MARKETS

Establishes and maintains standards for fair, orderly, and efficient markets. Regulates the major securities market participants, including broker-dealers, self-regulatory organizations (such as stock exchanges, FINRA, and clearing agencies), and transfer agents.

Director

Stephen Luparello . . . . (202) 551–5500

Deputy Directors

Gary Barnett . . . . (202) 551–5730

Gary Goldsholle . . . . (202) 551–5700

Chief Counsel

Heather Seidel . . . . (202) 551–5594

Associate Director (Analytics and Research)

Vacant . . . . (202) 551–5500

Associate Director (Broker-Dealer Finances)

Michael A. Macchiaroli . . . . (202) 551–5510

Assistant Director (Market Operations)

Vacant . . . . (202) 551–5670

Associate Director (Market Supervision)

David Shillman . . . . (202) 551–5668

Associate Director (Market Supervision)

Vacant . . . . (202) 551–5500

Associate Director (Trading Practices and Processing)

Joannne Swindler . . . . (202) 551–5750

Regional Offices

Atlanta Regional Office

(AL, GA, NC, SC, TN)

950 East Paces Ferry N.E., #900

Atlanta, GA 30326–1382

(404) 842–7600

E-mail: atlanta@sec.gov

Walter Jospin, regional director

Boston Regional Office

CT, MA, ME, NH, RI, VT)

33 Arch St., 23rd Floor

Boston, MA 02110–1424

(617) 573–8900

E-mail: boston@sec.gov

Paul Levenson, regional director

Chicago Regional Office

(IA, IL, IN, KY, MI, MN, MO, OH, WI)

175 W. Jackson Blvd., #900

Chicago, IL 60604

(312) 353–7390

E-mail: chicago@sec.gov

David A. Glockner, regional director

Denver Regional Office

(CO, KS, ND, NM, NE, SD, WY)

1961 Stout St. #1700

Denver, CO 80294

(303) 844–1000

E-mail: denver@sec.gov

Julie K. Lutz, regional director

Exam program administered from Denver regional office.

Fort Worth Regional Office

(AR, KS, OK, TX)

Burnett Plaza, #1900

801 Cherry St., Unit 18

Fort Worth, TX 76102

(817) 978–3821

E-mail: dfw@sec.gov

Marshall Gandy (acting), co-regional director

David Peavler (acting), co-regional director

Los Angeles Regional Office

(AZ, GU, HI, NV, Southern California [zip codes 93599 and below, except 93200–93299]

444 S. Flower St, #900

Los Angeles, CA 90071

(323) 965–3998

E-mail: losangeles@sec.gov

Michele Wein Layne, regional director

Miami Regional Office

(FL, LA, MS, PR, VI)

801 Brickell Ave., #1800

Miami, FL 33131

(305) 982–6300

E-mail: miami@sec.gov

Eric I. Bustillo, regional director

New York Regional Office

(NY, NJ)

200 Vesey St., #400

New York, NY 10281–1022

(212) 336–1100

E-mail: newyork@sec.gov

Andrew Calamari, regional director

Philadelphia Regional Office

(DC, DE, MD, PA, VA, WV)

One Penn Center

1617 JFK Blvd, #520
Philadelphia, PA 19103
(215) 597–3100
E-mail: philadelphia@sec.gov
Sharon Binger, regional director

Salt Lake Regional Office
(UT)
351 W. South Temple St., #6.100
Salt Lake City, UT 84101
(801) 524–5796
E-mail: saltlake@sec.gov
Richard Best, regional director

San Francisco Regional Office
(AK, ID, MT, WA, Northern California [zip codes 93600 and up, plus 93200–93299], OR)
44 Montgomery St., #2600
San Francisco, CA 94104
(415) 705–2500
E-mail: sanfrancisco@sec.gov
Jina Choi, regional director

■ CONGRESSIONAL ACTION

Congressional Liaison
Eric J. Spitler. (202) 551–2010

Committees and Subcommittees

HOUSE APPROPRIATIONS COMMITTEE
Subcommittee on Financial Services and General Government
B300 RHOB, Washington, DC 20515–6015
(202) 225–7245

HOUSE FINANCIAL SERVICES COMMITTEE
Subcommittee on Capital Markets and Government Sponsored Enterprises
2129 RHOB, Washington, DC 20515–6050
General information (202) 225–7502
Press (202) 226–0471

SENATE APPROPRIATIONS COMMITTEE
Subcommittee on Financial Services and General Government
SDOB-133, Washington, DC 20510
(202) 224–2104

SENATE BANKING, HOUSING, AND URBAN AFFAIRS COMMITTEE
Subcommittee on Securities, Insurance, and Investment
SDOB-239, Washington, DC 20510–6075
(202) 224–6142

Legislation
The SEC was created by the **Securities Exchange Act of 1934** (48 Stat. 881, 15 U.S.C. 78a). Signed by the president June 6, 1934. The act required any company whose securities are traded on national exchanges or over-the-counter to file registration applications and annual and periodic reports with the SEC that detail the economic health of the company. The act also set up the following requirements: proxy solicitations must disclose all information concerning the matter to be voted on; individuals or firms making a tender offer to buy up stock in a company, as well as individuals urging stockholders to accept or reject a tender offer, must provide full information to stockholders; corporate officers or insiders and large (10 percent) stockholders must report changes in their holdings; a company may recover profits earned by insiders on the sale or purchase of the company stock; and all national exchanges and all brokers and dealers who conduct business over-the-counter must register with the SEC and comply with principles of trade as enforced by the commission.

The legislation creating the SEC also gave the commission responsibility for administering the **Securities Act of 1933** (48 Stat. 74, 15 U.S.C. 77a). Signed by the president May 27, 1933. This act, originally administered by the Federal Trade Commission, required any firm or individual issuing securities for sale in interstate commerce or through the mail to file financial and other data about the issuer and the securities offered with the SEC before the securities can be placed on the market. Offerings exempt from the registration requirement include private offerings to a small number of individuals or institutions who are familiar with the securities being offered and who do not plan to redistribute them; offerings restricted to residents of the state in which the issuing company is located and engaged in business; securities of municipal, state, federal, and other governmental bodies (but not foreign governments or their instrumentalities), charitable institutions, banks, and carriers subject to the Interstate Commerce Act; offerings not in excess of certain amounts and made in compliance with SEC regulations (such as small business offerings under $500,000); and offerings of small business investment companies.

Public Utility Holding Company Act of 1935 (49 Stat. 803, 15 U.S.C. 79). Signed by the president Aug. 26, 1935. Required public utility (gas and electric) holding companies to register with the SEC and to file reports containing detailed data about organization, financial structure, and operations. Required the companies to operate as coordinated, integrated systems confined to a single area or region. Regulated the functions, activities, expansion, and operations of utility holding companies generally.

Trust Indenture Act of 1939 (53 Stat. 1149, 15 U.S.C. 77aaa). Signed by the president Aug. 3, 1939. Established conditions for the sale of debt securities issued under trust indentures; required that the indenture trustee be free from all conflicts of interest.

Investment Advisers Act of 1940 (54 Stat. 847, 15 U.S.C. 80b-1). Signed by the president Aug. 22, 1940. Required that all individuals engaged in the business of advising others on security transactions register with the commission and maintain books in accordance with commission rules. Empowered the SEC to enact rules to prevent fraudulent, deceptive, or manipulative acts and practices. Gave the SEC power to suspend or revoke registration of individuals found guilty of dishonest or illegal practices.

Investment Company Act of 1940 (54 Stat. 789, 15 U.S.C. 80a-1). Signed by the president Aug. 22, 1940. Required all investment companies to register with the SEC and regulated their activities to ensure fair treatment of all clients.

Securities Investor Protection Act of 1970 (84 Stat. 1636, 15 U.S.C. 780). Signed by the president Dec. 30, 1970. Established the Securities Investor Protection Corp. (SIPC) as an independent nongovernmental corporation, subject to close supervision by the SEC.

Securities Acts Amendments of 1975 (89 Stat. 97, 15 U.S.C. 78a note). Signed by the president June 4, 1975. Directed the SEC to encourage development of a national system for buying and selling stocks. Enlarged SEC oversight powers over the stock exchanges and its indirect oversight responsibility for over-the-counter markets.

Foreign Corrupt Practices Act of 1977 (91 Stat. 1494, 15 U.S.C. 78a note). Signed by the president Dec. 19, 1977. An amendment to the Securities Act. Prohibited U.S. companies from making payments to foreign officials for the purpose of winning business contracts or to influence laws or regulations of other governments. Required firms to maintain records that accurately reflect their transactions and dispositions of assets. The SEC was given responsibility for enforcing the bribery ban and could seek civil injunctions against violators.

Bankruptcy Reform Act of 1978 (92 Stat. 2625, 11 U.S.C. 1101 et seq.). Signed by the president Nov. 6, 1978. Authorized the SEC to aid the federal courts in the administration of corporations reorganizing as a result of bankruptcy.

Small Business Investment Incentive Act of 1980 (94 Stat. 2275, 15 U.S.C. 80a). Signed by the president Oct. 21, 1980. Amended the Securities Acts to exempt certain small- and medium-sized businesses from securities law registration requirements.

Insider Trading Sanctions Act of 1984 (98 Stat. 1264, 15 U.S.C. 78a note). Signed by the president Aug. 10, 1984. Authorized the SEC to seek a civil penalty of up to three times the profit gained or loss avoided as a result of insider trading. Allowed an increase in the maximum fine for a criminal violation.

Shareholder Communications Act of 1985 (99 Stat. 1737, 15 U.S.C. 78n note). Signed by the president Dec. 28, 1985. Required banks, associations, and fiduciaries to disseminate proxy materials.

Government Securities Act of 1986 (100 Stat. 3208, 15 U.S.C. 78a). Signed by the president Oct. 28, 1986. Tightened federal regulation of brokers and dealers who trade in government securities and mortgage pools.

Insider Trading and Securities Fraud Enforcement Act of 1988 (102 Stat. 4677, 15 U.S.C. 78a note). Signed by the president Nov. 19, 1988. Increased civil and criminal penalties for persons who trade stocks using substantive, nonpublic information.

Securities Enforcement Remedies and Penny Stock Reform Act of 1990 (Remedies Act) (104 Stat. 931, 15 U.S.C. 78a note). Signed by the president Oct. 15, 1990. Amended the federal securities laws to provide additional enforcement remedies for violations and to eliminate abuses in transactions in penny stocks.

Market Reform Act of 1990 (104 Stat. 963, 15 U.S.C. 78a note). Signed by the president Oct. 16, 1990. Provided measures to enhance financial market stability, authorized increased monitoring of risks posed to SEC-regulated firms by their holding company, and set provisions for the institution of a large trader reporting system by the SEC to facilitate analysis of market developments.

Futures Trading Practices Act of 1992 (106 Stat. 3590, 7 U.S.C. 1 note). Signed by the president Oct. 28, 1992. Amended the Commodity Exchange Act to improve the regulation of futures and options traded under rules and regulations of the Commodity Futures Trading Commission.

North American Free Trade Agreement Implementation Act (107 Stat. 2057, 19 U.S.C. 3301 note). Signed by the president Dec. 8, 1993. Implemented the North American Free Trade Agreement (NAFTA). Required each party (United States, Canada, and Mexico) to grant most-favored-nation (MFN) treatment to financial service providers and investors of the other parties.

Government Securities Act Amendments of 1993 (107 Stat. 2344, 15 U.S.C. 78a note). Signed by the president Dec. 17, 1993. Amended the government securities provisions of the Securities Exchange Act of 1934. Regulated sales practices and required disclosure by government securities dealers and brokers that are not financial institutions if their accounts are not insured by the Securities Investor Protection Corp.

Telemarketing and Consumer Fraud and Abuse Prevention Act (108 Stat. 1545, 15 U.S.C. 6101 et seq.). Signed by the president Aug. 16, 1994. Directed the SEC to prescribe rules that would prohibit deceptive telemarketing acts and practices by brokers and dealers.

Unlisted Trading Privileges Act of 1994 (108 Stat. 4081, 15 U.S.C. 78a note). Signed by the president Oct. 22, 1994. Amended the Securities Exchange Act of 1934 to enable a national securities exchange to extend unlisted trading privileges for corporate securities.

Private Securities Litigation Reform Act of 1995 (109 Stat. 737, 15 U.S.C. 78a note). Signed by the president. Amended the Securities Act of 1933 and the Securities Exchange Act of 1934. Prohibited the SEC from using disgorgement funds resulting from actions in the federal court to pay for legal expenses incurred by private parties seeking distribution of such funds. Authorized the SEC to seek injunctive relief or money penalties against those who commit securities laws violations. Directed the SEC to make recommendations to the Congress to protect senior citizens and qualified retirement plans from securities fraud and abusive or unnecessary securities fraud litigation.

Telecommunications Act of 1996 (110 Stat. 56, 47 U.S.C. 609 note). Signed by the president Feb. 8, 1996. Title I amended the Public Utility Holding Company Act of 1935 to allow the SEC to determine that a registered holding company providing telecommunications, information, and other related services through a single-purpose subsidiary is an "exempt telecommunications company" (ETC). The relationship between an ETC and a registered holding company will remain subject to SEC's jurisdiction. If a registered holding company or its subsidiary acquires or holds the securities or an interest in the business of an ETC, it must file with the SEC the following information: (1) investments and activities by the registered holding company, or any subsidiary thereof, with respect to the ETCs; and (2) any activities of an ETC within the holding company system that are reasonably likely to have a material impact on the financial or operational condition of the holding company system.

Capital Markets Efficiency Act of 1996 (110 Stat. 3417, 15 U.S.C. 78a note). Signed by the president Oct. 11, 1996. Part of a larger bill. Section 102 directs the SEC to study and to report to the Congress on the extent to which uniformity of state regulatory requirements for securities has been achieved for noncovered securities. Section 108 amended the Securities Exchange Act of 1934 to mandate the SEC and certain self-regulatory organizations to coordinate their examination functions according to prescribed guidelines in order to avoid duplication in the process.

Investment Company Act Amendments of 1996 (110 Stat. 3432, 15 U.S.C. 78a note). Signed by the president Oct. 11, 1996. Section 208 repealed the SEC's authority to bring an action in a U.S. district court for injunctive relief against a violator of unlawful adoption of a name that is materially deceptive or misleading. Section 210 authorized the SEC to provide exemptions from certain investment advisory performance fee contract restrictions to the extent that an exemption relates to a contract with any person that the SEC determines does not need the statutory protections.

Investment Advisers Supervision Coordination Act (110 Stat. 3437, 15 U.S.C. 78a note). Signed by the president Oct. 11, 1996. Section 303 amended the Investment Advisers Act of 1940 to exempt from SEC registration requirements investment advisers subject to a state securities regulator, unless they manage at least $25 million in assets and serve as advisers to certain federally registered investment companies.

Securities and Exchange Commission Authorization Act of 1996 (110 Stat. 3441, 15 U.S.C. 78a note). Signed by the president Oct. 11, 1996. Required the SEC to collect transaction fees and securities registration fees to recover federal costs related to securities registration and market regulation and supervision. Also required national securities exchanges to pay the SEC an annual exchange-traded securities fee and an off-exchange-trades of last-sale-reported securities fee. Fee rates and due dates are to be published in the *Federal Register. (See appendix for information on accessing and using this publication.)*

Gramm-Leach-Bliley Act (113 Stat. 1338, 12 U.S.C. 1811 note). Signed by the president Nov. 12, 1999. Repealed provisions of the Banking Act of 1933 and the Bank Holding Act of 1956 to allow affiliations between banks and any financial company, including brokerage and insurance firms. Amended the Securities Exchange Act of 1934 to extend SEC regulation of securities to the securities activities of banks.

Investor and Capital Markets Fee Relief Act (115 Stat. 2390, 15 U.S.C. 78a note). Signed by the president Jan. 16, 2002. Reduced fees on the purchase and sale of securities, on trades of single stock futures, on merger and tender offers, and on security registration fees. Eliminated fees on Trust Indenture applications. Required the SEC to adjust its fees annually after fiscal 2002 to account for changing market conditions. Increased SEC staff salaries by authorizing the SEC to establish an employee compensation system outside of the existing federal civil service system.

Uniting and Strengthening America by Providing Appropriate Tools Required to Intercept and Obstruct Terrorism Act of 2001 (USA Patriot Act) (115 Stat. 272, 18 U.S.C. 1 note). Signed by the president Oct. 26, 2001. Directed certain federal agencies to investigate and curtail money laundering and other activities that might be undertaken to finance terrorist actions. Required securities brokers and dealers to submit reports regarding suspected money-laundering transactions.

Sarbanes-Oxley Act (116 Stat. 745, 15 U.S.C. 7201 note). Signed by the president July 30, 2002. Established the Public Company Accounting Oversight Board (PCAOB) to police accounting firms and granted the SEC enforcement authority over the board. Amended the Securities Exchange Act of 1934 to prohibit accounting companies from conducting many consulting services for public companies they audit. Directed the SEC to establish rules requiring attorneys to report discovery of corporate wrongdoing to the company's chief legal counsel or CEO and, if necessary, its directors. Required the SEC to conduct a study of corporations' use of off-balance-sheet transactions.

Accountant, Compliance, and Enforcement Staffing Act of 2003 (117 Stat. 842, 5 U.S.C. 1). Signed by the president July 3, 2003. Provided for the protection of investors, increased confidence in the capital markets system, and allowed full implementation of the Sarbanes-Oxley Act of 2002 by streamlining the hiring process for certain employment positions in the SEC.

Fair and Accurate Credit Transactions Act of 2003 (FACT Act) (117 Stat. 1952, 15 U.S.C. 1681a). Signed by the president Dec. 4, 2003. Amended the Fair Credit Reporting Act, prescribing guidelines under which the federal banking agencies, including the SEC, are directed to establish guidelines and prescribe regulations for financial institutions and creditors regarding identity theft.

Emergency Securities Response Act of 2004 (118 Stat. 3638, 50 U.S.C. 401 note). Signed by the president Dec. 17, 2004. Amended the Securities Exchange Act of 1934 to expand the authority of the SEC to issue orders or take other actions to protect investors and markets in emergency situations.

Credit Rating Agency Reform Act of 2006 (120 Stat. 1327, 15 U.S.C. 780 et seq.). Signed by the president Sept. 29, 2006. Amended the Securities Exchange Act of 1934 to require nationally recognized statistical rating organizations to register with the SEC. Required a number of disclosures from credit rating agencies, including a list of subscribers and certification from institutional investors. Directed the SEC to use its rulemaking authority to allow for registration.

Financial Services Regulatory Relief Act of 2006 (120 Stat. 1966, U.S.C. 1811 note). Required the SEC to work with federal banking regulators in implementing exceptions to broker registration requirements for banks under the Securities Exchange Act of 1934 and the Gramm-Leach-Bliley Act. Provided for the final implementation of exceptions to the definition of broker for banks under the Gramm-Leach-Bliley Act.

Dodd-Frank Wall Street Reform and Consumer Protection Act of 2010 (124 Stat. 1376, 12 U.S.C. 5201 note). Signed by the president July 21, 2010. Created the Financial Stability Oversight Council, composed of federal regulators including the SEC chair, to assess potential threats to the financial system. Increased the SEC's enforcement authority to conduct investigations and bring lawsuits against violators of securities laws.

▦ INFORMATION SOURCES

Internet

Agency website: www.sec.gov. FTP Server: ftp.sec.gov

Both Internet addresses provide access to EDGAR (Electronic Data Gathering, Analysis, and Retrieval). For details about this system, see Reference Resources below. A wide range of contact information, including regional and district offices and a listing of e-mail addresses, is provided.

Telephone Contacts

Recorded Information . . . . (202) 942–8088
General Information . . . . (888) 732–6585
Federal Relay Service TTY . . . . (800) 877–8339
Publications. . . . . (202) 551–4040
Personnel Locator . . . . (202) 551–6000
Public Document Requests. . . . . (202) 551–8090
Investor Information Service . . . . (202) 551–6551
Toll-free . . . . (800) 732–0330
Fraud, waste, and abuse hotline . . . . . . (877) 442–0854

Information and Publications

KEY OFFICES

SEC Public Affairs
100 F St. N.E.
Washington, DC 20549
(202) 551–4120
Fax (202) 777–1026
John Nester, director and press contact

Issues news releases on important commission decisions, suspensions of trading, and other areas related to the SEC. Also issues the daily *SEC News Digest,* which is available through the SEC website, www.sec.gov.

Office of Freedom of Information and Privacy Act (FOIA) and Records Management Services
100 F St. N.E., MS 2736
Washington, DC 20549

(202) 551–7900
Fax (202) 772–9337
General e-mail: foiapa@sec.gov
Barry Walters, director of support operations and chief FOIA officer
John Livornese, public liaison, (202) 551–7900

The www.sec.gov/foia/howfo2.htm Web page provides information on how to make a FOIA or Privacy Act request.

SEC Publications Unit
100 F St. N.E.
Washington, DC 20549
(202) 551–4040
(800) 732–0330

Provides selected SEC forms and publications to the public.

DATA AND STATISTICS

The Office of Economic Analysis conducts research on various aspects of the securities markets and compiles statistics on the industry. The data are published in the SEC annual report. The Electronic Data Gathering, Analysis, and Retrieval (EDGAR) system contains lists of documents filed with the SEC and is available to the public for free (*see EDGAR in Reference Resources*).

MEETINGS

Advance notice of open commission meetings is published the preceding week in the *SEC News Digest.* The Office of the Secretary also provides information, as well as audiotapes of open meetings; (202) 551–5400.

Closed meetings also are announced in the *Digest.* Agendas generally are not published, although in some cases the subject of the meeting is made public. Agendas of open meetings also are available on the SEC website or at the meeting itself.

PUBLICATIONS

Visit the SEC Web page at www.sec.gov/investor.shtml to search for a publication by a specific topic, title, or general category; click on the site headings for "Publications and Alerts" and/or "Special Information for" to get specific information on SEC publications, documents, and information. Some of the more frequently requested information includes

▪ EDGAR, the SEC's electronic filing system; description of how companies can use it

▪ Seniors Care Package to help seniors save and invest wisely including: *Get the Facts on Savings and Investing; Ask Questions: Questions You Should Ask About Your Investments; Invest Wisely: An Introduction to Mutual Funds; and Variable Annuities: What You Should Know....*

▪ Teachers Care Package to help teachers get started on a path to saving and investing, including some of the pamphlets listed above and others.

Reference Resources

REFERENCE AND INFORMATION SERVICES

SEC Library

100 F St. N.E., MS 1520
Washington, DC 20549
(202) 551–5450
E-mail: library@sec.gov
Sheryl Rosenthal, director (Reference and
    Information Services)
Hours: 9:00 a.m. to 5:00 p.m.

Open to the public. Appointment required.

SEC Public Reference Room

100 F St. N.E., #1543
Washington, DC 20549
(202) 551–5450
Hours: 10:00 a.m. to 3:00 p.m.

Open to the public. No appointment required.

Provides access to filings submitted in paper by SEC registrants. Filings are required by statutes administered by the SEC. Maintains copies of paper filings for 60 days. Also provides access to all SEC filings available on www.sec.gov. Maintains reference copies of selected SEC publications.

ONLINE

EDGAR

The Electronic Data Gathering, Analysis, and Retrieval (EDGAR) system on the SEC website contains publicly available filings submitted to the SEC from 1994 to the present. It is accessible via the Internet for the public and via terminals in the Public Reference Room. It also can be accessed directly from LEXIS/NEXIS. Since 1994, all corporations and investment management companies that file information with the SEC have been required to use EDGAR. The website also contains the tutorial "Researching Public Companies through EDGAR: A Guide for Investors and How to Access Public Documents." Features include

■ EDGARLink and EDGARLite client applications, which are tools to assist filers in preparing their submissions on their own computers;
■ A website to allow filers to update their own entities' information;
■ Return notifications to filers via e-mail to update them on the status of their filings;
■ Automated Form ID process, which gives new filers an online capability to request access codes to file on EDGAR and gives current filers the ability to regenerate their access codes in case they are lost or compromised;
■ A website to allow the public to search for data about companies who file on EDGAR;
■ A website to assist in the filing process, check status of filings, download EDGARLink and EDGARLite, with links to other helpful sites and information; and

■ Instant dissemination of publicly filed documents to the SEC website and to subscribers throughout the world.

The public portion of these filings is available in hard copy or on microfiche in the Public Reference Room. Manuals on how to use this system and on how to file via EDGAR are available for reference use at the Public Reference Room or on the SEC website. More information on filings can be obtained by calling the SEC's Office of Information Technology Filer Support lines at (202) 551–8900. Queries about EDGAR data on the SEC website can be directed by e-mail to webmaster@sec.gov.

DOCKETS

The SEC makes dockets available on its website where users can review them and submit comments electronically. Federal dockets are also available at www.regulations.gov. (*See appendix for Searching and Commenting on Regulations: Regulations.gov.*)

RULES AND REGULATIONS

SEC rules and regulations are published in the *Code of Federal Regulations*, Title 17, Chapter II, Parts 200–399. Proposed rules, new final rules, and updates to the *Code of Federal Regulations* are published in the daily *Federal Register*. (*See appendix for information on how to obtain and use these publications.*) The *Federal Register* may be accessed at www.federalregister.gov and the *Code of Federal Regulations* at www.archives.gov/federal-register/cfr; also see the federal government's website www.regulations.gov (*see appendix*).

Other Information Sources

RELATED AGENCY

Securities Investor Protection Corp. (SIPC)

1667 K St. N.W., #1000
Washington, DC 20006–1620
(202) 371–8300
Fax (202) 223–1679
Bill Jasien, CEO and president
Stephen Harbeck, deputy president
Josephine Wang, general counsel
Internet: www.sipc.org

An independent nongovernmental corporation under the supervision of the SEC and Congress, which was set up in 1970 to protect customers against loss in the event of the financial failure of a securities dealer or broker.

The SIPC provides information to the public, including a pamphlet titled *How SIPC Protects You*.

NONGOVERNMENTAL RESOURCES

The following are some key resources for information on the SEC and securities issues.

American Institute of Certified Public Accountants

1211 Avenue of the Americas
New York, NY 10036–8775
(212) 596–6200
Fax (212) 596–6213

Washington office
1455 Pennsylvania Ave. N.W.
Washington, DC 20004–1081
(202) 737–6600
Fax (202) 638–4512
Internet: www.aicpa.org

American Law Institute–Continuing Legal Education (ALI–CLE)
4025 Chestnut St.
Philadelphia, PA 19104
(215) 243–1600
(800) CLE-NEWS (253–6397)
Fax (215) 243–1664
Internet: www.ali-aba.org

Bureau of National Affairs (Bloomberg BNA, a subsidiary of Bloomberg, Inc.)
1801 S. Bell St.
Arlington, VA 22202
(703) 341–3000
(800) 372–1033 (U.S. and Canada)
(703) 341–3500 (international)
Fax (800) 253–0332
Internet: www.bna.com

Council of Institutional Investors
888 17th St. N.W., #500
Washington, DC 20006
(202) 822–0800
Fax (202) 822–0801
Internet: www.cii.org

Dow Jones & Co.
(Owns *Wall Street Journal, Barron's, Factiva,* and *MarketWatch*)
Publications Dept.
84 2nd Ave.
Chicopee, MA 01020
(800) DOWJONES (369–5663)
(800) JOURNAL (568–7625)
Internet: www.dowjones.com

Financial Accounting Standards Board
401 Merritt
Box 5116
Norwalk, CT 06856–5116
(203) 847–0700
Fax (203) 849–9714
Internet: www.fasb.org

Financial Industry Regulatory FINRA
1735 K St.
Washington, DC 20006
(301) 590–6500
Internet: www.finra.org

Investment Company Institute (ICI)
1401 H St. N.W., #1200
Washington, DC 20005–2148
(202) 326–5800
Fax (202) 326–5806
Internet: www.ici.org

IPREO
1359 Broadway, 2nd Floor
New York, NY 10018
(212) 849–5000
Fax (212) 812–4447
Internet: www.ipreo.com
    Washington office
    4833 Rugby Ave., #600
    Bethesda, MD 20814
    (301) 760–2500
    Fax (301) 656–0983

The McGraw-Hill Companies
(Owns Standard & Poor's, J.D. Power & Associates, and Platts)
55 Water St.
New York, NY 10041
(212) 438–1000
Internet: www.mcgraw-hill.com; www.mhfi.com

Nasdaq Stock Market, Inc.
One Liberty Plaza
165 Broadway
New York, NY 10006
(212) 401–8700
Internet: www.nasdaq.com

New York Stock Exchange
11 Wall St.
New York, NY 10005
(212) 656–3000
Internet: www.nyse.com
    Washington office
    801 Pennsylvania Ave. N.W., #630
    Washington, DC 20004
    (202) 347–4300
    Fax (202) 347–4372

Value Line
485 Lexington Ave., 9th Floor
New York, NY 10017
(212) 907–1500
(800) 825–8354
Fax (212) 907–1913
Internet: www.valueline.com

Wolters Kluwer Law and Business
2700 Lake Cook Rd.
Riverwoods, IL 60015
(212) 771–0600
(800) 835–5224
Internet: www.wklawbusiness.com

Other Regulatory Agencies

Architectural and Transportation Barriers Compliance Board

1331 F St. N.W., #1000, Washington, DC 20004–1111
Internet: www.access-board.gov

The Architectural and Transportation Barriers Compliance Board (ATBCB), referred to as the Access Board, was created under Section 502 of the Rehabilitation Act of 1973 to enforce the provisions of the Architectural Barriers Act (ABA) of 1968. The ABA requires that all facilities owned, rented, or funded in any part by the federal government after September 1969 be accessible to and usable by persons with disabilities. The Access Board also sets standards for telecommunication equipment and standards as authorized under the Telecommunications Act of 1996.

The Access Board is an independent federal agency with twenty-five board members. The president appoints thirteen public members (a majority of whom must be people with disabilities) to four-year terms. The remaining twelve board members represent various federal agencies with responsibilities for ensuring equal access to programs and facilities. These agencies include the departments of Commerce, Defense, Education, Health and Human Services, Housing and Urban Development, Interior, Justice, Labor, Transportation, and Veterans Affairs; the General Services Administration; and the U.S. Postal Service. An executive director heads the Access Board staff.

Since enactment of the Americans with Disabilities Act (ADA) of 1990 (and subsequent amendments), the Access Board has been responsible for developing ADA accessibility guidelines, which include minimum accessibility guidelines for places of public accommodation, commercial facilities, state and local government facilities, transportation vehicles and facilities, Internet technology and electronic communications, voting accommodations and access to medical treatment.

The Access Board establishes minimum guidelines and requirements for standards under the ADA. It proposes alternative solutions to barriers facing persons with disabilities in housing, transportation, communications, education, recreation, and public attitudes. Along these lines, it also determines what federal, state, and local governments and other public or private agencies and groups are doing to eliminate barriers. The Access Board also

prepares plans for adequate transportation and housing for persons with disabilities, including proposals to cooperate with other agencies, organizations, and individuals working toward such goals. In addition, the Access Board reports annually to the president and Congress on investigations, actions, and extent of compliance with the ABA.

The ADA Amendments of 2008 changed the legal definition of disability for employment purposes. In several high-profile Supreme Court cases, plaintiffs were unable to demonstrate that their disabilities "substantially limited" major life activities. In reviewing these cases, Congress found that the Equal Employment Opportunity Commission ADA regulations defining the term "substantially limits" as "significantly restricted" set the standard too high and was inconsistent with congressional intent. The changes also cover impairments that are episodic or in remission that substantially limit a major life activity when active. The 2008 amendments make it easier for an individual seeking protection under the ADA to establish that he or she has a disability within the meaning of the ADA.

Public accommodation, commercial facilities, state and local government facilities. The Access Board, in conjunction with other federal agencies with governing jurisdiction, develops accessibility guidelines for public accommodation, commercial facilities, and state and local government facilities. The guideline development covers access to buildings and sites, recreational facilities, and sidewalks and streets.

In October 2000 the Access Board published accessibility guidelines for newly built or altered play areas under ADA. The guidelines address play areas provided at schools, parks, child care facilities (except those based in the operator's home, which are exempt), and other facilities subject to the ADA.

In September 2010, the Justice Department adopted new standards for accessible design, effective March 15, 2012. The standards apply to facilities covered by the ADA, including places of public accommodation, commercial facilities, and state and local government facilities. The 2010 ADA regulations address new construction and alterations. Title II regulation addresses state and local government facilities, and Title III regulations cover places of public accommodation and commercial facilities. Other sections of these regulations address program access (Title II) and removal of barriers in existing facilities (Title III).

The new standards are based on revised minimum guidelines previously established by the Access Board that include supplements for certain types of facilities and sites not previously addressed. The revised rules will cover recreational facilities such as amusement parks, marinas, gyms, golf facilities and swimming pools, and municipal facilities such as courtrooms and prisons.

Transportation. Under the ADA, the Access Board is responsible for developing and maintaining accessibility guidelines for transportation vehicles. When it originally issued the ADA Accessibility Guidelines for Transportation Vehicles, the Access Board reserved requirements for passenger vessels pending further study and gathering of information. Under the ADA, the Transportation Department issues and enforces accessibility standards for transportation vehicles that are based on the Access Board's ADA Accessibility Guidelines for Transportation Vehicles.

In August 1998 the Access Board created the Passenger Vessel Access Advisory Committee to provide recommendations for a proposed rule addressing accessibility guidelines for ferries, cruise ships, excursion boats, and other passenger vessels. Between December 2000 and June 2008, the Access Board and the Advisory Committee held public hearings and issued a report and draft guidelines. The Access Board released revised proposed guidelines for passenger vessels for public comment on June 18, 2013. Responding to industry request, the Access Board extended the deadline for public comment to January 24, 2014.

In July 2010, the board published a proposal for public comment to update sections of its ADA Accessibility Guidelines for Transportation Vehicles that cover access to buses and vans. The proposal contains revisions to the guidelines, which apply to new or remanufactured vehicles, to address new types of systems, such as bus rapid transit and low floor buses, and advances in technology, including automation of announcements.

The Rail Vehicles Access Advisory Committee (RVAAC), which the Access Board established in 2013, will develop consensus recommendations for updating sections of the guidelines that cover vehicles of fixed guideway systems, including rapid, light, commuter, intercity, and high-speed rail.

Access to Electronic Information. The Telecommunications Act of 1996 authorized the Access Board to set standards for accessibility, usability, and compatibility of telecommunications equipment and customer premises equipment. The Rehabilitation Act Amendments of 1998 covered access to federally funded programs and services. The Access Board also issued accessibility standards for electronic and information technology under Section 508 of the Rehabilitation Act, as amended. Enforcement of Section 508 began in June 2001.

The law strengthened Section 508 of the Rehabilitation Act and required access to electronic and information technology provided by the federal government. The law applied to all federal agencies when they develop, procure, maintain, or use electronic and information technology. Federal agencies had to ensure that this technology was accessible to employees and members of the public with disabilities. Section 508 listed various means for disseminating information, including federal websites. The law also empowered the Access Board to develop accessibility standards for such technology for incorporation into regulations that govern federal procurement practices.

Medical. The Access Board also is responsible for ensuring the medical community complies with access requirements for disabled patients. The Patient Protection and Affordable Care Act of 2010 required the Access Board to develop new access standards for medical diagnostic equipment used in medical settings, such as exam tables, weight scales, and radiological equipment. The Food and Drug Administration Safety and Innovation Act of 2012 required the Access Board to convene a stakeholder working group to develop best practices on access to information on prescription drug container labels for blind or visually impaired individuals.

Voting. The Help America Vote Act of 2002 contained key provisions on improving access to polling places and voting systems for persons with disabilities. The law required every precinct in the country to have at least one voting machine or system accessible to persons with disabilities, including those with vision impairments, by Jan. 1, 2006. The measure created a new independent entity, the Election Assistance Commission (*p. 392*), to oversee the development of guidelines for voting systems that were to include provisions for accessibility. The guidelines were to be developed through several advisory bodies, with the Access Board represented on some of these entities.

Training. The Access Board offers training and technical assistance to individuals and organizations on how to remove architectural, transportation, and communication barriers. Live trainings are usually delivered via seminars and workshops upon request and tailored to specific audiences, such as architects, public and private facility managers, the transportation community, and any other stakeholder group requiring such training. The Access Board also delivers training through webinars, with schedules listed on its website.

Regulatory and Enforcement Authority. The Access Board may conduct investigations, hold public hearings, and issue orders to comply with the ABA. An order is final and binding on any federal department, agency, or instrumentality of the United States. The Access Board responds to all complaints it receives about an inaccessible federally funded building or facility. The board first tries to resolve complaints informally. If necessary, legal proceedings before an administrative law judge may be initiated.

It is not necessary to file a complaint to obtain information and assistance from the Access Board. The agency maintains extensive files on bibliographies, products, and other resources on accessibility; it also may direct inquiries to officials in state, local, or other federal agencies or private organizations.

Under its rulemaking authority, the Access Board issues and updates guidelines. The Access Board website provides information on the rulemaking process and subsequent guidelines and regulations. Standards and guidelines are published on the agency's website.

■ KEY PERSONNEL

Executive Director
David M. Cappozzi . . . . (202) 272–0010
General Counsel
Gretchen Jacobs . . . . (202) 272–0040
Technical and Information Services
Marsha Mazz . . . . (202) 272–0020
TTY . . . . (202) 272–0076

■ INFORMATION SOURCES

Internet

Agency website: www.access-board.gov. Includes information on ATBCB guidelines and publications. E-mail: info@access-board.gov.

Telephone Contacts

General Information . . . . (202) 272–0080
Toll-free . . . . (800) 872–2253
Agency Fax . . . . (202) 272–0081
TTY . . . . (202) 272–0082
TTY (toll-free) . . . . (800) 993–2822

Information and Publications

KEY OFFICES

ATBCB Public Affairs
1331 F St. N.W., #1000
Washington, DC 20004–1111
(202) 272–0026
TTY (202) 272–0027
David Yanchulis, coordinator
E-mail: news@access-board.gov

Issues news releases, prepares and distributes the board's annual report, and answers or refers general questions.

Freedom of Information
1331 F St. N.W., #1000
Washington, DC 20004–1111
(202) 272–0046
TTY (202) 272–0082
Lisa Fairhall, deputy general counsel

Advisory Committee on Standards for Medical Diagnostic Equipment
(202) 272–0023
TTY (202) 272–0064
E-mail: pace@access-board.gov

Guidance on Prescription Drug Labels
(202) 272–0020
TTY (202) 272–0076
Marsha Mazz, director
E-mail: mazz@access-board.gov

MEETINGS

The board meets six times a year, usually in Washington, DC; public hearings may be held in different locations around the country to give stakeholders and interested parties outside the Washington area the opportunity to express their opinions to the board.

After each meeting, the board publishes *Access Currents* to cover actions taken at the meeting. It can be obtained through the Public Affairs office, or interested individuals can subscribe to it by e-mailing their names and mailing addresses to news@access-board.gov.

PUBLICATIONS

Various publications, including all ATBCB guidelines and standards, are available free from the ATBCB and its website. These publications include

About the Architectural Barriers Act and Other Disability Rights Laws

ADA Accessibility Guidelines and the *Uniform Federal Accessibility Standards*. Provides design criteria for the construction and alteration of buildings and facilities. Checklists, manuals, and technical bulletins related to these documents are also available.

ADA Accessibility Guidelines for Transportation Vehicles. Provides accessibility requirements for buses, vans, rail vehicles, and other modes of public transportation.

Telecommunications Act Accessibility Guidelines

Standards for Electronic and Information Technology

Access Currents. The Access Board's bimonthly newsletter.

Side by Side Comparison. New ADA guidelines, the original standards, and the International Building Code.

Securement of Wheelchairs and Other Mobility Aids.

A checklist of publications is available. For further information contact the ATBCB or visit its website.

Reference Resources

LIBRARY

ATBCB Library
1331 F St. N.W., #1000
Washington, DC 20004–1111
(202) 272–0021
Jim Pecht, librarian
Hours: 9:30 a.m. to 5:30 p.m., by appointment only

RESEARCH

The research program is focused on the study of accessibility relating to architecture and design, communication, and transportation.
E-mail: research@access-board.gov

DOCKETS

Hard copies of federal dockets are available for inspection at the ATBCB office. Appointment preferred. Dockets may also be viewed at www.regulations.gov. (*See appendix for information on Searching and Commenting on Regulations.*)

RULES AND REGULATIONS

ATBCB rules and regulations are published in the *Code of Federal Regulations,* Title 36, Chapter XI, Parts 1100–1199. Proposed rules, new final rules, and updates to the *Code of Federal Regulations* are published in the daily *Federal Register.* (*See appendix for information on how to obtain and use these publications.*)

Other Information Sources

NONGOVERNMENTAL RESOURCES

American Council of the Blind

2200 Wilson Blvd., #650
Arlington, VA 22201-3354
(202) 467–5081
(800) 424–8666
Fax (703) 465–5085
Kim Charlson, president
E-mail: kim.charlson@acb.org
Internet: www.acb.org

National Council on Aging

251 18th St. South, #500
Arlington, VA 22202
(571) 527-3900
Howard Bedlin, vice president
E-mail: howard.bedlin@ncoa.org
Internet: www.ncoa.org

■ LEGISLATION

The ATBCB administers the following laws:

Architectural Barriers Act of 1968 (82 Stat. 718, 42 U.S.C. 4151 et seq.). Signed by the president Aug. 12, 1968. Ensured that buildings and facilities designed, constructed, altered, or leased with certain federal funds after September 1969 are accessible to people with disabilities.

Rehabilitation Act of 1973 (87 Stat. 355, 29 U.S.C. 792). Signed by the president Sept. 26, 1973. Established the ATBCB to enforce disability access laws. Barred discrimination by the federal government against persons with disabilities.

Fair Housing Amendments Act of 1988 (102 Stat. 1619, 42 U.S.C. 3601 note). Signed by the president Sept. 13, 1988. Prohibited discrimination in the sale or rental of housing to persons with disabilities.

Americans with Disabilities Act of 1990 (104 Stat. 327, 42 U.S.C. 12101 note). Signed by the president July 26, 1990. Titles II and III provided Americans with disabilities, including those with AIDS, the same rights to jobs, public transportation, and public accommodations that women and racial, religious, and ethnic minorities receive under the Civil Rights Act of 1964.

Telecommunications Act of 1996 (110 Stat. 56, 47 U.S.C. 609 note). Signed by the president Feb. 8, 1996. Gave the ATBCB additional authority to set guidelines for telecommunications equipment and customer premises equipment.

Rehabilitation Act Amendments of 1998 (29 U.S.C. 794d). Signed by the president Aug. 7, 1998. Section 508, as amended by the Workforce Investment Act of 1998, required federal agencies to make their electronic and information technology accessible to people with disabilities. Applied to all federal agencies when they develop, procure, maintain, or use electronic and information technology.

Help America Vote Act of 2002 (116 Stat. 1666, 42 U.S.C. 15301 et seq.). Signed by the president Oct. 29, 2002. Required voting systems to be accessible for individuals with disabilities. Established the Election Assistance Commission (EAC) to serve as a national clearinghouse and resource for the compilation of information and review of procedures with respect to the administration of federal elections.

ADA Amendment Acts of 2008 (122 Stat. 3553, 42 U.S.C. 12101 note). Signed by the president Sept. 25, 2008. Amended the Americans with Disabilities Act of 1990 (ADA) to redefine the term "disability," including by defining "major life activities" and "being regarded as having such an impairment." Declared that nothing in the act altered the standards for determining eligibility for benefits under state workers' compensation laws or under state and federal disability benefit programs.

Patient Protection and Affordable Care Act (124 Stat. 119, 42 U.S.C. 18001 note). Signed by the president March 23, 2010. Amends the Rehabilitation Act of 1973 to require the Architectural and Transportation Barriers Compliance Board to promulgate standards setting forth the minimum technical criteria for medical diagnostic equipment used in medical settings to ensure that such equipment is accessible to, and usable by, individuals with accessibility needs.

Food and Drug Administration Safety and Innovation Act (126 Stat. 993, 29 U.S.C. 792 note). Signed by the president July 9, 2012. Title IX: Drug Approval and Patient Access required the Architectural and Transportation Barriers Compliance Board to convene a stakeholder working group to develop best practices on access to information on prescription drug container labels for blind or visually impaired individuals.

Commodity Futures Trading Commission

Three Lafayette Centre, 1155 21st St. N.W
Washington, DC 20581
Internet: www.cftc.gov

The Commodity Futures Trading Commission (CFTC) was established in 1975 as an independent agency to replace the Commodity Exchange Authority to administer the Commodity Exchange Act of 1936. The commission's mandate is to regulate commodity futures and options markets in the United States.

The purpose of the CFTC is to further the economic utility of futures markets by encouraging their efficiency, ensuring their integrity, and protecting participants against abusive trade practices, fraud, and deceit. The objective is to enable the markets to serve their designated function: to provide a price discovery mechanism and a means of offsetting price risk to contribute to better planning, more efficient distribution and consumption, and more economical marketing.

The commission is composed of five members appointed by the president and confirmed by the Senate, with one member designated as chair. Members serve five-year terms arranged so that one term expires each year. No more than three members of the commission may belong to the same political party.

The CFTC is funded by an annual appropriation by Congress. The CFTC has authority to charge the industry fees for services such as approval of contracts and the registration of leverage commodities.

The commission oversees futures and options trading on exchanges and trading in certain off-exchange trade options. A futures contract is a firm commitment to deliver or to receive a specified quantity and grade of a commodity during a designated month, with the price being determined by public auction among exchange members. A futures option is a unilateral contract that enables the holder to buy or sell a futures contract at a set price at a specified time, regardless of the market price of that commodity.

The commission monitors the trading in futures contracts, including physical commodities such as lumber, precious metals, petroleum products, coffee, livestock, grains, and pork bellies; financial instruments, such as currencies, Treasury bonds, and Eurodollars; various indices in stocks, currencies, and other commodities; and options on futures contracts and options on physical commodities. Futures contracts have been offered in various other nontraditional commodity areas such as seafood, dairy products, crop yields, and energy commodities, such as oil and natural gas.

The 1982 reauthorizing legislation, the Futures Trading Act of 1982, delineated the jurisdiction of the CFTC and the Securities and Exchange Commission (SEC), affirming exclusive CFTC authority over commodity futures contracts and options on futures, including futures and options on so-called exempted securities, such as instruments of the Government National Mortgage Association and Treasury bills, but not on municipal securities.

The 1982 law also required the industry's self-regulatory group, the National Futures Association (NFA), to begin actively sharing regulatory responsibilities with the CFTC. The CFTC later delegated to the NFA authority to register brokers and certain commodity professionals, to audit records and bank accounts, and to enforce compliance of member firms to rules and regulations of both the NFA and CFTC.

The Commodity Futures Modernization Act of 2000, passed as part of an omnibus appropriations bill, created a flexible structure for regulation of futures trading, codified an agreement between the CFTC and the Securities and Exchange Commission to repeal the eighteen-year-old ban on trading single stock futures, and provided legal certainty for the over-the-counter derivatives markets. The law clarified the Treasury Amendment exclusion and specifically granted the CFTC authority over retail foreign exchange trading. The flexibility sought by industry stakeholders concerned industry analysts, who believed the deregulatory effort could be harmful to the overall well-being of the U.S. economy. The most outspoken opponent of the legislation was then CFTC Chair Brooksley Born. The Patriot Act of 2001, which amended the Bank Secrecy Act, was passed in response to the 2001 terrorist attacks. The Patriot Act strengthened U.S. measures to prevent, detect, and prosecute international money laundering and the financing of terrorism. Under the act, persons who were required to be registered as futures commission merchants, including brokers, commodity pool operators, and commodity trading advisers, were subject to new requirements for establishing programs against money laundering.

The CFTC Reauthorization Act of 2008, which was Title XIII of the Food, Conservation, and Energy Act of 2008, was passed via congressional override of a presidential veto. The act amended the Commodity Exchange Act to give CFTC enhanced authority over off-exchange retail foreign currency. The act also provides the CFTC with enhanced oversight over contracts trading on exempt commercial markets (ECMs), a type of electronic trading facility offering energy derivatives and other products. The purpose was to provide transparency in the energy trading sector, closing what some analysts termed "the Enron loophole," created by the Commodity Futures Modernization Act of 2000, which exempted these trades from regulation.

Under the CFTC Reauthorization Act of 2008, the CFTC was required to issue a proposed rule regarding the significant price discovery standards within 180 days of the date of enactment and a final rule within 270 days. The CFTC also was required to complete a review of the agreements, contracts, and transactions of any electronic trading facility operating on the effective date of the final rule within 180 days after such date to determine whether such agreement, contract, or transaction performs a significant price discovery function. Final rules were published in March 2009.

The Dodd-Frank Wall Street Reform and Consumer Protection Act, signed into law in July 2010, gave the CFTC new regulatory authority over previously unregulated swaps markets, which was a contributing factor in the economic crisis that began in 2007. The Dodd-Frank Act requires the Securities and Exchange Commission (SEC) and the Commodities Futures Trading Commission (CFTC) to work with the prudential regulators—the Farm Credit Administration, the Federal Reserve Board, the Office of the Comptroller of the Currency, the Federal Deposit Insurance Corporation, and the Federal Housing Finance Agency—to develop regulations for margin requirements on non-cleared derivatives for each of the entities subject to regulation under each of the respective agencies. SEC and CFTC are authorized to establish margin requirements for swaps dealers that are not primarily regulated by the prudential regulators.

The Dodd-Frank Act also requires each federal agency to review certain regulations that refer to external credit ratings (such as those provided by Moody's, Standard & Poor's, and Fitch) and to replace such regulations with alternative credit standards, as appropriate.

Following passage of Dodd-Frank, the CFTC identified 38 areas where rules would be necessary. By the end of 2014, the CFTC had finalized 69 rules, exemptive orders, and guidance actions and five other actions required under Dodd-Frank.

The Dodd-Frank Act also requires the CFTC to conduct a number of studies and reports on a wide variety of issues that affect the derivatives market; the agency publishes these reports on its website as they become available. Published reports include "Abusive Swaps," "World Derivatives," "New Product Delegation," "Improving Clearing Oversight," and "Whistleblowers."

As the CFTC promulgated rules to address issues as required by Dodd-Frank, the agency was flexing its enforcement muscle regarding improprieties discovered in foreign markets. In July 2012 the CFTC issued an order against Barclays for manipulating the London Interbank Offered Rate (LIBOR), which is among the most important benchmark interest rates in the interconnected global economy; it is a key rate in the United States. These benchmark rates affect the cost of borrowing for consumers and corporations. The order against Barclays would be the first of several issued by CFTC (as well as financial regulators in other nations) against banks that rigged global benchmark interest rates. Between June 2012 and November 2014, the CFTC imposed penalties exceeding $3.34 billion on entities relating to acts of attempted manipulation, completed manipulation, and/or false reporting with respect to global benchmarks.

In the waning days of session, the 113th Congress debated the Consolidated and Further Continuing Appropriations Act of 2015. Tucked into the 1,600-plus-page omnibus appropriations bill was an amendment that repealed section 716 of the Dodd-Frank Act, which prohibited federal assistance to a swaps entity with respect to any swap, security-based swap, or other activity. The purpose of the Dodd-Frank section 716 provision was to prevent taxpayer bailouts of financial institutions that engaged in risky derivatives activities. Senator Elizabeth Warren strenuously objected to the repeal of this provision as the omnibus appropriations bill was debated on the Senate floor. However, Congress passed the spending bill to avoid a government shutdown and the president signed the bill into law on December 16, 2014.

As a new Congress took office in January 2015, it was clear that there was intent to continue to chip away at the Dodd-Frank provisions. In the first week, House Republicans, with some bipartisan support, attempted to fast-track legislation that would water down key Dodd-Frank provisions, including regulatory oversight of derivatives. Fast-tracking the legislation, which moves it through the House without debate, required a two-thirds majority approval of the House. The effort failed.

The commission has four divisions with primary oversight and regulatory responsibility: (1) The Division of Enforcement investigates allegations of fraud or manipulation and conducts all other enforcement proceedings; (2) the Division of Market Oversight has regulatory responsibility for initial recognition and continuing oversight of trade execution facilities, including new registered futures exchanges and derivatives transaction execution facilities; (3) the Division of Clearing and Risk oversees derivatives clearing organizations (DCOs) and other market participants in the clearing process, monitoring the clearing of futures, options on futures, and swaps by DCOs, assessing DCO regulatory compliance, and conducting risk assessment; and (4) the Division of Swap Dealer and Intermediary Oversight has oversight responsibility for the registration and compliance of intermediaries and futures industry self-regulatory organizations (SROs), including U.S. derivatives exchanges and the National Futures Association (NFA).

Specific responsibilities of the commission include

Regulating Exchanges. All exchanges on which commodities are traded for future delivery are regulated by the commission. The commission reviews and approves rules and may require a market to change its rules or practices. In emergencies the CFTC may direct an exchange to take action to maintain or restore orderly markets. Under commission rules, procedures must be developed to settle customer complaints against members and employees of exchanges.

Approving Futures Contracts. The commission must approve all futures and options contracts traded on exchanges. Contracts must reflect normal market flow and commercial trading practices in the actual commodity being traded and provide for a broad deliverable supply. A limit may be imposed on the number of contracts a single speculator may trade or hold.

Regulation of Futures Professionals. Companies and individuals who handle customer funds or give trading advice must apply for registration through the National Futures Association (NFA), a self-regulatory organization approved by the commission. The CFTC also seeks to protect customers by requiring registrants to disclose market risks and past performance information to prospective customers, by requiring that customer funds be kept in accounts separate from company funds, and by requiring customer accounts to be adjusted to reflect the current market value at the close of trading. In addition, the CFTC monitors registrant supervision systems, internal controls, and sales practice compliance programs. All registrants are also required to complete ethics training.

Protecting Customers. The commission sets minimum financial requirements for futures brokers and option dealers and requires that customer funds be segregated from company funds. The commission operates a reparation process to adjudicate and settle customer complaints.

Monitoring Information. The commission requires that information provided by exchanges, such as volume and open interest, be timely and accurate. It monitors market letters, reports, and statistics provided by traders, brokers, trading advisers, and commodity pool operators. The commission analyzes written complaints of staff-detected problems and enforces the law by filing cases in federal district court or through administrative proceedings before agency administrative law judges. Enforcement actions may lead to the loss of trading rights or a substantial fine.

Four CFTC divisions carry out the agency's business and regulatory functions:

Clearing and Risk (DCR). The Division of Clearing and Risk oversees derivatives clearing organizations (DCOs) and other market participants in the clearing process, including futures commission merchants, swap dealers, major swap participants, and large traders. It monitors the clearing of futures, options on futures, and swaps by DCOs, assesses DCO compliance with commission regulations, and conducts risk assessment and surveillance. DCR also makes recommendations on DCO applications and eligibility, rule submissions, and which types of swaps should be cleared.

Enforcement (DOE). The Division of Enforcement investigates and prosecutes alleged violations of the Commodity Exchange Act and commission regulations. Potential violations include fraud, manipulation, and other abuses concerning commodity derivatives and swaps that threaten market integrity, market participants, and the general public.

Market Oversight (DMO). The Division of Market Oversight fosters derivatives markets that accurately reflect the forces of supply and demand and are free of disruptive activity. It oversees trade execution facilities and data repositories, conducts surveillance, reviews new exchange applications, and examines existing exchanges to ensure compliance with applicable core principles. DMO also evaluates new products to ensure they are not susceptible to manipulation as well as rule filings by exchanges to ensure compliance with core principles.

Swap Dealer and Intermediary Oversight (DSIO). The Division of Swap Dealer and Intermediary Oversight oversees the registration and compliance of intermediaries and futures industry self-regulatory organizations (SROs), including U.S. derivatives exchanges and the National Futures Association (NFA). DSIO is responsible for developing and monitoring compliance with regulations addressing registration, business conduct standards, capital adequacy, and margin requirements for swap dealers and major swap participants.

■ KEY PERSONNEL

Chair and Commissioner
Timothy G. Massad. . . . . (202) 418–5050
Fax. . . . . (202) 418–5533
Commissioners
Mark P. Wetjen. . . . . (202) 418–5010
Sharon Y. Bowen . . . . (202) 418–5060
J. Christopher Giancarlo . . . . (202) 418–5030
Executive Director
Anthony C. Thompson. . . . . (202) 418–5697
Chief Economist
Sayee Srinivasan . . . . (202) 418–5309
Clearing and Risk
Phyllis Dietz (acting) . . . . (202) 418–5449
Enforcement
Aitan Goelman . . . . (202) 418–5000
Equal Employment Opportunity
Pamela Gibbs. . . . . (202) 418–5000
Financial Officer
Mary Jean Buhler . . . . (202) 418–5477
General Counsel
Jonathan L. Marcus. . . . . (202) 418–5120
Fax. . . . . (202) 418–5524
Human Resources
Catherine McCoy . . . . (202) 418–5003
Information Officer
John Rogers . . . . (202) 418–5240
Inspector General
A. Roy Lavik. . . . . (202) 418–5110
Fax. . . . . (202) 418–5522

International Affairs
   Sarah E. Josephson .... (202) 418–5645
      Fax......................... (202) 418–5548
Market Oversight
   Vince A. McGonagle .... (202) 418–5387
Secretariat
   Chris Kirkpatrick .... (202) 418–5100
Swap Dealer and Intermediary Oversight
   Thomas Smith (interim) .... (202) 418–6700

■ INFORMATION SOURCES

Internet
Agency website: www.cftc.gov.

Telephone Contacts
   Personnel Locator .... (202) 418–5000
   Fax .... (202) 418–5521
   TTY .... (202) 418–5514
   Consumer Assistance.............. (866) 366–2382

Information and Publications

KEY OFFICES

Office of External Affairs
Three Lafayette Centre
1155 21st St. N.W.
Washington, DC 20581
Toll-free complaint line (866) 366–2382
Fax (202) 418–5521
TTY (202) 418–5514
E-mail: questions@cftc.gov
Internet: www.cftc.gov
Steven W. Adamske, public affairs, (202) 418–5080
Cory Claussen, legislative affairs, (202) 418–5075

Issues press releases and media advisories; publishes newsletters and pamphlets of general information. Handles legislative matters.

Freedom of Information
FOIA Compliance Office
Three Lafayette Centre
1155 21st St. N.W.
Washington, DC 20581
(202) 418–5497
Linda J. Mauldin, paralegal specialist
Edwin J. Yoshimura, counsel, (312) 596–0562

Office of Proceedings
(formerly the Complaints Section)
Three Lafayette Centre
1155 21st St. N.W.
Washington, DC 20581
(202) 418–5250
Fax (202) 418–5532
Jason Gizzarelli, director

Reparation is available for any valid claim filed within two years after the violation occurs. To obtain a pamphlet detailing the reparation procedure or to file a claim, contact this office.

DATA AND STATISTICS
The commission releases a weekly *Commitments of Traders Compressed Reports* each Friday that shows, for each commodity traded, current trading statistics, including a breakdown of speculative and hedge positions among large (reportable) traders and aggregate positions for small (non-reporting) traders. Data from *Commitments of Traders Compressed Reports* are available to the public through a variety of intermediaries. For a list of providers or information on how to obtain historical COT data, contact the Division of Market Oversight, (202) 418–5260, or the CFTC website, www.cftc.gov. The Education Center found on the CFTC website answers basic questions about future markets and how they work, where to go if you need help, and other frequently asked questions.

MEETINGS
The CFTC meets in executive session in the Hearing Room at its headquarters. Meetings are open to the public unless the subject of the meeting is exempt under the Government in the Sunshine Act.

Notices of scheduled commission meetings are posted on the calendar of CFTC's website, www.cftc.gov. The office of the secretariat keeps an up-to-date list of meetings; (202) 418–5100.

REPORTS AND PUBLICATIONS
Trading reports, option reports, market reports, and other commission reports are available from the CFTC Office of External Affairs, (202) 418–5080. Book and brochure offerings include
   Ponzimonium: How Scam Artists are Ripping Off America
   Commodity Futures Trading Commission Overview
   Foreign Currency Trading Fraud
   Whistleblower Program

Reference Resources

LIBRARY

CFTC Library
Three Lafayette Centre
1155 21st St. N.W.
Washington, DC 20581
(202) 418–5254
Daniel May, librarian

Generally closed to the public. Interlibrary loan service is available to authorized libraries.

DOCKETS
Federal dockets are available at www.regulations.gov. (*See appendix for information on searching and commenting on regulations.*)

RULES AND REGULATIONS

Rules and regulations of the CFTC are published in the *Code of Federal Regulations,* Title 5, Chapter XLI, Part 5101; Title 17, Chapter I, Parts 1–199. Proposed regulations, new final regulations, and updates to the *Code of Federal Regulations* are published in the daily *Federal Register.* (*See appendix for details on how to obtain and use these publications.*)

■ LEGISLATION

The CFTC carries out its responsibilities under

Grain Futures Act (42 Stat. 998, 7 U.S.C. 1–17). Signed by the president Sept. 21, 1922. Empowered the secretary of agriculture to give markets the federal authority to trade commodities or to revoke markets' authority.

Commodity Exchange Act (49 Stat. 1491, 7 U.S.C. chap. 1). Signed by the president June 15, 1936. Established the Commodity Exchange Authority in the Agriculture Department to regulate commodity brokerage activities and commodity fraud.

Bank Secrecy Act (31 U.S.C. 5311 et seq.). Also known as the Currency and Foreign Transaction Reporting Act. Signed by the president Oct. 26, 1970. Required financial institutions to file reports to the United States Treasury for certain currency transactions. Designed to detect and prevent money laundering.

Commodity Futures Trading Commission Act of 1974 (88 Stat. 1389, 7 U.S.C. 4a). Signed by the president Oct. 23, 1974. Amended the Commodity Exchange Act and established the CFTC as an independent agency to replace the Commodity Exchange Authority.

Futures Trading Act of 1978 (92 Stat. 865, 7 U.S.C. chap. 1). Signed by the president Sept. 30, 1978. Reauthorized the CFTC to Sept. 30, 1982.

Futures Trading Act of 1982 (96 Stat. 2294, 7 U.S.C. chap. 1). Signed by the president Jan. 11, 1983. Reauthorized the CFTC to Sept. 30, 1986. Delineated more clearly the jurisdiction of the CFTC and Securities and Exchange Commission (SEC). Required the National Futures Association (NFA) to begin actively sharing regulatory responsibilities with the CFTC.

Futures Trading Act of 1986 (100 Stat. 3556, 7 U.S.C. chap. 1). Signed by the president Nov. 10, 1986. Reauthorized the CFTC to Sept. 30, 1989. Required the CFTC to maintain communication with the Securities and Exchange Commission, the Federal Reserve Board, and the Treasury Department.

Futures Trading Practices Act of 1992 (106 Stat. 3590, 7 U.S.C. 1 note). Signed by the president Oct. 28, 1992. Reauthorized the CFTC to Sept. 30, 1994. Required futures exchanges to put in place electronic or computerized systems to audit and monitor all floor trades. Authorized the CFTC to exempt certain new financial instruments, such as swaps or hybrids, from regulations applied to other futures products.

Commodity Futures Modernization Act (114 Stat. 2763, 7 U.S.C. chap. 1). Signed by the president Dec. 21, 2000. Created a flexible structure for the regulation of futures trading, codified an agreement between the CFTC and the SEC to repeal the ban on trading single stock futures, and provided regulation for the over-the-counter derivatives markets.

Uniting and Strengthening America by Providing Appropriate Tools Required to Intercept and Obstruct Terrorism Act of 2001 (USA Patriot Act) (115 Stat. 272, 18 U.S.C. 1 note). Signed by the president Oct. 26, 2001. Required registered securities brokers and dealers, futures commission merchants, commodity trading advisers, and commodity pool operators to file reports of suspicious financial transactions and share monetary instruments transactions records upon request of a U.S. intelligence agency for use in the conduct of intelligence or counter-intelligence activities to protect against international terrorism.

USA Patriot Act Additional Reauthorizing Amendments Act of 2006 (18 U.S.C. 1 note). Signed by the president March 9, 2006. Reauthorized the USA Patriot Act and made permanent fourteen of its sixteen sections. Placed a four-year sunset provision on the other two sections: the authority to conduct "roving" surveillance under the Foreign Intelligence Surveillance Act (FISA) and the authority to request production of business records under FISA.

CFTC Reauthorization Act of 2008 (122 Stat. 1651, 7 U.S.C. 1 et seq.). Title XIII of the Food, Conservation, and Energy Act of 2008. Vetoed by the president May 21, 2008; veto overridden May 22, 2008/June 18, 2008. Reauthorized the CFTC through 2013. Enhanced agency authority over off-exchange retail foreign currency. Strengthened the CFTC's oversight over contracts trading on exempt commercial markets. Required the CFTC to issue a proposed rule regarding the significant price discovery standards within 180 days of the date of enactment and a final rule within 270 days. Increased civil and criminal penalties for violations such as manipulation, attempted manipulation, and false reporting.

Dodd-Frank Wall Street Reform and Consumer Protection Act (124 Stat. 1376, 12 U.S.C. 5301 note). Signed by the president July 21, 2010. Authorizes the Commodity Futures Trading Commission (CFTC) to regulate the swaps marketplace, which was previously unregulated. With some exceptions, directs the CFTC and the Securities and Exchange Commission (SEC) to coordinate with each other and with the prudential regulators (the Federal Reserve Board, the Office of the Comptroller of the Currency, the Federal Deposit Insurance Corporation, the Farm Credit Administration, and the Federal Housing Finance Agency) before commencing any rulemaking or issuing an order regarding swaps, swap dealers, major swap participants, swap repositories, persons associated with a swap dealer or major swap participant, eligible contract participants, or swap execution facilities. SEC and CFTC are authorized to establish margin requirements for swaps dealers that are not primarily regulated by the prudential regulators. Other provisions.

Consolidated and Further Continuing Appropriations Act, 2015 (Public Law 113-235). Signed by the president Dec. 16, 2014. Section 630 of the omnibus appropriations bill repeals section 716 of the Dodd-Frank Wall Street Reform and Consumer Protection Act, which prohibits federal assistance to financial institutions that engage in certain derivatives activities.

▉ REGIONAL OFFICES

EASTERN REGION
140 Broadway, 19th Floor
New York, NY 10005
(646) 746–9700
Fax (646) 746–9938
TTY (646) 746–9820

CENTRAL REGION
525 W. Monroe St., #1100
Chicago, IL 60661
(312) 596–0700
Fax (312) 596–0716
TTY (312) 596–0565

SOUTHWESTERN REGION
4900 Main St. #500
Kansas City, MO 64112
(816) 960–7700
Fax (816) 960–7750
TTY (816) 960–7704

SELECTED SELF-REGULATORY ORGANIZATIONS

National Futures Association
300 S. Riverside Plaza, #1800
Chicago, IL 60606
(312) 781–1300
(800) 621–3570
Fax (312) 781–1467
Information center (312) 781–1410
E-mail: information@nfa.futures.org
Internet: www.nfa.futures.org

REGULATED MARKETS

Chicago Board Options Exchange
400 S. LaSalle St.
Chicago, IL 60605
(312) 786–5600
(877) THE-CBOE
Fax (312) 786–7409
Internet: www.cboe.com

CME Group
20 S. Wacker Dr.
Chicago, IL 60606
(312) 930–1000

(866) 716–7274
E-mail: info@cmegroup.com
Internet: www.cmegroup.com

ICEFutures U.S.
1 North End Ave.
New York, NY 10282–1101
(212) 748–4000
Ice Help Desk (770) 738–2101
E-mail: icehelpdesk@theice.com
Internet: www.theice.com

Kansas City Board of Trade
4800 Main St., #303
Kansas City, MO 64112
(816) 753–7500
Fax (816) 753–3944
E-mail: agriculture@cmegroup.com
Internet: www.cmegroup.com/trading/agricultural

Minneapolis Grain Exchange
400 S. Fourth St.
130 Grain Exchange Bldg.
Minneapolis, MN 55415
(612) 321–7101
(800) 827–4746
E-mail: mgex@mgex.com
Internet: www.mgex.com

NASDAQ
One Liberty Plaza
165 Broadway
New York, NY 10006
(212) 401–8700
Internet: www.nasdaq.com

New York Mercantile Exchange
World Financial Headquarters
One North End Ave.
New York, NY 10282–1102
(212) 299–2000
Fax: (212) 301–4711
Internet: www.cmegroup.com/company/
    nymex.html

OneChicago
311 S. Wacker Dr., #1700
Chicago, IL 60606
(312) 883-3410
Media (312) 883-3440
E-mail: info@OneChicago.com
Internet: www.onechicago.com

Consumer Financial Protection Bureau

1500 Pennsylvania Ave. N.W., Washington, DC 20220
Internet: www.consumerfinance.gov

The Consumer Financial Protection Bureau (CFPB) was authorized by Title X of the Dodd-Frank Wall Street Reform and Consumer Protection Act of 2010 as an independent agency in the Federal Reserve System, headed by a director nominated by the president and confirmed by the Senate. CFPB is not funded through a direct congressional appropriation—it is funded as a fixed percentage of the Federal Reserve's operating budget. CFPB was charged with regulating consumer financial products and services under federal consumer financial laws. The Treasury Secretary was responsible for setting up the CFPB. President Barack Obama appointed Harvard professor Elizabeth Warren as special Adviser to the Treasury secretary for the Consumer Financial Protection Bureau and on July 18, 2011, nominated Richard Cordray to be the CFPB's first director.

The CFPB was created in response to the economic crisis that began unfolding in 2007, fueled by the collapse of the housing market. A report released by U.S. Senate Permanent Subcommittee on Investigations in April 2011 pointed to several causes of the crisis, including high-risk mortgage lending, inflated credit ratings, structured products sold by investment banks, and repeated failures of regulatory agencies to provide adequate oversight of the financial services industry. The Senate report verified what many economists and financial analysts (and best-selling authors) had previously published in various media outlets.

The CFPB was intended to increase government oversight and accountability by consolidating various consumer financial protections, which had previously been charged among various other government entities. The Dodd-Frank Act transferred to the CFPB director specific consumer financial protection functions from the following entities: the Federal Reserve Board; the Comptroller of the Currency; the Office of Thrift Supervision director; the Federal Deposit Insurance Corporation (FDIC); the Federal Trade Commission (FTC); the National Credit Union Administration (NCUA); the Secretary of Housing and Urban Development (HUD) (relating to the Real Estate Settlement Procedures Act of 1974 and the Secure and Fair Enforcement for Mortgage Licensing Act of 2008); and the prudential regulators (Federal Reserve Board, the Office of the Comptroller of the Currency, the Federal Deposit Insurance Corporation, the Farm Credit Administration and the Federal Housing Finance Agency). CFPB reviews and streamlines regulations that it inherited from other agencies pursuant to a transfer of rulemaking authority under the Dodd-Frank Act.

The CFPB has exclusive rulemaking authority to the extent that a federal consumer financial law authorizes the CFPB and another federal agency to issue regulations to assure compliance with such law. CFPB is also responsible for supervision and rulemaking affecting certain nondepository covered persons, including those who offer or provide origination, brokerage, or servicing of loans secured by real estate for use by consumers primarily for personal, family, or household purposes or loan modification or foreclosure relief services in connection with such loans, including private education and payday loans.

Several entities and industries were exempted from CFPB supervisory or rulemaking authority: real estate brokers; retailers of manufactured and modular homes; certified public accountants and tax preparers; attorneys; persons regulated by state insurance regulators or state securities commissions; employee benefit and compensation plans and certain other arrangements; persons in offices or positions regulated by the Securities Exchange Commission (SEC), the Commodity Futures Trading Commission (CFTC), or the Farm Credit Administration; activities related to charitable contributions; and auto dealers.

The CFPB has three primary divisions: handling education, research, and enforcement. The CFPB also has administrative divisions (Operations, External Affairs, and Legal) that are responsible for day-to-day agency functions.

The Consumer Education and Engagement Division promotes financial education and manages a center to take consumer complaints. Within this division is the Office of Financial Education, which is required to establish a grants program for states or eligible entities to investigate and prosecute misleading and fraudulent marketing practices. In addition, the division addresses education for seniors to increase awareness and understanding of misleading or fraudulent marketing as well as address consumer crimes against seniors. This division manages the "Know Before You Owe" series of projects undertaken by CFPB to simplify some of the documents consumers rely on to make financial choices for themselves and their families. This includes mortgages, student loans, and credit cards.

The Research, Markets and Regulations Division conducts rulemaking for federal consumer financial protection laws and researches consumer behavior. The division also is responsible for monitoring financial markets for new risks to consumers. These markets include mortgage and home equity markets; credit cards and prepaid card markets; installment lending markets; deposit payment markets, and credit information markets.

The Supervision, Fair Lending, and Enforcement Division restricts unfair, deceptive, or abusive acts or practices and enforces laws that prohibit discrimination and fraudulent activity in consumer finance. The division implements and enforces protections under the Dodd-Frank Act that require mortgage lenders to determine that a borrower has the ability to repay a loan by adequately verifying income; prohibit prepayment penalties, which can make it expensive to refinance for high-cost loans and adjustable-rate mortgages; prohibit practices such as paying bonuses to mortgage brokers and loan officers who steer borrowers into higher-cost loans than they otherwise qualify for; and require clearer and simpler disclosure about international money transfers. In FY14, CFPB's enforcement efforts helped secure orders for more than $2.4 billion in relief for consumers who fell victim to various violations of consumer financial protection laws.

However, before the CFPB assumed full operations, ideological battles took place in Congress over the direction of the agency. A Republican-controlled House viewed the new CFPB as too powerful and sought to change the leadership structure and reduce the authority of the agency. Republicans sponsored legislation that would replace the director of the agency with a five-member bipartisan board. Another bill sought to make it easier for other banking regulators to veto regulations developed by the CFPB. Other bills sought to chip away at institutions and businesses that would be subjected to the regulations prescribed by the Dodd-Frank Act. In May 2011 forty-four Senate Republicans threatened to block President Obama's expected nomination of Elizabeth Warren as the director of the CFPB. Democrats called on the president to appoint Warren during a congressional recess. However, the president instead nominated Richard Cordray in July 2011; after contentious negotiations, he was confirmed by the Senate on July 17, 2013. Elizabeth Warren was elected to the Senate in 2012; she was appointed to the Banking Committee.

In January 2015 federal financial regulatory agencies, in partnership with the State Liaison Committee (SLC) of the Federal Financial Institutions Examination Council, issued guidance for financial institutions on private student loans with graduated repayment terms at origination. Graduated repayment terms are structured to provide for lower initial monthly payments that gradually increase. The agencies—the Board of Governors of the Federal Reserve System, the Consumer Financial Protection Bureau, the Federal Deposit Insurance Corporation, the National Credit Union Administration, and the Office of the Comptroller of the Currency—urged private student loan originators to adhere to six principles: ensure orderly repayment; avoid payment shock; align payment terms with a borrower's income; provide borrowers with clear disclosures; comply with all applicable federal and state consumer laws, regulations and reporting standards; and contact borrowers before reset dates.

Financial Stability Oversight Council

The Dodd-Frank Act also created the Financial Stability Oversight Council. The Financial Stability Oversight Council has ten voting members: secretary of the Treasury (chairs the council); comptroller of the currency; the Federal Reserve chairperson; director of the Consumer Financial Protection Bureau; SEC chairperson; FDIC chairperson; CFTC chairperson; director of the Federal Housing Finance Agency; NCUA chairperson; an independent insurance expert appointed by the president and approved by the Senate.

The council, among many responsibilities, is required to identify risks to U.S. financial stability that could arise from the material financial distress or failure, or ongoing activities, of large, interconnected bank holding companies or nonbank financial companies or that could arise outside the financial services marketplace. The council is also responsible for identifying gaps in regulation that could pose risks to U.S. financial stability. In addition, the council is charged with requiring supervision by the Federal Reserve Board for nonbank financial companies that may pose risks to U.S. financial stability in the event of their material financial distress or failure.

The council, on the petition of one of its member agencies, is authorized to set aside a final CFPB regulation or any of its provisions if the council decides via a two-thirds majority vote that the regulation or provision would put the safety and soundness of the U.S. banking system or the stability of the U.S. financial system at risk. The CFPB is the only banking regulatory agency subject to such a ruling.

■ KEY PERSONNEL

Director
  Richard Cordray . . . . (202) 435–7000
Deputy Director
  Steven Antonakes . . . . (202) 435–7000
Chief of Staff
  Christopher D'Angelo . . . . (202) 435–7000
Administrative Law Judge
  Cameron Elliot
Ombudsman
  Wendy Kamenshine . . . . (202) 435–9835
Associate Director for Consumer Education and Engagement
  Gail Hillebrand . . . . (202) 435–7937
  Consumer Engagement
    Gene Koo, assistant director . . . . . (202) 435–7937
  Financial Education
    Janneke Ratcliffe, assistant
       director . . . . (202) 435–7937
  Financial Empowerment
    Daniel Dodd-Ramierez,
       assistant director . . . . (202) 435–7485
  Older Americans
    Nora Dowd Eisenhower, assistant
       director . . . . (202) 435–7954

Servicemember Affairs
Hollister Petraeus, assistant
director . . . . (202) 435–7275
Students
Seth Frotman (acting), assistant
director . . . . (202) 435–7170
Associate Director for External Affairs
Zixta Martinez . . . . (202) 435–7204
Fax . . . . (202) 435–7244
Communications
Jennifer Howard, assistant
director . . . . (202) 435–7170
Community Affairs
Chris Vaeth, assistant director . . . . . (202) 435–7216
Office of Financial Institutions and Business Liaisons
Daniel Smith, assistant director . . . . (202) 435–7971
Consumer Advisory Board and Councils
Delicia Hand, staff director . . . . . . (202) 435–9348
Intergovernmental Affairs
Cheryl Parker-Rose, assistant director
Legislative Affairs
Catherine Galicia, assistant
director . . . . (202) 435–7960
Associate Director for Legal and General Counsel
Meredith Fuchs . . . . (202) 435–7091
Principal Deputy General Counsel
Vacant, deputy associate director
Deputy General Counsel for General Law and Ethics
Richard Lepley, assistant director . . . (202) 435–7091
Deputy General Counsel for Oversight, Litigation, and Enforcement Support
To-Quyen Truong, assistant director (202) 435–7434
Deputy General Counsel for Law and Policy
Stephen Van Meter, assistant
director . . . . (202) 435–7434
Associate Director for Operations (Chief Operating Officer)
Sartaj Alag . . . . (202) 435–7489
Chief Administrative Officer
Suzanne Tosini, assistant director . . . (202) 435–7209
Chief Financial Officer
Stephen Agostini, assistant
director . . . . (202) 435–7143
Chief Human Capital Officer
Jeffrey Sumberg, assistant director . . . .(202) 435–7143
Chief Information Officer for Technology and Innovation
Ashwin Vasan, assistant director . . . (202) 435–9575
Office of Consumer Response
Scott Pluta, assistant director . . . . (202) 435–7306
Office of Equal Employment Opportunity and Civil Rights
M. Stacey Bach, assistant director . . . (202) 435–9336
Office of Minority and Women Inclusion
Stuart Ishimaru, assistant director . . . .(202) 435–9012
Chief Procurement Officer
David Gragan, assistant
director . . . . (202) 435–7192
Associate Director for Research, Markets, and Regulations
David Silberman . . . . (202) 435–7700

Research
Christopher Carroll, assistant
director . . . . (202) 435–7381
Card Markets
William Wade-Gery, assistant
director . . . . (202) 435–7700
Deposits, Liquidity Lending, and Reporting Markets
Bayard Stone Jr., assistant director (202) 435–9734
Installment Lending and Collections Markets
Jeffrey Langer, assistant director . . (202) 435–9158
Mortgage Markets
Patricia McClung, assistant
director . . . . (202) 435–7150
Regulations
Kelly Cochran, assistant
director . . . . (202) 435–7149
Associate Director for Supervision, Enforcement, and Fair Lending
Steven Antonakes . . . . (202) 435–7000
Enforcement
Anthony Alexis, assistant director . . (202) 435–7944
Fair Lending and Equal Opportunity
Patrice Ficklin, assistant director . . . (202) 435–9599
Office of Supervision Examinations
Paul Sanford, assistant director. . . (202) 435–7000
Office of Supervision Policy
Peggy Twohig, assistant director. . . (202) 435–7168
Consumer Advisory Board
Delicia Hand . . . . (202) 552–6380
E-mail: CAB@cbpg.gov
Community Bank Advisory Council
Tyrone Fenderson . . . . (202) 435–9336
E-mail: CBAC@cfpb.gov
Credit Union Advisory Council
Rose Bartolomucci . . . . (202) 435–7176
E-mail: UAC@cfpb.gov
Academic Research Council
Raphael Bostic . . . . (202) 435–9064
E-mail: ARC@cfpb.gov
Financial Stability Oversight Council (U.S. Department of the Treasury)
Kathryn Blandford . . . . (202) 927–8776
Fax . . . . (202) 622–6415
Office of the Inspector General
Mark Bialek, inspector general . . . . . . (202) 973–5005
Fax . . . . (202) 973–5044
IG Hotline . . . . (202) 452–6400

■ INFORMATION SOURCES

Internet

Agency website: www.consumerfinance.gov. The user-friendly site includes financial literacy material covering credit issues, home ownership, student loans, debt collection, and more. The site also includes multimedia and social media: there is an archive of informational videos for consumers; a blog; and links to Facebook, Flickr, YouTube, and Twitter.

Telephone Contacts

Switchboard . . . .(202) 435–7000
Claire Shelton, CFPB initiation team .(202) 435–7220
Whistleblower hotline . . . .(855) 695–7974
Credit Card complaints. . . . .(855) 729–2372

Information and Publications

KEY OFFICES

Consumer Help

Consumer Financial Protection Bureau
P.O. Box 4503
Iowa City, IA 52244
(855) 411–CFPB (2372)
TTY (855) 729–CFPB (2372)
Fax (855) 237–2392
8:00 a.m. to 8:00 p.m. eastern time, Monday–Friday
180+ languages available

Communications Office

1700 G St. N.W.
Washington, DC 20552
(202) 435–7454
Fax (202) 435–7244
Jennifer Howard, assistant director, (202) 435–7170
E-mail: press@consumerfinance.gov

Freedom of Information

1700 G St. N.W.
Washington, DC 20552
(855) 444–FOIA (3642)
Fax: (855) FAX–FOIA (329–3642)
E-mail: FOIA@cfpb.gov
Mark Vugrinovich, public liaison

ADVISORY COMMITTEE MEETINGS

Agendas and records of all advisory committee meetings are available from the CFPB website, www.con sumer finance.gov. Details, including video recordings, of meetings of the Consumer Advisory Board are also available on the agency blog site, www.consumerfinance.gov/blog/category/consumer-advisory-board.

RULES AND REGULATIONS

Consumer Financial Protection Bureau rules and regulations are contained in the *Code of Federal Regulations,* Title 12, Chapter X. Proposed rules, updates to the *Code of Federal Regulations,* and new final rules are published in the daily *Federal Register.* (*See appendix for information on how to obtain and use these publications.*)

◼ LEGISLATION

The Consumer Financial Protection Bureau carries out its responsibilities under

Federal Deposit Insurance Act (12 U.S.C. 1831t[c]–[f]). Signed by the president Sept. 21, 1951. Section 43 set forth the guidelines whereby privately insured depository institutions must notify consumers that the institution is not federally insured and that if the institution fails, the federal government does not guarantee that the depositor will get back the depositor's money.

Truth in Lending Act (82 Stat. 146, 15 U.S.C. 1601). Signed by the president May 29, 1968. Required lenders and merchants to inform consumers of total cost of loans and installment purchase plans and to state annual percentage rate clearly. Also prohibited unsolicited distribution of credit cards.

Interstate Land Sales Full Disclosure Act (82 Stat. 590, 15 U.S.C. 1701). Signed by the president Aug. 1, 1968. Title XIV of the Housing and Urban Development Act of 1968. Established regulations for the sale or lease of subdivision lots to prevent consumer fraud. Required sellers to make available certain information about the land involved and to furnish purchasers with a property report approved by HUD.

Fair Credit Reporting Act (84 Stat. 1128, 15 U.S.C. 1681 et seq.). Signed by the president Oct. 26, 1970. Required that credit reports be accurate and allowed consumers to correct faulty information in their reports. Also required that credit reports be kept confidential and that only properly authorized entities be allowed access to the reports.

Equal Credit Opportunity Act (88 Stat. 1521, 15 U.S.C. 1691). Signed by the president Oct. 28, 1974. Prohibited credit discrimination against women; amended in 1976 to include discrimination based on age, race, religion, or national origin (90 Stat. 251).

Fair Credit Billing Act (88 Stat. 1521, 15 U.S.C. 1666 et seq.). Signed by the president Oct. 28, 1974. Amended the Truth in Lending Act by setting up a mechanism that consumers can use to dispute billing errors and requiring creditors to take steps to correct billing errors.

Real Estate Settlement Procedures Act (88 Stat. 1724, 12 U.S.C. 2601). Signed by the president Dec. 22, 1974. Minimized settlement charges for home buyers; confirmed the authority of the Department of Housing and Urban Development to set standards for settlement charges on homes financed through federally guaranteed mortgages.

Home Mortgage Disclosure Act (89 Stat. 1125, 12 U.S.C. 2801). Signed by the president Dec. 31, 1975. Required lending institutions within standard metropolitan statistical areas (SMSA) to disclose the number and amount of mortgage loans made yearly to determine if banks are discriminating against certain city neighborhoods by refusing to make mortgage loans regardless of the creditworthiness of the potential borrower (the practice known as "redlining").

Fair Debt Collection Practices Act (91 Stat. 874, 15 U.S.C. 1692). Signed by the president Sept. 20, 1977. Regulated methods used by debt collection agencies.

Consumer Leasing Act of 1976 (90 Stat. 257, 15 U.S.C. 1667 et seq.). Signed by the president March 23, 1976. Amended the Truth in Lending Act to regulate personal property leases that exceed four months in duration and that are made to consumers for personal, family, or household purposes. The statute requires that certain lease costs and terms be disclosed, imposes limitations on the size of penalties for delinquency or default and on the size of residual liabilities, and requires certain disclosures in lease advertising.

Electronic Fund Transfer Act of 1978 (92 Stat. 3728, 15 U.S.C. 1601 note). Signed by the president Nov. 10, 1978. Established rules relating to consumer liability for unauthorized use of an electronic fund transfer card and unsolicited issuance of cards by financial institutions. Prohibited creditors from making automatic repayment of loans a condition of extending credit; overdraft plans were exempted.

Garn–St. Germain Depository Institutions Act of 1982 (96 Stat. 1469, 12 U.S.C. 3801 et seq.). Signed by the president October 15, 1982. Title VIII: The Alternative Mortgage Transaction Parity Act of 1982 authorized all housing creditors to make, purchase, and enforce alternative mortgage transactions so long as the transactions are in conformity with the regulations issued by the federal banking regulatory agencies.

Truth in Savings Act (105 Stat. 2334, 12 U.S.C. 4301 note). Signed by the president Dec. 19, 1991. Subtitle F of the FDIC Improvement Act of 1991 provided uniformity in the disclosure of terms and conditions on which interest is paid and fees are assessed in connection with savings accounts.

Home Ownership and Equity Protection Act of 1994 (108 Stat 2160, 15 U.S.C. 1601 note.) Signed by the president Sept. 23, 1994. Amends the Truth in Lending Act to set forth disclosure requirements for certain (closed-end) consumer credit transactions secured by a consumer's principal dwelling (other than a residential mortgage transaction, a reverse mortgage transaction, or a transaction under an open-end credit plan) that meet specified criteria. Amends the Truth in Lending Act to require a creditor to conspicuously disclose specified lending data to a consumer in connection with reverse mortgage transactions.

Homeowners Protection Act of 1998 (112 Stat. 897, 12 U.S.C. 4901 et seq.). Signed by the president July 29, 1998. Prescribes guidelines for mandatory termination of private mortgage insurance (PMI) for a residential mortgage when the principal balance is first scheduled to reach or actually reaches 80 percent of the original value of the property securing the mortgage loan.

Gramm-Leach-Bliley Act (113 Stat. 1338, 12 U.S.C. 1811 note). Signed by the president Nov. 12, 1999. Sections 502–509 established protections for consumers against unauthorized release of nonpublic information to unaffiliated third parties for marketing purposes. Amends the Fair Credit Reporting Act enforcement guidelines to require federal banking agencies to jointly prescribe regulations governing dissemination by holding companies and their affiliates of customer nonpublic personal information.

Secure and Fair Enforcement (SAFE) for Mortgage Licensing Act of 2008 (122 Stat. 2654, 12 U.S.C. Sec. 5101 et seq.). Title V of the Housing and Economic Recovery Act. Signed by the president July 30, 2008. Required federal banking agencies jointly, through the Federal Financial Institutions Examination Council, to develop and maintain a national system to register loan originators. Defined "federal banking agencies" as the Federal Reserve System, the Comptroller of the Currency, the Office of Thrift Supervision, the National Credit Union Administration, and the Federal Deposit Insurance Corporation.

Omnibus Appropriations Act of 2009 (123 Stat. 524, 15 USC 1638 note). Signed by the president on March 11, 2009. Section 626 directs the Federal Trade Commission to issue rules relating to unfair or deceptive acts or practices regarding mortgage loans, including loan modification and foreclosure rescue services. It also authorizes the FTC to enforce the rules and obtain civil penalties for violations. The Dodd-Frank Act transfers the rulemaking authority to the Consumer Financial Protection Bureau.

Credit Card Accountability Responsibility and Disclosure Act (CARD Act) of 2009 (123 Stat. 1734, 15 U.S.C. 1601 note). Signed by the president May 22, 2009. Places restrictions on financial institutions regarding hikes in credit card interest rates. Required more transparency in credit card terms and transactions for consumers. Restricted financial institutions from using certain types of marketing practices on college campuses. Also made agreements between credit card issuers and institutions of higher education subject to public disclosure. The Dodd-Frank Act transferred regulatory authority of the CARD Act to the Consumer Financial Protection Bureau.

Dodd-Frank Wall Street Reform and Consumer Protection Act (124 Stat. 1376, 12 U.S.C. 5301 note). Signed by the president July 21, 2010. Title X (the Consumer Financial Protection Act) establishes an independent Bureau of Consumer Financial Protection in the Federal Reserve System, headed by a director nominated by the president and confirmed by the Senate, to regulate consumer financial products or services under federal consumer financial laws. Authorizes the Federal Reserve Board to delegate to the bureau the authority to examine persons subject to board jurisdiction for compliance with federal consumer financial laws. Grants the bureau exclusive rulemaking authority to the extent that a federal consumer financial law authorizes the bureau and another federal agency to issue regulations to assure compliance with such law. Transferred regulatory authority of various consumer financial protections laws to the CFPB.

FDIC Amendments (126 Stat. 1589). Signed by the president on Dec. 20, 2012. Amends the Federal Deposit Insurance Act to make the Consumer Financial Protection Bureau (CFPB) a covered agency that may share information with another covered agency or any other federal agency without waiving any privilege applicable to the information.

National Defense Authorization Act for Fiscal Year 2013; Military Lending Act amendments (126 Stat. 1785, 10 U.S.C. 987). Signed by the president Jan. 2, 2013. Subtitle G declared the Military Lending Act is enforceable in the same manner as the Truth in Lending Act by the Federal Deposit Insurance Corporation, member banks of the Federal Reserve System, Office of the Comptroller of the Currency, National Credit Union Administration, Consumer Financial Protection Bureau, Federal Trade Commission, and certain other specified agencies.

Examination and Supervisory Privilege Parity Act of 2014 (128 Stat. 1899, 12 U.S.C. 5301 note). Signed by the president Sept. 26, 2014. Requires the Consumer Financial Protection Bureau to coordinate its supervisory activities with the supervisory activities of the state agencies that license, supervise, or examine the offering of consumer financial products or services.

Election Assistance Commission

1335 East West Highway, #4300, Silver Spring, MD 20910
Internet: www.eac.gov

The Election Assistance Commission (EAC), an independent bipartisan agency, was created by the Help America Vote Act (HAVA) of 2002 to serve as a clearinghouse for the dissemination of election and voting information to all voters. The EAC also dispenses funds to states for the replacement of voting systems and for making election-related improvements, provides testing and certification of voting equipment and software, and produces voluntary voting system guidelines. The EAC assumed the clearinghouse function of the Federal Election Commission's Office of Election Administration, which for many years had been collecting information on election procedures and making it available to federal, state, and local election officials.

Under HAVA, the EAC is composed of four commissioners appointed by the president and subject to confirmation by the Senate. Only two commissioners can be of the same political party. The commissioners are required to brief the public on the EAC's activities and accomplishments on an ongoing basis.

Each January the commission submits an annual report to Congress detailing the commission's activities during the previous fiscal year, including detailed information on programs, grant payments, grant recipient reports, adoption of voluntary voting standards, and votes taken by the commission.

The executive director of the EAC serves a term of four years and may serve for a longer period if reappointed by a vote of the commission. The executive director's duties include managing the operations of the commission, preparing the commission's mission statements and long-term plans, developing voluntary voting system guidelines, reviewing all reports and study recommendations submitted by the commission, and appointing EAC staff members and consultants.

In the wake of the controversial 2000 presidential election, Congress passed HAVA to ensure that outdated voting systems and other obstacles did not infringe on the right of Americans to vote. The law was enacted to "establish a program to provide funds to states to replace punch-card voting systems, to establish the Election Assistance Commission to assist in the administration of Federal elections and to otherwise provide assistance with the administration of certain Federal election laws and programs, to establish minimum election administration standards for States and units of local government with responsibility for the administration of Federal elections, and for other purposes."

The act required that the EAC generate technical guidance on the administration of federal elections, produce voluntary voting systems guidelines, and research and report on matters affecting the administration of federal elections. One of the most important responsibilities of the EAC is to test and certify voting equipment and software and to disseminate this information so that states can decide what technology to purchase. The EAC also keeps the public informed on all issues related to voting through publications, mail, radio, television, and the Internet.

The 2004 national elections were the first in which the EAC provided voting assistance to the states. In that year 45.4 million people, or 29 percent of the nation's voters, used new electronic voting machines, up from just 12 percent in 2000. One provision of HAVA required the use of provisional ballots, and the EAC assisted many states before the 2004 election in setting up the procedure for the first time. A provisional ballot allows a voter to cast a ballot on a conditional basis. The ballot is not counted until the voter's eligibility is confirmed, often after Election Day. In 2009 the EAC reported that more than 189 million voters were eligible and registered for the November 2008 general election, in which 33 percent cast ballots via electronic voting machines.

The EAC also oversees the implementation of the National Voter Registration Act of 1993, also known as the "Motor Voter Act." Congress enacted the Motor Voter Act to enhance voting opportunities and simplify the registration process, thereby making it easier for Americans to vote. The act required that voter registration be made available when an individual applies for a driver's license or renewal. Voter registration opportunities must also be offered to every qualified applicant when requesting address changes or seeking services at all public assistance offices and from all state-funded programs that provide services to persons with disabilities. Also, under the act, voter registration must be accepted via mail-in forms developed by the Federal Election Commission.

Section 703 of HAVA also directs the EAC, following each federal election, to collect and publish comprehensive data from the states on all of the ballots sent and received by voters covered by the Uniformed and Overseas

Citizens Absentee Voting Act of 1986. Following the 2004 elections, the EAC published its first best-practices report in March 2006 to meet this mandate.

Specific program areas and responsibilities of the EAC include

- Voting systems—consults with the National Institute of Standards and Technology and the Technical Guidelines Committee to develop voluntary voting system guidelines and a national program for the testing, certification, and decertification of voting systems and equipment.
- Voter registration—maintains the national voter registration form required by the Motor Voter Act, provides information to the states concerning their legal responsibilities under the act, and submits congressional reports every two years on the effects of the act on federal elections.
- Payments and grants—administers programs that delegate federal funds to the states to meet HAVA requirements; finances the development of election technology and pilot programs to test new voting technology; funds programs to encourage youth participation and interest in the voting process; and audits persons who received federal funds authorized by HAVA from the General Services Administration or the EAC.
- Research—studies and reports on practices and other topics relevant to the effective administration of federal elections.
- Outreach—communicates information and technical guidance on the laws, procedures, technology, studies, and data relevant to the administration of federal elections to Congress, the media, and all interested persons; and keeps voters informed of local information, such as polling places and times.

HAVA provided for the establishment of two boards to advise the commission: the Standards Board and the Board of Advisors. The Standards Board (acting through its executive board) and the Board of Advisors review proposed voluntary voting system guidelines and EAC technical guidance. The boards may hold hearings and take testimony related to carrying out the HAVA provisions. The boards also recommend candidates for the EAC executive director.

The Standards Board is composed of 110 members drawn from state and local election officials. Terms of service for Standards Board members are not specified. The Standards Board is required to select nine of its members to serve as the executive board of the Standards Board. Members of the executive board serve two-year terms, and they may not serve more than three consecutive terms. The length of service for first members on the board was staggered, with three serving one term, three serving two consecutive terms, and three serving three consecutive terms.

The Board of Advisors is composed of thirty-seven members drawn from various national associations and governmental agencies involved in the implementation of the HAVA and from professionals in science and technology,

appointed by Congress. Members of the Board of Advisors serve two-year terms and may be reappointed.

HAVA required that all EAC boards have partisan and geographic balance. Members of the boards are not compensated for their services, but their travel costs are paid in accordance with federal law.

Although military and overseas voting programs are administered by the Defense Department, the EAC works with states to implement the requirements of and funding for the Uniformed and Overseas Citizens Absentee Voting Act (UOCAVA). The Military and Overseas Voter Empowerment (MOVE) Act amends the Help America Vote Act of 2002, regarding use of payment administered by EAC to implement new UOCAVA voting requirements as mandated by the MOVE Act. The MOVE Act authorizes the use of federal write-in absentee ballots in general, special, primary, and runoff elections for federal office and also requires a strategic plan to describe how the state will meet such requirements.

Commissioner Resignations and Suspension of Standards Board and Board of Advisors Activities

Following the 2010 elections, there were several attempts by House Republicans to eliminate the EAC. The Senate failed to act on presidential EAC nominations. The EAC was without a quorum of commissioners beginning in 2010; by the end of 2011, the executive director resigned as did the remaining two commissioners. On January 25, 2012, Mark Robbins, EAC's general counsel and acting executive director, issued a memo suspending all activities of the Standards Board and the Board of Advisors. The memo noted that a commission chair was required to appoint a Designated Federal Official (DFO) for the Standards Board and Board of Advisors (a requirement under the Federal Advisory Committee Act). Because EAC no longer had any commissioners, the commission did not have a chair to appoint the DFOs. As such, Robbins requested that "the EAC Standards Board and Board of Advisors refrain from all official business until further notice and that no expense be incurred to which EAC will be liable." Mr. Robbins noted in the memo that it was unlikely that the Senate would confirm any new commissioners in 2012. Mr. Robbins resigned in May 2012. As the EAC remained without commissioners, agency staff carried out various operational functions but could not make policy decisions.

Future of the EAC

With the EAC crippled, President Barack Obama issued Executive Order 13639, Establishment of the Presidential Commission on Election Administration (PCEA) in March 2013. The executive order was issued in response to voting difficulties and unusually long lines during the 2012 national elections. The PCEA issued a report in January 2014. Among its findings, PCEA noted that states were unable to upgrade technology because the non-functioning EAC could not promulgate new standards (existing standards dated back to 2005).

On December 16, 2014, the U.S. Senate voted unanimously to confirm EAC nominees Thomas Hicks, Matthew Masterson, and Christy McCormick as members of the commission. A fourth nominee, Matthew Butler, was awaiting confirmation as the 114th Congress convened.

▓ KEY PERSONNEL

Chair
Christy McCormick . . . . (202) 566–3100
Vice Chair
Thomas Hicks . . . . (202) 566–3100
Commissioners
Matthew Masterson . . . . (202) 566–2365
Vacant
Executive Director
Alice Miller (acting) . . . . (202) 566–3110
Chief Operating Officer
Alice Miller . . . . (202) 566–3110
Administrative Services
Diana M. Scott . . . . (202) 566–3119
Communications and Congressional Affairs
Bryan Whitener . . . . (202) 566–3118
Chief Financial Officer
Annette Lafferty . . . . (202) 566–3100
Chief Information Officer
Mohammed Maeruf . . . . (202) 566–3100
General Counsel
Vacant . . . . (202) 566–3100
Human Resources
Sheila Banks . . . . (202) 566–3100
Inspector General
Curtis Crider . . . . (202) 566–3125
Research
Karen Lynn-Dyson . . . . (202) 566–3100
Voting System Testing and Certification
Brian J. Hancock . . . . (202) 566–3122

▓ INFORMATION SOURCES

Internet

Agency website: www.eac.gov. Includes information on the U.S. federal election system, EAC publications and services, and payments made to states for the replacement of voting systems and other improvements. Also features advisories, guidance, and best practices in election administration, including EAC's Voluntary Voting System Guidelines and types of voting systems.

The EAC develops and maintains the Web-based National Mail Voter Registration Form, accepted in all states covered by the National Voter Registration Act.

Telephone Contacts

Main . . . . (301) 563–3919
Personnel Locator . . . . (202) 566–3100
Fax . . . . (301) 734–3108
Toll-free . . . . (866) 747–1471
Federal Relay Service TTY . . . . (800) 877–8339

Information and Publications

KEY OFFICES

EAC Communications Division
1335 East West Hwy., #4300
Silver Spring, MD 20910
(202) 566–3100
Bryan Whitener, director of communications

Responsible for liaison with the media and answers and refers questions from media representatives.

EAC Research Division
1335 East West Hwy., #4300
Silver Spring, MD 20910
(202) 566–3100
Karen Lynn-Dyson, director

Handles questions on research and reports regarding matters affecting the administration of federal elections.

EAC Voting System Testing and Certification Division
1335 East West Hwy., #4300
Silver Spring, MD 20910
(202) 566–3122
Brian J. Hancock, director

Provides for EAC accreditation of independent voting system test laboratories in conjunction with the National Voluntary Laboratory Accreditation Program of the National Institute of Standards and Technology. Provides procedures for testing, certification, decertification, and recertification of voting systems in accordance with applicable EAC Standards and Guidelines.

EAC Programs and Services Division
1335 East West Hwy., #4300
Silver Spring, MD 20910
(202) 566–3100
Karen Lynn-Dyson, director of research, programs, and policy
Monica Evans, director of payments and grants

Handles questions on grant programs and payments made to states for the replacement of voting systems and election-related improvements. Provides best practices resources to election officials and voters. Coordinates the EAC College Poll Worker Program and the Mock Election Grant Programs.

EAC General Counsel
1335 East West Hwy., #4300
Silver Spring, MD 20910
(202) 566–3100
Vacant, general counsel

Handles questions and comments on EAC advisories and guidance, ethics, compliance matters, the Help America

Vote Act of 2002, the National Voter Registration Act of 1993, and Freedom of Information Act requests. Coordinates public meetings and hearings and serves as legislative liaison to the U.S. Congress.

Freedom of Information

Contact the Communications Division, above.

DATA AND STATISTICS

Voter registration and turnout statistics, including demographic data, and other special reports are available on the EAC website or by calling (202) 566–3100.

MEETINGS

Public hearings and meeting information is available on the EAC website or by calling (202) 566–3100.

PUBLICATIONS

Publications offered by EAC include best practices documents, advisories and guidance regarding the implementation of the Help America Vote Act, surveys and reports such as the Election Day Survey, annual reports and congressional testimonies, toolkits for election administrators, and data on election administration. Other publications include the voluntary voting system guidelines and information about voting system certification and laboratory accreditation. The publications and reports are available on the EAC website or by calling (202) 566–3100.

Reference Resources

DOCKETS

Federal dockets are available at www.regulations.gov. (*See appendix for information on searching and commenting on regulations.*)

RULES AND REGULATIONS

Election Assistance Commission rules and regulations are published in Title 11, Parts 9405, 9407, and 9409 of the *Code of Federal Regulations*. The regulatory authority of the EAC is derived from the National Voter Registration Act (42 U.S.C. 1973gg-1 et seq.) as amended by the Help America Vote Act of 2002 and can be found in the *Code of Federal Regulations* under Title 11, Chapter I, Part 8, which predates the commission's independence from the FEC.

▮ LEGISLATION

National Voter Registration Act of 1993 (107 Stat. 77, 42 U.S.C. 1973gg-1 et seq.). Signed by the president May 20, 1993. Required states to establish federal election voter registration procedures by application made simultaneously with a driver's license application; by mail; and by application in person at a designated office or at the applicant's residential registration site in accordance with state law. Declared that each state motor vehicle license application (or renewal) shall simultaneously serve as a voter registration application with respect to federal elections, unless the applicant fails to sign the voter registration application.

Help America Vote Act of 2002 (116 Stat. 1666, 42 U.S.C. 15301 et seq.). Signed by the president Oct. 29, 2002. Established the EAC as an independent entity to serve as a national resource for information and review of procedures concerning federal elections. Established requirements for voting systems used in federal elections that would allow voters to verify and correct their selections before casting ballots, remove language barriers, and permit provisional voting where eligible voters were not listed on official registration lists. Established the EAC Standards Board and the Board of Advisors to review the EAC's voluntary voting system guidelines. Required the EAC to provide for the testing, certification, decertification, and recertification of voting system hardware and software by accredited laboratories.

Military and Overseas Voter Empowerment (MOVE) Act (123 Stat. 2318, 42 U.S.C. 1971 note). Signed by the president Oct. 28, 2009. Authorizes the use of federal write-in absentee ballots in general, special, primary, and runoff elections for federal office. Amends the Help America Vote Act of 2002 to mandate that states use payment administered by the EAC to meet Uniformed and Overseas Citizens Absentee Voting Act requirements imposed as a result of the MOVE Act amendments. Also requires a strategic plan to describe how the state will meet such requirements.

Farm Credit Administration

1501 Farm Credit Dr., McLean, VA 22102–5090
Internet: www.fca.gov

The Farm Credit Administration (FCA) was established in 1933 by executive order under President Franklin D. Roosevelt. FCA was independent until 1939, when it was moved under the U.S. Department of Agriculture (USDA). The Farm Credit Act of 1953 once again gave the FCA independent status.

The Farm Credit Act of 1971 superseded all prior legislation and recodified the farm credit laws. Today, the FCA is an independent agency responsible for examining and regulating the activities of the Farm Credit System (FCS), a nationwide system of borrower-owned financial institutions organized as cooperatives. Under the Farm Credit Act of 1971, the agency is empowered to issue cease-and-desist orders, levy civil money penalties, remove officers and directors of system institutions, and place such institutions into conservatorship or receivership. The FCA, however, does not mediate disputes between borrowers and FCS financial institutions.

The FCA is the safety and soundness regulator of the FCS. FCA charters, regulates, and examines the banks, associations, and service corporations of the FCS. FCS institutions make loans to agricultural producers and their cooperatives nationwide.

FCA policy is set by a three-member board, appointed by the president and confirmed by the Senate. The chair is designated the chief executive officer. Board members serve six-year terms and are not eligible for reappointment. The FCA board members also serve on the board of the Farm Credit System Insurance Corporation.

The Farm Credit System (FCS) is a network of borrower-owned lending institutions and related service organizations serving all fifty states, the District of Columbia, and Puerto Rico. These institutions specialize in providing credit and related services to farmers, ranchers, and producers or harvesters of aquatic products. Loans may also be made to finance the processing and marketing activities of these borrowers. In addition, loans may be made to rural homeowners; certain farm-related businesses; and agricultural, aquatic, and public utility cooperatives.

All FCS banks and associations are governed by boards of directors elected by the stockholders who are farmer-borrowers of each institution. Federal law also requires that at least one member of the board be elected from outside the FCS by the other directors. FCS institutions, unlike commercial banks or thrifts, do not take deposits.

The FCS is composed of the following lending institutions:

- Three Farm Credit Banks (FCBs) that provide loan funds to fifty Agricultural Credit Associations (ACAs) and one Federal Land Credit Association (FLCA). FCBs make short- and intermediate-term loans, ACAs make short-, intermediate-, and long-term loans, and FLCAs make long-term loans.
- One Agricultural Credit Bank (ACB) has the authority of an FCB and provides loan funds to twenty-six ACAs and one FLCA. In addition, the ACB makes loans of all kinds to agricultural, aquatic, and public utility cooperatives and is authorized to finance U.S. agricultural exports and provide international banking services for farmer-owned cooperatives.

The following FCS entities also are examined and regulated by FCA:

- The Federal Farm Credit Banks Funding Corporation (Funding Corporation) is an entity owned by the FCS banks that markets the securities the banks sell to raise loan funds. FCS institutions obtain the majority of their loan funds through the sale of these securities in the nation's capital markets. These securities, chiefly bonds and discount notes, are offered by the Funding Corporation through a nationwide group of securities dealers and dealer banks.
- The Federal Agricultural Mortgage Corporation, also known as Farmer Mac, provides a secondary market for agricultural real estate and rural housing mortgages. It guarantees the timely payment of principal and interest on securities representing interests in, or obligations backed by, mortgage loans secured by first liens on agricultural real estate or rural housing. It also guarantees securities backed by the "guaranteed portions" of farm ownership and operating loans, rural business and community development loans, and certain other loans guaranteed by the U.S. Department of Agriculture. Farmer Mac also purchases or commits to purchase qualified loans or securities backed by qualified loans directly from lenders.

The farming and agricultural financing crisis of the 1980s resulted in passage of the Farm Credit Act

Amendments of 1985 and the Agricultural Credit Act of 1987. The 1985 amendments gave the FCA more independent regulatory authority, increased enforcement powers, and created the Farm Credit System Capital Corporation to give technical and financial assistance to financially weak FCS institutions and their borrowers. However, this remedy was not strong enough to shore up weakened institutions and direct federal intervention was necessary.

The Agricultural Credit Act of 1987 authorized up to $4 billion in federal assistance to troubled institutions. The act also established the Farm Credit System Insurance Corporation and the Federal Agricultural Mortgage Corporation (Farmer Mac). In 1988 the Federal Land Bank and the Federal Intermediate Credit Bank in eleven of the twelve then-existing Farm Credit districts merged to become FCBs as authorized by the 1987 act. This act also created the Agricultural Credit Association (ACA) composed of Production Credit Associations (PCAs) and Federal Land Bank Associations (FLBAs).

The FCA formerly examined the Farm Credit System Financial Assistance Corporation (Assistance Corporation), which was created by the Agricultural Credit Act of 1987 and chartered in 1988 to provide needed capital to the FCS through the purchase of preferred stock issued by FCS institutions that received financial assistance authorized by the Farm Credit System Assistance Board. On Jan. 11, 2007, the FCA board canceled the charter and consequently the corporate existence of the Assistance Corporation retroactively to Dec. 31, 2006. The FCA Board determined that the Assistance Corporation "had completed its statutory mission, complied with applicable laws and regulations, and operated in a safe and sound manner."

Following the economic crisis that began in 2008, Congress passed the Dodd-Frank Wall Street Reform and Consumer Protection Act of 2010 to better regulate risk in the financial markets. The Dodd-Frank Act requires the Securities and Exchange Commission (SEC) and the Commodities Futures Trading Commission (CFTC) to work with the prudential regulators—the Farm Credit Administration, the Federal Reserve Board, the Office of the Comptroller of the Currency, the Federal Deposit Insurance Corporation, and the Federal Housing Finance Agency—to develop regulations for margin requirements on non-cleared derivatives for each of the entities subject to regulation under each of the respective agencies. SEC and CFTC are authorized to establish margin requirements for swaps dealers that are not primarily regulated by the prudential regulators. After several proposed rules and public comments dating from 2011, the final rules were pending in January 2015.

The Dodd-Frank Act also requires each federal agency to review certain regulations that refer to external credit ratings (such as those provided by Moody's, Standard & Poor's, and Fitch) and to replace such regulations with alternative credit standards, as appropriate. In June and September of 2011, FCA issued advance notices of proposed rulemaking to solicit comments on ways, other than using credit ratings, to measure the creditworthiness

of a security or money-market instrument. Final regulations were pending in January 2015.

FCA Organization

Service corporations organized under the Farm Credit Act of 1971 are also examined and regulated by the FCA. These include (1) the Farm Credit Leasing Services Corporation (Leasing Corporation), which provides equipment-leasing services to eligible borrowers, including agricultural producers, cooperatives, and rural utilities (the Leasing Corporation is owned by CoBank, ACB); (2) Farm Credit Financial Partners, Inc., which provides support services to the associations affiliated with CoBank, ACB, one association affiliated with AgriBank, FCB; the Farm Credit Leasing Services Corporation; and two FCS-related entities; (3) the FCS Building Association (FCSBA), which acquires, manages, and maintains facilities to house FCA's headquarters and field office staff (the FCSBA was formed in 1981, is owned by the FCS banks, and the FCA Board oversees the FCSBA's activities on behalf of its owners); (4) AgVantis Inc., which provides technology-related and other support services to the associations affiliated with the Farm Credit Bank of Wichita. AgVantis, which was chartered by the FCA in August 2001, is owned by the bank and its affiliated associations; and (5) Farm Credit Foundations, which provides human resource services to its employer-owners, including payroll processing, benefits administration, centralized vendor management, workforce management and operations, corporate tax and financial reporting services, and retirement workshops. It is owned by AgriBank, FCB, and each of its 17 affiliated associations, as well as 24 associations and one service corporation (AgVantis, Inc.) affiliated with CoBank, ACB.

The Office of Examination monitors the financial activities of the Farm Credit System. Field operations are managed by directors located in Bloomington, MN; Dallas, TX; Denver, CO; McLean, VA; Sacramento, CA; and the Special Examination and Supervision Division (SESD), located in McLean, VA. In addition, the SESD is responsible for managing the FCA's enforcement activities. The office examines the corporations within the FCS.

The regional offices examine the FCS institutions within their jurisdictions under the supervision of the Office of Examination. The Agricultural Credit Act of 1987 required the FCA to draft new examination regulations, update its examination manual, and analyze the quality of financial disclosure information provided to stockholders.

The Office of General Counsel (OGC) provides legal advice and services to the FCA Board and agency staff. OGC renders legal opinions relating to the powers, duties, and authorities of the agency and FCS institutions. It also provides legal support for the development and promulgation of FCA regulations and legislation affecting the agency. In addition, OGC represents the agency in enforcement proceedings initiated by the FCA, in proceedings before other administrative bodies, and, in coordination with the Department of Justice, in other litigation. OGC also processes requests under the Freedom of Information

Act and the Privacy Act and reviews agency compliance with other federal laws.

The Office of Inspector General is an independent office within FCA established by law to conduct, supervise, and coordinate audits, investigations, and operations reviews relating to FCA's programs and operations; review existing and proposed legislation and regulations and to make recommendations to the Congress concerning the impact on the economy and efficiency of programs and operations administered by FCA and the prevention and detection of fraud and abuse; and keep the chair of the agency and Congress fully up to date and informed.

The Office of Regulatory Policy manages all policy and regulation development, which ensure the safety and soundness of the FCS and support the FCA's mission. Policy and regulation development activities include the analysis of policy and strategic risks, consideration of economic trends, and study of other risk factors. The office also evaluates all regulatory and statutory prior approvals for system institutions, including chartering and other corporate approvals, as well as funding approvals on behalf of the FCA board.

The Office of Secondary Market Oversight provides for the examination, regulation, and supervision of the activities of Farmer Mac to ensure its soundness and adherence to its public policy purposes as authorized by Congress.

The FCA does not receive a federal appropriation. It is funded through assessments paid by system institutions.

■ KEY PERSONNEL

Board
Kenneth Spearman, chair . . . . (703) 883–4004
    Fax . . . . (703) 883–4151
Executive Assistant to Chair
Russell Middleton . . . . (703) 883–4016
Secretary to the Board
Dale L. Aultman . . . . (703) 883–4009
Members
Dallas Tonsager . . . . (703) 883–4006
Jeffery S. Hall . . . . (703) 883–4004
Chief Operating Officer
William Hoffman . . . . (703) 883–4340
Chief Examiner
S. Robert Coleman . . . . (703) 883–4246
Chief Human Capital Officer
Stephen G. Smith . . . . (703) 883–4200
Chief Information Officer
Vacant . . . . (703) 883–4166
General Counsel
Charles R. Rawls . . . . (703) 883–4021
Inspector General
Elizabeth Dean . . . . (703) 883–4036
Director of Management Services
Stephen G. Smith . . . . (703) 883–4200
Director of Equal Employment Opportunity
Thais Burlew . . . . (703) 883–4290
Director of Regulatory Policy
Gary K. Van Meter . . . . (703) 883–6000

Director of Secondary Market Oversight
Laurie A. Rea . . . . (703) 883–4237
Designated Agency Ethics Official
Wendy R. Laguarda . . . . (703) 883–4234

■ INFORMATION SOURCES

Internet
Agency website: www.fca.gov. Comprehensive website includes information on the FCA and its board members.

Telephone Contacts
Switchboard . . . . (703) 883–4000
TTY . . . . (703) 883–4056

Information and Publications

KEY OFFICES

FCA Congressional and Public Affairs
1501 Farm Credit Dr.
McLean, VA 22102–5090
(703) 883–4056
E-mail: info-line@fca.gov
Michael A. Stokke, director

Answers general questions about the FCA and the Farm Credit System and provides information and publications. Director serves as liaison to Congress.

Freedom of Information
1501 Farm Credit Dr.
McLean, VA 22102–5090
(703) 883–4071
Fax (703) 790–0052
Jane Virga, chief FOIA officer
Internet: www.fca.gov/home/submit_foia.html

PUBLICATIONS
Congressional and Public Affairs distributes a number of FCA publications, including the FCA annual performance and accountability report. All publications, reports, and documents are available on the website, at www.fca.gov/reports/index.html. Other published works include the *FCA Handbook,* a compilation of FCA regulations. You may also contact the publications office at info-line@fca.gov, or you may telephone (703) 883–4056 with questions.

DOCKETS
Federal dockets are available on the website and at www.regulations.gov. (*See appendix for information on searching and commenting on regulations.*)

REGULATIONS
FCA regulations are published in the *Code of Federal Regulations,* Title 5, Chapter XXXI, Parts 4100, 4199; Title 12, Chapter VI, Parts 600–699. Proposed regulations, new final regulations, and updates to the *Code of Federal*

Regulations are published in the daily *Federal Register.* (*See appendix for information on how to obtain and use these publications.*) FCA regulations and the Farm Credit Act of 1971, as amended, are available on FCA's website: www .fca.gov, in a searchable database posted under Legal Info.

LEGISLATION

The FCA carries out its responsibilities under

Farm Credit Act of 1971 (85 Stat. 583, 12 U.S.C. 2001). Signed by the president Dec. 10, 1971. Recodified all previous laws governing federal land banks, federal land bank associations, federal intermediate credit banks, production credit associations, and banks for cooperatives. Authorized loans to commercial fishermen and rural home owners. Reduced loan-to-value ratios and authorized variable rate loans, lease financing, and loans for farm-related services.

Farm Credit Act Amendments of 1980 (94 Stat. 3437, 12 U.S.C. 2012). Signed by the president Dec. 24, 1980. Amended the Farm Credit Act of 1971 to permit Farm Credit System institutions to improve their services. Authorized banks for cooperatives to engage in international lending transactions and authorized federal land banks and production credit associations to finance basic processing and marketing activities of farmers.

Farm Credit Act Amendments of 1985 (99 Stat. 1678, 12 U.S.C. 2001 note). Signed by the president Dec. 23, 1985. Amended the Farm Credit Act of 1971 to restructure and reform the Farm Credit System. Gave the Farm Credit System broader authority to use its own resources to shore up weak system units. Authorized the FCA to reorganize and regulate the Farm Credit System. Authorized the secretary of the Treasury to guarantee bonds issued by the Farm Credit System Financial Assistance Corporation.

Agricultural Credit Act of 1987 (101 Stat. 1568, 12 U.S.C. 2162). Signed by the president Jan. 6, 1988. Provided credit assistance to farmers, strengthened the Farm Credit System, and facilitated the establishment of secondary markets for agricultural loans. Provided for mandated and voluntary mergers between Farm Credit System institutions. Expanded borrower rights provisions of the 1971 act and established a corporation to insure rates and bonds issued by system institutions after 1993.

Food, Agriculture, Conservation, and Trade Act Amendments of 1991 (105 Stat. 1818, 7 U.S.C. 1421 note). Signed by the president Dec. 13, 1991. Gave the FCA regulatory control over the Federal Agricultural Mortgage Corporation (Farmer Mac), a secondary market for agricultural loans. Authorized Farmer Mac to borrow money with unsecured notes in order to purchase securities.

Farm Credit Banks and Associations Safety and Soundness Act of 1992 (106 Stat. 4102, 12 U.S.C. 2277a). Signed by the president Oct. 28, 1992. Amended Farm Credit System Insurance Corporation authority and provided for a separate board of directors, effective Jan. 1, 1996. Expanded the lending powers of banks for cooperatives.

Farm Credit System Reform Act of 1996 (110 Stat. 162, 12 U.S.C. 2001 note). Signed by the president Feb. 10, 1996. Reduced regulatory burdens on Farm Credit System institutions. Repealed a previous law to create a separate Farm Credit Insurance Corporation Board and authorized rebates of excess Insurance Fund interest earnings. Authorized the Federal Agricultural Mortgage Corporation to purchase and pool loans and to issue mortgage-backed securities with guaranteed payment of principal and interest.

Preserving Independence of Financial Institution Examinations Act of 2003 (117 Stat. 2899, 18 U.S.C. 201 note). Signed by the president Dec. 19, 2003. Amended federal criminal law to subject to criminal penalties personnel of a financial institution who offer a loan or gratuity to a financial institution examiner and a financial institution examiner who accepts such loan or gratuity. Authorized a federal financial institution regulatory agency to prescribe regulations establishing additional limitations on the application for and receipt of credit or mortgage loans.

Food, Conservation, and Energy Act of 2008 (Farm Bill) (7 U.S.C. 8701 note). Vetoed by the president May 21, 2008; veto overridden May 22, 2008/June 18, 2008. Title V (Credit) clarified rules governing financial obligations among members of Farm Credit System, including insurance assessments. Amended the Farm Credit Act to equalize lending authorities among certain FCS district associations and authorized the FCA to review these equalization policies within thirty days.

Secure and Fair Enforcement (SAFE) for Mortgage Licensing Act of 2008 (12 U.S.C. 5101 et seq.). Title V of the Housing and Economic Recovery Act. Signed by the president July 30, 2008. Required federal banking agencies jointly, through the Federal Financial Institutions Examination Council, to develop and maintain a national system to register loan originators. Defined "federal banking agencies" as the Board of Governors of the Federal Reserve System, the Comptroller of the Currency, the director of the Office of Thrift Supervision, the National Credit Union Administration, and the Federal Deposit Insurance Corporation.

Dodd-Frank Wall Street Reform and Consumer Protection Act (124 Stat. 1376, 12 USC 5301 note). Signed by the president July 21, 2010. Authorizes the Commodity Futures Trading Commission (CFTC) to regulate the swaps marketplace, which was previously unregulated. With some exceptions, directs the CFTC and the Securities and Exchange Commission (SEC) to coordinate with each other and with the prudential regulators (the Federal Reserve Board, the Office of the Comptroller of the Currency, the Federal Deposit Insurance Corporation, the Farm Credit Administration, and the Federal Housing Finance Agency) before commencing any rulemaking or issuing an order regarding swaps, swap dealers, major swap participants, swap repositories, persons associated with a swap dealer or major swap participant, eligible contract participants, or swap execution facilities. SEC and CFTC are authorized to establish margin requirements for swaps dealers that are not primarily regulated by the prudential regulators. Other provisions.

Biggert-Waters Flood Insurance Reform Act of 2012 (126 Stat. 916, 42 U.S.C. 4001 note). Signed by the president

July 6, 2012. Title II of Moving Ahead for Progress in the 21st Century Act (MAP-21). Biggert-Waters made changes to the flood insurance program, which included requiring banking regulatory agencies to draft regulations concerning forced-placed flood insurance and flood insurance escrow provisions.

Agricultural Act of 2014 (128 Stat. 841, 12 U.S.C. 2252 note). Signed by the president Feb. 7, 2014. Requires the Farm Credit Administration to review its rules to reflect congressional intent that a primary responsibility of the boards of directors of Farm Credit System institutions is to oversee compensation practices.

Consolidated and Further Continuing Appropriations Act, 2015 (P. L. 113-235). Signed by the president Dec. 16, 2014. Section 630 of the omnibus appropriations bill repeals section 716 of the Dodd-Frank Wall Street Reform and Consumer Protection Act, which prohibits federal assistance to financial institutions that engage in certain derivatives activities.

■ FARM CREDIT BANKS

These are federally chartered banks regulated by the FCA. Each Farm Credit Bank has numerous local lending associations and branches underneath it; detailed information about these is available on the FCA website, by contacting Public Affairs, or by contacting the regional banks, below.

MID-ATLANTIC AND SOUTHEAST REGION

(AL, DC, DE, FL, GA, KY, LA, MD, MS, NC, OH, PA, PR, SC, TN, VA, WV)
AgFirst Farm Credit Bank
1901 Main St.
P.O. Box 1499
Columbia, SC 29201
(803) 799–5000
Leon Amerson, president and chief executive officer

MIDWEST REGION

(AR, IA, IL, IN, KY, MI, MN, MO, ND, NE, OH, SD, TN, WI, WY)
AgriBank, FCB
30 East 7th St., #1600
St. Paul, MN 55101
(651) 282–8800
L. William York, chief executive officer

CENTRAL PLAINS AND SOUTHWEST REGION

(AZ, CA, CO, HI, eastern ID, KS, NM, NV, OK, UT)
CoBank's Wichita Operations Office
245 N. Waco St.
Wichita, KS 67201–2940
(316) 290–2000
David Janish, chief operations officer

SOUTH CENTRAL REGION

(Long-term financing for AL, LA, MS, TX; short-term financing for northwest LA, NM, TX)

Farm Credit Bank of Texas
4801 Plaza on the Lake Dr.
Austin, TX 78746
(512) 465–0400
Larry R. Doyle, chief executive officer

■ AGRICULTURAL CREDIT BANK

This is a federally chartered bank regulated by the FCA.

COBANK

(Serves cooperatives nationwide and associations in AK, CT, ID, MA, ME, MT, NH, NJ, NY, OR, RI, VT, WA)
5500 S. Quebec St.
Greenwood Village, CO 80111
Mailing address:
P.O. Box 5110
Denver, CO 80217
(303) 740–4000
Robert B. Engel, president and chief executive officer

■ FIELD OFFICES

NATIONAL HEADQUARTERS

1501 Farm Credit Dr.
McLean, VA 22102–5090
(703) 883–4246
S. Robert Coleman, director and chief examiner

BLOOMINGTON FIELD OFFICE

7900 International Dr., #200
Bloomington, MN 55425
(952) 854–7151
Chester Slipek, director

DALLAS FIELD OFFICE

500 East John Carpenter Freeway, #400
Irving, TX 75062–3930
(972) 869–0550
Sharon Wilhite, director

DENVER FIELD OFFICE

3131 S. Vaughn Way, #250
Aurora, CO 80014–3507
(303) 696–9737
Michael Anderson, director

McLEAN FIELD OFFICE

1501 Farm Credit Dr.
McLean, VA 22102–5090
(703) 883–4160
Ronald Boehr, director

SACRAMENTO FIELD OFFICE

2180 Harvard St., #300
Sacramento, CA 95815–3323
(916) 648–1118
David E. Kuhler, director

CORPORATIONS

FARM CREDIT LEASING SERVICES CORPORATION

600 Hwy. 169 South, #300
Minneapolis, MN 55426
(952) 417–7800
Russell D. Nelson, president and chief
    executive officer

FEDERAL FARM CREDIT BANKS FUNDING CORPORATION

10 Exchange Pl., #1401
Jersey City, NJ 07302
(201) 200–8131
Tracey McCabe, president

FARM CREDIT SYSTEM INSURANCE CORPORATION

1501 Farm Credit Dr.
McLean, VA 22102
(703) 883–4380
Dorothy L. Nichols, chief operating officer

FEDERAL AGRICULTURAL MORTGAGE CORPORATION (FARMER MAC)

1999 K St. N.W., 4th Floor
Washington, DC 20006
(202) 872–7700
(800) 879–3276
Timothy L. Buzby, president and chief
    executive officer

Federal Election Commission

999 E St. N.W., Washington, DC 20463
Internet: www.fec.gov

The Federal Election Commission (FEC) is an independent regulatory agency. It administers and enforces the provisions of the Federal Election Campaign Act of 1971, as amended. The act requires the disclosure of sources and uses of funds in campaigns for any federal office, limits the size of individual contributions, and provides for partial public financing of presidential elections. Partial funding is available to primary election candidates on a matching basis if they meet certain requirements. Full funding for the general election is available to qualified candidates.

The commission is composed of six members appointed by the president and confirmed by the Senate. The commissioners serve staggered six-year terms, and no more than three commissioners may be members of the same political party. The chair and vice chair must be members of different political parties; they are elected annually by their fellow commissioners.

The commission staff is headed by a staff director. Other senior staff members include a general counsel; inspector general; and assistant staff directors for audits, reports analysis, public disclosure, information, and administration.

Campaign Finance

The Presidential Election Campaign Fund Act (PECFA) of 1971 authorized the commission to certify payments to presidential campaigns from the Presidential Election Campaign Fund. (This money comes from taxpayers who have indicated on their federal tax returns that they wish $3 of their taxes to be contributed to the fund). These funds also were distributed in equal amounts to the two major parties for their respective national conventions. However, President Barack Obama signed a law in 2014 that transferred funds intended for political nominating conventions to a ten-year pediatric research initiative fund. The omnibus appropriations bill for fiscal year 2015 contained a section that increased contribution limits to national political party committees and permitted the committees to establish new accounts to support party conventions, facilities, and recounts or other legal matters. The FEC announced it would review the new provisions and assess their impact on existing regulations.

The PECFA, as amended, required campaign committees, political action committees (PACs), and parties to file periodic financial reports. It also established limits on the size and type of contributions a candidate may receive. Contributions from national banks, corporations, labor organizations, government contractors, and nonresident foreign nationals are prohibited. Also prohibited are contributions of cash (currency) in excess of $100, contributions from one person given in the name of another, and contributions exceeding legal limits (box, p. 404).

Any candidate for federal office and any political group or committee formed to support a candidate must register with the FEC; the committee treasurer must periodically file reports on campaign finances with the secretary of the Senate (candidates for Senate seats), the House clerk's office (candidates for House seats), or the FEC. Individuals and committees making independent expenditures on behalf of or against a candidate also must file reports. In addition, campaign reports must be submitted to the secretary of state (or equivalent office) in the state where the nomination or election is sought or where the political committee's headquarters is located. Reports are made available to the public within forty-eight hours of their receipt.

To register with the FEC, candidates and committees must submit a statement of candidacy that designates a principal campaign committee. (This committee must be registered by filing a statement of organization within ten days; PACs and party committees also register by filing a statement of organization.) Other financial disclosure documents submitted include a report of receipts and expenditures, a statement of independent expenditures on behalf of or against a candidate, and a statement of any debt settlements. Disclosure statements also must be filed showing costs incurred on behalf of candidates by corporations, labor organizations, membership organizations, and trade associations for certain partisan communication conducted within their own particular organization.

Independent expenditures are payments for communications that advocate the election or defeat of a candidate but made without the cooperation of the particular candidate or campaign committee. A PAC or party committee must report aggregate independent expenditures that exceed $10,000 per calendar year. Any other person (individual, partnership, qualified nonprofit corporation, or group of individuals) must report independent expenditures greater than $250 per calendar year to the FEC. Independent expenditures may not be regulated except for disclosure.

FEC staff members review the reports for errors or omissions; if any are found, the agency can request that the campaign or committee provide additional information. If this information is not supplied, the FEC has the authority to begin a formal investigation. If after the investigation, the commission decides that violations of the law did occur, it has the authority to negotiate a conciliation agreement with the party in question. Failure to negotiate an agreement within legal parameters allows the FEC to seek enforcement of the law and the imposition of civil penalties in U.S. District Court.

These procedures to enforce compliance also apply to cases in which the FEC discovers a violation of campaign finance law. FEC investigations of alleged violations can spring from an audit or routine review of a report or from a complaint sent to the FEC from another group or individual.

If candidates or committees have questions concerning the finance laws as they relate to specific campaigns, they may request an advisory opinion from the commission. Advisory opinion requests and advisory opinions are available for public inspection at the Public Records Office (p. 406).

The commission also administers provisions of the law covering the public financing of presidential primaries and general elections. Public funds are also made available to national party committees for their nominating conventions. Candidates who accept public campaign funds must adhere to spending limits imposed by the Federal Election Campaign Act Amendments of 1976 (FECA). The limits are adjusted each campaign season to account for inflation. To become eligible for matching funds, candidates must raise a threshold amount of $100,000 by collecting $5,000 in twenty different states in amounts no greater than $250 from any individual. Publicly funded candidates must agree to limit expenditures.

The FEC determines a candidate's eligibility for public funds. If eligible, the candidate or committee is certified by the commission to the Treasury Department. After receiving subsequent submissions for matching funds, the commission certifies specific amounts to be paid from the fund. The Treasury is responsible for the actual disbursement of money.

The Bipartisan Campaign Reform Act (BCRA) of 2002, also known as McCain-Feingold, made many substantial and technical changes to the federal campaign finance law. The law banned the national parties and federal candidates from raising and spending soft money. It also broadened the definition of issue ads to include any ad that referred to a specific federal candidate sixty days before a general election and thirty days before a primary. It barred the use of corporate or union money for such ads and required that the names of major backers of the ads be disclosed. Political parties were barred from making independent expenditures on behalf of a candidate if they made coordinated expenditures for that candidate. Most of the changes became effective November 6, 2002; however, changes involving contribution limits took effect with regard to contributions made on or after January 1, 2003. Later, court challenges would invalidate some of the BCRA provisions (see below).

The Honest Leadership and Open Government Act of 2007 amended the Lobbying Disclosure Act and made various changes to disclosure for lobbyists, PACs, and political campaigns. The act amended the Federal Election Campaign Act of 1971 to require the disclosure of information regarding certain bundled contributions. The FEC is required to publish the information about bundled contributions on its website in a searchable database.

For the 2008 presidential campaign, six candidates were eligible for public funding during their primary campaigns, but the two candidates who eventually won their respective party's nomination chose not to participate: Sen. Barack Obama, the Democratic nominee, and Sen. John McCain, the Republican nominee. McCain had initially pledged he would run a publicly supported campaign, but he later withdrew from the federal primary election matching funds program. Candidates could reject public funds for the general or primary campaigns, freeing them to spend as much as they liked. The limits on the size of contributions remained the same, however. For the 2008 general election campaign, only McCain accepted public funds, amounting to $84.1 million. Obama became the first president elected since the onset of public funding to have declined public funds in both the primary and general elections. In the 2012 elections, both presidential candidates, Barack Obama and Mitt Romney, declined public funds.

Legal Opposition to Campaign Finance Reform

When Congress passed Federal Election Campaign Act of 1971, as amended, the purpose was to bring transparency and limit corruption in the election process while balancing the rights of candidates to communicate with the public. In 1976, the U.S. Supreme Court ruling in *Buckley v. Valeo* upheld the contribution limits in the Federal Election Campaign Act of 1971 (but struck down candidate expenditure limits). Acknowledging the contribution limitations did restrict a particular type of political speech, the U.S. Supreme Court concluded that contribution limits "serve[d] the basic governmental interest in safeguarding the integrity of the electoral process without directly impinging upon the rights of individual citizens and candidates to engage in political debate and discussion."

Opponents of Bipartisan Campaign Reform Act (BCRA) of 2002 took the battle against campaign funding regulations back to court. The plaintiffs argued that such regulations were an unconstitutional limitation on free speech. Early efforts to overturn BCRA and related FEC regulations were largely unsuccessful. But BCRA opponents later found success with the U.S. Supreme Court under Chief Justice John Roberts. Notably, Justice Sandra Day O'Connor, who cast the swing vote to uphold BCRA provisions earlier, had been replaced by Justice Samuel Alito, who would cast the deciding votes to restrict BCRA.

In June 2007 the Supreme Court upheld (5-4) a district court ruling that the electioneering communication financing restrictions of the BCRA were unconstitutional as applied to ads that the nonprofit Wisconsin Right to Life, Inc. intended to run before the 2004 elections. The

CONTRIBUTION LIMITS (2015–2016)

Donors	Candidate committee	PAC[1]	State, district, and local party committee[2]	National party committee[3]	Special limits
Individual	$2,700* per election[4]	$5,000 per year	$10,000 per year combined limit	$33,400* per year	$100,200* per account, per year
State, district, and local party committee[2]	$5,000 per election combined limit	$5,000 per year combined limit	Unlimited transfers to other party committees		
National party committee[3]	$5,000 per election	$5,000 per year	Unlimited transfers to other party committees		
PAC (multicandidate)[6]	$5,000 per election	$5,000 per year	$5,000 per year combined limit	$15,000 per year	$45,000 per account, per year
PAC (not multicandidate)[6]	$2,700* per election	$5,000 per year	$10,000 per year combined limit	$33,400* per year	$100,200* per account, per year
Candidate committee	$2,000 per election[4]	$5,000 per year	Unlimited transfers		

Source: Federal Election Commission.

Notes: *These limits are indexed for inflation.

1. A contribution earmarked for a candidate through a political committee counts against the original contributor's limit for that candidate. In certain circumstances, the contribution may also count against the contributor's limit to the PAC.

2. A state party committee shares its limits with local and district party committees in that state, unless a local or district committee's independence can be demonstrated. These limits apply to multicandidates only.

3. A party's national committee, Senate campaign committee, and House campaign committee are each considered national party committees and each has separate limits except for contributions to Senate candidates. See "Special limits" column.

4. Each of the following is considered a separate election with a separate limit: primary election, caucus, or convention with authority to nominate, general election, runoff election, and special election.

5. A multicandidate committee is a political committee that has been registered for at least six months, has received contributions from more than fifty contributors, and, with the exception of a state party committee, has made contributions to at least five federal candidates.

Court held that advocacy (or issue) ads were exempt from BCRA restrictions as long as the ads did not expressly call for electing or defeating a particular candidate.

In 2008 the U.S. Supreme Court ruled 5–4 to overturn the "Millionaire's Amendment," a provision in BCRA that increased contribution limits for candidates facing a wealthy opponent who intended to make large expenditures from personal funds.

In January 2010 the U.S. Supreme Court, in a 5–4 vote, issued a decision in *Citizens United vs. FEC* and overturned campaign finance limits on corporate and union spending on advertisements and political communications during campaigns—communications to the public that advocate the election or defeat of a federal candidate. However, the political advertising consisting of independent expenditures or electioneering communications must contain a disclaimer clearly stating who paid for such communication. Although the restrictions for elections communications were overturned, the limits on campaign contributions to candidates remain.

Immediately after the Supreme Court decision, the FEC issued guidelines. The FEC will no longer enforce the statutory provisions or its regulations prohibiting corporations and labor organizations from making independent expenditures and electioneering communications. However, certain information about electioneering

communications and independent expenditures, and the contributions received for such spending, must be disclosed to the FEC.

On April 2, 2014, the Supreme Court issued a ruling in *McCutcheon v. FEC* that struck down the aggregate limits on the amount an individual may contribute during a two-year period to all federal candidates, parties, and political action committees combined. By a vote of 5–4, the Supreme Court ruled that the biennial aggregate limits are unconstitutional under the First Amendment. The ruling did not, however, change the base limits ($2,700 limit on direct donations to a single candidate and limit of $33,400 to a single party committee, as of 2015). As such, the ruling allows individuals to donate a limited amount of funds to an unlimited number of candidates, political parties, and PACs. On October 9, 2014, the FEC approved an interim final rule removing regulations that impose aggregate contribution limits the Supreme Court held were unconstitutional.

The Supreme Court rulings had tremendous impact on the amounts of money raised and spent during elections. The *Citizens United* decision gave rise to so-called super PACs, which raised unlimited money aimed at supporting or defeating particular candidates. Likewise, the ability for 501(c)(4) tax-exempt "social welfare" organizations to raise and expend large sums in politics without disclosing donors led critics to decry the influence of "dark money" in elections. The current climate for campaign reform appears to favor those who advocate fundraising as expression of free speech over those who express concern that such fundraising compromises the integrity of elections.

Other Responsibilities

The FEC's voluntary alternative dispute resolution (ADR) program is designed to promote compliance with the campaign finance law and FEC regulations by encouraging settlements outside the normal enforcement context. Bilateral negotiations through ADR are oriented toward reaching an expedient resolution with a mutually agreeable settlement that is both satisfying to the respondent(s) and in compliance with the Federal Election Campaign Act (FECA). Resolutions reached through direct and, when necessary, mediated negotiations are submitted to the commissioners for final approval. If a resolution is not reached in bilateral negotiation, the case proceeds to mediation. It should be noted that cases resolved through ADR are not precedent-setting cases.

The FEC and the Election Assistance Commission (EAC) (p. 392) serve as the primary federal agencies charged with providing assistance in the administration of federal elections by state and local governments. To aid election officials with the acquisition of reliable voting equipment, the FEC promulgated the 1990 Voting System Standards (VSS) to ensure that machines used for voting meet certain baseline criteria for accuracy, reliability, and durability. States adopt VSS on a voluntary basis as voting systems are subject to state regulation. After its creation in 2002, the EAC took on the role of testing and certifying voting equipment and software and disseminating that information to the states.

▓ KEY PERSONNEL

Chair (position rotates annually)
  Ann M. Ravel . . . . (202) 694–1010
Vice Chair
  Matthew S. Petersen . . . . (202) 694–1050
Commissioners
  Caroline C. Hunter . . . . (202) 694–1045
  Ellen L. Weintraub . . . . (202) 694–1011
  Steven T. Walther . . . . (202) 694–1053
  Lee E. Goodman . . . . (202) 694–1035
Staff Director
  Alec Palmer . . . . (202) 694–1007
Auditor
  Tom Hintermister . . . . (202) 694–1200
Chief Compliance Officer
  Patricia Orrock . . . . (202) 694–1130
Chief Financial Officer
  Judy Berning (acting) . . . . (202) 694–1215
Congressional Affairs
  Duane Pugh . . . . (202) 694–1006
Enforcement
  Daniel Petalas . . . . (202) 694–1650
Equal Employment Opportunity
  Kevin Salley . . . . (202) 694–1228

General Counsel
  Daniel A. Petalas (acting). . . . . (202) 694–1650
Human Resources
  Judy McLaughlin . . . . (202) 694–1080
Information Division
  Gregory J. Scott . . . . (202) 694–1100
Information Technology
  Alec Palmer . . . . (202) 694–1250
Inspector General
  Lynne A. McFarland . . . . (202) 694–1015
Litigation
  Kevin Deeley (acting) . . . . (202) 694–1650
Policy
  Adav Noti (acting) . . . . (202) 694–1650
Press
  Judith Ingram . . . . (202) 694–1220
Procurement
  Lorna Baptiste-Jones . . . . (202) 694–1225
Public Disclosure
  Patricia Young . . . . (202) 694–1120
Public Financing, Ethics, and Special Projects
  Gregory Baker . . . . (202) 694–1650
Reports Analysis
  Debbie Chacona . . . . (202) 694–1130
Secretary
  Shawn Worth . . . . (202) 694–1040

▓ INFORMATION SOURCES

Internet

Agency website: www.fec.gov. Includes information about FEC offices, activities, and services, as well as data and statistics and publications about elections, PACs, and campaigns, including guidelines for political contributions.

Telephone Contacts

General number, information, and
  publications. . . . . (202) 694–1000
Toll-free . . . . (800) 424–9530
Fax . . . . (202) 219–3880
Fax-on-demand . . . . (202) 501–3413
TTY . . . . (202) 219–3336
Federal Relay Service TTY . . . . (800) 877–8339

Information and Publications

KEY OFFICES

FEC Information Division
999 E St. N.W.
Washington, DC 20463
(202) 694–1250
Toll-free (800) 424–9530
E-mail: info@fec.gov
Alec Palmer, chief information officer

Provides all public information on the FEC, including publications. Handles inquiries from candidates and committees as well as the general public and operates a toll-free number for queries and publication orders from outside the Washington, DC, area.

FEC Press Office
999 E St. N.W., #107
Washington, DC 20463
(202) 694–1220
Judith Ingram, press officer

Handles all liaison with the media and answers and refers questions from media representatives. Also handles Freedom of Information requests from within the FEC. Press releases, the FEC *Weekly Digest,* campaign finance filings, and FEC e-mail alerts are also available at www.fec .gov/press/press.shtml.

FEC General Counsel
999 E St. N.W.
Washington, DC 20463
(202) 694–1650
Daniel A. Petalas (acting), general counsel

Handles complaints alleging violations of the Federal Election Campaign Act, as amended, or FEC regulations. Complaints must be in writing, sworn to, and notarized and must contain the name, address, and telephone number of the person making the complaint; a statement of the facts; and evidence concerning the complaint. Complaints must be signed by the person making the complaint and must include a statement indicating whether the complaint is made at the suggestion of or on behalf of any other person. Complaints must be submitted, in triplicate, to the Office of the General Counsel. For information on procedure, contact the Information Division, above.

Freedom of Information
FOIA Requester Center
999 E St. N.W., Room 408
Washington, DC 20463
(202) 694–1650
Fax (202) 219–1043
E-mail: FOIA@fec.gov
Internet: www.fec.gov/press/foia.shtml
Gregory R. Baker, FOIA officer
Katie Higginbothom, FOIA public liaison

DATA AND STATISTICS
Extensive statistical data on elections is available from the Public Records Office, state offices (see below), and on the website.

MEETINGS
The commission is required by law to meet once each month; however, it generally holds weekly meetings Thursdays at 10:00 a.m. Dates and agendas are published in the *Federal Register* and are available on the website at www.fec.gov/agenda/agendas.shtml. Commission meetings are open to the public unless they deal with pending compliance cases and personnel matters. Up-to-date information on changes in agenda or schedule may be obtained from the Information Division, the Public Records Office, the Press Office, or on the website.

PUBLICATIONS
Numerous FEC publications are available from the Information Division and on the website, including the annual report and a free monthly newsletter, *The FEC Record* (issues from 1996 to the present are available at www. fec.gov/pages/record.shtml). The commission also makes available numerous campaign guides for political committees, corporations, labor organizations, and candidates.

Several Bipartisan Campaign Reform Act resources, including the BCRA Campaign Guides and Supplements, are available for download at www.fec.gov/info/publica tions.shtml or by calling (800) 424–9530.

Reference Resources

LIBRARIES

FEC Law Library
999 E St. N.W.
Washington, DC 20463
(202) 694–1600
Leta Holley, librarian
Hours: 9:00 a.m. to 5:00 p.m.

FEC Public Records Office
999 E St. N.W., 1st Floor
Washington, DC 20463
(202) 694–1120
Fax-on-demand (202) 501–3413
E-mail: pubrec@fec.gov
Patricia Young, assistant staff director

Maintains and makes available to the public all campaign finance reports filed by federal candidates and committees since 1972. (The National Archives and Records Administration maintains records prior to 1972.) Copies of campaign reports may be requested in person, by mail, or by phone, and are available on the website and from state offices. There is a minimal charge for paper or microfilm. Fax-on-demand service provides automatic faxes of selected FEC documents.

Open to the public from 9:00 a.m. to 5:00 p.m., the office is open for extended hours during reporting periods.

The Public Records Office also makes available the following materials:

■ Names and addresses of presidential and congressional candidates and names and addresses of their authorized committees
■ Enforcement actions and litigation relating to campaigns
■ Audits of campaigns
■ Summary financial figures on total receipts, disbursements, contributions (individual, PAC, and party), cash on hand, and debts owed to and by campaigns
■ Extensive information on PACs

- Information on individuals who contribute more than $500 to a campaign
- Statistical summaries of campaign finance reports
- Computer indexes and cross indexes to help locate documents
- Advisory opinion requests and texts of advisory opinions
- Commission memoranda, agendas of all commission meetings, agenda items, and minutes.

Secretary of the Senate
Office of Public Records
SHOB-232
Washington, DC 20510
(202) 224–0758
Dana McCallum, superintendent
Internet: http://disclosure.senate.gov

Maintains for public inspection an electronic database of original campaign finance reports filed by candidates for the U.S. Senate and their committees. Also maintains lobbying disclosure reports and forms, senior senate staff public disclosure forms, legal expense fund disclosures, revised gift rule filings (including travel paid by nongovernmental organizations), and registration of mass mailings.

Legislative Resource Center
Office of the Clerk of the House
135 CHOB
Washington, DC 20515–6612
(202) 226–5200
Ronald Dale Thomas, director

Maintains copies of financial disclosure reports filed by candidates for the U.S. House of Representatives and their committees. Also maintains financial disclosure reports for members of the House and for federal agency staff.

State Records Offices
Campaign finance reports must also be filed with the secretary of state or equivalent official in each state. See list below.

DOCKETS
Federal dockets are available at www.regulations.gov. (*See appendix for information on searching and commenting on regulations.*)

RULES AND REGULATIONS
Effective September 1, 2014, the Federal Election Campaign Act (formerly 2 U.S.C. §431 et seq) and other laws relating to elections and voting were relocated to the new Title 52, Voting and Elections. Proposed rules, updates to the *Code of Federal Regulations,* and new final rules are published in the daily *Federal Register.* (*See appendix for information on how to obtain and use these publications.*)

A publication issued by the commission, *FEC Regulations,* is available from the Information Division.

▌ LEGISLATION
The FEC carries out its responsibilities under

Federal Election Campaign Act of 1971 (86 Stat. 3, 2 U.S.C. 431 note). Signed by the president Feb. 7, 1972. Established detailed spending limits and disclosure procedures. This act was the first comprehensive revision of federal campaign legislation since the Corrupt Practices Act of 1925.

Federal Election Campaign Act Amendments of 1974 (88 Stat. 1263, 2 U.S.C. 431 note). Signed by the president Oct. 15, 1974. Amended the Federal Election Campaign Act of 1971 by instituting limits on how much an individual can contribute to a candidate, how much candidates can spend in primary and general elections, and how much political parties are allowed to spend on candidates and nominating conventions. The amendments set up the FEC to enforce the provisions of the act. They also established public funding of presidential elections. Partial funding is available during the primaries to candidates who meet certain requirements. Full funding is available to qualified candidates for the general election. In the *Buckley v. Valeo* decision of 1976, the Supreme Court found parts of the 1974 act unconstitutional.

Federal Election Campaign Act Amendments of 1976 (90 Stat. 475, 2 U.S.C. 431 note). Signed by the president May 11, 1976. Reorganized the commission in a form that is constitutional. This law required that the commissioners be appointed by the president and confirmed by the Senate, established new contribution limits for individuals and political committees, and cut off matching funds for presidential candidates who receive less than a specific percentage of the votes cast during the primaries. No limit was imposed on spending for congressional races, and individual candidates were exempted from any limits on contributions they make to themselves.

Federal Election Campaign Act Amendments of 1979 (93 Stat. 1339, 2 U.S.C. 431 note). Signed by the president Jan. 8, 1980. Changed reporting and registration requirements that apply to political committees and candidates. Generally the amendments simplified paperwork requirements and removed some restrictions on party assistance to federal candidates and on volunteer activities.

Bipartisan Campaign Reform Act of 2002 (116 Stat. 81, 2 U.S.C. 441a and 441a-1). Signed by the president March 27, 2002. Amended the Federal Election Campaign Act of 1971 (FECA) with respect to soft money to prohibit candidates or political parties from soliciting or receiving contributions or making expenditures not subject to FECA. Restricted use of broadcast electioneering communication that was coordinated with a candidate (or his or her authorized committee) or a federal, state, or local political party or committee. Increased the limit on individual contributions to a federal candidate from $1,000 to $2,000 per election.

Consolidated Appropriations Act, 2005 (118 Stat. 3272, 2 U.S.C. 432[e][3][B]). Signed by the president Dec. 8, 2004. Authorized the use of campaign contributions for donations to state and local candidates (subject to state law) or any other lawful purpose not specifically prohibited by the Federal Election Campaign Act.

Honest Leadership and Open Government Act of 2007 (2 U.S.C. 1601 note). Signed by the president Sept. 14, 2007. Amended the Federal Election Campaign Act of 1971 to require the disclosure of information regarding certain bundled contributions. Required the FEC to publish the information about these bundled contributions in a searchable database on the FEC website. Placed new restrictions on the use of campaign funds for travel on noncommercial aircraft.

Federal Election Campaign Act Amendments (127 Stat. 1210, 2 U.S.C. 437g note). Signed by the president Dec. 26, 2013. Amended the Federal Election Campaign Act to extend through 2018 the authority of the Federal Election Commission to impose civil money penalties on the basis of a schedule of penalties established and published by FEC, to expand such authority to certain other violations, and for other purposes.

Gabriella Miller Kids First Research Act (128 Stat. 1085, 26 U.S.C. 1 note). Signed by the president April 3, 2014. Transfers funds from the Presidential Election Campaign Fund for the presidential nominating conventions to a ten-year pediatric research initiative fund.

Consolidated and Further Continuing Appropriations Act, 2015 (52 U.S.C. 30116[a]). Signed by the president Dec. 16, 2014. Division N, section 101 of the omnibus appropriation bill for FY15 increases contribution limits to national political party committees. Allows the committees to establish new accounts, each with separate contribution limits, to support party conventions, facilities, and recounts or other legal matters. Requires that the proposed convention accounts spend no more than $20 million per convention for the increased contribution limits to apply.

■ STATE RECORDS OFFICES

The FEC has no regional offices; however, campaign finance reports are available at the office of the secretary of state (or equivalent office) in the state or territory where a candidate is seeking nomination or election or where the campaign headquarters is located. The following state offices maintain copies of campaign records for public inspection; those marked by an asterisk (*) also offer direct computer access to the FEC disclosure database through www.fec.gov.

ALABAMA*
Elections Division
Office of the Secretary of State
State Capitol, #E-208
600 Dexter Ave.
Montgomery, AL 36130
(334) 242–7210 or (800) 274–8683

ALASKA*
Division of Elections
Office of the Lieutenant Governor
State Capitol, 315
Juneau, AK 99801
Mailing address:
P.O. Box 110015

Juneau, AK 99811–0017
(907) 465–3520
TTY (907) 465–3020

AMERICAN SAMOA
Election Office
P.O. Box 3970
Pago Pago, AS 96799
(684) 699–3570
E-mail: asgelect@samoatelco.com

ARIZONA*
Office of the Secretary of State
State Capitol, Executive Tower, 7th Floor
1700 W. Washington St.
Phoenix, AZ 85007–2808
(602) 542–8683

ARKANSAS*
Elections Division
Office of the Secretary of State
State Capitol Bldg., Room 026
Little Rock, AR 72201
(501) 682–5070

CALIFORNIA*
Political Reform Division
Office of the Secretary of State
1500 11th St., Room 495
Sacramento, CA 95814–2974
(916) 653–6224

COLORADO*
Elections Division
Office of the Secretary of State
1700 Broadway, 270
Denver, CO 80290
(303) 894–2200

CONNECTICUT*
Legislation and Election Administration Division
Office of the Secretary of State
20 Trinity St., # 101
Hartford, CT 06106
Mailing address:
P.O. Box 150470
Hartford, CT 06118–0470
(866) 733–2463
(860) 566–1776

DELAWARE*
Office of the Secretary of State
Townsend Bldg.
401 Federal St., #3
Dover, DE 19901
(302) 739–4111

DISTRICT OF COLUMBIA*
Board of Elections and Ethics
1 Judiciary Square

441 4th Street N.W., #250N
Washington, DC 20001–2745
(202) 727–2525
TTY (202) 639–8916

FLORIDA*

Division of Elections
Office of the Secretary of State
Room 316, R. A. Gray Bldg.
500 South Bronough St.
Tallahassee, FL 32399–0250
(850) 245–6200

GEORGIA*

Elections Division
Office of the Secretary of State
200 Piedmont Ave., S.E.
Suite 1402, West Tower
Atlanta, GA 30334–1505
(404) 463-1980
TTY (800) 551–8029

GUAM

Election Commission
414 W. Soledad Ave., 2nd Floor, Room #200
Hagatna, Guam 96910
(671) 477–9791
E-mail: director@gec.guam.gov

HAWAII*

Campaign Spending Commission
235 South Beretania Street, Room 300
Honolulu, HI 96813
(808) 586–0285
E-mail: elections@hawaii.gov

IDAHO*

Elections Division
Office of the Secretary of State
700 W. Jefferson St.
P.O. Box 83720
Boise, ID 83720–0080
(208) 334–2852

ILLINOIS*

State Board of Elections
2329 S. MacArthur Blvd.
Springfield, IL 62704
(217) 782–4141
TTY (217) 782–1518

State Board of Elections
100 W. Randolph St., #14–100
Chicago, IL 60601
(312) 814–6440

INDIANA*

Indiana Election Commission
302 W. Washington St., Room E204

Indianapolis, IN 46204–2767
(317) 232–3939 or (800) 622–4941

IOWA*

Ethics and Campaign Disclosure Board
510 E. 12th St., #1A
Des Moines, IA 50319
(515) 281–4028

KANSAS*

Elections Division
Office of the Secretary of State
Memorial Hall, 1st Floor
120 S.W. 10th Ave.
Topeka, KS 66612–1594
(785) 296–4561

KENTUCKY*

Registry of Election Finance
140 Walnut St.
Frankfort, KY 40601–3240
(502) 573–2226

LOUISIANA*

Elections Division
Office of the Secretary of State
8585 Archives Ave.
Baton Rouge, LA 70809
Mailing address:
P.O. Box 94125
Baton Rouge, LA 70804–9125
(225) 922–0900

MAINE*

Commission on Governmental Ethics
    and Election Practices
135 State House Station
Augusta, ME 04333–0135
(207) 287–4179

MARYLAND*

State Board of Elections
151 West St., #200
Annapolis, MD 21401–0486
Mailing address:
P.O. Box 6486
Annapolis, MD 21401
(800) 222–8683

MASSACHUSETTS*

Public Records Division
Office of the Secretary of the Commonwealth
One Ashburton Place, Room 1719
Boston, MA 02108
(617) 727–2832

MICHIGAN*

Elections Bureau
Office of the Secretary of State
430 W. Allegan St., 1st Floor

Lansing, MI 48918
Mailing address:
P.O. Box 20126
Lansing, MI 48901–0726
(517) 373–2540

MINNESOTA*
Elections Division
Office of the Secretary of State
180 State Office Bldg.
100 Rev. Dr. Martin Luther King Jr. Blvd.
St. Paul, MN 55155–1299
(651) 215–1440

MISSISSIPPI*
Office of the Secretary of State
401 Mississippi St.
Jackson, MS 39201
Mailing address:
P.O. Box 136
Jackson, MS 39205–0136
(601) 359–1350 or (800) 829–6786

MISSOURI*
Missouri Ethics Commission
3411-A Knipp Dr.
Jefferson City, MO 65109
Mailing address:
P.O. Box 1370
Jefferson City, MO 65102
(573) 751–2020 or (800) 392–8660

MONTANA*
Commissioner of Political Practices
1205 8th Ave.
P.O. Box 202401
Helena, MT 59620–2401
(406) 444–2942

NEBRASKA*
Accountability and Disclosure Commission
State Capitol, 11th Floor
Lincoln, NE 68509
Mailing address:
P.O. Box 95086
Lincoln, NE 68509–5086
(402) 471–2522

NEVADA*
Elections Division
Office of the Secretary of State
101 N. Carson Street, #3
Carson City, NV 89701–4786
(775) 684–5705

NEW HAMPSHIRE*
Office of the Secretary of State
71 S. Fruit St.
Concord, NH 03301
(603) 271–2236

NEW JERSEY*
Elections Division
Office of the Secretary of State
225 W. State St., 5th Floor
P.O. Box 304
Trenton, NJ 08625–0304
(609) 292–3760
TTY (800) 292–0039

NEW MEXICO*
Office of the Secretary of State
325 Don Gaspar, #300
Santa Fe, NM 87501
(505) 827–3600 or (800) 477–3632

NEW YORK*
State Board of Elections
40 North Pearl St., #5
Albany, NY 12207–2729
(518) 474–8100

NORTH CAROLINA*
State Board of Elections
441 N. Harrington St.
Raleigh, NC 27603
Mailing address:
P.O. Box 27255
Raleigh, NC 27611–7255
(919) 733–7173

NORTH DAKOTA*
Office of the Secretary of State
Capitol Bldg., Dept. 108
600 E. Boulevard Ave.
Bismarck, ND 58505–0500
(701) 328–2900 or (800) 352–0867

OHIO
Elections Division
Office of the Secretary of State
180 E. Broad St., 15th Floor
Columbus, OH 43215
(614) 466–2585

OKLAHOMA*
Ethics Commission
2300 N. Lincoln Blvd. Room B-5
Oklahoma City, OK 73105–4812
(405) 521–3451

OREGON*
Elections Division
Office of the Secretary of State
255 Capitol St. N.E., #501
Salem, OR 97310–0722
(503) 986–1518

PENNSYLVANIA*
Bureau of Commissions, Elections,
and Legislation

210 North Office Bldg.
Harrisburg, PA 17120–0029
(717) 787–5280

PUERTO RICO
State Elections Commission
235 Arterial Hostas Ave.,
North Tower, Box 1401
San Juan, PR 00919
(787) 332-2050

RHODE ISLAND*
Elections Civics Division
Office of the Secretary of State
138 W. River St.
Providence, RI 02904
(401) 222–2340 or (877) 222–2340

SOUTH CAROLINA*
State Election Commission
2221 Devine St., #105
Columbia, SC 29205
Mailing address:
P.O. Box 5987
Columbia, SC 29250
(803) 734–9060

SOUTH DAKOTA*
Office of the Secretary of State
500 E. Capitol Ave.
State Capitol Bldg., #204
Pierre, SD 57501–5070
(605) 773–3537

TENNESSEE*
Registry of Election Finance
404 James Robertson Pkwy., #1614
Nashville, TN 37243
(615) 741–7959

TEXAS*
Texas Ethics Commission
Sam Houston Office Bldg.
201 E. 14th St., 10th Floor
Austin, TX 78701
Mailing address:
P.O. Box 12070
Austin, TX 78711–2070
(512) 463–5800

UTAH*
Elections Office
Office of the Lieutenant Governor
350 North State St., #220
Salt Lake City, UT 84114–2325
(801) 538–1041 or (800) 995–8683

VERMONT*
Election Division
Office of the Secretary of State
128 State St.
Montpelier, VT 05633–1101
(802) 828–2363

VIRGIN ISLANDS
Board of Elections
93A Diamond Sunny Isle Shopping Center Annex
Christiansted, St. Croix
U.S. Virgin Islands 00823
Mailing address:
P.O. Box 1499
Kingshill, St. Croix, USVI 00851–1499
(340) 773–1021
E-mail: electionsys@unitedstatesvi

VIRGINIA*
State Board of Elections
Washington Bldg.
1100 Bank St., 1st Floor
Richmond, VA 23219
(804) 864–8901 or (800) 552–9745

WASHINGTON*
Public Disclosure Commission
711 Capitol Way, Room 206
P.O. Box 40908
Olympia, WA 98504–0908
(360) 753–1111 or (877) 601–2828

WEST VIRGINIA*
Office of the Secretary of State
Bldg. 1, #157-K
1900 Kanawha Blvd. East
Charleston, WV 25305–0770
(304) 558–6000 or (866) 767–8683

WISCONSIN*
Government Accountability Board
212 E. Washington Ave., 3rd Floor
Madison, WI 53703
Mailing address:
P.O. Box 7984
Madison, WI 53707–7984
(608) 266–8005

WYOMING
Elections Division
Office of the Secretary of State
Capitol Bldg.
200 W. 24th St.,
Cheyenne, WY 82002–0020
(307) 777–5860

Federal Housing Finance Agency

1700 G St. N.W., Washington, DC 20552
Internet: www.fhfa.gov

The Federal Housing Finance Agency (FHFA), established in July 2008 by the Housing and Economic Recovery Act of 2008 (HERA), regulates the Federal National Mortgage Association (Fannie Mae), the Federal Home Loan Mortgage Corporation (Freddie Mac), and the twelve Federal Home Loan Banks. The 2008 act created the FHFA by merging the Federal Housing Finance Board (the Finance Board) and the Office of Federal Housing Enterprise Oversight (OFHEO), an independent regulatory agency previously within the Department of Housing and Urban Development (HUD). The FHFA took over the regulatory authority of the two agencies.

Before the merger, the Finance Board was an independent regulatory agency that had supervised the Federal Home Loan Bank (FHLB) system. OFHEO had regulatory oversight over Fannie Mae and Freddie Mac, the government-sponsored enterprises (GSEs). The 2008 act gave the new FHFA increased regulatory oversight, including the authority to place the GSEs into conservatorship. The FHFA is headed by a director appointed by the president.

FHLBank Oversight

The FHFA's Division of FHLBank Regulation is responsible for ensuring that the Federal Home Loan Banks operate in a fiscally sound manner, have adequate capital, and are able to raise funds in the capital markets. To carry out FHLBank oversight duties, FHFA has implemented a program of FHLBank supervision to conduct on-site annual examinations and off-site monitoring of the FHLBanks and the Office of Finance. This includes programs for safety and soundness examinations, Affordable Housing Program (AHP) examinations, examination and supervisory policy and program development, FHLBank analysis, risk modeling, risk monitoring and information management, and risk analysis and research.

The FHLBank system, consisting of twelve district banks, is required to contribute funds to the AHP. This program lends money to member banks below market cost to finance purchase and renovation of housing for families with incomes at 80 percent or below the median for their communities. The members of the FHLBank system include commercial banks, insured savings and loan associations, mutual savings banks, credit unions, and insurance companies. Members must be primarily home-financing institutions that reinvest the funds as home mortgages.

In September 2014 the FHFA proposed a rule to revise FHFA's existing FHLBanks membership regulation to ensure that members maintain a commitment to housing finance and that only eligible entities can gain access to bank advances and the benefits of membership. The rule would establish a new quantitative test requiring all members to hold one percent of their assets in home mortgage loans (HML) and to do so on an ongoing basis. Also, the rule would require certain members that are subject to the 10 percent residential mortgage loans (RML) requirement to adhere to this requirement on an ongoing basis. In both cases, banks were required to meet this threshold only during the application period. The proposal also sought insurance changes as well. The comment period was extended into 2015.

Government Sponsored Enterprise (GSE) Oversight

The FHFA's Division of Enterprise Regulation is responsible for ensuring that Fannie Mae and Freddie Mac are adequately capitalized and operate in a safe and sound manner. To implement this statutory authority, the FHFA has implemented a supervision program to assess the overall safety and soundness of the GSEs. This includes programs for accounting and disclosure, capital adequacy, examination, financial analysis, and supervision infrastructure.

By summer 2008, with accounting scandals at Fannie Mae and Freddie Mac making headlines and the banking crisis rapidly unfolding, public confidence in the two agencies dropped sharply. On July 13, 2008, Treasury Secretary Henry Paulson announced a three-point plan to provide emergency assistance to Fannie Mae and Freddie Mac. First, the Treasury would provide a temporary increase in the line of credit to the GSEs. Second, the Treasury would have temporary authority to purchase equity in either of the two GSEs if they failed. Third, the Federal Reserve would have a consultative role in the new GSE regulator's process. This plan was unveiled in anticipation of the Housing and Economic Recovery Act (HERA) of 2008, passing Congress and being signed by the president later that month.

On Sept. 7, 2008, director James Lockhart announced the conservatorship of Fannie Mae and Freddie Mac.

Freddie Mac's inability to raise capital and the continuing deterioration in the mortgage market—home prices in free fall and mortgage delinquency rates rising—led to the decision to put the GSEs into conservatorship. At the time, the GSEs had $5.4 trillion of guaranteed mortgage-backed securities (MBS) and debt outstanding. Paulson and Federal Reserve Chair Ben Bernanke publicly endorsed the FHFA's conservatorship. By September 2010, the combined debt and obligations of these GSEs totaled $6.7 trillion.

When Lockhart announced the conservatorship, he outlined key changes in business practice, which included

■ Businesses would open as normal, only with stronger backing for the holders of MBS, senior debt, and subordinated debt.

■ The GSEs would be allowed to increase their guarantee MBS books without limits and continue to purchase replacement securities for their portfolios, about $20 billion per month without capital constraints.

■ As the conservator, FHFA would assume the power of the board and management.

■ The CEOs of both GSEs were dismissed and replaced; compensation for the new CEOs would be significantly lower than for the outgoing CEOs.

■ In order to conserve more than $2 billion in capital every year, the common stock and preferred stock dividends would be eliminated, but the common and all preferred stocks would continue to remain outstanding. Subordinated debt interest and principal payments would continue to be made.

■ Any other management action would be limited.

■ All political activities, including all lobbying, would be halted immediately. FHFA would review charitable activities.

■ There would be a continuing financing and investing relationship with the Treasury to provide critically needed support to Freddie Mac and Fannie Mae, and also to the liquidity of the mortgage market, which included the twelve Federal Home Loan Banks.

During the conservatorship period, FHFA continued to work on regulations necessary to implement HERA. By the end of 2010, FHFA published final rules. Key regulations include minimum capital standards, prudential safety and soundness standards, and portfolio limits.

In 2012 the FHFA released *A Strategic Plan for Enterprise Conservatorships*. This plan identified three strategic goals for the next phase of the conservatorships: (1) build a new infrastructure for the secondary mortgage market, (2) contract the GSEs' dominant presence in the marketplace gradually while simplifying and shrinking their operations, and (3) maintain foreclosure prevention activities and credit availability for new and refinanced mortgages.

Homeowners Assistance

The Emergency Economic and Stabilization Act of 2008 authorized FHFA, as conservator of the Fannie Mae and Freddie Mac, to implement a plan to maximize assistance for home owners and encourage the servicers

of the underlying mortgages to take advantage of the HOPE for Homeowners Program under the National Housing Act, or other available programs, to minimize foreclosures. FHFA mandated a moratorium on GSE foreclosures November 26, 2008, through January 31, 2009, to work with borrowers in foreclosure. In the first year, Fannie Mae and Freddie Mac implemented more than 405,000 trial and permanent loan modifications under the administration's Home Affordable Modification Program (HAMP) and refinanced four million loans.

The FHFA expanded the homeowner refinancing effort with the Home Affordable Refinance Program (HARP) in 2009. HARP, as introduced, allowed homeowners to refinance up to 105 percent of the value of the home's appraised value. This was an effort to assist homeowners who were underwater on their loans—the loan value was more than the home's current value. As the number of underwater loans increased and loan-to-value ratio (LTV) grew, HARP was modified to allow homeowners to refinance up to 125 percent of the home's appraised value. FHFA eventually eliminated the LTV ceiling for fixed-rate mortgages backed or guaranteed by Fannie Mae and Freddie Mac.

In 2013 the FHFA implemented a streamlined modification initiative requiring Freddie and Fannie servicers to offer eligible borrowers who are at least 90 days delinquent on their mortgages the ability to lower their monthly payments and modify their mortgages without requiring financial or hardship documentation.

By the end of 2014 the FHFA refinanced more than 3.2 million loans through HARP. FHFA loan modification programs prevented more than 3.3 million foreclosures by the end of 2014. FHFA extended the HARP, HAMP, and the streamlined modification program to the end of 2015. HARP loans, HAMP modifications, and FHFA-authorized streamlined modifications are available only to consumers whose loans are owned or guaranteed by Fannie Mae or Freddie Mac.

Dodd-Frank Wall Street Reform and Consumer Protection Act

Following the economic crisis that began in 2008, Congress passed the Dodd-Frank Wall Street Reform and Consumer Protection Act in 2010 to better regulate risk in the financial markets. The Dodd-Frank Act requires the Securities and Exchange Commission (SEC) and the Commodity Futures Trading Commission (CFTC) to work with the prudential regulators—the Farm Credit Administration, the Federal Reserve Board, the Office of the Comptroller of the Currency, the Federal Deposit Insurance Corporation, and the Federal Housing Finance Agency—to develop regulations for margin requirements on non-cleared derivatives for each of the entities subject to regulation under each of the respective agencies. SEC and CFTC are authorized to establish margin requirements for swaps dealers that are not primarily regulated by the prudential regulators.

The CFTC and the prudential regulators issued proposed rules in April 2011 for swaps markets and swaps participants. The proposed rules would require swap entities regulated by the prudential regulators to collect minimum amounts of initial margin and variation margin from counterparties to non-cleared swaps and non-cleared, security-based swaps.

The Dodd-Frank Act also requires each federal agency to review certain regulations that refer to external credit ratings (such as those provided by Moody's, Standard & Poor's, and Fitch) and to replace such regulations with alternative credit standards, as appropriate.

HERA also required the GSEs to set aside specified fund allocations for affordable housing programs for low-income families—a Housing Trust Fund within the Housing and Urban Development Department and the Capital Magnet Fund within the Treasury Department. HERA authorized FHFA to temporarily suspend GSE allocations if such a move would cause financial instability; as such, the GSEs did not allocate funds for several years. In December 2014 the FHFA issued a rule directing Fannie Mae and Freddie Mac to begin setting aside and allocating funds to the Housing Trust Fund and the Capital Magnet Fund.

FHFA Files Suit to Recover Losses Suffered by Fannie Mae and Freddie Mac

On July 27, 2011, FHFA, as conservator for Fannie Mae and Freddie Mac (the Enterprises), filed a lawsuit in federal court against UBS Americas, Inc. and related defendants alleging violations of federal securities laws in the sale of residential private-label, mortgage-backed securities (PLS) to the GSEs. The lawsuit alleged that UBS Americas made numerous material misstatements and omissions about the mortgage loans underlying the private-label MBS, including the creditworthiness of the borrowers and the quality of the origination and underwriting practices used to evaluate and approve such loans.

On September 2, 2011, FHFA filed lawsuits against 17 financial institutions, including some of their officers and various unaffiliated lead underwriters. The losses claimed under the suits total nearly $200 billion; the suit would require the institutions to buy back the bad loans. The suits alleged violations of federal securities laws and common law in the sale of residential private-label, mortgage-backed securities to the Enterprises. The complaints sought damages and civil penalties under the Securities Act of 1933. In addition, each complaint sought compensatory damages for negligent misrepresentation. Certain complaints also alleged state securities law violations or common law fraud.

Several of the institutions, led by UBS, sought to have the lawsuit dismissed. UBS argued that the three-year statute of limitations had expired. In May 2012, Judge Denise L. Cote, the presiding judge in the case, denied the banks' motions to dismiss the suit. UBS appealed the decision.

Rather than engaging in costly litigation, several of the defendants negotiated settlements with FHFA. In January 2013, FHFA reached settlement with General Electric (GE) and underwriters Morgan Stanley (MS) and

Credit Suisse Group AG (CS), which were among the 17 institutions listed in the September 2011 lawsuit. Other financial institutions listed in the lawsuit later settled as well. In addition, Wells Fargo, which was not one of the 17 institutions, entered into a non-litigation settlement. By September 2014, FHFA had settled all but two cases for roughly $18 billion. Settlements ranged from $6.5 million to $5.83 billion. The dispositions of the final two cases were in question in early 2015. Royal Bank of Scotland Group, PLC was expected to settle in 2015. After losing an appeal to have the case dismissed in 2014, Nomura Holding America continued to fight the lawsuit and the case was expected to go to trial in spring 2015.

■ KEY PERSONNEL

Director
Melvin Watt . . . . (202) 649–3800
    Fax. . . . . (202) 649–1072
    E-mail: Director@fhfa.gov

Board Members
Melvin Watt, director of
    the FHFA . . . .(202) 649–3800, ext. 2
Julian Castro, secretary of Housing
    and Urban Development . . . . (202) 708–0417
Jacob (Jack) L. Lew, secretary
    of the Treasury. . . . . (202) 622–1100
Mary Jo White, chair of the Securities
    and Exchange Commission . . . . . . (202) 551–2100

Senior Deputy Director and Chief Operating Officer
Lawrence Stauffer (acting). . . . . (202) 649–3800
    E-mail: coo@fhfa.gov

Senior Associate for Examination, Office of Conservatorship Operations
Wanda DeLeo . . . . (202) 649–3800

Deputy Director, Division of Federal Home Loan Bank Regulation
Fred C. Graham. . . . . (202) 649–3808
    E-mail: DeputyDirector-FHLBanks@fhfa.gov

Senior Associate Director, Monitoring and Analysis
Anthony G. Cornyn . . . . (202) 649–3800

Deputy Director, Division of Enterprise Regulation
Nina Nichols . . . . (202) 649–3809
    E-mail: DeputyDirector-Enterprises@fhfa.gov

Associate Director, Credit Risk
Maria Fernandez. . . . . (202) 649–3800

Senior Associate Director, Office of Financial Analysis & Modeling
Naa Awaa Tagoe . . . . (202) 649–3800

Associate Director, Minority and Women Inclusion
Sharron P. A. Levine . . . . (202) 649–3806
    E-mail: OMWIinfo@fhfa.gov

Chief Accountant
Nick Satriano. . . . . (202) 649–3800

Chief Economist/Associate Director for Policy Analysis and Research
Nayantara Hensel . . . . (202) 649–3800

Chief Financial Officer, Budget & Financial Management
Mark A. Kinsey . . . . (202) 649–3800

Senior Associate Director, Office of Congressional Affairs & Communication

    Meg Burns . . . . (202) 649–3802

General Counsel

    Alfred M. Pollard . . . . (202) 649–3804

        E-mail: GeneralCounsel@fhfa.gov

Housing and Regulatory Policy

    Sandra Thompson . . . . (202) 649–3800

Human Capital

    Polly Grago . . . . (202) 649–3807

Inspector General

    Laura S. Wertheimer . . . . (202) 730–0381

        E-mail: OIGhotline@fhfa.gov

Chief Information Officer, Office of Technology and Information Management

    Kevin Winkler . . . . (202) 649–3800

Ombudsman

    Mario Uholetti . . . . (202) 649–3805

    Fax . . . . (202) 649–2811

        E-mail: Ombudsman@fhfa.gov

■ INFORMATION SOURCES

Internet

Agency website: www.fhfa.gov. For general information, e-mail fhfainfo@fhfa.gov; for consumer complaints, consumer_complaints@fhfa.gov; and for media inquiries, mediainquiries@fhfa.gov.

Telephone Contacts

    Main Number and Personnel Locator (202) 649–3800

    Consumer Complaints . . . . (202) 649–3811

    Homeowners' Hope Hotline (Making

        Home Affordable.gov . . . . (888) 995–4673

    Inspector General's Hotline . . . . (800) 793–7724

    Media . . . . (202) 649–3700

Information and Publications

KEY OFFICES

Office of Congressional Affairs & Communications

400 7th St. S.W.
Washington, DC 20024
(202) 649–3802
E-mail: FHFAinfo@fhfa.gov; consumerhelp@fhfa.gov

Answers media inquiries; provides information about scheduled meetings and hearings; makes available congressional testimony, official statements, public notices, and guidelines for ensuring the integrity of the information disseminated by the agency; provides information on mortgage basics, mortgage- and housing-related fraud, avoiding foreclosure, housing-related discrimination, and consumer information from financial services regulators. All information is available on the website.

Freedom of Information

Requester Service Center
400 7th St S.W., 8th Floor
Washington, DC 20024
(202) 649–3803
Fax (202) 649–1073
E-mail: foia@fhfa.gov
David A. Lee, chief FOIA officer

PUBLICATIONS

Numerous publications, surveys, and data sets are available on the website and through the Office of External Relations, including *A Primer on the Secondary Mortgage Market,* a monthly *Foreclosure Prevention Report,* the monthly interest rate survey, and *U.S. Treasury Support for Fannie Mae and Freddie Mac,* which outlines the various facilities introduced by the Treasury Dept. to support Fannie Mae and Freddie Mac in conservatorship.

MEETINGS

The schedule may be obtained on the website or by contacting the Office of External Relations (*see above*).

Reference Resources

Information on FHFA decision documents of all kinds, plus information on such topics as board meetings, rules and regulations, the monthly interest rate survey, and Federal Home Loan Bank policies and programs is available at the FHFA website, www.fhfa.gov.

DOCKETS

Records of rulemakings, administrative proceedings, and docket information are available at www.regulations.gov. (*See appendix for information on searching and commenting on regulations.*) Information may also be obtained by contacting the Office of General Counsel:

Office of General Counsel

400 7th St. S.W.
Washington, DC 20024
(202) 649–3804
E-mail: GeneralCounsel@FHFA.gov
Alfred M. Pollard, general counsel

RULES AND REGULATIONS

FHFA rules and regulations are published in *Code of Federal Regulations,* Title 12, Chapter XII. Proposed regulations, new final regulations, and updates to the *Code of Federal Regulations* are published in the daily *Federal Register.* (*See appendix for details on how to obtain and use these publications.*)

■ LEGISLATION

The FHFA was created by the **Housing and Economic Recovery Act of 2008** (5 U.S.C. 301 and 552, 122 Stat. 2654), which merged the Federal Housing Finance Board (FHFB) and the Office of Federal Housing Enterprise Oversight (OFHEO). FHFB rules and regulations were codified in the *Code of Federal Regulations,* Title

12, Chapter IX, Parts 900–999. OFHEO rules and regulations were codified in the *Code of Federal Regulations,* Title 12, Chapter XVII.

Federal Home Loan Bank Act of 1932 (FHLBA) (47 Stat. 725, 12 U.S.C. 1421–1449). Signed by the president July 22, 1932. Created the Federal Home Loan Bank Board and the Federal Home Loan Bank System, which included federally chartered institutions insured by the Federal Savings and Loan Insurance Corporation and mutual savings banks.

Federal National Mortgage Association Charter Act of 1954 (Title III of National Housing Act, 12 U.S.C. 1716 et seq.). Signed by the president August 2, 1954. Chartered the Federal National Mortgage Association (Fannie Mae). Amended by the 1968 Charter Act, which divided Fannie Mae into two parts: a reformed Fannie Mae and Ginnie Mae, the Government National Mortgage Association. Ginnie Mae provides guarantees on mortgage-backed securities backed by federally insured or guaranteed loans.

Emergency Home Finance Act of 1970 (12 U.S.C. 1454[a][2]). Signed by the president July 24, 1970. Contained the Federal Home Loan Mortgage Act, which chartered the Federal Home Loan Mortgage Corporation (Freddie Mac) and authorized it to create a secondary market for conventional mortgages.

Financial Institutions Reform, Recovery, and Enforcement Act of 1989 (FIRREA) (101 Stat. 183, 12 U.S.C. 1811 note). Signed by the president Aug. 9, 1989. Abolished the Federal Home Loan Bank Board and distributed its responsibilities to other agencies; established the FHFB and the Office of Thrift Supervision. Created the Affordable Housing Program.

Federal Housing Enterprises Financial Safety and Soundness Act of 1992 (12 U.S.C. 4501 et seq.). Established the Office of Federal Housing Enterprise Oversight (OFHEO) as an independent entity within the Department of Housing and Urban Development. The OFHEO director was authorized to ensure that Fannie Mae and Freddie Mac (the enterprises) and their affiliates were adequately capitalized and operating safely. Authorized the director to establish and collect from the enterprises annual assessments for reasonable costs and expenses.

Financial Services Modernization Act of 1999 (Gramm-Leach-Bliley Act) (113 Stat. 1338, 12 U.S.C. 1811 note). Signed by the president Nov. 12, 1999. Title VI: Federal Home Loan Bank System Modernization Act of 1999 amended the FHLBA to expand FHLB membership parameters to make a federal savings association's membership in the FHLB system voluntary instead of mandatory. Empowered the FHFB to charge an FHLB or any executive officer or director with violation of the law or regulation in connection with the granting of any application or other request by the bank, or any written agreement between the bank and the FHFB and other provisions.

Preserving Independence of Financial Institution Examinations Act of 2003 (117 Stat. 2899, 18 U.S.C. 201 note). Signed by the president Dec. 19, 2003. Amended federal criminal law to subject to criminal penalties personnel of a financial institution who offer a loan or gratuity to a financial institution examiner and a financial institution examiner who accepts such loan or gratuity.

The Housing and Economic Recovery Act of 2008 (5 U.S.C. 301 and 552, 122 Stat. 2654). Signed by the president July 30, 2008. Merged the regulatory authority, employees, property, and facilities of the OFHEO and the Finance Board into the newly created FHFA. Authorized appointment of a director with oversight over the Office of Finance, the Federal Home Loan Banks, Fannie Mae, and Freddie Mac. Amended the Securities Exchange Act of 1934 to subject the regulated entities to its registration and reporting requirements. Prescribed regulatory actions for undercapitalized regulated entities. Empowered the FHFA director to place GSEs (Fannie Mae and Freddie Mac) into receivership or conservatorship. Prescribed the minimum capital level for each FHLB. Authorized community development financial institutions (CDFIs) that have been certified by the CDFI Fund of the U.S. Treasury Department to become members of Federal Home Loan Banks. Requires the GSEs to set aside specified funds allocations for affordable housing programs; authorized FHFA to temporarily suspend GSE allocations if such allocations would cause financial instability.

Emergency Economic Stabilization Act of 2008 (122 Stat. 3765, 12 U.S.C. 5201). Signed by the president Oct. 3, 2008. Authorized FHFA, as conservator of the Fannie Mae and Freddie Mac, to implement a plan to maximize assistance for home owners and encourage the servicers of the underlying mortgages to take advantage of the HOPE for Homeowners Program under the National Housing Act or other available programs to minimize foreclosures.

Dodd-Frank Wall Street Reform and Consumer Protection Act (124 Stat. 1376, 12 U.S.C. 5301 note). Signed by the president July 21, 2010. Authorizes the Commodity Futures Trading Commission (CFTC) to regulate the swaps marketplace, which was previously unregulated. With some exceptions, directs the CFTC and the Securities and Exchange Commission (SEC) to coordinate with each other and with the prudential regulators (the Federal Reserve Board, the Office of the Comptroller of the Currency, the Federal Deposit Insurance Corporation, the Farm Credit Administration, and the Federal Housing Finance Agency) before commencing any rulemaking or issuing an order regarding swaps and related actions. Prohibits a creditor from making a "higher-risk mortgage" to any consumer without first obtaining a written appraisal of the property involving a physical property visit by a licensed or certified appraisal. Directed banking regulators to implement minimum requirements for state registration and supervision of appraisal management companies. Other financial regulatory provisions.

Temporary Payroll Tax Cut Continuation Act of 2011 (125 Stat. 1280). Signed by the president Dec. 23, 2011. Title IV required the FHFA director to direct Freddie Mac and Fannie Mae (GSEs) to increase guarantee fees by 10 basis points on all mortgages delivered for inclusion into mortgage-backed securities pools. Additionally, Freddie Mac and Fannie Mae were directed to increase the credit fee on whole loans by a similar amount. Requires direct deposit into the Treasury of any amounts received from fee increases imposed by this act.

GOVERNMENT-SPONSORED ENTERPRISES REGULATED BY FHFA

FANNIE MAE

3900 Wisconsin Ave. N.W.
Washington, DC 20016
(800) 732–6643
(202) 752–7000
Internet: www.fanniemae.com
Timothy J. Mayopoulos, president and chief executive officer

FREDDIE MAC

8200 Jones Branch Dr.
McLean, VA 22102–3110
(703) 903–2000
(800) 424–5401
Internet: www.freddiemac.com
Donald H. Layton, chief executive officer

OFFICE OF FINANCE

1818 Library St., #200
Reston, VA 20190
(703) 467–3600
E-mail: info@fhlb-of.com
Internet: www.fhlb-of.com
John Fisk, chief executive officer

REGIONAL FEDERAL HOME BANK DISTRICTS

REGION 1

(CT, MA, ME, NH, RI, VT)
800 Boylston St., 9th Floor
P.O. Box 990411
Boston, MA 02199
(617) 292–9600
Internet: www.fhlbboston.com
E-mail: info@fhiboston.com
Donna L. Boulanger, president

REGION 2

(NJ, NY, PR, VI)
101 Park Ave., 5th Floor
New York, NY 10178–0599
(212) 681–6000
Fax (212) 441–6890
Internet: www.fhlbny.com
Jose Gonzalez, president

REGION 3

(DE, PA, WV)
601 Grant St.
Pittsburgh, PA 15219–4455

(800) 288–3400
Internet: www.fhlb-pgh.com
Winthrop Watson, president

REGION 4

(AL, DC, FL, GA, MD, NC, SC, VA)
1475 Peachtree St. N.E.
Atlanta, GA 30309
Mailing address:
P.O. Box 105565
Atlanta, GA 30348
(404) 888–8000
(800) 536–9650
Internet: www.fhlbatl.com
Wes McMullan, president

REGION 5

(KY, OH, TN)
P.O. Box 598
221 E. 4th St., #600
Cincinnati, OH 45202
(513) 852–7500
(888) 852–6500
E-mail: info@fhibcin.com
Internet: www.fhlbcin.com
Andrew S. Howell, president

REGION 6

(IN, MI)
8250 Woodfield Crossing Blvd.
Indianapolis, IN 46240
(317) 465–0200
(800) 442–2568
Internet: www.fhlbi.com
Cindy L. Konich, president

REGION 7

(IL, WI)
200 E. Randolph Dr., #1800
Chicago, IL 60601
(312) 565–5700
Internet: www.fhlbc.com
Matthew R. Feldman, president, (312) 565–5834

REGION 8

(AK, AS, GU, HI, ID, IA, MI, MN, MO, MN, ND, OR, SD, UT, WA, WY)
801 Walnut St., #200
Des Moines, IA 50309–3513
(515) 281–1000
(800) 544–3452
Fax (515) 699–1293
Internet: www.fhlbdm.com
Richard S. Swanson, president

REGION 9

(AR, LA, MS, NM, TX)
8500 Freeport Pkwy. South
Irving, TX 75063

Mailing address:
P.O. Box 619026
Dallas, TX 75261
(214) 441–8500
Internet: www.fhlb.com
E-mail: fhlb@fhbl.com
Sanjay Bhasin, president

REGION 10

(CO, KS, NE, OK)
One Security Benefit Place, #100
Topeka, KS 66606
Mailing address:
P.O. Box 176
Topeka, KS 66601
(785) 233–0507
Fax (785) 234–1716
Internet: www.fhlbtopeka.com
Andrew J. Jetter, president

REGION 11

(AZ, CA, NV)
600 California St.,
San Francisco, CA 94108
Mailing address:
P.O. Box 7948
San Francisco, CA 94120
(415) 616–1000
(800) 283–0700
Fax (415) 616–2626
Internet: www.fhlbsf.com
Dean Schultz, president

Federal Maritime Commission

800 N. Capitol St. N.W., Washington, DC 20573
Internet: www.fmc.gov

The Federal Maritime Commission (FMC) is an independent regulatory agency within the executive branch. It began operations Aug. 12, 1961, as the result of Reorganizational Plan No. 7 issued by President John F. Kennedy. The FMC has five commissioners nominated by the president and confirmed by the Senate. No more than three of the commissioners may be members of the same political party. The president designates one of the commissioners to serve as chair with all commissioners serving five-year terms.

The FMC is responsible for regulating the ocean commerce of the United States, a role formerly held by the Federal Maritime Board. The board was abolished by the reorganization that created the FMC. The other chief function of the former maritime board, promoting the nation's merchant marine, was transferred to the Transportation Department's Maritime Administration (p. 806).

The FMC consists of eight offices that report to the managing director. They are the offices of the secretary, general counsel, consumer affairs and dispute resolution services, administrative law judges, management services, human resources, budget and finance, and information technology. Two offices, the inspector general and equal employment opportunity, report directly to the chair. Three bureaus—Bureau of Trade Analysis, Bureau of Enforcement, and Bureau of Consumer Certification and Licensing—are organized under the managing director and are responsible for the direct administration and coordination of FMC regulatory functions and other activities. The FMC has area representatives in Los Angeles, South Florida, New Orleans, New York, Seattle, and Houston. The area representatives also serve other major port cities and transportation centers within their respective areas on a regular rotating basis.

Bureau of Trade Analysis. Formerly known as the Bureau of Economics and Agreement Analysis, this bureau reviews agreements and monitors the concerted activities of common carriers by water under the standards of the Shipping Act of 1984.

The bureau also reviews and analyzes service contracts, monitors rates of government-controlled carriers, reviews carrier published tariff systems under the accessibility and accuracy standards of the Shipping Act of 1984, and responds to inquiries or issues concerning service contracts or tariffs. The bureau also is responsible for competition oversight and market analysis, focusing on activity that is substantially anticompetitive and market distorting in violation of the Shipping Act of 1984.

An integral part of the bureau's responsibilities is the systematic surveillance of carrier activity and commercial conditions in the U.S. liner trades. Accordingly, the bureau administers a variety of monitoring programs, and other research efforts, designed to apprise the commission of current trade conditions, emerging commercial trends, and carrier pricing and service activities.

The Bureau of Trade Analysis also maintains an agreement library of carrier and terminal agreements on file with the commission and publishes Carrier Agreements in the U.S. Oceanborne Trades.

The Bureau of Enforcement. Formed through the merger of the former Hearing Counsel and Bureau of Investigations, this bureau participates as trial counsel in formal adjudicatory proceedings, nonadjudicatory investigations, rulemaking proceedings when designated by commission order, and other proceedings initiated by the commission. The bureau also participates in formal complaint proceedings where intervention is permitted and appropriate, and monitors all other formal proceedings in order to identify major regulatory issues and to advise the managing director and the other bureaus.

The bureau also participates in the development of commission rules and regulations. Through investigative personnel, the bureau conducts investigations into and monitors the activities of ocean common carriers, non-vessel operating common carriers (NVOCCs), freight forwarders, shippers, ports and terminals, and other persons to ensure compliance with the statutes and regulations administered by the commission. Investigations are conducted into alleged violations of the full range of statutes and regulations administered by the commission.

The Bureau of Certification and Licensing. This bureau is composed of two offices, the Office of Passenger Vessels and Information Processing and the Office of Transportation Intermediaries. The Office of Passenger Vessels and Information Processing issues certificates to operators of passenger vessels with fifty or more berths that embark passengers from U.S. ports. The Office of Transportation Intermediaries licenses ocean transportation intermediaries; administers the ocean transportation intermediary bonding program by setting policies and guidelines and reviewing financial instruments that evidence financial responsibility; and certifies that owners and operators of passenger vessels in U.S. trades have evidenced financial responsibility to satisfy liability incurred for nonperformance of voyages or death or injury to passengers and other persons. This bureau, formerly the Bureau of Consumer Complaints and Licensing, was responsible for responding to consumer inquiries and complaints and overseeing a program of alternative dispute resolution. Those responsibilities were moved to the Office of Consumer Affairs and Dispute Resolution Services located within the Office of the Secretary.

The Shipping Act of 1984 expedited FMC procedures so that agreements between U.S. ocean liner companies (also known as conferences) that met the act's requirements were automatically approved by the FMC. The Shipping Act deregulated the shipping industry because such conferences were no longer subject to prior review by the FMC, and the agreements were exempted from U.S. antitrust laws.

The 1984 act protects the rights of shippers and consumers by expanding the powers of shippers to bargain with shipping cartels (conferences) for the best rates. Under the Controlled Carrier Act, the FMC is authorized to review the rates of government-owned carriers to ensure that they are not artificially low to ensure that U.S. trade remains competitive and not hampered by unfair trading practices of foreign governments. The FMC publishes a list of controlled carriers on its Web site.

The FMC can still intervene if it believes the enactment of an agreement would exploit its grant of antitrust immunity and to ensure that agreements do not otherwise violate the 1984 act or result in an unreasonable increase in transportation cost or unreasonable reduction in service. However, the commission no longer has the authority to approve or disapprove general rate increases or individual commodity rate levels in U.S. foreign commerce except with regard to certain foreign government-owned carriers.

Charges of discriminatory treatment (by terminal operators, forwarders, and others) are initially filed with the Office of the Secretary. The charges are then investigated and may result in formal administrative proceedings adjudicated by an administrative law judge. In addition, formal complaints may be filed seeking reparations or other remedies. Formal complaint proceedings, investigations, and other administrative proceedings can include a prehearing conference, a formal hearing before an administrative law judge, the judge's decision, oral argument before the commissioners, and a final report. The decisions of the commission may be appealed to the U.S. Court of Appeals.

The FMC reported that the act's reform did not bring about the negative consequences that some opponents had predicted. There were no sharp rate increases and was no curtailment of shipping services or loss of independent carrier competition. In fact, ocean freight rates fell after the 1984 act. Most carriers advocate a renewal of the act with few amendments because it allows them to discuss rates with their competition without violating U.S. antitrust laws. Shippers approve of their ability to enter

into service contracts with the carriers. Service contracts provide valuable leverage to control shipping rates.

During 1995, the FMC increased its cooperation with the U.S. Customs Service. The FMC now has online access to Customs' Automated Commercial Environment database, the Automated Broker Interface module that provides investigators with information on shipping transactions that had been very difficult to obtain.

The Shipping Act of 1984 was amended by the Ocean Shipping Reform Act (OSRA) of 1998. OSRA was the culmination of a nearly four-year effort to update and revise the Shipping Act, with virtually all segments of the industry represented in the legislative reform process. The following are major provisions of OSRA:

- Provide shippers and common carriers greater choice and flexibility in entering into contractual relationships with shippers for ocean transportation and intermodal services, including allowing members of ocean carrier agreements to negotiate and enter into service contracts with one or more shippers independent of the agreement.
- Reduce the expense of the tariff filing system and privatize the function of publishing tariff information while maintaining current tariff enforcement and common carriage principles with regard to tariff shipments.
- Protect U.S. exporters from disclosure to their foreign competitors of their contractual relationships with common carriers and proprietary business information, including targeted markets.
- Exempt new assembled motor vehicles specifically from tariff and service contract requirements and provide the FMC with greater flexibility to grant general exemptions from provisions of the 1984 act.
- Reform the licensing and bonding requirements for ocean freight forwarders and NVOCCs and consolidate the definitions of those two entities under the term ocean transportation intermediary.

In September 2001 the commission issued its mandated study on the regulatory and economic impact of OSRA. The study provided a general regulatory and economic overview of ocean shipping and examined several key issues: service contract developments, agreement and voluntary service contract guideline activities, ocean transportation intermediary licensing and bonding, and tariff publication. Other issues covered included controlled carriers, restrictive shipping practices by foreign governments, port trucking, and e-commerce. The study's closing observations identify issues meriting continuing attention and offer several suggestions for possible legislative consideration. The study is available on the FMC Web site.

The FMC chair (or the chair's designee) serves on the U.S. Committee on the Marine Transportation System. The committee, established under the Coast Guard and Maritime Transportation Act of 2012, was created to assess the adequacy of the marine transportation system, promote integration with other modes of transportation and uses of the marine environment, and coordinate federal policy recommendations. Membership includes the chair of the Federal Maritime Commission as well as the secretary of Transportation, the secretary of Defense, the secretary of Homeland Security, the secretary of Commerce, the secretary of the Treasury, the secretary of State, the secretary of the Interior, the secretary of Agriculture, the Attorney General, the secretary of Labor, the secretary of Energy, the administrator of the Environmental Protection Agency, and the chairman of the Joint Chiefs of Staff.

◼ KEY PERSONNEL

Chair

Mario Cordero. . . . . (202) 523–5911

Commissioners

William P. Doyle . . . . (202) 523–5723

Rebecca F. Dye. . . . . (202) 523–5715

E-mail: rdye@fmc.gov

Michael A. Khouri . . . . (202) 523–5712

E-mail: mkhouri@fmc.gov

Richard A. Lidinsky Jr. . . . . (202) 523–5721

E-mail: rlidinsky@fmc.gov

Managing Director

Vern W. Hill . . . . (202) 523–5800

E-mail: OMD@fmc.gov

Strategic Planning and Regulatory Review

Austin L. Schmitt. . . . . (202) 523–5800

Administrative Law Judge

Clay G. Guthridge. . . . . (202) 523–5750

E-mail: judges@fmc.gov

Equal Employment Opportunity

Howard F. Jimenez . . . . (202) 523–5859

E-mail: eeo@fmc.gov

General Counsel

Tyler J. Wood . . . . (202) 523–5740

Inspector General

Jon Hatfield . . . . (202) 523–5863

E-mail: OIG@fmc.gov

Secretary

Karen V. Gregory. . . . . (202) 523–5725

E-mail: secretary@fmc.gov

Consumer Affairs and Dispute Resolution Services

Rebecca A. Fenneman . . . . (202) 523–5807

E-mail: complaints@fmc.gov

Budget and Finance

Karon E. Douglass. . . . . (202) 523–5770

E-mail: obfmmaritime@fmc.gov

Human Resources

Todd Cole . . . . (202) 523–5773

E-mail: humanresources@fmc.gov

Information Technology

Edward Anthony. . . . . (202) 523–5835

E-mail: oit@fmc.gov

Management Services

Kristian Jovanovic. . . . . (202) 523–5900

E-mail: mgmtservices@fmc.gov

Bureau of Certification and Licensing

Sandra L. Kusumoto . . . . (202) 523–5787

Bureau of Enforcement

Peter J. King . . . . (202) 523–5783

E-mail: boe@fmc.gov

Bureau of Trade Analysis

Florence A. Carr . . . . (202) 523–5796

Passenger Vessels and Information Processing

Tajuanda Singletary. . . . . (202) 523–5818

E-mail: bcl@fmc.gov

Transportation Intermediaries

Jeremiah D. Hospital . . . . (202) 523–5843

Agreements

Jason Guthrie. . . . . (202) 523–5793

E-mail: tradeanalysis@fmc.gov

Economics and Competition Analysis

Roy J. Pearson . . . . (202) 523–5845

E-mail: tradeanalysis@fmc.gov

Service Contracts and Tariffs

Gary Kardian . . . . (202) 523–5856

E-mail: tradeanalysis@fmc.gov

◼ INFORMATION SOURCES

Internet

Agency Web site: www.fmc.gov. Includes information on FMC offices and programs; FMC regulations, statutes and rules; cruise passenger information; and forms that can be downloaded.

Telephone Contacts

General number . . . . (202) 523–5800

Inspector General Hotline . . . . (202) 523–5865

Equal Opportunity Hotline. . . . . (202) 523–5806

Federal Relay Service TTY . . . . (800) 877–8339

Information and Publications

KEY OFFICES

FMC Public Information

Office of the Secretary
800 N. Capitol St. N.W., #1046
Washington, DC 20573
(202) 523–5725

Issues news releases and answers or refers general questions. Distributes the commission's annual reports.

Freedom of Information

Office of the Secretary
800 N. Capitol St. N.W., #1046
Washington, DC 20573
(202) 523–5725
Karen V. Gregory, chief FOIA officer
E-mail: FOIA@fmc.gov
FOIA Requester Service, (202) 523–5707

MEETINGS

The commissioners hold periodic meetings at 10:00 a.m. in the Main Hearing Room, 800 N. Capitol St. N.W., 1st Floor, Washington, DC 20573. The agenda for each meeting is posted in the Office of the Secretary, (202) 523–5725, on the agency's Web site at www.fmc.gov (listed on the home page under What's New), and in the *Federal Register* and trade publications.

PUBLICATIONS

The annual report is available from FMC Public Information (above) and the agency's Web site at www .fmc.gov.

Reference Resources

LIBRARY

FMC Library
800 N. Capitol St. N.W., #1085
Washington, DC 20573
(202) 523–5762
Charlotte White, librarian
E-mail: Libraryinquiries@fmc.gov

Collection specializes in maritime law. Open to the public from 8:00 a.m. to 4:30 p.m., Monday to Friday.

DOCKETS
800 N. Capitol St. N.W., #1049
Washington, DC 20573
(202) 523–5760
Magdalene Grant, manager
E-mail: secretary@fmc.gov

Maintains dockets for FMC rulemakings and other regulatory proceedings. Open to the public from 9:00 a.m. to 5:00 p.m. FMC dockets can be found online at www.fmc .gov, in the Electronic Reading Room. Federal dockets are also available at www.regulations.gov. (*See appendix for information on searching and commenting on regulations.*)

RULES AND REGULATIONS

FMC rules and regulations are published in the *Code of Federal Regulations,* Title 46, Chapter IV, Parts 500–599. Proposed rules, new final rules, and updates to the *Code of Federal Regulations* are published in the daily *Federal Register.* (*See appendix for information on how to obtain and use these publications.*)

◼ LEGISLATION

Legislation the FMC administers includes

Shipping Act of 1916 (46 App. U.S.C. 801 et seq.). Signed by the president Sept. 7, 1916. Created the five-member U.S. Shipping Board to regulate the rates and practices of common carriers under the U.S. flag. This applied to foreign and interstate commerce. Gave the board the ability to acquire and operate merchant vessels.

Merchant Marine Act of 1920 (41 Stat. 988, 46 U.S.C. 13). Signed by the president June 5, 1920. Section 19 empowered the commission to make rules and regulations to reduce the effect on U.S. shippers of unfavorable rules made by foreign countries.

Public Law 89-777 (80 Stat. 1356, 46 U.S.C. 362). Signed by the president Nov. 6, 1966. Authorized the FMC

to require evidence of adequate financial resources from owners or operators of vessels with accommodations for fifty or more passengers that take on passengers at U.S. ports to cover judgments for personal injury or death and to repay passengers if the voyage fails to take place.

Shipping Act of 1984 (98 Stat. 67, 46 U.S.C. 1701 note). Signed by the president March 20, 1984. Amended the Shipping Act of 1916. The Controlled Carrier Act of the Shipping Act authorized the FMC to review the rates and rules of government-controlled carriers to ensure that they are not unjust or unreasonable.

Omnibus Trade and Competitiveness Act of 1988 (102 Stat. 1107, 19 U.S.C. 2901 note). Signed by the president Aug. 23, 1988. Included the Foreign Shipping Practices Act of 1988 (102 Stat. 1570, 46 U.S.C. app. 1710a). Authorized the FMC to take action against foreign ocean carriers whose practices or whose government's practices result in adverse conditions affecting the operations of U.S. carriers.

Title I of the **Ocean Shipping Reform Act of 1998** (112 Stat. 1902), signed by the president Oct. 14, 1998, made comprehensive amendments to the Shipping Act of 1984. Granted carriers participating in conferences or cooperative agreements automatic immunity from antitrust prosecution. The FMC could seek a federal court injunction against any agreement that it believed unnecessarily raised transportation costs or limited services. The act also provided for licensing and bonding ocean transportation intermediaries, the confidential filing of service contracts, and the publication of ocean freight rates.

◼ REGIONAL OFFICES

FMC Office of Operations

In 1996 the FMC's five field offices were replaced with six area representatives. Appointments are required to meet with area representatives.

HEADQUARTERS
800 N. Capitol St. N.W., 10th Floor
Washington, DC 20573–0001
(202) 523–5800
Fax (202) 523–5785
Michael F. Carley, area representative at large

HOUSTON
650 Sam Houston Pkwy., #230
Houston, TX 77060
(281) 386–8211
Fax (281) 591–6099
Adam Sinko, area representative
E-mail: ASinko@fmc.gov

LOS ANGELES
P.O. Box 230
839 S. Beacon St., #320
San Pedro, CA 97033–0230
(310) 514–4905 (Clark)

(310) 514–8618 (Asandas)
Fax (310) 514–3931
Oliver E. Clark, area representative
E-mail: oclark@fmc.gov
Nash D. Asandas, area representative
E-mail: nasandas@fmc.gov

SOUTH FLORIDA

P.O. Box 813609
Hollywood, FL 33081–3609
(954) 963–5362 (Margolis)
(954) 963–5284 (Mintz)
Fax (954) 963–5630
Andrew Margolis, area representative
E-mail: amargolis@fmc.gov
Eric O. Mintz, area representative
E-mail: emintz@fmc.gov

NEW ORLEANS

P.O. 700
St. Rose, LA 70087
(504) 589–6662
Fax (504) 589–6663

Bruce N. Johnson Sr., area representative
E-mail: bjohnson@fmc.gov

NEW YORK

Building No. 75, Room 205B
JFK International Airport
Jamaica, NY 11430
(718) 553–2228 (Podlaskowich)
(718) 553–2223 (Forst)
Fax (718) 553–2229
Ronald Podlaskowich, area representative
E-mail: rpodlaskowich@fmc.gov
Matthew D. Forst, assistant area representative
E-mail: mforst@fmc.gov

SEATTLE

FMC c/o Customs and Border Protection
7 S. Nevada St., #100
Seattle, WA 98134
(253) 922–7622
Fax (253) 922–7859
Michael A. Moneck, area representative
E-mail: mmoneck@fmc.gov

National Credit Union Administration

1775 Duke St., Alexandria, VA 22314–3428
Internet: www.ncua.gov

The National Credit Union Administration (NCUA), an independent agency within the executive branch, was created by a 1970 amendment to the Federal Credit Union Act of 1934. Administration of the original Federal Credit Union Act, which authorized the federal government to charter credit unions, was shifted among several agencies before the creation of the NCUA in 1970.

A three-member board governs the agency. Members of the board are nominated by the president and confirmed by the Senate for six-year terms.

The credit union movement in the United States dates from 1909, when Massachusetts passed the first state credit union law. Since then, all states have passed similar laws. A credit union is a cooperative association designed to promote thrift among its members. Membership is limited to persons having a common bond of occupation or association and to groups within a well-defined neighborhood, community, or rural district. The credit union accumulates funds from savings to make loans to members for useful purposes at reasonable interest rates.

A credit union is managed by a board of directors and committees made up of members. After expenses and legal reserve requirements are met, most of the earnings of a credit union are returned to the members as dividends on share holdings.

There are two types of credit unions: federal credit unions, chartered by the NCUA; and state credit unions, chartered by state agencies.

The NCUA:

- Approves or disapproves applications for federal credit union charters.
- Issues charters when applications are approved.
- Examines federal credit unions to determine financial condition.
- Supervises and regulates all federally insured credit unions.
- Regulates the operations of the Central Liquidity Facility, the central bank for loans.
- Administers the National Credit Union Share Insurance Fund (NCUSIF), which was authorized in 1970. All federally chartered credit unions are insured by NCUSIF. The NCUA board formulates standards and requirements for insured credit unions.

- Manages and sells unprofitable assets and assets of liquidated credit unions.

In 1998 the banking industry and the credit unions battled over credit union membership. The banking industry sought to limit credit union membership to groups with a common bond of enterprise. In February 1998 the Supreme Court, in a 5–4 decision, ruled that credit unions had overstepped their bounds by accepting members and groups that did not have a common bond with the credit union's chartering organization. However, the credit unions won a major victory with passage of the Credit Union Membership Access Act in August 1998. This act amended the Federal Credit Union Act to add multiple common bond credit unions to the current permissible categories of single common bond and community credit unions. However, the act limited membership of multiple bond credit unions to 3,000.

The American Bankers Association filed suit against NCUA shortly after the NCUA adopted changes to the chartering and field of membership policies in compliance with the 1998 act. In November 2001 the U.S. Court of Appeals dismissed the American Bankers Association suit against NCUA's field of membership regulation issued pursuant to the Credit Union Membership Access Act.

The September 11, 2001, attacks prompted immediate efforts by the federal government to further restrict methods of moving funds internationally that could fund terrorist activities. On Oct. 26, 2001, President George W. Bush signed the Uniting and Strengthening America by Providing Appropriate Tools Required to Intercept and Obstruct Terrorism Act (USA Patriot Act) of 2001. Title III of the Patriot Act, International Money Laundering Abatement and Financial Anti-Terrorism Act of 2001, strengthened money-laundering laws established under the Bank Secrecy Act, including funds held in credit unions. The 2003 Fair and Accurate Credit Transactions Act amended the Fair Credit Reporting Act to prevent identity theft, improve resolution of consumer disputes, improve the accuracy of consumer records, and make improvements in the use of, and consumer access to, credit information. This legislation directed the federal banking agencies, the National Credit Union Administration (NCUA), and the Federal Trade Commission (FTC) to establish guidelines and prescribe regulations for financial institutions and creditors regarding identity theft.

On Oct. 13, 2006, the president signed the Financial Services Regulatory Relief Act (FSRRA) of 2006, which permitted a federal credit union to offer money transfer instruments, including international and domestic electronic fund transfers, to persons in the field of membership (previously limited to actual members). FSRRA also amended the Federal Deposit Insurance Act to grant enforcement authority to the state supervisor of either a private deposit insurer or a depository institution that received deposits insured by a private deposit insurer. In November 2006 the NCUA issued an interim final rule to implement amendments to the Federal Credit Union Act made by FSRRA.

The NCUA reviews a third of its existing regulations every year so that each NCUA regulation receives a review at least once every three years. The NCUA publishes the list of regulations that are up for review and invites public comment.

On June 29, 2007, responding to concern over a spike in foreclosures that many industry analysts tied to risky lending practices coupled with a national downturn in the housing market, the federal financial regulatory agencies—the Federal Reserve (*p. 206*), the Office of the Comptroller of the Currency (*p. 839*), the Federal Deposit Insurance Corporation (FDIC) (*p. 153*), the Office of Thrift Supervision, and the NCUA—issued a final *Statement on Subprime Mortgage Lending*. The formal guidelines were developed to address issues relating to certain risky adjustable-rate mortgage (ARM) products. The final statement urged lenders to

• Provide borrowers with clearly defined disclosures on the impact of rising interest rates for ARMs and for prepayment penalties.
• Use "low-documentation" loans, which require little borrower income documentation, only when mitigating circumstances warrant.
• Consider a borrower's ability to pay a loan back, at the fully indexed rate, before making a mortgage loan.
• Allow borrowers at least sixty days before the reset date of their loans to refinance their loans without being charged a prepayment fee.

The *Statement on Subprime Mortgage Lending* was a set of guidelines, not formal regulation. The guidelines applied only to banks, credit unions, and thrifts—not to nonbank lenders under state regulation, where many of the risky loans originated. Consumer groups expressed concern that the guidelines did not do enough to protect borrowers and called on Congress to pass comprehensive legislation to address predatory lending practices.

The mortgage meltdown continued in 2008 and contributed to a deepening national and international banking crisis by the fall of that year. In response, President George W. Bush signed the Secure and Fair Enforcement (SAFE) for Mortgage Licensing Act of 2008. This required the federal banking agencies—the Federal Reserve System, Comptroller of the Currency, Office of Thrift Supervision, National Credit Union Administration, and Federal Deposit Insurance Corporation—to work jointly through the Federal Financial Institutions Examination Council to develop and maintain a national system to register loan originators.

A few months later, Congress hastily passed and the president signed the Emergency Economic Stabilization Act of 2008, which included the Troubled Asset Relief Program (TARP). Known as the bank bailout bill, the legislation also increased the amount of deposit and share insurance coverage offered under the Federal Deposit Insurance Act and the Federal Credit Union Act from $100,000 to $250,000, until Dec. 31, 2009.

In May 2009, President Barack Obama signed the Credit Card Accountability Responsibility and Disclosure Act, which required financial institutions to notify customers forty-five days in advance of any rate increase or significant changes in credit card account terms. The act also required institutions to mail or deliver periodic statements for open-end consumer credit plans at least twenty-one days before the payment due date.

The same month, the president signed the Helping Families Save Their Homes and the Fraud Enforcement and Recovery Act, which extended the increased FDIC insurance coverage to Dec. 31, 2013. The legislation also directed the NCUA to establish a National Credit Union Share Insurance Fund Restoration Plan whenever it projects that the equity ratio of the National Credit Union Share Insurance Fund will fall below a designated minimum equity ratio; and to establish the Temporary Corporate Credit Union Stabilization Fund to make payments for the insurance and liquidation of insured credit unions.

The Dodd-Frank Wall Street Reform and Consumer Protection Act, enacted in July 2010, made the increased insurance coverage from $100,000 to $250,000 per account permanent. The legislation also directed the banking regulatory agencies (including NCUA) to promulgate regulations regarding real estate appraisals and minimum requirements for state registration and supervision of appraisal management companies.

The Federal Credit Union Act authorizes the NCUA Board to appoint itself as conservator when necessary to conserve the assets of a federally insured credit union, protect members' interests, or protect the National Credit Union Share Insurance Fund (NCUSIF). During conservatorship, members can continue to conduct normal financial transactions—deposit and access funds, make loan payments, and use shares—at the credit union.

Though government action preserved the banks deemed "too big to fail" through TARP, some corporate credit unions were crumbling under the weight of investment losses caused by toxic assets purchased from Wall Street firms. NCUA, as liquidating agent for the failed corporate credit unions, invoked its statutory duty to seek recoveries from responsible parties to minimize the cost of any failure to its insurance funds and the credit union industry. As such, NCUA began filing a series of lawsuits seeking compensation from the parties that created and sold the faulty mortgage-backed securities to several failed corporate credit unions.

By January 2015 NCUA had filed lawsuits against multiple Wall Street firms that underwrote these securities for failing to disclose significant risks. NCUA settled multiple suits; outcomes were pending in several other cases.

In January 2015 federal financial regulatory agencies, in partnership with the State Liaison Committee (SLC) of the Federal Financial Institutions Examination Council, issued guidance for financial institutions on private student loans with graduated repayment terms at origination. Graduated repayment terms are structured to provide for lower initial monthly payments that gradually increase. The agencies—the Board of Governors of the Federal Reserve System, the Consumer Financial Protection Bureau, the Federal Deposit Insurance Corporation, the National Credit Union Administration, and the Office of the Comptroller of the Currency—urged private student loan originators to adhere to six principles: ensure orderly repayment; avoid payment shock; align payment terms with a borrower's income; provide borrowers with clear disclosures; comply with all applicable federal and state consumer laws, regulations and reporting standards; and contact borrowers before reset dates.

◼ KEY PERSONNEL

Chair of the Board
Debbie Matz...................... (703) 518–6320
Board Members
Rick Metsger, vice chair .... (703) 518–6300
J. Mark McWatters................. (703) 518–6300
Secretary to the Board
Gerard Poliquin .... (703) 518–6300
Chief Financial Officer
Rendell L. Jones .... (703) 518–6570
Executive Director
Mark Treichel..................... (703) 518–6320
Deputy Director
John Kutchey..................... (703) 518–6320
Capital Markets and Planning
Owen Cole .... (703) 518–6620
Consumer Protection
Gail Laster .... (703) 518–6440
Corporate Credit Unions
Scott Hunt .... (703) 518–6640
Equal Opportunity Programs
S. Denise Hendricks .... (703) 518–6325
Examination and Insurance
Larry Fazio...................... (703) 518–6360
National Exams and Supervision
Scott Hunt .... (703) 518–6640
FOIA Public Liaison
Linda Dent...................... (703) 518–6540
General Counsel
Michael McKenna................. (703) 518–6540
Chief Economist
John D. Worth................... (703) 518–6660
Human Resources
Cheryl Eyre .... (703) 518–6498
Minority and Woman Inclusion
Wendy Angus (acting) .... (703) 518–1650

Inspector General
James Hagan...................... (703) 518–6350
Chief Information Officer
Ed Dorris .... (703) 518–6440
Public and Congressional Affairs
Todd M. Harper................... (703) 518–6330
Small Credit Union Initiatives
William Myers.................... (703) 518–6610
Asset Management and Assistance Center (Austin, Texas)
Mike Barton..................... (512) 231–7900
Ombudsman
Joy Lee .... (703) 518–1175

◼ INFORMATION SOURCES

Internet
Agency website: www.ncua.gov.

Telephone Contacts
Switchboard ....(703) 518–6300
Fax ....(703) 518–6671
TTY ....(703) 518–6332
Consumer Assistance Center ....(800) 755–1030
  (E-mail: consumerassistance@ncua.gov)
Inspector General's Hotline ....(800) 778–4806
  (E-mail: oigmail@ncua.gov)
Fraud ....(800) 827–9650
  (E-mail: ogcmail@ncua.gov)
Investments......................(800) 755–5999
  (E-mail: ocmpmail@ncua.gov)
OCIO Technical Support ....(800) 827–3255
  (E-mail: csdesk@ncua.org)

Information and Publications

KEY OFFICES

NCUA Public and Congressional Affairs
1775 Duke St.
Alexandria, VA 22314–3428
(703) 518–6330
E-mail: pacamail@ncua.gov
Todd M. Harper, director

Answers questions from the press and the public. NCUA news, fact sheets, press releases, legal opinions, regulatory alerts, and rules and regulations are also available on the website.

Freedom of Information
NCUA Office of General Counsel
1775 Duke St.
Alexandria, VA 22314–3428
(703) 518–6540
Linda Dent, FOIA public liaison
Lara Rodriguez, chief FOIA officer
E-mail: foia@ncua.gov

PUBLICATIONS

NCUA Office of Chief Financial Officer
Attn: Publications
1775 Duke St.
Alexandria, VA 22314–3428
(703) 518–6340 (paper-based)
Fax (703) 518–6417
Rendell L. Jones, chief financial officer

Handles publication orders. Brochures and publications may be ordered or downloaded from the website (some are free and charges vary). Titles include
Annual Report of the National Credit Union Administration
The Federal Credit Union Act
Federal Credit Union Handbook
Is a Credit Union Right for Me
NCUA–Credit Union Directory
You Have the Power to Stop ID Theft
Your Insured Funds (also available in Spanish)
Technical publications include
The Federal Credit Union Bylaws
NCUA Rules and Regulations Manual (compliance activities)

Reference Resources

LIBRARY

NCUA Library
1775 Duke St.
Alexandria, VA 22314–3428
(703) 518–6546
Jackie Minor, library technician

A legal library located in the Office of the General Counsel. Open to the public from 9:00 a.m. to 4:00 p.m. An appointment is required.

DOCKETS
Federal dockets are available at www.regulations.gov. (*See appendix for information on searching and commenting on regulations.*)

RULES AND REGULATIONS
NCUA rules and regulations are published in the *Code of Federal Regulations,* Title 12, parts 700–760. Proposed regulations, new final regulations, and updates to the *Code of Federal Regulations* are published in the daily *Federal Register.* (*See appendix for details on how to obtain and use these publications.*)

The *Annual Report* of the NCUA also reports on regulatory actions taken by the agency during the previous year.

▨ LEGISLATION
The NCUA carries out its responsibilities under
Federal Credit Union Act (48 Stat. 1216, 12 U.S.C. 1751). Signed by the president June 26, 1934. Authorized the federal government to charter credit unions.

National Housing Act (48 Stat. 1246, 12 U.S.C. 1701). Signed by the president June 27, 1934. Created the Federal Savings and Loan Insurance Corporation to insure accounts; establish reserves and regulate activities of insured institutions; prevent defaults by making loans, purchasing assets, or making contributions; and act as conservator in cases of default.

Truth in Lending Act (82 Stat. 146, 15 U.S.C. 1601). Signed by the president May 29, 1968. Required lenders and merchants to inform consumers of total cost of loans and installment purchase plans and to state annual percentage rate clearly. Also prohibited unsolicited distribution of credit cards.

Bank Protection Act of 1968 (82 Stat. 294, 12 U.S.C. 1881). Signed by the president July 7, 1968. Required the establishment of minimum security system standards for banking institutions.

Fair Credit Reporting Act (84 Stat. 1128, 15 U.S.C. 1681). Signed by the president Oct. 26, 1970. Regulated credit information and use.

Federal Credit Union Act Amendments of 1970 (84 Stat. 994, 12 U.S.C. 1781). Signed by the president Oct. 19, 1970. Provided insurance coverage for member accounts in state and federally chartered credit unions.

Bank Secrecy Act (31 U.S.C. 5311 et seq.). Also known as the Currency and Foreign Transaction Reporting Act. Signed by the president Oct. 26, 1970. Required financial institutions to file reports to the U.S. Treasury for certain currency transactions. Designed to detect and prevent money laundering.

NOW Accounts Act (87 Stat. 342, 12 U.S.C. 1832). Signed by the president Aug. 16, 1973. Regulated interest-bearing checking accounts.

Equal Credit Opportunity Act (88 Stat. 1521, 15 U.S.C. 1691). Signed by the president Oct. 28, 1974. Prohibited credit discrimination against women; amended in 1976 to include discrimination based on age, race, religion, or national origin (90 Stat. 251).

Real Estate Settlement Procedures Act (88 Stat. 1724, 12 U.S.C. 2601). Signed by the president Dec. 22, 1974. Minimized settlement charges for home buyers; confirmed the authority of the Department of Housing and Urban Development to set standards for settlement charges on homes financed through federally guaranteed mortgages.

Home Mortgage Disclosure Act (89 Stat. 1125, 12 U.S.C. 2801). Signed by the president Dec. 31, 1975. Required lending institutions within standard metropolitan statistical areas (SMSA) to disclose the number and amount of mortgage loans made yearly to determine if banks are discriminating against certain city neighborhoods by refusing to make mortgage loans regardless of the creditworthiness of the potential borrower (the practice known as "redlining").

Fair Debt Collection Practices Act (91 Stat. 874, 15 U.S.C. 1692). Signed by the president Sept. 20, 1977. Regulated methods used by debt collection agencies.

Housing and Community Development Act of 1977 (91 Stat. 1111, 42 U.S.C. 5301). Signed by the president Oct. 12, 1977. Amended the lending authority of federally chartered savings and loan associations, increasing the amount of money available for conventional home mortgages and home improvement loans.

Community Reinvestment Act of 1977 (91 Stat. 1147, 12 U.S.C. 2901). Signed by the president Oct. 12, 1977. Required financial institution regulators to encourage banks under their supervision to meet the credit needs of their communities, including low- and middle-income neighborhoods.

Financial Institutions Regulatory and Interest Rate Control Act of 1978 (92 Stat. 3641, 12 U.S.C. 226 note). Signed by the president Nov. 10, 1978. Reorganized the NCUA and expanded the authority of bank regulators.

Electronic Fund Transfer Act of 1978 (92 Stat. 3728, 15 U.S.C. 1601 note). Signed by the president Nov. 10, 1978. Established rules relating to consumer liability for unauthorized use of an electronic fund transfer card and unsolicited issuance of cards by financial institutions. Prohibited creditors from making automatic repayment of loans a condition of extending credit; overdraft plans were exempted.

Depository Institutions Deregulation and Monetary Control Act of 1980 (94 Stat. 132, 12 U.S.C. 226 note). Signed by the president March 31, 1980. Extended reserve requirements to all financial institutions, phased out interest rate ceilings over a six-year period, and allowed thrift institutions to offer a wide range of financial services.

Garn–St. Germain Depository Institutions Act of 1982 (96 Stat. 1469, 12 U.S.C. 226 note). Signed by the president Oct. 15, 1982. Expanded the power of federal regulatory agencies to assist troubled banks. Allowed either direct or merger-related assistance to prevent the closing of or to reopen any insured bank; also permitted assistance when severe financial conditions threatened the stability of a significant number of banks or banks with substantial financial resources. Authorized the NCUA Board to differentiate the activities of corporate credit unions (corporates) from natural person credit unions through rules, regulations, and orders of the NCUA Board.

Deficit Reduction Act of 1984 (98 Stat. 1203, 12 U.S.C. 1781). Signed by the president July 18, 1984. Clarified the guidelines of the National Credit Union Share Insurance Fund; Central Liquidity Fund given tax-exempt status.

Competitive Equality Banking Act of 1987 (101 Stat. 552, 12 U.S.C. 226 note). Signed by the president Aug. 10, 1987. Streamlined credit union operations; exempted the NCUA from Gramm-Rudman-Hollings budget restrictions.

Financial Institutions Reform, Recovery, and Enforcement Act of 1989 (103 Stat. 183, 12 U.S.C. 1881 note). Signed by the president Aug. 9, 1989. Enhanced the regulatory and enforcement powers of federal financial institutions' regulatory agencies; established internal pay scale system; clarified the NCUA's powers as a liquidating agent and conservator.

Truth in Savings Act (105 Stat. 2334, 12 U.S.C. 4301 note). Signed by the president Dec. 19, 1991. Subtitle F of the FDIC Improvement Act of 1991 provided uniformity in the disclosure of terms and conditions on which interest is paid and fees are assessed in connection with savings accounts.

Small Business Regulatory Enforcement Fairness Act (110 Stat. 857, 5 U.S.C. 601 note). Signed by the president March 29, 1996. Amended the Regulatory Flexibility Act of 1980 and the Equal Access to Justice Act of 1985. Required the NCUA to prepare an economic analysis outlining any major impact a regulation may have on a significant number of small credit unions; required the NCUA to publish a compliance guide regarding the rules covered by the act; and provided for congressional and GAO review of all agency regulations.

Examination Parity and Year 2000 Readiness for Financial Institutions Act (112 Stat. 32, 12 U.S.C. 1461 note, 12 U.S.C. 1811 note). Signed by the president March 20, 1998. Provided authority to the NCUA to supervise credit union organizations and institutions that provide services affected by the year 2000 computer problem.

Credit Union Membership Access Act (112 Stat. 918, 12 U.S.C. 1782(a)(6)(C)). Signed by the president Aug. 7, 1998. Amended the Federal Credit Union Act to add multiple common bond credit unions to the current permissible categories of single common bond and community credit unions. Limited a multiple common bond credit union group to fewer than 3,000 members. Directed the NCUA board to prescribe regulations defining "well-defined local community, neighborhood, or rural district" for the purposes of membership criteria.

Gramm-Leach-Bliley Act (113 Stat. 1338, 12 U.S.C. 1811 note). Signed by the president Nov. 12, 1999. Permitted affiliations between banks and any financial company, including brokerage and insurance firms. Amended the Home Owners' Loan Act of 1933 to prohibit new affiliations between savings and loan holding companies and certain commercial firms. Amended the Electronic Fund Transfer Act of 1978 to mandate fee disclosures to a consumer using an ATM machine. Title VI, the Federal Home Loan Bank System Modernization Act of 1999, amended the 1932 Federal Home Loan Bank Act to make a federal savings association's membership in the Federal Home Loan Bank system voluntary instead of mandatory.

Uniting and Strengthening America by Providing Appropriate Tools Required to Intercept and Obstruct Terrorism Act of 2001 (USA Patriot Act) (115 Stat. 272, 18 U.S.C. 1 note). Signed by the president Oct. 26, 2001. Title III amended federal law governing monetary transactions to prescribe procedural guidelines under which the secretary of the Treasury could require domestic financial institutions and agencies to take specified measures to combat money laundering. Required any credit union to record and report requirements for monetary instrument transactions.

Fair and Accurate Credit Transactions Act of 2003 (FACT Act) (117 Stat. 1952, 15 U.S.C. 1681a). Signed by the president Dec. 4, 2003. Amended the Fair Credit Reporting Act, prescribing guidelines under which the federal banking agencies, the NCUA, and the FTC are directed to establish guidelines and prescribe regulations for financial institutions and creditors regarding the accuracy and integrity of information furnished to credit bureaus and other consumer reporting agencies and to address identity theft.

USA Patriot Act Additional Reauthorizing Amendments Act of 2006 (18 U.S.C. 1 note). Signed by the president March 9, 2006. Reauthorized the USA Patriot Act.

Financial Services Regulatory Relief Act of 2006 (120 Stat. 1966, U.S.C. 1811 note). Signed by the president Oct. 13, 2006. Amended the Federal Credit Union Act to permit a federal credit union to offer money transfer instruments, including international and domestic electronic fund transfers, to persons in the field of membership. Amended the Federal Deposit Insurance Act to grant enforcement authority to the state supervisor of either a private deposit insurer or a depository institution that receives deposits insured by a private deposit insurer.

Secure and Fair Enforcement for Mortgage Licensing Act of 2008 (the SAFE Act) (122 Stat. 2654, 12 U.S.C. Sec. 5101 et seq.). Title V of the Housing and Economic Recovery Act. Signed by the president July 30, 2008. Required federal banking agencies jointly, through the Federal Financial Institutions Examination Council, to develop and maintain a national system to register loan originators. Defined "federal banking agencies" as the Federal Reserve System, the Comptroller of the Currency, the Office of Thrift Supervision, the National Credit Union Administration, and the Federal Deposit Insurance Corporation.

Emergency Economic Stabilization Act of 2008 (12 U.S.C. 5201–5261). Signed by the president Oct. 3, 2008. Title I, Troubled Asset Relief Program (TARP), increased the amount of deposit and share insurance coverage offered under the Federal Deposit Insurance Act and the Federal Credit Union Act from $100,000 to $250,000 until Dec. 31, 2009.

Helping Families Save Their Homes Act and the Fraud Enforcement and Recovery Act (123 Stat. 1632, 12 U.S.C. 5201 note). Signed by the president May 20, 2009. Expanded Department of Justice authority in prosecuting banking fraud. Created the Financial Crisis Inquiry Commission to investigate the financial practices that resulted in the 2008 banking crises. Extended increased deposit and share insurance coverage ($250,000) offered under the Federal Deposit Insurance Act and the Federal Credit Union Act to Dec. 21, 2013. Expanded federal fraud laws to include independent mortgage companies, previously not covered under the regulations that applied to traditional banking institutions. Amended the FCUA to require the NCUA Board to (1) establish a National Credit Union Share Insurance Fund Restoration Plan whenever it projects that the equity ratio of the National Credit Union Share Insurance Fund will fall below a designated minimum equity ratio and (2) establish the Temporary Corporate Credit Union Stabilization Fund to make payments for the insurance and liquidation of insured credit unions.

Credit Card Accountability Responsibility and Disclosure Act of 2009 (123 Stat. 1734, 15 U.S.C. 1601 note). Signed by the president May 22, 2009. Required financial institutions to notify customers forty-five days in advance of any rate increase or significant changes in credit card account terms. Required institutions to mail or deliver periodic statements for open-end consumer credit plans at least twenty-one days before the payment due date.

Dodd-Frank Wall Street Reform and Consumer Protection Act (124 Stat. 1376, 12 U.S.C. 5301 note). Signed by the president July 21, 2010. Increased the amount of deposit and share insurance coverage offered under the Federal Deposit Insurance Act and the Federal Credit Union Act from $100,000 to $250,000 permanently. With some exceptions, directs the Commodity Futures Trading Commission and the Securities and Exchange Commission (SEC) to coordinate with each other and with the prudential regulators before commencing any rulemaking or issuing an order regarding swaps and related actions. Prohibits a creditor from making a "higher-risk mortgage" to any consumer without first obtaining a written appraisal of the property involving a physical property visit by a licensed or certified appraisal. Directed banking regulators to implement minimum requirements for state registration and supervision of appraisal management companies. Other financial regulatory provisions.

Biggert–Waters Flood Insurance Reform Act of 2012 (126 Stat. 916, 42 U.S.C. 4001 note). Signed by the president July 6, 2012. Title II of Moving Ahead for Progress in the 21st Century Act (MAP-21). Biggert-Waters made changes to the flood insurance program, which included requiring banking regulatory agencies to draft regulations concerning forced-placed flood insurance and flood insurance escrow provisions. Some exceptions.

National Defense Authorization Act for Fiscal Year 2013 Military Lending Act amendments (126 Stat. 1785, 10 U.S.C. 987). Signed by the president Jan. 2, 2013. Subtitle G declared the Military Lending Act is enforceable in the same manner as the Truth in Lending Act by the Federal Deposit Insurance Corporation, member banks of the Federal Reserve System, Office of the Comptroller of the Currency, National Credit Union Administration, Consumer Financial Protection Bureau, Federal Trade Commission, and certain other specified agencies.

▪ REGIONAL OFFICES

REGION 1—Albany

(CT, MA, ME, MI, NH, NV, NY, RI, VT)
9 Washington Square
Washington Ave. Extension
Albany, NY 12205
(518) 862–7400
Fax (518) 862–7420
E-mail: region1@ncua.gov
L. J. Blankenberger, director

REGION 2—Capital

(CA, DC, DE, MD, NJ, PA, VA, WV)
1900 Duke St., #300
Alexandria, VA 22314–3437
(703) 519–4600
Fax (703) 519–4620
E-mail: region2@ncua.gov
Jane Walters, director

REGION 3—Atlanta

(AL, FL, GA, IN, KY, MS, NC,
    OH, PR, SC, TN, VI)
7000 Central Pkwy., #1600
Atlanta, GA 30328
(678) 443–3000
Fax (678) 443–3020
E-mail: region3@ncua.gov
Myra Toeppe, director

REGION 4—Austin

(AR, IA, IL, KS, LA, MN, MO, ND, NE,
    OK, SD, TX, WI)
4807 Spicewood Springs Rd., #5200
Austin, TX 78759–8490
(512) 342–5600
Fax (512) 342–5620
E-mail: region4@ncua.gov
C. Keith Morton, director

REGION 5—Tempe

(AK, AZ, CO, GU, HI, ID, MT, NM,
    OR, WA, UT, WY)
1230 W. Washington St., #301
Tempe, AZ 85281
(602) 302–6000
Fax (602) 302–6024
E-mail: region5@ncua.gov
Elizabeth Whitehead, director

**ASSET MANAGEMENT
ASSISTANCE CENTER (AMAC)**

4807 Spicewood Springs
    Rd., #5100
Austin, TX 78759–8490
(512) 231–7900
Fax (512) 231–7920
E-mail: amacmail@ncua.gov
Mike Barton, president

National Mediation Board

1301 K St. N.W., 250 East, Washington, DC 20005–7011
Internet: www.nmb.gov

The National Mediation Board (NMB), established by the 1934 amendments to the Railway Labor Act of 1926, is an independent agency that performs a central role in facilitating harmonious labor-management relations within two of the nation's key transportation modes—the railroads and airlines.

The board has three members who are nominated by the president and confirmed by the Senate to three-year terms. The board members select a chair annually among themselves.

The board is responsible for the mediation of disputes over wages, hours, and working conditions that arise between rail and air carriers and organizations representing their employees. If a dispute arises among the employees of a carrier concerning the representation of the employees in negotiations, the board investigates and determines to whom such powers should be granted.

Either the carriers or the employee organizations may request mediation, or the board may intercede on its initiative. The NMB mediates until the dispute is settled or until it determines that its efforts are unsuccessful, at which time it tries to persuade both parties to submit to arbitration. If either party refuses to arbitrate, the board states that mediation has failed. After a thirty-day cooling off period, the employer is entitled to change rates of pay, rules, or working conditions, and employees may strike.

If a labor dispute, in the NMB's opinion, seriously threatens to interrupt interstate commerce, the board notifies the president. The president may, in turn, appoint an emergency board to investigate the dispute. During an investigation a strike is barred. The appointment of a presidential emergency board (PEB) to resolve labor disputes within the airline industry is rare. Notably, in 1997, President Bill Clinton established a PEB as American Airlines pilots called for a strike. In March 2001 President George W. Bush created a PEB to resolve ongoing conflict between Northwest Airlines and its mechanics union. In December 2001 President Bush appointed members to a PEB to investigate a strike threatened at United Airlines. The airline and its union workers eventually reached agreement without a strike or lock-out. However, railroad PEBs are appointed more frequently.

Individual grievances arising under labor-management agreements in the railroad industry are handled by the National Railroad Adjustment Board and public law boards. These are paid for by the NMB. There are no publicly funded boards for the airline industry; the NMB merely appoints a neutral referee on request.

The elimination of the Interstate Commerce Commission (ICC) at the end of 1995 raised questions about the status of certain companies that the ICC categorized as "express carriers." In particular, Federal Express, a mail and package delivery company, had been covered by the Railway Labor Act, while its principal competitor, United Parcel Service (UPS), fell under the National Labor Relations Act. Legislation in 1996 preserved this controversial distinction, but in September 2000 the NMB certified that UPS flight dispatchers were covered under the Railway Labor Act. UPS aircraft mechanics also are covered under the Railway Labor Act.

In July 2010, the NMB issued a final rule regarding rail and airline union elections. The NMB's voting procedures for union representation elections was changed to add a "No" option and to provide that the majority of votes cast (rather than the majority of eligible voting workers) would determine the outcome of a union representation election. This was considered a win for labor union leadership. Previously, a majority of all eligible voting workers had to vote in favor of unionization in order for a union to be certified as a bargaining representative for that group of employees.

The Federal Aviation Administration Modernization and Reform Act of 2012 contained amendments to the Railway Labor Act that impacts the NMB's rulemaking and oversight of union elections in the rail and air industries. The FAA reform act required union organizers to affirm a showing of support from 50 percent of the employees in an unrepresented class or craft before the NMB could order a secret ballot election. Before the FAA reform act, union organizers were required to affirm a showing of support from a minimum of 35 percent of the employees in an unrepresented class or craft. Other changes to elections required a runoff election of the top two options (including the option of no representation) if one of the options failed to obtain more than 50 percent of the vote. The amendments did not overturn the NMB's 2010 rule mandating that election outcomes are determined by a majority of votes cast rather than a majority of eligible voters. The

FAA reform act also made administrative changes to the NMB's rulemaking processes and required congressional audits of the NMB.

■ KEY PERSONNEL

Chair
Harry Hoglander .... (202) 692–5082
Board Members
Linda A. Puchala.................. (202) 692–5082
Nicholas Geale.................... (202) 692–5082
Administration
Samantha Williams, assistant
    chief of staff.................. (202) 692–5010
General Counsel
Mary L. Johnson .... (202) 692–5040
Arbitration Services
Roland Watkins, director.......... (202) 692–5055
Alternative Dispute Resolution Services
LoValerie Mullins .... (202) 692–5043
Mediation Services
Michael Kelliher, deputy chief of
    staff......................... (202) 692–5000
Ombudsman
Denise Hedges, senior mediator..... (202) 692–5047

■ INFORMATION SOURCES

Internet
The NMB maintains its website at www.nmb.gov.

Telephone Contacts
Switchboard ....(202) 692–5000
Fax...(202) 692–5080
TTY...(202) 692–5001
Information hotline ....(202) 692–5050

Information and Publications

KEY OFFICES

NMB Information Contacts
1301 K St. N.W., #250 East
Washington, DC 20005–7011
E-mail: infoline@NMB.gov
Mary Johnson, general counsel
Tonya Kirksey, FOIA Requester Service Center
Angela Heverling, FOIA liaison
(202) 692–5000

PUBLICATIONS

NMB Publications
1301 K St. N.W., #250 East
Washington, DC 20005–7011
(202) 692–5000
E-mail: PDO@NMB.gov
Samantha Williams, contact

Titles available include
Annual Report of the National Mediation Board (including the Report of the National Railroad Adjustment Board)
Determinations of the National Mediation Board
The Railway Labor Act

Reference Resources

DOCUMENTS

Documents Office
1301 K St. N.W., #250 East
Washington, DC 20005–7011
(202) 692–5051
Samantha Williams, contact

Copies of collective bargaining agreements between labor and management of rail and air carriers, copies of the determinations issued by the board, air and rail union constitutions and bylaws, NMB rules, the NMB annual report, and numerous other documents are available for inspection. Documents are also available on the website at www.nmb.gov/resources/docs.

DOCKETS
Federal dockets are available from the Mediation Services office, on the website, and at www.regulations .gov. *(See appendix for information on searching and commenting on regulations.)*

RULES AND REGULATIONS
NMB rules and regulations are published in the *Code of Federal Regulations,* Title 29, Chapter X, Parts 1200–1299. Proposed regulations, new final rules, and updates to the *Code of Federal Regulations* are published in the daily *Federal Register.* (*See appendix for details on how to obtain and use these publications.*)

■ LEGISLATION
The National Mediation Board exercises its authority under amendments to the **Railway Labor Act** (48 Stat. 1185, 45 U.S.C. 151–158, 160–162). The amendments creating the board were signed by the president June 21, 1934. Amendments including airlines under RLA were signed by the president on April 10, 1936. An amendment establishing public law boards was signed by the president on April 20, 1966. An amendment establishing presidential emergency boards was signed by the president on Jan. 2, 1981. Amendments to change union elections and administrative procedures were signed by the president on Feb. 14, 2012.

■ REGIONAL OFFICE

NATIONAL RAILROAD ADJUSTMENT BOARD
844 N. Rush St.
Chicago, IL 60611
(312) 751–4688
Michael C. Lesnick, chair

National Transportation Safety Board

490 L'Enfant Plaza East S.W., Washington, DC 20594
Internet: www.ntsb.gov

The National Transportation Safety Board (NTSB) was created by the Department of Transportation Act of 1966 and began operations in April 1967. Originally, it was an autonomous agency within the Department of Transportation. In 1974 Congress passed the Independent Safety Board Act that granted NTSB independent status. The board began operations under the new act on April 1, 1975.

The board derives its authority from Title 49 of the United States Code, Chapter 11. The rules of the board are located in Chapter VIII, Title 49 of the *Code of Federal Regulations*.

The board is composed of five members appointed by the president and confirmed by the Senate. Board members serve five-year terms; two members are designated by the president to serve as chair and vice chair for two-year terms. No more than three members of the board may be of the same political party. At least three members must be appointed on the basis of demonstrated knowledge of accident reconstruction, safety engineering, human factors, transportation safety, or transportation regulation.

The NTSB headquarters are in Washington, DC. A managing director oversees five safety-related offices, which include the Office of Research and Engineering; the Office of Railroad, Pipeline, and Hazardous Materials Investigations; the Office of Aviation Safety; the Office of Highway Safety; and the Office of Marine Safety. Additional offices manage administrative and legal affairs. NTSB also maintains regional offices for aviation, highway, and railroad accidents. The NTSB

- Investigates, determines the cause of, makes safety recommendations for, and reports the facts and circumstances of all U.S. civil aviation accidents; all railroad accidents in which there is a fatality or substantial property damage, or which involve a passenger train; all pipeline accidents in which there is a fatality or substantial property damage; highway accidents involving matters of wide-ranging safety significance; major marine casualties and marine accidents involving a public vessel and a nonpublic vessel; and other catastrophic transportation accidents.
- Investigates and reports on the transportation of hazardous materials.
- Makes recommendations on matters pertaining to transportation safety and works to prevent accidents by conducting special studies.

- Assesses techniques of accident investigation.
- Publishes recommended procedures for accident investigations, establishing regulations governing the reporting of accidents and evaluating the effectiveness of the transportation safety efforts of other government agencies.
- Reviews on appeal the suspension, amendment, modification, revocation, or denial of any certificate or license issued by the secretary or any of the administrators of the Department of Transportation.

Following several highly publicized, mass casualty investigations in 1990s, the NTSB was assigned the role of coordinating the resources of the federal government and other organizations to support the efforts of the local and state authorities and the airlines to meet the needs of aviation disaster victims and their families. Family counseling, victim identification and forensic services, communication with foreign governments, and translation services are among the services with which the federal government can help local authorities and the airlines deal with a major aviation disaster.

In cases where criminal action is suspected, the NTSB works closely with the Federal Bureau of Investigation (FBI). Once sabotage has been proven, the FBI officially takes over the investigation. In the wake of the terrorist attacks of Sept. 11, 2001, the NTSB worked with the FBI in investigating the four flights that were hijacked and crashed by terrorists.

Although the NTSB does not have enforcement authority, the NTSB's administrative law judges conduct formal hearings and issue initial decisions on appeals by airmen filed with the NTSB. The NTSB serves as the "court of appeals" for any airman, mechanic or mariner, whenever certificate action is taken by the Federal Aviation Administration or the U.S. Coast Guard Commandant, or when civil penalties are assessed by the FAA. The Pilot's Bill of Rights, signed into law in 2012, requires the NTSB proceedings for the review of decisions of the administrator of the FAA to deny, amend, modify, suspend, or revoke an airman's certificate to be conducted, to the extent practicable, in accordance with the Federal Rules of Civil Procedure and Federal Rules of Evidence. NTSB issued its final rule implementing provisions of the Pilot's Bill of Rights in late 2013.

Passage of the Rail Safety Improvement Act of 2008 addressed some concerns NTSB had raised in the past regarding rail safety. Addressing "fatigue in the railroad industry," the act limited the number of railroad service hours and established fatigue management requirements. The new law also addressed positive train control, an anti-collision technology. The act required Class 1 railroads and regularly scheduled intercity or commuter rail passenger carriers to develop a plan for the implementation of a positive train control system by Dec. 31, 2015. The bill was signed into law just a few weeks after an accident involving a Metrolink passenger train and a Union Pacific freight train in Chatsworth, CA, claimed twenty-five lives and resulted in more than 100 injuries.

The NTSB can only make safety recommendations; it has no authority to impose them or to take action. The NTSB does, however, publicly advocate for safety changes through industry partnerships and public awareness campaigns. Each year, the NTSB releases its "Most Wanted List," a list of the top ten transportation safety issues the agency has identified. The list covers all transportation modes. NTSB included operational safety in rail mass transit for the first time on the 2014 list. NTSB added improvements to rail tank car safety to the list in 2015, just weeks before a train carrying crude derailed in West Virginia, spilling oil into a river. NTSB releases the list and the recommendations in an effort to drive policy at the national and state levels and to raise awareness among the public.

KEY PERSONNEL

Chair
 Christopher A. Hart . . . . (202) 314–6145
Vice Chair
 T. Bella Dinh-Zarr. . . . . (202) 314–6145
Board Members
 Robert L. Sumwalt. . . . . (202) 314–6021
 Earl F. Weener . . . . (202) 314–6024
 Vacant
Administrative Law Judges
 Alfonso J. Montano, chief judge . . . . . (202) 314–6150
Aviation Safety
 John DeLisi. . . . . (202) 314–6300
Chief Financial Officer
 Edward Benthall . . . . (202) 314–6210
Chief Information Officer
 Robert Scherer. . . . . (202) 314–6566
Communications
 Tom Zoeller . . . . (202) 314–6690
Equal Employment Opportunity, Diversity, and Inclusion
 Fara D. Guest . . . . (202) 314–6190
General Counsel
 David Tochon . . . . (202) 314–6080
Government and Congressional Affairs
 Jane Terry. . . . . (202) 314–6000
Highway Safety
 Don Karol. . . . . (202) 314–6440
Managing Director
 Tom Zoeller (acting) . . . . (202) 314–6690
Marine Safety
 Tracy Murrell. (202) 314–6224

Railroad, Pipeline, and Hazardous Materials Investigations
 Robert Hall. . . . . (202) 314–6500
Research and Engineering
 Joseph Kolly . . . . (202) 314–6500
Safety Recommendations and Quality Assurance
 Paula Sind-Prunier . . . . (202) 314–6426
Transportation Disaster Assistance
 Paul Sledzik . . . . (202) 314–6185
  Fax. . . . . (202) 459–9402
  E-mail: assistance@ntsb.gov

INFORMATION SOURCES

Internet
 Agency website: www.ntsb.gov. Offers press releases, the calendar of board meetings, as well as information on transportation accidents and a list of the improvements in transportation safety that are the highest priorities for the NTSB. Those interested in receiving press releases by e-mail may register on the website; an RSS feed is also available.

Telephone Contacts
 Switchboard . . . .(202) 314–6000
 Main Fax. . . . .(202) 314–6293
 TTY. . . . .(800) 877–8339
 Transportation Disaster
  Assistance (24/7) . . . .(800) 683–9369

Information and Publications

KEY OFFICES

NTSB Public Affairs
 490 L'Enfant Plaza S.W.
 Washington, DC 20594–2000
 (202) 314–6100
 Fax (202) 688–2566
 Kelly Nantel, director

 Provides information about the NTSB, including press releases.

Freedom of Information
 FOIA Requester Service Center, C10–40
 490 L'Enfant Plaza S.W.
 Washington, DC 20594–2000
 (202) 314–6540
 Robert Scherer, chief FOIA officer
 Melba D. Moye, FOIA public liaison, records
  management
 FOIA Requester Service, (800) 877–6799

DATA AND STATISTICS
 The NTSB's annual report contains statistical data on accidents, accident rates, and fatalities. All NTSB documents and information available to the public may be viewed on the website; in the Public Reference Room,

open from 8:45 a.m. to 4:45 p.m.; or by contacting the Records Management Division at (202) 314–6551 or (800) 877–6799.

PUBLICATIONS

Titles available include the annual report; accident report series; transportation accident briefs; transportation safety standards and recommendations; transportation special reports; initial decisions; board opinions and orders in safety enforcement and seafarer cases; TDA-related (transport disaster assistance) legislation and policies; the transportation abstract newsletter; and *We Are All Safer,* a review of NTSB-inspired improvements in transportation safety. Publications are available online through the NTSB website. Documents concerning preliminary and probable cause reports, factual investigation reports, hearing exhibit items, and videotapes may be ordered from the website at www.ntsb.gov/publications/Pages/default.aspx or from General Microfilm Inc. at (304) 267–5830 or through their website: www.general-microfilm.com.

E-mail and RSS-feed subscriptions are available on the website; those who wish to receive NTSB information on a continuing basis may also call the Public Inquiries Section at (202) 314–6551.

Reference Resources

DOCKETS

NTSB Public Inquiries Section

490 L'Enfant Plaza S.W.
Washington, DC 20594–2000
(202) 314–6551
Melba D. Moye, records management officer

Handles all requests for files on aviation, highway, rail, pipeline, and marine accidents investigated by the NTSB.

Federal dockets are also available on the website at www.ntsb.gov/info/foia_fri.htm and at www.regulations .gov. (*See appendix for information on searching and commenting on regulations.*)

NTSB Docket Management Section

490 L'Enfant Plaza S.W.
Washington, DC 20594–2000
(202) 314–6551
Internet: www.ntsb.gov/investigations/SitePages/
   dms.aspx

Handles all requests for information on appeals cases of air and marine personnel.

RULES AND REGULATIONS

NTSB rules and regulations are published in the *Code of Federal Regulations,* Title 49, Chapter VIII, Parts 800–999. Proposed regulations, new final regulations, and updates to the *Code of Federal Regulations* are published in the daily *Federal Register.* (*See appendix for details on how to obtain and use these publications.*)

The *National Transportation Safety Board Annual Report to Congress* reports on accident investigations and safety study actions taken by the agency during the previous year.

■ LEGISLATION

Federal Aviation Act of 1958 as amended (72 Stat. 731, 49 U.S.C. 1411). Signed by the president Aug. 23, 1958. Required the Civil Aeronautics Board to investigate and report on accidents involving civil aircraft. (These responsibilities were acquired by the NTSB in 1966.)

Department of Transportation Act of 1966 (80 Stat. 931, 49 U.S.C. 1651). Signed by the president Oct. 15, 1966. Created the Department of Transportation and established the National Transportation Safety Board as an independent agency within the department.

Independent Safety Board Act of 1974 (88 Stat. 2166, 49 U.S.C. 1901). Signed by the president Jan. 3, 1975. Established the NTSB as a entirely separate agency.

Independent Safety Board Act Amendments of 1981 (95 Stat. 1065, 49 U.S.C. 1901). Signed by the president Nov. 3, 1981. Gave board investigations priority over other federal agency investigations; allowed NTSB employees to examine or test any item necessary to investigations.

Aviation Insurance Program (96 Stat. 1453, 49 U.S.C. 1902 note). Signed by the president Oct. 14, 1982. Amended the Independent Safety Board Act of 1974 by requiring that at least three members of the board have expertise in the fields of accident reconstruction, safety engineering, human factors, transportation safety, or transportation regulation.

Aviation Drug-Trafficking Control Act (98 Stat. 2315, 49 U.S.C. app. 1301). Signed by the president Oct. 19, 1984. Authorized the board to review on appeal the revocation of certain certificates or licenses issued by the FAA administrator because of aircraft transportation of controlled substances.

Airport and Airway Safety and Capacity Expansion Act of 1987 (101 Stat. 1528, 49 U.S.C. app. 2201). Signed by the president Dec. 30, 1987. Authorized the board to require the reporting of accidents and aviation incidents involving public aircraft other than aircraft of the armed forces and the intelligence agencies.

Independent Safety Board Act Amendments of 1988 (102 Stat. 876, 877; 49 U.S.C. app. 1901). Signed by the president July 19, 1988. Authorized an emergency fund of $1 million for necessary expenses, not otherwise provided, for the purpose of accident investigations.

National Transportation Safety Board Amendments of 1996 (110 Stat. 3452, 49 U.S.C. 1101 note). Signed by the president Oct. 11, 1996. Prohibited the NTSB from disclosing records or information relating to its participation in foreign aircraft accident investigations. Authorized the NTSB to conduct training of its employees in subjects necessary for the proper performance of accident investigations.

Aviation Disaster Family Assistance Act of 1996 (110 Stat. 3264, 49 U.S.C. 3264). Signed by the president Oct. 9, 1996. Gave the NTSB the authority to coordinate federal services to victims of major aviation accidents and their families. Directed the NTSB to develop a system for classifying air carrier accident data. Directed the NTSB to develop a fully enhanced safety performance analysis system, including automated surveillance targeting systems.

Foreign Air Carrier Support Act of 1997 (111 Stat. 2681, 49 U.S.C. 41313). Signed by the president Dec. 16, 1997. Amended federal transportation law to require foreign air carriers to transmit to the NTSB a plan for addressing the needs of families of passengers involved in aircraft accidents involving foreign air carriers and a significant loss of life.

National Transportation Safety Board Reauthorization Act of 2003 (117 Stat. 2032, 49 U.S.C. 1118a). Signed by the president Dec. 6, 2003. Relieved the NTSB of the duty to render assistance to families of passengers involved in an aircraft accident if the NTSB has relinquished its investigative priority to another federal agency that is also able to provide such assistance.

Rail Safety Improvement Act of 2008 (122 Stat. 4848, 49 U.S.C. 20101 note). Signed by the president Oct. 16, 2008. Required railroads and intercity or commuter rail passenger carriers to develop and submit to the secretary of transportation, within eighteen months, plans for the implementation of a positive train control system by Dec. 31, 2015. Required the secretary of transportation to report annually to Congress on the specific actions taken to implement unmet statutory railroad safety mandates and railroad safety recommendations made by the NTSB or the Department of Transportation.

Pilot's Bill of Rights (126 Stat. 1159, 49 USC 44703 note). Signed by the president Aug. 3, 2012. Requires the National Transportation Safety Board (NTSB) proceedings for the review of decisions of the Administrator of the Federal Aviation Administration (FAA) to deny, amend, modify, suspend, or revoke an airman's certificate to be conducted, to the extent practicable, in accordance with the Federal Rules of Civil Procedure and Federal Rules of Evidence.

Nuclear Regulatory Commission

11555 Rockville Pike, Rockville, MD 20852
Mailing address: Washington, DC 20555–0001
Internet: www.nrc.gov

The Nuclear Regulatory Commission (NRC) was created by the Energy Reorganization Act of 1974 and began operation in January 1975. It took over the nuclear regulatory and licensing functions of the Atomic Energy Commission (AEC), which was abolished. The other functions of the AEC, primarily nuclear research and development, were taken over by the Energy Research and Development Administration (later incorporated into the Department of Energy).

The commission is headed by five commissioners appointed by the president and confirmed by the Senate. No more than three commissioners may be members of the same political party. Commissioners serve five-year terms; the president names one commissioner to serve as chair.

Specifically, the NRC

- Licenses the construction and operation of nuclear reactors and commercial fuel cycle facilities.
- Licenses the possession, use, transportation, handling, packaging, and disposal of nuclear materials.
- Regulates licensed activities including ensuring that measures are taken for the physical protection of nuclear facilities and materials.
- Develops and implements rules and regulations for licensed nuclear activities.
- Conducts public hearings on radiological safety, environmental, common defense, security, and antitrust matters.
- Develops effective working relationships with states and monitors their regulation of nuclear materials, including those used in medical therapy and research.
- Licenses the export and import of nuclear equipment and materials.

NRC Organization and Functions

The Energy Reorganization Act of 1974 mandated three offices within the commission responsible for the following areas: nuclear material safety and safeguards, nuclear regulatory research, and nuclear reactor regulation. Current structure to meet this mandate includes

The Office of Nuclear Material Safety and Safeguards (NMSS) ensures that public health and safety, national security, and environmental factors are considered in the licensing and regulation of nuclear facilities. Safeguards are reviewed and assessed against possible threats, thefts, and sabotage.

The NMSS manages Material Safety, State, Tribal, and Rulemaking Programs, which provides guidance to states intending to become agreement states and reviews Agreement State programs for continued adequacy to protect public health and safety and evaluates compatibility with NRC's regulatory program. This unit serves as the liaison between the NRC and states, local governments, other federal agencies, and tribal governments. The Office of Nuclear Regulatory Research conducts research in nuclear safety, safeguards, and environmental assessment to support agency licensing activities and the commission's decision-making process. Its functions include developing and recommending nuclear safety standards in the licensed uses of nuclear facilities and materials and preparing standards for the preparation of environmental impact statements.

The Office of Nuclear Reactor Regulation licenses nuclear reactors used for testing, research, and power generation. A construction permit must be granted before construction can begin on a nuclear facility, and an operating license must be issued before fuel can be loaded and the reactor started. License applications are reviewed to determine whether the proposed facility can be built and operated without undue risk to public safety and health. Environmental impact is also considered. Applicants are investigated to determine if they are properly insured against accidents.

An applicant may apply for a limited work authorization (LWA) if a favorable initial decision has been issued on environmental and site suitability issues but not on the possible effects on public health and safety. The LWA enables the applicant to begin work on plant construction, but there is no guarantee that the final construction permit will later be authorized. Complete construction of the site may be carried out only after a licensing board has made favorable findings regarding health and safety matters.

Public hearings on applications for construction permits are mandatory. The proceedings are conducted by an Atomic Safety and Licensing Board in communities near proposed nuclear facilities. Notices of hearings are published in the *Federal Register,* posted in the nearest public document room, and published in local newspapers. Interested parties petition the licensing board for the right to participate in public hearings.

The Office of New Reactors, which is responsible for regulatory activities in the primary program areas of site selection, licensing, and oversight for new commercial nuclear power reactors. Its Division of New Reactor Licensing manages design certification application reviews, combined license application (COL) reviews, and new reactor pre-application activities. By issuing a COL, the NRC authorizes the licensee to construct and operate a nuclear power plant at a specific site in accordance with established laws and regulations. COLs are valid for forty years.

Office of Nuclear Security and Incident Response, established in April 2002, develops overall agency policy and provides management direction for evaluation and assessment of technical issues involving security at nuclear facilities. The office operates as the agency interface on security matters with the Departments of Energy (*p. 601*) and Homeland Security (*p. 639*), the Federal Emergency Management Agency (FEMA), *(p. 640)* the intelligence and law enforcement communities, and other federal agencies.

Other offices within the NRC assist the agency in carrying out its mission but are not required under the commission's establishing legislation.

The Office of Enforcement monitors compliance with regulatory requirements. Current enforcement policy forbids operations by any licensees with inadequate levels of protection. The Office of Enforcement may issue written violation notices; assign civil penalties; order a licensee to "cease and desist"; and modify, suspend, or revoke licenses.

The Office of Investigations monitors the investigations of licensees, applicants, contractors, or vendors, including the investigation of all allegations of wrongdoing by other than NRC employees and contractors.

Elements of the NRC also serve an advisory function. The Advisory Committee on Reactor Safeguards provides advice on the safety of proposed and existing nuclear facilities. Licensing boards for the NRC are formed from members of the Atomic Safety and Licensing Board Panel. The Advisory Committee on the Medical Uses of Isotopes advises NRC on policy and technical issues that arise in the regulation of the medical uses of radioactive material in diagnosis and therapy.

Current Nuclear Energy Policy and Political Considerations

The economic, regulatory, and political climate discouraged construction of new plants after the Three Mile Island accident in 1979. That accident brought orders on new nuclear plants to a halt. Moreover, changes mandated after Three Mile Island greatly increased construction costs for the plants on order, adding to the financial burdens of an industry already plagued by cost overruns and construction mismanagement. This climate would last for nearly thirty years.

During the 1990s, the NRC saw several challenges and changes. Following media revelations of dangerously lax oversight at several facilities, NRC chair Shirley Jackson announced several major organizational changes within the NRC. Under Jackson, the NRC also moved to let nuclear plants conduct their own examinations of prospective reactor operators. This shift was projected to save the agency at least $3 million a year. Consumer advocates feared it could lower standards for operators at a time when the challenges to avert accidents were increasing.

In 1998 the NRC and the Department of Energy (DOE) began a pilot program to test the feasibility of NRC external regulation of DOE nuclear facilities. The pilot program tested regulatory concepts at specific DOE nuclear facilities, through simulated regulations, by evaluating a facility and its standards, requirements, procedures, practices, and activities against the standards that the NRC determined would ensure safety. The overall conclusion of the NRC task force was that most of the technical, policy, and regulatory issues involved in NRC oversight of the DOE nuclear facilities studied as part of the pilot program could be handled adequately within the existing NRC regulatory structure.

By 2000 the NRC was concerned that the race toward electric utility deregulation might compromise safety as well as bring about financial problems for nuclear power plants. Some industry watchers predicted that the deregulation of electricity prices would cause so much financial pressure that a large percentage of operating nuclear plants would be forced to shut down before the end of their forty-year licenses. Despite these dire predictions, nuclear plants have not shut down as some had predicted and have continued to apply for license renewal.

The problems of managing and storing nuclear waste from nuclear power plants and from facilities that are decommissioned have remained unsolved. The Nuclear Waste Policy Act of 1982 directed the Department of Energy to site, construct, and operate a geologic repository for high-level waste. In 2002, after many years of debate, Congress approved a permanent DOE nuclear waste repository at a site beneath Yucca Mountain in the Nevada desert. The DOE, after licensing from the NRC, would construct the repository, marking the first step in a process that would also require NRC approval to operate the facility. Besides the license application and other ongoing scientific studies, the DOE would implement a plan for transporting used nuclear fuel and defense waste to the Nevada site, approximately ninety miles north of Las Vegas.

In Sept. 8, 2008, the NRC docketed the DOE application for license and adopted the DOE Environmental Impact Study. From that date, the NRC had three years to reach a decision on whether to approve construction. Following the docketing, the NRC implemented a comprehensive review. In March 2009, the NRC published a final rule implementing the Environmental Protection Agency's radiation protection standard for the Yucca Mountain facility. EPA set standards for the period beyond 10,000 years after the facility is closed, supplementing its previous protection standards for the period up to 10,000 years.

In April 2011 funding for the development of the Yucca Mountain nuclear waste repository was canceled. The fight over Yucca Mountain is largely political. South Carolina and Washington have sued to force the federal government to abide by the law requiring the construction of the nuclear waste repository. Senator Harry Reid, the powerful Democrat from Nevada, used his position as Senate majority leader to cripple progress toward building the site. The U.S. Court of Appeals for the District of Columbia Circuit ordered the NRC in August 2013 to resume the licensing process using available funding appropriated from the Nuclear Waste Fund. In January 2015 the NRC released the last two volumes of a five-volume safety report, concluding that Yucca Mountain meets all technical and safety requirements. In an accompanying press release, the NRC noted, "Completion of the safety evaluation report does not represent an agency decision on whether to authorize construction. A final licensing decision, should funds beyond those currently available be appropriated, could come only after completion of a supplement to the Department of Energy's environmental impact statement, hearings on contentions in the adjudication, and Commission review."

Commercial spent fuel continues to be held in temporary storage at nuclear power plants across the country more than thirty years after Congress directed the federal government to site and license a facility for storage of nuclear waste. In June 2012 the U.S. Court of Appeals for the District of Columbia Circuit struck down the NRC's 2010 revision of its "waste confidence" rule, directing the agency to consider the possibility that a geologic repository for permanent disposal of spent fuel might never be built and to do further analysis of spent fuel pool leaks and fires. In August 2014 the NRC approved a final rule on the environmental effects of continued storage of spent nuclear fuel.

Security Issues

Following the terrorist attacks of Sept. 11, 2001, the NRC made a number of significant changes to its regulatory programs and issued orders to licensees to improve security in the interim period while the commission completed a comprehensive security review. The NRC established the Office of Nuclear Security and Incident Response to focus and coordinate the agency's efforts in the security and emergency preparedness areas. Since 2001 the NRC has increased the characteristics of the design basis threat—raising the level against which nuclear plants must provide protection. Plant protection capabilities and response strategies are protected from public disclosure.

In devising security measures against attacks on a nuclear facility or a dirty bomb attack on a U.S. city, the NRC works in conjunction with the Department of Homeland Security, the Department of Defense, and other agencies in developing a unified National Response Plan and National Incident Management System.

The Energy Policy Act of 2005 amended the Atomic Energy Act of 1954 to direct the NRC to evaluate the security at each licensed nuclear facility to assess its ability to defend against any type of threat. The act also expanded NRC's regulatory oversight to include additional radioactive materials, including certain sources of radium-226 and materials produced in accelerators rather than in reactors. The NRC promulgated rules under this act that included formalizing requirements for U.S. research and test reactors to perform fingerprint-based background checks on staff with unescorted access to their facilities and issued a final rule making it a federal crime to introduce, without authorization, weapons or explosives into specified classes of facilities designated by the NRC.

The act also required the NRC to develop a national tracking system for radioactive materials used in industry, academia, and medicine. By October 2006 the NRC had approved a final rule implementing a National Source Tracking System (NSTS). The NSTS covers radioactive sources typically used in radiothermal generators, irradiators, radiation therapy, industrial gamma radiography and high- and medium-dose-range brachytherapy cancer treatments. The system was implemented in 2009.

In March 2011 a tsunami struck the Fukushima Daiichi nuclear power plant in Japan. In the wake of that disaster, the NRC established a task force to review NRC regulations and processes to determine whether the agency should make additional improvements to programs in light of the events at Fukushima. Congress also directed the NRC to be proactive in ensuring nuclear power plants were able to withstand external hazards. Section 402 of the 2012 Consolidated Appropriations Act directs the NRC to require reactor licensees to reevaluate the seismic, tsunami, flooding, and other hazards at their sites against current NRC requirements and update the design basis of each reactor where necessary.

The agency established the Japan Lessons Learned Project Directorate, a group of more than twenty full-time employees focused exclusively on implementing the task force's recommendations and related activities. On March 12, 2012, based on the prioritized task force recommendations, the NRC issued the first regulatory requirements for the nation's 104 operating reactors based on the lessons-learned at Fukushima Daiichi. The NRC also provided guidance documents for performing a surge or seiche hazard assessment and for performing a tsunami hazard assessment.

▓ KEY PERSONNEL

Chair
> Stephen G. Burns . . . . (301) 415–1750
> > E-mail: Chairman@nrc.gov

Commissioners
> Kristine L. Svinicki . . . . (301) 415–1855
> > E-mail: CMRSVINICKI@nrc.gov
> William C. Ostendorff . . . . (301) 415–1800
> > E-mail: CMROSTENDORFF@nrc.gov
> Jeff Baran . . . . (301) 415–1839
> > E-mail: CMRBARAN@nrc.gov
> Vacant

Administration
> Cynthia Carpenter . . . . (301) 287–0863

Advisory Committee on Reactor Safeguards
> Edwin Hackett . . . . (301) 415–7360

Atomic Safety and Licensing Board Panel
E. Roy Hawkens................... (301) 415–5147
Chief Financial Officer
Maureen Wylie .... (301) 415–7322
Computer Security Office
Thomas Rich .... (301) 415–6596
Congressional Affairs
Eugene Dacus .... (301) 415–1776
Corporate Management
Darren B. Ash .... (301) 415–7443
Enforcement
Patricia K. Holahan .... (301) 415–2741
Executive Director for Operations
Mark A. Satorius .... (301) 415–1700
General Counsel
Margaret M. Doane................ (301) 415–1743
Human Capital
Miriam Cohen.................... (301) 287–0724
Information Services
James Flanagan .... (301) 415–8700
Inspector General
Hubert T. Bell.................... (301) 415–5930
International Programs
Nader Mamish................... (301) 415–1780
Investigations
Cheryl McCrary .... (301) 415–2373
**Materials, Waste, Research, State, Tribal, and
Compliance Programs**
Michael F. Weber................. (301) 415–1705
E-mail: Michael.weber@nrc.gov
New Reactors
Glenn Tracy..................... (301) 415–1897
Nuclear Material Safety and Safeguards
Catherine Haney................. (301) 415–0595
Nuclear Reactor Regulation
William M. Dean................. (301) 415–1270
Nuclear Regulatory Research
Brian W. Sheron................. (301) 251–7400
Nuclear Security and Incident Response
Brian E. Holian .... (301) 287–3734
Site Safety and Environmental Analysis
Scott Flanders .... (301) 415–1634
Reactor and Preparedness Programs
Michael R. Johnston .... (301) 415–1713
Secretary of the Commission
Annette L. Vietti-Cook............ (301) 415–1969
Small Business and Civil Rights
Vonna Ordaz .... (301) 415–7380

■ INFORMATION SOURCES

Internet

Agency website: www.nrc.gov. Includes a wide range of information on the NRC and on nuclear reactors and materials.

The NRC Public Document Room also operates the Agency-wide Documents Access and Management System (ADAMS), an online database that provides access to all image and text documents that the NRC has made public since November 1, 1999, as well as bibliographic records made public before November 1999. Instructions on accessing the database can be obtained via the Internet at www.nrc.gov/reading-rm/adams.html.

The NRC Public Participation page lists a variety of venues for public participation, including a daily blog at http://public-blog.nrc-gateway.gov.

Telephone Contacts

Switchboard ....(301) 415–7000
Toll-free.........................(800) 368–5642
TTY ....(301) 415–5575
Emergencies ....(301) 816–5100
Public Document Room ....(301) 415–4209
Toll-free.........................(800) 397–4209
TTY ....(800) 635–4512

Information and Publications

KEY OFFICES

NRC Public Affairs
11555 Rockville Pike
Rockville, MD 20852–2738
(301) 415–8200
Fax: (301) 415–3716
E-mail: OPA.Resource@nrc.gov
Eliot B. Brenner, director

Answers general questions from the public and the press; issues publications and news releases (also available by e-mail subscription); coordinates requests for speakers and/or participants for seminars and lectures.

Freedom of Information
NRC Office of Information Services
11555 Rockville Pike, MS T-5 F09
Rockville, MD 20852–2738
(301) 415–7169
Fax: (301) 415–5130
E-Mail: FOIA.resource@nrc.gov
Patricia Hirsch, FOIA public liaison

MEETINGS

Advisory Committee Meetings
Schedules of upcoming advisory committee meetings are available from NRC Public Affairs (*see above*) and are given on the website; schedules are also published in the *Federal Register* at least seven days in advance of the meeting (*see appendix for how to use the Federal Register*). Records of previous meetings are available for review in the NRC Public Document Room and on the website.

Commission Meetings
The commissioners usually meet several times a week in the commissioner's conference room at NRC

headquarters in Rockville, MD. Meetings are open to the public unless the subject of the meeting is exempt under the Government in the Sunshine Act. Remote participants may also see and hear meetings via live video feed and submit questions over the Internet.

Notices of meetings are posted on the NRC website; at http://meetings.nrc.gov/pmns/mtg. Subjects to be covered are published on the website at least one week before each meeting.

Meeting notice information is also available on the NRC website, by a recorded message service, (301) 415–1292, or by contacting Glenn Ellmers (301) 415–0442. To coordinate access for disabled persons, contact Kimberly Meyer-Chambers by phone at (301) 287–0727 or by e-mail at Kimberly.Meyer-Chambers@nrc.gov.

PUBLICATIONS

Contact the NRC Public Document Room (*see Libraries, below*) for help locating NRC publications, or access NRC publications on the website in the Electronic Reading Room at www.nrc.gov/reading-rm/pdr.html collections. Other sources include the National Technical Information Service (NTIS) and U.S. Government Printing Office (GPO). (*See appendix, Ordering Government Publications.*)

Publications include

Nuclear Regulatory Commission's Regulatory Guides. Description of methods acceptable for implementing specific requirements of NRC regulations; published in ten subject areas.

Nuclear Regulatory Commission's Rules and Regulations. Loose-leaf set of the information contained in Title 10, parts 0–199, *Code of Federal Regulations,* and replacement pages, issued as supplements, reflecting amendments to rules.

Reference Resources

LIBRARIES

NRC Public Document Room

1 White Flint North, 1st Floor
11555 Rockville Pike
Rockville, MD 20852–2738
(301) 415–4737
Fax (301) 415–3548
TTY (800) 635–4512
Internet: www.nrc.gov/reading-rm/pdr.html
E-mail: pdr.resource@nrc.gov
Hours: 7:45 a.m. to 4:15 p.m., Monday through Friday
Phone reference hours: 8:00 a.m. to 4:00 p.m., Monday
    through Friday
Anna McGowan, branch chief

Helps the public find and obtain NRC information in the agency's electronic, paper, and microfiche collections. Holdings are focused on unclassified documents related to the NRC's licensing and rulemaking activities, as well as documents from the regulatory activities of the former Atomic Energy Commission. Maintains the ADAMS online database. NRC documents available to the public may be accessed on the website in the Electronic Reading Room.

NRC Technical Library

11555 Rockville Pike, MS T2B9
Rockville, MD 20852–2738
(301) 415–6239
Hours: 8:00 a.m. to 4:00 p.m., Monday through Friday
Anna McGowan, branch chief

Maintains a collection of published materials from the scientific and technical fields related to nuclear energy, nuclear reactors, radiation safety, and other nuclear technology. The library is primarily for use by NRC staff but is open to the public by appointment, from 8:00 a.m. to 4:00 p.m.

DOCKETS

Contact the NRC Public Document Room (*see Libraries, above*) or access on the website at www.nrc.gov/public-involve/doc-comment.html. Federal dockets are also available at www.regulations.gov. (*See appendix for information on searching and commenting on regulations.*)

RULES AND REGULATIONS

NRC rules, regulations, and standards are published in the *Code of Federal Regulations,* Title 5, Chapter XLVIII, Part 5801; Title 10, Chapter I, Parts 0–199. Proposed regulations and standards, new final rules and standards, and updates to the *Code of Federal Regulations* are published in the daily *Federal Register.* (*See appendix for information on how to obtain and use these publications.*)

■ LEGISLATION

The NRC exercises authority under the following legislation, as amended:

Atomic Energy Act of 1954 as amended (68 Stat. 919, 42 U.S.C. 2011). Signed by the president Aug. 30, 1954. Established the Atomic Energy Commission, which was the forerunner of the NRC, and set out the basic authority for the regulation of nuclear energy.

Energy Reorganization Act of 1974 as amended (88 Stat. 1242, 42 U.S.C. 5841). Signed by the president Oct. 11, 1974. Abolished the Atomic Energy Commission, transferring its powers to the NRC and the Energy Research and Development Administration (now Department of Energy).

Clean Air Act Amendments (91 Stat. 685, 42 U.S.C. 7401). Signed by the president Aug. 7, 1977. Gave the Environmental Protection Agency and the NRC authority to set air quality standards for radioactive substances and emissions.

Nuclear Non-Proliferation Act of 1978 (92 Stat. 120, 22 U.S.C. 3201). Signed by the president March 10, 1978. Established a more effective framework to ensure worldwide development of peaceful nuclear activities and prevent the export by any nation of equipment, technology, or nuclear materials that contribute to proliferation.

Uranium Mill Tailings Radiation Control Act of 1978 as amended (92 Stat. 3021, 42 U.S.C. 7901 note). Signed by the president Nov. 8, 1978. Authorized the NRC to regulate the handling and disposal of wastes from the processing of uranium.

Reorganization Plan No. 1 (H. Doc. 96–288, as amended by H. Doc. 96–307). Effective June 16, 1980. Increased the authority of the NRC chair to oversee nuclear power plant emergencies and to control staff operations.

Low-Level Radioactive Waste Policy Act of 1980 (94 Stat. 3347, 42 U.S.C. 2021b). Signed by the president Dec. 23, 1980. Established a federal program for the interim storage of spent nuclear fuel away from the reactor. Title III established NRC's duties and policy regarding storage and licensing of waste storage facilities.

Nuclear Waste Policy Act of 1982 (96 Stat. 2201, 42 U.S.C. 10101 note). Signed by the president Jan. 7, 1983. Established a deadline for establishing a permanent underground repository for high-level nuclear waste.

Low-Level Radioactive Waste Policy Amendments Act of 1985 (99 Stat. 1842, 42 U.S.C. 2021). Signed by the president Jan. 15, 1986. Imposed strict deadlines for states or regions to set up disposal facilities for low-level radioactive wastes; approved compacts among thirty-seven states to join together for the disposal of such wastes.

Solar, Wind, Waste, and Geothermal Power Production Incentives Act of 1990 (104 Stat. 2834, 16 U.S.C. 791a note). Signed by the president Nov. 15, 1990. Amended the Atomic Energy Act of 1954 by providing a single-step process for licensing uranium enrichment. Directed the NRC to regulate the control, ownership, or possession of any equipment or device, or important component part, that is capable of separating uranium isotopes or enriching uranium.

Energy Policy Act of 1992 (106 Stat. 2776, 42 U.S.C. 13201). Signed by the president Oct. 24, 1992. Title VIII specifically dealt with the NRC's responsibilities regarding the disposal/storage of high-level radioactive waste. Section 801b established NRC requirements and criteria regarding nuclear waste disposal, particularly at the Yucca Mountain site. Section 803 required that the NRC, along with the DOE and the EPA, submit plans for the management of nuclear waste. Created the United States Enrichment Corporation (USEC), a government-owned corporation, as a first step in transferring the uranium enrichment business to the private sector.

USEC Privatization Act (110 Stat. 1321–335, 42 U.S.C. 2011 note). Signed by the president April 26, 1996. Required the board of directors of the USEC to sell the assets of the corporation to a private-sector entity. The new private owner would be responsible for the operation of two gaseous diffusion plants in Kentucky and Ohio, and the development of the atomic vapor laser isotope separation (AVLIS) technology. Amended the Atomic Energy Act of 1954, with respect to certification of

gaseous diffusion plants and licensing of an AVLIS enrichment facility. Provided that NRC would not license the corporation or its successor if the corporation is owned, controlled, or dominated by a foreign corporation or government.

Joint Resolution by the Senate and House of Representatives Approving the Site at Yucca Mountain (116 Stat. 735, 42 U.S.C. 10139). Signed by the president July 23, 2002. Approved the site at Yucca Mountain, NV, for the development of a repository for the disposal of high-level radioactive waste and spent nuclear fuel, pursuant to the Nuclear Waste Policy Act of 1982.

Energy Policy Act of 2005 (119 Stat. 594, 16 U.S.C. 8240). Signed by the president Aug. 8, 2005. Established a long-range, comprehensive national energy policy. Encouraged nuclear power plant construction. Required the NRC, before issuing a license for a nuclear power plant, to consult with the Department of Homeland Security regarding the vulnerability of the proposed location to terrorist attack. Gave NRC regulatory authority over additional radioactive materials, including certain sources of radium-226 and materials produced in accelerators rather than in reactors. Required the NRC to issue regulations establishing a mandatory tracking system for radiation sources in the United States.

Consolidated Appropriations Act, 2012 (125 Stat. 786). Signed by the president on Dec. 23, 2011. Sec. 402 directed the NRC to require reactor licensees to reevaluate the seismic, tsunami, flooding, and other hazards at their sites against current NRC requirements and update the design basis of each reactor where necessary.

■ REGIONAL OFFICES

REGION 1

(CT, DC, DE, MA, MD, ME, NH, NJ, NY, PA, RI, VT)
2100 Renaissance Blvd., #100
King of Prussia, PA 19406–2713
(610) 337–5000
(800) 432–1156
TTY (301) 415–5575
E-mail: OPA1.Resource@nrc.gov
Daniel Dorman, regional administrator
(610) 337–5000, ext. 2

REGION 2

(AL, FL, GA, KY, MS, NC, PR, SC, TN, VA, VI, WV)
Marquis One Tower
245 Peachtree Center Ave. N.E., #1200
Atlanta, GA 30303
(404) 997–4000
(800) 577–8510
TTY (301) 415–5575
E-mail: OPA2.Resource@nrc.gov
Victor McCree, regional administrator

REGION 3

(IA, IL, IN, MI, MN, OH, WI)

2443 Warrenville Rd., #210

Lisle, IL 60532–4352

(630) 829–9500

(800) 522–3025

TTY (301) 415–5575

Fax (630) 515–1078

E-mail: OPA3.Resource@nrc.gov

Cynthia Pedson, regional
  administrator

REGION 4

(AK, AR, AS, AZ, CA, CO, GU, HI, ID, KS, LA,
  MO, MT, ND, NE, NM, NV, OK, OR, SD, TX,
  UT, WA, WY)

1600 E. Lamar Blvd.

Arlington, TX 76011–4511

(817) 860–8100

(800) 952–9677

TTY (301) 415–5575

E-mail: OPA4@Resource@nrc.gov

Marc L. Dapas, regional administrator

Pension Benefit Guaranty Corporation

1200 K St. N.W., Washington, DC 20005–4026
Internet: www.pbgc.gov

The Employee Retirement Income Security Act of 1974 (ERISA) extended federal regulatory control of private pension and welfare plans. The Welfare and Pension Plans Disclosure Act of 1958 had required only the filing of annual reports and the disclosure of the operation and administration of pension plans. ERISA is administered by three government agencies: the Pension Benefit Guaranty Corporation (PBGC), the Employee Benefits Security Administration (EBSA) of the Department of Labor (*p. 753*), and the Internal Revenue Service of the Treasury Department (*p. 846*).

The EBSA administers and enforces ERISA's fiduciary standards and its requirements on reporting and disclosure, employee protection, and enforcement. The IRS administers and enforces standards for funding, participation, and vesting of individuals covered by pension plans. The PBGC is responsible for pension plan insurance programs.

ERISA does not require businesses to establish private pension and welfare plans; however, if an employer wishes to continue a plan or intends to establish a new plan, guidelines and standards promulgated under the statute must be followed. The basic provisions of ERISA are the following:

- Employees cannot be forced to work for an unreasonable amount of time before becoming eligible for participation in a pension plan.
- Benefit pension plans must meet minimum funding standards.
- Operators of pension and welfare plans must file a copy of the plan with the EBSA and must file an annual or triennial financial report; both the plan and the report may be inspected by the public (*see Information Sources, below*).
- Pension plan participants must be provided with summaries of the plan's provisions and be informed of any changes made regarding benefits.
- Individuals with a fiduciary responsibility for handling a pension plan's funds and assets must meet certain standards of conduct and avoid conflict of interest.

Pension plans not covered by the provisions of ERISA include government plans (including Railroad Retirement Act plans and plans of some international organizations); certain church plans; plans maintained solely to comply with workers' compensation laws, unemployment compensation laws, or disability insurance laws; plans operated outside the United States primarily for nonresident aliens; and excess benefit plans (those that provide benefits or contributions above those allowed for tax-qualified plans) that are unfunded. Tax-qualified plans are those in which the assets are not taxable until they are distributed.

The PBGC was created by Title IV of ERISA. The PBGC ensures that participants in the pension plans it insures will receive at least basic retirement benefits in the event that the plan does not have sufficient funds to pay. The PBGC's termination insurance program covers single-employer, private-defined benefit pension plans— plans whose benefits are determined by using a formula including factors such as age, length of service, and salary. The agency, under its insurance program, also protects the pension benefits of the approximately 10 million participants in multiemployer pension plans. Multiemployer plans are based on collective bargaining agreements involving a union and two or more employers. These plans usually cover an industry, skilled trade, or craft in a particular geographic area.

The PBGC is a nonprofit corporation wholly owned by the federal government. It is financed by premiums levied against covered pension plans, the assets of plans it places into trusteeship, and investment income. The corporation is administered by a board of directors and an executive director. The board is composed of the secretaries of labor, commerce, and the Treasury; the labor secretary serves as chair.

A seven-member advisory committee, made up of two labor representatives, two business representatives, and three public members, advises the corporation on various matters related to the PBGC's insurance programs. The committee is appointed by the president.

When a covered single-employer pension plan terminates, the PBGC determines whether the plan will be able to pay basic benefits to all entitled participants. If it can, the corporation ensures that the fund's assets are used properly; if it cannot pay the benefits, the PBGC takes over, makes up the difference in assets, administers the fund, and distributes the basic benefits.

In cases involving the termination of an insufficiently funded plan, the employer or plan sponsor is liable to the PBGC for the insufficiency. The PBGC also may force a plan to terminate if the plan is unable to pay benefits or if the long-term losses to the insurance program would be unreasonable. In that case, the corporation takes over the pension plan to assure continued payments of benefits to participants.

PBGC also works with companies that have underfunded pensions to keep them from failing. Through its Early Warning Program, PBGC monitors specific companies with underfunded defined benefit pension plans to identify corporate transactions that could endanger pensions. PBGC works with the companies to arrange suitable protections for those pensions and the pension insurance program. Under pension law, when layoffs or plant closures threaten a plan's funding status, PBGC can move to obtain protection for the plans with a guarantee, posting of collateral, or contribution to the plan. In FY14, PBGC helped to protect 163,000 people by encouraging companies to keep their plans when they emerged from bankruptcy and negotiated $464 million in financial assurance to protect 126,000 people in plans at risk from corporate transactions.

A Supreme Court ruling broadened the PBGC's powers to protect the pensions of American workers by affirming the government's authority to order corporations to reinstate terminated retirement plans. The ruling involved the LTV Corp., a Dallas-based steel and aerospace manufacturing company that filed for bankruptcy in 1986. Its pension plans were terminated by the PBGC, which assumed LTV's pension payment responsibilities. When LTV's financial condition improved, however, the PBGC in 1987 ordered the company to resume responsibility for its pension plans. LTV refused, saying it should be held liable only after it fully recovered financially. LTV's refusal was initially upheld by a federal district judge and a U.S. Court of Appeals.

In 1990 the Supreme Court's reversal of the two lower courts in the LTV case made it harder, if not impossible, for corporations to use bankruptcy laws to "dump" their unfunded pension liability on the PBGC in order to have more cash for their creditors. The ruling also improved the financial outlook for the PBGC; the government had warned that the agency's future was threatened if it could not order firms to restore abandoned pension benefits and that it could suffer a financial crisis similar to that facing the government's insurance program for the savings and loan industry.

Congress enacted legislation in 1980 to define PBGC liability in the event of multiemployer plan failures. If a multiemployer plan becomes insolvent, the PBGC can provide financial assistance for the period of insolvency but does not take over administration of the plan. An employer who contributes to a multiemployer plan and subsequently withdraws from that plan is liable to the plan for a portion of the plan's unfunded vested benefits. This is called the employer's "withdrawal liability." The legislation also increased the PBGC premium paid by a plan for each participant to $2.60 per year, with incremental increases in future years. The per-participant flat premium rate for plan years beginning in 2015 is $57 for single-employer plans (up from a 2014 rate of $49) and $26 for multiemployer plans (up from a 2014 rate of $12).

To protect the benefits of U.S. workers and retirees, President Bill Clinton signed the Retirement Protection Act of 1994, which accelerated funding for underfunded pension plans, improved disclosure, and strengthened the pension insurance program. The act required certain underfunded plans to notify participants and beneficiaries annually of the plan's funding status and the limits of PBGC's guarantee.

High-profile bailouts did not go unnoticed in Congress. A review of the plans taken over by PBGC indicates most of these have come from two industries: steel and airline. In his testimony before Congress in October 2004, PBGC director Bradley Belt noted that the steel and airline industries had accounted for more than 70 percent of PBGC's claims by dollar amount, while covering less than 5 percent of the insured base. Director Belt urged Congress to reform the PBGC. Specifically, Belt said that the risks stem from three categories: archaic funding laws that do not adjust premiums for high-risk companies; a "moral hazard" that allows companies to exploit the system and knowingly make pension promises it cannot keep, relying on PBGC for a bailout; and rules that allow companies to shield relevant information regarding the funding status of plans from participants, investors, and even regulators.

Congress passed a temporary fix in 2004. The Pension Funding Equity Act of 2004 amended the Employee Retirement Income Security Act of 1974 (ERISA) and the Internal Revenue Code to temporarily replace (for plan years 2004 and 2005) the thirty-year Treasury rate with a rate based on long-term corporate bonds for certain pension plan funding requirements. It also allowed applicable employers, defined as airlines and steel companies, to make deficit reduction payments to PBGC.

In September 2004 the Congressional Budget Office (CBO) estimated that the PBGC shortfall of $23 billion in 2004 would balloon to nearly $87 billion over the next decade. Also that month Delta and Northwest Airlines filed for bankruptcy, adding to the PBGC woes.

In fall 2005 both the House and Senate began working on PBGC overhaul bills. On Aug. 17, 2006, President George W. Bush signed the Pension Protection Act (PPA) of 2006. PPA provided for stronger pension funding rules, greater transparency, and a stronger pension insurance system. PPA made the PBGC's variable-rate premium payable by all underfunded plans; reformed the pension funding rules; established new limits on the PBGC's guarantee (for example, shut-down benefits); provided funding relief to certain companies, particularly those in the airline industry; and imposed new reporting and disclosure requirements.

However, as the U.S. economy sharply declined during fall 2008, companies faced difficulties in meeting the additional funding requirements under PPA. Plans suffered investment losses of 20 percent to 30 percent and nearly 1,000 plans, or two-thirds of all multiemployer plans, were certified to be in endangered or critical status. Congress passed the Worker, Retiree, and Employer Recovery Act of 2008. The act eased the increased funding requirements under PPA, which required employers to increase funding for single-employer pension plans from 90 percent to 100 percent over a seven-year period. The new law also provided relief to riskier multiemployer pension plans that had been required to provide additional funding and to set forth a funding improvement plan. The Preservation of Access to Care for Medicare Beneficiaries and Pension Relief Act of 2010 provided temporary funding relief for contributors to single-employer and multiemployer defined benefit plans. Plans that elect relief under the act are required to notify PBGC of the election.

Prompted by Executive Order 13563 in 2011, which mandated that agencies undertake a retrospective review of existing regulation, PBGC undertook a regulatory review of rules enforcing ERISA section 4062(e); this requires companies with pension plans to report to PBGC when they stop operations at a facility and employees lose their jobs. Stakeholder feedback during the review process resulted in PBGC rolling out a pilot program that relaxed enforcement of 4062(e) for some firms. The new approach screens out financially sound companies and small plans with fewer than 100 people, which excludes 92 percent of businesses that sponsor plans from the agency's enforcement efforts.

The Moving Ahead for Progress in the 21st Century Act (MAP-21), enacted in 2012, made changes to the funding requirements of single-employer pension plans. The Pension Funding Stabilization provision of MAP amends ERISA to allow for the segment rates to be adjusted if they are below or above specified (applicable) minimum and maximum percentages of the average of the rates for the preceding 25 years. MAP-21 increases premium rates for single- and multiemployer plans through calendar year 2015.

The PBGC currently guarantees payment of basic pension benefits for more than 33 million U.S. workers and retirees participating in private-sector benefit pension plans. PBGC is responsible for the current and future pensions of about 1.5 million people in failed plans. In FY14, PBGC assumed responsibility for an additional 97 single-employer plans with about 53,000 participants. The agency also began providing financial assistance to nine newly insolvent multiemployer plans with about 4,300 people. In FY14, PBGC paid $5.5 billion to almost 813,000 retirees in more than 4,600 failed single-employer plans and $97 million in financial assistance to 53 multiemployer plans covering 52,000 retirees. The maximum guarantee applicable to a plan is fixed; for single employer pension plans terminating in 2012, the maximum guaranteed amount is just over $5,000 per month ($60,000 yearly) for a participant retiring at age sixty-five. The guarantee limit for multiemployer plans is variable according to several factors, including years of service and dollar amount of the benefit.

At the close of fiscal year 2014, PBGC reported a $62 billion deficit, up from the previous record-setting deficit of $34 billion in 2012. PBGC's multiemployer insurance program's deficit rose to $42.4 billion, compared with $8.3 billion the previous year. The program's increased deficit is largely due to the fact that several additional large multiemployer plans are expected to become insolvent within the next decade. The FY14 financial condition of the single-employer program improved with a deficit of about $19.3 billion, down from $27.4 billion in the previous year.

Given the alarming condition of multiemployer pension plans and the impact to the PBGC, Congress passed the Multiemployer Pension Reform Act of 2014, which was included in the FY15 omnibus appropriations act signed by President Barack Obama. The reform act made multiple revisions to existing pension law designed to reduce the financial burden on PBGC. The act proscribes remediation measures for deeply troubled plans, including provisions that would allow for suspension of benefits for retirees in multiemployer pension plans in "critical and declining status" under specified circumstances. The act provides PBGC with increased flexibility with regard to mergers and partitions and more than doubled the per capita insurance premium for multiemployer pension plans.

The reform act tasks the Treasury Secretary with oversight and regulation promulgation, in consultation with PBGC and the Labor Department. PBGC published a page within its website as a clearinghouse for information pertaining to the Multiemployer Pension Reform Act of 2014.

■ KEY PERSONNEL

Chair
    Thomas E. Perez . . . . (202) 693–6000
Board Members
    Thomas E. Perez, secretary of labor . . (202) 693–6000
    Penny Pritzker, secretary of
        commerce. (202) 482–2112
    Jacob (Jack) Lew, secretary of the
        Treasury . . . . (202) 622–1100
Director
    Alice Maroni . . . . (202) 326–4010
Chief Counsel
    Israel Goldowitz . . . . (202) 326–4020
Chief Financial Officer
    Patricia Kelly . . . . (202) 326–4170
Chief Information Officer
    Robert Scherer. . . . . (202) 326–4010
Chief Management Officer
    Edgar Bennett . . . . (202) 326–4180
Chief Policy Officer
    Vacant. . . . . (202) 326–4010
Benefits Administration and Payment Department
    Cathy Kronopolus. . . . . (202) 326–4050
Budget and Organizational Performance
    Wayne Hobbs (acting) . . . . (202) 326–4120
Communications Outreach and Legislative Affairs
    Sanford McLaurin. . . . . (202) 326–4343
Corporate Controls and Reviews
    Martin Boehm. . . . . (202) 326–4161
Corporate Finance and Restructuring
    Dana Cann (acting) . . . . (202) 326–4070
Corporate Investments
    John Greenberg . . . . (202) 326–4592, ext. 4592
Director for Policy and External Affairs
    Vacant . . . . (202) 326–4010

Equal Employment Opportunity
Karen Margensey......... (202) 326–4000, ext. 4363
E-mail: eeo@pbgc.gov
Financial Operations
Theodore J. Winter Jr............... (202) 326–4060
General Counsel
Judith R. Starr .... (202) 326–4400
Human Resources Department
Arrie Etheridge .... (202) 326–4110
Information Technology and Business Modernization
Vidhya Shyamsunder .... (202) 326–4130
Information Technology Infrastructure Operations
Joshua Kossoy (acting) .... (202) 326–4130
Inspector General
Robert Westbrooks .... (202) 326–4030
Hotline .... (800) 303–9737
Fax.......................... (202) 326–4129
Negotiations and Restructuring
Sanford (Sandy) Rich .... (202) 326–4020
Policy, Research, and Analysis
Christopher Bone .... (202) 326–4080
Procurement Department
Arthur S. (Steve) Block............. (202) 326–4160
Quality Management
Diane Braunstein.................. (202) 326–4160

■ INFORMATION SOURCES

Internet

Agency website: www.pbgc.gov. Includes information on PBGC offices and programs, including news releases, publications, and all aspects of PBGC operations. Agency e-mail: mypension@pbgc.gov.

Telephone Contacts

Inspector General's Hotline......... (800) 303–9737

For worker or retiree:
8:00 a.m. to 7:00 p.m. EST, Mon. through Fri.
Switchboard .... (202) 326–4000
Toll-free .... (800) 400–7242
Federal Relay Service (FRS) TTY .... (800) 877–8339
FRS ask to be connected to .... (800) 400–7242

For plan sponsor, administrator, or other practitioner:
8:00 a.m. to 5:00 p.m. EST, Mon. through Fri.
Switchboard .... (202) 326–4242
Toll-free .... (800) 736–2444
Federal Relay Service (FRS) TTY .... (800) 877–8339
FRS ask to be connected to .... (800) 736–2444

Information and Publications

KEY OFFICES

PBGC Communications and Public Affairs
1200 K St. N.W.
Washington, DC 20005

(202) 326–4343
Fax (202) 326–4344
Sanford McLauren, director

Answers general questions from the media and the public and issues PBGC publications.

Freedom of Information (FOIA) Requester Service Center
1200 K St. N.W., #11125
Washington, DC 20005
(202) 326–4040
Fax (202) 326–4042
Michelle Chase, FOIA public liaison
Betty Gamez, FOIA public liaison

PBGC Customer Contact Center
(202) 326-4000
(800) 400–7242
Fax (202) 326-4047
P.O. Box 151750
Alexandria, VA 22315

Answers questions about specific pension plans that have been taken over by the PBGC.

PUBLICATIONS

Many publications are available on the website, in English and Spanish. Publishes a series of technical updates, specialized program brochures, interest rate updates, annual financial reports, and historical operating data. Titles available from the website and PBGC Communications and Public Affairs include
PBGC Annual Reports
Your Guaranteed Pension (answers to commonly asked questions about pension plans)
Finding a Lost Pension
Pension Insurance Data Book
Small Business Guide
Your Right to Appeal
Electronic Direct Deposit
Your PBGC Benefit Options: Questions and Answers for Participants
PBGC's 2011–2016 Strategic Plan
Qualified Domestic Relations Orders
A Predictable, Secure Pension for Life
My Plan Administration Account

DATA AND STATISTICS

See the *Annual Report to the President and Congress* for data and statistics on the operations of the PBGC. Information about pension plans trusted by the PBGC, state pension plans, the health coverage tax credit, and premium payment instructions is also available on the website.

Reference Resources

DOCKETS

PBGC Disclosure Room
1200 K St. N.W.
Washington, DC 20005

(202) 326–4040

Fax (202) 326–4042

Hours: 9:00 a.m. to 4:30 p.m.

D. Camilla Perry, disclosure officer

Dockets for selected PBGC regulations and rulings, litigated cases, news releases, and a list of all terminated pension plans may be inspected and copied at this office. Federal dockets are also available at www.regulations.gov. (*See appendix for information on searching and commenting on regulations.*)

RULES AND REGULATIONS

PBGC rules and regulations are published in the *Code of Federal Regulations,* Title 29, Chapter XL, Parts 4000–4999. Proposed rules, new final rules, and updates to the *Code of Federal Regulations* are published in the daily *Federal Register.* (*See appendix for information on how to obtain and use these publications.*)

▓ LEGISLATION

The legislation that established regulation of employee benefit plans is the **Employee Retirement Income Security Act of 1974** (88 Stat. 829, 29 U.S.C. 1001). Signed by the president Sept. 2, 1974, the statute, known as ERISA, authorized mandatory minimum federal standards for pension and welfare plans and created the PBGC.

ERISA did not require the establishment of pension plans; rather, it specified minimum requirements for existing or proposed plans. The requirements applied to vesting formulas, capitalization of the fund, participation in the fund, and the responsibilities of the fund's operators.

The law required that operators of pensions make reports on the conditions of their funds and inform participants of changes in the fund.

ERISA also provided for the establishment of tax-deferred plans for retirement income by individuals not covered by a pension plan.

Multi-Employer Pension Plan Amendments Act of 1980 (94 Stat. 1208, 29 U.S.C. 1001). Signed by the president Sept. 26, 1980, the amendments to ERISA and to the Internal Revenue Code of 1954 (68a Stat. 3, 26 U.S.C. 1) strengthened the funding requirements for multiemployer pension plans and replaced the termination insurance program with an insolvency-based benefit protection plan covering multiemployer plans only.

Retirement Equity Act of 1984 (98 Stat. 1426, 29 U.S.C. 1001 note). Signed by the president Aug. 23, 1984. Provided for greater equity in private pension plans for workers and their spouses and dependents.

Single-Employer Pension Plan Amendments Act of 1986 (100 Stat. 82, 29 U.S.C. 1001). Signed by the president April 7, 1986. Strengthened the PBGC single-employer insurance fund that covers individual firms and prevented companies from terminating their pension plans arbitrarily.

Pension Protection Act of 1987 (101 Stat. 1330–1333, 26 U.S.C. note 1). Signed by the president Dec. 22, 1987. Barred employers from deducting contributions to

"overfunded" pension funds, defined as funds with assets exceeding 150 percent of current liability.

Retirement Protection Act of 1994 (108 Stat. 4809, 26 U.S.C. 1 note). Signed by the president Dec. 8, 1994. Amended the Employee Retirement Income Security Act of 1974 (ERISA) requirements for pension plan funding, including minimum funding, revising additional funding requirements for single-employer plans; limitation on changes in current liability assumptions; anticipation of bargained benefit increases; modification of the quarterly contribution requirement; and exceptions to the excise tax on nondeductible contributions.

Pension Funding Equity Act of 2004 (118 Stat. 596, 15 U.S.C. 37b). Signed by the president April 10, 2004. Amended the Employee Retirement Income Security Act of 1974 (ERISA) and the Internal Revenue Code (Code) to temporarily replace (for plan years 2004 and 2005) the thirty-year Treasury rate with a rate based on long-term corporate bonds for certain pension plan funding requirements. Allowed applicable employers defined as airlines and steel companies to make deficit reduction payments to PBGC. Established ERISA requirements for multiemployer plan funding notices. Required plan administrators to send such notices to participants, beneficiaries, labor organizations, and employers for each plan year.

Deficit Reduction Act of 2005 (120 Stat. 4, 42 U.S.C. 1305 note). Signed by the president Feb. 8, 2006. Increased flat-rate premiums for single-employer and multiemployer pension plans and established a termination premium for certain single-employer plans. Stipulated that these premium rates were to be adjusted each year for inflation, based on changes in the national average wage index.

Pension Protection Act of 2006 (120 Stat. 780, 29 U.S.C. 1002). Signed by the president Aug. 17, 2006. Amended the Employee Retirement Income Security Act of 1974 to require companies that underfund their pension plans to pay additional premiums. Extended a requirement that companies that terminate their pensions provide extra funding for the pension insurance system. Closed loopholes that allow underfunded plans to skip pension payments.

Worker, Retiree, and Employer Recovery Act of 2008 (122 Stat. 5092, 29 U.S.C. 1001 note). Signed by the president Oct. 23, 2008. Eased some of the increased funding requirements for single-employer and multiemployer pension plans that were passed under the Pension Protection Act of 2006. Provides a waiver of minimum distribution requirements for certain retirement plans and accounts for 2009.

Preservation of Access to Care for Medicare Beneficiaries and Pension Relief Act of 2010 (124 Stat. 1280, 29 U.S.C. 1001 note). Signed by the president June 25, 2010. Provides single and multiemployer pension plan sponsors with temporary relief from pension funding requirements. Other provisions.

Moving Ahead for Progress in the 21st Century Act (MAP-21). (126 Stat. 405, 23 U.S.C. 101 note). Signed by the president July 6, 2012. The Pension Funding

Stabilization provision of MAP amends ERISA to allow for the segment rates to be adjusted if they are below or above specified (applicable) minimum and maximum percentages of the average of the rates for the preceding 25 years. Increases premium rates for single- and multi-employer plans through calendar year 2015.

Cooperative and Small Employer Charity Pension Flexibility Act of 2014 (128 Stat. 1101, 29 U.S.C. 1001 note). Signed by the president April 7, 2014. Defines and proscribes regulations for cooperative and small employer charity pension plans.

Multiemployer Pension Reform Act of 2014. (Public Law 113-235). Signed by the president December 16, 2014. Division O of the Consolidated and Further Continuing Appropriations Act, 2015. Made multiple revisions to existing pension law designed to reduce the financial burden on PBGC. This includes provisions that would allow for temporary suspension of benefits for retirees in multiemployer pension plans in "critical and declining" status under specified circumstances. More than doubled the per capita insurance premium for multiemployer pension plans.

Postal Regulatory Commission

901 New York Ave. N.W., #200, Washington, DC 20268–0001
Internet: www.prc.gov

The Postal Regulatory Commission (PRC), formerly the Postal Rate Commission, is an independent agency created by the Postal Reorganization Act of 1970, as amended by the Postal Reorganization Act Amendments of 1976 and the Postal Accountability and Enhancement Act (PAEA) of 2006. The PRC's main responsibility is to regulate the postal rates and mail classifications used by the U.S. Postal Service (USPS).

The PRC has five members nominated by the president and confirmed by the Senate. Members serve six-year terms. The president designates the chair, and the commission annually elects one of its members to be vice chair. No more than three commissioners can be members of the same political party.

The PRC is responsible for developing a system of rate regulation, consulting with the USPS on delivery service standards and performance measures, adjudicating complaints, soliciting comments, examining proposals for new products and services, and publishing proposals in the *Federal Register*. The PRC has appellate jurisdiction to review USPS decisions to close or consolidate small post offices. Rate and classification decisions made by the commission may be appealed to the U.S. Court of Appeals.

The Postal Reorganization Act's promise of a more businesslike approach to providing the nation's mail service prompted considerable concern over the fate of small post offices, particularly rural ones. Section 101(b) of the Postal Reorganization Act reflects this concern by providing that no small post office shall be closed simply for operating at a deficit, it being the specific intent of the Congress that effective postal services be ensured to residents of both urban and rural communities.

The Postal Reorganization Act as originally enacted did not provide any role for the commission in small post office closings. It contemplated only USPS involvement. However, the early-to-mid 1970s saw mounting concern and frustration over inflammatory GAO reports and USPS administrative proposals to close up to 6,000 small post offices. In response, Congress amended the Postal Reorganization Act in 1976 to provide for commission review of appeals of post office closings or consolidations brought to it by affected persons.

In March 2002 the PRC approved an unusual settlement that allowed postal rates to increase on June 30, 2002. The settlement was offered in a PRC proceeding considering a USPS request for rate increases. The request had been developed before the terrorist attacks of Sept. 11, 2001. However, the PRC recognized that the events of September and October 2001, in particular the disruption caused by the use of the mail to distribute lethal anthrax spores, had a significant impact on USPS operations and finances.

In the rate increase request, the USPS had joined with mailer groups, postal employee organizations, competitors, and the Office of Consumer Advocate that represents the interests of the general public to offer a proposal that increased rates by 7.7 percent. The settlement raised rates for first-class letters by three cents, to 37 cents. The postcard rate was increased by two cents to 23 cents.

This was the first time a postal rate case had been resolved through settlement. Normally, the numerous conflicting interests engage in complex litigation to determine whether rate increases are justified. Until passage of PAEA, federal law required the USPS to break even from operations (the PAEA allowed the USPS to retain earnings, or make a profit, though this was unlikely). As part of the settlement, the USPS agreed to defer any additional increases until summer 2003. However, in November 2002 the USPS announced good news about future postal hikes. A financial review of USPS contributions since 1971 to the Civil Service Retirement System revealed that the Postal Service had been paying too much into its retirement fund. Legislation passed in April 2003 corrected the imbalance and allowed the USPS to reduce its debt. This also allowed USPS to forecast that another postal rate increase would not be needed until 2006.

After more than a decade of negotiations, the PAEA was signed by the president on Dec. 20, 2006, to establish an updated system for regulating rates and classes for market-dominant products (all first-class mail, parcels, postcards, periodicals, standard mail, single-piece parcel post, media mail, bound printed matter, library mail, special services, and single-piece international mail). Future market-dominant product increases were not to exceed the increase of the Consumer Price Index.

Under the PAEA, the reconfigured Postal Regulatory Commission was directed to establish a modern system for regulating rates and classes for market-dominant postal products. The PAEA further authorized the PRC to set regulations for determining USPS rates for competitive postal products. The PRC released regulations for the price-setting process on Oct. 29, 2007. The new system consisted of three parts: (1) regulations related to price adjustments for market dominant products, including the formula for the calculation of the price cap; (2) regulations related to competitive products; and (3) establishment of a mail classification schedule, which categorized postal products as either market dominant or competitive.

The PAEA required USPS contributions to the civil service retirement system return the military service costs of its retirees to the Treasury, and at the same time the act mandated that the USPS significantly fund its liability for retiree health benefits. Along with a general decline in revenue and the national economic downturn, this proved to be a heavy financial burden, and the USPS suffered a net loss of $2.8 billion in fiscal year (FY) 2008. By the end of FY14, the USPS had amassed a total net deficit of more than $50 billion, even though it had increased revenues.

The act also established an Office of Inspector General (OIG) in the PRC and gave the PRC subpoena authority and a broader scope for regulation and oversight, including the authority to hear complaints from public and business interests that believe the USPS is in violation of the PAEA. In March 2009 the PRC issued new regulations for complaints and rate or service inquiries in accordance with PAEA.

In early 2011 the PRC began conducting the first five-year review of the PAEA. Section 701 of the PAEA requires the PRC, at least every five years, to submit a report to the president and Congress on the effectiveness of the PAEA and to provide recommendations for legislation or other policies to improve the efficiency of postal laws.

In March 2011 the PRC issued an advisory opinion on the USPS's request to eliminate Saturday mail delivery as a cost-cutting measure. The USPS analysis predicted a savings of $3 billion by eliminating Saturday delivery; the PRC predicted a savings of $1.7 billion, which would not be realized until the third year of implementation. Also, the PRC noted that the USPS did not take into consideration the impact of five-day delivery on rural postal customers.

The elimination of one mail delivery day had been considered in previous decades. In 1983, Congress adopted language requiring the USPS to maintain six-day delivery. In its advisory opinion, the PRC maintained a neutral stance. The USPS recommendation was not implemented.

In February 2013 the USPS proposed a six-day package delivery and five-day mail delivery schedule, which it planned to implement in August 2013. The USPS anticipated annual savings from this schedule would be approximately $2 billion dollars annually. In its announcement, USPS did not provide a detailed plan. The PRC noted it would need to review the plan before making a recommendation. However, when Congress passed a continuing resolution in March 2013, the bill contained language that prohibited implementation of a new national delivery schedule for mail and packages. The language prohibiting such schedule changes appeared in subsequent appropriations bills.

PRC continues its expanded regulatory role under PAEA. In 2014 the PRC adopted three final rules that streamline advisory opinions on nationwide changes in postal services requested by the USPS; clarify rate incentives and de minimis rate increases under the price cap; and implement regulations for market tests of experimental products.

■ KEY PERSONNEL

Chair
Robert Taub (acting) . . . . (202) 789–6868
Vice Chair
Tony Hammond . . . . (202) 789–6805
Commissioners
Mark Acton . . . . (202) 789–6866
Nanci E. Langley . . . . (202) 789–6813
Ruth Y. Goldway . . . . (202) 789–6872
Chief Administrative Officer and Secretary
Shoshana Grove. . . . . (202) 789–6800
   Fax. . . . . (202) 789–6886
General Counsel
David Trissell . . . . (202) 789–6820
Inspector General
Jack Callender . . . . (202) 789–6817
Accountability and Compliance
Margaret Cigno . . . . (202) 789–6850
Public Affairs and Government Relations
Ann C. Fisher. . . . . (202) 789–6800
   Fax. . . . . (202) 789–6891

■ INFORMATION SOURCES

Internet
Agency website: www.prc.gov. Includes information on PRC opinions and decisions, meetings, filings, rules of practice, and offices, as well as PRC reports and studies.

Telephone Contacts
Switchboard . . . . (202) 789–6800
Fax . . . . (202) 789–6861
Federal Relay Service TTY . . . . (800) 877–8339

Information and Publications

KEY OFFICES

PRC Public Affairs and Government Relations
901 New York Ave. N.W., #200
Washington, DC 20268–0001
(202) 789–6800
Fax (202) 789–6891
Ann C. Fisher, director
E-mail: Ann.Fisher@PRC.Gov
Internet: PRC-PAGR@prc.gov

Handles requests for information from the press and the general public. Correspondence and comments should be directed to this office.

**FOIA Requester Service
Center and Reading Room**
> 901 New York Ave., N.W., #200
> Washington, DC 20268
> (202) 789–6840
> Fax (202) 789–6891
> Jennie Jbara, FOIA public liaison
> (202) 789–6800

PUBLICATIONS

The PRC Public Affairs and Government Relations Office provides information on PRC studies and other publications; documents are also available from the commission's website.

DATA AND STATISTICS

Many PRC publications include data and statistics on specific aspects of the Postal Service.

Reference Resources

DOCKETS

PRC Dockets Section
> 901 New York Ave. N.W., #200
> Washington, DC 20268–3001
> (202) 789–6846
> Joyce Taylor, contact
> Hours: 8:30 a.m. to 4:30 p.m.

Docket information is available through the Postal Regulatory Commission's website. Federal dockets are available at www.regulations.gov. (*See appendix for information on searching and commenting on regulations.*)

RULES AND REGULATIONS

PRC rules and regulations are published in the *Code of Federal Regulations,* Title 5, Chapter XLVI, Part 5601; Title 39, Chapter III, Parts 3000–3099. Proposed rules, new final rules, and updates to the *Code of Federal Regulations* are published in the daily *Federal Register.* (*See appendix for information on how to obtain and use these publications.*)

◼ LEGISLATION

The PRC carries out its responsibilities under the following legislation:

Postal Reorganization Act of 1970 (84 Stat. 759, 39 U.S.C. 3601). Signed by the president Aug. 12, 1970. Created the USPS as an independent government corporation and abolished the cabinet-level Post Office Department. Established the PRC to advise the USPS on rates and mail classification.

Postal Reorganization Act Amendments of 1976 (90 Stat. 1303, 39 U.S.C. 101). Signed by the president Sept. 24, 1976. This act made some administrative changes in the PRC but had no effect on the regulatory powers of the commission.

Postal Accountability and Enhancement Act (120 Stat. 3243, 39 U.S.C. 3622e). Signed by the president Dec. 20, 2006. Changed the name of the Postal Rate Commission to the Postal Regulatory Commission. Directed the commission to establish a modern system for regulating rates and classes for market-dominant postal products. Required the commission to make annual determinations of USPS compliance with regulatory requirements and to evaluate annually whether the USPS met certain goals. Changed postal service retirement and health benefits funding. Established the Office of the Inspector General in the PRC.

Small Business Administration

409 3rd St. S.W., #7000, Washington, DC 20416
Internet: www.sba.gov

The Small Business Administration (SBA) is an independent federal agency created by the Small Business Act of 1953. The SBA operates under the Small Business Investment Act of 1958, which was enacted to "aid, counsel, assist and protect insofar as is possible the interests of small business concerns in order to preserve free competitive enterprise, to ensure that a fair proportion of the total purchases and contracts for supplies and services for the government be placed with small business enterprises, and to maintain and strengthen the overall economy of the nation."

SBA has established numerical definitions of small businesses, or size standards, for all for-profit industries. Size standards represent the maximum size that a business may be to remain classified as a small business concern. These size standards are used to determine eligibility for SBA's programs, as well as eligibility for federal government procurement programs designed to help small businesses. Also, the Small Business Act states that unless specifically authorized by statute, no other federal department or agency may prescribe a small business size standard, unless such proposed size standard meets certain criteria and is approved by the SBA administrator.

The SBA makes loan guaranties and offers management counseling and training to all types of small businesses. Eligibility for SBA assistance requires that the business be independently owned and operated, not dominate its field, and meet SBA's size standard. The SBA makes long-term and low-interest loans under the Physical Disaster Loan Program to small or large businesses and to homeowners who suffer uninsured losses in natural disasters declared by the president or SBA administrator. It also provides loan assistance to businesses to control or abate air and water pollution.

The SBA also provides venture capital to small businesses by licensing, regulating, and providing financial assistance to small business investment companies (SBICs) and section 301(d) licensees (formerly minority enterprise small business investment companies). SBICs are privately owned companies that provide management assistance, equity financing, and long-term loans.

The agency also operates the Small Business Answer Desk, a toll-free information center that handles inquiries and addresses the concerns of businesspeople. Key offices within the SBA are as follows:

- The Office of Government Contracting refers small businesses to prime government contractors and uses several options to ensure small business participation in assorted federal projects.
- The Office of Advocacy researches the economic role of small businesses, analyzes proposed laws and rules affecting small businesses, reports the results of its research to the government and the small business community, and interacts with state and local governments.
- The Office of Entrepreneurial Development provides training, counseling, and access to resources. Programs and services within OED include the following:
- The Office of Small Business Development Centers provides assistance and training to businesspeople through nearly 900 small business development center service locations.
- The Office of Women's Business Ownership provides support, training, and advocacy for women entrepreneurs and businesses owned primarily by women. This office also runs the women's business centers that provide assistance or training in finance, management, marketing, procurement, and the Internet, as well as addresses specialized topics such as home-based businesses, corporate executive downsizing, and welfare-to-work.
- The Office of Entrepreneurship Education administers programs and activities designed to provide information, education, and training to prospective and existing small business owners.
- The Office of Disaster Assistance provides low-interest disaster loans to homeowners, renters, businesses, and nonprofit organizations to repair or replace real estate, personal property, equipment, and business assets that have been damaged or destroyed in a declared disaster.
- The Office of International Trade provides information and assistance to small business owners new to exporting or those looking to expand their export business.
- The Office of Veterans Business Development maximizes the availability of all SBA programs for veterans, service-disabled veterans, reserve component members, and their dependents or survivors.

The 8(a) Program, named for Section 8(a) of the Small Business Act, is a business development program that assists small disadvantaged businesses in competing in the marketplace and assists such companies in gaining access to federal and private procurement markets. The SBA works alongside federal purchasing agents and program participants, functioning as the prime contractor, and subcontracts work assignments to small disadvantaged firms.

During the 1990s, Congress worked to facilitate the relationship between the federal government and small business. The most notable initiative was the passage of the Small Business Regulatory Enforcement Fairness Act of 1996, which required, among other things, that federal agencies promulgating a new regulation prepare a cost-benefit analysis of the proposed regulation, prepare a report outlining the economic impact of the proposed regulation on a significant number of small businesses, and submit these reports to Congress. After review Congress could pass a joint resolution of disapproval and bar the regulation from enactment. However, the president could enact the regulation if necessary to protect national security, protect the public health, or to implement an international trade agreement.

The 1996 act also required SBA to assist small businesses with compliance through community information clearinghouses and resource centers; to establish a Small Business and Agriculture Regulatory Enforcement Ombudsman; and to establish a Small Business Regulatory Fairness Board in each SBA regional office.

All federal agencies are subject to the requirements of the HUBZone (historically underutilized business zone) Empowerment Contracting program, which was enacted into law as part of the Small Business Reauthorization Act of 1997. The program, which falls under the auspices of the SBA, provides federal contracting opportunities for qualified small businesses located in distressed areas and encourages economic development in historically underutilized business zones through the establishment of preferences.

A small business must meet all of the following criteria to qualify for the HUBZone program: it must be owned and controlled at least 51 percent by U.S. citizens, or a Community Development Corporation, or an agricultural cooperative or an Indian tribe; its principal office must be located within a HUBZone; and at least 35 percent of its employees must reside in a HUBZone.

Responding to the economic crisis that hit small businesses, Congress enacted the Small Business Jobs Act of 2010. The legislation provided financial resources, including increased lending and new loan programs, and tax relief to assist small businesses during the economic recovery. The Jobs Act expansion saw record loan approval from SBA.

■ KEY PERSONNEL

Administrator
Maria Contreras-Sweet .... (202) 205–6605
Deputy Administrator
Vacant .... (202) 205–6605
Advocacy
Claudia Rodgers (acting) .... (202) 205–6533

Business Development
Jackquline Robinson-Burnette ...... (202) 205–5852
Fax .... (202) 205–7259
Capital Access
Ann Marie Mehlum .... (202) 205–6657
Communications and Public Liaison
Benjamin Chang .... (202) 205–7085
Congressional and Legislative Affairs
Thaddeus Inge .... (202) 205–6700
Credit Risk Management
Brent M. Ciurtino .... (202) 205–6600
Disaster Assistance
James Rivera .... (202) 205–6734
E-mail: james.rivera@sba.gov
E-mail: disastercustomerservice@sba.gov
Entrepreneurship Education
Ellen Thrasher .... (202) 205–6665
Faith Based and Community Initiatives
Sarah Bard .... (202) 205–6677
Economic Opportunity
Grady Hedgespeth .... (202) 205–7562
E-mail: dionna.martin@sba.gov
General Counsel
Melvin Williams Jr. .... (202) 205–6642
Government Contracting and Business Development
A. John Shoraka .... (202) 205–6459
Government Contracting and Business Development for HUBZone Empowerment Contracting
Mariana Pardo .... (202) 205–2985
E-mail: mariana.pardo@sba.gov
Government Contracting and Business Development for Non-contiguous States and Territories
Darryl K. Hairston .... (202) 205–5852
Hearings and Appeals
Delorice P. Ford .... (202) 205–7340
TTY .... (202) 205–6189
E-mail: delorice.ford@sba.gov
Information Office
Renee Macklin .... (202) 205–6708
E-mail: chase.garwood@sba.gov
Inspector General
Peggy E. Gustafson .... (202) 205–6586
Interagency Affairs
Charley Maresca .... (202) 205–6978
International Trade
Eileen Sanchez .... (202) 205–6720
Fax .... (202) 205–7272
Investment and Innovation
Javier Saade .... (202) 205–6510
National Ombudsman and Assistant Administrator for Regulatory Enforcement Fairness
Brian Castro .... (888) 734–3247
Native American Affairs
Christopher L. James .... (202) 205–7364
Small Business Development Centers
Carroll A. Thomas .... (202) 205–6766
Veterans Business Development
Barb Carson .... (202) 205–6773
Women's Business Ownership
Erin Andrew .... (202) 205–6673

■ INFORMATION SOURCES

Internet

Agency website: www.sba.gov. Comprehensive website includes information on SBA programs and activities and access to SBA publications. Information about the agency is available in thirteen languages at www.sba.gov/category/navigation-structure/about-sba. The Small Business Answer Desk may be contacted by phone (see below) or at answerdesk@sba.gov. For information about disaster loans, e-mail disastercustomerservice@sba.gov; and for information about the HUBZone Program, e-mail hubzone@sba.gov.

Telephone Contacts

Switchboard	(202) 205–6600
Small Business Answer Desk (also in Spanish)	(800) 827–5722
HUBZone Help Desk	(202) 205–8885
Disaster Assistance Customer Service	(800) 659–2955
National Ombudsman	(888) 734–3247
Federal Relay Service TTY	(800) 877–8339

Information and Publications

KEY OFFICES

SBA Communications and Public Liaison Office
409 3rd St. S.W., #7450
Washington, DC 20416
(202) 205–6740
Iris Argueta, deputy assistant administrator

Handles press inquiries and issues news releases. Interested persons may sign up on the website to receive e-mail alerts.

Freedom of Information
409 3rd St. S.W.
Washington, DC 20416
(202) 401–8203
E-mail: foia@sba.gov
Delorice P. Ford, FOIA assistant administrator
E-mail: delorice.ford@sba.gov

PUBLICATIONS

An extensive series of publications are available on the website, in English and Spanish, including a small business management series and a government contracting series. Numerous e-newsletters are available as well, at www.sba.gov/offices/headquarters/ocpl/resources/22161. The Office of Advocacy also has law journal articles, executive orders, GAO reports, statutes, and numerous other documents and publications available at www.sba.gov/ADVO. In addition, numerous reports and studies, statistics and research, laws and regulations, and standard operating procedures are available at www.sba.gov/about-sba/sba-performance/open-government/digital-sba/open-data. Some publications are available on paper or microfiche for purchase from the National Technical Information Service (*see appendix on Ordering Government Publications*).

Reference Resources

LIBRARY

SBA Law Library
409 3rd St. S.W.
Washington, DC 20416
(202) 205–6849
Imelda Kish, law librarian
Open to the public
Hours: 8:30 a.m. to 2:30 p.m.

DOCKETS

Federal dockets are available at www.regulations.gov. (*See appendix for information on searching and commenting on regulations.*)

RULES AND REGULATIONS

SBA rules and regulations are published in the *Code of Federal Regulations*, Title 13, Chapter I, Parts 101–199. Proposed regulations, new final regulations, and updates to the *Code of Federal Regulations* are published in the daily *Federal Register*. (*See appendix for details on how to obtain and use these publications.*)

■ LEGISLATION

The SBA carries out its responsibilities under the following legislation:

Small Business Act (72 Stat. 384, 15 U.S.C. 631). Signed by the president July 30, 1953. Created and organized the SBA, declared the agency's policy, and defined small business concerns.

Small Business Investment Act of 1958 (72 Stat. 689, 15 U.S.C. 661). Signed by the president Aug. 21, 1958. Made equity capital and long-term credit more readily available for small business concerns.

Disaster Relief Act of 1970 (84 Stat. 1744, 42 U.S.C. 4401). Signed by the president Dec. 31, 1970. Revised and expanded federal relief programs that deal with victims of natural disasters.

Consolidated Farm and Rural Development Act (87 Stat. 24, 7 U.S.C. 1969). Signed by the president April 20, 1973. Guaranteed and set interest rates for loans made as a result of natural disasters.

Regulatory Flexibility Act of 1980 (94 Stat. 1164, 5 U.S.C. 601 note). Signed by the president Sept. 19, 1980. Required the federal government to anticipate and reduce the impact of rules and paperwork requirements on small businesses.

Small Business Investment Incentive Act of 1980 (94 Stat. 2275, 15 U.S.C. 80a). Signed by the president Oct. 21, 1980. Amended the Securities Act to exempt certain small- and medium-sized businesses from securities laws registration requirements.

Business Opportunity Development Reform Act of 1988 (102 Stat. 3853, 15 U.S.C. 631 note). Signed by the president Nov. 15, 1988. Amended the Small Business Act to reform the Capital Ownership Development Program 8(a) to abolish the noncompetitive contract award system, stiffened criminal penalties for persons who establish "front companies" posing as minority businesses, and restricted minority business owners' ability to sell 8(a) contracts to nonminority enterprises.

Omnibus Trade and Competitiveness Act of 1988 (102 Stat. 1107, 19 U.S.C. 2901). Signed by the president Aug. 23, 1988. Enhanced SBA's ability to promote international trade among small businesses and provided new financing authority for export purposes.

Fair Labor Standards Amendments of 1989 (103 Stat. 938, 29 U.S.C. 201 note). Signed by the president Nov. 17, 1989. Amended the Fair Labor Standards Act of 1938 to increase the minimum wage.

Americans with Disabilities Act of 1990 (104 Stat. 327, 42 U.S.C. 12101). Signed by the president July 26, 1990. Declared that it was discriminatory, on the basis of disability, to deny opportunities or to afford them unequally, to provide opportunities less effectively, to assist an organization or individual that discriminates, or to otherwise limit opportunities enjoyed by others.

Civil Rights Act of 1991 (105 Stat. 1071, 42 U.S.C. 1981 note). Signed by the president Nov. 21, 1991. Amended the Civil Rights Act of 1964 to strengthen and improve federal civil rights laws, to provide for damages in cases of intentional employment discrimination, and to clarify provisions regarding disparate impact actions.

Small Business Credit and Business Opportunity Enhancement Act of 1992 (106 Stat. 986, 15 U.S.C. 631 note). Signed by the president Sept. 4, 1992. Amended Small Business Investment Act of 1958 to improve operations of small business investment companies.

Family and Medical Leave Act of 1993 (107 Stat. 6, 29 U.S.C. 2601 note). Signed by the president Feb. 5, 1993. Established certain requirements for family and medical leave for permanent employees.

Small Business Lending Enhancement Act of 1995 (109 Stat. 295, 15 U.S.C. 631 note). Signed by the president Oct. 12, 1995. Amended the Small Business Act to reduce the level of participation by the SBA in loans guaranteed under the act on a deferred basis. Directed the SBA, with respect to each guaranteed loan made from the proceeds of development company debentures issued by qualified state or local development companies, to assess and collect a fee for such loans.

Small Business Regulatory Enforcement Fairness Act of 1996 (110 Stat. 857, 5 U.S.C. 601 note). Signed by the president March 29, 1996. Required SBA to assist small businesses with regulatory compliance through community information clearinghouses and resource centers; to establish a regulatory enforcement ombudsman; and to establish a regulatory fairness board in each SBA regional office. Required all federal agencies promulgating new regulations to submit cost-benefit reports and small business economic impact reports to Congress for review.

Small Business Programs Reauthorization Act of 2000 (114 Stat. 2763, 2763A-691, 15 U.S.C. 631 note). Signed by the president Dec. 21, 2000. Amended the portions of the Small Business Act to qualify as a HUBZone small business concern: (1) an Alaska Native

Corporation owned and controlled by Alaska Natives; (2) a small business that is wholly owned by one or more Native American tribal governments; or (3) a small business owned in part by one or more tribal governments if all other owners are either U.S. citizens or small businesses. Reauthorized the National Women's Business Council.

Small Business Technology Transfer Program Reauthorization Act of 2001 (115 Stat. 263, 15 U.S.C. 631 note). Signed by the president Oct. 15, 2001. Amended the Small Business Act to increase and extend through 2009 the authorization of appropriations for the Small Business Technology Transfer Program.

Small Business Paperwork Relief Act of 2002 (116 Stat. 729, 44 U.S.C. 3520). Signed by the president June 28, 2002. Required the director of the Office of Management and Budget (OMB) to publish annually in the *Federal Register,* and make available on the Internet, a list of regulatory compliance assistance resources available to small businesses.

Executive Order 13272. Signed by the president Aug. 13, 2002. Each agency shall establish procedures and policies to promote compliance with the Regulatory Flexibility Act, as amended (5 U.S.C. 601 et seq.). Agencies shall thoroughly review draft rules to assess and take appropriate account of the potential impact on small businesses, small governmental jurisdictions, and small organizations.

Executive Order 13360. Signed by the president Oct. 20, 2004. Directed the SBA to assist federal agencies to meet the requirement that 3 percent of their contracts must be awarded to service-disabled veteran-owned small businesses.

Energy Independence and Security Act of 2007 (15 U.S.C. 657h). Signed by the president Dec. 19, 2007. Title XII: Small Business Energy Programs amended the Small Business Act to direct the SBA to make an Express Loan for purchasing a renewable energy system or carrying out an energy efficiency project for a small business concern. Amended the Small Business Act of 1958 to include among eligibility criteria for SBA loans various energy conservation efforts. Other provisions.

Military Reservist and Veteran Small Business Reauthorization and Opportunity Act of 2008 (122 Stat. 623, 15 U.S.C. 631 note). Signed by the president Feb. 14, 2008. Bolstered SBA veterans small business loan programs. Provided additional assistance to small businesses that have suffered or are likely to suffer substantial economic injury as the result of an essential employee being called to active duty.

Small Business Jobs Act of 2010 (124 Stat. 2504, 15 U.S.C. 631 note). Signed by the president Sept. 27, 2010. Provided financial resources, including increased lending and new loan programs, and tax relief to assist small businesses. Expanded the number of small businesses eligible for SBA loans by increasing the alternate size standard.

National Defense Authorization Act for FY 2013 (126 Stat. 2079, 15 U.S.C. 657s). Signed by the president Jan. 2, 2013. Amended the Small Business Act with regard to subcontracting and joint ventures. Removed caps on the contract thresholds for women-owned small businesses. Required revisions to SBA's regulations pertaining to the Nonmanufacturer rule. Authorizes the SBA administrator to establish a mentor-protégé program for all small businesses.

Carl Levin and Howard P. "Buck" McKeon National Defense Authorization Act of 2015 (Public Law 113-291). Signed by the president Dec. 19, 2014. Section 825 amends the Small Business Act to authorize federal agencies to award sole-source contracts to women-owned small businesses eligible for the Woman-Owned Small Business (WOSB) Federal Contract Program.

■ REGIONAL OFFICES

REGION 1
(CT, MA, ME, NH, RI, VT)
10 Causeway St., #265A
Boston, MA 02222–1093
(617) 565–8416
Fax (617) 565–8420
Seth A.Goodall, regional administrator
E-mail: seth.goddall@sba.gov

REGION 2
(NJ, NY, PR, VI)
26 Federal Plaza, #3108
New York, NY 10278
(212) 264–1450
Kellie LeDet, regional administrator

REGION 3
(DC, DE, MD, PA, VA, WV)
1150 First Ave., #1001
King of Prussia, PA 19406
(610) 382–3092
Natalia Olsen-Urtecho, regional administrator

REGION 4
(AL, FL, GA, KY, MS, NC, SC, TN)
233 Peachtree St. N.E., #1800
Atlanta, GA 30303
(404) 331–4999
Cassius Butts, regional administrator

REGION 5
(IL, IN, MI, MN, OH, WI)
500 W. Madison St., #1150
Chicago, IL 60661–2511
(312) 353–0357
Fax (312) 353–3426
Marianne O'Brien Markowitz, regional administrator

REGION 6
(AR, LA, NM, OK, TX)
4300 Amon Carter Blvd., #108
Fort Worth, TX 76155
(817) 684–5581
Fax (817) 684–5588
Yolanda Garcia Olivarez, regional administrator

REGION 7
(IA, KS, MO, NE)
1000 Walnut St., #530
Kansas City, MO 64106
(816) 426–4840
Fax (816) 426–4848
Pat Brown-Dixon, regional administrator

REGION 8
(CO, MT, ND, SD, UT, WY)
721 19th St., #400
Denver, CO 80202–2599
(303) 844–0500
Fax (303) 844–0506
Stan Nakano (acting), regional administrator

REGION 9
(AZ, CA, GU, HI, NV)
330 Brand Blvd., #1200
Glendale, CA 91203
(818) 552–3437
Donna Davis, regional administrator

REGION 10
(AK, ID, OR, WA)
2401 Fourth Ave., #400
Seattle, WA 98121
(206) 553–5676
Fax (206) 553–4155
Calvin Goings, regional administrator
E-mail: calvin.goings@sba.gov

Social Security Administration

6401 Security Blvd., Baltimore, MD 21235
Internet: www.ssa.gov

The Social Security Administration (SSA) administers the Social Security system that ensures eligible workers' income after they retire or become disabled. Some benefits also are provided to families of workers who die while employed. In addition, the SSA administers the supplemental security income (SSI) program for the aged, blind, and disabled. The SSA operates ten regional offices and more than 1,300 local offices. All SSA programs are administered through its local offices. In 2014 the SSA opened a centralized fraud prevention unit in New York City to identify potential fraud and detect fraud trends that can be applied to disability cases nationwide.

Legislation signed into law in August 1994 made the SSA independent from the Department of Health and Human Services as of March 1995. The administration is headed by a commissioner who is appointed by the president and confirmed by the Senate. The commissioner has a fixed six-year term and is not removable except for wrongdoing. The 1994 law also created a seven-member bipartisan advisory board that makes recommendations to the president and Congress. The president appoints three members and Congress appoints four.

The SSA is authorized to regulate eligibility requirements for the following programs:

- Social Security retirement benefits.
- Social Security disability payments.
- Social Security survivor benefits.
- Supplemental security income programs for the aged, blind, and disabled.
- Income maintenance payments in Puerto Rico, Guam, the Virgin Islands, and the Northern Marianas.

Individuals dissatisfied with a determination of eligibility may appeal to an SSA administrative law judge. The administrative law judge's opinion may, in turn, be appealed to the SSA Appeals Council.

The basic Social Security program is financed by contributions from employees, employers, and the self-employed paid into special trust funds. Funds are paid out on a regular basis when a worker retires, is disabled, or dies. Part of the contributions goes to a hospital trust fund to help finance the Medicare program administered by the Centers for Medicare and Medicaid Services (*see p. 622*).

The SSA also conducts research on the social, health, and financial problems of the aged, the blind, the poor, and the disabled.

Solvency Issues

The Supplementary Medical Insurance (SMI) Trust Fund, which pays doctors' bills and other outpatient expenses, is expected to remain adequately funded into the indefinite future, but only because current law sets financing each year to meet the next year's expected costs. Although the rate of growth of SMI costs has moderated in recent years, outlays have increased faster than the economy as a whole. Despite the improvement in the financial outlook for Medicare, the projected increases in medical care costs still make finding solutions to Medicare's financing problems more difficult than for Social Security.

The Balanced Budget Act of 1997 established the Bipartisan Commission on Medicare to address the future of Medicare. In March 1999 the commission recommended (1) designing a premium support system that would allow beneficiaries to choose from among competing comprehensive health plans in a system based on a blend of existing government protections and market-based competition; (2) improving the current Medicare program incrementally, including providing federal funding of pharmaceutical coverage through Medicaid for all seniors living at up to 135 percent of the poverty level; and (3) combining Part A and Part B Trust Funds into a single Medicare Trust Fund while developing a new concept of solvency for Medicare. Congress did not implement the commission's recommendations, although some of the concepts were models for later legislation

Under provisions of the Social Security Amendments of 1983, the normal retirement age for Social Security increased for 150 million working Americans beginning in January 2000. Although sixty-two remains the earliest age at which individuals can retire and collect reduced benefits, the age for collecting full Social Security benefits increased from age 65 to 67 over a 22-year period.

An additional provision of the 1983 law will give workers who continue working, and delay collecting Social Security benefits until after their normal retirement age, higher benefits. The amount of the increase, known as the "delayed retirement credit," is determined by a set percentage and increases the longer retirement is delayed. The increase stops at age seventy.

In 2005 President George W. Bush toured the country promoting the controversial use of private Social Security accounts for younger workers—allowing workers to divert up to 4 percent of their wages into personally managed retirement accounts that could include a combination of stocks and bonds. The plan was not well received by Congress, and opinion polls showed public opposition to these individual accounts. The administration's push for privatization effectively ended with the power shift to a Democratic-controlled Congress following the 2006 elections.

The solvency of the Social Security and Medicare trust funds continue to be a difficult issue. Each year the trustees of the Social Security and Medicare trust funds report in detail on their financial condition. In the 2014 annual report, the trustees projected that the combined assets of the Old-Age, Survivors, and Disability Insurance (OASDI) Trust Funds will be exhausted in 2033, a projection that was unchanged from the previous year. The DI Trust Fund was projected to be exhausted in 2016. However, Social Security reform is acknowledged to be the "third rail of politics," and as such, there have been no major reforms since the 1983 amendments.

Changes to Medicare

The Balanced Budget Act of 1997 established a Medicare+Choice program under which each Medicare +Choice eligible individual could elect to receive Medicare benefits either through the original Medicare fee-for-service program or through a Medicare+Choice plan, offered by group or private insurers. Medicare+Choice plans, referred to as Part C, covered Medicare Parts A (hospital insurance) and B (medical insurance).

The Medicare Prescription Drug, Improvement, and Modernization Act of 2003 created a voluntary prescription drug benefit program (Part D) for all individuals eligible for Medicare, under which participants pay a monthly premium for coverage in helping purchase prescription drugs. The legislation also replaced the Medicare+Choice program with Medicare Advantage, which covered Medicare Parts A and B and included the new Part D prescription drug plan.

In July 2008 Congress enacted the Medicare Improvements for Patients and Providers Act of 2008 over the president's veto. The legislation extended programs for low-income Medicare beneficiaries. The bill also provides Medicare mental health parity by phasing in reduced patient copayments for mental health care over a six-year period. The legislation required SSA to provide applicants for Medicare Part D Low-Income Subsidy (LIS) with information about Medicare Savings Programs, which help Medicare beneficiaries reduce their out-of-pocket costs. These programs include Qualified Medicare Beneficiaries (QMB), Specified Low-Income Medicare Beneficiaries (SLMB), Qualifying Individuals (QI), and Qualified Disabled Working Individuals (QDWI). SSA also is required, with the consent of those filing, to transmit LIS application data to the states to increase enrollment.

Patient Protection and Affordable Care Act

In March 2010, President Barack Obama signed the Patient Protection and Affordable Care Act, the controversial health care reform bill. SSA would have several responsibilities under this legislation:

Health Exchange and Affordability Tax Credits: Each state is required to establish an "American Health Benefit Exchange" to facilitate the purchase of qualified health plans for individuals and employees of small businesses. If states do not establish these exchanges, the federal government will administer the program. Illegal immigrants are prohibited from participating in an exchange and obtaining premium tax credits and reduced cost sharing. SSA, working with the Department of Health and Human Services (HHS), is required to determine whether an applicant's name, Social Security number, date of birth, and allegation of U.S. citizenship are consistent with SSA records and report such determination to the Secretary of HHS.

Medicare Coverage: Amends SSA title XVIII (Medicare) to allow certain individuals exposed to environmental health hazards to become eligible for Medicare. The legislation also freezes the current income thresholds for imposing income-related Medicare Part B premiums for the period of 2011 through 2019. It establishes a twelve-month Medicare Part B special enrollment period (SEP) for TRICARE beneficiaries who are entitled to Medicare Part A by virtue of entitlement to disability insurance benefits or End Stage Renal Disease benefits but who have declined Medicare Part B.

Tax Policies During the Great Recession

To address economic hardships facing U.S. workers, Congress passed tax relief legislation in 2010. The Hiring Incentives to Restore Employment (HIRE) Act provided exemptions for qualified employers from paying the employer share of Old Age and Survivors, and Disability Insurance (OASDI) tax for newly hired employees who had previously been unemployed. The Small Business Jobs Act of 2010 allowed business owners to deduct the cost of health insurance incurred in 2010 for themselves and their family members when calculating their 2010 self-employment tax, which was previously not allowed. The Tax Relief, Unemployment Insurance Reauthorization, and Job Creation Act of 2010 reduced the OASDI payroll tax by two percentage points for wages and salaries paid in calendar year 2011 and self-employment in calendar year 2011, applied to the portion of the tax paid by the worker. This temporary "tax holiday" was reauthorized for another year and then expired at the end of calendar year 2012.

U.S. Supreme Court Decision Regarding Same-Sex Marriage

On June 26, 2013, the U.S. Supreme Court ruled Section 3 of the Defense of Marriage Act (DOMA) unconstitutional in *Windsor v. the United States*. Section

3 of DOMA, signed into law in 1996, had defined marriage as a legal union of one man and one woman for the purposes of "any act of Congress . . . any ruling, regulation, or interpretation of the various administrative bureaus and agencies of the United States." While the *Windsor* ruling settled the matter of same-sex marriage with regard to federal government laws and regulations, it did not legalize same-sex marriage across the nation. However, several rulings in some federal district courts overturned state prohibitions against same-sex marriage, leaving a patchwork of state laws regulating marriage for same-sex couples.

In the weeks after the 5–4 *Windsor* ruling, the Justice Department provided guidance to various federal agencies to remove barriers to federal programs for same-sex spouses. The SSA is required by law to confer certain marriage-related benefits based on the law of the state in which the married couple resides or resided, preventing the extension of benefits to same-sex married couples living in states that do not allow or recognize same-sex marriages. By the end of 2013 the SSA was processing some claims for retirement benefits and survivor's benefits for same-sex spouses. In January 2014 the SSA published new instructions that allowed the agency to process some Supplemental Security Income (SSI) claims by individuals who are in a same-sex marriage.

By early 2015, 37 states permitted same-sex marriage, and while several same-sex marriage cases were pending in the federal court system that could impact the SSA and other legal benefits for same-sex spouses in the future, the SSA encouraged same-sex spouses "to apply now to protect you against the loss of any potential benefits. We will process claims as soon as additional instructions become finalized." On June 26, 2015, the U.S. Supreme Court ruled in *Obergefell v. Hodges* that state bans on same-sex marriage were unconstitutional, effectively legalizing same-sex marriage nationwide.

■ KEY PERSONNEL

Commissioner
Carolyn W. Colvin (acting)
(Baltimore office) . . . . (410) 965–3120
(Washington office) . . . . (202) 358–6000
Budget, Finance, Quality, and Management
Elizabeth Reich . . . . (410) 965–2910
Communications
Douglas Walker . . . . (410) 965–2982
Fax . . . . (410) 966–9973
Disability Adjudication and Review
(5107 Leesburg Pike, Falls Church, VA 22041)
Glenn E. Sklar . . . . (703) 605–8200
General Counsel
David F. Black . . . . (410) 965–0600
Human Resources
Reginald F. Wells . . . . (410) 965–0200
Inspector General
Patrick B. O'Carroll . . . . (410) 965–7427
Hotline . . . . (800) 269–0271
TTY . . . . (866) 501–2101

International Programs
Vance N. Teel, associate
commissioner . . . . (410) 965–7389
Legislative and Congressional Affairs
Judy Chesser, deputy commissioner
Royce B. Min, assistant deputy
commissioner . . . . (410) 965–3737
Operations
Nancy A. Berryhill . . . . (410) 965–3342
Retirement and Disability Policy
Virginia Reno . . . . (410) 965–0100/7295
Systems
William B. Zielinski . . . . (410) 965–7670

■ INFORMATION SOURCES

Internet
Agency website: www.ssa.gov. Includes information on specific SSA offices and programs and offers numerous SSA publications. Much of the information also is available in Spanish.

Telephone Contacts
Personnel Locator . . . . (410) 965–2982
Service Center . . . . (800) 772–1213
TTY . . . . (800) 325–0778

Information and Publications

KEY OFFICES

SSA Office of Public Inquiries
Windsor Park Bldg.
6401 Security Blvd.
Baltimore, MD 21235
(410) 965–2738
Fax (410) 966–6166
Steven L. Patrick, associate commissioner

The central point for consumer inquiries about the SSA and its various programs. (The administration encourages individuals to seek help by calling the Service Center at [800] 772–1213.)

SSA Press Office
440 Altmeyer Bldg.
6401 Security Blvd
Baltimore, MD 21235
(410) 965–8904
E-mail: press.office@ssa.gov
Washington office (202) 358–6000
LaVenia LaVelle, press officer

Serves as the central point for media inquiries about the SSA and its various programs. Issues news releases; arranges press conferences and interviews for SSA officials.

Freedom of Information
617 Altmeyer Bldg.
6401 Security Blvd.

Baltimore, MD 21235
(410) 965–1727
Fax (410) 966–4304
Deborah Verzi, FOIA director
E-mail: foia.pa.officers@ssa.gov
Joan Cooper, FOIA public liaison

DATA AND STATISTICS

SSA Office of Research, Evaluation, and Statistics

6401 Security Blvd.
Baltimore, MD 21235
(410) 965–2841
Ted Horan, deputy associate commissioner
(410) 966–2788

Washington Office

International Trade Commission Bldg.
500 E St. S.W., 8th Floor
Washington, DC 20254

Provides information on selected SSA reports and bulletins. These include the *Social Security Bulletin,* which contains data on employment and earnings, beneficiary and benefit payments, and other topics related to SSA programs; the SSA's *Annual Statistical Supplement;* and reports on specific topics.

PUBLICATIONS

All SSA local offices can provide SSA publications, including brochures on types of coverage available and the SSA annual report. Information regarding all SSA publications also may be obtained by calling (800) 772–1213 or (410) 965–2039; e-mail: op.publications@ssa.gov. SSA publications are available via the Internet at www.ssa.gov/pubs/index.html.

Reference Resources

DOCKETS

Federal dockets are available at www.regulations.gov. (*See appendix for information on searching and commenting on regulations.*)

RULES AND REGULATIONS

Most SSA rules and regulations are published in the *Code of Federal Regulations,* Title 20, Chapter III, Parts 400–499; Title 48, Chapter XXIII, Parts 2300–2399. Proposed regulations, new regulations, and updates to the *Code of Federal Regulations* are published in the *Federal Register.* (*See appendix for information on how to obtain and use these publications.*)

▓ LEGISLATION

The SSA carries out its responsibilities under

Social Security Act (49 Stat. 620, 42 U.S.C. 301). Signed by the president Aug. 14, 1935. Authorized the SSA to set, maintain, and enforce eligibility requirements for SSA-administered benefits. Amendments over the years have both expanded and restricted benefits available to various categories of recipients.

Social Security Administrative Reform Act of 1994 (108 Stat. 1464, 42 U.S.C. 1305 note). Signed by the president Aug. 15, 1994. Established the Social Security Administration as an independent agency and made other improvements in the old-age, survivors, and disability insurance program.

Contract with America Advancement Act of 1996 (110 Stat. 847, 5 U.S.C. 601 note). Signed by the president March 29, 1996. Prohibited the SSA from providing disability insurance and supplemental security income eligibility to individuals whose drug addiction or alcoholism is a contributing factor to the finding of disability. Established the position of chief actuary, to be appointed by, and report directly to, the commissioner, and be subject to removal only for cause.

Omnibus Consolidated Rescissions and Appropriations Act of 1996 (110 Stat. 1321, 31 U.S.C. 3701 note). Signed by the president April 26, 1996. Provided the SSA with permanent debt collection authorities. Required recurring federal payments to persons who began receiving them after July 1996 to be paid by electronic funds transfer (EFT).

Balanced Budget Act of 1997 (111 Stat. 251). Signed by the president Aug. 5, 1997. Established a Medicare+Choice program under which each Medicare+Choice eligible individual may elect to receive Medicare benefits (Parts A and B) either through the original Medicare fee-for-service program or through a Medicare+Choice plan (Part C). Established the Bipartisan Commission on Medicare to study the future solvency of Medicare and make policy recommendations.

Ticket to Work and Work Incentives Improvement Act of 1999 (113 Stat. 1860, 42 U.S.C. 1305 note). Signed by the president Dec. 17, 1999. Directed the commissioner to establish a Ticket to Work and Self-Sufficiency Program within one year that would provide Social Security disability beneficiaries with a ticket for obtaining vocational rehabilitation services, employment services, and other support services. Established a Work Incentives Advisory Panel within the SSA.

Medicare Prescription Drug, Improvement, and Modernization Act (117 Stat. 2066, 42 U.S.C. 1305 note). Signed by the president Dec. 8, 2003. Amended title XVIII of the Social Security Act to provide for a voluntary prescription drug benefit under the Medicare program. Established Health Savings Accounts to allow individuals covered by high-deductible health plans to receive tax-preferred treatment of money saved for medical expenses.

Social Security Protection Act of 2004 (118 Stat. 493, 42 U.S.C. 402x, 1382e). Signed by the president March 2, 2004. Amended the Social Security Act and the Internal Revenue Code of 1986 to provide additional safeguards for Social Security and SSI beneficiaries with representative payees, and to enhance program protections.

Medicare Improvements for Patients and Providers Act of 2008 (42 U.S.C. 1305 note). Vetoed by the president July 15, 2008; veto overridden July 15, 2008. Extended programs for low-income Medicare beneficiaries. Prohibited certain marketing activities of Medicare Advantage plans and Part D drug plans. Requires the Social Security Administration (SSA) to provide applicants for Medicare Part D Low-Income Subsidy (LIS) with information about Medicare Savings Programs (MSP). Requires SSA, with the consent of those filing, to transmit LIS application data to the states.

Children's Health Insurance Program Reauthorization Act of 2009 (123 STAT. 8, 42 U.S.C. 1305 note). Signed by the president Feb. 4, 2009. Gives states the option, as an alternative to the current documentation requirement, to verify a declaration of U.S. citizenship or nationality for purposes of Medicaid or CHIP eligibility through verification of a name and Social Security number with the Commissioner of Social Security. Prescribes a procedure for investigating any inconsistency between the name and number presented and the name and number in the records maintained by the commissioner.

Social Security Disability Applicants' Access to Professional Representation Act of 2010 (124 Stat. 38, 42 U.S.C. 1305 note). Signed by the president February 27, 2010. Provided a permanent extension of the attorney fee withholding procedures under Title II of the Social Security Act (SSA) to Title XVI of SSA (this provision was set to expire in 2010).

Hiring Incentives to Restore Employment (HIRE) Act (124 STAT. 71, 26 U.S.C. 1 note). Signed by the president March 18, 2010. Provided exemptions for qualified employers from paying the employer share of OASDI tax for newly hired employees who had previously been unemployed.

Patient Protection and Affordable Care Act (124 Stat. 119, 42 U.S.C. 18001 note). Signed by the president March 23, 2010. Health Exchange and Affordability Tax Credits: Requires each state to establish an "American Health Benefit Exchange" to facilitate the purchase of qualified health plans for individuals and employees of small businesses. Illegal immigrants are prohibited from participating in an exchange and obtaining premium tax credits and reduced cost sharing. Requires SSA to determine whether an applicant's name, SSN, date of birth, and allegation of U.S. citizenship are consistent with SSA records and report such determination to the Secretary of HHS. **Medicare Coverage**: Amends SSA Title XVIII (Medicare) to deem eligible for Medicare coverage certain individuals exposed to environmental health hazards. Freezes the current income thresholds for imposing income-related Medicare Part B premiums for the period of 2011 through 2019. Establishes a 12-month Medicare Part B special enrollment period (SEP) for TRICARE beneficiaries who are entitled to Medicare Part A by virtue of entitlement to disability insurance benefits or End Stage Renal Disease benefits but who have declined Medicare Part B. **Medicaid**: Expands Medicaid eligibility to non-elderly individuals who are not entitled to or enrolled in Medicare Part A, or enrolled in Medicare Part B, and whose income does not exceed 133 percent of the federal poverty level. Other provisions.

Small Business Jobs Act of 2010 (124 Stat. 2504, 15 U.S.C. 631 note). Signed by the president Sept. 27, 2010. Allows business owners to deduct the cost of health insurance incurred in 2010 for themselves and their family members when calculating their 2010 self-employment tax, which was previously not allowed.

Tax Relief, Unemployment Insurance Reauthorization, and Job Creation Act of 2010 (124 Stat. 3296, 26 U.S.C. 1 note). Signed by the president Dec. 17, 2010. Reduces the OASDI payroll tax by two percentage points for wages and salaries paid in calendar year 2011 and self-employment in calendar year 2011, applied to the portion of the tax paid by the worker. Excludes certain tax refunds paid to an individual from consideration as income (in the month received) or as a resource (for a period of 12 months from receipt) for federal or federally assisted program purposes, including SSI.

■ REGIONAL OFFICES

REGION 1
(CT, MA, ME, NH, RI, VT)
John F. Kennedy Federal Bldg., #1900
Boston, MA 02203–0003
(617) 565–2870
Fax (617) 565–2143
Linda Dorn, regional commissioner

REGION 2
(NJ, NY, PR, VI)
26 Federal Plaza, #40–102
New York, NY 10278
(212) 264–3915
Fax (212) 264–6847
Frederick Maurin, regional commissioner

REGION 3
(DC, DE, MD, PA, VA, WV)
300 Spring Garden St.
Philadelphia, PA 19123
Mailing Address:
P.O. Box 8788
Philadelphia, PA 19101
(215) 597–5157
Fax (215) 597–2827
Terry M. Stradtman, regional commissioner

REGION 4
(AL, FL, GA, KY, MS, NC, SC, TN)
61 Forsyth St. S.W.
Atlanta, GA 30303–8931
(404) 562–5600
Fax (404) 562–5608
Rodney Taylor, regional commissioner

REGION 5
(IL, IN, MI, MN, OH, WI)
600 W. Madison St., 10th Floor
Chicago, IL 60661
(312) 575–4000
Fax (312) 575–4016
Phyllis Smith (acting), regional commissioner

REGION 6

(AR, LA, NM, OK, TX)
1301 Young St., #500
Dallas, TX 75202–5433
(214) 767–4210
Fax (214) 767–4259
Sheila S. Everett, regional commissioner

REGION 7

(IA, KS, MO, NE)
601 E. 12th St., #1028
Kansas City, MO 64106–2817
(816) 936–5700
Fax (816) 936–5972
Ken Powell, regional commissioner

REGION 8

(CO, MT, ND, SD, UT, WY)
1500 Champa St.
Denver, CO 80202
(303) 844–2388
Fax (303) 844–6767

Wanda Colon-Mollfulleda (acting),
regional commissioner

REGION 9

(AS, AZ, CA, GU, HI, NV)
1221 Nevin Ave.
Richmond, CA 94804
Mailing Address:
P.O. Box 4201
Richmond, CA 94804
(510) 970–8400
Fax (510) 970–8216
E-mail: SF.RPA@ssa.gov
Grace M. Kim, regional commissioner

REGION 10

(AK, ID, OR, WA)
701 Fifth Ave., #2900
Seattle, WA 98104–7075
(206) 615–2100
Fax (206) 615–2193
Stanley Friendship, regional commissioner

United States International Trade Commission

500 E St. S.W., Washington, DC 20436
Internet: www.usitc.gov

The United States International Trade Commission (USITC) is an independent, nonpartisan, quasi-judicial federal agency created by an act of Congress on Sept. 8, 1916. Initially called the U.S. Tariff Commission, the agency's name was changed to the U.S. International Trade Commission by the Trade Act of 1974.

The USITC is headed by a staff of six commissioners. They are appointed by the president and confirmed by the Senate; the president also designates members to serve as chair and vice chair. The commissioners serve nine-year terms and are not eligible for reappointment, unless they have completed fewer than five years of a term. The chair serves a statutory two-year term. No more than three commissioners may be members of the same political party and the chair and vice chair must belong to different parties.

The USITC staff includes attorneys, economists, investigators, commodity analysts, computer specialists, and service and production personnel. The staff's primary function is to gather facts and evaluate data to aid the commission in its determinations.

As a fact-finding agency, the commission has broad powers to study and investigate all issues relating to U.S.-foreign trade: its effect on domestic production, employment, and consumption; the competitiveness of U.S. products; and foreign and domestic customs laws. The USITC does not set policy; however, its technical advice forms a basis for economic policy decisions on U.S. international trade. The commission may act on its initiative or at the request of the president; other government agencies; the Senate Finance Committee; the House Ways and Means Committee; or on behalf of an industry, a company, or a group of workers.

As imports have increased and many domestic producers face what they view as unfair foreign competition, industries continue to file petitions with the commission for relief from foreign competition.

The commission conducts three major types of investigations. First, it examines whether rapidly increasing imports are causing financial injury to U.S. industries. Workers, companies, or other industry representatives may request the investigation. The commission advises the president on what relief, if any, might be needed to help U.S. businesses. The president may decide to do nothing; provide adjustment assistance to workers, companies, or communities hurt by low-cost imports; restrict quantities of imports; negotiate market agreements; impose tariffs; or impose a combination of tariffs, quotas, or other remedies.

Second, the commission investigates whether importers are infringing U.S. patents, copyrights, or trademarks. The commission may begin the investigation on its own or after receiving a complaint under oath from an interested party. If the USITC finds that the unfair practices are harming U.S. businesses, it may issue cease-and-desist orders or ban the article from entering the United States. These orders are effective when issued and become final sixty days after issuance unless disapproved for policy reasons by the president within that sixty-day period.

Third, after receiving a petition from an industry representative or the Commerce Department, the commission investigates whether there are reasonable indications that U.S. industries are threatened or materially injured by imports that are subsidized or sold in the United States at prices lower than foreigners would charge in their home market (a practice known as dumping). At the same time, the International Trade Administration of the Commerce Department conducts a preliminary investigation to determine whether dumping actually is taking place.

If both preliminary investigations are affirmed, the commission must conduct a final investigation to determine whether a U.S. industry is being materially injured or threatened by unfairly priced imports. If the commission finds that such harm is occurring, the Commerce Department must order that a duty be placed on the imports equal to the amount of the unfair subsidy or price. That duty cannot be lifted by the president.

The USITC is responsible for continually reviewing the Harmonized Tariff Schedule of the United States (HTS), a list of all the specific items that are imported into and exported from the United States, and for recommending modifications to the HTS that it considers necessary or appropriate.

In addition, the USITC

- Advises the president on the effect of international trade negotiations on U.S. industries and consumers.
- Studies effects of lifting duties on imports from developing nations.
- Investigates the effects of trade with communist countries, including the effect of granting most-favored-nation status to those countries.

- Studies the potential effects of imports from nations with state-run economies.
- Advises the president whether agricultural imports interfere with the price support programs of the U.S. Department of Agriculture.
- Monitors import levels.
- Provides the president, Congress, other government agencies, and the general public with technical information on trade and tariff matters.
- Assists in the development of uniform statistical data on imports, exports, and domestic production.
- Conducts studies on trade and tariff issues relating to U.S. foreign trade.

The Trade Act of 2002 granted the president authority to negotiate trade agreements that can only be approved or disapproved (but not amended) by Congress. The law required the USITC to prepare a report that assessed the likely effect of a proposed free trade agreement on the U.S. economy as a whole and on specific industry sectors and the interests of U.S. consumers.

The Trade and Globalization Adjustment Assistance Act, part of the American Recovery and Reinvestment Act (ARRA), required the ITC to notify the labor, commerce, and agriculture secretaries of any findings regarding domestic industry market disruption; the initiation of proceedings under safeguard provisions enacted to implement a trade agreement; or injury, or threat of injury, to a domestic industry caused by subsidized imports subjected to an antidumping duty.

■ KEY PERSONNEL

Commissioners
Meredith Broadbent, chair . . . . (202) 205–2250
Dean Pinkert, vice chair . . . . (202) 708–2882
David S. Johanson . . . . (202) 205–2744
F. Scott Lieff . . . . (202) 708–5482
Rhonda Schmidtlein . . . . (202) 205–5990
Irving Williamson . . . . (202) 205–2051

Secretary to the Commission
Lisa Barton . . . . (202) 205–2000

Inspector General
Philip M. Heneghan . . . . (202) 205–2219

Chief Administration Officer
Stephen A. McLaughlin . . . . (202) 205–3182

Chief Financial Officer
John Ascienzo . . . . (202) 205–3098

Chief Information Officer
Kirit Armin . . . . (202) 205–2513

Administrative Law Judges
Charles Edward Bullock, chief . . . . . . (202) 205–2694
Theodore R. Essex . . . . (202) 205–2692
Thomas Pender . . . . (202) 205–2681
David Shaw . . . . (202) 708–4051
Dee Lord . . . . (202) 205–3352

Analysis and Research Services
James Kennedy . . . . (202) 205–1833

Economics
William Powers (acting) . . . . (202) 205–3216

Equal Employment Opportunity
Altivia Jackson . . . . (202) 205–2239

External Relations
Lyn M. Schlitt . . . . (202) 205–3141

General Counsel
Dominic Bianchi . . . . (202) 205–3061

Human Resources
Eric Mozie . . . . (202) 205–2651

Industries
Michael G. Anderson . . . . (202) 205–3296

Investigations
Douglas Corkran . . . . (202) 205–3160

Operations
Catherine DeFilippo . . . . (202) 205–2230

Security and Support Services
Bob Reiss . . . . (202) 205–1069

Tariff Affairs and Trade Agreements
James Holbein . . . . (202) 205–2593

Unfair Import Investigations
Margaret Macdonald . . . . (202) 205–2560

■ INFORMATION SOURCES

Internet

Agency website: www.usitc.gov. The ITC's website offers access to an extensive variety of ITC information resources and work products, including news releases; *Federal Register* notices; ITC reports and publications, including the Harmonized Tariff Schedule of the United States and congressional bill reports; the ITC DataWeb; the ITC Electronic Document Information System (EDIS—also accessible through https://edis.usitc.gov/edis3-external/app); information on recent petitions and complaints; the monthly calendar; a section focused on the ITC's five-year (sunset) reviews; the ITC's rules of practice and procedure, hearing guidelines, an introduction to APO practices at the ITC, and other investigation-related materials; information related to the Freedom of Information Act; and general information about the agency, its work, and its commissioners and staff.

Telephone Contacts

Switchboard . . . . (202) 205–2000
TTY . . . . (202) 205–1810

Information and Publications

KEY OFFICES

USITC Office of the Secretary
500 E St. S.W.
Washington, DC 20436
(202) 205–2000
Lisa Barton, secretary

The Office of the Secretary compiles and maintains the ITC's official records, including petitions, briefs, and other legal documents. The office issues ITC notices, reports, and orders, and it schedules and participates in all commission meetings and hearings. The office makes determinations on requests for confidential treatment of information, requests for information to be released under protective order, and requests under the Freedom of Information Act (FOIA). The Office of the Secretary manages distribution of ITC reports and studies.

USITC Office of External Relations

500 E St. S.W.
Washington, DC 20436
(202) 205–3141
Lyn M. Schlitt, director
Margaret (Peg) O'Laughlin, public affairs
(202) 205–1819
E-mail: margaret.olaughlin@usitc.gov
Maureen McLaughlin, congressional relations
(202) 205–3151
John Greer, trade remedy assistance
(202) 205–2200

The Office of External Relations develops and maintains liaison between the ITC and its varied external customers. The office is the focal point for contacts with the U.S. Trade Representative and other executive branch agencies; Congress; foreign governments; international organizations; the public; and international, national, and local news media.

Freedom of Information

Chief FOIA Officer
500 E St. S.W.
Washington DC 20436
(202) 205–2786
Lisa R. Barton, chief FOIA officer
Jackie Gross, FOIA liaison, (202) 205–1816
Internet: www.usitc.gov/secretary/foia

Certain FOIA requests may be submitted electronically on the commission's website.

DATA AND STATISTICS

The ITC DataWeb is an extensive tariff and trade computerized database. The system is relied upon for tariff and trade data by various federal government agencies, congressional offices, various U.S. trade negotiating groups, and U.S. embassies. The ITC DataWeb provides worldwide interactive access to current and historical U.S. trade data. Internet: http://dataweb.usitc.gov/; DataWeb contact: David Lundy, (202) 205–3439.

Harmonized Tariff Schedule of the United States is the legal document used by the importing business community to ascertain the appropriate commodity classification, dutiable status, statistical treatment, and other fundamental requirements for entry of foreign goods. Internet: www.usitc.gov/tata/hts/index.htm.

MEETINGS

Commission members meet in Room 101, 500 E St. S.W., Washington, DC. Meetings are not held on a regularly scheduled basis but are open to the public unless the subject of the meeting is considered private or is exempt under the Government in the Sunshine Act.

Notices of commission meetings are listed in the *Federal Register* and are available on the Internet site at www.usitc.gov/calendarpad/calendar.html. Agendas are published in the *Federal Register* and on the Internet site.

PUBLICATIONS

Order from the USITC Office of the Secretary, (202) 205–2000, or contact Mark Toye, (202) 205–2792. ITC publications are available via the Internet at www.usitc.gov/research_and_analysis/commission_publications.htm.

Reference Resources

LIBRARIES

USITC Law Library

500 E St. S.W.
Washington, DC 20436
(202) 205–3287
Hours: 8:30 a.m. to 5:00 p.m.
Maureen Bryant, law librarian

Primarily for the use of trade commission attorneys, the collection includes standard reference materials, domestic and international trade laws, and works on the history of trade relations. Open by appointment only.

USITC Research Library

500 E St. S.W.
Washington, DC 20436
(202) 205–2630
Hours: 8:45 a.m. to 5:15 p.m.
Robert Bauchspies, chief librarian

Maintains a general collection of books, theses, working papers, government reports, and periodicals on subjects relating to export-import and trade.

DOCKETS

500 E St. S.W., #112
Washington, DC 20436
(202) 205–1802
Katherine Hiner, supervisory attorney
Shannon Grace, docket services

The USITC Docket Office provides nonconfidential files of cases under investigation and recent determinations for public inspection. Also handles requests to inspect the files of older cases. Docket information can be obtained from the EDIS Document Filing Center located on the USITC's website. Federal dockets are also available at www.regulations.gov. (*See appendix for information on searching and commenting on regulations.*)

RULES AND REGULATIONS

USITC rules and regulations are published in the *Code of Federal Regulations,* Title 19, Chapter II, Parts 200–299. Proposed regulations, new final regulations, and updates to the *Code of Federal Regulations* are published in the daily *Federal Register.* (*See appendix for details on how to obtain and use these publications.*)

▓ LEGISLATION

The USITC administers the following laws in full or in part:

Revenue Act of 1916 (39 Stat. 795, 19 U.S.C. 1330 and note). Signed by the president Sept. 8, 1916. Established the U.S. Tariff Commission (later renamed the United States International Trade Commission).

Tariff Act of 1930 (46 Stat. 590, 19 U.S.C. 1202). Signed by the president June 17, 1930. Protected U.S. industry from unfair methods of competition and unfair acts in the importation of merchandise into the country.

Agricultural Adjustment Act (48 Stat. 31, 7 U.S.C. 601). Signed by the president May 12, 1933. Established and maintains orderly market conditions for agricultural commodities in interstate commerce.

Trade Expansion Act of 1962 (76 Stat. 872, 19 U.S.C. 1801). Signed by the president Oct. 11, 1962. Authorized adjustment assistance to industries and groups of workers who may be injured by increased imports resulting from foreign trade agreements.

Trade Act of 1974 (88 Stat. 1978, 19 U.S.C. 2101). Signed by the president Jan. 3, 1975. Provided adequate safeguards to American industry and labor against unfair or injurious import competition.

Trade Agreements Act of 1979 (93 Stat. 144, 19 U.S.C. 2501 note). Signed by the president July 26, 1979. Changed U.S. trade laws to carry out the agreements reached during multilateral trade talks in Tokyo. Amended the Tariff Act of 1930 to incorporate protection for U.S. industry against dumped or subsidized merchandise. Repealed the Anti-Dumping Act of 1921, which protected against dumping of goods.

Trade and Tariff Act of 1984 (98 Stat. 2498, 19 U.S.C. 54 note). Signed by the president Oct. 30, 1984. Specified several criteria that the commission must use in assessing the threat of injury to U.S. industries from imports. Created a Trade Remedy Assistance Office to inform the public of the remedies and benefits of trade laws. Stipulated that if the president does not follow the commission's advice on how to aid industries hurt by imports, Congress may enact the commission's recommendations by joint resolution. However, the president may veto that joint resolution.

Omnibus Trade and Competitiveness Act of 1988 (100 Stat. 1107, 19 U.S.C. 2901 note). Signed by the president Aug. 23, 1988. Amended Section 201 of the Trade Act of 1974 to place a greater emphasis on industry adjustment to import competition in granting relief. Changed the antidumping and countervailing duty law with respect to release of business proprietary information under protective orders.

Continued Dumping and Subsidy Offset Act of 2000 (Byrd Amendment) (114 Stat. 1549, 19 U.S.C. 1675c). Signed by the president Oct. 28, 2000. CDSOA is Title X of the Farm Bill. Amended the Tariff Act of 1930 to declare that the Customs Service shall disburse antidumping and countervailing duties collected by the agency to domestic producers injured by foreign dumping and subsidies. Under the act, ITC must forward to Customs within sixty days after issuance of an antidumping or countervailing duty order an initial list of potentially eligible "affected domestic producers" who publicly indicated support for the petition through a response to an ITC questionnaire during the investigation or by letter submitted to the ITC during that investigation.

Trade Act of 2002 (116 Stat. 933, 19 U.S.C. 2272). Signed by the president Aug. 6, 2002. Authorized the president to enter into trade agreements with foreign countries regarding tariff and nontariff barriers. Required the president to submit trade agreements for USITC assessment.

Dominican Republic–Central America–United States Free Trade Agreement Implementation Act (119 Stat. 462, 19 U.S.C. 4001). Signed by the president Aug. 2, 2005. Approved the U.S. free trade agreement with the governments of Costa Rica, the Dominican Republic, El Salvador, Guatemala, Honduras, and Nicaragua. Amended the Trade Agreements Act of 1979 to make products or services of any foreign country or instrumentality that is a party to the agreement eligible for U.S. government procurement.

American Recovery and Reinvestment Act (19 U.S.C. 2101 note). Signed by the president Feb. 13, 2009. Required the USITC to notify the secretaries of labor, commerce, and agriculture of any (1) serious market disruption, or threat of disruption, to a domestic industry; (2) initiation of proceedings under safeguard provisions of a trade agreement to which the United States is a party; or (3) injury, or threat of injury, to a domestic industry by reason of subsidized imports subjected to an antidumping duty. Required the three secretaries to notify the firms of the affected industry of the allowances, training, employment services, assistance in filing petitions, and other trade adjustment assistance benefits available through the USITC.

Leahy-Smith America Invents Act (125 Stat. 284, 35 U.S.C. 1 note). Signed by the president Sept. 16, 2011. Makes changes to legal proceedings in patent disputes. Prohibits the petitioner from asserting claims in certain proceedings before the U.S. Patent and Trademark Office (USPTO) and International Trade Commission (ITC) and in specified civil actions if such claims were raised or reasonably could have been raised in the respective reviews that result in a final board decision.

United States Postal Service

475 L'Enfant Plaza S.W., Washington, DC 20260
Internet: www.usps.gov

The United States Postal Service (USPS) is an independent agency in the executive branch. Created by the Postal Reorganization Act of 1970, it replaced the Post Office Department. The USPS regulates all aspects of the mail.

The service is administered by an eleven-member board of governors; nine members are appointed by the president and confirmed by the Senate. The nine members select and appoint the postmaster general, who serves as the tenth member of the board and as chief executive officer of the service. The ten board members then appoint a deputy postmaster, who serves as the eleventh board member. The appointed members serve staggered nine-year terms. No more than five of the nine appointees may belong to the same political party.

The authority to regulate the mail was given to the USPS through a group of federal laws known as the private express statutes. These statutes give the USPS the exclusive right to carry letters subject to certain exceptions and also protect USPS revenues, which enables the Postal Service to provide service throughout the country at uniform rates as mandated by law.

Violations of these statutes are punishable by fine, imprisonment, or both. The statutes also may be enforced by means of an injunction.

Although repeal of all, or part of, the private express statutes often has been considered, Congress is concerned that repealing postal monopoly laws could result in a significant decline of mail volume handled by the USPS. Private companies likely would concentrate on service to high-density areas and large-volume business mailers. Individuals, particularly those outside metropolitan areas, would not have alternative services available to them and would have to pay more for service.

The Postal Service provides information to consumers and businesses on mail rates and classification. Recommendations on domestic mail rates and classification matters are handled by the Postal Regulatory Commission (PRC) (*see p. 450*), another independent agency created by the Postal Reorganization Act of 1970.

The Postal Service also sets standards for several areas related to mail delivery, including the size of individual pieces of mail, bulk mailings, mail chutes, mail boxes in apartment houses, lockers for parcels, and postage meters.

The appropriations that the USPS receives from Congress are annual "revenue forgone" appropriations as authorized under the Postal Reorganization Act of 1970. Revenue forgone appropriations reimburse the USPS for handling certain public service second-, third-, and fourth-class mails at rates lower than those paid by regular commercial mailers as determined by Congress. These appropriations are not used to subsidize other postal operations.

The USPS enforces the laws and regulations governing the mail system through its Inspection Service. The Inspection Service is authorized by law to protect, audit, and police three areas of the postal service:

- The personnel, property, equipment, revenue, and technology that make up the assets of the USPS.
- The safety and security of the environment in which mail delivery and related postal business is conducted.
- The overall integrity of the postal system.

There are two divisions that are responsible for inspections and law enforcement activities within the USPS: the USPS Office of the Inspector General (OIG) and the US Postal Inspection Service (USPIS).

The OIG is an independent agency within USPS under the general supervision of nine presidentially appointed governors. OIG investigative efforts detect fraud, waste and misconduct by postal personnel and those who contract with the USPS. OIG audits evaluate and analyze USPS programs and operations.

The Postal Inspection Service (USPIS), the law enforcement arm of USPS, enforces more than 200 federal laws covering investigations of crimes that adversely affect or fraudulently use the U.S. mail, postal system and postal employees. USPIS uses forfeiture procedures as a law enforcement tool in child pornography, mail fraud, drug, and money-laundering cases. USPIS offices include national headquarters offices, 18 field divisions, two service centers, and the National Forensic Laboratory. The offices are staffed by more than 1,400 postal inspectors, about 700 Postal Police Officers, and approximately 600 support personnel.

During the late 1990s the USPS began investing more than $5 billion to improve and expand the capability of its operating systems. The five-year investment plan concentrated resources in two main categories: new technologies that produce labor savings or achieve cost avoidance; and customer service programs that generate revenue or enhance competitiveness in the marketplace. USPS implemented an overnight express mail service and a two-day (not guaranteed) priority mail service to compete with private express carriers. Technology that has improved postal operations includes barcoding flat mail, remote encoding technology, and handwriting recognition software.

In October 2001 the nation and the USPS were shocked by the discovery that deadly anthrax had been sent through the mail, resulting in the deaths of several people, including two Washington, DC, postal workers. The USPS shut down mail facilities and instituted precautionary procedures throughout its entire system, greatly increasing its costs. The administration provided an immediate $175 million in funding, with an additional $500 million coming through the Department of Defense Emergency Supplemental Appropriations Act and $87 million through the Supplemental Appropriations Act for Further Recovery From and Response To Terrorist Attacks on the United States. Congress also appropriated funds for the purchase of biohazard detection and prevention equipment.

In March 2002 the PRC approved an unusual settlement that allowed postal rates to increase on June 30, 2002. In the rate increase request, the USPS had joined with mailer groups, postal employee organizations, competitors, and the Office of Consumer Advocate, which represents the interests of the general public, to offer a proposal that increased rates by 7.7 percent. As part of the settlement, the USPS agreed to not raise rates again until summer 2003.

In November 2002, however, the USPS had to change that forecast. After completing a financial review of its contributions since 1971 to the Civil Service Retirement System, the Postal Service discovered that it had been overpaying into its retirement fund. Congress passed legislation in April 2003 to correct the imbalance, change the way the Postal Service calculated its retirement payments, and reduce the Postal Service debt.

The Postal Accountability and Enhancement Act (PAEA) of 2006, the first major legislative change to the Postal Service since 1971, mandated that the USPS significantly fund its liability for retiree health benefits. The PAEA also directed the USPS board of governors to establish rates and classes for products in the competitive category of mail (priority and expedited mail, bulk parcel post and bulk international mail, and mailgrams).

Facing decreasing business and billion-dollar deficits, in 2010 the USPS unveiled a cost-cutting plan to reduce delivery service from six days to five days, eliminating Saturday delivery to street addresses (post office boxes would receive mail on Saturday). Post offices would remain open on Saturday. In its plan, USPS noted that many activities formerly done by mail are now accomplished online, and as a result, the volume of mail delivered has plummeted, from 213 billion pieces in 2007 to 177 billion pieces in 2009. USPS estimated an eventual annual savings of $3 billion per year under this plan.

In March 2011, the Postal Regulatory Commission (PRC) issued an advisory opinion on the USPS's request to eliminate Saturday mail delivery as a cost-cutting measure. The USPS analysis predicted a savings of $3 billion by eliminating Saturday delivery; the PRC predicted a savings of $1.7 billion, which would not be realized until the third year of implementation. Also, the PRC noted that the USPS did not take into consideration the impact of five-day delivery on rural postal customers.

In February 2013, USPS announced a six-day package delivery and five-day mail delivery schedule, which it planned to implement in August 2013. The USPS anticipated savings from this schedule, when fully implemented, would be approximately $2 billion dollars annually. USPS did not provide a detailed plan at the time it made its announcement; the PRC noted it would need to review the plan before making a recommendation.

The elimination of one mail delivery day had been considered in previous decades. In 1983, Congress adopted language requiring the USPS to maintain six-day delivery. When Congress passed a continuing resolution in March 2013, the bill contained language that prohibited implementation of a new national delivery schedule for mail and packages. Subsequent appropriations bills have also prohibited such changes in mail delivery scheduling.

Since the passage of the PAEA, the USPS amassed a total net deficit of more than $50 billion by the end of FY14. USPS employed other efforts to reduce costs. Under its Network Rationalization Initiatives (NRI), USPS began closing processing centers following a study period that concluded in 2011. The USPS consolidated 141 mail processing facilities, without employee layoffs, in 2012 and 2013. The Office of the Inspector General (OIG) was critical of the fast pace of closures. The OIG issued a report in 2013 that noted, among other findings, that the savings predicted by the USPS was overstated and was revised downward frequently, and the USPS management must improve the communication process by ensuring accurate and consistent information is shared with stakeholders on consolidation impacts.

To further shrink its operations, USPS announced a plan to close more than 80 processing plants serving small cities and rural areas during 2015. Postal Regulatory Commission (PRC) Chair Ruth Goldway publicly criticized the plan, noting that the result would have a disparate impact on smaller cities and rural areas, which would see "degraded service."

A more controversial debt reduction policy was the sale of historic post office buildings. USPS awarded a contract to CB Richard Ellis, Inc., to be the sole provider of real estate management services for the sale of post office properties. Critics argued that these sales were conducted without adequate public input and lacked transparency (often buyers were not publicly disclosed). The OIG issued a report critical of the contract with CBRE, noting that there were conflicts of interest.

In November 2014 the City of Berkeley, California, sued the USPS to halt the sale of the Berkeley Main Post Office Building. The city alleged that USPS failed to adhere to the requirements under the National Historic Preservation Act and the National Environmental

Policy Act for evaluating historic impact. The National Trust for Historical Preservation also filed suit. In December a pending purchase for a real estate developer to buy the property fell through. In January 2015 the USPS filed a motion to dismiss the lawsuits. The City of Berkeley continued to pursue legal action to halt the sale. A hearing was set for March to determine whether the suit would continue without a buyer vying for the property.

▨ KEY PERSONNEL

Postmaster General and Chief Executive Officer
    Megan J. Brennan . . . . (202) 268–2550
    Fax. . . . . (202) 268–4860
Deputy Postmaster General
    Ronald A. Stroman . . . . (202) 268–2519
Director, Strategic Planning
    Emil Dzuray. (202) 268–6740
General Counsel and Executive Vice President
    Thomas J. Marshall. . . . . (202) 268–2950
Chief Sustainability Officer
    Thomas G. Day . . . . (202) 268–8020
Vice President, Corporate Communications
    Elizabeth Johnson (acting). . . . . (202) 268–2145
Chief Financial Officer and Executive Vice President
    Joseph Corbett. . . . . (202) 268–5272
Chief Human Resources Officer and Executive Vice President
    Jeffrey Williamson. . . . . (202) 268–2028
Chief Information Officer and Executive Vice President
    Randy Miskanic. . . . . (202) 268–5700
Chief Marketing & Sales Officer and Executive Vice President
    Jim Cochrane (acting) . . . . (202) 268–7536
Chief Operating Officer and Executive Vice President
    David E. Williams . . . . (202) 268–4841
Chief Postal Inspector
    Guy Cottrell . . . . (202) 268–4264

▨ INFORMATION SOURCES

Internet

Agency website: www.usps.gov. Comprehensive website includes consumer and business information on postal rates and regulations and an extensive series of manuals and handbooks about USPS procedures and activities. An interactive feature allows the user to check the correct zip code (ZIP+4) for any U.S. address.

Telephone Contacts

    Personnel Locator and Switchboard . . (202) 268–2000
    Information (also in Spanish). . . . . (800) 275–8777
    Inspector General's Hotline . . . . (703) 248–2100
    Mail Fraud and Counterfeit Money
        Order Hotline. . . . . (800) 372–8347
    Postal Inspection Service . . . . (877) 876–2455
    TTY . . . . (877) 889–2457

Information and Publications

KEY OFFICES

USPS Consumer and Industry Affairs
475 L'Enfant Plaza S.W., #4016
Washington, DC 20260–2200
(202) 268–6567
James Nemec, vice president

Provides information to consumers on USPS services and products. Receives and attempts to settle consumer grievances. Unresolved complaints are referred to Postal Service officials.

USPS Corporate Communications
475 L'Enfant Plaza S.W., #10341
Washington, DC 20260–3100
(202) 268–2145
Elizabeth Johnson (acting), vice president
David Partnerheimer, media relations

Provides the media with public information about the Postal Service.

USPS Government Relations and Public Policy
475 L'Enfant Plaza S.W.
Washington, DC 20260–3100
(202) 268–2505
Ronald A. Stroman, chief government relations
    officer

Provides primary liaison to government leaders and public policymakers

Forensic Laboratory Services
USPS Inspection Service
22433 Randolph Dr.
Dulles, VA 20104–1000
(703) 406–7100
(877) 876–2455
Fax (703) 406–7115
Patricia A. Manzolillo, director

Provides scientific expertise to the criminal and security investigations of the USPS. Processes information requests for all USPS crime labs.

Freedom of Information
475 L'Enfant Plaza S.W., Room 5821
Washington, DC 20260–1540
(202) 268–2608
Fax (202) 268–5353
Jane Eyre, FOIA contact
Internet: http://about.usps.com/who-we-are/foia/
    service-centers.htm

USPS Brand and Policy
475 L'Enfant Plaza S.W., #4646
Washington, DC 20260–1540

(202) 268–5225

Kevin Coleman, manager

Produces and provides information on many USPS publications (see below for ordering information).

DATA AND STATISTICS

USPS Records

475 L'Enfant Plaza S.W., #9431
Washington, DC 20260
(202) 268–2608
Jane Eyre, manager and records officer

Provides access to all postal records.

PUBLICATIONS

An extensive series of USPS publications is available on the website at https://about.usps.com/publications/welcome.htm. Directives and forms are listed in the *Directives and Forms Catalog* (Pub. 223), also available on the website and from:

Material Distribution Center

U.S. Postal Service
500 S.W. Gary Ormsby Dr.
Topeka, KS 66624–9998
(785) 861–2919

All USPS publications, manuals, and handbooks (some in Spanish) are available on the website, and selected items are available at main post offices. Publications include

A Consumer and Business Guide to Preventing Mail Fraud (Pub. 300)

A Customer's Guide to Mailing

A Directory of Postal Services and Products (Pub. 201)

Domestic Mail Manual

Hazardous, Restricted, and Perishable Mail (Pub. 52)

International Mail Manual

Let's Do Business (Pub. 5)

Mailing Free Matter for Blind and Visually Handicapped Persons (Pub. 347)

Postal Bulletin. Biweekly newspaper that contains current orders, new rates, classifications, and items of interest to USPS personnel and stamp collectors.

Comprehensive Statement on Postal Operations. An annual USPS report to Congress, available from USPS Government Relations, (202) 268–2505. The annual report also is available on the website.

Reference Resources

LIBRARY

USPS Library

475 L'Enfant Plaza S.W., #11800
Washington, DC 20260
(202) 268–2074
Jennifer M. Lynch, postal historian
Email: Jennifer.m.lynch@usps.gov

DOCKETS

Materials related to enforcement actions, rate cases, and other administrative proceedings are maintained at the USPS Library. Information on dockets and regulatory matters may also be obtained from Betty Sheriff, USPS Payroll Accounting/Records, (202) 268–2608. Federal dockets are also available at www.regulations.gov. (*See appendix for information on searching and commenting on regulations.*)

RULES AND REGULATIONS

USPS rules and regulations are published in the *Code of Federal Regulations,* Title 5, Chapter LX, Part 7001; Title 39, Chapter I, Parts 1–999. Proposed rules, new final rules, and updates to the *Code of Federal Regulations* are published in the daily *Federal Register.* (*See appendix for information on how to obtain and use these publications.*)

■ LEGISLATION

The Postal Service carries out its responsibilities under

Postal Reorganization Act (84 Stat. 719, 39 U.S.C. 101). Signed by the president Aug. 12, 1970. Created the USPS and the PRC. Transferred the powers to regulate the distribution of mail from the Post Office Department to the USPS. (A description of the private express statutes also can be found under these cites: 84 Stat. 727, 39 U.S.C. 601–606; 84 Stat. 727, 18 U.S.C. 1693–1699, 1724–1725.) The Postal Reorganization Act removed appointment of postmasters from the influence of Congress.

Mail Order Consumer Protection Amendments of 1983 (97 Stat. 1316–1317, 39 U.S.C. 3005, 3013). Signed by the president Nov. 30, 1983. Strengthened the investigatory and enforcement powers of the USPS by authorizing certain inspection authority by providing for civil penalties for misleading advertisements that use the mail. Required semiannual reports summarizing investigative activities.

Inspector General Amendments of 1988 (101 Stat. 2524, 5 U.S.C. appendix). Signed by the president Oct. 18, 1988. Elevated the Postal Inspector Office to an Office of Inspector General within the USPS. The inspector general reports to the postmaster general and Congress regarding problems and deficiencies relating to the USPS and suggests corrections.

Anti-Drug Abuse Act of 1988 (101 Stat. 4362, 18 U.S.C. 3061; 102 Stat. 4363, 21 U.S.C. 881). Signed by the president Nov. 18, 1988. Gave the Inspection Service additional civil and criminal forfeiture authority incident to postal-related drug and money-laundering investigations as agreed to by the attorney general. Proceeds from forfeiture activities are deposited in the Postal Service Fund.

Act of Dec. 12, 1989 (103 Stat. 1944, 39 U.S.C. 2005a). Signed by the president Dec. 12, 1989. Raised the USPS's borrowing authority limitations from $10 billion in fiscal year 1990 to $15 billion for fiscal year 1992 and each fiscal year thereafter.

Omnibus Reconciliation Act (103 Stat. 2133, 39 U.S.C. 2009a). Signed by the president Dec. 19, 1989. Excluded the

USPS from the federal budget and exempted it from inclusion in calculating the federal deficit under the Balanced Budget and Emergency Deficit Control Act of 1985.

Postal Civil Service Retirement System Funding Reform Act of 2003 (117 Stat. 624, 5 U.S.C. 101 note). Signed by the president April 23, 2003. Required that the USPS change the way it calculated its contributions to the Civil Service Retirement and Disability Fund.

Postal Accountability and Enhancement Act (120 Stat. 3198, 39 U.S.C. 3622e). Signed by the president Dec. 20, 2006. Authorized the USPS board of governors to establish reasonable and equitable classes of mail and rates of postage and fees for competitive products. Required the Postal Regulatory Commission to make annual determinations of USPS compliance with regulatory requirements. Changed the postal service retirement and health benefits funding.

Prevent All Cigarette Trafficking Act of 2009 (PACT)Act (124 STAT. 1087, 15 U.S.C 375 note). Signed by the president March 31, 2010. Amends the Jenkins Act to revise provisions governing the collection of taxes on, and trafficking in, cigarettes and smokeless tobacco. Establishes the PACT Postal Service Fund to which 50 percent of criminal and civil fines for mailing violations shall be transferred and made available to the postmaster general to enforce mailing restrictions on cigarettes and smokeless tobacco products.

■ AREA OFFICES

U.S. Postal Service

CAPITAL METRO AREA
(Atlanta; greater SC, mid-Carolinas, and Greensboro; DC; MD; northern, central, and Richmond, VA)
6 Montgomery Village Ave., #655
Gaithersburg , MD 20879
Mailing address:
16501 Shady Grove Rd.
Gaithersburg, MD 20898–9998
(301) 548–1410
Kristin Seaver, vice president

EASTERN AREA
(DE, part of IN, KY, central and southern NJ, OH, PA, western NY, TN, western VA, WV)
5315 Campbells Run Rd.
Pittsburgh, PA 15277–7010
(412) 494–2510
Joshua Colin, vice president

GREAT LAKES AREA
(IL, IN, MI, WI)
500 Fullerton Ave., #896

Carol Stream, IL 60199–1000
(630) 539–5885
Jacqueline Krage Strako, vice president

NORTHEAST AREA
(CT, MA, ME, NH, parts of NJ & NY, RI, VT, Puerto Rico, and U.S. Virgin Islands)
6 Griffin Rd. North
Windsor, CT 06006–7010
(860) 285–7040
Richard P. Uluski, vice president

PACIFIC AREA
(CA, HI, Guam, American Samoa, Trust Territories)
11255 Rancho Carmel Dr.
San Diego, CA 92197–0100
(858) 674–3100
Dean Granholm, vice president

SOUTHERN AREA
(AL, AR, FL, some of GA, LA, MS, OK, part of SC, TX)
7800 N. Stemmons Fwy.
Dallas, TX 75247
Mailing address:
P.O. Box 224748
Dallas, TX 75222–4748
(214) 819–8650
Jo Ann Feindt, vice president

WESTERN AREA
(AK, AZ, CO, IA, ID, KS, MN, MO, MT, southwest ND, NE, NM, NV, OR, SD, UT, WA, WY, and parts of IL, MI, and WI)
1745 Stout St., #1000
Denver, CO 80299–1000
(303) 313–5100
Drew Aliperto, vice president

Postal Inspection Service Centers

CHICAGO
Criminal Investigations Service Center
433 W. Harrison St., #3255
Chicago, IL 60699–3255
(312) 669–5650
Bryan Fleming (acting), manager

MEMPHIS
Security Investigation Service Center
225 N. Humphreys Blvd.
Memphis, TN 38161–0001
(901) 747–7700
Lewistine Brooks, manager

Departmental
Agencies

Agriculture Department

1400 Independence Ave. S.W., Washington, DC 20250
Internet: www.usda.gov

Agricultural Marketing Service

1400 Independence Ave. S.W., #3071S, MS 0201
Washington, DC 20250–0201
Internet: www.ams.usda.gov

In 1922 the Bureau of Markets was combined with another bureau to form the Bureau of Agricultural Economics. In 1939 this bureau was incorporated into the Agricultural Marketing Service (AMS). The AMS is one of several service and regulatory units within the U.S. Department of Agriculture (USDA). The AMS is under the jurisdiction of the assistant secretary of agriculture for marketing and regulatory programs and is headed by an administrator appointed by the secretary of agriculture. Serving under the administrator is a deputy administrator responsible for management and marketing programs.

Regulatory responsibilities at the AMS are shared by seven units; each unit supervises marketing and regulatory activities for a particular segment of the agriculture industry. The specific areas are dairy products; fruits and vegetables; livestock, poultry, and seed; cotton and tobacco; National Organic Program; science and technology; and transportation and marketing.

The regulatory activities of the AMS are the broadest of any of the agencies within the USDA. The agency administers programs designed to promote order and efficiency in marketing agricultural products and regulates fair trading of fruits and vegetables and truth-in-labeling of seeds. The agency also prohibits discrimination against members of producers' organizations and protects the rights of plant breeders. By agreement with groups of producers, the AMS issues marketing orders to manage the flow of agricultural commodities to the marketplace.

AMS regulatory programs include:

- Administration of the Perishable Agricultural Commodities Act, which prohibits unfair and fraudulent practices in the marketing of fresh and frozen fruits and vegetables. The act requires licensing of interstate dealers and specifies that any labels on containers be accurate.
- Administration of the Federal Seed Act, which requires that all agricultural and vegetable seeds shipped interstate be truthfully labeled. It prohibits false advertising and imports of seed lots containing undesirable components.
- Administration of the Plant Variety Protection Act, which protects the "inventions" of breeders of plants that reproduce sexually (by seed) or tuber-propagated. Protection extends for twenty years for a plant and twenty-five

years for a tree or vine and prohibits others from using the new plant without the breeder's permission.
- Administration of the Agricultural Fair Practices Act, which makes it unlawful for handlers of agricultural commodities to discriminate against farmers who belong to a producers association.
- Administration of the Export Fruit Acts, which authorizes regulation of the quality of exported apples, pears, grapes, and plums to protect the reputation of U.S.-produced fruit in international markets.
- Administration of the Egg Products Inspection Act, which assures that eggs and egg products that reach consumers are unadulterated, and provides continuous inspection in all plants that process liquid, dried, or frozen egg products.
- Administration of the Country of Origin Labeling (COOL) Program, a law requiring retailers to provide information to consumers regarding the source of certain foods. Covered commodities include beef, veal, pork, lamb, goat, and chicken; wild and farm-raised fish and shellfish; fresh and frozen fruits and vegetables; peanuts, pecans, and macadamia nuts; and ginseng.

The Transportation and Marketing Programs division assists in the development of an efficient transportation system for rural communities to move commodities through the nation's highways, railroads, airports, and waterways into the domestic and international marketplace. The division serves as the expert source for economic analysis on agricultural transportation from farm to markets, making recommendations to government policymakers regarding regulatory action, economic analysis and transportation disruption solutions.

The AMS National Organic Program (NOP) develops, implements, and administers national production, handling, and labeling standards for organic agricultural products. The NOP also accredits the certifying agents, foreign and domestic, who inspect organic production and handling operations to certify that they meet USDA standards. The National Organic Standards Board (NOSB) is a federal advisory committee whose members are appointed by the secretary of agriculture. NOSB provides recommendations to the secretary through the AMS's NOP deputy administrator.

The Science and Technology Program division provides centralized scientific support to AMS programs, including laboratory analyses and quality assurance, coordination of scientific research conducted by other agencies for the AMS, and statistical and mathematical consulting services. The Science and Technology Program division also issues certificates of protection for new varieties of sexually (by seed) reproduced plants. In addition, it administers USDA's pesticide record-keeping program.

The AMS also operates support programs to help producers and handlers market their products efficiently and ensure that high quality is maintained. These include a market news service, grading standardization and classification programs, commodity procurement programs, research and promotion programs, administration of a system of marketing orders and agreements, and farmer's market and local food marketing programs.

The Market News Service provides current information to the agricultural commodities industry to encourage an orderly marketing and distribution system. Information in the reports covers prices and demand, current supply, location, quality, and condition. Much of this information covers national trends.

The AMS develops standards to be used in classifying certain farm products. These include fresh and processed fruits and vegetables, livestock, wool, mohair, tobacco, cotton, and naval stores. Grading services are offered to buyers and sellers. AMS's quality grade standards, grading, certification, auditing, inspection, and laboratory analysis are voluntary tools that industry can use to promote and communicate quality to consumers. Industry pays for these services.

The AMS administers a commodity procurement program, which purchases domestically produced food for distribution through programs of the Food and Nutrition Service (p. 494), such as the school lunch program, nutrition programs for the elderly, and the supplemental food program for women, infants, and children. A government-wide food quality assurance program helps ensure the federal government buys its food as efficiently and economically as possible. The program eliminates overlap and duplication among federal agencies in government food purchases. It also encourages bidding by food processors on government contracts. In its procurement programs, the AMS applies federal law giving minority- and women-owned businesses certain preferences.

Research and promotion programs, designed to improve the quality of agricultural commodities and develop new markets, are sponsored by the agricultural industries monitored by the USDA and authorized by congressional acts for each commodity. The programs conducted under AMS supervision are funded by the producers, either through direct assessments or by deducting funds from price support payments. Laws have been passed authorizing research and promotion programs for beef, cotton, dairy products, fluid milk, eggs, floral products, honey, lamb, mohair, pork, potatoes, watermelon, and wool.

Authorized by the Agricultural Marketing Act of 1946, marketing orders and agreements are issued by the AMS to help stabilize markets for a number of farm commodities, chiefly milk, fruits, vegetables, and specialty crops such as peanuts, kiwifruit, and avocados. Through these programs individual farmers can organize to solve common marketing problems. AMS specialists make sure the orders operate in the public interest and within legal bounds.

The programs are voluntary and are initiated and designed by farmers. The secretary of agriculture may issue a marketing order only after a public hearing at which farmers, marketers, and consumers may testify, and after farmers vote approval through a referendum.

Marketing orders enable the agriculture industry to regulate the handling and marketing of its products to prevent market shortages and gluts without direct control over pricing. In addition, marketing orders can keep high-quality produce on the market, standardize packs or containers, regulate the weekly flow to the market, establish reserve pools for storable commodities, and authorize advertising, research, and development.

Farmer's market and local food marketing programs improve marketing opportunities for small and midsized producers through the combination of applied research and technical services. AMS administers four grant programs to help farmers and ranchers market the food they produce, including programs that further farmers markets, specialty crops such as fruit and vegetables, local food marketing, and cost-share programs to help farmers become organic.

The Dairy Market Enhancement Act of 2000 amended the Agricultural Marketing Act of 1946 to provide for timely, accurate, and reliable market information to facilitate more informed marketing decisions and promote competition in the dairy product manufacturing industry. Following a lengthy rulemaking process, the AMS established the Dairy Products Mandatory Reporting Program in June 2007.

The Farm Security and Rural Investment Act of 2002 adjusted many of the programs regulated under AMS. These included programs dealing with peanuts, dairy, commodity purchases, sheep research and promotion, caneberry marketing orders, farmers markets, organic classification, cotton classing, country of origin labeling, and salmon promotion.

The Agricultural Act of 2014 (known as the 2014 Farm Bill) reauthorized USDA programs through 2018. The most recent Farm Bill declared all certified organic production exempt from commodity assessment fees and reauthorized funding for organic certification cost-share assistance. The bill directed AMS to lift the stay on the research and promotion program for fresh cut Christmas trees.

■ KEY PERSONNEL

Administrator
    Ann Alonzo . . . . (202) 720–5115
Associate Administrator
    Rex Barnes . . . . (202) 720–5115
Compliance and Analysis Programs
    Sonia Jimenez . . . . (202) 720–6766
Cotton and Tobacco
    Darryl Earnest . . . . (901) 384–3060

Dairy
Dana H. Coale . . . . (202) 720–4392

Fruit and Vegetable
Chuck Parrott . . . . (202) 720–4722

Legislative and Regulatory Review Staff
Chris Sarcone. (202) 720–3203

Livestock, Poultry, and Seed
Craig Morris. (202) 720–5705

Public Affairs
Jim Brownlee . . . . (202) 690–3816

Science and Technology
Ruihong Guo . . . . (202) 720–5231

Transportation and Marketing
Arthur Neal . . . . (202) 690–1300

National Organic Program
Miles McEvoy . . . . (202) 720–3252

Farmers Market and Local Food Marketing
Debra Tropp. . . . . (202) 720–8326

■ INFORMATION SOURCES

Internet

Agency website: www.ams.usda.gov. Comprehensive website includes information on AMS programs, offices, and publications.

Telephone Contacts

Personnel Locator . . . . (202) 720–8732
Federal Relay Service TTY . . . . (800) 877–8339

Information and Publications

KEY OFFICES

AMS Public Affairs Staff

1400 Independence Ave. S.W.
South Bldg., #3933-S
Washington, DC 20250–0201
(202) 690–3816
Fax (202) 720–7135
Wayne Maloney, director

Issues publications, news releases, and speeches related to the AMS.

Market news on specific agricultural products is available from the following contacts and on the website, and e-mail subscriptions about agricultural products are also available on the website (see also *Publications*, below).

AMS Cotton and Tobacco Market News Branch

3275 Appling Rd.
Memphis, TN 38133–2701
(901) 384–3016
Barbara Meredith, chief

AMS Dairy Market Information Branch

USDA-AMS Dairy Programs
1400 Independence Ave. S.W., #2968-S
Washington, DC 20250–0225

(202) 720–4392
Joe Gaynor, chief

AMS Fruit and Vegetable Market News Branch

1400 Independence Ave. S.W.
South Bldg., #2077-S
Washington, DC 20250–0238
(202) 720–2745
Terry Long, director

AMS Livestock, Poultry, and Grain Market News Division

1400 Independence Ave. S.W.
South Bldg., #2619-S
Washington, DC 20250–0201
(202) 720–6231
Mike Lynch, director

Freedom of Information

AMS Legislative and Regulatory Review Staff
1400 Independence Ave. S.W.
South Bldg., #3521-S
Washington, DC 20250–0273
(202) 720–2498
Fax (202) 690–3767
Carrie Hyde-Michaels, FOIA officer

PUBLICATIONS

Contact the AMS Public Affairs Staff at (202) 720–8998. Publications are also available on the agency's website.

The USDA Economics, Statistics, and Market Information System (ESMIS) contains approximately 2,500 reports and datasets, covering U.S. and international agriculture. Available titles include both current and historical data, and many are available on the website and by e-mail subscription. (ESMIS is a collaborative project between the Albert R. Mann Library at Cornell University and several agencies of USDA.)

DATA AND STATISTICS

AMS statistical material on specific agricultural products is available from the appropriate news/information branch (*see above*).

MEETINGS

Notices of administrative proceedings—hearings before the administrative law judges, public hearings on marketing orders, and hearings on proposed rules and regulations—are published in the *Federal Register* and are available at www.federalregister.gov. Information about administrative hearings, marketing orders, and other programs also may be obtained from the website and from AMS legislative staff (202) 720–3203.

Reference Resources

LIBRARY

National Agricultural Library

10301 Baltimore Ave.
Beltsville, MD 20705–2351

(301) 504–5755
Stan Kosecki, director (acting)
Hours: 8:30 a.m. to 4:30 p.m.

The National Agricultural Library also maintains a reference center at the Agriculture Department's South Building. The collection consists primarily of reference volumes, databases, and other computer resources.

D.C. Reference Center

1400 Independence Ave. S.W.
South Bldg., #1052-S
Washington, DC 20250–0201
(202) 720–3434
Rebecca Mazur, coordinator of research services

DOCKETS

AMS Legislative and Regulatory Review Staff

1400 Independence Ave. S.W.
South Bldg., #3521-S
Washington, DC 20250–0201
(202) 720–3203
Chris Sarcone, director

Information on public dockets related to AMS rule-making and regulations may be obtained at this office. All federal dockets are also available at www.regulations.gov. (*See appendix for Searching and Commenting on Regulations: Regulations.gov.*)

RULES AND REGULATIONS

AMS rules and regulations are published in the *Code of Federal Regulations,* Title 7, Chapter I, Parts 27–209; Title 7, Chapters IX, X, XI, Parts 900–1299. Proposed rules, new final rules, and updates to the *Code of Federal Regulations* are published in the daily *Federal Register. (See appendix for information on how to obtain and use these publications.)*

▪ LEGISLATION

Legislation administered by the AMS includes:

U.S. Cotton Standards Act (42 Stat. 1517, 7 U.S.C. 51–65). Signed by the president March 4, 1923. Authorized the secretary of agriculture to establish and promote the use of official U.S. cotton standards.

Produce Agency Act (44 Stat. 1355, 7 U.S.C. 491–497). Signed by the president March 3, 1927. Prohibited destruction or dumping of farm products by commissions, merchants, and others.

Wool Standards Act (45 Stat. 593, 7 U.S.C. 415b–d). Signed by the president May 17, 1928. Authorized the use of certain funds for wool standardization and grading work.

Perishable Agricultural Commodities Act (46 Stat. 531, 7 U.S.C. 499a–499t). Signed by the president June 10, 1930. Prohibited unfair or fraudulent practices in the marketing of fresh or frozen fruits and vegetables. Required licenses for dealers, commission merchants, brokers, shippers, and agents who deal with fresh or frozen fruits and vegetables. It also impressed a trust on the commodities and sales proceeds for the benefit of unpaid sellers.

Export Apple Act (48 Stat. 123, 7 U.S.C. 581–590). Signed by the president June 10, 1933. Required inspection of fresh apples exported from the United States to determine that they meet minimum quality specifications.

Tobacco Inspection Act (49 Stat. 735, 7 U.S.C. 511–511q). Signed by the president Aug. 23, 1935. Established and maintained standards of classification for tobacco and provided for official tobacco inspections.

Act of August 24, 1935 (49 Stat. 750, 7 U.S.C. 612c). Signed by the president Aug. 24, 1935. Authorized purchase, export, and diversion programs to expand market outlets for surplus farm commodities. Provided for limited price assistance to farmers and for increased use of agricultural products among low-income groups.

Agricultural Marketing Agreement Act of 1937 (50 Stat. 246, 7 U.S.C. 601, 602, 608a–e, 610, 612, 614, 624, 627, 671–674). Signed by the president June 3, 1937. Authorized establishment of marketing orders and agreements to regulate milk handling and to set minimum prices for farmers; regulated quality and quantity of containers and shipments of certain fruits, vegetables, nuts, and hops. Regulated the import of certain of these commodities whenever domestic shippers are subject to quality regulations under marketing orders.

Federal Seed Act (53 Stat. 1275, 7 U.S.C. 1551–1611). Signed by the president Aug. 9, 1939. Required truth-in-labeling and advertising of seeds shipped in interstate commerce.

Agricultural Marketing Act of 1946 (60 Stat. 1087, 7 U.S.C. 1621–1627). Signed by the president Aug. 14, 1946. Provided basic authority for many AMS functions. Authorized federal standards for farm products, grading, and inspection services, market news services, cooperative agreements, transportation services, market expansion activities, and consumer education.

Export Grape and Plum Act (74 Stat. 734, 7 U.S.C. 591–599). Signed by the president Sept. 2, 1960. Required inspection of export shipments of fresh grapes and plums for which quality specifications have been established.

Agricultural Fair Practices Act (82 Stat. 93, 7 U.S.C. 2301–2306). Signed by the president April 16, 1968. Prohibited unfair trade practices by processors and handlers who deal with farmers, prohibiting discriminating activities against members of a producer association. Protected farmers' rights to organize and join cooperatives.

Plant Variety Protection Act (84 Stat. 1542, 7 U.S.C. 2321–2331). Signed by the president Dec. 24, 1970. Encouraged the development of novel varieties of sexually (by seed) reproduced or tuber propagated plants by providing protection to developers of such plants.

Egg Products Inspection Act (84 Stat. 1620, 21 U.S.C. 1031–1056). Signed by the president Dec. 29, 1970. Provided for a shell surveillance program to ensure the proper disposition of restricted (dirty, cracked, leaking) eggs.

International Carriage of Perishable Foodstuffs Act of 1982 (96 Stat. 1603, 7 U.S.C. 4401 note). Signed by the president Oct. 15, 1982. Designates the secretary of agriculture as the authority to implement the Agreement on the International Carriage of Perishable Foodstuffs.

Dairy and Tobacco Adjustment Act of 1983 (97 Stat. 1149, 7 U.S.C. 511r). Signed by the president Nov. 29, 1983. Required all imported tobacco, with the exception of cigar and oriental tobacco, be inspected for grade and quality.

Organic Foods Production Act of 1990 (104 Stat. 3935, 7 U.S.C. 6501–6522). Signed by the president Nov. 28, 1990. Authorized a program of national standards for the production and certification of organically produced foods. Established a National Organic Standards Board to provide recommendations on implementation of the act and to develop a list of allowed and prohibited substances.

Various **Commodity Research and Promotion Laws** authorizing self-help industry-financed programs to carry out national promotion and research efforts. These laws apply to avocados (7 U.S.C. 7801–7813), beef (7 U.S.C. 2901–2911), canola (7 U.S.C. 7441–7452), cotton (7 U.S.C. 2101–2118), dairy (7 U.S.C. 4501–4513), eggs (7 U.S.C. 2701–2718), flowers (7 U.S.C. 4301–4319), fluid milk (7 U.S.C. 6401–6417), fresh cut flowers and greens (7 U.S.C. 6801–6814), honey (7 U.S.C. 4601–4613), kiwifruit (7 U.S.C. 7461–7473), limes (7 U.S.C. 6201–6212), mushrooms (7 U.S.C. 6101–6112), pecans (7 U.S.C. 6001–6013), popcorn (7 U.S.C. 7481–7491), pork (7 U.S.C. 4801–4819), potatoes (7 U.S.C. 2611–2627), sheep (7 U.S.C. 7101–7111), soybeans (7 U.S.C. 6301–6311), watermelons (7 U.S.C. 4901–4916), and wheat (7 U.S.C. 3401–3417).

Dairy Market Enhancement Act of 2000 (114 Stat. 2541, 7 U.S.C. 1621 note). Signed by the president Nov. 22, 2000. Amended the Agricultural Marketing Act of 1946 to direct the secretary of agriculture to establish a program of mandatory dairy product information reporting.

Farm Security and Rural Investment Act of 2002 (116 Stat. 1348, 7 U.S.C. 7901 note). Signed by the president May 13, 2002. Provided that all peanuts marketed in the United States, including imported ones, be officially inspected and graded. Eliminated the termination date of the Fluid Milk Promotion Act. Required mandatory country of origin labeling (COOL) for beef, lamb, pork, fish, perishable agricultural commodities, and peanuts after a two-year voluntary program. Required the establishment of a national organic certification cost-share program.

Food, Conservation, and Energy Act of 2008 (Farm Bill) (122 Stat. 1651, 7 U.S.C. 8701 note). Vetoed by the president May 21, 2008; veto overridden June 18, 2008. Reauthorized Department of Agriculture programs through fiscal year 2012. Amended the Farm Bill of 2002 to include chicken (whole and in parts), goat meat, ginseng, pecans, honey, and macadamia nuts to the list of required mandatory country of origin labeling products. Mandated that the Dairy Order be amended to implement an assessment on imported dairy products to fund promotion and research.

Agricultural Act of 2014 (128 Stat. 649). Signed by the president Feb. 7, 2014. Title X Horticulture declared all certified organic production exempt from commodity assessment fees (7 U.S.C. 7401). Authorized funding for organic certification cost-share assistance (7 U.S.C. 6523(d)). Authorized Specialty Crop Block Grant Program (7 U.S.C. 1622) and Farmers Market and Local Food Promotion Program (7 U.S.C. 3005). Amended the Export Apple Act (7 U.S.C. 581-590) to exempt apples shipped in bulk bins weighing 101 pounds or more from USDA's inspection requirement. Directed AMS to lift the stay on the research and promotion program for fresh cut Christmas trees.

▓ FIELD OFFICES

Each of the Marketing Program Divisions has one or more field offices. For field office phone numbers, contact the program directors at the Washington headquarters office.

Marketing Program Divisions

The physical address in Washington, DC, is listed for each division. The mailing address for these offices is 1400 Independence Ave. S.W., Washington, DC 20250–0201.

COTTON AND TOBACCO

3275 Appling Rd.
Memphis, TN 38133–2701
(901) 384–3060
Darryl Earnest, deputy administrator

DAIRY

1400 Independence Ave. S.W., #2968-S
(202) 720–4392
Dana H. Coale, deputy administrator

FRUIT AND VEGETABLE

1400 Independence Ave. S.W., #2077-S
(202) 720–4722
Chuck Parrott, deputy administrator

LIVESTOCK, POULTRY, AND SEED

1400 Independence Ave. S.W., #0249-S
(202) 720–5705
Craig Morris, deputy administrator

SCIENCE AND TECHNOLOGY

1400 Independence Ave. S.W., #3543-S
(202) 720–8556
Ruihong Guo, deputy administrator

TRANSPORTATION AND MARKETING

1400 Independence Ave. S.W., #1098-S
(202) 690–1300
Arthur Neal, deputy administrator

Animal and Plant Health Inspection Service

1400 Independence Ave. S.W., #312E, MS 3401
Washington, DC 20250–3401
Internet: www.aphis.usda.gov

The Animal and Plant Health Inspection Service (APHIS) was created in 1972 as an agency within the U.S. Department of Agriculture (USDA). APHIS is under the jurisdiction of the assistant secretary of agriculture for marketing and regulatory programs; the agency is run by an administrator who is appointed by the secretary of agriculture. APHIS is responsible for programs to eradicate diseases and pests that affect animals and plants, for animal and plant health and quarantine programs, and for the control of depredating animals. The agency also regulates the agricultural products of biotechnology and enforces certain humane laws. Also, following the Sept. 11, 2011, attacks and the Hurricane Katrina disaster, the mission of APHIS expanded to include working with farmers and ranchers to implement a traceability program for livestock and emergency response programs affecting domestic animals.

Plant Health. APHIS Plant Protection and Quarantine (PPQ) regulates the importation of plants and plant products under the authority of the Plant Protection Act. PPQ and the Department of Homeland Security's Customs and Border Protection (CBP) *(p. 664)* work together to carry out all Agricultural Quarantine Inspection (AQI) program activities to intercept and keep out any foreign agricultural pests that could affect U.S. agriculture, trade, and commerce. CBP enforces APHIS regulations at ports of entry. CBP agriculture specialists inspect shipments of imported products and ensure that the required permits and certificates accompany each shipment.

PPQ also provides phytosanitary certification of both U.S. and foreign-origin agricultural commodities. The certification ensures U.S. agricultural and food products shipped to markets abroad meet the importing countries' entry requirements.

APHIS programs concerning plant pests and diseases concentrate on control and eradication. These programs usually are carried out in cooperation with the affected states.

Surveys are made of various areas throughout the country to determine pest activity, population, and spread. When evidence of a dangerous pest is found, an emergency may be declared; emergency regulations designed to prevent the spread of the pest may go into effect and an area-wide quarantine may be invoked.

APHIS control programs are carried out in cooperation with the states to prevent the spread of pests and plant diseases. Control efforts may take the form of chemical sprays, introduction of a pest's natural enemy into an infested area, and release of sterilized insect pests to reduce the population.

The 2008 Farm Bill (the Food, Conservation, and Energy Act of 2008) amended the Lacey Act to make it illegal to import, export, transport, sell, receive, acquire, or purchase, in interstate or foreign commerce, any plant—with limited exceptions—to be taken or traded in violation of domestic or international laws. The Act requires an import declaration for a broad range of plants and plant products that includes the scientific name of any plant and a description of the value, quantity, and the name of the country from where the plant was taken.

Animal Health. APHIS Veterinary Services performs similar functions to protect animal health. APHIS Veterinary Services reorganized in November 2013 into four strategically focused units:

Surveillance, Preparedness, and Response (SPRS), which is responsible for animal health incident management; disease program, surveillance, and animal disease traceability policy; emergency preparedness; epidemiologic investigations and tracing; veterinary accreditation; and veterinary stockpiling.

National Import Export Services (NIES), which is responsible for import animal and animal product inspection and quarantine; import and export policy; facility inspection; health certificate endorsement; World Organization for Animal Health (OIE) representation and disease reporting; permit issuance; and pre-export inspection.

Science, Technology, and Analysis (STAS), which is responsible for analysis of response options; animal disease modeling; animal health data analysis; animal health surveillance design; national animal health laboratory network coordination; risk assessments; and veterinary biologics approval and monitoring regulatory activities.

Program Support Services (PSS), which is responsible for guidance documents; regulatory coordination; the Secretary's Advisory Committee on Animal Health facilitation; and strategic planning.

Animal Welfare. APHIS also administers regulations under the Animal Welfare Act. In 1966, responding to complaints about suffering and neglected dogs and cats supplied to research institutions and focusing on the problem of "petnapping," Congress passed the Laboratory Animal Welfare Act. Four years later, a much more comprehensive piece of legislation—the Animal Welfare Act (AWA) of 1970—was enacted. This law expanded coverage to most other mammals used in research; to animals in zoos and circuses and marine mammals in sea life shows and exhibits; and to animals sold in the wholesale pet trade. The law does not cover retail pet shops, game ranches, livestock shows, rodeos, state or county fairs, or dog and cat shows. In 2013 APHIS revised the definition of "retail pet store" in its regulations to bring animals sold by breeders in Internet transactions under the Animal Welfare Act so that they can be monitored for health and humane treatment.

The AWA has been amended several times. A 1976 amendment extended the scope of the act to include care and treatment while animals are being transported via common carriers. It also outlawed animal fighting ventures, such as dog or cock fights, unless specifically allowed by state law. The Farm Security and Rural Investment Act of 2002 amended AWA to exclude rats, mice, and birds bred for research purposes from the definition of *animal* in the AWA.

Under the Horse Protection Act, APHIS protects horses by enforcing a statute that forbids "soring" of horses in interstate commerce. (Soring is the willful bruising of the front feet of a horse that causes the horse to lift the tender hooves high off the ground, creating a dancing step admired in horse shows.)

APHIS regulates the manufacture of biological products used in the treatment of animals, including genetically engineered biologics, to ensure that the products are safe, pure, potent, and effective. APHIS issues licenses to manufacturers of biologics, surveys production techniques, and inspects production facilities. The agency also regulates the interstate movement and import of genetically engineered plants and microorganisms that are or may be plant pests.

Wildlife Damage. The Animal Damage Control Program, now the Wildlife Services Program, was transferred in 1986 from the U.S. Fish and Wildlife Service to APHIS. Under the Animal Damage Control Act of 1931, APHIS is authorized to protect livestock and crops from depredating mammals and birds. This program protects forests, range lands, and many kinds of wildlife, including endangered species, from animal damage. In addition, the program helps protect human health and safety through control of animal-borne diseases and hazards to aircraft caused by birds.

Emergency Response. Following the attacks of September 11, 2001, and the anthrax attacks in the weeks that followed, Congress and the administration of George W. Bush enacted the Agricultural Bioterrorism Protection Act of 2002. The law required the Agriculture Department to establish and maintain a list of biological agents and toxins that could pose a severe threat to animal or plant health. The FBI was responsible for conducting security risk assessments of individuals seeking access to listed agents and toxins and individuals or entities seeking to register under the act.

As part of the increased focus on food safety, the Department of Agriculture established the National Animal Identification System (NAIS), a voluntary national program intended to identify animals and track them as they come into contact with animals other than herdmates from their premises of origin. Many of these animals can be identified through some sort of identification system within the states, but these systems are not consistent across the country. NAIS included three components—premises registration, animal identification, and animal tracking or tracing. By May 2009 APHIS had more than 520,000 premises registered—out of 1.4 million premises nationwide.

By 2010 it was clear that there was not enough support for NAIS. Because the system was not widely accepted by stakeholders, the agriculture secretary announced a new approach to animal disease traceability in February 2010. The new program would only apply to animals moved interstate; be administered by the states and tribal nations; encourage the use of lower-cost technology; and be implemented through federal regulations and rule-making processes.

The final rules for animal disease traceability were published in the *Federal Register* in January 2013. Public comments resulted in several changes to the proposed rule. Specifically, the final rule allowed for accepting the use of brands, tattoos, and brand registration as official identification when accepted by the shipping and receiving states or tribes; the use of backtags as an alternative to official eartags for cattle and bison moved directly to slaughter; accepting movement documentation other than an Interstate Certificate of Veterinary Inspection (ICVI) for all ages and classes of cattle when accepted by the shipping and receiving states or tribes; and clarifying that all livestock moved interstate to a custom slaughter facility are exempt from the regulations. Chicks moved interstate from a hatchery were exempted from the official identification requirements.

Lessons learned following Hurricane Katrina demonstrated that enabling pet evacuation promotes citizen evacuation, thereby saving human and animal lives. The Pets Evacuation and Transportation Standards Act required the federal government and state governments to develop disaster management plans for household pets. APHIS, along with the Federal Emergency Management Agency, works with states and tribal governments to develop and implement emergency plans that include evacuation and sheltering of pets.

■ KEY PERSONNEL

Administrator
    Kevin Shea . . . . (202) 799–7017
        Fax . . . . (202) 720–3054
Associate Administrator
    Michael Gregoire . . . . (202) 799–7000

Animal Care (Riverdale)
Chester Gipson . . . . (301) 851–3751
Biotechnology Regulatory Services
Michael Firko. . . . . (301) 851–3877
Civil Rights Enforcement and Compliance
Ken Johnson. (202) 799–7020
Executive Communications (Riverdale)
Christina Myers. . . . . (301) 851–4111
Information Technology
Gary Washington . . . . (301) 851–2900
International Services
Cheryle Blakely . . . . (202) 799–7132
Marketing and Regulatory Programs
Business Services
Marilyn Holland . . . . (202) 799–7065
Plant Health Programs
Scott Pfister (acting) . . . . (301) 851–2046
Plant Regulations, Permits, and Manuals
Emily Pullins . . . . (301) 851–2046
Plant Protection and Quarantine
Osama El-Lissy . . . . (202) 799–7163
Policy and Program Development
Christine Zakarka . . . . (301) 851–3098
Veterinary Services
John R. Clifford . . . . (202) 799–7146
Wildlife Services
William H. Clay. . . . . (202) 799–7095

▪ INFORMATION SOURCES

Internet

Agency website: www.aphis.usda.gov. Comprehensive website includes APHIS publications and information on program activities.

Telephone Contacts

See *APHIS Legislative and Public Affairs,* below.

Information and Publications

KEY OFFICES

APHIS Legislative and Public Affairs

1400 Independence Ave. S.W., #1147-S
Washington, DC 20250–3407
(202) 799–7030
Bethany Jones, deputy administrator

Answers general questions from the public, the media, and Congress. Refers specific questions on APHIS programs to the proper office. Divisions include:

APHIS Legislative Services

(202) 799–7030
James Ivy, associate deputy administrator

Provides liaison services between the agency and Congress.

APHIS Printing, Distribution, Mail, and Copier Solutions

4700 River Rd., Unit 1
Riverdale, MD 20737–1228
(301) 851–2632

Provides ordering information on APHIS publications and data.

APHIS Public Affairs

4700 River Rd., Unit 51
Riverdale, MD 20737
(301) 851–4100
Ed Curlett, director

Issues news releases on actions taken by APHIS and recent developments concerning plant and animal diseases.

Freedom of Information

Executive Communications
4700 River Rd., Unit 50
Riverdale, MD 20737
(301) 851–4102
Fax (301) 734–5941
E-mail: FOIA.officer@aphis.usda.gov
Tonya Woods, director

Handles or processes all APHIS correspondence.

DATA AND STATISTICS

Statistical information on the work of APHIS is available in various fact sheets at www.aphis.usda.gov/lpa/pubs/pubs.html or by calling (301) 734–7799. Issues covered include agricultural trade, animal health and welfare, biotechnology, international services, plant health, and wildlife management. Reports on animal health/management are prepared by the APHIS Veterinary Services' Centers for Epidemiology and Animal Health at Fort Collins, Colorado.

PUBLICATIONS

APHIS publishes pamphlets and brochures in four categories: fact sheets, frequently asked questions, and notices for travelers; popular publications; scientific and technical reports; and industry alerts and tech notes. Topics include agricultural quarantines, plant pest control, animal welfare, livestock and poultry diseases, foreign animal diseases, identification of cattle and swine, animal import and export, and veterinary biologics. Guidelines for travel are available at www.aphis.usda.gov/travel. Topics include travel alerts, traveling to the United States, traveling with pets, safeguarding American agriculture, and bringing agricultural products into the United States.

Reference Resources

LIBRARIES

APHIS Public Reading Room

1400 Independence Ave. S.W., #1141-S
MS 3499

Washington, DC 20250–3499
(202) 799–7039
Judy Lee, program specialist
Hours: 7:00 a.m. to 4:30 p.m.

Maintains records of APHIS public hearings and administrative proceedings for public inspection. Some materials concerning APHIS are also available from:

National Agricultural Library
10301 Baltimore Ave.
Beltsville, MD 20705–2351
(301) 504–5755
Stan Kosecki, director
Hours: 8:30 a.m. to 4:30 p.m.

The National Agricultural Library also maintains a reference center at the Agriculture Department's South Building. The collection consists primarily of reference volumes, databases, and other computer resources.

D.C. Reference Center
1400 Independence Ave. S.W., #1052-S
Washington, DC 20250–0201
(301) 504–5077
Rebecca Mazur, coordinator of research services

DOCKETS
All APHIS rulemaking materials are available in the APHIS Public Reading Room. Address comments on proposed regulations to:

APHIS Policy and Program Development Division
Regulatory Analysis and Development Branch
4700 River Rd., Unit 118
Riverdale, MD 20737–1238
(301) 851–3072
Stephen O'Neill, chief

Federal dockets are also available at www.regulations.gov. (*See appendix for Searching and Commenting on Regulations: Regulations.gov.*)

RULES AND REGULATIONS
APHIS rules and regulations are published in the *Code of Federal Regulations,* Title 7, Chapter III, Parts 300–399; Title 9, Chapter I, Parts 1–199. Proposed rules, new final rules, and updates to the *Code of Federal Regulations* are published in the daily *Federal Register.* (*See appendix for information on how to obtain and use these publications.*)

▋ LEGISLATION

Legislation administered by APHIS includes:
Act of Aug. 30, 1890 (26 Stat. 416, 21 U.S.C. 101). Signed by the president Aug. 30, 1890. Prohibited the importation of certain animals except at quarantine stations and authorized the slaughter of animals that have been diagnosed to be diseased.

Plant Quarantine Act of 1912 (37 Stat. 319, 7 U.S.C. 151). Signed by the president Aug. 20, 1912. Set standards for the importation of nursery stock and established procedures for importing plants; also known as the Nursery Stock Quarantine Act. This act was later amended by the **Plant Quarantine Act Amendment** (96 Stat. 2276, 7 U.S.C. 159). Signed by the president Jan. 8, 1983. Permitted APHIS to restrict the importation of plants without holding a public hearing.

Mexican Border Act of 1942 (56 Stat. 40, 7 U.S.C. 149). Signed by the president Jan. 31, 1942. Authorized inspection and cleaning of vehicles and materials that enter the country from Mexico.

Federal Plant Pest Act (71 Stat. 31, 7 U.S.C. 150aa). Signed by the president May 23, 1957. Authorized regulation of movement of any plant pest from a foreign country into or through the United States; authorized inspections and seizures.

Act of July 2, 1962 (76 Stat. 129, 21 U.S.C. 134). Signed by the president July 2, 1962. Established procedure standards for the interstate transportation of animals exposed to communicable diseases.

Animal Welfare Act (80 Stat. 350, 7 U.S.C. 2131). Signed by the president Aug. 24, 1966. Amended by the Animal Welfare Act of 1970 (84 Stat. 1560, 7 U.S.C. 2131), signed by the president Dec. 24, 1970, and the Animal Welfare Act Amendments of 1976 (90 Stat. 417, 7 U.S.C. 2131 note), signed by the president April 22, 1976. Established minimum standards for transportation, purchase, sale, housing, care, handling, and treatment of certain animals used for research experiments or exhibition.

Act of May 6, 1970 (84 Stat. 202, 21 U.S.C. 135). Signed by the president May 6, 1970. Authorized the establishment of an international quarantine station.

Horse Protection Act of 1970 (84 Stat. 1404, 15 U.S.C. 1821). Signed by the president Dec. 9, 1970. Prohibited the "soring" (the bruising of the front feet) of horses shipped interstate.

Food Security Act of 1985 (99 Stat. 1650, 7 U.S.C. 2131 note). Signed by the president Dec. 23, 1985. Established more stringent standards of care for regulated animals, including a suitable physical environment for primates and exercise for dogs.

Continuing Appropriations Act for Fiscal Year 1987 (100 Stat. 3341–3347, 7 U.S.C. 426). Signed by the president Oct. 30, 1986. Authorized the transfer of funds from the Interior Department to the USDA to carry out the responsibilities authorized in the Animal Damage Control Act of 1931 (46 Stat. 1468, 7 U.S.C. 426), signed by the president March 2, 1931. Authorized APHIS to conduct investigations and tests as necessary to determine the best methods of eradication or control in national areas of mountain lions, wolves, coyotes, bobcats, prairie dogs, gophers, ground squirrels, jack rabbits, and other animals injurious to agriculture, forestry, wild game animals, livestock, and other domestic animals.

Farm Security and Rural Investment Act of 2002 (116 Stat. 1348, 7 U.S.C. 7901 note). Signed by the president May 13, 2002. Established a grant program for security upgrades at colleges and universities. Established a felony provision under the Plant Protection Act. Amended definition of animal under the AWA to exclude rats, mice, and birds bred for research. Authorized APHIS to conduct research on transmissible spongiform encephalopathy in deer, elk, and moose, and chronic wasting disease.

Agricultural Bioterrorism Protection Act of 2002 (116 Stat. 647, 7 U.S.C. 8401). Signed by the president June 12, 2002. Directed the establishment of a list of biological agents and toxins that could pose a severe threat to animal or plant health. Set forth provisions for the regulation of transfers of listed agents and toxins; possession and use of listed agents and toxins; registration, identification, and maintenance of database of listed toxins; and security and safeguard of persons possessing, using, or transferring a listed agent or toxin. Expanded the APHIS's ability to conduct specified inspection activities. Authorized automated record keeping for APHIS.

Homeland Security Act of 2002 (116 Stat. 2135, 6 U.S.C. 551, 557). Signed by the president Nov. 25, 2002. Created the Department of Homeland Security. Section 421 transferred to the Department of Homeland Security the Agriculture Department functions relating to agricultural import and entry inspection activities under specified animal and plant protection laws.

Pets Evacuation and Transportation Standards Act of 2006 (120 Stat. 1725, 42 U.S.C. 5121 note). Signed by the president Oct. 6, 2006. Authorized federal agencies to provide assistance to ensure that state and local emergency preparedness operational plans address the needs of individuals with household pets and service animals following a major disaster or emergency.

Animal Fighting Prohibition Reinforcement Act (121 Stat. 88, 18 U.S.C. 1 note). Signed by the president May 3, 2007. Expanded scope of prohibitions against animal fighting. Amended the federal criminal code to impose a fine and/or prison term of up to three years for related violations.

Food, Conservation and Energy Act of 2008 (Farm Bill) (7 U.S.C. 8701 note). Vetoed by the president May 21, 2008; veto overridden June 18, 2008. Reauthorized Department of Agriculture programs through fiscal year 2012. Increased maximum fines for each violation of Animal Welfare Act to $10,000. Addressed livestock disease prevention and food safety concerns. Amended the Lacey Act by expanding its protection to a broader range of plants and plant products, making it unlawful to import certain plants and plant products without an import declaration.

Agricultural Act of 2014 (Farm Bill) (128 Stat. 947, 7 U.S.C. 7721). Signed by the president Feb. 7, 2014. Amends the Plant Protection Act to consolidate the plant pest and disease management and disaster prevention program and the National Clean Plant Network.

▇ REGIONAL OFFICES

Animal Care

EASTERN REGION
(AL, CT, DC, DE, FL, GA, IL, IN, KY, MA, MD, ME, MI, MN, MS, NC, NH, NJ, NY, OH, PA, PR, RI, SC, TN, VA, VI, VT, WI, WV)
920 Main Campus Dr., #200
Raleigh, NC 27606–5210
(919) 855–7100
Elizabeth Goldentyer, regional director

WESTERN REGION
(AK, AR, AZ, CA, CO, GU, HI, IA, ID, KS, MO, MT, ND, NE, NM, OK, OR, SD, TX, UT, WA, WY)
2150 Centre Ave., Bldg. B
MS 3W11
Ft. Collins, CO 80526–8117
(970) 494–7478
Robert M. Gibbons, regional director

Plant Protection and Quarantine Program

EASTERN REGION
(AL, CT, DE, FL, GA, IL, IN, KY, MA, MD, ME, MI, MN, MS, NC, NH, NJ, NY, OH, PA, PR, SC, TN, VA, VT, WI, WV)
920 Main Campus Dr., #200
Raleigh, NC 27606–5210
(919) 855–7300
Matthew Royer, regional director

WESTERN REGION
(AK, AR, AZ, CA, CO, GU, HI, IA, ID, KS, LA, MS, MT, ND, NE, NM, NV, OK, OR, SD, TX, UT, WA, WY)
2150 Centre Ave., Bldg. B
MS 3E101
Ft. Collins, CO 80526–8117
(970) 494–7500
Matthew Royer, executive director

Veterinary Services

EASTERN REGION
(AL, CT, DC, DE, FL, GA, IL, IN, KY, MA, MD, ME, MI, MN, MS, NC, NH, NJ, NY, OH, PA, PR, RI, SC, TN, VA, VI, VT, WI, WV)
920 Main Campus Dr., #200
Raleigh, NC 27606–5210
(919) 855–7250
Jack Shere, regional director

WESTERN REGION
(AK, AR, AS, AZ, CA, CO, GU, HI, IA, ID, KS, LA, MO, MT, ND, NE, NM, NV, OK, OR, SD, TX, UT, WA, WY)

2150 Centre Ave., Bldg. B
MS 3E13
Ft. Collins, CO 80526–8117
(970) 494–7400
Mark Davidson, regional director

Wildlife Services

EASTERN REGION
(AL, AR, CT, DC, DE, FL, GA, IA, IL, IN, KY,
LA, MA, MD, ME, MI, MN, MO, MS, NC,
NH, NJ, NY, OH, PA, PR, RI, SC, TN, VA,
VI, VT, WI, WV)

920 Main Campus Dr., #200
Raleigh, NC 27606–5210
(919) 855–7200
Charles S. Brown, regional director

WESTERN REGION
(AK, AS, AZ, CA, CO, GU, HI, ID, KS, MT, ND, NE,
NM, NV, OK, OR, SD, TX, UT, WA, WY)
2150 Centre Ave., Bldg. B
MS 3W9
Ft. Collins, CO 80526–8117
(970) 494–7453
Jason Suckow, regional director

Farm Service Agency

1400 Independence Ave. S.W., #3086, MS 0501
Washington, DC 20250–0501
Internet: www.fsa.usda.gov

The Farm Service Agency (FSA) was created in 1994 by a reorganization of the U.S. Department of Agriculture (USDA). It combines the farm loan section of the former Farmers Home Administration (FmHA) with the former Agricultural Stabilization and Conservation Service (ASCS). In addition, the FSA administers most functions of the government-owned and operated corporation, the Commodity Credit Corporation (CCC). The FSA formerly administered crop insurance programs through the Federal Crop Insurance Corporation (FCIC). In 1996 the Risk Management Agency (RMA) (*p. 535*) was created as a separate agency within USDA. RMA now administers the functions of the FCIC.

The FSA is headed by an administrator who reports to the under secretary of agriculture for farm and foreign agricultural services. The administrator is appointed by the president and confirmed by the Senate. After its creation in 1994, the FSA was briefly known as the Consolidated Farm Service Agency. Major program areas of the FSA include commodity programs, farm loans, conservation programs, price support, and disaster assistance. More than 2,300 state and county offices are the primary distributors of FSA programs in the 48 continental states. FSA is also represented in Hawaii and Puerto Rico.

Commodity Programs. The CCC operates commodity programs to stabilize the price and supply of agricultural products, in particular wheat, corn, cotton, peanuts, rice, tobacco, milk, sugar beets and sugar cane, wool, mohair, honey, barley, oats, grain sorghum, rye, soybeans, and other oilseeds.

The CCC is a wholly owned government corporation that is now administered by the FSA. It was created in 1933 and incorporated in 1948 as a federal corporation within the USDA by the Commodity Credit Corporation Charter Act. It is managed by an eight-member board of directors (including the secretary of agriculture) appointed by the president. The secretary of agriculture serves as chair of the CCC board of directors and as an *ex officio* director. The other seven board members are appointed by the president and designated according to their positions in the USDA. The corporation staff members, including president, executive vice president, secretary of the board, and general counsel, are also senior officials of the USDA.

The FSA makes CCC loans to eligible farmers using the stored crop as collateral. Many of these loans are "nonrecourse." When market prices are higher than the loan rate, a farmer may pay off the loan and market the commodity; when prices are below the loan levels, the farmer can forfeit or deliver the commodity to the government to discharge the loan in full. Hence the loans promote orderly marketing by providing farmers with income while they hold their crops for later sale. In most cases, to qualify for payments, commodity loans, and purchases, a farmer must participate in the acreage reduction, allotment, or quota programs in effect for the particular crop. The CCC also has authority to license and inspect warehouses and other facilities that store insured commodities.

Commodities acquired by the CCC under the various commodity stabilization programs are sold in this country and abroad, transferred to other government agencies, and donated to domestic and foreign agencies. The Foreign Agricultural Service (*p. 505*) administers CCC export activities.

The FSA also administers the Dairy Indemnity Payment Program, which provides payments to dairy producers when a regulatory agency directs them to remove their raw milk from the commercial market because it has been contaminated by pesticides, nuclear radiation or fallout, or toxic substances and chemical residues other than pesticides.

Farm Loans. The FSA makes direct and guaranteed loans to farmers who are temporarily unable to obtain private, commercial credit. Farmers who qualify receive loan guarantees, whereby a local agricultural lender makes and services the loan and the FSA guarantees the loan up to a maximum of 90 percent. For farmers who cannot qualify for loan guarantees, the FSA makes direct loans, which in most cases are administered by the FSA at the local level. This program provides loans for farm ownership, operations, emergencies, and conservation activities.

In support of its farm loan programs, the FSA provides credit counseling and supervision to its direct borrowers. The agency also assesses the feasibility of these borrowers' farming operations and provides further loan services to borrowers whose accounts are delinquent.

Unlike FSA's commodity loans, these loans can only be approved for those who have repayment ability; the farm loans are fully secured and are "nonrecourse." The goal of FSA farm credit operations is to graduate its customers to commercial credit.

Through the Emergency Loans Program, FSA also provides low-interest emergency loan assistance to eligible farmers to help cover production and physical losses in counties declared as disaster areas. The FSA administrator may also authorize emergency loan assistance to cover physical losses only. Emergency loans are traditionally made to producers in declared disaster areas where drought, floods, and other natural disasters have had devastating effects.

Conservation Programs. The FSA operates most of the programs of the former Agricultural Stabilization and Conservation Service (ASCS), many of which pertain to commodities and are discussed above. The FSA now administers two major voluntary land-use programs designed to protect, expand, and conserve farm lands, wetlands, and forests. The Conservation Reserve Program (CRP) targets the most fragile farmland by encouraging farmers to plant a permanent vegetative cover, rather than crops. In return, the farmer receives an annual rental payment for the term of the multiyear contract. The Conservation Reserve Enhancement Program (CREP) is a partnership among producers; tribal, state, and federal governments; and, in some cases, private groups. CREP is an offshoot of the Conservation Reserve Program.

The Farmable Wetlands Program (FWP) is a voluntary program to restore farmable wetlands and associated buffers by improving the land's hydrology and vegetation. Eligible producers in all states can enroll eligible land in the FWP through the Conservation Reserve Program (CRP).

The FSA also conducts the Emergency Haying and Grazing Assistance program. Haying and grazing of certain conservation reserve program acreage may be made available in areas suffering from weather-related natural disasters. Requests have to be made by the FSA county committees through the state committees and finally decided by the deputy administrator for farm programs.

Another is the Emergency Conservation Program (ECP). ECP shares with agricultural producers the cost of rehabilitating eligible farmlands damaged by a natural disaster. During severe drought, ECP also provides emergency water assistance for livestock and for existing irrigation systems, for orchards and vineyards. ECP may be made available in areas without regard to a presidential or secretarial emergency disaster designation.

Price Support. The Farm Service Agency Price Support Division (PSD) offers a variety of programs that assist farmers and ranchers in managing their businesses, from marketing loans to price support programs. This division also administers the Market Loss Assistance Payment Program, which provides assistance to farmers for market loss incurred because of imports and compensates dairy producers when domestic milk prices fall below a specified level.

The 2014 Farm Bill authorized the Margin Protection Program for Dairy (MPP-Dairy), a voluntary risk management program for dairy producers. The MPP-Dairy offers protection to dairy producers when the difference between the all-milk price and the average feed cost (the margin) falls below a certain dollar amount selected by the producer.

The 2014 Farm Bill established the Agriculture Risk Coverage (ARC) and the Price Loss Coverage (PLC) replaced the direct payment program, which paid farmers in good years and bad, with new initiatives based on market forces. Farmers choose between the programs, which include individual (ARC-IC) and county (ARC-CO) coverage options and offer farmers protection when market forces cause substantial drops in crop prices and/or revenues.

The PLC program provides payments when the market year average price for a covered commodity falls below the crop's reference price specified in the 2014 Farm Bill. The ARC-IC program provides revenue loss protection for revenue losses determined at the farm level. A determination regarding revenue loss for each covered commodity planted on the farm will be made after the market year average price is published by USDA. The ARC-CO program provides revenue loss protection for revenue losses at the county level. A determination regarding revenue loss for each covered commodity with enrolled bases acres in the county will be made after the market year average price is published by USDA.

To help farmers choose between ARC and PLC, USDA has online tools that allow farmers to enter information about their operation and see projections about what each program will mean for them under possible future scenarios. Producers were required to enroll by March 31, 2015. The election will remain in effect for 2014–2018 crop years.

Disaster Assistance. FSA offers a number of programs that assist farmers and ranchers in recovering from weather-related setbacks. The Noninsured Crop Disaster Assistance Program is for crops for which crop insurance is not available. It provides assistance for farmers who grow such crops, limiting their losses from natural disaster and helping to manage their overall business risk. Eligible crops include agricultural commodities that are grown for food; planted and grown for livestock consumption; grown for fiber, except for trees; and specialty crops, such as aquaculture, floriculture, ornamental nursery, Christmas trees, turf for sod, industrial crops, and seed crops.

The 2008 Farm Bill amended the Trade Act of 1974 to create five new disaster programs, collectively referred to as Supplemental Agriculture Disaster Assistance (SADA) programs. SADA provided disaster assistance payments to producers of eligible commodities in counties declared disaster counties by the agriculture secretary. The 2014 Farm Bill indefinitely extended the following four disaster programs that were previously authorized by the 2008 Farm Bill:

- Emergency Assistance for Livestock, Honey Bees, and Farm-Raised Fish (ELAP)
  - Livestock Forage Disaster Program (LFP)
  - Livestock Indemnity Program (LIP)
  - Tree Assistance Program (TAP).

The programs, which had lapsed, were made retroactive to Oct. 1, 2011. To be eligible for disaster assistance programs under the 2014 Farm Bill, producers are no longer required to purchase crop insurance or Noninsured Crop Disaster Assistance Program (NAP) coverage, which was the risk management purchase mandate under the 2008 Farm Bill.

Energy Programs. The 2008 Farm Bill authorized two programs that encourage biofuel renewable energy production, the Biomass Crop Assistance Program (BCAP) and Feedstock Flexibility Program for Bioenergy Producers. BCAP provides financial assistance to owners and operators of agricultural and non-industrial private forest land who wish to establish, produce, and deliver biomass feedstocks. Biomass includes all plants and plant-derived material and is a sustainable feedstock for the production of transportation fuels, products, and power.

The Feedstock Flexibility Program for Bioenergy Producers (FFP) was established to encourage the domestic production of biofuels from surplus sugar. USDA reviews the domestic sugar market every year to determine the level of sugar purchases needed to avoid forfeiture of CCC sugar price support loan collateral. The USDA first implemented the program in 2013.

The 2014 Farm Bill reauthorized energy programs established in the 2008 Farm Bill until 2018. The legislation made changes to the eligibility requirements for the Feedstock Flexibility Program for Bioenergy Producers program.

▩ KEY PERSONNEL

Administrator
Val Dolcini . . . . (202) 720–3467
Fax . . . . (202) 720–9105
Controller (Alexandria, VA)
Bruce Ward . . . . (703) 720–3674
Fax . . . . (703) 305–2842
General Counsel (Agriculture Dept.)
Jeffrey Prieto . . . . (202) 720–3351
Legislative Liaison
Mary Helen Askins . . . . (202) 720–7961
President
Michael Scuse . . . . (202) 720–3111
Fax . . . . (202) 720–8254
Secretary
Gary Crawford . . . . (202) 720–7068
Associate Administrator for Operations and Management
Chris Beyerhelm . . . . (202) 720–2056
Deputy Administrator for Management
Mark A. Rucker . . . . (202) 720–3436
Budget and Finance
Radha Sekar . . . . (202) 720–3674
Emergency Preparedness
Robert Haughton . . . . (202) 690–4161
Human Resources
Danny Sadler (acting) . . . . (202) 401–0069
Strategic Performance and Evaluation
Steve Mikkelson . . . . (202) 720–1068

Civil Rights (Agriculture Dept.)
Brian Garner . . . . (202) 401–7220
Commodity Operations
James Monahan . . . . (202) 720–3217
Fax . . . . (202) 720–8055
Commodity Credit Corporation Chair
Tom Vilsack . . . . (202) 720–3631
Fax . . . . (202) 720–2166
External Affairs
Todd Atkinson . . . . (202) 720–3865
Economic and Policy Analysis
Joy Harwood . . . . (202) 720–3451
Farm Programs
Mike Schmidt . . . . (202) 720–3175
Fax . . . . (202) 720–4726
Production, Emergency, and Compliance
Dan McGlynn (acting) . . . . (202) 720–7641
Price Support
Raellen Erickson . . . . (202) 720–7901
Conservation and Environmental Programs
Matt Ponish (acting) . . . . (202) 720–6221
Farm Loan Programs
Jim Radintz (acting) . . . . (202) 720–7597
Fax . . . . (202) 690–3573
Program Development and Economic Enhancement
Courtney Dixon . . . . (202) 720–1360
Loan Making
Connie Holman . . . . (202) 720–1632
Loan Servicing and Property Management
Mike Hinton . . . . (202) 720–4572
Field Operations
Gregory Diephouse . . . . (202) 690–2807
Fax . . . . (202) 690–3309
Kansas City Commodity Office (6501 Beacon Dr., Kansas City, MO 64133–4676)
Patrick Dardis (acting) . . . . (816) 926–6301

▩ INFORMATION SOURCES

Internet
Agency website: www.fsa.usda.gov. Comprehensive website includes news releases, publications, and extensive information on FSA programs.

Telephone Contacts
Information . . . . (202) 720–7163
Personnel Locator (USDA) . . . . (202) 720–7163
English-Language Federal
Relay (TTY) . . . . (866) 377–8642
Spanish-Language Federal
Relay (TTY) . . . . (800) 845–6136

Information and Publications

KEY OFFICES

FSA Public Affairs Staff
USDA/FSA
1400 Independence Ave. S.W., #4074-S

Washington, DC 20250–0506
(202) 720–7163
Fax (202) 720–2979
Kent Politsch, branch chief

Provides all public and press information on the FSA. Issues news releases on programs, actions, and decisions on pricing; maintains a mailing list. Produces publications, pamphlets, and fact sheets.

Freedom of Information

USDA Farm Service Agency
1400 Independence Ave. S.W., #4070-S
MS 0506
Washington, DC 20250–0506
(202) 720–1598
Fax (202) 690–2828
E-mail: FSA.FOIA@wdc.usda.gov

DATA AND STATISTICS

FSA statistical publications, including reports on the Commodity Credit Corporation and specific programs, are available from the FSA Public Affairs Staff.

Publications of special interest include:

- Annual Report of the Commodity Credit Corporation. Covers operations of the CCC during the preceding year.
- Commodity Fact Sheets. Includes provisions and selected basic data for individual agricultural commodity programs, including dairy, feed grains, sugar, tobacco, cotton, peanuts, and rice.

PUBLICATIONS

Contact the FSA Public Affairs Staff for leaflets and fact sheets on agricultural policies, problems, and programs; and pamphlets on FSA operations. FSA publications are also available on the website.

Reference Resources

LIBRARY

National Agricultural Library

10301 Baltimore Ave.
Beltsville, MD 20705–2351
(301) 504–5755
Stan Kosecki, director
Hours: 8:30 a.m. to 4:30 p.m.

The National Agricultural Library also maintains a reference center at the Agriculture Department's South Building. The collection consists primarily of reference volumes, databases, and other computer resources.

D.C. Reference Center

1400 Independence Ave. S.W.
South Bldg., #1052-S
Washington, DC 20250–0201
(301) 504–5077
Rebecca Mazur, coordinator of research services

DOCKETS

Federal dockets are available at www.regulations .gov. (*See appendix for Searching and Commenting on Regulations: Regulations.gov.*)

RULES AND REGULATIONS

FSA rules and regulations are published in the *Code of Federal Regulations,* Title 7, Chapter VII, Parts 700–799; Title 7, Chapter VIII, various parts. Proposed regulations, new final regulations, and updates to the *Code of Federal Regulations* are published in the daily *Federal Register.* (*See appendix for details on how to obtain and use these publications.*)

■ LEGISLATION

Following are the acts that established the FSA and the laws pertaining to the FSA's program areas:

Department of Agriculture Reorganization Act of 1994 (108 Stat. 3209, 7 U.S.C. 6901 note). Signed by the president Oct. 13, 1994. Consolidated the direct farm programs of the Agricultural Stabilization and Conservation Service and the Commodity Credit Corporation with those of the Federal Crop Insurance Corporation and the Farmers Home Administration into a new Agriculture Service Agency (now the FSA).

Crop Insurance

Federal Crop Insurance Corporation Act of 1938 (52 Stat. 72, 7 U.S.C. 1501 et seq.). Signed by the president Feb. 16, 1938. Established the FCIC as an agency of the USDA.

Federal Crop Insurance Reform Act of 1994 (108 Stat. 3178, 7 U.S.C. 1501 note). Signed by the president Oct. 13, 1994. Overhauled the crop insurance program. Established catastrophic level (CAT) coverage as a requirement to participate in certain FSA programs; also established the Noninsured Crop Disaster Assistance Program for crops not yet insurable.

Agricultural Market Transition Act (110 Stat. 896, 7 U.S.C. 7201). Signed by the president April 4, 1996. Part of the Federal Agriculture Improvement and Reform Act of 1996. Title I, Subtitle H, Section 193 amended the Federal Crop Insurance Act to offer catastrophic risk protection through state Department of Agriculture offices. Provided for the transfer of current policies to private insurers. Section 194 established the Office of Risk Management to oversee the Federal Crop Insurance Corporation and related crop insurance matters. Section 195 established a revenue insurance pilot program. Section 196 created a noninsured crop disaster assistance program for food or fiber crops not covered by the federal crop insurance catastrophic risk protection program.

Agricultural Research, Extension, and Education Reform Act of 1998 (112 Stat. 523). Signed by the president June 23, 1998. Title V (agricultural program adjustments), subtitle C (crop insurance) amended the Federal Crop Insurance Corporation Act of 1938 to make permanent the Federal Crop Insurance Corporation's authority to pay expenses from the insurance fund. Directed the corporation to establish and implement procedures for responding to regulatory inquiries.

Commodity and Price Support Programs

U.S. Warehouse Act (39 Stat. 486, 7 U.S.C. 241). Signed by the president Aug. 11, 1916. Authorized licenses for warehouses that store agricultural products; provides for inspection of warehouses and products. These functions formerly were carried out by the Agricultural Marketing Service; they were transferred to the ASCS (now the FSA) in January 1985. Amended by the Grain Standards and Warehouse Improvement Act of 2000 (7 U.S.C. 241 note), which gave the secretary authority over regulations governing electronic systems relating to the shipment, payment, and financing of the sale of agricultural products.

Commodity Credit Corporation Charter Act (62 Stat. 1070, 15 U.S.C. 714 note). Signed by the president June 29, 1948. Established the CCC as an agency of the USDA. The CCC originally was created in 1933 as an agency of the federal government under the corporation laws of Delaware; in 1939 it was transferred to the USDA by a reorganization plan. The 1948 act authorized the agency to support the prices of commodities through loans, purchases, and payments.

Agricultural Act of 1949 (63 Stat. 1051, 7 U.S.C. 1446a, 1427). Signed by the president Oct. 31, 1949. This act, together with the **Agricultural Act of 1956** (70 Stat. 188, 7 U.S.C. 1851a), signed by the president May 28, 1956, authorized the CCC to make domestic donations to the military, the Veterans Administration, schools, and nonprofit institutions.

Agricultural Trade Development and Assistance Act (68 Stat. 454, 7 U.S.C. 1427). Signed by the president July 10, 1954. Authorized the CCC to finance the sale and export of agricultural commodities for relief donations abroad; also authorized the CCC to trade excess commodities for materials required abroad by other federal agencies. This act was amended and later known as the **Food for Peace Act** (80 Stat. 1526, 7 U.S.C. 1691). Signed by the president Nov. 11, 1966. Promoted agricultural trade; donated food, fertilizers, and technology to foreign countries to combat hunger; and encouraged economic development in developing countries.

Agricultural Act of 1954 (68 Stat. 910, 7 U.S.C. 1781). Signed by the president Aug. 28, 1954. Included the **National Wool Act**, which established mohair and wool price stabilization by authorizing payments to producers.

Dairy Farmers Indemnity Payments, as amended (82 Stat. 750, 7 U.S.C. 450j). Signed by the president Aug. 13, 1968. Authorized indemnity payments to dairy farmers who had to remove their milk from commercial markets because it contained residues of chemicals, toxic substances, or nuclear radiation.

Food and Agriculture Act of 1977 (91 Stat. 913, 7 U.S.C. 1308). Signed by the president Sept. 23, 1977. Established revised price supports and loan levels for various agricultural commodities.

Food and Agriculture Act of 1977 (91 Stat. 953, 7 U.S.C. 1427). Signed by the president Sept. 29, 1977. Provided a farmer-owned grain reserve program for wheat and feed grains to isolate grain stocks from the market to counter the price-depressing effects of these surplus stocks.

Agricultural Trade Act of 1978 (92 Stat. 1685, 7 U.S.C. 1707a). Signed by the president Oct. 21, 1978. Authorized the CCC to finance agricultural export sales to expand and maintain foreign markets for certain U.S. agricultural commodities.

Agriculture and Food Act of 1981 (95 Stat. 1213, 7 U.S.C. 1281). Signed by the president Dec. 22, 1981. Basic statute administered by the ASCS. Extended, expanded, and revised the subsidy, allotment, and set-aside programs established by earlier legislation (including the Agricultural Act of 1949 and the farm bills of 1965, 1970, 1973, and 1977).

Extra Long Staple Cotton Act of 1983 (97 Stat. 494, 7 U.S.C. 1421 note). Signed by the president Aug. 26, 1983. Authorized the ASCS to make deficiency payments to producers of extra long staple cotton. Lowered the federal commodity loan rate for extra long staple cotton and authorized paid acreage reduction programs for the cotton crop.

Export Administration Amendments Act of 1985 (99 Stat. 158, 15 U.S.C. 4053). Signed by the president July 12, 1985. Authorized the CCC to exchange commodities for petroleum and petroleum products and other materials vital to the national interest.

Food Security Act of 1985 (99 Stat. 1354, 7 U.S.C. 1281 note). Signed by the president Dec. 23, 1985. Authorized new programs: Targeted Export Assistance, Conservation Reserve, and Export Enhancement. Amended the Food for Peace Act to allow the use of accrued foreign currencies to encourage development of private enterprise in developing countries. Extended, expanded, and revised income and price support programs, set-aside and acreage reduction programs, and voluntary paid land diversion programs.

Continuing Appropriations Act, Fiscal 1988 (101 Stat. 1329–1335, 15 U.S.C. 714). Signed by the president Dec. 22, 1988. Increased the CCC's borrowing authority from $25 billion to $30 billion.

Food, Agriculture, Conservation, and Trade Act of 1990 (104 Stat. 3359, 7 U.S.C. 1421 note). Signed by the president Nov. 28, 1990. Adjusted the formula for determining price supports on various commodities and the rules for the operation of grain reserves. Limited the total acreage eligible for diversion and deficiency payments on certain crops. Expanded planting flexibility.

Farm Security and Rural Investment Act of 2002 (116 Stat. 1348, 7 U.S.C. 7901 note). Signed by the president May 13, 2002. Amended the FAIRA to direct the secretary of agriculture to enter into contracts with eligible owners and producers of eligible cropland for both direct and countercyclical payments in crop years 2002 through 2006. Required owner or producer compliance with appropriate conservation, wetlands, planting flexibility, and agricultural use requirements. Authorized the Milk Income Loss Contract (MILC) Program for dairy producers. Required that USDA operate the sugar program at no net cost to taxpayers, thus avoiding forfeitures to the CCC.

Fair and Equitable Tobacco Reform Act of 2004 (7 U.S.C. 518). Signed by the president, Oct. 22, 2004. Title VI of the American Jobs Creation Act of 2004. Eliminated price supports and marketing quotas for all tobacco beginning with the 2005 crop year. Established the Tobacco Transition Payment Program to provide annual transitional payments for ten years to eligible tobacco farmers.

Food, Conservation and Energy Act of 2008 (Farm Bill) (7 U.S.C. 8701 note). Vetoed by the president May 21, 2008; veto overridden June 18, 2008. Reauthorized Department of Agriculture programs through fiscal year 2012. Provided income support, with new payment and eligibility limits, for wheat, feed grains, cotton, rice, oilseeds; countercyclical payments; marketing loan assistance program; and new average crop revenue election payments through fiscal year 2012. Adjusted sugar loan rates and added a program to use surplus sugar for bioenergy production. Revised dairy price support to operate with administered prices for manufactured products rather than fluid milk. Restricted the closing or relocating a USDA Farm Service Agency county or field office for first two years after enactment.

Presidential Appointment Efficiency and Streamlining Act of 2011 (126 Stat. 1283, 15 U.S.C. 714g(a)). Signed by the president Aug. 10, 2012. Eliminates the requirement of Senate approval (advice and consent) for presidential appointment of all members of the board of directors of the Commodity Credit Corporation.

Agricultural Act of 2014 (Farm Bill) (128 Stat. 659, 7 U.S.C. 9011). Signed by the president Feb. 7, 2014. Eliminates direct payments and continues crop insurance. Requires producers to choose between the price loss coverage and agricultural risk coverage. Restores livestock disaster assistance for losses dating back to 2011, and establishes a permanent livestock disaster program (7 U.S.C. 9081). Established the Dairy Margin Protection program (7 U.S.C. 9051).

Farm Loans

Bankhead-Jones Farm Tenant Act (50 Stat. 525, 7 U.S.C. 1010). Signed by the president July 22, 1937. Provided loan authorization to cover costs of resource conservation and development projects.

Farmers Home Administration Act (60 Stat. 1062, 7 U.S.C. 451 note). Signed by the president Aug. 14, 1946. Changed the name of the Farm Security Administration to the Farmers Home Administration and continued government loan programs established under that agency and the Resettlement Administration. Gave FmHA authority to insure loans made by banks, other agencies, and private individuals.

Consolidated Farm and Rural Development Act (75 Stat. 307, 7 U.S.C. 1921). Signed by the president Aug. 8, 1961. Authorized the FmHA to prescribe terms and conditions for making loans and grants and to require that the lender and the borrowers comply with applicable federal laws and regulations.

Rural Development Act of 1972 (86 Stat. 657, 7 U.S.C. 1006). Signed by the president Aug. 30, 1972. Empowered the FmHA to guarantee loans made by commercial lenders for farming and other purposes.

Agricultural Credit Act of 1978 (92 Stat. 420, 7 U.S.C. 1921 note). Signed by the president Aug. 4, 1978. Amended the Consolidated Farm and Rural Development Act to allow the FmHA to make or guarantee loans to farmers hurt by shortages of credit from normal sources or by a cost-price squeeze (when costs of producing goods rise faster than prices charged for them). It also expanded eligibility for farm loans to family corporations, cooperatives, and partnerships; and increased loan limits to $200,000 for insured and $300,000 for guaranteed real estate loans.

Emergency Agricultural Credit Act of 1984 (98 Stat. 138, 7 U.S.C. 1921). Signed by the president April 10, 1984. Authorized the FmHA to raise loan limits on new farm operating direct loans from $100,000 to $200,000, and on guaranteed loans from $200,000 to $400,000; and increased the maximum repayment period for rescheduled or consolidated emergency and operating loans from seven to fifteen years from the date of the original note.

Food Security Act of 1985 (99 Stat. 1518, 7 U.S.C. 1281 note). Signed by the president Dec. 23, 1985. Changed farm loan eligibility requirements and provided additional protections for borrowers undergoing serious financial difficulty. Two of three FmHA county committee members were to be elected by farmers in the community instead of being appointed.

Agricultural Credit Act of 1987 (101 Stat. 1568, 12 U.S.C. 2001 note). Signed by the president Jan. 6, 1988. Permitted FmHA farmer program loans to be reduced to the recovery value of the borrower's collateral if the farmer has a feasible plan to continue the farming operation. Expanded preservation loan servicing programs. Established an independent appeals unit. Authorized the USDA to certify and issue grants to assist agricultural loan mediation programs in states upon a governor's request.

Food, Agriculture, Conservation, and Trade Act of 1990 (104 Stat. 3359, 7 U.S.C. 1421 note). Signed by the president Nov. 28, 1990. Modified delinquent farm-borrower debt relief provisions of the 1987 Agricultural Credit Act and instituted new procedures to strengthen borrowers' prospects for success. Transferred some FmHA programs to the new Rural Development Administration.

Agricultural Credit Improvement Act of 1992 (106 Stat. 4142, 7 U.S.C. 1921 note). Signed by the president Oct. 28, 1992. Established a program of targeted farm ownership and operating assistance for qualified beginning farmers and ranchers. Limited the number of years that borrowers are eligible for FmHA assistance and created a new lender-certified program for guaranteed farm loans. Established safeguards to ensure against discrimination on the basis of gender in FmHA farm lending practices.

Federal Agriculture Improvement and Reform Act of 1996 (110 Stat. 888, 7 U.S.C. 7201 note). Signed by the president April 4, 1996. Amended the Consolidated Farm and Rural Development Act of 1961 (CFRDA). Title VI, subtitle A revised direct farm ownership loan provisions. Subtitle B revised farm operating loan provisions; authorized line-of-credit loans. Subtitle C revised emergency loan provisions. Subtitle D authorized the secretary to enter into farm loan service contracts with eligible financial institutions through

FY 2002; reduced loan service notice requirements; set property sale provisions; revised cash flow margin and loan termination provisions; prohibited direct operating loans to delinquent borrowers; and limited borrowing ability of persons who have received debt forgiveness. Title VII, Subtitle B authorized loan guarantees to family farmers for cooperative stock purchases.

Farm Security and Rural Investment Act of 2002 (116 Stat. 1348, 7 U.S.C. 7901 note). Signed by the president May 13, 2002. Amended FAIRA to direct the secretary of agriculture to make nonrecourse marketing assistance loans and loan deficiency payments available to producers of specified commodities through crop year 2006 (upland cotton through crop year 2007).

Food, Conservation and Energy Act of 2008 (Farm Bill) (7 U.S.C. 8701 note). Vetoed by the president May 21, 2008; veto overridden June 18, 2008. Reauthorized Department of Agriculture programs through fiscal year 2012. Authorized new conservation loan program, expanded programs and preferences for beginning and socially disadvantaged farmers and ranchers, increased loan limits for all borrowers, and made equine farmers eligible for emergency loans.

Conservation Programs

Food Security Act of 1985 (99 Stat. 1354, 7 U.S.C. 1281 note). Signed by the president Dec. 23, 1985. Established the Conservation Reserve program and other conservation provisions.

Food, Agriculture, Conservation, and Trade Act of 1990 (104 Stat. 3359, 7 U.S.C. 1421 note). Signed by the president Nov. 28, 1990. Incorporated previous conservation programs into the Agricultural Resource Conservation Program.

Federal Agriculture Improvement and Reform Act of 1996 (110 Stat. 888, 7 U.S.C. 7201 note). Signed by the president April 4, 1996. Title III amended the Food Security Act of 1985; the Food, Agriculture, Conservation, and Trade Act of 1990; the Cooperative Forestry Assistance Act of 1978; and the Agriculture and Food Act of 1981. Established the National Natural Resource Conservation Foundation, a conservation-related nonprofit corporation.

Farm Security and Rural Investment Act of 2002 (116 Stat. 1348, 7 U.S.C. 7901 note). Signed by the president May 13, 2002. Amended the Food Security Act of 1985 to establish a conservation security program from 2003 through 2006 to assist conservation practices on production land.

Food, Conservation and Energy Act of 2008 (Farm Bill) (7 U.S.C. 8701 note). Vetoed by the president May 21, 2008; veto overridden June 18, 2008. Reauthorized Department of Agriculture programs through fiscal year 2012. Amended the Trade Act of 1974 to create five new disaster programs, collectively referred to as Supplemental Agriculture Disaster Assistance programs.

Energy Programs

Food, Conservation and Energy Act of 2008 (Farm Bill) (7 U.S.C. 8701 note). Vetoed by the president May 21, 2008; veto overridden June 18, 2008. Authorizes a program to support establishment and production of eligible crops for conversion to bioenergy. Project sponsors apply for selection as Biomass Crop Assistance Program (BCAP) project areas. Secretary must purchase sugar (eligible for human consumption) that would otherwise be forfeited to CCC, and either sell it to eligible bioenergy producers or dispose of it by other specified means to ensure that the U.S. sugar program operates at no net cost to the government (authorization of the Feedstock Flexibility Program for Bioenergy Producers).

Agricultural Act of 2014 (Farm Bill) (128 Stat. 931, 7 U.S.C. 8110). Reauthorizes energy programs established in the 2008 Farm Bill. Made changes to eligibility requirements for the Feedstock Flexibility Program for Bioenergy Producers program.

▇ REGIONAL OFFICES

Provides information on commodity sales and purchases. Directs many of the functions of the Commodity Credit Corporation (CCC).

FSA operates state and county offices; a complete list is available on the website. FSA county offices are the primary points of contact for participation in programs and are also listed in telephone directories under "U.S. Department of Agriculture." FSA state offices supervise the county offices and are usually located in the state capital or near the state land-grant university.

FSA KANSAS CITY
COMMODITY OPERATIONS OFFICE

6501 Beacon Dr.
Kansas City, MO 64133–4676
(816) 926–6301
Patrick Dardis (acting), director

Food and Nutrition Service

3101 Park Center Dr., Alexandria, VA 22302
Internet: www.fns.usda.gov

The Food and Nutrition Service (FNS), formerly the Food and Consumer Service (FCS), was established in 1969 to administer the food assistance programs of the U.S. Department of Agriculture (USDA). The FNS is under the jurisdiction of the assistant secretary of agriculture for food, nutrition, and consumer services. The FNS is headed by an administrator who is appointed by the secretary of agriculture.

The agency administers fifteen nutrition programs and conducts nutrition education to inform consumers about the link between diet and health. FNS programs include the supplemental nutrition assistance program (SNAP, formerly the food stamp program); the supplemental food program for women, infants, and children (WIC); a nutrition program and a commodity supplemental food program for the elderly; commodity distribution to charitable institutions; the emergency food assistance program (TEFAP), which distributes food to soup kitchens and food banks; and the national school breakfast and lunch programs. In 2014 more than 30 million children participated in the FNS's school meals programs.

The FNS also administers programs that supply milk to school children free or at reduced prices, provide nutritional training for food service personnel and children, supply commodity foods to Native American families who live on or near reservations and to Pacific Islanders, provide cash and coupons to participants in Puerto Rico and the Northern Marianas, supply WIC participants with coupons to purchase fresh fruits and vegetables at authorized farmers markets, supply food for special children's summer programs, and provide food for child and adult day-care centers. As administrator of these programs, FNS sets eligibility requirements and works with states to implement the programs according to federal guidelines.

The Good Samaritan Food Donation Act, passed in October 1996, encouraged the donation of food and grocery products to nonprofit organizations such as homeless shelters, soup kitchens, and churches for distribution to needy individuals. Through the Food Recovery and Gleaning program, FNS joined with key nonprofit organizations and community-based groups to recover surplus food for distribution to food banks. The Good Samaritan act also limited liability for donors.

The Farm Security and Rural Investment Act of 2002 affected many of the functions of FNS, including the food stamp, child nutrition, special nutrition, food distribution, and supplemental nutrition programs. The act partially restored food stamp benefits to legal aliens, regardless of date of entry into the United States. Previously, legal aliens were required to have been in the country on Aug. 22, 1996. The bill also simplified food stamp eligibility requirements and established, as an independent entity of the legislative branch, the Congressional Hunger Fellows Program.

The Child Nutrition and WIC Reauthorization Act of 2004 extended the child nutrition programs through 2008. The legislation provided children with increased access to food and nutrition assistance and placed an emphasis on nutrition education. The legislation also qualified homeless and runaway children for free breakfast and lunch programs and reauthorized and revised requirements for the summer food service program for children.

The Agricultural Marketing Service (*p. 476*) acts as the purchasing agent for the FNS to obtain the commodities donated to schools and other institutions.

FNS programs are administered through the agency's regional offices. These offices coordinate all FNS programs through state agricultural, educational, welfare, and health agencies. The states determine most details regarding distribution of food benefits and eligibility, and FNS funding covers most of the states' administrative costs. Certain special nutrition programs are administered directly by FNS if states choose not to administer them.

In June 2008 Congress enacted the Food, Conservation, and Energy Act of 2008 (Farm Bill) via override of the president's veto. The 2008 Farm Bill continued agricultural and other programs of the Department of Agriculture through fiscal year 2012. The bill provided increased funding for nutrition programs. The legislation also required FNS to implement pilot projects to improve the dietary and health status of eligible or participating households and to reduce obesity (including childhood obesity) and associated co-morbidities in the United States.

As the nation plunged into economic freefall, newly elected President Barack Obama addressed the crisis upon taking office. On Feb. 13, 2009, the president signed an economic stimulus bill, the American Recovery and

Reinvestment Act (ARRA). Among its many provisions, the legislation provided additional appropriations for supplemental nutrition programs administered by FNS. The bill also temporarily relaxed the requirements for jobless workers without dependents to receive assistance under the supplemental nutrition assistance program (SNAP). Current law allows adults ages 18–50 without dependents to participate in SNAP if they live in areas of high unemployment.

The Healthy, Hunger-Free Kids Act of 2010 reauthorized the Child Nutrition and WIC programs. The legislation also sought to address the growing childhood obesity epidemic. The act required USDA to promulgate regulations to raise nutritional standards of school lunch and breakfast meals. The legislation also requires USDA to establish regulations for local wellness policies and to provide technical assistance to states/schools in consultation with the Education Department and the Centers for Disease Control. The legislation also sets forth the formula for setting the average price paid for school meals so that school meal prices are equitable between meals paid out-of-pocket by parents and the reimbursement rate provided by the federal government for free and reduced price lunches.

The act also contained a community eligibility provision as an alternative to household applications for free and reduced price meals and reduces the burden of collecting funds and maintaining accounts for the few students who pay for school meals. To qualify, schools or districts must have at least 40 percent of the total student enrollment directly certified for free meals, based on their participation in SNAP or other means-tested assistance programs. Meal costs are shared between the federal government and the school or district. The provision became available to eligible schools and districts nationwide beginning July 1, 2014. Districts now have until June 30 each year to elect to participate.

The 2014 Agricultural Act made several changes to the eligibility and administration requirements of the SNAP program. Many of these requirements were designed to strengthened the integrity of the program and reduce fraud and waste. Retailers were required to absorb the cost of equipment and services associated with Electronic Benefit Transfer (EBT) systems. The bill requires states to establish an immigration verification system to verify immigration status and ensure that affluent college students and lottery and gambling winners did not receive SNAP assistance. The legislation made several changes to the SNAP Employment and Training Program and disqualified some convicted felons from participating in SNAP. The law also requires states to phase out the participation of women, infants, and children in the Commodity Supplemental Food Program, which would then serve only low-income senior citizens.

▓ KEY PERSONNEL

Administrator
    Audrey Rowe . . . . (703) 305–2060

Associate Administrator
    Jeffrey Tribiano . . . . (703) 305–2064
Chief Financial Officer
    David Burr . . . . (703) 305–2046
Benefit Redemption
    Jeff Cohen. . . . . (703) 305–2434
Child Nutrition
    Cynthia Long . . . . (703) 305–2590
Civil Rights
    David Youngblood . . . . (703) 305–2060
Communications and Governmental Affairs
    Bruce Alexander . . . . (703) 305–2281
Emergency Management
    Brenda Lisi . . . . (703) 305–2062
Food Distribution
    Vacant . . . . (703) 305–2680
Information Technology
    Jonathan Alboum . . . . (703) 305–2759
Management, Technology, and Finance
    Jeffrey Tribiano . . . . (703) 305–2030
Policy Support, Research, and Analysis
    Steven Carlson . . . . (703) 305–2017
Program Accountability
    David Burr . . . . (703) 305–2022
Program Development
    Art Foley. . . . . (703) 305–2027
Public Affairs
    Jean Daniel . . . . (703) 305–2293
Regional Operations and Support
    Yvette Jackson . . . . (202) 305–2062
Retailer Operations
    Neva Terry . . . . (202) 305–2062
Special Nutrition Programs
    Tim O'Connor . . . . (703) 305–2054
State Systems
    Karen Painter-Jacquess (acting) . . . . . (202) 305–2062
Strategic Initiatives, Partnership, and Outreach
    Duke Storen . . . . (202) 305–2017
Supplemental Food Programs
    Debra Whitford . . . . (703) 305–2746
Supplemental Nutrition Assistance Program (SNAP)
    Jessica Shahin. (703) 305–2022

▓ INFORMATION SOURCES

Internet

Agency website: www.fns.usda.gov. FNS programs, news releases, publications, and fact sheets are all available on the comprehensive agency website. Links also are provided to reach other agencies within the USDA.

Telephone Contacts

    Main . . . . (703) 305–2060
    Personnel Locator (USDA) . . . . (202) 720–8732
    English-Language Federal
        Relay (TTY) . . . . (866) 377–8642
    Spanish-Language Federal
        Relay (TTY) . . . . (800) 845–6136

Information and Publications

KEY OFFICES

FNS Communications and Governmental Affairs

3101 Park Center Dr., #926
Alexandria, VA 22302
(703) 305–2281
Bruce Alexander, director

Issues news releases and publications, including a quarterly newsletter, *Commodity Foods,* which is directed toward school system food service directors (available on the website or call (703) 305–2662, the Food Distribution Division, for further information). News releases, reports, and publications are also available on the website. Refers questions on specific FNS programs to the appropriate office.

Freedom of Information

FNS Information Technology Division
3101 Park Center Dr., #302
Alexandria, VA 22302
(703) 605–0773
Email: foia@fns.usda.gov
Jennifer Weatherly, FOIA officer

DATA AND STATISTICS

News Branch
FNS Governmental Affairs and Public Information
3101 Park Center Dr., #926
Alexandria, VA 22302
(703) 305–2011

Provides information on how to obtain copies of reports and databases.

Data and statistics available to the public in FNS's *Food Program Update* include:

- Monthly report of food stamp participation and coupon issuance.
- Participation in school nutrition programs.
- Participation in special nutrition programs.
- Receipt and distribution of donated commodities by state agencies.

Statistics on the programs provided by the FNS also are available on the website.

PUBLICATIONS

Publishing and Audiovisual Branch FNS
Governmental Affairs and Public Information
3101 Park Center Dr., #928
Alexandria, VA 22302
(703) 305–2290
Christopher Kocsis, team leader

Edits, coordinates, designs, and prints FNS publications, most of which are about the food and nutrition programs the agency administers. Publications are also available on the website.

Reference Resources

LIBRARY

National Agricultural Library

10301 Baltimore Ave.
Beltsville, MD 20705–2351
(301) 504–5755
Stan Kosecki, director
Hours: 8:30 a.m. to 4:30 p.m.

The National Agricultural Library also maintains a reference center at the Agriculture Department's South Building. The collection consists primarily of reference volumes, databases, and other computer resources.

D.C. Reference Center

1400 Independence Ave. S.W.
South Bldg., #1052-S
Washington, DC 20250–0201
(301) 504–5077
Rebecca Mazur, coordinator of research services

DOCKETS

Regulatory Affairs Unit
Communications and Governmental Affairs
Food and Nutrition Service, USDA
3101 Park Center Dr.
Alexandria, VA 22302
(703) 305–2572
Jim Herbert, regulatory officer

Maintains dockets, containing all materials pertaining to FNS rulemakings and other regulatory proceedings, for public inspection. Federal dockets are also available at www.regulations.gov. (*See appendix for Searching and Commenting on Regulations: Regulations.gov.*)

RULES AND REGULATIONS

FNS (formerly FCS) rules and regulations are published in the *Code of Federal Regulations,* Title 7, Chapter II, Parts 210–299. Proposed rules, new final rules, and updates to the *Code of Federal Regulations* are published in the daily *Federal Register.* (*See appendix for information on how to obtain and use these publications.*) The *Federal Register* and the *Code of Federal Regulations* may be accessed online at www.gpoaccess.gov/fr/index.html; the site contains a link to the federal government's regulatory website at www .regulations.gov (*see appendix*).

▓ LEGISLATION

The FNS carries out its responsibilities under:

National School Lunch Act (60 Stat. 230, 42 U.S.C. 1751). Signed by the president June 4, 1946. Set standards for school lunch programs and established eligibility requirements for children and institutions participating in the program.

Food Stamp Act of 1964 (78 Stat. 703, 7 U.S.C. 2011). Signed by the president Aug. 31, 1964. Set eligibility requirements for food stamp program participants, including recipients, vendors, food stores, and states.

Child Nutrition Act of 1966 (80 Stat. 885, 42 U.S.C. 1771). Signed by the president Oct. 11, 1966. Authorized the regulation of school breakfast programs, established requirements for supplemental food programs, and provided for nutrition education and training programs for students and food service personnel.

Food Stamp Act of 1977 (91 Stat. 951, 7 U.S.C. 2011). Signed by the president Sept. 29, 1977. Tightened eligibility requirements for food stamps and allowed their free distribution.

Emergency Jobs Appropriations Act of 1983, Title II (97 Stat. 13, 7 U.S.C. 612c note). Signed by the president March 24, 1983. Authorized the FCS (now the FNS) to distribute the Commodity Credit Corporation's excess food supplies.

National Nutrition Monitoring and Related Research Act of 1990 (104 Stat. 1034, 7 U.S.C. 5301 note). Signed by the president Oct. 22, 1990. Directed the secretaries of agriculture and health and human services to develop a national nutrition-monitoring plan. Established an advisory council to publish dietary guidelines and coordinate nutritional advice issued by federal agencies.

Food, Agriculture, Conservation, and Trade Act of 1990 (104 Stat. 3359, 7 U.S.C. 1421 note). Signed by the president Nov. 28, 1990. Reauthorized the food stamp program for five years. Established new standards for the calculation of income in determining food stamp eligibility. Authorized online electronic benefit transfer systems as a replacement for food stamp coupons. Strengthened reporting requirements and imposed fines for fraud and misuse of food stamps by retail and wholesale food operations.

WIC Farmers' Market Nutrition Act of 1992 (106 Stat. 280, 42 U.S.C. 1771 note). Signed by the president July 2, 1992. Established a program to promote the use of fresh fruits and vegetables in the WIC program.

Child Nutrition Amendments of 1992 (106 Stat. 911, 42 U.S.C. 1751 note). Signed by the president Aug. 5, 1992. Authorized the FCS (now the FNS) to reimburse homeless shelters that provide meals to children under the age of six.

Mickey Leland Childhood Hunger Relief Act (107 Stat. 672, 7 U.S.C. 2011 note). Signed by the president Aug. 10, 1993. Expanded the food stamp program. Restructured benefit eligibility requirements to allow increased deductions for housing costs and removed reporting requirement on income earned by family members in high school.

Good Samaritan Food Donation Act (104 Stat. 3183, 42 U.S.C. 1791a). Signed by the president Oct. 1, 1996. Encouraged the donation of food and grocery products to nonprofit organizations such as homeless shelters, soup kitchens, and churches for distribution to needy individuals. Promoted food recovery by limiting the liability of donors to instances of gross negligence or intentional misconduct. Also established basic nationwide uniform definitions pertaining to donation and distribution of nutritious foods and helps ensure that donated foods meet all quality and labeling standards of federal, state, and local laws and regulations.

Farm Security and Rural Investment Act of 2002 (116 Stat. 1348, 7 U.S.C. 7901 note). Signed by the president May 13, 2002. Title IV simplified various food stamp eligibility requirements, including restoring eligibility to qualified aliens who were receiving disability benefits, regardless of date of entry. Authorized the president to provide U.S. agricultural commodities and financial and technical assistance for educational school food programs in foreign countries and for nutrition programs for pregnant women, nursing mothers, and infants and children.

Child Nutrition and WIC Reauthorization Act of 2004 (118 Stat. 729, 42 U.S.C. 1751 note). Signed by the president June 30, 2004. Amended the Child Nutrition Act of 1966 to provide children with increased access to food and nutrition assistance, to simplify program operations and improve program management, and to reauthorize child nutrition programs.

Food, Conservation, and Energy Act of 2008 (Farm Bill) (7 U.S.C. 8701 note). Vetoed by the president May 21, 2008; veto overridden June 18, 2008. Reauthorized Department of Agriculture programs through fiscal year 2012. Expanded eligibility for food stamps and renamed the supplemental nutrition assistance program; increased benefits; and made additional adjustments for inflation. Increased funding for Emergency Food Assistance Program, Fresh Fruit and Vegetable Program, and Senior Farmers' Market Nutrition Program. Created initiatives for community food security, promoting locally produced foods, and healthy eating patterns, including curbing obesity. Renamed the Food Stamp Act of 1977 as the Food and Nutrition Act of 2008, effective Oct. 1, 2008.

American Recovery and Reinvestment Act (123 Stat. 115, 26 U.S.C. 1 note). Signed by the president Feb. 13, 2009. Provided additional appropriations for supplemental nutrition programs administered by FNS. Amended eligibility requirements for jobless workers for supplemental nutrition assistance program (SNAP) benefits. Mandated that SNAP benefits of jobless workers without dependents were not to be limited under the Food and Nutrition Act of 2008 unless an individual did not comply with specified state work program provisions through Sept. 30, 2010. Beginning Oct. 1, 2010, with respect to such work-related provisions, a state agency could disregard any period during which an individual received supplemental nutrition assistance program benefits prior to Oct. 1, 2010.

Healthy, Hunger-Free Kids Act of 2010 (124 Stat. 3183, 42 U.S.C. 1751 note). Signed by the president Dec. 13, 2010. Reauthorized the Child Nutrition and WIC programs. Required USDA to promulgate regulations to raise nutritional standards of school lunch and breakfast meals. Requires USDA to establish regulations for local wellness policies and to provide technical assistance to states/schools in consultation with the Education Department and the Centers for Disease Control. Provides performance bonus in no more than fifteen states for "outstanding performance" and "substantial improvement" in direct certification. Establishes requirements regarding the nonfederal contribution required of school food authorities receiving federal reimbursement through the school lunch program. Sets forth the formula for setting the average price paid for school meals.

Agricultural Act of 2014 (128 Stat. 782, 7 U.S.C. 2012-2018). Signed by the president Feb. 7, 2014. Makes many changes to SNAP retailer qualifications and administration of SNAP own Electronic Benefit Transfer (EBT). Requires states to establish an immigration verification system to verify immigration status. Makes several changes to the SNAP Employment and Training Program and disqualifies some convicted felons from participating in SNAP. Requires FNS to carry out pilot projects to identify, investigate, and reduce retailer fraud in SNAP. Requires states to phase out the participation of women, infants, and children in the Commodity Supplemental Food Program.

▦ REGIONAL OFFICES

MID-ATLANTIC REGION
(DC, DE, MD, NJ, PA, PR, VA, VI, WV)
Mercer Corporate Park
300 Corporate Blvd.
Robbinsville, NJ 08691–1518
(609) 259–5025
Patricia N. Dombroski, regional administrator

MIDWEST REGION
(IL, IN, MI, MN, OH, WI)
77 W. Jackson Blvd., 20th Floor
Chicago, IL 60604–3507
(312) 353–6664
Timothy English, regional administrator

MOUNTAIN PLAINS REGION
(CO, IA, KS, MO, MT, ND, NE, SD, UT, WY)
1244 Speer Blvd., #903
Denver, CO 80204–3581
(303) 844–0300
Darlene L. Barnes, regional administrator

NORTHEAST REGION
(CT, MA, ME, NH, NY, RI, VT)
10 Causeway St., #501
Boston, MA 02222–1069
(617) 565–6370
Kurt Messner (acting), regional administrator

SOUTHEAST REGION
(AL, FL, GA, KY, MS, NC, SC, TN)
61 Forsyth St. S.W., #8T36
Atlanta, GA 30303–3427
(404) 562–1801
Robin Bailey, regional administrator

SOUTHWEST REGION
(AR, LA, NM, OK, TX)
1100 Commerce St., #555
Dallas, TX 75242–9800
(214) 290–9800
William Ludwig, regional administrator

WESTERN REGION
(AK, AS, AZ, CA, GU, HI, ID, MP, NV, OR, WA)
90 7th St., #10–100
San Francisco, CA 94103
(415) 705–1310
Jesus Mendoza, regional administrator

Food Safety and Inspection Service

1400 Independence Ave. S.W., #331E, Washington, DC 20250
Internet: www.fsis.usda.gov

The Food Safety and Inspection Service (FSIS) is an agency within the U.S. Department of Agriculture (USDA) under the jurisdiction of the under secretary for food safety. The FSIS is headed by an administrator appointed by the secretary of agriculture.

The FSIS regulates the meat, poultry, and egg products industries by inspecting all meat, poultry, and egg products plants that ship goods in interstate and foreign commerce. The service also administers laws that ensure these products are accurately labeled.

Slaughtering and processing plants must receive FSIS approval of facilities, equipment, and procedures before they may operate. The FSIS sets food standards for all products containing more than 3 percent fresh meat or at least 2 percent cooked poultry meat. The Food and Drug Administration (FDA) oversees the labeling of most other food products. Food standards set requirements on the kinds and amounts of ingredients used in the manufacture of processed foods and assure the consumer that a product sold under a particular name has certain characteristics.

The service cooperates with other USDA agencies, such as the Agricultural Marketing Service (*p. 476*) and the Animal and Plant Health Inspection Service (*p. 481*), and with other federal agencies with food safety responsibilities, such as the FDA (*p. 265*) and the Environmental Protection Agency (*p. 67*). FSIS entered into a Memorandum of Agreement with the Public Health Service (PHS) in the Department of Health and Human Services, under which PHS-commissioned corps officers can be assigned to scientific positions at FSIS. Flexible deployment rules allow the officers to assist FSIS staff in instantly responding to emergencies, such as a food-borne illness outbreak, and shifting priorities within the agency. These additional officers also enhance FSIS capabilities for rapid response during heightened security alerts or an actual threat to food security.

The Office of the Administrator oversees FSIS's major divisions:

Office of Data Integration and Food Protection. Manages all homeland security activities within FSIS. Prepares, prevents, and coordinates a response to intentional or suspected deliberate acts and major events threatening the U.S. food supply. Ensures that policymakers, scientists, field staff, and management are prepared to prevent and respond to any food security threat.

Office of Program Investigation, Enforcement, and Audit (OIEA). Responsible for the surveillance and investigation of regulated and in-commerce meat, poultry and processed egg products facilities; investigation of food-borne illness outbreaks; response to natural disaster and intentional contamination events. OIEA enforces FSIS criminal, civil, and administrative sanctions and verifies that meat, poultry, and egg products imported into the United States are produced under equivalent standards.

Office of Public Affairs and Consumer Education. Provides information to varied groups, including Congress, the media, and the public. Educates consumers about the importance of safe food handling. Manages educational programs including the USDA Food Safety Mobile.

Office of Public Health Science. Provides expert scientific analysis, advice, data, and recommendations on all matters involving public health and science of concern to FSIS. Designs, develops, and oversees passive and active surveillance systems to collect data and information regarding food-borne illness and pathogens and analyzes such information to assess the use and efficacy of prevention measures in the human population. Provides microbiological, chemical, and toxicological expertise, leadership, quality assurance, and control for the agency. Operates field service laboratories. In 2005 the office established the Food Emergency Response Network (FERN), an integrated network of laboratories across the United States to respond quickly to food-related emergencies.

Office of Management. Provides administrative services in the areas of budget and finance, personnel management, administrative services, employee and organizational development, automated information systems, labor management relations, civil rights, planning, and internal controls to meet the needs of the agency.

Office of Field Operations. Manages a program of regulatory oversight and inspection pursuant to meat, poultry, and egg products laws to ensure that covered products are safe, wholesome, and properly labeled. Plans and coordinates FSIS cooperative activities to assist states in administering meat, poultry, and egg products inspection. Coordinates all trace back and investigation recall activities whenever meat, poultry, and egg products are associated with food-borne illness outbreaks.

This office includes the Recall Division, which monitors recalls of meat and poultry products produced by federally inspected establishments, and the Office of Catfish Inspection Programs.

Office of Policy and Program Development. Develops domestic FSIS policies and inspection methods and administers programs to protect consumers from misbranded and economically adulterated meat, poultry, and egg products. Provides leadership for the analysis and development of all FSIS regulations, ensuring compliance with relevant legal requirements, program needs, and policy priorities. Also responsible for international policy development.

■ KEY PERSONNEL

Administrator
Alfred V. Almanza................ (202) 720–7025
Fax........................... (202) 205–0158
Chief of Staff
Carmen Rottenberg .... (202) 720–6618
Chief Financial Officer
Steven Fischer .... (202) 720–8700
Chief Information Officer
Janet Stevens .... (202) 205–9950
U.S. Codex Programs
Mary Frances Lowe............. (202) 205–7760
Data Integration and Food Protection
Terry Nintenmann .... (202) 690–6486
Fax........................... (202) 690–5634
Emergency Response Coordination
Mary Cutshall .... (202) 690–6523
Field Operations
William C. (Bill) Smith............. (202) 720–8803
Fax........................... (202) 720–5439
Recall Management and Technical Analysis
Regina Tan.................... (202) 690–1975
Regulatory Operations
Hany Sidrak................... (202) 720–3697
Fax........................... (202) 690–3287
Resource Management and Financial Planning
Robert Cooke.................. (202) 418–8928
Strategic Planning and Operations Management
Quita Bowman Blackwell........ (202) 720–8803
Management
Jacqueline Myers.................. (202) 720–4425
Administrative Services
Gabriel Jones .... (301) 504–3990
Human Resources
Sandra Burrell .... (202) 205–0699
Outreach, Employee Education, and Training
Michael Watts .... (202) 205–0194
Policy and Program Development
Daniel L. Englejohn .... (202) 205–0495
Fax........................... (202) 720–2025
Import/Export Coordination and Policy Development
Rita Kishore (acting) .... (202) 720–0082
International Coordination
Jane H. Doherty................ (202) 708–9543
Fax........................... (202) 690–3856

International Equivalence
Andreas Keller................. (202) 720–0082
International Relations and Strategic Planning
Mary Stanley .... (202) 690–4354
Labeling and Program Delivery
Rosalyn Murphy-Jenkins........ (301) 504–0879
Policy Analysis
Todd Furey.................... (301) 504–3374
Policy Development
Scott Seebohm (Omaha, NE) .... (402) 344–5000
Toll-free .... (800) 233–3935
Fax....................... (402) 344–5005
Policy Issuances
Charles Williams............... (202) 720–5627
Risk, Innovation, and Management
William Shaw.................. (301) 504–0889
Program Investigation, Enforcement, and Audit
Carl Mayes (acting)............... (202) 720–8609
Compliance and Investigations
Jerry Elliott.................... (202) 720–3781
Enforcement and Litigation
Scott Safian................... (202) 418–8872
Hearing and Appeals
Valerie Neris-Blankenship....... (202) 418–8846
International Audit
Shaukat Syed .... (202) 690–0997
Public Affairs and Consumer Education
Carole Blake................... (202) 720–3884
Fax....................... (202) 690–0550
Civil Rights
Angela Kelly................... (301) 504–7755
Congressional and Public Affairs
Alan Lang.................... (202) 720–9113
Food Safety Education
Maria Malagon .... (202) 720–9891
Fax....................... (202) 720–5704
Public Health Science
David P. Goldman................ (202) 720–2644
Fax....................... (202) 690–2980
USDA Chief Medical Officer
David P. Goldman (acting) ...... (202) 720–2644
Applied Epidemiology
Karen Becker .... (202) 690–6045
Resources and Program Management
Sherri Johnson................. (202) 690–6623
Risk Assessment and Analytics
Michelle Caitlin................ (202) 690–2680

■ INFORMATION SOURCES

Internet
Agency website: www.fsis.usda.gov. Links to various FSIS programs are available. Publications and the latest news are also maintained at the site.

Telephone Contacts
Personnel Locator (USDA)..........(202) 720–8732
Meat and Poultry Hotline......... (888) MPHotline
or ....(888) 674–6854

USDA English-Language Federal
Relay (TTY) . . . .(866) 377–8642
USDA Spanish-Language Federal
Relay (TTY) . . . .(800) 845–6136

Information and Publications

KEY OFFICES

Congressional and Public Affairs Staff
1400 Independence Ave. S.W.
South Bldg., #1175
Washington, DC 20250–3700
(202) 720–9113
Fax (202) 720–5704
Alan Lang, director

Answers general questions about inspection, food safety, and labeling, and refers technical queries to the appropriate office within the agency. Issues news releases and consumer publications on FSIS actions. Issues publications and other informational materials for consumers.

Freedom of Information
14th and Independence Ave. S.W.
South Bldg., #1142
Washington, DC 20250–3700
(202) 690–2760
Fax (202) 690–3023
E-mail: fsis.foia@usda.gov
Arianne Perkins (acting), FOIA director

DATA AND STATISTICS
For types of data and statistics available from the FSIS, contact the Food Safety Education Staff: (301) 344–4755.

PUBLICATIONS

FSIS Food Safety Education Staff
5601 Sunnyside Ave.
Mail Drop 5268
Beltsville, MD 20705
(202) 720–9891
Fax (202) 720–5704
Maria Malagon, director

Issues publications and other informational materials about FSIS programs and the safe handling of meat, poultry, and egg products. Publications are also available at the FSIS website.

Reference Resources

LIBRARY

National Agricultural Library
10301 Baltimore Ave.
Beltsville, MD 20705–2351
(301) 504–5755

Stan Kosecki, director
Hours: 8:30 a.m. to 4:30 p.m.

The National Agricultural Library also maintains a reference center at the Agriculture Department's South Building. The collection consists primarily of reference volumes, databases, and other computer resources.

D.C. Reference Center
1400 Independence Ave. S.W.
South Bldg., #1052
Washington, DC 20250–0201
(301) 504–5077
Rebecca Mazur, coordinator of research services

DOCKETS

Public Reading Room
5601 Sunnyside Ave., #2–2127
Beltsville, MD 20705–5000
(301) 504–0857
Fax (202) 205–0381
Suzette Rhodes, hearing clerk
Hours: 8:00 a.m. to 3:30 p.m.

Public dockets containing all public materials related to FSIS rulemaking, standard settings, and other regulatory proceedings may be inspected in this office. An electronic reading room is also available on the FSIS website. Federal dockets are also available at www.regulations.gov. (*See appendix for Searching and Commenting on Regulations: Regulations.gov.*)

RULES AND REGULATIONS
FSIS rules and regulations are published in the *Code of Federal Regulations,* Title 9, Chapter III, Parts 300–599. Proposed rules, standards, and guidelines are published in the daily *Federal Register. (See appendix for information on how to obtain and use these publications.)* The *Federal Register* and the *Code of Federal Regulations* may be accessed online at www.archives.gov/federal-register/cfr; the site contains a link to the federal government's regulatory website at www.regulations.gov (*see appendix*).

For specific handbooks of FSIS regulations, see *Publications* above.

▓ LEGISLATION
The FSIS administers the following statutes:

Poultry Products Inspection Act (71 Stat. 441, 21 U.S.C. 451). Signed by the president Aug. 28, 1957. Provided for regulation of the processing and distribution of poultry and poultry products. This act was amended by the Wholesome Poultry Products Act (82 Stat. 791, 21 U.S.C. 451). Signed by the president Aug. 18, 1968. Authorized the secretary of agriculture to assist state agencies in developing and administering poultry product inspection programs equal to federal inspection programs for poultry products sold as human food only within a particular state.

Talmadge-Aiken Act (76 Stat. 663, 7 U.S.C. 450). Signed by the president Sept. 28, 1962. Provided for coordination between the federal government and the states to regulate agricultural products and to control or eradicate plant and animal diseases and pests.

Wholesome Meat Act (81 Stat. 584, 21 U.S.C. 601). Signed by the president Dec. 15, 1967. Revised the Federal Meat Inspection Act of 1907. Provided for the regulation, by inspection and labeling, of meat and meat products in interstate and foreign commerce. Later amended by the Agriculture and Food Act of 1981, Title XVIII (95 Stat. 1213, 7 U.S.C. 1281 note). Signed by the president Dec. 22, 1981.

Humane Methods of Slaughter Act of 1978 (92 Stat. 1069, 21 U.S.C. 601). Signed by the president Oct. 10, 1978. Set standards for slaughtering livestock and poultry to ensure humane treatment; prohibited importation of meat or meat products unless such livestock were slaughtered in a humane manner.

Food Security Act of 1985 (99 Stat. 1633, 21 U.S.C. 466). Signed by the president Dec. 23, 1985. Title XVII required that imported poultry and meat products be subject to the same inspection, sanitary, quality, species verification, and residue standards applied to products produced in the United States. Any meat or poultry product not meeting U.S. standards was not permitted entry into the United States.

Omnibus Trade and Competitiveness Act of 1988 (102 Stat. 1408, 21 U.S.C. 620). Signed by the president Aug. 23, 1988. Known as the Reciprocal Meat Inspection Requirement, this section required that the agriculture secretary and the U.S. trade representative recommend that the president restrict the importation of meat products from foreign countries that apply standards for the importation of meat articles from the United States that were not based on public health concerns.

NAFTA Implementation Act (107 Stat. 2057, 19 U.S.C. 3301 note). Signed by the president Dec. 8, 1993. Implemented the North American Free Trade Agreement (NAFTA) between the United States, Mexico, and Canada. Required U.S. inspections to recognize "equivalent" sanitary meat and poultry inspection measures of both Canada and Mexico.

Department of Agriculture Reorganization Act of 1994 (108 Stat. 3209, 7 U.S.C. 6901 note). Signed by the president Oct. 13, 1994. Created the new position of under secretary for food safety.

Federal Agricultural Improvement and Reform Act of 1996 (110 Stat. 888, 7 U.S.C. 7201 note). Signed by the president April 4, 1996. Established the Safe Meat and Poultry Inspection Panel. However, funding for the panel was not included in the 1999 appropriations bill.

Farm Security and Rural Investment Act of 2002 (116 Stat. 1348, 7 U.S.C. 7901 note). Signed by the president May 13, 2002. Amended the Agricultural Marketing Act of 1946 to require a retailer of a covered commodity (beef, lamb, pork, wild or farm-raised fish, perishable agricultural commodities, or peanuts—but not processed beef, lamb, and pork items or frozen entrees containing beef, lamb, and pork) to inform consumers at the final point of sale of a commodity's country of origin.

Agricultural Bioterrorism Protection Act of 2002 (116 Stat. 647, 7 U.S.C. 8401). Signed by the president June 12, 2002. Sought to improve the ability of the United States to prevent, prepare for, and respond to bioterrorism and other public health emergencies. Expanded the capacity of the FSIS to conduct food safety inspections.

Food, Conservation, and Energy Act of 2008 (Farm Bill) (7 U.S.C. 8701 note). Vetoed by the president May 21, 2008; veto overridden June 18, 2008. Reauthorized Department of Agriculture programs through fiscal year 2012. Amended the Federal Meat Inspection Act (FMIA) and Poultry Products Inspection Act (PPIA) to create an option for state-inspected plants with twenty-five employees or less to ship in interstate commerce (but did not replace existing state inspection programs). Amended the FMIA to require the examination and inspection of catfish when processed for human food.

■ REGIONAL OFFICES

Food Safety and Inspection Service

POLICY DEVELOPMENT DIVISION

(formerly Technical Service Center)
Edward Zorinsky Federal Bldg.
1616 Capitol Ave., #620
Omaha, NE 68102–5908
(402) 344–5000
(800) 233–3935
Fax (402) 344–5005
Scott Seebohm (acting), director

DISTRICT 5

(AZ, CA, NV)
620 Central Ave., Bldg. 2C
Alameda, CA 94501–3222
(510) 337–5000, ext. 1
Fax (510) 337–5081
Emergency 24-Hour: (866) 729–9307
Yudhbir Sharma, district manager

DISTRICT 15

(AK, AS, AZ, CO, GU, HI, ID, MP, MT, NE, OR, UT, WA, WY)
1 Denver Federal Center
P.O. Box 25387, Bldg. 45
Denver, CO 80225
(303) 236–9800
Emergency 24-Hour: (303) 236–9800
Fax (303) 236–9794
Anna Gallegos, district manager

DISTRICT 25

(IA, ND, SD, WI)
Neil Smith Federal Bldg.
210 Walnut St., #985
Des Moines, IA 50309–2123
(515) 727–8960; (800) 990–9834
Emergency 24-Hour: (515) 343–4499; (402) 681–1556

Fax (515) 727–8992
Dawn Sprouls, district manager

DISTRICT 35

(AR, KS, MO)
Country Club Center, Bldg. B, #201
4700 S. Thompson
Springdale, AR 72764
(479) 751–8412
Emergency 24-Hour: (479) 751–8412
Fax (479) 751–9049
Paul Kiecker, district manager

DISTRICT 40

(LA, NM, OK, TX)
110 Commerce St., #516
Dallas, TX 75242-0598
(214) 767–9116
Emergency 24-Hour: (214) 767–9116, ext.
    250 Fax (214) 767–8230
Jennifer Beasley-McKean, district manager

DISTRICT 50

(IL, IN, MI, OH)
1919 S. Highland Ave., #115C
Lombard, IL 60148
(630) 620–7474
Emergency 24-Hour: (630) 544–9866;
    (630) 544–9805
Fax (630) 620–7599
Paul Wolseley, district manager

DISTRICT 60

(CT, MA, ME, NH, NY, PA, RI, VT)
USDA
Mellon Independence Center
701 Market St., #4100-A
Philadelphia, PA 19106
(215) 597–4219
Emergency 24-Hour: (800) 637–6681, ext. 6
Fax (215) 597–4217
Susan Scarcia, district manager

DISTRICT 80

(DC, DE, MD, NC, NJ, VA, WV)
6020 Six Forks Rd.
Raleigh, NC 27609
(919) 844–8400
Emergency 24-Hour: (919) 844–8400; (800) 662–7608
Fax (919) 844–8411
Steve Lalicker, district manager

DISTRICT 85

(FL, GA, PR, SC, VI)
100 Alabama St. S.W., Bldg. 1924, #3R90
Atlanta, GA 30303
(404) 562–5900
Emergency 24-Hour: (800) 282–7005
Fax (404) 562–5877
Phyllis Adams, district manager

DISTRICT 90

(AL, KY, MS, TN)
713 S. Pear Orchard Rd., #402
Ridgeland, MS 39157
(601) 965–4312
Emergency 24-Hour: (800) 647–2484
Fax (601) 965–5901
Paul Resweber, director

Regional Compliance and Investigations Division

NORTHEAST REGION

(CT, IN, MA, ME, MI, NH, NJ, NY, OH,
    PA, RI, VT, WI)
Mellon Independence Center
701 Market St., #4100C
Philadelphia, PA 19106
(215) 430–6222
Fax (215) 597–9099
James Borda, regional director

SOUTHEAST REGION

(AL, AR, DC, DE, FL, GA, KY, LA, MD, MS, NC, PR,
    SC, TN, VA, VI, WV)
100 Alabama St. S.W.
1924 Bldg., #3R95
Atlanta, GA 30303-3104
(404) 562–5962
Emergency: (215) 292–7696
Fax (404) 562–5935
Larry Hortert, regional director

SOUTHWEST REGION

(IA, IL, KS, MN, MO, NE, OK, SD, TX)
1100 Commerce St., #557
Dallas, TX 75242
(214) 767–9101
Emergency: (972) 632–7987
Fax (214) 767–3094
Luis Zamora, regional director

WESTERN REGION

(AK, AS, AZ, CA, CO, GU, HI, ID, MP, MT, ND, NM,
    NV, OR, UT, WA, WY)
620 Central Ave., Bldg. 2B
Alameda, CA 94501
(510) 769–5733
Emergency: (510) 207–3346
Fax (510) 337–5080
Alison Khroustalev, regional director

Northeast Import Field Office— Philadelphia

(CT, DE, MA, MD, ME, NJ, New York City, PA, RI,
    VA, WV)
Mellon Independence Center
701 Market St., #1400 B
Philadelphia, PA 19106

(215) 430–6215
Fax (215) 597–4219
Wendy Calkins, regional import field supervisor

Northern Import Field Office—Detroit

(IA, ID, IL, IN, MI, MN, MO, ND, NE, NH, NY
(along Canadian border), OH, SD, WI)
Crowne Pointe Bldg.
29500 Greenfield Rd., #203
Oak Park, MI 48237
(248) 967–2055
Fax (248) 967–2148
Deborah Curtis, regional import field supervisor

Northwestern Import Field Office—Los Angeles

(AK, northern CA, CO, GU, ID, MP, MT, NV, OR,
Trust Territories of the Pacific, UT, WA, WY)
Gateway Corporate Center
21660 Copley Dr., #175
Diamond Bar, CA 91765
(909) 396–9518, ext. 31

Fax (909) 396–9520
Carolyn Pearson, regional import field supervisor

Southern Import Field Office—Miami

(AL, AR, FL, GA, KS, LA, MS, NC, NM, OK, PR, SC,
TN, TX, VI)
7771 West Oakland Park Blvd., #142
Sunrise, FL 33351
(954) 578–1398
Fax (954) 578–1536
Angel Cruzafanador, regional import field
supervisor

Western Import Field Office—Los Angeles

(AS, AZ, southern CA, HI, NM, NV, El
Paso area of TX)
Gateway Corporate Center
21660 Copley Dr., #175
Diamond Bar, CA 91765
(909) 396–9518
Fax (909) 396–9520
Megan Potts, regional import field supervisor

Foreign Agricultural Service

1400 Independence Ave. S.W., MS 1001
Washington, DC 20250–1001
Internet: www.fas.usda.gov

The Foreign Agricultural Service (FAS) was established in 1953 as an agency within the U.S. Department of Agriculture (USDA). It is under the jurisdiction of the under secretary of agriculture for farm and foreign agricultural services. The FAS is primarily an information and promotion agency. The service represents U.S. agricultural interests overseas by gathering information about crop production and supply and demand abroad. It then distributes this data to U.S. producers and exporters. The FAS also provides information about U.S. products and supplies to foreign importers and cooperates with U.S. exporters on projects to establish and expand export markets.

The administrator of the FAS is appointed by the secretary of agriculture and is assisted by three associate administrators and six deputy administrators. The deputy administrators are responsible for commodity and marketing programs, export credits, international trade policy, and scientific affairs.

The main function of the FAS is to gather information about foreign agriculture to assist U.S. exporters of commodities. The FAS receives reports from agricultural attachés and officers in more than ninety locations around the world. Trade information sent to Washington from FAS personnel overseas is used to map strategies for improving market access, pursuing U.S. rights under trade agreements, and developing programs and policies to make U.S. farm products more competitive. The FAS publishes nearly 200 commodity reports annually that present a world picture of production, consumption, and trade flows for about 100 crop and livestock commodities. These reports analyze changes in international trading conditions and indicate market opportunities for U.S. exporters (*see Data and Statistics; Publications, p. 506*).

In addition, the agency collects information on export sales from private exporters of agricultural commodities; this material is compiled in weekly reports. To aid in the promotion of U.S. agricultural products abroad, the FAS operates several programs designed to stimulate contacts between domestic producers and foreign markets.

The largest FAS promotional programs are the Foreign Market Development Program, also known as the Cooperator Program, and the Market Access Program. FAS provides assistance to exporters through practical marketing information and services to help them locate buyers. Additionally, FAS supports U.S. participation in several major trade shows and a number of single-industry exhibitions each year, frequently coordinating these activities with states and industry representatives.

FAS cooperates with other USDA agencies, U.S. universities, and other organizations to promote U.S. agriculture's global competitiveness. FAS also coordinates USDA's international training and technical assistance programs and serves as the department's liaison with international food and agriculture organizations.

FAS coordinates and directs USDA's responsibilities in international trade negotiations, working closely with the U.S. Trade Representative's office in this effort. During international negotiations, FAS staff represents U.S. agricultural interests. This representation extends to bilateral and regional trade arrangements, as well as the World Trade Organization (WTO), successor to the General Agreement on Tariffs and Trade. The FAS also has a permanent representative at the WTO.

USDA FAS shares administration of U.S. international food aid programs with the U.S. Agency for International Development to help people in need around the world. The 2014 Farm Bill reauthorized through fiscal year 2018 four major international food aid programs: Food for Peace Act (P.L. 480); the Food for Progress Act of 1985; the McGovern-Dole International Food for Education and Child Nutrition Program; and the Local and Regional Procurement (LRP) Pilot Program. The legislation also reauthorized the Bill Emerson Humanitarian Trust (BEHT), which provides funding for emergency humanitarian food assistance to developing countries. Section 416(b) programs, authorized by the Agricultural Act of 1949, provide for donations of surplus Commodity Credit Corporation (CCC) commodities abroad. The Section 416(b) program, while permanently authorized, is currently inactive because of the lack of CCC surplus stock for international aid.

FAS administers the Commodity Credit Corporation Export Credit Sales Guarantee Program, designed to facilitate the export of U.S. agricultural commodities (other CCC activities are administered by the Farm Service Agency, *p. 487*). FAS also is responsible for all USDA export credit and market development programs and acts as principal foreign sales spokesperson for the department.

The Farm Security and Rural Investment Act of 2002 amended provisions of the 1996 Farm Bill and made adjustments to FAS's export credit guarantee programs, market development programs, the Export Enhancement Program, food aid and development programs, technical barriers to trade, and trade-related programs in other titles. The act also required an update to the long-term agricultural trade strategy.

The Food, Conservation, and Energy Act of 2008 (Farm Bill) reauthorized the 2002 farm bill programs, including Technical Assistance for Specialty Crops Program (TASC). The TASC program helps open, retain, and expand markets for U.S. specialty crops. Resources are provided to address barriers, including phytosanitary or related technical restrictions that prohibit or threaten the export of U.S. specialty crops. Specialty crops include all cultivated plants and their products produced in the United States except wheat, feed grains, oilseeds, cotton, rice, peanuts, sugar, and tobacco.

The 2014 Farm Bill required the FAS to promulgate regulations for the Pima Agriculture Cotton Trust and the Wool Apparel Manufacturers Trust for calendar years 2014–2018. Trust payments are designed to counter economic harm resulting from tariffs on the commodities being higher than tariffs on certain imported apparel made using cotton and wool. The Pima Agriculture Cotton Trust provides one annual payment disbursed by formula to trade associations, yarn spinners, and apparel manufacturers. The Wool Apparel Manufacturers Trust is a mechanism for four types of annual payments to manufacturers of certain worsted wool fabrics.

▓ KEY PERSONNEL

Administrator
  Phil Karsting . . . . (202) 720–3935
Associate Administrator
  Janet Nuzum . . . . (202) 720–3935
Administrative Operations
  Brock Howard . . . . (202) 720–0590
Agreements and Scientific Affairs
  Bob Macke (acting). . . . . (202) 720–3798
  Animal Division
    Casey Bean. (202) 720–1353
  International Regulations and Standards
    Cathy McKinnell. . . . . (202) 690–0929
  New Technologies and Production Methods
    Ed Porter . . . . (202) 720–6369
  Plant Division
    Dennis Voboril . . . . (202) 720–5100
  Processed Products and Technical Regulations
    Marianne McElroy . . . . (202) 720–0689
Budget
  Thomas Bellamy . . . . (202) 690–4052
Capacity Building and Development
  Jocelyn Brown . . . . (202) 720–6887
Civil Rights
  Daniel B. Whitley . . . . (202) 720–7061

Country and Regional Affairs
  Bonnie Borris. (202) 720–0997
  Western Hemisphere
    Lisa Anderson . . . . (202) 720–3223
  Europe
    Robert Hanson . . . . (202) 690–4057
  Africa/Middle East
    Frederick Giles . . . . (202) 690–4066
  North Asia
    Deanna Ayala. . . . . (202) 720–3080
  South Asia
    Susan Phillips. . . . . (202) 690–4053
Development Resources and Disaster Assistance
  Scott Lewis . . . . (202) 690–1927
Food Assistance (including LRP)
  Ron Croushorn . . . . (202) 720–3038
Foreign Service Operations
  James Higgiston. . . . . (202) 720–7562
General Sales Manager
  Asif Chaundhry. . . . . (202) 720–3935
Global Analysis
  Daniel Whitley. . . . . (202) 720–6301
Grants Programs
  Lona Powell . . . . (202) 720–8557
Legislative Affairs
  Chris Church . . . . (202) 720–6830
Monitoring and Evaluation
  Mary Ponomarenko . . . . (202) 720–4453
Policy Coordination and Planning
  Howard Anderson. . . . . (202) 720–4056
Public Affairs and Executive Correspondence
  Sally Klusaritz . . . . (202) 690–4064
Trade and Scientific Capacity Building
  Larry Trouba . . . . (202) 720–5337
Trade Programs
  Christian Foster. . . . . (202) 720–9516

▓ INFORMATION SOURCES

Internet

Agency website: www.fas.usda.gov. Comprehensive website includes information on FAS and on international agricultural trade.

Telephone Contacts

Personnel Locator (USDA). . . . .(202) 720–8732
USDA English-Language Federal
  Relay (TTY) . . . .(866) 377–8642
USDA Spanish-Language Federal
  Relay (TTY) . . . .(800) 845–6136

Information and Publications

KEY OFFICES

FAS Public Affairs Division
  1400 Independence Ave. S.W.
  MS 1004
  Washington, DC 20250–1004

(202) 720–3224

Fax (202) 720–1727

E-mail: sally.klusaritz@fas.usda.gov

Sally Klusaritz, director

Issues news releases and other items of interest to the public and the news media. News releases, information about FAS programs, and publications are also available on the website.

Freedom of Information

1400 Independence Ave. S.W.

MS 1004

Washington, DC 20250–1004

(202) 720–2936

Fax (202) 720–1727

Rochelle Foster, FOIA officer

DATA AND STATISTICS

The FAS collects and distributes information about foreign crop production and the demand for U.S. agricultural products abroad. Topics include trade, consumption of commodities, weather, and political and economic developments that affect U.S. agriculture. FAS also offers several databases, including PS&Donline, supplying data on international agricultural trade. Market data is available online at www.fas.usda.gov/data.

PUBLICATIONS

FAS publications, including reports, fact sheets, special feature reports, and circulars, are available online at www.fas.usda.gov. Subscription fulfillment and distribution is handled on the website and by the National Technical Information Service (NTIS) (*see appendix, Ordering Government Publications*).

PS&Donline. This database tracks production, supply, and distribution reports containing import and export data, statistics on foreign agricultural trade, world market and commodity analysis reports, and fact sheets on commodities.

Foreign Agriculture Circulars. Published periodically on various commodities and trade topics.

U.S. Export Sales. A weekly report that summarizes sales and exports of selected U.S. agricultural commodities by country, based on reports from private exporters.

Fact sheets. An extensive selection of fact sheets on trade issues can be found on the website.

Reference Resources

DOCKETS

FAS has limited regulatory authority; consequently there is no central place where FAS rulemaking dockets are kept. If a regulation applies to a particular commodity or function of the FAS, contact the office responsible for the commodity or function. Federal dockets are also available at www.regulations.gov. (*See appendix for Searching and Commenting on Regulations: Regulations.gov.*)

RULES AND REGULATIONS

FAS rules and regulations are published in the *Code of Federal Regulations*, Title 7, Chapter XV, Parts 1500–1599.

Proposed rules, new final rules, and updates to the *Code of Federal Regulations* are published in the daily *Federal Register. (See appendix for information on how to obtain and use these publications.)* The *Federal Register* and the *Code of Federal Regulations* may be accessed online at www.archives.gov/federal-register/cfr; the site contains a link to the federal government's regulatory website at www.regulations.gov (*see appendix*).

▪ LEGISLATION

The FAS carries out its responsibilities under the following legislation:

Agricultural Adjustment Act of 1933 (48 Stat. 31, 7 U.S.C. 601). Signed by the president May 12, 1933. Authorized the FAS to administer import quotas for several commodities whenever the president determines that imports pose a threat to the well-being of U.S. farmers.

Agricultural Trade Development and Assistance Act of 1954 (68 Stat. 454, 7 U.S.C. 1427). Signed by the president July 10, 1954. Granted authority to the general sales manager, authorized the sale and export of agricultural commodities for relief abroad, and authorized the trading of excess commodities for long-term credit with foreign governments.

Agriculture and Consumer Protection Act of 1973 (87 Stat. 221, 7 U.S.C. 1281 note). Signed by the president Aug. 10, 1973. Authorized the FAS to monitor the export sales contracts of certain designated commodities.

Meat Import Act of 1979 (93 Stat. 1291, 19 U.S.C. 1202 note). Signed by the president Dec. 31, 1979. Authorized the FAS to administer import quotas on beef. Under a "countercyclical" formula, quotas were to be imposed when domestic supplies were plentiful; when supplies declined, more foreign beef would be allowed to enter the country.

Federal Agriculture Improvement and Reform Act of 1996 (110 Stat. 888, 7 U.S.C. 7201 note). Signed by the president April 4, 1996. Capped funding for several agricultural export and market promotion programs. Gave statutory authority to the Foreign Market Development Program, which helps develop overseas markets.

Farm Security and Rural Investment Act of 2002 (116 Stat. 1348, 7 U.S.C. 7901 note). Signed by the president May 13, 2002. All trade programs were reauthorized through 2007. New programs included the McGovern-Dole International Food for Education and Nutrition Program, the Biotechnology and Agricultural Trade Program that addressed nontariff barriers to U.S. exports, a Technical Assistance for Specialty Crops Program, and an online Exporter Assistance Initiative.

Dominican Republic–Central America–United States Free Trade Agreement Implementation Act (P.L. 109–53). Signed by the president Aug. 2, 2005. Approved the U.S. free trade agreement with the governments of Costa Rica, the Dominican Republic, El Salvador, Guatemala, Honduras, and Nicaragua. Prescribed requirements for enforcement of textile and apparel rules of origin; retroactive application for certain liquidations and reliquidations of textile or apparel goods.

Food, Conservation, and Energy Act of 2008 (Farm Bill) (7 U.S.C. 8701 note). Vetoed by the president May 21, 2008; veto overridden June 18, 2008. Reauthorized Department of Agriculture programs through fiscal year 2012, including the FAS Technical Assistance for Specialty Crops (TASC) program. Extended the Caribbean Basin and Haitian textile and apparel trade preferences. Directs the secretary of agriculture to implement a local and regional purchase pilot program in developing countries from fiscal year (FY) 2009 through 2012.

Agricultural Act of 2014 (Farm Bill) (128 Stat. 993, 7 U.S.C. 2101 note). Signed by the president Feb. 7, 2014. Required the USDA Foreign Agriculture Service to promulgate regulations for the Pima Agriculture Cotton Trust and the Wool Apparel Manufacturers Trust for calendar years 2014–2018. Reauthorized food aid programs through FY 2018.

▓ REGIONAL OFFICES

The FAS does not have regional offices in the United States; however, it maintains 94 offices covering 154 countries overseas. FAS officers also monitor and report on agricultural trade matters in an additional 69 countries. All countries served along with FAS and locally employed personnel and contact information are listed on the website, along with a link to each overseas office's own website. All of the country, officers below can be reached via U.S. or APO addresses. For those listed as c/o FAS, the address is USDA Foreign Agricultural Service, Washington, DC 20250–6000.

ALGERIA

American Embassy
c/o FAS
05 Chemin Cheikh Bachir Ibrahami
E-Gar 16030
Algiers, Algeria
Nabila Hales, agricultural marketing specialist

Department of State (AGR)
6030 Algiers Pl.
Washington, DC 20521–6030
E-mail: agalgiers@fas.usda.gov
Charles Rush, attaché

ANGOLA

American Embassy
Rua Houari Boumedienne #32
Mirimar, Luanda
Ricardo Dias, agricultural specialist

Department of State (AGR)
2550 Luanda Pl.
Washington, DC 20521–2550
Eric Wenberg, minister-counselor

ARGENTINA

(Paraguay, Uruguay)
American Embassy, Buenos Aires
AV. Colombia 4300
Buenos Aires, Argentina
APO AA 34034–0001
Kenneth N. Joseph, agricultural specialist

Department of State (AGR)
3130 Buenos Aires Pl.
Washington, DC 20521–3130
E-mail: agbuenosaires@fas.usda.gov
Melinda Sallyards, agricultural counselor

AUSTRALIA

American Embassy, Canberra
Moonah Pl.
Yarraluma ACT 2600
Canberra, Australia
Roger Farrell, agricultural specialist

Office of Agricultural Affairs
Department of State (AGR)
7800 Canberra Pl.
Washington, DC 20521–7800
E-mail: agcanberra@fas.usda.gov
Hugh Maginnis, agricultural counselor

AUSTRIA

American Embassy A1020
Boltzmanngasse 16
A-1020 Vienna, Austria
Roswitha Krautgartner, agricultural specialist

Department of State (AGR)
9900 Vienna Pl.
Washington, DC 20521–9900
E-mail: agvienna@fas.usda.gov
Kelly Strange, attaché (resident in Berlin)

BANGLADESH

U.S. Embassy Annex
Bavidhara, Dhaka - 1212
Bangladesh
Vacant, agricultural specialist

Department of State (AGR)
6120 Dhaka Pl.
Washington, DC 20521–6120
E-mail: agdhaka@fas.usda.gov
Scott Sindelar, minister-counselor (resident in New Delhi)

BELGIUM

American Embassy, Brussels
FAS/USEU 27
Unit 7600, Box 6000 DPO AE 09710
27, Blvd du Regent
1000 Brussels, Belgium
Karin Bendz, agricultural specialist

Office of Agricultural Affairs
Department of State (AGR)

5770 The Hague Pl.
Washington, DC 20521–5770
E-mail: aguseubrussels@fas.usda.gov
James Higgiston, agricultural minister-counselor

BOSNIA AND HERZEGOVINA

American Embassy
Roberta Frasurea 1
71000 Sarajevo, Bosnia, and Herzegovina
Sanela Stanojcic-Eminagic, agricultural specialist

Department of State (AGR)
7130 Sarajevo Pl.
Washington, DC 20521–7130
E-mail: stanojcics@state.gov
Christine Sloop, attaché (resident in Rome)

BRAZIL

American Embassy
Office of Agricultural Affairs
Avenida das Nacoes Quadra 801 Lote 3
70403-900 Brasilia DF
Brazil
Joao Faustino da Silva, agricultural specialist

Office of Agricultural Affairs
Department of State (AGR)
7500 Brasilia Pl.
Washington, DC 20521–7500
E-mail: agbrasilia@usda.gov
Clay Hamilton, minister-counselor

BULGARIA

(Kosovo, the former Yugoslav Republic of Macedonia,
    Romania, and Serbia/Montenegro)
American Embassy, Sofia
16 Koziak Str
1408 Sofia
Bulgaria
Mila Boshnakova, agricultural specialist

Office of Agricultural Affairs
Department of State
5740 Sofia Pl.
Washington, DC 20521–5740
E-mail: agsofia@fas.usda.gov
Russ Nicely, attaché (resident in Warsaw)

BURMA (see MYANMAR)

CANADA

American Embassy
490 Promenade Sussex Dr.
K1N 1G8
Ottawa, Ontario
Darlene Dessureault, agricultural specialist

Office of Agricultural Affairs
American Consulate, Toronto
480 University Ave., Suite 602

Toronto, ON Canada M5G 1V2
American Embassy
P.O. Box 5000
Ogdensburg, NY 13669–0430
E-mail: agottowa@fas.usda.gov
Kathryn Ting, minister-counselor

CARIBBEAN BASIN COUNTRIES

(Anguilla, Antigua and Barbuda, Aruba, Bahamas,
    Barbados, Bermuda, Caribbean Dutch [Bonaire,
    Sint Eustatius, Saba], Cayman Islands, Curacao,
    Dominica, Grenada, Guadeloupe, Martinique,
    Montserrat, Saint Barthelemy, Saint Kitts and
    Nevis, Saint Lucia, Saint Martin, Saint Vincent
    and the Grenadines, Sint Maarten, Trinidad and
    Tobago, Turks and Caicos)

Agricultural Trade Office
909 S.E. 1st Ave., #720
Miami, FL 33131
E-mail: agcaribbeanbasin@fas.usda.gov
Michael Henney, director

CHILE

American Embassy, Santiago
Avda. Andres Bello 2800
Las Condes
Santiago, Chile
Luis Hennicke, agricultural specialist

Office of Agricultural Affairs
Department of State (AGR)
3460 Santiago Pl.
Washington, DC 20521–3460
E-mail: agsantiago@fas.usda.gov
Anita Katial, agricultural attaché

CHINA

Internet: www.usdachina.org
Beijing region
Office of Agricultural Affairs, Beijing
U.S. Embassy, Beijing
No. 55 An Jia Lou Rd., Chaoyang District
Beijing, China 100600
Ma Jie, agricultural specialist

Office of Agricultural Affairs
Department of State (AGR)
7300 Beijing Place
Washington, DC 20521–7300
E-mail: agbeijing@fas.usda.gov
Philip Shull, agricultural minister-counselor

Chengdu region
Western Tower, #1222
No. 19 4th Section, South Renmin Rd.
Chengdu, China 610041
Shuheng Shawn Shen, agricultural marketing specialist
Agricultural Trade Office

Department of State (AGR)
4080 Chengdu Place
Washington, DC 20521–4080
E-mail: atochengdu@fas.usda.gov
Morgan Haas, director

Guangzhou region
China Hotel Office Tower 14/F
Luhua Road
Guangzhou, China 510015
Kang Ken Chen, agricultural
    marketing specialist

Agricultural Trade Office
Department of State
4090 Guangzhou Pl.
Washington, DC 20521–4090
E-mail: atoguangzhou@fas.usda.gov
Hoa Van Huynh, director

Shanghai region
Agricultural Trade Office, Shanghai
U.S. Consulate General, Shanghai
Shanghai Centre, #331
1376 Nanjing West Rd.
Shanghai, China 200040
Min Xu, agricultural marketing specialist

Agricultural Trade Office
Department of State (AGR)
4100 Shanghai Place
Washington, DC 20521–4100
E-mail: ATOShanghai@fas.usda.gov
Valerie Brown-Jones, director

Shenyang region
North Media International Tower, #1903
No 167, Qing Nian St., Shenhe District
Shenyang, 110014
Rongsen Rex Zhang, agricultural
    marketing specialist

Agricultural Trade Office
4110 Shenyang Pl.
Washington, DC 20521–4110
Philip Jarrell, agricultural director

COLOMBIA
American Embassy Bogota
Calle 24 Bis No. 48–50
Bogota, D.C. Colombia
Juan Diaz, agricultural specialist

Office of Agricultural Affairs
Department of State (AGR)
3030 Bogota Pl.
Washington, DC 20521–3030
E-mail: agbogota@fas.usda.gov
Michael Conlon, counselor

COSTA RICA
American Embassy
Frente al Centro Comercial de Pavas
San Jose, Costa Rica
Victor Gonzalez, agricultural specialist

Office of Agricultural Affairs
Department of State (AGR)
3440 San Jose Pl.
Washington, DC 20521–3440
Erich Kuss, agricultural counselor

CROATIA
American Embassy Office of Agricultural Affairs
Ulica Thomasa Jeffersona 2
10 010 Zagreb, Croatia
Office of Agricultural Affairs
Andreja Misir, agricultural specialist

Department of State (AGR)
5080 Zagreb Pl.
Washington, DC 20521–5080
E-mail: andreja.misir@usda.gov
Christine Sloop, agricultural counselor (resident in
    Rome)

CZECH REPUBLIC
American Embassy
Trziste 15
118 01 Prague, Czech Republic
Jana Mikulasova, agricultural specialist

Department of State (AGR)
5630 Prague Pl.
Washington, DC 20521–5630
E-mail: agprague@fas.usda.gov
Russ Nicely, attaché (resident in Warsaw)

DENMARK
(see also NETHERLANDS)

DOMINICAN REPUBLIC
(also Haiti, Jamaica)
FAS, American Embassy
Office of Agricultural Affairs
 Ave. Republica de Colombia, #57 Altos de Arroyo
    Hondo II
Santo Domingo, Dominican Republic
Luis Gonzales, agricultural specialist

Office of Agricultural Affairs
Department of State (AGR)
3470 Santo Domingo Place
Washington, DC 20521–3470
E-mail: agsantodomingo@fas.usda.gov
Morgan Perkins, agricultural attaché

ECUADOR
Office of Agricultural Affairs
American Embassy

Servicio Agricola del Exterior
Ave. Avigiras E12–170 y Ave. Eloy Alfaro
Quito, Ecuador
Henry Vega, agricultural specialist

Office of Agricultural Affairs
Department of State (AGR)
3420 Quito Pl.
Washington, DC 20521–3420
E-mail: agquito@fas.usda.gov
Casey Bean, counselor (resident in Lima)

EGYPT

(Iraq, Israel, Jordan, Lebanon, Syria)
Office of Agricultural Affairs
Embassy of the United States of America
5 Tawfik Diab St.
Garden City, Cairo, Egypt
Mohammed Hamza, senior agricultural specialist

Office of Agricultural Affairs
Department of State (AGR)
7700 Cairo Pl.
Washington, DC 20521–7700
E-mail: agcairo@fas.usda.gov
Ronald Verdonk, minister-counselor

EL SALVADOR

American Embassy, Edif. AID, 3er. Piso
Final Boulevard Santa Elena
Antiguo Cuscatlan; La Libertad
El Salvador
Miguel Hererra, agricultural specialist

Office of Agricultural Affairs
3450 San Salvador Pl.
Washington, DC 20521–3450
Henry Schmick Jr., agricultural counselor (resident in Guatemala)

ETHIOPIA

(African Union, Djibouti, Eritrea, Somalia, South Sudan, Yemen)
American Embassy
Entoto Rd.
Addis Ababa, Ethiopia
Abu Tefera, agricultural specialist

Office of Agricultural Affairs
Department of State (AGR)
2030 Addis Ababa Pl.
Washington, DC 20521–2030
E-mail: agaddisababa@fas.usda.gov
Michael Francom, counselor

FRANCE

American Embassy
2, Avenue Gabriel
75382 Paris Cedex 08
France

Xavier Audran, agricultural specialist
Office of Agricultural Affairs
Department of State (AGR)
9200 Paris Pl.
Washington, DC 20521–9200
E-mail: agparis@fas.usda.gov
David Salmon, counselor

GEORGIA

Office of Agricultural Affairs
American Embassy
11 George Balanchine Street
Tbilisi, Georgia 0131
Demna Dzirkvadze, agricultural specialist

Department of State (AGR)
7060 Tbilisi Pl.
Washington, DC 20521–7060
E-mail: dzirkvadzed@state.gov
Kimberly Svec Sawatzki, agricultural minister-counselor (resident in Ankara)

GERMANY

(Austria, Hungary, Slovenia)
Office of Agricultural Affairs
American Embassy, Berlin
Clayallee 170
14195 Berlin, Germany
Sabine Lieberz, agricultural specialist

Office of Agricultural Affairs
Department of State (AGR)
5090 Berlin Pl.
Washington, DC 20521–5090
E-mail: agberlin@fas.usda.gov
Kelly Strange, attaché

GHANA

American Embassy
No. 24 Fourth Circular Rd.
Cantonments, Accra, Ghana
Elmasoeur Ashitey, agricultural specialist

Office of Agricultural Affairs
American Embassy, Accra
Department of State (AGR)
2020 Accra Pl.
Washington, DC 20521–2020
Kurt Seifarth, agricultural counselor

GREECE (see ITALY)

GUATEMALA

(Belize, El Salvador, Honduras)
Office of Agricultural Affairs
American Embassy, Guatemala City
Avenida La Reforma 7-01, Zona 1
Guatemala City, Guatemala 010010
Karla Tay, agricultural specialist

Office of Agricultural Affairs
Department of State (AGR)
3190 Guatemala Pl.
Washington, DC 20521–3190
E-mail: agguatemala@usda.gov
Henry Schmick Jr., counselor

HONDURAS

Office of Agricultural Affairs
American Embassy, Tegucigalpa
Avenida La Paz
Tegucigalpa, Honduras
Ana Gomez, agricultural specialist

Office of Agricultural Affairs
Department of State (AGR)
3480 Tegucigalpa Pl.
Washington, DC 20521–3480
E-mail: agtegucigalpa@usda.gov
Henry Schmick Jr., counselor (resident in Guatemala)

HONG KONG

U.S. Agricultural Trade Office
18 St. John's Bldg.
33 Garden Rd., Central
Hong Kong
Caroline Yee LingYuen, agricultural specialist

Agricultural Trade Office
Department of State (AGR)
8000 Hong Kong Pl.
Washington, DC 20521–8000
E-mail: ATOHongKong@fas.usda.gov
M. Melinda Meador, director

HUNGARY

American Embassy
Bank Center Bldg.
Szabadsag Ter 7
H-1054 Budapest, Hungary
Goyla Gellert, agricultural specialist

Office of Agricultural Affairs
Department of State (AGR)
5270 Budapest Pl.
Washington, DC 20521–5270
E-mail: agbudapest@fas.usda.gov
Kelly Strange, attaché (resident in Berlin)

INDIA

American Consulate General
C-49, G Block
Bandar Kural Complex
Mumbai 400 051
Dhruv Sood, agricultural specialist

Office of Agricultural Affairs
Department of State (AGR)
6240 Mumbai.
Washington, DC 20521–6240

E-mail: agmumbai@fas.usda.gov
Adam Branson, senior attaché

American Embassy
Shanti Path, Chanakyapuri
New Delhi 110021, India
Amit Aradhey, agricultural specialist

Office of Agricultural Affairs
Department of State (AGR)
9000 New Delhi Pl.
Washington, DC 20521–9000
E-mail: agnewdelhi@fas.usda.gov
Scott Sindelar, minister-counselor

INDONESIA

Office of Agricultural Affairs
American Embassy
Jl. Medan Merdeka Selatan, No 5
Jakarta 10110, Indonesia
Sugiarti Meylinah, agricultural specialist

Office of Agricultural Affairs
Department of State (AGR)
8200 Jakarta Pl.
Washington, DC 20521–8200
E-mail: agdakarta@fas.usda.gov
Ali Abdi, counselor

IRELAND (see UNITED KINGDOM)

ISRAEL

Office of Agricultural Affairs
American Embassy
71 Ha'Yarkon St.
63903 Tel Aviv, Israel
Yossi Barak, agricultural specialist

Office of Agricultural Affairs
Department of State (AGR)
9700 Tel Aviv Pl.
Washington, DC 20521–9700
E-mail: agtelaviv@fas.usda.gov
Ronald Verdonk, senior attaché (resident in Cairo)

ITALY

(Albania, Bosnia and Herzegovina, Croatia, Greece,
   Malta, Serbia)
Office of Agricultural Affairs
American Embassy
Via Vittorio Veneto 119/A
00187 Roma, Italy
Dana Biasetti, senior agricultural specialist

Office of Agricultural Affairs
Department of State (AGR)
9500 Rome Pl.
Washington, DC 20521–9500
E-mail: agrome@usda.gov
Christine Sloop, attaché

JAMAICA

American Embassy
142 Old Hope Rd.
Kingston 6, Jamaica
Courtland Grant, agricultural specialist

Office of Agricultural Affairs
American Embassy, Kingston
Department of State (AGR)
3210 Kingston Pl.
Washington, DC 20521–3210
E-mail: agkingston@fas.usda.gov
Mogran Perkins, agricultural attaché (resident in
Santo Domingo)

JAPAN

Internet: usdajapan.org
Agricultural Trade Office (ATO)
American Embassy, Tokyo
Office of Agricultural Affairs-FAS
1-10-5 Akasaka
Minato-ku, Japan 107-8420 Japan
Thomas Aoki, agricultural marketing specialist

Department of State (ATO)
9800 Tokyo Pl.
Washington, DC 20521–9800
E-mail: atotokyo@fas.usda.gov
Rachel Nelson, director (resident in Tokyo)

Agricultural Trade Office, Osaka
2-11-5, Nishitenma
Kita-ku, Osaka 530–8534 Japan
E-mail: atoosaka@fas.usda.gov
Akiko Kashiwagi, agricultural marketing specialist

Agricultural Trade Office
Department of State (ATO)
4330 Osaka-Kobe Pl.
Washington, DC 20521–4330
E-mail: atoosaka@fas.usda.gov
Rachel Nelson, director (resident in Tokyo)

JORDAN

American Embassy, Amman
Abdoun, Al-Umawyeen St.
Amman, Jordan
Mohamed Khraishy, agricultural specialist

Office of Agricultural Affairs
Department of State (AGR)
6050 Amman Pl.
Washington, DC 20521–6050
E-mail: agamman@fas.usda.gov
Ronald Verdonk, minister-counselor (resident
in Cairo)

KAZAKHSTAN

American Embassy, Astana
Ak Bulak 4 Str. 23-22, Bldg. #3

Astana 010010, Kazakhstan
Zhamal Zharmagambetova, agricultural specialist

Office of Agricultural Affairs
Department of State (AGR)
2230 Astana Pl.
Washington, DC 20521–2230
E-mail: zhamal.zharmagambetova@fas.usda.gov
Holly Higgins, minister-counselor (resident in
Moscow)

KENYA

(Burundi, Malawi, United Republic of Tanzania,
Uganda, Zambia)
Office of Agricultural Affairs
American Embassy, Nairobi
P.O. Box 606 Village Market
00621 Nairobi
Republic of Kenya
Caroline N. Kamau, agricultural marketing specialist

Office of Agricultural Affairs
Department of State (AGR)
8900 Nairobi Pl.
Washington, DC 20521–8900
E-mail: agnairobi@usda.gov
Kate Snipes, counselor

KOREA

Agricultural Trade Office, U.S. Embassy in Seoul
Rm. 303, Leema Bldg.
146–1 Jongro-gu, Susong-dong
Seoul 110–755, Korea
Sang Yong Oh, agricultural marketing specialist

Agricultural Trade Office
Department of State (AGR)
9600 Seoul Pl.
Washington, DC 20521–9600
E-mail: atoseoul@fas.usda.gov
Kevin Sage-El, director

MALAYSIA

(Brunei, Papua New Guinea, Singapore)
American Embassy
376 Jalan Tun Razak
50400 Kuala Lumpur
Malaysia
Abdul Ghani Wahab, agricultural specialist

Office of Agricultural Affairs
Department of State (AGR)
4210 Kuala Lumpur Pl.
Washington, DC 20521–4210
E-mail: agkualalumpur@fas.usda.gov
Joani Dong, attaché

MEXICO

Office of Agricultural Affairs
American Embassy, Mexico City

Paseo de la Reforma No. 305
Col Cuauhtemoc
Mexico, D.F. 06500
Dulce-M. Flores, agricultural specialist

U.S. Agricultural Trade Office Mexico City
Liverpool No. 31, Col. Juárez,
C.P. 06600 México D.F.
E-mail: atomexico@fas.usda.gov
Joseph Lopez, director

U.S. Agricultural Trade Office Monterrey
Prolongacion Ave. Alfonso Reyes No. 150,
Santa Catarina, , Nuevo Leon, Mexico 66196
E-mail: atomonterrey@fas.usda.gov
Eduardo Lozano, agricultural specialist

American Embassy, Mexico
Foreign Agricultural Service
P.O. Box 9000
Brownsville, TX 78520–0900
E-mail: agmexico@fas.usda.gov
Lloyd Harbert, minister-counselor

MOROCCO

American Embassy
Km 5.7, Avenue Mohamed VI
Soussi, Rabat 10170
Morocco
Vacant, agricultural specialist

Office of Agricultural Affairs
Department of State (AGR)
9400 Rabat Pl.
Washington, DC 20521–9400
E-mail: agrabat@fas.usda.gov
Sarah Hanson, attaché

MOZAMBIQUE

American Embassy, OAA
193 Ave. Kenneth Kaunda
Maputo, Mozambique
Almeida Zacarias, agricultural specialist

Embassy of Mozambique
2330 Maputo Pl.
Washington, DC 20521–2330
Eric Wenberg, minister-counselor (resident in Pretoria)

MYANMAR

(formerly Burma)
American Embassy
No: 110 University Ave.
Kamayut Township
Yangon, Myanmar
Swe Mon Aung, agricultural specialist

Office of Agricultural Affairs
Department of State (AGR)

4250 Rangoon Pl.
Washington, DC 20521–4250
E-mail: agrangoon@fas.usda.gov
Bobby Richey, counselor (resident in Bangkok)

NETHERLANDS

(Belgium, Denmark, Finland, Iceland, Luxembourg, Norway, Sweden)
American Embassy
Lange Voorhout 102
2514 EJ The Hague
The Netherlands
Robertus Flach, agricultural specialist

Office of Agricultural Affairs
Department of State (AGR)
5770 The Hague Pl.
Washington, DC 20521–5770
E-mail: agthehague@fas.usda.gov
Susan Phillips, attaché

NEW ZEALAND

American Embassy
29 Fitzherbert Terrace
Wellington, New Zealand
David Lee-Jones, agricultural attaché

Office of Agricultural Affairs
Department of State (AGR)
4360 Wellington Pl.
Washington, DC 20521–4360
E-mail: agwellington@fas.usda.gov
Hugh Maginnis, counselor (resident in Canberra)

NICARAGUA

Office of Agricultural Affairs
American Embassy
Km 5 1/2 Carretera Sur Frente Parque las
Managua, Nicaragua
Jimmy Bolanos, agricultural specialist

Office of Agricultural Affairs
Department of State (AGR)
3240 Managua Pl.
Washington, DC 20521–3240
E-mail: agmanagua@fas.usda.gov
Erich Kuss, counselor (resident in San Jose)

NIGERIA

(Benin, Cameroon, Ghana, Liberia)
Office of Agricultural Affairs
U.S. Consulate General
2 Walter Carrington Crescent
Victoria Island
Lagos
Uche Nzeka, agricultural marketing specialist

Office of Agricultural Affairs
Department of State (AGR)
8300 Lagos Pl.

Washington, DC 20521–8300
E-mail: aglagos@fas.usda.gov
Kurt Seifarth, counselor

PAKISTAN

Office of Agricultural Affairs,
  American Embassy
Diplomatic Enclave
Ramna-5
Islamabad, Pakistan
Asmat Raza, agricultural specialist

Office of Agricultural Affairs
Department of State (AGR)
8100 Islamabad Pl.
Washington, DC 20521–8100
E-mail: agislamabad@fas.usda.gov
David Williams, counselor

PANAMA

American Embassy, Panama City
Departamento de Agricultura
Calle Demetrio Basilio Lakas No. 783
Clayton, Panama
Arlene Villalaz, agricultural specialist

Office of Agricultural Affairs
Department of State (AGR)
9100 Panama City Pl.
Washington, DC 20521–9100
E-mail: agpanama@fas.usda.gov
Erich Kuss, counselor (resident in San José)

PARAGUAY (see ARGENTINA)

PERU

(Bolivia, Ecuador)
American Embassy, Lima
Office of Agricultural Affairs
Avenida La Encalada cdra. 17 s/n
Surco, Lima 33, Peru
Gaspar Nolte, agricultural specialist

Office of Agricultural Affairs
Department of State (AGR)
3230 Lima Pl.
Washington, DC 20521–3230
E-mail: aglima@fas.usda.gov
Casey Bean, agricultural counselor

PHILIPPINES

American Embassy, Manila
Office of Agricultural Affairs
Roxas Boulevard
Manila, Philippines
Pia Francesca Ang, agricultural specialist

Office of Agricultural Affairs
Department of State (AGR)
8600 Manila Pl.

Washington, DC 20521–8600
E-mail: agmanila@fas.usda.gov
Ralph Bean, counselor

POLAND

(Bulgaria, Czech Republic, Estonia, Latvia, Lithuania,
  Romania, Slovakia)
American Embassy, Warsaw
Office of Agricultural Affairs
Al. Ujazdowskie 29/31
00–540 Warsaw
Mira Kobuszynska, agricultural specialist

Office of Agricultural Affairs
Department of State (AGR)
5010 Warsaw Pl.
Washington, DC 20521–5010
E-mail: agwarsaw@fas.usda.gov
Russ Nicely, attaché

ROMANIA

American Embassy, Bucharest
7–9, Tudor Arghezi St.
District 2, Bucharest
020942 Romania
Monica Dobrescu, agricultural specialist

Office of Agricultural Affairs
Department of State (AGR)
5260 Bucharest Pl.
Washington, DC 20521–5260
E-mail: agbucharest@fas.usda.gov
Russ Nicely, attaché (resident in Warsaw)

RUSSIA

(Armenia, Belarus, Kazakhstan, Kyrgyzstan)
American Embassy
Bolshoi Devyatinskiy Pereulok, #8
121009 Moscow, Russia
Andrey Gryaznov, agricultural specialist OAA
Olga Ivanova, agricultural specialist ATO

American Consulate General
125 Ulitsa Furshtatskaya
St. Petersburg 191028, Russia
E-mail: atostpetersburg@state.gov
Svetlana Il'yina, agricultural marketing specialist

Office of Agricultural Affairs (OAA), or Agricultural
  Trade Office (ATO)
Department of State (AGR)
5430 Moscow Pl.
Washington, DC 20521–5430
E-mail: agmoscow@usda.gov, atomoscow@usda.gov
Holly Higgins, agricultural minister-counselor, OAA

Agricultural Trade Office
Department of State (ATO)
5880 Vladivostok Pl.
Washington, DC 20521–5880

E-mail: agvladivostok@fas.usda.gov
Erik Hanson, director

SAUDI ARABIA

Office of Agricultural Affairs
American Embassy, Riyadh
Abdulla Bin Huthfah Al Sahmy Rd.
Ad Dir'iyah 12523, Saudi Arabia
Hussein-B Mousa, agricultural specialist

Agricultural Trade Office
Department of State (ATO)
6300 Riyadh Pl.
Washington, DC 20521–6300
E-mail: agriyadh@fas.usda.gov
Hassan Ahmed, attaché

SENEGAL

(Burkina Faso, Chad, Côte d'Ivoire, The Gambia,
Mali, Niger)
American Embassy, Dakar
Office of Agricultural Affairs
Route des Almadies
BP 49 Dakar, Senegal
Fana Marie Sylla, agricultural specialist

Office of Agricultural Affairs
Department of State (AGR)
2130 Dakar Pl.
Washington, DC 20521–2130
E-mail: agdakar@fas.usda.gov
Jude Akhidenor, attaché

SERBIA

American Embassy, Belgrade
Kneza Aleksandra Karakjordjevica 92
11000 Belgrade, Serbia
Tatjana Maslac, agricultural specialist

Office of Agricultural Affairs
Department of State (AGR)
5070 Belgrade Pl.
Washington, DC 20521–5070
E-mail: agbelgrade@fas.usda.gov
Christine Sloop, agricultural attaché (resident in
Rome)

SINGAPORE

American Embassy
27 Napier Rd.
Singapore 258508
Alice Chai-Kwek, agricultural marketing specialist

Office of Agricultural Affairs
Department of State (AGR)
4280 Singapore Pl.
Washington, DC 20521–4280
E-mail: agsingapore@fas.usda.gov
Christopher Rittgers, agricultural attaché (resident in
Kuala Lumpur)

SOUTH AFRICA

(Angola, Botswana, Lesotho, Madagascar,
Mauritius, Mozambique, Namibia, Swaziland,
Zambia, Zimbabwe)
Office of Agricultural Affairs
American Embassy, Pretoria
877 Pretorius St.
Arcadia, Pretoria, 0083
Republic of South Africa
Dirk Esterhuizen, agricultural specialist

Department of State (AGR)
9300 Pretoria Pl.
Washington, DC 20521–9300
E-mail: agpretoria@fas.usda.gov
Eric Wenburg, minister-counselor

SPAIN

(Portugal)
Office of Agricultural Affairs
American Embassy
Serrano, 75
28006 Madrid, Spain
Marta Guerrero, agricultural specialist

Office of Agricultural Affairs
Department of State (AGR)
8500 Madrid Pl.
Washington, DC 20521–8500
E-mail: agmadrid@fas.usda.gov
Rachel Bickford, attaché

SWEDEN (see NETHERLANDS)

SWITZERLAND

Office of Agricultural Affairs
11 Route de Pregny
1292 Chambesy-Geneva
Switzerland

Office of Agricultural Affairs
Department of State (AGR/USTR)
5120 Geneva Pl.
Washington, DC 20521–5120
E-mail: aggeneva@fas.usda.gov
Suzanne Heinen, agricultural minister-counselor

SYRIA (see EGYPT)

TAIWAN

American Institute in Taiwan (AIT)
No. 7, Lane 134, Xinyi Rd., Sec. 3
Taipei, 10659 Taiwan
Rosemary Kao, agricultural specialist

ATO/American Institute in Taiwan
Suite 704 Lotus Mansion
7th Floor, No. 136, Renai Rd., Sec. 3
Taipei, Taiwan
Cleo W. Y. Fu, agricultural marketing specialist

Agricultural Trade Office
Department of State (AGR)
4170 AIT Taipei Pl.
Washington, DC 20521–4170
E-mail for AIT: atgaipei@fas.usda.gov
W. Garth Thorburn II, chief (AIT)
E-mail for ATO: agtaipei@fas.usda.gov
Mark Ford, director

TANZANIA
American Embassy
686 Old Bagamoyo Rd., Msasani
P.O. Box 9123
Dar es Salaam, Tanzania
Vacant, agricultural specialist
Kate Snipes, counselor
   (resident in Nairobi)

THAILAND
Office of Agricultural Affairs
U.S. Embassy
93/1 Wireless Rd.
Bangkok 10330
Ponnarong Prasertsri, agricultural specialist

Office of Agricultural Affairs
Department of State (AGR)
7200 Bangkok Pl.
Washington, DC 20521–7200
E-mail: agbangkok@usda.gov
Bobby Richey, counselor

TUNISIA
Office of Agricultural Affairs
American Embassy, Tunis
Les Berges du Lac
1053 Tunis, Tunisia
Vacant, agricultural specialist

Department of State (AGR)
6360 Tunis Pl.
Washington, DC 20521–6360
E-mail: agtunis@fas.usda.gov
Sarah Hanson, attaché (resident in Rabat)

TURKEY
(Azerbaijan, Georgia, Tajikistan,
   Turkmenistan)
Office of Agricultural Affairs
American Embassy, Ankara
110 Atatürk Bulvd.
Kavaklıdere, 06100 Ankara
Turkey
Nergiz Ozbag, senior agricultural specialist

Office of Agricultural Affairs
Department of State (AGR)
7000 Ankara Pl.
Washington, DC 20521–7000

E-mail: agankara@fas.usda.gov
Kimberly Svec Sawatzki, counselor

TURKEY
American Consulate General
Kaplicalar Mevkii No. 2
Istinye 34460
Istanbul, Turkey
Ibrahim Sirtioglu, agricultural
   marketing specialist

Office of Agricultural Affairs
Department of State (AGR)
5030 Istanbul Pl.
Washington, DC 20521–5030
E-mail: agistanbul@fas.usda.gov
Kimberly Svec Sawatzki, counselor (resident in
   Ankara)

UKRAINE
Office of Agricultural Affairs
American Embassy, Kyiv
4, Igor Sikorsky St.
Kyiv, 04112 Ukraine
Denys Sobolev, agricultural specialist

Office of Agricultural Affairs
Department of State (AGR)
5850 Kyiv Pl.
Washington, DC 20521–5850
E-mail: agkyiv@fas.usda.gov
Jorge Sanchez, agricultural attaché

UNITED ARAB EMIRATES
(Afghanistan, Kuwait, Oman, Qatar)
American Consulate General
Al Seef Road – Bur Dubai
Dubai, United Arab Emirates
Mohamed Taha, agricultural specialist

Office of Agricultural Affairs
Department of State (AGR)
6020 Dubai Pl.
Washington, DC 20521–6020
E-mail: atodubai@fas.usda.gov
Quintin Gray, counselor

UNITED KINGDOM
Office of Agricultural Affairs
American Embassy
24 Grosvenor Square
London, W1K 6AH, UK
Steven R. Knight, agricultural specialist

Office of Agricultural Affairs
Department of State (AGR)
8400 London Pl.
Washington, DC 20521–8400
E-mail: aglondon@fas.usda.gov
Stan Phillips, counselor

URUGUAY (see ARGENTINA)

UZBEKISTAN

American Embassy (OAA)
3 Moyqorghon St., 5th Block
Yunusobod District
100093 Tashkent
Uzbekistan
Nizam Yuldashbaev, agricultural specialist

Department of State (AGR)
7110 Tashkent Pl.
Washington, DC 20521–7110
E-mail: agtashkent@fas.usda.gov
Kimberly Svec Sawatzki, counselor (resident in Ankara)

VENEZUELA

Office of Agricultural Affairs
American Embassy
Calle F con Calle Suapure
Urb, Colinas de Valle Arriba
Caracas, Venezeula 1080
Clara Nunez, agricultural specialist

Office of Agricultural Affairs
Department of State (AGR)
3140 Caracas Pl.
Washington, DC 20521–3140
E-mail: agcaracas@fas.usda.gov
Richard Todd Drennan, attaché

VIETNAM

American Embassy OAA
3/F Rose Garden Tower
170 Ngoc Khanh St.
Hanoi, Vietnam
Thi Huong Bui, agricultural
    specialist

Office of Agricultural Affairs
Department of State (AGR)
4550 Hanoi Pl.
Washington, DC 20521–4550
E-mail: aghanoi@fas.usda.gov
Mark Dries, counselor

Ho Chi Minh City
Office of Agricultural Affairs
8th Floor, Diamond Plaza
34 Le Duan Blvd., District 1
Ho Chi Minh City, Vietnam
Kiet Vo, senior agricultural s
    pecialist

Office of Agricultural Affairs
Department of State (AGR)
7160 Ho Chi Minh City Pl.
Washington, DC 20521–7160
E-mail: atohochiminh@fas.usda.gov
Dwight Wilder, senior attaché

Forest Service

1400 Independence Ave. S.W., MS 1144
Washington, DC 20250–1144
Internet: www.fs.fed.us

Congress established the Forest Service (FS) in 1905 to provide quality water and timber for the nation's benefit. The Forest Service, an agency within the U.S. Department of Agriculture (USDA), is under the jurisdiction of the assistant secretary of agriculture for natural resources and the environment. The Forest Service is administered by a chief who is assisted by four deputy chiefs responsible for business operations, the National Forest System, research and development, and state and private forestry.

The Forest Service manages and regulates the use and protection of the nation's 193 million-acre National Forest System, with 154 national forests and twenty national grasslands in forty-four states, the Virgin Islands, and Puerto Rico. The agency operates under the concept of multiple use and administers statutes that are aimed at providing sustained yields of renewable resources such as water, livestock forage, wildlife habitat, and timber, as well as preserving wilderness and biodiversity for recreational and scenic purposes. Forest Service programs also oversee protection of national forest lands from wildfires, pest and disease epidemics, floods, erosion, and water and air pollution. The agency administers statutes that regulate:

- Construction of roads and trails through national forests to ensure closely regulated timber harvesting and give the public access to recreation areas.
- Construction and maintenance of facilities on National Forest System lands.
- Removal of oil, gas, uranium, and other minerals of strategic importance, as well as geothermal steam and coal.
- Timber harvesting methods and quantities.
- Use of national forests and range lands as a refuge for threatened and endangered species.
- Use of national forests and grasslands for grazing.

The Forest Service also works with state forestry agencies to develop multiple-use forestry practices on forests and adjacent lands. Through its cooperative state and private forestry programs, the agency provides financial and technical assistance to private landowners to protect and improve the quality of air, water, soil, and open space on nonfederal lands. The research division conducts extensive research on a wide range of forest-related subjects, including long-term natural resources issues of both national and international scope.

The USDA's Forest Service office of International Programs provides assistance to promote sustainable development and global environmental stability, particularly in countries important in global climate change. International Programs has three main staff units: Technical Cooperation, Policy, and Disaster. Technical Cooperation develops and manages natural resource projects overseas on a wide range of topics. There are two main disaster programs: Disaster Assistance Support Program (DASP) and the Disaster Mitigation Program. Both Technical Cooperation and DASP work closely with United States Agency for International Development (USAID). The International Program's policy unit is actively involved in sustainability roundtables and international fora, representing the United States on global forest policies and agreements.

Since 1908, 25 percent of the USDA's Forest Service revenues from timber receipts have been returned to states in which national forest lands are located to help pay for school services and road maintenance. As revenue from timber sales has steadily declined during the past decades, payments to communities have also declined, thus affecting communities' ability to provide necessary services.

The Secure Rural Schools and Community Self-Determination Act (SRS) of 2000 stabilized payment levels to their historic high. Instead of the annual flat 25 percent rate, the act directed the secretary of the Treasury to base future payments for fiscal year 2001 through 2006 for eligible states and counties on the average of the three highest annual payment amounts from fiscal year 1986 through 1999. The legislation also created citizen advisory committees and gave local communities the choice to fund restoration projects on federal lands or in counties. The act was reauthorized under the Emergency Economic Stabilization Act of 2008. Congress did not reauthorize SRS; the act expired at the end of fiscal year 2014. The 25 percent allocation was restored, which substantially reduced the payments to the states.

The Farm Security and Rural Investment Act of 2002 amended the Cooperative Forestry Assistance Act of 1978 to direct the secretary to establish in the Forest Service the Office of Tribal Relations. The Tribal Relations Program ensures indigenous perspectives are an integral part of maintaining and restoring healthy lands for future generations.

President George W. Bush's Healthy Forests Restoration Act of 2003 eased environmental restrictions for tree and brush clearing in the national forests with the hope that this would mitigate wildland fires. The new regulations promulgated under the act allowed for a predecisional objection process during the analysis phase of a project, before a final decision was rendered. This curtailed the often-lengthy appeal process. The Tribal Forest Protection Act of 2004 authorized the secretaries of agriculture and interior to enter into agreements for the purpose of protecting Native American forest lands from wildland fire and to assist with restoration projects.

Provisions in the Consolidated Appropriations Act of 2012 directed the Forest Service to establish a predecisional objection process for other projects in lieu of the postdecisional appeal procedures that had been in use with those projects since 1993. The Forest Service had successfully used this objection process since 2004 for hazardous-fuel reduction projects authorized under the Healthy Forests Restoration Act. The Agricultural Act of 2014 (Farm Bill) included provisions to modify the existing public notice, comment, and appeals process for land and resource management plans, exempting some USFS projects from the pre-decisional objection process under specific circumstances.

The 2001 Roadless Rule

In 1999 the administration of President Bill Clinton began to develop a comprehensive policy to protect specific wilderness areas in the National Forest System. On January 12, 2001, the Forest Service published the Roadless Rule. The 2001 Roadless Rule establishes prohibitions on road construction, road reconstruction, and timber harvesting on nearly 60 million acres of inventoried roadless areas on National Forest System lands.

President George W. Bush took office less than two weeks later, and the administration halted implementation of the Roadless Rule. The rule would be subject to litigation for more than 10 years. Some states sued the federal government, arguing that the administration's new regulations for forest road building and logging violated federal law because the government did not conduct a complete analysis of the environmental impact. The states also were concerned that the new forest rules would be costly to the states and adversely affect water quality.

In September 2006 a federal court ruling reinstated the 2001 Roadless Rule and required the Forest Service to comply with current law. The Forest Service and the timber industry appealed the decision in April 2007.

The administration of President Barack Obama took another look at the controversy. In May 2009 Agriculture Secretary Tom Vilsack announced an interim directive regarding inventoried roadless areas, allowing the Forest Service to carefully consider activities in these inventoried roadless areas while long-term roadless policy was being developed and related court cases move forward. Policies under the interim directive would align with the provisions under the rules during the Clinton administration.

Some states and industry interests continued to challenge the 2001 Roadless Rule. In March 2013 a federal court upheld the original 2001 Roadless Rule; the judge noted that the statute of limitations for challenging the 2001 roadless rule had run out. After more than 10 years of litigation, the authority of the 2001 Roadless Rule is firmly established.

State Roadless Rules

Two states, Idaho and Colorado, developed their own roadless rules. Idaho promulgated its own roadless rule through the Administrative Procedures Act. The Idaho Roadless Rule was developed through a collaborative effort that included conservation groups, timber companies, hunters, and recreation groups. Idaho Governor Jim Risch worked with stakeholders to develop a plan to manage various tracts within the 9.3 million acres of inventoried roadless areas in Idaho. Idaho's Roadless Rule was challenged, but a federal district court upheld the rules in 2011.

On July 3, 2012, after a six-year process, the Forest Service finalized the Colorado Roadless Rule, which was developed in cooperation with the state of Colorado. From July 2006 to June 2012, there were five public comment periods resulting in more than 310,000 comments. The rule applies to 4.2 million acres of National Forest roadless areas within Colorado.

▪ KEY PERSONNEL

Chief of the Forest Service
  Tom Tidwell . . . . (202) 205–8439
Associate Chief
  Mary Wagner . . . . (202) 205–1779
Chief of Staff
  Tim Decoster . . . . (202) 205–1661
Business Operations
  Steve Schlientz . . . . (703) 605–4891
Communication
  Erin O'Connor . . . . (202) 205–1470
  Chief Information Officer
    Douglas Nash . . . . (703) 605–4600
Legislative Affairs
  Doug Crandall . . . . (202) 205–1636
National Forest System
  Leslie A. C. Weldon . . . . (202) 205–1523
    Fax . . . . (202) 205–1758
  Lands and Realty Management
    Gregory Smith . . . . (202) 205–1769
  Ecosystem Management Coordination
    Leanne Marten . . . . (202) 205–0830
National Partnership Office
  Joe Meade . . . . (202) 205–1072
Policy Analysis
  Bill Lange . . . . (202) 205–1775
Press Officer
  Larry Chambers . . . . (202) 205–1005
Regulatory and Management Services
  Andria Weeks . . . . (202) 205–5102
Research and Development
  Jim Reaves . . . . (202) 205–1665
    Fax . . . . (202) 205–1530
  Engineering, Technical, and Geospatial Services
    Emilee Blount . . . . (703) 606–4962
State and Private Forestry
  James E. Hubbard . . . . (202) 205–1657
    Fax . . . . (202) 205–1174
  Forest Health Protection
    Monica Lear . . . . (703) 605–5344

Strategic Planning, Budget, and Accountability
Antoine Dixon.................... (202) 401–4470

INFORMATION SOURCES

Internet
Agency website: www.fs.fed.us. Provides information on the Forest Service and related topics. Includes a feature for customized information searches.

Telephone Contacts
Toll-free general information .... (800) 832–1355
Personnel Locator (USDA) .... (202) 720–8732
English-Language Federal
    Relay (TTY).................. (866) 377–8642
Spanish-Language Federal
    Relay (TTY)................. (800) 845–6136

Information and Publications

KEY OFFICES

Forest Service Office of Communication
1400 Independence Ave. S.W.
MS 1111
Washington, DC 20250–1111
(202) 205–1470
(800) 832–1355
Fax (202) 205–0885
Erin O'Connor, director

Communicates with the public about the Forest Service's people and their stewardship of the natural resources entrusted to them.

Visual Information and Publishing Services is responsible for the publication and distribution of Forest Service documents that are available to the public; for organizing and producing photographic, audiovisual, and other presentation products; and for managing and operating the National Forest Service Information Center. For more information, contact Mary Jane Senter (202) 205–1719.

Media Relations. For information concerning these areas contact press officer Larry Chambers (202) 205–1005.

Freedom of Information
Attn: FOIA officer
1400 Independence Ave. S.W.
MS 1143
Washington, DC 20250–1143
(202) 205–1542
Fax (703) 605–5221
E-mail: wo_foia@fs.fed.us
Raynell D. Lazier, FOIA officer
Requests must be submitted in writing.

DATA AND STATISTICS
The best source of statistics on the operations of the Forest Service is the agency's annual report, *Report of the Forest Service,* which is available from Visual Information and Publishing Services in Forest Service Office of Communication (202) 401–7784.

PUBLICATIONS
Produces publications on forestry, natural resources, wood utilization, recreation, and Forest Service programs, available on the website. Contact Visual Information and Publishing Services in Forest Service Office of Communication at (202) 205–1719.

Reference Resources

LIBRARY

National Agricultural Library
10301 Baltimore Ave.
Beltsville, MD 20705–2351
(301) 504–5755
Stan Kosecki, director
Hours: 8:30 a.m. to 4:30 p.m.

The National Agricultural Library also maintains a reference center at the main Agriculture Department's South Building. The collection consists primarily of reference volumes, databases, and other computer resources.

D.C. Reference Center
1400 Independence Ave. S.W.
South Bldg., #1052-S
Washington, DC 20250
(301) 504–5755
Rebecca Mazur, coordinator of research services

DOCKETS
Public dockets, containing records of all Forest Service rulemakings and other administrative proceedings, are maintained by the division responsible for the proceeding. Information on where a docket is kept is published in the *Federal Register* in the notice announcing the proceeding. Contact information for a particular docket may be obtained from:

Forest Service Directives and Regulations
1400 Independence Ave. S.W.
Yates Bldg., 1 S.E.
Washington, DC 20250
(202) 205–6560
Larenda King, director

Federal dockets are also available at www.regulations.gov. (*See appendix for Searching and Commenting on Regulations: Regulations.gov.*)

RULES AND REGULATIONS
Forest Service rules and regulations are published in the *Code of Federal Regulations,* Title 36, Chapter II, Parts 200–299. Proposed rules, new final rules, and updates to the *Code of Federal Regulations* are published in the *Federal Register.* (*See appendix for information on how to*

obtain and use these publications.) The *Federal Register* and the *Code of Federal Regulations* may be accessed online at www.archives.gov/federal-register/cfr; the site contains a link to the federal government's regulatory website at www.regulations.gov (*see appendix*).

▇ LEGISLATION

Laws administered by the Forest Service are listed in the publication *The Principal Laws Relating to Forest Service Activities*. Copies may be obtained from Creative Services in the Public Affairs Office.

The statutes authorizing the Forest Service to manage the National Forest System, conduct forestry research, and assist state and private forestries include:

Organic Administration Act (30 Stat. 34, 16 U.S.C. 473–482, 551). Signed by the president June 4, 1897. Provided basic authority for protecting and managing national forest lands.

Act of March 1, 1911 (Weeks Act) (36 Stat. 961, 16 U.S.C. 480). Signed by the president March 1, 1911. Authorized the secretary of agriculture to purchase forested, cutover, or denuded lands within watersheds of navigable streams necessary to the regulation and flow of navigable streams or for the production of timber. Lands acquired under this act were permanently reserved as national forest lands.

Clarke-McNary Act (43 Stat. 653, 16 U.S.C. 471b, 499, 505, 564–570). Signed by the president June 7, 1924. Established forest fire prevention programs in cooperation with the states and provided for the production and distribution of forest tree seeds and plants. Authorized the purchase of forests to protect navigable streams and to promote timber production.

Knutson-Vandenberg Act (46 Stat. 527, 16 U.S.C. 576–576b). Signed by the president June 9, 1930. Authorized the establishment of forest tree nurseries and other activities that are necessary to prepare for planting on national forests. The act also required purchasers of national forest timber to make deposits to cover the cost of replanting national forest land that is logged by the purchaser.

Anderson-Mansfield Reforestation and Revegetation Act (63 Stat. 762, 16 U.S.C. 581j). Signed by the president Oct. 11, 1949. Authorized funding for reforestation and revegetation of national forest lands.

Cooperative Forest Management Act (64 Stat. 473, 16 U.S.C. 568c). Signed by the president Aug. 25, 1950. Authorized cooperative efforts in forest management.

Multiple-Use Sustained-Yield Act of 1960 (74 Stat. 215, 16 U.S.C. 528). Signed by the president June 12, 1960. Decreed that national forests are established and administered for recreation, range, timber, watershed, and fish and wildlife purposes.

Wilderness Act (78 Stat. 890, 16 U.S.C. 1121). Signed by the president Sept. 3, 1964. Established a National Wilderness Preservation System composed of federally owned areas designed as "wilderness areas."

National Forest Roads and Trails Systems Act (78 Stat. 1089, 16 U.S.C. 532–538). Signed by the president Oct. 13, 1964. Authorized construction and regulation of roads and trails in national forests.

Wild and Scenic Rivers Act (82 Stat. 906, 16 U.S.C. 127, 1271–1287). Signed by the president Oct. 2, 1968. Protected selected rivers with remarkable scenic, geologic, fish and wildlife, and other values.

Forest and Range Land Renewable Resources Planning Act (88 Stat. 476, 16 U.S.C. 1600–1614). Signed by the president Aug. 17, 1974. A planning and budgetary procedure act that required the Forest Service to prepare long-term programs for the National Forest System. Amended by the National Forest Management Act of 1976 (90 Stat. 2949, 16 U.S.C. 472a). Signed by the president Oct. 22, 1976. Provided for a coordinated land management planning process that required full public participation in the development and revision of land management plans for each national forest or grassland. Provided comprehensive new authorities for managing, harvesting, and selling national forest timber; and provided direction for bidding on national forest timber, road building associated with timber harvesting, reforestation, salvage sales, and the handling of receipts from timber sales activities.

Federal Land Policy and Management Act of 1976 (90 Stat. 2743, 43 U.S.C. 1752). Signed by the president Oct. 21, 1976. Provided for the use of national forests and grasslands for grazing; authorized the secretary of agriculture to issue grazing permits; and authorized issuances of rights-of-way.

Cooperative Forestry Assistance Act of 1978 (92 Stat. 365, 16 U.S.C. 2101, 1606). Signed by the president July 1, 1978. Authorized the Forest Service to carry out cooperative forestry programs with state and other federal agencies that are directed at the sustained protection and development of all forestry resources.

Alaska National Interest Lands Conservation Act (94 Stat. 2371, 16 U.S.C. 3101 note). Signed by the president Dec. 2, 1980. Provided for the conservation of certain public lands in Alaska, including additional designations of national park, national wildlife refuge, national forest, and national wilderness areas.

Wood Residue Utilization Act of 1980 (94 Stat. 3257, 16 U.S.C. 1600 note). Signed by the president Dec. 19, 1980. Established a program to improve recovery of wood residue in national forests for use as fuel.

National Forest Foundation Act (104 Stat. 2969, 16 U.S.C. 583j note). Signed by the president Nov. 16, 1990. Established a nonprofit foundation to encourage and administer private donations of land to the Forest Service.

Forest Stewardship Act of 1990 (104 Stat. 3521, 16 U.S.C. 582 note). Signed by the president Nov. 28, 1990. Reauthorized the Cooperative Forestry Assistance Act of 1978 and established research and conservation programs to support better stewardship of private forests. Created a private foundation, America the Beautiful, to promote tree planting and conservation activities through grants for planting, protection, and cultivation of trees. Authorized the USDA to provide emergency reforestation assistance to landowners who suffered losses because of damaging weather or wildfire.

Tongass Timber Reform Act (104 Stat. 4426, 16 U.S.C. 539d note). Signed by the president Nov. 28, 1990. Withheld one million acres of the Alaskan Tongass National Forest from timber cutting. Required that long-term contracts between the Forest Service and pulp mills in the region be renegotiated to ensure that timber sales would be profitable for the federal government.

Pacific Yew Act (106 Stat. 859, 16 U.S.C. 4801 note). Signed by the president Aug. 7, 1992. Required the harvesting of Pacific yew trees on public lands before those lands are opened to commercial logging. Taxol, a cancer-fighting agent, is derived from the bark of the tree. Directed the Forest Service to inventory yew trees in federal forests and to ensure that yews be harvested in a way to promote new growth.

Omnibus Consolidated and Emergency Supplemental Appropriations Act of 1999 (112 Stat. 2681, 16 U.S.C. 2104 note). Signed by the president Oct. 21, 1998. Authorizes the Forest Service, until September 30, 2002, to enter into up to 28 contracts with private persons (of which Region One of the Forest Service shall have authority to enter into nine) to perform services to achieve land management goals for national forests that meet local and rural community needs. Reauthorized in 2003 to extend authority for stewardship contracting until September 30, 2013.

Secure Rural Schools and Community Self-Determination Act of 2000 (114 Stat. 1607, 16 U.S.C. 500 note). Signed by the president Oct. 30, 2000. Title I directed that timber-related and other revenue-sharing payments for eligible states and counties be recalculated based on the average of the three highest annual payment amounts from fiscal year 1986 through 1999. Directed the secretary to make payments to eligible states from Forest Service lands for affected counties to use for public education and transportation.

Farm Security and Rural Investment Act of 2002 (116 Stat. 1348, 7 U.S.C. 7901 note). Signed by the president May 13, 2002. Amended the Cooperative Forestry Assistance Act of 1978 to establish the Office of Tribal Relations. Authorized the secretary to provide financial, technical, educational, and related assistance to Native American tribes for Forest Service coordination respecting resource management, tribal land interests, and traditional and cultural matters; conservation activities; and tribal acquisition of conservation interests from willing sellers.

Healthy Forests Restoration Act of 2003 (117 Stat. 1887, 16 U.S.C. 6501 note). Signed by the president Dec. 3, 2003. Provided increased authority to the secretary of agriculture and the secretary of the interior to conduct hazardous fuels reduction projects on National Forest System lands aimed at protecting communities, watersheds, and certain other at-risk lands from catastrophic wildfire. Directed the secretary of agriculture to issue interim and final regulations establishing a process by which an eligible individual shall be able to seek administrative review regarding a project on Forest Service land.

Tribal Forest Protection Act of 2004 (118 Stat. 868, 25 U.S.C. 3101 note). Signed by the president Jan. 20, 2004. Authorized the secretary of agriculture and the secretary of the interior to enter into an agreement or contract with Native American tribes meeting certain criteria to carry out projects to protect Native American forest land from threats of wildland fire and restoration.

Federal Lands Recreation Enhancement Act (118 Stat. 3377, 16 U.S.C. 6801 note). Signed by the president Dec. 8, 2004. Title VIII of the Omnibus Appropriations Act. Beginning in FY 2005, and thereafter, the secretary may establish, modify, charge and collect recreation fees at federal recreation lands and waters as provided for in the act. Authority terminates ten years after the date of enactment.

Energy Policy Act of 2005 (119 Stat. 594, 42 U.S.C. 15801 note). Signed by the president Aug. 8, 2005. Directed the secretaries of agriculture, commerce, defense, energy, and the interior to designate energy transport corridors for oil, gas, and hydrogen pipelines and electricity transmission and distribution facilities on federal lands in portions of Arizona, California, Colorado, Idaho, Montana, Nevada, New Mexico, Oregon, Utah, Washington, and Wyoming.

The Food, Conservation, and Energy Act of 2008 (Farm Bill) (7 U.S.C. 8701 note). Vetoed by the president May 21, 2008; veto overridden June 18, 2008. Reauthorized Department of Agriculture programs through fiscal year 2012. Established a competitive research and development program to encourage the use of forest biomass for energy. Established the Community Wood Energy Program. Authorized tribal access to Forest Service lands for cultural activities. Amended the Cooperative Forestry Assistance Act of 1978 to set new priorities and planning standards and adjust rules governing cooperative federal, state, and private forest programs. Enhanced existing and established new forest preservation programs and tightened restrictions on importation of illegally harvested wood.

Emergency Economic Stabilization Act of 2008 (122 Stat. 3765, 12 U.S.C. 5201 note). Signed by the president Oct. 3, 2008. Reauthorized the Secure Rural Schools and Community Self-Determination Act through fiscal year 2011.

Omnibus Public Land Management Act of 2009 (123 Stat. 991, 16 U.S.C. 1 note). Signed by the president March 30, 2009. Authorized certain watershed restoration programs, created a new wildland fire safety program. Authorized a number of land conveyances and forest service designation studies. Designated three new units in the National Park System, enlarged the boundaries of several existing parks, and designated a number of National Heritage Areas.

Consolidated Appropriations Act of 2012 (125 Stat. 1046, 16 U.S.C. 6515). Signed by the president Dec. 23, 2011. Replaced the appeal process for most USFS actions with a pre-decisional objection process (a process implemented in the Healthy Forests Restoration Act of 2003 for hazardous fuel reduction). Applies the pre-decisional objection process to proposed USFS actions that implement land and resource management plans developed under the Forest and Rangeland Renewable Resources Planning Act of 1974.

Agricultural Act of 2014 (Farm Bill) (128 Stat. 913, 16 U.S.C. 6515 note). Signed by the president Feb. 7, 2014.

Includes provisions to modify the existing public notice, comment, and appeals process for land and resource management plans, exempting some USFS projects from the pre-decisional objection process under specific circumstances. Repealed and reauthorized various USFS programs.

■ REGIONAL OFFICES

ALASKA REGION
Federal Office Bldg.
709 W. 9th St., #559A
P.O. Box 21628
Juneau, AK 99802–1628
(907) 586–8806
Beth Pendleton, regional forester

EASTERN REGION
(CT, DE, IA, IL, IN, MA, MD, ME, MI, MN, MO,
     NH, NJ, NY, OH, PA, RI, VT, WI, WV)
626 E. Wisconsin Ave.
Milwaukee, WI 53202
(414) 297–3600
Fax (414) 297–3808
TTY (414) 297–3507
Kathleen Atkinson, regional forester

INTERMOUNTAIN REGION
(Southern ID, NV, UT, western WY)
Federal Bldg.
324 25th St.
Ogden, UT 84401–2310
(801) 625–5605
Fax (801) 625–5127
Nora Rasure, regional forester

NORTHERN REGION
(Northern ID, MT, ND, northwestern SD,
     northern WY)
Federal Bldg.
200 E. Broadway
P.O. Box 7669
Missoula, MT 59807
(406) 329–3511

Fax (406) 329–3347
Faye Krueger, regional forester

PACIFIC NORTHWEST REGION
(OR, WA)
333 S.W. 1st Ave.
P.O. Box 3623
Portland, OR 97204
(503) 808–2648
Kent P. Connaughton, regional forester

PACIFIC SOUTHWEST REGION
(CA, HI, GU, Pacific Trust Territories)
1323 Club Dr.
Vallejo, CA 94592–1110
(707) 562–8737
TTY (707) 562–9240
Randy Moore, regional forester

ROCKY MOUNTAIN REGION
(CO, KS, NE, southeastern SD, eastern WY)
740 Simms St.
Golden, CO 80401–5367
(303) 275–5350
TTY (303) 275–5367
Daniel Jirón, regional forester

SOUTHERN REGION
(AL, AR, FL, GA, KY, LA, MS, NC, OK,
     PR, SC, TN, TX, VA)
1720 Peachtree Rd. N.W., #760S
Atlanta, GA 30309
(404) 347–4095
Fax (404) 347–1781
Liz Agpaoa, regional forester

SOUTHWESTERN REGION
(AZ, NM)
333 Broadway S.E.
Albuquerque, NM 87102
(505) 842–3292
Fax (505) 842–3800
TTY (505) 842–3198
Cal Joyner, regional forester

Grain Inspection, Packers, and Stockyards Administration

1400 Independence Ave. S.W., Washington, DC 20250–3601
Internet: www.gipsa.usda.gov

The Grain Inspection, Packers, and Stockyards Administration (GIPSA) was created as a unit within the U.S. Department of Agriculture (USDA) in 1994, through the merger of the Federal Grain Inspection Service (FGIS) and the Packers and Stockyards Administration (PSA). GIPSA is headed by an administrator who is appointed by the president and confirmed by the Senate; the administrator reports to the assistant secretary of agriculture for marketing and regulatory programs. The FGIS and the renamed Packers and Stockyards Programs continue to function as distinct divisions of GIPSA.

Federal Grain Inspection Service. Created in 1976 to administer the provisions of the Grain Standards Act, the service establishes federal standards for grain and performs inspections to ensure compliance. It also regulates the weighing of all grain that is moved through any export facility in the country.

Standards have been established for corn, wheat, rye, oats, barley, flaxseed, grain sorghum, soybeans, triticale (a hybrid of durum wheat and rye), sunflower seed, and mixed grains.

The FGIS also has authority to establish and enforce standards for rice, dry beans, peas, lentils, and hops under the provisions of the Agricultural Marketing Act of 1946.

The FGIS is divided into four major divisions:

- Quality Assurance and Compliance ensures through reviews, evaluations, and enforcement actions that regulations are uniformly enacted and followed.
- Field Management directs the operation of FGIS field offices; establishes U.S. standards for grain, rice, and other commodities; and measures the quality of grain as it moves through the market.
- Technology and Science develops tests and methods to determine grain quality, recommends specifications and approves grain inspection instrumentation, develops quality control systems, and makes final decisions on inspection appeals.
- Office of Departmental Initiatives and International Affairs (OIA) represents GIPSA on committees and task forces concerned with international grain trade policies, and national policy issues relating to the World Trade Organization, the North American Free Trade Agreement (NAFTA), agricultural biotechnology, and sanitary and phytosanitary issues. The staff also serves as GIPSA's liaison with the Foreign Agricultural Service.

Nearly all grain exported from the United States is inspected during loading. The inspections are performed by FGIS personnel or state inspection agencies authorized by the FGIS. Domestic grain is examined by state inspectors or private firms certified by the FGIS administrator. If a buyer or seller disputes an inspection result, an appeal inspection from the FGIS field office can be requested. This, in turn, may be appealed to the FGIS Board of Appeals and Review.

FGIS personnel, or state inspectors approved by the service, inspect grain and certify weight at export facilities. This process is closely monitored by FGIS field employees. At nonexport facilities, FGIS-approved officials perform weighings on request under the supervision of the FGIS. Violations of FGIS standards are punishable by fines and imprisonment.

All individuals and companies engaged in large-scale grain export operations must register with the FGIS and supply ownership and management information. Registrants are granted a certificate that must be renewed annually. The certificate may be revoked or suspended by the FGIS administrator if a hearing determines that FGIS standards have been violated.

Packers and Stockyards Programs (PSP). This division of GIPSA carries out its responsibilities under the 1921 Packers and Stockyards Act, which charges the agency with the regulation of livestock and live poultry marketing practices as well as those of meat and poultry packers in interstate or foreign commerce.

The act safeguards farmers, ranchers, and consumers from unfair business practices and protects members of the livestock, poultry, and meat industries from unfair, deceptive, unjustly discriminatory, or monopolistic competition.

The 2008 Farm Bill authorized GIPSA to provide significant new protections for producers against unfair, fraudulent, or retaliatory practices in the marketing of livestock and poultry. GIPSA promulgated rules to address the inequity in prices paid to producers in relation to what processors made. In statements provided during the hearings, it was noted that in the poultry industry, a producer makes 34 cents per bird, while the processing company on average makes $3.23 a bird. In December 2011 USDA published the final rule implementing the 2008 Farm Bill provisions to better protect livestock producers and poultry growers.

The Business and Economic Analysis Division provides economic advice to agency officials on broad policy issues and the economic implications of various programs, policies, and practices of the livestock, meat, poultry, and grain industries. The division also administers Section 1324 of the Food Security Act of 1985 (Clear Title program) and certifies state central filing systems to notify buyers, commission merchants, and selling agents of lenders' security interests in farm products.

The Policy and Litigation Division is responsible for developing regulations, enforcement policies, and procedures and for providing litigation support to the Office of General Counsel. To accomplish these tasks, the office consists of three branches that focus on the core responsibilities of competition, fair trade practices, and financial protection.

The Regional Offices of Packers and Stockyards Programs are located in Atlanta, GA; Aurora, CO; and Des Moines, IA. Each office is responsible for carrying out the activities and functions of the Packers and Stockyards Programs and for investigating potential violations of the Packers and Stockyards Act within its assigned region. The regional offices are located near concentrations of livestock and poultry production and slaughter.

◼ KEY PERSONNEL

Administrator
Larry Mitchell . . . . (202) 720–0219
Fax. . . . . (202) 205–9237
Management and Budget Services
Marianne Plaus . . . . (202) 690–3460
Chief of Staff
R. Dexter Thomas (acting) . . . . . . (202) 720–6529
Public Affairs
R. Dexter Thomas. . . . . (202) 720–6529

FEDERAL GRAIN INSPECTION SERVICE

Deputy Administrator for Federal Grain Inspection
Randall D. Jones . . . . (202) 720–9170
Fax. . . . . (202) 690–2333
Departmental Initiatives and International Affairs
Byron Reilly . . . . (202) 690–3368
Quality Assurance and Compliance
Samantha Simon . . . . (202) 690–3206
Fax. . . . . (202) 720–7786
Investigation and Enforcement
Vacant . . . . (202) 720–0228

Field Management
Bob Lijewski. (202) 720–0228
Fax. . . . . (202) 720–1015
Policies, Procedures, and Market Analysis (Kansas City)
Patrick McCluskey . . . . (816) 659–8403
USDA FGIS Technical Center/Domestic Inspection Operations Office
10383 N. Ambassador Dr., Kansas City,
MO 64153–1394
Ronald G. Metz . . . . (816) 659–8400
Technology and Science
Mary Alonzo . . . . (816) 891–0463
Fax. . . . . (816) 891–1253
Board of Appeals and Review (BAR)
Brian Adam . . . . (816) 891–0421
Biotechnology and Analytical Services
Tandace Bell. . . . . (816) 891–0459
Analytical Chemistry
Tim Norden . . . . (816) 891–0470
Inspection Instrumentation
Vacant . . . . (816) 891–0430

PACKERS AND STOCKYARDS PROGRAM

Deputy Administrator for Packers and Stockyards Program
Susan Keith. (202) 720–7051
Fax. . . . . (202) 205–9237
Litigation and Economic Analysis Division
Brett Offutt. (202) 720–7362
Fax. . . . . (202) 690–3207

◼ INFORMATION SOURCES

Internet

Agency website: www.gipsa.usda.gov. Comprehensive website includes information about GIPSA offices and programs, news releases, and GIPSA publications.

Telephone Contacts

Personnel Locator (USDA) . . . . (202) 720–8732
Violations hotline . . . . (800) 998–FGIS
GIPSA idea hotline . . . . (800) 455–3447
E-mail: gipsa-ideas@usda.gov
English-Language Federal
Relay (TTY). . . . . (866) 377–8642
Spanish-Language Federal
Relay (TTY). . . . . (800) 845–6136

Information and Publications

KEY OFFICES

Freedom of Information
1400 Independence Ave. S.W., #1640-S
MS 3642
Washington, DC 20250–3642
(202) 720–8087
Joanne Peterson, FOIA officer

DATA AND STATISTICS

Contact the administrator's office at (202) 720–0219 for the FGIS annual report, which includes data on many of the agency's activities.

PUBLICATIONS

All GIPSA publications are available from the website or contact the administrator's office at (202) 720–0219.

Reference Resources

LIBRARY

National Agricultural Library

10301 Baltimore Ave.
Beltsville, MD 20705–2351
(301) 504–5755
Stan Kosecki, director
Hours: 8:30 a.m. to 4:30 p.m.

The National Agricultural Library also maintains a reference center at the Agriculture Department's South Building. The collection consists primarily of reference volumes, databases, and other computer resources.

D.C. Reference Center

1400 Independence Ave. S.W.
South Bldg., #1052-S
Washington, DC 20250–0201
(301) 504–5077
Rebecca Mazur, coordinator of research services

DOCKETS

GIPSA and Support Staff

1400 Independence Ave. S.W., #2055-S
MS 3604
Washington, DC 20250–3604
(202) 720–6529
R. Dexter Thomas, regulatory analyst
Hours: 8:30 a.m. to 4:00 p.m.

Maintains dockets containing the files for GIPSA rulemaking proceedings. Federal dockets are also available at www.regulations.gov. (*See appendix for Searching and Commenting on Regulations: Regulations.gov.*)

RULES AND REGULATIONS

GIPSA rules and regulations are published in the *Code of Federal Regulations,* Title 7, Chapter VIII, Parts 800–899; Title 9, Chapter II, Parts 200–299. Proposed regulations, new final regulations, and updates to the *Code of Federal Regulations* are published in the daily *Federal Register.* (*See appendix for information on how to obtain and use these publications.*)

▨ LEGISLATION

Department of Agriculture Reorganization Act of 1994 (7 U.S.C. 6901). Signed by the president Oct. 13, 1994. Merged the Federal Grain Inspection Service with the Packers and Stockyards Administration to form GIPSA.

The FGIS carries out its responsibilities under:

Agricultural Marketing Act of 1946 (60 Stat. 1087, 7 U.S.C. 1621). Signed by the president Aug. 14, 1946. Authorized the FGIS to provide official inspection and weighing services for rice, dry beans, peas, lentils, hay, straw, hops, and other processed grain products.

U.S. Grain Standards Act of 1976 (90 Stat. 2867, 7 U.S.C. 71 note). Signed by the president Oct. 21, 1976. Amended the U.S. Grain Standards Act of 1916 (39 Stat. 454, 7 U.S.C. 71), which was signed by the president Aug. 11, 1916. The 1976 act created the FGIS, strengthened the inspection provisions of the original legislation, required supervised weighing of grain, and added stiffer penalties for violations. This act was later amended by the Food and Agriculture Act of 1977 (91 Stat. 913, 7 U.S.C. 1281 note), the United States Grain Standards Act–Grain Exportation Amendments (94 Stat. 1870, 7 U.S.C. 75), the Agriculture and Food Act of 1981 (95 Stat. 1213, 7 U.S.C. 1281 note), the Omnibus Budget Reconciliation Act of 1981 (95 Stat. 357, 31 U.S.C. 1331), and the Federal Grain Inspection Program Amendments (98 Stat. 1831, 7 U.S.C. 79).

Futures Trading Act of 1986 (100 Stat. 3564, 7 U.S.C. 71 note). Signed by the president Nov. 10, 1986. Included the **Grain Quality Improvement Act of 1986.** Established four purposes for grades and standards to guide the work of the FGIS: to facilitate marketing, reflect storability, measure the end-product yield and quality, and provide market incentives.

U.S. Grain Standards Act Amendments of 1993 (107 Stat. 1525, 7 U.S.C. 71 note). Signed by the president Nov. 24, 1993. Authorized inspection and weighing activities in Canadian ports. Authorized a pilot program to permit more than one official agency to carry out inspections within a single geographic area. Extended inspector licensing authority to contract-supervised persons. Enabled the administrator of the FGIS to test weighing equipment and collect related fees. Established Sept. 30, 2000, as the date when the grain standards advisory committee will terminate.

Grain Standards and Warehouse Improvement Act of 2000 (114 Stat. 2058, 7 U.S.C. 71 note). Signed by the president Nov. 9, 2000. Authorized the collection of the tonnage portion of the original inspection and weighing fees, and the fee for supervising official agencies. Also extended authority to maintain an advisory committee.

The PSP carries out its responsibilities under:

Packers and Stockyards Act of 1921, as amended (42 Stat. 159, 7 U.S.C. 181–229). Signed by the president Aug. 15, 1921. Gave the secretary authority to regulate competition and trade practices in the livestock, meat packing, and poultry industries. The Packers and Stockyards Administration (PSA), the forerunner of the Packers and Stockyards Programs within GIPSA, was created to administer the act. A 1958 amendment (72 Stat. 1749) substantially expanded the secretary's jurisdiction over auction markets and dealers. A 1976 amendment (90 Stat. 1249) increased financial protection for livestock sellers and made meat wholesalers subject to regulation as packers.

Food Security Act of 1985 (99 Stat. 1354, 7 U.S.C. 1281 note). Signed by the president Dec. 23, 1985. Gave the PSA regulatory and certifying power over a new central filing system for notification of liens against farm products.

Poultry Producers Financial Protection Act of 1987 (101 Stat. 917, 7 U.S.C. 181 note). Signed by the president Nov. 23, 1987. Expanded the responsibilities of the PSA by adding statutory trust and payment provisions for poultry producers similar to those adopted in 1976 for livestock producers.

Livestock Mandatory Reporting Act of 1999 (113 Stat. 1188, 7 U.S.C. 1635 note). Title IX of the Agriculture, Rural Development, Food and Drug Administration, and Related Agencies Appropriations Act of 2000. Amends the Agricultural Marketing Act of 1946 to define specified terms relating to livestock reporting, including cattle, lamb, and swine reporting. Requires the secretary of agriculture to establish mandatory price reporting programs for live cattle and swine that: provide timely and accurate market information; facilitate informed marketing decisions; and promote competition in the slaughtering industry. Sets forth reporting provisions for the secretary and packers.

Farm Security and Rural Investment Act of 2002 (116 Stat. 1348, 7 U.S.C. 7901 note). Signed by the president May 13, 2002. Section 10502 amended the Packers and Stockyards Act to make any swine contractor subject to the jurisdiction of the act. Persons contracting with others to raise and care for feeder pigs or other swine that were not intended for slaughter were not covered.

Food, Conservation, and Energy Act of 2008 (Farm Bill) (7 U.S.C. 8701 note). Vetoed by the president May 21, 2008; veto overridden June 18, 2008. Reauthorized Department of Agriculture programs through fiscal year 2012. Allowed some interstate sales of state-inspected meat and poultry, established voluntary catfish grading and inspection, and amended rules for hog and poultry production contracts.

■ REGIONAL OFFICES

FEDERAL GRAIN INSPECTION SERVICE FIELD LOCATIONS (USDA, GIPSA, FGIS)

Domestic Inspection Operations Office
(CO, IA, IL, IN, KS, portions of MN, MS, ND, NE, NM, OK, SD, TX, WI, WY)
10383 N. Ambassador Dr.
Kansas City, MO 64153
(816) 659–8400
Fax (816) 872–1258
E-mail: Ronald.G.Metz@usda.gov
Ronald G. Metz, field office manager

Grand Forks Field Office
(ID, MT, portions of ND, UT)
2625 24th Ave. South, Suite C
P.O. Box 13427

Grand Forks, ND 58208–3427
(701) 772–3371
Fax (701) 772–0362
E-mail: Edward.R.Stallman@usda.gov
Ed Stallman, field office manager

League City Field Office
(Portions of TX)
1025 E. Main St., #104
League City, TX 77523–2483
(281) 338–2787
Fax (281) 338–2788
E-mail: Dave.Grady@usda.gov
Dave Grady, field office manager

New Orleans Field Office
(AL, FL, GA, LA, SC)
104 Campus Dr. East, #200
Destrehan, LA 70047–0640
(985) 764–2324
Fax (985) 764–2324
E-mail: Kerry.F.Petit@usda.gov
Kerry F. Petit, field office manager

Portland Field Office
(AZ, CA, HI, OR)
1100 N.W. Naito Pkwy.
Portland, OR 97209–2818
(503) 326–7887
Fax (503) 326–7896
E-mail: Andy.Ping@usda.gov
Andy Ping, field office manager

Stuttgart Field Office
(AK, CA rice, portions of IL, IN, KY, MS, MS rice, TN)
211 Leslie St.
Stuttgart, AR 72160–4340
(870) 673–2508
Fax (870) 673–2500
E-mail: Sandra.A.Metheny@usda.gov
Sandra Metheny, field office manager

Toledo Field Office
(CT, DC, DE, portions of IL, IN, KY, MA, MD, MI, NH, NY, OH, PA, RI, VI, VT, Milwaukee, WI, WV, Eastern Canada)
1910 Indian Wood Circle, #401
Maumee, OH 43537
(419) 893–3076
Fax (419) 893–2861
E-mail: Lynn.E.Thomas@usda.gov
Lynn Thomas, field office manager

Washington Federal/State Office
3939 Cleveland Ave. S.E.
Olympia, WA 98501–4079
(360) 753–9072

Lab (360) 753–6964
Fax (360) 586–5257
E-mail: Randall.R.Deike@usda.gov
Randall Deike, federal state manager

PACKERS AND STOCKYARDS PROGRAM REGIONAL LOCATIONS (USDA, GIPSA, P&SP)

Eastern Regional Office

(AK, AL CT, DC, DE, FL, GA,
LA, MA, MD, ME, MI, NC, NH, NJ,
NY, PA, RI, SC, TN, VA, VT, WV)
75 Spring St., #230
Atlanta, GA 30303
(404) 562–5840
Fax (404) 562–5848
E-mail: Elkin.W.Parker@usda.gov
Elkin Parker, regional director

Midwestern Regional Office

(IA, IL, IN, KY, MI, MN, MS, ND, NE, OH, SD, WI)
Federal Building, #317
210 Walnut St.
Des Moines, IA 50309
(513) 323–2579
Fax (513) 323–2590
E-mail: Stuart.D.Frank@usda.gov
Stuart Frank, regional director

Western Regional Office

(AR, AS, CA, CO, HI, ID, KS, MN, MT, NM, NV, OK,
OR, TX, UT, WA, WY)
1 Gateway Center
3950 Lewiston, #200
Aurora, CO 80011
(303) 375–4240
Fax (303) 371–4609
E-mail: Kraig.J.Roesch@usda.gov
Kraig Roesch, regional director

Natural Resources Conservation Service

1400 Independence Ave. S.W., #5105, Washington, DC 20250
Internet: www.nrcs.usda.gov

The Natural Resources Conservation Service (NRCS) was created in 1994 by a reorganization of the U.S. Department of Agriculture (USDA). It succeeded the former Soil Conservation Service, a USDA agency established by the Soil Conservation and Domestic Allotment Act of 1935, and combined its functions with various conservation programs previously administered by the Agricultural Stabilization and Conservation Service (ASCS) and the Farmers Home Administration (FmHA).

The NRCS provides technical and financial assistance to conserve natural resources. It works primarily with farmers and ranchers on private lands but also assists the conservation districts of rural and urban governments to reduce erosion, conserve and protect water, and solve other resource problems. Most NRCS employees work in the USDA's local county offices. To accomplish its conservation goals, the NRCS also works with environmental groups, AmeriCorps, and its Earth Team volunteers. The agency is headed by a chief who reports to the under secretary of agriculture for natural resources and environment.

In addition to technical assistance to landowners and governments, the NRCS conducts various other programs. Many of these involve cooperation with other government agencies and state land-grant universities.

Conservation Programs

The Agricultural Act of 2014 (Farm Bill) consolidated several conservation programs. The legislation established the Regional Conservation Partnership Program (RCPP), which consolidated four existing programs: the Agricultural Water Enhancement Program, the Chesapeake Bay Watershed Program, the Cooperative Conservation Partnership Initiative, and the Great Lakes Basin Program. RCPP promotes coordination between NRCS and its partners to support projects that improve wildlife habitat, soil quality, water quality, or in a specific area or region. NRCS provides assistance to producers through partnership agreements and through program contracts or easement agreements. Three previous easement programs—Wetlands Reserve Program, Grassland Reserve Program, and Farm and Ranch Lands Protection Program—were replaced with the Agricultural Conservation Easement Program (ACEP), which provides financial and technical assistance to help conserve agricultural lands and wetlands.

In addition to several watershed and flood prevention programs, NRCS programs authorized or reauthorized under the 2014 Farm Bill include:

- Agricultural Management Assistance Program provides cost share assistance to agricultural producers to voluntarily address issues such as water management, water quality, and erosion control by incorporating conservation into their farming operations.
- Conservation of Private Grazing Land Program provides technical assistance from the NRCS to owners and managers of private grazing land.
- Conservation Stewardship Program (formerly the Conservation Security Program) provides financial and technical assistance to conserve soil, water, air, energy, and plant and animal life on tribal and private working lands—cropland, grassland, prairie land, improved pasture and rangeland, as well as certain forested land that is an incidental part of an agriculture operation.
- Environmental Quality Incentive Program (EQIP) helps farmers and ranchers to treat identified soil, water, and related natural resource concerns on eligible land. Includes the Agricultural Water Enhancement Program and Conservation Innovation Grants.
- Farm and Ranch Land Protection Program provides matching funds to help purchase development rights to keep productive farm and ranch land in agricultural uses.

Healthy Forest Reserve Program is a voluntary program to restore and protect forest ecosystems, promote biodiversity, and promote the recovery of threatened and endangered species.The 2014 Farm Bill reauthorized the Voluntary Public Access and Habitat Incentive Program (VPA-HIP), often referred to as the "Open Fields" program. This program provides grants to states and tribal governments to encourage owners and operators of privately held farm, ranch, and forest land to voluntarily make land available for public access for wildlife-dependent recreation, including hunting or fishing, under programs administered by states and tribal governments.

The 2014 Farm Bill relinked highly erodible land conservation and wetland conservation compliance with eligibility for premium support paid under the federal crop insurance program. Changes mandated through the 2014 Farm Bill require producers to have on file a Highly

Erodible Land Conservation and Wetland Conservation Certification. The 2014 Farm Bill continues the requirement that producers adhere to conservation compliance guidelines to be eligible for most programs administered by Farm Service Agency (FSA) and NRCS. This includes the new price and revenue protection programs, the Conservation Reserve Program, the Livestock Disaster Assistance programs, and Marketing Assistance Loans implemented by FSA. It also includes the Environmental Quality Incentives Program, the Conservation Stewardship Program, and other conservation programs.

■ KEY PERSONNEL

Chief
Jason Weller . . . . (202) 720–7246
Fax. . . . . (202) 720–7690
Deputy Chief
Gayle Barry . . . . (202) 720–7847
Fax. . . . . (202) 720–2588
Budget Formulation
Selena Miller . . . . (202) 720–4209
Communications
Terry Bish . . . . (202) 720–8851
Community Planning
Avery Patillo. (202) 720–5974
Financial Management
Stephen Kunze . . . . (202) 720–5904
Information Technology
Mia Wright. . . . . (202) 720–6707
International Activities
Lillian Woods Shawver. . . . . (301) 504–2269
National Resources Inventory
Patrick Flanagan (national
statistician). . . . . (301) 504–2222
Outreach Programs and Project Activities
Larry Holmes. . . . . (202) 720–1986
Soil Science and Resource Assessment
David Smith. (301) 504–2302
Fax. . . . . (301) 504–3788
Science and Technology
Wayne Honeycutt . . . . (202) 720–4630
Fax. . . . . (202) 720–7710
Soil Climate Analysis Network (SCAN)
Tony Tolsdorf. . . . . (503) 414–3006
Strategic Planning and Accountability
Lesia Reed . . . . (301) 504–6297
Conservation Specialties
  Agricultural Water Management
  Rob Sampson. . . . . (202) 720–5356
  Agroforestry
  Eunice Padley . . . . (202) 720–3921
  Agronomy
  Norman Widman . . . . (202) 720–3783
  Air Quality
  Greg Johnson (acting) . . . . (503) 273–2424
  Animal Agriculture and Water Quality Regulations
  Glenn Carpenter. . . . . (301) 504–2293
  Animal Feeding Operations
  Glenn Carpenter. . . . . (301) 504–2293

Animal Husbandry
  Glenn Carpenter. . . . . (301) 504–2293
Animal Waste Management
  Glenn Carpenter. . . . . (301) 504–2293
Aquaculture
  Craig Goodwin . . . . (202) 205–7711
Aquatic Ecology
  Craig Goodwin . . . . (202) 205–7711
Atmospheric Resources
  Greg Johnson (acting) . . . . (503) 273–2424
Biology
  Danielle Flynn. . . . . (202) 690–0856
Botany
  Norman Melvin. . . . . (817) 509–3572
Cartography (Fort Worth, TX)
  Steve Nechero . . . . (817) 509–3366
Climate Data (Portland, OR)
  Rashawn Tama . . . . (503) 414–3010
Conservation Planning
  Dan Lawson. . . . . (202) 720–5322
Coral Reef Initiative
  Craig Goodwin . . . . (202) 205–7711
Cultural Resources
  Vacant. . . . . (202) 720–4912
Desertification
  Thomas Reinsch . . . . (301) 504–2289
Ecology
  Benjamin Smallwood. . . . . (202) 720–7838
Economics
  Janet Berry. . . . . (301) 720–7838
Energy (Portland, OR)
  Kenneth Phiel (acting). . . . . (503) 273–2437
Engineering
  Noller Herbert. . . . . (202) 720–2520
Fire Ecology
  Chuck Stanley . . . . (817) 509–3282
Fisheries
  Craig Goodwin . . . . (202) 205–7711
Forestry, Woodland Management
  Eunice Padley . . . . (202) 720–3921
Geographic Information Systems (GIS) (Fort Worth, TX)
  Bill Marken . . . . (817) 509–3524
Grazing Lands
  Sid Brantly . . . . (202) 720–5010
Historic Preservation
  Vacant. . . . . (202) 720–4912
Invasive Species
  Doug Holy . . . . (202) 720–0307
Land Health
  Norman Widman . . . . (202) 720–3782
Migratory Birds
  Danielle Flynn. . . . . (202) 690–0856
Nitrogen Management
  Norm Widman . . . . (202) 720–3783
Nutrient Management
  Chris Gross . . . . (301) 504–3954
  Glenn Carpenter. . . . . (301) 504–2293
Ocean Ecology
  Craig Goodwin . . . . (202) 205–7711

Organic Agriculture
  Benjamin Smallwood . . . . (202) 720–7838
Pasture Management
  Sid Brantly . . . . (202) 720–5010
Pest Management
  Benjamin Smallwood . . . . (202) 720–7838
Pesticides
  Benjamin Smallwood . . . . (202) 720–7838
  Joe Bagdon . . . . (413) 253–4376
Pollinators
  Doug Holy . . . . (202) 720–0307
Range Conservation
  Sid Brantly . . . . (202) 720–5010
Risk Assessment
  Richard Farnsworth . . . . (301) 504–2009
Soil Health
  David Lamm . . . . (336) 370–3339
Stream Restoration
  Jon Fripp. (817) 509–3771
Urban Conservation
  Avery Patillo . . . . (202) 720–7671
Waste Management
  Bill Reck . . . . (336) 370–3353
Water Quality
  Craig Goodwin . . . . (202) 205–7711
Programs
  Agriculture Management Assistance Program (AMA)
    Dave Mason. . . . . (202) 720–0673
  Chesapeake Bay Program
    Robert McAfee . . . . (443) 482–2953
  Conservation Effects Assessment Project (CEAP)
    Daryl Lund. . . . . (202) 384–2033
  Conservation Easement
    Kim Berns (acting) . . . . (202) 720–4527
    Fax. . . . . (202) 720–6559
  Conservation Reserve Program
    Sharif Branham . . . . (202) 720–1870
  Conservation Security Program (CSP)
    Richard Zetterberg (acting) . . . . . . (202) 720–3524
  **Global Climate Change Activities
    and Programs**
    Michael Wilson . . . . (402) 437–4134
  Great Lakes Programs
    Paul Younstrum. . . . . (312) 886–0261
  Mississippi River Basin Initiative
    Meghan Wilson . . . . (202) 720–9615
  Range Conservationist Partnership Program
    Lindsay Haines . . . . (202) 720–1873
  Small Watershed Program
    Dan Lawson. . . . . (202) 720–5322
  **Snow Survey and Water Supply Forecasting
    Program (Portland, OR)**
    Michael Strobel . . . . (503) 414–3055
  Waterbank Program
    Dave Mason. . . . . (202) 720–0673
  Watershed Programs
    Ildefonso Chavez. . . . . (202) 720–7730
  Wetlands Reserved Program
    Jessica Groves . . . . (202) 720–1067

World Soil Resources Program
  Thomas Reinsch . . . . (301) 504–2289
Regional Assistant Chiefs
  Central (IA, IL, IN, KS, MN, MO, ND, NE, OK, SD, TX, WI)
    Kevin Wickey. . . . . (202) 690–2196
  Northeast (CT, DE, MA, MD, ME, MI, NH, NJ, NY, OH, PA, RI, VT, WV)
    Tony Kramer (acting). . . . . (202) 690–2197
  Southeast (AK, AL, Caribbean area, FL, GA, KY, LA, MI, NC, SC, TN, VA)
    James Tillman . . . . (202) 690–2196
  West (AK, AZ, CA, CO, HI, ID, MT, NM, NV, OR, Pacific Basin, UT, WA, WY)
    Astor Boozer . . . . (202) 690–2196

■ INFORMATION SOURCES

Internet
  Agency website: www.nrcs.usda.gov. Provides information on NRCS offices, an programs, and updates on agency activities.

Telephone Contacts
  See *NRCS Conservation Communication Staff*, below.

Information and Publications

KEY OFFICES

NRCS Conservation Communication Staff
  1400 Independence Ave. S.W., #6121-S
  Washington, DC 20250
  (202) 720–3210
  Fax (202) 720–1564
  Kaveh Sadeghzadeh, director

NRCS Legislative Affairs Staff
  1400 Independence Ave. S.W., #5121
  Washington, DC 20250
  (202) 720–2771
  Fax (202) 690–0854
  Callie Eideberg (acting), director

Freedom of Information
  375 Jackson St., #600
  St. Paul, MN 55101
  (651) 602–7907
  Email: nrcs-foia@wdc.usda.gov
  Patrick McLoughlin, FOIA officer

DATA AND STATISTICS
  For data and statistics available from the NRCS, contact the Resource Inventory and Assessment Division: (301) 504–2311.

PUBLICATIONS
  Publications are available on the website. Electronic Field Office Technical Guides (eFOTG) contain technical

information about the conservation of soil, water, air, and related plant and animal resources, as well as information on conservation standards and specifications. For publications contact:

NRCS Publications and Forms Distribution Center
1–888-LANDCARE
5140 Park Ave., Suite C
Des Moines, IA 50321
(888) 526–3227

A selected number of publications can be found on the agency's website, www.nrcs.usda.gov.

Reference Resources

LIBRARY

National Agricultural Library
10301 Baltimore Ave.
Beltsville, MD 20705–2351
(301) 504–5755
Stan Kosecki, director
Hours: 8:30 a.m. to 4:30 p.m.

The National Agricultural Library also maintains a reference center at the Agriculture Department's South Building. The collection consists primarily of reference volumes, databases, and other computer resources.

D.C. Reference Center
1400 Independence Ave. S.W., South Bldg., #1052-S
Washington, DC 20250–0201
(301) 504–5077
Rebecca Mazur, coordinator of research services

DOCKETS
Federal dockets are available at www.regulations.gov. (*See appendix for Searching and Commenting on Regulations: Regulations.gov.*)

RULES AND REGULATIONS
NRCS rules and regulations are published in Title 7, Chapter VI, Parts 600–699 of the *Code of Federal Regulations.* Proposed rules, new final rules, and updates to the *Code of Federal Regulations* are published in the *Federal Register.* (*See appendix for information on how to obtain and use these publications.*)

■ LEGISLATION
Soil Conservation and Domestic Allotment Act (49 Stat. 163, 16 U.S.C. 590a). Signed by the president April 27, 1935. Created the Soil Conservation Service, now NRCS. Authorized the secretary of agriculture to provide loans and payments to farmers and others to improve conservation efforts and prevent erosion.

Watershed Protection and Flood Prevention Act (68 Stat. 666, 16 U.S.C. 1001 note). Signed by the president Aug. 4, 1954. Empowered the FmHA to make loans to state or local organizations to carry out watershed and flood prevention measures.

Water Bank Act (84 Stat. 1468, 16 U.S.C. 1301). Signed by the president Dec. 19, 1970. Provided funds for the improvement and maintenance of wetlands and adjacent natural resource areas; the control of runoff, erosion, and floods; and the promotion of water management techniques.

Soil and Water Conservation Act of 1977 (91 Stat. 1407, 16 U.S.C. 2001 et seq.). Signed by the president Nov. 18, 1977. Directed the secretary of agriculture to conduct an appraisal and develop a National Conservation Program every five years.

Cooperative Forestry Assistance Act of 1978 (92 Stat. 367, 16 U.S.C. 2103). Signed by the president July 1, 1978. Authorized the Forestry Incentives Program to provide cost-sharing incentives to encourage development, management, and protection of nonindustrial private forest lands.

Agriculture, Rural Development, and Related Agencies Appropriations Act for Fiscal Year 1980 (93 Stat. 835, 16 U.S.C. 590e-1). Signed by the president Nov. 9, 1979. Authorized the experimental Rural Clean Water program to provide cost-sharing and technical assistance for installing measures that control nonpoint source pollution and improve water quality in rural America.

Food Security Act of 1985 (99 Stat. 1518, 7 U.S.C. 1281 note). Signed by the president Dec. 23, 1985. Began a program in which a farmer can sell an easement on highly erodible land for conservation for 50 years in exchange for a reduction of FmHA debt. Required farmers and ranchers who have highly erodible crop land to have a conservation plan to remain eligible for program benefits.

Food, Agriculture, Conservation, and Trade Act of 1990 (104 Stat. 3359, 7 U.S.C. 1421 note). Signed by the president Nov. 28, 1990. Established standards for protection of wetlands in the FmHA inventory.

Department of Agriculture Reorganization Act of 1994 (108 Stat. 3209, 7 U.S.C. 6901 note). Signed by the president Oct. 13, 1994. Established the NRCS by combining the Soil Conservation Service with conservation programs from the former ASCS and FmHA.

Federal Agriculture Improvement and Reform Act of 1996 (110 Stat. 888, 7 U.S.C. 7201 note). Signed by the president April 4, 1996. Authorized more than $2.2 billion in additional funding for conservation programs, extended the Conservation Reserve Program and the Wetlands Reserve Program, and created new programs to address high priority environmental protection goals.

Farm Security and Rural Investment Act of 2002 (116 Stat. 1348, 7 U.S.C. 7901 note). Signed by the president May 13, 2002. Authorized several new conservation programs. Amended the Food Security Act of 1985 to establish a conservation security program through 2006 to assist conservation practices on production land. Amended the Cooperative Forestry Management Act of

1978 to permit local governments or qualified organizations to acquire forest legacy program conservation easements and enhance community fire protection and tree and forest growth and resource conservation.

Food, Conservation, and Energy Act of 2008 (Farm Bill) (7 U.S.C. 8701 note). Vetoed by the president May 21, 2008; veto overridden June 18, 2008. Reauthorized USDA conservation programs through fiscal year 2012. Created the Voluntary Public Access and Habitat Incentive Program. Instructed the agriculture secretary to use 5 percent of Environmental Quality Incentive Program (EQIP) funds to assist new farmers and ranchers, and 5 percent for socially disadvantaged farmers and ranchers.

Agricultural Act of 2014 (Farm Bill) (128 Stat. 713, 16 U.S.C. 3831 et seq.). Signed by the president Feb. 7, 2014. Consolidated several conservation programs and links basic conservation practices to crop insurance premium subsidies for highly erodible lands and wetlands as well as eligibility for federal conservation funding.

Risk Management Agency

1400 Independence Ave. S.W., #6092S, MS 0801
Washington, DC 20250–0801
Internet: www.rma.usda.gov

In 1996 the Risk Management Agency (RMA) was created to administer Federal Crop Insurance Corporation programs and other noninsurance-related risk management and education programs that help support U.S. agriculture. Many of these functions were formerly covered under the Farm Service Agency.

Today, the crop insurance program, which is administered by the RMA, helps farmers survive a major crop loss. Nearly ninety percent of insurable acreage planted on major U.S. farms is insured, covering more than 100 commodities and many of their varieties. Livestock risk protection insurance plans also are available. Crop insurance is sold and serviced by nineteen insurance companies authorized by the USDA to sell polices within the crop insurance program. The effectiveness of this partnership is evident in that virtually all indemnities are paid within thirty days of a claim.

Federal Crop Insurance Corporation. Through the Federal Crop Insurance Corporation (FCIC), the RMA offers all-risk crop insurance to cover unavoidable losses because of insect infestation, adverse weather conditions, plant disease, flood, wildlife, fire, and earthquake.

The management of the corporation is vested in a board of directors subject to the general supervision of the secretary of agriculture. The board consists of the manager of the corporation, the under secretary of agriculture responsible for the federal crop insurance program, USDA chief economist, one member who is experienced in crop insurance but not otherwise employed by the federal government, an individual knowledgeable about reinsurance or regulation, and four active farmers, one of whom grows specialty crops.

Congress first authorized federal crop insurance in the 1930s along with other initiatives to help agriculture recover from the combined effects of the Great Depression and the Dust Bowl. The FCIC was created in 1938 to carry out the program. Crop insurance activities were mostly limited to major crops in the main producing areas.

The Federal Crop Insurance Act of 1980 expanded the crop insurance program to many more crops and regions of the country. It encouraged expansion to replace the free disaster coverage (compensation to farmers for prevented planting losses and yield losses) offered under farm bills enacted in the 1960s and 1970s, because the free coverage competed with the experimental crop insurance program.

However, there was not a high rate of participation in the new insurance program. Several years of drought and other natural disasters ensued during the1980s and into the early 1990s. Congress responded to each crisis with emergency appropriations to assist farmers. After several years of ad hoc assistance, Congress passed the Federal Crop Insurance Reform Act of 1994.

The Federal Crop Insurance Reform Act of 1994 significantly changed the way in which government assisted producers suffering a major crop loss. Under the program, producers were required to purchase at least the catastrophic level (CAT) of crop insurance of economic significance to participate in other assistance programs through the Farm Service Agency (see p. 487), such as price support and production adjustment programs and certain farm loans. CAT coverage provides per-acre return similar to the coverage under most previous ad hoc disaster programs. It is fully subsidized by the federal government, apart from a nominal processing fee, and is available from both commercial insurance agents and local USDA offices.

The FCIC also provides money and policy incentives for producers to purchase additional coverage from commercial insurance agents. For crops that are not yet insurable, the Federal Crop Insurance Reform Act has established a Noninsured Crop Disaster Assistance Program (NAP), which provides benefits similar to CAT coverage. NAP is administered through the Farm Service Agency.

In 1996 Congress repealed the mandatory participation requirement. However, farmers who accepted other benefits were required to purchase crop insurance or otherwise waive their eligibility for any disaster benefits that might be made available for the crop year.

Participation in the crop insurance program increased significantly following enactment of the 1994 act. In 1998 more than 180 million acres of farmland were insured under the program, more than three times the acreage insured in 1988, and more than twice the acreage insured in 1993. The liability (or value of the insurance in force) in 1998 was $28 billion. The total premium, which includes subsidy, and the premium paid by insured persons (nearly $950 million) were also record figures.

Since 2000 farmer purchases of higher levels of protection and revenue coverage policies have increased. In 2012 RMA managed nearly $117 billion in liability insurance covering more than 282 million acres.

2014 Farm Bill

The Agricultural Act of 2014 (Farm Bill) made significant changes to risk management direction and programs. The policy guiding the 2014 Farm Bill sought to move producers away from price supports and into crop insurance as the preferred risk management tool. The 2014 Farm Bill continues the growth of the crop insurance program and expands farm safety net options for organic farmers and specialty crop producers. New products to help producers expand their protection against losses due to natural disasters or price declines include:

Supplemental Coverage Option (SCO) is a county-level revenue or yield-based optional endorsement that covers a portion of losses not covered by the same crop's underlying crop insurance policy. Indemnities will be payable once a 14 percent loss has occurred in the county, and individual payments will depend upon coverage levels selected by producers. Crops on a farm enrolled in Agriculture Risk Coverage (ARC, offered through FSA) will not be eligible for SCO coverage. However, a crop on a farm may be enrolled in both SCO and Price Loss Coverage (PLC), another program administered by FSA.

Stacked Income Protection Plan, or STAX, is a stand-alone/supplemental insurance policy for cotton only. STAX protects against countywide revenue losses and can supplement a producer's underlying cotton policy, or be purchased as a stand-alone policy. Cotton producers are not eligible for ARC or PLC.

RMA is developing a new whole-farm insurance product to target highly diversified farms and farms selling two to five commodities to wholesale markets. Whole-farm insurance covers all commodities on the farm including specialty crops. The 2014 Farm Bill also provided additional assistance for beginning farmers, peanut producers, and organic producers.

In order to receive premium assistance from the federal government for crop insurance, producers must comply with highly erodible land and wetland conservation requirements that most already have to comply with as a result of participating in FSA and Natural Resources Conservation Service (NRCS) programs.

RMA Pilot Programs. New RMA programs are tested on a pilot basis in selected counties to allow the agency to gain insurance experience and test the programs' components. Most pilot programs operate for about two to three years before they are made more broadly available or are converted to permanent program status. However, during a new program's pilot period, expansion into new counties may be approved by the FCIC board of directors. RMA routinely develops, implements, and monitors pilot programs for new crops, new plans of insurance, and new management strategies. The 2014 Farm Bill eliminated the requirement that the FCIC evaluate pilot programs.

Congress mandated risk management education in the Federal Agriculturel Improvement and Reform (FAIR) Act of 1996. RMA provides training to farmers to help them acquire the risk management skills needed to compete and win in the global marketplace. The agency is leading a risk management education initiative in cooperation with USDA's Cooperative State Research, Education, and Extension Service; USDA's National Office of Outreach; and the Commodity Futures Trading Commission. With public and private partners, RMA works to find improved risk management strategies, develop educational curricula and materials, and train producers in effective use of risk management tools. The 2014 Farm Bill requires crop insurance and risk management education programs to emphasize farm financial benchmarking as a risk management strategy.

■ KEY PERSONNEL

Administrator
   Brandon Willis . . . . (202) 690–2803
      Fax . . . . (202) 690–2818
Associate Administrator
   Michael Alston . . . . (202) 690–2533
      Fax . . . . (202) 690–2818
Strategic Data Acquisition and Analysis
   Ken Lanclos . . . . (202) 205–3933
Insurance Services
   Heather Manzano (acting) . . . . (202) 690–4494
Risk Management Education
   Lana Cusick . . . . (202) 720–3325
Risk Management Services
   Robert Ibarra . . . . (202) 260–8286
Program Support
   Wes Azama . . . . (202) 260–0080
Risk Compliance
   Heather Manzano . . . . (202) 720–9146
Appeals, Litigation, and Legal Liaison Staff
   Donna Gibson . . . . (202) 720–0642
Regulatory Liaison
   Robert Ibarra . . . . (202) 260–8286
Product Management (Kansas City, MO)
   Timothy B. Witt . . . . (816) 926–7394
Reinsurance Services
   David L. Miller . . . . (202) 720–9830

■ INFORMATION SERVICES

Internet
   Agency website: www.rma.usda.gov.

Information and Publications

KEY OFFICES

Public Affairs
   USDA-RMA
   1400 Independence Ave. S.W.
   MS 0801

Washington, DC 20250–0801
John Shea, director
(202) 260–0080
Bill Crews, FOIA officer
(202) 720–9507

DATA AND STATISTICS

National Ag Risk Education Library

The National Ag Risk Education Library is an online, searchable resource maintained by the Digital Center for Risk Management Education at the University of Minnesota, and is supported by the Extension Regional Risk Management Education Centers. It is accessible at www.agrisk.umn.edu.

PUBLICATIONS

RMA publications, reports, and bulletins are available online at www.rma.usda.gov/pubs. For more information, contact Shirley Pugh at (202) 690–0437.

DOCKETS

Federal dockets are available at www.regulations .gov. (*See appendix for Searching and Commenting on Regulations: Regulations.gov.*)

RULES AND REGULATIONS

RMA rules and regulations are published in the *Code of Federal Regulations,* Title 7, Chapters IV–VI, Parts 400–699. Proposed rules, new final rules, and updates to the *Code of Federal Regulations* are published in the daily *Federal Register.* (*See appendix for information on how to obtain and use these publications.*) The *Federal Register* and the *Code of Federal Regulations* may be accessed online at www.archives.gov/federal-register/cfr; the site contains a link to the federal government's regulatory website at www.regulations.gov (*see appendix*).

■ LEGISLATION

Federal Crop Insurance Corporation Act of 1938 (52 Stat. 72, 7 U.S.C. 1501 et seq.). Signed by the president Feb. 16, 1938. Established the FCIC as an agency of the USDA.

Federal Crop Insurance Reform Act of 1994 (108 Stat. 3179, 7 U.S.C. 1501 note). Signed by the president Oct. 13, 1994. Overhauled the crop insurance program. Established catastrophic level (CAT) coverage as a requirement to participate in certain FSA programs; also established the Noninsured Crop Disaster Assistance Program (NAP) for crops not yet insurable.

Federal Agriculture Improvement and Reform Act of 1996 (110 Stat. 888, 7 U.S.C. 7201 note). Signed by the president April 4, 1996. Title I, subtitle H, section 193 amended the Federal Crop Insurance Act to direct the secretary of agriculture to offer catastrophic risk protection in a state through the local Department of Agriculture offices if sufficient coverage is unavailable. Provided for the transfer of current policies to private insurers and established a crop insurance pilot project.

Section 194 established the Office of Risk Management to oversee the Federal Crop Insurance Corporation and related crop insurance matters. Section 196 directed the secretary to operate a noninsured crop disaster assistance program through the FSA for food or fiber crops not covered by the federal crop insurance catastrophic risk protection program. Mandated education for farmers and agribusiness producers in management of the financial risks inherent in the production and marketing of agricultural commodities.

Agricultural Research, Extension, and Education Reform Act of 1998 (112 Stat. 523, 7 U.S.C. 7926). Signed by the president June 23, 1998. Title V, subtitle C amended the Federal Crop Insurance Corporation Act of 1938 to make permanent the Federal Crop Insurance Corporation's authority to pay expenses from the insurance fund. Directed the corporation to establish and implement procedures for responding to regulatory inquiries.

Agricultural Risk Protection Act of 2000 (114 Stat. 358, 7 U.S.C. 1501 note). Signed by the president June 20, 2000. Amended the Federal Crop Insurance Act to provide greater access to more affordable risk management tools and to improve the efficiency and integrity of the federal crop insurance program. Directed the Commodity Credit Corporation to offer optional quality adjustment crop insurance policies (with reduced premiums for nonelecting producers) and to conduct crop insurance-related research and pilot programs. Amended the Agricultural Research, Extension, and Education Reform Act of 1998 to establish an educational program to improve agricultural producers' risk management skills.

Farm Security and Rural Investment Act of 2002 (116 Stat. 1348, 7 U.S.C. 7901 note). Signed by the president May 13, 2002. Amended the Federal Agricultural Improvement and Reform Act of 1996 to restrict commodity and crop insurance payments, loans, and benefits to qualifying previously cropped land, including conservation reserve land. Amended the Food Security Act of 1985 to include farm storage facility loans, disaster payments, and indemnity payments for producers of commodities on highly erodible land.

Food, Conservation, and Energy Act of 2008 (Farm Bill) (7 U.S.C. 8701 note). Vetoed by the president May 21, 2008; veto overridden June 18, 2008. Reauthorized Department of Agriculture programs through fiscal year 2012. Reduced subsidies to insurance companies and increased administrative fees paid by farmers for minimum insurance coverage level. Allowed the FCIC to renegotiate the Standard Reinsurance Agreement with insurance companies effective in reinsurance year 2011 and once every five years thereafter unless adverse circumstances exist.

Agricultural Act of 2014 (128 Stat. 954, 7 U.S.C. 1508). Signed by the president Feb. 7, 2014. Made substantive changes to the crop insurance program to move producers from price supports to crop insurance as the primary risk management tool. Expanded program options for underserved producers.

■ REGIONAL OFFICES

BILLINGS, MT
(MT, ND, SD, WY)
3490 Gabel Rd., #100
Billings, MT 59102–7302
(406) 657–6447
Fax (406) 657–6573
E-mail: rsomt@rma.usda.gov
Eric Bashore, director

DAVIS, CA
(AZ, CA, HI, NV, UT)
430 G St., #4168
Davis, CA 95616–4168
(530) 792–5870
Fax (530) 792–5893
E-mail: rsoca@rma.usda.gov
Jeffrey Yasui, director

JACKSON, MS
(AR, KY, LA, MS, TN)
803 Liberty Rd.
Flowood, MS 39232
(601) 965–4771
Fax (601) 965–4517
E-mail: rsmos@rma.usda.gov
Michael Davis, director

OKLAHOMA CITY, OK
(NM, OK, TX)
215 Dean A. McGee Ave., #342
Oklahoma City, OK 73102
(405) 879–2700
Fax (405) 879–2741
E-mail: rsook@rma.usda.gov
Grant James, director

RALEIGH, NC
(CT, DE, MA, MD, ME, NC, NH, NJ, NY,
PA, RI, VA, VT, WV)
4405 Bland Rd., #160
Raleigh, NC 27609
(919) 875–4880
Fax (919) 875–4915
E-mail: rsonc@rma.usda.gov
Scott Lucas, director

ST. PAUL, MN
(IA, MN, WI)
30 7th St. East, #1890
St. Paul, MN 55101–4937
(651) 290–3304
Fax (651) 290–4139
E-mail: rsmon@rma.usda.gov
Duane Voy, director

SPOKANE, WA
(AK, ID, OR, WA)
11707 E. Sprague Ave., #201
Spokane, WA 99206–6125
(509) 228–6320
Fax (509) 228–6321
E-mail: rsowa@rma.usda.gov
Ben Thiel, director

SPRINGFIELD, IL
(IL, IN, MI, OH)
3500 Wabash Ave.
Springfield, IL 62711–8287
(217) 241–6600
Fax (217) 241–6618
E-mail: rsoil@rma.usda.gov
Brian Frieden, director

TOPEKA, KS
(CO, KS, MO, NE)
2641 S.W. Wanamaker, #201
Topeka, KS 66614
(785) 228–5512
Fax (785) 228–1456
E-mail: rsoks@rma.usda.gov
Rebecca Davis, director

VALDOSTA, GA
(AL, FL, GA, PR, SC)
106 S. Patterson St., #250
Valdosta, GA 31601–5673
(229) 219–7235
Fax (229) 242–3566
E-mail: rsoga@rma.usda.gov
Davina Lee (acting), director

Regional Compliance Offices

CENTRAL REGIONAL COMPLIANCE OFFICE
(CO, KS, MO, NE)
USDA/RMA/CRCO
Beacon Facility MS 0833
9240 Trost Ave.
P.O. Box 419205
Kansas City, MO 64141–6205
(816) 926–7363
Fax (816) 926–5186
E-mail: CFOMO@rma.usda.gov
Alvin Gilmore, director

EASTERN REGIONAL COMPLIANCE OFFICE
(AL, CT, DE, FL, GA, MA,
MD, ME, NC, NH, NJ, NY, PA,
PR, RI, SC, VA, VT, WV)
4405 Bland Rd., #165

Raleigh, NC 27609–6872
(919) 875–4930
Fax (919) 875–4928
E-mail: CFONC@rma.usda.gov
Jessica Dedrick, director

MIDWEST REGIONAL COMPLIANCE OFFICE

(IL, IN, MI, OH)
6045 Lakeside Blvd.
Indianapolis, IN 46278
(317) 290–3050
Fax (317) 290–3065
E-mail: CFOIN@rma.usda.gov
Ronie C. Griffin, director

NORTHERN REGIONAL COMPLIANCE OFFICE

(IA, MN, MT, ND, SD, WI, WY)
3440 Federal Dr., #200
Eagan, MN 55122–1301
(651) 452–1688
Fax (651) 452–1689

E-mail: CFPMN@rma.usda.gov
Scott Tincher, director

SOUTHERN REGIONAL COMPLIANCE OFFICE

(AR, KY, LA, MS, NM, OK, TN, TX)
1111 W. Mockingbird Lane, #280
Dallas, TX 75247–5016
(214) 767–7700
Fax (214) 767–7721
E-mail: CFOTX@rma.usda.gov
Billy M. Pryor, director

WESTERN REGIONAL COMPLIANCE OFFICE

(AK, AZ, CA, HI, ID, NV, OR, UT, WA)
430 G St., #4167
Davis, CA 95616–4167
(530) 792–5850
Fax (530) 792–5865
E-mail: CFOCA@rma.usda.gov
Susan Choy, director

Rural Development

1400 Independence Ave. S.W., #206-W, MS 0107
Washington, DC 20250–0107
Internet: www.rd.usda.gov

The Rural Development (RD) mission area was created in 1994 by a reorganization of the U.S. Department of Agriculture (USDA). Rural Development is the successor to two former USDA agencies, the Rural Development Administration (RDA) and the Rural Electrification Administration (REA), and it also took over the rural housing programs of a third former agency, the Farmers Home Administration (FmHA). Following the 1994 reorganization, Rural Development was initially known as Rural Economic and Community Development.

Three agencies make up Rural Development: the Rural Business-Cooperative Service, the Rural Housing Service, and the Rural Utilities Service. Each of these is primarily a lending agency and is headed by an administrator who reports to the under secretary of agriculture for rural development. Administrators for the Rural Business-Cooperative Service and the Rural Housing Service are appointed by the president and confirmed by the Senate. The administrator for Rural Utilities Service also is appointed by the president but does not require Senate confirmation.

Rural Business-Cooperative Service (RBS). The RBS inherited the business development programs of the RDA and the REA. Through its business programs, the RBS makes or guarantees a wide range of loans and grants to improve, develop, or finance business, industry, and employment in rural communities. Loans are made primarily through the existing private credit structure.

Intermediary Relending Program loans are available to nonprofit corporations, public agencies, Native American tribes, and cooperatives: these entities serve in turn as "intermediaries" to provide loans to "ultimate recipients" to finance business and community development projects.

The Rural Economic Development Loan and Grant program provides funding to rural projects through local utility organizations. Under the REDLoan program, USDA provides zero interest loans to local utilities that they, in turn, pass through to local businesses for projects that will create and retain employment in rural areas. The Rural Business Investment Program promotes economic development in mostly rural areas by helping to meet the equity capital investment needs of smaller enterprises located in such areas.

The Business and Industry Guaranteed Loan Program bolsters the existing private credit structure through the guarantee of quality loans for specified purposes.

Permitted uses of the loan include: business and industrial acquisitions when the loan will keep the business from closing, prevent the loss of employment opportunities, or provide expanded job opportunities; business conversion, enlargement, repair, modernization, or development; purchase and development of land, easements, rights-of-way, buildings, or facilities; and purchase of equipment, leasehold improvements, machinery, supplies, or inventory.

Rural Housing Service (RHS). The RHS inherited the rural housing programs of the FmHA and the rural community loan programs of the RDA and the REA. The RHS provides direct and guaranteed loans to individuals and local sponsoring organizations for various purposes in rural areas, including community facilities; rental and congregate housing; and the construction, purchase, or improvement of housing by rural residents. The RHS also provides grants for many of these projects as well as rental assistance to low-income families in rural areas. Most loans and grants have either an income requirement for individuals or a population requirement for participating communities, two exceptions being the watershed and resource conservation programs.

The 2014 Farm Bill revised eligibility standards for Rural Housing programs. Areas with populations of up to 35,000 that are rural in character are now eligible for USDA rural housing programs, with certain provisions. If an area has a population greater than 35,000, it will no longer be eligible. The legislation made some narrow exceptions for areas that had been "grandfathered" at any time between January 1, 2000 and December 31, 2010.

Rural Utilities Service (RUS). The RUS inherited the electric and telecommunications programs of the REA and the water and waste disposal programs of the RDA. Under the Rural Electrification Act of 1936, as amended, the RUS Electric Program ensures adequate electric service to rural areas by making or guaranteeing loans to nonprofit and cooperative associations and to public bodies for construction and operation of generating plants and transmission and distribution lines.

The RUS Telecommunications Program similarly ensures adequate telephone service in rural areas through loans to commercial companies, public bodies, and cooperative, nonprofit, limited dividend, or mutual associations. The program assists in modernizing rural telecommunications, particularly to accommodate use of the Internet.

The Telecommunications Infrastructure Loan Program improves the quality of life in rural America by providing investment capital, in the form of loans, for the deployment of rural telecommunications infrastructure at a rate consistent with the bank's cost in obtaining the money from the U.S. Treasury.

The RUS Water and Environmental Program makes or guarantees loans to develop water and waste disposal systems in rural areas and towns. Funds are available to public entities such as municipalities, counties, special-purpose districts, Native American tribes, and nonprofit corporations. The Water and Waste Disposal Program also distributes a variety of related grants, including for repair and replacement of facilities, and provides technical assistance to rural water systems.

The Farm Security and Rural Investment Act of 2002 authorized creation of the Rural Broadband Loan and Loan Guarantee Program (Broadband Program), which provides financing to telecommunications providers in rural areas where traditional financing is not otherwise available. Funds are used for the construction, improvement, and acquisition of facilities and equipment to provide broadband service to eligible rural communities. The 2014 Farm Bill reauthorized the broadband program and revised priority and eligibility requirements. The legislation also required data collection and evaluation related to these programs. The 2008 Farm Bill also established the Rural Energy for America Program to help farmers, ranchers, and rural small businesses reduce energy costs through energy efficiency and renewable energy initiatives. To achieve this goal, RDA would provide grants and guaranteed loans to farmers, ranchers, and rural small businesses; total program participation in a project may not exceed 75 percent of eligible project costs.

The 2008 Farm Bill authorized other renewable energy programs. The Advanced Biofuel Payment Program makes payments to eligible producers based on the amount of advanced biofuel produced from renewable biomass, other than corn kernel starch. Examples of eligible feedstocks include but are not limited to: crop residue; animal, food, and yard waste; vegetable oil; and animal fat. The Biorefinery Assistance Program provides loan guarantees for up to 80 percent of the project costs to develop, construct, and retrofit commercial-scale biorefineries. These programs were reauthorized in the 2014 Farm Bill. The bill also authorized a new Rural Energy Savings Program to fund loans to qualified consumers to implement energy efficiency measures.

■ KEY PERSONNEL

Under Secretary
Lisa Mensah . . . . (202) 720–4581
Fax . . . . (202) 720–2080
Deputy Under Secretaries
Patricia Kunesh . . . . (202) 720–4581
Fax . . . . (202) 720–2080
Chief of Staff
Kathryn Ferguson . . . . (202) 690–1533
Alternative Dispute Resolution
Derek Allen . . . . (202) 692–0204

Budget Division
Roger Glendenning . . . . (202) 692–0122
Chief Financial Officer
Roger Glendenning . . . . (202) 692–0122
Financial Management Division
John Dunsmuir . . . . (202) 692–0082
Native American Coordinator
Tedd Buelow (in Colorado) . . . . (720) 544–2911

RURAL BUSINESS-COOPERATIVE SERVICES
Administrator
Lillian Salerno . . . . (202) 690–4730
Fax . . . . (202) 690–4737

Business Programs
Deputy Administrator
Chad Parker . . . . (202) 720–7287
Assistant Deputy Administrator
William Smith . . . . (202) 720–0813
Business and Industry Division
John Broussard . . . . (202) 690–4103
Specialty Programs Division
Claudette Fernandez . . . . (202) 720–1394

Cooperative Programs
Deputy Administrator
Tom Hannah . . . . (202) 720–7558
Fax . . . . (202) 720–4641
Education, Research, and Development Division
John H. Wells . . . . (202) 720–3350
Cooperative Marketing
Charles Ling . . . . (202) 690–1410
Statistics Staff
Eldon Eversull . . . . (202) 690–1415

RURAL HOUSING SERVICE
Administrator
Tony Hernandez . . . . (202) 690–1533

Single-Family Housing
Deputy Administrator
Joyce Allen . . . . (202) 720–5177
Direct Loan Division
Cathy Glover . . . . (202) 720–1474
Director, Guaranteed Loan Division
Joaquin Tremols . . . . (202) 720–1465

Multi-Family Housing
Deputy Administrator
Bryan Hooper . . . . (202) 720–3773
Director, Guaranteed Loan Division
Michael Steininger . . . . (202) 720–1604
Portfolio Management Division
Stephanie White . . . . (202) 720–1615

Community Programs
Deputy Administrator
Rich Davis . . . . (202) 720–1500
Direct Loan and Grant Processing Division
Joseph Ben-Israel . . . . (202) 720–1505

Guaranteed Loan Division
Joseph Ben-Israel . . . . (202) 720–1505

RURAL UTILITIES SERVICE
Administrator
Brandon McBride . . . . (202) 720–9540
Fax . . . . (202) 720–1725
Chief of Staff
Michele Brooks (acting) . . . .(202) 690-1078
Policy Analysis and Risk Management
Gary Bojes . . . . (202) 720–1265
Program Accounting and Regulatory Analysis
Kenneth M. Ackerman . . . . (202) 720–9450

Electric Program
Assistant Administrator
Christopher A. McLean . . . . (202) 720–9545
Loan Origination and Approval
Annie Holloway-Jones . . . . (202) 720–1900
Portfolio Management and Risk Assessment
Victor T. Vu . . . . (202) 720–6436
Policy, Outreach, and Standards
Joseph Badin . . . . (202) 720–1420

Telecommunications Program
Assistant Administrator
Keith Adams . . . . (202) 720–9556
Deputy Assistant Administrator
Sami Zarour . . . . (202) 720–9556

Water and Environmental Programs
Assistant Administrator
Jacqueline Ponti-Lazaruk . . . . (202) 690–2670
Fax . . . . (202) 720–0718
Water Programs Division
Kent Evans . . . . (202) 720–9643
Program Operations Branch
Cheryl Francis . . . . (202) 720–1937
Portfolio Management Branch
Stephen Saulnier . . . . (202) 720–9631
Engineering and Environmental Staff
Vacant . . . . (202) 720–1649

COMMUNITY AND ECONOMIC DEVELOPMENT
Deputy Administrator
Claudette Fernandez . . . . (202) 720–4581
Fax . . . . (202) 401–7311

OPERATIONS AND MANAGEMENT
Deputy Administrator
Edna Primrose . . . . (202) 692–0200
Chief Information Officer
Francisco Salguero . . . . (202) 692–0212
Civil Rights Staff
Angilla Denton . . . . (202) 692–4109
Cultural Transformation
Gail Lacey . . . . (202) 692–0118
Emergency Preparedness
John Pavek . . . . (202) 720–2078
Human Resources
Anita Adkins . . . . (202) 692–0222

Legislative and Public Affairs
David Sandretti . . . . (202) 720–4323
Procurement and Administrative Services
Sharon Randolph . . . . (202) 692–0207

▓ INFORMATION SOURCES

Internet
Agency website: www.rd.usda.gov Includes information on Rural Development agencies and programs and links to related economic development Internet sites.

Telephone Contacts
Personnel Locator (USDA) . . . .(202) 720–8732
General Information . . . .(202) 720–4323
Toll-free . . . .(800) 670–6553
English-Language Federal
Relay (TTY) . . . .(866) 377–8642
Spanish-Language Federal
Relay (TTY) . . . .(800) 845–6136

Information and Publications

KEY OFFICES

Legislative and Public Affairs
USDA Rural Development
1400 Independence Ave. S.W., #4801-S
MS 0705
Washington, DC 20250–0705
(202) 720–1019
Fax (202) 690–4083
TTY (800) 877–8339
David Sandretti, director

Provides public information and responds to general queries.

Freedom of Information
USDA Rural Development
1400 Independence Ave. S.W.
MS 0742
Washington, DC 20250–0742
(202) 690–5394
Fax (202) 692–0034
Email: ssd.foia@usda.gov
Vacant, FOIA officer

Records also may be requested at the state offices.

PUBLICATIONS
The Legislative and Public Affairs Staff provides USDA Rural Development fact sheets: (202) 720–4323. The fact sheets and other publications are also available from the Rural Development website at www.rd.usda.gov/publications .

Information and applications for financial assistance are available through state USDA Rural Development offices and on the website. This information is available for persons with disabilities (in media including Braille, large print, and audiotape) from the USDA Office of Communications: (202) 720–4623.

Economic Research Service

1800 M St. N.W.
Washington, DC 20036
(202) 694–5478
Marca Weinberg, director
Hours: 7:30 a.m. to 4:00 p.m.

Reference Resources

LIBRARY

National Agricultural Library

10301 Baltimore Ave.
Beltsville, MD 20705–2351
(301) 504–5755
Stan Kosecki, director
Hours: 8:30 a.m. to 4:30 p.m.

The National Agricultural Library also maintains a reference center at the Agriculture Department's South Building. The collection consists primarily of reference volumes, databases, and other computer resources.

D.C. Reference Center

1400 Independence Ave. S.W.
South Bldg., #1052-S
Washington, DC 20250–0201
(301) 504–5755
Rebecca Mazur, coordinator of research services

DOCKETS

Regulations and Paperwork Management

USDA Rural Development
Reporters Bldg., 7th Floor
1400 Independence Ave. S.W.
Washington, DC 20250
(202) 692–0040
Jeanne Jacobs, branch chief
Hours: 8:00 a.m. to 4:30 p.m.

Maintains dockets containing all information and materials pertaining to Rural Development administrative proceedings for public inspection. Rulemaking materials are also available on the Rural Development website at www.rd.usda.gov. Federal dockets are also available at www.regulations.gov. (*See appendix for Searching and Commenting on Regulations: Regulations.gov.*)

RULES AND REGULATIONS

USDA Rural Development rules and regulations are published in the *Code of Federal Regulations,* Title 7, Chapter XLII, various parts. Proposed rules, new final rules, and updates to the *Code of Federal Regulations* are published in the *Federal Register.* (*See appendix for information on how to obtain and use these publications.*) The *Federal Register* and the *Code of Federal Regulations* may be accessed online at www.archives.gov/federal-register/cfr; the site contains a link to the federal government's regulatory website at www.regulations.gov (*see appendix*).

■ LEGISLATION

Legislation administered by USDA Rural Development includes:

Cooperative Marketing Act of 1926 (44 Stat. 802, 7 U.S.C. 451). Signed by the president July 2, 1926. Authorized the Division of Cooperative Marketing in the Agriculture Department. Allowed farmers, through associations, to exchange prospective crop, market, statistical, economic, and other related information without violating antitrust laws.

Federal Housing Act of 1949 (63 Stat. 413, 42 U.S.C. 1401). Signed by the president July 15, 1949. Empowered the FmHA to make rural housing loans and to require that buildings constructed comply with federal housing regulations.

Consolidated Farm and Rural Development Act (75 Stat. 307, 7 U.S.C. 1921). Signed by the president Aug. 4, 1961. Authorized the FmHA to prescribe terms and conditions for making loans and grants and to require that lenders and borrowers comply with applicable federal laws and regulations.

Senior Citizens Housing Act (76 Stat. 670, 42 U.S.C. 1471). Signed by the president Sept. 28, 1962. Established a loan program for low-rent apartments for individuals age sixty-two and over and authorized loans for establishment of recreational facilities.

Rural Development Act of 1972 (86 Stat. 657, 7 U.S.C. 1006). Signed by the president Aug. 30, 1972. Authorized the FmHA to guarantee loans made by commercial lenders for farming, housing, and rural business and industry in cities up to 50,000 population. Authorized loans for construction of community facilities, as well as youth loans and industrial site improvement grants.

Rural Housing Amendments of 1983 (97 Stat. 1240, 42 U.S.C. 1441). Signed by the president Nov. 30, 1983. Required the FmHA to revise income definitions to be consistent with the Department of Housing and Urban Development (HUD), and to accept any of the voluntary national model building codes and HUD minimum property standards, in addition to FmHA construction standards. Empowered the FmHA to extend eligible single-family home mortgages from thirty-three years to thirty-eight years, and required the administration to give more priority to persons in the low-income classification.

Housing and Community Development Technical Amendments Act of 1984 (98 Stat. 2218, 42 U.S.C. 5301). Signed by the president Oct. 17, 1984. Authorized the FmHA to lend 60 percent of its single-family housing funds to persons in the low-income classification and 40 percent to those in the very low-income classification.

Food, Agriculture, Conservation, and Trade Act of 1990 (104 Stat. 3359, 7 U.S.C. 1421 note). Signed by the president Nov. 28, 1990. Established the RDA as a new agency within the USDA. Consolidated and transferred to the RDA rural development responsibilities previously under the FmHA and other agencies. Authorized the RDA to administer technical assistance and credit programs for rural community facilities, water and waste systems, and business and industry.

Cranston-Gonzalez National Affordable Housing Act (104 Stat. 4079, 42 U.S.C. 12701 note). Signed by the president Nov. 28, 1990. Authorized a guaranteed loan program for rural single-family home ownership. Mandated special targeted housing assistance to underserved areas and modified the rural population standard for housing program eligibility. Created a demonstration program for mortgage payment deferral.

Housing and Community Development Act of 1992 (106 Stat. 3672, 43 U.S.C. 5301 note). Signed by the president Oct. 28, 1992. Increased the income level for applicants eligible to apply for single-family home ownership loans and the percentage of a state's rural multifamily rental housing allocation reserved for nonprofit organizations. Authorized FmHA to require a 5 percent equity contribution by rental housing developers receiving assistance from the agency. Provided housing preservation grant funds for replacement housing. Established a rural housing voucher program and expanded the underserved areas assistance program.

Omnibus Budget Reconciliation Act of 1993 (107 Stat. 312). Signed by the president Aug. 10, 1993. Subchapter C: Empowerment Zones, Enterprise Communities, Rural Development Investment Areas provided for the designation of ninety-five tax enterprise communities and nine empowerment zones during calendar years after 1993 and before 1996. Provided for the issuance of enterprise zone facility bonds in enterprise communities and empowerment zones in a manner similar to exempt facility bonds. Allowed a general business tax credit for contributions to selected community development corporations to provide employment of, and business opportunities for, low-income individuals who are residents of the operational area of the community.

Department of Agriculture Reorganization Act of 1994 (108 Stat. 3209, 7 U.S.C. 6901 note). Signed by the president Oct. 13, 1994. Consolidated the missions of the RDA and REA, and the rural housing programs of the FmHA.

Federal Agriculture Improvement and Reform Act of 1996 (110 Stat. 888, 7 U.S.C. 7201 note). Signed by the president April 4, 1996. Title VI (credit), subtitles A, B, and C, revised farm loan provisions with regard to farm ownership loans, operating loans, and emergency loans. Title VII (rural development), subtitle A repealed the rural investment partnerships program, the water and waste facility loan, and the rural wastewater circuit rider programs. Subtitle B established a program under which the secretary may guarantee rural development loans made by a certified lender, and established a rural community advancement program of grants, loans, guarantees, and other assistance to local communities and federally recognized Native American tribes.

Farm Security and Rural Investment Act of 2002 (116 Stat. 1348, 7 U.S.C. 7901 note). Signed by the president May 13, 2002. Amended the Consolidated Farm and Rural Development Act to establish the National Rural Cooperative and Business Equity Fund Act. Authorized qualifying private investors to establish a nonfederal entity, the National Rural Cooperative and Business Equity Fund, to generate and provide equity capital for rural businesses. Authorized the establishment of the Rural Endowment Program. Made grants and loans available for improvement of rural broadband service and for rural economic development. Title VI, National Rural Development Partnership Act of 2002, established the National Rural Development Partnership composed of the National Rural Development Coordinating Committee and state development councils.

Food, Conservation, and Energy Act of 2008 (Farm Bill) (7 U.S.C. 8701 note). Vetoed by the president May 21, 2008; veto overridden June 18, 2008. Reauthorized Department of Agriculture programs through fiscal year 2012. Established the Rural Energy for America Program to help farmers, ranchers, and rural small businesses reduce energy costs. Authorized biofuels programs. Authorizes RUS to make loans to rural electric cooperatives for electric generation from renewable energy sources. Established the Rural Collaborative Investment Program (RCIP). Revised definition of "rural" for program eligibility. Extended all REAP zones until Sept. 30, 2012.

Tax Relief, Unemployment Insurance Reauthorization, and Job Creation Act of 2010 (124 Stat. 3321, 26 U.S.C. 1367 note). Signed by the president Dec. 17, 2010. Extends through December 31, 2011, the period for designation of empowerment zones for purposes of allowing certain tax incentives for investment in such zones.

Agricultural Act of 2014 (Farm Bill) (128 Stat. 841, 7 U.S.C. 1926). Signed by the president Feb. 7, 2014. Reauthorized most existing programs established by the Consolidated Farm and Rural Development Act and the Rural Electrification Act. Consolidates several business loan and grant programs (with various definition and eligibility changes). Reauthorized energy programs. Directed USDA to evaluate program effectiveness for specific broadband programs.

■ STATE OFFICES

ALABAMA
Sterling Center
4121 Carmichael Rd., #601
Montgomery, AL 36106–3683
(334) 279–3400
Fax (334) 279–3403
Ronald Davis, director

ALASKA
800 W. Evergreen, #201
Palmer, AK 99645
(907) 761–7707
Fax (907) 761–7783
Jim Nordlund, director

ARIZONA
230 N. 1st Ave., #206
Phoenix, AZ 85003
(602) 280–8701
Fax (602) 280–8881
Ernie Wetherbee (acting), director

ARKANSAS
Federal Bldg.
700 W. Capitol, #3416
Little Rock, AR 72201–3225
(501) 301–3200
Fax (855) 747–7793
Lawrence McCullough, director

CALIFORNIA
430 G St., #4169
Davis, CA 95616–4169
(530) 792–5800
Fax (530) 792–5837
Glenda Humiston, director

COLORADO
Denver Federal Center
Bldg. 56, #2300
P.O. Box 25426
Denver, CO 80225–0246
(720) 544–2903
Fax (720) 544–2981
Colorado Relay Service
(TTY) (800) 659–3656
Trudy Kareus, director

DELAWARE/MARYLAND
1221 College Park Dr., #200
Dover, DE 19904–8713
(302) 857–3580
Fax (855) 389–2241
Bill McGowan, director

FLORIDA/VIRGIN ISLANDS
4440 N.W. 25th Pl.
Gainesville, FL 32606
(352) 338–3402
Fax (352) 328–3405
Richard Machek, director

GEORGIA
355 E. Hancock Ave., MS 300
Athens, GA 30601–2768
(706) 546–2162
Fax (706) 546–2152
Quinton Robinson, director

HAWAII
Federal Bldg.
154 Waianuenue Ave., #311
Hilo, HI 96720–2452
(808) 933–8380
Fax (808) 933–8327
Chris Kanazawa, director

IDAHO
9173 W. Barnes Dr., #A1
Boise, ID 83709
(208) 378–5600
(800) 632–5991
Fax (208) 378–5643
Wallace Hedrick, director

ILLINOIS
2118 W. Park Court, Suite A
Champaign, IL 61821
(217) 403–6200
Fax (217) 403–6243
Colleen Callahan, director

INDIANA
5975 Lakeside Blvd.
Indianapolis, IN 46278–1996
(317) 290–3100, ext. 4
Fax (317) 290–3127
Philip G. Lehmkuhler, director

IOWA
210 Walnut St., #873
Des Moines, IA 50309–2196
(515) 284–4663
Fax (515) 284–4859
William Menner, director

KANSAS
1303 S.W. First American Pl., #100
Topeka, KS 66604–4040
(785) 271–2700
Fax (785) 271–2708
Patricia Clark, director

KENTUCKY
771 Corporate Dr., #200
Lexington, KY 40503–5477
(859) 224–7300
Fax (859) 224–7340
Thomas G. Fern, director

LOUISIANA
3727 Government St.
Alexandria, LA 71302
(318) 473–7920
Fax (318) 473–7661
Clarence W. Hawkins, director

MAINE
967 Illinois Ave., #4
Bangor, ME 04402–0405
(207) 990–9160
Fax (855) 589–1060
Virginia Manuel, director

MASSACHUSETTS/RHODE ISLAND/CONNECTICUT
451 West St., #2
Amherst, MA 01002–2999
(413) 253–4300;
(800) 352–8015
Fax (413) 253–4347
Scott Soares, director

MICHIGAN
3001 Coolidge Rd., #200
East Lansing, MI 48823

(517) 324–5190
Fax (855) 813–7741
James J. Turner, director

MINNESOTA
375 Jackson St., #410
St. Paul, MN 55101–1853
(651) 602–7800
Fax (651) 602–7824
Mary Collen Landkamer, director

MISSISSIPPI
100 West Capitol St., #831
Jackson, MS 39269
(601) 965–4316
Fax (601) 965–4088
Trina George, director

MISSOURI
601 Business Loop 70 West
Parkade Center, #235
Columbia, MO 65203
(573) 876–0976
Fax (855) 830–0684
Anita J. (Janie) Dunning, director

MONTANA
2229 Boot Hill Court.
Bozeman, MT 59715
(406) 585–2580
Fax (855) 576–2674
Janelle Gustafson (acting), director

NEBRASKA
100 Centennial Mall North, #308
Lincoln, NE 68508
(402) 437–5551
Fax (402) 437–5408
Maxine Moul, director

NEVADA
1390 S. Curry St.
Carson City, NV 89703–5146
(775) 887–1222
Fax (775) 885–0841
Sarah Mersereau-Adler, director

NEW JERSEY
5th Floor North, #500
8000 Midlantic Dr.
Mt. Laurel, NJ 08054
(856) 787–7700
Fax (856) 787–7783
Howard Henderson, director

NEW MEXICO
6200 Jefferson St. N.E., #255
Albuquerque, NM 87109
(505) 761–4950

Fax (505) 761–4976
Terrence Brunner, director

NEW YORK
441 S. Salina St., #357
Syracuse, NY 13202
(315) 477–6400
Fax (315) 477–6438
Stanley Telega, director

NORTH CAROLINA
4405 Bland Rd., #260
Raleigh, NC 27609
(919) 873–2000
Fax (919) 8873–2075
Randall Gore, director

NORTH DAKOTA
220 E. Rosser, #208
P.O. Box 1737
Bismarck, ND 58502–1737
(701) 530–2037
Fax (701) 530–2111
Bill Davis (acting), director

OHIO
200 N. High St., #507
Columbus, OH 43215–2477
(614) 255–2400
Fax (614) 255–2561
Tony Logan, director

OKLAHOMA
100 USDA, #108
Stillwater, OK 74074–2654
(405) 742–1000
Fax (405) 742–1005
David Ryan McMullen, director

OREGON
1201 N.E. Lloyd Blvd., #801
Portland, OR 97232–1274
(503) 414–3300
(800) 923–5626
Fax (855) 824–6180
Vicki L. Walker, director

PENNSYLVANIA
1 Credit Union Pl., #330
Harrisburg, PA 17110–2996
(717) 237–2299
Fax (717) 237–2191
Thomas Williams, director

PUERTO RICO
IBM Bldg., #601
654 Munoz Rivera Ave.
San Juan, PR 00918
(787) 766–5095

Fax (787) 766–5844
José A. Otero, director

SOUTH CAROLINA
1835 Assembly St., #1007
Columbia, SC 29201
(803) 765–5163
Fax (803) 765–5633
Vernita F. Dore, director

SOUTH DAKOTA
200 4th St. S.W., #210
Huron, SD 57350
(605) 352–1100
(800) 670–6553
Fax (605) 352–1146
Bruce Jones (acting), director

TENNESSEE
3322 West End Ave., #300
Nashville, TN 37203–1071
(615) 783–1300
Fax (615) 783–1301
Bobby Goode, director

TEXAS
101 S. Main, #102
Temple, TX 76501
(254) 742–9700
Fax (254) 742–9709
Francisco Valentin Jr., director

UTAH
125 S. State St., #4311
Salt Lake City, UT 84138
(801) 524–4321
Fax (801) 524–4406
Wilson (David) Conine, director

VERMONT/NEW HAMPSHIRE
City Center, 3rd Floor
87 Main St., #324
P.O. Box 249

Montpelier, VT 05602
(802) 828–6000
Fax (802) 828–6018
Ted Brady, director

VIRGINIA
1606 Santa Rosa Rd., #238
Richmond, VA 23229–5014
(804) 287–1552
Fax (804) 287–1718
Basil I. Gooden, director

WASHINGTON
1835 Black Lake Blvd. S.W., Suite B
Olympia, WA 98501–5715
(360) 704–7740
Fax (360) 704–7742
Mario Villanueva, director

WEST VIRGINIA
1550 Earl Core Rd., #101
Morgantown, WV 26505
(304) 284–4860
(800) 295–8228
Fax (304) 284–4891
Robert Lewis, director

WISCONSIN
5417 Clem's Way
Stevens Point, WI 54482
(715) 345–7600
Fax (715) 345–7669
Stan Gruszynski, director

WYOMING
100 East B St., #1005
Casper, WY 82601
Mailing address:
P.O. Box 11005
Casper, WY 82602
(307) 233–6700
Fax (855) 415–3411
Connie Baker Wolfe, director

Commerce Department

14th St. and Constitution Ave. N.W., Washington, DC 20230
Internet: www.commerce.gov

Bureau of Industry and Security

14th St. and Constitution Ave. N.W., Washington, DC 20230
Internet: www.bis.doc.gov

The Commerce Department's Bureau of Export Administration (BXA) was established in 1987 to stem proliferation of weapons of mass destruction without unnecessarily impeding U.S. export growth. In 2002 the BXA changed its name to the Bureau of Industry and Security (BIS) to reflect more accurately the broad scope of the agency's responsibilities. The change in name did not substantively affect its activities, nor those of its sister organization, the International Trade Administration (*p. 464*), which remained responsible for the Commerce Department's trade promotion and policy activities.

To accomplish its mission, the BIS controls exports and reexports of dual-use commodities and technical data from the United States and its territories and possessions. Dual-use commodities are items of a primarily civilian nature that also have potential military applications. Under the authority of the Export Administration Act (EAA), controls on these commodities and technologies are maintained for reasons of national security, foreign policy, and short supply. For example, the EAA includes export controls designed to address national security and foreign policy issues, such as protecting human rights and combating terrorism.

The BIS administers the Export Administration Regulations (EAR), which specify rules for the submission of export license applications. The BIS also administers export controls on commercial encryption products under EAR. These regulations were extensively revised in 1995 for the first time in more than forty years.

The BIS maintains controls for purposes of nuclear nonproliferation pursuant to section 309(C) of the Nuclear Nonproliferation Act of 1978, as well as limiting the proliferation of chemical and biological weapons and missile technology, in cooperation with other governments.

BIS implements the controls that the United States agreed to in the four multilateral export control regimes: the Nuclear Suppliers Group, the Missile Technology Control Regime, the Australia Group (chemical and biological nonproliferation), and the Wassenaar Arrangement (conventional arms and dual-use goods and technologies). BIS plays a significant role in implementing three treaties: the Chemical Weapons Convention, the Additional Protocol to the U.S.-International Atomic Energy Agency Safeguards Agreement (nuclear weapons nonproliferation), and the Biological Weapons Convention.

The agency is divided into two principal divisions: Export Administration, which serves as the federal government's licensing agency for dual-use commodities and technical data; and Export Enforcement, which executes administrative, civil, and criminal sanctions against parties who violate U.S. export control laws, including the antiboycott provisions of the EAA. Within enforcement is the BIS Information Triage Unit (ITU), which is responsible for assembling and disseminating relevant export and trade information and coordinating reviews of separate stove-piped processes across government.

Export Controls and Technology Growth

The decade that began in 1990 saw exponential growth in computer technology. In 1995 President Bill Clinton announced a new policy for controlling the export of high-performance computers (HPCs). The new policy focused on limiting the acquisition of computational capabilities by potential adversaries and countries of proliferation concern. Balanced against national security was the assurance that U.S. domestic industries supporting computing capabilities important for national security could compete in markets of limited security or proliferation risks.

In 1998 the White House swiftly directed the BIS to implement far-reaching sanctions against India and Pakistan following nuclear weapons tests by both countries. Export and reexport licenses for dual-use items relating to nuclear or missile proliferation, such as computers and software, were denied indefinitely to both countries' governments and nongovernment entities. During this same time period, the United States also limited exports of HPCs, commercial satellites, and related technology to China and a host of other countries. Concerns had been raised about such exports assisting in weapons research.

Following a review in 1999 by all relevant security and nonproliferation agencies and private-sector experts, it was apparent that the growth in widely available computer hardware capabilities was outpacing the ability of export control policy to keep up. The greatest challenge to the ability to control computer hardware effectively was the capabilities of endusers to network large clusters of computers.

The dawn of the twenty-first century saw the beginning of a more practical approach to export technology review and licensing. In January 2003 the Commerce Department announced a new regulation to streamline export controls on general purpose microprocessors that were used worldwide in technology and commercial applications, such as personal computers and cell phones. Under the new rule, a license would only be required to export general-purpose microprocessors to terrorist countries or for military uses in countries posing national security concerns. The BIS published the regulation after consultation with the State and Defense Departments.

In September 2006 the commerce secretary appointed twelve business and academic leaders to the newly formed Deemed Export Advisory Committee (DEAC). The DEAC had no regulatory power and was set up to advise BIS on how to address the complex issues surrounding "deemed exports"—sensitive technology transfers that involve the release of closely monitored dual-use technology to foreign nationals in the United States.

In December 2007 the DEAC issued a report that recommended that BIS establish an Emerging Technologies Advisory Committee, composed of representatives from leading research universities, government research labs, and industry, to make recommendations to BIS regarding emerging technologies on a regular basis. In response, BIS announced the new Emerging Technology and Research Advisory Committee (ETRAC) in May 2008. The committee was charged with assessing new and existing regulatory controls that have the greatest impact on U.S. national security and study the implications of the release of dual-use technology to foreign nationals under current deemed exports licensing requirements.

The success of the ETRAC later resulted in the establishment of additional Technical Advisory Committees (TACs). TACs advise the Commerce Department on the technical parameters for export controls applicable to dual-use commodities and technology and on the administration of those controls. The TACs are composed of representatives from industry and government. TAC members are appointed by the commerce secretary and serve terms of not more than four consecutive years; members must obtain secret-level clearances prior to appointment. In addition to the Emerging Technology and Research Advisory Committee, other TACs include:

- President's Export Council Subcommittee on Export Administration provides advice on matters pertinent to the Export Administration Act, the Export Administration Regulations, and related statutes and regulations.
- Regulations and Procedures Technical Advisory Committee, which offers advice about the Export Administration Regulations (EAR) and procedures implementing these regulations.
- Materials Technical Advisory Committee evaluates articles, materials, and supplies for radar absorption, jet engine turbines blades, super-conductivity, fluids, lubricants, composites, and for nuclear, missile, chemical, and biological weapons, including technical data and other information.
- Transportation and Related Equipment Technical Advisory Committee evaluates articles, materials, and supplies of transportation and related equipment and assesses any potential security issues.

Export Control Reforms under the Obama Administration

In August 2009 President Barack Obama directed a broad-based interagency review of the current export control system to ensure that the system addressed emerging security issues while protecting the competitiveness of U.S. industries. The review determined that the export control system was overly complicated, contained too many redundancies, and was overly broad, diminishing the ability to focus efforts on the most critical national security priorities.

In August 2010 the president outlined a plan based upon the review: the Export Control Reform (ECR) initiative. This initiative addressed the two export control lists: the dual-use Commerce Control List (CCL) administered by the Commerce Department (BIS) and the United States Munitions List (USML) administered by the State Department. One of the key aspects of ECR has been the effort to move less sensitive items (primarily parts and components) from the less flexible USML to the more flexible CCL of the Export Administration Regulations (EAR). Under the revised approach, regulatory agencies apply a common set of policies for determining when an export license is required. Control list criteria are tiered to distinguish the types of items that should be subject to stricter or more permissive levels of control for different destinations, end uses, and end users. The government places a higher priority and more controls on the most sensitive items in order to enhance national security. The final rules published by BIS and the State Department that provided for the initial implementation of ECR became effective in October 2013.

In November 2010 President Barack Obama issued Executive Order 13558, which established an interagency Export Coordination Enforcement center within the Department of Homeland Security. The center, which opened in March 2012, serves as a primary point of contact between enforcement authorities and agencies engaged in export licensing.

In June 2011 BIS issued a final rule implementing a new License Exception Strategic Trade Authorization (License Exception STA) under the Export Administration Regulations (EAR). The final rule allows conditional license-free treatment of items to specific countries where there are lower risks of diversion to end uses and end users of concern to the United States. The implementation of STA furthered the administration's ECR policy goals.

The National Defense Authorization Act for FY 2013 allowed certain satellites and related items to be removed from the State Department's USML and transferred back to the CCL upon certain determinations. The legislation prohibits any satellites or related items subject to the EAR from being exported or transferred to China, North Korea, or a state sponsor of terrorism. A provision of the law allows the president to waive such prohibition in the national security interest upon congressional notification.

On March 8, 2013, the president issued Executive Order 13637 to update delegated presidential authorities over the administration of certain export and import controls, which had not been comprehensively updated in 36 years. This action makes the necessary changes to implement the new export control system.

BIS proactively works to inform the regulated community about revisions under ECR through outreach efforts that include seminars, webinars, and teleconferences with industry groups. BIS provides web-based decision tools to assist exporters with order of review and classifying items subject to the EAR.

■ KEY PERSONNEL

Under Secretary
Eric L. Hirschhorn . . . . (202) 482–1455
Deputy Under Secretary
Daniel O. Hill. (202) 482–1427
Administration
Vacant . . . . (202) 482–1054
Chief Counsel for Industry and Security
John T. Masterson Jr. . . . . (202) 482–5301

Export Administration Division
Assistant Secretary
Kevin J. Wolf . . . . (202) 482–5491
Fax. . . . . (202) 482–3911
Deputy Assistant Secretary for Export Administration
Matthew S. Borman . . . . (202) 482–5491
Exporter Services
Karen Nies-Vogel . . . . (202) 482–3811
National Security and Technology Transfer Controls
Eileen Albanese. . . . . (202) 482–0092
Nonproliferation and Treaty Compliance
Alexander Lopes . . . . (202) 482–3825
Strategic Industries and Economic Security
Michael Vaccaro . . . . (202) 482–4506
Technology Evaluation
Gerard Horner. . . . . (202) 482–2078

Export Enforcement Division
Assistant Secretary
David W. Mills. . . . . (202) 482–3618
Deputy Assistant Secretary
Richard Majauskas . . . . (202) 482–3618
Antiboycott Compliance
Ned Weant . . . . (202) 482–5914
Enforcement Analysis
Kevin Kurland . . . . (202) 482–4255
Information Triage Unit
Gregory Lee . . . . (202) 482–1881
Export Enforcement
Douglas Hassebrock . . . . (202) 482–1208

■ INFORMATION SOURCES

Internet
Agency website: www.bis.doc.gov. The agency also operates the Export License Application and Information Network, which accepts export license applications electronically. The Agency's website contains extensive information on Denied Persons and Entities; encryption guidelines; antiboycotting; defense industry export guidelines; international programs; and BIS offices, personnel, activities, regulations, and publications at www.bis.doc.gov/sitemap.html. The Online Training Room includes instruction manuals and modules, online seminars ("webinars"), and information about seminars around the country at www.bis.doc.gov/index.php/compliance-a-training/export-administration-regulations-training/online-training-room.

The website also links to the Government Printing Office's Export Administration Regulation website, www.bis.doc.gov/index.php/regulations#ear, which contains an up-to-date database of the entire Export Administration Regulations (EAR), including the Commerce Control List and General Prohibitions. EAR revisions are incorporated into this site. Questions may be directed to the GPO Access User Support Team at (202) 512–1800 or (866) 512–1800.

The NTIS website www.ntis.gov/products/export-regs also offers an up-to-date EAR database, with downloadable and searchable versions of the Entity List, the Debarred List, and the Specially Designated Nationals List, the Denied Persons List, the Unverified List, and Nonproliferation Sanctions.

Telephone Contacts
Personnel Locator . . . .(202) 482–2000
Antiboycott Advice Line . . . .(202) 482–2381
Enforcement Hotline . . . .(800) 424–2980
Federal Relay Service TTY . . . .(800) 877–8339
Exporter Counseling Center
Outreach and Educational Services . . (202) 482–4811
System for Tracking Export
License Applications (STELA) . . . (202) 482–4811

Information and Publications

BIS Congressional and Public Affairs
14th St. and Constitution Ave. N.W., #3897
Washington, DC 20230
(202) 482–2721
Eugene Cottilli, liaison
Internet: www.bis.doc.gov/index.php/about-bis/newsroom/press-releases

Provides information and responds to questions about the BIS.

BIS Exporter Services
Outreach and Educational Services
14th and Pennsylvania Ave. N.W., #1099-B
Washington, DC 20230

(202) 482–3811

Karen Nies-Vogel, director

Programs advise the exporting community on export control, export licensing, and defense conversion issues. For Western Region programs, call (949) 660–0144 or check the Internet site at www.bis.doc.gov/index.php/compliance-a-training/export-administration-regulations-training/online-training-room.

PUBLICATIONS

The following are available at the BIS website, www.bis.doc.gov/index.php/about-bis/newsroom/publications:

BIS Annual Report and *BIS Brochure*

Don't Let It Happen to You!

Exporter User Manual

How to Request an Export Control Classification Number (ECCN)

Introduction to the Commerce Department's Export Controls

Reference Resources

LIBRARY

Commerce Department

1401 Constitution Ave. N.W.

Washington, DC 20230

(202) 482–1154

Karen Krugman, director

Public access by appointment only.

DOCKETS

Federal dockets are available at www.regulations.gov. (*See appendix for Searching and Commenting on Regulations: Regulations.gov.*)

RULES AND REGULATIONS

BIS rules and regulations are published in the *Code of Federal Regulations,* Title 15, Chapter VII, Parts 700–799 and at www.bis.doc.gov/regulations database. Proposed regulations are published in the daily *Federal Register.* (*See appendix for details on how to obtain and use these publications.*) The *Federal Register* may be accessed at www.federalregister.gov and the *Code of Federal Regulations* at www.archives.gov/federal-register/cfr; also see the federal government's website www.regulations.gov (*see appendix*).

■ LEGISLATION

The BIS carries out its trade regulation responsibilities under:

International Emergency Economic Powers Act (IEEPA) (50 U.S.C. 1701–1706). Signed by the president Oct. 28, 1977. Granted the president authority, if a national emergency is declared, to regulate a comprehensive range of commercial and financial transactions with other countries to manage a threat to the national security, foreign policy, or economy of the United States.

Export Administration Act of 1979 (93 Stat. 503, 50 U.S.C. 4001 note). Signed by the president Sept. 29, 1979. Extended the earlier act of 1969, which prohibited export of goods, including technology, that could threaten U.S. national security. Prohibited participation in unsanctioned foreign boycotts.

Export Administration Amendments of 1985 (99 Stat. 120, 50 U.S.C. app. 2401 note). Signed by the president July 12, 1985. Reauthorized and amended the Export Administration Act of 1979 to make American exporters more competitive and to protect U.S. national security. To make U.S. exporters more competitive, the law decontrolled the export of low-tech items and liberalized licensing where similar products are available in the international market. To protect U.S. national security interests, the law expanded export enforcement authority.

Omnibus Trade and Competitiveness Act of 1988 (100 Stat. 1170, 19 U.S.C. 2901 note). Signed by the president Aug. 23, 1988. Amended Section 201 of the Trade Act of 1974 to place a greater emphasis on industry adjustment to import competition in granting relief. Changed the antidumping and countervailing duty law to provide new provisions relating to the release of business proprietary information under protective orders.

1998 National Defense Authorization Act (111 Stat. 1029, 50 U.S.C. app. 2404 note). Signed by the president Nov. 18, 1997. Set export controls on high performance computers. Required exporters to give the BIS advance notice of all exports and reexports of certain HPCs from the United States to Tier 3 countries (as listed in the *Code of Federal Regulations*). The BIS must refer the notice to the Defense, Energy, and State Departments.

Strom Thurmond National Defense Authorization Act for FY 1999 (112 Stat. 1920, 22 U.S.C. 2778 note). Signed by the president Oct. 17, 1998. Requires all satellites and related items on the Commerce Control List to be transferred to the U.S. Munitions List and controlled under provisions of the Arms Export Control Act.

Export Administration Modification and Clarification Act of 2000 (114 Stat. 2360, 50 U.S.C. app. 2419). Signed by the president Nov. 13, 2000. Reauthorized the Export Administration Act. Amended the Export Administration Act of 1979 to increase the civil penalties for violations of the export control requirements contained in such act.

Executive Order 13558 Export Coordination Enforcement Center. Signed by the president Nov. 9, 2010. Established within the Department of Homeland Security (for administrative purposes) an interagency Federal Export Enforcement Coordination Center to coordinate matters relating to export enforcement among cabinet-level departments. The center serves as a primary point of contact between enforcement authorities and agencies engaged in export licensing.

National Defense Authorization Act for FY 2013 (126 Stat. 1632). Signed by the president January 2, 2013. Allowed certain satellites and related items to be removed from the United States Munitions List (USML) and transferred back to the Commerce Control List (CCL) upon certain determinations and a report to Congress by the president. The legislation prohibits any satellites or related items that are made subject to the Export Administration Regulations (EAR) from being exported or transferred to China, North Korea, or a state sponsor of terrorism. A provision of the law allows the president to waive such prohibition in the national security interest upon congressional notification.

Executive Order 13637 Administration of Reformed Export Controls. Signed by the president March 8, 2013. Updated delegated presidential authorities over the administration of certain export and import controls.

◼ FIELD OFFICES

Office of Export Enforcement

CALIFORNIA
2601 Main St., #310
Irvine, CA 92714
(949) 251–9001
Fax (949) 251–9103
Anthony Levey, special agent in charge

160 W. Santa Clara St., #725
San Jose, CA 95113
(408) 291–4204
Fax (408) 291–4320
Julie Salcido, special agent in charge

FLORIDA
200 E. Las Olas Blvd., #1800
Fort Lauderdale, FL 33301
(954) 356–7540
Fax (954) 356–7549
Robert Luzzi, special agent in charge

ILLINOIS
1 Oakbrook Terrace, #804
Oakbrook Terrace, IL 60181

(630) 705–7010
Fax (630) 424–0118
Ronald Orzel, special agent in charge

MASSACHUSETTS
10 Causeway St., #253
Boston, MA 02222
(617) 565–6030
Fax (617) 565–6039
John McKenna, special agent in charge

NEW YORK
1200 South Ave., #104
Staten Island, NY 10314
(718) 370–0070
Fax (718) 370–0826
Sidney Simon, special agent in charge

TEXAS
225 E. John Carpenter Freeway, # 820
Irving, TX 75062
(214) 296–1060
Fax (214) 767–9299
Tracy Martin, special agent in charge

15109 Heathrow Forest Pkwy., #170
Houston, TX 77032
(281) 372–7130
Fax (281) 590–3931
Tracy Martin, special agent in charge

VIRGINIA/WASHINGTON, DC
381 Elden St., #1125
Herndon, VA 20170
(703) 487–9300
Fax (703) 487–9463
Rick Shimon, special agent in charge

Economic Development Administration

14th St. and Constitution Ave. N.W., Washington, DC 20230
Internet: www.eda.gov

The Economic Development Administration (EDA), an agency within the Commerce Department, was created by the Public Works and Economic Development Act of 1965 to administer programs providing assistance to states, counties, cities, and communities suffering from substantial, persistent, or potential unemployment and underemployment. The EDA provides assistance to local and state governments as well as to private nonprofit organizations.

EDA programs include planning grants, technical assistance, public works, research grants, economic adjustment assistance, trade adjustment assistance, post-disaster economic recovery, and sudden and severe economic dislocations, such as military base closings. The EDA also responds to community needs and priorities that create private-sector jobs and leverage private-sector capital.

The EDA is headed by the assistant secretary of commerce for economic development, who is supported by a deputy assistant secretary and six regional directors. The six regional directors are responsible for coordinating with local communities in economic planning and development of overall economic development programs, which are related to the needs of designated areas and districts served by the regional offices; managing EDA resources available for the economic development of designated areas and districts; and processing and approving applications for assistance. The regional directors monitor approved projects.

The EDA has economic development representatives, primarily located away from the regional offices, who are responsible for providing information about the agency's programs and activities. They also assist prospective applicants in preparing applications for financial assistance. The economic development representatives report to their respective regional directors.

Conservatives, who criticized the EDA's efforts as inappropriate interference in the private sector, sought to eliminate the agency in the 1980s and 1990s. However, Rep. Harold K. Rogers (R-KY), then-chair of the Appropriations subcommittee that provided funding for the Commerce Department, resisted those efforts. Rogers, who represented an economically troubled district, was a determined champion of the program's efforts to generate economic development through public works projects and technical assistance grants.

The Economic Development Administration Reauthorization Act of 2004 reauthorized Public Works and Economic Development Act economic assistance programs through 2008. The 2004 legislation also revised the definition of eligible EDA recipients. With the economy faltering in 2008 and 2009, newly elected President Barack Obama signed the American Recovery and Reinvestment Act (ARRA) in February 2009; the bill provided funding to the EDA. The agency was tasked to give grants to the states to spur job growth and development, targeting areas of the country hit the hardest by the recession. In FY 2009, EDA awarded approximately $579 million, including ARRA monies and disaster supplemental funds; most of this funding paid for construction and infrastructure projects.

EDA funds regional activities through seven competitive investment programs: Public Works, Economic Adjustment, Partnership Planning, Trade Adjustment Assistance for Firms, University Centers, Research and National Technical Assistance, and Local Technical Assistance. Public Works investments support a variety of specific economic development strategies, including specialized workforce development, diversification of natural resource dependent economies, and community and faith-based social entrepreneurship. The Economic Adjustment Assistance program provides loans and project planning to communities and regions hard-hit by severe economic difficulties, such as an economic dislocation caused by a plant closing that changes the local or regional economic base. Partnership Planning supports local organizations (Economic Development Districts, Indian tribes, and other eligible areas) with long-term planning efforts. Under the Trade Adjustment Assistance for Firms program, a national network of Trade Adjustment Assistance Centers work to strengthen the competitiveness of American companies that have lost domestic sales and employment because of increased imports of similar goods and services. The University Centers program promotes the vast resources of universities available to the economic development community. The Research and National Technical Assistance program focuses on applied research to provide technical assistance to public and private-sector organizations with the goal of enhancing local economic development. The Local Technical Assistance program provides research and technical assistance to local public and economic leaders in distressed areas.

The America Creating Opportunities to Meaningfully Promote Excellence in Technology, Education, and Science Reauthorization Act of 2010 (COMPETES Act) established an Office of Innovation and Entrepreneurship within the EDA. The Office of Innovation and Entrepreneurship administers the i6 Challenge competitive grant, which supports innovative projects demonstrating excellence in technology commercialization and entrepreneurship in six different regions of the country. The bill also supports EDA's Jobs and Innovation Partnership framework through the establishment of a Regional Innovation Program to encourage and support the development of regional innovation strategies, including regional innovation clusters and science and research parks.

▧ KEY PERSONNEL

Assistant Secretary of Commerce for Economic Development
    Jay Williams . . . . (202) 482–5081
Deputy Assistant Secretary of Commerce for Economic Development / Chief Operating Officer
    Matthew Erskine . . . . (202) 482–5081
Deputy Assistant Secretary for Regional Affairs
    Thomas Guevara . . . . (202) 482–5081
Chief Counsel
    Stephen Kong. (202) 482–4687
Chief Financial Officer / Chief Administrative Officer
    Andy Baldus. . . . . (202) 482–5892
External Affairs and Communications
    Angela Martinez . . . . (202) 482–2900
Deputy Chief Information Officer
    Mark Johnson . . . . (202) 482–2507
Legislative and Intergovernmental Affairs
    Angela Ewell-Madison (director) . . . . (202) 482–2900
Innovation and Entrepreneurship
    Julie Lenzer Kirk . . . . (202) 482–2042

▧ INFORMATION SOURCES

Internet

Agency website: www.eda.gov. Includes information about EDA personnel and offices, investment programs, regulations, application requirements, and current issues.

Telephone Contacts

    Personnel Locator . . . .(202) 482–2000
    Federal Relay Service TTY . . . .(800) 877–8339

Information and Publications

KEY OFFICES

EDA External Affairs and Communications

    14th St. and Constitution Ave. N.W., #7814A
    Washington, DC 20230

    (202) 482–2900
    Breelyn Pete, public affairs director

Provides public information. Issues news releases and publications.

Freedom of Information

    FOIA and Privacy Act Officer
    14th St. and Constitution Ave. N.W., #72023
    Washington, DC 20230
    (202) 482–3085
    Stephen Kong, chief counsel

DATA AND STATISTICS

    See *Publications*, below.

PUBLICATIONS

    EDA External Affairs and Communications provides publications, including the *Program Description Book* and the *EDA Annual Report.* Publications, reports, speeches, and documents may also be found on the Agency's Internet site.

Reference Resources

LIBRARY

Commerce Department

    1401 Constitution Ave. N.W.
    Washington, DC 20230
    (202) 482–1154
    Karen Krugman, director
    Public access by appointment only.

DOCKETS

    Federal dockets are available at www.regulations .gov. (*See appendix for Searching and Commenting on Regulations: Regulations.gov.*)

RULES AND REGULATIONS

    EDA rules and regulations are published in the *Code of Federal Regulations,* Title 13, Chapter III, Parts 300–399 and at www.regulations.gov. Proposed rules, new final rules, and updates to the *Code of Federal Regulations* are published in the daily *Federal Register.* (*See appendix for information on how to obtain and use these publications.*) The *Federal Register* and the *Code of Federal Regulations* may be accessed online at www .federalregister.gov; the site contains a link to the federal government's regulatory website at www.regulations.gov (*see appendix*).

▧ LEGISLATION

The EDA carries out its responsibilities under:

Public Works and Economic Development Act of 1965 (79 Stat. 552, 42 U.S.C. 312). Signed by the president Aug. 26, 1965. Established the EDA to provide aid to economically distressed areas of the country.

Trade Act of 1974 (19 U.S.C. 2341). Signed by the president Jan. 3, 1975. Provided for trade adjustment assistance for firms and industries adversely affected by foreign firms.

Economic Development Administration and Appalachian Regional Development Reform Act of 1998 (112 Stat. 3596, 42 U.S.C. 3121 note). Signed by the president Nov. 13, 1998. Title I, Economic Development Administration Reform Act of 1998, amended the Public Works and Economic Development Act of 1965 to replace Titles I through VI with the provisions of this act. Directed the secretary of commerce to cooperate with states and other entities to ensure that federal economic development programs are compatible with and further the objectives of state, regional, and local economic development plans and comprehensive economic development strategies. Directed the secretary to promulgate regulations for intergovernmental review of proposed economic development projects. Authorized the secretary to enter into economic development cooperation agreements with two or more adjoining states. Set forth provisions similar to existing provisions of law authorizing grants to eligible recipients for acquisition or development of public works and development of facilities.

Economic Development Administration Reauthorization Act of 2004 (118 Stat. 1756, 42 U.S.C. 3121 et seq.). Signed by the president Oct. 27, 2004. Reauthorized EDA programs through 2008. Amended the Public Works and Economic Development Act of 1965 to revise the definition of an eligible recipient to (1) remove the reference to an eligible recipient as an area having a low per capita income, an unemployment rate that is above the national average, or actual or threatened severe unemployment or economic adjustment problems; and (2) include as a city or other political subdivision of a state a special purpose unit of a state or local government engaged in economic or infrastructure development activities.

American Recovery and Reinvestment Act (19 U.S.C. 2101 note). Signed by the president Feb. 13, 2009. Appropriated $150 million to be distributed through the EDA's regional offices in the form of state grants to create jobs and encourage new development, especially in areas facing severe economic disruption and job loss.

America Creating Opportunities to Meaningfully Promote Excellence in Technology, Education, and Science Reauthorization Act of 2010 (COMPETES Act). (124 Stat. 3982, 42 U.S.C. 1861 note). Signed by the president Jan. 4, 2011. Established an Office of Innovation and Entrepreneurship and a regional innovation program within the EDA.

■ REGIONAL OFFICES

ATLANTA
(AL, FL, GA, KY, MS, NC, SC, TN)
401 W. Peachtree St. N.W., #1820
Atlanta, GA 30308–3510
(404) 730–3002
Fax (404) 730–3025
H. Phillip Paradice Jr., regional director

AUSTIN
(AR, LA, NM, OK, TX)
903 San Jacinto, #206
Austin, TX 78701
(512) 381–8144
Fax (512) 381–8177
Jorge Ayala (acting), regional director

CHICAGO
(IL, IN, MI, MN, OH, WI)
230 S. Dearborn St., 3280
Chicago, IL 60604
(312) 353–8143
Fax (312) 353–8575
Jeannette Tamayo, regional director

DENVER
(CO, IA, KS, MO, MT, ND, NE, SD, UT, WY)
1244 Speer Blvd., #431
Denver, CO 80204
(303) 844–4715
Fax (303) 844–3968
Robert E. Olson, regional director

PHILADELPHIA
(CT, DC, DE, MA, MD, ME, NH, NJ, NY, PA, PR, RI, VA, VI, VT, WV)
601 Walnut St., #140 South
Philadelphia, PA 19106–3323
(215) 597–4603
Fax (215) 597–1063
Tonia Williams (acting), regional director

SEATTLE
(AK, AS, AZ, CA, GU, HI, ID, NV, OR, WA, Marshall Islands, Federated States of Micronesia, Northern Marianas, Palau)
915 Second Ave., #1890
Seattle, WA 98174–1001
(206) 220–7660
Fax (206) 220–7669
A. Leonard Smith, regional director

International Trade Administration

14th St. and Constitution Ave. N.W., Washington, DC 20230
Internet: www.trade.gov

The International Trade Administration (ITA), formerly the Industry and Trade Administration, was established Jan. 2, 1980. The ITA grew out of a presidential directive aimed at consolidating the federal government's nonagricultural trade functions, particularly export promotion, into a single agency. The functions of the ITA are to expand exports, to improve enforcement of U.S. trade laws, and to upgrade government trade activities in line with the Multilateral Trade Negotiations agreements signed by the United States in 1979.

Supervision of the ITA is vested in the under secretary for international trade and a deputy under secretary. The agency's role in export promotion includes the responsibility for U.S. commercial attachés in most major countries; the secretary of commerce is an *ex officio* nonvoting member of the board of the Export-Import Bank. In addition, the ITA has responsibility for implementing trade agreements, antidumping investigations, imposition of countervailing duties and embargoes, and national security trade investigations.

ITA activities are divided into three principal areas, each directed by an assistant secretary.

Enforcement and Compliance. This section investigates dumping complaints to determine whether foreign goods are being sold in the United States at less than fair price and investigates countervailing duty petitions to determine whether foreign governments are subsidizing their exports to the United States. It administers the foreign trade zones program and conducts an industrial mobilization program to ensure availability of materials essential to national defense.

Industry and Analysis (I&A). This section undertakes industry trade analysis, shapes U.S. trade policy, participates in trade negotiations, organizes trade capacity building programs, and evaluates the impact of domestic and international economic and regulatory policies on U.S. manufacturers and service industries. I&A works with other U.S. agencies to develop a public policy environment that advances the competitiveness of U.S. industry. The section works with U.S. businesses on domestic and international economic and regulatory policies through its Office of Advisory Committees, which oversees four advisory groups: the Manufacturing Council, the Industry Trade Advisory Center, the Travel and Tourism Board, and the President's Export Council.

U.S. Foreign Commercial Service (USFCS) and Global Markets. This service assists U.S. traders in countries around the world and gathers information on foreign commercial and industrial trends for the benefit of U.S. businesses. The service, through its district offices, furnishes information, technical assistance, and counseling to the local business community. With a network of trade promotion and policy professionals located in more than 70 countries and 100 U.S. locations, USFCS and Global Markets promotes U.S. exports, especially among small and medium-sized enterprises; advances and protects U.S. commercial interests overseas; and attracts investment into the United States.

▓ KEY PERSONNEL

Under Secretary for International Trade
  Stefan Selig .... (202) 482–2867
Deputy Under Secretary
  Kenneth E. Hyatt.................. (202) 482–3917
Chief Counsel for Enforcement and Compliance
  John D. McInerney .... (202) 482–5589
Chief Counsel for International Commerce
  John F. Cobau.................... (202) 482–0937
Chief Financial and Administration Officer
  Tim Rosado .... (202) 482–5855
Chief Information Officer
  Joe Paiva .... (202) 482–3801
Legislative and Intergovernmental Affairs
  Jordan Haas .... (202) 482–3015

ENFORCEMENT AND COMPLIANCE
Assistant Secretary
  Paul Piquado .... (202) 482–1780
Deputy Assistant Secretary
  Ronald K. Lorentzen.............. (202) 482–2104
Foreign Trade Zone Staff
  Andrew McGilvray .... (202) 482–2862
Operations Support
  Robert Goodyear................. (202) 482–5194
Policy and Negotiations
  Lynn Fischer Fox................. (202) 482–6199
Trade Agreements, Negotiations, and Compliance
  John Liuzzi (acting) .... (202) 482–0539
Accounting
  Neal Halper .... (202) 482–2989

Policy
Carole Showers .... (202) 482–4412
Anti-Dumping Countervailing Duty Operations
Christian Marsh. .... (202) 482–5497

INDUSTRY AND ANALYSIS
Assistant Secretary
Marcus Jadotte. .... (202) 482–1461
Fax. .... (202) 482–5697
Deputy Assistant Secretary
Maureen Smith .... (202) 482–1461
Planning, Coordination, and Management
J. Slade Broom .... (202) 482–4921
Trade Programs and Strategic Partnerships
Anne Grey (acting). .... (202) 482–5927
Advisory Committees and Industry Outreach
Shannon Roche .... (202) 482–4501
Trade Promotion Programs
Anne Grey .... (202) 482–4501
Strategic Partnerships
Vacant .... (202) 482–5226
Textiles, Consumer Goods, and Materials
Josh Teitelbaum. .... (202) 482–3737
Textiles and Apparel
Janet Heinzen. .... (202) 482–5078
Materials
Gary Stanley. .... (202) 482–0376
Consumer Goods
James Rice .... (202) 482–1176
Manufacturing
Chandra Brown. .... (202) 482–1872
Energy and Environmental Industries
Adam O'Malley .... (202) 482–5225
Transportation and Machinery
Vacant. .... (202) 482–0554
Health and Information Technology
Ellen Bohon. .... (202) 482–0539
Trade Policy and Analysis
Praveen Dixit. .... (202) 482–5241
Investment Policy
Chris Rosettie .... (202) 482–3227
Trade and Economic Analysis
Joseph Flynn .... (202) 482–1606
Negotiations and Analysis
Jean Janicke .... (202) 482–5947
Intellectual Property Rights
Stevan Mitchell .... (202) 482–5751
National Travel and Tourism
Kelly Craighead Mullen .... (202) 482–4931
Travel and Tourism Industries
Isabel Hill. .... (202) 482–5120
Services
Ted Dean .... (202) 482–5261
Financial and Insurance Industries
Paul Thanos. .... (202) 482–3277
Digital Service Industries
Krysten Jenci .... (202) 482–0551
Supply Chain, Professional, and Business Services
David F. Long. .... (202) 482–3575

U.S. AND FOREIGN COMMERCIAL SERVICES AND GLOBAL MARKETS
Assistant Secretary
Arun Kumar. .... (202) 482–5777
Fax. .... (202) 482–5013
Deputy Director General
Judy Reinke .... (202) 482–5777
Advocacy Center
Jenna Pilat .... (202) 482–3896
Global Markets
Vacant .... (202) 482–6228
Western Hemisphere
John M. Andersen. .... (202) 482–5324
Asia
Holly Vineyard .... (202) 482–4651
Europe, the Middle East, and Africa
Matthew Murray. .... (202) 482–5638
China
Patrick Santillo .... (202) 482–4527
Domestic Operations
Antwaun Griffin .... (202) 482–4767

■ INFORMATION SOURCES

Internet

Agency website: www.trade.gov. A comprehensive site providing information on trade agency programs and services, trade statistics, publications, and links to Internet sites devoted to specific countries and regions.

The Trade Information enter (TIC) is a comprehensive resource for information on federal government export assistance programs. The center is operated by the ITA for the twenty federal agencies that make up the Trade Promotion Coordinating Committee (TPCC). These agencies are responsible for managing the government's export promotion programs and activities. The TIC can be reached at (800) 872–8723 (800-USA-TRADE), or e-mail tic@ita.doc.gov; trade specialists are available for assistance with questions on exporting. Current foreign tariff rates on exports are also available. The center is open Monday through Friday from 8:30 a.m. to 5:30 p.m. More information is available via its website at www.export.gov.

Telephone Contacts
Personnel Locator .... (202) 482–2000
Federal Relay Service TTY .... (800) 877–8339
Trade Information Center. .... (800) USA–TRADE
or .... (800) 872–8723

Information and Publications

KEY OFFICES

ITA Public Affairs
1401 Constitution Ave. N.W., #3416
Washington, DC 20230
(202) 482–3809
Mary L. Trupo, director

ITA Legislative and Intergovernmental Affairs
1401 Constitution Ave. N.W., #3424
Washington, DC 20230
(202) 482–3015
Jordan Haas, director

ITA Publications Division
1401 Constitution Ave. N.W.
Washington, DC 20230
(202) 482–5487
Mary L. Trupo, director
Internet: www.trade.gov/publications

Produces and distributes ITA publications.

ITA Trade Information Center
1401 Constitution Ave. N.W.
Washington, DC 20230
(202) 482–0543
Toll-free (800) USA–TRADE or (800) 872–8723
Susan Lusi, director
Internet: www.export.gov

Counsels U.S. businesses on exporting. Services are also provided by ITA's Export Assistance Centers (*see below*).

DATA AND STATISTICS
ITA data and statistics may be obtained from the Industry Trade Data and Analysis section of the agency's Internet site http://trade.gov/data.asp. Most information available from the ITA can also be obtained from the National Trade Data Bank, which can be accessed via the agency's main Internet site www.trade.gov/mas/ian/tradestatistics. Data also are available from the National Technical Information Service (*see appendix, Ordering Government Publications*).

PUBLICATIONS
The ITA Publications Division (*see above*) can provide information on obtaining books, magazines, and reports; publications are also available on the website, www.trade.gov/publications. Titles available include:

Annual Report of the Foreign-Trade Zones Board
Assessing Trends and Policies of Foreign Direct Investment in the United States
A Basic Guide to Exporting, 10th ed.
Business Ethics: A Manual for Managing a Responsible Business Enterprise in Emerging Market Economies
Clean Technology: An Exporter's Guide to China
Clean Technology: An Exporter's Guide to India
Commercial Outlook for U.S. Small Modular Nuclear Reactors
Electric Current Abroad
Exports Support American Jobs
The Impact of Exporting on the Stability of U.S. Manufacturing Industries
National Export Strategy, 2012 ed.
Packaging Machinery: Sustainability and Competitiveness
Protect Your Intellectual Property: Stop Trade in Fakes

U.S. Foreign Trade Highlights. Annual; contains statistics on U.S. foreign trade.

Reference Resources

LIBRARY

Commerce Department
1401 Constitution Ave. N.W.
Washington, DC 20230
(202) 482–1154
Karen Krugman, director
Public access by appointment only.

DOCKETS
Federal dockets are available at www.regulations.gov. (*See appendix for Searching and Commenting on Regulations: Regulations.gov.*)

RULES AND REGULATIONS
ITA rules and regulations are published in the *Code of Federal Regulations,* Title 15, Chapter III, Parts 300–399; Title 19, Chapter III, Parts 300–399; and at www.export.gov. Proposed regulations are published in the daily *Federal Register.* (*See appendix for details on how to obtain and use these publications.*) The *Federal Register* and the *Code of Federal Regulations* may be accessed online at www.federalregister.gov; the site contains a link to the federal government's regulatory website at www.regulations.gov (*see appendix*).

The annual report of the secretary of commerce reports on regulatory actions taken during the previous year.

▩ LEGISLATION
The ITA carries out its trade regulation responsibilities under:

Trade Agreements Act of 1979 (93 Stat. 144, 19 U.S.C. 2051). Signed by the president July 26, 1979. Approved and implemented the agreements reached in the Multilateral Trade Negotiations; its purpose is to expand U.S. foreign trade. The law overhauled the U.S. countervailing duty law, which was designed to protect domestic industry against foreign government subsidies on imported goods; and speeded up investigations and imposition of penalties under both the countervailing duty law and antidumping statutes.

Export Trading Company Act of 1982 (96 Stat. 1233, 15 U.S.C. 4001 note). Signed by the president Oct. 8, 1982. Encouraged exports by facilitating the formation of export trading companies, export trade associations, and the export trade services generally.

Trade and Tariff Act of 1984 (98 Stat. 2948, 19 U.S.C. 1654 note). Signed by the president Oct. 30, 1984. Amended the laws that govern international trade and investment, authorized the negotiation of trade agreements, extended trade preferences, and changed the tariff treatment of certain articles. Three of the act's titles are especially pertinent to the ITA. Title VI changed trade laws concerning antidumping and countervailing duties. Title VIII gave the president enforcement authority for bilateral steel agreements. Title IX gave the president the authority to seek the reduction or elimination of international trade barriers to U.S. wine exports.

Omnibus Trade and Competitiveness Act of 1988 (100 Stat. 1107, 19 U.S.C. 2901 note). Signed by the president Aug. 23, 1988. Amended section 201 of the Trade Act of 1974 to place a greater emphasis on industry adjustment to import competition in granting relief. Changed the antidumping and countervailing duty law to provide new provisions relating to release of business proprietary information under protective orders.

Export Enhancement Act of 1992 (106 Stat. 2199, 15 U.S.C. 4727). Signed by the president Oct. 21, 1992. Established the Trade Promotion Coordinating Committee to coordinate and promote the export financing activities of the United States, develop trade promotion policies and programs, and act as a central source of information on federal export promotion and export financing programs.

Freedom Support Act (106 Stat. 3322, 22 U.S.C. 5812). Signed by the president Oct. 24, 1992. Enhanced opportunities for trade and facilitated foreign investment in the independent states of the former Soviet Union.

Trade and Development Act of 2000 (114 Stat. 251, 19 U.S.C. 3701 note). Signed by the president May 18, 2000. Directed the ITA to take specified action to encourage the export of U.S. goods and services to sub-Saharan African countries.

Dominican Republic–Central America–United States Free Trade Agreement Implementation Act (119 Stat. 462, 19 U.S.C. 4001). Signed by the president Aug. 2, 2005. Approved the U.S. free-trade agreement with the governments of Costa Rica, the Dominican Republic, El Salvador, Guatemala, Honduras, and Nicaragua. Amended the Trade Agreements Act of 1979 to make products or services of any foreign country or instrumentality that is a party to the agreement eligible for U.S. government procurement. Prescribed requirements for enforcement of textile and apparel rules of origin; retroactive application for certain liquidations and reliquidations of textile or apparel goods; and presidential actions with regard to USITC findings on whether imports of articles are a substantial cause of serious injury or threat to U.S. articles and industries.

■ EXPORT ASSISTANCE CENTERS

A complete listing of export assistance centers and U.S. Commercial Service offices, including district and local offices, can be found at http://export.gov/usoffices/index.asp. Information is also available by phone at 1-800-USA-TRADE (1-800-872-8723). Website addresses for each state are formed as follows: http://export.gov/arkansas[state name]. Individuals' e-mail addresses follow the format firstname.lastname@trade.gov. There are also U.S. Commercial Service offices in many countries and at international banks; complete listings are available at http://export.gov/worldwide_us/index.asp.

ALABAMA
950 22nd St. North, #773
Birmingham, AL 35203–5309
(205) 731–1331
Robert Stackpole, director

ALASKA
431 W. 7th Ave., #108
Anchorage, AK 99501–0700
(907) 271–6237
Greg Wolf, consultant
(907) 278–7233

ARIZONA
2828 N. Central Ave., #800
Phoenix, AZ 85004
(602) 640–2513
Kristian Richardson, director

ARKANSAS
425 W. Capitol Ave., #425
Little Rock, AR 72201
(501) 324–5794
James Aardappel, director

CALIFORNIA
55 S. Market St., #1040
San Jose, CA 95113
(408) 535–2757
Joanne Vliet, director

2302 Martin Court., #315
Irvine, CA 92612
(949) 660–1688
Richard Swanson, regional director
(949) 660–8871

COLORADO/WYOMING
1625 Broadway, #680
Denver, CO 80202
(303) 844–6623
Paul G. Bergman, director
(303) 844–6001

CONNECTICUT
213 Court St., #903
Middletown, CT 06457–3382
(860) 638–6950
Anne S. Evans, director
(860) 638–6953

FLORIDA
5835 Blue Lagoon Dr., #203
Miami, FL 33126–3009
(305) 526–7425
Sarah Fox, commercial officer
(305) 526–7434

GEORGIA

111 E. Liberty St., #202
Savannah, GA 31401
(912) 652–4204
Todd Gerken, director

HAWAII

521 Ala Moana Blvd., #214
Honolulu, HI 96813
(808) 522–8040
John Holman, director
(808) 522–8041

IDAHO

700 W. State St., 2nd Floor
Boise, ID 83720
(208) 364–7791
Amy Benson, director

ILLINOIS

200 W. Adams St., #2450
Chicago, IL 60606
(312) 353–8040
Julie Carducci, director
(312) 353–8490

INDIANA

11405 N. Pennsylvania St., #106
Carmel, IN 46032
(317) 582–2300
Mark A. Cooper, director

IOWA

210 Walnut St., #749
Des Moines, IA 50309
(515) 284–4590
Patricia Cook, director

KANSAS

150 N. Main St., #200
Wichita, KS 67202–4012
(316) 263–4067
Andrew J. Anderson, director

KENTUCKY

601 W. Broadway, #634B
Louisville, KY 40202
(502) 582–5066
E-mail: Peggy.Pauley@trade.gov
Margaret (Peggy) Pauley, director

LOUISIANA

423 Canal St., #419
New Orleans, LA 70130
(504) 589–6546
Brittany Banta, director
(504) 589–6530

MAINE

511 Congress St.
Portland, ME 04101
(207) 541–7430
Jeffrey Porter, director

MARYLAND

300 W. Pratt St., #300
Baltimore, MD 21201–6504
(410) 962–4539
Bill F. Burwell, director

MASSACHUSETTS

JFK Federal Building
55 New Sudbury St., #1826A
Boston, MA 02203
(617) 565–4301
James Paul, director
(619) 565–4304

MICHIGAN

440 Burroughs St., #315
Detroit, MI 48202
(313) 872–6791
Sara Coulter, director
(313) 226–3652

MINNESOTA

100 N. 6th St., #210C
Minneapolis, MN 55403
(612) 348–1638
Ryan Kanne, director
(612) 348–1637

MISSISSIPPI

1230 Raymond Rd.
Box 600
Jackson, MS 39204
(601) 373–0773
Carol Moore, director

MISSOURI

4300 Goodfellow Blvd.
Bldg. 110, #1100A
St. Louis, MO 63120
(314) 260–3780
Cory Simek, director
(314) 260–3782

MONTANA

The University of Montana
Gallagher Business Bldg., #257
Missoula, MT 59812
(406) 370–0097
Carey Hester, international
 trade specialist

NEBRASKA

6708 Pine St.
Mammel Hall, #200
Omaha, NE 68182–0248
(402) 597–0193
Meredith Bond, director

NEVADA
400 South Forest St., #250
Las Vegas, NV 89101
(702) 388–6694
Andrew Edlefsen, director

NEW HAMPSHIRE
121 Technology Dr., #2
Durham, NH 03824
(603) 953–0212
Justin Oslowski, director
(603) 953–0210

NEW JERSEY
Princeton Pike Corporate Center
Lawrenceville, NJ 08648–2311
(609) 896–2732
Debora Sykes, director
(609) 896–2734

NEW MEXICO
c/o New Mexico Dept. of Economic Development
P. O. Box 20003
1100 St. Francis Dr.
Santa Fe, NM 87504–5003
(505) 231–0075
Sandra Necessary, director

NEW YORK
290 Broadway, #1312
New York, NY 10007
(212) 809–2675
Carmela Mammas, director
(212) 809–2676

NORTH CAROLINA
521 E. Morehead St., #435
Charlotte, NC 28202
(704) 333–4886
Greg Sizemore, director

NORTH DAKOTA
Fargo, ND 58102
(701) 552–0792
Heather Andrea Ranck, director

OHIO
600 Superior Ave. East, #700
Cleveland, OH 44114
(216) 522–4750
Susan Whitney, director
(216) 522–4755

OKLAHOMA
301 N.W. 63rd St., #330
Oklahoma City, OK 73116
(405) 608–5302
Marcus Verner, director

OREGON
121 S.W. Salmon St., #242
Portland, OR 97204
(503) 326–3001
Scott Goddin, director
(503) 326–5156

PENNSYLVANIA/DELAWARE
601 Walnut St., #580W
Philadelphia, PA 19106–3304
(215) 597–6101
Antonio Ceballos, director
(215) 597–7141

PUERTO RICO
Centro International de Mercado
Tower II, #702
Street 165
Guaynabo, PR 00968–8058
(787) 775–1992
Jose F. Burgos, director

RHODE ISLAND
315 Iron Horse Way, #101
Providence, RI 02908
(401) 528–5104
Keith Yatsuhashi, director

SOUTH CAROLINA
1705 College St., #600
Columbia, SC 29208
(803) 777–2571
Dorette Coetsee, director
(803) 397–4590

SOUTH DAKOTA
2001 S. Summit Ave.
Sioux Falls, SD 57197
(605) 330–4265
Cinnamon King, director

TENNESSEE
312 Rosa Parks Blvd., 10th Floor
Nashville, TN 37243
(615) 736–2222
Brie Knox, director
(615) 736–2223

TEXAS
4300 Amon Carter Blvd., #114
Fort Worth, TX 76155
(817) 684–5347
Daniel Swart, director

1919 Smith St., #1026
Houston, TX 77002
(713) 209–3104
Eric Nielson (acting), director
(713) 209–3105

UTAH

9690 S. 300 W., #201
Sandy, UT 84070
(801) 255–1871
David Fiscus, director
(801) 255–1873

VERMONT

1 National Life Dr.
National Life Bldg., 6th Floor
Montpelier, VT 05620–0501
(802) 828–4508
Susan Murray, director

VIRGINIA/WASHINGTON, DC

2800 S. Randolph St., #800
Arlington, VA 22206
(703) 235–0331
William Fanjoy, director
(703) 235–0327

800 E. Leigh St.
Richmond, VA 23219

(804) 771–2246
Eric McDonald, director

WASHINGTON

2001 6th Ave., #2610
Seattle, WA 98121
(206) 553–5615
Diane Mooney, director

WEST VIRGINIA

1116 Smith St., #302
Charleston, WV 25301
(304) 347–5123
Leslie Drake, director

WISCONSIN

1235 N. Milwaukee St., #R-01
Milwaukee, WI 53202
(414) 297–3473
Damian Felton, director
(414) 297–3457

National Oceanic and Atmospheric Administration

14th St. and Pennsylvania Ave. N.W., Washington, DC 20230
Internet: www.noaa.gov

The National Oceanic and Atmospheric Administration (NOAA), within the Commerce Department, was established by Reorganization Plan No. 4 on Oct. 3, 1970. The agency's principal functions are to explore, map, and chart the global ocean and its living resources and to manage, use, and conserve those resources.

The agency describes, monitors, and predicts conditions in the atmosphere, ocean, sun, and space environment; reports the weather of the United States and its possessions; issues warnings about impending destructive natural events; disseminates environmental data through a system of meteorological, oceanographic, geophysical, and solar-terrestrial data centers; manages and conserves living marine resources and their habitats, including certain endangered species and marine mammals; and develops policy on ocean management and use along the coastline of the United States and provides grants for marine research, education, and advisory services. The agency also plays a substantial role in the federal research effort on the potential for global climate change.

The National Ocean Service (NOS) coordinates coastal zone management and information; conducts marine environmental quality and pollution research, development, and monitoring; and directs programs to produce charts and related information for safe navigation of the nation's waterways, territorial seas, and national airspace.

Within NOS, the Office of Coastal Management has the primary responsibility of developing resource management plans for the nation's coastal zone. The office administers the provisions of the Coastal Zone Management Act of 1972 and is responsible for designating and managing the nation's network of marine sanctuaries. It also administers the National Estuarine Research Reserve System, the Coral Reef Conservation Program, and the National Marine Protected Areas (MPA) Center. CRM oversees the licensing of Ocean Thermal Energy Conversion projects, a renewable energy technology that uses temperature gradients in the ocean water to generate electricity.

In an effort to help the Gulf of Mexico region recover from damage caused by the Deepwater Horizon oil spill, Congress passed the Resources and Ecosystems Sustainability, Tourist Opportunities, and Revived Economies of the Gulf Coast States Act of 2012 (RESTORE Act). The legislation requires a percentage of the penalties paid by responsible parties in connection with oil spills to be deposited into a Gulf Coast Restoration Trust Fund for ecological and economic recovery efforts. NOAA was authorized to establish and administer the program in consultation with the U.S. Fish and Wildlife Service. The program will be administered by NOAA's National Ocean Service, National Centers for Coastal Ocean Science (NCCOS). In October 2014, NOAA released for public comment the draft science plan for the NOAA RESTORE Act Science Program, which was later followed by an announcement funding priorities for 2015.

The National Weather Service (NWS) program prepares and delivers weather predictions and warnings, as well as exchanging information with international organizations such as the World Meteorological Organization and the International Civil Aviation Organization. NWS also manages the NOAA Weather Radio broadcasting service. NOAA Weather Radio All Hazards, a component of the nation's Emergency Alert System, is comprised of a nationwide network of transmitters directly linked with one of the more than 100 local offices of NOAA's National Weather Service, which issues weather warnings and relays civil emergency messages on behalf of law enforcement agencies. The broadcasts cannot be heard on a simple AM/FM radio receiver. The public may purchase NOAA radio receivers at electronics and sporting goods stores or via the Internet.

The NOAA Fisheries, formerly the National Marine Fisheries Service, works to rebuild and maintain sustainable fisheries, promote the recovery of protected species, and protect and maintain the health of coastal marine habitats. To advance these goals, the service measures the social and economic effects of fishing practices and regulations, enforces fishing laws, and manages fish and marine mammals. Fisheries service scientists also research the biology and population status of marine animals and assess their habitat needs. During the 1990s, marine conservation laws were strengthened with major revisions to the Marine Mammal Protection Act in 1994 and the Magnuson-Stevens Fishery Conservation and Management Act in 1996.

Within Fisheries is NOAA's Office of Law Enforcement (OLE), which protects marine wildlife and habitat by enforcing domestic laws and international treaty requirements. OLE works to prevent the illegal, unregulated, and unreported harvesting and trafficking of fish and wildlife. The Office of the General Counsel is NOAA's civil prosecutor.

The National Environmental Satellite, Data, and Information Service (NESDIS) is responsible for NOAA's environmental satellite and data management programs. The program includes management services to develop and operate civilian satellite systems for observing land, ocean, atmospheric, and solar conditions required by governments, commerce, industry, and the general public. The office operates the Satellite Operational Control Center in Maryland and Command and Data Acquisition facilities in Virginia and Alaska to control and track the satellites and to read their data. NOAA's satellite service operates the mission control center for an international search and rescue network. NESDIS also operates satellites in the Defense Department's Defense Meteorological Satellite Program (DMSP is managed by the Space and Missile Systems Center, Los Angeles Air Force Base in California; daily operations is provided by the NESDIS in Maryland).

The Office of Oceanic and Atmospheric Research is responsible for coordinating NOAA's oceanic and atmospheric research and development programs. The office conducts research to further the understanding of phenomena such as the El Niño ocean current, global warming, and ozone depletion. The office also coordinates NOAA programs with other federal agencies, universities, international scientific organizations, and other stakeholder groups.

NOAA also houses the nation's seventh uniformed service, the NOAA Corps, a force of commissioned officers who operate a research fleet and pilot NOAA research and hurricane-tracking aircraft. A high-profile responsibility of NOAA is tracking and forecasting major storms and hurricanes. One of the most frequently visited features on NOAA's website is the National Hurricane Center, which allows the public to follow tropical storms and hurricanes. This data is available at www.nhc.noaa.gov.

Following the devastating tsunami that struck the nations surrounding the Indian Ocean in December 2004, NOAA worked with foreign governments to improve tsunami warning systems. NOAA joined the government of Thailand in deploying the first Deep-ocean Assessment and Reporting of Tsunami (DART) buoy station in the Indian Ocean. NOAA built and provided the DART station with funding from the U.S. Agency for International Development. In 2006 the U.S. Tsunami Warning Program reached its initial operating capability with the deployment of the twenty-third DART buoy in the western Pacific Ocean.

The National Integrated Drought Information System Act of 2006 authorized a National Integrated Drought Information System (NIDIS) within NOAA to improve drought monitoring and forecasting capabilities. In response, NOAA established the NIDIS Office at the Earth System Research Laboratory in Boulder, CO, to provide a real-time status report on the current levels and future risks of drought.

◼ KEY PERSONNEL

Under Secretary and Administrator
Kathryn Sullivan . . . . (202) 482–3436

Assistant Secretary and Deputy Administrator, Environmental Observation and Prediction
Manson Brown . . . . (202) 482–6236
Assistant Secretary, Conservation and Management
Holly A. Bamford . . . . (301) 713–3074, ext. 222
Deputy Assistant Secretary, International Fisheries
Russell Smith . . . . (202) 482–5682
Deputy Under Secretary, Operations
Michael Devany . . . . (202) 482–4569
Chief Scientist
Richard Spinrad . . . . (202) 482–5688
General Counsel
Lois J. Schiffer . . . . (202) 482–4627
Senior Advisor
Christine Blackburn . . . . (202) 482–2351
Chief of Staff
Renee Stone . . . . (202) 482–3436
Acquisitions and Grants
Mitchell Jay Ross . . . . (301) 713–0325
Chief Administrative Officer
Edward Horton . . . . (301) 713–0836
Chief Financial Officer
Mark Seiler . . . . (202) 482–4022
Chief Information Officer
Zach Goldstein . . . . (301) 713–9600
Civil Rights
Joseph E. Hairston . . . . (301) 713–0500, ext. 189
Education
Louisa Koch . . . . (202) 482–3384
International Affairs
Brenda Pierce . . . . (202) 482–6196
Legislative and Intergovernmental Affairs
Amanda Hallberg Greenwell . . . . (202) 482–4981
Meteorology
Dave McCarren (acting) . . . . (301) 427–9247
Military Affairs
Capt. Gary Joseph
Brenner . . . . (301) 427–2300, ext. 150
Col. Paul Roelle . . . . (301) 628–0056
Program Planning and Integration
Pat Montanio . . . . (301) 713–1632
Communications and External Affairs
Ciaran Clayton . . . . (202) 482–0199
Marine and Aviation Operations and NOAA Corps
Rear Adm. David Score . . . . (301) 713–7600
  Aircraft Operations Center
  Capt. Harris B. Halverson . . . . (813) 828–4048
  Marine Operations
  Capt. Todd A. Bridgeman . . . . (514) 867–8801
National Environmental Satellite, Data, and Information Service
  Assistant Administrator
  Stephen Volz . . . . (301) 713–3578
  Center for Satellite Applications and Research
  Al Powell . . . . (301) 683–3487
  National Center for Environmental Information
  Thomas R. Karl . . . . (828) 271–4476
  Commercial Remote Sensing Regulatory Affairs
  Tahara Dawkins . . . . (301) 713–3385

Geostationary Operational Environmental Satellites–R Series (GOES-R)
Gregory Mandt . . . . (303) 286–1355
International and Intragency Affairs Division
D. Brent Smith. . . . . (301) 713–2024, ext. 203
Joint Polar Satellite System Program
Harry Cikanek. . . . . (301) 713–4782
Projects, Planning, and Analysis
Suzanne Hilding . . . . (301) 713–0100
Satellite and Product Operations
Vanessa Griffin . . . . (301) 713–7311
Satellite Ground Services
Steven Petersen . . . . (301) 713–7111
Space Commercialization
Mark S. Paese (acting) . . . . (301) 713–2010
Fisheries
Assistant Administrator
Eileen Sobeck . . . . (301) 427–8000
Deputy Assistant Administrator for Regulatory Programs
Samuel Rauch . . . . (301) 427–7000
Aquaculture
Michael Rubino. . . . . (301) 427–8325
Habitat Conservation
Buck Sutter. . . . . (301) 427–8600
International Affairs and Seafood Inspection
John Henderschedt. . . . . (301) 427–8350
Law Enforcement
Logan Gregory. . . . . (301) 427–2300
Management and Budget
Brian Pawlak . . . . (301) 427–8720
Protected Resources
Donna S. Wieting . . . . (301) 427–8400
Science and Technology
Ned Cyr . . . . (301) 427–8100
Sustainable Fisheries
Alan Risenhoover . . . . (301) 427–8500
National Ocean Service
Assistant Administrator
Russell Callender
(acting) . . . . (301) 713–3074, ext. 222
Center for Operational Oceanographic Products and Services
Richard Edwing. . . . . (301) 713–2981 ext. 123
Coast Survey
Rear Adm. Gerd Glang. . . . . (301) 713–2770
Coastal Management
Jeff Payne (acting). . . . . (843) 740–1220
National Geodetic Survey
Juliana Blackwell . . . . (301) 713–3222, ext. 141
National Center for Coastal Ocean Science
Mary Erickson. . . . . (301) 713–3020
National Marine Sanctuaries
Dan Basta. (301) 713–7235
Response and Restoration
David Westerholm . . . . (301) 713–2989
National Weather Service
Assistant Administrator
Louis W. Uccellini. . . . . (301) 713–9095
Deputy Assistant Administrator for Weather Services
Laura K. Furgione. . . . . (301) 713–0711

Analyze, Forecast, and Support
Andrew Stern (acting) . . . . (301) 427–9120
National Centers for Environmental Prediction
William Lapenta . . . . (301) 683–1315
National Hurricane Center (11691 S.W. 17th St., Miami, FL 33165)
Richard (Rick) Knabb. . . . . (305) 229–4470
National Water Center
John Murphy . . . . (301) 427–9119
Oceanic and Atmospheric Research
Assistant Administrator
Craig McLean . . . . (301) 713–2458
Chief Science Advisor
Alexander E. MacDonald. . . . . (303) 497–6378
Climatic Program
Wayne Higgins . . . . (301) 734–1263
National Sea Grant College Program
Nikola Garber (acting). . . . . (301) 734–1088
Ocean Exploration and Research
Alan Leonardi. . . . . (301) 734–1016
Unmanned Aircraft Systems Program
Robbie Hood . . . . (301) 734–1102
Weather and Air Quality
John Cortinas. . . . . (301) 734–1198
Laboratories and Cooperative Institutes
Mike Uhart. . . . . (301) 734–1177

▓ INFORMATION SOURCES

Internet

Agency website: www.noaa.gov. Provides information on NOAA programs, with links to data centers and other divisions of NOAA.

Telephone Contacts

General number . . . . (202) 482–3436
Toll-free Coastal Survey;
Nautical Charting Program . . . . . . (888) 990–6622
Federal Relay Service TTY . . . . (800) 877–8339
Fisheries Tipline (violations) . . . . (800) 853–1964

Information and Publications

KEY OFFICES

NOAA Communications

1401 Constitution Ave. N.W., #6217
Washington, DC 20230
(202) 482–5647
Ciaran Clayton, director
Scott Smullen, deputy director
(202) 482–6090

Answers questions, distributes publications, and issues news releases.

Freedom of Information

1315 East-West Hwy., #9718
Silver Spring, MD 20910
(301) 628–5658

Fax (301) 713–4040
Robert Swisher, FOIA officer
E-mail: FOIA@noaa.gov

DATA AND STATISTICS

National Environmental Satellite, Data, and Information Service (NESDIS)

1335 East-West Hwy.
Silver Spring, MD 20910
(301) 713–3578
Fax (301) 713–1249
Stephen Volz, director

Manages all U.S. civil operational remote-sensing satellite systems and provides a variety of space-derived and environmental data and information products and services. Operates polar-orbiting, geostationary, and land satellites to provide real-time products to users. Also gathers data collected by global and national organizations for processing and dissemination by the National Centers for Environmental Information, listed below.

National Centers for Environmental Information (NCEI)

325 Broadway
Boulder, CO 80305–3328
(303) 497–6215
Thomas R. Karl, director
General E-mail: ncei.info@noaa.gov

Provides solid earth geophysical data on accelerograms, earthquakes, tsunamis, volcanoes, and magnetic surveys. Provides marine geology and geophysical data on seismic reflection, bathymetry, gravimetrics, geomagnetic total field measurements, cores, samples, sediments, and heat flow. Provides weather and climate data, including sky cover, visibility, precipitation, pressure, high and low temperature, wind direction, wind speed, degree days, and humidity, as well as worldwide satellite cloud photos and analyses, infrared imagery, and data and computer-derived products from operational and experimental environmental satellites. Provides oceanographic data, including temperature, salinity, conductivity, oxygen, inorganic phosphate, total phosphorus, nitrite-nitrogen, silicate-silicon, and pH, as well as information on ocean pollution and on surface currents, plankton standing crop, chlorophyll concentrations, and rates of primary productivity. Also provides solar-terrestrial physics data on the ionosphere, solar activity, geomagnetic variation, auroras, cosmic rays, airglow, and ice and snow.

PUBLICATIONS

Distribution Division

10201 Good Luck Rd.
Glen Dale, MD 20769
(800) 638–8972
DC area (301) 436–8301
Fax orders (301) 436–6829

Offers nautical and aeronautical charts and publications, which are also available free of charge from www.faacharts.faa.gov. (The Federal Aviation Administration now manages the website.) Chart catalogs are free on request at www.nauticalcharts.noaa.gov/index.html. An extensive series of reports and publications is available on the Internet site, listed under each center or office. Requests for formal and informal educational resources may be directed to (301) 713–1208 or outreach@noaa.gov.

Reference Resources

LIBRARY

NOAA Library and Information Services Division

1315 East-West Hwy.
55MC3, 2nd Floor, E/OC4
Silver Spring, MD 20910
(301) 713–2600
Fax (301) 713–4599
Open from 9:00 a.m. to 4:00 p.m.

Headquarters library; maintains a collection of current books, journals, and monographs dealing with oceanic and atmospheric phenomena. A virtual library including e-journals, e-books, and e-reference, as well as numerous databases, is also available on the Internet site. An Ask-the-Librarian service is available by telephone or e-mail at Library.Reference@noaa.gov. NOAA also maintains specialty libraries at its regional offices.

DOCKETS

Federal dockets are available at www.regulations.gov. (*See appendix for Searching and Commenting on Regulations: Regulations.gov.*)

RULES AND REGULATIONS

NOAA rules and regulations are published in the *Code of Federal Regulations,* Title 15, Chapter IX, Parts 900–999. Proposed regulations, new final regulations, and updates to the *Code of Federal Regulations* are published in the *Federal Register* and at www.regulations.gov. (*See appendix for details on how to obtain and use these publications.*) The *Federal Register* and the *Code of Federal Regulations* may be accessed online at www.federalregister.gov; the site contains a link to the federal government's regulatory website at www.regulations.gov (*see appendix*).

■ LEGISLATION

The NOAA carries out its responsibilities under:

Whaling Convention Act of 1949 (64 Stat. 421, 16 U.S.C. 916). Signed by the president Aug. 9, 1950. Provided for the licensing, enforcement of regulations, and research to assist the International Whaling Commission, established in 1946.

Tuna Convention Acts of 1950 (64 Stat. 777, 16 U.S.C. 951). Signed by the president Sept. 7, 1950. Provided authority to the secretary of commerce to issue regulations to protect the tuna population to ensure the maximum sustained catch.

Fur Seal Act of 1966 (80 Stat. 1149, 16 U.S.C. 1151). Signed by the president Nov. 2, 1966. Amended earlier laws providing for management of the fur seal herd and administration of the Pribilof Islands. Implemented the protocol on fur seals signed by the United States, Canada, Japan, and the Soviet Union.

Public Law 92–205 (85 Stat. 735, 15 U.S.C. 330). Signed by the president Dec. 18, 1971. Required persons engaged in weather modification activities to submit to the secretary of commerce reports describing these activities. A 1976 amendment to the act provided for research into weather modification technology.

Marine Mammal Protection Act of 1972 (86 Stat. 1027, 16 U.S.C. 1361). Signed by the president Oct. 21, 1972. Established a moratorium on the taking of marine mammals and a ban on the importation of marine mammals and marine mammal products with certain exceptions. Amended in 1994 to strengthen the law's provisions protecting marine mammals from incidental harm in commercial fishing.

Marine Protection, Research, and Sanctuaries Act of 1972 (86 Stat. 1052, 32 U.S.C. 1401). Signed by the president Oct. 23, 1972. Established a system for regulating the dumping of materials into ocean waters and for the transportation of these materials. Authorized research into ocean dumping, including the long-range effects of pollution, overfishing, and human-induced changes of ocean ecosystems.

Coastal Zone Management Act of 1972 (86 Stat. 1280, 16 U.S.C. 1451). Signed by the president Oct. 27, 1972. Authorized the secretary of commerce to make grants and contracts with any coastal state for developing and implementing a management program for the coastal zone and for acquiring and operating estuarine sanctuaries. Later amendments dealt with impacts resulting from coastal energy activities.

Endangered Species Act of 1973 (87 Stat. 884, 16 U.S.C. 1531). Signed by the president Dec. 28, 1973. Provided for the conservation of endangered species of fish, wildlife, and plants by identifying these species and implementing plans for their survival.

Magnuson Fishery Conservation Management Act of 1976 (Magnuson Act) (90 Stat. 331, 16 U.S.C. 1801). Signed by the president April 13, 1976. Extended the U.S. exclusive fishery zone to 200 from 12 nautical miles and set limits on foreign vessels fishing within these waters. This act has been amended numerous times. Last reauthorized in 2006.

Deep Seabed Hard Minerals Resources Act (94 Stat. 553, 30 U.S.C. 1401). Signed by the president June 28, 1980. Established a framework for the development and deployment of deep seabed mining technologies and authorized NOAA to issue licenses for exploration and permits for commercial recovery.

Ocean Thermal Energy Conversion Act of 1980 (94 Stat. 974, 42 U.S.C. 9109). Signed by the president Aug. 3, 1980. Authorized NOAA to issue licenses and regulations for research into the conversion to energy of differences in ocean temperatures. Research and development authority was left to the Energy Department.

Comprehensive Environmental Response, Compensation, and Liability Act of 1980 (94 Stat. 2767, 42 U.S.C. 9601 note). Signed by the president Dec. 11, 1980. This act, commonly referred to as "Superfund," designated the president as trustee for natural resources. The president delegated his trusteeship for marine resources to NOAA.

Oceans Act of 1992 (106 Stat. 5039, 16 U.S.C. 1431). Signed by the president Nov. 4, 1992. Amended the Marine Mammal Protection Act of 1972. Title III established a program to examine trends of marine mammal populations and ensure effective responses to strandings and catastrophic events involving marine mammals.

Airport and Airways Improvement Act (108 Stat. 698, 26 U.S.C. 9502). Signed by the president Aug. 23, 1994. Authorized the secretary of transportation to reimburse NOAA from the Airport and Airway Trust Fund for the cost of providing the Federal Aviation Administration with aviation weather reporting services.

Sustainable Fisheries Act (110 Stat. 3559, 16 U.S.C. 1801 note). Signed by the president Oct. 11, 1996. Amended the Magnuson Act to revise requirements regarding the review and taking effect of fishery management plans, amendments, and regulations. Modified foreign fishing prohibitions and requirements. Provided for an international agreement on bycatch reduction standards and measures.

Hydrographic Services Improvement Act of 1998 (112 Stat. 3454, 33 U.S.C. 892 et seq.). Signed by the president Nov. 13, 1998. Authorized NOAA to acquire and disseminate hydrographic data, promulgate hydrographic services standards, and ensure comprehensive geographic coverage of hydrographic services. Reauthorized and amended under the Hydrographic Services Improvement Act Amendments of 2008.

Homeland Security Act of 2002 (116 Stat. 2135, 6 U.S.C. 551, 557). Signed by the president Nov. 25, 2002. Transferred to Homeland Security the functions, personnel, assets, and liabilities of the Integrated Hazard Information System of NOAA, which was renamed FIRESAT.

National Oceanic and Atmospheric Administration Commissioned Officers Corps Act of 2002 (116 Stat. 3094, 10 U.S.C. 1293 note). Signed by the president Dec. 19, 2002. Applied certain specified provisions of federal law pertaining to the armed forces to the NOAA Commissioned Officer Corps, including ones dealing with leave, retirement, or separation for physical disability, and with computation of retired pay. Allowed the president to transfer NOAA vessels, equipment, stations, and officers to a military department in times of emergency, and prescribed rules for such cooperation.

Marine Debris Research, Prevention, and Reduction Act (120 Stat. 3333, 33 U.S.C. 1951 note). Signed by the president Dec. 22, 2006. Establishes a Marine Debris Prevention and Removal Program within NOAA to reduce and prevent the occurrence and adverse impacts of marine debris on the marine environment and navigation safety.

National Integrated Drought Information System Act of 2006 (120 Stat. 2918, 15 U.S.C. 311 note, 15 U.S.C. 313d note). Signed by the president Dec. 22, 2006. Established a National Integrated Drought Information System within NOAA to improve drought monitoring and forecasting capabilities.

America Creating Opportunities to Meaningfully Promote Excellence in Technology, Education, and Science Act (121 Stat. 572, 20 U.S.C. 9801 note). Signed by the president Aug. 9, 2007. Title IV, Ocean and

Atmospheric Programs, directed NOAA to establish a program of ocean, coastal, Great Lakes, and atmospheric research and development, in collaboration with academic institutions and other nongovernmental entities to promote U.S. leadership in ocean and atmospheric science, as well as competitiveness in applied uses of such research and development.

Omnibus Public Land Management Act of 2009 (123 Stat. 991, 16 U.S.C. 1 note). Signed by the president March 30, 2009. Directed the interior secretary to coordinate with the U.S. Geological Survey (USGS) and NOAA to ensure that the secretary has access to the best available scientific information regarding presently observed and projected future impacts of climate change on water resources.

Resources and Ecosystems Sustainability, Tourist Opportunities, and Revived Economies of the Gulf Coast States Act (RESTORE) of 2012 (126 Stat. 588, 33 U.S.C. 1321 note). Signed by the president July 12, 2014. Established a Gulf Coast Restoration Trust Fund for deposit of administrative and civil penalties paid in connection with the Deepwater Horizon incident. Directed NOAA to establish and administer the program.

Coast Guard and Maritime Transportation Act of 2012 (126 Stat. 1540, 33 U.S.C. 1951). Signed by the president Dec. 20, 2012. Replaces NOAA's Marine Debris Prevention and Removal Program with a Marine Debris Program to identify, determine sources of, assess, prevent, reduce, and remove marine debris and its adverse impacts on the U.S. economy, the marine environment, and navigation safety. Provisions of the Marine Debris Program require NOAA to provide national and regional coordination to assist states, Indian tribes, and regional organizations in the identification, determination of sources, assessment, prevention, reduction, and removal of marine debris.

▓ REGIONAL OFFICES

National Marine Fisheries Service

ALASKA REGION
709 W. 9th St., #420
P.O. Box 21668
Juneau, AK 99802–1668
(907) 586–7235
James W. Balsiger, regional administrator

GREATER ATLANTIC REGION
(CT, DC, DE, IL, IN, MA, MD, ME, MI, MN, NH, NJ, NY, OH, PA, RI, VA, WV)
55 Great Republic Dr.
Gloucester, MA 01930–2276
(978) 281–9300
John K. Bullard, regional administrator

Pacific Regions
(AS, GU, HI, MP)
1845 Wasp Blvd., Bldg. 176
Honolulu, HI 96818
(808) 725–5000
Michael D. Tosatto, regional administrator

SOUTHEAST REGION
(AL, FL, GA, LA, MS, NC, PR, SC, TX)
263 13th Ave. South
St. Petersburg, FL 33701
(727) 824–5301
Roy Crabtree, regional administrator

WEST COAST REGION
(AZ, CA, CO, GU, HI, ID, MT, ND, NV, OR, SD, UT, WA, WY)
7600 Sand Point Way N.E.
Seattle, WA 98115–0070
(206) 526–6150
Willian W. Stelle Jr., regional administrator

National Weather Service

ALASKA REGION
222 W. Seventh Ave., #23
Anchorage, AK 99513–7575
(907) 271–5088
Aimee Devaris, director

CENTRAL REGION
(CO, IA, IL, IN, KS, KY, MI, MN, MO, ND, NE, SD, WI, WY)
7220 N.W. 101st Terrace
Kansas City, MO 64153
(816) 891–8914
John Ogren, director

EASTERN REGION
(CT, DC, DE, MA, MD, ME, NC, NH, NJ, NY, OH, PA, RI, SC, VA, VT, WV)
630 Johnson Ave.
Bohemia, NY 11716–2626
(631) 244–0101
Jason Tuell, director

PACIFIC REGION
(GU, HI)
1845 Wasp Blvd., Bldg. 176
Honolulu, HI 96818
(808) 532–6416
Jeffrey LaDouce, director

SOUTHERN REGION
(AL, AR, FL, GA, LA, MS, NM, OK, PR, TN, TX, VI)
819 Taylor St., #10A06
Fort Worth, TX 76102
(817) 978–2651
Michael Coyne (acting), director

WESTERN REGION
(AZ, CA, ID, MT, NV, OR, UT, WA)
125 S. State St.
Salt Lake City, UT 84103
(801) 524–5122
Grant Cooper, director

United States Patent and Trademark Office

600 Dulany St., Alexandria, VA 22314
Mailing address: P.O. Box 1450, Alexandria, VA 22313
Internet: www.uspto.gov

On April 10, 1790, President George Washington signed the first patent bill. Three years earlier, the Constitutional Convention had given Congress the power to "promote the process of science and useful arts by securing for limited times to authors and inventors the exclusive right to their respective writings and discoveries."

The U.S. Patent Office became an actual entity in 1802 when an official in the State Department was designated as superintendent of patents. In 1849 the Patent Office was moved to the Interior Department, and in 1925 its authority was transferred to the Commerce Department. The name of the agency was changed on Jan. 2, 1975, to the Patent and Trademark Office (USPTO). The functions of the USPTO are to examine and issue patents on new and useful inventions and to examine and register trademarks used with goods and services in interstate commerce. The American Inventors Protection Act of 1999 established the USPTO as an agency within the Department of Commerce.

The USPTO examines applications for three kinds of patents: design patents (issued for fourteen years from the date of application), plant patents (issued for twenty years from the date of application), and utility patents (issued for twenty years). Patents provide inventors with exclusive rights to the results of their creative efforts. The patent system is intended to give incentive to invent, to invest in research and development, to commercialize new technology, and to make public inventions that otherwise would be kept secret.

The USPTO no longer files paper copies of trademark applications; the agency now relies exclusively on trademark data submitted or captured electronically to support trademark examination, publication of documents, and granting of registrations. A trademark consists of any distinctive word, name, symbol, or device used by manufacturers, merchants, or businesses to identify goods or services or to distinguish them from those manufactured or sold by others. Trademarks, registered for twenty years with renewal rights, are examined by the USPTO to ensure compliance with various statutory requirements to prevent unfair competition and consumer deception.

In 2003 the United States became a member of the Madrid Protocol, which allows U.S. business owners to file a single application with the USPTO and have their mark protected in any or all of the countries that are members of the protocol. In a similar manner trademark owners of member countries may seek an extension of protection of their international registration in the United States by filing through the World Intellectual Property Organization.

The USPTO also sells printed copies of issued documents, hears and decides appeals from prospective inventors and trademark applicants, participates in legal proceedings involving the issue of patent or trademark registration, and helps to represent the United States in international patent policy matters. The USPTO maintains a list of agents and attorneys who are qualified to practice before it.

In 2011 Congress passed the Leahy-Smith America Invents Act (AIA), the most extensive reform to patent law in more than fifty years. The legislation moves the invention precedence standard from first-to-invent to a first-inventor-to-file system, which is more aligned with global intellectual property standards. AIA also makes changes to legal proceedings involving patent disputes. It authorizes USPTO to revise the fee schedule. The first-inventor-to-file provisions went into effect on March 16, 2013.

Following the AIA reforms, President Barak Obama issued five executive actions in June 2013 to address abusive litigation by patent-assertion entities, so-called patent trolls. Patent trolls often buy vague patents, then sue targets with the intent of forcing a settlement. Because these lawsuits are very expensive, the target often settles, even if the case is weak. Patent trolls often set up shell companies to hide their activities, which prevent defendants from knowing the full extent of the patents that their adversaries hold when negotiating settlements.

USPTO is responsible for implementing four of these actions. USPTO was directed to stop issuing overly broad patents and must require a company to be more specific about exactly what its patent(s) covers and how it is being infringed. Another action directed USPTO to curb patent-infringement lawsuits against "Main Street" retailers, consumer, and small-business owners that are end users of products containing patented technology (such as Wi-Fi). Also, USPTO was directed to open patent applications for public scrutiny during the approval stage to help examiners locate prior art and assist with analyzing patent claims. Finally, USPTO expands public outreach efforts and empirical research. Within a year, USPTO had made notable progress on these directives.

The Patent Law Treaties Implementation Act of 2012 amends federal patent law to implement the Geneva Act of the Hague Agreement Concerning the International Registration of Industrial Designs (Hague Treaty) and the Patent Law Treaty. Both treaties were ratified by the Senate on December 7, 2007. The Hague system for the protection of industrial designs allows inventors the ability to register for a maximum of 100 designs in more than 62 territories with the filing of one single international application. United States membership became effective on May 13, 2015. U.S. design patents resulting from applications filed after that date have a fifteen-year term.

■ KEY PERSONNEL

Under Secretary of Commerce for Intellectual Property and Director
Michelle K. Lee . . . . (571) 272–8600
    Fax . . . . (571) 273–0464
Deputy Under Secretary of Commerce for Intellectual Property and Deputy Director
Russell Slifer . . . . (571) 272–8600
    Intellectual Property, Senior Advisor
    Justin Hughes . . . . (571) 272–8700
Chief Communications Officer
Todd Elmer . . . . (571) 272–8400
Chief Information Officer
John B. Owens II . . . . (571) 272–9400
Chief Policy Officer
Shira Perlmutter . . . . (571) 272–9300
Congressional Liaison
Paul Zanowski . . . . (571) 272–8308
Equal Employment Opportunity and Diversity
Bismarck Myrick . . . . (571) 272–8292
Enrollment and Discipline
William R. (Will) Covey . . . . (571) 272–4097
Governmental Affairs
Dana Roberts Colarulli . . . . (571) 272–6434
General Counsel
Sarah Harris . . . . (571) 272–7000
General Law
James Payne . . . . (571) 272–3000
Chief Financial Officer
Anthony P. (Tony) Scardino . . . . (571) 272–9200
Chief Administrative Officer
Frederick Steckler . . . . (571) 272–9660
Enforcement
Michael L. Smith . . . . (571) 272–8495
Human Resources
Karen Karlinchak . . . . (571) 272–6000
Policy and International Affairs
Shira Perlmutter . . . . (571) 272–9300
Patents Commissioner
Margaret A. (Peggy) Focarino . . . . (571) 272–8800
    Fax . . . . (571) 273–0125

Trademarks Commissioner
Mary Boney Denison . . . . (571) 272–8901
    Fax . . . . (571) 273–0029

■ INFORMATION SOURCES

Internet

Agency website: www.uspto.gov. Includes agency information, forms that can be downloaded, searchable databases of patents, electronic patent application processing, and links to other intellectual property office websites. The website includes a Kids' Page and section, which explains and illustrates patent and trademark legal terms and codes in simple terms.

Telephone Contacts

General Inquiries and
    Technical Support . . . . (571) 272–1000
or . . . . (800) 786–9199
TTY . . . . (571) 272–9950
Patent Electronic Business Center . . . . (866) 217–9197
or . . . . (571) 272–4100
E-mail ebc@uspto.gov
Inspector General's Hotline . . . . (866) 999–4258

Information and Publications

KEY OFFICES

Mailing address for USPTO offices is P.O. Box 1450, Alexandria, VA 22313–1450.

USPTO Office of Chief Communications Officer

600 Dulany St.
Madison West Bldg.
Alexandria, VA 22314–1450
(571) 272–8400
Fax (571) 273–0340
Todd Elmer, chief communications officer
E-mail: USPTOinfo@uspto.gov

Answers questions, distributes publications, issues news releases, and responds to press inquiries.

Freedom of Information

USPTO FOIA
P.O. Box 1450
Alexandria, VA 22313–1450
(571) 270–7420
Fax (571) 273–0099
Ricou Heaton, FOIA officer
E-mail: foiarequests@uspto.gov

USPTO Patent Application Processing

2800 S. Randolph St.
Arlington, VA 22206
(571) 272–4000
Kevin Little, director

Pre-examination processing of new patent applications.

USPTO Data Management
2800 S. Randolph St.
Arlington, VA 22206
(571) 272–4000
Thomas L. (Tom) Koontz, director

Oversees contractor servicing.

USPTO Patent Information Management
600 Dulany St.
Madison West Bldg.
Alexandria, VA 22314
(571) 272–5450
Internet: PATFT.uspto.gov
Debra Stephens, director

Publishes reports on patent activity; maintains patent files and databases.

DATA AND STATISTICS
USPTO Patent Information Management maintains a patent file that contains more than 7 million distinct U.S. patents. These are classified and cross-referenced into approximately 158,000 categories of technology. The technology assessment and forecast program maintains a master database covering all U.S. patents.

PUBLICATIONS
USPTO publications are available on the website at www.uspto.gov/about-us/organizational-offices/office-policy-and-international-affairs/office-chief-econo mist-5. Publications include *Mumbo Jumbo Gumbo,* which explains patent and trademark legal terms and codes in simple terms as part of the USPTO Kids' Page.

Reference Resources

LIBRARIES
See also *Data and Statistics,* above. For Patent and Trademark Depository Libraries, contact the USPTO Library, call (800) 786–9199, or visit the website at www .uspto.gov/learning-and-resources/support-centers.

USPTO Library
Remsen Bldg., Lobby level #1D58
400 Dulany St.
Alexandria, VA 22314
(571) 272–2520
Anne Hendrickson, manager
(571) 272–3490
Hours: 8:00 a.m. to 5:00 p.m.

Contains material of a scientific or biotechnology nature or dealing with intellectual property law.

Public Patent Search Facility
600 Dulany St.
Madison East Bldg., 1st Floor
Alexandria, VA 22314
(571) 272–3275

Terry Howard, manager
(571) 272–3258
Hours: 8:00 a.m. to 8:00 p.m. (no staff assistance after 5:00 p.m.)

Free training is available to search for patent and trademark information. Write to USPTO, Att: PSF Public Training, Box 1450, Alexandria VA 22315–1450, or call (571) 272–3275.

Library of Congress Copyright Office
101 Independence Ave. S.E.
Washington, DC 20559–6000
(202) 707–5959 or (877) 476–0778
website: www.copyright.gov
Maria A. Pallante, register of copyrights
Hours: Monday–Friday, 8:30 a.m. to 5:00 p.m.

Provides information on copyright registration procedures, requirements, and copyright law. Registers copyright claims; maintains records of copyright registrations and transfers; and processes copyright applications, whether submitted electronically or on paper. Copyright files are open to the public for research, or searches may be conducted by the library staff for a fee. The Copyright Office is not permitted to give legal advice. For information on copyrights contact the Library of Congress.

DOCKETS
Federal dockets are available at www.regulations. gov. (*See appendix for Searching and Commenting on Regulations: Regulations.gov.*)

RULES AND REGULATIONS
USPTO proposed regulations, new final regulations, and updates are published in the *Code of Federal Regulations,* Title 37, Chapter I, Parts 1–199, and in the *Federal Register.* (*See appendix for details on how to obtain and use these publications.*) The *Federal Register* and the *Code of Federal Regulations* may be accessed online at www.federalregister.gov; the site contains a link to the federal government's regulatory website at www.regulations .gov (*see appendix*).

▪ LEGISLATION
The USPTO carries out its responsibilities under authority granted in the following legislation:

Trademark Act of 1946, as amended (60 Stat. 427, 15 U.S.C. 1051). Signed by the president July 5, 1946. Revised and codified earlier statutes pertaining to the protection of trademarks used in interstate commerce.

Title 35 of the U.S. Code. Established the USPTO and the U.S. patent system. All amendments related to patent legislation were covered under this title. Authorized the administration of patent laws, derived from the act of July 19, 1952, and subsequent enactment. Made available revenues from fees, to the extent provided for in appropriations acts, to the commissioner to carry out the activities of the office. Authorized the USPTO to charge international fees for activities undertaken pursuant to the Patent Cooperation Treaty. Authorized the deployment of automated search systems of the office to the public.

44 U.S.C. 1337–1338 of the U.S. Code. Authorized the USPTO to print patents, trademarks, and other matters relating to the business of the office.

Government Patent Policy Act of 1980 (94 Stat. 3018, 35 U.S.C. 200 note). Signed by the president Dec. 12, 1980. Also known as the Bayh-Dole Act. Created a uniform patent policy among federal agencies that fund research, allowing small businesses and nonprofit organizations (including universities) to retain title to inventions made under federally funded research programs.

Intellectual Property and Communications Omnibus Reform Act of 1999 (113 Stat. 1536, 1501A–521, 35 U.S.C. 1 note). Signed by the president Nov. 29, 1999. Title III, Anticybersquatting Consumer Protection Act, amended the Trademark Act of 1946 to make liable in a civil action by the owner of a trademark any person who, with a bad faith intent to profit from that trademark, registers or uses a domain name that is (1) identical or confusingly similar to a distinctive mark; (2) dilutive of a famous mark; or (3) is a protected trademark, word, or name. Title IV, American Inventors Protection Act of 1999, provided protection for inventors against deceptive practices of certain invention promotion companies. Reduced certain patent fees and emphasized that trademark fees could only be used for trademark-related activities. Established the USPTO as an agency within the Department of Commerce. Provided authority for the electronic filing, maintenance, and publication of documents.

Technology, Education, and Copyright Harmonization Act of 2002 (116 Stat. 1758, 28 U.S.C. 351 note). Signed by the president Nov. 2, 2002. Amended federal patent and trademark law to specify that third-party requesters were persons who may invoke reexamination of a patent in light of new evidence affecting its patentability. Set forth the Madrid Protocol concerning the international registration of trademarks. Authorized the owner of a basic application for trademark registration pending before, or of a basic registration granted by, the USPTO who is a U.S. national, is domiciled in the United States, or has a real and effective industrial or commercial establishment in the United States to file an international application with the USPTO.

Prioritizing Resources and Organization for Intellectual Property Act of 2008 (122 Stat. 4256, 15 U.S.C. 8101 note). Signed by the president Oct. 13, 2008. Enhanced civil and criminal intellectual property laws. Provided for the forfeiture and destruction of any property used to commit a criminal offense involving copyrighted works.

Trademark Technical and Conforming Amendment Act of 2010 (124 Stat. 66, 15 U.S.C. 1051 note). Signed by the president March 17, 2010. Allows the holder of an international registration to appeal to the U.S. Court of Appeals for the Federal Circuit if the holder is dissatisfied with the decision of the USPTO director or Trademark Trial and Appeal Board.

Leahy-Smith America Invents Act (125 Stat. 284, 35 U.S.C. 1 note). Signed by the president Sept. 16, 2011. Converted the patent process from a first-to-invent system to a first-inventor-to-file system. Makes changes to legal proceedings in patent disputes. Other provisions.

Patent Law Treaties Implementation Act of 2012 (126 Stat. 1527, 35 U.S.C. 1 note). Signed by the president Dec. 18, 2012. Amends federal patent law to implement the Geneva Act of the Hague Agreement Concerning the International Registration of Industrial Designs (Hague Treaty) and the Patent Law Treaty. Allows applicants to file a single international design application to acquire global protection.

Defense Department

1400 Defense Pentagon, Washington, DC 20301
Internet: www.defense.gov

Army Corps of Engineers

441 G St. N.W., Washington, DC 20314
Internet: www.usace.army.mil

The Army Corps of Engineers (USACE) regulates all construction projects in the navigable waterways of the United States. It also regulates the use of special areas, designating both danger zones (areas that may be used by the Defense Department for military exercises), and restricted areas (areas that are reserved for special uses). In addition, the corps promulgates regulations governing the transportation and dumping of dredged materials in navigable waters.

The corps is a division of the Army Department within the Defense Department. The chief of engineers is the army's chief engineer and the commander of the corps of engineers and is appointed by the president and confirmed by the Senate.

The majority of the corps' responsibilities involve water resource development projects. The corps develops, plans, and builds various structures—dams, reservoirs, levees, harbors, waterways, and locks—to protect areas from floods, reduce transportation costs, supply water for municipal and industrial use, generate hydroelectric power, create recreational areas, improve water and wildlife quality, and protect the shorelines of oceans and lakes. The USACE also provides assistance to state, local, and non-federal water resource management groups, as well as to foreign countries.

USACE regulatory activities are administered by the Directorate of Civil Works. The directorate has primary responsibility for granting permits for structures or work in or affecting the navigable waters of the United States, for the discharge of dredged or fill materials in navigable waters, and for the transportation of dredged material to ocean dumping grounds. This nationwide civil works organization, consisting of almost 800 officers and nearly 33,000 employees (including civilians), works to ensure, through administrative proceedings and the solicitation of public comments, that proposed construction projects are not contrary to the public interest. The directorate is located in nine divisions, more than forty districts, and hundreds of area, project, and resident engineer offices worldwide.

Public benefit is determined by judging each proposal against several factors, including conservation, economics, aesthetic and cultural value, navigation, recreation, agricultural and mineral value, and private property rights.

The Directorate of Military Programs manages all army construction, installations, family housing, real estate, facilities requirements, and real property maintenance. The directorate also is responsible for a major portion of construction programs for the U.S. Air Force.

The corps is authorized under the Flood Control and Coastal Emergency Act to respond to emergencies caused by flooding. The corps provides technical and direct assistance to communities to reduce risk to the public, property, or the environment, with the emphasis on public safety. The corps coordinates efforts with other federal agencies (such as the Federal Emergency Management Agency) and state and local authorities.

In the wake of Hurricane Katrina's destructive blow to the Gulf Coast in 2005, the corps was a major part of the federal response to the devastated areas. In New Orleans the corps repaired the city's broken levee system and helped pump the flooded city dry. The corps had an initial budget of $3 billion for repairing levees and other structures and removing storm debris throughout the region.

In 2006, the corps created its Levee Safety Program to assess the integrity and viability of levees and recommend courses of action to ensure that levee systems do not present unacceptable risks to the public, property, and environment. There are more than 14,000 miles of levee systems in Army Corps of Engineers programs.

The Disaster Relief Appropriations Act of 2013 provided USACE with $5.35 billion to assist with disaster recovery following Hurricane Sandy. The legislation provided supplemental appropriations to address damages caused by Hurricane Sandy and to reduce future flood risk in ways that will support the long-term sustainability of the coastal ecosystem and communities and reduce the economic costs and risks associated with large-scale flood and storm events.

The Water Resources Reform and Development Act of 2014 (WRRDA 2014) authorized thirty-four new Army Corps projects. The legislation expedited the project delivery process, limiting feasibility studies to three years and requiring USACE to concurrently conduct reviews of a feasibility study. WRRDA 2014 authorized USACE to accept funds from non-federal public interests to expedite the processing of permits within the USACE regulatory framework.

The USACE hosted four listening sessions to receive public input on the development of implementation guidance for WRRDA 2014. Subsequently, USACE developed a Web page where guidance is posted and updated.

■ KEY PERSONNEL

Commander
Lt. Gen. Thomas P. Bostick . . . . (202) 761–0001
Fax. . . . . (202) 761–1683
Deputy Commander
Maj. Gen. Richard L. Stevens . . . . . . (202) 761–0002
Chief Audit Executive
Sandra L. Pack . . . . (202) 761–1985
Chief Counsel
Earl H. Stockdale. . . . . (202) 761–0018
Civil and Emergency Operations
Maj. Gen. John W. Peabody . . . . (202) 761–5859
Civil Works
Steven L. Stockton. . . . . (202) 761–0099
Contingency Operations
Karen Durham-Aguilera . . . . (202) 761–5903
Contracting
Stuart A. Hazlett . . . . (202) 761–0567
Corporate Information and Chief Information Officer
Robert V. Kazimer. . . . . (202) 761–0273
Engineer Inspector General
Frank D. Ellis . . . . (703) 428–6572
Toll-free . . . . (800) 328–6572
Engineering and Construction
James C. Dalton. . . . . (202) 761–8826
Environmental
Karen J. Baker (acting) . . . . (202) 761–5642
Equal Employment Opportunity
James C. Braxton. . . . . (202) 761–0095
History
John C. Lonnquest . . . . (703) 428–6563
Human Resources
Susan A. Engelhardt . . . . (202) 761–0559
Interagency and International Services
Charles R. Alexander . . . . (202) 761–8656
Logistics
Robert Gosciewski . . . . (202) 761–5455
Military and International Operations
Brig. Gen. Donald E. Jackson . . . . (202) 761–0379
Military Programs
Lloyd Caldwell. . . . . (202) 761–0838
Real Estate
Brenda M. Johnson-Turner . . . . (202) 761–0579
Research and Development
Jeffrey P. Holland. . . . . (202) 761–1839
Resource Management
Wesley C. Miller . . . . (202) 761–0077
Safety and Occupational Health
Richard L. Wright . . . . (202) 761–8567
Small Business
Grace K. Fontana. . . . . (202) 761–8789

■ INFORMATION SOURCES

Internet

Agency website: www.usace.army.mil. Provides information on Corps of Engineers activities, news releases, and links to related government Internet sites.

Telephone Contacts

Information, maps, charts,
permits, publications . . . . (202) 761–0011
Switchboard/Locator . . . . (202) 761–0005
TTY . . . . (800) 877–8339
Chief of Engineers Hotline . . . . (800) 328–2207

Information and Publications

KEY OFFICES

Office of Public Affairs
441 G St. N.W.
Washington, DC 20314–1000
(202) 761–0010
Fax (202) 761–1803
Curry Graham, director
(202) 761–4715
Internet: www.usace.army.mil/Media.aspx
E-mail: hq-publicaffairs@usace.army.mil

Provides information on operations of the Army Corps of Engineers. Answers or refers questions about the corps and issues news releases and publications.

Freedom of Information
Attn: CECC-G
441 G St. N.W.
Washington, DC 20314–1000
(202) 761–8557
Fax (202) 761–0270
Richard Frank, FOIA liaison
E-mail: foia-liaison@usace.army.mil

DATA AND STATISTICS

The best source of data and statistics related to the corps is through the website at www.usace.army.mil, including information from its expertise centers at www.usace.army.mil/About/CentersofExpertise.aspx. The Army Corps of Engineers collection is the only repository of all its official regulations, circulars, and manuals. In addition, the corps produces many reports on its projects; contact the Directorate of Civil Works or the Office of Public Affairs to find out which office within the corps has specific types of information needed.

PUBLICATIONS

Information about corps publications may be obtained from the Office of Public Affairs or the nearest regional office. Army Corps of Engineers publications are also available on the website at www.publications.usace.army.mil this collection is the only repository of all official ACE engineering regulations, circulars, and manuals. Listings of publications are available on the website at publications.usace.army.mil, or for assistance in obtaining publications contact Hector Hunt by e-mail at hector.n.hunt@usace.army.mil or by phone at (301) 394–0124.

Reference Resources

LIBRARY

Humphreys Engineer Center

7701 Telegraph Rd.
110 Casey Bldg.
Alexandria, VA 22315
(703) 428–6388
Connie Wiley, library director
Internet: www.usace.army.mil/Library/
    HeadquartersLibrary.aspx and
    www.usace.army.mil/library
E-mail: HECSA.library@usace.army.mil

The library is not open to the public but participates in the international cooperative resources sharing system OCLC. The website's Electronic Library provides more than 4,600 online resources, available to HQ USACE, HECSA, IWR, and 249th Engineer Battalion but not to the general public.

DOCKETS

Federal dockets are available at www.regulations .gov. (*See appendix for Searching and Commenting on Regulations: Regulations.gov.*)

RULES AND REGULATIONS

Army Corps of Engineers rules and regulations are published in the *Code of Federal Regulations,* Title 33, Chapter II, Parts 200–399; Title 36, Chapter III, Parts 300–399, and on the website. Proposed rules, final rules, and updates to the *Code of Federal Regulations* are published in the daily *Federal Register.* (*See appendix for information on how to obtain and use these publications.*)

Corps of Engineers regulations and policies are outlined in the *Digest of Water Resources Policies,* available from the Office of Public Affairs and on the website.

▦ LEGISLATION

Regulatory statutes administered by the Army Corps of Engineers include:

Rivers and Harbors Act of 1899 (30 Stat. 1151, 33 U.S.C. 403). Signed by the president March 3, 1899. Authorized regulation of all construction work in the navigable waters of the United States.

Rivers and Harbors Act of 1917 (40 Stat. 250, 33 U.S.C. 1). Signed by the president Aug. 8, 1917. Authorized the secretary of the army to regulate navigable waters of the United States as public necessity may require for the protection of life, property, and operations of the United States in channel improvement.

Army Act of July 9, 1918, Chapter XIX (40 Stat. 892, 33 U.S.C. 3). Signed by the president July 9, 1918. Authorized issuance of danger zone regulations to protect lives and property on navigable waters.

Flood Control and Coastal Emergency Act (69 Stat. 186, 33 U.S.C. 701 note). Signed by the president June 28,

1955. Authorized the Army Corps of Engineers to provide emergency repair or rehabilitation of eligible federally authorized flood control works damaged by floods and to participate in an intergovernmental levee task force.

Federal Water Pollution Control Act Amendments of 1972 (Clean Water Act) (86 Stat. 816, 33 U.S.C. 1251). Vetoed by the president Oct. 17, 1972; veto overridden Oct. 18, 1972. Empowered the Army Corps of Engineers to issue permits for the disposal of dredged or fill material at specified sites. Amended in 1977.

Marine Protection, Research, and Sanctuaries Act of 1972 (86 Stat. 1052, 33 U.S.C. 1401). Signed by the president Oct. 23, 1972. Authorized the corps to issue permits for transportation of dredged material to be dumped in ocean waters.

Water Resources Development Act of 1996 (110 Stat. 3658, 33 U.S.C. 2201 note). Signed by the president on Oct. 12, 1996. Allowed a project sponsor of a levee to seek a variance from Corps standards to allow additional vegetation on or near levees when such vegetation would preserve, protect, and/or enhance natural resources.

Water Resources Development Act of 1999 (113 Stat. 269, 33 U.S.C. 2201 note). Signed by the president Aug. 17, 1999. Provided for the conservation and development of water and related resources. Authorized the secretary of the army to construct various projects for improvements to rivers and harbors of the United States, and for other purposes.

Estuary Restoration Act of 2000 (114 Stat. 1958, 33 U.S.C. 2901 note). Signed by the president Nov. 7, 2000. Establishes an estuary habitat restoration program under which the secretary of the army may carry out estuary habitat restoration projects and provide technical assistance.

Water Resources Development Act of 2007 (121 Stat. 1041, 33 U.S.C. 2201 note). Signed by the president Nov. 8, 2007. Reauthorized the Water Resources Development Act (WRDA). Authorized flood control, navigation, and environmental projects and studies by the Army Corps of Engineers. Title IX National Levee Safety Act established a Committee on Levee Safety to develop recommendations for a national levee safety program.

Water Resources Reform and Development Act of 2014 (128 Stat. 1193, 33 U.S.C. 2201 note). Signed by the president June 10, 2014. Authorized 34 new Army Corps projects. Reformed process for USACE feasibility studies and permit processing.

▦ REGIONAL DIVISIONS AND HEADQUARTERS

The areas served by most of these offices are determined by watersheds rather than political boundaries.

GREAT LAKES AND OHIO RIVER DIVISION

550 Main St., #10032
Cincinnati, OH 45202–3222
(513) 684–6228
www.lrd.usace.army.mil
Brig. Gen. Richard Kaiser, commander

MISSISSIPPI VALLEY DIVISION

1400 Walnut St.
P.O. Box 80
Vicksburg, MS 39180–0080
(601) 634–5760
www.mvd.usace.army.mil
Maj. Gen. Michael C. Wehr, commander

NORTH ATLANTIC DIVISION

Fort Hamilton
302 General Lee Ave.
Brooklyn, NY 11252
(347) 370–4500
www.nad.usace.army.mil
Col. William Graham, commander

NORTHWESTERN DIVISION

1125 N.W. Couch St., #500
P. O. Box 2870
Portland, OR 97209
(503) 808–3705
www.nwd.usace.army.mil
Brig. Gen. John Kern, commander

PACIFIC OCEAN DIVISON

Bldg. 525, #300
Fort Shafter, HI 96858–5440
(808) 438–4715
www.pod.usace.army.mil
Brig. Gen. Jeffrey Milhorn, commander

SOUTH ATLANTIC DIVISION

60 Forsyth St. S.W., #9M15
Atlanta, GA 30303–8801
(404) 562–5006
Brig. Gen. David Turner, commander

SOUTH PACIFIC DIVISION

1455 Market St., #9M15
San Francisco, CA 94103–1398
(415) 503–6503
www.spd.usace.army.mil
Brig. Gen. Mark Toy, commander

SOUTHWESTERN DIVISON

1100 Commerce St., #831
Dallas, TX 75242–1317
(469) 487–7007
www.swd.usace.army.mil
Brig. Gen. David C. Hill, commander

TRANSATLANTIC DIVISION

255 Fort Collier Rd.
Winchester, VA 22603–5776
(540) 662–3502
www.tad.usace.army.mil
Maj. Gen. Robert Carlson, commander
Col. Vincent Quarles, commander, Middle
     East district

Education Department

400 Maryland Ave. S.W., Washington, DC 20202
Internet: www.ed.gov

Office for Civil Rights

400 Maryland Ave. S.W., Washington, DC 20202
Internet: www.ed.gov/about/offices/list/ocr

The Department of Education's Office for Civil Rights (OCR) enforces several federal civil rights laws that prohibit discrimination in programs or activities receiving federal financial assistance from the Department of Education. Discrimination on the basis of race, color, and national origin is prohibited by Title VI of the Civil Rights Act of 1964; sex discrimination is prohibited by Title IX of the Education Amendments of 1972; discrimination on the basis of disability is prohibited by Section 504 of the Rehabilitation Act of 1973; and age discrimination is prohibited by the Age Discrimination Act of 1975.

These civil rights laws enforced by OCR extend to all state education agencies, elementary and secondary school systems, colleges and universities, vocational schools, proprietary schools, state vocational rehabilitation agencies, libraries, and museums that receive U.S. Department of Education funds. Areas covered include admissions, recruitment, financial aid, academic programs, student treatment and services, counseling and guidance, discipline, classroom assignment, grading, vocational education, recreation, physical education, athletics, housing, and employment. OCR also has responsibilities under Title II of the Americans with Disabilities Act of 1990 (prohibiting disability discrimination by public entities, whether or not they receive federal financial assistance).

The OCR also enforces the Boy Scouts of America Equal Access Act, which was included in the No Child Left Behind Act of 2001. Under this law, no public elementary school or state or local education agency that provides an opportunity for one or more outside youth or community groups to meet on school premises or in school facilities could deny equal access or a fair opportunity to meet to, or discriminate against, any group officially affiliated with the Boy Scouts of America, or any other youth group listed in Title 36 of the United States Code as a patriotic society.

In 2011 the Education Department issued guidance advising schools, colleges, and universities that their responsibilities under Title IX include protecting students from sexual violence. The guidance included enforcement strategies that schools and the OCR could use to end sexual violence, prevent its recurrence, and remedy its effects. In 2014 the Education Department followed up with additional guidance to curb sexual violence and other forms of sex discrimination; the department issued a report that publicly named more than 80 colleges and universities that were currently under investigation for Title IX violations in relation to sexual violence.

Most of OCR's activities are conducted by its twelve enforcement offices throughout the country. These enforcement offices are organized into four divisions. Two enforcement directors in the office of the assistant secretary oversee the work of, respectively, the Eastern and Southern and the Midwestern and Western Divisions. OCR administrative offices in Washington, DC, provide additional administrative support, coordination, policy development, and overall leadership.

■ KEY PERSONNEL

Assistant Secretary
　　Catherine Lhamon . . . . (202) 453–6048
Policy
　　John DiPaolo . . . . (202) 453–6594
Enforcement
　　Sandra Battle . . . . (202) 453–5900
Program Legal Group
　　Polly Hayes. . . . . (202) 453–6639
Resource Management
　　Diedre Windsor. . . . . (202) 453–5512
Budget and Planning Support Team
　　Lavern Jordan . . . . (202) 453–5993
Human Resources Team
　　Diane Blumenthal. . . . . (202) 453–5971
Customer Service and Technology Team
　　Corwin Jennings . . . . (202) 453–5686

■ INFORMATION SOURCES

Internet
The agency's comprehensive website (www.ed.gov/about/offices/list/ocr/index.html) provides information on OCR offices, programs, and news releases and offers links to numerous resources including legislation, policy guidelines, and publications. The agency's e-mail address is ocr@ed.gov.

Telephone Contacts
　　Main Office. . . . . (202) 453–5900
　　Fax . . . . (202) 453–6012/6013
　　Toll-free . . . . (800) 421–3481
　　TTY . . . . (877) 521–2172

Information and Publications

KEY OFFICES

U.S. Department of Education
Communications and Outreach
Information Resource Center
400 Maryland Ave. S.W.
Washington, DC 20202–0498
(202) 401–2000
(800) 872–5327
TTY (800) 437–0833
E-mail: education@custhelp.com

Answers questions from parents, educators, students, and citizens about all aspects of the Department of Education.

Freedom of Information
U.S. Department of Education
Office of Management
Privacy Information and Records Management
  Services (PIRMS)
400 Maryland Ave. S.W., LBJ 2E321
Washington, DC 20202–4536
Attn: FOIA Public Liaison
(202) 401–8365
Fax (202) 401–0920
E-mail: EDFOIAManager@ed.gov
Kathleen Styles, PIRMS director
Gregory Smith, FOIA director (202) 453–6362

DATA AND STATISTICS
The OCR's electronic reading room provides data collections that supply information about the enrollment of—and educational services to—students in public schools in every state by race/ethnicity, sex, and disability.

For statistical publications, fast facts, survey and program areas, and other education-related resources, contact the National Center for Education Statistics (NCES) or the Institute of Education Sciences through the OCR website or by mail, phone, fax, or Internet as follows:

National Center for Education Statistics
1990 K St. N.W.
Washington, DC 20006
(202) 502–7300
Fax (202) 502–7466
Internet: http://nces.ed.gov

Institute of Education Sciences
555 New Jersey Ave. N.W.
Washington, DC 20208
(202) 219–1385
E-mail: Contact.IES.ed.gov
Internet: http://ies.ed.gov

PUBLICATIONS
Publications are available from EDPubs Online Ordering System through the OCR website or by mail, phone, TTY, or fax as follows:

EDPubs
P.O. Box 22207
Alexandria, VA 22304
(877) 433–7827
TTY (877) 576–7734
Fax (703) 605–6794
Para Español (877) 433–7827

Reference Resources

ONLINE
Resources available through the OCR website include:
Educational Resources Information Center (ERIC). Provides access to an extensive body of education-related literature via website, http://eric.ed.gov, or phone (202) 208–2321.

ED Legislation, Regulations, and Policy Guidance. Legislation, regulations, guidance, and other policy documents can be found here for The Civil Rights Act of 1964 as well as for other education-related legislation: www2.ed.gov/policy/landing.jhtml?src-rt.

DOCKETS
Federal dockets are available at www.regulations.gov. (*See appendix for Searching and Commenting on Regulations: Regulations.gov.*)

RULES AND REGULATIONS
The Office for Civil Rights rules and regulations are published in the *Code of Federal Regulations,* Title 34, Chapter I, Parts 100–199. Proposed regulations, new final regulations, and updates are published in the daily *Federal Register.* (*See appendix for details on how to obtain and use these publications.*) The *Federal Register* and the *Code of Federal Regulations* may be accessed online at www.archives.gov/federal-register/cfr; the site contains a link to the federal government's regulatory website at www.regulations.gov (*see appendix*).

■ LEGISLATION
Civil Rights Act of 1964 (42 U.S.C. 2000a et seq.). Signed by the president July 2, 1964. Title VI prohibited discrimination based on race, color, or national origin in programs or activities receiving federal financial assistance.

Elementary and Secondary Education Act (ESEA) of 1965 (108 Stat. 3519, 20 U.S.C. 6301 et seq.). Signed by the president April 11, 1965. Provided federal funding for public and private education for elementary and secondary educational institutions. Targeted at high-poverty areas. Title I provided for basic-skills instruction in disadvantaged urban neighborhoods. Title II provided funds for library books and textbooks, including aid to parochial schools. Title III offered grants for local-level program innovations. Title IV created federal research and development programs. Title V enhanced state departments of education.

Bilingual Education Act of 1968 (81 Stat. 799, 803, 816, 819, 20 U.S.C. 3381). Signed by the president Jan. 2, 1968. Established Title VII of ESEA. Authorized funds for local school districts for programs for students who spoke languages other than English.

Education Amendments of 1972 (20 U.S.C. 1681 et seq.). Signed by the president June 23, 1972. Title IX prohibited discrimination based on gender in programs and activities of educational institutions that receive federal financial assistance.

Rehabilitation Act of 1973 (87 Stat. 394, 29 U.S.C. 794.). Signed by the president Sept. 26, 1973. Mandated that no qualified individual who had a disability should be excluded from participation in, be denied the benefits of, or be subjected to discrimination under any program or activity receiving federal financial assistance. This included publicly funded educational institutions.

Family Educational Rights and Privacy Act (FERPA) (20 U.S.C. 1232g). Signed by the president Aug. 21, 1974. Granted parents and students the right to privacy of student education records. The law applied to all educational institutions, public and private, that receive funds under any applicable Department of Education program.

Age Discrimination Act of 1975 (42 U.S.C. 6101 et seq.). Signed by the president Nov. 28, 1975. Prohibited discrimination based on age in programs or activities that receive federal financial assistance (it did not cover employment discrimination).

Education for All Handicapped Children Act (20 U.S.C. 1400 et seq.). Signed by the president Dec. 2, 1975. Stated that all children with disabilities were entitled to receive a free and appropriate public school education. Encouraged states receiving federal education funds to create policies and practices facilitating the needs of special needs students.

Education Amendments of 1978 (92 Stat. 2143, 20 U.S.C. 6301 note). Signed by the president Nov. 11, 1978. Reauthorized ESEA through 1983. Amended ESEA by adding a new Title V, State Leadership, which required that each state desiring to participate in ESEA programs submit a general application. Added a new Title IX, Gifted and Talented Children's Education Act, which authorized funds for gifted and talented children's programs; and a new Title XI, Indian Education, which established a method for computing the entitlements of local school districts that provide public education to Native American children.

Department of Education Organization Act (93 Stat. 668, 20 U.S.C. 3401 note). Signed by the president Oct. 17, 1979. Established the Education Department as a cabinet-level agency to be directed by a secretary of education. Authorized local education authorities to inform the under secretary of conflicts between federal regulations. Prohibited the withholding of funds from schools on the basis of any requirement imposed by the secretary or the department with which a state fails to comply.

Education of the Deaf Act of 1986 (20 U.S.C. 4301 et seq.). Signed by the president Aug. 4, 1986. Established the Commission on Education of the Deaf. Authorized appropriations for the National Technical Institute for the Deaf (Rochester, NY) and Gallaudet University (Washington, DC) to provide postsecondary education and training for deaf individuals.

Americans with Disabilities Act of 1990 (104 Stat. 327, 42 U.S.C. 12101 et seq.). Signed by the president July 26, 1990. Title II prohibited discrimination against people based on disability in public entities, including elementary, secondary, and postsecondary educational institutions.

Individuals with Disabilities Education Act (IDEA) (20 U.S.C. 1400 et seq.). Signed by the president Oct. 3, 1990. Reauthorized, renamed, and recodified the Education for All Handicapped Children Act. Required that public schools create an individualized education program for each student who is found to be eligible under both the federal and state eligibility standards. Law applied to eligible children between the ages of three and twenty-one and required special education services because of the disability.

Improving America's Schools Act of 1994 (108 Stat. 3518, 20 U.S.C. 6301 note). Signed by the president Oct. 20, 1994. Revised and reauthorized ESEA. Established Title I program for Helping Disadvantaged Children Meet High Standards. Established the Fund for the Improvement of Education.

Individuals with Disabilities Education Act amendments of 1997 (IDEA) (111 Stat. 37, 20 U.S.C. 1400 note). Signed by the president June 4, 1997. Revises the program of assistance for education of all children with disabilities. Sets forth state eligibility requirements for placement of students.

Education of the Deaf Amendments of 1998 (112 Stat. 1581, 20 U.S.C. 1001 note). Signed by the president Oct. 7, 1998. Included in the Higher Education Amendments of 1998. Amended the Education of the Deaf Act to require elementary and secondary programs to comply with certain requirements under the Individuals with Disabilities Education Act.

No Child Left Behind Act (NCLB) (115 Stat. 1425, 20 U.S.C. 6301). Signed by the president Jan. 8, 2002. Reauthorized and amended ESEA. Established requirements for schools to test students annually and report on the progress. Set forth corrective actions for schools that failed to meet standards for two consecutive years. Provided alternatives for students at failing schools and supplementary educational services for low-income children who remained at such schools. Replaced Title III, the Bilingual Education Act, with the English Language Acquisition Act. Changed Title V, Promoting Informed Parental Choice and Innovative Programs, which revised formulas relating to distribution of federal innovative program funds. The Boy Scouts of America Equal Access Act prohibited discrimination against any group officially affiliated with the Boy Scouts of America.

Individuals with Disabilities Education Improvement Act of 2004 (118 Stat. 2647, 20 U.S.C. 1400 et seq.). Signed by the president Dec. 3, 2004. Allowed a state or local educational agency to determine if a child needs special education and related services. Provided definitions of core academic subject, highly qualified teacher, and limited English proficient individual to conform to requirements under ESEA, as amended by NCLB.

ADA Amendments of 2008 (122 Stat. 3553, 42 U.S.C. 12101 note). Signed by the president Sept. 25, 2008. Amends the Disabilities Act of 1990 (ADA) to redefine the term "disability," by defining "major life activities" and "being regarded as having such an impairment."

Office for Federal Student Aid

400 Maryland Ave. S.W., Washington, DC 20202
Internet: www2.ed.gov/about/offices/list/fsa

The Higher Education Amendments of 1998 (HEA) authorized the establishment of a performance-based organization within the Education Department for the delivery of student financial assistance authorized under Title IV—the Office for Federal Student Aid (OFSA). OFSA administers Federal Student Aid programs, including Pell grants, Stafford loans, PLUS loans, and the campus-based programs: Federal Work Study, Perkins loans, and Federal Supplemental Educational Opportunity grants.

The OFSA advises the education secretary on issues related to the department's operation of student financial assistance programs under Title IV of the Higher Education Act. The office recommends policies and promulgates regulation for programs that provide financial assistance to eligible students enrolled in postsecondary educational institutions; delivers grants, loans, and work-study assistance to eligible students; and collects outstanding loans. In fiscal year 2014 the OFSA provided nearly $134 billion of financial aid to more than 13 million college students through Title IV programs that included loans, grants, and work study.

In June 2013 the U.S. Supreme Court ruled in *Windsor v. the United States* that Section 3 of the Defense of Marriage Act (DOMA), which had defined marriage as a legal union of one man and one woman for the purposes of federal programs, was unconstitutional. In the weeks after the 5-4 *Windsor* ruling, the Justice Department provided guidance to various federal agencies to remove barriers to federal programs for same-sex spouses. In December 2013 the Education Department announced new guidance on the use of "marriage" and "spouse" in the federal student aid programs, including on the completion of the Free Application for Federal Student Aid (FAFSA). Under the new guidance, the department recognizes a student or a parent as legally married if the couple was legally married in any jurisdiction that recognizes the marriage, regardless of whether the marriage is between a couple of the same sex or opposite sex, and regardless of where the student or couple lives or where the student is attending school.

Student Loan and Debt Collection Reforms

In response to the tightening of the credit markets in 2008, President George W. Bush signed the Ensuring Continued Access to Student Loans Act. The legislation created significant changes to the Academic Competitive Grant and Science and Mathematics Access to Retain Talent (SMART) Grant programs and increased annual and aggregate Stafford loan limits. Also in 2008, President Bush signed the Higher Education Opportunity Act, which reauthorized the HEA. The legislation authorized additional aid and benefits for students and required new disclosures and reports to assist students and parents in making decisions about obtaining and financing higher education and authorized government regulation of private educational lending (federal student loan programs were already regulated).

The Health Care and Education Reconciliation Act of 2010 made several significant student loan reforms. The legislation ended the practice of subsidizing banks and other financial institutions to make guaranteed federal student loans. Instead, students apply for Direct Loans from the federal government. Students complete one application, the FAFSA, for all FSA programs, including Direct Loans.

The bill lowered the cap on student loan payments under the Income-Based Repayment (IBR) plan, which previously allowed borrowers to limit their loan payments to 15 percent of their discretionary income and forgives all remaining debt after 25 years. New borrowers who assumed loans after July 1, 2014, may cap their student loan repayments at 10 percent of their discretionary income and, if they keep up with their payments over time, will have the balance forgiven after 20 years. Public service workers—such as teachers, nurses, and those in military service—will see any remaining debt forgiven after just 10 years. IBR currently helps more than 1 million borrowers manage their student loan payments.

In December 2012 the Education Department announced a new student loan payment assistance program: Pay As You Earn (PAYE). The PAYE plan caps payments for federal Direct Loans at 10 percent of discretionary income for eligible borrowers; the plan will forgive the balance of their debt after 20 years of payments. The public service provisions of the IBR are the same for PAYE. The Education Department estimates as many as 1.6 million Direct Loan borrowers could reduce their monthly payments with this plan.

PAYE allowed the Obama administration to provide student loan relief before the reduction in payments for the IBR program becomes effective in July 2014. The option under PAYE complements the IBR repayment plan. Borrowers who are not eligible for PAYE may qualify for the IBR program. Direct Loans and Federal Family Education Loans (FFEL) are eligible for IBR; only Direct Loans are eligible under PAYE. To qualify for PAYE or IBR, eligible borrowers must demonstrate a Partial Financial Hardship (a defined high debt-to-income ratio). Borrowers must qualify annually for the program, which will result in payments increasing or decreasing relative to the borrower's (and spouse's) income.

Responding to consumer complaints and widespread criticism of private education and career training institutes that ensnared students in student loan debt but did little to prepare them for careers, the Education Department undertook a regulatory process in 2010 to hold such institutions accountable. In June 2011, the Education Department issued final regulations requiring career college programs to better prepare students for gainful employment or risk losing access to federal student aid. The regulations were adopted after the most extensive public input in the Education Department's history; the department received more than 90,000 written comments and hosted several stakeholder meetings with widespread participation. Under the new regulations, a program would be considered to lead to gainful employment if it meets at least one of the following three metrics: at least 35 percent of former students are repaying their loans; the estimated annual loan payment of a typical graduate does not exceed 30 percent of his or her discretionary income; or the estimated annual loan payment of a typical graduate does not exceed 12 percent of his or her total earnings.

In June 2012, the Education Department released a progress report of schools under the regulations. The data, which covered career training programs at public, for-profit, and nonprofit schools, showed that 5 percent of them—all located at for-profit colleges—did not meet any of the three key requirements of the department's Gainful Employment regulation. The report covered 3,695 programs in 1,336 schools over a two-year period, comprising 43 percent of students in career training programs (the report was for informational purposes only). Eventually, these for-profit programs could lose access to federal student aid if they do not improve performance. No program would lose eligibility before 2015.

Following a 2012 court decision that affirmed the Education Department's regulatory authority with regard to this issue, the agency undertook more rigorous rulemaking. In October 2014 the Education Department published a revised gainful employment rule after a process that once again received more than 90,000 public comments. The revised regulations set a higher passing requirement and lay out a shorter path to ineligibility for the poorest-performing programs.

Under the new regulations, a program would be considered to lead to gainful employment if the estimated annual loan payment of a typical graduate does not exceed 20 percent of his or her discretionary income or 8 percent of his or her total earnings. Programs that exceed these levels would be at risk of losing their ability to participate in taxpayer-funded federal student aid programs. In 2012 the department estimated that 193 programs would not have passed the previous regulations; the department estimated that about 1,400 programs would not pass the accountability metric under the new regulations.

Tackling abusive student loan debt collectors was also a reform priority. Following a review of 22 private collection agencies under contract with the department, the Education Department announced in 2014 it would move to wind down contracts with five private debt collection agencies that were providing inaccurate information to borrowers. In its review, the department found that agents of the companies made materially inaccurate representations to borrowers about the loan rehabilitation program and had engaged in other deceptive practices at unacceptably high rates. The department also announced that it would provide enhanced monitoring and guidance to ensure that contracted debt collectors are consistently providing borrowers with accurate information regarding their loans.

■ KEY PERSONNEL

Chief Operating Officer
James Runcie . . . . (202) 377–3003
Chief of Staff
James Manning . . . . (202) 377–3007
Ombudsman
Joyce DeMoss. (202) 377–3992
Policy Liaison and Implementation Staff
Jeff Baker . . . . (202) 377–4009
Communications and Outreach Staff
Chris Greene . . . . (202) 377–4003
Customer Experience
Brenda Wensil . . . . (202) 377–4671

■ INFORMATION SOURCES

Internet
The FSA's comprehensive website (www.ed.gov/about/offices/list/fsa/index.html) provides information on lender programs and scholarships, academic planning (through its student portal), as well as news, publications, and links to other relevant sites. The Free Application for Federal Student Aid (FAFSA) can be filed and processed through FSA's website at http://fafsa.ed.gov.

Telephone Contacts
Main Office . . . . (202) 377–3000
Federal Student Aid Information
    Center (FSAIC) . . . . (800) 433–3243
TTY . . . . (800) 730–8913
Callers in locations without access to toll-free
    numbers. . . . . (319) 337–5665
FSA Research and Customer
    Care Center. . . . . (800) 433–7327

Information and Publications

KEY OFFICES

U.S. Department of Education
Communications and Outreach
Information Resource Center
400 Maryland Ave. S.W.
Washington, DC 20202–0498
(202) 401–2000
(800) 437–0833
E-mail: education@custhelp.com

Answers questions from parents, educators, students, and the public about all aspects of the Department of Education.

Freedom of Information
U.S. Department of Education
Office of Management
Privacy Information and Records Management
    Services (PIRMS)
400 Maryland Ave. S.W., LBJ 2E321
Washington, DC 20202–4536
Attn: FOIA Public Liaison
(202) 401–8365
Fax (202) 401–0920
E-mail: EDFOIAManager@ed.gov
Kathleen Styles, PIRMS director
Gregory Smith, FOIA director, (202) 453–6362

DATA AND STATISTICS
The National Student Loan Data System (NSLDS) is the U.S. Department of Education's central database for student aid. NSLDS receives data from schools; guaranty agencies; and the Direct Loan, Pell grant, and other Department of Education programs. The NSLDS is available through FSA's website at www.nslds.ed.gov. At NSLDS Student Access, aid recipients can view information on their loans and grants.

Federal Student Aid provides Federal Student Aid data and information about the major Title IV aid programs. May be reached by phone at (800) 433–3243, or online at http://studentaid.ed.gov.

For statistical publications, fast facts, survey and program areas, and other education-related resources, contact the National Center for Education Statistics (NCES) or the Institute of Education Sciences through the OPE website or via mail, phone, fax, or Internet as follows:

National Center for Education Statistics
1990 K St. N.W.
Washington, DC 20006
(202) 502–7300
Fax (202) 502–7466
Internet: http://nces.ed.gov

Institute of Education Sciences
555 New Jersey Ave. N.W.
Washington, DC 20208
(202) 219–1385
E-mail: Contact.IES@ed.gov
Internet: http://ies.ed.gov

PUBLICATIONS
The publications section of the FSA website provides access to free publications and application tools. It includes guides, brochures, and fact sheets, such as *College Preparation Checklist, Federal Student Aid: Proud Sponsor of the American Mind,* and *2013–2014 FAFSA.*

All FSA publications (including special bulk orders available to postsecondary institutions, high schools, libraries, and nonprofit counseling centers) can be ordered through the FSA website at www.fsapubs.org. Free publications can be ordered by calling (800) 394–7084 or via e-mail at orders@FSAPubs.org.

Publications are also available from EDPubs Online Ordering System (http://edpubs.ed.gov) or by mail, phone, TTY, or fax as follows:

ED Pubs
P.O. Box 22207
Alexandria, VA 22304
(877) 433–7837
TTY (877) 576–7734
Fax (703) 605–6794
Para Español (877) 433–7827

Reference Resources

ONLINE
StudentAid.ed.gov. Offers encouragement and specific steps to help students plan and pay for college.

Fafsa.ed.gov. Provides a free online application for federal student aid. The FAFSA4caster helps students find out how much aid they may receive.

Opportunity.gov. In conjunction with the Department of Labor, provides information on educational opportunities for unemployed workers. Website available at federal studentaid.ed.gov/opportunity.

DOCKETS
Federal dockets are available at www.regulations.gov. (*See appendix for Searching and Commenting on Regulations: Regulations.gov.*)

RULES AND REGULATIONS
The Office for Federal Student Aid rules and regulations are published in the *Code of Federal Regulations,* Title 34, Chapter VI, various parts. Proposed regulations, new final regulations, and updates are published in the daily *Federal Register.* (*See appendix for details on how to obtain and use these publications.*) The *Federal Register* and the *Code of Federal Regulations* may be accessed online at www.archives.gov/federal-register/cfr; the site contains a link to the federal government's regulatory website at www.regulations.gov (*see appendix*).

■ LEGISLATION
Higher Education Act of 1965 (20 U.S.C. 1001 et seq.). Signed by the president Nov. 8, 1965. Title IV established the federal student financial aid programs.

Education Amendments of 1972 (20 U.S.C. 1681 et seq.). Signed by the president June 23, 1972. Title IX prohibited discrimination based on gender in education programs and activities that receive federal financial assistance.

Rehabilitation Act of 1973 (87 Stat. 394, 29 U.S.C. 794). Signed by the president Sept. 26, 1973. No otherwise qualified individual with a disability shall be excluded from participation in, be denied the benefits of, or be subjected to discrimination under any program or activity receiving federal financial assistance solely by reason of his or her disability. This includes publicly funded educational institutions.

Family Educational Rights and Privacy Act (FERPA) (20 U.S.C. 1232g). Signed by the president Aug. 21, 1974. Granted parents and students rights to privacy of student education records. The law applies to all educational institutions, public and private, that receive funds under any applicable program of the U.S. Department of Education.

Age Discrimination Act of 1975 (42 U.S.C. 6101 et seq.). Signed by the president Nov. 28, 1975. Prohibits discrimination based on age in programs or activities that receive federal financial assistance (it does not cover employment discrimination).

Department of Education Organization Act (93 Stat. 668, 20 U.S.C. 3401 note). Signed by the president Oct. 17, 1979. Established the Education Department as a cabinet-level agency to be directed by a secretary of education.

Higher Education Amendments of 1998 (112 Stat. 1581, 20 U.S.C. 1001 note). Signed by the president Oct. 7, 1998. Reauthorization of the Higher Education Act of 1965. Established a performance-based organization for the delivery of student financial assistance authorized under Title IV. Made various changes to student loan programs, including lowering interest rates on student loans for a five-year period. Authorized the suspension of a student's federal loan eligibility if the student has been convicted of a drug-related offense.

Executive Order 13445 (Strengthening Adult Education). Signed by the president Sept. 27, 2007. Established an Interagency Adult Education Working Group consisting of the education secretary, who served as chair; the treasury secretary; the attorney general; and the secretaries for interior, labor, health and human services, housing and urban development, and veterans affairs. The group focused on federal programs that work to improve the basic education skills of adults and have the goal of transitioning adults from basic literacy to postsecondary education, training, or employment.

College Cost Reduction and Access Act (121 Stat. 784, 20 U.S.C. 1001 note). Signed by the president Sept. 27, 2007. Reauthorized HEA Title IV federal student financial aid programs. Repealed the formula for calculating an individual Pell grant. Reduces the interest rate on undergraduate loans under the Federal Family Education Loan and Direct Loan programs. Establishes the College Access Challenge Grant program to provide formula matching grants to states to improve student access to postsecondary education. Established the Public Service Loan Forgiveness program.

Ensuring Continued Access to Student Loans Act of 2008 (122 Stat. 740, 20 U.S.C. 1001 note). Signed by the president May 7, 2008. Authorized the Education Department to purchase Federal Family Education Loan Program (FFELP) loans. Increased amount of Stafford loans available to undergraduate students. Made significant changes to other FSA grant programs.

Higher Education Opportunity Act (122 Stat. 3078, 20 U.S.C. 1001 note). Signed by the president Aug. 14, 2008. Reauthorized HEA. Authorized additional aid and benefits for students, and requires new disclosures and reports to assist students and parents in making decisions about obtaining and financing higher education. Authorized government regulation of private educational lending (federal student loan programs were previously regulated).

American Recovery and Reinvestment Act of 2009 (123 Stat. 115, 26 U.S.C. 1 note). Signed by the president Feb. 17, 2009. Title I, the State Fiscal Stabilization Fund, provided more than $100 billion to states for the support of elementary, secondary, and postsecondary education as well as early childhood education. To obtain the education funds, governors are required to sign assurances to improve the quality of standardized tests and raise standards and include a plan for evaluating the state's progress in closing achievement gaps.

Health Care and Education Reconciliation Act of 2010 (124 Stat.1029, 20 U.S.C. 1087a et seq.). Signed by the president March 30, 2010. Ended the practice of subsidizing banks and other financial institutions to make guaranteed federal student loans. Instead, students apply for Direct Loans from the federal government. Reduced the cap on student loan payments under the Income-Based Repayment (IBR) plan. Increased Pell grant funding.

Office of Elementary and Secondary Education

400 Maryland Ave. S.W., Washington, DC 20202
Internet: www2.ed.gov/about/offices/list/oese

The Department of Education Organization Act of 1979 established the Department of Education as a cabinet-level agency that began operation in 1980. The department was formed by transferring to it the educational responsibilities from other agencies, most notably those from the Health, Education and Welfare Department, which was redesignated as the Health and Human Services Department. The Education Department was charged with ensuring equal access for educational opportunities and improving the coordination of federal education programs.

The Office of Elementary and Secondary Education (OESE) provides financial assistance to state and local education agencies for elementary and secondary education (K–12), including public and private preschools. The OESE promotes academic excellence and provides funding and policy guidance to enhance educational opportunities and improve the quality of teaching and learning.

The assistant secretary for elementary and secondary education is the principal adviser to the secretary of education on all matters related to elementary and secondary education. The department provides direction, coordination, and leadership for Impact Aid programs, student achievement and school accountability programs, academic improvement and teacher quality programs, school support and rural programs, safe and healthy students program, school turnaround program, and the Office of Migrant Education, the Office of Early Learning, and Office of Indian Education. The OESE is responsible for directing, coordinating, and recommending policy for programs designed to do the following:

- Assist state and local educational agencies to improve the achievement of elementary and secondary school students.
- Ensure equal access to services leading to such improvement for all children, particularly the educationally disadvantaged, Native Americans, children of migrant workers, or the homeless.
- Foster educational improvement at the state and local levels.

- Provide financial assistance to local educational agencies whose local revenues are affected by federal activities.

The Elementary and Secondary Education Act (ESEA) of 1965 and its reauthorizations direct much of OESE's policy. The Bilingual Education Act of 1968 established Title VII of ESEA. Title VII authorized funds for local school districts for programs for students who speak languages other than English. Controversy over Title VII funding arose in 1996 when the Oakland, CA, school board passed a resolution defining Ebonics as the native language of 28,000 African American students in the school district. Reacting quickly, Congress declared that Ebonics was not a separate language eligible for Title VII money.

The greatest controversy in recent years, however, has been legislation and policy dealing with standardized testing at public elementary and secondary schools. President Bill Clinton made voluntary national testing a top priority of his second term, but his education initiative was defeated by the Republican-led Congress.

George W. Bush was more successful in passing his education reform: the No Child Left Behind Act (NCLB), passed in 2002, reauthorized ESEA and made sweeping changes that affected local school authorities. Under the regulatory authority of the NCLB, schools were to be held accountable for student achievement levels, requiring annual testing of students in grades three through eight. The reform act imposed penalties for schools that did not make adequate yearly progress toward meeting the goals. Penalties included requiring school districts to pay for tutoring and requiring school districts to offer transfers for students to private schools.

NCLB established requirements for:

- Yearly testing and assessments of student performance.
- State standards for and assessments of adequate yearly progress (AYP).
- Local educational agency (LEA) identification of schools for improvement and corrective actions.
- Reports to parents and the public on school performance and teacher quality.

- Eligibility requirements for schoolwide programs.
- Increased qualifications of teachers and paraprofessionals.

NCLB requires all U.S. public schools to meet annual AYP targets designed to ensure all students are 100 percent proficient in reading or language arts and math by 2014; not one state met the requirements. Under pressure from states and local jurisdictions, as well as teachers' unions, the Education Department has allowed for flexibility in some regulations implemented under NCLB. This has included easing the requirement that 95 percent of all students in each subgroup in a school must take the test for the school to make adequate yearly progress; assessing students with disabilities; assessing limited English proficient students; and easing requirements regarding "highly qualified teachers."

Nonetheless, some states and local school districts have viewed NCLB as an unfunded mandate, claiming that Congress has made increased demands of the schools but has not provided the adequate level of funding to implement the provisions of NCLB. States sued claiming the federal government fell billions short in necessary funding to implement NCLB; the lawsuits were unsuccessful.

As the legal battles against the NCLB played out in the courts, the act itself came up for reauthorization in fall 2007. The presence of a Democratic-led Congress signaled that the Bush administration would not get everything it wanted in the reauthorization. Although Democrats announced a desire to rework the core testing components of the NCLB, even some Republican lawmakers said the original law gave the federal government too much authority over state and local jurisdictions.

Shortly after President Barack Obama took office, he announced that his K–12 education policy would largely follow that established under NCLB, with an emphasis on standardized testing and teacher qualification. Congress in 2009 began another attempt at reauthorizing ESEA. In early 2009, nearly 6,000 of the nation's 95,000 schools were labeled as needing restructuring or corrective action because they failed to achieve testing targets under NCLB.

In an attempt to drive education policy via the appropriations process, the American Recovery and Reinvestment Act (2009 stimulus bill) provided more than $100 billion to states for the support of elementary, secondary, and postsecondary education as well as early childhood education programs. To obtain the education funds, governors were required to sign assurances to improve the quality of standardized tests, raise standards, and include a plan for evaluating the state's progress in closing achievement gaps.

By June 2011 ESEA reauthorization legislation had not been introduced and the Obama administration announced plans to provide regulatory flexibility around NCLB; on Oct. 23, 2011, the Education Department announced the ESEA waiver program. States could request flexibility from specific NCLB mandates by complying with a strict set of requirements. Schools were required to transition students, teachers, and schools to a system aligned with college and career-ready standards

for all students; develop differentiated accountability systems, and undertake reforms to support effective classroom instruction and school leadership. The flexibility package, developed with input from chief state school officers from forty-five states, was allowable under the waiver authority explicitly granted to the Education Department under the ESEA.

The flexibility provided under the waiver system would usher in one of the greatest controversies for federal education policy: adoption of the Common Core standards. The K–12 standards were developed under a joint partnership of the National Governors Association and the Council of Chief State School Officers to meet the requirement of preparing K–12 students for college and career. States were required to adopt the Common Core math and language arts standards or demonstrate that their own standards were equally rigorous (most states did not meet this benchmark). To further incentivize states to adopt Common Core standards, the Education Department made adoption of college and career-ready standards a requirement to obtain a competitive federal Race to the Top grant. Forty-four states adopted the Common Core standards; Virginia and Texas each had standards that were internationally benchmarked as college and career ready. Each state was required to adopt an assessment to measure effectiveness of the new college and career ready standards.

The perceived top-down push of a common set of standards for states set off a political firestorm. Conservatives decried it as a federal takeover of local schools. Educators and some parents pushed back against the "one size fits all" approach. Some education advocates were unhappy with the continued reliance on standardized tests. Politicians who supported Common Core came under fire, with some high-level officials losing reelection. Some states that initially adopted the standards later repealed or dropped them.

By the end of the 2013–2014 school year, one full cohort had begun kindergarten and graduated high school since the signing of No Child Left Behind. Not a single state was in compliance with the terms of the legislation. Eight years after ESEA was scheduled to be reauthorized, Congress has failed to send a reauthorization bill to the president.

■ KEY PERSONNEL

Assistant Secretary
    Deborah S. Delisle.................. (202) 401–0113
        Fax.......................... (202) 205–0303
Chief of Staff
    Heather Rieman .... (202) 260–1700
Academic Improvement and Teacher Quality Programs
    Sylvia Lyles...................... (202) 260–8230
Policy and Early Learning
    Libby Doggett .... (202) 401–0113
Impact Aid Programs
    Alfred Lott .... (202) 260–3858
Indian Education
    Joyce Silverthorne................. (202) 401–0767

Management and Planning Deputy Assistant Secretary
Alexander Goniprow . . . . (202) 401–9090
Migrant Education Programs
Lisa Ramirez . . . . (202) 260–1164
Policy and School Turnaround Deputy Assistant Secretary
Scott Sargrad . . . . (202) 453–7254
Technical Assistance Deputy Assistant Secretary
Vacant . . . . (202) 401–0113
Safe and Healthy Students
David Esquith . . . . (202) 245–7896
School Support and Rural Programs
Lisa Ramirez (acting) . . . . (202) 401–0039
School Support Program Group
Collette Fisher . . . . (202) 260–2544
State Support
Monique M. Chism. . . . . (202) 260–0826

▓ INFORMATION SOURCES

Internet

Agency website: www.ed.gov/about/offices/list/oese/index.html. Offers links to legislation, *Federal Register* notices, policy guidance, and grant applications for the *No Child Left Behind Act of 2001*. Also maintains links to legislation, regulations, and policy guidance for programs still being implemented under the *Improving America's Schools Act.*

Telephone Contacts

Information. . . . .(202) 401–0113
Toll-free . . . .(800) 872–5327
Federal Relay Service TTY . . . .(800) 877–8339

Information and Publications

KEY OFFICES

U.S. Department of Education
Communications and Outreach
Information Resource Center
400 Maryland Ave. S.W.
Washington, DC 20202–0498
(202) 401–2000
(800) 872–5327
TTY (800) 437–0833
E-mail: education@custhelp.com

Answers questions from parents, educators, students, and citizens about all aspects of the Department of Education.

Freedom of Information
U.S. Department of Education
Office of Management
Privacy Information and Records Management
 Services (PIRMS)
400 Maryland Ave. S.W., LBJ 2E321
Washington, DC 20202–4536
Attn: FOIA Public Liaison

(202) 401–8365
Fax (202) 401–0920
E-mail: EDFOIAManager@ed.gov
Kathleen Styles, PIRMS director
Gregory Smith, FOIA director, (202) 453–6362

DATA AND STATISTICS

For statistical publications, fast facts, survey and program areas, and other education-related resources, contact the National Center for Education Statistics (NCES) or the Institute of Education Sciences through the OPE website, or by mail, phone, fax, or Internet as follows:

National Center for Education Statistics
1990 K St. N.W.
Washington, DC 20006
(202) 502–7300
Fax (202) 502–7466
Internet: http://nces.ed.gov

Institute of Education Sciences
555 New Jersey Ave. N.W.
Washington, DC 20208
(202) 219–1385
E-mail: Contact.IES@ed.gov
Internet: http://ies.ed.gov

PUBLICATIONS

Publications are available from EDPubs Online Ordering System through the OESE's website, or by mail, phone, TTY, or fax as follows:

EDPubs
P.O. Box 22207
Alexandria, VA 22304
(877) 433–7827
TTY (877) 576–7734
Fax (703) 605–6794
Para Español (877) 433–7827

Reference Resources

ONLINE

The following resources are available through the OESE's website:

Educational Resources Information Center (ERIC). Provides access to an extensive body of education-related literature at http://eric.ed.gov.

Education Resources Organization Directory (EROD). Identifies organizations that provide information and assistance on a broad range of education-related topics at www2.ed.gov/about/contacts/state/index.html.

OESE Listserv. Subscribers automatically receive periodic notification of K–12 education issues published on the Office of Elementary and Secondary Education's website, www2.ed.gov/about/offices/list/oese/oeselistserv.html.

ED Initiatives. Up-to-date information about new educational initiatives at www2.ed.gov/about/inits/ed/index.html.

DOCKETS

Federal dockets are available at www.regulations .gov. (*See appendix for Searching and Commenting on Regulations: Regulations.gov.*)

RULES AND REGULATIONS

The No Child Left Behind Act rules and regulations are published in the *Code of Federal Regulations,* Title 34, Chapter II, Parts 200–299. Proposed regulations, new final regulations, and updates are published in the daily *Federal Register. (See appendix for details on how to obtain and use these publications.)* The *Federal Register* and the *Code of Federal Regulations* may be accessed online at www.gpoaccess.gov/fr/index.html; the site contains a link to the federal government's regulatory website at www.regulations.gov (*see appendix*).

▓ LEGISLATION

Mutual Educational and Cultural Exchange Act (Fulbright Hays Act) (75 Stat. 527, 22 U.S.C. 2451 et seq.). Signed by the president September 21, 1961. Regulates foreign exchange students, scholars, and related programs.

Higher Education Act (HEA) of 1965 (20 U.S.C. 1001 et seq.). Signed by the president Nov. 8, 1965. Title IV established the federal student financial aid programs.

Education Amendments of 1972 (20 U.S.C. 1681 et seq.). Signed by the president June 23, 1972. Title IX prohibited discrimination based on gender in education programs and activities that receive federal financial assistance.

Rehabilitation Act of 1973 (87 Stat. 394, 29 U.S.C. 794). Signed by the president Sept. 26, 1973. Mandated that no qualified individual who had a disability should be excluded from participation in, be denied the benefits of, or be subjected to discrimination under any program or activity receiving federal financial assistance. This included publicly funded educational institutions.

Family Educational Rights and Privacy Act (20 U.S.C. 1232g). Signed by the president Aug. 21, 1974. Granted parents and students the right to privacy of student education records. Applied to all educational institutions, public and private, that received funds under any applicable Department of Education program.

Age Discrimination Act of 1975 (42 U.S.C. 6101 et seq.). Signed by the president Nov. 28, 1975. Prohibited discrimination based on age in programs or activities that receive federal financial assistance (it did not cover employment discrimination).

Department of Education Organization Act (93 Stat. 668, 20 U.S.C. 3401 note). Signed by the president Oct. 17, 1979. Established the Education Department as a cabinet-level agency to be directed by a secretary of education.

The McKinney–Vento Homeless Assistance Act of 1987 (101 Stat. 482, 42 U.S.C. 11301 et seq.). Signed by the president July 22, 1987. Requires each state to adopt a homeless children education plan.

Americans with Disabilities Act of 1990 (104 Stat. 327, 42 U.S.C. 12101 et seq.). Signed by the president July 26, 1990. Title II prohibited discrimination against people based on disability in public entities, including elementary, secondary, and postsecondary educational institutions.

Individuals with Disabilities Education Act (IDEA) (20 U.S.C. 1400 et seq.). Signed by the president Oct. 3, 1990. Reauthorized, renamed, and recodified the Education for All Handicapped Children Act. Required that public schools create an individualized education program for each student who is eligible under both the federal and state eligibility standards. Applied to eligible children between the ages of three and twenty-one who require special education services because of the disability. The 1997 amendments established formula and discretionary grants to assist states in providing education to eligible children with special needs.

College Cost Reduction and Access Act (121 Stat. 784, 20 U.S.C. 1001 note). Signed by the president Sept. 27, 2007. Reauthorized HEA Title IV federal student financial aid programs. Repealed the formula for calculating an individual Pell grant. Reduced the interest rate on undergraduate loans under the Federal Family Education Loan and Direct Loan programs. Established the College Access Challenge Grant program to provide formula matching grants to states to improve student access to postsecondary education. Established the Public Service Loan Forgiveness program.

Ensuring Continued Access to Student Loans Act of 2008 (122 Stat. 740, 20 U.S.C. 1001 note). Signed by the president May 7, 2008. Authorized the Department of Education to purchase Federal Family Education Loan Program (FFELP) loans. Increased amount of Stafford loans available to undergraduate students. Made significant changes to other FSA grant programs.

Higher Education Opportunity Act (122 Stat. 3078, 20 U.S.C. 1001 note). Signed by the president Aug. 14, 2008. Reauthorized HEA. Authorized additional aid and benefits for students and required new disclosures and reporting requirements to assist students and parents to make better-informed decisions about obtaining and financing higher education. Authorized government regulation of private educational lending (federal student loan programs were previously regulated). Established, in the department's Office of Postsecondary Education, a deputy assistant secretary for International and Foreign Language Education with extensive experience in international and foreign language instruction.

American Recovery and Reinvestment Act of 2009 (123 Stat. 115, 26 U.S.C. 1 note). Signed by the president Feb. 17, 2009. Title I, the State Fiscal Stabilization Fund, provided more than $100 billion to states for the support of elementary, secondary, and postsecondary education as well as early childhood education. To obtain the education funds, governors were required to sign assurances to improve the quality of standardized tests and raise standards and include a plan for evaluating the state's progress in closing achievement gaps.

Office of Postsecondary Education

1990 K St. N.W., Washington, DC 20006
Internet: www2.ed.gov/about/offices/list/ope

The Department of Education's Office of Postsecondary Education (OPE) formulates federal postsecondary education policy and administers programs to increase access to postsecondary education. OPE includes three divisions: Higher Education Programs (HEP), International and Foreign Language Education (IFLE), and Policy, Planning, and Innovation (PPI).

Higher Education Programs (HEP) administers programs to increase access to higher education. HEP also coordinates a variety of higher education-related activities with states. HEP grant projects are awarded primarily to institutions of higher education, nonprofit organizations and agencies, and state agencies. HEP components include Institutional Service and Student Service.

Institutional Service administers programs that increase access to postsecondary education for disadvantaged students and strengthen the capacity of colleges and universities that serve a high percentage of minority students. This program area administers the Fund for the Improvement of Postsecondary Education (FIPSE), which provides grants to colleges and universities to promote reform, innovation, and improvement in postsecondary education. FIPSE also administers awards for Higher Education Disaster Relief.

Student Service performs planning, program development, and grant administration functions for the Federal TRIO programs, the Child Care Access Means Parents in School program, the Thurgood Marshall Legal Educational Opportunity program, Gaining Early Awareness and Readiness for Undergraduate Programs (GEAR UP), the Graduate Fellowships Programs (Title VII, Part A, HEA), and the Erma Byrd Scholarship Program.

International and Foreign Language Education (IFLE) advises the assistant secretary for postsecondary education on matters affecting postsecondary, international, and foreign language education. IFLE administers the international special focus programs authorized under Title VII of the HEA. These international programs are designed to support student exchange, faculty cooperation and exchange, mutual recognition of credits, acquisition of host country language, and apprenticeships and other work activities.

Policy, Planning, and Innovation (PPI) develops postsecondary education policy and legislative proposals and is responsible for budget formulation and forecasting for programs administered by OPE. PPI leads OPE strategic planning efforts, is responsible for developing OPE program performance measures, and conducts a number of data collections. Report topics include the Student Financial Assistance Program, Equity in Athletics Disclosure Act, and Title II Reports on the Quality of Teacher Preparation Programs. PPI is responsible for coordinating activities and reporting under the Campus Security and Safety Act (Clery Act), which requires postsecondary institutions receiving federal aid to publish an annual campus crime report and comply with other provisions regarding notification and disciplinary proceedings resulting from student crime.

Within PPI, the Accreditation Group has responsibility for the accrediting agency recognition process and for the coordination of activities between states and the Education Department that affect institutional participation in the federal financial assistance programs. The Accreditation Group provides a list of postsecondary educational institutions and programs accredited by accrediting agencies and state approval agencies recognized by the U.S. secretary of education.

▓ KEY PERSONNEL

Assistant Secretary
    Erika Miller . . . . (202) 502–7750
Executive Office
    Daniel Miller . . . . (202) 502–7889

POLICY, PLANNING, AND INNOVATION
Deputy Assistant Secretary
    Lynn Mahaffie . . . . (202) 502–7950
Policy Coordination, Development and Accreditation Service
    Policy Coordination Development
        Lynn Mahaffie . . . . (202) 502–7903
    Policy Coordination Group
        Gail McLarnon . . . . (202) 219–7048
    Policy Development Group
        Carney McCullough . . . . (202) 502–7693
    Accreditation Group
        Chuck Mula . . . . (202) 219–7036
Strategic Planning, Analysis, and Initiatives Service
    Strategic Planning Group
        Janie Funkhouser . . . . (202) 502–7517
    Policy Analysis and Forecasting Group
        Robert Lewis . . . . (202) 502–7713

Strategic Initiatives Group
Pamela Moran-Lewis . . . . (202) 502–7732

INTERNATIONAL AND FOREIGN LANGUAGE EDUCATION
Deputy Assistant Secretary
Mohamed Abdel-Kader . . . . (202) 502–7697
International Studies Group
Michelle Guilfoil . . . . (202) 502–7625
Advanced Training and Research Group
Kimonanh Nquyan-Lam . . . . (202) 219–7020

HIGHER EDUCATION PROGRAMS
Deputy Assistant Secretary
James Minor . . . . (202) 219–7027
Student Service
Linda Byrd Johnson . . . . (202) 502–7729
Student Group A
Gaby Watts. . . . . (202) 502–7545
Student Group B
Eileen Bland. . . . . (202) 502–7730
Student Group C
James Davis . . . . (202) 502–7802
Student Programs Development Group
Frances Bergeron . . . . (202) 502–7528
Institutional Services
Leonard Haynes . . . . (202) 502–7549
Institutional Group A
Nancy Regan . . . . (202) 219–7018
Institutional Group B
Don Watson. . . . . (202) 219–7037
Institutional Group C
Ralph Hines (acting). . . . . (202) 502–7618
Institutional Programs Development Group
John Clement. . . . . (202) 502–7520
Fund for the Improvement of Postsecondary Education
Ralph Hines . . . . (202) 502–7618

◼ INFORMATION SOURCES

Internet

OPE's website, www.ed.gov/about/offices/list/ope/index .html, is a comprehensive resource for information on all aspects of higher education including accreditation and student funding sources as well as legislation, regulations, and policy guidance for the Higher Education Opportunity Act of 2008. Free reports as well as links to other relevant sources can also be found on this website.

Telephone Contacts

Information. . . . .(202) 502–7750
Federal Relay Service TTY . . . .(800) 877–8339

Information and Publications

KEY OFFICES

U.S. Department of Education
Communications and Outreach
Information Resource Center

400 Maryland Ave. S.W.
Washington, DC 20202–0498
(202) 401–2000
Toll-free (800) 437–0833
E-mail: education@custhelp.com

Answers questions from parents, educators, students, and citizens about all aspects of the Department of Education.

Freedom of Information
U.S. Department of Education
Office of Management
Privacy Information and Records Management
Services (PIRMS)
400 Maryland Ave. S.W., LBJ 2E321
Washington, DC 20202–4536
Attn: FOIA Public Liaison
(202) 401–8365
Fax (202) 401–0920
E-mail: EDFOIAManager@ed.gov
Kathleen Styles, PIRMS director
Gregory Smith, FOIA director, (202) 453–6362

DATA AND STATISTICS

OPE collects and disseminates student financial assistance program data as well as data in several key areas relating to postsecondary education. Data books and other statistical reports for the Pell Grant Program, Campus-Based Programs, and the student loan programs can be downloaded from the OPE website. Resources include:

▪ Federal Student Financial Assistance Programs Data

▪ Annual Reports on Teacher Quality

▪ Federal TRIO Programs: Program Profiles and Other Reports

For statistical publications, fast facts, survey and program areas, and other education-related resources, contact the National Center for Education Statistics (NCES) or the Institute of Education Sciences through the OPE website, direct website, or by mail, phone, or fax as follows:

National Center for Education Statistics
1990 K St. N.W.
Washington, DC 20006
(202) 502–7300
Fax (202) 502–7466
Website: nces.ed.gov

Institute of Education Sciences
555 New Jersey Ave. N.W.
Washington, DC 20208
(202) 219–1385
E-mail: Contact.IES@ed.gov
Website: ies.ed.gov

PUBLICATIONS

Publications are available from EDPubs Online Ordering System through the OPE website, or by mail, phone, TTY, or fax, as follows:

EDPubs

P.O. Box 22207

Alexandria, VA 22304

(877) 433–7827

TTY (877) 576–7734

Fax (301) 470–1244

Para Español (877) 433–7827

Reference Resources

ONLINE

The following resources are available through the OPE website:

Database of Accredited Postsecondary Institutions and Programs. A database of approximately 6,900 postsecondary educational institutions and programs, each of which is accredited by an accrediting agency or state approval agency recognized by the U.S. secretary of education. website: www.ope.ed.gov/accreditation.

Diploma Mills and Accreditation. Helps consumers gain a better understanding of accreditation in the United States. website: www2.ed.gov/students/prep/college/diplomamills/diploma-mills.html.

Career Colleges and Technical Schools. Provides information for those interested in postsecondary education or training for a specific career, trade, or profession. website: www2.ed.gov/students/prep/college/consumerinfo/index.html.

Career Voyages. A collaboration between the U.S. Department of Labor and the U.S. Department of Education that provides information on high-growth, high-demand occupations along with the skills and education needed to attain those jobs. Twitter: Career Voyager@ CareerVoyager.

College Navigator (from the National Center for Education Statistics). Provides information on colleges based on location, programs, tuition, distance learning, evening courses, and more. website: nces.ed.gov/collegenavigator.

Saving for College—The College Savings Plan Network. This network was formed as an affiliate to the National Association of State Treasurers. Intended to make higher education more attainable, the Network serves as a clearinghouse for information among existing college savings programs. website: www.collegesavings.org/index.aspx.

Students.gov. A student resource link for information and services from the U.S. government on colleges, financial assistance, and educational benefits. website: https://studentaid.ed.gov/sa/redirects/college-gov.

International Educational Mobility. The U.S. Network for Education Information, developed by the National Library of Education, provides information to help Americans contemplating an educational experience abroad, including extensive links to foreign education systems. It also presents information about education in the United States, its structure and organization, from the primary through the postgraduate levels, including a wide array of links to useful sites in the U.S. education community. website: www2.ed.gov/about/offices/list/OUS/international/usnei/edlite-index.html.

General Education Online. Database of links to higher education facilities worldwide. website: www.findaschool.org

Web U.S. Higher Education. Links to colleges and universities, including community colleges. website: www.utexas.edu/world/univ

Mapping Your Future. A public-service website that provides career, college, financial aid, and financial literacy information and services. website: mappingyourfuture.org

Tax Benefits for Higher Education. IRS website with tax information for students. website: www.irs.gov/individuals/students

NASFAA (National Association of Student Financial Aid Administrators). Financial aid resources for parents and students. website: www. nasfaa.org

Student Portal Website (Federal Student Aid). This site provides information on academic planning and preparation, choosing a school, applying for college, federal student aid options, and more. website: studentaid.ed.gov.

DOCKETS

Federal dockets are available at www.regulations.gov. (*See appendix for Searching and Commenting on Regulations: Regulations.gov.*)

RULES AND REGULATIONS

The Office of Postsecondary Education rules and regulations are published in the *Code of Federal Regulations,* Title 34, Chapter VI, Parts 600–699. Proposed regulations, new final regulations, and updates are published in the daily *Federal Register.* (*See appendix for details on how to obtain and use these publications.*) The *Federal Register* and the *Code of Federal Regulations* may be accessed online at www.archives.gov/federal-register/cfr; the site contains a link to the federal government's regulatory website at www.regulations.gov (*see appendix*).

◼ LEGISLATION

Mutual Educational and Cultural Exchange Act (Fulbright Hays Act) (75 Stat. 527, 22 U.S.C. 2451 et seq.). Signed by the president September 21, 1961. Regulates foreign exchange students, scholars, and related programs.

Higher Education Act of 1965 (HEA) (20 U.S.C. 1001 et seq.). Signed by the president Nov. 8, 1965. Title IV established the federal student financial aid programs.

Education Amendments of 1972 (20 U.S.C. 1681 et seq.). Signed by the president June 23, 1972. Title IX prohibits discrimination based on gender in programs and activities of educational institutions that receive federal financial assistance.

Rehabilitation Act of 1973 (87 Stat. 394, 29 U.S.C. 794). Signed by the president Sept. 26, 1973. Mandated that no qualified individual who had a disability should be excluded from participation in, be denied the benefits of, or be subjected to discrimination under any program or activity receiving federal financial assistance. This includes publicly funded educational institutions.

Family Educational Rights and Privacy Act (20 U.S.C. 1232g). Signed by the president Aug. 21, 1974. Granted parents and students the right to privacy of student education records. Applied to all educational institutions, public and private, that received funds under any applicable Department of Education program.

Age Discrimination Act of 1975 (42 U.S.C. 6101 et seq.). Signed by the president Nov. 28, 1975. Prohibits discrimination based on age in programs or activities that receive federal financial assistance (it does not cover employment discrimination).

Department of Education Organization Act (93 Stat. 668, 20 U.S.C. 3401 note). Signed by the president Oct. 17, 1979. Established the Education Department as a cabinet-level agency to be directed by a secretary of education.

Crime Awareness and Campus Security Act (104 Stat. 2381, 20 U.S.C. 1092 note). Signed by the president Nov. 8, 1990. Allowed postsecondary institutions to share the results of any student disciplinary proceedings resulting from a campus crime with the victim. Amended HEA to require postsecondary institutions receiving federal aid to publish an annual campus crime report.

Higher Education Amendments of 1998 (112 Stat. 1581, 20 U.S.C. 1001 note). Signed by the president Oct. 7, 1998. Reauthorization of the Higher Education Act of 1965. Established a performance-based organization for the delivery of student financial assistance authorized under Title IV. Made various changes to student loan programs, including lowering interest rates on student loans for a five-year period. Authorized the suspension of a student's federal loan eligibility if the student has been convicted of a drug-related offense. Amended and renamed the Campus Crime and Security Act as the Jeanne Clery Disclosure of Campus Security Policy and Campus Crime Statistics Act.

Executive Order 13445 (Strengthening Adult Education). Signed by the president Sept. 27, 2007. Established an Interagency Adult Education Working Group consisting of the education secretary, who served as chair; the treasury secretary, the attorney general, and the secretaries of interior, labor, health and human services, housing and urban development, and veterans affairs. The group focused on federal programs that work to improve the basic education skills of adults and have the goal of transitioning adults from basic literacy to postsecondary education, training, or employment.

College Cost Reduction and Access Act (121 Stat. 784, 20 U.S.C. 1001 note). Signed by the president Sept. 27, 2007. Reauthorized HEA Title IV federal student financial aid programs. Repealed the formula for calculating an individual Pell grant. Reduced the interest rate on undergraduate loans under the Federal Family Education Loan and Direct Loan programs. Established the College Access Challenge Grant program to provide formula matching grants to states to improve student access to postsecondary education. Established the Public Service Loan Forgiveness program.

Ensuring Continued Access to Student Loans Act of 2008 (122 Stat. 740, 20 U.S.C. 1001 note). Signed by the president May 7, 2008. Authorized the Department of Education to purchase Federal Family Education Loan Program (FFELP) loans. Increased amount of Stafford loans available to undergraduate students. Made significant changes to other FSA grant programs.

Higher Education Opportunity Act (122 Stat. 3078, 20 U.S.C. 1001 note). Signed by the president Aug. 14, 2008. Reauthorized HEA. Authorized additional aid and benefits for students and required new disclosures and reporting requirements to assist students and parents to make better-informed decisions about obtaining and financing higher education. Authorized government regulation of private educational lending (federal student loan programs were previously regulated). Established, in the department's Office of Postsecondary Education, a deputy assistant secretary for International and Foreign Language Education with extensive experience in international and foreign language instruction.

American Recovery and Reinvestment Act of 2009 (123 Stat. 115, 26 U.S.C. 1 note). Signed by the president Feb. 17, 2009. Title I, the State Fiscal Stabilization Fund, provided more than $100 billion to states for the support of elementary, secondary, and postsecondary education as well as early childhood education. To obtain the education funds, governors are required to sign assurances to improve the quality of standardized tests and raise standards and include a plan for evaluating the state's progress in closing achievement gaps.

Health Care and Education Reconciliation Act of 2010 (124 Stat.1029, 20 U.S.C. 1087a et seq.). Signed by the president March 30, 2010. Ended the practice of subsidizing banks and other financial institutions to make guaranteed federal student loans. Instead, students apply for Direct Loans from the federal government. Reduced the cap on student loan payments under the Income-Based Repayment (IBR) plan. Increased Pell grant funding.

Violence Against Women Reauthorization Act of 2013 (127 Stat. 89, 20 U.S.C. 1092(f)). Signed by the president Mar. 7, 2013. Amended HEA to expand requirements for the disclosure of campus security policy and crime statistics by postsecondary institutions. Included provisions for awareness activities and disciplinary procedures.

Office of Special Education and Rehabilitative Services

400 Maryland Ave. S.W., Washington, DC 20202
Internet: www2.ed.gov/about/offices/list/osers

The Department of Education's Office of Special Education and Rehabilitative Services (OSERS) directs, coordinates, and recommends policy for programs that are designed to meet the needs and develop the full potential of children with disabilities through the provision of special educational programs and services. This includes providing independent living and vocational rehabilitation services and disseminating information about services, programs, and laws affecting persons with disabilities. To accomplish these goals, OSERS provides support to parents and individuals, school districts, and states in three main areas: special education, vocational rehabilitation, and research. To accomplish this mission, OSERS carries out these functions under three offices, the latter of which is transferring to the Health and Human Services Department:

OSERS Office of Special Education Programs works to improve educational results for children and youth with disabilities from birth through age twenty-one via financial support to assist states and local districts. The Individuals with Disabilities Education Act (IDEA) authorized formula grants to states, and discretionary grants to institutions of higher education and other nonprofit organizations to support research, technical assistance and dissemination, personnel development and parent-training, and information centers. IDEA programs serve approximately 7 million children and youth with disabilities.

OSERS Rehabilitation Services Administration (RSA) is the principal federal agency authorized to carry out Titles I, III, VI, and VII, as well as specified portions of Title V of the Rehabilitation Act of 1973, as amended. RSA oversees grant programs that help individuals with physical or mental disabilities to obtain employment and live more independently through support programs that include medical and psychological services, job training, and other individualized services. RSA's Title I formula grant program provides funds to state vocational rehabilitation agencies to provide employment-related services for individuals with disabilities.

OSERS National Institute on Disability and Rehabilitation Research (NIDRR) conducts comprehensive and coordinated programs of research and related activities to maximize the full inclusion, social integration, employment, and independent living of individuals of all ages with disabilities. NIDRR's research focuses on employment; health and function; technology for access and function; independent living and community integration; and other associated disability research areas. NIDRR coordinates with the other federal agencies that conduct disability research through the Interagency Committee on Disability Research (ICDR), which the director of NIDRR chairs. In addition, NIDRR co-sponsors research programs with other federal government agencies and with foreign governments and international agencies.

The Workforce Innovation and Opportunity Act (WIOA) of 2014 renamed the National Institute on Disability and Rehabilitation Research (NIDRR) as the National Institute on Disability, Independent Living, and Rehabilitation Research (NIDILRR), and transferred it to the Health and Human Services Department (HHS); the Education Department was working with HHS to transfer the office in 2015.

▧ KEY PERSONNEL

Assistant Secretary
 Sue Swenson (acting) . . . . (202) 245–8021
Deputy Assistant Secretary
 Sue Swenson. . . . . (202) 245–8021
Executive Administrator
 Andrew J. Pepin. . . . . (202) 245–7476
Special Institutions Liaison
 Annette Reichman . . . . (202) 245–7489
Management and Support Staff
 Melanie Winston. . . . . (202) 245–7419
Communications and Customer Service Team
 Paul Steenen. . . . . (202) 245–6721
Policy and Planning Staff
 Mary Louise Dirrigl . . . . (202) 245–7324
Grants and Contracts Services Team
 Melanie Winston. . . . . (202) 245–7419
Special Education Programs
 Director
  Melody Musgrove . . . . (202) 245–7459

Deputy Director
Ruth Ryder . . . . (202) 245–7459
Program Support Services Group
Bill Wolf . . . . (202) 245–7580
Monitoring and State Improvement Planning
Gregg Corr . . . . (202) 245–7309
Research to Practice
Larry Wexler . . . . (202) 245–7571
National Institute on Disability, Independent Living, and Rehabilitation Research*
Director
John Tschida . . . . (202) 245–7640
Deputy Director
Kristi Wilson-Hill . . . . (202) 245–7640
Research Sciences
Ruth Brannon . . . . (202) 245–7278
Program, Budget, and Evaluation
Timothy Muzzio . . . . (202) 245–7458
*Formerly the National Institute on Disability and Rehabilitation Research. Transferred to the Administration for Community Living (ACL) in the U.S. Department of Health and Human Services in 2015, but information can continue to be found at ed.gov until the transfer is complete.
Rehabilitation Services Administration
Commissioner
Janet LaBreck . . . . (202) 245–7488
Deputy Commissioner
Edward Anthony . . . . (202) 245–7256
Program Support Staff
Mary Lovley . . . . (202) 245–7423
State Monitoring and Program Improvement
Sue Rankin-White . . . . (202) 245–7312
Training and Services Program
Thomas Finch . . . . (202) 245–7343

▓ INFORMATION SOURCES

Internet

Agency website: www.ed.gov/about/offices/list/osers/index.html. Provides information on programs, news, and funding as well as on legislation, regulations, and policy guidance for programs being implemented under the No Child Left Behind Act (NCLB) and the Individuals with Disabilities Education Improvement Act (IDEA). Makes available tools and publications. Maintains links to disability-related and employment-related resources.

Telephone Contacts

Information . . . .(202) 245–7468
Federal Relay Service TTY . . . .(800) 877–8339

Information and Publications

KEY OFFICES

U.S. Department of Education
Communications and Outreach
Information Resource Center
400 Maryland Ave. S.W.

Washington, DC 20202–0498
(202) 401–2000
(800) 437–0833
E-mail: education@custhelp.com

Answers questions from parents, educators, students, and the public about all aspects of the Department of Education.

Freedom of Information
U.S. Department of Education
Office of Management
Privacy Information and Records Management
   Services (PIRMS)
400 Maryland Ave. S.W., LBJ 2E321
Washington, DC 20202–4536
Attn: FOIA Public Liaison
(202) 401–8365
Fax (202) 401–0920
E-mail: EDFOIAManager@ed.gov
Kathleen Styles, PIRMS director
Gregory Smith, FOIA director, (202) 453–6362

DATA AND STATISTICS
The OSERS website provides information to parents and other individuals, school districts, and states in three main areas: special education, vocation rehabilitation, and research information.

For statistical publications, fast facts, survey and program areas, and other education-related resources, contact the National Center for Education Statistics (NCES) or the Institute of Education Sciences through the OPE website, or by mail, phone, fax, or Internet as follows:

National Center for Education Statistics
1990 K St. N.W.
Washington, DC 20006
(202) 502–7300
Fax (202) 502–7466
Internet: http://nces.ed.gov

Institute of Education Sciences
555 New Jersey Ave. N.W.
Washington, DC 20208
(202) 219–1385
E-mail: Contact.IES.ed@gov
Internet: http://ies.ed.gov

PUBLICATIONS
Publications are available from EDPubs Online Ordering System through the OSERS website or by mail, phone, TTY, or fax as follows:

EDPubs
P.O. Box 22207
Alexandria, VA 22304
(877) 433–7827
TTY (877) 576–7734

Fax (703) 605–6794

Para Español (877) 433–7827

OSER Titles include:

Learning Opportunities for Your Child Through Alternate Assessments

Disability Employment 101

Opening Doors: Technology and Communication Options for Children with Hearing Loss.

Some publications can be downloaded free of charge from the OSERS website.

Reference Resources

ONLINE

The OSERS website provides information to parents and other individuals, school districts, and states in three main areas: special education, vocation rehabilitation, and research information.

DOCKETS

Federal dockets are available at www.regulations.gov. (*See appendix for Searching and Commenting on Regulations: Regulations.gov.*)

RULES AND REGULATIONS

The Office of Special Education and Rehabilitative Services rules and regulations are published in the *Code of Federal Regulations,* Title 34, Chapter III, Parts 300–399. Proposed regulations, new final regulations, and updates are published in the daily *Federal Register.* (*See appendix for details on how to obtain and use these publications.*) The *Federal Register* and the *Code of Federal Regulations* may be accessed online at www.archives.gov/federal-register/cfr; the site contains a link to the federal government's regulatory website at www.regulations.gov (*see appendix*).

▥ LEGISLATION

Elementary and Secondary Education Act (ESEA) of 1965 (108 Stat. 3519, 20 U.S.C. 6301 et seq.). Signed by the president April 11, 1965. Provided federal funding for public and private education for elementary and secondary educational institutions, especially in high-poverty areas. Title I provided for basic-skills instruction in disadvantaged urban neighborhoods. Title II provided funds for library books and textbooks, including aid to parochial schools. Title III offered grants for local-level program innovations. Title IV created federal research and development programs. Title V enhanced state departments of education.

Helen Keller National Center Act (29 U.S.C. 1901 et seq.). Signed by the president Oct. 3, 1967. Contained within the Vocational Rehabilitation Amendments of 1967. Provided for the establishment, operation, and funding of the Helen Keller National Center for Deaf-Blind Youths and Adults.

Bilingual Education Act of 1968 (81 Stat. 799, 803, 816, 819, 20 U.S.C. 3381). Signed by the president Jan. 2, 1968. Established Title VII of ESEA. Authorized funds for local school districts for programs for students who speak languages other than English.

Rehabilitation Act of 1973 (87 Stat. 394, 29 U.S.C. 794.). Signed by the president Sept. 26, 1973. Stated that no otherwise qualified individual with a disability in the United States shall, solely by reason of her or his disability, be excluded from participation in, be denied the benefits of, or be subjected to discrimination under any program or activity receiving federal financial assistance. This includes publicly funded educational institutions.

Family Educational Rights and Privacy Act (FERPA) (20 U.S.C. 1232g). Signed by the president Aug. 21, 1974. Granted parents and students the right to privacy of student education records. The law applies to all educational institutions, public and private, that receive funds under any applicable Department of Education program.

The Randolph-Sheppard Act (20 U.S.C. section 107 et seq.). Signed by the president Dec. 7, 1974. The Vending Facility Program authorized by the Randolph-Sheppard Act provides persons who are blind with remunerative employment and self-support through the operation of vending facilities on federal and other property.

Education for All Handicapped Children Act (20 U.S.C. 1400 et seq.). Signed by the president Dec. 2, 1975. Stated that all children with disabilities are entitled to receive a free and appropriate public school education. Encouraged states receiving federal education funds to create policies and practices facilitating the needs of special needs students.

Education Amendments of 1978 (92 Stat. 2143, 20 U.S.C. 6301 note). Signed by the president Nov. 11, 1978. Reauthorized ESEA through 1983. Amended ESEA by adding Title V, State Leadership, which required that each state desiring to participate in ESEA programs submit a general application. Added Title IX, Gifted and Talented Children's Education Act, which authorized funds for gifted and talented children's programs; and Title XI, Indian Education, which established a method for computing the entitlements of local school districts that provide public education to Native American children.

Department of Education Organization Act (93 Stat. 668, 20 U.S.C. 3401 note). Signed by the president Oct. 17, 1979. Established the Education Department as a cabinet-level agency to be directed by a secretary of education. Transferred education and related civil rights functions from the former Health, Education and Welfare Department to the department. Authorized local education authorities to inform the under secretary of conflicts between federal regulations. Prohibited the withholding of funds from schools on the basis of any requirement imposed by the secretary or the department with which a state fails to comply.

Education of the Deaf Act of 1986 (20 U.S.C. 4301 et seq.). Signed by the president Aug. 4, 1986. Established the Commission on Education of the Deaf. Authorized appropriations for the National Technical Institute for the Deaf (Rochester, NY) and Gallaudet University (Washington, DC) to provide postsecondary education and training for deaf individuals.

Americans with Disabilities Act of 1990 (104 Stat. 327, 42 U.S.C. 12101 et seq.). Signed by the president July 26, 1990. Title II prohibited discrimination based on disability in public entities, including elementary, secondary, and postsecondary educational institutions.

Individuals with Disabilities Education Act (IDEA) (20 U.S.C. 1400 et seq.). Signed by the president Oct. 3, 1990. Reauthorized, renamed, and recodified the Education for All Handicapped Children Act. Required that public schools create an individualized education program for each student who is eligible under both the federal and state eligibility standards. Applied to eligible children between the ages of three and twenty-one who require special education services because of the disability. The 1997 amendments established formula and discretionary grants to assist states in providing education to eligible children with special needs.

Goals 2000: Educate America Act (108 Stat. 125–191, 200–211, 265–280, 20 U.S.C. 5801 note). Signed by the president March 31, 1994. Established the National Education Standards and Improvement Council to develop and certify voluntary national standards for content areas, student performance, and fair opportunity-to-learn. Created the National Skill Standards Board to facilitate development of rigorous occupational standards. Made provisions with regard to school safety.

Improving America's Schools Act of 1994 (108 Stat. 3518, 20 U.S.C. 6301 note). Signed by the president Oct. 20, 1994. Revised and reauthorized ESEA. Established Title I program for Helping Disadvantaged Children Meet High Standards. Established the Fund for the Improvement of Education.

Individuals with Disabilities Education Act amendments of 1997 (IDEA) (111 Stat. 37, 20 U.S.C. 1400 note). Signed by the president June 4, 1997. Revises the program of assistance for education of all children with disabilities. Sets forth state eligibility requirements for placement of students.

Education of the Deaf Amendments of 1998 (112 Stat. 1581, 20 U.S.C. 1001 note). Signed by the president Oct. 7, 1998. Included in the Higher Education Amendments of 1998. Amended the Education of the Deaf Act to require elementary and secondary programs to comply with certain requirements under the Individuals with Disabilities Education Act and to revise requirements relating to agreements with Gallaudet University and the National Technical Institute for the Deaf.

No Child Left Behind Act (115 Stat. 1425, 20 U.S.C. 6301). Signed by the president Jan. 8, 2002. Reauthorized and amended ESEA. Established requirements for schools to test students annually and report on the progress. Set forth corrective actions for schools that fail to meet standards for two consecutive years. Provided alternatives for students at failing schools and supplementary educational services for low-income children who remain at such schools. Replaced Title III, the Bilingual Education Act, with the English Language Acquisition Act. Changed Title V, Promoting Informed Parental Choice and Innovative Programs, which revised formulas relating to distribution of federal innovative program funds.

Assistive Technology Act of 2004 (118 Stat. 1707, 29 U.S.C. 3001 et seq.). Signed by the president Oct. 25, 2004. Directed the secretary of education to make assistive technology (AT) grants to states to maintain comprehensive statewide programs designed to (1) maximize the ability of individuals with disabilities, and their family members, guardians, advocates, and authorized representatives, to obtain assistive technology and (2) increase access to assistive technology.

Individuals with Disabilities Education Improvement Act of 2004 (118 Stat. 2647, 20 U.S.C. 1400 et seq.). Signed by the president Dec. 3, 2004. Allowed a state or local educational agency to determine if a child needed special education and related services. Provided definitions of core academic subject, highly qualified teacher, and limited English proficient individual to conform with requirements under ESEA, as amended by NCLB.

ADA Amendments of 2008 (122 Stat. 3553, 42 U.S.C. 12101 note). Signed by the president Sept. 25, 2008. Amends the Americans with Disabilities Act of 1990 (ADA) to redefine the term "disability," including by defining "major life activities" and "being regarded as having such an impairment."

American Recovery and Reinvestment Act of 2009 (123 Stat. 115, 26 U.S.C. 1 note). Signed by the president Feb. 17, 2009. Title I, the State Fiscal Stabilization Fund, provided more than $100 billion to states for the support of elementary, secondary, and postsecondary education as well as early childhood education programs. To obtain the education funds, governors are required to sign assurances to improve the quality of standardized tests and raise standards and include a plan for evaluating the state's progress in closing achievement gaps.

The Workforce Innovation and Opportunity Act (WIOA) of 2014 (128 Stat. 1425, 29 U.S.C. 702). Signed by the president July 22, 2014. Made various changes to Rehabilitation Act programs administered by the Education Department; some programs required joint administration with the Labor Department. Imposed unified strategic planning requirements and common performance accountability measures for state participation in programs. Renamed the National Institute on Disability and Rehabilitation Research (NIDRR) as the National Institute on Disability, Independent Living, and Rehabilitation Research (NIDILRR) and transferred it to the Health and Human Services Department.

Other Education Department Offices

▪ FAMILY POLICY COMPLIANCE OFFICE

400 Maryland Ave. S.W.
Washington, DC 20202
Internet: http://familypolicy.ed.gov

The Family Policy Compliance Office (FPCO) is responsible for implementing two laws that seek to ensure student and parental rights in education: the Family Educational Rights and Privacy Act (FERPA) and the Protection of Pupil Rights Amendment (PPRA).

FERPA is a federal law that protects the privacy of student education records. The law applies to all schools that receive funds under an applicable program of the Education Department. FERPA gives parents certain rights with respect to their children's education records. These rights transfer to the student when he or she reaches the age of 18 or attends a school beyond the high school level.

In January 2013 Congress passed the Uninterrupted Scholars Act, which amended FERPA to permit educational agencies and institutions to disclose education records of students in foster care to state and county social service agencies or child welfare agencies. The statute also amended the requirement that educational agencies and institutions notify parents before complying with judicial orders and subpoenas in certain situations.

The PPRA governs the administration to students of a survey, analysis, or evaluation that concerns one or more of the following eight protected areas:

- political affiliations or beliefs of the student or the student's parent;
- mental or psychological problems of the student or the student's family;
- sex behavior or attitudes;
- illegal, antisocial, self-incriminating, or demeaning behavior;
- critical appraisals of other individuals with whom respondents have close family relationships;
- legally recognized privileged or analogous relationships, such as those of lawyers, physicians, and ministers;
- religious practices, affiliations, or beliefs of the student or student's parent; or,

- income (other than that required by law to determine eligibility for participation in a program or for receiving financial assistance under such program).

PPRA also concerns marketing surveys and other areas of student privacy, parental access to information, and the administration of certain physical examinations to minors. The rights under PPRA transfer from the parents to a student who is 18 years old or an emancipated minor under state law. The PPRA applies to the programs and activities of a state educational agency (SEA), local educational agency, or other recipient of funds under any program funded by the Education Department.

Director
    Dale King . . . . (202) 453–5549
        E-mail: dale.king2@ed.gov
Deputy Director
    Frank Miller . . . . (202) 260–3887
        E-mail: frank.e.miller@ed.gov

▪ OFFICE OF CAREER, TECHNICAL, AND ADULT EDUCATION

400 Maryland Ave. S.W.
Washington, DC 20202
Internet: www2.ed.gov/about/offices/list/ovae

The Office of Career, Technical, and Adult Education (OCTAE) administers and coordinates programs that are related to adult education and literacy, career and technical education, and community colleges. OCTAE accomplishes its mission through three divisions.

The Division of Adult Education and Literacy (DAEL) promotes and administers adult literacy and education programs. The major areas of support are Adult Basic Education, Adult Secondary Education, and English Language Acquisition. These programs emphasize basic skills such as reading, writing, math, English language competency, and problem solving. DAEL provides formula funding to states for adult education and literacy programs. States distribute funds to local eligible entities to provide adult education and literacy services.

The Division of Academic and Technical Education is responsible for establishing national initiatives that help states implement rigorous career and technical education programs. This division administers state formula and discretionary grant programs under the Carl D. Perkins Career and Technical Education Act.

OCTAE's Community College Division works to promote and facilitate the role of community colleges in expanding access to postsecondary education for youth and adults and advancing workforce development. OCTAE's community college initiatives are designed to build public support for community colleges as providers of affordable education and training and promote the development of strategies that support students in the completion of their postsecondary certification and degree programs.

The Workforce Innovation and Opportunity Act (WIOA) of 2014 reauthorized the Adult Education and Family Literacy Act (AEFLA) with several major revisions.

WIOA became effective on July 1, 2015, the first full program year after its enactment. However, the act includes several provisions that become effective on other dates. OCTAE is responsible for working with states to implement several mission-related initiatives under this legislation.

Assistant Secretary
  Johan Uvin (acting). . . . . (202) 245–6352
Deputy Assistant Secretary for Community Colleges
  Mark Mitsui . . . . (202) 245–7812
Chief of Staff
  Carmen Drummond (acting) . . . . (202) 245–7759
Executive Director
  Dan Miller (acting) . . . . (202) 245–7777
Adult Education and Literacy
  Cheryl Keenan . . . . (202) 245–7721
Academic and Technical Education
  Sharon Miller . . . . (202) 245–7846
Policy, Research, and Evaluation
  Braden Goetz . . . . (202) 245–7405

Energy Department

1000 Independence Ave. S.W., Washington, DC 20585
Internet: www.energy.gov

Office of Energy Efficiency and Renewable Energy

1000 Independence Ave. S.W., Washington, DC 20585
Internet: www.eere.energy.gov

The Office of Energy Efficiency and Renewable Energy (EERE) is responsible for developing and directing Department of Energy (DOE) programs to increase the production and use of renewable energy such as solar, biomass, wind, geothermal, and alternative fuels. Headed by an assistant secretary, EERE works to improve the energy efficiency of buildings, transportation, and industrial systems through financial and technological support of long-term research and development.

EERE carries out its mission through a variety of offices, programs, and initiatives:

Advanced Manufacturing Office. Partners with industry, small business, regional entities, and other stakeholders to identify and invest in emerging advanced manufacturing and clean energy technologies, provide energy-related leadership in the national and interagency Advanced Manufacturing Partnership through targeted manufacturing institutes.

Bioenergy Technologies Office. Supports targeted research, development, demonstration, and deployment activities to pursue an energy policy that will include sustainable, nationwide production of advanced biofuels that will displace a share of petroleum-derived fuels. This includes programs utilizing feedstock, algae, and lignocellulosic (plant-based) biomass sources.

Building Technologies Program. Conducts research and development on technologies and practices for energy efficiency, working closely with the building industry and manufacturers. Promotes energy- and money-saving opportunities to builders and consumers. Works with state and local regulatory groups to improve building codes and appliance standards.

Fuel Cells Technologies Office. Integrates activities in hydrogen production, storage, and delivery with transportation and stationary fuel cell activities. Administers state and local financial incentive programs to encourage the installation of fuel cells and hydrogen fueling infrastructure.

Government Energy Management Program. Provides information and technical assistance, creates partnerships, and leverages resources for reducing energy use in federal buildings and operations. Provides information on project financing and guidelines for federal procurement of energy efficient products. Also provides formula grant funding and technical assistance for state, local, and tribal governments to manage weatherization and clean energy programs.

Geothermal Technologies Program. Offers research and development support for U.S. industry to establish geothermal and hydrothermal energy as an economically competitive contributor to the U.S. energy supply. Geothermal resources range from shallow ground to hot water and rock several miles below Earth's surface, and even farther down to the extremely high temperatures of molten rock (magma).

Solar Energy Technologies Program. Accelerates the development of solar technologies as energy sources. Administers funding programs to support collaborative partnerships among industry, universities, national laboratories, federal, state, and local governments, and non-government agencies and advocacy groups to develop cost-effective solutions to develop and distribute solar technology.

Strategic Programs Office. Increases the effectiveness and impact of all EERE activities by funding cross-cutting activities and initiatives, analysis, and engagement functions with key stakeholders, the media, and the public.

Sustainability Performance Office. Supports DOE's internal activities to meet goals related to sustainability, including energy, water, land, and paper conservation and use, greenhouse gas emission reductions, and other objectives related to sustainability, such as the development of DOE's annual Strategic Sustainability Performance Plan (SSPP).

Vehicle Technologies Program. Develops and deploys efficient and environmentally sound highway transportation technologies to reduce reliance upon petroleum. This unit also maintains the Alternative Fuels Data Center (AFDC), which provides information, data, and tools to help fleets managers reduce petroleum consumption through the use of alternative and renewable fuels, advanced vehicles, and other fuel-saving measures.

Weatherization and Intergovernmental Programs. Provides consumers and decision makers with information on cost, performance, and financing energy efficiency and renewable energy projects. The Weatherization Assistance Program offers financial assistance to improve energy efficiency in low-income housing. This office administers the Tribal Energy Program, which offers financial and technical assistance to Indian tribes to evaluate and develop renewable energy resources and reduce their energy consumption through efficiency and weatherization.

Wind and Water Power Technologies Programs. Conducts and coordinates research and development with industry and other federal agencies for wind energy research programs, wind turbine research and development, and hydropower projects.

The Energy Policy Act of 2005 provided $2.2 billion for research on renewable energy technologies such as wind, solar, and geothermal power. The bulk of the funding was to promote the construction of new wind farms, and the remainder was to assist biomass, geothermal, and hydroelectric research. The act extended tax credits for companies that produce power from renewable sources.

The Energy Policy Act also required new federal buildings to achieve at least 30 percent greater energy efficiency over prevailing building codes. In January 2007 the Energy Department released the final regulations to meet this mandate.

In 2009 President Barack Obama announced that clean, renewable energy would be a centerpiece of his energy policy. The American Recovery and Reinvestment Act (ARRA) provided nearly $8 billion for energy efficiency and conservation projects through several energy grant programs, including the Weatherization Assistance Program, the Energy Efficiency Community Block Grants Program, and grants made to state energy offices and state energy programs.

▓ KEY PERSONNEL

Assistant Secretary
David Danielson . . . . (202) 586–9220
Principal Deputy Assistant Secretary
Michael S. Carr . . . . (202) 586–9220
Chief of Staff
Matthew Nelson . . . . (202) 586–9220
Chief Science Officer
Sam Baldwin . . . . (202) 586–0927
Deputy Assistant Secretary for Business Administration
William Valdez . . . . (202) 586–4479
Deputy Assistant Secretary for Energy Efficiency
Kathleen Hogan . . . . (202) 586–5523
Deputy Assistant Secretary for Renewable Energy
Steven Chalk . . . . (202) 586–9220
Advanced Manufacturing
Mark Johnson . . . . (202) 586–6912
Bioenergy Technologies
Jonathan Male . . . . (202) 586–5188
Building Technologies
Roland Risser . . . . (202) 586–9127

Fuel Cells Technologies
Sunita Satyapal . . . . (202) 586–2336
Government Energy Management Program
Timothy Unruh . . . . (202) 586–5772
Geothermal Technologies Program
Douglas Hollett . . . . (202) 586–1818
Planning, Budget Formulation, and Analysis
Leshawn Sutton (acting) . . . . (202) 586–9258
Project Management Coordination
Scott Hine . . . . (202) 586–9744
Solar Energy Technologies Program
Minh Le . . . . (202) 287–1372
Strategic Programs
John Lushetsky . . . . (202) 586–4276
Sustainability Performance
Drew Campbell . . . . (202) 586–8645
Technology-to-Market Program
Jennifer DeCesaro . . . . (202) 586–9258
Tribal Energy Program
Younes Masiky . . . . (202) 586–3160
Vehicle Technologies
Patrick Davis . . . . (202) 586–8055
Weatherization and Intergovernmental Programs
Anna Garcia . . . . (202) 586–1762
Weatherization Assistance Program
Robert Adams . . . . (202) 586–1591
Wind and Water Power Technologies
Jose Zayas . . . . (202) 586–3463
Workforce Management
Robin Sweeney (acting) . . . . (202) 586–5264

▓ INFORMATION SOURCES

Internet
Agency website: www.eere.energy.gov. Comprehensive website includes information on offices, personnel, research, publications, and national laboratories, as well as information on fuel efficiency and renewable energy. The Energy Information Administration (EIA) offers data and statistics on energy efficiency and renewable energy at www.eia.gov. For energy saving tips, visit http://energy.gov/energysaver/energy-saver.

Telephone Contacts
Switchboard and Personnel Locator . . (202) 586–5000
National Energy Information Center . (202) 586–8800
Toll-free . . . . (877) 337–3463
Federal Relay Service TTY . . . . (800) 877–8339

Information and Publications

KEY OFFICES

DOE Office of Public Affairs
1000 Independence Ave. S.W., #7A145
Washington, DC 20585
(202) 586–4940
Rick Borchelt, director

Freedom of Information

DOE Freedom of Information Reading Room
1000 Independence Ave. S.W.
Washington, DC 20585
(202) 586–5955
Kevin Hagerty, FOIA public liaison

The FOI Reading Room is open from 9:00 a.m. to 4:00 p.m. Visitors are required to call the Reading Room for a DOE escort.

DATA AND STATISTICS

Office of Communications

Energy Information Administration
1000 Independence Ave. S.W., #1E-30
Washington, DC 20585
(202) 586–8800
Karla Olsen, director
E-mail: InfoCtr@eia.gov
Internet: www.eia.gov
Hours: 9:00 a.m. to 5:00 p.m.

The Energy Information Administration (EIA), which was created in 1977 as the DOE's independent statistical and analytical agency, collects and publishes data; prepares analyses on energy production, consumption, and prices; and makes energy supply and demand projections. For more information, see the website at www.eia.gov.

PUBLICATIONS

For publications go to www.eere.energy.gov/library.

Reference Resources

LIBRARY

Energy Department Electronic Library

Email: Forrestal.library@hq.doe.gov
Courtney L. Byrd, supervisor
(202) 586–6021
E-mail: lashawn.byrd@hq.doe.gov

DOE publications and databases are available on the website.

DOCKETS

Federal dockets are available at www.regulations .gov. (*See appendix for Searching and Commenting on Regulations: Regulations.gov.*)

RULES AND REGULATIONS

Conservation and renewable energy rules and regulations are published in the *Code of Federal Regulations,* Title 10, various parts. Proposed rules, final rules, and updates to the *Code of Federal Regulations* are published in the daily *Federal Register. (See appendix for information on how to obtain and use these publications.)* The *Federal Register* and the *Code of Federal Regulations* may be accessed online at www.archives.gov/federal-register/cfr; the site contains a link to the federal government's regulatory website at www .regulations.gov (*see appendix*).

◼ LEGISLATION

EERE's responsibilities fall under the following legislation:

Federal Energy Administration Act of 1974 (88 Stat. 96, 15 U.S.C. 761). Signed by the president May 7, 1974. Created the Federal Energy Administration.

Federal Non-nuclear Energy Research and Development Act of 1974 (88 Stat. 1878, 42 U.S.C. 5901). Signed by the president Dec. 31, 1974. Provided federal support for programs of research and development of fuels and energy.

Energy Policy and Conservation Act (89 Stat. 871, 42 U.S.C. 6201 note). Signed by the president Dec. 22, 1975. Authorized the DOE to coordinate activities among the federal agencies to reduce energy consumption in federal buildings and operations.

Energy Conservation and Production Act (90 Stat. 1125, 42 U.S.C. 6801 note). Signed by the president Aug. 14, 1976. Encouraged implementation of energy conservation measures and reauthorized the Federal Energy Administration.

Energy Research and Development Administration Appropriations (91 Stat. 191, 42 U.S.C. 7001 note). Signed by the president June 3, 1977. Included the **National Energy Extension Service Act** (Title V), which established a federal/state partnership to provide small-scale energy users with technical assistance to facilitate energy conservation and the use of renewable resources.

Department of Energy Organization Act (91 Stat. 566, 42 U.S.C. 7101 note). Signed by the president Aug. 4, 1977. Established the Department of Energy within the executive branch.

Department of Energy Act of 1978–Civilian Applications (92 Stat. 47, codified in scattered sections of 42 U.S.C.). Signed by the president Feb. 25, 1978. Authorized funds for fiscal year 1978 for energy research and development programs of the DOE.

National Energy Conservation Policy Act (92 Stat. 3206, 42 U.S.C. 8201 note). Signed by the president Nov. 9, 1978. Authorized federal matching grant programs to assist public or nonprofit schools and hospitals to make energy-conserving improvements in their facilities and operating practices.

Public Utility Regulatory Policies Act of 1978 (92 Stat. 3117, 16 U.S.C. 2601). Signed by the president Nov. 9, 1978. Required utilities to give customers information about energy conservation devices. Provided funds to schools and hospitals to install energy-saving equipment and provided grants and government-backed loans to low-income families for home energy conservation.

Emergency Energy Conservation Act of 1979 (93 Stat. 749, 42 U.S.C. 8501 note). Signed by the president Nov. 5, 1979. Granted authority to the president to create an emergency program to conserve energy.

Department of Interior Appropriations (93 Stat. 970, 42 U.S.C. 5915). Signed by the president Nov. 27, 1979. Established the Energy Security Reserve of $19 billion until expended to stimulate domestic commercial production of alternative fuels such as ethanol and ammonia fertilizer plants.

Energy Security Act of 1980 (94 Stat. 611, 42 U.S.C. 8701). Signed by the president June 30, 1980. Established a five-year multibillion-dollar program for developing synthetic fuels, including the establishment of the U.S. Synthetic Fuels Corporation; expanded the use of biomass, alcohol fuels, and urban waste; ordered the president to set energy targets; instituted renewable energy initiatives; expanded the use of geothermal energy; and established a program to study the problems of acid rain and carbon dioxide associated with coal burning.

Ocean Thermal Energy Conversion Act of 1980 (94 Stat. 974, 42 U.S.C. 9101). Signed by the president Aug. 3, 1980. Established a legal framework to govern operations of ocean thermal energy conversion plants and extended to such facilities the federal financing aid, including loan guarantees, available to shipbuilders.

Ocean Thermal Energy Conversion Research, Development, and Demonstration Act (94 Stat. 941, 42 U.S.C. 9001). Signed by the president Aug. 17, 1980. Provided funds for an accelerated research and development program by the DOE on ocean thermal energy conversion.

Wind Energy System Act of 1980 (94 Stat. 1139, 42 U.S.C. 9201). Signed by the president Sept. 8, 1980. Authorized spending to accelerate the development of wind energy systems.

Renewable Energy Industry Development Act (98 Stat. 1211, 42 U.S.C. 6201 note). Signed by the president July 18, 1984. Established the Committee on Renewable Energy Commerce and Trade to promote and assist U.S.-developed renewable energy technology to compete within the international marketplace.

Energy Policy Act of 1992 (106 Stat. 2776, 42 U.S.C. 13201 note). Signed by the president Oct. 24, 1992. Set strategy for economic growth and national security by promoting conservation and efficient use of energy along with increased domestic production.

Biomass Research and Development Act of 2000 (114 Stat. 428, 7 U.S.C. 7624 note). Signed by the president on June 22, 2000. Directed the secretary of agriculture and the secretary of energy to cooperate and coordinate research and development activities with respect to production of biobased industrial products. Established the Biomass Research and Development Board to coordinate federal programs for the promotion and use of biobased industrial products. Also established the Biomass Research and Development Technical Advisory Committee.

Energy Act of 2000 (114 Stat. 2029, 42 U.S.C. 6201 note). Signed by the president Nov. 9, 2000. Reauthorized a program under the Energy Policy and Conservation Act that provided for continued operation of U.S. strategic petroleum reserves.

Energy Policy Act of 2005 (119 Stat. 594). Signed by the president Aug. 8, 2005. Provided incentives for the development of energy-efficient technologies and conservation methods. Provided two-year extension of a tax credit for companies that produce power from renewable sources. Authorized federal grants for state energy conservation programs and for energy-efficient buildings. Required modernization of the national electric grid. Required new federal buildings to achieve at least 30 percent greater energy efficiency over prevailing building codes.

Energy Independence and Security Act of 2007 (121 Stat. 1492, 42 U.S.C. 17001 note). Signed by the president Dec. 19, 2007. Increased fuel efficiency standards effective in 2020. Authorized competitive grants for emerging electric vehicle technologies. Established the Energy Efficiency and Conservation Block Grant Program for state, local, and tribal governments.

American Recovery and Reinvestment Act of 2009 (123 Stat. 115, 26 U.S.C. 1 note). Signed by the president Feb. 17, 2009. Amended Title XVII Energy Policy Act to create new loan guarantee authority for renewable energy systems that generate electricity or thermal energy, electric power transmission systems, and certain biofuel projects. Authorized additional funds for several energy grant programs, including the Weatherization Assistance Program, the Energy Efficiency Community Block Grants Program, and grants made to the state energy offices and state energy programs.

American Energy Manufacturing Technical Corrections Act (126 Stat. 1514, 42 U.S.C. 6201 note). Signed by the president Dec. 18, 2012. Allowed for innovations and alternative technologies that meet or exceed desired energy efficiency goals. Made technical corrections to existing federal energy efficiency laws.

▪ FIELD OFFICE

Supports DOE's Office of Energy Efficiency (EE) and Renewable Energy through research and development partnerships, outreach to stakeholders nationwide to further the use of EE technologies, and laboratory contract administration.

GOLDEN FIELD OFFICE

1617 Cole Blvd.
MS 1501
Golden, CO 80401–3393
(720) 356–1800
Timothy J. Meeks, business services director

Office of Environment, Health, Safety, and Security

1000 Independence Ave. S.W., Washington, DC 20585
Internet: http://energy.gov/ehss/
environment-health-safety-security

The Office of Environment, Safety, and Health, created in 1985, became the Office of Health, Safety, and Security (HSS) in August 2006. In 2014 the HSS was divided into two separate organizations: the Office of Environment, Health, Safety and Security (EHSS) and the Office of Enterprise Assessment (EA). HSS environment, health, safety, and security policy, and programs transferred to the EHSS. HSS assessment, enforcement, and outreach functions were transferred to EA. Headed by an assistant secretary, the EHSS is responsible for ensuring the compliance of Department of Energy (DOE) facilities with applicable environmental laws and regulations and protecting the safety and health of DOE employees and the public. The EHSS also develops DOE policy regarding the effects of national environmental policy on U.S. energy industries and energy supply and demand. The EHSS has several offices dedicated to environment, health, safety, and security, including:

Office of Environmental Protection, Sustainability Support, and Corporate Safety Analysis establishes environmental protection policy and implements sustainability programs and requirements. Promotes environmental justice in all its activities in keeping with Executive Order 12898: Federal Actions to Address Environmental Justice in Minority Populations and Low-Income Populations. Provides assistance to support all DOE organizations in the resolution of many Resource Conservation and Recovery Act hazardous waste issues.

Office of Worker Health and Safety establishes worker safety and health requirements and expectations for the department to ensure protection of workers from the hazards associated with department operations.

Office of Nuclear Safety establishes nuclear safety and environmental protection requirements and expectations for the department to ensure protection of workers and the public from the hazards associated with nuclear operations, and protection of the environment from the hazards associated with all department operations. The office provides assistance to field elements in implementation of policy and resolving nuclear safety and environmental protection issues.

Office of Nuclear Facility Safety Programs works with headquarters and field offices to ensure nuclear safety through implementation of nuclear safety management programs and fire protection and natural phenomena hazard control requirements.

Office of Security provides security expertise to assist field elements in planning site protection strategies and by coordinating with domestic authorities to provide safeguards and security technical assistance, technical systems support, and technology development and deployment opportunities.

Office of Classification manages the government-wide program to classify and declassify nuclear weapons-related technology, implements the requirements of Executive Order 12958 regarding the classification and declassification of information that is vital to national security, and manages the department-wide programs to control unclassified but sensitive information.

▓ KEY PERSONNEL

Associate Under Secretary
  Matthew Moury. . . . . (202) 586–1285
Corporate Security, Strategy, Analysis and Special Operations
  Robert Lingan . . . . (202) 586–1461
Departmental Representative
  Joseph Olencz . . . . (301) 903–4516
Classification
  Andrew Weston-Dawkes . . . . (301) 903–3526
Environmental Protection, Sustainability Support, and Corporate Safety Analysis
  Andrew Lawrence. . . . . (202) 586–5680
Health and Safety
  Patricia R. Worthington . . . . (301) 903–5926
Worker Safety and Health Policy
  Bill R. McArthur . . . . (301) 903–9674
Worker Safety and Health Assistance
  Bradley K. Davy. . . . . (301) 903–2473
Domestic and International Health Studies
  Gerald R. Petersen. . . . . (301) 903–2340

Worker Screening and Compensation Support
Gregory S. Lewis . . . . (301) 586–2784
Nuclear Safety
James B. O'Brien . . . . (301) 903–4586
Nuclear Facility Safety Programs
William M. Blackburn . . . . (301) 903–8396
Resource Management
Richard Updegrove (acting) . . . . (301) 903–1832
Security Operations
Michael Zimmerman . . . . (301) 903–2177
Information Security
Michael Zimmerman . . . . (301) 903–2177
Personnel Security Operations
Stephanie Grimes . . . . (301) 903–4175
Security
Robert Lingan (acting) . . . . (301) 903–4516
Cyber and Security Assessments
John Boulden III . . . . (301) 903–2178
Security Policy
Marc Brooks. . . . . (301) 903–4291
National Training Center (Albuquerque, NM)
Karen Boardman . . . . (505) 845–6444

▣ INFORMATION SOURCES

Internet

Agency website: http://energy.gov/hss/office-health-safety-and-security.

Telephone Contacts

Personnel Locator . . . . (202) 586–5000
Environmental Hotline . . . . (800) 541–1625
Washington, DC, area . . . . (202) 586–4073
Federal Relay Service TTY . . . . (800) 877–8339

Information and Publications

KEY OFFICES

DOE Office of Public Affairs

Office of Public Information
1000 Independence Ave. S.W.
Washington, DC 20585
Rick Borchelt, director
(202) 585–4940

Answers questions from the public and news organizations.

Environmental Hotline

DOE Office of the Inspector General
Attention: IG Hotline
1000 Independence Ave. S.W., #5D-031
Washington, DC 20585
(800) 541–1625
(202) 586–4073 (Washington, DC, area)
Fax (202) 586–4902
Gregory Friedman, inspector general
Hours: 8:00 a.m. to 4:00 p.m.

To facilitate the reporting of allegations of fraud, waste, abuse, or mismanagement in U.S. DOE programs or operations.

Freedom of Information

DOE Freedom of Information Reading Room
1000 Independence Ave. S.W.
Washington, DC 20585
(202) 586–5955
Kevin Hagerty, FOIA public liaison

The FOI Reading Room is open from 9:00 a.m. to 4:00 p.m. Visitors are required to call the Reading Room for a DOE escort.

DATA AND STATISTICS

Office of Communications

Energy Information Administration
1000 Independence Ave. S.W., #EI-30
Washington, DC 20585
(202) 586–8800
Gina Pearson, assistant administrator
E-mail: Infoctr@eia.gov
Internet: www.eia.gov

The Energy Information Administration, created in 1977 as the DOE's independent statistical and analytical agency, collects and publishes data; prepares analyses on energy production, consumption, prices, and resources; and makes energy supply and demand projections. For more information, see the website at www.eia.gov.

PUBLICATIONS

Contact specific offices for publications. In addition, a number of publications are available for viewing and downloading on the website at http://energy.gov/hss/office-health-safety-and-security.

Reference Resources

LIBRARY

Energy Department Electronic Library

Email: Forrestal.library@hq.doe.gov
Courtney L. Byrd, supervisor
(202) 586–6021
E-mail: lashawn.byrd@hq.doe.gov

DOE publications and databases are available on the website.

DOCKETS

Federal dockets are available at www.regulations .gov. (*See appendix for Searching and Commenting on Regulations: Regulations.gov.*)

RULES AND REGULATIONS

EHSS rules and regulations are published in the *Code of Federal Regulations,* Title 10, Chapters II, III, X, Parts 200–1060. Proposed rules, final rules, and updates to the *Code of Federal Regulations* are published in the daily *Federal Register.* (*See appendix for information on how to obtain and use these publications.*) The *Federal Register* and the *Code of Federal Regulations* may be accessed online at www.archives.gov/federal-register/cfr; the site contains a link to the federal government's regulatory website at www.regulations.gov (*see appendix*).

▓ LEGISLATION

The EHSS carries out its responsibilities under:

Resource Conservation and Recovery Act of 1976 (RCRA) (90 Stat. 2807, 42 U.S.C. 6923). Signed by the president Oct. 21, 1976. Authorized the Environmental Protection Agency to regulate the treatment, storage, transportation, and disposal of hazardous wastes. Set standards for the transportation of certain types of hazardous wastes and the cleanup of hazardous waste sites.

Department of Energy Organization Act (91 Stat. 566, 42 U.S.C. 7101 note). Signed by the president Aug. 4, 1977. Established the DOE within the executive branch.

Executive Order 12038. Issued by the president Feb. 7, 1978. Transferred responsibilities of the Federal Energy Administration, the Energy Research and Development Administration, and the Federal Power Commission to the DOE.

Executive Order 12088. Issued by the president Oct. 13, 1978. Required that all federal facilities and activities comply with applicable pollution control standards and required each agency to submit an annual pollution control plan to the president.

Comprehensive Environmental Responses, Compensation, and Liability Act of 1980 (Superfund) (94 Stat. 2767, 42 U.S.C. 9601). Signed by the president Dec. 11, 1980. Required the identification and cleanup of inactive hazardous waste sites by responsible parties. Allowed state cleanup standards to be substituted for federal standards if the state imposed more stringent requirements. Amended by the **Superfund Amendments and Reauthorization Act of 1986** (100 Stat. 1613, 42 U.S.C. 9601 note). Signed by the president Oct. 17, 1986. These two acts limited or prohibited many formerly acceptable waste management practices.

Price-Anderson Amendments Act of 1988 (102 Stat. 1066, 43 U.S.C. 2011 note). Signed by the president Aug. 20, 1988. Amended the Atomic Energy Act of 1954 to establish a comprehensive, equitable, and efficient mechanism for full compensation of the public in the event of a DOE accident involving nuclear materials.

Energy Policy Act of 1992 (106 Stat. 2776, 42 U.S.C. 13201 note). Signed by the president Oct. 24, 1992. Set strategy for economic growth and national security by promoting the conservation and efficient use of energy along with increased domestic production.

Executive Order 12898. Issued by the president Feb. 16, 1994. Directs federal agencies to identify and address the disproportionately high and adverse human health or environmental effects of their actions on minority and low-income populations and to develop a strategy for implementing environmental justice.

Executive Order 12958. Issued by the president April 17, 1995. Prescribed a uniform system for classifying, safeguarding, and declassifying national security information.

Energy Policy Act of 2005 (119 Stat. 594). Signed by the president Aug. 8, 2005. Required the DOE to use sound and objective scientific practices in assessing risks to human health and the environment from energy technology or conservation activities; consider the best available science (including peer reviewed studies); and include a description of the weight of the scientific evidence concerning such risks. Instructed the DOE to study and report to Congress on direct and significant health impacts to persons living in proximity to petrochemical and oil refinery facilities.

Office of Environmental Management

1000 Independence Ave. S.W., Washington, DC 20585
Internet: http://energy.gov/em/office-environmental-management

The Office of Environmental Management (EM) was established by the secretary of energy in October 1989 to consolidate responsibility within the Department of Energy (DOE) for environmental management activities. EM was originally called the Office of Environmental Restoration and Waste Management until 1994. EM is headed by an assistant secretary and is responsible for environmental cleanup, compliance, and waste management activities.

The DOE and the Environmental Protection Agency (EPA) share responsibility for transportation of hazardous wastes or radioactive and hazardous waste mixtures generated at facilities operated by the DOE under the authority of the Atomic Energy Act. These responsibilities are delineated in the 1984 DOE/EPA Memorandum of Understanding on Responsibilities for Hazardous and Radioactive Mixed Waste Management. The DOE complies with Resource Conservation and Recovery Act requirements for hazardous waste transporters that require transporters to obtain an EPA identification number for the waste, adhere to the manifest system, and deal with hazardous waste discharges. These regulations incorporate and require compliance with Department of Transportation provisions for labeling, marking, placarding, proper container use, and discharge reporting.

The EM program is responsible for cleaning up sites involved with research, development, production, and testing of nuclear weapons. Taken together, these sites encompassed an area of more than 2 million acres—equal to the combined size of Rhode Island and Delaware. By the end of fiscal year 2013, EM had completed legacy waste cleanup at 90 of 107 total sites. This included cleanup and closure of 85 smaller sites and five major nuclear sites in 24 states. Legacy sites remain in 11 states.

Environmental Management accomplishes its mission through four broad mission areas:

Waste Management. Carries out planning and optimizing tank waste processing and nuclear materials, including spent nuclear fuel. EM offices that focus on waste management develop policy and guidance and provide technical advice on the tank waste system and nuclear materials.

Site and Facility Restoration. Performs program management functions to identify and advance strategies to plan and optimize EM soil and groundwater remediation, deactivation and decommissioning (D&D), and facility engineering projects and processes.

Program Management. Provides program management support across the EM organization. Assures effective project, acquisition, and contract management; manages the safeguards, security, and emergency preparedness activities; and manages, integrates, and coordinates planning and budget support for the EM.

Communications and Engagement. Manages EM's interactions with intergovernmental groups, advisory boards, tribal nations, and other affected entities, communities, and stakeholders.

Seven offices, headed by deputy assistant secretaries, carry out mission functions and program support:

Office of Acquisition and Project Management is responsible for acquisition, contract, and project management in executing the EM program. The office accomplishes this by working closely with senior level officials in HQ and field managers, external stakeholders, and major contractors.

Office of Program Planning and Budget manages, integrates, and coordinates planning and budget support for EM. This support includes budget development and execution, strategic planning and analysis, and materials and waste disposition planning.

Office of Human Capital and Corporate Services oversees the EM human resource development programs to provide technical expertise and capabilities of employees in EM programs. The office provides essential business services for EM employees and the EM program.

Office of Safety, Security, and Quality Programs implements DOE/EM-wide Integrated management oversight activities, standards assurance for major project planning and execution, operational safety and awareness programs, and quality assurance programs. The office manages the safeguards and security and emergency preparedness activities for EM.

Office of Site Restoration manages strategies to plan and optimize EM soil and groundwater remediation, deactivation and decommissioning (D&D), and facility engineering projects and processes to ensure technically sound environmental and public health risk evaluations and performance assessments in selecting remedies and disposal sites and to ensure environmental compliance.

Office of Tank Waste and Nuclear Materials manages strategies to plan and optimize tank waste processing and nuclear materials, including spent nuclear fuel.

Office of Waste Management manages strategies to plan and optimize EM waste management projects and processes to ensure optimized management and disposition of certain excess material inventories having potential asset value and to ensure safe and efficient packaging and transportation systems necessary to achieve waste and materials disposition. It takes the lead on matters related to EM's legal and regulatory responsibilities defined by law, negotiated or stipulated compliance agreements, DOE policies and orders, and Defense Nuclear Facilities Safety Board (DNFSB) milestones. This Office also supports the implementation of EM waste and materials disposition activities in the field.

The Energy Policy Act of 2005 provided another boost to EM's cleanup and closure programs. The act made technical corrections to regulations governing low-activity wastes and permitted timely disposal of the wastes in a licensed commercial disposal facility. The act also instructed the DOE to develop a comprehensive plan for permanent disposal of low-level radioactive waste.

EM received a boost for its cleanup operations via the American Recovery and Reinvestment Act (ARRA), which provided nearly $6 billion for projects focusing on accelerating cleanup of soil and groundwater, transportation and disposal of waste, and demolishing former weapons complex facilities.

▪ KEY PERSONNEL

Assistant Secretary
Mark Whitney . . . . (202) 586–7709
Fax . . . . (202) 586–9100
Principal Deputy Assistant Secretary
Monica Regalbuto . . . . (202) 586–7709
Chief Business Officer
Frank Marcinowski III . . . . (202) 586–0370
Acquisition and Project Management
Jack Surash . . . . (202) 586–3867
Communications and External Affairs
Candice Trummell (acting) . . . . (202) 586–5591
Human Capital and Corporate Services
Melody C. Bell (acting) . . . . (202) 586–3087
Large Sites Support
Tammey Johnson . . . . (301) 903–4845
Program, Planning, and Budget
Connie Flohr (acting) . . . . (301) 903–0393
Safeguards, Security, and Emergency Management
Jimmy McMillian . . . . (301) 903–5498
Safety, Security, and Quality Programs
James A. Hutton . . . . (202) 586–5151
Site Restoration
Mark Gilbertson . . . . (202) 586–5042
Small Site Projects
Stacy Charboneau . . . . (509) 376–7411

Tank Waste and Nuclear Materials Management
Kenneth G. Picha . . . . (202) 586–2281
Waste Support
Frank Marcinowski III . . . . (202) 586–0370

▪ INFORMATION SOURCES

Internet

Agency website: http://energy.gov/em/office-environmental-management. Features schedules for conferences and courses, press releases and regulatory news, and information on job opportunities and relocation assistance.

Telephone Contacts

Personnel Locator . . . . (202) 586–5000
Environmental Hotline
(Inspector General) . . . . (800) 541–1625
Washington, DC, Area . . . . (202) 586–4073
Federal Relay Service TTY . . . . (800) 877–8339

Information and Publications

KEY OFFICES

DOE Office of Public Affairs
1000 Independence Ave. S.W.
Washington, DC 20585
(202) 586–4940
Rick Borchelt, director

Answers questions from the public and news organizations.

DOE Press Office
1000 Independence Ave. S.W.
Washington, DC 20585
(202) 586–4940
Aoife McCarthy, press secretary

Handles press inquiries and issues press releases.

Environment, Safety, Health, National Energy Policy Act (NEPA) Hotline
DOE Office of the Inspector General
Attention: IG Hotline
1000 Independence Ave. S.W., #5D-031
Washington, DC 20585
(800) 541–1625
(202) 586–4073 (Washington, DC, area)
Gregory Friedman, inspector general
Hours: 8:00 a.m. to 4:00 p.m.

To facilitate the reporting of allegations of fraud, waste, abuse, or mismanagement in U.S. DOE programs or operations.

Freedom of Information
DOE Freedom of Information Reading Room
1000 Independence Ave. S.W.

Washington, DC 20585
(202) 586–5955
Kevin Hagerty, FOIA public liaison

The FOIA Reading Room is open from 9:00 a.m. to 4:00 p.m. Visitors are required to arrange for a DOE escort to use the Reading Room.

DATA AND STATISTICS

Office of Communications
Energy Information Administration
1000 Independence Ave. S.W., #1E-238
Washington, DC 20585
(202) 586–8800
TTY (202) 586–1181
Gina Pearson, assistant administrator
E-mail: infoctr@eia.gov
Internet: www.eia.gov

The Energy Information Administration (EIA), which was created in 1977 as the DOE's independent statistical and analytical agency, collects and publishes data; prepares analyses on energy production, consumption, prices, and resources; and makes energy supply and demand projections. For more information, visit the website: www.eia.gov.

PUBLICATIONS
Publications can be obtained from specific offices, from the website, and from the Energy Information Administration's Office of Communications.

Reference Resources

LIBRARY

Energy Department Electronic Library
Email: Forrestal.library@hq.doe.gov
Courtney L. Byrd, supervisor
(202) 586–6021
E-mail: Lashawn.byrd@hq.doe.gov

DOE publications and databases are available on the website.

DOCKETS
Federal dockets are available at www.regulations .gov. (*See appendix for Searching and Commenting on Regulations: Regulations.gov.*)

RULES AND REGULATIONS
EM rules and regulations are published in the *Code of Federal Regulations,* Title 10, Chapters II, III, X, XVII, and XVIII, Parts 200 to the end; Title 40, Chapter I, Part 260; Title 40, Chapter I, Part 300. Proposed rules, final rules, and updates to the *Code of Federal Regulations* are published in the daily *Federal Register.* (*See appendix for information on how to obtain and use these publications.*) The *Federal Register* and the *Code of Federal Regulations* may be accessed online at www.archives.gov/federal-register/cfr;

the site contains a link to the federal government's regulatory website at www.regulations.gov (*see appendix*).

■ LEGISLATION
Environmental Management carries out its responsibilities under:

National Environmental Policy Act of 1969 (83 Stat. 852, 42 U.S.C. 4321). Signed by the president Jan. 1, 1969. Established a broad national environmental policy and required that federal agencies provide environmental impact statements regarding any major federal action or legislative proposal.

Toxic Substances Control Act, as amended (90 Stat. 2003, 15 U.S.C. 2601). Signed by the president Oct. 11, 1976. Required the federal government to regulate the manufacture, processing, distribution in commerce, use, or disposal of chemical substances and mixtures that may present an unreasonable risk to the public health or the environment.

Resource Conservation and Recovery Act of 1976 (RCRA) (90 Stat. 2807, 42 U.S.C. 6923). Signed by the president Oct. 21, 1976. Authorized the Environmental Protection Agency to regulate the treatment, storage, transportation, and disposal of hazardous wastes. Set standards for the transportation of certain types of hazardous wastes and the cleanup of hazardous waste sites.

Department of Energy Organization Act (91 Stat. 566, 42 U.S.C. 7101 note). Signed by the president Aug. 4, 1977. Established the DOE within the executive branch.

Executive Order 12038. Issued by the president Feb. 7, 1978. Transferred responsibilities of the Federal Energy Administration, the Energy Research and Development Administration, and the Federal Power Commission to the DOE.

Uranium Mill Tailings Radiation Control Act of 1978, as amended (92 Stat. 3021, 42 U.S.C. 7901). Signed by the president Nov. 8, 1978. Provided a remedial action program to stabilize, dispose of, and control uranium mill tailings to prevent or minimize radon diffusion into the environment and other health hazards.

Comprehensive Environmental Response, Compensation, and Liability Act of 1980 (Superfund) (94 Stat. 2767, 42 U.S.C. 9601). Signed by the president Dec. 11, 1980. Required the identification and cleanup of inactive hazardous waste sites by responsible parties. Allowed state cleanup standards to be substituted for federal standards if the state imposed more stringent requirements. Amended by the **Superfund Amendments and Reauthorization Act of 1986** (100 Stat. 1613, 42 U.S.C. 9601 note). Signed by the president Oct. 17, 1986. These two acts limited or prohibited many formerly acceptable waste management practices.

Nuclear Waste Policy Act of 1982, as amended (96 Stat. 2201, 42 U.S.C. 10101 note). Signed by the president Jan. 7, 1983. Provided for the development of federal repositories for the disposal of high-level radioactive waste and spent fuel, and established a research program regarding the disposal of high-level radioactive waste and spent nuclear fuel.

Low-Level Radioactive Waste Policy Amendments Act of 1985 (99 Stat. 182, 42 U.S.C. 2021). Signed by the president Jan. 15, 1986. Imposed strict deadlines for states or regions to set up disposal facilities for low-level radioactive wastes; approved compacts among thirty-seven states to join together for the disposal of such wastes.

Energy Policy Act of 1992 (106 Stat. 2276, 42 U.S.C. 13201 note). Signed by the president Oct. 24, 1992. Set strategy for economic growth and national security by promoting conservation and efficient use of energy along with increased domestic production.

Energy Policy Act of 2005 (119 Stat. 594). Signed by the president Aug. 8, 2005. Allowed the DOE to dispose of nuclear wastes in a facility regulated by the Nuclear Regulatory Commission (NRC) or by a state. Directed the DOE to develop a new or use an existing facility for safely disposing of all low-level radioactive waste and to develop a comprehensive plan for permanent disposal of low-level radioactive waste.

American Recovery and Reinvestment Act of 2009 (123 Stat. 115, 26 U.S.C. 1 note). Signed by the president Feb. 17, 2009. Provided nearly $6 billion to the Office of Environmental Management for projects focusing on accelerating cleanup of soil and groundwater, transportation and disposal of waste, and cleaning and demolishing former weapons complex facilities.

▓ REGIONAL AND FIELD OFFICES

The Office of Environmental Management has six field offices and numerous cleanup site locations. For information on cleanup sites under the purview of Environmental Management, go to the website http://energy.gov/em/office-environmental-management and select "Sites/Locations."

CARLSBAD FIELD OFFICE
4021 National Parks Hwy.
Carlsbad, NM 88220
(800) 336–9477
E-mail: infocntr@wipp.ws
Joe Franco, manager

CONSOLIDATED BUSINESS CENTER
250 E. 5th St., #500
Cincinnati, OH 45202
(513) 246–0500
Jack R. Craig Jr., director

OFFICE OF RIVER PROTECTION
P.O. Box 450 MSIN: H6–60
2440 Stevens Center Pl.
Richland, WA 99354
(509) 376–7411
E-mail: webmaster@ri.gov
Kevin Smith, manager

PORTSMOUTH/PADUCAH PROJECT OFFICE
1017 Majestic Dr., #200
Lexington, KY 40513
(859) 219–4000
William Murphie, manager

RICHLAND OPERATIONS
825 Jadwin Ave.
P.O. Box 550
Richland, WA 99352
(509) 376–7411
Stacy Charboneau, manager

SAVANNAH RIVER OPERATIONS OFFICE
P.O. Box A
Aiken, SC 29802
(803) 952–7697
E-mail: DOE-SROEA@srs.gov
David Moody, manager

Office of Fossil Energy

1000 Independence Ave. S.W., Washington, DC 20585
Internet: http://energy.gov/fe/office-fossil-energy

The Department of Energy's (DOE) Office of Fossil Energy is responsible for research and development programs involving fossil fuels. The regulatory responsibilities of the Fossil Energy Office are carried out primarily by three divisions: Oil and Natural Gas, Clean Coal and Carbon Management, and Petroleum Reserves.

Oil and Natural Gas develops policy and regulations, conducts administrative law proceedings to determine whether to authorize imports and exports of natural gas, and intervenes in Federal Energy Regulatory Commission proceedings involving natural gas issues (*p. 181*). This office also supports numerous research and development activities to ensure environmentally sustainable domestic and global supplies of oil and natural gas. Some of these initiatives include Hydraulic Fracturing & Shale Gas Research (fracking), Methane Hydrate Research and Development, and Offshore Drilling Research and Development.

Oil and Gas Global Security and Supply regulates natural gas imports and exports, maintains statistics on North American natural gas trade, and oversees Fossil Energy's international programs pertaining to natural gas and petroleum. Oil and Natural Gas carries out its responsibilities under the Natural Gas Act.

Clean Coal and Carbon Management authorizes the export of electricity and issues permits for the construction and operation of electric transmission lines that cross international borders. (The federal government does not regulate the import of electric energy or commercial arrangements between the United States and foreign utilities.) Clean Coal also is responsible for certifying that new electric power plants are constructed or operated with the capability to use coal or another alternate fuel as a primary energy source. This provision was required by the Power Plant and Industrial Fuel Use Act. In 1989 the regulatory authority to implement provisions of the act was transferred from the Economic Regulatory Administration to Fossil Energy. This division also administers the Clean Coal Technology Program.

Fossil Energy administers carbon capture and storage (CCS) research and development initiatives. CCS is technology that captures carbon dioxide emissions, transporting it and storing is securing (usually very deep underground). Key programs include Industrial Carbon Capture and Storage, a cost-shared collaboration with industry to demonstrate large-scale industrial carbon capture and storage technology and the Regional Carbon Sequestration Partnerships, a nationwide network of federal, state, and private sector partnerships to determine the most suitable technologies, regulations, and infrastructure for future carbon capture, storage, and sequestration in different areas of the country.

Petroleum Reserves oversees the Strategic Petroleum Reserve (SPR) and the Naval Petroleum Reserves. The Office of Strategic Petroleum Reserves is authorized by the Energy Policy and Conservation Act of 1975, which was enacted following the energy crisis in the United States that resulted from the OPEC oil embargo of 1973–1974. The SPR was established to give the United States a backup supply if it lost access to foreign oil markets. The Office of Naval Petroleum Reserves is authorized by the Naval Petroleum Reserves Production Act of 1976. The president is authorized to draw down from the reserve under the Energy Policy and Conservation Act.

The SPR, with the capacity to hold 727 million barrels of crude oil, is the largest emergency oil stockpile in the world. In the event of an energy emergency, SPR oil is distributed by competitive sale. The SPR has been used for emergency purposes three times: in 1991 during Operation Desert Storm; in 2005 after hurricanes Katrina and Rita disrupted the oil industry on the Gulf Coast; and in 2011 following political and military unrest in the Middle East.

The Energy Policy Act of 2005 sought to promote energy research and development, to increase energy efficiency, to diversify supplies, to reduce U.S. dependence on foreign energy sources, and to improve U.S. energy security. The act included $14.6 billion in tax incentives for the energy industry over the following decade, most of which went to developers and producers of fossil fuels. The law authorized the expansion of SPR capacity to one billion barrels. Other provisions funded coal research, including the Clean Coal Technology Program, and required an inventory of offshore oil and gas resources, including areas that were off limits to drilling.

In 2005 Congress directed the SPR to take actions to fill its authorized size of one billion barrels. This required developing a new storage site and expanding existing SPR storage sites. On Dec. 8, 2006, the DOE identified the salt domes at Richton, near Hattiesburg, MS, as the preferred new site. However, efforts to expand the SPR to one billion barrels were terminated in late 2011.

Petroleum Reserves also administers the Northeast Home Heating Oil Reserve. Established in 2000, the Northeast Home Heating Oil Reserve is a supply of emergency fuel oil (two million barrels) for homes and businesses in the northeast United States. The Heating Oil Reserve as an emergency buffer that can supplement commercial fuel supplies should the heavily oil-dependent region be hit by a severe heating oil supply disruption. In February 2011, DOE sold the entire inventory of the reserve for the purpose of converting its high sulfur stocks to cleaner-burning ultra-low sulfur distillate. DOE used the proceeds of the sale to purchase ultra-low sulfur distillate for the reserve for a reduced reserve of one million barrels.

In summer 2014 domestic oil production was at its highest level in more than two decades; the United States overtook Russia and Saudi Arabia as the world's leading producer of oil and natural gas. The boom in domestic oil production followed technological advances in hydraulic fracturing (fracking), which made it economically viable to extract oil from shale. Saudi Arabia increased exports, which resulted in drastic drops in oil on the world market. In a matter of months, oil dropped from more than $100 a barrel to less than $50 a barrel.

■ KEY PERSONNEL

Assistant Secretary
    Christopher A. Smith . . . . (202) 586–6660
    Principal Deputy Assistant Secretary for Clean Coal and Carbon Management
    Julio Friedmann . . . . (202) 586–6660
    Chief Operating Officer
    Vacant . . . . (202) 586–6600
    Communications
    Vacant . . . . (202) 586–6803
    Budget and Financial Management
    Robert Pafe . . . . (202) 586–4026
    Management and Field Operations
    Alan Perry (acting) . . . . (202) 586–4484
    Environment, Security, Safety, and Health
    Mark Matarrese . . . . (202) 586–0491
Clean Coal and Carbon Management
    David Mohler . . . . (202) 586–1650
    Advanced Fossil Technology Systems
    Darren Mollot . . . . (202) 586–6837
    Clean Energy Research
    Sam Tam . . . . (301) 903–9699
    Strategic Planning and Global Engagement
    Jarad Daniels . . . . (202) 586–7355
Oil and Natural Gas
    Paula Gant . . . . (202) 586–9684
    Oil and Gas Resources
    Guido DeHoratiis . . . . (202) 586–7296
    Oil and Gas Global Security and Supply
    John Anderson
Petroleum Reserves
    Robert Corbin . . . . (202) 586–9460

Economic Planning, Policy, and Finance
    Rick Hoffman . . . . (202) 586–4401
Management and Administration
    Shenee Meredith . . . . 202) 586–4669
Operations and Readiness
    Patrick Willging (acting) . . . . (202) 586–4692
Planning and Engineering
    Wayne Elias . . . . (202) 586–1533
Reserve Lands Management
    Wayne Elias (acting) . . . . (202) 586–1533

■ INFORMATION SOURCES

Internet
    Agency website: http://energy.gov/fe/office-fossil-energy Includes information on offices and activities, speeches and events, scientific and technical reports, and budgets.

Telephone Contacts
    Personnel Locator . . . . (202) 586–5000
    Federal Relay Service TTY . . . . (800) 877–8339

Information and Publications

KEY OFFICES

Fossil Energy Office of Communications
    1000 Independence Ave. S.W., #4G-085
    Washington, DC 20585
    (202) 586–5616
    Jenny Hakun, media contact

Handles questions from the public and media about fossil energy issues.

Freedom of Information
    DOE Freedom of Information Reading Room
    1000 Independence Ave. S.W.,
    Washington, DC 20585
    (202) 586–5955
    Kevin Hagerty, FOIA public liaison

The FOI Reading Room is open from 9:00 a.m. to 4:00 p.m. Visitors are required to arrange for a DOE escort to use the Reading Room.

DATA AND STATISTICS
    See the website for databases and statistics for each project area; data and statistics for projects are also available by state.

Office of Communications and Public Affairs
    Energy Information Administration
    1000 Independence Ave. S.W., #1E-210
    Washington, DC 20585
    (202) 6537
    TTY (202) 586–0114
    Gina Pearson, assistant administrator

E-mail: InfoCtr@eia.gov
Internet: www.eia.gov

The Energy Information Administration (EIA), which was created in 1977 as the DOE's independent statistical and analytical agency, collects and publishes data; prepares analyses on energy production, consumption, prices, and resources; and makes energy supply and demand projections. For more information, visit the website: www.eia.gov.

PUBLICATIONS

Publications are available on the website and from specific offices.

Reference Resources

LIBRARY

Energy Department Electronic Library

Email: Forrestal.Library@hq.doe.gov
Courtney L. Byrd, supervisor
(202) 586–6021
E-mail: lashawn.byrd@hq.doe.gov

DOE publications and databases are available on the website.

DOCKETS

Natural Gas Docket Room

1000 Independence Ave. S.W., #3E-042
Washington, DC 20585
(202) 586–9478
Larine Moore, manager
Hours: 8:00 a.m. to 4:30 p.m.

Federal dockets are also available at http://energy.gov/fe/services/natural-gas-regulation or at www.regulations.gov. (*See appendix for Searching and Commenting on Regulations: Regulations.gov.*)

RULES AND REGULATIONS

Fossil Energy rules and regulations are published in the *Code of Federal Regulations,* Title 10, Chapter II, Parts 205, 500–516, and 590. Proposed regulations, new final regulations, and updates to the *Code of Federal Regulations* are published in the daily *Federal Register.* (*See appendix for details on how to obtain and use these publications.*) These are also available at www.regulations.gov (*see appendix*).

▦ LEGISLATION

Fossil Energy carries out its responsibilities under:

Federal Power Act, as amended (49 Stat. 839, 16 U.S.C. 824a(e)). Signed by the president Aug. 26, 1935. Required any person desiring to transmit any electric energy from the United States to a foreign country to obtain an authorizing order from the Federal Power Commission.

Natural Gas Act (52 Stat. 822, 15 U.S.C. 717b). Signed by the president June 21, 1938. Required any person desiring to export any natural gas from the United States to a foreign country or to import any natural gas from a foreign country to the United States to obtain an authorizing order from the Federal Power Commission.

Executive Order 10485. Issued by the president Sept. 3, 1953. Empowered the Federal Power Commission to receive and approve all applications of permits for facilities to transmit electric energy or natural gas between the United States and a foreign country provided that the construction and operation of such facility is in the public interest.

Energy Supply and Environmental Coordination Act of 1974, as amended (88 Stat. 246, 15 U.S.C. 791). Signed by the president June 22, 1974. To encourage the use of coal and alternative fuels instead of petroleum and natural gas, this act required the Federal Energy Administration to prohibit certain existing power plants from using petroleum and natural gas as primary energy sources.

Energy Policy and Conservation Act (89 Stat. 881, 42 U.S.C. 6231). Signed by the president Dec. 22, 1975. Authorized the creation of the Strategic Petroleum Reserve to reduce the disruptions in petroleum supplies and to carry out the obligations of the United States in the event of a national emergency.

Naval Petroleum Reserves Production Act of 1976 (90 Stat. 303, 42 U.S.C. 6501 note). Signed by the president April 5, 1976. Directed that the reserves be produced at their maximum efficient rates of production for six years with a provision that the president could extend production in three-year increments if continued production was determined to be in the national interest.

Department of Energy Organization Act (91 Stat. 566, 42 U.S.C. 7101 note). Signed by the president Aug. 4, 1977. Established the DOE within the executive branch.

Executive Order 12038. Issued by the president Feb. 7, 1978. Transferred responsibilities of the Federal Energy Administration and the Federal Power Commission to the DOE.

Power Plant and Industrial Fuel Use Act of 1978 (92 Stat. 3289, 42 U.S.C. 8301 et seq.). Signed by the president Nov. 9, 1978. Prohibited the use of petroleum and natural gas by power plants and major fuel-burning installations. Much of the act was repealed by the **1987 Amendments** (101 Stat. 310, 42 U.S.C. 8301 et seq.). Signed by the president May 21, 1987. The amendments limited the act's application to new baseload power plants that generate electricity for resale. Currently, no new electric power plant may be operated as a baseload power plant without the capability to use coal or another alternate fuel as a primary energy source. The act was amended again by the **Omnibus Budget Reconciliation Act of 1981** (95 Stat. 614, 42 U.S.C. 8341). Signed by the president Aug. 13, 1981. Required the DOE to monitor natural gas consumption by every U.S. electric utility and to publish biannual summaries.

Public Utility Regulatory Policies Act of 1978 (PURPA) (92 Stat. 3117, 16 U.S.C. 2601 note). Signed by the president Nov. 9, 1978. Required annual reports to Congress on the rate-reform initiatives of state regulatory commissions and nonregulated utilities.

Energy Policy Act of 1992 (106 Stat. 2775, 42 U.S.C. 13201 note). Signed by the president Oct. 24, 1992. Set strategy for economic growth and national security by promoting the conservation and efficient use of energy along with increased domestic production.

Energy Policy Act of 2000 (114 Stat. 2029, 42 U.S.C. 6201 note). Signed by the president Nov. 9, 2000. Reauthorized a program under the Energy Policy and Conservation Act that provided for continued operation of U.S. strategic petroleum reserves. Established the Northeast Home Heating Oil Reserve.

Energy Policy Act of 2005 (119 Stat. 594, 42 U.S.C. 15801 note). Signed by the president Aug. 8, 2005. Established long-range, comprehensive national energy policies. Provided incentives for increased domestic oil and natural gas production. Funded coal research, including methods for improving existing plants but also new technologies such as gasification and sequestration. Authorized a clean-coal technology program, which aimed at developing clean-coal technologies that reduce pollutants such as carbon dioxide, mercury, and sulfur dioxide.

Strategic Petroleum Reserve Fill Suspension and Consumer Protection Act of 2008 (122 Stat. 879). Signed by the president May 19, 2008. Temporarily suspended petroleum acquisition for the Strategic Petroleum Reserve (SPR) from May 19 to Dec. 31, 2008 (or until crude oil prices fell below $75 per barrel for more than ninety days) because of historically high consumer fuel prices.

▣ FIELD OFFICES

NATIONAL ENERGY TECHNOLOGY LABORATORY

Albany Research Center

1450 Queen Ave. S.W.
Albany, OR 97312–2198
(541) 967–5892
Cynthia Powell, director

Arctic Energy Office

420 L St., #305
Anchorage, AK 99501
(907) 271–3618
E-mail: joel.lindstrom@contr.netl.doe.gov
Jared Ciferno, regional director

Houston Office

13131 Dairy Ashford Rd., #225
Sugar Land, TX 77478
(412) 386–6023
Anthony V. Cugini, director

Morgantown Center

3610 Collins Ferry Rd.
P.O. Box 880
Morgantown, WV 26507–0880
(412) 386–6023
Cynthia Powell, director

Pittsburgh Center

626 Cochrans Mill Rd.
P.O. Box 10940
Pittsburgh, PA 15236–0940
(412) 386–6023
Cynthia Powell, director

ROCKY MOUNTAIN OILFIELD TESTING CENTER

907 N. Poplar, #150
Casper, WY 82601
(307) 233–4800
(888) 599–2200
Clarke D. Turner, director

STRATEGIC PETROLEUM RESERVE PROJECT MANAGEMENT OFFICE

900 Commerce Rd. East
New Orleans, LA 70123
(504) 734–4200
William C. Gibson Jr., project manager

Health and Human Services Department

200 Independence Ave. S.W., Washington, DC 20201
Internet: www.hhs.gov

Administration for Children and Families

370 L'Enfant Promenade S.W., Washington, DC 20447
Internet: www.acf.hhs.gov

The Administration for Children and Families (ACF), within the Department of Health and Human Services, is responsible for federal programs that promote the economic and social well-being of families, children, individuals, and communities. Originally created by the secretary of Health and Human Services (HHS) in 1986 as the Family Support Administration (FSA), the ACF was created when the FSA merged with the Office of Human Development Services in 1991.

Office of Family Assistance

The most prominent division of the ACF, the Office of Family Assistance (OFA), is the principal agency designated to carry out the federal programs that provide temporary financial assistance to needy families with dependent children. This office saw its mission transformed by the Personal Responsibility and Work Opportunity Reconciliation Act of 1996, commonly known as the welfare reform bill. The law replaced the Aid to Families with Dependent Children (AFDC), which had provided direct cash assistance to families, with Temporary Assistance for Needy Families (TANF), block grants to states, territories and tribes. States, territorie, and tribes use TANF funds to provide cash assistance to families with children in accordance with federal regulations.

Welfare reform placed conditions upon recipients regarding work requirements, denied most federal benefits to noncitizen legal immigrants as well as to both legal and illegal aliens, and placed a lifetime limit of five cumulative years of cash assistance for each family. The legislation also provided for stronger child support enforcement through a computer registry of child support cases against which employers must check new hires.

The Deficit Reduction Act (DRA) of 2005 reauthorized TANF through fiscal year 2010 and made changes to work activity requirements for TANF eligibility. DRA provided for a state penalty for failure to establish or comply with work participation verification procedures. In 2008 the ACF reported that since welfare reform had become law in 1996, welfare rolls for families had declined by 62 percent.

The economic meltdown that began in 2008 resulted in an increase in unemployment and subsequent requests for TANF benefits. The American Recovery and Reinvestment Act (ARRA) established the Emergency Contingency Fund for State TANF programs. ARRA provided up to $5 billion to help states, territories, and tribes that had an increase in assistance caseloads and basic assistance expenditures, or in expenditures related to short-term benefits or subsidized employment.

OFA also administers the Native Employment Works (NEW) program, the Healthy Marriage and Responsible Fatherhood discretionary grant program, the Tribal TANF-Child Welfare Coordination discretionary grant program, and the Health Profession Opportunities discretionary grant program.

Other ACF Programs

The ACF also performs its regulatory responsibilities through the following offices:

Community Services. This office is responsible for the distribution of Community Services Block Grants, which are used to provide services to local communities to assist low-income persons, including the elderly. It also administers the Social Service Block Grant program and carries out the Low Income Home Energy Assistance Program (LIHEAP) to assist low-income households in meeting the costs of home energy.

Child Support Enforcement. This office administers the program to ensure that children are supported by their parents. It locates absent parents, establishes paternity when necessary, establishes child support obligations, and enforces child support orders. The 1996 law required states to establish a computerized registry of child support orders and a registry of new hires by employers (to verify compliance with child support responsibilities). The law authorized states to suspend driver's licenses and professional licenses of deadbeat parents. The law also provides for centralized collection and disbursement of payments within states.

Refugee Resettlement. This office helps refugees achieve economic self-sufficiency within the shortest time possible. It provides a comprehensive program of cash, medical assistance, and social services. Unlike other noncitizens, refugees and those granted asylum are exempted from restrictions on welfare benefits. Victims of human trafficking also are eligible for benefits. Unaccompanied children apprehended by the Department of Homeland Security immigration officials are transferred to the care and custody of Office of Refuge Settlement.

Administration on Children, Youth, and Families (ACYF). ACYF is responsible for several programs that affect the well-being of low-income children and their families. ACYF is divided into two bureaus, each of which is responsible for different issues involving children, youth, and families, and a cross-cutting unit responsible for research and evaluation: Children's Bureau and Family and Youth Services Bureau. The Children's Bureau provides grants to states, tribes, and communities to operate a range of child welfare services including child protective services (child abuse and neglect), family preservation and support, foster care, adoption, and independent living. The Family and Youth Services Bureau assists at-risk youth, particularly runaway and homeless youth. Most of the federal child care and family preservation programs are administered through the block grants to states.

Administration for Native Americans. This office promotes social and economic self-sufficiency of Native Americans, Alaska Natives, Native Hawaiians, and other Native American Pacific Islanders, including Native Samoans. Assistance is provided through discretionary grant funding for community-based projects and training and technical assistance to eligible tribes and native organizations.

Early Childhood Development (ECD). ECD promotes a joint approach to improving the availability of high-quality early learning and development programs. This office includes the Office of Head Start, the Office of Child Care, and the Interagency Team. ECD coordinates with other federal agencies, state and tribal councils and administrators, and national organizations and nonprofit partners to deliver early childhood learning and development services. ECD administers grant funding for the Maternal, Infant, and Early Childhood Home Visiting Programs established by the Patient Protection and Affordable Care Act. In FY 2014, states reported serving approximately 115,500 parents and children.

Office of Child Care. This office supports low-income working families through child care financial assistance and promotes children's learning by improving the quality of early care and education and after-school programs.

Office of Head Start. Head Start promotes school readiness for children, ages three to five, in low-income families by offering educational, nutritional, health, social, and other services. Early Head Start provides support to low-income infants, toddlers, pregnant women, and their families. The Office of Head Start (OHS) provides grants to local public and private nonprofit and for-profit agencies to provide Head Start and Early Head Start services.

Human Services Emergency Preparedness and Response (HSEPR). In emergency preparedness, response, and recovery, HSEPR works in partnership with the ACF Immediate Offices of the Regional Administrators in the ten HHS regions. HSEPR and the Immediate Office of the Regional Administrators provide technical assistance and support to state, grantees, local, tribal, and territorial governments in their preparedness planning efforts.

▓ KEY PERSONNEL

Assistant Secretary
 Mark Greenberg (acting) . . . . (202) 401–5383

Deputy Assistant Secretary, External Affairs
 Marianne McMullen. . . . . (202) 401–1822
Deputy Assistant Secretary, Administration
 Robert Noonan . . . . (202) 401–9238
Deputy Assistant Secretary and Interdepartmental Liaison, Early Childhood Development
 Linda K. Smith . . . . (202) 401–9204
Administration on Children, Youth, and Families
 (1250 Maryland Ave. S.W., Washington, DC 20024; Mailing address: 370 L'Enfant Promenade S.W., Washington, DC 20447)
 Commissioner
  Bryan Samuels. . . . . (202) 205–8347
  Fax. . . . . (202) 205–9721
 Children's Bureau
  JooYeun Chang . . . . (202) 205–8618
   E-mail: info@childwelfare.gov
 Child Abuse and Neglect
  Catherine Nolan . . . . (202) 260–5140
 Family and Youth Services Bureau
  William Bentley. . . . . (202) 205–2360
Administration for Native Americans
Commissioner
 Lillian Sparks Robinson . . . . (202) 690–7776
  Toll-free . . . . (877) 922–9262
  E-mail: anacomments@acf.hhs.gov
Child Care
 Rachel Schumaker. . . . . (202) 401–6984
Child Support Enforcement
 Vicki Turetsky . . . . (202) 401–9368
Community Services
 Jeannie Chaffin . . . . (202) 401–9333
Early Childhood Development
Deputy Assistant Secretary and Interdepartmental Liaison
 Linda K. Smith. . . . . (202) 401–9204
Family Assistance
 Nisha Patel . . . . (202) 401–9275
TANF (Temporary Assistance for Needy Families) Bureau
 Nisha Patel . . . . (202) 401–9275
Head Start
 Blanca Enriquez. . . . . (202) 205–8573
Human Services Emergency Preparedness Response
 Capt. Mary Riley . . . . (202) 401–9306
Legislative Affairs and Budget
 Matthew McKearn . . . . (202) 401–9222
Planning, Research, and Evaluation
 Naomi Goldstein . . . . (202) 401–9220
Refugee Resettlement
 Robert (Bob) Carey. . . . . (202) 401–9246
Regional Operations
 James Murray (acting) . . . . (202) 401–4802

▓ INFORMATION SOURCES

Internet
 Agency website: www.acf.hhs.gov. Includes information about ACF programs and administrative services, as well as links to child support information from various states.

Telephone Contacts

Child Abuse Hotline . . . .(800) 4-A-CHILD
. . . .(800) 422–4453
Child Care Aware . . . .(800) 424–2246
Missing and Exploited Children . . . (800) THE-LOST
. . . .(800) 843–5678
Domestic Violence Hotline . . . . (800) 799–SAFE
. . . .(800) 799–7233
TTY . . . .(800) 787–3224
National Human Trafficking
Resource Center . . . .(888) 373–7888
National Runaway Safeline . . . . (800) RUN-AWAY
. . . . (800) 786–2929

Information and Publications

KEY OFFICES

ACF Public Affairs

370 L'Enfant Promenade S.W.
Washington, DC 20447
(202) 401–9215
Kenneth Wolfe, deputy director

Handles or refers general inquiries about ACF programs.

DATA AND STATISTICS

Requests can be referred by ACF Public Affairs. Statistics are available via the agency's website.

PUBLICATIONS

Fact sheets, the annual report, studies, publications, and a FOIA electronic reading room are available on the agency's website.

DOCKETS

Federal dockets are available at www.regulations.gov. (*See appendix for Searching and Commenting on Regulations: Regulations.gov.*)

RULES AND REGULATIONS

ACF rules and regulations are published in the *Code of Federal Regulations,* Title 45, Chapter II, Parts 200–299; Title 45, Chapter III, Parts 300–399; Title 45, Chapter IV, Parts 400–499; Title 45, Chapter X, Parts 1000–1099. Proposed regulations, new final regulations, and updates to the *Code of Federal Regulations* are published in the daily *Federal Register.* (*See appendix for details on how to obtain and use these publications.*) The *Federal Register* and the *Code of Federal Regulations* may be accessed online at www.archives.gov/federal-register/cfr; the site contains a link to the federal government's regulatory website at www.regulations.gov (*see appendix*).

■ LEGISLATION

The ACF carries out its responsibilities under the following major laws:

Social Security Act, Title IV (49 Stat. 627, 42 U.S.C. 601). Signed by the president Aug. 14, 1935. Established the Aid to Families with Dependent Children (AFDC) program. Amendments over the years both expanded and restricted benefits available to various categories of recipients. This legislation and its amendments also provided for most other programs administered by the ACF.

Immigration and Nationality Act, as amended (66 Stat. 163, 8 U.S.C. 1101). Signed by the president June 27, 1952. Contained virtually all of the law relating to the entry of aliens and to the acquisition and loss of U.S. citizenship.

Refugee Act of 1980 (94 Stat. 102, 8 U.S.C. 1101 note). Signed by the president March 17, 1980. Established the Office of Refugee Resettlement within the Department of Health and Human Services.

Child Care and Development Block Grant Act of 1990 (104 Stat. 1388–236, 42 U.S.C. 9801 note). Signed by the president Nov. 5, 1990. Established the child care block grants to states to allow for subsidized child care for low-income families.

Personal Responsibility and Work Opportunity Reconciliation Act of 1996 (42 U.S.C. 1305 note). Signed by the president Aug. 22, 1996. Overhauled the AFDC program, replacing it with Temporary Assistance for Needy Families (TANF). Established time limits and work requirements for receipt of welfare assistance. Shifted funding of welfare to block grants to states. Required states to establish welfare plans by July 1, 1997. Strengthened enforcement of child support payments.

Child Abuse Prevention and Enforcement Act (114 Stat. 35, 42 U.S.C. 3711 note). Signed by the president March 10, 2000. Amended the Crime Identification Technology Act of 1998 to authorize the use of funds to upgrade the capability of the criminal justice system to deliver timely and accurate criminal record information to child welfare agencies and programs related to the protection of children, including protection against child sexual abuse and placement of children in foster care.

Strengthening Abuse and Neglect Courts Act of 2000 (114 Stat. 1266, 42 U.S.C. 670 note). Signed by the president Oct. 17, 2000. Directed the attorney general to award grants to help improve the data collection and case-tracking systems of state and local abuse and neglect courts.

Trafficking Victims Protection Act of 2000 (114 Stat. 1466, 22 U.S.C. 7101 note). Signed by the president Oct. 28, 2000. Allowed victims of a severe form of trafficking in persons to be eligible for federally funded or administered benefits and services to the same extent as refugees.

Homeland Security Act of 2002 (116 Stat. 2202, 6 U.S.C. 279). Signed by the president Nov. 25, 2002. Transferred responsibilities for the care and placement of unaccompanied children from the Commissioner of the Immigration and Naturalization Service to the Director of the Office of Refugee Resettlement within the Department of Health and Human Services.

Victims Protection Reauthorization Act of 2003 (117 Stat. 2875, 22 U.S.C. 7101 note). Signed by the president Dec. 19, 2003. Amended the Trafficking Victims Protection Act to extend to nonimmigrant alien family members the same benefits and services available to a trafficking victim.

Deficit Reduction Act of 2005 (120 Stat. 4, 42 U.S.C. 1305 note). Signed by the president Feb. 8, 2006. Reauthorized TANF through fiscal year 2010. Provided for a state penalty for failure to establish or comply with work participation verification procedures. Expanded the use of Federal Tax Refund Offset to more child support cases. Ended federal matching of state spending of federal child support incentive payments. Provides funding for healthy marriage promotion and fatherhood programs.

Improving Head Start for School Readiness Act of 2007 (121 Stat. 1363, 42 U.S.C. 9801 note). Signed by the president Dec. 12, 2007. Altered rules regarding eligible Head Start program participants (allows homeless children to participate). Revised Head Start quality standards and monitoring requirements. Prioritized expansion for Early Head Start, which serves children from birth to age three.

American Recovery and Reinvestment Act of 2009 (123 Stat. 115, 26 U.S.C. 1 note). Signed by the president Feb. 17, 2009. Established the Emergency Contingency Fund for State TANF programs. Temporarily reversed a provision in the Deficit Reduction Act of 2005 that ended the practice of providing federal matching funds for the state expenditure of child support incentive payments.

Patient Protection and Affordable Care Act (124 Stat. 119, 42 U.S.C. 18001 note). Signed by the president March 23, 2010. Amends SSA title V (Maternal and Child Health Services) to direct the secretary to make grants to eligible entities for early childhood home visitation programs.

■ REGIONAL OFFICES

While the Administration for Children and Families maintains the following offices, a list of regional offices that serve all HHS agencies is also provided on p. 632.

REGION 1
(CT, MA, ME, NH, RI, VT)
John F. Kennedy Federal Bldg., #2000
Boston, MA 02203
(617) 565–1020
E-mail: ACF.region1@acf.hhs.gov
Mary Ann Higgins, regional administrator

REGION 2
(NJ, NY, PR, VI)
26 Federal Plaza, #4114
New York, NY 10278
(212) 264–2890
Joyce A. Thomas, regional administrator

REGION 3
(DC, DE, MD, PA, VA, WV)
150 S. Independence Mall West, #864

Philadelphia, PA 19106
(215) 861–4000
Essey Workie, regional administrator

REGION 4
(AL, FL, GA, KY, MS, NC, SC, TN)
61 Forsyth St. S.W., #4M60
Atlanta, GA 30303–8909
(404) 562–2800
Carlis V. Williams, regional administrator

REGION 5
(IL, IN, MI, MN, OH, WI)
233 N. Michigan Ave., #400
Chicago, IL 60601–5519
(312) 353–4237
Kathie Gray (acting), regional administrator

REGION 6
(AR, LA, NM, OK, TX)
1301 Young St., #914
Dallas, TX 75202–5433
(214) 767–9648
E-mail: dallas@acf.hhs.gov
Leon R. McCowan, regional administrator

REGION 7
(IA, KS, MO, NE)
601 E. 12th St., #349
Kansas City, MO 64106–2808
(816) 426–3981
Nancy Thoma Groetken (acting), regional administrator

REGION 8
(CO, MT, ND, SD, UT, WY)
999 18th St., South Terrace, #499
Denver, CO 80202
(303) 844–3100
E-mail: region8@acf.hhs.gov
Thomas F. Sullivan, regional administrator

REGION 9
(AS, AZ, CA, GU, HI, NV, other
    Pacific Islands)
90 7th St., 9th Floor
San Francisco, CA 94103
(415) 437–8400
Robert E. (Bob) Garcia, regional administrator

REGION 10
(AK, ID, OR, WA)
2201 6th Ave., #300
Seattle, WA 98121
(206) 615–2547
Cathy Adams-Bomar, regional administrator

Centers for Medicare and Medicaid Services

7500 Security Blvd., Baltimore, MD 21244
Internet: www.cms.gov

The Centers for Medicare and Medicaid Services (CMS) are responsible for oversight of the Medicare program, the federal portion of the Medicaid program, and related federal medical care quality control activities. Originally created as the Health Care Financing Administration in 1977, the administration of President George W. Bush renamed the agency as the CMS on July 1, 2001.

In October 2001 the CMS launched its toll-free phone number (800-633–4227), which provides service to beneficiaries twenty-four hours a day, seven days a week. The CMS also launched a national media campaign to give seniors and other Medicare beneficiaries more information about their Medicare and Medicaid benefits.

Medicare helps pay hospital and supplementary medical bills for people aged sixty-five or older. Medicare also pays for medical services for persons with permanent kidney failure or persons who have been Social Security or Railroad Retirement Board disability beneficiaries for more than two years.

The Medicare Prescription Drug, Improvement, and Modernization Act of 2003 created a voluntary prescription drug benefit program (Part D) for all individuals eligible for Medicare, under which participants pay a monthly premium for coverage in helping purchase prescription drugs.

In July 2008 Congress enacted the Medicare Improvements for Patients and Providers Act of 2008 over the president's veto. The legislation extended programs for low-income Medicare beneficiaries. The bill also provides Medicare mental health parity by phasing in reduced patient copayments for mental health care over a six-year period.

Medicaid, enacted in 1965 through amendments to the Social Security Act, is a health and long-term care coverage program that is jointly financed by states and the federal government. The federal government's portion is determined under a statutory formula known as the Federal Medical Assistance Percentage (FMAP). The FMAP varies by state according to respective per capita income levels. A state with lower income rates receives a more generous portion of federal assistance. The average FMAP is 57 percent.

Each state establishes and administers its own Medicaid program and determines the type, amount, duration, and scope of services covered within broad federal guidelines. States must cover certain mandatory benefits and may choose to provide other optional benefits.

CMS also administers the Children's Health Insurance Program (CHIP), which provides health coverage to nearly 8 million children in families with incomes too high to qualify for Medicaid, but who can't afford private coverage. Signed into law in 1997, CHIP provides federal matching funds to states to provide this coverage.

CMS also regulates all laboratory testing (except research) performed on humans through the Clinical Laboratory Improvement Amendments (CLIA). CLIA covers approximately 200,000 laboratory entities to ensure compliance with accepted laboratory testing standards.

The CMS has several offices dedicated to client service:

The Center for Medicare Management focuses on the management of the traditional fee-for-service Medicare program, including development and implementation of payment policy and management of the Medicare carriers and fiscal intermediaries.

The Center for Medicaid and CHIP Services implements and evaluates policies and operations relating to Medicaid, the State Children's Health Insurance Program (CHIP), and survey and certification.

The Center for Consumer Information and Insurance Oversight develops and implements policies and rules governing state-based exchanges; implements, monitors compliance with, and enforces the new rules governing the insurance market such as the prohibition on rescissions and on pre-existing condition exclusions for children.

The Center for Clinical Standards and Quality coordinates quality, clinical, and medical science issues and policies for the agency's programs and monitors the quality of Medicare, Medicaid, and Clinical Laboratory Improvement Amendments (CLIA).

The Medicare-Medicaid Coordination Office manages integration of benefits under Medicare and Medicaid for individuals eligible for both programs and manages coordination between the federal government and states in the delivery of benefits. The office also performs policy and program analysis of federal and state statutes, policies, rules, and regulations impacting the dual eligible population.

Health Care Reform

In March 2010 President Barack Obama signed the Patient Protection and Affordable Care Act (ACA). The legislation sought to reform the health insurance industry through a wide variety of changes and to allow access to health insurance to a majority of the 50 million uninsured Americans. The wide-ranging legislation was designed to be implemented in stages, with most provisions implemented by 2014.

Some key provisions include:

▪ Allows young adults to stay on their parent's plan until they turn twenty-six years old unless their employers offer an insurance plan (effective 2010).

▪ Provides small businesses with a tax credit to provide coverage (effective 2010).

▪ Prohibits health insurance companies from rescinding insurance (effective for health plan years beginning on or after September 23, 2010).

▪ Prohibits insurance companies from imposing lifetime dollar limits on essential benefits and regulates annual limits (effective for health plan years beginning on or after September 23, 2010).

▪ Provides consumers with a way to appeal coverage determinations or claims to their insurance company, and establishes an external review process (effective 2010).

▪ Provides a 50 percent discount to seniors who reach the coverage gap, when buying Medicare Part D covered brand-name prescription drugs (effective 2011).

▪ Requires that at least 85 percent of all premium dollars collected by insurance companies for large employer plans are spent on health care services and health care quality improvement. For plans sold to individuals and small employers, at least 80 percent of the premium must be spent on benefits and quality improvement. If insurance companies do not meet these goals, because their administrative costs or profits are too high, they must provide rebates to consumers (effective 2011).

▪ Makes changes to student health plans: no pre-existing condition exclusions for students under age nineteen, no lifetime limits on coverage, and no arbitrary rescissions of insurance coverage (effective 2011).

▪ Establishes the Community First Choice Option, which allows states to offer home- and community-based services to disabled individuals through Medicaid rather than institutional care in nursing homes (effective 2011).

▪ Establishes a Hospital Value-Based Purchasing program (VBP) in Medicare. This program offers financial incentives to hospitals to improve the quality of care (effective 2012).

▪ Institutes a series of changes to standardize billing and requires health plans to begin adopting and implementing rules for the secure electronic exchange of health information in order to cut costs and improve quality (effective 2012).

▪ Establishes a system for payment bundling wherein hospitals, doctors, and providers are paid a flat rate for an episode of care rather than the current system where each service or test is billed separately to Medicare (effective 2013).

▪ Requires states to establish health insurance exchanges that provide market-based coverage options for individuals and small businesses. If states do not establish these exchanges, the federal government will administer the program (effective 2014).

▪ Prohibits annual dollar limits on essential benefits for new plans in the individual market and all group plans (effective 2014).

▪ Requires most individuals who can afford it to obtain basic health insurance coverage or pay a penalty (effective 2014).

The Affordable Care Act was passed amid controversy and via partisan voting in Congress. Several states and individuals sued the federal government to prevent the legislation from taking effect, challenging the constitutionality of the law.

One of the more controversial policy issues concerned expanding Medicaid roles. The Affordable Care Act mandated Medicaid coverage for all children and adults with family incomes under 133 percent of the federal poverty level, effective January 1, 2014. This was expected to result in an additional 16 million persons enrolled in Medicaid. Because this program is a shared expense between the federal government and the states, governors from several states were concerned that the costs would strain budgets at a time when nearly every state was running a budget deficit. For many states, Medicaid spending consumed more than 20 percent of state budgets prior to enactment of the Affordable Care Act.

The Affordable Care Act required states to maintain their Medicaid and CHIP eligibility methods, standards, and procedures, or risk losing all of their federal Medicaid matching funds. This maintenance of effort restriction placed a heavier burden on states with more generous programs. However, this requirement was placed in a section of Medicaid law that the secretary of Health and Human Services may waive. The maintenance of effort was required only until the states' insurance exchanges were operational. Some states applied for waivers to circumvent the maintenance of effort requirement. Arizona, a state that allowed coverage for childless adults who earn up to 100 percent of the federal poverty level, petitioned HHS for a waiver to eliminate services to childless adults. Secretary Kathleen Sebelius determined that the state's benefit rules for childless adults, previously established under a waiver set to expire in September 2011, was in place prior to the requirements of the Affordable Care Act and, therefore, not subject to the maintenance of efforts provisions. Secretary Sebelius also notified states that if a state had or was projecting a budget deficit, the maintenance of effort provision would not apply to adults who are not eligible for coverage on the basis of pregnancy or disability and whose incomes are above 133 percent of the federal poverty level.

On October 1, 2013, consumers began applying for health insurance coverage in the health insurance marketplaces. The CMMS online portal, HealthCare.gov, was immediately overwhelmed, and consumers reported long waiting times and system crashes. It was a political setback for the Obama administration, and took two months to fix the problems, and the CMMS had to offer alternative methods of enrollment, including telephone and paper applications. In April 2014 Kathleen Sebelius resigned as secretary.

U.S. Supreme Court and the Affordable Care Act

In June 2012 the U.S. Supreme Court, in a 5–4 vote, upheld most provisions in the Affordable Care Act, ruling that the penalties for not purchasing insurance amounted to a tax and Congress had the authority to levy taxes. The Supreme Court upheld Medicaid expansion, but limited the federal government's ability to penalize noncompliant states by withholding all Medicaid funds. The court found that the ACA created a new Medicaid program for newly eligible adults. This effectively made Medicaid expansion optional rather than mandatory. However, the generous increase in the Federal Medical Assistance Percentage (FMAP), which covers 100 percent of the costs for the newly eligible population for the first three years, provided an incentive for states to expand coverage. The FMAP is gradually reduced to 90 percent. By the end of 2014, 28 states and the District of Columbia had expanded Medicaid coverage.

In June 2014 the U.S. Supreme Court ruled 5–4 in *Burwell v. Hobby Lobby* that some closely held for-profit companies could not be forced to provide contraceptive coverage as mandated under ACA if the company leadership had moral objections. HSS responded by issuing regulations complying with the Supreme Court ruling weeks later, allowing women to obtain coverage directly from the insurer when their employers notified them in writing of their religious objections.

In *King v. Burwell*, four plaintiffs in Virginia who did not want to buy health insurance filed suit, arguing that the law only authorizes subsidies through exchanges established by the state. Supported by financial backing from a libertarian think tank, the plaintiffs challenged a rule issued by the IRS that provided subsidies to low-income consumers in 34 states did not establish their own marketplaces. At the heart of the argument was the wording in the language of the legislation and whether the intent of Congress was to provide subsidies to low-income consumers who purchased only through the state marketplaces or whether the intent was to cover consumers in the federal marketplace as well. In a 5–4 decision on June 25, 2015, the U.S. Supreme Court upheld the ACA subsidies in states that opted to use the federal exchange, preserving insurance coverage for an estimated eight million people who were expected to have lost their insurance coverage if the plaintiffs had prevailed in *King*.

On June 26, 2013, the U.S. Supreme Court ruled Section 3 of the Defense of Marriage Act (DOMA) unconstitutional in *Windsor v. the United States*. Section 3 of DOMA, signed into law in 1996, had defined marriage as a legal union of one man and one woman for the purposes of "any act of Congress . . . any ruling, regulation, or interpretation of the various administrative bureaus and agencies of the United States." The *Windsor* ruling settled the matter of same-sex marriage with regard to federal government laws and regulations, and in the weeks after the *Windsor* ruling, the Justice Department provided guidance to various federal agencies to remove barriers to federal programs for same-sex spouses. Because of this ruling, Medicare is no longer prevented by DOMA from recognizing same-sex marriages for determining entitlement to, or eligibility, for Medicare. Also, beneficiaries in private Medicare plans have access to equal coverage when it comes to care in a nursing home where their same-sex spouse lives.

Same-sex marriage was legalized across the nation on June 26, 2015, in a 5–4 ruling in *Obergefell v. Hodges*, which asked the court to decide whether the Fourteenth Amendment requires states to issue marriage licenses to same-sex couples and whether states are required to recognize same-sex marriages lawfully performed out-of-state. This decision will lead to the further removal of barriers regarding health care coverage for married same-sex couples in the months to come.

■ KEY PERSONNEL

Administrator
Andy Slavitt (acting) . . . . (202) 690–6726
Fax . . . . (202) 690–6262
Principal Deputy Administrator
Patrick Conway (acting) . . . . (202) 690–6301
Center for Clinical Standards and Quality
Patrick Conway . . . . (410) 786–6841
Center for Consumer Information and Insurance Oversight
Kevin Counihan . . . . (301) 492–4400
Center for Medicaid and CHIP Services
Victoria Wachino (acting) . . . . (202) 690–7428
Center for Medicare
Sean Cavanaugh . . . .(202) 690–6301; (410) 786–4164
Fax . . . . (410) 786–0192
Center for Medicare and Medicaid Innovation
Patrick Conway . . . . (410) 786–3316
Actuary
Paul Spitalnic . . . . (410) 786–6374
Acquisition and Grants Management
Daniel Kane . . . . (410) 786–1391
Communications
Lori Lodes . . . . (202) 205–9450
Enterprise Data and Analytics
Niall Brennan . . . . (410) 786–1800
Equal Opportunity and Civil Rights
Anita Pinder . . . . (410) 786–5110
Financial Management
Deborah Taylor . . . . (410) 786–5448
Legislation
Megan O'Reilly . . . . (202) 690–5960
Media Relations
Aaron Albright . . . . (202) 690–6145
Operations Management
Jim Weber . . . . (410) 786–1051
Strategic Operations and Regulatory Affairs
Kathleen Cantwell . . . . (202) 690–8390
Freedom of Information
Hugh Gilmore . . . . (410) 786–5352
Fax . . . . (410) 786–0474

■ INFORMATION SOURCES

Internet

Agency website: www.cms.gov. Includes information about CMS programs and administrative services, as well as links to various stand-alone websites for programs. Information about the Affordable Health Care Act can be found at: www.healthcare.gov. A CMS YouTube channel features a catalog of educational videos on an array of health care–related topics. Two Twitter accounts, @IKNGov and @CMSGov, will tweet breaking news and educational resources.

Telephone Contacts

General Information . . . . (877) 267–2323
TTY General Information . . . . (800) 877–8339
Medicare Service Center . . . . (800) 633–4227
Medicare Service Center TTY . . . . . . (877) 486–2048
Report Medicare Fraud and Abuse . . . (800) 447–8477

Information and Publications

KEY OFFICES

Medicare Ombudsman

7500 Security Blvd.
Baltimore, MD 21244
(800) MEDICARE
(800) 633–4227
Lois Serio, Medicare ombudsman
(202) 690–7418

DATA AND STATISTICS

Information is available from the CMS website as well as from the general Health and Human Services Department site, www.hhs.gov.

PUBLICATIONS

A variety of publications may be accessed on the CMS website, including *Publications for Partners*, a list of publications of interest to partners, such as *Prescription Drug Coverage Basics* and *Protecting Your Choice of Healthcare Providers*. A product ordering website, http://product ordering.cms.hhs.gov, and partnership e-mail updates are also available.

DOCKETS

Federal dockets are available at www.regulations.gov. (*See appendix for Searching and Commenting on Regulations: Regulations.gov.*)

RULES AND REGULATIONS

CMS rules and regulations are published in the *Code of Federal Regulations,* Title 42, Chapter IV, Parts 400–429, Chapter V, Parts 430–end. Proposed regulations, new final regulations, and updates to the *Code of Federal Regulations* are published in the daily *Federal Register. (See appendix for details on how to obtain and use these publications.)* The *Federal Register* and the *Code of Federal Regulations* may be accessed online at www.archives.gov/federal-register/cfr; the site contains a link to the federal government's regulatory website at www.regulations.gov (*see appendix*).

▓ LEGISLATION

Social Security Act Amendments of 1965 (79 Stat. 286, 42 U.S.C. 1305 note). Signed by the president July 30, 1965. Amended SSA: Title XVIII established Medicare to provide medical assistance to the elderly and the disabled. Title XIX requires states to establish Medicaid programs to provide medical assistance to low-income individuals and families.

Medicare-Medicaid Anti-Fraud and Abuse Amendments (91 Stat. 1175, 42 U.S.C. 1305 note). Signed by the president Oct. 25, 1977. Established and provided funding for state Medicaid anti-fraud units to investigate and prosecute Medicaid fraud. HHS, by regulation, shall define those costs that may be charged to the personal funds of patients in skilled nursing facilities who are individuals receiving benefits under the provisions of SSA Title XVIII.

Emergency Medical Treatment and Labor Act (100 Stat. 164, 42 U.S.C. 1395dd). Signed by the president April 7, 1986. Part of the Consolidated Omnibus Budget Reconciliation Act (COBRA). Mandates public access to emergency medical services regardless of citizenship, legal status, or ability to pay.

Health Care Quality Improvement Act of 1986 (100 Stat. 3784, 42 U.S.C. 11101 et seq.). Signed by the president Nov. 14, 1986. Title IV required the secretary of HHS to establish a national health care fraud and abuse data collection program for the reporting of final adverse actions (not including settlements in which no findings of liability have been made) against health care providers, suppliers, or practitioners.

Clinical Laboratory Improvement Amendments (102 Stat. 2903, 42 U.S.C. 201 note). Signed by the president Oct. 31, 1988. Established HHS regulatory authority of clinical laboratory testing over human subjects.

Health Insurance Portability and Accountability Act of 1996 (110 Stat. 1936, 42 U.S.C. 201 note). Signed by the president Aug. 21, 1996. Directed the secretary of health and human services to submit to specified congressional committees detailed recommendations on standards with respect to the privacy of individually identifiable health information. Title II requires the HHS to adopt national standards for electronic health care transactions and national identifiers for providers, health plans, and employers. Established a Medical Savings Account (MSA) pilot program.

Balanced Budget Act of 1997 (111 Stat. 552, 42 U.S.C. 1397aa). Signed by the president Aug. 5, 1997. Amended the Social Security Act to add a new title XXI (State Children's Health Insurance Program) to provide funds to states to expand the provision of child health assistance to uninsured, low-income children.

Medicare Prescription Drug, Improvement, and Modernization Act of 2003 (117 Stat. 2066, 42 U.S.C. 1305 note). Signed by the president December 8, 2003. Provides seniors and individuals with disabilities with a prescription drug benefit. Established health savings accounts.

Deficit Reduction Act of 2005 (120 Stat. 4, 42 U.S.C. 1305 note). Signed by the president Feb. 8, 2006. Makes changes to Medicare payments for various service provider groups, including doctors, hospitals, ambulatory surgical centers, home health care providers, and therapy providers. Makes changes to other fees.

Tax Relief and Health Care Act of 2006 (120 Stat. 2975, 42 U.S.C. 1305 note). Signed by the president

Dec. 20, 2006. Division B, the Medicare Improvements and Extension Act of 2006, directed HHS to establish a quality reporting system and a Physician Assistance and Quality Initiative Fund available for physician payment and quality improvement initiatives. Other provisions.

Medicare Improvements for Patients and Providers Act of 2008 (42 U.S.C. 1305 note). Vetoed by the president July 15, 2008; veto overridden July 15, 2008. Extended programs for low-income Medicare beneficiaries. Provided Medicare mental health parity by phasing in reduced patient copayments for mental health care over a six-year period. Offered financial incentives for Medicare physicians to adopt electronic prescription technology. Prohibited certain marketing activities of Medicare Advantage plans and Part D drug plans.

Patient Protection and Affordable Care Act (124 Stat. 119, 42 U.S.C. 18001 note). Signed by the president March 23, 2010. Made sweeping changes to the health insurance industry regarding products, pricing, and availability. Expanded Medicaid eligibility to all children and adults with family incomes under 133 percent of the federal poverty level, effective January 1, 2014. Mandated that individuals obtain health insurance by 2014 or face a financial penalty.

Health Care and Education Reconciliation Act of 2010 (124 Stat. 1029, 42 U.S.C. 1305 note). Signed by the president March 30, 2010. Amended portions of the Patient Protection and Affordable Care Act, including fees, payments, and deadlines. Set schedules for Medicaid matching rates to states for newly covered populations.

▪ REGIONAL OFFICES

While the Centers for Medicare and Medicaid Services maintain the following offices, a list of regional offices that serve all HHS agencies is also provided on p. 632.

Atlanta
(AL, FL, GA, KY, MS, NC, SC, TN)
Atlanta Federal Center
61 Forsyth St. S.W., #4T20
Atlanta, GA 30303–8909
(404) 562–7150
E-mail: ROATLORA@cms.hhs.gov
David Wright (acting), regional administrator

Boston
(CT, MA, ME, NH, RI, VT)
JFK Federal Bldg. #2325
Boston, MA 02203–0003
(617) 565–1188
E-mail: ROBOSORA@cms.hhs.gov
Raymond Hurd, regional administrator

Chicago
(IL, IN, MI, MN, OH, WI)
233 N. Michigan Ave., #600
Chicago, IL 60601
(312) 886–6432

E-mail: ROCHIORA@cms.hhs.gov
John Hammarlund, regional administrator

Dallas
(AR, LA, NM, OK, TX)
1301 Young St., #714
Dallas, TX 75202
(214) 767–6427
E-mail: RODALORA@cms.hhs.gov
David Wright (acting), regional administrator

Denver
(CO, MT, ND, SD, UT, WY)
1600 Broadway, #700
Denver, CO 80202–4367
(303) 844–7481
E-mail: ROREAORA@cms.hhs.gov
Jeff Hinson, regional administrator

Kansas City
(IA, KS, MO, NB)
601 E. 12th St., #335
Kansas City, MO 64106
(816) 426–5233
E-mail: ROKCMORA@cms.hhs.gov
Jeff Hinson, regional administrator

New York
(NJ, NY, PR, VI)
Jacob K. Javits Federal Bldg.
26 Federal Plaza, #3811
New York, NY 10278–0063
(212) 616–2205
E-mail: ROBOSORA@cms.hhs.gov
Raymond Hurd, regional administrator

Philadelphia
(DC, DE, MD, PA, VA, WV)
The Public Ledger Bldg., #216
150 S. Independence Mall West
Philadelphia, PA 19106
(215) 861–4140
E-mail: ROPHIORA@cms.hhs.gov
Nancy B. O'Connor, regional administrator

San Francisco
(AZ, CA, HI, NV, Pacific Territories)
90 7th St., #5–300
San Francisco, CA 94103–6706
(415) 744–3501
E-mail: ROSFOORA@cms.hhs.gov
David Sayen, regional administrator

Seattle
(AK, ID, OR, WA)
2201 6th Ave., #801
Seattle, WA 98121
(206) 615–2306
E-mail: ROSEA_ORA2@cms.hhs.gov
John Hammarlund, regional administrator

Office for Civil Rights

200 Independence Ave. S.W., Washington, DC 20201
Internet: www.hhs.gov/ocr/office

The Office for Civil Rights (OCR) in the Department of Health and Human Services (HHS) is responsible for ensuring, through the enforcement of various civil rights laws and regulations, that the beneficiaries of federal financial assistance provided by HHS receive services and benefits without discrimination. Services and benefits are provided through state agencies, nursing homes, skilled nursing facilities, medical laboratories, hospitals, day care centers, social service agencies, and other providers. OCR teaches health and social service workers about civil rights, health information privacy, and patient safety confidentiality laws that they must follow.

Any person who believes that he or she has been discriminated against in the provision of services because of age, race, color, disability, national origin, religion, or sex may file a complaint with the OCR. Discrimination in the provision of services includes the denial of services, the provision of services in a different manner, segregation in the provision of services, and otherwise providing services and benefits in a manner that treats groups of individuals receiving assistance under the same program differently.

The OCR is under the supervision of a director, who reports to the secretary of HHS. The director is responsible for the overall coordination of the agency's civil rights activities. The director is also the HHS secretary's special assistant for civil rights and serves as the secretary's chief adviser on all departmental civil rights matters. The office comprises policy and procedural staff headquartered in Washington, DC, and local staff in ten regional offices (*addresses below*).

The OCR conducts compliance reviews of institutions that receive HHS funds. These reviews determine whether policies or practices exist that are discriminatory in nature. If the review indicates that probable discrimination exists, the OCR staff notifies the institution in writing, indicating the particular areas of noncompliance, and advising the institution of its responsibility to prepare and submit a plan for correcting the situation. If an institution submits a plan that is unsatisfactory in any respect, the OCR will inform the institution of its deficiency.

If an institution refuses to correct discriminatory practices, the HHS will either initiate proceedings for the termination of the institution's federal financial assistance or refer the matter to the Department of Justice with a recommendation for appropriate legal action.

Termination proceedings begin with an administrative hearing before a federal administrative law judge. The judge's initial decision is subject to review by a departmental reviewing authority. A final appeal may be made to the secretary of HHS. Before becoming effective, termination orders are reported to the congressional committees with authority over the affected funds. Termination orders may be appealed to the U.S. District Court.

OCR has been designated to receive complaints of discrimination based on the Federal Health Care Conscience Protection Statutes, a collection of statutes enacted to protect health care workers from facing discrimination or retaliation if they choose to not provide health care services (such as abortion or sterilization) that conflict with the health care provider's religious or moral views.

Complaints

Any person with a complaint that discrimination exists in any program funded by HHS should notify the OCR. Complaints involving schools, colleges, and universities should be filed with the Department of Education. A written complaint usually should be filed with the regional office that serves the state in which the alleged discrimination occurred. Complaints may also be filed at OCR headquarters office.

Patient Privacy Protection

Recognizing the rapid evolution of health information systems, Congress moved to protect the privacy of health information by passing the Health Insurance Portability and Accountability Act of 1996 (HIPAA). HIPAA's administrative simplification provisions were designed to improve the health care system by facilitating the electronic exchange of information with respect to certain financial and administrative transactions carried out by health plans, health care clearinghouses, and health care providers. To implement these provisions, the statute directed HHS to adopt uniform, national standards for transactions, unique health identifiers, code sets for the data elements of the transactions, security of health information, and electronic signature. HHS issued a final rule on Dec. 28, 2000, establishing "Standards for Privacy of Individually Identifiable Health Information." The OCR is the HHS office responsible for implementing and enforcing the privacy regulation. OCR has six educational programs for health care providers on compliance with various aspects of the HIPAA Privacy and Security Rules. Each of these programs is available with free Continuing Medical Education credits for physicians and Continuing Education credits for health care professionals.

The HIPAA protections give patients greater access to their medical records and more control over how their personal information is used by their health plans and health care providers. Consumers receive a notice explaining how their health plans, doctors, pharmacies, and other health care providers use, disclose, and protect their personal information. In addition, consumers have the ability to see and copy their health records and to request corrections of any errors included in their records. Consumers may file complaints about privacy issues with their health plans or providers or with the OCR.

The Patient Safety and Quality Improvement Act of 2005 (PSQIA) established a voluntary reporting system designed to enhance the data available to assess and resolve patient safety and health care quality issues. PSQIA provides federal privilege and confidentiality protections for patient safety information, called patient safety work product. To implement PSQIA, the DHHS issued the Patient Safety Rule, which became effective on Jan. 19, 2009.

The Health Information Technology for Economic and Clinical Health (HITECH) Act, Title XIII of the American Recovery and Reinvestment Act of 2009, amended HIPPA by allowing patients the right to get a report on who has electronically accessed their protected health information and requiring HIPAA-covered entities and their business associates to provide notification following a breach of unsecured protected health information. In May 2011, HHS opened the rulemaking process to address these provisions. Although covered entities were required by the HIPAA Security Rule to track access to electronic protected health information, they were not required to share this information with patients. The act also requires regulations establishing safeguards for the protection of electronic protected health information to business associates of a covered entity.

In January 2014 HHS issued a Notice of Proposed Rulemaking (NPRM) to modify the HIPAA Privacy Rule to permit certain HIPAA-covered entities to disclose to the National Instant Criminal Background Check System (NICS) the identities of persons prohibited by federal law from possessing or receiving a firearm for reasons related to mental health. NICS helps to ensure that guns are not sold to prohibited possessors, including felons, those convicted of domestic violence, and individuals involuntarily committed to a mental institution.

The proposed rule would give states and certain covered entities flexibility to ensure accurate but limited information is reported to the NICS, which would not include clinical, diagnostic, or other mental health information. Instead, certain covered entities would be permitted to disclose the minimum necessary identifying information about individuals who have been involuntarily committed to a mental institution or otherwise have been determined by a lawful authority to be a danger to themselves or others or to lack the mental capacity

to manage their own affairs. The proposed permission focuses on those entities performing relevant commitments, adjudications, or data repository functions.

In February 2014 HHS announced a final rule amending the Clinical Laboratory Improvement Amendments of 1988 (CLIA) regulations to allow laboratories to give a patient, or a person designated by the patient, access to the patient's completed test reports on the patient's request. The final rule eliminated the exception under the HIPAA Privacy Rule to an individual's right to access his or her protected health information when it is held by a CLIA-certified or CLIA-exempt laboratory. While patients may continue to get access to their laboratory test reports from their doctors, these changes give patients a new option to obtain their test reports directly from the laboratory. The final rule was issued jointly by three agencies within HHS: the Centers for Medicare and Medicaid Services (CMS), which is generally responsible for laboratory regulation under CLIA; the Centers for Disease Control and Prevention (CDC), which provides scientific and technical advice to CMS related to CLIA; and the Office for Civil Rights (OCR), which is responsible for enforcing the HIPAA Privacy Rule.

■ KEY PERSONNEL

Director
    Jocelyn Samuels . . . . (202) 619–0403
Executive Staff Assistant to the Director
    Gwen Irby . . . . (202) 619–0403
Chief of Staff and Senior Advisor
    A.J. Pearlman . . . . (202) 619–0403
General Counsel for Civil Rights
    Edwin Woo . . . . (202) 619–0900
Deputy Director, Civil Rights
    Robinsue Frohboese . . . . (202) 619–0403
Centralized Case Management Operations
    Kurt Temple . . . . (202) 619–0403
**Deputy Director, Planning and Business
Administrative Management**
    Steven Novy . . . . (202) 619–0403
Deputy Director, Health Information Privacy
    Christina Heide (acting) . . . . (202) 619–0403

■ INFORMATION SOURCES

Internet
    Agency website: www.hhs.gov/ocr/office. Features information on regulations and how to file a complaint, the health privacy act (HIPAA), the patient safety and quality improvement act (PSQIA), fact sheets on legal rights of various groups, and frequently asked questions.

Telephone Contacts
    Toll-free . . . . (877) 696–6775
    General Information (recording) . . . . . (800) 368–1019
    TTY . . . . (800) 537–7697
    Fax . . . . (202) 619–3437
    Press Office . . . . (202) 690–6343

Information and Publications

DATA AND STATISTICS

Contact the OCR director's office. Information is available from the OCR website and also from the general Health and Human Services website, www.hhs.gov.

PUBLICATIONS

Contact the OCR director's office for specific publications or to receive information on a regular basis, or sign up on the website to receive regular e-mail news alerts. Publications may also be accessed at www.hhs.gov/news/reports/index.html.

Reference Resources

LIBRARY

The OCR director's office handles reference requests.

DOCKETS

Federal dockets are available at www.regulations.gov. (*See appendix for Searching and Commenting on Regulations: Regulations.gov.*)

RULES AND REGULATIONS

OCR rules and regulations are published in the *Code of Federal Regulations,* Title 45, Chapter I, Parts 80–86. Proposed regulations, new final regulations, and updates to the *Code of Federal Regulations* are published in the daily *Federal Register.* (*See appendix for details on how to obtain and use these publications.*) The *Federal Register* and the *Code of Federal Regulations* may be accessed online at www.archives.gov/federal-register/cfr; the site contains a link to the federal government's regulatory website at www.regulations.gov (*see appendix*).

▪ LEGISLATION

The OCR administers the following laws in full or in part:

Public Health Service Act (42 U.S.C. 201). Signed by the president July 1, 1944. Consolidated existing legislation pertaining to the Public Health Service. Subsequent amendments addressed discrimination in the public health system. Section 1908 prohibited discrimination on the basis of age, race, color, national origin, disability, gender, or religion in programs, services, and activities funded by Preventative Health and Health Services Block Grants. Section 542 barred discrimination in admission or treatment against substance abusers by federally assisted hospitals and outpatient facilities.

Hospital Survey and Construction Act (78 Stat. 447, 42 U.S.C. 291c(e)). Signed by the president Aug. 13, 1946. Also known as the Hill-Burton Act. Ensured that federally assisted hospital or health care facilities provide services to all persons residing in the community without discrimination based on race, color, national origin, or method of payment.

Civil Rights Act of 1964, Title VI (78 Stat. 241, 42 U.S.C. 2000d). Signed by the president July 2, 1964. Prohibited discrimination based on race, color, or national origin in programs receiving federal financial assistance.

Comprehensive Alcohol Abuse and Alcoholism Prevention Treatment and Rehabilitation Act of 1970, Section 321 (84 Stat. 1848, 42 U.S.C. 4581). Signed by the president Dec. 30, 1970. Prohibited hospital discrimination against alcoholics in admissions or treatment solely because of alcohol abuse.

Health Manpower Training Act of 1971, Title VII (84 Stat. 1355, 42 U.S.C. 292d). Signed by the president Nov. 18, 1971. Amended the Public Health Service Act to bar sex discrimination in admissions to health training programs.

Drug Abuse Offense and Treatment Act of 1972 (86 Stat. 65, 21 U.S.C. 1171–1180). Signed by the president March 21, 1972. Prohibited hospitals receiving federal assistance from refusing admission or treatment to anyone needing emergency care solely because that person is dependent on or addicted to drugs.

Education Amendments of 1972, Title IX (86 Stat. 235, 20 U.S.C. 1681–1686). Signed by the president June 23, 1972. Prohibited sex discrimination in federally assisted education programs.

Health Programs Extension Act of 1973, Church Amendments (87 Stat. 9142 U.S.C. 300a-7). Enacted as a conscience clause to protect health care providers, the amendments prohibited any entity receiving federal public health funding from requiring individuals to perform abortion or sterilization procedures if the processes are in conflict with the health care provider's religious or moral convictions.

Rehabilitation Act of 1973, Title V, Section 504 (87 Stat. 355, 29 U.S.C. 701). Signed by the president Sept. 26, 1973. Prohibited discrimination against the handicapped in programs receiving federal financial assistance.

Age Discrimination Act of 1975 (89 Stat. 713, 42 U.S.C. 3001). Signed by the president Nov. 28, 1975. Prohibited discrimination because of age in programs receiving federal financial assistance.

Omnibus Budget Reconciliation Act of 1981 (95 Stat. 357, 31 U.S.C. 1331). Signed by the president Aug. 31, 1981. Established block grant programs to be administered by the HHS secretary. Authorizations for six of the seven grant programs included sex and religion provisions along with the existing nondiscrimination requirements.

Child Abuse Amendments of 1984 (98 Stat. 1761, 42 U.S.C. 10406). Signed by the president Oct. 9, 1984. Extended and improved provisions of laws relating to child abuse, neglect, and adoption. Section 307(a) prohibited discrimination on the basis of age, handicap, sex, race, color, or national origin in participating in programs or receiving funds made available under this act.

Americans with Disabilities Act of 1990 (104 Stat. 327, 42 U.S.C. 12101 et seq.). Signed by the president July 26, 1990. Title II prohibits discrimination based on disability in public entities.

Civil Rights Act of 1991 (105 Stat. 1071, 42 U.S.C. 1981 note). Signed by the president Nov. 21, 1991. Promoted the goals of ridding the workplace of discrimination on the basis of race, color, sex, religion, national origin, and disability.

Multiethnic Placement Act of 1994 (108 Stat. 4056, 42 U.S.C. 1305). Signed by the president Oct. 20, 1994. Prohibited an agency or entity receiving federal assistance that is involved in adoptive or foster care placements from delaying or denying the placement of a child solely on the basis of race, color, or national origin of the adoptive or foster parent, or the child, involved. Permitted consideration of the child's cultural, ethnic, or racial background when such factors are considered in conjunction with other factors, and relevant to the child's best interest.

Health Insurance Portability and Accountability Act of 1996 (110 Stat. 1936, 42 U.S.C. 201 note). Signed by the president Aug. 21, 1996. Directed the secretary of health and human services to submit to specified congressional committees detailed recommendations on standards with respect to the privacy of individually identifiable health information.

Consolidated Appropriations Act of 2005, Weldon Amendment (118 Stat. 3163). Signed by the president December 8, 2004. Section 508(d) of the Labor-HHS Division prohibits federal agencies and programs, and state and local governments that receive federal funding, from discriminating against health care entities because they do not offer abortion services, or provide coverage or referral for abortions.

Patient Safety and Quality Improvement Act of 2005 (119 Stat. 424, 42 U.S.C. 299 et seq.). Signed by the president July 29, 2005. Amended the Public Health Service Act to establish a voluntary reporting system designed to enhance the data available to assess and resolve patient safety and health care quality issues. Provided federal privilege and confidentiality protections for patient safety information.

Genetic Information Nondiscrimination Act of 2008 (122 Stat. 881, 42 U.S.C. 2000ff note). Signed by the president May 21, 2008. Clarifies that genetic information is protected under the HIPAA Privacy Rule and prohibits most health plans from using or disclosing genetic information for underwriting purposes.

Health Information Technology for Economic and Clinical Health (HITECH) Act (123 Stat. 226, 42 U.S.C. 201 note). Signed by the president Feb. 17, 2009. Title XIII of the American Recovery and Reinvestment Act. Amends HIPAA to require regulations establishing safeguards for the protection of electronic protected health information to business associates of a covered entity. Gives individuals a right to an accounting of the disclosures of their electronic health record, including disclosures to carry out treatment, payment, and health care operations.

Patient Protection and Affordable Care Act (124 Stat. 119, 42 U.S.C. 18001 note). Signed by the president March 23, 2010. Prohibits any qualified health plan offered through an exchange from discriminating against any individual health care provider or health care facility because of its unwillingness to provide, pay for, provide coverage of, or refer for abortions.

◼ REGIONAL OFFICES

While the Office for Civil Rights maintains the following offices, a list of regional offices that serve all HHS agencies is also provided on p. 632.

REGION 1
(CT, MA, ME, NH, RI, VT)
John F. Kennedy Federal Bldg., #1875
Boston, MA 02203
(617) 565–1340
TTY (617) 565–1343
Susan Rhodes, regional manager

REGION 2
(NJ, NY, PR, VI)
Jacob Javits Federal Bldg.
26 Federal Plaza, #3312
New York, NY 10278
(212) 264–3313
TTY (800) 537–7697
Linda Colon, regional manager

REGION 3
(DC, DE, MD, PA, VA, WV)
Public Ledger Bldg., #372
150 S. Independence Mall West
Philadelphia, PA 19106–9111
(215) 861–4441
TTY (800) 537–7697
Barbara Holland, regional manager

REGION 4
(AL, FL, GA, KY, MS, NC, SC, TN)
Atlanta Federal Center, #16T70
61 Forsyth St. S.W.
Atlanta, GA 30303–8909
(404) 562–7886
TTY (404) 331–2867
Tim Noonan, regional manager

REGION 5
(IL, IN, MI, MN, OH, WI)
233 North Michigan Ave., #240
Chicago, IL 60601
(312) 886–2359
TTY (312) 353–5893
Art Garcia (acting), regional manager

REGION 6
(AR, LA, NM, OK, TX)
1301 Young St., #1169
Dallas, TX 75202
(214) 767–4056
TTY (214) 767–8940
Vaniecy Nwigwe (acting), regional manager

REGION 7
(IA, KS, MO, NE)
601 E. 12th St., #353

Kansas City, MO 64106
(816) 426–7277
TTY (800) 537–7697
Steven Mitchell (acting), regional manager

REGION 8
(CO, MT, ND, SD, UT, WY)
999 18th St., South Terrace, #417
Denver, CO 80202
(303) 844–2024
TTY (303) 844–3439
Andrea Olliver, regional manager

REGION 9
(AS, AZ, CA, GU, HI, NV)
90 7th St., #4–100

San Francisco, CA 94103
(415) 437–8310
TTY (415) 437–8311
Michael Leoz, regional manager

REGION 10
(AK, ID, OR, WA)
2201 6th Ave.
MS RX–11
Seattle, WA 98121–1831
(206) 615–2290
TTY (206) 615–2296
Linda Yuu Connor, regional manager

Other Health and Human Services Department Offices

ADMINISTRATION FOR COMMUNITY LIVING
One Massachusetts Ave. N.W.
Washington, DC 20201
Internet: www.acl.gov

In 2012 the Department of Health and Human Services (HHS) combined the Administration on Aging, the Office on Disability, and the Administration on Developmental Disabilities into the Administration for Community Living (ACL), a single agency that supports cross-cutting initiatives and efforts focused on the unique needs of individual groups, such as children with developmental disabilities or seniors with dementia. ACL works to increase access to community support and to achieve full community participation for people with disabilities and seniors. Support needs include health care, the availability of appropriate housing, employment, education, and social participation.

ACL administers programs under several authorizing statutes. The Older Americans Act is administered by the Administration on Aging. The Developmental Disabilities Assistance and Bill of Rights Act of 2000 is administered by the Administration on Intellectual and Developmental Disabilities. In addition, ACL is also responsible for administering other authorizing statutes relevant to older Americans and individuals with disabilities.

ACL is headed by an administrator, who reports directly to the secretary. The administrator is also the assistant secretary for aging. In addition to the administrator, the ACL consists of the principal deputy administrator, who also serves as the senior advisor to the secretary on HHS activities relating to disabilities.

ACL is comprised of the following program units:

- Administration on Aging (AoA)
- Administration on Intellectual and Developmental Disabilities (AIDD)
- Center for Disability and Aging Policy (CDAP)
- Center for Consumer Access and Self-Determination (BD)

ACL has ten Regional Support Centers located across the United States.

Administrator
Kathy Greenlee . . . . (202) 401–4634
Principal Deputy Administrator, Administration for Community Living
Sharon Lewis . . . . (202) 401–4634
Deputy Assistant Secretary, Administration on Aging
Edwin L. Walker . . . . (202) 401–4634
Commissioner, Administration on Intellectual and Developmental Disabilities
Aaron Bishop . . . . (202) 401–4634
Deputy Administrator, Center for Consumer Access and Self-Determination
John Wren . . . . (202) 401–4634
Deputy Administrator, Center for Management and Budget
Dan Berger . . . . (202) 357–3419
Administration and Personnel
Terry Nicolosi . . . . (202) 357–3413
American Indian, Alaska Native, and Native Hawaiian Programs
Cynthia LaCounte . . . . (202) 357–0148
Center for Policy and Evaluation
Vicki Gottlich . . . . (202) 401–4634
External Affairs
Christine Phillips . . . . (202) 357–3547
Elder Justice and Adult Protective Services
Vacant . . . . (202) 357–0139
Grants Management
Rimas Liogys . . . . (202) 357–3454
Home and Community Based Services
Greg Case . . . . (202) 357–3442
Independent Living
Jamie Kendall . . . . (202) 357–3421
Integrated Programs
Lori Gerhard . . . . (202) 357–3443
Regional Support Operations
Aviva Sufian . . . . (202) 357–3585

Other Telephone Contacts
Eldercare Locator . . . . (800) 677–1116
Public Inquiries . . . . (202) 619–0724
TTY . . . . (800) 877–8339

■ CENTERS FOR DISEASE CONTROL AND PREVENTION

1600 Clifton Road
Atlanta, GA 30333
Internet: www.cdc.gov

The Centers for Disease Control and Prevention (CDC) is the primary federal agency for conducting and supporting public health activities in the United States. Composed of the Office of the Director, the National Institute for Occupational Safety and Health, and several coordinating centers or offices—including noncommunicable diseases, injury, and environmental health; infectious diseases; global health; surveillance, epidemiology, and laboratory services; state, tribal, local, and territorial support; and public health preparedness and response—CDC has more than 14,000 employees, including more than 280 assignees in fifty-plus countries, with approximately forty staff detailed to international organizations.

The Office of Scientific Integrity leads the agency in protecting the rights and welfare of people who participate in research. This office coordinates CDC's institutional review boards (IRBs), exemptions from human subject research, and joint review arrangements with research partners. The office also is responsible for ensuring compliance with federal laws and principles in the care and use of laboratory animals at CDC. In addition, the office is responsible for establishing newly required oversight and regulatory activities and works with CDC National Centers and other federal agencies to protect the privacy of individuals when records are maintained by a federal agency by applying the Privacy Act as required.

Director
　　Thomas R. Frieden . . . . (404) 639–7000
　　Fax. . . . . (404) 639–7111
Principal Deputy Director
　　Ileana Arias . . . . (404) 639–7000
Associate Director for Communication
　　Katherine Lyon Daniel . . . . (404) 639–7540
Associate Director for Policy
　　John Auerbach. . . . . (404) 639–0600
Associate Director for Program Performance and Evaluation
　　Kathleen E. Ethier . . . . (404) 639–7061
Associate Director for Science
　　Harold Jaffe . . . . (404) 639–7220
Chief Operating Officer
　　Sherri A. Berger. . . . . (404) 639–7000
Chief of Staff
　　Carmen Villar . . . . (404) 639–7000
Diversity Management and Equal Employment Opportunity
　　Reginald Mebane. . . . . (770) 488–3210
Public Health Preparedness and Emergency Response
　　Stephen C. Redd . . . . (404) 639–7405
Scientific Integrity
　　Ron Otten. . . . . (404) 639–7570

Animal Care and Use Program
　　Tim Barrett . . . . (404) 639–4879
Human Research Protection
　　Barbara DeCausey . . . . (404) 639–7570
Information Collection Review
　　Tony Richardson . . . . (404) 639–7570
Infectious Diseases
　　Rima Khabbaz . . . . (404) 639–2100
National Center for Immunization and Respiratory Diseases
　　Anne Schuchat. . . . . (404) 639–8200
National Center for Emerging and Zoonotic Infectious Diseases
　　Beth P. Bell . . . . (404) 639–3967
National Center for HIV, Viral Hepatitis, STD, and TB Prevention
　　Jonathan Mermin . . . . (404) 639–8000
Media Relations
　　Llelwyn Grant . . . . (404) 639–3286
Noncommunicable Diseases, Injury, and Environmental Health
　　Robin Ikeda . . . . (770) 488–0608
National Center on Birth Defects and Developmental Disabilities
　　Coleen Boyle . . . . (404) 498–3800
National Center for Chronic Disease Prevention and Health Promotion
　　Ursula Bauer . . . . (770) 488–5401
National Center for Environmental Health / Agency for Toxic Substances and Disease Registry
　　Patrick Breysse. . . . . (770) 488–0604
National Center for Injury Prevention and Control
　　Debra Houry . . . . (770) 488–4696
Public Health Scientific Services
　　Chesley Richards. . . . . (770) 498–6001
Office of Surveillance, Epidemiology, and Laboratory Services
　　Michael F. Iademarco . . . . (404) 498–6010
National Center for Health Statistics
　　Charles J. Rothwell . . . . (301) 458–4500
State, Tribal, Local, and Territorial Support
　　Judith A. Monroe . . . . (404) 498–0300
Public Health Preparedness and Response
　　Stephen C. Redd . . . . (404) 469–7663
National Institute for Occupational Safety and Health
　　John Howard . . . . (202) 245–0674
Center for Global Health
　　Tom Kenyon. (404) 718–4713

Other Telephone Contacts
　　Information (24 hrs.) . . . . (800) 232–4636
　　TTY. . . . . (888) 232–6348

■ INDIAN HEALTH SERVICE

The Reyes Bldg.
801 Thompson Ave.
Rockville, MD 20852
Internet: www.ihs.gov

The Indian Health Service (IHS) is responsible for providing federal health services to Native Americans and Alaska Natives. The Snyder Act of 1921 was the principal legislation authorizing federal funds for health services to Native American tribes.

Tribes may contract with the IHS through self-determination contracts and annual funding agreements under Title I or self-governance compacts and funding agreements under Title V of the Indian Self-Determination and Education Assistance Act. As of January 2015 the IHS and tribes have negotiated 85 self-governance compacts that are funded through 111 funding agreements with more than 350 federally recognized tribes.

IHS services are administered through a system of twelve area offices and 170 IHS and tribally managed service units, providing health services for approximately 2.2 million Native Americans and Alaska Natives who belong to 566 federally recognized tribes in thirty-five states.

Under its Urban Indian Health Service program, IHS funds thirty-three urban programs in 59 locations, ranging from community health to comprehensive primary health care services. Approximately 60 percent of American Indians and Alaska Natives live in urban areas, with 25 percent of them residing in counties served by urban Indian health programs.

Director
   Robert McSwain (acting) . . . . (301) 443–1083
Deputy Director
   Sandra Pattea . . . . (301) 443–1083
Chief Medical Officer
   Susan V. Karol . . . . (301) 443–1083
Executive Secretariat Staff
   Julie A. Czajkowski . . . . (301) 443–1011
Congressional and Legislative Affairs
   June Tracy (acting) . . . . (301) 443–7261
Clinical and Preventive Services
   Alec Thundercloud . . . . (301) 443–4644
Direct Service and Contracting Tribes
   Chris Buchanan . . . . (301) 443–1104
Diversity Management / Equal Employment Opportunity
   Pauline Bruce . . . . (301) 443–1108
Environmental Health and Engineering
   Gary J. Hartz . . . . (301) 443–1247
Field Operations
   Randy Grinnell . . . . (301) 443–1083
Finance and Accounting
   Kenneth Cannon (acting) . . . . (301) 443–1270
Information Technology
   Mark Rives . . . . (301) 443–0750
Management Operations
   Elizabeth A. Fowler . . . . (301) 443–1083
Management Services
   Terri Schmidt (acting) . . . . (301) 443–6290
Public Affairs
   Constance James . . . . (301) 443–3593
Public Health Support
   Richard Church . . . . (301) 443–0222
Resource Access and Partnerships
   Carl L. Harper . . . . (301) 443–3216

Tribal Self-Governance
   P. Benjamin Smith . . . . (301) 443–7821
Urban Indian Health Programs
   Phyllis S. Wolfe . . . . (301) 443–4680
Regional Offices
   Aberdeen Area
      Ron Cornelius . . . . (605) 226–7581
   Alaska Area
      Christopher Mandregan Jr. . . . . . . (907) 729–3686
   Albuquerque Area
      Leonard Thomas (acting) . . . . (505) 248–8003
   Bemidji Area
      Keith Longie . . . . (218) 444–0452
   Billings Area
      Dorothy Dupree (acting) . . . . (406) 247–7107
   California Area
      Beverly Miller (acting) . . . . (916) 930–3927
   Nashville Area
      Martha Ketcher . . . . (615) 467–1500
   Navajo Area
      John Hubbard Jr . . . . (928) 871–5811
   Oklahoma City Area
      Adm. Kevin Meeks . . . . (405) 951–3774
   Phoenix Area
      Rose Weahkee (acting) . . . . (602) 364–5039
   Portland Area
      Dean Seyler . . . . (503) 414–5555
   Tucson Area
      Dixie Gaikowski . . . . (520) 295–2405

■ OFFICE FOR HUMAN RESEARCH PROTECTIONS
1101 Wootton Parkway, #200
Rockville, MD 20852
Internet: www.hhs.gov/ohrp

The Office for Human Research Protections (OHRP) guides policy for the protection of the rights, welfare, and well-being of subjects involved in biomedical and behavioral research conducted or supported by HHS. OHRP maintains regulatory oversight of applicable research, provides clarification of and guidance on policy, and provides advice on ethical and regulatory issues.

Basic regulations governing the protection of human subjects in research supported or conducted by the Department of Health, Education, and Welfare (now HHS) were first published at 45 *CFR* part 46 in 1974. The current version of the regulations includes five subparts. Subpart A is the basic set of protections for all human subjects of research conducted or supported by HHS (revised in 1981 and 1991, with technical amendments made in 2005). Three of the other subparts provide added protections for specific vulnerable groups of subjects. Subpart B (issued in1975 and most recently revised in 2001) provides additional protections for pregnant women, human fetuses, and neonates involved in research. Subpart C (issued in 1978) provides additional protections pertaining to biomedical and behavioral research involving prisoners as subjects. Subpart D (issued in 1983) provides additional protections for children involved as subjects in research. Subpart E (issued in 2009) requires registration of institutional review boards (IRBs), which conduct review of human research studies conducted or supported by HHS.

OHRP's Division of Compliance Oversight evaluates all suspected incidents of noncompliance with HHS regulations. OHRP asks the institution involved to investigate the allegations and to provide OHRP with a written report of its investigation. OHRP then determines what, if any, regulatory action needs to be taken to protect human research subjects.

OHRP's Division of Education and Development provides guidance to individuals and institutions conducting HHS-supported human subject research; conducts national and regional conferences; participates in professional, academic, and association conferences; and develops and distributes resource materials in an effort to improve protections for human research subjects. OHRP also helps institutions assess and improve their human research protection programs through quality improvement consultations.

OHRP's Division of Policy and Assurances prepares policies and guidance documents and interpretations of requirements for human subject protections and disseminates this information to the research community.

Director
Jerry Menikoff . . . . (240) 453–6900
Compliance Oversight
Kristina Borror . . . . (240) 453–8132
Education and Development
Yvonne Lau . . . . (240) 453–8236
International Activities
Edward Bartlett . . . . (240) 453–8249
Policy and Assurances
Irene Stith-Coleman . . . . (240) 453–8138
Secretary's Advisory Committee on Human Research Protections
Julia Gorey . . . . (240) 453–8141
Other Contacts
Main switchboard . . . . (866) 447–4777
Fax. . . . . (240) 453–6909
Freedom of Information. . . . . (301) 492–4800
Fax. . . . . (301) 492–4848
E-mail: foiarequest@psc.hhs.gov

OFFICE OF GLOBAL HEALTH AFFAIRS
200 Independence Ave. S.W., Room 639H
Washington, DC 20201
Internet: www.globalhealth.gov

The Office of Global Health Affairs (OGHA) develops U.S. policy and strategy positions related to global health issues. The office represents the HHS to other governments, other federal departments and agencies, international organizations, and the private sector on international health issues.

It also provides policy guidance and coordination on refugee health policy issues, in collaboration with the U.S. Public Health Service (PHS), the Office of Refugee Resettlement in the Administration for Children and Families, the State Department, and other agencies. OGHA provides leadership and coordination for bilateral programs with selected countries, such as the U.S.-Russia Biotechnology Engagement Program and U.S.-India Cooperation in Health and Biomedical Research.

The Department of Health and Human Services (HHS) has a range of relationships with most of the world's ministries of health. Multilateral partners include the World Health Organization; the Pan American Health Organization; the Global Fund to Fight AIDS, Tuberculosis, and Malaria; and UNICEF. OGHA Multilateral Affairs maintains a health attaché at the U.S. Mission in Geneva who serves as the HHS liaison to the World Health Organization and other UN bodies.

OGHA supports an information portal on global health issues, including reports, statistics, and links to international organizations at www.globalhealth.gov.

Assistant Secretary
Jimmy Kolker. (202) 690–6174
Fax. . . . . (202) 690–7127

OFFICE OF THE ASSISTANT SECRETARY FOR HEALTH
200 Independence Ave. S.W., Room 716G
Washington, DC 20201
Internet: www.hhs.gov/ash

The Office of the Assistant Secretary for Health (ASH), formerly the Office of Public Health and Science, provides advice on broad-based health assessments to better define public health problems; assists in the design and implementation of strategies to sustain and improve national health conditions; recommends policy and analyzes legislation; and maintains specialized staffs who examine major public health and science issues. ASH oversees twelve core public health offices—including the Office of the Surgeon General and the U.S. Public Health Service Commissioned Corps (USPHSCC)—as well as ten regional health offices across the nation and ten presidential and secretarial advisory committees.

The following offices under the assistant secretary for health comprise elements of the Public Health Services.

Office of the Surgeon General (OSG). Provides Americans the best scientific information available on how to improve their health and reduce their risk of illness and injury. The office also manages the operations of the Commissioned Corps of the U.S. Public Health Service.

National Vaccine Program Office (NVPO). Ensures collaboration among the many federal agencies involved in vaccine and immunization activities.

Office of Adolescent Health (OAH). Coordinates adolescent health promotion and disease prevention initiatives across HHS.

Office of Disease Prevention and Health Promotion (ODPHP). Provides leadership, coordination, and policy development for public health and prevention activities. Leads the Healthy People initiative for HHS.

Office of HIV/AIDS and Infectious Disease Policy. The Office of HIV/AIDS policy is responsible for coordinating, integrating, and directing the department's policies, programs, and activities related to HIV/AIDS.

Office for Human Research Protections (OHRP). Maintains regulatory oversight of applicable research, provides clarification of and guidance on policy, and provides advice on ethical and regulatory issues related to protecting volunteers in research conducted or supported by HHS.

Office of Minority Health (OMH). Addresses health status and quality of life for minority populations in the United States.

Office of Population Affairs (OPA). Advises on issues related to family planning and population affairs.

Office of Research Integrity (ORI). Oversees and directs Public Health Service (PHS) research integrity activities, with the exception of the regulatory research integrity activities of the Food and Drug Administration. Responds to allegations of research misconduct.

Office on Women's Health (OWH). Improves the health of American women by advancing a comprehensive women's health agenda throughout HHS.

President's Council on Fitness, Sports, and Nutrition (PCFSN). Advises on issues related to fitness, sports, and nutrition in the United States.

Other Public Health Services components include the Indian Health Service, Agency for Toxic Substances and Disease Registry, Centers for Disease Control and Prevention, Food and Drug Administration (*p. 265*), Health Resources and Services Administration, National Institutes of Health, and Substance Abuse and Mental Health Services Administration.

The Patient Protection and Affordable Care Act created the Ready Reserve Corps, a new component of the USPHS Commissioned Corps. The Ready Reserve Corps provides additional Commissioned Corps personnel who will be available on short notice (similar to the other uniformed services' reserve programs) to assist regular Commissioned Corps personnel with both routine public health and emergency response missions.

Assistant Secretary for Health
Karen B. DeSalvo (acting) . . . . (202) 690–7694
Fax. . . . . (202) 690–7425
E-mail: ASH@hhs.gov

Principal Deputy Assistant Secretary for Health
Wanda K. Jones . . . . (202) 690–7694

Deputy Assistant Secretary for Health (Science and Medicine)
Anand K. Parekh . . . . (202) 690–7694

Adolescent Health
(1101 Wootton Pkwy., #700, Rockville, MD 20852)
Evelyn Kappeler. . . . . (240) 453–2846
Website: www.hhs.gov/ash/oah

Advisory Committee on Blood Safety and Availability
(1101 Wootton Pkwy., #250, Rockville, MD 20852)
James Berger . . . . (240) 453–8803
Fax. . . . . (240) 453–8456
E-mail: ACBSA@hhs.gov

Disease Prevention and Health Promotion
(1101 Wootton Pkwy., #LL100, Rockville, MD 20852)

Don Wright . . . . (240) 453–8280
Website: http://odphp.hhs.gov

HIV / AIDS and Infectious Disease Policy
Ronald O. Valdiserri . . . . (202) 690–5560
Website: www.hhs.gov/ash/ohaidp

Human Research Protections
(1101 Wootton Pkwy., #200, Rockville, MD 20852)
Jerry Menikoff. . . . . (240) 453–6900
Website: www.hhs.gov/ohrp

Minority Health
(1101 Wootton Pkwy., #600, Rockville, MD 20852)
J. Nadine Gracia (acting) . . . . (240) 453–2882
Website: http://minorityhealth.hhs.gov

National Vaccine Program
Bruce Gellin. . . . . (202) 690–5566
Fax. . . . . (202) 690–4631
Website: www.hhs.gov/nvpo

Population Affairs
(1101 Wootton Pkwy., #700, Rockville, MD 20852)
Susan Moskosky (acting) . . . . (240) 453–2800
Website: www.hhs.gov/opa

Presidential Commission for the Study of Bioethical Issues
(1425 New York Ave. N.W., #C100, Washington, DC 20005)
Lisa Lee. . . . . (202) 233–3960

President's Council on Fitness, Sports, and Nutrition
(1101 Wootton Pkwy., #560, Rockville, MD 20852)
Shellie Pfohl. . . . . (240) 276–9567
Website: www.fitness.gov

Research Integrity
(1101 Wootton Pkwy., #750, Rockville, MD 20852)
Don Wright (acting) . . . . (240) 453–8200
Website: http://ori.hhs.gov

Surgeon General
(1101 Wootton Pkwy., #100, Plaza Level, Rockville, MD 20852)
Vice Adm. Vivek H. Murthy . . . . (301) 443–4000
Website: www.surgeongeneral.gov

U.S. Public Health Service Commissioned Corps
(1100 Wootton Pkwy., Plaza Level, Rockville, MD 20852)
General . . . . (800) 279–1605
Vice Adm. Vivek H. Murthy, Surgeon General
Vacant, Assistant Secretary for Health

Women's Health
Nancy C. Lee . . . . (202) 690–7650
Fax. . . . . (202) 401–4005
Website: www.womenshealth.gov

■ SUBSTANCE ABUSE AND MENTAL HEALTH SERVICES ADMINISTRATION

1 Choke Cherry Rd.
Rockville, MD 20857
Internet: www.samhsa.gov

The Substance Abuse and Mental Health Services Administration (SAMHSA) was founded in 1992 through the reorganization of the federal administration of mental health services. SAMHSA provides various services related to substance abuse and mental health treatment, including grants to state and local agencies, policy promulgation, and program analysis. SAMHSA carries out these functions via its four centers and supporting offices.

SAMHSA's Center for Mental Health Services guides policy to ensure the application of scientifically established findings in the prevention and treatment of mental disorders; to improve access to effective programs and services for people with, or at risk for, these disorders; and to promote an improved state of mental health within the nation, as well as the rehabilitation of people with mental disorders.

SAMHSA's Center for Substance Abuse Prevention develops policies, programs, and services to prevent the onset of illegal drug, underage alcohol, and tobacco use. This center disseminates effective substance abuse prevention practices and works with states, local communities, and other organizations to apply prevention strategies.

SAMHSA's Center for Substance Abuse Treatment promulgates policy to expand the availability of effective treatment and recovery services for alcohol and drug problems; and to improve access, reduce barriers, and promote high-quality effective treatment and recovery services for people with substance abuse problems, as well as for their families and communities.

SAMHSA's Center for Behavioral Health Statistics and Quality (formerly the Office of Applied Studies) collects, analyzes, and disseminates behavioral health data. This includes alcohol, tobacco, marijuana, and other drug abuse; drug-related emergency department episodes and medical examiner cases; and the nation's substance abuse treatment system.

Some of the policies, guidelines, and regulations developed and/or implemented by SAMHSA include Regulations on the Substance Abuse Prevention and Treatment Block Grant, Mandatory Guidelines for Federal Workplace Drug Testing Programs, Confidentiality of Alcohol and Drug Abuse Patient Records, and Regulations on the Protection and Advocacy Program.

Administrator
Pamela S. Hyde . . . . (240) 276–2000
Deputy Principal Administrator, Policy
Kana Enomoto. . . . . (240) 276–2000
Center for Behavioral Health Statistics and Quality
Peter Delany. . . . . (240) 276–1250
Center for Mental Health Services
Paolo del Vecchio . . . . (240) 276–1310
Center for Substance Abuse Prevention
Frances M. Harding . . . . (240) 276–2420
Center for Substance Abuse Treatment
Daryl W. Kade (acting). . . . . (240) 276–1660
Communications
Marla Hendriksson . . . . (240) 276–2130
Financial Resources
Deepa Avula (acting) . . . . (240) 276–2200
Management Technology and Operations
Michael E. Etzinger. . . . . (240) 276–1110
Policy, Planning and Innovation
Mary Flemming. . . . . (240) 276–2230

Other Contacts
National Clearinghouse for Alcohol and Drug Information . . . . (800) 729–6686
Workplace Helpline (English and Spanish) . . . . (800) 662–4357
TTY. . . . . (800) 457–4889
Freedom of Information. . . . . (240) 276–2137
Publications, Office of Applied Statistics, website: www.samhsa.gov/data

■ REGIONAL OFFICES

The following regional offices serve all HHS agencies. Information about the regional offices is available at www .hhs.gov/iea/regional/index.html.

REGION 1
(CT, MA, ME, NH, RI, VT)
Government Center
John F. Kennedy Federal Bldg., #2100
Boston, MA 02203–0001
(617) 565–1505
A. Kathryn Power, regional health administrator
Internet: www.hhs.gov/region1

REGION 2
(NJ, NY, PR, VI)
Jacob Javits Federal Bldg.
26 Federal Plaza, #3835
New York, NY 10278–0022
(212) 264–4600
Dennis Romero, regional health administrator
Internet: www.hhs.gov/region2

REGION 3
(DC, DE, MD, PA, VA, WV)
Public Ledger Bldg., #1172
150 S. Independence Mall West
Philadelphia, PA 19106–3499
(215) 861–4639
Jean Bennett, regional health administrator
Internet: www.hhs.gov/region3

REGION 4
(AL, FL, GA, KY, MS, NC, SC, TN)
Sam Nunn Atlanta Federal Center
61 Forsyth St. S.W., #5B95
Atlanta, GA 30303–8909
(404) 562–7890
Stephanie McCladdie, regional health administrator
Internet: www.hhs.gov/region4

REGION 5
(IL, IN, MI, MN, OH, WI)
233 N. Michigan Ave
Chicago, IL 60601
(312) 353–1385
Jeffrey A. Coady, regional health administrator
Internet: www.hhs.gov/region5

REGION 6

(AR, LA, NM, OK, TX)
1301 Young St., #1030
Dallas, TX 75202
(214) 767–3879
Michael Duffy, regional health administrator
Internet: www.hhs.gov/region6

REGION 7

(IA, KS, MO, NE)
Bolling Federal Bldg.
601 E. 12th St., #S-1801
Kansas City, MO 64106–2898
(816) 426–3291
Kimberly Brown (acting), regional health
    administrator
Internet: www.hhs.gov/region7

REGION 8

(CO, MT, ND, SD, UT, WY)
999 18th St., South Tower, #4-342
Denver, CO 80202

(303) 844–6163
Charles Smith, regional health administrator
Internet: www.hhs.gov/region8

REGION 9

(AS, AZ, CA, GU, HI, NV, other
    Pacific Islands)
90 Seventh St., 8th Floor
San Francisco, CA 94103
(415) 437–8096
Jon Perez, regional
    health administrator
Internet: www.hhs.gov/region9

REGION 10

(AK, ID, OR, WA)
701 Fifth Ave., #1520
Seattle, WA 98104
(206) 615–2469
David Dickinson, regional
    health administrator
Internet: www.hhs.gov/region10

Homeland Security Department

3801 Nebraska Ave. N.W., Washington, DC 20528
Internet: www.dhs.gov

Federal Emergency Management Agency

500 C St. S.W., Washington, DC 20472
Internet: www.fema.gov

The Federal Emergency Management Agency (FEMA) was established by presidential executive order in 1979 as an independent agency of the federal government. The Homeland Security Act of 2002 transferred FEMA into the Department of Homeland Security (DHS) in 2003.

Under the authority of the Robert T. Stafford Act, FEMA is responsible for providing assistance to maintain and enhance the nation's all-hazards emergency management capability and coordinates federal emergency recovery and response operations. FEMA programs include response to and recovery from major natural disasters and human-made emergencies, emergency management planning, flood-plain management, hazardous materials planning, and dam safety. Other activities include off-site planning for emergencies at commercial nuclear power plants and the Army's chemical stockpile sites, emergency food and shelter funding for the homeless, plans to ensure the continuity of the federal government during national security emergencies, coordination of the federal response to major terrorist incidents, and coordinating disaster mitigation programs. In addition, FEMA manages the National Flood Insurance Program.

FEMA also houses the U.S. Fire Administration and the National Fire Academy. The Fire Research and Safety Act of 1968 established the National Commission on Fire Prevention and Control, which was charged with analyzing the fire threat in the United States. In 1973 this commission issued a report titled "America Burning," which made recommendations to reduce and mitigate the U.S. fire threat. It also called for the establishment of a United States Fire Administration and a national fire-training academy. Following the commission's recommendations, Congress passed the Federal Fire Prevention and Control Act of 1974 and established the National Fire Prevention and Control Administration, which is now the United States Fire Administration (USFA), and the National Fire Academy in Emmitsburg, MD.

More than 14,000 employees work to accomplish the agency's disaster preparedness and response mission. Many are full-time employees working at agency headquarters in Washington, DC, at regional and area offices across the country, at the Mount Weather Emergency Operations Center, and at the FEMA training centers in Emmitsburg, MD. However, the majority of FEMA employees are standby disaster assistance experts who are available to deploy after disasters. Often FEMA works in partnership with other organizations that are part of the nation's emergency management system. These partners include state and local emergency management agencies, federal agencies, tribal governments, and the American Red Cross.

In late summer 2005 FEMA received intense criticism for its flawed response to Hurricane Katrina, which devastated the Gulf Coast and toppled levees in New Orleans, flooding the city. Across four states the storm killed more than 1,200 people and forced more than 1.5 million people to evacuate. Within two weeks of the storm, President George W. Bush replaced FEMA director Michael Brown with R. David Paulison, director of the U.S. Fire Administration.

Government officials later acknowledged that FEMA was underprepared for the enormity of the disaster. The heaviest criticism was leveled at the former FEMA director Brown, who had no previous emergency management experience before being named to head the agency. As a result, the Post-Katrina Emergency Management Reform Act of 2006 required the president to appoint the FEMA director from among individuals who have a demonstrated ability in and knowledge of emergency management and homeland security and not less than five years of executive leadership and management experience in the public or private sector.

In October 2012, Hurricane Sandy struck the mid-Atlantic and New England seaboard, with the heaviest destruction in New York and New Jersey. It was the second-costliest storm in U.S. history, but partisan bickering in Congress delayed additional disaster relief aid for the hardest-hit areas. On January 29, 2013, three months after the storm hit, President Barack Obama signed the Sandy Recovery Improvement Act of 2013 (SRIA). In addition to providing more than $50 billion in aid, the law authorized several significant changes to the way FEMA may deliver disaster assistance under a variety of programs. Some of the streamlining efforts included the following:

- Expediting hazard mitigation projects by establishing an expedited and unified environmental and historic preservation (EHP) process.
- Permitting debris removal grants to be based on fixed estimates, with applicants accepting responsibility for any actual costs above the estimate.

- Providing local governments greater flexibility to consolidate or rebuild facilities by allowing FEMA to issue fixed price grants on the basis of damage estimates instead of a traditional reimbursement process.
- Allowing FEMA to make limited repairs, instead of lease payments, for the purpose of providing housing when less expensive than traditional FEMA trailers.
- Establishing a limited dispute resolution pilot to resolve disputes over assistance to drive projects to closure and avoid cost overruns.
- Allowing tribal nations to petition the president to declare an emergency or continue with the process of seeking assistance under a declaration for a state.
- Requiring FEMA to review and update factors for individual assistance disaster declarations to make them less subjective.

In 2013 FEMA developed specific implementation procedures for each new authority and provided additional guidance through a combination of rulemaking and the development of policy or other guidance documents. By the end of 2014 FEMA had issued guidance and regulations for more than a dozen SRIA-authorized initiatives and several programs were in pilot phase. These initiatives included public assistance program changes, emergency transportation coordination, new authorities for tribal governments, and several changes to financial and reporting requirements for disaster aid. A phased implementation plan for the unified EHP process was developed as well.

▓ KEY PERSONNEL

Administrator
W. Craig Fugate . . . . (202) 646–3900
Deputy Administrator
Joseph Nimmich . . . . (202) 646–3900
External Affairs
Joshua C. Batkin . . . . (202) 646–4600
Federal Insurance and Mitigation
David L. Miller . . . . (202) 646–2781
Grant Programs
Brian E. Kamoie. . . . . (202) 786–9847
Logistics
Jeffrey Dorko . . . . (202) 646–4508
National Capital Region Coordination
Kim Kadesch . . . . (202) 212–1500
National Continuity Programs
Damon Penn . . . . (202) 646–4145
Protection and National Preparedness
Timothy W. Manning . . . . (202) 646–3100
Recovery
Alex Amparo (assistant
administrator) . . . . (202) 646–3642
Response and Recovery
Elizabeth Zimmerman (associate
administrator) . . . . (202) 646–3888
U.S. Fire Administration
Ernest (Ernie) Mitchell Jr. . . . . (301) 447–1018

▓ INFORMATION SOURCES

Internet
Agency website: www.fema.gov
Blog: www.fema.gov/blog

Telephone Contacts
General Questions . . . . (202) 646–2500
Disaster Relief. (800) 621–3362
TTY . . . . (800) 462–7585
Technical Assistance
(Online Registration) . . . . (800) 745–0243
Inspector General. . . . . (800) 323–8603
Federal Relay Service TTY . . . . (800) 877–8339
News Desk. . . . . (202) 646–3272
E-mail: FEMA-News-Desk@dhs.gov

Reference Resources
Library
www.fema.gov/reference-library

Building Codes and Building Science
www.fema.gov/building-science

DOCKETS
Federal dockets are available at www.regulations.gov. (*See appendix for Searching and Commenting on Regulations: Regulations.gov.*)

RULES AND REGULATIONS
FEMA rules and regulations are published in the *Code of Federal Regulations,* Title 44, Chapter I, Parts 0–399. Proposed rules, final rules, and updates to the *Code of Federal Regulations* are published in the daily *Federal Register. (See appendix for information on how to obtain and use these publications.)* The *Federal Register* and the *Code of Federal Regulations* may be accessed online at www.archives.gov/federal-register/cfr; the site contains a link to the federal government's regulatory website at www.regulations.gov (*see appendix*).

▓ LEGISLATION
FEMA carries out its responsibilities under:
Disaster Relief Act (64 Stat. 1109). Signed by the president Sept. 30, 1950. Authorized the president to declare a major disaster and to provide supplementary federal assistance when a governor requested help. Authorized federal agencies to coordinate intergovernmental relief efforts.
National Flood Insurance Act of 1968 (82 Stat. 572, 42 U.S.C. 4001 note). Signed by the president Aug. 1, 1968. Created the National Flood Insurance Program (NFIP). Through strategic risk management, NFIP provides federally backed flood insurance to homeowners, renters, and business owners.
Robert T. Stafford Disaster Relief and Emergency Assistance Act (88 Stat. 143, 42 U.S.C. 5121 note). Signed by the president May 22, 1974. Broadened provisions of the Disaster Act of 1950. Encouraged and assisted states and local governments with comprehensive disaster

preparedness and assistance plans. Provided for greater coordination between federal government and the states for disaster management and recovery.

Federal Fire Prevention and Control Act of 1974 (88 Stat. 1535, 15 U.S.C. 2201 note). Signed by the president Oct. 29, 1974. Established the National Fire Prevention and Control Administration (now the United States Fire Administration) and established the National Fire Academy.

Antiterrorism and Effective Death Penalty Act of 1996 (110 Stat. 1214, 18 U.S.C. 1 note). Signed by the president Oct. 11, 1996. Authorized the attorney general, in consultation with FEMA, to provide specialized training and equipment for enhancing the capabilities of metropolitan fire and emergency service departments to respond to terrorist attacks.

Disaster Mitigation Act of 2000 (114 Stat. 1552, 42 U.S.C. 5121 note). Signed by the president Oct. 30, 2000. Amended the Stafford Act to focus on mitigation planning to prepare for and avoid disasters. Required state, tribal, and local agencies to coordinate mitigation planning and implementation efforts and linked the preplanning requirements to eligibility for several categories of disaster recovery funding.

Homeland Security Act of 2002 (116 Stat. 2135, 6 U.S.C. 551, 557). Signed by the president Nov. 25, 2002. Established the Department of Homeland Security (DHS). Transferred FEMA to the new department.

Flood Insurance Reform Act of 2004 (118 Stat. 712, 42 U.S.C. 4001 note). Signed by the president June 30, 2004. Amended the National Flood Insurance Act of 1968 to reduce losses to properties for which repetitive flood insurance claim payments have been made.

Post-Katrina Emergency Management Reform Act of 2006 (120 Stat. 1394, 6 U.S.C. 701 note). Signed by the president Oct. 6, 2006. Title VI of the 2007 appropriations bill, the legislation required the president to appoint the FEMA director from among individuals who have a demonstrated ability in and knowledge of emergency management and homeland security and not less than five years of executive leadership and management experience in the public or private sector. Required the FEMA Administrator, in coordination with other federal agencies, state, local, and tribal governments, and organizations, to develop, coordinate, and maintain the National Disaster Housing Strategy.

Pets Evacuation and Transportation Standards Act (120 Stat. 1725, 42 U.S.C. 5121 note). Signed by the president Oct. 6, 2006. Title V of the 2007 appropriations bill, the legislation amends the Stafford act to require DHS, in approving standards for state and local emergency preparedness operational plans, to account for the needs of individuals with household pets and service animals.

Moving Ahead for Progress in the 21st Century Act (MAP-21) (126 Stat. 916, 42 U.S.C. 4001 note). Signed by the president July 6, 2012. Title II, Biggert-Waters Flood Insurance Reform Act of 2012, made changes to the flood insurance program. Amended the National Flood Insurance Act of 1968 to direct the DHS secretary, acting through the FEMA administrator, to establish a standard formula (COASTAL formula) to determine and allocate wind losses and flood losses for claims involving indeterminate losses.

Sandy Recovery Improvement Act of 2013 (127 Stat. 39, 42 U.S.C. 5121 note). Signed by the president Jan. 29, 2013. Amended the Stafford Act to authorize the president, acting through the FEMA Administrator, to approve public assistance projects for major disasters or emergencies under alternative procedures. Provided federally recognized tribal governments the option to choose whether to make a request directly to the president for a federal emergency or major disaster declaration or continue to seek assistance under a declaration for a state.

Homeowner Flood Insurance Affordability Act of 2014 (128 Stat. 1020, 42 U.S.C. 4001 note). Signed by the president March 21, 2014. Repeals and modifies certain provisions of the Biggert-Waters Flood Insurance Reform Act (BWFIRA) of 2012. Delays the flood insurance premium increases mandated under the BWFIRA.

Immigration and Customs Enforcement

425 Eye St. N.W., Washington, DC 20536
Internet: www.ice.gov

The Homeland Security Act of 2002 created the Department of Homeland Security (DHS). On March 1, 2003, the act transferred the enforcement and investigation arms of the U.S. Customs Service, the investigative and enforcement functions of Immigration and Naturalization Service (INS), and the entire operation of Federal Protective Services into Immigration and Customs Enforcement (ICE). ICE is a component of the Directorate of Border and Transportation Security established within the DHS.

The service and benefit functions of the INS transferred into U.S. Citizenship and Immigration Services (*see p. 652*); the inspection functions of the U.S. Customs Service were organized as U.S. Customs and Border Protection (*see p. 664*).

Backed by a workforce of more than 20,000 employees in each state and in forty-eight foreign countries, ICE is the investigative arm of the DHS. The agency combines the investigative, detention and removal, and intelligence functions of the former INS with the investigative, intelligence, and air and marine functions of the former Customs Service.

ICE is led by an assistant secretary who reports directly to the DHS under secretary for border and transportation security. The organizational structure of ICE supports three distinct operational divisions:

Office of Homeland Security Investigations (HSI) is charged with investigating violations of the criminal and administrative provisions of the Immigration and Nationality Act, as well as other related immigration law provisions. The special agents, immigration agents, and support personnel perform their duties at field offices, in task force offices, and at domestic and foreign duty posts.

Several mission-related offices carry out the investigation activities of HSI. National Security Investigations investigates vulnerabilities in the nation's borders. It also works to prevent acts of terrorism. Investigative Programs conducts operations in areas including cybercrime, financial and narcotics violations, transnational crime, and public safety. Office of Intelligence conducts broad intelligence operations. It also develops data for use by ICE, the Department of Homeland Security and other law enforcement partners. International Operations oversees HSI attaché offices and builds relationships with foreign law enforcement

partners while Domestic Operations oversees all investigative activities of HSI's domestic field offices.

On December 7, 2012, President Barack Obama signed into law the Jaime Zapata Border Enforcement Security Task Force (BEST) Act, which authorized the secretary of homeland security to establish a Border Enforcement Security Task Force program to enhance border security by fostering coordinated efforts among federal, state, and local border and law enforcement officials. These teams are comprised of members representing more than 100 law enforcement agencies that investigate transnational criminal activity along the southwest and northern U.S. borders.

Office of Enforcement and Removal Operations is charged with the supervision, detention, and removal of aliens who are in the United States unlawfully or who are found to be deportable or inadmissible by enforcing the nation's immigration laws.

This office administers the 287(g) program, one of ICE's top partnership initiatives, which allows a state and local law enforcement entity to enter into a partnership with ICE, under a joint Memorandum of Agreement (MOA). The state or local entity receives delegated authority for immigration enforcement within their jurisdictions.

Office of Management and Administration is responsible for ICE's budget, accounting and finance, procurement, human resources, information technology systems, property, and equipment needs.

At the field level, ICE is organized into a special-agent-in-charge (SAC) structure for investigations, following the model of other federal law enforcement agencies. There are twenty-six principal field offices responsible for directing ICE investigative operations and resources in specific geographic areas of the United States.

ICE's immigration enforcement component deters illegal migration, prevents immigration-related crimes, and removes individuals, especially criminals, who are unlawfully present in the United States. This mandate is carried out by the Immigration Investigations and Enforcement and Removal divisions.

Operational and tactical control of investigative and intelligence operations is divided geographically by areas of responsibility. The SACs are responsible for the administration and management of all investigative-related customs enforcement activities within the geographic boundaries of the office.

Traditionally, the primary mission of customs enforcement has been to combat various forms of smuggling. Over time, however, this mission has been expanded to other violations of law including terrorist financing, money laundering, arms trafficking (including weapons of mass destruction), technology exports, commercial fraud, and child pornography. Customs enforces more than 400 different laws and regulations including those of forty other agencies. High-profile operations include:

Operation Predator, an international initiative to protect children from sexual predators, including those who travel overseas for sex with minors; Internet child pornographers; criminal alien sex offenders; and child sex traffickers. In 2014 ICE agents arrested more than 2,000 individuals under Operation Predator, bringing the total of arrests to more than 12,000 since the launch of Operation Predator in 2003.

Community Shield, established in February 2005, is a national law enforcement initiative that targets violent transnational street gangs through the use of ICE's broad law enforcement powers, including the ability to deport criminal aliens, including illegal aliens and legal permanent resident aliens.

Project Shield America focuses on preventing illegal exporters, targeted foreign countries, terrorist groups, and international criminal organizations from trafficking in weapons of mass destruction and their components; obtaining and illegally exporting licensable commodities, technologies, conventional munitions, and firearms; exporting stolen property; and engaging in financial and other transactions that support these activities or that violate U.S. sanctions and embargoes. ICE enforces provisions of the Arms Export Control Act that relate to illegal smuggling and sales of military components and technology.

Secure Communities prioritizes the removal of criminal aliens, those who pose a threat to public safety, and repeat immigration violators via a federal information-sharing partnership between ICE and the Federal Bureau of Investigation (FBI) that helps to identify criminal aliens. Local jurisdictions share the fingerprints of individuals who are booked into jails with the FBI to check for criminal history. Under Secure Communities, the FBI automatically sends the fingerprints to ICE to check against its immigration databases. ICE takes enforcement action against those individuals who have criminal records and are unlawfully present in the United States.

ICE also works in conjunction with other federal agencies as well as state and local law enforcement on issues of national security. To facilitate these joint investigations and operations, ICE works through several centers:

National Intellectual Property Rights Coordination Center (IPR Center) focuses on keeping counterfeit products out of the United States, as well as identifying and dismantling the criminal organizations behind this activity. The IPR Center serves as a fusion point for intelligence on IPR violations from other government agencies, industry, and stakeholder groups. The IPR Center is led by an HSI director, along with deputy directors from HSI, the FBI, and U.S. Customs and Border Protection. The center consists of law enforcement groups including Interpol, Europol, and the governments of Canada and Mexico.

Law Enforcement Support Center (LESC) is a national enforcement operations facility administered by ICE. The primary users of LESC are state and local law enforcement officers seeking information about aliens encountered in the course of their daily enforcement activities. Law enforcement officers have immediate access to alien records entered with the National Crime Information Center (NCIC) and immigration information from every alien file maintained by DHS.

Human Rights Violators and War Crimes Unit (HRVWCU) prevents the admission of foreign war crimes suspects, persecutors, and human rights abusers into the United States. It also identifies, prosecutes, and ultimately removes such offenders who are already unlawfully in the United States.

■ KEY PERSONNEL

Director
Sarah Saldaña. . . . . (202) 732–3000
Chief of Staff
Leonard Joseph . . . . (202) 732–3000
Chief Operating Officer
Daniel Ragsdale. . . . . (202) 732–5100
Congressional Relations and GAO/OIG Audit Liaison
Jason M. Yanussi . . . . (202) 732–3000
Human Rights Violators and War Crimes Unit
Mark Shaffer . . . . (202) 732–4213
Toll-free . . . . (866) DHS-2-ICE
Email: HRV.ICE@ice.dhs.gov
Law Enforcement Support Center
David Palmatier. . . . . (802) 872–6050
National Intellectual Property Rights Coordination Center (IPR Center)
Lev Kubiak . . . . (703) 603–3900
Toll-free . . . .(866) IPR-2060
Email: IPRCenter@dhs.gov
Detention Policy and Planning
Kevin Landy. . . . . (202) 732–5500
Enforcement and Removal Operations
Thomas Homan. . . . . (202) 732–3100
Homeland Security Investigations
Peter Edge. . . . . (202) 732–5100
Intelligence
Patricia F. S. Cogswell. . . . . (202) 732–5200
International Affairs
Lev Kubiak . . . . (202) 732–8000
Principal Legal Adviser
Riah Ramlogan (acting) . . . . (202) 732–5000
Management and Administration
Tracey Bardorf (acting) . . . . (202) 732–3000
Chief Information Officer
Steven Smith (acting) . . . . (202) 732–2000
Acquisition Management
Bill Weinberg . . . . (202) 732–2600

Diversity and Civil Rights
Scott Lanum . . . . (202) 732–0190
TTY . . . . (202) 732–0097
Firearms and Tactical Programs
Bert Medina . . . . (202) 732–3937
Human Capital
Staci Barrera (acting) . . . . (202) 732–7770
Policy
Tracey Bardorf . . . . (202) 732–5904
Training and Development
Donato W. Coyer . . . . (202) 732–7800
Public Affairs
Pedro Ribeiro . . . . (202) 732–4242

■ INFORMATION SOURCES

Internet

Agency website: www.ice.gov. Includes an overview of the agency, frequently asked questions, press releases, ICE regulations, employer information, and links to other federal Internet sites.

Telephone Contacts

Personnel Locator
(DHS Switchboard) . . . . (202) 282–8000
General Information/Immigration Information
(English and Spanish) . . . . (800) 375–5283
Suspicious Activities/Immigration or Customs
Violations . . . . (866) 347–2423
Internet: www.ice.gov/webform/hsi-tip-form
Federal Protective Service . . . . (202) 242–2300
Toll-free . . . . (877) 437–7411
SEVC (Student and Exchange Visitors Program)
Response Center . . . . (703) 603–3400
Federal Relay Service TTY . . . . (800) 877–8339
Human Rights Violators and War
Crimes Unit (HRVWCU) . . . . . (866) DHS–2–ICE
Operation Predator . . . . (866) 347–2423

Information and Publications

KEY OFFICES

ICE Public Affairs

500 12th St. S.W.
Washington, DC 20536
(202) 732–4242
Pedro Ribeiro, assistant director
Internet: www.ice.gov/news/media-resources

Answers questions from the press. Issues news releases and media information materials.

Freedom of Information

500 12th St. S.W., STOP 5009
Washington, DC 20536
(202) 732–0600
(866) 633–1182
E-mail: ICE-FOIA@dhs.gov
Catrina M. Pavlik-Keenan, FOIA officer

**Delegation of Immigration
Authority Section 287(g)**
Internet: www.ice.gov/287g

**ICE Agreements of Cooperation in
Communities to Enhance Safety
and Security**
Internet: www.ice.gov/factsheets/287g

**Human Rights Violators and War
Crimes Unit (HRVWCU)**
E-mail: HRV.ICE@ice.dhs.gov

Operation Predator
Internet: www.ice.gov/predator
Internet: www.missingkids.com/cybertipline

DOCKETS

Federal dockets are available at www.regulations.gov. (*See appendix for Searching and Commenting on Regulations: Regulations.gov.*)

RULES AND REGULATIONS

Immigration and Customs Enforcement rules and regulations are published in the *Code of Federal Regulations,* Title 8, Chapter I, Parts 1–499, and Title 19, Chapter I, Parts 1–199. Proposed rules, final rules, and updates to the *Code of Federal Regulations* are published in the daily *Federal Register. (See appendix for information on how to obtain and use these publications.)* The *Federal Register* and the *Code of Federal Regulations* may be accessed online at www.archives.gov/federal-register/cfr; the site contains a link to the federal government's regulatory website at www.regulations.gov (*see appendix*).

■ LEGISLATION

ICE carries out its immigration investigation and enforcement responsibilities under:

Immigration and Nationality Act, as amended (66 Stat. 163, 8 U.S.C. 1101). Signed by the president June 27, 1952. Contained virtually all of the law relating to the entry of aliens and to the acquisition and loss of U.S. citizenship.

Immigration and Nationality Technical Corrections Act of 1994 (108 Stat. 4305, 8 U.S.C. 1101). Signed by the president Oct. 25, 1994. Made numerous specific changes to the Immigration and Nationality Act. Allowed U.S. visas for visits from officials of Taiwan; gave equal treatment to women in conferring U.S. citizenship to children born abroad.

Amendments to the Violent Crime Control and Law Enforcement Act of 1994 (110 Stat. 1214, 18 U.S.C. 1). Signed by the president April 24, 1996. Directed the criminal alien identification system to be used to identify and locate deportable aliens who have committed aggravated felonies; the system was to be transferred from the attorney general to the commissioner of the INS.

Trafficking Victims Protection Act of 2000 (114 Stat. 1464, 22 U.S.C. 7101 note). Signed by the president Oct. 28, 2000. Legislation authorized strategies to combat trafficking of persons, especially into the sex trade, slavery, and slavery-like conditions in the United States and around the world through prevention, through prosecution and enforcement against traffickers, and through protection and assistance to victims of trafficking.

Homeland Security Act of 2002 (116 Stat. 2135, 6 U.S.C. 551, 557). Signed by the president Nov. 25, 2002. Created the DHS and transferred to ICE all old INS functions performed under the following programs: (1) the Border Patrol program; (2) the detention and removal program; (3) the intelligence program; (4) the investigations program; and (5) the inspections program. Granted the secretary of homeland security exclusive authority to issue regulations with respect to the Immigration and Nationality Act.

Prosecutorial Remedies and Other Tools to End the Exploitation of Children Today Act (PROTECT Act) (117 Stat. 650). Signed by the president on April 30, 2003. Made it a crime for U.S. citizens to travel to foreign countries for the purpose of engaging in sex with minor children (sex tourism). Increased the criminal penalties for other forms of child abuse and sexual exploitation.

Intelligence Reform and Terrorism Prevention Act of 2004 (118 Stat. 3638, 8 U.S.C. 1155, 1201). Signed by the president Dec. 17, 2004. Established the Human Smuggling and Trafficking Center, to be operated by the DHS secretary, secretary of state, and the attorney general. The center served as a clearinghouse for federal agency information relating to terrorist travel and migrant smuggling and trafficking of persons.

ICE carries out its customs investigation and enforcement responsibilities through authority granted in:

Tariff Act of 1930 (46 Stat. 763, 19 U.S.C. 1202). Signed by the president June 17, 1930. Established rules and regulations relating to assessment and collection of duty, protection of revenue, entry of vessels, clearance of passengers, exclusion of prohibited merchandise, and regulation of customhouse brokers.

Arms Export Control Act of 1976 (90 Stat. 729, 22 U.S.C. 2778). Signed by the president June 30, 1976. Expanded congressional authority over U.S. arms sales and exports by requiring the president to report arms sales to Congress and by allowing Congress to deny arms sales and exports to certain countries.

Money Laundering Control Act of 1986 (100 Stat. 3207, 18 U.S.C. 981). Signed by the president Oct. 27, 1986. Prohibited the transport or attempted transport of funds obtained through the commission of a crime or intended for use in a crime. Prohibited the structuring of financial transactions in order to evade federal reporting requirements. Authorized the seizure and forfeiture of cash or other property derived from criminal activity.

United States–Canada Free-Trade Agreement Implementation Act of 1988 (102 Stat. 1851, 19 U.S.C. 2112 note). Signed by the president Sept. 28, 1988. Set a ten-year schedule to phase out tariffs between the United States and Canada. Provided new mechanisms for solving trade disputes.

North American Free Trade Agreement Implementation Act (107 Stat. 2057, 19 U.S.C. 3301 note).

Signed by the president Dec. 8, 1993. Title VI, the Customs Modernization Act, amended the Tariff Act of 1930 to revise customs procedures with respect to electronic transmission of forged, altered, or false data to the Customs Service with regard to the entry of imported merchandise; to set penalties for failure to declare imported controlled substances and for fraud, gross negligence, and negligence; to restrict unlawful unloading or transshipment; and to handle the seizure of imported merchandise.

Anticounterfeiting Consumer Protection Act of 1996 (110 Stat. 1836, 18 U.S.C. 2311 note). Signed by the president July 2, 1996. Made trafficking in goods or services bearing counterfeit marks a predicate offense under the Racketeer Influenced and Corrupt Organizations Act (RICO). Gave the U.S. Customs Service authority to establish civil penalties and fines for importing, selling, or distributing merchandise bearing a counterfeit American trademark.

Civil Asset Forfeiture Reform Act of 2000 (114 Stat. 202, 18 U.S.C. 981 note). Signed by the president April 25, 2000. Authorizes both the criminal and civil forfeiture of the proceeds of all specified unlawful activities. Amended the Immigration and Nationality Act provisions regarding the smuggling and harboring of aliens to authorize the seizure and forfeiture of the gross proceeds of a violation and any property traceable to such conveyance or proceeds. Amended code provisions regarding search warrant requirements for civil forfeiture.

Trade Act of 2002 (116 Stat. 933, 19 U.S.C. 3801 note). Signed by the president Aug. 6, 2002. Title III, the Customs Border Security Act of 2002, provided customs officers with immunity from lawsuits stemming from personal searches of people entering the country, as long as the officers conducted the searches in good faith and followed federal inspection procedures. Allowed officers to search unsealed, outbound U.S. mail and packages weighing sixteen ounces or more for unreported monetary instruments, weapons of mass destruction, firearms, and other contraband.

Uniting and Strengthening America by Providing Appropriate Tools Required to Intercept and Obstruct Terrorism Act of 2002 (USA Patriot Act) (115 Stat. 272, 18 U.S.C. 1 note). Signed by the president Oct. 26, 2001. Allows for the inclusion of foreign corruption offenses as predicate offenses to money laundering crimes.

Homeland Security Act of 2002 (116 Stat. 2135, 6 U.S.C. 551, 557). Signed by the president Nov. 25, 2002. Established the DHS. Transferred to ICE the U.S. Customs Service from the Department of the Treasury, but with certain customs revenue functions remaining with the secretary of the Treasury.

Intelligence Reform and Terrorism Prevention Act of 2004 (118 Stat. 3739, 8 U.S.C. 1182(a)(3)(E)). Signed by the president Dec. 17, 2004. Renders inadmissible and deportable those aliens who commit, order, incite, assist, or participate in acts of torture, extrajudicial killing, or genocide as defined by U.S. law.

Executive Order 13627: Strengthening Protections against Trafficking in Persons in Federal Contracts. Signed by the president Sept. 25, 2012. Directs the Federal Acquisition Regulatory (FAR) Council, working with the appropriate agencies (including DHS), to amend federal contracting regulations to prohibit contractors and sub-contractors from engaging in specific trafficking-related activities; apply new, tailored compliance measures for larger contracts performed abroad; establish a process to identify industries and sectors that have a history of human trafficking, to enhance compliance on domestic contracts; and augment training and heighten agencies' ability to detect and address trafficking violations.

Jaime Zapata Border Enforcement Security Task Force (BEST) Act (126 Stat. 1487, 6 U.S.C. 101 note). Signed by the president Dec. 7, 2012. Amended the Homeland Security Act of 2002 to authorize the secretary of homeland security to establish a Border Enforcement Security Task Force program to enhance border security by fostering coordinated efforts among federal, state, and local border and law enforcement officials.

■ REGIONAL OFFICES

Office of Investigations

SPECIAL-AGENT-IN-CHARGE (SAC) OFFICES

SAC Atlanta
1100 Centre Pkwy.
Atlanta, GA 30344
(404) 346-2300
Fax (404) 346-2374

SAC Baltimore
40 S. Gay St., 3rd Floor
Baltimore, MD 21202
(410) 962-2620
Fax (410) 962-3469

SAC Boston
10 Causeway St., #722
Boston, MA 02222-1054
(617) 565-3100
Fax (617) 565-7422

SAC Buffalo
1780 Wehrle Dr., Suite D
Williamsville, NY 14221
(716) 565-2039
Fax (716) 565-9509

SAC Chicago
1 N. Tower Lane, #1600
Oakbrook Terrace, IL 60181
(630) 574-4600
Fax (630) 574-2889

SAC Dallas
125 E. John Carpenter Freeway, #800
Irving, TX 75062-2224
(972) 444-7300
Fax (972) 444-7461

SAC Denver
5445 DTC Pkwy., #600
Englewood, CO 80111
(303) 721-3000
Fax (303) 721-3003

SAC Detroit
477 Michigan Ave., #1850
Detroit, MI 48226
(313) 226-0500
Fax (313) 226-6282

SAC El Paso
4191 N. Mesa
El Paso, TX 79902
(915) 231-3200
Fax (915) 231-3227

SAC Honolulu
595 Ala Moana Blvd.
Honolulu, HI 96813
(808) 532-3746
Fax (808) 532-4689

SAC Houston
4141 N. Sam Houston Pkwy. East, #300
Houston, TX 77032
(281) 985-0500
Fax (281) 985-0505

SAC Los Angeles
501 W. Ocean Blvd., #7200
Long Beach, CA 90802-4213
(562) 624-3800
Fax (562) 590-7352

SAC Miami
11226 N.W. 20th St.
Miami, FL 33172
(305) 597-6000
Fax (305) 597-6227

SAC Minneapolis/St. Paul
2901 Metro Dr., #100
Bloomington, MN 55425
(952) 853-2940
Fax (612) 313-9045

SAC New Orleans
1250 Poydras St., #2200
New Orleans, LA 70113-1807
(504) 310-8800
Fax (504) 310-8900

SAC New York
601 W. 26th St., 7th Floor
New York, NY 10001
(646) 230-3200
Fax (646) 230-3255

SAC Newark

620 Frelinghuysen Ave.
Newark, NJ 07114–2534
(973) 776–5500
Fax (973) 776–5365

SAC Philadelphia

220 Chestnut St., #200
Philadelphia, PA 19106
(215) 717–4800
Fax (215) 597–4200

SAC Phoenix

4041 N. Central Ave., #1650
Phoenix, AZ 85012
(602) 200–2200
Fax (602) 277–0038

SAC San Antonio

40 N.E. Loop 410, #501
San Antonio, TX 78216
(210) 321–2800
Fax (210) 321–2832

SAC San Diego

185 W. F St., #600
San Diego, CA 92101–6086
(619) 744–4600
Fax (619) 557–7275

SAC San Francisco

630 Sansome St., #890
San Francisco, CA 94111
(415) 844–5455
Fax (415) 844–5451

SAC San Juan

Capitol Office Bldg., 12th Floor
800 Ponce de Leon Ave.
Santurce, PR 00908
(787) 729–5151
Fax (787) 729–6646

SAC Seattle

1000 Second Ave., #2300
Seattle, WA 98104–1048
(206) 442–2200
Fax (206) 442–2201

SAC Tampa

2203 N. Lois Ave., #600
Tampa, FL 33607
(813) 357–7000
Fax (813) 348–1877

SAC Washington, DC

2675 Prosperity Ave.
Fairfax, VA 22031
(703) 285–6700
Fax (703) 285–6709

Transportation Security Administration

601 S. 12th St., TSA-1, Arlington, VA 20598
Internet: www.tsa.gov

Soon after the September 11, 2001, attacks on New York and Washington, DC, the Aviation and Transportation Security Act created the Transportation Security Administration (TSA), on Nov. 19, 2001. Placed within the Department of Transportation, the TSA's initial focus was on aviation security; the agency was also given the responsibility of providing security for the entire national transportation system, including rail, land, maritime, transit, and pipeline elements. The Homeland Security Act of 2002 transferred the TSA into the newly created Department of Homeland Security (DHS). By the end of 2003 the TSA was screening 100 percent of checked and unchecked baggage at U.S. airports.

The TSA works with other DHS agencies, including the U.S. Coast Guard, the U.S. Customs and Border Protection office, the Information Analysis and Infrastructure Protection Directorate, and the Science and Technology Directorate to address surface and maritime transportation security issues. The TSA also maintains a close alliance with the Transportation Department.

On May 5, 2003, the TSA and the Transportation Department issued an interim final rule on the transport of hazardous materials. The rule required background checks on commercial drivers before certification to transport hazardous materials. During the first two years of the rule's implementation, approximately 3.5 million commercial drivers underwent background checks that included a review of criminal, mental health, and FBI records. The checks also verified that the driver was a U.S. citizen or a lawful permanent resident.

The TSA issues and administers Transportation Security Regulations (TSRs). Many TSRs are former rules of the Federal Aviation Administration (FAA) that were transferred to the TSA when the TSA assumed FAA's civil aviation security function on Feb. 17, 2002.

Under the direction of the **Office of Security Policy and Industry Engagement**, the TSA enhances national transportation security by maintaining a systemwide awareness of potential threats and setting standards to prevent and protect the transportation system and its users from harm or disruption by terrorists. The office consists of the following divisions:

Commercial Aviation works with industry stakeholders to develop and implement aviation security policies and programs based on evolving threats. These functions were previously carried out under two different offices: Commercial Airlines and Commercial Airports. In 2009, the Offices of Commercial Airports and Airlines were consolidated under the newly formed office of Commercial Aviation.

Air Cargo evaluates risks associated with supply chain stakeholders, cargo, critical supply chains, and key nodes/systems, with an emphasis on air cargo supply chains.

Freight Rail works with industry and government experts to facilitate assessments of threat vulnerabilities related to the freight rail environment and how to best address them.

General Aviation develops strategies, policies, and programs to reduce the security risks and vulnerabilities associated with general aviation operations.

Highway and Motor Carriers focuses on security of the movement of people, goods, and services through the highway transportation infrastructure, which includes highways, roads, intermodal terminals, bridges, tunnels, trucks, buses, and maintenance facilities.

Mass Transit and Passenger Rail develops security policies and plans that reduce the risk of terrorist attacks on mass transit systems, including commuter rail, subways and metros, long-distance rail (Amtrak and Alaska Railroad) and intracity buses.

Pipeline Security focuses on security for pipeline infrastructure and the security of movement of hazardous materials through the national pipeline infrastructure.

Cross Modal manages and guides the national transportation system counterterrorism protection mission, including developing strategies, plans, and performance reports. This division also provides economic analyses and regulatory evaluations.

Maritime works with the U.S. Coast Guard (the lead agency for maritime security) and Customs and Border Protection, in order to secure the nation's ports and shipping transportation network.

The TSA works to maintain two-way communications with all of its partners, including federal, state, and local governments and agencies; Congress; trade and industry associations and organizations; public organizations and private businesses; foreign governments; international businesses and organizations; and the general public.

The TSA's **Office of Law Enforcement/Federal Air Marshal Service**, through its Federal Flight Deck Officer training, provides intensive forty-eight-hour training to volunteer commercial pilots who function as federal law enforcement officers, with jurisdiction limited to the flight deck, or cockpit. These pilots complement the federal air marshals deployed within the aircraft and are authorized to act only if the cockpit is threatened. The TSA also manages the Federal Air Marshal Service that deploys air marshals to detect, deter, and defeat hostile acts targeting U.S. air carriers, airports, passengers, and crews.

In addition, the Office of Law Enforcement/Federal Air Marshal Service maintains oversight of the Law Enforcement Officers Flying Armed training program. This training program is mandatory for all law enforcement officers flying armed under the Code of Federal Regulation Carriage of Accessible Weapons. State, local, and territorial law enforcement officers who are flying armed must submit a National Law Enforcement Telecommunications System (NLETS) message prior to travel.

TSA was mandated by Congress to implement provisions recommended by the 9/11 Commission to enhance transportation security. Among the provisions TSA has implemented:

Secure Flight program requires airlines to collect a passenger's full name (as it appears on government-issued ID), date of birth, gender, and Redress Number (if applicable). TSA compares the names to the terrorist watch list.

Certified Cargo Screening Program fulfills the requirement that all cargo transported on a passenger aircraft be screened for explosives. TSA certifies cargo screening facilities in the United States to screen cargo prior to providing it to airlines for shipment on passenger flights. Certified cargo screening facilities must carry out a TSA-approved security program and adhere to a strict chain of custody requirements.

Visible Intermodal Prevention and Response (VIPR) teams enhance security by working in aviation, mass transit, rail, and other transportation modes alongside local law enforcement agencies. VIPR teams work with local law enforcement officials to supplement existing security resources, provide deterrent presence and detection capabilities, and introduce an element of unpredictability to disrupt potential terrorist planning activities.

From its inception, TSA has been charged with balancing security needs and customer service. TSA allowed expedited screening for travelers that participate in any of the Trusted Travelers programs administered by Customs and Border Protection (see *p. 664*). TSA also administers its own Precheck program for frequent travelers to expedite the screening process. After several highly publicized gaffes involving screening of small children, elderly, and disabled passengers, TSA modified requirements for screening these passengers. Congress stepped in and mandated changes as well. The Risk-Based Security Screening for Members of the Armed Forces Act directed the TSA to develop and implement a plan for expedited security screening services for a uniformed Armed Forces member. The No-Hassle Flying Act of 2012 authorized TSA to waive rescreening requirements for flights from international preclearance airports that install U.S. equivalent checked baggage screening processes and equipment.

■ KEY PERSONNEL

Administrator
 Melvin Carraway (acting) . . . . (571) 227–2801
Deputy Administrator
 Mark Hatfield Jr. (acting) . . . . (571) 227–2801
Law Enforcement / Federal Air Marshal Service
 Roderick Allison . . . . (703) 487–3100
Legislative Affairs
 Sarah Dietch . . . . (571) 227–2717
Security Operations
 Kelly C. Hoggan . . . . (571) 227–5560
Security Policy and Industry Engagement
 Eddie Mayenschein . . . . (571) 227–4640

■ INFORMATION SOURCES

Internet
 Agency website: www.tsa.gov. Includes an overview of the agency, frequently asked questions, press releases, regulations, employer information, traveler and consumer information, and links to other federal Internet sites.
 E-mail: TSA-ContactCenter@dhs.gov

Telephone Contacts
 TSA Contact Center . . . . (866) 289–9673
 Hotline (for reporting suspicious
  behavior at airports) . . . . (866) 427–3287
 TSA Recruitment Center . . . . (877) 872–7990
 TTY . . . . (877) 872–7992
 Federal Relay Service TTY . . . . (800) 877–8339

TSA Strategic Communications and Public Affairs
 601 S. 12th St., 11th Floor
 Arlington, VA 20598
 (571) 227–2829
 LuAnn Canipe, assistant administrator
 E-mail: tsamedia@tsa.dhs.gov

Answers questions from the press. Issues news releases and media information materials.

Freedom of Information
 Freedom of Information Act Office, TSA-20
 601 South 12th St., 11th Floor
 Arlington, VA 20598
 (571) 227–2300
 (866) 364–2872
 E-mail: FOIA@tsa.dhs.gov
 Teri Miller (acting), FOIA officer

DOCKETS
 Federal dockets are available at www.regulations.gov. (*See appendix for Searching and Commenting on Regulations: Regulations.gov.*)

RULES AND REGULATIONS

TSA rules and regulations are published in the *Code of Federal Regulations,* Title 49, Chapter XII, Parts 1500–1699. Proposed rules, final rules, and updates to the *Code of Federal Regulations* are published in the daily *Federal Register. (See appendix for information on how to obtain and use these publications.)* The *Federal Register* and the *Code of Federal Regulations* may be accessed online at www.archives.gov/federal-register/cfr; the site contains a link to the federal government's regulatory website at www.regulations.gov *(see appendix).*

▇ LEGISLATION

Uniting and Strengthening America by Providing Appropriate Tools Required to Intercept and Obstruct Terrorism Act of 2002 (USA Patriot Act) (115 Stat. 272, 18 U.S.C. 1 note). Signed by the president Oct. 26, 2001. Amended the federal transportation code to require background checks on individuals before certification to transport hazardous materials.

Aviation and Transportation Security Act (115 Stat. 597, 49 U.S.C. 40101 note). Signed by the president Nov. 19, 2001. Amended federal transportation law to establish the TSA within the Transportation Department. Authorized the TSA to provide for civil aviation security; day-to-day federal security screening operations for passenger air transportation; maritime, rail, and other surface transportation security, especially during a national emergency; and the management of security information, including notifying airports of possible terrorists.

Maritime Transportation Security Act of 2002 (116 Stat. 2064, 46 U.S.C. 2101 note). Signed by the president Nov. 25, 2002. Required the creation of a National Maritime Transportation Security Plan for deterring and responding to a transportation security incident. Established the Transportation Worker Identification Credential program to issue tamper-resistant biometric credentials to workers who require unescorted access to secure areas of ports, vessels, outer continental shelf facilities, and credentialed merchant mariners.

Homeland Security Act of 2002 (116 Stat. 2135, 6 U.S.C. 551, 557). Signed by the president Nov. 25, 2002. Transferred the TSA to the DHS. Title XIV amended federal law to establish a two-year pilot program to deputize volunteer pilots of air carriers as federal law enforcement officers and provide training, supervision, and equipment for such officers.

Intelligence Reform and Terrorism Prevention Act of 2004 (118 Stat. 3638, 50 U.S.C. 401 note). Signed by the president Dec. 17, 2004. Required the TSA to incorporate biometric technology in law enforcement identification. Directed the TSA to provide a passenger prescreening system of persons who rent charter or rental aircraft with a maximum takeoff weight of more than 12,500 pounds.

Directed the TSA to establish an appeals process for persons included on the federal government's terrorist watch list to correct erroneous information. Made other requirements with regard to strengthening screening procedures.

USA Patriot Act Additional Reauthorizing Amendments Act of 2006 (18 U.S.C. 1 note). Signed by the president March 9, 2006. Reauthorized the USA Patriot Act and made permanent fourteen of its sixteen sections. Placed a four-year sunset provision on the other two sections: the authority to conduct "roving" surveillance under the Foreign Intelligence Surveillance Act (FISA), and the authority to request production of business records under FISA.

Implementing Recommendations of the 9/11 Commission Act of 2007 (121 Stat. 266, 6 U.S.C. 101 note). Signed by the president Aug. 3, 2007. Authorized the TSA to develop Visible Intermodal Prevention and Response (VIPR) teams to augment the security of any mode of U.S. transportation. Increased security measures regarding cargo screening and directed the DHS secretary to promulgate a system to compare passenger information to "no fly" lists using the consolidated and integrated terrorist watch list.

Supplemental Appropriations Act, 2010 (124 Stat. 2317). Signed by the president July 29, 2010. Requires TSA to issue a security directive that requires a commercial foreign air carrier that operates flights in and out of the United States to check the list of individuals who TSA has prohibited from flying not later than 30 minutes after such list is modified and provided to such carrier, except for such carriers that are enrolled in the Secure Flight program or that are Advance Passenger Information System Quick Query compliant.

Risk-Based Security Screening for Members of the Armed Forces Act (125 Stat. 1874, 49 U.S.C. 40101 note). Signed by the president Jan. 3, 2012. Directs the TSA to develop and implement a plan for expedited security screening services for a uniformed Armed Forces member and, to the extent possible, accompanying family, if the member, while in uniform, presents documentation indicating official orders for air transportation departing from a primary airport.

No-Hassle Flying Act of 2012 (126 Stat. 1593, 49 U.S.C. 40101 note). Signed by the president Dec. 20, 2012. Authorizes TSA administrator to waive rescreening requirements for flights from international preclearance airports that install U.S. equivalent checked baggage screening processes and equipment.

Honor Flight Act (128 Stat. 2094, 49 U.S.C. 40101 note). Signed by the president Dec. 16, 2014. Directs the Transportation Security Administration administrator to establish a process for providing expedited passenger screening services for veterans traveling on an Honor Flight Network private charter, or another not-for-profit organization that honors veterans.

U.S. Citizenship and Immigration Services

20 Massachusetts Ave. N.W., Washington, DC 20529
Internet: www.uscis.gov

The Homeland Security Act of 2002 established the bureau of U.S. Citizenship and Immigration Services (USCIS) within the Department of Homeland Security (DHS) on March 1, 2003. The USCIS assumed the service and benefit functions of the old Immigration and Naturalization Service (INS). The investigation and enforcement activities of INS transferred to the Immigration and Customs Enforcement (ICE) (*p. 643*); the Border Patrol transferred to U.S. Customs and Border Protection (CBP) (*p. 664*).

The agency is headed by the director of USCIS, who reports directly to the deputy secretary for homeland security.

Immigration and Related Services

The DHS improves the administration of benefits and immigration services for applicants by exclusively focusing on immigration and citizenship services. USCIS includes approximately 19,000 employees and contractors working in approximately 223 headquarters and field offices around the world. The USCIS is responsible for processing benefits that range from work authorization documents, to asylum and refugee applications, to petitions for immediate relatives to immigrate to the United States.

Immigration has been a highly politicized issue for many years. Between 1993 and 2000, nearly 6.9 million immigrants applied for citizenship, more than the total in the previous forty years combined. The pending caseload of naturalization applications grew to more than 2 million in 1998. Faced with this unprecedented workload, INS undertook a two-year initiative to clear the naturalization backlog and restore timely processing of citizenship applications. By the end of 2002 (before its transition to the USCIS), the pending caseload had dropped to nearly 600,000—the lowest it had been since November 1996.

The reconstituted agency went through a similar cycle. By September 2005 the USCIS had successfully reduced its backlog to 1.5 million cases, down from a high of 3.8 million cases in January 2004. The agency was working toward a six-month processing time for each case.

Immigration continues to be a hot-button issue. After failed attempts at passing comprehensive immigration reform through Congress, President Barack Obama announced on June 15, 2012, a program through DHS that would allow persons brought to the U.S. illegally as children to remain in the country without the fear of deportation through a two-year deferred action program. Though widely reported at the time as an executive order, this was not the case. The legal premise for this program was the authority of the DHS to exercise "prosecutorial discretion." Such discretion is usually administered on a case-by-case basis, but this action made it policy for a group of immigrants that met set requirements that mirrored provisions of the DREAM Act. Specifically, the deferral action applied to immigrants who came to the United States before age sixteen and were not older than thirty, had lived in the United States for at least five years, were in school or graduated high school, or served in the military. The applicants for the deferral program had to have a clean criminal history. The policy, known as Deferred Action for Childhood Arrivals (DACA), did not grant permanent legal status but provided the young immigrants a path to work legally and obtain driver's licenses.

The action came just months before the 2012 elections and prompted outcry from conservatives, who called the action an end-run around Congress to apply amnesty to a select group of immigrants. Following the results of the 2012 presidential race, whereby President Obama received more than 70 percent of the Hispanic vote, pragmatic Republicans took up the cause of immigration reform when the 113th Congress convened in 2013.

As Congress prepared to take up the issue in early 2013, President Obama continued to exercise executive authority to further his immigration agenda. On January 2, 2013, DHS announced the posting of a final rule in the *Federal Register* that reduced the time U.S. citizens are separated from their immediate relatives (spouse, children, and parents) who are in the process of obtaining visas to become lawful permanent residents of the United States under certain circumstances. The final rule established a process that allows certain individuals to apply for a provisional unlawful presence waiver before they depart the United States to attend immigrant visa interviews in their countries of origin. The process took effect on March 4, 2013. Previously, an immediate relative of a U.S. citizen who was in the country illegally (including overstaying a visa) faced deportation and a waiting period of up to 10 years before being able to return.

Also in November 2014 the Obama administration expanded the provisions of DACA to allow more applicants and extended the deferral time from two years to three. The administration also announced another program, Deferred Action for Parental Accountability (DAPA), which would allow parents of U.S. citizens and lawful permanent residents to request deferred action and employment authorization for three years. In December the state of Texas filed a lawsuit questioning the constitutionality of President Obama's executive action. In February 2015 a U.S. District Court in Texas granted an injunction halting the expanded programs until the case could be heard. A ruling by the 5th Circuit Court of Appeals was expected in late spring.

USCIS manages the process that allows individuals from other countries to work in the United States. All foreign workers must obtain permission to work legally in the United States. Each employment category for admission has different requirements, conditions, and authorized periods of stay. Some of the opportunities are temporary and some provide a path to a green card (permanent residence). A temporary worker is an individual seeking to enter the United States temporarily for a specific purpose. Nonimmigrants enter the United States for a temporary period of time; they are restricted to the activity or reason for which their nonimmigrant visa was issued. A permanent worker is an individual who is authorized to live and work permanently in the United States. Students and exchange visitors may, under certain circumstances, be allowed to work in the United States. They must obtain permission from an authorized official at their school.

USCIS administers E-Verify, an Internet-based system that compares information from an employee's Form I-9, Employment Eligibility Verification, to data from U.S Department of Homeland Security and Social Security Administration records to confirm employment eligibility. While participation in E-Verify is voluntary for most businesses, some companies may be required by state law or federal regulation to use E-Verify. E-Verify is also mandatory for employers with federal contracts or subcontracts that contain the Federal Acquisition Regulation E-Verify clause.

USCIS also administers a program to verify immigration status for the purpose of granting public benefits to qualified immigrants. The Systematic Alien Verification for Entitlements (SAVE) Program is an inter-governmental initiative designed to aid benefit-granting agencies in determining an applicant's immigration status, thereby ensuring that only entitled applicants receive federal, state, or local public benefits and licenses. The program is an information service for benefit-granting agencies, institutions, licensing bureaus, and other governmental entities.

Each year, USCIS services assists thousands of U.S. citizens to adopt children from overseas. USCIS is responsible for determining the eligibility and suitability of the prospective adoptive parents looking to adopt and determining the eligibility of the child to immigrate to the United States. There are three processes for adopting a child internationally: the Hague Convention treaty; orphan adoptions from non-Hague convention countries; and Petition for Alien Relative filing. Each process is governed by its own set of regulations.

Homeland Security and Humanitarian Assistance

The Intelligence Reform and Terrorism Prevention Act of 2004 required aliens to submit to in-person interviews with consular officers in specified circumstances. It also precluded judicial review of visa revocations or revocations of other travel documents by consular officers or the secretary of state.

In May 2005 the REAL ID Act was passed. Among its provisions, the REAL ID Act amended the Immigration and Nationality Act to deny entry to the United States to persons who committed acts of terrorism or associated with terrorist organizations. The legislation also provided for the deportation of aliens who committed acts of terrorism or who associated with terrorist organizations.

The REAL ID Act placed a burden on states to incorporate new federal standards for driver licenses and non-driver identification cards. Governors and state legislatures balked at the unfunded mandate. By 2011 none of the fifty states was in compliance with the REAL ID Act. In December 2013 DHS announced a phased enforcement plan for the REAL ID Act. States and other jurisdictions began making progress to enhance the security of their driver's licenses. Some states began implementing a two-tier system that offers federally compliant identification as well as allows individuals to keep their non-compliant identification. In April 2014 the federal government began restricting access to federal facilities and nuclear power plants for individuals unless they had the federally approved identification. The final phase of implementation would restrict passengers from boarding commercial flights unless they had compliant identification; the deadline for this final phase was slated for January 2016. Passengers from states that did not implement the provisions of the REAL ID Act would have the option to use a passport to board commercial flights (including domestic flights).

USCIS also administers humanitarian programs that provide protection to individuals inside and outside the United States who are displaced by war, famine, and civil and political unrest, and those who are forced to flee their countries to escape the risk of death and torture. Refugee status or asylum may be granted to people who have been persecuted or fear they will be persecuted on account of race, religion, nationality, and/or membership in a particular social group or political opinion. A battered spouse, children, and/or parents of U.S. citizens or permanent residents may file for immigration benefits without the abuser's knowledge. Also, victims of human trafficking and other crimes may receive immigration status in certain circumstances.

■ KEY PERSONNEL

Director
      Leon Rodriguez.................. (202) 272–1000
Deputy Director
      Lori Scialabba .... (202) 272–8000

Chief Counsel
Ur Mendoza Jaddou . . . . (202) 272–1400
Office of Citizenship
Laura Patching. . . . . (202) 272–1310
Office of Communications
Angelica Alfonso-Royals . . . . (202) 272–1215
Office of Legislative Affairs
James McCament . . . . (202) 272–1940
Office of Performance and Quality
David Garner. (202) 272–1000
Office of Policy and Strategy
Denise Vanison . . . . (202) 272–1470
Office of Privacy
Donald Hawkins . . . . (202) 272–8404
Office of Transformation Coordination
Kathleen Stanley . . . . (202) 223–2300
Customer Service and Public Engagement
Mariela Melero . . . . (202) 272–1191
Enterprise Services
Tammy Meckley . . . . (202) 272–1000
Field Operations
Daniel Renaud. . . . . (202) 272–1001
Fraud Detection and National Security
Sarah Kendall. (202) 272–8448
Management
Tracy Renaud. (202) 272–8120
Refugee, Asylum, and International Operations
Joseph E. Langlois. . . . . (202) 272–1663
Service Center Operations
Donald Neufeld . . . . (202) 272–1710

■ INFORMATION SOURCES

Internet

Agency website: www.uscis.gov. Includes an overview of the agency, frequently asked questions, press releases, USCIS regulations, and links to other federal Internet sites. Data and statistics on immigration and the foreign-born population are also accessible through the agency's website. USCIS forms may be downloaded from the USCIS website.

Telephone Contacts

General Information
(Human Capital) . . . .(202) 272–1560
USCIS Forms Request Line . . . .(800) 870–3676
Federal Relay Service TTY . . . .(800) 877–8339
National Human Trafficking
Resource Center. . . . .(888) 373–7888
E-mail: nhtrc@polarisproject.org
National Benefits Center (Adoptions) . .(877) 424–8374
General Employer Information . . . . . .(800) 357–2099

Information and Publications

KEY OFFICES

USCIS National Customer Service Center
(800) 375–5283
TTY (800) 767–1833

Phone service providing information and assistance on immigration services and benefits.

USCIS Office of Communications
20 Massachusetts Ave. N.W., #3100
Washington, DC 20529
(202) 272–1200
Angie Alfonso-Royals, deputy chief
Christopher Bentley, press secretary
Blog: http://blog.uscis.gov

Answers questions from the press. Oversees and coordinates official USCIS communications to both internal and external audiences. Issues news releases and media information materials. Those interested may subscribe to receive free e-mail updates and press releases.

Freedom of Information
U.S. Citizenship and Immigration Services
National Record Center/FOIA/PA Office
P.O. Box 648010
Lee's Summit, MO 64064–8010
(800) 375–5283
Fax (816) 350–5785
E-mail: uscis.foia@uscis.dhs.gov
Jill Eggleston, FOIA officer
Hours: 7:00 a.m. to 2:15 p.m. (central time)

PUBLICATIONS

Immigration handbooks, manuals, and the *USCIS Monthly* newsletter are available through the USCIS website, by calling the USCIS National Customer Service Center at (800) 375–5283, or by contacting the Office of Communications at (202) 272–1200.

Reference Resources

LIBRARIES

USCIS Public Reading Room
111 Massachusetts Ave. N.W., 1st Floor
Washington, DC 20529–2180
(202) 587–9720
Hours: 8:00 a.m. to 4:30 p.m.
Internet: www.uscis.gov/library

Maintains USCIS annual reports, statistical reports on aliens and immigrants, interim decisions of the Board of Immigration Appeals, booklets describing immigration forms, and information on immigration regulations. The Reading Room also maintains two computers for viewing information maintained in the Electronic Reading Room. Call ahead for appointment.

USCIS History Office
111 Massachusetts Ave. N.W., 1st Floor
Washington, DC 20529
(202) 272–8370
E-mail: CISHistory.library@dhs.gov

Maintains a collection on the history of USCIS and immigration in general. Open to the public by appointment only.

DOCKETS

Federal dockets are available at www.regulations.gov. (*See appendix for Searching and Commenting on Regulations: Regulations.gov.*)

RULES AND REGULATIONS

USCIS rules and regulations are published in the *Code of Federal Regulations,* Title 8, Chapter I, Parts 1–499. Proposed rules, final rules, and updates to the *Code of Federal Regulations* are published in the daily *Federal Register. (See appendix for information on how to obtain and use these publications.)* The *Federal Register* and the *Code of Federal Regulations* may be accessed online at www.archives.gov/federal-register/cfr; the site contains a link to the federal government's regulatory website at www.regulations.gov (*see appendix*).

▨ LEGISLATION

The USCIS carries out its responsibilities under:

Immigration and Nationality Act (INA), as amended (66 Stat. 163, 8 U.S.C. 1101). Signed by the president June 27, 1952. Contained virtually all of the law relating to the entry of aliens and to the acquisition and loss of U.S. citizenship.

Immigration Control and Reform Act of 1986 (100 Stat. 3359). Signed by the president Nov. 6, 1986. Amended the Immigration and Nationality Act to make it unlawful for an employer to hire or recruit any alien knowing that such person is unauthorized to work. Established an employment verification system. Provided "amnesty" clause for agricultural seasonal workers and immigrants who had been continuously and illegally present in the United States since Jan. 1, 1982, allowing them to apply for citizenship (excluding criminal aliens) within eighteen months of enactment.

Immigration Act of 1990 (104 Stat. 4978, 8 U.S.C. 1101 note). Signed by the president Nov. 29, 1990. Implemented major changes affecting immigrants and nonimmigrants, Filipino World War II veterans desiring U.S. citizenship, and El Salvadoran nationals, and others with immigration concerns. Revised the numerical limits and preference system regulating immigration, empowered the attorney general to issue final determinations on applications for U.S. citizenship, and charged INS with issuing certificates of naturalization.

Immigration and Nationality Technical Corrections Act of 1994 (108 Stat. 4305, 8 U.S.C. 1101). Signed by the president Oct. 25, 1994. Made numerous specific changes to the Immigration and Nationality Act. Allowed U.S. visas for visits from officials of Taiwan; gave equal treatment to women in conferring U.S. citizenship to children born abroad.

Antiterrorism and Effective Death Penalty Act of 1996 (110 Stat. 1214, 18 U.S.C. 1 note). Signed by the president April 24, 1996. Amended the INA to establish procedures for the removal of alien terrorists.

Personal Responsibility and Work Opportunity Reconciliation Act of 1996 (The Welfare Reform Act) (110 Stat. 2260, 8 U.S.C. 1601). Signed by the president Aug. 22, 1996. Restricted the access of legal and illegal immigrants to many public benefits.

Illegal Immigration Reform and Immigration Responsibility Act of 1996 (110 Stat. 3009–5468, U.S.C. 1101 note). Signed by the president Sept. 30, 1996. Changed the public charge of inadmissibility standard for prospective immigrants and greatly strengthened the financial responsibility of petitioners for family-based immigrants as well as for some employment-based immigrants. Required the INS to establish a verification system for most federal public benefits. Required INS to verify status of aliens and naturalized citizens for federal, state, or local government agencies.

An Act to Require the Attorney General to Establish a Program in Local Prisons to Identify, Prior to Arraignment, Criminal Aliens and Aliens Who Are Unlawfully Present in the United States (111 Stat. 2647, 8 U.S.C. 1226 note). Signed by the president Dec. 5, 1997. Directs the attorney general to implement a program to identify aliens held in local incarceration facilities prior to criminal arraignment who are illegally in the United States or who are deportable on criminal or security grounds. Requires that at least one INS employee with identification expertise be assigned to each program facility.

Torture Victims Relief Act of 1998 (13 Stat. 1301, 22 U.S.C. 2151 note). Signed by the president Oct. 30, 1998. Recognized that a significant number of refugees and asylum-seekers entering the United States have been victims of torture and required INS to give those claiming asylum prompt consideration of their applications for political asylum.

Immigration and Naturalization Service Data Management Improvement Act of 2000 (114 Stat. 337, 8 U.S.C. 1101 note). Signed by the president June 15, 2000. Amended the Illegal Immigration Reform and Immigrant Responsibility Act of 1996 regarding the automated entry-exit control system to require that such system be an integrated entry and exit data system using available data. Stated that that no additional data collection authority was authorized.

Intercountry Adoption Act of 2000 (114 Stat. 825, 42 U.S.C. 14901 note). Signed by the president Oct. 6, 2000. Amended the Immigration and Nationality Act to include under its definition of "child," an adopted child.

Trafficking Victims Protection Act of 2000 (114 Stat. 1464, 22 U.S.C. 7101 note). Signed by the president Oct. 28, 2000. Amends the Immigration and Nationality Act to create a new nonimmigrant "T" visa for an alien whom the attorney general determines is a victim of a severe form of trafficking in persons.

Child Citizenship Act (CCA) (114 Stat. 1631, 8 U.S.C. 1101 note). Signed by the president Oct. 30, 2000. Amended the Immigration and Nationality Act to provide automatic U.S. citizenship for a child born outside the United States when the following conditions are met: (1) at least one parent is a U.S. citizen; (2) the child is under eighteen years old; and (3) the child is residing in the United States in the legal and physical custody of the citizen parent pursuant to a lawful admission for permanent residence.

Legal Immigration Family Equity Act (LIFE Act) (114 Stat. 2762, 2762A-142, 8 U.S.C. 1101 note). Signed by the president Dec. 21, 2000. Amended the Immigration and Nationality Act to accord nonimmigrant status to certain aliens: (1) with pending or approved but unavailable visa petitions who are the spouses or unmarried sons and daughters of permanent resident aliens; and (2) with approved but unavailable visa petitions who are the spouses of U.S. citizens or minor children of such spouses.

Food Stamp Reauthorization Act of 2002 (116 Stat. 1348, 7 U.S.C. 7901 note). Signed by the president May 13, 2002. Amended the Personal Responsibility and Work Opportunity Reconciliation Act of 1996 to make all legal immigrant children, regardless of U.S. entry date, eligible for the Supplemental Security Income and food stamp programs, beginning in fiscal year 2004.

Homeland Security Act of 2002 (116 Stat. 2135, 6 U.S.C. 551, 557). Signed by the president Nov. 25, 2002. Created the DHS. Gave the department exclusive authority to issue, administer, and enforce regulations with respect to the Immigration and Nationality Act (INA). Authorized the USCIS to (1) establish policies for performing and administering transferred INS functions; (2) establish national immigration services policies and priorities; and (3) implement a managerial rotation program.

Consolidated Appropriations Act, 2005 (118 Stat. 2809). Signed by the president Dec. 8, 2004. Title IV: L-1 Visa and H-1B Visa Reform Act. The L-1 visa provisions, which applied to foreign companies with offices in the United States, were tightened to prevent abuse of blanket L-1 visas by prohibiting the placement of L-1 visa holders at unrelated companies. The H-1B visa provisions raised the cap on the number of H-1B visas allowed for highly skilled, educated workers.

Intelligence Reform and Terrorism Prevention Act of 2004 (118 Stat. 3638, 8 U.S.C. 1155, 1201). Signed by the president Dec. 17, 2004. Amended the Immigration and Nationality Act to require aliens to submit to in-person interviews with consular officers in specified circumstances. Precluded judicial review of visa revocations or revocations of other travel documents by consular officers or the secretary of state. Added to the list of deportable aliens those nonimmigrants whose visas or other documentation authorizing admission were revoked.

REAL ID Act of 2005 (119 Stat. 231, 8 U.S.C. 1211 note). Signed by the president May 11, 2005. Amended the Immigration and Nationality Act to exclude immigration benefits to persons who engaged in or supported terrorist activities or organizations. Allowed for the deportation of aliens from the United States for terrorism-related offenses.

Violence Against Women and Department of Justice Reauthorization Act of 2005 (119 Stat. 2960, 42 U.S.C. 13701). Signed by the president Jan. 5, 2006. Amended the Immigration and Nationality Act (INA) respecting T-visa (victims of trafficking) nonimmigrant aliens to replace references to the attorney general with references to the secretary of homeland security. Eliminated language requiring "extreme hardship" for the admission of specified family members accompanying or following to join such an alien. Exempted an alien from the requirement to assist in a trafficking investigation if the person is unable to do so because of psychological or physical trauma.

Consolidated Natural Resources Act of 2008 (122 Stat. 853, 48 U.S.C. 1806 note). Signed by the president May 8, 2008. Title VII Extends U.S. immigration laws, as defined by the Immigration and Nationality Act, to the Commonwealth of the Northern Mariana Islands, subject to a transition period through December 31, 2014.

SSI Extension for Elderly and Disabled Refugees Act (122 Stat. 3567, 8 U.S.C. 1612(a)(2)). Signed by the president Sept. 30, 2008. Amended the Personal Responsibility and Work Opportunity Reconciliation Act of 1996 to extend supplemental security income (SSI) for refugees, asylees, and certain other humanitarian immigrants in fiscal years 2009 through 2011.

Child Soldiers Accountability Act of 2008 (122 Stat. 3735, 18 U.S.C. 1 note). Signed by the president Oct. 3, 2008. Amended the Immigration and Nationality Act to render any alien who has recruited or used child soldiers inadmissible or deportable.

Military Personnel Citizenship Processing Act (122 Stat. 4087, 8 U.S.C. 1101 note). Signed by the president Oct. 9, 2008. Established a liaison with the Federal Bureau of Investigation in United States Citizenship and Immigration Services to expedite naturalization applications filed by members of the armed forces.

Employ American Workers Act (123 Stat. 305). Signed by the president Feb. 17, 2009. Title XVI of the American Recovery and Reinvestment Act makes it unlawful for any recipient of Troubled Asset Relief Program (TARP) funding under the Emergency Economic Stabilization Act of 2008 or under the Federal Reserve Act to hire any nonimmigrant with an H-1B visa unless the recipient is in compliance with the requirements for an H-1B dependent employer.

Human Rights Enforcement Act of 2009 (123 Stat. 3480, 28 U.S.C. 1 note). Signed by the president Dec. 22, 2009. Amends the Immigration and Nationality Act to broaden the basis for rendering aliens participating in genocide inadmissible.

Patient Protection and Affordable Care Act (124 Stat. 119, 42 U.S.C. 18001 note). Signed by the president March 23, 2010. Made sweeping changes to the health insurance industry regarding products, pricing, and availability. Extended some provisions to immigrants lawfully present in the United States.

International Adoption Simplification Act (124 Stat. 3058, 8 U.S.C. 1101 note). Signed by the president Nov. 30, 2010. Amends the Immigration and Nationality Act to include in the definition of "child," and thus in the exemption from required admissions vaccination documentation, certain children who have been adopted in a foreign country that is a signatory to the Hague Convention or who are emigrating from such a country for U.S. adoption.

Help HAITI Act of 2010 (124 Stat. 3175, 8 U.S.C. 1255 note). Signed by the president Dec. 9, 2010. Authorizes USCIS to grant lawful permanent resident status to certain orphaned children from Haiti.

Asia-Pacific Economic Cooperation Business Travel Cards Act of 2011 (125 Stat. 550, 8 U.S.C. 1185). Signed by the president Nov. 12, 2011. Authorized the DHS secretary, in coordination with the secretary of state, to issue Asia-Pacific Economic Cooperation Business Travel Cards to eligible persons during the seven-year period ending on September 30, 2018.

Public Law 112–58 (125 Stat. 747, 8 U.S.C. 1186a). Signed by the president Nov. 23, 2011. Amended the Immigration and Nationality Act to toll, during active-duty service abroad in the Armed Forces, the 90-day period of time for an alien spouse or petitioning spouse to file a petition and appear for an interview to remove the conditional basis for permanent resident status.

Violence Against Women Reauthorization Act of 2013 (127 Stat. 54, 42 U.S.C. 13701 note). Signed by the president March 7, 2013. Amended the Immigration and Nationality Act to expand the definition of nonimmigrant U-visa (aliens who are victims of certain crimes) to include victims of stalking. Amended the Immigration and Nationality Act to make eligible for a nonimmigrant T-visa (trafficking victims cooperating with law enforcement) adult or minor children of certain derivative family members of a T-visa alien. Amended the Illegal Immigration Reform and Immigrant Responsibility Act of 1996 to authorize the DHS secretary to disclose information relating to aliens who are victims of domestic violence to law enforcement officials.

U.S. Coast Guard

2100 2nd St. S.W., Washington, DC 20593
Internet: www.uscg.mil

The U.S. Coast Guard (USCG) is the federal government's primary maritime law enforcement agency. The Coast Guard is a branch of the armed forces formerly under the jurisdiction of the Department of Transportation (DOT). It was transferred to the jurisdiction of the Department of Homeland Security (DHS) with enactment of the Homeland Security Act of 2002. During time of war, or by presidential order, the Coast Guard operates as a part of the U.S. Navy. The primary mission of the Coast Guard is the protection of U.S. maritime resources and infrastructure, which includes 95,000 miles of coastline, more than 300 ports, more than 10,000 miles of navigable rivers, and 3.4 million square miles of ocean.

The Coast Guard regulates vessels, sets and enforces safety standards, and prescribes license requirements for merchant marine personnel. Standards apply to vessels built in or under the jurisdiction of the United States.

The president appoints the commandant of the Coast Guard, and the Senate confirms the nomination. The Marine Safety Council, chaired by the Coast Guard's chief counsel, provides oversight and guidance for the Coast Guard's regulatory activity. Units within the Coast Guard bring proposals for regulations to the council, whose members also include the assistant commandants of three other Coast Guard offices: Marine Safety and Environmental Protection; Operations; and Systems. The council determines whether or not the proposed regulation will be approved.

Areas for which the Coast Guard is responsible include:

Boating safety. Regulations are issued by the Coast Guard to establish minimum boating safety standards, to require use of safety equipment, and to prevent damage to vessels and structures in navigable waters.

Bridges. The Coast Guard regulates the construction, maintenance, and operation of bridges across U.S. navigable waters.

Deep-water ports. The construction, ownership, and operation of deep-water ports (offshore installations used to transfer oil from supertankers to shore facilities) are regulated by the Coast Guard.

Great Lakes. Registration is required of pilots of domestic and foreign vessels on the Great Lakes. There also are regulations that prescribe permissible rates and charges for pilot services.

Merchant marine personnel. The Coast Guard develops and regulates licensing procedures for masters, mates, chief engineers, and assistant engineers of merchant ships. It also certifies merchant mariners.

Navigation. Navigation aids, including lighthouses, fog signals, lightships, buoys, and beacons, are installed and maintained by the Coast Guard.

The Coast Guard also operates a fleet of ice-breaking vessels to assist marine transportation, prevent flooding, and aid U.S. polar installations and research teams.

Outer continental shelf (OCS). The Coast Guard regulates the design, construction, and maintenance of structures built on the OCS.

Passenger vessels. Vessels that carry passengers must pass Coast Guard inspections. In addition, the design, construction, and alteration of passenger ships are regulated, and limits are established on the number of passengers cargo vessels may carry. Operators are licensed by the Coast Guard.

Search and rescue. The Coast Guard operates a search and rescue network that is responsible for saving lives and protecting property on the high seas. It enforces federal laws and treaties related to the high seas and conducts investigations.

Vessel documentation. The Coast Guard administers vessel documentation statutes and operates a system to register U.S. vessels sold or transferred to U.S. citizens abroad.

Water pollution. The Coast Guard boards and examines vessels carrying oil and other hazardous materials. It requires proof and issues certificates of responsibility to owners and operators of vessels that may be liable to the United States for the costs of removing oil and other hazardous materials from the navigable waters of the United States, adjoining shorelines, and waters of the contiguous zone.

The Homeland Security Act of 2002 specifies five homeland security missions for the Coast Guard:

- Ports, waterways, and coastal security: Protecting ports, the flow of commerce, and the marine transportation system from terrorism.
- Drug interdiction: Maintaining maritime border security against illegal drugs.
- Migrant interdiction: Maintaining maritime border security against illegal aliens and weapons of mass destruction.

- Defense readiness: Keeping Coast Guard units at a high state of readiness and keeping marine transportation open for the transit of assets and personnel from other branches of the armed forces.
- Other law enforcement: Protecting against illegal fishing and indiscriminate destruction of living marine resources; coordinating efforts and intelligence with federal, state, and local agencies.

As part of its homeland security mission, the Coast Guard implemented provisions of the Maritime Transportation Security Act of 2002. The legislation requires port security committees, security plans for privately owned port facilities, vessel security plans, and other measures. The act standardizes security measures of the domestic port security team of federal, state, local, and private authorities, and authorized the creation of Coast Guard Maritime Safety and Security Teams. The act also requires the Coast Guard to issue regulations for the issuance of merchant mariner qualification credentials. In March 2009 the Coast Guard announced final rules for the Transportation Worker Identification Credentials (TWIC) program for workers who require unescorted access to secure areas of ports, vessels, outer continental shelf facilities, and credentialed merchant mariners.

In late summer 2005 the Coast Guard was among the first federal agencies to arrive on the Gulf Coast to assist in the aftermath of Hurricane Katrina. Using helicopters to pluck stranded residents from their rooftops in flooded areas, the Coast Guard rescued 22,000 people and assisted with the evacuation of 9,400 patients and medical personnel from hospitals in the region. Overall the Coast Guard deployed more than forty helicopters, twenty-five ships, and 2,400 personnel to conduct search, rescue, response, waterway reconstitution, and environmental impact assessment operations.

The Coast Guard was mandated by the SAFE Port Act of 2006 to track all large commercial vessels within U.S. waters. The Coast Guard met the April 1, 2007, deadline for rolling out the mandated system.

Under the current regulatory system, both the U.S. Coast Guard and the Interior Department Bureau of Safety and Environmental Enforcement (BSEE) (p. 705) have shared responsibilities for the regulation of safety management systems on the OCS. In 2013 the two agencies signed a memorandum of agreement (MOA) for regulating MODUs on the OCS. The MOA outlined the responsibilities of each agency for inspection and oversight of the systems and subsystems associated with mobile offshore drilling units (MODU) engaged in offshore drilling operations.

The Coast Guard was the first responding agency to the BP *Deepwater Horizon* oil spill in April 2010. The Coast Guard continued to lead the federal government's response efforts, with a deployment of forty-six cutters and twenty-two aircraft. Coast Guard regulations call for an Incident Specific Preparedness Review (ISPR) following a major oil spill. The *Deepwater Horizon* ISPR panel, comprised of retired Coast Guard officers and government officials,

released a report that acknowledged the enormity of the problem, but also noted that the Coast Guard mission of environmental protection and response had been eroded since the agency's focus was directed on homeland security functions. The report also indicated that increased funding and government oversight were necessary to prevent and mitigate such disasters in the future.

In 2014 the Coast Guard issued notice of recommended interim voluntary guidelines concerning fire and explosion analyses for mobile offshore drilling units (MODUs) and manned fixed and floating offshore facilities engaged in activities on the U.S. outer continental shelf (OCS). The guidelines are voluntary because there was no requirement in the current OCS regulations that requires a fire and explosion analysis. The Coast Guard also noted that recommendations in the 2009 International Maritime Organization MODU Code on the parameters of fire and explosion risk analysis were not sufficiently specific to adequately address these recommendations from the Coast Guard *Deepwater Horizon* report.

KEY PERSONNEL

Commandant
Adm. Paul F. Zukunft . . . . (202) 372–4411
Fax . . . . (202) 372–4960
Vice Commandant
Vice Adm. Peter V. Neffenger . . . . (202) 372–4422
Chief Administrative Law Judge
Walter J. Brudzinski . . . . (202) 372–4440
Acquisitions
Rear Adm. Bruce D. Baffer . . . . (202) 475–3000
Chief of Staff
Vice Adm. John P. Currier . . . . (202) 372–4546
Civil Rights
Terri Dickerson . . . . (202) 372–4500
Command, Control, Communications, Computers, and Information Technology
Rear Adm. Marshall B. Lytle III . . . . . (202) 475–3500
Congressional and Government Affairs
Rear Adm. Karl L. Schultz . . . . (202) 372–4620
Engineering and Logistics
Rear Adm. Ronald Rabago. . . . . (202) 475–5554
Human Resources
Rear Adm. David Callahan . . . . (202) 475–5000
Intelligence and Criminal Investigations
Rear Adm. Christopher J. Tomney . . . (202) 372–2700
International Affairs and Foreign Policy
Kelli Seybolt . . . . (202) 372–4453
Judge Advocate General
Rear Adm. Steven D. Poulin . . . . (202) 372–3726
Marine Transportation Systems
Gary C. Rasicot . . . . (202) 372–1001
Regulations and Standards
Jeff Lantz. . . . . (202) 372–1351
Operational Logistics
Rear Adm. Thomas W. Jones. . . . . (757) 628–4488
Resources
Rear Adm. Todd A. Sokalzuk . . . . (202) 372–3470

▥ INFORMATION SOURCES

Internet

Agency website: www.uscg.mil. Features news releases and information on programs and services, the history of the Coast Guard, recruiting, and Coast Guard personnel, as well as publications, forms, and regulations. The Commandant also maintains a Web log (blog) on the Coast Guard's website.

Telephone Contacts

Personnel Locator . . . .(202) 493–1713
Toll-free . . . .(866) 634–0574
National Command Center
(Emergencies Only) . . . .(202) 372–2100
Toll-free . . . . (800) DAD–SAFE
Maritime Safety Operations
(North-East) . . . .(800) 682–1796
Merchant Mariner Licensing and
Documentation . . . .(888) 427–5662
Coast Guard Academy. . . . .(800) 883–8724
Federal Relay Service TTY . . . .(800) 877–8339

Information and Publications

KEY OFFICES

USCG Governmental and Public Affairs
2100 2nd St. S.W., MS 7362
Washington, DC 20593–7362
(202) 372–4620
(202) 372–4627
Rear Adm. Peter Gautier, director
Internet: www.uscg.mil/history/default.asp

Provides information on operations, answers or refers questions, and issues news releases. The Office of the Coast Guard Historian can also answer questions, and its website contains detailed information about individuals within the Coast Guard and the history of the organization.

USCG Community Relations
Community Relations Branch
Office of Public Affairs
2703 Martin Luther King Jr. Ave. S.E., MS 7362
Washington, D.C. 20593
(202) 372–4620
Pride Sanders (acting), chief
(202) 372–4641
E-mail: pride.l.sanders@uscg.mil

Works to cultivate relationships within local communities. Provides information about air shows, public speakers, honor guard ceremonies, and other events. For more information, see the website at www.uscg.mil/community/index.htm.

USCG Office of Boating Safety
2703 Martin Luther King Jr. Ave., S.E., MS 7501
Washington, DC 20593–0001

(202) 372–1062
Jeffrey Hoedt, chief

The office maintains a list of publications relating to boating safety, standards, and regulations, available on the website at www.uscgboating.org.

Freedom of Information
Commandant (CG-611)
U.S. Coast Guard
2703 Martin Luther King Jr. Ave. S.E., MS 7710
Washington, DC 20593–7710
(202) 475–3525
Donald Taylor, FOIA officer
(202) 475–3516
Internet: www.uscg.mil/foia
E-mail: EFOIA@uscg.mil

PUBLICATIONS

USCG Public Affairs provides publications on boating safety, the merchant marine, environmental topics, and related subjects. Consumer publications are also available through the Coast Guard's district offices and on the website at www.uscg.mil/top/library/magazines.asp. These include the *Coast Guard Magazine* and journals such as "The Leadership News," "On Scene," and "USCG Search and Rescue." The Commandant of the Coast Guard maintains a blog on the website as well.

The Coast Guard publishes a monthly magazine, *Proceedings of the Marine Safety and Security Council,* intended for the maritime industry, which reports on new and proposed Coast Guard regulations and provides other articles on the promotion of maritime safety. Readers may subscribe to *Proceedings* online at www.uscg.mil/proceedings or by mailing a request to *Proceedings,* 2100 2nd St. S.W., Washington, DC 20593, or call (202) 372–2316. *Proceedings* magazine is free of charge.

Reference Resources

LIBRARY

USCG Library
Hours: 8:30 a.m. to 4:30 p.m., by appointment only
Internet: www.uscg.mil/top/library

DOCKETS
Federal dockets are available at www.regulations.gov. (*See appendix for Searching and Commenting on Regulations: Regulations.gov.*)

RULES AND REGULATIONS
Major Coast Guard rules and regulations are published in the *Code of Federal Regulations,* Title 33, Chapter I, Parts 1–199; Title 46, Chapter I, Parts 1–199; Title 46, Chapter III, Parts 400–404; Title 49, Chapter IV, Parts 400–499. Proposed rules, final rules, notices, and updates to the *Code of Federal Regulations* are

published in the daily *Federal Register*. (*See appendix for information on how to obtain and use these publications.*) The *Federal Register* and the *Code of Federal Regulations* may be accessed online at www.archives.gov/federal-register/cfr; the site contains a link to the federal government's regulatory website at www.regulations.gov (*see appendix*).

▣ LEGISLATION

The Coast Guard was established under Title 14 of the United States Code. It administers the following statutes:

Dangerous Cargo Act (R.S. 4472, 46 U.S.C. 170). Signed by the president Feb. 28, 1871. Provided authority to regulate the carriage of explosives and hazardous substances on vessels.

Bridge Laws (34 Stat. 84, 28 Stat. 362, 54 Stat. 467, 60 Stat. 847; 33 U.S.C. 491, 499, 511, 525). Signed by the president March 3, 1899. As amended, authorized the Coast Guard to approve the location and navigational clearance of bridges built across navigable waters. Also authorized the regulation of drawbridges and provided partial funding for the costs of altering obstructive bridges.

Merchant Marine Act of 1920 (41 Stat. 998, 46 U.S.C. 882). Signed by the president June 5, 1920. Set the number of passengers cargo vessels may carry and established rules of behavior for corporate-owned U.S. vessels.

Anti-Smuggling Act (49 Stat. 517, 19 U.S.C. 1701). Signed by the president Aug. 5, 1935. Gave the U.S. Customs Service special enforcement authority to cope with smuggling.

Act of June 25, 1936 (49 Stat. 1922, 46 U.S.C. 738). Signed by the president June 25, 1936. Established the ice patrol service under the administration of the Coast Guard; required that vessel operators crossing the north Atlantic Ocean give public notice of regular routes and any changes in routes.

Motorboat Act of 1940 (54 Stat. 163, 46 U.S.C. 526). Signed by the president April 25, 1940. Established safety regulations for motorboats and required licensing of motorboat operators.

Outer Continental Shelf Lands Act (67 Stat. 462, 43 U.S.C. 1333). Signed by the president Aug. 7, 1953. Authorized the Coast Guard to establish and enforce safety standards on the outer continental shelf lands.

Act of May 10, 1956 (70 Stat. 151, 46 U.S.C. 390). Signed by the president May 10, 1956. Authorized the Coast Guard periodically to inspect passenger vessels and to establish guidelines for design, construction, alteration, and repair of vessels.

Great Lakes Pilotage Act of 1960 (74 Stat. 259, 46 U.S.C. 216). Signed by the president June 30, 1960. Required registration of pilots of foreign and domestic vessels on the Great Lakes; set rates and charges for pilot services.

Oil Pollution Act of 1961 (75 Stat. 402, 33 U.S.C. 1001). Signed by the president Aug. 30, 1961. Prohibited discharge of oil or oily mixtures into navigable waters.

Department of Transportation Act (80 Stat. 931, 49 U.S.C. 1655). Signed by the president Oct. 15, 1966.

Transferred the Coast Guard to the DOT. Established lighting requirements, provided procedures for ships passing one another, established anchorage grounds for safe navigation, required alteration of bridges obstructing navigation, established regulations governing the operation of drawbridges, set reasonable rates for tolls, and required approval of plans and locations for the construction of bridges.

Federal Boat Safety Act of 1971 (85 Stat. 213, 46 U.S.C. 1451 et seq.). Signed by the president Aug. 10, 1971. Empowered the Coast Guard to issue regulations to establish minimum boating safety standards and to require the installation of safety equipment.

Ports and Waterways Safety Act of 1972 (86 Stat. 424, 33 U.S.C. 1221). Signed by the president July 10, 1972. Established safety measures to prevent damage to vessels and structures on navigable waters.

Port and Tanker Safety Act (92 Stat. 1471, 33 U.S.C. 1221, 46 U.S.C. 391a). Signed by the president July 10, 1972. Provided for the port safety program, which includes the establishment of vessel traffic services, issuance of regulations to protect the environment, and authority to regulate various activities in the nation's ports. Also authorized inspection and regulation of tank vessels.

Federal Water Pollution Control Act Amendments of 1972 (86 Stat. 816, 33 U.S.C. 1251 et seq.). Signed by the president Oct. 18, 1972. Authorized inspections of vessels carrying oil or other hazardous materials; required cleanup of spills in navigable waters of oil or other hazardous materials; and established standards of performance for marine sanitation devices.

Marine Mammal Protection Act of 1972 (86 Stat. 1027, 16 U.S.C. 1361). Signed by the president Oct. 21, 1972. Established a moratorium on the taking and importation of marine mammals as well as products taken from them (with some exceptions). Established procedures for waiving the moratorium and transferring management responsibility to the states.

Marine Protection, Research, and Sanctuaries Act of 1972 (86 Stat. 1052 and 1061, 33 U.S.C. 1401–1445). Signed by the president Oct. 23, 1972. Regulated ocean dumping activities. Authorized the commerce secretary to designate national marine sanctuaries.

Federal-Aid Highway Act of 1973 (87 Stat. 267, 33 U.S.C. 526a). Signed by the president Aug. 13, 1973. Established guidelines for toll increases used for bridge construction.

Intervention on the High Seas Act (33 U.S.C. 1471–1487). Signed by the president Feb. 5, 1974. Authorized measures to prevent and mitigate oil pollution and other noxious damage on the high seas that affected U.S. coastlines and related interests. The act implemented the International Convention Relating to Intervention on the High Seas in Cases of Oil Pollution Casualties and the Protocol Relating to Intervention on the High Seas in Cases of Marine Pollution by Substances other than Oil.

Robert T. Stafford Disaster Relief and Emergency Assistance Act (88 Stat. 143, 42 U.S.C. 5121 note). Signed by the president May 22, 1974. Broadened provisions of the Disaster Act of 1950. Encouraged and assisted states and local governments with comprehensive disaster preparedness and assistance plans. Provided for greater coordination between federal government and the states for disaster management and recovery.

Deepwater Port Act of 1974 (88 Stat. 2126, 33 U.S.C. 1501). Signed by the president Jan. 3, 1975. Required licensing and regulation of deepwater port facilities.

Hazardous Materials Transportation Act (88 Stat. 2156). Signed by the president Jan. 3, 1975. Authorized the transportation secretary to issue regulations for the safe transportation in commerce of hazardous materials, in cooperation with the Interstate Commerce Commission. Authorized the Coast Guard to enforce maritime shipping regulations with regard to hazardous material.

Fishery Conservation Management Act (90 Stat. 331, 16 U.S.C. 1801). Signed by the president April 13, 1976. Authorized enforcement and regulation of fishery conservation management zones.

Clean Water Act of 1977 (91 Stat. 1566, 33 U.S.C. 1251). Signed by the president Dec. 27, 1977. Raised liability limit on oil spill cleanup costs. Amended the Federal Water Pollution Control Act Amendments of 1972.

Outer Continental Shelf Lands Act Amendments of 1978 (92 Stat. 629, 43 U.S.C. 1811). Signed by the president Sept. 18, 1978. Imposed liabilities for oil spills associated with the ocean's outer continental shelf.

Deep Seabed Hard Mineral Resources Act of 1980 (94 Stat. 553, 30 U.S.C. 1401). Signed by the president June 28, 1980. Established an interim program to encourage and regulate the development of hard mineral resources of the deep seabed by the United States.

Drug Interdiction Act of 1980 (94 Stat. 1159, 21 U.S.C. 955). Signed by the president Sept. 15, 1980. Facilitated enforcement by the Coast Guard of laws relating to the importation of illegal drugs.

Recreational Boating and Safety and Facilities Act of 1980 (94 Stat. 1983, 46 U.S.C. 1451). Signed by the president Oct. 14, 1980. Amended the Federal Boat Safety Act of 1971 to improve recreational boating safety and facilities through the development, administration, and financing of a national recreational safety and facilities improvement program.

Act to Prevent Pollution from Ships (33 U.S.C. 1901–1915). Signed by the president Oct. 21, 1980. Authorized the secretary of the department in which the Coast Guard was operating to administer, enforce, and prescribe regulations to carry out the provisions of the MARPOL Protocol and this act, utilizing other federal departments and agencies as necessary.

Oil Pollution Act of 1990 (104 Stat. 484, 33 U.S.C. 2701 note). Signed by the president Aug. 18, 1990. Provided for environmental safeguards in oil transportation and addressed wide-ranging problems associated with preventing, responding to, and paying for oil spills.

Executive Order 12807. Signed by the president May 24, 1992. Directed the Coast Guard to interdict undocumented aliens at sea.

Maritime Transportation Security Act of 2002 (116 Stat. 2064, 46 U.S.C. 2101 note). Signed by the president Nov. 25, 2002. Required the DOT to develop antiterrorism plans at U.S. ports and foreign ports where U.S.-bound shipments originate. Required the identification of suspicious vessels before they enter U.S. ports. Authorized the Coast Guard to block the entry of ships that failed to meet security standards. Amended the Ports and Waterways Safety Act to authorize Coast Guard personnel to act as sea marshals to respond to acts of terrorism. Established the Transportation Worker Identification Credential program to issue tamper-resistant biometric credentials to workers who require unescorted access to secure areas of ports, vessels, outer continental shelf facilities and all credentialed merchant mariners.

Homeland Security Act of 2002 (116 Stat. 2135, 6 U.S.C. 551, 557). Signed by the president Nov. 25, 2002. Transferred to the DHS the authorities, functions, personnel, and assets of the Coast Guard, which was to be maintained as a distinct entity within the DHS. Required the commandant of the Coast Guard to report directly to the secretary of homeland security. Prohibited any of the above conditions and restrictions from applying to the Coast Guard when it was operating as a service in the navy.

Coast Guard Maritime Transportation Act of 2004 (118 Stat. 1028, 14 U.S.C. 1 note). Signed by the president Aug. 9, 2004. Authorizes the secretary to promulgate inland navigation regulations. Authorized regulations requiring an owner or operator of a tank vessel, a nontank vessel, or an onshore or offshore facility that transfers noxious liquid substances in bulk to or from a vessel to prepare and submit a disaster response plan.

SAFE Port Act of 2006 (120 Stat. 1884). Signed by the president Oct. 13, 2006. Implemented a long-range vessel tracking system. Authorized the secretary to issue regulations to establish a voluntary long-range automated vessel tracking system prior to the issuance of final regulations for such system.

Marine Debris Research, Prevention, and Reduction Act (120 Stat. 3333, 33 U.S.C. 1951 note). Signed by the president Dec. 22, 2006. Directed the commandant of the Coast Guard to take actions to reduce violations of and improve implementation of MARPOL Annex V (Annex V of the International Convention for the Prevention of Pollution from Ships, 1973) and the Act to Prevent Pollution from Ships with respect to the discard of plastics and other garbage from vessels.

Maritime Pollution Prevention Act of 2008 (122 Stat. 2611, 33 U.S.C. 1901 et seq.). Signed by the president July 21, 2008. Amended the Act to Prevent Pollution from Ships to provide for the adoption of MARPOL Annex VI (Prevention of Air Pollution from Ships Enforcement).

Drug Trafficking Vessel Interdiction Act of 2008 (122 Stat. 4296, 18 U.S.C. 1 note). Signed by the president Oct. 13, 2008. Amended the federal criminal code to impose a fine and/or prison term of up to fifteen years for knowingly operating any submersible or semi-submersible vessel that is without nationality in waters beyond the outer limit of the territorial sea of a single country with the intent to avoid detection. Granted extraterritorial federal jurisdiction over an offense under this act and imposed a civil penalty of up to $1 million for a violation of this act.

Coast Guard Authorization Act of 2010 (124 Stat. 2905). Signed by the president Oct. 15, 2010. Requires regulations to reduce the risks of oil spills in operations involving the transfer of oil from, or to, a tank vessel. Allows enforcement of certain state laws or regulations that are at least as stringent as such regulations. Authorizes the secretary to issue port security regulations. Directs the commandant to establish, by regulation, national standards for training and credentialing law enforcement personnel to enforce a security zone or assist in such enforcement. Authorizes promulgation and clarification of commercial fishing vessel safety standards.

Coast Guard and Maritime Transportation Act of 2012 (126 Stat. 1540, 14 U.S.C. 1 note). Signed by the president Dec. 20, 2012. Required that the USCG conduct dockside safety examinations for certain uninspected fishing industry vessels (that operate beyond three nautical miles of the shoreline) at least once every five years (instead of two years). A vessel's first examination must be completed no later than October 15, 2015.

▪ REGIONAL OFFICES

ATLANTIC AREA
431 Crawford St.
Portsmouth, VA 23704–5004
(757) 398–6287
Vice Adm. William Lee, commander

PACIFIC AREA
Bldg. 51–6
1 Eagle Rd., Coast Guard Island
Alameda, CA 94501–5100
(510) 437–3522
Vice Adm. Charles W. Ray, commander

District Command Centers

DISTRICT 1
(CT, MA, ME, NH, northeast NJ, eastern NY, RI, VT)
Capt. John Foster Williams Bldg.
408 Atlantic Ave.
Boston, MA 02110–3350
(617) 223–8555
Rear Adm. Linda Fagan, commander

DISTRICT 5
(MD, NC, southern NJ, eastern PA, VA)
431 Crawford St., Federal Bldg.
Portsmouth, VA 23704–5004
(757) 398–6641
Rear Adm. Steven P. Metruck, commander

DISTRICT 7
(most of FL, GA, SC, VI)
Brickell Plaza Federal Bldg.
909 S.E. First Ave.
Miami, FL 33131–3050
(305) 415–6670 or (305) 415–6683
Rear Adm. Scott A. Buschman, commander

DISTRICT 8
(AL, AR, CO, FL panhandle, IA, KS,
    KY, LA, MO, MS, ND, NE, NM, OK,
    SD, TN, TX, WV, WY; areas of IL, IN,
    MN, OH, and WI not adjacent to
    Great Lakes)
Hale Boggs Federal Bldg.
500 Poydras St., #1324
New Orleans, LA 70130
(504) 589–6298
Rear Adm. David R. Callahan, commander

DISTRICT 9
(MI, Great Lakes area of IL, IN, MN,
    NY, OH, PA, and WI)
Anthony J. Celbrezze Federal Bldg.
1240 E. 9th St.
Cleveland, OH 44199–2060
(216) 902–6000
Rear Adm. June Ryan, commander

DISTRICT 11
(AZ, CA, NV, UT)
Coast Guard Island Bldg. 50-6
Alameda, CA 94501
(510) 437–3968
Rear Adm. Joseph A. Servidio, commander

DISTRICT 13
(ID, MT, OR, WA)
Henry M. Jackson Federal Bldg.
915 Second Ave.
Seattle, WA 98174–1067
(800) 982–8813
Rear Adm. Richard T. Gromlich, commander

DISTRICT 14
(GU, HI, Pacific islands)
Prince Kalanianaole Federal Bldg.
300 Ala Moana Blvd., #9–204
Honolulu, HI 96850–4982
(800) 818–8724
Rear Adm. Vincent B. Atkins, commander

DISTRICT 17
(AK)
P.O. Box 25517
Juneau, AK 99802–5517
(907) 463–2065
Rear Adm. Daniel B. Abel, commander

U.S. Customs and Border Protection

1300 Pennsylvania Ave. N.W., Washington, DC 20229
Internet: www.cbp.gov

U.S. Customs and Border Protection (USCBP) became an agency of the Department of Homeland Security (DHS) on March 1, 2003, combining employees from the Department of Agriculture (Agriculture and Quarantine Inspections), the Immigration and Naturalization Service (INS) inspection services, the Border Patrol, and the U.S. Customs Service (USCS), which was organized within the DHS Border and Transportation Directorate. The investigative and enforcement functions of the Customs Service were transferred to the office of Immigration and Customs Enforcement (ICE) (*p. 643*). USCBP is headed by a commissioner who is appointed by the president and confirmed by the Senate. The Customs Service commissioner originally transferred as the commissioner for USCBP.

To accomplish its mission of inspecting goods and people crossing the U.S. borders, USCBP has a workforce of nearly 60,000 employees, including inspectors, canine enforcement officers, border patrol agents, trade specialists, and mission support staff.

USCBP works with the trade community to develop, enhance, and maintain security processes throughout the global supply chain and to stem the illegal export of equipment, technology, and munitions to unauthorized destinations. Cooperation between the United States and other nations is needed to allow placement of U.S. inspectors in foreign ports to screen containers before they enter the United States.

As the single unified U.S. border agency, USCBP's mission is to improve security and facilitate the flow of legitimate trade and travel. The strategy to accomplish this mission includes:

- Improving targeting systems and expanding advance information regarding people and goods arriving in the United States.
- Partnering with foreign governments as well as with the private sector.
- Deploying advanced inspection technology and equipment.
- Increasing staffing for border security.
- Working in concert with other agencies to coordinate activities with respect to trade fraud, intellectual property rights violations, controlled deliveries of illegal drugs, and money laundering.

In addition to administrative and policy units, key USCBP operations offices include the following:

Office of Field Operations. Manages more than 28,000 employees with nearly 24,000 inspectors that protect U.S. borders. Operates twenty field operations offices; 328 ports of entry; fifteen preclearance stations in six countries; and agricultural quarantine inspection at all ports of entry to protect the health of U.S. plant and animal resources. Manages core USCBP programs such as border security and facilitation, which handle interdiction and security, passenger operations, targeting and analysis, and canine enforcement.

Office of Air and Marine (OAM). Uses a coordinated air and marine force to deter, interdict, and prevent crimes, including acts of terrorism, arising from the unlawful movement of people and goods across the U.S. borders. OAM has three core competencies: air and marine interdiction, air and marine law enforcement, and airspace security. Formerly part of ICE, the OAM moved to USCBP in 2005.

Office of Border Patrol. Responsible for monitoring the border for illegal transportation of human beings and smuggling of drugs (including pharmaceuticals), counterfeit goods, and other contraband.

Office of International Affairs. Operates international activities and programs for conducting customs bilateral and multilateral relations with other countries. Manages the operations of the USCBP foreign attachés and advisory teams.

Office of Intelligence. Produces all-source intelligence products for USCBP and serves as the agency's liaison to the intelligence community and other federal law enforcement agencies. Detects and identifies criminal, drug, and alien smuggling; monitors, coordinates, recommends, assesses, and participates in the development of all policy, programs, training, and matters relating to terrorism; and disseminates strategic, operational, and tactical intelligence on criminal and terrorist groups to USCBP border security units for use in targeting and interdiction.

USCBP facilitates international travel while maintaining security through various programs:

Western Hemisphere Travel Initiative (WHTI) requires all citizens of the United States, Canada, Mexico, and Bermuda to have a passport or other accepted document that establishes the bearer's identity and nationality to enter or depart the United States from within the Western Hemisphere. The travel document requirements make up the Departments of State and Homeland Security's Western Hemisphere Travel Initiative.

Electronic System for Travel Authorization (ESTA) requires travelers under the Visa Waiver Program (VWP) to apply for and receive an approved travel authorization to board a plane or vessel bound for the United States. The VWP allows nationals of participating countries to travel to the United States for tourism or business for stays of 90 days or less without obtaining a visa.

CBP's Trusted Traveler Programs provide expedited travel for preapproved, low-risk travelers through dedicated lanes and kiosks. Trusted Traveler programs include the following:

- Global Entry program allows program participants to proceed to Global Entry kiosks at participating airports, present their machine-readable passport or U.S. permanent resident card, place their fingertips on the scanner for fingerprint verification, and make a customs declaration. The kiosk issues the traveler a transaction receipt and directs the traveler to baggage claim and the exit. All applicants undergo a rigorous background check and interview before enrollment.

- NEXUS program issues cards that are WHTI-compliant documents for land and sea travel, as well as air travel when traveling to and from airports using the NEXUS program and provides expedited travel via land, air, or sea to approved members between the U.S. and Canada border.

- FAST: Free and Secure Trade Program allows U.S./Canada and U.S./Mexico partnering importers expedited release for qualifying commercial shipments.

- SENTRI program issues cards that are WHTI-compliant documents for entry into the United States by land or sea, and also provides expedited travel to approved members between the U.S. and Mexico border.

■ KEY PERSONNEL

Commissioner
R. Gil Kerlikowski . . . . (202) 344–2001
Fax . . . . (202) 344–1380

Deputy Commissioner
Kevin K. McAleenan . . . . (202) 344–1010

Chief of Staff
Vacant . . . . (202) 344–1080

Chief Counsel
Scott Falk . . . . (202) 344–2940
Fax . . . . (202) 344–2950

Air and Marine
Gen. Randolph D. Alles . . . . (202) 344–3950

Border Patrol
Michael J. Fisher . . . . (202) 344–2050

Congressional Affairs
Michael J. Yeager . . . . (202) 344–1760
E-mail: OCAInquiry@cbp.dhs.gov

Diversity and Civil Rights
Franklin C. Jones . . . . (202) 344–1610

Field Operations
Todd C. Owen . . . . (202) 344–1620

Finance and Chief Financial Officer
Eugene H. Schied . . . . (202) 344–2300

Human Resources Management
Katherine Coffman . . . . (202) 863–6100

Information and Technology
Charles R. Armstrong . . . . (202) 344–1680

Intelligence
David J. Glawe . . . . (202) 344–1150

Internal Affairs
Vacant . . . . (202) 863–8100

International Affairs
Charles E. Stallworth . . . . (202) 344–3000
Fax . . . . (202) 344–2064

International Trade
Brenda Smith . . . . (202) 863–6000
Fax . . . . (202) 863–6080

Policy and Planning
Benjamin E. Webb . . . . (202) 344–2700

Public Affairs
Philip LaVelle . . . . (202) 344–1700

Technology Innovation and Acquisition
Mark S. Borkowski . . . . (571) 468–7500

Trade Relations
Maria Luisa Boyce . . . . (202) 340–1440

Training and Development
Chris Hall . . . . (202) 325–7100

■ INFORMATION SOURCES

Internet

Agency website: www.cbp.gov. Offers information on border security mission, importing and exporting in the United States, traveling internationally, CBP's enforcement activities, and access to quota reports, forms, and press releases. Also provides the quarterly magazine *Frontline*. Information on Trusted Traveler programs is available at www.cbp.gov/travel/trusted-traveler-programs.

Telephone Contacts

Personnel Locator (commissioner's office) . . . . (202) 344–2001
Customer Service and Inquiries . . . . . (877) 227–5511
TTY . . . . (866) 880–6582
International Callers . . . . (703) 526–4200
Hotline (to report suspicious activity) . . . . (800) BE-ALERT
Public Affairs . . . . (202) 344–1770
Federal Relay Service TTY . . . . (800) 877–8339

Information and Publications

KEY OFFICES

National Issues–HQ Press Officers

E-mail: cbpmediarelations@dhs.gov (outside business hours only)

Media Division, Anti-Terrorism
Michael Friel, director
(202) 344–1780
E-mail: Michael.friel@dhs.gov

Southwest Border Field, Border Fence
Carlos Diaz, chief
(202) 325–3018
E-mail: carlos.a.diaz@cbp.dhs.gov

Technology, Acquisition, Cargo and Conveyance, International Trade
Jenny Burke, press secretary
(202) 344–1313
E-mail: Jenny.L.Burke@dhs.gov

Admissibility and Passenger Programs, Agriculture
Carlos Lazo, public affairs specialist
(202) 344–1862
E-mail: Stephanie.mailin@dhs.gov

Freedom of Information
FOIA Division
799 9th St. N.W., Mint Annex
Washington, DC 20229–1177
(202) 325–0150
Sabrina Burroughs, FOIA officer
Internet: www.cbp.gov/site-policy-notices/foia

CBP Legal Reference Staff
1300 Pennsylvania Ave. N.W.
Washington, DC 20229
(202) 325–0073
Stephanie Talton, branch chief

Maintains a legal precedent retrieval system.

PUBLICATIONS
Contact the CBP Public Information staff for information on CBP travel and trade publications and brochures, at (202) 344–1770; publications are also available on the website. "Trusted Traveler" publications are available through the Web page www.cbp.gov/xp/cgov/travel/trusted_traveler. Publications available on the website and in print include:

Know Before You Go (No. 0000–0512)
Importing into the United States (No. 0000–0504)
Welcome to the United States (No. 0000–0146)
CBP Traveler Entry Forms (No. 0000–0602)
Currency Reporting Flyer (No. 0000–0503)
Snapshot: A Summary of CBP Facts and Figures (No. 0000–0508)

The agency's annual report and its quarterly magazine, *Frontline*, are also available, as well as performance and accountability reports and fact sheets on CBP activities and initiatives. CBP publications may be obtained via the website, www.cbp.gov, or by e-mail request to CBP.PAR@dhs.gov. For more information on publications, contact Jennifer Evanitsky, Office of Public Affairs, at (202) 344–1355.

Reference Resources

LIBRARY

CBP Library
90 K St. N.E
Washington, DC 20229
(202) 325–0130
Linda B. Cullen, director
Hours: 9:00 a.m. to 5:00 p.m.
Open to the public by appointment only

DOCKETS
Federal dockets are available at www.regulations.gov. (*See appendix for Searching and Commenting on Regulations: Regulations.gov.*)

RULES AND REGULATIONS
CBP rules and regulations are published in the *Code of Federal Regulations,* Title 19, Chapter I, Parts 1–199. Proposed regulations, new final regulations, and updates to the *Code of Federal Regulations* are published in the daily *Federal Register.* (*See appendix for details on how to obtain and use these publications.*) The *Federal Register* and the *Code of Federal Regulations* may be accessed online at www.archives.gov/federal-register/cfr; the site contains a link to the federal government's regulatory website at www.regulations.gov (*see appendix*).

■ LEGISLATION
The USCBP carries out its responsibilities through authority granted in:

Unfair Competition Act (39 Stat. 798, 15 U.S.C. 71). Signed by the president Sept. 8, 1916. Restricted the importation of articles at less than market value and established import restrictions against countries that prohibit the importation of U.S. goods.

Customs Bureau Act (44 Stat. 1381, 19 U.S.C. 2071). Signed by the president March 3, 1927. Established the Customs Bureau as an agency within the Treasury Department to assess and collect duties on imports.

Tariff Act of 1930 (46 Stat. 763, 19 U.S.C. 1202). Signed by the president June 17, 1930. Established rules and regulations relating to assessment and collection of duty, protection of revenue, entry of vessels, clearance of passengers, exclusion of prohibited merchandise, and regulation of customhouse brokers.

Anti-Smuggling Act (49 Stat. 517, 19 U.S.C. 1701). Signed by the president Aug. 5, 1935. Gave the Customs Bureau special enforcement authority to cope with smuggling.

Customs Courts Act of 1970 (84 Stat. 274, 28 U.S.C. 1541). Signed by the president June 2, 1970. Streamlined the judicial machinery of the customs courts by allowing formerly separate appeals of customs court decisions concerning classification of merchandise and collection of customs revenues to be handled by one court.

Trade Act of 1974 (88 Stat. 1978, 19 U.S.C. 2101). Signed by the president Jan. 3, 1975. Gave the Customs

Bureau additional enforcement responsibilities with respect to antidumping, countervailing duties, and unfair import practices.

Customs Procedural Reform and Simplification Act (92 Stat. 888, 19 U.S.C. 1654 note). Signed by the president Oct. 3, 1978. Streamlined the Customs Service's procedures to expedite international travel and trade. Allowed the Customs Service to release goods to importers immediately upon presentation of appropriate entry documents, raised the personal duty exemption for returning U.S. residents, and amended the Tariff Act of 1930 to remove unduly harsh penalty assessments.

Trade Agreements Act of 1979 (93 Stat. 144, 19 U.S.C. 2501 note). Signed by the president July 26, 1979. Transferred dumping and countervailing duties authority from the Customs Service to the Commerce Department.

Money Laundering Control Act of 1986 (100 Stat. 3207, 18 U.S.C. 981). Signed by the president Oct. 27, 1986. Prohibited the transport or attempted transport of funds obtained through the commission of a crime or intended for use in a crime. Prohibited the structuring of financial transactions in order to evade federal reporting requirements. Authorized the seizure and forfeiture of cash or other property derived from criminal activity.

United States-Canada Free-Trade Agreement Implementation Act of 1988 (102 Stat. 1851, 19 U.S.C. 2112 note). Signed by the president Sept. 28, 1988. Set a ten-year schedule to phase out tariffs between the United States and Canada. Provided new mechanisms for solving trade disputes.

North American Free Trade Agreement (NAFTA) Implementation Act (107 Stat. 2057, 19 U.S.C. 3301 note). Signed by the president Dec. 8, 1993. Implemented NAFTA, which opened trade borders with Canada, the United States, and Mexico. Title VI, the Customs Modernization Act, amended the Tariff Act of 1930 to revise customs procedures with respect to electronic transmission of forged, altered, or false data to the Customs Service with regard to the entry of imported merchandise; to set penalties for failure to declare imported controlled substances and for fraud, gross negligence, and negligence; to restrict unlawful unloading or transshipment; and to handle the seizure of imported merchandise.

Anticounterfeiting Consumer Protection Act of 1996 (110 Stat. 1836, 18 U.S.C. 2311 note). Signed by the president July 2, 1996. Made trafficking in goods or services bearing counterfeit marks a predicate offense under the Racketeer Influenced and Corrupt Organizations Act. Gave the Customs Service authority to establish civil penalties and fines for importing, selling, or distributing merchandise bearing a counterfeit American trademark.

Continued Dumping and Subsidy Offset Act of 2000 (CDSOA) (114 Stat. 1549, 19 U.S.C. 1675c). Signed by the president Oct. 28, 2000. CDSOA is Title X of the Farm Bill. Amended the Tariff Act of 1930 to declare that the Customs Service shall disburse antidumping and countervailing duties collected by the agency to domestic producers injured by foreign dumping and subsidies. Directed the Customs Service commissioner to prescribe offset disbursement procedures.

Trade Act of 2002 (116 Stat. 933, 19 U.S.C. 3801 note). Signed by the president Aug. 6, 2002. Title III, the Customs Border Security Act of 2002, provided the Customs Service officers with immunity from lawsuits stemming from personal searches of people entering the country, as long as the officers conduct the searches in good faith and follow federal inspection procedures. Allowed officers to search unsealed, outbound U.S. mail and packages weighing sixteen ounces or more for unreported monetary instruments, weapons of mass destruction, firearms, and other contraband.

Maritime Transportation Security Act of 2002 (116 Stat. 2064, 46 U.S.C. 2101 note). Signed by the president Nov. 25, 2002. Required the Department of Transportation to develop antiterrorism plans at U.S. ports and foreign ports where U.S.-bound shipments originate. Authorized funds for research and development to improve the inspecting of cargo, including inspecting merchandise on vessels arriving in U.S. ports; purchasing equipment to detect explosives, chemical and biological agents, and nuclear materials; and improving tags and seals on shipping containers. Authorized rules requiring shippers to electronically provide information on cargo shipped to or from the United States before it arrives.

Homeland Security Act of 2002 (116 Stat. 2135, 6 U.S.C. 551, 557). Signed by the president Nov. 25, 2002. Established the DHS. Transferred the INS inspection services, the Border Patrol, the Agriculture and Quarantine Inspections program, and inspection elements of the Customs Service into the USCBP within the DHS.

Clean Diamond Trade Act (117 Stat. 631, 19 U.S.C. 3901 et seq.). Signed by the president on April 25, 2003. Prohibited the importation into, or exportation from, the United States of any rough diamond that has not been controlled through the international Kimberley Process Certification Scheme. Designated the USCBP as the importing authority.

Intelligence Reform and Terrorism Prevention Act of 2004 (118 Stat. 3638, 50 U.S.C. 401 note). Signed by the president Dec. 17, 2004. Created a national intelligence director to oversee U.S. intelligence programs and intelligence-related activities. Established a national counter-terrorism center to serve as a clearinghouse for terrorism intelligence. Expanded immigration and border security laws, including the addition of 10,000 border patrol agents over five years. Authorized plan to require that U.S. citizens and foreign nationals present a passport, or other secure document, when entering the United States.

SAFE Port Act of 2006 (120 Stat. 1884). Signed by the president Oct. 13, 2006. Authorized the DHS secretary, acting through the USCBP commissioner to establish the Customs-Trade Partnership Against Terrorism, as a voluntary program between the government and the private sector to strengthen the security of the international supply chain and U.S. border security and to facilitate the movement of secure cargo.

Implementing Recommendations of the 9/11 Commission Act of 2007 (121 Stat. 266, 6 U.S.C. 101 note). Signed by the president Aug. 3, 2007. Established the Electronic System for Travel Authorization (ESTA), which requires travelers under the Visa Waiver Program (VWP) to apply for and receive an approved travel authorization to board a plane or vessel bound for the United States.

Prioritizing Resources and Organization for Intellectual Property Act of 2008 (122 Stat. 4256, 15 U.S.C. 8101 note). Signed by the president Oct. 13, 2008. Authorized the DHS secretary to issue regulations by which any performer may, upon payment of a specified fee, be entitled to notification by USCBP of the importation of bootleg copies of musical performances. Imposes criminal penalties, in intentionally trafficking in counterfeit goods or services, if an offender knowingly or recklessly causes serious bodily injury or death.

Travel Promotion Act of 2009 (124 Stat. 56, 22 U.S.C. 2131). Signed by the president March 4, 2010. Amends the Immigration and Nationality Act to authorize the DHS secretary to establish and collect a fee for the use of an electronic data sharing system concerning the admissibility of certain aliens into the United States, which will ensure recovery of the full costs of providing and administering such system.

Consolidated Appropriations Act, 2014 (128 Stat. 279, 6 U.S.C. 211 note). Signed by the president Jan. 17, 2014. Sec. 559 authorized the Commissioner of U.S. Customs and Border Protection, in collaboration with the Administrator of General Services, to conduct a pilot program in accordance with this section to permit USCBP to enter into partnerships with private sector and government entities at ports of entry for certain services and to accept certain donations.

Sean and David Goldman International Child Abduction Prevention and Return Act of 2014 (128 Stat. 1822, 6 U.S.C. 241). Signed by the president Aug. 8, 2014. Directed Homeland Security secretary to establish within U.S. Customs and Border Protection a child abduction prevention program.

▪ REGIONAL OFFICES

Field Operations Offices

There are 20 field operations offices in the United States that provide centralized management oversight and operational assistance to 328 ports of entry and 15 preclearance offices.

ATLANTA, GA
1699 Phoenix Pkwy., #400
College Park, GA 30349
(678) 284–5900
Reginald Manning, director

BALTIMORE, MD
217 E. Redwood St., 12th Floor
Baltimore, MD 21202
(410) 962–6200
Michael Lovejoy, director

BOSTON, MA
10 Causeway St., #801
Boston, MA 02222–1059
(617) 565–6208
Kevin Weeks, director

BUFFALO, NY
300 Airborne Pkwy., #300
Buffalo, NY 14225
(716) 626–0400
James T. Engleman, director

CHICAGO, IL
610 S. Canal St., #900
Chicago, IL 60607
(312) 542–5700
David J. Murphy, director

DETROIT, MI
211 W. Fort St., #1200
Detroit, MI 48226
(313) 496–2155
Christopher Perry, director

EL PASO, TX
9400 Viscount Blvd., #104
El Paso, TX 79925–7040
(915) 633–7300 ext. 100
Hector A. Mancha, director

HOUSTON, TX
2323 S. Shepherd St., #1300
Houston, TX 77019
(713) 387–7200
Judson Murdock, director

LAREDO, TX
109 Shiloh Dr., #300
Laredo, TX 78045
(956) 753–1700
David Higgerson, director

LOS ANGELES, CA
1 World Trade Center, #705
Long Beach, CA 90831
(562) 980–3100
Vacant, director

MIAMI, FL
909 S.E. First Ave., #980
Miami, FL 33131–3030
(305) 810–5120
Vernon Foret, director

NEW ORLEANS, LA
423 Canal St., #350
New Orleans, LA 70130
(504) 670–2404
Reginald Manning, director

NEW YORK, NY
1 Penn Plaza, 11th Floor
New York, NY 10119
(646) 733–3100
Robert E. Perez, director

PORTLAND, OR
33 New Montgomery, #1600
San Francisco, CA 94105
(415) 744–1530
Brian Humphrey, director
Daniel Wagner, area port director

SAN DIEGO, CA
610 W. Ash St., #1200
San Diego, CA 92101
(619) 652–9966, ext. 100
Pete Flores, director

SAN FRANCISCO, CA
33 New Montgomery St., 16th Floor
San Francisco, CA 94105
(415) 744–1530 ext. 221
Brian Humphrey, director

SAN JUAN, PR
City View Plaza, #3000
#48 Rd. 165 Km.1.2
Guaynabo, PR 00968-8000
(787) 729–6950
Marcelino Borges, director

SEATTLE, WA
1000 Second Ave., #2200
Seattle, WA 98104–1049
(206) 553–6944
Michele James, director

TAMPA, FL
1624 E. Seventh Ave., #300
Tampa, FL 33605–3769
(813) 712–6100
Vernon Foret, director

TUCSON, AZ
4740 N. Oracle Rd., #316
Tucson, AZ 85705
(520) 407–2300
William K. Brooks, director

Housing and Urban Development Department

451 7th St. S.W., Washington, DC 20410
Internet: www.hud.gov

Office of Fair Housing and Equal Opportunity

451 7th St. S.W., Washington, DC 20410
Internet: www.hud.gov/offices/fheo

The Department of Housing and Urban Development (HUD) is the primary federal agency responsible for programs concerned with housing needs and improving and developing the nation's communities. The assistant secretary for fair housing and equal opportunity is the principal adviser to the HUD secretary on matters concerning civil rights and equal opportunity in housing, employment, lending, and business.

The office administers the fair housing program authorized by Title VI and Title VII of the Civil Rights Act of 1964; Title VIII of the Civil Rights Act of 1968; Sections 501, 504, and 505 of the Rehabilitation Act of 1973; the Age Discrimination Act of 1975, as amended; Executive Orders 11063, 11246, 11478, 12259, 12432, and 12892; the Age Discrimination Act of 1967; Section 3 of the Housing and Urban Development Act of 1968, as amended; Section 109 of the Housing and Community Development Act of 1974; the Fair Housing Amendments Act of 1988; and the Americans with Disabilities Act of 1990. The Violence Against Women Reauthorization Act of 2013 affords housing protections to victims of domestic violence participating in HUD programs.

These laws ensure that HUD programs operate to further the goals of equal opportunity by providing for the coordination, planning, monitoring, and review of programs to increase training, employment, and business opportunities for lower income and minority group residents of HUD-assisted housing programs.

Persons who believe they have been victims of discrimination prohibited by the Fair Housing Act may file a complaint with the Office of Fair Housing and Equal Opportunity (FHEO). FHEO will investigate to determine if there has been a violation of the Fair Housing Act. If FHEO finds that the act has been violated, several actions may be taken.

First, HUD will try to reach an agreement with the person or parties named in the complaint (the respondent). A conciliation agreement must protect both the victim and the public interest. If an agreement is signed, HUD will take no further action. However, if HUD has reasonable cause to believe that a conciliation agreement is breached, HUD will recommend that the attorney general file a suit.

If, after investigating a complaint, HUD finds reasonable cause to believe that discrimination occurred, the case will be heard in an administrative hearing within 120 days, unless the complainant or the respondent wants the case to be heard in federal district court. Either way, there is no cost to the complainant. Both the administrative law judge and the federal district court may award actual and punitive damages. In addition, the attorney general may file a suit in a federal district court if there is reasonable cause to believe a pattern or practice of housing discrimination is occurring.

The federal Fair Housing Act prohibits housing discrimination based on race, color, national origin, religion, sex, disability, and familial status. The Fair Housing Act does not specifically include sexual orientation and gender identity as prohibited bases. However, HUD issued policies to address housing discrimination against the lesbian, gay, bisexual, and transgender (LGBT) community as related to HUD programs:

- Required grantees and those who participate in the HUD's programs to comply with local and state nondiscrimination laws that cover sexual orientation or gender identity;
- Specified that any FHA-insured mortgage loan must be based on the creditworthiness of a borrower and not on unrelated factors or characteristics such as sexual orientation or gender identity;
- Published the Equal Access Rule in 2012 intended to ensure that its core housing programs are open to all eligible persons, regardless of sexual orientation or gender identity;
- Commissioned the first-ever national study of discrimination against members of the LGBT community in the rental and sale of housing;
- Updated the Equal Access Rule in 2015 to provide guidance to recipients and subrecipients receiving emergency housing funds regarding how best to provide shelter to transgender persons in a single-sex facility.

HUD participates in a national media campaign to educate the public and housing providers about their rights and responsibilities under the Fair Housing Act. The campaign is launched in April to recognize Fair Housing Month when the nation marks the passage of the 1968 Fair Housing Act. The campaign includes radio and print public service advertisements (PSAs) in multiple languages that feature examples of actions that violate the

Fair Housing Act and let the public know what to do if they experience housing discrimination. HUD also incorporates social media in the Fair Housing public awareness efforts.

■ KEY PERSONNEL

Assistant Secretary
Gustavo Velasquez . . . . (202) 708–4252
    Fax . . . . (202) 708–4483
General Deputy Assistant Secretary
Bryan Greene . . . . (202) 708–4211
Enforcement Programs Deputy Assistant Secretary
Sara Pratt . . . . (202) 402–6322
Economic Opportunity
Staci N. Gilliam . . . . (202) 402–3468
Operations and Management Deputy Assistant Secretary
David Ziaya . . . . (202) 708–0768
Policy, Legislative Initiatives, and Outreach Deputy Assistant Secretary
George D. Williams . . . . (202) 402–3983

■ INFORMATION SOURCES

Internet

Agency website: www.hud.gov/offices/fheo. Includes information about the Fair Housing Act and on what to do if your rights have been violated. HUD also maintains the following online service:

HUD USER
P.O. Box 23268
Washington, DC 20026–3268
(800) 245–2691
(202) 708–3178
TTY (800) 927–7589
E-mail: helpdesk@huduser.org
Internet: www.huduser.org
Jennie Simpson, project manager
(703) 742–7881, ext. 211
Email: Jsimpson@sagecomputing.com

Provides an extensive list of HUD publications and datasets pertaining to fair housing.

Telephone Contacts

Personnel Locator . . . . (202) 708–1420
Housing Discrimination Hotline . . . . . (800) 669–9777
Counseling Agency Locator . . . . (800) 569–4287
TTY . . . . (800) 927–9275

Information and Publications

KEY OFFICES

HUD Public Affairs
451 7th St. S.W., #10130
Washington, DC 20410

(202) 708–0980
Jaime Castillo (acting), assistant secretary for public affairs

Issues news releases and answers questions from the public and the press.

Freedom of Information
HUD Office of the Executive Secretary
451 7th St. S.W., #10139
Washington, DC 20410
(202) 708–3054
E-mail: foia_hud@hud.gov
Deborah R. Snowden, FOIA branch chief
(202) 402–7606

PUBLICATIONS

HUD Customer Service/Distribution Center
451 7th St. S.W., Room BS-11
Washington, DC 20410–3000
(800) 767–7468
Fax orders: (202) 708–2313
E-mail orders: on_demand_mail@hud.gov

Distributes over 7,000 HUD publications, including brochures. Titles available include:
Fair Housing—Equal Opportunity for All
Equal Housing Posters
Are You a Victim of Housing Discrimination?
Many titles, forms, research studies, handbooks, and notices are also available on the website under Hudclips, http://portal.hud.gov/hudportal/HUD?src=/program_offices/administration/hudclips as well as from www.huduser.org (see *Information Sources,* above).

Reference Resources

LIBRARY

Housing and Urban Development Department
451 7th St. S.W., #8141
Washington, DC 20410
(202) 708–2370

Related materials are also available at regional offices and from the website's Online Library. Library materials may be used on site only, and a limited number of publications are available. The headquarters library is open to the public from 8:30 a.m. to 4:30 p.m.

DOCKETS
Federal dockets are available at www.regulations.gov. (*See appendix for Searching and Commenting on Regulations: Regulations.gov.*)

RULES AND REGULATIONS
FHEO rules and regulations are published in the *Code of Federal Regulations,* Title 24, Chapter I, Parts 100–199. Proposed regulations, new final regulations, and updates

to the *Code of Federal Regulations* are published in the daily *Federal Register.* (*See appendix for details on how to obtain and use these publications.*) The *Federal Register* and the *Code of Federal Regulations* may be accessed online at www.archives.gov/federal-register/cfr; the site contains a link to the federal government's regulatory website at www.regulations.gov (*see appendix*). FHEO rules and regulations are also available at www.hudclips.org.

▓ LEGISLATION

FHEO exercises its authority under:

Executive Order 11063. Issued by the president Nov. 20, 1962. Directed HUD to institute policies and actions to prevent discrimination because of race, color, creed, national origin, or sex in the sale, leasing, rental, or other disposition of residential property and related facilities owned, operated, or assisted financially by the federal government and in housing loans insured or guaranteed by the federal government.

Title VI of the Civil Rights Act of 1964 (78 Stat. 241, 42 U.S.C. 2000d). Signed by the president July 2, 1964. Prohibited discrimination in programs or activities receiving federal financial assistance on the basis of race, color, religion, national origin, or sex.

Executive Order 11246. Issued by the president Sept. 24, 1965. Provided for nondiscrimination in employment by government contractors and subcontractors.

Civil Rights Act of 1968, Title VIII (82 Stat. 81, 42 U.S.C. 3601). Signed by the president April 11, 1968. Also known as the Fair Housing Act. Prohibited discrimination in the sale or rental of most housing.

Section 3 of the Housing and Urban Development Act of 1968, as amended (82 Stat. 476, 12 U.S.C. 1701u). Signed by the president Aug. 1, 1968. Provided for maximum employment and training opportunities on HUD-assisted housing projects for lower-income residents of the metropolitan areas where these projects are located. The act also gave maximum work contract opportunities on these projects to individuals and firms located in or owned by persons residing in the housing project areas.

Architectural Barriers Act of 1968 (82 Stat. 718, 42 U.S.C. 4151 et seq.). Signed by the president Aug. 12, 1968. Ensured that buildings and facilities designed, constructed, altered, or leased with certain federal funds after September 1969 were accessible to people with disabilities.

Education Amendments of 1972 (20 U.S.C. 1681 et seq.). Signed by the president June 23, 1972. Title IX prohibited discrimination based on gender in education programs and activities that receive federal financial assistance.

Section 504 of the Rehabilitation Act of 1973 (87 Stat. 355, 29 U.S.C. 794). Signed by the president Sept. 16, 1973. Prohibited discrimination based on handicap in federally assisted and conducted programs and activities.

Section 109 of the Housing and Community Development Act of 1974 (88 Stat. 633, 42 U.S.C. 5309). Signed by the president Aug. 22, 1974. Prohibited discrimination in any federally funded activity, including employment, benefits, and services, and any program or activity that receives a loan guarantee under the title.

Age Discrimination Act of 1975 (42 U.S.C. 6101 et seq.). Signed by the president Nov. 28, 1975. Prohibited discrimination based on age in programs or activities that receive federal financial assistance (it does not cover employment discrimination).

Executive Order 12259. Issued by the president Dec. 31, 1980. Provided the secretary of HUD with a leadership role in the administration of any federal programs and activities relating to housing and urban development to further new housing throughout the nation.

Fair Housing Amendments Act of 1988 (102 Stat. 1619, 42 U.S.C. 3601 note). Signed by the president Sept. 13, 1988. Amended Title 8 of the Civil Rights Act of 1968 to prohibit housing discrimination against disabled people and families with young children.

Americans with Disabilities Act of 1990 (104 Stat. 327, 42 U.S.C. 12101 et seq.). Signed by the president July 25, 1990. Ensured that all programs, services, and regulatory activities relating to state and local public housing and housing assistance are available to people with disabilities.

Executive Order 12892. Issued by the president Jan. 17, 1994. Required all federal executive agencies to administer HUD programs in a manner that affirmatively furthers fair housing.

Executive Order 12898. Issued by the president Feb. 11, 1994. Required that each federal agency conduct its program, policies, and activities that substantially affect human health or the environment in a manner that does not exclude persons based on race, color, or national origin.

Multifamily Property Disposition Reform Act of 1994 (108 Stat. 342, 12 U.S.C. 1701). Signed by the president April 11, 1994. Amended Section 203 of the Housing and Community Development Amendments of 1978 to provide for the disposition of multifamily properties owned by HUD.

Home Ownership and Equity Protection Act of 1994 (108 Stat. 2190, 15 U.S.C. 1601 note). Signed by the president Sept. 23, 1994. Amended the Truth in Lending Act to require a creditor to disclose specified lending data to a consumer in connection with reverse mortgage transactions. Directed the Federal Reserve to conduct periodic public hearings on the home equity loan market and the adequacy of existing consumer protection laws.

Housing for Older Persons Act of 1995 (HOPA) (46 U.S.C. 3601 note). Signed by the president Dec. 28, 1995. Amended the Fair Housing Act definition of housing for older persons by deleting the "significant facilities and services" requirement and requiring at least 80 percent of occupied units to be occupied by at least one person fifty-five years of age or older.

Executive Order 13166. Issued by the president Aug. 11, 2000. Eliminated limited English proficiency as a barrier to participation by beneficiaries in all federally assisted and federally conducted programs and activities.

Executive Order 13217. Issued by the president June 18, 2001. Required federal agencies to evaluate and revise their policies and programs to improve the availability of community-based living arrangements for persons with disabilities.

Violence Against Women Reauthorization Act of 2013 (127 Stat. 102, 42 U.S.C. 14043e-113). Signed by the president Mar. 7, 2013. Affords rights and protections to survivors of domestic and dating violence, stalking, and sexual assault who are residing in housing assisted by HUD, including women living with HIV/AIDS.

▪ REGIONAL OFFICES

Housing and Urban Development Department

The Office of Fair Housing and Equal Opportunity does not have its own regional offices, but the Housing and Urban Development Department maintains the following regional offices to serve all HUD agencies.

REGION I

(CT, MA, ME, NH, RI, VT)
New England Office
10 Causeway St., #308
Boston, MA 02222–1092
(617) 994–8300
(800) 827–5005
Susan Forward, regional director

REGION II

(NJ, NY)
New York and New Jersey Office
26 Federal Plaza, #3541
New York, NY 10278–0068
(212) 542–7507
Jay Golden, regional director

REGION III

(DC, DE, MD, PA, VA, WV)
Mid-Atlantic Office
100 Penn Square East, 12th Floor
Philadelphia, PA 19107–3380
(215) 861–7643
(888) 799–2085
Melody Taylor-Blancher, regional director

REGION IV

(AL, FL, GA, KY, MS, NC, PR, SC, TN, VI)
Southeast Office
40 Marietta St.
Atlanta, GA 30303–2806
(678) 732–2905
(800) 440–8091
Carlos Osegueda, regional director

REGION V

(IL, IN, MI, MN, OH, WI)
Midwest Office
77 W. Jackson Blvd., #2101
Chicago, IL 60604–3507
(312) 353–7776
(800) 765–9372
Maurice McGough, regional director

REGION VI

(AR, LA, NM, OK, TX)
Southwest Office
801 Cherry St., Unit 45, #2500
Fort Worth, TX 76102
(817) 978–5868
(888) 560–8913
Gary Sweeney, regional director

REGION VII

(IA, KS, MO, NE)
Great Plains Office
400 State Ave.
Kansas City, KS 66101–2406
(913) 551–6857
(800) 743–5323
Betty Bottiger, regional director

REGION VIII

(CO, MT, ND, SD, UT, WY)
Rocky Mountain Office
1670 Broadway
Denver, CO 80202–4801
(303) 672–5151
(800) 877–7353
Amy Frisk, regional director

REGION IX

(AS, AZ, CA, GU, HI, NV)
Pacific/Hawaii Office
1 Sansome St., #1200
San Francisco, CA 94104
(415) 489–6526
(800) 347–3739
Anne Quesada, regional director

REGION X

(AK, ID, OR, WA)
Northwest/Alaska Office
909 First Ave., #205
Seattle, WA 98104–1000
(206) 220–5312
(800) 877–0246
Vacant, regional director

Office of Housing

451 7th St. S.W., Washington, DC 20410
Internet: www.hud.gov/offices/hsg

The assistant secretary for housing, who is also the federal housing commissioner, directs the Department of Housing and Urban Development (HUD) housing and mortgage insurance programs. These include the federally insured Federal Housing Administration (FHA) loans. These programs include the building, financing, and management of new and substantially rehabilitated housing and the conservation and rehabilitation of existing housing. The Office of Housing insures mortgages on single-family homes; multifamily rental, condominium, and cooperative projects; land purchased for residential development; nursing homes; group practice facilities and hospitals; and loans for property improvements and the purchase of manufactured (mobile) homes. The office directs special programs for the housing needs of low-income families, the elderly, disabled and mentally ill individuals, veterans, disaster victims, and prospective home buyers who are marginal credit risks.

The Office of Housing's basic missions are to create homeownership opportunities and to provide affordable rental housing for low- and moderate-income families. The National Homeownership Strategy, created in 1994, promotes homeownership through the cooperative effort of HUD, state and local governments, and private nonprofit and profit-making entities. The 2004 homeownership rate reached 69 percent—the highest annual rate in U.S. history. That level held steady until it began to dip with the 2007–2009 housing downturn and resulting financial crisis. By the first quarter of 2015, 63.7 percent of Americans owned their homes, the lowest level since 1990. The Office of Housing also works to ensure the availability of affordable rental housing through the administration of the multifamily insurance programs and Housing Choice Voucher Programs (formerly called Section 8) rental assistance programs.

As previously underserved borrowers were able to buy homes for the first time, many were falling victim to predatory lending practices in a segment of the mortgage lending market. Predatory mortgage lending practices strip borrowers of home equity and threaten families with foreclosure. The Home Ownership and Equity Protection Act of 1994 was enacted to prevent low-income consumers from losing their homes as a result of predatory lending practices.

The Housing Office is authorized to issue federal construction and safety standards to protect manufactured homeowners by Title VI of the Housing and Community Development Act of 1974 and the Housing and Community Development Act of 1977. HUD issues these standards to improve the quality of manufactured homes and to decrease property damage, insurance costs, and the number of personal injuries resulting from manufactured home accidents. The standards, which apply to mobile homes built after June 1976, preempt existing state and local codes and standards that do not meet federal standards. HUD standards cover body and frame requirements, thermal protection, plumbing, electrical, fire safety, and more. These standards are published in the *Code of Federal Regulations* at 24 *CFR* 3280.

HUD-authorized inspection agencies must approve every manufactured home design and inspect construction operations in manufactured housing plants. Standards may be enforced either by HUD or by various state agencies set up for the program. The manufacturer is required to notify the consumer if a manufactured home does not conform to federal standards. The manufacturer must correct any defects that might present an unreasonable risk of injury or death. Use of the mail or interstate commerce to sell or lease substandard manufactured homes is prohibited and may result in civil and criminal penalties.

In May 2003 HUD issued a final rule addressing property flipping, the practice in which a property recently acquired is resold at an artificially inflated value, often abetted by a lender's collusion with the appraiser. The final rule established requirements regarding the eligibility of properties to be financed with FHA mortgage insurance. The new requirements made flipped properties ineligible for FHA-insured mortgage financing, thus precluding FHA home purchasers from becoming victims of predatory flipping activity.

In August 2004 HUD issued a final ruling, Lender Accountability for Appraisals, which strengthened HUD's regulations concerning the responsibilities of FHA-approved lenders in the selection of appraisers for properties that would be the security for FHA-insured mortgages. The rule held lenders strictly accountable for the quality of their appraisals. The rule also required appraisals that do not meet FHA requirements to be subject to the imposition of sanctions by the HUD Mortgage Review Board.

For the first time in more than thirty years, HUD published new Real Estate Settlement Procedures Act (RESPA) regulations on Nov. 17, 2008. The updated rules required loan originators to provide borrowers with the new standard Good Faith Estimate and required closing agents to provide borrowers with the new HUD-1 settlement statement. HUD estimated the new regulations, designed to help consumers shop for the lowest-cost mortgage, would save consumers nearly $700 in closing costs.

Beginning in 2007 and continuing into 2009, a housing crisis hit nearly all of the nation's major metropolitan areas, affecting low-income as well as middle-class homeowners. Many housing markets saw plummeting prices and increased foreclosures. To help combat the crisis, Congress passed and President George W. Bush signed in July 2008 the Housing and Economic Recovery Act to enhance consumer protection, reduce fraud, and help struggling homeowners refinance mortgages through the HOPE for Homeowners program. The act included the FHA Modernization Act of 2008, which increased the cash down payment for an FHA loan from 3 percent to 3.5 percent of the appraised value of the property. The act also called for the Conference of State Bank Supervisors and the American Association of Residential Mortgage Regulators to establish and maintain a nationwide mortgage licensing system and registry for the residential mortgage industry.

Less than a month after taking office in 2009, President Barack Obama outlined his Homeowner Affordability and Stability Plan, which gave rise to the Making Homes Affordable program. The Making Homes Affordable program offered incentives to lenders to refinance home loans or offer distressed consumers loan modifications in order to prevent foreclosure. HUD counselors assisted homeowners in determining eligibility for the programs and warned consumers against firms that fraudulently offered the same services for high fees, generally without obtaining a loan modification for the consumer.

In May the passage of the Helping Families Save Their Homes Act of 2009 expanded the Making Homes Affordable programs and streamlined the FHA's HOPE for Homeowners program. The law sought further consumer protections through provisions to prevent predatory lending entities from participating in the FHA home mortgage insurance program, and the law established a Nationwide Mortgage Fraud Task Force. The legislation also provided protection for tenants renting homes that went into foreclosure by requiring a ninety-day notice for eviction.

HUD also took steps to address risk management and oversight of FHA lenders. In 2009, HUD announced a set of credit policy changes to enhance FHA's risk management function, including the hiring of a Chief Risk Officer for the first time in the agency's seventy-five-year history. HUD promulgated rules to increase the net worth requirements of FHA-approved lenders, strengthen lender approval criteria, and make lenders liable for the oversight of mortgage brokers.

Government assistance to homeowners continued into 2011 as the housing market showed anemic signs of stabilizing in some states. The Dodd-Frank Wall Street Reform and Consumer Protection Act authorized HUD to administer a $1 billion Emergency Homeowners Loan Program (EHLP) to provide assistance for up to twenty-four months to homeowners who have experienced a substantial reduction in income due to involuntary unemployment, underemployment, or a medical condition, and are at risk of foreclosure.

In accordance with the Dodd-Frank Wall Street Reform and Consumer Protection Act, the following programs were transferred from HUD to the new Consumer Financial Protection Bureau (CFPB) (p. 387) on July 21, 2011: Real Estate Settlement Procedures Act (RESPA); Interstate Land Sales; and Secure and Fair Enforcement for Mortgage Licensing Act of 2008 (SAFE Act). CFPB assumes regulatory authority under the authorizing statutes of the programs.

In 2012 HUD and the Justice Department announced that the federal government and forty-nine state attorneys general had reached a $25 billion agreement with the nation's five largest mortgage servicers to address mortgage loan servicing and foreclosure abuses. The joint agreement was the largest federal-state civil settlement ever obtained. This was the result of extensive investigations by federal agencies, state attorneys general, and state banking regulators across the country. The joint agreement with Bank of America Corporation, JPMorgan Chase, Wells Fargo, Citigroup Inc., and Ally Financial Inc. (formerly GMAC) provided financial relief to homeowners and established additional homeowner protections.

In December 2014 the Federal Housing Finance Agency (FHFA) (p. 412) directed Fannie Mae and Freddie Mac to begin setting aside and allocating funds to the Housing Trust Fund pursuant to the Housing and Economic Recovery Act of 2008. In January 2015 HUD issued an interim rule providing guidance to state and local entities for the implementation of the National Housing Trust Fund (HTF), which will complement existing federal, state, and local efforts to increase affordable housing for extremely low-income and very low-income households, including homeless families.

The Office of Housing carries out its responsibilities through four business areas:

Single-family housing programs include mortgage insurance on loans to purchase new or existing homes, condominiums, manufactured housing, houses needing rehabilitation, and for reverse equity mortgages to elderly homeowners. This unit also administers the Home Equity Conversion Mortgage (HECM) program, the FHA's reverse mortgage program for eligible homeowners aged 62 or older.

Multifamily housing programs provide mortgage insurance to HUD-approved lenders to facilitate the construction, substantial rehabilitation, purchase, and refinancing of multifamily housing projects.

Health care programs provide mortgage insurance on loans that finance the construction, renovation, acquisition, or refinancing of health care facilities such as hospitals and residential care facilities.

Regulatory programs assist homeowners and homebuyers, and regulate real estate transactions.

■ KEY PERSONNEL

Assistant Secretary for Housing—Federal Housing Administration Commissioner

Vacant . . . . (202) 708–2601

Fax . . . . (202) 708–2580

Principle Deputy Assistant Secretary
Edward Golding . . . . (202) 708–2601
Deputy Assistant Secretary for Finance and Budget
George Rabil . . . . (202) 708–2004
Asset Sales
John Lucey . . . . (202) 708–2625
Budget and Field Resources
Brenda Davis . . . . (202) 401–8975
FHA Comptroller
Susan Betts (acting) . . . . (202) 401–8800
Financial Services
Kathleen Malone . . . . (202) 708–1046
Financial Analysis and Reporting
Carol Britton . . . . (202) 401–0450
Systems and Technology
William F. Fuentevilla. . . . . (202) 401–1577
Deputy Assistant Secretary for Health Care Programs
Roger Miller. (202) 708–0599
Associate Deputy Assistant Secretary for Health Care Programs
Roger Lukoff . . . . (202) 708–0599
Hospital Facilities
Geoffrey Papsco . . . . (202) 402–2436
Residential Care Facilities
Roger Lewis . . . . (206) 220–6465
Architecture and Engineering
Robin Senator (acting). . . . . (212) 542–7874
Deputy Assistant Secretary for Housing Counseling
Sarah Gerecke . . . . (202) 708–0317
Associate Deputy Assistant Secretary for Housing Counseling
Danberry Carmon . . . . (202) 402–2462
Policy and Grant Administration
Brian Siebenlist . . . . (202) 402–5415
Outreach and Capacity Building
Jerrold Mayer. . . . . (714) 955–0888
Oversight and Accountability
Cheryl Appline . . . . (678) 732–2696
Deputy Assistant Secretary for Multifamily Housing
Benjamin Metcalf . . . . (202) 708–2495
Associate Deputy Assistant Secretary for Multifamily Housing
Vacant . . . . (202) 708–2495
Field Support and Operations
Peter Duklis . . . . (202) 402–4432
Multifamily Asset Management and Portfolio Oversight
Nancie-Ann Bodell (acting) . . . . . (202) 402–2472
Multifamily Production
Ted Toon . . . . (202) 402–8386
Program Administration
Priya Jayachandran. . . . . (202) 402–2314
Program Systems Management
Carolyn Cockrell. . . . . (202) 402–6038
Recapitalization
Janet Golrick (acting) . . . . (202) 402–3998
Deputy Assistant Secretary for Single Family Housing
Kathleen Zadareky . . . . (202) 708–3175

Associate Deputy Assistant Secretary for Single Family Housing
Robert Mulderig . . . . (202) 708–3175
Lender Activities and Program Compliance
Joy Hadley . . . . (202) 708–1515
Mortgage Review Board Division
Nancy Murray . . . . (202) 708–2224
Single Family Asset Management
Ivory Himes. . . . . (202) 708–1672
Single Family Program Development
Elissa Saunders . . . . (202) 708–2121
Deputy Assistant Secretary for Risk Management and Regulatory Affairs
Frank Vetrano . . . . (202) 402–3134
Chief Risk Officer
Rob Ryan . . . . (202) 402–6203
Evaluation
Shawn Jones (acting) . . . . (202) 402–6914
Manufactured Housing
Pamela Danner . . . . (202) 402–6423
Risk Management and Assessment
Nandini Bhaskara . . . . (202) 402–2398
Deputy Assistant Secretary for Housing Operations
Lori Michalski . . . . (202) 708–1104
Associate Deputy Assistant Secretary for Housing Operations
Kevin Perkins. . . . . (202) 708–1104
Business Development
Richard Kurtz (acting) . . . . (202) 708–2598
Environmental Clearance
Vacant . . . . (202) 708–1104
Management
E. Neil Brown . . . . (202) 708–1014

■ INFORMATION SOURCES

Internet

Agency website: www.hud.gov/offices/hsg. Comprehensive website features general information on renting and buying single-family and multifamily homes; also includes information on neighborhood networks and the Real Estate Settlement Procedures Act. HUD also maintains the following online service:

HUD USER
P.O. Box 23268
Washington, DC 20026–3268
(800) 245–2691
(202) 708–3178
TTY (800) 927–7589
E-mail: helpdesk@huduser.org
Internet: www.huduser.org
E-mail: Jsimpson@sagecomputing.com

More than 1,000 reports, resource guides, kits, executive summaries, case studies, and guidebooks published by HUD are available from HUD USER, most for a nominal fee.

Telephone Contacts

Personnel Locator . . . .(202) 708–1420
Housing Discrimination Hotline . . . . .(800) 669–9777
Counseling Agency Locator . . . .(800) 569–4287
TTY . . . .(202) 708–1455

Information and Publications

KEY OFFICES

HUD Public Affairs

451 7th St. S.W., #10130
Washington, DC 20410
(202) 708–0980
Jaime Castillo (acting), assistant secretary for public
    affairs

Answers questions from the public and the press about
the Housing Office and its activities, distributes several
publications and policy amendments, and issues news
releases.

Freedom of Information

HUD Office of the Executive Secretary
451 7th St. S.W., #10139
Washington, DC 20410
(202) 708–3054
Deborah R. Snowden, FOIA branch chief
(202) 402–7606

PUBLICATIONS

HUD Customer Service/Distribution Center

451 7th St. S.W., Room BS-11
Washington, DC 20410
(800) 767–7468
Fax orders: (202) 708–2313
E-mail: on_demand_mail@hud.gov

Distributes more than 7,000 publications including
brochures on manufactured housing standards, real estate
settlement procedures, and interstate land sales.
Publications available include:
Manufactured Housing
Minimum Property Standards
Programs of HUD. Describes HUD programs including the nature of the programs, eligibility requirements,
distribution of aid, information sources, current status,
and the funding of the programs. Lists regional and field
offices. Many publications, research studies, and forms are
also available at the website, www.hudclips.org, as well as
from www.huduser.org (*see Information Sources, above*).

Reference Resources

LIBRARY

Housing and Urban Development Department

451 7th St. S.W., #8141
Washington, DC 20410

(202) 708–2370
Hours: 8:30 a.m. to 4:30 p.m.
Internet: www.hud.gov/library/index.cfm

Materials related to the Office of Housing are available
here and at regional offices. All materials must be used on
site, and only a limited number of resources are available.

REGULATORY BARRIERS CLEARINGHOUSE

HUD's Regulatory Barriers Clearinghouse (RBC) was
created to support state and local governments and other
organizations seeking information about laws, regulations, and policies affecting all aspects of affordable housing. RBC supports the collection and dissemination of
resources that can help identify and address regulatory
barriers in each individual state and community. RBC is
available at www.huduser.org/portal/rbc/home.html.

DOCKETS

Federal dockets are available at www.regulations.gov.
(*See appendix for Searching and Commenting on Regulations:
Regulations.gov.*)

RULES AND REGULATIONS

Office of Housing rules and regulations are published
in the *Code of Federal Regulations,* Title 24, Chapter II,
Parts 200–299; Title 24, Chapter IV, Parts 400–499; Title
24, Chapter X, Parts 1700–1799; Title 24, Chapter XX, Parts
3200–3899. Proposed regulations, new final regulations,
and updates to the *Code of Federal Regulations* are published
in the daily *Federal Register.* (*See appendix for details on how
to obtain and use these publications.*) The *Federal Register*
and the *Code of Federal Regulations* may be accessed online
at www.archives.gov/federal-register/cfr; the site contains a
link to the federal government's regulatory website at www
.regulations.gov (*see appendix*). FHEO rules and regulations are also published at www.hudclips.org.

▤ LEGISLATION

The Office of Housing carries out its responsibilities
under numerous pieces of legislation; among the most
important are the following:

National Housing Act of 1934 (48 Stat. 1246, 12 U.S.C.
1702). Signed by the president June 27, 1934. Authorized
mortgage insurance, rehabilitation, health facilities, and
other financial and related assistance programs.

U.S. Housing Act of 1937 (50 Stat. 888, 42 U.S.C.
1401). Signed by the president Sept. 1, 1937. Authorized
the low-income housing programs.

Housing Act of 1959 (73 Stat. 654, 12 U.S.C. 1701q).
Signed by the president Sept. 23, 1959. Strengthened laws
governing programs to improve housing and renew urban
communities such as the FHA Insurance Program, urban
renewal, and low-rent public housing. Section 202 provided for a direct-loan program for the construction of
housing for the elderly.

Housing and Urban Development Act of 1965 (79
Stat. 451, 42 U.S.C. 3535). Signed by the president Aug.
10, 1965. Strengthened financial assistance provisions

for low- and moderate-income families in existing housing laws to promote orderly urban development and to improve living conditions in urban areas. Title I authorized the rent supplement programs.

Housing and Urban Development Act of 1968 (82 Stat. 476, 12 U.S.C. 1701 note). Signed by the president Aug. 1, 1968. Amended the National Housing Act of 1934. Section 106(a) authorized HUD to provide advice and technical assistance with regard to construction, renovation, and operation of low- and moderate-income housing.

Interstate Land Sales Full Disclosure Act (82 Stat. 590, 15 U.S.C. 1701). Signed by the president Aug. 1, 1968. Title XIV of the Housing and Urban Development Act of 1968. Established regulations for the sale or lease of subdivision lots. Required sellers to make available certain information about the land involved and to furnish purchasers with a property report approved by HUD. Regulatory authority for this law was transferred from HUD to the Consumer Financial Protection Bureau under the Dodd-Frank Wall Street Reform and Consumer Protection Act in July 2011.

Lead-Based Paint Poisoning Prevention Act (84 Stat. 2078, 42 U.S.C. 4801). Signed by the president Jan. 13, 1971. Provided for federal assistance to communities to develop local programs to eliminate causes of lead-based paint poisoning. Prohibited the use of lead-based paint in federal or federally assisted construction or renovation.

Housing and Community Development Act of 1974 (88 Stat. 633, 42 U.S.C. 5301). Signed by the president Aug. 22, 1974. Section 8 created the Housing Assistance Payments Program, which provided housing assistance payments to participating private owners and public housing agencies to provide decent housing for low-income families at affordable costs.

National Mobile Home Construction and Safety Standards Act of 1974 (88 Stat. 700, 42 U.S.C. 5401). Signed by the president Aug. 22, 1974. Title VI of the Housing and Community Development Act of 1974 established federal standards for the construction, design, performance, and safety of mobile homes.

Real Estate Settlement Procedures Act of 1974 (88 Stat. 1724, 12 U.S.C. 2601). Signed by the president Dec. 22, 1974. Provided for disclosure of the nature and costs of real estate settlement services. Regulatory authority for this law was transferred from HUD to the Consumer Financial Protection Bureau under the Dodd-Frank Wall Street Reform and Consumer Protection Act in July 2011.

Housing and Community Development Act of 1987 (101 Stat. 1815, 42 U.S.C. 5301 note). Signed by the president Feb. 5, 1988. Authorized funding for housing and community development for fiscal years 1988 and 1989. Permanently extended Federal Housing Administration authority to insure home mortgage loans. Provided incentives and rules to improve maintenance and safety of public housing.

Omnibus Budget Reconciliation Act of 1990 (104 Stat. 1388, 42 U.S.C. 1437f). Signed by the president Nov. 5, 1990. Authorized a series of reforms to FHA single-family programs to ensure the actuarial soundness of the Mutual Mortgage Insurance Fund.

Cranston-Gonzalez National Affordable Housing Act of 1990 (104 Stat. 4079, 42 U.S.C. 12701). Signed by the president Nov. 28, 1990. Reformed low-income housing programs to expand home ownership. Brought state and local government into a new housing investment partnership with the federal government and the private sector to provide for affordable housing.

Housing and Community Development Act of 1992 (106 Stat. 3672, 42 U.S.C. 5301 note). Signed by the president Oct. 28, 1992. Increased the maximum mortgage amount in FHA single-family insurance programs; provided for a regulatory structure for government-sponsored enterprises; and implemented programs to reduce the risk of lead-based paint poisoning in public housing.

Multifamily Property Disposition Reform Act of 1994 (108 Stat. 342, 12 U.S.C. 1701). Signed by the president April 11, 1994. Amended Housing and Community Development Amendments of 1978 to provide for the disposition of multifamily properties owned by HUD.

Home Ownership and Equity Protection Act of 1994 (108 Stat. 2190, 15 U.S.C. 1601 note). Signed by the president Sept. 23, 1994. Sought to prohibit predatory lending practices against low-income and minority consumers by amending the Truth in Lending Act to require a creditor to disclose specified lending data to a consumer in connection with reverse mortgage transactions. Directed the Federal Reserve to conduct periodic public hearings on the home equity loan market and the adequacy of existing consumer protection laws.

FHA Downpayment Simplification Act of 2002 (116 Stat. 2792, 13 U.S.C. 1709). Signed by the president Dec. 4, 2002. Amended the National Housing Act to make the existing FHA single-family home down payment provisions permanent. Required that original lenders, in conjunction with an FHA-insured loan, provide prospective borrowers with a one-page analysis of other mortgage products for which they would qualify, including information about rates, insurance premiums, other costs and fees, and mortgage insurance premium termination.

Servicemembers Civil Relief Act (117 Stat. 2835, 50 U.S.C. App. 501 et seq.). Signed by the president Dec. 19, 2003. Mandates that military personnel on active duty in wartime are entitled to mortgage relief, including a lower interest rate (not more than 6 percent) on their mortgages and foreclosure protection.

Housing and Economic Recovery Act (42 U.S.C. 4501 note, 122 Stat. 2654). Signed by the president July 30, 2008. Division B, Title I, FHA Modernization Act of 2008, increased the cash down payment for an FHA loan from the 3 percent to 3.5 percent of the appraised value of the property. Authorized the HOPE for Homeowners program, which refinanced mortgages for borrowers who were having difficulty making their payments but qualified for a loan insured by the FHA. Required Fannie Mae and Freddie Mac (GSEs) to set aside specified funds allocations for affordable housing trust fund programs; authorized FHFA to temporarily suspend GSE allocations if such allocations would cause financial instability. Instructed the HUD secretary to establish a Housing Trust Fund to provide grants to states to increase the supply of housing for low-income families.

Helping Families Save Their Homes Act of 2009 (123 Stat. 1632, 12 U.S.C. 5201 note). Signed by the president May 20, 2009. Amended the HOPE for Homeowners Program to reduce excessive fee levels. Provided greater incentives for mortgage servicers to engage in modifications. Reduced administrative burdens to loan underwriters by making the requirements more consistent with standard FHA practices. Established a Nationwide Mortgage Fraud Task Force to address mortgage fraud. Contained provisions to prevent predatory lending entities from participating in the FHA home mortgage insurance program. Required a ninety-day notice for eviction for tenants renting homes that go into foreclosure.

Dodd-Frank Wall Street Reform and Consumer Protection Act (124 Stat. 1376, 12 U.S.C. 5301 note). Signed by the president July 21, 2010. Requires federal banking agencies, the SEC, the secretary of Housing and Urban Development (HUD), and the Federal Housing Finance Agency (FHFA), to jointly prescribe regulations to require sponsors of asset-backed securities to retain a percentage of the credit risk of the assets underlying the securities and would not permit sponsors to transfer or hedge that credit risk. Transfers the consumer protection regulatory functions of the Real Estate Settlement Procedures Act (RESPA), Interstate Land Sales, and SAFE Mortgage Licensing Act of 2008 from HUD to the Consumer Financial Protection Bureau. Authorizes HUD to administer an Emergency Homeowners Loan Program to provide temporary assistance to homeowners who have experienced a substantial reduction in income due to involuntary unemployment, underemployment, or a medical condition and are at risk of foreclosure.

■ REGIONAL OFFICES

The Office of Housing does not maintain its own regional offices, but a list of regional offices that serve all Housing and Urban Development Department agencies can be found on p. 674.

Office of Public and Indian Housing

451 7th St. S.W., Washington, DC 20410
Internet: www.hud.gov/offices/pih

The Office of Public and Indian Housing (PIH) is responsible for directing the low-income public housing program, including housing for low-income seniors, of the Department of Housing and Urban Development (HUD) and coordinating all departmental housing and community development programs for Native Americans and Alaska Natives. The low-income housing program provides financial and technical assistance for the development, operation, and management of public housing, including assistance to Indian Housing Authorities (IHAs) for low-income Native American families residing in Native American areas and reservations. PIH also provides operating subsidies for Public Housing Authorities (PHAs) and IHAs.

PIH is responsible for administering the following programs:

- The Capital Fund to provide funds to PHAs for the development, financing, and modernization of public housing projects
- The Resident Opportunities and Self-Sufficiency (ROSS) Program to help public housing residents become economically self-sufficient
- The HOPE VI Program, which provides funding for physical improvements and community services to public housing authorities (Congress has not appropriated funds for this program since FY 2010)
- Housing Choice Voucher Programs (formerly Section 8)
- Demolition/Disposition program to help eliminate old, rundown public housing
- Mixed-Finance Public Housing allows HUD to mix public, private, and nonprofit funds to develop and operate housing development.

Indian Housing

The provision of assistance for Indian Housing Authorities is authorized by the U.S. Housing Act of 1937, as amended. IHAs must be established before they can receive any HUD assistance. IHAs are corporate, public bodies established by tribal ordinance or state law. They plan, construct, purchase, lease, and manage properties. HUD's role is to administer the federal government's participation in the Indian Housing Program.

Within PIH, the Office of Native American Programs (ONAP) administers housing and community development programs that benefit American Indian and Alaska Native tribal governments, tribal members, the Department of Hawaiian Home Lands, Native Hawaiians, and other Native American organizations, including the following:

- Indian Home Loan Guarantee Program (Section 184) is a home mortgage for American Indian and Alaska Native families, Alaska Villages, Tribes, or tribally designated housing entities. Section 184 loans can be used for new construction, rehabilitation, purchase of an existing home, or refinance, on and off native lands.
- Indian Housing Block Grant Program, a formula grant that provides a range of affordable housing activities on Indian reservations and Indian areas.
- The Indian Community Development Block Grant Program to develop Native American and Alaska Native communities and to aid families with low and moderate income.
- Native Hawaiian Housing Block Grant fund use is limited to eligible affordable housing activities for low-income native Hawaiians eligible to reside on Hawaiian home lands. Housing can be either rental or homeownership.
- Native Hawaiian Home Loan Guarantee Program (Section 184A) offers home ownership, property rehabilitation, and new construction opportunities for eligible Native Hawaiian individuals and families wanting to own a home on Hawaiian home lands.
- Title VI Loan Guarantee Program provides an additional source of financing for affordable tribal housing activities, including costs related to land acquisition and construction and rehabilitation.

Housing and Community Development Act of 1992 established the Section 184 Indian Housing Loan Guarantee Program. The program is designed to offer homeownership and housing rehabilitation opportunities for eligible Native American individuals or families, tribes, and tribally designated entities (including Indian Housing Authorities) on their native lands. Before 2005 these opportunities were restricted to home ownership on federally recognized reservations. Under new guidelines established in 2005, tribes and tribal housing entities can provide Section 184 homeownership opportunities beyond their reservations.

The Native American Housing Assistance and Self-Determination Act of 1996 established the Title IV Loan Guarantee assistance program. The Title VI program allows tribes to leverage their Indian Housing Block Grants by pledging current and future block grants to finance affordable housing activities within the tribal community, such as buying and rehabilitating homes. The Title VI program also allows tribes to use the leverage funds as seed money to build facility infrastructure that supports the housing, such as community centers, health clinics, and public utilities.

The Quality Housing and Work Responsibility Act of 1998 authorized a new public housing homeownership program. PIH's rule outlining the program's regulations went into effect in April 2003. The program makes public housing dwelling units available for purchase by low-income Native American families as their principal residence.

■ KEY PERSONNEL

Assistant Secretary for Public and Indian Housing
 Lourdes Ramirez .... (202) 708–0950
  Fax .... (202) 619–8478
General Deputy Assistant Secretary
 Jemine Bryon..................... (202) 708–0950
Chief Risk Officer
 Wendell Conner .... (336) 255–4821
Budget/Chief Financial Officer
 Ricky Valentine .... (202) 402–6073
Coordination and Compliance
 Marcia Martin (acting) .... (202) 402–4256
Field Operations
 Unabyrd Wadhams .... (202) 402–6296
Grants Management Center
(550 12th St. S.W., Washington, DC 20410)
 Toll-free .... (888) 404–3893
Housing Vouchers Financial Management Center
(2345 Grand Blvd., #1150, Kansas City, MO 64108)
 Tamara Gray..................... (312) 886–9754
Native American Programs
 Roger Boyd...................... (202) 401–7914
Planning, Resource Management, and Administrative Services
 Edward Turner................... (202) 402–4440
Policy, Programs, and Legislative Initiatives
 Danielle Bastarache .... (202) 402–4673
Procurement and Contract Services
 Keia Neal .... (202) 402–8312
Public Housing and Voucher Programs
 Milan Ozdinec .... (202) 708–1380
Public Housing Investments
 Dominique Blom .... (202) 401–8812
Real Estate Assessment Center
 Donald LaVoy .... (202) 475–7949
Receivership and Oversight
 Kimberly Wize................... (317) 957–7345
Recovery and Prevention Corps
(Renaissance on Playhouse Square, 1350 Euclid Ave., #900, Cleveland, OH 44115)
 Patricia A. Knight .... (216) 522–4300

Section 8 Financial Management Center
(2345 Grand Blvd., #1150, Kansas City, MO 64108–2603)
 Jacquelyn Lunn, director .... (816) 426–6251
Special Applications Center
(77 W. Jackson Blvd., 24th Floor, Chicago, IL 60604)
 Tamara Gray...................... (312) 886–9754

■ INFORMATION SOURCES

Internet
Agency website: www.hud.gov/offices/pih. Comprehensive website includes general information on public housing, application kits, and frequently asked questions. The website also includes Code Talk, which delivers electronic information for Native American communities (for Code Talk support, call 800–561–5913). HUD also maintains the following service:

HUD USER
 P.O. Box 23268
 Washington, DC 20026–3268
 (800) 245–2691
 (202) 708–3178
 TTY (800) 927–7589
 E-mail: helpdesk@huduser.org
 Internet: www.huduser.org

Provides numerous HUD publications pertaining to public and Indian housing.

Telephone Contacts
 Personnel Locator ....(202) 708–1420
 Native American Programs ....(800) 735–3239
 Public and Indian Information Resource
  Center (includes the Senior Housing
  Information Center) ....(800) 955–2232
 Housing Discrimination Hotline ....(800) 669–9777
 Counseling Agency Locator ....(800) 569–4287
 TTY ....(202) 708–1455

Information and Publications

KEY OFFICES

HUD Public Affairs
 451 7th St. S.W., #10130
 Washington, DC 20410
 (202) 708–0980
 Jaime Castillo (acting), assistant secretary for public affairs

Issues news releases and answers questions from the public and the press.

Freedom of Information
 HUD Office of the Executive Secretary
 451 7th St. S.W., #10139
 Washington, DC 20410

(202) 708–3054
Deborah R. Snowden, FOIA branch chief
(202) 402–7606

PUBLICATIONS

HUD Customer Service/Distribution Center
451 7th St. S.W., Room BS-11
Washington, DC 20410
(800) 767–7468
Fax orders: (202) 708–2313
E-mail orders: on_demand_mail@hud.gov

Distributes over 7,000 HUD publications, including brochures, research studies, and datasets. Publications, forms, handbooks, research studies, and notices are also available at the website, www.hudclips.org, as well as from www.huduser.org (*see Information Sources, above*).

Reference Resources

LIBRARY

Housing and Urban Development Department
451 7th St. S.W., #8141
Washington, DC 20410
(202) 708–2370

Related materials are also available at regional offices and the Online Library on the website, at www .hud.gov/library/index.cfm. Materials must be used on site, and the library has a limited collection. The headquarters library is open to the public from 8:30 a.m. to 4:30 p.m.

DOCKETS
Federal dockets are available at www.regulations.gov. (*See appendix for Searching and Commenting on Regulations: Regulations.gov.*)

RULES AND REGULATIONS
PIH rules and regulations are published in the *Code of Federal Regulations,* Title 24, Chapter VII, Parts 700–1699; Title 24, Chapter IX, Parts 900–999. Proposed regulations, new final regulations, and updates to the *Code of Federal Regulations* are published in the daily *Federal Register.* (*See appendix for details on how to obtain and use these publications.*) The *Federal Register* and the *Code of Federal Regulations* may be accessed online at www.archives.gov/ federal-register/cfr; the site contains a link to the federal government's regulatory website at www.regulations.gov (*see appendix*). PIH rules and regulations are also available from www.hudclips.org.

■ LEGISLATION
U.S. Housing Act of 1937 (50 Stat. 888, 42 U.S.C. 1401). Signed by the president Sept. 1, 1937. Authorized HUD to provide financial and technical assistance to Indian Housing Authorities for the operation, development, and management of housing for low-income Native American families living in Indian areas or reservations.

Housing and Community Development Act of 1974 (88 Stat. 633, 42 U.S.C. 5301). Signed by the president Aug. 22, 1974. Established the Section 8 Rental Certificate Program, which provided housing assistance payments to participating private owners and public housing agencies to provide decent housing for low-income families at affordable costs. Also authorized the Indian Community Development Block Grant Programs.

Cranston-Gonzalez National Affordable Housing Act (104 Stat. 4079, 42 U.S.C. 12701). Signed by the president Nov. 28, 1990. Created the Home Investment Partnership to expand the supply of decent and safe affordable housing. Funds are awarded competitively to state and local governments and federally recognized Indian tribes and Alaska Native villages.

Public and Assisted Housing Drug Elimination Act of 1990 (101 Stat. 4245, 42 U.S.C. 11901 note). Signed by the president Nov. 28, 1990. Authorized HUD to make grants to PHAs and IHAs for use in eliminating drug-related crime in public housing projects.

Housing and Community Development Act of 1992 (106 Stat. 3672, 42 U.S.C. 5301 note). Signed by the president Oct. 28, 1992. Section 184 established an Indian Housing Loan Guarantee Fund to guarantee loans for the construction, acquisition, or rehabilitation of one- to four-family homes that are standard housing located on trust or restricted land or land located in a Native American or Alaska Native area, and for which an Indian Housing Plan has been submitted and approved.

Native American Housing Assistance and Self-Determination Act of 1996 (110 Stat. 4016, 25 U.S.C. 4101 note). Signed by the president Oct. 26, 1996. Provided grants to carry out affordable housing programs for Native Americans. Established Title IV loan guarantee program. Reauthorized in 2008.

Multifamily Assisted Housing Reform and Affordability Act of 1997 (111 Stat. 1344). Signed by the president Oct. 27, 1997. Title V of the 1998 HUD appropriations bill. Amended the Social Security Act to make permanent provisions authorizing disclosure by states of certain income and unemployment records of housing assistance participants or applicants to HUD. Authorized the HUD secretary to issue regulations to carry out these provisions.

Quality Housing and Work Responsibility Act of 1998 (112 Stat. 2518, 42 U.S.C. 1437 note). Signed by the president Oct. 21, 1998. Amended the Public and Assisted Housing Drug Elimination Act of 1990 to make Native American tribes eligible to receive grants for elimination of drug-related crime in public housing. Established Native American housing grants and loan guarantees. Mandated that a public housing authority establish minimum rent of not more than $50 per month (with some exceptions). Required adult residents of public housing to contribute no less than eight hours of community service per month or to participate in an economic self-sufficiency or job-training program.

Housing and Urban Development Fiscal Year 2000 Appropriations (113 Stat. 1047). Signed by the president

Oct. 20, 1999. Amended the Housing Act of 1937 to authorize the HUD secretary to establish income ceilings, with respect to eligibility for public housing or project-based Section 8 assistance, that are higher or lower than 30 percent of the area median income.

Omnibus Fiscal Year 2009 Appropriations (123 Stat. 524). Signed by the president March 11, 2009. Placed Section 8 rental assistance restrictions on certain groups of persons, including any person who is enrolled in college, under age twenty-four, not a veteran, unmarried, does not have a dependent child, and not a person with disabilities.

■ REGIONAL OFFICES

Office of Public and Indian Housing

An additional list of regional offices that serve all Housing and Urban Development Department agencies can be found on p. 674.

ALASKA

Office of Native American Programs
3000 C St., #401
Anchorage, AK 99503
(907) 677–9836
TTY (907) 667–9825
Toll-free within Alaska (877) 302–9800
Bill Zachares, administrator
(907) 677–9860

EASTERN/WOODLANDS

(All states east of the Mississippi River and IA, MN, and WI)
Office of Native American Programs
77 W. Jackson Blvd., #2404
Chicago, IL 60604–3507
(800) 735–3239
Mark Butterfield, administrator
(312) 913–8750

HAWAII

Covers Native Hawaiian Programs, including Native Hawaiian Housing Block Grant and the Section 184A Native Hawaiian Housing Loan Guarantee.

Office of Native American Programs, Native Hawaiian Housing
1132 Bishop St., #1400
Honolulu, HI 96813
(808) 457–4674
Claudine Allen, program specialist

NORTHERN PLAINS

(CO, MT, ND, NE, SD, UT, WY)
Office of Native American Programs
1670 Broadway, 22nd Floor
Denver, CO 80202–4801
(303) 672–5465
(888) 814–2945
TTY (303) 672–5116
Randall R. Akers, administrator
(303) 672–5160

NORTHWEST

(ID, OR, WA)
Office of Native American Programs
909 First Ave., #300
Seattle, WA 98104–1000
(206) 220–5270
Ken Bowring, administrator
(206) 220–5391

SOUTHERN PLAINS

(AR, KS, LA, MO, OK, TX except Isleta del Sur)
Office of Native American Programs
301 N.W. 6th St., #200
Oklahoma City, OK 73102
(405) 609–8520
(800) 609–8400
Wayne Sims, administrator
(405) 609–8520

SOUTHWEST

(AZ, CA, NM, NV; Isleta del Sur, TX)
Office of Native American Programs
1 North Central Ave., #600
Phoenix, AZ 85004–2361
(602) 379–7200
Carolyn O'Neil, administrator
(602) 379–7200

Other Housing and Urban Development Department Offices

■ GOVERNMENT NATIONAL MORTGAGE ASSOCIATION
550 12th St. S.W., #300
Washington, DC 20024
Mailing address: 451 7th St. S.W., B-133
Washington, DC 20410
Internet: www.ginniemae.gov

The Government National Mortgage Association, also known as Ginnie Mae, is a U.S. government corporation created in 1968 through an amendment to Title III of the National Housing Act. Ginnie Mae was established to support the government's housing objectives by providing liquidity in the secondary mortgage market for federally insured mortgages originating from the Federal Housing Administration and Department of Veterans Affairs. As a government corporation, Ginnie Mae and its program are governed by a set of regulations published in the *Code of Federal Regulations* at Title 24, Parts 300–310.

Ginnie Mae's principal activity in supporting those objectives is with its Mortgage-Backed Securities (MBS) Program, which provides the necessary liquidity and attempts to attract new sources of financing for residential loans. Through this program, Ginnie Mae facilitates the use of mortgage collateral for securities by guaranteeing the payment of principal and interest in a timely manner.

In 1993 Congress authorized Ginnie Mae to undertake a Real Estate Mortgage Investment Conduit, a trust consisting of mortgage-backed securities. In March 2005 Ginnie Mae announced its first rural housing project loan securitization. This project marked the first time Ginnie Mae securitization was used to support affordable multifamily housing through the USDA Rural Development's Section 538 program. The program provides a government guarantee for certain loans made in rural areas. The Department of Housing and Urban Development's Office of Public and Indian Housing (PIH) loans also are eligible as collateral for Ginnie Mae MBS.

The 2008 collapse of the subprime loan market dramatically changed the housing industry: credit tightened, home prices fell, and foreclosures rose to record levels. In April 2008 Ginnie Mae added a new multiple-issuer security under the Ginnie Mae MBS program to accommodate the jumbo loans insured by the Federal Housing Administration (FHA).

In fiscal year 2014, Ginnie Mae generated $1.5 billion in profits for the federal government and managed guarantees on more than $1.5 trillion in mortgage-backed securities.

The agency's Internet site provides links to various programs and products, industry reports, and a list of pertinent statutes and regulations.

President
Theodore Tozer . . . . (202) 708–0926
    Fax . . . . (202) 708–0490
    Hotline . . . . (888) 446–6434
Executive Vice President
Mary Kinney . . . . (202) 708–0926
Chief Financial Officer
Thomas R. Weakland . . . . (202) 708–2648
Chief Risk Officer
Gregory A. Keith . . . . (202) 475–4918
Administration
Deborah A. Hernandez . . . . (202) 475–8945
Issuer and Portfolio Management
Michael R. Drayne . . . . (202) 475–7836
Enterprise Data and Technology Solutions
Barbara Cooper Jones . . . . (202) 475–7817
Capital Markets
John F. Getchis . . . . (202) 475–8855
Securities Operations
John T. Daugherty (acting) . . . . (202) 475–7848

■ OFFICE OF COMMUNITY PLANNING AND DEVELOPMENT
451 7th St. S.W.
Washington, DC 20410
Internet: www.hud.gov/offices/cpd
Information (HUD Public Affairs): (202) 708–0980

The Office of Community Planning and Development (CPD) administers economic and community development grant programs, housing rehabilitation programs, special purpose grants, and homeless assistance programs. Community Development Block Grants are used to develop urban areas. Grants are given to state or local governments primarily to benefit people of low and moderate income. The CPD provides a number of financial and technical assistance programs to state and local governments to stimulate effective planning and management of community development programs. The agency also administers the Uniform Relocation Assistance and Real Property Acquisitions Policy Act of 1970.

In another capacity, the CPD is coordinator of environmental duties that the Department of Housing and Urban Development (HUD) shares with other federal agencies and with the Council on Environmental Quality. In particular, the CPD stresses the prudent use of energy by HUD clients, especially those with low and moderate incomes. The CPD assistant secretary ensures departmental compliance with the National Environmental Policy Act of 1969, the National Historic Preservation Act of 1966, and other laws and executive orders.

Within CPD is the Office of HIV/AIDS Housing. This office manages the Housing Opportunities for Persons with AIDS program, which addresses housing needs of persons living with HIV/AIDS and their families. HIV/AIDS housing includes short- and long-term rental assistance, live-in medical facilities, and housing sites developed exclusively for people living with AIDS.

CPD, in consultation with national veteran service organizations, operates a veteran resource center, HUDVet, which provides veterans and their family members with information on HUD's community-based programs and services.

CPD's Office of Affordable Housing administers three separate programs to address affordable housing. The HOME Investment Partnerships, Self-Help Homeownership, and National Housing Trust Fund direct federal resources to the state and local level to develop affordable housing units, or to assist income-eligible households in purchasing, rehabilitating, or renting safe and decent housing.

HUD, along with other federal agencies, funds programs to help persons who are homeless. CPD is responsible for administering HUD's homeless assistance programs, which were created by the McKinney-Vento Homeless Assistance Act and later amended under the Homeless Emergency Assistance and Rapid Transition to Housing (HEARTH) Act. The HEARTH Act created the Rural Housing Stability Assistance Program and consolidated the McKinney-Vento competitive grants programs: the Shelter Plus Care Program, the Supportive Housing Program, and the Section 8 Moderate Rehabilitation Single Room Occupancy Program are now collectively the Continuum of Care (CoC) Program.

Assistant Secretary
    Harriet Tregoning . . . . (202) 708–2690
        Fax . . . . (202) 708–3336
General Deputy Assistant Secretary
    Cliff Taffet . . . . (202) 708–2690
Deputy Assistant Secretary for Economic Development
    Valerie Piper . . . . (202) 708–4445
    Community Renewal
        Vacant . . . . (202) 708–4445
    Economic Development
        Vacant . . . . (202) 708–4445
    Rural Housing and Economic Development
        Jackie Williams . . . . (202) 402–2290
Deputy Assistant Secretary for Grant Programs
    Marion Mollegen McFadden . . . . (202) 708–2111

Affordable Housing Programs
    Virginia Sardone . . . . (202) 402–2684
Block Grant Assistance
    Stan Gimont. . . . . (202) 402–3587
Environment and Energy
    Danielle Schopp . . . . (202) 402–4442
Deputy Assistant Secretary for Operations
    Frances Bush. . . . . (202) 401–6367
    Field Management
        Renee Ryles . . . . (202) 708–2565
    Policy Development and Coordination
        Steven Washington . . . . (202) 402–4142
    Technical Assistance and Management
        David Enzel . . . . (202) 402–5557
Deputy Assistant Secretary for Special Needs
    Ann Oliva . . . . (202) 402–4300
    HIV / AIDS Housing
        William Rudy (acting) . . . . (202) 402–1934
    Special Needs Assistance Programs
        Norman Suchar . . . . (202) 402–5015

■ OFFICE OF LEAD HAZARD CONTROL AND HEALTHY HOMES

451 7th St. S.W., Room P-3202
Washington, DC 20410
Internet: www.hud.gov/offices/lead

The Office of Lead Hazard and Control Healthy Homes, established by the Residential Lead-Based Paint Hazard Reduction Act of 1991, provides overall direction to HUD's lead-based paint activities and works closely with other HUD offices to develop regulations, guidelines, and policies applicable to departmental programs. Ten years after the establishment of the office, HUD estimated there were 26 million fewer homes with lead-based paint.

The office also undertakes programs to increase public awareness of the dangers of lead-based paint poisoning. It conducts demonstrations, studies, and standards development; promotes technology improvements in lead-hazard reduction; and encourages, through a grant program, local and state officials to develop cost-effective methods for the reduction of lead-based paint hazards in private housing for both low- and moderate-income families.

Congress established HUD's Healthy Homes Initiative in 1999 to develop and implement a program of research and demonstration projects that would address multiple housing-related problems affecting the health of children.

In 2009 and again in 2012 HUD sent notices to local Public Housing Authorities (PHAs) encouraging them to implement nonsmoking policies in some or all of their public housing units. In multifamily units, nonsmokers are exposed to secondhand smoke. Also, HUD was concerned about the increase fire risk associated with smoking. Since 2000 more than 500 PHAs have adopted and implemented smoke-free policies.

The agency's website features downloadable community outreach materials in multiple languages, as well as general information about the office and the

Lead-Based Paint Hazard Control Grant Program. The webpage devoted to outreach includes healthy homes fact sheets about asthma, carbon monoxide, and radon as well as information about the hazards caused by moisture and mold in homes.

Director
  Matthew Ammon . . . . (202) 708–0310, ext. 4337
    Fax . . . . (202) 708–0014
Lead Programs Enforcement
  Robert Weisberg . . . . (202) 402–7687
Policy and Standards
  Peter Ashley . . . . (202) 402–7595

Programs
  Eric Hornbuckle . . . . (202) 402–7599
Regional Management and Technical Support
  Martin Nee . . . . (202) 402–6087
Information and Regulations Line . . . . (800) 424-LEAD;
  . . . . (202) 402–7698

■ REGIONAL OFFICES

A list of regional offices that serve all Housing and Urban Development Department agencies can be found on p. 674.

Interior Department

1849 C St. N.W., Washington, DC 20240
Internet: www.doi.gov

Bureau of Indian Affairs

1849 C St. N.W., Washington, DC 20240
Internet: www.bia.gov

The Bureau of Indian Affairs (BIA), an agency within the Interior Department, was established as part of the War Department in 1824 and transferred to the Interior Department in 1849. In 1977 the office of the assistant secretary for Indian affairs was created in the Interior Department to centralize the federal government's policy making and advocacy functions with respect to Native Americans. The bureau is directed by the assistant secretary of the interior for Indian affairs, who is appointed by the president and confirmed by the Senate.

The BIA is organized into area offices and field offices under the control of headquarters in Washington, DC. The central office is responsible for policy and program administration. Twelve regional offices assist the central office with budget allocation and service delivery.

The BIA is the principal link between the federal government and the Native American tribes. The BIA has administrative responsibility for nearly 56 million acres of land held in trust for tribes and individuals by the government. Working with tribal governments, the BIA also provides a range of services and programs for approximately 1.9 million American Indians and Alaska natives from 566 federally recognized tribes and native villages in Alaska.

To be eligible for participation in programs administered by the BIA, a Native American tribe must have a statutory relationship with the U.S. government. The tribe is required to have an elected governing body and a constitution subject to approval by the secretary of the interior.

Each tribe sets its rules to determine who is eligible to vote and to be an enrolled member of the tribe. Only those enrolled members living on or near trust lands, currently half of the nation's total Native American population, are considered part of the service population of the bureau.

The BIA encourages each tribe to assume administration of reservation programs. Under the Indian Self-Determination and Education Assistance Act of 1975, the individual tribes may assume control of reservation programs.

The BIA also seeks to offer Native Americans educational opportunities responsive to their individual needs and cultural backgrounds. In 2006 the BIA Office of Indian Education Programs was reorganized and renamed as the Bureau of Indian Education (BIE) headed by a director. The BIA funds a federal Native American school system and gives financial assistance to public school systems that have substantial Native American enrollment. A total of 183 BIE-funded elementary and secondary schools serve approximately 42,000 Native American students. The BIE also funds or operates off-reservation boarding schools and peripheral dormitories near reservations for students attending public schools.

BIA schools are subject to the provisions of the No Child Left Behind Act, which establishes separate geographic attendance areas for BIA-funded schools, establishes a formula for determining minimum annual funding for BIA-funded schools, establishes guidelines to ensure constitutional and civil rights of Native American students, and establishes a method for administering grants to tribally controlled schools. The BIA published the final rules for the No Child Left Behind Act in 2005.

The BIA Office of Justice Services (OJS) is responsible for the overall management of the Bureau's law enforcement program. OJS fulfills this mandate through seven program areas: Criminal Investigations and Police Services, Detention/Corrections, Inspection/Internal Affairs, Tribal Law Enforcement and Special Initiatives, the Indian Police Academy, Tribal Justice Support, and Program Management.

The BIA Division of Law Enforcement Operations consists of six regional districts with 208 BIA and tribal law enforcement programs. Of these programs, forty-three are operated by the BIA. The Division of Law Enforcement Operations provides telecommunications, uniformed police, and criminal investigations services. Along with providing direct oversight of BIA law enforcement programs, the division also provides technical assistance and oversight to law enforcement programs contracted by tribes under Self-Determination and Self-Government Policy.

The Tribal Law and Order Act of 2010 (TLOA) was enacted to strengthen tribal law enforcement on American Indian reservations. TLOA strengthens law enforcement in Indian Country by authorizing the appointment of Special Assistant U.S. Attorneys to prosecute crimes in tribal communities in federal court; providing tribal courts tougher sentencing powers; and allowing some tribal police officers to enforce federal laws on Indian lands.

The BIA Branch of Wildland Fire Management is one of five federal agencies that fight wildfires in cooperation with state agencies and local fire departments. The other federal agencies are the Agriculture Department's Forest Service (*p. 519*) and the Interior Department's Fish and Wildlife Service (*p. 714*), Bureau of Land Management (*p. 695*), and National Park Service (*p. 723*). The Branch is responsible for managing fire operations, aviation, preparedness (fuels management and prevention), fire planning, training, and communication and outreach. The Branch supports tribes through suppression activities, as well as policies regarding the integration of wildland fire procedures into natural resource management.

The BIA Office of Indian Energy and Economic Development (IEED) works to provide access to energy resources and assists tribes with stimulating job creation and economic development. The Office of Indian Energy Policy and Programs is responsible for developing regulations for Tribal Energy Resource Agreements (TERAs). A TERA provides a tribe with the option of entering into energy-related business agreements and leases and for granting rights-of-way without the review and approval of the interior secretary for each proposed project.

The BIA oversees the development of mineral resources on Native American lands. The Interior Department's Office of Natural Resources Revenue (formerly the Minerals Management Service) (*p. 710*) collects royalties from mineral leasing on Native American lands. During the final decades of the twentieth century, Native Americans questioned the Interior Department's accounting of their land royalties. Since the passage of the Dawes Act in 1887, which allowed the government to take over the management of 90 million acres of land belonging to individual Native Americans and set up individual trust accounts for them, some records have been lost, destroyed, or not kept in the first place.

In 1996 a group of Native Americans filed a lawsuit against the Interior Department to recover what they claimed were lost royalties owed to trust fund beneficiaries. Elouise Cobell was the lead plaintiff in the case that spanned fourteen years and included hundreds of motions, seven full trials, and dozens of rulings and appeals. The case was settled at the end of 2010, with terms and funding authorized included in the Claims Resolution Act of 2010. The $3.4 billion Cobell settlement addresses the federal government's responsibility for trust accounts and trust assets maintained by the United States on behalf of more than 300,000 individual Native Americans. A fund of $1.5 billion will be used to compensate class members for their historical accounting, trust fund, and asset mismanagement claims.

In addition, to address the continued proliferation of thousands of new trust accounts caused by the "fractionation" of land interests through succeeding generations, the settlement established a $1.9 billion fund for the voluntary buy-back and consolidation of fractionated land interests. The land consolidation program provides individual Native Americans with an opportunity to obtain cash payments for divided land interests and free up the land for the benefit of tribal communities. The settlement also authorized a set-aside of some funding from the buy-back program into the Cobell Education Scholarship Fund, which provides financial assistance through scholarships to American Indian and Alaska Native students wishing to pursue post-secondary and graduate education and training.

The Helping Expedite and Advance Responsible Tribal Homeownership (HEARTH) Act of 2012 allows federally recognized tribes to develop and implement their own regulations governing certain leasing on Indian lands. With approval from the secretary of the Interior Department of these tribal regulations, tribes will have the authority to process land leases without BIA approval.

■ KEY PERSONNEL

OFFICE OF THE ASSISTANT SECRETARY
Assistant Secretary for Indian Affairs
Kevin K. Washburn . . . . (202) 208–7163
Fax . . . . (202) 208–5320
Principal Deputy Assistant Secretary
Larry Roberts . . . . (202) 208–7163
Solicitor (Interior Dept.)
Hilary Tompkins . . . . (202) 208–4423
Associate Solicitor for Indian Affairs
Michael Berrigan . . . . (202) 208–3401
Congressional and Legislative Affairs
Darren Pete . . . . (202) 208–5706
Equal Employment Opportunity
Vanessa Green . . . . (202) 208–6120
Deputy Assistant Secretary, Management
Thomas Thompson . . . . (202) 408–6418
Chief Financial Officer
James Schock . . . . (703) 390–6583
Chief Information Officer
Sylvia Burns (acting) . . . . (202) 208–3508
Human Capital Management
Jim Burckman . . . . (202) 208–2643
Facilities, Environmental, and Cultural Resources
Jack Rever . . . . (703) 390–6433
Planning and Policy Analysis
Curtis Faust . . . . (202) 208–5104
Indian Energy and Economic Development
Deputy Assistant Secretary
Ann Marie Bledsoe Downes . . . . . (202) 208–7163
Capital Investment
David B. Johnson (acting) . . . . (202) 208–3026
E-mail: david.johnson3@bia.gov
Economic Development
Jack R. Stevens . . . . (202) 219–6764
E-mail: jack.stevens@bia.gov
Energy and Mineral Development
Stephen Manydeeds . . . . (720) 407–0600
E-mail: stephen.manydeeds@bia.gov
Capital Investment
David Johnson (acting) . . . . (202) 219–0740
E-mail: david.johnson3@bia.gov
Indian Gaming
Paula L. Hart . . . . (202) 219–4066

BUREAU OF INDIAN AFFAIRS

Director
Michael S. Black .... (202) 208–5116

Indian Services
Hankie Ortiz .... (202) 513–7640

Human Services
Sue Settles........................ (202) 513–7642

Tribal Government Services
Vacant........................... (202) 513–7641

Transportation
LeRoy Gishi .... (202) 513–7714

Self-Determination
Sharee Freeman................... (202) 219–0240

Justice Services
Darren A. Cruzan .... (202) 208–5787

Indian Police Academy
Steve Juneau...................... (575) 748–8151

Corrections
Vincente Anchondo ...... (602) 379–6958, ext. 1809

Law Enforcement Services
Jason Thompson .... (602) 379–6958, ext. 1811

Professional Standards
Monty K. Gibson.................. (505) 563–3950

Tribal Justice Support
Tricia Tingle..................... (202) 208–5787

Regulatory Affairs and Collaborative Action
(1001 Indian School Rd. N.W., #312, Albuquerque, NM 87104)
Elizabeth Appel .... (202) 273–4680
E-mail: elizabeth.appel@bia.gov

Trust Services
Helen Riggs .... (202) 208–5831

Real Estate Services
Sharlene Round Face .... (202) 208–3615

Natural Resources
Ira New Breast .... (202) 208–7373

Land Titles and Records
Beth Wenstrom .... (202) 208–3842

Probate Services
Charlene Toledo .... (505) 563–3371

Water and Power
Yulan Jin........................ (202) 219–0941

Forestry and Wildland Fire Management
Bill Downes .... (202) 208–4837

Wildland Fire Management (3833 S. Development Ave., Boise, ID 83705)
Gini Broyles .... (208) 387–5696

BUREAU OF INDIAN EDUCATION

Director
Charles M. Roessel .... (202) 208–6123

Performance and Accountability
Jeffrey Hamley.................... (505) 563–5260

Planning and Research
Brian Bough...................... (505) 563–5283

Policy and Evaluation & Post-Secondary Education
Stephanie Birdwell. .... (202) 208–6407

School Operations
Bart Stevens .... (505) 563–5235

■ INFORMATION SOURCES

Internet

Agency website: www.bia.gov. Includes general information about the bureau and the Indian Health Service, a list of tribal leaders, information on Indian ancestry, and the *Bureau of Indian Education National Directory* of schools.

For questions or comments on law enforcement in general, e-mail ojs.lawenforcement@bia.gov; on detention or corrections issues, ojs.divisionofcorrections@bia.gov; and on Tribal Law and Order Act of 2010 consultations, ojs.tloa2010.comments@bia.gov.

Telephone Contacts

Personnel Locator ....(202) 208–3100
Federal Relay Service TTY ....(800) 877–8339

Information and Publications

KEY OFFICES

BIA Public Affairs

1849 C St. N.W
MS 3658-MIB
Washington, DC 20240
(202) 208–3710
(202) 219–4152, media
Media (202) 219–4152
Nedra Darling, director

Provides information and publications to the media, the Indian community, and the general public.

Freedom of Information

1849 C St. N.W., #3070-MIB
Washington, DC 20240
(202) 208–3135
Daniel Largo, FOIA officer

PUBLICATIONS

Contact BIA Public Affairs for fact sheets, brochures, pamphlets, and a newsletter for Indian tribes and organizations; many publications are also available on the agency's website.

Reference Resources

LIBRARY

Interior Department

1849 C St. N.W.
Washington, DC 20240
(202) 208–5815
George Franchois, director
Hours: 7:45 a.m. to 5:00 p.m.
Internet: www.doi.gov/library/index.cfm
E-mail: library@ios.doi.gov

The BIA does not have its own library, but material on Indian affairs is housed in the Interior Department Library, with a million volumes and numerous databases.

Only Interior Department employees may check out materials, but interlibrary loan services are available. BIA has an electronic library on its website at www.bia.gov/DocumentLibrary/index.htm.

DOCKETS

Federal dockets are available at www.regulations.gov. (*See appendix for Searching and Commenting on Regulations: Regulations.gov.*)

RULES AND REGULATIONS

BIA rules and regulations are published in the *Code of Federal Regulations,* Title 25, Chapter I, Parts 1–299; Title 25, Chapter V, Part 900; Title 25, Chapter VI, Parts 1000–1001. Proposed regulations, new final regulations, and updates to the *Code of Federal Regulations* are published in the daily *Federal Register.* (*See appendix for details on how to obtain and use these publications.*) The *Federal Register* and the *Code of Federal Regulations* may be accessed online at www.archives.gov/federal-register/cfr; this site also contains a link to the federal government's regulatory website at www.regulations.gov (*see appendix*).

■ LEGISLATION

The BIA carries out its responsibilities under:

Snyder Act of 1921 (42 Stat. 208, 25 U.S.C. 13). Signed by the president Nov. 2, 1921. Authorized general, nonspecific funding for the benefit, care, and assistance of Native Americans.

Indian Reorganization Act of 1934 (48 Stat. 984, 25 U.S.C. 461). Signed by the president June 18, 1934. Allowed Native Americans to reorganize as constitutional governments with elected governing bodies.

Indian Self-Determination and Education Assistance Act of 1975 (88 Stat. 2203, 25 U.S.C. 450). Signed by the president Jan. 4, 1975. Gave Native American parents and communities greater control over education and training designed to promote further self-determination. Allowed Native American tribes to run programs previously run for them by the federal government.

Tribally Controlled Community College Assistance Act of 1978 (92 Stat. 1325, 25 U.S.C. 1801). Signed by the president Oct. 17, 1978. Provided financial assistance to Native American–controlled institutions of higher education.

Education Amendments of 1978 (92 Stat. 2143, 20 U.S.C. 2701). Signed by the president Nov. 1, 1978. Amended the **Elementary and Secondary Education Act of 1965** (91 Stat. 911, 20 U.S.C. 241). Title IX increased control of Native American tribes in determining educational needs of children.

Indian Child Welfare Act of 1978 (92 Stat. 3069, 25 U.S.C. 1901). Signed by the president Nov. 8, 1979. Strengthened tribal and parental rights in the custody of children. Promoted the continuation of Native American culture by discouraging the forced placement of tribal children in nontribal foster homes.

Indian Gaming Regulatory Act of 1988 (102 Stat. 2467, 25 U.S.C. 2701 note). Signed by the president Oct. 17, 1988. Prohibited casino gambling and parimutuel betting on reservations unless the tribe enters into a compact with the state for the operation of such activities.

Indian Law Enforcement Reform Act (25 U.S.C. 2801). Signed by the president Aug. 18, 1990. Authorized the secretary of the interior, acting through the Bureau of Indian Affairs (BIA), to provide law enforcement services in Native American areas. Established within BIA a Division of Law Enforcement Services. Authorized the interior secretary, after consultation with the attorney general, to prescribe regulations relating to the enforcement of criminal statutes and to consideration of applications for contracts awarded under the Indian Self-Determination Act to perform the functions of the branch of criminal investigations.

Indian Employment, Training, and Related Services Demonstration Act of 1992 (106 Stat. 2302, 25 U.S.C. 3401). Signed by the president Oct. 23, 1992. Authorized tribal governments to integrate all federally funded employment, training, and related services programs into a single, comprehensive program.

Indian Tribal Justice Act (107 Stat. 2004, 25 U.S.C. 3601). Signed by the president Dec. 3, 1993. Created an office of Tribal Justice Support within the BIA to assist tribes in developing and maintaining tribal justice systems.

American Indian Trust Fund Management Reform Act of 1994 (108 Stat. 4239, 25 U.S.C. 42). Signed by the president Oct. 25, 1994. Amended federal law to provide for the proper management of Native American trust funds. Required the Interior Department to account for daily and annual balances of trust funds and provide periodic performance statements. Established the Office of the Special Trustee for American Indians to develop a comprehensive reform plan of the secretary's trust responsibilities to Native American tribes.

No Child Left Behind Act (115 Stat. 1425, 20 U.S.C. 6301). Signed by the president Jan. 8, 2002. Reauthorized and amended the Elementary and Secondary Education Act. Established requirements for schools to test students annually and report on the progress. Amended the Education Amendments of 1978 to revise provisions for BIA programs. Required BIA schools to be accredited within a specified period.

American Indian Probate Reform Act of 2004 (118 Stat. 1773, 15 U.S.C. 2201 note). Signed by the president Oct. 27, 2004. Authorized federal probate code for inheritance of trust land among Native American population. Authorized the interior secretary to adopt regulations necessary to implement the provisions of this act. Amended in 2006.

Buy Indian Act (36 Stat. 861, 25 U.S.C. 47). Signed by the president June 25, 2010. Authorized BIA to promulgate rules for set-aside procurement contracts for qualified Indian-owned businesses.

Tribal Law and Order Act (124 Stat. 2261, 25 U.S.C. 2801 note). Signed by the president July 29, 2010. Strengthens law enforcement in Indian Country by authorizing the appointment of Special Assistant U.S. Attorneys to prosecute crimes in tribal communities in federal court; providing tribal courts tougher sentencing powers; and allowing some tribal police officers to enforce federal laws on Indian lands. Requires federal investigators and prosecutors to maintain information on cases that occur on Indian lands that are closed or declined for prosecution in federal court and share that information with tribal justice officials. Requires the secretary of interior to establish the Indian Law Enforcement Foundation.

Claims Resolution Act of 2010 (124 Stat. 3064, 42 U.S.C. 1305 note). Signed by the president Dec. 8, 2010. Provided settlement in the Cobell class-action lawsuit brought against the Department of Interior for decades of mismanaged mineral royalties to Native Americans. Also provided settlement in four separate Indian water claims.

Moving Ahead for Progress in the 21st Century Act (MAP-21) (126 Stat. 473, 23 U.S.C. 201, 202). Signed by the president July 6, 2012. Revises requirements for making authorized funds available for the tribal transportation, federal lands transportation, and federal lands access programs for various transportation planning and highway improvement projects. Established Tribal Transportation Program (TTP), which replaced the Indian Reservation Roads program.

Helping Expedite and Advance Responsible Tribal Home Ownership Act of 2012 (HEARTH Act) (126 Stat. 1150, 25 U.S.C. 415 note). Signed by the president July 30, 2012. Authorizes federally recognized tribes to develop and implement their own land-leasing regulations. Upon approval of these tribal regulations by the secretary of the interior, tribes will have the authority to process land leases without Bureau of Indian Affairs approval.

Violence Against Women Reauthorization Act of 2013 (127 Stat. 120, 25 U.S.C. 1304). Signed by the president Mar. 7, 2013. Gives Indian tribes jurisdiction over domestic violence, dating violence, and violations of protective orders that occur on their lands. Makes that jurisdiction concurrent with federal and state jurisdiction.

■ REGIONAL OFFICES

ALASKA
(AK except Metlakatla)
3601 C St., #1100
Anchorage, AK 99503–5947
(907) 271–1735
Weldon (Bruce) Loudermilk, regional director

EASTERN OKLAHOMA
3100 W. Peak Blvd.
Muskogee, OK 74401–6206
Mailing address:
P.O. Box 8002
Muskogee, OK 74401–6201
(918) 781–4608
Eddie Streater (acting), regional director

EASTERN REGIONAL OFFICE
(AL, CT, FL, LA, MA, ME, MS, NC, NY, RI, TN, VA)
545 Marriott Dr., #700
Nashville, TN 37214
(615) 564–6500
Johnna Blackhair, deputy regional director

GREAT PLAINS
(ND, NE, SD)
115 Fourth Ave. S.E., # 400
Aberdeen, SD 57401–4384
(605) 226–7343
Timothy LaPointe, regional director

MIDWEST
(IA, MI, MN, WI)
Norman Pointe 11 Bldg.
5600 W. American Blvd., #5600
Bloomington, MN 55347
(612) 713–4400
E-mail: diane.rosen@bia.gov
Diane Rosen, regional director

NAVAJO
(Navajo reservations in AZ, NM, UT)
Navajo Regional Office
301 West Hill St.
Gallup, NM 87301
Mailing address:
P.O. Box 1060
Gallup, NM 87305
(505) 863–8314
Sharon A. Pinto, regional director

NORTHWEST
(AK, ID, MT, OR, WA)
911 Northeast 11th Ave.
Portland, OR 97232–4169
(503) 231–6702
E-mail: Stanley.Speaks@bia.gov
Stanley M. Speaks, regional director

PACIFIC
(CA)
2800 Cottage Way
Sacramento, CA 95825
(916) 978–6000
E-mail: amy.dutschke@bia.gov
Amy Dutschke, regional director

ROCKY MOUNTAIN
(MT, WY)
2021 4th Ave. North
Billings, MT 59101
(406) 247–7943
Darryl LaCounte, regional director

SOUTHERN PLAINS
(KS, western OK, TX)
WCD Office Complex

P.O. Box 368
Anadarko, OK 73005–0368
(405) 247–6673
E-mail: dan.deerinwater@bia.gov
Dan Deerinwater, regional director

SOUTHWEST

(CO, NM)
1001 Indian School Rd. N.W.
Albuquerque, NM 87104

(505) 563–3103
Bill Walker, regional director

WESTERN

(AZ, NV, UT—except Navajo reservations)
2600 N. Central Ave. 4th Floor
Phoenix, AZ 85004–3050
(602) 379–6789
E-mail: bryan.bowker@bia.gov
Bryan L. Bowker, regional director

Bureau of Land Management

1849 C St. N. W., Washington, DC 20240
Internet: www.blm.gov

The Bureau of Land Management (BLM), an agency within the Department of the Interior, was created in 1946 when Congress combined the functions of the General Land Office (created in 1812) and the U.S. Grazing Service (created in 1934) into a single bureau.

The BLM consists of a headquarters staff in Washington, DC, and twelve state offices. It is headed by a director appointed by the president who works under the supervision of the assistant secretary of the interior for land and minerals management.

Resources managed by the BLM include timber, minerals, oil and gas, geothermal energy, wildlife habitats, endangered plant and animal species, range land vegetation, recreation areas, lands with cultural importance, wild and scenic rivers, designated conservation and wilderness areas, and open-space lands.

The BLM is responsible for administering more than 245 million acres of public lands, located mainly in twelve western states. Most of these lands are original public domain lands, which became federal property in territorial expansions, such as the Louisiana Purchase in 1803 or the Mexican Cession in 1848, and have never been privately owned.

Energy Development and Mineral Resources. The BLM leases lands for development of designated mineral deposits and grants rights of way through federal lands for pipelines and other uses. The BLM is responsible for inspection and enforcement of oil, gas, and geothermal wells and other development operations to ensure that lessees and operators comply with the lease requirements and BLM's regulations.

In March 2015 BLM issued a final rule regarding hydraulic fracturing (fracking). There are more than 100,000 oil and gas wells on federally managed lands. Of wells currently being drilled, over 90 percent use hydraulic fracturing. The rule applies only to development on public and tribal lands and includes a process so that states and tribes may request variances from provisions if they have an equal or more protective regulation in place. The rule process spanned four years and included more than 1.5 million public comments following publication of the initial draft rule and a supplemental draft rule.

In April 2015 BLM issued an Advance Notice of Proposed Rulemaking (ANPR) to seek public comment on potential updates to BLM rules governing oil and gas royalty rates, rental payments, lease sale minimum bids, civil penalty caps, and financial assurances. The ANPR also sought comment on the adequacy of bonding requirements and civil penalty assessments. Discussing the adequacy of the bonding requirements, a bureau official noted that the current bonding rates "were set when Dwight D. Eisenhower was president."

Because the BLM manages federal sources of oil and gas, coal, and increasingly, renewable sources of energy such as geothermal, wind, and biomass, the BLM is active in implementing the Energy Policy Act of 2005. The 2005 act provided incentives to develop dependable, affordable, and environmentally sound energy production while reducing U.S. dependence on foreign oil.

The BLM issued a wind energy policy in December 2008 to provide guidance on best management practices to mitigate potential impacts on birds, wildlife habitat, and other resource values; and guidance on administering wind energy authorizations. The BLM manages 20.6 million acres of public lands with wind potential; BLM has authorized 39 wind energy development projects.

In 2012 BLM finalized a program for initiating development of solar energy on public lands in six western states. The Programmatic Environmental Impact Statement (PEIS) for solar energy development provides a blueprint for utility-scale solar energy permitting in Arizona, California, Colorado, Nevada, New Mexico, and Utah. The plan established solar energy zones with access to existing or planned transmission, incentives for development within those zones, and a process through which to consider additional zones and solar projects. The Solar PEIS establishes an initial set of seventeen Solar Energy Zones (SEZs), totaling about 285,000 acres of public lands. In fiscal year 2014 BLM was processing thirteen renewable energy projects (eleven solar and two wind).

BLM, as administrator of the Federal Helium Program, is responsible for the conservation and sale of federally owned helium. The BLM operates and maintains a helium storage reservoir, enrichment plant, and pipeline system near Amarillo, Texas, that supplies over 40 percent of domestic demand and 30% percent of global demand for helium.

Conservation and Recreation. Approximately 250 million acres of public lands are available to the public to enjoy outdoor activities such as camping, hunting, fishing, hiking, horseback riding, boating, whitewater rafting, mountain biking, climbing, all types of winter sports, and visiting natural and cultural heritage sites. The number of visitors to recreation sites on BLM-managed lands and waters continues to increase in recent years; visitors to public lands now number about 59 million.

The BLM's National Landscape Conservation System (NLCS) includes more than 874 federally recognized areas and approximately 30 million acres of National Conservation Areas, National Monuments, Wilderness Areas, Wilderness Study Areas, Wild and Scenic Rivers, National Scenic and Historic Trails, and Conservation Lands of the California Desert. The program was first established by the BLM in 2000; the Omnibus Public Land Management Act of 2009 legislatively authorized the program and designated specific areas under the NLCS.

In July 2009, Interior Secretary Salazar reversed a policy passed in the waning days of the Bush administration to intensify logging in western Oregon, known as the Western Oregon Plan Revisions (WOPR). Claiming that the previous administration failed to follow established administrative procedure before leaving office, Salazar declared WOPR to be legally indefensible. With the withdrawal of the WOPR, management of BLM forests in western Oregon again was directed by the Northwest Forest Plan, which guided BLM timber sales from 1994 until 2008. Salazar directed the BLM—in coordination with the U.S. Fish and Wildlife Service— to identify ecologically sound timber sales under the Northwest Forest Plan.

Grazing and Wild Mustang and Burro Management. The BLM regulates federal grazing lands, protects and preserves timberland for permanent forest production, manages and protects wild horses and burros living on public lands, controls erosion on public lands, and issues permits for mineral exploration purposes.

Under the authority of the Wild Free-Roaming Horse and Burro Act of 1971, the BLM also managed programs protecting and allowing for the adoption of wild horses and burros. However, the protection granted to such animals under this act—protection from being sold to meat-processing plants—was rescinded under the 2004 Omnibus Appropriations Act. In 2007 Congress took up legislation to reinstate the protection for these animals, but the legislation was never signed into law.

Wildfire Management and Suppression. The BLM is one of five federal agencies that fight wildfires in cooperation with state agencies and local fire departments. The other federal agencies are the Agriculture Department's Forest Service (*p. 519*) and the Interior Department's Fish and Wildlife Service (*p. 714*), National Park Service (*p. 723*), and Bureau of Indian Affairs (*p. 689*). The agencies' wildland fire-fighting activities are coordinated through the National Interagency Fire Center in Boise, ID. The Healthy Forests Restoration Act of 2003 sought to address the issue of wildland fire mitigation through fuels reduction. The legislation expanded the stewardship contracting authority to allow federal agencies, such as the Agriculture Department and the Interior Department, to enter into long-term (up to ten years) contracts with private organizations or businesses to remove forest products, such as trees for lumber, in return for fuels reduction services that removes rotted trees and undergrowth.

■ KEY PERSONNEL

Assistant Secretary, Land and Minerals Management
Janice Schneider . . . . (202) 208–6734
Director
Neil Kornze . . . . (202) 208–3801
Fax . . . . (202) 208–5242
E-mail: Director@blm.gov
Deputy Director, Operations
Steven A. Ellis . . . . (202) 208–3801
E-mail: director@blm.gov
Deputy Director, Programs and Policy
Linda Lance . . . . (202) 208–3801
Business and Fiscal Resources
Janine Velasco . . . . (202) 208–4864
E-mail: jvelasco@blm.gov
Communications
Craig Leff (acting) . . . . (202) 208–6913
E-mail: cleff@blm.gov
Legislative Affairs and Correspondence
Patrick Wilkinson . . . . (202) 912–7429
E-mail: p2wilkin@blm.gov
Regulatory Affairs
Ian Senio . . . . (202) 912–7440
E-mail: isenio@blm.gov
Energy, Minerals, and Realty Management
Michael Nedd . . . . (202) 208–4201
E-mail: mnedd@blm.gov
Fluid Minerals
Steve Wells . . . . (202) 912–7143
E-mail: s1wells@blm.gov
Solid Minerals
Mitchell Leverette . . . . (202) 912–7113
E-mail: mleveret@blm.gov
Lands, Realty, and Cadastral Survey
Lucas Lucero (acting) . . . . (202) 912–7088
National Renewable Energy Coordination
Ray A. Brady . . . . (202) 912–7312
E-mail: rbrady@blm.gov
Fire and Aviation
Ron Dunton . . . . (202) 208–5440
E-mail: rdunton@blm.gov
Human Capital Management
Carole Carter-Pfisterer . . . . (202) 501–6723
E-mail: capfiste@blm.gov
Civil Rights
Alexie Rogers . . . . (202) 912–7484
E-mail: alrogers@blm.gov
Human Resources Policy and Programs
Vickki Johnson . . . . (202) 912–7489
Safety, Health, and Emergency Management
Edward Jerome . . . . (202) 912–7494
Law Enforcement and Security
Salvatore R. Lauro . . . . (202) 208–3269
E-mail: Slauro@blm.gov

National Landscape Conservation System and Community Programs
    Tim Murphy . . . . (202) 208–3516
        E-mail: tmurphy@blm.gov

Renewable Resources and Planning
    Edwin Roberson . . . . (202) 208–4896
        E-mail: eroberson@blm.gov

Cultural, Paleontological Resources, and Tribal Consultation
    Byron Loosle . . . . (202) 912–7208
        E-mail: bloosle@blm.gov

Environmental Quality and Protection
    McKinley Ben Miller (acting) . . . . (202) 912–7165
        E-mail: mbmiller@blm.gov

Fish, Wildlife, and Plant Conservation
    Stephen Small . . . . (202) 912–7366
        E-mail: ssmall@blm.gov

Forests and Woodlands
    Kathy Radigan (acting) . . . . (202) 912–7261

Planning and NEPA
    Joe Stout . . . . (202) 912–7275
        E-mail: j2stout@blm.gov

Rangeland Resources
    Melvin Tague . . . . (202) 912–7222
        E-mail: jtague@blm.gov

Recreation and Visitor Services
    Andy Tenney . . . . (202) 912–7094
        E-mail: atenney@blm.gov

Wild Horses and Burros
    Mary D'Aversa . . . . (202) 912–7260
        E-mail:mdaversa@blm.gov

■ INFORMATION SOURCES

Internet

Agency website: www.blm.gov. Features state-by-state information, a national map, a calendar of events, and a directory of public contacts.

Telephone Contacts

    Personnel Locator . . . . (202) 208–3100
    Federal Relay Service TTY . . . . (800) 877–8339

Information and Publications

KEY OFFICES

BLM Public Affairs
1849 C St. N.W., #406-LS
Washington, DC 20240
(202) 912–7415
Jeffrey Krauss, chief, (202) 912–7410
E-mail: jkrauss@blm.gov

Answers questions for the press and the public. Distributes publications and issues news releases; maintains a mailing list.

Freedom of Information
1849 C St. N.W., #2134
Washington, DC 20240

Ryan Witt, FOIA officer
(202) 912–7562
Fax (202) 245–0027
E-mail: BLM_WO_FOIA@blm.gov

Write and underline "Freedom of Information Request" on the envelope address or follow directions on the website to file online.

PUBLICATIONS

BLM Public Affairs distributes single copies of bureau publications to individuals free of charge, and publications are available from the website.

Publications cover the following subject areas: cadastral (land) surveying; forest resource management; lands studies; public lands law and statistics; range management; wildlife habitat management; watershed management; minerals management; mineral, oil, gas, and geothermal leasing; minerals operations; the history, development, administration, conservation, and use of public lands; and hydropower, solar, and wind energy. There is also a brochure on the Bureau of Land Management generally.

Reference Resources

LIBRARIES

BLM Library Services, National Operations Center
Bldg. 50
Denver Federal Center
Denver, CO 80225–0047
(303) 236–6650
Deborah Harnke, reference librarian, (303) 236–6648
E-mail: dharnke@blm.gov
Hours: 7:30 a.m. to 4:00 p.m.
E-mail: blm_library@blm.gov

Collection includes monographs, serials, periodicals, technical reports, government documents, directives, and an extensive collection of pamphlets and reprints. Makes interlibrary loans and provides both in-person and telephone reference service.

Interior Department Library
1849 C St. N.W.
Washington, DC 20240
(202) 208–5815
George Franchois, director
Hours: 7:45 a.m. to 5:00 p.m.
Internet: www.doi.gov/library/index.cfm
E-mail: library@ios.doi.gov

Houses material on land management and databases.

DOCKETS

Federal dockets are available at www.regulations.gov. (*See appendix for Searching and Commenting on Regulations: Regulations.gov.*)

RULES AND REGULATIONS

BLM rules and regulations are published in the *Code of Federal Regulations,* Title 43, Chapter II, Parts 1000 to end. Proposed regulations, new final regulations, and updates to the *Code of Federal Regulations* are published in the daily *Federal Register.* (*See appendix for details on how to obtain and use these publications.*) The *Federal Register* and *Code of Federal Regulations* may also be accessed online at www.archives.gov/federal-register/cfr; the site also contains a link to the federal government's regulatory website at www.regulations.gov (*see appendix*).

◾ LEGISLATION

The BLM administers public lands through a framework of public laws, the most comprehensive being:

Federal Land Policy and Management Act of 1976 (90 Stat. 2744, 43 U.S.C. 1701). Signed by the president Oct. 21, 1976. Restated the policy of the United States to retain and manage federal land for its protection, preservation, and use by the public. Directed land use planning, governed grants and use of right of way over public land, directed review of lands for possible wilderness designation, and amended the Taylor Grazing Act with respect to livestock management, *inter alia.*

The BLM also administers the following laws in full or in part:

Act of May 18, 1796, as amended (1 Stat. 465, 43 U.S.C. 751 et seq.). Signed by the president May 18, 1796. Established the public land survey system of square mile sections and thirty-six-section townships for use in the settlement, disposal, and use of public lands.

Act of May 10, 1872 (R.S. 2319, 30 U.S.C. 22 et seq.). Signed by the president May 10, 1872. Permitted entry on public lands for location of hard rock minerals.

Allotted Indian Land Leasing Act of 1909 (35 Stat. 783, 25 U.S.C. 396). Signed by the president March 3, 1909. Provided for leasing and management of allotted Native American mineral lands through Interior Department regulations.

Mineral Leasing Act (41 Stat. 437, 30 U.S.C. 181). Signed by the president Feb. 25, 1920. Permitted the leasing of public lands for the exploration and development of specified minerals, chiefly oil, gas, and coal.

Recreation and Public Purposes Act (44 Stat. 741, 43 U.S.C. 869). Signed by the president June 14, 1926. Allowed the sale or lease of public lands to federal instrumentalities, territories, states, counties, municipalities, and political subdivisions and to nonprofit organizations and associations for recreational and other uses. Reserved mineral rights on leased lands for the U.S. government.

Right-of-Way Leasing Act of 1930 (46 Stat. 373, 30 U.S.C. 301). Signed by the president May 21, 1930. Provided for the leasing of oil and gas deposits in or under railroads and other rights of way.

Taylor Grazing Act (48 Stat. 1269, 43 U.S.C. 315). Signed by the president June 28, 1934. Provided the basic legislative authority governing the management and protection of the vacant public land of the United States.

Omnibus Tribal Leasing Act of 1938 (52 Stat. 347, 25 U.S.C. 396a). Signed by the president May 11, 1938. Provided for leasing of unallotted (tribal) lands through Interior Department regulations.

Materials Act (61 Stat. 681, 30 U.S.C. 601). Signed by the president July 31, 1947. Authorized the secretary of the interior to dispose of certain surface mineral materials and timber found on public land.

Mineral Leasing Act for Acquired Lands (61 Stat. 13, 30 U.S.C. 351–359). Signed by the president Aug. 7, 1947. Permitted the leasing of acquired lands for exploration and development of specified minerals.

Submerged Lands Act of 1953 (67 Stat. 29, 43 U.S.C. 1301). Signed by the president May 22, 1953. Extended the boundaries of coastal states seaward for three miles.

Outer Continental Shelf Lands Act (67 Stat. 462, 43 U.S.C. 1331). Signed by the president Aug. 7, 1953. Established Interior Department authority for leasing and managing minerals in the Outer Continental Shelf.

Wilderness Act of 1964 (78 Stat. 890, 16 U.S.C. 1131). Signed by the president Sept. 3, 1964. Directed the secretary of the interior to review areas within the National Wildlife Refuge and National Park Systems in order to recommend to the president new additions for the National Wilderness Preservation System.

Wild and Scenic Rivers Act (82 Stat. 906, 16 U.S.C. 1271). Signed by the president Oct. 2, 1968. Described procedures and limitations for control of lands in federally administered components of the National Wild and Scenic Rivers System and for dealing with disposition of lands and minerals under federal ownership.

National Trails System Act (82 Stat. 919, 16 U.S.C. 1241). Signed by the president Oct. 2, 1968. Established the National Recreational and National Scenic Trails Systems.

National Environmental Policy Act of 1969 (83 Stat. 852, 42 U.S.C. 4321). Signed by the president Jan. 1, 1969. Established a broad national environmental policy and required that federal agencies provide environmental impact statements regarding any major federal action or legislative proposal.

Geothermal Steam Act of 1970 (84 Stat. 1566, 30 U.S.C. 1001). Signed by the president Dec. 24, 1970. Regulated the leasing of lands for the development and utilization of geothermal steam and associated geothermal resources.

Mining and Minerals Policy Act of 1970 (84 Stat. 1876, 30 U.S.C. 21a). Signed by the president Dec. 31, 1970. Authorized the interior secretary to establish a coordinated policy of fostering development of economically stable mining and minerals industries, their orderly and economic development, and studying methods for disposal of waste and reclamation.

Wild Free-Roaming Horse and Burro Act of 1971 (85 Stat. 649, 16 U.S.C. 1331–1340). Signed by the president Dec. 15, 1971. Protected all unclaimed horses and burros on public lands from capture, branding, harassment, or death. Directed the Forest Service or the BLM to manage all such horses and burros as components of the public lands in a manner that was designed to achieve a thriving natural ecological balance on the public lands.

Alaska Native Claims Settlement Act (85 Stat. 688, 43 U.S.C. 1601 et seq.). Signed by the president Dec. 18, 1971. Established right and method for Alaska natives to form local and regional corporations to receive title to 40 million acres of public land.

Federal Coal Leasing Act of 1976 (90 Stat. 1083, 30 U.S.C. 201). Signed by the president Aug. 4, 1976. Amended the coal leasing provision of the 1920 Mineral Leasing Act. Provided for a coal exploration program by the Interior Department and for issuance of coal exploration licenses.

Payments in Lieu of Taxes Act (90 Stat. 1032, 31 U.S.C. 6901). Signed by the president Oct. 20, 1976. Directed the interior secretary to make payments to local jurisdictions where entitled land is located.

Federal Land Policy and Management Act of 1976 (90 Stat. 2744, 43 U.S.C. 1701 note). Signed by the president Oct. 21, 1976. Required that public lands be retained in federal ownership unless it is determined that disposal of a particular parcel will serve the national interest.

Public Range Lands Improvement Act of 1978 (92 Stat. 1803, 43 U.S.C. 1901). Signed by the president Oct. 25, 1978. Provided for the protection and improvement of public range lands. Amended the Wild Free-Roaming Horse and Burro Act to establish the BLM adoption program for excess wild horses and burros, stipulating that the animals were not to be sold for slaughter.

Archaeological Resources Protection Act of 1979 (93 Stat. 721, 92 U.S.C. 4151). Signed by the president Oct. 31, 1979. Established civil and criminal penalties for damaging or removing archaeological resources found on public and Native American lands.

Alaska National Interest Lands Conservation Act of 1980 (94 Stat. 2430, 43 U.S.C. 1631 et seq.). Signed by the president Dec. 2, 1980. Divided public lands in Alaska into national parks and wildlife refuges, and areas subject to special management and study. Established provisions for disposing of Alaska lands to Native Corporations and the state of Alaska.

Mineral Lands—Production of Oil from Tar Sand Act of 1981 (95 Stat. 1070, codified in scattered sections of 30 U.S.C.). Signed by the president Nov. 16, 1981. Provided for the leasing of tar sand deposits and oil and gas leasing.

Federal Oil and Gas Royalty Management Act of 1982 (96 Stat. 2447, 30 U.S.C. 1701). Signed by the president Jan. 12, 1983. Ensured that all energy and mineral resources originating on public lands and on the Outer Continental Shelf are accounted for under the secretary of the interior.

Omnibus Budget Reconciliation Act/Federal Reform Oil and Gas Leasing Act of 1987 (101 Stat. 1330–256, 30 U.S.C. 226b). Signed by the president Dec. 22, 1987. Overhauled the system of leasing federal lands, other than those offshore, for oil and gas drilling and production.

Federal Land Exchange Facilitation Act of 1988 (102 Stat. 1086, 43 U.S.C. 1716). Signed by the president Aug. 20, 1988. Streamlined land-exchange procedures between the BLM and the U.S. Forest Service.

Uranium Mill Tailings Remedial Action Amend ments Act of 1988 (102 Stat. 3192, 42 U.S.C. 7916). Signed by the president Nov. 5, 1988. Allowed the Interior Department to transfer BLM lands to the Department of Energy for surveillance and maintenance of slightly radioactive mill tailings.

Federal Land Transaction Facilitation Act (114 Stat. 613, 43 U.S.C. 2301 et seq.). Signed by the president July 25, 2000. Allows a portion of the proceeds from BLM public land sales to be used to purchase certain qualified private properties.

Healthy Forests Restoration Act of 2003 (117 Stat. 1887, 16 U.S.C. 6501 note). Signed by the president Dec. 3, 2003. Provided increased authority to the secretary of agriculture and the secretary of the interior to conduct hazardous fuels reduction projects on National Forest System and BLM lands, with emphasis on protecting communities, watersheds, and certain other at-risk lands from catastrophic wildfire.

Omnibus Appropriations Bill 2005 (118 Stat. 2924, 35 U.S.C. 41 note). Signed by the president Dec. 8, 2004. Amended to the 1971 Wild Free-Roaming Horse and Burro Act to allow for the sale of wild horses to foreign markets, including for meat processing, under certain requirements.

Energy Policy Act of 2005 (119 Stat. 594, 42 U.S.C. 15801 note). Signed by the president Aug. 8, 2005. Established long-range, comprehensive national energy policies. Provided incentives for increased domestic oil and natural gas production. Amended the Geothermal Steam Act of 1970 to revise competitive lease sale requirements. Directed the interior secretary to promulgate final royalty incentive regulations for natural gas production from wells in certain shallow waters of the Gulf of Mexico.

Omnibus Public Land Management Act of 2009 (123 Stat. 991, 16 U.S.C. 1 note). Signed by the president March 30, 2009. Established in the BLM the National Landscape Conservation System (thus enacting into law the National Landscape Conservation System created by the BLM in 2000) in order to conserve, protect, and restore nationally significant landscapes that have outstanding cultural, ecological, or scientific value. Designated specific areas under the NLCS.

The Helium Stewardship Act of 2013 (127 Stat. 534, 50 U.S.C. 167 note). Signed by the president Oct. 2, 2013. Makes significant changes to the Federal Helium Program. Requires secretary of the interior credit all proceeds received from the sale or disposition of helium on federal land from sale or auction to the Helium Production Fund (established in this act).

■ STATE OFFICES

ALASKA

222 W. Seventh Ave., #13
Anchorage, AK 99513–7504
(907) 271–5960
E-mail: bcribley@blm.gov
Bud C. Cribley, director

ARIZONA

One N. Central Ave., #800
Phoenix, AZ 85004–4427
(602) 417–9200
Fax (602) 417–9398

E-mail: rmsuazo@blm.gov
Ray Suazo, associate director

CALIFORNIA

2800 Cottage Way, #W-1623
Sacramento, CA 95825–1886
(916) 978–4400
E-mail: jkenna@blm.gov
Jim Kenna, director
(916) 978–4600

COLORADO

2850 Youngfield St.
Lakewood, CO 80215–7093
(303) 239–3600
E-mail: hhankins@blm.gov
Ruth Welch, director
(303) 239–3700

EASTERN STATES

(All states east of the Mississippi River)
20 M St. S.E., #950
Washington, DC 20003
(202) 912–7700
Fax (202) 912–7186
John Ruhs, director

IDAHO

1387 S. Vinnell Way
Boise, ID 83709–1657
(208) 373–4000
E-mail: BLM_ID_StateOffice@blm.gov
Tim Murphy, director
(208) 373–4001

MONTANA

(MT, ND, SD)
5001 Southgate Dr.
Billings, MT 59101
(406) 896–5000
E-mail: jconnell@blm.gov
Jamie Connell, director
(406) 896–5012

NEVADA

1340 Financial Blvd.
Reno, NV 89502

(775) 861–6400
E-mail: alueders@blm.gov
Amy Lueders, director
(775) 861–6583

NEW MEXICO

(KS, NM, OK, TX)
301 Dinosaur Trail
Santa Fe, NM 87508
Mailing address:
P.O. 27115
Santa Fe, NM 87502–0115
(505) 954–2000
Aden Seidlitz (acting), director
(505) 954–2222

OREGON

(OR, WA)
333 S.W. First Ave.
Portland, OR 97204
Mailing address:
P.O. Box 2965
Portland, OR 97208
(503) 808–6001
E-mail: jperez@blm.gov
Jerome E. Perez, director
(503) 808–6026

UTAH

440 W. 200 South, #500
Salt Lake City, UT 84101–1345
(801) 539–4001
E-mail: jwhitloc@blm.gov
Jenna Whitlock (acting), director
(801) 539–4010

WYOMING

(NE, WY)
5353 Yellowstone Rd.
Cheyenne, WY 82009
Mailing address:
P.O. Box 1828
Cheyenne, WY 82003–1828
(307) 775–6256
Mary Jo Rugwell (acting), director

Bureau of Ocean Energy Management

1849 C St. N.W., Washington, DC 20240
Internet: www.boem.gov

The Department of the Interior's Minerals Management Service (MMS) was renamed the Bureau of Ocean Energy Management, Regulation and Enforcement (BOEMRE) in June 2010. On October 1, 2010, the revenue collection arm of the former MMS became the Office of Natural Resources Revenue (*p. 710*). Effective October 1, 2011, BOEMRE was divided into two separate organizations: the Bureau of Ocean Energy Management (BOEM) and the Bureau of Safety and Environmental Enforcement (BSEE) (*p. 705*).

Reorganization of the Former MMS

The reorganization followed high-profile scandals at MMS. In late 2008 the Department of Interior Inspector General released a report that documented misconduct and unethical behavior by Interior Department employees in the Denver office. Among the accusations: employees accepted expensive gifts and money from the industries they were charged with regulating; had improper personal relationships with industry representatives; rigged oil contract bidding; and mismanaged millions of dollars in royalties.

But the scandal was not enough to restructure the agency; it would take an epic disaster to force the breakup of MMS. In April 2010, after years of allowing the oil industry to self-regulate on issues of safety and environmental management, disaster struck: BP's Transocean *Deepwater Horizon* offshore oil rig exploded in the Gulf of Mexico, killing 11 workers and unleashing the worst environmental disaster in the nation's history. Within weeks, the MMS was renamed and leadership at the new BOEMRE began undertaking reforms as an independent commission investigated the causes of the BP disaster. The blowout well continued spilling oil into the Gulf for three months before BP was able to successfully cap the well, which was 5,000 feet below the surface.

In January 2011 the National Commission on the BP *Deepwater Horizon* Oil Spill and Offshore Drilling released its report. The commission, established by presidential executive order in May 2010, was comprised of former government officials and academic and environmental leaders. While acknowledging that the well blew out because a number of separate risk factors, oversights, and mistakes combined to overwhelm the safeguards meant to prevent just such an event from happening, the report determined that most of the mistakes and oversights could be traced back to a single overarching failure—a failure of management. The commission also noted the conflict of interest that existed between industry and the government agency authorized to regulate the industry. The commission released a list of recommendations to improve safety and reduce conflict of interest within the Interior Department's management of some of the nation's most valuable natural resources and regulation of the industry permitted to extract those resources from federally controlled areas (for a list of the commission's recommendations, see BSEE, *p. 705*).

Establishment of BOEM

To fulfill the commission's recommendations following the explosion of BP's *Deepwater Horizon* drilling rig, BOEMRE was divided into two separate organizations on October 1, 2011: the Bureau of Ocean Energy Management (BOEM) and the Bureau of Safety and Environmental Enforcement (BSEE). The purpose of the split was to further reduce conflict of interest between resource management and environmental and safety regulators. BOEM is responsible for managing development of the nation's offshore resources. BOEM operations include leasing, plan administration, environmental studies, National Environmental Policy Act (NEPA) analysis, resource evaluation, economic analysis, and the renewable energy program. BSEE enforces safety and environmental regulations. BSEE operations include all field operations, including permitting and research, inspections, offshore regulatory programs, oil spill response, training, and environmental compliance functions.

BOEM's Office of Strategic Resources, which is responsible for the development of the Five-Year Outer Continental Shelf (OCS) Oil and Natural Gas Leasing Program, oversees assessments of the oil, gas, and other mineral resource potential of the OCS; inventories oil and gas reserves; develops production projections; and conducts economic evaluations that ensure the receipt of fair market value by U.S. taxpayers for OCS leases. BOEM handles the actual oil and gas lease sales, along with sand and gravel negotiated agreements and official maps and GIS data. The leased OCS acres contribute about 15 percent of America's domestic natural gas production and about 27 percent of America's domestic oil production.

As required by the OCS Lands Act, BOEM published a Request for Information (RFI) in the *Federal Register* on June 16, 2014, to begin development of a new five-year program to cover the years 2017 to 2022. On January 27, 2015, the Interior Department announced the Draft Proposed Program (DPP) for the U.S. OCS Oil and Gas Leasing Program for 2017 to 2022. The DPP includes offshore planning areas in the Gulf of Mexico, in the Atlantic (from coastal Virginia to Georgia), and in Alaska.

BOEM's Office of Renewable Energy is responsible for offshore Renewable Energy Programs. The Renewable Energy Program grants leases, easements, and rights-of-way for orderly, safe, and environmentally responsible renewable energy development activities, including offshore wind energy and hydrokinetic (ocean wave and ocean current) energy development.

The Energy Policy Act of 2005 earlier had granted MMS the authority to regulate renewable energy development on the Outer Continental Shelf. The act required the Interior Department to issue rules and regulations within nine months to guide the development of wind, wave, and tidal power. However, by January 2009, the agency had issued only a proposed rule. In April 2009 the Interior Department and the Federal Energy Regulatory Commission (FERC) (*p. 181*) signed an agreement that clarified their agencies' jurisdictional responsibilities for leasing and licensing renewable energy offshore projects, clearing the way for publication of the final rules.

Under the agreement, the BOEM has exclusive jurisdiction with regard to the production, transportation, or transmission of energy from non-hydrokinetic renewable energy projects, including wind and solar. FERC has exclusive jurisdiction to issue licenses for the construction and operation of hydrokinetic projects (including wave and current), but companies would be required to first obtain a lease through BOEM.

Later in 2009 the administration announced final regulations for the Outer Continental Shelf (OCS) Renewable Energy Program. The framework establishes a program to grant leases, easements, and rights-of-way for orderly, safe, and environmentally responsible renewable energy development activities, such as the siting and construction of off-shore wind farms, on the OCS. The program also establishes methods for sharing revenues generated from OCS renewable energy projects with adjacent coastal states.

In the fall of 2010 Secretary Salazar launched the "Smart from the Start" wind energy initiative to expedite development of wind energy projects off the Atlantic coast. In coordination with the relevant states, BOEM has identified Wind Energy Areas (WEAs) offshore on the Atlantic coast as ideal for renewable energy development. A number of states on the Atlantic coast have initiated planning for renewable energy projects and developers are pursuing leases. By early 2015 BOEM had issued nine commercial wind energy leases on the OCS, including those offshore Delaware, Maryland, Massachusetts, Rhode Island, Virginia, and Massachusetts.

BOEM's Office of Environmental Programs conducts environmental reviews, including NEPA analyses and compliance documents for energy development planning. These analyses inform the BOEM's decisions on the five-year program, and conventional and renewable energy leasing and development activities. BOEM's scientists also conduct and oversee environmental studies to guide policy decisions relating to the management of energy and marine mineral resources on the OCS.

BOEM is supported by three regional offices in New Orleans, LA; Camarillo, CA; and Anchorage, AK. The regional offices manage oil and gas resource evaluations, environmental studies and assessments, leasing activities, fair market value determinations, and geological and geophysical permitting.

■ KEY PERSONNEL

Director
 Abigail Ross Hopper . . . . (202) 208–6300
Deputy Director
 Walter D. Cruikshank . . . . (202) 208–6300/3505
Chief Environmental Officer, Environmental Programs
 William Yancey Brown . . . . (703) 787–1087
Chief, Environmental Science
 Rodney E. Cluck . . . . (202) 208–6249
Budget and Program Coordination
 Jim Anderson . . . . (202) 208–3826
Policy Regulation and Analysis
 Peter Meffert . . . . (703) 787–1610
Renewable Energy
 Jim Bennett . . . . (703) 787–1300
Strategic Resources
 Renee L. Orr . . . . (202) 208–3515
Leasing Division (381 Elden St., Herndon, VA 20170)
 Vacant . . . . (703) 787–1215

■ INFORMATION SOURCES

Internet
Agency website: www.boem.gov.

Telephone Contacts
 Personnel Locator . . . . (202) 208–3100
 Federal Relay Service TTY . . . . (800) 877–8339

Information and Publications

KEY OFFICES

Office of Public Affairs
 1849 C St. N.W., #4230
 Washington, DC 20240
 (202) 208–6474
 Connie Gillette, press secretary
 (202) 208–5387
 E-mail: connie.gillette@boem.gov
 E-mail: BOEMPublicAffairs@boem.gov

Office of Congressional Affairs

1849 C St. N.W.
Washington, DC 20240
Lee Tilton, congressional affairs specialist
(202) 208–3788

Freedom of Information

45600 Woodland Rd.
Sterling, VA 20166
Rosemary Melendy, public liaison
(703) 787–1315
Fax (703) 787–1209
FOIA Requester Service Center
(703) 787–1818
E-mail: boemfoia@boem.gov

Requests must be in writing; write "Freedom of Information Request" on the envelope. Requests may also be made online at the website.

DATA AND STATISTICS

PUBLICATIONS

For manuals, bulletins, videos, scientific and technical publications, and the quarterly magazine *Ocean Science,* visit the Web page www.boem.gov/BOEM-Newsroom/Library/Library.aspx.

Reference Resources

LIBRARY

Interior Department

1849 C St. N.W.
Washington, DC 20240
(202) 208–5815
George Franchois, director
Hours: 7:45 a.m. to 5:00 p.m.
Internet: www.doi.gov/library/index.cfm
E-mail: library@ios.doi.gov

Materials on mineral leasing and royalty management are kept in the Interior Department Library, housing more than a million volumes and numerous databases.

DOCKETS

Federal dockets are available on the website in the Electronic Reading Room and at www.regulations.gov. (*See appendix for Searching and Commenting on Regulations: Regulations.gov.*)

RULES AND REGULATIONS

Bureau of Ocean Energy Management rules and regulations are published in the *Code of Federal Regulations,* Title 30, Chapter II, Parts 500–599. Proposed regulations, new final regulations, and updates to the *Code of Federal Regulations* are published in the daily *Federal Register.* (*See appendix for details on how to obtain and use these publications.*) The *Federal Register* and the *Code of Federal Regulations* may also be accessed online at www.archives.gov/federal-register/cfr; this site also provides a link to the federal government's regulatory website at www.regulations.gov (*see appendix*).

▣ LEGISLATION

BOEM administers the following laws in full or in part:

Submerged Lands Act (43 U.S.C. 1301–1315). Signed by the president May 22, 1953. Granted title to coastal states to the natural resources located within three miles of their coastline. Authorized the federal government to regulate offshore activities for national defense, commerce, international affairs, and navigation. Maintained federal control of the seabed and resources therein of the Outer Continental Shelf beyond state boundaries and authorized leasing by the interior secretary.

Outer Continental Shelf Lands Act of 1953 (43 U.S.C. 1331–1356). Signed by the president Aug. 7, 1953. Defined the Outer Continental Shelf as all submerged lands lying seaward of state coastal waters (three miles offshore) as being under U.S. jurisdiction. Authorized the interior secretary to promulgate regulations to lease the underwater area.

National Environmental Policy Act of 1969 (83 Stat. 852, 42 U.S.C. 4321). Signed by the president Jan. 1, 1969. Established a broad national environmental policy and required that federal agencies provide environmental impact statements regarding any major federal action or legislative proposal.

Outer Continental Shelf Lands Act Amendments of 1978 (92 Stat. 629, 43 U.S.C. 1801). Signed by the president Sept. 18, 1978. Gave the secretary of the interior authority to expedite exploration and development of Outer Continental Shelf minerals.

Oil Pollution Prevention, Response, Liability, and Compensation Act (104 Stat. 484, 33 U.S.C. 2701). Signed by the president Aug. 18, 1990. Established limitations on liability for damages from oil spillage. Created a fund to pay for cleanup and compensation costs not covered otherwise.

Energy Policy Act of 2005 (119 Stat. 594, 42 U.S.C. 15801 note). Signed by the president Aug. 8, 2005. Established long-range, comprehensive national energy policies. Provided incentives for increased domestic oil and natural gas production. Authorized MMS to develop renewable energy projects such as wave, wind, and current energy on the Outer Continental Shelf. Directed MMS to disburse 25 percent of receipts from geothermal energy production directly to counties where that production occurs.

Gulf of Mexico Energy Security Act of 2006 (120 Stat. 3000, 43 U.S.C. 1331 note). Signed by the president Dec. 20, 2006. Instructed the interior secretary to offer specified areas within the Gulf of Mexico for oil and gas leasing. Placed a moratorium on oil and gas leasing in any area east of the Military Mission Line in the Gulf of Mexico; any area in the Eastern Planning Area that was within 125 miles of the Florida coastline; or areas within 100 miles of the Florida coastline.

Executive Order 13547 Stewardship of the Ocean, Our Coasts, and the Great Lakes (July 19, 2010). Set forth policy directive on ocean, coastal, and Great Lakes resource management that incorporates regional efforts on coastal and marine spatial planning (CMSP).

Established an interagency National Ocean Council to oversee its implementation.

■ REGIONAL OFFICES

ALASKA REGION

3801 Centerpoint Dr., #500
Anchorage, AK 99503–5820
(907) 334–5200
Fax (907) 334–5202
James Kendall, BOEM regional director
(907) 334–5200
E-mail: james.kendall@boam.gov
John Callahan, public affairs
(907) 334–5208
E-mail: john.callahan@boem.gov

GULF REGION

1201 Elmwood Park Blvd.
New Orleans, LA 70123–2394

(504) 736–0557
Vacant, BOEM regional director
E-mail: gulfpublicinfo@boem.gov
John Filostrat, public affairs
(504) 731–7815
E-mail: john.filostrat@boem.gov

PACIFIC REGION

770 Paseo Camarillo, 2nd Floor
Camarillo, CA 93010
(805) 384–4706
Fax: (805) 389–7505
Ellen G. Aronson, BOEM
    regional director
(805) 389–7511
E-mail: ellen.aronson@boem.gov
John Romero, public affairs
(805) 384–6324
Email: john.romero@boem.gov

Bureau of Safety and Environmental Enforcement

1849 C St. N.W., Washington, DC 20240
Internet: www.bsee.gov

The Department of the Interior's Minerals Management Service (MMS) was renamed the Bureau of Ocean Energy Management, Regulation and Enforcement (BOEMRE) in June 2010. On October 1, 2010, the revenue collection arm of the former MMS became the Office of Natural Resources Revenue (p. 710). Effective October 1, 2011, BOEMRE was divided into two separate organizations; the Bureau of Ocean Energy Management (BOEM) (p. 701) and the Bureau of Safety and Environmental Enforcement (BSEE).

Reorganization of the Former MMS

The reorganization followed high-profile scandals at MMS. In late 2008, the Department of Interior inspector general released a report that documented misconduct and unethical behavior by Interior Department employees in the Denver office. Among the accusations: employees accepted expensive gifts and money from the industries they were charged with regulating; had improper personal relationships with industry representatives; rigged oil contract bidding; and mismanaged millions of dollars in royalties.

But the scandal was not enough to restructure the agency; it would take an epic disaster to force the breakup of MMS. In April 2010, after years of allowing the oil industry to self-regulate on issues of safety and environmental management, disaster struck: BP's Transocean *Deepwater Horizon* offshore oil rig exploded in the Gulf of Mexico, killing 11 workers and unleashing the worst environmental disaster in the nation's history. Within weeks, the MMS was renamed and leadership at the new BOEMRE began undertaking reforms as an independent commission investigated the causes of the BP disaster.

Events Leading to Disaster

In July 2008, with the cost of oil at record highs, President George W. Bush withdrew an executive order that prohibited offshore drilling along the east and west coasts of the United States; the executive order banning offshore drilling had been signed by his father, President George H. W. Bush, in 1990. In September 2008, Congress also allowed a twenty-seven-year-old moratorium on offshore

drilling along the East and West coasts and in the eastern Gulf of Mexico to expire. The moratorium had prevented offshore drilling.

In the final hours of the Bush administration, the Interior Department published a proposed five-year plan for oil and gas development on the U.S. Outer Continental Shelf. A focal point of the draft plan proposed oil and gas drilling along the Atlantic seaboard, from Maine to Florida. The proposal was published in the *Federal Register* Jan. 21, 2009, with a public comment deadline of March 23, 2009. Interior Secretary Ken Salazar, of the incoming administration of President Barack Obama, extended the deadline for another 180 days. The delay gave the new administration, which favored an energy policy focused on renewable sources, time to chart a new direction in offshore minerals management.

Although the new administration did pursue a high-profile, ambitious renewable energy policy initiative supported with funding from Congress, the administration did not reverse course on expanding offshore drilling. On March 31, 2010, President Obama announced the expansion of offshore oil and gas exploration in the mid and south Atlantic and the Gulf of Mexico. The news was immediately criticized by environmentalists.

Three weeks later, the BP Transocean *Deepwater Horizon* rig exploded. The U.S. Coast Guard (p. 658) was the responding agency and set up incident command, but the incident was catastrophic beyond what the government and industry were capable of containing. The blown-out well continued spilling oil into the Gulf for three months before BP was able to successfully cap the well, which was 5,000 feet below the surface.

In fall 2010 the Interior Department announced two new rules, the Drilling Safety Rule and the Workplace Safety Rule. The rules sought to improve drilling safety by strengthening requirements for safety equipment, well control systems, and blowout prevention practices on offshore oil and gas operations, and improve workplace safety by reducing the risk of human error.

In January 2011 the National Commission on the BP *Deepwater Horizon* Oil Spill and Offshore Drilling released its report. The commission, established by presidential executive order in May 2010, was comprised of former government officials and academic and environmental leaders. While acknowledging that the well blew out because a number of separate risk factors, oversights, and mistakes combined to overwhelm the safeguards meant to prevent just such an event from happening, the report determined that most of the mistakes and oversights could be traced back to a single overarching failure—a failure of management. The commission also noted the conflict of interest that existed between industry and the government agency authorized to regulate the industry.

Key recommendations from the commission included:

• Congress and the administration should create an independent safety agency within the Department of the Interior, headed by an official shielded from political interference with energy and engineering experience and expertise, with enforcement authority to oversee all aspects of offshore drilling safety.

• U.S. offshore drilling regulations and enforcement practices should be the most advanced in the world. The U.S. should lead an international effort to develop global best practices for safety that can be adopted and applied worldwide.

• These new regulations should be supplemented by a risk-based regulatory approach that requires all offshore drilling companies to demonstrate that they have thoroughly evaluated all of the risks associated with an operation and are prepared to address any and all risks pertaining to that operation.

• Broader consultations among federal agencies, including the Coast Guard and the National Oceanic and Atmospheric Administration (NOAA), prior to leasing and exploration will help identify and address risks.

• Congress and Interior should enhance environmental protection review by creating a distinct environmental science office within Interior headed by a chief scientist with specified environmental protection review responsibilities.

• Adequate and predictable funding for regulatory oversight is essential for these reforms to be effective. Budgets for the regulatory agencies that oversee offshore drilling should come directly from fees paid by the companies that are being granted access to a publicly owned resource.

• Drilling operators should be financially responsible for the consequences of failure. The current $75 million cap on liability for offshore facility accidents is inadequate and places the economic risk on the backs of the victims and the taxpayers.

• The oil and gas industry must adopt a culture of safety.

• Spill response planning by both government and industry must improve. Industry spill response plans must provide realistic assessments of response capability, including well containment. Government review of those plans must be rigorous and involve all federal agencies with responsibilities for oil spill response.

At the end of 2010 the area in the Eastern Gulf of Mexico remained under an oil drilling moratorium, mandated by Congress, and the mid and south Atlantic planning areas were no longer under consideration for potential development through 2017. The Interior Department announced a plan that included environmental analysis to determine whether seismic studies should be conducted in the mid and south Atlantic and rigorous scientific analysis of the Arctic to determine if future oil and gas development could be conducted safely. On January 27, 2015, the Interior Department announced the Draft Proposed Program (DPP) for the U.S. OCS Oil and Gas Leasing Program for 2017–2022. The DPP includes offshore planning areas in the Gulf of Mexico, in the Atlantic (from coastal Virginia to Georgia), and in Alaska.

Establishment of BSEE

To fulfill the Commission's recommendations following the explosion of BP's *Deepwater Horizon* drilling rig, BOEMRE was divided into two separate organizations on October 1, 2011: the Bureau of Ocean Energy Management (BOEM) and the Bureau of Safety and Environmental Enforcement (BSEE). The purpose of the split was to further reduce conflict of interest between resource management and environmental and safety regulators. BOEM is responsible for managing development of the nation's offshore resources. BOEM operations include leasing, plan administration, environmental studies, National Environmental Policy Act (NEPA) analysis, resource evaluation, economic analysis, and the renewable energy program. BSEE enforces safety and environmental regulations. BSEE operations include all field operations, including permitting and research, inspections, offshore regulatory programs, oil spill response, training, and environmental compliance functions.

The bureau undertook comprehensive reforms to offshore oil and gas regulation and oversight that included enhanced drilling safety, enhanced workplace safety, and ongoing improvements to the offshore regulator.

The drilling safety rule had been undertaken prior to the *Deepwater Horizon* disaster, but BOEMRE released an interim rule in 2010. On Aug. 15, 2012, BSEE released the Final Drilling Safety Rule, which refines the Interim Final Rule by addressing requirements for compliance with documents incorporated by reference. Operators must demonstrate that they are prepared to deal with the potential for a blowout and worst-case discharge. Permit applications for drilling projects must meet new standards for well design, casing, and cementing and be independently certified by a professional engineer.

The Workplace Safety Rule covers all offshore oil and gas operations in federal waters and makes mandatory the previously voluntary practices in the American Petroleum Institute's (API) Recommended Practice 75 (RP 75). A mandatory oil and gas SEMS (Safety and Environmental Management System) program enhances the safety and environmental protection of oil and gas drilling operations on the Outer Continental Shelf (OCS).

BSEE imposed requirements that offshore operators maintain comprehensive safety and environmental programs. This includes performance-based standards for offshore drilling and production operations, including equipment, safety practices, environmental safeguards, and management oversight of operations and contractors. Companies will now have to develop and maintain a SEMS per the new Workplace Safety Rule. The Workplace Safety Rule was extensive in its requirements and will address human factors behind accidents not covered by previous regulations. BSEE continued issuing regulations to implement *Deepwater Horizon* commission recommendations in 2015.

Ongoing improvements to the offshore regulator address issues of transparency and seek to prevent the types of behavior that resulted in scandal and disaster prior to reorganization. An Investigations and Review Unit (IRU) was established under BOEMRE to identify and correct ethical problems within the regulatory agency and target companies that exploited the previous system. IRU is comprised of professionals with law enforcement backgrounds or technical expertise whose mission is to respond to allegations or evidence of misconduct and unethical behavior by bureau employees and pursue allegations of misconduct by oil and gas companies involved in offshore energy projects; and ensure the bureau's ability to respond swiftly to emerging issues and crises, including significant incidents such as spills and accidents. BSEE has implemented a recusal policy for employees to deal with real and perceived conflicts of interest.

BSEE accomplishes its mission through programs and divisions centered on enhanced safety and regulatory enforcement:

The Offshore Regulatory Program develops standards and regulations to enhance operational safety and environmental protection for the exploration and development of offshore oil and natural gas on the U.S. OCS. Under the current regulatory system, both the U.S. Coast Guard *(p. 658)* and BSEE share jurisdiction over the regulation of mobile offshore drilling units (MODU) activities on the OCS.

The Environmental Enforcement Division was established to provide regulatory oversight focuses on operator compliance with all applicable environmental regulations, as well as ensuring that operators honor their contractual obligations in their leases, submit their plans, and apply for their permits.

The Oil Spill Response Division is responsible for developing standards and guidelines for offshore operators' Oil Spill Response Plans (OSRP), which must comply with regulatory requirements and include coordination of oil spill drill activities. This division guides creation of policy, direction, and oversight of activities related to the agency's oil spill response. The division oversees the Unannounced Oil Spill Drill program and works closely with sister agencies such as the U.S. Coast Guard and Environmental Protection Agency to continually enhance response technologies and capabilities.

BSEE is supported by three regional offices: New Orleans, LA; Camarillo, CA; and Anchorage, AK. The regional offices are responsible for reviewing applications for permit to drill to ensure all safety requirements are met. These offices also are responsible for conducting inspections of drilling rigs and production platforms using multi-person, multidiscipline inspection teams. BSEE's inspectors issue incidents of noncompliance and have the authority to levy civil penalties for regulatory infractions. Regional and field operations personnel also investigate accidents and incidents.

■ KEY PERSONNEL

Director
Brian Salerno .... (202) 208–3500
Deputy Director
Margaret Schneider................ (202) 208–3500
Environmental Enforcement Division
Charles Barbee.................... (703) 787–1567
Offshore Regulatory Program
Doug Morris .... (202) 208–3974
Oil Spill Response
David Moore .... (703) 787–1637
Associate Director for Administration
Scott Mabry .... (202) 208–3220

■ INFORMATION SOURCES

Internet
Agency website: www.bsee.gov. For information on the agency's collaboration with national and international government and industry organizations, see the website for the International Committee on Regulatory Authority Research and Development (ICRARD): www.ICRARD.org.

Telephone Contacts
Personnel Locator .... (202) 208–3100
Federal Relay Service TTY .... (800) 877–8339
News Room....................... (202) 208–3985
Public Information Office.......... (800) 200–4853

Information and Publications

KEY OFFICES

Office of Public Affairs
1849 C St. N.W., #4230
Washington, DC 20240
(202) 208–3985
Greg Julian, press secretary
(202) 208–6184

Office of Congressional Affairs
1849 C St. N.W.
Washington, DC 20240
Julie Fleming, congressional affairs specialist
(202) 208–3827

Freedom of Information
45600 Woodland Rd.
Sterling, VA 20166

Debbie Kimball, FOIA officer
(703) 787–1689
Fax (703) 787–1207
FOIA Requester Service Center
(703) 787–1404
E-mail: bseefoia@bsee.gov
Internet FOIA reading room: www.bsee.gov/About-
    BSEE/FOIA/BSEE-FOIA-Reading-Room

Requests must be in writing; write "Freedom of Information Request" on the envelope. Requests may also be made online at the website.

PUBLICATIONS

Reports, studies, and other publications are available on the agency website at www.bsee.gov/BSEE-Newsroom/Publications-Library/Index

The Office of Communications operates a scientific and technical publications program. Informal documents are published that by law must be released quickly; these are short-term documents with a narrow focus. Formal documents—more in-depth materials of a wider ranging and longer term interest—also are published. To obtain such documents contact:

Office of Communications
381 Elden St.
Herndon, VA 20170–4817
(703) 787–1460

Reference Resources

LIBRARY

Interior Department
1849 C St. N.W.
Washington, DC 20240
(202) 208–5815
George Franchois, director
Hours: 7:45 a.m. to 5:00 p.m.
Internet: www.doi.gov/library/index.cfm
E-mail: library@ios.doi.gov

DOCKETS

Federal dockets are available on the website in the Electronic Reading Room and at www.regulations.gov. (*See appendix for Searching and Commenting on Regulations: Regulations.gov.*)

RULES AND REGULATIONS

Bureau of Safety and Environmental Management, Regulation, and Enforcement rules and regulations are published in the *Code of Federal Regulations,* Title 30, Chapter II, Parts 200–299. Proposed regulations, new final regulations, and updates to the *Code of Federal Regulations* are published in the daily *Federal Register.* (*See appendix for details on how to obtain and use these publications.*) The *Federal Register* and the *Code of Federal Regulations* may also be accessed online at www.archives.gov/federal-register/cfr; this site also provides a link to the federal government's regulatory website at www.regulations.gov (*see appendix*).

▦ LEGISLATION

BSEE administers the following laws in full or in part:

Submerged Lands Act (43 U.S.C. 1301–1315). Signed by the president May 22, 1953. Granted title to coastal states to the natural resources located within three miles of their coastline. Authorized the federal government to regulate offshore activities for national defense, commerce, international affairs, and navigation. Maintained federal control of the seabed and resources therein of the Outer Continental Shelf beyond state boundaries and authorized leasing by the interior secretary.

Outer Continental Shelf Lands Act of 1953 (43 U.S.C. 1331–1356). Signed by the president Aug. 7, 1953. Defined the Outer Continental Shelf as all submerged lands lying seaward of state coastal waters (three miles offshore) as being under U.S. jurisdiction. Authorized the interior secretary to promulgate regulations to lease the underwater area.

National Environmental Policy Act of 1969 (83 Stat. 852, 42 U.S.C. 4321). Signed by the president Jan. 1, 1969. Established a broad national environmental policy and required that federal agencies provide environmental impact statements regarding any major federal action or legislative proposal.

Outer Continental Shelf Lands Act Amendments of 1978 (92 Stat. 629, 43 U.S.C. 1801). Signed by the president Sept. 18, 1978. Gave the secretary of the interior authority to expedite exploration and development of Outer Continental Shelf minerals.

Federal Oil and Gas Royalty Management Act of 1982 (96 Stat. 2447, 30 U.S.C. 1701 note). Signed by the president Jan. 12, 1983. Requires that oil and gas facilities be built in a way that protects the environment and conserves federal resources.

Oil Pollution Prevention, Response, Liability, and Compensation Act (104 Stat. 484, 33 U.S.C. 2701). Signed by the president Aug. 18, 1990. Established limitations on liability for damages from oil spillage. Created a fund to pay for cleanup and compensation costs not covered otherwise.

Energy Policy Act of 2005 (119 Stat. 594, 42 U.S.C. 15801 note). Signed by the president Aug. 8, 2005. Established long-range, comprehensive national energy policies. Provided incentives for increased domestic oil and natural gas production. Authorized MMS to develop renewable energy projects such as wave, wind, and current energy on the Outer Continental Shelf. Directed MMS to disburse 25 percent of receipts from geothermal energy production directly to counties where that production occurs.

Gulf of Mexico Energy Security Act of 2006 (120 Stat. 3000, 43 U.S.C. 1331 note). Signed by the president Dec. 20, 2006. Instructed the interior secretary to offer specified areas within the Gulf of Mexico for oil and gas leasing. Placed a moratorium on oil and gas leasing in any area east of the Military Mission Line in the Gulf of

Mexico; any area in the Eastern Planning Area that was within 125 miles of the Florida coastline; or areas within 100 miles of the Florida coastline.

▥ REGIONAL OFFICES

ALASKA REGION
3801 Centerpoint Dr., #500
Anchorage, AK 99503–5820
(907) 334–5300
Fax (907) 334–5202
Mark Fesmire, regional director

GULF REGION
1201 Elmwood Park Blvd.
New Orleans, LA 70123–2394
(504) 736–0557
Press (504) 736–2485
Lars Herbst, regional director

PACIFIC REGION
770 Paseo Camarillo, 2nd Floor
Camarillo, CA 93010
(800) 672–2627
Jaron E. Ming, regional director
(805) 389–7514

Office of Natural Resources Revenue

1849 C St. N.W., Washington, DC 20240
Mailing address: 1801 Pennsylvania Ave. N.W.,
Washington, DC 20006
Internet: www.onrr.gov

The Department of the Interior's Minerals Management Service (MMS) was reorganized in 2010. The Bureau of Ocean Energy Management, Regulation, and Enforcement (BOEMRE), which was responsible for the environmental and safety regulation functions of MMS, was established in June 2010; the final stage of the reorganization of BOEMRE became effective October 1, 2011, when it split into two independent entities: the Bureau of Ocean Energy Management (BOEM) (*p. 701*) and the Bureau of Safety and Environmental Enforcement (BSEE) (*p. 705*). On October 1, 2010, the revenue collection arm of the former MMS became the Office of Natural Resources Revenue (ONRR). ONRR is responsible for collecting and disbursing revenues from energy production on federal and American Indian lands and offshore on the Outer Continental Shelf. This revenue management effort is one of the federal government's greatest sources of non-tax revenues.

In 2014 the program disbursed more than $13 billion. Some of this revenue is distributed to Native American tribes and to states in which the minerals were found. Annually the agency distributes funds to thirty-five states for mineral production on federal lands located within their borders and from federal offshore lands adjacent to their shores. Other recipients of funds include the Land and Water Conservation Fund, the Historic Preservation Fund, and the Reclamation Fund of the Treasury.

The Bureau of Land Management (*p. 695*) within the Interior Department oversees the leasing of minerals management on federal lands; the Interior Department's Bureau of Indian Affairs (*p. 689*) works with the ONRR on royalty management functions on Native American lands.

Terminating the Royalty-in-Kind Program

Companies that develop and produce oil and gas from federal lands and waters are required to report their production volumes and other data to the Interior Department's ONRR and to pay royalties. Previously, royalties could be paid either in value (cash) or in kind (oil or gas). Through the Royalty-in-Kind (RIK) program,

energy companies paid royalties in the form of oil or gas production rather than cash. MMS then sold the oil and gas in the marketplace and disbursed the revenues or provided oil to the Energy Department for the Strategic Petroleum Reserve (SPR).

The RIK program was a source of controversy, and lawmakers tried, unsuccessfully, to reform or eliminate the program, an effort that the oil and gas industry vigorously fought. Then scandal hit the MMS. In 2008 the Interior Department Inspector General released a report that documented misconduct and unethical behavior by Interior Department employees in the Denver office who managed the RIK program. Among the accusations: employees accepted expensive gifts and money from the industries they were charged with regulating; had improper personal relationships with industry representatives; rigged oil contract bidding; and mismanaged millions of dollars in royalties.

In August 2009 the General Accounting Office released a report, "MMS Does Not Provide Reasonable Assurance It Receives Its Share of Gas, Resulting in Millions in Forgone Revenue." The report noted that MMS had failed to adequately account for and manage the resources under this program, costing the taxpayers millions of dollars in lost revenue.

In September 2009 Interior Secretary Ken Salazar announced he was reforming and restructuring the department's management of U.S. energy resources, starting with the termination of the MMS controversial Royalty-in-Kind program. The RIK program would transition to a more transparent and accountable royalty collection program. Through a phased-out plan, the Interior Department honored the existing contracts, which terminated in 2010.

Updating Regulations and Enforcement Activities

In January 2011 ONRR proposed to establish a negotiated rulemaking committee to replace outdated regulations governing the valuation of oil produced on American Indian lands. The negotiated rulemaking committee would make recommendations to replace existing regulations governing the valuation of oil production from American Indian leases, which had been in place since March 1, 1988.

In May 2011 Secretary Salazar announced that the department was evaluating the potential streamlining of regulations that govern the calculation of royalties owed to the United States from oil and natural gas produced offshore and on federal lands. The regulations required complex, transaction-by-transaction evaluations of the negotiated price for the oil and gas produced on public lands, followed by an analysis of the costs associated with the transportation and gas processing. In December 2014 the Interior Department released a draft proposed federal regulation by the ONRR governing the valuation of federal oil and gas, and federal and American Indian coal resources, as well as expanded guidance on the production of coal on public lands issued by the Bureau of Land Management (BLM) *(p. 695)*. The new rules updated regulations put in place more than two decades earlier.

The Indian Oil Valuation Negotiated Rulemaking Committee, established in December 2011, began meeting in 2012 to develop specific recommendations regarding proposed revisions to the existing regulations for oil production from Indian leases, especially the major portion requirement. The committee membership includes representatives from Indian tribes, individual Indian mineral owner organizations, minerals industry representatives, and other federal agencies. On June 19, 2014, ONRR published the draft rule in the Federal Register; the final rule is effective July 1, 2015.

The ONRR civil penalties program is a tool ONRR uses to encourage compliance. ONRR issues civil penalties when companies fail to comply with, or knowingly violate, applicable regulations or laws. For administrative violations, ONRR works with the offender to correct the action. However, knowingly violating and refusing to take corrective action will earn a company a civil penalty, as authorized by the Federal Oil and Gas Royalty Management Act of 1982. Some violations are also crimes under Title 18 U.S.C. or under the False Claims Act. ONRR works in partnership with the department's Office of the Inspector General and the U.S. Attorney's Office in pursuing these violations.

In 2012 ONRR promulgated regulations to establish procedures governing collection of delinquent royalties, rentals, bonuses, and other amounts due under leases and other agreements for the production of oil, natural gas, coal, geothermal energy, other minerals, and renewable energy from federal lands onshore, Indian tribal and allotted lands, and the Outer Continental Shelf.

KEY PERSONNEL

Director
    Gregory (Greg) J. Gould. . . . . (202) 208–3415
Audit and Compliance Management
    Theresa Walsh Bayani. . . . . (303) 231–3701
Congressional Liaison
    Anita Gonzalez-Evans . . . . (202) 513–0607

Media Contact
    Pat Etchart . . . . (303) 231–3162
Royalty Policy Committee, Program Analyst
    Shirley Conway . . . . (202) 254–5554
        E-mail: Shirley.Conway@onrr.gov
        Internet: www.onrr.gov/Laws_R_D/RoyPC/
        default.htm

▪ INFORMATION SOURCES

Internet
Agency website: www.onrr.gov.

Telephone Contacts
    Information. . . . .(303) 231–3162
    Federal Relay Service TTY . . . .(800) 877–8339

Information and Publications

KEY OFFICES
Public Affairs
1849 C St. N.W., MS 4211
Washington, DC 20006
Anita Gonzalez-Evans, (202) 513–0600
Pat Etchart, (303) 231–3162

Freedom of Information
P.O. Box 25165, MS 60541A
Denver, CO 80225–0165
(303) 231–3078
Fax (303) 445–4288
E-mail: onrrfoia@onrr.gov
Clarice Julka, FOIA officer

DATA AND STATISTICS
Detailed state-by-state information on disbursement, lease data, and reported royalty revenues is available on the website or by contacting Public Affairs.

PUBLICATIONS

Handbooks and Manuals
    Internet: www.onrr.gov/FM/Handbooks/default.htm

Reference Resources

LIBRARY

Interior Department
1849 C St. N.W.
Washington, DC 20240
(202) 208–5815
Fax (202) 208–6773
George Franchois, director
Hours: 7:45 a.m. to 5:00 p.m.
Internet: www.doi.gov/library/about/index.cfm
E-mail: library@ios.doi.gov

The ONRR has an electronic reading room (eFOIA) but does not have its own library. Materials on mineral leasing and royalty management are kept in the Interior Department Library, housing over a million volumes and numerous databases.

DOCKETS

Federal dockets are available at www.regulations.gov. (*See appendix for Searching and Commenting on Regulations: Regulations.gov.*)

RULES AND REGULATIONS

MMS rules and regulations were published in the *Code of Federal Regulations*, Title 30, Chapter II, Parts 200–299. Proposed regulations, new final regulations, and updates to the *Code of Federal Regulations* are published in the daily *Federal Register*. (*See appendix for details on how to obtain and use these publications.*) The *Federal Register* and the *Code of Federal Regulations* may also be accessed online at www.archives.gov/federal-register/cfr; this site also provides a link to the federal government's regulatory website at www.regulations.gov (*see appendix*).

■ LEGISLATION

The ONRR administers the following laws in full or in part:

False Claims Act (12 Stat. 696, 31 U.S.C. 3729–3733). Signed by the president March 2, 1863. Knowingly presenting or causing to be presented a false claim for payment or approval by the federal government. Excludes tax fraud.

Submerged Lands Act (43 U.S.C. 1301–1315). Signed by the president May 22, 1953. Granted title to coastal states to the natural resources located within three miles of their coastline. Authorized the federal government to regulate offshore activities for national defense, commerce, international affairs, and navigation. Maintained federal control of the seabed and resources therein of the Outer Continental Shelf beyond state boundaries and authorized leasing by the interior secretary.

Outer Continental Shelf Lands Act of 1953 (43 U.S.C. 1331–1356). Signed by the president Aug. 7, 1953. Defined the Outer Continental Shelf as all submerged lands lying seaward of state coastal waters (three miles offshore) as being under U.S. jurisdiction. Authorized the interior secretary to promulgate regulations to lease the underwater area.

Federal Oil and Gas Royalty Management Act of 1982 (96 Stat. 2447, 30 U.S.C. 1701 note). Signed by the president Jan. 12, 1983. Sought to ensure that all oil and gas originating on public lands and on the Outer Continental Shelf are properly accounted for under the direction of the secretary of the interior.

Outer Continental Shelf Lands Act Amendments of 1985 (100 Stat. 147, 43 U.S.C. 1301 note). Signed by the president April 7, 1986. Mandated that the federal government share with affected coastal states 27 percent of revenues generated from the leasing and development of oil and natural gas resources located within three miles of the state's coastline.

Federal Oil and Gas Royalty Simplification and Fairness Act of 1996 (110 Stat. 1700, 30 U.S.C. 1701 et seq.). Signed by the president Aug. 13, 1996. Amended the Federal Oil and Gas Royalty Management Act of 1982 to revise and expand the guidelines for delegating the collection of oil and gas receipts and related activities to a state upon its request. Excluded Native American lands and privately owned minerals from the purview of this act.

Mineral Revenue Payments Clarification Act of 2000 (114 Stat. 1624, 30 U.S.C. 181 note). Signed by the president Oct. 30, 2000. Amended the Mineral Leasing Act respecting federal oil and gas revenue distributions to prohibit state amounts from being reduced by federal administrative or other costs.

Energy Policy Act of 2005 (119 Stat. 594, 42 U.S.C. 15801 note). Signed by the president Aug. 8, 2005. Established long-range, comprehensive national energy policies. Directed MMS to disburse 25 percent of receipts from geothermal energy production directly to counties where that production occurs.

Gulf of Mexico Energy Security Act of 2006 (120 Stat. 3000, 43 U.S.C. 1331 note). Signed by the president Dec. 20, 2006. Instructed the interior secretary to offer specified areas within the Gulf of Mexico for oil and gas leasing. Placed a moratorium on oil and gas leasing in any area east of the Military Mission Line in the Gulf of Mexico; any area in the Eastern Planning Area that was within 125 miles of the Florida coastline; or areas within 100 miles of the Florida coastline.

Department of the Interior, Environment, and Related Agencies Appropriations Act, 2010 (123 Stat. 2915). Signed by the president Oct. 30, 2009. Directs MMS to collect $10 million for safety and environmental compliance inspections that occur on Outer Continental Shelf oil and gas facilities in the Gulf of Mexico and off the coast of California. The law establishes the fee for inspection activities based on the number of wells per facility.

■ REGIONAL OFFICES

COLORADO

(Handles all disbursement and royalty collection.)
Sixth Ave. and Kipling St.
P.O. Box 25165
Bldg. 85, Denver Federal Center, Suite A-614
Denver, CO 80225
(303) 231–3162
Deborah (Debbie) Gibbs Tschudy, deputy director

NEW MEXICO

(Handles problems with disbursements to local Native American populations.)
Farmington Indian Minerals Office
6251 College Blvd., Suite B
Farmington, NM 87401–1783
(505) 564–7640
(800) 238–2839

OKLAHOMA

Oklahoma City

4013 N.W. Expressway, #230
Oklahoma City, OK 73116–1697
Audit and Compliance (405) 879–6000
State and Indian Outreach (405) 879–6050
(800) 354–7015

Tulsa

1603 S. 101st East Ave., #129
Tulsa, OK 74128–4629
(918) 610–6500

TEXAS

Dallas

4050 Alpha Rd., #420
Farmers Branch, TX 75244–4201
(214) 640–9030

Houston

15109 Heathrow Forest Pkwy., #200
Houston, TX 77032–3843
(281) 987–6800

United States Fish and Wildlife Service

1849 C St. N.W., Washington, DC 20240
Internet: www.fws.gov

The U.S. Fish and Wildlife Service (FWS) was created within the Interior Department by Reorganization Plan No. 3 in 1940. Its predecessor agency, the Bureau of Fisheries, was created in 1871, initially as an independent agency and later within the Department of Commerce. A second agency, the Bureau of Biological Survey, was established in 1885 in the Department of Agriculture. The two bureaus and their functions were transferred to the Department of the Interior in 1939 and were consolidated into one agency in 1940. The FWS is under the jurisdiction of the assistant secretary of the interior for fish, wildlife, and parks.

The service is the lead federal agency for fish and wildlife and is composed of a headquarters staff in Washington, DC, seven regional offices, and field units. FWS manages the 93 million-acre National Wildlife Refuge System of more than 551 National Wildlife Refuges and thousands of small wetlands and other special management areas. Under the fisheries program it also operates seventy National Fish Hatcheries, sixty-five fishery resource offices, and ecological services field stations throughout the United States. FWS enforces wildlife laws through a nationwide network of wildlife law enforcement agents.

The service is responsible for conservation and management of fish and wildlife resources and their habitats, including migratory birds, endangered species, certain marine mammals, and fresh water and anadromous fisheries. It regulates hunting of migratory birds and preserves wetlands for waterfowl and other species within the National Wildlife Refuge System.

The FWS Division of Law Enforcement focuses on potentially devastating threats to wildlife resources—illegal trade, unlawful commercial exploitation, habitat destruction, and environmental contaminants. The division investigates wildlife crimes, regulates wildlife trade, and works in partnership with international, state, and tribal counterparts to conserve wildlife resources.

In 1993 some of the research, monitoring, and information transfer programs of the service were consolidated in a new nonregulatory Interior Department bureau, the National Biological Survey (NBS). Subsequently renamed the National Biological Service, the NBS was transferred to the U.S. Geological Survey in 1996.

The United States is a signatory of the Convention of International Trade in Endangered Species of Wild Fauna and Flora (CITES), a treaty among party nations dedicated to protecting endangered fish, wildlife, and plants from commercial exploitation and illegal global trade. The Office of Law Enforcement of the FWS administers CITES through the Endangered Species Act. In 2007 FWS announced it would be publishing the first major update and compilation of regulations implementing the CITES since 1977; the regulations became effective Sept. 24, 2007. The office also enforces the Lacey Act, which makes it unlawful to sell any wildlife taken, possessed, transported, or sold in violation of any law, treaty, or regulation of the United States.

An amendment to the Credit Card Accountability Responsibility and Disclosure Act of 2009 contained a provision that allows an individual to lawfully possess a firearm within the boundaries of a National Wildlife Refuge and in the National Park System in accordance with federal, state, and local firearms laws. The law repealed Interior Department regulations that had previously prohibited firearms in these areas. Similarly, the 2015 omnibus appropriations bill contained a rider that prohibits the U.S. Fish and Wildlife Service from writing and issuing rules related to sage grouse. FWS was in the process of finalizing ESA protections for the bird.

The FWS Fire Management division is one of five federal agencies that fight wildfires in cooperation with state agencies and local fire departments. The other federal agencies are the Agriculture Department's Forest Service (p. 519) and the Interior Department's Bureau of Indian Affairs (p. 689), Bureau of Land Management (p. 695), and National Park Service (p. 723).

◼ KEY PERSONNEL

Assistant Secretary for Fish, Wildlife, and Parks
Rachel Jacobson (acting) . . . . (202) 208–5347
Deputy Assistant Secretary
Michael Bean . . . . (202) 208–4416
Director
Daniel (Dan) M. Ashe . . . . (202) 208–4717
Fax. . . . . (202) 208–6965
Deputy Director of Policy
Steve Guertin . . . . (202) 208–4545

Deputy Director of Operations
Jim Kurth . . . . (202) 208–4545
Solicitor (Interior Dept.)
Hilary Tompkins . . . . (202) 208–4423
Assistant Solicitor for Fish and Wildlife
Vacant . . . . (202) 208–6172
Budget, Planning, and Human Capital
Denise Sheehan . . . . (703) 358–2400
Congressional and Legislative Affairs
Martin Kodis . . . . (703) 358–2243
Duck Stamp Office
Laurie Shaffer . . . . (703) 358–1784
E-mail: laurie_shaffer@fws.gov
E-mail: duckstamps@fws.gov
Ecological Services
Gary Frazer . . . . (202) 358–2171
Endangered Species
Gary Frazer . . . . (202) 208–4646
External Affairs
Betsy Hildebrandt . . . . (202) 208–3971
Fish and Aquatic Conservation
David Hoskins . . . . (202) 208–3517
In Arlington, Va. . . . . (703) 358–1829
International Affairs
Bryan Arroyo . . . . (202) 208–6394
Law Enforcement
William C. Woody . . . . (703) 358–1949
Migratory Birds
Jerome Ford . . . . (202) 208–1050
National Wildlife Refuge System
Cynthia Martinez . . . . (202) 208–5333
Policies, Permits, and Regulations
George T. Allen . . . . (703) 358–1825
Science Applications
Paul Souza . . . . (202) 208–3884
Wildlife and Sport Fish Restoration Programs
Hannibal Bolton . . . . (703) 208–7337
E-mail: Hannibal_Bolton@fws.gov

▦ INFORMATION SOURCES

Internet
Agency website: www.fws.gov. Features the mission of the service, locations of offices, and information on activities nationwide.

Telephone Contacts
Personnel Locator . . . .(800) 344–WILD; (9453)
Federal Relay Service TTY . . . .(800) 877–8339

Information and Publications

KEY OFFICES

FWS Division of Communications
5275 Leesburg Pike
Falls Church, VA
(703) 358–2220
Gavin Shire, chief of communications

(703) 358–2649
E-mail: gavin_shire@fws.gov

Answers questions for the press and the public, distributes publications and photographs, and issues news releases. Provides information on public use of wildlife refuges and fish hatcheries; also issues information on the annual Duck Stamp art competition and annual migratory bird hunting regulations.

FWS Conservation Library
Publications Unit
National Conservation Training Center
698 Conservation Way
Shepherdstown, WV 25443–9713
(304) 876–7263
Anne Post, director
Internet: www.library.fws.gov
E-mail: library@fws.gov

Distributes scientific and technical reports, refuge leaflets, and general interest materials. These materials are also available on the website, as are Resources for Environmental Educators, the National Digital Library, and the NCTC Image Library. Technical reports are available from the National Technical Information Service (NTIS) at www.ntis.gov (*see appendix for ordering NTIS publications*).

DATA AND STATISTICS
FWS Public Affairs maintains data and statistics on topics including endangered and threatened wildlife and plants; hunting and fishing license sales by the states; federal aid for fish and wildlife restoration; and results of National Survey of Fishing, Hunting, and Wildlife Associated Recreation.

PUBLICATIONS
A large collection of reports, books, journals, newsletters, and posters is available from the FWS Publications Unit at http://nctc.fws.gov/resources/knowledge-resources (or by calling (800) 344–WILD) including:
Annals of Botany (journal)
Careers
Conserving the Nature of America
Contaminated Military Sites on Refuges of Southwestern Alaska (poster)
The Duck Stamp Story
Endangered and Threatened Wildlife and Plants
Facts about Federal Wildlife Laws
50 Years Restoring America's Wildlife
Fish and Wildlife News
Freshwater Mussels: America's Hidden Treasure
Marine Ornithology
Pollination Equation (poster)
Restoring America's Sport Fisheries
Visitor's Guide to the National Wildlife Refuge System
Weird and Wonderful Wildlife (poster)
World of Pollinators (poster)

Reference Resources

LIBRARY

Interior Department
1849 C St. N.W.
Washington, DC 20240
(202) 208–5815
George Franchois, director
Hours: 7:45 a.m. to 5:00 p.m.
Internet: www.doi.gov/library/index.cfm
E-mail: library@ios.doi.gov

DOCKETS

Federal dockets are available at www.regulations.gov.
(*See appendix for Searching and Commenting on Regulations: Regulations.gov.*)

RULES AND REGULATIONS

FWS rules and regulations are published in the *Code of Federal Regulations,* Title 50, Chapter I, Parts 1–199; Title 50, Chapter IV, Parts 400–499. Proposed regulations, new final regulations, and updates to the *Code of Federal Regulations* are published in the daily *Federal Register.* (*See appendix for details on how to obtain and use these publications.*) The *Federal Register* and the *Code of Federal Regulations* may also be accessed online at www.archives .gov/federal-register/cfr; this site also contains a link to the federal government's regulatory website at www.regula tions.gov (*see appendix*).

▓ LEGISLATION

The FWS exercises its authority under:
Lacey Act of 1900 (31 Stat. 187, 16 U.S.C. 667). Signed by the president May 25, 1900. Stated that the duties of the Department of the Interior include conservation, preservation, and restoration of birds and other wildlife.

Migratory Bird Treaty Act (40 Stat. 755, 16 U.S.C. 703). Signed by the president July 3, 1918. Implemented the 1916 Convention between the U.S. and Great Britain (for Canada) for the protection of migratory birds, thereby establishing a federal responsibility for protection of this natural resource.

Migratory Bird Conservation Act (45 Stat. 1222, 16 U.S.C. 715). Signed by the president Feb. 28, 1929. Implemented treaties between the United States and other countries for the protection of migratory birds.

Fish and Wildlife Coordination Act (48 Stat. 401, 16 U.S.C. 661). Signed by the president March 10, 1934. Authorized the secretary of the interior to assist federal, state, and other agencies in development, protection, rearing, and stocking fish and wildlife on federal lands, and to study effects of pollution on fish and wildlife.

Migratory Bird Hunting and Conservation Stamp Act (48 Stat. 452, 16 U.S.C. 718). Signed by the president March 16, 1934. Also known as the Duck Stamp Act. Required waterfowl hunters to have a valid federal hunting stamp.

Refuge Revenue Sharing Act (49 Stat. 383, 16 U.S.C. 715). Signed by the president June 15, 1935. Established

the procedure for sharing with counties the revenue derived from sales of products from refuges located within the counties.

Federal Aid in Wildlife Restoration Act (50 Stat. 917, 16 U.S.C. 699). Signed by the president Sept. 2, 1937. Provided federal aid to states for game restoration work.

Bald Eagle Protection Act (54 Stat. 250, 16 U.S.C. 668). Signed by the president June 8, 1940. Provided for the protection of bald eagles and golden eagles by prohibiting, except under specified conditions, the taking, possession of, and commerce in such birds.

Federal Aid in Sport Fish Restoration Act (64 Stat. 430, 16 U.S.C. 777). Signed by the president Aug. 9, 1950. Provided federal aid to the states for management and restoration of sport fish.

Fish and Wildlife Act of 1956 (70 Stat. 1119, 16 U.S.C. 742). Signed by the president Aug. 8, 1956. Established a comprehensive national fish and wildlife policy; directed a program of continuing research, extension, and information services on fish and wildlife.

Sikes Act (74 Stat. 1052, 16 U.S.C. 670a-o). Signed by the president Sept. 15, 1960. Provided for cooperation by the Interior and Defense Departments with state agencies in planning, development, and maintenance of fish and wildlife resources on military reservations throughout the United States.

Refuge Recreation Act (76 Stat. 653, 16 U.S.C. 460). Signed by the president Sept. 28, 1962. Permitted recreational use of refuges, hatcheries, and other conservation areas when such use does not interfere with the area's primary purpose.

Anadromous Fish Conservation Act (79 Stat. 1125, 16 U.S.C. 757). Signed by the president Oct. 30, 1965. Authorized the secretaries of commerce and the interior to enter into agreements with the states and other interests for conservation, development, and enhancement of anadromous fish.

National Wildlife Refuge System Administration Act of 1966 (80 Stat. 927, 16 U.S.C. 668). Signed by the president Oct. 15, 1966. Provided guidelines and directives for administration and management of all areas in the National Wildlife Refuge System.

National Environmental Policy Act of 1969 (83 Stat. 852, 42 U.S.C. 4321). Signed by the president Jan. 1, 1969. Established a broad national environmental policy and required that federal agencies provide environmental impact statements regarding any major federal action or legislative proposal.

Marine Mammal Protection Act of 1972 (86 Stat. 1027, 16 U.S.C. 1361). Signed by the president Oct. 21, 1972. Established a federal responsibility for conservation of marine mammals and vested in the Department of the Interior responsibility for management of certain animals.

Endangered Species Act of 1973 (87 Stat. 884, 16 U.S.C. 1531). Signed by the president Dec. 28, 1973. Provided for the conservation of threatened and endangered species of fish, wildlife, and plants by federal action and establishment of state programs.

Executive Order 11987. Issued by the president May 24, 1977. Required federal agencies to restrict the introduction of exotic species into the natural ecosystems on lands and waters owned or leased by the United States. Encouraged states, local governments, and private citizens to prevent the introduction of exotic species into U.S. ecosystems.

Fish and Wildlife Improvement Act of 1978 (92 Stat. 3110, 16 U.S.C. 7421). Signed by the president Nov. 8, 1978. Authorized establishment of a law enforcement training program for state fish and wildlife law enforcement personnel and research to improve enforcement.

Fish and Wildlife Conservation Act of 1980 (94 Stat. 1322, 16 U.S.C. 2901). Signed by the president Sept. 29, 1980. Provided federal aid to the states for the management and restoration of nongame species.

Alaska National Interest Lands Conservation Act of 1980 (94 Stat. 2371, 16 U.S.C. 3101 note). Signed by the president Dec. 2, 1980. Designated certain public lands in Alaska as units of the national park, national wildlife refuges, wild and scenic rivers, national wilderness preservation, and national forest systems.

National Fish and Wildlife Foundation Establishment Act (98 Stat. 107, 16 U.S.C. 3701). Signed by the president March 26, 1984. Established the National Fish and Wildlife Foundation to encourage and administer donations of real or personal property in connection with fish and wildlife programs and activities in the United States.

North American Wetlands Conservation Act (103 Stat. 1968; 16 U.S.C. 4401–4412). Signed by the president Dec. 13, 1989. Implemented the North American Waterfowl Management Plan and the Tripartite Agreement on wetlands between the United States, Canada, and Mexico.

Coastal Barrier Improvement Act of 1990 (104 Stat. 2931, 16 U.S.C. 3501 note). Signed by the president Nov. 16, 1990. Added 700,000 acres along the Atlantic and Gulf coasts, Great Lakes shores, Florida Keys, Puerto Rico, and Virgin Islands to the national barrier island system. Established mechanisms to allow states and localities to bring coastal areas into the system for protection.

Nonindigenous Aquatic Nuisance Prevention and Control Act of 1990 (104 Stat. 4761, 16 U.S.C. 4701 note). Signed by the president Nov. 29, 1990. Established a program to monitor and control the spread of introduced aquatic nuisance species such as the zebra mussel in the Great Lakes.

Coastal Wetlands Planning, Protection, and Restoration Act (104 Stat. 4761, 16 U.S.C. 3953). Signed by the president Nov. 29, 1990. Established a conservation and restoration program for Louisiana coastal wetlands. Authorized a national program matching grants for state wetlands conservation projects.

Wild Bird Conservation Act of 1992 (106 Stat. 2224, 16 U.S.C. 4901 note). Signed by the president Oct. 23, 1992. Established a federal system to limit or prohibit the importation of endangered exotic wild birds.

Rhinoceros and Tiger Conservation Act of 1994 (108 Stat. 4094, 16 U.S.C. 5306). Signed by the president Oct. 22, 1994. Prohibited the sale, import, or export of any product derived from any species of rhinoceros or tiger. Established the Rhinoceros and Tiger Conservation Fund.

Executive Order 12996: Management and General Public Use of the National Wildlife Refuge System. Issued by the president March 25, 1996. Established guiding principles to help ensure the long-term sustainability of the National Wildlife Refuge System. Directed the interior secretary to recognize compatible wildlife-dependent recreational activities involving hunting, fishing, wildlife observation and photography, and environmental education as priority general public uses in the refuge system.

National Wildlife Refuge System Improvement Act of 1997 (111 Stat. 1252, 16 U.S.C. 668dd note). Signed by the president Oct. 9, 1997. Amended the National Wildlife Refuge System Administration Act of 1966 to reinforce the National Wildlife Refuge System's authority to administer the national networks of lands and waters under its protection. Recognized and supported wildlife-dependent recreation.

Migratory Bird Treaty Reform Act of 1998 (112 Stat. 2956, 16 U.S.C. 710 note). Signed by the president Oct. 30, 1998. Amended the Migratory Bird Treaty Act to make it unlawful for persons to take migratory birds with the aid of baiting.

Marine Turtle Conservation Act of 2004 (118 Stat. 791, 16 U.S.C. 6601 note). Signed by the president July 2, 2004. Authorized projects that help recover and sustain viable populations of marine turtles in the wild by assisting conservation programs in foreign countries. Established the Marine Turtle Conservation Fund.

Credit Card Accountability Responsibility and Disclosure Act of 2009 (123 Stat. 1765). Signed by the president May 22, 2009. Sec. 512 prohibits the secretary of the interior from promulgating or enforcing any regulation that prohibits an individual from possessing a firearm, including an assembled or functional firearm, in any unit of the National Park System (NPS) or the National Wildlife Refuge System (NWRS) if (1) the individual is not otherwise prohibited by law from possessing the firearm; and (2) the possession of the firearm complies with the law of the state in which the NPS or NWRS unit is located.

Consolidated and Further Continuing Appropriations Act, 2015 (Public Law 113-235). Signed by the president Dec. 16, 2014. Section 122 prohibits the U.S. Fish and Wildlife Service from writing and issuing rules related to sage-grouse.

▪ REGIONAL OFFICES

REGION 1

(AS, HI, ID, MP, PI, OR, WA)
911 N.E. 11th Ave.
Portland, OR 97232–4181
(503) 231–6120
Internet: www.fws.gov/pacific
Robyn Thorson, regional director
(503) 231–6118

REGION 2

(AZ, NM, OK, TX)
500 Gold Ave. S.W., #8016
Albuquerque, NM 87102

Mailing address:
P.O. Box 1306
Albuquerque, NM 87103–1306
(505) 248–6888
Internet: www.fws.gov/southwest
E-mail: RDTuggle@fws.gov
Benjamin N. Tuggle, regional director
(505) 248–6282

REGION 3

(IA, IL, IN, MI, MN, MO, OH, WI)
5600 American Blvd. West, #990
Bloomington MN 55437–1458
(612) 713–5360
Internet: www.fws.gov/midwest
Tom Melius, regional director
(612) 713–5301

REGION 4

(AL, AR, FL, GA, KY, LA, MS, NC, PR, SC, TN, VI)
1875 Century Blvd., #400
Atlanta, GA 30345
(404) 679–7397
Internet: www.fws.gov/southeast
Cynthia (Cindy) Dohner, regional director
(404) 679–4000

REGION 5

(CT, DC, DE, MA, MD, ME, NH, NJ, NY, PA,
    RI, VA, VT, WV)
300 Westgate Center Dr.
Hadley, MA 01035–9589
(413) 253–8402
Internet: www.fws.gov/northeast

E-mail: northeast@fws.gov
Wendi Weber, regional director
(413) 253–8300

REGION 6

(CO, KS, MT, ND, NE, SD, UT, WY)
134 Union Blvd., #400
Lakewood, CO 80228
Mailing Address:
P.O. Box 25486 DFC
Denver, CO 80225
(303) 236–7920
Internet: www.fws.gov/mountain-prairie
E-mail: mountainprairie@fws.gov
Noreen Walsh, regional director
(303) 236–7905

REGION 7

(AK)
1011 E. Tudor Rd., MS 235
Anchorage, AK 99503
(907) 786–3309
Internet: www.fws.gov/alaska
Geoffrey Haskett, regional director
(907) 786–3542

REGION 8

(CA, NV, Oregon's Klamath Basin)
2800 Cottage Way, W-2606
Sacramento, CA 95825
(916) 414–6464
Internet: www.fws.gov/cno
Ren Lohoefener, regional director
Alexandra Pitts, deputy regional director

United States Geological Survey

National Center, 12201 Sunrise Valley Dr., Reston, VA 20192
Internet: www.usgs.gov

The U.S. Geological Survey (USGS) was established in the Interior Department by the Act of March 3, 1879, which provided for "the classification of the public lands and the examination of the geological structure, mineral resources, and products of the national domain." Authorization was expanded in 1962 to include activities outside the limits of the United States.

With headquarters staffed in Reston, VA, other offices include seven regional centers; water resources offices in fifty states, Puerto Rico, the Virgin Islands, and Guam; and various science and research centers. The USGS operates under the jurisdiction of the assistant secretary of the interior for water and science.

The objectives of the USGS are to perform surveys, investigations, and research covering topography, geology, the identification of potential natural hazards (such as earthquakes and landslides), the mineral, water, and energy resources of the United States, water quality assessment, and water use.

The USGS prepares and publishes reports and maps, including topographic, orthophoto, geologic, geospatial, and mineral resource maps and various databases related to cartography and the earth sciences. The survey cooperates with other agencies in researching mineral and water resources and other earth science activities.

In October 1996 the USGS absorbed the National Biological Service (NBS), a nonregulatory Interior Department bureau that was created in 1993 as the National Biological Survey. It was renamed the Biological Resources division (BRD) of the USGS and continued to perform the same research, monitoring, and information transfer programs that it was charged with as a separate agency. In 2010 BRD was absorbed into other mission areas at USGS. Realignment at USGS established the Ecosystems Mission Area, which comprised the Fisheries, Wildlife, Status and Trends, Environments and Invasive Species Programs, and the Cooperative Research Units, all former programs of the BRD. Contaminant Biology moved to the Environmental Health Mission Area. Biological Information Management and Delivery moved to the Core Science Systems Mission Area. Other key divisions include Climate and Land-Use Change, Water, Natural Hazards, and Energy and Minerals.

■ KEY PERSONNEL

Assistant Secretary for Water and Science
Anne Castle . . . . (202) 208–3186
Deputy Assistant Secretary
Jennifer Gimbal . . . . (202) 208–3186
Solicitor (Interior Dept.)
Hilary Tompkins . . . . (202) 208–4423
Director
Suzette M. Kimball (acting) . . . . (703) 648–7412
    Fax . . . . (703) 648–4454
    E-mail: suzette_kimball@usgs.gov
Deputy Director
Mark Sogge (acting) . . . . (703) 648–7411
    E-mail: mark_sogge@usgs.gov
Budget, Planning, and Integration
Cynthia Lodge . . . . (703) 648–4430
Climate and Land-Use Change
Doug Beard (acting) . . . . (703) 648–4215
    E-mail: dbeard@usgs.gov
Congressional Liaison Officer
Timothy J. West . . . . (703) 648–4300/4455
    E-mail: twest@usgs.gov
Core Science Systems
Kevin Gallagher . . . . (703) 648–5747
    E-mail: kgallagher@usgs.gov
Diversity and Equal Opportunity
Jim Mays (acting) . . . . (703) 648–7787
    E-mail: jmmays@usgs.gov
Energy and Minerals, and Environmental Health
Geoffrey Plumlee (acting) . . . . (703) 648–7419
    E-mail: gplumlee@usgs.gov
Environmental Health
Geoffrey Plumlee (acting) . . . . (703) 648–7419
    E-mail: gplumlee@usgs.gov
Ecosystems
Anne Kinsinger . . . . (703) 648–4051
    E-mail: akinsinger@usgs.gov
International Programs
Vic Labson . . . . (703) 648–6206
    E-mail: vlabson@usgs.gov
Natural Hazards
David Applegate . . . . (703) 648–6600
    E-mail: applegate@usgs.gov

Science Quality and Integrity
Alan Thornhill. . . . . (703) 648–6601
E-mail: athornhill@usgs.gov

Water
William Werkheiser . . . . (703) 648–4557
E-mail: whwerkhe@usgs.gov

▌ INFORMATION SOURCES

Internet

Agency website: www.usgs.gov. Includes fact sheets, selected data and publications, and information on ordering products. The USGS library and access to its publications may be reached at http://library.usgs. gov ("www" should not be used to reach this site). The USGS Electronic Reading Room, at www.usgs.gov/foia, also contains many documents, reports, and manuals. USGS maps, photos, atlases, and earth science data are available on the website as well as information on recent earthquakes, volcanic hazard areas, water resources, and geographic place names, at www.usgs.gov/pubprod/ data.html. The USGS's National Map website also contains more than 200,000 topographic maps, including historical maps dating back to 1884, as well as information about the geospatial mapping program, at http:// nationalmap.gov.

Telephone Contacts

Personnel Locator . . . . (202) 208–3100
Information, Map Orders,
    and Publications . . . . (888) ASK–USGS
Fax-on-Demand . . . . (703) 648–4888
Federal Relay Service TTY . . . . (800) 877–8339

Information and Publications

KEY OFFICES

USGS Office of Communications and Publishing
12201 Sunrise Valley Dr.
MS 119
Reston, VA 20192–0002
(703) 648–5750
E-mail: bwainman@usgs.gov
Barbara W. Wainman, director

Public Affairs Office
12201 Sunrise Valley Dr.
MS 119
Reston, VA 20192–0002
(703) 648–4460
E-mail: abwade@usgs.gov
Anne-Berry Wade, public affairs officer
(703) 648–4483

Prepares news releases, feature articles, and related visual material describing the survey's activities. Maintains a mailing list.

Freedom of Information
12201 Sunrise Valley Dr.
MS 807
Reston, VA 20192–0002
FOIA Requester Service Center
(703) 648–7197
E-mail: foia@usgs.gov
Brian May, FOIA public liaison
(443) 498–5521

DATA AND STATISTICS

Earth Resources Observation and Science (EROS) Data Center
47914 252nd St.
Sioux Falls, SD 57198–0001
(605) 594–6151; (800) 252–4547
Frank Kelly, director
Barbara Morrison, ABS and Facilities contact for
    director
(605) 594–6090
E-mail: bmorrison@usgs.gov
John Hahn, deputy director

Receives, processes, and distributes remote sensing data acquired by satellite and aircraft. Conducts and sponsors research to apply data findings in areas including mapping, geography, mineral and land resources, water resources, and environmental monitoring. For more information, visit the Internet home page at http://eros.usgs.gov.

National Earthquake Information Center (NEIC)
1711 Illinois St.
Golden, CO 80401
Mailing Address:
Box 25046, DFC, MS 966
Denver, CO 80225–0046
(303) 273–8500 (24 hours)
Fax (303) 273–8600
Internet: www.earthquake.usgs.gov
Jill McCarthy, chief scientist
(303) 273–8595

Provides information on earthquakes and earthquake-locating technology to the media, disaster agencies, research scientists, and the public. The National Earthquake Information Center is part of the Advanced National Seismic System, which also includes the Rapid Response Program. For more information, visit the Internet home page at http://earthquake.usgs.gov.

PUBLICATIONS
Technical and scientific reports and maps are listed in the permanent catalogues, *Publications of the Geological Survey.* Volumes cover 1879–1961, 1962–1970, 1971–1981, and 1981–2000, annually. More recent publications from the USGS can be found in New Publications of the United States Geological Survey at www.usgs.gov/ pubprod/index.html.

These reports and maps are available by calling 1-888-ASK-USGS and on the USGS website. In addition, USGS's National Map website contains more than 200,000 topographical maps, including historical maps dating from 1884, at http://nationalmap.gov. The USGS Library also offers publications at its website: http://library.usgs.gov.

Reference Resources

LIBRARY

USGS Science Information and Library Center
12201 Sunrise Valley Dr.
MS 950
Reston, VA 20192–0002
(703) 648–4302
(888) ASK-USGS (option # 5)
Brenda Graff and Bruce Wallace, reference/
   information team
Hours: 8:00 a.m. to 4:00 p.m.
Internet: http://library.usgs.gov
E-mail: library@usgs.gov
Cate Canevari, director of library services
(703) 648–7182
E-mail: ccanevari@usgs.gov

Facilities for examining reports, maps, field records, photographs, atlases, and publications of the USGS are located here and at the following locations:

Central Region
Denver Federal Center, Bldg. 20
C-2002
Denver, CO 80225
Mailing Address:
Box 25046, MS 914
Denver Federal Center
Denver, CO 80225–0046
(303) 236–1000
E-mail: den_lib@usgs.gov
Keith Van Cleave, branch manager
(303) 236–1004
E-mail: kvancleave@usgs.gov
April Kobayashi and Emily Wild, reference/
   information team
(303) 236–1095/1003

Southwestern Region and Astrogeology Collection
2255 N. Gemini Dr.
Flagstaff, AZ 86001
(928) 556–7008
E-mail: flg_lib@usgs.gov
Donita Polly, reference and circulation librarian
E-mail: dpolly@usgs.gov

Western Region
345 Middlefield Rd.
MS 955
Menlo Park, CA 94025–3591

E-mail: men_lib@usgs.gov
Susie Bravos, reference
(650) 329–5027
E-mail: abravos@usgs.gov
Chuck Wenger, information
(650) 329–5025
E-mail: cwenger@isgs.gov

The USGS Library also maintains its own website with access to numerous publications: http://library.usgs.gov. In addition, more than 200,000 topographic maps of the United States, including historical maps dating back to 1884, are available on The National Map website, at http://nationalmap.gov.

DOCKETS
Federal dockets are available on the website by agency, at http://minerals.usgs.gov/dockets/search.htm, and at www.regulations.gov. (*See appendix for Searching and Commenting on Regulations: Regulations.gov.*)

RULES AND REGULATIONS
USGS rules and regulations are published in the *Code of Federal Regulations,* Title 30, Chapter IV, Part 400–499. Proposed regulations, new final regulations, and updates to the *Code of Federal Regulations* are published in the daily *Federal Register.* (*See appendix for details on how to obtain and use these publications.*) The *Federal Register* and the *Code of Federal Regulations* may be accessed online at www.archives.gov/federal-register/cfr; this site also provides a link to the federal government's regulatory website at www.regulations.gov (*see appendix*).

▪ LEGISLATION
The USGS carries out its responsibilities under:
Act of March 3, 1879, as amended (20 Stat. 394, 43 U.S.C. 31A). Signed by the president March 3, 1879. Established the USGS.
Water Resources Research Act of 1964 (78 Stat. 1, 42 U.S.C. 1961-1961c-7). Signed by the president July 17, 1964. Established a Water Resources Research Institute in each state and Puerto Rico.
Earthquake Hazards Reduction Act of 1977 (91 Stat. 1098, 42 U.S.C. 7701). Signed by the president Oct. 7, 1977. Designed to reduce the risks of life and property from future earthquakes in the United States through the establishment and maintenance of an effective earthquake hazards reduction program.
Alaska National Interest Lands Conservation Act of 1980 (94 Stat. 2371, 16 U.S.C. 3101 note). Signed by the president Dec. 2, 1980. Required that the Geological Survey assess the oil and gas potential of specific federal lands in Alaska and participate in a review of the wilderness characteristics of the area.
Water Resources Research Act of 1984 (98 Stat. 97, 42 U.S.C. 10301). Vetoed by the president Feb. 21, 1984; veto overridden March 22, 1984. Authorized Interior Department grants for water research projects and programs at land grant colleges.

Continental Scientific Drilling and Exploration Act of 1988 (102 Stat. 1760, 43 U.S.C. 31 note). Signed by the president Sept. 22, 1988. Established an interagency program to research the composition, structure, dynamics, and evolution of the continental crust, and how such processes affect natural phenomena such as earthquakes and volcanic eruptions.

National Geologic Mapping Act of 1992 (106 Stat. 166, 43 U.S.C. 31a). Signed by the president May 18, 1992. Established the National Cooperative Geologic Mapping Program. Also established a national geologic map database to be a national archive.

National Geologic Mapping Reauthorization Act of 1997 (111 Stat. 1107, 43 U.S.C. 31a note). Signed by the president Aug. 5, 1997. Amended the National Geologic Mapping Act of 1992 to establish a national cooperative geologic mapping program between the USGS and state geological surveys. Established a geologic mapping advisory committee to advise the director of the USGS on the planning and the implementation of the program.

Omnibus Public Land Management Act of 2009 (123 Stat. 991, 16 U.S.C. 1 note). Signed by the president March 30, 2009. Title XI, United States Geological Survey Authorizations, amended the National Geologic Mapping Act of 1992 to extend deadlines for development of a five-year strategic plan for the geologic mapping program. Modified the advisory committee and required it, at the request of the president or Congress, to provide a report on the quality, utility, and appropriateness of geologic maps intended for federal use.

▨ REGIONAL OFFICES

ALASKA

4210 University Dr.
Anchorage, AK 99508–4626
(907) 786–7055
E-mail: nlee@usgs.gov
Nancy Lee (acting), regional director

MIDWEST AREA

(IA, IL, IN, KY, MI, MN, MO, ND, NE, OH, SD, WI)
1451 Green Rd.
Ann Arbor, MI 48105
(734) 214–7207
E-mail: lcarl@usgs.gov
Leon Carl, regional director

NORTHEAST AREA

(CT, DE, MA, MD, ME, NH, NJ, NY, PA, RI, VA, VT, WV)
12201 Sunrise Valley Dr.
MS 953
Reston, VA 20192
(703) 648–5953
E-mail: mrbennett@usgs.gov
Mark Bennett (acting), regional director
(703) 648–6660

NORTHWEST AREA

(ID, MT, OR, WA, WY)
909 1st Ave., #800
Seattle, WA 98104
(206) 220–4578
E-mail: rferrero@usgs.gov
Rich Ferrero, regional director
(206) 795–4527

PACIFIC

(CA, NV, HI)
Modoc Hall USGS
3020 State University Dr. East, #3005
Sacramento, CA 95819
E-mail: colin@usgs.gov
Colin Williams (acting), regional director
(650) 329–4881

SOUTHEAST AREA

(AL, AR, FL, GA, LA, MS, PR, NC, SC, TN, VI)
1700 Corporate Dr., # 500
Norcross, GA 30093
(678) 924–6609
E-mail: jdweaver@usgs.gov
Jess Weaver, regional director
(303) 236–5440

SOUTHWEST AREA

(AZ, CO, KS, OK, NM, TX, UT)
West 6th Ave. and Kipling St.
DFC Bldg. 25
Lakewood, CO 80225–0046
Mailing address:
P.O. Box 25046
Denver, CO 80225–0046
E-mail: methridge@usgs.gov
Max Ethridge, regional director
(303) 236–5440

Other Interior Department Offices

▨ BUREAU OF RECLAMATION
1849 C St. N.W.
Washington, DC 20240
Internet: www.usbr.gov

In 1902, when Congress authorized "the reclamation of arid and semi-arid lands in the West," the secretary of the interior gave this task to the U.S. Geological Survey (USGS). In 1907 the Reclamation Service (now the Bureau of Reclamation) was separated from the USGS.

The bureau is responsible for water and power resource development protection and management in seventeen western states. Projects include municipal and industrial water services, irrigation water service, hydropower generation, flood control, river regulation, outdoor recreational opportunities, fish and wildlife enhancement, and water quality improvement. Programs are financed both through taxes levied upon direct beneficiaries of these projects and from the Treasury Department's Reclamation Fund.

The bureau's fifty-three power plants annually provide almost 40 billion kilowatt hours generating nearly $1 billion in power revenues and produce enough electricity to serve nearly 3.5 million homes. The bureau is the largest wholesaler of water in the United States, providing water to more than 31 million people, and providing one out of five western farmers with irrigation water for 10 million acres of farmland.

In cooperation with other agencies, the Bureau of Reclamation prepares and reviews environmental impact statements for proposed federal water resource projects and provides technical assistance to foreign countries in water resource development and utilization.

The bureau has offices in six regions in the western United States. The agency's website includes organizational information, searchable databases, law and policy information, and a searchable index.

Information . . . .(202) 208–4215
Commissioner
    Estevan Lopez . . . . (202) 513–0501
        Fax. . . . . (202) 513–0309
Chief of Staff
    Robert Quint . . . . (202) 513–0542
Public Affairs
    Dan DuBray. . . . . (202) 513–0570

Library (Denver Federal Center)
    Dianne H. Powell . . . . (303) 445–2061
        Internet: www.usbr.gov/library
        E-mail: library@usbr.gov

▨ NATIONAL PARK SERVICE
1849 C St. N.W.
Washington, DC 20240
Internet: www.nps.gov

The National Park Service (NPS) was established in the Interior Department in 1916. Its fundamental objective is to conserve the scenery, natural and historic objects, and wildlife in the nation's parks, and to provide for the enjoyment of these resources without impairing them for future generations. The service administers an extensive system of 400 national parks, monuments, historic sites, and recreation areas. It develops park management plans and staffs the areas under its administration with more than 20,000 employees.

The NPS includes more than 84 million acres in forty-nine states, the District of Columbia, American Samoa, Guam, Puerto Rico, Saipan, and the Virgin Islands. The system includes the historic Civil War battlefields on the East Coast; the unique Everglades water park in south Florida; Alaska's Glacier Bay, which is accessible only by boat; the active volcanoes on the island of Hawaii; and the storied parks of Yosemite, Yellowstone, and the Grand Canyon. In total the system attracts 275 million visitors annually.

The service seeks to convey the natural values and the historical significance of these areas to the public through talks, tours, films, exhibits, and publications. It operates campgrounds and other visitor facilities and provides lodging, food, and transportation services in many areas. The service also manages historic preservation and recreation programs.

The Service Center in Denver provides planning, architectural, engineering, and other professional services. A center for production of museum exhibits, audiovisual materials, and publications is located in Harpers Ferry, WV.

The NPS website provides general information on the Park Service, maps and descriptions of specific park properties, and multimedia presentations on park properties and park wildlife. The site also provides resources for school teachers.

Information . . . .(202) 208–3818

Director

Jon Jarvis. . . . . (202) 208–4621

E-mail: jon_jarvis@nps.gov

Public Affairs

April Slayton . . . . (202) 208–4995

Fax. . . . . (202) 219–0910

E-mail: april_slayton@nps.gov

Resources for teachers are available on the Internet at www.nps.gov/teachers

▒ OFFICE OF SURFACE MINING RECLAMATION AND ENFORCEMENT

1951 Constitution Ave. N.W.
Washington, DC 20240
Internet: www.osmre.gov

The Office of Surface Mining Reclamation and Enforcement was established in the Interior Department by the Surface Mining Control and Reclamation Act of 1977 (SMCRA).

Its primary mission is to administer a nationwide program that protects society and the environment from the adverse effects of coal mining operations, set national standards for regulating surface effects of coal mining, and assist states in implementing regulatory programs.

In addition, the Office of Surface Mining Reclamation and Enforcement (OSMRE) supports reclamation of coal mines abandoned prior to the passage of the 1977 act. The Abandoned Mine Land (AML) Reclamation Program is OSMRE's largest program under SMCRA. Since SMCRA's enactment in 1977, the AML program has collected over $10.1 billion in fees from present-day coal production and distributed more than $7.6 billion in grants to states and tribes, mandatory distributions to the United Mine Workers of America (UMWA) and OSMRE's operation of the national program to reclaim land and waters damaged by coal mining before the law's passage.

The responsibilities of the office are carried out through monitoring the activities of coal-producing states and providing technical support and research capabilities.

The headquarters are in Washington, DC, with regional offices in Pittsburgh, PA; Alton, IL; and Denver, CO; and field offices in coal-producing states.

The agency's website includes news releases, information on the environment and citizen involvement, and lists of state and federal regulations. Each region has an individual website.

Director

Joseph Pizarchik . . . . (202) 208–4006

E-mail: Director_Pizarchik@osmre.gov

Fax. . . . . (202) 219–3106

Communications

Cynthia Johnson (acting). . . . . (202) 208–2730

E-mail: cjohnson@osmre.gov

TTY. . . . . (202) 208–2694

AML regulatory (Title V) programs (abandoned mine lands) contact information is available on the Internet at www.osmre.gov/programs/AML.

Justice Department

10th St. and Constitution Ave. N.W., Washington, DC 20530
Internet: www.justice.gov

_____

Antitrust Division

950 Pennsylvania Ave. N.W., Washington, DC 20530
Internet: www.usdoj.gov/atr

The Antitrust Division, a unit within the Justice Department, is headed by the assistant attorney general for antitrust, who is responsible for investigating and prosecuting cases under federal antitrust laws.

Many actions that restrain and monopolize trade or reduce competition are violations of antitrust laws. Enforcement activities of the division include investigating possible antitrust violations by the civil investigative process and by conducting grand jury proceedings, preparing and prosecuting antitrust cases, prosecuting appeals, and negotiating and enforcing final judgments. Two major areas of enforcement activity are (1) investigation, detection, and criminal prosecution of price fixing; and (2) investigation and civil litigation to prevent anticompetitive mergers and bid rigging.

The division represents the United States in judicial proceedings to review certain orders of the Federal Communications Commission (FCC) (*p. 122*), the Federal Maritime Commission (*p. 419*), and the Nuclear Regulatory Commission (*p. 437*).

The Antitrust Division serves as the administration's principal authority for competition policy in regulated industries and advises government departments and agencies on the competitive implications of their policies. From time to time the division participates in regulatory proceedings involving competition in transportation, energy, agriculture, communication, banking, health care, and professional and occupational licensing.

In certain circumstances, and at the written request of interested parties, the division reviews proposed private business plans and offers a statement of its enforcement intentions under the antitrust law with regard to the proposed conduct.

The Antitrust Division provides guidance to the business community, much of it jointly with the Federal Trade Commission (*p. 239*). This guidance includes new and subsequently revised and expanded joint statements of policy regarding the health care industry, the licensing of intellectual property, international operations, and an accelerated individual business review process.

Staff members of the Antitrust Division participate in interagency committees on government trade policy. The division represents the United States on the Competition Committee of the Organisation for Economic Co-operation and Development (OECD) and the International Competition Network. It also maintains, through the State Department, a liaison with foreign governments on antitrust enforcement matters that have an impact on trade with other nations. The website features links to foreign antitrust enforcement agencies.

In 1993 the Antitrust Division implemented a Corporate Leniency Policy under which a corporation can avoid criminal prosecution for antitrust violations by confessing its role in the illegal activities, fully cooperating with the division, and meeting other specified conditions. In 1994 the division also implemented a Leniency Policy for Individuals under which persons who approach the division on their own behalf, not as part of a corporate proffer or confession, may seek leniency for reporting illegal antitrust activity of which the division has not previously been made aware. In 2004 the Antitrust Criminal Penalty Enhancement and Reform Act of 2004 encouraged corporations to report illegal conduct by limiting the damages recoverable from a corporate amnesty applicant that also cooperates with private plaintiffs in their damage actions against remaining cartel members. The Antitrust Division's Leniency Program remains its most important investigative tool for detecting cartel activity.

In May 1998, in one of the most noted antitrust cases in years, the department and attorneys general for nineteen states plus the District of Columbia filed suit against Microsoft, alleging the software giant had violated the Sherman Antitrust Act. After lengthy legal proceedings and unsuccessful mediation efforts, a federal district court judge in April 2000 held that Microsoft had engaged in a series of anticompetitive acts to protect and maintain its Windows operating system monopoly and to monopolize the market for Web browsers and other "middleware" software products. The court ordered Microsoft to submit a plan to reorganize itself into two separate firms: an operating system business and an applications business.

In 2001 a federal appeals court overturned the breakup order but still ruled that Microsoft was an illegal monopoly. The software giant then cut a deal with the Justice Department in 2002. Under the agreement, Microsoft remained whole in exchange for lifting license restrictions on its operating system, which would allow Microsoft competitors to gain more equal footing within the software market. In May 2011 the division announced that the measures taken by Microsoft had satisfactorily addressed the issues and the final judgment was expired.

Anticompetitive conduct by criminal cartels such as price fixing, bid rigging, and procurement fraud remains the highest enforcement priority of the division. Under the administration of President Barack Obama, the Antitrust Division saw a significant increase in the criminal penalties assessed. Between 2009 and 2014 the division topped more than $1 billion in fines. The average prison sentence increased more than three-fold, from eight months to twenty-five months.

In 2011 the division announced fines and prison sentences for auto parts manufacturing executives for bid-rigging and price fixing. This was the beginning of the most extensive criminal investigation in the Antitrust Division's history. By the beginning of 2015, thirty executives and thirty-five corporations had pleaded guilty or agreed to do so and to pay more than $2.5 billion in criminal fines.

The Antitrust Division pursues legal action against companies that conspire to limit employment competition among workers. In late 2012 the department filed a civil antitrust lawsuit against eBay, alleging that it violated antitrust laws by entering into an agreement not to recruit or hire Intuit's employees, asserting that the agreement eliminated a significant form of competition to the detriment of affected employees who were likely deprived of access to better job opportunities and salaries. The suit sought to prevent eBay from enforcing the agreement and from entering into any similar agreements with any other companies. Intuit had already settled a similar case with the department. Several other tech companies, including Adobe, Apple, Google, Intel, and Pixar, had settled similar cases with the department prior to the suit against eBay.

The Antitrust Division is an active participant in the Financial Fraud Enforcement Task Force. President Barack Obama established the Financial Fraud Enforcement Task Force in November 2009 to pursue legal action against individuals and organizations whose illegal activity contributed to the financial crisis as well as those who would attempt to fraudulently take advantage of economic recovery efforts. The task force is chaired by the attorney general and is comprised of a coalition of law enforcement, investigatory, and regulatory agencies. More than twenty federal agencies, ninety-four U.S. Attorneys Offices, and state and local partners participate in an effort to combat fraud.

▓ KEY PERSONNEL

Assistant Attorney General
William J. Baer................... (202) 514–2401
Fax.......................... (202) 616–2645
General E-mail: antitrust.atr@usdoj.gov
Operations
Patricia Brink................. (202) 514–2562
Executive Office
Thomas D. King .... (202) 514–4005
Deputy Assistant Attorneys General
for Civil Enforcement
Leslie Overton................... (202) 353–4651

Renata Hesse .... (202) 353–1535
Networks and Technology Enforcement
James J. Tierney............... (202) 307–6640
Telecommunications and Media Enforcement
Scott A. Scheele................ (202) 616–5924
Fax........................ (202) 514–0306
Transportation, Energy, and Agriculture
William H. Stallings .... (202) 514–9323
Litigation I
Peter J. Mucchetti .... (202) 307–0001
Litigation II
Maribeth Petrizzi .... (202) 307–0924
Litigation III
David C. Kully................. (202) 305–9969
Deputy Assistant Attorney General for Criminal Enforcement
Brent C. Snyder .... (202) 514–3543
Fax........................... (202) 307–9978
Deputy Assistant Attorney General for Economic Analysis
Nancy L. Rose .... (202) 514–0163
Competition Policy and Intergovernmental Relations
Caroline N. Holland............ (202) 307–6603
Economic Litigation
Norman Familant .... (202) 307–6323
Economic Regulatory Section
Elizabeth Armington .... (202) 307–6332
Appellate
James J. Fredericks .... (202) 514–2886
Foreign Commerce
Edward T. Hand .... (202) 514–2464
Legal Policy
Robert A. Potter .... (202) 514–2512

▓ INFORMATION SOURCES

Internet
Agency website: www.justice.gov/atr. The site contains updated information on the most recent antitrust news or issues.

Telephone Contacts
Justice Dept. Switchboard...........(202) 514–2000
Personnel Locator ....(202) 514–2469
Federal Relay Service TTY ....(800) 877–8339

Information and Publications

KEY OFFICES

Freedom of Information
Antitrust Division
Liberty Square Bldg.
450 Fifth St. N.W., #1000
Washington, DC 20530–0001
(202) 514–2692
Fax (202) 616–4529
E-mail: antitrust.foia@usdoj.gov
Sue Ann Slates, FOIA officer

Antitrust Documents Group

Antitrust Division
450 5th St. N.W.
Washington, DC 20530
(202) 514–2481
Fax (202) 514–3763
E-mail: atrdocs.grp@usdoj.gov
Janie Ingalls, contact

Provides Antitrust Division publications, which are also available on the website.

DOJ Public Affairs

950 Pennsylvania Ave. N.W., #1220
Washington, DC 20530
(202) 514–2007
Fax (202) 514–5331

Maintains an e-mail list for antitrust issues.

PUBLICATIONS

Contact the Antitrust Division's Antitrust Documents Group; publications are also available on the website. Titles include:

Annual Accountability Reports
Enforcement Policy Statements
International Property Rights: Promoting Innovational Competition

Reference Resources

LIBRARY

Antitrust Division Library

450 5th St. N.W.
Washington, DC 20530
(202) 514–5870
Fax (202) 514–9099
Bridget Gilhool, librarian
Hours: 8:30 a.m. to 5:30 p.m.

Houses legal, business, and reference materials. May be used by the public only with prior permission.

DOCKETS

Federal dockets are available at www.regulations.gov. (*See appendix for Searching and Commenting on Regulations: Regulations.gov.*)

RULES AND REGULATIONS

Antitrust Division rules and regulations are published in the *Code of Federal Regulations,* Title 28, Chapter I, Parts 0.40A–0.49. Proposed regulations, new final regulations, and updates to the *Code of Federal Regulations* are published in the daily *Federal Register.* (*See appendix for details on how to obtain and use these publications.*) The *Federal Register* and the *Code of Federal Regulations* may be accessed online at www.gpoaccess.gov/fr/index.html; this site also contains a link to the federal government's regulatory website at www.regulations.gov (*see appendix*).

The annual report of the attorney general details the regulatory actions taken by the division during the previous year. Single copies of the report are available from DOJ Public Affairs or the website.

■ LEGISLATION

The Antitrust Division exercises its responsibilities under:

Sherman Antitrust Act (26 Stat. 209, 15 U.S.C. 1). Signed by the president July 2, 1890. Prohibited restraint of trade and the monopolization of interstate trade or commerce.

Wilson Tariff Act of 1894 (28 Stat. 570, 15 U.S.C. 8 note). Declared illegal the importation of any article into the United States that was in restraint of lawful trade or free competition in lawful trade or commerce.

Clayton Act (38 Stat. 730, 15 U.S.C. 12). Signed by the president Oct. 15, 1914. Outlawed mergers or acquisitions that could substantially lessen competition or help to create monopolies.

Antitrust Procedures and Penalties Act (88 Stat. 1706, 15 U.S.C. 16(b)(h)). Signed by the president Dec. 23, 1974. Amended the Sherman Act to reclassify antitrust violations such as price fixing from misdemeanors to felonies; increased the maximum sentences. Required any proposal for a consent judgment in any civil proceeding brought by or on behalf of the United States under the antitrust laws to be filed with the district court before which such proceeding is pending and published in the *Federal Register* at least sixty days prior to the effective date of such judgment.

Hart-Scott-Rodino Antitrust Improvement Act of 1976 (90 Stat. 1383, 15 U.S.C. 1311 note). Signed by the president Sept. 30, 1976. Required enterprises to notify the Antitrust Division and the Federal Trade Commission before engaging in mergers or acquisitions exceeding certain minimum sizes.

Export Trading Company Act of 1982 (96 Stat. 1233, 15 U.S.C. 40001). Signed by the president Oct. 8, 1982. Encouraged exports by facilitating the formation and operation of export trade companies, associations, and services. Authorized the Antitrust Division and the secretary of commerce to determine if appropriate standards are met for the issuance of a certificate conferring a limited antitrust exemption.

Antitrust Amendments Act of 1990 (104 Stat. 2879, 15 U.S.C. 1 note). Signed by the president Nov. 16, 1990. Amended the Sherman Antitrust Act to increase the maximum criminal fines for corporations from $1 million to $10 million.

National Cooperative Research and Production Act of 1993 (NCRPA) (107 Stat. 117, 15 U.S.C. 4301 note). Signed by the president June 10, 1993. Permitted parties participating in joint research and development ventures to limit their possible antitrust damage exposure to actual damages if they filed notification with the attorney general and the Federal Trade Commission.

International Antitrust Enforcement Assistance Act of 1994 (108 Stat. 4597, 15 U.S.C. 6201 note). Signed by the president Nov. 2, 1994. Authorized the Justice Department and the FTC to negotiate reciprocal assistance agreements with foreign antitrust enforcement authorities.

Charitable Gift Annuity Antitrust Relief Act of 1995 (109 Stat. 687, 15 U.S.C. 1 note). Signed by the president Dec. 5, 1995. Provided antitrust protection to qualified charities that issue charitable gift annuities by creating a specific statutory exemption.

Telecommunications Act of 1996 (110 Stat. 56, 47 U.S.C. 609 note). Signed by the president Feb. 8, 1996. Gave the Antitrust Division a role in FCC proceedings on "Baby Bell" applications to provide in-region long-distance telephone services.

Antitrust Technical Corrections Act of 2002 (116 Stat. 1762). Signed by the president Nov. 2, 2002. Repealed provisions requiring depositions for use in lawsuits filed under the Sherman Act to be open to the public. Repealed provisions of the Wilson Tariff Act that authorized any person injured by reason of anything prohibited by such act to sue to recover damages. Amended the Sherman Act to apply the prohibitions against monopolizing trade or commerce among the states or with foreign nations to monopolizing trade or foreign commerce in or among any U.S. territories and the District of Columbia.

Antitrust Modernization Commission Act of 2002 (116 Stat. 1758, 1856, 15 U.S.C. 1 note). Signed by the president Nov. 2, 2002. Established the Antitrust Modernization Commission to study and report to Congress and the president on issues and problems relating to the modernization of the antitrust laws.

Antitrust Criminal Penalty Enhancement and Reform Act of 2004 (118 Stat. 665, 668, 15 U.S.C. 1–3). Signed by the president June 22, 2004. Increased the maximum Sherman Act corporate fine to $100 million, the maximum individual fine to $1 million, and the maximum Sherman Act jail term to ten years. Enhanced the incentive for corporations to report illegal conduct by limiting the damages recoverable from a corporate amnesty applicant that also cooperates with private plaintiffs in their damage actions against remaining cartel members.

Antitrust Criminal Penalty Enhancement and Reform Act of 2004 Extension Act (123 Stat. 1775, 15 U.S.C. 1 note). Signed by the president June 19, 2009. Amended the Criminal Penalty Enhancement and Reform Act of 2004 to extend, through June 22, 2020, provisions of that act limiting civil damages in antitrust enforcement actions.

▧ FIELD OFFICES

CHICAGO
(CO, IA, IL, IN, KS, western MI, MO, MN, ND, NE, SD, WI)
Rookery Bldg.
209 S. LaSalle St., #600
Chicago, IL 60604–1204
(312) 984-7200
E-mail: Chicago.ATR@usdoj.gov
Frank J. Vondrak, chief

NEW YORK
(CT, MA, ME, NH, northern NJ, NY, RI, VT)
26 Federal Plaza, #3630
New York, NY 10278–0004
(212) 335–8000
E-mail: NewYork.ATR@usdoj.gov
Jeffrey Martino, chief

SAN FRANCISCO
(AK, AZ, CA, HI, ID, MT, NV, OR, UT, WA, WY)
450 Golden Gate Ave., #10–0101
Box 36046
San Francisco, CA 94102–3478
(415) 934-5300
E-mail: SanFran.ATR@usdoj.gov
Marc Siegel, chief

Bureau of Alcohol, Tobacco, Firearms, and Explosives

99 New York Ave. N.E., #5S 100, Washington, DC 20226
Internet: www.atf.gov

The Bureau of Alcohol, Tobacco, and Firearms (ATF), a law enforcement and regulatory bureau within the Treasury Department since 1972, became the Bureau of Alcohol, Tobacco, Firearms, and Explosives (also ATF), within the Justice Department on Jan. 24, 2003. The Homeland Security Act of 2002, which created the Department of Homeland Security, also reorganized the ATF. The old ATF's law enforcement functions relating to firearms, explosives, and arson were transferred to the Justice Department, while the functions relating to the regulation and collection of revenue from the alcohol and tobacco industries remained at Treasury in the form of a new agency, the Alcohol and Tobacco Tax and Trade Bureau (*p. 836*).

The ATF director is appointed by the attorney general. Although the headquarters of the ATF are in Washington, DC, most of its personnel are stationed in area and district offices nationwide and in some overseas offices. The ATF field operations offices across the country are responsible for investigating the illegal use of firearms, ammunition, and explosives; operations carried on without a license or permit; and crimes of arson with an interstate nexus.

Under the Justice Department, the ATF continues to perform the law enforcement and regulatory functions relating to firearms, explosives, and arson, which were originally transferred to the bureau from the Internal Revenue Service in 1972 legislation. The ATF works closely with other Justice Department law enforcement agencies, especially the Federal Bureau of Investigation. It also administers the U.S. Criminal Code provisions concerning alcohol and tobacco smuggling and diversion.

In addition, the ATF enforces federal explosives laws and develops methods to locate bombs before an explosion and to trace the source of explosives after detonation. The Church Arson Prevention Act of 1996 authorized funds for additional ATF agents for the investigation of church fires.

ATF maintains National Response Teams (NRTs) of highly trained and well-equipped special agents, forensic chemists, and professional support staff that can be deployed within twenty-four hours to major explosion and fire scenes anywhere in the United States. ATF also operates a similar International Response Team.

The bureau provides technical and scientific services to state and local law enforcement officials. It is the central agency for all gun tracing; approximately half of all ATF gun traces are for state and local law enforcement officials. The bureau's National Integrated Ballistic Information Network (NIBIN) provides for the nationwide installation and networking of automated ballistic imaging equipment in partnership with state and local law enforcement agencies.

ATF maintains four national crime labs in Maryland, Georgia, and California to perform alcohol, tobacco, firearms, explosives, and fire debris analysis. Each ATF laboratory also has a mobile laboratory to support examination of evidence at the scene of a fire or explosion. ATF lab technicians also are available to perform ink analysis and other technical operations to aid local law enforcement agencies in gathering evidence for criminal prosecutions. In 2006 ATF established a DNA analysis capability at the National Laboratory Center, which was operational in 2007.

The NICS Improvement Amendments Act (NIAA) was passed following the Virginia Tech massacre. The Virginia Tech shooter was able to purchase firearms from licensed firearms dealers because information about his prohibiting mental health history was not available to the National Instant Criminal Background Check System (NICS), which is administered nationally by the Federal Bureau of Investigation. The system was therefore unable to deny the transfer of the firearms used in the shootings. The bill sought to address the gap in information available to NICS about such prohibiting mental health adjudications and commitments and other prohibiting backgrounds. NICS is comprised of criminal history records and other information pertaining to prohibited possessors, most of which is provided by the states.

Included in the NIAA was a provision, section 105, to allow a person who had been adjudicated mentally incompetent the ability to petition the court to have his or her firearms rights restored. This provision was pursued by the gun lobby. In order for states to qualify for federal funding under NIAA to improve NICS records, the state must statutorily allow for such relief. ATF is authorized to promulgate NICS regulations, including rules to ensure states are in compliance with section 105 provisions.

This issue once again was the focus of national attention when a gunman opened fire at a public event hosted by U.S. Representative Gabrielle Giffords in Tucson, AZ. The congresswoman was critically wounded and survived; six people were killed and thirteen others were injured. Prior to the incident, the gunman had displayed erratic behavior indicative of mental illness, but he had never been adjudicated as such. Congress did not pursue additional gun control legislation, but President Barack Obama wrote an editorial for the *Arizona Daily Star*, published in Tucson, that encouraged states to participate more fully in the NICS system. Gun control advocates, however, were quick to point out that the NICS system does not apply to purchases at gun shows.

The gun control debate resurfaced following two high-profile mass casualty incidents involving firearms in 2012. The first took place in July, when a gunman opened fire, killing twelve people and injuring dozens more at a movie theater in Aurora, Colorado. In December, twenty-six people, mostly five- and six-year-old children, were murdered at Sandy Hook Elementary School in Connecticut. The gunman killed himself as police entered the school.

President Barack Obama designated a gun control task force, led by Vice President Joe Biden. The president's goal was legislation that would require universal background checks for all gun buyers (current law only applied to purchasers who bought weapons from federally licensed firearms dealers). The president also called for bans on assault weapons and high-capacity ammunition magazines.

The National Rifle Association (NRA) aggressively pushed back against any attempts at expanding background checks or renewing the ban on assault weapons. The NRA instead called for funding to place armed police officers in every school.

As President Obama waited for Congress to respond, he took executive action to improve enforcement of existing laws. Following a presidential directive, the Justice Department required federal agencies to file reports documenting improved procedures for submitting records to the NICS database. The department also opened grants to states to improve their records contribution to the NICS database. A NICS Consultation and Coordination Working Group was formed to coordinate efforts to improve background checks under existing law. Another directive required the Justice Department to prepare a report analyzing information on lost and stolen guns and to make the report widely available to law enforcement. However, Congress took no legislative action to expand background checks.

ATF also issues regulations and enforces federal laws pertaining to alcohol and tobacco distribution. Enforcement activities primarily focus on criminal and terrorist organizations by identifying, investigating, and arresting offenders who traffic in contraband cigarettes and illegal liquor. ATF conducts financial investigations

in conjunction with alcohol and tobacco diversion investigations in order to seize and deny further access to assets and funds utilized by criminal enterprises and terrorist organizations. ATF also works with local, state, and other federal law enforcement and tax agencies in order to thoroughly investigate the interstate trafficking of contraband cigarettes and liquor.

▪ KEY PERSONNEL

Director
Thomas A. Brandon (acting). . . . . (202) 648–8700
  Fax. . . . . (202) 648–9622
Deputy Director
Ronald B. Turk (acting) . . . . (202) 648–8710
Chief Counsel
Charles Gross. . . . . (202) 648–7000
  Fax. . . . . (202) 648–9600
Arson and Explosives Programs
Debra Satkowiak . . . . (202) 648–7100
Disclosure
Peter Chisholm . . . . (202) 648–7386
Enforcement Programs and Services
Marvin Richardson. . . . . (202) 648–7080
Field Operations
Charles E. Smith . . . . (202) 648–8410
Field Management Staff
Russell Vanderwers (acting) . . . . (202) 648–8400
Financial Investigative Services Division
Francis Frande. . . . . (202) 648–7968
Financial Management
David Horn . . . . (202) 648–7704
Firearms and Explosives Industry Division
Chad Yoder . . . . (202) 648–7090
Human Resources Professional Development
Theresa Stoop . . . . (202) 648–8460
Litigation
John Manfreda. . . . . (202) 648–7000
Management
Mark Potter . . . . (202) 648–7800
National Laboratory Center (Ammendale, MD)
Greg Czarnopys. . . . . (202) 648–6000
Professional Responsibility and Security Operations
Joel Roessner . . . . (202) 648–7500
Public and Government Affairs
Richard Marianos . . . . (202) 648–8500
Science and Technology
Richard (Rick) Holgate. . . . . (202) 648–8390
Strategic Intelligence and Information
James McDermond. . . . . (202) 648–7600
Strategic Planning
Ronald Humphries . . . . (202) 648–8720

▪ INFORMATION SOURCES

Internet
Agency website: www.atf.gov. Offers access to many ATF publications, including the agency newsletter; information on ATF program areas, including firearms,

explosives, tobacco, and alcohol; the ATF most wanted persons list; and a link to the ATF Victim/Witness Protection Program.

Telephone Contacts

Toll-free . . . .(800) 800–3855
Local. . . . .(202) 648–7777
Personnel Locator (Labor Dept.) . . . . .(866) 487–2365
Arson Hotline . . . . (888) ATF-FIRE;
. . . .(888) 283–3473
Bomb Hotline . . . . (888) ATF-BOMB
. . . .(888) 283–2662
Report Illegal Firearms
Activity . . . . . . (800) ATF-GUNS; (800) 283–4867
Explosives Theft Hotline . . . .(800) 461–8841
Federal Firearms Licensee
Theft Hotline . . . .(888) 930–9275
Report Stolen, Hijacked,
or Seized Cigarettes . . . .(800) 659–6242
Other Criminal
Activity . . . .(888) ATF-TIPS; (888) 283–8477
Federal Relay Service TTY . . . .(800) 877–8339

Information and Publications

KEY OFFICES

Public Affairs

99 New York Ave. N.E.
Washington, DC 20226
(202) 648–8500
Ginger Colbrun, chief

Answers questions for the press and the public. Distributes publications and issues news releases.

Firearms Tracing Center

Serves all local, state, and federal agencies upon request. A gun trace by the bureau provides law enforcement officials with the history of the firearm, from the manufacturer or importer through wholesale and retail dealers to the first retail purchase. Firearms retailers are required by the bureau to maintain files on purchasers, including name, address, physical characteristics, and form of identification used to verify identity.

To request a firearms trace, call (304) 260–1500 or (800) 788–7133. (Only law enforcement agents may request a firearms trace.)

For information pertaining to Title II weapons that fall under the National Firearms Act, call (800) 788–7133.

For information on firearms applications and licensing, call the Federal Firearms Licensing Center at (404) 417–2750 or (866) 662–2750.

Freedom of Information

ATF Disclosure Division
99 New York Ave. N.E., # 4E-301
Washington, DC 20226
(202) 648–8740
Fax (202) 648–9619

E-mail: foiamail@atf.gov
Stephanie Boucher, chief

Maintains a reading room in Suite 1E360, open to the public between 9:00 a.m. and 5:00 p.m., and an Electronic Reading Room on the ATF website.

PUBLICATIONS

ATF Distribution Center

1519 Cabin Branch Rd.
Hyattsville, MD 20785
(202) 648–6420
Internet: www.atf.gov/forms/dcof

Handles requests for publications, pamphlets, posters, and audiovisual materials. Titles include:
ATF: Explosives Laws and Regulations
Explosives License Application
Federal Firearms Regulations
Firearms Curios and Relics List
Firearms Transaction Record, Over-the-Counter
Report of Multiple Sale or Disposal of Pistols and Revolvers
State Laws and Published Ordinances: Firearms

Many publications are also available on the ATF website, at www.atf.gov/resource-center/publications-library. For publications covering distilled spirits and alcohol fuels, see the Alcohol and Tobacco Tax and Trade Bureau publications at www.ttb.gov/publications.

DOCKETS

Federal dockets are available at www.regulations.gov. (*See appendix for Searching and Commenting on Regulations: Regulations.gov.*)

RULES AND REGULATIONS

ATF rules and regulations are published in the *Code of Federal Regulations*, Title 27, Chapters I and II, Parts 1 to end. Proposed regulations, new final regulations, and updates to the *Code of Federal Regulations* are published in the daily *Federal Register*. (*See appendix for details on how to obtain and use these publications.*) The *Federal Register* and the *Code of Federal Regulations* may be accessed online at www.archives.gov/federal-register/cfr; this site also contains a link to the federal government's regulatory website at www.regulations.gov (*see appendix*).

■ LEGISLATION

The ATF exercises its authority under:
National Firearms Act (48 Stat. 1236, 26 U.S.C. 53). Signed by the president June 26, 1934. Authorized regulation of sales and registration of firearms.
Title VII of Omnibus Crime Control and Safe Streets Act of 1968 (82 Stat. 197, 18 U.S.C. app., sec. 1201). Signed by the president June 19, 1968. Prohibited the shipment of firearms in interstate or foreign commerce by convicted felons.
Gun Control Act of 1968 (82 Stat. 1213, 18 U.S.C. 921). Signed by the president Oct. 22, 1968. Amended the National Firearms Act of 1934 that regulated machine

guns and shotguns used by gangsters. Repealed the Federal Firearms Act of 1938 and set record-keeping and eligibility requirements for the purchase and sale of firearms.

Organized Crime Control Act of 1970 (84 Stat. 922, 18 U.S.C. 841). Signed by the president Oct. 15, 1970. Title XI Explosive Control Act of 1970 established a system of federal controls over the interstate and foreign commerce of explosive materials through licenses and permits to curb the misuse of explosives.

Arms Export Control Act of 1976 (90 Stat. 744, 22 U.S.C. 2778, sec. 38). Signed by the president June 30, 1976. Gave the president discretionary authority to control the import and export of defense articles and services. Empowered him to designate which items were to be considered as defense related, and authorized him to promulgate regulations for the import and export of such items.

Contraband Cigarette Trafficking Act (18 U.S.C. Chapter 114). Signed by the president Nov. 2, 1978. Makes it unlawful for any person, other than an "exempt person," to ship, transport, receive, possess, sell, distribute, or purchase contraband cigarettes.

Anti-Arson Act of 1982 (96 Stat. 1319, 18 U.S.C. 1124). Signed by the president Oct. 12, 1982. Amended Title 18 of the U.S. Code and Title XI of the Organized Crime Control Act of 1970 to clarify crimes and penalties involving explosives and fire.

Comprehensive Crime Control Act of 1984 (98 Stat. 1837, 18 U.S.C. 921). Signed by the president Oct. 12, 1984. Required federal judges to follow new sentencing guidelines and restricted use of the insanity defense. Increased penalties for drug trafficking and reestablished anticrime grants for states.

Brady Handgun Violence Prevention Act (107 Stat. 1536, 18 U.S.C. 921). Signed by the president Nov. 30, 1993. Provided a waiting period before purchasing a handgun and established a background check system for the transfer of any firearm.

Violent Crime Control and Law Enforcement Act of 1994 (108 Stat. 1796, 42 U.S.C. 13701 note). Signed by the president Sept. 13, 1994. Increased funding for police hiring, prison construction, and prevention programs. Banned the possession and manufacture of nineteen types of assault weapons (this provision expired in September 2004). Adopted mandatory life sentences for federal offenders with three or more convictions for serious violent felonies or drug trafficking crimes ("three strikes and you're out" provision).

Church Arson Prevention Act (109 Stat. 1492, 18 U.S.C. 242). Signed by the president Aug. 6, 1996. Expanded the circumstances under which the federal government can become involved in prosecuting those who damage religious property. Authorized funds for additional ATF agents for investigation of church fires.

Homeland Security Act of 2002 (116 Stat. 2135, 6 U.S.C. 101 note). Signed by the president Nov. 25, 2002. Created the Bureau of Alcohol, Tobacco, Firearms, and Explosives by transferring the Bureau of Alcohol, Tobacco, and Firearms' law enforcement functions relating to firearms, explosives, and arson from the Treasury Department to the Justice Department. Contained Safe

Explosives Act, a re-write of federal criminal code provisions regarding the purchase of explosives.

USA PATRIOT Improvement and Reauthorization Act of 2005 (120 Stat. 247, 6 U.S.C. 531(a)(2)). Signed by the president March 9, 2006. Amends the Homeland Security Act of 2002 to provide that the president (previously, the attorney general) shall appoint the director of the Bureau of Alcohol, Tobacco, and Firearms, with Senate confirmation required.

NICS Improvement Amendments Act of 2007 (121 Stat. 2559, 18 U.S.C. 922 note). Signed by the president January 8, 2008. Section 105 requires states, as a condition of grant eligibility, to establish procedures to allow persons with disabilities relating to mental health status or commitment to obtain relief from such disabilities for purposes of firearms eligibility. Requires states to allow *de novo* review in state courts of denials of relief. ATF promulgates regulations for this program.

Prevent All Cigarette Trafficking Act of 2009 (PACT Act) (124 Stat. 1087, 15 U.S.C. 375 note). Signed by the president March 31, 2010. Revises provisions governing the collection of taxes on, and trafficking in, cigarettes and smokeless tobacco. Authorizes the Bureau of Alcohol, Tobacco, Firearms, and Explosives (ATF) to enter the business premises of delivery sellers and inspect their records and information and any cigarettes or smokeless tobacco stored at such premises.

◼ REGIONAL OFFICES

Law Enforcement District Offices

ATLANTA
(GA)
2600 Century Pkwy., #300
Atlanta, GA 30345–3104
(404) 417–2600
E-mail: AtlantaDiv@atf.gov

BALTIMORE
(DE, MD)
31 Hopkins Plaza, 5th Floor
Baltimore, MD 21201
(443) 965–2000
E-mail: BaltimoreDiv@atf.gov

BOSTON
(CT, MA, ME, NH, RI, VT)
10 Causeway St., #791
Boston, MA 02222–1047
(617) 557–1200
E-mail: BostonDiv@atf.gov

CHARLOTTE
(NC, SC)
6701 Carmel Rd., #200
Charlotte, NC 28226
(704) 716–1800
E-mail: CharlotteDiv@atf.gov

CHICAGO
525 W. Van Buren St., #600
Chicago, IL 60607
(312) 846–7200
E-mail: ChicagoDiv@atf.gov

COLUMBUS
(IN, OH)
230 West St., #400
Columbus, OH 43215–4167
(614) 827–8400
E-mail: ColumbusDiv@atf.gov

DALLAS
(OK, northwest TX)
1114 Commerce St., #303
Dallas, TX 75242
(469) 227–4300
E-mail: DallasDiv@atf.gov

DENVER
(CO, MT, UT, WY)
950 17th St., #1800
Denver, CO 80202
(303) 575–7600
E-mail: DenverDiv@atf.gov

DETROIT
(MI)
1155 Brewery Park Blvd., #300
Detroit, MI 48207–2602
(313) 202–3400
E-mail: DetroitDiv@atf.gov

HOUSTON
(southeast TX)
5825 N. Sam Houston Pkwy., #300
Houston, TX 77086
(281) 716–8200
E-mail: HoustonDiv@atf.gov

KANSAS CITY
(IA, KS, MO, NE)
1251 Briarcliff Pkwy., #600
Kansas City, MO 64116
(816) 559–0700
E-mail: KansascityDiv@atf.gov

LOS ANGELES
(southern CA)
550 N. Brand Blvd., #800
Glendale, CA 91203
(818) 265–2500
E-mail: LosangelesDiv@atf.gov

LOUISVILLE
(southern IN, KY, western WV)
600 Dr. Martin Luther King Jr. Pl., #500
Louisville, KY 40202

(502) 753–3400
E-mail: LouisDiv@atf.gov

MIAMI
(southeastern FL, PR, VI)
11410 N.W. 20th St., #200
Miami, FL 33172
(305) 597–4800
E-mail: MiamiDiv@atf.gov

NASHVILLE
(AL, TN)
5300 Maryland Way, #200
Brentwood, TN 37027
(615) 565–1400
E-mail: NashDiv@atf.gov

NEW ORLEANS
(AR, LA, MS)
One Galleria Blvd., #1700
Metairie, LA 70001
(504) 841–7000
E-mail: NewOrleansDiv@atf.gov

NEW YORK
(NY)
Financial Square
32 Old Slip, #3500
New York, NY 10005
(646) 335–9000
E-mail: NYDiv@atf.gov

NEWARK
(NJ)
1 Garret Mountain Plaza, #400
Woodland Park, NJ 07424
(973) 413–1179
E-mail: NJDivision@atf.gov

PHILADELPHIA
(PA)
601 Walnut St., #1000E
Philadelphia, PA 19106
(215) 446–7800
E-mail: PhilDiv@atf.gov

PHOENIX
(AZ, NM)
201 E. Washington St., #940
Phoenix, AZ 85004
(602) 776–5400
E-mail: PhoenixDiv@atf.gov

ST. PAUL
(MN, ND, SD, WI)
30 E. 7th St., #1900
St. Paul, MN 55101
(651) 726–0200
E-mail: StPaulDiv@atf.gov

SAN FRANCISCO

(northern CA, NV)
5601 Arnold Rd., #400
Dublin, CA 94568
(925) 557–2800
E-mail: SanFranciscoDiv@atf.gov

SEATTLE

(AK, GU, HI, ID, OR, WA)
915 Second Ave., #790
Seattle, WA 98174–1093
(206) 204–3205
E-mail: SeattleDiv@atf.gov

TAMPA

(all but southeastern FL)
400 N. Tampa St., #2100
Tampa, FL 33602
(813) 202–7300
E-mail: TampaDiv@atf.gov

WASHINGTON, DC

(DC, VA, eastern WV)
1401 H St. N.W., #900
Washington, DC 20005
(202) 648–8010
E-mail: WashDiv@atf.gov

Civil Rights Division

950 Pennsylvania Ave. N.W., Washington, DC 20530
Internet: www.justice.gov/crt

The Civil Rights Division is a unit within the Justice Department that was established in 1957 in response to the need to ensure effective enforcement of federal civil rights laws. The division is headed by an assistant attorney general appointed by the president and confirmed by the Senate.

The division enforces the federal civil rights laws that prohibit discrimination on the basis of race, color, religion, sex, or national origin in the areas of voting, education, employment, credit, and housing; in the use of public facilities and accommodations; and in the administration of all federally assisted programs. Laws prohibiting discrimination on the basis of disability in the areas of employment and education are enforced by this division. It is responsible for protecting the constitutional rights of the mentally disabled, state prisoners, and psychiatric hospital patients. It also prosecutes federal hate crimes.

The division also enforces federal criminal statutes that prohibit violations of individual civil rights and interference with federally secured rights. It is responsible for coordinating the civil rights enforcement programs of federal agencies and offers assistance to agencies to help them identify and eliminate policies and programs that discriminate on the basis of sex. The division also works on civil rights issues with other federal agencies including the Equal Employment Opportunity Commission (EEOC) (*p. 97*), the Department of Education's Office for Civil Rights (*p. 580*), the Department of Health and Human Services Office for Civil Rights (*p. 627*), and the Department of Housing and Urban Development's Office of Fair Housing and Equal Opportunity (*p. 671*).

The division's Voting Section is responsible for the enforcement of the Voting Rights Act of 1965, the National Voter Registration Act of 1993, the Voting Accessibility for the Elderly and Handicapped Act, the Uniformed and Overseas Citizens Absentee Voting Act, and other statutory provisions designed to safeguard the right to vote.

The division's Special Litigation Section enforces federal civil rights statutes in six major areas: conditions of institutional confinement; law enforcement misconduct; access to reproductive health facilities and places of religious worship; protection of institutionalized persons' religious exercise rights; the rights of individuals with disabilities to receive services in their communities, rather than in institutions; and the rights of justice-involved youth.

The Criminal Section prosecutes cases involving the violent interference with liberties guaranteed under federal law. These cases include federal hate crimes and violent and intimidating acts motivated by hatred based on race, ethnicity, national origin, religious beliefs, gender, sexual orientation, or disability. This section also prosecutes cases of violent conduct targeting religious houses of worship, usually involving the arson of churches or synagogues. This includes cases of official misconduct, whereby a person acting "under color of any law" willfully deprives a person of a right or privilege protected by the Constitution or federal laws. This pertains to a federal, state, or local official acting within his or her lawful authority as well as acts done beyond the bounds of that official's lawful authority.

The Criminal Section prosecutes crimes that violate the Freedom of Access to Clinic Entrances Act. This act established federal criminal penalties and civil remedies for "certain violent, threatening, obstructive, and destructive conduct that is intended to injure, intimidate, or interfere with persons seeking to obtain or provide reproductive health care services."

The section helps enforce the Trafficking Victims Protection Act of 2000. Since 2001, the Civil Rights Division, in conjunction with U.S. Attorneys' Offices, has sharply increased the number of human trafficking cases filed and the number of defendants charged and convicted. On Jan. 31, 2002, the Justice Department issued a regulation enabling certain trafficking victims to live and work legally in the United States for three years while their cases are investigated and prosecuted; these victims are issued T visas. The Civil Rights Division participates in an interagency center to coordinate intelligence information on human trafficking and migrant smuggling.

The division's Employment Litigation Section enforces against state and local government employers the provisions of Title VII of the Civil Rights Act of 1964, as amended, and other federal laws prohibiting employment practices that discriminate on grounds of race, sex, religion, and national origin. The section also enforces against state and local government employers and private employers the Uniformed Services Employment and Reemployment Rights Act of 1994, which prohibits employers from discriminating against or firing employees because of their military obligations. The division saw increased violations of the Uniformed Services Employment and Reemployment Rights Act following deployment of reservists and National Guard members to Afghanistan and Iraq.

The Office of Special Counsel for Immigration-Related Unfair Employment Practices (OSC) enforces the anti-discrimination provision of the Immigration and Nationality Act. The office takes action against companies engaged in a pattern or practice of discrimination by imposing unnecessary documentary requirements on non-U.S. citizens when establishing their authority to work in the United States or engages in a pattern of hiring only U.S. workers while excluding authorized immigrant workers.

KEY PERSONNEL

Assistant Attorney General
Vanita Gupta . . . . (202) 514–4609
Fax. . . . . (202) 514–0293
TTY. . . . . (202) 514–0716
Principal Deputy Assistant Attorney General
Vanita Gupta . . . . (202) 514–2151
Chief of Staff
Emily Loeb (acting) . . . . (202) 307–2502
Deputy Assistant Attorneys General
Greg Friel . . . . (202) 353–9418
Eve Hill . . . . (202) 353–9390
Policy and Strategy Section
Aaron Schuham. . . . . (202) 514–4224
Fax. . . . . (202) 514–1783
Appellate
Diana K. Flynn. . . . . (202) 514–2195
Fax. . . . . (202) 514–8490
E-mail: crt.appellate@usdoj.gov
Complaint Adjudication
Mark Gross. . . . . (202) 305–0079
Fax. . . . . (202) 514–0655
Criminal
Robert Moossy. . . . . (202) 514–3204
Fax. . . . . (202) 514–8336
TTY. . . . . (202) 305–4566
Disability Rights
Rebecca Bond . . . . (202) 307–0663
Fax. . . . . (202) 307–1197
TTY. . . . . (800) 514–0383
Educational Opportunities
Anurima Bhargava . . . . (202) 514–4092
Toll-free . . . . (877) 292–3804
Fax. . . . . (202) 514–8337
E-mail: education@usdoj.gov
Employment Litigation
Delora L. Kennebrew . . . . (202) 514–3831
Fax. . . . . (202) 514–1105
TTY. . . . . (202) 514–6780
Federal Coordination and Compliance
Deeana Jang . . . . (202) 307–2222
Fax. . . . . (202) 307–0595
TTY. . . . . (202) 307–2676

Housing and Civil Enforcement
Steven H. Rosenbaum. . . . . (202) 514–4713
Fax. . . . . (202) 514–1116
TTY. . . . . (202) 305–1882
TTY. . . . . (202) 305–1882
Policy and Strategy
Aaron Schuham. . . . . (202) 616–3315
Special Counsel for Immigration-Related Unfair Employment Practices
Alberto Ruisanchez (deputy). . . . . (202) 616–5594
Fax. . . . . (202) 616–5509
TTY. . . . . (800) 237–2515
E-mail: osccrt@usdoj.gov
Special Litigation
Judy Preston (acting) . . . . (202) 514–6255
Toll-free . . . . (877) 218–5228
Fax. . . . . (202) 514–6273
E-mail: Special.Litigation@usdoj.gov
Voting
Vacant . . . .
Toll-free . . . . (800) 253–3931
Fax. . . . . (202) 307–3961
TTY. . . . . (800) 253–3931
E-mail: Voting.Section@usdoj.gov

INFORMATION SOURCES

Internet
Agency website: www.justice.gov/crt. Includes general agency information, selected speeches, and legal cases.

Telephone Contacts
General Information . . . .(202) 514–4609
TTY . . . .(202) 514–0716
ADA Information. . . . .(800) 514–0301
TTY . . . .(800) 514–0383
Personnel Locator . . . .(202) 514–3934
Employer Hotline. . . . .(800) 255–8155
TTY . . . .(800) 237–2515
Fair Housing Tip Line . . . .(800) 896–7743
Title VI Hotline . . . .(888) 848–5306
Voting. . . . .(800) 253–3931
Worker Hotline. . . . .(800) 255–7688
TTY . . . .(800) 237–2515

Information and Publications

KEY OFFICES

DOJ Public Affairs
950 Pennsylvania Ave. N.W., #1220
Washington, DC 20530
(202) 514–2007
Fax (202) 514–5331

Answers questions about the Civil Rights Division for the press. Distributes publications and issues news releases. Maintains a mailing list for news releases and other reports on civil rights.

Freedom of Information

FOIA/PA Branch
DOJ Civil Rights Division
BICN, #3234
950 Pennsylvania Ave. N.W.
Washington, DC 20530
(202) 514–4209
Fax (202) 514–6195
E-mail: CRT.FOIArequests@usdoj.gov
Nelson D. Hermilla, chief

Call (202) 514–4210 for access instructions to the reading room. The electronic reading room at www.justice.gov/crt/foia/readingroom provides frequently requested records created by the Civil Rights Division from November 1, 1996.

PUBLICATIONS

Contact DOJ Public Affairs. Publications are also available on the website at the Electronic Reading Room. ADA technical assistance materials and regulations, as well as *Disability Rights Online News* are also available on the website.

Reference Resources

LIBRARY

The Department of Justice maintains an internal library and a Federal Depository Library that is open to the public by appointment; call (202) 514–3775.

DOCKETS

Federal dockets are available at www.regulations .gov. (*See appendix for Searching and Commenting on Regulations: Regulations.gov.*)

RULES AND REGULATIONS

Civil Rights Division rules and regulations are published in the *Code of Federal Regulations,* Title 28, Chapter I, parts 0.50–0.52. Proposed regulations, new final regulations, and updates to the *Code of Federal Regulations* are published in the daily *Federal Register.* (*See appendix for details on how to obtain and use these publications.*) The *Federal Register* and the *Code of Federal Regulations* may be accessed online at www .archives.gov/federal-register/cfr; the site also contains a link to the federal government's regulatory website at www.regulations.gov (*see appendix*).

▪ LEGISLATION

The Civil Rights Division carries out its responsibilities under:

Civil Rights Act of 1960 (74 Stat. 88, 42 U.S.C. 1971). Signed by the president May 6, 1960. Strengthened provisions of the Civil Rights Act of 1957 for court enforcement of voting rights and required preservation of voting records. Contained limited criminal penalty provisions relating to bombing and to obstruction of federal court orders (aimed primarily at school desegregation orders).

Civil Rights Act of 1964 (78 Stat. 243, 42 U.S.C. 2000a). Signed by the president July 2, 1964. Prohibited discrimination in public accommodations and in programs receiving federal assistance. Prohibited discrimination by employers and unions. Established the Equal Employment Opportunity Commission and strengthened enforcement of voting laws and desegregation of schools and public facilities.

Voting Rights Act of 1965 (79 Stat. 445, 42 U.S.C. 1971). Signed by the president Aug. 6, 1965. Authorized the attorney general to appoint federal examiners to register voters in areas of marked discrimination. Strengthened penalties for interference with voter rights.

Civil Rights Act of 1968 (82 Stat. 81, 42 U.S.C. 3601). Signed by the president April 11, 1968. Prohibited discrimination in the sale or rental of approximately 80 percent of all housing. Protected persons exercising specified rights, such as attending school or working, and civil rights workers urging others to exercise their rights. Included anti-riot provisions.

Equal Credit Opportunity Act (88 Stat. 1521, 15 U.S.C. 1691). Signed by the president Oct. 28, 1974. Prohibited credit discrimination against women. Amended in 1975 to include discrimination based on age, race, color, religion, or national origin.

Civil Rights of Institutionalized Persons Act of 1980 (94 Stat. 349, 42 U.S.C. 1997). Signed by the president May 23, 1980. Authorized the federal government to file suit against states to protect the rights of persons confined in state institutions.

Executive Order 12250. Issued by the president Nov. 2, 1980. Empowered the attorney general to coordinate the implementation and enforcement by executive agencies of Title VI of the Civil Rights Act of 1964, Title IX of the Education Amendments of 1972, and Section 504 of the Rehabilitation Act of 1973. Federal agencies that provide federal financial assistance are subject to these nondiscrimination statutes.

The **Voting Accessibility for the Elderly and Handicapped Act of 1984** (98 Stat. 1680, 42 U.S.C. 1973ee et seq.). Signed by the president Sept. 28, 1984. Requires polling places across the United States to be physically accessible to people with disabilities.

Uniformed and Overseas Citizens' Absentee Voting Act (100 Stat. 924, 42 U.S.C. 1973). Signed by the president Aug. 28, 1986. Enacted to improve absentee registration and voting for members of the military and U.S. citizens living abroad and to consolidate existing laws.

Americans with Disabilities Act (104 Stat. 327, 42 U.S.C. 1201 note). Signed by the president July 26, 1990. Provided disabled Americans, including those with AIDS, the same rights to jobs, public transportation, and public accommodations that women and racial, religious, and ethnic minorities receive under the Civil Rights Act of 1964.

Civil Rights Act of 1991 (105 Stat. 1071, 42 U.S.C. 1981 note). Signed by the president Nov. 21, 1991. Strengthened protection in the workplace against bias and harassment on the basis of race, color, sex, religion, national origin, or disability. Allowed for greater damage awards in successful lawsuits.

EEOC Education, Technical Assistance, and Training Revolving Fund Act of 1992 (106 Stat. 2102, 42 U.S.C. 200a). Signed by the president Oct. 14, 1992. Amended the Civil Rights Act of 1964 to establish the EEOC Education, Technical Assistance, and Training Revolving Fund.

Freedom of Access to Clinic Entrances Act (18 U.S.C. 248). Signed by the president May 26, 1994. Made it a federal crime to injure, intimidate, or interfere with any person obtaining or providing reproductive health services or seeking to exercise the right of religious freedom at a place of religious worship. Also criminalized intentionally damaging or destroying the property of a facility because such facility provides reproductive health services, or intentionally damaging or destroying the property of a place of religious worship. Included civil remedies, injunctive relief, compensatory and punitive damages, and costs.

Violent Crime Control and Law Enforcement Act of 1994 (108 Stat. 1796, 42 U.S.C. 13701 note). Signed by the president Sept. 13, 1994. Prohibited any federal law enforcement officers from depriving persons of their constitutional or federal rights. Authorized the attorney general to bring a civil action against such officers to eliminate such practices.

Uniformed Services Employment and Reemployment Rights Act of 1994 (108 Stat. 3149, 38 U.S.C. 101 note). Signed by the president Oct. 13, 1994. Prohibited the denial of initial employment, reemployment, retention in employment, promotion, or any benefit of employment by an employer against a person who is a member of, applies for membership in, or performs, has performed, applies to perform, or has an obligation to perform service in a uniformed service on the basis of such service or obligation.

Congressional Accountability Act of 1995 (109 Stat. 3, 2 U.S.C. 1301 note). Signed by the president Jan. 23, 1995. Applied provisions of several laws to the legislative branch, including the Fair Labor Standards Act of 1938, Title VII of the Civil Rights Act of 1964, and the Age Discrimination in Employment Act of 1967. Required all personnel actions affecting covered employees to be made free from any discrimination based on race, color, religion, sex, national origin, age, or disability.

Presidential and Executive Office Accountability Act (110 Stat. 4053, 3 U.S.C. 401 note). Signed by the president Oct. 26, 1996. Provided for the application of several laws to the Executive Office of the President, the Executive Residence, and the Official Residence of the Vice President. These laws included the Fair Labor Standards Act of 1938, Title VII of the Civil Rights Act of 1964, Title I of the Americans with Disabilities Act of 1990, and the Age Discrimination in Employment Act of 1967. Amended the Government Employee Rights Act of 1991 to repeal its rights, protections, and remedies with respect to employment of presidential appointees.

Executive Order 13160. Issued by the president June 23, 2000. Prohibited discrimination on the basis of race, sex, color, national origin, disability, religion, age, sexual orientation, and status as a parent in federally conducted education and training programs.

Executive Order 13166. Issued by the president Aug. 11, 2000. Required federal agencies to assess and address the needs of otherwise eligible persons seeking access to federally conducted programs and activities who, because of limited English proficiency, cannot fully and equally participate in or benefit from those programs and activities.

Victims of Trafficking and Violence Protection Act of 2000 (114 Stat. 1464, 22 U.S.C. 7101 note). Signed by the president Oct. 28, 2000. Enacted to combat trafficking of persons, especially into the sex trade, slavery, and slavery-like conditions in the United States and countries around the world through prevention, through prosecution and enforcement against traffickers, and through protection and assistance to victims of trafficking.

Help America Vote Act of 2002 (116 Stat. 1666, 42 U.S.C. 15301 note). Signed by the president Oct. 29, 2002. Required voting systems to be accessible for individuals with disabilities.

The Servicemembers Civil Relief Act (117 Stat. 2835, 50 U.S.C. App. 501 et seq.). Signed by the president Dec. 19, 2003. Formerly known as the Soldiers' and Sailors' Civil Relief Act. Provides certain protections for servicemembers against default judgments while in military service, including a minimum 90-day stay of proceedings, with respect to the payment of any tax, fine, penalty, insurance premium, or other civil obligation or liability.

Emmett Till Unsolved Civil Rights Crime Act of 2007 (122 Stat. 3934, 28 U.S.C. 509 note). Signed by the president Oct. 7, 2008. Directed the attorney general to designate a deputy chief in the Criminal Section of the Civil Rights Division. Authorized the deputy chief to investigate and prosecute violations of criminal civil rights statutes in which the alleged violation occurred before Jan. 1, 1970, and resulted in death.

Drug Enforcement Administration

700 Army Navy Dr., Arlington, VA 22202
Mailing Address: Washington, DC 20537
Internet: www.dea.gov

The Drug Enforcement Administration (DEA) was established as an agency within the Justice Department by Reorganization Plan No. 2 of 1973. The reorganization merged into one agency the Bureau of Narcotics and Dangerous Drugs, the Office for Drug Abuse Law Enforcement, the Office of National Narcotic Intelligence, divisions of the Bureau of Customs that had drug investigative responsibilities, and divisions of the Office of Science and Technology related to drug enforcement. The DEA administrator reports to the U.S. attorney general.

The DEA coordinates the drug enforcement activities of other federal agencies and works with them to control the supply of illicit drugs. These agencies include the Federal Aviation Administration (p. 783); Federal Bureau of Investigation, Immigration and Customs Enforcement (p. 643); Internal Revenue Service (p. 846); Bureau of Alcohol, Tobacco, Firearms, and Explosives (p. 730); U.S. Coast Guard (p. 658); U.S. Customs and Border Protection (p. 664); the U.S. Marshals Service; and the U.S. Army Criminal Investigation Command.

In carrying out its responsibilities the DEA:

- Acts as the lead agency responsible for the development of overall federal drug enforcement strategy, programs, planning, and evaluation.
- Investigates and prepares for the prosecution of major violators of controlled substances laws operating at the interstate and international levels.
- Manages a national narcotics intelligence system in cooperation with federal, state, and foreign officials to collect, analyze, and disseminate strategic and operational intelligence information.
- Seizes and forfeits assets derived from, traceable to, or intended to be used for illicit drug trafficking.
- Enforces the provisions of the Controlled Substances Act that pertain to the manufacture, distribution, and dispensing of legally produced controlled substances, including Internet sales.
- Maintains liaison with the United Nations, INTERPOL, and other foreign organizations on matters relating to international narcotics control programs.

- Coordinates programs associated with drug law enforcement counterparts in foreign countries under the policy guidance of the secretary of state and U.S. ambassadors abroad.
- Coordinates and cooperates with federal, state, and local law enforcement officials on mutual drug enforcement efforts, including interstate and international investigations.
- Coordinates and cooperates with other federal, state, and local agencies, and with foreign governments, in programs designed to reduce the availability of illicit drugs on the U.S. market through nonenforcement methods such as crop eradication, crop substitution, and training of foreign officials.

The DEA has twenty-one domestic field divisions, each managed by a special agent in charge (SAC). Subordinate to these divisions are more than 200 domestic offices (at least one office located in every state). SACs also manage the El Paso Intelligence Center in Texas and the Office of Training at Quantico, VA.

The DEA operates several regional forensic laboratories, a special testing and research laboratory, and an aviation unit that provides air support throughout the United States and in foreign countries. Overseas, the DEA maintains eighty-six offices in sixty-six countries.

The DEA State and Local Task Force Program manages state and local task forces, which include Program Funded, Provisional, High Intensity Drug Trafficking Area (HIDTA), and Tactical Diversion Squads. Participating state and local task force officers are deputized to perform the same functions as DEA special agents.

The Secure and Responsible Drug Disposal Act of 2010 authorized DEA to develop and implement regulations that outline methods to transfer unused or unwanted pharmaceutical controlled substances to authorized collectors for the purpose of disposal. In 2014 the DEA published a final rule for the disposal of controlled substances. Prior to the passage of the Act, the Controlled Substances Act made no legal provisions for the public to dispose of unwanted pharmaceutical controlled substances except to give them to law enforcement. Pharmacies, doctors' offices, and hospitals were prohibited from accepting them. As a result, most people flushed their unused drugs down the toilet, threw them in the trash, or kept them in the household medicine cabinet. To curtail this activity, the DEA, along with local law enforcement agencies, would hold public prescription drug take-back events. The DEA held its final take-back event prior to issuing the disposal regulations. The DEA take-back initiative removed from circulation 2,411 tons of unused prescription drugs in four years.

KEY PERSONNEL

Administrator
Charles (Chuck) Rosenberg (acting) . (202) 307–8000
Deputy Administrator
Vacant . . . . (202) 307–7345
Chief of Staff
Vacant . . . . (202) 307–8003
Administration
Mary Colarusso . . . . (202) 307–7708
Administrative Law Judge
John J. Mulrooney II . . . . (202) 307–8188
Board of Professional Conduct
Christopher Quaglino . . . . (202) 307–8980
Chief Counsel
Wendy H. Goggin . . . . (202) 307–7322
Chief Inspector
Vacant . . . . (202) 307–7358
Deputy Chief Inspector, Professional Responsibility
Vacant . . . . (202) 307–8235
Congressional and Public Affairs
Eric Akers (acting) . . . . (202) 307–7988
Demand Reduction
Eric Akers . . . . (202) 307–7988
Diversion Control
Joseph Rannazzisi . . . . (202) 307–7165
Equal Employment Opportunity
Oliver C. Allen Jr. . . . . (202) 307–8888
Financial Management
Frank M. Kalder Jr. . . . . (202) 307–7330
Forensic Sciences
Nelson Santos . . . . (202) 307–8866
Global Enforcement
Jim Soiles . . . . (202) 307–7927
Human Resources
Raymond A. Pagliarini Jr. . . . . (202) 307–4195
Information Systems
Dennis R. McCrary . . . . (202) 307–3653
Intelligence Division
Rodney G. Benson . . . . (202) 307–3607
Intelligence Plans and Program
Patrick Lowry . . . . (202) 307–8541
Operational Support Division
Preston L. Grubbs . . . . (202) 307–4730
Operations Division
Vacant . . . . (202) 307–7340
Special Operations
Derek Maltz . . . . (703) 488–4205

INFORMATION SOURCES

Internet
Agency website: www.dea.gov Features general information about the administration, trends and statistics, a list of DEA fugitives, and employment opportunities.

Telephone Contacts
Personnel Locator and Information . . (202) 307–1000
Federal Relay Service TTY . . . . (800) 877–8339
Drug Registrant Information . . . . (800) 882–9539

Information and Publications

KEY OFFICES

DEA Public Affairs Section
700 Army Navy Dr.
Arlington, VA 22202
(202) 307–7977
Eric Akers (acting), chief

Responds to media inquiries; serves as entertainment industry liaison and speakers bureau for the DEA.

Freedom of Information
DEA Freedom of Information Operations Unit
8701 Morrissette Dr.
Springfield, VA 22152
(202) 307–7596
Kathy Myrick, chief
Internet: www.dea.gov/FOIA/FOIA.shtml

DATA AND STATISTICS
Data and statistics are available on the website.
The DEA Media Affairs Section also provides information to the media (i.e., data is not designed for the general public) from the following computer data bank systems:
Asset Seizures and Forfeitures. Information includes statistics on seizures and forfeitures of assets seized by the Drug Enforcement Administration or referred to the DEA by another agency. System is being expanded to provide data by judicial districts.
Defendant Data. Data includes statistics on arrests, dispositions, and sentencing of defendants arrested by the Drug Enforcement Administration. Reports can be generated in a variety of formats.
Drug Removals. Drug removal statistics reflect the total of all drugs purchased, seized, or otherwise obtained through DEA investigations. Data are reported by net weight and displayed in four major categories: heroin, cocaine, cannabis, and dangerous drugs.

PUBLICATIONS
For information, contact the DEA Demand Reduction Section: (202) 307–7936; publications are also available on the website.

Reference Resources

LIBRARY

DEA Library
700 Army Navy Dr., W-7216
Arlington, VA 22202
(202) 307–8932
RoseMary Russo, chief librarian
Hours: 8:00 a.m. to 5:00 p.m.

Maintains an extensive collection of research materials related to the history, study, and control of narcotic and dangerous drugs. Materials for research purposes are available only for DEA employees. The website's Electronic Reading Room contains many publications.

DOCKETS
Federal dockets are available at www.regulations.gov. (*See appendix for Searching and Commenting on Regulations: Regulations.gov.*)

RULES AND REGULATIONS
DEA rules and regulations are published in the *Code of Federal Regulations,* Title 21, Chapter II, Parts 1300–1399. Proposed regulations, new final regulations, and updates to the *Code of Federal Regulations* are published in the daily *Federal Register.* (*See appendix for details on how to obtain and use these publications.*) The *Federal Register* and the *Code of Federal Regulations* may also be accessed online at www.archives.gov/federal-register/cfr; the site contains a link to the federal government's regulatory website at www.regulations.gov (*see appendix*).

▓ LEGISLATION
The DEA carries out its responsibilities under:

Controlled Substances Act of 1970 (84 Stat. 1236, 21 U.S.C. 801). Signed by the president Oct. 27, 1970. Required registration of persons engaged in the manufacture and distribution of controlled substances; established criteria for determining abuse potential of drugs; provided for increased research into drug abuse and development of drug abuse prevention programs; strengthened existing drug laws.

Reorganization Plan No. 2 of 1973 (Executive Order No. 11727, 38 F.R. 18357). Signed by the president July 6, 1973. Established the DEA within the Department of Justice.

Narcotic Addict Treatment Act of 1974 (88 Stat. 124, 125, 42 U.S.C. 801). Signed by the president May 14, 1974. Required registration of narcotic treatment and drug rehabilitation programs with the DEA; established record-keeping and security requirements for these programs.

Comprehensive Crime Control Act of 1984, Title II (98 Stat. 2044, 21 U.S.C. 853). Signed by the president Oct. 12, 1984. Gave the attorney general emergency authority to require tight control of new chemical substances. Authorized the attorney general to establish programs to help states reduce the amount of drugs diverted from medical channels to the black market. Gave federal prosecutors new authority to seize the assets and profits of drug traffickers. Increased maximum fines and prison sentences for certain drug offenses.

Anti-Drug Abuse Act of 1988 (102 Stat. 4181, 21 U.S.C. 1501 note). Signed by the president Nov. 18, 1988. Created the Office of National Drug Control Policy and allowed for the death penalty for major drug traffickers who intentionally killed someone as part of their drug-related transactions.

Domestic Chemical Diversion Control Act of 1993 (107 Stat. 2333, 21 U.S.C. 801). Signed by the president Dec. 17, 1993. Modified the so-called legal exemption of the 1988 act. Established a registration system for distributors, importers, and exporters of listed chemicals.

Combat Methamphetamine Epidemic Act of 2005 (120 Stat. 256, 21 U.S.C. 801 note). Signed by the president Mar. 9, 2006. Amended the Controlled Substance Act to authorize regulation of methamphetamine precursor drugs.

Ryan Haight Online Pharmacy Consumer Protection Act of 2008 (122 Stat. 4820, 21 U.S.C. 801). Signed by the president Oct. 15, 2008. Amended the Controlled Substances Act to prohibit the delivery, distribution, or dispensing of a controlled substance that is a prescription drug over the Internet without a valid prescription. Exempted telemedicine practitioners. Required the DEA to report to Congress on the foreign supply chains and sources of controlled substances offered for sale on the Internet; DEA efforts and strategy to decrease such foreign supply chains; and DEA efforts to work with domestic and multinational pharmaceutical companies in combating the sale of controlled substances over the Internet without a valid prescription.

Combat Methamphetamine Enhancement Act of 2010 (124 Stat. 2847, 21 U.S.C. 801 note). Signed by the president Oct. 12, 2010. Requires retail sellers of products containing precursors for methamphetamine to submit a self-certification of compliance with the requirements of such Act to the attorney general. Requires the attorney general to establish criteria for certifications of mail order-distributors that are consistent with the criteria for the certifications of regulated sellers.

Secure and Responsible Drug Disposal Act of 2010 (124 Stat. 2858, 21 U.S.C. 801 note). Signed by the president Oct. 12, 2010. Authorizes persons who have legally obtained a controlled substances to deliver unused portions of that controlled substance to another entity for destruction without a DEA registration if the drug is disposed of in accordance with regulations issued by the DEA.

▓ FIELD DIVISIONS
The DEA has 227 domestic offices and 886 foreign offices in sixty-three countries. The main offices follow.

ATLANTA
(GA, NC, SC, TN)
75 Spring St. S.W., #800

Atlanta, GA 30303
(404) 893–7000
Daniel R. Salter, special agent in charge

CARIBBEAN
(PR, VI (Caribbean except Bahamas, PR, VI))
Metro Office Park
Millenium Park Plaza
15 Calle 2, #710
Guaynabo, PR 00968–1743
(787) 277–4700
Vito S. Guarino, special agent in charge

CHICAGO
(most of IL, IN, MN, ND, WI)
230 S. Dearborn St., #1200
Chicago, IL 60604
(312) 353–7875
Dennis A. Wichern, special agent in charge

DALLAS
(OK, northern TX)
10160 Technology Blvd. East
Dallas, TX 75220
(214) 366–6900
Calvin C. Bond (acting), special agent in charge

DENVER
(CO, MT, UT, WY)
12154 E. Easter Ave.
Centennial, CO 80112–6740
Barbara M. Roach, special agent in charge

DETROIT
(KY, MI, OH)
431 Howard St.
Detroit, MI 48226
(313) 234–4000
Joseph P. Reagan, special agent in charge

EL PASO
(NM, western TX)
660 Mesa Hills Dr., #2000
El Paso, TX 79912
(915) 832–6000
Will R. Glaspy, special agent in charge

EL PASO INTELLIGENCE CENTER
11339 SSG Sims St.
El Paso, TX 79918–8033
(915) 760–2000
Timothy Jennings, director

HOUSTON
(southern TX)
1433 W. Loop South, #600
Houston, TX 77027–9506
(713) 693–3000
Joseph M. Arabit, special agent in charge

LOS ANGELES
(southern CA, GU, HI, NV)
255 E. Temple St., 17th Floor
Los Angeles, CA 90012
(213) 621–6700
Anthony Williams, special agent in charge

MIAMI
(Bahamas, FL)
2100 N. Commerce Pkwy.
Weston, FL 33326
(954) 660–4500
Adolphus P. Wright, special agent in charge

NEW ENGLAND
(CT, MA, ME, NH, RI, VT)
15 New Sudbury St., Suite E400
Boston, MA 02203–0402
(617) 557–2100
Michael J. Ferguson, special agent in charge

NEW JERSEY
(NJ)
80 Mulberry St., 2nd Floor
Newark, NJ 07102–4206
(973) 776–1100
Carl J. Kotowski, special agent in charge

NEW ORLEANS
(AL, AR, LA, MS)
3838 N. Causeway Blvd., #1800
3 Lakeway Center
Metairie, LA 70002
(504) 840–1100
Raymond (Keith) Brown, special agent in charge

NEW YORK
(NY)
99 10th Ave.
New York, NY 10011
(212) 337–3900
James J. Hunt, special agent in charge

OFFICE OF TRAINING
DEA Training Academy
P.O. Box 1475
Quantico, VA 22134–1475
(703) 632–5000
James R. Gregorious, special agent in charge

PHILADELPHIA
(DE, PA)
600 Arch St., #10224
Philadelphia, PA 19106
(215) 861–3474
Gary Tuggle, special agent in charge

PHOENIX
(AZ)
3010 N. Second St., #100

Phoenix, AZ 85012
(602) 664–5600
Douglas W. Coleman, special agent in charge

ST. LOUIS

(IA, southern IL, KS, MO, NE, SD)
317 S. 16th St.
St. Louis, MO 63103
(314) 538–4600
James P. Shroba, special agent in charge

SAN DIEGO

(San Diego and Imperial Co. in CA, Mexican border)
4560 Viewridge Ave.
San Diego, CA 92123–1672
(858) 616–4100
William R. Sherman, special agent in charge

SAN FRANCISCO

(northern CA)
450 Golden Gate Ave.

P.O. Box 36035
San Francisco, CA 94102
(415) 436–7900
Bruce C. Balzano (acting), special agent in
charge

SEATTLE

(AK, ID, OR, WA)
300 5th Ave., #1300
Seattle, WA 98104
(206) 553–5443
Keith R. Weis, special agent in
charge

WASHINGTON, DC

(DC, MD, VA, WV)
800 K St. N.W., #500
Washington, DC 20001
(202) 305–8500
Karl C. Colder, special agent
in charge

Office of Justice Programs

810 7th St. N.W., Washington, DC 20531
Internet: www.ojp.gov

Formerly the Office of Justice Assistance, Research, and Statistics, and the Law Enforcement Assistance Administration before that, the Office of Justice Programs (OJP) was established by the Justice Assistance Act of the Comprehensive Crime Control Act of 1984. It is headed by an assistant attorney general nominated by the president and confirmed by the Senate.

The OJP is responsible for the coordination of the Bureau of Justice Assistance, the Bureau of Justice Statistics, the National Institute of Justice, the Office of Juvenile Justice and Delinquency Prevention, the Office for Victims of Crime; and the Sex Offender Sentencing, Monitoring, Apprehending, Registering, and Tracking (SMART) Office.

Through the programs developed and financed by its bureaus and offices, the OJP works to form partnerships among federal, state, and local government officials. Program bureaus and offices award formula grants to state agencies, which, in turn, subgrant funds to units of state and local government.

Formula grant programs—drug control and system improvement, juvenile justice, victims' compensation, and victims' assistance—are administered by state agencies. Discretionary grant funds are announced in the *Federal Register,* and applications are made directly to the sponsoring OJP bureau or office.

The Violent Crime and Law Enforcement Act of 1994 significantly expanded the responsibilities of the Office of Justice Programs. The bureaus and program offices of the OJP implemented the majority of the act's provisions, which included the Violent Crime Reduction Trust Fund to provide for 100,000 new police officers and strengthen community policing; a ban on the manufacture of various military-type assault weapons; the expansion of the federal death penalty to cover more than sixty offenses; and enactment of mandatory life sentences for federal offenders with three or more convictions for serious violent felonies or drug trafficking crimes. Some of these provisions, such as the ban on assault rifles, had time limits and were not reauthorized.

The Bureau of Justice Assistance (BJA) is authorized to provide federal financial and technical assistance to states, local governments, and private nonprofit organizations for criminal justice programs. The BJA administers the Justice Department's programs for the donation of surplus federal property for correctional purposes and the payment of benefits to the survivors of public safety officers killed in the line of duty. The BJA also administers the Edward Byrne Memorial Justice Assistance Grants program, which provides funds to state and local jurisdictions for various criminal justice programs. A clearinghouse of information is maintained by the BJA.

The Bureau of Justice Statistics compiles, analyzes, and distributes a number of criminal justice statistical reports, including the reports on capital punishment, crime victimization, deaths in custody, recidivism, and other criminal justice issues.

The National Institute of Justice (NIJ) is the principal research and development agency in the Justice Department. NIJ's principal authorities are derived from the Omnibus Crime Control and Safe Streets Act of 1968 and Title II of the Homeland Security Act of 2002.

NIJ responsibilities include evaluating the effectiveness of justice programs and supporting basic research and development on criminal justice issues. The institute administers the National Criminal Justice Reference Service, which distributes information about the OJP and the Office of National Drug Control Policy and maintains a computerized database on law enforcement and criminal justice information.

In addition to managing research and evaluation grants programs, the NIJ also manages DNA backlog reduction grants programs.

The Court Security Improvement Act of 2007 required the NIJ to conduct a study to determine the collateral consequences of convictions for criminal federal offenses and criminal offenses in each state, U.S. territory, and the District of Columbia. The survey was to identify any provision in the Constitution, law, or administrative rules of each jurisdiction that imposed a collateral sanction or authorized the imposition of a disqualification, and any such provision that might afford relief from such sanction or disqualification.

The Office of Juvenile Justice and Delinquency Prevention (OJJDP) administers federal programs relating to missing and exploited children and to juvenile delinquency. The OJJDP's missing children's assistance program maintains a national resource center and clearinghouse to provide technical assistance to public and private agencies in locating and recovering missing children.

It awards federal grants and contracts for research and service projects and operates a national toll-free hotline to assist in locating missing children.

The federal Coordinating Council on Juvenile Justice and Delinquency Prevention reviews federal policies on juvenile justice and advises the OJJDP administrator. As designated by the Juvenile Justice and Delinquency Prevention Act of 1974, the council is composed of nine statutory members representing the following federal agencies: Departments of Justice, Education, Health and Human Services, Housing and Urban Development, and Labor; the Office of National Drug Control Policy; U.S. Citizenship and Immigration Service; the Corporation for National Service; and the Office of Juvenile Justice and Delinquency Prevention. The council also includes nine practitioner members representing disciplines that focus on youth.

The Victims of Crime Act of the Comprehensive Crime Control Act of 1984 established a crime victims fund in the Treasury Department to be administered by the attorney general through the OJP's Office for Victims of Crime (OVC). Sources for the fund include federal criminal fines, penalty assessment fees, and forfeited bonds and collateral. Grants from the fund are given to the states both to finance their crime victim compensation programs and to allow them to award funds to local crime victim assistance programs. In addition, OVC sponsors training to sensitize criminal justice practitioners to victims' needs.

Crime victim compensation is a direct reimbursement to, or on behalf of, a crime victim for the following crime-related expenses: medical costs, mental health counseling, funeral and burial costs, lost wages, or loss of support. Other expenses that may be compensated include eyeglasses or other corrective lenses, dental services and devices, prosthetic devices, and crime scene cleanup.

The Public Safety Officer Medal of Valor Act, enacted in 2001, established the Public Safety Medal of Valor as the highest national award for valor by a public safety officer. The president awards the Public Safety Officer Medal of Valor to public safety officers cited by the attorney general and recommended by the Medal of Valor Review Board. The OJP manages the medal of valor program.

The Adam Walsh Child Safety and Protection Act of 2006 established within the OJP the Sex Offender Sentencing, Monitoring, Apprehending, Registering, and Tracking (SMART) Office. The act mandated a comprehensive national system for the registration of sex offenders and offenders against children under Title I, Sex Offender Registration and Notification Act (SORNA). The SMART Office promulgated regulations to implement the provisions of SORNA. States are required to establish registries, policies, and procedures to meet the provisions of the act or risk losing 10 percent of their Byrne grants funding. Tribal nations also were required to establish registries either through the state or on their own. After initial regulations were released, only one state, Ohio, was able to comply with the provisions by the 2010 deadline. Governors and state legislatures believed the regulations were too narrowly written and too expensive to implement; many states had already invested millions in their own sex offender registration systems. In January 2011 the SMART Office revised the regulations and several more states were deemed to be in "substantial compliance" based on the revised guidelines. By early 2015 eighteen states were in compliance with SORNA.

■ KEY PERSONNEL

Assistant Attorney General
Karol Mason. . . . . (202) 307–5933
Fax. . . . . (202) 514–7805
Principal Deputy Assistant Attorney General
Beth McGarry . . . . (202) 307–5933
Deputy Assistant Attorney General
Maureen Henneberg. . . . . (202) 307–5933
Administration
Phillip Merkle . . . . (202) 307–0087
Chief Financial Officer
Leigh Benda. . . . . (202) 307–0623
Chief Information Officer
Angel Santa (acting) . . . . (202) 305–9071
Civil Rights
Michael Alston. (202) 307–0690
General Counsel
Rafael A. Madan . . . . (202) 307–6325
Bureau of Justice Assistance
Main office. . . . . (202) 616–6500
    Director
    Denise E. O'Donnell. . . . . (202) 616–6500
        Fax. . . . . (202) 514–6323
    Policy
    Kristen Mahoney. . . . . (202) 616–5139
    Planning
    Eileen Garry. . . . . (202) 307–6226
    Programs
    Tracy Trautman. . . . . (202) 305–1491
Bureau of Justice Statistics
Main office. . . . . (202) 307–0765
    Director
    William J. Sabol. . . . . (202) 307–0765
        Fax. . . . . (202) 307–5846
    Corrections Statistics Unit
    Vacant. . . . . (202) 616–5164
    Criminal Justice Data Improvement Program
    Devon Adams . . . . (202) 514–9157
    Law Enforcement Prosecution, Courts, and Special Projects Division
    Vacant. . . . . (202) 307–0765
    Publication and Dissemination Unit
    Doris J. James. . . . . (202) 616–3625
    Recidivism, Reentry, and Special Projects Unit
    Howard Snyder . . . . (202) 616–8305
    Statistical Collections and Analysis
    Allen J. Beck. . . . . (202) 616–3277
    Statistical Planning, Policy, and Operations Division
    Gerard (Jerry) Ramker. . . . . (202) 307–0759
    Victimization Statistics Unit
    Michael Planty. . . . . (202) 514–9746

National Institute of Justice
    Main office . . . . (202) 307–2942
    Director
        Nancy Rodriguez . . . . (202) 307–2942
    Research and Evaluation
        Seri Irazola . . . . (202) 616–0685
    Communications
        Jolene Hernon . . . . (202) 307–1464
    Operations
        Portia Graham . . . . (202) 307–2964
    Science and Technology
        Chris Tillery . . . . (202) 305–9829
    Investigative and Forensic Sciences
        Gerald LaPorte (acting) . . . . (202) 305–1106
Office for Victims of Crime
    Main office . . . . (202) 307–5983
    Director
        Joye E. Frost . . . . (202) 307–5983
        Fax . . . . (202) 514–6383
    Deputy
        James Cantrell . . . . (202) 305–1696
Office of Juvenile Justice and Delinquency Prevention
    Main Office . . . . (202) 307–5911
    Administrator
        Robert L. Listenbee . . . . (202) 307–5911
        Fax . . . . (202) 307–2093
Office of Sex Offender Sentencing, Monitoring, Apprehending, Registering, and Tracking (SMART)
    Main office . . . . (202) 514–4689
    Director
        Luis C.deBaca . . . . (202) 514–4689
        Fax . . . . (202) 354–4200

▉ INFORMATION SOURCES

Internet

Agency website: www.ojp.gov. Features information on OJP divisions and programs.

Telephone Contacts

Personnel Locator (Justice Dept.) . . . . (202) 514–2000
Family Assistance/Victims of Crime
    Call Center . . . . (800) 331–0075
OJP Customer Service Center . . . . (800) 458–0786
TTY . . . . (202) 616–3867

See Publications (*below*) for toll-free order numbers and information numbers.

Information and Publications

KEY OFFICES

OJP Communications

810 7th St. N.W., #6338
Washington, DC 20531
(202) 307–0703
Fax (202) 514–5958
E-mail: ojp.ocom@usdoj.gov
Silas Darden (acting), director

Answers questions about the OJP and its activities. Distributes publications and issues news releases. Maintains a mailing list.

Freedom of Information

Office of the General Counsel
Attn: FOIA Staff
810 7th St. N.W., #5400
Washington, DC 20531
(202) 307–0790
Fax (202) 307–1419
Dorothy A. Lee, FOIA contact
Carolyn Kennedy, FOIA public liaison
(202) 307–6235
E-mail: FOIAOJP@usdoj.gov

The OJP reading room is in Room 5430; the electronic reading room is at www.ojp.usdoj.gov/about/foia/reading_room.htm.

DATA AND STATISTICS

National Criminal Justice Reference Service (NCJRS)

2277 Research Blvd.
P.O. Box 6000
Rockville, MD 20849–6000
(800) 851–3420
Fax (301) 519–5212
TTY (301) 947–8374
Internet: www.ncjrs.gov
E-mail: library@ncjrs.org

A clearinghouse for information on criminal justice, juvenile justice, and drug policy, serves the offices of the U.S. Department of Justice, Office of Justice Programs, Office on Violence Against Women, National Institute of Corrections, and Office of Community Oriented Policing Services, as well as the Office of National Drug Control Policy under the Executive Office of the President. Conducts searches of its database to provide information requested by organizations or individuals. Information is available in the following forms: automated matching of a user's interest area with literature in the NCJRS system; library services, interlibrary loan, and photocopy; hardcopy and electronic documents; search and retrieval on specific and general questions; referral to other information and reference services; indexes; and Internet services.

The NCJRS distributes research titles, including government and final grant reports, journal articles, and monographs; manuals; law enforcement equipment studies; statistics on custody, prisoners, and other corrections issues; community crime prevention programs; juvenile justice; crime victim services; illicit drugs; and audiovisual materials listings.

NCJRS's information resources, databases, and services can be accessed through the NCJRS home page at www.ncjrs.gov, with hundreds of publications and abstracts available. Access to the information resources and databases is free of charge. However, shipping and handling fees may apply to hard-copy document requests and charges apply to some services.

National Law Enforcement and Corrections Technology Center

700 N. Frederick Ave., Bldg. 181, #1L30
Gaithersburg , MD 20879
(800) 248–2742
Fax (301) 240–6730
Internet: www.justnet.org
E-mail: asknlectc@justnet.org

Administered by the National Institute of Justice. Provides information about law enforcement and corrections equipment and technology. Helps identify needs; initiates partnerships among private and public organizations to develop technologies; and tests and evaluates products.

PUBLICATIONS

Data and publications are available from the following toll-free numbers and from the website.

National Criminal Justice Reference Service/Office for Victims of Crime

Response Center.................. (800) 851–3420
TTY ....(877) 712–9279

Reference Resources

LIBRARIES

OJP Online Research and Information Center

810 7th St. N.W., #6304
Washington, DC 20531
(202) 307–6742
James Fort, librarian

Resources available to Justice Department staff only, though many publications and databases are available through the NCJRS Research and Information Center and its website (*below*).

NCJRS Research and Information Center

2277 Research Blvd.
MS-2A
P.O. Box 6000
Rockville, MD 20849–6000
(800) 851–3420
Kreg Purcell, library services manager
Internet: www.ncjrs.gov

Houses the main library collection of the National Criminal Justice Reference Service. The library is not open to the public. The website's online library includes hundreds of publications and their abstracts, which may be accessed by the public. Paper copies (whether books, articles, or photocopies) are also available for a fee.

DOJ Community Oriented Policing Services (COPS)

145 N St. N.E.
Washington, DC 20530

(202) 307–1480; (800) 421–6770
E-mail: askcopsRC@usdoj.gov
Internet: www.cops.usdoj.gov

Advances the practice of community policing in state, local, and tribal law enforcement agencies. Provides technical information to applicants for grants administered by COPS.

DOCKETS

Federal dockets are available at www.regulations .gov. (*See appendix for Searching and Commenting on Regulations: Regulations.gov.*)

RULES AND REGULATIONS

OJP rules and regulations are published in the *Code of Federal Regulations,* Title 28, Chapter 1, Parts 18–20, 30, and 32. Proposed regulations, new final regulations, and updates to the *Code of Federal Regulations* are published in the daily *Federal Register.* (*See appendix for details on how to obtain and use these publications.*) The *Federal Register* and the *Code of Federal Regulations* May also be accessed online at www.archives.gov/federal-register/cfr; this site also contains a link to the federal government's regulatory website at www.regulations.gov (*see appendix*).

◾ LEGISLATION

The OJP carries out its responsibilities under:

Civil Rights Act of 1964 (78 Stat. 252, 42 U.S.C. 2000d). Signed by the president July 2, 1964. Title IV barred discrimination based on race, color, or national origin in any program or activity receiving federal assistance.

Omnibus Crime Control and Safe Streets Act of 1968 (82 Stat. 197, 42 U.S.C. 3701). Signed by the president June 19, 1968. Provided grants to law enforcement agencies (through the now-defunct Law Enforcement Assistance Administration).

Rehabilitation Act of 1973 (87 Stat. 357, 29 U.S.C. 701). Signed by the president Sept. 26, 1973. Extended basic federal aid programs to the disabled.

Juvenile Justice and Delinquency Prevention Act of 1974 (88 Stat. 1109, 42 U.S.C. 5601). Signed by the president Sept. 7, 1974. Established the Office of Juvenile Justice and Delinquency Prevention. Amended in 1984 to establish a program for missing and exploited children.

Public Safety Officers' Benefits Act of 1976 (90 Stat. 1346, 42 U.S.C. 3701 note). Signed by the president Sept. 29, 1976. Authorized the provision of a $100,000 benefit to the survivors of public safety officers killed as a result of a personal injury sustained in the line of duty. Currently administered by the Bureau of Justice Assistance.

Justice System Improvement Act of 1979 (93 Stat. 1167, 42 U.S.C. 3711). Signed by the president Dec. 27, 1979. Created the Office of Justice Assistance, Research, and Statistics and brought under its jurisdiction the Law Enforcement Assistance Administration (now defunct), the National Institute of Justice, and the Bureau of Justice Statistics. Also provided for grants to states, local governments, and nonprofit organizations for criminal justice purposes.

Comprehensive Crime Control Act of 1984 (98 Stat. 1837, 18 U.S.C. 1 note). Signed by the president Oct. 12, 1984. Provisions of the act included those under the Justice Assistance Act (98 Stat. 2077, 42 U.S.C. 3711 note), which established the OJP to coordinate the activities of several units within the Department of Justice. Also created the Bureau of Justice Assistance to administer a new program of block grants for anticrime projects. The Victims of Crime Act (98 Stat. 2170, 42 U.S.C. 10601 note) established a crime victims fund in the Treasury to provide financing for victim compensation and victim assistance programs.

Anti-Drug Abuse Act of 1988 (102 Stat. 4181, 21 U.S.C. 1501 note). Signed by the president Nov. 18, 1988. Authorized more than $2 billion to prevent the manufacturing, distribution, and use of illegal drugs; to increase drug treatment and education programs; and to strengthen local law enforcement efforts. Created a cabinet-level "drug czar" position.

Crime Control Act of 1990 (104 Stat. 4789, 18 U.S.C. 1 note). Signed by the president Nov. 29, 1990. Provided for federal debt collection and prosecution of fraud at financial institutions. Also provided further protection for children from child abuse and child pornography.

Violent Crime Control and Law Enforcement Act of 1994 (108 Stat. 1796, 42 U.S.C. 13701 note). Signed by the president Sept. 13, 1994. Provided funding to hire 100,000 police officers and build boot camps and prisons. Expanded the federal death penalty and enacted mandatory life imprisonment for federal offenders with three or more serious violent felonies or drug trafficking crimes.

Juvenile Justice and Delinquency Prevention Act of 2002 (116 Stat. 1758, 42 U.S.C. 3711 note). Signed by the president Nov. 2, 2002. Amended the Juvenile Justice and Delinquency Prevention Act to repeal certain provisions and to establish the Juvenile Delinquency Prevention Block Grant Program.

Justice For All Act of 2004 (118 Stat. 2260, 42 U.S.C. 13701 note). Signed by the president Oct. 30, 2004. An omnibus criminal justice bill that established new programs and amended existing programs within the OJP and other provisions. This included the Debbie Smith Act of 2004 to provide funding for timely analyses of DNA samples, including samples from rape kits; DNA Sexual Assault Justice Act of 2004, which amended standards for DNA entered into CODIS; Innocence Protection Act of 2004, which amended the federal criminal code to establish procedures for post-conviction DNA testing in federal court; and authorized the Kirk Bloodsworth Post-Conviction DNA Testing Grant Program to award grants to states to help defray the costs of post-conviction DNA testing.

Adam Walsh Child Protection and Safety Act of 2006 (120 Stat. 587, 42 U.S.C. 16901 note). Signed by the president July 20, 2006. Title I (Sex Offender Registration and Notification Act) established a comprehensive national system for the registration of sex offenders and offenders against children.

Court Security Improvement Act of 2007 (121 Stat. 2534, 28 U.S.C. 1 note). Signed by the president Jan. 7, 2008. Required the National Institute of Justice to conduct a study of the collateral consequences of convictions for criminal offenses in the states, District of Columbia, and U.S. territories. Defined "collateral consequences" as sanctions against an individual or disqualifications resulting from a felony or misdemeanor conviction that were not part of the original judgment of the sentencing court. Directed the Office of Justice Programs to give grants to enable the highest court in each state to establish and maintain a threat assessment database.

Prioritizing Resources and Organization for Intellectual Property Act of 2008 (122 Stat. 4256, 15 U.S.C. 8101 note). Signed by the president Oct. 13, 2008. Authorized the Office of Justice Programs to give grants for training, prevention, enforcement, and prosecution of intellectual property theft and infringement crimes.

Other Justice Department Offices

■ CRIMINAL DIVISION
950 Pennsylvania Ave. N.W.
Washington, DC 20530
Internet: www.justice.gov/criminal

The Criminal Division of the Department of Justice (DOJ) is the unit responsible for coordinating the development and enforcement of the majority (more than 900) of federal criminal statutes (except those specifically assigned to the Antitrust, Civil Rights, Environment and Natural Resources, or Tax Divisions). It is headed by an assistant attorney general, who is appointed by the president with confirmation by the Senate.

The division handles certain civil matters related to its criminal jurisdiction under federal liquor, narcotics, counterfeiting, gambling, firearms, customs, and immigration laws. It investigates and prosecutes criminal offenses involving subversive activities, including treason, espionage, sedition, and Nazi war crimes. The division approves or monitors sensitive areas of law enforcement such as participation in the Witness Security Program and the use of electronic surveillance. The Criminal Division also is responsible for civil litigation resulting from petitions for writs of habeas corpus by members of the Armed Forces, actions brought on behalf of federal prisoners, and legal issues concerning national security, such as counterespionage.

Divisions include the Public Integrity Section, Asset Forfeiture and Money Laundering Section, Capital Case Unit, Organized Crime and Gang Section, Fraud Section, Computer Crime and Intellectual Property Section, Human Rights and Special Prosecution Section, Narcotics and Dangerous Drugs Section, Appellate Section, and the Child Exploitation and Obscenity Section.

Prosecution of cases usually is handled in the field by one or more of the division's ninety-four U.S. attorneys. The division focuses most of its prosecution efforts on organized crime, white-collar crime and fraud, official corruption and public integrity, and major narcotics trafficking.

The agency's website provides an overview of the Criminal Division.

Assistant Attorney General
Leslie R. Caldwell . . . . (202) 514–2601
    E-mail: Criminal.Division@usdoj.gov
DOJ Public Affairs
Emily Pierce (acting) . . . . (202) 514–2007

Administration
    Tracy Melton (acting) . . . . (202) 514–2001
Appellate
    Patty M. Stemler . . . . (202) 514–2611
Asset Forfeiture and Money Laundering
    M. Kendall Day . . . . (202) 514–1263
Capital Case
    P. Kevin Carwile . . . . (202) 514–3705
Child Exploitation and Obscenity
    Andrew G. Oosterbaan. . . . . (202) 514–5780
Computer Crime & Intellectual Property
    John Lynch . . . . (202) 514–1026
Enforcement Operations
    Monique Perez Roth . . . . (202) 514–6809
Fraud
    Andrew Weissmann . . . . (202) 514–7023
Human Rights and Special Prosecutions
    Teresa McHenry . . . . (202) 616–2492
International Affairs
    Mary Roderiguez (acting) . . . . (202) 514–0000
International Criminal Investigative Training Assistance Program
    Richard W. Miller (acting) . . . . (202) 305–8190
Narcotic and Dangerous Drugs
    Arthur Wyatt . . . . (202) 514–0917
Organized Crime
    James M. Trusty. . . . . (202) 514–3594
Overseas Prosecutorial Development, Assistance, and Training
    Faye Ehrenstamm . . . . (202) 514–1323
Policy and Legislation
    Jonathan J. Wroblewski . . . . (202) 514–4194
Public Integrity
    Raymond Hulser (acting). . . . . (202) 514–1412

■ FEDERAL BUREAU OF PRISONS
320 1st St. N.W.
Washington, DC 20534
Internet: www.bop.gov

The Federal Bureau of Prisons was established in 1930 to provide more progressive and humane care for federal inmates, to professionalize the prison service, and to ensure consistent and centralized administration of the federal prison system. The bureau is respon-sible for the custody and care of federal offenders. The agency confines these offenders in bureau-operated correctional institutions or detention centers, as well as through agreements with state and local governments and through contracts with privately operated commu-nity correction centers, detention centers, prisons, and juvenile facilities. In 2015 the bureau operated 119 insti-tutions and was responsible for the confinement of more than 208,000 federal offenders in bureau-operated and privately operated facilities.

The Bureau of Prisons' headquarters, or Central Office, is located in Washington, DC. The Central Office is com-posed of nine divisions that are responsible for establish-ing national policy; developing and reviewing programs; providing training and technical assistance to the field; and coordinating agency operations in the various disciplines (administration; correctional programs; health services; industries, education, and vocational training; human resources management; legal issues, information, policy and public affairs; program review; and re-entry services). The bureau has created six regions and has given direct responsibility for overseeing day-to-day operations of the prisons to a regional office, headed by a regional director. In conjunction with the central office, the regional offices also provide administrative oversight and support to the institutions and community corrections offices. Institution wardens have responsibility for managing the prisons and report to their respective regional directors. Community corrections offices oversee community corrections centers and home confinement programs.

The bureau uses two training centers for bureau staff. Introductory training is conducted at the bureau's Staff Training Academy at the Federal Law Enforcement Training Center in Glynco, GA; specialized professional training is conducted at the Management and Specialty Training Center in Aurora, CO.

The National Institute of Corrections (NIC), an agency within the Bureau of Prisons, was established in 1974 as a result of the attention to prison conditions brought about by the Attica prison uprising in 1971. NIC provides tech-nical assistance, training, and information to state and local correctional agencies throughout the country. NIC has four divisions (Jails, Prisons, Community Corrections, and Academy), and it operates a clearinghouse known as the NIC Information Center. NIC provides training to state and local correctional personnel and to bureau employees at its academy in Aurora, CO.

The agency's website features an inmate locator that allows users to search the location and status of inmates incarcerated since 1982.

Director

Charles E. Samuels Jr. . . . . (202) 307–3250
    Fax. . . . . (202) 514–6878

BOP Public Affairs

Traci Billingsley. . . . . (202) 514–6551
    General Information. . . . . (202) 307–3198
    Inmate Locator Service . . . . (202) 307–3126
    National Institute of Corrections
      Information Center . . . . (800) 877–1461

■ OFFICE ON VIOLENCE AGAINST WOMEN

145 N Street NE, 10th Floor
Washington, DC 20530
Internet: www.justice.gov/ovw

The Office on Violence Against Women (OVW) was created specifically to implement the Violence Against Women Act (VAWA). VAWA, part of the Violent Crime Control and Law Enforcement Act of 1994, was enacted to address the crimes associated with domestic violence, sexual assault, and stalking. OVW administers funding and technical assistance to communities that are develop-ing programs and policies with the goal of ending domestic violence, dating violence, sexual assault, and stalking.

Passage of VAWA was the result of an organized grass-roots effort comprised primarily of advocates who worked on behalf of women in national, state, and local juris-dictions. In the two decades prior to VAWA, rape crisis centers and women's shelters were established in commu-nities. In this time, state and local laws changed to address the severity of domestic and sexual violence against women. However, progress addressing these crimes had not reached all parts of the nation. As such, advocates sought a national solution and worked with Congress to craft and pass VAWA to fill that void.

Currently, OVW administers four formula-based and twenty discretionary grant programs, established under VAWA and subsequent legislation. The three formula programs include STOP (Services, Training, Officers, Prosecutors), SASP (Sexual Assault Services Program), State Coalitions and Tribal Coalitions. The discretion-and ary programs support victims and hold perpetrators accountable through promoting a coordinated com-munity response. Funding is provided to local and state and tribal governments, courts, nonprofit organizations, community-based organizations, secondary schools, institutions of higher education, and state and tribal coalitions. These agencies, organizations, and coalitions work toward developing more effective responses to violence against women through activities that include direct services, crisis intervention, transitional hous-ing, legal assistance to victims, court improvement, and training for law enforcement and courts. They also serve specific populations such as elderly victims, persons with disabilities, college students, teens, and culturally and lin-guistically specific populations.

Since its inception, OVW has awarded more than $6 billion in grants and cooperative agreements. By forging state, local, and tribal partnerships among police, pros-ecutors, judges, victim advocates, health care providers, faith leaders, and other professionals, OVW grant pro-grams help provide victims with the services they need to recover, while enabling communities to hold offend-ers accountable. VAWA was most recently reauthorized in 2013.

Director

Bea Hanson (acting) . . . . (202) 307–6026
    Fax. . . . . (202) 305–2589

Telephone Contacts

National Domestic Violence
Hotline. . . . . . (800) 799–SAFE or (800) 799–7223
TTY . . . .(800) 787–3224
National Sexual Assault
Hotline. . . . . .(800) 656–HOPE or (800) 656–4673
National Teen Dating Abuse
Hotline. . . . .(866) 331–9474
TTY . . . .(866) 331–8453

▓ UNITED STATES PAROLE COMMISSION

90 K St. N.E., 3rd Floor
Washington, D.C. 20530
Internet: www.justice.gov/uspc

The U.S. Parole Commission is an independent unit within the Justice Department. The agency was created by Congress in 1930 as the U.S. Board of Parole. The commission administers the parole system for federal prisoners and is responsible for developing a federal parole policy. The commission:

- Determines parole eligibility for federal prisoners.
- Imposes conditions on the release of any prisoner from custody.
- Revokes parole or mandatory release judgments.
- Discharges offenders from supervision and terminates prison sentences prior to expiration of the supervision period.

Hearing examiners at headquarters conduct hearings with eligible prisoners and make parole recommendations to the commission. The Bureau of Prisons (p. 750) makes arrangements for hearings and implements release orders.

The parole process begins at sentencing. Unless the court has specified a minimum time for the offender to serve, or has imposed an "indeterminate" type of sentence, parole eligibility occurs on completion of one-third of the term. If an offender is serving a life sentence or a term or terms of thirty years or more, he or she will become eligible for parole after ten years.

Appeals for parole revocation decisions may be taken up with the regional commissioner and then with the National Appeals Board. The commission also is required to review periodically cases of all released prisoners to determine the appropriateness of terminating future sentences earlier than the term imposed by the court.

With passage of the Sentencing Reform Act of 1984 and implementation of the U.S. Sentencing Guidelines on Nov. 1, 1987, the commission began to be phased out. The commission closed its former regional offices; in February 1996 all functions were consolidated at the Chevy Chase, MD, headquarters. The number of commissioners was also reduced, from the original nine to three in October 1996, with corresponding reductions in staff. However, by 2005 the commission had grown to five commissioners.

The Parole Phaseout Act of 1996 extended the life of the commission until Nov. 1, 2002, but provided for further reductions. The law also required the attorney general to report to Congress yearly, beginning in 1998, whether it is more cost-effective for the commission to remain a separate agency or whether its functions and personnel should be assigned elsewhere.

The Department of Justice Appropriations Authorization Act of 2002 extended the commission for an additional three years. The legislation directed the attorney general to establish a committee within the DOJ to evaluate the merits and feasibility of transferring the commission's functions regarding the supervised release of District of Columbia offenders to other entities outside the DOJ. Congress passed extensions of the commission in 2005 and 2008, with a phaseout date of Oct. 31, 2011. Just ten days before the phaseout deadline, the United States Parole Commission Extension Act of 2011 was signed into law, which extended the USPC for two more years. In 2013 Congress reauthorized USPC for another five years.

Chair
J. Patricia Wilson Smoot (acting) . . . . (202) 346–7000
Fax. . . . . (202) 357–1085
E-mail: public.inquiries@usdoj.gov
USPC Public Affairs
Anissa Hunter Banks . . . . (202) 346–7000
Fax. . . . . (202) 357–1085

Labor Department

200 Constitution Ave. N.W., Washington, DC 20210
Internet: www.dol.gov

Employee Benefits Security Administration

200 Constitution Ave. N.W., Washington, DC 20210
Internet: www.dol.gov/ebsa

The Employee Benefits Security Administration (EBSA) is responsible for administering the Title I provisions of the Employee Retirement Income Security Act (ERISA) of 1974. Before January 1986, EBSA was known as the Pension and Welfare Benefits Administration. At the time of its name change, EBSA was upgraded to a subcabinet position with the establishment of assistant secretary and deputy assistant secretary positions.

The EBSA has primary responsibility for ERISA's requirements on fiduciary standards, reporting and disclosure, employee protection, and enforcement. The agency develops rules and regulations on the standards of conduct of individuals who operate employee benefit plans or manage pension plan funds. It also oversees requirements designed to protect the benefits of workers, including health plan benefits, and employees' rights to information about their plans. These requirements include continuation of health care benefits as established by the Consolidated Omnibus Budget Reconciliation Act (COBRA) of 1985 and extended by the Health Insurance Portability and Accountability Act (HIPAA) of 1996. The office also is responsible for processing requests for exemptions from ERISA's prohibited transaction provisions.

The Mental Health Parity Act (MHPA) of 1996 required that annual or lifetime dollar limits on mental health benefits be no lower than any such dollar limits for medical and surgical benefits offered by a group health plan or health insurance issuer offering coverage in connection with a group health plan. The act had exemptions for small businesses and for increased costs. MHPA was reauthorized in 2008 and included parity for chemical substance and substance abuse disorders, which were not previously covered under the 1996 act.

In response to complaints against health insurance plans that provided scant benefits under maternity plans—so-called drive-through deliveries—Congress enacted the Newborns' and Mothers' Health Protection Act of 1996. This act requires plans that offer maternity coverage to pay for at least a forty-eight-hour hospital stay following childbirth (ninety-six-hour stay in the case of a caesarean section). This law went into effect Jan. 1, 1998. In 1998 the Department of Labor, in conjunction with the Departments of the Treasury and Health and Human Services (HHS), published interim regulations clarifying issues arising under the newborns' act.

The Child Support Performance and Incentive Act of 1998 is intended to help children gain access to coverage under their noncustodial parents' employer-based group health plans. The act provides a uniform National Medical Support Notice to be used by the states in carrying out their responsibilities in child support enforcement. The National Medical Support Notice also allows administrators of group health plans to determine readily that medical child support orders are qualified under section 609(a) of ERISA.

Under its enforcement authority, the EBSA monitors and investigates the administration of these plans to ensure compliance with the requirements of ERISA. The agency has authority to enforce ERISA through voluntary compliance to resolve any violations of law or by bringing civil actions in federal courts. EBSA's oversight authority extends to nearly 684,000 retirement plans, approximately 2.4 million health plans, and a similar number of other welfare benefit plans, such as those providing life or disability insurance. These plans cover about 141 million workers and their dependents and include assets of approximately $.6 trillion. EBSA enforcement efforts recovered nearly $600 million in fiscal year 2014.

The Abandoned Plan Program facilitates the termination of, and distribution of benefits from, individual account pension plans that have been abandoned by their sponsoring employers. The program was established pursuant to three final regulations and a related class exemption and is administered by EBSA national and regional offices.

Criminal prosecutions based on violations of ERISA are directed by the U.S. Attorney's Offices. *(For further information on regulation of pension plans, see Pension Benefit Guaranty Corporation, p. 444.)*

In 2010 President Barack Obama signed the Patient Protection and Affordable Care Act (Affordable Care Act). The legislation made sweeping changes to the health insurance industry regarding products, pricing, and availability, including employer-sponsored health insurance plans. The wide-ranging legislation was designed to be implemented in stages, with most provisions implemented by 2014. The law required that the secretary of health and human services, in consultation with the secretaries of Labor and the Treasury, promulgate regulations to carry out various provisions *(see Centers for Medicare and Medicaid Services, p. 622).*

This includes regulations governing claims and appeals, preexisting condition exclusions, lifetime and annual limits, rescissions, extension of coverage for adult children, and patient protections. This also included authority to establish the Early Retiree Reinsurance Program (ERRP), which became operational in 2010. The ERRP was designed to help employers and other sponsors of employment-based health plans continue to provide coverage for early retirees until 2014, at which time insurance companies may no longer deny coverage based on preexisting conditions or charge more based on an individual's health status. ERRP provided nearly $5 billion in reinsurance payments to approximately 2,900 employers and other sponsors of retiree plans.

In 2015 EBSA issued a proposed rule to expand the number of persons who are subject to fiduciary best interest standards when they provide retirement investment advice. The rule was proposed to mitigate conflict of interest in the retirement investment marketplace between financial advisors and their clients.

▓ KEY PERSONNEL

Assistant Secretary
Phyllis C. Borzi . . . . (202) 693–8300
Fax. . . . . (202) 219–5526
Deputy Assistant Secretary
Judy Mares . . . . (202) 693–8300
Deputy Assistant Secretary for Program Operations
Timothy D. Hauser . . . . (202) 693–8315
Chief Accountant
Ian Dingwall. . . . . (202) 693–8361
Outreach, Education, and Assistance
Mark Connor. (202) 693–8337
Enforcement
Mabel Capolongo . . . . (202) 693–8443
Exemption Determinations
Lyssa Hall . . . . (202) 693–8540
Health Plan Standards and Compliance Assistance
Amy Turner (acting). . . . . (202) 693–8335
Policy and Research
Joseph Piacentini. . . . . (202) 693–8410
Program Planning, Evaluation, and Management
Joe Lovelace . . . . (202) 693–8480
Regulations and Interpretations
Joe Canary . . . . (202) 693–8500
Regulations
Vacant. . . . . (202) 693–8513
Regulatory Policy Analysis
G. Christopher Cosby . . . . (202) 693–8425
Technology and Information Services
Diane Schweizer . . . . (202) 693–8595

▓ INFORMATION SOURCES

Internet
Agency website: www.dol.gov/ebsa. Information about EBSA includes publications, media releases, and regulations the agency enforces. The site also includes user-friendly fact sheets that outline rights and protections afforded under the law.

Telephone Contacts
National Contact Center
(Labor Dept.) . . . . (866) 487–2365
TTY . . . . (877) 889–5627
EBSA Toll-free Hotline . . . . (866) 444–EBSA
or . . . . (866) 444–3272

Information and Publications

KEY OFFICES

EBSA Office of Outreach, Education, and Assistance
200 Constitution Ave. N.W., Room N-5623
Washington, DC 20210
(202) 693–8337
Mark Connor, director

Administers the Participant and Compliance Outreach, Education, and Assistance Program. Employee benefits advisors may be reached at (202) 693–8700, or toll-free (866) 444–3272.

Freedom of Information
Contact FOIA officer Mark Connor in the *EBSA Office of Education, Outreach, and Assistance*, above.

DATA AND STATISTICS

Policy and Research
200 Constitution Ave. N.W., Room N-5718
Washington, DC 20210
(202) 693–8410
Joseph Piacentini, director

PUBLICATIONS
The EBSA Office of Participant Assistance distributes a list of available publications and studies of the agency. Subjects are primarily related to health and retirement, addressed to small businesses and consumers. Compliance assistance publications, health and pension reports, ERISA Advisory Counsel reports, and funded research papers are available. EBSA publications are available through the request line at (866) 444–3272 or on the agency website at www.dol.gov/ebsa/publications.

EBSA titles include:
An Employees' Guide to Health Benefits Under COBRA
401(k) Plans for Small Businesses
How to Obtain Employee Benefit Documents from the Labor Department
New Employee Savings Tips—Time Is on Your Side
Payroll Deduction IRAs for Small Businesses
Savings Fitness: A Guide to Your Money and Your Financial Future
Taking the Mystery Out of Retirement Planning
Understanding Your Fiduciary Responsibilities Under A Group Health Plan

What You Should Know About Your Retirement Plan Your Health Plan and HIPAA–Making the Law Work for You

Reference Resources

LIBRARIES

Wirtz Labor Library

200 Constitution Ave. N.W., Room N-2445
Washington, DC 20210
(202) 693–6600
Macaire Carroll-Gavula, director
Internet: www.dol.gov/oasam/wirtzlaborlibrary
E-mail: library@dol.gov
Open to the public.
Hours: 8:15 a.m. to 4:45 p.m., Mon.–Fri.

The DOL library's large collection includes a 30,000 volume Labor Law library, over 200 journals, trade union periodicals, and the Folio Collection, over 750 items dating to the 1890s about the rise of the labor movement. The Digital Library and library catalogue are also available on the website.

EBSA Public Disclosure Room

200 Constitution Ave. N.W., Room N-1513
Washington, DC 20210
(202) 693–8673
Hours: 8:15 a.m. to 4:45 p.m., Mon.–Fri.

Maintains annual financial reports and descriptions of plan requirements for pension and welfare plans required by ERISA for public inspection. The agency sends copies of specific reports to individuals upon phone request (such requests taken until 3:30 p.m.). A nominal fee is charged for copying.

DOCKETS

Federal dockets are available at www.regulations.gov. (*See appendix for Searching and Commenting on Regulations: Regulations.gov.*)

RULES AND REGULATIONS

EBSA rules and regulations are published in the *Code of Federal Regulations,* Title 29, Chapter XXV, Parts 2500–2599. Proposed rules, new rules, and updates to the *Code of Federal Regulations* are published in the daily *Federal Register.* (*See appendix for information on how to obtain and use these publications.*) The *Federal Register* and the *Code of Federal Regulations* may be accessed online at www.archives.gov/federal-register/cfr; this site also contains a link to the federal government's regulatory website at www.regulations.gov (*see appendix*).

▉ LEGISLATION

The EBSA is responsible for the following statutes:

Employee Retirement Income Security Act of 1974 (ERISA) (88 Stat. 829, 29 U.S.C. 1001). Signed by the president Sept. 2, 1974. Authorized the agency to enforce provisions regulating individuals who operate pension funds.

Multi-Employer Pension Plan Amendments of 1980 (94 Stat. 1208, 29 U.S.C. 1001). Signed by the president Sept. 26, 1980. Amended ERISA to strengthen the funding requirements for multi-employer pension plans.

Retirement Equity Act of 1984 (98 Stat. 1426, 29 U.S.C. 1001). Signed by the president Aug. 23, 1984. Provided for greater equity in private pension plans for workers and their spouses and dependents.

Consolidated Omnibus Budget Reconciliation Act of 1985 (COBRA) (10 Stat. 82, 29 U.S.C. 1162). Signed by the president April 7, 1986. Guaranteed continuation of health care coverage for eighteen months for workers who lose their jobs (twenty-nine months for disabled workers), and for the worker's spouse and dependent children if they are covered when employment is terminated.

Single-Employer Pension Plan Amendments of 1986 (100 Stat. 82, 29 U.S.C. 1001). Signed by the president April 7, 1986. Prevented companies from terminating their pension plans arbitrarily.

Pension Protection Act of 1987 (101 Stat. 1330–1333, 26 U.S.C. note 1). Signed by the president Dec. 22, 1987. Barred employers from the act of deducting contributions to "overfunded" pension funds, which are defined as funds with assets exceeding 150 percent of current liability.

Retirement Protection Act of 1994 (108 Stat. 4809, 26 U.S.C. 1 note). Signed by the president Dec. 8, 1994. Amended the Employee Retirement Income Security Act of 1974 (ERISA) requirements for pension plan funding, including (1) minimum funding, revising additional funding requirements for single-employer plans; (2) limitation on changes in current liability assumptions; (3) anticipation of bargained benefit increases; (4) modification of the quarterly contribution requirement; and (5) exceptions to the excise tax on nondeductible contributions.

Health Insurance Portability and Accountability Act of 1996 (110 Stat. 1936, 42 U.S.C. 201 note). Signed by the president Aug. 21, 1996. Limited the circumstances in which employers can use preexisting conditions to deny new workers health care benefits. Extended COBRA coverage to workers who become disabled within the first sixty days of coverage and to children born to or adopted by workers during the period of coverage.

Newborns' and Mothers' Health Protection Act of 1996 (110 Stat. 2935). Signed by the president Sept. 26, 1996. Title VI of the VA, HUD, and Independent Agencies Appropriations bill. Amended ERISA and the Public Health Service Act to require a health plan that provided maternity benefits to provide coverage for a minimum hospital stay of forty-eight hours for normal vaginal delivery, and ninety-six hours for caesarian section. Prohibited plans from using certain types of penalties regarding participants, beneficiaries, policyholders, or providers to circumvent this act.

Mental Health Parity Act of 1996 (110 Stat. 2945, 29 U.S.C. 1185a). Signed by the president Sept. 26, 1996. Title VII of the VA, HUD, and Independent Agencies Appropriations bill. Amended ERISA and the Public

Health Service Act to require group health plans, if they choose to offer mental health benefits, to provide the same financial conditions for such mental health benefits that they provide for medical and surgical benefits, including the same aggregate lifetime limits and the same annual limits.

Child Support Performance and Incentive Act of 1998 (112 Stat. 645, 42 U.S.C. 1305 note). Signed by the president July 16, 1998. Directed the enforcement of a child support order for health care coverage. Prescribed enforcement guidelines for enrollment of the child in the health care coverage of the noncustodial parent's employer.

Women's Health and Cancer Rights Act of 1998 (112 Stat. 2681–337, 2681–436, 42 U.S.C. 201 note). Signed by the president Oct. 21, 1998. Contains protections for patients who elect breast reconstruction in connection with a mastectomy.

Pension Funding Equity Act of 2004 (118 Stat. 596, 15 U.S.C. 37b). Signed by the president April 10, 2004. Amended the Employee Retirement Income Security Act of 1974 (ERISA) and the Internal Revenue Code (IRC) to replace temporarily (for plan years 2004 and 2005) the thirty-year Treasury rate with a rate based on long-term corporate bonds for certain pension plan funding requirements. Allowed applicable employers defined as airlines and steel companies to make deficit reduction payments to the Pension Benefit Guaranty Corporation. Established ERISA requirements for multiemployer plan funding notices. Required plan administrators to send such notices to participants, beneficiaries, labor organizations, and employers for each plan year.

Pension Protection Act of 2006 (120 Stat. 780). Signed by the president Aug. 17, 2006. Required greater disclosure of retirement plan performance to participants. The provision of investment advice to a plan and its participants was exempted from prohibited transaction rules, if such advice is given by fiduciary advisors meeting specified requirements. Permitted an employer maintaining a defined benefit plan to transfer excess pension assets to cover current retirees future health liabilities. Directed the labor secretary to issue regulations relating to the time and order of issuance of qualified domestic relations orders under ERISA and IRC provisions.

Genetic Information Nondiscrimination Act of 2008 (122 Stat. 881, 42 U.S.C. 2000ff note). Signed by the president May 21, 2008. Amended ERISA, the Public Health Service Act, and the Internal Revenue Code to prohibit a group health plan from adjusting premium or contribution amounts for a group on the basis of genetic information.

Paul Wellstone and Pete Domenici Mental Health Parity and Addiction Equity Act of 2008 (122 Stat. 3881). Signed by the president Oct. 3, 2008. Modified the original definition of mental health benefits created by MHPA in 1996 and added a definition of substance use disorder benefits. Required a group health plan that provides both medical and surgical benefits and mental health or substance use disorder benefits to ensure that the financial requirements, such as deductibles and copayments, are no more restrictive than the predominant financial requirements applied to substantially all medical and surgical benefits covered by the plan.

Worker, Retiree, and Employer Recovery Act of 2008 (122 Stat. 5092). Signed by the president Oct. 23, 2008. Eased some of the increased funding requirements for single-employer and multiemployer pension plans that were passed under the Pension Protection Act of 2006. Provided a waiver of minimum distribution requirements for certain retirement plans and accounts for 2009.

Patient Protection and Affordable Care Act (124 Stat. 119, 42 U.S.C. 18001 note). Signed by the president March 23, 2010. Made sweeping changes to the health insurance industry regarding products, pricing, and availability. Amends ERISA to direct the secretary of labor to adopt regulatory standards and/or issue orders to subject multiple employer welfare arrangements to state law relating to fraud and abuse. Provides consumers with a way to appeal coverage determinations or claims to their insurance company and establishes an external review process. Other provisions.

Health Care and Education Reconciliation Act of 2010 (124 Stat. 1029, 42 U.S.C. 1305 note). Signed by the president March 30, 2010. Amended portions of the Patient Protection and Affordable Care Act, including fees, payments, and deadlines.

■ REGIONAL AND DISTRICT OFFICES

ATLANTA REGIONAL OFFICE
(AL, northern FL, GA, MS, NC, SC, TN)
61 Forsyth St. S.W., #7B54
Atlanta, GA 30303
(404) 302–3900
Isabel Colon, regional director

BOSTON REGIONAL OFFICE
(CT, MA, ME, NH, central and western NY, RI, VT)
JFK Bldg.
15 New Sudbury St., #575
Boston, MA 02203
(617) 565–9600
Susan Hensley, regional director

CHICAGO REGIONAL OFFICE
(northern IL, northern IN, WI)
John C. Kluczynksi Federal Bldg.
230 S. Dearborn St., #2160
Chicago, Il 60604
(312) 353–0900
Jeffrey Monhart, regional director

CINCINNATI REGIONAL OFFICE
(southern IN, KY, MI, OH)
1885 Dixie Hwy., #210
Fort Wright, KY 41011–2664
(859) 578–4680
Joe Rivers, regional director

DALLAS REGIONAL OFFICE

(AR, LA, NM, OK, TX)
525 S. Griffin St., #900
Dallas, TX 75202–5025
(972) 850–4500
Deborah Perry, regional director

KANSAS CITY REGIONAL OFFICE

(CO, IA, southern IL, KS, MN, MO, MT, ND, NE, SD, WY)
2300 Main St., #1100
Kansas City, MO 64108
(816) 285–1800
James Purcell, regional director

LOS ANGELES REGIONAL OFFICE

(AS, AZ, southern CA, GU, HI, Wake Island)
1055 E. Colorado Blvd., #200
Pasadena, CA 91106–2357
(626) 229–1000
Crisanta Johnson, regional director

MIAMI DISTRICT OFFICE

(southern FL, PR)
1000 S. Pine Island Rd., #100
Plantation, FL 33324
(954) 424–4022
Norma Rivera, supervisor

NEW YORK REGIONAL OFFICE

(northern NJ, eastern NY)
33 Whitehall St., #1200
New York, NY 10004–2112
(212) 607–8600
Jonathan Kay, regional director

PHILADELPHIA REGIONAL OFFICE

(DE, southern NJ, PA)
Curtis Center, #870W
170 S. Independence Mall West
Philadelphia, PA 19106–3317
(215) 861–5300
Marc Machiz, regional director

SAN FRANCISCO REGIONAL OFFICE

(northern CA, NV, UT)
90 7th St., #11–300
San Francisco, CA 94103
(415) 625–2481
Jean Ackerman, regional director

SEATTLE DISTRICT OFFICE

(AK, ID, OR, WA)
300 5th Ave., #1110
Seattle, WA 98104
(206) 757–6781
Judy Owen, supervisor

WASHINGTON, DC, DISTRICT OFFICE

(DC, MD, VA, WV)
1335 East-West Hwy., #200
Silver Spring, MD 20910
(202) 693–8700
Elizabeth Bond, supervisor

Employment and Training Administration

200 Constitution Ave. N.W., Washington, DC 20210
Internet: www.doleta.gov

The Employment and Training Administration (ETA) is an agency within the Department of Labor under the jurisdiction of the assistant secretary of labor for employment and training. The ETA funds and regulates training and employment programs administered by state and local agencies and is responsible for the employment service and the unemployment insurance systems.

Following passage of the Personal Responsibility and Work Opportunity Reconciliation Act of 1996 (Welfare Reform Act), greater emphasis was placed on welfare-to-work and job training. As a result of the act, welfare recipients have been required to move into the workforce. The welfare-to-work initiative is administered at the state level through block grants, allowing each state to design and implement a program to move people from public assistance to gainful employment. In the years immediately following the Welfare Reform Act, training programs administered by the Employment and Training Administration experienced increased enrollment and increased funding during the economic boom of the 1990s. This included ETA programs implemented to support the goals of the Welfare Reform Act. However, as the economic crisis took hold in 2008 and eroded state budgets, welfare-to-work programs were scaled back, along with other social services.

Legislation was passed and signed into law to address high rates of unemployment and economic duress that began in 2008. The Trade and Globalization Adjustment Assistance Act of 2009, a title within the American Recovery and Reinvestment Act, amended the Trade Act of 1974 to extend trade adjustment assistance (TAA) to adversely affected workers. Also, the Emergency Unemployment Compensation (EUC) program was created via congressional appropriation in 2008 and was a 100 percent federally funded program that provided benefits to individuals who had exhausted regular state benefits.

The EUC program was modified several times. The Middle Class Tax Relief and Job Creation Act of 2012 extended EUC to Jan. 2, 2013. The act required an unemployment insurance beneficiary to be able to work, available to work, and actively seeking work. The American Taxpayer Relief Act of 2012 extended the expiration date of the EUC program to Jan. 1, 2014; the EUC program was not reauthorized.

Programs administered by ETA include the following:

Apprenticeship. ETA establishes standards for apprenticeship programs and promotes the development of such programs in industry and among individuals. It provides technical assistance and advisory services to private industry in establishing and registering high-skill quality training programs, protects the welfare of apprentices, ensures equal employment opportunity, and provides for credentialing of training programs and participants.

Employment and Training Programs. The ETA administers basic employment and training programs through One-Stop Career Centers. Core services include outreach, as well as job search and placement assistance. Intensive services include more comprehensive assessments, development of individual employment plans, and counseling and career planning. Training services link job seekers with opportunities in their communities, including both occupational training and training in basic skills. Additional services are provided as needed. Support services such as transportation, childcare, dependent care, housing, and needs-related payments are provided under certain circumstances to allow an individual to participate in the program.

All adults and some disadvantaged youth are eligible for core services, but priority for intensive and training services is given to recipients of public assistance and other low-income individuals. The One-Stop Career Centers also provide employment and training services to veterans as authorized under the Jobs for Veterans Act. Veterans receive priority referral to jobs and training as well as special employment services and assistance.

The ETA also administers national employment and training programs for targeted groups such as persons with disabilities and the economically disadvantaged, as well as programs for Native Americans and migrant workers. The ETA administers the Senior Community Service Employment Program for older workers, which is authorized by Title V of the Older Americans Act Amendments of 2006. The ETA also administers reentry programs for inmates leaving prison. These programs make grants to nonprofit and faith-based organizations to provide mentoring, job training, and placement services to assist nonviolent offenders in obtaining and retaining employment. This includes programs that assist adult offenders as well as justice-involved youth. In addition, the ETA makes grants and provides resources to assist with large-scale unemployment resulting from military base closures or mass layoffs.

ETA's Youth Services division coordinates training programs for youth. The Workforce Investment Act (WIA) of 1998 enacted a formula-funded youth program serving eligible low-income youth, ages fourteen to twenty-one, who face barriers to employment. Funds for youth services are allocated to state and local areas based on a formula distribution to prepare youth for employment and/or postsecondary education.

ETA and federal law assists employer partners through tax incentives as well. Since 1979, employers under the Work Opportunity Tax Credit (formerly the Targeted Jobs Tax Credit) have received an income tax break by hiring workers the ETA has designated as hard to employ, such as individuals with disabilities or economically disadvantaged individuals.

Unemployment Insurance. The ETA monitors state unemployment insurance programs to ensure compliance with federal laws and regulations; assists states with administration of unemployment programs; and establishes formulas to determine the amount of money needed to administer state unemployment services.

Trade Act Programs. The Trade Adjustment Assistance (TAA) program assists U.S. workers who have lost or may lose their jobs as a result of foreign trade. This program seeks to provide adversely affected workers with opportunities to obtain the skills, credentials, resources, and support necessary to become reemployed. Displaced workers must file a petition with the Labor Department to receive services. Upon receiving a petition, the department initiates an investigation to determine whether the circumstances of the layoff meet the group eligibility criteria established by the Trade Act of 1974, as amended.

The trade act program offers on-site services to workers threatened by layoffs, such as employment counseling, job placement, job training, income support, and relocation allowances. The American Recovery and Reinvestment Act (ARRA) of 2009 expanded Trade Act Programs and established the Re-employment Trade Adjustment Assistance program for workers aged fifty and older. ARRA also authorized the Trade Adjustment Assistance Community College and Career Training (TAACCCT) grant program to expand capacity among community colleges and technical training institutions to provide two-year training to TAA recipients. The program was implemented in partnership with the Education Department.

The Workforce Innovation and Opportunity Act, signed into law in 2014, amends the Workforce Investment Act of 1998 (WIA) to revise requirements and reauthorize appropriations for WIA title I, workforce development systems for job training and employment services; and WIA title II, adult education and family literacy education programs.

▨ KEY PERSONNEL

Assistant Secretary
    Portia Wu . . . . (202) 693–2700
           Fax . . . . (202) 693–2725
Deputy Assistant Secretary
    Gerri Fiala . . . . (202) 693–2700

Deputy Assistant Secretary
    Eric Seleznow . . . . (202) 693–2700
Deputy Assistant Secretary
    Byron Zuidema . . . . (202) 693–2700
Apprenticeship
    John Ladd . . . . (202) 693–3812
Financial Administration
    Ron Sissel . . . . (202) 693–2700
Foreign Labor Certification
    William Thompson (acting) . . . . (202) 693–3010
Management and Administrative Services
    Lisa Lahrman (acting) . . . . (202) 693–2800
    Human Resources
        Crystal Kelly . . . . (202) 693–3922
National Response
    Erica Cantor . . . . (202) 693–3500
    Worker Dislocation and Special Response
        Greg Hitchcock . . . . (202) 693–3500
Policy, Development, and Research
    Adele Gagliardi . . . . (202) 693–3700
    Policy, Legislation, and Regulation
        Vacant . . . . (202) 693–3201
    Research and Evaluation
        Wayne Gordan . . . . (202) 693–3179
    Strategic Planning and Performance
        Karen Staha . . . . (202) 693–2917
Regional Management
    Carrie Snidar . . . . (202) 693–3690
Trade Adjustment Assistance
    Gerri Fiala . . . . (202) 693–3560
Unemployment Insurance
    Gay M. Gilbert . . . . (202) 693–3029
    Fiscal and Actuarial Services
        Ronald Wilus . . . . (202) 693–2931
    Legislation
        Suzanne Simonetta . . . . (202) 693–3225
    Performance Management
        Subri Raman . . . . (202) 693–3058
    Unemployment Insurance Operations
        Betty Castillo . . . . (202) 693–3209
Workforce Investment
    Amanda Ahlstrand . . . . (202) 693–3980
    Adult Services and Workforce Systems
        Robert L. Kight . . . . (202) 693–3046
    Strategic Investments
        Robin Fernkas . . . . (202) 693–3949
    National Programs, Tools, and Technical Assistance
        Kim Vitelli . . . . (202) 693–3045
    Youth Services
        Jennifer Troke . . . . (202) 693–3030
    Indian and Native Americans
        Athena Brown . . . . (202) 693–3737

▨ INFORMATION SOURCES

Internet

Agency website: www.doleta.gov. Features general information about the ETA and specific information about ETA programs.

Telephone Contacts

National Contact Center
(Labor Dept.) ....(866) 487–2365
TTY ....(877) 889–5627
ETA Toll-free Help Line ....(877) US2–JOBS
or ....(877) 872–5627

Information and Publications

KEY OFFICES

ETA Office of Trade Adjustment Assistance

200 Constitution Ave. N.W., Room N-5428
Washington, DC 20210
(202) 693–3560
Gerri Fiala, director

Provides information on the Trade Adjustment Assistance Program.

Freedom of Information

200 Constitution Ave. N.W., Room N-4653
Washington, DC 20210
Paula Lynch, (202) 693–3556, FOIA coordinator

DATA AND STATISTICS

The ETA Research Publication Database provides access to a collection of research and evaluation reports commissioned by ETA. Lists of publications and ordering details are available on the website, www.doleta.gov. Publications may also be ordered by calling the ETA Publications Order Line at (202) 693–3666.

Reference Resources

LIBRARY

Wirtz Labor Library

200 Constitution Ave. N.W., Room N-2445
Washington, DC 20210
(202) 693–6600
Macaire Carroll-Gavula, director
Internet: www.dol.gov/oasam/wirtzlaborlibrary
E-mail: library@dol.gov
Open to the public.
Hours: 8:15 a.m. to 4:45 p.m., Mon.–Fri.

The DOL library's large collection includes a 30,000 volume Labor Law library, over 200 journals, trade union periodicals, and the Folio Collection, over 750 items dating to the 1890s about the rise of the labor movement. The Digital Library and library catalogue are also available on the website.

DOCKETS

Each main office within the ETA keeps copies of dockets containing materials and information related to rulemakings and other administrative proceedings for which it is responsible. Federal dockets are also available at www.regulations.gov. (*See appendix for Searching and Commenting on Regulations: Regulations.gov.*)

RULES AND REGULATIONS

ETA rules and regulations are published in the *Code of Federal Regulations,* Title 20, Chapter V, Parts 600–699. Proposed rules, new final rules, and updates to the *Code of Federal Regulations* are published in the daily *Federal Register.* (*See appendix for information on how to obtain and use these publications.*) The *Federal Register* and the *Code of Federal Regulations* may be accessed online at www.archives.gov/federal-register/cfr; this site also contains a link to the federal government's regulatory website at www.regulations.gov (*see appendix*).

▦ LEGISLATION

Statutes administered by the ETA include:

Wagner-Peyser Act (48 Stat. 113, 29 U.S.C. 49). Signed by the president June 3, 1933. Established a national system of ETA employment offices and authorized the secretary of labor to establish the system's operating standards.

Social Security Act (49 Stat. 620, 42 U.S.C. 301). Signed by the president Aug. 14, 1935. Certified states that had unemployment compensation laws approved under the Federal Unemployment Tax Act to receive payments from the Treasury Department.

Immigration and Nationality Act, as amended (66 Stat. 163, 8 U.S.C. 1101). Signed by the president June 27, 1952. Established requirements relating to the entry of aliens and to the acquisition and loss of U.S. citizenship. Authorized the conditions under which foreign nationals may be employed to work in the United States.

Federal Unemployment Tax Act (68A Stat. 439, 26 U.S.C. 23). Signed by the president Aug. 16, 1954. Established a state system providing unemployment compensation to eligible individuals. The ETA would ensure state compliance with national program standards.

Trade Act of 1974 (88 Stat. 1978, 19 U.S.C. 2101). Signed by the president Jan. 3, 1975. Authorized the ETA to certify for benefit payments workers unemployed because of U.S. trade agreements.

Job Training Partnership Act (96 Stat. 1322, 29 U.S.C. 1501). Signed by the president Oct. 13, 1982. Authorized the ETA to provide job training and other employment services to economically disadvantaged and unskilled youths and adults and to dislocated workers. Replaced the Comprehensive Employment and Training Act, which expired Sept. 30, 1982.

Immigration Reform and Control Act of 1986 (100 Stat. 3359, 8 U.S.C. 1101 note). Signed by the president Nov. 6, 1986. Title I amended the Immigration and Nationality Act and the Migrant and Seasonal Agricultural Worker Protection Act to make it unlawful for a person or other entity to knowingly hire, recruit, or refer for a fee any alien workers who are unauthorized to work in the United States.

Worker Adjustment and Retraining Notification Act (29 U.S.C. 2101 et seq.). Sent to National Archives and Records Administration unsigned, became Public Law No. 100–379 on Aug. 4, 1988. Required most employers with 100 or more employees to provide notification (sixty calendar days) in advance of plant closings and mass layoffs. Includes proscribed penalties.

Economic Dislocation and Worker Adjustment Assistance Act (102 Stat. 1524, 29 U.S.C. 1501 note). Signed by the president Aug. 23, 1988. Replaced Title III of the Job Training Partnership Act and created a new training program for workers who lose their jobs because of economic factors, including plant closings and mass layoffs, and for divorced or widowed displaced homemakers with no salable job skills.

Indian Employment, Training, and Related Services Demonstration Act of 1992 (106 Stat. 2302, 25 U.S.C. 3401). Signed by the president Oct. 23, 1992. Authorized tribal governments to integrate all federally funded employment, training, and related services programs into a single, comprehensive program.

North American Free Trade Agreement Implementation Act (107 Stat. 2057, 19 U.S.C. 3301 note). Signed by the president Dec. 8, 1993. Title V established a Transitional Adjustment Assistance program for workers in companies affected by imports from Canada or Mexico or by shifts of U.S. production to those countries because of NAFTA.

Workforce Investment Act of 1998 (112 Stat. 936, 20 U.S.C. 9201 note). Signed by the president Aug. 7, 1998. Established federal aid programs for vocational education, adult education, and job training at state and local levels. Also established the Twenty-First Century Workforce Commission to study information technology in the U.S. workforce.

Jobs for Veterans Act of 2002 (JVA) (116 Stat. 2033, 38 U.S.C. 4215). Signed by the president Nov. 7, 2002. Required workforce development programs funded in whole or in part by the Labor Department to provide priority of service to veterans and, under certain circumstances, spouses of veterans. Removed "disabled and Vietnam-era veterans" from coverage under Vietnam Era Veterans Readjustment Assistance Act of 1974 and replaced the language with "qualified covered veterans" as defined in the JVA, which included disabled and specified combat veterans.

Older Americans Act Amendments of 2006 (120 Stat. 2563, 42 U.S.C. 3056 et seq.). Signed by the president Oct. 17, 2006. Title V Community Service Senior Opportunities Act established Senior Community Service Employment Program for older workers with the Labor Department.

Veterans' Benefits, Health Care, and Information Technology Act of 2006 (120 Stat. 3403, 38 U.S.C. 4215 note). Signed by the president Dec. 22, 2006. Required the labor secretary, within two years after enactment, to prescribe regulations to implement provisions concerning the priority of service for veterans in the Labor Department's job training programs.

Second Chance Act of 2007 (122 Stat. 681, 42 U.S.C. 17501). Signed by the president April 9, 2008. Authorized the labor secretary to make grants to nonprofit organizations to provide mentoring, job training and placement services, and other services to assist certain convicted nonviolent offenders in obtaining and retaining employment.

Supplemental Appropriations Act, 2008 (122 Stat. 2323, 26 U.S.C. 3304 note). Signed by the president June 30, 2008. Title IV Emergency Unemployment Compensation authorizes a state to enter into an agreement with the secretary of labor under which the state agency will make emergency unemployment compensation payments to individuals under specified conditions.

American Recovery and Reinvestment Act (19 U.S.C. 2101 note). Signed by the president Feb. 17, 2009. Subtitle I Trade and Globalization Adjustment Assistance Act of 2009 amended the Trade Act of 1974 to extend trade adjustment assistance (TAA) to adversely affected workers. Authorized funding for national emergency grants for adversely affected workers. Revised group eligibility requirements for TAA. Directed the labor secretary to establish standards for investigations of TAA petitions and criteria for making determinations. Established the Re-employment Trade Adjustment Assistance program for workers aged fifty and older. Revised the prohibition against determining an adversely affected worker for unemployment insurance or TAA program benefits because of training or other specified reasons.

Middle Class Tax Relief and Job Creation Act of 2012 (126 Stat. 156, 26 U.S.C. 1 note). Signed by the president Feb. 22, 2012. Extended the end date for the Emergency Unemployment Compensation (EUC) program to Jan. 2, 2013. Requires an unemployment insurance beneficiary to be able to work, available to work, and actively seeking work. Allowed states to enact legislation to require an applicant for unemployment compensation to submit to and pass a drug test for the unlawful use of controlled substances under specified conditions. Authorized the secretary of labor to enter into agreements with up to ten states for demonstration projects that are designed to assist and expedite the reemployment of the long-term unemployed.

American Taxpayer Relief Act of 2012 (126 Stat. 2313, 26 U.S.C. 1 note). Signed by the president Jan. 2, 2013. Extended the expiration date of the Emergency Unemployment Compensation (EUC) program to Jan. 1, 2014.

Workforce Innovation and Opportunity Act (128 Stat. 1425, 29 U.S.C. 3101 note). Signed by the president July 22, 2014. Amends the Workforce Investment Act of 1998 (WIA) to revise requirements and reauthorize appropriations for WIA title I, workforce development systems for job training and employment services; and WIA title II, adult education and family literacy education programs.

▪ REGIONAL OFFICES

REGION 1—BOSTON

(CT, MA, ME, NH, NJ, NY, PR, RI, VI, VT)
JFK Federal Bldg., Room E-350
35 New Sudbury St.
Boston, MA 02203
(617) 788–0170
Holly O'Brien, regional administrator

REGION 2—PHILADELPHIA

(DC, DE, MD, PA, VA, WV)
The Curtis Center
170 S. Independence Mall West, #825-East
Philadelphia, PA 19106–3315
(215) 861–5205
Leo Miller (acting), regional administrator

REGION 3—ATLANTA

(AL, FL, GA, KY, MS, NC, SC, TN)
Atlanta Federal Center
61 Forsyth St. S.W., #6M12
Atlanta, GA 30303
(404) 302–5300
Les Range, regional administrator

REGION 4—DALLAS

(AR, CO, LA, MT, ND, NM, OK, SD, TX, UT, WY)
Federal Building
525 Griffin St., #303
Dallas, TX 75202
(972) 850–4600
Nicholas Lalpuis, regional administrator

REGION 5—CHICAGO

(IA, IL, IN, KS, MI, MN, MO, NE, OH, WI)
230 S. Dearborn St., 6th Floor
Chicago, IL 60604
(312) 596–5400
Rose Zibert (acting), regional administrator

REGION 6—SAN FRANCISCO

(AK, AZ, CA, GU, HI, ID, NV, OR, WA)
90 7th St., #17–300
San Francisco, CA 94103
(415) 625–7900
Virginia Hamilton, regional administrator

Mine Safety and Health Administration

1100 Wilson Blvd., 21st Floor, Arlington, VA 22209–3939
Internet: www.msha.gov

In 1910, following a decade in which the number of coal mine fatalities exceeded 2,000 annually, Congress established the Bureau of Mines as a new agency in the Interior Department. The bureau was charged with the responsibility to conduct research and to reduce accidents in the coal mining industry, but the agency was given no inspection authority until 1941, when Congress empowered federal inspectors to enter mines. In 1947 Congress authorized the formulation of the first code of federal regulations for mine safety. The Federal Coal Mine Safety Act of 1952 provided for annual inspections in certain underground coal mines and gave the bureau limited enforcement authority, including power to issue violation notices and imminent danger withdrawal orders. The last incarnation under the Interior Department was the Mining Enforcement and Safety Administration.

The Federal Mine Safety and Health Amendments Act of 1977 (the Mine Act) established the Mine Safety and Health Administration (MSHA) as an agency within the Labor Department under the jurisdiction of the assistant secretary of labor for mine safety and health.

The MSHA develops and promulgates mandatory safety and health standards, ensures compliance with such standards, proposes penalties for violating standards, investigates accidents, and cooperates with the states in developing mine safety and health programs. While health and safety standards apply to all types of mining, coal mining and metal and nonmetal mining are administered separately.

MSHA technical support engineers investigate and survey conditions that affect mine workers' health and safety, such as ventilation, radiation, dust, noise, industrial hygiene, ground support, and mine wastes. The agency also operates the National Mine Health and Safety Academy in Beckley, WV, to train its inspectors and technical support personnel as well as professionals from the mining industry. MSHA also works with the National Institute of Occupational Safety and Health on various safety and health research projects.

The Mine Act provides that MSHA inspectors shall inspect each surface mine at least twice a year and each underground mine at least four times a year (seasonal or intermittent operations are inspected less frequently) to determine whether an imminent danger exists and whether there is compliance with health and safety standards or with any citation, order, or decision issued under the Mine Act. The Mine Act provides for criminal sanctions against mine operators who willfully violate safety and health standards. MSHA initially investigates possible willful violations; if evidence of such a violation is found, the agency turns its findings over to the Justice Department for prosecution.

Before any citation or order is assessed, the operator or miners' representative can confer with an MSHA supervisor about any disagreement with the inspector's findings. If the disagreement cannot be resolved on this level, the operator is entitled to a hearing before an administrative law judge with the Federal Mine Safety and Health Review Commission. An operator or miners' representative who disagrees with any other enforcement action by MSHA also is entitled to a hearing. The administrative law judge's decision can be appealed to the commissioners and thereafter to the U.S. Court of Appeals.

In January 2006 the nation was transfixed by the coal mine disaster in Sago, WV that killed twelve miners. Some criticized MSHA for perceived failures in its disaster response oversight. After the tragedy, MSHA instituted several rule changes, including requiring mine owners to add lifelines to escape routes to help guide miners to safety in poor visibility; to provide additional self-contained self-rescue devices (SCSRs) in underground storage areas for quick use in an emergency; and to increase emergency evacuation drills in miner training. The disaster was one factor behind Congress passing the Mine Improvement and New Emergency Response (MINER) Act of 2006. The MINER Act directed MSHA to establish and update criteria to certify the qualifications of mine rescue teams and to require that mine operators have one employee knowledgeable in emergency response on each shift and two certified mine rescue teams available at each mine within one hour. In June 2009 MSHA published a final rule for mine rescue teams regarding underground coal mines in accordance with the Mine Improvement and New Emergency Response (MINER) Act of 2006.

All MSHA activities are aimed at preventing and reducing mine accidents and occupational diseases. While the nation has been well aware of the large mining tragedies, such as the six miners and three rescue workers lost at Crandall Canyon Mine in Utah in August 2007, what is less known is that fifty to seventy coal and metal/nonmetal miners have perished each year in all mining accidents from 2001 to 2007. In 2008 forty-three fatalities were reported, a record low.

Despite the attention focused on mining safety following the Sago and Utah multiple mine fatalities, the worst was yet to come. On April 5, 2010, the United States experienced its worst mining disaster since 1970: an explosion killed twenty-nine miners at the Big Branch Mine, owned and operated by Massey Energy in West Virginia. Poor ventilation in the mines caused a build-up of methane, which was ignited into a coal dust explosion; these are well-known safety risks in the industry. The hazardous conditions made rescue and recovery operations exceptionally difficult. The conditions were so hazardous that it took two months before an underground investigation team could begin its work.

Public scrutiny immediately focused on Massey Energy's multiple safety violations. The mine had had hundreds of violations in the previous year, a pattern that continued up until the explosion. Concerns were raised about the mine's safety record and MSHA's process for identifying mines with a pattern of violations (POV). POV authority allows MSHA to take enhanced enforcement actions when a mine demonstrates recurring safety violations that could significantly increase health and safety risks. The Department of Labor inspector general released a report regarding MSHA's failure to utilize its POV authority, noting: "MSHA has not successfully exercised its POV authority in 32 years. Administration of this authority has been hampered by a lack of leadership and priority in the Department across various administrations." The Big Branch Mine had been excluded from receiving a POV violation letter—an action that MSHA officials attributed to a computer programming error. Labor Secretary Hilda Solis responded that the department would work on new regulations to govern the POV system and would change its administrative policies regarding POV to the extent permitted under the law.

MHSA released preliminary findings from its investigation into the causes of the disaster in June 2011. The evidence supported the physical causes of the explosion as outlined in earlier findings, including the Governor's Independent Investigation Panel report commissioned by West Virginia Governor Joe Manchin III. The MSHA also presented findings that painted Massey Energy as a business that callously disregarded the safety of its employees, with tactics that included intimidating managers for shutting down production to address safety issues. A section foreman was fired for delaying production for an hour to fix ventilation problems. Company examiners were pressured not to list hazards in their records, and investigators discovered that two sets of books containing safety information were kept in order to conceal potential violations from federal regulators. Eighteen former Massey officials refused to assist the investigation, invoking their Fifth Amendment right against self-incrimination. In 2011 Alpha Natural Resources acquired Massey Energy.

MSHA released its final report in December 2011. The report upheld the preliminary findings that the twenty-nine miners died in a massive coal dust explosion that started as a methane ignition and concluded that Massey's corporate culture was the root cause of the tragedy. MSHA issued 369 citations and orders, including twenty-one flagrant violations, against Massey and Performance Coal Company, a subsidiary of Massey Energy Company. MSHA fined Massey $10.8 million, the largest in agency history.

MSHA's report followed a nonprosecution agreement reached among the U.S. Attorney's Office for the Southern District of West Virginia, the U.S. Department of Justice, Alpha Natural Resources Inc., and Alpha Appalachia Holdings Inc., formerly known as Massey Energy Company. The agreement, which included nearly $210 million for remedial safety measures at all Alpha mines, a trust fund for improvements in mine safety and health, payment of outstanding civil penalties for all former Massey mines and restitution payments for the victims' families, resolved criminal liability for Alpha but did not provide protection against criminal prosecution of any individuals.

In May 2010 federal prosecutors announced a criminal investigation into the mine explosion. In the ensuing years, several employees, including management, were sentenced to prison for various violations, including lying during the investigation and attempts to cover up the company's malfeasance. In November 2014 a federal grand jury indicted former Massey Energy CEO Don Blankenship on counts of conspiring to violate mine safety and health regulations and impeding mine safety inspectors. He also faced charges related to securities fraud. The trial was set for January 2015 but later moved back to July 2015.

In January 2013, MSHA announced a final rule that revises the pattern of violations (POV) regulation. Under the Federal Mine Safety and Health Act of 1977, MSHA is required to issue a POV notice to any mine operator that demonstrates a disregard for the health and safety of miners through a pattern of significant and substantial (S&S) violations that are likely to result in a reasonably serious injury or illness. The new rule promotes consistency in applying the POV notice as an enforcement tool, provides for a more open and transparent process, emphasizes operators' responsibility to comply with safety and health standards and monitor their own compliance, and more effectively achieves the statutory intent of the Mine Act.

The new POV regulations had an impact. Between the 2010 and 2014 screenings, there was a 30 percent drop in S&S violations among the top 200 mines ranked by number of S&S issuances. Those mines also saw a 24 percent drop in total violations and a 27 percent drop in elevated enforcement actions, such as closure orders for imminent dangers or unwarrantable failures to comply with health and safety standards.

In 2014 MSHA released a final rule to lower miners' exposure to respirable coal mine dust in all underground and surface coal mines. Prolonged exposure to respirable coal mine dust causes lung diseases, referred to as black lung, which can lead to permanent disability and death. Since 1969 more than $45 billion in federal compensation benefits have been paid out to coal miners disabled by black lung and their survivors.

■ KEY PERSONNEL

Assistant Secretary
Joseph A. Main . . . . (202) 693–9414
Fax. . . . . (202) 693–9401
Deputy Assistant Secretary for Operations
Patricia W. Silvey. . . . . (202) 693–9414
Deputy Assistant Secretary for Policy
Stephen Weatherford . . . . (202) 693–9414
Diversity and Equal Opportunity
Darlene Farrar-Warren. . . . . (202) 693–9880
Administration and Management
Eugene F. Hubbard . . . . (202) 693–9800
Budget and Finance
Thomas Charboneau . . . . (202) 693–9812
Human Resources
Nancy Crawford . . . . (202) 693–9808
Assessments
Jay Mattos. . . . . (202) 693–9700
Special Assessments
Margaret Bishop . . . . (202) 693–9710
Technical Compliance and Investigations
Carolyn James . . . . (202) 693–9620
Coal Mine Safety and Health
Kevin Stricklin. . . . . (202) 693–9500
Health
Robert Thaxton. . . . . (202) 693–9515
Safety
Stephen Gigliotti . . . . (202) 693–9479
Accident Investigation
Terry Bentley . . . . (202) 693–9521
Metal and Nonmetal Mine Safety and Health
Neal Merrifield . . . . (202) 693–9600
Accident Investigation
Michael Hancher. . . . . (202) 693–9760
Safety and Health
Brian Goepfert. . . . . (202) 693–9640
Management
Nancy Wilson . . . . (202) 693–9607
Educational Policy and Development
Jeffrey Duncan. . . . . (202) 693–9570
Qualifications and Certifications Unit
Kerbi Jacobson. . . . . (303) 231–5473
National Mine Safety and Health Academy
Janet Bertinuson . . . . (304) 256–3265
Small Mine Office
Kevin Burns. (202) 693–9594
Program Evaluation and Information Resources
Syed Hafeez (acting) . . . . (202) 693–9750
Standards, Regulations, and Variances
George Triebsch. . . . . (202) 693–9440

Technical Support
George Fesak . . . . (202) 693–9470
Safety and Health Technology Center
William Francart. . . . . (412) 386–6902
Approval and Certification
Dennis Ferlich . . . . (304) 547–2029

■ INFORMATION SOURCES

Internet

Agency website: www.msha.gov. Includes news releases, speeches, special reports, and congressional testimony; information on safety and health, including mining accidents and injuries; and employment opportunities with MSHA.

Telephone Contacts

Main Office. . . . .(202) 693–9899
Immediately Reportable Accidents
and Injuries. . . . .(800) 746–1553
Fax-on-Demand. . . . .(202) 693–9801
Federal Relay Service TTY . . . .(800) 877–8339

Information and Publications

KEY OFFICES

MSHA Office of Program Education and Outreach Services

1100 Wilson Blvd., #2317
Arlington, VA 22209
(202) 693–9400
Vacant, director
Rodney Brown, deputy director

Provides general information to the public on mine safety issues.

MSHA Office of Public Affairs

1100 Wilson Blvd
Arlington, VA 22209
(202) 693–9423
Amy Louviere, director
E-mail: louviere.amy@dol.gov

Issues press releases, decisions, reports, and statements for use by the media and handles all media requests.

Freedom of Information

1100 Wilson Blvd., #2311
Arlington, VA 22209
(202) 693–9542
Lanesia Washington, FOIA officer
Internet: www.msha.gov/readroom/readroom.htm
E-mail: foiarequest@dol.gov

RELATED MINING AGENCIES

Federal Mine Safety and Health Review Commission

601 New Jersey Ave. N.W., #9500
Washington, DC 20001–2021

(202) 434–9900
Fax (202) 434–9906
Internet: www.fmshrc.gov

Handles disputes arising under the Federal Mine Safety and Health Act.

DOL Workers' Compensation Programs

The Coal Mine Workers' Compensation division administers the black lung benefits program, certifies benefit payments, and maintains beneficiary rolls. Contact (202) 693–0046 or (800) 638–7072.

DATA AND STATISTICS

Statistics are posted on MSHA's website at www.msha .gov/stats/statinfo.htm. MSHA offices that gather data and statistics include:

Civil Penalty Program. Determines assessments and keeps track of the status of cases and the collection of fines. Contact William Wilson, MSHA Office of Assessments, 1100 Wilson Blvd., Arlington, VA 22209; (202) 693–9700.

Program Evaluation and Informational Resources (PEIR). Conducts internal reviews and evaluates the effectiveness of agency programs and conducts follow-up reviews to ensure that appropriate corrective actions have been taken. Another function of PEIR is to collect, analyze, and publish statistical data obtained from mine operators on the prevalence of work-related injuries and illnesses in the mining industry. PEIR is also responsible for support and training for all MSHA automated information systems, data communications networks, and ADP equipment.

PUBLICATIONS

MSHA Office of Program Education and Outreach Services provides various fact sheets on mining health and safety; many publications are obtainable via the MSHA website. Technical reports, instruction guides, safety manuals, and the *Catalog of Training Products for the Mining Industry* are also available from:

National Mine Health and Safety Academy
1301 Airport Rd.
Beaver, WV 25813–9426
Cheryl Stevens, coordinator
(304) 256–3200
Fax (304) 256–3299

Reference Resources

LIBRARIES

MSHA Technical Information Center and Library
1301 Airport Rd.
Beaver, WV 25813–9426
(304) 256–3266

The technical information center and reference library maintains books, journals, newspapers, technical reports,

audiovisual materials, and other information related to mine health and safety. The library gives academy students, clients, and the general public immediate and easy access to information sources. Many library resources are available online, through the MSHA website.

Wirtz Labor Library
200 Constitution Ave. N.W., Room N-2445
Washington, DC 20210
(202) 693–6600
Macaire Carroll-Gavula, director
Internet: www.dol.gov/oasam/wirtzlaborlibrary
E-mail: library@dol.gov
Open to the public.
Hours: 8:15 a.m. to 4:45 p.m., Mon.–Fri.

The DOL library's large collection includes a 30,000 volume Labor Law library, over 200 journals, trade union periodicals, and the Folio Collection, over 750 items dating to the 1890s about the rise of the labor movement. The Digital Library and library catalogue are also available on the website.

DOCKETS

Federal dockets are available at www.regulations.gov. (*See appendix for Searching and Commenting on Regulations: Regulations.gov.*)

RULES AND REGULATIONS

A full listing of all current regulations is published in the *Code of Federal Regulations,* Title 30, Chapter I, Parts 1–199. Proposed rules, new final rules, and updates to the *Code of Federal Regulations* are published in the daily *Federal Register.* (*See appendix for information on how to obtain and use these publications.*) The *Federal Register* and the *Code of Federal Regulations* may be accessed online at www.archives.gov/federal-register/cfr; this site also contains a link to the federal government's regulatory website at www.regulations.gov (*see appendix*).

■ LEGISLATION

The MSHA exercises authority under the following legislation:

Federal Mine Safety and Health Act of 1977, as amended (91 Stat. 1290, 30 U.S.C. 801). Signed by the president Nov. 9, 1977. Combined metal and nonmetal mines under the same authority as coal mines, transferred the Mining Enforcement and Safety Administration from the Interior Department to the Labor Department and reorganized it as the MSHA. Established the Mine Safety and Health Review Commission to adjudicate disputes.

Waste Isolation Pilot Plant Land Withdrawal Act (106 Stat. 4777). Signed by the president Oct. 30, 1992. Required periodic inspections of the Waste Isolation Pilot Plant project by the MSHA. Required the results to be submitted for review to the secretary of energy.

Mine Improvement and New Emergency Response Act of 2006 (MINER Act) (120 Stat. 493–505, 30 U.S.C. 801). Signed by the president June 15, 2006. Directed

MSHA to establish and update criteria to certify the qualifications of mine rescue teams. Required mine operators to have one employee knowledgeable in emergency response on each shift and two certified mine rescue teams available at each mine within one hour.

■ REGIONAL OFFICES

MSHA/Metal and Nonmetal Mine Safety and Health

NORTH CENTRAL DISTRICT
(IA, IL, IN, MI, MN, WI)
Federal Bldg., U.S. Courthouse
515 W. First St., #333
Duluth, MN 55802–1302
(218) 720–5448
Christopher Hensler, district manager

NORTHEASTERN DISTRICT
(CT, DC, DE, MA, MD, ME, NH, NJ,
    NY, OH, PA, RI, VT, WV)
178 Thorn Hill Rd., #100
Warrendale, PA 15086
(724) 772–2334
Vacant, district manager

ROCKY MOUNTAIN DISTRICT
(AZ, CO, portions of ID, KS, MT, ND, NE, SD,
    UT, WY)
Denver Federal Center, 6th and Kipling
2nd St., Bldg. 25, E-16
Denver, CO 80225
Mailing address:
P.O. Box 25367, DFC
Denver, CO 80225–0367
(303) 231–5465
Richard Laufenberg, district manager

SOUTH CENTRAL DISTRICT
(AR, LA, MO, portions of MS, NM, OK, TX)
1100 Commerce St., #462
Dallas, TX 75242–0499
(214) 767–8401
Michael A. Davisd district manager

SOUTHEASTERN DISTRICT
(AL, FL, GA, KY, portions of MS, NC, PR, SC, TN,
    VA, VI)
1030 London Dr., #400
Birmingham, AL 35211
(205) 290–7296
Samuel Pierce, district manager

WESTERN DISTRICT
AK, Mohave Co. AZ, CA, HI, portions of ID, NV, OR,
    Washington Co. UT, WA)
991 Nut Tree Rd.

Vacaville, CA 95687–6696
(707) 447–9844
Wyatt Andrews, district manager

MSHA/Coal Mine Safety and Health

DISTRICT 2
(Bituminous and anthracite coal
    regions of PA)
631 Excel Dr., #100
Mt. Pleasant, PA 15666
(724) 925–5150
Thomas Light, district manager

DISTRICT 3
(MD, OH, northern WV)
604 Cheat Rd.
Morgantown, WV 26508
(304) 225–6800
Carlos Mosley, district manager

DISTRICT 4
(Southern WV)
100 Bluestone Rd.
Mt. Hope, WV 25880
(304) 877–3900
David Mandeville, district manager

DISTRICT 5
(VA)
Wise County Bldg.
147 Plaza Rd., 2nd Floor
Norton, VA 24273
Mailing address:
P.O. Box 560
Norton, VA 24273
(276) 679–0230
Clayton Sparks, district manager

DISTRICT 6
(Eastern KY)
100 Fae Ramsey Lane
Pikeville, KY 41501–3211
(606) 432–0944
Norman G. Page, district manager

DISTRICT 7
(Central KY, NC, SC, TN)
3837 S. U.S. Hwy. 25E
Barbourville, KY 40906
(606) 546–5123
Jim Langley, district manager

DISTRICT 8
(IA, IL, IN, MI, MN, northern MO, WI)
2300 Willow St., #200
Vincennes, IN 47591
(812) 882–7617
Ronald Burns, district manager

DISTRICT 9

(All states west of the Mississippi River except IA,
MN, and northern MO)
Denver Federal Center
P.O. Box 25367, DFC
Denver, CO 80225–0367
(303) 231–5458
Riley Russell, district manager

DISTRICT 10

(Western KY)
100 YMCA Dr.
Madisonville, KY 42431–9019
(270) 821–4180
Ronald Burns (acting), district manager

DISTRICT 11

(AL except northeast corner,
FL, central and southern GA,
MS, PR, VI)
1030 London Dr., #400
Birmingham, AL 35211
(205) 290–7300
Richard Gates, district manager

DISTRICT 12

(Southern WV)
1301 Airport Rd.
Beaver, WV 25813
(304) 253–5237
Timothy Watkins, district manager

Veterans' Employment and Training Service

200 Constitution Ave. N.W., #S-1325, Washington, DC 20210
Internet: www.dol.gov/vets

The Veterans' Employment and Training Service (VETS), a component of the Department of Labor, is administered by the assistant secretary for veterans' employment and training. The assistant secretary is responsible for ensuring that the policies of the secretary of labor regarding national employment and training programs for veterans are carried out by the local public employment services and private-sector contractors. The assistant secretary also is responsible for promulgating policies, procedures, and training opportunities mandated by legislation for veterans and other eligible persons, with priority services given to qualified covered veterans as defined in the Jobs for Veterans Act of 2002, which included disabled and specified combat veterans.

Nationwide field staff provides supervision and technical assistance to state job services and private contractors to ensure that counseling, referral, and placement services are provided to all veterans and to other eligible persons. Service to veterans is provided by Disabled Veterans' Outreach Program specialists and local veterans' employment representatives, who are stationed in many local offices throughout the state job service system.

VETS and the Office of Veterans' Reemployment Rights within the Department of Veterans Affairs (VA) (*p. 853*) assist veterans, reservists, members of the National Guard, and rejectees in exercising reinstatement rights to the jobs they left to enter military service and to the right to any increased wages or benefits added during their absence, while in military service.

Cooperative agreements with the VA provide other services and benefits to veterans.

The effort to place veterans in federal jobs got a boost from the president. On Nov. 9, 2009, President Barack Obama signed Executive Order 13518, Employment of Veterans in the Federal Government. The order established the Interagency Council on Veterans Employment (Council), which is co-chaired by the secretaries of labor and veterans affairs and is comprised of twenty-four cabinet-level and other independent agencies. The council established Veterans Employment Program Offices in twenty-four participating federal agencies by March 2010.

By mid-2011, veterans comprised roughly one-third of new federal hires. The council launched a website to market the program and facilitate federal employment opportunities for veterans: www.FedsHireVets.gov.

The VOW to Hire Heroes Act of 2011 established the Veterans Retraining Assistance Program (VRAP) for unemployed veterans aged thirty-five to sixty who were discharged other than dishonorably and are not eligible for other education benefits and are not receiving unemployment compensation. The act mandated that the Department of Labor and the VA would jointly administer the process for determining an applicant's VRAP eligibility.

▇ KEY PERSONNEL

Assistant Secretary
    Teresa W. Gerton (acting) . . . . (202) 693–4700
        Fax. . . . . (202) 693–4754
Deputy Assistant Secretary, Policy
    Teresa Gerton. . . . . (202) 693–4700
Deputy Assistant Secretary, Operations
    Ralph Charlip. . . . . (202) 693–4700
Administration and Budget
    Maria E. Temiquel. . . . . (202) 693–4706
Compliance Programs
    Kenan Torrans . . . . (202) 693–4731
Employment Programs
    Emmanuel Ekwo . . . . (202) 693–4717
Field Operations
    Bill Metheny. (202) 693–4700
National Programs
    Ruth Samardick . . . . (202) 693–4700
Strategic Outreach
    Timothy Green . . . . (202) 693–4723

▇ INFORMATION SOURCES

Internet
Agency website: www.dol.gov/vets. Features media releases, statutory and regulatory information, and information about grants and VETS activities.

Telephone Contacts

National Contact Center
(Labor Dept.) . . . . (866) 487–2365
TTY . . . . (877) 889–5627

Information and Publications

KEY OFFICES

Freedom of Information

Contact Carrie Timus, FOIA coordinator, (202) 693–4718.

DATA AND STATISTICS

Contact William (Kenan) Torrans at (202) 693–4731 for the Veterans' Employment and Training Service's USERRA (Uniformed Services Employment and Reemployment Rights Act) annual report, the best source of data and statistics on VETS. The annual report and other data and statistics are also available on the Internet site.

PUBLICATIONS

Publications are available via the agency's Internet site at www.dol.gov/vets/media or can be located through the Labor Department's referral line: (866) 487–2365.

Reference Resources

LIBRARY

Wirtz Labor Library

200 Constitution Ave. N.W., Room N-2445
Washington, DC 20210
(202) 693–6600
Macaire Carroll-Gavula, director
Internet: www.dol.gov/oasam/wirtzlaborlibrary
E-mail: library@dol.gov
Open to the public.
Hours: 8:15 a.m. to 4:45 p.m., Mon.–Fri.

The DOL library's large collection includes a 30,000 volume Labor Law library, over 200 journals, trade union periodicals, and the Folio Collection, over 750 items dating to the 1890s about the rise of the labor movement. The Digital Library and library catalogue are also available on the website.

DOCKETS

Federal dockets are available at www.regulations.gov. (*See appendix for Searching and Commenting on Regulations: Regulations.gov.*)

RULES AND REGULATIONS

VETS rules and regulations are published in the *Code of Federal Regulations* under Title 20, Chapter IX, Parts 1000–1099; Title 41, Chapter 61, Parts 61–1–61–999 and 61–250. Proposed rules, new rules, and updates to the *Code of Federal Regulations* are published in the daily *Federal Register*. (*See appendix for information on how to obtain and use these publications.*) The *Federal Register* and the *Code of Federal Regulations* may be accessed online at www.archives.gov/federal-register/cfr; this site also contains a link to the federal government's regulatory website at www.regulations.gov (*see appendix*).

■ LEGISLATION

VETS is responsible for:

Vietnam Era Veterans Readjustment Assistance Act of 1974 (VEVRAA) (88 Stat. 1578, 38 U.S.C. 4232). Vetoed by the president Nov. 26, 1974; veto overridden Dec. 3, 1974. Required federal government contractors and subcontractors to take affirmative action to employ and advance in employment veterans and prohibited discrimination against veterans.

Veterans Compensation, Education, and Employment Amendments of 1982 (96 Stat. 1429, 38 U.S.C. 101 note). Signed by the president Oct. 14, 1982. Transferred responsibility for enforcement of the Vietnam Era Veterans Readjustment Assistance Act of 1974 to the office of the assistant secretary of labor for veterans' employment and training.

Veterans' Employment, Training, and Counseling Amendments of 1988 (102 Stat. 556, 38 U.S.C. 101 note). Signed by the president May 20, 1988. Extended a veteran's job-training program for two years and provided additional funding for 1,600 local veterans' employment representatives nationwide.

Veterans' Education and Employment Programs (105 Stat. 48, 38 U.S.C. 2010). Signed by the president March 22, 1991. Established within the Department of Labor an Advisory Committee on Veterans Employment and Training.

Uniformed Services Employment and Reemployment Rights Act of 1994 (108 Stat. 3149, 38 U.S.C. 101 note). Signed by the president Oct. 13, 1994. Guaranteed the rights of veterans to return to their former jobs with no loss of status, pay, or seniority.

Workforce Investment Act of 1998 (112 Stat. 936, 20 U.S.C. 9201 note). Signed by the president Aug. 7, 1998. Veterans Workforce Investment Program established a grant program designed to meet the employment and training needs of service-connected disabled veterans, Vietnam veterans, and veterans recently separated from military service, as well as veterans awarded a campaign or expedition medal or badge.

Veterans Employment Opportunities Act of 1998 (112 Stat. 3182, 5 U.S.C. 2101 note). Signed by the president Oct. 31, 1998. Provided that veterans or other preference eligible individuals who believed that their rights under any law or regulation related to veterans' preference were violated may file a written complaint with the Veterans' Employment and Training Service.

Jobs for Veterans Act of 2002 (JVA) (116 Stat. 2033, 38 U.S.C. 4215). Signed by the president Nov. 7, 2002. Required workforce development programs funded in whole or in part by the Labor Department to provide priority of service to veterans and, under certain circumstances, spouses of veterans. Removed "disabled and Vietnam-era veterans" from coverage under VEVRAA and replaced the language with "qualified covered veterans" as defined in the JVA, which included disabled and specified combat veterans.

Veterans' Benefits, Health Care, and Information Technology Act of 2006 (120 Stat. 3403, 38 U.S.C. 4215 note). Signed by the president Dec. 22, 2006. Required the labor secretary, within two years after enactment, to prescribe regulations to implement provisions concerning the priority of service for veterans in the Labor Department's job training programs.

Veterans' Benefits Improvement Act of 2008 (122 Stat. 4145, 38 U.S.C. 4322). Signed by the president Oct. 10, 2008. Amended provisions concerning veterans' employment and reemployment rights and benefits under the Uniformed Services Employment and Reemployment Rights Act of 1994 to require (1) complainants to be notified of their rights within five days after receipt of the complaint by the VETS; (2) complaint investigation and resolution to be completed within ninety days; and (3) the Office of Special Counsel or attorney general, within sixty days after receiving a complaint referral, to determine whether to provide legal representation to the claimant.

VOW to Hire Heroes Act of 2011 (125 Stat. 711, 38 U.S.C. 101 note). Signed by the president Nov. 21, 2011. Established the Veterans Retraining Assistance Program (VRAP) for unemployed veterans aged thirty-five to sixty (who met certain conditions) to provide eligible veterans with up to twelve months of Department of Veterans Affairs (VA)-funded retraining assistance to pursue an associate degree or certificate in a high-demand occupation. Mandated that the VA and Department of Labor (DOL) shall jointly administer the process for determining an applicant's VRAP eligibility.

◼ REGIONAL OFFICES

ATLANTA REGION

(AL, FL, GA, KY, MS, NC, SC, TN)
Sam Nunn Atlanta Federal Center
61 Forsyth St. S.W., #6T85
Atlanta, GA 30303
(404) 665–4330
Maurice Buchanan, regional administrator

BOSTON REGION

(CT, MA, ME, NH, NJ, NY, PR, RI, VI, VT)
JFK Federal Bldg., #E-315
Boston, MA 02203
(617) 565–2080
Vacant, regional administrator

CHICAGO REGION

(IA, IL, IN, KS, MI, MN, MO, NE, OH, WI)
230 S. Dearborn St., #1064
Chicago, IL 60604
(312) 353–0970
Heather Higgins, regional administrator

DALLAS REGION

(AR, CO, LA, MT, ND, NM, OK, SD, TX, UT, WY)
525 Griffin St., #858
Dallas, TX 75202–5028
(972) 850–4715
Robert Creel, regional administrator

PHILADELPHIA REGION

(DC, DE, MD, PA, VA, WV)
The Curtis Center, #770W
170 S. Independence Mall
Philadelphia, PA 19106–3310
(215) 861–5390
Tim Crowley, regional administrator

SAN FRANCISCO REGION

(AK, AZ, CA, GU, HI, ID, NV, OR, WA)
90 7th St., #2–600
San Francisco, CA 94103
(415) 625–7671
Alfred Kwok, regional administrator

Other Labor Department Offices

The following offices comprised the Employment Standards Administration (ESA) until ESA was eliminated on November 8, 2009. These offices now report directly to the secretary of labor.

■ OFFICE OF FEDERAL CONTRACT COMPLIANCE PROGRAMS
200 Constitution Ave. N.W.
Washington, DC 20210
Internet: www.dol.gov/ofccp

The Office of Federal Contract Compliance Programs (OFCCP) administers Executive Order 11246, Section 503 of the Rehabilitation Act of 1973, and Section 402 of the Vietnam-Era Veterans Readjustment Assistance Act of 1974.

Executive Order 11246 prohibits discrimination by federal contractors and subcontractors against employees on the basis of race, color, religion, national origin, and sex. It also directs federal contractors and subcontractors to take affirmative action to hire and promote groups that have been targets of previous discrimination.

Executive Order 11246, as amended, applies to employers in any of the following groups: contractors or subcontractors that provide the federal government with more than $10,000 worth of supplies, services, or labor; contractors or subcontractors that have had more than $10,000 worth of government contracts in any twelve-month period; any firm that serves as an issuing or paying agent of U.S. savings bonds and notes; and any firm that serves as a depository of federal funds in any amount.

On July 21, 2014, President Barack Obama signed Executive Order 13672, amending Executive Order 11246, to prohibit federal contractors and subcontractors from discriminating on the basis of sexual orientation or gender identity. The Department of Labor published a final rule on December 9, 2014, changing OFCCP's regulations to require federal contractors and subcontractors to treat applicants and employees without regard to their sexual orientation or gender identity.

In addition, the order applies to all contractors and subcontractors who hold federally assisted contracts in excess of $10,000 and to a construction contractor's or subcontractor's construction employees who are engaged in on-site construction, including those construction employees who work on a nonfederal or non-federally assisted construction site.

Contractors with fifty or more employees who also have a contract of $50,000 or more must develop a written affirmative action program. Contractors with contracts or subcontracts of $2,500 or more are covered by rules for persons with disabilities, and those with contracts of $10,000 or more are covered by rules for veterans.

The office also administers programs under Section 503 of the Rehabilitation Act of 1973, as amended, which requires federal contractors and subcontractors to take affirmative action to hire and promote qualified persons with disabilities, Vietnam-era veterans, and disabled veterans.

The Americans with Disabilities Act (ADA) prohibits discrimination against persons with disabilities. The office enforces provisions under ADA with regard to government contractors.

Enforcement actions can result from either compliance reviews or complaints. Violations of federal compliance standards can result in partial or total cancellation or suspension of contracts, and violators may be declared ineligible for further government contract work. The agency may order remedies such as reimbursement of back pay or imposition of retroactive seniority.

Complaints against employers should be filed with the OFCCP regional offices. The regional offices also offer technical assistance to government contractors and subcontractors to help them comply with employment laws.

Director
    Patricia A. Shiu . . . . (202) 693–0101
Deputy Director
    Patrick O. Patterson . . . . (202) 693–0101
Senior Civil Rights Advisor
    Donna R. Lenhoff . . . . (202) 693–0101
Senior Program Advisor
    Pamela Coukos . . . . (202) 693–0101
Management and Administrative Programs
    Heidi Casta (acting) . . . . (202) 693–0119
Policy, Planning, and Program Development
    Heidi Casta. . . . . (202) 693–0105
Program Operations
    Marika Litras . . . . (202) 693–0106

■ OFFICE OF LABOR-MANAGEMENT STANDARDS
200 Constitution Ave. N.W.
Washington, DC 20210
Internet: www.dol.gov/olms

The Office of Labor-Management Standards (OLMS) safeguards the financial integrity and internal democracy of labor unions by working cooperatively with unions in the areas of administration and regulation.

The OLMS administers the Labor-Management Reporting and Disclosure Act (LMRDA) of 1959, which requires labor organizations to file copies of their constitutions, bylaws, and annual financial reports. All of these materials are available for public inspection.

Unions are required to follow certain rules in election of union officers, administration of labor union trusteeships, protection of the rights of union members, and handling of union funds. In addition, employers must report any expenditures intended to interfere with or restrain the right of employees to form a union or bargain collectively.

Employers must file reports if they arrange with labor relations consultants to obtain certain information about employees' union activities. Labor relations consultants must file reports if they agree to perform these services for employers.

The OLMS attempts, through technical assistance, to encourage compliance with the act. The office can, however, bring suit in U.S. District Court to force compliance.

The OLMS also enforces portions of the Civil Service Reform Act of 1978 and the Foreign Service Act of 1980, which established standards of conduct for federal employee unions similar to those established for public unions by the Labor-Management Reporting and Disclosure Act. Unions representing U.S. Postal Service employees became subject to the LMRDA with the passage of the Postal Reorganization Act of 1970. Mass transit employees are protected as well under the Urban Mass Transportation Act of 1964 and under Section 5333(b) of Title 49 U.S. Code.

Executive Order 13496 requires that federal contractors provide notice to their employees of their rights under federal labor laws. Specifically, the order requires that covered contractors provide notice of employee rights under the National Labor Relations Act (NLRA), the law that governs relations between unions and employers in the private sector.

Formerly part of the Office of the American Workplace, the OLMS retains its network of regional offices.

Director
Michael J. Hayes .... (202) 693–0122
Enforcement
Patricia Fox .... (202) 693–0143
Interpretations and Standards
Andrew R. Davis.................. (202) 693–0123
Planning, Management, and Technology
Deborah M. Becker............... (202) 693–0127
Reports, Disclosure, and Audits
Larry King .... (202) 693–0124

Statutory Programs
Ann Comer .... (202) 693–0126

■ OFFICE OF WORKERS' COMPENSATION PROGRAMS
200 Constitution Ave. N.W.
Washington, DC 20210
Internet: www.dol.gov/owcp

The Office of Workers' Compensation Programs (OWCP) administers claims under four major disability programs, each aimed at mitigating—through income replacement and medical benefit payments—the financial burden on certain workers, their dependents, or survivors resulting from work-related injury, disease, or death.

These four programs include:

The Division of Federal Employees' Compensation provides workers' compensation coverage to 3 million federal and postal workers around the world for employment-related injuries and occupational diseases.

The Division of Longshore and Harbor Workers' Compensation compensates for lost wages, medical benefits, and rehabilitation services to longshore, harbor, and other maritime workers who are injured during their employment or who contract an occupational disease related to employment.

Division of Coal Mine Workers' Compensation, or Federal Black Lung Program, administers claims filed under the Black Lung Benefits Act. The Act provides benefits to the nation's coal miners who are totally disabled by black lung disease and to their eligible survivors. Benefits include monthly compensation for disabled miners and survivors of miners whose deaths are attributable to black lung and medical coverage for disabled miners' lung disease.

The Division of Energy Employees Occupational Illness Compensation administers the Energy Employees Occupational Illness Compensation Program Act (EEOICPA), which provides compensation and medical benefits to employees of the Department of Energy (DOE), its predecessor agencies, its contractors and subcontractors, and employees of DOE designated Atomic Weapons Employers (AWE) and Beryllium Vendors who became ill as a result of work performed in the production and testing of nuclear weapons. Uranium miners, millers, and ore transporters (or their eligible survivors) under the Radiation Exposure Compensation Act (RECA) administered by the Department of Justice may also be eligible for benefits under the EEOICPA.

Director
Leonard J. Howie III.............. (202) 343–5970
Federal Employees' Compensation
Douglas C. Fitzgerald............. (202) 693–0040
Energy Employees Occupational Illness Compensation
Rachel P. Leiton................... (202) 693–0081
Longshore and Harbor Workers' Compensation
Antonio Rios .... (202) 693–0038
Coal Miners Workers' Compensation (Black Lung)
Michael A. Chance .... (202) 693–0046

▤ WAGE AND HOUR DIVISION

200 Constitution Ave. N.W.
Washington, DC 20210
Internet: www.dol.gov/WHD

The Wage and Hour Division (WHD) administers the Fair Labor Standards Act (FLSA) and a number of other labor standards statutes. The FLSA is the federal law of most general application concerning wages and hours of work. In May 2007 President George W. Bush signed an emergency spending bill that, among other things, amended the FLSA to increase the federal minimum wage in three steps: to $5.85 per hour effective July 24, 2007; to $6.55 per hour effective July 24, 2008; and to $7.25 per hour effective July 24, 2009. Workers also were to be paid not less than one-and-a-half times their regular rates of pay for all hours worked in excess of forty in a work week. Executive Order 13658, signed by President Barack Obama in 2014, raised the minimum wage to $10.10 for workers on federal construction and service contracts.

The child labor provisions of the FLSA set a basic sixteen-year minimum age for employment; however, individuals of the ages fourteen and fifteen may be employed outside school hours in a variety of nonmanufacturing and nonhazardous occupations. Minors under age fourteen may engage only in employment that is exempt from the FLSA or that is not covered by its child labor provisions.

The FLSA requires that employers keep records on all employees and make the records available on request. Although the FLSA does not specify the form of these records, it does require that the records contain certain types of information identifying the employee and listing hours worked and wages paid. Records must be kept for three years.

The division receives complaints from workers across the country; compliance officers in regional and local offices investigate and, if necessary, correct the situation.

The division also prohibits the following practices: the withholding of more than a limited amount of money from a worker's wages to settle a debt (garnishment) and the firing of an employee because earnings have been garnished for only one debt; the payment by federal contractors of less than the prevailing wage rates and fringe benefits for workers on government construction projects or contracts for goods and services; and the exploitation of migrant workers. Farm labor contractors are required to register with the ESA; contractors, their employees, and other employers of migrant workers must observe certain rules in the employment of migrant workers.

Administrator
    David Weil . . . . (202) 693–0051
Deputy Administrator
    Laura A. Fortman . . . . (202) 693–0051
Enforcement Strategy and Support
    Bruce Clark . . . . (202) 693–0051
Enforcement Policy and Procedures
    Vacant . . . . (202) 693–0051
Regulations, Legislation, and Interpretation
    Mary Ziegler . . . . (202) 693–0051
Wage Determinations
    Bezarah Gaither (acting) . . . . (202) 693–0051
Help Line . . . . (866) 487–9243

State Department

2201 C St. N.W., Washington, DC 20520
Internet: www.state.gov

Bureau of Consular Affairs   777

Bureau of Consular Affairs

2201 C St. N.W., Washington, DC 20520
Internet: http://travel.state.gov

The purpose of the Bureau of Consular Affairs is to administer laws, formulate regulations, and implement policies relating to the broad range of consular services provided to U.S. citizens abroad. Three main offices implement these responsibilities: the Passport Services Office, the Visa Services Office, and the Office of Overseas Citizens Services.

The Passport Services Office issues passports to U.S. citizens and is responsible for administering laws, formulating regulations, and recommending and implementing policies relating to the determination of U.S. citizenship and nationality. The Passport Services Office serves the public through twenty-five regional offices and centers and a network of more than 9,100 public offices across the United States designated to accept passport applications.

The Intelligence Reform and Terrorism Prevention Act of 2004 mandated that the Departments of State and Homeland Security implement a plan to require U.S. citizens and foreign nationals to present a passport or other secure document when entering the United States. The result of this mandate was the Western Hemisphere Travel Initiative, and on Jan. 23, 2007, U.S. citizens were required to have a passport, or other appropriate security identity and citizen document, to reenter the United States when traveling via air travel from Canada, Mexico, and the Caribbean.

The second part of the Western Hemisphere Travel Initiative required that all U.S. citizens, Canadians, Mexicans, and citizens of Bermuda have a passport or other approved secure document to enter or reenter the United States by sea or land ports by Jan. 1, 2008, but that date was pushed back. In the interim, U.S. citizens could present documents proving citizenship, such as a birth certificate, and government-issued documents proving identity to gain U.S. reentry. Effective June 1, 2009, all U.S. citizens reentering the country by land or sea are required to present a passport book, passport card, or a government-issued document.

The Implementing Recommendations of the 9/11 Commission Act of 2007 required the secretary of state to develop proposals for reducing the proposed execution fee charged for the passport card. The legislation also directed the homeland security secretary and the secretary of state to initiate a pilot program to determine if an enhanced driver's license that is machine-readable, tamper proof, and issued by such state may permit an individual to meet documentation requirements for entry into the United States from Canada. The Homeland Security Department took the lead and works with states to issue enhanced drivers licenses, which provide proof of identity and U.S. citizenship, are issued in a secure process, and include technology that makes travel easier.

The Office of Visa Services oversees the issuance of immigrant and nonimmigrant visas to the United States by consular officers as governed by the Immigration and Nationality Act, as amended. Visa Services provides liaison between the State Department and Foreign Service posts on visa matters, interprets visa laws and regulations, and acts as a point of contact for the public. Visa Services publishes an annual report that provides statistics on recent immigration into the United States.

The Office of Overseas Citizens Services advises and supports U.S. embassies and consulates around the world in such matters as deaths, arrests, robberies, citizenship and nationality, federal benefits, and notarization of documents. To assist the traveling public, the office issues consular information sheets, travel warnings, and public announcements concerning conditions in countries where Americans may be planning to visit or reside.

Within the Office of Overseas Citizens Services, the Office of Children's Issues formulates, develops, and coordinates policies and programs and provides direction to Foreign Service posts on international parental child abduction, international adoption, and child support issues. It also fulfills U.S. treaty obligations relating to the abduction of children.

The office offers general information and assistance regarding the adoption process in more than sixty countries. Because adoption is a private legal matter within the judicial sovereignty of the nation where the child resides, the State Department cannot intervene on behalf of an individual U.S. citizen in foreign courts.

Since the late 1970s the Bureau of Consular Affairs has taken action in thousands of cases of international parental child abduction. The Office of Children's Issues works closely with parents, attorneys, other government agencies, and private organizations in the United States to prevent international abductions. Eighty countries (including the United States) have joined the Hague Convention on the Civil Aspects of International Child Abduction. The convention discourages abduction as a means of resolving a custody matter, by requiring (with few exceptions) that the abducted child be returned to the country where he or she resided before the abduction.

The office also enforces child support orders. U.S. citizens who are more than $2,500 in arrears in child support will not be issued a passport. The office also negotiates bilateral child support enforcement agreements with other countries. The United States is also participating in the Hague Convention on the International Recovery of Child Support to achieve a new multilateral treaty on child support enforcement.

The Bureau of Consular Affairs informs the public of its activities through publications on international travel through its hotline numbers and through its website.

■ KEY PERSONNEL

Assistant Secretary
Michele T. Bond (acting) . . . . (202) 647–9584
Principal Deputy Assistant Secretary
Michelle T. Bond . . . . (202) 647–9584
Executive Director
Marjorie Arnes . . . . (202) 485–8400
Deputy Assistant Secretary, Overseas Citizens Services (also American Citizens Services and Crisis Management)
Karen L. Christensen . . . . (202) 647–9584
Managing Director
Michelle Bernier-Toth . . . . (202) 485–6046
Children's Issues
Henry Hand. (202) 485–6262
Legal Affairs
Corrin Ferber. . . . . (202) 485–6180
Deputy Assistant Secretary, Passport Services
Brenda Sprague . . . . (202) 647–9584
Fax. . . . . (202) 647–0341
Managing Director
Florence Fultz . . . . (202) 485–6379
Legal Affairs and Law Enforcement Liaison
Jonathan Rolbin. . . . . (202) 485–6590
Planning and Program Support
Winnie Fuentes (acting). . . . . (202) 485–6604
Special Issuance Agency
Christine Harold-Aluyen . . . . (202) 485–8202
Deputy Assistant Secretary, Visa Services
Edward Ramotowski. . . . . (202) 647–9584
Fax. . . . . (202) 647–0341
Managing Director
Karen King. . . . . (202) 485–7560
Field Support and Liaison
Vacant. . . . . (202) 485–7578
Legislation, Regulation, and Advisory Assistance
David Newman . . . . (202) 485–7642
Diplomatic and Public Liaison
Jill Esposito. (202) 485–7425
Director, Fraud Prevention
Josh Glazeroff . . . . (202) 485–6754

■ INFORMATION SOURCES

Internet

Agency website: http://travel.state.gov. Includes passport and visa information, travel warnings, the text of selected publications, and links to many U.S. embassies and consulates abroad. For assistance, call Public Affairs at (202) 647–1488.

Telephone Contacts

Personnel Locator . . . .(202) 647–4000
Federal Relay Service TTY . . . .(800) 877–8339

OVERSEAS CITIZENS SERVICES

Toll-free from U.S. and Canada . . . . . .(888) 407–4747
From Overseas . . . .(202) 501–4444
Children's
Issues . . . . (202) 501–4444; (888) 407–4747
E-mail: askCI@state.gov

PASSPORT SERVICES

General Information . . . .(877) 487–2778
E-mail: NPIC@state.gov

VISA SERVICES

General Information . . . .(202) 663–1225
National Visa Center (immigrant
visa inquiries). . . . .(603) 334–0700

Information and Publications

KEY OFFICES

Public Affairs and Policy Coordination
Bureau of Consular Affairs
2201 C St. N.W.
Washington, DC 20520–4818
(202) 485–7702
Fax (202) 647–6074
State Dept. press office: (202) 647–2492, or outside
regular office hours, (202) 647–1512
Marie C. Damour, director

Handles press inquiries, legislative affairs, and public outreach on consular issues. Publishes country-specific information, current travel warnings, travel alerts, and other travel information. The website www.travel.state .gov contains information about passports, visas, and overseas citizens services.

Visa Services
Bureau of Consular Affairs
2201 C St. N.W., #6811
Washington, DC 20520–4818
(202) 663–1153
Fax (202) 647–0341
Edward Ramotowski, deputy assistant secretary

Publishes an annual report providing statistical information on immigrant and nonimmigrant visa issuances by consular offices, as well as information on the use of visa numbers in numerically limited categories. See http://travel.state.gov/content/visas/english/law-and-policy/statistics.html for the annual report of the Visa Office.

Freedom of Information/Privacy
Department of State
CA/GIS/IPS
515 22nd St. N.W.
Washington, DC 20522–8100
FOIA requester service center (202) 261–8484
Marianne Manheim, FOIA coordinator

DATA AND STATISTICS
Contact Visa Services, above, for the annual report on immigration.

PUBLICATIONS
Country-specific information, travel warnings, and travel alerts are available on www.travel.state.gov. The *Report of the Visa Office,* the *Hague Abduction Convention Compliance Report,* the *Consular Notification and Access Manual,* and the *Report of Death of U.S. Citizens Abroad by Non-Natural Causes* are published online at www.travel.state.gov. The *Annual Report on Intercountry Adoptions* is available at www.adoption.state.gov.

Reference Resources

LIBRARY

Ralph J. Bunche Library
2201 C St. N.W.
Washington, DC 20520
(202) 647–1099
Fax (202) 647–2971
Hugh Howard, librarian
E-mail: library@state.gov
Hours: 8:15 a.m. to 5:00 p.m.

Open to State Department employees only. Some exceptions for unusual circumstances may be made.

DOCKETS
Federal dockets are available at www.regulations.gov. (*See appendix for Searching and Commenting on Regulations: Regulations.gov.*)

RULES AND REGULATIONS
Bureau of Consular Affairs rules and regulations are published in the *Code of Federal Regulations,* Title 8, Part 1101 et seq. Proposed rules, new final rules, and updates to the *Code of Federal Regulations* are published in the daily *Federal Register.* (*See appendix for information on how to obtain and use these publications.*) The *Federal Register* and the *Code of Federal Regulations* may be accessed online at www.federalregister.gov; this site also contains a link to the federal government's regulatory website at www.regulations.gov (*see appendix*).

■ LEGISLATION
The Bureau of Consular Affairs carries out its responsibilities under:

Social Security Act, as amended (42 U.S.C. 659). Signed by the president Aug. 14, 1935. Title IV-D authorized the secretary of state, with the concurrence of the secretary of health and human services, to declare any foreign country to be a foreign reciprocating country if the foreign country established procedures for the enforcement of child support owed to persons who are residents of the United States.

Immigration and Nationality Act, as amended (66 Stat. 163, 8 U.S.C. 1101). Signed by the president June 27, 1952. Contained virtually all of the law relating to the entry of aliens and to the acquisition and loss of U.S. citizenship.

Immigration Act of 1990 (104 Stat. 4978, 8 U.S.C. 1101 note). Signed by the president Nov. 29, 1990. Implemented major changes affecting immigrants and nonimmigrants, Filipino World War II veterans desiring U.S. citizenship, El Salvadoran nationals, and others with immigration concerns.

Child Support Recovery Act of 1992 (18 U.S.C. 228). Signed by the president Oct. 25, 1992. Created a federal offense for traveling in interstate or foreign commerce with the intent to evade a child support obligation, if the obligation has remained unpaid for longer than one year or is greater than $5,000.

Immigration and Nationality Technical Corrections Act of 1994 (108 Stat. 4305, 8 U.S.C. 1101). Signed by the president Oct. 25, 1994. Made numerous specific changes to the Immigration and Nationality Act. Allowed U.S. visas for visits from officials of Taiwan. Gave equal treatment to women in conferring U.S. citizenship to children born abroad.

Personal Responsibility and Work Opportunity Reconciliation Act of 1996 (42 U.S.C. 1305 note). Signed by the president Aug. 22, 1996. Required the secretary of state to deny, revoke, or limit a passport upon certification of nonpayment of child support. Authorized the secretary of state to negotiate reciprocal agreements with foreign nations regarding international enforcement of child support obligations.

Child Citizenship Act (CCA) (114 Stat. 1631, 8 U.S.C. 1101 note). Signed by the president Oct. 30, 2000. Amended the Immigration and Nationality Act to provide automatic U.S. citizenship for a child born outside the United States when the following conditions are met: (1) at least one parent is a U.S. citizen; (2) the child is under eighteen years old; and (3) the child is residing in the United States in the legal and physical custody of the citizen parent pursuant to a lawful admission for permanent residence.

Intelligence Reform and Terrorism Prevention Act of 2004 (118 Stat. 3638, 50 U.S.C. 401 note). Signed by the president Dec. 17, 2004. Created a national intelligence director to oversee U.S. intelligence programs and intelligence-related activities. Established a national counter-terrorism center to serve as a clearinghouse for terrorism intelligence. Expanded immigration and border security laws, including the addition of 10,000 border patrol agents over five years. Authorized plan to require that U.S. citizens and foreign nationals present a passport, or other secure document, when entering the United States. Authorized the secretary of state to increase the number of consular officers by 150 per year through 2009.

Implementing Recommendations of the 9/11 Commission Act of 2007 (121 Stat. 266, 6 U.S.C. 101 note). Signed by the president Aug. 3, 2007. Directed the homeland security secretary and the secretary of state to initiate a pilot program to determine if an enhanced driver's license that was machine-readable, tamper proof, and state-issued could be used by an individual to meet documentation requirements for entry into the United States from Canada. Required the secretary of state to develop proposals for reducing the proposed execution fee charged for a passport card.

Refugee Crisis in Iraq Act of 2007 (122 Stat. 395, 8 U.S.C. 1101 note). Signed by the president Jan. 28, 2008. Authorized the issuance of Special Immigrant Visas (SIVs) to Iraqi nationals who meet certain requirements and who were employed in Iraq.

Afghan Allies Protection Act of 2009 (123 Stat. 807, 8 U.S.C. 1101 note). Signed by the president March 11, 2009. Authorized the issuance of Special Immigrant Visas (SIVs) to Afghan nationals who meet certain requirements and who were employed in Afghanistan.

International Adoption Simplification Act (124 Stat. 3058, 8 U.S.C. 1101 note). Signed by the president Nov. 30, 2010. Amends the Immigration and Nationality Act to include in the definition of "child," and thus in the exemption from required admissions vaccination documentation, certain children who have been adopted in a foreign country that is a signatory to the Hague Convention or who are emigrating from such a country for U.S. adoption.

Help HAITI Act of 2010 (124 Stat. 3175, 8 U.S.C. 1255 note). Signed by the president Dec. 9, 2010. Authorizes USCIS to grant lawful permanent resident status to certain orphaned children from Haiti.

▩ REGIONAL OFFICES

Passport Services

The National Passport Information Center at (877) 487–2778, TTY (888) 874–7793, is available twenty-four hours a day, seven days a week. E-mail: NPIC@state.gov

Representatives can be reached from 8:00 a.m. to 10:00 p.m. Eastern time, Monday–Friday, excluding federal holidays, to provide assistance in applying for, renewing, or amending a U.S. passport; making an appointment at a regional passport agency; checking the status of an application; obtaining information on birth records issued for U.S. citizens born abroad; reporting lost or stolen passports; providing specific travel information to a foreign country; offering assistance for U.S. citizens overseas; providing information on international adoptions; and preventing child abductions. Information is also available on the agency's website.

ARKANSAS PASSPORT CENTER
191 Office Park Dr.
Hot Springs, AR 71913
Automated Appointment Number: (877) 487–2778

ATLANTA PASSPORT AGENCY
230 Peachtree St. N.W., #1000
Atlanta, GA 30303
Automated Appointment Number: (877) 487–2778

BOSTON PASSPORT AGENCY
Tip O'Neill Federal Bldg.
10 Causeway St., #247
Boston, MA 02222–1094
Automated Appointment Number: (877) 487–2778
Issues the U.S. Passport Card on-site.

BUFFALO PASSPORT AGENCY
Genesee Gateway Bldg.
111 Genesee St., #101
Buffalo, NY 14203
Automated Appointment Number: (877) 487–2778
Issues the U.S. Passport Card on-site.

CHICAGO PASSPORT AGENCY
Kluczynski Federal Bldg.
230 S. Dearborn St., 18th Floor
Chicago, IL 60604–1564
Automated Appointment Number: (877) 487–2778
Issues the U.S. Passport Card on-site.

COLORADO PASSPORT AGENCY
Cherry Creek III
3151 S. Vaughn Way, #600
Aurora, CO 80014
Automated Appointment Number: (877) 487–2778

CONNECTICUT PASSPORT AGENCY
850 Canal St.
Stamford, CT 06902
Automated Appointment Number: (877) 487–2778

DALLAS PASSPORT AGENCY
Earle Cabell Federal Bldg.
1100 Commerce St., #1120
Dallas, TX 75242
Automated Appointment Number: (877) 487–2778
Issues the U.S. Passport Card on-site.

DETROIT PASSPORT AGENCY
211 W. Fort St., 2nd Floor
Detroit, MI 48226–3269
Automated Appointment Number: (877) 487–2778
Issues the U.S. Passport Card on-site.

EL PASO PASSPORT AGENCY
Anson Mills Bldg.
303 N. Oregon St.
El Paso, TX 79901
Automated Appointment Number: (877) 487–2778
Issues the U.S. Passport Card on-site.

HONOLULU PASSPORT AGENCY
Prince Kuhio Federal Bldg.
300 Ala Moana Blvd., #1–330
Honolulu, HI 96850
Automated Appointment Number: (877) 487–2778

HOUSTON PASSPORT AGENCY
Mickey Leland Federal Bldg.
1919 Smith St., 4th Floor
Houston, TX 77002–8049
Automated Appointment Number: (877) 487–2778
Issues the U.S. Passport Card on-site.

LOS ANGELES PASSPORT AGENCY
Federal Bldg.
11000 Wilshire Blvd., #1000
Los Angeles, CA 90024–3615
Automated Appointment Number: (877) 487–2778

MIAMI PASSPORT AGENCY
Omni Center
1501 Biscayne Blvd., #210
Miami, FL 33132
Automated Appointment Number: (877) 487–2778
Issues the U.S. Passport Card on-site.

MINNEAPOLIS PASSPORT AGENCY
212 3rd Ave. South
Minneapolis, MN 55401
Automated Appointment Number: (877) 487–2778
Issues the U.S. Passport Card on-site.

NATIONAL PASSPORT CENTER
207 International Dr.
Portsmouth, NH 03801
Automated Appointment Number: (877) 487–2778

NEW ORLEANS PASSPORT AGENCY
1 Canal Place (corner of Canal and North Peters Sts.)
365 Canal St., #1300
New Orleans, LA 70130–6508
Automated Appointment Number: (877) 487–2778

NEW YORK PASSPORT AGENCY
Greater New York Federal Bldg.
376 Hudson St.
New York, NY 10014–4896
Automated Appointment Number: (877) 487–2778
Serves customers who are traveling within two weeks or who need foreign visas for travel. Issues the U.S. Passport Card on-site.

PHILADELPHIA PASSPORT AGENCY
U.S. Customs House
200 Chestnut St., #103
Philadelphia, PA 19106–2970
Automated Appointment Number: (877) 487–2778

SAN DIEGO PASSPORT AGENCY
401 West A St., 10th Floor
San Diego, CA 92101
Automated Appointment Number: (877) 487–2778
Issues the U.S. Passport Card on-site.

SAN FRANCISCO PASSPORT AGENCY
95 Hawthorne St., 5th Floor
San Francisco, CA 94105–3901
Automated Appointment Number: (877) 487–2778

SEATTLE PASSPORT AGENCY
5th and Yesler Bldg.
300 5th Ave., #600
Seattle, WA 98104
Automated Appointment Number: (877) 487–2778
Serves customers who are traveling within two weeks or who need foreign visas for travel.

SPECIAL ISSUANCE AGENCY
600 19th St. N.W. (South entrance)
Washington, DC 20006
Automated Appointment Number: (877) 487–2778
Applications for diplomatic, official, no-fee, and congressional referral customers only, who are traveling within two weeks or who need foreign visas for travel.

VERMONT PASSPORT AGENCY
50 S. Main St., #101
St. Albans, VT 05478
Automated Appointment Number: (877) 487–2778
Issues the U.S. Passport Card on-site.

WASHINGTON PASSPORT AGENCY
600 19th St., N.W. (1st Floor, Sidewalk Level)
Washington, DC 20006
Automated Appointment Number: (877) 487–2778

WESTERN PASSPORT AGENCY
Western Passport Center
7373 E. Rosewood St.
Tucson, AZ 85710
Automated Appointment Number: (877) 487–2778
Issues the U.S. Passport Card on-site.

Transportation Department

400 7th St. S.W., Washington, DC 20590
Internet: www.dot.gov

Federal Aviation Administration

800 Independence Ave. S.W., Washington, DC 20591
Internet: www.faa.gov

The Federal Aviation Administration (FAA), an agency within the Department of Transportation (DOT), establishes and enforces rules and regulations for safety standards covering all aspects of civil aviation. Major areas under FAA regulatory control are the manufacture, maintenance, and operation of aircraft; the training and certification of air personnel (pilots, flight engineers, navigators, aviation mechanics, air traffic controllers, parachute riggers, and aircraft dispatchers); security measures at airports; domestic and international air traffic; and noise and exhaust emissions from aircraft (in cooperation with the Environmental Protection Agency). The FAA also develops air traffic rules and regulations and allocates the use of U.S. airspace, known as the National Airspace System (NAS).

The FAA also inspects commercial aircrafts for safety violations.

The FAA promotes civil aviation abroad by the assignment of technical groups, the training of foreign nationals, and the exchange of information with foreign governments. It provides technical representation at conferences, including participation in the International Civil Aviation Organization and other international organizations.

Drug testing of pilots, flight attendants, and other personnel became mandatory in December 1989. Legislation passed that same year prohibited smoking on almost all flights in the United States.

Managing the National Airspace System (NAS)

The FAA opened the national Air Traffic Control System Command Center near Dulles International Airport in northern Virginia in 1994. The center tracks and manages the flow of more than 50,000 daily flights within the United States.

The Vision 100—Century of Aviation Reauthorization Act, passed in 2003, required the transportation secretary to create an integrated plan for a Next Generation Air Transportation System (NextGen), a modernization of the NAS. Modernization of the NAS requires updates in equipment and aviation fleets as well.

NextGen will replace radar with a satellite-based Global Positioning System (GPS) network. In November 2008 the FAA announced the nationwide deployment of a NextGen system that allows aircraft to be tracked by satellite rather than radar. Automatic Dependent Surveillance–Broadcast (ADS-B) will reduce the risk of midair collisions and weather-related accidents, provide more efficient routes in adverse weather, and improve situational awareness for pilots. The FAA announced completion of the infrastructure in August 2014. The FAA published a rule requiring ADS-B transmitters in many types of airspace effective Jan. 1, 2020.

Another component of NextGen is Data Communications. Data Communications (Data Comm) will enable a transition from analog voice systems to an International Civil Aviation Organization (ICAO) compliant digital communications system. Data Comm will enable controllers to send digital instructions and clearances to pilots, and will eventually supplant voice communications as the primary means of communication between controllers and flight crews. Data communications between aircraft and air traffic management is projected to increase safety and efficiency. In 2014 the FAA began limited trials using existing avionics on airline aircraft to send departure clearances to the cockpit by data instead of voice.

The FAA first authorized use of unmanned aircraft in the NAS in 1990. Since then, the FAA has authorized limited use of unmanned aircraft systems (UAS or drones) for critical missions in the public interest, such as firefighting, disaster relief, search and rescue, law enforcement, border patrol, military training, and testing and evaluation. Federal, state, and local government entities must obtain an FAA Certificate of Waiver or Authorization (COA) before flying UAS in the NAS. Operations potentially range from ground level to above 50,000 feet, depending on the specific type of aircraft. However, routine operation of UAS over densely populated areas is prohibited.

The FAA Modernization and Reform Act of 2012 required the transportation secretary to develop a plan to integrate UAS into the national airspace system by Sept. 30, 2015. The FAA was required to establish a program to integrate UAS into the national airspace system at six test ranges.

In 2014 the FAA gave approval for energy corporation BP and UAS manufacturer AeroVironment to fly an AeroVironment Puma AE for aerial surveys in Alaska, marking the first time the FAA had authorized a commercial UAS operation over land. Later that year, the FAA granted regulatory exemptions to six aerial photo and video production companies.

In February 2015 the FAA released a proposed set of regulations that would allow routine use of certain small UAS in the current aviation system, while maintaining flexibility to accommodate future technological innovations. The FAA proposal offered safety rules for small UAS (under 55 pounds) conducting non-recreational operations. The rule would limit flights to daylight and visual-line-of-sight operations. It also addressed height restrictions, operator certification, optional use of a visual observer, aircraft registration and marking, and operational limits.

Airline Safety

Passenger safety on domestic and international flights is a major focus of the FAA. The deaths of 270 people in the 1988 explosion of a Pan Am 747 over Lockerbie, Scotland, caused by a bomb hidden in a portable tape player, initiated a reassessment of airport security. The Aviation Security Improvement Act of 1990 mandated the implementation of several recommendations from the President's Commission on Aviation Security and Terrorism, set up to investigate the Lockerbie disaster. Provisions included the establishment of federal security managers as the FAA liaison with airport managers and law enforcement officials, and provisions for notifying passengers of terrorist threats to flights.

Following the terrorist attacks of Sept. 11, 2001, the FAA instituted additional in-flight security measures. By April 2003 the agency required airlines to install reinforced, bulletproof doors to protect cockpits from intrusion and small arms fire. The FAA also required that the doors remain locked during flights, with only the pilots having the ability to unlock them from inside the cockpit. The FAA also proposed a new in-flight security measure—placing video cameras and wireless devices in the cabin to enable the cockpit crew to monitor unfolding emergencies.

After the rate of commercial pilots failing sobriety tests doubled, the FAA established new procedures for dealing with intoxicated pilots in 2003. Regulations since then require that pilots who fail sobriety tests have their medical and airman's certificates revoked immediately, effectively grounding them. Grounded pilots must then wait a year and go through rehabilitation to restore their medical certificates, and they must retake all the required written and flight tests to restore their airman's certificates.

Passenger safety once again became the focal point of legislation following the crash of a Colgan Air commuter flight in Buffalo, NY, in 2009. NTSB investigated and determined the accident was the result of pilot error. During the investigation, it was determined that the pilot was not adequately trained to handle emergency situations. Safety issues identified included pilot training, hiring, and fatigue problems. The FAA cited a need for improvements in the practices of regional carriers, which were not subject to the same regulations that governed larger commercial carriers.

Following the findings of the Colgan Air crash investigation, the Airline Safety and Federal Aviation Administration Extension Act of 2010 was enacted to address the safety issues identified. The FAA was authorized to develop and implement an aviation safety action program and a flight operational quality assurance program for use by commercial air carriers. The FAA was required to conduct a rulemaking proceeding to require commercial air carriers to implement a safety management system and develop methods for ensuring that flight crew members have proper qualifications and experience. The law required the FAA to issue regulations to limit the number of flight and duty time hours allowed for pilots to address pilot fatigue. In 2013 the FAA announced a rule increasing the qualification requirements for first officers who fly for U.S. passenger and cargo airlines.

Additional safety requirements were included in the FAA Modernization and Reform Act of 2012, which sought to improve aviation safety and capacity of the NAS, provide a framework for integrating new technology safely into the NAS and advance the implementation of Next Gen. The bill established in the FAA an Aviation Safety Whistleblower Investigation program. The act directed the FAA to initiate rulemaking proceedings regarding duty periods and flight time limitations for flight crew members. The act directed the FAA to initiate rules to implement regulations that permit flight crews of transportation aircraft to use wireless devices for operational, emergency safety-related, or employment-related communications, or another purpose directly related to operation of the aircraft; all other crew uses of wireless devices on the flight deck are prohibited. The legislation also required the FAA to issue a final rule to improve the safety of flight crewmembers, medical personnel, and passengers on board helicopters providing helicopter air ambulance services. The FAA issues progress reports on the regulatory requirements under this legislation.

To ensure that pilots who were the subject of an FAA action received due process, Congress passed the Pilot's Bill of Rights, which requires National Transportation Safety Board (NTSB) proceedings for the review of FAA decisions to deny, amend, modify, suspend, or revoke an airman's certificate to be conducted in accordance with the Federal Rules of Civil Procedure and Federal Rules of Evidence. The legislation requires the FAA to provide timely, written notification to the subject of such an investigation and requires the FAA to provide him or her with access to relevant air traffic data.

Major FAA offices include the following:

Air Traffic Organization. The Air Traffic Organization manages an important function of the FAA: the operation and maintenance of the air traffic control network. The network consists of air-route traffic control centers and airport control towers, staffed by air traffic controllers, and flight service stations, which provide weather briefings and other aeronautical information. The office is staffed by 35,000 controllers, technicians, engineers, and support personnel.

Policy, International Affairs, and Environment. This office leads the agency's strategic policy and planning efforts, coordinates the agency's reauthorization before Congress, and is responsible for national aviation policies and strategies in the environment and energy arenas, including aviation activity forecasts, economic analyses, aircraft noise and emissions research and policy, environmental policy, aviation insurance, and employee safety and health. Within this office, the Office of Aviation Policy and Plans develops policies, goals, and priorities; forecasts future aviation technology and demand; and analyzes the economic impact of regulations. The Office of Environment and Energy develops, recommends, and coordinates national aviation policy relating to environmental and energy matters, which includes noise and emissions. The Office of International Affairs provides leadership of the agency's international programs for coordination of global standards, training, and infrastructure planning.

Office of Aviation Safety. Aviation Safety serves as the principal organization of the FAA responsible for the certification, production approval, and continued airworthiness of aircraft; and the certification of pilots, mechanics, and others in safety-related positions. Aviation Safety is also responsible for certification of all operational and maintenance enterprises in domestic civil aviation; certification and safety oversight of approximately 7,300 U.S. commercial airlines and air operators; civil flight operations; and developing regulations.

Office of Security and Hazardous Materials. This office ensures the integrity of those who work in or support the National Airspace System. The office is responsible for preventing criminal acts such as air piracy, hijacking, sabotage, and extortion. The administration requires all airports to maintain security systems to screen airline passengers. The office is also responsible for enforcement of hazardous materials regulations and runs training programs to reduce the number of hazardous materials incidents.

Office of Commercial Space Transportation. This office regulates the commercial space transportation industry to ensure compliance with international obligations of the United States and to protect public safety. It issues FAA licenses for commercial launches of orbital rockets and suborbital rockets and regulates amateur rocket activities.

NextGen Office. The NextGen Office provides leadership in planning and developing the Next Generation Air Transportation System (NextGen). The NextGen Office coordinates NextGen initiatives, programs, and policy development across the various FAA lines of business and staff offices. The office also works with other federal and state government agencies, the FAA's international counterparts, and members of the aviation community to ensure harmonization of NextGen activities.

▪ KEY PERSONNEL

Administrator
  Michael Huerta . . . . (202) 267–8111
Deputy Administrator
  Michael G. Whitaker . . . . (202) 267–8111
Chief of Staff
  Chris Rocheleau (acting) . . . . (202) 267–3180
  Fax. . . . . (202) 267–5047

Chief Counsel
  Reginald C. Govan . . . . (202) 267–3222
  International Law, Legislation, and Regulations
    Mark Bury . . . . (202) 267–3110
  Enforcement
    Peter J. Lynch. . . . . (202) 267–5158
Civil Rights
  Mamie Mallory . . . . (202) 267–8087
Air Traffic Organization
  Teri Bristol . . . . (202) 493–5602
  Fax. . . . . (202) 267–5716
  Air Traffic Services
    Terri Biggio . . . . (202) 267–5202
  Management Services
    Nancy Kalinowski (acting) . . . . . . (202) 267–4395
  Mission Support
    Elizabeth Lynn Ray. . . . . (202) 267–8261
  Navigation Programs
    James C. Johns. . . . . (202) 385–6724
  Program Management
    James Eck (acting). . . . . (202) 267–8626
  Safety Management System
    Paula Martinez . . . . (202) 267–7602
  Safety and Technical Training
    Joseph S. Teixeira . . . . (202) 267–3341
  Satellite Navigation, Global Positional Satellites (GPS)
    Calvin Miles. . . . . (202) 267–3200
  System Operations Services
    Dan Smiley (acting) . . . . (202) 267–9205
  Technical Operations Services
    Vaughn Turner . . . . (202) 267–8181
  Terminal Services
    Walt Cochran. . . . . (202) 385–8802
    Fax . . . . (202) 554–9837
Airports
  Eduardo Angeles. . . . . (202) 267–9471
  Airport Planning and Programming
    Elliot Black. (202) 267–8775
  Airport Safety and Standards
    Michael J. O'Donnell . . . . (202) 267–3053
  Compliance and Management Analysis
    Randall Fiertz . . . . (202) 267–3085
Aviation Safety
  Margaret Gilligan . . . . (202) 267–3131
  Fax. . . . . (202) 267–9675
  Accident Investigation and Prevention
    Wendell Griffin . . . . (202) 267–9612
  Aerospace Medicine
    Dr. James R. Fraser, federal
      air surgeon. . . . . (202) 267–3535
  Air Traffic Safety Oversight Service
    Anthony Ferrante . . . . (202) 267–5205
  Aircraft Certification
    Dorenda Baker . . . . (202) 267–8235
  Flight Standards Service
    John Duncan . . . . (202) 267–8237
  Quality, Integration, and Executive Services
    Sunny Lee-Fanning. . . . . (202) 493–5717

Rulemaking
Lirio Liu . . . . (202) 267–9677
Commercial Space Transportation
George C. Nield. . . . . (202) 267–7793
Fax. . . . . (202) 267–5450
Licensing and Evaluation Division
Ken Wong. (202) 267–8465
Regulations and Analysis Division
Stewart Jackson . . . . (202) 267–7903
Space Integration
Michael Romanowski. . . . . (202) 267–7793
Space Transportation Development Division
Daniel Murray. . . . . (202) 267–7859
Strategic Planning
Charles Leader. . . . . (202) 267–8737
Finance and Management
Victoria B. Wassmer, assistant
administrator. . . . . (202) 267–8627
Financial Services
Mark House, chief financial officer . . (202) 267–9105
Acquisitions and Business Services
Nathan Tash, chief acquisitions
officer . . . . (202) 267–7222
Information Services
Tina Amereihn, chief information
officer . . . . (202) 493–4570
Regions and Center Operations Services
Ray Towels, chief logistics officer . . (202) 267–7369
Fax. . . . . (202) 267–5015
Government and Industry Affairs
Molly Harris (acting) . . . . (202) 267–3277
Human Resource Management
Rickie P. Cannon (acting) . . . . (202) 267–3456
NextGen
Edward Bolton. . . . . (202) 267–7111
Fax. . . . . (202) 267–5621
Portfolio Management and Technology Development
Paul Fontaine. . . . . (202) 267–9251
Chief Scientist
Steve Bradford. . . . . (202) 493–4245
Systems Analysis and Modeling
Joseph Post. . . . . (202) 385–7111
NAS Systems Engineering Services
Michele Merkle . . . . (202) 385–7100
Policy, International Affairs, and Environment
Rich Swayze . . . . (202) 267–3927
Fax. . . . . (202) 267–5800
Aviation Insurance
Scott Hubbard . . . . (202) 267–0976
Aviation Policy and Plans
Nan Shellabarger. . . . . (202) 267–9954
Environment and Energy
Lourdes Maurice . . . . (202) 267–3866
International Affairs
David S. Burkholder. . . . . (202) 385–8900
Security and Hazardous Materials
Claudio Manno . . . . (202) 267–7211
William J. Hughes Technical Center
(Atlantic City International Airport, Atlantic City, NJ 08405)

Dennis Filler. . . . . (609) 485–6641
En Route and Oceanic
Olethia Lawson-Brown . . . . (609) 485–6669

■ INFORMATION SOURCES

Internet

Agency website: www.faa.gov. Comprehensive website includes information on FAA divisions, centers, and regions; news releases; publications; data and statistics; and links to other FAA Internet sites.

Telephone Contacts

Personnel Locator . . . . (202) 366–4000
TTY . . . . (800) 877–8339
Public Inquiry Center, Consumer Issues,
Statistics, and Publications . . . . (202) 267–3484
Public Information. . . . . (800) 322–7873
Consumer Protection Hotline . . . . (202) 366–2220
Inspector General's Hotline . . . . (800) 424–9071
Safety Hotline . . . (866) TELL-FAA or (866) 835–5322
Whistleblower Protection Program. . . (800) 255–1111

Information and Publications

KEY OFFICES

FAA Communications

800 Independence Ave. S.W., #908
Washington, DC 20591
(202) 267–3883
Jenny Rosenberg, assistant administrator

Provides general information. DOT Public Affairs maintains e-mail lists for DOT advisories; e-mail list may be joined at www.dot.gov/affairs/index.html.

FAA Public Information Line

800 Independence Ave. S.W., #908
Washington, DC 20591
(202) 267–3484
(800) 322–7873
(866) TELL-FAA or (866) 835–5322

Distributes FAA publications and provides assistance and answers to complaints and inquiries. Publications are also available on the website, www.faa.gov/air_traffic/publications and at http://bookstore.gpo.gov.

Freedom of Information Office

National FOIA Staff, ARC-140
800 Independence Ave. S.W.
Washington, D.C. 20591
(202) 267–7799
Fax (202) 267–6514
E-mail: 7-awa-arc-foia@faa.gov
Douglas Taylor, FOIA public liaison
FOIA Service Center (202) 267–9165

HOTLINES

The FAA operates a number of hotlines, listed above under Telephone Contacts; some functions formerly under the FAA now fall under the Department of Homeland Security's Transportation Security Administration (866) 289–9673.

FAA Consumer Hotline

Handles complaints about carry-on baggage restrictions, airport security procedures, and child safety seats. Also handles complaints about user services of the FAA, including examinations, aircraft certification, and facility operations. All calls are picked up by an answering machine; calls are returned by an FAA official if the caller leaves a name and telephone number. Questions regarding airline service, such as flight delays, lost luggage, and ticketing, are handled by DOT Aviation Consumer Protection Division (202) 366–2220.

FAA Safety Hotline

For the public and aviation industry employees with specific knowledge of possible violations of FAA regulations. Callers' identities are confidential. Operates weekdays 8:00 a.m. to 4:00 p.m. Callers may leave a message after business hours; calls are returned by an FAA official if the caller leaves a name and telephone number. Online form is available at www.faa.gov/contact/safety_hotline.

DATA AND STATISTICS

The FAA publishes statistical and financial reports as well as economic studies on domestic and international air traffic activity, the aviation industry, aviation safety, and air personnel. Data and statistics, reports, and publications are available on the website at www.faa.gov (search "Publications" and "Data and Statistics"), at www.faa.gov/data_research, and www.faa.gov/pilots, as well as at http://bookstore.gpo.gov.

PUBLICATIONS

Publications are available on the website at www .faa.gov/data_research and www.faa.gov/pilots as well as from the Government Printing Office Bookstore online (http://bookstore.gpo.gov). FAA publications may also be ordered from the U.S. Government Printing Office (GPO) (*see appendix, Ordering Government Publications*). *FAA Safety Briefing* is a bimonthly periodical devoted to aviation safety, written by the staff of the Flight Standards Service, available on a subscription basis. Current issues are also available on the website.

Reference Resources

LIBRARY

FAA Library

800 Independence Ave. S.W.
Washington, DC 20590
(202) 267–3174
Terry Dempsey, legal information officer
Hours: 8:00 a.m. to 4:00 p.m.

Law library that is open to the public. Collection includes copies of FAA rules, regulations, and guidelines, as well as law reports and compilations. The FAA website also includes a Regulatory and Guidance Library, at http://rgl.faa.gov, and a Technical Library, at www.faa.gov/about/office_org/headquarters_offices/ang/offices/tc/library

DOCKETS

Rules Docket

FAA Office of the Chief Counsel
800 Independence Ave. S.W., #900
East Washington, DC 20591
(202) 267–3222
Reggie Govan, chief counsel

Maintains dockets containing official FAA records, correspondence, and materials related to rulemaking and regulations. Most material in the dockets is available for public inspection and copying. Copies of requested material can be mailed; there is a charge for copying. Two other DOT offices also have FAA-related dockets:

U.S. Department of Transportation— Docket Management Facility

1200 New Jersey Ave. S.E., West Bldg.
Ground Floor, #W12–140
Washington, DC 20590
(202) 366–9329
Hours: 9:00 a.m.–5:00 p.m.
Barbara Hairston, program manager
Docket Management System Website: http://docketsinfo.dot.gov

Maintains docket information concerning air routes. Releases official opinions and orders. Files are open to the public for inspection and copying; an index to the dockets is on file.

Regulatory Affairs

DOT Office of International Aviation
1200 New Jersey Ave. S.E., #W88–316
Washington, DC 20590
(202) 366–2423
Paul L. Gretch, director
E-mail: paul.gretch@dot.gov

Holds complete listings of all the tariffs (fares) currently in effect for all air carriers operating international passenger service.

Included in the filings are all the regular and promotional fares that are charged by airlines for international service. The material is arranged by air carrier.

Federal dockets are also available at www.regulations .gov. (*See appendix for Searching and Commenting on Regulations: Regulations.gov.*)

RULES AND REGULATIONS

FAA rules and regulations are published on the website and in the *Code of Federal Regulations,* Title 14, Chapter I,

Parts 1–199. Proposed rules, final rules, and updated rules and regulations are published in the daily *Federal Register*. (*See appendix for information on how to obtain and use these publications.*) The *Federal Register* and the *Code of Federal Regulations* may also be accessed online at www.archives.gov/federal-register/cfr; the site contains a link to the federal government's regulatory website at www.regulations.gov (*see appendix*).

■ LEGISLATION

The FAA is responsible for the administration of parts of several statutes, most of which are related to aviation safety. The FAA carries out its responsibilities under:

Federal Aviation Act of 1958 (72 Stat. 737, 49 U.S.C. 1301). Signed by the president Aug. 23, 1958. Created the Federal Aviation Agency and gave the agency authority to regulate aviation safety standards, control the nation's navigable airspace, operate air navigation facilities, formulate air traffic rules and regulations, issue certificates of standards for air personnel and aircraft, establish grant programs for the construction and improvement of airports, require registration of aircraft, and establish security provisions for aircraft and airports.

Department of Transportation Act (80 Stat. 931, 49 U.S.C. 1651). Signed by the president Oct. 15, 1966. Created the cabinet-level Department of Transportation; placed the functions, powers, and authorities of the Federal Aviation Agency in one of the three separate administrations within the DOT; changed the name of the Federal Aviation Agency to the Federal Aviation Administration.

Airport and Airway Improvement Act of 1982 (96 Stat. 671, 49 U.S.C. 2201). Signed by the president Sept. 3, 1982. Authorized the FAA to issue operating certificates to airports to ensure safe operation. Authorized a long-range program of planning and construction grants for expansion and improvement of the nation's airports and navigation facilities.

Tax Equity and Fiscal Responsibility Act of 1982 (96 Stat. 324, 26 U.S.C. 1 note). Signed by the president Sept. 3, 1982. Established certain taxes imposed on users of the aviation system to fund construction and improvement projects.

Commercial Space Launch Act of 1984 (98 Stat. 3055, 49 U.S.C. 701). Signed by the president Oct. 30, 1984. Authorized the transportation secretary to promulgate regulations regarding the procedures and requirements applicable to the authorization and supervision of commercial space transportation activities conducted in the United States or by a U.S. citizen.

Airport and Airway Safety and Capacity Expansion Act of 1987 (101 Stat. 1486, 49 U.S.C. app. 2201 note). Signed by the president Dec. 30, 1987. Amended the Airport and Airway Improvement Act of 1982 to reauthorize funding for airport programs, including expansion grants, through fiscal year 1992, and airway programs, including funding for air traffic control equipment, through 1990.

Department of Transportation and Related Agencies Appropriations Act (103 Stat. 1098, 49 U.S.C. app. 1374d). Signed by the president Nov. 21, 1989. Banned smoking on virtually all domestic air flights.

Miscellaneous Aviation Amendments (103 Stat. 2060, 49 U.S.C. app. 1475d). Signed by the president Dec. 15, 1989. Extended the authorization for the penalty assessment program.

Aviation Security Improvement Act of 1990 (104 Stat. 3066, 49 U.S.C. app. 2152 note). Signed by the president Nov. 16, 1990. Amended Title III of the Federal Aviation Act of 1958 to add sections 318 and 319, which included measures to strengthen air transport security and ensure the safety of passengers of U.S. air carriers against terrorist threat. Established the position of Civil Aviation Security associate administrator within the FAA.

Department of Transportation and Related Agencies Appropriations Act of 1992 (105 Stat. 917, 49 U.S.C. app. 1301 note). Signed by the president Oct. 28, 1991. Required air carriers and foreign air carriers to conduct pre-employment, reasonable suspicion, random, and postaccident testing of pilots, crew members, airport security, and air carrier employees to test for alcohol and controlled substances. This law also required testing of FAA employees whose duties include responsibility for safety-sensitive functions.

FAA Civil Penalty Administrative Assessment Act of 1992 (106 Stat. 923, 49 U.S.C. app. 1301 note). Signed by the president Aug. 26, 1992. Amended the Federal Aviation Act of 1958 to authorize the FAA administrator to assess a civil penalty for violations pertaining to civil air flights over security zones, aviation safety regulations, and regulations requiring public notice of existing or proposed construction or repairs that will promote safety in air commerce.

Antiterrorism and Effective Death Penalty Act of 1996 (110 Stat. 1214, 18 U.S.C. 1 note). Signed by the president April 24, 1996. Title III, International Terrorism Prohibitions, required the FAA administrator to approve security programs used by foreign air carriers operating in the United States. Required foreign carriers to meet standards used by U.S. carriers and airports.

Air Traffic Management System Performance Improvement Act of 1996 (110 Stat. 3227, 49 U.S.C. 106 note, 40101 note). Signed by the president Oct. 9, 1996. Authorized the administrator to use personnel of other federal agencies. Established the Federal Aviation Management Advisory Council to provide advice and counsel on operational issues and act as an oversight resource for management, policy, spending, and regulatory matters. Established the National Civil Aviation Review Commission to analyze alternative financing means for meeting the needs of the aviation system and aviation safety in the United States.

Aviation Medical Assistance Act of 1998 (112 Stat. 47, 49 U.S.C. 44701 note). Signed by the president April 24, 1998. Directed the administrator to reevaluate the medical equipment and supplies carried by air carriers and the training of flight attendants in the use of such equipment.

Aviation and Transportation Security Act (115 Stat. 597, 49 U.S.C. 40101 note). Signed by the president Nov. 19, 2001. Created a Transportation Security Administration within the DOT. Gave the TSA jurisdiction over airport security, federalized airport security workers, and mandated random deployment of armed federal sky marshals on commercial flights. Also permitted pilots to carry guns after specialized training. Required physical security improvements in planes and airports, including strengthened cockpit doors, mandatory training for flight crews on how to deal with hijacking attempts, and screening of all checked and carry-on baggage. Created a Transportation Security Oversight Board to review emergency security regulations and other actions of the TSA.

Homeland Security Act of 2002 (116 Stat. 2135, 6 U.S.C. 101 note). Signed by the president Nov. 25, 2002. Established the Department of Homeland Security (DHS) and transferred all or significant portions of twenty-two existing agencies to the new department, which is responsible for protecting the United States from terrorist attacks. Integrated the Transportation Security Administration into the border and transportation security division of DHS.

Vision 100—Century of Aviation Reauthorization Act (117 Stat. 2490, 49 U.S.C. 40101 note). Signed by the president Dec. 12, 2003. Directed the secretary of transportation to establish in the FAA the Next Generation Air Transportation System Joint Planning and Development Office to create an integrated plan for a Next Generation Air Transportation System.

Intelligence Reform and Terrorism Prevention Act of 2004 (118 Stat. 3638, 50 U.S.C. 401 note). Signed by the president Dec. 17, 2004. Requires the FAA to issue plastic, tamper-resistant pilot certificates with photos.

Commercial Space Launch Amendments Act of 2004 (118 Stat. 3974, 49 U.S.C. 40101 note). Signed by the president Dec. 23, 2004. Authorized the transportation secretary to promulgate regulations for the safety of launch vehicles designed to carry humans. Authorized the transportation secretary to issue additional regulations setting reasonable requirements for space flight participants, including medical and training requirements. Established an experimental permit program for developmental reusable suborbital rockets for testing purposes.

Safe, Accountable, Flexible, and Efficient Transportation Equity Act of 2005 (SAFETEA) (23 U.S.C. 134). Signed by the president Aug. 10, 2005. Expanded the scope of federal safe transportation of hazardous materials regulations to include shipping and packaging companies.

Fair Treatment for Experienced Pilots Act (121 Stat. 1450, 49 U.S.C. 44729). Signed by the president Dec. 13, 2007. Allowed both the pilot and copilot on a domestic flight to be up to age sixty-five. For international flights, one pilot may be up to age sixty-five provided the other is under age sixty.

Executive Order 13479. Issued Nov. 18, 2008. Established an executive advisory committee to accelerate the implementation of the Next Generation Air Transportation System, authorized under Vision 100—Century of Aviation Reauthorization Act.

Airline Safety and Federal Aviation Administration Extension Act of 2010 (124 Stat. 2348, 49 U.S.C. 40101 note). Signed by the president Aug. 1, 2010. Authorized various actions to improve airline safety and pilot training.

Requires the FAA to issue regulations to limit the number of flight and duty time hours allowed for pilots to address pilot fatigue. Directs the FAA to develop and implement an aviation safety action program and a flight operational quality assurance program by commercial air carriers. Directs the FAA to conduct a rulemaking proceeding to require commercial air carriers to implement a safety management system and develop methods for ensuring that flight crewmembers have proper qualifications and experience.

FAA Modernization and Reform Act of 2012 (126 Stat. 11, 49 U.S.C. 40101 note). Signed by the president Feb. 14, 2012. Directed the Federal Aviation Administration (FAA) to initiate rulemaking proceedings regarding duty periods and flight time limitations for flight crewmembers. Directed the FAA to issue a final rule to improve the safety of flight crewmembers, medical personnel, and passengers on board helicopters providing helicopter air ambulance services. Directed the FAA to initiate a rule to implement regulations that permit flight crews of transportation aircraft to use wireless devices for operational, emergency safety-related, employment-related communications, or another purpose directly related to operation of the aircraft. All other uses are prohibited. Required the transportation secretary to develop a plan to integrate civil unmanned aircraft systems (UAS or drones) into the national airspace system by Sept. 30, 2015. Directed the FAA to establish a program to integrate UAS into the national airspace system at six test ranges. Required the FAA to promulgate a proposed rule to require alcohol and controlled substances testing of specific foreign repair station employees responsible for safety-sensitive maintenance functions on specified air carrier aircraft. Established in the FAA an Aviation Safety Whistleblower Investigation Office.

Pilot's Bill of Rights (126 Stat. 1159, 49 U.S.C. 44703 note). Signed by the president Aug. 3, 2012. Requires National Transportation Safety Board (NTSB) proceedings for the review of Federal Aviation Administration (FAA) decisions to deny, amend, modify, suspend, or revoke an airman's certificate to be conducted in accordance with the Federal Rules of Civil Procedure and Federal Rules of Evidence, to the extent practicable. The legislation requires the FAA to provide timely, written notification to the subject of such an investigation, and requires FAA to provide him or her with access to relevant air traffic data.

◼ REGIONAL OFFICES

ALASKA
222 W. Seventh Ave., #14
Anchorage, AK 99513
(907) 271–5645
Kerry Long, regional administrator

CENTRAL
(IA, KS, MO, NE)
901 Locust St., #335

Kansas City, MO 64106–2641
(816) 329–3050
Joe Miniace, regional administrator

EASTERN
(DC, DE, MD, NJ, NY, PA, VA, WV)
159–30 Rockaway Blvd.
Jamaica, NY 11434–4848
Mailing address:
1 Aviation Plaza
Jamaica, NY 11434–4809
(718) 553–3001
Carmine Gallo, regional administrator

GREAT LAKES
(IL, IN, MI, MN, ND, OH, SD, WI)
2300 E. Devon Ave.
Des Plaines, IL 60018–4686
(847) 294–7294
Barry Cooper, regional administrator

NEW ENGLAND
(CT, MA, ME, NH, RI, VT)
12 New England Executive Park
Burlington, MA 01803–5299
(781) 238–7020
Amy Lind Corbett, regional administrator

NORTHWEST MOUNTAIN
(CO, ID, MT, OR, UT, WA, WY)
1601 Lind Ave. S.W.
Renton, WA 98057
(425) 227–2001; (800) 220–5715
Kathryn Vernon, regional administrator

SOUTHERN
(AL, FL, GA, KY, MS, NC, PR, SC, TN, VI)
1701 Columbia Ave.
College Park, GA 30337–2747
Mailing address:
P.O. Box 20636

Atlanta, GA 30320
(404) 305–5000
Dennis Roberts, regional administrator

SOUTHWEST
(AR, LA, NM, OK, TX)
2601 Meacham Blvd.
Fort Worth, TX 76137–4298
(817) 222–5001
Kevin L. Solco, regional administrator

WESTERN-PACIFIC
(AZ, CA, HI, NV)
15000 Aviation Blvd.
Lawndale, CA 90261
(310) 725–3550
Mailing address:
P.O. Box 92007
Los Angeles, CA 90009
Package delivery address:
15000 Aviation Blvd.
Hawthorne, CA 90250
Glen A. Martin, regional administrator

Other Field Offices

MIKE MONRONEY AERONAUTICAL CENTER
6500 South MacArthur Blvd.
Oklahoma City, OK 73169
Mailing address:
P.O. Box 25082
Oklahoma City, OK 73125
(405) 954–4521
Michelle Coppedge, director

WILLIAM J. HUGHES TECHNICAL CENTER
Atlantic City International Airport
Atlantic City, NJ 08405
(609) 485–6641
Dennis Filler, director

Federal Highway Administration

1200 New Jersey Ave. S.E., Washington, DC 20590
Internet: www.fhwa.dot.gov

The Federal Highway Administration (FHWA), an agency within the Department of Transportation (DOT), sets functional safety standards for the design, construction, and maintenance of the nation's highways. The FHWA administers the federal highway program, which distributes federal funds to the states to construct and improve the federal-aid highway systems. The National Highway System Designation Act of 1995 designated roughly 160,000 miles of interstate highways and other heavily traveled roads as the National Highway System (NHS). Routes on the NHS receive slightly more than 30 percent of all federal highway aid.

The FHWA is headed by an administrator who is appointed by the president and confirmed by the Senate. Serving under the administrator are the deputy administrator, the executive director, and associate administrators with functional responsibilities for administration; operations; planning, environment, and realty; infrastructure; policy and government affairs; research, development, and technology; and safety. Also reporting to the administrator are the chief counsel, the director of civil rights, and the director of public affairs, and five regional resource centers.

The FHWA regulates highway design and construction to reduce traffic deaths, injuries, and damage to property and to increase the efficiency of traffic movement. FHWA rules and regulations must be followed by the states and communities that receive FHWA matching funds to construct or improve highways.

The FHWA operates the National Highway Institute, which administers a training program for state and local highway employees. The institute offers both classroom-based and online learning as well as free Web-based seminars. In addition, it offers fellowships in highway safety and transportation research and education, and a highway technician scholarship.

The FHWA's Office of Federal Lands Highway (OFLH) is responsible for highway beautification programs, the Darien Gap and Alaska Highway programs, the highway construction portions of the Appalachian regional development project, and the territorial highway program. It designs and builds forest highways, national defense access roads, and roads in national parks and on Native American reservations, and administers training programs in highway construction for unskilled workers. The OFLH also provides highway engineering services and assistance to other federal agencies and foreign governments.

The FHWA's annual budget is primarily funded by fuel and motor vehicle excise taxes. The budget is primarily divided between two programs: funding to state and local governments, and funding for national parks, national forests, Native American lands, and other land under federal stewardship.

In 2002 President George W. Bush issued an executive order that authorized expedited environmental review processes for a select group of high-priority transportation projects. The executive order established an interagency task force to oversee the implementation of the order's provisions and monitor the environmental reviews of the fast-tracked projects.

In 2005 the $286.5 billion Safe, Accountable, Flexible, and Efficient Transportation Equity Act (SAFETEA) reauthorized federal highway programs through fiscal year 2009. The American Recovery and Reinvestment Act of 2009 appropriated an additional $26 billion for highway infrastructure improvements. However, Congress has not passed a transportation reauthorization bill since SAFTEA expired. As work continues on the omnibus transportation reauthorization bill, Congress continues to appropriate money to fund transportation programs via short-term reauthorization bills.

Although Congress failed to pass an omnibus transportation reauthorization bill, it did enact the Moving Ahead for Progress in the 21st Century Act (MAP-21) in 2012. The bill reauthorized several surface transportation programs for two years and included significant reforms. Provisions of the bill restructured core highway formula programs and consolidated funding programs, eliminating many discretionary programs. To measure success, the bill established national performance goals for federal highway programs.

MAP-21 includes provisions to improve efficiency, effectiveness, and accountability at every stage of a transportation project. This includes streamlining the environmental review process. Projects stalled in the environmental review process can get technical assistance to speed completion within four years.

MAP-21 directs the transportation secretary to establish a national freight network to improve movement of freight on highways, including freight intermodal connectors and national highway and aerotropolis transportation systems. States are encouraged to develop individual freight plans and establish freight advisory committees.

By May 2015 Congress had not passed an omnibus transportation reauthorization bill and funding for transportation infrastructure was set to expire by the end of the month. Days before the deadline, Congress passed a two-month stop-gap measure. The lack of a multiyear budget and policy priorities places a hardship on states for long-term transportation infrastructure planning.

■ KEY PERSONNEL

Administrator
Gregory G. Nadeau . . . . (202) 366–2240
Fax . . . . (202) 366–3244
Deputy Administrator
Vacant . . . . (202) 366–2240
Executive Director
Jeffrey Paniati . . . . (202) 366–2242
Chief Counsel
Thomas Echikson . . . . (202) 366–0740
Fax . . . . (202) 366–7499
Chief Financial Officer
Elissa Konove . . . . (202) 366–0622
Administration
Sarah Shores . . . . (202) 366–5154
Civil Rights
Warren Whitlock . . . . (202) 366–0693
Federal Lands Highway Program
Robert Arnold (acting) . . . . (202) 366–1285
Fax . . . . (202) 366–7495
Policy and Program Review
Karen A. Pinell . . . . (202) 366–9478
Program Development
Scott T. Johnson . . . . (202) 366–9480
Infrastructure
Walter Waidelich Jr. . . . . (202) 366–0371
Fax . . . . (202) 493–0099
Program Administration
Thomas Everett . . . . (202) 366–5530
Bridges and Structures
Joseph Hartmann . . . . (202) 366–4599
Asset Management, Pavements, and Construction
Grant Zammit (acting) . . . . (404) 562–3575
Transportation Performance Management
Peter Stephanos . . . . (202) 366–0027
Innovative Program Delivery
Regina McElroy . . . . (202) 366–8006
Intelligent Transportation Systems
Kenneth Leonard . . . . (202) 366–9536
National Highway Institute . . . . (703) 235–0500
(1310 N. Court House Rd., #30, Arlington, VA 22201)
Valerie Briggs . . . . (703) 235–0500
Operations
Jeffrey A. (Jeff) Lindley . . . . (202) 366–8753
Freight Management and Operations
Caitlin H. Rayman . . . . (202) 493–0457
Transportation Management
Robert E. Arnold . . . . (202) 366–1285

Transportation Operations
Mark R. Kehrli . . . . (202) 366–0600
Planning, Environment, and Realty
Gloria M. Shepherd . . . . (202) 366–0116
Human Environment
Shari M. Schaftlein . . . . (202) 366–5570
Natural Environment
April L. Marchese . . . . (202) 366–2074
Planning
Kenneth (Ken) N. Petty II . . . . (202) 366–6654
Project Development and Environmental Review
Gerald (Gerry) L. Solomon . . . . . . (202) 366–2037
Real Estate Services
Virgil R. Pridemore . . . . (202) 366–2058
Policy and Governmental Affairs
David Kim . . . . (202) 366–8169
Highway Policy Information
David R. Winter . . . . (202) 366–4631
International Programs
Ian C. Saunders . . . . (202) 366–4044
Legislative Affairs and Policy Communication
Cheryl J. Walker . . . . (202) 366–6378
Transportation Policy Studies
E. Ross Crichton (acting) . . . . (202) 366–5027
Public Affairs
Jane Mellow . . . . (202) 366–9910
Research, Development, and Technology
(6300 Georgetown Pike, McLean, VA 22101)
Michael F. Trentacoste . . . . (202) 493–3259
Fax . . . . (202) 493–3170
Safety
Anthony (Tony) Furst . . . . (202) 366–2288
Fax . . . . (202) 366–3222
Safety Programs
Elizabeth Alicandri . . . . (202) 366–6409
Safety Technologies
Michael Griffith . . . . (202) 366–9469

■ INFORMATION SOURCES

Internet
Agency website: www.fhwa.dot.gov. Comprehensive website includes information on publications and statistics, procurement, legislation and regulations, and conferences and training.

Telephone Contacts
Personnel Locator . . . . (202) 366–0537
Federal Relay Service TTY . . . . (800) 877–8339

Information and Publications

KEY OFFICES

FHWA Public Affairs
1200 New Jersey Ave. S.E.
Washington, DC 20590
(202) 366–9910
Jane Mellow, director

Provides public information, answers or refers general questions, and acts as media liaison.

FHWA Office of Highway Policy Information

1200 New Jersey Ave. S.E., #E83–310
Washington, DC 20590
(202) 366–4631
David Winter, director

Handles statistical reports on highway systems.

FHWA Office of Chief Counsel

1200 New Jersey Ave. S.E.
Washington, DC 20590
(202) 366–0740
Thomas G. Echikson, chief counsel

Serves as principal FHWA legal officer and adviser, rendering legal services and providing legal advice to headquarters and field offices concerning all aspects of FHWA programs, functions, and activities.

Freedom of Information

1200 New Jersey Ave. S.E. (HCC-40)
Washington, DC 20590
FOIA Service Center (202) 366–6131
E-mail: foia.officer@fhwa.dot.gov
Manizheh Boehm, FOIA public liaison
(202) 366–0948

DATA AND STATISTICS

See the website or contact FHWA Public Affairs or the FHWA Office of Highway Policy Information.

PUBLICATIONS

FHWA reports and publications are available from the Electronic Reading Room on the website and at www .fhwa.dot.gov/publications. E-Cal (Electronic Centralized Agreement Library), www.fhwa.dot.gov/agreements, lists publications according to office within the FHWA. Other materials may be obtained from the Government Printing Office (online at http://bookstore.gpo.gov or see appendix on *Ordering Government Publications*).

The Research, Development, and Technology Office handles requests for research publications; these are also available on the website.

Reference Resources

LIBRARIES

FHWA Research Library

Turner-Fairbank Highway Research Center
6300 Georgetown Pike
McLean, VA 22101–2296
(202) 493–3172
E-mail: fhwalibrary@dot.gov
Dawn Vanlandingham, information management
   specialist
Internet: www.fhwa.dot.gov/research/library
Hours: 8:00 a.m. to 4:00 p.m.

DOT Library

1200 New Jersey Ave. S.E., #W12–300
Washington, DC 20590
(202) 366–3282
(800) 853–1351
Law Library (202) 366–0749
Amanda Wilson, director
(202) 366–2480
Internet: www.ntl.bts.gov
E-mail: library@dot.gov
Hours: 8:00 a.m. to 5:00 p.m.

The National Transportation Library is the primary repository for DOT technical and legal information and research, maintaining both digital and traditional library environments. Resources include book and journal collections, reference services (including the website's Ask-a-Librarian service), electronic database access, and interlibrary loan services. The library's website also provides an extensive list of libraries across the United States that have significant resources on transportation issues.

DOCKETS

Contact the FHWA Law Library, Docket Room (above). Federal dockets are also available at www.regulations .gov. (*See appendix for Searching and Commenting on Regulations: Regulations.gov.*)

RULES AND REGULATIONS

FHWA rules and regulations are published in the *Code of Federal Regulations,* Title 23, Chapter I, Parts 1–999, and Title 23, Chapter II, Parts 1200–1299. Proposed rules, new final rules, and updates to the *Code of Federal Regulations* are published in the daily *Federal Register.* (*See appendix for details on how to obtain and use these publications.*) The *Federal Register* and the *Code of Federal Regulations* may also be accessed online at www.archives .gov/federal-register/cfr; this site also contains a link to the federal government's regulatory website at www .regulations.gov (*see appendix*).

▦ LEGISLATION

The FHWA carries out its responsibilities under:

Interstate Commerce Act (24 Stat. 379, 49 U.S.C. 1). Signed by the president Feb. 4, 1887. Empowers the FHWA to establish safety standards for all commercial motor carriers engaged in interstate or foreign commerce.

Crimes and Criminal Procedures Act (62 Stat. 738, 18 U.S.C. 831). Signed by the president June 25, 1948. Authorized the FHWA to regulate transportation of dangerous cargo on U.S. highways.

Highway Safety Act of 1966 (80 Stat. 731, 23 U.S.C. 401). Signed by the president Sept. 9, 1966. Required each state to have a highway safety program that meets federal standards for driver and pedestrian performance and bicycle safety. Authorized the FHWA to provide incentive grants to states that reduce traffic fatalities and to enact legislation requiring the use of seat belts.

Department of Transportation Act (80 Stat. 931, 49 U.S.C. 1651). Signed by the president Oct. 15, 1966. Created the cabinet-level Department of Transportation; transferred authority for safety standards for motor carriers from the Interstate Commerce Commission to the FHWA.

Highway Safety Act of 1970 (84 Stat. 1739, 23 U.S.C. 144). Signed by the president Dec. 31, 1970. Divided responsibility for the Highway Safety Act of 1966 between the National Highway Traffic Safety Administration (NHTSA) and the FHWA. The FHWA was given responsibility for highway safety and design programs and the NHTSA was given authority over vehicle and pedestrian safety.

Intermodal Surface Transportation Efficiency Act of 1991 (ISTEA) (105 Stat. 1914, 49 U.S.C. 101 note). Signed by the president Dec. 18, 1991. Increased funding to enhance transportation efficiency. Authorized implementation and evaluation of value pricing pilot projects to manage congestion on highways through tolling and other pricing mechanisms. Authorized funding for incentive programs to improve passenger safety and to prevent drunk driving.

National Highway System Designation Act of 1995 (109 Stat. 568, 23 U.S.C. 101 note). Signed by the president Nov. 28, 1995. Designated roughly 160,000 miles of interstate highways and other heavily traveled roads as the NHS. Repealed the federal cap on highway speed limits, allowing states to set their own speed limits for all roadways.

Transportation Equity Act for the 21st Century (TEA-21) (112 Stat. 154, 23 U.S.C. 143). Signed by the president June 9, 1998. Reauthorized the federal highway, transit, safety, research, and motor carrier programs under the ISTEA from fiscal year 1998 through 2003. Provided incentives for states to adopt tough.08 blood alcohol concentration standards for drunk driving.

Motor Carrier Safety Improvement Act of 1999 (113 Stat. 1748). Signed by the president Dec. 9, 1999. Title I established the Federal Motor Carrier Safety Administration within the DOT, to be headed by an administrator appointed by the president and confirmed by the Senate.

Executive Order 13274. Issued Sept. 18, 2002. Authorized expedited environmental review processes for a select group of high-priority transportation projects. Established an interagency task force to oversee the implementation of the executive order and monitor the environmental reviews of its fast-tracked projects.

Safe, Accountable, Flexible, and Efficient Transportation Equity Act of 2005 (SAFETEA) (23 U.S.C. 134). Signed by the president Aug. 10, 2005. Reauthorized federal surface transportation programs through fiscal year 2009. Authorized appropriations for the Interstate Maintenance Program and the NHS. Removed the actions of the FHWA administrator from judicial reviewability.

American Recovery and Reinvestment Act of 2009 (123 Stat. 115, 26 U.S.C. 1 note). Signed by the president Feb. 17, 2009. Appropriated more than $26 billion for highway infrastructure improvements. Set forth maintenance of effort and reporting requirements for state or state agency awarded funds.

Moving Ahead for Progress in the 21st Century Act (MAP-21) (126 Stat. 405, 23 U.S.C. 101 note). Signed by the president July 6, 2012. Restructured core highway formula programs and consolidated funding programs, eliminating many discretionary programs. Established national performance goals for federal highway programs. Streamlines the environmental review process. Requires the transportation secretary, upon request, to provide additional technical assistance to resolve within four years any project issues and project delays related to environmental review under the National Environmental Policy Act of 1969 (NEPA). Directs the secretary to establish a national freight network to improve movement of freight on highways, including freight intermodal connectors and national highway and aerotropolis transportation systems.

■ REGIONAL OFFICES

CENTRAL RESOURCE CENTER

12300 West Dakota Ave., #340
Lakewood, CO 80228
(720) 963–3500
Bernetta Collins, director
(720) 963–3243

EASTERN RESOURCE CENTER

10 S. Howard St., #4000
Baltimore, MD 21201–1819
(410) 962–0093
Joyce A. Curtis, director
Shay Burrows, team manager

MIDWESTERN RESOURCE CENTER

One Prairie Office Center
4749 Lincoln Mall Dr., #600
Matteson, IL 60443
(708) 283–3500
Dan Ghere, team manager

SOUTHERN RESOURCE CENTER

61 Forsyth St. S.W., #17T26
Atlanta, GA 30303–3104
(404) 562–3570
Rob Elliott, team leader
(404) 562–3941

WESTERN RESOURCE CENTER

201 Mission St., #1700
San Francisco, CA 94105
(415) 744–3100
Robert M. O'Loughlin, team leader

Federal Motor Carrier Safety Administration

1200 New Jersey Ave. S.E., Washington, DC 20590
Internet: www.fmcsa.dot.gov

The Federal Motor Carrier Safety Administration (FMCSA) was established within the Department of Transportation on Jan. 1, 2000, pursuant to the Motor Carrier Safety Improvement Act of 1999. Formerly a part of the Federal Highway Administration, the Federal Motor Carrier Safety Administration's primary mission is to prevent commercial motor vehicle fatalities and injuries.

FMCSA promotes safety in motor carrier operations through strong enforcement of safety regulations, targeting high-risk carriers and commercial motor vehicle drivers; improving safety information systems and commercial motor vehicle technologies; strengthening commercial motor vehicle equipment and operating standards; and increasing safety awareness. To accomplish these activities, FMCSA works with federal, state, and local enforcement agencies, the motor carrier industry, labor safety interest groups, and others.

The Motor Carrier Safety Advisory Committee (MCSAC) is charged with providing advice and recommendations to the FMCSA Administrator on motor carrier safety programs and motor carrier safety regulations. MCSAC is comprised of twenty experts from the motor carrier industry, safety advocates, and safety enforcement sectors. Initially chartered by the secretary of transportation on September 8, 2006, the current charter runs through September 30, 2015.

The following are programs administered by FMCSA.

Motor Carrier Safety Assistance Program. This is a federal grant program that provides states with financial assistance for roadside inspections and other commercial motor vehicle safety programs. It promotes detection and correction of commercial motor vehicle safety defects, commercial motor vehicle driver deficiencies, and unsafe motor carrier practices before they become contributing factors in crashes and hazardous materials incidents. The program also promotes the adoption and uniform enforcement by the states of safety rules, regulations, and standards compatible with the federal motor carrier safety regulations and federal hazardous materials regulations.

Commercial Driver's License Program. FMCSA develops, issues, and evaluates standards for testing and licensing commercial motor vehicle drivers. These standards require states to issue a commercial driver's license only after drivers pass knowledge and skill tests that pertain to the type of vehicle operated. States are audited every three years to monitor compliance with federal standards; noncompliance could result in loss of federal funding.

Research and Analysis. The Office of Analysis, Research, and Technology (ART) seeks to reduce the number and severity of commercial motor vehicle crashes. The office conducts scientific studies aimed at understanding and adopting, testing, and deploying innovative driver, carrier, vehicle, and roadside best practices and technologies. ART collects and disseminates a wide variety of data in technical and analytical briefs.

International Programs. FMCSA supports the development of compatible motor carrier safety requirements and procedures in the context of the North American Free Trade Agreement (NAFTA). The agency supports programs to improve the safety performance of motor carriers operating in border areas through special grants to states for enforcement activities and, in cooperation with other federal agencies, it supports the development of state safety inspection facilities. FMCSA participates in international technical organizations and committees to share best practices in motor carrier safety.

Hazardous Materials Regulations. FMCSA enforces regulations for the safe transportation of hazardous materials by highway and rules governing the manufacture and maintenance of cargo tank motor vehicles, as set forth in Chapter 51 of Title 49 of the U.S. Code.

Passenger Carrier Safety. FMCSA provides resources for consumers and industry regarding passenger carrier safety programs and regulations. Resources include online searchable carrier safety records, federal regulation fact sheets and mobile safety apps for smartphones.

Performance & Registration Information Systems Management (PRISM). PRISM, a federal-state partnership links federal motor carrier safety records with the state's vehicle registration system. Safety performance is continuously monitored, and carriers prohibited by FMCSA from operating in interstate commerce may have their ability to register vehicles denied.

Household Goods Program. FMCSA regulates interstate household goods movers and requires them to register with the agency. FMCSA has developed a website, www.ProtectYourMove.gov, to assist consumers moving across state lines.

■ KEY PERSONNEL

Administrator
Thomas F. (Scott) Darling (acting)... (202) 366–1927
Deputy Administrator
Daphne Jefferson............... (202) 366–1927
Assistant Administrator and Chief Safety Officer
Jack Van Steenburg............ (202) 366–1927
Administration
Vacant......................... (202) 366–1314
Analysis, Research, and Technology
Steven Smith .... (202) 493–0145
Chief Counsel
Thomas F. (Scott) Darling .... (202) 493–0349
Civil Rights
Kennie J. May Sr. .... (202) 366–8810
Commercial Passenger Carrier Safety Division
Loretta Bitner.................. (202) 385–2428
Regulatory Affairs
Suzanne O'Malley .... (202) 366–0834
Regulatory Ombudsman
Steven LaFreniere .... (202) 366–0596
Enforcement and Program Delivery
William Quade .... (202) 366–4553
Policy and Program Development
Larry Minor.................... (202) 366–2551
Research and Information Technology
Kelly Leone..................... (202) 366–2525

■ INFORMATION SOURCES

Internet
Agency website: www.fmcsa.dot.gov.

Telephone Contacts
DOT Main Line .... (202) 366–4000
Information Line .... (800) 832–5660
Federal Relay Service TTY .... (800) 877–8339
Vehicle Safety Hotline .... (888) 327–4236

Information and Publications

KEY OFFICES

FMCSA Office of Communications
1200 New Jersey Ave. S.E.
Washington, DC 20590
(202) 366–9999
E-mail: fmcsa.publicaffairs@dot.gov
DaRonda McDuffie, public affairs specialist

Many publications, documents, reports, and webinars are available on the FMCSA website.

Freedom of Information
FOIA Team
1200 New Jersey Ave. S.E.
Washington, DC 20590
(202) 366–2960
Fax (202) 385–2335

Tiffanie Coleman, FOIA public liaison
FOIA Requester Service Center (202) 366–2960
Internet: www.fmcsa.dot.gov/foia

DOCKETS
Federal dockets are available at www.regulations.gov. (*See appendix for Searching and Commenting on Regulations: Regulations.gov.*)

RULES AND REGULATIONS
FMCSA rules and regulations are published in the *Code of Federal Regulations,* Title 49, Chapter III, Parts 300–399. Proposed rules, new final rules, and updates to the *Code of Federal Regulations* are published in the daily *Federal Register.* (*See appendix for details on how to obtain and use these publications.*) The *Federal Register* and the *Code of Federal Regulations* may also be accessed online at www.archives.gov/federal-register/cfr; this site contains a link to the federal government's regulatory website at www .regulations.gov (*see appendix*).

■ LEGISLATION
Tandem Truck Safety Act of 1984/Motor Carrier Safety Act of 1984 (98 Stat. 2829, 49 U.S.C. app. 2311). Signed by the president Oct. 30, 1984. Allowed states to ban large tandem trucks from unsafe sections of interstate highways. Improved uniformity of truck safety laws and broadened DOT enforcement powers to regulate truck safety.

Commercial Motor Vehicle Safety Act of 1986 (100 Stat. 3207–170, 49 U.S.C. app. 2701). Signed by the president Oct. 27, 1986. Required the DOT to issue and enforce state testing and licensing of commercial vehicle operators.

Truck and Bus Safety and Regulatory Reform Act of 1988 (102 Stat. 4527, 49 U.S.C. 2501 note). Signed by the president Nov. 18, 1988. Eliminated exemptions from safety rules for trucks and buses operating in metropolitan commercial zones and required rulemaking from the DOT secretary on the need and methods available to improve operator compliance.

Intermodal Surface Transportation Efficiency Act of 1991 (ISTEA) (105 Stat. 1914). Signed by the president Dec. 18, 1991. Authorized a pilot project to explore the potential benefits of using state commercial vehicle registration sanctions as an incentive to improve motor carrier safety. The pilot project was later adopted as the Performance and Registration Information Systems Management Program (PRISM).

Transportation Equity Act for the 21st Century (TEA-21) (112 Stat. 154, 23 U.S.C. 143). Signed by the president June 9, 1998. Reauthorized the federal highway, transit, safety, research, and motor carrier programs under the ISTEA. Provided incentives for states to adopt tough .08 blood alcohol concentration standards for drunk driving.

Motor Carrier Safety Improvement Act of 1999 (113 Stat. 1748, 49 U.S.C. 101 note). Signed by the president Dec. 9, 1999. Title I established the Federal Motor Carrier Safety Administration within the DOT, to be headed by an administrator appointed by the president and confirmed by the Senate.

Safe, Accountable, Flexible, and Efficient Transportation Equity Act of 2005 (SAFETEA) (23 U.S.C. 134). Signed by the president Aug. 10, 2005. Reauthorized federal surface transportation programs through fiscal year 2009. Directed FMCSA to provide training to state personnel engaged in the enforcement of FMCSA safety regulations. Required FMCSA to study the degree to which Canadian and Mexican commercial motor vehicles operating in the United States comply with the U.S. standards. Established a Medical Review Board to provide FMCSA with recommendations for driver qualification medical standards and guidelines. Required drivers of commercial motor vehicles to submit to inspections by authorized FMCSA employees. Included the Household Goods Movers Oversight Enforcement and Reform Act of 2005, authorizing FMCSA to regulate commercial movers. Included the Unified Carrier Registration Act of 2005, which directs the transportation secretary to issue regulations to establish an online federal Unified Carrier Registration System. Expanded the scope of federal safe transportation of hazardous materials regulations to include shipping and packaging companies.

Implementing Recommendations of the 9/11 Commission Act of 2007 (121 Stat. 467, 49 U.S.C. 13908 note). Signed by the president Aug. 3, 2007. Established a deadline of Oct. 1, 2007, for the FMCSA to issue final regulations to establish the Unified Carrier Registration System as directed under SAFETEA.

Moving Ahead for Progress in the 21st Century Act (MAP-21) (126 Stat. 405, 23 U.S.C. 101 note). Signed by the president July 6, 2012. Div. C, Title II: Commercial Motor Vehicle Safety Enhancement Act of 2012 directs the secretary to issue final regulations establishing minimum entry-level training requirements for individual operators of commercial motor vehicles. Revises the commercial driver's license (CDL) information system program. Directs the secretary to prescribe regulations to require commercial motor vehicles involved in interstate commerce, and operated by a driver subject to both federal hours-of-service and record of duty status requirements, to be equipped with an electronic logging device meeting certain performance and design standards and requirements. Requires the secretary to establish a national registry of medical examiners who conduct physical examinations on commercial drivers. Div. C, Title III: Hazardous Materials Transportation Safety Improvement Act of 2012 requires revised regulations to address transportation of hazardous materials. Directs the secretary to issue regulations that establish standard operating procedures for the administration of the special permit and approval programs for hazmat transportation, and objective criteria for the evaluation of special permit and approval applications.

■ REGIONAL OFFICES

Aside from the regional offices that follow, the FMCSA also maintains division offices in each state.

EASTERN

(CT, DC, DE, MA, MD, ME, NH, NJ, NY, PA, PR, RI, VA, VI, VT, WV)
802 Cromwell Park Dr., Suite N
Glen Burnie, MD 21061
(443) 703-2240
Curtis Thomas, field administrator

MIDWESTERN

(IA, IL, IN, KS, MI, MN, MO, NE, OH, WI)
4749 Lincoln Mall Dr., # 300A
Matteson, IL 60443
(708) 283-3577
Darin G. Jones, field administrator

SOUTHERN

(AL, AR, FL, GA, KY, LA, MS, NC, NM, OK, SC, TN, TX)
1800 Century Blvd. N.E., #1700
Atlanta, GA 30345-3220
(404) 327-7400
Dariell Ruban, field administrator

WESTERN

(AK, AS, AZ, CA, CO, GU, HI, ID, Northern Mariana Islands, MT, ND, NV, OR, SD, UT, WA, WY)
12600 W. Colfax Ave., #B-300
Lakewood, CO 80215
(303) 407-2350
William Paden, field administrator

Federal Railroad Administration

1200 New Jersey Ave. S.E., Washington, DC 20590
Internet: www.fra.dot.gov

The Federal Railroad Administration (FRA) is an agency within the Department of Transportation (DOT). It has the authority to regulate the safety aspects of U.S. rail transportation.

The FRA is headed by an administrator appointed by the president and confirmed by the Senate. Serving under the administrator are a deputy administrator, an executive director, and three associate administrators responsible for administration, railroad safety, and railroad policy and development. Other divisions include the offices of policy and communications, chief counsel, chief financial officer, and civil rights.

The Office of Administration is the business center and customer service for FRA headquarters and regional offices. This includes human resources, information technology, and acquisitions.

The Office of Railroad Safety is the principal regulatory unit in the FRA. The regulatory responsibility of the FRA extends to the safety of locomotives, signals, train safety appliances, power brakes, hours of service, operating practices (including drug and alcohol), and transportation of dangerous articles by railway.

In 2008 Los Angeles commuter rail Metrolink experienced one of the nation's worst rail disasters. The train's engineer had been sending text messages on his cell phone, and ran through a red signal and collided with a freight train in the Chatsworth district. Twenty-five people were killed and more than 100 others were injured. The transportation company paid $200 million to settle a lawsuit. In response to this crash, Congress passed the Rail Safety Improvement Act of 2008, which required major freight railroads and intercity and commuter rail operators to submit their plans for Positive Train Control (PTC) to FRA for approval by April 16, 2010. PTC technology is capable of automatically controlling train speeds and movements if a locomotive engineer fails to take appropriate action.

The legislation mandated that PTC systems must be fully in place by the end of 2015. Industry experts indicated that less than 30 percent of commuter railroads would meet the deadline. In addition to the substantial costs, some railroad companies indicated they have been hobbled by a lack of access to wireless spectrum required for implementing the safety system. The Federal Communications Commission (FCC) is charged with regulating spectrum use as well as some of the equipment needed for PTC infrastructure. Railroads complained that the FCC moved too slowly to accommodate the congressionally mandated deadline.

At a cost of more than $200 million, Metrolink was the first commuter rail to install PTC, which went active in 2014 on segments of the rail. Metrolink expects to meet the December 2015 deadline for systemwide implementation.

The act also increased safety and security requirements related to shipping of hazardous materials. This included addressing employee hours of service and requiring training standards and plans for categories of railroad employees. It also addressed safety issues at public and private highway-rail grade crossings.

The Implementing Recommendations of the 9/11 Commission Act of 2007 directed the transportation secretary to publish a final rule for the railroad routing of security-sensitive materials that requires railroads to perform the safety and security risk analyses and then to make an appropriate route selection for transporting hazardous materials. On Nov. 26, 2008, the Pipeline and Hazardous Materials Safety Administration (PHMSA) (*p. 818*), in coordination with the Transportation Security Administration (*p. 649*), announced the final rule implementing the requirements under the 9/11 Commission Act.

The FRA Office of Railroad Safety employs about 400 inspectors in eight regional offices to monitor safety equipment and procedures. Regulations require that all rail accidents be reported to and investigated by the Office of Railroad Safety.

The Office of Railroad Policy and Development (RPD) is responsible for federal investment and assistance to the rail industry as well as the development and implementation of administration policy concerning intercity rail passenger service and high-speed rail.

RPD programs include rail transportation research and development, financial assistance in the form of grants to the National Railroad Passenger Corporation (Amtrak), and financial assistance (loans and loan guarantees) to railroads and others to promote safe operation and preserve the public interest in the nation's rail system.

Financial assistance takes the form of grant and loan programs for Amtrak and railroads in reorganization in the Midwest and Northeast, grants for state rail safety programs, and subsidies to small freight lines so that they will be able to continue service.

The Transportation Equity Act for the 21st Century (TEA-21) passed in 1998, funded high-speed rail technology activities (including corridor planning). High-speed rail refers to a series of technologies involving trains traveling at top speeds of 90 to 300 miles per hour. A 1997 report to Congress concluded that each of these technologies has potential to solve passenger transportation problems in the nation's most well-traveled intercity corridors. The FRA administers programs to help develop high-speed rail systems in such corridors.

In December 2000 Amtrak unveiled its new high-speed train service, Acela Express, in the Boston–New York–Washington northeast corridor. During its first four weeks, Acela Express attracted more than 11,000 customers and earned more than $1.25 million in ticket sales.

FRA programs related to high-speed rail include research and development on high-speed rail safety and several activities authorized under TEA-21: the Next Generation High-Speed Rail Technology program, which develops and demonstrates technology elements that are important for reducing the cost or improving the effectiveness of high-speed rail through partnerships with states and industry; the Grade Crossing Hazard Elimination Program, which provides grants to states with designated high-speed rail corridors; and the Maglev Deployment Program, which aims to select one rail project for possible construction subsequent to preconstruction planning efforts by several competing states. The 2009 American Recovery and Reinvestment Act appropriated $8 billion for FRA for high-speed rail corridors and intercity passenger rail service.

High-speed rail—and the FRA—suffered a setback under the fiscal year 2011 appropriations bill. Funding was reduced to several key FRA programs, but high-speed rail funding was targeted by conservatives in Congress who do not support the program. The bill eliminated appropriations for FRA capital assistance for high speed rail corridors and intercity passenger rail service, with a rescission of prior year unobligated balances, for a total reduction of $2.9 billion from the fiscal year 2010 level.

By summer 2015 Congress had not passed an omnibus transportation reauthorization bill since SAFETEA expired in 2009. Congress continued to appropriate money to fund transportation programs via short-term extension bills.

◼ KEY PERSONNEL

Administrator
Sarah Feinberg (acting) . . . . (202) 493–6014
Fax. . . . . (202) 493–6481
Deputy Administrator
Vacant. . . . . (202) 493–6015
Civil Rights
Calvin Gibson . . . . (202) 493–6012
Public Affairs
Kevin Thompson . . . . (202) 493–6024
Fax . . . . (202) 493–6013

Public Engagement
Timothy Barkley . . . . (202) 493–6405
Chief Counsel
Melissa Porter . . . . (202) 493–6052
Chief Financial Officer
Rebecca Pennington . . . . (202) 440–2870
Budget
Erin McCartney. . . . . (202) 493–6454
Financial Services
Tiwalade (Tiwa) Bello . . . . (202) 493–6163
Administration
Tamela Riggs . . . . (202) 493–6014
Human Resources
William (Bill) Tito. . . . . (202) 493–6110
Information Technology
Arnel Rivera . . . .(202) 493–1331
Railroad Policy and Development
Paul Nissenbaum. . . . . (202) 493–6381
Fax. . . . . (202) 493–6330
Passenger and Freight Programs
Corey Hill. (202) 493–6373
Policy and Development
Neil Moyer . . . . (202) 493–6365
Fax . . . .(202) 493–6401
Research and Development
John Tunna . . . . (202) 493–1300
Railroad Safety
Robert Lauby . . . . (202) 493–6474
Fax. . . . . (202) 493–6309
Safety Compliance and Program Implementation
Mark Hartong . . . . (202) 493–6300
Regulatory and Legislative Operations
Jamie Rennert . . . . (202) 493–6404
Safety Analysis
Brenda Moscoso . . . . (202) 493–6282
Safety Assurance and Compliance
Jerry Powers. . . . . (202) 493–6404

◼ INFORMATION SOURCES

Internet

Agency website: www.fra.dot.gov. Comprehensive website includes general agency information, publications, and links to specific FRA offices.

Telephone Contacts

DOT Main Line . . . .(202) 366–4000
Federal Relay Service TTY . . . .(800) 877–8339
Inspector General's Hotline . . . .(800) 424–9071

Information and Publications

KEY OFFICES

FRA Public Affairs
1200 New Jersey Ave. S.E., MS 5
Washington, DC 20590
(202) 493–6024
Kevin Thompson, director

Provides public information on the FRA and distributes all FRA publications and news releases.

Freedom of Information

1200 New Jersey Ave. S.E., MS 10
Washington, DC 20590
FOIA Requester Service: (202) 493–6065
Timothy Barkley, FOIA public liaison
(202) 493–1305
Denise Kollehlon, FOIA officer
(202) 493–6039

DATA AND STATISTICS

The FRA annually produces reports and studies that are available to the public. In particular, the Office of Safety releases accident reports and data, including an annual analysis of railroad accidents and incidents. Contact the Office of Safety or the Office of Public Affairs. Data and statistics are also available on the FRA's website.

PUBLICATIONS

An extensive collection of FRA reports, studies, and publications is available on the website, at www.fra.dot .gov/eLib/Find. FRA Public Affairs can also provide information on publications. *(See above.)*

Reference Resources

LIBRARY

DOT Library

1200 New Jersey Ave. S.E., #W12–300
Washington, DC 20590
(202) 366–0746
(800) 853–1351
Law Library (202) 366–0749
Amanda Wilson, director
(202) 366–2480
Internet: www.ntl.bts.gov
E-mail: library@dot.gov
Hours: 8:00 a.m. to 5:00 p.m.

DOCKETS

FRA Office of the Chief Counsel

1200 New Jersey Ave. S.E.
MS 10
Washington, DC 20590
(202) 493–6052
Melissa Porter, chief counsel
Michelle Silva, docket clerk, (202) 493–6030
Hours: 8:30 a.m. to 5:00 p.m.

Maintains dockets, containing all material related to FRA rulemakings and other administrative proceedings, for inspection. Federal dockets are also available at www .regulations.gov. (*See appendix for Searching and Commenting on Regulations: Regulations.gov.*)

RULES AND REGULATIONS

FRA rules and regulations are published in the *Code of Federal Regulations,* Title 49, Chapter II, Parts 200–299.

Proposed rules, new final rules, and updates to the *Code of Federal Regulations* are published in the daily *Federal Register. (See appendix for information on how to obtain and use these publications.)* The *Federal Register* and the *Code of Federal Regulations* may also be accessed online at www.archives.gov/federal-register/cfr; the site also contains a link to the federal government's regulatory website at www.regulations.gov (*see appendix*).

▉ LEGISLATION

Statutes administered by the FRA include:

Department of Transportation Act (80 Stat. 931, 49 U.S.C. 1652). Signed by the president Oct. 15, 1966. Created the FRA and set rail safety standards; provided for inspection of locomotives, signal systems, and mail cars; and set standards for reporting railroad accidents.

Federal Railroad Safety and Hazardous Materials Transportation Control Act of 1970 (84 Stat. 971, 45 U.S.C. 431). Signed by the president Oct. 16, 1970. Required establishment of safety standards for railroads and provided grants to states for safety programs.

Regional Rail Reorganization Act of 1973 (87 Stat. 986, 45 U.S.C. 701). Signed by the president Jan. 2, 1974. Provided funds for rail service continuation, property acquisition, and construction or improvement of facilities.

Railroad Revitalization and Regulatory Reform Act of 1976 (90 Stat. 31, 45 U.S.C. 801). Signed by the president Feb. 5, 1976. Provided financial assistance to rehabilitate and improve railroads.

Staggers Rail Act of 1980 (94 Stat. 1895, 49 U.S.C. 10101 note). Signed by the president Oct. 14, 1980. Provided railroads more pricing rate flexibility and contract provisions.

Rail Safety Improvement Act of 1988 (102 Stat. 624, 45 U.S.C. 421 note). Signed by the president June 22, 1988. Amended the Federal Railroad Safety and Hazardous Materials Transportation Control Act of 1970 by increasing penalties and liabilities of individuals. Established a program requiring licensing or certification of engineers. Gave the FRA jurisdiction over high-speed rail systems.

Transportation Equity Act for the 21st Century (TEA-21) (112 Stat. 154, 23 U.S.C. 143). Signed by the president June 9, 1998. Amended federal railroad law to authorize appropriations for high-speed rail technology activities. Amended the Railroad Revitalization and Regulatory Reform Act of 1976 to authorize direct loans and loan guarantees to state and local governments, government-sponsored authorities and corporations, railroads, and joint ventures that include at least one railroad.

Safe, Accountable, Flexible, and Efficient Transportation Equity Act of 2005 (SAFETEA) (23 U.S.C. 134). Signed by the president Aug. 10, 2005. Reauthorized federal surface transportation programs through fiscal year 2009. Directed the FRA to improve its railroad track inspection procedures, validate a predictive accident model for railroad tank cars, and implement appropriate design standards for pressurized tank cars. Required the FRA to study the impact resistance of the steels in the shells of pressure tank cars constructed before 1989 and establish a program to rank the cars according to their risk of catastrophic fracture and implement measures to mitigate such risk.

Implementing Recommendations of the 9/11 Commission Act of 2007 (121 Stat. 444). Signed by the president Aug. 3, 2007. Directed the transportation secretary to publish a final rule with respect to the railroad routing of security-sensitive hazardous materials.

Rail Safety Improvement Act of 2008 (122 Stat. 4848–4906). Signed by the president Oct. 16, 2008. Required Class 1 railroads and regularly scheduled intercity or commuter rail passenger carriers to develop and submit to the transportation secretary, within eighteen months, their plans for the implementation of a positive train control system to prevent train-to-train collisions by Dec. 31, 2015. Mandates increased security for hazardous materials rail transportation.

Passenger Rail Investment and Improvement Act of 2008 (122 Stat. 4907). Signed by the president Oct. 16, 2008. Directed the FRA to establish an alternative passenger rail service program that allowed a rail carrier or carriers that own a route over which Amtrak operated to petition FRA to become a passenger rail carrier for that route in lieu of Amtrak for a period of up to five years. Authorized a program to establish a public-private partnership for high-speed rail development.

American Recovery and Reinvestment Act of 2009 (123 Stat. 208, 49 U.S.C. 24401 and 24405). Signed by the president Feb. 17, 2009. Appropriated $8 billion to FRA for high-speed rail corridors and intercity passenger rail service.

▥ REGIONAL OFFICES

REGION 1
(CT, MA, ME, NH, NJ, NY, RI, VT)
55 Broadway, #1077
Cambridge, MA 02142
(617) 494–2302
(800) 724–5991
Les Fiorenzo, regional administrator

REGION 2
(DC, DE, MD, OH, PA, VA, WV)
Baldwin Tower, #660
1510 Chester Pike
Crum Lynne, PA 19022
(610) 521–8200
(800) 724–5991
Brian Hontz, regional administrator

REGION 3
(AL, FL, GA, KY, MS, NC, SC, TN)
61 Forsyth St. S.W., #16T20
Atlanta, GA 30303–3104
(404) 562–3800
(800) 724–5993
Patrick Plumb, regional administrator

REGION 4
(IL, IN, MI, MN, WI)
200 W. Adams St., #310
Chicago, IL 60606
(312) 353–6203
(800) 724–5040
Michael Long, regional administrator

REGION 5
(AR, LA, NM, OK, TX)
4100 International Plaza, #450
Fort Worth, TX 76109–4820
(817) 862–2200
(800) 724–5995
Vence Haggard, regional administrator

REGION 6
(CO, IA, southern Illinois, KS, MO, NE, southeastern Wyoming)
901 Locust St., #464
Kansas City, MO 64106
(816) 329–3840
(800) 724–5996
Steven J. Fender, regional administrator

REGION 7
(AZ, CA, HI, NV, UT)
801 I St., #466
Sacramento, CA 95814
(916) 498–6540
(800) 724–5997
James Jordan, regional administrator

REGION 8
(AK, ID, MT, ND, OR, SD, WA, WY)
500 Broadway, #240
Vancouver, WA 98660
(360) 696–7536
(800) 724–5998
Mark Daniels, regional administrator

Federal Transit Administration

1200 New Jersey Ave. S.E., Washington, DC 20590
Internet: www.fta.dot.gov

The federal government became actively involved in mass transportation with the enactment of the Housing Act of 1961, which provided limited loans and grants to state and local governments for transit development. The first comprehensive transit legislation, the Federal Transit Act, was signed by President Lyndon B. Johnson in 1964, but the actual forerunner to the Federal Transit Administration (FTA), the Urban Mass Transit Administration (UMTA), was not established until 1968. The UMTA became one of the five modal administrations in the newly created Department of Transportation (DOT).

The various transit act laws authorize FTA to promulgate regulations for various mass transportation issues, including school bus operations; transportation for the elderly and disabled; charter service; rail fixed guideway systems; state safety oversight; and bus testing. The Federal Transit Act of 1964 established the first comprehensive program of federal assistance for mass transportation, including provisions for matching grants, technical assistance, and research and development. The Federal Transit Assistance Act of 1970 included substantially increased funding and officially designated the FTA to provide consolidated management of all federal mass transit programs.

The Surface Transportation Assistance Act of 1982 included a penny-a-gallon gas tax dedicated to transit. Other major provisions established a separate Mass Transit Account (under the Highway Trust Fund), authorized discretionary contract authority for the trust fund, and created a block grant program funded from the general fund apportionments. Most grant recipients are states and public transit agencies. Major research and demonstration projects are carried out by the FTA under contract to private organizations and public institutions, including state and local governments.

FTA projects include new techniques of traffic management, crime reduction and safety studies, new computerized techniques for planning needs, and special features to facilitate the use of mass transportation systems by the elderly and disabled.

In 1991 the Intermodal Surface Transportation Efficiency Act (ISTEA) authorized funding for highways, highway safety, and mass transportation through fiscal year 1997. In 1998 ISTEA was reauthorized through 2003 with a budget authority totaling $215 billion.

Following the passage of welfare reform legislation in 1996, the DOT recognized that most welfare recipients (94 percent) did not own automobiles. The 1998 ISTEA reauthorization established the Job Access and Reverse Commute Grant program designed to assist states and localities in developing new or expanded transportation services that connect welfare recipients and other low-income persons to jobs and other employment-related services.

The FTA's discretionary New Starts program is the federal government's primary financial resource for supporting local major transit capital investments, including heavy to light rail, commuter rail, and bus rapid transit systems. The New Starts program has helped to make possible hundreds of new or extended transit fixed guideway systems across the country.

The Safe, Accountable, Flexible, and Efficient Transportation Equity Act (SAFETEA) of 2005, at a cost of $286.5 billion, reauthorized federal highway programs through fiscal year 2009. The American Recovery and Reinvestment Act of 2009 (ARRA) appropriated an additional $8.4 billion for transit capital assistance, fixed guideway infrastructure investment, and capital investment grants. ARRA authorized the Transportation Investment Generating Economic Recovery (TIGER) grants program, which awards competitive discretionary grants for road, rail, transit, bicycle/pedestrian, port, and multimodal projects.

On July 6, 2012, President Barack Obama signed the Moving Ahead for Progress in the 21st Century Act (MAP-21). While this was not an omnibus bill, MAP-21 authorized funding for surface transportation programs at more than $105 billion for fiscal years 2013 and 2014. MAP-21 also included consolidation of some funding programs and regulatory reforms for programs administered by FTA, the Federal Highway Administration (p. 791), the Pipeline and Hazardous Materials Safety Administration (p. 818), the Federal Motor Carrier Safety Administration (p. 795), and the National Highway Traffic Safety Administration (p. 811).

MAP-21 replaced the fixed guideway modernization program under the New Starts discretionary grants program with a grants program to maintain public transportation systems in a state of good repair. Other programs that were repealed or consolidated under MAP-21 included Alternatives Analysis, Clean Fuels, Job Access and Reverse Commute, New Freedom, Transit in the Parks, and Over the Road Bus.

However, the FTA announced a new jobs access transportation program in 2014: the Ladders of Opportunity Initiative. The program was funded through remaining discretionary grant funds originally available prior to the enactment of MAP-21. The funds were made available as grants to modernize and expand transit bus service specifically for the purpose of connecting disadvantaged and low-income individuals, veterans, seniors, and youth with local workforce training, employment centers, health care, and other vital services.

MAP-21 also addressed public transit safety issues. The legislation granted FTA the authority to establish and enforce a new comprehensive framework to oversee the safety of public transportation nationwide. MAP-21 directed FTA to develop safety performance criteria for all modes of public transportation and required all recipients of FTA funding to develop agency safety plans that include performance targets, strategies, and staff training.

By summer 2015 Congress had not passed a transportation reauthorization bill since SAFETEA expired in 2009. Congress continued to appropriate money to fund transportation programs via short-term extension bills. The lack of a multiyear budget and policy priorities places hardship on states for long-term transportation infrastructure planning.

KEY PERSONNEL

Administrator
Therese W. McMillan (acting)....... (202) 366–4040
    Fax........................... (202) 366–9854
Deputy Administrator
Vacant....................... (202) 366–4040
Executive Director
Matthew Welbes .... (202) 366–4040
Senior Advisor
Carolyn Flowers.................. (202) 366–4550
Administration
Matthew M. Crouch .... (202) 366–4007
Budget and Policy
Robert J. Tuccillo.................. (202) 366–4050
Chief Counsel
Dana Nifosi (acting) .... (202) 366–4011
    Fax........................... (202) 366–3809
Civil Rights
Linda Ford .... (202) 366–4018
Communications and Congressional Affairs
Nathan J. Robinson (acting) ..... (202) 366–4043
Planning and Environment
Lucy Garliauskas............... (202) 366–4033
Program Management
Henrika Buchanan-Smith .... (202) 366–4020
Research, Demonstration, and Innovation
Vincent Valdes.................... (202) 366–4052
Transit Safety and Oversight
Thomas Littleton.................. (202) 366–1783

■ INFORMATION SOURCES

Internet
Agency website: www.fta.dot.gov. Comprehensive website includes a search feature, news releases, publications, reports, regulations, and information organized by subject and by office.

Telephone Contacts
FTA Main ....(202) 366–4043
Toll-free..........................(866) 377–8642
DOT Main.........................(202) 366–4000
Federal Relay Service TTY ....(800) 877–8339

Information and Publications

KEY OFFICES

Office of Communications and Congressional Affairs
1200 New Jersey Ave. S.E.
Washington, DC 20590
(202) 366–4043
Nathan J. Robinson, associate administrator

FTA Office of Research, Demonstration, and Innovation
1200 New Jersey Ave. S.E.
Washington, DC 20590
(202) 366–4052
Vincent Valdes, associate administrator

Distributes FTA publications and technical information; maintains a reference collection.

Freedom of Information
1200 New Jersey Ave. S.E.
4th Floor East Bldg.
Washington, DC 20590
(202) 366–4022
Fax (202) 366–7164
Nancy Sipes, FOIA public liaison
E-mail: FTA.FOIA@dot.gov

DATA AND STATISTICS
Technical information is available from the website and from the FTA Office of Research, Demonstration, and Innovation: (202) 366–4052.

PUBLICATIONS
Publications are available on the website, or contact the FTA Office of Research, Demonstration, and Innovation for pamphlets and brochures, including bibliographies, abstracts of project reports, conference proceedings, and the annual directory of research, development, and demonstration projects.

Technical reports and publications on particular mass transit projects are available on the website and through the National Technical Information Service (see appendix, Ordering Government Publications).

Reference Resources

LIBRARIES

The FTA online library can be found at www.fta.dot .gov/about/library.html.

DOT Library

1200 New Jersey Ave. S.E., #W12–300
Washington, DC 20590
(202) 366–0746
(800) 853–1351
Law Library (202) 366–0749
Amanda Wilson, director
(202) 366–2480
Internet: www.ntl.bts.gov
E-mail: library@dot.gov
Hours: 8:00 a.m. to 5:00 p.m.

DOCKETS

DOT Office of Docket Management

1200 New Jersey Ave. S.E., #W12–140
Washington, DC 20590
(800) 647–5527
Hours: 9:00 a.m. to 5:00 p.m.
Barbara Hairston, program manager

Paper and electronic reading room records are available. Federal dockets are also available at www.regulations .gov. (*See appendix for Searching and Commenting on Regulations: Regulations.gov.*)

RULES AND REGULATIONS

FTA rules and regulations are published in the *Code of Federal Regulations,* Title 49, Chapter VI, Parts 600–699. Proposed regulations, new final regulations, and updates to the *Code of Federal Regulations* are published in the daily *Federal Register. (See appendix for details on how to obtain and use these publications.)* The *Federal Register* and the *Code of Federal Regulations* may be accessed online at www.archives.gov/federal-register/cfr; the site also contains a link to the federal government's regulatory website at www.regulations.gov (*see appendix*).

▆ LEGISLATION

The FTA carries out its responsibilities under:

Federal Transit Act of 1964 (78 Stat. 302, 49 U.S.C. 1601). Signed by the president July 9, 1964. Authorized the Housing and Home Finance Administration to provide additional assistance for the development of comprehensive and coordinated mass transportation systems.

Reorganization Plan No. 2 of 1968 (82 Stat. 1369, 49 U.S.C. 1608 note). Signed by the president June 30, 1968. Established the FTA as an agency within the DOT.

Federal Transit Assistance Act of 1970 (84 Stat. 962, 49 U.S.C. 1601 note). Signed by the president Oct. 15, 1970. Provided long-term financing for expanded urban mass transportation programs.

Federal Transit Assistance Act of 1974 (88 Stat. 1567, 49 U.S.C. 1604a). Signed by the president Nov. 26, 1974. Authorized grants to state and local agencies to ensure adequate commuter transportation service in urban areas.

Federal Public Transportation Act of 1978 (92 Stat. 2735, 49 U.S.C. 1601 note). Signed by the president Nov. 6, 1978. Authorized mass transit funding for five years. Reorganized the mass transit discretionary grant program.

Surface Transportation Assistance Act of 1982 (96 Stat. 2097, 23 U.S.C. 104 note). Signed by the president Jan. 6, 1983. Amended the Federal Transit Act of 1964. Established mass transit accounts in the Highway Trust Fund for discretionary capital grants and a new Section 9 formula program to replace the Section 5 formula program.

Surface Transportation and Uniform Relocation Assistance Act of 1987 (101 Stat. 133, 49 U.S.C. 1601). Vetoed by the president March 27, 1987; veto overridden April 2, 1987. Authorized mass transit funding through Sept. 30, 1991. Reauthorized existing highway and mass transit policies and programs.

Americans with Disabilities Act of 1990 (104 Stat. 327, 42 U.S.C. 12101 note). Signed by the president July 26, 1990. Titles II and III provided Americans with disabilities the same rights to jobs, public transportation, and public accommodations that women and racial, religious, and ethnic minorities receive under the Civil Rights Act of 1964.

Intermodal Surface Transportation Efficiency Act of 1991 (ISTEA) (105 Stat. 1914, 49 U.S.C. 104 note). Signed by the president Dec. 18, 1991. Authorized funding for highways, highway safety, and mass transportation through fiscal year 1997. Set policy to develop a national intermodal transportation system that is economically efficient and environmentally sound. Title III changed the agency name from the UMTA to the FTA.

Transportation Equity Act for the 21st Century (TEA-21) (112 Stat. 154, 23 U.S.C. 143). Signed by the president June 9, 1998. Reauthorized the federal highway, transit, safety, research, and motor carrier programs under the ISTEA from fiscal year 1998 through 2003. Provided incentives for states to adopt tough .08 blood alcohol concentration standards for drunk driving.

Safe, Accountable, Flexible, and Efficient Transportation Equity Act of 2005 (SAFETEA) (23 U.S.C. 134). Signed by the president Aug. 10, 2005. Reauthorized federal mass transit programs from fiscal year 2005 through 2009. Authorized a program to establish a public-private partnership for certain new fixed guideway capital projects—public transit systems that use rail or a dedicated road, such as a bus rapid transit system. Revised enforcement requirements for violations of conditions on charter bus transportation service and school bus transportation. Directed the transportation secretary to issue a final rule on implementation of Buy America requirements.

American Recovery and Reinvestment Act of 2009 (123 Stat. 209). Signed by the president Feb. 17, 2009. Appropriated $8.4 billion to FTA for transit capital assistance, fixed guideway infrastructure investment, and capital investment grants.

Moving Ahead for Progress in the 21st Century Act (MAP-21) (126 Stat. 405, 23 U.S.C. 101 note). Signed by the president July 6, 2012. Restructured and consolidated public transit funding programs. Authorized funding for surface transportation programs through fiscal year 2014. MAP-21 grants FTA the authority to establish and enforce a new comprehensive framework to oversee the safety of public transportation nationwide. Directs FTA to develop safety performance criteria for all modes of public transportation. Requires all recipients of FTA funding to develop agency safety plans that include performance targets, strategies, and staff training.

■ REGIONAL OFFICES

LOWER MANHATTAN RECOVERY OFFICE
1 Bowling Green, #436
New York, NY 10004
(212) 668–1770
Stephen Goodman, administrator

REGION 1
(CT, MA, ME, NH, RI, VT)
55 Broadway, #920
Cambridge, MA 02142–1093
(617) 494–2055
Mary Beth Mello, regional administrator

REGION 2
(NJ, NY,)
1 Bowling Green, #429
New York, NY 10004–1415
(212) 668–2170
Marilyn G. Shazor, regional administrator

REGION 3
(DC, DE, MD, PA, VA, WV)
1760 Market St., #500
Philadelphia, PA 19103–4124
(215) 656–7100
Terry Garcia-Crews, regional administrator

REGION 4
(AL, FL, GA, KY, MS, NC, PR, SC, TN, VI)
230 Peachtree N.W., #800
Atlanta, GA 30303

(404) 865–5600
Yvette G. Taylor, regional administrator

REGION 5
(IL, IN, MI, MN, OH, WI)
200 W. Adams St., #320
Chicago, IL 60606–5232
(312) 353–2789
Marisol Simon, regional administrator

REGION 6
(AR, LA, NM, OK, TX)
819 Taylor St., #8A36
Fort Worth, TX 76102
(817) 978–0550
Robert C. Patrick, regional administrator

REGION 7
(IA, KS, MO, NE)
901 Locust St., #404
Kansas City, MO 64106
(816) 329–3920
Mokhtee Ahmad, regional administrator

REGION 8
(CO, MT, ND, SD, UT, WY)
12300 W. Dakota Ave., #310
Lakewood, CO 80228–2583
(720) 963–3300
Linda Gehrke, regional administrator

REGION 9
(AS, AZ, CA, GU, HI, Northern Mariana Islands, NV)
201 Mission St., #1650
San Francisco, CA 94105–1839
(415) 744–3133
Leslie T. Rogers, regional administrator

REGION 10
(AK, ID, OR, WA)
Jackson Federal Bldg.
915 Second Ave., #3142
Seattle, WA 98174–1002
(206) 220–7954
Richard F. (Rick) Krochalis, regional administrator

Maritime Administration

1200 New Jersey Ave. S.E., Washington, DC 20590
Internet: www.marad.dot.gov

The Maritime Administration (MARAD) was transferred to the Department of Transportation (DOT) in 1981. It had been a Commerce Department agency since its establishment under the Reorganization Plan No. 21 of 1950. MARAD is responsible for programs that aid the development, promotion, and operation of the U.S. merchant marine. The fleet serves the nation's foreign and domestic shipping needs and provides support as a naval auxiliary to the armed forces in times of national emergency.

MARAD is headed by a maritime administrator assisted by one deputy maritime administrator, a chief counsel, and six associate administrators. The associate administrators are responsible for administration, budget and programs, environment and compliance, intermodal system development, strategic sealift, and business and finance development.

Financial Assistance. MARAD provides financial assistance programs to the U.S. shipping industry. As originally enacted in 1936, the Federal Ship Financing Guarantees (Title XI) program authorized the federal government to insure private-sector loans or mortgages made to finance or refinance the construction or reconstruction of U.S.-flag vessels in American shipyards. Title XI was amended in 1972 to provide direct government guarantees of the underlying debt obligations for future transactions, with the government holding a mortgage on the equipment financed. The government insures or guarantees full payment of the unpaid principal, interest, mortgage, or obligation in the event of default by the vessel owner.

The 2009 American Recovery and Reinvestment Act appropriated $100 million to MARAD for the Small Shipyards Grant Program for capital improvements and related infrastructure improvements and for maritime training programs. The grants program had been funded at $10 million in 2008.

Capital Construction Fund (CCF). Administered by MARAD, it was authorized by the Merchant Marine Act of 1970. This program enables operators to deposit tax-deferred earnings and other monies in CCF accounts to accumulate the large amounts of capital necessary to build, reconstruct, or acquire large ships.

U.S.-flag vessels that are involved in essential foreign trade are eligible for an operating-differential subsidy from MARAD. This subsidy is designed to offset the higher cost of operating U.S.-flag vessels in foreign trade compared to operating vessels under foreign flags.

Ships and Shipping. MARAD is responsible for formulating, directing, and coordinating national policies and programs for developing and reviewing the designs of proposed ships; assisting in the administration of MARAD's shipbuilding contracts; and administering programs that collect, analyze, and maintain data on the relative costs of shipbuilding in the United States and foreign countries.

- *Reserve Fleet.* MARAD also maintains a National Defense Reserve Fleet (NDRF) of 100 merchant ships at Ft. Eustis, VA; Beaumont, TX; and Suisun Bay, CA. The ships are preserved for reactivation if needed during a national emergency. In 1975 MARAD established the Ready Reserve Fleet (RRF) with the U.S. Navy. The RRF provides merchant vessels that can be activated for military sealift duties within five to twenty days.

- *Emergency Operations.* During a national emergency MARAD directs the operation of merchant ships through the National Shipping Authority. The American merchant marine has transported approximately 90 percent of sealift cargoes in U.S. war efforts of the past.

Maritime Security Program (MSP). On a contingency basis, an active, privately owned, U.S.-flagged, and U.S.-crewed liner fleet is available to assist the Department of Defense (DOD). The MSP was established by the Maritime Security Act of 1996 and reauthorized in 2003. The reauthorized program covers fiscal years 2006–2015 and provides funding for sixty ships (including up to five product tankers). Annual funding authorization in fiscal year 2006 was $156 million, which was to increase to $186 million by fiscal year 2012. In 2006 MARAD approved sixty vessel operating agreements for fifteen different carriers.

Ship Disposal Program. MARAD serves as the federal government's disposal agent for merchant type vessels of 1,500 gross tons or more. MARAD's Ship Disposal Program employs vessel sales and ship recycling services as the primary means to dispose of obsolete NDRF vessels. The program has included artificial reefing, ship donation, and sink at-sea live-fire training exercises as additional vessel disposal options. Additionally, MARAD disposes of vessels through a ship donation program.

Maritime Subsidy Board. The Maritime Subsidy Board, whose membership includes the administrator, the administrator's deputy, and the chief counsel, has authority to award, amend, and terminate subsidy contracts for the construction and operation of vessels in the foreign commerce of the United States. It also performs investigations, gathers data from the industry, and holds public hearings. All of the board's decisions are subject to review by the secretary of transportation.

Ports. MARAD coordinates port security policy with stakeholders and other government agencies. MARAD also provides expertise and resources for port financing and port infrastructure and has assisted major ports in their redevelopment plans. MARAD is the government's licensing agency for Deepwater Liquefied Natural Gas (LNG) Ports.

Other Responsibilities. MARAD also is responsible for promoting the U.S. merchant marine and for a variety of other programs. These include the training of officers at the U.S. Merchant Marine Academy at Kings Point, NY, and administering the Cargo Preference Act, which requires at least 50 percent of all federal government-generated cargoes to be shipped in U.S.-flag vessels. The agency also operates a National Maritime Research Center at Kings Point.

The Maritime Administration is charged under the American Fisheries Act (AFA) of 1998 with the responsibility of determining whether vessels of 100 feet or greater comply with the new ownership, control, and financing requirements. The AFA raised the U.S. citizen ownership and control threshold that U.S.-flag vessels must meet to be eligible to operate in U.S. waters from 50 percent to 75 percent.

The Maritime Transportation Act of 2002 was one of the most extensive maritime laws in decades. The act required the DOT to improve security at U.S. ports and foreign ports where U.S.-bound shipments originate. The legislation was originally introduced in July 2001 to protect ports from illegal activity, including drug trafficking, cargo theft, and smuggling of contraband and aliens. Following the 2001 terrorist attacks on the United States, concerns about the vulnerability of ports to terrorism accelerated passage of the bill.

▓ KEY PERSONNEL

Maritime Administrator
    Paul N. Jaenichen .... (202) 366–5823
    Fax.......................... (202) 366–3890
Deputy Maritime Administrator
    Michael Rodriguez .... (202) 366–5823
Executive Director
    Joel Szabat .... (202) 366–5772
    Civil Rights
        Pattie Tom .... (202) 366–3449
    Policy and Plans
        Douglas McDonald............ (202) 366–4894
    International Activities
        Lonnie Kishiyama.............. (202) 366–5493
Administration
    Delia Davis...................... (202) 366–2332

    Fax......................... (202) 366–3889
Acquisition
    Wayne Leong .... (202) 366–5620
Management and Administrative Services
    Steven Snipes.................. (202) 366–2811
Human Resources
    Kim Norris.................... (202) 366–4141
Budget and Programs
    Lydia Moschkin.................. (202) 366–3071
Business and Finance Development
    Owen Doherty .... (202) 366–5737
Cargo Preference
    Dennis Brennan .... (202) 366–1029
Financial Approvals and Marine Insurance
    Vacant........................ (202) 366–5737
Chief Counsel
    Franklin R. Parker................. (202) 366–5320
    Chief Counsel, Legislation and Regulations
        Christine S. Gurland........... (202) 366–5157
    Chief Counsel, Maritime Programs
        Ryan Kabacinski .... (202) 366–5320
Deepwater Ports and Offshore Activities
    Yvette M. Fields............... (202) 366–0926
        E-mail: Yvette.Fields@dot.gov
Environment and Compliance
    John P. Quinn.................... (202) 366–1931
    Environment
        Michael S. Carter............... (202) 366–9431
    Safety
        Christopher McMahon .... (202) 366–7018
        E-mail: Chris.Mcmahon@dot.gov
    Security
        Cameron Naron .... (202) 366–1883
Intermodal System Development
    Lauren K. Brand .... (202) 366–0678
    Marine Transportation System
        Richard Lolich................. (202) 366–0704
    Marine Highways and Passenger Services
        Scott Davies (acting)........... (202) 366–7057
    Infrastructure Development and Congestion Mitigation
        Robert Bouchard............... (202) 366–5076
Strategic Sealift
    Kevin M. Tokarski................. (202) 366–5400
    Cargo and Commercial Sealift
        Dennis Brennan .... (202) 366–4610
    Emergency Preparedness
        Thomas M. P. Christensen....... (202) 366–5900
    Ship Operations
        William H. Cahill .... (202) 366–1875
Maritime Workforce Development
    Anne Wehde .... (202) 493–0029
Ship Disposal Programs
    Curt J. Michanczyk............. (202) 366–2624
Ship Operations
    William H. Cahill .... (202) 366–1875
Strategic Communications and Public Engagement
    Michael Novak .... (202) 366–4105
U.S. Merchant Marine Academy
    Rear Adm. James A. Helis .... (516) 726–5812

▓ INFORMATION SOURCES

Internet

Agency website: www.marad.dot.gov. Comprehensive website includes news and features, programs and initiatives, publications, education, data and statistics, and doing business with MARAD.

Telephone Contacts

MARAD Main	(202) 366–9445
DOT Main	(202) 366–4000
Toll-free	(800) 996–2723
Federal Relay Service TTY	(800) 877–8339
Cargo Preference and Domestic Trade (laws and regulations)	(202) 366–4610

Information and Publications

KEY OFFICES

MARAD Congressional and Public Affairs

1200 New Jersey Ave. S.E.
Washington, DC 20590
(202) 366–5807
Michael Novak, director
(202) 366–5067
Susan Clark, media relations and public affairs officer
E-mail: pao.marad@dot.gov

Issues news releases, publications, and texts of speeches given by administration officials.

Freedom of Information

1200 New Jersey Ave. S.E., W24–233
Second Floor, West Bldg.
Washington, DC 20590
(800) 986–9678, ext. 65181
Fax (202) 366–7485
Anne Herchenrider, FOIA public liaison
(202) 366–5165
FOIA Service Center (202) 366–2666
E-mail: FOIA.Marad@dot.gov

DATA AND STATISTICS

Reports and data and statistics are available from the website (see "Library" and subheadings) and from MARAD Congressional and Public Affairs. Sections within the offices of Policy and Plans and National Security (202–366–2277) also offer data analysis.

PUBLICATIONS

MARAD Congressional and Public Affairs makes available numerous publications, including policy papers, fact sheets, reports, and *Federal Register* notices via the website; the Marine Highway Reference Library is also available on the website. Some publications may also be obtained from NTIS (see appendix, *Ordering Government Publications*).

Reference Resources

LIBRARY

DOT Library

1200 New Jersey Ave. S.E., #W12–300
Washington, DC 20590

(202) 366–0746
(800) 853–1351
Law Library (202) 366–0749
Amanda Wilson, director
(202) 366–2480
Internet: www.ntl.bts.gov
E-mail: library@dot.gov
Hours: 8:00 a.m. to 5:00 p.m.

DOCKETS

DOT Dockets Office
1200 New Jersey Ave. S.E., #W12–140
Washington, DC 20590
(202) 366–9322
(202) 366–9826
(800) 647–5527
Hours: 9:00 a.m. to 5:00 p.m.
Barbara Hairston, program manager

Maintains dockets for MARAD rules, orders, and regulations. Records on or after November 1, 1996, are available online via the Electronic Reading Room at www.marad.dot.gov/about-us/foia/electronic-reading-room. Federal dockets are also available at www.regulations.gov. (*See appendix for Searching and Commenting on Regulations: Regulations.gov.*)

RULES AND REGULATIONS

MARAD rules and regulations are published in the *Code of Federal Regulations*, Title 46, Chapter II, Parts 200–499. Proposed rules, new final rules, and updates to the *Code of Federal Regulations* are published in the daily *Federal Register*. (*See appendix for information on how to obtain and use these publications.*) The *Federal Register* and the *Code of Federal Regulations* may be accessed online at www.archives.gov/federal-register/cfr; this site also contains a link to the federal government's regulatory website at www.regulations.gov (*see appendix*).

▓ LEGISLATION

MARAD carries out its responsibilities under:

Merchant Marine Act of 1920 (41 Stat. 988, 46 U.S.C. 861). Signed by the president June 5, 1920. Section 867 of this act authorized support for the development of ports and other facilities connected with transport by water.

Merchant Marine Act of 1936 (49 Stat. 1985, 46 U.S.C. 1101). Signed by the president June 29, 1936. Established the subsidy program for the construction and operation of U.S. vessels.

Merchant Ship Sales Act (60 Stat. 41, 50 U.S.C. 1735). Signed by the president March 8, 1946. Gave MARAD authority to approve all sales or transfers of U.S.-flag vessels to a foreign country.

Cargo Preference Act (68 Stat. 832, 46 U.S.C. 1241). Signed by the president Aug. 26, 1954. Required that at least 50 percent of certain government cargoes be shipped on U.S. vessels.

Merchant Marine Act of 1970 (84 Stat. 1018, 46 U.S.C. 1101). Signed by the president Oct. 21, 1970. Overhauled the 1936 act to revitalize the merchant marine.

Shipping Act of 1984 (98 Stat. 67, 46 U.S.C. app. 1701 note). Signed by the president March 20, 1984. Reformed the regulation of liner shipping in U.S. foreign trade.

Food Security Act of 1985 (99 Stat. 1491, 46 U.S.C. 1241f). Signed by the president Dec. 23, 1985. Required that at least 75 percent of certain agricultural cargoes be shipped on U.S. vessels and that the DOT finance any resulting increase in ocean freight charges.

Intermodal Surface Transportation Efficiency Act of 1991 (ISTEA) (105 Stat. 1914, 49 U.S.C. 104 note). Signed by the president Dec. 18, 1991. Set the national policy plan for an economically and environmentally efficient intermodal transport system.

National Maritime Heritage Act of 1994 (16 U.S.C. 5401). Signed by the president Nov. 2, 1994. Allocated specified percentages of funds attributed to the sale and scrapping of obsolete vessels sold by Sept. 30, 2006, to the maintenance of the National Defense Reserve Fleet; the facility and training ship maintenance for state maritime academies or the United States Merchant Marine Academy; and the National Maritime Heritage Grants program.

Maritime Security Act of 1996 (110 Stat. 3118, 46 U.S.C. app. 1245 note). Signed by the president Oct. 8, 1996. Amended the Merchant Marine Act of 1936 to mandate establishment of a fleet of active, militarily useful, privately owned vessels to meet national defense and other security requirements and maintain a U.S. presence in international commercial shipping, establishing the Maritime Security Program within MARAD. Reauthorized in 2003.

American Fisheries Act (112 Stat. 2681–616, 46 U.S.C. 2101 note). Signed by the president Oct. 21, 1998. Amended federal law with regard to eligibility requirements for vessels to operate in certain fisheries.

Floyd D. Spence National Defense Authorization Act (114 Stat. 1654A-490, 16 U.S.C. 5405). Signed by the president Oct. 30, 2000. Amended the National Maritime Heritage Act of 1994 to extend through fiscal year 2006 the period for disposal of obsolete vessels in the National Defense Reserve Fleet. Authorized the transportation secretary to scrap obsolete vessels through qualified scrapping facilities.

Maritime Transportation Security Act of 2002 (116 Stat. 2064, 46 U.S.C. 2101). Signed by the president Nov. 25, 2002. Amended the Merchant Marine Act of 1936 to require the DOT to develop antiterrorism plans at U.S. ports and foreign ports where U.S.-bound shipments originate. Required the DOT to develop and maintain an antiterrorism cargo identification, tracking, and screening system. Required the DOT to establish a maritime intelligence program to help identify suspicious vessels before they entered U.S. ports. Authorized the DOT to establish a long-range vessel tracking system using satellite technology. Established a DOT National Maritime Security Advisory Committee to make recommendations for port security improvements.

National Defense Authorization Act (122 Stat. 591). Signed by the president Jan. 28, 2008. Amended the Merchant Ship Sales Act of 1946 to allow the transportation secretary to charter to any U.S. state, locality, or territory any vessel of the Ready Reserve Force or National Defense Reserve Fleet.

Duncan Hunter National Defense Authorization Act (122 Stat. 4761, 46 U.S.C. 57102 note). Signed by the president Oct. 14, 2008. Prohibited (with an exception) any U.S. vessel from being approved for export to a foreign country for purposes of dismantling, recycling, or scrapping. Directed MARAD's administrator to execute agreements with shipyards to provide assistance in the form of grants, loans, and loan guarantees to small shipyards for capital improvements and for maritime training programs.

American Recovery and Reinvestment Act of 2009 (123 Stat. 212). Signed by the president Feb. 17, 2009. Appropriated $100 million to MARAD for the Small Shipyards Grant Program for capital improvements and related infrastructure improvements and for maritime training programs.

Cruise Vessel Security and Safety Act of 2010 (124 Stat. 2243, 46 U.S.C. 101 note). Signed by the president July 27, 2010. The transportation secretary, in consultation with the director of the Federal Bureau of Investigation and the Maritime Administration, shall develop training to allow for the certification of passenger vessel security personnel, crew members, and law enforcement officials on the appropriate methods for prevention, detection, evidence preservation, and reporting of criminal activities in the international maritime environment.

Coast Guard and Maritime Transportation Act of 2012 (126 Stat. 1540, 14 U.S.C. 1 note). Signed by the president Dec. 20, 2012. Reauthorizes the national security aspects of the Maritime Administration for fiscal year 2013. Amended federal shipping laws that require a determination by the Administrator of the Maritime Administration regarding the nonavailability of qualified U.S. flag capacity to meet national defense requirements.

▪ REGIONAL OFFICES

EASTERN GULF/LOWER MISSISSIPPI
(AL; AR; FL panhandle; LA; MS; TN; and
internationally, the Gulf of Mexico)
500 Poydras St., #1223
New Orleans, LA 70130–3394
(504) 589–2000, ext. 229
E-mail: James.Murphy@dot.gov
James Murphy, gateway director

GREAT LAKES
(northern IL, IN, MI, northern MN, portion of NY,
OH, northwestern PA, WI)
500 W. Madison St., #1110
Chicago, IL 60661
(312) 353–1032
E-mail: Floyd.Miras@dot.gov
Floyd Miras, gateway director

INLAND WATERWAYS
(portions of 15 states adjacent to navigable rivers in
the region, including the Upper Mississippi, and
portions of the Missouri and Ohio Rivers, and
Illinois Waterway)

1222 Spruce St., #2.202F
St. Louis, MO 63103–2818
(314) 539–6783
E-mail: William.Paape@dot.gov
William Paape, director

MID-ATLANTIC

(DE, MD, NC, most of PA, VA, WV)
7737 Hampton Blvd., Bldg. 19, #300
Norfolk, VA 23505–1204
(757) 322–5800
E-mail: Jeffrey.Flumignan@dot.gov
Jeffrey Flumignan (acting), gateway director

NORTH ATLANTIC

(CT, MA, ME, NH, NJ, NY, RI, VT)
1 Bowling Green, #418
New York, NY 10004–1415
(212) 668–2064
E-mail: Jeffrey.Flumignan@dot.gov
Jeffrey Flumignan, gateway director

NORTHERN CALIFORNIA

(northern CA, GU, HI, NV, UT, U.S. Marianas)
201 Mission St., #1800
San Francisco, CA 94105–1905
(415) 310–8062
E-mail: John.Hummer@dot.gov
John Hummer, gateway director
(415) 744–2924

PACIFIC NORTHWEST/ALASKA

(AK, ID, OR, WA, western Canada)
Henry M. Jackson Federal Bldg.
915 2nd Ave., 26th Floor, #2608
Seattle, WA 98174
(206) 220–7717
E-mail: Robert.Loken@dot.gov
Robert Loken, director

SOUTH ATLANTIC

(FL except panhandle, GA, PR, SC, VI)
51 S.W. 1st Ave., #1305
Miami, FL 33130
(305) 530–6420

E-mail: Frances Bohnsack@dot.gov
Frances Bohnsack, director

SOUTHERN CALIFORNIA

(AZ, southern CA, and west
coast of Mexico)
501 W. Ocean Blvd., #5190
Long Beach, CA 90802
(415) 744–2924
E-mail: John.Hummer@dot.gov
John Hummer (acting), gateway director

WESTERN GULF

(CO, NM, OK, TX)
8701 S. Gessler Rd., #1235
Houston, TX 77074
(713) 272–2864
E-mail: Brian.P.Hill@dot.gov
Brian Hill, gateway director

GREAT LAKES FIRE TRAINING ACADEMY

2600 S. Eber Rd.
Swanton, OH 43558
(419) 574–1965
(419) 259–6362
E-Mail: glfireschool@dot.gov
Michael Romstadt, director and
senior instructor

U.S. MERCHANT MARINE ACADEMY

300 Steamboat Rd.
Kings Point, NY 11024–1699
(516) 726–5800
Rear Adm. James A. Helis, superintendent
(516) 726–5812
Web: www.usmma.edu

In addition, there are six state Maritime Academies for which the Maritime Administration provides funding: California Maritime Academy, Maine Maritime Academy, Massachusetts Maritime Academy, Great Lakes Maritime Academy, Texas Maritime Academy, and the State University of New York Maritime College.

National Highway Traffic Safety Administration

1200 New Jersey Ave. S.E., Washington, DC 20590
Internet: www.nhtsa.dot.gov

The National Highway Traffic Safety Administration (NHTSA) is an agency within the Department of Transportation (DOT). It administers federal programs designed to increase motor vehicle safety and combat the deaths, injuries, and economic losses caused by highway crashes. The administration has authority to issue standards for vehicle safety, fuel economy, damage liability, and theft protection.

The NHTSA is headed by an administrator appointed by the president and confirmed by the Senate. Three senior associate administrators serve under the administrator. The senior associate administrators are responsible for policy and operations, traffic injury control, and vehicle safety.

The NHTSA:

- Develops mandatory minimum safety standards for domestic and foreign vehicles and vehicle equipment (tires, lights, child restraints) sold in the United States.
- Establishes corporate average fuel economy standards for passenger cars and light-duty vehicles (vans and pickup trucks).
- Administers state and community highway safety grant programs with the Federal Highway Administration (FHWA) (*p. 791*).
- Undertakes research, development, and demonstration of new state and community highway safety grant programs, particularly against drunk driving.
- Enforces compliance with safety and fuel economy standards, identifies safety defects in vehicles and administers manufacturer-recall campaigns for corrective action, enforces federal odometer tampering laws, and operates a toll-free auto safety hotline.
- Issues bumper standards designed to minimize consumer losses associated with low-speed crashes.
- Issues standards requiring certain parts on high-theft vehicle lines to be marked to reduce vehicle thefts.

Vehicles. NHTSA safety standards for vehicles are based on research performed by the agency. The research determines which parts of the vehicle can be improved to provide greater protection in the event of a crash or to reduce the incidence of crashes. The administration also investigates vehicle defects and can order manufacturers to repair flaws that affect the safe performance of the vehicle.

The agency can order manufacturers to include certain safety features in the design of a motor vehicle. In the past, safety features ordered by the NHTSA have included seat belts, safety windshields, dual brake systems, air bags, steering columns able to absorb impact, and high-mounted stop lamps.

The NHTSA operates a toll-free auto safety hotline through which it receives most of its information and complaints on vehicle defects from consumers.

Copies of all complaints not covered by an agency standard are forwarded to vehicle manufacturers and to the NHTSA's Office of Defects Investigation. This office enters complaints into a computer database. If a pattern of complaints develops that points to a possible safety defect, an investigation is conducted to confirm the defect and to determine its cause and severity. The manufacturer may voluntarily recall and repair the product at any time during this agency process. If the process reaches the formal investigation stage without a recall, the NHTSA will issue a public announcement and request comments from the public and the manufacturer. After analysis of this information, the agency will (if it appears necessary) issue an initial determination that a safety defect exists and schedule a public meeting. The public meeting is announced in the *Federal Register* and in the news media, allowing comments from the manufacturer, consumer groups, and other interested parties.

Based on findings from the public meeting, the agency may issue a final determination of a defect and then may order the manufacturer to recall the product. The manufacturer is required to supply the NHTSA with information on how the recall will be carried out and what corrective action will be taken. Consumers must be notified by mail and the defect must be corrected at no charge to the consumer. NHTSA recall orders may be contested by the manufacturer in U.S. District Court. Most investigations leading to a recall are resolved in the early stages with a voluntary recall, but the NHTSA has been to court on several occasions to try to force involuntary recalls.

Compliance with NHTSA standards is achieved through the annual outlay of funds for the selected purchase of motor vehicles of all classes as well as the procurement of automotive parts and components, including tires, for testing. Using a precise procedure prepared by agency engineers, compliance testing is accomplished under agency supervision, principally through the use of private (nonfederal) testing facilities. Motor vehicle equipment and motor vehicles that do not comply with the standards are subject to manufacturer recall and substantial civil penalties.

The NHTSA manages programs to ensure that nonconforming foreign vehicles (gray market) are properly modified and certified in conformity with the Federal Motor Vehicle Safety Standards. This is principally accomplished through the engineering review of certification data submitted by registered importers as evidence of compliance and by physical inspections of selected vehicles. The NHTSA can recommend the forfeiture of customs bonds, impose civil penalties, or enter into litigation in its efforts to support certification.

In 1998 NHTSA officials signed an international agreement in Geneva that made possible the development of global regulations concerning the safety performance of motor vehicles and motor vehicle equipment.

Enforcement of the Federal Odometer Tampering Law and Regulations also is a NHTSA responsibility. Investigators at agency headquarters and in regional offices refer cases of odometer fraud to the Department of Justice for criminal prosecution. In addition, each investigator works closely with state agencies in each enforcement region in odometer fraud investigations.

The Cameron Gulbransen Kids Transportation Safety Act of 2007 (KT Safety Act) addressed vehicle hazards to small children. The law required the transportation secretary to initiate a rulemaking for motor vehicles to require: automatic reversal of direction by power windows and panels when they detect an obstruction; an expanded rearward field of view to prevent backing incidents; and automatic transmissions to have an anti-rollaway system that requires the service brake to be depressed before the transmission can be shifted out of park. In 2010 NHTSA proposed rules to prevent backing-over deaths. This included a rule for power windows and a rule requiring automobiles to have backup cameras installed in all cars by 2014.

NHTSA issued a rule requiring all vehicles with automatic transmission with a park position, manufactured for sale after September 1, 2010, to have brake transmission shift interlock (BTSI), a technology that prevents vehicles from being put into gear unless the brake is depressed.

In February 2011 NHTSA formally terminated rulemaking regarding the power windows automatic reversal provision. The KT Safety Act provided the secretary with discretion whether to issue a final rule. After the agency analyzed and considered the benefits and costs of installing automatic reversal systems for all types of vehicle windows, NHTSA decided to propose requiring automatic reversal systems on only one type of power window, the "one-touch" windows, which close with a single activation rather than continuous activation. NHTSA also noted that it had previously issued rules requiring safer "pull to close" window switches that would address this safety issue.

The rule for backup cameras was delayed several times. NHTSA estimated that a final rule requiring the installation of rearview cameras would cost the auto industry up to $2.7 billion; cost was widely believed to be the cause of delay. In 2014 NHTSA issued a final rule requiring rear visibility technology in all new vehicles under 10,000 pounds by May 2018. Aftermarket backup cameras are available for consumers who want to add the cameras to older cars.

Traffic Safety. The NHTSA supervises a program of grants to states to set up motor vehicle, driver, and pedestrian safety programs. Areas covered by safety programs include effects of alcohol and other drugs on driving ability, occupant protection, emergency medical services, police traffic services, motorcycle safety, and traffic records.

The NHTSA, through its National Driver Register, maintains a nationwide file on drivers with license sanctions for drunk driving and other serious violations.

In 1995 Congress repealed the federal cap on highway speed limits, allowing states to set their speed limits for all roadways.

Distracted driving related to cell phone use, texting, and other personal electronic communications equipment, continues to be a top concern for traffic safety advocates. NHTSA statistics revealed that nearly 5,000 traffic fatalities and nearly a half million injuries result from distracted driving each year. NHTSA has implemented distracted driver regulations for commercial drivers; NHTSA enacted rules banning commercial bus and truck drivers from texting on the job and restricted train operators from using electronic devices while operating a train.

States must enact distracted driver legislation for noncommercial drivers. NHTSA serves as a resource to states that desire to participate in distracted driving campaigns or pass legislation to prohibit such activity. NHTSA provides data and statistics, as well as public service announcements and hosts an annual distracted driving summit. The Transportation Department launched a website to serve as a clearinghouse on the issue, www.distraction.gov. By 2011 more than thirty states had enacted some sort of distracted driver legislation. By 2015, forty-three states and the District of Columbia banned text messaging for all drivers.

In August 2014 NHTSA released an advanced notice of proposed rulemaking (ANPRM) and a supporting comprehensive research report on vehicle-to-vehicle (V2V) communications technology. The ANPRM initiated rulemaking that would propose to create a new Federal Motor Vehicle Safety Standard to require V2V communication capability for light vehicles and to create minimum performance requirements for V2V devices and messages. NHTSA research indicated the technology would significantly reduce collisions.

Fuel Economy Standards. The NHTSA has authority to prescribe fuel use economy standards—the average number of miles per gallon a manufacturer's fleet has to achieve. The agency has established average fuel economy standards for passenger cars beginning with the 1978 model year and nonpassenger motor vehicles beginning with the 1979 model year. The NHTSA has developed an economic, marketing, and technological database to support and provide information on the fuel economy program.

Fuel economy standards are enforced through tests, inspections, and investigations. The Environmental Protection Agency (*p. 67*) is responsible for the actual testing of automobiles for gas mileage performance. The NHTSA recommends enforcement and compliance actions in conjunction with the Department of Justice and the Federal Trade Commission (*p. 239*), the agencies that enforce the law requiring that fuel economy rating labels be affixed to new vehicles. The NHTSA has the authority to fine manufacturers who fail to comply with standards; it offers credits to offset fines to manufacturers who exceed average fuel economy standards.

After twelve temporary extensions of the 1998 surface transportation law to keep highway and transit programs running at their fiscal 2004 levels, Congress passed a full reauthorization in summer 2005. The Safe, Accountable, Flexible, and Efficient Transportation Equity Act (SAFETEA) appropriated $286.5 billion for federal transportation programs. The bill earmarked $24.1 billion for special transportation projects across the country—about 6,000 projects in all.

SAFETEA also provided incentives to states to institute safety belt laws. States would get additional funding under the act if they had recently adopted, or adopted during the life of the act, a primary safety belt law, which would allow drivers to be fined for not wearing a seat belt even if they were not violating other traffic laws. SAFETEA also instructed the NHTSA to follow tighter deadlines for issuing rules or reports on several pending safety issues, including vehicle rollover prevention and side impact protection.

SAFETEA requires new passenger vehicles to be labeled with safety rating information published by the NHTSA under its New Car Assessment Program. In November 2006 the NHTSA issued its final rule regarding the regulations to ensure that the labeling requirements were implemented by Sept. 1, 2007.

The Energy Independence and Security Act of 2007 directed the transportation secretary to promulgate rules establishing a national tire fuel efficiency consumer information program. NHTSA issued final rules in March 2010.

In an effort to boost the sagging economy and provide an incentive to consumers to buy more fuel-efficient vehicles, President Barack Obama in June 2009 signed the Consumer Assistance to Recycle and Save Act of 2009, which established the "Cash for Clunkers" program at NHTSA. The legislation authorized the transportation secretary to establish rules for the program, which issued vouchers to consumers to trade in older vehicles for more fuel efficient vehicles. The act also directed the secretary to establish and provide for the enforcement of measures to prevent and penalize fraud under the program. The program was funded at $1 billion; the popularity of the program ran through the appropriated money in less than one week. Congress authorized another $2 billion for the program, which ended in August 2009.

Congress did not pass an omnibus transportation reauthorization bill after SAFETEA expired in 2009. Congress continued to appropriate money to fund transportation programs via short-term extension bills. In 2012, Congress passed Moving Ahead for Progress in the 21st Century Act (MAP-21). While not an omnibus bill, the legislation reauthorized various NHTSA programs for two years. MAP-21 also required rulemaking to increase transparency and accountability regarding vehicle safety information and increased civil penalties for violations. The bill also established within NHTSA a Council for Vehicle Electronics, Vehicle Software, and Emerging Technologies to build and integrate NHTSA expertise in passenger motor vehicle electronics and other new and emerging technologies.

By summer 2015 Congress had not passed an omnibus transportation reauthorization bill since SAFETEA's expiration in 2009. Congress continued to appropriate money to fund transportation programs via short-term extension bills.

■ KEY PERSONNEL

Administrator
Mark R. Rosekind . . . . (202) 366–1836
Fax . . . . (202) 366–2106
Deputy Administrator
David Friedman . . . . (202) 366–2775
Chief Counsel
Kevin Vincent . . . . (202) 366–9511
Civil Rights
Regina Morgan . . . . (202) 366–1836
Governmental Affairs, Policy, and Strategic Planning
Alison Pascale . . . . (202) 366–1836
Communications
Gordon Trowbridge . . . . (202) 366–1836
Policy and Operations
Vacant . . . . (202) 366–5925
Planning, Administrative, and Financial Management
Mary Sprague . . . . (202) 366–3564
Chief Information Officer
Colleen Coggins . . . . (202) 366–1199
Communications and Consumer Information
Susan Gorcowski . . . . (202) 366–9550
Traffic Injury Control
Vacant . . . . (202) 366–2121
Behavioral Safety Research
Richard Compton . . . . (202) 366–2699
Emergency Medical Service
Drew Dawson . . . . (202) 366–9966

Impaired Driving and Occupant Protection
Michael Brown .... (202) 366–4913
Research and Program Development
Jeffrey Michael. .... (202) 366–1755
Safety Programs
John Marshall .... (202) 366–4016
Vehicle Safety
Daniel C. Smith................... (202) 366–0361
Crashworthiness Standards
Lori Summers .... (202) 366–1810
Crash Avoidance Standards
David Hines................... (202) 366–1810
International Policy, Fuel Economy, and Consumer Programs
Vacant....................... (202) 366–1810
Rulemaking
Ryan Posten .... (202) 366–1810
National Center for Statistics and Analysis
Terry Shelton .... (202) 366–1503
Regulatory Analysis and Evaluation
Larry Blincoe.................. (202) 366–2555
Vehicle Safety Research
Nat Beuse .... (202) 366–4862
Vehicle Research and Test Center
Vacant....................... (937) 666–4511
Vehicle Crash Worthniness Research
Stephan Ridella .... (202) 366–5662
Vehicle Crash Avoidance and Electronic Controls Research
Tim Johnson .... (202) 366–5663
Enforcement
Nancy Lewis..................... (202) 366–3217
Defects Investigation
Frank Borris................... (202) 366–8087
Vehicle Safety Compliance
Vacant....................... (202) 366–5203
Odometer Fraud Investigation
David Sparks .... (202) 366–5953

■ INFORMATION SOURCES

Internet

Agency website: www.nhtsa.dot.gov. Topics covered include vehicle testing, regulations and standards, and research; also injury prevention, driver performance, and crash information. Crash test results and safety ratings for particular vehicles are also available on the website. The NHTSA also hosts several websites containing information about related subjects, including www.SaferCar.gov, www.TrafficSafetyMarketing.gov, www.Distraction.gov, www.nhtsa.gov/Impaired, www.EMS.gov, and www.911.gov.

Telephone Contacts

Information, Publications, and Data Request Line
(NCSA) .... (800) 934–8517
DOT Vehicle Safety Hotline .... (888) 327–4236
TTY .... (800) 424–9153
DOT Main....................... (202) 366–4000

Information and Publications

KEY OFFICES

Communications and Consumer Information

1200 New Jersey Ave. S.E.
Washington, DC 20590
(202) 366–9550
Susan Gorcowski, associate administrator

Provides public information, issues news releases and other materials, and answers general questions on vehicle safety.

Consumer information division responds to consumer complaints and questions, acts as a clearinghouse for consumer publications on vehicle and pedestrian safety, issues *NHTSA Consumer Advisories* (press releases that contain information on investigations and recalls), and solicits reports from consumers on problems under investigation. Specific questions and complaints concerning vehicle safety should be directed to the DOT toll-free Vehicle Safety Hotline *(see above)*.

Freedom of Information

NHTSA Office of the Chief Counsel
1200 New Jersey Ave. S.E., #W41–304
Washington, DC 20590
(202) 366–3564
Mary Sprague, FOIA public liaison

DATA AND STATISTICS

NHTSA National Center for Statistics and Analysis (NCSA)

1200 New Jersey Ave. S.E., West Bldg.
Washington, DC 20590
(202) 366–1503
Publications, information, and data request line
(800) 934–8517
Terry Shelton, associate administrator

Publications, reports, statistics, and datasets on highway traffic safety are available on the website. See also *Internet,* above, for websites containing related information.

PUBLICATIONS

An extensive collection of NHTSA consumer and technical publications and reports are available on the website. See also *Internet,* above, for websites containing related information.

NHTSA Publications

Resource Center
3341 E. 75th Ave., Suite F
Landover, MD 20785
Fax (301) 386–2194
Internet: www-nrd.nhtsa.dot.gov/CATS

Materials are available on multiple highway safety topics, including antilock brake systems; alcohol and impaired driving; booster and child safety seats; pedestrian, bicycle, and motorcycle safety; occupant protection; cell phone use; emergency medical services; traffic law enforcement; traffic safety; crash statistics; vehicle safety; and numerous other topics.

Reference Resources

LIBRARIES

NHTSA Technical Information Services

Reference Reading Room
1200 New Jersey Ave. S.E., E12–100
Washington, DC 20590
(202) 366–2588
E-mail: tis@nhtsa.dot.gov
Hours: 9:30 a.m. to 4:00 p.m.

Contains a collection of technical literature on highway and vehicle safety, rulemaking docket files, investigation files, and Internet and microfiche workstations. Many technical reports available for viewing in the reading room are available on the website or may be purchased through the National Technical Information Services (*see appendix, Ordering Government Publications*).

DOT Library/National Transportation Library

1200 New Jersey Ave. S.E., #W12–300
Washington, DC 20590
(202) 366–0746
(800) 853–1351
Law Library (202) 366–0749
Amanda Wilson, director
(202) 366–2480
Internet: www.ntl.bts.gov
E-mail: library@dot.gov
Hours: 8:00 a.m. to 5:00 p.m.

DOCKETS

DOT Dockets Office
1200 New Jersey Ave. S.E., #W12–140
Washington, DC 20590
(202) 366–9322
(202) 366–9826
(800) 647–5527
Hours: 9:00 a.m. to 5:00 p.m.
Barbara Hairston, program manager

Maintains dockets for NHTSA rulemakings and other administrative proceedings for copying and inspection. Federal dockets are also available at www.regulations.gov. (*See appendix for Searching and Commenting on Regulations: Regulations.gov.*)

RULES AND REGULATIONS

NHTSA rules and regulations are published in the *Code of Federal Regulations,* Title 23, Chapter II, Parts 1200–1299; Title 23, Chapter III, Parts 1300–1399; and Title 49, Chapter V, Parts 500–599. Proposed rules, new final rules, and updates to the *Code of Federal Regulations* are published in the daily *Federal Register.* (*See appendix for information on how to obtain and use these publications.*) The *Federal Register* and the *Code of Federal Regulations* may be accessed online at www.archives.gov/federal-register/cfr; this site also contains a link to the federal government's regulatory website at www.regulations.gov (*see appendix*).

▨ LEGISLATION

The NHTSA carries out its responsibilities under:

National Traffic and Motor Vehicle Safety Act of 1966 (80 Stat. 718, 15 U.S.C. 1381). Signed by the president Sept. 9, 1966. Required the establishment of safety standards for all tires and vehicles, domestic and imported, sold in the United States. Authorized research and development programs on auto safety and expanded the national driver registration service to record the names of drivers whose licenses have been suspended or revoked.

Highway Safety Act of 1966 (80 Stat. 731, 23 U.S.C. 401). Signed by the president Sept. 9, 1966. Required states to establish highway safety programs that meet federal standards. Established a grant program to assist states and communities in creating highway safety programs.

Highway Safety Act of 1970 (84 Stat. 1739, 23 U.S.C. 144). Signed by the president Dec. 31, 1970. Divided responsibility for the Highway Safety Act of 1966 between the NHTSA and the FHWA. The FHWA was given responsibility for highway safety and design programs and the NHTSA was given authority over vehicle and pedestrian safety.

Motor Vehicle Information and Cost Savings Act of 1972 (86 Stat. 947, 15 U.S.C. 1901). Signed by the president Oct. 20, 1972. Authorized the NHTSA to enforce the national speed limit of fifty-five miles per hour and to set mandatory fuel use standards for motor vehicles. Authorized the agency to impose fines on manufacturers who fail to meet standards. Authorized the agency to perform research on reducing economic losses in car crashes by using diagnostic inspection techniques and prohibited any form of tampering with motor vehicle odometers.

Imported Vehicle Safety Compliance Act of 1988 (102 Stat. 2818, 15 U.S.C. 1381 note). Signed by the president Oct. 31, 1988. Required importers to prove that they are capable of modifying foreign-manufactured vehicles to meet U.S. safety standards.

Intermodal Surface Transportation Efficiency Act of 1991 (ISTEA) (105 Stat. 1914, 49 U.S.C. 101 note). Signed by the president Dec. 18, 1991. Authorized funding for incentive programs to improve occupant safety and to prevent drunk driving. Increased funding to enhance transportation efficiency.

National Highway System Designation Act of 1995 (109 Stat. 568, 23 U.S.C. 101 note). Signed by the president Nov. 28, 1995. Designated roughly 160,000 miles of interstate highways and other heavily traveled roads as the National Highway System (NHS). Routes on the NHS receive 30 percent of all federal highway aid initially, with increases to follow. Repealed the federal cap on highway speed limits, allowing states to set their own speed limits for all roadways.

Transportation Equity Act for the 21st Century (TEA-21) (112 Stat. 154, 23 U.S.C. 143). Signed by the president June 9, 1998. Reauthorized the federal highway, transit, safety, research, and motor carrier programs under the ISTEA from 1998 through 2003. Provided incentives for states to adopt tough .08 blood alcohol concentration standards for drunk driving.

Transportation Recall Enhancement, Accountability, and Documentation Act (TREAD) (114 Stat. 1806, 49 U.S.C. 3016 note). Signed by the president Nov. 1, 2000. Directed the DOT to undertake certain activities to improve highway safety.

Safe, Accountable, Flexible, and Efficient Transportation Equity Act of 2005 (SAFETEA) (23 U.S.C. 134). Signed by the president Aug. 10, 2005. Reauthorized federal surface transportation and highway programs through fiscal year 2009. Authorized the NHTSA to participate and cooperate in international activities to enhance highway safety. Required collection of motor vehicle collision data to determine crash causation and the study of the safety of highway toll collection facilities. Directed the NHTSA to train state law enforcement personnel in police chase guidelines. Directed the NHTSA to require the testing of fifteen-passenger vans for rollover prevention and side impact protection. Required new passenger vehicles to be labeled with safety rating information published by the NHTSA under its New Car Assessment Program.

Energy Independence and Security Act of 2007 (121 Stat. 1506, 49 U.S.C. 32304). Signed by the president Dec. 19, 2007. Directed the transportation secretary to promulgate rules establishing a national tire fuel efficiency consumer information program. Set forth a civil penalty for noncompliance with the national tire fuel efficiency information program.

The Cameron Gulbransen Kids Transportation Safety Act of 2007 (KT Safety Act) (122 Stat. 639, 49 U.S.C. 30111 note). Signed by the president Feb. 28, 2008. Directs the secretary of transportation to initiate a rulemaking for motor vehicles to require automatic reversal of direction by power windows and panels when they detect an obstruction; an expanded rearward field of view to prevent backing incidents; and automatic transmissions to have an anti-rollaway system that requires the service brake to be depressed before the transmission can be shifted out of park. Provided the secretary with discretion as to whether to issue a final rule.

Consumer Assistance to Recycle and Save Act of 2009 (123 Stat. 1909, 49 U.S.C. 32901 note). Signed by the president June 24, 2009. Title XIII of the Supplemental Appropriations Act established a voluntary Consumer Assistance to Recycle and Save Program (Cash for Clunkers), authorizing the transportation secretary to establish rules for the program that issued vouchers to consumers to trade in older vehicles for more fuel efficient vehicles.

Pedestrian Safety Enhancement Act of 2010 (124 Stat. 4086, 49 U.S.C. 30111 note). Signed by the president Jan. 4, 2011. Mandates a rule to establish a standard requiring electric and hybrid vehicles to be equipped with a pedestrian alert sound system that would activate in certain vehicle operating conditions to aid visually impaired and other pedestrians in detecting the presence, direction, location, and operation of those vehicles.

Moving Ahead for Progress in the 21st Century Act (MAP-21) (126 Stat. 405, 23 U.S.C. 101 note). Signed by the president July 6, 2012. Required rulemaking to increase transparency and accountability regarding vehicle safety information. Increased civil penalties for violations. Reauthorized various programs for two years. Established within NHTSA a Council for Vehicle Electronics, Vehicle Software, and Emerging Technologies to build and integrate NHTSA expertise in passenger motor vehicle electronics and other new and emerging technologies.

■ REGIONAL OFFICES

REGION 1
(CT, MA, ME, NH, RI, VT)
55 Broadway
Kendall Square, Code 8E
Cambridge, MA 02142
(617) 494–3427
Fax (617) 494–3646
Michael Geraci, regional administrator

REGION 2
(NJ, NY, PA, PR, VI)
245 Main St., #210
White Plains, NY 10601–2442
(914) 682–6162
Fax (914) 682–6239
Thomas Louizou, regional administrator

REGION 3
(DC, DE, KY, MD, VA, WV)
10 S. Howard St., #6700
Baltimore, MD 21201
(410) 962–0090
Fax (410) 962–2770
Elizabeth A. Baker, regional administrator

REGION 4
(AL, FL, GA, SC, TN)
61 Forsyth St. S.W., #17T30
Atlanta, GA 30303
(404) 562–3739
Fax (404) 562–3763
Carmen Hayes, regional administrator

REGION 5
(IL, IN, MI, MN, OH, WI)
4749 Lincoln Mall Dr., #300B
Matteson, IL 60443–3800
(708) 503–8822
Fax (708) 503–8991
Darin Jones, regional administrator

REGION 6
(Indian Nations, LA, MS, NM, OK, TX)
819 Taylor St., #8A38
Fort Worth, TX 76102–6177
(817) 978–3653
Fax (817) 978–8339
Georgia S. Chakiris, regional administrator

REGION 7
(AR, IA, KS, MO, NE)
901 Locust St., #466
Kansas City, MO 64106
(816) 329–3900
Fax (816) 329–3910
Susan DeCourcy, regional administrator

REGION 8
(CO, ND, NV, SD, UT, WY)
12300 W. Dakota Ave., #140
Lakewood, CO 80228–2583

(720) 963–3100
Fax (720) 963–3124
Bill R. Watada, regional administrator

REGION 9
(AS, AZ, CA, GU, HI, Northern Marianas)
John E. Moss Federal Bldg.
650 Capitol Mall, #5–400
Sacramento, CA 95814
(916) 498–5058
Chris Murphy, regional administrator

REGION 10
(AK, ID, MT, OR, WA)
3140 Jackson Federal Bldg.
915 Second Ave.
Seattle, WA 98174
(206) 220–7640
Fax (206) 220–7651
John Moffat, regional administrator

Pipeline and Hazardous Materials Safety Administration

1200 New Jersey Ave. S.E., Washington, DC 20590
Internet: www.phmsa.dot.gov

The Pipeline and Hazardous Materials Safety Administration (PHMSA), an agency within the Department of Transportation (DOT), is responsible for safe and secure movement of hazardous materials to industry and consumers by all transportation modes, including the nation's pipelines. The PHMSA was formed in February 2005 when DOT's Research and Special Programs Administration (RSPA) was split between the PHMSA and the Research and Innovative Technology Administration (RITA) (p. 823).

The PHMSA oversees the safety of the nearly one million daily shipments of hazardous materials in the United States and the nation's energy that is transported via a 2.6 million mile pipeline transportation system. The agency is dedicated solely to safety by working toward the elimination of transportation-related deaths and injuries in hazardous materials and pipeline transportation, and by promoting transportation solutions that enhance communities and protect the natural environment. The PHMSA is required by law to respond to safety recommendations issued by the National Transportation Safety Board (NTSB) (p. 433); the PHMSA lists open and closed NTSB recommendations on its website.

The PHMSA's main hazmat and pipeline safety functions are carried out by the following offices: Hazardous Materials Safety and Pipeline Safety.

Office of Hazardous Materials Safety (OHMS). The OHMS regulates the transportation of hazardous materials by all modes of transportation except bulk transport by water. The office designates substances as hazardous materials; monitors shipping and carrier operations and packaging and container specifications in cooperation with the modal offices of the DOT; and operates a centralized system for reporting accidents involving hazardous materials. Hazmat incidents must be reported by telephone within twelve hours; written reports must be submitted to OHMS within thirty days. The OHMS has the authority to impose civil penalties and refer cases for criminal prosecution.

The OHMS also sponsors outreach programs to foster cooperation among federal, state, and local agencies and the private sector, with responsibilities for maintaining hazardous materials transportation safety. OHMS Training and Outreach programs provide publications, self-training products, and in-person training opportunities to help the regulated community comply with the requirements of the hazardous materials regulations. The Hazardous Materials Emergency Preparedness (HMEP) grant program provides financial and technical assistance to enhance state, tribal, and local hazardous materials emergency planning and training.

The Implementing Recommendations of the 9/11 Commission Act of 2007 directed the transportation secretary to publish a final rule for the railroad routing of security-sensitive materials that requires railroads to perform the safety and security risk analyses and then to make an appropriate route selection for transporting hazardous materials. On Nov. 26, 2008, the PHMSA, in coordination with the Federal Railroad Administration (p. 798) and the Transportation Security Administration (p. 649), announced the final rule implementing the requirements under the 9/11 Commission Act.

In May 2015 PHMSA announced a final rule for the safe transportation of flammable liquids by rail. The final rule, developed by PHMSA and Federal Railroad Administration (FRA) in coordination with Canada, focuses on safety improvements that are designed to prevent accidents, mitigate consequences in the event of an accident, and support emergency response. These enhanced regulations were developed in response to several serious, high profile rail disasters resulting from an exponential increase in petroleum transported by rail from the Bakken region in North Dakota. The regulations cover rail tank design, reduced operating speed, classification of unrefined petroleum-based products, and rail routing risk assessment and information access.

Office of Pipeline Safety (OPS). The OPS develops and enforces design, construction, operations, and maintenance safety regulations for the transportation of gas and hazardous materials by pipeline. The OPS also formulates and issues special exemptions to regulations.

Under the Natural Gas Pipeline Safety Act of 1968, states may acquire regulatory jurisdiction over some or all of their intrastate gas facilities. To enable a state to carry out an effective safety program, the OPS administers a program to pay states up to 50 percent of the actual cost incurred in regulating natural gas pipelines. The Pipeline Safety Act of 1979 authorized the establishment of a similar grant program for liquid gas facilities.

The OPS also reviews state regulation certificates for intrastate pipeline transportation, requires annual examination of pipelines and associated facilities on federal lands, and establishes and enforces standards and regulations to ensure safe construction and operation of pipelines on the Outer Continental Shelf.

The OPS has authority to impose civil penalties and refer cases for criminal prosecution. In fiscal year 2013 PHMSA initiated 266 enforcement cases against pipeline operators for problems involving their integrity management programs, risk assessments, failure prevention and mitigation programs, and several other possible regulatory violations identified during failure investigations and routine inspections.

The Pipeline Inspection, Protection, Enforcement, and Safety Act of 2006 required that PHMSA issue regulations subjecting low-stress hazardous liquid pipelines to the same standards and regulations as other hazardous liquid pipelines with some limited exceptions. The act also required the secretary to provide for pipeline safety enforcement transparency, including a monthly updated summary to the public of all gas and hazardous liquid pipeline enforcement actions taken by the secretary or the PHMSA.

In 2012 two laws were enacted that directed PHMSA to revise safety regulations and increased civil penalties for violations. The Pipeline Safety, Regulatory Certainty, and Job Creation Act of 2011 directed the transportation secretary to revise regulations pertaining to communications of hazmat incidents, enforcement hearings, national pipeline mapping system requirements, and gas and liquid pipeline integrity management improvements. The Moving Ahead for Progress in the 21st Century Act (MAP-21) requires revised regulations to address transportation of hazardous materials. MAP-21 includes provision to improve training for first responders and hazmat inspectors and investigators and includes new requirements for data collection of hazmat incidents. The law also mandates new state responsibilities relating to highway routing disclosures

Other PHMSA functions include investigations and enforcement, research and development (R&D), and data and statistics. Investigations and enforcement staff inspect entities that offer hazardous materials for transportation and manufacturers of products used to transport hazardous materials. This unit is responsible for ensuring that pipeline operators are in full compliance with pipeline safety regulations. The Office of Hazardous Materials Safety's R&D program directs basic and applied research for the purpose of minimizing risks associated with the transportation of hazardous materials. PHMSA's Pipeline Safety R&D Program conducts and supports research to support regulatory and enforcement activities and to

provide the technical and analytical foundation necessary for planning, evaluating, and implementing the pipeline safety program. PHMSA tracks data on the frequency of failures, incidents, and accidents. PHMSA also analyzes the causes and the resulting consequences and reports these data in various categories such as year, state, type, cause, and result.

■ KEY PERSONNEL

Administrator
    Marie Therese Dominguez . . . . (202) 366–4433
        Fax. . . . . (202) 366–3666
Deputy Administrator
    Vacant. . . . . (202) 366–3666
Assistant Administrator and Chief Safety Officer
    Stephen L. Domotor . . . . (202) 366–4595
Chief Counsel
    Vanessa Sutherland . . . . (202) 366–4400
        Fax. . . . . (202) 366–7041
Chief Financial Officer
    Scott Poyer . . . . (202) 366–5608
Civil Rights
    Rosanne Goodwill. . . . . (202) 366–9638
Governmental, International, and Public Affairs
    Artealia Gilliard. . . . . (202) 366–4831
Hazardous Materials Safety
    Magdy El-Sibaie. . . . . (202) 366–0656
Approvals and Permits
    Ryan Paquet . . . . (202) 366–4511
Enforcement
    Rod Dyck . . . . (202) 366–3844
Engineering and Research
    Harpreet Singh. . . . . (202) 366–4545
Field Operations
    William Schoonover . . . . (202) 366–0656
Field Services Support
    Richard Raksins. . . . . (202) 366–4700
Fitness
    Margaret Carson . . . . (202) 366–4700
International Standards
    Shane Kelley (acting) . . . . (202) 366–0656
Outreach, Training, and Grants
    Aaron Mitchell. . . . . (202) 366–1109
Program Development
    Ben Supko (acting) . . . . (202) 366–1017
Regulatory Review and Reinvention
    Glenn Foster. . . . . (202) 366–8553
Standards and Rulemaking
    Charles Betts . . . . (202) 366–8553
Pipeline Safety
    Jeffrey D. Wiese. . . . . (202) 366–4595

■ INFORMATION SOURCES

Internet
    Agency website: www.phmsa.dot.gov. Comprehensive website includes general information about the PHMSA, as well as PHMSA publications, reports, data and statistics,

and regulations. The Office of Hazardous Materials Safety also hosts its own website, http://phmsa.dot.gov/hazmat

Telephone Contacts

PHMSA Main . . . . (202) 366–4433
DOT Main. . . . . (202) 366–4000
Federal Relay Service TTY . . . . (800) 877–8339
Hazardous Materials Safety Information
    Center . . . . (800) 467–4922; (202) 366–4488
National Response Center—Hazardous Materials
    Transportation and Pipeline
    Safety . . . . (800) 424–8802

Information and Publications

KEY OFFICES

PHMSA Governmental, International, and Public Affairs

1200 New Jersey Ave. S.E.
East Bldg., 2nd Floor, MS E27–303
Washington, DC 20590
(202) 366–4831
Fax (202) 366–7431
Artealia Gilliard, director

Answers general inquiries from the public, the press, members of Congress, and state and local officials about offices within the PHMSA.

Freedom of Information

PHMSA Office of Chief Counsel
1200 New Jersey Ave. S.E.
East Bldg., 2nd Floor, E23–306
Washington, DC 20590
(202) 366–4831
Patricia Klinger, FOIA public liaison
Madeline Bush, FOIA officer
(202) 366–0273

DATA AND STATISTICS

Data and statistics concerning pipelines and hazardous materials are available through the PHMSA website, at www.phmsa.dot.gov/resources/data-stats and www.phmsa.dot.gov/library/reading-room, or by calling PHMSA Governmental, International, and Public Affairs (*see above*).

PUBLICATIONS

Pipeline and hazardous materials publications are available through the PHMSA website, including the Electronic Reading Room, or by calling PHMSA Governmental, International, and Public Affairs (*see above*).

Reference Resources

LIBRARY

DOT Library

1200 New Jersey Ave. S.E., #W12–300
Washington, DC 20590
(202) 366–0746

(800) 853–1351
Law Library: (202) 366–0749
Amanda Wilson, director
(202) 366–2480
Internet: www.ntl.bts.gov; www.dotlibrary.dot.gov
E-mail: library@dot.gov
Hours: 8:00 a.m. to 5:00 p.m.

DOCKETS

DOT Dockets Office

1200 New Jersey Ave. S.E., #W12-140
Washington, DC 20590
(202) 366–9322
(202) 366–9826
(800) 647–5527
Hours: 9:00 a.m. to 5:00 p.m.
Barbara Hairston, program manager

All PHMSA rulemaking materials are available through the DOT's Dockets Office, open to the public from 10:00 a.m. to 5:00 p.m. (call from the front desk for building escort); these are also available at the Electronic Reading Room on the PHMSA website, www.phmsa.dot.gov/library/reading-room. Federal dockets are also available from the online Docket Management System at http://docketsinfo.dot.gov and at www.regulations.gov. (*See appendix for Searching and Commenting on Regulations: Regulations.gov.*)

RULES AND REGULATIONS

PHMSA rules and regulations are published in the *Code of Federal Regulations,* Title 49, Chapter I, Parts 100–199. Proposed regulations, new final regulations, and updates to the *Code of Federal Regulations* are published daily in the *Federal Register.* (*See appendix for details on how to obtain and use these publications.*) The *Federal Register* and the *Code of Federal Regulations* may be accessed online at www.archives.gov/federal-register/cfr; the site contains a link to the federal government's regulatory website at www.regulations.gov (*see appendix*).

■ LEGISLATION

The Office of Hazardous Materials Safety and the Office of Pipeline Safety carry out their responsibilities under authority granted in the following laws:

Mineral Leasing Act of 1920 (41 Stat. 437, 30 U.S.C. 185). Signed by the president Feb. 25, 1920. Authorized inspections of pipelines that have right-of-way through federal lands.

Department of Transportation Act (80 Stat. 937, 49 U.S.C. 1655). Signed by the president Oct. 15, 1966. Created the cabinet-level Department of Transportation.

Natural Gas Pipeline Safety Act of 1968 (82 Stat. 720, 49 U.S.C. 1671). Signed by the president Aug. 12, 1968. Authorized the secretary of transportation to prescribe safety standards for the transportation of natural and other gas by pipeline.

Deepwater Port Act of 1974 (88 Stat. 2126, 33 U.S.C. 1501). Signed by the president Jan. 3, 1975. Established a licensing and regulatory program governing offshore deepwater ports development.

Hazardous Materials Transportation Act (HMTA) (88 Stat. 2156, 49 U.S.C. 1801). Signed by the president Jan. 3, 1975. Strengthened the laws governing the transportation of hazardous materials.

Hazardous Liquid Pipeline Safety Act of 1979 (93 Stat. 989, 49 U.S.C. 2001). Signed by the president Nov. 30, 1979. Clarified and expanded the authority of the DOT over liquefied natural gas and transportation safety. Established a statutory framework to regulate the transport of hazardous liquids.

Nuclear Waste Policy Act of 1982 (96 Stat. 2241, 42 U.S.C. 10157). Signed by the president Jan. 7, 1982. Assigned responsibility for licensing and regulating the transport of spent nuclear fuel to the DOT.

Comprehensive Omnibus Budget Reconciliation Act of 1986 (100 Stat. 140, 49 U.S.C. app. 1682a). Signed by the president April 7, 1986. Placed responsibility on the DOT for the establishment and collection of fees for natural gas and hazardous materials pipelines.

Comprehensive Environmental Response, Compensation, and Liability Act of 1986 (Superfund) (100 Stat. 1695, 42 U.S.C. 9656). Signed by the president Oct. 17, 1986. Made common or contract carriers liable for damages or remedial actions resulting from the release of hazardous materials in transport, unless the carrier can demonstrate a lack of knowledge of the identity or nature of the substance.

Sanitary Food Transportation Act of 1990 (104 Stat. 1213, 49 U.S.C. app. 2801 note). Signed by the president Nov. 3, 1990. Prohibited transportation of most solid waste in refrigerated vehicles used to transport food, and transportation of some nonfood products in cargo tanks used to transport food.

Hazardous Materials Transportation Uniform Safety Act of 1990 (104 Stat. 3244, 49 U.S.C. app. 1801 note). Signed by the president Nov. 16, 1990. Strengthened the HMTA to include creation of a grant program to provide assistance to state and local governments. Authorized establishing regulations for the safe transportation of hazardous materials in intrastate, interstate, and foreign commerce.

Pipeline Safety Act of 1992 (106 Stat. 3289, 49 U.S.C. app. 1671 note). Signed by the president Oct. 24, 1992. Authorized the DOT to take several near-term actions to protect the environment, increased pipeline inspection requirements, and instituted a national program to inspect underwater pipelines.

Transportation Equity Act for the 21st Century (TEA-21) (112 Stat. 154, 23 U.S.C. 143). Signed by the president June 9, 1998. Reauthorized the federal research and safety programs under the Intermodal Surface Transportation Efficiency Act of 1991 (ISTEA) from 1998 through 2003.

Pipeline Safety Improvement Act of 2002 (116 Stat. 2985, 49 U.S.C. 60101). Signed by the president Dec. 17, 2002. Required the inspection of all major natural gas pipelines in densely populated areas within ten years, followed by reinspections every seven years. Authorized funds for research and development to improve all aspects of pipeline quality. Increased the DOT's authority to require operators to fix pipelines that have a potentially unsafe condition. Gave DOT the authority to increase states' involvement in the oversight of interstate pipeline transportation.

Norman Y. Mineta Research and Special Programs Improvement Act (118 Stat. 2423, 41 U.S.C. 1). Signed by the president Nov. 30, 2004. Amended federal transportation law to replace the RSPA with the PHMSA and RITA.

Safe, Accountable, Flexible, and Efficient Transportation Equity Act of 2005 (SAFETEA) (23 U.S.C. 134). Signed by the president Aug. 10, 2005. Reauthorized federal surface transportation programs through fiscal year 2009. Directed the PHMSA to transmit certain hazardous material information to FMCSA. Authorized the DOT to enter into grants, cooperative agreements, and other transactions with federal agencies, state and local governments, other public entities, private organizations, and persons to conduct transportation research. Expanded the scope of federal safe transportation of hazardous materials regulations to include shipping and packaging companies.

The Pipeline Inspection, Protection, Enforcement, and Safety Act of 2006 (49 U.S.C. 60102, 60115). Signed by the president Dec. 29, 2006. Required that PHMSA issue regulations subjecting low-stress hazardous liquid pipelines to the same standards and regulations as other hazardous liquid pipelines with some limited exceptions.

Implementing Recommendations of the 9/11 Commission Act of 2007 (121 Stat. 444). Signed by the president Aug. 3, 2007. Directed the transportation secretary to publish a final rule with respect to the railroad routing of security-sensitive hazardous materials.

The Pipeline Safety, Regulatory Certainty, and Job Creation Act of 2011 (125 Stat. 1904, 49 U.S.C. 60101 note). Signed by the president Jan. 3, 2012. Directed the transportation secretary to revise regulations pertaining to communications of hazmat incidents, enforcement hearings, national pipeline mapping system requirements, and gas and liquid pipeline integrity management improvements. Increased civil penalties for violations. Reauthorized PHMSA's federal pipeline safety programs through fiscal year 2015.

Moving Ahead for Progress in the 21st Century Act (MAP-21) (126 Stat. 405, 23 U.S.C. 101 note). Signed by the president July 6, 2012. Div. C, Title III: Hazardous Materials Transportation Safety Improvement Act of 2012 requires revised regulations to address transportation of hazardous materials. Includes provision to improve training for first responders and hazmat inspectors and investigators. Includes new requirements for data collection of hazmat incidents. Mandates new state responsibilities relating to highway routing disclosures. Increases civil penalties for violations.

■ REGIONAL OFFICES

Office of Hazardous Materials Safety

CENTRAL

(IA, IL, IN, KS, MI, MN, MO, ND, NE, OH, SD, WI)
2300 E. Devon Ave., #478

Des Plaines, IL 60018–4696
(847) 294–8580
Kip Wills, regional chief

EASTERN
(CT, DC, DE, MA, MD, ME, NH, NJ, NY, PA, RI, VA,
VT, WV)
820 Bear Tavern Rd., #306
West Trenton, NJ 08628
(609) 989–2256
Marc Nichols (acting), regional chief

SOUTHERN
(AL, FL, GA, KY, MS, NC, PR, SC, TN, VI)
233 Peachtree St. N.E., #602
Atlanta, GA 30303
(404) 832–1140
John Heneghan, regional chief

SOUTHWEST
(AR, LA, NM, OK, TX)
8701 S. Gessner Rd., #900
Houston, TX 77074
(713) 272–2820
Jay Sorah, regional chief

WESTERN
(AK, AS, AZ, CA, CO, GU, HI, ID, Northern Mariana
Islands, MT, NV, OR, UT, WA, WY)
3401 Centrelake Dr., #550B
Ontario, CA 91761
(909) 937–3279
Sean E. Lynum, regional chief

Office of Pipeline Safety

CENTRAL
(IA, IL, IN, KS, MI, MN, MO, ND, NE, OH, SD, WI)
901 Locust St., #462

Kansas City, MO 64106–2641
(816) 329–3800
Allan Beshore, director

EASTERN
(CT, DC, DE, MA, MD, ME, NH, NJ, NY, PA, RI, VA,
VT, WV)
820 Bear Tavern Road, #103
West Trenton, NJ 08628
(609) 989–2171
Byron Coy, director

SOUTHERN
(AL, FL, GA, KY, MS, NC, PR, SC, TN)
233 Peachtree St., #600
Atlanta, GA 30303
(404) 832–1147
Wayne Lemoi, director

SOUTHWEST
(AR, LA, NM, OK, TX)
8701 S. Gessner, #1110
Houston, TX 77074
(713) 272–2859
Rodrick M. Seeley, director

WESTERN
(AK, AS, AZ, CA, CO, GU, HI, ID, MT, Northern
Mariana Islands, NV, OR, UT, WA, WY)
12300 W. Dakota Ave., #110
Lakewood, CO 80228
(720) 963–3160
Christopher Hoidal, director

PHMSA Pipeline Safety Training Center
3700 South MacArthur Blvd., Suite B
Oklahoma City, OK 73179
(405) 686–2310
Charlie Helm (acting), director

Research and Innovative Technology Administration

1200 New Jersey Ave. S.E., Washington, DC 20590
Internet: www.rita.dot.gov

The Research and Innovative Technology Administration (RITA) enables the Department of Transportation (DOT) to manage more effectively the DOT's research activities, expedite implementation of innovative technologies, and assist in the training of DOT personnel and the formulation of regulations. RITA was formed when the Norman Y. Mineta Research and Special Programs Improvement Act of 2004 split the Research and Special Programs Administration (RSPA) into two new administrations: the RITA and the Pipeline and Hazardous Materials Safety Administration (PHMSA) (*p. 818*).

Under the reorganization, RITA's resources are used to coordinate and advance transportation research efforts within the DOT; support transportation professionals in their research efforts through grants and consulting services, as well as professional development through training centers; inform transportation decision makers on intermodal and multimodal transportation topics through the release of statistics, research reports, and a variety of information products; and train DOT personnel in how to work with regulations.

RITA issues notices of proposed rulemaking for data collection and other related agency functions. In July 2011 RITA proposed a new rule to require airlines to report sixteen additional categories of fee revenue in addition to the baggage and reservation change fees; this includes sources such as food, entertainment, seating assignments, and other ancillary fees. The rule also requires airlines to report the number of checked bags and mishandled wheelchairs. The proposal would revise reporting requirements to improve data collection on the amount airlines receive from different, specific types of fees. Identification of all ancillary fees and the amounts collected by each airline would improve information available to the public and help determine the impact of the increasing use of these fees on the Airport and Airways Trust Fund.

The following are major RITA research and training offices:

Bureau of Transportation Statistics (BTS). The Intermodal Surface Transportation Efficiency Act (ISTEA) of 1991 created the BTS to administer data collection, analysis, and reporting, and to ensure the most cost-effective use of transportation-monitoring resources. Some of the BTS data collection and reporting includes airline traffic data, airfares data, airline on-time data, freight data and statistics, border crossing/entry data, transportation indicators, and national transportation statistics. BTS became a part of RITA in 2005.

Transportation Safety Institute (TSI). The TSI is a federal cost recovery agency that conducts worldwide safety, security, and environmental training, and develops products and/or services for both the public and private sectors. RITA is the institute's parent organization within the DOT.

The TSI was established in 1971 to help DOT modal administrations accomplish their mission-essential training requirements. Since its inception, the TSI has expanded its clientele to keep up with the needs of the department and the transportation industry. The TSI offers premier transit, aviation, pipeline, motor carrier, highway safety, hazardous material, and risk management training nationally and internationally.

University Transportation Centers (UTCs). The 1987 Surface Transportation and Uniform Relocation Assistance Act initiated the UTC program at ten sites across the country to advance U.S. expertise and technology transfer. The UTC program has been reauthorized several times under various omnibus transportation bills. The Intermodal Surface Transportation Efficiency Act (ISTEA) of 1991 added four national centers and six university research institutes (URI). Each URI had a specific transportation research and development mandate. The Transportation Equity Act for the 21st Century (TEA-21) of 1998 established thirteen new UTCs. The Safe, Accountable, Flexible, Efficient Transportation Equity Act (SAFETEA) expanded the UTC program and authorized up to sixty UTCs throughout the United States. Twenty of these centers were chosen in a competitive selection and forty centers are located at institutions named in the legislation.

By 2011 Congress had not passed an omnibus transportation reauthorization bill since SAFETEA expired in 2009. In 2012 Congress passed a limited two-year transportation bill, the Moving Ahead for Progress in the 21st Century Act (MAP-21). MAP-21 authorized additional funds for grants to establish and operate up to thirty-five UTCs throughout the United States. The UTC grants program has not been reauthorized and the future of the program is uncertain.

Intelligent Transportation System (ITS). The ITS research program focuses on intelligent vehicles, intelligent infrastructure, and the creation of an intelligent transportation system. The program supports the overall advancement of ITS through investments in major research initiatives, exploratory studies, and a deployment support program.

Volpe National Transportation Systems Center (TSC). Headquartered in Cambridge, MA, the TSC is the DOT's research, analysis, and systems engineering facility. Funding is generated through project agreements with various clients within the DOT and other federal agencies, such as the Federal Aviation Administration (*p. 783*), the Federal Highway Administration (*p. 791*), the Office of the Secretary of Transportation, the Environmental Protection Agency (*p. 67*), and the Departments of Defense, Energy, and State. State and local governments also use the center's resources.

The Volpe Center is organized into four technical centers. Each technical center applies its technical capabilities to Transportation Department strategic goals and national transportation priorities:

Infrastructure Systems and Technology monitors demands placed on the existing and future transportation infrastructure and provides technical support in inspection, maintenance, and rehabilitation, including vehicles, guideways, and intermodal facilities. It also addresses issues including physical and cyber security, logistics management systems, and maritime domain awareness, covering local, regional, national, and global freight logistics and transportation infrastructure. Further, the center researches innovative applications of advanced communications, navigation, and information technologies to enhance transportation safety, mobility, and energy/environmental performance, including vehicle crash avoidance, electronic systems safety and resilience, technology assessment, field test and evaluation, and strategic planning and research program management.

Safety Management and Human Factors improves transportation safety by developing and applying innovative safety management and human factors processes and principles to sponsored research and demonstration projects.

Policy, Planning, and Environment informs transportation decision makers regarding the planning, development, management, operations, and financing of transportation systems and agencies. It also provides critical data and analyses to support energy independence, transportation innovations, and transportation-related climate-change mitigation and adaptation.

Center for Air Traffic Systems and Operations supports the development of aviation systems and procedures that alleviate air traffic congestion, improve safety, and mitigate environmental impacts. The center specializes in planning, research, testing, and evaluation activities in support of the development of the Next-Generation Air Transportation System (NextGen) at the Federal Aviation Administration (*p. 783*).

KEY PERSONNEL

Assistant Secretary
Gregory D. Winfree . . . . (202) 366–4180

Fax. . . . . (202) 366–3759
Deputy Assistant Secretary
Ellen Partridge. . . . . (202) 366–4180
Chief Counsel
Ellen Partridge. . . . . (202) 366–1580
Executive Director
Audrey Farley. (202) 366–4112
Budget and Finance
Vacant . . . . (202) 366–0314
Bureau of Transportation Statistics
Patricia S. Hu . . . . (202) 366–6268
Civil Rights
Daryl Hart. . . . . (202) 366–0288
Governmental, International, and Public Affairs
Jane Mellow . . . . (202) 366–4792
Intelligent Transportation Systems, Joint Program Office
Kenneth Leonard. . . . . (202) 366–5719
National Space-Based PNT Coordination
Harold W. Martin III . . . . (202) 482–5809
National Transportation Library
Amanda Wilson. . . . . (202) 366–3492
Positioning, Navigation and Timing, and Spectrum Management
Karen Van Dyke . . . . (202) 366–3180
Research, Development, and Technology
Kevin Womack . . . . (202) 366–5447
Transportation Safety Institute
(P.O. Box 25082, Oklahoma City, OK 73125–5050)
Christine Lawrence. . . . . (405) 954–3153
University Transportation Centers
Kevin Womack . . . . (202) 366–5447
Volpe National Transportation Systems Center
(55 Broadway Cambridge, MA 02142)
Robert C. Johns . . . . (617) 494–2306
Air Traffic Systems and Operations
Steven Lang . . . . (617) 494–2357
Infrastructure Systems and Technology
Luisa Paiewonsky . . . . (617) 494–2364
Policy, Planning, and Environment
Gregg Fleming. . . . . (617) 494–2018
Safety Management and Human Factors
Stephen Popkin . . . . (617) 494–3532

INFORMATION SOURCES

Internet
Agency website: www.rita.dot.gov. Comprehensive website includes information about RITA, as well as publications, reports, news releases, data and statistics, and links to related Internet sites.

Telephone Contacts
RITA Main . . . . (202) 366–4180
DOT Main. . . . . (202) 366–4000
Reference Service . . . . (800) 853–1351
Fax . . . . (202) 366–3759
Federal Relay Service TTY . . . . (800) 877–8339

Information and Publications

KEY OFFICES

RITA Public Affairs
Bureau of Transportation Statistics
1200 New Jersey Ave. S.E.
Washington, DC 20590
(202) 366–5128
David (Dave) Smallen, director
(202) 366–5568

Answers general inquiries from the press. Public inquiries should be directed to the RITA Reference Service at (800) 853–1351 or e-mail: answers@bts.gov.

Transportation Safety Institute
6500 S. MacArthur Blvd.
P.O. Box 25082
Oklahoma City, OK 73125–0082
(405) 954–3153
Christine Lawrence, director
Internet: www.tsi.dot.gov

Provides training in transit, aviation, pipelines, motor carriers, highway safety, hazardous material, and risk management in both the public and private sectors.

Freedom of Information
Research and Innovative Technology Administration
Office of Chief Counsel (RTC)
1200 New Jersey Ave. S.E., E35–330, RTC
Washington, DC 20590
Kathy Ray, FOIA officer
(202) 366–1580

DATA AND STATISTICS

Bureau of Transportation Statistics
1200 New Jersey Ave. S.E.
Washington, DC 20590
(202) 366–3282
(800) 853–1351
Patricia S. Hu, director
Internet: www.bts.gov

Collects, analyzes, and publishes a comprehensive, cross-modal set of transportation statistics.

Volpe National Transportation Systems Center
55 Broadway
Cambridge, MA 02142
(617) 494–2000
(617) 494–2306
Robert C. Johns, director
Internet: www.volpe.dot.gov

Provides data and statistics on transportation research, as well as transportation systems engineering and analysis services.

Reference Resources

LIBRARY

DOT Library/National Transportation Library
1200 New Jersey Ave. S.E., #W12–300
Washington, DC 20590
(202) 366–0746
(800) 853–1351
Law Library (202) 366–0749
Amanda Wilson, director
(202) 366–2480
Internet: www.ntl.bts.gov
E-mail: library@dot.gov
Hours: 8:00 a.m. to 5:00 p.m.

The National Transportation Library is the primary repository for DOT technical and legal information and research, maintaining both digital and traditional library environments. Resources include book and journal collections, reference services (including the website's Ask-a-Librarian service), electronic database access, and interlibrary loan services. The library's website also provides an extensive list of libraries across the United States that have significant resources on transportation issues.

DOCKETS
DOT Dockets Office
1200 New Jersey Ave. S.E., #W12–140
Washington, DC 20590
(202) 366–9322
(202) 366–9826
(800) 647–5527
Hours: 9:00 a.m. to 5:00 p.m.
Barbara Hairston, program manager

All RITA rulemaking materials are available through the DOT's Docket Office. Federal dockets are also available at www.regulations.gov. (*See appendix for Searching and Commenting on Regulations: Regulations.gov.*)

RULES AND REGULATIONS
RITA's Office of Airline Information, in conjunction with its Office of Chief Counsel and the Office of the assistant secretary for Aviation and International Affairs, issues rules and regulations in the *Code of Federal Regulations,* Title 49, Chapter XI, Part 1420. RITA has not yet exercised any independent rulemaking capabilities but is not precluded from doing so in the future. Proposed regulations, new final regulations, and updates to the *Code of Federal Regulations* are published daily in the *Federal Register.* (*See appendix for details on how to obtain and use these publications.*) The *Federal Register* and the *Code of Federal Regulations* may be accessed online at www.archives.gov/federal-register/cfr; the site contains a link to the federal government's regulatory website at www.regulations.gov (*see appendix*).

▊ LEGISLATION
Department of Transportation Act (80 Stat. 937, 49 U.S.C. 1655). Signed by the president Oct. 15, 1966. Created the cabinet-level Department of Transportation.

Surface Transportation and Uniform Relocation Assistance Act of 1987 (101 Stat. 133, 49 U.S.C. 1601). Vetoed by the president March 27, 1987; veto overridden April 2, 1987. Authorized mass transit funding through Sept. 30, 1991. Reauthorized existing highway and mass transit policies and programs. Established the UTC program.

Intermodal Surface Transportation Efficiency Act of 1991 (ISTEA) (105 Stat. 1914, 49 U.S.C. 101 note). Signed by the president Dec. 18, 1991. Authorized funding for incentive programs to improve occupant safety and to prevent drunk driving. Increased funding to enhance transportation efficiency. Established the Bureau of Transportation Statistics.

Transportation Equity Act for the 21st Century (TEA-21) (112 Stat. 154, 23 U.S.C. 143). Signed by the president June 9, 1998. Reauthorized the federal research and safety programs under the Intermodal Surface Transportation Efficiency Act of 1991 from 1998 through 2003.

Norman Y. Mineta Research and Special Programs Improvement Act (118 Stat. 2423, 41 U.S.C. 1). Signed by the president Nov. 30, 2004. Amended federal transportation law to replace the RSPA with RITA and the PHMSA. Transferred the Bureau of Transportation Statistics (BTS) to RITA. Transferred the powers and duties of the RSPA administrator to the RITA administrator. Established the Office of Intermodalism within RITA.

Safe, Accountable, Flexible, and Efficient Transportation Equity Act of 2005 (SAFETEA) (23 U.S.C. 134). Signed by the president Aug. 10, 2005. Reauthorized federal transportation programs through fiscal year 2009. Authorized the DOT to enter into grants, cooperative agreements, and other transactions with federal agencies, state and local governments, other public entities, private organizations, and persons to conduct transportation research.

Moving Ahead for Progress in the 21st Century Act (MAP-21) (126 Stat. 405, 23 U.S.C. 101 note). Signed by the president July 6, 2012. Codifies federal law concerning the Bureau of Transportation Statistics (BTS) in the Research and Innovative Technology Administration (RITA).

Saint Lawrence Seaway Development Corporation

Massena Office: 180 Andrews St., #1, Massena, NY 13662
Washington Office: 1200 New Jersey Ave. S.E.,
Washington, DC 20590
Internet: www.seaway.dot.gov

The Saint Lawrence Seaway Development Corporation (SLSDC) is a government-owned corporation. Created by an act of Congress in 1954 to oversee the construction of U.S. facilities for the Saint Lawrence Seaway project, it joined the Department of Transportation (DOT) under the Department of Transportation Act of 1966.

The corporation is headed by an administrator who is appointed by the president. The agency's offices are divided between Washington, DC, and Massena, NY. Funding for the corporation is appropriated by Congress.

The corporation is responsible for the operation and maintenance of the section of the Saint Lawrence Seaway within U.S. territorial limits, between the port of Montreal and Lake Erie. It conducts trade development programs and coordinates all activities with its Canadian counterpart, the Saint Lawrence Seaway Management Corporation (successor to the Saint Lawrence Seaway Authority [SLSA] of Canada). Together they develop safety standards and set toll rates for vessels and cargoes passing through the seaway, manage vessel traffic, publish transit regulations, and maintain navigational aids. The SLSDC also encourages the development of trade through the Great Lakes Seaway System.

In 1997 the SLSDC, along with the U.S. Coast Guard *(see p. 658)* and the SLSA, began to inspect all vessels making their first inbound transit of the seaway in compliance with new environmental laws, including the Oil Pollution Act and the Nonindigenous Aquatic Nuisance Prevention and Control Act of 1990.

The Maritime Transportation Security Act of 2002 amended the Ports and Waterways Safety Act of 1972 to authorize the use of Coast Guard personnel to deter or respond to acts of terrorism. The act also amended the Ports and Waterways Safety Act to require all commercial vessels entering U.S. waters to provide specified information, including name, route, and a description of any hazardous conditions or cargo.

■ KEY PERSONNEL

Administrator
Betty Sutton . . . . (202) 366–0091
Fax. . . . . (202) 366–7147
Deputy Administrator
Craig H. Middlebrook . . . . (202) 366–0105
Associate Administrator
Salvatore (Sal) Pisani. . . . . (315) 764–3209
Fax . . . .(315) 764–3235
Chief Counsel
Carrie Mann Lavigne . . . . (315) 764–3231
Senior Advisor
Anita K. Blackman . . . . (202) 366–0091
Congressional Affairs and Public Relations
Nancy Alcalde . . . . (202) 366–6114
Budget and Economic Development
Kevin O'Malley . . . . (202) 366–8982
Finance and Administration
Nancy Scott (acting) . . . . (315) 764–3273
Trade Development
Rebecca A. Spruill. . . . . (202) 366–5418

■ INFORMATION SOURCES

Internet
Agency website: www.seaway.dot.gov. Includes agency news, the current toll schedule, a link to the Saint Lawrence Seaway Management Corporation, and general information about the seaway.

Telephone Contacts
SLSDC Main Contact . . . .(202) 366–0091
General Information . . . .(800) 785–2779
Massena Office. . . . .(315) 764–3200
Eisenhower Lock Visitors' Center
  (open late May through early
  September) . . . .(315) 769–2422
Federal Relay Service TTY . . . .(800) 877–8339

Information and Publications

KEY OFFICES

SLSDC Office of Congressional and Public Relations

1200 New Jersey Ave. S.E.
Washington, DC 20590
(202) 366–6114
Nancy Alcalde, director

Handles policy matters and general inquiries with a national scope. Most questions concerning the immediate region will be referred to the Massena Public Information Office.

Freedom of Information

1200 New Jersey Ave. S.E.
Washington, DC 20590
FOIA Requester Center: (202) 366–6510
Fern Kaufman, FOIA public liaison
E-mail: foia.request@dot.gov

PUBLICATIONS

The SLSDC website and the Office of Congressional and Public Relations provide extensive information on the seaway, as well as numerous reports, studies, maps, fact sheets, and the annual report of the agency. For further special requests or information, e-mail publications@seaway.ca.

Reference Resources

LIBRARY

DOT Library

1200 New Jersey Ave. S.E., #W12–300
Washington, DC 20590
(202) 366–0746
(800) 853–1351
Law Library (202) 366–0749
Amanda Wilson, director
(202) 366–2480
Internet: www.ntl.bts.gov
E-mail: library@dot.gov
Hours: 8:00 a.m. to 5:00 p.m.

DOCKETS

DOT Dockets Office
1200 New Jersey Ave. S.E., #W12–140
Washington, DC 20590
(202) 366–9322
(202) 366–9826
(800) 647–5527
Hours: 9:00 a.m. to 5:00 p.m.
Barbara Hairston, program manager

The SLSDC maintains an electronic reading room containing materials related to agency rulemakings and other administrative proceedings. Dockets and other records may also be examined, in paper form, at the DOT Reading Room, located at the above address. A computer terminal and printer are available at this location, where Electronic Reading Room records may be accessed. The best source of information is the director of the office that has jurisdiction over a particular rule. Notices of rulemakings listed in the *Federal Register* include the name of a staff member to contact for additional information and the location where the docket may be inspected. Federal dockets are also available at www.regulations.gov. (*See appendix for Searching and Commenting on Regulations: Regulations.gov.*)

RULES AND REGULATIONS

SLSDC rules and regulations are published in the *Code of Federal Regulations,* Title 33, Chapter IV, Parts 400–499. Proposed regulations, new final regulations, and updates to the *Code of Federal Regulations* are published in the daily *Federal Register. (See appendix on how to obtain and use these publications.)* The *Federal Register* and the *Code of Federal Regulations* may be accessed online at www. archives.gov/federal-register/cfr; this site also contains a link to the federal government's regulatory website at www .regulations.gov *(see appendix).*

■ LEGISLATION

The SLSDC carries out its responsibilities under authority granted by:

Saint Lawrence Seaway Act, as amended (68 Stat. 92, 33 U.S.C. 981 et seq.). Signed by the president May 13, 1954. Created the Saint Lawrence Seaway Development Corporation.

Ports and Waterways Safety Act of 1972 (86 Stat. 424, 33 U.S.C. 1221). Signed by the president July 10, 1972. Authorized establishment of standards and regulations to promote safety of ports, harbors, and navigable waters of the United States.

Port and Tanker Safety Act of 1978 (92 Stat. 1471, 33 U.S.C. 1221). Signed by the president Oct. 17, 1978. Expanded and strengthened regulations concerning vessel safety standards.

Water Resources Development Act of 1986 (100 Stat. 4102, 33 U.S.C. 2234a). Signed by the president Nov. 17, 1986. Instituted a tax on cargo loaded or unloaded in U.S. ports; revenue from this tax is held by the Harbor Maintenance Trust Fund and appropriated by Congress for the costs of maintaining and operating the Saint Lawrence Seaway.

Maritime Transportation Security Act of 2002 (116 Stat. 2064, 46 U.S.C. 2101). Signed by the president Nov. 25, 2002. Amended the Merchant Marine Act of 1936 to require the DOT to develop antiterrorism plans at U.S. ports and foreign ports where U.S.-bound shipments originate. Amended the Ports and Waterways Safety Act of 1972 to authorize the use of qualified armed Coast Guard personnel to deter or respond to acts of terrorism. Amended the Ports and Waterways Safety Act to require all commercial vessels entering U.S. waters to provide specified information, including name, route, and a description of any hazardous conditions or cargo.

Surface Transportation Board

395 E St. S.W., Washington, DC 20423–0001
Internet: www.stb.dot.gov

The Surface Transportation Board (STB), an agency within the Department of Transportation (DOT), was created on Jan. 1, 1996, by the ICC Termination Act of 1995. The STB is the successor to the Interstate Commerce Commission (ICC), an independent agency that had been established in 1887. The STB consists of a chair, a vice chair, and an additional board member, who are appointed by the president and confirmed by the Senate. Each board member serves a five-year term. The STB is decisionally independent, although it is administratively affiliated with the Department of Transportation.

The STB is an adjudicatory and economic regulatory agency; it adjudicates disputes and regulates interstate surface transportation through various laws pertaining to different modes of surface transportation. The STB's general responsibilities include the oversight of firms engaged in transportation in interstate and in foreign commerce to the extent that it takes place within the United States, or between or among points in the contiguous United States and points in Alaska, Hawaii, or U.S. territories or possessions. The principal mission of the board, however, is to facilitate commerce by providing an effective forum for efficient dispute resolution and facilitation of appropriate market-based business transactions through rulemakings and case disposition.

The STB is responsible for several aspects of the railroad industry: review of railroad mergers, settlement of railroad rate disputes, regulation of some new rail line construction, transfer of rail lines or trackage rights, rate regulation, and approval of rail line abandonment proposals. Regulation of abandonments has been reduced, although the STB remains involved in the transition of railroad routes to trails or other public rights-of-way. Under the National Trails System Act, the STB is authorized to assist carriers who wish to rail-bank their corridors as an alternative to a complete abandonment of the line. Under the rail-banking status, the railroad may enter into an agreement with an entity that would like to use the banked rail line as a trail or park until it is again needed for rail use. The STB also has jurisdiction over certain trucking company, moving van, and noncontiguous ocean shipping company rate matters; certain intercity passenger bus company structure, financial, and operational matters; and rates and services of certain pipelines not regulated by the Federal Energy Regulatory Commission (*p. 181*).

The following offices carry out the functions of the STB:

Office of Environmental Analysis (OEA) is responsible for directing the environmental review process in pertinent cases before the agency, conducting independent analyses of all environmental data, and making environmental recommendations to the board members.

Office of Economics (OE) supports the STB's decision-making process through economic, cost, financial, and engineering analyses in railroad maximum-rate proceedings, mergers, line abandonments, and line-construction and trackage-rights cases before the agency.

Office of Public Assistance, Governmental Affairs, and Compliance (OPAGAC) serves as the STB's primary contact point with the public. The office interacts with members of Congress, executive agencies, state and local governments, news media, stakeholders, and other interested persons to provide information and informal guidance as to the STB's procedures, regulations, and actions. OPAGAC also serves as the agency's compliance arm, overseeing the actions of transportation carriers subject to the agency's jurisdiction to ensure that these carriers are operating in compliance with their statutory responsibilities.

Office of Proceedings (OP) has primary responsibility for developing the public record in formal cases filed with the STB, making recommendations regarding the resolution of issues presented in those cases, and preparing the decisions issued by the board. OP is a legal office, consisting almost entirely of attorneys and paralegal specialists.

■ KEY PERSONNEL

Chair
  Daniel R Elliott III. . . . . (202) 245–0220
    Fax. . . . . (202) 245–0450
Vice Chair
  Ann D. Begeman. . . . . (202) 245–0200
Board Member
  Debra L. Miller . . . . (202) 245–0210
Administration
  Cynthia T. Brown . . . . (202) 245–0384
Congressional Liaison
  Mary Turek. . . . . (202) 245–0233

Economics

    William F. Huneke . . . . (202) 245–0325

Environmental Analysis

    Victoria J. Rutson . . . . (202) 245–0295

Financial Services

    Marcin Skomial (acting). . . . . (202) 245–0346

General Counsel

    Craig Keats . . . . (202) 245–0260

    Fax . . . . (202) 245–0460

Management Information and Legal Support Services

    Andrea Pope-Matheson . . . . (202) 245–0363

    Legal Counsel I

        Julia Farr. . . . . (202) 245–0359

    Legal Counsel II

        Joseph H. Dettmar . . . . (202) 245–0395

Managing Director

    Leland L. Gardner . . . . (202) 245–0324

    Fax . . . . (202) 245–0454

Proceedings

    Rachel D. Campbell . . . . (202) 245–0357

    Fax . . . . (202) 245–0464

Public Assistance, Government Affairs, and Compliance

    Lucille Marvin . . . . (202) 245–0238

■ INFORMATION SOURCES

Internet

    Agency website: www.stb.dot.gov. Comprehensive website maintains information on the function of the STB. Publications, news releases, dockets, and data and statistics are available for viewing or for downloading.

Telephone Contacts

    General Information . . . .(202) 245–0245

    Federal Relay Service TTY . . . .(800) 877–8339

Information and Publications

KEY OFFICES

STB Public Assistance, Government Affairs, and Compliance

    395 E St. S.W., #1202

    Washington, DC 20423–0001

    (202) 245–0238

    Lucille Marvin, director

    Mary Turek, congressional liaison, (202) 245–0233

    Provides information for Congress, the press, and the public. Helps businesses resolve surface transportation regulation problems. Informs the STB of the nature and status of these problems and advises it of the public-interest aspects of rail regulatory actions. Assists individuals, consumer groups, small communities, small shippers, and public utility commissioners participating in STB proceedings.

STB Office of Proceedings

    395 E St. S.W., #1002

    Washington, DC 20423–0001

    (202) 245–0350

    Rachel D. Campbell, director

    Provides legal and policy advice to the board. Responsible for accepting, docketing, and processing applications to construct or abandon railroad lines, to consolidate, or to merge. Also processes various exemptions, complaints about carrier practices and rates, and rulemaking proceedings approved by the board.

Freedom of Information

    395 E St. S.W., #1263

    Washington, DC 20423–0001

    (202) 245–0269

    Marilyn R. Levitt, FOIA public liaison

    E-mail: FOIA.Privacy@stb.dot.gov

DATA AND STATISTICS

STB Office of the Managing Director

    395 E St. S.W., #1100

    Washington, DC 20423–0001

    (202) 245–0324

    Leland L. Gardner, director

    Contact this office for information about available statistical reports and publications. Reports, statistics, and data also are available on the agency's website.

MEETINGS

    Under the Government in the Sunshine Act, board meetings are open to the public unless the subject of the meeting is specific litigation or discussion of an opinion on a pending court case. Notices of scheduled board meetings are listed on the website and in the *Federal Register*. (*See website for a link to the Federal Register website or see the appendix for information on how to obtain and use the Federal Register.*)

PUBLICATIONS

    For information and publications, visit the STB website or contact STB Congressional and Public Services. Publications available include *STB Annual Report to Congress; Abandonments and Alternatives to Abandonments; So You Want to Start a Small Railroad; Request for Interim Trail Use;* as well as numerous reports and studies.

Reference Resources

LIBRARY/DOCKETS

STB Library and Docket Room

    395 E St. S.W., #131

    Washington, DC 20423

    (202) 245–0406

    Fax (202) 245–0461

    Christine L. Glaab, librarian

    Hours: 8:30 a.m. to 5:00 p.m.

    Assists the STB and the general public in researching court cases involving surface transportation problems and cross-referencing significant information such as date, decision, and precedent. Dockets and recordations may be examined and are also available on the website at www.stb.dot.gov/service%20list/servicelist.nsf/svclist caller?OpenForm and www.stb.dot.gov/recordations.nsf. Library and Docket Room open to the public. Federal dockets are also available at www.regulations.gov. (*See appendix for Searching and Commenting on Regulations: Regulations.gov.*)

RULES AND REGULATIONS

STB rules and regulations are published in the *Code of Federal Regulations,* Title 49, Chapter X, Parts 1000–1399. Proposed rules, new final rules, and updates to the *Code of Federal Regulations* are published in the daily *Federal Register. (See appendix for information on how to obtain and use these publications.)* The *Federal Register* and the *Code of Federal Regulations* may be accessed online at www.archives.gov/federal-register/cfr; this site also contains a link to the federal government's regulatory website at www.regulations.gov *(see appendix).*

▉ LEGISLATION

The STB exercises its authority under:

Interstate Commerce Act of 1887 (24 Stat. 379, 49 U.S.C. 1). Signed by the president Feb. 4, 1887. **Revised Interstate Commerce Act** (92 Stat. 1337, Subtitle IV, 49 U.S.C. 10101). Signed by the president Oct. 13, 1978. The revision was a recodification of existing laws and did not make any substantive changes in the powers and authority of the ICC. Obsolete language was changed and superseded statutes removed. The following references to the U.S. Code reflect the 1978 revision.

Hepburn Act of 1906 (34 Stat. 584, 49 U.S.C. 10501). Signed by the president June 29, 1906. Extended ICC jurisdiction over express companies, pipelines (except water and gas), and sleeping car companies. It also gave the commission the power to prescribe and enforce reasonable rates, charges, and regulations for the industries it regulated at that time.

Mann-Elkins Act of 1910 (36 Stat. 539, 49 U.S.C. 10501). Signed by the president June 18, 1910. Authorized the commission to suspend and investigate new rate proposals.

Panama Canal Act of 1912 (37 Stat. 566, 15 U.S.C. 31, 46 U.S.C. 11, 49 U.S.C. 10503, 11321, 11914). Signed by the president Aug. 24, 1912. Prohibited railroads from continuing ownership or operation of water lines when competition would be reduced.

Esch Car Service Act of 1917 (40 Stat. 101, 49 U.S.C. 10102). Signed by the president May 29, 1917. Authorized the commission to determine the reasonableness of freight car service rules; to prescribe rules in place of those found unreasonable; and, in time of emergency, to suspend car service rules and direct the car supply to fit the circumstances.

Transportation Act of 1920 (41 Stat. 474, 49 U.S.C. 10501). Signed by the president Feb. 28, 1920. Granted the commission authority to fix minimum as well as maximum rates, to prescribe intrastate rates if necessary to remove discrimination against interstate commerce, and to require that railroads obtain ICC approval for construction and operation of new lines as well as abandonment of existing lines.

Transportation Act of 1940 (54 Stat. 898, 49 U.S.C. 10501). Signed by the president Sept. 18, 1940. Brought coastal, intercoastal, and inland water carriers and freight forwarders under ICC jurisdiction.

Reed-Bullwinkle Act of 1948 (62 Stat. 472, 49 U.S.C. 10706). Signed by the president June 17, 1948. Allowed common carriers by rail, motor, and water, and freight forwarders to join in collective ratemaking activities.

Transportation Act of 1958 (72 Stat. 568, 49 U.S.C. 10501). Signed by the president Aug. 12, 1958. Gave the ICC authority to determine reasonable minimum railroad rates, enlarged ICC jurisdiction over curtailment of railroad services, and exempted truckers of certain agricultural products from ICC rules.

Department of Transportation Act of 1967 (81 Stat. 224, 49 U.S.C. 1652). Signed by the president Sept. 11, 1967. Created the cabinet-level Department of Transportation and transferred to it jurisdiction over carrier safety practices.

National Trails System Act (82 Stat. 919, 16 U.S.C. 1247 (d)). Signed by the president Oct. 2, 1968. Authorized a national system of trails and defined four categories of national trails.

Rail Passenger Service Act of 1970 (84 Stat. 1327, 26 U.S.C. 250, 45 U.S.C. 501). Signed by the president Oct. 30, 1970. Gave the ICC authority to establish standards of adequate rail passenger service.

Regional Rail Reorganization Act of 1973 (87 Stat. 985, 31 U.S.C. 856, 45 U.S.C. 11124). Signed by the president Jan. 2, 1974. Reorganized bankrupt railroads in the northeast United States and created the Rail Services Planning Office within the ICC. The new office was responsible for ensuring public participation in the Northeast redevelopment project.

Railroad Revitalization and Regulatory Reform Act of 1976 (90 Stat. 31, 15 U.S.C. 77c, 31 U.S.C. 11, 45 U.S.C. 543, 49 U.S.C. 10501). Signed by the president Feb. 5, 1976. Reduced the degree of regulation imposed on rail industry by the ICC. Allowed railroad management more flexibility to raise and lower individual freight rates; imposed strict time limits on the ICC for the processing and disposition of rail-related proceedings; and gave permanent status to the Rail Services Planning Office.

Staggers Rail Act of 1980 (94 Stat. 1895, 49 U.S.C. 10101 note). Signed by the president Oct. 14, 1980. Gave railroads increased price-setting flexibility with less regulation by the ICC, limited railroad carriers' immunity from antitrust laws to set rates collectively, and expedited procedures for railroad abandonment of service.

Surface Freight Forwarder Deregulation Act of 1986 (100 Stat. 2993, 49 U.S.C. 10101 note). Signed by the president Oct. 22, 1986. Rescinded licensing requirement for general commodities freight forwarders but maintained requirement for filing cargo liability insurance information. Excluded household goods freight forwarders from this deregulation.

Negotiated Rates Act of 1993 (107 Stat. 2044, 49 U.S.C. 10101 note). Signed by the president Dec. 3, 1993. Set up mechanisms for settlements between bankrupt carriers and former shippers based on the weight of the shipment. Reduced the statute of limitations for filing undercharge claims and exempted from claims those shippers who transported charitable or recyclable goods.

Interstate Commerce Commission Termination Act of 1995 (49 U.S.C. 101 note). Signed by the president Dec. 29, 1995. Abolished the ICC, establishing the STB within the DOT to handle most of the ICC's surviving regulatory functions.

Transportation Equity Act for the 21st Century (TEA-21) (112 Stat. 154, 23 U.S.C. 143). Signed by the president June 9, 1998. Reauthorized the federal highway, transit, safety, research, and motor carrier programs under the Intermodal Surface Transportation Efficiency Act of 1991 (ISTEA) from 1998 through 2003. Provided incentives for states to adopt tough .08 blood alcohol concentration standards for drunk driving.

Safe, Accountable, Flexible, and Efficient Transportation Equity Act of 2005 (SAFETEA) (23 U.S.C. 134). Signed by the president Aug. 10, 2005. Reauthorized federal surface transportation programs through fiscal year 2009. Authorized appropriations for the STB. Directed the STB to complete a review of federal regulations regarding the level of liability protection required by motor carriers providing transportation of household goods; and revised the regulations to provide enhanced protection in the case of loss or damage.

Passenger Rail Investment and Improvement Act of 2008 (122 Stat. 4925, 49 U.S.C. 24308). Signed by the president Oct. 16, 2008. Enhanced the STB's responsibilities in various types of disputes between Amtrak, commuter rail operators, host railroads over which they operate, or states that seek to use Amtrak equipment or services, with respect to cost allocations, quality of service, compensation, liability, and other terms for provision of service

Other Transportation Department Offices

■ AVIATION AND INTERNATIONAL AFFAIRS

1200 New Jersey Ave. S.E.
Washington, DC 20590
Internet: www.transportation.gov/policy/assistant-secretary-aviation-international-affairs

The Office of the Assistant Secretary for Aviation and International Affairs develops and coordinates policy related to economic regulation of the airline industry, and the office administers the laws and regulations governing U.S. and foreign carrier economic authority to engage in air transportation. The following divisions are key regulatory offices within Aviation and International Affairs.

Office of Aviation Analysis. This office sets and renews subsidy and service levels for essential air service and monitors air carriers' reliability and performance. It represents the public interest in formal hearings concerning carrier fitness, mergers and acquisitions, and employee protection cases. It evaluates applications from companies for new air carrier authority; researches and monitors aviation industry performance; and develops and administers operating authority policies for services by scheduled, charter, cargo, air taxi, commuter, and indirect air carriers. It also aids in rulemaking and legislative proposals concerning essential air service.

Office of International Aviation. This office formulates, coordinates, and executes the international aviation policy of the United States and administers economic regulatory functions related to foreign air travel. The office originates international aviation negotiating positions, coordinates negotiating policy and strategy with government agencies and air carriers, and conducts or participates in those negotiations. It also receives complaints from U.S. carriers experiencing difficulties in foreign markets and intervenes to resolve those problems.

International Aviation also receives, processes, and makes or recommends disposition of all U.S. and foreign carrier requests for economic operating authority between the U.S. and foreign points, and of all tariff filings and fare and rate agreements from these carriers.

Office of International Transportation and Trade. This office is responsible for developing international transportation policy and carrying out the department's international responsibilities in a timely manner. The office promotes international cooperation and trade by facilitating open global transportation markets via in-depth analysis and by providing policy recommendations to address emerging and ongoing international transportation issues.

Assistant Secretary
  Susan Kurland . . . . (202) 366–4551
Aviation Analysis
  Todd Homan . . . . (202) 366–5903
  Fax . . . . (202) 366–7638
International Aviation
  Paul Gretch . . . . (202) 366–2423
  Fax . . . . (202) 366–3694
  E-mail: Paul.Gretch@dot.gov
Regulatory Affairs
  Jeffrey Gaynes . . . . (202) 366–2424
  E-mail: Jeffrey.Gaynes@dot.gov
International Transportation and Trade
  Julie Abraham . . . . (202) 366–4398
  E-mail: David.DeCarme@dot.gov

■ AVIATION ENFORCEMENT AND PROCEEDINGS

Office of the General Counsel
1200 New Jersey Ave. S.E.
Washington, DC 20590
Internet: www.transportation.gov/airconsumer

The Office of the Assistant General Counsel for Aviation Enforcement and Proceedings provides legal support to offices that handle airline functions. This includes enforcing Department of Transportation (DOT) rules and regulations governing the obligations of air carriers under the Federal Aviation Act, except those dealing with safety, which are enforced by the Federal Aviation Administration.

The office also conducts administrative proceedings in cases in which airlines have failed to follow DOT rules and regulations concerning consumer affairs. The

Consumer Protection Division takes action when it believes an airline or charter operator has engaged in unfair or deceptive practices, such as when there is evidence of "bait and switch" sales tactics, or when violations of advertising and overbooking regulations occur and when other consumer-related matters are concerned. The department is charged with prohibiting discrimination, and this office is responsible for civil rights enforcement in air transportation.

General Counsel

 Kathryn Thompson . . . . (202) 366–4702

  Fax. . . . . (202) 366–3388

Deputy General Counsel

 Kristin Amerling. . . . . (202) 366–4702

Deputy General Counsel

 Judy Kaleta. . . . . (202) 366–4713

Assistant General Counsel for Aviation Enforcement and Proceedings

 Samuel Podbereskey. . . . . (202) 366–9342

Assistant General Counsel for Office of Regulations and Enforcement

 Jonathan Moss. . . . . (202) 366–4723

Deputy Assistant General Counsel

 Brett A. Jortland . . . . (202) 366–9342

Aviation Consumer Protection

 Norman A. Strickman . . . . (202) 366–5960

  Hotline . . . .(202) 366–2220; (202) 366–5957

  Fax. . . . . (202) 366–5944

  TTY. . . . . (202) 366–0511

■ OFFICE OF HEARINGS

1200 New Jersey Ave. S.E.
Washington, DC 20590
Internet: www.transportation.gov/mission/
administrations/administration/hearings

The Office of Hearings conducts formal proceedings requiring oral evidence concerning the regulatory powers of the DOT. The Office of Hearings is composed of administrative law judges, who hold hearings under the Administrative Procedure Act (APA) for the department's Office of the Secretary (primarily in aviation matters) and DOT's component modal administrations that need formal APA hearings, including the Federal Aviation Administration (*p. 783*), Federal Motor Carrier Safety Administration (*p. 795*), Federal Railroad Administration (*p. 798*), Maritime Administration (*p. 806*), National Highway Traffic Safety Administration (*p. 811*), and the Pipeline and Hazardous Materials Safety Administration (*p. 818*).

The DOT office prosecuting the case normally prepares the exhibits, analyses, and written testimony. At the end of the hearing, the presiding administrative law judge issues an initial recommended decision on the case at hand.

Chief Administrative Law Judge

 Ronnie A. Yoder . . . . (202) 366–2142

  Fax. . . . . (202) 366–7536

Administrative Law Judges

 Richard C. Goodwin. . . . . (202) 366–5121

 J. E. Sullivan . . . . (202) 366–2132

Treasury Department

15th St. and Pennsylvania Ave. N.W., Washington, DC 20220
Internet: www.treasury.gov

Alcohol and Tobacco Tax and Trade Bureau

1310 G St. N.W., #300, Washington, DC 20220
Internet: www.ttb.gov

The Homeland Security Act of 2002, which created the Department of Homeland Security, also created the Alcohol and Tobacco Tax and Trade Bureau (TTB) within the Treasury Department on Jan. 24, 2003. The TTB's authority to regulate and collect revenue from the alcohol and tobacco industries had been within the Treasury Department's Bureau of Alcohol, Tobacco, and Firearms (ATF) since 1972. The Homeland Security Act also transferred the ATF's law enforcement functions relating to firearms, explosives, and arson to the Justice Department (*p. 725*).

The TTB continues to regulate and collect revenue from the alcohol and tobacco industries. The agency also provides assistance to states for certain programs and develops consumer protection programs. Offices within the agency are responsible for investigating trade practice violations, issuing licenses and permits, and overseeing tax collection on alcohol and tobacco products. The bureau makes periodic inspections of tobacco manufacturing plants, breweries, and wineries. TTB designates viticultural areas to allow vintners to better describe the origin of their wines and to allow consumers to better identify wines they may purchase. TTB personnel also monitor the advertising, packaging, and formulation of alcoholic beverages to ensure that the products are safe and that they are accurately labeled.

The regulatory inspectors monitor the annual collection of more than $15 billion in excise taxes on distilled spirits, beer, wine, tobacco products, and firearms. They investigate trade practices that could result in alcohol law violations and administer certain environmental protection programs, such as efforts by regulated industries to curb water pollution.

The TTB also is responsible for regulating the manufacture of alcohol fuels. It issues permits for small-scale and commercial production of alcohol fuels—including gasohol production—for heating and for operating machinery.

Major TTB divisions include the following:

Advertising, Labeling, and Formulation Division (ALFD). Implements and enforces a broad range of statutory and compliance provisions of the Internal Revenue Code and the Federal Alcohol Administration (FAA) Act, with regard to the formulation and labeling of alcoholic beverages. The FAA Act requires importers and bottlers of beverage alcohol to obtain certificates of label approval or certificates of exemption from label approval for most alcoholic beverages before their introduction into interstate commerce. ALFD ensures that products are labeled in accordance with federal laws and regulations. In addition, ALFD examines alcohol products to ensure that they are manufactured in accordance with federal laws and regulations.

International Affairs Division. Ensures industry compliance with international trade regulations—inclusive of the FAA Act and the Internal Revenue Code. Assists other TTB divisions by providing technical support in matters relating to international trade investigations. Works with the Office of the United States Trade Representative (USTR) and other federal executive departments to further economic development and technological progress. Functions as an adviser to industry members, the various federal government branches, and the embassies of international governments.

Scientific Services Division. Provides scientific and technical services to the TTB, as well as to other federal, state, and local agencies and the regulated industries. The laboratory has two locations: Walnut Creek, CA, and Beltsville, MD. There are four laboratories: the Compliance Laboratory, the Beverage Alcohol Laboratory, the Nonbeverage Alcohol Laboratory, and the Tobacco Laboratory. The office traces its history back to the first Treasury laboratory, established in 1886 for the enforcement of the Oleomargarine Act.

National Revenue Center. Based in Cincinnati, OH, the center reconciles returns, reports, and claims; screens applications and promptly issues permits; and provides expert technical assistance for industry, the public, and government agencies to ensure fair and proper revenue collection and public safety.

Regulations and Rulings Division. Drafts new and revised regulations under the Internal Revenue Code and the FAA Act. Considers requests for alternate methods of complying with the law and regulations and acts on petitions to change the regulations. Issues rulings, procedures, and informational documents to clarify the law and regulations. In conjunction with the Scientific Services Division, resolves technical questions affecting tax classification of regulated products and advises field offices and industry members of findings. Responds to Freedom of Information Act (FOIA) requests.

Trade Investigations Division (TID). This division provides assistance and advice concerning the provisions of the Federal Alcohol Administration Act, the Internal Revenue Code, and all related regulations. TID investigators ensure industry compliance with the laws and regulations administered by the TTB. The division investigates allegations of trade practice violations in the marketplace and conducts investigations of suspected alcohol or tobacco tax evasion. TID also examines Certificates of Label Approvals (COLAs) to deter unauthorized usage.

Intelligence Division (ID). Collects, analyzes, and shares intelligence with other TTB divisions to enforce laws and regulations. ID includes the Risk Management Branch (RM), which develops, implements, and analyzes risk for Field Operations. ID coordinates intelligence efforts with counterparts from other state, federal, and foreign intelligence and law enforcement organizations.

■ KEY PERSONNEL

Administrator
John J. Manfreda . . . . (202) 453–2176
Deputy Administrator
Mary G. Ryan. . . . . (202) 453–2182
Chief of Staff
Liz Kann . . . . (202) 453–2000
Congressional and Public Affairs
Thomas Hogue . . . . (202) 453–2182
Equality, Diversity, and Inclusion
Tram-Tiara Ngo . . . . (202) 453–2054
Executive Liaison for Industry and State Matters
Susan Evans . . . . (202) 453–2176
Chief Counsel
Anthony Gledhill . . . . (202) 453–2240
Field Operations
Thomas R. Crone . . . . (202) 453–2119
Deputy Assistant Administrator
Ronald N. Hancock . . . . (202) 453–2000
Intelligence
Jerry D. Bowerman . . . . (202) 453–2107
National Revenue Center
Thurla F. Skora . . . . (513) 684–3334
Toll-free . . . . (877) 882–3277
Trade Investigations
Robert M. Angelo . . . . (202) 453–9200
Tax Audit
Allen F. Leftwich . . . . (202) 453–9595
Headquarters Operations
Theresa McCarthy. . . . . (202) 453–2181
Advertising, Labeling, and Formulation
Janet Scalese . . . . (202) 453–2250
Customer Service . . . . (866) 927–2533
International Affairs
John Lom . . . . (202) 453–2260
Knowledge Management Staff
Barbara M. Pearson . . . . (202) 927–8210
Regulations and Rulings
Amy Greenberg. . . . . (202) 453–2265
Scientific Services
Abdul Mabud. . . . . (240) 264–1661

Information Resources/Chief Information Officer
Robert J. Hughes . . . . (202) 453–2128
Management/Chief Financial Officer
Cheri D. Mitchell. . . . . (202) 453–2057

■ INFORMATION SOURCES

Internet

Agency website: www.ttb.gov. Includes an overview of federal alcohol, tobacco, tax, and trade matters; press releases; regulations; employer information; and links to other federal websites. A state-by-state listing of field and district offices is available on the website at www.ttb.gov/about/locations.shtml.

Telephone Contacts

Information and Switchboard . . . .(202) 453–2000
Toll-free Help Line. . . . .(877) 882–3277
TTY . . . .(202) 882–9914

KEY OFFICES/LABORATORIES

Laboratory, Scientific Services Division
Abdul Mabud, director. . . . . (240) 264–1661
Fax. . . . . (240) 264–1581

Beverage Alcohol Laboratory and Nonbeverage Products Laboratory
6000 Ammendale Rd.
Beltsville, MD 20705–1250
(202) 264–1496
Beverage Alcohol Laboratory
Jeffrey Ammann, chief . . . . (240) 264–1596
Fax. . . . . (240) 264–1583
Nonbeverage Products Laboratory
Vanessa Kinton, chief . . . . (240) 264–1591
Fax. . . . . (240) 264–1583
Tobacco Laboratory
Dawit Bezabeh. . . . . (240) 264–1594

Compliance Laboratory
490 N. Wiget Lane, Walnut Creek, CA 94598
Patricia Nedialkova, chief . . . .(513) 684–3356
Fax . . . .(925) 280–3651

National Revenue Center
Alcohol and Tobacco Tax and Trade Bureau
National Revenue Center
550 Main St., #8002
Cincinnati, OH 45202
Thurla F. Skora, director
(513) 684–3334
(877) 882–3277

Reconciles returns, reports, and claims; screens applications and promptly issues permits; provides expert technical assistance for the industry, the public, and government agencies to ensure fair and proper revenue collection and public safety.

Freedom of Information

Freedom of Information Act/Privacy Act
FOIA/Disclosure Officer
1310 G St. N.W., Box 12
Washington, DC 20220
(202) 882–9904
Fax (202) 453–2331
Brodi Fontenot, chief FOIA Officer

Instructions on how to make a freedom of information act request can be found on the website, http://ttb.gov/foia/make_request.shtml, or e-mail ttbfoia@ttb.gov.

PUBLICATIONS

Publications offered on the agency website cover a wide range of document types: industry guidance publications, newsletters, industry circulars, TTB white papers, Treasury decisions, procedures, rulings, delegation orders, and *Federal Register* documents (www.ttb.gov/publications/publications.shtml). For information about accessibility and for older publications call (202) 453–2270 or e-mail TTBWebmaster@ttb.gov. Industry guidance publications include:

Information for Tax-Free Alcohol Applicants
Liquor Laws and Regulations for Retail Dealers
Laws and Regulations under the Federal Alcohol Administration Act
What You Should Know about Grape Wine Labels

DOCKETS

Federal dockets are available at www.regulations.gov. (*See appendix for Searching and Commenting on Regulations: Regulations.gov.*)

RULES AND REGULATIONS

Alcohol and Tobacco Tax and Trade Bureau rules, regulations, and standards are published in the *Code of Federal Regulations,* Title 27, Chapter I, Parts 1–end. Proposed regulations and standards, new final rules, and standards and updates to the *Code of Federal Regulations* are published in the daily *Federal Register. (See appendix for information on how to obtain and use these publications.)* The *Federal Register* and the *Code of Federal Regulations* may be accessed online at www.archives.gov/federal-register/cfr; the site contains a link to the federal government's regulatory website at www.regulations.gov (*see appendix*).

▦ LEGISLATION

The TTB exercises its authority under:

Webb-Kenyon Act (37 Stat. 699, 27 U.S.C. 122 note). Signed by the president March 1, 1913. Regulated interstate sales of alcohol.

Federal Alcohol Administration Act (49 Stat. 977, 27 U.S.C. 201). Signed by the president Aug. 29, 1935. Defined unlawful trade practices in the alcoholic beverage industry.

Internal Revenue Code of 1954 (68A Stat. 595, 26 U.S.C. 5001). Signed by the president Aug. 16, 1954. Set limits on the tax collected on the manufacture of alcoholic beverages, tobacco products, and firearms.

Trafficking in Contraband Cigarettes Act (92 Stat. 2463, 18 U.S.C. 2341). Signed by the president Nov. 2, 1978. Prohibited the possession or transportation of contraband cigarettes.

Distilled Spirits Tax Revision Act of 1979 (93 Stat. 273, 26 U.S.C. 1 et seq.). Signed by the president July 26, 1979. Provided that liquor be taxed solely on the basis of alcohol content and allowed an additional deferral period for payment on spirits bottled in the United States.

Crude Oil Windfall Profits Tax of 1980 (94 Stat. 278, 26 U.S.C. 5181). Signed by the president April 2, 1980. Amended the Internal Revenue Code and established a new category of distilled spirits plant—the alcohol fuel plant. The TTB is responsible for the licensing of these plants.

Alcohol Beverage Labeling Act (102 Stat. 4181, 21 U.S.C. 1501 note). Signed by the president Nov. 18, 1988. Mandates that a government warning statement appear on all alcohol beverages for sale or distribution in the United States.

Homeland Security Act of 2002 (116 Stat. 2135, 6 U.S.C. 101 note). Signed by the president Nov. 25, 2002. Created the Alcohol and Tobacco Tax and Trade Bureau (TTB) within the Treasury Department. Transferred the ATF's authority to regulate and collect revenue from the alcohol and tobacco industries to the TTB. Transferred the ATF's law enforcement functions to the Justice Department.

Public Health Security and Bioterrorism Preparedness and Response Act of 2002 (116 Stat. 594, 42 U.S.C. 201 note). Signed by the president June 12, 2003. Authorized the secretary of health and human services, acting through the Food and Drug Administration (FDA), to issue regulations to protect the nation's food and drug supplies, including alcohol beverages, against bioterrorism and food-borne illness.

Children's Health Insurance Program Reauthorization of 2009 (123 Stat. 106, 26 U.S.C. 5701). Signed by the president Feb. 4, 2009. Amended the Internal Revenue Code to increase excise tax rates on cigars, cigarettes, cigarette papers and tubes, smokeless tobacco, pipe tobacco, and roll-your-own tobacco, effective April 1, 2009. Imposed a floor stocks tax on all tobacco products (except large cigars), cigarette papers, and cigarette tubes held for sale on April 1, 2009. Applied administrative tax law provisions relating to permits, inventories, reporting, and record keeping to manufacturers and importers of processed tobacco.

Family Smoking Prevention and Tobacco Control Act of 2009 (P.L. 111–31, 123 Stat. 1776). Signed by the president June 22, 2009. Provided the FDA with the authority to restrict and regulate the marketing and manufacturing of tobacco products.

Prevent All Cigarette Trafficking Act of 2009 (PACT Act) (124 Stat. 1087, 15 U.S.C. 375 note). Signed by the president March 31, 2010. Revises provisions governing the collection of taxes on, and trafficking in, cigarettes and smokeless tobacco.

Comptroller of the Currency

400 7th Street S.W., Washington, DC 20219
Internet: www.occ.treas.gov

The Office of the Comptroller of the Currency (OCC) is a bureau of the Treasury Department. Established by the National Bank Act of 1863, it was the first federal agency created to regulate financial institutions (*see also Federal Reserve System, p. 206, and Federal Deposit Insurance Corporation, p. 153*).

The comptroller of the currency is nominated by the president and confirmed by the Senate for a five-year term.

The OCC does not receive any appropriations from Congress. Instead, its operations are funded primarily by assessments on national banks. National banks pay for their examinations, and they pay for the OCC's processing of their corporate applications. The OCC also receives revenue from its investment income, primarily from U.S. Treasury securities.

In carrying out its regulatory functions the OCC:

- Grants charters to national banks.
- Supervises and examines nationally chartered banks.
- Takes supervisory actions against national banks that do not conform to laws and regulations or otherwise engage in unsound banking practices.
- Regulates the foreign activities of national banks.
- Issues charters to foreign banks that wish to operate branches in the United States if those branches operate like national banks.
- Approves mergers and consolidations if the resulting financial institution is a nationally chartered bank.
- Approves the conversion of state-chartered banks to national banking institutions.
- Reports on national bank operations and financial conditions.
- Approves plans of national banks to open branches, relocate headquarters, and expand services and facilities.

The comptroller of the currency is required by law to be an *ex officio* member of the Federal Deposit Insurance Corporation board of directors and the Neighborhood Reinvestment Corporation (dba NeighborWorks® America).

The OCC schedules examinations and visitations according to a bank's condition. National bank examinations are designed to determine the condition and performance of a bank, the quality of operations, and compliance with federal laws. The examination policy of the comptroller places greater emphasis on analysis and interpretation of financial data and banks' internal control systems than on detailed verification procedures. By law, the OCC is prohibited from releasing information from its bank safety and soundness examinations to the public. National banks must, however, submit a Report of Condition and Income (call report) four times a year to the FDIC.

The comptroller rates banks on a uniform numerical scale of 1 to 5, representing healthy to increasingly troubled banks. Banks with ratings of 3, 4, or 5 are subject to special supervisory action by the OCC, including removal of officers, negotiation of agreements to change existing bank practices, and issuance of cease-and-desist orders to prevent further deterioration.

More than national banks, federal branches of foreign banks, uninsured national trust companies, federal savings associations, and District of Columbia banks are subject to regulation by the comptroller's office. In addition, nationally chartered financial institutions are required to be members of the Federal Reserve System and must be insured by the FDIC.

National banks may hold investments in foreign financial institutions either directly or through subsidiaries known as Edge Corporations, which are named after Sen. Walter Edge, the sponsor of the legislation that allowed their creation.

The OCC is responsible for supervising this international activity. Examiners evaluate the quality of international loan and investment portfolios and analyze foreign exchange activities, reporting procedures, accounting and bookkeeping systems, and the adequacy of internal controls and audit programs.

In June 2007 the OCC joined with the Federal Reserve, the Federal Deposit Insurance Corporation (FDIC), the Office of Thrift Supervision (OTS), and the National Credit Union Administration (NCUA) to issue a final *Statement on Subprime Mortgage Lending*. This statement was not official regulation but rather guidance on how to address issues concerning certain adjustable-rate mortgages (ARMs).

By fall 2008, led by a collapsing housing market, the U.S. economy was in crisis with many banking and other financial institutions on the brink of failure. The Emergency Economic Stabilization Act of 2008 authorized the Treasury to establish the Troubled Asset Relief Program (TARP) to purchase troubled assets from financial institutions. After Barack Obama became president in 2009, Treasury Secretary Timothy Geithner launched increased oversight of financial institutions with the aim of keeping them solvent. The administration's Financial Stability Plan included a stress test for major banks, increased balance sheet transparency and disclosure, a Capital Assistance Program, and a Public-Private Investment Fund.

In late February 2009 the Treasury Department, the FDIC, the OCC, OTS, and the Federal Reserve Board outlined the Capital Assistance Program, which was developed to ensure that banking institutions are appropriately capitalized. By the second quarter of the calendar year, banks were beginning to return TARP money to the Treasury.

Although these actions mitigated the impact of the economic crisis, by summer 2009 there were no substantive regulatory reforms in place. The financial regulators looked to improve accountability through the regulatory authority already vested in them—that is, enhancing accounting practices and transparency. In June 2009 the Obama administration announced a regulatory reform plan that would include a consumer financial protection agency. Some of the heads of the financial regulatory agencies expressed concern about the proposed agency, including Comptroller of the Currency John C. Dugan, who was concerned that the rules would not be uniform because states could adopt different laws and regulations, and national bank preemption would be repealed. Consumer advocates argued that the OCC and Dugan, a former banking industry lobbyist, frequently decided its rules preempted state laws with stronger consumer protections, which contributed to the economic crisis.

In July 2010 President Obama signed the Dodd-Frank Wall Street Reform and Consumer Protection Act. The issue of preemption—that federal banking laws supersede state banking laws—again took center stage. On July 21, 2011, OCC issued a final rule implementing some of the provisions of the Dodd-Frank Act. The final rule incorporated the OTS responsibilities and includes amendments to OCC rules pertaining to preemption and visitorial powers. These amendments eliminate preemption for operating subsidiaries of national banks and operating subsidiaries of federal savings associations. The rule applies to federal thrifts the same preemption standard as applied to national banks and applies to federal thrifts the visitorial powers standards applicable to national banks. The rule also revises the OCC's visitorial powers rule to conform to the Supreme Court's *Cuomo* decision, recognizing the ability of state attorneys general to bring enforcement actions in court to enforce applicable laws against national banks as authorized by such laws.

The Dodd-Frank Act transfered specific consumer financial protection functions from OCC to the Consumer Financial Protection Bureau (CFPB) (*p. 387*). This includes adjustable-rate mortgages (but only as applied to nonfederally chartered housing creditors under the Alternative Mortgage Transaction Parity Act); registration of residential mortgage loan originators; privacy of consumer financial information; and fair credit reporting (with some exceptions).

Dodd-Frank abolished the OTS and transferred to the Office of the Comptroller of the Currency all OTS functions relating to federal savings associations and all rule-making authority relating to savings associations. Other OTS functions were transferred to the Federal Reserve Board, the FDIC, and the CFPB.

On Oct. 9, 2012, the OCC published a final rule that implements provisions of the Dodd-Frank that requires certain companies to conduct annual stress tests pursuant to regulations prescribed by their respective primary financial regulatory agencies. Specifically, this rule requires national banks and federal savings associations with total consolidated assets in excess of $10 billion (covered institutions) to conduct an annual stress test as prescribed by the rule. The OCC published similar rules for medium-sized firms in March 2014.

On December 10, 2013, the OCC, jointly with the FDIC, Federal Reserve Board, and the Securities and Exchange Commission (SEC), adopted final regulations implementing the requirements of section 619 of the Dodd-Frank Act, also known as the Volcker Rule. The final rules prohibit insured depository institutions and companies affiliated with insured depository institutions (banking entities) from engaging in short-term proprietary trading of certain securities, derivatives, commodity futures, and options on these instruments, for their own account. The final rules also impose limits on banking entities' investments in, and other relationships with, hedge funds or private equity funds. The final rules provide exemptions for certain activities, including market making, underwriting, hedging, trading in government obligations, insurance company activities, and organizing and offering hedge funds or private equity funds. The final rules also clarify that certain activities are not prohibited, including acting as agent, broker, or custodian. Banking organizations covered by section 619 were required to fully align their activities and investments by July 21, 2015.

By the end of fiscal year 2014 the OCC had completed all rules it was required to issue under the Dodd-Frank Act (those for which it had independent authority to issue). Also, the OCC had finalized many of the regulations that the Dodd-Frank Act required the OCC to issue jointly or on a coordinated basis with other federal financial regulators. This included integrating the functions of the former Office of Thrift Supervision, risk retention, financial firm stress testing, and minimum requirements for state registration and supervision of appraisal management companies.

In January 2015 federal financial regulatory agencies, in partnership with the State Liaison Committee (SLC) of the Federal Financial Institutions Examination Council, issued guidance for financial institutions on private student loans with graduated repayment terms at origination. Graduated repayment terms are structured to provide for lower initial monthly payments that gradually increase. The agencies—the Federal Reserve Board, the Consumer Financial Protection Bureau, the Federal

Deposit Insurance Corporation, the National Credit Union Administration, and the Office of the Comptroller of the Currency—urged private student loan originators to adhere to six principles: ensure orderly repayment; avoid payment shock; align payment terms with a borrower's income; provide borrowers with clear disclosures; comply with all applicable federal and state consumer laws, regulations, and reporting standards; and contact borrowers before reset dates.

The Financial Stability Oversight Council

The Dodd-Frank Act also created the Financial Stability Oversight Council. The Financial Stability Oversight Council has ten voting members: secretary of the treasury (chairs the Council); comptroller of the currency; the Federal Reserve chairperson; director of the Consumer Financial Protection Bureau; Security and Exchange Commission chairperson; FDIC chair; Commodity Futures Trading Commission chairperson; director of the Federal Housing Finance Agency; National Credit Union chairperson; and an independent insurance expert appointed by the president and approved by the Senate.

The Council, among many responsibilities, is required to identify risks to U.S. financial stability that could arise from the material financial distress or failure, or ongoing activities, of large, interconnected bank holding companies or nonbank financial companies, or that could arise outside the financial services marketplace. The Council is also responsible for identifying gaps in regulation that could pose risks to U.S. financial stability. The Council is also charged with requiring supervision by the Federal Reserve Board for nonbank financial companies that may pose risks to U.S. financial stability in the event of their material financial distress or failure.

■ KEY PERSONNEL

Comptroller of the Currency
Thomas J. Curry . . . . (202) 649–6400
Senior Advisor to the Comptroller
Kenyon T. Kilber . . . . (202) 649–6400
Senior Deputy Comptroller and Chief Counsel
Amy S. Friend . . . . (202) 649–5400
Legislative and Regulatory Activities
Stuart Feldstein . . . . (202) 649–5490
Senior Deputy Comptroller and Chief of Staff
Paul M. Nash . . . . (202) 649–6480
Deputy Comptroller for Public Affairs
Robert M. Garsson Jr. . . . . (202) 649–6870
Banking Relations
Gregory C. Golembe . . . . (202) 649–6490
FDIC Liaison
William A. Rowe . . . . (202) 649–6480
Communications
Oliver A. Robinson . . . . (202) 649–6700
Congressional Liaison
Carrie Moore . . . . (202) 649–6440
Public Affairs Operations
Bryan Hubbard . . . . (202) 649–6747

Senior Deputy Comptroller for Bank Supervision Policy and Chief National Bank Examiner
Jennifer C. Kelly . . . . (202) 649–6770
Compliance Operations and Policy
Grovetta Gardineer . . . . (202) 649–5470
Regulatory and Capital Policy
Charles Taylor . . . . (202) 649–6987
Senior Deputy Comptroller for Economics
David Nebhut . . . . (202) 649–5410
Senior Deputy Comptroller for Enterprise Governance and Ombudsman
Larry L. Hattix . . . . (202) 649–5530
Senior Deputy Comptroller for Large Bank Supervision
Martin Pfinsgraff . . . . (202) 649–5590
Senior Deputy Comptroller for Management and Chief Financial Officer
Kathy K. Murphy . . . . (202) 649–4900
Information Technology Services and Chief Information Officer
Vacant . . . . (202) 649–6000
Senior Deputy Comptroller for Midsize and Community Bank Supervision
Toney Bland . . . . (202) 649–5420

■ INFORMATION SOURCES

Internet
Agency website: www.occ.treas.gov. website offers press releases, an organizational directory, access to OCC publications, a complete publications list, and links to related Internet sites.

Telephone Contacts
Personnel Locator . . . . (202) 649–6800
Customer Assistance
Group . . . . (800) 613–6743; (713) 336–4350
Customer Assistance Group TTY . . . . (713) 658–0340
Federal Relay Service TTY . . . . (800) 877–8339

Information and Publications

KEY OFFICES

OCC Public Affairs
250 E St. S.W.
Washington, DC 20219
(202) 649–6870
Bryan Hubbard, director

Serves as the general information and freedom of information office for the OCC. Distributes material on administrative, legal, regulatory, and economic aspects of banking.

Freedom of Information
Office of the Comptroller of the Currency
Disclosure Officer
400 7th St. S.W., #3E–218

Washington, DC 20219
(202) 649–6700
E-mail: FOIA-PA@occ.treas.gov
Frank Vance, FOIA manager

Provides access to public OCC documents and publications; these are also available on the website in the Electronic Reading Room.

DATA AND STATISTICS

Contact the Communications Division at (202) 649–6700 or check the website at www.occ.gov.

PUBLICATIONS

Contact the OCC Communications Division at (202) 649–6700 for specific publications or a list of publications and reports. A complete list of publications is also available on the agency's website at www.occ.gov/publications/index-publications.html.

Publications available include:
Building Healthy Communities Through Bank Small Business Finance
Comptroller's Handbook for Asset Management
Comptroller's Handbook for Compliance
Consumer Rights
Detecting Red Flags in Board Reports
Licensing Manuals

Reference Resources

LIBRARY

OCC Library

400 7th St. S.W.
Washington, DC 20219
(202) 649–5520
Rebecca Aftowicz, reference librarian
(202) 649–6977

Contains reference volumes dealing with banking legislation and regulation. Open to the public by appointment only.

DOCKETS

Consult the OCC Library and contact the FOIA office, above. Federal dockets are also available at www.regulations.gov. (*See appendix for Searching and Commenting on Regulations: Regulations. gov.*)

RULES AND REGULATIONS

OCC rules and regulations are published in the *Code of Federal Regulations,* Title 12, Chapter I, Parts 1–end. They are also available on CD ("E-File"). Proposed regulations, new final regulations, and updates to the *Code of Federal Regulations* are published in the daily *Federal Register.* (*See appendix for details on how to obtain and use these publications.*) The *Federal Register* and the *Code of Federal Regulations* may be accessed online at www.archives.gov/federal-register/cfr; the site contains a link to the federal government's regulatory website at www.regulations.gov (*see appendix*).

▎ LEGISLATION

The OCC administers the following legislation in full or in part:

Fair Housing Act of 1968 (82 Stat. 81, 42 U.S.C. 3601). Signed by the president April 11, 1968. Prohibited discrimination in the sale or rental of housing.

Truth in Lending Act (82 Stat. 146, 15 U.S.C. 1601). Signed by the president May 29, 1968. Required lenders and merchants to inform consumers of total cost of loans and installment purchase plans and to clearly state annual percentage rate. Also prohibited unsolicited distribution of credit cards.

Bank Protection Act of 1968 (82 Stat. 294, 12 U.S.C. 1881). Signed by the president July 7, 1968. Required establishment of minimum security system standards for banking institutions.

Fair Credit Reporting Act (84 Stat. 1128, 15 U.S.C. 1681). Signed by the president Oct. 26, 1970. Regulated credit information and use.

Bank Secrecy Act (31 U.S.C. 5311 et seq.). Also known as the Currency and Foreign Transaction Reporting Act. Signed by the president Oct. 26, 1970. Required financial institutions to file reports to the U.S. Treasury for certain currency transactions. Designed to detect and prevent money laundering.

NOW Accounts Act (87 Stat. 342, 12 U.S.C. 1832). Signed by the president Aug. 16, 1973. Regulated interest-bearing checking accounts.

Equal Credit Opportunity Act (88 Stat. 1521, 15 U.S.C. 1691). Signed by the president Oct. 28, 1974. Prohibited credit discrimination against women. Amended in 1976 to include discrimination based on age, race, religion, or national origin (90 Stat. 251).

Real Estate Settlement Procedures Act (88 Stat. 1724, 12 U.S.C. 2601). Signed by the president Dec. 22, 1974. Minimized settlement charges for home buyers; confirmed the authority of the Department of Housing and Urban Development to set standards for settlement charges on homes financed through federally guaranteed mortgages.

Home Mortgage Disclosure Act (89 Stat. 1125, 12 U.S.C. 2801). Signed by the president Dec. 31, 1975. Required lending institutions within standard metropolitan statistical areas (SMSAs) to disclose the number and amount of mortgage loans made yearly to determine if banks were discriminating against certain city neighborhoods by refusing to make loans regardless of the creditworthiness of the potential borrower (a practice known as "redlining").

Fair Debt Collection Practices Act (91 Stat. 874, 15 U.S.C. 1692). Signed by the president Sept. 20, 1977. Regulated methods used by debt collection agencies.

Community Reinvestment Act of 1977 (CRA) (91 Stat. 1147, 12 U.S.C. 2901). Signed by the president Oct. 12, 1977. Required financial institution regulators to encourage the banks under their supervision to meet the credit needs of their communities, including low- and moderate-income neighborhoods.

International Banking Act of 1978 (92 Stat. 607, 12 U.S.C. 3101). Signed by the president Sept. 17, 1978. Provided for the federal regulation of foreign banks in domestic financial markets.

Financial Institutions Regulatory and Interest Rate Control Act of 1978 (92 Stat. 3641, 12 U.S.C. 226 note). Signed by the president Nov. 10, 1978. Prohibited interlocking management and director relationships among financial institutions.

Depository Institutions Deregulation and Monetary Control Act of 1980 (94 Stat. 132, 12 U.S.C. 226 note). Signed by the president March 31, 1980. Extended reserve requirements to all financial institutions; provided for phaseout of interest ceilings by 1986 and allowed thrift institutions to offer an expanded range of financial services; increased federal deposit insurance to $100,000 per depositor.

Garn–St. Germain Depository Institutions Act of 1982 (96 Stat. 1469, 12 U.S.C. 226 note). Signed by the president Oct. 15, 1982. Increased or repealed certain statutory ceilings affecting lending and borrowing by national banks. Simplified statutory restrictions on transactions by bank officials. Permitted the comptroller to dispose of certain unclaimed property recovered from closed national banks and banks in the District of Columbia. Permitted the chartering of certain limited-purpose banks and expanded the powers of bank service corporations (subsidiaries of banks) to deal with the public.

Competitive Equality Banking Act of 1987 (101 Stat. 552, 12 U.S.C. 226 note). Signed by the president Aug. 10, 1987. Granted the Federal Savings and Loan Insurance Corporation (FSLIC) new borrowing authority to reimburse depositors as it shut down bankrupt thrifts. Suspended the expansion of banks into insurance, securities underwriting, and real estate. Eased regulatory requirements for savings and loans in economically depressed areas and required faster clearing of depositors' checks.

Financial Institutions Reform, Recovery, and Enforcement Act of 1989 (FIRREA) (103 Stat. 183, 12 U.S.C. 1811 note). Signed by the president Aug. 9, 1989. Approved the use of $50 billion to finance the closing of insolvent savings and loans. Created the Resolution Trust Corporation to manage the disposal of the assets of bankrupt thrifts. FIRREA also dissolved the Federal Home Loan Bank Board, assigning its regulatory responsibilities to the Department of the Treasury and assigning its role in insuring depositors through the Federal Savings and Loan Insurance Corporation to the FDIC. Savings and loans were required to maintain a minimum amount of tangible capital equal to 1.5 percent of total assets.

Resolution Trust Corporation Refinancing, Restructuring, and Improvement Act of 1991 (105 Stat. 1761, 12 U.S.C. 1421). Signed by the president Dec. 12, 1991. Provided funding to resolve failed savings associations and working capital for restructuring the Oversight Board and the Resolution Trust Corporation.

Federal Deposit Insurance Corporation Improvement Act of 1991 (FDICA) (105 Stat. 2236, 12 U.S.C. 1811). Signed by the president Dec. 19, 1991. Required the most cost-effective resolution of insured depository institutions and improved supervision and examinations. It also made available additional resources to the Bank Insurance Fund.

Removal of Regulatory Barriers to Affordable Housing Act of 1992 (106 Stat. 3938, 42 U.S.C. 12705a). Signed by the president Oct. 28, 1992. Encouraged state and local governments to identify and remove regulatory barriers to affordable housing.

Government Securities Act Amendments of 1993 (107 Stat. 2344, U.S.C. Title 15 various parts). Signed by the president Dec. 17, 1993. Extended and revised the government's rulemaking authority under the federal securities laws.

Riegle-Neal Interstate Banking and Branching Efficiency Act of 1994 (108 Stat. 2338, 12 U.S.C. 1811 note). Signed by the president Sept. 29, 1994. Permitted banks to operate networks of branch offices across state lines without having to set up separately capitalized subsidiary banks.

Riegle-Neal Amendments Act of 1997 (111 Stat. 238, 12 U.S.C. 36). Signed by the president July 3, 1997. Required the comptroller of the currency to review actions taken during the preceding year regarding the applicability of state law to national banks and to include review results in the annual report.

Gramm-Leach-Bliley Act (113 Stat. 1338, 12 U.S.C. 1811 note). Signed by the president Nov. 12, 1999. Permitted affiliations between banks and any financial company, including brokerage and insurance firms. Amended the CRA to allow regulators to block banks' applications for mergers or acquisitions if they do not have satisfactory CRA ratings.

American Homeownership and Economic Opportunity Act of 2000 (114 Stat. 2944, 12 U.S.C. 1701). Signed by the president Dec. 27, 2000. Established programs to make home ownership more affordable for low- and moderate-income families, the elderly, and the disabled. Title XII, the Financial Regulatory Relief and Economic Efficiency Act of 2000, amended the FDICA to increase to 100 percent of fair-market value the permissible valuation of readily marketable, purchased mortgage servicing rights that may be included in calculating a bank's tangible capital, risk-based capital, or leverage limit.

Uniting and Strengthening America by Providing Appropriate Tools Required to Intercept and Obstruct Terrorism Act of 2001 (USA Patriot Act) (115 Stat. 272, 18 U.S.C. 1 note). Signed by the president Oct. 26, 2001. Title III, the International Money Laundering Abatement and Financial Anti-Terrorism Act of 2001, provided enhanced authority to identify, deter, and punish international money laundering. Required additional record keeping for particular transactions and the identification of foreign owners of certain accounts at U.S. financial institutions. Required banks to have minimum antimoney-laundering due diligence standards for private bank accounts. Barred U.S.

depository institutions from establishing, maintaining, administering, or managing correspondent accounts for certain foreign shell banks.

Check Clearing for the 21st Century Act (Check 21 Act) (117 Stat. 1177, 12 U.S.C. 5001 note). Signed by the president Oct. 28, 2003. Enabled banks to lawfully convert paper checks to purely electronic formats and to generate substitute paper checks in lieu of the original when requested by customers or other banks. Imposed new requirements on all banks.

Fair and Accurate Credit Transactions Act of 2003 (117 Stat. 1952, 15 U.S.C. 1601 note). Signed by the president Dec. 4, 2003. Amended the Fair Credit Reporting Act to extend consumer rights related to credit reporting, as well as federal preemption of state credit reporting laws. Placed requirements on financial institutions that provide adverse credit information to a consumer reporting agency or are party to a transaction involving alleged identity theft. Required users of credit scores to make disclosures to consumers and required users of consumer credit reports to notify consumers of less favorable credit terms. Stated that consumers must have an opportunity to "opt out" before a financial institution uses information provided by an affiliated company to market its products and services to the consumer.

Controlling the Assault of Non-Solicited Pornography and Marketing Act of 2003 (CAN-SPAM Act) (117 Stat. 2699, 15 U.S.C. 7701 note). Signed by the president Dec. 16, 2003. Authorized criminal and civil penalties for any company, including a national bank, that sends deceptive, unsolicited e-mail advertisements, or spam. Directed companies to clearly state the source and content of nonsolicited commercial electronic mail and honor the requests of recipients who do not want to receive additional nonsolicited electronic mail.

Preserving Independence of Financial Institution Examinations Act of 2003 (117 Stat. 2899, 18 U.S.C. 201 note). Signed by the president Dec. 19, 2003. Amended federal law to subject to criminal penalties (1) personnel of a financial institution who offer a loan or gratuity to personnel of a financial institution; and (2) a financial institution examiner who accepts such loan or gratuity. Declared that the term "loan" does not include any credit card account or mortgage loan.

Servicemembers Civil Relief Act (117 Stat. 2835, 50 U.S.C. App. 501 et seq.). Signed by the president Dec. 19, 2003. Mandates that military personnel on active duty in wartime are entitled to postponement or suspension of certain civil obligations, including mortgage payments, credit card payments, termination of lease, and eviction from housing.

USA Patriot Act Additional Reauthorizing Amendments Act of 2006 (18 U.S.C. 1 note). Signed by the president March 9, 2006. Reauthorized the USA Patriot Act and made permanent fourteen of its sixteen sections. Placed a four-year sunset provision on the other two sections: the authority to conduct "roving" surveillance under the Foreign Intelligence Surveillance Act (FISA), and the authority to request production of business records under FISA.

Financial Services Regulatory Relief Act of 2006 (120 Stat. 1966). Signed by the president Oct. 13, 2006.

Amended the Securities Exchange Act of 1934 and the Investment Advisers Act of 1940 to exempt savings associations from the same investment adviser and broker-dealer registration requirements as banks. Amended the Federal Reserve Act and the Bank Holding Company Act Amendments of 1970 to repeal specified reporting requirements regarding loans to bank executive officers and principal shareholders (insider lending).

Housing and Economic Recovery Act (42 U.S.C. 4501 note, 122 Stat. 2654). Signed by the president July 30, 2008. Division A, Title V, **Secure and Fair Enforcement for Mortgage Licensing Act** of 2008 **(SAFE)**, encouraged states to establish a Nationwide Mortgage Licensing System and Registry. Required federal banking agencies jointly, through the Federal Financial Institutions Examination Council, to develop and maintain a national system to register loan originators. Defined "federal banking agencies" as the Federal Reserve System, the Comptroller of the Currency, the Office of Thrift Supervision, the National Credit Union Administration, and the Federal Deposit Insurance Corporation.

Emergency Economic Stabilization Act of 2008 (122 Stat. 3765, 12 U.S.C. 5201 note). Signed by the president Oct. 3, 2008. Authorized the treasury secretary to establish the Troubled Asset Relief Program (TARP) to purchase troubled assets from any financial institution. Provided tax relief to banking organizations that suffered losses on certain holdings of Federal National Mortgage Association (Fannie Mae) and Federal Home Loan Mortgage Corporation (Freddie Mac).

Helping Families Save Their Homes Act of 2009 (123 Stat. 1632, 12 U.S.C. 5201 note). Signed by the president May 20, 2009. Amended the HOPE for Homeowners Program to reduce excessive fee levels, provide greater incentives for mortgage servicers to engage in modifications, and reduce administrative burdens to loan underwriters. Required the OCC and the Office of Thrift Supervision (OTS) to report jointly to Congress on the volume of mortgage modifications reported to their agencies. Required that borrowers be informed whenever their loan is sold or transferred.

Credit Card Accountability, Responsibility, and Disclosure Act of 2009 (P.L. 111–24, 123 Stat. 1734). Signed by the president May 22, 2009. Required banks to notify customers forty-five days in advance of any rate increase or significant changes in credit card account terms.

Dodd-Frank Wall Street Reform and Consumer Protection Act (124 Stat. 1376, 12 U.S.C. 5301 note). Signed by the president July 21, 2010. Sets guidelines for securitizations, derivatives, and large bank capital. Affirms the authority of state securities regulators and state insurance regulators to take action with respect to a person whose institution they regulate; and the Comptroller of the Currency and the Director of the Office of Thrift Supervision (OTS) regarding the applicability of state law under federal banking law to existing contracts entered into by the national banks and federal savings associations they regulate and supervise. Title III **Enhancing Financial Institution Safety and Soundness Act of 2010** transfers to the Office of the Comptroller of the Currency all Office of Thrift Supervision functions relating to federal savings associations, and all rulemaking authority relating to savings associations. Established the Financial Stability Oversight Council (FSOC) to provide comprehensive monitoring of and reporting on the nation's financial system. FSOC is comprised of nine heads of financial regulatory agencies (including the Comptroller of the Currency) and an insurance expert.

Biggert-Waters Flood Insurance Reform Act of 2012 (126 Stat. 916, 42 U.S.C. 4001 note). Signed by the president July 6, 2012. Title II of Moving Ahead for Progress in the 21st Century Act (MAP-21). Biggert-Waters made changes to the flood insurance program, which included requiring banking regulatory agencies to draft regulations concerning forced-placed flood insurance and flood insurance escrow provisions.

Honoring America's Veterans and Caring for Camp Lejeune Families Act of 2012 (126 Stat. 1165, 50 U.S.C. app. 533). Signed by the president Aug. 6, 2012. Amended the Servicemembers Civil Relief Act (SCRA) to extend from nine to twelve months after a servicemember's period of military service both the stay of proceedings to enforce an obligation on real or personal property owned by the servicemember prior to such military service, as well as the protection against sale, foreclosure, or seizure of such property. Provisions expire at the end of 2014.

National Defense Authorization Act for Fiscal Year 2013 Military Lending Act amendments (126 Stat. 1785, 10 U.S.C. 987). Signed by the president Jan. 2, 2013. Subtitle G declared the Military Lending Act is enforceable in the same manner as the Truth in Lending Act by the Federal Deposit Insurance Corporation, member banks of the Federal Reserve System, Office of the Comptroller of the Currency, National Credit Union Administration, Consumer Financial Protection Bureau, Federal Trade Commission, and certain other specified agencies.

◾ REGIONAL OFFICES

CENTRAL DISTRICT

(IL, IN, KY, MI, MN, eastern MO, ND, OH, WI)
One Financial Plaza
440 S. LaSalle St., #2700
Chicago, IL 60605
(312) 360–8800
Fax (312) 435–0951
Blake Paulson, deputy comptroller

NORTHEASTERN DISTRICT

(CT, DC, DE, eastern KY, MA, MD, ME, NC, NH, NJ,
  NY, PA, RI, SC, VA, VI, VT, WV)
340 Madison Ave., 5th Floor
New York, NY 10173–0002
(212) 790–4000
Fax (212) 790–4098
Kristin Kiefer, deputy comptroller

SOUTHERN DISTRICT

(AL, AR, FL, GA, LA, MS, OK, TN, TX)
500 N. Akard St., #1600
Dallas, TX 75201
(214) 720–0656
Fax (214) 720–7000
Gilbert T. Barker, deputy comptroller

WESTERN DISTRICT

(AK, AZ, CA, CO, HI, IA, ID, KS, western MO, MT,
  NE, NM, NV, OR, SD, UT, WA, WY, Guam)
1225 17th St., #300
Denver, CO 80202
(720) 475–7600
Fax (720) 475–7690
Kay E. Kowitt, deputy comptroller

Internal Revenue Service

1111 Constitution Ave. N.W., Washington, DC 20224
Internet: www.irs.gov

The Internal Revenue Service (IRS) is the largest bureau within the Treasury Department. It is responsible for enforcing internal revenue laws, except those falling under the jurisdiction of the Alcohol and Tobacco Tax and Trade Bureau (p. 836).

The office of the commissioner of the Internal Revenue was established in 1862, and Congress first received authority to levy taxes on the income of individuals and corporations in 1913 under the Sixteenth Amendment to the Constitution.

The IRS is headed by a commissioner nominated by the president and confirmed by the Senate. The commissioner is assisted by two deputy commissioners. Each deputy commissioner is responsible for a specific area: Services and Enforcement and Operations Support. The national office develops policies and programs for the administration of internal revenue laws; most of the day-to-day operations are carried out by regional offices, district offices, and service centers across the United States.

The primary responsibility of the IRS is to determine, assess, and collect taxes. The IRS provides services to taxpayers, including help with income tax questions or problems. It also determines pension plan qualifications and rules on the tax status of exempt organizations. To supplement the provisions of the Internal Revenue Code, the service prepares and issues additional rules and regulations. The IRS also conducts research on taxpayer opinions, the simplification of federal tax reporting, and tax compliance.

The IRS encourages the resolution of tax disputes through an independent administrative appeals system rather than through litigation. The appeals system is administered by the office of the regional director of appeals in each region.

The major sources of revenue collected are the individual income, social insurance, and retirement taxes. Other sources of revenue are the corporation income, excise, estate, and gift taxes.

In an effort to increase the effectiveness of the services provided by the IRS, the Citizen Advocacy Panel program was established in 1998. The Citizen Advocacy Panel (CAP) was replaced with the Taxpayer Advocacy Panel (TAP), a federal advisory committee made up of volunteers representing all fifty states, the District of Columbia, and Puerto Rico. Established in 2002, TAP provides a forum for taxpayers to raise concerns about

IRS service and offer suggestions for improvement. The TAP reports annually to the secretary of the Treasury, the IRS Commissioner, and the National Taxpayer Advocate. Members serve three-year terms.

The Internal Revenue Service Restructuring and Reform Act of 1998 brought about the agency's most sweeping overhaul since 1952. At the management level, then Commissioner Charles O. Rossotti added two new deputy commissioner posts for operations and modernization. Also, the Joint Committee on Taxation was given oversight authority of the IRS with regard to reviewing all requests for investigations of the IRS by the General Accounting Office (now the Government Accountability Office) and to approve such requests when appropriate. The act also placed the burden of proof regarding income tax liability upon the IRS rather than the taxpayer.

In October 2000 the IRS officially unveiled its new organizational structure. The agency's old standard of dividing the nation's taxpayers by geographic boundaries was replaced with a new system centered on four customer-focused divisions, a major reduction from the IRS's thirty-three districts and ten service centers of past years. The organizational structure also permits the agency to work quickly to solve problems and to meet the needs of specific taxpayer groups. More IRS resources are now devoted to prefiling activities, such as education and outreach to help taxpayers comply with tax law. Postfiling activities focus on problem prevention, with targeted enforcement activities for noncompliance.

A key component of the reorganization required computer modernization. The IRS worked to overhaul its 1960s-era, tape-based computer system with a state-of-the-art system. To address these issues, the IRS released its Information Technology Modernization Vision and Strategy document in 2006 as a blueprint for upgrading computer technology to enhance business and customer service operations. The IRS continues to encourage taxpayers to file electronically. Enhanced technology has allowed the IRS to direct deposit taxpayer refunds to e-file customers in less than two weeks.

The four customer service divisions of the IRS include the following:

- **Wage and Investment Division**. Serves individual taxpayers with wage and investment incomes. Members of the division, headquartered in Atlanta, GA, focus on educating and assisting taxpayers during all interactions with the IRS.

- **Small Business/Self-Employed Division**. Headquartered in New Carrollton, MD. This diverse group covers taxpayers who are fully or partially self-employed or who own small businesses with assets of less than $10 million. Taxpayers in this group (approximately 45 million) face some of the most complex tax law requirements and file twice as many forms and schedules as individual taxpayers. This division also focuses on increased education and communication efforts with taxpayers and external stakeholder organizations, such as tax practitioners.
- **Large Business and International Division**. Serves corporations and partnerships that have assets greater than $10 million. This division, headquartered in Washington, DC, works with businesses that employ large numbers of employees, deal with complex tax law and accounting principles, and conduct business in a global environment.
- **Tax-Exempt/Government Entities**. Headquartered in Washington, DC. The division serves three distinct customer segments—employee plans, tax-exempt organizations, and government entities—representing 3 million customers. These groups controlled more than $8 trillion in assets.

The Tax Increase Prevention and Reconciliation Act of 2005 made various changes to the tax code affecting taxes, long-term capital gains, and qualified dividends; raised the alternative minimum tax limits; and extended the tax cutoff from age fourteen to eighteen for a child's investment income. The legislation now requires individuals making an offer-in-compromise to settle their IRS debt to make a 20 percent payment on the anticipated compromise amount.

The economic crisis resulted in various stimulus packages that included tax incentives and tax relief. Some of these legislative initiatives included:

- The Mortgage Forgiveness Debt Relief Act of 2007, which amended the Internal Revenue Code to exclude from gross income amounts attributable to a discharge, prior to Jan. 1, 2010, of indebtedness incurred to acquire a principal residence.
- The Economic Stimulus Act of 2008, which provided tax rebate stimulus checks in 2008 to qualifying individuals ($600), married couples filing jointly ($1,200), and a dependent child credit ($300). Also provided tax breaks to businesses.
- The Emergency Economic Stabilization Act of 2008, while better known for its bank bailout provisions, contained legislation that provided tax relief to victims of natural disaster and to those individuals who made charitable contributions to disaster victims.
- The American Recovery and Reinvestment Act of 2009 contained a variety of tax incentives for businesses, as well as a tax credit for individuals via changes to the federal income tax withholding tables. The legislation also

provided a range of tax incentives to individuals and businesses for energy efficiency initiatives.
- Small Business Jobs Act of 2010, which contained tax provisions designed to encourage investment and provide access to capital for businesses.

In March 2009 the IRS announced an Offshore Voluntary Disclosure Program (OVDP) to allow voluntary disclosures by taxpayers with unreported income from hidden offshore accounts. The program allowed taxpayers some terms of amnesty if they voluntarily reported this income, including avoiding higher penalties and criminal prosecution. The 2009 program ended in October that year. The IRS announced a second OVDP in 2011, but the terms of the second program were not as generous as the 2009 program. In 2012 the IRS extended the OVDP indefinitely but noted it may end the program at any time in the future. In 2014 the IRS reports that self-reporting efforts had resulted in more than 45,000 voluntary disclosures from individuals who paid about $6.5 billion in back taxes, interest, and penalties.

Congress targeted institutions that helped U.S. citizens conceal income from the IRS. The Foreign Account Tax Compliance Act (FATCA) targets noncompliance by U.S. taxpayers through foreign accounts. FATCA was enacted in 2010 as part of the Hiring Incentives to Restore Employment (HIRE) Act. FATCA requires foreign financial institutions (FFIs) to report to the IRS information about financial accounts held by U.S. taxpayers, or by foreign entities in which U.S. taxpayers hold a substantial ownership interest.

In order to avoid financial penalties under FATCA, a participating FFI will have to enter into an agreement with the IRS to identify U.S. accounts, report certain information to the IRS regarding U.S. accounts, and withhold a 30 percent tax on certain payments to nonparticipating FFIs and account holders who are unwilling to provide the required information. FFIs that do not enter into an agreement with the IRS will be subject to withholding on certain types of payments, including U.S. source interest and dividends, gross proceeds from the disposition of U.S. securities, and pass-through payments. The IRS and the Treasury Department issued guidelines to implement FATCA by January 1, 2014.

The Patient Protection and Affordable Care Act of 2010 contains tax provisions that will be implemented over several years. Some of these provisions include:

- With some exceptions, a 10-percent excise tax on indoor UV tanning services went into effect on July 1, 2010.
- The Small Business Health Care Tax Credit is available to small employers who pay at least half the cost of single coverage for their employees and is specifically targeted for businesses with low- and moderate-income workers.
- The cost of an over-the-counter medicine or drug can no longer be reimbursed from Flexible Spending Arrangements or health reimbursement arrangements unless a prescription is obtained (some exceptions).

- Health coverage for an employee's children under twenty-seven years of age is now generally tax-free to the employee.

- Starting in 2011 the Affordable Care Act established an annual fee payable by certain manufacturers and importers of brand-name pharmaceuticals.

- Starting in tax year 2011 the Affordable Care Act required employers to report the cost of coverage under an employer-sponsored group health plan; to give employers more time to update their payroll systems, the IRS made this requirement optional for all employers in 2011.

- A new Net Investment Income Tax goes into effect starting in 2013. The 3.8 percent Net Investment Income Tax applies to individuals, estates, and trusts that have certain investment income above certain threshold amounts.

- A new Additional Medicare Tax goes into effect in 2013. The 0.9 percent Additional Medicare Tax applies to an individual's wages, Railroad Retirement Tax Act compensation, and self-employment income that exceeds a threshold amount based on the individual's filing status.

- Certain employers must offer health coverage to their full-time employees or a shared responsibility payment may apply; exempts small firms that have fewer than fifty full-time employees. The employer shared responsibility provisions are first effective on January 1, 2015, but transition relief from certain requirements is available for 2015.

The IRS website publishes information pertaining to the Affordable Care Act and the related tax provisions.

In August 2013 the IRS ruled that same-sex couples, legally married in jurisdictions that recognize their marriages, would be treated as married for federal tax purposes. The ruling applies regardless of whether the couple lives in a jurisdiction that recognizes same-sex marriage or a jurisdiction that does not recognize same-sex marriage. The ruling implements federal tax aspects of the June 26 Supreme Court decision invalidating a key provision of the 1996 Defense of Marriage Act, which had defined marriage as a legal union of one man and one woman for the purposes of "any act of Congress . . . any ruling, regulation, or interpretation of the various administrative bureaus and agencies of the United States."

■ KEY PERSONNEL

Commissioner
John Koskinen . . . . (202) 622–9511
    Fax . . . . (202) 622–5756
Chief of Staff
Crystal Philcox . . . . (202) 622–9511
Chief Counsel
William J. Wilkins . . . . (202) 622–3300
Chief, Appeals
Kristin Weilobob . . . . (202) 435–5600
Chief, Communications and Liaison
Tracy Lemons . . . . (202) 622–5440

Director, Compliance Analytics
Vacant
Director, Equity, Diversity, and Inclusion
Monica Davy . . . . (202) 622–5400
Director, Research, Analysis, and Statistics
Rosemary Marcuss . . . . (202) 874–0100
National Taxpayer Advocate
Nina E. Olson . . . . (202) 622–6100
Deputy Commissioner, Services and Enforcement
John Dalrymple . . . . (202) 622–6860
Commissioner, Large Business and International
Heather Maloy . . . . (202) 283–8710
Commissioner, Small Business/Self-Employed
Karen Schiller . . . . (202) 622–0600
Commissioner, Tax Exempt and Government Entities
Sunita B. Lough . . . . (202) 622–2500
Commissioner, Wage and Investment
Debra Holland . . . . (202) 622–9106
Chief, Criminal Investigations
Richard Weber . . . . (202) 622–3200
Director, Professional Responsibility
Karen L. Hawkins . . . . (202) 927–3397
Director, Return Preparer Office
Carol A. Campbell . . . . (202) 927–6428
Deputy Commissioner, Operations Support
Stuart Burns (acting) . . . . (202) 622–4255
  Chief Financial Officer
  Robin Canady . . . . (202) 622–6400
  Chief Technology Officer
  Terence Milholland . . . . (202) 622–6800
  Chief, Agency-Wide Shared Services
  Kevin McIver (acting) . . . . (202) 622–7500
  Chief, Human Capital
  Daniel Riorden . . . . (202) 622–7676

■ INFORMATION SOURCES

Internet
Agency website: www.irs.gov. website offers access to IRS publications and forms, including all tax forms and instruction manuals, tax tips and tax information for both businesses and individuals, and a register of tax regulations.

Telephone Contacts
General Information and Taxpayer
    Assistance . . . . (800) 829–1040
TTY . . . . (800) 829–4059
International Line (taxpayers calling
    from outside U.S.) . . . . (267) 941–1000
IRS Business and Specialty
    Help Line . . . . (800) 829–4933
IRS Refund Hotline . . . . (800) 829–1954
IRS Tele-Tax Recorded Information . . (800) 829–4477
Electronic Filing ("e-filing")
    Information . . . . (512) 941–1000
Personnel Locator . . . . (202) 622–3028
Publications and Tax Forms . . . . (800) 829–3676
Taxpayer Advocate Service
    Assistance . . . . (877) 777–4778

Information and Publications

KEY OFFICES

IRS Communications and Liaison Division

1111 Constitution Ave. N.W.
Washington, DC 20224
(202) 622–5440
Tracy Lemons, chief

Answers questions from the press and media, and issues news releases.

Freedom of Information

IRS Freedom of Information Reading Room
1111 Constitution Ave. N.W., #1621
Washington, DC 20224
Fax (877) 807–9215; (877) 891–6035
Candice Cromling, national public liaison
(202) 622–3359
Monday–Friday, 9:00 a.m. to 4:00 p.m.
Internet: www.irs.gov/foia

Contains IRS public records and documents; not set up to respond to written requests for agency materials. Written requests are handled by IRS Disclosure Offices; call the General Information and Taxpayer Assistance number, above, or see the agency website for Disclosure Office contact information at www.irs.gov/uac/IRS_Disclosure_Offices. Public records and documents are available on the Internet in the IRS Electronic Reading Room.

PUBLICATIONS

IRS publications are available online at the IRS website, www.irs.gov/publications. Publications can also be ordered by calling (800) 829–3676 or (800) 829–1040.

The *Instructions for Form 1040* booklet contains help, updates, and information taxpayers need to prepare and file tax returns. Form 1040 is available by typing "1040" on the IRS website's search screen.

IRS Guide to Free Tax Services (Publication No. 910) gives information on IRS filing options, helpful tips, publications, and seminars. The guide lists all free tax services, such as Community-Based Outlet Programs (CBOP), E-News subscription services, and taxpayer advocate services; FOIA and privacy information; taxpayer education and assistance programs; IRS Tele-Tax telephone services; exploration of IRS e-file; copies of transcripts of prior year returns; installment plans for paying taxes; small business tax workshops; IRS telephone numbers; and tax publications.

There are several hundred IRS publications available, including:

Your Rights as a Taxpayer (No. 1)
Tax Guide for Small Business (No. 334)
Medical and Dental Expenses (No. 502)
Business Use of Your Home (No. 587)
Individual Retirement Accounts (IRAs) (No. 590)
The IRS Collection Process (No. 594)

The weekly *Internal Revenue Bulletin* contains official IRS rulings and procedures as well as Treasury decisions, executive orders, tax conventions, legislation, and court decisions. The *Internal Revenue Bulletin* can be accessed on the IRS website. Weekly bulletins are indexed twice a year and published as the *Cumulative Bulletin*.

Reference Resources

Taxpayer Assistance Centers

Taxpayer Assistance Centers (TACs) are available for personal, face-to-face tax help for individuals who believe their tax issues cannot be handled online or by phone. A list of all Taxpayer Assistance Centers is available on the IRS website by selecting "Contact IRS" from the home page. While appointments are not necessary, taxpayers may call ahead to get hours and request appointments.

The IRS maintains local, toll-free tax assistance numbers to answer tax questions and to aid in the preparation of returns. During the filing season, the TACs extend their hours of telephone assistance and walk-in assistance. Extended hours vary according to location.

The IRS also has a toll-free telephone service called Tele-Tax, which provides pre-recorded tax messages covering tax topics ranging from "IRS assistance" to "who must file." Customers can also check the status of tax refunds on Tele-Tax.

Telephone assistance is available for:

Individuals.......................(800) 829–1040
    Hours: Monday–Friday, 7:00 a.m. to 7:00 p.m.,
    local time
Businesses ....(800) 829–4933
    Hours: Monday–Friday, 7:00 a.m. to 7:00 p.m.,
    local time
Exempt Organizations, Retirement Plan
    Administrators, and
    Government Entities............(877) 829–5500
    Hours: Monday–Friday, 8:00 a.m. to 5:00 p.m.,
    central time
Electronic filing ("e-filing")
    questions.....................(512) 416–7750
Identity Theft (for those who believe they may be
    victims of identity theft).........(800) 908–4490
    Hours: Monday–Friday, 7:00 a.m. to 7:00 p.m.
International Line (for taxpayers and businesses
    outside the U.S.)................(267) 941–1000
Fax ....(267) 941–1055
TTY ....(800) 829–4059
Tele-Tax Rcorded Information.......(800) 829–4477

Taxpayer Education and Assistance

The IRS conducts programs to help taxpayers obtain, understand, and complete their income tax returns:

Community Based Outlet Programs (CBOP). Tax materials are available from the IRS website. The IRS also supplies federal tax materials to other public and private institutions, including post offices, libraries, copy centers, and office supply stores. Businesses that want to participate in a CBOP can call (800) 829–2765.

Volunteer Income Tax Assistance (VITA). Offers free tax help to people who cannot afford professional assistance. Also trains people to become VITA volunteers. For information about the VITA program, call the IRS at (800) 829–1040.

Tax Counseling for the Elderly (TCE). Provides free tax counseling and tax preparation services for individuals 60 years of age or older. For information on the TCE program, locations, dates, and hours of nearest TCE site, call the IRS toll-free at (800) 829–1040.

Low Income Taxpayer Clinics (LITCs) and LITC Grant Program. Represent low-income taxpayers and individuals for whom English is a second language for free or for a nominal charge. Provide tax education and outreach. IRS Publication No. 4134, *Low Income Taxpayer Clinic List,* provides information on local clinics; available through the agency's website or local IRS offices.

Understanding Taxes. An online educational program for teachers and students accessed via the agency's website by selecting "Students" from the home page, then "Understanding Taxes."

Taxpayer Advocate Service. An independent organization within the IRS whose employees assist taxpayers who are experiencing economic harm and are seeking help in resolving tax problems they believe have not been resolved through normal IRS channels. Individuals must qualify for this service. Eligibility requirements and other information about the Taxpayer Advocate Service is available on the IRS website or by calling (877) 777–4778.

DOCKETS

Consult the IRS Freedom of Information Reading Room, above. Federal dockets are also available at www.regulations.gov. (*See appendix for Searching and Commenting on Regulations: Regulations.gov.*)

RULES AND REGULATIONS

IRS rules and regulations are published in the *Code of Federal Regulations,* Title 26, Chapter I, Parts 1–end. Proposed regulations, new final regulations, and updates to the *Code of Federal Regulations* are published in the daily *Federal Register.* (*See appendix for details on how to obtain and use these publications.*) The *Federal Register* and the *Code of Federal Regulations* may be accessed online at www.archives.gov/federal-register/cfr; the site contains a link to the federal government's regulatory website at www.regulations.gov (*see appendix*).

■ LEGISLATION

The IRS carries out its responsibilities under:

Tax Reform Act of 1986 (100 Stat. 2085, 26 U.S.C. 1 et seq.). Signed by the president Oct. 22, 1986. Reduced income tax rates for corporations and individuals, lowering the top rate to 34 percent and 28 percent, respectively. Curtailed or eliminated dozens of tax breaks, including the lower tax rate on capital gains.

Revenue Reconciliation Act of 1993 (107 Stat. 416, 26 U.S.C. 1 et seq.). Signed by the president Aug. 10, 1993. Amended the Tax Reform Act of 1986. Increased income tax top rates to 36 percent for individuals and to 35 percent for corporations.

Taxpayer Bill of Rights 2 (110 Stat. 1452, 26 U.S.C. 1 note). Signed by the president July 30, 1996. Increased from $100,000 to $1 million the maximum amount of damages taxpayers can recover if wrongly accused in IRS collections actions. Increased the amount taxpayers can recover in attorney's fees if they win a dispute with the IRS. Extended the interest-free period for delinquent payments under $100,000 from ten days to twenty-one days.

Small Business Job Protection Act of 1996 (110 Stat. 1755, 26 U.S.C. 1 note). Signed by the president Aug. 20, 1996. Increased the tax deduction limit on equipment purchased by small businesses. Expanded the tip credit for owners of bars and restaurants. Provided a $5,000 tax credit for adoptive parents. Allowed nonworking spouses to save up to $2,000 a year in tax-deferred IRAs.

Health Insurance Portability and Accountability Act of 1996 (110 Stat. 1936, 42 U.S.C. 201 note). Signed by the president Aug. 21, 1996. Established rules for a pilot program for medical savings accounts. Increased the deduction for health insurance costs for self-employed individuals.

Personal Responsibility and Work Opportunity Reconciliation Act (110 Stat. 2105, 42 U.S.C. 1305 note). Signed by the president Aug. 22, 1996. Amended the Internal Revenue Code to deny the Earned Income Credit (EIC) to individuals who are not authorized to work in the United States and to those who do not have Social Security numbers. Authorized the IRS to deny the EIC without appeal.

Internal Revenue Service Restructuring and Reform Act of 1998 (112 Stat. 689, 26 U.S.C. 7801 note). Signed by the president July 22, 1998. Directed the development of a plan to reorganize the IRS by eliminating or modifying the existing national, regional, and district structures. Directed the establishment of organizational units serving particular groups of taxpayers with similar needs. Established the Internal Revenue Service Oversight Board within the Department of the Treasury.

Taxpayer Bill of Rights 3 (112 Stat. 726, 26 U.S.C. 1 note). Signed by the president July 22, 1998. Placed any burden of proof in any court proceeding regarding the income tax liability of a taxpayer on the government if the taxpayer has met substantiation requirements. Increased the award cap on the hourly rate of attorney's fees from $110 to $125. Permitted civil damages of up to $100,000 for negligent actions by IRS employees. Suspended the statute of limitations for claiming a refund or credit during periods of a medically determined physical or mental impairment. Required the establishment of procedures to alert married taxpayers of their joint liabilities on all appropriate publications and instructions. Authorized the secretary to make grants to provide matching funds for the development, expansion, or continuation of qualified low-income taxpayer clinics.

Ticket to Work and Work Incentives Improvement Act of 1999 (113 Stat. 1860, 42 U.S.C. 1305). Signed by the president Dec. 17, 1999. Expanded health care benefits for the working disabled, extended a variety of business tax breaks, and postponed the implementation of new regulations for organ transplant recipients. Amended the Internal Revenue Code to provide a package of business tax-break extensions, including credits for employers who provide workers with educational assistance or who hire disadvantaged workers or former welfare beneficiaries.

Economic Growth and Tax Relief Reconciliation Act of 2001 (115 Stat. 38, 26 U.S.C. 1 note). Signed by the president June 7, 2001. Reduced marginal tax rates, reduced taxes for married couples, and increased contribution limits on retirement savings plans. Amended the Internal Revenue Code to create a 10 percent tax bracket, modified the 15 percent bracket, and gradually reduced rates for the 28, 31, 36, and 39.6 percent brackets. Increased the child tax credit over ten years. Allowed taxpayers to deduct higher-education expenses from their taxable incomes. Increased the student loan–interest deduction income limitation. Phased out estate, gift, and generation-skipping taxes over ten years. Changed the way capital gains are taxed. Increased the limit on annual contributions to traditional and Roth IRAs by 2008. Increased the amounts employers and employees can put into defined-contribution plans.

Victims of Terrorism Tax Relief Act of 2001 (115 Stat. 2427, 26 U.S.C. 1 note). Signed by the president Jan. 23, 2002. Amended the Internal Revenue Code of 1986 to provide tax relief to families of terrorist victims. Applied to victims of the Sept. 11, 2001, terrorist attacks on the United States; the 1995 Oklahoma City bombing; and anthrax-related deaths between September 2001 and January 2002.

Job Creation and Worker Assistance Act of 2002 (116 Stat. 21, 26 U.S.C. 1 note). Signed by the president March 9, 2002. Authorized funds in fiscal 2002 for a thirteen-week extension of unemployment benefits for workers who exhausted their normal twenty-six weeks of benefits. Title II, the Temporary Extended Unemployment Compensation Act of 2002, allowed businesses to deduct 30 percent of the cost of equipment purchases made from Sept. 11, 2001, through Sept. 10, 2004, and to deduct losses in 2001 and 2002 to offset profits in the previous five years. Established tax breaks and tax-exempt bonds for businesses in New York's "Liberty Zone," the area around the World Trade Center site.

Uniting and Strengthening America by Providing Appropriate Tools Required to Intercept and Obstruct Terrorism Act of 2002 (USA Patriot Act) (115 Stat. 272, 18 U.S.C. 1 note). Signed by the president Oct. 26, 2002. Title III provided enhanced authority to identify, deter, and punish international money laundering. Required additional record keeping for particular transactions and the identification of foreign owners of certain accounts at U.S. financial institutions.

Military Family Tax Relief Act of 2003 (117 Stat. 121, 26 U.S.C. 1 note). Signed by the president Nov. 11, 2003. Provided tax breaks to military personnel and their families. Doubled the death gratuity payment to survivors. Expanded the definition of those eligible for tax relief to include the survivors of astronauts who died during space missions. Granted members of the military assigned to noncombat zone contingency operations an extended time to file federal tax returns.

Working Families Tax Relief Act of 2004 (118 Stat. 1166, 26 U.S.C. 1 note). Signed by the president Oct. 4, 2004. Amended the Internal Revenue Code of 1986 to end certain abusive tax practices and to extend numerous expiring tax breaks for individuals and businesses.

American Jobs Creation Act of 2004 (118 Stat. 1418, 26 U.S.C. 1 note). Signed by the president Oct. 22, 2004. Amended the Internal Revenue Code of 1986 to make U.S. manufacturing, service, and high-technology businesses and workers more competitive and productive both at home and abroad. Repealed an export trade subsidy and offered new corporate tax deductions.

USA Patriot Act Additional Reauthorizing Amendments Act of 2006 (18 U.S.C. 1 note). Signed by the president March 9, 2006. Reauthorized the USA Patriot Act and made permanent fourteen of its sixteen sections. Placed a four-year sunset provision on the other two sections: the authority to conduct "roving" surveillance under the Foreign Intelligence Surveillance Act (FISA), and the authority to request production of business records under FISA.

Tax Increase Prevention and Reconciliation Act of 2005 (120 Stat. 345, 26 U.S.C. 7805). Signed by the president May 17, 2006. Made various changes to the tax code affecting long-term capital gains and qualified dividends. Raised the alternative minimum tax limits. Extended the tax cutoff from age fourteen to eighteen for a child's investment income. Required individuals making an offer-in-compromise to settle their IRS debt to make a 20 percent payment on the anticipated compromise amount.

Mortgage Forgiveness Debt Relief Act of 2007 (121 Stat. 1803, 26 U.S.C. 1 note). Signed by the president Dec. 20, 2007. Amended the Internal Revenue Code to exclude from gross income amounts attributable to a discharge, prior to Jan. 1, 2010, of indebtedness incurred to acquire a principal residence ($2 million limit).

Tax Increase Prevention Act of 2007 (121 Stat. 2461, 26 U.S.C. 55 note). Signed by the president Dec. 26, 2007. Amended the Internal Revenue Code to extend through 2007 for individual taxpayers the increased alternative minimum tax (AMT) exemption amounts.

Economic Stimulus Act of 2008 (122 Stat. 613, 26 U.S.C. 6428, 26 U.S.C. 179). Signed by the president Feb. 13, 2008. Amended the Internal Revenue Code to grant tax rebates in 2008 of the lesser of net income tax liability or $600 to individual taxpayers ($1,200 for married taxpayers filing joint returns). Allowed additional rebates of $300 for each child of an eligible taxpayer. Provided incentives to businesses including a special 50 percent depreciation allowance for 2008 purchases.

Emergency Economic Stabilization Act of 2008 (122 Stat. 3765, 12 U.S.C. 5201 note). Signed by the president Oct. 3, 2008. Title VII, National Disaster Relief Act of 2008, provided tax relief for victims of federally declared disasters occurring after Dec. 31, 2007, and before Jan. 1, 2010. Also included the Heartland Disaster Tax Relief Act, which allowed a taxpayer to deduct qualifying cash contributions up to 100 percent of his or her adjusted gross income. A corporation may deduct qualifying cash contributions up to 100 percent of its taxable income.

American Recovery and Reinvestment Act (ARRA) of 2009 (123 Stat. 115, 26 U.S.C. 1 note). Signed by the president Feb. 17, 2009. Provided a number of tax incentives for businesses, including faster write-offs for certain capital expenditures, expanded net operating loss carryback, exclusion of gain on the sale of certain small business stock, and COBRA credit. Included tax incentives for various energy efficiency improvements for businesses and homeowners. Provided tax credit to individuals via changes to the federal income tax withholding tables. Provided an $8,000 first-time homebuyer's tax credit for homes purchased in 2009.

Hiring Incentives to Restore Employment (HIRE) Act (124 Stat. 71, 26 U.S.C. 1 note). Signed by the president March 18, 2010. Provides tax incentives to employers hiring workers who were previously unemployed or working part-time only. Title V **Foreign Account Tax Compliance** amends the Internal Revenue Code to revise and add reporting and other requirements relating to U.S. citizens' income from assets held abroad.

Patient Protection and Affordable Care Act (124 Stat. 119, 42 U.S.C. 18001 note). Signed by the president March 23, 2010. Made sweeping changes to the health insurance industry regarding products, pricing, and availability. The act also contained a myriad of changes to taxes, including new taxes, tax credits, and tax exemptions related to health care financing.

Small Business Jobs Act of 2010 (124 Stat. 2504, 15 U.S.C. 631 note). Signed by the president September 27, 2010. Contained tax provisions designed to encourage investment and provide access to capital for businesses.

American Taxpayer Relief Act of 2012 (126 Stat. 2313, 26 U.S.C. 1 note). Signed by the president Jan. 3, 2013. Extended some of the tax credits and other related provisions enacted under ARRA. Changed various tax rates.

Tax Increase Prevention Act of 2014 (128 Stat. 4010, 26 U.S.C. 1 note). Signed by the president Dec 19, 2014. Renewed a number of "extender" provisions of the tax law that expired at the end of 2013 through the end of 2014.

Division B: Achieving A Better Life Experience Act of 2014 (ABLE) established tax-free savings accounts to help individuals and families finance disability needs.

Veterans Affairs Department

810 Vermont Ave. N.W., Washington, DC 20420
Internet: www.va.gov

Veterans Affairs Department   854

Veterans Affairs Department

810 Vermont Ave. N.W., Washington, DC 20420
Internet: www.va.gov

The Department of Veterans Affairs (VA) was elevated to cabinet status on March 15, 1989. The VA was created from the Veterans Administration, which was established as an independent agency in July 1930. The secretary of veterans affairs is appointed by the president and confirmed by the Senate.

The VA administers programs to assist the nation's veterans, their families, and dependents. Most of the programs provide health care to veterans and pensions or other compensation to veterans, their dependents, and survivors. Other programs assist veterans in continuing their education. The department also guarantees loans made by commercial lenders to veterans for new homes, condominiums, and mobile or manufactured homes. Three units within the VA administer veterans programs: The Veterans Benefits Administration, the Veterans Health Administration, and National Cemetery Administration.

Veterans Benefits Administration administers veterans' benefits programs, including disability compensation, pension, education and training, home loans, life insurance as well as programs for survivors and dependents.

The education program provides funds to veterans to pay for education at any high school, vocational, correspondence, or business school; junior or teachers college; college or university; professional, scientific or technical institution; or any other institution that furnishes education at the secondary school level or above. These schools must be approved by a state approval agent. The VA reviews the state approval procedure to ensure that the state standards measure up to VA criteria. The VA has no authority to force a state to use its approval standards; it can only refuse to provide the funds to a veteran who wishes to attend a non-approved school.

The Improving Transparency of Education Opportunities for Veterans Act of 2012 mandated transparency improvements among institutions of higher learning that offered postsecondary education to veterans and members of the military. The legislation was enacted to curb abuses by for-profit institutions. The Veterans Access, Choice, and Accountability Act of 2014 (VACAA) expands the Fry Scholarship to include the surviving spouses of service members who died in the line of duty after September 10, 2001. VACAA also requires VA to disapprove payment for education at public institutions of higher learning if the school charges qualifying veterans and dependents tuition and fees in excess of the rate for resident students for terms beginning after July 1, 2015.

VetSuccess on Campus places experienced VA counselors directly on college campuses, which strengthens VA's partnership with institutions of higher learning to help veterans succeed. Counselors maintain close relationships with local VA Centers and VA medical facilities, referring veterans as needed for counseling or medical services and providing assistance enrolling in and applying for VA medical and nonmedical benefits. Partner schools provide on-campus office space for the VA counselors.

The VA ensures that schools and training institutions comply with VA rules and regulations; with the Civil Rights Act of 1964, which prohibits discrimination because of race, color, or national origin in any program that receives federal financial assistance; and with Title IX of the Education Amendments of 1972, which prohibits sex discrimination by an education program that receives federal funds.

The VA guarantees or insures part of each home loan and requires the lending institution to make the loan at a specific rate of interest (usually below the market rate). The department also has authority to provide grants to veterans with permanent disabilities to purchase houses adapted to their needs.

VA officials appraise properties, supervise construction of new homes, and ensure that lenders comply with federal laws and regulations governing access to credit.

The online eBenefits website, administered jointly by the VA and the Department of Defense, is a web portal that provides active-duty service members, veterans, their families, and authorized caregivers with a single sign-on, central access point to clinical and benefits information. The portal provides applications for disability compensation and various benefits and access to employment resources.

Veterans Health Administration is the nation's largest integrated health care system with more than 1,700 sites of care serving 8.76 million veterans each year. The VA arranges for the care of some veterans in nonveteran hospitals and homes when space in VA facilities is not available. The VA also performs a wide variety of research and assists in the training of physicians and dentists.

Following a highly publicized scandal of lengthy waiting periods and falsified scheduling data for medical appointments at the Phoenix VA Health Care System in April 2014, Congress passed and the president signed the Veterans Access, Choice, and Accountability Act of 2014 (VACAA). Under VACAA, the VA established the Choice Program, a new, temporary benefit that allows some veterans to receive health care in their communities rather than waiting for a VA appointment or traveling to a VA facility. VACAA also expanded eligibility for veterans in need of mental health care due to sexual assault or sexual harassment that occurred during their military service.

The VA also issued a Request for Proposal for a new medical appointment scheduling system to improve access to care for veterans by providing schedulers with state-of-the-art, management-based scheduling software. The new system will replace a legacy scheduling system that has been in use at VA since 1985.

National Cemetery Administration. The VA also operates the National Cemetery System. Qualified veterans are eligible for a headstone and burial in any national cemetery where space is available. The eligible veteran's next of kin also can receive allowances for private burial, plot, and headstone.

The Honoring America's Veterans and Caring for Camp Lejeune Families Act of 2012 contained provisions that placed restrictions on protests at military funerals. The legislation prohibited disruptions of funerals of members or former members of the Armed Forces two hours before and after a military funeral and restricted the protests from occurring within 500 feet of the boundary of a funeral location, or on or near the boundary of the residence of a surviving member of a deceased's immediate family. The legislation provided civil remedies, including actual and statutory damages.

In June 2013 the U.S. Supreme Court issued a decision invalidating a key provision of the 1996 Defense of Marriage Act, which had defined marriage as a legal union of one man and one woman for the purposes of "any act of Congress . . . any ruling, regulation, or interpretation of the various administrative bureaus and agencies of the United States." While the ruling settled the matter of same-sex marriage with regard to federal government laws and regulations, it did not legalize same-sex marriage across the nation. However, several rulings in some federal district courts overturned state prohibitions against same-sex marriage, leaving a patchwork of state laws regulating marriage for same-sex couples.

Federal law requires the VA to use residency to determine whether a Veteran's marriage is recognized for the purposes of VA benefits. In June 2014 the VA announced it was providing guidance to same-sex married couples on the benefits and services to which they are entitled under current laws and regulations. Following the Supreme Court decision, VA worked with Justice Department to develop guidance to process claims and applications for same-sex married couples while still following the statutory requirement to look to the place of residency.

■ KEY PERSONNEL

Secretary
    Robert A. McDonald . . . . (202) 461–4800
        Fax. . . . . (202) 495–5463
Deputy Secretary
    Sloan D. Gibson. . . . . (202) 461–4800
Chief of Staff
    Jill Draime (acting) . . . . (202) 461–7016
General Counsel
    Leigh A. Bradley . . . . (202) 273–6660
Board of Veterans Appeals
    Laura H. Eskenazi, executive and
        vice chair . . . . (202) 565–4644
    Bruce Gipe, principal deputy
        vice chair . . . . (202) 565–5436
Inspector General
    Linda A. Halliday . . . . (202) 565–8620
Acquisition, Logistics, and Construction
    Gregory L. Giddens. . . . . (202) 632–4606
Center for Faith-Based and Neighborhood Partnerships
    Rev. E. Terri LaVelle . . . . (202) 273–7499
Center for Minority Veterans
    Barbara Ward. . . . . (202) 461–6191
Center for Women Veterans
    Elisa Basnight. . . . . (202) 461–6193
Employment Discrimination Complaint Adjudication
    Maxanne R. Witkin. . . . . (202) 254–0065
Interagency Care and Benefits Coordination
    Margarita Devlin. . . . . (202) 461–6776
Small and Disadvantaged Business Utilization
    Tom Leney . . . . (202) 461–4300
Survivors Assistance
    Wendy Yeldell (acting) . . . . (202) 632–7702
        Toll-free . . . . (800) 827–1000
Veterans Service Organization Liaison
    Kevin Secor . . . . (202) 273–4835
Veterans Benefits Administration
    Allison A. Hickey, under secretary. . . (202) 461–9300
        Fax. . . . . (202) 495–5761
    Asset Enterprise Management
        James M. Sullivan . . . . (202) 461–9200
    Compensation and Pension Service
        Thomas Murphy . . . . (202) 461–9700
    Education Service
        Robert Worley . . . . (202) 461–9800
    Facilities, Access, and Administration
        Vacant. . . . . (202) 461–9430
    Loan Guaranty Service
        Michael Frueh . . . . (202) 461–9500
    Public Affairs
        Steve Westerfeld . . . . (202) 461–9310
    Vocational Rehabilitation and Counseling Service
        Vacant. . . . . (202) 461–9600

Under Secretary for Health, Veterans Health Administration
David J. Shulkin . . . . (202) 461–7000
Fax . . . . (202) 273–5787
Communications Officer
Todd Livick . . . . (202) 273–6409
National Cemetery Administration
Ronald E. Walters (acting), under secretary for
memorial affairs . . . . (202) 461–6112
Fax . . . . (202) 273–6709
Public Affairs
Mike Nacincik . . . . (202) 461–6240
Assistant Secretary, Congressional and Legislative Affairs
Christopher E. O'Connor (acting) . . . (202) 461–6490
Fax . . . . (202) 273–6791
Director of Operations
William Delaney . . . . (202) 461–6491
Assistant Secretary, Human Resources and Administration
Gina S. Farrisee . . . . (202) 461–7750
Fax . . . . (202) 273–4914
Administration
Roy Herndon . . . . (202) 461–5000
Diversity and Inclusion
Georgia Coffey . . . . (202) 461–4131
Human Resources Management
Vacant . . . . (202) 461–7765
Labor-Management Relations
Kimberly D. Moseley . . . . (202) 461–4122
Assistant Secretary, Information and Technology
Stephen Warren (acting) . . . . (202) 461–6911
Assistant Secretary, Management
Ed Murray (acting) . . . . (202) 461–6600
Fax . . . . (202) 273–6892
Acquisition and Logistics Management
Jim Sullivan . . . . (202) 461–6669
Budget and Finance
Santos Cordero-Rivera . . . . (202) 461–6630
Assistant Secretary, Operations, Security, and Preparedness
Kevin T. Hanretta . . . . (202) 461–4980
Assistant Secretary, Policy and Planning
Linda Spoonster Schwartz . . . . (202) 461–5800
Fax . . . . (202) 273–5993
Data Governance and Analysis
Dat Tran . . . . (202) 461–5788
Interagency Collaboration and Integration
John Medve . . . . (202) 461–5626
Policy
Susan Sullivan . . . . (202) 461–5801
Program Management
Greg Giddens . . . . (202) 461–6986
Assistant Secretary, Public and Intergovernmental Affairs
Maura Sullivan . . . . (202) 495–7500
Fax . . . . (202) 273–0954
Intergovernmental Affairs
Jason Cain . . . . (202) 461–7400

■ INFORMATION SOURCES

Internet

Agency website: www.va.gov. Includes information on benefits, facilities, and special programs, with links to related Internet sites.

Telephone Contacts

General Information . . . . (202) 273–5400
Fraud, Waste, Abuse, and
Mismanagement Hotline . . . . (800) 488–8244
Veterans Benefits Hotline . . . . (800) 827–1000
Education (GI Bill) Hotline . . . . (888) 442–4551
Health Care Benefits Hotline . . . . (877) 222–8387
Debt Management Hotline . . . . (800) 827–0648
Life Insurance Hotline . . . . (800) 669–8477
Veterans Crisis Hotline . . . . (800) 273–TALK (273–8255)
Women Veterans
Hotline . . . . (855) VA–Women (829–6636)
VHA Mammography Helpline . . . . (888) 492–7844
TTY . . . . Dial 711

Information and Publications

KEY OFFICES

VA Public Affairs

810 Vermont Ave. N.W.
Washington, DC 20420
General public (202) 461–7700
Press (202) 461–7600
Fax (202) 273–5719
Josh Taylor (acting), assistant secretary

Provides general information, issues news releases, and answers queries from the media.

VA Intergovernmental Affairs

810 Vermont Ave. N.W.
Washington, DC 20420
(202) 461–7400
Jason Cain, deputy assistant secretary

Serves as liaison to state and local governments, veterans service organizations, and faith-based and community organizations.

Veterans Benefits Administration

810 Vermont Ave. N.W.
Washington, DC 20420
(800) 827–1000
Fax (202) 495–5790

Provides publications on veterans' benefits.

Freedom of Information

VA Information and Technology
810 Vermont Ave. N.W., 005R1C
Washington, DC 20420

(202) 632–7641

Fax (202) 632–7581

Email: vacofoiaservice@va.gov

Jim Horan, director

DATA AND STATISTICS

A good source of data and statistics on the VA is the agency website, www.va.gov/vetdata

PUBLICATIONS

Each unit within the VA (e.g., Veterans Benefits Administration, Veterans Health Administration, National Cemetery Association) publishes and distributes publications. For availability of material on specific topics, contact the appropriate division or unit, or the nearest regional office.

The popular VA publication *Federal Benefits for Veterans, Dependents, and Survivors* is available via the agency's website or from the U.S. Government Printing Office (GPO) (*see appendix, Ordering Government Publications*).

Reference Resources

LIBRARIES

VA Central Office Library

810 Vermont Ave. N.W., #975

MS 10P2C2

Washington, DC 20420

(202) 461–7573

Caryl Kazen, director

Holdings include material on VA and military history, biomedicine, business, and women veterans. Visitors may obtain more information about the collection by arranging an appointment with the director's office.

VA Law Library

Office of the General Counsel

810 Vermont Ave. N.W

Washington, DC 20420

(202) 461–7623

Fax (202) 273–6645

Susan Sokoll, law librarian

Collection consists of legal materials related to veterans programs. The library is connected to the Lexis computerized database system. Public use is restricted and must be arranged through the office of the chief librarian.

DOCKETS

Federal dockets relating to the Department of Veterans Affairs are available at www.regulations.gov. (*See appendix for Searching and Commenting on Regulations: Regulations.gov.*)

RULES AND REGULATIONS

VA rules and regulations are published in the *Code of Federal Regulations,* Title 38, Chapter I, Parts 0–end.

Proposed regulations and standards, new final rules, and standards and updates to the *Code of Federal Regulations* are published in the daily *Federal Register. (See appendix for information on how to obtain and use these publications.)* The *Federal Register* and the *Code of Federal Regulations* may also be accessed online at www.archives.gov/federal-register/cfr; the site contains a link to the federal government's regulatory website at www.regulations.gov (*see appendix*).

■ LEGISLATION

Legislation for which the VA has regulatory responsibility includes:

Veterans Benefits Act (72 Stat. 1105, 38 U.S.C. 101). Signed by the president Sept. 2, 1958. Detailed the full range of veterans benefits. Authorized the VA to establish standards for loans it guarantees or insures.

Veterans Readjustment Benefits Act of 1966 (80 Stat. 12, 38 U.S.C. 101). Signed by the president March 3, 1966. Authorized a system of educational assistance to veterans.

Veterans Health Care Amendments of 1979 (93 Stat. 47, 38 U.S.C. 101 note). Signed by the president June 13, 1979. Established a readjustment counseling program for veterans of the Vietnam era.

Veterans Administration Health Care Amendments of 1980 (94 Stat. 1048, 38 U.S.C. Title III). Vetoed by the president Aug. 22, 1980; veto overridden Aug. 26, 1980. Improved and expanded the capability of VA health care facilities to respond to the needs of older veterans.

Veterans Rehabilitation and Education Amendments of 1980 (94 Stat. 2171, 38 U.S.C. 101 note). Signed by the president Oct. 17, 1980. Revised and expanded veterans employment and training programs.

Veterans Health Care, Training, and Small Business Loan Act of 1981 (95 Stat. 1047, 38 U.S.C. 101 note). Signed by the president Nov. 3, 1981. Provided health care for veterans exposed to Agent Orange, a toxic defoliant used in Vietnam.

Veterans Education and Employment Assistance Act of 1984 (98 Stat. 2553, 38 U.S.C. 101 note). Signed by the president Oct. 19, 1984. Established a new educational assistance program for veterans as part of the Department of Defense Authorization Act of 1985.

Veterans Dioxin and Radiation Exposure Compensation Standards Act (98 Stat. 2725, 38 U.S.C. 354 note). Signed by the president Oct. 24, 1984. Required the VA to pay compensation to some veterans exposed to Agent Orange, or to ionizing radiation from atmospheric nuclear tests or from the U.S. occupation of Hiroshima or Nagasaki, Japan.

Department of Veterans Affairs Act (100 Stat. 2635, 38 U.S.C. 201 note). Signed by the president Oct. 25, 1988. Renamed the VA the Department of Veterans Affairs and elevated the agency to an executive department.

Veterans Home Loan Program Amendments of 1992 (106 Stat. 3633, 38 U.S.C. 101 note). Signed by the president Oct. 28, 1992. Authorized the VA to provide home loan benefits for veterans, including guaranteeing adjustable rate mortgages.

Veterans Health Care Act of 1992 (106 Stat. 4943, 38 U.S.C. 101 note). Signed by the president Nov. 4, 1992. Established the Persian Gulf War Veterans Health Registry within the VA. Authorized the VA to provide counseling services to women who suffer the trauma of sexual assault or harassment during their military service.

Persian Gulf War Veterans Benefits Act (108 Stat. 4647, 38 U.S.C. 101 note and 1117 note). Signed by the president Nov. 2, 1994. Authorized the VA to provide disability benefits to veterans suffering from Persian Gulf Syndrome. Established a Center for Women Veterans within the VA to coordinate women's programs. Expanded eligibility for VA-guaranteed home loans.

Veterans' Health Care Eligibility Reform Act of 1996 (110 Stat. 3177, 38 U.S.C. 101 note). Signed by the president Oct. 9, 1996. Established the Advisory Committee on the Readjustment of Veterans. Required the Veterans Health Administration to establish a peer review panel to assess the scientific and clinical merit of proposals dealing with mental health and behavioral sciences of veterans.

Veterans' Benefits Improvements Act of 1996 (110 Stat. 3322, 32 U.S.C. 101 note). Signed by the president Oct. 9, 1996. Relaxed some of the requirements needed for veterans to obtain benefits relating to education, housing, memorial affairs, employment, and training.

Veterans' Millennium Health Care and Benefits Act (113 Stat. 1545, 38 U.S.C. 101 note). Signed by the president Nov. 30, 1999. Established a four-year plan requiring the VA to provide institutional care and extended care services to veterans with 70 percent or more service-connected disabilities. Authorized the VA to pay for emergency treatment for uninsured veterans. Required the VA to operate a sexual trauma program through 2004 and to establish specialized mental health treatments for post-traumatic stress and drug abuse. Authorized benefits to spouses of former prisoners of war who were rated completely disabled because of service-connected disabilities. Directed the VA to establish six additional national veterans' cemeteries and to commission a study on improvements to veterans' cemeteries and benefits.

Veterans Claims Assistance Act of 2000 (114 Stat. 2096, 38 U.S.C. 101 note). Signed by the president Nov. 9, 2000. Authorized the VA to help veterans find evidence to use in establishing benefits claims. Required the VA to assist veterans in obtaining medical records and other relevant data at other federal agencies.

Homeless Veterans Comprehensive Assistance Act of 2001 (115 Stat. 903, 38 U.S.C. 101 note). Signed by the president Dec. 21, 2001. Authorized and expanded assistance programs for homeless veterans.

Veterans Education and Benefits Expansion Act of 2001 (115 Stat. 976, 38 U.S.C. 101 note). Signed by the president Dec. 27, 2001. Increased the amounts of veterans' education benefits covered by the Montgomery GI Bill. Repealed the thirty-year presumptive period for respiratory cancers associated with exposure to herbicide agents in Vietnam. Expanded the definition of "undiagnosed illnesses" for Persian Gulf War veterans. Provided a service pension to low-income veterans. Required the VA to give benefit applicants, within three months of their application, information on all benefits available to veterans, dependents, and survivors. Increased the maximum VA home loan guarantee amount.

Department of Veterans Affairs Emergency Preparedness Act of 2002 (116 Stat. 2024, 38 U.S.C. 101 note). Signed by the president Nov. 7, 2002. Created four national medical-preparedness centers to conduct research on the detection, diagnosis, prevention, and treatment of illnesses that could result from a biological, chemical, or radiological attack. Authorized the centers to provide laboratory and other medical support services to federal, state, and local authorities during a national emergency. Authorized the VA to provide medical care for people affected by president-declared emergencies or disasters.

Veterans Benefits Improvement Act of 2002 (116 Stat. 2820, 38 U.S.C. 101 note). Signed by the president Dec. 6, 2002. Expanded veterans' benefits, including a retroactive increase in the Medal of Honor pension. Extended special monthly compensation to women who have at least partial breast loss as a result of military service.

Veterans Health Care, Capital Asset, and Business Improvement Act of 2003 (117 Stat. 2042, 38 U.S.C. 101 note). Signed by the president Dec. 6, 2003. Enhanced the provision of long-term health care for veterans and authorized funding for construction of numerous medical facilities.

Veterans Benefits Act of 2003 (117 Stat. 2651, 38 U.S.C. 101 note). Signed by the president Dec. 16, 2003. Authorized economic incentives for veterans who participate in apprenticeship programs, and increased assistance to disabled veterans who need adaptive equipment for their homes or vehicles. Expanded the GI Bill program by authorizing educational assistance for on-the-job training in certain self-employment training programs.

Veterans Health Programs Improvement Act of 2004 (118 Stat. 2379, 38 U.S.C. 101 note). Signed by the president Nov. 30, 2004. Authorized changes to a variety of medical benefit programs administered by the VA, including assistance for homeless veterans, nursing, and hospice and education benefits.

Veterans' Benefits Improvements Act of 2004 (118 Stat. 3598, 38 U.S.C. 101 note). Signed by the president Dec. 10, 2004. Provided a variety of education, employment, housing, and other benefits to veterans and their families, including increasing the monthly educational assistance allowance; extending the period of time that the surviving spouse of a service member or veteran is eligible for educational assistance; and extending eligibility for specially adapted housing grants to veterans with permanent and total service-connected disabilities.

Veterans Benefits, Health Care, and Information Technology Act of 2006 (38 U.S.C. 501(a), 5902, 5903, 5904). Signed by the president Dec. 22, 2006. Amended regulations concerning the appointment of legal counsel in claim proceedings before the VA. Expanded mental health services for veterans. Expanded eligibility under the Survivors' and Dependents' Educational Assistance Program to include the spouse or child of a disabled veteran.

Wounded Warrior Act (122 Stat. 447, 10 U.S.C. 1071 note). Signed by the president Jan. 28, 2008. Required the VA and the Department of Defense (DOD) to coordinate care for injured veterans, including the prevention, diagnosis, treatment, research, and rehabilitation of traumatic brain injury and post-traumatic stress disorder (PTSD), and other mental health conditions in members of the Armed Forces. Required VA and DOD to jointly develop and implement procedures and standards for the transition of recovering service members from DOD to VA.

Post-9/11 Veterans Educational Assistance Act of 2008 (122 Stat. 2357, 38 U.S.C. 101 note). Signed by the president June 30, 2008. Allowed eligible veterans who served at least ninety days active duty after Sept. 11, 2001, to receive an in-state, undergraduate education at a public institution at no cost. Allowed certain members of the armed forces to transfer benefits to a spouse or dependent children.

Veterans' Benefits Improvement Act of 2008 (122 Stat. 4145, 38 U.S.C. 101 note). Signed by the president Oct. 10, 2008. Enhanced compensation and pension, housing, labor and education, and insurance benefits for veterans. Set forth provisions to allow veterans to convert subprime loans from the private sector to VA loans.

American Recovery and Reinvestment Act of 2009 (123 Stat. 199). Signed by the president Feb. 17, 2009. Appropriated more than $1.4 billion to the VA to improve its medical facilities and national cemeteries; to provide grants to assist states in acquiring or constructing state nursing home and domiciliary facilities and to remodel, modify, or alter existing facilities; and to administer one-time payments of $250 to eligible veterans and their survivors or dependents. Authorized benefits for Filipino veterans who aided American troops in World War II.

VOW to Hire Heroes Act of 2011 (125 Stat. 711, 38 U.S.C. 101 note). Signed by the president Nov. 21, 2011. Established the Veterans Retraining Assistance Program (VRAP) for unemployed veterans aged thirty-five to sixty (who met certain conditions) to provide eligible veterans with up to twelve months of Department of Veterans Affairs (VA)-funded retraining assistance to pursue an associate degree or certificate in a high-demand occupation. Mandated that the VA and Department of Labor (DOL) shall jointly administer the process for determining an applicant's VRAP eligibility.

Honoring America's Veterans and Caring for Camp Lejeune Families Act of 2012 (126 Stat. 1165, 50 U.S.C. app. 533). Signed by the president Aug. 6, 2012. Provides extended medical care for veterans and their families who were based in Camp Lejeune in the years the water was contaminated there. Included provisions to improve access to health care for veterans, streamline VA services, and expand support for homeless veterans. Placed restrictions on protesting at military funerals.

Improving Transparency of Education Opportunities for Veterans Act of 2012 (126 Stat. 2398, 38 U.S.C. 36980. Signed by the president Jan. 10, 2013. Directs Veterans Affairs (VA) to develop a comprehensive policy to improve transparency and accountability of institutions of higher learning. The policy would include consumer protection provisions and information for veterans to assist with selection of postsecondary education programs. Included additional provisions for health care and transition services.

Dignified Burial and Other Veterans' Benefits Improvement Act (126 Stat. 2417, 38 U.S.C. 101 note). Signed by the president Jan. 10, 2013. Mandates proper burial for veterans who die without next of kin or do not have ability to pay for a proper burial.

Veterans Access, Choice, and Accountability Act of 2014 (128 Stat. 1754, 38 USC 101 note). Signed by the president Aug. 7, 2014. Allows for increased veterans access to, and eligibility for, non-VA health care. Expanded eligibility for veterans in need of mental health care due to sexual assault or sexual harassment that occurred during their military service. Expands the Fry Scholarship to include the surviving spouses of service members who died in the line of duty after Sept. 10, 2001. Requires VA to disapprove payment for education at public institutions of higher learning if the school charges qualifying veterans and dependents tuition and fees in excess of the rate for resident students for terms beginning after July 1, 2015.

Clay Hunt Suicide Prevention for American Veterans Act (129 Stat. 30, 38 U.S.C. 101 note). Signed by the president Feb. 12, 2015. Makes provisions to expand VA mental services. Provides a one-year window of enhanced VA health care enrollment for combat veterans who are not enrolled in the VA health care system and who were discharged or released from active military service after January 1, 2009 and before January 1, 2011.

◼ REGIONAL OFFICES

VA Public Affairs Offices

The Department of Veterans Affairs also maintains benefits offices in each state. For information on these offices, call (800) 827–1000.

REGION 1
(CT, MA, ME, NH, NJ, NY, RI, VT)
245 W. Houston St., #213
New York, NY 10014
(212) 807–3429
James Blue, regional director

REGION 2
(DC, DE, MD, PA, NC, VA, WV except Huntington)
1722 Eye St. N.W., #306
Washington, DC 20421
(202) 530–9360
Ramona Joyce, regional director

REGION 3
(AL, FL except Pensacola, GA, KY, PR, SC, TN,
Huntington WV Medical Center, VI)
1700 Clairmont Rd.
Decatur, GA 30033
(404) 929–5880
Jan Northstar, regional director

REGION 4

(Most of IL, IN except Evansville, MI, OH, WI except
Superior)
2122 W. Taylor St., #320
Chicago, IL 60612
(312) 980–4235
Craig Larson, regional director

REGION 5

(CO, IA, parts of ID and IL, KS, MN, MO, MT, ND,
NE, SD, UT, WY)
155 Van Gordon St.
Lakewood, CO 80228
(303) 914–5855
Paul S. Sherbo, regional director

REGION 6

(AK, CA, GU, HI, Pocatello, ID; NV, OR, WA;
Philippines)
c/o VA Greater LA Health Care System
11301 Wilshire Blvd., Bldg. 506
Los Angeles, CA 90073
(310) 268–4207
David S. Bayard, regional director

REGION 7

(AR, AZ, LA, MS, NM, OK, TX)
2301 E. Lamar Blvd., #350
Arlington, TX 76006
(817) 385–3720
Oziel Garza, regional director

Regulatory Oversight and Coordination Agencies

Regulatory Oversight and Coordination Agencies

▨ CONGRESSIONAL BUDGET OFFICE

Ford House Office Bldg., 4th Floor
2nd and D Sts. S.W.
Washington, DC 20515–6925
Internet: www.cbo.gov

The Congressional Budget and Impoundment Control Act of 1974 established the Congressional Budget Office (CBO) as a nonpartisan agency in the legislative branch. The CBO provides Congress with objective, timely, nonpartisan analyses needed for economic and budget decisions and with the information and estimates required for the congressional budget process. The CBO supports the work of the House and Senate Budget Committees, which also were created by the 1974 Congressional Budget Act. The CBO's services can be grouped in four categories: helping Congress formulate a budget plan, helping it stay within that plan, assessing the impact of federal mandates, and studying issues related to the budget and to economic policy. It also is responsible for producing the budget and economic outlook and midsession updates each year. The budget projections and economic forecast are generally issued each January and updated in August. The budget projections are also usually updated each March. The CBO is the only part of the legislative branch whose mandate includes making economic forecasts and projections.

Director
    Keith Hall . . . . (202) 226–2700
    Fax . . . . (202) 225–7509
Deputy Director
    Robert A. Sunshine . . . . (202) 226–2700
Communications
    Deborah Kilroe . . . . (202) 226–2602
Economic Analysis
    Jeffrey Kling . . . . (202) 226–0210
Legislative Affairs
    Edward (Sandy) Davis . . . . (202) 226–2837
General Counsel
    Mark P. Hadley . . . . (202) 226–2839
Budget Analysis
    Theresa A. Gullo . . . . (202) 226–2800
Financial Analysis
    Damien Moore . . . . (202) 226–2258
Health, Retirement, and Long-Term Analysis
    Linda Bilheimer . . . . (202) 226–2666

Macroeconomic Analysis
    Wendy Edelberg . . . . (202) 226–2750
Management, Business, and Information Services
    Joseph E. Evans Jr. . . . . (202) 226–2600
Microeconomic Studies
    Joseph Kile . . . . (202) 226–2940
National Security
    David E. Mosher . . . . (202) 226–2900
Tax Analysis
    David Weiner . . . . (202) 226–2680

▨ CORPORATION FOR NATIONAL AND COMMUNITY SERVICE

1201 New York Ave. N.W.
Washington, DC 20525
Internet: www.nationalservice.gov

The Corporation for National and Community Service provides opportunities for Americans of all ages and backgrounds to serve their communities and country through nonprofit organizations, faith-based groups, schools, and local agencies. Volunteers help meet needs in education, the environment, public safety, homeland security, and other critical areas.

The Corporation operates the following programs:

AmeriCorps. AmeriCorps provides volunteers with opportunities to serve their communities on a full- or part-time basis, while earning educational awards for college or vocational training. Participants are sponsored and trained by national, state, or local nonprofit organizations to meet the specific needs of the communities they serve. In addition to these local programs, AmeriCorps also offers two national programs, the AmeriCorps National Civilian Community Corps (NCCC) program and the AmeriCorps Volunteers in Service to America (VISTA) program. NCCC is a full-time program in which members work in teams and live together in housing complexes on NCCC campuses. Members help meet the nation's critical needs in education, public safety, the environment, and other human needs. In Americorps VISTA, individuals work in nonprofit organizations. Rather than providing direct service, such as tutoring or housing renovation, VISTA members work to expand the organization's services by training and recruiting volunteers and helping to establish new community activities.

Senior Corps. Senior Corps is a network of three programs designed to help older Americans find service opportunities in their communities. The Retired and Senior Volunteers Program encourages older citizens to use their talents and experience in community service. The Foster Grandparent Program offers older citizens opportunities to work with exceptional children and children with special needs. The Senior Companion Program recruits older citizens to help homebound adults, especially seniors with special needs.

Social Innovation Fund. The fund is a public-private partnership grant program that was established in 2009 by the Kennedy Serve America Act, which was co-authored by Senators Edward M. Kennedy, D-Mass., and Orrin Hatch, R-Utah. The fund provides federal money for up to five years to other grantmaking institutions, which fully match the federal money and then direct the resources through competitions to community-based nonprofit organizations, or "subgrantees," that support youth development, economic opportunity, and healthy futures in low-income communities.

General Information ....(202) 606–5000
Inspector General Hotline............(800) 452–8210
Chief Executive Officer
    Wendy Spencer .... (202) 606–6636
Chief Operating Officer
    Jeffrey Page....................... (202) 606–6632
    TTY.......................... (800) 833–3722
AmeriCorps
    Bill Basl.......................... (202) 606–6790
AmeriCorps Recruiting Information.... (800) 942–2677
    AmeriCorps NCCC
        José Phillips .... (202) 606–6706
    AmeriCorps VISTA
        Paul Monteiro .... (202) 606–6943
    Senior Corps
        Erwin Tan..................... (202) 606–3237
    Senior Corps Recruiting
    Information...................... (800) 424–8867

■ COUNCIL OF ECONOMIC ADVISERS
1800 G St. N.W., 8th Floor
Washington, DC 20502
Internet: www.whitehouse.gov/cea

The Employment Act of 1946 created the Council of Economic Advisers. The office, within the Executive Office of the President, consists of three members, one designated as chair, who are appointed by the president and confirmed by the Senate. The council and its staff of economists analyze the national economy and its various segments, including economic programs and policies of the federal government; advise the president on economic matters both domestic and international; and prepare the annual *Economic Report of the President* for Congress.

Chair
    Jason Furman.................... (202) 456–4779
    Fax........................... (202) 456–3080

Members
    Maurice Obstfeld................. (202) 456–4775
    Betsey Stevenson.................. (202) 456–4775

■ COUNCIL ON ENVIRONMENTAL QUALITY
722 Jackson Pl. N.W.
Washington, DC 20506–0003
Internet: www.whitehouse.gov/
administration/eop/ceq

The National Environmental Policy Act (NEPA) of 1969 established the Council on Environmental Quality (CEQ), and the Environment Quality Improvement Act of 1970 assigned additional responsibilities to it. The council, within the Executive Office of the President, is headed by a chair who is appointed by the president and confirmed by the Senate. Specific functions of the CEQ include formulating and recommending policies to the president that further environmental quality; analyzing changes and trends in the national environment; reviewing environmental programs of the federal government to determine their soundness; overseeing implementation of NEPA; approving agency environmental regulations; and preparing the president's annual environmental quality report to Congress. CEQ also oversees the Office of the Federal Environmental Executive, which encourages sustainable environmental stewardship throughout the federal government.

Deputy Director
    Christy Goldfuss (acting) .... (202) 456–9636
        Fax........................... (202) 456–6546
General Counsel
    Vacant.......................... (202) 456–4317
    Deputy General Counsel
        Manisha Patel .... (202) 456–2464
Managing Director
    Christy Goldfuss .... (202) 456–9636
Chief of Staff
    Vacant.......................... (202) 456–3360
    Deputy Chief of Staff
        Lowry Crook.................... (202) 456–3360
Communications
    Taryn Tuss .... (202) 456–6998
Legislative Affairs
    Trent Bauserman................. (202) 456–1574
Land and Water Ecosystems
    Vacant.......................... (202) 395–2025
Energy and Climate Change
    Rick Duke....................... (202) 456–5190
Policy Outreach
    Tom Elson .... (202) 456–3621
NEPA Oversight
    Horst Greczmiel .... (202) 395–0827
Federal Environmental Executive
    Kate E. Brandt .... (202) 564–2659

▨ DOMESTIC POLICY COUNCIL
1600 Pennsylvania Ave. N.W.
Washington, DC 20502
Internet: www.whitehouse.gov/dpc

The Domestic Policy Council (DPC) was established by an executive order on Aug. 16, 1993. The council is within the Executive Office of the President. It is composed of the vice president, cabinet officials, administrators of federal agencies that deal with the issues addressed by the DPC. The principal functions of the council include coordinating the domestic policy-making process; ensuring domestic policy decisions and programs are consistent with the president's stated goals; and monitoring the implementation of the domestic policy agenda. The Office of National AIDS Policy, the Office of Social Innovation and Civic Participation, and the Office of Faith-Based and Neighborhood Partnerships are also affiliated with the Domestic Policy Council. All executive departments and agencies, whether or not represented on the council, coordinate their domestic policy through the council.

Director
Cecilia Muñoz . . . . (202) 456–5594
Executive Assistant
Lauren Dunn . . . . (202) 456–5594

▨ GOVERNMENT ACCOUNTABILITY OFFICE
441 G St. N.W.
Washington, DC 20548
(202) 512–6000
TTY (202) 512–2537
Internet: www.gao.gov

The Government Accountability Office (GAO) was established in 1921 as the General Accounting Office. The office's current name was adopted in 2004. The GAO is the investigative arm of Congress, charged with examining all matters relating to the receipt and disbursement of public funds. The GAO is under the control and direction of the comptroller general of the United States, who is nominated by the president and confirmed by the Senate for one nonrenewable fifteen-year term.

The GAO's mission is to support the Congress in meeting its constitutional responsibilities and to help improve the performance and accountability of the federal government for the benefit of the American people. Nearly all its work is mandated in legislation requested by committee or subcommittee chairs, ranking minority members, or individual members of appropriations, authorizing, budget, or oversight committees.

Most of the GAO's work is based on original data collected and analyzed. All of the office's work is conducted in accordance with applicable professional audit and investigation standards.

The GAO supports congressional oversight in several ways. It evaluates federal policies and the performance of agencies and programs to determine how well they are working. It oversees government operations through financial and other management audits to determine whether public funds are being spent efficiently, effectively, and in accordance with applicable laws. It conducts investigations to assess whether illegal or improper activities are occurring. It analyzes financing for government activities. It provides legal opinions to determine whether agencies are in compliance with laws and regulations. It conducts analyses to assess needed actions and the implications of proposed actions.

The GAO's role is both to meet short-term needs for information and to help the Congress better understand issues that are newly emerging, longer-term in nature, broad in scope, and cutting across government. The Congress looks to the GAO to turn assertions and information into facts and knowledge.

Copies of unclassified GAO reports are available on the website, www.gao.gov.

Comptroller General
Gene L. Dodaro . . . . (202) 512–5500
Fax . . . . (202) 512–5507
Chief Administrative Officer/Chief Financial Officer
Karl Maschino . . . . (202) 512–5800
Chief Information Officer
Howard Williams Jr . . . . (202) 512–5589
Applied Research and Methods
Nancy Kingsbury . . . . (202) 512–2700
Audit Policy and Quality Assurance
Timothy P. Bowling . . . . (202) 512–7680
Congressional Relations
Katherine Siggerud . . . . (202) 512–4400
Federal Accounting Standards Advisory Board
Wendolyn M. Payne . . . . (202) 512–7357
Field Operations
Linda Calbom (Seattle, WA) . . . . (206) 287–4809
Financial Management and Assurance
Greg Marchand . . . . (202) 512–6082
Forensic Audits and Investigative Services
Stephen M. Lord . . . . (202) 512–4379
General Counsel
Susan Poling . . . . (202) 512–5400
Human Capital
Carolyn Taylor . . . . (202) 512–2974
Inspector General
Adam Trzeciak . . . . (202) 512–8110
Personnel Appeals Board
William Persina . . . . (202) 512–6137
Public Affairs
Charles Young . . . . (202) 512–4800
Strategic Planning/External Liaison
James-Christian Blockwood . . . . (202) 512–2639
Other Telephone Contacts
Locator . . . . (202) 512–3000
Publications . . . . (202) 512–6000; (202) 512–3992
Fraud Hotline . . . . (202) 512–7470
(outside Washington, DC) . . . . (800) 424–5454

**U.S. Government Accountability Office
Document Ordering System**
700 4th St. N.W., Room 1100
Washington, DC 20548

(202) 512–6000
(866) 801–7077
TTY (202) 512–2537

All GAO reports are available at no cost via the GAO website (www.gao.gov/ordering.htm). Office hours are 8:00 a.m. to 7:00 p.m. Eastern time.

▓ NATIONAL ECONOMIC COUNCIL
1600 Pennsylvania Ave. N.W.
Washington, DC 20502
Internet: www.whitehouse.gov/nec

The National Economic Council (NEC) was created by an executive order on Jan. 25, 1993. The NEC is within the Executive Office of the President and is composed of cabinet members and other high-ranking executive branch officials. The principal functions of the council include coordinating the economic policy-making process; coordinating economic policy advice to the president; ensuring economic policy decisions and programs are consistent with the president's stated goals; and monitoring the implementation of the president's economic policy agenda. The NEC director is supported by a staff of policy specialists in various fields including agriculture, commerce, energy, financial markets, fiscal policy, health care, labor, and Social Security.

Assistant to the President and Director, National Economic Council
Jeffrey Zients . . . . (202) 456–2800
Fax . . . . (202) 456–0127

▓ NATIONAL SECURITY COUNCIL
1600 Pennsylvania Ave. N.W.
Washington, DC 20504
Internet: www.whitehouse.gov/nsc

The National Security Act of 1947 established the National Security Council (NSC), which was placed within the Executive Office of the President by Reorganization Plan No. 4 of 1949. The NSC is composed of the president, who chairs the council, the vice president, and the secretaries of defense, state, and the Treasury. The chair of the joint chiefs of staff and the Director of National Intelligence serve as advisers to the NSC, with other high-ranking executive branch officials, including the assistant to the president for national security affairs (also referred to as the national security adviser), attending council meetings. The chief of staff, counsel to the president, and the assistant to the president for economic policy are among the advisors routinely invited to attend meetings.

The NSC advises and assists the president in integrating all aspects of national security policy as it affects the United States—domestic, foreign, military, intelligence, and economic—in conjunction with the National Economic Council.

National Security Advisor
Susan Rice . . . . (202) 456–9491
Fax . . . . (202) 456–9490
Deputy National Security Advisor
Lisa Monaco . . . . (202) 456–9481

▓ NATIONAL TELECOMMUNICATIONS AND INFORMATION ADMINISTRATION
Herbert C. Hoover Bldg.
Department of Commerce
1401 Constitution Ave. N.W., #4898
Washington, DC 20230
Internet: www.ntia.doc.gov

The National Telecommunications and Information Administration (NTIA), created in 1978, is an agency within the Department of Commerce that serves as the president's principal adviser on telecommunications and information policy. NTIA manages and coordinates the use of the federal radio frequency spectrum; advances the interests and international competitiveness of the United States through policy analysis, technical guidance, and international representation; provides grants to further the national information infrastructure; maintains the Institute for Telecommunication Sciences, which offers scientific, engineering, and technical expertise to NTIA; and works to bring the benefits of advanced telecommunications technologies to millions of Americans in rural and underserved urban areas.

General Information . . . . (202) 482–2000
Assistant Secretary
Lawrence E. Strickling . . . . (202) 482–1840
Fax . . . . (202) 501–0536
Institute for Telecommunication Sciences
(325 Broadway, Boulder, CO 80305–3328)
Brian D. Lane (acting) . . . . (303) 497–5216
International Affairs
Fiona Alexander . . . . (202) 482–1890
Policy Analysis and Development
John Morris . . . . (202) 482–1880
Policy Coordination and Management
Len Bechtel . . . . (202) 482–1056
Public Safety Communications
Stephen Fletcher . . . . (202) 482–5802
Spectrum Management
Paige R. Atkins . . . . (202) 482–1850
Telecommunications and Information Applications
Douglas Kinkoph . . . . (202) 482–5802
Chief Counsel
Kathy Smith . . . . (202) 482–1816
Public Affairs
Heather Phillips . . . . (202) 482–7002
Congressional Affairs
James Waslilewski . . . . (202) 482–1840

■ OFFICE OF COMPLIANCE
110 2nd St. S.W., Room LA 200
Washington, DC 20540–1999
Internet: www.compliance.gov

The Congressional Accountability Act of 1995 estab-lished the Office of Compliance as an independent and neutral agency within the legislative branch. The office extends federal workplace laws to the employees of Congress and the agencies under its jurisdiction. The office enforces laws pertaining to worker safety, public access, civil rights, overtime pay, fair labor standards, family medical leave, polygraph protection, and plant closing notification. The office has a five-member, non-partisan Board of Directors and is led by four statutory executive staff members who carry out its day-to-day functions.

General Information ....(202) 724–9250
Recorded Information ....(202) 724–9260
Executive Director
    Barbara Sapin.....................(202) 724–9250
      Fax...........................(202) 426–1913
General Counsel
    Amy Dunning ....(202) 724–9250
    TTY ....(202) 426–1912
Deputy Executive Director, House
    Vacant..........................(202) 724–9270
Deputy Executive Director, Senate
    Woody Anglade...................(202) 724–9228
Chair
    Barbara L. Camens ....(202) 724–9250
Board Members
    Alan V. Friedman ....(202) 724–9250
    Roberta L. Holzwarth.............(202) 724–9250
    Susan S. Robfogel ....(202) 724–9250
    Barbara Childs Wallace ....(202) 724–9250

■ OFFICE OF GOVERNMENTWIDE POLICY
General Services Administration
1800 F St. N.W.
Washington, DC 20405
Internet: www.gsa.gov/ogp

The Office of Governmentwide Policy (OGP) was established within the General Services Administration (GSA) in December 1995 to consolidate several of the GSA's policy-making activities within one central office. The OGP promotes collaboration between government and the private sector in developing policy; better inte-gration of acquisition, management, and disposal of gov-ernment property; and the adaptation of private-sector management techniques to government agencies. In recent years, the office has been involved deeply in elec-tronic government initiatives.

Associate Administrator
    Giancarlo Brizzi..................(202) 501–8880

■ OFFICE OF INTERGOVERNMENTAL AFFAIRS
1600 Pennsylvania Ave. N.W., #106
Washington, DC 20502
Internet: www.whitehouse.gov/
administration/eop/iga

The Office of Intergovernmental Affairs serves as a liaison between the Executive Office of the President and state and local governments. The office answers questions and provides information to state and local governments on administration programs and policies.

Assistant to the President and Senior Advisor,
Intergovernmental Affairs and Public Engagement
    Valerie Jarrett.....................(202) 456–1414
Deputy Assistant
    Jerry Abramson...................(202) 456–2896

■ OFFICE OF MANAGEMENT AND BUDGET
Eisenhower Executive Office Bldg., #252
725 17th St. N.W.
Washington, DC 20503
Internet: www.whitehouse.gov/omb

The Bureau of the Budget, created in 1939 within the Executive Office of the President, became the Office of Management and Budget (OMB) in 1970. The OMB's pre-dominant mission is to assist the president in overseeing the preparation of the federal budget and to supervise its administration in executive branch agencies. OMB is the largest part of the Executive Office of the President.

In helping to formulate the president's budget plan, the OMB evaluates the effectiveness of agency pro-grams, policies, and procedures; assesses competing funding demands among agencies; and sets funding pri-orities. In addition, the OMB oversees and coordinates development of regulatory reform proposals, programs for paperwork reduction, and measures for improved agency performance. OMB also oversees correspon-dence with Congress, executive orders, and presidential memoranda.

The Office of Information and Regulatory Affairs (OIRA) within the OMB was created in 1981 and is pri-marily responsible for the management of federal infor-mation resources, including the collection of information from the public, and for carrying out presidential oversight responsibilities in federal rulemaking activities. It also works to expand interagency coordination by reviewing significant executive agency rules before releasing them to the public and works to reduce unnecessary paperwork and excessive reporting requirements of federal agencies.

The Paperwork Reduction Act of 1980 consolidated within the jurisdiction of the OMB director and the OIRA the following information management functions: general information, paperwork clearance, statistical activities, records management, privacy, and automatic data processing and telecommunications related to the collection of information.

The Paperwork Reduction Act also transferred the functions of the former Regulatory Reports Review Group from the General Accounting Office (GAO) to the OIRA. Those functions include reviewing information requests issued by federal departments and agencies (including independent federal regulatory agencies) to ensure that the proposed data collection is necessary, does not duplicate existing federal collections of information, and does not impose undue or excessive burdens on the public. Any information request sent to nine or more respondents by a federal department must be reviewed by this office.

The OIRA also oversees federal information policy, information technology management, and statistical policy activities. The purpose of joining these functions within one single office was to establish a governmentwide policy framework for "information resources management."

President Ronald Reagan's Executive Orders 12291 and 12498, which gave the OMB broad oversight responsibilities over most federal regulatory agencies, were revoked by President Bill Clinton's Executive Order 12866, issued Sept. 30, 1993. Executive Order 12866 provided a comprehensive guide for the writing and issuance of regulations. It listed the responsibilities of the regulating agencies, the vice president, and other policy advisers in the regulatory process (*for text of order, see p. 931*). Like Reagan's Executive Order 12291, Clinton's executive order gave the OMB authority to identify duplication, overlap, and conflict in rules, which agencies then were required to rectify; to develop procedures for cost-benefit analysis; to recommend changes in laws authorizing regulatory activity; to monitor compliance with the executive order; and to schedule existing rules for agency review. President Barack Obama added a few executive orders affecting regulatory affairs. Those included Executive Order 13563 in 2011, which called on executive agencies to "use the best, most innovative, and least burdensome tools for achieving regulatory ends" and "ensure that regulations are accessible, consistent, written in plain language, and easy to understand." The executive order asked each executive agency to determine if any existing rules "should be modified, streamlined, expanded, or repealed so as to make the agency's regulatory program more effective or less burdensome." Obama's Executive Order 13579 expressed the administration's hope that independent regulatory agencies would also choose to modify any rules that are "outmoded, ineffective, insufficient, or excessively burdensome."

As part of its regulatory oversight responsibilities, OMB prepares reports on government agencies for the president. These fact sheets are available to the public and can be downloaded from the OMB website at www.whitehouse.gov/omb.

Director
Shaun Donovan . . . . (202) 395–3080
Deputy Director
Beth Cobert (acting) . . . . (202) 395–1117
Deputy Director for Management
Beth Cobert . . . . (202) 395–1117

Budget Review
Courtney Timberlake . . . . (202) 395–4630
Economic Policy
Vacant . . . . (202) 395–7279
General Counsel
Geovette Washington . . . . (202) 395–5044
E-Government and Information Technology
Tony Scott . . . . (202) 395–3018
Information and Regulatory Affairs
Howard Shelanski . . . . (202) 395–4852

■ OFFICE OF NATIONAL AIDS POLICY

The White House
Washington, DC 20502
Internet: www.whitehouse.gov/
administration/eop/onap

The Office of National AIDS Policy was established within the Executive Office of the President in 1993. The office advises the president and formulates policy on matters related to HIV and AIDS. It coordinates the continuing domestic effort to reduce the number of new infections in the United States, in particular in segments of the population that are experiencing new or renewed increases in the rate of infection. The office also emphasizes the integration of domestic and international efforts to combat HIV/AIDS, and its Interdepartmental Task Force on HIV/AIDS helps to facilitate better communication among the various federal departments and agencies involved in HIV/AIDS policy.

Director
Douglas M. Brooks . . . . (202) 456–7320
Fax . . . . (202) 456–7315

■ OFFICE OF NATIONAL DRUG CONTROL POLICY

750 17th St. N.W.
Washington, DC 20503
Internet: www.whitehouse.gov/ondcp

The Office of National Drug Control Policy was established within the Executive Office of the President by the Anti-Drug Abuse Act of 1988. The office is headed by a director, who is appointed by the president and confirmed by the Senate. Responsibilities of this office include establishing policies and overseeing implementation of a national and international drug control strategy; recommending changes in the organization, management, budgeting, and personnel allocation of federal agencies involved in drug enforcement activities; and advising the president and National Security Council on drug control policy. These objectives and strategies, along with a budget summary, are published annually in the *National Drug Control Strategy*.

Director
Michael Botticelli . . . . (202) 395–6700
Fax . . . . (202) 395–6708

Deputy Director of Demand Reduction
David K. Mineta . . . . (202) 395–6751
Deputy Director of Supply Reduction
James C. Olson (acting) . . . . (202) 395–6741
Deputy Director of State, Local, and Tribal Affairs
Mary Lou Leary. . . . . (202) 395–4693

▣ OFFICE OF SCIENCE AND TECHNOLOGY POLICY
725 17th St. N.W., Room 5228
Washington, DC 20502
Internet: www.whitehouse.gov/
administration/eop/ostp

The National Science and Technology Policy, Organization, and Priorities Act of 1976 established the Office of Science and Technology Policy (OSTP) within the Executive Office of the President. The OSTP provides expert advice to the president in all areas of science and technology. Through the National Science and Technology Council, the OSTP coordinates science, space, and technology policy and programs across the federal government. OSTP's duties include advising the president and other executive agencies in policy and budget development on questions related to science and technology; coordinating the government's research and development efforts to maximize the return on the public's investment; and advancing international cooperation in science and technology.

Director
John P. Holdren . . . . (202) 456–7116
Fax. . . . . (202) 456–6021
Environment and Energy
Tamara Dickinson, deputy director . . (202) 456–7116
National Security and International Affairs
Vacant. . . . . (202) 456–7116
Science
Jo Handelsman . . . . (202) 456–4444
Technology and Innovation
Tom Kalil, deputy director. . . . . (202) 456–7116

▣ OFFICE OF THE U.S. TRADE REPRESENTATIVE
600 17th St. N.W.
Washington, DC 20508
Internet: www.ustr.gov

The Trade Expansion Act of 1962 created the Office of the U.S. Trade Representative (USTR). Originally named the Office of the Special Trade Representative, the Trade Act of 1974 established the office as a cabinet-level agency within the Executive Office of the President. The USTR sets and administers overall trade policy, serves as the nation's chief trade negotiator, and represents the United States in all major international trade organizations. The USTR has offices in Washington, DC, and in Geneva, Switzerland. The office in Geneva is organized to cover general World Trade Organization (WTO) affairs, nontariff agreements,

agricultural policy, commodity policy, and the harmonized code system. The Geneva deputy USTR is the U.S. ambassador to the WTO and to the United Nations Conference on Trade and Development. USTR also serves as vice chair of the Board of Directors of the Overseas Private Investment Corporation, on the Board of Directors of the Millennium Challenge Corporation, as a nonvoting member of the Export-Import Bank Board of Directors, and a member of the National Advisory Council on International Monetary and Financial Policies.

U.S. Trade Representative
Michael Froman . . . . (202) 395–6890
Fax. . . . . (202) 395–4549
Deputy U.S. Trade Representatives
Michael W. Punke (Geneva) . . .011–41–22–749–5253
Wendy Cutler (acting) . . . . (202) 395–5114
Robert Holleyman. . . . . (202) 395–9484
General Counsel
Timothy Reif . . . . (202) 395–3150
Fax. . . . . (202) 395–3639

▣ REGULATORY INFORMATION SERVICE CENTER
1275 1st St. N.E.
Washington, DC 20417
Internet: www.gsa.gov/risc

The Regulatory Information Service Center was established in June 1981 as part of the General Services Administration. The center works closely with the Office of Management and Budget to provide the president, Congress, and the public with information on federal regulatory policies. Its major project has been to coordinate the development and publication of agency agendas in the *The Unified Agenda of Federal Regulatory and Deregulatory Actions,* published twice yearly (typically in April and October) in the *Federal Register.* The purpose of the agenda is to list governmentwide regulatory agendas in a consistent format and to include a comprehensive listing of upcoming regulations, not simply those considered "major." The agenda includes all executive branch regulatory agencies as well as most independent commissions.

Since December 1995 the center has officially been a division of the GSA's Office of Governmentwide Policy; however, its mission in support of the OMB remains unchanged. The center, working with OMB's Office of Information and Regulatory Affairs, created the www.reginfo.gov website to provide the public information about regulations.

Executive Director
John C. Thomas . . . . (202) 482–7340
Fax. . . . . (202) 482–7360

▣ NONGOVERNMENTAL ORGANIZATIONS
The following are some important organizations that monitor issues of federal regulation, including reform initiatives and proposals to regulate emerging technologies.

AMERICAN ENTERPRISE INSTITUTE FOR PUBLIC POLICY RESEARCH
1150 17th St. N.W.
Washington, DC 20036
(202) 862–5800
Fax (202) 862–7177
Internet: www.aei.org

THE BROOKINGS INSTITUTION
1775 Massachusetts Ave. N.W.
Washington, DC 20036
(202) 797–6000
Internet: www.brookings.edu

CATO INSTITUTE
1000 Massachusetts Ave. N.W.
Washington, DC 20001–5403
(202) 842–0200
Fax (202) 842–3490
Internet: www.cato.org

CENTER FOR AMERICAN PROGRESS
1333 H St. N.W., 10th Floor
Washington, DC 20005
(202) 682–1611
Fax (202) 892–2590
Internet: www.americanprogress.org

CENTER FOR EFFECTIVE GOVERNMENT
2040 S St. N.W., 2nd Floor
Washington, DC 20009
(202) 234–8494
Fax (202) 234–8584
Internet: www.foreffectivegov.org

CITIZENS AGAINST GOVERNMENT WASTE
1301 Pennsylvania Ave. N.W., #1075
Washington, DC 20004
(202) 467–5300
Fax (202) 467–4253
Internet: www.cagw.org

GOVERNMENT ACCOUNTABILITY PROJECT
1612 K St. N.W., #1100
Washington, DC 20006
(202) 457–0034
E-mail: info@whistleblower.org
Internet: www.whistleblower.org

HERITAGE FOUNDATION
214 Massachusetts Ave. N.E.
Washington, DC 20002–4999
(202) 546–4400

Fax (202) 546–8328
Internet: www.heritage.org

INDEPENDENT INSTITUTE
100 Swan Way, #200
Oakland, CA 94621–1428
(510) 632–1366
Fax (510) 568–6040
Internet: www.independent.org

NATIONAL CENTER FOR POLICY ANALYSIS
14180 Dallas Parkway, # 350
Dallas, TX 75251
(972) 386–6272
Fax (972) 386–0924
Internet: www.ncpa.org
   Washington Office:
   600 Pennsylvania S.E., #310
   Washington, DC 20003
   (202) 830–0177

PACIFIC RESEARCH INSTITUTE
1 Embarcadero Center, #350
San Francisco, CA 94111
(415) 989–0833
Fax (415) 989–2411
Internet: www.pacificresearch.org

PROPUBLICA
155 Avenue of the Americas, 13th Floor
New York, NY 10013
(212) 514–5250
Fax (212) 785–2634
E-mail: communications@propublica.org
Internet: www.propublica.org

PUBLIC CITIZEN
1600 20th St. N.W.
Washington, DC 20009
(202) 588–1000
Internet: www.citizen.org

REASON FOUNDATION
5737 Mesmer Ave.
Los Angeles, CA 90230
(310) 391–2245
Fax (310) 391–4395
Internet: www.reason.org
   Washington office:
   1747 Connecticut Ave. N.W.
   Washington, DC 20009
   (202) 986–0916
   Fax (202) 315–3623

Appendix

Federal World Wide Websites

▨ MAJOR REGULATORY AGENCIES

Consumer Product Safety Commission,
  www.cpsc.gov
Environmental Protection Agency,
  www.epa.gov
Equal Employment Opportunity Commission,
  www.eeoc.gov
Federal Communications Commission,
  www.fcc.gov
Federal Deposit Insurance Corporation,
  www.fdic.gov
Federal Energy Regulatory Commission,
  www.ferc.gov
Federal Reserve System,
  www.federalreserve.gov
Federal Trade Commission,
  www.ftc.gov
Food and Drug Administration,
  www.fda.gov
National Labor Relations Board,
  www.nlrb.gov
Occupational Safety and Health Administration,
  www.osha.gov
Securities and Exchange Commission,
  www.sec.gov

▨ OTHER REGULATORY AGENCIES

Architectural and Transportation Barriers Compliance Board (United States Access Board),
  www.access-board.gov
Commodity Futures Trading Commission,
  www.cftc.gov
Consumer Financial Protection Bureau
  www.consumerfinance.gov
Election Assistance Commission,
  www.eac.gov
Farm Credit Administration,
  www.fca.gov
Federal Election Commission,
  www.fec.gov
Federal Housing Finance Agency,
  www.fhfa.gov

Federal Maritime Commission,
  www.fmc.gov
National Credit Union Administration,
  www.ncua.gov
National Mediation Board,
  www.nmb.gov
National Transportation Safety Board,
  www.ntsb.gov
Nuclear Regulatory Commission,
  www.nrc.gov
Pension Benefit Guaranty Corporation,
  www.pbgc.gov
Postal Regulatory Commission,
  www.prc.gov
Small Business Administration,
  www.sba.gov and www.business.usa.gov
Social Security Administration,
  www.ssa.gov
United States International Trade Commission,
  www.usitc.gov
United States Postal Service,
  www.usps.com

Federal Relay Service Online (FRSO) is a service offered to deaf and hard of hearing federal/military employees that allows them to place relay calls over the Internet between locations in the United States (including its territories). The service is also available to members of the general public who are deaf or hard of hearing trying to communicate with federal or military agencies. A TTY machine is not required, and a video relay service is available.

www.frso.us

▨ DEPARTMENTAL AGENCIES

Agriculture Department
  www.usda.gov
Agricultural Marketing Service,
  www.ams.usda.gov
Animal and Plant Health Inspection Service,
  www.aphis.usda.gov

Farm Service Agency,
www.fsa.usda.gov

Food and Nutrition Service,
www.fns.usda.gov

Food Safety and Inspection Service,
www.fsis.usda.gov

Foreign Agricultural Service,
www.fas.usda.gov

Forest Service,
www.fs.fed.us

Grain Inspection, Packers, and Stockyards Administration,
www.gipsa.usda.gov

Natural Resources Conservation Service,
www.nrcs.usda.gov

Risk Management Agency,
www.rma.usda.gov

Rural Development,
www.rurdev.usda.gov

Commerce Department
www.commerce.gov

Bureau of Industry and Security,
www.bis.doc.gov

Economic Development Administration,
www.eda.gov

International Trade Administration,
www.trade.gov

National Oceanic and Atmospheric Administration,
www.noaa.gov

United States Patent and Trademark Office,
www.uspto.gov

Defense Department
www.defense.gov

Army Corps of Engineers,
www.usace.army.mil

Education Department
www.ed.gov

Office for Civil Rights,
www.ed.gov/about/offices/list/ocr

Office for Federal Student Aid,
www.ed.gov/about/offices/list/fsa

Office for Postsecondary Education,
www.ed.gov/about/offices/list/ope

Office of Elementary and Secondary Education,
www.ed.gov/about/offices/list/oese

Office of Special Education and Rehabilitative Services,
www.ed.gov/about/offices/list/osers

Energy Department
www.energy.gov

Office of Energy Efficiency and Renewable Energy,
www.energy.gov/eere

Office of Environmental Management,
www.energy.gov/em

Office of Environment, Health, Safety and Security,
www.energy.gov/ehss

Office of Fossil Energy,
www.energy.gov/fe

Health and Human Services Department
www.hhs.gov

Administration for Children and Families,
www.acf.hhs.gov

Administration for Community Living,
www.acl.gov

Administration on Aging,
www.aoa.gov and www.acl.gov

Administration on Intellectual and Developmental Disabilities,
www.acf.gov/Programs/AIDD

Advisory Committee on Blood and Tissue Safety and Availability,
www.hhs.gov/ash/bloodsafety

Center for Disability and Aging Policy,
www.acl.gov/Programs/CDAP

Centers for Disease Control and Prevention,
www.cdc.gov

Centers for Medicare and Medicaid Services,
www.cms.hhs.gov

Indian Health Service,
www.ihs.gov

National Vaccine Program Office,
www.hhs.gov/nvpo

Office for Civil Rights,
www.hhs.gov/ocr

Office for Human Research Protections,
www.hhs.gov/ohrp

Office of Adolescent Health,
www.hhs.gov/ash/oah

Office of Disease Prevention and Health Promotion,
www.health.gov

Office of Global Health Affairs,
www.globalhealth.gov

Office of HIV/AIDS and Infectious Disease Policy,
www.hhs.gov/ash/ohaidp

Office of Minority Health,
www.minorityhealth.hhs.gov

Office of Population Affairs,
www.hhs.gov/opa

Office of Research Integrity,
www.ori.dhhs.gov

Office of the Assistant Secretary for Health,
www.hhs.gov/ash

Office of the Inspector General,
www.oig.hhs.gov

Office of the Surgeon General,
www.surgeongeneral.gov

Office on Women's Health,
www.womenshealth.gov

Presidential Commission for the Study of Bioethical Issues,
www.bioethics.gov

President's Council on Fitness, Sports, and Nutrition,
www.fitness.gov
Substance Abuse and Mental Health Services Administration,
www.samhsa.gov
U.S. Public Health Service Commissioned Corps,
www.usphs.gov

Homeland Security Department
www.dhs.gov
Federal Emergency Management Agency,
www.fema.gov
Immigration and Customs Enforcement,
www.ice.gov
Transportation Security Administration,
www.tsa.gov
U.S. Citizenship and Immigration Services,
www.uscis.gov
U.S. Coast Guard,
www.uscg.mil
U.S. Customs and Border Protection,
www.cbp.gov

Housing and Urban Development Department
www.hud.gov
Office of Community Planning and Development,
www.hud.gov/offices/cpd
Office of Fair Housing and Equal Opportunity,
www.hud.gov/offices/fheo
Office of Housing,
www.hud.gov/offices/hsg
Office of Lead Hazard Control and Healthy Homes,
www.hud.gov/offices/lead
Office of Public and Indian Housing,
www.hud.gov/offices/pih

Interior Department
www.doi.gov
Bureau of Indian Affairs,
www.bia.gov
Bureau of Land Management,
www.blm.gov
Bureau of Ocean Energy Management,
www.boem.gov
Bureau of Reclamation,
www.usbr.gov
Bureau of Safety and Environmental Enforcement,
www.bsee.gov
National Park Service,
www.nps.gov
Office of Natural Resources Revenue,
www.onrr.gov
Office of Surface Mining, Reclamation and Enforcement,
www.osmre.gov
United States Fish and Wildlife Service,
www.fws.gov
United States Geological Survey,
www.usgs.gov

Justice Department
www.justice.gov
Antitrust Division,
www.justice.gov/atr
Bureau of Alcohol, Tobacco, Firearms, and Explosives,
www.atf.gov
Civil Rights Division,
www.justice.gov/crt
Criminal Division,
www.justice.gov/criminal
Drug Enforcement Administration,
www.dea.gov
Federal Bureau of Prisons,
www.bop.gov
Office of Justice Programs,
www.ojp.gov
United States Parole Commission,
www.justice.gov/uspc

Labor Department
www.dol.gov
Employee Benefits Security Administration,
www.dol.gov/ebsa
Employment and Training Administration,
www.doleta.gov
Mine Safety and Health Administration,
www.msha.gov
Office of Federal Contract Compliance Programs,
www.dol.gov/ofccp
Office of Labor-Management Standards,
www.dol.gov/olms
Office of Workers' Compensation Programs,
www.dol.gov/owcp
Veterans' Employment and Training Service,
www.dol.gov/vets
Wage and Hour Division,
www.dol.gov/WHD

State Department
www.state.gov
Bureau of Consular Affairs,
www.travel.state.gov

Transportation Department
www.transportation.gov
Aviation Consumer Protection,
www.transportation.gov/airconsumer
Federal Aviation Administration,
www.faa.gov
Federal Highway Administration,
www.fhwa.dot.gov
Federal Motor Carrier Safety Administration,
www.fmcsa.dot.gov
Federal Railroad Administration,
www.fra.dot.gov
Federal Transit Administration,
www.fta.dot.gov
Maritime Administration,
www.marad.dot.gov

National Highway Traffic Safety Administration,
www.nhtsa.gov

Office of Assistant Secretary for Aviation and International Affairs,
www.transportation.gov/policy/assistant-secretary-aviation-international-affairs

Office of Aviation Analysis,
www.transportation.gov/policy/aviation-policy/office-aviation-analysis

Office of International Aviation,
www.transportation.gov/policy/aviation-policy/office-international-aviation

Office of International Transportation and Trade,
www.transportation.gov/policy/international-policy-and-trade/about-us

Office of Hearings,
www.transportation.gov/mission/administrations/administration/hearings

Pipeline and Hazardous Materials Safety Administration,
www.phmsa.dot.gov

Research and Innovative Technology Administration,
www.rita.dot.gov

Saint Lawrence Seaway Development Corporation,
www.seaway.dot.gov

Surface Transportation Board,
www.stb.dot.gov

Treasury Department
www.treasury.gov

Alcohol and Tobacco Tax and Trade Bureau,
www.ttb.gov

Comptroller of the Currency,
www.occ.treas.gov

Internal Revenue Service,
www.irs.gov

Veterans Affairs Department
www.va.gov

▪ REGULATORY OVERSIGHT AND COORDINATION

Congressional Budget Office,
www.cbo.gov

Corporation for National and Community Service,
www.nationalservice.gov

Council of Economic Advisers,
www.whitehouse.gov/administration/eop/cea

Council on Environmental Quality,
www.whitehouse.gov/administration/eop/ceq

Domestic Policy Council,
www.whitehouse.gov/dpc

Government Accountability Office,
www.whitehouse.gov/administration/eop/dpc

National Economic Council,
www.whitehouse.gov/administration/eop/nec

National Security Council,
www.whitehouse.gov/administration/eop/nsc

National Telecommunications and Information Administration,
www.ntia.doc.gov

Office of Compliance,
www.compliance.gov

Office of Government-wide Policy,
www.gsa.gov/portal/content/104550

Office of Information and Regulatory Affairs,
www.reginfo.gov

Office of Management and Budget,
www.whitehouse.gov/omb

Office of National AIDS Policy,
www.whitehouse.gov/administration/eop/onap

Office of National Drug Control Policy,
www.whitehouse.gov/ondcp

Office of Science and Technology Policy,
www.whitehouse.gov/administration/eop/ostp

Office of the U.S. Trade Representative,
https://ustr.gov

Regulatory Information Service Center,
www.gsa.gov/portal/content/104622

▪ GOVERNMENT INFORMATION

Federal Citizen Information Center,
www.publications.usa.gov

Federal Data Catalogs (searchable datasets),
www.data.gov

National Technical Information Service,
www.ntis.gov

THOMAS: Legislative Information from the Library of Congress website,
http://thomas.loc.gov/home/thomas.php

U.S. Government Printing Office,
www.gpo.gov

Ordering Government Publications

In addition to the publications contacts listed in each agency profile, the federal government maintains the following general offices for the distribution of publications:

■ FEDERAL CITIZEN INFORMATION CENTER (FCIC)
(Pueblo office)
31451 United Ave.
Pueblo, CO 81009
E-mail: Pueblo@gpo.gov
Questions only (no new orders):
(719) 295–2675
Internet: www.publications.usa.gov

(Washington office)
General Services Administration Number:
(1800) 488–3111
1800 F St. N.W., Room G–142 (XCC)
Washington, DC 20405

Part of the General Services Administration. Distributes free publications, including the *Consumer Information Catalog* and consumer booklets from many federal agencies. Also distributes new releases on consumer issues to the media, consumer organizations, and state and local consumer agencies. Orders for publications and catalogs are filled by the Pueblo office; orders are no longer accepted by phone and can be placed online via the FCIC's website at www.publications.usa.gov. The Washington office provides services to the U.S. Government Printing Office and other federal agencies.

■ NATIONAL TECHNICAL INFORMATION SERVICE (NTIS)
U.S. Department of Commerce
5301 Shawnee Rd.
Alexandria, VA 22312
Agency Phone: (703) 605–6000

Customer Service Phone: (888) 584–8332
Website Support Phone: (703) 605–6585
E-mail: orders@ntis.gov
Internet: www.ntis.gov
Orders: (800) 553–6847

Part of the Commerce Department. Distributes or sells publications, subscriptions, and other information from most federal departments, many independent agencies, and a number of foreign governments. Publications can be retrieved online, in print, and in various electronic formats. Publication catalogs are available for download at the NTIS website.

In addition to the main order lines above, key telephone contacts include:
Rush Service . . . . (800) 553–NTIS

FEDWORLD
Internet: http://fedworld.ntis.gov
A division of NTIS and a central access point for federal online information, including government jobs, scientific and technical publications, 30 million government Web pages, the text of Supreme Court decisions issued between 1937 and 1975, and archived Internal Revenue Service forms and publications.

NATIONAL AUDIOVISUAL CENTER (NAC)
Internet: www.ntis.gov/products/nac
A division of the NTIS that distributes over 9,000 federal media-based products, including videotapes, audiocassettes, and CD-ROMs. Training materials cover occupational safety and health, foreign languages, law enforcement, and fire services. Educational materials cover topics in history, health, agriculture, and natural resources.

■ U.S. GOVERNMENT PRINTING OFFICE (GPO)
732 N. Capitol St. N.W.
Washington, DC 20401

Orders: (202) 512–1800;
(866) 512–1800
Internet: http://bookstore.gpo.gov

Produces publications for Congress and the federal departments and agencies. The superintendent of documents distributes or sells products, including catalogs, books, and subscriptions; booklets and other frequently requested publications are generally available from the agencies themselves. An increasing number of GPO products are available in electronic formats. The agency's website provides indexes of GPO products and access to a variety of government databases. The GPO also maintains two government bookstores in the DC metropolitan area, which stock selected government publications, and a network of Regional Federal Depository Libraries, which receive a copy of all federal government documents that must be made available for public inspection. For the location of these libraries, please go to www.gpoaccess.gov/ libraries.html.

In addition to the main order lines above, some key GPO contacts include:

MAIL ORDERS

U.S. Government Printing Office
P.O. Box 979050
St. Louis, MO 63197–9000

GPO Bookstore
710 N. Capitol St. N.W.
Washington, DC 20401–0001
(202) 512–0132

How to Use the *Federal Register* and the *CFR*

The basic tool for finding out about agency rulings, proposed rules, meetings, and adjudicatory proceedings is the *Federal Register,* which is published daily. The *Federal Register* system of publication was established by the Federal Register Act of 1935 (44 U.S.C. Ch. 15) and was further enlarged and amended by the Administrative Procedure Act of 1946 (5 U.S.C. 551).

Contained in the *Federal Register* are federal agency regulations and other legal documents of the executive branch, including presidential documents (among them the texts of proclamations and executive orders).

The system of codifying federal regulations parallels that of legislation. Laws enacted by Congress are compiled annually in the *U.S. Statutes at Large* and are then codified in the U.S. Code by subject titles. Rules and regulations to implement the legislation are published daily in the *Federal Register* and are then codified by subject title in the *Code of Federal Regulations* (*CFR*), which is updated annually. Working with the *Federal Register* and the *CFR,* a person may find an up-to-date account of all regulations pertaining to a particular agency or subject.

Organization of the *CFR*

The *CFR*, a compilation of the current general and permanent regulations of federal agencies, is divided into fifty titles, according to broad subject areas affected by regulatory action. For example, Title 1 concerns "General Provisions"; Title 3, "The President"; Title 12, "Banks and Banking"; Title 15, "Commerce and Foreign Trade"; Title 21, "Food and Drugs"; and so forth. (The subject of a title may change as regulations are rescinded and different regulations are issued. Not all titles are in use at one time.)

Within each title (consisting of one or more volumes), subjects are further broken down into chapters (numbered in roman capitals as I, II, III, etc.). Chapters are further subdivided into parts, numbered in Arabic numerals (1, 2, 3, etc.). Parts are normally assigned to chapters as follows: Chapter I, Parts 1 to 199; Chapter II, Parts 200 to 299; and so forth. Each part contains a number of sections, set off by a decimal point preceded by the symbol §. The notation "§ 32.5" would refer to section 5 of part 32. The "section"

is the basic unit of the *CFR* and ideally consists of a short, simple presentation of one proposition.

As an example: Title 36 of the *CFR*, composed of one volume, concerns all regulations pertaining to "Parks, Forests, and Public Property." The table of contents of the volume divides the title into fourteen chapters. Chapter I contains regulations affecting the "National Park Service, Department of the Interior." There is a table of contents for each chapter, giving the subject matter of each part and the page number on which it may be found. Part 4 of Chapter I, for example, concerns "Vehicles and Traffic Safety." Within Part 4, there are a number of sections. Section 4.30, for example, concerns "Bicycles."

Each *CFR* volume contains front matter on how to use the code, effective dates, and whom to contact for further information. The "*CFR* Index and Finding Aids" is revised annually and is contained in a separate volume. The index section contains a list of *CFR* titles, chapters, and parts; an alphabetical listing of agencies appearing in the *CFR*; and lists of current and superseded *CFR* volumes. The finding aids section consists of additional information and guides to material in the *CFR*. Included is a parallel table of statutory authorities and rules that lists all sections of the U.S. Code and the *United States Statutes at Large,* cited as the rulemaking authority for *CFR* regulations. The publication "*CFR* Index and Finding Aids" is available for purchase via the Government Printing Office bookstore, at http://bookstore.gpo.gov.

The *CFR* also publishes monthly a cumulative list of changes in regulations since they were published in the latest annual code. The listing contains the title, chapter, part, and section of the amended regulation and the page number in the *Federal Register* where the change was published. There is no single annual issue of the cumulative list; rather, four of the monthly issues include cumulative lists for certain titles. The December issue contains changes for Titles 1–16; the March issue is the annual revision for Titles 17–27; the June issue contains changes in Titles 28–41; and the September issue notes changes in Titles 42–50.

The entire *CFR* is revised annually according to the following schedule: Titles 1–16, as of January 1; Titles

17–27, as of April 1; Titles 28–41, as of July 1; Titles 42–50, as of October 1.

The *Federal Register*

Published daily, the *Federal Register* serves to update the *Code of Federal Regulations*. In order to determine the most recent version of a rule, the latest edition of the *CFR*, the *CFR* cumulative list of revisions, and the *Federal Register* must be used together.

Each issue of the *Federal Register* includes preliminary pages of finding aids. Documents are arranged under various headings: "Presidential Documents," "Rules and Regulations," "Proposed Rules," "Notices," and "Sunshine Act Meetings."

Final Rules. This section on final rules usually contains for each entry the following information: the part (title, chapter, etc.) of the *CFR* affected; a brief descriptive heading for the change; the agency proposing the action; the type of action involved (e.g., a final rule, a termination of rulemaking or proceeding, or a request for further public comment); a brief summary of the nature of the action; the effective date; and the person to contact for further information. This is followed by more or less detailed supplementary information, including the text of the change in the regulation.

Agencies are required to publish rules in the *Federal Register* thirty days before they are to take effect. Exceptions to this requirement, found in section 553 of the Administrative Procedure Act, include: "(1) a substantive rule which grants or recognizes an exemption or relieves a restriction; (2) interpretative rules and statements of policy; or (3) as otherwise provided by the agency for good cause found and published with the rule."

In publishing the supplementary information on the final rule, agencies must summarize comments received about the rule, what action was taken on them, and why. On occasion, agencies may allow further comment on a final rule and will give notice of such in the *Federal Register*.

Proposed Rules. The format for publishing a proposed rule is similar to that for final rules. The entry is headed by the name of the agency initiating the action; the *CFR* sections affected; a brief descriptive title of the action; the nature of the action (proposed rulemaking, extension of public comment period, etc.); a summary of the proposed rule; the deadlines for receiving public comments and/or dates of public hearings; the person to contact for further information; and a more detailed supplementary section. Also included is the agency's "docket" number under which its files on the proposed action may be identified and examined.

Occasionally, agencies will publish an "advance notice of proposed rulemaking" in cases where a rule is being considered but where the agency has not developed a concrete proposal.

Requests may be made for an extension of the deadline for public comment, but agencies are not required to grant them.

Notices. Contained in this section of the *Federal Register* are documents other than rules or proposed rules that are applicable to the public. Notices of hearings and investigations, committee meetings, agency decisions and rulings, delegations of authority, filing of petitions and applications, issuance or revocation of licenses, and grant application deadlines are examples. Announcements of advisory committee meetings are also required to be published in the "Notices" section. An example of an application notice is a request by an airline company to establish a new route or service. Notice of filings of environmental impact statements are also included in this section.

Sunshine Act Meetings. Notices of open agency meetings are printed in the *Federal Register* in accordance with the provisions of the Government in the Sunshine Act *(see p. 902)*. Each entry contains the name of the agency; time, date, and place of the meeting; a brief description of the subject; status (open or closed); the person to contact; and supplementary information. Agencies that have closed a meeting are required to list those that are closed, citing the relevant exemption under the Sunshine Act.

Finding Aids. There are several kinds of finding aids that are published each day in the *Federal Register*. These include:

- Selected Subjects: a list of the subjects affected by rules and proposed rules included in each issue.
- Contents: a comprehensive list of documents in the issue and their page numbers arranged by agency and type of document (rule, proposal, or notice).
- List of *CFR* parts affected: a numerical guide listing each title of the *CFR* affected by documents published in the day's issue, giving the citation to the *CFR* and the page number in that day's *Federal Register* where the action may be found.
- Cumulative list of *CFR* parts affected; monthly: rules and proposals that have appeared so far in that month's *Federal Register*, arranged in similar fashion to the above.
- *Federal Register* pages and dates: a parallel table of the inclusive pages and corresponding dates for the *Federal Registers* of the month.

In addition to information provided in each daily *Federal Register,* there are other monthly, quarterly, and annual publications. The first *Federal Register* of each month contains a table of effective dates and time periods for the month. The first issue of each week includes the *CFR* checklist, which shows the revision date and price of *CFR* volumes issued to date. The *Federal Register* also publishes a monthly index of all the documents appearing in a given month arranged alphabetically by agency name and thereunder by rules, proposed rules, and notices; broad subject headings are inserted alphabetically among agency headings. The index also includes a list of Freedom of Information Act indexes and a table showing the relationship between *Federal Register* dates and pages. The index is cumulated quarterly and annually.

The *List of CFR Sections Affected* (*LSA*) directs users to changes to the *CFR* that were published in the *Federal Register*. Entries for rules are arranged numerically by *CFR* title, chapter, part, section, and paragraph. A descriptive word or phrase indicates the nature of the amendatory action such as additions, revisions, or removals. The number at the end of each entry gives the page in the *Federal Register* where the amendatory action appears. Proposed rules are listed at the end of the appropriate titles. The proposed rule entries are to the part number. They do not contain a descriptive word or phrase.

The *LSA* is published monthly in cumulative form and keyed to the annual revision schedule of the *CFR* volumes. The issues of December, March, June, and September are annual cumulations for certain *CFR* titles. If a particular *LSA* is an annual cumulation, a notation appears on the cover.

Each *LSA* also contains a detailed introductory explanation on how to use the publication. In addition, the *LSA* contains a parallel table of authorities and rules, which shows additions and removals of authorities, and a table of *Federal Register* issue pages and dates.

The Office of the Federal Register has published a booklet, "The *Federal Register:* What It Is and How to Use It," which may be obtained from the Government Printing Office, and also offers seminars on how to use the *Federal Register.* These are announced in the *Federal Register.*

Federal Digital System (FDsys)

Federal Digital System (FDsys) is an online information-dissemination service that provides access to the *Federal Register* (www.gpo.gov/fdsys) using multiple browse and search features. The electronic version of the *Federal Register* is updated daily and includes volumes from fifty-nine (1994) to the present. *CFR* volumes are added to the online service concurrent with the release of the print editions. Issues are available from 1996 (partial) to the current year. Both publications' documents are available in PDF and ASCII text files. Also available is the *Electronic Code of Federal Regulations* (e-CFR) (www.ecfr .gov), a daily updated version of the *CFR* that incorporates information from the *CFR, Federal Register,* and the *List of CFR Sections Affected.* The e-CFR is not an official legal edition of the *CFR.*

Searching and Commenting on Regulations: Regulations.gov

The President's Management Agenda was launched in 2001 as a collection of governmentwide initiatives for improving the management and performance of the federal government. One of the five main initiatives was Expanded Electronic Government, known as the E-Government Act of 2002. It is an ongoing effort by federal agencies to use Internet-based technology to make it easier for citizens and businesses to interact with the government and modernize citizen-to-government communications.

The E-Government Act (116 Stat. 2899, 44 U.S.C. 3601 et seq.) authorized the eRulemaking Initiative, which focuses on improving citizen access and participation in the rulemaking process and streamlining the efficiency of internal agency processes. The three key objectives are:

- To expand public understanding of the rulemaking process.
- To improve the quality of rulemaking decisions.
- To increase the amount, breadth, and ease of citizen and intergovernmental participation in rulemaking by using the Internet to enhance public access to information.

The eRulemaking Initiative continues to consolidate existing federal information technology systems into a single federal system and integrate 135 federal agencies that use or used paper-based rule-writing processes.

Background

Rulemaking is the process followed by federal departments and agencies to formulate, amend, or repeal a regulation. The rulemaking process generally consists of two stages: the proposed and the final regulation. More than 8,000 rules are created each year by approximately 300 different federal agencies, with as many as 500 regulations open for comment at any given time. For most categories of rulemaking, the department or agency provides notice of a proposed regulation and any person or organization may review this document and submit comments on it during a specified period (usually thirty, sixty, or ninety days).

As part of the rulemaking process, the department or agency is required to consider the public comments received on the proposed regulation.

A docket serves as the depository for documents or information related to an agency's rulemaking activities. Agencies most commonly use dockets for rulemaking actions, but dockets may also be used for various other activities. The docket generally contains the materials referenced in the *Federal Register,* any received public comments, or other information used by decision makers related to the agency rulemaking activity. Some agencies maintain their dockets electronically with access via the Internet, while other agencies maintain hard copies of materials submitted to their docket.

REGULATIONS.GOV

Internet: www.regulations.gov
Help Desk Phone: (877) 378–5457

Regulations.gov, a federal regulatory clearinghouse, was launched in January 2003 as the first achievement of the eRulemaking Initiative—a cross-agency effort authorized under the E-Government Act. The initial goal of Regulations.gov was to provide online access to every open rule published by the federal agencies. The eRulemaking Initiative is managed by the Environmental Protection Agency in conjunction with more than twenty-five federal departments and agency partners.

In fall 2005 Regulations.gov launched its Federal Docket Management System (FDMS). FDMS enables the public to access entire rulemaking dockets from participating federal departments and agencies. With this system, federal departments and agencies can post *Federal Register* documents, supporting materials, and public comments on the Internet. The public can search, view, and download these documents.

Regulations.gov initially made available the dockets for the Department of Housing and Urban Development, the Animal and Plant Health Inspection Service of the Department of Agriculture, a portion of the Department of Homeland Security, and the Office of Personnel Management. In 2005 Regulations.gov began adding federal departments and agencies, including the following:

- Additional sections of the Department of Homeland Security
- Department of Housing and Urban Development
- Environmental Protection Agency
- Federal Emergency Management Agency, Department of Homeland Security
- Federal Trade Commission
- Internal Revenue Service
- National Archives and Records Administration
- U.S. Citizenship and Immigration Services, Department of Homeland Security
- U.S. Customs and Border Protection, Department of Homeland Security

Regulations.gov allows the public to view a description of rules currently open for comment, read full texts of the accompanying documents, and submit comments to the appropriate federal department or agency. This interactive site now provides online access to every rule published and open for comment, from more than 300 different federal agencies. This includes all federal documents that are open for comment and published in the *Federal Register,* the official daily publication for final regulations, proposed regulations, and other notices of federal departments and agencies and organizations, as well as executive orders and other presidential documents. Through the website, some agencies post comments back to the public site.

The Regulations.gov website allows users to:

- Search for open regulations and documents.
- Comment on open regulations and documents.
- Request e-mail notifications on dockets.
- Access further help in using the Regulations.gov website.

The website also provides visitors with a variety of means to search for and retrieve those documents and also allows visitors to submit a comment on any open rulemaking, which is then forwarded to the appropriate agency. All public comments received are then reviewed by that department or agency and taken into account when the final regulation is developed.

Each *Federal Register* regulatory action that is open for comment through the Regulations.gov website contains specific instructions on how to submit comments for that particular rulemaking action.

Regulations.gov provides four predefined searches to access documents and regulations open for comment:

- All documents open for comment.
- Documents published for comment today.
- Regulations open for public comment by topic.
- All documents for which the comment period closes today.

Regulations.gov is updated daily by the National Archives and Records Administration using electronic versions of the same *Federal Register* documents printed every business day to ensure that regulations open for comment are available for public access.

Administrative Procedure Act

The Administrative Procedure Act (APA) had its genesis in the proliferation of regulatory agencies during the New Deal. Passed in 1946, the act was the product of a nine-year study of administrative justice by congressional committees, the Justice Department, and lawyers' organizations. On enactment, Pat McCarran, D-NV, chair of the Senate Judiciary Committee, described it as a "bill of rights for the hundreds of thousands of Americans whose affairs are controlled or regulated in one way or another by agencies of the federal government" and said it was designed "to provide guaranties of due process in administrative procedure."

Major provisions of the act:

- Required agencies to publish in the *Federal Register* a description of their organization and rulemaking procedures and to hold hearings or provide other means of public comment on proposed rules.
- Prescribed standards and procedures for agency adjudications, including licensing and injunctive orders. (Among the requirements: adequate notice to parties concerned; separation of prosecution and decision functions through a ban on investigatory or prosecuting officials deciding cases; discretionary authority for agencies to issue declaratory orders.)
- Spelled-out hearing procedures, including a requirement that the proponent of a rule or order should have the burden of proof and that no decision could be made except as supported by "relevant, reliable and probative evidence."
- Provided that any person suffering legal wrong because of any agency action would be entitled to judicial review, except where statutes precluded judicial review or where agency action was by law committed to agency discretion, but required the aggrieved party to exhaust administrative remedies first. The court was to set aside agency actions "unsupported by substantial evidence," and was to review the whole record and take "due account" of the rule of prejudicial error.
- Directed each agency to appoint competent examiners to act as hearing officers and to make, or recommend, decisions.

The act established minimum requirements that all agencies would have to meet. Based on these requirements,

agencies have developed their own procedures, which are spelled out in statutes contained in the *Code of Federal Regulations*. Amendments to the APA include the Government in Sunshine Act, the Freedom of Information Act, and the Privacy Act.

The APA divides administrative proceedings into two categories: rulemaking and adjudication. A "rule" is defined by Section 551 as "the whole or a part of an agency statement of general or particular applicability and future effect designed to implement, interpret, or prescribe law or policy or describing the organization, procedure, or practice requirements of an agency." "Adjudication" is the process of formulating an order, which is defined as a "final disposition . . . of an agency in a matter other than rulemaking but including licensing."

Rulemaking

Section 553 sets forward the basic requirements for rulemaking. General notice of a proposed rulemaking is to be published in the *Federal Register,* unless persons subject to the rule "are named and either personally served or otherwise have actual notice thereof in accordance with law. The notice shall include (1) a statement of the time, place, and nature of public rule making proceedings; (2) reference to the authority under which the rule is proposed; and (3) either the terms or substance of the proposed rule or a description of the subjects and issues involved." The APA provides an opportunity for public participation through written or oral comment (the act does not require agencies to hold hearings).

There are two kinds of rulemaking: formal and informal. If a particular statute calls for "on the record" or formal rulemaking, the agency must go through a trial-type procedure. Decisions must be based on the record of transcripts of oral testimony or written submissions. Unlike adjudicatory proceedings, however, the initial and recommended decision of the hearing examiner may be omitted. Under the informal rulemaking process, the decision need not be based on the record and, unless the agency decides otherwise, only the minimum requirements of the APA must be met.

Under Section 553 of the Administrative Procedure Act, a "substantive rule which grants or recognizes an exemption or relieves a restriction" must be published at least thirty days before it becomes effective. However, there are many exceptions to this, among them interpretative rules or general statements of policy. Such notice is not required if it would defeat the purpose of the rule or if immediate action is required to protect property.

Formal Hearings

Where the APA requires a formal hearing—as in a formal rulemaking or adjudicatory proceeding—usually an administrative law judge (hearing examiner) presides and receives evidence. (However, the act also provides that the agency or one or more members of the body that constitutes the agency may do so.) The act requires that each agency "shall appoint as many hearing examiners as are necessary for proceedings required to be conducted" under adjudicatory or formal rulemaking procedures. Hearing examiners, or presiding officers, have the power to administer oaths and affirmations; issue subpoenas authorized by law; rule on offers of proof and receive relevant evidence; regulate the hearings; hold conferences to settle or simplify issues; handle procedural requests; make or recommend decisions; and take other action authorized by agency rules.

Following the hearing, the examiner makes an initial or recommended decision, but the agency makes the final determination.

Adjudication

In contrast to the more generalized character of rulemaking, adjudication usually involves a more limited number of parties (between the agency and a private party, or among two or more private parties) and is more judicial in nature. Section 554 of the APA requires that the agency notify the affected parties of the hearing's time and place, the statute involved, and the factual dispute that will be decided. The parties involved may submit oral or written evidence, present a defense and rebuttal, and cross-examine witnesses. The hearing examiner is prohibited from consulting any party on an issue of fact unless all parties have a chance to participate.

Judicial Review

Section 702 of the APA provides that: "A person suffering legal wrong because of agency action, or adversely affected or aggrieved by agency action within the meaning of a relevant statute, is entitled to judicial review thereof." The reviewing court may "compel agency action unlawfully withheld or unreasonably delayed," and rule unlawful any agency action found to be "arbitrary, capricious, an abuse of discretion, or otherwise not in accordance with law"; unconstitutional; "in excess of statutory jurisdiction, authority, or limitations, or short of statutory right"; taken "without observance of procedure required by law"; and unsupported by substantial evidence.

The provisions of the Administrative Procedure Act are contained in the U.S. Code, Title 5, Chapter 5, Subchapter II, and Title 5, Chapter 7.

The following text includes Subchapter II, section 551 and sections 553–559 as well as Chapter 7.

Section 552, known as the Freedom of Information Act, may be found on p. 891; section 552a, known as the Privacy Act, may be found on p. 914; and section 552b, known as the Government in the Sunshine Act, may be found on p. 902.

SUBCHAPTER II ADMINISTRATIVE PROCEDURE § 551. Definitions

For the purpose of this subchapter—

(1) "agency" means each authority of the Government of the United States, whether or not it is within or subject to review by another agency, but does not include—

(A) the Congress;

(B) the courts of the United States;

(C) the governments of the territories or possessions of the United States;

(D) the government of the District of Columbia; or except as to the requirements of section 552 of this title—

(E) agencies composed of representatives of the parties or of representatives of organizations of the parties to the disputes determined by them;

(F) courts martial and military commissions;

(G) military authority exercised in the field in time of war or in occupied territory; or

(H) functions conferred by sections 1738, 1739, 1743, and 1744 of title 12; chapter 2 of title 41; or sections 1622, 1884, 1891–1902, and former section 1641(b)(2), of title 50, appendix;

(2) "person" includes an individual, partnership, corporation, association, or public or private organization other than an agency;

(3) "party" includes a person or agency named or admitted as a party, or properly seeking and entitled as of right to be admitted as a party, in an agency proceeding, and a person or agency admitted by an agency as a party for limited purposes;

(4) "rule" means the whole or a part of an agency statement of general or particular applicability and future effect designed to implement, interpret, or prescribe law or policy or describing the organization, procedure, or practice requirements of an agency and includes the approval or prescription for the future of rates, wages, corporate or financial structures or reorganizations thereof, prices, facilities, appliances, services or allowances therefor or of valuations, costs, or accounting, or practices bearing on any of the foregoing;

(5) "rule making" means agency process for formulating, amending, or repealing a rule;

(6) "order" means the whole or a part of a final disposition, whether affirmative, negative, injunctive, or declaratory in form, of an agency in a matter other than rule making but including licensing;

(7) "adjudication" means agency process for the formulation of an order;

(8) "license" includes the whole or a part of an agency permit, certificate, approval, registration, charter, membership, statutory exemption, or other form of permission;

(9) "licensing" includes agency process respecting the grant, renewal, denial, revocation, suspension, annulment, withdrawal, limitation, amendment, modification, or conditioning of a license;

(10) "sanction" includes the whole or a part of an agency—

(A) prohibition, requirement, limitation, or other condition affecting the freedom of a person;

(B) withholding of relief;

(C) imposition of penalty or fine;

(D) destruction, taking, seizure, or withholding of property;

(E) assessment of damages, reimbursement, restitution, compensation, costs, charges, or fees;

(F) requirement, revocation, or suspension of a license; or

(G) taking other compulsory or restrictive action;

(11) "relief" includes the whole or a part of an agency—

(A) grant of money, assistance, license, authority, exemption, exception, privilege, or remedy;

(B) recognition of a claim, right, immunity, privilege, exemption, or exception; or

(C) taking of other action on the application or petition of, and beneficial to, a person;

(12) "agency proceeding" means an agency process as defined by paragraphs (5), (7), and (9) of this section;

(13) "agency action" includes the whole or a part of an agency rule, order, license, sanction, relief, or the equivalent or denial thereof, or failure to act; and

(14) "ex parte communication" means an oral or written communication not on the public record with respect to which reasonable prior notice to all parties is not given, but it shall not include requests for status reports on any matter or proceeding covered by this subchapter.

§ 553. Rule making

(a) This section applies, according to the provisions thereof, except to the extent that there is involved—

(1) a military or foreign affairs function of the United States; or

(2) a matter relating to agency management or personnel or to public property, loans, grants, benefits, or contracts.

(b) General notice of proposed rulemaking shall be published in the *Federal Register,* unless persons subject thereto are named and either personally served or otherwise have actual notice thereof in accordance with law. The notice shall include—

(1) a statement of the time, place, and nature of public rule making proceedings;

(2) reference to the legal authority under which the rule is proposed; and

(3) either the terms or substance of the proposed rule or a description of the subjects and issues involved. Except when notice or hearing is required by statute, this subsection does not apply—

(A) to interpretative rules, general statements of policy, or rules of agency organization, procedure, or practice; or

(B) when the agency for good cause finds (and incorporates the finding and a brief statement of reasons therefor in the rules issued) that notice and public procedure thereon are impracticable, unnecessary, or contrary to the public interest.

(c) After notice required by this section, the agency shall give interested persons an opportunity to participate in the rule making through submission of written data, views, or arguments with or without opportunity for oral presentation. After consideration of the relevant matter presented, the agency shall incorporate in the rules adopted a concise general statement of their basis and purpose. When rules are required by statute to be made on the record after opportunity for an agency hearing, sections 556 and 557 of this title apply instead of this subsection.

(d) The required publication or service of a substantive rule shall be made not less than 30 days before its effective date, except—

(1) a substantive rule which grants or recognizes an exemption or relieves a restriction;

(2) interpretative rules and statements of policy; or

(3) as otherwise provided by the agency for good cause found and published with the rule.

(e) Each agency shall give an interested person the right to petition for the issuance, amendment, or repeal of a rule.

§ 554. Adjudications

(a) This section applies, according to the provisions thereof, in every case of adjudication required by statute to be determined on the record after opportunity for an agency hearing, except to the extent that there is involved—

(1) a matter subject to a consequent trial of the law and the facts de novo in a court;

(2) the selection or tenure of an employee, except a hearing examiner appointed under section 3105 of this title;

(3) proceedings in which decisions rest solely on inspections, tests, or elections;

(4) the conduct of military or foreign affairs functions;

(5) cases in which an agency is acting as an agent for a court; or

(6) the certification of worker representatives.

(b) Persons entitled to notice of an agency hearing shall be timely informed of—

(1) the time, place, and nature of the hearings;

(2) the legal authority and jurisdiction under which the hearing is to be held; and

(3) the matters of fact and law asserted.

When private persons are the moving parties, other parties to the proceeding shall give prompt notice of issues controverted in fact or law; and in other instances agencies may by rule require responsive pleading. In fixing the time and place for hearings, due regard shall be had for the convenience and necessity of the parties or their representatives.

(c) The agency shall give all interested parties opportunity for—

(1) the submission and consideration of facts, arguments, offers of settlement, or proposals of adjustment when time, the nature of the proceeding, and the public interest permit; and

(2) to the extent that the parties are unable so to determine a controversy by consent, hearing and decision

on notice and in accordance with sections 556 and 557 of this title.

(d) The employee who presides at the reception of evidence pursuant to section 556 of this title shall make the recommended decision or initial decision required by section 557 of this title, unless he becomes unavailable to the agency. Except to the extent required for the disposition of ex parte matters as authorized by law, such an employee may not—

(1) consult a person or party on a fact in issue, unless on notice and opportunity for all parties to participate; or

(2) be responsible to or subject to the supervision or direction of an employee or agent engaged in the performance of investigative or prosecuting functions for an agency.

An employee or agent engaged in the performance of investigative or prosecuting functions for an agency in a case may not, in that or a factually related case, participate or advise in the decision, recommended decision, or agency review pursuant to section 557 of this title, except as witness or counsel in public proceedings. This subsection does not apply—

(A) in determining applications for initial licenses;

(B) to proceedings involving the validity or application of rates, facilities, or practices of public utilities or carriers; or

(C) to the agency or a member or members of the body comprising the agency.

(e) The agency, with like effect as in the case of other orders, and in its sound discretion, may issue a declaratory order to terminate a controversy or remove uncertainty.

§ 555. Ancillary matters

(a) This section applies, according to the provisions thereof, except as otherwise provided by this subchapter.

(b) A person compelled to appear in person before an agency or representative thereof is entitled to be accompanied, represented, and advised by counsel or, if permitted by the agency, by other qualified representative. A party is entitled to appear in person or by or with counsel or other duly qualified representative in an agency proceeding. So far as the orderly conduct of public business permits, an interested person may appear before an agency or its responsible employees for the presentation, adjustment, or determination of an issue, request, or controversy in a proceeding, whether interlocutory, summary, or otherwise, or in connection with an agency function. With due regard for the convenience and necessity of the parties or their representatives and within a reasonable time, each agency shall proceed to conclude a matter presented to it. This subsection does not grant or deny a person who is not a lawyer the right to appear for or represent others before an agency or in an agency proceeding.

(c) Process, requirement of a report, inspection, or other investigative act or demand may not be issued, made, or enforced except as authorized by law. A person compelled to submit data or evidence is entitled to retain or, on payment of lawfully prescribed costs, procure a copy or transcript thereof, except that in a nonpublic investigatory proceeding the witness may for good cause be limited to inspection of the official transcript of his testimony.

(d) Agency subpoenas authorized by law shall be issued to a party on request and, when required by rules of procedure, on a statement or showing of general relevance and reasonable scope of the evidence sought. On contest, the court shall sustain the subpoena or similar process or demand to the extent that it is found to be in accordance with law. In a proceeding for enforcement, the court shall issue an order requiring the appearance of the witness or the production of the evidence or data within a reasonable time under penalty of punishment for contempt in case of contumacious failure to comply.

(e) Prompt notice shall be given of the denial in whole or in part of a written application, petition, or other request of an interested person made in connection with any agency proceeding. Except in affirming a prior denial or when the denial is self-explanatory, the notice shall be accompanied by a brief statement of the grounds for denial.

§ 556. Hearings; presiding employees; powers and duties; burden of proof; evidence; record as basis of decision

(a) This section applies, according to the provisions thereof, to hearings required by section 553 or 554 of this title to be conducted in accordance with this section.

(b) There shall preside at the taking of evidence—

(1) the agency;

(2) one or more members of the body which comprises the agency; or

(3) one or more hearing examiners appointed under section 3105 of this title.

This subchapter does not supersede the conduct of specified classes of proceedings, in whole or in part, by or before boards or other employees specially provided for by or designated under statute. The functions of presiding employees and of employees participating in decisions in accordance with section 557 of this title shall be conducted in an impartial manner. A presiding or participating employee may at any time disqualify himself. On the filing in good faith of a timely and sufficient affidavit of personal bias or other disqualification of a presiding or participating employee, the agency shall determine the matter as a part of the record and decision in the case.

(c) Subject to published rules of the agency and within its powers, employees presiding at hearings may—

(1) administer oaths and affirmations;

(2) issue subpoenas authorized by law;

(3) rule on offers of proof and receive relevant evidence;

(4) take depositions or have depositions taken when the ends of justice would be served;

(5) regulate the course of the hearing;

(6) hold conferences for the settlement or simplification of the issues by consent of the parties;

(7) dispose of procedural requests or similar matters;

(8) make or recommend decisions in accordance with section 557 of this title; and

(9) take other action authorized by agency rule consistent with this subchapter.

(d) Except as otherwise provided by statute, the proponent of a rule or order has the burden of proof. Any oral or documentary evidence may be received, but the agency as a matter of policy shall provide for the exclusion of irrelevant, immaterial, or unduly repetitious evidence. A sanction may not be imposed or rule or order issued except on consideration of the whole record of those parts thereof cited by a party and supported by and in accordance with the reliable, probative, and substantial evidence. The agency may, to the extent consistent with the interests of justice and the policy of the underlying statutes administered by the agency, consider a violation of section 557(d) of this title sufficient grounds for a decision adverse to a party who has knowingly committed such violation or knowingly caused such violation to occur. A party is entitled to present his case or defense by oral or documentary evidence, to submit rebuttal evidence, and to conduct such cross-examination as may be required for a full and true disclosure of the facts. In rule making or determining claims for money or benefits or applications for initial licenses an agency may, when a party will not be prejudiced thereby, adopt procedures for the submission of all or part of the evidence in written form.

(e) The transcript of testimony and exhibits, together with all papers and requests filed in the proceeding, constitutes the exclusive record for decision in accordance with section 557 of this title and, on payment of lawfully prescribed costs, shall be made available to the parties. When an agency decision rests on official notice of a material fact not appearing in the evidence in the record, a party is entitled, on timely request, to an opportunity to show the contrary.

§ 557. Initial decisions; conclusiveness; review by agency; submissions by parties; contents of decisions; record

(a) This section applies, according to the provisions thereof, when a hearing is required to be conducted in accordance with section 556 of this title.

(b) When the agency did not preside at the reception of the evidence, the presiding employee or, in cases not subject to section 554(d) of this title, an employee qualified to preside at hearings pursuant to section 556 of this title, shall initially decide the case unless the agency requires, either in specific cases or by general rule, the entire record to be certified to it for decision. When the presiding employee makes an initial decision, that decision then becomes the decision of the agency without further proceedings unless there is an appeal to, or review on motion of, the agency within time provided by rule. On appeal from or review of the initial decision, the agency has all the powers which it would have in making the initial decision except as it may limit the issues on notice or by rule. When the agency makes the decision without having presided at the reception of the evidence, the presiding employee or an employee qualified to preside at hearings pursuant to section 556 of this title shall first recommend a decision, except that in rule making or determining applications for initial licenses—

(1) instead thereof the agency may issue a tentative decision or one of its responsible employees may recommend a decision; or

(2) this procedure may be omitted in a case in which the agency finds on the record that due and timely execution of its functions imperatively and unavoidably so requires.

(c) Before a recommended, initial, or tentative decision, or a decision on agency review of the decision of subordinate employees, the parties are entitled to a reasonable opportunity to submit for the consideration of the employees participating in the decisions—

(1) proposed findings and conclusions; or

(2) exceptions to the decisions or recommended decisions of subordinate employees or to tentative agency decisions; and

(3) supporting reasons for the exceptions or proposed findings or conclusions. The record shall show the ruling on each finding, conclusion, or exception presented. All decisions, including initial, recommended, and tentative decisions, are a part of the record and shall include a statement of—

(A) findings and conclusions, and the reasons or basis therefor, on all the material issues of fact, law, or discretion presented on the record; and

(B) the appropriate rule, order, sanction, relief, or denial thereof.

(d)(1) In any agency proceeding which is subject to subsection (a) of this section, except to the extent required for the disposition of ex parte matters as authorized by law—

(A) no interested person outside the agency shall make or knowingly cause to be made to any member of the body comprising the agency, administrative law judge, or other employee who is or may reasonably be expected to be involved in the decisional process of the proceeding, an ex parte communication relevant to the merits of the proceeding;

(B) no member of the body comprising the agency, administrative law judge, or other employee who is or may reasonably be expected to be involved in the decisional process of the proceeding, shall make or knowingly cause to be made to any interested person outside the agency an ex parte communication relevant to the merits of the proceeding;

(C) a member of the body comprising the agency, administrative law judge, or other employee who is or may reasonably be expected to be involved in the decisional process of such proceeding who receives, or who makes or knowingly causes to be made, a communication prohibited by this subsection shall place on the public record of the proceeding:

(i) all such written communications;

(ii) memoranda stating the substance of all such oral communications; and

(iii) all written responses, and memoranda stating the substance of all oral responses, to the materials described in clauses (i) and (ii) of this subparagraph;

(D) upon receipt of a communication knowingly made or knowingly caused to be made by a party in violation of this subsection, the agency, administrative law judge, or other employee presiding at the hearing may, to the extent consistent with the interests of justice and the policy of the underlying statutes, require the party to show cause why his claim or interest in the proceeding should not be dismissed, denied, disregarded, or otherwise adversely affected on account of such violation; and

(E) the prohibitions of this subsection shall apply beginning at such time as the agency may designate, but in no case shall they begin to apply later than the time at which a proceeding is noticed for hearing unless the person responsible for the communication has knowledge that it will be noticed, in which case the prohibitions shall apply beginning at the time of his acquisition of such knowledge.

(2) This subsection does not constitute authority to withhold information from Congress.

§ 558. Imposition of sanctions; determination of applications for licenses; suspension, revocation, and expiration of licenses

(a) This section applies, according to the provisions thereof, to the exercise of a power or authority.

(b) A sanction may not be imposed or a substantive rule or order issued except within jurisdiction delegated to the agency and as authorized by law.

(c) When application is made for a license required by law, the agency, with due regard for the rights and privileges of all the interested parties or adversely affected persons and within a reasonable time, shall set and complete proceedings required to be conducted in accordance with sections 556 and 557 of this title or other proceedings required by law and shall make its decision. Except in cases of willfulness or those in which public health, interest, or safety requires otherwise, the withdrawal, suspension, revocation, or annulment of a license is lawful only if, before the institution of agency proceedings therefor, the licensee has been given—

(1) notice by the agency in writing of the facts or conduct which may warrant the action; and

(2) opportunity to demonstrate or achieve compliance with all lawful requirements.

When the licensee has made timely and sufficient application for a renewal or a new license in accordance with agency rules, a license with reference to an activity of a continuing nature does not expire until the application has been finally determined by the agency.

§ 559. Effect on other laws; effect of subsequent statute

(a) This subchapter, chapter 7, and sections 1305, 3105, 3344, 4301(2)(E), 5372, and 7521 of this title, and the provisions of section 5335(a)(B) of this title that relate to hearing examiners, do not limit or repeal additional requirements imposed by statute or otherwise recognized by law. Except as otherwise required by law, requirements or privileges relating to evidence or procedure apply equally to agencies and persons. Each agency is granted the authority necessary to comply with the requirements of this subchapter through the issuance of rules or otherwise. Subsequent statute may not be held to supersede or modify this subchapter, chapter 7, sections 1305, 3105, 3344, 4301(2)(E), 5372, or 7521 of this title, or the provisions of section 5335(a)(B) of this title that relate to hearing examiners, except to the extent that it does so expressly.

CHAPTER 7—JUDICIAL REVIEW

§ 701. Applications; definitions

(a) This chapter applies, according to the provisions thereof, except to the extent that—

(1) statutes preclude judicial review; or

(2) agency action is committed to agency discretion by law.

(b) For the purpose of this chapter—

(1) "agency" means each authority of the Government of the United States, whether or not it is within or subject to review by another agency, but does not include—

(A) the Congress;

(B) the courts of the United States;

(C) the governments of the territories or possessions of the United States;

(D) the government of the District of Columbia;

(E) agencies composed of representatives of the parties or of representatives of organizations of the parties to the disputes determined by them;

(F) courts martial and military commissions;

(G) military authority exercised in the field in time of war or in occupied territory; or

(H) functions conferred by sections 1738, 1739, 1743, and 1744 of title 12; chapter 2 of title 41; or sections 1622, 1884, 1891–1902, and former section 1641(b)(2), of title 50, appendix; and

(2) "person," "rule," "order," "license," "sanction," "relief," and "agency action" have the meanings given them by section 551 of this title.

§ 702. Right of review

A person suffering legal wrong because of agency action, or adversely affected or aggrieved by agency action within the meaning of a relevant statute, is entitled to judicial review thereof. An action in a court of the United States seeking relief other than money damages and stating a claim that an agency or an officer or employee thereof acted or failed to act in an official capacity or under color of legal authority shall not be dismissed nor relief therein denied on the ground that it is against the United States or that the United States is an indispensable party. The United States may be named as a defendant in any such action, and a judgment or decree may be entered against the United States: *Provided,* That any mandatory or injunctive decree shall specify the Federal officer or officers (by name or by title), and their successors in office, personally responsible for compliance. Nothing herein (1) affects other limitations on judicial review or the power or duty of the court to dismiss any action or deny relief on any other appropriate legal or equitable ground; of (2) confers authority to grant relief if any other statute that grants consent to suit expressly or impliedly forbids the relief which is sought.

§ 703. Form and venue of proceeding

The form of proceeding for judicial review is the special statutory review proceeding relevant to the subject matter in a court specified by statute or, in the absence or inadequacy thereof, any applicable form of legal action, including actions for declaratory judgments or writs of prohibitory or mandatory injunction or habeas corpus, in a court of competent jurisdiction. If no special statutory review proceeding is applicable, the action for judicial review may be brought against the United States, the agency by its official title, or the appropriate officer. Except to the extent that prior, adequate, and exclusive opportunity for judicial review is provided by law, agency action is subject to judicial review in civil or criminal proceedings for judicial enforcement.

§ 704. Actions reviewable

Agency actions made reviewable by statute and final agency action for which there is no other adequate remedy in a court are subject to judicial review. A preliminary, procedural, or intermediate agency action or ruling not directly reviewable is subject to review on the review of the final agency action. Except as otherwise expressly required by statute, agency action otherwise final is final for the purposes of this section whether or not there has been presented or determined an application for a declaratory order, for any form of reconsiderations, or, unless the agency otherwise requires by rule and provides that the action meanwhile is inoperative, for an appeal to superior agency authority.

§ 705. Relief pending review

When an agency finds that justice so requires, it may postpone the effective date of action taken by it, pending judicial review. On such conditions as may be required and to the extent necessary to prevent irreparable injury, the reviewing court, including the court to which a case may be taken on appeal from or on application for certiorari or other writ to a reviewing court, may issue all necessary and appropriate process to postpone the effective date of an agency action or to preserve status or rights pending conclusion of the review proceedings.

§ 706. Scope of review

To the extent necessary to decision and when presented, the reviewing court shall decide all relevant questions of law, interpret constitutional and statutory provisions, and determine the meaning or applicability of the terms of an agency action. The reviewing court shall—

(1) compel agency action unlawfully withheld or unreasonably delayed; and

(2) hold unlawful and set aside agency action, findings, and conclusions found to be—

(A) arbitrary, capricious, an abuse of discretion, or otherwise not in accordance with law;

(B) contrary to constitutional right, power, privilege, or immunity;

(C) in excess of statutory jurisdiction, authority, or limitations, or short of statutory right;

(D) without observance of procedure required by law;

(E) unsupported by substantial evidence in a case subject to sections 556 and 557 of this title or otherwise reviewed on the record of an agency hearing provided by statute; or

(F) unwarranted by the facts to the extent that the facts are subject to trial de novo by the reviewing court. In making the foregoing determinations, the court shall review the whole record or those parts of it cited by a party, and due account shall be taken of the rule of prejudicial error.

Freedom of Information Act

The 1966 Freedom of Information Act (100 Stat. 3207–48, 5 U.S.C. 552 note) requires executive branch agencies and independent commissions to make available to citizens, upon request, all documents and records—except those that fall into the following exempt categories:

- Secret national security or foreign policy information;
- Internal personnel practices;
- Information exempted by law;
- Trade secrets or other confidential commercial or financial information;
- Interagency or intra-agency memos;
- Personal information, personnel, or medical files;
- Law enforcement investigatory information;
- Information related to reports on financial institutions; and
- Geological and geophysical information.

Following passage of the FOIA, studies of its operation noted that major problems in obtaining information were bureaucratic delay, the cost of bringing suit to force disclosure, and excessive charges levied by the agencies for finding and providing the requested information. Congress in 1974 amended the act to remove some of the obstacles to public access.

Chief among the provisions of the amendments were those allowing a federal judge to review a decision of the government to classify certain material. Another provision set deadlines for the agency to respond to a request for information under the law. Another amendment permitted judges to order payment of attorneys' fees and court costs for plaintiffs who won suits brought for information under the act.

As amended in 1974, the act:

- Required federal agencies to publish their indexes of final opinions on settlements of internal cases, policy statements, and administrative staff manuals—or, if the indexes were not published, to furnish them on request to any person for the cost of duplication. The 1966 law simply required agencies to make such indexes available for public inspection and copying.
- Reworded a provision of the 1966 law to require agencies to release unlisted documents to someone requesting them with a reasonable description. This change was to ensure that an agency could not refuse to provide material simply because the applicant could not give its precise title.
- Directed each agency to publish a uniform set of fees for providing documents at the cost of finding and copying them; the amendment allowed waiver or reduction of those fees when in the public interest.
- Empowered federal district courts to order agencies to produce improperly withheld documents—and to examine the contested materials privately (*in camera*) to determine if they were properly exempted under one of the nine categories. This amendment removed the barrier to court review, which the Supreme Court had pointed out, giving courts the power to hold that a document had been improperly classified and therefore should be released. The government was required to prove that contested material was properly classified.
- Set time limits for agency responses to requests: ten working days for an initial request; twenty working days for an appeal from an initial refusal to produce documents; a possible ten working-day extension that could be granted only once in a single case.
- Set a thirty-day time limit for an agency response to a complaint filed in court under the act, provided that such cases should be given priority attention by the courts at the appeal, as well as at the trial, level.
- Allowed courts to order the government to pay attorneys' fees and court costs for persons winning suits against it under the act.
- Authorized a court to find if an agency employee acted capriciously or arbitrarily in withholding information. Such a finding would set into action Civil Service Commission proceedings to determine the need for disciplinary action. If the commission found such a need, the relevant agency would take the disciplinary action which the commission recommended.
- Amended the wording of the national defense and national security exemption to make clear that it applied only to properly classified information, clarifying congressional intent to allow review of the decision to stamp something "classified."
- Amended the wording of the law enforcement exemption to allow withholding only of information which, if disclosed, would interfere with enforcement

proceedings, deprive someone of a fair trial or hearing, invade personal privacy in an unwarranted way, disclose the identity of a confidential source, disclose investigative techniques, or endanger law enforcement personnel. Also protected from disclosure all information from a confidential source obtained by a criminal law enforcement agency or by an agency conducting a lawful national security investigation.

- Provided that segregable nonexempt portions of requested material be released after deletion of the exempt portions.

- Required an annual agency report to Congress including a list of all agency decisions to withhold information requested under the act, the reasons, the appeals, the results, all relevant rules, the fee schedule, and the names of officials responsible for each denial of information.

- Required an annual report from the attorney general to Congress listing the number of cases arising under the act, the exemption involved in each case, and the disposition, costs, fees, and penalties of each case.

All agencies of the executive branch have issued regulations to implement the Freedom of Information Act, which may be found in the *Code of Federal Regulations* (consult the general index of the code under "Freedom of Information").

FOIA and presidential records. During the Nixon administration, Congress enacted legislation to protect presidential papers for historical reason, the Presidential Recordings and Materials Preservation Act of 1974. In 1978, Congress expanded the protection of historic presidential documents by passing the Presidential Records Act, which authorized the preservation of all presidential records and declared public ownership of such documents. Various executive orders have amended public access to presidential documents. In 1989, President Ronald Reagan issued Executive Order 12667, which established policies and procedures governing the assertion of executive privilege by incumbent and former presidents in connection with the release of presidential records by the National Archives and Records Administration pursuant to the Presidential Records Act. In November 2001 President George W. Bush issued Executive Order 13233, which expanded the executive privilege coverage and revoked President Reagan's Executive Order 12667. The move was denounced by open government advocates. Upon his first day in office, Jan. 21, 2009, President Barack Obama issued Executive Order 13489, which revoked Executive Order 13233 and reinstated the text of President Reagan's Executive Order 12667.

Electronic FOIA provisions. The passage of the Electronic Freedom of Information Act of 1996 amended the FOIA by expanding coverage to government information stored electronically. In addition, the act specified that federal data should be placed in electronic form when possible. The 1996 act also set about to improve the public's access to government data by speeding up the time government agencies are allowed to take in responding to a request, and by requiring that indexes of government records be made available to the public.

FOIA and Homeland Security. The Homeland Security Act of 2002, which established the Department of Homeland Security (DHS), granted broad exemption to the FOIA in exchange for the cooperation of private companies in sharing information with the government regarding vulnerabilities in the nation's critical infrastructure. Subtitle B of the act (the Critical Infrastructure Information Act) exempted from the FOIA and other federal and state disclosure requirements any critical infrastructure information that is voluntarily submitted to a covered federal agency for use in the security of critical infrastructure and protected systems, analysis, warning, interdependency study, recovery, reconstitution, or other informational purpose when accompanied by an express statement that such information is being submitted voluntarily in expectation of such nondisclosure protection. The Homeland Security Act required the secretary of DHS to establish specified procedures for the receipt, care, and storage by federal agencies of such critical infrastructure information and to provide criminal penalties for the unauthorized disclosure of such information.

After passage of the Homeland Security Act in 2002, many lawmakers voiced concern that the new law might limit disclosure of some government information. Initial attempts to update the FOIA were not successful in 2003. With Democrats in majority in the 110th Congress, Sen. Patrick Leahy (D-VT) reintroduced the Openness Promotes Effectiveness in Our National (OPEN) Government Act of 2007, on Dec. 14 2007; the president signed it Dec. 31, 2007. The legislation did not include any new information to be released under the FOIA but instead focused on making it easier for the public to make FOIA requests. Among the legislation's provisions:

- Provides definitions of "representative of the news media" and "news" for purposes of request processing fees.
- Provides that, for purposes of awarding attorney fees and litigation costs, a FOIA complainant has substantially prevailed in a legal proceeding to compel disclosure if such complainant obtained relief through either a judicial order or an enforceable written agreement or consent decree; or a voluntary or unilateral change in position by the agency if the complainant's claim is not insubstantial.
- Directs the attorney general to notify the Special Counsel of civil actions taken for arbitrary and capricious rejections of requests for agency records; and submit annual reports to Congress on such civil actions. Directs the Special Counsel to submit an annual report on investigations of agency rejections of FOIA requests.
- Requires the twenty-day period during which an agency must determine whether to comply with a FOIA request to begin on the date the request is received by the appropriate component of the agency, but no later than ten days after the request is received by any component that is designated to receive FOIA requests in the agency's FOIA regulations. Prohibits the tolling of the twenty-day period by the agency (with some exceptions). Prohibits an agency from assessing search or duplication fees if it fails to comply with time limits, provided that no unusual or exceptional circumstances apply to the processing of the request.

- Requires agencies to establish a system to assign an individualized tracking number for each FOIA request received that will take longer than ten days to process and a telephone line or Internet service that provides information on the status of a request.
- Revises annual reporting requirements on agency compliance with FOIA to require information on: (1) FOIA denials based upon particular statutes; (2) response times; and (3) compliance by the agency and by each principal component thereof.
- Redefines "record" under FOIA to include any information maintained by an agency contractor.
- Establishes within the National Archives and Records Administration (NARA) an Office of Government Information Services to (1) review compliance with FOIA policies; (2) recommend policy changes to Congress and the President; and (3) offer mediation services between FOIA requesters and administrative agencies as a nonexclusive alternative to litigation. Authorizes the office to issue advisory opinions if mediation has not resolved the dispute.
- Requires each agency to designate a chief FOIA officer and authorizes responsibilities for this position.
- Requires the Office of Personnel Management (OPM) to report to Congress on personnel policies related to FOIA.
- Sets forth requirements to describe exemptions authorizing deletions of material provided under FOIA.

Prior to congressional revisions to the FOIA, President George W. Bush issued Executive Order 13392: Improving Agency Disclosure of Information on Dec. 14, 2005 (see p. 938). The order sought to streamline the effectiveness of government agencies in responding to FOIA requests and to reduce backlogs of FOIA requests. The order did not expand the information available under FOIA.

The executive order provided that

- A chief FOIA officer (at the assistant secretary or equivalent level) of each government agency monitor FOIA compliance throughout the agency. The chief FOIA officer was required to inform agency heads and the attorney general of the agency's FOIA compliance performance.
- A FOIA Requester Service Center serve as the first point of contact for a FOIA requester seeking information concerning the status of the person's FOIA request and appropriate information about the agency's FOIA response.
- FOIA public liaisons or supervisory officials facilitate further action if a requester has concerns regarding how an initial request was handled by the center staff.
- The chief FOIA officer review and evaluate the agency's implementation and administration of FOIA pursuant to the executive order. The agency head was mandated to report the findings to the attorney general and to the director of the Office of Management and Budget. The report also must be published on the agency's website or in the Federal Register. Annual reports are posted on the Justice Department website.
- The attorney general review the agency-specific plans and submit to the president a report on government-wide FOIA implementation.

On December 29, 2009, President Obama signed Executive Order 13526, which prescribes a uniform system for classifying, safeguarding, and declassifying national security information, including information relating to defense against transnational terrorism. It replaces the provisions of previous Executive Order 12958 (signed by President Bill Clinton) and Executive Order 13292 (signed by President George W. Bush). Executive Order 13526 established a National Declassification Center at the National Archives and Records Administration. The center is tasked with clearing the backlog of referrals in reviewed documents both in federal records and in presidential materials.

Congress also addressed transparency and classification regarding information shared among federal, state, local, and tribal agencies and private-sector partners. In 2010 the Reducing Over-Classification Act was enacted to increase transparency, decrease over-classification, and promote information sharing across the federal government and with state, local, tribal, and private sector entities. The legislation was in response to the 9/11 Commission report, which noted that over-classification and inadequate information sharing contributed to the government's failure to prevent the attacks of September 11, 2001.

Legislation Addressing Exemptions

The OPEN FOIA Act of 2009, a title within the Department of Homeland Security Appropriations Act, 2010, amended FOIA to require statutory exemptions to its disclosure requirements to specifically cite its provision that authorizes such exemptions. These exemptions are known as (3)(b) exemptions, or exemption 3. The OPEN FOIA Act impacts statutes enacted after October 28, 2009, the date the OPEN FOIA Act was signed into law. For any statute enacted after that date to qualify as an exemption 3 statute, it must satisfy one of the original requirements: It must "require that the matters be withheld from the public in such a manner as to leave no discretion on the issue" or "establish particular criteria for withholding or refer to particular types of matters to be withheld." If enacted after October 28, 2009, the statute must meet one additional requirement—it must specifically cite to exemption 3 in order to qualify as a withholding statute.

The Protected National Security Documents Act of 2009, also included in the Department of Homeland Security Appropriations Act, 2010, was Congress's response to litigation under FOIA to obtain photographs of prisoner abuse in Iraq and Afghanistan. The legislation exempts from disclosure under FOIA any "protected document," defined as any record for which the secretary of defense has issued a certification stating that its disclosure would endanger U.S. citizens, members of the U.S. Armed Forces, or U.S. government employees deployed outside the United States, and that is a photograph that was taken between September 11, 2001, and January 22, 2009, relating to the treatment of individuals engaged, captured, or detained after September 11, 2001, by the U.S. Armed Forces in operations outside of the United States. The law provides that such a certification shall expire three years after issuance or renewal.

In 2010 Congress passed the Dodd-Frank Wall Street Reform and Consumer Protection Act to expand federal oversight of financial markets, including trading in derivatives, hedge funds, and municipal bonds. Section 929I of the Dodd-Frank Act exempted the Security and Exchange Commission's (SEC) regulatory and oversight activities from the Freedom of Information Act. The intent was to shield institutional and trade-secret information, such as client lists, from competitors. This was included to cover entities that were not previously subject to SEC regulation, such as hedge funds. Other financial institutions previously regulated by the SEC did enjoy some protections through the FOIA exemption 8, which allows exemption for information "contained in or related to examination, operating, or condition reports prepared by, on behalf of, or for the use of an agency responsible for the regulation or supervision of financial institutions."

However, critics said the language was too broad and could potentially exempt all of the SEC's regulatory and investigative activity and related documents. The critics garnered bi-partisan support for their position; just three months after the Dodd-Frank Act was signed, Congress passed legislation to repeal the SEC's exemption from disclosing records or information obtained from registered persons pursuant to its regulatory or oversight activities. The legislation broadened the definition of "financial institution" to include new entities that the SEC will regulate under the Dodd-Frank Act to allow for FOIA exemption 8 protections.

The following is the text of the Freedom of Information Act, as amended, as it appears in the U.S. Code, Title 5, Chapter 5, Subchapter II, section 552.

§ 552. Public information; agency rules, opinions, orders, records, and proceedings

(a) Each agency shall make available to the public information as follows:

(1) Each agency shall separately state and currently publish in the *Federal Register* for the guidance of the public—

(A) descriptions of its central and field organization and the established places at which, the employees (and in the case of a uniformed service, the members) from whom, and the methods whereby, the public may obtain information, make submittals or requests, or obtain decisions;

(B) statements of the general course and method by which its functions are channeled and determined, including the nature and requirements of all formal and informal procedures available;

(C) rules of procedure, descriptions of forms available or the places at which forms may be obtained, and instructions as to the scope and contents of all papers, reports, or examinations;

(D) substantive rules of general applicability adopted as authorized by law, and statements of general policy or interpretations of general applicability formulated and adopted by the agency; and

(E) each amendment, revision, or repeal of the foregoing.

Except to the extent that a person has actual and timely notice of the terms thereof, a person may not in any manner be required to resort to, or be adversely affected by, a matter required to be published in the *Federal Register* and not so published. For the purpose of this paragraph, matter reasonably available to the class of persons affected thereby is deemed published in the *Federal Register* when incorporated by reference therein with the approval of the Director of the *Federal Register.*

(2) Each agency, in accordance with published rules, shall make available for public inspection and copying—

(A) final opinions, including concurring and dissenting opinions, as well as orders, made in the adjudication of cases;

(B) those statements of policy and interpretations which have been adopted by the agency and are not published in the *Federal Register;*

(C) administrative staff manuals and instructions to staff that affect a member of the public;

(D) copies of all records, regardless of form or format, which have been released to any person under paragraph (3) and which, because of the nature of their subject matter, the agency determines have become or are likely to become the subject of subsequent requests for substantially the same records; and

(E) a general index of the records referred to under subparagraph (D); unless the materials are promptly published and copies offered for sale. For records created on or after November 1, 1996, within one year after such date, each agency shall make such records available, including by computer telecommunications or, if computer telecommunications means have not been established by the agency, by other electronic means. To the extent required to prevent a clearly unwarranted invasion of personal privacy, an agency may delete identifying details when it makes available or publishes an opinion, statement of policy, interpretation, staff manual, instruction, or copies of records referred to in subparagraph (D). However, in each case the justification for the deletion shall be explained fully in writing, and the extent of such deletion shall be indicated on the portion of the record which is made available or published, unless including that indication would harm an interest protected by the exemption in subsection (b) under which the deletion is made. If technically feasible, the extent of the deletion shall be indicated at the place in the record where the deletion was made. Each agency shall also maintain and make available for public inspection and copying current indexes providing identifying information for the public as to any matter issued, adopted, or promulgated after July 4, 1967, and required by this paragraph to be made available or published. Each agency shall promptly publish, quarterly or more frequently, and distribute (by sale or otherwise) copies of each index or supplements thereto unless it determines by order published in the *Federal Register* that the publication would be unnecessary and impracticable, in which case the agency shall nonetheless provide copies of an index on request at a cost not to exceed the direct cost of duplication. Each agency shall make the index referred to in subparagraph (E) available by computer telecommunications by December 31, 1999. A final order, opinion, statement of policy, interpretation, or staff manual or instruction that affects a member of the public may be relied on, used, or cited as precedent by an agency against a party other than an agency only if—

(i) it has been indexed and either made available or published as provided by this paragraph; or

(ii) the party has actual and timely notice of the terms thereof.

(3)(A) Except with respect to the records made available under paragraphs (1) and (2) of this subsection, and except as provided in subparagraph (E), each agency, upon any request for records which (i) reasonably describes such records and (ii) is made in accordance with published rules stating the time, place, fees (if any), and procedures to be followed, shall make the records promptly available to any person.

(B) In making any record available to a person under this paragraph, an agency shall provide the record in any form or format requested by the person if the record is readily reproducible by the agency in that form or format. Each agency shall make reasonable efforts to maintain its records in forms or formats that are reproducible for purposes of this section.

(C) In responding under this paragraph to a request for records, an agency shall make reasonable efforts to search for the records in electronic form or format, except when such efforts would significantly interfere with the operation of the agency's automated information system.

(D) For purposes of this paragraph, the term "search" means to review, manually or by automated means, agency records for the purpose of locating those records which are responsive to a request.

(E) An agency, or part of an agency, that is an element of the intelligence community (as that term is defined in section 3(4) of the National Security Act of 1947 (50 U.S.C. 401a(4))) shall not make any record available under this paragraph to—

(i) any government entity, other than a State, territory, commonwealth, or district of the United States, or any subdivision thereof; or

(ii) a representative of a government entity described in clause (i).

(4)(A)(i) In order to carry out the provisions of this section, each agency shall promulgate regulations, pursuant to notice and receipt of public comment, specifying the schedule of fees applicable to the processing of requests under this section and establishing procedures and guidelines for determining when such fees should be waived or reduced. Such schedule shall conform to the guidelines which shall be promulgated, pursuant to notice and receipt of public comment, by the Director of the Office of Management and Budget and which shall provide for a uniform schedule of fees for all agencies.

(ii) Such agency regulations shall provide that—

(I) fees shall be limited to reasonable standard charges for document search, duplication, and review, when records are requested for commercial use;

(II) fees shall be limited to reasonable standard charges for document duplication when records are not sought for commercial use and the request is made by an educational or noncommercial scientific institution, whose purpose is scholarly or scientific research; or a representative of the news media; and

(III) for any request not described in (I) or (II), fees shall be limited to reasonable standard charges for document search and duplication.

In this clause, the term "a representative of the news media" means any person or entity that gathers information of potential interest to a segment of the public, uses its editorial skills to turn the raw materials into a distinct work, and distributes that work to an audience. In this clause, the term "news" means information that is about current events or that would be of current interest to the public. Examples of news-media entities are television or radio stations broadcasting to the public at large and publishers of periodicals (but only if such entities qualify as disseminators of "news") who make their products available for purchase by or subscription by or free distribution to the general public. These examples are not all-inclusive. Moreover, as methods of news delivery evolve (for example, the adoption of the electronic dissemination of newspapers through telecommunications services), such alternative media shall be considered to be news-media entities. A freelance journalist shall be regarded as working for a news-media entity if the journalist can demonstrate a solid basis for expecting publication through that entity, whether or not the journalist is actually employed by the entity. A publication contract would present a solid basis for such an expectation; the Government may also consider the past publication record of the requester in making such a determination.

(iii) Documents shall be furnished without any charge or at a charge reduced below the fees established under clause (ii) if disclosure of the information is in the public interest because it is likely to contribute significantly to public understanding of the operations or activities of the government and is not primarily in the commercial interest of the requester.

(iv) Fee schedules shall provide for the recovery of only the direct costs of search, duplication, or review. Review costs shall include only the direct costs incurred during the initial examination of a document for the purposes of determining whether the documents must be disclosed under this section and for the purposes of withholding any portions exempt from disclosure under this section. Review costs may not include any costs incurred in resolving issues of law or policy that may be raised in the course of processing a request under this section. No fee may be charged by any agency under this section—

(I) if the costs of routine collection and processing of the fee are likely to equal or exceed the amount of the fee; or

(II) for any request described in clause (ii)(II) or (III) of this subparagraph for the first two hours of search time or for the first one hundred pages of duplication.

(v) No agency may require advance payment of any fee unless the requester has previously failed to pay fees in a timely fashion, or the agency has determined that the fee will exceed $250.

(vi) Nothing in this subparagraph shall supersede fees chargeable under a statute specifically providing for setting the level of fees for particular types of records.

(vii) In any action by a requester regarding the waiver of fees under this section, the court shall determine the matter de novo: Provided, That the court's review of the matter shall be limited to the record before the agency.

(viii) An agency shall not assess search fees (or in the case of a requester described under clause (ii)(II), duplication fees) under this subparagraph if the agency fails to comply with any time limit under paragraph (6), if no unusual or exceptional circumstances (as those terms are defined for purposes of paragraphs (6)(B) and (C), respectively) apply to the processing of the request.

(B) On complaint, the district court of the United States in the district in which the complainant resides, or has his principal place of business, or in which the agency records are situated, or in the District of Columbia, has jurisdiction to enjoin the agency from withholding agency records and to order the production of any agency records improperly withheld from the complainant. In such a case the court shall determine the matter de novo, and may examine the contents of such agency records in camera to determine whether such records or any part thereof shall be withheld under any of the exemptions set forth in subsection (b) of this section, and the burden is on the agency to sustain its action. In addition to any other matters to which a court accords substantial weight, a court shall accord substantial weight to an affidavit of an agency concerning the agency's determination as to technical feasibility under paragraph (2)(C) and subsection (b) and reproducibility under paragraph (3)(B).

(C) Notwithstanding any other provision of law, the defendant shall serve an answer or otherwise plead to any complaint made under this subsection within thirty days after service upon the defendant of the pleading in which such complaint is made, unless the court otherwise directs for good cause is shown.

[(D) Repealed. Pub. L. 98–620, title IV, Sec. 402(2), Nov. 8, 1984, 98 Stat. 3357.]

(E)(i) The court may assess against the United States reasonable attorney fees and other litigation costs reasonably incurred in any case under this section in which the complainant has substantially prevailed.

(ii) For purposes of this subparagraph, a complainant has substantially prevailed if the complainant has obtained relief through either—

(I) a judicial order, or an enforceable written agreement or consent decree; or

(II) a voluntary or unilateral change in position by the agency, if the complainant's claim is not insubstantial.

(F)(i) Whenever the court orders the production of any agency records improperly withheld from the complainant and assesses against the United States reasonable attorney fees and other litigation costs, and the court additionally issues a written finding that the circumstances surrounding the withholding raise questions whether agency personnel acted arbitrarily or capriciously with respect to the withholding, the Special Counsel shall promptly initiate a proceeding to determine whether disciplinary action is warranted against the officer or employee who was primarily responsible for the withholding. The Special Counsel, after investigation and consideration of the evidence submitted, shall submit his findings and recommendations to the administrative authority of the agency concerned and shall send copies of the findings and recommendations to the officer or employee or his representative. The administrative authority shall take the corrective action that the Special Counsel recommends.

(ii) The Attorney General shall—

(I) notify the Special Counsel of each civil action described under the first sentence of clause (i); and

(II) annually submit a report to Congress on the number of such civil actions in the preceding year.

(iii) The Special Counsel shall annually submit a report to Congress on the actions taken by the Special Counsel under clause (i).

(G) In the event of noncompliance with the order of the court, the district court may punish for contempt the responsible employee, and in the case of a uniformed service, the responsible member.

(5) Each agency having more than one member shall maintain and make available for public inspection a record of the final votes of each member in every agency proceeding.

(6)(A) Each agency, upon any request for records made under paragraph (1), (2), or (3) of this subsection, shall—

(i) determine within 20 days (excepting Saturdays, Sundays, and legal public holidays) after the receipt of any such request whether to comply with such request and shall immediately notify the person making such request of such determination and the reasons therefor, and of the right of such person to appeal to the head of the agency any adverse determination; and

(ii) make a determination with respect to any appeal within twenty days (excepting Saturdays, Sundays, and legal public holidays) after the receipt of such appeal. If on appeal the denial of the request for records is in whole or in part upheld, the agency shall notify the person making such request of the provisions for judicial review of that determination under paragraph (4) of this subsection.

The 20-day period under clause (i) shall commence on the date on which the request is first received by the appropriate component of the agency, but in any event not later than ten days after the request is first received by any component agency that is designated in the agency's regulations under this section to receive requests under this section. The 20-day period shall not be tolled by the agency except—

(I) that the agency may make one request to the requester for information and toll the 20-day period while it is awaiting such information that it has reasonably requested from the requester under this section; or

(II) if necessary to clarify with the requester issues regarding fee assessment. In either case, the agency's receipt of the requester's response to the agency's request for information or clarification ends the tolling period.

(B)(i) In unusual circumstances as specified in this subparagraph, the time limits prescribed in either clause (i) or clause (ii) of subparagraph (A) may be extended by written notice to the person making such request setting forth the unusual circumstances for such extension and the date on which a determination is expected to be dispatched. No such notice shall specify a date that would result in an extension for more than ten working days, except as provided in clause (ii) of this subparagraph.

(ii) With respect to a request for which a written notice under clause (i) extends the time limits prescribed under clause (i) of subparagraph (A), the agency shall notify the person making the request if the request cannot be processed within the time limit specified in that clause and shall provide the person an opportunity to limit the scope of the request so that it may be processed within that time limit or an opportunity to arrange with the agency an alternative time frame for processing the request or a modified request. To aid the requester, each agency shall make available its FOIA Public Liaison, who shall assist in the resolution of any disputes between the requester and the agency. Refusal by the person to reasonably modify the request or arrange such an alternative time frame shall be considered as a factor in determining whether exceptional circumstances exist for purposes of subparagraph (C).

(iii) As used in this subparagraph, "unusual circumstances" means, but only to the extent reasonably necessary to the proper processing of the particular requests—

(I) the need to search for and collect the requested records from field facilities or other establishments that are separate from the office processing the request;

(II) the need to search for, collect, and appropriately examine a voluminous amount of separate and distinct records which are demanded in a single request; or

(III) the need for consultation, which shall be conducted with all practicable speed, with another agency having a substantial interest in the determination of the request or among two or more components of the agency having substantial subject-matter interest therein.

(iv) Each agency may promulgate regulations, pursuant to notice and receipt of public comment, providing for the aggregation of certain requests by the same requestor, or by a group of requestors acting in concert, if the agency reasonably believes that such requests actually constitute a single request, which would otherwise satisfy the unusual circumstances specified in this subparagraph, and the requests involve clearly related matters. Multiple requests involving unrelated matters shall not be aggregated.

(C)(i) Any person making a request to any agency for records under paragraph (1), (2), or (3) of this subsection shall be deemed to have exhausted his administrative remedies with respect to such request if the agency fails to comply with the applicable time limit provisions of this paragraph. If the Government can show exceptional circumstances exist and that the agency is exercising due diligence in responding to the request, the court may retain jurisdiction and allow the agency additional time to complete its review of the records. Upon any determination by an agency to comply with a request for records, the records shall be made promptly available to such person making such request. Any notification of denial of any request for records under this subsection shall set forth the names and titles or positions of each person responsible for the denial of such request.

(ii) For purposes of this subparagraph, the term "exceptional circumstances" does not include a delay that results from a predictable agency workload of requests under this section, unless the agency demonstrates reasonable progress in reducing its backlog of pending requests.

(iii) Refusal by a person to reasonably modify the scope of a request or arrange an alternative time frame for processing a request (or a modified request) under clause (ii) after being given an opportunity to do so by the agency to whom the person made the request shall be considered as a factor in determining whether exceptional circumstances exist for purposes of this subparagraph.

(D)(i) Each agency may promulgate regulations, pursuant to notice and receipt of public comment, providing for multitrack processing of requests for records based on the amount of work or time (or both) involved in processing requests.

(ii) Regulations under this subparagraph may provide a person making a request that does not qualify for the fastest multitrack processing an opportunity to limit the scope of the request in order to qualify for faster processing.

(iii) This subparagraph shall not be considered to affect the requirement under subparagraph (C) to exercise due diligence.

(E)(i) Each agency shall promulgate regulations, pursuant to notice and receipt of public comment, providing for expedited processing of requests for records—

(I) in cases in which the person requesting the records demonstrates a compelling need; and

(II) in other cases determined by the agency.

(ii) Notwithstanding clause (i), regulations under this subparagraph must ensure—

(I) that a determination of whether to provide expedited processing shall be made, and notice of the determination shall be provided to the person making the request, within 10 days after the date of the request; and

(II) expeditious consideration of administrative appeals of such determinations of whether to provide expedited processing.

(iii) An agency shall process as soon as practicable any request for records to which the agency has granted expedited processing under this subparagraph. Agency action to deny or affirm denial of a request for expedited processing pursuant to this subparagraph, and failure by an agency to respond in a timely manner to such a request shall be subject to judicial review under paragraph (4), except that the judicial review shall be based on the record before the agency at the time of the determination.

(iv) A district court of the United States shall not have jurisdiction to review an agency denial of expedited processing of a request for records after the agency has provided a complete response to the request.

(v) For purposes of this subparagraph, the term "compelling need" means—

(I) that a failure to obtain requested records on an expedited basis under this paragraph could reasonably be expected to pose an imminent threat to the life or physical safety of an individual; or

(II) with respect to a request made by a person primarily engaged in disseminating information, urgency to inform the public concerning actual or alleged Federal Government activity.

(vi) A demonstration of a compelling need by a person making a request for expedited processing shall be made by a statement certified by such person to be true and correct to the best of such person's knowledge and belief.

(F) In denying a request for records, in whole or in part, an agency shall make a reasonable effort to estimate the volume of any requested matter the provision of which is denied, and shall provide any such estimate to the person making the request, unless providing such estimate would harm an interest protected by the exemption in subsection (b) pursuant to which the denial is made.

(7) Each agency shall do the following:

(A) Establish a system to assign an individualized tracking number for each request received that will take longer than 10 days to process and provide each person making a request the tracking number assigned to the request; and

(B) Establish a phone line or Internet service that provides information about the status of a request to the person making the request using the assigned tracking number, including

(i) the date on which the agency originally received the request and

(a) an estimated date on which the agency will complete action on the request.

(b) This section does not apply to matters that are

(1)(A) specifically authorized under criteria established by an Executive order to be kept secret in the interest of national defense or foreign policy and (B) are in fact properly classified pursuant to such Executive order;

(2) related solely to the internal personnel rules and practices of an agency;

(3) specifically exempted from disclosure by statute (other than section 552b of this title), if that statute

(A)(i) requires that the matters be withheld from the public in such a manner as to leave no discretion on the issue, or

(ii) establishes particular criteria for withholding or refers to particular types of matters to be withheld;

(B) if enacted after the date of enactment of the OPEN FOIA Act of 2009, specifically cites to this paragraph.

(4) trade secrets and commercial or financial information obtained from a person and privileged or confidential;

(5) inter-agency or intra-agency memorandums or letters which would not be available by law to a party other than an agency in litigation with the agency;

(6) personnel and medical files and similar files the disclosure of which would constitute a clearly unwarranted invasion of personal privacy;

(7) records or information compiled for law enforcement purposes, but only to the extent that the production of such law enforcement records or information (A) could reasonably be expected to interfere with enforcement proceedings, (B) would deprive a person of a right to a fair trial or an impartial adjudication, (C) could reasonably be expected to constitute an unwarranted invasion of personal privacy, (D) could reasonably be expected to disclose the identity of a confidential source, including a State, local, or foreign agency or authority or any private institution which furnished information on a confidential basis, and, in the case of a record or information compiled by a criminal law enforcement authority in the course of a criminal investigation or by an agency conducting a lawful national security

intelligence investigation, information furnished by a confidential source, (E) would disclose techniques and procedures for law enforcement investigations or prosecutions, or would disclose guidelines for law enforcement investigations or prosecutions if such disclosure could reasonably be expected to risk circumvention of the law, or (F) could reasonably be expected to endanger the life or physical safety of any individual;

(8) contained in or related to examination, operating, or condition reports prepared by, on behalf of, or for the use of an agency responsible for the regulation or supervision of financial institutions; or

(9) geological and geophysical information and data, including maps, concerning wells.

Any reasonably segregable portion of a record shall be provided to any person requesting such record after deletion of the portions which are exempt under this subsection. The amount of information deleted, and the exemption under which the deletion is made, shall be indicated on the released portion of the record, unless including that indication would harm an interest protected by the exemption in this subsection under which the deletion is made. If technically feasible, the amount of the information deleted, and the exemption under which the deletion is made, shall be indicated at the place in the record where such deletion is made.

(c)(1) Whenever a request is made which involves access to records described in subsection (b)(7)(A) and—

(A) the investigation or proceeding involves a possible violation of criminal law; and

(B) there is reason to believe that (i) the subject of the investigation or proceeding is not aware of its pendency, and (ii) disclosure of the existence of the records could reasonably be expected to interfere with enforcement proceedings, the agency may, during only such time as that circumstance continues, treat the records as not subject to the requirements of this section.

(2) Whenever informant records maintained by a criminal law enforcement agency under an informant's name or personal identifier are requested by a third party according to the informant's name or personal identifier, the agency may treat the records as not subject to the requirements of this section unless the informant's status as an informant has been officially confirmed.

(3) Whenever a request is made which involves access to records maintained by the Federal Bureau of Investigation pertaining to foreign intelligence or counterintelligence, or international terrorism, and the existence of the records is classified information as provided in subsection (b)(1), the Bureau may, as long as the existence of the records remains classified information, treat the records as not subject to the requirements of this section.

(d) This section does not authorize the withholding of information or limit the availability of records to the public, except as specifically stated in this section. This section is not authority to withhold information from Congress.

(e)(1) On or before February 1 of each year, each agency shall submit to the Attorney General of the United States a report which shall cover the preceding fiscal year and which shall include—

(A) the number of determinations made by the agency not to comply with requests for records made to such agency under subsection (a) and the reasons for each such determination;

(B)(i) the number of appeals made by persons under subsection (a)(6), the result of such appeals, and the reason for the action upon each appeal that results in a denial of information; and

(ii) a complete list of all statutes that the agency relies upon to authorize the agency to withhold information under subsection (b)(3), the number of occasions on which each statute was relied upon, a description of whether a court has upheld the decision of the agency to withhold information under each such statute, and a concise description of the scope of any information withheld;

(C) the number of requests for records pending before the agency as of September 30 of the preceding year, and the median and average number of days that such requests had been pending before the agency as of that date;

(D) the number of requests for records received by the agency and the number of requests which the agency processed;

(E) the median number of days taken by the agency to process different types of requests, based on the date on which the requests were received by the agency;

(F) the average number of days for the agency to respond to a request beginning on the date on which the request was received by the agency, the median number of days for the agency to respond to such requests, and the range in number of days for the agency to respond to such requests;

(G) based on the number of business days that have elapsed since each request was originally received by the agency—

(i) the number of requests for records to which the agency has responded with a determination within a period up to and including 20 days, and in 20-day increments up to and including 200 days;

(ii) the number of requests for records to which the agency has responded with a determination within a period greater than 200 days and less than 301 days;

(iii) the number of requests for records to which the agency has responded with a determination within a period greater than 300 days and less than 401 days; and

(iv) the number of requests for records to which the agency has responded with a determination within a period greater than 400 days;

(H) the average number of days for the agency to provide the granted information beginning on the date on which the request was originally filed, the median number of days for the agency to provide the granted information, and the range in number of days for the agency to provide the granted information;

(I) the median and average number of days for the agency to respond to administrative appeals based on the date on which the appeals originally were received by the agency, the highest number of business days taken by the agency to respond to an administrative appeal, and the lowest number of business days taken by the agency to respond to an administrative appeal;

(J) data on the 10 active requests with the earliest filing dates pending at each agency, including the amount of time that has elapsed since each request was originally received by the agency;

(K) data on the 10 active administrative appeals with the earliest filing dates pending before the agency as of September 30 of the preceding year, including the number of business days that have elapsed since the requests were originally received by the agency;

(L) the number of expedited review requests that are granted and denied, the average and median number of days for adjudicating expedited review requests, and the number adjudicated within the required 10 days;

(M) the number of fee waiver requests that are granted and denied, and the average and median number of days for adjudicating fee waiver determinations;

(N) the total amount of fees collected by the agency for processing requests; and

(O) the number of full-time staff of the agency devoted to processing requests for records under this section, and the total amount expended by the agency for processing such requests.

(2) Information in each report submitted under paragraph (1) shall be expressed in terms of each principal component of the agency and for the agency overall.

(3) Each agency shall make each such report available to the public including by computer telecommunications, or if computer telecommunications means have not been established by the agency, by other electronic means. In addition, each agency shall make the raw statistical data used in its reports available electronically to the public upon request.

(4) The Attorney General of the United States shall make each report which has been made available by electronic means available at a single electronic access point. The Attorney General of the United States shall notify the Chairman and ranking minority member of the Committee on Government Reform and Oversight of the House of Representatives and the Chairman and ranking minority member of the Committees on Governmental Affairs and the Judiciary of the Senate, no later than April 1 of the year in which each such report is issued, that such reports are available by electronic means.

(5) The Attorney General of the United States, in consultation with the Director of the Office of Management and Budget, shall develop reporting and performance guidelines in connection with reports required by this subsection by October 1, 1997, and may establish additional requirements for such reports as the Attorney General determines may be useful.

(6) The Attorney General of the United States shall submit an annual report on or before April 1 of each calendar year which shall include for the prior calendar year a listing of the number of cases arising under this section, the exemption involved in each case, the disposition of such case, and the cost, fees, and penalties assessed under subparagraphs (E), (F), and (G) of subsection (a)(4). Such report shall also include a description of the efforts undertaken by the Department of Justice to encourage agency compliance with this section.

(f) For purposes of this section, the term—

(1) "agency" as defined in section 551(1) of this title includes any executive department, military department, Government corporation, Government controlled corporation, or other establishment in the executive branch of the Government (including the Executive Office of the President), or any independent regulatory agency; and

(2) "record" and any other term used in this section in reference to information includes—

(A) any information that would be an agency record subject to the requirements of this section when maintained by an agency in any format, including an electronic format; and

(B) any information described under subparagraph (A) that is maintained for an agency by an entity under Government contract, for the purposes of records management.

(g) The head of each agency shall prepare and make publicly available upon request, reference material or a guide for requesting records or information from the agency, subject to the exemptions in subsection (b), including—

(1) an index of all major information systems of the agency;

(2) a description of major information and record locator systems maintained by the agency; and

(3) a handbook for obtaining various types and categories of public information from the agency pursuant to chapter 35 of title 44, and under this section.

(h)(1) There is established the Office of Government Information Services within the National Archives and Records Administration.

(2) The Office of Government Information Services shall—

(A) review policies and procedures of administrative agencies under this section;

(B) review compliance with this section by administrative agencies; and

(C) recommend policy changes to Congress and the President to improve the administration of this section.

(3) The Office of Government Information Services shall offer mediation services to resolve disputes between persons making requests under this section and administrative agencies as a non-exclusive alternative to litigation and, at the discretion of the Office, may issue advisory opinions if mediation has not resolved the dispute.

(i) The Government Accountability Office shall conduct audits of administrative agencies on the implementation of this section and issue reports detailing the results of such audits.

(j) Each agency shall designate a Chief FOIA Officer who shall be a senior official of such agency (at the assistant secretary or equivalent level).

(k) The Chief FOIA Officer of each agency shall, subject to the authority of the head of the agency—

(1) have agency-wide responsibility for efficient and appropriate compliance with this section;

(2) monitor implementation of this section throughout the agency and keep the head of the agency, the chief legal officer of the agency, and the Attorney General appropriately informed of the agency's performance in implementing this section;

(3) recommend to the head of the agency such adjustments to agency practices, policies, personnel, and funding as may be necessary to improve its implementation of this section;

(4) review and report to the Attorney General, through the head of the agency, at such times and in such formats as the Attorney General may direct, on the agency's performance in implementing this section;

(5) facilitate public understanding of the purposes of the statutory exemptions of this section by including concise descriptions of the exemptions in both the agency's handbook issued under subsection (g), and the agency's annual report on this section, and by providing an overview, where appropriate, of certain general categories of agency records to which those exemptions apply; and

(6) designate one or more FOIA Public Liaisons.

(1) FOIA Public Liaisons shall report to the agency Chief FOIA Officer and shall serve as supervisory officials to whom a requester under this section can raise concerns about the service the requester has received from the FOIA Requester Center, following an initial response from the FOIA Requester Center Staff. FOIA Public Liaisons shall be responsible for assisting in reducing delays, increasing transparency and understanding of the status of requests, and assisting in the resolution of disputes.

Government in the Sunshine Act

A four-year campaign to open the government to more public scrutiny achieved its goal in 1976, with enactment of legislation requiring most federal agencies to open their meetings to the public.

Called "Government in the Sunshine Act," the bill (90 Stat. 1241, 5 U.S.C. 552b note) required for the first time that all multiheaded federal agencies—about fifty of them—conduct their business regularly in public session. The unprecedented open-door requirements embraced regulatory agencies, advisory committees, independent offices, the Postal Service—almost all executive branch agencies except the cabinet departments.

The only exception to the rule of openness was for discussion of ten kinds of matters, such as court proceedings or personnel problems, specifically listed in the bill.

A separate section of the legislation also placed a ban on informal—*ex parte*—contacts between agency officials and interested outsiders to discuss pending agency business. Calling that provision a sleeper, some Washington lawyers suggested that it could have a broad impact on what had come to be an accepted practice in regulatory proceedings.

The final version of the bill represented a victory for advocates of tough open-meeting requirements. The definition of meetings included almost any gathering, formal or informal, of agency members, including conference telephone calls. Agencies also were required to keep transcripts of closed meetings. However, the bill did allow agencies discussing very sensitive matters, such as monetary policy, to keep either minutes or transcripts.

Among its key features, the bill:

- Required all agencies headed by two or more persons, a majority of whom were appointed by the president and confirmed by the Senate, to open all meetings to the public unless a majority voted to close a meeting. (The Environmental Protection Agency is among the single-headed agencies not covered by the act.)
- Defined a "meeting" as the deliberations of at least the number of members required to take action for an agency where such deliberations determined or resulted in the joint conduct or disposition of agency business.
- Specified that a meeting could be closed only for discussion of the following ten matters: (1) national defense, foreign policy, or matters classified by executive order; (2) agency personnel rules and practices; (3) information required by other laws to be kept confidential; (4) trade secrets or financial or commercial information obtained under a pledge of confidentiality; (5) accusation of a crime or formal censure; (6) information whose disclosure would constitute an unwarranted invasion of personal privacy; (7) certain law enforcement investigatory records; (8) bank examination records and similar financial audits; (9) information whose premature disclosure could lead to significant financial speculation, endanger the stability of a financial institution, or frustrate a proposed agency action; or (10) the agency's involvement in federal or state civil actions or similar legal proceedings where there was a public record.

- Allowed a meeting to be closed by a majority record vote of all members, barring use of proxies; permitted a single vote to be taken to close a series of meetings on the same subject to be held within a thirty-day period.
- Permitted an agency to close a meeting at the request of a person affected by the agency's deliberations if the discussion could be exempted under exemptions 5, 6, or 7.
- Required an agency to disclose its vote to close a meeting within one day of the vote and to make public in advance of a closed meeting a written explanation of the closing, with a list of all persons expected to attend the closed meeting.
- Permitted agencies that regularly must meet in closed session to devise general regulations to expedite closed meetings and exempted such agencies from many procedural requirements for closed meetings.
- Required advance public notice (seven days) of the date, place, subject matter, and open-closed nature of all meetings, as well as the person to contact for information.
- For closings of meetings, required the general counsel or chief legal officer of an agency to certify it was properly closed according to a specific exemption under the bill.
- Required all agencies to keep and make public complete verbatim transcripts of closed meetings, with deletions of material exempted under the act; agencies closing meetings under exemptions 8, 9, or 10 could elect to keep minutes instead of a transcript.
- Provided for district court enforcement and review of the open-meeting requirements and placed the burden of proof in disputes upon the agency; permitted the court

to assess an agency found in violation of the act for the plaintiff's attorneys' fees and court costs and permitted the court to charge a plaintiff for such costs if his suit was found to be "frivolous or dilatory."

- Allowed federal courts reviewing a non-Sunshine agency action, upon request of a party in the proceeding, to inquire into a Sunshine law violation and afford appropriate relief.

- Specified that the provision of this act would take precedence over the Freedom of Information Act (100 Stat. 3207–48, 5 U.S.C. 552 note) in cases of information requests.

- Required each agency to report annually to Congress the numbers of open and closed meetings, reasons for closings, and descriptions of any litigation against an agency under the bill.

- Prohibited *ex parte* communications between agency officials and outsiders affected by pending agency business, required an official to make public any such contact, and made *ex parte* communications grounds for ruling against a party in an agency proceeding.

Agencies covered by the act have established their own regulations to implement it. They are required by the act to publish notice of all meetings—open and closed—in the *Federal Register*.

The following is the text of the Government in the Sunshine Act as it appears in the U.S. Code, Title 5, Chapter 5, Subchapter II, section 552b.

§ 552b. Open meetings

(a) For purposes of this section—

(1) the term "agency" means any agency, as defined in section 552(e) of this title, headed by a collegial body composed of two or more individual members, a majority of whom are appointed to such position by the President with the advice and consent of the Senate, and any subdivision thereof authorized to act on behalf of the agency;

(2) the term "meeting" means the deliberations of at least the number of individual agency members required to take action on behalf of the agency where such deliberations determine or result in the joint conduct or disposition of official agency business, but does not include deliberations required or permitted by subsection (d) or (e); and

(3) the term "member" means an individual who belongs to a collegial body heading an agency.

(b) Members shall not jointly conduct or dispose of agency business other than in accordance with this section.

(c) Except as provided in subsection (c), every portion of every meeting of an agency shall be open to public observation. Except in a case where the agency finds that the public interest requires otherwise, the second sentence of subsection (b) shall not apply to any portion of an agency meeting, and the requirements of subsections (d) and (e) shall not apply to any information pertaining to such meeting otherwise required by this section to be disclosed to the public, where the agency properly determines that such portion or portions of its meeting or the disclosure of such information is likely to—

(1) disclose matters that are (A) specifically authorized under criteria established by an Executive order to be kept secret in the interests of national defense or foreign policy and (B) in fact properly classified pursuant to such Executive order;

(2) relate solely to the internal personnel rules and practices of an agency;

(3) disclose matters specifically exempted from disclosure by statute (other than section 552 of this title), provided that such statute (A) requires that the matters be withheld from the public in such a manner as to leave no discretion on the issue, or (B) establishes particular criteria for withholding or refers to particular types of matters to be withheld;

(4) disclose trade secrets and commercial or financial information obtained from a person and privileged or confidential;

(5) involve accusing any person of a crime, or formally censuring any person;

(6) disclose information of a personal nature where disclosure would constitute a clearly unwarranted invasion of personal privacy;

(7) disclose investigatory records compiled for law enforcement purposes, or information which if written would be contained in such records, but only to the extent that the production of such records or information would (A) interfere with enforcement proceedings, (B) deprive a person of a right to a fair trial or an impartial adjudication, (C) constitute an unwarranted invasion of personal privacy, (D) disclose the identity of a confidential source and, in the case of a record compiled by a criminal law enforcement authority in the course of a criminal investigation, or by an agency conducting a lawful national security intelligence investigation, confidential information furnished only by the confidential source, (E) disclose investigative techniques and procedures, or (F) endanger the life or physical safety of law enforcement personnel;

(8) disclose information contained in or related to examination, operating, or condition reports prepared by, on behalf of, or for the use of an agency responsible for the regulation or supervision of financial institutions;

(9) disclose information the premature disclosure of which would—

(A) in the case of an agency which regulates currencies, securities, commodities, or financial institutions, be likely to (i) lead to significant financial speculation in currencies, securities, or commodities, or (ii) significantly endanger the stability of any financial institution; or

(B) in the case of any agency, be likely to significantly frustrate implementation of a proposed agency action except that subparagraph (B) shall not apply in any instance where the agency has already disclosed to the public the content or nature of its proposed action, or where the agency is required by law to make such disclosure on its own initiative prior to taking final agency action on such proposal; or

(10) specifically concern the agency's issuance of a subpoena, or the agency's participation in a civil action or proceeding, an action in a foreign court or international

tribunal, or an arbitration, or the initiation, conduct, or disposition by the agency of a particular case of formal agency adjudication pursuant to the procedures in section 554 of this title or otherwise involving a determination on the record after opportunity for a hearing.

(d)(1) Action under subsection (c) shall be taken only when a majority of the entire membership of the agency (as defined in subsection (a)(1)) votes to take such action. A separate vote of the agency members shall be taken with respect to each agency meeting, a portion or portions of which are proposed to be closed to the public pursuant to subsection (c), or with respect to any information which is proposed to be withheld under subsection (c). A single vote may be taken with respect to a series of meetings, a portion or portions of which are proposed to be closed to the public, or with respect to any information concerning such series of meetings, so long as each meeting in such series involves the same particular matters and is scheduled to be held no more than thirty days after the initial meeting in such series. The vote of each agency member participating in such vote shall be recorded and no proxies shall be allowed.

(2) Whenever any person whose interests may be directly affected by a portion of a meeting requests that the agency close such portion to the public for any of the reasons referred to in paragraph (5), (6), or (7) of subsection (c), the agency, upon request of any one of its members, shall vote by recorded vote whether to close such meeting.

(3) Within one day of any vote taken pursuant to paragraph (1) or (2), the agency shall make publicly available a written copy of such vote reflecting the vote of each member on the question. If a portion of a meeting is to be closed to the public, the agency shall, within one day of the vote taken pursuant to paragraph (1) or (2) of this subsection, make publicly available a full written explanation of its action closing the portion together with a list of all persons expected to attend the meeting and their affiliation.

(4) Any agency, a majority of whose meetings may properly be closed to the public pursuant to paragraph (4), (8), (9)(A), or (10) of subsection (c), or any combination thereof, may provide by regulation for the closing of such meetings or portions thereof in the event that a majority of the members of the agency votes by recorded vote at the beginning of such meeting, or portion thereof, to close the exempt portion or portions of the meeting, and a copy of such vote, reflecting the vote of each member on the question, is made available to the public. The provisions of paragraphs (1), (2), and (3) of this subsection and subsection (e) shall not apply to any portion of a meeting to which such regulations apply: *Provided,* That the agency shall, except to the extent that such information is exempt from disclosure under the provisions of subsection (c), provide the public with public announcement of the time, place, and subject matter of the meeting and of each portion thereof at the earliest practicable time.

(e)(1) In the case of each meeting, the agency shall make public announcement, at least one week before the meeting, of the time, place, and subject matter of the meeting, whether it is to be open or closed to the public, and the name and phone number of the official designated by the agency to respond to requests for information about the meeting. Such announcement shall be made unless a majority of the members of the agency determines by a recorded vote that agency business requires that such meeting be called at an earlier date, in which case the agency shall make public announcement of the time, place, and subject matter of such meeting, and whether open or closed to the public, at the earliest practicable time.

(2) The time or place of a meeting may be changed following the public announcement required by paragraph (1) only if the agency publicly announces such change at the earliest practicable time. The subject matter of a meeting, or the determination of the agency to open or close a meeting, or portion of a meeting, to the public, may be changed following the public announcement required by this subsection only if (A) a majority of the entire membership of the agency determines by a recorded vote that agency business so requires and that no earlier announcement of the change was possible, and (B) the agency publicly announces such change and the vote of each member upon such change at the earliest practicable time. Immediately following each public announcement required by this subsection, notice of the time, place, and subject matter of a meeting, whether the meeting is open or closed, any change in one of the preceding, and the name and phone number of the official designated by the agency to respond to requests for information about the meeting, shall also be submitted for publication in the *Federal Register.*

(f)(1) For every meeting closed pursuant to paragraphs (1) through (10) of subsection (c), the General Counsel or chief legal officer of the agency shall publicly certify that, in his or her opinion, the meeting may be closed to the public and shall state each relevant exemptive provision. A copy of such certification, together with a statement from the presiding officer of the meeting setting forth the time and place of the meeting, and the persons present, shall be retained by the agency. The agency shall maintain a complete transcript or electronic recording adequate to record fully the proceedings of each meeting, or portion of a meeting, closed to the public, except that in the case of a meeting, or portion of a meeting, closed to the public pursuant to paragraph (8), (9) (A), or (10) of subsection (c), the agency shall maintain either such a transcript or recording, or a set of minutes. Such minutes shall fully and clearly describe all matters discussed and shall provide a full and accurate summary of any actions taken, and the reasons therefore, including a description of each of the views expressed on any item and the record of any roll call vote (reflecting the vote of each member on the question). All documents considered in connection with any action shall be identified in such minutes.

(2) The agency shall make promptly available to the public, in a place easily accessible to the public, the transcript, electronic recording, or minutes (as required by paragraph (1)) of the discussion of any item on the agenda, or of any item of the testimony of any witness received at the meeting, except for such item or items of

such discussion or testimony as the agency determines to contain information which may be withheld under subsection (c). Copies of such transcript, or minutes, or a transcription of such recording disclosing the identity of each speaker, shall be furnished to any person at the actual cost of duplication or transcription. The agency shall maintain a complete verbatim copy of the transcript, a complete copy of the minutes, or a complete electronic recording of each meeting, or portion of a meeting, closed to the public, for a period of at least two years after such meeting, or until one year after the conclusion of any agency proceeding with respect to which the meeting or portion was held, whichever occurs later.

(g) Each agency subject to the requirements of this section shall, within 180 days after the date of enactment of this section, following consultation with the Office of the Chairman of the Administrative Conference of the United States[1] and published notice in the *Federal Register* of at least thirty days and opportunity for written comment by any person, promulgate regulations to implement the requirements of subsections (b) through (f) of this section. Any person may bring a proceeding in the United States District Court for the District of Columbia to require an agency to promulgate such regulations if such agency has not promulgated such regulations within the time period specified herein. Subject to any limitations of time provided by law, any person may bring a proceeding in the United States Court of Appeals for the District of Columbia to set aside agency regulations issued pursuant to this subsection that are not in accord with the requirements of subsections (b) through (f) of this section and to require the promulgation of regulations that are in accord with such subsections.

(h)(1) The district courts of the United States shall have jurisdiction to enforce the requirements of subsections (b) through (f) of this section by declaratory judgment, injunctive relief, or other relief as may be appropriate. Such actions may be brought by any person against an agency prior to, or within sixty days after, the meeting out of which the violation of this section arises, except that if public announcement of such meeting is not initially provided by the agency in accordance with the requirements of this section, such action may be instituted pursuant to this section at any time prior to sixty days after any public announcement of such meeting. Such actions may be brought in the district court of the United States for the district in which the agency meeting is held or in which the agency in question has its headquarters, or in the District Court for the District of Columbia. In such actions a defendant shall serve his answer within thirty days after the service of the complaint. The burden is on the defendant to sustain his action. In deciding such cases the court may examine in camera any portion of the transcript, electronic recording, or minutes of a meeting closed to the public, and may take such additional evidence as it deems necessary. The court, having due regard for orderly administration and the public interest, as well as the interests of the parties, may grant such equitable relief as it deems appropriate, including granting an injunction against future violations of this section or

ordering the agency to make available to the public such portion of the transcript, recording, or minutes of a meeting as is not authorized to be withheld under subsection (c) of this section.

(2) Any Federal court otherwise authorized by law to review agency action may, at the application of any person properly participating in the proceeding pursuant to other applicable law, inquire into violations by the agency of the requirements of this section and afford such relief as it deems appropriate. Nothing in this section authorizes any Federal court having jurisdiction solely on the basis of paragraph (1) to set aside, enjoin, or invalidate any agency action (other than an action to close a meeting or to withhold information under this section) taken or discussed at any agency meeting out of which the violation of this section arose.

(i) The court may assess against any party reasonable attorney fees and other litigation costs reasonably incurred by any other party who substantially prevails in any action brought in accordance with the provisions of subsection (g) or (h) of this section, except that costs may be assessed against the plaintiff only where the court finds that the suit was initiated by the plaintiff primarily for frivolous or dilatory purposes. In the case of assessment of costs against an agency, the costs may be assessed by the court against the United States.

(j) Each agency subject to the requirements of this section shall annually report to Congress regarding its compliance with such requirements, including a tabulation of the total number of agency meetings open to the public, the total number of meetings closed to the public, the reasons for closing such meetings, and a description of any litigation brought against the agency under this section, including any costs assessed against the agency in such litigation (whether or not paid by the agency).

(k) Nothing herein expands or limits the present rights of any person under section 552 of this title, except that the exemptions set forth in subsection (c) of this section shall govern in the case of any request made pursuant to section 552 to copy or inspect the transcripts, recordings, or minutes described in subsection (f) of this section. The requirements of chapter 33 of title 44, United States Code, shall not apply to the transcripts, recordings, and minutes described in subsection (f) of this section.

(l) This section does not constitute authority to withhold any information from Congress, and does not authorize the closing of any agency meeting or portion thereof required by any other provision of law to be open.

(m) Nothing in this section authorizes any agency to withhold from any individual any record, including transcripts, recordings, or minutes required by this section, which is otherwise accessible to such individual under section 552a of this title.

[1] The Administrative Conference of the United States was abolished by Congress in 1995; the consultation requirement of this provision was not transferred to any other agency.

Paperwork Reduction Act

The Paperwork Reduction Act of 1980 (94 Stat. 2812, 44 U.S.C. 101 note) was enacted during the administration of Jimmy Carter on the recommendation of the Commission on Federal Paperwork, which issued a report in 1977 calling for major reforms of federal information collection practices. The act was intended to reduce the burden of federal government paperwork, to ensure that information collected by the federal government was necessary, and to establish uniform federal policies and efficient procedures for the collection, storage, and dissemination of information. It established the Office of Information and Regulatory Affairs within the Office of Management and Budget (OMB) to carry out the provisions of the act.

Major provisions of the Paperwork Reduction Act:

- Authorized OMB to develop and implement federal information policies, principles, standards, and guidelines.
- Required agencies to submit to OMB for review and approval any requests for information that will be solicited from ten or more individuals or businesses.
- Provided that agencies must submit to OMB copies of any proposed rule that contains a request for information for review no later than when the rule is published in the *Federal Register*.
- Established a requirement that requests for information must include a control number issued by OMB and must state why the information is being collected.
- Exempted members of the public from penalties for failing to comply with an information request issued after Dec. 31, 1981, that does not display a current OMB control number.
- Required agencies to designate a senior official to carry out their responsibilities under the act.
- Prohibited agencies from requesting information unless they had determined that: the information is necessary for their mission; it is unavailable elsewhere in the federal government; and they have reduced the burden of the request as much as possible.
- Set a goal for reduction of the paperwork burden by 15 percent by Oct. 1, 1982, and by an additional 10 percent by Oct. 1, 1983.
- Established a Federal Information Locator System at OMB to serve as a directory of information resources and an information referral service.
- Required OMB to complete actions on recommendations of the Commission on Federal Paperwork.
- Authorized OMB to oversee compliance with records management provisions of the act and to coordinate records management policies and programs with information collection policies and programs.
- Permitted OMB to monitor compliance with the Privacy Act and to develop and implement policies concerning information disclosure, confidentiality, and security.
- Authorized OMB to develop policies for automatic data processing and telecommunications within the federal government.
- Required OMB to report to Congress annually on implementation of the act.

The following is the text of the Paperwork Reduction Act as it appears in the U.S. Code, Title 44, Chapter 35, section 3501.

§ 3501. Purpose

The purpose of this chapter is—

(1) to minimize the Federal paperwork burden for individuals, small businesses, State and local governments, and other persons;

(2) to minimize the cost to the Federal Government of collecting, maintaining, using, and disseminating information;

(3) to maximize the usefulness of information collected by the Federal Government;

(4) to coordinate, integrate and, to the extent practicable and appropriate, make uniform Federal information policies and practices;

(5) to ensure that automatic data processing and telecommunications technologies are acquired and used by the Federal Government in a manner which improves service delivery and program management, increases productivity, reduces waste and fraud, and, wherever practicable and appropriate, reduces the information processing burden for the Federal Government and for persons who provide information to the Federal Government; and

(6) to ensure that the collection, maintenance, use and dissemination of information by the Federal Government is consistent with applicable laws relating to confidentiality, including section 552a of title 5, United States Code, known as the Privacy Act . . .

§ 3503. Office of Information and Regulatory Affairs

(a) There is established in the Office of Management and Budget an office to be known as the Office of Information and Regulatory Affairs.

(b) There shall be at the head of the Office an Administrator who shall be appointed by, and who shall report directly to, the Director. The Director shall delegate to the Administrator the authority to administer all functions under this chapter, except that any such delegation shall not relieve the Director of responsibility for the administration of such functions. The Administrator shall serve as principal adviser to the Director on Federal information policy.

§ 3504. Authority and functions of Director

(a) The Director shall develop and implement Federal information policies, principles, standards, and guidelines and shall provide direction and oversee the review and approval of information collection requests, the reduction of the paperwork burden, Federal statistical activities, records management activities, privacy of records, interagency sharing of information, and acquisition and use of automatic data processing telecommunications, and other technology for managing information resources. The authority under this section shall be exercised consistent with applicable law.

(b) The general information policy functions of the Director shall include—

(1) developing and implementing uniform and consistent information resources management policies and overseeing the development of information management principles, standards, and guidelines and promoting their use;

(2) initiating and reviewing proposals for changes in legislation, regulations, and agency procedures to improve information practices, and informing the President and the Congress on the progress made therein;

(3) coordinating, through the review of budget proposals and as otherwise provided in this section, agency information practices;

(4) promoting, through the use of the Federal Information Locator System, the review of budget proposals and other methods, greater sharing of information by agencies;

(5) evaluating agency information management practices to determine their adequacy and efficiency, and to determine compliance of such practices with the policies, principles, standards, and guidelines promulgated by the Director; and

(6) overseeing planning for, and conduct of research with respect to, Federal collection, processing, storage, transmission, and use of information.

(c) The information collection request clearance and other paperwork control functions of the Director shall include—

(1) reviewing and approving information collection requests proposed by agencies;

(2) determining whether the collection of information by an agency is necessary for the proper performance of the functions of the agency, including whether the information will have practical utility for the agency;

(3) ensuring that all information collection requests—

(A) are inventoried, display a control number and, when appropriate, an expiration date;

(B) indicate the request is in accordance with the clearance requirements of section 3507; and

(C) contain a statement to inform the person receiving the request why the information is being collected, how it is to be used, and whether responses to the request are voluntary, required to obtain a benefit, or mandatory;

(4) designating as appropriate, in accordance with section 3509, a collection agency to obtain information for two or more agencies;

(5) setting goals for reduction of the burdens of Federal information collection requests;

(6) overseeing action on the recommendations of the Commission on Federal Paperwork; and

(7) designing and operating, in accordance with section 3511, the Federal Information Locator System.

(d) The statistical policy and coordination functions of the Director shall include—

(1) developing long range plans for the improved performance of Federal statistical activities and programs;

(2) coordinating, through the review of budget proposals and as otherwise provided in this section, the functions of the Federal Government with respect to gathering, interpreting, and disseminating statistics and statistical information;

(3) developing and implementing Government-wide policies, principles, standards, and guidelines concerning statistical collection procedures and methods, statistical data classifications, and statistical information presentation and dissemination; and

(4) evaluating statistical program performance and agency compliance with Government-wide policies, principles, standards, and guidelines.

(e) The records management functions of the Director shall include—

(1) providing advice and assistance to the Administrator of General Services in order to promote coordination in the administration of chapters 29, 31, and 33 of this title with the information policies, principles, standards, and guidelines established under this chapter;

(2) reviewing compliance by agencies with the requirements of chapters 29, 31, and 33 of this title and with regulations promulgated by the Administrator of General Services thereunder; and

(3) coordinating records management policies and programs with related information programs such as information collection, statistics, automatic data processing and telecommunications, and similar activities.

(f) The privacy functions of the Director shall include—

(1) developing and implementing policies, principles, standards, and guidelines on information disclosure and confidentiality, and on safeguarding the security of information collected or maintained by or on behalf of agencies;

(2) providing agencies with advice and guidance about information security, restriction, exchange, and disclosure; and

(3) monitoring compliance with section 552a of title 5, United States Code, and related information management laws.

(g) The Federal automatic data processing and telecommunications functions of the Director shall include—

(1) developing and implementing policies, principles, standards, and guidelines for automatic data processing and telecommunications functions and activities of the Federal Government, and overseeing the establishment of standards under section 111(f) of the Federal Property and Administrative Services Act of 1949;

(2) monitoring the effectiveness of, and compliance with, directives issued pursuant to sections 110 and 111 of such Act of 1949 and reviewing proposed determinations under section 111(g) of such Act;

(3) providing advice and guidance on the acquisition and use of automatic data processing and telecommunications equipment, and coordinating, through the review of budget proposals and other methods, agency proposals for acquisition and use of such equipment;

(4) promoting the use of automatic data processing and telecommunications equipment by the Federal Government to improve the effectiveness of the use and dissemination of data in the operation of Federal programs; and

(5) initiating and reviewing proposals for changes in legislation, regulations, and agency procedures to improve automatic data processing and telecommunications practices, and informing the President and the Congress of the progress made therein.

(h)(1) As soon as practicable, but no later than publication of a notice of proposed rulemaking in the *Federal Register,* each agency shall forward to the Director a copy of any proposed rule which contains a collection of information requirement and upon request, information necessary to make the determination required pursuant to this section.

(2) Within sixty days after the notice of proposed rulemaking is published in the *Federal Register,* the Director may file public comments pursuant to the standards set forth in section 3508 on the collection of information requirement contained in the proposed rule.

(3) When a final rule is published in the *Federal Register,* the agency shall explain how any collection of information requirement contained in the final rule responds to the comments, if any, filed by the Director or the public, or explain why it rejected those comments.

(4) The Director has no authority to disapprove any collection of information requirement specifically contained in an agency rule, if he has received notice and failed to comment on the rule within sixty days of the notice of proposed rulemaking.

(5) Nothing in this section prevents the Director, in his discretion—

(A) from disapproving any information collection request which was not specifically required by an agency rule;

(B) from disapproving any collection of information requirement contained in an agency rule, if the agency failed to comply with the requirements of paragraph (1) of this subsection; or

(C) from disapproving any collection of information requirement contained in a final agency rule, if the Director finds within sixty days of the publication of the final rule that the agency's response to his comments filed pursuant to paragraph (2) of this subsection was unreasonable.

(D) from disapproving any collection of information requirement where the Director determines that the agency has substantially modified in the final rule the collection of information requirement contained in the proposed rule where the agency has not given the Director the information required in paragraph (1), with respect to the modified collection of information requirement, at least sixty days before the issuance of the final rule.

(6) The Director shall make publicly available any decision to disapprove a collection of information requirement contained in an agency rule, together with the reasons for such decision.

(7) The authority of the Director under this subsection is subject to the provisions of section 3507(c).

(8) This subsection shall apply only when an agency publishes a notice of proposed rulemaking and requests public comments.

(9) There shall be no judicial review of any kind of the Director's decision to approve or not to act upon a collection of information requirement contained in an agency rule.

§ 3505. Assignment of tasks and deadlines

In carrying out the functions under this chapter, the director shall—

(1) upon enactment of this Act—

(A) set a goal to reduce the then existing burden of Federal collections of information by 15 per centum by October 1, 1982; and

(B) for the year following, set a goal to reduce the burden which existed upon enactment by an additional 10 per centum;

(2) within one year after the effective date of this Act—

(A) establish standards and requirements for agency audits of all major information systems and assign responsibility for conducting Government-wide or multi-agency audits, except the Director shall not assign such responsibility for the audit of major information systems used for the conduct of criminal investigations or intelligence activities as defined in section 4–206 of Executive Order 12036, issued January 24, 1978, or successor orders, or for cryptologic activities that are communications security activities;

(B) establish the Federal Information Locator System;

(C) identify areas of duplication in information collection requests and develop a schedule and methods for eliminating duplication;

(D) develop a proposal to augment the Federal Information Locator System to include data profiles of major information holdings of agencies (used in the conduct of their operations) which are not otherwise required by this chapter to be included in the System; and

(E) identify initiatives which may achieve a 10 per centum reduction in the burden of Federal collections of information associated with the administration of Federal grant programs; and

(3) within two years after the effective date of this Act—

(A) establish a schedule and a management control system to ensure that practices and programs of information handling disciplines, including records management, are appropriately integrated with the information policies mandated by this chapter;

(B) identify initiatives to improve productivity in Federal operations using information processing technology;

(C) develop a program to (i) enforce Federal information processing standards, particularly software language standards, at all Federal installations; and (ii) revitalize the standards development program established pursuant to section 759(f)(2) of title 40, United States Code, separating it from peripheral technical assistance functions and directing it to the most productive areas;

(D) complete action on recommendations of the Commission on Federal Paperwork by implementing, implementing with modification or rejecting such recommendations including, where necessary, development of legislation to implement such recommendations;

(E) develop, in consultation with the Administrator of General Services, a five-year plan for meeting the automatic data processing and telecommunications needs of the Federal Government in accordance with the requirements of section 111 of the Federal Property and Administrative Services Act of 1949 (40 U.S.C. 759) and the purposes of this chapter; and

(F) submit to the President and the Congress legislative proposals to remove inconsistencies in laws and practices involving privacy, confidentiality, and disclosure of information.

§ 3506. Federal agency responsibilities

(a) Each agency shall be responsible for carrying out its information management activities in an efficient, effective, and economical manner, and for complying with the information policies, principles, standards, and guidelines prescribed by the Director.

(b) The head of each agency shall designate, within three months after the effective date of this Act, a senior official or, in the case of military departments, and the Office of the Secretary of Defense, officials who report directly to such agency head to carry out the responsibilities of the agency under this chapter. If more than one official is appointed for the military departments the respective duties of the officials shall be clearly delineated.

(c) Each agency shall—

(1) systematically inventory its major information systems and periodically review its information management activities, including planning, budgeting, organizing, directing, training, promoting, controlling, and other managerial activities involving the collection, use, and dissemination of information;

(2) ensure its information systems do not overlap each other or duplicate the systems of other agencies;

(3) develop procedures for assessing the paperwork and reporting burden of proposed legislation affecting such agency;

(4) assign to the official designated under subsection (b) the responsibility for the conduct of and accountability for any acquisitions made pursuant to a delegation of authority under section 111 of the Federal Property and Administrative Services Act of 1949 (40 U.S.C. 759); and

(5) ensure that information collection requests required by law or to obtain a benefit, and submitted to nine or fewer persons, contain a statement to inform the person receiving the request that the request is not subject to the requirements of section 3507 of this chapter.

(d) The head of each agency shall establish such procedures as necessary to ensure the compliance of the agency with the requirements of the Federal Information Locator System, including necessary screening and compliance activities.

§ 3507. Public information collection activities—submission to Director; approval and delegation

(a) An agency shall not conduct or sponsor the collection of information unless, in advance of the adoption or revision of the request for collection of such information—

(1) the agency has taken actions, including consultation with the Director, to—

(A) eliminate, through the use of the Federal Information Locator System and other means, information collections which seek to obtain information available from another source within the Federal Government;

(B) reduce to the extent practicable and appropriate the burden on persons who will provide information to the agency; and

(C) formulate plans for tabulating the information in a manner which will enhance its usefulness to other agencies and to the public;

(2) the agency (A) has submitted to the Director the proposed information collection request, copies of pertinent regulations and other related materials as the Director may specify, and an explanation of actions taken to carry out paragraph (1) of this subsection, and (B) has prepared a notice to be published in the *Federal Register* stating that the agency has made such submission; and

(3) the Director has approved the proposed information collection request, or the period for review of information collection requests by the Director provided under subsection (b) has elapsed.

(b) The Director shall, within sixty days of receipt of a proposed information collection request, notify the agency involved of the decision to approve or disapprove the request and shall make such decisions publicly available. If the Director determines that a request submitted for review cannot be reviewed within sixty days, the Director may, after notice to the agency involved, extend the review period for an additional thirty days. If the Director does not notify the agency of an extension, denial, or approval within sixty days (or, if the Director has extended the review period for an additional thirty days and does not notify the agency of a denial or approval within the time of the extension), a control number shall be assigned without further delay, the approval may be inferred, and the agency may collect the information for not more than one year.

(c) Any disapproval by the Director, in whole or in part, of a proposed information collection request of an independent regulatory agency, or an exercise of authority under section 3504(h) or 3509 concerning such an agency, may be voided, if the agency by a majority vote of its members overrides the Director's disapproval or exercise of authority. The agency shall certify each override to the Director, shall explain the reasons for exercising the override authority. Where the override concerns an information collection request, the Director shall without further delay assign a control number to such request, and such override shall be valid for a period of three years.

(d) The Director may not approve an information collection request for a period in excess of three years.

(e) If the Director finds that a senior official of an agency designated pursuant to section 3506(b) is sufficiently independent of program responsibility to evaluate fairly whether proposed information collection requests should be approved and has sufficient resources to carry out this responsibility effectively, the Director may, by rule in accordance with the notice and comment provisions of chapter 5 of title 5, United States Code, delegate to such official the authority to approve proposed requests in specific program areas, for specific purposes, or for all agency purposes. A delegation by the Director under this section shall not preclude the Director from reviewing individual information collection requests if the Director determines that circumstances warrant such a review. The Director shall retain authority to revoke such delegations, both in general and with regard to any specific matter. In acting for the Director, any official to whom approval authority has been delegated under this section shall comply fully with the rules and regulations promulgated by the Director.

(f) An agency shall not engage in a collection of information without obtaining from the Director a control number to be displayed upon the information collection request.

(g) If an agency head determines a collection of information (1) is needed prior to the expiration of the sixty-day period for the review of information collection requests established pursuant to subsection (b), (2) is essential to the mission of the agency, and (3) the agency cannot reasonably comply with the provisions of this chapter within such sixty-day period because (A) public harm will result if normal clearance procedures are followed, or

(B) an unanticipated event has occurred and the use of normal clearance procedures will prevent or disrupt the collection of information related to the event or will cause a statutory deadline to be missed, the agency head may request the Director to authorize such collection of information prior to expiration of such sixty-day period. The Director shall approve or disapprove any such authorization request within the time requested by the agency head and, if approved, shall assign the information collection request a control number. Any collection of information conducted pursuant to this subsection may be conducted without compliance with the provisions of this chapter for a maximum of ninety days after the date on which the Director received the request to authorize such collection.

§ 3508. Determination of necessity for information; hearing

Before approving a proposed information collection request, the Director shall determine whether the collection of information by an agency is necessary for the proper performance of the functions of the agency, including whether the information will have practical utility. Before making a determination the Director may give the agency and other interested persons an opportunity to be heard or to submit statements in writing. To the extent, if any, that the Director determines that the collection of information by an agency is unnecessary, for any reason, the agency may not engage in the collection of the information.

§ 3509. Designation of central collection agency

The Director may designate a central collection agency to obtain information for two or more agencies if the Director determines that the needs of such agencies for information will be adequately served by a single collection agency, and such sharing of data is not inconsistent with any applicable law. In such cases the Director shall prescribe (with reference to the collection of information) the duties and functions of the collection agency so designated and of the agencies for which it is to act as agent (including reimbursement for costs). While the designation is in effect, an agency covered by it may not obtain for itself information which it is the duty of the collection agency to obtain. The Director may modify the designation from time to time as circumstances require. The authority herein is subject to the provisions of section 3507(c) of this chapter.

§ 3510. Cooperation of agencies in making information available

(a) The Director may direct an agency to make available to another agency, or an agency may make available to another agency, information obtained pursuant to an information collection request if the disclosure is not inconsistent with any applicable law.

(b) If information obtained by an agency is released by that agency to another agency, all the provisions of law (including penalties which relate to the unlawful disclosure of information) apply to the officers and employees of the agency to which information is released to the same extent and in the same manner as the provisions apply to the officers and employees of the agency which originally obtained the information. The officers and employees of the agency to which the information is released, in addition, shall be subject to the same provisions of law, including penalties, relating to the unlawful disclosure of information as if the information had been collected directly by that agency.

§ 3511. Establishment and operation of Federal Information Locator System

(a) There is established in the Office of Information and Regulatory Affairs a Federal Information Locator System (hereafter in this section referred to as the System) which shall be composed of a directory of information resources, a data element dictionary, and an information referral service. The System shall serve as the authoritative register of all information collection requests.

(b) In designing and operating the System, the Director shall—

(1) design and operate an indexing system for the System;

(2) require the head of each agency to prepare in a form specified by the Director, and to submit to the Director for inclusion in the System, a data profile for each information collection request of such agency;

(3) compare data profiles for proposed information collection requests against existing profiles in the System, and make available the results of such comparison to—

(A) agency officials who are planning new information collection activities; and

(B) on request, members of the general public; and

(4) ensure that no actual data, except descriptive data profiles necessary to identify duplicative data or to locate information, are contained within the System.

§ 3512. Public protection

Notwithstanding any other provision of law, no person shall be subject to any penalty for failing to maintain or provide information to any agency if the information collection request involved was made after December 31, 1981, and does not display a current control number assigned by the Director, or fails to state that such request is not subject to this chapter.

§ 3513. Director review of agency activities; reporting; agency response

(a) The Director shall, with the advice and assistance of the Administrator of General Services, selectively review, at least once every three years, the information management activities of each agency to ascertain their adequacy and efficiency. In evaluating the adequacy and efficiency of such activities, the Director shall pay particular attention to whether the agency has complied with section 3506.

(b) The Director shall report the results of the reviews to the appropriate agency head, the House Committee on Government Operations, the Senate Committee on Governmental Affairs, the House and Senate Committees on Appropriations, and the committees of the Congress having jurisdiction over legislation relating to the operations of the agency involved.

(c) Each agency which receives a report pursuant to subsection (b) shall, within sixty days after receipt of such report, prepare and transmit to the Director, the House Committee on Government Operations, the Senate Committee on Governmental Affairs, the House and Senate Committees on Appropriations, and the committees of the Congress having jurisdiction over legislation relating to the operations of the agency, a written statement responding to the Director's report, including a description of any measures taken to alleviate or remove any problems or deficiencies identified in such report.

§ 3514. Responsiveness to Congress

(a) The Director shall keep the Congress and its committees fully and currently informed of the major activities under this chapter, and shall submit a report thereon to the President of the Senate and the Speaker of the House of Representatives annually and at such other times as the Director determines necessary. The Director shall include in any such report—

(1) proposals for legislative action needed to improve Federal information management, including, with respect to information collection, recommendations to reduce the burden on individuals, small businesses, State and local governments, and other persons;

(2) a compilation of legislative impediments to the collection of information which the Director concludes that an agency needs but does not have authority to collect;

(3) an analysis by agency, and by categories the Director finds useful and practicable, describing the estimated reporting hours required of persons by information collection requests, including to the extent practicable the direct budgetary costs of the agencies and identification of statutes and regulations which impose the greatest number of reporting hours;

(4) a summary of accomplishments and planned initiatives to reduce burdens of Federal information collection requests;

(5) a tabulation of areas of duplication in agency information collection requests identified during the preceding year and efforts made to preclude the collection of duplicate information, including designations of central collection agencies;

(6) a list of each instance in which an agency engaged in the collection of information under the authority of section 3507(g) and an identification of each agency involved;

(7) a list of all violations of provisions of this chapter and rules, regulations, guidelines, policies, and procedures issued pursuant to this chapter; and

(8) with respect to recommendations of the Commission on Federal Paperwork—

(A) a description of the specific actions taken on or planned for each recommendation;

(B) a target date for implementing each recommendation accepted but not implemented; and

(C) an explanation of the reasons for any delay in completing action on such recommendations.

(b) The preparation of any report required by this section shall not increase the collection of information burden on persons outside the Federal Government.

§ 3515. Administrative powers

Upon the request of the Director, each agency (other than an independent regulatory agency) shall, to the extent practicable, make its services, personnel, and facilities available to the Director for the performance of functions under this chapter.

§ 3516. Rules and regulations

The Director shall promulgate rules, regulations, or procedures necessary to exercise the authority provided by this chapter.

§ 3517. Consultation with other agencies and the public

In development of information policies, plans, rules, regulations, procedures, and guidelines and in reviewing information collection requests, the Director shall provide interested agencies and persons early and meaningful opportunity to comment.

§ 3518. Effect on existing laws and regulations

(a) Except as otherwise provided in this chapter, the authority of an agency under any other law to prescribe policies, rules, regulations, and procedures for Federal information activities is subject to the authority conferred on the Director by this chapter.

(b) Nothing in this chapter shall be deemed to affect or reduce the authority of the Secretary of Commerce or the Director of the Office of Management and Budget pursuant to Reorganization Plan No. 1 of 1977 (as amended) and Executive order, relating to telecommunications and information policy, procurement and management of telecommunications and information systems, spectrum use, and related matters.

(c)(1) Except as provided in paragraph (2), this chapter does not apply to the collection of information—

(A) during the conduct of a Federal criminal investigation or prosecution, or during the disposition of a particular criminal matter;

(B) during the conduct of (i) a civil action to which the United States or any official or agency thereof is a party or (ii) an administrative action or investigation involving an agency against specific individuals or entities;

(C) by compulsory process pursuant to the Antitrust Civil Process Act and section 13 of the Federal Trade Commission Improvements Act of 1980; or

(D) during the conduct of intelligence activities as defined in section 4–206 of Executive Order 12036, issued January 24, 1978, or successor orders, or during the conduct of cryptologic activities that are communications security activities.

(2) This chapter applies to the collection of information during the conduct of general investigations (other than information collected in an antitrust investigation to the extent provided in subparagraph (C) of paragraph (1)) undertaken with reference to a category of individuals or entities such as a class of licensees or an entire industry.

(d) Nothing in this chapter shall be interpreted as increasing or decreasing the authority conferred by Public Law 89–306 on the Administrator of the General Services Administration, the Secretary of Commerce, or the Director of the Office of Management and Budget.

(e) Nothing in this chapter shall be interpreted as increasing or decreasing the authority of the President, the Office of Management and Budget or the Director thereof, under the laws of the United States, with respect to the substantive policies and programs of departments, agencies and offices, including the substantive authority of any Federal agency to enforce the civil rights laws.

§ 3519. Access to information

Under the conditions and procedures prescribed in section 313 of the Budget and Accounting Act of 1921, as amended, the Director and personnel in the Office of Information and Regulatory Affairs shall furnish such information as the Comptroller General may require for the discharge of his responsibilities. For this purpose, the Comptroller General or representatives thereof shall have access to all books, documents, papers, and records of the Office.

§ 3520. Authorization of appropriations

There are hereby authorized to be appropriated to carry out the provisions of this chapter, and for no other purpose, sums—

(1) not to exceed $8,000,000 for the fiscal year ending September 30, 1981;

(2) not to exceed $8,500,000 for the fiscal year ending September 30, 1982; and

(3) not to exceed $9,000,000 for the fiscal year ending September 30, 1983.

(b) The item relating to chapter 35 in the table of chapters for such title is amended to read as follows: "35. Coordination of Federal Information Policy."

(c)(1) Section 2904(10) of such title is amended to read as follows:

"(10) report to the appropriate oversight and appropriations committees of the Congress and to the Director of the Office of Management and Budget annually and at such other times as the Administrator deems desirable (A) on the results of activities conducted pursuant to paragraphs (1) through (9) of this section, (B) on evaluations of responses by Federal agencies to any recommendations resulting from inspections or studies conducted under paragraphs (8) and (9) of this section, and (C) to the extent practicable, estimates of costs to the Federal Government resulting from the failure of agencies to implement such recommendations."

(2) Section 2905 of such title is amended by redesignating the text thereof as subsection (a) and by adding

at the end of such section the following new subsection: "(b) The Administrator of General Services shall assist the Administrator for the Office of Information and Regulatory Affairs in conducting studies and developing standards relating to record retention requirements imposed on the public and on State and local governments by Federal agencies."

SEC. 3. (a) The President and the Director of the Office of Management and Budget shall delegate to the Administrator for the Office of Information and Regulatory Affairs all functions, authority, and responsibility under section 103 of the Budget and Accounting Procedures Act of 1950 (31 U.S.C. 18b).

(b) The Director of the Office of Management and Budget shall delegate to the Administrator for the Office of Information and Regulatory Affairs all functions, authority, and responsibility of the Director under section 552a of title 5, United States Code, under Executive Order 12046 and Reorganization Plan No. 1 for telecommunications, and under section 111 of the Federal Property and Administrative Services Act of 1949 (40 U.S.C. 759).

SEC. 4. (a) Section 400A of the General Education Provisions Act is amended by (1) striking out "and" after "institutions" in subsection (a)(1)(A) and inserting in lieu thereof "or," and (2) by amending subsection (a)(3)(B) to read as follows:

"(B) No collection of information or data acquisition activity subject to such procedures shall be subject to any other review, coordination, or approval procedure outside of the relevant Federal agency, except as required by this subsection and by the Director of the Office of Management and Budget under the rules and regulations established pursuant to chapter 35 of title 44, United States Code. If a requirement for information is submitted pursuant to this Act for review, the timetable for the Director's approval established in section 3507 of the Paperwork Reduction Act of 1980 shall commence on the date the request is submitted, and no independent submission to the Director shall be required under such Act."

(b) Section 201(e) of the Surface Mining Control and Reclamation Act of 1977 (30 U.S.C. 1211) is repealed.

(c) Section 708(f) of the Public Health Service Act (42 U.S.C. 292h(f)) is repealed.

(d) Section 5315 of title 5, United States Code, is amended by adding at the end thereof the following:

"Administrator, Office of Information and Regulatory Affairs, Office of Management and Budget."

SEC. 5. This Act shall take effect on April 1, 1981.

Approved December 11, 1980.

Privacy Act

While the Freedom of Information Act was designed to provide the public access to agency documents and proceedings, the 1974 Privacy Act (88 Stat. 1896, 5 U.S.C. 552a note) was designed to give individuals an opportunity to find out what files the government has about them and to challenge, correct, or amend the material. In addition, provisions of the act were designed to protect individual privacy by preventing a person from looking at records involving another individual. The Privacy Act protects only U.S. citizens and permanent residents.

The Privacy Act authorizes the director of the Office of Management and Budget to develop and, after notice and opportunity for public comment, prescribe guidelines and regulations for the use of agencies in implementing the provisions of this section. All executive branch agencies have developed their own regulations and procedures for handling the act (consult the *Code of Federal Regulations* under "Privacy Act"), and each agency publishes its procedures for appeal following the denial of a request.

Major provisions of the Privacy Act:

- Permitted an individual access to personal information contained in federal agency files and to correct or amend the information.
- Prevented an agency maintaining a file on an individual from using it or making it available to another agency for a second purpose without the individual's consent.
- Required agencies to maintain records that were necessary and lawful as well as current and accurate and to disclose the existence of all data banks and files they maintain containing information on individuals.
- Prohibited agencies from keeping records that described an individual's exercise of First Amendment rights unless the records were authorized by statute or approved by the individual or were within the scope of an official law enforcement activity.
- Permitted an individual to seek injunctive relief to correct or amend a record maintained by an agency and permitted the individual to recover actual damages when an agency acted in a negligent manner that was "willful or intentional."
- Provided that an officer or employee of an agency who willfully violated provisions of the act should be subject to a fine of not more than $5,000.

- Exempted from disclosure provisions: records maintained by the Central Intelligence Agency; records maintained by law enforcement agencies; Secret Service records; statistical information; names of persons providing material used for determining the qualification of an individual for federal government service; federal testing material; and National Archives historical records.
- Prohibited an agency from selling or renting an individual's name or address for mailing list use.
- Required agencies to submit to Congress and to the Office of Management and Budget any plan to establish or alter any system of records.
- Established a privacy protection study commission composed of seven members to provide Congress and the president information about problems related to privacy in the public and private sectors. The commission issued a report in 1977, *Personal Privacy in an Information Society*.
- Made it illegal for any federal, state, or local agency to deny an individual any benefit provided by law because he refused to disclose his Social Security account number to the agency. (The provision did not apply to disclosure required by federal statute or to government agencies requiring disclosure of the number before Jan. 1, 1975.)

The Computer Matching and Privacy Protection Act of 1988 amended the Privacy Act by adding new provisions regulating the use of computer matching of records maintained by the government. Computer matching is the computerized comparison of databases to determine the status, rights, or benefits of the individuals within those systems of records. Computer matching allows federal, state, and local government agencies to compare computerized information about individuals for the purpose of determining eligibility for federal benefit programs. Every agency that uses a matching program must have a Data Integrity Board. The Data Integrity Board reviews and approves the data matching agreements to ensure that the agency is in compliance with laws, guidelines, and regulations.

Following the 2001 terrorist attacks, Congress enacted two laws that affected privacy issues: the Homeland Security Act of 2002 and the USA Patriot Act.

The Homeland Security Act of 2002, which established the Department of Homeland Security, exempted from criminal penalties any disclosure made by an electronic communication service to a federal, state, or local governmental entity if made in the good faith belief that an emergency involving danger of death or serious physical injury to any person required disclosure without delay. It also required any government entity receiving such a disclosure to report it to the U.S. attorney general. The act directed the Homeland Security secretary to appoint a senior department official to assume primary responsibility for information privacy policy.

The USA Patriot Act amended the federal criminal code to authorize the interception of wire, oral, and electronic communications for the production of evidence of specified chemical weapons or terrorism offenses and computer fraud and abuse. The act also amended the Foreign Intelligence Surveillance Act of 1978 (FISA) to require an application for an electronic surveillance order or search warrant to certify that a significant purpose (formerly, the sole or main purpose) of the surveillance was to obtain foreign intelligence information.

Some provisions of the USA Patriot Act were set to expire at the end of 2005. After a lengthy battle Congress voted to reauthorize the Patriot Act with some of the more controversial provisions intact, including the FISA amendments and the electronic wiretap provisions. Civil libertarians were concerned over four provisions: sections 206 (roving wiretaps), 213 (delayed notice warrants), 215 (business records), and 505 (national security letters). The Senate addressed some of these concerns in a separate bill, USA Patriot Act Additional Reauthorizing Amendments Act of 2006. On March 9, 2006, President George W. Bush signed into law the USA Patriot Improvement and Reauthorization Act of 2005 as well as the USA Patriot Act Additional Reauthorizing Amendments Act of 2006.

The reauthorized Patriot Act allows for greater congressional oversight and judicial review of section 215 orders, section 206 roving wiretaps, and national security letters. In addition, the act includes requirements for high-level approval for section 215 FISA orders for library, bookstore, firearm sale, medical, tax return, and educational records. The act also provides for greater judicial review for delayed notice ("sneak and peak") search warrants. Fourteen of sixteen Patriot Act provisions were made permanent, with a sunset date of Dec. 31, 2009, for sections 206 and 215.

On May 26, 2011, President Barack Obama signed PATRIOT Sunsets Extension Act of 2011. This extended provisions concerning roving electronic surveillance orders and requests for the production of business records and other tangible items, as well as a provision revising the definition of an "agent of a foreign power" to include any non-U.S. person who engages in international terrorism or preparatory activities ("lone wolf" provision). These extensions expired June 1, 2015, and attempts to either reauthorize section 215 or enact new legislation are in discussion. In the meantime, the FBI can still obtain phone records issuing subpoenas to phone companies.

Controversy over the U.S. government's surveillance methods erupted when a national security contractor revealed the details of a telecommunications surveillance program in June 2013. Under the program, code named PRISM, the Foreign Intelligence Surveillance Court issued FISA orders to telecommunications companies to collect Internet and telephone data from foreigners, but there were no failsafe methods that prevented spying on U.S. citizens. PRISM was established in 2007; that same year, Congress enacted the Protect America Act of 2007. The law removed the requirement for a warrant for electronic surveillance and provided telecommunications firms with immunity from liability for cooperating with the U.S. government on FISA orders. The law had a sunset date of 180 days from enactment. The FISA Amendments Act of 2008 reauthorized these provisions.

Consistent with the authority granted to U.S. Customs and Border Protection (CBP) under the Aviation and Transportation Security Act of 2001 and its interim implementing regulations, each air carrier operating passenger flights in foreign air transportation to or from the United States must provide CBP with electronic access to passenger name record (PNR) data to the extent it is collected and contained in the air carrier's automated reservation and departure control systems for each person traveling to and from the United States.

After working through privacy concerns, President George W. Bush signed agreements in May 2004 with the European Union (EU) to exchange PNR data collected by airlines. The agreement took into account the privacy laws of both the United States and the EU. However, the European Court of Justice struck down the agreement in 2006 based on technical issues not pertaining to privacy.

In 2007 the Bush administration negotiated another agreement that collected less data on individuals. After the agreement was signed, the Department of Homeland Security (DHS) published a Privacy Act system of records notice (SORN) for the Arrival and Departure Information System (ADIS), claiming exemption from certain requirements of the Privacy Act for ADIS. DHS stated these exemptions were needed to protect information relating to DHS investigatory and enforcement activities from disclosure to subjects or others related to these activities. In December 2008 the DHS published an additional SORN for legacy records for the Immigration and Customs Enforcement (ICE) Search, Arrest, and Seizure Records system of records. Although these DHS SORN national security and law enforcement exemptions are routine and covered under the Privacy Act, civil libertarians in the United States and abroad expressed concern over the amount of information being collected, the length the information was being held, and the inability of individuals to access information about themselves.

The following is the text of the Privacy Act, as amended, as it appears in the U.S. Code, Title 5, Chapter 5, Subchapter II, section 552a.

§ 552a. Records maintained on individuals
(a) Definitions

For purposes of this section—(1) the term "agency" means agency as defined in section 552(e) of this title;

(2) the term "individual" means a citizen of the United States or an alien lawfully admitted for permanent residence;

(3) the term "maintain" includes maintain, collect, use, or disseminate;

(4) the term "record" means any item, collection, or grouping of information about an individual that is maintained by an agency, including, but not limited to, his education, financial transactions, medical history, and criminal or employment history and that contains his name, or the identifying number, symbol, or other identifying particular assigned to the individual, such as a finger or voice print or photograph;

(5) the term "system of records" means a group of any records under the control of any agency from which information is retrieved by the name of the individual or by some identifying number, symbol, or other identifying particular assigned to the individual;

(6) the term "statistical record" means a record in a system of records maintained for statistical research or reporting purposes only and not used in whole or in part in making any determination about an identifiable individual, except as provided by section 8 of title 13;

(7) the term "routine use" means, with respect to the disclosure of a record, the use of such record for a purpose which is compatible with the purpose for which it was collected.

(8) the term "matching program"—

(A) means any computerized comparison of—

(i) two or more automated systems of records or a system of records with non-Federal records for the purpose of—

(I) establishing or verifying the eligibility of, or continuing compliance with statutory and regulatory requirements by, applicants for, recipients or beneficiaries of, participants in, or providers of services with respect to, cash or in-kind assistance or payments under Federal benefit programs, or

(II) recouping payments or delinquent debts under such Federal benefit programs, or

(ii) two or more automated Federal personnel or payroll systems of records or a system of Federal personnel or payroll records with non-Federal records,

(B) but does not include—

(i) matches performed to produce aggregate statistical data without any personal identifiers;

(ii) matches performed to support any research or statistical project, the specific data of which may not be used to make decisions concerning the rights, benefits, or privileges of specific individuals;

(iii) matches performed, by an agency (or component thereof) which performs as its principal function any activity pertaining to the enforcement of criminal laws, subsequent to the initiation of a specific criminal or civil law enforcement investigation of a named person or persons for the purpose of gathering evidence against such person or persons;

(iv) matches of tax information (I) pursuant to section 6103(d) of the Internal Revenue Code of 1986, (II) for purposes of tax administration as defined in section 6103(b)(4) of such Code, (III) for the purpose of intercepting a tax refund due

an individual under authority granted by section 404(e), 464, or 1137 of the Social Security Act; or (IV) for the purpose of intercepting a tax refund due an individual under any other tax refund intercept program authorized by statute which has been determined by the Director of the Office of Management and Budget to contain verification, notice, and hearing requirements that are substantially similar to the procedures in section 1137 of the Social Security Act;

(v) matches—

(I) using records predominantly relating to Federal personnel, that are performed for routine administrative purposes (subject to guidance provided by the Director of the Office of Management and Budget pursuant to subsection (v)); or

(II) conducted by an agency using only records from systems of records maintained by that agency; if the purpose of the match is not to take any adverse financial, personnel, disciplinary, or other adverse action against Federal personnel;

(vi) matches performed for foreign counter-intelligence purposes or to produce background checks for security clearances of Federal personnel or Federal contractor personnel;

(vii) matches performed incident to a levy described in section 6103(k)(8) of the Internal Revenue Code of 1986; or

(viii) matches performed pursuant to section 202(x)(3) or 1611(e)(1) of the Social Security Act (42 U.S.C. §402(x)(3), §1382(e)(1));

(9) the term "recipient agency" means any agency, or contractor thereof, receiving records contained in a system of records from a source agency for use in a matching program;

(10) the term "non-Federal agency" means any State or local government, or agency thereof, which receives records contained in a system of records from a source agency for use in a matching program;

(11) the term "source agency" means any agency which discloses records contained in a system of records to be used in a matching program, or any State or local government, or agency thereof, which discloses records to be used in a matching program;

(12) the term "Federal benefit program" means any program administered or funded by the Federal Government, or by any agent or State on behalf of the Federal Government, providing cash or in-kind assistance in the form of payments, grants, loans, or loan guarantees to individuals; and

(13) the term "Federal personnel" means officers and employees of the Government of the United States, members of the uniformed services (including members of the Reserve Components), individuals entitled to receive immediate or deferred retirement benefits under any retirement program of the Government of the United States (including survivor benefits).

(b) Conditions of disclosure

No agency shall disclose any record which is contained in a system of records by any means of communication to any person, or to another agency, except pursuant to a written request by, or with the prior written consent of, the individual to whom the record pertains, unless disclosure of the record would be—

(1) to those officers and employees of the agency which maintains the record who have a need for the record in the performance of their duties;

(2) required under section 552 of this title;

(3) for a routine use as defined in subsection (a)(7) of this section and described under subsection (e)(4)(D) of this section;

(4) to the Bureau of the Census for purposes of planning or carrying out a census or survey or related activity pursuant to the provisions of title 13;

(5) to a recipient who has provided the agency with advance adequate written assurance that the record will be used solely as a statistical research or reporting record, and the record is to be transferred in a form that is not individually identifiable;

(6) to the National Archives and Records Administration as a record which has sufficient historical or other value to warrant its continued preservation by the United States Government, or for evaluation by the Archivist of the United States or the designee of the Archivist to determine whether the record has such value;

(7) to another agency or to an instrumentality of any governmental jurisdiction within or under the control of the United States for a civil or criminal law enforcement activity if the activity is authorized by law, and if the head of the agency or instrumentality has made a written request to the agency which maintains the record specifying the particular portion desired and the law enforcement activity for which the record is sought;

(8) to a person pursuant to a showing of compelling circumstances affecting the health or safety of an individual if upon such disclosure notification is transmitted to the last known address of such individual;

(9) to either House of Congress, or, to the extent of matter within its jurisdiction, any committee or subcommittee thereof, any joint committee of Congress or subcommittee of any such joint committee;

(10) to the Comptroller General, or any of his authorized representatives, in the course of the performance of the duties of the Government Accounting Office;

(11) pursuant to the order of a court of competent jurisdiction; or

(12) to a consumer reporting agency in accordance with section 3711(e) of Title 31.

(c) Accounting of certain disclosures

Each agency, with respect to each system of records under its control, shall—

(1) except for disclosures made under subsections (b)(1) or (b)(2) of this section, keep an accurate accounting of—

(A) the date, nature, and purpose of each disclosure of a record to any person or to another agency made under subsection (b) of this section; and

(B) the name and address of the person or agency to whom the disclosure is made;

(2) retain the accounting made under paragraph (1) of this subsection for at least five years or the life of the record, whichever is longer, after the disclosure for which the accounting is made;

(3) except for disclosures made under subsection (b)(7) of this section, make the accounting made under paragraph (1) of this subsection available to the individual named in the record at his request; and

(4) inform any person or other agency about any correction or notation of dispute made by the agency in accordance with subsection (d) of this section of any record that has been disclosed to the person or agency if an accounting of the disclosure was made.

(d) Access to records

Each agency that maintains a system of records shall—

(1) upon request by any individual to gain access to his record or to any information pertaining to him which is contained in the system, permit him and upon his request, a person of his own choosing to accompany him, to review the record and have a copy made of all or any portion thereof in a form comprehensible to him, except that the agency may require the individual to furnish a written statement authorizing discussion of that individual's record in the accompanying person's presence;

(2) permit the individual to request amendment of a record pertaining to him and—

(A) not later than ten days (excluding Saturdays, Sundays, and legal public holidays) after the date of receipt of such request, acknowledge in writing such receipt; and

(B) promptly, either—

(i) make any correction of any portion thereof which the individual believes is not accurate, relevant, timely, or complete; or

(ii) inform the individual of its refusal to amend the record in accordance with his request, the reason for the refusal, the procedures established by the agency for the individual to request a review of that refusal by the head of the agency or an officer designated by the head of the agency, and the name and business address of that official;

(3) permit the individual who disagrees with the refusal of the agency to amend his record to request a review of such refusal, and not later than thirty days (excluding Saturdays, Sundays, and legal public holidays) from the date on which the individual requests such review, complete such review and make a final determination unless, for good cause shown, the head of the agency extends such thirty-day period; and if, after his review, the reviewing official also refuses to amend the record in accordance with the request, permit the individual to file with the agency a concise statement setting forth the reasons for his disagreement with the refusal of the agency, and notify the individual of the provisions for judicial review of the reviewing official's determination under subsection (g)(1)(A) of this section;

(4) in any disclosure, containing information about which the individual has filed a statement of disagreement, occurring after the filing of the statement under paragraph

(3) of this subsection, clearly note any portion of the record which is disputed and provide copies of the statement and, if the agency deems it appropriate, copies of a concise statement of the reasons of the agency for not making the amendments requested, to persons or other agencies to whom the disputed record has been disclosed; and

(5) nothing in this section shall allow an individual access to any information compiled in reasonable anticipation of a civil action or proceeding.

(e) Agency requirements

Each agency that maintains a system of records shall—

(1) maintain in its records only such information about an individual as is relevant and necessary to accomplish a purpose of the agency required to be accomplished by statute or by executive order of the President;

(2) collect information to the greatest extent practicable directly from the subject individual when the information may result in adverse determinations about an individual's rights, benefits, and privileges under Federal programs;

(3) inform each individual whom it asks to supply information, on the form which it uses to collect the information or on a separate form that can be retained by the individual—

(A) the authority (whether granted by statute, or by executive order of the President) which authorizes the solicitation of the information and whether disclosure of such information is mandatory or voluntary;

(B) the principal purpose or purposes for which the information is intended to be used;

(C) the routine uses which may be made of the information, as published pursuant to paragraph (4) (D) of this subsection; and

(D) the effects on him, if any, of not providing all or any part of the requested information;

(4) subject to the provisions of paragraph (11) of this subsection, publish in the *Federal Register* upon establishment or revision a notice of the existence and character of the system of records, which notice shall include—

(A) the name and location of the system;

(B) the categories of individuals on whom records are maintained in the system;

(C) the categories of records maintained in the system;

(D) each routine use of the records contained in the system, including the categories of users and the purpose of such use;

(E) the policies and practices of the agency regarding storage, retrievability, access controls, retention, and disposal of the records;

(F) the title and business address of the agency official who is responsible for the system of records;

(G) the agency procedures whereby an individual can be notified at his request if the system of records contains a record pertaining to him;

(H) the agency procedures whereby an individual can be notified at his request how he can gain access to any record pertaining to him contained in the system of records, and how he can contest its content; and

(I) the categories of sources of records in the system;

(5) maintain all records which are used by the agency in making any determination about any individual with such accuracy, relevance, timeliness, and completeness as is reasonably necessary to assure fairness to the individual in the determination;

(6) prior to disseminating any record about an individual to any person other than an agency, unless the dissemination is made pursuant to subsection (b)(2) of this section, make reasonable efforts to assure that such records are accurate, complete, timely, and relevant for agency purposes;

(7) maintain no record describing how any individual exercises rights guaranteed by the First Amendment unless expressly authorized by statute or by the individual about whom the record is maintained or unless pertinent to and within the scope of an authorized law enforcement activity;

(8) make reasonable efforts to serve notice on an individual when any record on such individual is made available to any person under compulsory legal process when such process becomes a matter of public record;

(9) establish rules of conduct for persons involved in the design, development, operation, or maintenance of any system of records, or in maintaining any record, and instruct each such person with respect to such rules and the requirements of this section, including any other rules and procedures adopted pursuant to this section and the penalties for noncompliance;

(10) establish appropriate administrative, technical, and physical safeguards to insure the security and confidentiality of records and to protect against any anticipated threats or hazards to their security or integrity which could result in substantial harm, embarrassment, inconvenience, or unfairness to any individual on whom information is maintained;

(11) at least thirty days prior to publication of information under paragraph (4)(D) of this subsection, publish in the *Federal Register* notice of any new use or intended use of the information in the system, and provide an opportunity for interested persons to submit written data, views, or arguments to the agency; and

(12) if such agency is a recipient agency or a source agency in a matching program with a non-Federal agency, with respect to any establishment or revision of a matching program, at least 30 days prior to conducting such program, publish in the *Federal Register* notice of such establishment or revision.

(f) Agency rules

In order to carry out the provisions of this section, each agency that maintains a system of records shall promulgate rules, in accordance with the requirements (including general notice) of section 553 of this title, which shall—

(1) establish procedures whereby an individual can be notified in response to his request if any system of records named by the individual contains a record pertaining to him;

(2) define reasonable times, places, and requirements for identifying an individual who requests his record or

information pertaining to him before the agency shall make the record or information available to the individual;

(3) establish procedures for the disclosure to an individual upon his request of his record or information pertaining to him, including special procedure, if deemed necessary, for the disclosure to an individual of medical records, including psychological records pertaining to him;

(4) establish procedures for reviewing a request from an individual concerning the amendment of any record or information pertaining to the individual, for making a determination on the request, for an appeal within the agency of an initial adverse agency determination, and for whatever additional means may be necessary for each individual to be able to exercise fully his rights under this section; and

(5) establish fees to be charged, if any, to any individual for making copies of his record, excluding the cost of any search for and review of the record.

The Office of the Federal Register shall biennially compile and publish the rules promulgated under this subsection and agency notices published under subsection (e)(4) of this section in a form available to the public at low cost.

(g)(1) Civil remedies

Whenever any agency

(A) makes a determination under subsection (d)(3) of this section not to amend an individual's record in accordance with his request, or fails to make such review in conformity with that subsection;

(B) refuses to comply with an individual request under subsection (d)(1) of this section;

(C) fails to maintain any record concerning any individual with such accuracy, relevance, timeliness, and completeness as is necessary to assure fairness in any determination relating to the qualifications, character, rights, or opportunities of, or benefits to the individual that may be made on the basis of such record, and consequently a determination is made which is adverse to the individual; or

(D) fails to comply with any other provision of this section, or any rule promulgated thereunder, in such a way as to have an adverse effect on an individual, the individual may bring a civil action against the agency, and the district courts of the United States shall have jurisdiction in the matters under the provisions of this subsection.

(2)(A) In any suit brought under the provisions of subsection (g)(1)(A) of this section, the court may order the agency to amend the individual's record in accordance with his request or in such other way as the court may direct. In such a case the court shall determine the matter de novo.

(B) The court may assess against the United States reasonable attorney fees and other litigation costs reasonably incurred in any case under this paragraph in which the complainant has substantially prevailed.

(3)(A) In any suit brought under the provisions of subsection (g)(1)(B) of this section, the court may enjoin the agency from withholding the records and order the production to the complainant of any agency records improperly withheld from him. In such a case the court shall determine the matter de novo, and may examine the contents of any agency records in camera to determine whether the records or any portion thereof may be withheld under any of the exemptions set forth in subsection (k) of this section, and the burden is on the agency to sustain its action.

(B) The court may assess against the United States reasonable attorney fees and other litigation costs reasonably incurred in any case under this paragraph in which the complainant has substantially prevailed.

(4) In any suit brought under the provisions of subsection (g)(1)(C) or (D) of this section in which the court determines that the agency acted in a manner which was intentional or willful, the United States shall be liable to the individual in an amount equal to the sum of—

(A) actual damages sustained by the individual as a result of the refusal or failure, but in no case shall a person entitled to recovery receive less than the sum of $1,000; and

(B) the costs of the action together with reasonable attorney fees as determined by the court.

(5) An action to enforce any liability created under this section may be brought in the district court of the United States in the district in which the complainant resides, or has his principal place of business, or in which the agency records are situated, or in the District of Columbia, without regard to the amount in controversy, within two years from the date on which the cause of action arises, except that where an agency has materially and willfully misrepresented any information required under this section to be disclosed to an individual and the information so misrepresented is material to establishment of the liability of the agency to the individual under this section, the action may be brought at any time within two years after discovery by the individual of the misrepresentation. Nothing in this section shall be construed to authorize any civil action by reason of any injury sustained as the result of a disclosure of a record prior to September 27, 1975.

(h) Rights of legal guardians

For the purposes of this section, the parent of any minor, or the legal guardian of any individual who has been declared to be incompetent due to physical or mental incapacity or age by a court of competent jurisdiction, may act on behalf of the individual.

(i) Criminal penalties

(1) Any officer or employee of an agency, who by virtue of his employment or official position, has possession of, or access to, agency records which contain individually identifiable information the disclosure of which is prohibited by this section or by rules or regulations established thereunder, and who knowing that disclosure of the specific material is so prohibited, willfully discloses the material in any manner to any person or agency not entitled to receive it, shall be guilty of a misdemeanor and fined not more than $5,000.

(2) Any officer or employee of any agency who willfully maintains a system of records without meeting the notice requirements of subsection (e)(4) of this section shall be guilty of a misdemeanor and fined not more than $5,000.

(3) Any person who knowingly and willfully requests or obtains any record concerning an individual from an agency under false pretenses shall be guilty of a misdemeanor and fined not more than $5,000.

(j) General exemptions

The head of any agency may promulgate rules, in accordance with the requirements (including general notice) of sections 553(b)(1), (2), and (3), (c), and (e) of this title, to exempt any system of records within the agency from any part of this section except subsections (b), (c)(1) and (2), (e)(4)(A) through (F), (e)(6), (7), (9), (10), and (11), and (i) if the system of records is—

(1) maintained by the Central Intelligence Agency; or

(2) maintained by an agency or component thereof which performs as its principal function any activity pertaining to the enforcement of criminal laws, including police efforts to prevent, control, or reduce crime or to apprehend criminals, and the activities of prosecutors, courts, correctional, probation, pardon, or parole authorities, and which consists of (A) information compiled for the purpose of identifying individual criminal offenders and alleged offenders and consisting only of identifying data and notations of arrests, the nature and disposition of criminal charges, sentencing, confinement, release, and parole and probation status; (B) information compiled for the purpose of a criminal investigation, including reports of informants and investigators, and associated with an identifiable individual; or (C) reports identifiable to an individual compiled at any stage of the process of enforcement of the criminal laws from arrest or indictment through release from supervision.

At the time rules are adopted under this subsection, the agency shall include in the statement required under section 553(c) of this title, the reasons why the system of records is to be exempted from a provision of this section.

(k) Specific exemptions

The head of any agency may promulgate rules, in accordance with the requirement (including general notice) of sections 553(b)(1), (2), and (3), (c), and (e) of this title, to exempt any system of records within the agency from subsections (c)(3), (d), (e)(1), (e)(4)(G), (H), and (I) and (f) of this section if the system of records is—

(1) subject to the provisions of section 552(b)(1) of this title;

(2) investigatory material compiled for law enforcement purposes, other than material within the scope of subsection (j)(2) of this section: *Provided, however,* That if any individual is denied any right, privilege, or benefit that he would otherwise be entitled by Federal law, or for which he would otherwise be eligible, as a result of the maintenance of such material, such material shall be provided to such individual, except to the extent that the disclosure of such material would reveal the identity of a source who furnished information to the Government under an express promise that the identity of the source would be held in confidence, or, prior to the effective date of this section, under an implied promise that the identity of the source would be held in confidence;

(3) maintained in connection with providing protective services to the President of the United States or other individuals pursuant to section 3056 of title 18;

(4) required by statute to be maintained and used solely as statistical records;

(5) investigatory material compiled solely for the purpose of determining suitability, eligibility, or qualifications for Federal civilian employment, military service, Federal contracts, or access to classified information, but only to the extent that the disclosure of such material would reveal the identity of a source who furnished information to the Government under an express promise that the identity of the source would be held in confidence, or, prior to the effective date of this section, under an implied promise that the identity of the source would be held in confidence;

(6) testing or examination material used solely to determine individual qualifications for appointment or promotion in the Federal service the disclosure of which would compromise the objectivity or fairness of the testing or examination process; or

(7) evaluation material used to determine potential for promotion in the armed services, but only to the extent that the disclosure of such material would reveal the identity of a source who furnished information to the Government under an express promise that the identity of the source would be held in confidence, or, prior to the effective date of this section, under an implied promise that the identity of the source would be held in confidence. At the time rules are adopted under this subsection, the agency shall include in the statement required under section 553(c) of this title, the reasons why the system of records is to be exempted from a provision of this section.

At the time rules are adopted under this subsection, the agency shall include in the statement required under section 553(c) of this title, the reasons why the system of records is to be exempted from a provision of this section.

(l) Archival records

(1) Each agency record which is accepted by the Archivist of the United States for storage, processing, and servicing in accordance with section 3103 of title 44 shall, for the purposes of this section, be considered to be maintained by the agency which deposited the record and shall be subject to the provisions of this section. The Archivist of the United States shall not disclose the record except to the agency which maintains the record, or under rules established by that agency which are not inconsistent with the provisions of this section.

(2) Each agency record pertaining to an identifiable individual which was transferred to the National Archives of the United States as a record which has sufficient historical or other value to warrant its continued preservation by the United States Government, prior to the effective

date of this section, shall, for the purposes of this section, be considered to be maintained by the National Archives and shall not be subject to the provisions of this section, except that a statement generally describing such records (modeled after the requirements relating to records subject to subsections (e)(4)(A) through (G) of this section) shall be published in the *Federal Register.*

(3) Each agency record pertaining to an identifiable individual which is transferred to the National Archives of the United States as a record which has sufficient historical or other value to warrant its continued preservation by the United States Government, on or after the effective date of this section, shall, for the purposes of this section, be considered to be maintained by the National Archives and shall be exempt from the requirements of this section except subsections (e)(4)(A) through (G) and (e)(9) of this section.

(m) Government contractors

(1) When an agency provides by a contract for the operation by or on behalf of the agency of a system of records to accomplish an agency function, the agency shall, consistent with its authority, cause the requirements of this section to be applied to such system. For purposes of subsection (i) of this section any such contractor and any employee of such contractor, if such contract is agreed to on or after the effective date of this section, shall be considered to be an employee of an agency.

(2) A consumer reporting agency to which a record is disclosed under section 3711(e) of Title 31 shall not be considered a contractor for the purposes of this section.

(n) Mailing lists

An individual's name and address may not be sold or rented by an agency unless such action is specifically authorized by law. This provision shall not be construed to require the withholding of names and addresses otherwise permitted to be made public.

(o) Matching agreements

(1) No record which is contained in a system of records may be disclosed to a recipient agency or non-Federal agency for use in a computer matching program except pursuant to a written agreement between the source agency and the recipient agency or non-Federal agency specifying—

(A) the purpose and legal authority for conducting the program;

(B) the justification for the program and the anticipated results, including a specific estimate of any savings;

(C) a description of the records that will be matched, including each data element that will be used, the approximate number of records that will be matched, and the projected starting and completion dates of the matching program;

(D) procedures for providing individualized notice at the time of application, and notice periodically thereafter as directed by the Data Integrity Board of such agency (subject to guidance provided by the Director of the Office of Management and Budget pursuant to subsection (v)), to—

(i) applicants for and recipients of financial assistance or payments under Federal benefit programs, and

(ii) applicants for and holders of positions as Federal personnel, that any information provided by such applicants, recipients, holders, and individuals may be subject to verification through matching programs;

(E) procedures for verifying information produced in such matching program as required by subsection (p);

(F) procedures for the retention and timely destruction of identifiable records created by a recipient agency or non-Federal agency in such matching program;

(G) procedures for ensuring the administrative, technical, and physical security of the records matched and the results of such programs;

(H) prohibitions on duplication and redisclosure of records provided by the source agency within or outside the recipient agency or the non-Federal agency, except where required by law or essential to the conduct of the matching program;

(I) procedures governing the use by a recipient agency or non-Federal agency of records provided in a matching program by a source agency, including procedures governing return of the records to the source agency or destruction of records used in such program;

(J) information on assessments that have been made on the accuracy of the records that will be used in such matching program; and

(K) that the Comptroller General may have access to all records of a recipient agency or a non-Federal agency that the Comptroller General deems necessary in order to monitor or verify compliance with the agreement.

(2)(A) A copy of each agreement entered into pursuant to paragraph (1) shall—

(i) be transmitted to the Committee on Governmental Affairs of the Senate and the Committee on Government Operations of the House of Representatives; and

(ii) be available upon request to the public.

(B) No such agreement shall be effective until 30 days after the date on which such a copy is transmitted pursuant to subparagraph (A)(i).

(C) Such an agreement shall remain in effect only for such period, not to exceed 18 months, as the Data Integrity Board of the agency determines is appropriate in light of the purposes, and length of time necessary for the conduct, of the matching program.

(D) Within 3 months prior to the expiration of such an agreement pursuant to subparagraph (C), the Data Integrity Board of the agency may, without additional review, renew the matching agreement for a current, ongoing matching program for not more than one additional year if—

(i) such program will be conducted without any change; and

(ii) each party to the agreement certifies to the Board in writing that the program has been conducted in compliance with the agreement.

(p) Verification and opportunity to contest findings

(1) In order to protect any individual whose records are used in a matching program, no recipient agency, non-Federal agency, or source agency may suspend, terminate, reduce, or make a final denial of any financial assistance or payment under a Federal benefit program to such individual, or take other adverse action against such individual, as a result of information produced by such matching program, until—

(A)(i) the agency has independently verified the information; or

(ii) the Data Integrity Board of the agency, or in the case of a non-Federal agency the Data Integrity Board of the source agency, determines in accordance with guidance issued by the Director of the Office of Management and Budget that—

(I) the information is limited to identification and amount of benefits paid by the source agency under a Federal benefit program; and

(II) there is a high degree of confidence that the information provided to the recipient agency is accurate;

(B) the individual receives a notice from the agency containing a statement of its findings and informing the individual of the opportunity to contest such findings; and

(C)(i) the expiration of any time period established for the program by statute or regulation for the individual to respond to that notice; or

(ii) in the case of a program for which no such period is established, the end of the thirty-day period beginning on the date on which notice under subparagraph (B) is mailed or otherwise provided to the individual.

(2) Independent verification referred to in paragraph (1) requires investigation and confirmation of specific information relating to an individual that is used as a basis for an adverse action against the individual, including where applicable investigation and confirmation of—

(A) the amount of any asset or income involved;

(B) whether such individual actually has or had access to such asset or income for such individual's own use; and

(C) the period or periods when the individual actually had such asset or income.

(3) Notwithstanding paragraph (1), an agency may take any appropriate action otherwise prohibited by such paragraph if the agency determines that the public health or public safety may be adversely affected or significantly threatened during any notice period required by such paragraph.

(q) Sanctions

(1) Notwithstanding any other provision of law, no source agency may disclose any record which is contained in a system of records to a recipient agency or non-Federal agency for a matching program if such source agency has reason to believe that the requirements of subsection (p), or any matching agreement entered into pursuant to subsection (o), or both, are not being met by such recipient agency.

(2) No source agency may renew a matching agreement unless—

(A) the recipient agency or non-Federal agency has certified that it has complied with the provisions of that agreement; and

(B) the source agency has no reason to believe that the certification is inaccurate.

(r) Report on new systems and matching programs

Each agency that proposes to establish or make a significant change in a system of records or a matching program shall provide adequate advance notice of any such proposal (in duplicate) to the Committee on Government Operations of the House of Representatives, the Committee on Governmental Affairs of the Senate, and the Office of Management and Budget in order to permit an evaluation of the probable or potential effect of such proposal on the privacy or other rights of individuals.

(s) [Biennial report] Repealed.

(t) Effect of other laws

(1) No agency shall rely on any exemption contained in section 552 of this title to withhold from an individual any record which is otherwise accessible to such individual under the provisions of this section.

(2) No agency shall rely on any exemption in this section to withhold from an individual any record which is otherwise accessible to such individual under the provisions of section 552 of this title.

(u) Data integrity boards

(1) Every agency conducting or participating in a matching program shall establish a Data Integrity Board to oversee and coordinate among the various components of such agency the agency's implementation of this section.

(2) Each Data Integrity Board shall consist of senior officials designated by the head of the agency, and shall include any senior official designated by the head of the agency as responsible for implementation of this section, and the inspector general of the agency, if any. The inspector general shall not serve as chairman of the Data Integrity Board.

(3) Each Data Integrity Board—

(A) shall review, approve, and maintain all written agreements for receipt or disclosure of agency records for matching programs to ensure compliance with subsection (o), and all relevant statutes, regulations, and guidelines;

(B) shall review all matching programs in which the agency has participated during the year, either as a source agency or recipient agency, determine compliance with applicable laws, regulations, guidelines, and agency agreements, and assess the costs and benefits of such programs;

(C) shall review all recurring matching programs in which the agency has participated during the year, either as a source agency or recipient agency, for continued justification for such disclosures;

(D) shall compile an annual report, which shall be submitted to the head of the agency and the Office of Management and Budget and made available to the public on request, describing the matching activities of the agency, including—

(i) matching programs in which the agency has participated as a source agency or recipient agency;

(ii) matching agreements proposed under subsection (o) that were disapproved by the Board;

(iii) any changes in membership or structure of the Board in the preceding year;

(iv) the reasons for any waiver of the requirement in paragraph (4) of this section for completion and submission of a cost-benefit analysis prior to the approval of a matching program;

(v) any violations of matching agreements that have been alleged or identified and any corrective action taken; and

(vi) any other information required by the Director of the Office of Management and Budget to be included in such report;

(E) shall serve as a clearinghouse for receiving and providing information on the accuracy, completeness, and reliability of records used in matching programs;

(F) shall provide interpretation and guidance to agency components and personnel on the requirements of this section for matching programs;

(G) shall review agency recordkeeping and disposal policies and practices for matching programs to assure compliance with this section; and

(H) may review and report on any agency matching activities that are not matching programs.

(4)(A) Except as provided in subparagraphs (B) and (C), a Data Integrity Board shall not approve any written agreement for a matching program unless the agency has completed and submitted to such Board a cost-benefit analysis of the proposed program and such analysis demonstrates that the program is likely to be cost effective.

(B) The Board may waive the requirements of subparagraph (A) of this paragraph if it determines in writing, in accordance with guidelines prescribed by the Director of the Office of Management and Budget, that a cost-benefit analysis is not required.

(C) A cost-benefit analysis shall not be required under subparagraph (A) prior to the initial approval of a written agreement for a matching program that is specifically required by statute. Any subsequent written agreement for such a program shall not be approved by the Data Integrity Board unless the agency has submitted a cost-benefit analysis of the program as conducted under the preceding approval of such agreement.

(5)(A) If a matching agreement is disapproved by a Data Integrity Board, any party to such agreement may appeal the disapproval to the Director of the Office of Management and Budget. Timely notice of the filing of such an appeal shall be provided by the Director of the Office of Management and Budget to the Committee on Governmental Affairs of the Senate and the Committee on Government Operations of the House of Representatives.

(B) The Director of the Office of Management and Budget may approve a matching agreement notwithstanding the disapproval of a Data Integrity Board if the Director determines that

(i) the matching program will be consistent with all applicable legal, regulatory, and policy requirements;

(ii) there is adequate evidence that the matching agreement will be cost-effective; and

(iii) the matching program is in the public interest.

(C) The decision of the Director to approve a matching agreement shall not take effect until 30 days after it is reported to committees described in subparagraph (A).

(D) If the Data Integrity Board and the Director of the Office of Management and Budget disapprove a matching program proposed by the inspector general of an agency, the inspector general may report the disapproval to the head of the agency and to the Congress.

(6) The Director of the Office of Management and Budget shall, annually during the first 3 years after the date of enactment of this subsection and biennially thereafter, consolidate in a report to the Congress the information contained in the reports from the various Data Integrity Boards under paragraph (3)(D). Such report shall include detailed information about costs and benefits of matching programs that are conducted during the period covered by such consolidated report, and shall identify each waiver granted by a Data Integrity Board of the requirement for completion and submission of a cost-benefit analysis and the reasons for granting the waiver.

(7) In the reports required by paragraph (3)(D), agency matching activities that are not matching programs may be reported on an aggregate basis, if and to the extent necessary to protect ongoing law enforcement or counterintelligence investigations.

(v) Office of Management and Budget responsibilities
The Director of the Office of Management and Budget shall—

(1) develop and, after notice and opportunity for public comment, prescribe guidelines and regulations for the use of agencies in implementing the provisions of this section; and

(2) provide continuing assistance to and oversight of the implementation of this section by agencies.

Executive Orders

▪ **EXECUTIVE ORDER 12044**
(Revoked Feb. 17, 1981)

Improving Government Regulations

As President of the United States of America, I direct each Executive Agency to adopt procedures to improve existing and future regulations.

Section 1. *Policy*. Regulations shall be as simple and clear as possible. They shall achieve legislative goals effectively and efficiently. They shall not impose unnecessary burdens on the economy, on individuals, on public or private organizations, or on State and local governments.

To achieve these objectives, regulations shall be developed through a process which ensures that:

(a) the need for and purposes of the regulation are clearly established;

(b) heads of agencies and policy officials exercise effective oversight;

(c) opportunity exists for early participation and comment by other Federal agencies, State and local governments, businesses, organizations and individual members of the public;

(d) meaningful alternatives are considered and analyzed before the regulation is issued; and

(e) compliance costs, paperwork and other burdens on the public are minimized.

Sec. 2. *Reform of the Process for Developing Significant Regulations*. Agencies shall review and revise their procedures for developing regulations to be consistent with the policies of this Order and in a manner that minimizes paperwork.

Agencies' procedures should fit their own needs but, at a minimum, these procedures shall include the following:

(a) *Semiannual Agenda of Regulations*. To give the public adequate notice, agencies shall publish at least semiannually an agenda of significant regulations under development or review. On the first Monday in October, each agency shall publish in the *Federal Register* a schedule showing the times during the coming fiscal year when the agency's semiannual agenda will be published. Supplements to the agenda may be published at other times during the year if necessary, but the semiannual agendas shall be as complete as possible. The head of each agency shall approve the agenda before it is published.

At a minimum, each published agenda shall describe the regulations being considered by the agency, the need for and the legal basis for the action being taken, and the status of regulations previously listed on the agenda.

Each item on the agenda shall also include the name and telephone number of a knowledgeable agency official and, if possible, state whether or not a regulatory analysis will be required. The agenda shall also include existing regulations scheduled to be reviewed in accordance with Section 4 of this Order.

(b) *Agency Head Oversight*. Before an agency proceeds to develop significant new regulations, the agency head shall have reviewed the issues to be considered, the alternative approaches to be explored, a tentative plan for obtaining public comment, and target dates for completion of steps in the development of the regulation.

(c) *Opportunity for Public Participation*. Agencies shall give the public an early and meaningful opportunity to participate in the development of agency regulations. They shall consider a variety of ways to provide this opportunity, including (1) publishing an advance notice of proposed rulemaking; (2) holding open conferences or public hearings; (3) sending notices of proposed regulations to publications likely to be read by those affected; and (4) notifying interested parties directly.

Agencies shall give the public at least 60 days to comment on proposed significant regulations. In the few instances where agencies determine this is not possible, the regulation shall be accompanied by a brief statement of the reasons for a shorter time period.

(d) *Approval of Significant Regulations*. The head of each agency, or the designated official with statutory responsibility, shall approve significant regulations before they are published for public comment in the *Federal Register*. At a minimum, this official should determine that:

(1) the proposed regulation is needed;

(2) the direct and indirect effects of the regulation have been adequately considered;

(3) alternative approaches have been considered and the least burdensome of the acceptable alternatives has been chosen;

(4) public comments have been considered and an adequate response has been prepared;

(5) the regulation is written in plain English and is understandable to those who must comply with it;

(6) an estimate has been made of the new reporting burdens or recordkeeping requirements necessary for compliance with the regulation;

(7) the name, address and telephone number of a knowledgeable agency official is included in the publication; and

(8) a plan for evaluating the regulation after its issuance has been developed.

(e) *Criteria for Determining Significant Regulations.* Agencies shall establish criteria for identifying which regulations are significant. Agencies shall consider among other things: (1) the type and number of individuals, businesses, organizations, State and local governments affected; (2) the compliance and reporting requirements likely to be involved; (3) direct and indirect effects of the regulation including the effect on competition; and (4) the relationship of the regulations to those of other programs and agencies. Regulations that do not meet an agency's criteria for determining significance shall be accompanied by a statement to that effect at the time the regulation is proposed.

Sec. 3. *Regulatory Analysis.* Some of the regulations identified as significant may have major economic consequences for the general economy, or for individual industries, geographical regions or levels of government. For these regulations, agencies shall prepare a regulatory analysis. Such an analysis shall involve a careful examination of alternative approaches early in the decision-making process.

The following requirements shall govern the preparation of regulatory analyses:

(a) *Criteria.* Agency heads shall establish criteria for determining which regulations require regulatory analyses. The criteria established shall:

(1) ensure that regulatory analyses are performed for all regulations which will result in (a) an annual effect on the economy of $100 million or more; or (b) a major increase in costs or prices for individual industries, levels of government or geographic regions; and

(2) provide that in the agency head's discretion, regulatory analysis may be completed on any proposed regulation.

(b) *Procedures.* Agency heads shall establish procedures for developing the regulatory analysis and obtaining public comment.

(1) Each regulatory analysis shall contain a succinct statement of the problem; a description of the major alternative ways of dealing with the problems that were considered by the agency; an analysis of the economic consequences of each of these alternatives and a detailed explanation of the reasons for choosing one alternative over the others.

(2) Agencies shall include in their public notice of proposed rules an explanation of the regulatory approach that has been selected or is favored and a short description of the other alternatives considered. A statement of how the public may obtain a copy of the draft regulatory analysis shall also be included.

(3) Agencies shall prepare a final regulatory analysis to be made available when the final regulations are published.

Regulatory analyses shall not be required in rulemaking proceedings pending at the time this Order is issued if an Economic Impact Statement has already been prepared in accordance with Executive Orders 11821 and 11949.

Sec. 4. *Review of Existing Regulations.* Agencies shall periodically review their existing regulations to determine whether they are achieving the policy goals of this Order. This review will follow the same procedural steps outlined for the development of new regulations.

In selecting regulations to be reviewed, agencies shall consider such criteria as:

(a) the continued need for the regulation;

(b) the type and number of complaints or suggestions received;

(c) the burdens imposed on those directly or indirectly affected by the regulations;

(d) the need to simplify or clarify language;

(e) the need to eliminate overlapping and duplicative regulations; and

(f) the length of time since the regulation has been evaluated or the degree to which technology, economic conditions or other factors have changed in the area affected by the regulation.

Agencies shall develop their selection criteria and a listing of possible regulations for initial review. The criteria and listing shall be published for comment as required in Section 5. Subsequently, regulations selected for review shall be included in the semiannual agency agendas.

Sec. 5. *Implementation.*

(a) Each agency shall review its existing process for developing regulations and revise it as needed to comply with this Order. Within 60 days after the issuance of the Order, each agency shall prepare a draft report outlining (1) a brief description of its process for developing regulations and the changes that have been made to comply with this Order; (2) its proposed criteria for defining significant agency regulations; (3) its proposed criteria for identifying which regulations require regulatory analysis; and (4) its proposed criteria for selecting existing regulations to be reviewed and a list of regulations that the agency will consider for its initial review. This report shall be published in the *Federal Register* for public comment. A copy of this report shall be sent to the Office of Management and Budget.

(b) After receiving public comment, agencies shall submit their revised report to the Office of Management and Budget for approval before final publication in the *Federal Register.*

(c) The Office of Management and Budget shall assure the effective implementation of this Order. OMB shall report at least semiannually to the President on the effectiveness of the Order and agency compliance with its provisions. By May 1, 1980, OMB shall recommend to the President whether or not there is a continued need for the Order and any further steps or actions necessary to achieve its purpose.

Sec. 6. *Coverage.*

(a) As used in this Order, the term regulation means both rules and regulations issued by agencies including those which establish conditions for financial assistance. Closely related sets of regulations shall be considered together.

(b) This Order does not apply to:

(1) regulations issued in accordance with the formal rulemaking provisions of the Administrative Procedure Act (5 U.S.C. 556, 557);

(2) regulations issued with respect to a military or foreign affairs function of the United States;

(3) matters related to agency management or personnel;

(4) regulations related to Federal Government procurement;

(5) regulations issued by the independent regulatory agencies; or

(6) regulations that are issued in response to an emergency or which are governed by short-term statutory or judicial deadlines. In these cases, the agency shall publish in the *Federal Register* a statement of the reasons why it is impracticable or contrary to the public interest for the agency to follow the procedures of this Order. Such a statement shall include the name of the policy official responsible for this determination.

Sec. 7. This Order is intended to improve the quality of Executive Agency regulatory practices. It is not intended to create delay in the process or provide new grounds for judicial review. Nothing in this order shall be considered to supersede existing statutory obligations governing rulemaking.

Sec. 8. Unless extended, this Executive Order expires on June 30, 1980.

JIMMY CARTER

The White House,
March 23, 1978.

■ EXECUTIVE ORDER 12291

(Revoked Sept. 30, 1993)

Federal Regulation

By the authority vested in me as President by the Constitution and laws of the United States of America, and in order to reduce the burdens of existing and future regulations, increase agency accountability for regulatory actions, provide for presidential oversight of the regulatory process, minimize duplication and conflict of regulations, and insure well-reasoned regulations, it is hereby ordered as follows:

Section 1. *Definitions.* For the purposes of this Order:

(a) "Regulation" or "rule" means an agency statement of general applicability and future effect designed to implement, interpret, or prescribe law or policy or describing the procedure or practice requirements of an agency, but does not include:

(1) Administrative actions governed by the provisions of Sections 556 and 557 of Title 5 of the United States Code;

(2) Regulations issued with respect to a military or foreign affairs function of the United States; or

(3) Regulations related to agency organization, management, or personnel.

(b) "Major rule" means any regulation that is likely to result in:

(1) An annual effect on the economy of $100 million or more;

(2) A major increase in costs or prices for consumers, individual industries, Federal, State, or local government agencies, or geographic regions; or

(3) Significant adverse effects on competition, employment, investment, productivity, innovation, or on the ability of United States-based enterprises to compete with foreign-based enterprises in domestic or export markets.

(c) "Director" means the Director of the Office of Management and Budget.

(d) "Agency" means any authority of the United States that is an "agency" under 44 U.S.C. 3502(1), excluding those agencies specified in 44 U.S.C. 3502(10).

(e) "Task Force" means the Presidential Task Force on Regulatory Relief.

Sec. 2. *General Requirements.* In promulgating new regulations, reviewing existing regulations, and developing legislative proposals concerning regulation, all agencies, to the extent permitted by law, shall adhere to the following requirements:

(a) Administrative decisions shall be based on adequate information concerning the need for and consequences of proposed government action;

(b) Regulatory action shall not be undertaken unless the potential benefits to society from the regulation outweigh the potential costs to society;

(c) Regulatory objectives shall be chosen to maximize the net benefits to society;

(d) Among alternative approaches to any given regulatory objective, the alternative involving the least net cost to society shall be chosen; and

(e) Agencies shall set regulatory priorities with the aim of maximizing the aggregate net benefits to society, taking into account the condition of the particular industries affected by regulations, the condition of the national economy, and other regulatory actions contemplated for the future.

Sec. 3. *Regulatory Impact Analysis and Review.*

(a) In order to implement Section 2 of this Order, each agency shall, in connection with every major rule, prepare, and to the extent permitted by law consider, a Regulatory Impact Analysis. Such Analyses may be combined with any Regulatory Flexibility Analyses performed under 5 U.S.C. 603 and 604.

(b) Each agency shall initially determine whether a rule it intends to propose or to issue is a major rule, *provided that,* the Director, subject to the direction of the Task Force, shall have authority, in accordance with Sections 1(b) and 2 of this Order, to prescribe criteria for making such determinations, to order a rule to be treated as a major rule, and to require any set of related rules to be considered together as a major rule.

(c) Except as provided in Section 8 of this Order, agencies shall prepare Regulatory Impact Analyses of major rules and transmit them, along with all notices of proposed rulemaking and all final rules, to the Director as follows:

(1) If no notice of proposed rulemaking is to be published for a proposed major rule that is not an emergency rule, the agency shall prepare only a final Regulatory Impact Analysis, which shall be transmitted, along with the proposed rule, to the Director at least 60 days prior to the publication of the major rule as a final rule;

(2) With respect to all other major rules, the agency shall prepare a preliminary Regulatory Impact Analysis, which shall be transmitted, along with a notice of proposed rulemaking, to the Director at least 60 days prior to the publication of a notice of proposed rulemaking, and a final Regulatory Impact Analysis, which shall be transmitted along with the final rule at least 30 days prior to the publication of the major rule as a final rule;

(3) For all rules other than major rules, agencies shall submit to the Director, at least 10 days prior to publication, every notice of proposed rulemaking and final rule.

(d) To permit each proposed major rule to be analyzed in light of the requirements stated in Section 2 of this Order, each preliminary and final Regulatory Impact Analysis shall contain the following information:

(1) A description of the potential benefits of the rule, including any beneficial effects that cannot be quantified in monetary terms, and the identification of those likely to receive the benefits;

(2) A description of the potential costs of the rule, including any adverse effects that cannot be quantified in monetary terms, and the identification of those likely to bear the costs;

(3) A determination of the potential net benefits of the rule, including an evaluation of effects that cannot be quantified in monetary terms;

(4) A description of alternative approaches that could substantially achieve the same regulatory goal at lower cost, together with an analysis of this potential benefit and costs and a brief explanation of the legal reasons why such alternatives, if proposed, could not be adopted; and

(5) Unless covered by the description required under paragraph (4) of this subsection, an explanation of any legal reasons why the rule cannot be based on the requirements set forth in Section 2 of this Order.

(e)(1) The Director, subject to the direction of the Task Force, which shall resolve any issues raised under this Order or ensure that they are presented to the President, is authorized to review any preliminary or final Regulatory Impact Analysis, notice of proposed rulemaking, or final rule based on the requirements of this Order.

(2) The Director shall be deemed to have concluded the review unless the Director advises an agency to the contrary under subsection (f) of this Section:

(A) Within 60 days of a submission under subsection (c)(1) or a submission of a preliminary Regulatory Impact Analysis or notice of proposed rulemaking under subsection (c)(2);

(B) Within 30 days of the submission of a final Regulatory Impact Analysis and a final rule under subsection (c)(2); and

(C) Within 10 days of the submission of a notice of proposed rulemaking or final rule under subsection (c)(3).

(f)(1) Upon the request of the Director, an agency shall consult with the Director concerning the review of a preliminary Regulatory Impact Analysis or notice of proposed rulemaking under this Order, and shall, subject to Section 8(a)(2) of this Order, refrain from publishing its preliminary Regulatory Impact Analysis or notice of proposed rulemaking until such review is concluded.

(2) Upon receiving notice that the Director intends to submit views with respect to any final Regulatory Impact Analysis or final rule, the agency shall, subject to Section 8(a)(2) of this Order, refrain from publishing its final Regulatory Impact Analysis or final rule until the agency has responded to the Director's views, and incorporated those views and the agency's response in the rulemaking file.

(3) Nothing in this subsection shall be construed as displacing the agencies' responsibilities delegated by law.

(g) For every rule for which an agency publishes a notice of proposed rulemaking, the agency shall include in its notice:

(1) A brief statement setting forth the agency's initial determination whether the proposed rule is a major rule, together with the reasons underlying that determination; and

(2) For each proposed major rule, a brief summary of the agency's preliminary Regulatory Impact Analysis.

(h) Agencies shall make their preliminary and final Regulatory Impact Analyses available to the public.

(i) Agencies shall initiate reviews of currently effective rules in accordance with the purposes of this Order, and perform Regulatory Impact Analyses of currently effective major rules. The Director, subject to the direction of the Task Force, may designate currently effective rules for review in accordance with this Order, and establish schedules for reviews and Analyses under this Order.

Sec. 4. *Regulatory Review.* Before approving any final major rule, each agency shall:

(a) Make a determination that the regulation is clearly within the authority delegated by law and consistent with congressional intent, and include in the *Federal Register* at the time of promulgation a memorandum of law supporting that determination.

(b) Make a determination that the factual conclusions upon which the rule is based have substantial support in the agency record, viewed as a whole, with full attention to public comments in general and the comments of persons directly affected by the rule in particular.

Sec. 5. *Regulatory Agendas.*

(a) Each agency shall publish, in October and April of each year, an agenda of proposed regulations that the agency has issued or expects to issue, and currently effective rules that are under agency review pursuant to this Order. These agendas may be incorporated with the agendas published under 5 U.S.C. 602, and must contain at the minimum:

(1) A summary of the nature of each major rule being considered, the objectives and legal basis for the issuance of the rule, and an approximate schedule for completing action on any major rule for which the agency has issued a notice of proposed rulemaking;

(2) The name and telephone number of a knowledgeable agency official for each item on the agenda; and

(3) A list of existing regulations to be reviewed under the terms of this Order, and a brief discussion of each such regulation.

(b) The Director, subject to the direction of the Task Force, may, to the extent permitted by law:

(1) Require agencies to provide additional information in an agenda; and

(2) Require publication of the agenda in any form.

Sec. 6. *The Task Force and Office of Management and Budget.*

(a) To the extent permitted by law, the Director shall have authority, subject to the direction of the Task Force, to:

(1) Designate any proposed or existing rule as a major rule in accordance with Section 1(b) of this Order;

(2) Prepare and promulgate uniform standards for the identification of major rules and the development of Regulatory Impact Analyses;

(3) Require an agency to obtain and evaluate, in connection with a regulation, any additional relevant data from any appropriate source;

(4) Waive the requirements of Sections 3, 4, or 7 of this Order with respect to any proposed or existing major rule;

(5) Identify duplicative, overlapping and conflicting rules, existing or proposed, and existing or proposed rules that are inconsistent with the policies underlying statutes governing agencies other than the issuing agency or with the purposes of this Order, and, in each such case, require appropriate interagency consultation to minimize or eliminate such duplication, overlap, or conflict;

(6) Develop procedures for estimating the annual benefits and costs of agency regulations, on both an aggregate and economic or industrial sector basis, for purposes of compiling a regulatory budget;

(7) In consultation with interested agencies, prepare for consideration by the President recommendations for changes in the agencies' statutes; and

(8) Monitor agency compliance with the requirements of this Order and advise the President with respect to such compliance.

(b) The Director, subject to the direction of the Task Force, is authorized to establish procedures for the performance of all functions vested in the Director by this Order. The Director shall take appropriate steps to coordinate the implementation of the analysis, transmittal, review, and clearance provisions of this Order with the authorities and requirements provided for or imposed upon the Director and agencies under the Regulatory Flexibility Act, 5 U.S.C. 601 *et seq.,* and the Paperwork Reduction Plan Act of 1980, 44 U.S.C. 3501 *et seq.*

Sec. 7. *Pending Regulations.*

(a) To the extent necessary to permit reconsideration in accordance with this Order, agencies shall, except as provided in Section 8 of this Order, suspend or postpone the effective dates of all major rules that they have promulgated in final form as of the date of this Order, but that have not yet become effective, excluding:

(1) Major rules that cannot legally be postponed or suspended;

(2) Major rules that, for good cause, ought to become effective as final rules without reconsideration. Agencies shall prepare, in accordance with Section 3 of this Order, a final Regulatory Impact Analysis for each major rule that they suspend or postpone.

(b) Agencies shall report to the Director no later than 15 days prior to the effective date of any rule that the agency has promulgated in final form as of the date of this Order, and that has not yet become effective, and that will not be reconsidered under subsection (a) of this Section:

(1) That the rule is excepted from reconsideration under subsection (a), including a brief statement of the legal or other reasons for that determination; or

(2) That the rule is not a major rule.

(c) The Director, subject to the direction of the Task Force, is authorized, to the extent permitted by law, to:

(1) Require reconsideration, in accordance with this Order, of any major rule that an agency has issued in final form as of the date of this Order and that has not become effective; and

(2) Designate a rule that an agency has issued in final form as of the date of this Order and that has not yet become effective as a major rule in accordance with Section 1(b) of this Order.

(d) Agencies may, in accordance with the Administrative Procedure Act and other applicable statutes, permit major rules that they have issued in final form as of the date of this Order, and that have not yet become effective, to take effect as interim rules while they are being reconsidered in accordance with this Order, *provided that,* agencies shall report to the Director, no later than 15 days before any such rule is proposed to take effect as an interim rule, that the rule should appropriately take effect as an interim rule while the rule is under reconsideration.

(e) Except as provided in Section 8 of this Order, agencies shall, to the extent permitted by law, refrain from promulgating as a final rule any proposed major rule that has been published or issued as of the date of this Order until a final Regulatory Impact Analysis, in accordance with Section 3 of this Order, has been prepared for the proposed major rule.

(f) Agencies shall report to the Director, no later than 30 days prior to promulgating as a final rule any proposed rule that the agency has published or issued as of the date of this Order and that has not been considered under the terms of this Order:

(1) That the rule cannot legally be considered in accordance with this Order, together with a brief explanation of the legal reasons barring such consideration; or

(2) That the rule is not a major rule, in which case the agency shall submit to the Director a copy of the proposed rule.

(g) The Director, subject to the direction of the Task Force, is authorized, to the extent permitted by law, to:

(1) Require consideration, in accordance with this Order, of any proposed major rule that the agency has published or issued as of the date of this Order; and

(2) Designate a proposed rule that an agency has published or issued as of the date of this Order, as a major rule in accordance with Section 1(b) of this Order.

(h) The Director shall be deemed to have determined that an agency's report to the Director under subsections (b), (d), or (f) of this Section is consistent with the purposes of this Order, unless the Director advises the agency to the contrary:

(1) Within 15 days of its report, in the case of any report under subsections (b) or (d); or

(2) Within 30 days of its report, in the case of any report under subsection (f).

(i) This Section does not supersede the President's Memorandum of January 29, 1981, entitled "Postponement of Pending Regulations," which shall remain in effect until March 30, 1981.

(j) In complying with this Section, agencies shall comply with all applicable provisions of the Administrative Procedure Act, and with any other procedural requirements made applicable to the agencies by other statutes.

Sec. 8. *Exemptions.*

(a) The procedures prescribed by this Order shall not apply to:

(1) Any regulation that responds to an emergency situation, *provided that,* any such regulation shall be reported to the Director as soon as is practicable, the agency shall publish in the *Federal Register* a statement of the reasons why it is impracticable for the agency to follow the procedures of this Order with respect to such a rule, and the agency shall prepare and transmit as soon as is practicable a Regulatory Impact Analysis of any such major rule; and

(2) Any regulation for which consideration or reconsideration under the terms of this Order would conflict with deadlines imposed by statute or by judicial order, *provided that,* any such regulation shall be reported to the Director together with a brief explanation of the conflict, the agency shall publish in the *Federal Register* a statement of the reasons why it is impracticable for the agency to follow the procedures of this Order with respect to such a rule, and the agency, in consultation with the Director, shall adhere to the requirements of this Order to the extent permitted by statutory or judicial deadlines.

(b) The Director, subject to the direction of the Task Force, may, in accordance with the purposes of this Order, exempt any class or category of regulations from any or all requirements of this Order.

Sec. 9. *Judicial Review.* This Order is intended only to improve the internal management of the Federal government, and is not intended to create any right or benefit, substantive or procedural, enforceable at law by a party against the United States, its agencies, its officers or any person. The determinations made by agencies under Section 4 of this Order, and any Regulatory Impact Analyses for any rule, shall be made part of the whole record of agency action in connection with the rule.

Sec. 10. *Revocations.* Executive Orders No. 12044, as amended, and No. 12174 are revoked.

RONALD REAGAN

The White House,
February 17, 1981.

EXECUTIVE ORDER 12498

(Revoked Sept. 30, 1993)

Regulatory Planning Process

By the authority vested in me as President by the Constitution and laws of the United States of America, and in order to create a coordinated process for developing on an annual basis the Administration's Regulatory Program, establish Administration regulatory priorities, increase the accountability of agency heads for the regulatory actions of their agencies, provide for Presidential oversight of the regulatory process, reduce the burdens of existing and future regulations, minimize duplication and conflict of regulations, and enhance public and Congressional understanding of the Administration's regulatory objectives, it is hereby ordered as follows:

Section 1. General Requirements.

(a) There is hereby established a regulatory planning process by which the Administration will develop and publish a Regulatory Program for each year. To implement this process, each Executive agency subject to Executive Order No. 12291 shall submit to the Director of the Office of Management and Budget (OMB) each year, starting in 1985, a statement of its regulatory policies, goals, and objectives for the coming year and information concerning all significant regulatory actions underway or planned; however, the Director may exempt from this Order such agencies or activities as the Director may deem appropriate in order to achieve the effective implementation of this Order.

(b) The head of each Executive agency subject to this Order shall ensure that all regulatory actions are consistent with the goals of the agency and of the Administration, and will be appropriately implemented.

(c) This program is intended to complement the existing regulatory planning and review procedures of agencies and the Executive branch, including the procedures established by Executive Order No. 12291.

(d) To assure consistency with the goals of the Administration, the head of each agency subject to this Order shall adhere to the regulatory principles stated in Section 2 of Executive Order No. 12291, including those elaborated by the regulatory policy guidelines set forth in the August 11, 1983, Report of the Presidential Task Force on Regulatory Relief, "Reagan Administration Regulatory Achievements."

Sec. 2. *Agency Submission of Draft Regulatory Program.*

(a) The head of each agency shall submit to the Director an overview of the agency's regulatory policies, goals, and objectives for the program year and such information concerning all significant regulatory actions of the agency, planned or underway, including actions taken to consider whether to initiate rulemaking; requests for public comment; and the development of documents that may influence, anticipate, or could lead to the commencement of rulemaking proceedings at a later date, as the Director deems necessary to develop the Administration's Regulatory Program. This submission shall constitute the agency's draft regulatory program. The draft regulatory program shall be submitted to the Director each year, on a date to be specified by the Director, and shall cover the period from April 1 through March 31 of the following year.

(b) The overview portion of the agency's submission should discuss the agency's broad regulatory purposes, explain how they are consistent with the Administration's regulatory principles, and include a discussion of the significant regulatory actions, as defined by the Director, that it will take. The overview should specifically discuss the significant regulatory actions of the agency to revise or rescind existing rules.

(c) Each agency head shall categorize and describe the regulatory actions described in subsection (a) in such format as the Director shall specify and provide such additional information as the Director may request; however, the Director shall, by Bulletin or Circular, exempt from the requirements of this Order any class or category of regulatory action that the Director determines is not necessary to review in order to achieve the effective implementation of the program.

Sec. 3. *Review, Compilation, and Publication of the Administration's Regulatory Program.*

(a) In reviewing each agency's draft regulatory program, the Director shall (i) consider the consistency of the draft regulatory program with the Administration's policies and priorities and the draft regulatory programs submitted by other agencies; and (ii) identify such further regulatory or deregulatory actions as may, in his view, be necessary in order to achieve such consistency. In the event of disagreement over the content of the agency's draft regulatory program, the agency head or the Director may raise issues for further review by the President or by such appropriate Cabinet Council or other forum as the President may designate.

(b) Following the conclusion of the review process established by subsection (a), each agency head shall submit to the Director, by a date to be specified by the Director, the agency's final regulatory plan for compilation and publication as the Administration's Regulatory Program for that year. The Director shall circulate a draft of the Administration's Regulatory Program for agency comment, review, and interagency consideration, if necessary, before publication.

(c) After development of the Administration's Regulatory Program for the year, if the agency head proposes to take a regulatory action subject to the provisions of Section 2 and not previously submitted for review under this process, or if the agency head proposes to take a regulatory action that is materially different from the action described in the agency's final Regulatory Program, the agency head shall immediately advise the Director and submit the action to the Director for review in such format as the Director may specify. Except in the case of emergency situations, as defined by the Director, or statutory or judicial deadlines, the agency head shall refrain from taking the proposed regulatory action until the review of this submission by the Director is completed. As to those regulatory actions not also subject to Executive Order No. 12291, the Director shall be deemed to have concluded that the proposal is consistent with the purposes of this Order, unless he notifies the agency head to the contrary within 10 days of its submission. As to those regulatory actions subject to Executive Order No. 12291, the Director's review shall be governed by the provisions of Section 3(e) of that Order.

(d) Absent unusual circumstances, such as new statutory or judicial requirements or unanticipated emergency situations, the Director may, to the extent permitted by law, return for reconsideration any rule submitted for review under Executive Order No. 12291 that would be subject to Section 2 but was not included in the agency's final Regulatory Program for that year; or any other significant regulatory action that is materially different from those described in the Administration's Regulatory Program for that year.

Sec. 4. *Office of Management and Budget.*

The Director of the Office of Management and Budget is authorized, to the extent permitted by law, to take such actions as may be necessary to carry out the provisions of this order.

Sec. 5. *Judicial Review.*

This Order is intended only to improve the internal management of the Federal government, and is not intended to create any right or benefit, substantive or procedural, enforceable at law by a party against the United States, its agencies, its officers or any person.

RONALD REAGAN

The White House,
January 4, 1985.

EXECUTIVE ORDER 12866
(Amended Feb. 26, 2002, and Jan. 18, 2007)

Regulatory Planning and Review

The American people deserve a regulatory system that works for them, not against them; a regulatory system that protects and improves their health, safety, environment, and well-being and improves the performance of the economy without imposing unacceptable or unreasonable costs on society; regulatory policies that recognize that the private sector and private markets are the best engine for economic growth; regulatory approaches that respect the role of State, local, and tribal governments; and regulations that are effective, consistent, sensible, and understandable. We do not have such a regulatory system today.

With this Executive order, the Federal Government begins a program to reform and make more efficient the regulatory process. The objectives of this Executive order are to enhance planning and coordination with respect to both new and existing regulations; to reaffirm the primacy of Federal agencies in the regulatory decision-making process; to restore the integrity and legitimacy of regulatory review and oversight; and to make the process more accessible and open to the public. In pursuing these objectives, the regulatory process shall be conducted so as to meet applicable statutory requirements and with due regard to the discretion that has been entrusted to the Federal agencies.

Accordingly, by the authority vested in me as President by the Constitution and the laws of the United States of America, it is hereby ordered as follows:

Section 1. Statement of Regulatory Philosophy and Principles.

(a) *The Regulatory Philosophy.* Federal agencies should promulgate only such regulations as are required by law, are necessary to interpret the law, or are made necessary by compelling public need, such as material failures of private markets to protect or improve the health and safety of the public, the environment, or the well-being of the American people. In deciding whether and how to regulate, agencies should assess all costs and benefits of available regulatory alternatives, including the alternative of not regulating. Costs and benefits shall be understood to include both quantifiable measures (to the fullest extent that these can be usefully estimated) and qualitative measures of costs and benefits that are difficult to quantify, but nevertheless essential to consider. Further, in choosing among alternative regulatory approaches, agencies should select those approaches that maximize net benefits (including potential economic, environmental, public health and safety, and other advantages; distributive impacts; and equity), unless a statute requires another regulatory approach.

(b) *The Principles of Regulation.* To ensure that the agencies' regulatory programs are consistent with the philosophy set forth above, agencies should adhere to the following principles, to the extent permitted by law and where applicable:

(1) Each agency shall identify the problem that it intends to address (including, where applicable, the failures of private markets or public institutions that warrant new agency action) as well as assess the significance of that problem.

(2) Each agency shall examine whether existing regulations (or other law) have created, or contributed to, the problem that a new regulation is intended to correct and whether those regulations (or other law) should be modified to achieve the intended goal of regulation more effectively.

(3) Each agency shall identify and assess available alternatives to direct regulation, including providing economic incentives to encourage the desired behavior, such as user fees or marketable permits, or providing information upon which choices can be made by the public.

(4) In setting regulatory priorities, each agency shall consider, to the extent reasonable, the degree and nature of the risks posed by various substances or activities within its jurisdiction.

(5) When an agency determines that a regulation is the best available method of achieving the regulatory objective, it shall design its regulations in the most cost-effective manner to achieve the regulatory objective. In doing so, each agency shall consider incentives for innovation, consistency, predictability, the costs of enforcement and compliance (to the government, regulated entities, and the public), flexibility, distributive impacts, and equity.

(6) Each agency shall assess both the costs and the benefits of the intended regulation and, recognizing that some costs and benefits are difficult to quantify, propose or adopt a regulation only upon a reasoned determination that the benefits of the intended regulation justify its costs.

(7) Each agency shall base its decisions on the best reasonably obtainable scientific, technical, economic, and other information concerning the need for, and consequences of, the intended regulation.

(8) Each agency shall identify and assess alternative forms of regulation and shall, to the extent feasible, specify performance objectives, rather than specifying the behavior or manner of compliance that regulated entities must adopt.

(9) Wherever feasible, agencies shall seek views of appropriate State, local, and tribal officials before imposing regulatory requirements that might significantly or uniquely affect those governmental entities. Each agency shall assess the effects of Federal regulations on State, local, and tribal governments, including specifically the availability of resources to carry out those mandates, and seek to minimize those burdens

that uniquely or significantly affect such governmental entities, consistent with achieving regulatory objectives. In addition, as appropriate, agencies shall seek to harmonize Federal regulatory actions with related State, local, and tribal regulatory and other governmental functions.

(10) Each agency shall avoid regulations that are inconsistent, incompatible, or duplicative with its other regulations or those of other Federal agencies.

(11) Each agency shall tailor its regulations to impose the least burden on society, including individuals, businesses of differing sizes, and other entities (including small communities and governmental entities), consistent with obtaining the regulatory objectives, taking into account, among other things, and to the extent practicable, the costs of cumulative regulations.

(12) Each agency shall draft its regulations to be simple and easy to understand, with the goal of minimizing the potential for uncertainty and litigation arising from such uncertainty.

Sec. 2. *Organization.* An efficient regulatory planning and review process is vital to ensure that the Federal Government's regulatory system best serves the American people.

(a) *The Agencies.* Because Federal agencies are the repositories of significant substantive expertise and experience, they are responsible for developing regulations and assuring that the regulations are consistent with applicable law, the President's priorities, and the principles set forth in this Executive order.

(b) *The Office of Management and Budget.* Coordinated review of agency rulemaking is necessary to ensure that regulations are consistent with applicable law, the President's priorities, and the principles set forth in this Executive order, and that decisions made by one agency do not conflict with the policies or actions taken or planned by another agency. The Office of Management and Budget (OMB) shall carry out that review function. Within OMB, the Office of Information and Regulatory Affairs (OIRA) is the repository of expertise concerning regulatory issues, including methodologies and procedures that affect more than one agency, this Executive order, and the President's regulatory policies. To the extent permitted by law, OMB shall provide guidance to agencies and assist the President, the Vice President, and other regulatory policy advisors to the President in regulatory planning and shall be the entity that reviews individual regulations, as provided by this Executive order.

(c) *The Vice President.* The Vice President is the principal advisor to the President on, and shall coordinate the development and presentation of recommendations concerning regulatory policy, planning, and review, as set forth in this Executive order. In fulfilling their responsibilities under this Executive order, the President and the Vice President shall be assisted by the regulatory policy advisors within the Executive Office of the President and by such agency officials and personnel as the President and the Vice President may, from time to time, consult.

Sec. 3. *Definitions.* For purposes of this Executive order:

(a) "Advisors" refers to such regulatory policy advisors to the President as the President and Vice President may from time to time consult, including, among others: (1) the Director of OMB; (2) the Chair (or another member) of the Council of Economic Advisors; (3) the Assistant to the President for Economic Policy; (4) the Assistant to the President for Domestic Policy; (5) the Assistant to the President for National Security Affairs; (6) the Assistant to the President for Science and Technology; (7) the Assistant to the President for Intergovernmental Affairs; (8) the Assistant to the President and Staff Secretary; (9) the Assistant to the President and Chief of Staff to the Vice President; (10) the Assistant to the President and Counsel to the President; (11) the Deputy Assistant to the President and Director of the White House Office on Environmental Policy; and (12) the Administrator of OIRA, who also shall coordinate communications relating to this Executive order among the agencies, OMB, the other Advisors, and the Office of the Vice President.

(b) "Agency," unless otherwise indicated, means any authority of the United States that is an "agency" under 44 U.S.C. 3502(1), other than those considered to be independent regulatory agencies, as defined in 44 U.S.C. 3502(10).

(c) "Director" means the Director of OMB.

(d) "Regulation" or "rule" means an agency statement of general applicability and future effect, which the agency intends to have the force and effect of law, that is designed to implement, interpret, or prescribe law or policy or to describe the procedure or practice requirements of an agency. It does not, however, include:

(1) Regulations or rules issued in accordance with the formal rulemaking provisions of 5 U.S.C. 556, 557;

(2) Regulations or rules that pertain to a military or foreign affairs function of the United States, other than procurement regulations and regulations involving the import or export of non-defense articles and services;

(3) Regulations or rules that are limited to agency organization, management, or personnel matters; or

(4) Any other category of regulations exempted by the Administrator of OIRA.

(e) "Regulatory action" means any substantive action by an agency (normally published in the *Federal Register*) that promulgates or is expected to lead to the promulgation of a final rule or regulation, including notices of inquiry, advance notices of proposed rulemaking, and notices of proposed rulemaking.

(f) "Significant regulatory action" means any regulatory action that is likely to result in a rule that may:

(1) Have an annual effect on the economy of $100 million or more or adversely affect in a material way the economy, a sector of the economy, productivity, competition, jobs, the environment, public health or safety, or State, local, or tribal governments or communities;

(2) Create a serious inconsistency or otherwise interfere with an action taken or planned by another agency;

(3) Materially alter the budgetary impact of entitlements, grants, user fees, or loan programs or the rights and obligations of recipients thereof; or

(4) Raise novel legal or policy issues arising out of legal mandates, the President's priorities, or the principles set forth in this Executive order.

Sec. 4. *Planning Mechanism.* In order to have an effective regulatory program, to provide for coordination of regulations, to maximize consultation and the resolution of potential conflicts at an early stage, to involve the public and its State, local, and tribal officials in regulatory planning, and to ensure that new or revised regulations promote the President's priorities and the principles set forth in this Executive order, these procedures shall be followed, to the extent permitted by law:

(a) *Agencies' Policy Meeting.* Early in each year's planning cycle, the Vice President shall convene a meeting of the Advisors and the heads of agencies to seek a common understanding of priorities and to coordinate regulatory efforts to be accomplished in the upcoming year.

(b) *Unified Regulatory Agenda.* For purposes of this subsection, the term "agency" or "agencies" shall also include those considered to be independent regulatory agencies, as defined in 44 U.S.C. 3502(10). Each agency shall prepare an agenda of all regulations under development or review, at a time and in a manner specified by the Administrator of OIRA. The description of each regulatory action shall contain, at a minimum, a regulation identifier number, a brief summary of the action, the legal authority for the action, any legal deadline for the action, and the name and telephone number of a knowledgeable agency official. Agencies may incorporate the information required under 5 U.S.C. 602 and 41 U.S.C. 402 into these agendas.

(c) *The Regulatory Plan.* For purposes of this subsection, the term "agency" or "agencies" shall also include those considered to be independent regulatory agencies, as defined in 44 U.S.C. 3502(10).

(1) As part of the Unified Regulatory Agenda, beginning in 1994, each agency shall prepare a Regulatory Plan (Plan) of the most important significant regulatory actions that the agency reasonably expects to issue in proposed or final form in that fiscal year or thereafter. The Plan shall be approved personally by the agency head and shall contain at a minimum:

(A) A statement of the agency's regulatory objectives and priorities and how they relate to the President's priorities;

(B) A summary of each planned significant regulatory action including, to the extent possible, alternatives to be considered and preliminary estimates of the anticipated costs and benefits;

(C) A summary of the legal basis for each such action, including whether any aspect of the action is required by statute or court order;

(D) A statement of the need for each such action and, if applicable, how the action will reduce risks to public health, safety, or the environment, as well as how the magnitude of the risk addressed by the action relates to other risks within the jurisdiction of the agency;

(E) The agency's schedule for action, including a statement of any applicable statutory or judicial deadlines; and

(F) The name, address, and telephone number of a person the public may contact for additional information about the planned regulatory action.

(2) Each agency shall forward its Plan to OIRA by June 1st of each year.

(3) Within 10 calendar days after OIRA has received an agency's Plan, OIRA shall circulate it to other affected agencies, the Advisors, and the Vice President.

(4) An agency head who believes that a planned regulatory action of another agency may conflict with its own policy or action taken or planned shall promptly notify, in writing, the Administrator of OIRA, who shall forward that communication to the issuing agency, the Advisors, and the Vice President.

(5) If the Administrator of OIRA believes that a planned regulatory action of an agency may be inconsistent with the President's priorities or the principles set forth in this Executive order or may be in conflict with any policy or action taken or planned by another agency, the Administrator of OIRA shall promptly notify, in writing, the affected agencies, the Advisors, and the Vice President.

(6) The Vice President, with the Advisors' assistance, may consult with the heads of agencies with respect to their Plans and, in appropriate instances, request further consideration or inter-agency coordination.

(7) The Plans developed by the issuing agency shall be published annually in the October publication of the Unified Regulatory Agenda. This publication shall be made available to the Congress; State, local, and tribal governments; and the public. Any views on any aspect of any agency Plan, including whether any planned regulatory action might conflict with any other planned or existing regulation, impose any unintended consequences on the public, or confer any unclaimed benefits on the public, should be directed to the issuing agency, with a copy to OIRA.

(d) *Regulatory Working Group.* Within 30 days of the date of this Executive order, the Administrator of OIRA shall convene a Regulatory Working Group ("Working Group"), which shall consist of representatives of the heads of each agency that the Administrator determines to have significant domestic regulatory responsibility, the Advisors, and the Vice President. The Administrator of OIRA shall chair the Working Group and shall periodically advise the Vice President on the activities of the Working Group. The Working Group shall serve as a forum to assist agencies in identifying and analyzing important regulatory issues (including, among others (1) the development of innovative regulatory techniques, (2) the methods, efficacy, and utility of comparative risk assessment in regulatory decision-making, and (3) the development of short forms and other streamlined regulatory approaches for small businesses and other entities). The Working Group shall meet at least quarterly and may meet as a whole or in subgroups of agencies with an interest in particular issues or subject areas. To inform its discussions, the Working Group may commission analytical studies and reports by OIRA, the Administrative Conference of the United States, or any other agency.

(e) *Conferences.* The Administrator of OIRA shall meet quarterly with representatives of State, local, and tribal governments to identify both existing and proposed regulations that may uniquely or significantly affect those governmental entities. The Administrator of OIRA shall also convene, from time to time, conferences with representatives of businesses, nongovernmental organizations, and the public to discuss regulatory issues of common concern.

Sec. 5. *Existing Regulations.* In order to reduce the regulatory burden on the American people, their families, their communities, their State, local, and tribal governments, and their industries; to determine whether regulations promulgated by the executive branch of the Federal Government have become unjustified or unnecessary as a result of changed circumstances; to confirm that regulations are both compatible with each other and not duplicative or inappropriately burdensome in the aggregate; to ensure that all regulations are consistent with the President's priorities and the principles set forth in this Executive order, within applicable law; and to otherwise improve the effectiveness of existing regulations:

(a) Within 90 days of the date of this Executive order, each agency shall submit to OIRA a program, consistent with its resources and regulatory priorities, under which the agency will periodically review its existing significant regulations to determine whether any such regulations should be modified or eliminated so as to make the agency's regulatory program more effective in achieving the regulatory objectives, less burdensome, or in greater alignment with the President's priorities and the principles set forth in this Executive order. Any significant regulations selected for review shall be included in the agency's annual Plan. The agency shall also identify any legislative mandates that require the agency to promulgate or continue to impose regulations that the agency believes are unnecessary or outdated by reason of changed circumstances.

(b) The Administrator of OIRA shall work with the Regulatory Working Group and other interested entities to pursue the objectives of this section. State, local, and tribal governments are specifically encouraged to assist in the identification of regulations that impose significant or unique burdens on those governmental entities and that appear to have outlived their justification or be otherwise inconsistent with the public interest.

(c) The Vice President, in consultation with the Advisors, may identify for review by the appropriate agency or agencies other existing regulations of an agency or groups of regulations of more than one agency that affect a particular group, industry, or sector of the economy, or may identify legislative mandates that may be appropriate for reconsideration by the Congress.

Sec. 6. *Centralized Review of Regulations.* The guidelines set forth below shall apply to all regulatory actions, for both new and existing regulations, by agencies other than those agencies specifically exempted by the Administrator of OIRA:

(a) Agency Responsibilities.

(1) Each agency shall (consistent with its own rules, regulations, or procedures) provide the public with meaningful participation in the regulatory process. In particular, before issuing a notice of proposed rulemaking, each agency should, where appropriate, seek the involvement of those who are intended to benefit from and those expected to be burdened by any regulation (including, specifically, State, local, and tribal officials). In addition, each agency should afford the public a meaningful opportunity to comment on any proposed regulation, which in most cases should include a comment period of not less than 60 days. Each agency also is directed to explore and, where appropriate, use consensual mechanisms for developing regulations, including negotiated rulemaking.

(2) Within 60 days of the date of this Executive order, each agency head shall designate a Regulatory Policy Officer who shall report to the agency head. The Regulatory Policy Officer shall be involved at each stage of the regulatory process to foster the development of effective, innovative, and least burdensome regulations and to further the principles set forth in this Executive order.

(3) In addition to adhering to its own rules and procedures and to the requirements of the Administrative Procedure Act, the Regulatory Flexibility Act, the Paperwork Reduction Act, and other applicable law, each agency shall develop its regulatory actions in a timely fashion and adhere to the following procedures with respect to a regulatory action:

(A) Each agency shall provide OIRA, at such times and in the manner specified by the Administrator of OIRA, with a list of its planned regulatory actions, indicating those which the agency believes are significant regulatory actions within the meaning of this Executive order. Absent a material change in the development of the planned regulatory action, those not designated as significant will not be subject to review under this section unless, within 10 working days of receipt of the list, the Administrator of OIRA notifies the agency that OIRA has determined that a planned regulation is a significant regulatory action within the meaning of this Executive order. The Administrator of OIRA may waive review of any planned regulatory action designated by the agency as significant, in which case the agency need not further comply with subsection (a)(3)(B) or subsection (a)(3)(C) of this section.

(B) For each matter identified as, or determined by the Administrator of OIRA to be, a significant regulatory action, the issuing agency shall provide to OIRA:

(i) The text of the draft regulatory action, together with a reasonably detailed description of the need for the regulatory action and an explanation of how the regulatory action will meet that need; and

(ii) An assessment of the potential costs and benefits of the regulatory action, including an explanation of the manner in which the regulatory action is consistent with a statutory mandate and, to the extent permitted by law, promotes the President's priorities and avoids undue interference with State, local, and tribal governments in the exercise of their governmental functions.

(C) For those matters identified as, or determined by the Administrator of OIRA to be, a significant regulatory action within the scope of section 3(f)(1), the agency shall also provide to OIRA the following additional information developed as part of the agency's decision-making process (unless prohibited by law):

(i) An assessment, including the underlying analysis, of benefits anticipated from the regulatory action (such as, but not limited to, the promotion of the efficient functioning of the economy and private markets, the enhancement of health and safety, the protection of the natural environment, and the elimination or reduction of discrimination or bias) together with, to the extent feasible, a quantification of those benefits;

(ii) An assessment, including the underlying analysis, of costs anticipated from the regulatory action (such as, but not limited to, the direct cost both to the government in administering the regulation and to businesses and others in complying with the regulation, and any adverse effects on the efficient functioning of the economy, private markets (including productivity, employment, and competitiveness), health, safety, and the natural environment), together with, to the extent feasible, a quantification of those costs; and

(iii) An assessment, including the underlying analysis, of costs and benefits of potentially effective and reasonably feasible alternatives to the planned regulation, identified by the agencies or the public (including improving the current regulation and reasonably viable non-regulatory actions), and an explanation why the planned regulatory action is preferable to the identified potential alternatives.

(D) In emergency situations or when an agency is obligated by law to act more quickly than normal review procedures allow, the agency shall notify OIRA as soon as possible and, to the extent practicable, comply with subsections (a)(3)(B) and (C) of this section. For those regulatory actions that are governed by a statutory or court-imposed deadline, the agency shall, to the extent practicable, schedule rulemaking proceedings so

as to permit sufficient time for OIRA to conduct its review, as set forth below in subsection (b)(2) through (4) of this section.

(E) After the regulatory action has been published in the *Federal Register* or otherwise issued to the public, the agency shall:

(i) Make available to the public the information set forth in subsections (a)(3)(B) and (C);

(ii) Identify for the public, in a complete, clear, and simple manner, the substantive changes between the draft submitted to OIRA for review and the action subsequently announced; and

(iii) Identify for the public those changes in the regulatory action that were made at the suggestion or recommendation of OIRA.

(F) All information provided to the public by the agency shall be in plain, understandable language.

(b) *OIRA Responsibilities.* The Administrator of OIRA shall provide meaningful guidance and oversight so that each agency's regulatory actions are consistent with applicable law, the President's priorities, and the principles set forth in this Executive order and do not conflict with the policies or actions of another agency. OIRA shall, to the extent permitted by law, adhere to the following guidelines:

(1) OIRA may review only actions identified by the agency or by OIRA as significant regulatory actions under subsection (a)(3)(A) of this section.

(2) OIRA shall waive review or notify the agency in writing of the results of its review within the following time periods:

(A) For any notices of inquiry, advance notices of proposed rulemaking, or other preliminary regulatory actions prior to a Notice of Proposed Rulemaking, within 10 working days after the date of submission of the draft action to OIRA;

(B) For all other regulatory actions, within 90 calendar days after the date of submission of the information set forth in subsections (a)(3)(B) and (C) of this section, unless OIRA has previously reviewed this information and, since that review, there has been no material change in the facts and circumstances upon which the regulatory action is based, in which case, OIRA shall complete its review within 45 days; and

(C) The review process may be extended (1) once by no more than 30 calendar days upon the written approval of the Director and (2) at the request of the agency head.

(3) For each regulatory action that the Administrator of OIRA returns to an agency for further consideration of some or all of its provisions, the Administrator of OIRA shall provide the issuing agency a written explanation for such return, setting forth the pertinent provision of this Executive order on which OIRA is relying. If the agency head disagrees with some or all of the bases for the return, the agency head shall so inform the Administrator of OIRA in writing.

(4) Except as otherwise provided by law or required by a Court, in order to ensure greater openness, accessibility, and accountability in the regulatory review process, OIRA shall be governed by the following disclosure requirements:

(A) Only the Administrator of OIRA (or a particular designee) shall receive oral communications initiated by persons not employed by the executive branch of the Federal Government regarding the substance of a regulatory action under OIRA review;

(B) All substantive communications between OIRA personnel and persons not employed by the executive branch of the Federal Government regarding a regulatory action under review shall be governed by the following guidelines:

(i) A representative from the issuing agency shall be invited to any meeting between OIRA personnel and such person(s);

(ii) OIRA shall forward to the issuing agency, within 10 working days of receipt of the communication(s), all written communications, regardless of format, between OIRA personnel and any person who is not employed by the executive branch of the Federal Government, and the dates and names of individuals involved in all substantive oral communications (including meetings to which an agency representative was invited, but did not attend, and telephone conversations between OIRA personnel and any such persons); and

(iii) OIRA shall publicly disclose relevant information about such communication(s), as set forth below in subsection (b)(4)(C) of this section.

(C) OIRA shall maintain a publicly available log that shall contain, at a minimum, the following information pertinent to regulatory actions under review:

(i) The status of all regulatory actions, including if (and if so, when and by whom) Vice Presidential and Presidential consideration was requested;

(ii) A notation of all written communications forwarded to an issuing agency under subsection (b)(4)(B)(ii) of this section; and

(iii) The dates and names of individuals involved in all substantive oral communications, including meetings and telephone conversations, between OIRA personnel and any person not employed by the executive branch of the Federal Government, and the subject matter discussed during such communications.

(D) After the regulatory action has been published in the *Federal Register* or otherwise issued to the public, or after the agency has announced its decision not to publish or issue the regulatory action, OIRA shall make available to the public all documents exchanged between OIRA and the agency during the review by OIRA under this section.

(5) All information provided to the public by OIRA shall be in plain, understandable language.

Sec. 7. *Resolution of Conflicts.* To the extent permitted by law, disagreements or conflicts between or among agency heads or between OMB and any agency that cannot be resolved by the Administrator of OIRA shall be resolved by the President, or by the Vice President acting at the request of the President, with the relevant agency head (and, as appropriate, other interested government officials). Vice Presidential and Presidential consideration of such disagreements may be initiated only by the Director, by the head of the issuing agency, or by the head of an agency that has a significant interest in the regulatory action at issue. Such review will not be undertaken at the request of other persons, entities, or their agents.

Resolution of such conflicts shall be informed by recommendations developed by the Vice President, after consultation with the Advisors (and other executive branch officials or personnel whose responsibilities to the President include the subject matter at issue). The development of these recommendations shall be concluded within 60 days after review has been requested.

During the Vice Presidential and Presidential review period, communications with any person not employed by the Federal Government relating to the substance of the regulatory action under review and directed to the Advisors or their staffs or to the staff of the Vice President shall be in writing and shall be forwarded by the recipient to the affected agency(ies) for inclusion in the public docket(s). When the communication is not in writing, such Advisors or staff members shall inform the outside party that the matter is under review and that any comments should be submitted in writing.

At the end of this review process, the President, or the Vice President acting at the request of the President, shall notify the affected agency and the Administrator of OIRA of the President's decision with respect to the matter.

Sec. 8. *Publication.* Except to the extent required by law, an agency shall not publish in the *Federal Register* or otherwise issue to the public any regulatory action that is subject to review under section 6 of this Executive order until (1) the Administrator of OIRA notifies the agency that OIRA has waived its review of the action or has completed its review without any requests for further consideration, or (2) the applicable time period in section 6(b)(2) expires without OIRA having notified the agency that it is returning the regulatory action for further consideration under section 6(b)(3), whichever occurs first. If the terms of the preceding sentence have not been satisfied and an agency wants to publish or otherwise issue a regulatory action, the head of that agency may request Presidential consideration through the Vice President, as provided under section 7 of this order. Upon receipt of this request, the Vice President shall notify OIRA and the Advisors. The guidelines and time period set forth in section 7 shall apply to the publication of regulatory actions for which Presidential consideration has been sought.

Sec. 9. *Agency Authority.* Nothing in this order shall be construed as displacing the agencies' authority or responsibilities, as authorized by law.

Sec. 10. *Judicial Review.* Nothing in this Executive order shall affect any otherwise available judicial review of agency action. This Executive order is intended only to improve the internal management of the Federal Government and does not create any right or benefit, substantive or procedural, enforceable at law or equity by a party against the United States, its agencies or instrumentalities, its officers or employees, or any other person.

Sec. 11. *Revocations.* Executive Orders Nos. 12291 and 12498; all amendments to those Executive orders; all guidelines issued under those orders; and any exemptions from those orders heretofore granted for any category of rule are revoked.

WILLIAM J. CLINTON

The White House,
September 30, 1993.

EXECUTIVE ORDER 13258
(Revoked Jan. 30, 2009)

Amending Executive Order 12866 on Regulatory Planning and Review

By the authority vested in me as President by the Constitution and the laws of the United States of America, it is hereby ordered that Executive Order 12866, of September 30, 1993, is amended as follows:

Section 1. Section (2)(b) is amended by striking "the Vice President, and other regulatory policy advisors" and inserting in lieu thereof "and regulatory policy advisors."

Sec. 2. Section (2)(c) is amended by:
(a) striking in the heading the words "The Vice President" and inserting in lieu thereof "Assistance";
(b) striking the sentence that begins "The Vice President is";
(c) striking "In fulfilling their responsibilities" and inserting in lieu thereof "In fulfilling his responsibilities"; and
(d) striking "and the Vice President" both times it appears.

Sec. 3. Section 3(a) is amended by:
(a) striking "and Vice President";
(b) striking "the Assistant to the President for Science and Technology" and inserting in lieu thereof "the Director of the Office of Science and Technology Policy";
(c) striking "the Assistant to the President for Intergovernmental Affairs" and inserting in lieu thereof "the Deputy Assistant to the President and Director for Intergovernmental Affairs";
(d) striking "the Deputy Assistant to the President and Director of the White House Office of Environmental Policy" and inserting in lieu thereof "the Chairman of the

Council on Environmental Quality and Director of the Office of Environmental Quality"; and
(e) striking "and (12)" and inserting in lieu thereof "(12) the Assistant to the President for Homeland Security; and (13)."

Sec. 4. Section 4(a) is amended by striking "the Vice President shall convene" and inserting in lieu thereof "the Director shall convene."

Sec. 5. Section 4(c)(3) is amended by striking "the Advisors, and the Vice President" and inserting in lieu thereof "and the Advisors."

Sec. 6. Section 4(c)(4) is amended by striking "the Advisors, and the Vice President" and inserting in lieu thereof "and the Advisors."

Sec. 7. Section 4(c)(5) is amended by striking "the Advisors, and the Vice President" and inserting in lieu thereof "and the Advisors."

Sec. 8. Section 4(c)(6) is amended by striking "Vice President, with the Advisors' assistance," and inserting in lieu thereof "Director."

Sec. 9. Section 4(d) is amended by:
(a) striking "the Advisors, and the Vice President" and inserting in lieu thereof "and the Advisors"; and
(b) striking "periodically advise the Vice President" and inserting in lieu thereof "periodically advise the Director."

Sec. 10. Section 5(c) is amended by striking "Vice President" and inserting in lieu thereof "Director."

Sec. 11. Section 6(b)(4)(C)(i) is amended by striking "Vice Presidential and."

Sec. 12. Section 7 is amended by:
(a) striking "resolved by the President, or by the Vice President acting at the request of the President" and inserting in lieu thereof "resolved by the President, with the assistance of the Chief of Staff to the President ("Chief of Staff ")";
(b) striking "Vice Presidential and Presidential consideration" and inserting in lieu thereof "Presidential consideration";
(c) striking "recommendations developed by the Vice President" and inserting in lieu thereof "recommendations developed by the Chief of Staff ";
(d) striking "Vice Presidential and Presidential review period" and inserting in lieu thereof "Presidential review period";
(e) striking "or to the staff of the Vice President" and inserting in lieu thereof "or to the staff of the Chief of Staff";
(f) striking "the President, or the Vice President acting at the request of the President, shall notify" and insert in lieu thereof "the President, or the Chief of Staff acting at the request of the President, shall notify."

Sec. 13. Section 7 is also amended in the first paragraph by inserting the designation "(a)" after the words "Resolution of Conflicts," and by designating the following three paragraphs as "(b)," "(c)," and "(d)" in order.

Sec. 14. Section 8 is amended by striking "Vice President" both times it appears and inserting in lieu thereof "Director."

GEORGE W. BUSH

The White House,
February 26, 2002.

■ EXECUTIVE ORDER 13392

Improving Agency Disclosure of Information

By the authority vested in me as President by the Constitution and the laws of the United States of America, and to ensure appropriate agency disclosure of information, and consistent with the goals of section 552 of title 5, United States Code, it is hereby ordered as follows:

Section 1. *Policy.*

(a) The effective functioning of our constitutional democracy depends upon the participation in public life of a citizenry that is well informed. For nearly four decades, the Freedom of Information Act (FOIA) has provided an important means through which the public can obtain information regarding the activities of Federal agencies. Under the FOIA, the public can obtain records from any Federal agency, subject to the exemptions enacted by the Congress to protect information that must be held in confidence for the Government to function effectively or for other purposes.

(b) FOIA requesters are seeking a service from the Federal Government and should be treated as such. Accordingly, in responding to a FOIA request, agencies shall respond courteously and appropriately. Moreover, agencies shall provide FOIA requesters, and the public in general, with citizen centered ways to learn about the FOIA process, about agency records that are publicly available (e.g., on the agency's website), and about the status of a person's FOIA request and appropriate information about the agency's response.

(c) Agency FOIA operations shall be both results-oriented and produce results. Accordingly, agencies shall process requests under the FOIA in an efficient and appropriate manner and achieve tangible, measurable improvements in FOIA processing. When an agency's FOIA program does not produce such results, it should be reformed, consistent with available resources appropriated by the Congress and applicable law, to increase efficiency and better reflect the policy goals and objectives of this order.

(d) A citizen-centered and results-oriented approach will improve service and performance, thereby strengthening compliance with the FOIA, and will help avoid disputes and related litigation.

Sec. 2. *Agency Chief FOIA Officers.*

(a) *Designation.* The head of each agency shall designate within 30 days of the date of this order a senior official of such agency (at the Assistant Secretary or equivalent level), to serve as the Chief FOIA Officer of that agency. The head of the agency shall promptly notify the Director of the Office of Management and Budget (OMB Director) and the Attorney General of such designation and of any changes thereafter in such designation.

(b) *General Duties.* The Chief FOIA Officer of each agency shall, subject to the authority of the head of the agency:

(i) have agency-wide responsibility for efficient and appropriate compliance with the FOIA;

(ii) monitor FOIA implementation throughout the agency, including through the use of meetings with the public to the extent deemed appropriate by the agency's Chief FOIA Officer, and keep the head of the agency, the chief legal officer of the agency, and the Attorney General appropriately informed of the agency's performance in implementing the FOIA, including the extent to which the agency meets the milestones in the agency's plan under section 3(b) of this order and training and reporting standards established consistent with applicable law and this order;

(iii) recommend to the head of the agency such adjustments to agency practices, policies, personnel, and funding as may be necessary to carry out the policy set forth in section 1 of this order;

(iv) review and report, through the head of the agency, at such times and in such formats as the Attorney General may direct, on the agency's performance in implementing the FOIA; and

(v) facilitate public understanding of the purposes of the FOIA's statutory exemptions by including concise descriptions of the exemptions in both the agency's FOIA handbook issued under section 552(g) of title 5, United States Code, and the agency's annual FOIA report, and by providing an overview, where appropriate, of certain general categories of agency records to which those exemptions apply.

(c) *FOIA Requester Service Center and FOIA Public Liaisons.* In order to ensure appropriate communication with FOIA requesters:

(i) Each agency shall establish one or more FOIA Requester Service Centers (Center), as appropriate, which shall serve as the first place that a FOIA requester can contact to seek information concerning the status of the person's FOIA request and appropriate information about the agency's FOIA response. The Center shall include appropriate staff to receive and respond to inquiries from FOIA requesters;

(ii) The agency Chief FOIA Officer shall designate one or more agency officials, as appropriate, as FOIA Public Liaisons, who may serve in the Center or who may serve in a separate office. FOIA Public Liaisons shall serve as supervisory officials to whom a FOIA requester can raise concerns about the service the FOIA requester has received from the Center, following an initial response from the Center staff. FOIA Public Liaisons shall seek to ensure a service-oriented response to FOIA requests and FOIA-related inquiries. For example, the FOIA Public Liaison shall assist, as appropriate, in reducing delays, increasing transparency and understanding of the status of requests, and resolving disputes. FOIA Public Liaisons shall report to the agency Chief FOIA Officer on their activities and shall perform their duties consistent with applicable law and agency regulations;

(iii) In addition to the services to FOIA requesters provided by the Center and FOIA Public Liaisons, the agency Chief FOIA Officer shall also consider what other FOIA-related assistance to the public should appropriately be provided by the agency;

(iv) In establishing the Centers and designating FOIA Public Liaisons, the agency shall use, as appropriate, existing agency staff and resources. A Center shall have appropriate staff to receive and respond to inquiries from FOIA requesters;

(v) As determined by the agency Chief FOIA Officer, in consultation with the FOIA Public Liaisons, each agency shall post appropriate information about its Center or Centers on the agency's website, including contact information for its FOIA Public Liaisons. In the case of an agency without a website, the agency shall publish the information on the Firstgov.gov website or, in the case of any agency with neither a website nor the capability to post on the Firstgov.gov website, in the *Federal Register;* and

(vi) The agency Chief FOIA Officer shall ensure that the agency has in place a method (or methods), including through the use of the Center, to receive and respond promptly and appropriately to inquiries from FOIA requesters about the status of their requests. The Chief FOIA Officer shall also consider, in consultation with the FOIA Public Liaisons, as appropriate, whether the agency's implementation of other means (such as tracking numbers for requests, or an agency telephone or Internet hotline) would be appropriate for responding to status inquiries.

Sec. 3. *Review, Plan, and Report.*

(a) *Review.* Each agency's Chief FOIA Officer shall conduct a review of the agency's FOIA operations to determine whether agency practices are consistent with the policies set forth in section 1 of this order. In conducting this review, the Chief FOIA Officer shall:

(i) evaluate, with reference to numerical and statistical benchmarks where appropriate, the agency's administration of the FOIA, including the agency's expenditure of resources on FOIA compliance and the extent to which, if any, requests for records have not been responded to within the statutory time limit (backlog);

(ii) review the processes and practices by which the agency assists and informs the public regarding the FOIA process;

(iii) examine the agency's:

(A) use of information technology in responding to FOIA requests, including without limitation the tracking of FOIA requests and communication with requesters;

(B) practices with respect to requests for expedited processing; and

(C) implementation of multi-track processing if used by such agency;

(iv) review the agency's policies and practices relating to the availability of public information through websites and other means, including the use of websites to make available the records described in section 552(a)(2) of title 5, United States Code; and

(v) identify ways to eliminate or reduce its FOIA backlog, consistent with available resources and taking into consideration the volume and complexity of the FOIA requests pending with the agency.

(b) *Plan.*

(i) Each agency's Chief FOIA Officer shall develop, in consultation as appropriate with the staff of the agency (including the FOIA Public Liaisons), the Attorney General, and the OMB Director, an agency-specific plan to ensure that the agency's administration of the FOIA is in accordance with applicable law and the policies set forth in section 1 of this order. The plan, which shall be submitted to the head of the agency for approval, shall address the agency's implementation of the FOIA during fiscal years 2006 and 2007.

(ii) The plan shall include specific activities that the agency will implement to eliminate or reduce the agency's FOIA backlog, including (as applicable) changes that will make the processing of FOIA requests more streamlined and effective, as well as increased reliance on the dissemination of records that can be made available to the public through a website or other means that do not require the public to make a request for the records under the FOIA.

(iii) The plan shall also include activities to increase public awareness of FOIA processing, including as appropriate, expanded use of the agency's Center and its FOIA Public Liaisons.

(iv) The plan shall also include, taking appropriate account of the resources available to the agency and the mission of the agency, concrete milestones, with specific timetables and outcomes to be achieved, by which the head of the agency, after consultation with the OMB Director, shall measure and evaluate the agency's success in the implementation of the plan.

(c) Agency Reports to the Attorney General and OMB Director.

(i) The head of each agency shall submit a report, no later than 6 months from the date of this order, to the Attorney General and the OMB Director that summarizes the results of the review under section 3(a) of this order and encloses a copy of the agency's plan under section 3(b) of this order. The agency shall publish a copy of the agency's report on the agency's website or, in the case of an agency without a website, on the Firstgov.gov website, or, in the case of any agency with neither a website nor the capability to publish on the Firstgov.gov website, in the *Federal Register*.

(ii) The head of each agency shall include in the agency's annual FOIA reports for fiscal years 2006 and 2007 a report on the agency's development and implementation of its plan under section 3(b) of this order and on the agency's performance in meeting the milestones set forth in that plan, consistent with any related guidelines the Attorney General may issue under section 552(e) of title 5, United States Code.

(iii) If the agency does not meet a milestone in its plan, the head of the agency shall:

(A) identify this deficiency in the annual FOIA report to the Attorney General;

(B) explain in the annual report the reasons for the agency's failure to meet the milestone;

(C) outline in the annual report the steps that the agency has already taken, and will be taking, to address the deficiency; and

(D) report this deficiency to the President's Management Council.

Sec. 4. *Attorney General.*

(a) *Report.* The Attorney General, using the reports submitted by the agencies under subsection 3(c)(i) of this order and the information submitted by agencies in their annual FOIA reports for fiscal year 2005, shall submit to the President, no later than 10 months from the date of this order, a report on agency FOIA implementation. The Attorney General shall consult the OMB Director in the preparation of the report and shall include in the report appropriate recommendations on administrative or other agency actions for continued agency dissemination and release of public information. The Attorney General shall thereafter submit two further annual reports, by June 1, 2007, and June 1, 2008, that provide the President with an update on the agencies' implementation of the FOIA and of their plans under section 3(b) of this order.

(b) *Guidance.* The Attorney General shall issue such instructions and guidance to the heads of departments and agencies as may be appropriate to implement sections 3(b) and 3(c) of this order.

Sec. 5. *OMB Director.* The OMB Director may issue such instructions to the heads of agencies as are necessary to implement this order, other than sections 3(b) and 3(c) of this order.

Sec. 6. *Definitions.* As used in this order:

(a) the term "agency" has the same meaning as the term "agency" under section 552(f)(1) of title 5, United States Code; and

(b) the term "record" has the same meaning as the term "record" under section 552(f)(2) of title 5, United States Code.

Sec. 7. *General Provisions.*

(a) The agency reviews under section 3(a) of this order and agency plans under section 3(b) of this order shall be conducted and developed in accordance with applicable law and applicable guidance issued by the President, the Attorney General, and the OMB Director, including the laws and guidance regarding information technology and the dissemination of information.

(b) This order:

(i) shall be implemented in a manner consistent with applicable law and subject to the availability of appropriations;

(ii) shall not be construed to impair or otherwise affect the functions of the OMB Director relating to budget, legislative, or administrative proposals; and

(iii) is intended only to improve the internal management of the executive branch and is not intended to, and does not, create any right or benefit, substantive or procedural, enforceable at law or in equity by a party against the United States, its departments, agencies, instrumentalities, or entities, its officers or employees, or any other person.

GEORGE W. BUSH

The White House,
December 14, 2005.

EXECUTIVE ORDER 13422
(Revoked Jan. 30, 2009)

Further Amendment to Executive Order 12866 on Regulatory Planning and Review

By the authority vested in me as President by the Constitution and laws of the United States of America, it is hereby ordered that Executive Order 12866 of September 30, 1993, as amended, is further amended as follows:

Section 1. Section 1 is amended as follows:

(a) Section 1(b)(1) is amended to read as follows:

"(1) Each agency shall identify in writing the specific market failure (such as externalities, market power, lack of information) or other specific problem that it intends to address (including, where applicable, the failures of public institutions) that warrant new agency action, as well as assess the significance of that problem, to enable assessment of whether any new regulation is warranted."

(b) by inserting in section 1(b)(7) after "regulation" the words "or guidance document."

(c) by inserting in section 1(b)(10) in both places after "regulations" the words "and guidance documents."

(d) by inserting in section 1(b)(11) after "its regulations" the words "and guidance documents."

(e) by inserting in section 1(b)(12) after "regulations" the words "and guidance documents."

Sec. 2. Section 2 is amended as follows:

(a) by inserting in section 2(a) in both places after "regulations" the words "and guidance documents."

(b) by inserting in section 2(b) in both places after "regulations" the words "and guidance documents."

Sec. 3. Section 3 is amended as follows:

(a) by striking in section 3(d) "rule" after "Regulation";

(b) by striking in section 3(d)(1) "or rules" after "Regulations";

(c) by striking in section 3(d)(2) "or rules" after "Regulations";

(d) by striking in section 3(d)(3) "or rules" after "Regulations";

(e) by striking in section 3(e) "rule or" from "final rule or regulation";

(f) by striking in section 3(f) "rule or" from "rule or regulation";

(g) by inserting after section 3(f) the following:

"(g) "Guidance document" means an agency statement of general applicability and future effect, other than a regulatory action, that sets forth a policy on a statutory, regulatory, or technical issue or an interpretation of a statutory or regulatory issue."

(h) "Significant guidance document"—

(1) Means a guidance document disseminated to regulated entities or the general public that, for purposes of this order, may reasonably be anticipated to:

(A) Lead to an annual effect of $100 million or more or adversely affect in a material way the economy, a sector of the economy, productivity, competition, jobs, the environment, public health or safety, or State, local, or tribal governments or communities;

(B) Create a serious inconsistency or otherwise interfere with an action taken or planned by another agency;

(C) Materially alter the budgetary impact of entitlements, grants, user fees, or loan programs or the rights or obligations of recipients thereof; or

(D) Raise novel legal or policy issues arising out of legal mandates, the President's priorities, or the principles set forth in this Executive order; and

(2) Does not include:

(A) Guidance documents on regulations issued in accordance with the formal rulemaking provisions of 5 U.S.C. 556, 557;

(B) Guidance documents that pertain to a military or foreign affairs function of the United States, other than procurement regulations and regulations involving the import or export of non-defense articles and services;

(C) Guidance documents on regulations that are limited to agency organization, management, or personnel matters; or

(D) Any other category of guidance documents exempted by the Administrator of OIRA.

Sec. 4. Section 4 is amended as follows:

(a) Section 4(a) is amended to read as follows: "The Director may convene a meeting of agency heads and other government personnel as appropriate to seek a common

understanding of priorities and to coordinate regulatory efforts to be accomplished in the upcoming year."

(b) The last sentence of section 4(c)(1) is amended to read as follows: "Unless specifically authorized by the head of the agency, no rulemaking shall commence nor be included on the Plan without the approval of the agency's Regulatory Policy Office, and the Plan shall contain at a minimum::"

(c) Section 4(c)(1)(B) is amended by inserting "of each rule as well as the agency's best estimate of the combined aggregate costs and benefits of all its regulations planned for that calendar year to assist with the identification of priorities" after "of the anticipated costs and benefits."

(d) Section 4(c)(1)(C) is amended by inserting "and specific citation to such statute, order, or other legal authority" after "court order."

Sec. 5. Section 6 is amended as follows:

(a) by inserting in section 6(a)(1) "In consultation with OIRA, each agency may also consider whether to utilize formal rulemaking procedures under 5 U.S.C. 556 and 557 for the resolution of complex determinations" after "comment period of not less than 60 days."

(b) by amending the first sentence of section 6(a)(2) to read as follows: "Within 60 days of the date of this Executive order, each agency head shall designate one of the agency's Presidential Appointees to be its Regulatory Policy Officer, advise OMB of such designation, and annually update OMB on the status of this designation."

Sec. 6. Sections 9–11 are redesignated respectively as sections 10–12.

Sec. 7. After section 8, a new section 9 is inserted as follows:

"Sec. 9. *Significant Guidance Documents.* Each agency shall provide OIRA, at such times and in the manner specified by the Administrator of OIRA, with advance notification of any significant guidance documents. Each agency shall take such steps as are necessary for its Regulatory Policy Officer to ensure the agency's compliance with the requirements of this section. Upon the request of the Administrator, for each matter identified as, or determined by the Administrator to be, a significant guidance document, the issuing agency shall provide to OIRA the content of the draft guidance document, together with a brief explanation of the need for the guidance document and how it will meet that need. The OIRA Administrator shall notify the agency when additional consultation will be required before the issuance of the significant guidance document."

Sec. 8. Newly designated section 10 is amended to read as follows:

"Sec. 10. *Preservation of Agency Authority.* Nothing in this order shall be construed to impair or otherwise affect the authority vested by law in an agency or the head thereof, including the authority of the Attorney General relating to litigation."

GEORGE W. BUSH

The White House,
January 18, 2007.

▣ EXECUTIVE ORDER 13497

Revocation of Certain Executive Orders Concerning Regulatory Planning and Review

By the authority vested in me as President by the Constitution and the laws of the United States of America, it is hereby ordered that:

Section 1. Executive Order 13258 of February 26, 2002, and Executive Order 13422 of January 18, 2007, concerning regulatory planning and review, which amended Executive Order 12866 of September 30, 1993, are revoked.

Sec. 2. The Director of the Office of Management and Budget and the heads of executive departments and agencies shall promptly rescind any orders, rules, regulations, guidelines, or policies implementing or enforcing Executive Order 13258 or Executive Order 13422, to the extent consistent with law.

Sec. 3. This order is not intended to, and does not, create any right or benefit, substantive or procedural, enforceable at law or in equity by any party against the United States, its departments, agencies, or entities, its officers, employees, or agents, or any other person.

BARACK OBAMA

The White House,
January 30, 2009.

▣ EXECUTIVE ORDER 13563

Improving Regulations and Regulatory Review

By the authority vested in me as President by the Constitution and the laws of the United States of America, and in order to improve regulation and regulatory review, it is hereby ordered as follows:

Section 1. General Principles of Regulation.

(a) Our regulatory system must protect public health, welfare, safety, and our environment while promoting economic growth, innovation, competitiveness, and job creation. It must be based on the best available science. It must allow for public participation and an open exchange of ideas. It must promote predictability and reduce uncertainty. It must identify and use the best, most innovative, and least burdensome tools for achieving regulatory ends. It must take into account benefits and costs, both quantitative

and qualitative. It must ensure that regulations are accessible, consistent, written in plain language, and easy to understand. It must measure, and seek to improve, the actual results of regulatory requirements.

(b) This order is supplemental to and reaffirms the principles, structures, and definitions governing contemporary regulatory review that were established in Executive Order 12866 of September 30, 1993. As stated in that Executive Order and to the extent permitted by law, each agency must, among other things: (1) propose or adopt a regulation only upon a reasoned determination that its benefits justify its costs (recognizing that some benefits and costs are difficult to quantify); (2) tailor its regulations to impose the least burden on society, consistent with obtaining regulatory objectives, taking into account, among other things, and to the extent practicable, the costs of cumulative regulations; (3) select, in choosing among alternative regulatory approaches, those approaches that maximize net benefits (including potential economic, environmental, public health and safety, and other advantages; distributive impacts; and equity); (4) to the extent feasible, specify performance objectives, rather than specifying the behavior or manner of compliance that regulated entities must adopt; and (5) identify and assess available alternatives to direct regulation, including providing economic incentives to encourage the desired behavior, such as user fees or marketable permits, or providing information upon which choices can be made by the public.

(c) In applying these principles, each agency is directed to use the best available techniques to quantify anticipated present and future benefits and costs as accurately as possible. Where appropriate and permitted by law, each agency may consider (and discuss qualitatively) values that are difficult or impossible to quantify, including equity, human dignity, fairness, and distributive impacts.

Sec. 2. *Public Participation.*

(a) Regulations shall be adopted through a process that involves public participation. To that end, regulations shall be based, to the extent feasible and consistent with law, on the open exchange of information and perspectives among State, local, and tribal officials, experts in relevant disciplines, affected stakeholders in the private sector, and the public as a whole.

(b) To promote that open exchange, each agency, consistent with Executive Order 12866 and other applicable legal requirements, shall endeavor to provide the public with an opportunity to participate in the regulatory process. To the extent feasible and permitted by law, each agency shall afford the public a meaningful opportunity to comment through the Internet on any proposed regulation, with a comment period that should generally be at least 60 days. To the extent feasible and permitted by law, each agency shall also provide, for both proposed and final rules, timely online access to the rulemaking docket on regulations.gov, including relevant scientific and technical findings, in an open format that can be easily searched and downloaded. For proposed rules, such access shall include, to the extent feasible and permitted by law, an opportunity for public comment on all pertinent parts of the rulemaking docket, including relevant scientific and technical findings.

(c) Before issuing a notice of proposed rulemaking, each agency, where feasible and appropriate, shall seek the views of those who are likely to be affected, including those who are likely to benefit from and those who are potentially subject to such rulemaking.

Sec. 3. *Integration and Innovation.* Some sectors and industries face a significant number of regulatory requirements, some of which may be redundant, inconsistent, or overlapping. Greater coordination across agencies could reduce these requirements, thus reducing costs and simplifying and harmonizing rules. In developing regulatory actions and identifying appropriate approaches, each agency shall attempt to promote such coordination, simplification, and harmonization. Each agency shall also seek to identify, as appropriate, means to achieve regulatory goals that are designed to promote innovation.

Sec. 4. *Flexible Approaches.* Where relevant, feasible, and consistent with regulatory objectives, and to the extent permitted by law, each agency shall identify and consider regulatory approaches that reduce burdens and maintain flexibility and freedom of choice for the public. These approaches include warnings, appropriate default rules, and disclosure requirements as well as provision of information to the public in a form that is clear and intelligible.

Sec. 5. *Science.* Consistent with the President's Memorandum for the Heads of Executive Departments and Agencies, "Scientific Integrity" (March 9, 2009), and its implementing guidance, each agency shall ensure the objectivity of any scientific and technological information and processes used to support the agency's regulatory actions.

Sec. 6. *Retrospective Analyses of Existing Rules.*

(a) To facilitate the periodic review of existing significant regulations, agencies shall consider how best to promote retrospective analysis of rules that may be outmoded, ineffective, insufficient, or excessively burdensome, and to modify, streamline, expand, or repeal them in accordance with what has been learned. Such retrospective analyses, including supporting data, should be released online whenever possible.

(b) Within 120 days of the date of this order, each agency shall develop and submit to the Office of Information and Regulatory Affairs a preliminary plan, consistent with law and its resources and regulatory priorities, under which the agency will periodically review its existing significant regulations to determine whether any such regulations should be modified, streamlined, expanded, or repealed so as to make the agency's regulatory program more effective or less burdensome in achieving the regulatory objectives.

Sec. 7. *General Provisions.*

(a) For purposes of this order, "agency" shall have the meaning set forth in section 3(b) of Executive Order 12866.

(b) Nothing in this order shall be construed to impair or otherwise affect:

(i) authority granted by law to a department or agency, or the head thereof; or

(ii) functions of the Director of the Office of Management and Budget relating to budgetary, administrative, or legislative proposals.

(c) This order shall be implemented consistent with applicable law and subject to the availability of appropriations.

(d) This order is not intended to, and does not, create any right or benefit, substantive or procedural, enforceable at law or in equity by any party against the United States, its departments, agencies, or entities, its officers, employees, or agents, or any other person.

BARACK OBAMA

The White House,
January 18, 2011.

▮ EXECUTIVE ORDER 13579

Regulation and Independent Regulatory Agencies

By the authority vested in me as President by the Constitution and the laws of the United States of America, and in order to improve regulation and regulatory review, it is hereby ordered as follows:

Section 1. *Policy.* (a) Wise regulatory decisions depend on public participation and on careful analysis of the likely consequences of regulation. Such decisions are informed and improved by allowing interested members of the public to have a meaningful opportunity to participate in rulemaking. To the extent permitted by law, such decisions should be made only after consideration of their costs and benefits (both quantitative and qualitative).

(b) Executive Order 13563 of January 18, 2011, "Improving Regulation and Regulatory Review," directed to executive agencies, was meant to produce a regulatory system that protects "public health, welfare, safety, and our environment while promoting economic growth, innovation, competitiveness, and job creation." Independent regulatory agencies, no less than executive agencies, should promote that goal.

(c) Executive Order 13563 set out general requirements directed to executive agencies concerning public participation, integration and innovation, flexible approaches, and science. To the extent permitted by law, independent regulatory agencies should comply with these provisions as well.

Sec. 2. *Retrospective Analyses of Existing Rules.*
(a) To facilitate the periodic review of existing significant regulations, independent regulatory agencies should consider how best to promote retrospective analysis of rules that may be outmoded, ineffective, insufficient, or excessively burdensome, and to modify, streamline, expand, or repeal them in accordance with what has

been learned. Such retrospective analyses, including supporting data and evaluations, should be released online whenever possible.

(b) Within 120 days of the date of this order, each independent regulatory agency should develop and release to the public a plan, consistent with law and reflecting its resources and regulatory priorities and processes, under which the agency will periodically review its existing significant regulations to determine whether any such regulations should be modified, streamlined, expanded, or repealed so as to make the agency's regulatory program more effective or less burdensome in achieving the regulatory objectives.

Sec. 3. *General Provisions.* (a) For purposes of this order, "executive agency" shall have the meaning set forth for the term "agency" in section 3(b) of Executive Order 12866 of September 30, 1993, and "independent regulatory agency" shall have the meaning set forth in 44 U.S.C. 3502(5).

(b) Nothing in this order shall be construed to impair or otherwise affect:

(i) authority granted by law to a department or agency, or the head thereof; or

(ii) functions of the Director of the Office of Management and Budget relating to budgetary, administrative, or legislative proposals.

(c) This order shall be implemented consistent with applicable law and subject to the availability of appropriations.

(d) This order is not intended to, and does not, create any right or benefit, substantive or procedural, enforceable at law or in equity by any party against the United States, its departments, agencies, or entities, its officers, employees, or agents, or any other person.

BARACK OBAMA

The White House,
July 11, 2011.

▥ EXECUTIVE ORDER 13609

Promoting International Regulatory Cooperation

By the authority vested in me as President by the Constitution and the laws of the United States of America, and in order to promote international regulatory cooperation, it is hereby ordered as follows:

Section 1. *Policy.* Executive Order 13563 of January 18, 2011 (Improving Regulation and Regulatory Review), states that our regulatory system must protect public health, welfare, safety, and our environment while promoting economic growth, innovation, competitiveness, and job creation. In an increasingly global economy, international regulatory cooperation, consistent with domestic law and prerogatives and U.S. trade policy, can be an important means of promoting the goals of Executive Order 13563.

The regulatory approaches taken by foreign governments may differ from those taken by U.S. regulatory agencies to address similar issues. In some cases, the differences between the regulatory approaches of U.S. agencies and those of their foreign counterparts might not be necessary and might impair the ability of American businesses to export and compete internationally. In meeting shared challenges involving health, safety, labor, security, environmental, and other issues, international regulatory cooperation can identify approaches that are at least as protective as those that are or would be adopted in the absence of such cooperation. International regulatory cooperation can also reduce, eliminate, or prevent unnecessary differences in regulatory requirements.

Sec. 2. *Coordination of International Regulatory Cooperation.* (a) The Regulatory Working Group (Working Group) established by Executive Order 12866 of September 30, 1993 (Regulatory Planning and Review), which was reaffirmed by Executive Order 13563, shall, as appropriate:

(i) serve as a forum to discuss, coordinate, and develop a common understanding among agencies of U.S. Government positions and priorities with respect to:

(A) international regulatory cooperation activities that are reasonably anticipated to lead to significant regulatory actions;

(B) efforts across the Federal Government to support significant, cross-cutting international regulatory cooperation activities, such as the work of regulatory cooperation councils; and

(C) the promotion of good regulatory practices internationally, as well as the promotion of U.S. regulatory approaches, as appropriate; and

(ii) examine, among other things:

(A) appropriate strategies for engaging in the development of regulatory approaches through international regulatory cooperation, particularly in emerging technology areas, when consistent with section 1 of this order;

(B) best practices for international regulatory cooperation with respect to regulatory development, and, where appropriate, information exchange and other regulatory tools; and

(C) factors that agencies should take into account when determining whether and how to consider other regulatory approaches under section 3(d) of this order.

(b) As Chair of the Working Group, the Administrator of the Office of Information and Regulatory Affairs (OIRA) of the Office of Management and Budget (OMB) shall convene the Working Group as necessary to discuss international regulatory cooperation issues as described above, and the Working Group shall include a representative from the Office of the United States Trade Representative and, as appropriate, representatives from other agencies and offices.

(c) The activities of the Working Group, consistent with law, shall not duplicate the efforts of existing interagency bodies and coordination mechanisms. The Working Group shall consult with existing interagency bodies when appropriate.

(d) To inform its discussions, and pursuant to section 4 of Executive Order 12866, the Working Group may commission analytical reports and studies by OIRA, the Administrative Conference of the United States, or any other relevant agency, and the Administrator of OIRA may solicit input, from time to time, from representatives of business, nongovernmental organizations, and the public.

(e) The Working Group shall develop and issue guidelines on the applicability and implementation of sections 2 through 4 of this order.

(f) For purposes of this order, the Working Group shall operate by consensus.

Sec. 3. *Responsibilities of Federal Agencies.* To the extent permitted by law, and consistent with the principles and requirements of Executive Order 13563 and Executive Order 12866, each agency shall:

(a) if required to submit a Regulatory Plan pursuant to Executive Order 12866, include in that plan a summary of its international regulatory cooperation activities that are reasonably anticipated to lead to significant regulations, with an explanation of how these activities advance the purposes of Executive Order 13563 and this order;

(b) ensure that significant regulations that the agency identifies as having significant international impacts are designated as such in the Unified Agenda of Federal Regulatory and Deregulatory Actions, on RegInfo.gov, and on Regulations.gov;

(c) in selecting which regulations to include in its retrospective review plan, as required by Executive Order 13563, consider:

(i) reforms to existing significant regulations that address unnecessary differences in regulatory requirements between the United States and its major trading partners, consistent with section 1 of this order, when stakeholders provide adequate information to the agency establishing that the differences are unnecessary; and

(ii) such reforms in other circumstances as the agency deems appropriate; and

(d) for significant regulations that the agency identifies as having significant international impacts, consider, to the extent feasible, appropriate, and consistent with law, any regulatory approaches by a foreign government that the United States has agreed to consider under a regulatory cooperation council work plan.

Sec. 4. *Definitions.* For purposes of this order:

(a) "Agency" means any authority of the United States that is an "agency" under 44 U.S.C. 3502(1), other than those considered to be independent regulatory agencies, as defined in 44 U.S.C. 3502(5).

(b) "International impact" is a direct effect that a proposed or final regulation is expected to have on international trade and investment, or that otherwise may be of significant interest to the trading partners of the United States.

(c) "International regulatory cooperation" refers to a bilateral, regional, or multilateral process, other than processes that are covered by section 6(a)(ii), (iii), and (v) of this order, in which national governments engage in various forms of collaboration and communication with respect to regulations, in particular a process that is reasonably anticipated to lead to the development of significant regulations.

(d) "Regulation" shall have the same meaning as "regulation" or "rule" in section 3(d) of Executive Order 12866.

(e) "Significant regulation" is a proposed or final regulation that constitutes a significant regulatory action.

(f) "Significant regulatory action" shall have the same meaning as in section 3(f) of Executive Order 12866.

Sec. 5. *Independent Agencies.* Independent regulatory agencies are encouraged to comply with the provisions of this order.

Sec. 6. *General Provisions.* (a) Nothing in this order shall be construed to impair or otherwise affect:

(i) the authority granted by law to a department or agency, or the head thereof;

(ii) the coordination and development of international trade policy and negotiations pursuant to section 411 of the Trade Agreements Act of 1979 (19 U.S.C. 2451) and section 141 of the Trade Act of 1974 (19 U.S.C. 2171);

(iii) international trade activities undertaken pursuant to section 3 of the Act of February 14, 1903 (15 U.S.C. 1512), subtitle C of the Export Enhancement Act of 1988, as amended (15 U.S.C. 4721 et seq.), and Reorganization Plan No. 3 of 1979 (19 U.S.C. 2171 note);

(iv) the authorization process for the negotiation and conclusion of international agreements pursuant to 1 U.S.C. 112b(c) and its implementing regulations (22 C.F.R. 181.4) and implementing procedures (11 FAM 720);

(v) activities in connection with subchapter II of chapter 53 of title 31 of the United States Code, title 26 of the United States Code, or Public Law 111–203 and other laws relating to financial regulation; or

(vi) the functions of the Director of OMB relating to budgetary, administrative, or legislative proposals.

(b) This order shall be implemented consistent with applicable law and subject to the availability of appropriations.

(c) This order is not intended to, and does not, create any right or benefit, substantive or procedural, enforceable at law or in equity by any party against the United States, its departments, agencies, or entities, its officers, employees, or agents, or any other person.

BARACK OBAMA

The White House,
May 1, 2012.

EXECUTIVE ORDER 13610

Identifying and Reducing Regulatory Burdens

By the authority vested in me as President by the Constitution and the laws of the United States of America, and in order to modernize our regulatory system and to reduce unjustified regulatory burdens and costs, it is hereby ordered as follows:

Section 1. *Policy.* Regulations play an indispensable role in protecting public health, welfare, safety, and our environment, but they can also impose significant burdens and costs. During challenging economic times, we should be especially careful not to impose unjustified regulatory requirements. For this reason, it is particularly important for agencies to conduct retrospective analyses of existing rules to examine whether they remain justified and whether they should be modified or streamlined in light of changed circumstances, including the rise of new technologies.

Executive Order 13563 of January 18, 2011 (Improving Regulation and Regulatory Review), states that our regulatory system "must measure, and seek to improve, the actual results of regulatory requirements." To promote this goal, that Executive Order requires agencies not merely to conduct a single exercise, but to engage in "periodic review of existing significant regulations." Pursuant to section 6(b) of that Executive Order, agencies are required to develop retrospective review plans to review existing significant regulations in order to "determine whether any such regulations should be modified, streamlined, expanded, or repealed." The purpose of this requirement is to "make the agency's regulatory program more effective or less burdensome in achieving the regulatory objectives."

In response to Executive Order 13563, agencies have developed and made available for public comment retrospective review plans that identify over five hundred initiatives. A small fraction of those initiatives, already finalized or formally proposed to the public, are anticipated to eliminate billions of dollars in regulatory costs and tens of millions of hours in annual paperwork burdens. Significantly larger savings are anticipated as the plans are implemented and as action is taken on additional initiatives.

As a matter of longstanding practice and to satisfy statutory obligations, many agencies engaged in periodic review of existing regulations prior to the issuance of Executive Order 13563. But further steps should be taken, consistent with law, agency resources, and regulatory priorities, to promote public participation in retrospective review, to modernize our regulatory system, and to institutionalize regular assessment of significant regulations.

Sec. 2. *Public Participation in Retrospective Review.* Members of the public, including those directly and indirectly affected by regulations, as well as State, local, and tribal governments, have important information about the actual effects of existing regulations. For this reason, and consistent with Executive Order 13563, agencies shall invite, on a regular basis (to be determined by the agency head in consultation with the Office of Information and Regulatory Affairs (OIRA)), public suggestions about regulations in need of retrospective review and about appropriate modifications to such regulations. To promote an open exchange of information, retrospective analyses of regulations, including supporting data, shall be released to the public online wherever practicable.

Sec. 3. *Setting Priorities.* In implementing and improving their retrospective review plans, and in considering retrospective review suggestions from the public, agencies shall give priority, consistent with law, to those initiatives that will produce significant quantifiable monetary savings or significant quantifiable reductions in paperwork burdens while protecting public health, welfare, safety, and our environment. To the extent practicable and permitted by law, agencies shall also give special consideration to initiatives that would reduce unjustified regulatory burdens or simplify or harmonize regulatory requirements imposed on small businesses. Consistent with Executive Order 13563 and Executive Order 12866 of September 30, 1993 (Regulatory Planning and Review), agencies shall give consideration to the cumulative effects of their own regulations, including cumulative burdens, and shall to the extent practicable and consistent with law give priority to reforms that would make significant progress in reducing those burdens while protecting public health, welfare, safety, and our environment.

Sec. 4. *Accountability.* Agencies shall regularly report on the status of their retrospective review efforts to OIRA. Agency reports should describe progress, anticipated accomplishments, and proposed timelines for relevant actions, with an emphasis on the priorities described in section 3 of this order. Agencies shall submit draft reports to OIRA on September 10, 2012, and on the second Monday of January and July for each year thereafter, unless directed otherwise through subsequent guidance from OIRA. Agencies shall make final reports available to the public within a reasonable period (not to exceed three weeks from the date of submission of draft reports to OIRA).

Sec. 5. *General Provisions.* (a) For purposes of this order, "agency" means any authority of the United States that is an "agency" under 44 U.S.C. 3502(1), other than those considered to be independent regulatory agencies, as defined in 44 U.S.C. 3502(5).

(b) Nothing in this order shall be construed to impair or otherwise affect:

(i) the authority granted by law to a department or agency, or the head thereof; or

(ii) the functions of the Director of the Office of Management and Budget relating to budgetary, administrative, or legislative proposals.

(c) This order shall be implemented consistent with applicable law and subject to the availability of appropriations.

(d) This order is not intended to, and does not, create any right or benefit, substantive or procedural, enforceable at law or in equity by any party against the United States, its departments, agencies, or entities, its officers, employees, or agents, or any other person.

BARACK OBAMA

The White House, May 10, 2012.

Name Index

Subject Index

CQ Press, an imprint of SAGE, is the leading publisher of books, periodicals, and electronic products on American government and international affairs. CQ Press consistently ranks among the top commercial publishers in terms of quality, as evidenced by the numerous awards its products have won over the years. CQ Press owes its existence to Nelson Poynter, former publisher of the *St. Petersburg Times,* and his wife Henrietta, with whom he founded *Congressional Quarterly* in 1945. Poynter established CQ with the mission of promoting democracy through education and in 1975 founded the Modern Media Institute, renamed The Poynter Institute for Media Studies after his death. The Poynter Institute (*www.poynter.org*) is a nonprofit organization dedicated to training journalists and media leaders.

In 2008, CQ Press was acquired by SAGE, a leading international publisher of journals, books, and electronic media for academic, educational, and professional markets. Since 1965, SAGE has helped inform and educate a global community of scholars, practitioners, researchers, and students spanning a wide range of subject areas, including business, humanities, social sciences, and science, technology, and medicine. A privately owned corporation, SAGE has offices in Los Angeles, London, New Delhi, and Singapore, in addition to the Washington DC office of CQ Press.